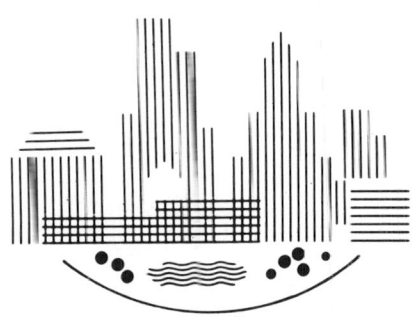

THE RISE OF URBAN AMERICA

ADVISORY EDITOR

Richard C. Wade

PROFESSOR OF AMERICAN HISTORY
UNIVERSITY OF CHICAGO

REPORT
ON THE
SOCIAL STATISTICS
OF CITIES

PART II

THE SOUTHERN AND THE WESTERN STATES

George E. Waring, Jr.

ARNO PRESS

&

The New York Times

NEW YORK • 1970

Reprint Edition 1970 by Arno Press Inc.

Reprinted from a copy in The State Historical Society of Wisconsin Library

LC# 74-112577

ISBN   Set 0-405-02481-9
Part II 0-405-02483-5

THE RISE OF URBAN AMERICA
ISBN for complete set 0-405-02430-4

Manufactured in the United States of America

DEPARTMENT OF THE INTERIOR,
CENSUS OFFICE.

FRANCIS A. WALKER, Superintendent,
Appointed April 1, 1879; resigned November 3, 1881.

CHAS. W. SEATON, Superintendent,
Appointed November 4, 1881.   Office of Superintendent
abolished March 3, 1885.

REPORT

ON THE

SOCIAL STATISTICS OF CITIES,

COMPILED BY

GEORGE E. WARING, Jr.,

EXPERT AND SPECIAL AGENT.

PART I.

THE NEW ENGLAND AND THE MIDDLE STATES.

PART II.

THE SOUTHERN AND THE WESTERN STATES

PART II.

WASHINGTON:
GOVERNMENT PRINTING OFFICE.
1887.

PART II.

SOCIAL STATISTICS OF CITIES.

SOUTHERN AND WESTERN STATES.

TABLE OF CONTENTS.

SOUTHERN STATES.

WESTERN STATES.

THE SOUTHERN STATES.

MARYLAND.
BALTIMORE.

DISTRICT OF COLUMBIA.
WASHINGTON.

VIRGINIA.
ALEXANDRIA,   NORFOLK,   PORTSMOUTH,
LYNCHBURG,   PETERSBURG,   RICHMOND.

WEST VIRGINIA.
WHEELING.

NORTH CAROLINA.
WILMINGTON.

SOUTH CAROLINA.
CHARLESTON,   COLUMBIA.

KENTUCKY.
COVINGTON,   LEXINGTON,   LOUISVILLE,   NEWPORT.

TENNESSEE.
CHATTANOOGA,   MEMPHIS,   NASHVILLE.

GEORGIA.
ATLANTA,   AUGUSTA,   MACON,   SAVANNAH.

FLORIDA.
JACKSONVILLE,   PENSACOLA.

ALABAMA.
MOBILE,   MONTGOMERY,   SELMA.

MISSISSIPPI.
VICKSBURG.

ARKANSAS.
LITTLE ROCK.

LOUISIANA.
NEW ORLEANS,   SHREVEPORT.

TEXAS.
AUSTIN,   DALLAS,   GALVESTON,   HOUSTON,   SAN ANTONIO.

MARYLAND.

BALTIMORE,

MARYLAND.

POPULATION

IN THE

AGGREGATE,

1800-1880.

	Inhab.
1790	13,503
1800	26,514
1810	46,555
1820	62,738
1830	80,620
1840	102,313
1850	169,054
1860	212,418
1870	267,354
1880	332,313

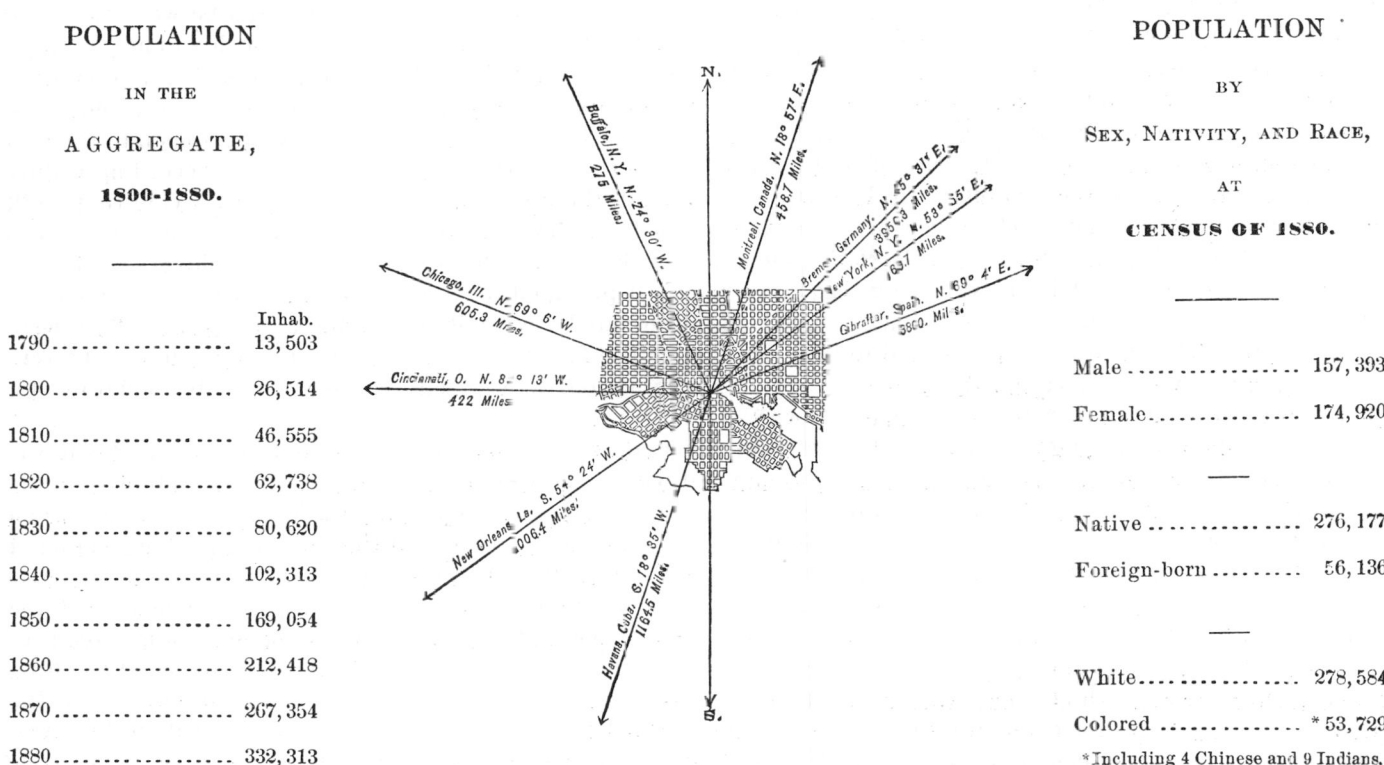

POPULATION

BY

SEX, NATIVITY, AND RACE,

AT

CENSUS OF 1880.

Male	157,393
Female	174,920
Native	276,177
Foreign-born	56,136
White	278,584
Colored	*53,729

*Including 4 Chinese and 9 Indians.

Latitude: 39° 17′ North; Longitude: 76° 37′ (west from Greenwich); Altitude: 0 to 250 feet.

FINANCIAL CONDITION:

Total Valuation: $244,043,181; per capita: $734 00.   Net Indebtedness: $854,466; per capita: $2 57.   Tax per $100: $1 22.

HISTORICAL SKETCH. (a)

Captain John Smith, the famous explorer, was beyond doubt the first white man whose eye rested upon the site of Baltimore. It was as far back as 1606, as appears from his history of Virginia, that he penetrated the Patapsco, a river marked, on the wonderfully accurate map that he constructed, as the "Bolus" river, and so called by him "for the red clay resembling bole Armoniack" After this visit a long time intervened before the coming of any other of the European race to the Patapsco. It is probable that in 1628 Lord Baltimore explored the

---

a The following sketch of Baltimore was compiled by Robert Luce, esq., from notes furnished by J. H. B. Latrobe, esq., and **from** *The Chronicles of Baltimore,* by Colonel J. Thomas Scharf.

surrounding country, of which he afterward procured a grant and which became Maryland, and it is possible that he might have penetrated to this spot at that time; but nothing is positively known of the presence of white men in the vicinity after Smith's departure up to the year 1659. In that year several patents were issued for land in the neighborhood, and plantations were established. In the same year Baltimore county was organized, with limits far more extensive than it has at present, embracing not only all of Harford and Carroll counties, but large portions of Anne Arundel, Howard, and Frederick counties. At that time the population of all Maryland was only 12,000, and that of the newly erected county was probably less than one-sixth of that number.

During the next few years many lands or farms, known by various names and titles, were taken up, and among them, in 1668, the land known as "Cole's harbor", on which the town of Baltimore was subsequently laid out. These farms, or rather plantations, were occupied by planters, a class which made far the larger portion of the inhabitants of the colony. The principal planters were also the merchants, who traded with London and the other great ports of England. The large plantations, with their groups of storehouses and other buildings, assumed the appearance and performed the office of little towns.

Amid the creeks and marshes and under the hills of the northwestern branch of the Patapsco a number of planters gradually gathered and a very significant settlement sprang up. To the point of land between the south and middle branches of the river was directed the main road from the west, and this, with such an anchorage for vessels, had brought it into notice as a possible site for a future metropolis. The owner, however, set prodigious store by certain iron mines which he believed to be situated on his territory, and by his opposition prevented the plan of using it for a town site from being carried out. Excluded from the level land, those persons interested in the project were obliged to seek the site of Baltimore, on the northwestern branch of the river. Accordingly, July 14, 1729, the petition of the inhabitants of Baltimore was read in the upper house of assembly, "praying that a bill may be brought in for the building of a town on the north side of the Patapsco river, upon the land supposed to belong to Messrs. Charles and Daniel Carroll". On the 30th the bill was finally passed, and on the 8th of August it was signed by Benedict Leonard Calvert, esq., governor. It provided for the laying out of 60 acres of land "in and about the place where one John Fleming" lived, and designated 7 commissioners for the purpose. There were to be 60 equal lots, the owner of the land to have the first choice for one lot, after which the remaining lots were to be taken up by others, paying the owner of the land its valuation, determined by agreement or by valuation of a jury. The town was to be called "Baltimore Town".

In the following January it was duly laid out and disposed of. Compared with the Baltimore of to-day it was a most insignificant affair, the whole of it being comprised within the westernmost branch of the Patapsco on the south, the chalk-hills of Charles and Saratoga streets on the north, the deep drain and gully which swept down about the present course of Liberty street and McClellan's alley on the west, and the big swamp which bordered Jones' falls on the east. From the small quantity of ground originally taken for the town, and from the difficulty of extending it in any direction, as it was surrounded by hills, water-courses, or marshes, it is evident that the commissioners did not anticipate either its present commerce or population. The expense of extending streets, of building bridges, and of leveling hills and filling marshes to which their successors have been subjected has been an obstacle to growth which most other American cities have scarcely felt, and one against which nothing but the great local advantages for trade of all kinds would have enabled the citizens to contend. The situation, however, afforded the most direct communication with the surrounding country, and also had in its favor the great security presented by the harbor, and the abundance of stone, lime, iron, and timber. On the other hand, it was unhealthful, and would continue to be so until a large marsh adjacent to it was reclaimed. Another unfavorable circumstance was that the alluvium of the falls, spreading from the shore from Harford run to South street, already limited the channel of the river on the north side of it, and formed some islands which continued to be overflowed by high tides until the islands and shoals were made fast lands, as they now are.

The character of the founders of the town is illustrated by the fact that in the very first year of its existence, in June, 1730, they secured the passage of an act by the general assembly "for the building of a church in Baltimore county, and in a town called Baltimore Town, in Saint Paul's parish". A lot was at once secured—on the northwest corner of which the present Saint Paul's church now stands—and a church edifice was immediately started, 50 feet by 23 feet in the clear, and with walls 18 feet high; but, owing to failure in fulfilling contracts and other delays, it was not completed until 1739. This, the first church in Baltimore, stood for 45 years, being succeeded in 1784 by a more elegant and costly edifice.

In August, 1732, the assembly passed an act erecting a town on the other side of the creek from Baltimore, on the land where Edward Fell kept store, to be known as "Jonas Town". This name was afterward changed to "Jones Town", in compliment to one of the former owners of the land. It was laid off in November into 20 lots, valued at 150 pounds of tobacco each. (Tobacco was long the most common currency of the province, as it also was its greatest product. Taxes were often laid in it, and most values were reckoned in it.) Improvements were soon made here by which, and from certain early settlements, it obtained the name which it now bears of "Old Town". The communication with Baltimore Town given by the ford was so inconvenient that the respective inhabitants of the towns soon erected a bridge where Gay Street bridge now stands.

In 1745, on the joint petition of the inhabitants of Baltimore and Jones Town, the assembly of Maryland incorporated them into one town, to be known as Baltimore Town. Seven commissioners were appointed "to see the present and former acts, relating to the towns before mentioned, put in execution", etc. In case of any vacancy occurring, the remaining commissioners should fill it, thus making the government of the town a close corporation. As to finances, the act provided that the commissioners might "levy, assess, and take by way of distress, if needful, from the inhabitants of the town, by even and equal proportion, the sum of 3 pounds yearly", but what was to be done with this money does not seem to have been mentioned.

Two years later another act was passed in regard to the town, enlarging it by the addition of about 18 acres which had been brought into notice by the building of the bridge; it lay principally on the west side of the falls, and contained all the fast land between the eastern limits of the first town and the falls. By the same act the commissioners were authorized to open and widen streets or alleys, with the consent of the proprietors, and to remove nuisances, and also to hold two annual fairs, on the first Thursdays of May and October, with exemption from civil process during the fairs. Housekeepers were to be subject to a fine of 10 shillings if they did not "keep ladder high enough to extend to the top of the roof of such house, or if their chimnies blazed out at top".

The early history of Baltimore is conspicuously wanting in events that are worth noting. The various additions to the town made by legislative enactments, and the founding of those various social institutions which spring up during the growth of any community, make up the mass of its early chronicles. In 1750, 25 acres of land on the north and east were surveyed and laid out into lots and streets and incorporated into the town. In the same year a house for the inspection of tobacco was erected, and the construction of a public wharf was begun. It is probable that in or about this year the First German Reformed Congregation was established.

In 1752 Baltimore had 200 inhabitants, 25 houses (4 of them brick, 1 two-storied without a hip roof), 1 church, and 2 taverns. There was one school-master in the place, but, according to the *Maryland Gazette* of February 27, 1752, another was wanted. The population of the county of Baltimore at this time consisted of 2,692 white men, 3,115 white boys, 2,587 white women, 2,951 white girls, 595 servant men, 126 servant boys, 200 servant women, 49 servant girls, 470 men convicts, 6 boy convicts, 87 women convicts, 6 girl convicts, being 569 convicts in all, designed for compulsory labor in the county, and sold for certain terms; and there were 116 mulatto slaves, 196 free mulattoes, 4,027 black slaves, and 8 free blacks, making a total-population of 17,231. Servants in Maryland at this time may properly be classed as the "redemptioners", provided for by Lord Baltimore in his original scheme of colonization. Much of the early emigration was thus effected, the emigrant binding himself to five years' service in the province, in consideration of his transportation thither at the cost of the contractor. In 1638 the term of service was reduced to four years. At the end of their term these "redemptioners", or indentured servants, received one whole year's provision of corn and 50 acres of land. These servants, therefore, are not to be confounded with the negro slaves or with the convicts, the latter of whom were also sold to labor for terms.

In 1753 another addition was made to the town, this time it being 32 acres of "Cole's harbor" that was annexed. The next year 450 "pieces of eight", or dollars, were raised by means of a lottery toward building a public wharf.

The event of 1755 in the history of Baltimore—and it was one which was of general importance to the country—was the defeat of Braddock by the French and Indians, who, after this terrible disaster, penetrated the country past forts Frederick and Cumberland, and pushed their plundering and marauding parties to within 50 miles of Baltimore. In the next year the assembly passed an act to raise supplies and to protect the province. The tax imposed by this act was a most curious one. All bachelors of twenty-five years of age and upward, worth £100 and under £300, were to pay 5 shillings; if worth £300 or upward, 20 shillings; all freehold estates, 1 shilling per 100 acres; if belonging to Roman Catholics, 2 shillings. This slight record throws much light on the times. It tells us that the Marylanders of the middle of the last century advocated marriage, and knew how to put a premium on it; that they thought the sin of being a bachelor increased out of proportion to his wealth; and, most important of all, it tells us that as late as 1756 the idea of perfect religious freedom and equality in the eyes of the law did not prevail in this colony.

In this year there was an influx of inhabitants, sent hither by an event which belongs to a most melancholy page of history—the expulsion of the Acadian French from Nova Scotia upon the conquest of that province by the British. There is nothing in human chronicles more tender or more touching than the story of that little colony, a band of simple, virtuous peasants driven from their homes, and thrust almost penniless upon the world by the pitiless, cruel invader. A fragment of that band of exiles came to Baltimore and was received with a ready and generous hospitality. At first they were lodged in private quarters, but it was not long before their frugality and industry enabled them to build some small but comfortable houses on South Charles street, near Lombard street, giving to that quarter its designation as "French town", which it preserved for a long time.

There is no doubt that the growth of Baltimore was promoted by the continuation of this war, since it prevented for a time the extension of the settlement westward. Within a year after peace the town came to be acknowledged as the greatest mart of trade in the province.

In 1763 the sum of £510 was raised by means of a lottery and applied toward completing the market-house, buying two fire-engines and a parcel of leathern buckets, enlarging the existing public wharf and building a new one. In 1766 a law was passed compelling Messrs. Marrison, Lawson, and Philpot to fill up the marsh between

Frederick street and the falls, and commissioners were appointed to lay it off as an addition to the town. A law was also passed prescribing quarantine, at the discretion of the governor, on all passenger ships infected by diseases, and another relating to the roads of the county. The resistance to the stamp act, which was so universal in this year throughout the country, was equally spirited in Baltimore, and her citizens took an active share in the nullification of the act in Maryland.

Down to 1768 Joppa was the shire town of Baltimore county when there was any shire town. It is a singular fact that no living man can tell with any degree of certainty at what spot in the wilderness the county-seat was first located. The court-house was on Bush river till some period between 1683 and 1707, when it was abandoned, and a second one was erected on Gunpowder river at a place called Forster's neck. In 1712 it was again removed, this time to a place which reached the dignity of being a town, and which was known as Joppa. Its population was never large, but it was one of the most important and prosperous seaports of Maryland before a single house had been erected in Baltimore. The courts were held here down to 1768, when Baltimore was made the shire town. From this time may be dated "the decline and fall" of the ancient town of Joppa. The old court-house has long since crumbled away; her wharves, at which hundreds of the largest merchantmen were laden, have disappeared; her dwellings have fallen one by one, until scarcely their foundations can be traced; and a solitary antique tenement is all that now remains to mark the spot where the shire town of Baltimore county once stood.

Commissioners were appointed in 1768 to build the county court-house and prison "on the uppermost part of Calvert street next to Jones' falls". The court-house was erected on a bluff overhanging the falls, precisely where the "Battle monument" now stands.

In 1769 a number of gentlemen, aided by general subscription, procured an engine for the extinguishing of fires, and formed "the Mechanical company". This was the first engine of the kind in Baltimore, and cost £99. This was the first of a long line of kindred associations.

An interesting contemporaneous account of the early growth of Baltimore is found in a letter dated January 18, 1771, written from Annapolis by Mr. William Eddis to his friends in London. After describing how the spot happened to become a commercial port, he said:

The commencement of a trade so lucrative to the first adventurers soon became an object of universal attention. Persons of a commercial and enterprising spirit emigrated from all quarters to this new and promising scene of industry. Wharves were constructed; elegant and convenient habitations were rapidly erected; marshes were drained; spacious fields were occupied for the purposes of general utility; and within 40 years from its first commencement, Baltimore became not only the most wealthy and populous town in the province, but inferior to few on this continent, either in size, number of inhabitants, or the advantages arising from a well-conducted and universal and commercial connection.

Baltimore had indeed grown wonderfully, but yet to a Baltimorean of to-day the town of a little over a century ago would appear very insignificant in comparison with the present city. At this time the hills on which the cathedral and the hospital now stand, and the grounds west of Greene street, where Mr. Lux had established a rope-walk, and the south shore of the river from Lee street, where Mr. Thomas Moore set up the frame of a vessel, to the fort point, were covered with forest trees or small plantations. The grounds between the town and the point called Philpot's hill yet remained an open common. Most of the timber fell a prey to the wants of necessitous inhabitants during the cold winters of 1779 and 1783, and improvements did not begin, even on Mr. Philpot's grounds, for some years after. When, in 1773, two new bridges were built, one at Baltimore street and the other on Water, now Lombard street, causeways had to be built to them from Frederick street across the marsh. The elevated and beautiful site of the county almshouse, situated at the head of North Howard street and containing 20 acres, which was purchased about this time, cost only £350.

It was at this prosperous period that first appeared in Baltimore what have become two of the most important elements in American social life, viz, the newspaper and the drama. Their nearly simultaneous appearance is significant as to the point in its growth which the town had now reached. Up to this time the newspapers of Philadelphia and Annapolis were the sole medium of information for the citizens of this place, and the only means of advertising their wares or their wants. One of the Philadelphia papers, *The Pennsylvania Chronicle*, had been ably edited by William Goddard. It gained great circulation, but, becoming at last too tory in its bias to stand the times, was discontinued early in 1773. In June of that year Mr. Goddard removed to Baltimore, and on the 20th of the following August issued the first newspaper in Baltimore. It was called *The Maryland Journal and Baltimore Advertiser*, and was a weekly. It was published with varying merit and success until 1797. In 1775 appeared the first number of Dunlap's *Maryland Gazette, or the Baltimore General Advertiser*, which was discontinued four years later on account of lack of support. Many other papers since those days have flourished and died in Baltimore, making the history of the press in that city long and varied.

Scharf well says that the history of the American theater is a subject of importance as connected with the history of our literature and manners. The rise, progress, and cultivation of the drama have a significant relation to the degree of refinement and the general condition of society at any given period in any country. The first company of players that crossed the Atlantic arrived at Yorktown, Virginia, in the summer of 1752. Williamsburg was then the capital of that colony, and thither the players proceeded, performing there on the 5th of September, 1752, the first play performed in America by a regular company of comedians. The first theater, in point of time, erected in this country, was built in Annapolis in the same year. The drama did not, however, reach Baltimore until some years afterward. In 1773 a large warehouse that stood at the corner of Baltimore and Frederick streets was occasionally converted into a theater, on the boards of which the company of Messrs. Douglas & Hallam performed plays from time to time for the edification of the colonists. It was Hallam who brought over the first company from England 21 years before. The encouragement given them was enough to induce them to erect a small theater at the intersection of Water and Albemarle streets, where they performed until the outbreak of the Revolution. All amusements of the kind being then prohibited, they removed to the British West India islands. The first brick theater in Baltimore was built in 1781, and was formally opened January 15, 1782. Another theater was built in 1786, and still another in 1794.

In 1773 the first Methodist and the first Baptist church were erected. It is a curious coincidence that these most ascetic of evangelical churches, the newspaper, the theater, and the almshouse should all have appeared in Baltimore for the first time in the same year.

The news of the passage by the British parliament of the Boston port bill—a bill intended to shut out the people of Boston from commercial intercourse with every part of the world—was received in Baltimore with the greatest indignation. Spirited resolutions were at once passed by earnest meetings of the citizens, and committees were appointed to correspond with those of other towns and colonies. Later on their sympathies found substantial expression in bountiful aid furnished to the persecuted Massachusetts town.

A Boston paper, under date of August 29, 1774, says:

Yesterday arrived at Marblehead, Captain Perkins, from Baltimore, with 3,000 bushels of Indian corn, 20 barrels of rye, and 21 barrels of bread, sent by the inhabitants of that place for the benefit of the poor of Boston, etc.

During the Revolutionary war the citizens of Baltimore took the greatest interest in the struggle, furnishing their just quota of men to the colonial armies and doing all that lay in their power to keep up the courage and enthusiasm which were so necessary in those who stayed at home. The place and its vicinity was never the actual scene of warfare, but it was threatened by the British once or twice, and throughout those years of turmoil it did not escape the general confusion. In the autumn of 1775 the mouth of the Chesapeake was watched by British ships of war, and the merchants of Baltimore, doubtful whether their most peaceful and legitimate intentions of trade would be respected, for the most part laid up their vessels. It was about this time that the water battery on Whetstone point was begun; also three massive chains of wrought iron, passing through floating blocks, were stretched across the river, leaving a small passage on either side next the fort, and the channel was protected by sunken vessels. At that time the inhabitants of Baltimore were incorporated into seven military companies.

In the next year Baltimore, from its peculiar fitness for the building and equipment of vessels, was selected as one of the sites for naval construction, and many ships that afterward became celebrated for the injury they inflicted on the enemy were built here. In March the British sloop of war "Otter" made a demonstration in the Patapsco river with various boats, which produced great alarm in the town. Captain Nicholson, the commander of the "Defence", who happened to be in Baltimore at the time, drove these marauders from the river and captured four or five of their boats. The result of this affair was the throwing up of batteries on Fell's point, the fortifying of Whetstone point with 18 guns, etc.

On the approach of the royal troops toward the Delaware in 1776, Congress, then in session in Philadelphia, adjourned to Baltimore, where it sat from December 20 to February 20 of the following year.

It is under date of 1777 that we find notice of the first of a long series of mobs that irreparably stain the history of Baltimore. Perhaps no large city of the United States has suffered so many times from mob violence. Perhaps no other city of our country has witnessed scenes so nearly similar to those enacted in the worst days of the French revolution. The cause of the first lawless outbreak was the publication by Mr. Goddard, in the *Maryland Journal* of February 25, 1777, of a communication congratulating the people on the terms of peace just offered to the colonists by General Howe, and lauding King George and the parliament to the skies. The "Whig Club", a revolutionary society that had just been formed of the more radical members of the old committees, took offense at this article, and ordered Goddard to leave the town. That gentleman entirely disregarded this order, and in consequence was, on the 25th of March, dragged from his office by a mob, carried to the meeting-room of the club, where he was treated with great indignity, and finally forced to flee the town. The legislature, however, took his part, and by its order the governor issued a proclamation censuring the club and sustaining Mr. Goddard, the first vindication of the liberty of the press in Maryland.

Two years later Mr. Goddard was again the victim of mob violence, a communication in the *Maryland Journal* being again the cause. In the issue of July 6, 1779, there were published a number of queries, styled "political and military", evidently tending to bring in question the military qualifications of General Washington for the august station he then occupied, and to create a prejudice against the French nation, which a short time before had entered into an alliance with the United States. It was afterward found out that their author was General Charles Lee. Their appearance was followed by the greatest excitement. This reached its climax on the night of July 8, when a mob broke into Goddard's house and demanded his immediate appearance before their main body in the coffee-house. He succeeded in getting this lawless trial postponed till the next morning, but then he was forced to leave the town. His house was pillaged, and two of his neighbors were subjected to insulting treatment for trying to befriend him.

The last serious alarm that excited the people of Baltimore during the war was caused by the movements of Earl Cornwallis in August, 1780, which gave the people reason to apprehend that he meant to make an invasion of Maryland and possess himself of Baltimore. In consequence of this apprehension there assembled in the town a force of about 2,800 men. These came from this and adjacent counties within two days after the alarm. Advice was soon received that the destination of Cornwallis was Virginia, in consequence of which these troops were dismissed.

Such troubled times were those of the Revolution, and of such general import were all the events of the period, that of local and internal history there is little to record. At the outbreak of the war there were 564 houses and 5,934 inhabitants in Baltimore proper, and 821 inhabitants in Fell's point, or Deptford hundred, as it was called. At the close of the war, in 1782, the town was said to contain 8,000 inhabitants. In the growth of Baltimore from 1752 up to the Revolution, there seems to have been quite a decided tendency toward settlements east of Jones' falls. There are parts of Old Town and Fell's point which to the present day retain the outward character of the oldest portions of the city. The streets there indicate by their names the colonial era to which they belong. The growth on the west of the falls, though of a later period, was much more rapid.

When the constitution of 1776 was adopted, Baltimore had so much increased in population that it was thought that she should be allowed the privilege of electing two delegates to the general assembly, the same number given to Annapolis. But the members who formed the constitution seem to have been suspicious that the prosperity of Baltimore was an ephemeral one, and that she might possibly soon begin to decay like her neighbor, Joppa, and they added a proviso that when for seven years the number of voters should be less than one-half those in some one county of the state, the town should lose the right of sending two representatives. They had much more confidence in the likelihood of the continual growth of Annapolis, and therefore thought it unnecessary to insert any such condition in regard to her.

Like the other wars which this country has experienced, that of the Revolution had an influence on the manufactures of the land, giving those that already existed fresh impetus and causing many new ones to spring up. Baltimore came in for her share of these results. As the war went on, British goods became scarce, and several manufactures that had hitherto been forbidden in the colonies were now established in or near this town. Among others were a bleach-yard, a linen factory, a paper-mill, a slitting-mill, a card factory, a woolen and linen factory, and two nail factories.

In 1780 an act was passed by the general assembly "to seize, confiscate, and appropriate all British property within this state". A large number of valuable lots in Baltimore and of estates in the neighborhood were confiscated under this law, and by their sale internal improvements received valuable aid. One of these sales was that of the entire property on Whetstone point, then called "Upton court", containing 400 acres, and belonging to the Principio company. It was disposed of during 1781 on the same terms with all the rest, viz, "one-half in specie, one-half in paper at its value; one-half in ten days, residue in six weeks".

Up to this time none of the streets of Baltimore town were paved, and the main street during some parts of the spring and fall seasons, owing to the depth of the soil, was actually impassable from the market-house at Gay street to Calvert street. It is said that when the army passed through Baltimore in 1781 a mounted drummer boy nearly swamped in Baltimore street opposite North street, in a deep mud-hole from which the rider and his horse were with difficulty extricated. In this year pavements began to be laid, especially on the main or Market street. Sidewalks also were built, and the width of the cellar doors and of the old-fashioned porches of front doors was limited, so that the burghers, while enjoying their evening chat or pipe before their dwellings, could not take up too much of the space allowed for pedestrians. Wharves, too, were built, and laws were made to guard the street from nuisances and the harbor from street drainage, while the streets themselves were to be used only by vehicles of a certain breadth of wheel. To defray these expenses an auction tax was laid on the sales of the only auctioneer in the town; a tax was also imposed on public exhibitions and on assessed property; and that common panacea, an annual lottery, was authorized to bring up the arrears of deficiencies in municipal expenses. The executive of this system was a board of commissioners, with ample powers to aid the town commissioners, a sort of body politic and corporate, authorized to fill its own vacancies, to appoint a treasurer, to collect fines for the use of the town, to appoint constables, and to report its accounts to the town commissioners. At the ensuing session of the legislature it was thought that the powers thus conferred on a self-appointing and irresponsible body were too extensive; and accordingly provision was made for the removal of the first set of commissioners and the selection of others every five years by elected electors. The existing government had already become unsatisfactory to a portion of the citizens, as is shown by the *Maryland Journal* of April 2, 1782, in which appeared a notice "that the inhabitants of Baltimore intend petitioning the ensuing general assembly to incorporate said town". This was defeated, however, by the laboring classes.

Another commission was that of nine gentlemen appointed in 1783 to be wardens of the port of Baltimore for five years, this commission to be renewed by election of the same electors that chose the special commissioners above mentioned. They were authorized to make a survey and chart of the basin, the harbor, and the Patapsco river; also to ascertain the depth and course of the channel, and provide for cleaning the same. To defray the expenses the sum of 1 penny per ton was imposed on every vessel entering or clearing; this tax was raised to 2 cents, and was sanctioned by Congress after the adoption of the Constitution.

Wharves and wharfage also came under the jurisdiction of these wardens. There was as yet no public wharf save that of about 100 feet on Calvert street, and only three private wharves, extending about 200 feet, so that the space occupied by the water at that time was perhaps equal to double the surface of the present basin and dock.

A hundred years ago, as Mr. John P. Kennedy pleasantly said in a lecture delivered some years back, Baltimore was fast emerging from its village state into a thriving commercial town. Lots were not yet sold by the foot, except, perhaps, in the denser marts of business; rather by the acre. It was in the *rus in urbe* category. The town had its hills then, which have been rounded off since; and that locality which is now described as lying between the two parallels of North Charles street and Calvert street, presented a steep and barren hillside, broken by rugged cliffs and deep ravines, washed out by the storms of winter into chasms, which were threaded by paths of toilsome and difficult ascent. Market street had shot, like a Nuremburg snake out of its toy box, as far as Congress hall, with its line of low-browed, high-roofed wooden houses in disorderly array, standing forward and back, after the manner of a regiment of militia with many an interval between the files. Some of these structures were painted blue and white and some yellow; and here and there sprang up a more magnificent mansion of brick, with windows like a multiplication-table, and great wastes of wall between the stories, with occasional court-yards before them.

Jones' falls was then a pretty rural stream rippling over a bed now laden with rows of comfortable dwellings, and meandering through meadows garnished with shrubbery and filled with browsing cattle, where now are produced steam-engines, soap and candles and lager beer.

The account of the manners and customs of those times reads strangely to-day. The daily routine of life has changed wonderfully in a century. "Early to bed and early to rise" was the universal rule. Afternoon visits were made, not at night, as now, but at so early an hour as to permit matrons to go home and see their children put to bed. The young part of the family, and especially the feminine portion, used to dress up neatly toward the close of the day and sit in the street porch. It was customary to go from porch to porch in the neighborhood and sit and converse. This custom still prevails during the hot summer seasons, when the whole population is out of doors in the evening, a sight which always excites the attention of strangers from the North.

It was usual for persons to live on the same spot where they pursued their business, a useful custom now generally departed from by the traders. Wives and daughters very often served in the stores of their husbands or parents. If a citizen in those days failed in business, it was a cause of deep and general regret, probably because of the rarity of the occurrence. Tradesmen before the Revolution were an entirely different species of mankind from those of to-day. They did not then, as now, present the appearance in dress of gentlemen. Between them and what were termed the hereditary gentlemen there was a marked difference. The leather apron was omnipresent among the workmen. Dingy buckskin breeches, check shirts, and a red flannel jacket were their common apparel; and men and boys from the country were seen in the streets in leather breeches and aprons; they would have been deemed out of character without them. Men and women then hired by the year; men got £16 to £20, and servant-women £8 to £10.

Prior to 1800 there were not over half a dozen four-wheeled carriages kept in the city. Livery-stables and hacks were unknown. Pacers were preferred to trotters. Street-lamps were not introduced until 1783. In the same year policemen were first employed. So exemplary in their demeanor were the 8,000 townsfolk of that time, that but 3 constables were required during business hours, and but 14 watchmen for the night.

Up to this period the old market-house at the corner of Gay and Baltimore streets had sufficed for the town, but now the inhabitants of Old Town and Fell's point, those on Howard's hill and those in the center of the settlement began to dispute about the site for enlarged accommodations for the traffic in provisions. It was wisely decided, however, to build three new market-houses, one in Hanover street, one at Fell's point, and the largest of the three on Harrison street, upon the bed of the old swamp which Mr. Harrison generously appropriated for the purpose. The successful drainage of this marsh was a great benefit to the town.

A new survey was now ordered to be made of the town, and the inhabitants began to discuss the necessity of a charter.

In 1785, John O'Donnell, esq., arrived from Canton in the ship "Pallas", with a full cargo of china goods, the value of which he realized here. This was the first direct importation thence into this port. Mr. O'Donnell gave the name of "Canton" to that section of Baltimore still so called. Three years later the ship "Chesapeake", of Baltimore, had the honor of being the first American vessel allowed to hoist the colors of the United States in the river Ganges and to trade there.

The first anti-slavery society in the state of Maryland—the fourth in the United States and the sixth in the world—was inaugurated in Baltimore September 8, 1789. It was called "The Maryland Society for Promoting the Abolition of Slavery, and the Relief of Free Negroes and Others Unlawfully Held in Bondage". On the 4th of July, 1791, George Buchanan, M. D., delivered before it ' An oration upon the moral and political evil of slavery", in which he advanced the most philanthropic and the most extreme opinions, yet it created not a ripple on the surface of southern society. The records of the society prove that the ideas expressed did not in the least offend those to whom it was addressed. Such an oration, in such a place, with such a reception, only four years after the adoption of the Constitution, is an incident pregnant with historical significance.

In the course of the year 1791 there arrived in Baltimore 68 ships and barges, 159 scows and brigs, 94 schooners, 45 sloops, and 370 coasters, making in all 746 vessels entered at the custom-house; and there cleared at that office 387 for foreign ports, and 662 coasters.

Men of the present age, seeing the immense use of cigars, might think they had always been so used since the civilized world became addicted to the use of tobacco; but that is not the fact. Their use began with the fevers which were very prevalent about this time, and they began to be smoked along the streets to keep off the yellow fever. This disease made its appearance in Baltimore in the summer of 1794. There were 344 deaths by the fever and other diseases during the months of August and September. The malady did not cease until the 15th of October. It was at this period, and particularly on account of the fever, that many citizens fled from the town with their families, and some of them erected country residences which now ornament the vicinity.

In 1795, Judge Jones, who resided at North Point, on the Patapsco, counted, in passing to Baltimore, no less than "109 ships, 162 brigs, 350 sloops and schooners, and 5,464 of the 'bay craft'", or small coasters, so well known in the traffic between the eastern and western coasts of the Chesapeake. The shad, herring, oyster, and other fisheries had grown to consequence, as may be judged from the large number of these smaller vessels. According to the published reports, the value of merchandise entered at the custom house for exportation from October 1, 1794, to October 1, 1795, was $4,421,924; in the five years of which this was the last the value was $13,444,796, and the exports from the whole state of Maryland for the same time were $20,026,126, showing that Baltimore already exported two-thirds of the whole amount sent forward by the state.

On the last day of the year 1796 a law was passed to constitute the town a city, and to incorporate the inhabitants by the name of "the mayor and city council of Baltimore". It required no little exertion on the part of the senators and delegates of the time to reconcile the citizens to the charter, such as it was. Those of the point, or Deptford hundred, were especially hard to conciliate, but they were won over by an exception from any tax toward deepening the upper harbor or basin. The act was introduced as an experiment for a year only, and another was passed the ensuing session to give it perpetual duration, with an enumeration of some of the principal powers. The new city was divided into 8 wards.

Up to 1799 the multitudes of people that assembled at the single polling-place of the town and county elections caused much turbulence and confusion. The legislature then changed the constitution, dividing both city and county into election districts, and later the manner of voting was limited to ballots, instead of by voice, and the elections ceased to be riotous, as they had been.

According to an account in a paper of the year 1799, there were then in Baltimore about 130 lanes, streets, and alleys, but several of them were yet without a building. The number of houses was about 3,500, the greater part of which were of brick. The number of warehouses was about 170. The manufacturing interest was concentrated in sugar, rum, tobacco, snuff, cordage, paper, wool and cotton cards, nails, saddles, boots and shoes, and ship-building in all its various branches. Within 18 miles of the city there were 50 "capital merchant-mills", 1 powder-mill, and 2 paper-mills, besides several furnaces and 2 forges.

The city was peopled from various parts of the Union, and from different countries in Europe. It was then said to contain "more men of wealth and probity in commercial transactions than any of the seaport towns in the Union".

In 1801 the legislature authorized the building of a lazaretto, which was accordingly put up by the corporation on the point opposite fort McHenry, which has since become one of the bounds of the city eastward.

About this time the necessity of a supply of water began to be felt in Baltimore. Accordingly, April 30, 1804, a company was formed, with a capital of $250,000, for the purpose of introducing water into the city. So great was the demand for the stock of this company that shares were sold for more than 900 per cent. above par, which produced a scene of speculation for a few days almost equal to the great "South Sea bubble" in England.

Congress declared war on Great Britain on the 18th of June, 1812. Two days later an article was published in the *Federal Republican*, a Baltimore newspaper, deploring this action, severely criticising the administration, and announcing it to be the purpose of the paper to oppose the war by "every constitutional argument and legal means". This article caused great irritation throughout the city, which was strongly in favor of the war, and on the 22d the headquarters of the editors of the obnoxious paper were mobbed, their printing-office was pulled down, and their press destroyed. All of this, the editors claimed, was done in the presence of the mayor, the judge of the criminal court, and several other magistrates and police officers, whose authority was not exerted to save the printing apparatus and to preserve the peace of the city. Mr. Hanson, one of the editors, who lived in Rockville, Montgomery county, thereupon determined to come to Baltimore and start the paper again, regardless of consequences. A number of his friends, being aware of the danger that would attend such an attempt, volunteered to accompany him and give him what aid and protection they could. They were eight in number, among them being General James M. Lingan, General Harry Lee—"Light Horse Harry"—and John Howard Payne. On reaching Baltimore they took possession of the house of one of the editors which he had vacated, and when they had early seen that reliance on the civil authorities was useless, the mayor having peremptorily refused to interfere, they supplied themselves with arms and prepared to resist the expected attack.

On the 27th of July the distribution of the paper was begun, and on that evening a mob assailed the house, but was repulsed by its defenders, who were about thirty in number. The military were called out, but their officers made no effort to disperse the mob. Early the next morning the mayor succeeded in inducing the brave defenders, by this time reduced in number from various causes to less than twenty, to put themselves under the protection of the civil authority. They were accordingly escorted to the jail, where they stayed during the day. At nightfall the military were dismissed, which proved to be for the mob the signal for a furious attack on the jail. After some delay they reached the prisoners, and a horrible scene ensued. About half the prisoners succeeded in escaping in the confusion, but the rest were recognized, beaten, trampled on, and then pitched for dead down the high stairs in front of the jail. There they lay in a heap for nearly three hours, the mob continuing all this time to torture their mangled bodies by beating first one and then the other, sticking pen-knives into their faces and hands, and opening their eyes and dropping hot candle-grease into them, etc. Strange to relate, only one man, the brave General Lingan, actually suffered death at their hands. Some were rendered insensible and were afterward restored by friends, and others, by feigning death and undergoing all their tortures without a groan, saved their lives.

The French Massacre-in-the-Prisons occurred on the famous days of September, in 1792. Notice that this Baltimore affair happened in the land of liberty just twenty years later.

Presentments were found against many individuals of each party in this affair, but all were acquitted and discharged—those who defended the house, at Annapolis, to which their trial was removed from Baltimore, the others in the city.

The British appeared at the mouth of the Patapsco in the spring of 1813, and preparations were made to give them a warm reception. It proved, however, to be a false alarm.

The next year the enemy again threatened the place, and this time with more serious consequences. On the morning of the 10th of September their ships were seen at the mouth of the Patapsco, in number from forty to fifty. Some of the vessels entered the river, while others proceeded to North point (at the mouth of the Patapsco), distant 12 miles from the city, and there landed their troops, which were about 9,000 in number, viz, 5,000 soldiers, 2,000 marines, and 2,000 sailors, the first under Major General Ross, the latter commanded by the famous Admiral Cockburn. The troops were a part of Wellington's "Invincibles". The expedition was fresh from the sacking of Washington.

For 4 miles the enemy marched toward the city uninterrupted, except by a few flying shots from the cavalry. Here they were met by General Stricker with his entire Baltimore brigade (except that he had only one company of the regiment of artillery), all but four companies being city troops, and the whole amounting to about 3,200 men. The rest of the American forces were judiciously stationed in or near the various defenses, etc.

As the enemy advanced the artillery opened a destructive fire on them, and the action soon became general. The men took deliberate aim, and the carnage was great—the "invincibles" dodging to the ground and crawling in a bending posture to avoid the militia—the "yeomen" they were taught so much to despise. When the Americans were outflanked by the much greater force of the enemy, they retired reluctantly at the repeated command of their officers, and in much better order than could have been expected. The whole number of Americans actually engaged did not exceed 1,700.

Nearly as much, perhaps, being done at this point as was expected, the brigade retreated toward the city. The British followed slowly, and approached within two miles of the intrenchments. Preparations were at once made to cut them off, but before the plan could be carried out they decamped suddenly in the night and embarked with great precipitation.

The attack on fort McHenry, a couple of miles below the city, was terribly grand and magnificent. The enemy's vessels formed a great half-circle in front of the works and began an active bombardment. This was kept up all day on the 12th, and with less vigor during the night. *Niles' Register*, from which this account is taken, says:

The houses in the city were shaken to their foundations, for never, perhaps, from the time of the invention of cannon to the present day [that was sixty-six years ago], were the same number of pieces fired with so rapid succession. * * * In about twenty-four hours there were blown not less that 1,500 great bombs, besides many rockets and some round shot.

Nevertheless, the damage to the fort was insignificant. The admiral had fully calculated on taking it in two hours. Never was the mortification of an invader more complete.

It was on this occasion that our national anthem, "The Star-Spangled Banner," was written. During the fearful night of the bombardment, Francis S. Key, a distinguished son of Maryland, was a prisoner on the British fleet, having gone on board under a flag of truce and been detained. It was under these circumstances that he composed that immortal song, descriptive of the scenes of that doubtful night and of his own excited feelings.

In memory of the brave defenders of the city who fell in the battle at North Point and at the bombardment of fort McHenry, "Battle monument" was afterward erected. The corner-stone was laid on the 12th of September, 1815, and the statue was placed on the monument on the 12th of September, 1822.

Baltimore plays an important part in the naval history of the war of 1812, especially in that portion of it relating to privateers and letters of marque. Within about four months after the declaration of war, Baltimore had sent to sea 42 armed vessels, carrying about 330 guns and from 2,800 to 3,000 men. Of the 250 privateers and private-armed ships commissioned by the United States as cruising-vessels during the war, 58 were from Baltimore, being more than sailed from any other one port in the country.

In 1817 a charter was granted to a gas-light company, but it did not get fairly under way until 1820.

In the summers of 1819 and 1821 Baltimore was visited by that dreadful scourge, yellow fever. Its ravages were principally confined to that section called Fell's point. Business was in a great measure suspended. Most of those whose means enabled them to remove from the infected district sought refuge in the country or in distant parts of the city, and the poor and the sick remained almost its sole inhabitants. Great distress in the winters that followed was the natural consequence, the misery being heightened by the failure of the City Bank, and the mismanagement of the office of the United States and other banks, accompanied by the fall of the price of flour and tobacco in foreign markets, affecting the prices of all kinds of property.

But Baltimore was to take a fresh start in the race for prosperity. She had been temporarily disheartened and crippled, but not destroyed; for her natural resources could not be taken away, and the people who had improved them in earlier days were still at hand to engage in new operations. These people saw that enterprise, to be repaid, must be content with slower processes than had been resorted to in the past, and that the clipper of their bay was no longer the Aladdin of their counting-houses. The merchants of Baltimore realizing these facts, an auspicious change took place in the commercial affairs of the city between 1820 and 1825. Capital and enterprise again became active. The extensive establishments and ventures became more limited, but were still more significant in both foreign and domestic trade. Baltimore was then undoubtedly the largest flour market in the world, sending forth 205,345 barrels in 1822 and 244,950 in 1823. Of tobacco the city shipped to foreign countries 19,250 hogsheads in 1822 and 21,733 hogsheads in 1823, as well as large quantities of provisions and manufactured goods.

At that time Baltimore ships went principally to the Spanish main, to Buenos Ayres, to Brazil, to Chili, Peru, and Mexico. The trade was well established with these countries, but less reliance seems to have been placed on it than on the magical change which the "internal-improvement" system was to produce as soon as fresh communications were opened with the growing West and its dependencies. Baltimore people seem to have been impressed since then with the idea that their first duty was to recover possession of the internal trade of the country. Certain it is that ever since 1825–'28 their minds have been greatly concerned with canals and railways, and the supreme results they were to produce for Baltimore and Maryland. It is very probable that the commerce and manufactures of the city have not advanced in that time as rapidly as they might have done under different inspirations.

Although no one then anticipated the growth of the country beyond the Alleghanies as it has since been developed, yet everybody felt that good things were in store there, and New York, Philadelphia, Boston, and Baltimore all essayed to grasp them. Railroads were not then thought of. Canals were the means relied on. Already New York had her Erie canal, and there was a canal constructed in Pennsylvania which actually afforded a water communication, imperfect, it is true, but still a communication, between the East and the West. Baltimore had a hope at one time of doing the same thing in the same way, but the report of General Bernard proved that a canal in this direction was impracticable, except at an immense cost. A large portion of the trade of Baltimore with the West had been drawn to Philadelphia and New York by the public works mentioned, and now emigration was not only spoken of among the merchants, but in some cases it actually took place to the successful rival cities.

Up to this time no railroad had been constructed either in Europe or in this country for the general conveyance of passengers or produce between distant points. A few railroads had been constructed in England for local purposes, such as the conveyance of coal and other heavy articles from the mines and places of production to navigable water, but for general purposes of travel and transportation they were regarded as an untried experiment.

Messrs. Philip E. Thomas and George Brown, two public-spirited citizens of Baltimore, frequently talked over, in the fall of 1826, the loss of trade the city had sustained, and came to the conclusion that unless some early means could be devised to draw it back, it would be lost to the city forever. They also concluded that the railroad seemed most likely to attain the desired end. In February, 1827, their ideas were laid before a meeting of citizens, who grew enthusiastic over them. They immediately went to work to secure a charter, and on the 24th of April, 1827, the first railroad company in the United States was chartered, with a capital of $1,500,000, with liberty to increase it; and the city of Baltimore and the state of Maryland were authorized to subscribe to the stock. Thus started the pioneer railroad company of America—the Baltimore and Ohio.

By this time public excitement had gone far beyond fever-heat and reached the boiling-point. Everybody wanted stock. The number of shares subscribed were to be apportioned if the limit of the capital should be exceeded, and every one set about obtaining proxies. Even before a survey was made the possession of stock in any quantity was regarded as a possession for old age, and great was the scramble to obtain it. Subscription books were opened on Tuesday, March 20, and were closed on the 31st. There were taken 41,781 shares, inclusive of the 5,000 allotted to and taken by the city of Baltimore. The amount of money subscribed therefor by this city alone was $4,178,000, divided among 22,000 people.

Presently the surveys were so far completed that the choice of a route might be made. At this time the wise men of the city council came to the aid of the company's engineering talent, and refused to pay a dollar of their subscription of $50,000 unless the road was at an elevation of 66 feet above tide; and the railroad company—which would otherwise in all probability have brought the work in to the city line, which, after a lapse of forty years, it completed from the deep cut to Ostend street—was forced to come to Pratt street at its junction with Amity alley, where Mount Clare station now covers acres of grounds with its shops and engine-houses.

As soon as the grading was completed for a mile west of Mount Clare the iron strap then called a rail was laid down and a car was built, not unlike a country market wagon without a top, and mounted upon wheels whose flanges were on the outside. After the directors were served, the public were permitted to enjoy the luxury of riding back and forth in the car for 12½ cents for the round trip. And this was the first money ever earned on a railroad constructed for general purposes in America.

In the beginning no one dreamed of steam upon the road: horses were to do all the work; and even after the line was completed to Frederick, December 1, 1831, relays of horses pulled the cars from place to place. When steam made its appearance on the Liverpool and Manchester railroad it attracted great attention here. But there was this difficulty about introducing an English engine on a American road. An English road was virtually a straight road; an American road had curves sometimes of as small a radius as 200 feet. For a brief season it was believed that this feature of the early American roads would prevent the use of locomotive engines. But Mr. Peter Cooper, of New York, was satisfied that this difficulty might be overcome, and to vindicate his belief he came to Baltimore, which then had the only road on which he could experiment. Here he made the first locomotive for railroad purposes ever built in America The trial trip was made on the 28th of August, 1830, and though a race with a stage-coach on the return trip was won by the latter, owing to a pulley-band slipping off a drum, nevertheless the real victory was with Mr. Cooper, for he had demonstrated that his engine could pass curves without difficulty at a speed of 15 miles an hour, and could ascend grades with comparative ease.

To Mr. Ross Winans, of Baltimore, were due other inventions almost equal in importance to that of Peter Cooper. The friction wheel, "the outside bearing", and the 8-wheeled car were among the results of his genius.

A rival project to the Baltimore and Ohio railroad was the Chesapeake and Ohio canal. Congress had been induced to vote $1,000,000 for a canal from Georgetown to Pittsburgh; and Virginia and Maryland, as well as the cities of Washington and Alexandria, having subscribed $1,250,000 more, the work was put under way in 1828, being begun on the same day on which the railroad was, and with similar ceremonies, President Adams himself first breaking the ground. This company fought the progress of the railroad as well as it could, delaying its completion considerably by means of litigation. The railroad was finished to Point of Rocks, April, 1832; to Harper's Ferry, December, 1834; to Washington, August, 1834. In March, 1836, the city subscribed $3,000,000 more to the capital stock of the road in the name of the mayor and city council of Baltimore. The line was finished to Wheeling in in January, 1853. At this time the Baltimore and Ohio railroad was the longest in the world.

Subscriptions for the Baltimore and Susquehanna railroad were opened in March, 1828. Much more than the requisite number of shares were taken in the city, besides a few shares at York, although the legislature of Pennsylvania had refused to aid or countenance the undertaking by continuance of the contemplated road within that state. The 8th of August, 1829, the hundredth anniversary of the passage of the act by the assembly creating Baltimore town, was chosen as a most suitable date for laying the corner-stone of this great work. The ceremonies on that occasion were fully as imposing as those when the Baltimore and Ohio was begun. This railroad was opened for public travel on the 4th of July, 1831, the rails on one track, being laid for more than 6 miles through the valley of Jones' falls.

For several years previous to 1826 a number of intelligent and zealous citizens of Baltimore, feeling great solicitude for the education of the rising generation, determined to make provision for establishing a system of public instruction. Giving all their energies and feelings to the cause, they established in its behalf an influence that procured the passage of a law by the legislature of the state, in February, 1826, authorizing the city of Baltimore to establish a system of public schools. In 1827 the city council took some favorable action in the matter, but no schools were put in operation until 1829, when 4 schools were opened. In 1838 and 1839 many modifications and improvements were made in the school system; between 1840 and 1843, 5 schools were added, and in subsequent years the system was much enlarged.

In 1832 Baltimore, in common with other cities of the Union, was visited by the cholera. The mayor and the officers of health made all preparations for it which the nature of the circumstances and the means placed in their hands would permit. However, it raged during the summer season, and during the month of September the number of deaths which it caused was appalling. At the almshouse its ravages were terrible. On the breaking out of the disease the inmates were about 500; of these, 125 perished.

The history of the Bank of Maryland is that of one of the most stupendous and general frauds ever committed. On the 24th of March, 1834, its directors declared its inability to prosecute its business longer, an announcement that fell with a heavy shock on the community. A local financial crisis ensued. Fuel was added to the flames by the bankruptcy of the Susquehanna Bank, the Maryland Savings Institution, and the United States Insurance Company. In all, the people were plundered of more than $2,000,000, perhaps $3,000,000. This bore especially hard on the industrious poor.

The long delay which occurred in obtaining a precise statement of the officers of the Bank of Maryland, and the fierce controversy which was carried on over the causes of the failure, brought on a riot in August, 1835, which continued for several days, causing a great destruction of private and public property and involving a suspension of all authority. The rioters were finally put down by the general uprising of the law-and-order classes.

The state indemnified the sufferers by these riots; the awards of damages made by the commissioners appointed amounted to $102,552 82.

Nothing more in the shape of a riot occurred till August 18, 1839, when a great excitement was caused by the escape of a nun from the Carmelite nunnery on Aisquith street. The prompt action of the mayor in calling out the regiment of city guards probably saved the nunnery from destruction.

On the occasion of the Presidential election of 1840 excitement ran very high. On the evening of the 3d of November, the day after the election, a serious riot took place in the neighborhood of the *Patriot* office, by which a number of respectable citizens were severely injured. It was, however, of short duration.

Baltimore was not again conspicuous for rioting till the fall of 1847, when a series of disgraceful conflicts between the rival fire-companies took place.

In October, 1848, two more riots occurred, one the result of a local election, the other a firemen's riot.

August 18, 1855, the firemen had another disgraceful *mêlée*, in which two men were mortally wounded and a great number severely hurt.

In the next year the city was again the scene of ruffianly riots; and in both the city and the Presidential election of 1856, contests, amounting almost to battles, were fought between contending factions.

May 2, 1857, the military was called out to suppress rioting among the strikers along the eastern end of the Baltimore and Ohio railroad.

Wholesale intimidation characterized the municipal election in October, 1858, although no serious affrays occurred.

The best people in the city now began to realize what a reputation Baltimore was making for herself. They became convinced that some movement was necessary to secure the peace and restore the good name of the city. Accordingly they united to form a "reform association". This was the first organization of what was formerly known as the "Reform" party.

Of all the riots that have occurred in Baltimore, the most famous as well as the most significant was that of the 19th of April, 1861, when a mob attacked the Massachusetts troops passing through the city. On this and on the events of the civil war as affecting Baltimore, it is not necessary to dwell.

On the 13th of May, 1861, the United States forces marched by night to the city and took possession of Federal hall, no one offering the slightest resistance. On the 27th of June, by order of General Banks, Colonel John H. Kenly suspended the board of police, and assumed command of the police force of the city. The troops which had been quartered in the heart of the city were withdrawn on the 11th of July. But the United States government, being resolved on permanently holding Baltimore during the war, made extensive additions to its fortifications from time to time, a number of forts being built in and about it. The city was, however, never attacked either by land or by sea.

In the course of this sketch no mention has been made of the floods, fires, and other calamities of a similar nature with which Baltimore has been afflicted. They may well be grouped together at this point. Naturally the narrative must be more or less in the nature of a catalogue.

The first great flood seems to have occurred October 5, 1786, when the damage in the city and within a radius of 25 miles was estimated at £100,000. Several lives were lost.

The first fire of any consequence took place December 4, 1796, when six buildings were burned, among them the Baltimore academy and the Methodist meeting-house.

On the 9th of August, 1817, Jones' falls, which is a stream about 14 miles long with a very rapid descent, and which flows through Baltimore, was swollen by rain to a great height. Two bridges were carried away; they formed with other *débris* a dam against a third, and caused the water to overflow the surrounding territory. Other bridges gave way, and a second dam was formed. The damage was very great.

The flood of July 14, 1837, was by far the most extensive calamity with which Baltimore had been afflicted up to that time. It was caused by heavy showers of rain filling the bed of Jones' falls to overflowing. About twenty lives were lost, many bridges and dams were carried away, and the damage to property was very great.

On the 15th of April, 1842, a beautiful steamboat called the "Medora", belonging to the Baltimore Steam Packet Company, started on a trial excursion down the bay. The wheel had made only two revolutions when the boiler exploded with terrible force. Of the 82 people on board 27 were killed and 40 wounded.

July 13, 1852, three bridges over Harford's run, in the northeastern section of the city, were carried away by a flood, six new houses were undermined and fell to the ground, and many other houses were damaged.

One of the most terrible railroad accidents that ever occurred in this country took place on the afternoon of the 4th of July, 1854, by which over 30 persons were killed and nearly 100 were wounded. Two trains returning over the Baltimore and Susquehanna railroad from probably the largest celebration ever held in the neighborhood of Baltimore collided, with the fatal result above indicated.

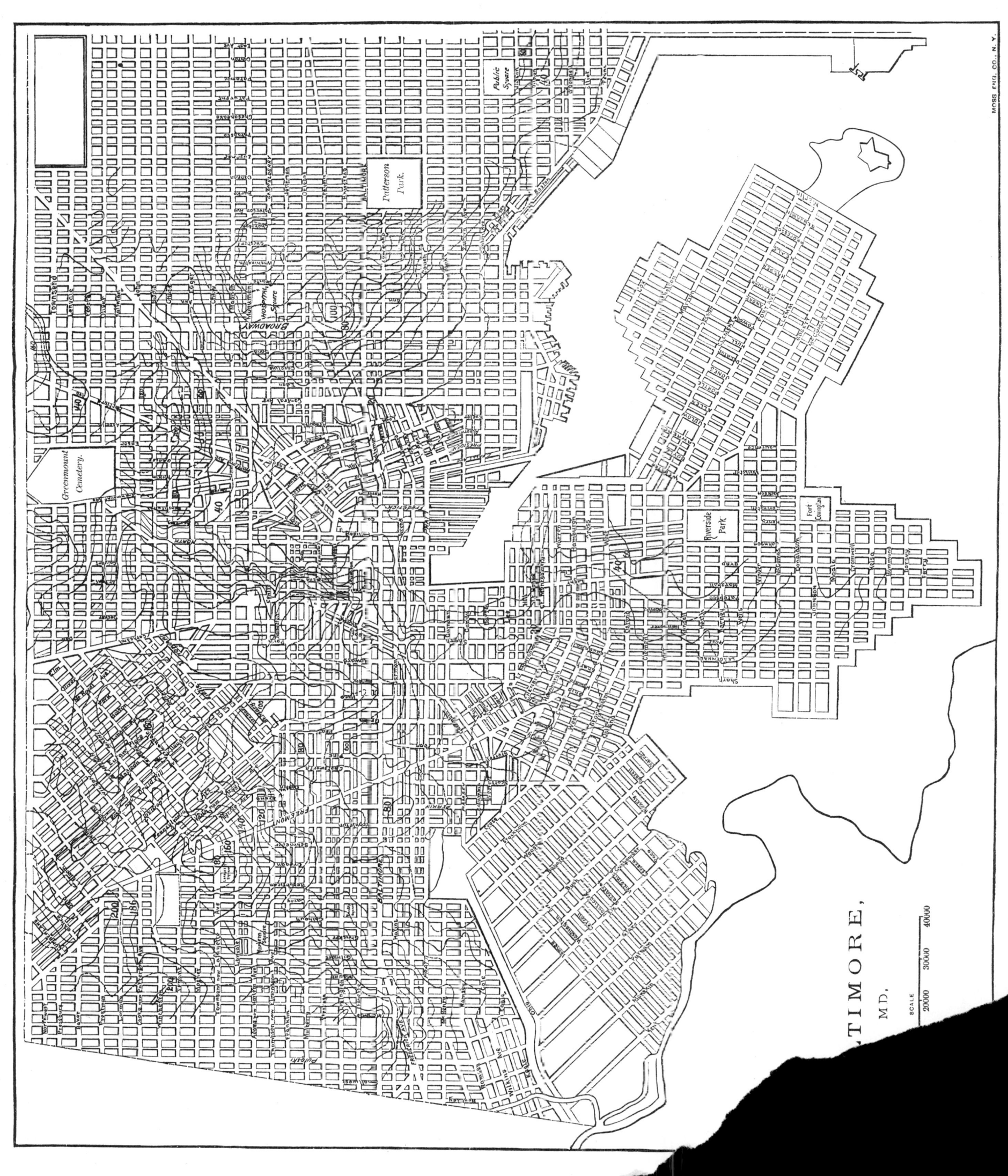

BALTIMORE,
MD.

SCALE

20000 30000 40000

Patterson Park.

Public Square

Riverside Park.

Fort McHenry

Greenmount Cemetery.

MOSS ENG. CO., N. Y.

A fire on the evening of the 14th of April, 1857, destroyed 7 or 8 large stores; 13 men were killed by the falling of a floor.

The city was visited on the afternoon of June 12, 1858, by a flood almost equal to that of 1837. The amount of property destroyed could not be estimated; one bridge was carried away.

July 16, 1868, was an exceedingly warm day in Baltimore, the thermometer ranging from 97 to 101 degrees in the shade, and 30 cases of sunstroke were reported, 21 of which proved fatal.

On the 24th of the same month a flood destroyed even more property than did the famous one of 1837. Had the rise occurred at night the loss of life could not but have been very great. Of the bridges over the falls 8 were swept away, and the 3 in the center of the city were all badly damaged.

On July 25, 1873, occurred the most extensive conflagration ever known in Baltimore. It threatened at one time to rival the previous disasters of Chicago and Boston. One hundred and thirteen buildings were destroyed, including 2 churches, 2 mills, 1 silk factory, and 3 school-houses. The loss amounted to about $750,000, and the insurance was about one-third that amount.

BALTIMORE IN 1880.

LOCATION.

Baltimore, the chief city of Maryland, lies in latitude 39° 17′ north, longitude 76° 37′ west from Greenwich, at the head of tide-water and navigation on the Patapsco river, about 14 miles from the Chesapeake bay, and 200 miles from the Atlantic ocean by ship-channel. The Patapsco to this point is a broad estuary; above, it is a small stream with a sufficient fall to furnish water-power to many mills and manufactories. The area of the city comprises $12\frac{1}{2}$ square miles of land and 2 of water. The site was originally very hilly, and, notwithstanding all the grading rendered necessary by improvements, much of the original inequality still exists. The elevations are from sea-level to 250 feet above; a point in Druid Hill park, just outside the corporate limits, rising 360 feet above the level of the sea. The surrounding country is of a character similar to that on which the city is built, and is intersected by many swift streams that afford ample facilities for surface-drainage.

The entrance to the harbor, between fort McHenry and Lazaretto Light-house point, is narrow, but inside the river widens out, while one arm of the Patapsco river stretches far into the business center and forms an inner harbor known as the "basin", used by passenger steamboats and coastwise and bay craft in large numbers. The channels leading to the harbor are kept at a depth of 25 feet, and from 200 to 300 feet wide. The deep water of the harbor, where the larger foreign and other vessels lie, is at Fell's point and Canton on the north side, and Locust point on the south side, above fort McHenry. The large manufactories and canning establishments are situated at Canton, while Locust point is the terminal tide-water outlet for the Baltimore and Ohio railroad, the large elevators and ocean-steamship piers being located here. Situated at the head-waters of the Chesapeake, and nearer to the navigable waters of the West than any other of the Atlantic cities, the advantages of Baltimore in this respect have long been understood; and now that the channel of the Patapsco has been so much improved that vessels of the same draught of water as those that visit New York can be brought alongside the elevators of the city, it is easily seen why it is that Baltimore is second only to New York in the exportation of grain to Europe.

RAILROAD COMMUNICATIONS.

The following railroad lines afford to Baltimore ample railroad communication with the country at large:

The Baltimore and Ohio railroad, one of the great trunk-lines, connects the city with Wheeling, Pittsburgh, Cincinnati, Chicago, and Saint Louis, and has also a line to Washington and Richmond.

The Northern Central railway, from Baltimore to Canandaigua, New York, and from there, by connections, to the ports on the great lakes.

The Baltimore and Potomac railroad, operated by the Pennsylvania railroad, to Washington, and from there to Quantico and Richmond.

The Philadelphia, Wilmington, and Baltimore railroad, between the points named, forms a link of the through line between Washington and New York.

The Western Maryland railroad to Frederick and Hagerstown, Maryland, and Martinsburg, Virginia, terminating at Williamsport on the Potomac.

By the expenditure of nearly $5,000,000, a system of underground communication has been constructed, by which all the above-named roads (except the Baltimore and Ohio, which has Locust point) are connected and brought to tide-water at Canton. The Baltimore and Potomac tunnel is, with the exception of the Hoosac tunnel, the largest on this side of the Atlantic. The western entrance is at Gilmor street, and the tunnel extends through the city in a northwesterly direction, passing under the bed of 29 streets, until it emerges at North avenue, the northern boundary of the city. The arch is built of five rings of brick, backed up with rubble masonry, and is 22 feet in height by 27 feet in width. The Union tunnel extends from Greenmount avenue on the west, under 13 streets, is built of brick, and is of the same interior dimensions as the Potomac tunnel. The aggregate length of these two tunnels is 10,379 feet.

TRIBUTARY COUNTRY.

It may be said that this is best described by referring to the termini of the roads branching in all directions from the city. In a more restricted sense, it may be confined to a circle whose radius is some 10 or 12 miles, embracing Ellicott City, Cockeysville, Towsontown, etc. To the northwest and north and northeast the country is extremely beautiful, thickly populated, and, where land is very valuable, commanding high prices, and where not occupied by villa residences and market gardens, highly cultivated as farm land. Less is to be said of the country lying to the southeast and southwest. To the southeast the Patapsco flows into the broad estuary of the Chesapeake. But in all directions, save to the south, the country tributary to Baltimore can not be better described than in the words used by Captain John Smith in 1606:

The country is not mountainous, nor yet low, but with pleasant hills and fertile valleys, one prettily crossing another, and watered so conveniently with fresh brooks and springs no less commodious and delightsome.

A distinguishing characteristic is the torrent-like nature of the streams which are to be found in this part of Maryland. The Patapsco itself is almost a mountain stream until it reaches tide, 7 miles from Baltimore. The well-known Jones' falls deserves its descriptive name. Gwynn's falls is another stream falling into the Patapsco near the city limits; and the name of Gunpowder falls is equally descriptive.

On all these streams there were formerly numerous mills and furnaces. A great many of them are still in operation, although in some instances the diminishing supply of water as the country is cleared of timber has made the use of steam necessary as an auxiliary.

Within the radius of 10 or 12 miles there have been found, from the earliest settlement of the country, inexhaustible supplies of iron ore of the purest quality, which even now supply iron-works in Baltimore. In going through the iron-ore districts east and west of Baltimore, are to be found the remains of furnaces built before the Revolution, and the spoil-banks of mines from which the ore that supplied them was excavated. This was at a time when the laws of England prohibited the refining of iron in the province, and required the pig-iron to be sent to the old country for the purpose. Indeed, so important was the iron product of this vicinage regarded, that there is an old law which permitted a party willing to build a furnace to obtain a writ of *ad quod damnum*, and to take the land he required at the valuation of a jury, without the owner's consent.

Nor is iron the only metal produced from the mines in the neighborhood. The copper mines of the Barehills, only 6 miles from the city, have long been known and worked; and the bichromate of potash is the product of the deposits of the chrome ore not much farther off.

CLIMATE.

From tables prepared by the Smithsonian Institution, and covering observations extending over a period of 36 years, the years of extreme heat were 1819, 1820, 1850, 1851, when the temperature was 98°, and the year of extreme cold was 1852, the mercury falling to —9°. The mean annual temperature during this period is given at 53.46°. From the same authority it is seen that the mean amount of precipitation in rain and melted snow is 42.87 inches per annum.

The variation of the compass at Baltimore since the year 1700 has been as follows:

Year.	Variation.	Year.	Variation.	Year.	Variation.
1700....	+5.4	1770....	1.46	1830....	1.23
1710...	5.0	1780....	1.04	1840....	1.70
1720....	4.5	1790....	+0.76	1850....	2.27
1730....	3.9	1800....	+0.64	1860....	2.90
1740....	3.2	1810....	0.68	1870....	3.55
1750....	2.6	1820....	0.88	1880....	+4.17
1760....	2.0				

STREETS.

The total length of streets is 290 miles. The following, regarding the streets of Baltimore, is taken from the annual message of the mayor for the year 1880:

Baltimore has long suffered from bad pavements; the antiquated and elsewhere almost obsolete cobble-stones are here a characteristic of our reverence for the relics of the past. The principal reason for laying cobble-stones in a new street is the indisposition of the adjacent property-owners, who are assessed for its paving, to incur the expense of an improved pavement. For the public good this policy should be changed, and I therefore recommend the passage of an ordinance requiring all new streets, when opened, to be paved with Belgian blocks or some other kind of improved pavement. * * * While the first cost of the Belgian blocks is larger, it will be found that its durability renders it more economical. Since 1874, 5,405,349 square feet of cobble-stones have been laid, and 86,628 square yards of Belgian blocks. Any kind of cobble-stone pavement is bad enough, but the system of laying it in Baltimore produces the very poorest of its kind. Most of it requires repairing within two years after it is laid. The fact that the adjacent property-holder pays his portion of the work, requires it to be contracted for to the lowest bidder, and in most cases the price paid is not sufficient to give good material or creditable work. If it was done by the city itself, or given out at fair prices, the cobble-stone pavement would be better, and therefore more economical.

The amount appropriated for repaving during the past year was $72,500. This was expended judiciously and economically in repairing, as far as practicable, the old cobble-stones and resetting or removing the old curbstones. The work was done by the city better and cheaper than when alone under contract, the amount for repairing during the year being equal to 2,709,605 square feet of paving and 27,640 linear feet of curbing, requiring 24,300 loads of sand and 5,930 perches of new stone. The difficulty about repairing the old pavements is the fact that many of the cobble-stones are completely worn out. I therefore suggest that in making the appropriations for repairs, authority be given to make them with Belgian blocks, by repaving with these blocks the center of the streets where travel is heaviest.

From the annual report of the city commissioners it appears that the total amount of paving done in the city, up to December 31, 1880, was 36,470,958 superficial feet.

HORSE-RAILROADS.

There are at this time four passenger railways using horse-power in the city:

The City Passenger railway, which unites the northern with the southern as well as the eastern with the western parts of the city, with collateral branches.

The Citizens' Passenger railway, which also connects the eastern and western sections of Baltimore.

The People's line, which connects the part of the city on Locust point with the western section.

The North Baltimore Passenger Railway line, which extends from the center of the city to its northwest portion, besides lines to Towsontown, Waverly, Catonsville, and suburban villages.

Other railways of this description, permeating the city in all directions, are projected, and are about being constructed under authority obtained already from the mayor and city council.

WATER-WORKS.

The water-supply of the city is governed by a board of six commissioners appointed biennially, who, with the mayor, receive no compensation. They have power to appoint and fix the compensation of a water engineer, a civil engineer, a water registrar, clerks, and collectors. The supply is derived from Jones' falls and the Gunpowder falls, the work connected with the latter being now (1880) on the eve of completion. The minimum supply from the former is 15,000,000 gallons per day, and from the latter 165,000,000, the two affording an aggregate daily supply of 190,000,000 gallons. The Gunpowder tunnel is capable of passing 170,000,000 gallons per diem. That of New York is limited to 100,000,000.

There are four reservoirs connected with Jones' falls supply, of 8½, 5, 53, and 4½ acres, respectively, storing in the aggregate 535,000,000 gallons; and two reservoirs connected with the Gunpowder supply, of 60 and 30 acres, respectively, with an aggregate storage of 765,000,000 gallons, making the entire storage supply 1,300,000,000 gallons.

The board is styled "the water-board of the city of Baltimore". The supply from the Gunpowder involved the construction of a tunnel 7 miles in length and 12 feet in diameter, the greater part of which is through rock, and the excellence of all the works appertaining to which have already become noted in the engineering world. It is the third largest tunnel in the world, being surpassed only by the Mont Cenis and the Saint Gothard tunnels.

The receipts for water-rents during the past year were $579,326 36, and the working expenses during the same period were $87,419 13. There are 278 miles of mains in the city, with 48,669 water-takers. There are 524 meters in use, and the registered consumption of water by them during 1880 was 629,680,175 gallons, the revenue from which amounted to $72,483 52. The charge for metered water has been 15 and 12 cents per 1,000 gallons, and this has been reduced to 8 cents per 1,000 gallons for the coming year (1880). The average consumption of water in the city is estimated at 45 gallons per day to each head of the population.

GAS.

The city is supplied with gas by three private corporations, but no statistics regarding them were furnished. The number of street-lamps in the city, exclusive of those in parks and squares, is 5,032 gas and 1,115 gasoline. The city pays $1 85 per 1,000 feet of gas used.

PUBLIC BUILDINGS.

Though there are many municipal buildings in Baltimore, as well as considerable property owned by the city and rented, no detailed account of them could be obtained. Among the principal public buildings may be mentioned the following:

The city hall, finished about four years ago, is built of white marble, and covers a block of land in the central part of the city. The area of the block within the building line is 35,000 square feet, and the total cost of the structure, including grounds and furniture, was $2,271,135, leaving an unexpended balance of $228,865 out of the $2,500,000 that was appropriated for the purpose. The building is 4 stories high, French roof, with iron dome reaching 260 feet above the pavement, and is used wholly for municipal purposes, all the departments of the city government being gathered here.

In addition to the above may be mentioned the Bay View asylum, a large brick building outside the corporate limits, with accommodations for 650 paupers; the house of refuge; the Spring Grove asylum, a state institution for the insane; the Maryland institute for the blind, and the United States custom-house. The Peabody institute, donated to the city by the late George Peabody, esq., who gave $1,000,000 for the purpose, is handsomely located near Washington monument, and is built of white marble. It has a free library of over 60,000 volumes, an art gallery, a musical conservatory, lecture-room, etc. The Johns Hopkins university, endowed by the late Johns Hopkins, esq., by a gift of over $3,000,000, can justly be classed with the public buildings of the city, and the Johns Hopkins hospital and the Johns Hopkins colored orphan asylum, also founded by the same gentleman, are handsome structures.

MONUMENTS.

Baltimore has earned her title of the "Monumental city" chiefly from the beautiful doric column to the "Father of his Country", which was erected between the years 1815 and 1830. The monument, which is called Washington monument, formerly stood alone in the midst of a handsome forest, but now it is in the center of the fashionable quarters of the city. It is of white marble, surmounted by a statue of Washington 16 feet high, the whole being 212 feet above the pavement and 280 feet above tide-water. A spiral staircase winds up inside the column, and visitors are allowed to ascend on the payment of a nominal sum. From the four sides of the square base of the monument grass plots radiate north, south, east, and west, and as there are many fine dwellings in the vicinity the architectural effect of the surroundings is striking.

Battle monument, erected by the city to the memory of her citizens who fell in the defense of Baltimore during the war with Great Britain, is near the center of the city, on Calvert street, not far from Baltimore street. The structure is 52 feet high, and is designed to be allegorical. The shaft surmounting the monumental base is in the form of fasces, to represent strength and union. Lachrymal urns indicate the purpose of the monument, and the names of those who lost their lives are inscribed on the entablature. The whole is crowned by a female figure representing the city of Baltimore, having a wreath of laurel in one hand uplifted.

Wells and McComas monument, on Ashland square, formed by the intersection of Monument, Aisquith, and Gay streets, is a simple marble obelisk on a square die-block and pedestal, the whole being about 30 feet high. It was erected as a tribute to the memory of two youths, Wells and McComas, who fell during the repulse of the British in the land attack at North Point, September 14, 1814. These two young men are said to have killed the English general, Ross, who led the attack.

Wildey monument, or the "Odd Fellows' memorial", was erected by the Odd Fellows to Thomas Wildey, a native of England, who is regarded as the founder of that order in the United States. It is a Grecian Doric column rising from a pedestal, the whole being 52 feet high, and is situated on Broadway, in the eastern part of the city.

The Poe monument, erected by the public schools of Baltimore to Edgar Allan Poe, is simply a pedestal or die-block, with an ornamental cap wholly of marble, resting on two marble slabs and a granite base. A medallion portrait of the poet is chiseled on the front of the die-block.

PUBLIC PARKS AND PLEASURE-GROUNDS.

The parks of Baltimore consist of *Druid Hill Park*, containing 693 acres; *Patterson Park*, of 56 acres; *Riverside Park*, 17¼ acres; *Federal Hill Park*, 8½ acres; and other smaller areas called squares, which are in charge of unpaid commissioners appointed from persons residing in the respective neighborhoods.

The first four parks are in charge of a board of four persons, also unpaid, of which the mayor is *ex officio* chairman. They hold their offices during good behavior, with power to fill vacancies occurring in their body, subject to the approval of the city councils. Their style is "The public park commissioners of the city of Baltimore".

The parks are supported by a tax of 12 per cent. on the gross earnings of the city passenger railways, from which there is deducted the interest on the bonds issued for the purchase of Druid Hill and Patterson parks. One-fifth of what remains is then invested as a sinking-fund to redeem the bonds at maturity, and the balance is expended by the park commissioners in the maintenance and improvements of the parks. They appoint an engineer and general superintendent, superintendents of the particular parks, a naturalist, a gardener, and generally the laboring force required. Riverside and Federal Hill parks are maintained by special appropriations from time to time, as necessary.

All of the above parks, as well as the public squares, are noted for their quiet beauty.

Druid Hill park, about 2½ miles from the center of the city, is a park in every sense of the word, having herds of deer ranging in thick green woods, and flocks of sheep feeding on the grassy hillsides. Art is not needed for embellishment, and the few structures required are generally well placed, and harmonize with the natural surroundings. The main approach from Madison avenue is a broad way, through a stone gateway, the carriage roads winding all over the park, and being 20 miles in length. Fine views are obtained at different points, not only over the city and the harbor beyond, but also over the surrounding country. One of the attractions in the park is a fountain in Druid lake (owned by the water-works) that sends a jet of water 100 feet into the air from a 5-inch nozzle. Park carriages are always in waiting at the Madison Avenue entrance, and visitors can be taken to any point they may desire at moderate charges. The park was originally 475 acres, and cost in 1858 $1,000 per acre.

Patterson park, in the eastern section of the city, is a great popular resort, owing to the fine view it affords of the river, harbor, and bay. Strictly speaking, the ground is not a park, there being but a few small trees, principally catalpas, that afford but little shade. Judicious gardening and engineering have given to the spot distinctive characteristics, and the work of improvement is steadily going on.

PLACES OF AMUSEMENT.

Baltimore is fairly well furnished with places of amusement, the principal theaters being as follows:
The Academy of Music, on North Howard street near Franklin street, with a seating capacity of 2,000.
Ford's Grand opera-house, on Fayette street near Eutaw street, seating 2,000.
Holliday Street theater, opposite the city hall, seating 1,500.
Front Street theater, on Front street near Gay street.
Concordia opera-house, on South Eutaw street near Baltimore street.
The Central theater, on Baltimore street near the bridge.
There are also many halls, art galleries, museums, etc., in various parts of the city, but no detailed information regarding them was furnished.

DRAINAGE.

So far as the question of drainage is concerned, Baltimore is mainly still in the condition of a small country town with paved streets.

Owing to the considerable and very general undulation of its surface, superficial drainage is easy, and, except in very dry seasons, tolerably efficient in removing the filth of the gutters. As the paved and covered area has extended, the accumulation of surface-water at various points has become so troublesome as to require the construction of a few main outlet sewers leading to the harbor, or to Jones' falls, which is the natural drainage outlet for most of the city. These sewers aggregate a length of 11⅔ miles. They have in all cases been built with an exclusive view to the removal of storm-water. In very many of the streets, where the flow of storm-water is considerable during heavy rains, high stepping-stones have long been in use, to enable foot-passengers to cross the flood from one side of the street to the other, these stones being so placed that the wheels of vehicles pass between them.

Practically, all excremental matter is delivered into cesspools and privy-vaults, of which it is estimated that about 80,000 are in use. Laundry waste, kitchen waste, and all foul liquids except urine are delivered across or under the sidewalk into the gutters at the sides of the streets, finding their way in the open air to the natural outlets or to recently constructed sewers leading to these.

In his report for 1880, Dr. McShane, assistant commissioner of health and general superintendent of streets, says:

Baltimore has no regular system of sewers, the present sewers of the city being constructed simply for the removal of storm-water. The outlet for the whole system is the river-front, which is in the direction of the prevailing winds; the outlets are usually partly submerged, consequently they are not self-cleansing, and are frequently obstructed, causing deposits which this department is compelled to remove. The sewers are imperfectly ventilated, and most of the ventilation is through the inlets and interiors of houses connected therewith. The sewers, with few exceptions, as at present ventilated, afford encouragement to the development of preventable diseases, and so long as they remain improperly trapped and ventilated a prejudice will exist against their construction, and will produce serious annoyance and detriment to health.

The Hon. F. C. Latrobe, mayor of the city, in his report for the same year says:

The city of Baltimore requires a system of sewerage. The continuance of the plan of digging the cesspools now honeycombing the surface of the ground upon which the city is built—there being on an average about one to each of its eighty thousand houses—must be discontinued if the health of the community is to be considered. To substitute a general system of sewerage is merely a question of time and expense. The modern plan of sewering cities now being adopted in Memphis, New Orleans, and elsewhere is that of using comparatively small pipes, not intended to carry off the storm-water, which in a great measure is left to flow over the surface of the streets. This, in my judgment, is what we require here. The cost will be large, and, should the city undertake the work, it can only be done by an enabling act of the legislature authorizing the creation of a loan for the purpose.

This suggestion of the mayor was adopted by the city council, and Charles H. Latrobe, esq., C. E., has been employed to investigate the whole subject, giving special consideration to the relative merits of different systems of sewerage, and instructed to prepare a plan for the complete sewerage of the city.

CEMETERIES.

It is to be regretted that a full report of the cemeteries of Baltimore can not be given here, but very little statistical information has been received on the subject, and therefore a bare enumeration of the principal ones only is available.

Greenmount Cemetery, on the York road, is the principal cemetery connected with the city, and in all parts of the ground may be seen the names of the noted dead of Baltimore. One of its distinguishing characteristics is a beautiful mound, from which it takes its name, that is crowned with an ornamental brownstone Gothic chapel. A fine diversity of hill and dale, valley and grove, affords a good basis for ornamentation, which has been utilized to the utmost.

Baltimore Cemetery, on an elevated situation at the northern boundary of the city, is reached by the Gay Street cars.

Mount Olivet Cemetery, situated 2 miles west of the city on the Frederick road, commands a fine view of the city and bay.

Western Cemetery, 1½ mile west of the city, on the banks of Gwynn's falls, is reached by way of West Baltimore street extended.

Loudon Park Cemetery, situated 3 miles from Baltimore, on the Catonsville road, is well wooded and handsomely laid out in drives, walks, etc. Here are interred the remains of the confederate soldiers, belonging to the city, who fell on distant battle-fields; while the remains of over 1,600 Union soldiers rest in another part of the same cemetery.

The New Catholic Cemetery (Bonny Brae), situated on the old Frederick road, is beautifully laid out.

MARKETS.

In the annual report of the inspector of buildings for the year 1880 the following public markets are mentioned:

Broadway market, on Broadway, between Lancaster street and Canton avenue.

Center market, from Baltimore to Pratt street, near Jones' falls.

Belair market, at the intersection of North Gay and Forest streets.

Lexington market, corner of Eutaw and Lexington streets.

Richmond market, at the junction of Eutaw and Richmond streets.

Hanover, Cross Street, and Hollins markets.

No statistics regarding these markets were furnished, but the register of the city shows that, during 1880, $45,000 was received from the market-rents.

SANITARY AUTHORITY—HEALTH DEPARTMENT.

"The health department of the city and port of Baltimore" is the full title of the chief sanitary organization of the city. It consists of a commissioner of health and registrar, and an assistant commissioner of health. In its employ are a resident physician at the Marine hospital, a secretary, a nuisance clerk, a permit clerk, and a clerk to the registrar; also a messenger, 6 sanitary inspectors, 5 superintendents of streets, 2 inspectors of sewers, and 2 superintendents of city public cemeteries. Ten vaccine physicians (one of whom is assigned for each two wards in the city) are appointed for the purpose of affording free (and compulsory) vaccination. The commissioner of health and assistant, both being physicians, are appointed annually by the mayor and confirmed by the city council, as are also the 5 superintendents of streets and the 10 vaccine physicians. All the rest of the force is appointed by the commissioner of health.

The scope of the department's work is large, embracing the removal of garbage, the cleaning of streets and sewers, the maintenance of the Marine hospital, etc. Its expenses for 1880 were, in total, $246,347 28. In case of an epidemic the city government is asked for an extra appropriation. In the absence of epidemics the board has authority to abate all nuisances, by order or by legal process, or, failing in this, at its own expense; and also has entire control of the street and garbage force and of the vaccine physicians, and indirect control over the quarantine department. During epidemics their power is practically unlimited.

The commissioner of health receives a salary of $2,500 per year. He has control of the department and is responsible for the sanitation of the city. He and his assistant are daily in attendance from 10 a. m. to 2 p. m. for the hearing of all matters complained of or reported by the sanitary inspectors, deciding vexed questions, looking after the registration department, etc. The employés of the department have not police powers.

Inspections of the city are made regularly, and as nuisances are reported. In the latter case an immediate inspection is made and reported, followed, if the report proves true, by a notice to the parties concerned to abate the same when necessary. This is followed by a later report of their abatement; or, otherwise, the parties are summoned before a city magistrate for the purpose of having them fined. In the case of defective public pumps, these are condemned and their use is discontinued; but the city water is not under the department's control. The department inspects, and corrects as in other matters, defective house-drainage, privy-vaults, cesspools, street-cleaning, etc. Defective sewerage is reached and corrected only so far as the removal of filth and deposits of sewers is concerned; the repair of sewers is under the control of the city commissioner's department. As above indicated, the department assumes the removal of the entire garbage of the city.

Small-pox patients are given the option of going to the pest hospital, distant 4 miles on the other side of the Patapsco river from the city, or, if they do not, of having a yellow warning-flag placed upon the house. Scarlet-fever patients are not isolated in any way.

An accurate register of births and deaths is kept by the commissioner of health, through the secretary. Physicians, or attendants, or coroners are required to furnish to the undertaker within forty-eight hours a full statement of the cause of death. No sexton may allow a dead body to be interred without first procuring such certificate, or, if from any cause this can not be procured, a certificate of death from the commissioner of health.

Every sexton or other person having charge of any vault, burying-ground, or cemetery within the city of Baltimore, and every undertaker or other person who shall remove any dead body, which had not been buried, from or out of the said city, shall return the certificate of death to the board of health before 12 o'clock m. on the Saturday next succeeding the date of burial or removal of the body out of the city.

For the proper registration of births, every person practicing midwifery shall keep a register of all births, with their details, occurring under their care. These are to be returned monthly on a blank schedule furnished for the purpose to the commissioner of health, between the first and third days of the month. Failure to report is punishable by a fine of $10. From the returns of deaths and the causes thereof a weekly mortuary report is made up and published in leaflet form by the department. To this is added a table of meteorological observations taken during the same week at the United States signal office. In the annual report of the health department to the mayor and city council these weekly mortuary tables are consolidated into a yearly table. The commissioner of health, James A. Steuart, M. D., in his annual report for 1880 says:

It is with no small pride that I call the attention of your honorable body to the department of vital statistics which was inaugurated in the year 1875, and is now brought to the highest perfection under the laborious and faithful conduct of Mr. A. R. Carter, secretary of the board of health, and of Mr. F. W. Raborg, recording clerk. The promptness and accuracy with which the weekly mortuary records are made up is, I may justly say, in advance of any other of the sixty odd cities with which we now correspond.

The returns of births by physicians and midwives have, during the past year, greatly improved, as shown by the increased number reported under that head in this report. The undoubtedly increasing population of Baltimore is thus demonstrable, and is a source of profound gratification to the board, as I am sure it must be to the public.

The vaccine physicians have done a fair amount of work during the year, and deserve especial praise for the energy displayed during the excitement of last spring. With the exception of the 14 or 15 cases which occurred at that period, our city has been free from small-pox for a number of years. Exemption from this disease can only be insured by attention to vaccination.

In addition to its regular annual reports, the department reports informally from time to time to the mayor and city council.

MUNICIPAL CLEANSING.

Street-cleaning, and removal of ashes and garbage.—This work is performed under the direction of the assistant health commissioner, who is the general superintendent of streets. The streets are cleaned by the regular force, hired for the purpose, and the work is done wholly by hand, no sweeping-machines being used. There is no stated time for the cleaning, the work going on constantly, the object being to keep the streets in good condition. The city is divided into districts, and a superintendent is appointed in each, who is under the direction of the general superintendent, and is required to keep his district clean. The men go through all the streets and alleys of the city scraping and sweeping the dirt into piles, when it is removed by teams. Garbage—which means kitchen-offal—and coal and other ashes, are removed daily (Sundays excepted) from May 1 to November 1, and three times a week, on alternate days, during the remainder of the year. Householders are required to have their garbage placed in vessels not exceeding in capacity one bushel each (kitchen-offal and ashes not being allowed in the same vessel), and to be placed near their premises, or in some convenient place of access. The garbage-carts have a capacity of at least 40 cubic feet, are strongly built, and, when loaded, are required to be covered. The driver of each cart carries a horn, which is sounded at intervals as a warning to householders to have their garbage ready. The final disposal of both street-sweepings and garbage is the same, viz, such of it as is salable is sold (this includes all the offal, etc.), while the remainder is used in filling low lots to grade. The following, from the report of the general superintendent of streets, will show the number of loads removed, cost of the service, etc., during the year 1880:

Number of loads of garbage and ashes removed	145,485
Number of loads of street-dirt, ice, sand, snow, etc., removed	162,092
Total number of loads of all kinds removed	307,577
Cost of removal of garbage and ashes	$87,355 50
Cost of removal of street-dirt, etc	86,852 85
Cost of dumps	3,471 00
Cost of tools and incidentals	2,100 06
Total cost	179,779 41
Amount of annual appropriation for street and garbage department	178,500 00
Deficiency	1,279 41

Average cost per load, 58½ cents.

Dr. James F. McShane, general superintendent, further says in his report, regarding the efficiency of the service:

Every endeavor has been made to keep the city in a cleanly condition, but the annual appropriation for this purpose is insufficient; consequently the work of scavengering has not approached the standard desired. * * * There is no more important service performed

by this department than the cleaning of streets and the removal of garbage and ashes. The immense
within the limits of the city makes it a deficient service in consequence of the insufficient force emp
compelled to carry the refuse; yet notwithstanding these drawbacks, there is a satisfaction i
performed has been generally commended.

Dead animals.—The carcass of any animal dying within the
once removed to the bone-dust factories by the regula
salaries and $500 for expenses, but no account
the system works satisfactorily, there h

Liquid household wastes
chamber-slops are dep
kitchen-slops
with

SOCIAL STATISTICS OF CITIES.

The number of alarms during the past twelve months was 343, of which 205 were telegraph alarms and 138
were extinguished without a telegraphic alarm. There were 8 second alarms and 7 general alarms. The losses
amounted to $580,290 43, of which amount $320,547 09 was caused by 2 fires, and $158,193 was caused by fires in
Baltimore county, outside the city limits.

In connection with the fire department there a salvage corps and a fire-alarm telegraph.

COMMERCE AND NAVIGATION.

[From the reports of the Bureau of Statistics for the fiscal years ending June 30.]

Customs district of Baltimore, Maryland.	1879.	1880.
Total value of imports	$14,042,768	$19,956,989
Total value of exports:		
Domestic	$57,478,495	$76,220,870
Foreign	$84,027	$32,696
Total number of immigrants	4,713	17,394

Customs district of Baltimore, Maryland.	1879.		1880.	
	Number.	Tons.	Number.	Tons.
Vessels in foreign trade:			1,794	1,502,713
			1,770	1,491,060
Entered	1,778	1,374,554		
Cleared	1,728	1,345,747	1,455	1,021,887
Vessels in coast trade and fisheries:			2,143	1,505,733
Entered	1,463	997,923	1,013	102,139
Cleared	1,871	1,269,074	24	445
Vessels registered, enrolled, and licensed in district.	1,006	100,008		
Vessels built during the year	24	1,977		

MANUFACTURES.

The following is a summary of the statistics of the manufactures of Baltimore for 1880, being taken from table
prepared for the Tenth Census by N. H. Creager, chief special agent:

Mechanical and manufacturing industries.	No. of establishments.	Capital.	AVERAGE NUMBER OF HANDS EMPLOYED.			Total amount paid in wages during the year.	Value of materials.	V pr
			Males above 16 years.	Females above 15 years.	Children and youths.			
All industries	3,683	$38,586,773	34,086	18,137	4,115	$15,117,489	$47,974,297	
Agricultural implements		106,000	118	30	15	49,250	101,0
Awnings and tents	5	4,600	11	22	4	7,900	16,
Bags, paper	3	78,500	24	14		17,704	159
Baking and yeast powders (see also Drugs and chemicals)	3	70,600	12		2	16,000	1
Baskets, rattan and willow ware	4	5,110	16		6	5,168	
Blacksmithing (see also Wheelwrighting)	16		270	83	25	123,894	
Bookbinding and blank-book making		127,520	99	18	1	61,593	
Boot and shoe uppers		91,756	27	507	70	11,755	
Boots and shoes, including custom work and repairing	116	7,700	2,117	19	9	939,861	32,0
Boxes, cigar	17	865,337	22			15,163	147,
Boxes, fancy and paper	11	19,325		169	10		16
Boxes, wooden packing	623		28		44		2
Brass castings	13	34,020	318		1		
Bread and other bakery products		139,012	32	73	58		
Brick and tile	8	19,500	625		69		
Brooms and brushes	13	832,372	1,460	22	32		
Carpentering	10	640,000			9		
Carpets, rag	316		210		4		
Carriages and sleds, children's	28		1,226	2	3		
Carriages and wagons (see also Wheelwrighting)		83,115	28	2	8		
Clothing, men's	28	1,107,800	31				
Clothing, women's	114	23,525	364				
Coffee and spices, roasted and ground	17	15,600		5,915			
Coffins, burial cases, and undertakers' goods	3	223,700		482			
Confectionery	37		5,184	22	23		
		3,848,851		46			
	188	136,250		73	87		
	27	124,750		222			
	13	91,275					
	52	339,765					
	53						

by this department than the cleaning of streets and the removal of garbage and ashes.

two
the c
wards,
power

Wh
taxation,

No del
mayor and
and city coun
in granting an
or credit be au
submitted to tl
majority of the
deficiency in the
safety and sanitar
whole or in part, o

Except whe
subordinate office

The collector
taxes of every desc
He gives bond in th
the state taxes colle
for the performance o

In this connection
with a clerk at a sala
assess the property of al
or deductions in assessn
permits for the erection o

Mechanical and manufacturing industries.	No. of establishments.	Capital.	AVERAGE NUMBER OF HANDS EMPLOYED.			Total amount paid in wages during the year.	Value of materials.	Value of products.
			Males above 16 years.	Females above 15 years.	Children and youths.			
Cooperage	43	$220,860	364	....	7	$146,382	$325,432	$560,696
Coppersmithing (see also Tinware, copperware, and sheet-iron ware)	8	20,200	21	....	....	11,900	15,600	32,250
Cotton goods (see also Mixed textiles)	3	699,000	209	225	103	80,738	182,283	327,366
Cutlery and edge tools (see also Hardware)	10	22,550	23	....	1	9,200	11,156	30,596
Dentistry, mechanical	14	12,260	11	1	1	6,323	4,313	32,788
Drugs and chemicals (see also Baking and yeast powders; Patent medicines and compounds).	17	652,300	189	47	....	78,144	529,485	873,125
Dyeing and cleaning	26	40,785	31	19	....	19,031	11,060	58,662
Electroplating	5	17,525	29	....	2	10,166	7,350	36,600
Engraving and die-sinking	7	1,925	6	....	....	3,300	1,450	14,059
Engraving, wood	4	1,250	4	....	....	1,800	905	6,900
Fertilizers	18	3,241,370	655	....	6	254,055	2,689,223	4,287,398
Files (see also Saws)	4	31,850	26	....	16	15,206	9,850	31,330
Flavoring extracts	5	8,200	15	4	....	5,274	16,360	31,100
Flouring- and grist-mill products	8	562,000	95	....	....	46,118	1,173,988	1,327,584
Food preparations	3	4,650	12	2	1	2,415	16,000	26,000
Foundery and machine-shop products	63	2,240,004	2,643	....	33	1,333,841	1,887,421	3,939,717
Fruits and vegetables, canned and preserved	41	1,959,100	2,324	6,753	1,846	815,013	3,854,550	5,201,268
Furniture (see also Mattresses and spring beds; Upholstering)	63	721,552	941	15	22	401,065	772,233	1,512,634
Furniture, chairs	3	150,250	64	30	2	47,200	130,200	278,500
Furs, dressed	4	30,000	6	17	....	8,125	10,635	33,913
Gas machines and meters	5	62,000	82	1	17	42,748	118,250	206,620
Glass	7	406,000	524	....	88	234,254	239,682	587,000
Gold and silver leaf and foil	3	6,000	16	29	2	10,500	26,000	49,200
Grease and tallow	6	101,500	22	....	....	10,254	213,449	258,021
Hairwork	11	12,250	4	29	....	5,654	16,575	34,298
Hardware (see also Cutlery and edge tools)	5	18,100	31	....	4	13,844	14,100	37,504
Hats and caps, not including wool hats	6	26,900	22	33	....	13,415	33,000	63,380
Instruments, professional and scientific	6	49,000	25	2	4	18,244	3,850	31,600
Iron and steel	10	1,632,125	1,343	....	65	532,579	1,303,209	2,672,940
Iron railing, wrought	6	5,900	19	....	....	8,200	13,000	32,800
Jewelry	4	11,300	16	1	3	9,744	12,860	33,100
Kindling wood	11	36,925	42	....	22	18,256	36,245	72,296
Leather, curried	18	115,017	74	....	2	29,117	310,527	405,317
Leather, tanned	17	134,768	93	9	4	39,379	266,654	287,980
Liquors, malt	21	1,143,490	203	....	....	97,851	488,752	888,644
Lock- and gun-smithing	20	28,100	35	....	1	15,932	12,143	42,286
Looking-glass and picture-frames	31	118,550	271	70	25	98,653	167,492	402,423
Lumber, planed (see also Sash, doors, and blinds; Wood, turned and carved).	3	36,000	20	....	....	15,500	33,000	60,700
Malt	6	705,000	58	....	....	52,060	547,000	752,000
Mantels, slate, marble, and marbleized	3	23,000	13	....	2	8,388	10,784	30,205
Marble and stone work	40	651,701	815	....	10	323,480	447,030	954,285
Masonry, brick and stone	47	203,600	655	....	1	266,889	399,777	767,946
Mattresses and spring beds (see also Furniture)	5	6,825	10	2	....	4,442	32,443	44,125
Millinery and lace goods	11	79,100	24	133	41	35,896	148,240	229,460
Millstones	3	34,700	24	....	....	11,293	14,242	38,319
Mineral and soda waters	17	66,900	84	....	....	33,753	108,035	199,607
Mixed textiles (see also Cotton goods; Silk and silk goods)	3	4,900	6	11	5	4,000	7,850	20,240
Models and patterns	3	1,450	5	....	....	2,050	1,700	8,100
Musical instruments and materials (not specified)	6	4,900	4	....	....	2,395	1,975	7,400
Musical instruments, organs and materials	3	16,250	21	....	2	8,000	24,810	41,000
Musical instruments, pianos and materials	4	638,382	380	....	5	200,988	157,699	534,099
Painting and paperhanging	89	99,505	265	....	3	144,861	168,898	453,943
Paints	10	367,200	93	....	7	39,941	192,185	338,658
Patent medicines and compounds (see also Drugs and chemicals)	33	222,650	103	109	45	68,467	438,027	646,493
Perfumery and cosmetics	5	23,410	11	27	1	7,902	15,251	42,409
Photographing	25	70,150	51	15	2	25,005	22,426	95,228
Pickles, preserves, and sauces	6	21,850	7	14	6	5,532	48,250	71,300
Plated and britannia ware	3	29,200	43	....	....	20,780	18,500	52,000
Plumbing and gasfitting	89	198,185	194	....	9	82,042	176,186	412,886
Printing and publishing	47	1,954,200	671	21	99	409,251	560,657	1,374,168

Mechanical and manufacturing industries.	No. of establishments.	Capital.	AVERAGE NUMBER OF HANDS EMPLOYED.			Total amount paid in wages during the year.	Value of materials.	Value of products.
			Males above 16 years.	Females above 15 years.	Children and youths.			
Pumps, not including steam-pumps	9	$8,475	16	....	1	$8,460	$14,550	$39,050
Refrigerators	3	16,200	24	....	....	7,099	13,040	27,990
Roofing and roofing materials	6	89,625	46	....	1	16,769	30,450	78,917
Saddlery and harness	76	304,625	461	2	81	223,187	388,092	857,810
Sash, doors, and blinds (see also Lumber, planed; Wood, turned and carved).	9	354,525	359	....	34	190,111	334,113	681,755
Saws	3	6,500	8	....	....	2,321	2,744	10,281
Scales and balances	3	9,200	7	....	....	4,181	2,819	11,077
Sewing-machines and attachments	6	20,500	22	1	2	11,620	9,450	35,595
Shipbuilding	62	1,493,275	887	....	....	524,873	707,026	1,445,080
Shirts	33	313,930	328	1,284	84	307,867	425,947	949,524
Show-cases	5	14,300	38	....	1	15,785	27,389	74,320
Silk and silk goods (see also Mixed textiles)	4	20,900	12	56	14	11,000	15,760	35,415
Silversmithing	4	98,703	38	....	....	26,979	49,542	112,061
Slaughtering and meat-packing, not including retail butchering	6	705,000	194	....	....	85,300	2,559,662	2,742,645
Soap and candles	7	250,432	77	....	6	43,145	215,238	323,350
Stencils and brands	3	2,800	6	....	1	3,526	2,200	9,500
Stone- and earthen-ware	6	125,700	194	10	62	115,004	74,923	254,594
Straw goods	3	160,800	107	422	15	57,761	264,507	362,982
Sugar and molasses, refined	3	260,000	106	....	....	31,000	756,703	840,986
Surgical appliances	3	5,700	35	5	....	17,000	15,600	61,500
Tinware, copperware, and sheet-iron ware (see also Coppersmithing)	154	1,071,360	1,231	124	298	569,642	2,250,500	3,371,081
Tobacco, chewing, smoking, and snuff (see also Tobacco, cigars and cigarettes).	10	602,600	187	740	128	165,107	1,152,906	1,531,424
Tobacco, cigars and cigarettes (see also Tobacco, chewing, smoking, and snuff).	329	568,282	1,050	115	84	462,099	617,585	1,551,014
Trunks and valises	15	24,150	51	....	4	19,228	36,810	75,463
Umbrellas and canes	3	8,550	4	6	....	2,080	8,500	17,400
Upholstering (see also Furniture)	19	22,725	42	7	2	16,820	51,781	98,539
Vinegar	8	47,750	17	1	1	7,012	58,112	87,012
Watch and clock repairing	23	18,500	25	....	4	14,883	6,454	41,115
Wheelwrighting (see also Blacksmithing; Carriages and wagons)	44	77,445	148	....	3	54,057	54,013	166,525
Whips	3	21,300	31	6	1	13,936	25,800	52,925
Window blinds and shades	3	5,500	24	....	....	3,200	11,500	18,900
Wirework	4	33,500	42	....	2	24,000	26,000	77,000
Wood, turned and carved (see also Lumber, planed; Sash, doors, and blinds).	8	2,660	17	....	4	8,203	9,020	26,436
All other industries (a)	81	2,790,664	1,564	271	293	766,948	4,945,900	6,655,810

a Embracing artificial limbs; babbitt metal and solder; bags, other than paper; bells; belting and hose, leather; billiard tables and materials; blacking; bluing; bridges; carpets, other than rag; carriage and wagon materials; cars, railroad, street, and repairs; cleansing and polishing preparations; cloth-finishing; cork cutting; cordage and twine; corsets; explosives and fireworks; fancy articles; fire extinguishers, chemical; flags and banners; furnishing goods, men's; glass, cut, stained, and ornamented; hand-knit goods; hosiery and knit goods; iron bolts, nuts, washers, and rivets; iron forgings; iron nails and spikes, cut and wrought; iron work, architectural and ornamental; ivory and bone work; japanning; kaolin and ground earths; lamps and reflectors; lard, refined; lasts; lead, bar, pipe, sheet, and shot; leather, dressed skins; lightning rods; lime; liquors, distilled; lithographing; lumber, sawed; oil, illuminating, not including petroleum refining; oil, lard; oleomargarine; pipes, tobacco; printing materials; regalia and society banners and emblems; rubber and elastic goods; safes, doors, and vaults, fire-proof; shoddy; spectacles and eyeglasses; sporting goods; stationery goods; telegraph and telephone apparatus; toys and games; type founding; upholstering materials; and wooden ware.

From the foregoing table it appears that the average capital of all establishments is $10,477; that the average wages of all hands employed is $268 34 per annum; that the average outlay in wages, in materials, and in interest (at 6 per cent.) on capital employed is $17,759 16.

DISTRICT OF COLUMBIA.

NOTE.—In June, 1878, Congress passed a law (which went into effect July 1, 1878) establishing a form of government for all of that territory which had been ceded by the state of Maryland to the national government as a permanent capital, and designated the same as the "DISTRICT OF COLUMBIA". This act says: "The District of Columbia shall remain and continue a municipal corporation; * * * all laws * * * not inconsistent with the provisions of this act shall remain in full force and effect." Existing corporate names are not now recognized in official acts. By strictly following out this law (so far as this report is concerned), there would be no city of Washington shown in the social statistics of the Tenth Census, and the capital of the country would figure under the name of the "District of Columbia". As Washington and Georgetown are, in any case, physical and social facts, it is deemed better to indicate by the accompanying map the condition of the whole District of Columbia, and to describe Washington and Georgetown separately.

G. E. W., JR.

WASHINGTON,
DISTRICT OF COLUMBIA.

POPULATION
IN THE
AGGREGATE,
1800-1880.

	Inhab.
1790	......
1800	3,210
1810	8,208
1820	13,247
1830	18,826
1840	23,364
1850	40,001
1860	61,122
1870	109,199
1880	147,293

POPULATION
BY
SEX, NATIVITY, AND RACE,
AT
CENSUS OF 1880.

Male	68,310
Female	78,983
Native	133,051
Foreign-born	14,242
White	98,895
Colored	*48,398

* Including 13 Chinese, 3 Japanese, and 5 Indians.

Latitude: 38° 53′ North; Longitude: 77° 2′ (west from Greenwich); Altitude: 0 to 103.7 feet. (a)

FINANCIAL CONDITION:
[Embracing the entire District of Columbia.]

Total Valuation: $99,401,787; per capita: $560 00.   Net Indebtedness: $22,675,459; per capita: $127 66.   Tax per $100: $1 48.

HISTORICAL SKETCH. (b)

The early history of the region now covered by the District of Columbia is extremely meager. It was visited in 1608 by Captain John Smith, who, as usual, left a narrative of his adventures. There seemed to be at that time a large aboriginal population, the seat of whose council-fire was on the point of land now occupied by the Arsenal, at the confluence of the Potomac and Anacostia rivers.

---

a Above ordinary low water in the Potomac river.
b Minor incidents of the history may be found in Keim's *Illustrated Hand-Book of Washington and its Environs*, and in the article on "Washington City", by A. R. Spofford, esq., in Johnson's *Cyclopedia*.

The country was early visited by Calvert's settlers, and in 1663 tracts were assigned to Robert Troop, Francis Pope, and William Langworth.

At the time of the selection of this site for the federal city the lands were owned mainly by Daniel Carroll, Notley Young, and David Burns. The residence of the latter is still standing on the Van Ness estate, south of the executive grounds. There were several small settlements along the Potomac and the Anacostia, but the whole region was a purely agricultural one.

After the cessation of hostilities between the colonies and the mother country, the subject of a permanent capital was discussed in Congress. New York and Maryland at once offered to cede sites for the purpose. In October, 1783, a vote was taken, in which New Jersey and Maryland received the highest number of votes; but the assignment of the capital was not yet secured. The next day, on motion of Elbridge Gerry, the federal city was located on or near the falls of the Delaware, near Trenton, and a committee was appointed to examine the locality and report upon it. Later in the same month the erection of buildings was authorized at or near the lower falls of the Potomac or Georgetown, and a committee was appointed to examine and report on that site. Two sites were now provided. Meanwhile Congress was to meet alternately at Trenton and Annapolis.

The Delaware committee reported favorably; the Potomac committee reported unfavorably, though they thought better of a site above Georgetown.

The Constitution had given Congress power "to exercise exclusive legislation, in all cases whatsoever, over such district (not exceeding ten miles square) as may by cession of particular states, and the acceptance of Congress, become the seat of the government of the United States".

During the first session of Congress assembled under the Constitution, the question of locating the federal city came up as one of great interest, and with it arose a sectional spirit which had never before been so strongly exhibited. The resolutions of the legislatures of states, petitions, and memorials urged each its own locality, and frequently offered great inducements. Petitions came from the people of Trenton, New Jersey; from Philadelphia, Lancaster, York, Carlisle, Harrisburg, Reading, and Germantown, Pennsylvania, and from Baltimore and Georgetown, Maryland.

At its next session the question of the location of the capital was again agitated, and the above-named and other localities were urged. Finally an act was passed, approved by President Washington July 16, 1790, establishing the temporary capital in Philadelphia from the first Monday in September, 1790, and the permanent site on the Potomac, to be made ready for the session of Congress by the first Monday in December, 1800. The vote in the Senate was, yeas 14, nays 12; and in the House, yeas 32, nays 29. In 1791 commissioners were appointed to superintend the affairs of the new city, and the President issued a proclamation directing them to establish four experimental boundary-lines as follows:

"Beginning at Jones' point, being the upper cape of Hunting creek, in Virginia, and at an angle in the outset of 45° west of the north, and moving in a direct line ten miles for the first line; then beginning again at the same Jones' point, and running another direct line at a right angle with the first, across the Potomac, ten miles for the second line; then from the terminations of the said first and second lines, running two other direct lines, of ten miles each, the one crossing the Potomac, and the other the eastern branch aforesaid, and meeting each other in a point." These lines were approved by Congress. By the act of Congress above referred to, the public buildings were required to be erected on the Maryland side of the Potomac.

Under the personal direction of President Washington, the three commissioners, with Andrew Ellicott and Major Peter Charles L'Enfant, made arrangements for laying out the site of the city. Some obstacles arose from the unwillingness of some of the proprietors to make reasonable concessions. The counsel of Washington had its effect, and the general terms were accepted by the principal proprietors. The President issued a proclamation defining the limits of the federal district, and directed the commissioners to have the lines permanently marked. The commissioners held their first regular meeting at Georgetown on the 12th of April. On the 13th they received information from President Washington, who had gone to Richmond to consult with Governor Randolph respecting the payment of $120,000 appropriated by Virginia toward the building of the capitol, that the money could be advanced at earlier periods than had been agreed. On the 15th the initial corner-stone of the lines of the federal territory was planted, and on June 29 the final settlement was effected by which the lands ceded to the government were conveyed to trustees for the United States. The streets, public squares, and certain parcels and lots were to be laid out and conveyed by the trustees to the United States. These were charged with the subdivision and sale of other lands. Owing to some disagreement, the streets and reservations were never formally conveyed to the commissioners. The title of the United States, however, has been confirmed by the Supreme Court.

The state of Maryland, December 19, 1791, ratified the cession of its portion of the federal territory, and defined certain powers and duties of the commissioners as to taking possession of lands in different parts of the district under an agreement with the proprietors.

The city was laid out according to plans made by Major L'Enfant, based on the plan of the city of Versailles, France. This was substantially a plan for a regular network of rectangular streets, traversed diagonally by broad avenues intersecting the streets obliquely, and giving occasion for many square, circular, and triangular reservations. The plan was carried out under the direction of Andrew Ellicott, who later laid out the city of Buffalo on a somewhat similar plan.

The central lines of the streets, both north and south and east and west, pass through the center of the capitol. They are placed according to the true meridian.

The system of street enumeration is simple and useful rather than artistic. The streets leading directly from the capitol are called North Capitol, East Capitol, and South Capitol streets. The north and south streets are numbered, the first street east being next east of North and South Capitol streets, and the first street west being the next street west of North and South Capitol streets.

The streets north and south of the capitol are indicated by letters, as North B, North C, North (or South) D, etc.

The houses in the blocks are numbered with reference to the street nomenclature. Thus, 1015 K street northwest is west of Tenth street, in K street, in the district northwest of the capitol; and 710 Fifth street northeast is in Fifth street between G and H streets in the district northeast of the capitol. A corresponding system of house-numbering applies also to the diagonal avenues.

These diagonal avenues are very wide—generally each 160 feet. They constitute the real thoroughfares and landmarks of the city. On them, or near them, are located most of the finer public and private buildings, and the more finished municipal decoration and ornamentation are generally to be found at their points of intersection, where are circular, triangular, or rectangular parks.

We who see Washington in its relatively finished condition to-day can have little idea of its appearance during the early years of its establishment. We have hardly yet forgotten the title given to it in derision, "the city of magnificent distances"

The city was subjected very early to the speculative fever which sooner or later takes all promising settlements, and more than one fortune was sunk in an attempt to take advantage of the promise held out by the future capital of the republic. One of the most undaunted of the early undertakers arranged for the erection of a great hotel on funds to be raised by a lottery, the hotel being the first prize. When partly erected it was drawn by a person who had not the means to complete it. It remained unfinished until, years after, it was taken by the government for public use.

The failure of some of these speculations, such as that of Robert Morris, James Greenleaf, and John Nicholson to take 6,000 lots at $80 a lot, and to pay for them in seven annual installments, erecting annually twenty 2-story brick houses, caused serious financial embarrassments to the commissioners. They were authorized in 1796 to borrow $300,000, but they were not successful in negotiating the loan in Europe, where the first effort was made. The assembly of Maryland came to their relief with a loan of $100,000. In 1799 Congress voted them another $100,000, which was advanced by Maryland. The next year they obtained $50,000 from the same source, but on the personal security of the commissioners. In February, 1800, they secured all loans and advances from the state of Maryland and from the national government to the amount of $300,000, leaving only the last $50,000 to be provided for.

At this time, the spring of the year 1800, the north wing of the capitol, begun in 1797, the President's house, and the War and Treasury offices were ready for occupation. A number of dwellings had been erected by private owners near the capitol, near the President's house, and on Greenleaf's point.

It has been stated by several writers that the reason why the city has extended itself so generally to the westward, in spite of the building of the capitol with its front to the east, is that speculators, anticipating a quick demand for land in that high and attractive part of the city, placed the price of their lots even as high as $1 per foot, while land could be bought elsewhere for from 10 to 25 cents per foot. Doubtless this had its influence; but the experience of most other cities, here and in Europe, seems almost to establish a law of municipal growth which leads the best of its population to occupy the western quarters. Whatever the motive, it is clear that the finest and most "fashionable" part of the city is its western part. Other influences, doubtless, in this case tended in the same direction. In early days the best accommodation for members of Congress was found in Georgetown. Later, the establishment of the War and Navy departments near the President's house induced officers of the permanent staff to build in that portion of the city. Whatever the general rule, or whatever the special influence operating in this particular instance, it is very clear that, while there are many fine residences and many prominent residents on Capitol hill, a wide stretch of respectable but unfashionable territory separates them from those whose building-lots are worth the highest price per foot—perhaps, after all, the best index of what is and what is not most fashionable.

During all the early part of the century the great plateau stretching from the capitol to the President's grounds was an exceedingly unpromising, unreclaimed swamp. We are told by one historian that "among the earliest improvements was the ditching of Pennsylvania avenue, the thoroughfare between the capitol and the President's house, and the planting of the reservations around these two buildings". The wife of President John Adams, the first occupant of the President's house, describes the rude and uncomfortable condition of the city when Congress first came to sit there. Before the public offices were removed from Philadelphia the population of the capital was hardly more than 500. John Cotton Smith, M. C., wrote: "The Pennsylvania avenue was then nearly the whole distance a deep morass covered with alder-bushes."

Washington was simply a backwoods town in the wilderness. Members of Congress lodged 3 miles away in Georgetown.

In 1839 George Combe wrote: "The town looks like a large straggling village reared in a drained swamp."

It was not until the middle of the century that any attempt was made to carry out the scheme projected by L'Enfant sixty years before. In 1851 Downing, the landscape-gardener, was employed by President Fillmore—a small appropriation having been made for the purpose—for the laying out and planting of the park occupied by the Smithsonian institution. Downing's death in the next year suspended these improvements, and nothing further was done until 1871.

On November 21, 1800, Congress began its sessions in the north wing of the capitol. Congress assumed jurisdiction over the District of Columbia in 1801, and declared that the laws of Virginia and Maryland should continue, respectively, in force in the portions of the district ceded by those states.

In 1802 the board of commissioners was abolished, and was succeeded by a superintendent, Thomas Munroe, who was required to settle up all accounts, and to sell a sufficient number of the lots pledged for the repayment of the loan of $200,000 from Maryland, to meet all obligations of interest and installments. In the event of an unwarrantable sacrifice of the property to meet these demands, the sale was to cease, and the balance was to be paid out of the Treasury of the United States. Lots not paid for were also to be sold to meet the loan of $50,000 from Maryland, or, if not sufficient, the residue was to be paid also from the Treasury. May 3, 1802, a municipal government was created by Congress, to consist of a mayor and council, Congress reserving supreme jurisdiction. The affairs of the county and the construction of roads outside of the city were intrusted to a board known as the "levy court".

At this time the crude and unkempt condition of the capitol grounds and the neglected aspect of the approaches to all the noble public buildings which adorn the capital were very noticeable. The streets and avenues were in a chronic state of neglect, the drifting of dust alternating with the deepest mud, and rendering them almost impassable. At length, in 1871, under the combined influence of a more liberal spirit in Congress, and the energetic determination of some of the private citizens, a new order of things was inaugurated. Congress, having abolished the municipal governments of Washington and Georgetown, created, by act approved February 21, 1871, all that part of the territory of the United States included within the limits of the district into a government under the name of the "District of Columbia", the executive power to be vested in a governor, to be nominated by the President and confirmed by the Senate, to hold office for four years, and the legislative power in a legislative assembly, composed of a council of eleven members, nominated by the President and confirmed by the Senate, to hold office for two years, and a house of delegates of twenty-two members, elected by the people, and to meet annually. There were a board of public works for improvements, a board of health charged with the sanitary care of the district, and a delegate in Congress. The first-named board became invested with exclusive power over the streets, sewers, and avenues of Washington and Georgetown, with authority to improve the same on a comprehensive plan. Endowed with these great powers and the ability to raise money by tax and loan, the new government went vigorously into the business of improving the federal city. An extensive system of sewerage and of street pavements was drawn up, through which the greater portion of the city was reclaimed from neglect and filth, the great ditch known as the Washington canal was filled up, and about 160 miles of streets and avenues were paved with wood, stone, or concrete. Many streets were completely regraded, the public squares were all fenced and planted with shade-trees, while in the streets and avenues about 29,000 trees were set out. The magnitude and extent of these improvements, carried on with a vigor and rapidity almost without precedent in American municipal history, of course entailed a corresponding amount of extravagance.

The territorial government made Washington in many respects the most beautiful city in the country, and prepared the way for it to become the best paved and one of the best built. It also encumbered the district with a debt of $20,000,000. The interest is paid annually, one-half by Congress and one-half by the city.

The territorial government lived too fast to live long. In June, 1874, Congress abolished the territorial form of government, retaining only the board of health, and created a provisional government of three commissioners, to be appointed by the President and Senate until a permanent government should be devised by Congress. The affairs of the city and of the district still continue to be managed by such commissioners, acting under direct legislation of Congress, and having its financial operations administered directly by the Treasury department.

One of these commissioners is the chief civil officer of the District; another is specifically the police commissioner; and the third, an officer of the United States engineer corps not below the rank of major, is engineer commissioner:

Thus far the system has worked extremely well, and since Washington has been governed by this board it has added much to the knowledge of the proper administration of municipal affairs in cities throughout the country generally.

In the course of the city's history its progress has been disturbed or stimulated by the incidents of two wars.

During the last war with Great Britain the city was captured and almost completely destroyed. The following account of these events is condensed from Keim's *Hand-Book of Washington:*

President Madison and his cabinet, over-confident of the safety of the capital or of the indisposition of the British, who controlled the Chesapeake, to attack, had neglected to make suitable provision for defense. As a consequence, about 3,500 raw militia, hastily concentrated and badly handled, were suddenly called upon to confront the enemy, 4,000 strong, at Bladensburg, 5 miles from the capital, on August 24, 1814. Commodore Barney, with a few hundred sailors and marines, and Beall's Maryland militia made a stubborn resistance.

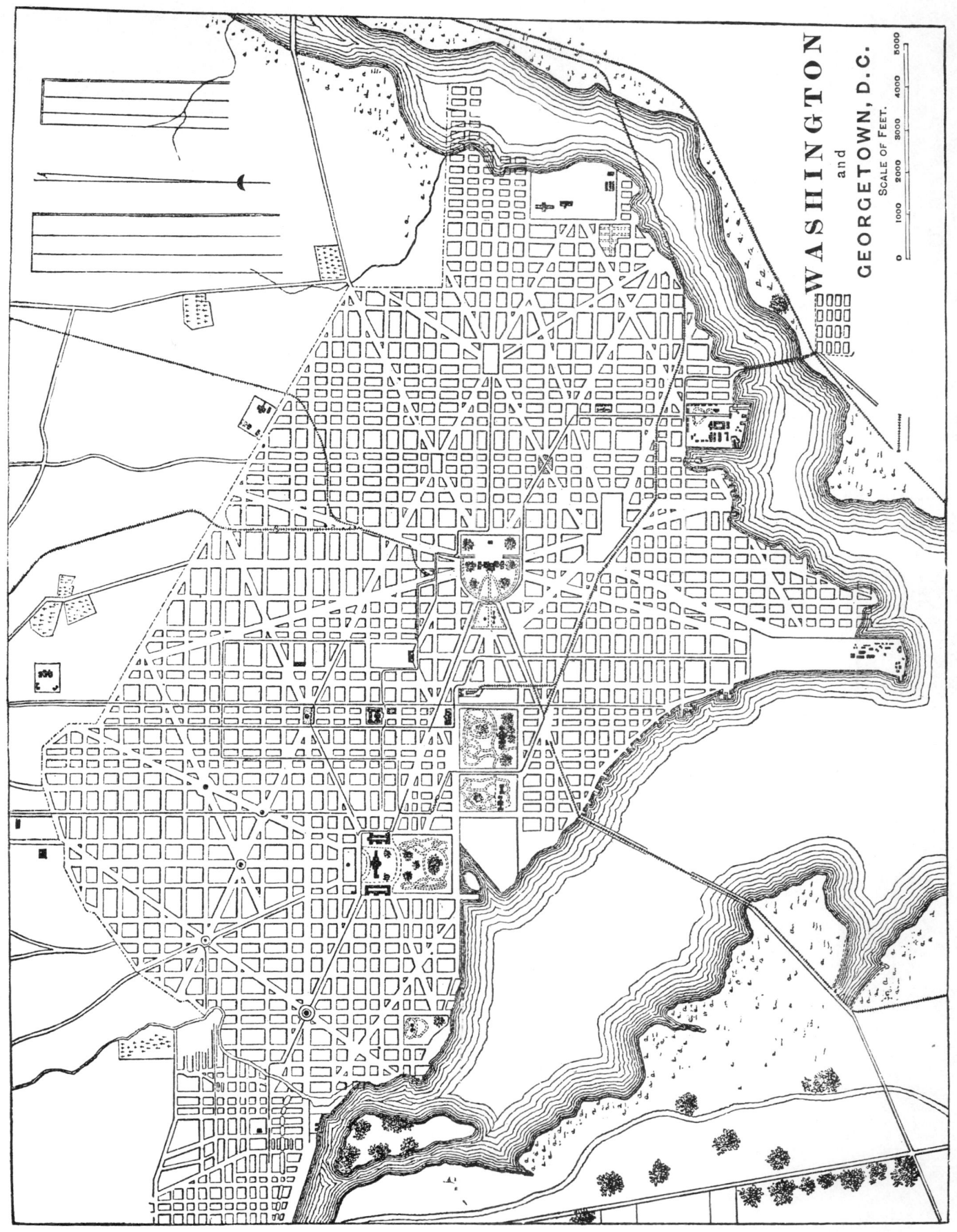

WASHINGTON
and
GEORGETOWN, D.C.

SCALE OF FEET.

0 1000 2000 3000 4000 5000

on the turnpike, but, unsupported by the rest of the troops, who had fled precipitately, fell back to the capital, proposing to defend that point. From here he was ordered to retire and take position behind Georgetown, leaving the city entirely defenseless. The American troops retreated toward Montgomery court-house, having been preceded by the President and cabinet and other prominent officers of the government. The total force of Americans available was 7,000 men, but, through mismanagement, the incapacity of General Winder, the commander, and the interference of the President and cabinet, not more than half that number reached the field, and even then were out-numbered at the point of attack. The whole British force which landed on the "Pautuxent" numbered 5,123 men, of which 4,500 took part in the fight. The American loss was 26 killed and 51 wounded, and the British 150 killed and 300 wounded.

At 8 p. m. on the day of the battle the British bivouacked on Capitol hill. The capitol, library of Congress, President's house, arsenal, Treasury and War offices, Long bridge, and office of the *National Intelligencer* newspaper were burned the same night, as well as some private buildings. The navy-yard and frigate "Columbia", on the stocks, the "Argus", 5 barges, and 2 gunboats were destroyed by order of the Secretary of the Navy. An explosion of powder in a well at the arsenal killed 15 and wounded 30 of the British.

On the evening of August 25 the British evacuated the capital. To use the words of one of the British officers, the retreat "was as cautious and stealthy and precipitate as was natural for a retreating army under such circumstances". On the retreat many died of fatigue or were taken prisoners by the cavalry harassing the rear. Nearly 200 of the dead left by the enemy were buried by the citizens. It was estimated that their aggregate loss was not less than 1,000 men. They reached Benedict on the evening of August 29, and re-embarked the next day.

The sight of the capital in flames had aroused the inhabitants of the surrounding country, who were being rallied by the Secretary of State, Mr. Monroe. It was resolved to cut off the enemy's retreat to his ships; but his haste frustrated the patriotic proceedings.

When the question of the restoration of the public buildings was under discussion a long and bitter debate ensued, evincing not only a strong disposition to abandon the city, but a dangerous sectional feeling. For a time the most serious consequences were threatened. Calmer counsels, however, prevailed, and an appropriation of $500,000 was made for the repair or re-erection of the buildings on their old sites, the estimated loss being $1,000,000.

In 1846 so much of the district as had been ceded by the state of Virginia as far as low-water line on the west shore of the Potomac river was returned to that state.

WASHINGTON IN 1880.

The capital of the nation is situated just above the confluence of the Potomac river and the Anacostia or "Eastern branch", 106 miles by river above the mouth of the Potomac and 105 miles due west of the Atlantic ocean. The distance by air-line to the mouth of the Potomac is 60 miles, and to the mouth of Chesapeake bay 143 miles.

The latitude of the city is 38° 53′ 39″ north, and the longitude 77° 2′ 48″ west from Greenwich. Exclusive of Georgetown, it lies 4 miles along the Potomac and 3¼ miles along the Anacostia. It is 14 miles in circumference, covering a little over 9½ square miles of the western side of the district. Its mean altitude is about 40 feet above ordinary low tide of the Potomac, the highest point being 103.7 feet above. The District of Columbia, originally 100 square miles in area, was reduced to 70 square miles by the retrocession of the Virginia portion. It is bounded on the north by Montgomery county, Maryland, on the east and south by Prince George county, and on the west by low-water mark of the Virginia shore of the Potomac.

Northwest of Washington, separated from it by Rock creek, but forming a continuous town with it, lies Georgetown, or West Washington, the head of navigation of the Potomac. Much of its site, like most of the country north of Washington, is high and broken. The northern portion of the district generally is of diversified surface and well wooded.

THE RIVER.

The Potomac rises in the Alleghany mountains, and its entire length is about 400 miles. At Washington the hills, by which it has been confined, recede, and it becomes a broad stream. The Anacostia is a much smaller river, though at Washington it spreads out into a tidal estuary nearly as wide as the Potomac itself. Each has a maximum depth of 18 feet. Where it reaches the Chesapeake bay the Potomac is 7½ miles wide. Salt water reaches up to within 50 miles of the city. The average rise of the tide is 3 feet. The available harbor consists of a channel extending from Greenleaf's, or Arsenal, point, the upper point at the junction of the two rivers, to the foot of Seventeenth street west, a distance of four-fifths of a mile, together with a small channel in the Anacostia. The wharves of Georgetown are on the main channel of the river. The Potomac channel has an average width of 400 feet up to Long bridge, with a minimum depth of 6 feet. At the Arsenal wharf it narrows to 250 feet. The average width of the Anacostia channel is 350 feet between the depths of 6 feet on either side, and it also narrows to 250 feet. The greatest depth of water up to the navy-yard is 14 feet. One mile above there it is but 6 feet.

RAILROAD COMMUNICATIONS.

Washington is on what is now the main line of the Baltimore and Ohio railroad, formerly known as the Washington branch of the same; on the Baltimore and Potomac railroad, and on the Virginia Midland railroad, using the Baltimore and Potomac's track between Washington and Alexandria.

Street-railroads.—There are five companies of street-railroads in Washington, having an aggregate length of 30.8 miles, and traversing the city in all directions. The usual rate of fare is 5 cents for each passenger. Six tickets are sold for 25 cents, and those of any line are good on all lines. Transfers are made free at certain crossings of lines owned by the same company. There is a short line charging only 3 cents. The names of the companies are as follows:

	Length of track.
Washington and Georgetown railroad	9.5 miles.
Metropolitan railroad	10.9 miles.
Capitol railroad	4.7 miles.
Columbia railroad	2.8 miles.
Anacostia railroad	2.9 miles.
Total	30.8 miles.

In addition to the street-cars, Herdic coaches run on regular routes, the fare being 5 cents. Omnibuses belonging to the several hotels of the city convey passengers to and from the depots.

WATER COMMUNICATION.

Steamers ply between Washington or Georgetown and landings on the Potomac river and Chesapeake bay, and Baltimore, Norfolk, Philadelphia, New York, and Boston.

TRIBUTARY COUNTRY.

The market supplies of Washington are mainly raised in the country adjacent, the products of the upper belt of the north temperate zone being here cultivated with success. Fruits and vegetables are grown in great abundance, and the supplying of the city with vegetables, poultry, hay, etc., constitutes an important industry.

TOPOGRAPHY.

The surface of Washington is gently undulating, sloping on either side to the rivers which sweep by it or to the low level land forming the delta between them. From the elevations bordering Rock creek the high land crosses the northern portion of the city, save where it has been cut through by the Tiber, at times a strong river, but ordinarily insignificant. East of the Tiber it rises and spreads out into the extensive plateau of Capitol hill, which overlooks the city and extends nearly to the Anacostia on the east. Within this circling ridge the surface falls away in terraces and gentle slopes to the river-banks. All of the more important public buildings are built on land considerably higher than the delta.

From the lower falls of the Potomac above Georgetown, where are outlying spurs of the Blue ridge, a chain of low wooded hills surrounds the city on the north, and continues on the opposite shores of the Anacostia. The hills on the Virginia side are of corresponding height. They inclose a vast amphitheater, in the center of which the city lies. The Tiber is a small river, whose sources are in the hills to the north. It enters the city in several branches, all of which have now been diverted into the main channels of the sewerage system. Although the stream traverses one of the most populous sections of the city, its course is beneath heavy brick arches, upon which buildings have been erected and avenues, streets, and parks laid out.

The soil of the district bordering the Potomac is alluvial. The elevated lands consist almost exclusively of yellow clay, interspersed with sand and gravel. Occasionally a mixture of loam and clay is met. Rock creek divides the primitive from the alluvial soil; above it the shores of the Potomac are lined with primitive rock. Some miles above the district an outcrop of sandstone appears. In some parts the rock frequently contains fossils of leaves of trees and ligneous fragments. A species of gneiss is abundant and constitutes the underlying rock of the entire district.

CLIMATE.

The climate of Washington is generally salubrious, though subject, especially in spring, to sudden changes. During summer intense heat is not unusual, and while much of the winter weather is moderate and pleasant, excessive cold is by no means unknown. During a period of forty-eight years, the highest temperature reached (July, 1838) was 103°, and the lowest (January, 1835),—14°. The storms of winter are largely rain; snow sometimes lies for a few days, but seldom long enough for sleighing. From autumn until spring the climate is, on the whole, one of the most agreeable of the Atlantic slope. Very violent thunder-storms are frequent in summer.

STREETS.

The streets and avenues of the capital are wider than those of any other great city of the world. Originally there were thirteen avenues, named after the original states; others, undesignated on the first plan, were named after states subsequently admitted, though not in the order of their admission. The avenues radiate from principal centers or connect different parts of the city. They are crossed by an independent series of streets intersecting each other at right angles running in the directions of the cardinal points of the compass. With the alleys, and the open spaces at intersections, the highways occupy, according to Keim, about 2,500 acres, or nearly one-half of the area of the city. The streets running east and west are designated by letters of the alphabet, and by the word "north" or "south", according as they are situated north or south of the capitol. The streets running north and south are designated numerically and by the word "east" or "west", according to their position with respect to the capitol. Thus: 309 K street N.W. is on the eleventh street north of the capitol, between the third and fourth streets west of it. The same system of naming the streets has been extended over Georgetown, the ancient names being also temporarily retained for convenience. The four quarters of the city are designated N.W., N.E., S.E., and S.W. Most of the avenues are from 120 to 160 feet wide; two, Missouri and Maine, are but 85 feet. The avenues running, as they do, diagonally across the city, effect quite an economy in travel between extreme points thereof. Since the improvements inaugurated in 1871, the streets of Washington have become the best paved of any in the country. On the 1st of July, 1880, the 230.05 miles of streets of the city were paved as follows:

Material.	Square yards.	Miles.
Asphalt and concrete (coal-tar)..	981,348	40.66
Stone blocks	411,774	14.87
Rough stone	559,051	18.04
Macadam	215,330	7.45
Gravel	644,993	31.31
Wood	509,481	22.10
Unimproved	1,799,541	95.62
Total	5,121,518	230.05

During the year ending June 30, 1880, the wooden paving was replaced to the following extent:

Material.	Cost.	Square yards.
Asphalt	$104,143 17	67,962.91
Granite	87,390 42	45,084.28
Asphalt block	6,349 51	3,214.08
Total	197,883 10	116,261.27

Since the 1st of July (to October 20) there have been executed or placed under contract 86,000 square yards of repaving.

As a temporary expedient, during the last few months, on some streets, the wood has been taken up in the center and replaced with gravel, well rolled, the amount of this being about 38,000 square yards. After all these deductions have been made, there will remain, on the 1st of January next, 17 miles, containing 385,000 square yards of wood pavement. This pavement has been gradually becoming more and more intolerable with each month, until now, in the whole 17 miles, there is hardly a single square on which a carriage can be driven with safety at a speed greater than a slow walk. The wooden streets are far less passable than those marked as unimproved.

There can hardly be any duty more important for a city government than to keep its streets in a passable and healthy condition. The streets now covered with wood are not in such a condition, and they should be disposed of within another fiscal year (i. e., by June, 1882), at the latest. Many of them are in outlying sections of the city, where there is but little travel. These could, with little expense, be replaced with gravel, which would answer their purpose perfectly well until the streets are more built up; about 120,000 square yards could then be disposed of. The remaining 265,000 square yards could be repaved with the balance [$115,000] of this year's appropriation and an appropriation of $400,000 for next year. If this amount is appropriated, the wood can all be removed in eighteen months from this date. If a less amount is appropriated, some of the wooden streets will have to remain in the same miserable condition that they are now until funds are provided for repairing them.(a)

A careful examination of the records of the old corporation and board of public works shows that there were laid, in all, 1,188,597.47 square yards of wooden pavement, aggregating a length of nearly 50 miles, and costing $4,003,744. When the present commissioners came into office, in 1878, there were on the streets, exclusive of paving between railway-tracks, 34 miles (790,000 square yards) of wooden pavements. On the 30th of June, 1880, these pavements had been partially replaced to the following extent, viz:

Years.	TOTAL.		WITH ASPHALT.		WITH GRANITE.		WITH ASPHALT BLOCK.	
	Square yards.	Cost.	Square yards.	Cost.	Square yards.	Cost.	Square yards.	Cost.
1878 and 1879	162,109.11	$333,219 11	104,022.52	$200,900 18	56,993.24	$129,657 32	1,093.35	$2,661 61
1879 and 1880	116,261.27	197,883 10	67,962.91	104,143 17	45,084.28	87,390 42	3,214.08	6,349 51
Total	278,370.38	531,102 21	171,985.43	305,043 35	102,077.52	217,047 74	4,307.43	9,011 12

a Report of Lieutenant Greene, assistant to the Engineer Commissioner, for year ending June 30, 1880.

The following extracts from Lieutenant Greene's report are of value as stating the results gained by long and careful experience:

In replacing the wood the two standard kinds of pavements, asphalt and granite block, have been strictly adhered to, except at the intersection of Seventh street and Louisiana avenue, where a second piece of compressed asphalt block was laid as an experiment. This class of pavement looks reasonably well after the traffic which it has had (one year and two years, respectively), but it is too soon yet to give any positive opinion as to its merits, and it would not be well to lay any large quantities until it has had a five years' test, and then only in case its cost can be brought down to compete with the standard pavements.

The granite-block pavement, laid on a foundation of gravel and sand, and filled in the joints with a cement of coal-tar, gives great satisfaction in business streets, where the travel is heavy. The experience in Paris and London puts the life of this character of pavement (when laid without cement in the joints) at about thirty years, with an annual expense of about 10 cents a yard for maintenance and repairs. There is every reason to believe that the stone pavement laid in this city will prove equally durable, and that the cement in the joints, by making the pavement water-tight and giving the blocks mutual support, will reduce the annual cost of maintenance to 2 or 3 cents a yard.

The only objection which is ever made to this class of pavement arises from the noise made by heavy teams. In several cases it has been necessary to lay it on streets where there are no business houses or heavy travel, but where the grade is heavy (above 2 in 100), or where the carriage-way is very narrow between the railroad track and the curb. In all such cases it has been laid against the vigorous protest of the residents, on account of the noise; but there is no question that it is much better suited to such streets than the smooth asphaltum. * * *

During the present fiscal year, owing to the difficulty formerly experienced in compelling contractors to furnish blocks of a suitable shape, the district has bought its own blocks, subject to careful inspection, and then made contracts in the usual manner for laying the blocks furnished by the district. The blocks were bought by contract awarded to the lowest bidder. The result of this change has been a much better grade of blocks, and a reduction in the total cost of the pavement of from 10 to 15 cents a yard. It now averages about $1 79 a yard, as against $1 92 for last year. The contracts for asphalt pavements averaged $1 47 per square yard last year and $1 85 this year. * * *

The oldest pavement of asphalt is the one laid by the paving commission of 1876, on Pennsylvania avenue between Sixth and Fifteenth streets. This has now been on the street between three and four years, and the repairs (made at the expense of the contractors) are understood to have cost $2,142 50, or at the rate of $714 16 per annum, the number of yards being 53,198.80. The annual expense for repairs has been less than 1½ cents per square yard. On the compressed asphalt pavement, laid by the Neuchatel Paving Company on Pennsylvania avenue, between First and Sixth streets, the repairs are reported to have cost about $1,867, or $622 33 per annum, the number of yards being 25,322.28. The annual expense for repairs has been about 2½ cents per square yard. This pavement of the Neuchatel company is of the same character as those laid on the roadways in Paris. It is composed of natural bituminous limestone, which is broken and reduced to powder by heat, placed on the streets in form of powder, and compressed by large iron rammers. The pavements which we are now laying in this city under the name of "asphalt" are artificial mixtures or mastics. Our investigations and practice are therefore on an entirely different line from those in Paris. The objections made to the Paris pavements are well known to be its slipperiness during a light rain or in damp weather, and the difficulty of cleaning. The contracts for maintenance provide for sanding the pavement when slippery, and for flushing it with a large amount of water and scrubbing with a rubber mop or "squeegee" in order to clean it. The same objections apply to the compressed asphalt pavement on Pennsylvania avenue, while the mastics as laid here are almost free from these objections, owing to the gritty nature of the sand which forms a large portion of the ingredients. It is too soon as yet to affirm any thing positive as to the wear of the mastics. Where cut by plumbers, for making connections with pipes and sewers, the surface-coat does not show any appreciable wear. The pavements are all to be repaired at the contractor's expense during the period of five years from date of completion, but as yet no repairs have been necessary except for cuts made by plumbers.

The entire surface of asphalt pavements on a concrete base in this city on the 1st of January, 1881, will amount to 360,000 square yards; of the so-called concrete pavements, of which the cementing substances was a product of coal-tar, the amount is 700,000 square yards, giving a total of 1,060,000 square yards of monolithic or smooth-surface pavements, extending over a length of 44 miles. This is considerably more than exists on the roadways of all other cities in the world taken together, the amounts for other cities being as follows:

Cities.	Square yards.	Miles.
Paris	370,000	19¾
London	150,000	6½
New York	20,000	1
Other cities (estimated)	60,000	2¾
Total	600,000	30

The so-called concrete pavements are, as a general rule, in a fair state of preservation; they were generally laid on a base of broken stone from 4 to 6 inches thick, covered with a layer of "binder" about 1 inch thick, composed of pebbles and a cement of coal-tar. The wearing-surface was made in various ways according to the patent, but consisted essentially of small gravel, sand, or stone-dust, cemented by a product of coal-tar. In the later pavements of this variety a certain proportion of asphalt was mixed with the coal-tar, and with beneficial results. Several of these pavements have stood the test of five years' wear, with little or no repairs, and are to-day in perfect condition; others were of inferior quality. When the top surface has worn off, these pavements begin to go to pieces very rapidly, and in order to save them from destruction they must be promptly covered with a new wearing-surface. During the year 1879–'80, 53,436 yards were thus resurfaced, and 17,863 yards were entirely condemned, taken up, and replaced with the standard asphalt pavement on a concrete base. During the current year about 15,000 yards have been resurfaced or are under contract.

Experience has, however, shown that by careful attention and constant repairs of small quantities in each, these pavements can be made to last much longer than was anticipated. Pavements, for example, which seemed on the point of destruction two years since have by constant patching been maintained up to the present time and still present good surfaces. These pavements, however, were all laid within a few years of each other, and there is a possibility that after a few years more of wear they might all break up at the same time, during a severe winter for example. It is therefore economical to gradually resurface a certain portion every year, and an appropriation of about $100,000 should be made annually for this purpose. A summary of these pavements is shown in the following table:

Repairs, etc.	Square yards.	Cost.
Resurfaced 1875–'78	218, 842. 69	$329, 378 69
Resurfaced 1878–'80	53, 436. 33	59, 187 40
Replaced 1879	17, 863. 75	29, 691 90
Minor repairs 1875–'78		3, 099 62
Minor repairs 1878–'79		13, 618 22
Minor repairs 1879–'80		3, 206 26
Total for repairs		443, 182 09
Laid 1871–'75	741, 415. 44	2, 281, 304 91

These repairs extended over a period of seven years, i. e., from 1873, the average time of laying, to 1880, and the average annual expense of repairs is therefore $64,026, or at the rate of 8½ cents per yard. This is certainly not an expensive rate for the luxury of smooth pavements. The asphalt pavements being composed of less perishable materials and being laid in a more substantial manner, it may be confidently expected that the cost of maintenance will be still less.

The minor repairs of concrete and asphalt pavements are made by contract let to the lowest bidder, and running for one year. These repairs include the damage done to pavements by plumbers' cuts, the actual cost of which is paid by the plumbers. The work to be done is specified by this office, and the whole city is carefully examined and repaired about four times a year, or oftener if necessary. The work is done under careful inspection of experienced inspectors employed by the district.

The rough-stone pavements (rubble and cobble) remain in the same condition as mentioned in the last annual report. They are uncomfortable for travel, but their replacement is of secondary importance, on sanitary grounds as well as others, to the replacement of the wooden pavements.

The macadam pavements, when laid in the center of a city and subject to heavy travel, have proved very unserviceable here as elsewhere. The pavement of this character on Four-and-a-half street is in very bad order, and to properly repair it would cost not less than 60 to 70 cents per square yard, or more than $20,000 for the whole street. It would be cheaper in the end and better to replace it with granite blocks and sell the macadam metal for use in making concrete. On streets of lighter travel, such as Boundary, T, and Eleventh streets, the macadam, when well laid and compressed, has lasted reasonably well, but it is an expensive pavement to keep up, and requires constant repairs. For five years these pavements have had little or no repairs and the ruts and holes have become very numerous. * * *

The total length of streets opened and improved during the year was 3¼ miles. All of this work has been done entirely at the cost of the district, there being no special assessments on property-owners for improving the streets in front of their property.

The general funds being, however, quite insufficient to make all the improvements desired, a considerable amount of work has been done, partly at the expense of the persons benefited and partly at the expense of the district, under what is known as the "permit system". Under this system the district pays for all the materials used (curb, flagging, cobble, bricks, etc.), and the persons benefited pay for the labor. The district also lays out, free of cost, the line of the street and furnishes the grade. A deposit is required when the material is issued, as a guarantee that it will be properly used; this deposit is returned after the work has been inspected and found satisfactory.

Under this system, during the past fiscal year, 2.1 miles of streets were improved, i. e., the curbs, gutters and sidewalks were laid, requiring 11,031 feet of gutter-flag, 3,677 square yards of cobble-stones, and nearly 700,000 paving-bricks. Nearly 60,000 bricks were also furnished for the repair of old sidewalks, and about 3,500 square yards of alleys were graded and paved.

During the current year the demand for materials for improvements under the above conditions has been still more active, and fully as much work has been done in the four months of the present fiscal year as during the whole of last year. The advantages of this system are obvious. * * *

It should be remembered that Washington is one of the most thinly built-up cities in existence, for the length of its streets and the area within its limits. It has 164 miles of streets improved or partially improved, in an area of 9½ square miles, and for a population [of 147,293] whose total revenues, including that contributed by the general government, amount only to $3,280,000 per annum. * * * It is evident that Washington has comparatively a very small population and small revenue to the amount of streets required to be kept up.

While this lack of density has great advantages for sanitary reasons, and in a measure adds to the beauty of the city, yet it renders the proper care of the streets extremely difficult under any reasonable rate of taxation. With the current revenues on the present basis, and without special assessments for improvements, it will therefore be many years before the outlying streets can be paved or even improved with gravel roadways. * * *

In addition to the 102 miles of paved streets, there are 33 miles of graveled streets in the city, the cleaning and repair of which is conducted by days' labor, as well as the miscellaneous repairs on the streets, alleys, and sewers of every character not specially provided for. All of this work is placed under the immediate charge of the very efficient superintendent of repairs, Dr. E. M. Chapin, who has under his direction a force of overseers and workmen which varies according to the amount of work to be done, but averages during the summer months 10 overseers, 50 laborers of various grades, and 40 carts.

STREET-SWEEPING.

The streets are swept by contract, according to schedule prepared in the engineer's office. During the past year the contract was held by L. P. Wright, at the rate of $33,000 per annum, for an amount not less than 92,000,000 yards. The work was satisfactorily performed with machines.

In May last proposals were invited for doing this work for the period of three years from July 1, 1880, subject to annual appropriations by Congress. The specifications required the work to be done according to schedule furnished by the engineer commissioner, and to be paid for at a fixed rate for each 1,000 yards actually swept, the total amount to be about 110,000,000 yards per annum. The lowest bidder was H. L. Cranford, at 23¾ cents per 1,000 yards, and the contract was awarded to him at that rate.

For 110,000,000 yards per annum the cost will be $26,675. The new contract, therefore, performs 20 per cent. more work, and saves the district about $7,000 a year.

The new contractor was required to execute an indemnity bond holding the district harmless from any suits growing out of patent rights in street-sweeping machines.

The work under the new contract is progressing favorably and satisfactorily. The frequency of sweeping depends on the amount of traffic on the street. Under the present schedule the 2,500,000 square yards of paved streets are swept as follows: Daily, about 4 per cent.; twice per week, 6 per cent.; once per week, 50 per cent.; and once in two weeks, 40 per cent. It is found by experience that bad weather prevents sweeping on about forty days in the year. As previously stated, the contractor is paid for the amount actually swept.

ALLEY-CLEANING.

The alleys are cleaned also by contract. The number of paved alleys is 303, and of graded but not paved, about 200. They are of very different sizes, but average about 1,200 square yards each. These alleys are all swept and cleaned once in every week during the eight months from April to November, and once in two weeks during the four months from December to March. Owing to the small width of the majority of them it is not practicable to use machines, and the sweeping is all done by hand. The alleys are thoroughly sprinkled, however, before sweeping, in order to avoid creating a dust during the operation. The lowest bidder for the current year was R. Carns, at $4,275 per annum, to whom the work was awarded.

During the past year the alleys were swept once in a week during six months, and once in two weeks during the remaining six months of the year. The cost of the work was $4,160 43 for the year.

STREET-LIGHTING.

There are at present on the streets of Washington 3,681 street-lamps, and in Georgetown 387 lamps, lighted at the expense of the district. The contract with the Washington company is $28 70 per annum, and with the Georgetown company $32 per annum for each lamp, to burn 2,200 hours per annum with a 6-foot burner. The companies also light, extinguish, clean, and repair the lamps, as part of their contract, without extra expense.

During the past year 80 new lamps were erected. On Pennsylvania avenue the lamps are placed at intervals of every 100 feet of curb; on the other streets the intervals vary up to 250 feet. About 5 miles of improved streets have no lamps at all.

During the past year the street signs of the new pattern were placed on the corner lamps throughout the city. These consist of a light iron frame, rectangular in shape, resting on the frame of the lamp, and inclosing on each side a piece of glass 16 inches long and 3¼ inches high. On these glasses the names or numbers of the streets were cut by sand-blast. The advantage of this arrangement lies in the fact that the signs are independent of the lamp proper, and are not liable to be broken in cleaning the panes. Twelve hundred and twenty-three signs were placed on the lamps, at a cost of $2,140 25.

The district is connected with the Virginia shore by three bridges across the Potomac. Long bridge, which has a track for the Baltimore and Potomac railroad and a carriage-way for vehicles and pedestrians, is laid on piers. The Aqueduct bridge, at Georgetown, is the only toll-bridge in the district. The Chain bridge, a suspension bridge, at Little falls, 4 miles above, has given place to an iron truss bridge, erected in 1874, but generally designated by the old name. Across the Anacostia runs the Navy-yard bridge, an iron structure, erected in 1875, and Benning's bridge, of wood, lies about a mile above the navy-yard.

Tree-planting.—The planting, care, and protection of trees in the streets, squares, reservations, and parks of Washington are in charge of a parking commission, consisting of three members. They report to the engineer commissioner for the year ending June, 1880, as follows:

During the year 3,000 trees were planted, and 248 old and decaying ones removed.

The planting of trees has now become a small item in the expenditures of the commission. So much is required for the ordinary care and keep of those already planted, that comparatively few can be added to the number with the present appropriations. The materials for repairing and reconstructing old tree-boxes and the purchase of 3,500 new ones cost $4,298 82, while the cost of labor for setting and repairing boxes amounts to $3,079 07. Other items of expenditure may be noted, such as for pruning, $418 23; watering, $540 75; mowing and cleaning reservations and parks, $169 87; taking out old trees, $78 75; whitewashing boxes and trees, $114 37; paving around trees, $583 11; weeding and cultivating around trees, $326 14.

The expenses incurred in the purchase and repairs of boxes could now be largely reduced if it were practicable to discontinue their use. Perhaps two-thirds of all the trees in the city would be improved by removal of the boxes, but where this has been attempted the trees have suffered from horses being allowed to gnaw the bark, and also from the malicious use of knives and hatchets in the hands of evil-disposed persons, by which the bark is cut and torn away in strips, so that it has been found necessary to replace the boxes in order to save the trees from total destruction. This vandalism is much to be regretted, as it would improve the appearance of the city far beyond ordinary expectation if the tree-boxes could be dispensed with.

With regard to horses, we would renew our suggestion of inserting rings in the curbstones for securing horses in the absence of drivers. It would be an economical measure to do so, as the cost of repairing broken boxes and replacing broken trees, caused by runaway and stray horses for one year, would go far toward supplying these rings. * * *

It may be remarked that after midsummer the insects are more unsightly than injurious to the trees; the young growths have then acquired a considerable degree of maturity and solidity, and they are not materially injured by the destruction of the leaves; in fact, the tree is much more permanently injured from the removal of infested branches by the pruning-shears.

WATER-WORKS. (a)

The water-supply of the city is brought from the Great falls of the Potomac, along the east bank of the river, by the aqueduct, a distance of 12 miles, to its termination in a distributing reservoir, 2 miles from Rock creek and 4½ miles from the capitol. The aqueduct is a cylindrical conduit of 9 feet interior diameter, constructed of stone and brick laid in hydraulic cement, and covered by an embankment or tunneled through the hills, and is carried across the streams flowing into the Potomac by magnificent bridges, and has a fall of 9½ inches to the mile. Some

---

a From Keim's *Hand-Book of Washington.*

2 miles before the distributing reservoir is reached there is a receiving reservoir used for the storage of water. This is a natural basin, formed by an embankment 65 feet high across Powder Mill creek, and retains the water within the encircling arms of the surrounding hills. It has a surface area of 52 acres, a greatest depth of 53 feet, and drains 40,000 acres of the adjacent country. In the south end is the sluice-tower. A conduit extends around the south end, connecting the aqueduct without passing through the receiving reservoir, the capacity of which is 163,000,000 gallons. The height of water herein is controlled by a channel cut in rock. The aqueduct here passes through a tunnel 800 feet long, pierced through the solid rock.

In the effluent screen-well at the distributing reservoir are laid four 48-inch mouth-pieces for the supply of the city, three of which are reduced in the pipe-vault to 36, 30, and 12 inches, respectively. Leaving the vault, these three mains run parallel across the country to a small stream known as Foundry branch. Near this point they strike the road along the Chesapeake and Ohio canal, which they follow through Bridge and Aqueduct streets, in Georgetown, to Rock creek, a distance of 2 miles. On the way the 30-inch and 12-inch mains cross College pond over an arch of 120 feet span, composed of two 30-inch pipes. The 36-inch main is laid in the bottom of the creek. At Rock creek two of the three mains are joined, so that the water is conveyed through two 48-inch pipes, which form an arch of 200 feet span across that stream. These arches also sustain a roadway for general traffic between Washington and Georgetown. Crossing this bridge, at the east abutment the three mains are resumed, and thence the vast water-supply for the public and private buildings and fountains of the capital is distributed by mains of 36, 30, 20, 12, 10, and 8 inches. The total length of mains in the District of Columbia is a little over 175 miles; there are 826 fire-plugs and 317 hydrants (268 in Washington and 49 in Georgetown), and there are in the neighborhood of 20,000 water-takers. The daily supply is about 30,000,000 gallons, and the consumption of water is about 17,000,000 gallons. The full capacity of the aqueduct is 80,000,000 gallons.

In Georgetown, at the head of Market street, is the Georgetown high-service reservoir, supplying all that part of Georgetown which lies at an elevation of over 100 feet above tide. It consists of a domical reservoir of brick, 120 feet in diameter, with a capacity of 1,000,000 gallons, and is fed from the aqueduct mains at the bridge over Rock creek by two pumps. The surface-water is 215 feet above tide and 70 feet above the distributing reservoir. There is also a stand-pipe of limited capacity on the hill north of Sixteenth street west for the supply of that high-lying neighborhood.

By statute the water-rates are limited to the cost of laying new pipes, keeping the old ones in repair, and the current expenses of administration. The expenses of the water department for the year ending June 30, 1880, were, including $74,025 interest paid to the sinking fund, $166,338 18.

GAS. (a)

The city is lighted by two private companies, the Washington Gas Light Company and the Georgetown Gas Light Company.

The United States government provides for the lighting of all public buildings and grounds, and the District of Columbia for the lighting of the avenues and streets. The average daily production of the Georgetown company is 45,924 feet; of the Washington company, 884,731 feet; together 930,655 feet. The charge per 1,000 feet of the former to private consumers is $2 50, of the latter $2 25, and for public buildings $2. These figures are for the year 1879.

The number of miles of lighted streets is	112. 38
The number of lamps on streets and alleys	4,163
The number of lamps on United States reservations	663
The total number of lamps	4,826

On January 1, 1880, a district contract was made with each company which reduced the price of gas 25 cents per 1,000 feet.

PUBLIC BUILDINGS.

The government of the District of Columbia hires rooms for offices, etc. The more important of the national public buildings may be described briefly as follows:

The Capitol occupies a position near the center of the city, and stands 89½ feet above ordinary low tide in the Potomac. It is constructed with a central building and two projecting wings of great extent, and is ornamented on the east front with 68 Corinthian columns of marble. The entire length of the building is 751 feet and 4 inches, with a width of from 121 to 324 feet in the different portions. The material of the central building, the original structure, is Virginia freestone; that of the wings is Massachusetts marble. The whole edifice covers nearly 3½ acres. The height of the center and wings from the ground to the roof is 70 feet. From the main or central building springs a lofty iron dome, 287 feet high and 135½ feet in diameter at its base, and containing 3,575 tons of cast and wrought iron. The apex of the dome is surmounted by a lantern 15 feet in diameter and 50 feet high, and

---

a From Keim's *Hand-book of Washington.*

this is crowned by a bronze statute of Freedom, designed by Crawford, and facing the east, the height of which is 19½ feet. The extreme height of the crest of the statue from the base-line is 307½ feet. The Senate chamber occupies the center of the north wing, is 81 by 113 feet in dimensions, and has seats for 76 senators. The south wing of the capitol is occupied by the House of Representatives and its offices and committee-rooms. The hall of the House measures 139 by 93 feet, and is 36 feet in height. The galleries will accommodate about 1,500 persons, while the floor affords ample space for 300 members. The Library of Congress occupies the main portion of the western projection of the central building. The Supreme Court room and offices occupy the old Senate chamber in the central building and rooms adjacent. The total expenditure upon the capitol for erection, extension, and repair has been a little more than $13,000,000. The present central structure dates from 1818 (completed 1827), and the extension or wings from 1851. The first capitol, begun on the same site, was destroyed by the British in August, 1814.

The Treasury department is at the corner of Pennsylvania avenue and Fifteenth street. It is an imposing edifice, Ionic in style, and with a stone balustrade running around its entire roof. It has four fronts. The eastern, constructed 1836-'41, of Virginia freestone, is the oldest part of the building. The other three, built 1855-'64, are of solid Maine granite. The monolithic columns of the south front are among the largest in the world, being 31½ feet high and 4½ feet in diameter. The whole building measures 468 by 264 feet, exclusive of porticos and stairways, contains some 200 rooms, exclusive of attic and sub-basement, and cost $6,000,000. The bureau of Engraving and Printing, a branch of the Treasury, occupies a separate building on the mall, corner of Fourteenth and B streets southwest. It is built in Romanesque style, and is 220 by 135 feet, costing $300,000. It is of pressed and molded brick, and is fire-proof.

The structure accommodating the departments of State, War, and the Navy is located just west of the Executive Mansion, and consists of three great buildings united by connecting wings. Its dimensions, exclusive of projections and steps, are 471 by 253 feet, the greatest length running north and south. The extreme height from the level of the terrace is 128 feet. The building was begun in 1871, and the south pavilion was finished and occupied by the State department four years later. The entire structure contains 150 rooms, and cost $5,000,000.

The department of the Interior, better known as the Patent Office building, stands near the center of the city, occupying the entire square between F and G streets, and running from Seventh to Ninth street. This building is massive, though simple, in its proportions, and in the Doric style. It measures 453 feet from east to west, and 331 feet from north to south, including the projections of the portico. Its height is 75 feet. The older part, built in 1837-'42 and fronting on F street, is of freestone; the three remaining fronts, built 1850-'64, are of Maryland marble; and the interior, fronting on an open court, is of New England granite. In this building are located, besides the Patent office, which occupies by far the largest portion of its 191 rooms, the Indian office and the office of the public lands, together with the offices of the Secretary of the Interior and clerks. The patent business of the United States is of enormous extent, and the models exhibited in this building just previous to the fire in 1877, by which 80,000 were destroyed, numbered upward of 160,000. The building cost $2,700,000. The reservation on which it stands covers 4⅑ acres, while the structure itself covers 2¾ acres.

The Postoffice Department building is directly opposite the Patent Office, occupying the square between Seventh and Eighth streets, and E and F streets. The E-street portion, begun in 1839, is of marble from New York quarries. The extension of the building over the northern portion of the square to F street was built in 1855, of Maryland marble. The style is Corinthian. The building is 300 feet north and south, by 204 feet east and west, and is two stories high. In the center is a court measuring 195 feet by 95 feet. The cost was $1,700,000.

The building for the department of Agriculture is of brick, with brownstone trimmings, in the renaissance style. It is 170 feet by 61 feet, and stands on the public reservation adjoining the Smithsonian Institution. It was erected in 1868, at a cost of $140,000. Connected with it are green-houses, graperies, and experimental grounds, covering about 10 acres. The ground is terraced in front and planted with beds of assorted flowers.

The Naval Observatory occupies grounds to the extent of 19 acres on the bank of the Potomac, east of Analostan island. The main building was erected in 1844.

The Army Medical Museum, formerly Ford's theater, where Lincoln was assassinated, is on Tenth street, between E and F streets. It contains the hospital records of the army, in over 10,000 manuscript volumes, as well as the library of the surgeon-general's office, embracing about 40,000 volumes, and a vast assemblage of curious and instructive specimens representing the effects upon the human body of wounds, morbid conditions of the mind, surgical operations, and other matters incident to army life.

The Government Printing-office and bindery occupies a plain painted brick building at the corner of North Capitol and H streets. It is L-shaped, 243 by 175 feet in size, 61½ feet deep, and is four stories high. The printing of Congress and of the executive and judicial departments is done here. Its equipment is very complete.

The Washington Navy-yard, established in 1804, embraces 27 acres, on the Anacostia river, at the foot of Eighth street. There are within it two ship-houses, several boat-houses, and shops for the manufacture of ordnance, together with buildings for officers' quarters. This yard, though practically no longer used for ship-building, is an important depot for the manufacture of naval supplies. Near it are Marine barracks, an extensive though unattractive building, forming the headquarters of the Marine Corps of the United States Navy.

The President's house, known as the Executive Mansion, or White House, built in 1815–'29, is on Pennsylvania avenue, on a reservation of about 20 acres, between the Treasury and the State departments. It is of freestone painted white, 170 feet long by 86 feet wide, two stories high, and has a colonnade of eight simple Ionic columns in front, and a semi-circular portico in rear. The grounds about it are laid out with walks, trees, shrubbery, and fountains, and a conservatory stands to the west. The first President's house, built in 1792, was occupied by President Adams in 1800, but was among the buildings burned by the British army in 1814.

The city hall, occupied until 1871 jointly by the municipal government of Washington and the United States courts for the District of Columbia, became, by purchase in 1873, the sole property of the United States. It is now devoted entirely to district judicial purposes. It stands on the south line of Judiciary square, fronting Four-and-a-half street west. Its erection was begun in 1820, and the east wing was finished in 1826, and the west wing in 1849. It is of two stories, is 47 feet high, and consists of a recessed center 150 feet long, with two projecting wings, each of 50 feet front and 166 feet deep, the entire frontage being 250 feet. It is built of brick, stuccoed, and painted white.

The Smithsonian Institution, founded on the bequest of James Smithson of England, for the "increase and diffusion of knowledge among men", stands in a reservation of 52½ acres, about 1 mile west of the capitol. The extreme length of the building, including the porch of the east wing, is 447 feet; the breadth of the center of the main building and towers, including the carriage-porch, is 160 feet. It is built of freestone found in the red sandstone formation on the Potomac, about 23 miles from Washington. The corner-stone was laid in 1847, and the building was completed nine years later. Its cost was $450,000, leaving in the Treasury of the nation a fund of $650,000, from the income of which the expenses of the institution are paid. The institution devotes its energies to ascertaining and publishing scientific information, as well as to conducting exchanges between the government and scientific bodies of this and foreign countries. It also has the care of the National Museum. This latter is a brick building, 327 feet square, standing east of the Smithsonian Institution some 50 feet.

Besides the public offices occupying buildings erected by the government there are others in rented buildings in various quarters of Washington, notably the department of Justice, the Pension Office, the Census Office, the Coast Survey, and the Signal Service.

Among the minor public buildings erected by the government are the Naval Hospital, at the corner of Pennsylvania avenue and Ninth street southeast; the Columbia Institution for the Deaf and Dumb, founded in 1857, accommodating 100 pupils and occupying 100 acres of ground at Kendall Green; the Government Hospital for the Insane, a large building, opened in 1855, on the east bank of the Anacostia, opposite Washington, surrounded by 419 acres of ground, belonging to the Army and Navy and the District of Columbia conjointly; and the Reform School of the District of Columbia (established in 1871), with 150 acres of ground, 3 miles from the capitol, on the Bladensburg turnpike.

In 1848 the erection of the Washington National Monument was begun, on a plateau south of the Executive Mansion and west of the mall near the bank of the Potomac, by an association incorporated by Congress. After an outlay of $230,000, raised by voluntary subscriptions, the work came to a standstill, but in 1876 Congress undertook its completion. It is a plain obelisk, 70 feet square at the base, and when finished will be 555 feet in height. It is built of great blocks of crystalline Maryland marble, lined with blue gneiss stone.

The Soldiers' Home, established in 1851 by the purchase of 200 acres of land 3 miles north of the capitol with the residue of the money levied by General Scott on the city of Mexico, is a national institution for the invalid soldiers of the regular army. It is sustained by a fund derived from retaining 12½ cents a month from the pay of each private in the army, and since its establishment its grounds have been more than doubled in extent. These grounds, laid out in groves and meadows, and dotted with lakes, afford 7 miles of beautiful drives, serving as a free public park for the city of Washington. The buildings are handsome, and form an attractive feature in themselves.

There are many charitable institutions in Washington, not a few of which have received continuous or occasional aid from the national treasury by act of Congress. Those most worthy of mention are Providence Hospital, a large building accommodating 200 patients, standing on Capitol hill; the Louise Home, for indigent gentlewomen, on Massachusetts avenue, erected and endowed in 1871 by W. W. Corcoran, esq.; the Columbia Hospital for Women, the National Soldiers' and Sailors' Orphans' Home, the Washington Orphan Asylum, Saint Joseph's and Saint Vincent's orphan asylums, Saint John's Hospital for Children, the Freedmen's Hospital, the Home for the Aged, under the care of the Little Sisters of the Poor, and the Washington Eye and Ear Infirmary.

PUBLIC PARKS AND PLEASURE-GROUNDS.

In the plan of the city numerous desirable localities were set apart for parks, for sites of public buildings, and for other purposes of the government. These reservations had a total area of 541 acres 109 rods, and were numbered from 1 to 17. Several have been sold or granted away, but the rest, amounting to 513 acres, are designated on the maps of the city by their original numbers, though they are popularly known by the name of the buildings situated on them or to the ones to which they are assigned, as "the Capitol grounds and mall", etc. Most of the grounds attached to public buildings have already been described. There are, however, numerous beautiful squares in different parts of the city, as follows:

Franklin Square, lying between Thirteenth and Fourteenth streets west, and I and K streets north, has an area of 4 acres, planted with trees and shrubs, and contains a fountain in its center, together with several drinking-fountains. In order to secure control of a fine spring located thereon, and whose waters were considered superior to that of the Potomac, the government purchased the ground in 1829, and pipe connection was made with the Executive Mansion in 1832, since which time the water has continued to be used there for drinking.

Scott Circle, with an area of 1 acre, lies at the intersection of Sixteenth street and Massachusetts and Rhode Island avenues. It is adorned by a bronze equestrian statue of General Winfield Scott, 10 feet in height (total height, 15 feet), weighing 12,000 pounds, and cost $20,000.

McPherson Square, area 1⅛ acre, located on Vermont avenue, between I and K streets north and Fifteenth street west, is laid out in walks, with shrubbery and drinking-fountains. In its center is a bronze equestrian statue of General James McPherson. It weighs 7,000 pounds and cost $23,500.

Lafayette Square, north of the President's house, between Fifteen-and-a-half and Sixteen-and-a-half streets, contains 7 acres, tastefully laid out with gravel walks and seats, and adorned with trees and choice shrubbery. Clark Mills' equestrian statue of Andrew Jackson stands in its center. It is a colossal figure, weighing 15 tons, and cost $50,000.

Farragut Square, area 1⅓ acre, lies on Connecticut avenue, between I and K streets north and Seventeenth street west. In it is a colossal bronze statue of Admiral David Glasgow Farragut. The figure is 10 feet high, weighs 1,500 pounds, and cost $20,000.

Lincoln Square is 1 mile east of the capitol, on East Capitol street. It is 6¼ acres in extent, and is beautifully laid out. In it stands the bronze group "Emancipation", representing Abraham Lincoln standing, and holding in his right hand the proclamation of emancipation. A slave kneeling at his feet, with chains broken, is about to rise. On his left is the trunk of a tree, with manacles and a lash strewn about. The group is 12 feet high, weighs 3,000 pounds, and cost $17,000.

Judiciary Square, with 19⅕ acres, extends south from G street north to the intersection of Louisiana and Indiana avenues and Four-and-a-half street west. This latter front is occupied by the city hall. Originally this square was known as reservation No. 9, and was set apart for the buildings then under contemplation for the accommodation of the judicial branch of the government.

Greene Square, situated at the intersection of Massachusetts and Maryland avenues, is handsomely laid out, and contains a colossal equestrian statue in bronze of General Nathaniel Greene. The figure is 13½ feet high and weighs 6,000 pounds. The whole structure cost $50,000.

Mount Vernon Place, lying at the intersection of Massachusetts and New York avenues and K and Eighth streets northwest, is well laid out and planted. In the center, on a raised circular space, is a bronze fountain.

Rawlins Square is on New York avenue, southwest of the State department. Its acre and a quarter of ground is handsomely laid out with walks, trees and shrubbery, and rustic fountains. It contains a heroic statue in bronze of Brigadier General John A. Rawlins, 8 feet in height, weighing 1,400 pounds and costing $2,500.

Stanton Place, comprising 3¼ acres, adjoins Greene square.

At the convergence of New Jersey and North Carolina and South Carolina avenues, and but a short distance south of the capitol, is a tract of land, 23½ acres in extent, on which it was originally designed to erect the town house or city hall, but nothing has as yet been done, and it is still without improvement.

There are in the southeastern part of the city other squares, but they are vacant and unimproved. The spaces at the intersections of the avenues and streets are called triangular reservations, while those at the intersection of the more important avenues are termed circles. Many of the former, east and west of the capitol, are planted with trees and shrubs and adorned with small fountains.

Among the circles may be mentioned *Washington Circle*, at the junction of Pennsylvania and New Hampshire avenues. It contains an equestrian statue of Washington cast from guns donated by Congress, and cost $50,000.

Thomas Circle is at the intersection of Massachusetts and Vermont avenues, and contains the bronze heroic statue of Major General George H. Thomas. This is 16 feet high, weighs 7,500 pounds, and cost $50,000.

Dupont Circle is at the intersection of Massachusetts, Connecticut, and New Hampshire avenues. Congress appropriated, in 1872, the sum of $10,000 for the erection here of a base and pedestal for a proposed statue of Rear Admiral Samuel Francis Du Pont, United States navy.

PLACES OF AMUSEMENT.

The principal places of amusement in Washington are Ford's opera-house, on Ninth street west, and the National theater, on E street north. Stock companies appear here during the season, varied at intervals by the presence of the operatic and theatrical stars. No further information upon this subject was furnished.

DRAINAGE.

Washington was adopted as the site for a city for reasons among which sanitary advantages had no conspicuous place, and it has grown to be a great capital without reference to these sanitary advantages, indeed largely in spite of their absence. Aside from the heavy rainfall to which the locality is subject, it lies across the outlets of a wide

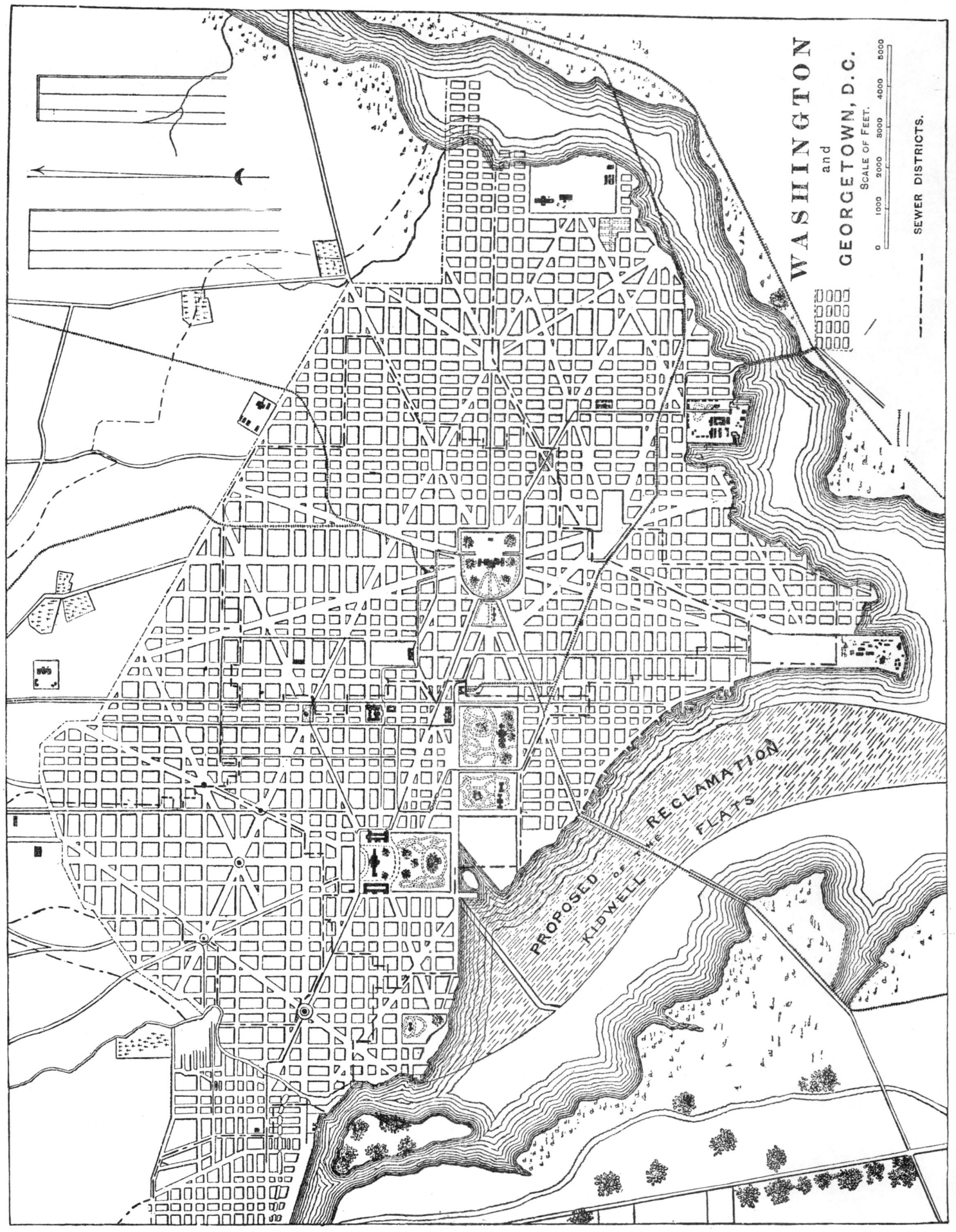

WASHINGTON
and
GEORGETOWN, D.C.
SCALE OF FEET.

0   1000 2000 3000 4000 5000

- - - - - SEWER DISTRICTS.

PROPOSED OF THE KIDWELL RECLAMATION FLATS

outlying drainage area whose storm-waters pour upon it in torrents. Much of the city is level, and its heavy soil at different points retains moisture almost to the point of saturation, while a large part of its area lies so near the level of tide-water as to prevent satisfactory drainage even were the soil more porous. In addition the streets of the city are, and probably will be, mainly paved with asphaltum and water-proof stone-block pavements, with no power of absorption.

The rivers by which the borders of the city are swept in addition to the degree to which their shoal shores prevent the requisite drainage of the city, accumulate deposits which, exposed at low tide, maintain in the immediate neighborhood a most prejudicial decomposition of organic matter fouled by the overflow of the sewers. The emanations from this decomposition in such close proximity to the heart of the city are a recognized and palpable source of ill-heath.

In 1878 the defects in the main system of sewerage of Washington became so pronounced that means for their relief was sought. Lieutenant R. L. Hoxie, of the United States Engineer Corps, made a report on the condition of the principal main sewers, and at the same time presented a plan of relief, which is now in part being carried out.

The most serious defect noted was the failure to discharge the sewage into the deep water of the Potomac river. To remedy this the extension of the main sewers through the marshes bordering the river-front and the reclamation of the latter was suggested, but as this work of improving the harbor rests with the general government, Lieutenant Hoxie recommended a temporary bulkhead inside the line of the new water-front, to be constructed down stream to a point where an open canal could be made to meet the B-street sewer. This was intended to enable this sewer to discharge into deep water, and as the improvement of the harbor-front was perfected, all the sewers would finally discharge their lighter flow into the deep running-water channel of the Potomac and into the Anacostia, as far up as the Navy-yard bridge. The deposits in the sewers themselves must remain considerable. Lieutenant Hoxie further said:

That defect of the present sewer system which has provoked most complaint is the want of capacity to discharge the rainfall of the violent storms which are of common occurrence in the District of Columbia. The remedy is in the construction of auxiliary sewers, and the use of certain temporary expedients for keeping the storm-water out of the present sewers until the latter can be constructed.

The present sewers will not carry off the storm-water. The surface of the streets, smoothly paved as most of them are, affords an ample water-way. If the water is allowed to enter the sewers they become gorged, and the back-flow through the house-connections inundates the cellars and basements of houses. If turned upon the streets the most serious inconvenience will be the condition of the streets during the storms, for any permanent injury from this may be readily prevented, and at a small expense. This is at least the case in the higher parts of the city, where the declivity of the streets is such as to throw off the water rapidly. In the lower areas, where the grade is flat and only a few feet above tide, in part submerged by freshets in the river, the accumulation of water is greater and special treatment is required.

The two principal drainage areas then under consideration were that of the B-street sewer and that of the main Tiber sewer. These two sewers were flooded at every heavy storm, notably in 1875 and again in 1878, the former backing up into its several branches, so that cellars and streets were flooded, while the latter overflowed into the Botanical Gardens, and at last burst and deluged the city along Third street and Missouri avenue toward Sixth and B streets. The bursting of the Tiber sewer occurred on August 5, 1878, during a rain-storm in which 2 inches of water fell in 40 minutes, equivalent to a rate of 3 inches per hour. An examination of the sewer after this storm showed that the arch had been lifted bodily, breaking at the crown, and with marked uniformity at the haunches on either side, about 6 feet from the springing-line, for a distance of about 400 feet, and in falling again into position with the subsidence of the head of water had been broken apart midway between the crown and the fracture at the haunch. This part of the sewer was therefore covered by two brick beams, resting on the haunches of the arch, and abutting against each other at the crown. The pieces had settled more or less out of position, so that the abutting surfaces were in some places 9 inches less than the thickness of the arch, the fractured ends projecting this distance into the sewer.

For the relief of these two drainage areas Lieutenant Hoxie recommended a plan that would include, for the Tiber district, an intercepting sewer on Boundary street, from Eighth street west to the Eastern branch, varying in diameter from 8 to 22 feet, with an open canal 1,600 feet in length; and for the B-street district an intercepting sewer on New York avenue, and another on B street, to terminate at the canal through the Kidwell flats to deep water in the Potomac. The estimated cost of this work was a little over $670,000.

The present sewerage system of Washington is divided into 5 districts, as follows: All the northwest portion of the city, including what was formerly known as Georgetown, is drained by 7 miles of brick and 30 miles of pipe sewers, with a main sewer one-half mile long, with its outfall at Rock creek. The Boundary district includes all that portion of the city between the Boundary, N, and Fourteenth streets, and the sewer here is intended to relieve the Tiber sewer by intercepting the storm-waters coming down from the hills back of the Soldiers' Home. There are 5 miles of brick and 15 miles of pipe sewers. The Tiber district has an area of about 5 square miles, with 16 miles of brick and 30 miles of pipe sewers, and includes all that part of the city lying east of Sixth street. The main sewer here is the largest in the city, the Tiber creek passing through part of its length. That portion of the city between the foot of Capitol hill and Seventeenth street, north and south of the mall, is drained by the B-street sewer. There are about 30 miles of laterals—13 miles being brick and 17 miles being pipe sewers.

That portion of the city contiguous to the two rivers forms another district, with 24 miles of sewers, draining into the two streams at different points.

In his report for the year ending June 30, 1880, Lieutenant Hoxie has the following regarding the present system of sewerage:

The sewerage of Washington and Georgetown is to be turned into deep water of the Potomac at the natural outlets of the sewers at four points on the Potomac front, where the storm-water of the corresponding drainage areas has its exit. The boundary intercepting sewer is to convey, ordinarily, no sewage whatever to its outlet. It is simply a water-course to the Eastern branch, into which the sewers of its drainage area will overflow in time of storms. An intercepting sewer along the Eastern branch, with overflows for storm-water, will carry the dry-weather flow of the sewers in the contiguous drainage areas to deep water below the bridge, and a similar intercepting sewer along the basin below the Long bridge will turn the corresponding dry-weather flow into the James Creek canal.

Under this plan each of the principal main sewers, following the line of natural drainage, discharges through a broad and deep channel into deep water at intervals along the water-front. This is advantageous in diffusing the sewage through the water in the main channel. The sewage is checked for a time in the outlet canals by the influx of the tide, which dilutes, while the efflux diffuses it.

The action of the James Creek canal, the outlet of the Tiber sewer, which is nearly completed to deep water, may be cited as illustrative of the present working of the canals. The canal is 7,450 feet long, and should have a depth of 6 feet at low tide, but has been silted up to much less than this, and requires dredging. The tide makes up into the Tiber sewer above the head of a canal about 5,000 feet. The sewer is an elliptical arch, 30 feet span, on side-walls 3 feet high, with a plank floor, which, in the lower part of the sewer, is horizontal and about 3 feet below mean low tide. It is not of recent construction, and may require modification.

About 3,000 feet above the head of the canal, bars of sand and gravel form at certain short curves in the sewer, and while these bars remain, mud, consisting of firm sand and clay, will accumulate. With the removal of the bars the mud disappears. Some of it is arrested in the canal, but a large proportion of the deposit here is sand, which is dredged up and used for building purposes. The ordinary flow of Tiber creek through the sewer is insignificant, but the storms are of great violence and bring down large quantities of coarse detritus. Sand and gravel are taken from the sewer and from the canal in large quantities, and are perfectly inoffensive when taken out for some time after a storm, or after a few days' exposure to the air at any time. It is all used for building or paving, and its value for this purpose more than pays the cost of removal. The dredging of the mud in the canal will be all outlay, but it is prevented from entering the river, and can be conveniently removed.

The ample water-way of the canals lowers the flood surface of water in the sewers by giving ready exit through the low grounds, and at all times performs to the best advantage the office of a settling tank for the protection of the river-channel, arresting sand, gravel, and the detritus of the streets.

Above the influence of the tides the sewers have all a constant overflow, and a size adapted to storm-water. Their oval shape concentrates the dry-weather flow of sewage in the invert, and the large air-space above this is favorable to the prompt oxidation of such gases as may form during the short time occupied in flowing to tide-water. The grated manhole-covers at short intervals effect a perpetual renewal of the air.

The principal main sewer of Georgetown furnishes an example of the successful working of the system upon which London still depends—air and water cure—without a distant outfall, and with very imperfect sewer construction. This is a large semi-circular sewer on vertical side-walls, with a flat wooden floor. It is more than fifty years old, and requires constant repair. It follows the bed of the original water-course, and is of a size to carry the storm-water, draining the greater part of the most thickly settled district of Georgetown. The fall is very rapid—about 150 feet in four-fifths of a mile. In its lower part the stream becomes a cataract which plunges under the water-wheels of two large mills, and receives the waste water from the tail-race of the mills before rushing over a rocky bed into the river-channel where the latter has a depth of 30 feet. The outlet of this sewer presents no evidence whatever of its character. The sewage disappears forever without a sign.

To recapitulate: The work now projected and in progress contemplates the reclamation of the flats along the water-front of Washington and the rectification of the channel of the river. It provides for the effective drainage of Washington and Georgetown, and the adaptation of the system of drainage to sewerage as well; providing in such manner for the possible separation of the systems at some future time, that, while the combination of the two shall be made to the best possible advantage, all of the work done in that direction shall be applicable to the separate system of sewerage. It contemplates, as the indispensable prerequisite of any system of sewerage by water-carriage, and of any reasonable condition of health and comfort consistent with modern civilization, the introduction of a liberal water-supply at a sufficient elevation.

The modifications described in Lieutenant Hoxie's report—some of which are now in course of execution—hardly compass the real evils of the case.

Like the proposed method of reclaiming the Kidwell flats, they will secure superficial improvement rather than the radical sanitary reformation that is so urgently demanded.

CEMETERIES.

Early in the present century two squares, known as the Eastern and the Western burial-grounds, were allotted by the government for the interment of the dead. The first, which stood in the eastern part of the city, was removed a few years since; the same thing is about being done with the western, later known as the Holmead, cemetery, which is located on Nineteenth street, between S and T streets northwest.

Congressional (or *Washington Parish*) *Cemetery* is situated on the banks of the Anacostia. This cemetery was laid out in 1807, and originally embraced about 10 acres, but additions have increased this to 30 acres. The name "Congressional" originated from the fact that a number of sites are set apart for the interment of members of Congress, in return for government donations of land and money. The small freestone cenotaphs to the memory of deceased members of Congress form a conspicuous feature. The grounds are adorned with drives, walks, trees, shrubs, evergreens, and a large fountain.

Oak Hill Cemetery is situated on the north side of Georgetown, on the northern slope of the heights. The original area, 10 acres, incorporated by Congress in 1849, was the gift of W. W. Corcoran, esq., from whom it has an endowment of $120,000. The present area is 30 acres, occupying a romantic spot, formerly Parrott's woods. It has a fine chapel and a public vault.

Glenwood Cemetery is situated at the head of Lincoln avenue, 1½ mile north of the capitol. It was incorporated in 1854, and contains 90 acres. The grounds are beautifully laid out in walks and drives. The public vault is a fine structure. Outside the gateway are *Prospect Hill Cemetery*, area 17 acres, incorporated in 1860, and *Saint Mary's* (Roman Catholic) *Burying-ground*, with an area of 3 acres.

Mount Olivet Cemetery lies just outside the city, to the northeast of the capitol, and covers 70 acres. It was incorporated in 1862 in the names of the parish priests of the four Roman Catholic churches of Washington. The grounds are well laid out and shaded with oak and evergreens.

Graceland Cemetery is situated immediately outside of the eastern limits of the city. It was opened in 1872, and comprises about 40 acres.

Rock Creek Cemetery (with church) lies northwest of and contiguous to the Soldiers' home, which lies about 3 miles north of the capitol. The cemetery comprises about one-half of "the Globe", of 100 acres, the gift of John Bradford in about 1819.

National Military Cemetery lies north of and adjoins the Soldiers' home, being just east of Rock Creek cemetery. It was established in 1861, and contains nearly 5,500 bodies. Here are a fine keeper's lodge and conservatory.

National Cemetery is located on Arlington heights, opposite Georgetown, and across the Potomac. It comprises about 200 acres of land, set apart out of the estate of General Lee when it was taken possession of by the government in 1864 for the interment of deceased soldiers of the army. The cemetery was formally established in 1867. To the rear of Arlington house is an amphitheater capable of accommodating 5,000 persons, erected in 1873, and designed for use in the ceremonies annually observed here on Decoration day. The grounds are laid out with special reference to the purpose. The bodies of nearly 16,000 soldiers, from battle-fields around Washington and hospitals in the city, here find rest. The west cemetery is devoted to white and the north to colored troops. A short distance south of the mansion is a granite sarcophagus, surmounted by cannon and balls, placed in 1866 over the grave of 2,111 unknown soldiers gathered after the war from the fields of Bull run and the route to the Rappahannock. The carriage entrance on the southeast is through a freestone gateway of composite order. On the frieze are suitable inscriptions, and over the arch the words "Here rest 15,585 of the 315,558 citizens who died in defense of our country from 1861 to 1865".

MARKETS.

There are 8 public markets in the district—2 being in the city of Georgetown and 6 in Washington. The largest is the Center market, situated between Seventh and Ninth streets, and Pennsylvania and Louisiana avenues and B street northwest. The retail-market building covers 60,175 square feet of ground, and is a one-story brick structure. It has also a wholesale market connected with it, a two-story brick building, 270 by 36 feet. The retail market contains 666 stalls—192 for butchers, 72 for butter and cheese mongers, 30 fish-stalls, 36 bacon-stalls, and 336 used for miscellaneous purposes. The buildings cost $350,000, and the average monthly rental of stalls is $8 35 each. The market is open daily, except Sunday, from 4 o'clock a. m. to 1 o'clock p. m., and is owned by a private company.

The Northern Liberty market, next in size, is situated on the corner of Fifth and K streets northwest. It is a one-story, arched-roof, brick structure, covering 41,600 square feet of ground, and containing 284 stalls, distributed as follows: 104 butcher-stalls, 16 bacon-stalls, 10 fish-stalls, 104 vegetable-stalls, and 50 used for miscellaneous purposes. This structure, owned and managed by a private company, cost $152,000, and the average monthly rental of stalls is $5 90 each.

The Riggs market, another private institution, is situated on P street, between Fourteenth and Fifteenth streets northwest, and is a one-story frame structure, 130 feet long by 70 feet wide. It contains 60 stalls—20 for butchers, 4 for fish, and 36 for vegetables and miscellaneous purposes. The building cost $5,000, and the average monthly rental of stalls is $4 33⅓ each; market days, Tuesday, Thursday, and Saturday, from 4 a. m. to 1 p. m.

The Corcoran market is a low frame structure, or rather collection of old sheds, belonging to the district, and located on O, near Seventh street northwest. It contains 187 stalls—25 butcher, 27 bacon, 70 vegetable, 9 butter and cheese, 14 fish, and 42 used for miscellaneous purposes.(a) The average monthly rental is $3 56 each. The market days are Monday, Wednesday, and Friday; also Saturday night.

The Western market is owned by the district, and is located on the southeast corner of Twenty-first and K streets northwest. It is a one-story brick structure. It contains 105 stalls—38 for butchers, 6 butter and cheese, 5 fish, 4 bacon, 31 vegetable, and 21 used for miscellaneous purposes. The market days are Monday, Tuesday, and Friday, from 4 o'clock a. m. to 1 o'clock p. m., and also Saturday night. The average monthly rental of stalls is $3 63 each.

The Butchers' market, situated on High between First and Second streets, Georgetown, is a one-story brick structure, 80 by 60 feet, owned by a private company, and cost $5,000. It contains 48 stalls, of which number 16 are for butchers, 4 butter and cheese, 15 vegetable, 8 bacon, and 5 miscellaneous. The average monthly rental is $3 80 each. The market is open every week-day.

---

a These sheds were torn down down later, in 1880, and a high-school building was erected on its site. A market building was put up on the next corner at the same time.

The Georgetown market is situated on Bridge street, fronting Market street. It is a one-story brick structure, 36 by 240 feet, owned by the district, and containing 75 stalls—28 butcher, 8 bacon, 24 huckster, 11 butter, and 4 fish. The average monthly rental is $1 92 each. The building cost $60,000.

The Eastern market, situated at the corner of Seventh and C streets southeast, is a one-story brick structure, 205 by 47 feet, covering 75,774 square feet of ground, and cost—ground and building—$90,000. It contains 85 stalls— 20 for butchers, 8 butter and cheese, 5 fish, 39 vegetable, 6 bacon, and 7 miscellaneous. The market-days are Monday, Wednesday, and Friday, from 4 a. m. to 1 p. m., and also Saturday night, the average monthly rental per stall being $3 75.

There are two food-inspectors appointed at a salary of $1,200 per annum each, and two privates of police are detailed to act in conjunction with these officers. It is the duty of each inspector of food to attend the market or markets within his inspection every morning at the time when sales begin, and carefully inspect all meats, fowl, game, and vegetables offered for sale, and condemn, seize, and cause to be removed such as may be diseased, or from any other cause rendered unfit for food; also to visit, as early as practicable each day, every green-grocery or other place within the district where articles of food are kept for sale, and perform his duty of inspection, condemnation, seizure, and removal, as hereinbefore described. He reports his official proceedings daily to the health officer, and in the performance of his duties is under the direction of said officer.

SANITARY AUTHORITY. (a)

The sanitary condition of the city and of the district is in the care of the "health department of the District of Columbia", which is represented by one official, known as the health officer, who is appointed by and under the direction of the commissioners of the district, and is a physician. The ordinary annual expenses of the health department are $25,000, incurred for the salaries of employés and contingent or office expenses. No provision is made for increasing the expenditures of the department in case of an epidemic. The salary of the health officer is $3,000 a year, and he is always on duty. His powers and duties require him to provide for the removal of all nuisances dangerous to health; to secure full and correct records of the vital statistics of the district; to prevent the sale of unwholesome food and drink; to prevent, so far as possible, the introduction or spread of contagions and infections; to prevent the running at large of domestic animals; and, generally, to preserve the healthfulness of the district.

There are employed six sanitary inspectors and two food-inspectors; two of these are physicians, and none have police powers. The city is divided into sanitary districts, inspections and reports being made daily. Each inspector is held responsible for the condition of the territory under his charge. When nuisances are found and reported the responsible parties are notified to abate them; on failure so to do they are taken before the police court and fined. Constant inspection is extended to defective house-drainage, privy-vaults, cesspools, and sources of drinking-water, and when such are found, notices are issued allowing a certain number of days for correction; if these are not complied with the subsequent proceedings are the same as for other nuisances. In the case of defective sewerage, street-cleaning, etc., streets and sewers being under the charge of the engineer department of the district, the health department can only request the abatement of such defects. The table following shows nuisances to the number of 25,587 reported and abated during the year ending June 30, 1880:

Alleys	448	Hydrants	26	Sewers, house-connection	109
Alleys needing repair	18	Lots, filthy	163	Stables	156
Areas	35	Lots, stagnant water	83	Stables, cow	119
Ashes	425	Manure	293	Streets, filthy	48
Cellars	136	Markets, public	6	Streets needing repair	5
Drainage, defective	645	Miscellaneous	965	Traps, sewer	225
Excavations	5	Pumps	4	Yards	3,438
Factories, soap	2	Pipes, water	27	Yards, cow	23
Garbage	241	Ponds	23	Vaults, privy	2
Gutters	208	Privies, filthy	6,517	Water-closets	133
Hog-pens	119	Privies, dilapidated	87	Wharves	14
Houses, filthy	191	Privies, full	8,532		
Houses unfit for habitation	139	Privies, leaky boxes	1,518	Total	25,587
Houses, slaughter	19	Roofs, leaky	111		
Houses, no privy	59	Sewers	270		

Concerning garbage, the health officer superintends its removal, which is done (very imperfectly) by contract.

In case of death, the department issues the necessary permit for burial upon the proper certificate of a registered physician.

The pollution of waters, other than those used for drinking purposes, does not seem to be definitely forbidden. None but those authorized by the health department may clean and remove the contents of privy-vaults. When done this must be by means of some air-tight apparatus or pneumatic process whereby the contents are not agitated or exposed to the open air during the operation; and said contents may be deposited only as and where directed by the department.

---

a Information on this subject is furnished chiefly by Smith Townshend, M. D., health officer of the district.

If premises in which small-pox patients are found are so situated that proper isolation can be had, it is allowed; otherwise they are removed to the small-pox hospital. There are no regulations touching the isolation of scarlet-fever patients. The department does not take cognizance of the breaking out of any contagious disease in the public schools, except small-pox, in which case the patient is at once isolated or removed to the hospital. Vaccination is made compulsory when it is considered necessary, and among the poorer classes is done at the public expense.

No record is kept of such diseases as do not result fatally; but what is believed to be a very complete registration is made of births and deaths, the data for such being required to be returned to the health officer—in the case of births, by the attending physician, midwife, or other person in charge, within six days; and in the case of deaths, by the attending physician or coroner, through the undertaker, within twenty-four hours in ordinary cases, but within eight hours in cases of contagious or infectious disease. Monthly reports of births, marriages, and deaths are published by the health officer, who also makes an annual report to the commissioners of the district, which is by them forwarded to the President, who transmits it to Congress, by which body it is printed as a public document.

The following summary of the work of the health department for the year ending June 30, 1880, is from the annual report of the health officer:

The work of the health department has progressed during the past year under more favorable circumstances, with probably one exception, than in any year since the inauguration of the service. Every year the number of persons who appreciate the labors of the health officials is increased, and assistance is now often lent where obstruction was formerly put forth. The masses begin to recognize the fact that no means so surely promotes the elevation of the lower classes as does the promotion of public and private cleanliness, and agitators of sanitary reform are no longer confined to the medical fraternity alone. The seed implanted in the minds of the public during latter years is beginning to bear fruit, and many who do not place the strongest recognition upon godliness are attending to cleanliness. It is encouraging to those engaged in the good work to find many who had to be forced formerly to abate nuisances existing on their premises, now conforming strictly to sanitary laws, and urging like action upon those around them.

The following synopsis shows, in condensed form, the nature and amount of work performed:

There were 25,587 nuisances reported and abated; 43,064 pounds of meat, 13,942 bushels of fruit and vegetables, 112,501 pounds of fish, and 11,236 bushels of oysters condemned as unfit for food; examinations and reports made on 2,134 citizens' complaints; orders issued for burial at public expense in 597 cases; examinations made to ascertain local cause of disease in 112 cases; 2,160 official letters written; 2,584 official notices issued; 99 cases referred to the attorney for prosecution under the health ordinances; 2,625 animals impounded; 4,338 dead animals, 7,456$\frac{8}{20}$ tons of garbage, and 22,153 barrels of night-soil removed; 254 deaths referred to the coroner for investigation; 4,720 permits for burial issued, and the office work of registry, compilation, etc., conducted.

MUNICIPAL CLEANSING.

Street-cleaning.—The district commissioners assume the cleaning of streets, and have the work performed by contract. Sweeping-machines are used entirely except in narrow alleys and on those rotten wooden streets where the holes and ruts are too deep for their use, when hand-cleaning is necessitated. The streets are divided into classes, the three principally used being swept daily, as follows:

Pennsylvania avenue, from First street to Seventeenth street.
C street, from Seventh street to Eighth street (Market space).
Fifteenth street, from Pennsylvania avenue to New York avenue.

The following are swept twice per week:

Seventh street northwest, from B street to Q street.
Ninth street northwest, from B street to K street.

Others are swept once per week, others twice per month, and the remainder once per month. The following statement shows the number of square yards of each class:

Total square yards swept daily	99,844
Total square yards swept twice in each week	57,277
Total square yards swept once in each week	889,328
Total square yards swept twice in each month	570,566
Total square yards swept once in each month	638,732
Total	2,255,747

The following is a yearly summary of street-sweeping:

Total square yards swept daily for one year	36,443,060
Total square yards swept twice in each week for one year	5,956,808
Total square yards swept once in each week for one year	46,245,056
Total square yards swept twice in each month for one year	13,693,584
Total square yards swept once in each month for one year	7,664,784
Total square yards swept annually	110,003,292

The service is said to be very thoroughly performed. Its annual cost to the city is 23¾ cents per 1,000 yards, or $26,125. The sweepings are deposited temporarily on vacant lots, being sold as manure, and removed thence within 48 hours. In reply to the request to specify merits and defects of the system and of the mode or place of final deposit it is stated:

The system has no defects except in the method of dumping. The deposits sometimes remain longer than 48 hours. There is, however, very little complaint about this.

Garbage and ashes.—The removal of garbage appears to be very incomplete. There are no regulations as to the conservancy of garbage while awaiting removal, except that it must be kept separate from ashes. It is taken to a point 15 miles below the city, and there utilized in the manufacture of fertilizers. The cost of removing garbage is $10,355 per annum. The following, from the report of the health officer for the year 1879–'80, seems to cover the whole case:

The garbage question.—I do not approach the discussion of this subject with any extra degree of pleasant reflection thereon. Indeed, I have become so thoroughly disgusted in ceaseless, untiring, and, withal, unavailing effort to secure some improvement in this service of the collection of garbage, that the very mention of the word is almost sufficient to nauseate.

It seems strange that we of the District of Columbia should have so much trouble with a service which is satisfactorily performed in almost every other city, yet the fact remains; and during the past two years the public has been forced to submit to the greatest discomfort and doubtless, at times, injury to health, resulting from accumulations of decaying animal and vegetable matter allowed to remain for days, and even weeks, upon premises throughout our cities. This, too, when parties had entered into contract, under bond, with the authorities, guaranteeing a prompt semi-weekly and tri-weekly removal of garbage from all dwellings.

I find, however, that the history of the sufferings of the community from neglect in the removal of offal dates back as far as the records of the health organization, and proves rather interesting as a study of the patience which people will sometimes exert. In the first report of the late board of health (1872) I find reference made to this subject in the following language: "There is no nuisance that has given more trouble and has been more inefficiently removed than this." The failure at that time was charged to insufficient number of collectors, and it was urged upon the legislature to increase the number from sixteen to thirty-two. The next year trouble seems to have continued, and it was claimed that collectors, having been appointed for political services, had employed irresponsible boys or men, who knew little or cared less about the work they had to perform. The force, it seems, was deemed too small, as I find the following assertion: "To impose upon twenty-one collectors of garbage the burden of work requiring forty, and then complain that the work is not thoroughly done, is manifestly unjust, but such has been the burden imposed during the past year." In 1874 a change for the better seems to have occurred, as the health officer says:

"The garbage service probably never was as satisfactorily and economically performed as at the present time. Being directly under control of this office, and not subject to the whims of politics or personal prejudice, we have been able to select faithful and efficient men, who are anxious to excel in their labor, knowing that their position depends upon their excellence as garbage-collectors.

"Twenty men are now employed, the city having been divided into as many garbage districts, so defined as to place each collector under the direct superintendence of one of the nine sanitary inspectors, and each inspector is held responsible for the condition of his district in regard to garbage as to other nuisances injurious to health, so that virtually there are nine superintendents of the work."

The delightful state of affairs depicted in the above did not last long; it seems to have been entirely too good to last, and in the year following we find that the spirit of economy has come into their dreams, and the garbage service has fallen into the hands of a contractor who is to experiment with a new system.

The experiment inaugurated in 1875 is, I regret to say, still in progress. During the interim between that time and this the different ones engaged in the work of conducting this experiment seem to have been actuated by a determination to ascertain who could perform the least labor in getting through with the contract. * * * Now, however, I think an opportunity is afforded for securing a change for the better, and I would urge with all the earnestness possible that it be not allowed to pass again. It is generally accepted as a fact that the contract for this work was taken at too low a figure to enable the contractor to comply with its terms and pay expenses. Now if a sufficient sum is appropriated for securing a proper performance of the work the trouble may be avoided in future.

There were removed during the year ending June 30, 1880, 7,456.4 tons of garbage.

Concerning the removal of ashes, the same officer says:

This is a subject of no small importance, and one upon which action has, I think, been too long delayed. No provision is made for the removal of ashes by the authorities, and as a consequence large accumulations are found in alleys, yards, and vacant spaces over the entire area of the two cities. These accumulations of ashes become also a place of deposit for filth and refuse of all kinds, and entice the creating and maintaining of numberless nuisances. On a majority of premises in Washington and Georgetown you will find in cellar, area, or yard such an accumulation. In some cases it is kept in box or barrel, in others it is dumped on the ground or pavement in one corner of the yard. To it is added daily some portion of refuse, animal or vegetable, potato-parings, egg-shells, dish-water, and other refuse. If in the cellar—which you will find in many instances is the case—the foul odors and noxious gases emanating therefrom permeate the entire house, and their constant inhalation by the inmates results in some form of low fever, which no one can account for, and which is accordingly set down in case of death therefrom as a "visitation of Divine Providence". The ash of wood or coal is not set down in the category of nuisances, and taken alone there is nothing in either to prove injurious to health; but, as I said before, the accumulation invites deposits of animal and vegetable matter, and these decaying do create a nuisance, and one which, if within a building used as a dwelling, is liable to prove injurious to the health of the inmates.

I think, therefore, it would be a wise measure for the authorities to take steps looking to the regular removal of ashes from dwellings. This is a work performed in many cities, and one which, I think, could be inaugurated and successfully conducted here at no very great expense. It will be noticed, by reference to the table, that 425 nuisances resulting from accumulations of ashes are recorded thereon.

Dead animals.—Dead animals are reported to the health department by the police, or by persons on whose premises they have died, and are at once collected and removed by persons who utilize their carcasses in various ways. The work is performed without cost to the city. In the year 1879–'80, 6,415 carcasses were removed, and the system is said to work very satisfactorily.

Liquid household wastes.—Nearly all of the liquid household wastes of the city are run into public sewers. Cesspools or dry wells are not allowed. A close box above ground for night-soil is the only receptacle allowed, except the sewers, for such matters.

Human excreta.—It is estimated that about three-fifths of the houses of Washington have water-closets; the remainder depend upon privy-boxes, vaults not being allowed. All water-closets deliver into sewers, and all privy-boxes are water-tight. The following is the ordinance regulating the construction of these boxes:

Any privy within the cities of Washington or Georgetown, or the more densely populated suburbs of said cities, including Uniontown or Anacostia and Mount Pleasant, in the District of Columbia, constructed of other material than brick, cement, or wood, or which is not provided with a sufficient box, bucket, or vessel for the reception of filth, and the inside of which is not at least 5 feet distant from the line of any adjoining lot, and at least 2 feet distant from any street, lane, alley, camp, square, or public place, or public or private passage-way; and any privy so constructed that it can not be conveniently approached and cleaned, or in such manner that each and every vault, box, bucket, or vessel thereof is not made tight and close, so that the contents thereof can not escape therefrom, except as may be permitted by means of a passage-way or conduit under ground, for the purpose of carrying away the contents of such vault, box, or vessel into any common sewer or drain, is hereby declared a nuisance injurious to health; and any person who shall create, maintain, or continue such nuisance, and shall fail, after due notice from this board, to abate or remedy the same, shall, upon conviction, be fined not less than $5 nor more than $25 for every such offense.

The regulation concerning their emptying is this, having been in force from the 5th of October, 1873:

No part of the contents (except substances not soluble in water) of any privy, privy-box, vault, sink, or cesspool, within said cities [of the District of Columbia] or their said suburbs, shall be removed therefrom, nor shall the same be transported through any of the streets, avenues, alleys, or other public places of said cities or of their said suburbs, except as the same shall be removed and transported by means of some air-tight apparatus, pneumatic or other process, so as to prevent the said contents from being agitated or exposed in the open air during said process of removal or transportation.

The dry-earth system is not in use. Night-soil is manufactured into poudrette and used as a fertilizer. There is no law prohibiting its use as such within the gathering-ground of the public water-supply, but, as the latter is taken from the Potomac, danger from this source is hardly to be apprehended.

Manufacturing wastes.—As Washington is not a large manufacturing city, there are no special regulations controlling the treatment or disposition of manufacturing wastes.

POLICE.

The Metropolitan police force, as distributed among the 8 precincts of the city, consists of 238 members, including the head of the department. Their positions and annual salaries are as follows:

1 major and superintendent	$2,610
1 captain and inspector	1,800
6 detectives (each)	1,320
10 lieutenants (each)	1,200
20 sergeants (each)	1,140
7 acting sergeants (each)	1,080
120 privates, class 2 (each)	1,080
73 privates, class 1 (each)	900

There are also connected with the force—

1 secretary and property clerk	1,800
1 clerk	1,500
1 messenger	900
3 telephone operators (each)	780
1 ambulance driver	600
16 station-keepers (each)	516
3 surgeons (each)	450
8 laborers (each)	420
1 messenger	360
1 major and superintendent, mounted service (additional allowance)	360
2 drivers (additional allowance to each)	300
1 captain and inspector, mounted (additional allowance)	240
50 lieutenants, sergeants, and privates, mounted (additional allowance to each)	240

During the year ending June 30, 1880, the force made 13,558 arrests, the chief causes for which were: Intoxication, 4,391; violation of ordinances, 1,421; petit larceny, 1,029; assault and battery, 1,020; disorderly conduct, 965; vagrancy, 811; suspicious, 645; drunk and disorderly, 463; profanity, 426; threatening, 385; assault, 290; affray, 217; witnesses, 127; carrying concealed weapons, 105; fugitives, 103.

These arrests were classified as follows:

Total number of arrests	13,558
Males	11,432
Females	2,126
Married	4,520
Single	9,038
Could read and write	6,130
Could not read and write	7,428

Offenses against the person were committed by 8,315 males and 1,741 females.
Offenses against property were committed by 3,117 males and 385 females.

The cases were disposed of as follows: Dismissed, 6,188; fined, 3,364; sent to workhouse, 1,784; sent to jail, 1,158; bonds (personal), 216; bonds (to keep the peace), 155; *nol. pros.* entered, 128; bonds (for grand jury), 110; variously disposed of, 346; remaining, 109.

The following list indicates the nature of the miscellaneous work performed by the department:

Attempted suicides	6
Accidents reported	323
Assistance rendered	284
Abandoned infants found	26
Broken lamps reported	174
Dead infants found	47
Dangerous holes in carriageways and sidewalks	106
Doors and windows found open and secured	176
Dead bodies found	14
Dead animals reported	445
Deaths where coroner was notified and no inquest held	20
Fire-plugs reported out of repair	31
Fires attended	172
Filthy alleys reported	67
Horses and vehicles found and returned to owners	196
Hydrants out of repair	123
Inquests attended	29
Loads of coal weighed	1,171
Lost children restored to parents	195
Lodgers accommodated	7,461
Nuisances reported	177
Owners of insecure buildings notified	13
Pumps out of repair	157
Permits examined	94
Sudden deaths reported	45
Sewers in bad condition	46
Suicides reported	9
Sunstroke	1
Trees and tree-boxes reported broken	1,121
Telegrams sent and received	48,434
Water-notices served by police	7,017

The mounted force consists of the major and superintendent, the captain and inspector, 4 of the lieutenants, 3 of the sergeants, and 43 of the privates. With the help of this force county beats are more thoroughly patrolled. Their services are also very valuable in the city, where they are kept constantly moving throughout their several precincts.

The district government owns the station-houses in the 3d, 4th, and 8th precincts; all others, including the police headquarters, and a substation at Uniontown, are rented at an annual rental of $5,960.

In his annual report for the year ending June 30, 1880, the superintendent of police says:

A great objection to the rented station-houses is the close proximity of the cells, lodging-rooms, and water-closets to the rooms occupied as sleeping-rooms by the officers and privates, and although the greatest attention is paid to the cleanliness of the cells and water-closets, it is found nearly impossible to keep them so clean, especially at night, when occupied by prisoners and lodgers, as to prevent them from being extremely offensive to the sense of smell. The noise, too, very often prevents the tired-out patrolman and sergeant from taking the rest and sleep so much needed after their tour of duty, or equally required to perform that on which they are preparing to enter. More especially is this the case during the summer months.

This matter of station-houses is one of the greatest importance to the health and comfort of the force, and I therefore earnestly call the attention of the commissioners to the great necessity of erecting buildings for such purposes to take the place of those now rented. On economical principles, too, it would also be desirable, as suitable buildings could be built that would cost much less than the district has to pay at present.

It is confidently believed that the discipline of the force is as near perfection as any similar organization in this country. To enforce it, there have been cited before the trial committee during the past year, on complaints preferred, eighty-one members of the force, as is shown in the table:

Conduct unbecoming an officer of police	1
Conduct unbecoming a policeman	10
Gross neglect of duty	12
Intoxication	10
Intoxication and insubordination	1
Insubordination and neglect of duty	1
Malicious arrest	1
Neglect of duty	17
Neglect of duty and disobedience of orders	1
Unlawful arrest	2
Violation of rules and regulations	25
Total	81

A branch of the police department is the sanitary office. The following from the report of the sanitary officer for the same period (1879–'80) sufficiently explains its province:

The daily duties of this office are principally to provide for the sick and poor, especially those who have no friends and are compelled to go to hospital for treatment, which includes not only the indigent sick poor and insane persons residents of the District of Columbia, but many transient sick and insane persons who are found in our midst in a destitute and deplorable condition, belonging to the different states and territories. Each case is carefully examined into, and, if found to be a fit subject for treatment, the patient is promptly conveyed to the hospital [to] which he or she is entitled to admission under the law. In connection with the removal of these sick and insane cases to the several hospitals and asylums, I wish to call attention to the great amount of service performed by the ambulance during the past year. * * * A great many of those cases are found to reside a great distance from the hospital to which they are assigned, some even in the extreme end of the county, and it frequently occurs that a patient is removed in the morning from a certain locality and another reported from near the same place in the afternoon; each case is generally reported to be urgent, and consequently must be removed without delay. It will thus be perceived the hard work the horses attached to the ambulance, as well as the driver, have to perform, traveling often without even having time to partake of food; frequently, after having worked hard all day, there is an urgent call at night, owing to accidents, etc., and the ambulance is * * * brought into service, as though it had done no duty during the day. The consequences are that the horses break down from overwork. * * * I therefore suggest that a light single-horse wagon, suitable for conveying such sick patients as are able to sit up (though unable to walk), and those residing outside of the city limits, be provided for the use of the office. * * *

In my last annual report I referred to the fact that a number of non-resident insane paupers were found by the officers of this department wandering about the streets, and that under the law the district was compelled to defray the expenses of their support in the government hospital for the insane until their legal place of residence is ascertained, a matter which is sometimes impossible, owing to the fact that many of them are not possessed of mind enough to give any account of their friends or place of residence. Those who can, are conveyed under escort to their homes, while the others are retained at the asylum, both at the entire expense of the district. I therefore suggest that Congress be requested to make special appropriation out of the United States Treasury to defray both the cost of their support while in hospital as well as transporting them to their homes, as they have no claim whatsoever upon the district, inasmuch as they belong [to] and are residents of the different states.

This office is also charged with furnishing transportation to persons who come here to this city in hopes of getting employment, or who have some claim against the government—for instance, soldiers and widows of soldiers applying for pensions, and who * * * find that they not only fail to obtain the object of their mission, but that the general government has made no provision whatsoever with which they could be sent to their homes. The result is, they apply, like all others, to the police department for assistance; and as they are not tramps, and can not be classed as such, being simply subjects of adverse circumstances, they must be treated with the consideration due to humanity, and therefore it has been the practice of this office to extend to those people, or at least to the most distressed ones among the number, relief by way of transportation to or toward their homes. Owing to the small amount appropriated, relief can not be extended to one applicant out of ten. The cost of such transportation is borne by the district, though the beneficiaries are residents of the different states, and with few exceptions have some claim on the general government, inasmuch as the greater number of them have been soldiers or [are] the widows or orphans of soldiers who served in the late war. I therefore suggest that the amount be increased to $5,000, as there is no money appropriated by Congress which does more good in relieving persons in distress than that expended in transporting this class of worthy people to their homes

The number of sick and destitute persons sent to the several hospitals and asylums by this department during the year was as follows:

To Washington asylum	327
To Freedmen's hospital	313
To Providence hospital	144
To Government hospital for the insane	73
To Children's hospital	8
To Columbia hospital	7
To Women's Christian Association home	2
Total	874

The number of non-resident paupers furnished with transportation to other cities, procured from the commissioners of the District of Columbia, was 372.

The number of cases removed in police ambulance from the scene of accident, and from the several dispensaries, to their respective homes, averaged about 4 per week.

The total cost of the Metropolitan police department for the year ending June 30, 1880, was $301,926 25.

FIRE DEPARTMENT.

The fire department of Washington is divided into 6 engine companies and 2 truck companies. The apparatus consists of 8 engines, 8 hose-carriages, 3 hook-and-ladder trucks, and 1 fuel-wagon. Of the engines, 5 are in good order and the rest in fair condition. The hose-carriages are all in good condition, and 2 of the trucks with ordinary repairs will last several years. There are on hand 15,600 feet of fabric hose in good, 3,700 feet in fair, and 3,400 feet in bad condition. The houses are 8 in number, and 6 of them are in excellent condition; but No. 4, in south Washington, and No. 5, in Georgetown, are really unfit for fire purposes, the latter, especially, being too old and small, and so dilapidated as to render it unsafe. The department has 38 horses, 32 of which are in active service. The *personnel* of the force and their salaries are:

2 commissioners at	$200	8 hostlers at	$800
1 commissioner and secretary at	400	6 firemen at	800
1 chief engineer at	1,800	2 tillermen at	800
1 assistant chief engineer at	1,400	54 privates at	720
8 foremen at	1,000	3 watchmen at	720
6 engineers at	1,000		

During the year ending June 30, 1880, there were 120 alarms, of which 109 were for actual fires, 4 false alarms, 6 chimney fires, and 1 test alarm. The actual fires involved an alleged loss of $133,450, with an insurance of $100,050.

The fire-alarm telegraph is used in connection with the department, and gives great satisfaction, though 50 additional signal-boxes are recommended by the superintendent.

The cost of the fire department for the year closing June 30, 1880, is $109,659 38.

The following is copied from the annual report of the fire commissioners for the same year:

Without a proper water-supply the services of the fire department are of but little avail. Particular attention is therefore asked to that portion of the chief engineer's report which suggests the erection of new and the change of old fire-plugs, the increase in size of water-mains, and the construction of cisterns in certain exposed and illy supplied sections of the district.

We are again constrained to call attention to the fact that no provision is made for members of the department rendered unfit for active service by disability incurred in the line of duty. We are compelled to carry these men on the rolls, or else discharge them from the force, broken in health and unable to make a living for themselves or families. We again recommend that provision be made for such men in other branches of the public service better suited to their physical condition. Where men are so far broken in health or maimed by accident as to be totally unfit for any duty whatever, they should be retired upon pay sufficient to keep them comfortably during the continuance of their disability. There are men now on the rolls who will never be able to perform active duty as firemen, and provision should be made at once for them, and their places on the force filled by active men.

The general good conduct of the officers and men is notable in so large a force, and seems to increase from year to year, as shown by the decreasing number of punishments inflicted for violations of the rules, while the efficiency of the department is also increasing, as shown by its almost uniform success in confining fires to the structures in which they originated.

The following is from the report of the chief engineer for the same period:

On this topic [water-supply] I can not do better than renew my recommendation of last year, as follows:

I beg leave to call your attention to the comparatively unknown fact that in the business portions of the city the present supply of water, or water-fixtures, is inadequate to properly work the full force of the department in the event of a large fire. This is a most important subject, and the proper and permanent remedy would be either in larger water-mains, or in reopening the old and constructing new cisterns in several sections of the city. This can be done at a comparatively small cost, and the advantages to be derived will be great.

It is useless to ask for the erection of additional fire-plugs along the line of 6- or 4-inch mains, for those now up can not supply sufficient water for our engines working at a high pressure, and for this reason I urge either cisterns or large mains, or both.

In addition to this, the old plugs with 9-inch outlets should be at once altered to 10 inch, as this will secure uniformity, and in many cases secure a larger flow of water.

A special point in the city to which I beg leave to call your attention is the Government Printing Office, a building which, in addition to the host of persons who are employed there day and night, contains so much valuable property. This building is old, illy constructed, and, although crowded with inflammable material, was constructed without any regard to safety from fire. In its vicinity there are but few plugs, and they are small mains. I beg that a 12- or 20-inch main be placed around the building, additional plugs erected, and that at least two cisterns be dug in that locality; for, besides the printing-office, there are in that vicinity several hundred buildings, built in rows, many of them without even brick partition-walls, and all liable to rapid destruction in the event of a fire without a full supply of water.

For the fifth time I call attention to the necessity of fire-escapes in all large buildings where numbers of persons congregate.

In addition to fire-escapes I would recommend that on all government buildings and hotels in the city iron ladders, reaching from the ground to the roof, be constructed and kept in position at all times, thus providing a mode of reaching or escaping from the roof in time of fire. Such ladders could be placed against the inside or court-yard walls of the public buildings, and in the others suitable places could be found so as to prevent their interfering with the appearance of the building. I notice with regret that many of the merchants have been permitted to erect upon the tops of their buildings large sign-boards, mostly of wood. This is a most dangerous practice, for in the event of a large fire they are liable to be lifted up by the heat and in this burning condition carried squares distant, to the imminent danger of other property. Further than this, in the business portion of the city, all large mercantile houses should be furnished with iron shutters. If these suggestions could be incorporated in the building laws I am sure they would add greatly to the security of property in the event of fires.

PUBLIC SCHOOLS.

The number of youth of school age (6 to 17, inclusive) in the District of Columbia, according to the census of 1878, was: White, 26,426; colored, 12,374; total, 38,800. The whole number of pupils enrolled in the public schools for the school year ending June 30, 1880, was: White, 16,914; colored, 9,505; total, 26,419; increase over the enrollment of last year, 1,289.

The average number of pupils enrolled in the public schools for the school year ending June 30, 1880, was: White, 13,978; colored, 7,602; total, 21,580. The increase over last year was 1,191.

The number of teachers employed for the school year ending June 30, 1880, was: In the white schools, 281; in the colored schools, 152; total, 433.

The total payment for the support of the public schools for the school year ending June 30, 1880, was $438,567 42.

The number of school-rooms owned is, for white schools, 166; for colored schools, 98; total, 264.

The number of school-rooms rented is, for white schools, 93; for colored schools, 27; total, 120.

An appropriation for two buildings of twelve rooms each, one for the white schools and one for the colored schools of Washington, has been made, and the work on them is already begun, and will be finished by the end of the present school year.

Estimating the average cost of a site and school-building of twelve rooms at $40,000, the following is the estimated cost of buildings needed to supply the place of the rented rooms:

For white schools: In Washington, $281,250; in Georgetown, $7,500; in the county, $15,000; total, $303,750.

For colored schools: In Washington, $45,000; in the county, $11,250; total $56,250. Grand total, $360,000.

An accurate register of births and deaths is kept by the commissioner of health, through the secretary. Physicians, or attendants, or coroners are required to furnish to the undertaker within forty-eight hours a full statement of the cause of death. No sexton may allow a dead body to be interred without first procuring such certificate, or, if from any cause this can not be procured, a certificate of death from the commissioner of health.

> Every sexton or other person having charge of any vault, burying-ground, or cemetery within the city of Baltimore, and every undertaker or other person who shall remove any dead body, which had not been buried, from or out of the said city, shall return the certificate of death to the board of health before 12 o'clock m. on the Saturday next succeeding the date of burial or removal of the body out of the city.

For the proper registration of births, every person practicing midwifery shall keep a register of all births, with their details, occurring under their care. These are to be returned monthly on a blank schedule furnished for the purpose to the commissioner of health, between the first and third days of the month. Failure to report is punishable by a fine of $10. From the returns of deaths and the causes thereof a weekly mortuary report is made up and published in leaflet form by the department. To this is added a table of meteorological observations taken during the same week at the United States signal office. In the annual report of the health department to the mayor and city council these weekly mortuary tables are consolidated into a yearly table. The commissioner of health, James A. Steuart, M. D., in his annual report for 1880 says:

> It is with no small pride that I call the attention of your honorable body to the department of vital statistics which was inaugurated in the year 1875, and is now brought to the highest perfection under the laborious and faithful conduct of Mr. A. E. Carter, secretary of the board of health, and of Mr. F. W. Raborg, recording clerk. The promptness and accuracy with which the weekly mortuary records are made up is, I may justly say, in advance of any other of the sixty odd cities with which we now correspond.
>
> The returns of births by physicians and midwives have, during the past year, greatly improved, as shown by the increased number reported under that head in this report. The undoubtedly increasing population of Baltimore is thus demonstrable, and is a source of profound gratification to the board, as I am sure it must be to the public.
>
> The vaccine physicians have done a fair amount of work during the year, and deserve especial praise for the energy displayed during the excitement of last spring. With the exception of the 14 or 15 cases which occurred at that period, our city has been free from small-pox for a number of years. Exemption from this disease can only be insured by attention to vaccination.

In addition to its regular annual reports, the department reports informally from time to time to the mayor and city council.

MUNICIPAL CLEANSING.

Street-cleaning, and removal of ashes and garbage.—This work is performed under the direction of the assistant health commissioner, who is the general superintendent of streets. The streets are cleaned by the regular force, hired for the purpose, and the work is done wholly by hand, no sweeping-machines being used. There is no stated time for the cleaning, the work going on constantly, the object being to keep the streets in good condition. The city is divided into districts, and a superintendent is appointed in each, who is under the direction of the general superintendent, and is required to keep his district clean. The men go through all the streets and alleys of the city scraping and sweeping the dirt into piles, when it is removed by teams. Garbage—which means kitchen-offal—and coal and other ashes, are removed daily (Sundays excepted) from May 1 to November 1, and three times a week, on alternate days, during the remainder of the year. Householders are required to have their garbage placed in vessels not exceeding in capacity one bushel each (kitchen-offal and ashes not being allowed in the same vessel), and to be placed near their premises, or in some convenient place of access. The garbage-carts have a capacity of at least 40 cubic feet, are strongly built, and, when loaded, are required to be covered. The driver of each cart carries a horn, which is sounded at intervals as a warning to householders to have their garbage ready. The final disposal of both street-sweepings and garbage is the same, viz, such of it as is salable is sold (this includes all the offal, etc.), while the remainder is used in filling low lots to grade. The following, from the report of the general superintendent of streets, will show the number of loads removed, cost of the service, etc., during the year 1880:

Number of loads of garbage and ashes removed	145,485
Number of loads of street-dirt, ice, sand, snow, etc., removed	162,092
Total number of loads of all kinds removed	307,577
Cost of removal of garbage and ashes	$67,355 50
Cost of removal of street-dirt, etc	66,852 85
Cost of dumps	3,471 00
Cost of tools and incidentals	2,100 06
Total cost	179,779 41
Amount of annual appropriation for street and garbage department	178,500 00
Deficiency	1,279 41

Average cost per load, 58½ cents.

Dr. James F. McShane, general superintendent, further says in his report, regarding the efficiency of the service:

> Every endeavor has been made to keep the city in a cleanly condition, but the annual appropriation for this purpose is insufficient; consequently the work of scavengering has not approached the standard desired. * * * There is no more important service performed

by this department than the cleaning of streets and the removal of garbage and ashes. The immense amount of territory embraced within the limits of the city makes it a deficient service in consequence of the insufficient force employed, and the distance to which we are compelled to carry the refuse; yet notwithstanding these drawbacks, there is a satisfaction in knowing that during the past year the work performed has been generally commended.

Dead animals.—The carcass of any animal dying within the limits of the city, is reported to the police, and at once removed to the bone-dust factories by the regular scavengers. The annual cost of the service is $3,000 for salaries and $500 for expenses, but no account is kept of the number of dead animals removed. It is stated that the system works satisfactorily, there being only small defects.

Liquid household wastes and human excreta.—There being no sewers to speak of in Baltimore, as a rule all chamber-slops are deposited in cesspools or privy-vaults, while the principal portions of the laundry wastes and kitchen-slops find their way into the street-gutters. The cesspools and privy-vaults are porous, are not provided with overflows, and receive the wastes from water-closets. It is estimated that there are fully 80,000 cesspools and privy-vaults in the city, many of them being dug down to either quicksand or running water. There do not appear to be any special rules as to their construction. They are cleaned by regular scavengers, who are under bond to conduct their business in a manner that will not offend the sight or cause a smell, and before any cesspool or privy-well is opened a permit must be obtained from the board of health. These permits must be used within twenty-four hours after issue. The night-soil, which used to be carried to the city dumps or disposed of to gardeners, is now all taken by a contractor who converts it into a fertilizer. The honeycombing of the soil under the city by the numerous privy-wells and cesspools, and the disposal of much of the household wastes by surface drainage, has had its influence on the well-water in a marked degree. In 1879 William P. Tonry, Ph. D., under direction of the board of health, made an extended examination into the condition of the pump (well) and spring water in the different sections of the city. Of the 35 samples taken from different points west of Jones' falls, 23 were found to be filthly, 5 bad, 7 suspicious, and only 1 sample that could be classed as good. This section of Baltimore is supposed to be much more liberally supplied than the eastern section, with all the modern conveniences, among which may be included privy-wells sunk to water. In that portion of the city east of Jones' falls 10 samples were found to be filthy, 5 bad, 15 suspicious, and 5 good. Professor Tonry says:

The 23 worst samples from West [Baltimore] and the 10 worst samples from East Baltimore show such very large amounts of ammonia as to point unmistakably to direct and close contact with privy refuse; and it is more than probable that these wells or springs have been drawing part at least of their supply of water from some of the privy-wells that have been sunk to water. Of these 33 filthy samples, 11 from West Baltimore and 4 from East Baltimore contain more free ammonia than a mixture of distilled water and wine, one-tenth of which was wine. As for the bad and suspicious samples, the source of contamination will be found in excrementary matter which has had to pass through the earth for a greater or less distance before oozing into the well or spring.

CITY GOVERNMENT.

The city government is vested in a mayor, elected biennially, with a salary of $5,000, and a city council of two branches—the first and second. The first branch consists of 1 member from each of the 20 wards into which the city is divided, elected annually, while the second branch consists of 10 members, each member representing 2 wards, elected biennially. The members of both branches receive each $1,000 per annum. The mayor has a veto power that it requires a vote of three-fourths of each branch to overcome.

While the mayor and city council have all the usual authority of municipal corporations to raise money by taxation, a provision of the constitution of the state declares that—

No debt (except as hereinafter excepted) shall be created by the mayor and the city council of Baltimore; nor shall the credit of the mayor and city council of Baltimore be given or loaned to or in aid of any individual, association, or corporation; nor shall the mayor and city council of Baltimore have the power to involve the city of Baltimore in the construction of works of internal improvement, nor in granting any aid thereto, which shall involve the faith and credit of the city, nor make any appropriation therefor, unless such debt or credit be authorized by an act of the general assembly of Maryland and by an ordinance of the mayor and city council of Baltimore, submitted to the legal voters of the city of Baltimore at such time and place as may be fixed by said ordinance, and approved by a majority of the votes at such time and place; but the mayor and city council may temporarily borrow any amount of money to meet any deficiency in the city treasury, or to provide for any emergency arising from the necessity of maintaining the police or preserving the safety and sanitary condition of the city, and may make due and proper arrangements and agreements for the removal and extension, in whole or in part, of any and all debts and obligations created according to law before the adoption of this constitution [1860].

Except where otherwise provided by ordinance or by the legislature of the state, the mayor appoints all subordinate officers by and with the advice and consent of the two branches of the council in convention.

The collector of state and city taxes is appointed annually " as other city officers are appointed, to collect all taxes of every description, levied or assessed by the mayor and city council or by the general assembly of Maryland". He gives bond in the sum of $75,000, and has a salary of $2,000, in addition to which he is allowed 1 per cent. of the state taxes collected by him. He appoints a deputy at a salary of $1,800, a cashier, and other officers required for the performance of his duties, as prescribed by the ordinance concerning the collection of taxes.

In this connection there is an appeal-tax court, consisting of three judges, who receive a salary each of $1,800, with a clerk at a salary of $1,600, an assessor, and other officers provided for by law. They are authorized to assess the property of all persons failing to make their own returns, and are authorized to make alterations, additions, or deductions in assessments, as they may deem proper. A part of the duty of the appeal-tax court is to grant permits for the erection of buildings within the city limits without charge.

There is a register, who is elected biennially by the two branches of the council in convention. The duties of the register are numerous. Generally stated, he has charge of the moneys and securities of the corporation and is its accounting officer; he gives bond in the sum of $50,000, and has a salary of $3,000. No money can be paid, however, except through a warrant of the comptroller.

The comptroller is appointed biennially by the mayor. He performs the duties indicated by his title; gives bond in the sum of $10,000, and has a salary of $2,500. The comptroller, although appointed by the mayor, can be removed only by the joint action of the city council.

The public debt of Baltimore January 1, 1880, was $35,017,151 13, against which, including a sinking-fund of $7,423,727 11, there are interest-bearing securities of $28,092,389 09, leaving a balance of debt over and above interest-bearing securities of $6,924,762 04, for which the city holds unproductive assets of more or less value amounting to $4,807,472 57, besides a large amount of real estate in its court-house, record office, city hall, jail, police-stations, fire-engine houses and apparatus, school-houses, almshouse, steam-tugs, Marine Hospital grounds, public parks, etc.

The public debt of the city, its investments and finances generally, are in charge of a board consisting of the mayor and two citizens, who are elected by the councils in convention annually, and styled "the commissioners of finance". No salary is attached to the office.

POLICE.

A police commission of three persons, known as the "board of police commissioners of the city of Baltimore", who hold their offices for six years, is elected by the state legislature, one at each biennial session. They give a bond to the state in the penalty of $10,000 each, and there is a salary of $2,500 attached to the office. They choose their own president, and a treasurer, who must be one of their number; a clerk, with a salary of $1,500, who gives bond in the penalty of $5,000, and is virtually the treasurer; a marshal, with a salary of $2,500, and a deputy marshal, whose salary is $2,000. They enroll and organize a permanent police force of 500 men. The captains on the force receive $22 per week; the lieutenants, $20; the sergeants, $19; and the privates, $18. Including officers, sergeants, keepers of stations, turnkeys, etc., the whole regular police force consists of about 600 men, and is maintained at an annual expense of about $590,000. The police commissioners are authorized to increase the force on special occasions, when the pay of each person added to the force is $2 50 per diem while he remains in service. While the state appoints the police commissioners, the expense of supporting the board is borne by the city. To enumerate the powers of the commission would extend this notice too far. They may be inferred from the title. It reports to the legislature at each session, and its books and papers are open at all times to the city authorities.

From the report of the board of police commissioners to the general assembly of Maryland, it seems that during 1880 there were 22,021 arrests made by the force, the principal causes being as follows: Assault (various), 2,998; disorderly conduct; 9,542; intoxication, 2,530; larceny, 1,152; suspicion of larceny, 412; threatening assault, 452; and violating ordinances, 1,262. The final disposition of the arrests was: Committed, 8,631; bailed, 6,027; fined, 917; and discharged, 6,446. During the same time the total amount of lost or stolen property secured by the police was $85,850 40, and of this $85,386 91 was returned to the owners. The total number of station-house lodgers during the year was 13,041.

FIRE DEPARTMENT.

The fire department of Baltimore is under the control of an unpaid commission of her citizens, styled "the fire commissioners of the city of Baltimore", of which the mayor is *ex officio* a member. They hold their offices for four years, two going out of office every second year. They appoint a chief engineer at a salary of $2,000, and two assistant engineers with a salary of $1,400 each. The power of the board of fire commissioners is ample in all matters connected with the most efficient service of the department. If a fireman is injured while on duty so as to be prevented from following his daily occupation, or attending to his duties in the department, he is paid his salary for one year, if his disability so long continues. If a fireman loses his life while in the discharge of his duties, the family of the deceased, including father and mother, are to be paid $500. In addition to this, the fire commissioners are authorized to effect insurances on the lives of the firemen.

A part of the force of the department is always on duty, day and night. Other members, although required to be at the engine-houses at night, are permitted to pursue (except during a fire) other occupations through the day. The annual expense of the fire department is $175,000.

From the annual report of the chief engineer for the year ending December 31, 1880, it is seen that the working force of the department consists of 17 foremen, 13 enginemen and 13 assistant engineers, 17 hostlers, 4 tillermen, 1 horseman, 104 firemen, and 39 laddermen, making a total of 208, exclusive of the general officers. They are divided into 17 companies, and each company, in addition to the above, has 5 substitutes, who give their services to the department for no compensation except when on duty, but who are always in the line of promotion. At the present time the department has in service the following apparatus, manned and equipped: 13 steam fire-engines, 26 four-wheeled hose-carriages, 10 steam-heaters, 4 hook-and-ladder trucks, 4 fuel-tenders, 1 supply-wagon, 24 fire-extinguishers, 5 covered wagons, and 1 jagger-wagon; while in reserve there are 4 steam fire-engines and equipments. There are now in service 73 horses and 25,900 feet of hose, 15,800 feet being good and 10,100 feet medium.

The number of alarms during the past twelve months was 343, of which 205 were telegraph alarms and 138 were extinguished without a telegraphic alarm. There were 8 second alarms and 7 general alarms. The losses amounted to $580,290 43, of which amount $320,547 09 was caused by 2 fires, and $158,193 was caused by fires in Baltimore county, outside the city limits.

In connection with the fire department there a salvage corps and a fire-alarm telegraph.

COMMERCE AND NAVIGATION.

[From the reports of the Bureau of Statistics for the fiscal years ending June 30.]

Customs district of Baltimore, Maryland.	1879.	1880.
Total value of imports	$14,042,768	$19,956,989
Total value of exports:		
Domestic	$57,478,495	$76,220,870
Foreign	$84,027	$32,696
Total number of immigrants	4,713	17,394

Customs district of Baltimore, Maryland.	1879.		1880.	
	Number.	Tons.	Number.	Tons.
Vessels in foreign trade:				
Entered	1,778	1,374,554	1,794	1,502,713
Cleared	1,728	1,345,747	1,770	1,491,060
Vessels in coast trade and fisheries:				
Entered	1,463	997,923	1,455	1,021,887
Cleared	1,871	1,269,074	2,143	1,505,733
Vessels registered, enrolled, and licensed in district..	1,006	100,008	1,013	102,139
Vessels built during the year	24	1,977	24	445

MANUFACTURES.

The following is a summary of the statistics of the manufactures of Baltimore for 1880, being taken from tables prepared for the Tenth Census by N. H. Creager, chief special agent:

Mechanical and manufacturing industries.	No. of establishments.	Capital.	AVERAGE NUMBER OF HANDS EMPLOYED.			Total amount paid in wages during the year.	Value of materials.	Value of products.
			Males above 16 years.	Females above 15 years.	Children and youths.			
All industries	3,683	$38,586,773	34,086	18,137	4,115	$15,117,489	$47,974,297	$78,417,304
Agricultural implements	5	106,000	118	....	15	49,250	101,000	229,550
Awnings and tents	3	4,600	11	30	....	7,900	16,800	36,100
Bags, paper	3	78,500	24	22	4	17,704	152,270	236,700
Baking and yeast powders (see also Drugs and chemicals)	4	70,600	12	14	....	16,000	111,040	167,808
Baskets, rattan and willow ware	16	5,110	16	....	2	5,168	5,335	18,826
Blacksmithing (see also Wheelwrighting)	116	127,520	270	....	6	123,894	98,225	348,835
Bookbinding and blank-book making	17	91,756	99	83	25	61,593	59,304	163,988
Boot and shoe uppers	11	7,700	27	18	1	11,755	17,375	37,675
Boots and shoes, including custom work and repairing	623	865,337	2,117	507	70	939,861	1,632,492	3,411,736
Boxes, cigar	13	19,325	22	19	9	15,163	28,883	58,822
Boxes, fancy and paper	8	34,020	28	169	10	32,617	82,883	140,625
Boxes, wooden packing	13	139,012	318	....	44	147,077	300,573	531,000
Brass castings	10	19,500	32	....	1	16,279	33,741	71,101
Bread and other bakery products	316	832,372	625	73	58	261,463	1,449,459	2,172,062
Brick and tile	28	640,000	1,460	....	69	322,839	156,648	626,813
Brooms and brushes	28	83,115	210	22	32	74,758	156,978	293,619
Carpentering	114	1,107,800	1,226	....	9	674,964	1,906,239	3,216,028
Carpets, rag	17	23,525	28	2	4	10,521	23,078	48,506
Carriages and sleds, children's	3	15,600	31	2	3	10,740	33,500	53,080
Carriages and wagons (see also Wheelwrighting)	37	223,700	364	....	8	147,201	155,573	397,849
Clothing men's	188	3,848,851	5,184	5,915	58	1,822,501	6,013,863	9,446,793
Clothing, women's	27	136,250	22	482	23	84,908	265,192	469,718
Coffee and spices, roasted and ground	13	124,750	46	23	....	24,503	221,108	299,874
Coffins, burial cases, and undertakers goods	52	91,275	73	....	1	31,984	73,103	184,423
Confectionery	53	339,765	222	87	13	110,718	781,752	1,108,638

MANUFACTURES.

The following is a summary of the statistics of manufactures of Washington for 1880, being taken from tables prepared for the Tenth Census by William H. Boyd, chief special agent:

Mechanical and manufacturing industries.	No. of establishments.	Capital.	AVERAGE NUMBER OF HANDS EMPLOYED.			Total amount paid in wages during the year.	Value of materials.	Value of products.
			Males above 16 years.	Females above 15 years.	Children and youths.			
All industries	971	$5,552,526	5,496	1,389	261	$3,924,612	$5,335,400	$11,882,316
Awnings and tents	3	2,050	4	6	....	3,581	4,643	13,924
Blacksmithing (see also Wheelwrighting)........	77	31,165	113	....	1	45,408	39,474	146,219
Bookbinding and blank-book making	4	4,200	9	1	2	4,332	2,280	10,731
Boots and shoes, including custom work and repairing	73	49,220	66	1	2	31,111	42,225	127,107
Brass castings	2	132,038	61	....		22,087	67,152	96,769
Bread and other bakery products	62	120,340	164	7	8	73,148	400,608	606,236
Brick and tile	13	330,600	576	....	120	123,161	62,575	314,298
Carpentering	58	48,145	245	....	8	135,626	247,006	486,702
Carriages and wagons (see also Wheelwrighting)...	25	173,792	149	....	6	69,496	53,277	183,205
Clothing, men's	35	104,550	157	68	2	98,778	178,302	376,065
Coffee and spices, roasted and ground	3	17,600	14	....		6,356	84,680	100,020
Coffins, burial-cases, and undertakers' goods...	14	61,425	32	....		19,631	41,440	92,640
Confectionery	27	85,575	80	24	2	40,131	122,263	221,902
Cooperage	3	6,700	28	....		11,300	10,770	25,770
Dentistry, mechanical	6	4,975	6	....		2,632	5,600	19,200
Drugs and chemicals (see also Patent medicines and compounds)....	5	54,000	25	....	1	10,190	31,836	63,025
Engraving and die-sinking	3	3,900	5	....	1	1,965	3,900	12,375
Fertilizers	3	95,000	87	....		29,600	156,250	207,250
Flouring- and grist-mill products	9	230,400	40	....		21,508	1,071,600	1,172,375
Foundery and machine-shop products	10	236,000	198	....	9	75,102	155,098	358,166
Furniture (see also Mattresses and spring beds; Upholstering)	19	46,125	72	....		39,385	39,005	113,375
Grease and tallow	3	25,000	7	....		3,422	47,918	69,400
Hairwork.................................	12	6,600	....	27		3,276	6,500	14,800
Instruments, professional and scientific......	5	36,100	14	2	1	13,724	7,750	37,561
Iron railing, wrought	5	3,275	11	....		3,912	4,685	13,403
Jewelry	11	19,600	21	....	2	12,444	11,310	37,533
Kindling wood.............................	6	18,465	28	....	7	11,114	21,969	40,650
Lime	5	19,100	24	....		11,952	17,424	51,648
Liquors, malt.............................	10	208,300	60	....	4	30,186	162,739	275,232
Lithographing (see also Printing and publishing) ...	5	33,200	40	....	3	23,164	16,860	52,334
Lock- and gun-smithing	6	11,700	10	....		5,585	3,745	13,546
Looking-glass and picture frames...........	10	15,000	32	....		16,308	28,706	65,227
Lumber, planed	10	96,200	86	....	5	40,950	124,925	192,792
Marble and stone work	25	113,745	137	....	1	60,400	91,806	198,699
Masonry, brick and stone	31	10,500	190	....		68,750	90,050	200,970
Mattresses and spring beds (see also Furniture)........	3	8,250	6	2		2,000	12,640	17,440
Mineral and soda waters	3	19,200	24	....	8	13,432	10,100	33,700
Models and patterns......................	7	7,200	12	....		6,338	2,605	16,440
Painting and paperhanging................	37	16,600	101	....	2	50,044	49,387	143,471
Patent medicines and compounds (see also Drugs and chemicals).....	5	5,600	9	....		7,098	7,200	20,454
Paving materials	5	56,000	259	....		99,500	171,250	316,500
Photographing	16	34,750	34	5		16,291	10,515	55,551
Plumbing and gasfitting	31	47,750	129	....	6	66,194	102,799	225,193
Printing and publishing (see also Lithographing)	28	971,800	1,026	688	28	1,475,880	827,519	2,896,312
Saddlery and harness	26	30,400	45	....		13,471	33,157	80,349
Soap and candles	5	60,966	22	....	1	7,735	41,678	66,563
Tinware, copperware, and sheet-iron ware....	42	66,965	7	....	3	4,857	96,472	192,081
Tobacco, cigars and cigarettes.............	43	25,950	81	....	8	31,628	45,692	118,318
Umbrellas and canes	5	1,150	3	3	1	785	2,070	6,218
Upholstering (see also Furniture)	10	18,550	25	5	1	12,341	27,016	56,191
Watch and clock repairing	32	17,460	40	....	5	24,361	6,345	42,360
Wheelwrighting (see also Blacksmithing; Carriages and wagons)...	10	6,565	7	....	1	2,252	3,230	11,323
All other industries (a)...................	60	1,702,785	795	550	13	871,113	459,354	1,572,703

a Embracing artificial limbs; bags, paper; baskets, rattan and willow ware; bluing; boxes, cigar; boxes, fancy and paper; brooms and brushes; carpets, rag; cars, railroad, street, and repairs; cheese and butter; clothing, women's; cordage and twine; dyeing and cleaning; electroplating; engraving, steel; engraving, wood; files; fruits and vegetables, canned and preserved; furniture, chairs; glass; glass, cut, stained, and ornamented; gloves and mittens; ink; iron and steel; iron work, architectural and ornamental; leather, curried; leather, dressed skins; leather, tanned; lumber, sawed; mantels, slate, marble, and marbleized; musical instruments and materials (not specified); oil, neat's-foot; paints; paper; perfumery and cosmetics; shirts; spectacles and eyeglasses; stationery goods; stereotyping and electrotyping; stone- and earthen-ware; taxidermy; terra-cotta ware; type-founding; vinegar; wirework; and wood, turned and carved.

From the foregoing table it appears that the average capital of all establishments is $5,718 36; that the average wages of all hands employed is $549 20 per annum; that the average outlay in wages, in materials, and in interest (at 6 per cent.) on capital employed is $9,910 57

PECULIARITIES OF LIFE IN WASHINGTON.

Early in the present century Washington had little else than a temporary population, brought together by the needs of government administration, and changing more or less with each Presidential term. Congress and the families of members, with their social associations, have been a part of Washington scarcely twelve months in each two years, while government employés have retained their legal residence in the localities to which they are accredited. At the present time there are not less than 15,000 persons busy or resident in Washington connected in one way or another with the government, together with the representatives of foreign nations. The local attachments of these people and of their families, which may aggregate 50,000, are elsewhere, and some of them are not even enumerated in Washington, but at their legal residences.

A considerable portion of those occupied in Washington leave their families, at least a part of the time, at their legal homes. The great mass of those employed by the government are adults, the number of pages and messengers yet minors being small. This has given peculiar form to household life in Washington. On every hand are rooms to rent, furnished and unfurnished, with or without board. The price paid for furnished rooms usually includes their care, fuel, and lights. Furnaces, heating- and cooking-stoves, and ranges are to an unusual extent a part of the fixed equipment of rented houses. The great majority of household servants do not sleep at their places of service, but return to their homes at night. Many people prepare coffee or tea and the simpler dishes at their rooms for breakfast, under the name of "light housekeeping", taking a full meal once a day at a boarding-house. Others have meals sent by caterers. The ordinary unit of board- and rent-bills is the calendar month. The duties in the offices confine thousands from 9 a. m. to 4 p. m., with a half-hour at noon for lunch. Thus the chief meal of the day is dinner after office hours, varying from 4 to 6 p. m. The midday meal is necessarily a trifling refreshment taken within the building occupied, or close by. The following list of cheap dishes furnished for such calls in many places about the city is not a mere matter of cash economy, but grows largely out of the inadequacy of time to take a full meal at midday, although such lunches can be had at all hours:

LUNCHES.

	Cents.
French coffee, with cream, rolls, and butter	10
French coffee and pie	10
Toast and tea	10
Oat-meal and milk	10
Oat-meal and cream	15
Soup, bread, and butter	10
Baked beans, bread, and butter	10
Cold meats, coffee, bread, and butter	15
Milk toast	10
Cream toast	20

The list given above might be considerably enlarged, but is a fair sample in the matter of prices. An individual or a family may find comfortable, neat quarters for a day, for a week, or for a month, securing lodgings and board under the same roof or under separate roofs. Numerous coffee-houses support themselves as business enterprises. One may live wholesomely at a small cost, or he may command the attendance and luxury of hotels and boarding-houses equipped for the wealthy. Good board is obtainable as follows: 3 meal-tickets, $1; 16 meal-tickets, $5; table board per month, $20.

GEORGETOWN,
DISTRICT OF COLUMBIA.

POPULATION IN THE AGGREGATE,
1800-1880.

	Inhab.
1790	......
1800	2,993
1810	4,948
1820	7,360
1830	8,441
1840	7,312
1850	8,366
1860	8,733
1870	11,384
1880	12,578

POPULATION BY SEX, NATIVITY, AND RACE,
AT
CENSUS OF 1880.

Male	5,847
Female	6,731
Native	11,763
Foreign-born	815
White	8,819
Colored	*3,759

* Including 1 Japanese.

[For "Financial Condition", see *Washington*.]

HISTORICAL SKETCH.

It is believed that the ground now occupied by the city of Georgetown was visited as early as 1608 by Captain John Smith, and that the famous navigator met the Indians in conference at or a little above this point. In 1748 the legislature of Maryland formed Frederick county, and, by an act passed May 15, 1751, created a commission, composed of 5 members, for the purpose of laying out a town on the Potomac river, above the mouth of Rock creek, in the new county. The land at this place was owned by two persons, but the act gave the commission power to purchase 60 acres, and, in case of failure to agree on satisfactory prices with the owners, to have the land appraised. After some little trouble with one of the proprietors, the necessary ground was acquired, and a survey and plat of the proposed town were completed February 27, 1752, the town being laid out in 80 lots, with streets and lanes. The town was called "Georgetown", not, as many suppose, after the first President of the republic, but in honor of George II, king of England, whose faithful subjects the colonists then were.

The town seems to have remained under the jurisdiction of a commission for several years, as the early records show that the "commissioners" met and appointed a "flour inspector" in February, 1772. In 1783 the town was increased by the addition of 61 acres, and, in 1784, 20 acres, divided into 65 lots, were added. In 1789 Georgetown was incorporated by an act of the Maryland assembly, with a mayor, recorder, board of aldermen, and common councilmen, and some years later the charter was changed so as to bring Georgetown into existence as a city. However, even before the incorporation, Georgetown had become a place of some importance, and as early as 1779 pupils from Bladensburg and the adjacent country came here to take advantage of the educational facilities that then existed.

It was believed that the Potomac would become a great thoroughfare for both foreign and domestic commerce. In 1784 the Potomac Company was chartered for the improvement of navigation up the river, and the work was begun at once, a canal being constructed around the falls of the Potomac. At the Great falls, where the difference of level is 76 feet 9 inches, there were 5 locks on the Virginia side, 2 being cut in the solid rock and 3 lined with red sandstone, while at the Little falls there were 4 locks, to surmount the 37 feet of difference of level. The red sandstone used in the locks was obtained at Seneca creek, a few miles distant, and was of such endurance that even now these locks may be seen with the tool-marks as plain as if just made.

In 1790 Georgetown was made a port of entry, and on October 1 of that year a collector of customs was appointed. In 1790 there were not more than 75 post-offices in the United States, and one of them was located here. Georgetown, however, is said to have had a post-office as early as 1776.

The completion of the locks and canal around the falls soon had an effect on the business of Georgetown, and the laying out of the city of Washington, with the work incident thereto, materially increased the population of the older town. For many years after the removal of the national government to the District of Columbia, part, and sometimes nearly all, of the officials lived in Georgetown. In 1801 Georgetown passed from the jurisdiction of the state of Maryland to that of the District of Columbia, retaining, however, its separate corporate existence. In early years the trade of Georgetown was with the surrounding country; later a large traffic was done on the upper Potomac, during the full stage of water; and then a brisk trade was carried on with European ports, as well as with Baltimore, New York, Boston, etc. In 1825 the Potomac Company was succeeded by a canal company, under which the Chesapeake and Ohio canal was begun in 1828, and completed for a distance of 134 miles in 1839, the remaining 50 miles to Cumberland, Maryland, its present terminus, being finished in 1850. In addition to the tobacco trade, which grew to quite large proportions, the flour and produce trade became of great importance, and until the completion of a railroad to Washington, in 1835, Georgetown supplied the district and the country adjacent. From 1815 to 1835 the value of produce exported to foreign markets from Georgetown amounted to $4,077,708, while the total value of American produce shipped from the port coastwise from 1826 to 1835 amounted to $5,190,540. The average tonnage engaged here during this time amounted to 170,158 per annum.

The progress of Georgetown from 1830 to 1860 was slow, owing in a great measure to the rapid growth of Washington. Business languished, houses ceased to be built, and during the three decades the total increase of population was only about $3\frac{1}{2}$ per cent. In 1833 work was begun on the Alexandria aqueduct and canal (connecting the Chesapeake and Ohio canal at Georgetown with Alexandria), and completed in 10 years, water being turned into the aqueduct July 4, 1843. The aqueduct was continued in use until 1861, when it was seized by the government, the water drawn off, and the aqueduct used as a military road. After the war it was restored to the company, but not in a condition for the use for which it was originally intended.

In 1853 an act was passed by the legislature of Maryland incorporating the Metropolitan Railroad Company, and authorizing the construction of a road from Point of Rocks, on the Baltimore and Ohio railroad, to Georgetown. In order to have the terminus of the road here, the city subscribed for 5,000 shares of the stock, equal to $250,000, and the first installment was paid in 1855. On June 21, 1856, the city passed an ordinance to provide for the payment of the second installment, then due, but the ordinance was vetoed by the mayor. The ordinance was at once passed over the veto, and then the mayor, finding his opposition to the measure becoming a law useless, refused to sign the bonds. This refusal prevented the payment of the second installment, and the railroad company, not being able to go on with its work, lost its charter. By this action Georgetown lost the advantage of becoming a railroad terminus with direct all-rail communication with the West.

Georgetown college, under control of the Society of Jesus, was planned in 1785. Its first building was erected in 1789, and three years later pupils were admitted. In 1815 the college was raised to the rank of a university, with power of conferring degrees in any of the faculties. During the war, 1861–'65, its grounds, at times, were occupied as camps, and its buildings, after the first battle of Bull Run, were used as hospitals. At present there are about 200 pupils, 40 being day scholars, and 14 instructors. Its age and literary standing give the institution prominence.

GEORGETOWN IN 1880.

Georgetown is situated on the left bank of the Potomac river, adjoining the northwest boundary of Washington, from which it is separated by Rock creek, a small stream that enters the Potomac at this point. The position of the city is favorable to good natural drainage, being elevated on hills that slope toward the creek and the river. Just above Georgetown the channel of the Potomac is obstructed by the rapids called the Little falls, to which the tide extends. Between these rapids and the city the channel is so rocky and narrow that practically Georgetown may be considered at the head of tide-water navigation. The harbor, which is here formed by the channel of the Potomac, has an average width of 800 feet, with an average depth of 25 feet. The depth of water over the bar in the channel, just below the city, is only 10 feet at mean low water, but this has been increased to 15 feet by dredging. This gives Georgetown water communication with the Chesapeake bay and the Atlantic ocean, while the Chesapeake and Ohio canal affords a water-route to Cumberland, Maryland, and the coal-fields of that region.

There are several fine buildings in the city, among which may be mentioned the custom-house, the post-office, the market-house, and the public school on Second street. Two street-car lines, running beyond the capitol in Washington, traverse the city and afford ample means of communication with the larger town.

All reports of the commissioners being made for the "district", no separate reports on the internal improvements, etc., of Georgetown can be shown here, and therefore such information regarding these subjects as was available is included under the present condition of Washington city.

VIRGINIA.

ALEXANDRIA,

ALEXANDRIA COUNTY, VIRGINIA.

POPULATION

IN THE

AGGREGATE,

1800-1880.

	Inhab.
1790	......
1800	4,971
1810	7,227
1820	8,218
1830	8,241
1840	8,459
1850	8,734
1860	12,652
1870	13,570
1880	13,659

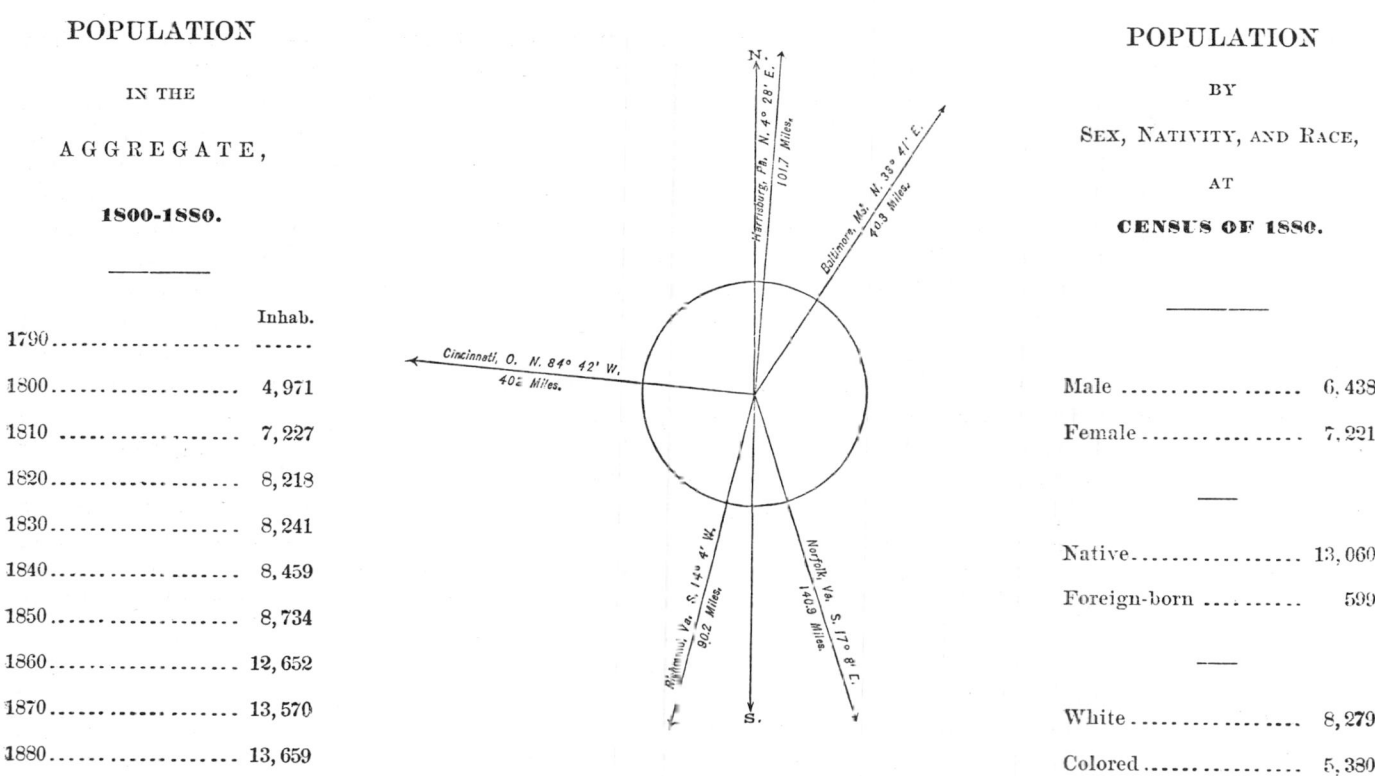

POPULATION

BY

SEX, NATIVITY, AND RACE,

AT

CENSUS OF 1880.

Male	6,438
Female	7,221
Native	13,060
Foreign-born	599
White	8,279
Colored	5,380

Latitude: 38° 48′ North; Longitude: 77° 2′ (west from Greenwich); **Altitude: 56 feet.** (a)

FINANCIAL CONDITION:

Total Valuation: $3,673,674; per capita: $269 00.   Net Indebtedness: $1,037,088; per capita: $75 93.   Tax per $100: $2 73.

HISTORICAL SKETCH.

In 1608 Captain John Smith and 14 companions explored the Potomac and saw, first of all white men, the site of Alexandria. It was occupied by a small tribe of Indians, called "Toags". Captain Smith's account of the place is very short, but sufficiently bespeaks the hospitality of the inhabitants: "At Toags they did their best to content us." Other Indians inhabited localities near, but all were driven away or killed, in 1676, by the fierce onslaught made upon the red men, which originated to protect the settlement against savage inroads. A few years before,

---

a At Smithsonian station.

in 1669, Robert Howison had obtained a patent for the land on which Alexandria stands, and had sold the patent to John Alexander, a Stafford planter, for 6,000 pounds of tobacco. The first known settlement on this patent was made in 1695 by Thomas Pearson, upon Pearson's island. The principal product of the time and locality was tobacco, and fields of the weed soon succeeded the original growth. Tobacco-growing required a warehouse, and in 1731 the Hunting Creek warehouse was built by the county authorities of Prince William county, on the high bluff overlooking the river, near where the gas-works now stand. Around this warehouse gathered the hamlet of Belhaven. With this hamlet for a nucleus, in 1749, William Ramsey, John Carlyle, and their associates founded the town of Alexandria. The town thus originated was laid out and gradually spread over old fields from which the first fertility had been sucked by tobacco.

The town plot was the very picture of colonial loyalty, the "Royal" and "Fairfax" family names ran side by side in its two long streets, which were crossed by the short streets bearing the Fairfax title.

The town grew up amid restrictions on commerce and fetters on manufactures which it now seems incredible that any community schooled in *Magna Charta* could have borne; but the colonists in Alexandria, like Anglo-Saxons everywhere, had a profound respect for law. They submitted to these restrictions because they were accustomed to them, and as they were pressed by French power, and in constant dread of the Indians, which still lingered near, they expected British aid, and thought the profits which England made by a monopoly of their trade was a high price to pay for such assistance, but at least it was a price paid for something. But when Braddock came, and the British troops, instead of protecting the colonists, had been compelled to rely on the colonial troops to protect them, the feeling changed.

The British monopoly of their trade and the restrictions on navigation and manufactures annoyed them. They felt the yoke, and when the time came for throwing it off, it found the people of Alexandria radically for it.

Before the close of the Revolution the political changes already effected demanded new municipal organizations. On the 9th of March, 1790, the first municipal government went into operation, with Robert Townshend Hooe as mayor. The first business of the new government was to grade the streets so as to make an easy approach to the river. The town had been built upon a bluff overlooking the Potomac river, and the inclines to the shore were rough and steep. As the future of the city was deemed to be a commercial one, it was considered wise to cut down this bluff, and it was done, reducing the level here from 10 to 15 feet. The town having been graded, the work of paving streets was begun in 1795. Before the close of the century Alexandria was ceded by Virginia to the federal government as a part of the District of Columbia, and, on the 27th of February, 1801, the exclusive legislation of Congress was extended over the town, but the charter of 1779, with the subsequent acts of Virginia in relation thereto, were continued in force until the 25th of February, 1804, when Congress enacted a new charter for the town.

After the close of the war, Alexandria's commerce grew apace; but soon—1799—came the war with France, and many of her finest vessels were captured by French cruisers. After this blow there came the terrible yellow fever in 1803, "which made a lazar house of the river-front and carried off one in ten of the Alexandrians that dwelt between Fairfax street and the river". The shipping business had scarcely recovered from this when the embargo act, in 1809, fell upon it like a paralytic stroke. In a few years more came the war with Great Britain, "making the port and its commerce a prey to the British frigates 'Euryalus' and 'Sea Horse', which, in August, 1814, sailed up the Potomac with bomb-ketches and captured the town". The captors plundered the warehouses of all the tobacco, flour, cotton, and liquor they found there, and, loading these on to vessels which they seized, sailed away. When peace came in 1815, Alexandria had lost all chance of competition with Baltimore, and she had, too, a nearer rival in the presence of Washington city, which was already drawing trade and population from the Virginia side. The wealth of the nation was used to build up its capital, but very little money was spent on the Virginia portion of the District of Columbia. Deprived of the aid which a connection with Virginia would have afforded, the town remained in a corner of the district, a useless adjunct to the federal territory. Whatever favors Congress conferred were given to Washington, and Alexandria beheld the growth of other cities without power to imitate them. Under these circumstances the town authorities did all that was within their power. Streets were extended and improved, the town was lighted, in the manner then usual, with oil-lamps, and, in 1817, the market building with the cupola and town clock was erected. On January 18, 1827, began a very destructive fire, which burned through the city to the foot of Duke street, destroying 53 houses and causing a loss of $103,000.

In 1828 the Ohio and Chesapeake canal was begun, and in 1829-'30 the Alexandria aqueduct, crossing the Potomac on granite piers, was begun, thus connecting Alexandria by a lateral canal with the Chesapeake and Ohio canal. It was completed in ten or twelve years, but Georgetown, 9 miles nearer the sources of its commerce, reaped the benefit. The place seemed doomed to decay. It was then that Alexandria, isolated in one corner of the District of Columbia, was about to decrease instead of increasing her population; an earnest appeal was made to the state of Virginia, and in 1846 the general assembly opened the arms of the commonwealth to her long-estranged child; the federal government consented and the voters of the town approved, and in September, 1846, with processions, bonfires, and illuminations, and a celebration extending over three days, Alexandria again became a Virginia town. The state began at once to extend substantial aid to the town. It purchased at par the valueless bonds of the Alexandria canal held by the town, thus taking off three-fifths of its debt. With state aid the Orange and Alexandria railroad, with its extensions, the Manassas Gap, and the Alexandria, Loudoun, and Hampshire railroads, were begun, and hundreds of miles were constructed. An era of prosperity began. Over 100 houses were built in a single year; many large and fine ones, including the Pioneer mills, cotton factory, and large warehouses along the river-front, were erected. On May 7, 1852, the general assembly granted to Alexandria a city charter, and the same was accepted by the people on the 4th of the following August. In June, 1860, there were 77 manufacturing establishments in operation, employing 785 hands, and producing, from raw material valued at $91,000, manufactured articles worth $860,000. Trade, both with foreign ports and coastwise, increased and assumed most encouraging proportions. The future was full of promise. The main reliance for commercial prosperity was on the valley of Virginia, of which Alexandria is the natural trade outlet. But, in the presence of railways, water-channels became valueless, and the contest for the trade of the valley became a matter of railroad enterprise. To reach Harrisonburg or Staunton was thought to be all that was needed to put Alexandria's commercial future beyond the reach of chance. The hope, the expectation, seemed well founded, and Alexandria, strong in the favor of the commonwealth, which her trade would help to build up, was sure of protection until the Manassas road was completed to Harrisonburg and commercial connections made that would never be broken. This was the outlook of the city in 1860. The iron rails to make the connection with Harrisonburg complete were piled on her wharves, where stood, on May 25, 1861, the Virginia pickets, whose warning guns announced the movement in force of the troops of the United States who occupied the place. Alexandria became, as it had been during the Revolutionary war, a hospital town. Thenceforward her commerce was ended. A blockade was declared, and the iron rails, bought to finish the Manassas road, were seized and sent off to make a military railroad near Bethel and Fortress Monroe. When the war ended, all chance of Alexandria's exclusive connection with the valley of Virginia was ended too. Baltimore helped to rebuild the road and controlled it. The connection between Winchester and Strasburg was made and managed also for the interest of that great city.

On the 27th of January, 1865, a new charter was granted, by which the government of the city was committed to a single body, called the city council, composed of four members from each ward, alternating by pairs, each two years. Under this charter all officers of the city except the mayor were chosen by the council. But this charter was in turn superseded by another, adopted on the 25th of the next January (1866), which arranged the legislative government of the city into two branches—a board of aldermen and a common council—together composing the city council. This remained in force until superseded by a new one, approved February 20, 1871, but not changing the form of government.

The census of 1870 found Alexandria with a slight decrease in her white population. Since that time, with many discouraging circumstances, Alexandria's progress has been measurably satisfactory; and, with a solid basis in the shape of additional trade and manufactures, which she is gaining, and her most favorable situation, she may reasonably expect yet more flattering corporate gains.

ALEXANDRIA IN 1880.

The following statistical accounts, collected by the Census Office, indicate the present condition of Alexandria:

LOCATION.

The city lies in latitude 38° 48′ north, longitude 77° 2′ west from Greenwich, on the west bank of the Potomac river, 7 miles below Washington, 100 miles above the Chesapeake bay, where the river empties, and 200 miles from the Atlantic ocean. The situation of the Smithsonian Observatory station at Alexandria is 56 feet above mean sea-level. The river is here 1 mile wide, and accommodates vessels drawing 30 feet of water, thus affording water communication with Washington and, via the Chesapeake bay, the ports of the world.

RAILROAD COMMUNICATIONS.

Alexandria is touched by the following railroads:
The Virginia Midland railroad, running to Lynchburg and Danville, Virginia, and its connections.
The Alexandria and Fredericksburg railroad, running to Richmond.
The Alexandria and Washington railroad, to Washington and the North.
The Washington and Ohio railroad, to Point Pleasant, on the Ohio river (completed only to Round Hill, a distance of 56 miles).

TRIBUTARY COUNTRY.

Alexandria has a large trade with neighboring counties, by way of the river, in grain of all kinds; from the Maryland side much tobacco is also received. Steamers ply daily between this place and Norfolk, connecting with steamers on the James river and to the North; and for the accommodation of local river trade three lines of steamers are engaged. There is a considerable growth of new timber in the country surrounding, which has grown up since the cutting of the old growth during the rebellion.

STREETS.

The city's streets are 35 miles in length, of which 20 miles are paved with cobble-stones, at a cost of 60 cents per square yard. Sidewalks are paved with brick, and gutters are paved with cobble-stones, with brick centers. Tree-planting is very generally carried out by property-owners on the street lines. Street-repairing is done by day work, under the supervision of an officer of the city specially delegated for the purpose. As between the contract system and day work it is stated that the contract system is regarded as the better, as under the day's-work system inefficient laborers are never gotten rid of. At the same time, it is thought that the latter method secures more thorough work.

WATER-WORKS.

The water-works are owned by a private corporation, and their total cost was $95,700. The pumping system is used, the pressure in the pipes being 30 pounds to the square inch. The average amount of water pumped per diem is about 288,000 gallons. The yearly cost of maintenance, aside from the cost of pumping, is $4,916 05, and the yearly income from water-rates is $14,500. Water-meters are not used.

GAS.

The gas-works are owned by the city. The daily average production is, in winter 70,000, and in summer 20,000 cubic feet. The charge per 1,000 feet is $2. The city pays $30 for each street-lamp, 150 in number.

PUBLIC BUILDINGS.

The city's municipal offices are contained in its large and fine market building, being the council-chamber and station-house, and mayor's, corporation counsel's, and other offices. The total cost of the municipal buildings belonging to the city is $260,000. The city hall, including market buildings, cost $58,000. It was rebuilt in 1872, and the income up to the present year has repaid the cost. This resource now constitutes a portion of the sinking-fund for the extinguishment of the city's debt.

PUBLIC PARKS AND PLEASURE-GROUNDS.

There are no public parks or pleasure grounds in the city.

PLACES OF AMUSEMENT.

Alexandria has the following concert-halls and lecture-rooms, but no theaters: Sarepta hall, seating 400; Alexandria Light Infantry hall, seating 800; Peabody School Building hall, seating 400; Burney's hall, seating 600; and Harmonic hall, seating 350. Halls used for amusements pay a yearly license fee of $25 each. There are the following concert- and beer-gardens: Englehardt's beer-garden and Portner's beer-garden.

DRAINAGE; CEMETERIES; MARKETS.

No information on any of these subjects was furnished by the city authorities.

SANITARY AUTHORITY—BOARD OF HEALTH.

The board of health is Alexandria's chief sanitary organization. It is an independent board, having twelve members, appointed annually by the city council, but one of whom, the health officer, who is president *ex officio*, is a physician. When there is no declared epidemic the annual expense of the board does not exceed $50, incurred in inquests on the bodies of persons drowned. During an epidemic the expenses of the board are limited by the appropriations of the city council. In the absence of an epidemic the board is authorized to do all such acts as it shall consider necessary to carry into execution the laws in relation to the removal of nuisances and the preservation of the health of the city. During an epidemic, either in the city or at points with which it has communication, the board may establish quarantine. It may order the removal of patients sick with contagious diseases to a temporary hospital. It may provide accommodations for persons who belong on board vessels undergoing quarantine, and generally exert a power over those matters influencing the sanitary condition of the city commensurate with the exigencies of the occasion. The health officer is the chief executive officer of the board, though the superintendent of police is required directly to serve all written orders to remove or abate nuisances which may be given him by any member of the board. The salary of the health officer is $50 per annum. The business of the board is transacted at meetings held monthly, or oftener if necessary, at which a majority of all the members makes a quorum, and a majority of the quorum may act. Only in case of epidemics are assistant health officers or inspectors employed. When necessary, extraordinary powers are given to them by the council. Inspections are not made regularly, but only as nuisances are reported, in the event of which the superintendent of police is ordered to have the nuisance removed at once. The recommendations of the city council, by which the board is appointed, are also invariably observed and acted upon. All interments must be made in the public burying-ground, and graves must be 6 feet deep.

INFECTIOUS DISEASES.

Small-pox patients are isolated either in their own home, when a yellow flag is placed at the door, or by removal to a hospital provided for the purpose. Scarlet-fever patients are not isolated. When necessary, vaccination is made compulsory, and, in the case of paupers, it is done at the public expense.

A register of the births, marriages, and deaths is kept by the clerk of the council.

REPORTS.

No stated reports are required of the board, but it occasionally makes reports in the city newspapers.

MUNICIPAL CLEANSING.

Street-cleaning.—This work is done by the city's force, wholly by hand, and at the public cost. The cleaning is done on the different streets when their condition requires it, and is well done. The cost of this work to the city in 1879 was $812 03. The sweepings are deposited on the outskirts of the city.

Removal of garbage and ashes.—Garbage is removed daily by the city's own force. While awaiting removal garbage must be stored in suitable vessels, ashes not being kept in the same receptacle. It is taken to the almshouse, and there fed to swine. Ashes are used for street-filling in the suburbs. The annual cost to the city for the removal of both is about $1,100. No nuisance or injury to health is reported to result from the improper handling or disposal of garbage and ashes, and the system pursued is considered a good one.

Dead animals.—These are removed and buried by the owners, or by the superintendent of police at their expense, if they can be found; if not, then at the expense of the city. Such animals, if they exceed the size of a cat, must be buried beyond the inhabited parts of the corporation; if they do not, they may be buried on the premises. The annual cost of this service is trifling.

Liquid household wastes.—It is reported that nearly all the liquid household wastes of the city are delivered into the public sewers. No other information on this subject was reported.

Human excreta.—Privy-vaults are cleared out, and the contents are removed, only by the annually appointed night-scavenger, and he can perform his duties only between the hours of 11 p. m. and 4 a. m. The carts employed in this service must be tight and have a suitable cover. For his services he receives fixed sums, differing according to the sizes of the vaults. The night-soil is carried out of the city and used as a fertilizer, but not on land within the gathering-ground of the city's water-supply.

POLICE.

The police force consists of a captain at a salary of $550 per year; a lieutenant at a salary of $500 per year; and 15 patrolmen at a salary each of $480 per year. The men provide their own uniforms. The force is appointed by the city council, and is directly controlled by the mayor. A number of extra policemen, for special occasions, are appointed. There are also 4 candidates on the list for appointment to vacancies occurring on the force. These are called "ready men". The total cost of the department for the year ending March 31, 1880, was $8,374 90, including $124 90 for extra police service.

LYNCHBURG,

CAMPBELL COUNTY, VIRGINIA.

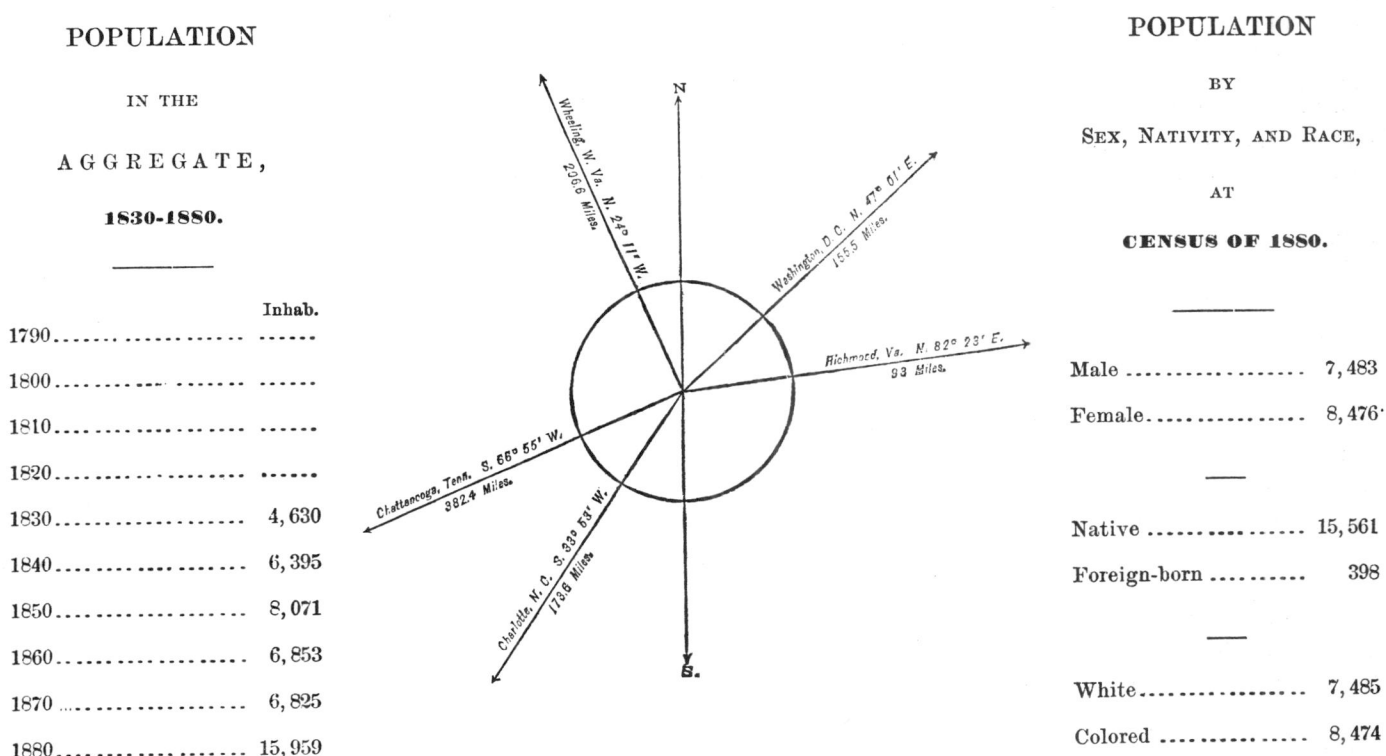

POPULATION

IN THE

AGGREGATE,

1830-1880.

	Inhab.
1790	......
1800	......
1810	......
1820	......
1830	4,630
1840	6,395
1850	8,071
1860	6,853
1870	6,825
1880	15,959

POPULATION

BY

SEX, NATIVITY, AND RACE,

AT

CENSUS OF 1880.

Male	7,483
Female	8,476
Native	15,561
Foreign-born	398
White	7,485
Colored	8,474

Latitude: 37° 22' North; Longitude: 79° 7' (west from Greenwich); Altitude: 528 to 858 feet.

FINANCIAL CONDITION:

Total Valuation: $8,405,610; per capita: $527 00.   Net Indebtedness: $794,837; per capita: $49 80.   Tax per $100: $1 97.

HISTORICAL SKETCH.

Lynchburg owes its foundation to the legislature of Virginia, which, in October, 1786, appointed certain trustees to lay out 45 acres of the land of John Lynch "lying contiguous to Lynch's ferry", in the county of Campbell. The trustees proceeded to sell the land, in half-acre lots, first at public auction, and later by private sale, for the benefit of Lynch, in whose honor they named the village they had laid out "Lynchburg". Starting with an area of 45 acres, the village was increased as fast as new lots could be laid out, and its bounds have been extended from time to time, as these additions made changes necessary. In 1805, when it was incorporated as a town, a considerable addition to its territory was made; and as late as 1870, when the present bounds were assigned, the last and most extensive annexation took place. The trustees continued in the execution of their duty until 1817, but had no other control of the town than in regard to the title of unsold lots.

The first attempt at a water-supply was made by the Lynchburg fire company, which in 1799 obtained permission to sink wells and put pumps in them for the general use. They made little use of the privilege, however; and a public supply of water being greatly needed, the council granted to John Lynch the right to convey water in wooden pipes through the streets, from springs on his farm near the head of Horseford branch, and to charge the citizens who used the water a certain price. The town reserved to itself the right to take water free of charge for use in case of fire. This was the only supply used—a very inadequate one; so in 1827 an agitation of the question began, and finally in 1830 new water-works were completed. They consisted of a dam and a pump-house, where, by means of a double force-pump driven by a breast-wheel, water from the James river was raised to a reservoir capable of holding 400,000 gallons, situated on Clay street, 253 feet above the level of the town. The works cost $50,000, and to pay for them Lynchburg contracted its first debt. It was supposed at the time that ample provision had been made for an indefinite future, but the growth of the city in the last few years has compelled the construction of a large reservoir on College hill. A bequest of $20,000, left by Mr. Samuel Miller in 1869 for additions to the water-works, contributed largely to meet the cost of this work.

The first court-house was built in 1812, and a market in 1813. Both these buildings have now disappeared, the first having been replaced by the present court-house in 1852, and the last, after receiving many additions, was demolished in 1872. A new market-house was built in the next year. In 1816 the town had a population of about 3,000. Its growth in wealth far outstripped the increase in numbers, for in 1850, while the population was only 8,071, the trade was reckoned in millions, and the value of its manufactures exceeded $700,000 a year.

The construction of the James River and Kanawha canal and the Virginia and Tennessee railroad added greatly to the advantages of Lynchburg as a trading center. In 1850 it had about 30 tobacco factories, several large flouring-mills, a cotton-mill, and an iron foundery. Lynchburg was made a city in 1852, but in the decade from 1850 to 1860 the population fell off more than 1,000, and during the war and the reconstruction period was nearly stationary. At the breaking out of the civil war the city sent nearly 1,000 men to the confederate army, and hardly a battle was fought in which Lynchburg was not called to lament the loss of some of her citizens. The city was not entered by the federal forces until after the capture of Appomattox Court-House.

After the war Lynchburg entered upon a new period of growth, and is to-day one of the most flourishing cities of Virginia. The James, which is here about 600 feet wide and 4 feet deep, offers a magnificent water-power, which only needs to be completely developed to make Lynchburg a very important manufacturing city. Since 1870 the population has increased from 6,825 to 15,959, nearly 134 per cent. The city has about 30 large tobacco factories and 6 warehouses, 3 large iron founderies, 3 large flouring-mills, and many other industries. As an inducement to the establishment of new industries the city exempts from taxes, for a space of ten years, all capital so employed. The region about Lynchburg is very rich in coal and other mineral deposits, and the development of these is destined vastly to increase the city's wealth. The present valuation of real and personal estate is over $8,000,000. There are 16 churches and chapels; 4 banks, with an aggregate capital of $525,000; 2 newspapers; and good schools, partly maintained by the Peabody fund.

The location is a peculiarly beautiful one. The James, which 20 miles to the west has broken through the Blue ridge, reaches along its beautiful valley by the city; the wooded country stretching out on all sides leads the eyes gently upward, until in the distant southern horizon they rest upon the famed peak of the Otter; and when one remembers that this beautiful prospect covers deposits of coal and minerals of great value, and that the James furnishes the power necessary to reduce these minerals to usefulness, he may well believe, with the energetic and prosperous people of Lynchburg, that a future of increasing wealth and importance lies open before the city.

LYNCHBURG IN 1880.

The following statistical accounts, collected by the Census Office, indicate the present condition of Lynchburg:

LOCATION.

Lynchburg is situated in latitude 37° 22' north, and longitude 79° 7' west, on the right or south bank of the James river, about 100 miles west by south from Richmond. The lowest point is about 528 and the highest 858 feet above the sea-level, the average level being about 651.5 feet. The James, which is here about 600 feet wide and 4 feet deep, is not navigable, the only means of water communication being by the James River and Kanawha canal, termini Richmond and Buchanan, the former 147 and the latter 50 miles from Lynchburg by the canal.

RAILROAD COMMUNICATIONS.

The Atlantic, Mississippi, and Ohio railroad, termini Bristol, Tennessee, and Norfolk, Virginia, and the Washington City, Virginia Midland, and Great Southern railroad, termini Alexandria and Danville, Virginia, connect the city with this terminal point, and put the city on the trunk-lines connecting the South with the seaboard.

TRIBUTARY COUNTRY.

The country about Lynchburg is mainly devoted to agriculture, tobacco being the principal crop. Market-gardening is carried on to a considerable extent.

TOPOGRAPHY.

The soil is red clay and gravel, with occasional immense bowlders of water-worn sandstone. The general rock formation is gneiss, with outcroppings of mica-schist and bastard granite. The variations of level are very abrupt, frequently as much as 24 feet in 100. The natural drainage is excellent—on one side directly into the river, and on the other into a small creek or natural course, which the city is fast making into a sewer.

The surrounding country is more elevated than the general level of the city. There are no marshes, ponds, or lakes of any consequence in the vicinity. Within a radius of 5 miles of the city, the forests, which used to be quite extensive, have been nearly all cut off.

CLIMATE.

The highest recorded summer temperature since 1873 is 100°, the temperature in average years reaching its highest point at 97.21°. The lowest recorded winter temperature in the same period is —5°, the lowest in average years being 2.75°. The climate is regarded as especially beneficial to invalids suffering from debility or pulmonary disease. The extreme heat of summer is tempered by cool breezes from the south, and the nights are always cool. Malarial fevers are very rare.

STREETS.

Lynchburg has 47½ miles of streets, 3 miles of which are paved with cobble-stones, about one-half mile with Belgian stone-block paving, and three-quarters of a mile with broken stone. The remaining 43¼ miles are unpaved. The cost of the Belgian pavement per square yard is $2 65; of the broken stone, 60 to 75 cents; and of cobble-stone, $1 to $1 25. The Belgian blocks are most easily kept in repair, the cobbles next, and the broken stone last in the scale of ease. No statement of the cost of repairs per year can be made, as no separate account of the expense is kept. The sidewalks are of flat stones of gneiss. The street-way extends from curb to curb, no separate gutter being made. The curbstones are generally of gneiss, sometimes of granite. The abutters have planted trees along the sides of the streets, placing them, by the direction of the city engineers, 12 inches back from the curb. The cost of constructing and repairing the streets varies from year to year. In 1878–'79 it was $21,613; in 1879–'80, $18,857; and in 1880–'81, $28,297. The total length of the horse-railroads is about 2 miles. There are 6 cars in all, drawn by 12 horses and 12 mules, and employing 8 men. The cash-fare is 6 cents; tickets, 5 cents. There are no omnibus lines.

WATER-WORKS.

No more detailed account of the water-works can be given than the information embodied in the "historical sketch" of the city.

GAS.

The city is supplied with gas by a private corporation. No information as to the amount of gas produced, or of the rates charged, could be obtained.

PUBLIC BUILDINGS.

The city owns and uses for municipal purposes a court-house, 6 engine-houses, and 4 school-houses. No record of the value of these buildings could be found. The city hires one engine-house and a building for the use of the city treasurer and other officers.

PUBLIC PARKS AND PLEASURE-GROUNDS.

Lynchburg owns a lot of about 10 acres, known as the "Fair grounds", which it leases to the Agricultural Society, by which all improvements have been made. When not in use by the society, these grounds are open to the public. They are situated just beyond the southwestern part of the city, and were a gift to it. No expense is incurred by Lynchburg in maintaining them. They are controlled by a committee of the city council and the city engineer.

PLACES OF AMUSEMENT.

The Lynchburg opera-house, which has a seating capacity of about 1,500, is the only theater in the city. Holcombe hall, seating about 600, is used for concerts, lectures, and entertainments. Theaters pay a license of $100 per annum to the city, and to the state $3 and 1 per cent. of the receipts for each entertainment. A concert- and beer-garden is in process of erection.

DRAINAGE.

The city has as yet no system of public sewers. No information of the present system of drainage could be obtained.

CEMETERIES.

Lynchburg has 5 cemeteries, as follows:

The Old Methodist or *Public Cemetery*, situated in the western part of the city—area about 12 acres—has been in use about 60 years. No charge is made for interment in this ground, which is controlled by the city council through a superintendent.

Presbyterian Cemetery, situated in the southern part of the city—area 12 acres—is controlled by a board of trustees. It has been in use about 45 years. Lots 16 by 20 feet in size are sold to private persons at a uniform price of $50.

Spring Hill Cemetery, just beyond the corporate limits to the southwest, contains 30 acres, which are laid off in lots varying in price from $40 to $250. It has been in use 26 years.

Saint Francis Xavier Cemetery (Catholic) contains 4 acres. It is a private enterprise of the priest, who sells lots, 16 by 17 feet, at $50. It is situated north of the city, and has been in use 8 years.

White Rock Cemetery is a new burial-ground, lying to the south of Lynchburg, and owned by colored people. It contains 8 acres.

The number of interments in these cemeteries is estimated at 18,000.

MARKETS.

The city owns a market-building, which cost $26,000, and controls an area of 15,312 square feet around it, which is used for wagon-stands. Stalls are rented at various prices according to their location and the use which is to be made of them. Butchers' stalls cost $220, $230, $240, $270, and $300; hucksters', from $30 to $75. The total rental is about $4,000. They are open from daylight until 12 m., and on Saturday all day. The gross amount of the annual sales could not be obtained.

SANITARY AUTHORITY—BOARD OF HEALTH.

The city council elects annually 3 physicians to serve as a board of health, who have the general charge of the sanitary condition of the city. This board, which meets regularly once a month, has unlimited power, both during and in the absence of an epidemic, to take such steps as seem necessary to prevent the origin and spread of any contagious or infectious diseases, to abate nuisances and, in general, to preserve the public health. Each of the members receives a salary of $100 a year, and all have equal authority, except that only the president of the board can summon a meeting. No health officers or assistants are regularly employed, but if their services are necessary the council will allow them to be appointed.

The police are the regular agents of the board, and visit all parts of the city, reporting to the president of the board any thing prejudicial to the public health. Inspections are regularly made only when complaint is entered. If on examination a nuisance is found to exist, the owner of the premises is ordered to abate it; if he refuses, the abatement is made by the mayor's orders, and the expense, with 20 per cent. additional as a penalty, is collected from the estate. Defective house-drainage, privy-vaults, cesspools, and sources of drinking-water are treated as nuisances, as are also defects in street-cleaning and in the few sewers.

The board has full control of the conservation and removal of garbage. The pollution of the river and streams is prohibited.

BURIAL OF THE DEAD.

Interments are generally made from 24 to 36 hours after the death has occurred. A permit must be obtained from the board of health before an interment will be allowed or the removal of a body from the city permitted. This permit is granted on receiving from the undertaker a certificate of death, signed by the attending physician, or the coroner when the case comes under his notice, stating the name of the deceased, sex, color, occupation, civil condition (single, married, or widowed), birthplace, etc. Graves in the cemeteries are dug 4 feet 8 inches deep for adults, and somewhat less deep for children.

INFECTIOUS DISEASES.

Small-pox patients are removed if possible to a small-pox hospital; if not possible, then the patient is quarantined at home. No action is taken in regard to scarlet-fever patients. All physicians are required to report any cases of infectious, contagious, or malignant disease coming under their notice. The authority of the board is sufficiently extensive to close the schools should contagious diseases break out in them. A pest-house is now in process of construction beyond the city limits, the old one, which was within the city, having been demolished. Vaccination is compulsory only for the children in the public schools, and is done at the public expense. The city ordinances require that the board of health shall always have vaccine matter at hand, and vaccinate, free of charge, all desiring it.

REPORTS.

The board reports monthly to the city council, but only the mortuary records are published.

No system of registering births has been in use. Diseases are registered by the board from the physicians' report, and deaths from the certificates of death in the hands of the undertakers.

MUNICIPAL CLEANSING.

Street-cleaning.—Along the paved streets the abutters are compelled to clean one-half the width of the streets opposite their premises, depositing the dirt in heaps in the middle of the street. These heaps are then removed by a contractor paid by the city. The unpaved streets are not cleaned at all. The city pays the contractor $1,800 a year; the cost of the cleaning to the abutters can not be stated. Such of the sweepings as are inoffensive are used for filling; the offensive part is dumped into the river below the city.

Removal of garbage and ashes.—Garbage, which is defined by the board of health as kitchen offal, and coal or other ashes, are removed by the person who takes away the street-dirt, and are included in the contract for that service. The garbage must be kept in vessels, placed where the contractor can easily get at them, and is removed twice in each week. The garbage is finally disposed of by dumping it into the river below the city. Ashes, when separate from offal, are used as filling, but if mixed with it are dumped into the river.

Dead animals are removed by the owners beyond the city limits. No estimate of the cost can be found, and no record of the number removed is kept.

Liquid household wastes.—Chamber-slops and kitchen and laundry wastes are disposed of alike, by running them into the public drains where these exist. A small amount is run into the street-gutters, which are flushed occasionally by the city during the summer months. The property-owners are required to keep the gutters clean. There are said to be no cesspools in the city.

Human excreta.—Less than one-fifth the houses are provided with water-closets, all of which empty into public drains or sewers. In those houses where privies are used the vaults are generally wooden boxes. No privy-vaults can be nearer than 10 feet to the line of any street or to any property line without the consent of the owner of the adjoining premises. The vaults must be cleaned when necessary, the work being done by licensed persons between 10 p. m. and daylight. The dry-earth system is rarely used. Night-soil is frequently buried in gardens in the suburbs, but is sometimes taken beyond the city limits, and in occasional cases is thrown into the river below the city. No regulation has as yet been necessary to prevent the use of night-soil as a manure on lands within the gathering-ground of the public water-supply.

Manufacturing wastes.—Lynchburg has no manufactures having wastes likely to become a nuisance, and so has made no regulation regarding the disposal of waste product.

NORFOLK,

NORFOLK COUNTY, VIRGINIA.

POPULATION

IN THE

AGGREGATE,

1800-1880.

	Inhab.
1790	......
1800	6,926
1810	......
1820	8,478
1830	9,814
1840	10,920
1850	14,326
1860	14,620
1870	19,229
1880	21,966

POPULATION

BY

SEX, NATIVITY, AND RACE,

AT

CENSUS OF 1880.

Male	10,069
Female	11,897
Native	21,131
Foreign-born	835
White	11,898
Colored	10,068

Latitude: 36° 51′ North; Longitude: 76° 17′ (west from Greenwich); **Altitude: 0 to 20 feet.**

FINANCIAL CONDITION:

Total Valuation: $11,057,249; per capita: $503 00.   Net Indebtedness: $2,187,371; per capita: $99 58.   Tax per $100: $3 35.

HISTORICAL SKETCH.

In 1680 the colonial assembly passed an act entitled "An act for the cohabitation and encouragement of trade and manufactures". It authorized the establishment of several towns on the various water-courses of the state, and, among others, "the town of Norfolk, in lower Norfolk, on Nicholas Wise his land on the eastern branch of the Elizabeth river, at the entrance of the branch". The town was first planted on its present eastern terminus, and for many years Bermuda street was its main avenue of trade and commerce, the principal wharves being in its immediate vicinity. On the 15th of September, 1736, Norfolk was raised to the dignity of a borough by letters patent from King George II, the preamble of the charter reciting that "the place was healthful and commodious for trade and navigation".

In the early days of its boroughship Norfolk grew and flourished, and at the breaking out of the Revolution was one of the most prosperous ports of the colonies. The Revolution, however, brought ruin to Norfolk. On the 1st of January, 1776, six months before the declaration of independence, an English fleet, consisting of five vessels, under Lord Dunmore, opened a heavy cannonade upon the town, and every house in it was burned, with the exception of an outhouse used as a dairy, situated near Market square. In a short time, however, the people had rebuilt the borough, and it again advanced on its onward course. In 1780, 1,000 houses had been built since the fire, and the trade of the place was assuming the most important proportions. In 1805, 1806, and 1807 the annual exports of the place varied from $5,000,000 to $7,000,000, and the imports were correspondingly large. At this time it was the center of the West India trade with the country, did a large business in tobacco and naval stores, and promised to be the commercial emporium of the whole country. But the embargo proclamation, in 1807, closed the harbor of Norfolk, in common with all other American ports, to all foreign ships, and reduced its commerce to a coasting trade. In 1809 the embargo was raised, and the commerce of Norfolk again revived and prospered until it was again suspended by the war of 1812. The navigation act of 1820, which prohibited commerce between British colonies and American ports, struck a heavy blow at Norfolk, and produced a panic and bankruptcy among many of the merchants, and brought general distress and depression upon the people. The commerce of the town began to decline, and for many years continued to do so.

On February 12, 1845, Norfolk ceased to be a borough, and by virtue of the amended charter of that date became a city. The increase in the value of real estate during the year following was $122,048, and the tonnage entered and cleared at the custom-house showed a gain of 100 per cent. In 1847 the famine in Ireland produced an extraordinary demand for corn, and the export of this article from Norfolk was very great. From 1847 to 1855 Norfolk advanced slowly. In the summer of the latter year the city was afflicted with an outbreak of yellow fever, and before the disease was checked about 2,000 of the population fell victims to the deadly character of the epidemic.

From 1855 to the breaking out of the civil war the people of Norfolk were bravely engaged in recuperating their shattered energies, and by 1860 had nearly succeeded in recovering their lost ground. The war put a stop to all business, and at its close Norfolk found her capital impaired and her trade destroyed. Nothing daunted, the inhabitants went to work with a will, and in a few years the city was more prosperous than ever. The railroad and canal connections were reopened and extended, and large quantities of cotton came in. The market-gardens for supplying the northern cities with fruits and vegetables and the oyster fisheries have contributed much to the wealth and advancement of the city. Norfolk also handles the greater portion of the peanut crop of the country. During the year 1878 the value of the exports was $10,052,062, and the total tonnage cleared for foreign ports during the same time was 91,624 tons. Detailed tables, showing the industries, etc., of Norfolk, will be found a few pages farther on.

NORFOLK IN 1880.

The following statistical accounts, collected by the Census Office, indicate the present condition of Norfolk:

LOCATION.

The city lies in latitude 36° 51' north, longitude 76° 17' west from Greenwich, on the north bank of the Elizabeth river, at the confluence of the eastern and western branches of that river, 8 miles from Hampton road, and 23 miles from capes Charles and Henry, on the Atlantic coast. The altitude above average high-water mark ranges from 10 to 20 feet. The channel capacity of the river is between 1,000 and 1,200 feet, with a draught of water of 22 feet, and the current is about 1 mile per hour.

RAILROAD COMMUNICATIONS.

Norfolk is touched by the following railroads:
The Norfolk and Western railroad, to Bristol, Tennessee.
The Elizabeth City and Norfolk railroad, to Elizabeth City, North Carolina.
The Norfolk and Ocean View railroad, to Ocean View, Virginia.

TRIBUTARY COUNTRY.

The country immediately tributary to the city, and with which it has a local trade, is agricultural, being entirely devoted to "truck-farming". The principal products are hay, cabbages, strawberries, and all early vegetables, and large quantities are annually shipped to the northern cities from Norfolk. The oyster fisheries and canning establishments employ a large number of persons. The location of the city and its climatic advantages have already earned for it the title of the "Atlantic Garden".

NORFOLK,
VA.
SCALE OF MILES.
1/16   1/8   1/4

MOSS ENG. CO. N.Y.

TOPOGRAPHY.

The site of the city is low. The strata met with in boring a well to the depth of 100 feet at the head of Market square were superficial soil, vegetable detritus, etc., a few inches; clay mixed with a little sand, about 7 feet; quicksand, from 12 to 20 feet; marl, firm and dry, composed chiefly of water-shells, about 30 feet; and decomposed marl, loose and interrupted at distances of 7 or 8 feet by strata of sand and gravel a foot or more in depth, the latter becoming coarser with the increase in depth, assuming the size of bowlders at the lowest point. The variations of level are from 0 to 20 feet above mean sea-level. Natural drainage is good. The elevation of the surrounding country is about the same as that of the city. There are no lakes or ponds. The salt-marshes are on the tributary of the river.

CLIMATE.

Highest recorded summer temperature, $102\frac{1}{2}°$; highest summer temperature in average years, 99°. Lowest recorded winter temperature, 6°; lowest winter temperature in average years, 11°. The lands nearest salt-water courses are less liable to injury from frost than others. The Chesapeake bay to the north, and the ocean, with the nearness of the Gulf stream, modify the climate, rendering it milder here than on the same parallel a few miles in the interior. Marshes that are covered by the salt tides are considered innocuous; those above tide-water, or where the tides have no influence, are malarious. The winds from the north, south, and west are most salubrious, while those from the east are damp and charged with malaria.

STREETS.

The total length of streets approximates 26 miles, paved as follows: Cobble-stones, 6 miles; stone blocks, $\frac{1}{5}$ mile; oyster-shells, 5 miles; rubble-stone, 3 miles; and dirt, $11\frac{4}{5}$ miles. The cost per square yard of each, as near as it may be estimated, is, for cobble-stones, by contract, 36 cents; for rubble, by contract, 64 cents; for stone blocks, by day work, $1 57; and for oyster-shell, by day work, 12 cents. The relative facility with which each is kept clean is given as stone blocks first, and then rubble, cobble-stone, shell, and finally the dirt roads. The stone blocks are preferred for heavy traffic and the shell for light traffic. The sidewalks are of brick and flag, and are reported as bad, particularly with reference to grades. There is no system of tree-planting. The work of construction and repairs of streets is at present done by the day. The cost last year, by contract, was about $10,000. For work of any magnitude contract is preferred, but for repairs, day work. There is one horse-railroad with a total length of $3\frac{3}{4}$ miles. It has 12 cars and 32 horses, and gives employment to 21 men. The rates of fare are 4 and 5 cents.

WATER-WORKS.

The water-works are owned by the city, and their total cost is $500,000. The Holly system, or direct pumping, is used; the pressure in the mains per square inch, for domestic purposes is 40 pounds, and for fire purposes 90 to 110 pounds. The average amount pumped per diem is 350,000 gallons, the greatest being 800,000 and the least 460,000 gallons. The average cost of raising 1,000,000 gallons 1 foot high is 7 cents. The yearly cost of maintenance is $15,240, and the yearly income from water-rates is $22,866. There are about 62 water-meters in use, and it is reported that they pay for themselves in a very short time in saving water. There are $24\frac{1}{2}$ miles of street-mains and 110 hydrants.

GAS.

The gas-works are owned by a private corporation. The daily average production is 76,279 cubic feet, and the charge per thousand feet is $2 40. The city pays $30 per annum for each street-lamp, 259 in number.

PUBLIC BUILDINGS.

The city owns and occupies for municipal uses, wholly or in part, 1 city hall, 1 jail, and 1 station-house, 1 fire-department building, 1 almshouse, 1 pest-house, and 7 school-houses. The total cost of these is given as $184,000. The city hall is owned entirely by the city, and cost $70,000.

PUBLIC PARKS AND PLEASURE-GROUNDS.

There are no parks in Norfolk.

PLACES OF AMUSEMENT.

There are 3 theatres in the city:
The Varieties, seating capacity 400, gives a performance every night.
The Norfolk opera-house, seating capacity 1,350, is hired by traveling shows.

The Academy of Music, seating capacity 1,500, hired occasionally for shows.

These theaters pay a license to the city of $1 for each performance, or $5 a week, and a license to the state of $3, and 1 per cent. of the gross receipts for each performance.

In addition to the theaters there are Masonic hall, Mechanics' hall, Oliver's hall and Dalten's hall, used for concerts, lectures, etc.

DRAINAGE.

There is no system of sewerage in Norfolk, but the whole matter is now under advisement. From the reports of the city officials, and the general feeling of the citizens, at the close of the census year, it is evident that the city will be sewered on the "separate system" now in use at Memphis, Tennessee.

CEMETERIES.

There are 3 public cemeteries belonging to the city, one near the northern boundary, area $8\frac{1}{4}$ acres; one just north of the city limits, area about 24 acres; and one in a northeasterly direction, area 12 acres.

Saint Paul's Church-yard, corner of Church and Cove streets, area 2 acres, is now no longer used for interments. From 1875 to 1880 there were 2,418 interments made in the 3 public cemeteries. No interment can be made except upon a physician's certificate of death. The depth of grave is 4 feet.

MARKETS.

There is one public market in the city. It is an iron building, in fair condition, with a ground space 200 by 40 feet, has 42 stalls, and cost $18,000. There is a space 200 by 25 feet reserved for hucksters, and the street is also used for this purpose. The stalls are all of one class, and the annual rent for each one is $150. The total rental of the market is $13,000. The hours during which the market is open are from 4 a. m. to 12 noon, every day except Saturday, when the closing hour is extended to 9 p. m. Meats, poultry, fish, and vegetables are principally sold at the market.

SANITARY AUTHORITY—BOARD OF HEALTH.

The chief sanitary authority of Norfolk is vested in the board of health, composed of 5 members, 3 of whom are physicians. They are appointed annually by the common council and are subject to its control. The annual expense of the board when there is no epidemic varies from $3,500 to $4,000, expended for drainage, sewerage, and sanitary measures generally. During an epidemic there is no limit to the increase of expense. Either in the absence or during an epidemic the board has entire control over all sanitary measures, and its authority is pre-eminent. The president is the chief executive officer; he receives no salary; he presides at all meetings, enforces all rules and regulations of the board, approves the accounts, and has general supervision over sanitation. One sanitary inspector is employed; he has no police powers. The board meets weekly during the summer and every two weeks during the winter. The sanitary inspector is constantly on duty and makes inspections in all parts of the city. When a nuisance is discovered it is ordered to be abated, a reasonable number of days being given for the purpose, and if the parties responsible fail to comply with the order they are dealt with according to law. The board has control over the removal of excrement.

INFECTIOUS DISEASES.

Small-pox patients are removed to the pest-house, half a mile outside the city limits. Scarlet-fever patients are not isolated. Vaccination is not compulsory, but it is done at the public expense.

The record of diseases, births, and deaths is kept by the physician to the almshouse, and he makes monthly returns to the board.

REPORTS.

The board makes an annual report to the mayor, and this is published with his message to the city council.

MUNICIPAL CLEANSING.

Street-cleaning.—The streets are cleaned at the expense of the city and with its own force. The work is done wholly by hand, no sweeping-machines being used. There is no stated time for cleaning the streets of different classes, a gang of men being at work all the time. The principal streets receive attention about once a week or once in ten days, and the efficiency of the work is reported as satisfactory. The annual cost to the city is about $11,000, which includes the removal of garbage, and the sweepings are sold and taken out of the city.

Removal of garbage and ashes.—All garbage and ashes are removed by the city with its own force. It is kept in boxes or barrels, and put out on the sidewalk every other day for removal, the empty vessels being at once taken in. Garbage and ashes are allowed to be kept in the same vessels. They are dumped outside of the city, and are taken by farmers for agricultural purposes. The cost of the service is included in the street-cleaning.

Dead animals.—Dead horses and cows are removed by the owners at their own expense. Dead dogs, cats, etc., are removed by the city, and the police are required to inform the street inspector of all dead animals they find on their beats. The annual cost of this service is included in the removal of garbage. No account of the number of large animals was kept, but during the year 161 dogs and 26 cats were removed from the streets.

Liquid household wastes.—There being no sewers in Norfolk, all laundry wastes are run into the gutters, while all offensive wastes are run into tight boxes or cesspools. The cesspools are generally porous, are not provided with overflows, receive the wastes from water-closets, and are allowed to be emptied only by the odorless-excavator process. The sanitary inspector can order the cesspools cleaned whenever he deems it necessary. During the summer season the gutters are flooded every other day, and in winter they are swept about as often.

Human excreta.—About one-eighth of the houses in the city have water-closets, and the remainder depend on privy-vaults. All of the water-closets deliver into cesspools or tight boxes, except a few that are connected with private sewers or drains. All the old privy-vaults are porous, but the law now requires that they shall be water-tight. They are emptied by the odorless-excavator process, and the night-soil is taken beyond the city limits; none of it is allowed on land within the gathering-ground of the public water-supply.

Manufacturing wastes.—There are no regulations regarding manufacturing wastes, but it is reported that they are generally carried into the street-gutters. The system is said to be objectionable.

POLICE.

The police force of Norfolk is appointed by the board of police commissioners, with the exception of the chief and assistant chief, whose appointments are confirmed by the city council, and is governed by the same authority. The chief of police is the executive officer, and has general supervision over the force; his salary is $3 a day. The remainder of the force consists of 1 assistant chief at $2 75 per day, 2 sergeants at $2 50 per day each, and 2 turnkeys and 31 patrolmen at $2 a day each. The uniform is the same as that worn by the New York police, with the exception of the hat, which is a black derby in winter and a white one in summer. The average cost of the uniform is $125, and each man provides his own. The patrolmen are equipped with a club, a revolver, nippers, and a "black-jack". The hours of service are 6 on and 12 off, and the force patrols 26 miles of streets and alleys.

During the past year there were 2,509 arrests made, the principal causes for such being drunk, or drunk and disorderly. The principal portion of those arrested paid fines, and the rest were committed in default. The total amount of property lost or stolen during the year and reported to the police was $200, and of this, two-thirds was recovered and one-third returned to the owners. The number of station-house lodgers during the year was 173, as against 93 in 1879. Nothing but crackers, at a cost of $12 annually, is given to the lodgers in the shape of free meals. The force is required to co-operate with the fire, health, and building departments, by rendering any assistance necessary. Special policemen are appointed only in cases of emergency, and they are under the supervision of the chief and the board of police commissioners. The yearly cost of the force (1880) is $28,534 93. A portion of this amount was paid as salaries to the chain-gang guards, viz, $1 50 each per day, whenever the chain-gang went out to work. There are also three substitutes on the force, who attend all roll-calls, and are available for vacancies.

COMMERCE AND NAVIGATION.

[From the reports of the Bureau of Statistics for the fiscal years ending June 30.]

Customs district of Norfolk and Portsmouth, Virginia.	1879.	1880.
Total value of imports	$33,814	$47,057
Total value of exports:		
Domestic	$9,830,352	$14,065,455
Foreign		
Total number of immigrants		

Customs district of Norfolk and Portsmouth, Virginia.	1879.		1880.	
	Number.	Tons.	Number.	Tons.
Vessels in foreign trade:				
Entered	64	64,451	53	62,802
Cleared	112	92,599	120	118,880
Vessels in coast trade and fisheries:				
Entered	1,022	988,794	1,206	1,164,117
Cleared	1,001	1,002,428	1,057	1,091,475
Vessels registered, enrolled, and licensed in district	377	13,422	407	14,521
Vessels built during the year	11	232	12	145

MANUFACTURES.

The following is a summary of the statistics of the manufactures of Norfolk for 1880, being taken from tables prepared for the Tenth Census by D. P. Morris, special agent:

Mechanical and manufacturing industries.	No. of establishments.	Capital.	AVERAGE NUMBER OF HANDS EMPLOYED.			Total amount paid in wages during the year.	Value of materials.	Value of products.
			Males above 16 years.	Females above 15 years.	Children and youths.			
All industries..	105	$570,276	668	61	23	$317,528	$861,026	$1,455,987
Agricultural implements	3	71,000	19	....	....	8,250	31,200	49,500
Blacksmithing...	8	2,550	23	....	....	8,350	9,200	23,800
Boots and shoes, including custom work and repairing	4	2,500	7	....	....	3,069	6,450	12,750
Bread and other bakery products.........................	9	38,200	66	15	7	25,921	144,000	200,700
Carpentering	6	15,300	57	....	1	25,900	32,100	74,500
Carriages and wagons....................................	4	81,200	68	....	5	27,500	75,500	123,800
Clothing, men's..	9	22,800	40	39	....	37,305	39,200	100,800
Cooperage	3	906	6	....	....	2,443	1,950	6,500
Flouring- and grist-mill products........................	5	96,500	24	....	....	8,762	287,060	336,737
Foundery and machine-shop products.....................	4	73,000	83	....	2	35,800	33,236	82,850
Plumbing and gasfitting.................................	3	3,700	18	....	1	8,700	9,900	25,200
Printing and publishing	5	55,600	73	....	....	41,000	27,300	94,400
Shipbuilding...	3	26,600	18	....	....	12,100	15,300	34,300
Tinware, copperware, and sheet-iron ware...............	9	31,000	71	....	3	33,600	54,173	108,400
Tobacco, cigars and cigarettes..........................	7	5,500	24	....	1	9,850	9,294	25,000
Watch and clock repairing	3	10,000	14	....	....	9,052	4,100	18,000
All other industries (a)	20	32,920	57	7	3	19,926	81,063	138,750

a Embracing coffee and spices, roasted and ground; coffins, burial cases, and undertakers' goods; confectionery; iron railing, wrought; kindling wood; leather, tanned; lumber, planed; marble and stone work; masonry, brick and stone; painting and paperhanging; pumps; saddlery and harness; shirts; stationery goods; and wheelwrighting.

From the foregoing table it appears that the average capital of all establishments is $5,431 20; that the average wages of all hands employed is $422 24 per annum; that the average outlay in wages, in materials, and in interest (at 6 per cent.) on capital employed is $11,550 20.

PETERSBURG,

DINWIDDIE COUNTY, VIRGINIA.

POPULATION

IN THE

AGGREGATE,

1800–1880.

	Inhab.
1790	......
1800	3,521
1810	5,668
1820	6,690
1830	8,322
1840	11,136
1850	14,010
1860	18,266
1870	18,950
1880	21,656

POPULATION ·

BY

SEX, NATIVITY, AND RACE,

AT

CENSUS OF 1880.

Male	9,779
Female	11,877
Native	21,300
Foreign-born	356
White	9,950
Colored	*11,706

* Including 5 Indians.

Latitude: 37° 14′ North; Longitude: 77° 24′ (west form Greenwich).

FINANCIAL CONDITION:

Total Valuation: $9,132,330; per capita: $422 00.   Net Indebtedness: $1,136,100; per capita: $52 46.   Tax per $100: $1 95.

HISTORICAL SKETCH.[a]

Petersburg, the capital of Dinwiddie county, is 23 miles south of Richmond, on the right bank of the Appomattox river, 12 miles from its mouth. It is picturesquely situated on the declivities of a hill sloping gradually to the river-bank, affording good natural drainage. It is located on the site of an Indian village, burnt by Nathaniel Bacon in 1676. The place was laid out simultaneously with Richmond, in 1733, by Colonel William Byrd; was incorporated in 1748, and reincorporated in 1781, and was twice during the Revolutionary war occupied as the headquarters of the British forces. A gallant company of Petersburg volunteers, in the war of

---

a No data for the history of Petersburg being furnished by the city authorities, the present brief sketch was gleaned from other sources.

1812, earned for it the title of "Cockade City of the South". Its heroic defense during the closing scenes of the late war has rendered it memorable as the "last citadel of the confederacy". The limits of the city include its quondam rival, the now decayed village of Blanford, the ruins of whose church are among the most interesting and picturesque of Virginia's possessions. In 1815 a great fire occurred here, by which 400 houses were consumed. A good water-power is furnished by the falls near the city, which stop tide-water. A canal around them continues the means of communication more than 100 miles for flat-boats. Petersburg is connected with Richmond, Norfolk, Lynchburg, Weldon, and City Point by means of the Atlantic, Mississippi, and Ohio; the Petersburg; and the Richmond and Petersburg railroads. It is well supplied with churches, schools, and newspapers, and has a large interest in manufactories, including many of tobacco, several of cotton goods, and iron and wooden ware. It is an important shipping point for southern agricultural staples, as flour, cotton, peanuts, and tobacco, the exportation of which in 1874 was 46 per cent. of the entire freight export of the latter article from the United States. The population remained nearly stationary during the decade 1860 to 1870, but since then it has increased and improved in many ways, and the place may justly be termed one of the most flourishing cities of the South..

PETERSBURG IN 1880.

No information was furnished regarding the following topics: Altitude, railroad communications, tributary country, topography, and climate.

STREETS.

Petersburg has about 60 miles of streets, of which 5 or 6 miles are paved with cobble-stones and 3 or 4 miles with broken stones. The cost of cobble-stone pavement is from 55 to 60 cents per square yard, and of broken stone from 20 to 30 cents per square yard. The annual cost of keeping streets in repair is from $12,000 to $15,000. Sidewalks are paved in a portion of the city with granite flagging and bricks, while in the rest of the city they are simply of gravel. Gutters are laid with cobble-stones and broken granite. There are no horse-railroads or omnibus lines.

WATER-WORKS.

The water-works are owned by the city, and their total cost was $125,000. The water is pumped into a reservoir elevated 110 feet. The average cost of raising 1,000,000 gallons 1 foot high is 6 cents. The average yearly cost of maintenance, aside from the cost of pumping, is $100, and the yearly income from water-rates is $8,000. No water-meters are used.

GAS.

The gas-works are owned by a private company. The daily average production is 30,000 cubic feet, and the charge per 1,000 feet is $2 85. The city pays annually $23 $16\frac{2}{3}$ for each street-lamp, 265 in number.

PUBLIC BUILDINGS.

The city owns and occupies for municipal purposes, wholly or in part, 1 court-house, city clerk's office, city jail, almshouse, and the fire-engine houses. Their total cost was not given.

PUBLIC PARKS AND PLEASURE-GROUNDS.

Petersburg has a public park, called "*Poplar Lawn*", area 10 acres, which is situated near the center of the city. Its total cost was $40,000. It is in the care of a keeper, under the control of a committee of the common council.

PLACES OF AMUSEMENT.

The Academy of Music, with a seating capacity for 650 persons, is used as a theater. All theaters are required to pay a license to the city of $3 for each performance. There are no concert- and beer-gardens.

DRAINAGE; CEMETERIES; MARKETS.

No information on these subjects was furnished.

SANITARY AUTHORITY—BOARD OF HEALTH.

The sanitary interests of the city are in the hands of a board of health, consisting of the mayor, president of the council, chief of police, and the four physicians to the poor—seven members in all. It is elected by and is responsible to the city council. The ordinary annual expense of the board is $500, for disinfectants and removing nuisances. There is no restriction, within the monthly appropriation of the council, to the expense of the board during epidemics. In absence of an epidemic the board has general supervision over the sanitary condition of the city, and during an epidemic can take all steps necessary to check and control the disease. The health officer is president of the board and chief executive officer. His powers and duties are defined by the state laws. He is also secretary of the board. He receives no salary for his services. All the members of the board are clothed with police powers. A regular inspector is employed, with necessary details from the police force as assistants. The board holds monthly meetings, and has special sittings upon the call of the president. The city is divided into districts, each one being in charge of a physician, and inspections are made regularly therein, as well as when nuisances are reported. When a nuisance is reported the inspector investigates and reports; if found to be such the health officer orders the party causing the same to remove it; and if this is not done it is removed by the city and the expense is charged to the property. The regular inspections include the correction of all defective house-drainage, privy-vaults, cesspools, and sources of drinking-water. The board has charge of the conservation and removal of garbage. The board issues burial permits, on certificates of cause of death, made by the attending physician; and sextons are required to report all interments made by them to the board. The board controls the removal of excrement, and appoints a scavenger for that purpose.

INFECTIOUS DISEASES.

Small-pox patients are removed to the hospital. Scarlet-fever patients are not isolated. By ordinance, vaccination is made compulsory, but it does not seem to be enforced; periodically it is done at the public expense.

REPORTS.

The board reports annually to the city council, and the report is published with the regular city documents. Mayor Cameron, who communicated the foregoing regarding health, adds:

Theoretically the board has all necessary power; but the city has no system of sewerage, and the surface drainage is defective, except in rainy weather; therefore the board is powerless to go beneath the surface of evils with which it has to deal.

MUNICIPAL CLEANSING.

Street-cleaning.—The streets are cleaned at the expense of the city and with its regular force. The work is done wholly by hand. The paved streets are cleaned weekly, and the work is reported as well done. The board of health may require, for sanitary precautions, the draining or cleaning out of the ditches, gutters, or low places in the streets or public grounds. Abutters are required to keep foot-ways clean and gutters open and free from obstructions.

Removal of garbage and ashes.—Garbage is removed by the city with its own force. While awaiting removal it must be kept in boxes and barrels. It is taken away four times a week in summer and once a week in winter. Light dirt, paper, ashes, etc., are removed, along with the street-sweepings, once a week, by the city's carts. The estimated cost of the removal to the city is $2,000 annually. The system is reported as fairly efficient.

Dead animals are removed by the city scavenger under a regular schedule of prices, and the cost is paid by the owner or person upon whose property the carcass is found. The animals are buried outside the city. The cost of the service to the city is only nominal.

Liquid household wastes.—But a small portion of these wastes are run into the sewers, as the city has none except on four of the principal streets; much is run into street-gutters, especially wash-water—including some surreptitious chamber-slops; in the thickly built-up portions of the city much is run into dry wells, and but comparatively little into privy-vaults. Dry wells are not regulated, but privy-vaults, or "cesspools" (as the term is here used), are required by ordinance to be laid with brick or stone, in hydraulic cement, and to be at least 10 feet deep; they are unprovided with overflows. When the water-supply is sufficient, gutters receiving household wastes are flushed when needful; when the supply is short, as has been the case for the last two summers, no flushing is done. There is no absolute knowledge that drinking-water is contaminated by the overflowing or leakage of privy-vaults or dry wells. Fortunately but few drinking-water wells exist in those parts of the city where dry wells most abound.

Human excreta.—About 8 per cent. of the houses in the city have water-closets, and the rest depend on receptacles for holding the excrement. It is the policy of the board of health to abolish privy-vaults, and to substitute therefor "surface privies" where water-closets can not be had for want of sewerage. Three fifths of the water-closets deliver into the public sewers, one-fifth into private sewers, and one-fifth into privy-vaults. All privy-vaults constructed after the passage of the ordinance of April 1, 1879, are nominally water-tight. They are cleaned out by the city scavenger between the hours of 11 p. m. and 4 a. m., and the contents must be deodorized before being removed in close carts. The night-soil is taken to the country and used for manure.

Manufacturing wastes.—These, both solid and liquid, are run into the Appomattox river.

Concerning the handling and disposal of the wastes of the city, Mayor Cameron says:

The whole system is defective—not in minor regulations nor in efficiency of subordinate administration, but on account of absence of proper surface drainage and insufficient supply of water for flushing drains. Movement now under way to sewer the city.

POLICE.

No information on this subject was returned by the city authorities.

FIRE DEPARTMENT.

The force of the fire department in 1879 consisted of 33 men, and the apparatus of 2 steam fire-engines, 6 hose-reels, 1 hook-and-ladder truck, and 1,500 feet of good hose; there were 4 horses in the department. During the year ending July 1, 1879, the cost of the department was $9,207 96. During the same time it responded to 31 alarms, including 3 false alarms, and the total loss by fire was about $110,000.

PUBLIC SCHOOLS.

The following statistics are for the school year ending June 15, 1879:

Petersburg has 1 white high school, 2 white graded schools, and 2 colored graded schools. The total enrollment (white and colored) is 1,985; average monthly enrollment, 1,578, and average daily attendance, 1,494. The number of teachers employed, including principal of schools and writing-master, is 29. The total cost of the schools for the year was $14,154 25.

MANUFACTURES.

The following is a summary of the statistics of the manufactures of Petersburg for 1880, being taken from tables prepared for the Tenth Census by S. S. Northington, special agent:

Mechanical and manufacturing industries.	No. of establishments.	Capital.	AVERAGE NUMBER OF HANDS EMPLOYED.			Total amount paid in wages during the year.	Value of materials.	Value of products.
			Males above 16 years.	Females above 15 years.	Children and youths.			
All industries	115	$1,755,415	2,209	1,245	742	$602,749	$3,290,116	$4,643,015
Agricultural implements	3	31,000	68	....	....	21,430	22,490	50,565
Blacksmithing (see also Wheelwrighting)	7	3,080	9	....	....	2,400	2,625	9,000
Boots and shoes, including custom work and repairing	15	680	28	....	....	4,860	5,104	15,116
Bread and other bakery products	8	6,750	32	2	1	7,462	40,600	57,900
Carpentering	7	5,975	63	....	....	17,850	27,600	52,700
Clothing, men's	5	6,130	16	9	....	8,186	18,380	36,280
Cotton goods	5	855,100	201	368	167	111,052	458,899	747,812
Flouring- and grist-mill products	4	107,500	28	....	....	8,400	181,360	210,545
Painting and paperhanging	3	1,050	8	....	....	2,075	3,000	5,923
Photographing	3	1,300	....	....	....	....	1,400	4,200
Printing and publishing	3	12,000	29	....	2	15,252	14,800	37,000
Tinware, copperware, and sheet-iron ware	4	6,200	20	....	....	6,600	16,100	33,600
Tobacco, chewing, smoking, and snuff	14	658,500	1,516	864	562	347,345	2,395,196	3,194,245
Watch and clock repairing	3	800	2	....	....	250	1,000	3,325
Wheelwrighting (see also Blacksmithing)	5	2,225	11	....	....	2,595	2,720	8,400
All other industries (a)	26	57,125	183	2	10	46,992	98,851	176,404

a Embracing brick and tile; brooms and brushes; carriages and wagons; coffins, burial cases, and undertakers' goods; cooperage; foundery and machine-shop products; lock- and gun-smithing; lumber, planed; marble and stone work; masonry, brick and stone; patent medicines and compounds; plumbing and gasfitting; saddlery and harness; sash, doors, and blinds; slaughtering and meat-packing; soap and candles; tobacco, cigars and cigarettes; upholstering, and upholstering materials.

From the foregoing table it appears that the average capital of all establishments is $15,624 48; that the average wages of all hands employed is $143 65 per annum; that the average outlay in wages, in materials, and in interest (at 6 per cent.) on capital employed is $34,766 87.

PORTSMOUTH,

NORFOLK COUNTY, VIRGINIA.

POPULATION

IN THE

AGGREGATE,

1840-1880.

	Inhab.
1790	......
1800	......
1810	......
1820	......
1830	......
1840	6,477
1850	8,122
1860	9,496
1870	10,590
1880	11,390

N.

Washington, D. C. N. 14° 53' W. 146.6 Miles.

Richmond, Va. N. 51° 53' W. 79.1 Miles.

Greensboro, N. C. S. 75° 54' W. 198.4 Miles.

Charleston, S. C. S. 37° 26' W. 347.4 Miles.

S.

POPULATION

BY

SEX, NATIVITY, AND RACE,

AT

CENSUS OF 1880.

Male	5,489
Female	5,901
Native	10,864
Foreign-born	526
White	7,554
Colored	*3,836

* Including 7 Indians.

Latitude: 36° 50' North; Longitude: 76° 18' (west from Greenwich); **Average Altitude: 10 feet.**

FINANCIAL CONDITION:

Total Valuation: $2,906,324; per capita: $255 00.   Net Indebtedness: $283,014; per capita: $24 85.   Tax per $100: $2 01.

HISTORICAL SKETCH.

Few places of the size and importance of Portsmouth have a history so destitute of interesting events. From its foundation in 1752 to the present time it has pursued its way in silence, while its history has been lost in that of its more prosperous neighbor, Norfolk. The city has a magnificent harbor, one of the finest on the Atlantic coast; and in Gosport, one of its suburbs, is situated the celebrated Norfolk navy-yard. No period of rapid growth either in population or in wealth has marked the progress of the city. Its exports are cotton, lumber, oak-staves, naval stores, pig-iron, and early vegetables for the northern markets. A single daily newspaper is published in Portsmouth. There are several churches and many public and private schools.

PORTSMOUTH IN 1880.

The following statistical accounts, collected by the Census Office, indicate the present condition of Portsmouth:

LOCATION.

Portsmouth is situated in latitude 36° 50' north, longitude 76° 18' west from Greenwich, on the west bank of the Elizabeth river as it enters Chesapeake bay. It is opposite Norfolk, 1 mile away, 8 miles from Hampton roads, and 105 miles east-southeast from Richmond. The lowest point is level with the tide-water, and the average altitude 10 feet above this mark. The harbor has a channel varying in width from 1,000 to 1,200 feet, and the depth of water is about 22 feet. The tidal current flows at the rate of 1 mile per hour. Lines of steamboats connect the city with important points on the Atlantic coast, and by river with Richmond.

RAILROAD COMMUNICATIONS.

The Seaboard and Roanoke railroad, termini Portsmouth, and Weldon, North Carolina, connects the city with lines of railroads offering almost direct communication with the important cities of the south Atlantic seaboard.

TRIBUTARY COUNTRY.

The country immediately surrounding the city is devoted exclusively to agriculture. Strawberries, peanuts, cabbages, potatoes, etc., are raised in large quantities, and sent, by way of Portsmouth and Norfolk, to the northern markets.

TOPOGRAPHY.

Portsmouth is situated on the land between the South and East branches of the Elizabeth river. Its general geological structure is the same as that of Norfolk, which see.

CLIMATE.

The climate is the same as that of Norfolk.

STREETS.

Portsmouth has about 17 miles of streets, of which 1⅗ mile is paved with cobble-stones and 2 miles with oyster-shells, while the rest are simple dirt roads. About half the sidewalks are of brick and the other half of dirt. The gutters are generally paved with cobble-stones and supported by 4-inch bluestone curbs. All the new streets have gutters 5 feet wide. No trees are planted along the streets by the city. The construction of the streets is generally done by contract, the repairs by day labor. The annual expense for repairs is about $4,500. Neither steam stone-crusher nor roller is used. There are no horse-railroads or omnibus lines.

WATER-WORKS.

There is no public water-supply. Cistern-water is generally used.

GAS.

Gas is supplied by a private corporation. The average daily production is about 23,000 feet; the charge per 1,000 feet is $3, but persons using more than 1,000 feet pay at the rate of $2 50. The city pays $22 a year for each of the 83 gas street-lamps in use.

PUBLIC BUILDINGS.

The city owns a mayor's office, and 3 engine-houses for the fire department. The total value of these buildings is $11,500. In addition, Portsmouth, jointly with Norfolk county, owns a court-house, valued at $30,000, and a jail worth $6,000.

PUBLIC PARKS AND PLEASURE-GROUNDS.

There are no public parks in the city.

PLACES OF AMUSEMENT.

Oxford hall, seating 600, is used by traveling shows, and for concerts and entertainments. The only other hall in the city is Maupin's hall. Theaters pay a license of $15 per annum to the city, and to the state $3 50 per night or $10 per week, and 1 per cent. on the gross receipts. There are no concert- and beer-gardens.

DRAINAGE.

The city has no public system of sewerage, and no information as to its drainage was furnished.

CEMETERIES.

There are 2 public cemeteries and 3 private or corporation cemeteries in Portsmouth. The public cemeteries are situated one in the northwestern, the other in the southwestern part of the city, and have an area, respectively, of 8 and 4 acres. One of the private cemeteries is situated to the northwest of the city, and about three-quarters of a mile beyond its limits; it contains about 10 acres. The other two private burial-grounds are no longer used; one, *Trinity Church-yard*, is on the south side of Glascow street, between Dinwiddie and Court streets. No record of the number of interments in these grounds has been kept. A certificate of death and a permit for interment must be obtained before any burial will be allowed. Graves are required to be 4 feet deep.

MARKETS.

There are 3 markets in the city. The meat market is a low wooden structure, 200 feet by 30 feet in size, and contains 28 stalls; the rental varies from $60 to $150. The vegetable market has no building, but controls a space of 245 feet by 22 feet, which is divided into 31 hucksters and farmers' stalls, the former renting at $25 a year, the latter at 10 cents a day. The fish market controls a space 16 by 80 feet, and has no stalls. Fish-carts pay 25 cents a day for their stands. The total rental of the fish market is $1,960; of the two others $2,950. They are open from daylight until 12 m. every day except Saturday, when they do not close until 10 p. m. No estimate of the gross annual sales can be given.

SANITARY AUTHORITY—BOARD OF HEALTH.

The chief sanitary authority of the city is vested in a board of health consisting of 5 members appointed annually by the city council, and the city physician, who is *ex officio* health officer and a member of the board. The annual expense of the board in the absence of an epidemic is about $4,000, which is expended in removing night-soil and garbage, in paying the salary of an inspector ($600), and in meeting incidental expenses. The city clerk is *ex officio* clerk of the board. Meetings are held weekly from March to November, and fortnightly from November to March. In case of an epidemic the board may increase its expenses to any necessary amount. The authority of the board both during and in the absence of an epidemic is unlimited in all ways to protect and insure the maintenance of the public health. The chief executive officer is the health officer, whose salary is $600; besides being city physician, he is also registrar of vital statistics. A single inspector is employed. He has, like the members of the board, authority to enter and examine premises, but has no other police powers. Inspections are made regularly in all parts of the city.

NUISANCES.

Nuisances are inspected when reported or found by the inspector, and the owner or occupant of the premises is ordered to remove them. If this order is not complied with in twenty-four hours, the person offending incurs a fine of not less than $5, and the inspector, health officer, or member of the board sues to recover the penalty, which increases not less than $5 for every day of neglect.

The board has authority to compel the rectification of all defective house-drainage, privy-vaults, cesspools, and sources of drinking-water. The cleaning of the streets is not under the charge of the board.

GARBAGE.

The board of health controls the conservation and removal of garbage.

BURIAL OF THE DEAD.

A burial permit must be obtained before any interment is allowed to be made. This permit is issued by the health officer on receiving a certificate of death signed by the attending physician when there is one, or by a competent person. The ordinances of the city forbid an interment in any private lot, garden, or other parcel of ground, or any burying-ground within the city, unless the person so interred has a father, mother, husband, wife, brother, sister, or child already interred therein.

INFECTIOUS DISEASES.

Small-pox patients are removed to a pest-house about 4 miles beyond the city limits. Scarlet-fever patients are quarantined at home.

Should contagious diseases break out in the public or private schools, the board of health has authority to close the schools, or to take such other precautions as it deems best. Vaccination is compulsory whenever ordered by the board, but is done at the public expense only for those who are unable to pay for it. A strict quarantine is maintained at all times for vessels from infected ports, or those on which any one has been sick or has died, or the cargoes of which have been damaged. Any breach of quarantine law is punished by a fine of not less than $20 nor more than $500.

REPORTS.

No regular report is made by the board. Accounts of its regular meetings are published by the city newspapers. The registrar of vital statistics records all births, diseases, and deaths.

MUNICIPAL CLEANSING.

Street-cleaning is done by the city with its own force and entirely by hand labor. The principal business streets are cleaned twice a week, the others about once a month, and the work is very efficiently done. The annual cost to the city is $2,000. The sweepings are deposited on the ends of streets extending into a salt-marsh. The system is regarded as excellent.

Removal of garbage and ashes.—Garbage is removed by a contractor hired by the board of health and paid by the city. While awaiting removal, garbage, which must not be mixed with ashes, must be kept in water-tight vessels until called for by the contractor's carts, which visit every part of the city every day. It is disposed of by using it as manure. Ashes are also removed by a city contractor, and are disposed of in the same way as the street-sweepings. No injury to the public health has arisen under this system of disposing of garbage.

Dead animals.—No system has been formed for the removal of the carcasses of dead animals. They are generally taken by the street department and buried. The number is very small.

Liquid household wastes.—Kitchen and laundry wastes and chamber-slops are disposed of alike. A large amount is run into the street-gutters, and a little into cesspools, which are porous and nearly always without overflows. They rarely receive the wastes of water-closets. There is no practice in regard to flushing the street-gutters. Cesspools are ignored by the city ordinances, which, however, require that privy-vaults shall be cleaned every three months, or oftener if necessary.

Human excreta.—The houses almost without exception depend on privy-vaults, which are generally tubs or boxes of various sizes. The work of cleaning the privies is done by a city scavenger appointed by the board of health. They must be cleaned four times a year, or oftener if necessary, and between the hours of 11 p. m. and 3 a. m. The fees for this service are determined by the board of health. The night-soil is removed beyond the city limits, and is used in manuring land. Its use within a quarter of a mile of the city limits is occasioning complaint.

Manufacturing wastes.—There are no manufactures carried on in the city producing wastes needing to be disposed of.

RICHMOND,

HENRICO COUNTY, VIRGINIA.

POPULATION

IN THE

AGGREGATE,

1790–1880.

	Inhab.
	3,761
	5,737
	9,736
	12,067
20	16,060
30	20,153
1840	27,570
1850	37,910
1860	51,038
1870	63,600
1880	

POPULATION

BY

SEX, NATIVITY, AND RACE,

AT

CENSUS OF 1880.

Male	29,483
Female	34,117
Native	60,260
Foreign-born	3,340
White	35,765
Colored	*27,835

*Including 3 Chinese.

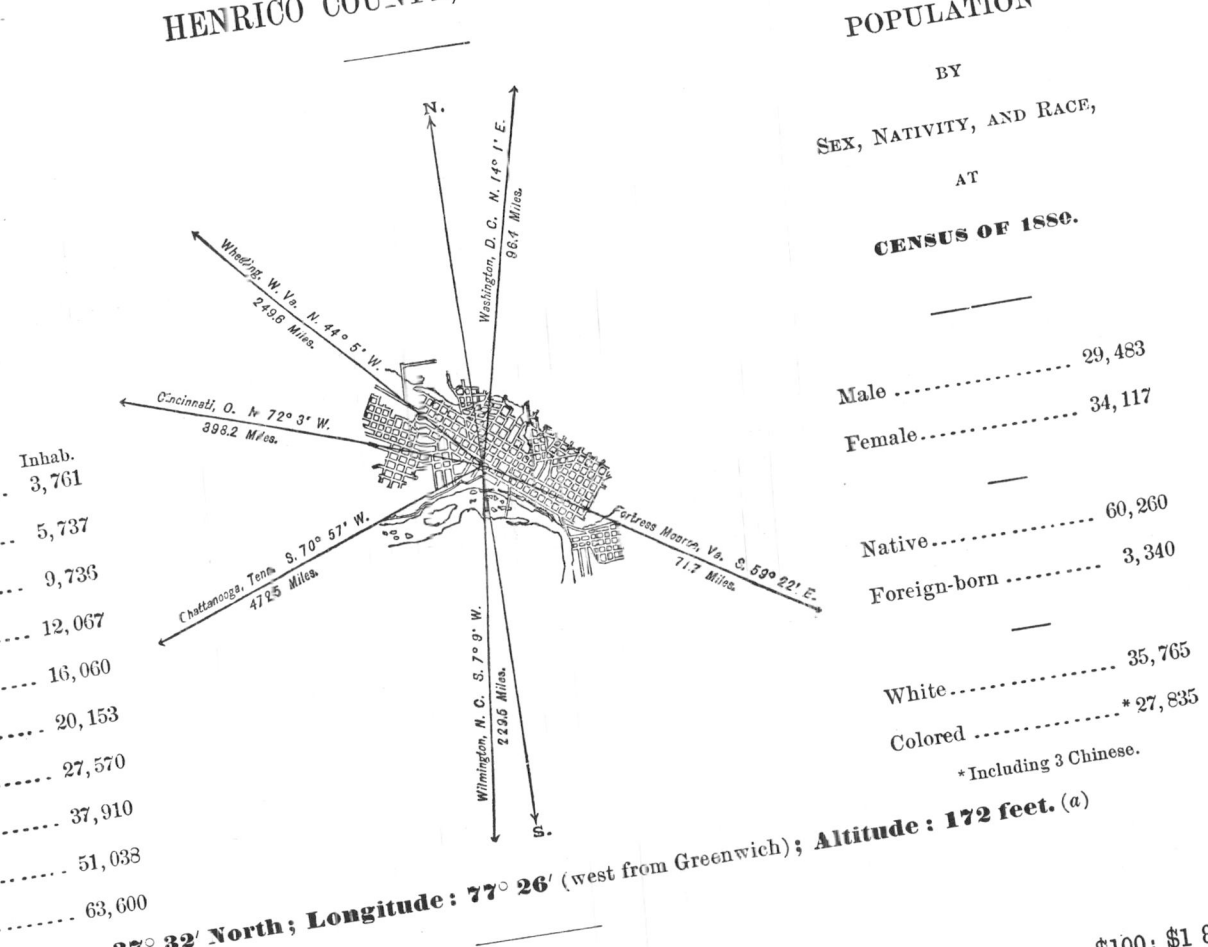

Latitude: 37° 32' North; Longitude: 77° 26' (west from Greenwich); **Altitude: 172 feet.** (a)

FINANCIAL CONDITION:

Net Indebtedness: $4,399,021; per capita: $69 17. Tax per $100: $1 85.

Total Valuation: $39,522,356; per capita: $621 00.

HISTORICAL SKETCH.

Although, from its eminence in the past, the capital of the Old Dominion deserves an extended notice, it is impossible here to give more than a cursory sketch of its history. The first settlement was made in 1609, when a small party sent out from Jamestown established themselves at this point. The settlement thus founded was only an outpost against the Indians, and its frontier character was illustrated by the erection of "Fort Charles", in 1644–'45, as a still further protection to the other settlements. The spot was the scene of a bloody contest in 1656 between a party of border rangers, under Colonel Hill, and the Indians, in which the former were defeated; and during the time of Bacon's rebellion, in 1676, it was again brought into prominence.

A mill was erected here by William Byrd in 1679, and some years later a warehouse was built here, which gave to the little place the name of "Byrd's Warehouse", by which it was known until its incorporation as the town of

a At Smithsonian station.

Richmond in 1742. It was laid out in streets and lots in 1737 by Colonel William Byrd, the real founder of the city, and was designed to cover about 3 square miles. It was in Saint John's church that Patrick Henry, addressing the Virginia convention in 1775, uttered his ever memorable "Give me liberty or give me death!"; and this convention is the only incident of general interest which marks the history of the town from its until 1779, when it was made the capital of Virginia in place of Williamsburg, 1698. Little more than a year after being made the capital of V 300 houses, was burnt by Arnold and Simsoe during mishap, it advanced in wealth The corner-st

navi
lowe
corp
part
Phila

RAILROAD COMMUNICATIONS.

Richmond is connected by the following-named railroads with the principal cities of the state, and, through their connections, with the leading places in the whole country:

The Richmond, Fredericksburg, and Potomac railroad, termini Richmond and Quantico.

The Richmond and Danville railroad, termini Richmond, and Charlotte, North Carolina.

The Chesapeake and Ohio railroad, termini Richmond, and Huntington, West Virginia.

The Richmond and Petersburg railroad, termini Richmond and Petersburg.

The Richmond and Alleghany railroad, termini Richmond and Columbia.

The Richmond, York River, and Chesapeake railroad, termini Richmond and West Point.

Nearly all are parts of trunk-lines, and have aided greatly in increasing the city's prosperity.

TRIBUTARY COUNTRY.

The country tributary to Richmond is rich in all kinds of mineral and agricultural wealth. Iron, copper, and manganese ores are found in abundance; the finest of sand for glass-making, and kaolin, granite, and slate, are found within the region tributary to the city, while lumber and coal are easily reached. The agricultural products are tobacco, grain, and vegetables.

TOPOGRAPHY.

The city is built upon two undulating plateaus, resting on granite, divided by the valley of the Shockoe creek, and subdivided by smaller valleys and ravines, through one of which flows Gillie's creek. The country for miles around is hilly.

CLIMATE.

No information as to the highest and lowest recorded temperatures could be obtained. The mean temperature for the year is about 60°. The elevation of the city above the sea makes its air pure and healthful.

STREETS.

The principal streets are laid out from east to west roughly parallel with the river, the cross-streets intersecting them at right angles. The total length of the streets can not be given, and no detailed information as to the cost of paving and repairs was furnished. The paving is either of broken stone or of stone blocks where the streets are paved at all. In the year ending February, 1879, the total cost of the construction and repairs of the streets and sewers was $65,159 13. The sidewalks are of brick or flagstone when they are paved at all, and are from 10 to 12 feet in width.

The Richmond City Passenger railway is the only horse-railroad in the city. It passes through Main and Broad streets, the two principal thoroughfares, and has a total length of about 8 miles. Omnibuses run to and from the railroad depots and the steamboat landings.

WATER-WORKS.

The city owns both the water- and the gas-works. The total cost of the water-works from the beginning, in 1830, to February, 1879, was $2,258,801 03, and the receipts during the same period were $1,490,163 46.

The water is taken from the James river. The maximum pumping capacity is 24,000,000 gallons per day, and the total storage capacity of the reservoirs is 52,000,000 gallons. There are over 50 miles of pipes and mains, varying from 30 to 1½ inches in diameter. The annual income is from $25,000 to $30,000.

GAS.

The gas-works were built in 1851. There are about 50 miles of mains, and nearly 90,000,000 cubic feet of gas are manufactured annually. The income is about $50,000 annually.

PUBLIC BUILDINGS.

The buildings owned by the city and used in whole or part for municipal purposes include a city hall, a jail, an almshouse, 2 police stations, 2 markets, and 3 engine-houses. The school-houses are valued at about $250,000. No information as to the value of the other public buildings was furnished.

PUBLIC PARKS AND PLEASURE-GROUNDS.

The total area of the public parks and pleasure-grounds is about 40 acres. *Chimborazo Park*, 29 square acres, and *Libby Hill Park*, 3½ acres, are in the eastern part of the city, about 150 feet above the river, and command a fine view of the James and the surrounding country. *Capitol Park*, 13 acres, is situated in the center of the city, and contains the state-house and the celebrated equestrian statue of Washington designed by Crawford. This statue rests upon a massive granite pedestal, surrounded by bronze statues of Patrick Henry, Thomas Jefferson,

John Marshall, George Mason, Thomas Nelson, and Andrew Lewis. A marble statue of Henry Clay, and Foley's statue of "Stonewall" Jackson, are among the other adornments of this park. *Gamble's Hill Park*, 8½ acres, on the south and river front of the city, and *Monroe Park*, nearly 9 acres, in the western part of Richmond, complete the list of public parks.

The *Old Reservoir* grounds, just on the western edge of the city, form another public pleasure-ground; and the *New Reservoir Park*, a mile beyond the city limits, embracing 160 acres, is the driving-park of the Richmond people.

PLACES OF AMUSEMENT.

The Richmond theater and Mozart hall are the principal places of amusement. Virginia hall and Assembly hall are used as concert- and lecture-rooms. No information was furnished of the seating capacity of these.

DRAINAGE.

No information on this subject was furnished.

CEMETERIES.

Richmond has 12 cemeteries which are now in use, 1 now no longer used, and 3 national cemeteries, where the federal soldiers killed during the attacks on the city in the civil war lie buried. The following are the cemeteries now in use:

Hollywood Cemetery, situated on Cherry street, in the western extremity of the city, near the river, contains about 77 acres, and is owned and managed by a corporation consisting of the lot-owners. It was first used in 1848, and 9,858 interments have been made in it, besides the 12,000 or 13,000 soldiers who lie buried there.

Shockoe Hill Cemetery, situated near the northern bounds of the city on Shockoe hill, contains 12½ acres, in which only white persons are buried, and 2½ acres where colored persons are interred. It was established in 1822, and contains the bodies of 16,989 white and 2,470 colored persons. It is open only to the inhabitants of the city of Richmond or of Henrico county.

Hebrew Cemetery, area not stated, adjoins the latter on the east.

Saint Mary's Cemetery lies about half a mile north of the city limits, on the Henrico turnpike, and contains 2½ acres. Since its establishment in 1874, there have been 169 interments made in it, and 71 bodies have been moved thither from other places.

Oakwood Cemetery is situated about half a mile east of the city, on Oakwood avenue, and contains 66¼ acres. Only white persons are allowed to be interred in it. There have been 20,300 interments. It is owned and maintained by the city.

The following 6 cemeteries are all owned and used by colored persons:

Ham's Cemetery, area 3 acres, contains 2,314 bodies; *Sycamore Cemetery*, 3 acres, contains 1,312 bodies; *Ebenezer Cemetery*, 1 acre; *Mechanics' Cemetery*, 5 acres; *Cedar Wood Cemetery*, ½ acre; and *Methodist Cemetery*, ½ acre. These are all situated about a quarter of a mile north of the city, on Saint James road.

The *Catholic Cemetery* is situated about half a mile east of the city, on the Mechanicsville road. No information as to its area or the number of interments made in it was furnished.

Saint John's Cemetery, the church-yard around Saint John's church, is now full and is no longer used. The 3 national cemeteries are situated far beyond the city limits, one about 1½ mile to the east of the city; the second, on the same road, 5 or 6 miles below, near Seven Pines; and the third, about 5 or 6 miles below the city, on the River road, near fort Harrison. All have been highly improved, but no statistics in regard to them could be obtained.

Hollywood, Oakwood, and Shockoe Hill cemeteries are finely laid out. Graves in Oakwood are required to be 6 feet deep; the depth in the others was not ascertained. No undertaker is allowed to make any interment until he has received a certificate from the attending physician stating the cause of the death and such other information as the schedules of the board of health call for.

MARKETS.

There are two markets in the city, each having a meat, vegetable, and fish department, and controlling a number of curbstone-stands. The First market contains in all 78 stalls. The meat department is 350 by 50 feet in size, and contains 40 stalls, which rent at from $9 to $9 50 per month; the vegetable department is 150 by 50 feet, and has 28 stalls, renting at from $2 to $5 per month; the fish department is 40 by 50 feet, and has 10 stalls, the rent of which is from $2 to $3 50 a month. The curb-stands rent at from $2 to $5 per month. In addition, there is a large open space beyond the market, used exclusively by farmers and truckers, who pay a small sum each. The total monthly rental is $805 50.

The meat market of the Second market has an area of 150 by 67 feet, and contains 32 stalls, the rent of which is from $6 to $12 50 a month; the vegetable market is 165 by 60 feet, and has 42 stalls, renting at from $2 33 to $4 a month; and the fish market is 60 by 28 feet, and has 12 stalls, the monthly rent of which is from $2 33 to $3 33.

There are 48 curbstone-stands, the rent of which is from $2 50 to $4 a month. The average monthly rental is $625.

Both markets are open from daylight until noon every week day except Saturday, when they do not close until 10 p. m. A large amount of business is done by private stores outside the markets.

SANITARY AUTHORITY—BOARD OF HEALTH.

The chief health organization of the city is a board of health, elected by the municipal authorities for a term of two years, and consists of three members, all of them physicians. The board is advisory to the municipal authorities; it can not make ordinances nor enforce them, and is charged with the duty of recommending measures for the general health of the community, of reporting all violations of the health ordinances and seeing that all causes of complaint under this head are removed, and of taking charge of street-cleaning and the removal of garbage. The expenses of the board are about $1,400 a year, $900 of which is for the salary of the president, $100 each for the other two members of the board, and the balance for incidental expenses. The board can under no circumstances exceed the appropriation placed at its disposal by the city councils, and its authority is the same both in the absence of and during an epidemic. The president is the chief health officer, and is also quarantine officer, while the other members are his assistants. Should quarantine be established, he is entitled to an additional compensation of $5 per day. Since 1865 there have been but two occasions when quarantine was established.

The board has no regular time of meeting, but is called together when occasion demands, and the president has the entire management of the department.

The committee on health, consisting of 2 members of the board of aldermen and 3 members of the council, constitutes another branch of the sanitary authority. This committee meets quarterly, or oftener if necessary. The president of the board of health is expected to be present to give the views of the board on any question. The committee has special charge of the small-pox hospital, and directs the disbursement of the amount appropriated to the board of health; it is expected to examine questions relating to the public health, and to be the exponent of the board of health before the aldermen and council.

Three policemen from the regular police force are detailed for duty as sanitary inspectors, to act under the orders of the president of the board. The city is divided into 3 sanitary districts, and 1 inspector is assigned to each. He makes inspections regularly in all parts of his district, and especially where nuisances are reported.

NUISANCES.

The list of nuisances includes all things, other than diseases, injurious to the health or comfort of the citizens. Nuisances are inspected whenever discovered or reported, and a notice is served on the owner or occupant of the premises requiring a removal within a specified number of days. · If this is not complied with, the party is reported to the police court. Cases of defective house-drainage, cesspools, privy-vaults, and sources of drinking-water are treated as nuisances. Defective sewerage when reported by the board is rectified by the city authorities, or by private persons if the defect is on their premises. Defective street-cleaning is directly remedied by the board so far as their appropriation will allow.

GARBAGE.

Garbage is defined as kitchen offal alone, and is removed by collectors appointed and governed by the board of health. The regulations of the garbage service require that householders shall keep the garbage in water-tight vessels, in places convenient for the collectors, but not on the sidewalks or in any public place, and separate from other refuse matter.

BURIAL OF THE DEAD.

No interment is allowed until the undertaker has received from the attending physician, the coroner, or, in their absence, from any competent person, a certificate stating the cause of death, the age, sex, color, civil condition (single, married, or widowed), residence, occupation, birthplace, place of death, and length of residence in the city of the deceased. The sextons receive these certificates, and are required to make a weekly return of all interments made by them, the return stating the information contained in the certificate of death. Graves must be not less than 5 feet in depth, and must in all cases be 6 feet deep, unless in the "public portion" of any cemetery the board of health permits a less depth. No body is allowed to be removed from the city without a permit from the board of health.

INFECTIOUS DISEASES.

Small-pox patients are removed to a small-pox hospital in the western part of the city in a completely isolated spot, unless perfectly safe arrangements can be made to care for the patient at home. Scarlet-fever patients are not isolated or quarantined in any way, and attempts by the board to obtain favorable action from the councils looking toward better precautions in cases of scarlet fever have proved fruitless. The school-board acts in thorough harmony with the board of health, and, when contagious diseases appear among the pupils in the public schools, immediately requires the absence of the pupils and all from the same family from school, until a physician has certified that danger of contagion no longer exists. The clergy of the city have consented to abandon public funerals for persons dying of small-pox, scarlet fever, and diphtheria. Vaccination is not compulsory, but is performed without charge at the city almshouse and dispensary for those wishing it.

REPORTS.

The board of health reports annually to the mayor and city council, and this report is published in pamphlet form. When occasion demands, special written reports are made, and these are generally printed.

The registration of births, diseases, and deaths is under the charge of the board, and is carefully attended to, the records being compiled weekly in cases of diseases and deaths.

MUNICIPAL CLEANSING.

Street-cleaning.—The streets are cleaned by the city with its own force and entirely by hand labor. The work is entirely under the control of the board of health, and is done whenever the condition of the streets makes it necessary. The great defect of the system is stated by the president of the board to lie in the fact that an insufficient and inefficient force of men is placed at the disposal of the board of health for that purpose. Such of the sweepings as can be used for manure are sold to farmers; the rest is used in filling up ravines in the extension of new streets. The cost of the street-cleaning and removal of garbage and ashes is $8,700 a year.

Removal of garbage and ashes.—Garbage is removed at the expense of the city by collectors licensed and controlled by the board of health. It must be kept in water-tight vessels, entirely separate from ashes, and placed where the collector can easily get at it. The collections are made twice in each week. It is finally disposed of by removing it beyond the city limits. Ashes are also removed at the city's expense, and are either sold or used in filling up ravines. The defect of the system is the unfrequent removal of the garbage, from which some discomfort and possibly some injury to health arises.

Dead animals.—The carcasses of animals dying within the city are removed by a contractor, who pays a small bonus to the city for the privilege. He must remove the carcasses within six hours after notification by the owner, under penalty of a fine. During the past year 148 horses, 24 mules, and 58 cows were removed beyond the city limits. The system has proved an excellent one.

Liquid household wastes.—When there are public sewers the chamber-slops and kitchen and laundry wastes all run alike into the sewers; but in other places the kitchen and laundry wastes pass into the street-gutters, and chamber-slops are thrown into cesspools. The number of cesspools is small; those that exist are porous, and are unprovided with overflows, which are not allowed by the city. The gutters are flushed whenever the supply of water will justify such a use of it. Chemical examination of some of the wells in the city has shown that they are nearly all polluted by the overflow or inflow from cesspools and privy-vaults.

Human excreta.—About one-third of the houses in the city depend on water-closets, while the other two-thirds make use of privy-vaults. The water-closets in almost every case deliver into the public sewers. None of the privy-vaults are even nominally water-tight. They must be cleansed when full or offensive, the work being done by scavengers licensed by the board of health. The rates charged for cleansing are fixed by the board. The night-soil is removed beyond the city limits and utilized there. It is not allowed to be used in manuring land within the gathering-ground of the public water-supply.

Manufacturing wastes.—Liquid wastes are allowed to pass into the sewers; solid wastes are removed beyond the city limits, and in many cases utilized there. No ill effects have resulted from the system.

COMMERCE AND NAVIGATION.

[From the reports of the Bureau of Statistics for the fiscal years ending June 30.]

Customs district of Richmond, Virginia.	1879.	1880.
Total value of imports	$188,459	$111,061
Total value of exports:		
Domestic	$2,932,597	$2,326,915
Foreign	None.	None.
Total number of immigrants	None.	None.

Customs district of Richmond, Virginia.	1879.		1880.	
	Number.	Tons.	Number.	Tons.
Vessels in foreign trade:				
Entered	47	15,380	42	14,512
Cleared	148	48,935	135	45,741
Vessels in coast trade and fisheries:				
Entered	446	426,118	618	494,360
Cleared	504	470,951	549	516,089
Vessels registered, enrolled, and licensed in district.	49	6,733	39	4,657
Vessels built during the year	3	155		

MANUFACTURES.

The following is a summary of the statistics of the manufactures of Richmond for 1880, being taken from tables prepared for the Tenth Census by James A. Cabell, special agent:

Mechanical and manufacturing industries.	No. of establishments.	Capital.	AVERAGE NUMBER OF HANDS EMPLOYED. Males above 16 years.	Females above 15 years.	Children and youths.	Total amount paid in wages during the year.	Value of materials.	Value of products.
All industries	598	$6,884,386	9,218	2,872	1,957	$3,006,456	$12,141,512	$20,790,106
Agricultural implements	5	219,530	246	....	2	82,904	114,972	320,988
Blacksmithing (see also Wheelwrighting)	8	1,925	15	....	....	2,410	2,430	8,170
Boots and shoes, including custom work and repairing	78	30,900	224	13	3	38,046	104,060	208,681
Boxes, cigar	3	6,100	15	9	5	5,700	21,500	35,600
Boxes, fancy and paper	3	18,000	52	87	102	48,596	26,210	107,410
Boxes, wooden packing	8	97,600	121	....	12	51,671	114,482	206,011
Bread and other bakery products	20	59,000	74	14	1	30,311	148,540	232,060
Brick and tile	4	21,500	64	....	19	17,900	9,125	36,460
Carpentering	34	41,000	158	....	2	58,055	136,410	272,000
Carriages and wagons (see also Wheelwrighting)	9	63,000	101	....	2	31,750	56,900	140,000
Clothing, men's	24	155,367	163	405	2	80,308	169,511	359,022
Coffee and spices, roasted and ground	5	46,000	36	1	1	13,060	143,000	241,000
Confectionery	13	69,700	63	7	6	23,687	98,624	151,450
Cooperage	15	33,700	238	....	9	36,765	89,722	155,282
Drugs and chemicals (see also Patent medicines and compounds)	7	142,500	247	....	3	39,200	160,250	247,790
Dyeing and cleaning	5	5,150	12	7	1	4,800	10,400	23,600
Fertilizers	5	298,000	172	3	....	28,900	326,450	476,600
Flouring- and grist-mill products	5	1,226,500	191	....	....	79,565	2,147,762	2,443,432
Foundery and machine-shop products	13	523,500	1,044	....	61	287,993	541,898	1,056,351
Furniture	26	108,650	124	10	13	55,605	96,570	232,010
Hairwork	4	7,500	5	36	....	8,200	16,900	33,000
Iron and steel	3	702,000	1,004	....	50	336,311	1,173,801	1,973,916
Lock- and gun-smithing	4	4,400	11	....	....	4,200	5,650	16,700
Looking-glass and picture frames	7	8,950	28	....	9	10,400	21,850	50,500
Marble and stone work	7	20,400	56	....	....	24,200	28,600	71,100
Oil, lubricating	3	12,000	7	....	1	990	11,300	20,500
Painting and paperhanging	9	14,200	36	....	....	12,250	19,500	47,850
Patent medicines and compounds (see also Drugs and chemicals)	8	37,000	32	1	....	10,150	25,900	52,900
Photographing	9	21,000	36	1	2	17,444	9,900	49,300
Plumbing and gasfitting	5	22,000	28	....	7	15,230	40,500	79,500
Printing and publishing	17	177,300	241	4	24	131,495	112,834	328,325
Saddlery and harness	12	38,100	74	....	9	37,644	71,020	141,400
Sash, doors, and blinds	6	73,500	100	....	....	39,092	201,513	311,184
Shipbuilding	4	3,500	23	....	....	9,300	8,900	23,500
Soap and candles	3	26,000	17	1	....	7,100	19,400	38,000
Tinware, copperware, and sheet-iron ware	26	88,050	143	....	3	55,800	135,700	265,500
Tobacco, chewing, smoking, and snuff (see also Tobacco, cigars and cigarettes)	39	1,333,100	2,838	1,704	1,179	895,657	3,109,076	6,580,984
Tobacco, cigars and cigarettes (see also Tobacco, chewing, smoking, and snuff)	26	140,430	261	19	78	76,770	152,980	343,702
Tobacco stemming	27	435,184	369	470	202	81,215	767,973	1,074,005
Watch and clock repairing	10	15,700	16	....	3	10,361	7,030	28,300
Wheelwrighting (see also Blacksmithing; Carriages and wagons)	24	27,450	77	....	1	17,976	25,210	69,000
All other industries (a)	55	509,000	456	80	145	187,385	1,657,159	2,237,023

a Embracing bagging, flax, hemp, and jute; bags, other than paper; bags, paper; baskets, rattan and willow ware; bookbinding and blank-book making; boot and shoe uppers; brass castings; brooms and brushes; coppersmithing; engraving, wood; food preparations; furs, dressed; grease and tallow; instruments, professional and scientific; iron bolts, nuts, washers, and rivets; iron forgings; iron work, architectural and ornamental; kindling wood; leather, tanned; liquors, vinous; lithographing; lumber, planed; mineral and soda waters; musical instruments, organs and materials; masonry, brick and tile; nets and seines; paints; paper; pumps; regalia and society banners and emblems; saws; slaughtering and meat-packing; stencils and brands; stone- and earthen-ware; trunks and valises; type founding; umbrellas and canes; upholstering; and wire work.

From the foregoing table it appears that the average capital of all establishments is $11,512 35; that the average wages of all hands employed is $214 03 per annum; that the average outlay in wages, in materials, and in interest (at 6 per cent.) on capital employed is $26,021 79.

WEST VIRGINIA.

WHEELING,
OHIO COUNTY, WEST VIRGINIA.

POPULATION

IN THE

AGGREGATE,

1810-1880.

	Inhab.
1790	......
1800	......
1810	914
1820	1,567
1830	5,221
1840	7,385
1850	11,435
1860	14,083
1870	19,280
1880	30,737

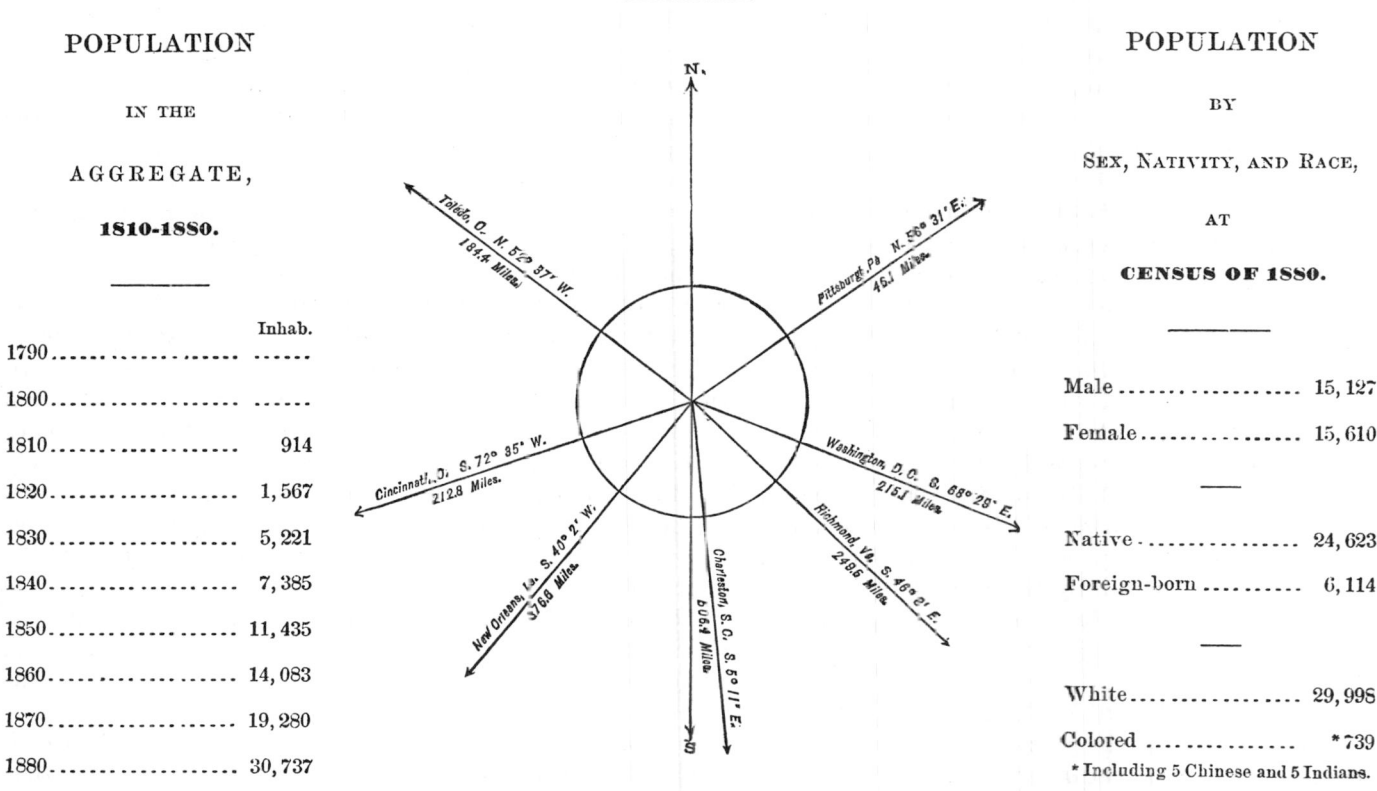

POPULATION

BY

SEX, NATIVITY, AND RACE,

AT

CENSUS OF 1880.

Male	15,127
Female	15,610
Native	24,623
Foreign-born	6,114
White	29,998
Colored	*739

* Including 5 Chinese and 5 Indians.

Latitude: 40° 5′ North; Longitude: 80° 43′ (west from Greenwich); **Altitude: 650 feet.**

FINANCIAL CONDITION:

Total Valuation: $14,173,600; per capita: $461 00.   Net Indebtedness: $531,882; per capita: $17 30.   Tax per $100: $1 68.

HISTORICAL SKETCH.(a)

The settlement of Wheeling is claimed to have begun in 1769, when Colonel Ebenezer Zane, Elias Zane, and Jonathan Zane, three brothers, then living on what is now known as the south branch of the Potomac river, near the present town of Moorfield, West Virginia, moved farther west, with the intention of relocating and settling on lands supposed to be more desirable.   They followed a trail frequented by Indians and traders to Redstone fort, the present site of Brownsville, Pennsylvania, and there, learning of a beautiful and fertile country bordering the

---

a By Dana L. Hubbard, esq.

waters of the Ohio river, they crossed the intervening country to the head-waters of the stream now known as Wheeling creek, and traveled along its banks to its confluence with the river. Here they marked out in three divisions a strip of territory including nearly all of the present site of Wheeling. In the following spring, Colonel Ebenezer Zane brought his family from the South branch of the Potomac by way of Redstone fort to the new settlement, coming from Redstone in canoes and pirogues, which were floated down the Ohio. Other families speedily joined the settlement, and in 1774, for its protection against hostile Indians, a well-constructed work of defense was built, called "Fort Fincastle", which name, in 1776, was changed to "Fort Henry." Constantly recurring warfare with the Indians checked the growth of the settlement, which in 1782 consisted of the fort, and a few log cabins surrounding it. Its early history was made up of almost continuous struggles against the efforts of the savages to destroy it, and the name "Wheeling" is said to have been derived from the killing of a white settler by the Delaware Indians, and the placing of his head on a pole near the center of the site of the present city, the word *wheeling* signifying "head" in the dialect of the Delaware tribe. Another tradition states that the place was named after a Catholic priest named Whalen, and still another that it took its name from the creek which pursued a wheeling or winding course through its boundaries.

The development of Wheeling as a municipality began in January, 1806, when it was incorporated as a village. In 1810 it had 914 inhabitants. The building of the Cumberland road to the Ohio river in 1818, and its subsequent extension through the state of Ohio about this time, gave Wheeling additional prominence as an avenue and distributing-point for passengers and freight east and west, until the national turnpike was superseded by railroads. The population increased rapidly. In 1836 Wheeling was incorporated as a city and the present city water-works were built. In 1847 the project of building a bridge over the Ohio river at Wheeling, which had been previously advocated unsuccessfully by some of the western states as a national measure before Congress, was revived by the people of Wheeling as a private enterprise, and under a charter from the state of Virginia a suspension bridge with a clear span of 1,010 feet was in 1849 built over the main channel, and connected with the Ohio shore by a pier-bridge previously built—the two structures being subsequently protected by an act of Congress declaring them post-roads. The suspension span was blown down in 1853, and was rebuilt during the same year.

In 1831 the city was made a port of delivery, and boat-building, which had been carried on to some extent previously, became one of its important industries. From 1849 to 1879, 99 steamboats, varying from 651 to 14 tons burden, were launched from Wheeling boat-yards. The quality, abundance, and location of the coal strata adjacent to Wheeling induced the establishment of other manufactures, notably of glass and iron, at an early day, and wagons, furniture, and other similar products were turned out in considerable quantities for western and southern markets. With the establishment of such manufactures came a further proportionate increase in the population of the city, besides a very considerable increase in its suburban towns and villages. This growth was assisted largely by the opening of the Baltimore and Ohio railroad to Wheeling in 1853, and the completion of its branch connections with the West, Northwest, and South; the completion of the Cleveland and Pittsburgh railroad and other branches of the Pennsylvania system, and of minor roads, opening up communication with adjacent territory. In 1848 the gas-works, now owned by the city, were begun by a private corporation. In 1851–'52 the building known as Washington hall, which was subsequently burnt and replaced by the present structure, was erected, and in 1859 the present custom-house, post-office, and United States court building was built. Street-cars were introduced in 1866, and at this time connect the extremities of the city and furnish a means of communication with all towns lying within a radius of 5 miles from its center.

Subsequently to the passage of the ordinance of secession by the state of Virginia, and the beginning of the civil war, a provisional government, called the "restored government of Virginia", was formed (June 19, 1861) by citizens of Virginia opposed to the secession of that state, which fixed its capital in the city of Wheeling. After the formation of the new state of West Virginia in 1863 the capital of the restored government of Virginia was removed to Alexandria, Virginia, and the capital of the new state was established at Wheeling. It remained here until removed to Charleston, in Kanawha county, by the legislature of the new state, in 1870. In 1875 it was again removed by the legislature to Wheeling, the taxpayers of the latter city building, at a cost of $160,000, and furnishing to the state gratuitously, so long as it desired to occupy it, a handsome and commodious capitol building in the central portion of the city. In 1877, by a vote of the people of the state, taken under regulations provided by the legislature, it was determined that the capitol should be removed to Charleston at the expiration of 8 years, and, unless future changes are made by the legislature, Wheeling will cease to be the capital May 1, 1885.

Wheeling suffered considerably from some of the periods of business depression which have affected the country at various times since its settlement, but they do not seem to have interfered with its steady growth. During the hard times closely following the war of 1812–'15, between the United States and Great Britain—from 1817 to 1825—her manufactures, trade, and industries of every character were more or less prostrated. The subsidence of the western land speculation, and the panic of 1837, produced similar disastrous effects, and the monetary troubles of 1842, 1857, 1861–'62, and 1873–'75 were severely felt; but their bad effects appear to have been only temporary. Notwithstanding these adverse years, there was a steady increase in the population from 1820 to 1880. The city has been singularly free from ravages by fire, for at no one time has it suffered the loss of more than two or three buildings.

WHEELING IN 1880.

The following statistical accounts, collected by the Census Office, indicate the present condition of Wheeling:

LOCATION.

Wheeling, the present capital of West Virginia, and the county-seat of Ohio county, is in the extreme northwestern portion of the state, on the east bank of the Ohio river, 92 miles below Pittsburgh, in latitude 40° 5′ north, longitude 80° 43′ west from Greenwich, and at an average altitude of 650 feet above the sea-level, and from 40 to 95 feet above low-water mark in the Ohio river. The depth of water in the river varies from 20 inches at the lowest stage to 30 or 40 feet during the spring and fall freshets. The harbor capacity is 1,250 feet, length of levee. The channel capacity (width) is from 100 feet at low water to 1,000 feet at high water. The current varies from 2 to 8 miles per hour, according to the stage of water, the current at the ordinary boating stage being 5½ miles per hour.

RAILROAD COMMUNICATIONS.

Wheeling is touched by two of the largest trunk lines between the East and the West—the Baltimore and Ohio railroad, to Baltimore on the east, and, via the Central Railroad of Ohio, to Chicago, Cincinnati, and Saint Louis on the west, and the Wheeling, Pittsburgh, and Baltimore branch to Washington, Pennsylvania; and the Pennsylvania railroad, with its connections, to all the large cities in the country. The Cleveland, Tuscarawas Valley, and Wheeling railroad, from Cleveland, terminates here.

TRIBUTARY COUNTRY.

The character of the surrounding country with which Wheeling has local dealings is, so far as agriculture is concerned, principally grain-growing, although grazing and tobacco-growing are carried on to a considerable extent in West Virginia, eastern Ohio, and western Pennsylvania. The industries are mainly iron and glass manufacturing and coal mining. There are no distinctive features in the commercial interests, they being made up of dealings in the usual supplies furnished to farming and manufacturing communities.

TOPOGRAPHY.

Wheeling is divided into 8 wards, which include Wheeling island in the Ohio river opposite the central portion of the city, making up the 7th ward, and Ritchietown, which was annexed to the city in 1870, comprised in the 8th ward. The main portion of the city, bounded on the east by a chain of hills averaging 400 feet in height above the river, extends along the eastern bank of the Ohio a distance of 4 miles, with a breadth of from two to eight squares, and, including the island, covers an area of about 4 square miles. A small portion of Main and Market streets, its principal business avenues, and a part of the island ward, which is mainly used for residences, are lower than the immediate banks of the river, but the surface drainage in other parts of the city is carried without difficulty into Wheeling creek and the Ohio river, and the current in both is sufficient to prevent any serious inconvenience to residents from accumulation of impurities in either. There are no lakes, ponds, or marshes in or about the city. The surrounding country is open, the hillsides only being wooded. The geological characteristics of the site are thus described by Dr. James E. Reeves:

"Geological stratification of Wheeling hill"—ascending. The dip of all the strata is southeast, 12.07 feet per mile. Bed of Wheeling creek, magnesian limestone containing fossil, ferruginous clay, and blue clay; depth of strata unknown.

	Total depth, feet.
1. Sandstone, containing pyrites; 25 feet of this is good building-stone, the remainder loose and of no practical value	100
2. Limestone bowlders, blue clay, yellow clay, nodular sandstone	25
3. Bituminous coal, with strata of basic, central, and roofing slate	6
4. Reddish-yellow soapstone, blue clay, limestone	25
5. Bituminous shale in thin layers; sandstone, with deposit of oxide of iron; fire-clay	10
6. Bluish or mottled clay-slate, soft, without minerals; sand- or flagging-stone, with deposit of oxide of iron	28
7. Limestone, yellow clay, yellow soapstone, fire-clay	70
8. Sandstone of different qualities, some very hard and fine-grained; limestone of different quality and color; yellow clay; bituminous shale	48
9. Brown limestone and gray sandstone, stratified	35
10. Cannel coal	1½
11. Sandstone, different varieties stratified; limestone, hydraulic; sandstone, micaceous, with carbonate of iron	55
12. Remainder to subsoil, irregular and non-primitive superstrata	180
13. Subsoil, tough yellow clay	14

CLIMATE.

Highest recorded summer temperature, 104° (1854); mean summer temperature in average years, 72°. Lowest recorded winter temperature, —15° (1856); mean winter temperature in average years, 33°. Frosts do not occur later than May, nor earlier than the first or middle of October. The direction of the winds is almost constantly from the southeast and northwest, rarely from the south—a fact accounted for by the comparatively open country on the west and north and the presence of the Alleghany mountains on the east.

STREETS.

The city contains 35¾ miles of streets, and about the same length of alleys. With few exceptions the streets intersect at right angles, and have a width of from 60 to 66 feet. Of the streets, 4½ miles are paved with cobble-stones and 5¼ miles with broken stone. The cost of the cobble-stone paving is $1 15, and of the broken stone 90 cents per square yard. The cobble-stone is preferred for quality, permanent economy, and the relative facility with which it is kept clean. The sidewalks are from 11 to 14 feet in width and are paved with brick and flagstone. The alleys are from 12 to 20 feet in width, and, with the exception of about 2 miles of paving, are unimproved. The gutters on the streets paved with cobble-stones are paved in the same manner, while on the streets with broken stone they are of the same material though in much larger blocks. No trees are planted along the streets by the city. Some few are set out by the abutters at their own cost, and are placed only in front of their residences, at the curbstone. There are no grass-plots in the streets or along the sidewalks. The construction and repairs of streets are done almost entirely by day labor, at an average annual cost of $30,000. For construction, contract work is deemed best, while for repairs the preference is given to day labor. There is no steam stone-crusher, but a 5-ton horse-roller is used on the macadamized streets. The total length of horse-railroads in the city is 6 miles, with 36 cars and 96 horses and mules. The number of men employed is 46, and the number of passengers carried during the year is 1,125,000. The rates of fare are 5 and 6 cents within the city limits. There are no regular street omnibus lines, but 13 vehicles, with 19 horses, and giving employment to 9 men, run from the several railroad stations, and carry passengers to different parts of the city for 25 cents for each fare.

WATER-WORKS.

The water-works are owned by the city, but their total cost is not given. The system is by direct pumping, with high-pressure, double-acting, piston pump, the pressure per square inch being 92 pounds on the pump-valves and 47 pounds on the distributing mains. The greatest amount pumped in 24 hours is 3,417,500 gallons, and the least 1,370,800 gallons. The average cost of raising 1,000,000 gallons 1 foot high, estimated in only the actual working expense, is 11.16 cents. The yearly cost of maintenance, aside from the cost of pumping, is $13,755.99, and the yearly income from water-rates averages $45,000. Water-meters are not used.

GAS.

The gas-works are owned by the city. The average daily production is 146,180 cubic feet, and the charge per 1,000 feet is $1 08 net. There are 311 street lamps.

PUBLIC BUILDINGS.

The city owns and occupies for municipal uses, wholly or in part, the city hall, the market-house, the city prison, and the court-house. The city hall, built originally for a Masonic temple, was purchased by the city for $10,000. The city and county buildings are not owned in common, although the city uses the basement of the county court-house as a lockup. The state capitol building will revert to the city in 1885, and will then be used for municipal purposes.

PUBLIC PARKS AND PLEASURE-GROUNDS.

There are no public parks or pleasure-grounds in Wheeling.

PLACES OF AMUSEMENT.

There are two theaters in the city—the opera-house, with a seating capacity of 900, and the Academy of Music, with a seating capacity of 1,000. These pay an annual license of $150 each to the city. There are, also, Assembly hall, Franzheim's hall, Germania hall, Harmom's hall, Koch's hall, La Belle hall, Mozart hall, Nolte's hall, Otto hall, Parker's hall, Turner hall, Walter's hall, and Westwood's hall. These are principally controlled by private societies, which frequently give public concerts, balls, lectures, etc. Most of them hold government licenses for the sale of beer and wine. When an admission fee is charged to persons who are not members of the society giving the entertainment, the city charges a license fee of $5 for each evening's entertainment.

DRAINAGE; CEMETERIES; MARKETS.

No information on either of these subjects was furnished.

SANITARY AUTHORITY—HEALTH COMMITTEE.

The chief sanitary organization of Wheeling is the health committee, composed of five members of the common council, selected annually from that body, and one health officer, a physician, elected biennially by the common council. The committee is controlled by the common council, and if any members of that body happen to be physicians, they are generally appointed on the committee. The annual expense of the committee in ordinary times is $1,500, expended for salaries, sanitary inspections, etc. The extent to which the committee may increase its expense in the presence of an epidemic is limited to the amount authorized by the common council. The health officer, however, has authority during an epidemic, or the threatened approach of one, to purchase disinfectants, to order the street commissioner to clean such localities as he may deem necessary for the health of the city, and to have the gutters of such streets and alleys flushed as may in his judgment require it. He also has discretionary power to remove to the pest-house persons afflicted with contagious disease. The health officer is also chief executive officer of the committee. His duties are to exercise general supervision over the sanitary condition of the city; to see that nuisances are abated; to prevent the accumulation of filth and garbage; and to attend, free of cost, the prisoners in the city prison and the city patients in the hospital. His salary is $600 per annum. Two or three health inspectors are employed during a short time each spring. They are under the orders of the health officer, as a rule are not physicians, and have no police power. The committee meets once a month and reports all business to the common council, which acts on its reports. The inspectors report all nuisances to the health officer, who orders them abated. When private persons report nuisances the health officer makes a personal inspection. The custom concerning the inspection and correction of defective house-drainage, privy-vaults, cesspools, sources of drinking-water, sewerage, street-cleaning, etc., is the same as that observed toward nuisances. The committee exercises no control over the conservation and removal of garbage, but the place for its final disposal is designated by the health officer. All burial permits are issued by the health officer. The committee has no regulations regarding the pollution of rivers or streams, or the removal of excrement.

INFECTIOUS DISEASES.

Small-pox patients are either sent to the pest-house in the extreme northeast part of the city and well isolated, or quarantined at home, the place being watched by persons appointed for the purpose by the health officer. As a rule, only the friendless poor are sent to the pest-house. Scarlet-fever cases are not isolated, except in very rare instances. On the breaking out of contagious diseases in the schools the committee requests that they be closed, and the board of education generally grants the request. Vaccination is compulsory, when the health officer thinks it is necessary, and in cases where persons are unable to pay it is done at the public expense.

The record of diseases and deaths is kept by the health officer, who publishes the same in the city papers once a month.

REPORTS.

The health committee reports to the common council at its own pleasure or by request of that body. These reports are published in the daily papers.

MUNICIPAL CLEANSING.

Street-cleaning.—The streets are cleaned at the expense of the city, and, since May 1, 1880, with its own force. Prior to this date the work was done by contract. The work is done wholly by hand. The paved streets are cleaned once a month, macadamized streets twice a year, and crossings once a week. Since the expiration of the contract the cleaning has been very inefficiently done. The annual cost of the work is $2,500 to the city, and the sweepings are deposited on the river-bank or on vacant lots. The system, while the contract lasted, is reported as nearly perfect. The only disadvantage in the place of deposit is that the sweepings are sometimes washed into the river and may assist in making bars in the channel.

Removal of garbage and ashes.—All garbage is removed at the expense of the city and under contract. It is required to be kept in suitable vessels, unmixed with ashes, in places convenient for removal. It is taken away every day in warm weather and twice a week in cool weather. It is finally dumped into the Ohio river. The annual cost to the city for this work is $2,300. Ashes are removed by the householders, and they are placed in back alleys or lots and used for grading. Temporary nuisances from the improper handling of garbage are reported. The system is good if enforced properly; but, owing to the negligence of householders to report omissions, the collectors are careless.

Dead animals.—The carcasses of dead animals are thrown, by the owners, into the Ohio river, at such distance from shore as to be carried away by the current. A failure to comply with the ordinance regarding this matter subjects the owner to a fine. The system is good so far as the city is concerned; its defect is the deleterious effect it may have on the water of the Ohio river.

Liquid household wastes.—In those parts of the city where sewers extend, all household wastes pass into them. Where there are no sewers, the chamber-slops are thrown into vaults or cesspools, while the laundry wastes and kitchen-slops run into the street-gutters. About two-fifths of the city has no sewers. The cesspools are porous at the bottom, are not provided with overflows, in some cases receive the wastes from water-closets, and are cleaned out in the same manner as privy-vaults. The street-gutters depend almost entirely on rain for flushing.

Human excreta.—Hardly 5 per cent. of the houses in the city have water-closets; nearly all of these deliver into the sewers, and the remainder depend on privy vaults. The vaults must be not less than 10 feet deep, lined on the sides with either brick or stone, and slushed with mortar, so that the sides shall be water-tight. About 20 per cent. of them are nominally water-tight. They must be cleaned when full, or when ordered to be so by the health officer, and the contents must be disinfected. The odorless-excavator apparatus is generally used; where night-carts and buckets are used, the work must be done between 10 p. m. and 5 a. m. The dry-earth system is reported as used to a considerable extent—about 30 per cent. The night-soil is deposited in the Ohio river, outside the city limits, and not within 100 feet of the shore.

Manufacturing wastes are deposited either in Wheeling creek or in the Ohio river. The defects of this system are great. Most of the wastes from slaughter-houses, gas-works, and oil-refineries go into a creek which passes through the city. In summer the creek has little or no current, and at such times the odor arising from it is extremely offensive.

No information concerning police or fire department was furnished.

MANUFACTURES.

The following is a summary of the statistics of the manufactures of Wheeling for 1880, being taken from tables prepared for the Tenth Census by Dana L. Hubbard, special agent:

Mechanical and manufacturing industries.	No. of establishments.	Capital.	AVERAGE NUMBER OF HANDS EMPLOYED.			Total amount paid in wages during the year.	Value of materials.	Value of products.
			Males above 16 years.	Females above 15 years.	Children and youths.			
All industries....................................	227	$4,868,288	4,658	196	658	$2,192,255	$5,203,931	$9,259,844
Baskets, rattan and willow ware.............	3	2,200	3	....	....	1,580	1,100	4,700
Blacksmithing...............................	7	15,200	14	....	....	5,820	5,575	18,721
Brick and tile	7	32,000	77	....	18	11,149	2,664	24,560
Carpentering	4	27,000	25	....	....	16,450	46,648	85,700
Carriages and wagons	4	172,000	78	....	1	36,234	54,000	145,000
Clothing, men's............................	27	85,000	160	10	15	47,500	108,000	220,684
Confectionery..............................	5	9,050	18	2	....	6,002	51,300	64,964
Cooperage.................................	5	25,800	63	....	32	42,608	38,339	89,900
Foundery and machine-shop products	6	221,500	198	....	1	89,339	69,471	228,762
Furniture..................................	3	48,000	103	....	2	40,616	31,342	98,827
Glass	3	500,522	525	87	206	296,450	192,564	714,000
Iron and steel.............................	7	2,214,425	2,327	....	246	1,098,296	2,472,053	4,306,567
Leather, curried	4	123,200	58	....	....	34,800	377,258	447,972
Leather, tanned	4	166,000	61	1	....	21,422	334,740	378,152
Liquors, malt	5	203,017	85	....	....	33,329	153,982	256,588
Lumber, planed............................	4	148,000	83	....	2	38,990	173,500	237,400
Marble and stone work	3	14,750	30	....	....	12,860	9,600	33,334
Masonry, brick and stone...................	3	2,000	30	....	....	11,940	5,869	22,700
Painting and paperhanging	3	1,500	9	....	....	4,066	6,167	12,850
Plumbing and gasfitting....................	6	54,015	45	....	....	23,288	58,113	99,453
Printing and publishing	7	122,500	127	15	35	67,392	41,864	165,356
Roofing and roofing materials...............	3	1,200	6	....	1	1,400	6,000	11,100
Saddlery and harness.......................	6	13,100	18	....	....	9,572	23,750	43,450
Shipbuilding...............................	3	7,500	9	....	....	6,850	16,800	27,550
Shirts.....................................	4	1,200	....	40	....	9,200	20,240	33,890
Slaughtering and meat-packing, not including retail butchering.....	4	97,361	25	....	....	11,350	243,440	270,500
Tinware, copperware, and sheet-iron ware......	11	40,373	49	....	5	23,393	49,461	94,405
Tobacco, cigars and cigarettes..............	45	124,965	232	3	19	86,294	217,521	366,984
All other industries (a)	31	391,910	200	38	75	104,065	392,570	755,775

a Embracing agricultural implements; baking and yeast powders; boots and shoes; boxes, fancy and paper; brass castings; bread and other bakery products; brooms and brushes; carriage and wagon materials; coffee and spices, roasted and ground; coke; dyeing and finishing textiles; files; flouring- and grist-mill products; food preparations; gloves and mittens; hardware; iron nails and spikes, cut and wrought; lamps and reflectors; lock- and gun-smithing; lumber, sawed; patent medicines and compounds; sash, doors, and blinds; soap and candles; stencils and brands; vinegar; wirework; and wheelwrighting.

From the foregoing table it appears that the average capital of all establishments is $21,446 20; that the average wages of all hands employed is $397 72 per annum; that the average outlay in wages, in materials, and in interest (at 6 per cent.) on capital employed is $33,869 09.

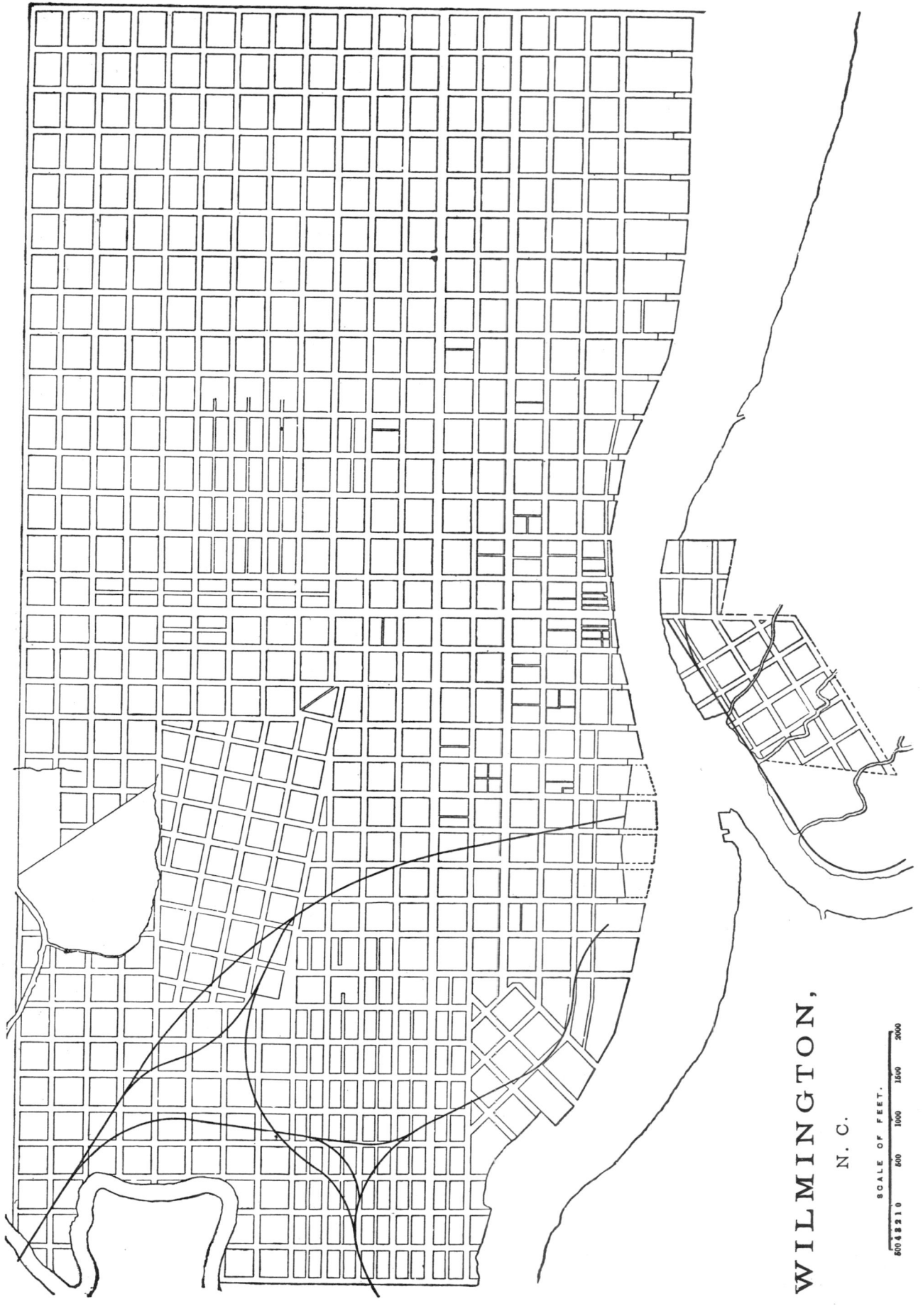

WILMINGTON,
N. C.

SCALE OF FEET.
500 1000 1500 2000

NORTH CAROLINA.

WILMINGTON,

NEW HANOVER COUNTY, NORTH CAROLINA.

POPULATION

IN THE

AGGREGATE,

1840-1880.

	Inhab.
1790	......
1800	......
1810	......
1820	......
1830	......
1840	4,744
1850	7,264
1860	9,552
1870	13,446
1880	17,350

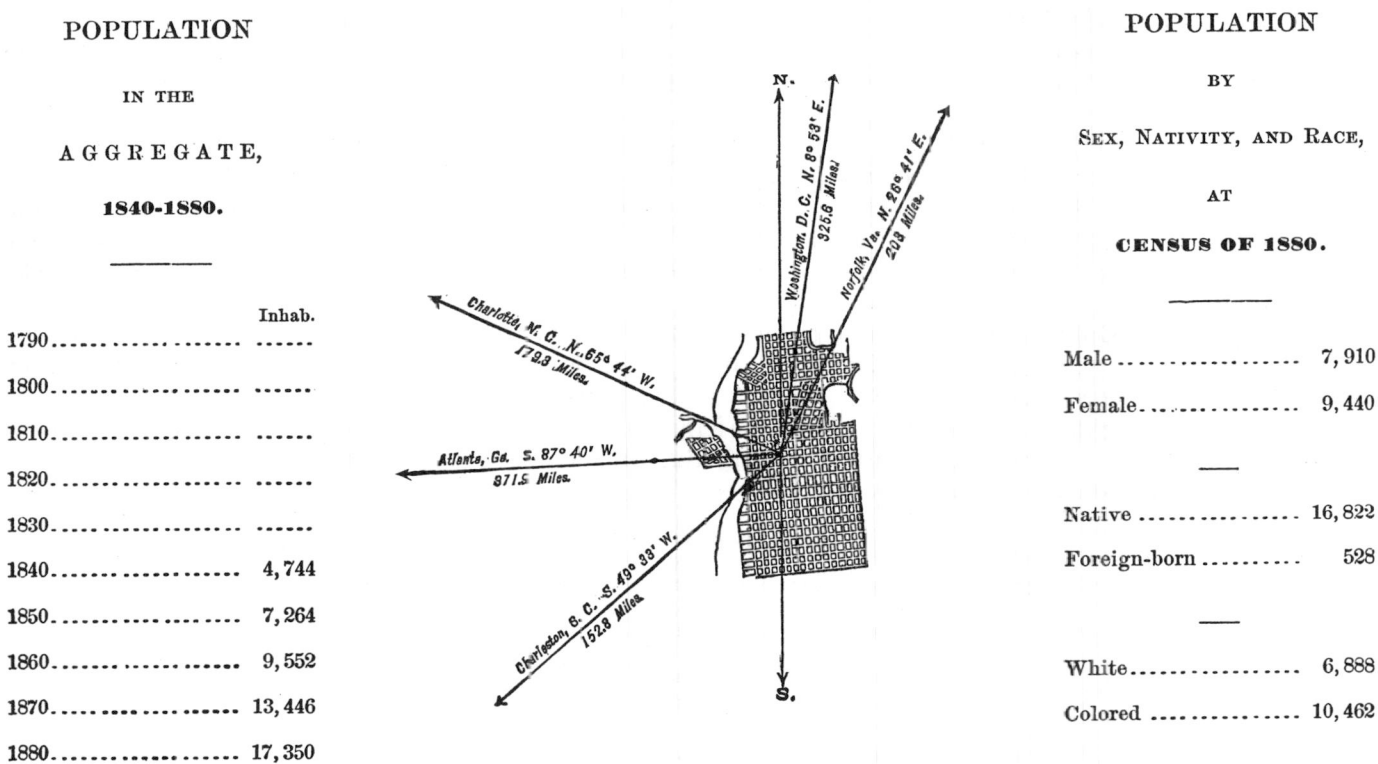

POPULATION

BY

SEX, NATIVITY, AND RACE,

AT

CENSUS OF 1880.

Male	7,910
Female	9,440
Native	16,822
Foreign-born	528
White	6,888
Colored	10,462

Latitude: 34° 14′ North; Longitude: 77° 56′ (west from Greenwich); **Altitude: 26 feet.** (a)

FINANCIAL CONDITION:

Total Valuation: $4,759,890; per capita: $274 00.   Net Indebtedness: $539,845; per capita: $31 11.   Tax per $100: $3 13.

WILMINGTON IN 1880. (b)

Wilmington, the capital of New Hanover county, is the principal seaport and the largest city in the state. It is on the east bank of the Cape Fear river, and 30 miles from the ocean. It has an extensive commerce, by sailing vessels, with all parts of the world. The draught of water at the entrance to the river, and of the river itself, has been much improved during the past decade. It has in fair proportions the usual concomitants of modern

---

a At Smithsonian station.

b Of the schedules of interrogatories, 10 in number, sent to Wilmington, but 2—that relating to *places of amusement*, and that relating to *municipal cleansing*—were returned with the information asked for.

American cities in the way of schools, churches, newspapers, etc. Of manufactories of different kinds it has a considerable number. The principal exports of the place are naval stores, lumber, shingles, and cotton. The exports for 1875, of which about one-half went to foreign ports, aggregated about $10,000,000 in value. Wilmington has long been a leading market for naval stores.

PLACES OF AMUSEMENT.

Wilmington has 1 opera-house, 1 concert-hall seating 600, and 3 lecture-halls seating from 250 to 300 each. There are 2 beer-gardens in the city; one, established 13 years ago, seats 200 persons, covers about 4 acres, and cost $10,000; and one, established 5 years ago, covers about the same number of acres and cost about the same amount.

MUNICIPAL CLEANSING.

Street-cleaning.—The city cleans the streets with its own force, and entirely by hand. The cleaning is constantly going on, under the direction of the chief of police, aided by the superintendent of streets, and its annual cost is $10,000. The sweepings are deposited half a mile beyond the city limits. The doing of the work by the city, as compared with contract work, finds favor on account of its greater efficiency.

Removal of garbage and ashes.—Garbage is removed by the city with its own force. While awaiting removal it is required to be kept in barrels or vessels, and unmixed with ashes. Some of the garbage which is fit for the purpose is used as manure by the truckers. Ashes are generally taken by those desiring to make soap.

Dead animals.—The carcasses of all the larger animals dying within the city are required to be removed by the owners, when they are able to do it; otherwise the city does it. The carcasses of small animals, as cats, dogs, etc., are removed by the city.

Liquid household wastes.—Almost all the liquid household wastes of the city are run into the sewers. None are allowed in the street-gutters, and but little passes into cesspools. When such cesspools do exist they are nominally water-tight. In some localities it is noticeable that drinking-water has been contaminated by the overflowing or the underground escape of the contents of cesspools and privy-vaults; hence these are now required to be built above ground and cleaned out in the winter or early spring, whenever the health officer thinks it necessary.

Human excreta.—Only a small proportion of the houses of the city have water-closets, some have privy-vaults, and many use boxes above ground. About two-thirds of the water-closets deliver into the sewers, and the remainder into cesspools. As yet the earth-closet is but little used, but the dry-earth system is thought to be growing in favor. Night-soil is removed beyond the city limits, where it is taken by truck-farmers and used as manure; but such use is not permitted within the gathering-ground of the public water-supply.

Manufacturing wastes are run into the public sewers.

COMMERCE AND NAVIGATION.

[From the reports of the Bureau of Statistics for the fiscal years ending June 30.]

Customs district of Wilmington, North Carolina.	1879.	1880.
Total value of imports	$73,832	$100,657
Total value of exports:		
Domestic	$4,748,931	$3,940,228
Foreign	None.	$1,437
Total number of immigrants	None.	None.

Customs district of Wilmington, North Carolina.	1879.		1880.	
	Number.	Tons.	Number.	Tons.
Vessels in foreign trade:				
Entered	313	100,538	215	67,757
Cleared	338	104,337	310	95,099
Vessels in coast trade and fisheries:				
Entered	154	75,596	None.	None.
Cleared	130	78,794	None.	None.
Vessels registered, enrolled, and licensed in district	77	5,929	78	6,171
Vessels built during the year	2	56	1	83

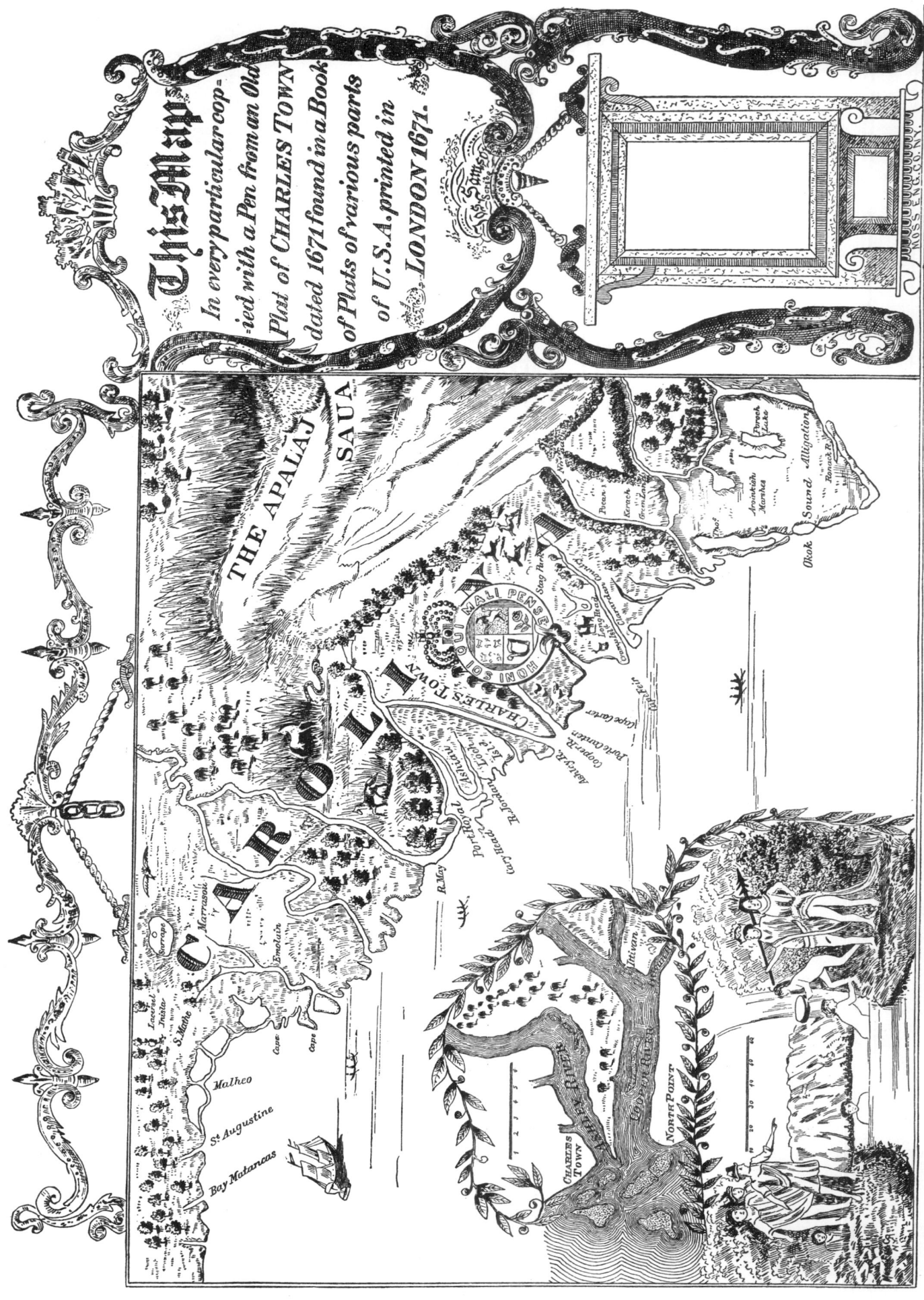

This Map

In every particular cop=
=ied with a Pen from an Old
Plat of CHARLES TOWN
dated 1671 found in a Book
of Plats of various parts
of U.S.A. printed in
LONDON 1671.

MOSS ENG. CO. N.Y.

THE APALAJ SAUA

CAROLI

CHARLES TOWN

HONI SOIT QUI MALI PENSE

Perseh Lake

Aroinebishi Marsha

Okok. Sound Alligation

Ronack R.

Stag Park

New

Pecan I.

Koaluin

Kerack

Green Lake

Chos.

Ashley R.

Cooper R.

Port Garden

Port Garden

Cape Carter

Linden

Jordan

Landgrave Smith

Isl.

Port Royal

Cart Head

R. May

Emelaita

Marrasoli

Burrage

S. Mathe

Laceras

Tristo

Malheo

St Augustine

Bay Matancas

Cape

Cape

CHARLES TOWN

NORTH POINT

COOPER RIVER

ASHLEY RIVER

Sullivan

SOUTH CAROLINA.

CHARLESTON,

CHARLESTON COUNTY, SOUTH CAROLINA.

POPULATION

IN THE

AGGREGATE,

1790-1880.

	Inhab.
1790	16,359
1800	18,924
1810	24,711
1820	24,780
1830	30,289
1840	29,261
1850	42,985
1860	40,519
1870	48,956
1880	49,984

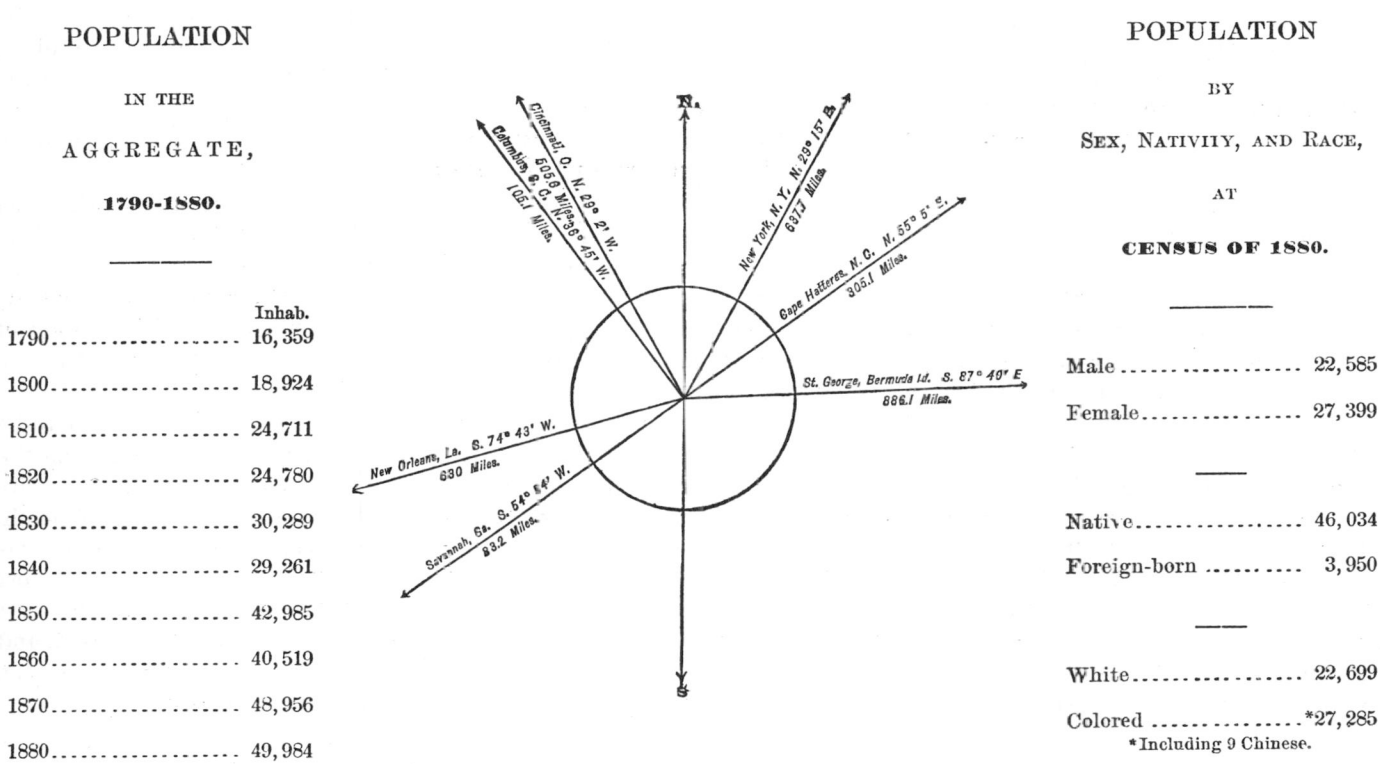

POPULATION

BY

SEX, NATIVITY, AND RACE,

AT

CENSUS OF 1880.

Male	22,585
Female	27,399

Native	46,034
Foreign-born	3,950

White	22,699
Colored	*27,285

*Including 9 Chinese.

Latitude: 32° 47′ North; Longitude: 79° 56′ (west from Greenwich); Altitude: 8 to 15 feet.

FINANCIAL CONDITION:

Total Valuation: $22,543,423; per capita: $451 00.   Net Indebtedness: $4,129,102; per capita: $82 61.   Tax per $100: $3 10.

HISTORICAL SKETCH.

The first attempt of the English lords proprietors to establish settlements in Carolina was made at Port Royal. This name, given by Ribault, about 1562, was remembered by the English, and thither William Sayle, with a number of colonists, directed his course in 1670. They reached this their desired port and laid the foundation of a town. They continued, however, only some months at Port Royal, and then removed to the western bank of Ashley river. Several reasons led to this change. Port Royal was too near the Spanish settlements and too accessible from the sea, Spain being then a great maritime power. The new site on Ashley river was also more convenient for pasturage and tillage. Here a new town was begun and named "Charles-town". Sayle died within the year. The colonists elected as his successor Joseph West. Upon Sayle's death becoming known in England, Sir John Geamans was appointed governor, and was commissioned December 26, 1671.

Lands were soon taken up on the east side of the Ashley river, and settlements were formed in other parts of the neighborhood. The first popular election known of in South Carolina was in April, 1672, under a proclamation from the grand council requiring all of the freeholders "to elect a new parliament". From this body five counsellors were chosen, who, with the governor and the deputies of the lords proprietors, formed the grand council. Arrangements were now made for the improvement of Charles-town. It was laid out and divided into lots. The settlers then surrendered to the grand council, July 22, 1672, the lots they had previously occupied, and received others according to the new arrangement. The town was fortified, and additional works of defense were erected in 1674.

It soon began to appear that the site was ill-adapted to the growing commerce and prosperity of the town. As early as 1672 settlements had been made on the neck of land opposite the town and called "Oyster Point". Some of the land had been taken up by Henry Hughes and John Corning. They offered to give up one-half, "to be employed in and toward enlarging of a town and commons of pasture, then intended to be erected". From this it would seem that there was an early design to found a town upon the spot. Mr. Hughes' offer was accepted, and his land was retained by the grand council for the purpose indicated. The settlement continuing to increase, it was known in 1677 as "Oyster Point town". The neck of land on which this town was begun was formed by the confluence of the two rivers, originally Kiawah and Etiwan, but named, in compliment to Lord Shaftesbury, "Ashley" and "Cooper". The superior advantages of this situation led gradually to a removal from the original site on the western bank of the Ashley. This last could not be reached by large vessels at low water. In 1679 it was ordered to remove the public offices, and in that and the following year the order was executed. In 1680 we find the town called in some official papers "New Charles-town", and in 1682 "Charles-town".

The town as originally laid out was of small extent, bounded by Meeting street on the west, Market street on the north, Water street on the south, and the bay on the east. It was surrounded by a line of fortifications. The settlers consisted both of Cavaliers and of Puritans. Old strifes and divisions reappeared and marred the harmony which might have been expected among a people having the same hardships to encounter, the same enemies to fear, and a common object to promote, viz, the prosperity of the colony. To these troubles must be added another of very serious character—wars with the surrounding Indians. One occurred in 1712, another in 1715. Both were savage and destructive. In the last, all the tribes from the Cape Fear river to Florida joined.

For the first thirty years the exports consisted chiefly of staves, furs, lumber, and peltry. Rice began to be exported about 1700. It had been introduced about 1693 by Landgrave Smith, who obtained a small bag from the captain of a vessel from Madagascar, and planted it in his garden, near what is now known as Longitude lane. By the year 1720 it was exported in considerable quantity. According to Ramsey the historian, the exports of rice in 1740 amounted to 91,110 barrels. At the beginning of the Revolution, 1776, the average annual export was about 142,000 barrels. According to Dayton (*View of South Carolina*) cotton was noticed as an article of export about the middle of the century, but it was not exported largely till after the Revolution. Indigo was planted first about 1741–'42. In 1747 there were sent to England about 200,000 pounds. In 1754, 216,924 pounds were sent, and just before the Revolution 1,107,660 pounds. Near the close of the century it gave place to cotton. From the valuable compilation of Drs. Dawson and De Saussure, published in 1849, the following statement is taken:

Year.	FOR SOUTH CAROLINA.		FOR THE OTHER COLONIES.	
	Exports.	Imports.	Exports.	Imports.
1725	£91,942	£39,132	£323,708	£510,511
1750	191,607	134,037	623,159	1,180,046
1774	432,302	378,116	941,544	2,212,321
1775	579,349	6,245	1,341,701	189,917

Early Indian wars have already been mentioned. In 1728 a hurricane threatened the entire destruction of the town. The streets were inundated, and 23 ships were driven ashore, most of which were destroyed. The storm was followed by yellow fever, which swept off multitudes. A fire in 1740 laid half the town in ashes; 300 buildings were consumed. Parliament voted £20,000 for the relief of the sufferers. In 1765 the population is stated as about 6,000 whites and from 7,000 to 8,000 colored.

The courts were all held in Charles-town. During the colonial period there does not appear to have been any organization entitled to the name, strictly speaking, of a municipal government. At an early date, 1704, an act of assembly was passed "to settle a patroll" and regulate a town-watch. Each captain of the town companies was required to mark off a certain number of men for the patrol service, to appoint one of these as commander, and to give notice what night every commander, with the men belonging to his list of the watch, was to take his turn.

A Plan of Charles Town from a Survey of Edw. Crisp, Esqr. in 1704.

Fac-simile of drawing.

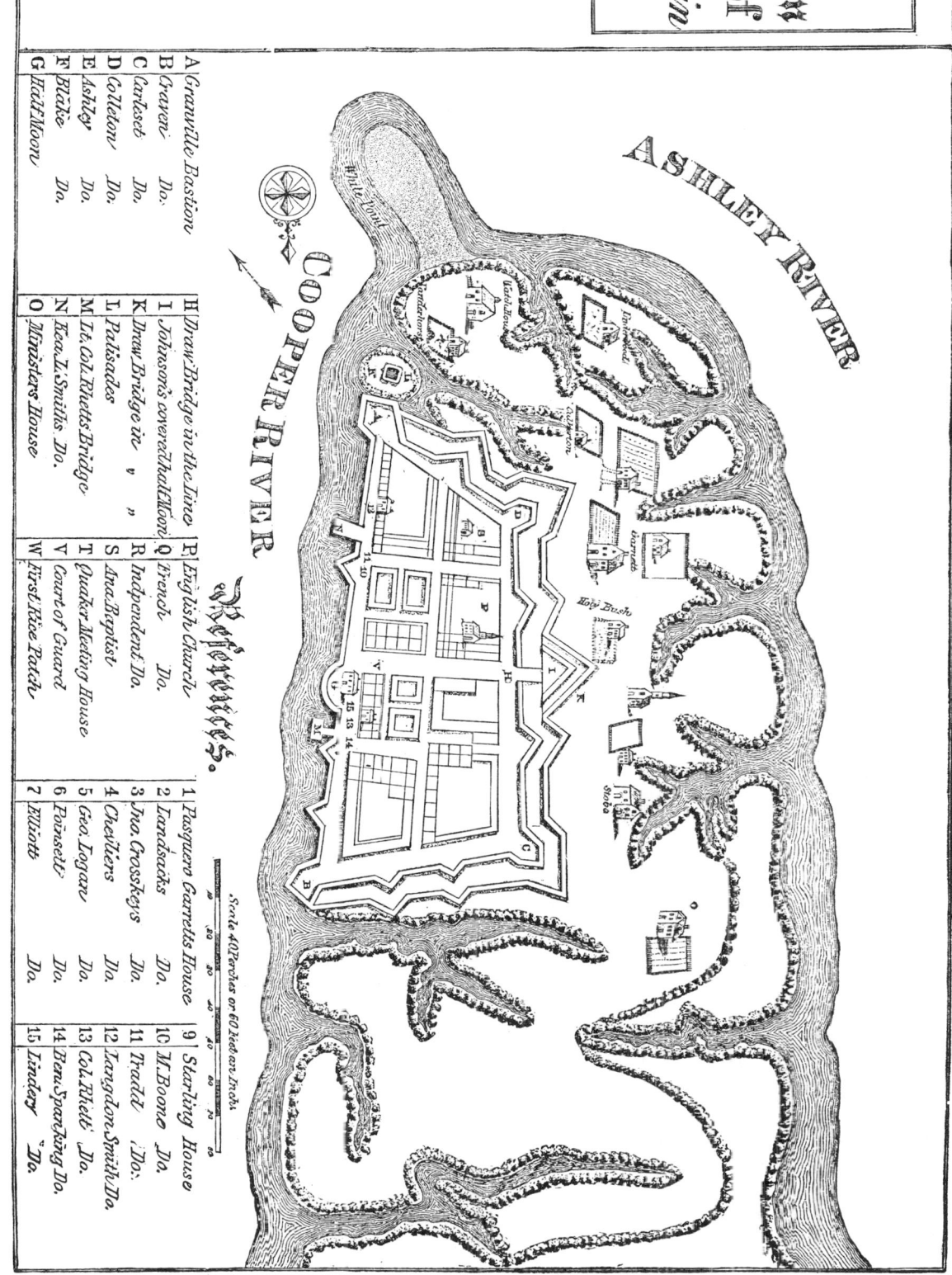

ASHLEY RIVER

COOPER RIVER

White Point

Holy Bush

References.

A Granville Bastion
B Craven.   Do.
C Carteret   Do.
D Colleton   Do.
E Ashley   Do.
F Blake   Do.
G Half Moon

H Draw Bridge in the Line
I Johnson's covered Half Moon.
K Draw Bridge in ,,
L Palisades
M Lt. Col. Rhetts Bridge
N Revd. L. Smiths. Do.
O Ministers' House

P English Church
Q French.   Do.
R Independent Do.
S Ana Baptist
T Quaker Meeting House
V Court of Guard
W First Rice Patch

1 Pasquero Garretts House
2 Landsacks   Do.
3 Jno. Grosskeys   Do.
4 Chevliers   Do.
5 Geo. Logan   Do.
6 Poinsett   Do.
7 Elliott   Do.
9 Starling House
10 M. Boone   Do.
11 Trott   Do.
12 Langdon Smith Do.
13 Col. Rhett   Do.
14 Ben. SparKing Do.
15 Lindsey   Do.

Scale 40 Perches or 60 inches an inch.

The management and regulation of town institutions appear to have been in the hands of commissioners, appointed by act of assembly. There were commissioners of the streets, of the markets, of the work-house, of pilotage, etc.; also there was a board of fire-masters. The charge and relief of the poor belonged to parish vestries, who had power to make assessments on the taxable inhabitants for the purpose, and to call on them for returns to be made to the assessor. The administration of this fund constituted a large portion of the business of each vestry. Abundant evidence of this may be found in the old journals of vestries. Shelter, food, clothing, and medical attendance were provided. Children received education. The poor were divided into two classes, viz, the parish poor and the transient poor. Lists of these, made out from time to time, may be seen in the journals of the vestries as late as 1783.

Education had received early attention. Contributions were made by the royal government, and liberal bequests by individuals. In 1711 a school was established by the English society for the propagation of the gospel. The success of this school led to the passage of an act the next year ordering a free school, which act applied not only to Charles-town, but to all the parishes.

The following particulars regarding the laying out of the town are extracted from Dalcho's *Church History*:

It is asserted by Rousseau (*Confessions*, tome II, p. 80) that his uncle superintended the building of Charles-town, of which he had given the plan. This is a mistake. Rousseau was born in 1712, and speaks of residing with his uncle in Switzerland after he was twelve years of age; consequently his uncle could not have come to Carolina before 1724. The map of Charles-town prefixed to the second volume of Ramsey's *South Carolina* is from a survey taken in 1704. The model of the town was sent out by the lords proprietors in May, 1671; and we have seen a warrant for laying out "one town at the Oyster point, observing the rules established in reference to the building of a town there". This was dated April 21, 1677. We find by act of general assembly "for the repairing the old and building of new fortifications", etc., passed in 1736, that Gabriel Bernard was then appointed chief engineer: "SECTION 10. And be it further enacted * * * that Mr. Gabriel Bernard shall be and he is hereby appointed chief engineer, who shall constantly attend, direct, and inspect the raising and repairing such fortifications as the said commissioners shall think fit, and shall be allowed at and after the rate of £700 per annum, nevertheless subjected to be displaced and the said salary taken away by vote or order of the general assembly." This person probably was Rousseau's uncle.

Toward the close of the colonial period, Charles-town was second to no city in North America in prosperity and social comfort, and even in luxury. European fashions and manners prevailed, and, as the historian Hewit tells us, "the people were not only blessed with plenty, but with a disposition to share it among friends and neighbors". Hewit adds, further:

Many will bear me witness when I say that travelers could scarcely go into any city where they could meet with a society of people more agreeable, intelligent, and hospitable than at Charles-town. In point of industry the town is like a beehive, and there are none that reap not advantage more or less from the flourishing trade and commerce.

The following extract from the journal of Josiah Quincy, who, in the year 1773, visited Charles-town, describes the place at that period:

This town (Charles-town) makes the most beautiful appearance as you come up to it, and in many respects a magnificent. * * * I can only say in general that in grandeur, splendour of buildings, decorations, equipages, numbers, commerce, shipping, and indeed almost everything, it far surpasses all I ever saw or ever expect to see in America. * * * All seems at present to be trade, riches, magnificence, and great state in everything; much gaiety and dissipation. * * * State and magnificence, the natural attendant on great riches, are conspicuous among this people. * * * There being but one chief place of trade, its increase is amazingly rapid. The stories you are everywhere told of the rise in the value of lands seems romantic; but I was assured that they were facts.

The part taken by Charles-town in the Revolutionary war and the progress of events within her territory during the present century are so much matters of history that a detailed account of them is not deemed necessary here. In 1783 the city was incorporated by an act of the legislature under the name of "Charleston", and divided into thirteen wards. In 1809 the former division into thirteen wards was abolished and the number was reduced to four, which number in 1849 was increased to eight, and so remains.

The city on several occasions has suffered severely from fires. One, in 1740, has already been mentioned. In 1778 another occurred, which burned more than 250 buildings, besides stores and outbuildings. Among the buildings destroyed was the house, with the greater portion of its contents, in which were deposited the books, apparatus, etc., of the Charleston Library Society. Again, in 1796, a large portion of the town was laid in ruins. "Five hundred chimneys were counted from which the buildings had been burnt, and it is believed that 150,000 pounds sterling would be far short of the value of these buildings." The French Protestant church was burnt, and the Saint Philip's (the oldest Episcopal church) was on fire, but was saved by the exertions of a brave negro, who climbed to the top of the belfry and tore away the shingles. For this service the negro received his freedom. In 1810 some 200 houses were burnt. In 1835 another terrible conflagration occurred, which is memorable because of the destruction of the venerable Saint Philip's church, finished in 1723. The interior of this church, of imposing architecture, was filled with monuments of citizens prominent both in church and in state, the date beginning as early as 1722. But of all these destructive fires the most destructive was that of 1861. Beginning at the eastern extremity of Hasel street, it burned diagonally through the city to its southwestern end, consuming a large number of fine dwellings, some noted for historical associations and some for their splendor. Of late years, however, a large portion of the area laid waste has been rebuilt. In addition to these fires, others, not so disastrous in their effect, occurred in 1800, 1819, 1838, 1875, and 1876.

Slight shocks of earthquake were felt in the years 1811 and 1812. The vibratory motion was east and west, but so slight that no damage ensued. Shocks were also felt in 1754, 1799, 1843, and 1857. Besides the hurricane of 1728, previously mentioned, Charleston suffered more or less from others in 1713, 1752, 1764, 1797, 1800, 1804, 1810, 1811, 1813, 1822, 1854, and 1873.

The early settlers, English, Irish, Scotch, French, and German, were never supplanted, and are represented by their descendants to the present time. They shared the fortunes and the hardships of those among whom they came.

CHARLESTON IN 1880.

The following statistical accounts, collected by the Census Office, indicate the present condition of Charleston:

LOCATION.

The city is situated in the middle of the low country and center of the sea-coast of the state, and is distant about 7 miles from the Atlantic ocean. It is built on a neck of land formed by the junction of the Ashley and Cooper rivers, is surrounded on two sides by the Sea islands, and, when approached by water, it appears to rise from the sea. The strip of land on which it is situated widens northward into a broad and extended plane, the surface of which is occupied by fruit, vegetable, and floral farms, dotted with farm-houses, manufactories, orchards, and patches of woodland, covered with a growth of timber of nearly every variety known in the state. The level of its streets is from 8 to 15 feet above the mark of the highest tides.

HARBOR AND WATER-COURSES.

The city lies upon navigable water; it has a tidal harbor, spacious and convenient, occupying a basin-like space 15 miles square. The harbor is land-locked, the city being on a peninsula, the east side facing Cooper river and the west side facing Ashley river, the point looking out upon the bay. There is no safer harbor to enter, as the bed of the ocean is here an inclined plane, gradually shallowing on its approach to the bar, the tide rising and falling 5.1 feet. The current formed by the outlet of the two rivers is obstructed by a sand-bar, and is approached by the main or ship channel, opposite to and distant about 2 miles from Morris Island beach on the south side of the entrance to the harbor, and by Moffit's channel, running parallel to Sullivan's island; also by the direct or middle channel. The draught of water on the bar at high tide is $17\frac{1}{2}$ feet, with a depth inside of the channel of 23 to 50 feet. The capacity of the harbor is sufficient to afford shelter for the navy of the strongest maritime nation on the globe, with good anchorage up the rivers on either side of the city. The United States government is now constructing jetties to increase the depth of water on the bar, and Pumpkin Hill channel, now being used, will be deepened to give 25 feet when the works are completed. The channel capacity is good, being considered sufficient for all purposes, except just at the bar, which is measurably circumscribed in width and in depth. The river or tidal current is very slight, not exceeding 2 miles an hour, and very steady, unless interrupted by heavy rains or storms, and is seldom materially affected by these unless they come from the east.

RAILROAD COMMUNICATIONS.

Three railroads give Charleston communication with all parts of the United States. They are as follows:

The South Carolina railroad, to Augusta, Georgia, 133 miles, with the Columbia branch, 68 miles, connecting with the railroad to Spartansburg and Hurdum, North Carolina, also with the Columbia and Charlotte railroad and the Camden branch, 37 miles; at Augusta this road connects with the Georgia railroad.

The North Eastern railroad, to Florence, 102 miles, connects with the Wilmington, Augusta, and Columbia railroad, the Cheraw and Darlington railroad, and the Wadesborough railroad.

The Charleston and Savannah railroad, to Savannah, 104 miles, connects with the Port Royal railroad from Beaufort to Augusta.

TRIBUTARY COUNTRY.

Charleston is the center of supply for the rice- and cotton-fields of South Carolina, northern Georgia, and the coast islands. The principal trade is in rice and sea-island cotton, the latter pertaining exclusively to this region. The trade with the surrounding country is chiefly supplies for plantations, etc. Small fruits and vegetables are largely raised and sent to the city for shipment. A large and growing trade is springing up in naval stores, lumber, and phosphates. Concerning the last-named industry, which is of recent creation, there were in 1875 five phosphate companies in active operation in Charleston, their works being located on the Ashley and Cooper rivers, within 5 miles of the city.

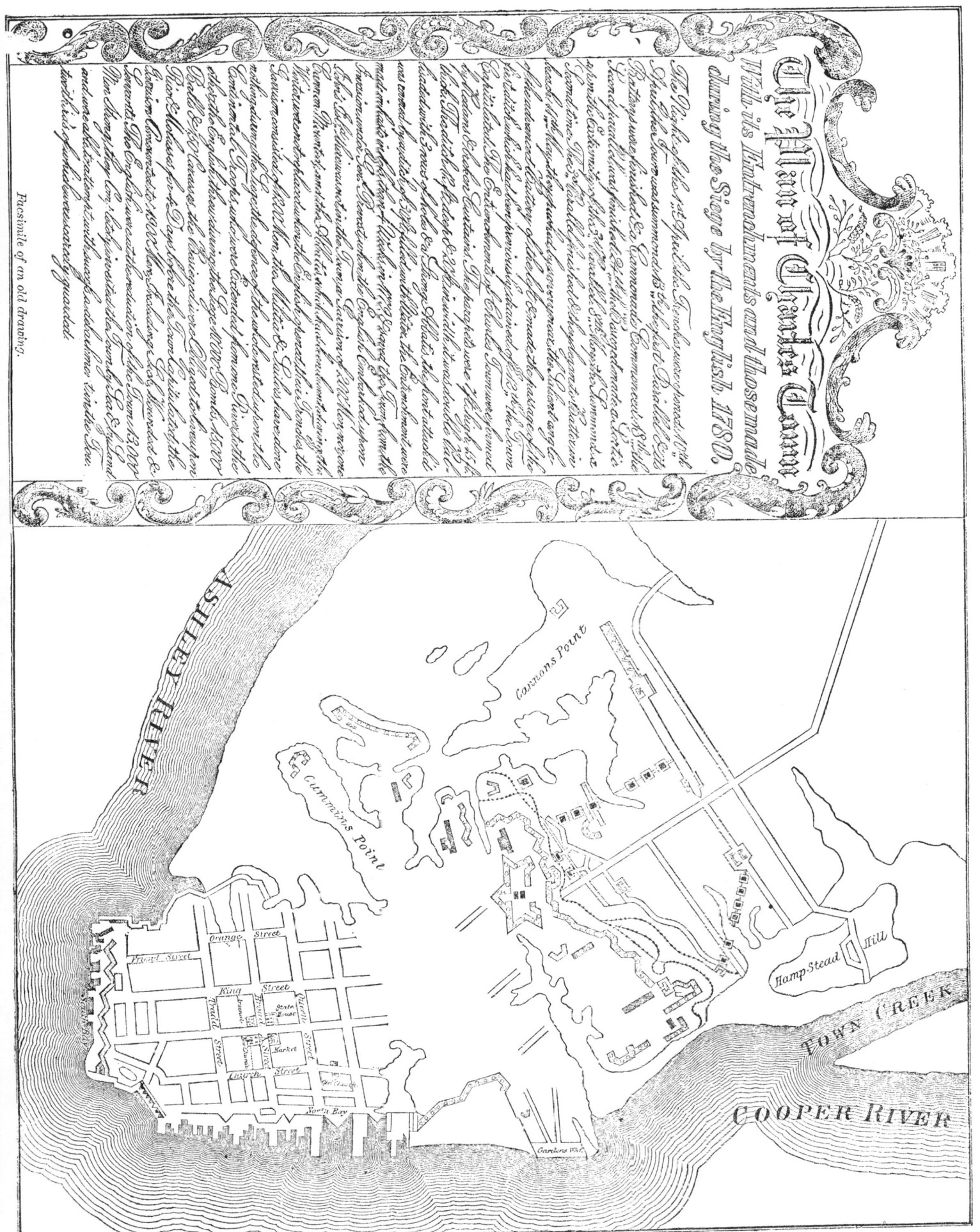

Facsimile of an old drawing.

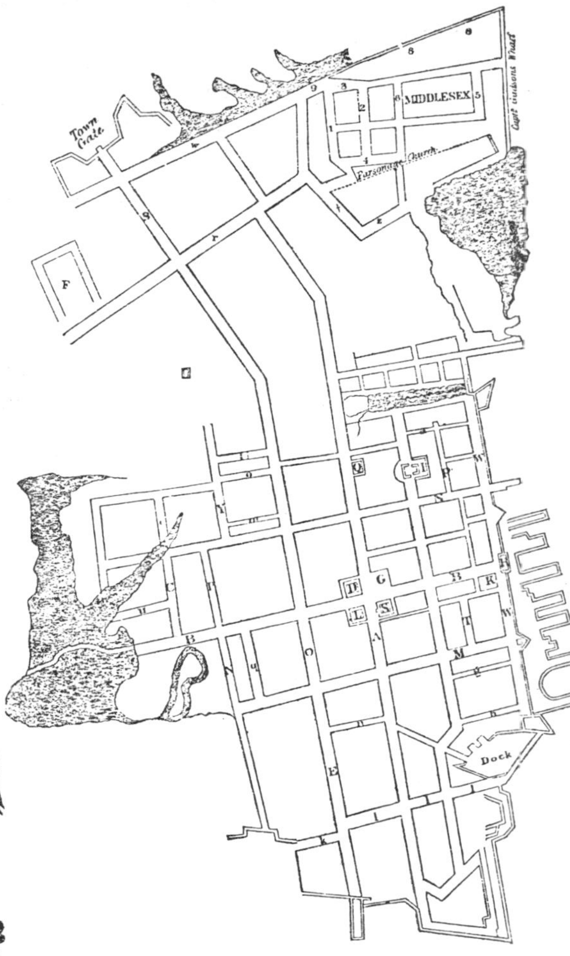

Town Gate
MIDDLESEX
Dock

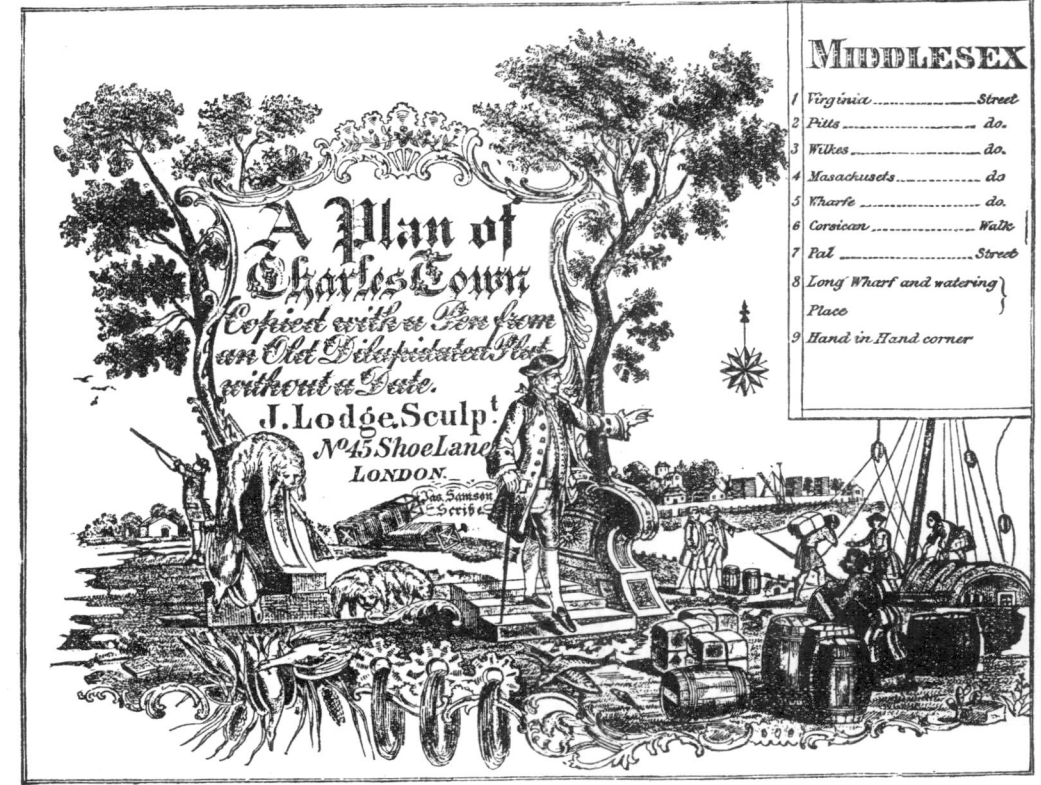

REFERENCES

A	Old Church Street	z	Centurion Street
B	Broad do	a	Chambers Alley
C	Mazicks do	b	Beresford do
D	State House	c	Union Street
E	Johnston do	d	Amen do
F	New Barracks	e	Unity Alley
G	Beef Market	f	Elliots Street
H	Church do	g	Longitude Lane
I	St. Philips Church	h	Stalls Alley
K	Gadsden Alley	i	Linches Lane
L	Armoury	k	Lambulls Street
M	Tradd do	l	Smiths Lane
N	Queen do	m	Bottle Alley
O	King do	n	Prices do
P	Union (Continued) do	o	Clifford Street
Q	Presbiterian Meeting	p	Allen do
R	Exchange	q	Orange do
S	St. Michael Church and Church Yard	r	George do
T	Bedons Alley	s	Squirrel do
U	Beresford do	t	Anson do
W	Bay do	u	Short do
X	Friend do	v	West do
Y	Archdale do	w	Boundary do

A Plan of
Charles Town
Copied with a Pen from
an Old Dilapidated Plat
without a Date.
J. Lodge Sculp.t
No. 45 Shoe Lane
LONDON.
Jas. Samson Scribe
MIDDLESEX
1 Virginia Street
2 Pitts do.
3 Wilkes do.
4 Masachusets do
5 Wharfe do.
6 Corsican Walk
7 Pal Street
8 Long Wharf and watering Place
9 Hand in Hand corner

Fac-simile of the original.

TOPOGRAPHY.

The site of the city originally contained 1,800 acres, and was intersected by ten large and several smaller creeks, besides ponds and lowlands. It was divided into a number of perinsulas by these creeks and marshes, which indented it on three sides so as to leave but little unbroken high land in the middle, and as the first buildings extended along East Bay street, they had a marsh along their entire front. Zanderhort's creek occupied the foundation of Water street, and another creek ran westwardly nearly parallel to East bay. From McLord's lots, the same kind of low ground ran up Queen street (then Dock street), and the north end of Union street (now State street) was planted with rice until the middle of the eighteenth century. It required time and perseverance, with much labor and expense, to change this quagmire into high, dry, and solid land; but it was finally accomplished.

The soil of the site is diversified, varying from the richest vegetable mold to the poorest yellow sand. Under this is a calcareous bed which rests upon rock of Cretaceous formation. The drainage is bad, and heavy rains saturate the soil to a depth of 18 feet. The surrounding country is low, and for the most part either marsh- or wood-land or sea-coast; it is all under cultivation. The Sea islands surrounding Charleston are composed of slight ridges of yellow sand, and in appearance resemble the ground swells of the ocean.

CLIMATE.

Highest recorded summer temperature, 102°; highest summer temperature in average years, 90°. Lowest recorded winter temperature, 18°; lowest winter temperature in average years, 28°. The seasons here are very equally divided between heat and cold, the former beginning about the last of April and ending with September, while the latter follows from the last of October to the end of March. Frosts never occur before October, and seldom, if ever, after April. The winters are not uniformly cold, but are marked by alternate spells of warm and cold weather from three to five days in duration. The changes, though more frequent than in colder climes, are seldom so sudden or severe. In summer the usual range of the thermometer during the day is from 84° to 90°, and at night from 60° to 78°. The heat is moderated by daily sea-breezes, which spring up about noon and continue till night. Cases of sunstroke are reported as extremely rare in Charleston. The marshes near the city are covered at each high tide, so no bad influences from them are perceptible. The only disagreeable wind is from the east; all others are pleasant and salubrious.

STREETS.

Total length of streets, 53½ miles, paved as follows: Cobble-stones, 9.25 miles; stone blocks, 1.60 mile; wood, 5.25 miles; and shell, 1.40 mile. The remainder, 36 miles, are of dirt. The cost per square yard, as near as may be estimated, is, for stone blocks, $1 65. The cost of the other kinds of pavement was not given. In point of quality and permanent economy stone blocks are considered best, and cobble-stones next. The sidewalks are of flagstone, brick, shell, and earth. The gutters are laid with stone, brick, and wood. Shade-trees are planted all over the city. The property-owners place them in front of their residences, on the curb-line, and the city plants in the parks.

The annual cost of construction and repairs is $80,000, the new work being done by contract and the repairs by day labor. The city authorities express a preference for day labor on the street work, as it is more easily controlled, is much cheaper in the end, and by it the public interests are much better served. A steam-roller and a steam stone-crusher have been tried, but as it has been decided to pave with stone blocks, the crusher is no longer used.

There are 20½ miles of horse-railroads in the city, using 57 cars and 125 horses, and giving employment to 89 men. The total number of passengers carried during the year is 1,516,428, and the rate of fare is 5 cents. The omnibus lines have 10 vehicles and 20 horses, and give employment to 10 men. They carry annually 75,000 passengers, at rates of fare varying from 50 to 75 cents.

WATER-WORKS.

The water-works are owned by a private corporation. The water is taken from artesian wells, and pumped either into a stand-pipe or into a reservoir of 3,200,000 gallons capacity, or direct into the mains. The pressure in the pumps varies from 54 pounds to the square inch when the stand-pipe is used, to 185 pounds to the square inch when pumping direct into the mains. The yearly cost of maintenance is $3,500. The yearly income from water-rates was not stated. Water-meters are not used. There are now completed 12 miles of mains. There are 165 fire-hydrants, and many others for private use. The wells, from which the water-supply is obtained, vary in depth from 1,230 to 1,965 feet. The stand-pipe gives sufficient head to force the water over any building in the city.

GAS.

The gas-works are owned by a private company. The daily average production is 50,000 cubic feet. The charge per 1.000 feet is $3 09 net. The city pays annually $19 50 for each street-lamp, 1,136 in number.

PUBLIC BUILDINGS.

The city owns and occupies for municipal purposes, wholly or in part, 1 city hall, 1 almshouse, 1 orphan house, 1 house of correction, 13 engine-houses, 2 markets, and 2 powder-magazines. Their total cost was not given.

PUBLIC PARKS AND PLEASURE-GROUNDS.

The city owns and has in use about 33 acres of public grounds, and 20 acres more, within the populous limits, available in the future.

White Point Garden, or "the Battery", area 10 acres, is situated at the eastern end of the city, facing the harbor, and is the general place of resort. It is laid out in walks, with trees, and provided with seats. Neither the total cost nor the annual cost of maintenance for any of the parks was given.

PLACES OF AMUSEMENT.

There is one theater in Charleston, the Academy of Music, seating 900, and the following halls, used for concerts, lectures, etc.: South Carolina hall, Freundschafts-Bund hall, Hibernia hall, Bruederlicher Bund hall, and Harmony Circle hall, with a total seating capacity of 2,300. Besides these there are 8 halls used by military companies, Free Masons, etc., with a total capacity of 3,700. There are no concert- or beer-gardens in the city.

DRAINAGE.

The sewers of Charleston drain into a system of tidal drains, built in 1856–'57, about 5½ miles in length, laid level, and at an elevation of 20 inches above mean tide. They extend across the city, and usually connect at both ends. They consist of a semi-circular arch 3 feet in diameter, resting on solid walls 3 feet high, supported on a platform of plank forming a flat bottom. Connecting with these are laterals, usually of the same shape but smaller in size, and laid at a slight inclination according to the grade of the streets.

Drainage from yards and slops from houses reach the street-drains sometimes by covered drains or pipes and sometimes by open gutters. Owing to defective foundations the tidal drains have gone out of shape in many places, and having been laid in level lines they are not self-cleansing in any part. In the years 1879–'80 there were 14,156 loads of sediment removed from them. The entire expenditure for this purpose in 15 years has been $93,106.

The street-drains are but little better. The health officer in his report of 1880, page 37, says:

The street-drains are open to several objections. Built from time to time, varying in form according to the constantly changing administrations, wanting in uniformity of grade and connection, not a harmonious whole, but a series of disjointed sections, they represent an aggregate outlay of money which, if applied under the direction of an intelligent engineer officer, would have long since developed into a complete whole. As an illustration of this, the Franklin Street drain recently cleaned is 18 inches below the level of the Broad Street drain into which it should discharge; and, at the intersection of State and Market streets, also recently opened, a net-work of drains were found of all sizes and shapes intersecting each other in different directions, and some drains actually under the others, are badly planned, and, of course, very filthy. * * * As regards the system of yard-drains, while there may be exceptions, as a whole they are as defective in operation as such constructions can well be. No attempt seems to have been made to secure uniformity in form, size, or material, in depth, level, inclination, or other necessary requisites, and the consequence is that a large proportion of these so-called yard-drains are mere shams choked up to the top, forming stench-traps, where malarial gases are contributed every hour to the atmosphere we breathe.

The superintendent of streets, in his report of the same date, page 168, says: "The following drains have been opened and cleaned; they were found for the most part filled to the crown of the arch." He then gives a list of nine streets, many of which are in the best part of the city. Water-closets are not much used, but the old-fashioned privy may be found in almost every back yard.

CEMETERIES.

The following cemeteries, graveyards, and burying-grounds are connected with Charleston, namely:

First Presbyterian, southwest corner of Tradd and Meeting streets; area, 1½ acre.

Saint Michael's, Episcopal, southeast corner of Meeting and Broad streets; area, 1½ acre.

First Baptist, west side of Church street, opposite Longitude lane; area, 1 acre.

Saint Peter's, Episcopal, east side of Logan street, between Broad and Tradd streets; area, 1 acre.

Huguenot, southeast corner of Church and Green streets; area, ¼ acre.

Saint Philip's, Episcopal, east side of Church street, between Queen and Cumberland streets; area, 2½ acres.

Circular Presbyterian, independent, Meeting street, east side, between Queen and Cumberland streets; area, 1½ acre.

Saint John, Lutheran, southeast corner of Clifford and Archdale streets; area, 2 acres.

Unitarian, Archdale street, east side, next south of Saint John.

Saint Mary, Catholic, south side of Hasel street, between King and Meeting streets; area, 1½ acre.

Bethel, Methodist, southwest corner of Calhoun and Pitt streets; area, 2 acres.

Flynn Church, Presbyterian, on Mogg square; area, about 3 acres.

Saint John Chapel, Methodist, corner of Amherst and Hanover streets; area, 1 acre.

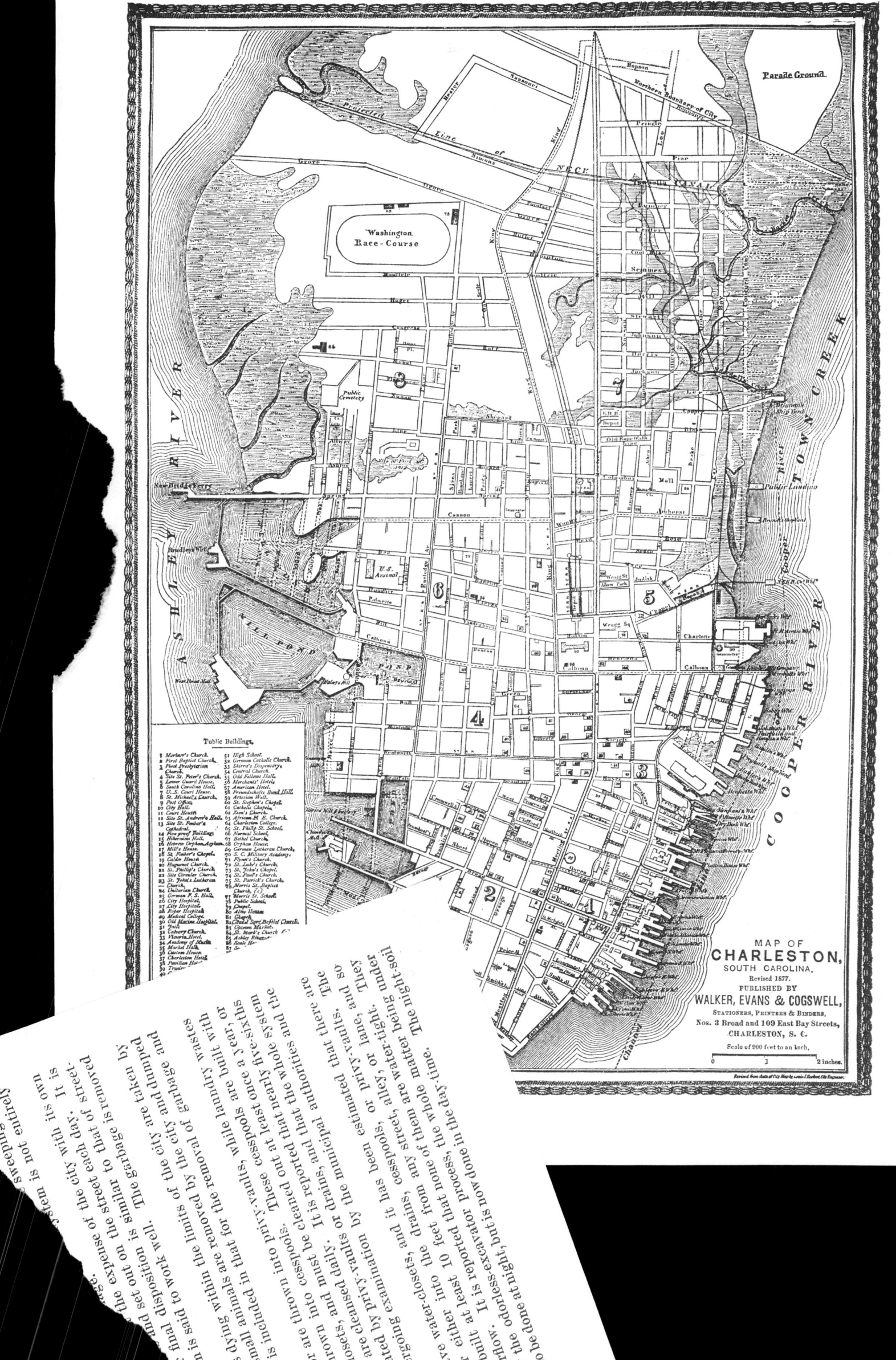

Map of Charleston, South Carolina. Revised 1877. Published by Walker, Evans & Cogswell.

efficiency are
sweepings are
system is not entirely
system with its own
It is
expense of the street each day.
the street that of street-
similar to that is removed
The garbage is taken by
and final disposition and
and set out on similar well.
their system is said to work well.
mules, and cows dying within the limits of the city and dumped and
small animals that for the removal of garbage and
carcasses is included in that
The cost of this service is within the limits of the city garbage and wastes
food", go into drains or are thrown into privy-vaults. These cesspools once a year, or
ter-stops gutters, or street-closets are cleansed daily. or drains, municipal that there are
rains or wastes of gutters are cleansed by privy-vaults by the estimated that whole system and so
receive the expense of water-closets, and it has been, or privy-lane, and so. They
ard of health. or less now undergoing examination by it cesspools, alley, or privy-vaults. under
wells is more and is now undergoing water-closets, drains, any street, are water-tight, under
is defective, and is now have water into feet from, of them are matter being night-soil
e houses in the city either at least 10 feet that none the whole matter. The night-time
About 500 water-closets in deliver at least. It is reported process, in the day-time.
The privy-vaults must be built. It is reported excavator now done in the
vaults. all privy-vaults or overflow. odorless excavator, but is now done in the
that contents can not escape, by the done at night, or if necessary, to be
e a year, or oftener. The work used to
the board of health.

of the old ...
burial-ground is ...
except the church-yards ...
tracts of land near the city for the ...

vo public markets in Charleston, ...
ter *Market,* and the other in ward one ...
The former contains 28 and the other in ward 3, on ...
each; vegetable stalls, 50 cents ...
The two markets during the latter 112 stalls, ...
urday in Market ...
market, the past year was $10,474 44 ...
. market, the opened daily, except Sunday, from ...
or farmers' and adjoining streets are occasionally in ...
ne 30 years ago.

SANITARY AUTHORITY—BOARD OF HEALTH.
zation of Charleston is the board of health, composed of the ...
1 the physician of the city orphan house, with 1 physician ...
trar, also a physician of the city orphan house, a member *ex officio.*
rolled when inside the law. In ordinary times the board is ent...
disinfectants, coffins, ambulance, stationery, printing, city hospi...
se its expenses, coffins, ambulance, stationery, but no limit is specified.
rd has full authority to any amount necessary, printing, city expens...
all things needful for the sanitary con...

Saint Paul's, Episcopal, northeast corner of Vanderhorst and Corning streets; area, 2¼ acres.

Saint Patrick, Catholic, northeast corner of Saint Philip and Radcliff streets; area, 2 acres.

Central, Presbyterian, northwest corner of West and Archdale streets; area, 1 acre (closed).

German Burying-ground, Protestant, south side of Amherst, next to corner of Hanover street; area, 2 acres (closed).

Hebrew, southeast corner of Amherst and Hanover streets; area, ¼ acre (closed).

These 18 are for white persons, and the following 15 are for colored persons:

Circular Burying-ground, Methodist, south side of Calhoun street, between Pitt and Smith streets; area, 1½ acre.

Bethel, Methodist, west side of Pitt, next to corner of Calhoun street; area, 1 acre.

Methodist Episcopal, east side of South street; area, ¼ acre.

McPhelin, Episcopal, east side of Pitt street, between Bull and Calhoun streets; area, ½ acre.

Brown Fellowship, Episcopal, Pitt street, next to above, south; area, ½ acre.

Baptist Burying-ground, north side of Line street, between Corning street and Rutledge avenue; area, ¼ acre (closed).

Mariners' Colored, general, adjoining the preceding (closed).

Saint John's, Catholic, southwest corner of Shepard and Corning streets; area, 1½ acre.

Lutheran Colored, northwest corner of Columbia and Aiken streets; area, ½ acre.

Calvary, Episcopal, north side of Line street, between Corning street and Rutledge avenue; area, 1¼ acre.

Field of Rest, Methodist, east side of Hanover street, between Hampton court and Amherst street; area, 2 acres (closed).

Scotch Colored Presbyterian, north side of Amherst street, between Hanover and America streets; area, 1 acre.

Beersheba, Presbyterian, northeast corner of Reid and Hanover streets; area, ¾ acre.

Zion Hill, Methodist, northeast corner of Hanover and Columbus streets; area, ½ acre (closed).

Methodist, west side of Pitt street, between Bull and Calhoun streets (closed).

In addition to the 33 cemeteries and burying-grounds just enumerated, there are the following just beyond the northern boundary of the city: *Magnolia Cemetery, Saint Lawrence Cemetery, German Cemetery, Hebrew Cemetery*, and 2 others for white persons, and 2, one on either side of the *Hebrew Cemetery*, for colored persons.

Owing to the imperfections in many of the records, the total number of interments can not be given. Burial permits are issued by the board of health on certificates of death signed by the attending physician, and graves may not be less than 6 feet in depth. A committee of the board of health has general supervision over all the burial-grounds in the city.

About 30 years ago extra-mural cemeteries were strongly advocated from hygienic motives, and very generally concurred in, Magnolia (Protestant), Saint Lawrence (Roman Catholic), Bethany (German Protestant), and Hebrew cemeteries being established. Most of the white interments are now made in these cemeteries, though a number of the old families owning lots in the burial-grounds attached to the churches in the city still bury there. No new burial-ground is allowed to be opened in the city, and no one is allowed to be buried in any city burial-ground, except the church-yards, and then only an owner or pew-holder. The colored people are also purchasing convenient tracts of land near the city for the burial of their dead.

MARKETS.

There are two public markets in Charleston, one in ward 6, corner of Vanderhorst and Saint Philips streets, known as the *Upper Market*, and the other in ward 3, on Market street, from Meeting street to Cooper river, known as the *Lower Market*. The former contains 28 and the latter 112 stalls, the rental per week for each class being as follows: Beef stalls, $1 10 each; vegetable stalls, 50 cents each; fish stalls, $1 50 each; and fruit stalls, 50 cents each. The total rental for the two markets during the past year was $10,474 44; amount expended, $4,793 73; and net receipts, $5,680 69. The markets are opened daily, except Sunday, from sunrise to 11 a. m., and on Saturdays, all day from the first Saturday in October to the first Saturday in June. The markets are built on a wide area, and, in the case of the lower market, the adjoining streets are occasionally used for the sale of hogs, calves, and sheep, and for standing-room for farmers' and hucksters' wagons. The lower market was established about 75 years ago, and the upper market some 30 years ago.

SANITARY AUTHORITY—BOARD OF HEALTH.

The chief health organization of Charleston is the board of health, composed of the president of the Medical Society of South Carolina, and the physician of the city orphan house, with 1 physician and 8 citizens appointed by the mayor, and the city registrar, also a physician, a member *ex officio*. The board is entirely an independent body, and its action is not controlled when inside the law. In ordinary times the annual expenses of the board are $28,335, for salaries, medicine, disinfectants, coffins, ambulance, stationery, printing, city hospital, etc. During an epidemic the board may increase its expenses to any amount necessary, but no limit is specified. In the absence of any declared epidemic the board has full authority to do all things needful for the sanitary condition of the city, and during an epidemic to take all measures necessary to check and control the same. The chief executive officer of the board is the city registrar, with a salary of $1,000 per annum. His duties are to see that all health regulations and ordinances are enforced, and to execute all orders coming from the board. There are 7 health physicians, 4 sanitary inspectors, and 1 health detective employed. They have power sufficient to carry out the instructions of the board and to make arrests. The board transacts its business as a deliberative body. The regular meetings are weekly, and the office hours are from 9 a. m. to 8 p. m., the registrar being required to attend from 12 to 2 daily.

Inspections are made regularly in all parts of the city, from house to house and from yard to yard. When nuisances are discovered, the owner of the property if private, or the city inspector if public, are notified to have the same corrected within a specified time, and if this is not done, the board has the necessary labor performed, charging the cost to the property on which the nuisance existed. When defective house-drainage exists, owners are notified to remedy the same. Privy-vaults are cleaned and disinfected and cesspools are ordered abated. There is no inspection of the water-supply. The artesian-well water is examined from time to time. Defective sewerage is, on being discovered, at once remedied, either by private parties, or, if in street-drains, by the superintendent of streets. The conservation and removal of garbage are controlled by the board, and the sanitary inspectors have supervision over the same. All matters pertaining to the burial of the dead are regulated by the board, and a standing committee on burial-grounds, sextons, and hearses is always appointed. The pollution of streams and harbors is prohibited, and the removal of excrement is under the control of the board.

INFECTIOUS DISEASES.

Small-pox patients are isolated by being sent to the pest-house, the board promptly providing one in case of need. Scarlet-fever patients are not isolated. The board takes cognizance of the breaking out of contagious diseases in public and private schools, but has no control over the treatment. Vaccination is not compulsory, but is done at the public expense for the poor, when requested.

The registration of marriages, births, diseases, and deaths is systematically done by the clerk of the board.

REPORTS.

The board of health reports annually to the city council, through the city registrar, and the report is published with the regular city documents.

MUNICIPAL CLEANSING.

Street-cleaning.—The streets are cleaned at the expense of the city and with its regular force. The work is done wholly by hand, no sweeping-machines being used. The paved streets are cleaned about once a month, and the unpaved ones three or four times a year, while certain low spots receive attention weekly. The efficiency of the work is reported as being "medium". The annual cost of this work is $3,000. Some of the sweepings are sold to farmers, and the remainder are used for filling in new streets in the marsh. The system is not entirely satisfactory, on account of the looseness of the surface and the difficulty of drainage.

Removal of garbage and ashes.—All garbage and ashes are removed at the expense of the city with its own force. While awaiting removal, garbage is kept in boxes and barrels and set out on the street each day. It is allowed to keep ashes and garbage in the same vessels, and their final disposition is similar to that of street-sweepings. The annual cost of this removal is $12,000. The system is said to work well. The garbage is removed every morning, and there are no complaints.

Dead animals.—The carcasses of all horses, mules, and cows dying within the limits of the city are taken by the neighboring farmers and used as manure. The carcasses of small animals are removed by the city and dumped in the marsh-lands with the garbage. The cost of this service is included in that for the removal of garbage and ashes. The system is reported as " good".

Liquid household wastes.—Chamber-slops go into drains or are thrown into privy-vaults, while laundry wastes and kitchen-slops are run into drains or street-gutters, or thrown into cesspools. These cesspools are built with brick sides and open bottoms, receive the wastes of water-closets, and must be cleaned out at least once a year, or oftener if so ordered by the board of health. Street-gutters are cleansed daily. It is reported that nearly five-sixths of the drinking-water from wells is more or less contaminated by privy-vaults or drains, and that the whole system of disposal of liquid wastes is defective, and is now undergoing examination by the municipal authorities and the board of health.

Human-excreta.—About 500 houses in the city have water-closets, and it has been estimated that there are nearly 7,000 privy-vaults. The water-closets deliver either into the drains, cesspools, or privy-vaults. The ordinances provide that all privy-vaults must be built at least 10 feet from any street, alley, or lane, and so constructed that their contents can not escape or overflow. It is reported that none of them are water-tight. They are cleaned once a year, or oftener if necessary, by the odorless-excavator process, the whole matter being under the control of the board of health. The work used to be done at night, but is now done in the day-time. The night-soil is taken out of the city, and is not used in the vicinity of the public water-supply. Mayor Courtenay reports: "The system of night-soil cleaning is defective and prejudicial to health. The subject of reform is now before the council and board of health."

POLICE.

The police force of Charleston is appointed by the chief of police, subject to confirmation by the mayor, and is governed by him. In addition to the government of the force the chief of police is required to maintain the peace and order of the city. His salary is $1,800 per annum. The force consists of:

	Salary, each.
2 first lieutenants	$950
2 second lieutenants	900
10 sergeants	600
3 detectives	600
80 privates	576
6 turnkeys	480
4 hostlers	480
5 steeplemen	480
3 day-men	300

The uniform consists in winter of a dark-blue military frock coat, with brass buttons stamped with the city crest and the words, "Charleston police", and black helmet hat, and in summer of a blue flannel suit, sack coat, and Panama hat. White gloves are worn while on duty. The winter suit costs $38, and the summer suit $16, and each man is required to provide his own uniform. Each patrolman is equipped with a rosewood baton, a revolver, a five-pointed star, and a Winchester rifle in reserve. The tours of duty are 4 hours day and 6 hours night, and all the streets of the city are patrolled by the force.

During the past year 3,452 arrests were made by the force, the principal causes being for disorderly conduct, drunkenness, larceny, and violation of the city ordinances. Their final disposition was by fine and imprisonment. In the same period the total value of lost or stolen property recovered by the police and returned to the owners was $23,402 73. The total number of station-house lodgers for the year was 445, as against 564 in 1879. No free meals are furnished to lodgers. The force is required to keep order at fires and protect property from theft; to report and arrest for violations of the health ordinances, and to report all violations of the building ordinances. Special policemen are appointed by the mayor for times of emergency, elections, etc., and as private watchmen. They are under the command of the chief of police and the rules and regulations of the police department. The yearly cost of the police force (1880) is $68,602 03.

FIRE DEPARTMENT.

The annual report of the chief of the fire department for the year ending December 31, 1880, states:

During the year there were 19 fires and 10 chimney and other alarms. The total amount of losses paid by insurance agencies located in this city this year is $151,842 48. The largest amount paid was $120,260 60. This was the fire that occurred on the 17th of October at Commercial wharves, which destroyed several thousand bales of cotton, also a number of buildings, and damaging wharf property and shipping in its course. The force numbers 14 steamers and 3 truck companies. The steamers are required by ordinance to have each 800 feet of good serviceable hose, making the total amount of hose 11,200 feet. The amount appropriated for the support of the department was $26,000. The fire-alarm telegraph, as small as it is, has worked quite satisfactorily. The introduction of water has been the means of facilitating the management of fires, as well as affording the fire department such relief and advantages as to enable them to control sudden fires much quicker than before its introduction.

PUBLIC SCHOOLS.

The following regarding the public schools of Charleston is taken from the last annual message (1880) of Mayor Courtenay:

The number of pupils registered at the five city public schools is as follows: Bennett school, 1,179—754 boys and 425 girls; Memminger school, 617, all girls; Meeting Street school, 275—109 boys and 166 girls; Morris Street school (colored), 1,403—646 boys and 757 girls; and Shaw Memorial school (colored), 318 boys and 348 girls. Grand total, 4,140—1,827 boys and 2,313 girls. These schools give employment to 91 teachers, 6 males and 85 females. Each school is divided into three departments—primary, intermediate, and grammar—and the minimum age for the admission of pupils is 6 years, and the maximum 16 years.

COMMERCE AND NAVIGATION.

[From the reports of the Bureau of Statistics for the fiscal years ending June 30.]

Customs district of Charleston, South Carolina.	1879.	1880.
Total value of imports	$131,185	$202,799
Total value of exports:		
Domestic	$19,607,897	$19,590,627
Foreign	None.	$500
Total number of immigrants	None.	4

COMMERCE AND NAVIGATION—continued.

Customs district of Charleston, South Carolina.	1879.		1880.	
	Number.	Tons.	Number.	Tons.
Vessels in foreign trade:				
Entered	320	160,669	255	116,283
Cleared	325	170,143	282	148,218
Vessels in coast trade and fisheries:				
Entered	383	306,395	424	375,819
Cleared	252	158,301	311	213,320
Vessels registered, enrolled, and licensed in district.	178	12,587	182	9,712
Vessels built during the year	8	117	11	153

MANUFACTURES.

The following is a summary of the statistics of the manufactures of Charleston for 1880, being taken from tables prepared for the Tenth Census by B. R. Stuart, special agent:

Mechanical and manufacturing industries.	No. of establishments.	Capital	AVERAGE NUMBER OF HANDS EMPLOYED.			Total amount paid in wages during the year.	Value of materials.	Value of products.
			Males above 16 years.	Females above 15 years.	Chi'dren and youths.			
All industries	194	$1,718,300	1,788	150	208	$639,030	$1,468,375	$2,732,590
Blacksmithing (see also Wheelwrighting)	6	10,050	10		5	6,058	3,855	13,727
Boots and shoes, including custom work and repairing	9	1,120	11		2	4,256	4,100	13,191
Bread and other bakery products	10	59,850	65		16	28,695	120,860	172,185
Carpentering	14	31,050	448		15	97,738	130,998	268,565
Clothing, men's	6	40,100	35	4	4	11,500	25,700	47,300
Confectionery	4	2,500	4		3	1,630	6,750	11,240
Cotton compressing	4	530,000	230			62,900	65,000	198,000
Dentistry, mechanical	7	2,800					3,785	9,800
Flouring- and grist-mill products	5	61,000	27			12,070	141,300	167,750
Foundery and machine-shop products	5	111,700	177		28	59,150	96,100	174,900
Lock- and gun-smithing	7	2,330	5		3	2,708	2,100	11,418
Lumber, planed	6	82,000	167		34	35,450	121,950	189,000
Lumber, sawed	4	115,000	37		12	21,420	139,509	254,550
Marble and stone work	5	14,700	16		4	10,900	17,000	34,000
Mineral and soda water	3	4,500	13			4,059	7,800	20,250
Painting and paperhanging	7	5,550	44			9,629	10,228	25,450
Photographing	3	4,800	4			1,800	1,500	8,100
Plumbing and gasfitting	6	3,900	10		8	9,086	19,050	33,176
Printing and publishing	10	116,700	144	33	9	88,772	80,150	249,320
Saddlery and harness	6	5,150	19		4	9,030	27,001	43,650
Shipbuilding	11	44,350	85			52,810	53,350	138,650
Tinware, copperware, and sheet-iron ware	10	7,300	35		3	9,296	16,576	36,176
Tobacco, cigars and cigarettes	8	8,600	33		1	13,411	9,240	30,520
Upholstering	4	13,400	11	4		6,000	30,420	49,600
Watch and clock repairing	8	4,700	11		3	9,996	2,030	16,900
Wheelwrighting (see also Blacksmithing)	8	18,050	26		22	14,388	7,685	31,066
All other industries (a)	18	417,100	121	109	32	56,278	324,338	484,106

a Embracing axle-grease; bagging, flax, hemp, and jute; bags, other than paper; baskets, rattan and willow ware; carriages and wagons; cars, railroad, street, and repairs; coppersmithing; cotton-ties; fertilizers; furnishing goods, men's; furniture; liquors, malt; soap and candles; and stencils and brands.

From the foregoing table it appears that the average capital of all establishments is $8,857 22; that the average wages of all hands employed is $297 78 per annum: that the average outlay in wages, in materials, and in interest (at 6 per cent.) on capital employed is $11,394 35.

COLUMBIA,

RICHLAND COUNTY, SOUTH CAROLINA.

POPULATION

IN THE

AGGREGATE,

1830-1880.

	Inhab.
1790	......
1800	......
1810	......
1820	......
1830	3,310
1840	4,340
1850	6,060
1860	8,052
1870	9,298
1880	10,036

POPULATION

BY

SEX, NATIVITY, AND RACE,

AT

CENSUS OF 1880.

Male	4,639
Female	5,397
Native	9,698
Foreign-born	338
White	4,338
Colored	5,698

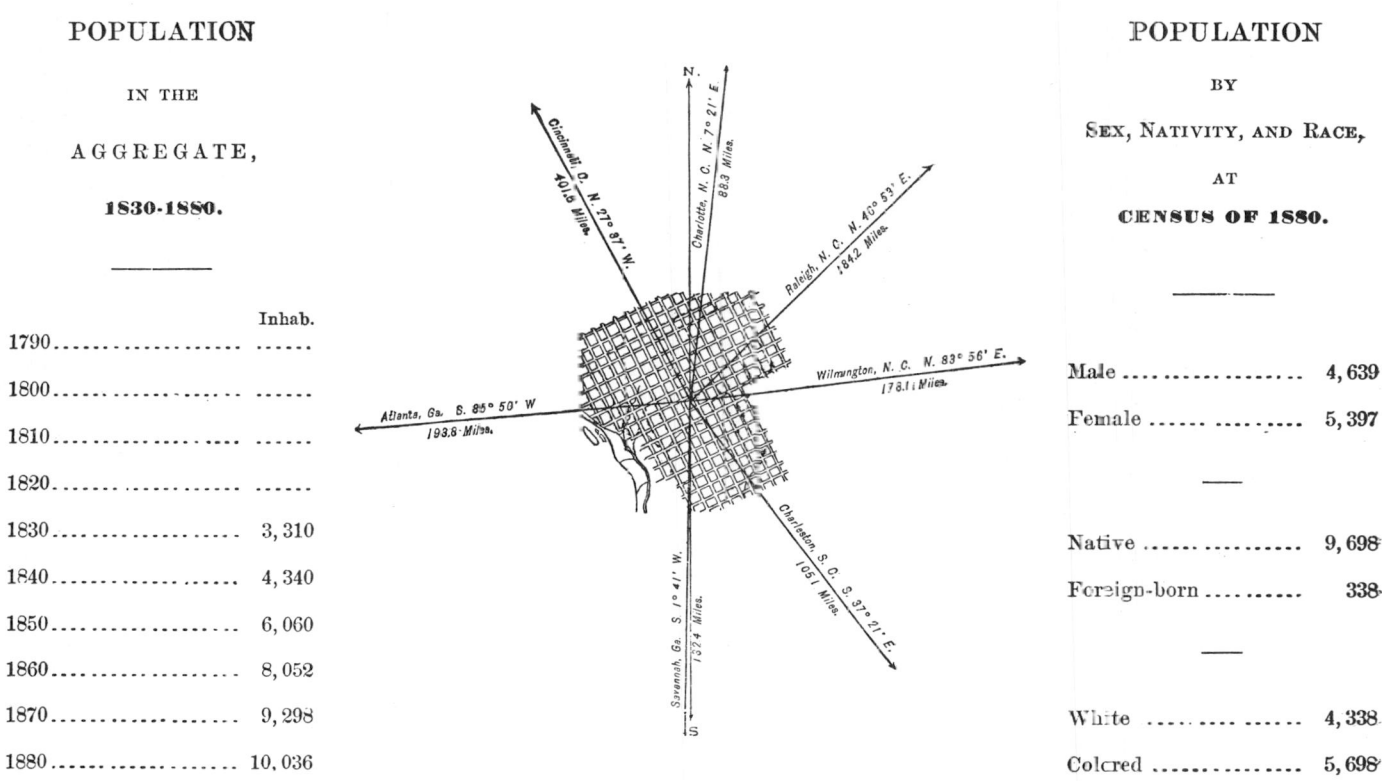

Latitude: 34° 2' North; Longitude: 80° 57' (west from Greenwich); **Altitude: 250 to 360 feet.**

FINANCIAL CONDITION:

Total Valuation: $2,600,000; per capita: $259 00.   Net Indebtedness: $854,850; per capita: $85 18.   Tax per $100: $2 42.

HISTORICAL SKETCH.

The demands of the people of South Carolina for a centrally located capital occasioned the founding of Columbia, and commissioners were appointed to select a site for the proposed city. By an act of the general assembly, ratified March 22, 1786, these commissioners were authorized "to lay off a tract of land 2 miles square near Friday's ferry, on the Congaree river, * * * into lots of half an acre each, and the streets shall be of such dimensions, not less than 60 feet wide, as they shall think convenient and necessary, with two principal streets running through the center of the town, at right angles, of 150 feet wide". They were also fairly to reimburse the proprietors of this land, and, after reserving one or more squares for the use of the public buildings, to sell one-fifth of the remainder of the lots to the highest bidder at a price not less than £20 each. The proceeds of this sale were to be applied to the construction of a state-house, executive mansion, and other necessary public buildings. The purchasers of these lots were required to erect upon each of them a house, not less than 30 by 18 feet in dimensions, within 3 years of the time of purchase, or, failing to comply with these conditions, to pay a forfeit of 5 per cent. per annum upon the purchase money until they did comply with them. Three years after the passage of the act the public records were removed to Columbia from Charleston, and 12 months later, exactly 120 years after the first European settlement in Carolina, the legislature convened here for the first time. However, not to make too sudden a change, the business of the state treasurer, secretary, and surveyor-general was for a time conducted both in Charleston and in Columbia.

The situation selected for the new capital was a good one. Columbia is very nearly in the center of the state, on the Congaree river; is pleasantly situated on a high and commanding plain in a productive and healthful region, and has very many of the inherent essentials of a prosperous and healthy growth. These qualities were effective, and up to the beginning of the civil war Columbia steadily fulfilled the just expectations of her people.

The educational facilities of Columbia are exceptionally good. Here, in 1804, was founded the South Carolina college, called since 1865 South Carolina university, on which $200,000 were expended in the original purchase of the site and the erection of the buildings. The university consists of 10 distinct schools, and has a fine library of about 30,000 volumes. It possesses, also, all the apparatus necessary for the illustration of philosophical, astronomical, chemical, and other studies, including that of medicine. The theological seminary of the synod of South Carolina and Georgia is also located within the city limits. This institution originated in a project set on foot as early as 1824. Its seat was originally at Lexington, Georgia, being removed hither in 1830. The doors of the seminary are open to students of all denominations who are church-members. Here, also, are the Ursuline Institute of the Immaculate Conception, located at Valle Crucis, about 2 miles from the city, and the Columbia male academy, founded in 1785 and under the control of a board of five trustees. The land was the gift of a citizen; the cost of the building was defrayed by subscriptions.

In 1821 the Columbia canal was constructed, to avoid the falls of the river, and originally ran from about half a mile above the city to Gravely, about 2 miles below. This canal, with the aid of a dam at its head creating considerable back-water, enabled produce, principally cotton, to be brought down in small boats from the northern or "Saluda" country. The canal was subsequently extended upward nearly 2 miles. In 1868 it was sold to the A. & W. Sprague Manufacturing Company, and was to be so improved as to form a fine water power, but it is still undeveloped. In 1830 a serious fire destroyed about $100,000 worth of property. From the financial panics of 1825 and 1857 Columbia recovered rapidly. In 1852 the new state-house was begun, and in 1854 Columbia was incorporated as a city.

The civil war fell with a very heavy hand on Columbia, inflicting a blow from which it has not yet recovered. On February 17, 1865, it was abandoned by the confederate forces and occupied by General Sherman's army, and during these operations a very large portion of the city was destroyed by fire. Columbia was completely prostrated, and only now may be said to have reached her *ante bellum* point in municipal growth. Being the capital of the state, the city has secured considerable state aid in the way of new buildings, and being the shire-town of Richland county has also been in its favor. Within its limits are the state lunatic asylum and the state penitentiary, the United States court-house, and a public market-house. It has also the usual modern lighting facilities and water-supply. The manufactories of the city are fair in number and importance, those of building-lumber and iron, perhaps, leading.

COLUMBIA IN 1880.

The following statistical accounts, collected by the Census Office, indicate the present condition of Columbia:

LOCATION.

Columbia lies in latitude 34° 2′ north, longitude 80° 57′ west from Greenwich, on the east bank of the Congaree river, just below the confluence of the Saluda and Broad rivers, which unite to form it. The altitudes of the city above mean sea-level are: Lowest point, 250 feet; highest point, Taylor's hill, 360 feet, and the city hall, 331 feet. The Congaree river is navigable for steamboats to this point, or very near it. Vessels used to ply between here and Charleston, but the much shorter distance made by land-routes has led to the almost total disuse of the river for such travel, the extent of which is now slight.

RAILROAD COMMUNICATIONS.

Columbia is touched by the following railroads:
The South Carolina railroad, to Charleston.
The Wilmington, Columbia, and Augusta railroad, running from Wilmington, North Carolina, on the north, to Augusta, Georgia, on the south.

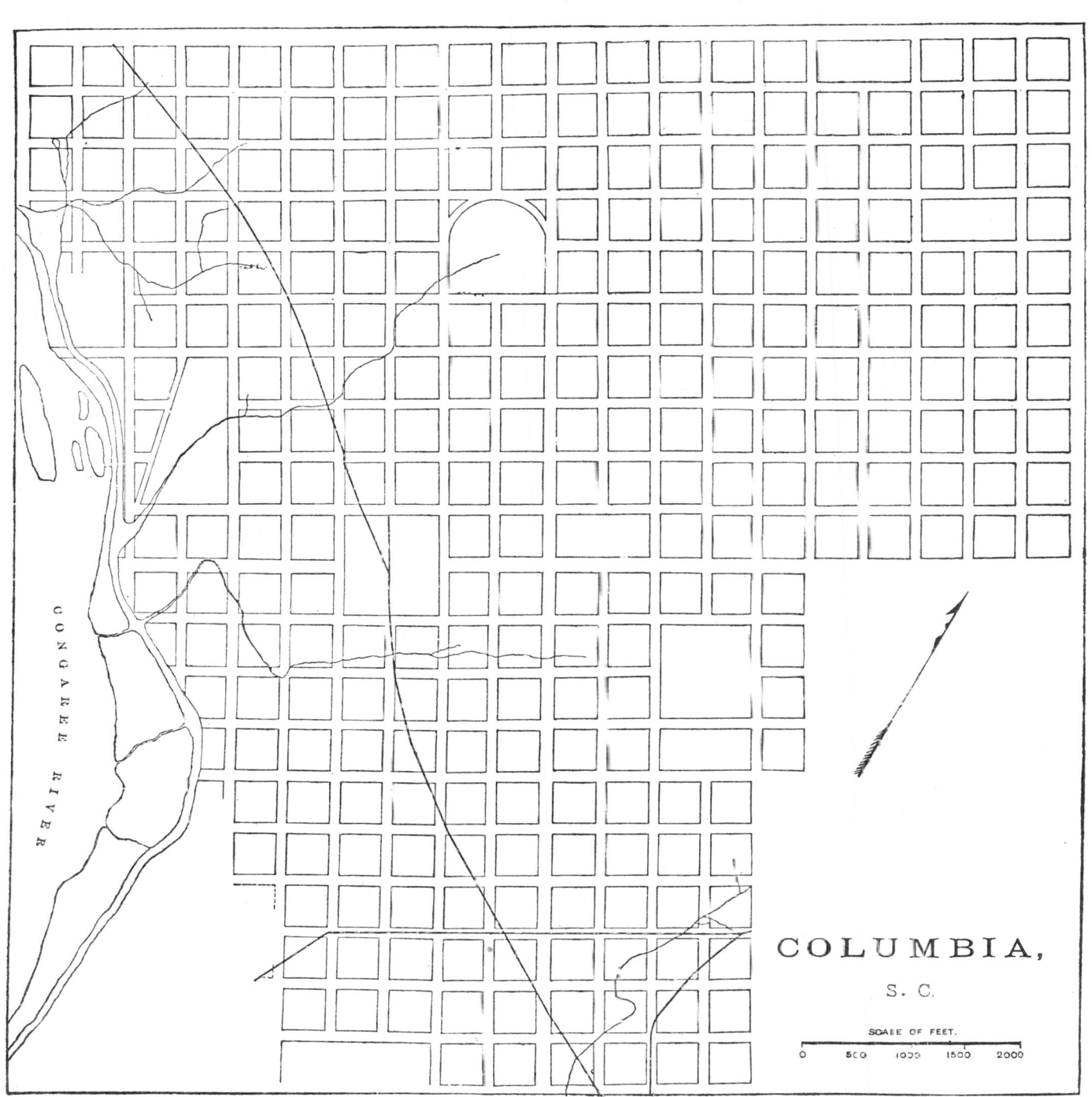

CONGAREE RIVER

COLUMBIA,
S. C.

SCALE OF FEET.

0   500   1000   1500   2000

The Charlotte, Columbia, and Augusta railroad, with Charlotte, North Carolina, as the northern, and Augusta, Georgia, as the southern terminus.

The Greenville and Columbia railroad, running to Greenville, South Carolina.

TRIBUTARY COUNTRY.

The country surrounding and tributary to the city is fertile and agricultural.

TOPOGRAPHY.

The soil of the site is sandy in the east and southeast, elsewhere it is clayey and loamy. The underlying rock is chiefly a first-class granite. The site is elevated, with considerable differences in level. The natural drainage is good. The surrounding country is very hilly, with considerable wood, which is fast disappearing. There are no near ponds or marshes.

CLIMATE.

Highest recorded summer temperature (July 12, 1879), 102°; highest summer temperature in average years, 95°. Lowest recorded winter temperature (January 4, 1879), 18°; lowest winter temperature in average years, 46°.

STREETS.

Columbia's streets cover a length of 68 miles, of which about 10 miles are paved with gravel and macadam. The annual cost of repairs is $4,000. This is not enough to keep them all in repair, and scarcely one-half of the streets can be considered in good order. The streets are all 100 feet wide, except the four boundary and two center intersecting streets, which are 150 feet wide, and all run at right angles to the streets crossing them. Sidewalks are paved with brick, tiles, flags, some artificial flags, and a little cast iron; but the major portion of the walks are unpaved. About half the street-gutters are paved with brick or granite; another portion, about 2 miles, is paved only with gravel and sand mixed and rammed hard. Nearly all the streets have shade-trees along their sides, and many of them have trees also planted in their centers. All street repairs are made by day work, which is considered by the authorities to be cheaper and better than by contract. No steam stone-crusher or roller is used in street work. There are no horse-railroads in the city at present, but a company has been chartered, and the stock partly raised, for the purpose. There are no regular omnibus lines, but conveyances run between the depots and hotels, etc.

WATER-WORKS.

The water-works are owned by the city, and cost $40,000. The water is pumped by steam- and water-power, and the pressure is 30 pounds to the square inch. The average amount pumped per diem is 300,000 gallons. The yearly cost of maintenance is $3,750, and the yearly income from water-rates is $8,000. Water-meters are not used.

GAS.

The gas-works are owned by a private company. The daily average production is 20,000 cubic feet. The charge per 1,000 feet is $4 50. The city pays $2 50 a month each for street-lamps, 33 in number.

PUBLIC BUILDINGS.

The city owns or occupies for municipal uses, wholly or in part, the city hall, mayor's court, council-chamber, and clerk's and treasurer's office; also that part of the county jail known as the police-station. The city hall (not quite finished) cost $100,000.

PUBLIC PARKS AND PLEASURE-GROUNDS.

Columbia has one public park, called *Sidney Park*. Its area is 25 acres, and its total cost is $50,000. There is annually spent on its maintenance $300. The annual visitors to it on foot number about 100,000; in carriages about 15,000, and on horseback about 2,000. The park is controlled by the city. A gardener is appointed, who acts as keeper, assisted by the police.

PLACES OF AMUSEMENT.

There is one opera-house in the city, fitted up as a theater, and seating 800; Parker's hall, seating 600, is also fitted with stage and scenery; Carolina hall, seating 400, and one or two smaller halls but little used. Theaters do not, but entertainments do, pay a license to the city of from $10 to $25 per day, amounting annually to about $300. There are no concert- or beer-gardens in the place.

DRAINAGE.

Columbia is entirely without sewers. Storm-water is carried off by surface drains in the streets.

CEMETERIES.

Columbia has 3 public and 7 private cemeteries and burying-grounds connected with it. The 3 public cemeteries are located on the corporation line; the others belong to churches. Up to the present year, 1880, burials in new lots were not prohibited, but now the opening of any new lot for interments within the city limits has been interdicted. There has been no system of registration which would make it possible to give the total number of interments in the cemeteries and graveyards. When interments are made a certificate of the cause of death, etc., in each case, is furnished to the sexton of the burial-ground. The annual number of deaths is stated to be about 200.

MARKETS.

Columbia has a good market-house, about 150 by 50 feet in size, the cost of which was $4,000. There are also connected with it outside grounds upon which hucksters or farmers may sell, after taking out the required license therefor. The stalls rent for $100 each, and the total rental of the market is $3,000 per annum. The market is open daily from 5 to 9 a. m., except Saturdays, when it is open from 5 a. m. to 10 p. m. The gross amount of the annual sales from within the market is not given.

SANITARY AUTHORITY—BOARD OF HEALTH.

The chief sanitary organization of the city is the board of health, which is composed of 12 members, 3 from each ward, 2 of whom at present are physicians. The board is elected and controlled by the city council. The board incurs no direct expense, its present powers being only advisory and the execution of its recommendations devolving upon the mayor. The chief of police, by the mayor's direction, executes the orders of the board and abates nuisances. The business of the board is transacted at meetings held twice a month between May 1 and November 1; a physician is selected as chairman of the board, and the city clerk acts as secretary, and transmits all orders to the chief of police. The chief directs the policemen to act as inspectors and report all nuisances, or pertinent matters, to the chairman. Inspections are not made regularly, but are made upon report or suspicion of a nuisance, either by members of the board or by policemen. When reported and found to exist, nuisances are abated by the chief of police. The scope of the board's work extends also to the inspection and correction of defective house-drainage, privy-vaults, cesspools, sources of drinking-water, etc. Under the direction of the board the chief of police superintends the removal of garbage. There is said to exist no pollution of streams. Excrement must be removed when it becomes offensive.

INFECTIOUS DISEASES.

Small-pox patients are removed to the pest-house, situated in the extreme limits of the city, remote from habitations. The care and regulation of cases of scarlet fever are left to the attending physician. At present the board does not take cognizance of the breaking out of contagious diseases in public or private schools. Vaccination is not compulsory, nor is it done at the public expense.

There is no system of registration of births, diseases, and deaths.

REPORTS.

At present the board reports to no one. A bill is about to be presented to the legislature regulating more thoroughly the whole subject of sanitary authority and its systematic working.

MUNICIPAL CLEANSING.

Street-cleaning.—The streets of Columbia, which are not paved, are cleaned by the city's own force, and by hand. This work is largely confined to the cleansing of the open surface-drains, which take the place of storm-water sewers. Some of them require daily or weekly sweeping and washing out. This cleaning is efficiently done, except on certain streets which require the most attention. The sweepings are deposited outside of the city. The annual cost of the work, including the removal of garbage, is $5,000.

Removal of garbage and ashes.—Garbage is removed daily by the city in its street-carts, though some is destroyed on the premises by fire. Householders are required to place their garbage in suitable vessels and, between certain hours, upon the street, when it is removed. No disinfectants are used upon garbage, and garbage and ashes may be kept in the same vessel. Both are disposed of by being dumped upon some vacant field. It is reported that garbage is frequently allowed to become a nuisance, and that more carts could with advantage be used in this work.

Dead animals.—The carcasses of larger animals, as horses and cows, are removed by their owners. Those of smaller size, as dogs, cats, etc., are removed by the city carts, and the cost thereof is included in the sum expended for street-cleaning. The number of such animals annually removed is from 75 to 100. The manner of disposal of the larger animals is very offensive, for they "are always carried outside of the city and deposited near the road leading to the same, to the annoyance, etc., of travelers".

Liquid household wastes.—Owing to the lack of a system of sewerage each householder is required to dispose of all the liquid wastes of the house upon the premises, either by pouring them into dry wells or cesspools or by throwing them upon the surface of their yards and gardens the running them into the street-gutters or drains not being permitted. About 2 per cent. of the houses have no cesspools. The cesspools are porous, as the desire is to dig deep enough to reach the sand underlying the red clay. They are not provided legitimately with overflows, but when these occur they run into the surface-drains, creating a nuisance along the streets. When street-gutters become foul from any cause they are flushed at the request of the board of health. Cesspools receive the wastes of such water-closets as are used in the city. Though no direct case of contamination of drinking-water by the escape of the contents of cesspools and privy-vaults is reported, the opinion is expressed that it does occur. It is the policy of the board of health to dissuade people from using for drinking purposes the water from wells in the more thickly settled parts of the city, or those near stables or cesspools. There are no regulations for the cleaning of cesspools.

Human excreta.—Two per cent. of the houses in the city have water-closets. The remainder depend either upon privy-vaults or upon privies without vaults—in which case the deposits fall on the surface of the ground—or upon the use of the dry-earth system. As a rule, privy-vaults are not tight. There are no regulations as to the construction and emptying of privy-vaults, except that they must not become a nuisance. Most of the night-soil is carried away by farmers and used for manure, none of it being allowed on land within the gathering-ground of the public water supply.

Manufacturing wastes.—The disposal of solid and liquid manufacturing wastes is not regulated.

POLICE.

The police force of the city is appointed and governed by the city council. The chief of police is the chief executive officer, has direct control of the force, and sees that all laws and ordinances are properly enforced; his salary is $900 per annum. The remainder of the force consists of 2 sergeants at $40 a month each, and 15 patrolmen at $35 a month each. The uniform in summer is a blue sack coat and trousers, and black felt hat with wreath and number, and in winter a frock coat, overcoat, and rubber "reliable." The uniforms are furnished by the city at an annual cost of $50 per man. The patrolmen are equipped with 20-inch hickory club, belt, pistol, and "duplex call". They serve 12 hours per day, and patrol in all 20 miles of streets.

The arrests during the year numbered 1,300, the chief causes being drunkenness, disorderly conduct, and profanity. Their final disposition was not stated. During the year property to the amount of $1,000 was reported to the police as lost or stolen, and about one-half of this was recovered and returned to the owners. The station-house lodgers for the same period numbered about 50, and some free meals were furnished to these at a trifling cost. In 1879 the number of station-house lodgers was about the same. The force is required to co-operate with and assist the fire department at fires by protecting property and preserving order, and with the health department by inspecting, reporting, and removing nuisances. Special policemen are appointed by the mayor on public occasions, as at elections, holidays, and when there are large concourses of people. Their duties and pay are the same as those of the regular force. The yearly cost of the police force (1880) is $10,000.

KENTUCKY.

COVINGTON,

KENTON COUNTY, KENTUCKY.

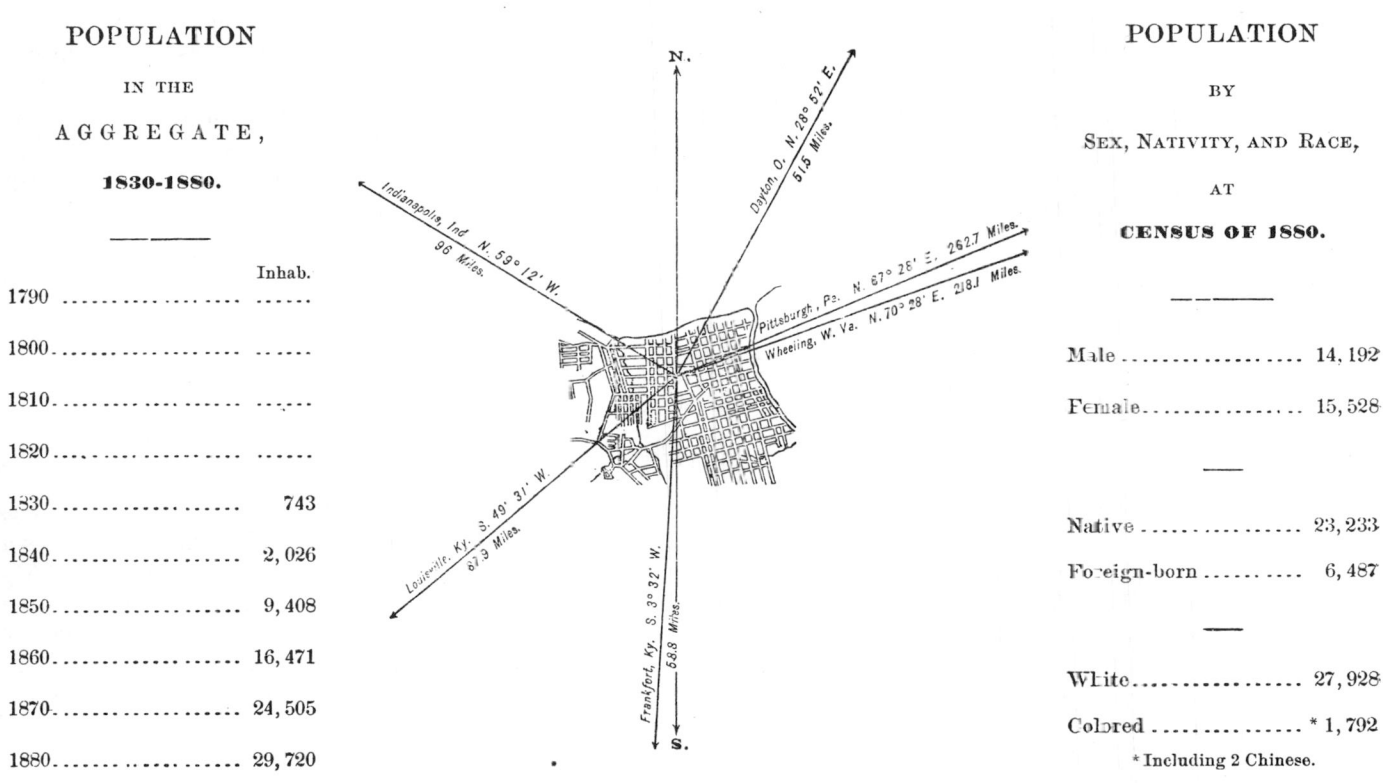

POPULATION

IN THE

AGGREGATE,

1830-1880.

	Inhab.
1790	......
1800	......
1810	......
1820	......
1830	743
1840	2,026
1850	9,408
1860	16,471
1870	24,505
1880	29,720

POPULATION

BY

SEX, NATIVITY, AND RACE,

AT

CENSUS OF 1880.

Male	14,192
Female	15,528
Native	23,233
Foreign-born	6,487
White	27,928
Colored	* 1,792

* Including 2 Chinese.

Latitude: 39° 5′ North; Longitude: 84° 36′ (west from Greenwich); Altitude: 440 to 545 feet.

FINANCIAL CONDITION:

Total Valuation: $14,521,725; per capita: $489 00. Net Indebtedness: $1,030,000; per capita: $34 66. Tax per $100: $2 17.

HISTORICAL SKETCH.

Information regarding the first settlement of Covington is of a somewhat traditional character. As early as 1771 Simon Kenton with others arrived and explored the country around the junction of the Licking with the Ohio river. About the year 1788 Thomas Kennedy built the first store house. In 1815 Covington was incorporated as a town, the streets and lots being laid out by Mr. A. R. Powell, and the boundaries were made to include about 150 acres. The next year the town contained 6 buildings. In 1820, when it had about 25 buildings, a log school-

111

house was built. A bank (Leather's Bank) had been created, and in 1829 a factory for making cotton yarn was erected; while in the following year the first iron-works—a rolling-mill—was started. At this date (1830) the inhabitants numbered 743, and the taxable valuation of the town's property was $170,220. In 1832 the first church (Methodist) was built. The next year a turnpike leading to Lexington was begun. In 1834 the town had so materially increased that it was given a city charter, and its boundaries were so extended as to include about 176 acres. In 1836 street-paving was begun. In 1839 appeared the first brewery, and 1840 found Covington with a population of more than 2,000, with property assessed at $634,805. Extensions of the city's limits took place again in 1841, 1850, 1860, and 1873. After the last-mentioned year the area of the city covered about 1,350 acres.

About the year 1847, in which another rolling-mill was added to the industries of the city, the beginning of a rapid advance, both in population and in the price of real estate, was noticeable. The valuation of property within the city rose from $170,220 in 1830 to $14,521,725 in 1880. The rate of taxation per $100 of valuation has risen from 40 cents in 1834, to $2 in 1876.

From 1818 to 1826 Covington suffered from a lack of money. The little specie in circulation was "cut money", or coins cut into pieces. Notes of the Commercial Bank were good for face value for the payment of town taxes, but in other transactions were accepted only at a discount of 50 per cent. From 1836 to 1842 was another period of financial depression, also from 1858 to 1862, and again the late depression caused by the panic of 1873. The first settlers of the place were from Virginia and Pennsylvania, and although the population has been somewhat increased by foreign immigration, at the present time the large majority of the inhabitants are native-born.

Covington's first railroad, the Kentucky Central, was begun in 1852. The erection of a suspension bridge across the Ohio river, to connect with Cincinnati, was begun in 1856 and completed in 1866; while one across the Licking river, to connect with Newport, was built in 1854 and rebuilt in 1855. Besides manufactures of iron, stoves, wood-work, tobacco, etc., Covington has glass-works, and a factory for the making of retorts, for gas-generation, out of fire-clay. The place is lighted with gas, and in 1871 it constructed water-works. The material growth of the city, up to the last depression at least, has been continuous. It has also been fortunate enough to escape any serious fires.

COVINGTON IN 1880.

The following statistical accounts, collected by the Census Office, indicate the present condition of Covington:

LOCATION.

Covington is situated on the Ohio river, opposite Cincinnati, and just below the mouth of the Licking river, which separates it from Newport, in latitude 39° 5' north, longitude 84° 36' west from Greenwich. It occupies a nearly level site, the altitudes above ocean-level being, lowest point, at the Ohio river, 440 feet; highest point, 545 feet; and average, about 520 feet. Its position, on the left bank of the Ohio river, gives it ample communication by water with all cities and points on the Ohio and Mississippi rivers and their navigable tributaries. The channel capacity of the river varies greatly. The minimum stage of water is stated to be 4 feet 2 inches, while the mean of the lowest stages, between 1858 and 1878, is nearly 4 feet. The highest stage was recorded in 1832 as 62 feet 11½ inches, while the mean of the highest stages, between 1832 and 1878, is about 50 feet. Licking river is also navigable for steamboats near its mouth when its water is backed up by high stages of the Ohio.

RAILROAD COMMUNICATIONS.

Covington is touched by the following railroads:
The Kentucky Central railroad, termini Covington, Lexington, and Paris.
The Cincinnati Southern railroad, termini Cincinnati, and Chattanooga, Tennessee.
The Louisville, Cincinnati, and Lexington railroad, from Cincinnati to Louisville.

TRIBUTARY COUNTRY.

The surrounding country, especially the valley portion, is largely engaged in raising garden-produce for Cincinnati, Covington, and the suburbs around these cities, while the hilly part is used, besides extensive fruit-culture, for common farming and dairying, considerable land being in pasture. Much of the product of this territory finds a sale or exchange for domestic supplies in the cities and suburbs centering around Cincinnati.

TOPOGRAPHY.

The underlying rock of the site of Covington is the blue limestone of the Cincinnati group of the Silurian. These rocks support the alluvium, forming the gently undulating site of the city. Its altitude above the low-water mark of the Ohio is about 80 feet. The Ohio and Licking rivers receive the creeks which drain the gradually rising

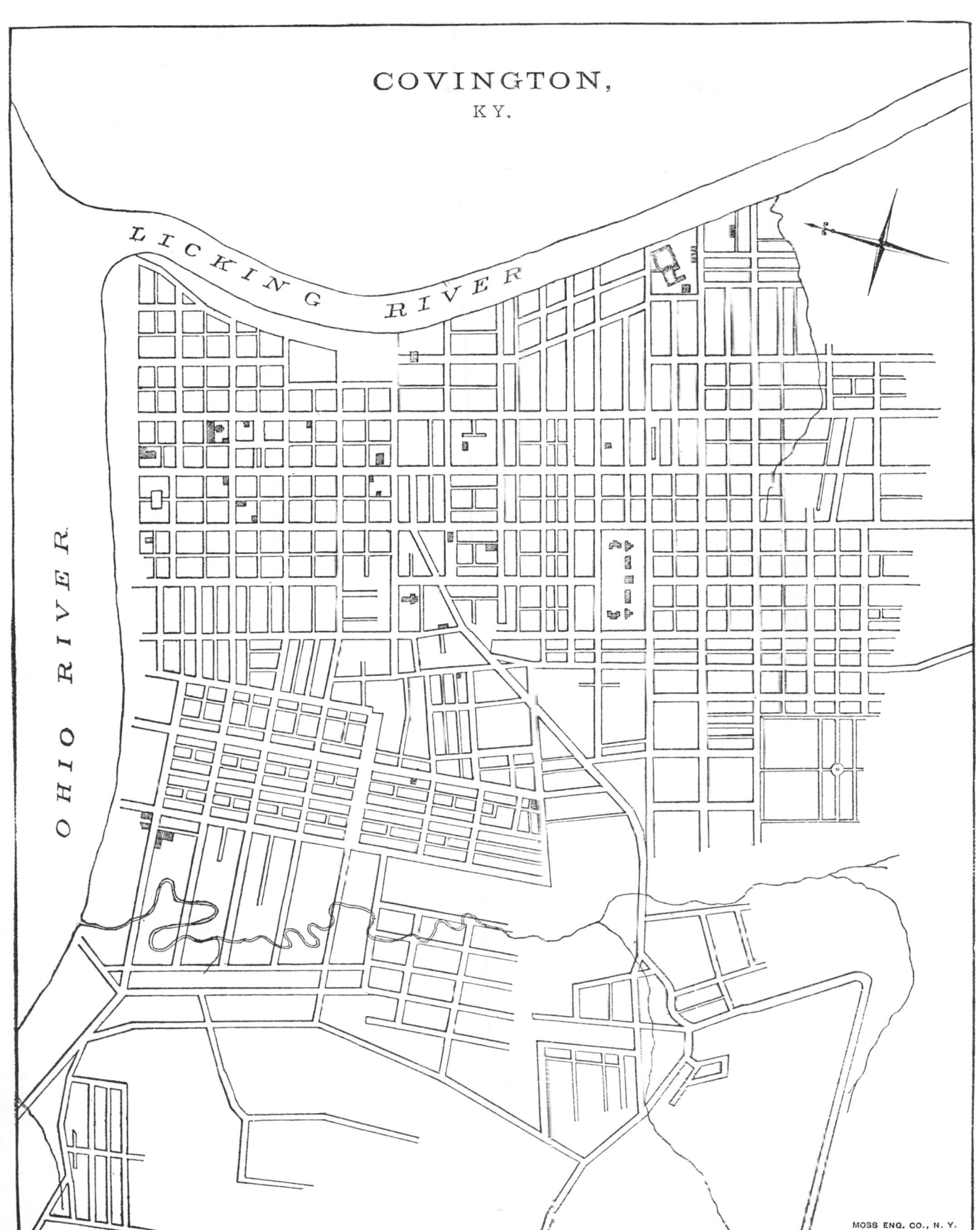

COVINGTON,
KY.

LICKING RIVER

OHIO RIVER.

hills outside the city proper. Near the top of these are some ponds of clear water. Most of the surrounding timber has been cut off for its own value and to make the highly fertile land available for agricultural use. The soil, except the alluvium, is a derivation of the Silurian rocks; hence it is of excellent quality, fertile, easy to work, and very fit for the famous bluegrass pasturage. Professor John R. Proctor, who superintended the collection of the above information, adds the following:

I am satisfied that the terrace of the river-valley on which Cincinnati and Covington and Louisville are built is the loess or bluff formation, and is synchronous with the same formation in the valley of the Mississippi. The gravel at the base (sometimes wanting) corresponds to the Paducah gravel of western Kentucky, partaking, however, in its composition, more of the character of the rocks of the Ohio valley, with many pebbles brought into the Ohio drainage by the swollen floods at the close of the last glacial era. The rocks under this terrace and above belong to the Cincinnati group of the Lower Silurian.

The gravel extends above high-water mark, and was deposited when the river was at a high level.

CLIMATE.

Highest recorded summer temperature, 102°; highest summer temperature in average years, 98°. Lowest recorded winter temperature, —20°; lowest winter temperature in average years, —6°. The climatic influence of the adjacent waters is not thought to be great, and there are no contiguous marshes. The adjacent hills shelter the city against winds. The prevailing winds are the southwest, generally bringing rain, and the west and northwest, sometimes strong and very cold.

STREETS.

The total length is 48.3 miles, paved as follows: Cobble-stones, 1,600 feet; broken stone, only 960 feet; broken stone and curbed, 29½ miles; wood (locust), 1.2 mile; and the remainder unpaved. The cost of each sort of paving, per square yard, as nearly as may be estimated, is: For cobble-stones, $1; for broken stone, 70 cents; and for wood, $1 25. The macadamized streets are the most difficult to keep clean, while the durability and economy of the wooden pavement used in Covington far surpasses that of any other material used. For suburban streets the broken stone is regarded as the best. Sidewalks are paved principally with hard-burned bricks, some with freestone, and some with artificial stone made of cement and sand; gutters are largely paved with stone. Shade-trees are planted on the curb-line of the streets, between the gutters and the sidewalks. The construction and repair of streets is usually done by contract, under the daily supervision of the superintendent of public works and the city engineer. No steam-roller is used, but one of 6,000 pounds' weight, and drawn by horses, is used for macadamizing streets. There are 6½ miles of street-railroads, with 32 cars and 152 horses, giving employment to 61 men. During the year, 1,070,000 passengers were carried, the rate of fare being 4 cents per mile. The omnibus lines have 5 vehicles and 10 horses, and employ 6 men. Passengers are carried at rates of fare varying from 25 to 50 cents.

WATER-WORKS.

The water-works are owned by the city, and their total cost is $427,253 21. The Holly system is used. The pressure is kept at the works at about 78 pounds per square inch, about 28 pounds of this being required to lift the water from the river; hence about 50 pounds is the pressure in the main pipe at the works. In 1878 the amount of water pumped per diem, in gallons, was, average, 1,377,083; greatest, 1,475,000; least, 1,200,000. For the same year the average cost of raising 1,000,000 gallons 1 foot high was 16 cents; yearly cost of maintenance, aside from cost of pumping, was $3,696 12; and the annual income from water-rates, $20,510 48. Water-meters are not used.

GAS.

The gas-works are owned privately. The daily average production is 75,000 cubic feet, and 25,000 of this goes to Newport. The charge per 1,000 cubic feet is, to the city, $1 25, to private persons, $2 25. There are 435 street-lamps, for the gas used in which the city pays its special rates.

PUBLIC BUILDINGS.

The city owns and occupies for municipal purposes, wholly or in part, the city hall or court-house, the city jail, and 4 engine-houses. The total cost of the city buildings is $95,000. The cost of the city hall is estimated at $4,000.

PUBLIC PARKS AND PLEASURE-GROUNDS.

Covington has no parks, but has a small grass-plot and walk now in course of construction, the probable cost of which will be $3,500.

PLACES OF AMUSEMENT.

There are here no theaters, but of halls there are Odd Fellows' hall, with 2 rooms, one seating 500 and the other 200; Drexler's hall, used frequently for public meetings, balls, etc., and Green hall. Concerts pay a license to the city of $10 for each performance. There are no concert- and beer-gardens in the city.

DRAINAGE.

The sewerage works of Covington are of recent date, and embrace only about 2½ miles of sewers, built principally of brick, with circular cross-sections. No comprehensive plan has been adopted providing for the whole city, but sewers are built according to the requirements in each case. In general features and in most details of construction the sewers of Covington are like those of Cincinnati, Ohio. The natural drainage is very good, as the city is situated between two streams—the Licking river on one side, next to Newport, and Wilson run on the west—with the Ohio river in front. The general surface is level, being what is known as the "second bottom", and is high enough above the river to secure ample fall for sewers by increasing somewhat the depth of cuttings toward the outlet. The cost of sewers built so far has been paid, one-half by the city and one-half by assessment upon abutting property, laid on the basis of frontage.

The following statement shows the character and cost of sewers built in 1880 by contract, each sewer being contracted for separately:

	Per linear foot.
4 feet diameter, brick	$4 60
3 feet diameter, brick	3 00
18 inches diameter vitrified pipe	1 60
12 inches diameter vitrified pipe	1 00

Average cost of catch-basins, $35 each.
Average cost of manholes, of average depth, $15 each.

CEMETERIES.

Covington has 4 cemeteries, public and private, as follows:

Highland Cemetery contains 114$\frac{17}{160}$ acres, is about 3½ miles west of the city, has existed since 1863, and is now the one most used.

Adjoining it is the Catholic *Saint Mary's Cemetery*, now the most used of the cemeteries belonging to that church.

Mother of God Cemetery, Catholic, contains about 8 acres.

Saint John's Cemetery, Catholic, contains 42 acres, only 10 of which are now used, is about 3½ miles southwest of the city, and has a vault for temporary use, also a chapel for services.

The number of interments in the several cemeteries since 1869, and including the present year, are, Highland cemetery, 1,898; Saint John's cemetery, 279; Saint Mary's cemetery, 1,130, and Mother of God cemetery, about 50 annually. For burials a permit must be obtained, and between April 1 and November 1 only four days may elapse between death and burial, but during winter, if the body is deposited in a vault, an indefinite time is allowed. Graves must be dug from 5 to 6 feet deep. Lots sold must, in all the cemeteries, be kept in nice order. Improvements are continually going on, and, as a general thing, all the incomes are spent in this way. In Saint John's cemetery lots 15 feet square sell for from $30 to $50.

MARKETS.

Covington has 3 market-houses, each about 250 by 40 feet in dimensions, arranged as follows:

Seventh Street market, 15 butcher-stalls, 20 huckster-stands, and about 2,000 feet in length outside for wagons.

Eleventh Street market, 8 butcher-stalls, 35 huckster-stands, and about 4,000 feet in length outside for wagons.

Sixth Street market, 8 butcher-stalls, 35 huckster-stands, and about 4,000 feet in length outside for wagons.

Butcher-stalls, 9 feet in width, rent for $18 per annum; the other stands are sold at auction, and bring from $5 to $36 yearly. The total rental of all the markets for 1880 was $2,000. The markets are open daily from daylight to 10 or 11 o'clock a. m. The gross annual sales from each stall will average about $2,000. Nearly 75 per cent. of the retail supply of meats, poultry, fish, and vegetables for the city is sold in these markets. The market-houses are brick piers, covered with roofs. The wholesale distribution of meats is done early in the morning. Beef is killed the previous evening or during the night, put on ice, and kept there till sold. There is no meat-inspector at the slaughter-houses. Some of the meat is brought from Cincinnati. Some vegetables, etc., are sold by peddlers.

SANITARY AUTHORITY—BOARD OF HEALTH.

The title of the chief health organization of Covington is the "board of health", which consists of 5 members of the city council, appointed by that body, none of whom need be physicians. The board is controlled by the city council. In ordinary times the board incurs no expense, and during an epidemic the expenses are regulated by the council. In the absence of an epidemic the board has authority only to direct the street commissioners to keep the streets clean and to have the garbage collected. During epidemics its authority is limited to the directions of the city council. The chief executive officer of the board is the health officer, whose duties are to carry out and enforce all sanitary laws and the orders of the board; to serve notices for the abatement of nuisances, and, in addition, to report all contagious diseases. His salary is $60 per month. He has all the powers of a policeman, and, in addition, power to act as overseer of the poor. The street commissioner acts as a sanitary inspector to a certain extent, as do all the policemen, but beyond these no assistant health officers or inspectors are employed. The mode of transacting the business of the board is very informal; ordinarily they come together at rare intervals in committee, during summer only, on call of the chairman. Inspections are not made regularly. When nuisances are reported they are ordered to be abated, and if this is not done the parties responsible are prosecuted in the mayor's court. In cases of defective house-drainage, privy-vaults, cesspools, or sources of drinking-water, if the evil is flagrant, the sanitary policeman reports the same to the board and mayor and corrective action is taken.

INFECTIOUS DISEASES.

If possible, small-pox patients are removed to the pest-house belonging to the city, situated 3 miles distant on the poor-house farm, or the house is blockaded and intercourse with the inmates is interdicted. Scarlet-fever patients are not isolated. In case of the breaking out of contagious diseases either in public or in private schools the board takes cognizance of the fact, but exercises no control. Should circumstances seem to require it, the school board would close the schools. Vaccination is compulsory, and in the case of the indigent is done at the public expense by the district physicians. The city is divided into 4 sanitary districts, each having a physician who attends to the calls of the poor, and who receives a small salary from the city.

There is no system for the registration of births, diseases, and deaths.

REPORTS. .

The board reports to the city council, but there has rarely been any need for a report.

MUNICIPAL CLEANSING.

Street-cleaning.—Streets are cleaned wholly by hand by the city's own force, under direction of the street commissioner. This cleaning is done irregularly as it seems to be needed, and is done reasonably well. The annual cost of the work to the city is $8,000, and the sweepings are used as filling for low places.

Removal of garbage and ashes.—Garbage is removed by the city, the work being done under contract. There are no regulations concerning the conservancy of garbage while awaiting removal, but it is usually put in barrels or other vessels, and must be kept separate from the ashes. Garbage and ashes are taken outside of the city limits and dumped in the places assigned for them. The removal cost the city during 1879, $4,095 61. No nuisance or injury to health is known to be caused by the improper handling or disposal of the garbage.

Dead animals.—Dogs and cats are usually buried on the premises; hogs, cattle, and horses are sold to a fertilizing company. A city ordinance requires that dead animals left by their owners unremoved for a longer period than five hours shall be forfeited to the city. The possession of these carcasses falls to the garbage contractor, but as they represent a certain value, the owners generally remove them before the five hours expire.

Liquid household wastes.—In the case of houses connected with the public sewers the wastes are disposed of through the sewers; but most of the wastes, including chamber-slops, are deposited in privy-vaults on the premises, though kitchen and laundry wastes usually run into the gutters. No dry wells or cesspools to speak of are in use in Covington. Street-gutters receive no artificial flushing. Wells for drinking-water are not used, the supply for this purpose being obtained either from the water-works or from rain-water cisterns.

Human excreta.—Only a small portion of the houses in the city have water-closets, the greater number depending on privy-vaults. Very few of the water-closets deliver into sewers, most of them running into privy-vaults, none of which are water-tight. There are no regulations as to the construction of privy-vaults; in some cases it is aimed to dig them so deep as to strike a substratum of gravel. In case of a vault becoming dangerously full its emptying would be ordered by the health officer. A city ordinance requires the cleaning of privies and vaults by licensed persons alone during May, June, July, August, and September, only between the hours of 11 p. m. and 4 a. m., and during the balance of the year between the hours of 10 p. m. and 5 a. m. Night-soil is not allowed to be deposited within the city limits except in the Ohio river below Ferry street, and none is allowed on land within the gathering-ground of the public water-supply. The dry-earth system is not used.

Manufacturing wastes.—Liquid and solid manufacturing wastes are either run into sewers or some ravine, or thrown into the Ohio river.

POLICE.

No report on this subject was received.

MANUFACTURES.

The following is a summary of the statistics of the manufactures of Covington for 1880, being taken from tables prepared for the Tenth Census by **J. M. Blackburn**, special agent:

Mechanical and manufacturing industries.	No. of establishments.	Capital.	AVERAGE NUMBER OF HANDS EMPLOYED.			Total amount paid in wages during the year.	Value of materials.	Value of products.
			Males above 16 years.	Females above 15 years.	Children and youths.			
All industries..	181	$3,182,141	2,251	223	451	$1,033,463	$3,935,727	$5,864,530
Blacksmithing..	8	14,700	27	....	....	10,878	6,500	24,200
Boots and shoes, including custom work and repairing	11	19,650	28	4	....	8,120	8,450	23,100
Boxes, wooden packing..	4	2,350	9	....	2	3,372	7,172	14,350
Bread and other bakery products	20	39,050	24	7	3	9,176	52,458	88,840
Brick and tile	9	6,200	73	....	21	14,650	15,100	40,795
Carpentering	8	12,750	29	....	....	14,486	66,400	93,600
Carriages and wagons..	4	40,700	39	....	....	18,156	22,200	51,500
Cooperage	6	2,660	35	....	....	10,265	18,340	34,070
Flouring- and grist-mill products	5	73,000	33	....	....	12,433	223,224	246,312
Furniture, chairs	4	1,850	6	....	1	2,500	3,450	7,600
Iron and steel...	3	730,000	533	....	32	281,925	663,705	1,012,004
Iron railing, wrought	3	7,500	26	....	....	8,200	10,560	25,480
Leather, tanned	3	37,000	39	....	....	15,900	301,106	330,150
Liquors, distilled	3	255,000	91	....	1	38,775	425,500	635,000
Liquors, malt...	4	319,129	94	....	....	43,912	188,395	313,659
Marble and stone work..	7	12,500	33	....	....	15,417	28,600	67,330
Saddlery and harness	4	13,500	20	....	1	7,600	14,700	27,421
Slaughtering and meat-packing, not including retail butchering	3	30,500	10	....	....	5,384	98,900	111,000
Tinware, copperware, and sheet-iron ware	5	16,700	15	1	....	5,223	8,921	17,558
Tobacco, chewing, smoking, and snuff (see also Tobacco, cigars and cigarettes).	13	581,500	279	88	161	150,202	1,057,339	1,395,533
Tobacco, cigars and cigarettes (see also Tobacco, chewing, smoking, and snuff).	15	40,627	57	1	21	22,453	56,659	100,422
All other industries (a)	39	925,275	751	122	208	334,436	658,048	1,204,606

a Embracing agricultural implements; brooms and brushes; carpets, rag; clothing, men's; coffee and spices, roasted and ground; cordage and twine; foundery and machine-shop products; furniture; glass; grease and tallow; hardware; iron nails and spikes, cut and wrought; iron work, architectural and ornamental; leather, curried; lumber, planed; lumber, sawed; mineral and soda waters; painting and paperhanging; patent medicines and compounds; pickles, preserves, and sauces; pumps; shipbuilding; sporting goods; stationery goods; upholstering; vinegar; wirework; wood, turned and carved; and woolen goods.

From the foregoing table it appears that the average capital of all establishments is $17,580 89; that the average wages of all hands employed is $353 32 per annum; that the average outlay in wages, in materials, and in interest (at 6 per cent.) on capital employed is $28,508 94.

LEXINGTON,
FAYETTE COUNTY, KENTUCKY.

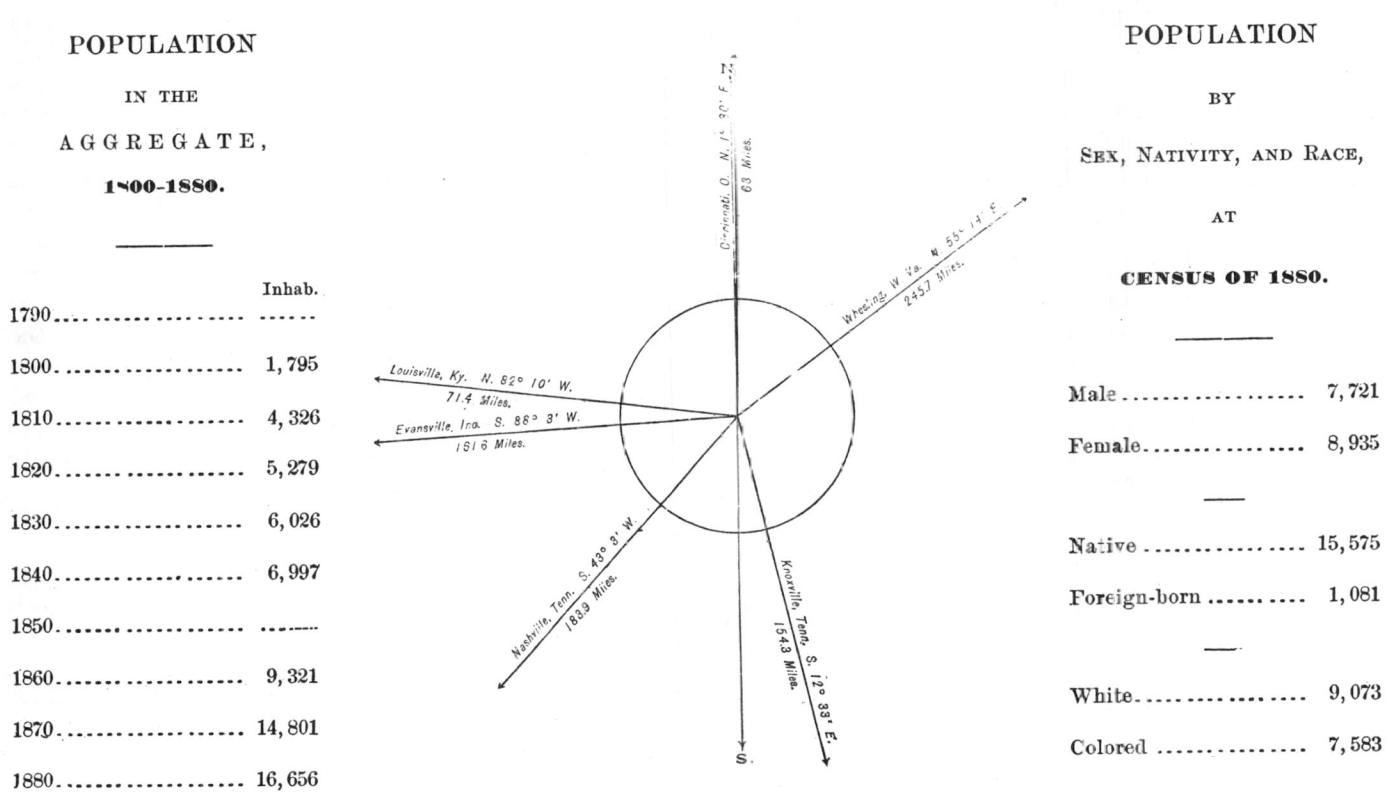

POPULATION
IN THE
AGGREGATE,
1800-1880.

	Inhab.
1790	......
1800	1,795
1810	4,326
1820	5,279
1830	6,026
1840	6,997
1850	......
1860	9,321
1870	14,801
1880	16,656

POPULATION
BY
SEX, NATIVITY, AND RACE,
AT
CENSUS OF 1880.

Male	7,721
Female	8,935
Native	15,575
Foreign-born	1,081
White	9,073
Colored	7,583

Latitude: 38° 7' North; Longitude: 84° 32' (west from Greenwich); Altitude: 906 to 1,025 feet.

FINANCIAL CONDITION:

Total Valuation: $4,964,005; per capita: $298 00.   Net Indebtedness: $112,000; per capita: $6 72.   Tax per $100: $1 63.

HISTORICAL SKETCH.

In May, 1775, a party of hunters, encamped on the Town fork of the Elkhorn river, Kentucky, were startled and shocked by the news of the battle of Lexington, Massachusetts. So much impressed by the news were they that they gave the name "Lexington" to the place of their encampment, and when, four years later, a regular settlement was begun there, the name thus given was retained. Lexington was settled by a party of Virginians, and in its beginning was sufficiently humble. The future city then contained only a block-house and three rows of cabins. It was incorporated in 1782 by the legislature of Virginia, and after an interval of bitter warfare with the Indians entered upon a period of steady and uninterrupted growth, which lasted until 1810, when the population had increased to about 3,000. The location of the town in the center of the richest and fairest part of Kentucky,

117

and the business enterprise of its citizens, promised to make Lexington not only the capital of Kentucky, but also the metropolis of the state, and in 1810 it was the most important town in the state, and the business center of a district which included the now far greater cities of Cincinnati and Louisville.

Only a year after the settlement the Transylvania seminary was founded, and the basis was thus laid of the reputation for educational facilities which the city still retains. In 1798 the seminary was united with the Kentucky academy to form the Transylvania university, the oldest of the western colleges. In the same year a Mr. West is claimed to have succeeded in propelling a boat by steam in the river at Lexington, thus antedating the voyage of the "Clermont" by nine years.

Whether or not the honor of inventing the steamboat belongs to Lexington, the introduction of steam navigation on the western rivers influenced its future greatly. The inland situation of the town prevented it from reaping the advantages which accrued to Louisville and Cincinnati from the introduction of steamboats. Its trade was drawn away, and a period of great depression followed. Since 1820 the growth has been slow, and in the sixty years which have intervened since then the population has only little more than tripled, a rate of increase which, however satisfactory in itself, is far below that of most of the western cities.

A little more than a mile from Lexington, at his beautiful home, Ashland, lived Henry Clay, the great son of Kentucky.

The manufactures of Lexington began in 1801, with the establishment of a cut-nail factory; and in 1810 this small beginning had already been followed by great results. There were 3 nail factories, 4 paper-mills, 4 cabinet-shops, 6 powder-mills, 7 brick-yards, 5 hat factories, 13 ropewalks, 7 distilleries, 5 bagging factories, and many other prosperous manufacturing establishments. In 1831 Lexington was incorporated as a city. Two years later it suffered severely from a visitation of cholera, which for a time put a stop to all trade and communication; and yet more severely in 1849, when the same plague again fell upon the city. These have been the only great misfortunes of Lexington, which has escaped almost entirely from losses by fire and flood. The building of the Lexington and Ohio railroad from Lexington via Frankfort to Louisville, and another somewhat later to Covington, increased the importance of the city, and in some degree compensated for its lack of direct water communication with the Mississippi valley. In 1865 the Kentucky state university was moved from Harrodsburg, where it had been founded in 1858, to Lexington, and Transylvania university was consolidated with it. This university in 1872 had a library of 20,000 volumes, a corps of 20 professors, and 6 other officers, while the names of 579 students were enrolled on its books. The schools of Lexington maintain their early excellence. Its churches are numerous, its charities are large. There are several newspapers, daily, semi-weekly, and weekly, published in the city.

LEXINGTON IN 1880.

The following statistical accounts, collected by the Census Office, indicate the present condition of Lexington.

LOCATION.

Lexington, the fourth city in size of Kentucky, and once the capital of the state, is situated in latitude 38° 7' north, longitude 84° 32' west from Greenwich, on the Town fork of the Elkhorn river. The lowest point is 906 feet, the highest 1,025 feet, above the level of the sea. The city is not on navigable water.

RAILROAD COMMUNICATIONS.

The Louisville, Cincinnati, and Lexington railroad connects the city with Cincinnati and Louisville; the Kentucky Central with Covington; the Lexington and Big Sandy with Mount Sterling; and the Cincinnati Southern with Cincinnati, and Chattanooga, Tennessee.

TRIBUTARY COUNTRY.

Lexington is situated in the so-called "blue-grass region" of Kentucky, a region celebrated for its fertility. The surrounding country is devoted almost exclusively to agriculture. The principal crop is hemp; corn is extensively cultivated, and wheat and oats are raised in a smaller degree. Fruit is neglected. The pasture-lands are very fine, and stock-raising is a well-established industry. The manufacturing interests are small, and principally devoted to preparing the raw product for finished manufacture elsewhere.

TOPOGRAPHY.

Lexington is situated on the axis of the so-called Cincinnati anticlinal, which in this region is comparatively unbroken, though rolling enough to give a good natural drainage. The rock—blue limestone—furnishes a rich red soil, and, being somewhat cavernous, makes the streams small and the living springs few. The land slopes to a lawn-level in the country to the east and west. Marshes are rarely found, and there are no lakes, though artificial ponds are numerous. The country is wooded in places where the old forests have been left standing, but in general is open.

CLIMATE.

No authentic record of the temperature has been kept. The highest summer temperature in average years is about 98° F., while the lowest winter temperature in such years rarely falls below —8°. The prevailing wind in summer comes from the southwest, while the winter winds are changeable, bringing frequent sudden changes. The city is higher than the surrounding country within a radius of about 100 miles, and is therefore unprotected by elevated lands in its vicinity.

STREETS.

The total length of the streets of Lexington is 31 miles, and of this distance only 18.7 miles are paved. The cost of this pavement (macadam) is 35 cents per square yard. A few short alleys are paved in the middle with stone blocks, to allow the flow of drainage through them. The cost of repairs on the streets in 1879 was $7,289 27. Turnpike companies kept 5½ miles of road in repair, and this expense is not included in the above amount. The sidewalks are almost exclusively of brick laid in coal-ashes, and rendered uneven by constant wear and the growth of tree-roots underneath them. The gutters are mostly square drains with curbs on both sides; some are flat slabs of limestone, laid at an angle to the curbstone, while newly laid gutters are made of blocks forming a concave drain. All are open, except at street-crossings. Trees, largely white maple, are planted along the streets. There are no horse-railroads. The omnibus lines have 6 omnibuses, 3 baggage-wagons, and 18 horses, and employ 13 men. The fare for a single passenger is 25 cents; if he has a trunk the fare is 40 cents. These lines run from the railway depot to various parts of the city.

WATER-WORKS.

The city has no public water-supply.

GAS.

Lexington is supplied with gas by a private corporation. The average daily production is 14,000 cubic feet; the charge per 1,000 feet is $3. The city pays $35 a year for each of its 218 gas street-lamps.

PUBLIC BUILDINGS.

The city owns a city hall, valued at $20,000. No information in regard to other municipal buildings belonging to the city was furnished.

PUBLIC PARKS AND PLEASURE-GROUNDS.

No information on this subject was furnished.

PLACES OF AMUSEMENT.

Lexington has but one theater, the Opera House, capable of seating 800 persons. No license is paid by theaters. There is one hall used for lecture and concert purposes. There are no concert- and beer-gardens.

DRAINAGE.

The drainage is naturally into the Elkhorn river, a branch of which flows through the city. For a distance of one or two squares on either side of the branch the lots are drained by an irregular system of sewers emptying into the branch. The rest of the city has no sewers. Such sewers as exist are about 18 inches square, are built of limestone, and follow no regular plan of construction. The gutters on the streets are simply open drains, and deliver direct into the sewers at the crossings. There are no manholes. No sewers have been built for a number of years. The mouths of the sewers are exposed; they empty direct into the branch, and the deposits formed at the mouths are washed away only whenever the branch gets high enough. The mouths are scraped once a month to keep the outlet open. No artificial flushing is resorted to. The cost of the scraping is about $12 per month, and the entire cost of construction and maintenance is paid by the city.

CEMETERIES.

There are 2 cemeteries now in use, and 5 in which interments are no longer made.

Lexington Cemetery, area 60 acres, is situated at the city limits, about 1 mile from the center, on the Lexington and Leestown turnpike. It is the property of a corporation, and is divided into lots, which are sold at an average price of $100. There have been 7,347 interments in this cemetery.

New Catholic Cemetery, area 20 acres, is situated near Lexington cemetery, and, like that, is beautifully laid out. It is owned and controlled by the Catholic church. It was opened in 1875, and since then 524 interments have been made within it.

The following burial grounds are no longer in use, and no statement of the number of interments within them can be made:

Old Episcopal Grave-yard, area 1 acre, situated on Winchester street, on the eastern edge of the city.

The *Catholic Cemetery*, area 2 acres, adjoining Episcopal.

Presbyterian, on Mulberry street near the city limits, and near the two preceding grounds.

Baptist Church-yard, area about 1 acre, situated on Main and Short streets near the city center.

The *Old City Grave-yard*, area 1 acre, situated in the southwestern part of the city.

All these are very old. Many of the bodies have been removed to the other cemeteries.

Graves in all the cemeteries must be 6 feet deep. There is no limit of time after death within which burials must be made; bodies will be kept twenty-one days during the summer in a public vault, and during the winter for an unlimited time. No burial permits are necessary.

MARKETS.

There is but one public market. This occupies the entire lower story of the city-hall building, is about 300 feet long and 50 feet wide, and contains 54 stalls. It is situated near the center of the city between Upper, Vine, Limestone, and Water streets. The space along Water and Vine streets on either side of the building is occupied by wagons. Meat-stalls rent at $40 per annum, vegetable-stalls at $30. The total rental averages about $1,500 per annum. It is open Tuesdays, Thursdays, and Saturdays; in the winter from 9 a. m. until noon; in the summer from 4 a. m. to 9 a. m. The gross amount of the annual sales can not be ascertained. About one-third of the retail supply of meat, poultry, fish, and vegetables is obtained from the market.

SANITARY AUTHORITY.

The chief sanitary authority of the city is a committee on health, one of the regular standing committees of the city council. Its authority is such as the council gives it from time to time, and its expenses are whatever the council allows. The chief officer is the chairman of the committee; he receives no salary, and his powers are only to preside at meetings of the committee and to report to the city council. No regular time for the meetings is established. A health officer is employed by the committee, who has police powers, and makes regular inspections throughout the city. The ordinances of the city empower the council to appoint a regular board of health, but it has never done so.

NUISANCES.

Nuisances are inspected by the health officer, and orders are issued to the owner or occupant of the premises to remove or abate them. If this order is disregarded, a fine is incurred for each day of delay. Defective house-drainage, privy-vaults, cesspools, and sources of drinking-water are treated as nuisances. The health officer sees that the streets are kept clean. The city ordinances do not prohibit casting filth into the stream which flows through the city, but compel the persons living on the banks to remove any obstructions in it and keep it clean.

BURIAL OF THE DEAD.

No interment is allowed to be made in any place except the burial-grounds authorized by the mayor and council. Graves must be at least 6 feet deep. No other regulations exist.

INFECTIOUS DISEASES.

Small-pox patients are removed to a small-pox hospital, unless proper arrangements can be made for caring for them at home. Scarlet-fever patients are neither isolated nor quarantined in any way. Any person who knows of the existence of any case of small-pox, yellow fever, or other dangerous, contagious, or infectious disease in the city is required to give notice of it to the mayor. The city has at present no pest-house, a former building for the purpose having been destroyed by fire. Vaccination, under the city ordinances, is compulsory whenever the city council thinks it necessary; and no pupil is admitted to the public schools until he has been successfully vaccinated. Vaccination is done at public expense for those unable to pay for it.

REPORTS.

The committee reports to the city council from time to time, and the health officer reports each month.

The law requires that physicians shall make an annual report of births, diseases, and deaths to the county clerk, to be transmitted to the secretary of the state board of health; but this law is not fully complied with.

MUNICIPAL CLEANSING.

Street-cleaning.—The streets are cleaned by the property-owners, and the dirt is then removed by a contractor paid by the city. The work is done wholly by hand, and whenever ordered by the chief of police. The cleaning is done only at long intervals and very poorly. The sweepings are used in grading out lots.

Removal of garbage and ashes.—Garbage and ashes are removed by the householders and dumped outside the city. No regulations govern the conservancy of garbage, which may be kept in the same vessel with ashes. The city authorities claim that no injury to the public health is known to have resulted under this system.

Dead animals are removed by the owners to the potter's field and there buried. No record of the number so disposed of is kept.

Liquid household wastes.—Only a small part of the liquid household wastes of the city passes into the public sewers; considerable is run directly into the street-gutters, and the rest goes into cesspools which are porous, and, if provided with overflows, deliver into the street-gutters and sewers. The gutters are flushed by the rain. In some cases the cesspools receive the wastes of water-closets. A number of wells have been contaminated by the overflow and soakage from cesspools, but no particular attention is paid to it. The contents of the cesspools, in cleaning them, are emptied into a fresh hole dug close by the pool, and the hole is then filled in with clay. The system is confessedly poor.

Human excreta.—There are only a few water-closets in the city, nearly all the houses depending on privy-vaults, which by the city ordinances must be at least 5 feet deep, unless resting on solid rock, in which case they must be 4 feet deep. The vaults must be walled up with stone, brick, or wood. They must be well limed in May and June, and again in August and September. Some of the water-closets, chiefly those in the business portion of the city, deliver into the public sewers. The dry-earth system is used to a small extent.

Manufacturing wastes.—There are very little of these to dispose of.

POLICE.

The police force of Lexington is sometimes appointed by the city council, sometimes elected by the people, the determination of the method resting with the council, and is governed by the council. The chief executive officer is the chief of police and city marshal, who acts also as captain of the day police; his salary is $25 per month and fees. The rest of the force consists of a captain of night police, salary $60 per month; a lieutenant, salary $52 50; and 14 patrolmen, salary $52 50 each. Of the patrolmen there are 3 privates from each of the 4 wards, and 2 extra men. The uniform is of dark blue cloth, and provided by the men, the suits costing $30 each. The men are armed with revolver and club, furnished by the men, and are on duty 12 hours each day, patrolling about 6 miles of streets. No record has been kept of the number of arrests, the amount of property lost or stolen and reported to the police, or the number of station-house lodgers. The force co-operates with the fire department at fires. Special policemen are appointed by the mayor on election days, and have the same position as members of the regular force. During 1880 one member of the force was killed. No record of the cost of the police force in 1880 could be obtained. The expense in 1879 was $11,080 76.

LOUISVILLE,

JEFFERSON COUNTY, KENTUCKY.

POPULATION

IN THE

AGGREGATE,

1800-1880.

	Inhab.
1790	......
1800	359
1810	1,357
1820	4,012
1830	10,341
1840	21,210
1850	43,194
1860	68,033
1870	100,753
1880	123,758

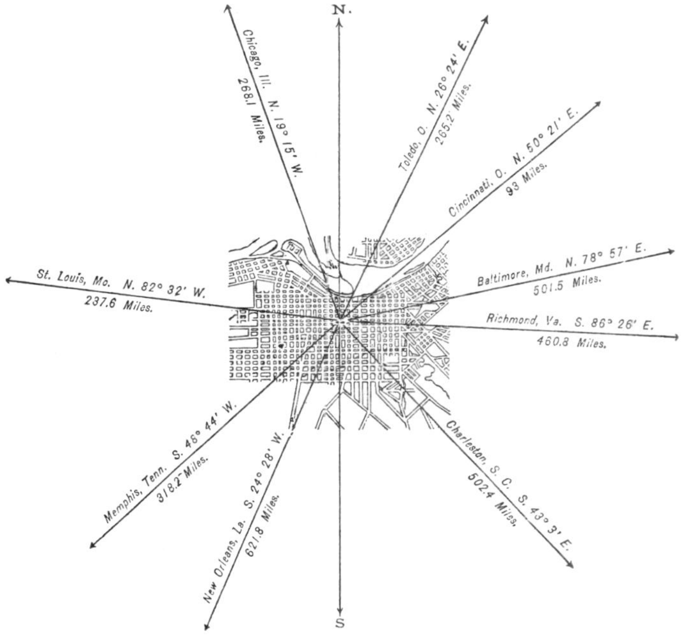

POPULATION

BY

SEX, NATIVITY, AND RACE,

AT

CENSUS OF 1880.

Male	58,982
Female	64,776
Native	100,602
Foreign-born	23,156
White	102,847
Colored	*20,911

* Including 5 Chinese and 1 Indian.

Latitude: 38° 15′ North; Longitude: 85° 50′ (west from Greenwich); **Average altitude: 456.5 feet.**

FINANCIAL CONDITION:

Total Valuation: $65,809,000; per capita: $532 00.   Net Indebtedness: $4,849,935; per capita: $39 19.   Tax per $100: $2 28.

HISTORICAL SKETCH.

The site of Louisville was occupied as early as 1773 by a surveying party under Captain Thomas Bullitt. The first settlement of Louisville was made by 13 families who accompanied Colonel George R. Clarke on his expedition down the Ohio in 1778. The situation was so exposed to Indian attacks that the settlers first established themselves on Corn island, an island at the head of the falls near the Kentucky shore, which has since disappeared. On the reception of the news of the capture of Vincennes by Colonel Clarke's forces, the colony removed to the mainland and built a station. In 1780 the town was laid out and called Louisville, in honor of Louis XVI of France, whose troops were then aiding the Americans in their struggle for independence. It was incorporated as a city in 1828, when its population was about 10,000. Its growth since then has been generally steady, even rapid. In 1822 the

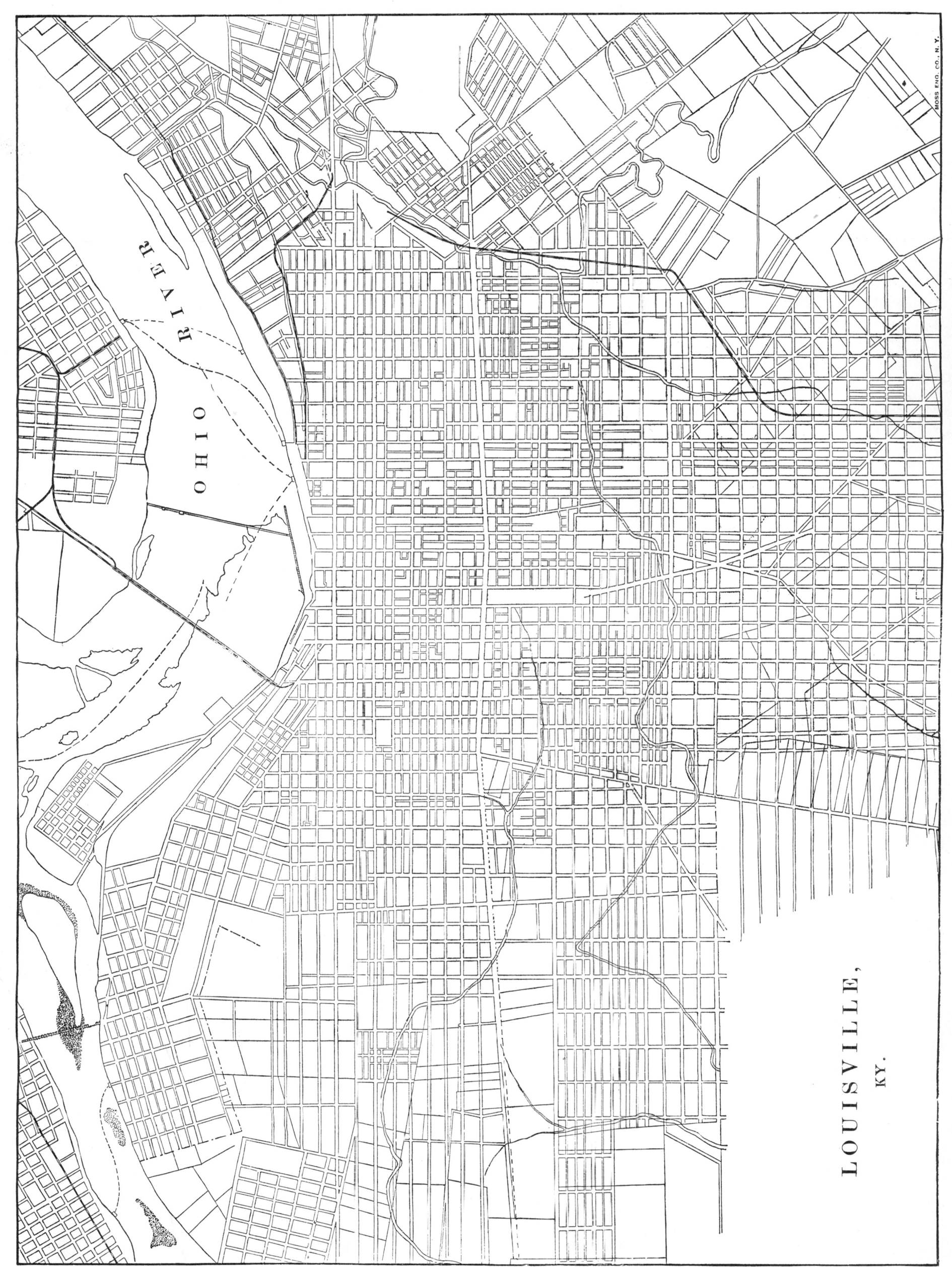

OHIO RIVER

LOUISVILLE, KY.

MOSS ENG. CO., N. Y.

place suffered from an epidemic of fever, being almost depopulated thereby. The recovery took several years, and business suffered severely, as it did also 10 years later after the flood of 1832. The city suffered more or less from the general panic in business from 1837 to 1840, and the great fire in the latter year, by which 30 stores and factories were destroyed (loss $300,000), augmented and prolonged its effect.

The first settlers were Pennsylvanians and Virginians. The Virginia or southern element has always been in the ascendency, at first owing to the facts of its settlement, and, since emancipation, owing to the intimate relations which have sprung up with the South by reason of the location and the railroad connections of the city. The German element has recently exerted large influence in forming the character of the city. The German language is taught in public schools.

LOUISVILLE IN 1880.

The following statistical accounts, collected by the Census Office, indicate the present condition of Louisville:

LOCATION.

Louisville, the chief city of Kentucky and the capital of Jefferson county, lies on the south side of the Ohio river at the upper end of the "falls of the Ohio", where Bear Grass creek enters the river, in latitude 38° 15' north, longitude 85° 50' west. The city has about 8 miles of water-front. Except in extremely dry seasons, when boats can not pass even the canal, navigation is always open. In high stages of the river the falls almost disappear, and steamboats pass over them; but when the water is low the whole width of the river has the appearance of a great many broken cascades of foam making their way over the rapids. To obviate the obstruction to navigation caused by these falls, a canal 2½ miles long was cut around them on the Kentucky side to Shipping Port, now included in Louisville. This was a work of vast labor, the canal, for the greater part of its course, being cut through the solid rock, and cost nearly $100,000. Louisville has thus communication by water with the great cities of Cincinnati, Pittsburgh, etc., above, and with all the river towns of the Mississippi and Ohio below.

RAILROAD COMMUNICATIONS.

Louisville has ample railroad facilities, as is shown by the following list of her roads:

The Ohio and Mississippi railroad, from Cincinnati to Saint Louis, connecting with Louisville by a branch from North Vernon, Indiana.

The Jeffersonville, Madison, and Indianapolis railroad, from Louisville to Indianapolis (operated by the Pennsylvania Railroad Company).

The Louisville, New Albany, and Chicago railroad, from Louisville to Michigan City.

The Louisville and Nashville railroad, one line of which runs from Louisville to Memphis, one to New Orleans, one to Saint Louis, and several minor branches to different points in the South.

The Louisville, Cincinnati, and Lexington railroad, to the cities named.

TRIBUTARY COUNTRY.

In the country tributary to Louisville, corn, wheat, rye, oats, hay, tobacco, hemp, and barley are largely raised, finding here a market. Much whisky is manufactured in the district, and large quantities of lumber from the interior of the state are shipped to and from here. As a matter of fact, much of the famed blue-grass region of the state may be considered as tributary to its chief city.

TOPOGRAPHY.

The city is situated on an alluvial plain, in a bend of the river, above which it is not greatly elevated. A few feet from the surface is found a deposit of sand and gravel sometimes 30 feet in thickness. Near the east and southern limits the land rises, and for miles away is undulating uplands. At the base of the hills, and in the bed of the river at low water, a fine limestone crops out, and is largely quarried for local building use and for making cement. At one time many ponds existed, to which were ascribed the existence of malarial fevers, but these have since been drained. In the immediate vicinity the soil is very fertile and has been mostly cleared of its original growth of trees; enough of these are left, however, on spots reserved for pasturage and around the farm-houses to make a pleasing landscape.

CLIMATE.

From records extending from 1874 to 1879, inclusive, the following figures are obtained: Highest summer temperature (July and August, 1874), 102°; highest mean summer temperature (1879), 82.5°. Lowest winter temperature (January, 1875 and 1879), −10°; lowest mean winter temperature (1876), 30.8°. Highest mean temperature of any year (1874), 58°. The prevailing winds are from the south. These moderate the temperature in winter, and cause frequent rains in summer; hence excessive droughts, as well as long cold periods, are rare.

STREETS.

The paved streets of Louisville are of a total length of 130.18 miles, and her alleys are about 25 miles in length. The streets are paved with the following materials: Cobble-stones, 13.55 miles; stone blocks (1 square), 0.1 mile; asphalt or other composition (2 squares), 0.2 mile; broken stone, 106.03 miles; wood, 7.64 miles; gravel, 2.76 miles.

The cost per square yard of most of this, which may be estimated, is: Cobble-stones, $1 15; broken stone, $0 63. No late contracts have been made for wooden paving. That first laid was by the Nicholson system, but repairs to it are made by the Wyckoff method, and, being laid on the original foundation, cost $0 45 per square yard. Street-making is done by contract.

The total cost of street repairs in 1879 was $26,501 16, and was divided among the different sorts of pavement thus: Broken stone, $12,303 50; cobble-stones, $2,917 88; wooden pavement, $2,887 06; gutters and alleys, $8,392 72, the work being performed by contract.

As to the relative facility with which each is kept clean it is stated that "wood pavement, until it begins to wear out, is most easily kept clean. Bowlders (cobble-stone) rank next. Broken stone always dirty". Street-cleaning costs annually about $40,000.

Concerning quality and permanent economy of each it is stated:

Experience here has been in favor of macadam for economy, though the tendency is now to change to bowlder and wood, as the street-cleaning bill (a constant outlay) is much less.

Sidewalks are laid with brick, and vary in width from 8 to 20 feet, while gutters are paved with stone blocks. The planting of trees is practiced upon the outer edge of the sidewalks. On residence streets these occur at intervals of not more than 20 or 30 feet, and often less. In the street work a steam stone-crusher and a roller are used, it is stated, with the following good effect:

[It] saves 33 per cent. of repairs on macadam streets; drainage is largely facilitated, sanitation, in consequence, advanced, and transportation economized, by securing more speed and less wear and tear.

From a report on "Street pavements", made by R. T. Scowden, city engineer, to the mayor, dated May 1, 1880, the following extract is taken:

I desire to call attention to two grievous abuses to which our thoroughfares are subjected: One is excessive street-sprinkling and the other excessive loading. Instead of dampening the streets to lay the dust, they are literally flooded with water. Neither bowlder nor wooden pavements can withstand the injurious effects of such treatment, and our broken-stone repairs are so softened by saturation that they are resolved into mud almost as soon as made.

The destructive effects of heavy hauling can be better appreciated when it is known that, upon our saturated streets, it is not uncommon for wagons with narrow tires to carry as much freight as an ordinary railroad-car. Granite would soon succumb to such heavy burdens.

The ordinance regulating the loads of vehicles used in hauling merchandise, with a view to the protection of street pavements, very prudently fixed the maximum loads for four-wheeled wagons with tires of 6 inches at not to exceed 8,000 pounds, or 4 tons, and 3,500 pounds, or 1¾ tons, for tires of 2½ inches in width. Drays and carts, or two-wheeled vehicles, are limited to 5,000 pounds, or 2½ tons, for 6-inch tires, and 2,500 pounds, or 1¼ tons, for 2½-inch tires. No ordinance is more persistently violated than this one. Wagons with loads exceeding 12,000 pounds, or 6 tons, upon 2½- and 3-inch tires, and drays with 3-inch tires, having loads exceeding 4,000 pounds, or 2 tons, daily traverse Main street and cut it into ruts, depressions, and ruptures. And there are frequent instances where blocks of marble weighing 12 and 16 tons, or 24,000 and 32,000 pounds, are hauled over the streets.

Economy to the business man in transportation is a heavy drain upon the tax-payer for street repairs. Iron rails have been found too weak to withstand such severe traffic. Bowlder pavements, therefore, which are the most difficult streets to keep in repair, are continually broken up from the injurious effects of excessive loading. If the ordinance regulating loading is correct, it should be enforced, or if the business interests would suffer from its enforcement, the ordinance should be changed. One fact, however, must be remembered, and that is that cheap transportation obtained from excessive loading is at the constant and increased cost of street repairs. No street yet invented has been able to resist such heavy burdens; and no city in Europe or America permits one-half the weight, upon narrow tires, to be hauled over their streets to which ours are subjected.

HORSE-RAILROADS, ETC.

The horse-railroads of Louisville lack but 383 yards of being 50 miles in length. They employ 173 cars, 726 horses and mules, and 323 men. The fare charged is 5 cents, and during a year about 8,000,000 passengers are carried.

There are no regular omnibus lines in the city, but vehicles to the number of 20 ply between the railroad stations and the hotels and all parts of the city. These employ 40 men and 50 horses, carry during a year about 110,000 passengers, and charge a fare of 50 cents with baggage and of 25 cents without.

WATER-WORKS.

The water-works are owned by the Louisville Water Company. The water is taken from the Ohio river, and is pumped into 2 reservoirs and a stand-pipe. The pressure is from 43 to 60 pounds. The average amount pumped per diem is 5,000,000 gallons, the greatest 7,500,000, and the least 4,000,000 gallons. The average cost of raising 1,000,000 gallons 1 foot high is 5.35 cents. The total yearly expenses (except interest, $54,000) is $23,500. The yearly income from water-rates is $175,000. Many double-piston and a few rotary water-meters are used; 3.4 per cent. of the water-takers use them, while 27 per cent. of the volume of water distributed is metered. Waste of water is undoubtedly restrained thereby. The total cost of the works has been $3,500,000.

GAS.

The gas-works are owned by a private company. The daily average production is 462,825 cubic feet. The charge per 1,000 feet is $2 35. The city pays for each street-lamp, exclusive of lighting and maintenance, $19 03; there are 2,500 of these lamps. The income from meter-rents is $1,249 35; from the total sales of gas, $316,871 41.

PUBLIC BUILDINGS.

The city owns the city hall and a number of station-houses. The former cost about $500,000.

PUBLIC PARKS AND PLEASURE-GROUNDS.

Louisville has no large public parks. *Central Park*, area 4 acres, and *Floral Park*, area 2 acres, both near the center of the city, are pleasant spots and are largely resorted to during the hot weather of summer. An entrance fee is charged at these grounds. The streets of the city, being wide (from 50 to 200 feet), are very liberally planted with shade-trees, and the lots in the resident localities being large—minimum size 6,000 square feet—the want of parks has not been very severely felt. A zoological garden is about being started, the grounds to have an area of 166 acres. Buildings have already been erected thereon at a cost of $58,000. These grounds are easy of access and are distant from the business center. The water-works company is also improving its grounds of about 100 acres as a park.

PLACES OF AMUSEMENT.

The following is a list of the theaters, with their seating capacities: Macauley's, 1,500 to 2,000; Opera-house (public library), 1,500; Knickerbocker (variety), 1,200; Metropolitan (variety), 1,300, and the Masonic temple, 1,200.

Of concert-halls and lecture-rooms there are: Liederkranz hall, Young Men's Christian Association hall, Eclipse hall, Avenue hall, and Exposition building.

Of concert- and beer-gardens there are three: Woodlawn garden, Phœnix hill, and National garden. These are patronized largely on Sundays. Concerts are given in the evening. They are situated in the suburbs of the city, and the grounds of each are ample for the accommodation of thousands. The better class attend these places only on special occasions, when the grounds are exclusively secured by contract with the proprietors.

DRAINAGE.

The ground on which Louisville is built is like the bottom-lands all along the Ohio river. Its surface is quite even and about 50 feet above the ordinary level of the river. The natural soil is a light loam over a hard stiff clay, in all about 15 feet deep, resting on a stratum of sand and gravel extending to a depth of from 40 to 60 feet. Water is found at various depths, according to the level of the water in the river, and affords an ample supply to numerous wells, both public and private. The stratum of sand and gravel is also made to serve another purpose, both useful and convenient. If cellars are damp or hold water, a small well or pipe sunk through the clay to the sand will usually afford relief. Sometimes in grading streets the natural surface drainage is interrupted and ponds of water accumulate in low lots. By driving a tube-well into the sand the pool soon disappears, and the low ground is relieved for a time, until the well gets filled with mud. Cesspools and vaults are also sunk into the gravel, or abandoned wells are converted to the same use, and will dispose of house-drainage for many years, with danger to the water-supply of those who depend on wells.

Beneath the sand and gravel is a layer of stiff blue clay, supposed to extend under the whole city, and usually found to be about 15 feet thick. This rests on a foundation of coarse gravel and cobbles very different from the upper sand and gravel, being much coarser and more compact, and probably composed of an ancient deposit, into which the present bed of the river has been worn, and which is often found in the upper terraces, sometimes, as at Cincinnati, being 100 feet above the present bottom of the river and extending to an unknown depth. Most of the public wells at the street-corners are now supplied with water from the lower stratum by driving a tube from 80 to 100 feet or more below the surface of the stream. Distilleries get their supply of water from the same source, and an ice-manufacturing company has been pumping a constant stream for several years from a 4-inch pipe without any apparent diminution of the supply. The water is used both for condensing purposes and for freezing into blocks of clear ice.

A number of natural water-courses traverse the bottom-lands; some take their rise within the city limits and flow away toward the south and west. The principal stream, known as Bear Grass creek, flows along the foot of the bluffs in the easterly part of the city till it comes within half a mile of the Ohio river, whence it discharges through an artificial channel to the river, nearly 2 miles above the public landing. The natural course of this stream was quite different, as it made a sharp turn at the place where the cut-off was made, and flowed almost back upon its course, running about midway between Main street and the river-shore, and discharged into the Ohio near the present location of the public landing at the foot of Fourth street. Its former outlet at this place is described by writers as making a large, safe, and commodious harbor for river-boats just above the falls. This outlet has been closed, a sewer has been built along the course of the stream, and the gradual filling in of the bed of the old creek to a height of from 20 to 30 feet forms an important feature of the geological structure of that part of the city.

The sewerage works of Louisville consist of 40½ miles of sewers, of which those 18 inches or less in diameter are of vitrified clay pipes, and those of larger size are of brick masonry. There are no stone sewers in use, except perhaps a short length of old drains in a few places, but not to any considerable extent. Brick sewers are laid in the hydraulic cement manufactured in the city and vicinity, some of which is of excellent quality. No stone inverts have been found necessary, as the flow of water is not remarkably rapid, but perhaps chiefly for the reason that sewage contains but little sand or gravel to wear away the masonry; the adjacent soil, being clay, loam, and mud, is carried along by the current or deposited quietly in the bottom, without much tendency to scour or wear out the brick-work.

Information relative to the size, cross-section, and rates of sewers may be found in the annual reports of the department of public works, which are unusually explicit and complete. The usual cross-section of pipe-sewers is circular, and Y-branches are laid at the time of construction in all situations where house-drain connections are at all likely to be wanted. Brick sewers are circular in cross-section where the flow of water is likely to be large, but in situations where the constant flow is small and the sewers are required to carry much water only at rare intervals, they are built egg-shaped, the distinction being made according to the judgment of the chief engineer, and not in accordance with any fixed rule.

The size of sewers constructed within recent years has been regulated according to the areas to be drained and the inclination of the sewers by the use of Adams' formula, assuming a rainfall of 1 inch per hour, of which one-half only would reach the sewer within the hour. The surface of the city is very nearly level, and from 45 to 55 feet above the river. The length of its sewers is generally not great, so that ample fall can be secured by increasing the depth of cutting on approaching the outfall. That part of the city lying between Walnut street and the river is usually drained directly into the Ohio by a sewer in each street. The uniformity of this rule, however, is interrupted above Third street, where the sewers, instead of flowing directly to the river, are discharged into an intercepting sewer along the shore in the old channel of Bear Grass creek and discharged to one outlet nearly opposite the city gas-works on Preston street. Those sewers which discharge into the Ohio have their outfalls so near the entrance to the canal that their contents are probably almost wholly drawn into and through the canal and locks. The drainage of that part of the city below Twelfth street would naturally go into the canal, and sewers have been constructed in Seventeenth, Twenty-first, and Twenty-sixth streets, discharging into it; but the authorities of the United States have forbidden the construction of any more outfall sewers into the canal, so that it will be necessary for the city to build an intercepting sewer to receive the contents of the sewers in all that part of the city and conduct and discharge it below the locks. The drainage of all the lower portion of the city below Twelfth street is now very incomplete.

The drainage of the western part of the city below Third street and south of Walnut has been provided for by a large trunk-sewer, in Broadway extension and other streets. This is circular in cross-section, made of brick, and is intended as the outlet for a large area of the city. The principal tributaries to it at present are a brick sewer in Twentieth street from Main, one in Fifteenth street from Grayson on the north and from Ormsby street on the south. Tributaries of less extent have also been built in Thirteenth from Chestnut, Ninth from Walnut, Seventh from Magazine, and Fifth from Chestnut street. These afford all the drainage there is in this part of the city up to the present time, but the natural water-courses have been taken into the sewer wherever they come to it, and a large area of suburban and rural district has been tile-drained, discharging into the sewer, thus greatly improving its condition and value for agricultural and building purposes. The part of the city beyond the Louisville and Nashville Railroad shops and in the vicinity of the Louisville Bridge works is sparsely settled, and many streets are not opened or improved. That part of the city lying south of Walnut and east of Fifth street is now drained into the stream, already mentioned, known as Bear Grass creek.

There are two principal outfalls, one for the main sewer in Kentucky street and the other at the crossing of Broadway. Other sewers of less extent discharge into the creek below Broadway, the principal one being in Green street, but of short extent only. These main sewers and their branches have been as carefully examined as they could be in the limited time devoted to the subject. The one in Broadway is at a higher level, and has a better flow at this time than the one in Kentucky street. Broadway is carried across the stream on a cut-stone arch with curved wing-walls to support the banks on each side. The water from the gutters reaches the creek by four separate culverts, each passing through the masonry in a square opening. The sewer is circular and made of brick, and its course is deflected and brought to the creek just at the lower edge of the bridge masonry. The outfall was about half submerged and inaccessible at the time the examination was made, but the sewer was examined in several places along its course and the flow of water was seen to be rapid and strong. There was more water than usual in both the main and branches when the examination was made—January 26, 1882—as it was raining slightly at the time, and had rained at intervals during the past forty-eight hours, but not enough to cause much addition to the usual flow. The sewers appeared to be clear, and in no case obstructed, with the single exception of a pipe sewer 15 inches in diameter in Floyd street near Gray, where some street-dirt had formed a slight obstruction at a manhole. The main sewer in Kentucky street is built at a lower level than any of the other main outlets, and was, on January 26, 1882, about half full of water for nearly half a mile from its outfall. It also contains a considerable deposit of clay and mud, which will probably be removed when the flood in the river subsides so that this sewer can be entered.

These two sewers last described drain a part of the city quite thickly populated.

CEMETERIES.

No information was furnished upon this subject.

MARKETS.

There are no public or corporation markets in Louisville, and no information as to the city's food-supply and the system of distributing it was given.

SANITARY AUTHORITY—BOARD OF HEALTH.

The official sanitary organization of the city is the board of health. This is a board of 12 members—9 of them being physicians—appointed by the general council, and responsible to it. The expenses of the board for 1879 were $3,900, of which $1,700 was used for quarantine purposes and the remainder for salaries and incidental purposes, including the registration of vital statistics. The board is limited in its expenditures to the appropriation made by the council; the amount is annually about $4,000. The board has power at all times to enforce such measures as may be necessary to protect the city from danger without in the way of infection, and to maintain within a healthful and cleanly condition. The chief executive is the health officer; his salary is $100 per month, and his chief duty is to attend to the abatement of nuisances.

The police act as sanitary inspectors, making and reporting inspections regularly, these covering all parts of the city. Inspections are also made as nuisances are reported. In all cases of nuisances the health officer orders the same abated; if this is not done within the time given, he procures a warrant against the offender, and proceeds to enforce his order. The nuisances under the surveillance of the board may relate to defective house-drainage, privy-vaults, cesspools, or sources of drinking-water; but defective sewerage, street-cleaning, etc., are under the control of the sewer and street-cleaning departments. Over the conservation and removal of garbage the board has authority "only to see that no nuisance is committed". Before burials are permitted the board requires its permit therefor to be obtained, and this is granted only upon the presentation of a certificate properly filled and signed by the physician and the undertaker. The board has thus far taken cognizance of the breaking out of contagious diseases in schools only in the case of small-pox. Small-pox patients are either isolated at their homes, upon which warning flags are placed, or they are removed to Saint John's eruptive hospital, which is located one-half mile outside and southeast of the city limits. Scarlet-fever patients are not isolated. Vaccination is compulsory, and is done at the public expense in the case of indigent persons. A registry of deaths is kept by the board, embracing in each case the name, sex, color, age, cause, duration of illness, physician, birthplace, residence, cemetery, and officiating undertaker.

The board of health meets once a month, or oftener upon call. It makes yearly reports to the general council, which are published with the other municipal reports.

The following table shows the nuisances reported to the health office and ordered abated during the year 1880, with comparative figures for 1879:

Nature of nuisance.	1880.	1879.	Nature of nuisance.	1880.	1879.
Foul cellars	101	131	Filthy slaughter-houses	20	15
Filthy cisterns	49	53	Filthy alleys, streets, and gutters	175	193
Filthy yards	200	217	Filthy ponds	25	73
Foul privy-vaults	76	75	Filthy dry wells	9	6
Foul and full privy-vaults	1,116	1,347	Dangerous flues	5	2
Dangerous privy-vaults	51	63	Dangerous houses	3	1
Hog- and cow-pens	82	93	Foul water-closets	20	5
Filthy stables	25	44	Totals	2,080	2,450
Filthy premises	95	103			
Filthy houses and sheds	19	29			

The following extract from the report of the health officer for 1880 upon the subject of the wells of Louisville is suggestive:

There is no subject of more importance than our water-supply. The formation of our soil is as follows: From 4 to 5 feet, sand and gravel; 30 to 50, blue clay; compact and water-proof, 8 to 15 feet; and then a coarse gravel and sand. Our wells now are from 30 to 45 feet deep, and the bottoms are located in the first sand and gravel. The custom in sinking is to stop as soon as a sufficient

Mechanical and manufacturing industries.	No. of establishments.	Capital.	Average number of hands employed.			Total amount paid in wages during the year.	Value of materials.	Value of products.
			Males above 16 years.	Females above 15 years.	Children and youths.			
Ink	3	$9,500	9	2	....	$3,908	$5,600	$11,800
Instruments, professional and scientific	3	11,500	6	....	....	3,820	1,800	11,000
Iron and steel	8	392,000	468	....	2	149,187	305,784	514,623
Iron work, architectural and ornamental (see also Foundery and machine-shop products).	4	33,500	31	....	....	12,004	19,940	48,493
Jewelry	7	25,099	31	2	1	14,794	28,384	53,703
Leather, curried	5	94,000	43	....	....	11,825	228,090	275,400
Leather, tanned	13	1,610,000	374	1	10	160,653	1,261,931	1,855,590
Liquors, distilled	15	1,049,000	218	....	1	89,855	953,900	1,382,500
Liquors, malt	20	712,000	275	1	2	134,291	575,533	959,221
Lithographing (see also Printing and publishing)	4	26,200	43	12	10	22,324	22,526	59,270
Lock- and gun-smithing	3	2,100	10	....	....	4,458	11,500	19,400
Looking-glass and picture frames	4	3,162	6	....	....	2,130	4,510	12,040
Lumber, planed (see also Wood, turned and carved)	9	268,768	235	....	2	106,475	336,997	611,204
Lumber, sawed	3	300,000	70	....	7	25,582	126,375	212,500
Marble and stone work	17	140,375	167	....	....	80,714	133,846	319,500
Masonry, brick and stone	4	50,650	78	....	7	35,674	53,300	113,150
Mattresses and spring beds (see also Furniture)	10	15,450	35	6	....	15,573	40,280	75,800
Millinery and lace goods	7	61,000	3	79	5	20,240	96,600	149,900
Mineral and soda waters	7	19,900	15	....	4	7,872	10,100	30,592
Mixed textiles (see also Woolen goods)	3	410,000	79	154	112	100,862	446,570	654,329
Musical instruments, pianos and materials	5	40,700	26	....	....	12,833	13,800	42,200
Painting and paperhanging	23	26,850	111	....	5	43,248	37,550	116,727
Patent medicines and compounds (see also Drugs and chemicals)	9	119,500	33	10	5	14,186	166,000	352,800
Photographing	11	27,900	32	4	1	18,306	27,650	68,685
Plumbing and gasfitting	17	35,650	81	....	3	34,560	54,421	123,975
Printing and publishing (see also Lithographing)	36	1,333,500	668	104	65	416,551	433,164	1,188,067
Pumps, not including steam-pumps	5	22,250	24	....	2	11,160	12,010	33,789
Roofing and roofing materials	8	16,300	26	....	2	11,687	32,700	58,350
Saddlery and harness	35	396,150	398	19	23	159,571	520,525	882,542
Shirts	8	64,300	9	100	....	19,594	30,774	65,315
Show-cases	3	2,100	6	....	2	1,950	2,650	6,900
Slaughtering and meat-packing, not including retail butchering	23	2,144,500	358	....	8	141,092	3,438,459	4,287,158
Stone- and earthen-ware	4	10,900	23	....	4	8,900	4,950	18,400
Tinware, copperware, and sheet-iron ware	45	178,900	151	....	5	73,548	228,395	419,030
Tobacco, chewing, smoking and snuff (see also Tobacco, cigars and cigarettes).	9	460,000	742	436	203	188,517	1,162,891	2,312,802
Tobacco, cigars and cigarettes (see also Tobacco, chewing, smoking, and snuff).	54	248,237	336	67	111	141,148	245,863	684,842
Trunks and valises	7	59,800	98	....	17	44,101	72,300	164,100
Upholstering (see also Furniture)	4	13,100	13	3	....	5,000	22,900	38,200
Vinegar	3	42,500	15	....	....	5,210	64,805	89,000
Watch and clock repairing	9	5,200	5	....	....	3,300	1,885	15,650
Wheelwrighting (see also Blacksmithing; Carriages and wagons)	16	26,750	35	....	....	17,534	19,250	64,500
Wood, turned and carved (see also Lumber, planed)	6	93,000	62	....	36	36,299	50,756	114,767
Woolen goods (see also Mixed textiles)	4	425,000	92	154	114	102,212	451,970	669,079
All other industries (a)	76	2,826,140	1,155	445	86	495,267	2,412,485	3,686,539

a Embracing artificial limbs; awnings and tents; axle-grease; bagging, flax, hemp, and jute; baking and yeast powders; bells; belting and hose, leather; bluing; boxes, cigar; boxes, fancy and paper; bridges; buttons; carriage and wagon materials; carriages and sleds, children's; cars, railroad, street, and repairs; cement; coppersmithing; cordage and twine; cork cutting; cotton goods; drain and sewer pipe; dyeing and finishing textiles; electrical apparatus and supplies; electroplating; files; glass, cut, stained, and ornamented; grease and tallow; handles, wooden; hats and caps; iron bolts, nuts, washers, and rivets; iron forgings; labels and tags; lapidary work; lightning rods; malt; models and patterns; musical instruments, organs and materials; nets and seines; oil, linseed; oleomargarine; paints; paper; pickles, preserves, and sauces; refrigerators; sash, doors, and blinds; saws; scales and balances; shipbuilding; soap and candles; sporting goods; stencils and brands; stereotyping and electrotyping; toys and games; umbrellas and canes; and wirework.

From the foregoing table it appears that the average capital of all establishments is $19,645 32; that the average wages of all hands employed is $334 45 per annum; that the average outlay in wages, in materials, and in interest (at 6 per cent.) on capital employed is $25,585 45.

NEWPORT,

CAMPBELL COUNTY, KENTUCKY.

POPULATION

IN THE

AGGREGATE,

1800-1880.

	Inhab.
1790	....
1800	106
1810	413
1820	....
1830	715
1840	....
1850	5,895
1860	10,046
1870	15,087
1880	20,433

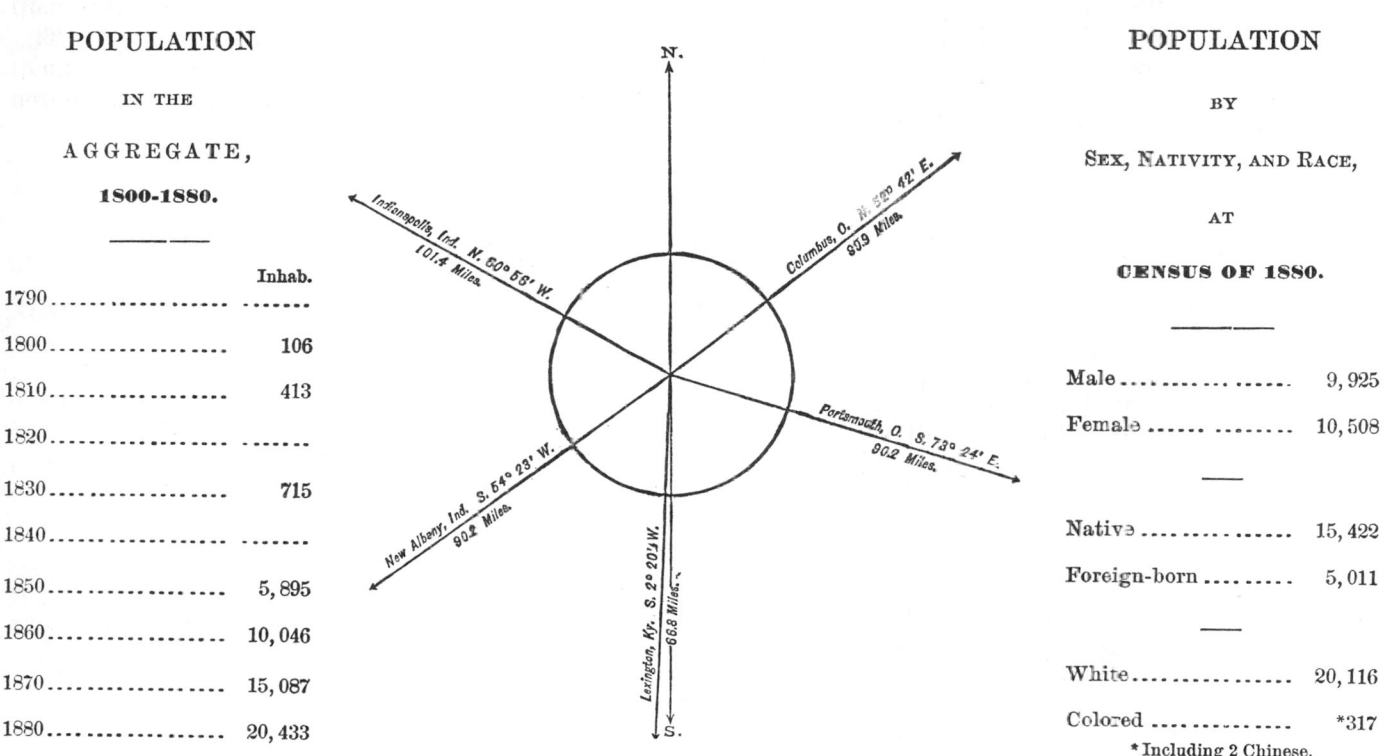

POPULATION

BY

SEX, NATIVITY, AND RACE,

AT

CENSUS OF 1880.

Male	9,925
Female	10,508
Native	15,422
Foreign-born	5,011
White	20,116
Colored	*317

* Including 2 Chinese.

Latitude: 39° 6' North; Longitude: 84° 29' (west from Greenwich).

FINANCIAL CONDITION:

Total Valuation: $6,588,653; per capita: $322 00.   Net Indebtedness: $966,618; per capita: $47 31.   Tax per $100: $2 36.

HISTORICAL SKETCH.

Newport was settled in 1791, but the spot had been visited before that time by various persons. In 1771 Simon Kenton came to the mouth of the Licking river, and he is thought to be the first white man who ever came to the spot, which had long been a favorite station for the Indians when on the war-path. It was the scene of a bloody encounter with the whites in 1779, in which nearly all the latter were killed. In the year 1780 it was visited by Hubbard Taylor, who located lands here for his father, Colonel James Taylor, of Virginia, who thus became proprietor of the land on which the city of Newport now stands. He again visited the place in 1791, accompanying thus far the Kentucky troops, who were on their way to join General St. Clair's expedition, and laid out a regular village, to which he gave the name of Newport, in honor of Captain Lord Newport, one of those who came in the first ship to old Jamestown.

In 1792, when Kentucky was made a state, Newport was only a little cluster of rude cabins. It was incorporated as a town in 1795, and in the next year was made the county-seat of Campbell county in the place of Wilmington, an honor it now shares with Alexandria, the courts being held alternately in the two places. Only three years after the incorporation of the town its citizens manifested their interest in the cause of education by procuring from the general assembly of Kentucky the incorporation of the Newport academy, and a year later a school-board was organized. In the year 1803 the United States purchased lands from General James Taylor, and in the next year completed the Newport barracks, which has since been a regular station of the United States army, with the exception of a short period in 1875-'76, when the troops were removed and stationed at Columbus, Ohio. It was an important post during the wars with the Indians, and the war of 1812 with Great Britain.

In 1830 Newport was made a city, and in the few following years received many additions to its population. It owes its prosperity and importance to its proximity to Cincinnati, which is situated just across the Ohio river. Newport is connected with Cincinnati by an iron railroad bridge, with foot- and carriage-ways, completed in 1872. A wire suspension bridge across the Licking connects the city with Covington. This bridge was built in 1854, but had hardly been opened to travel before it fell; it was rebuilt at once. The first railroad meeting was held in 1836, but the plan then projected of a railroad from Newport to Lexington, to form part of the Charleston and Cincinnati railroad, was not carried out. The Cincinnati Southern railroad of to-day very nearly realizes this plan of 1836.

Newport is now the third city of Kentucky in size. Its beautiful situation and its nearness to Cincinnati render it a favorite place of residence for business men. Its manufacturing interests are quite important, the iron and steel industries taking the lead.

NEWPORT IN 1880.

The following statistical accounts, collected by the Census Office, indicate the present condition of Newport:

LOCATION.

Newport is situated in latitude 39° 6' north, longitude 84° 29' west from Greenwich, on the east bank of the Licking river at its junction with the Ohio. It is separated by the former river from the city of Covington, and by the latter from Cincinnati, of which it practically is a suburb. Both rivers are navigable at this point, and an account of the draught of water, harbor capacity, and river current may be found under "Cincinnati, Ohio".

RAILROAD COMMUNICATIONS.

The Louisville, Cincinnati, and Lexington railroad connects Newport with Louisville and Lexington. This is the only railroad passing through the city, but is not the only means of railroad communication, as the vast system centering in Cincinnati is easily reached from Newport.

TRIBUTARY COUNTRY; TOPOGRAPHY; CLIMATE.

See, for these subjects, "Covington, Kentucky."

STREETS.

The total length of the city streets could not be obtained. Sixteen and four-tenths miles are paved with limestone set on edge, and $3\frac{3}{10}$ miles with broken stone; the other streets are unpaved. The limestone paving costs about 65 cents per square yard, but is now no longer used, as it is regarded as a very unsatisfactory pavement. The broken stone costs about 45 cents per square yard. The total cost of the streets, exclusive of the cost of cleaning, was $12,577 33 in 1880. Construction is done by contract, repairing by day labor. The sidewalks, when paved, are made of bricks or limestone; and an inspection made during the present year disclosed the fact that a large number were in very bad condition. On all the old streets the gutters were made of limestone set on edge; but along the recently improved streets they are of Indiana limestone flags, 12 inches wide and 3 or 4 feet long. Trees are planted at the edge of the sidewalks next the curbstones along most of the streets. A $5\frac{1}{2}$-ton roller is used on the streets and gives excellent results. It requires from 6 to 8 horses to haul it.

The Newport Street Railway Company has 24 cars and 100 horses. It carries passengers across the Licking to Covington, and thence via the suspension bridge over the Ohio to Cincinnati. The fares are 5 and 10 cents, according to distance. There are no omnibus lines.

WATER-WORKS.

The total cost of the public water-works was about $700,000. They are owned by the city. Water is pumped to a reservoir, and from this distributes itself through the city, yielding a pressure, varying with the locality, from 56 to 76 pounds to the square inch.

The average amount pumped daily is 475,000 gallons, and the average cost of raising one million gallons one foot high is $9\frac{7}{10}$ cents. The yearly cost of maintenance, aside from pumping, in 1880 was about $8,000. The income from water-rates was $16,063 11, and the total expenditure was $14,514 77. There are 16 water-meters in use.

GAS.

The city is supplied with gas by the Covington Gas Light Company, which charges $2 50 per 1,000 feet to private persons and $1 50 to the city. There are 227 gas street-lamps used.

PUBLIC BUILDINGS.

The buildings owned by the city, and used for municipal purposes only, are a court-house, a clerk's office, and a jail, together valued at $20,000. No other buildings are reported by the mayor.

PUBLIC PARKS AND PLEASURE-GROUNDS.

There are no public parks in the city.

PLACES OF AMUSEMENT.

There is no theater, and but one concert-hall, in the city. This hall has a seating capacity of 400. The city ordinances require a payment of an annual license of $50 by all halls that are let for the purpose of holding therein concerts, panoramas, theatrical or other shows; and each concert, circus, theatrical or other exhibition, and each menagerie, held in other places than a licensed hall, must pay a license of $5 for concerts and theatrical exhibitions, and $50 for the others, for every day of 24 hours or less.

DRAINAGE.

There is no system of sewerage in the city. All storm-water and most of the liquid household wastes run through the street-gutters into the rivers.

CEMETERIES.

No information on this subject was furnished.

MARKETS.

The city has a public market, a brick building, situated at the corner of Bellevue and Columbia streets. The building is 90 by 20 feet in area, and contains a number of meat-stalls, which rent at from $25 to $40 per annum. The Columbia Street front is taken up by hucksters' stands, and along both this and Bellevue street are wagon-stands for hucksters and farmers. The hucksters pay from $10 to $25 per annum for their stands, the farmers from 50 to 75 cents per month.

The total rental of the market is $1,150. It is open Tuesdays, Thursdays, and Saturdays from 4 to 10 a. m., and on Saturday afternoons from 4 to 9 o'clock. Only a small part of the retail supply of meat, fish, and vegetables is obtained from the market, private stores supplying most of the city. Every person carrying on a business in fresh meats in any other place than the market is compelled to obtain a license, costing $30 per annum, from the city. Hucksters peddling with wagons through the streets pay a license of $10 a year. The income from the licenses to meat-stores in 1880 was $780.

SANITARY AUTHORITY.

The charter of the city of Newport provides that the mayor and council shall have power and authority to appoint one or more health officers, to establish regulations necessary and proper to prevent the introduction of any disease, and to eradicate the same when it shall have made its appearance in said town; but no board of health has ever been appointed. The annual reports mention four "district physicians", but these do not seem to make any reports, nor are their duties defined by any ordinance.

When nuisances are reported to the mayor and council, as they become cognizant of them in any way, the owner or agent of the premises on which the nuisance exists is required to abate or remove it. If this order is disregarded the cost of making the abatement is estimated by the city engineer, and if it does not exceed 25 per cent. of the value of the entire property the removal is made by the city and the expense is charged upon the estate. If the cost of abatement exceeds 25 per cent. of the value, the owner or agent is liable to a fine for every day of delay after the time set in the notification has expired. Small-pox patients are isolated at home; the sidewalk is closed, and a large placard is placed upon the house to warn persons of their danger. Vaccination is not compulsory, nor is it done at public expense. There is no system of registration of births, diseases, and deaths, although the ordinances compel physicians to report all cases of small-pox to the mayor.

MUNICIPAL CLEANSING.

Street-cleaning.—The streets are supposed to be cleaned at the expense of the city by contractors, who receive $3,500 and are required to clean the streets thoroughly. The following, from the report of Mr. B. R. Morton, city engineer, for 1880, shows how the work is done:

Apparently the time has arrived when a change should be made in the present crude and unsatisfactory method of cleaning the streets. At present the only way of disposing of garbage, ashes, and other refuse which is constantly accumulating at every residence and business house is to dump the same in the streets or alleys, where, in the course of time, after being rooted by hogs in search of dainties, and spread by passing wheels, piles are formed, sometimes two or more feet in height, detracting from the appearance of streets already bad enough, and requiring considerable skill in driving along the winding way to prevent overturning. Twice each year the street-cleaning contractors are supposed to remove these piles and give the streets a thorough scraping and sweeping. The effect, however, even when well done, is not lasting, and within a short time, especially after the fall cleaning, the appearance is as bad as ever. The sweepings when removed are dumped on the river-bank and carried away by the rise of the river, or are deposited on vacant lots.

Removal of garbage and ashes.—No system for the removal of garbage and ashes has been formed. The account just quoted from the city engineer shows the practical methods resorted to in disposing of them.

Dead animals are removed and buried at the expense of the city; 300 dead animals are removed annually.

Liquid household wastes.—All the liquid household wastes run into the street-gutters, which are flushed occasionally.

Human excreta.—All the houses of the city depend upon privy-vaults. The construction of these is not regulated by law; they must be cleansed when the contents reach within 11 inches of the top, and the contents removed by licensed scavengers in water-tight carts. They are ultimately disposed of by being dumped into the Ohio river.

Manufacturing wastes are run into the Ohio and Licking rivers.

POLICE.

The police force of Newport is appointed and governed by a board of three police commissioners, the latter appointed by the city council. The chief executive officer is a chief of police, whose salary is $800 a year, and whose duty is the general supervision of his department. In addition to his salary he receives fees which amount to about $400 annually. The rest of the force consists of a lieutenant and 9 patrolmen, each of whom receives $2 per day. The uniform is of blue cloth with brass buttons, and a black felt hat with cord and metal wreath; each man supplies his own. The men are armed with a club and a revolver; they are on duty 12 hours and patrol 18 miles of streets. During 1880 the police made 486 arrests, (a) the principal causes being drunkenness and breaches of the peace.

Property valued at $4,000 was lost or stolen during the year and reported to the police; of this, $700 was recovered and returned to the owners. One hundred and ninety-three station-house lodgers were accommodated during 1880, as against 311 in 1879. No free meals are given to these.

Special police are appointed by the mayor for cases of emergency, and are treated as regular members of the force while on duty. The total cost of the department in 1880 was $8,236 50.

MANUFACTURES.

The following is a summary of the statistics of the manufactures of Newport for 1880, being taken from tables prepared for the Tenth Census by John H. Bodley, special agent:

Mechanical and manufacturing industries.	No. of establishments.	Capital.	AVERAGE NUMBER OF HANDS EMPLOYED.			Total amount paid in wages during the year.	Value of materials.	Value of products.
			Males above 16 years.	Females above 15 years.	Children and youths.			
All industries	94	$1,700,715	1,608	35	105	$711,019	$2,526,936	$3,996,995
Boots and shoes, including custom work and repairing	8	20,300	29	8	6	15,330	19,200	43,875
Bread and other bakery products	14	17,500	19	....	4	7,611	8,925	19,600
Carpentering	11	45,300	46	....	4	16,335	47,236	103,836
Carriages and wagons (see also Wheelwrighting)	3	31,000	25	....	....	11,120	18,500	45,000
Foundery and machine-shop products	3	117,500	280	....	3	89,011	309,707	471,349
Iron and steel	3	640,000	760	....	....	305,500	1,359,990	2,033,950
Marble and stone work	3	5,500	16	....	....	7,500	5,000	17,000
Tinware, copperware, and sheet-iron ware	4	5,500	12	....	1	3,700	3,500	9,400
Tobacco, cigars and cigarettes	23	16,800	51	....	13	17,600	22,360	49,000
Wheelwrighting (see also Carriages and wagons)	4	2,300	11	....	....	3,503	2,200	7,550
All other industries (a)	18	799,015	359	27	74	233,809	729,718	1,196,435

a Embracing agricultural implements; awnings and tents; boxes, cigar; brick and tile; clothing, men's; confectionery; flouring- and grist-mill products; gold and silver leaf and foil; liquors, malt; lumber, planed; lumber, sawed; mineral and soda waters; printing and publishing; saddlery and harness; watch cases; and wheelbarrows.

From the foregoing table it appears that the average capital of all establishments is $18,092 71; that the average wages of all hands employed is $406 76 per annum; that the average outlay in wages, in materials, and in interest (at 6 per cent.) on capital employed is $35,531 89.

---

a This does not include arrests made by constables on warrants.

TENNESSEE.

CHATTANOOGA,
HAMILTON COUNTY, TENNESSEE.

POPULATION

IN THE

AGGREGATE,

1860-1880.

	Inhab.
1790	......
1800	......
1810	......
1820	......
1830	......
1840	......
1850	......
1860	2,545
1870	6,093
1880	12,892

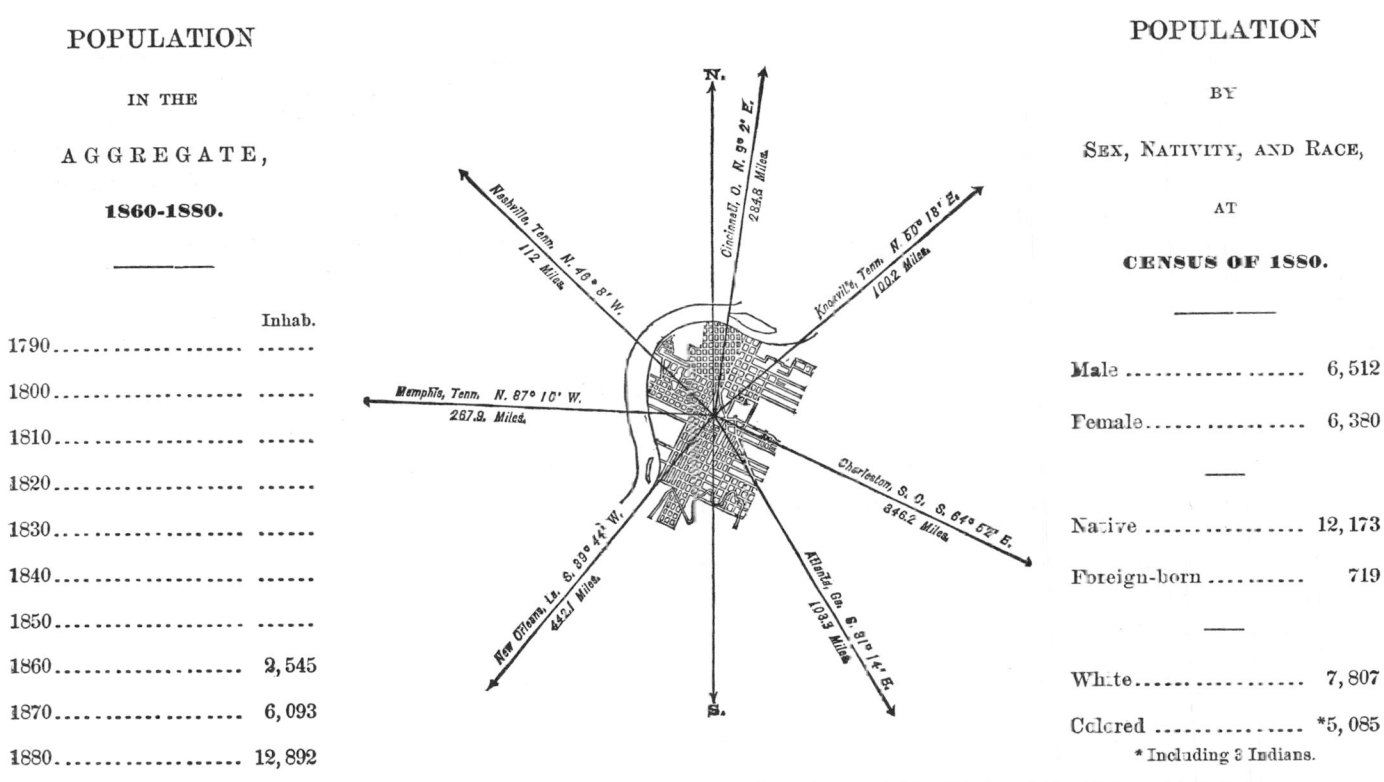

POPULATION

BY

SEX, NATIVITY, AND RACE,

AT

CENSUS OF 1880.

Male	6,512
Female	6,380
Native	12,173
Foreign-born	719
White	7,807
Colored	*5,085

* Including 3 Indians.

Latitude: 35° 2' North; Longitude: 85° 21' (west from Greenwich); Altitude: 630 to 971 feet.

FINANCIAL CONDITION:

Total Valuation: $3,600,925; per capita: $279 00.   Net Indebtedness: $116,264; per capita: $9 02.   Tax per $100: $2 75.

HISTORICAL SKETCH.

The first settlement of the site of Chattanooga by whites was made in 1836, immediately after the cession of the lands by the Cherokee nation of Indians. The first sale of lots took place April 20, 1839. The first charter of incorporation was granted in 1841, and on November 5, 1851, a new charter was granted by the legislature, giving city privileges and extending the limits. The population gradually increased by immigration from the adjoining states. The facilities afforded by the navigation of the river, and the building of some three different railways, gave the city considerable trade—a trade in grain and provisions superior to that of any other inland city of the state—and it had, in 1860, more than 2,500 inhabitants.

Chattanooga was the theater of some of the most important events in the civil war. Its trade was interrupted, its people were scattered, and a great portion of its buildings destroyed, so that at the close of the war it was but a wreck of its former importance and prosperity. A great many northern soldiers settled here permanently, others moved here from the north and the south, and so patent were the advantages of the place that by 1870 the population amounted to 6,093. Owing to the rapid development of the mineral resources of the adjoining country the population is fast increasing, and is about equally divided between settlers from the northern and from the southern states.

The principal periods of business depression were during the war, and in and since 1873. A very destructive fire occurred in 1871, when two squares of business houses were destroyed; but they were speedily replaced by superior buildings.

CHATTANOOGA IN 1880.

The following statistical accounts, collected by the Census Office, indicate the present condition of Chattanooga:

LOCATION.

Chattanooga lies in latitude 35° 2' north, longitude 85° 21' west from Greenwich, in the southeastern part of the state, and on the left bank of the Tennessee river, about 200 miles, by water, below Knoxville. The altitudes above sea-level are, lowest point 630, and highest 971 feet. The draught of water in the Tennessee river at the city, except at extreme low stages, is 3 feet, and improvements are now in progress for securing this depth at all times. The landing is sufficient for the accommodation of the 8 or 10 steamboats, of from 55 to 260 tons capacity, now navigating the river, and can readily be increased almost indefinitely. This part of the river is navigable from Knoxville, Tennessee, to Decatur, Alabama, a distance of 349 miles, and, on the completion of the work now on hand at the Muscle shoals, the river will be navigable to the Ohio, and thus be connected with the Mississippi and its tributaries. Water communication is now open to Knoxville, Loudon, Kingston, and Charleston, Tennessee, and with Guntersville, Bridgeport, and Decatur, in Alabama.

RAILROAD COMMUNICATIONS.

Chattanooga is touched by the following lines of railroad:

The Nashville, Chattanooga, and Saint Louis railroad, to Saint Louis, Missouri.

The Memphis and Charleston railroad, to Memphis, Tennessee.

The Alabama Great Southern railroad, to Meridian, Mississippi.

The Western and Atlantic railroad, to Atlanta, Georgia.

The East Tennessee, Virginia, and Georgia railroad, to Bristol, Tennessee, and the Norfolk and Western connections.

The Cincinnati Southern, to Cincinnati, Ohio.

These lines give to the city the most ample connections with all points in the country.

TRIBUTARY COUNTRY.

The soil immediately surrounding the city is light, and poor for general agriculture, except the river bottom-lands, which are very productive, yielding large crops of corn, wheat, and hay. The ridge-lands are very favorable for orchards and vineyards, whose cultivation is growing here to important proportions. There are in this vicinity several extensive coal-mines, beds of iron ore, and quarries of limestone, which give employment to a large number of men. The commercial interests of the city with the country immediately adjoining are not large, most of the products of Chattanooga's mills and factories finding more distant markets.

TOPOGRAPHY.

The general surface of the city is hilly, the hills varying in height from a slight rise to 300 feet. The soil is mainly a red clay; the hills are, in part, of a drift of gravel, iron ore, shale, blue and white clay, flint-gravel, and veins of a poor quality of bituminous coal. The rock immediately underlying a great part of the city, and cropping out in many places, is limestone. The surrounding country, within a radius of 3 miles, is generally open; outside of this the region is mountainous; the Lookout mountains, Raccoon mountains, Wallen's ridge (a spur of the Cumberland mountains), and Missionary ridge surround the city on all sides but one, and are all well wooded.

CLIMATE.

Highest recorded summer temperature, 104°; highest summer temperature in average years, 95°. Lowest recorded winter temperature, −3°; lowest winter temperature in average years, 16°.

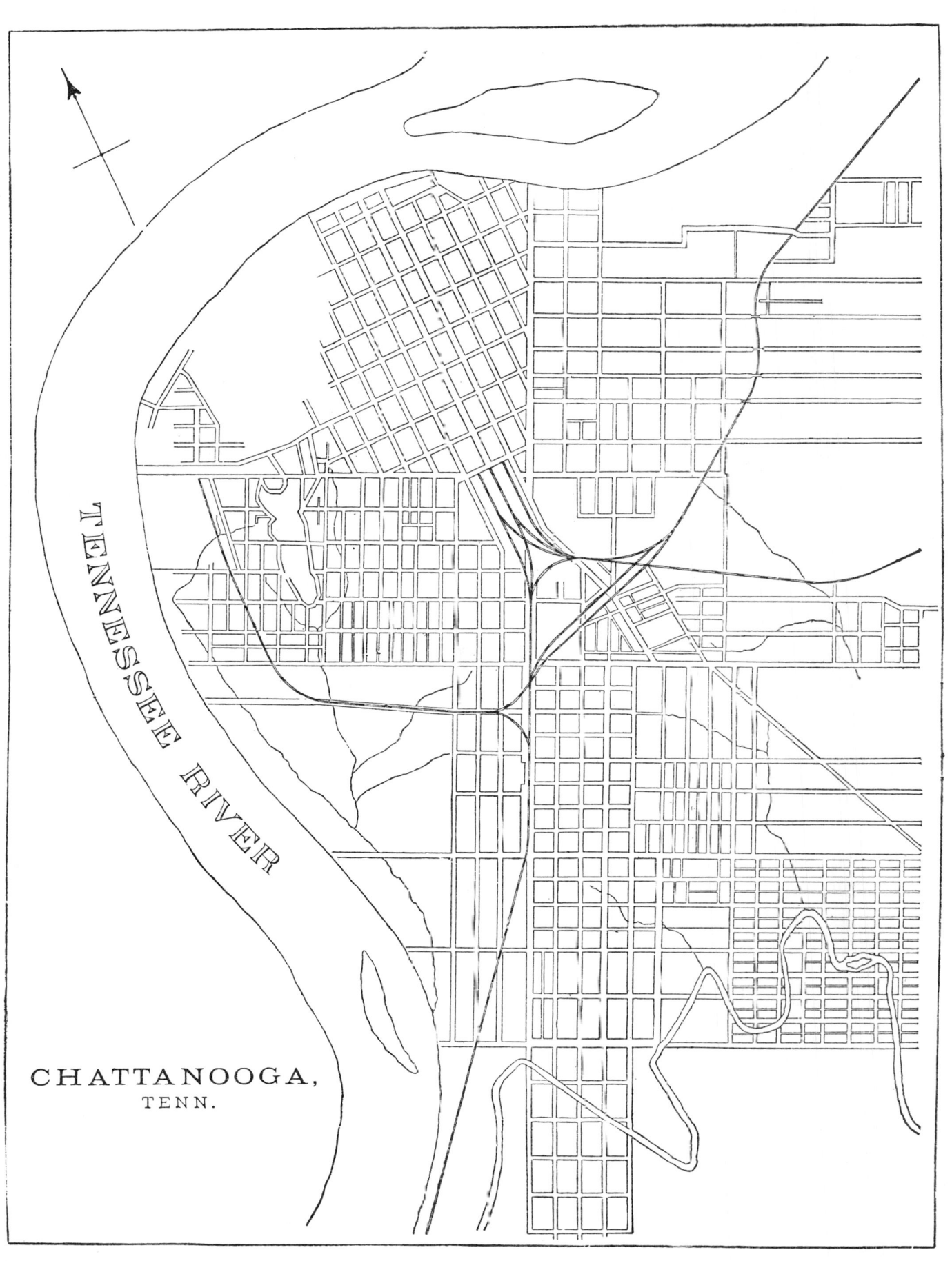

TENNESSEE RIVER

CHATTANOOGA,
TENN.

STREETS.

Total length, 65 miles, of which 4 miles are paved with broken stone and 1½ mile with gravel. The cost per square yard for each, as nearly as may be estimated, is, for broken stone 33⅓ cents, and for gravel 12½ cents. Each is kept clean with about equal facility. Gravel paving, with a good stone foundation, is preferred for durability and economy. The city is deficient in sidewalks; what it has are made of stone, brick, gravel, cinders, asphaltum, and plank. Gutters are paved with riprap and flagstones, the former predominating. Except on business streets, citizens are allowed to plant trees on the margin of the sidewalks. The work of construction and repair of streets is sometimes done by contract, but more frequently by the city's own force. About $7,000 is annually expended in this work. As a rule, day work is preferred. At present neither a steam stone-crusher nor a roller is used, though the use of the former is contemplated for future work.

HORSE-RAILROADS.

There are 2¾ miles of horse-railroads in the city, using 7 cars and 20 horses, and giving employment to 11 men. The rate of fare is 5 cents. There are no regular omnibus lines.

WATER-WORKS.

The water-works are owned by a private corporation called the "Lookout Water Company", organized in 1866, and their total cost was $130,000. The water is pumped into a reservoir in the northern part of the city, and 175 feet above low water in the Tennessee river (the source of supply), giving a pressure of 80 pounds to the square inch. From 1,250,000 to 2,000,000 gallons are pumped daily through about 12 miles of pipe. There are 58 fire-plugs, for which the city pays annually $50 each. No extra charge is made for water for flushing sewers, but the city pays for the use of water in the public buildings about $100 per year; also, under the present contract, as additional compensation, the water-works are exempt from municipal taxation. No water-meters are used. Street-sprinkling is done by private parties, who make their own contracts. The annual cost for maintenance of the works is $15,500, and the yearly income is about $19,500.

GAS.

The gas-works are owned by a private corporation. The daily average production is 25,000 feet; the charge per 1,000 feet is $2 70. The city pays $30 per annum for each street-lamp, 100 in number. The total length of pipe laid is 6 miles.

PUBLIC BUILDINGS.

The city owns no public buildings of any consequence, but occupies for municipal purposes the buildings owned by the county.

PUBLIC PARKS AND PLEASURE-GROUNDS.

Chattanooga is without public parks.

PLACES OF AMUSEMENT.

While without theaters, Chattanooga has the following halls: James' hall, used for theatrical purposes, seating capacity, 800; and Phœnix hall, Poss' hall, Concordia hall, and Cliffinger's hall, used for festivals, lectures, armories, churches, etc. James' hall pays an annual license fee of $75.

DRAINAGE.

A general plan for the drainage of this city was adopted in 1880. It provides for a sewer in every street throughout the principal part of the city, and establishes the location, grade, size, and character of each sewer at all points. Most of the laterals will deliver into a main sewer at Broad street, about the middle of the city, which is to discharge into the Tennessee river; 2,840 feet of this sewer have been built between Third and Ninth streets; the remaining three blocks to the river have not yet been constructed.

This main is described in a report of the street committee as "an egg-shaped sewer, built of vitrified brick, two thick, and well laid in cement-mortar". Its size varies from 60 by 40 inches to 75 by 50 inches. The lateral sewers in each street have, at their connection with the main, an oval section of 30 by 20 inches; the size is to be reduced as they recede from the main; 1,620 feet of laterals of this size have been built, also 451 feet of vitrified-pipe sewer, making the total length constructed, including the main, 4,911 feet. The cost of this work, including inlet-basins, was $23,146 60.

The street committee in its report of this work says:

Our experience this year, in being compelled to abandon pipe heretofore laid, especially the 24-inch pipe on Eighth street, which was put down at heavy expense, taught the lesson that not one foot of sewer should be built in any part of the town until the system has been established, and then all sewers should be built in conformity therewith. * * * It has also demonstrated that no street should be permanently improved until the sewer is built, where there is any probability of its construction within a reasonable time.

CEMETERIES.

Chattanooga has 5 cemeteries, as follows:

Old City Cemetery, on the northeastern side of the city.

Confederate Cemetery, connected with the above.

Jewish Cemetery, adjoining the above two on the east.

National Cemetery, on the city's eastern outskirts.

Forest Hills Cemetery, 1½ mile distant from the city in a southerly direction.

The total number of interments in each is about as follows: Old City cemetery, 2,000; Confederate cemetery, 400; Jewish cemetery, 50; National cemetery, 13,000, and Forest Hills cemetery, new, 50. There are no burial-grounds where interments are no longer permitted. Forest Hills cemetery belongs to a private corporation and comprises 116 acres. It was laid out this year, and, in general, the regulations of Spring Grove cemetery, Cincinnati, have been adopted. The price of lots ranges from 12½ to 20 cents per square foot. The cost of the property, with improvements, is about $10,000. The City cemetery continues to be the last resting-place of the greater portion of Chattanooga's dead. This is a public cemetery and belongs to the city. A superintendent has charge of the grounds under the direction of a board of directors. The National cemetery is owned by the United States government, and contains the bodies of 13,000 Union soldiers who fell in the late war. Before burials can be made, permits must be obtained. Except during epidemics there are no restrictions as to the time of burial after death. The usual depth given to graves is 6 feet.

MARKETS.

Chattanooga has no public or corporation markets.

SANITARY AUTHORITY—BOARD OF HEALTH.

The chief sanitary organization of the city is vested in a board of health, composed of 5 physicians, elected by the mayor and board of aldermen, with the mayor, city physician, city engineer, and 1 alderman (who is chairman of the hospital committee) as members *ex officio*—9 in all. The members serve without compensation. The board is under the control of the mayor and aldermen, who can abolish it at any time. The ordinary annual expense of the board is about $50, $36 being for salary of the secretary, and the balance for stationery. During an epidemic the board may increase its expenses to $250. In the absence of epidemics the board recommends health measures to the city council; it may declare and remove nuisances, and may establish and enforce such sanitary regulations as it may deem best calculated to guard against epidemics or malignant diseases; "but this does not authorize it to establish quarantine". During epidemics the board, through its quarantine officer (a member and physician), may apply directly to the board of mayor and aldermen for enactment of quarantine. The chief executive officer of the board is the secretary and registrar of vital statistics. This term indicates his duties, and his only compensation appears to be the $36 paid him for registration. One sanitary inspector is employed constantly, and an additional one is employed during four months in the year; neither of them is a physician; they have police powers, and execute the orders of the board regarding nuisances. The business of the board is transacted at regular monthly meetings, or called sessions if necessary, and five members constitute a quorum.

Inspections are made regularly and constantly, and reports are made upon every house and lot. When nuisances are reported, and are ascertained to be such, inspectors direct the abatement and the mode; if it is not done, the parties responsible are arrested and tried, either before a justice of the peace or the city recorder. Concerning the inspection and correction of defective house-drainage, privy-vaults, cesspools, sources of drinking-water, sewerage, street-cleaning, etc., action is taken only when these are reported to the board or its officers. As to the conservation and removal of garbage, the board has only advisory powers. For burial of the dead, a physician's certificate and a permit issued by the registrar of vital statistics must first be obtained. The board has no special regulations concerning the pollution of streams or the removal of excrement.

INFECTIOUS DISEASES.

Small-pox patients are removed to the pest-house, situated 3 miles south of the city, but not owned by it. Scarlet fever is of such rare occurrence (but 6 deaths from it in fifteen years) that no special regulations governing the disease are found necessary; nor has the board ever taken action upon the breaking out of contagious diseases in schools. Upon public-school children vaccination is compulsory, but the same is not done at the public expense.

A register is kept by the registrar of vital statistics of deaths, but not of diseases and births.

REPORTS.

The board reports annually to the city council, but the reports are published only as matters of news by the local papers. Dr. E. M. Wight, who furnishes the foregoing information regarding sanitary matters, adds the following: "Public interest since 1878—yellow fever—has been alert, and all respectable medical men are in harmony and awake to the interests of the public health and the work of health boards."

MUNICIPAL CLEANSING.

Street-cleaning.—The work of street-cleaning is done by the city's prison force, by hand, and is done as often as occasion requires. This work is not done as well as it should be; on macadamized streets considerable mud, etc., accumulate. The sweepings are deposited on unimproved streets. The cost of the work is not made a separate item.

Removal of garbage and ashes.—Garbage is removed by the city with its own force. It must be put in boxes or barrels, and before 8 a. m. of each day the same must be placed convenient for loading and removal by the city scavenger. Ashes and garbage may be kept in the same vessel, and both are disposed of outside of the city limits. The annual cost of removal to the city is $700. Occasionally nuisances result from the improper handling and disposal of garbage.

Dead animals.—The carcass of any animal dying within the city must be removed by the owner to a designated locality beyond the limits. If the owner can not be found, the city removes the carcass at its own expense.

Liquid household wastes.—Household slops, including the waste-water from sleeping-rooms, are disposed of in various ways; in some cases they are run into street-gutters, in others into cesspoools; and, in case of houses connected with the public sewers, into these. The dry wells and cesspools in use are porous. Though offensive household wastes are run into the street-gutters, there is no system of flushing them in vogue. In some instances cesspools receive the wastes from water-closets. It is not believed that the drinking-water is contaminated in any way from the contents of privy-vaults or cesspools.

Human excreta.—Only about 5 per cent. of the houses in the city have water-closets, the remainder depending on privies. Privy-vaults must be dug not less than 6 feet deep, and at least 4 feet from any street, etc., or from the property of another except with his consent; when dry-earth privies are used, the contents are removed at least twice each month. When privy-vaults become full or offensive, their contents are required to be removed beyond the city limits. The dry-earth system is used to a limited extent. Night-soil is not allowed to be used for manuring land within the gathering-ground of the public water-supply.

Manufacturing wastes.—No information was furnished as to the disposal of liquids, but the solid wastes from iron-works are used largely by railroad companies as road bed ballast, and by the city as a covering for the surface of the less-used streets.

POLICE.

The police force of the city of Chattanooga is elected by the city council and governed by a board of police commissioners. The title of the chief executive officer is "the city marshal". He has direct control of the force as its head. His salary is $1,000 per annum and the fees attached to the office. The rest of the force consists of one lieutenant at $900 a year and fees, and 12 patrolmen at $600 a year each. The uniform is of blue cloth, and is provided by the men themselves. The patrolmen are armed with club and pistol; they serve each 12 hours per day, and they patrol all the streets in the city. The arrests for 1880 numbered about 1,300, the principal causes being fighting, drunkenness, and carrying concealed weapons. No free meals were given to station-house lodgers during the year. The force is required to co-operate with the health department by noting the sanitary condition of the several wards and reporting all nuisances. The yearly cost of the police force (1880) is $11,000.

FIRE DEPARTMENT.

The manual force of the department consists of 102 men and the apparatus. They are divided as follows: 1 fire company with 1 fourth-class Ahrends steam fire-engine, 2 four-wheeled and 1 two-wheeled hose-carriages, 950 feet of unreliable hose, and 36 men; 1 fire company with 1 two-wheeled hose-carriage, 500 feet of good hose, and 36 men, and 1 hook-and-ladder company with 1 hook-and-ladder truck complete and 30 men. The expenses of the department for the year ending November 1, 1879, were $5,433. The loss by fires, 3 in number, during the same period, as given in the report of the chief of the fire department (and from which the foregoing is taken), was $15,500.

PUBLIC SCHOOLS.

The following school statistics are for the school year ending July 31, 1879: The city owns 3 and rents 5 school-houses, having 29 rooms, and employs 6 male and 21 female teachers. There are of school age in the city 2,807 children, and of these are enrolled 1,887. The highest monthly enrollment is 1,552. The percentage of enrollment on enumeration is 74.82. The average number belonging is 1,170.90. The percentage of attendance on number belonging is 94.41. The estimated total value of school property is $22,100.

MEMPHIS,

SHELBY COUNTY, TENNESSEE.

POPULATION

IN THE

AGGREGATE,

1850–1880.

	Inhab.
1790	
1800	
1810	
1820	
1830	
1840	
1850	8,841
1860	22,621
1870	40,226
1880	33,592

POPULATION

BY

SEX, NATIVITY, AND RACE,

AT

CENSUS OF 1880.

Male	16,302
Female	17,290
Native	29,621
Foreign-born	3,971
White	18,677
Colored	*14,915

* Including 17 Chinese and 2 Indians.

Latitude: 35° 8′ North; Longitude: 90° 4′ (west from Greenwich); Altitude: 220 to 280 feet.

FINANCIAL CONDITION:

Total Valuation: $16,784,314; per capita; $500 00.   Net Indebtedness: $4,554,355; per capita: $135 58.   Tax per $100: $1 79.

HISTORICAL SKETCH.(a)

Though one of the most modern cities of the United States, Memphis contains within its limits the oldest historic point in this country.   Saint Augustine, Florida, was founded in 1566, and Santa Fé, New Mexico, in 1582; but before either had been dreamed of, the site of Memphis had become historic.   De Soto had linked it with his name, for, in April, 1541, from the high bluff just below Memphis, he first saw the great river which was to make him famous, and was finally to be his grave.   He took possession of the country in the name of Spain, calling the great stream "The River of the Holy Ghost".   The site of Memphis was then occupied by an Indian village called

---

a The material for the following "historical sketch" of Memphis as far as the year 1827 was kindly furnished by Colonel J. M. Keating, of that city, and only lack of space forbids the insertion of the sketch entire as it came from the author's hands.

Chisca. More than a century rolled away before the spot was again visited by a European, but in July, 1673, the famed Father Marquette landed at Chisca while on his journey down the Mississippi. He remained many days, ministering to the Indians. Returning later, he established a mission at Chisca; and Joliet, who accompanied him by order of Frontenac, then governor of Canada, established there a trading post, the last in a chain extending from Quebec along the Saint Lawrence, the great lakes, and the Illinois river.

These posts were maintained by the French with little risk, as the traders adapted themselves to the life of the Indians, sometimes intermarried with them, and always avoided any opposition to their prejudices. In 1680 Chisca was visited by Father Hennepin, and two years later La Salle took formal possession of the territory in the name of France. La Salle made a treaty with the Chickasaw Indians, and established a fort and cabins at the mouth of the Margot, now the Wolf, river. This was the first permanent military occupation by any European nation on the Mississippi. La Salle returned to Europe in 1683, and then came back to America with a company of 280 colonists, intending to reach fort Prudhomme, as he had called the fort at Chisca. But he missed the mouth of the Mississippi, and finally landed at Matagorda bay, Texas. In January, 1687, after great suffering and loss, La Salle started overland, with the few of his men still living, for fort Prudhomme, and had advanced as far as Trinity river when he was murdered by his desperate and despairing followers. While La Salle was still at Matagorda bay, Tanti, one of his lieutenants, came to fort Prudhomme, expecting to meet his commander there. After waiting as long as he could he departed, leaving a letter, which was opened thirteen years after—in 1699—by Iberville, the last of the noted French discoverers to visit Chisca.

After this, fort Prudhomme is but little heard of. It was a dull, sleepy place, the monotony of its life being only occasionally broken by the arrival of a new commander, an inspection of posts, the coming of a courier or of a missionary.

In 1722, Charlevoix, the Jesuit historian and traveler, stopped at fort Prudhomme on his way to New Orleans. He found the place peaceful and prosperous; but this peace and prosperity were not to last long.

The rapid spread of the English settlements alarmed the French government, and in 1726 orders were sent to Bienville, then governor of Louisiana, to occupy the interior and consolidate the posts. In pursuance of his orders, Bienville, an able and courageous man, directed D'Artagnette, who was in command of the posts along the Illinois river, to collect a large force and join him at fort Prudhomme. Bienville was delayed at Mobile, and D'Artagnette, reaching the rendezvous and impatient at the delay, engaged the Indians in a battle, in which he was utterly defeated and fort Prudhomme was destroyed. When Bienville approached he too was defeated, and returned to New Orleans with only the wreck of his army. Another expedition was organized, and in 1739 Bienville reached the site of the old fort and built a new one, which he called fort Assumpsion, near the ruins of the old. While encamped here his army was decimated by an epidemic of dengue, and he was finally compelled to make a treaty with the Indians, dismantle his fort, and withdraw, taking with him the settlers at Chisca, Arkansas Post, and Natchez.

The treaty of Paris of 1763, which put an end to the French and Indian war, transferred to England all the possessions of France east of the Mississippi; and the treaty of Versailles, twenty years later, which terminated the Revolution, in its turn transferred the title to this territory to the United States. The Indians refused to acknowledge their transfer to England, and the Spaniards, to whom the French had ceded the territory protected by fort Prudhomme in 1762, supported them in their refusal. Accordingly, in 1782, Don Gayoso, the Spanish governor of New Orleans, sent a force to occupy Chisca. Whether or not the Indians resisted them is not clearly known, but it was not until after a year that the Spanish took possession and erected fort San Fernando, ready to dispute the possession of the country and the free use of the Mississippi river.

The flood of American immigration was, however, extending westward with irresistible force, and at the very time when fort San Fernando was being built, John Rice, of North Carolina, full of confidence in the power of the United States to maintain its title, purchased from his state 5,000 acres of the land on which Memphis now stands. A fellow-citizen, John Ramsey, followed his example, and purchased 5,000 acres adjoining and north of Rice's purchase. Both tracts were surveyed, one in 1786, while the Spanish flag was still waving over fort San Fernando. Rice was killed by Indians in 1791, while on a trading expedition, and his lands were thus placed upon the market. They were purchased in 1794 by John Overton, then a young lawyer, for himself and Andrew Jackson. Three years later, and a year after Tennessee had been admitted as a state into the Union (1796), Jackson sold three-fourths of his land to General James Winchester and his two brothers.

The claim of Spain to exclusive control of the Mississippi river was a source of constant annoyance to the settlers, and in 1795, by the treaty of Saint Lorenzo, the United States acquired free navigation of the river and the control of New Orleans for 10 years; and in 1803, by the Louisiana purchase, all the vast tract beyond the great river came into American possession. Immediately on notice of this, General Pike took formal possession of fort San Fernando, and unfurled the stars and stripes over fort Pike. In January, 1819, the cession of west Tennessee by the Chickasaw Indians was ratified by Congress, and in November the legislature of Tennessee organized Shelby county, and made Memphis, which had been laid out in the preceding May, the county-seat. The name "Memphis" was given, it is said, by Andrew Jackson. In 1825 the first religious congregation—Methodist—was organized; and in the following year Memphis was incorporated. This caused great surprise and indignation, for it was alleged that the charter had been smuggled through the legislature and passed in the interests of the proprietors, to whom it secured most of the profits to come from the growth of the place. A public meeting was called, denunciation was indulged in, and finally an amendment to the charter, fixing limits to the city, was passed. This was ratified by the legislature in 1827, and in March the organization of the city was completed by the election of aldermen, who chose M. B. Winchester, one of their number, mayor.

Such was the beginning of the city of Memphis, now "The Taxing District of Shelby County". A census taken at the time of incorporation showed that the population had increased from the 53 of 1819 to 308. The trade of the new city was, of course, small, money was scarce, and cotton-gin receipts were as good as gold. In July a severe blow was dealt to Memphis by the removal of the courts to Raleigh, which then became the county-seat; and its misfortune was increased by an epidemic of dengue, or break-bone fever, precursor of the plagues that were to come.

In 1828 the yellow fever made its first appearance in the city and carried away 53 inhabitants, one-sixth of the entire population. Owing to the reputation for unhealthfulness thus acquired, and to the somewhat riotous character of the flat-boatmen who frequented the city, Memphis acquired a bad name, which her neighbors did not disdain to turn to their own advantage. Steamboats rarely tied up at its landings, preferring Randolph, a few miles above. Its growth was therefore slow for many years.

The situation of the city on the Mississippi and its excellent landing facilities, combined with the energy of the inhabitants, gained for Memphis importance in spite of its unhealthfulness. In twenty-two years the population had increased to 8,841, and by that time Memphis was the most important place on the river between Saint Louis and New Orleans. Large quantities of cotton came there for shipment, its trade with the surrounding country increased, and the United States government recognized the importance of the city by making it a naval station and building a large ropewalk there.

In 1860 the population was 22,621, an increase of 13,780 in ten years; but the civil war brought a period of great loss. Memphis was taken by the Federal forces in June, 1862, and was held by them during the rest of the war, except for a few hours in 1864. With the close of the war the rapid growth began again, and the rate of increase established between 1850 and 1860 was fully maintained, as the census enumeration of 1870 showed a population of 40,226. Within the past ten years, however, misfortunes have come thick and fast upon the city. A considerable portion of its territory was set off in 1871–'72, and the population was thus diminished. A loss of this kind was, however, comparatively easy to bear, and had it not been for the frightful epidemics of yellow fever in 1873, 1878, and 1879, Memphis in 1880 would have shown a large increase in population and a larger one in wealth. Immediately after 1870 business was brisk and prosperity apparently assured. The number of bales of cotton received in the year 1870–'71 was larger than ever before in the history of the city, reaching a total of 511,432 bales, valued at $39,552,356. This prosperous beginning of the decade was followed by another year of good trade, and an era of unexampled good fortune seemed to have begun, when it was suddenly checked.

In September, 1873, just as the great commercial crisis was beginning, a severe epidemic of yellow fever, small-pox, and cholera came upon the city. A panic ensued. The frightened people fled the city and the population was reduced to about 20,000; 7,000 cases of yellow fever were reported and 2,000 deaths. Cholera carried away 276 from 1,000 it attacked, and small-pox was very prevalent among the negroes. Five years later came the most terrible of all the many epidemics. The yellow fever raged with unprecedented violence. The people fled in terror until a quarantine was established and the 19,500 persons then in the city were compelled to remain. It would be vain to attempt to portray the sufferings in the city; 17,600 of the 19,500 left in Memphis were attacked by the disease, and 5,150 succumbed to it.

Roused at last to their danger, the citizens took energetic means to prevent a return of the plague. The city was built on land naturally saturated with water, and the filth accumulated in years by the disregard of all sanitary rules rendered this moist soil a constant source of disease, a perfect arsenal of the weapons of death. No health could be hoped for until this land was drained and the constant sources of pollution were removed. The national, state, and municipal boards of health co-operated in investigating the causes of disease and in recommending improvements. Finally (January, 1808) a system of sewers and one of drainage-tiles was begun, and up to the present time (September, 1880), 20½ miles of sewers and 30 miles of drain-tiles have been laid, soon to be extended to 30 and 50 miles, respectively. This has so far been attended with excellent results, although an epidemic of yellow fever occurred in 1879, during which there were 1,532 cases and 485 deaths. No epidemic has visited the place during the present year, and it is hoped that now Memphis is freed from the fearful visitations which have so often desolated her.

Although these epidemics injured trade greatly, the prosperity of the citizens was able to meet the strain, and the yearly receipts of cotton averaged 404,485 bales, and a large trade with the South and Southwest was maintained. The wealth of the citizens, however, did not imply that the city corporation was financially sound. The debt of the city had increased to such an extent that it was impossible to meet the demands of creditors. The latter were accordingly about to take legal steps to obtain possession of the city property, when the citizens, to avoid paying their just debts, petitioned the legislature to deprive them of their charter as a city. This the legislature consented

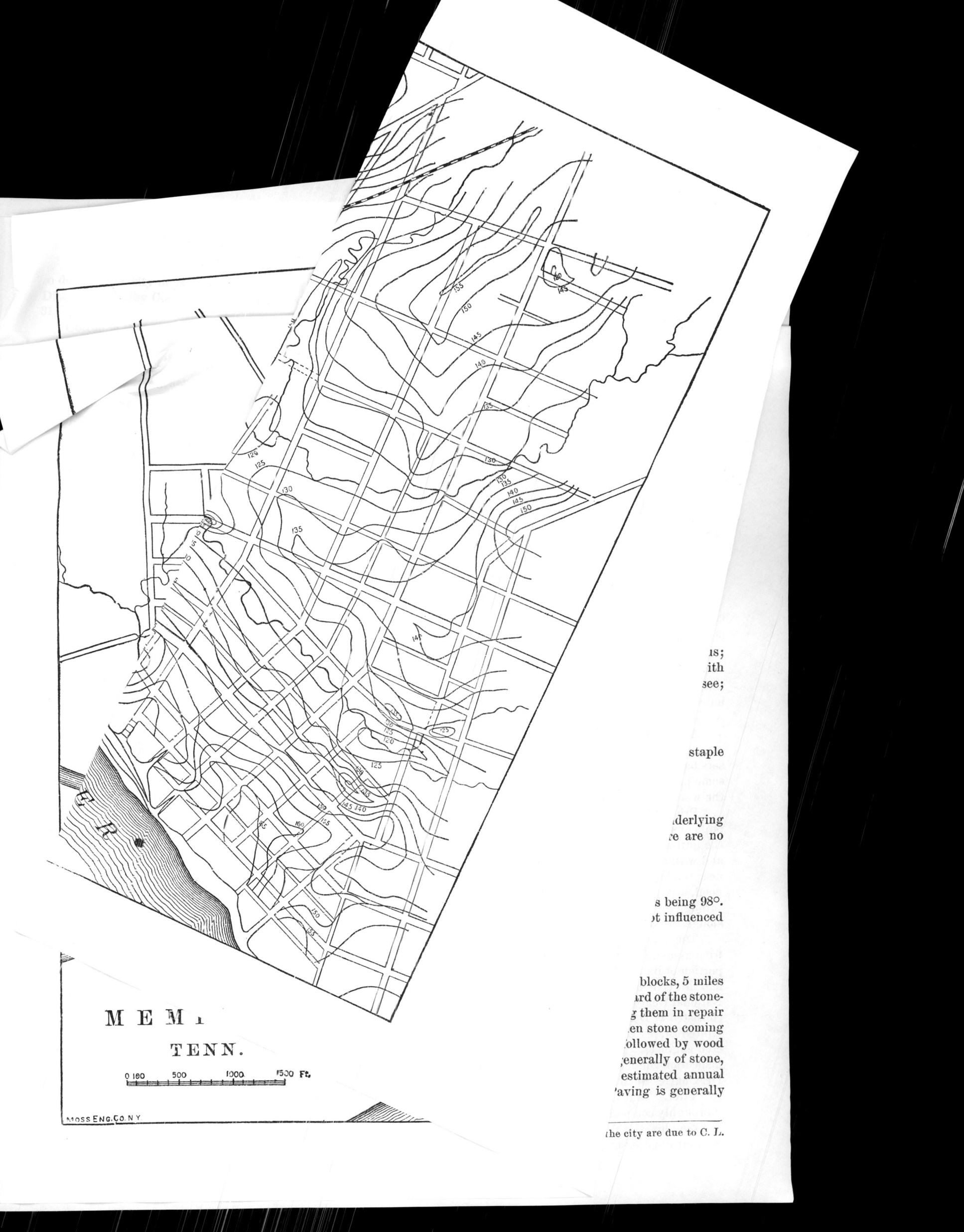

MEMﹾ

TENN.

0 180   500   1000   1500 Ft.

is;
ith
see;

staple

derlying
re are no

s being 98°.
t influenced

blocks, 5 miles
rd of the stone-
g them in repair
en stone coming
ollowed by wood
enerally of stone,
estimated annual
aving is generally

the city are due to C. L.

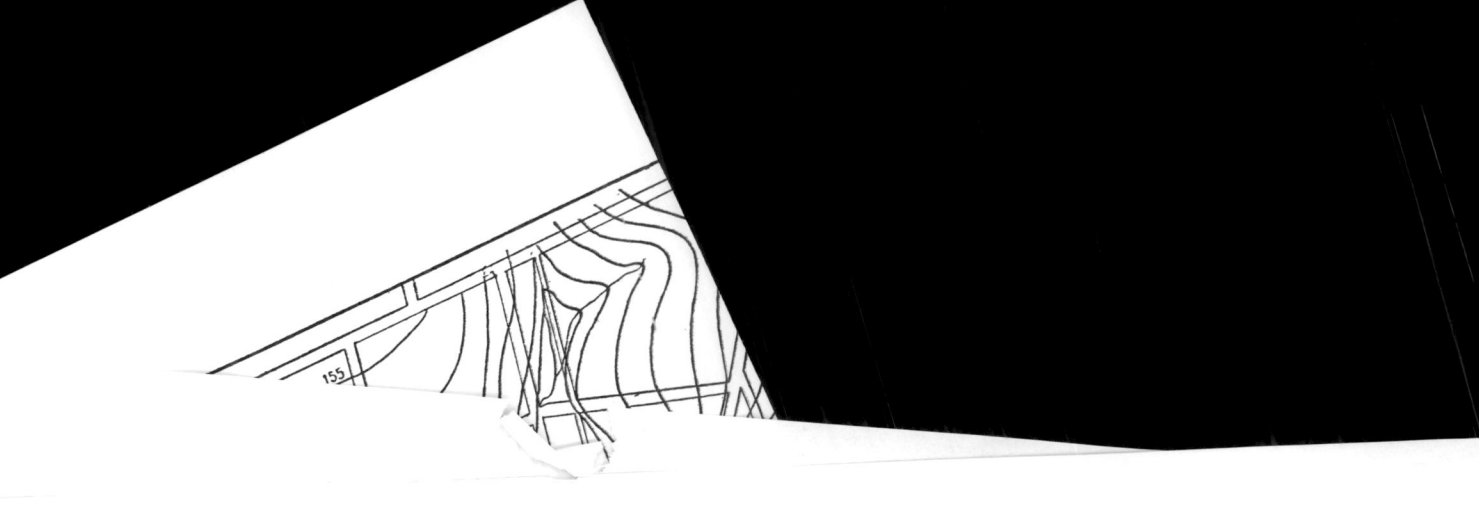

There is one horse-railroad company; this.has 15 miles of track, 80 cars, and 250 horses and mules, and employs 150 men; the rate of fare is 5 cents. Omnibuses ply between the depots and landings; 30 vehicles and 100 horses are in use; the number of men employed is 30, and the rate of fare is 25 cents.

WATER-WORKS.
GAS.

The gas supply is obtained from a private corporation, which refused to give any detailed information a... average daily production, annual income, etc. The charge per 1,000 feet is $3, and the city pays $27 a year f... each of its 580 gas street-lamps.

PUBLIC BUILDINGS.

The buildings owned by the city and used in whole or in part for municipal purposes, include 5 steam fire-engine houses, a police-station, and a city hall, together valued at $100,000. The present value of the city hall is $20,000.

PUBLIC PARKS AND PLEASURE-GROUNDS.

There are several small parks in the center of the city, nicely laid out and carefully kept. The total area is about 4 acres. They were gifts to the city, and are controlled by the city government.

PLACES OF AMUSEMENT.

Leubrie's theater and Greenlow's opera-house, each seating about 2,500, are the only theaters in the city. They pay an annual license of $500 to the city. Memphis Club, Männerchor, Tennessee Club, and Assembly halls, each of which has a seating capacity of about 1,000, are used for concerts, lectures, etc. There are a few beer-gardens outside the city limits.

DRAINAGE.

The natural drainage of Memphis, with the exception of a very small portion which has an inclination toward the Mississippi, is discharged into a deep-cut bayou—bayou Gayoso—which empties into Wolf river about half a mile from its outlet. The inclination of the surface toward the bayou and its various branches is uniform and somewhat rapid.

At the ordinary stages of the Mississippi, the bayou discharges at shallow depth, and its bottom is mainly exposed. During high stages of the river, usually from May to July, and occasionally at other seasons, the water sets back in the bayou quite half-way through the city, and toward Wolf river it overflows wide areas, including some built-up districts where the houses stand on piles, and only artificially graded streets are above the level of the water.

Prior to 1880 there had been built only about 4 miles of sewerage, mainly 12- and 15-inch pipes, in the compactly built business portion of the town, laid at the cost of private individuals. All surface-water was delivered through the gutters to the bayou or to the river. In the better-built streets these gutters were of brick, nearly semi-circular, and with a width of several feet, being bridged for a foot-way in front of each house. The population along and near the bayou delivered its entire filth, including excrementitious matters, over the bank of the stream or into its flood, according as its water might be high or low. A large proportion of the household wastes were discharged through gutters, also into the bayou, which was thus made to constitute an inexpressibly foul and objectionable slough through the heart of the city, and in many cases adjacent to its most most fashionable quarters.

The devastating epidemic of yellow fever in 1878, succeeded in 1879 by another epidemic, which was prevented from assuming like proportions largely by the removal into camps outside of the city of nearly the whole susceptible portion of its population, and which still found about 500 victims, led to the adoption of more active measures than had hitherto been carried out for the permanent improvement of the city. At the request of the authorities the National Board of Health appointed a special committee to advise as to permanent improvements. This committee consisted of Doctors Billings, Mitchell, and Johnson of the national board. To these were joined Major Benyaurd, United States Engineer, Dr. C. F. Folsom, secretary of the Massachusetts board of health, and G. E. Waring, jr., civil engineer. A thorough investigation of the condition of the city was made, including a careful house-to-house inspection conducted by Dr. F. W. Reilly, and a chemical examination of the various sources of water-supply by Dr. Charles Smart, U. S. A. The following is a summary of the recommendations made by this committee:

First. That the "superintendence and subsequent care of the sanitary work" be placed in the hands of a thoroughly competent sanitary officer, independent of politics, to direct "a large amount of sanitary work to be done in Memphis, the details of which must be left to a great extent discretionary, in order to secure the best results without unnecessary expense".

Notwithstanding the provision made for the constant cleanliness of the sewers, it was thought that permanent and efficient ventilation should be a prominent feature of the plan. It was therefore provided that every house-drain should be extended through an open-mouthed soil-pipe of not less than 4 inches diameter to the top of each house served, and that there should be nowhere in the course of this house-drain and soil-pipe any trap, contraction, or other obstruction to the free movement of the air. This to the end that under the varying influences of different winds, of different exposure to the rays of the sun, and of the different temperature of the buildings through which the soil-pipes passed, there should be maintained a constant movement up or down through these various pipes. It was found in practice that the ventilation of the sewers is greatly facilitated by the discharge of the flush-tanks, this discharge passing through the pipes with a sufficient volume to force the air before it and to establish a partial vacuum behind it, so that, as each wave moved forward, the soil-pipes in front of it became outlets for the sewer-air, and those behind it inlets for fresh air. The further provision was made in the original plan that there should be constructed at the lower end of each branch sewer a fresh-air inlet, opening to the surface of the street; this serving also as an inspection-hole to observe the flow of the sewers. As the work went rapidly forward, the construction of these fresh-air inlets was postponed, and a subsequent inspection of the sewers from which they had been omitted showed that they were not necessary to the maintenance of a complete ventilation; only some half a dozen of them in all were built, and these have been chiefly useful in enabling the inspectors to determine the rapidity and regularity of the flow, the efficiency of the capacity of the sewers, and the rapidity of movement of the discharge from the flush-tanks, experimental requirements which have been sufficiently satisfied by the small number of inlets constructed. It was found as the work went on that it was entirely safe to continue the sewers of a diameter of 6 inches, even through closely built streets, for a length of about 3,000 feet. The indications are that, so far at least as the branch sewers are concerned, they will never run more than half full, even during the hours of greatest use (from 8 to 11 in the morning), except momentarily, during the discharge of the flush-tanks.

In the construction of the work it was found that many of the lines crossed the beds of old branches of the bayou which had been filled with all manner of rubbish, and which afforded a most insecure foundation for the laying of the pipes. In such places the device was adopted of supporting each pipe on the ends of two board piles driven to a firm holding, and sawed out to fit the exterior circumference of the pipes. This was found in all cases to be a successful device. In one instance, where the ground was of such unstable character that the pipe-layers sank to their knees in the bottom of the ditch, subsequent examination showed the pipes to be undisturbed, the ground to the level of their bottoms having become perfectly solidified by the action of the adjoining tile-drain.

The flush-tanks used in the Memphis sewerage are the invention of Rogers Field, an English engineer of eminence, and are patented to him in this country. They are fed by a small, constant stream from the water-works supply, sufficient to fill them (112 gallons only) once or twice in 24 hours. They are discharged by an annular siphon, which becomes sealed against the outer atmosphere when they begin to overflow. The dripping through the inner limb of the slight stream added to the tank removes little by little the confined air, causing the flow to increase gradually until it becomes sufficient to exhaust all of the air and cause the contents of the tank to be discharged with great rapidity (in from 35 to 45 seconds).

Observations made on a sewer running eastward from the Court Square showed that when the tank discharged, the sewer was filled nearly half full with a very strong and rapid stream at the fresh-air inlet, about 1,000 feet down the line.

More because of the need for great economy than because of other considerations, the construction of manholes and lamp-holes and lateral sewers was entirely omitted; except at the few fresh-air inlets, no provision was made for inspecting the condition of the interior of the sewer. Experience has demonstrated great advantages resulting from this omission. Openings into the street, of whatever character, greatly enhance the likelihood of the admission of substances large enough to obstruct such small pipes. And with such small pipes the efficiency of manholes in removing obstructions is much less than it would be with even 12-inch sewers. As at present arranged, nothing can enter the sewer which does not reach it through a 4-inch house-drain. The work was carried out with the assumption that, ordinarily, whatever had passed through this drain would be swept forward in the 6-inch sewer by the discharge of the flush-tank. This assumption has thus far been well sustained, but few obstructions having occurred. Where these have occurred they have been easily located by the failure of the house-drain above them to discharge, and have been quickly and cheaply removed by excavation from the surface.

It is usual, where manholes are used, to build the sewers in straight lines vertically and laterally between these, so that their condition may be inspected by sighting a lantern through them, and to confine the curves needed for a change of direction to a very short area of the bottom of the manhole. In Memphis, as this restriction is not imposed, all corners are passed on curves of large radius, so that the lessening of the flow due to change of direction is reduced to the minimum.

Ground was broken for the work on the 21st of January, 1880, and at the beginning of June about 18½ miles of sewers had been laid, and the high-water outlet into Wolf river had been completed. Practically the whole city between the west main and the Mississippi had been sewered, and the branch main on the east side of the bayou, with some of its laterals, had been laid.

The improvement, as recommended to be carried out by the committee, and as adopted by the local authorities, includes a dam across Gayoso bayou, at Second street, with a flood-gate for the discharge of the waters of the bayou during low stages of the Mississippi. The purpose of the dam is to exclude the back-water of the high river, the flow of the bayou at such times being removed by a steam-pump. The completion of this part of the work will not only prevent the overflow and saturation of large areas of land bordering the bayou, but will also make it possible to extend the sewerage system to a large population whose houses are too low for connection with the main gravity outflow. The high-water outlet into Wolf river was first constructed because requiring less time in its execution, and as affording an immediate outlet for the flow. At ordinary stages of the river the entire flow will be delivered through a 20-inch iron pipe delivering into the Mississippi about half a mile below the high-water outlet, and at a point where the natural currents will carry the sewage away from the shore.

HOUSE-DRAINAGE.

Up to the time when the work above described was undertaken, the only method adopted for the disposal of household wastes was to deliver excrementitious matters into vaults and to discharge house-water into the street-gutters, or, more commonly, to flow it over the surface of the back yard. Some of the vaults were curiosities. In the business parts of the town they were excavated in the cellars, and were carried down to the level of the water-bearing stratum, sometimes 30 feet below the cellar-bottom. These served for a long time for the complete disposal of all that was delivered into them; but little by little their outlets became clogged, and they gradually filled nearly to the surface. They were then but slightly excavated, their upper portions being filled with earth, and a fresh pit being dug near by. In one case there were five of such accumulations of fecal matter in the cellar of a single house.

In connection with isolated houses, the ordinary privy-vault was constructed.

When the sewerage improvement was undertaken, the power of the local authorities being absolute, a rigid rule was enforced, not only compelling every house to connect with the sewers, but requiring that the connection be made under the supervision of the proper officer, both with reference to the laying of the main drain and the erection of the untrapped soil-pipe above referred to, but controlling every portion of the plumbing work. Memphis is probably at this time (1880) the only city in the world in which the use of the pan water-closet is prohibited, it being required that no water-closet shall be used which has an unventilated space of more than 100 cubic inches capacity between two water-seals.

While there is no trap on the main drain or soil-pipe, it is of course required that every fixture in the house shall be separated from these by its own trap, placed as close as possible to the fixture. Before the final connection with the sewer can be made, every part of the system must be approved by the inspecting engineer in charge of all such work. It is too early to determine with certainty what is to be the future of this system of sewerage, and much too early to determine its influence upon the sanitary condition of Memphis. In itself as it stands, it is to be regarded only as an experiment in sewerage. Its influence on the public health will hardly be perceptible until it shall have been extended not only to all of the higher-lying parts of the city, but equally to those portions to which it can be applied only after the exclusion of the Mississippi floods from the bayou, after the attendant purification of the bayou, and after the carrying out of the other sanitary recommendations of the National Board of Health committee, as recited above, including especially the completion of the outlet to the Mississippi river, and the consequent removal of the sewage from the vicinity of the intake of the water-works.

CEMETERIES.

There are 4 cemeteries connected with the city:

Jewish Cemetery, area 3 acres, situated a little beyond the city limits, about a mile from the center of the city.

Saint Peter's Cemetery, Catholic, quite near the Jewish cemetery.

Elmwood Cemetery, on Broadway, 2 miles from the city center, and beyond the limits, containing 100 acres.

A negro cemetery, neither the area nor location of which was furnished.

There are 2 other cemeteries within the city, in which interments are no longer allowed: *Winchester Cemetery*, situated on Winchester avenue, in the eastern part of the city, has an area of 10 acres. *Catholic Orphan Cemetery* contains 3 acres.

No information as to the number of interments in these cemeteries was furnished. A permit must be obtained before any burial will be allowed.

MARKETS.

Memphis has 2 markets, each of which cost about $6,000, contains 50 stalls, and controls a space of about 10,000 square feet used by farmers and hucksters as wagon-stands. The stalls rent at from $5 to $50 per annum. The total annual rental was not furnished. The markets are each under the charge of a market-master appointed by the legislative council, and are opened in winter from 5 to 9 p. m. and in summer from 4 to 10 a. m. The ordinances of the city require all dealers in fresh meat, fish, and vegetables outside the markets to pay an annual license, and prohibit the opening of new stores within one-fourth of a mile from the markets. About one-third of the retail supply of meat, fish, and vegetables is obtained in the markets.

SANITARY AUTHORITY—BOARD OF HEALTH.

The chief health organization of Memphis is a board of health, appointed by the legislative council, but independent in its action. It consists of the president of the taxing district *ex officio*, the chief of police, a secretary, who must be a physician, a health officer, and a physician. It meets when called together by the president. The board was organized in 1879, and its annual expenses have been $20,000, incurred in the inspection and cleaning of streets and the removal of garbage. A very large amount of work was done in removing accumulations of filth created in past years, and in cleaning and filling up privy-vaults. Assistance was also given to the city engineer in removing the Nicholson wood pavement. From these causes the total expenses of the board from February, 1879, to November, 1880, amounted to $35,108 51. In case of an epidemic the board seems to have the power to increase its expenses to any necessary amount. Its authority, both during and in the absence of an epidemic, is ample to meet all the requirements of sanitary science. The board constantly employs 3 assistant health officers and inspectors, and can at any time employ as many more as it deems necessary. The entire police force is at its disposal. All these assistants are members of the police force and retain their police authority, while any member of the board has power to enter and examine any premises. Inspections are made regularly in all parts of the city.

NUISANCES.

When nuisances are found or reported, an inspection is made, and orders are issued to the owner, occupant, or agent of the property to remove or abate it within a reasonable time. If this order is disregarded, the person so disregarding it is liable to a fine of not less than $5 nor more than $50, and the abatement or removal is made at once by the health officer, all expense so incurred being collected from the estate by the attorney of the city. The list of nuisances includes every thing, except disease, which may be an injury to the public health or a cause of offense to the citizens. Defective house-drainage, cesspools, etc., are treated as nuisances. Defective sources of drinking-water are inspected and ordered to be cleaned, while, if it seems impossible to render them safe, they are filled up and a supply of drinking-water is obtained in some other way. In cases of defective sewerage and street-cleaning, the board calls the attention of the proper officers to the defects, or in some cases makes the necessary changes itself.

GARBAGE.

The board has full control of the removal and conservation of garbage, prescribing the manner in which it shall be kept and the method of its removal. A detailed account of the regulations will be found under the heading "Removal of garbage and ashes" in the account of "Municipal cleansing".

BURIAL OF THE DEAD.

No interment is allowed until a burial permit has been obtained of the board of health. The application for a permit must be accompanied with a certificate of death signed by the attending physician or by some competent person, and this is placed on file at the office of the board. All sextons or other persons having charge of any burial-ground, tomb, or vault must make a weekly return of all burials coming under their charge.

INFECTIOUS DISEASES.

The regulations in regard to infectious and contagious diseases are very strict, care being taken to guard against all possible means of introducing or spreading them. Street-cars are forbidden to have cushions on the seats or backs of seats; the introduction of infected persons or articles is prohibited; the contents of privies and cesspools must be disinfected when removed; and buildings the sanitary condition of which is bad are torn down, and the construction of new ones is forbidden unless sanitary rules are observed. A quarantine can be established at any time by the board of public works on the recommendation of the board of health, and the legislative council may declare what boats and persons, and from what points, shall be subject to quarantine regulations. Boats from such infected places must stop at the quarantine grounds and be thoroughly inspected, and, if necessary, passengers or cargo must be removed to the places provided for infected persons or goods. A permanent quarantine station is established on President's island, a number of miles below the city, and here all steamers passing up the river are stopped and inspected. Infected goods are removed to the island and disinfected, and persons who are infected or who have been exposed to disease are retained there, although no one not absolutely sick may be detained at the station more than ten days. Any attempt to pass the station without stopping for inspection is a misdemeanor, and the captain, mate, engineers, pilots, and clerks of the boat so passing are arrested and fined.

Small-pox patients are removed to a small-pox hospital on the river, 4 miles below the city. In some cases, however, they are quarantined at home, and the house is placarded to warn passers of danger. Scarlet-fever patients are quarantined at home, and the house is placarded, and care is taken to prevent the spread of the disease. If contagious diseases make their appearance in the schools, the pupils from infected families are forced to absent themselves till all danger is passed. Should the case demand it the schools are closed. Vaccination is compulsory and is done at the public expense. All persons knowing the existence of any contagious, infectious, or malignant disease are required to report it to the board of health.

The registration of births, diseases, and deaths is in charge of the board of health, to which all births, diseases, and deaths must be reported.

REPORTS.

The board reports monthly to the legislative council, and these reports are published. An annual report is also published.

MUNICIPAL CLEANSING.

Street-cleaning.—Each householder is compelled to clean the streets and alleys, sidewalks and gutters adjoining his premises as far as the middle of the street or alley, placing the refuse in piles in the middle of the way, where it can be collected by the city's force. The work is done entirely by hand. The collection is under the charge of the board of health, which, from February 1, 1879, to November 30, 1880, expended $4,382 16 in this work. The annual cost to private persons is estimated at $2,000. The ordinances require the streets to be cleaned twice in each week; in practice, the work is done only when necessary. The sweepings are deposited on board a boat prepared to receive them, which finally empties them into the Mississippi below the city.

Removal of garbage and ashes.—The board of health has full control of the removal of garbage and ashes. Garbage, while awaiting removal, must be kept in suitable and sufficient boxes, barrels, or tubs, capable of holding, without being filled to within 4 inches of the top, the accumulations of 36 hours. They must be placed within the grounds of the householder, and can be allowed on the sidewalks only for such a time as is needful for the removal of the contents. Ashes must be kept in vessels either entirely of metal or lined with metal, and must not be mixed with garbage. The removal of garbage is made in tight carts, which must not be so loaded as to spill the contents. Both ashes and garbage are dumped into the boat which receives the street-sweepings, and are thrown with them into the river. The cost of the service in 1880 was $8,636 61.

Dead animals are removed by a contractor under the direction of the board of health. The annual cost is stated at $240.

Liquid household wastes.—Chamber-slops and kitchen and laundry wastes are disposed of alike, nearly all going into the public sewers. No wastes are allowed to run into the street-gutters, and only very little goes into cesspools, which are fast being abandoned and filled up. The few that remain are cleaned when full by the odorless-excavator process, and the contents thrown into the Mississippi river.

Human excreta.—Three-fourths of the houses in the city are provided with water-closets, all of which empty into the public sewers. The board of health has enforced the ordinances of the city which require that all privy-vaults shall be cleaned out and filled up. During the period of transition from privy-vaults to water-closets, the dry-earth system was in use, the city ordinances requiring that instead of privy-vaults a water-tight receptacle, holding from three pecks to a bushel, should be let in under the privy-seat and the contents covered at least once a day with dry earth or dry ashes. Once in every two weeks at least, the contents of these receptacles were removed. All vaults were required to be filled up by April 1, 1880, but a few are still left. None of these are absolutely water-tight, though nearly all are walled with bricks. They are cleaned in the same manner as cesspools, and the night-soil is thrown into the Mississippi.

Manufacturing wastes.—No information in regard to the disposal of manufacturing wastes was furnished.

POLICE.

The police force is appointed and governed by the board of fire and police commissioners. The chief executive officer is the chief of police, whose salary is $125 a month and whose duty is the general supervision and management of the force. The rest of the force consists of 2 captains, salary $90 a month each; 2 sergeants, salary $80 a month each; and 37 men, salary $60 each per month. Not all the latter are patrolmen; 2 are detectives, 2 market-keepers, and 3 sanitary inspectors. The uniform is of blue cloth with brass buttons. Each man supplies his own uniform, except the star and buttons, and purchases his arms, which consist of a baton and a revolver. The men are on duty twelve hours each day, and patrol 65 miles of streets. No record of the number of arrests, of the amount of property lost or stolen and reported to the police, or of the number of station-house lodgers was furnished. The force is expected to co-operate with the fire and health departments; each patrolman is a sanitary officer. Special policemen are appointed by the board of fire and police commissioners, and while on duty are treated as regular members of the force. The total cost of the department from February 1, 1879, to November 1, 1880, was $58,533 31; the annual expense is about $35,000.

MANUFACTURES.

The following is a summary of the statistics of the manufactures of Memphis for 1880, being taken from the tables prepared for the Tenth Census by William A. Hill, special agent:

Mechanical and manufacturing industries.	No. of establishments.	Capital.	AVERAGE NUMBER OF HANDS EMPLOYED.			Total amount paid in wages during the year.	Value of materials.	Value of products.
			Males above 16 years.	Females above 15 years.	Children and youths.			
All industries	138	$2,313,975	2,130	69	69	$845,672	$2,419,341	$4,413,422
Boots and shoes, including custom work and repairing	3	5,000	12			4,800	3,376	10,600
Bread and other bakery products	7	16,800	33		1	10,650	37,200	68,000
Carpentering	5	12,750	29			17,300	29,700	64,500
Carriages and wagons (see also Wheelwrighting)	6	178,400	158	2	1	51,250	55,250	176,500
Clothing, men's	8	32,100	85	39		63,600	65,000	175,500
Confectionery	5	32,500	53	3	2	18,050	110,500	160,000
Foundery and machine-shop products	9	140,800	189	2	9	83,114	91,274	252,400
Lock- and gun-smithing	5	4,600	9		1	4,150	3,300	11,200
Lumber, sawed	5	196,000	166		2	22,500	212,400	300,660
Marble and stone work	6	22,200	26			9,100	12,150	38,900
Oil, cottonseed and cake	5	535,000	415	2	18	120,000	550,000	835,000
Painting and paperhanging	3	13,500	26			5,653	7,300	20,500
Plumbing and gasfitting	6	17,400	58		6	19,500	30,400	73,000
Printing and publishing	4	92,000	101	6	5	67,246	52,939	165,714
Saddlery and harness	4	17,950	39			18,400	35,450	75,020
Tinware, copperware, and sheet-iron ware	10	104,500	88	10		42,899	99,500	203,000
Upholstering	4	55,000	22	3		11,445	7,308	34,000
Wheelwrighting (see also Carriages and wagons)	5	1,400	16			3,500	2,200	7,700
All other industries (a)	38	836,075	605	2	24	272,515	1,014,094	1,741,228

a Embracing agricultural implements; blacksmithing; bookbinding and blank-book making; brick and tile; brooms and brushes; cars, railroad, street, and repairs; clothing, women's; corsets; cotton compressing; cotton goods; cotton-ties; flouring- and grist-mill products; furnishing goods, men's; liquors, malt; looking-glass and picture frames; lumber, planed; masonry, brick and stone; mineral and soda waters; musical instruments and materials (not specified); photographing; sash, doors, and blinds; scales and balances; sewing machines and attachments; shipbuilding; slaughtering and meat-packing; soap and candles; stencils and brands; stone- and earthen-ware; tobacco, cigars and cigarettes; and trunks and valises.

From the foregoing table it appears that the average capital of all establishments is $16,767 93; that the average wages of all hands employed is $372 87 per annum; that the average outlay in wages, in materials, and in interest (at 6 per cent.) on capital employed is $24,665 59.

NASHVILLE,

DAVIDSON COUNTY, TENNESSEE.

POPULATION

IN THE

AGGREGATE,

1800-1880.

	Inhab.
1790	.....
1800	345
1810	.....
1820	.....
1830	5,566
1840	6,929
1850	10,165
1860	16,988
1870	25,865
1880	43,350

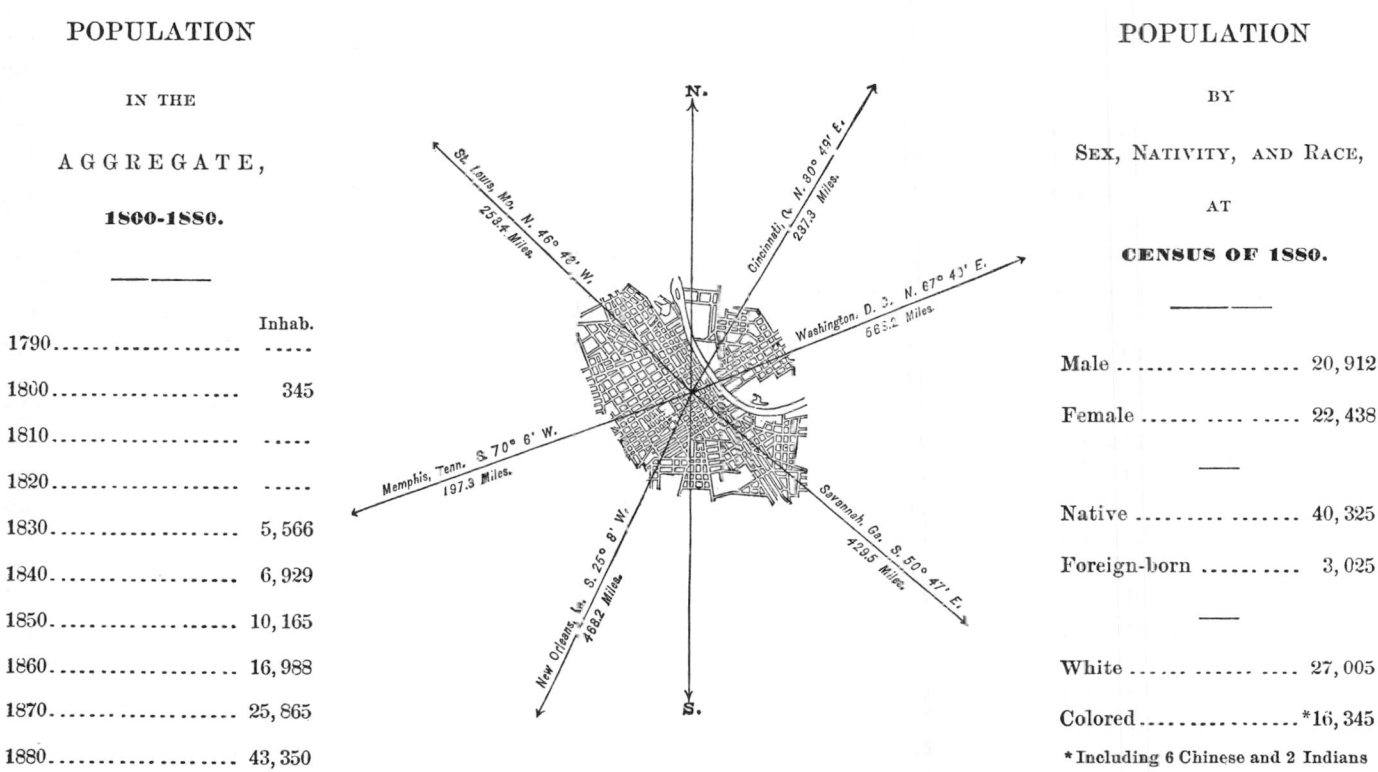

POPULATION

BY

SEX, NATIVITY, AND RACE,

AT

CENSUS OF 1880.

Male	20,912
Female	22,438
Native	40,325
Foreign-born	3,025
White	27,005
Colored	*16,345

* Including 6 Chinese and 2 Indians

Latitude: 36° 9′ North; Longitude: 86° 47′ (west from Greenwich); Altitude: 500 feet.

FINANCIAL CONDITION:

Total Valuation: $13,336,760; per capita: $308 00.   Net Indebtedness: $1,606,200; per capita: $37 05.   Tax per $100: $3 00.

HISTORICAL SKETCH.(a)

Previous to 1780, hunters from the Watauga settlement in East Tennessee came into the Cumberland country on trading and exploring expeditions. Among those who came in the spring of 1779 were James Robertson, Kasper Mauska, and several others, who planted a field of corn in what is now known as North Nashville, for the use of the colonists they intended to bring into the country the ensuing fall and winter. The whole country to the north, and as far south as the Tennessee river, was free from any settled tribe of Indians, though previously large numbers of red men had lived there, as the burial-places all around the city testify. Thousands and thousands of Indian graves have been opened or plowed over by the farmers in the neighborhood. The Indians made this part of the

a Prepared for the Tenth Census by Anson Nelson, esq.

country, as well as the present state of Kentucky, a common hunting-ground. Robertson made up a party in the Watauga settlement, to come by land; while John Donelson formed another party a little later, to come by water, and to bring the women and children of some of those who had gone with Robertson. The water-route was long, almost unknown, and full of dangers. The party traveling by land met a band of Virginian emigrants, under the leadership of John Raine, *en route* for Kentucky, whom they urged to join them. This was done, and the two bands reached the present site of Nashville in the latter part of 1779 or in the first part of 1780, the cattle and wagons being taken across the river on the ice. This winter is known as the *cold winter*, the temperature not having fallen so low here since then. Soon after this another company arrived from North Carolina, making the total number of persons at this point about 200. On the 24th of April, 1780, the Donelson party landed, and, several small stations having been established in the surrounding country, it was decided to make the Nashville station a headquarters. The settlers found here a French trading-post that had been established as early as 1710, and the "lick" at this place, where the buffalo and other wild animals obtained the saline nutriment they required, was therefore called the "French Salt Lick". This lick is within the present city limits, and adjoins the sulphur spring, whose waters are well known. These early settlers found a land of surpassing beauty and richness of soil. The trees of the forest were large and of almost endless variety, with a luxuriant undergrowth of cane. The woods were full of game. The streams abounded with fish, and in winter the water in the vicinity was covered with wild fowl.

On the 1st day of May, 1780, the different stations entered into a compact for their protection and government. The parent government of North Carolina was too far off to attempt any exercise of her guardian care. The compact or form of constitutional government established a court known as "judges, general arbiters, or triers", who had power to punish crime, to aid the needy, to assess fines, to regulate military defenses, land entries, etc.

The Indians on the south and west soon became jealous of the occupation of their hunting-grounds by the whites, and killed several of the settlers, one by one, as they would expose themselves, or be caught too far from the stations. A battle with the Indians took place in 1781 on Broad street, remembered as the "battle of the bluff". It was a hard fight, although the whites lost but few men. A number of the settlers, first and last, left here for "the Natchez", "the Illinois", etc., thinking they would find more attractive and profitable locations, and be free from the depredations of the Indians; and consequently the number of actual settlers in Nashville was considerably reduced in the beginning of 1783. In June of this year a treaty was entered into at General Robertson's house between commissioners from Virginia, Robertson, and the settlers, on one side, and a body of Indians on the other, the result being a better understanding between the races. Comparative peace prevailed for a short time. The Revolutionary struggle was over, there was general good feeling, and life and property were more secure. Commissioners from North Carolina came out, escorted by 100 soldiers, to look into the pre-emption rights of the new inhabitants, and to lay off a tract of 25,000 acres of land which the legislature proposed to give to General Greene for his extraordinary services in the war with Great Britain. North Carolina established an inferior court of pleas and quarter-sessions and invested it with considerable powers, not unlike those which the government of notables, arbiters, and triers had previously exercised. A court-house, prison, and stocks were erected, the town was laid off by commissioners, and Nashville assumed her place as a municipality. Two hundred acres was the quantity of land first laid off into town lots of 1 acre each, surveyed by Thomas Molloy in 1784. A ferry was established to cross the Cumberland, and provision was made for the institution of Davidson County academy, afterward the University of Nashville. This section of country was called Mero district, as a compliment to the Spanish governor of Louisiana at that time.

In 1790 North Carolina ceded all the territory west of the top of Stone mountain to the United States, and President Washington appointed William Blount territorial governor. Governor Blount appointed Andrew Jackson district attorney and John Donelson justice of the peace for Davidson county. These appointments were for the district of Mero, in the territory south of the Ohio river. The country prospered greatly, although the town grew slowly. A considerable trade was carried on by the Indians, who exchanged furs, skins, etc., for powder, lead, bright and gaudy colored handkerchiefs, and coarse blankets. Wheeled vehicles came into general use before the beginning of the present century.

Keel-boats and barges were used as early as 1810, and they took away large amounts of peltry to Pittsburgh, Natchez, and New Orleans, and brought back dry-goods, sugar, coffee, molasses, etc. The trips to either of the points named were long, tedious, and hazardous. The bargemen were stout and rough, and generally did as they pleased in every place where they landed. Their lawlessness was notorious. In the course of time, however, steamboats took the place of barges, and Nashville men very soon became either entire or part owners of steamers that navigated the Cumberland, the Ohio, and the Mississippi. In 1838, and for some years after, the finest and most costly steamboats that plowed the Mississippi river were owned by Nashville capitalists.

The panic of 1819 was very disastrous to the business men of Nashville. Many of them were utterly ruined, and this brought suffering to many others. The city finally recovered from this trouble, and was never in a more active, flourishing, and hopeful condition than in 1831-'32, about which time the city water-works were built, two banks, with large capital, were established, a house-insurance office was opened, and several steamboats were placed in the river trade. But the disastrous panic of 1837 checked all these things, and ruined many of

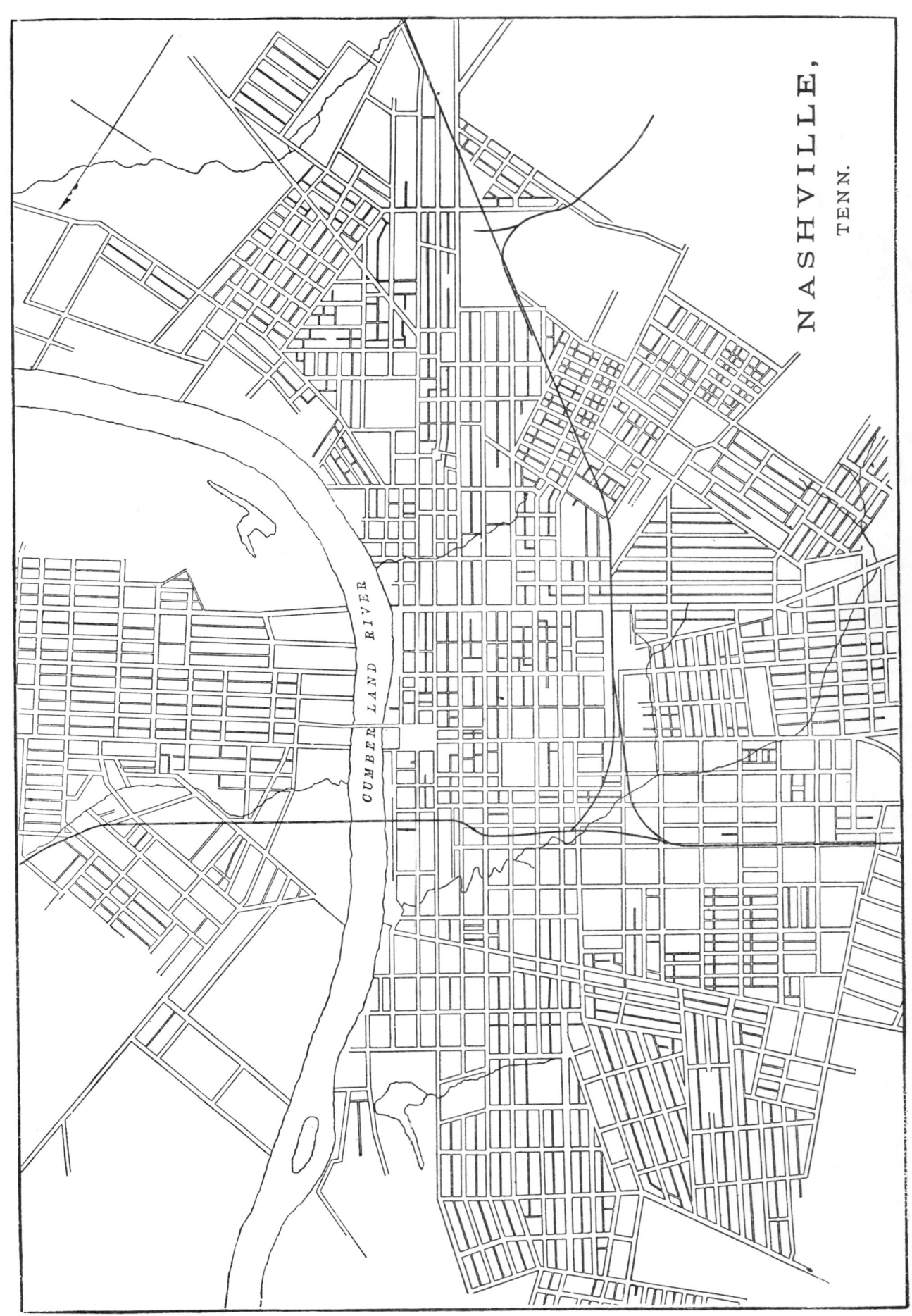

NASHVILLE, TENN.

CUMBERLAND RIVER

the best and most progressive business men. A considerable number of people removed to the then republic of Texas and began life anew. Real estate declined rapidly in value, and those who held on to what they had and bought more realized considerable profits in the course of a few years. The panic of 1857 did not very seriously affect the city. The panic of 1873, the effects of which continued for five years, greatly depressed business and labor; but most of the business men and all the banks successfully weathered the storm.

In 1806 the town was divided into six wards, containing nearly 533 acres. The municipality of South Nashville was organized, but subsequently was annexed to the old city, thus creating two more wards; then a large slice of territory in the northern part of the city came into the corporation, and the 9th ward was added; then the western suburb was annexed as the 10th ward, extending the area to 1,824 acres; then the corporation of Edgefield, on the eastern side of the Cumberland river, came into the city proper, making three more wards; then another slice of territory north of the city voted itself in, but the majority was so small that a lawsuit, known as the "fourteenth-ward case", was begun in court, and the matter is not yet decided—and the 14th ward is not yet incorporated as a part of the city. Then another slice of territory, on the western and southwestern portion of the city, was annexed as the 15th ward. The total area of the city now amounts to 3,483 acres, or nearly 5½ square miles.

During the civil war Nashville was at different times the storehouse for both armies, and was occupied by the Union as well as the Confederate forces.

NASHVILLE IN 1880.

The following statistical accounts, collected by the Census Office, indicate the present condition of Nashville:

LOCATION.

Nashville, the capital of Tennessee and seat of justice of Davidson county, lies in latitude 36° 9′ north, longitude 86° 47′ west from Greenwich, on the south bank of the Cumberland river, 200 miles above its mouth. The city is built on the river bluffs, that here rise 80 feet above low-water mark. The Cumberland river, which has its source among the Cumberland mountains near the southwestern boundary of Kentucky, flows at first nearly westward, and then making a wide circuit in middle Tennessee, it passes by Nashville, returns to Kentucky, flows northward, and finally enters the Ohio near Smithland. It is navigable from its mouth to Nashville during nine months in the year, and, for part of the time, to Carthage, about 200 miles above.

RAILROAD COMMUNICATIONS.

Nashville is touched by the following railroad lines:

The Louisville and Nashville railroad, to Louisville, Saint Louis, Hickman (Kentucky), Memphis, and New Orleans.

The Nashville, Chattanooga, and Saint Louis railroad, between the points named, with connections to Atlanta, and, via Lynchburg, Virginia, to the North.

TRIBUTARY COUNTRY.

Nashville is the chief commercial center and wholesale market south of the Ohio. In addition to the railroads that center here, twelve macadamized turnpikes enter the city, and give it great facilities for handling the trade with the surrounding country. The country immediately tributary to the city is agricultural, the principal crops being tobacco and cotton.

TOPOGRAPHY.

A chain or circle of beautiful conical-shaped hills rises on the north and northwest and on the south and southwest. Two streams—Lick branch and Wilson Spring branch—run through the old city, about 1 mile apart. A stream runs through the eastern part of the city. All of these waters flow into the river. The city is about 500 feet above the level of the sea. The rim of highlands around the city is about 1,000 feet above sea-level. The rock underlying the city—for the place is called the "City of Rocks"—is limestone, which is mostly of a bluish color, and generally very fossiliferous. The mass of rock is made up of several distinct, nearly horizontal beds or strata, which differ in texture, in amount of impurity, and in fossiliferous character. All belong to one of the oldest ages of geology—the Lower Silurian—and to the upper division of this, called the Nashville epoch. The sulphur spring at old French Salt Lick, is one of the finest sulphur springs in the country, and is situated within the city limits. A good chalybeate spring is at the east end of the suspension bridge which connects East Nashville with the old city.

WATER-WORKS.

The city has excellent water-works, established in 1832, and enlarged from time to time to suit the wants of the growing town, until now 50 miles of water-pipe are laid, furnishing 5,000 families and business houses with water. The water-works have cost about $1,500,000 in all.

GAS.

Gas-works have been for many years in successful operation, and the streets are lighted by 697 public lamps, at a cost of about $14,000 per annum.

PUBLIC BUILDINGS.

Among the public buildings of Nashville may be mentioned the insane asylum, situated 7 miles outside the city limits; the institution for the blind, near the water-works; the state capitol, situated on the highest point within the city; the United States custom-house, and many school-houses, etc.

PARKS; PLACES OF AMUSEMENT; DRAINAGE; STREETS; HEALTH; MUNICIPAL CLEANSING, ETC.

No information on any of these subjects was furnished.

MARKETS.

There is one public market in the city, situated on College street, near the city hall. The area of the grounds is 280 by 110 feet, the north and south ends being covered, with ample space on all sides for farmers' and hucksters' wagons, carts, etc. The total cost of the market, including land, was about $60,000. There are 32 butchers' stalls that rent for $150 per annum each; 88 vegetable stalls that rent for $75 per annum each; and 7 fish stalls that each rent for $25 a year. The annual amount received for rentals, including public scales, 2 ice-houses, and 2 restaurants, is $14,450. The hours during which the market is open are from 3 to 9 a. m. from April 1 to October 1, and from 4 to 11 a. m. during the remainder of the year; on Saturday the hours are from 4 a. m. to 9 p. m. all the year round. It is estimated that one-third of the retail supply of meats, poultry, fish, and vegetables is obtained by the public from this market, the remaining two-thirds being obtained from private shops and stores.

CEMETERIES.

There are 6 cemeteries used by the citizens of Nashville; 2 are general cemeteries for the Protestants, 2 are used by the Roman Catholics, 1 by the colored people, and 1 by the Jews.

City Cemetery, area 25 acres, situated in the southern part of the city, near the junction of the Louisville and Nashville, and the Nashville, Chattanooga and Saint Louis railroads, is not much used now. From 1822 to date there have been 21,589 interments made in this cemetery.

Mount Olivet Cemetery, 2 miles south of the city, contains 120 acres, and so far 6,079 interments have been made in it since 1859.

Mount Cavalry Cemetery, adjoining the above, has an area of 47 acres, and since 1869, 1,336 persons have been buried here.

The *Old Catholic Cemetery* has an area of 10 acres, but is not much used now.

Mount Ararat Cemetery, 1½ mile outside the city, has an area of 35 acres, and the number of interments averages 350 a year. This cemetery is owned and managed by the colored people.

The *Jewish Cemetery* is about 1 mile north of the city, and has an area of about 2 acres; but few interments have been made here.

There are no church-yards or private burying-grounds in the city in which interments are made.

PUBLIC SCHOOLS.

Nashville has ever been noted as an educational center in the South, and never more so than at the present time. A grant of 240 acres adjoining the town was made by the state of North Carolina as early as 1785, through the efforts of General James Robertson, the founder of the city. From this grant Davidson academy was established, which grew into Davidson college, and subsequently into the University of Nashville. By the legislature of the state, one-half of one per cent. of the capital stock of the Planters' Bank of Tennessee, and of the Farmers' and Merchants' Bank of Memphis, was appropriated, in 1833, to the support of common schools, to be divided among all the counties, according to the free white population. Of the net profits of the Tennessee Fire and Marine Insurance Company, located at Nashville, 5 per cent. was appropriated to these schools. In 1837 the school-fund was ordered to be placed in the hands of the directors of the State Bank of Tennessee, as capital in the bank, upon which they were to issue certificates of stock to the superintendent of public instruction. In 1841 one-half of the fund arising from the sale of public lands to which the state was entitled by act of Congress of that year, was appropriated for the benefit of common schools. Besides the revenue from banking and insurance companies, the school-fund was increased $11,700 by the proceeds of the sale of lands appropriated in 1849, and invested in state bonds. In 1853 a tax of 25 cents on polls and 2½ cents on each $100 of property was assigned by the legislature for annual distribution to the different counties, through their county trustees, if two-thirds of the justices of the peace did not object, in which case the people were to adopt or reject the law by a general election. By the act of

1840, three school commissioners were elected in each county, and all children between the ages of 6 and 21 years were allowed to attend school. Thus common schools were in operation all over the state for many years before the war. The war destroyed these schools, and a new common-school system was established in 1867, and provision was made for the education of colored as well as white people. At this time the system is in very general operation throughout the state. The amount now annually received from the state and county to support the public schools of Nashville, which is the first civil district of Davidson county, is about $25,000. But Nashville could not afford to wait for slow legislative enactments, and her people saw that the amount realized would not be half sufficient to sustain a good system of such schools as she needed, and therefore had a system established by municipal ordinance, and erected suitable buildings, employed a competent superintendent and capable and efficient teachers. The result is that now, in 1880, the city of Nashville owns, in her corporate capacity, 7 good large school-houses, and rents several small ones, in which to teach her school population of 6,098, at a cost of $65,000 per annum. The schools are divided into primary, intermediate, grammar, and high-school departments. Vocal music, drawing, etc., are taught. Of the 6,098 pupils, 4,883 are white and 1,215 colored. The schools are taught 10 months in the year.

In addition to the public schools and the University of Nashville, already noted, may be mentioned the state normal school, the Nashville female academy, the Vanderbilt university, the Fisk university (the principal school for the colored people of the South), the Nashville normal and theological institute (also for colored people), the Central Tennessee college, and quite a number of private schools, etc., all situated in the city or in its immediate neighborhood.

MANUFACTURES.

The following is a summary of the statistics of the manufactures of Nashville for 1880, being taken from tables prepared for the Tenth Census by Franz M. Paul, special agent:

Mechanical and manufacturing industries.	No. of establishments.	Capital.	AVERAGE NUMBER OF HANDS EMPLOYED.			Total amount paid in wages during the year.	Value of materials.	Value of products.
			Males above 16 years.	Females above 15 years.	Children and youths.			
All industries..	268	$3,892,330	3,815	538	438	$1,312,735	$5,312,527	$8,597,278
Blacksmithing.....	22	7,625	38	....	2	13,995	19,126	51,038
Bookbinding and blank-book making........................	4	49,000	20	21	3	12,650	41,125	74,200
Boots and shoes, including custom work and repairing............	27	17,225	71	1	4	28,633	37,685	95,159
Bread and other bakery products	9	90,700	77	6	7	32,040	165,674	250,967
Brick and tile..........................	4	57,000	164	....	51	38,920	27,060	80,938
Carpentering	17	56,450	213	....	....	92,142	162,190	302,205
Carriages and wagons	9	385,500	515	....	....	68,550	404,400	780,331
Clothing, men's.....................	4	15,500	20	203	10	22,600	57,200	97,875
Coffins, burial cases, and undertakers' goods....................	4	6,850	10	....	....	4,750	14,250	38,550
Confectionery	3	24,000	14	73	10	11,500	113,000	146,225
Cooperage	6	6,500	53	....	....	19,105	24,140	63,650
Flouring- and grist-mill products.....................	6	385,000	96	....	....	51,172	1,315,721	1,542,516
Foundery and machine-shop products	13	143,300	206	....	7	69,755	288,786	487,407
Furniture	7	189,000	278	7	105	105,178	244,445	489,625
Leather, curried	3	36,000	18	....	....	7,300	169,362	187,010
Leather, tanned	4	59,000	31	....	3	18,000	121,735	174,791
Lock- and gun-smithing.....................	5	3,400	2	....	1	1,025	3,000	7,925
Looking-glass and picture frames	4	11,500	25	....	4	8,164	15,375	31,675
Lumber, sawed.....................	7	330,000	458	....	44	114,600	248,836	520,125
Marble and stone work	5	25,500	92	....	....	32,240	36,425	114,446
Painting and paperhanging.....................	7	11,000	40	....	....	20,615	25,275	66,468
Patent medicines and compounds.....................	7	61,500	31	....	3	11,769	27,750	80,300
Plumbing and gasfitting.....................	6	20,000	52	....	1	20,725	64,358	101,950
Printing and publishing	17	495,400	222	32	40	163,314	144,437	436,981
Saddlery and harness.....................	11	32,600	131	1	10	42,975	133,450	235,430
Tinware, copperware, and sheet-iron ware.....................	12	118,150	148	....	2	47,003	101,870	254,698
Tobacco, cigars and cigarettes	3	2,500	11	....	2	4,110	3,800	14,310
Watch and clock repairing	8	7,500	13	....	....	12,125	10,095	31,080
All other industries (a).....................	34	1,245,380	766	194	129	237,810	1,291,957	1,839,403

a Embracing bags, paper; baskets, rattan and willow ware; boxes, wooden packing; brooms and brushes; coffee and spices, roasted and ground; corsets; cotton goods; electroplating; furniture, chairs; instruments, professional and scientific; liquors, distilled; liquors, malt; masonry, brick and stone; mattresses and spring beds; mineral and soda waters; oil, cottonseed and cake; pumps; sash, doors, and blinds; show-cases; slaughtering and meat-packing; stencils and brands; trunks and valises; wooden ware; and woolen goods.

From the foregoing table it appears that the average capital of all establishments is $14,523 81; that the average wages of all hands employed is $274 01 per annum; that the average outlay in wages, in materials, and in interest (at 6 per cent.) on capital employed is $25,592 67.

GEORGIA.

ATLANTA,

FULTON COUNTY, GEORGIA.

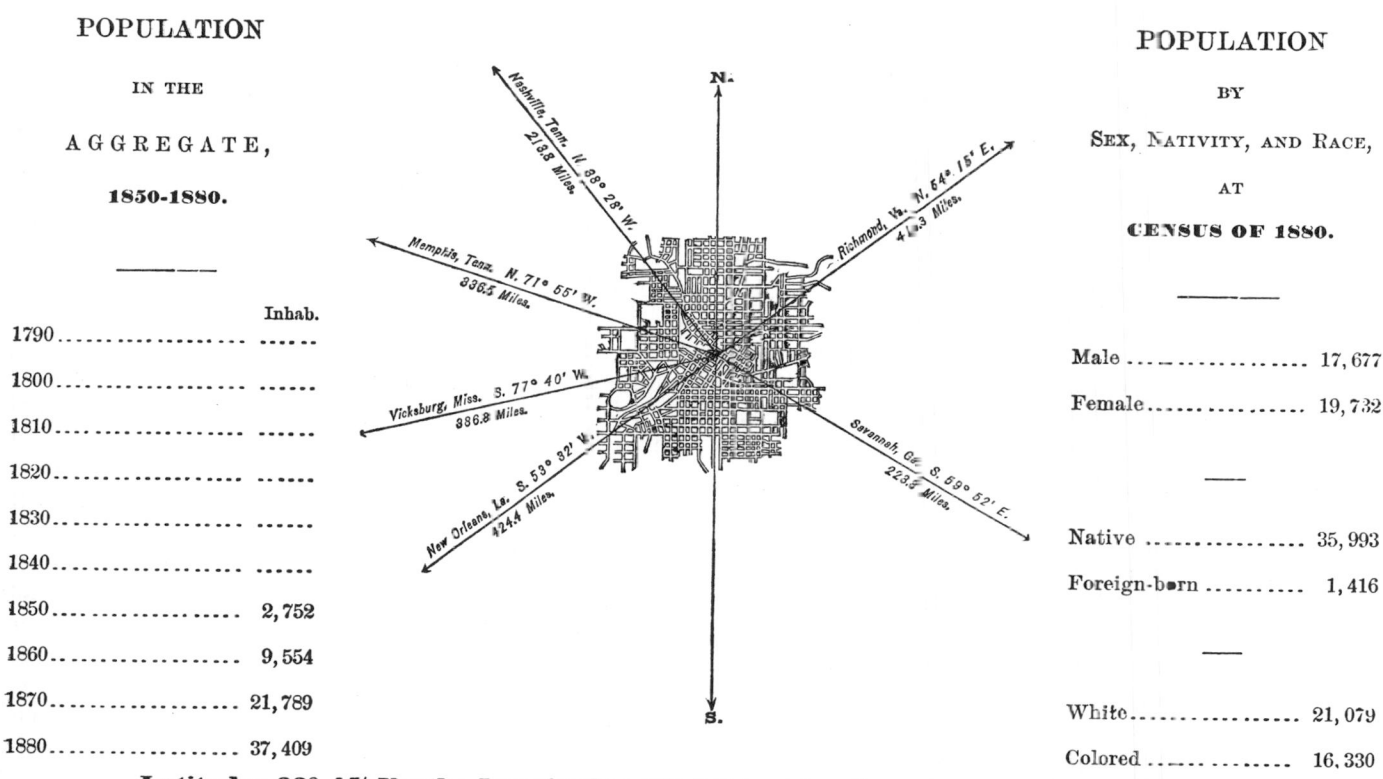

<table>
<tr><td colspan="2">POPULATION
IN THE
AGGREGATE,
1850-1880.</td></tr>
<tr><td></td><td>Inhab.</td></tr>
<tr><td>1790</td><td>......</td></tr>
<tr><td>1800</td><td>......</td></tr>
<tr><td>1810</td><td>......</td></tr>
<tr><td>1820</td><td>......</td></tr>
<tr><td>1830</td><td>......</td></tr>
<tr><td>1840</td><td>......</td></tr>
<tr><td>1850</td><td>2,752</td></tr>
<tr><td>1860</td><td>9,554</td></tr>
<tr><td>1870</td><td>21,789</td></tr>
<tr><td>1880</td><td>37,409</td></tr>
</table>

POPULATION BY SEX, NATIVITY, AND RACE, AT CENSUS OF 1880.	
Male	17,677
Female	19,732
Native	35,993
Foreign-born	1,416
White	21,079
Colored	16,330

Latitude: 33° 45' North; Longitude: 84° 24' (west from Greenwich); Altitude: 1,050 feet.

FINANCIAL CONDITION:

Total Valuation: $18,000,000; per capita: $481 00.   Net Indebtedness: $2,180,000; per capita: $58 27.   Tax per $100: $2 20.

HISTORICAL SKETCH.

On the 21st of December, 1835, an act of the legislature of Georgia was approved by the governor, authorizing the "construction of a railroad from the Tennessee line, near the Tennessee river, to the southwestern bank of the Chattahoochee river, at a point most eligible for the running of branch roads thence to Athens, Madison, Milledgeville, Forsyth, and Columbus". In 1837 the eastern terminus was established, not at the Chattahoochee, but 7 miles east of it, near the site of the present passenger depot at Atlanta. At first, and until 1843, the place was called

"Terminus". The first house erected here was the work of Hardy Ivy, in 1836. To John Thrasher belongs the credit of erecting, in 1839, the second dwelling. In 1841, '42, and '43, a few more people moved here. In June of 1842 Willis Carlisle arrived and established a store near the present location of the First Presbyterian church. At the close of the year very little progress had been made, there being not more than half a dozen dwellings and three or four families; but the construction of the Western and Atlantic railroad had been pushed steadily forward, the Chattahoochee had been spanned and Marietta reached. The completion of the road to Terminus was soon accomplished.

In 1844, the settlement having made some growth, application was made to the legislature for a charter, which was granted on December 23, incorporating the village under the name of "Marthasville", in compliment to the daughter of ex-Governor Lumpkin, a gentleman distinguished in developing the railroad interests of the state. In 1845 appeared, under the editorship of Rev. Joseph Baker, *The Luminary*, Atlanta's first newspaper. Another event was the completion of the entire line of the Georgia railroad, the first train running through from Augusta to Marthasville on the 15th of September, 1845. A third important step taken during this year was the construction, by general subscription, of a small building for church and school purposes; it was used during the week as a school-house, and on Sunday as a union church. Still the population was scanty, numbering probably not more than 100 souls.

The year 1846 ushered in the third great railroad event in the life of Marthasville—the arrival of a train from Macon, on the Macon and Western railroad. The depot and junction of this road was fixed near the terminus of the "State" road and present passenger depot. This fact undoubtedly determined the exact location of the coming city. In this year three more newspapers made their appearance. They were all short-lived. While possessing many of the requirements of a large city, Marthasville contained but few people, and the number increased slowly. Nevertheless, while the village did not contain 300 inhabitants, some of the ambitious citizens began to feel too large for a village incorporation, and in the same year (1846) an effort was made to obtain a city charter; but the opposition of some of the more conservative people defeated the measure. In the following year, however, the attempt was more successful and the charter was obtained, giving the place the name of "Atlanta". The legislature passed the act December 29, 1847. A more rapid growth now began. The Baptists began the erection of a church edifice, and J. O. and P. C. McDaniel built the first block of brick stores, the only other brick buildings being the Atlanta hotel, erected by the Georgia railroad the previous year, and the railroad depots.

Atlanta's first city election occurred on Saturday, January 29, 1848, and the city council met for the first time on the 2d of February following. A fresh impetus was diffused through the body politic, and manifested itself in all directions. An excellent class of people moved in and new enterprises sprang up. In three years 5 churches were organized and buildings were erected. The estimated population of Atlanta at the beginning of its municipal career was not far from 500. There was a large class at this time, composed chiefly of workmen employed on the various railways, and adventurers, usual with new and thriving places, which was lawless and disposed to disorder. There were occasional conflicts between this class and the better citizens reinforced by the law; but the lawless element was gradually suppressed by the influx of better classes.

The year 1854 found Atlanta a busy and growing little city of about 6,000 inhabitants, showing a late rapid increase. There were 60 stores, and the sales of goods ran up to $1,500,000. The onward march of Atlanta was not impaired by the commercial crisis of 1857, and the United States Census of 1860 showed it to be the fourth city of the state. Up to the beginning of the civil war the history of Atlanta is but a record of new enterprises and of the introduction of city improvements. Gas was introduced and the streets were lighted December 25, 1855, and in 1856 the Bank of Fulton was established, with a capital of $125,000. The opening of the war was the first serious check which Atlanta had sustained. But during the war, though building mostly ceased and many of the best citizens left for the field, the aggregate population and business increased. Atlanta, of necessity, became one of the military centers and supply depots of the Confederacy. The manufacture of arms, ammunition, and war material in general was conducted here on the most extensive scale. In 1862 the city passed under martial law, and at once became the headquarters of quartermasters and commissaries; it was also made a chief hospital point.

On July 9, 1864, the confederate army and the Union army had both reached the Atlanta side of the Chattahoochee, and on September 1 the city was evacuated, and was occupied the following day by the Union army. Two days later, September 4, General Sherman issued an order requiring the departure of all citizens within 8 days, which was complied with. Sherman held the city until November 16, when he began his famous march to the sea. What could not be consumed by fire was blown up, torn down, or otherwise destroyed. No other city during the war was so nearly annihilated. The center of the city was a mass of ruins, there being but a solitary structure standing on the main (Whitehall) street between its extreme commercial limits. At least three-fourths of the buildings in the city were destroyed.

The people of Atlanta began to return in November and December, 1864, and the work of rehabilitation began at once. Before the end of 1865 the old citizens had very generally returned, and many others ruined by the war, and forced again to choose a home site, came also. The work of rebuilding and restoring went on very rapidly, and in 1866 a census of the city showed that its population had passed the highest figure reached before the confederate evacuation, being 20,228 souls. In that year the legislature enlarged the limits of the city to a circle

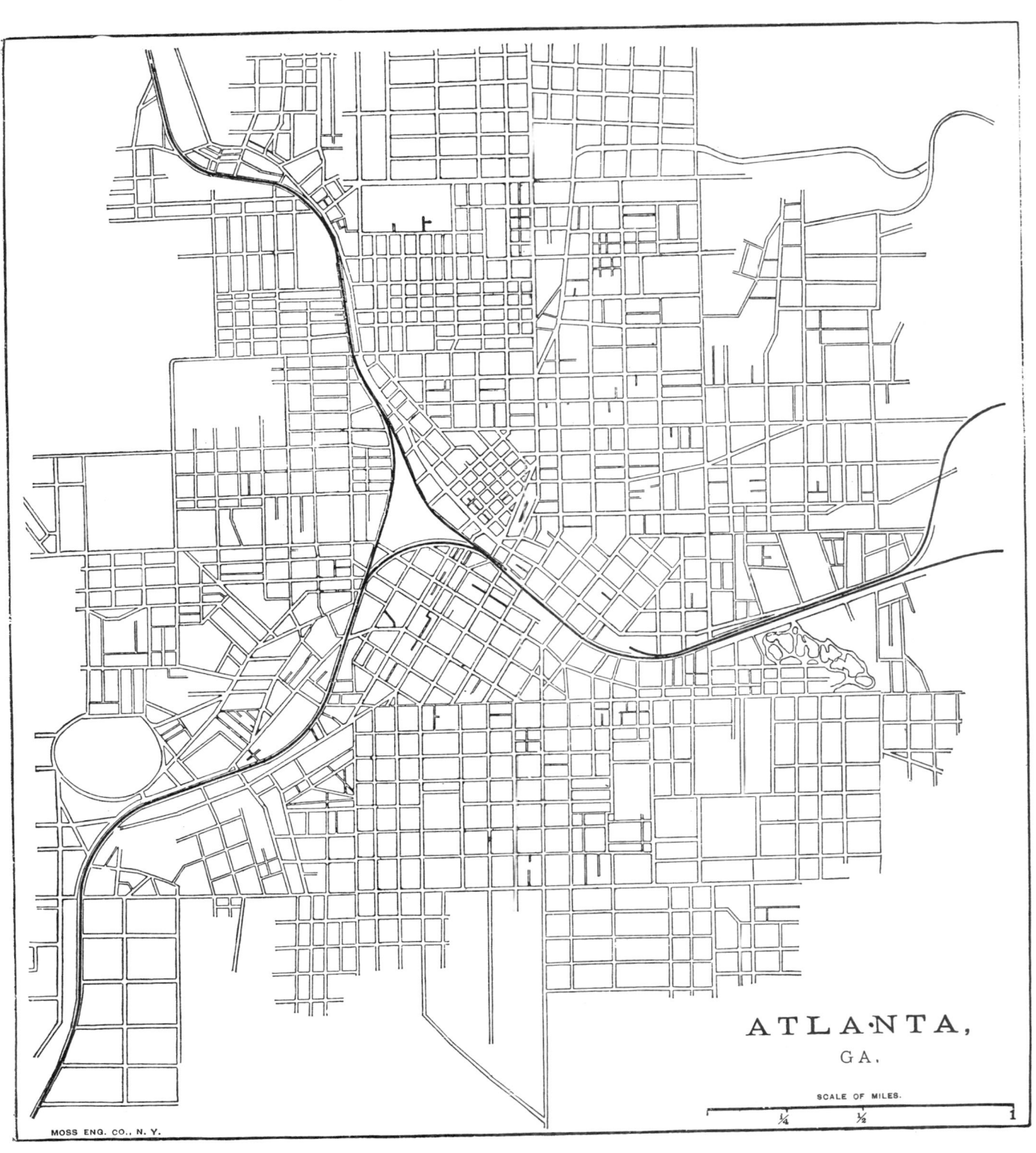

ATLANTA,
GA.

SCALE OF MILES.

¼   ½   1

3 miles in diameter. The new growth of the city was marvelous. The United States Census of 1870 found Atlanta exceeded in population by but one city of Georgia—Savannah—the figures being 21,789 and 28,235, respectively. In 1870 the need for a free-school system had become so pressing that the city charter was amended to empower the establishment and maintenance of the system. In the latter part of the previous year a board of education had been elected, and to this board was now by ordinance given full power to construct or lease school-buildings. The erection of 3 school-houses was begun at once, and finished by January, 1872. In February they were opened, and at the end of the first year showed 2 high and 7 grammar schools, with an attendance of 2,075 white scholars taught by 30 teachers.

The financial crisis of 1873 was severely felt in Atlanta, but its recovery was almost as marvelous as its previous rehabilitation. No bank in Atlanta fell, though one was obliged to suspend for a short time. Soon progress was again noticeable, and Atlanta seemed on the full tide of prosperity before many other places began to feel recovery. Certain abuses having crept into the municipal government, and the existence of a large and increasing public debt being noted with alarm, a "committee of forty-nine" was chosen which thoroughly revised the city charter. The legislature passed the revision, and it was approved by the governor on February 28, 1874. From this date to 1880 Atlanta's story is but a succession of forward steps. Its manufactures, trade, and resources are very large; in size it is now without a rival in the state, while the vote of Georgia in 1877, making it the capital, is destined to add still further to the importance of this rapidly growing city.

ATLANTA IN 1880.

The following statistical accounts, collected by the Census Office, indicate the present condition of Atlanta:

LOCATION.

Atlanta lacks the advantage of a situation upon navigable water, its nearest considerable stream being the Chattahoochee, about 7 miles distant. It lies in latitude 33° 45' north, longitude 84° 24' west from Greenwich, nearly equidistant from New York and from New Orleans, near the northern central part of the state, and is the capital of Fulton county. Its average altitude above sea-level is 1,050 feet.

RAILROAD COMMUNICATIONS.

The city has long had much importance as a railroad center. It is the terminus of the following lines: The Western and Atlantic ("State") railroad, running to Chattanooga, Tennessee; the Georgia railroad, running to Augusta, Georgia; the Central railroad, running to Savannah, Georgia; the Atlanta and West Point railroad, to the latter place; and the Atlanta and Richmond Air Line, to Charlotte, North Carolina. Other roads are projected.

TRIBUTARY COUNTRY.

The country surrounding Atlanta is not rich, but under good cultivation yields very well. Most of the land has a clay subsoil and retains fertilizers readily, producing good crops of both northern and southern staples, including fruits of all kinds, vegetables, and cotton. The region has many fine water-powers, only a part of which are utilized, and contains a number of mines of coal, iron, copper, and other metals, including gold. The city is the leading market for upper Georgia, and is a great distributing point for the products of the West.

TOPOGRAPHY.

Atlanta is situated on the ridge which divides the waters of the Chattahoochee from those of the Savannah, Oconee, Ocmulgee, and Flint rivers. The geological formation is metamorphic. The rocks are granite, gneiss, and micaceous, and hydro-mica schists, which are decomposed generally to a depth of from 5 to 100 feet, affording a soil retentive of moisture. The surface of the site is varied by hills and valleys, affording fine building sites and perfect drainage—on the north into the Chattahoochee, and on the south into the South and Ocmulgee rivers. There are no adjacent ponds or marshes, though in the vicinity are some good chalybeate and magnesian springs. The surrounding country is still mostly covered with the original forest growth of oak, hickory, gum, etc.

CLIMATE.

Highest recorded summer temperature, 102°; highest summer temperature in average years, 96°. Lowest recorded winter temperature, 4°; lowest winter temperature in average years, 10°. There is no body of water near enough to have any appreciable climatic influence. Atlanta's prevailing breeze is from the mountains, and is pure and pleasant.

STREETS.

The total length of streets in the city is 100 miles, of which only 3 miles are paved with broken stone. Sidewalks are paved with brick, stone, flagging, and asphalt, with stone curbing, and have a width of 10 feet. Gutters are paved with rough stone. Trees are planted along the sidewalks 8 feet from the street line. The work of street construction and repairs is done both by contract and by day work, at an annual cost of $15,000. No steam stone-crusher or roller is used.

HORSE RAILROADS.

There are 10½ miles of horse-railroads in the city, using 21 cars and 80 horses, and giving employment to 45 men. The number of passengers carried annually is 800,000, and the rate of fare is 5 cents. There are no omnibus lines.

WATER-WORKS.

The water-works are owned by the city, and their total cost is $320,785. The Holly system of pumping is used, the pressure at the works being 115 pounds and in the city 45 pounds to the square inch. The average amount of water pumped per diem is 1,430,000 gallons—least amount, 1,298,000; greatest, 1,753,000 gallons. The average cost of raising 1,000,000 gallons one foot high is $12\frac{1}{10}$ cents. The yearly cost of maintenance, aside from the cost of pumping, is $600, and the yearly income from water-rates is $21,000. A few water-meters, in the case of large consumers, are used, tending, it is believed, to reduce the consumption of water. The charge per 1,000 gallons is, to ordinary consumers, 17 cents, and to large manufacturing establishments 10 cents. There are 17 miles of water-pipes and 119 hydrants. The income from the works, after deducting operating expenses, is spent in extending water-mains and in other improvements.

GAS.

The gas-works are owned by a private company. The average daily production is from 50,000 to 60,000 cubic feet. The charge per 1,000 feet is $3. The city pays $30 annually for each street-lamp, 300 in number.

PUBLIC BUILDINGS.

The city owns and occupies for municipal purposes, wholly or in part, the city hall, station-house, engine-rooms, etc., also the "exposition building". The total cost of the municipal buildings owned by the city is $150,000. The city hall alone cost about $25,000.

PUBLIC PARKS AND PLEASURE-GROUNDS.

The total area of the parks already opened is 32 acres. *Oglethorpe Park*, located on the Western Atlantic railroad, 2 miles from the center of the city, contains 27 acres, and is used mainly for agricultural expositions. It has been considerably improved by terracing, turfing, etc., and has a fine lake. *City Hall Park* is in the center of the city, contains 5 acres, and has been regularly laid out in walks, trees planted, and the ground grassed; it also has seats. *Ponce de Leon Springs*, 2 miles from the city, is approached by a street railway, and is, though open to the public, owned by a private person; it contains about 15 acres. The water-works grounds, owned by the city, are not yet laid out. They are about 4 miles from the city's center, and contain 318 acres. The parks are under the control of the mayor and general council. Oglethorpe park has been leased to the North Georgia stock and fair association for a term of years.

PLACES OF AMUSEMENT.

Atlanta has one theater, the Opera House, seating 1,600 persons; it pays a license of $250 annually, or $10 for each exhibition. There is also a hall—Concordia hall—with a seating capacity of 500, belonging to a German society, and used for concerts, lectures, balls, etc. There are no concert- and beer-gardens.

DRAINAGE.

Sewers are laid according to the requirements of each case as it comes up. They discharge into the natural water-courses. No information is furnished in regard to the size, material, extent, or cost of sewers, beyond the fact that inlet-basins cost $20 and manholes $30 each; brick-work laid in sewers $16 50, and in manholes $14 50 per thousand. Stone sewers are said to cost $3 25 per perch. The whole cost of the sewers is paid by the city by general tax. Trenching and back-filling is done by day work. The 15,369 feet of sewers laid in 1878 cost $9,793, but nothing is said of their size or material.

CEMETERIES.

There is one large public cemetery, called *Oakland Cemetery*, belonging to Atlanta. It contains about 100 acres of land, and is situated 1½ mile southeast of the center of the city. The total number of interments made in the cemetery is 22,313. Of this number, 5,000 were regularly interred or removed up to January 1, 1870, and since that time 9,147. There have also been 8,166 confederate soldiers interred or removed here since the war. Before an interment can take place a certificate by the attending physician is required, setting forth the cause of death, etc., which is recorded by the sexton. When such certificate can not from any cause be obtained, an order for burial may be given by the mayor or a member of the relief committee of the ward. A body may not be kept before burial longer than 6 days. Graves are dug 6 feet deep. Lots in the cemetery are sold at from $25 to $100 each. The charge for digging a grave for a person under 10 years of age is $2; over 10 years, $4. Lot-owners are unrestricted in the beautifying and improving of their lots. The gates of the cemetery are open from 8 a. m. to 6 p. m. A watchman employed by the city is constantly on duty. A section is set apart in which the city buries its pauper dead.

MARKETS.

Atlanta has no public market, supplies being sold by private stores and stands scattered over the city. The mayor reports that this method is not satisfactory, and the erection of a market-house is in contemplation.

SANITARY AUTHORITY—BOARD OF HEALTH.

The chief sanitary organization of the city is the board of health, composed of 5 members, one from each ward, 3 of whom are physicians, elected annually by the general council. Each member, including the chairman, receives $100 annually. The board incurs no direct expense, its province being chiefly to advise and recommend measures to the general council. Its work consists largely in reporting and removing nuisances. When the council adopts any health measure, it appropriates the money needed to carry it out. As yet the city has escaped epidemics; should one occur the council would doubtless appropriate the additional funds needed for the board's work. It does not appear that the powers of the board are increased during an epidemic. The board has 2 executive officers, who are policemen detailed for the duty. The board meets every two weeks, or oftener if necessary, is presided over by a chairman, and considers in the usual way matters pertaining to its department.

Inspections are made regularly in all parts of the city, and particular attention is paid to reported nuisances, in which case, if the report is found to be true, the causing person or owner on whose lot the nuisance is found is required to abate it. In case of defective house-drainage, if the fault lies in the sewer, the city remedies it; if in a private lot, the owner must rectify it. All privy-vaults and cesspools have been abolished by cleaning out their contents and filling them with fresh earth. To prevent the contamination of drinking-water, the gathering-ground of the reservoir is inspected regularly for the detection and removal of nuisances. Street-cleaning is inspected by the inspectors of the board. Atlanta has no streams, except a few from small springs, and some houses deliver their sewage into these runs. Excrement is carted away from the center of the city, but, as yet, in an imperfect manner.

INFECTIOUS DISEASES.

Small-pox patients are sent to the pest-house, situated just outside the city limits. Cases of scarlet fever are rare, and patients are not isolated. Schools have never suffered from epidemics, other than those of measles and hooping-cough. School-children only are required to be vaccinated, but this is not done at the public expense.

Births and diseases are not registered, but the deaths reported by the sextons are recorded by the board.

REPORTS.

The board makes semi-annual reports to the general council, and the same are published.

MUNICIPAL CLEANSING.

Street-cleaning.—The streets are cleaned at the expense of the city and with its regular force. The work is done wholly by hand, no sweeping-machines being used. In the thickly built-up portions of the city this cleaning is done daily, in other parts only as often as necessary. The work is reported as reasonably well done. The cost of the work is not kept separate from that of the street department. The sweepings are deposited outside the city, such as are suitable being made into fertilizers. The system is under the supervision of inspectors, and is said to work well.

Removal of garbage and ashes.—Within certain defined central limits, the city with its own force removes garbage; outside of this district it is done by the householders. The city requires such garbage as it removes to be placed in suitable receptacles at certain hours, for removal by the daily carts. Ashes and garbage may be kept in the same vessel, and both are removed outside of the city and made into fertilizers. The cost of the service is not separated in the accounts of the street department, to which the work belongs. The whole system is under rigid inspection, and is thus kept up to a good degree of efficiency and freedom from menace to health, though the opinion is expressed that there should be a more uniform system of final disposition. At present it is given to private individuals.

Dead animals.—The carcasses of all animals dying within the city must be removed outside the limits and buried by the owners; if the owners can not be found the city does the work. Neither the cost of the service nor the number of carcasses removed is stated. The system is not entirely satisfactory, as the owners of dead animals are inclined to throw upon the city the trouble and cost of removal.

Liquid household wastes.—A large part of the liquid household wastes of the city are delivered into the public sewers; where sewer connection is not had, a recent ordinance requires a water-tight receptacle under privies, into which the wastes are poured. No wastes are run into street-gutters, and all privy-vaults and cesspools have been abolished as dangerous to health.

Human excreta.—About one-third of the houses in the city have water-closets, all of which deliver into the public sewers, and the rest depend on privy receptacles. The city removes the contents of the privies in the thickly built part twice a week; elsewhere the owners are required to empty them. In the operation of cleaning out, dry earth or other disinfectants must be used. The night-soil is carried out of the city and given to private parties, who manufacture it into fertilizers. It is not allowed to be used for manuring land within the gathering-ground of the public water-supply.

Manufacturing wastes are said to be removed outside the city.

POLICE.

The police force of Atlanta is appointed and governed by a board of 5 police commissioners. The chief of police is at the head of the force, and has direct control of the same; his salary is $1,500 per annum. The remainder of the force consists of 4 captains at $900 each per annum; 1 clerk and station-house keeper at $900 per annum; and 1 assistant clerk and station-house keeper, 2 sanitary officers, and 26 patrolmen, at $54 a month each. The uniform is of blue cloth; for officers double-breasted and for privates single-breasted frock coats. Patrolmen are equipped with 22-inch clubs, and furnish their own pistols. They serve 12 hours per day and patrol 7½ square miles of territory.

During 1880 the arrests numbered 4,345. Of these, 3,619 had violated city ordinances, and 726 had transgressed state laws. Their disposition was: city cases fined, 1,969; dismissed, 1,650; state cases prosecuted, 505; released, 221. The force is required to assist firemen at fires and protect property; the members are also required to report all nuisances coming to their knowledge. The yearly cost of the police force (1880) is $27,668 35.

MANUFACTURES.

The following is a summary of the statistics of the manufactures of Atlanta for 1880, being taken from tables prepared for the Tenth Census by Moses T. Simmons, special agent:

Mechanical and manufacturing industries.	No. of establishments.	Capital.	AVERAGE NUMBER OF HANDS EMPLOYED.			Total amount paid in wages during the year.	Value of materials.	Value of products.
			Males above 16 years.	Females above 15 years.	Children and youths.			
All industries	196	$2,468,456	2,753	533	394	$889,282	$3,159,267	$4,861,727
Blacksmithing	16	5,300	29	....	2	7,650	10,360	24,950
Boots and shoes, including custom work and repairing	11	1,800	23	....	....	8,438	10,467	26,080
Bread and other bakery products	6	36,900	42	13	9	19,260	115,500	161,100
Brick and tile	14	31,240	230	....	83	42,230	33,915	102,200
Carpentering	10	85,500	318	....	5	92,800	220,000	382,200
Carriages and wagons	8	22,000	86	....	4	32,800	30,700	81,500
Clothing, men's	3	13,400	12	28	....	8,465	17,000	32,500
Confectionery	4	78,300	50	23	1	18,146	215,000	263,000
Dyeing and cleaning	3	7,600	7	4	....	3,614	2,624	10,000
Flouring- and grist-mill products	4	125,000	34	....	....	15,000	474,000	527,800
Foundery and machine-shop products	7	314,866	172	....	7	72,393	114,784	252,908
Furniture (see also Mattresses and spring beds)	3	22,350	85	3	3	17,558	28,759	82,014
Lumber, planed	5	81,000	235	....	10	56,789	179,000	285,000
Marble and stone work	4	14,400	25	....	....	8,950	7,800	33,100
Mattresses and spring beds (see also Furniture)	3	1,400	5	5	1	1,860	2,600	6,200
Painting and paperhanging	6	2,650	23	....	....	6,920	6,400	18,650
Patent medicines and compounds	9	102,500	59	15	7	30,492	52,700	128,500
Printing and publishing	10	183,500	163	10	15	71,112	96,549	229,883
Saddlery and harness	3	12,200	15	....	....	8,000	17,100	32,000
Slaughtering and meat-packing, not including retail butchering	9	25,700	35	....	6	9,473	269,077	309,093
Tinware, copperware, and sheet-iron ware	7	44,300	86	....	6	25,250	80,400	127,900
Watch and clock repairing	4	5,200	7	....	2	4,524	4,000	14,800
All other industries (a)	47	1,251,350	1,012	432	233	327,558	1,170,532	1,730,349

a Embracing agricultural implements; bags, paper; baking and yeast powders; bookbinding and blank-book making; boxes, fancy and paper; boxes, wooden packing; brass castings; coal-tar; coffee and spices, roasted and ground; coffins, burial cases, and undertakers' goods; cooperage; coppersmithing; cotton goods; dyeing and finishing textiles; ice, artificial; instruments, professional and scientific; iron and steel; liquors, distilled; liquors, malt; lithographing; looking-glass and picture frames; masonry, brick and stone; millstones; mineral and soda waters; models and patterns; musical instruments, organs and materials; paints; paving materials; perfumery and cosmetics; plumbing and gasfitting; stencils and brands; straw goods; tobacco, cigars and cigarettes; trunks and valises; and upholstering.

From the foregoing table it appears that the average capital of all establishments is $12,594 16; that the average wages of all hands employed is $241 65 per annum; that the average outlay in wages, in materials, and in interest (at 6 per cent.) on capital employed is $21,411 51.

AUGUSTA,
RICHMOND COUNTY, GEORGIA.

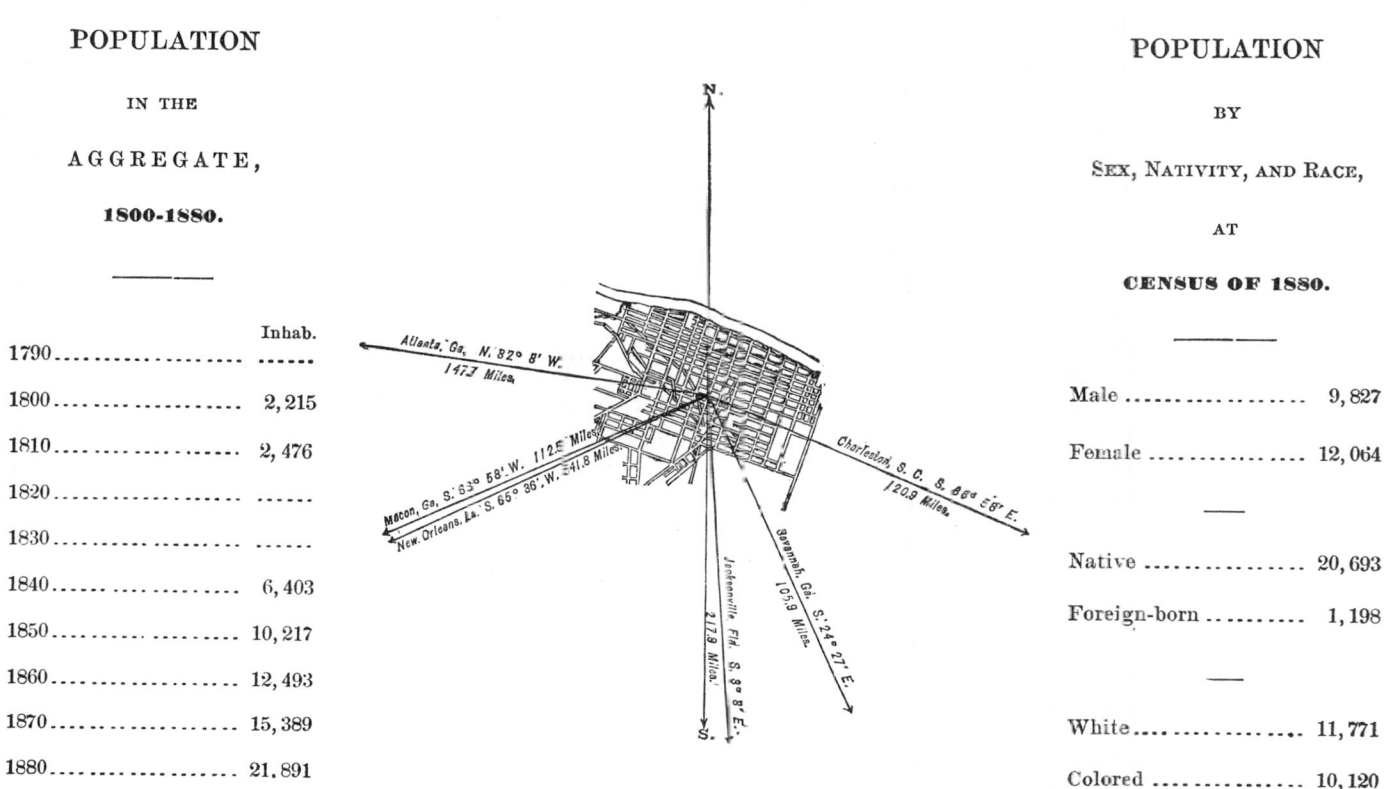

POPULATION
IN THE
AGGREGATE,
1800-1880.

	Inhab.
1790	......
1800	2,215
1810	2,476
1820	......
1830	......
1840	6,403
1850	10,217
1860	12,493
1870	15,389
1880	21,891

POPULATION
BY
SEX, NATIVITY, AND RACE,
AT
CENSUS OF 1880.

Male	9,827
Female	12,064
Native	20,693
Foreign-born	1,198
White	11,771
Colored	10,120

Latitude: 33° 29′ North; Longitude: 81° 51′ (west from Greenwich); **Average altitude: 147 feet.**

FINANCIAL CONDITION:

Total Valuation: $13,730,681; per capita: $627 00.   Net Indebtedness: $1,959,519; per capita: $89 51.   Tax per $100: $1 93.

HISTORICAL SKETCH.

Augusta was settled by English colonists under Oglethorpe, and was laid out in 1735 under royal charter, being named in honor of one of the English princesses. It was again chartered in January, 1798, and incorporated as a city in December, 1817. It was for many years the most important inland town of the colony. It had acquired a considerable trade at the commencement of the Revolutionary war, but in the beginning of 1779 was captured by the British and loyalists, who held possession of it till the spring of 1781, the British force being then commanded by a loyalist by the name of Brown. On May 23, 1781, an American force under command of General Henry Lee—"Light-Horse Harry"—laid siege to it, and, on the 5th of June, Brown surrendered. The Americans lost 51 killed and wounded; the British lost 52 killed, and 334, including the wounded, taken prisoners. During the war of 1812 or the Indian wars Augusta was not molested. During the war of the rebellion the city was not visited by the Union army, though General Sherman made a feint against that place in his march through the state. The water-power

163

of Augusta has contributed much to her present prosperity. As early as 1844 a project was started for the building of the Augusta canal, and a board of commissioners was appointed by the city council for "the purpose of constructing a canal from a point in the Savannah river, about 7 miles above, to the city of Augusta, for manufacturing purposes, and for the better securing of an abundant supply of water to the city". The work was begun in 1845, and was completed early in 1847. The canal had a width of 40 feet at surface and 20 feet at bottom, and was 5 feet deep, giving a total mechanical effect of about 600 horse-power. It soon became evident that the canal was too small, and, after several temporary expedients had been tried, the city council decided on its enlargement. The new work, which stands to-day, was begun in March, 1872, and completed in July, 1875, making the dimensions and capacity of the canal as follows: Length of main canal or first level, 7 miles, and, including second and third levels, 9 miles; minimum water-way, 150 feet at surface, 106 feet at bottom, and 11 feet deep, making an area of cross-section of 1,408 square feet. The bulkhead, locker, dam, and other structures are of stone masonry laid in hydraulic cement, and are of the most substantial character. The area of the openings for the supply of the canal amounts to 1,463 square feet, and the entire waters of the Savannah river are made available for maintaining the supply. There are about 275 acres of reservoirs, exclusive of the canal proper and the pond above the bulkhead of of the dam. There is a bottom grade or descent in the main canal of 0.01 foot in 100 feet, giving a theoretical mean velocity of 2.74 feet per second, or a mechanical effect under the minimum fall between the first and third levels, or between the first level and the Savannah river, of upward of 14,000 horse-power, not including the available supply from the reservoir. Of this immense power only 1,900 horse-power is contracted for. The present price per horse-power, conveyed on perpetual lease, is $5 50. The canal is owned and operated by the city, which sells the land along the canal to those leasing the water-power. From first to last there has been nearly $2,000,000 expended on the works, the last enlargement costing $822,866 69, and its completion seems to assure the manufacturing future of Augusta, several cotton-mills being now in operation.

On April 3, 1829, a fire occurred in the city that consumed between 400 and 500 houses and entailed a loss of $1,000,000. The people, however, quickly recuperated, and better buildings were erected in the place of those destroyed. Since the "great fire", as it is called, Augusta has not been visited by any severe conflagrations. At one time the population seemed to decrease and business depreciated, but the work on the canal and the erection of factories arrested the downward progress. The first settlers were originally English, who were afterward supplanted by a strong northern element, which still exists. Quite a large Irish population came in during the construction of the canal. Augusta was for some years the capital of the state.

AUGUSTA IN 1880.

The following statistical accounts, collected by the Census Office, indicate the present condition of Augusta:

LOCATION.

Augusta lies in latitude 33° 29′ north, longitude 81° 51′ west from Greenwich, on the right bank of the Savannah river, at the head of steamboat navigation, and distant 213 miles by river above the city of Savannah. Its average altitude above mean sea-level is 147 feet. Hamburg, South Carolina, is on the opposite bank of the river, and is reached by a bridge. The draught of water in the river varies from 4 to 10 feet.

RAILROAD COMMUNICATIONS.

The city is touched by the following-named railroads:
The Macon and Brunswick railroad, to Macon, and from there to the coast.
The Georgia railroad, to Atlanta.
The South Carolina railroad, to Charleston.
The Port Royal railroad, to Port Royal.
The Central Railroad of Georgia, to Savannah.
The Charlotte, Columbia, and Augusta railroad, to Charlotte, North Carolina.
These roads give Augusta communication with all parts of the country.

TRIBUTARY COUNTRY.

The country immediately tributary to Augusta is agricultural, with cotton as the chief staple. About 200,000 bales of this product are brought into the city annually, part of which is used in the manufactories in and around the place, while the remainder is shipped to Charleston and Savannah. The numerous railroads running from here give the city excellent facilities for a great wholesale business with most of the towns in the state and with the "hill country" of South Carolina, drawing, in return, the produce from those regions.

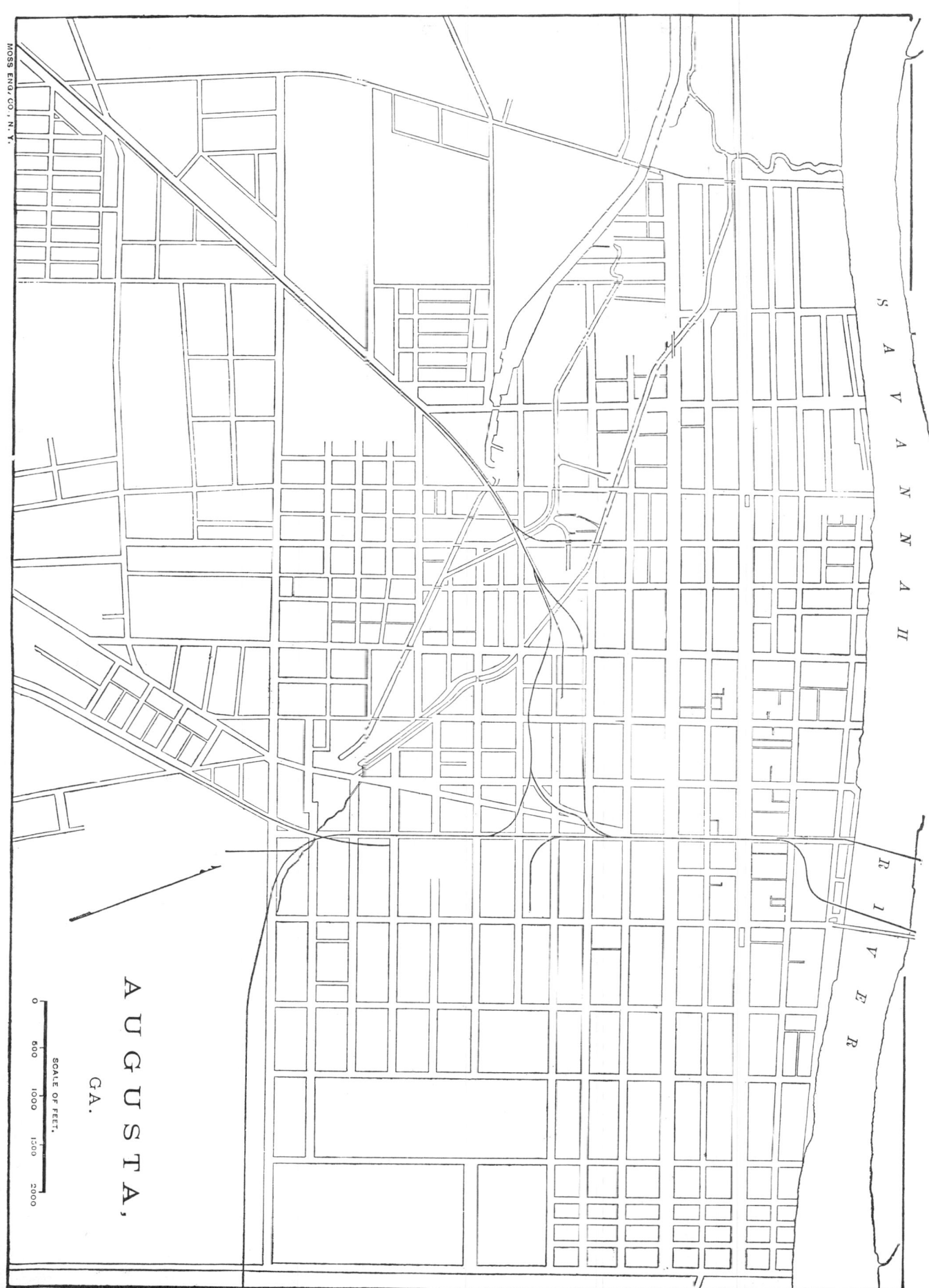

AUGUSTA,
GA.

SCALE OF FEET.

0
500
1000
1500
2000

SAVANNAH

RIVER

TOPOGRAPHY.

The site of the city is on a bluff of the Savannah river, averaging about 20 feet in height from the surface of the river at low water. The variations of level are but small, and the natural drainage is not good, but a large sewer or canal, soon to be built (at a cost of $30,000), will give sufficient drainage for the city. The character of the soil is a mixture of clay and sand-loam, while back from the river, on the hills, it is nothing but sand. The adjacent country is considerably wooded.

CLIMATE.

Highest recorded summer temperature, 104°; highest summer temperature in average years, 86.5°. Lowest recorded winter temperature, 17°; lowest winter temperature in average years, 29°. The marshes in the vicinity have but little influence on the climate. Westerly winds are considered healthful, and easterly winds the reverse.

STREETS.

There are 46 miles of streets in the city, none of which are paved. The sidewalks are of brick, 15 to 20 feet in width. Nearly all the streets in the city have trees growing at the sides, at the edge of the sidewalks, and there are about 5 miles of avenues in the centers of the different streets. The work of repairing streets is done by the day, at an annual cost of $16,000.

STREET-RAILWAYS.

There are 4½ miles of horse-railroads in the city, using 7 cars and 34 horses, and giving employment to 37 men. The number of passengers carried during the year is 377,309, and the rate of fare is 5 cents. There are 5 omnibuses in the city, with 14 horses and 7 men, that carry annually 12,000 passengers for 25 cents each.

WATER-WORKS.

The water-works are owned by the city, but their total cost was not given. The water is pumped by water-power, either directly into the main or into a stand-pipe, with no expense, except for keeping the pumps in repair and the engineer's salary. The pressure in pumping is 45 pounds to the square inch. The amount of water pumped per diem varies from 2,000,000 to 3,000,000 gallons. The annual cost of maintenance is $7,500, and the yearly income from water-rates is $16,000; water-meters are not used.

GAS.

The gas-works are owned by a private corporation. The charge per 1,000 feet is $3 50. The city pays $20 annually for each street-lamp, 370 in number.

PUBLIC BUILDINGS.

The city owns and occupies for municipal uses, wholly or in part, city hall, jail, engine-houses, and treasury building. Their total cost is given at $300,000. The city hall is owned entirely by the city, but it is also used for county purposes. Its original cost was $100,000.

PUBLIC PARKS AND PLEASURE-GROUNDS.

The fair-grounds, situated in the southeastern portion of the city, cover an area of 47 acres, and are owned by the city. Their total cost was $60,000. The grounds are controlled by the city council.

PLACES OF AMUSEMENT.

The Augusta opera-house, seating capacity 1,000; Masonic hall, seating capacity, 800; and Market hall, seating capacity, 1,800, are used for theatrical performances, concerts, and lectures. Theaters pay an annual license of $100 to the city. There are no concert- or beer-gardens.

DRAINAGE.

The few sewers now used in the city were originally built for drainage purposes and are not adapted for sewerage. They are flushed monthly, and obstructions, as a rule, are removed annually, or oftener if occasion requires. In the building of these old drains the property-owner furnished the brick or pipe and the city did the work. A complete system of sewerage has been adopted, and work will soon be begun. The city will issue 6 per cent. bonds to defray the cost.

CEMETERIES.

There are 2 cemeteries and 1 church-yard in Augusta:

City Cemetery, for whites, situated in the southeastern portion of the city, adjoining the fair-grounds, contains 41.61 acres.

Colored Cemetery, also adjoining the fair-grounds, is used by the colored people, and contains 17.16 acres.

Saint Paul Church-yard, between Reynold and Bay streets, is now no longer used for interments.

The total number of interments since 1813, including 2,000 in the Church-yard, so far as can be learned from past records, is 13,383. The two cemeteries are owned and controlled by the city, and are in charge of the city sexton, appointed annually by the city council. An assistant keeper for the Colored cemetery is also appointed by the city council, who is subordinate to the city sexton. Interments are made under the direction of the sexton, and in all cases a certificate of death, signed by the attending physician, must be furnished. No grave may be dug less than 5 feet deep. Burial fees, price of lots, etc., are regulated by the city council and existing ordinances. Lots are sold for burial purposes, and the owners can improve and inclose the same, in accordance with the rules and regulations of the cemeteries.

MARKETS.

There are 2 public markets in the city. They are both situated in the center of Broad street, and the street outside of them is used as standing-ground by farmers' and hucksters' wagons. The Lower market, at 5th street, is a new building, erected four years ago at a cost of $25,000, and is in perfect order. It contains 32 stalls—19 meat, 12 vegetable, and 1 fish—and the total yearly rental to July 1, 1880, was $4,055 87. The Upper market, near 12th street, is an old building, or rather shed, on brick pillars, and its yearly rental was but $100. The markets are opened from one hour before sunrise to sunset, and on Saturdays from the same hour in the morning till 10 p. m. The gross amount of annual sales from the stalls within the markets is $100,000. It is estimated that double the quantity of meats, fish, and poultry are sold either from private stores or from huckster wagons than are sold from the markets. There is only one fish-stall in the Lower, and none in the Upper market, the most of this trade being done on the streets from wagons.

SANITARY AUTHORITY—BOARD OF HEALTH.

The chief sanitary authority of Augusta is the board of health, created by the state laws, an independent body appointed by the city council. It is composed of 4 citizens, one from each ward, 2 physicians from the city at large, and 1 chemist, holding office for four years each, with the mayor and committee of health as members *ex officio*. The members of the board serve without pay or emoluments. A secretary is appointed to serve for four years. The expenses of the board in ordinary times are $5,000, for salaries, disinfectants, etc., and in case of an epidemic this sum may be increased to such amount as the city council may deem proper. The authority of the board in the absence of epidemics extends over all sanitary measures necessary to the public health and for the prevention of the generation and introduction of all contagious diseases. During an epidemic the board has power to establish hospitals, to declare what are infected portions of the city, to establish and enforce quarantine, and, in general, to do every thing necessary to check and control the disease. The chief executive officer is the president, who presides at all meetings, and between meetings enforces all the rules and regulations of the board; he receives no salary. One or two inspecting officers are appointed from each ward, when necessary, and they have full police powers. The board meets once a month, or oftener on call of the president, and transacts its business as a deliberative body. Inspections are made regularly in all parts of the city, and the inspectors are enjoined carefully to note the condition of all buildings, privies, yards, streets, lanes, sewers, etc., in their respective districts. When a nuisance is discovered the party responsible for the same is notified to remove it, and if this is not done the inspector has the nuisance removed by order of the mayor, the cost and fine being collected in the recorder's court. All defective house-drainage, privy-vaults, cesspools, sources of drinking-water, sewerage, etc., are noted and corrected by the inspectors. The board exercises no control over the removal of garbage, other than that it must not become a nuisance. Burials are made by the city sexton on physicians' certificate of death, but no body can be disinterred except by permission of the board. The board forbids the pollution of all streams or canals, and regulates the removal of excrement.

INFECTIOUS DISEASES.

Small-pox patients are at once isolated in the small-pox hospital. Scarlet-fever patients are either quarantined at home or sent to the hospital. In case of the breaking out of a contagious disease in either public or private schools, the board forbids the attendance of children from infected families. Vaccination is compulsory, and is done at the public expense when the people are unable to pay.

A record of the vital statistics of the city is kept by the secretary of the board. The sexton is required to make a return of all deaths, and physicians or others to report all cases of contagious diseases.

REPORTS.

The board reports annually to the city council, and the report is published in pamphlet form.

MUNICIPAL CLEANSING.

Street-cleaning.—The streets are cleaned at the expense of the city and with its regular force. The work is done wholly by hand, no sweeping-machines being used. The streets are cleaned daily, and the work is reported as efficiently done. The cost is included in the repair of streets. The sweepings are taken to South common and burned, after which they are hauled into the country for manure. The system is good, but the place of disposal is too near the city limits.

Removal of garbage and ashes.—All garbage is removed at the expense of the city with its own force. It is set out in suitable vessels, and removed daily from June 1 to November 1, and three times a week during the remainder of the year. It is disposed of in the same way as street-sweepings. Ashes are either thrown into the streets or used for filling up sunken lots. The cost of the removal is included in the repair of streets. Owing to the frequency of the removal of garbage, no injury to health arises from the system.

Dead animals.—The carcasses of all animals dying within the city are removed by the street force and buried on South common. No record is kept of the number, and the cost is included in the street-work. The system is faulty, and it is recommended that the carcasses be either thrown into the river or buried outside the city limits.

Liquid household wastes.—About one-tenth of the wastes are run into the sewers, and the balance are thrown into privy-vaults, cesspools, or surface privies, but very little ever reaching the street-gutters. The cesspools are porous, are not provided with overflows, and frequently receive the wastes from water-closets. When cleansing is necessary, 100 or 200 gallons of copperas-water are thrown in, and then the contents are removed and buried in a pit dug in the adjacent soil for the purpose. Street-gutters are flushed twice a month. Many cases have been known where well-water has been contaminated by the overflowing and underground escape of the contents of vaults and cesspools, and these will be abolished.

Human excreta.—About one-sixth of the houses in the city are provided with water-closets, two-thirds of which deliver into the sewers and one-third into cesspools, and the remainder depend either on privy-vaults or on surface privies. Privy-vaults must be at least 2 feet from any party-line and 5 feet from any street or alley. None of them are water-tight. They are required to be disinfected every two weeks, and are cleaned out in the same manner as cesspools, between the hours of 11 p. m. and 4 a. m. The night-soil is buried in holes dug near the privies.

Manufacturing wastes.—The liquid wastes are thrown into the canal, while the solid wastes are treated in the same manner as garbage.

POLICE.

The police force of Augusta is appointed and governed by the board of police commissioners, appointed by the state legislature. The board consists of five members, with the mayor as a member *ex officio*. The chief of police is the executive officer, and has full charge, under the board, of the entire force. His salary is $1,300 per annum. The remainder of the force consists of 1 first lieutenant at $1,100 a year; 1 second lieutenant at $950 a year; 1 orderly sergeant at $820 a year; 4 patrol sergeants at $720 a year each; and 38 patrolmen at $600 a year each. The uniform is the same as that worn by the police of New York city, and each man provides his own. The men are equipped with clubs and belts and revolvers. The hours of service are six on and six off, and all the streets in the city are patrolled by the force.

During the past year 3,540 arrests were made by the police, the principal causes being for drunkenness, disorderly conduct, larceny, etc. Those for drunkenness and disorderly conduct were sent before the recorder, while the others were turned over to higher courts. During the year the amount of stolen property reported to the police was $2,557 15, and of this sum $2,35 415 was recovered and returned to the owners. In the same period there were 326 station-house lodgers. The police department is subject to the orders of the chief of the fire department during all fires, and co-operates with the board of health at all times. Extra men are appointed by the board of commissioners when deemed necessary for the public good. They have all the powers of the regular force while on duty. The yearly cost of the police force (1880) is about $30,000.

MANUFACTURES.

The following is a summary of the statistics of the manufactures of Augusta for 1880, being taken from tables prepared for the Tenth Census by Ernest E. Doscher, special agent:

Mechanical and manufacturing industries.	No. of establishments.	Capital.	AVERAGE NUMBER OF HANDS EMPLOYED.			Total amount paid in wages during the year.	Value of materials.	Value of products.
			Males above 16 years.	Females above 15 years.	Children and youths.			
All industries	60	$2,069,275	867	511	302	448,825	$2,247,665	$3,139,029
Blacksmithing	5	2,075	11			3,221	5,730	12,539
Carpentering	5	14,350	81			30,585	68,033	111,016
Carriages and wagons	4	80,450	62		2	24,456	52,750	91,746
Cotton goods	6	1,360,000	222	493	234	223,633	1,038,466	1,460,982
Flouring- and grist-mill products	3	144,000	50		6	18,360	770,000	869,950
Foundery and machine-shop products	4	56,000	107	4	14	37,620	79,699	146,250
Tinware, copperware, and sheet-iron ware	4	4,100	14		1	4,250	17,200	27,700
All other industries (a)	29	408,300	320	14	45	106,700	215,787	418,846

a Embracing bread and other bakery products; brick and tile; coffins, burial cases, and undertakers' goods; confectionery; fertilizers; ice, artificial; looking-glass and picture frames; marble and stone work; mattresses and spring beds; mineral and soda waters; painting and paperhanging; patent medicines and compounds; plumbing and gasfitting; printing and publishing; saddlery and harness; sash, doors, and blinds; stencils and brands; tobacco, chewing, smoking, and snuff; tobacco, cigars and cigarettes; wheelwrighting; and woolen goods.

From the foregoing table it appears that the average capital of all establishments is $34,487 92; that the average wages of all hands employed is $267 16 per annum; that the average outlay in wages, in materials, and in interest (at 6 per cent.) on capital employed is $47,010 78.

MACON,

BIBB COUNTY, GEORGIA.

POPULATION

IN THE

AGGREGATE,

1840-1880.

	Inhab.
1790	
1800	
1810	
1820	
1830	
1840	3,927
1850	5,720
1860	8,247
1870	10,810
1880	12,749

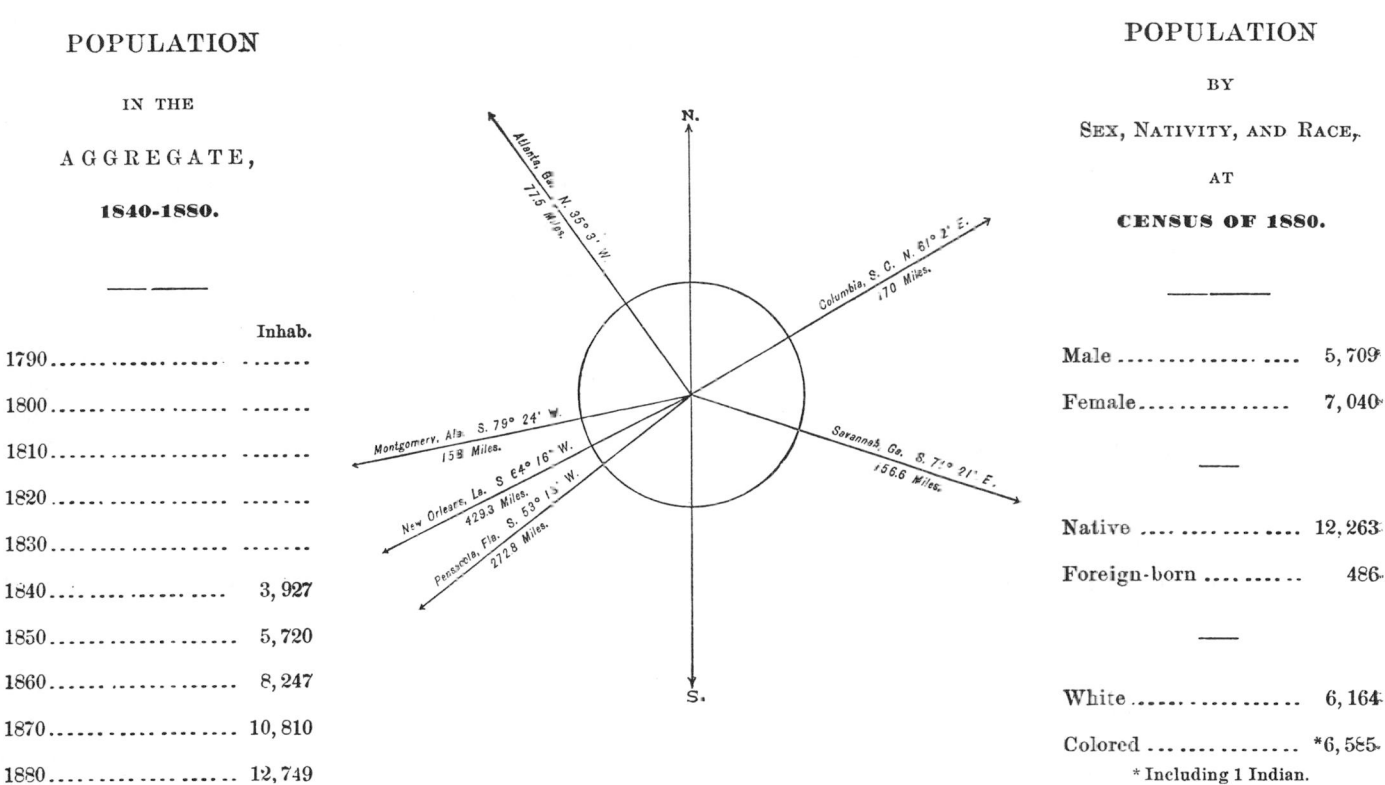

POPULATION

BY

SEX, NATIVITY, AND RACE,

AT

CENSUS OF 1880.

Male	5,709
Female................	7,040
Native	12,263
Foreign-born	486
White	6,164
Colored	*6,585

* Including 1 Indian.

Latitude: 32° 50′ North; Longitude: 83° 40′ (west from Greenwich); Altitude: 330 to 480 feet.

FINANCIAL CONDITION:

Total Valuation: $6,222,000; per capita: $488 00.   Net Indebtedness: $743,000; per capita: $55 28.   Tax per $100: $2 05.

MACON IN 1880.

In 1822 there was but one cabin on the ground now occupied by the city of Macon. Since then its increase has been steady and at times rapid.

The following statistical accounts, collected by the Census Office, indicate the present condition of Macon:

LOCATION.

Macon, the capital of Bibb county, is situated on both sides of the Ocmulgee river, at the head of steamboat navigation, in latitude 32° 50′ north, longitude 83° 40′ west from Greenwich, and about 80 miles southwest from Atlanta. Its altitudes above sea-level are, average, 350 feet; lowest point, 330 feet; and highest, 480 feet. At one time 8 or 10 steamboats were engaged in the river trade from here, but of late years the Ocmulgee has become so filled with logs and mud that navigation has been abandoned.

RAILROAD COMMUNICATIONS.

Macon is touched by the following-named railroads:

The Central Railroad of Georgia, between Columbus and Savannah.

The Western division, to Atlanta.

The Georgia railroad, to Camack, and from there to Augusta.

The Southwestern railroad, to Eufaula, Alabama.

The Macon and Brunswick railroad, to the places named.

These roads, and their terminal connections, give to Macon communication with all parts of the country.

TRIBUTARY COUNTRY.

The country immediately tributary to Macon is level, and is generally devoted to agriculture, cotton being the principal production.

TOPOGRAPHY.

The site of the city is hilly, with sandy soil and underlying rock, in some portions of limestone, in others sandstone. The city is rather more elevated than the surrounding country, which, within a radius of 5 miles, is considerably wooded. Lakes and swamps lie below the city.

CLIMATE.

Highest recorded summer temperature, 104°; highest summer temperature in average years, 96°. Lowest recorded winter temperature, 4°; lowest winter temperature in average years, 20°. The influence of the adjacent waters is not considered injurious to health, but the marshes are said to give rise to malaria.

STREETS.

There are 135 miles of streets in the city, none of which are paved. Sidewalks are of brick and granite. But few gutters have been placed, and they are of stone. Trees are planted in the middle of streets, and grass is also allowed to grow there. All construction and repairs are done by the city's force and the chain-gang, the annual cost being about $5,000. Day work is reported to be better done than contract work. At present there is no horse-railroad in operation, but one is being built. The only omnibus lines are those from the hotels.

WATER-WORKS.

The water-works are owned by a private company, and no statistics regarding them were furnished.

GAS.

The gas-works are owned by the city. The charge per 1,000 feet is $3. The city pays $25 a year for each street-lamp, 100 in number.

PUBLIC BUILDINGS.

The city owns or occupies for municipal uses, wholly or in part, the city hall and the police barracks. The total cost of the city buildings is given as $80,000, and the cost of the city hall as $20,000.

PUBLIC PARKS AND PLEASURE-GROUNDS.

There is but one park in Macon, called "*Central City Park*", with a total area of 720 acres. It is mostly in large forest trees, the race-course and the fair-ground building occupying about 100 acres of it. The land was donated to the city by the state, and the total cost of improvements is $300,000; the annual cost of maintenance is $2,000. Ex-mayor W. A. Huff was the designer of the park. It is controlled by the mayor and council, through a park-keeper.

PLACES OF AMUSEMENT.

Ralston's opera-house and Masonic hall, each with a seating capacity of about 800, are used for theatrical purposes, concerts, etc. They pay no license as buildings, but each performance pays a license of $5 to the city. There are no other halls in the city unconnected with churches, and there are no concert- and beer-gardens.

DRAINAGE.

No maps or surveys of the surface of Macon have ever been made, and therefore no detailed account of the system can be given here. There has been no regular plan followed with the sewers already constructed, the chairman of the street committee having had them built according to his own ideas. A city ordinance places the sewerage of the city in the hands and under the control of the city engineer, but the city council has always put the matter into the hands of the chairman of the street committee.

The mouths of the sewers now in use are fully exposed, and deliver the sewage on the swamps below the city, to the injury of the same in point of healthfulness. What flushing the sewers receive is due to rain, the deposits not being removed in any artificial way. When sewers are built the city pays the whole cost, no assessments on abutters being made.

CEMETERIES.

There are 2 cemeteries in Macon. No church-yards or private grounds for interments have ever been allowed in the city. The absence of any data renders it impossible to give the number of interments.

MARKETS.

There are no public or corporation markets in the city, supplies being obtained from private stores or from hucksters' wagons. Farmers are allowed to sell their own produce, from wagons, without paying a license.

SANITARY AUTHORITY—BOARD OF HEALTH.

The chief health organization in Macon is the board of health, composed of 9 members, one of whom is a physician, appointed annually by the mayor and council, and under full control of the mayor and aldermen. In ordinary times the expenses of the board are included in the street appropriation, and during an epidemic the expenses may be increased to such extent as the mayor and council may deem best for the interests of the city. In the absence of epidemics the board is required to keep the city in a cleanly condition and abate all nuisances, and during epidemics to have the city properly quarantined and otherwise reduce the chances of contagion. The president of the board is the executive officer; he serves without compensation. One assistant health officer or inspector is employed, who has full police powers. The clerk of the council is also clerk of the board. The city carts and chain-gang are placed under an inspector, who is controlled by the board. In summer, inspections are made regularly, and in winter, only as nuisances are reported. When a nuisance is reported or discovered, the inspector orders the same abated, and if his orders are not complied with, the party responsible is summoned before the mayor's court. The inspector notes all defective house-drainage, privy-vaults, cesspools, sources of drinking-water, etc., and orders these corrected. The board exercises no control over the conservation and removal of garbage, except to report all cases of neglect.

INFECTIOUS DISEASES.

Small-pox patients are usually placed in the hospital, situated some distance from the city. Scarlet-fever patients are neither isolated nor quarantined at home. The board takes no cognizance of the breaking out of contagious diseases in either public or private schools, as the matter is under the control of the city physician. Vaccination is compulsory, and among the poor is done at the public expense.

There is no regular system of registration of births, diseases, and deaths.

REPORTS.

The board reports to the city council, but its reports are not formally published.

MUNICIPAL CLEANSING.

Street-cleaning.—The streets are cleaned at the expense of the city and with its own force. The work is done wholly by hand. The streets are cleaned whenever they need it, and the work is reported as well done. The annual cost is from $1,000 to $1,500, and the sweepings are deposited below the city.

Removal of garbage and ashes.—The garbage is removed by the city with its own force. Pending removal it must be kept in boxes or barrels, and it is allowed to keep ashes in the same vessel with the garbage. The garbage is hauled below the city, and the final disposition of the ashes is the same. No nuisance or probable injury to health is reported to result from the improper keeping, infrequent removal, improper handling, or improper final disposal of the garbage.

Dead animals.—The carcasses of any animals dying within the city must be removed by the owner and hauled to certain localities selected by the mayor and council. The total number of dead animals removed annually is about 500 or 600.

Liquid household wastes.—But a small portion of these go into sewers. They are mostly thrown into vaults or cesspools, or emptied in the yards on the premises. The cesspools are porous, are not provided with overflows, do not receive the wastes from water-closets, and when cleaned, the contents are buried on the premises. The house-lots are very large, and the streets are from 120 to 180 feet wide; hence there has been very little contamination of drinking-water from the escape of the contents of either vaults or cesspools.

Human excreta.—Water-works having just been erected, the city may be said to depend exclusively on privy-vaults. About 5 per cent. of the houses in the city have water-closets, all of which deliver into the sewers. About 20 per cent. of the vaults are nominally water-tight. The privy-vaults are cleaned twice a year, the health-inspector having the matter in charge. The night-soil is buried on the premises.

Manufacturing wastes.—The wastes from founderies are used for filling washouts and cuts in the streets, while the wastes from cotton factories are sold or hauled away.

POLICE.

The police force of Macon is appointed by the mayor, subject to confirmation by the board of aldermen, and governed by the mayor and council. The executive officer is the chief of police, with a salary of $1,000 per annum. He has immediate control of the police force, and collects all executions issued by the mayor and council. The remainder of the force consists of 1 first lieutenant at $780 a year; 1 second lieutenant at $720 a year; and 18 privates (patrolmen) at $600 a year each. The uniform is blue in summer and gray in winter, and is furnished by the city at a cost of about $45 to each man. The men are equipped with clubs and pistols, and their hours of service are 12 on and 12 off. The force patrols 116 miles of streets.

During the past year there were about 1,600 arrests made, the principal causes being for drunkenness, fighting, shooting in the city, and violations of license ordinance. The cases were either dismissed or the parties were fined or put to labor on the streets. There was but little property reported to the police as lost or stolen during the year, and what was recovered was returned to the owners. The force is required to co-operate with the fire department so far as to protect property from theft at fires. Special policemen for duty at railroads, etc., are appointed by the mayor, but they have no connection with the regular force. The yearly cost of the police force is something over $14,000.

SAVANNAH,

CHATHAM COUNTY, GEORGIA.

POPULATION IN THE AGGREGATE, 1800-1880.

	Inhab.
1790	......
1800	5,166
1810	5,215
1820	7,523
1830	7,776
1840	11,214
1850	15,312
1860	22,292
1870	28,235
1880	30,709

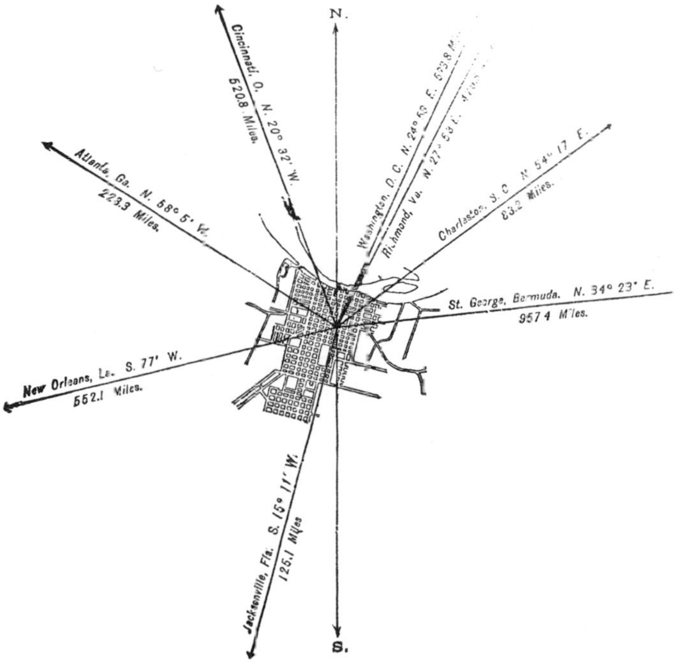

POPULATION BY SEX, NATIVITY, AND RACE, AT CENSUS OF 1880.

Male	13,936
Female	16,773
Native	27,715
Foreign-born	2,994
White	15,041
Colored	*15,668

*Including 2 Chinese and 12 Indians.

Latitude: 32° 5' North; Longitude: 81° 6' (west from Greenwich); **Altitude: 1 to 50 feet.**

FINANCIAL CONDITION:

Total Valuation: $15,060,445; per capita: $490 00. Net Indebtedness: $3,425,000; per capita: $111 53. Tax per $100: $2 93.

HISTORICAL SKETCH.

On June 9, 1732, George II, King of England, granted to a company of benevolent gentlemen, among whom James Oglethorpe was a leading spirit, a charter for a province to lie between the Savannah and the Altamaha rivers, to which they wished to send certain poor people as colonists. A party was organized with great care, and in November, 1732, under the charge of Oglethorpe, it sailed in the galley "Nan" for America. After a long voyage they reached Charleston January 13, 1733, where they were hospitably received, the citizens doing all in their power to make the colonists comfortable. Leaving his party in Charleston, Oglethorpe, in company with Colonel William Bull, of South Carolina, sailed in a small vessel for the Savannah river, to select a site for his colony. Ascending the river about 18 miles, his attention was attracted by a bluff about 50 feet high, on the south side of the river, and covered with a thick growth of pine trees. Here he landed, and ascending the bluff found the top partly cleared of trees; a small party of Indians and a single white trader were the only inhabitants of the place. Oglethorpe was so pleased with the location that he determined to establish his party there. Considerable difficulty was experienced in obtaining the consent of the Indians to a settlement, but a conditional assent was finally given, and Oglethorpe returned to Charleston to conduct his emigrants to their new home.

The party reached the bluff on February 1, 1733, and immediately began to prepare the spot for their town, which they decided to call "Savannah", from the river which flowed at their feet. No time was lost. The land was cleared, timber was hewn, and palisades were erected; the colonists in the mean while living in tents, which they had pitched around four large pine trees that stood not far from the edge of the bluff. Scarcely had the tents been pitched when a party of Indians came with friendly greetings, and the friendship thus begun was strengthened by a treaty made in May with the chiefs of the Creek nation. The party on leaving England included about 125 persons, and in July the number was increased by the arrival of 150 new-comers. A meeting was held July 7, 1733, and names were assigned to the wards, streets, and squares, for the streets had already been marked out, running at right angles, with spaces left at the intersection of every other street for public squares. The town and its people were divided into 4 wards, and each of these into 16 tithings. The 5 streets which had already been laid out were named Bull, Whittaker, Drayton, Saint Julian, and Bryan, in honor of South Carolinians who had greatly assisted the colonists. Lots were drawn for the land, a town court of record was established, bailiffs were appointed, a jury was empaneled, and the first court in Georgia was held. Four days later a party of Hebrews arrived and were welcomed by Oglethorpe. This act caused considerable dissatisfaction in England, but the leader refused to ask these new-comers to depart, though eventually all but 3 families were attracted away by the superior advantages of Charleston. In March, 1734, a party of Salzburgers arrived, and were established at a place 24 miles distant, which they called "Ebenezer".

After seeing his colony firmly established, Oglethorpe left for Europe, leaving behind him a town of 91 houses and a prosperous company. During his absence one of the three bailiffs left in charge drew all the authority into his own hands, and so mismanaged affairs that Oglethorpe, on his return in 1736, had much difficulty in allaying dissatisfaction. He was accompanied at this time by Charles Wesley and John Wesley, the founders of Methodism, and a year later the Rev. George Whitfield came to Savannah. Three laws of the town deserve mention, as they show the spirit of the founders of Georgia: All distilled liquors and brandies were prohibited under heavy penalties; no slavery or negroes were allowed; and all persons going among the Indians were compelled to give bonds for good behavior. The estates of the settlers were entailed, and this was regarded as very fortunate, for otherwise the lands might have fallen into the hands of a few men. The security of Savannah was threatened by an invasion of the Spaniards from Florida, but Oglethorpe, with a band of colonists, determined to protect their homes, met and repulsed the invaders. After this the progress of the town was not again threatened, and went on rapidly, though not in the direction the trustees desired.

It was the intention of the company in England which held the charter, to devote the colony to raising wine and silk, and, in spite of the want of success which attended the attempt, this object was persisted in, and commerce and agriculture of other kinds were discouraged as long as the company held its charter. As late as 1750 large bounties were offered to those who would raise silk and wine, and in 1751 a factory was built for the manufacture of silk goods. One enterprising citizen, however, established a commercial business in 1744, and by 1749 the exports of the town were valued at $10,000, while the culture of rice and indigo became of such value that the trustees began to doubt the wisdom of persisting in their first design. On January 15, 1751, a general assembly of Georgia met at Savannah and drew up a list of complaints which they presented to the council of the trustees, and in 1752, the charter having expired, no effort was made to renew it, and Georgia became a royal province. The first royal governor, John Reynolds, was sent to the colony in 1734 and remained until 1737, when he was replaced by Henry Ellis, who, at his own request, was recalled in 1760, and Sir James Wright was appointed. These three men were the only royal governors of Georgia, for during the term of the last the Revolution began.

The stamp act was very unpopular in Savannah, and the agent for the sale of stamps was compelled to flee the town; but in 1775, when a provincial congress met in Savannah and delegates were elected to the Continental Congress, they refused to go, saying that the convention which elected them did not represent a majority of the people of the province. Many of the townspeople were apathetic in regard to resistance to England, as it would injure their commerce, which in 1773 amounted in export alone to $379,422, while not a few openly favored the mother country; yet when the news of the battle of Lexington reached Savannah all thought of submission to England vanished. The town was destined to be the scene of much fighting. In January, 1776, an attempt was made by the British to capture Savannah, but it failed of success; and the town was the meeting-place of the convention which framed the constitution of Georgia, adopted finally February 5, 1777. A second attack by the British in December, 1778, proved successful; and, in spite of the determined attempt of a combined force of French and Continentals under Estaing and Lincoln, in 1779, to recapture the town, during which Count Pulaski lost his life, it remained in British hands until July, 1782, when it was evacuated.

View of Savannah, as it stood the 29th March, A.D. 1734.

1. The Stairs going up.
2. Mr. Oglethorpe's Tent.
3. The Crane and Well.
4. The Tabernacle & Court House.
5. The Publick Mill.
6. The House for Strangers.
7. The Publick Oven.
8. The Stone Well.

9. The Lott for the Church.
10. The Publick Stores.
11. The Fort
12. The Parsonage House.
13. The Pallisadoes.
14. The Guard House and
    Battery of Cannon.
15. Hutchinsons Island.

To the Hon. the Trustees for establishing the Colony of Georgia in America.

This View of the Town of Savannah, is humbly dedicated by their Honours

Obliged and most Obedient Servant,

Peter Gordon.

VUE de Savanah dans la Georgie.

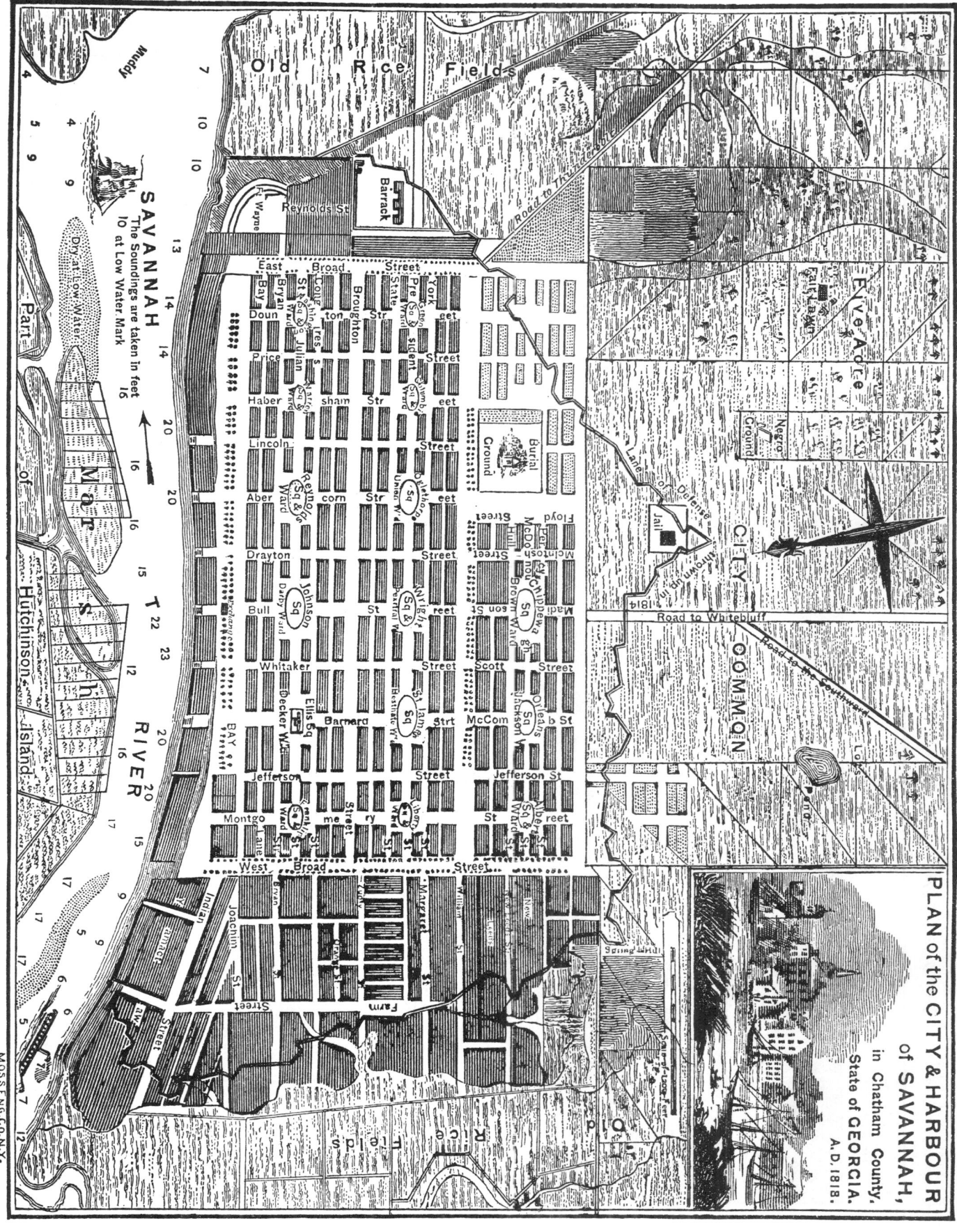

PLAN of the CITY & HARBOUR of SAVANNAH,
in Chatham County, State of GEORGIA. A.D. 1818.

SAVANNAH
The Soundings are taken in feet
10 at Low Water Mark

MOSS ENG. CO. N.Y.

The rule of the British had done great injury to the commerce of the town, and under the terms of the capitulation the British merchants already established there had been allowed to remain unmolested; yet the people overcame all obstacles placed in their way, and Savannah was soon as prosperous as ever. In 1789 it was incorporated as a city. Seven years later it met with a great misfortune, the first of a series of severe losses. On November 26, 1796, a fire broke out, and before it could be extinguished 229 buildings had been destroyed. The loss was more than $1,000,000, but courage and energy soon enabled the citizens to recover their position. A census taken in 1798 showed a population of 6,226, and the exports in 1800 were valued at $2,155,982. The first shipment of cotton was made in 1788, a single bale being exported by Thomas Miller. The city suffered considerable loss from a storm, September 8, 1804, which destroyed many public and private buildings, while the river carried 18 vessels on to the wharves and injured many others. During the war of 1812 the city was in constant fear of attack, and was carefully fortified, but no attempt was made to take it.

The first steamship built in America was owned and projected in Savannah, and bore the name of the city. It was built in the north, and April, 1819, arrived in the city from New York. A few days later it steamed for Liverpool, arriving there after a passage of 22 days, on only 8 of which sails were used. The "Savannah" was the first steamship which crossed the Atlantic, and its arrival created great surprise in England.

A second great fire occurred in January, 1820, destroying 463 houses and entailing a loss of $4,000,000; and the city had hardly recovered from the shock when an epidemic of yellow fever broke out. The disease was brought from the West Indies and spread rapidly, attacking 239 persons before it could be checked. A census taken in October showed that only 1,494, from a population of 7,523, still remained in the city. The year 1825 was memorable for the visit of Lafayette. During his stay the distinguished guest assisted in laying the corner-stones of the Pulaski and the Greene monuments.

The importance of Savannah as a cotton port came principally with the construction of railroads to the city, and notably by the building of the Georgia Central railroad. This road was projected in 1834, and a company was formed in the following year; the trains began running regularly in 1838, but the line was not completed to Macon, the terminus, until 1843. This railroad greatly increased the cotton receipts of Savannah, and, with the roads since constructed, has made the city second only to New Orleans in the amount and value of its shipment. In 1854 the yellow fever appeared again, and in a short time spread throughout the city. It reached its height September 12, when 51 interments were reported; 591 deaths from the fever occurred. While the fever was still raging a severe storm caused great damage to buildings and shipping.

The city early in the civil war became an object of attack by the Federal army, and in February, 1862, fort Pulaski was taken by it. Savannah, however, remained in confederate hands until December, 1864, when it was taken by General Sherman at the end of his "march to the sea". A large fire in 1865 laid part of the city in ashes.

With the close of the civil war the prosperity of the city soon returned, and in 1873 its exports were valued at $52,644,053 75. Cotton is, of course, the staple of the export trade, but rice, timber, and naval stores enter largely into the trade. Indeed, the growth of Savannah since the war has been phenomenal. It has large manufacturing establishments; three important railroad systems center in the city; it has three horse-railroads; while regular lines of steamships run to New York, Philadelphia, Boston, and Baltimore. The inland trade is large and important. Savannah is a beautiful city. The streets are laid out regularly, intersecting one another at right angles, while at the intersection of every other street small parks are made, which are planted with fine trees and add greatly to the beauty and healthfulness of the city. It is lighted with gas, and a good water-supply was introduced in 1854. Many fine buildings add to the attractiveness of the city, among them several church edifices. Within easy reach are a number of pleasant resorts; and Bonaventure cemetery, the resting-place of Savannah's dead, is a spot of remarkable beauty. The schools of the city are well regulated and good. The Chatham County academy was founded in 1788, and early became a leading institution. Free schools were begun in 1816, and the system of to-day is considered a good one. The churches are many, the various charities large, and societies of all kinds numerous. The first newspaper was published in 1763, and to-day there are several dailies and weeklies published in the city. The health of the city in the early part of the century was not good; but the marshes have been largely cleared, under the operation of the dry-system contract, which began in 1817 and was ended in 1870, putting an end to the wet cultivation of rice in the immediate vicinity of the city; and Savannah may now be called a healthy city, though somewhat of malaria still remains. The advantages of the city, both as a place of residence and of business, are great, and the rapid growth of the past few years seems only a promise of greater things in the future.

SAVANNAH IN 1880.

The following statistical accounts, collected by the Census Office, indicate the present condition of Savannah:

LOCATION.

Savannah is situated in latitude 32° 5' north, longitude 81° 6' west from Greenwich, on the south bank of the Savannah river, about 18 miles from the ocean. The city is located upon a bluff about 45 feet above the river-level, while the wharves extend along the river-front under the bluff. The lowest point is covered by 1 foot of water at high tide, while the highest point is 50 feet above mean low water, which corresponds very nearly with the sea-level. The water over the bar at the mouth of the river is 26 feet deep at mean high tide, while at mean low tide it is 19 feet deep. At Tybee island, inside the bar, the depth is 38 and 31 feet, and at the city wharves it is 16 feet. The river is navigable for steamboats to Augusta, 203 miles from Savannah. The tide flows about 45 miles up the river, the rise and fall at Savannah being about 6½ feet. Regular lines of steamers run to and from New York, Philadelphia, Boston, and Baltimore, while many steamers ply between the city and other southern ports.

RAILROAD COMMUNICATIONS.

Three important railroad lines center in Savannah, connecting it closely with the southeastern states and cities. The Central Railroad of Georgia, terminus Macon; the Savannah, Florida, and Western railroad, terminus Bainbridge, Georgia; and the Charleston and Savannah railroad, terminus Charleston, connect with other lines at their terminal points, thus affording to the city communication with the entire country.

TRIBUTARY COUNTRY.

The country tributary to the city is devoted entirely to agriculture. Vegetables are raised in great abundance for the northern markets, and on the tide-lands near the city rice is extensively cultivated.

TOPOGRAPHY.

Savannah is situated on a plain of sandy land, about 45 feet above low-water mark, extending about a mile along the river and back from it 8 or 9 miles, varying in width from three-quarters of a mile to 2 miles. On the east and west the plain slopes gently to the level of the tide-lands, which, if unprotected by embankments, would be covered 1 foot by the tide at high water. Large marshes once hedged in the city on the east and west, but they have been drained to a large extent. The country for a radius of 2 miles is open, but beyond that distance it is well wooded.

CLIMATE.

The highest recorded summer temperature is 102°; highest summer temperature in average years, 96°. Lowest recorded winter temperature, 15°; lowest winter temperature in average years, 30°. The series from which these figures are taken extends from 1839 to 1874. The elevation of the city above the low lands frees it somewhat from the malarial influences of the marshes, but a mild type of malaria is present at all times. Previous to 1817, when the rice-lands adjacent to the city were regularly flooded, the malaria was very injurious; but the draining of the swamp and the introduction of the dry-culture system for rice have greatly improved the health of the city. The nearness of the Gulf stream keeps the climate warm, while the winds from the south are rendered soft and mild by it. The cold and dry winds are from the north and west. The rainfall in June, July, and August is very large.

STREETS.

Of the streets of Savannah, 3¼ miles are paved with cobble-stones, one-half mile with stone blocks, and one-half mile with broken stone. In some streets wood pavement was laid at one time, but it has since been removed. The cost per square yard of the cobble-stone pavement is $1; of the stone blocks the cost has differed; at present it is $2 50, but at one time it was $4 per square yard. The stone-block pavement is found to be both more economical than any other and easier to keep clean, only the gutters needing to be scraped in the climate of Savannah. The sidewalks are of flagstone, Philadelphia and Baltimore paving-brick, and Savannah gray brick. The gutters are of cobble-stones. Trees are planted along the sidewalks, 1 foot within the curbstone and about 30 feet apart. From 200 to 300 are planted yearly. The streets are kept in repair by day labor, at an annual cost of between $25,000 and $30,000. No steam stone-crusher or roller is used. There are three horse-railroad lines, each about 1⅓ mile in length. The estimated number of cars is 50, and of horses 100. About 100 men are employed. The fare on all the lines is 5 cents. Omnibuses run from the hotels to the railroad stations and steamboat landings.

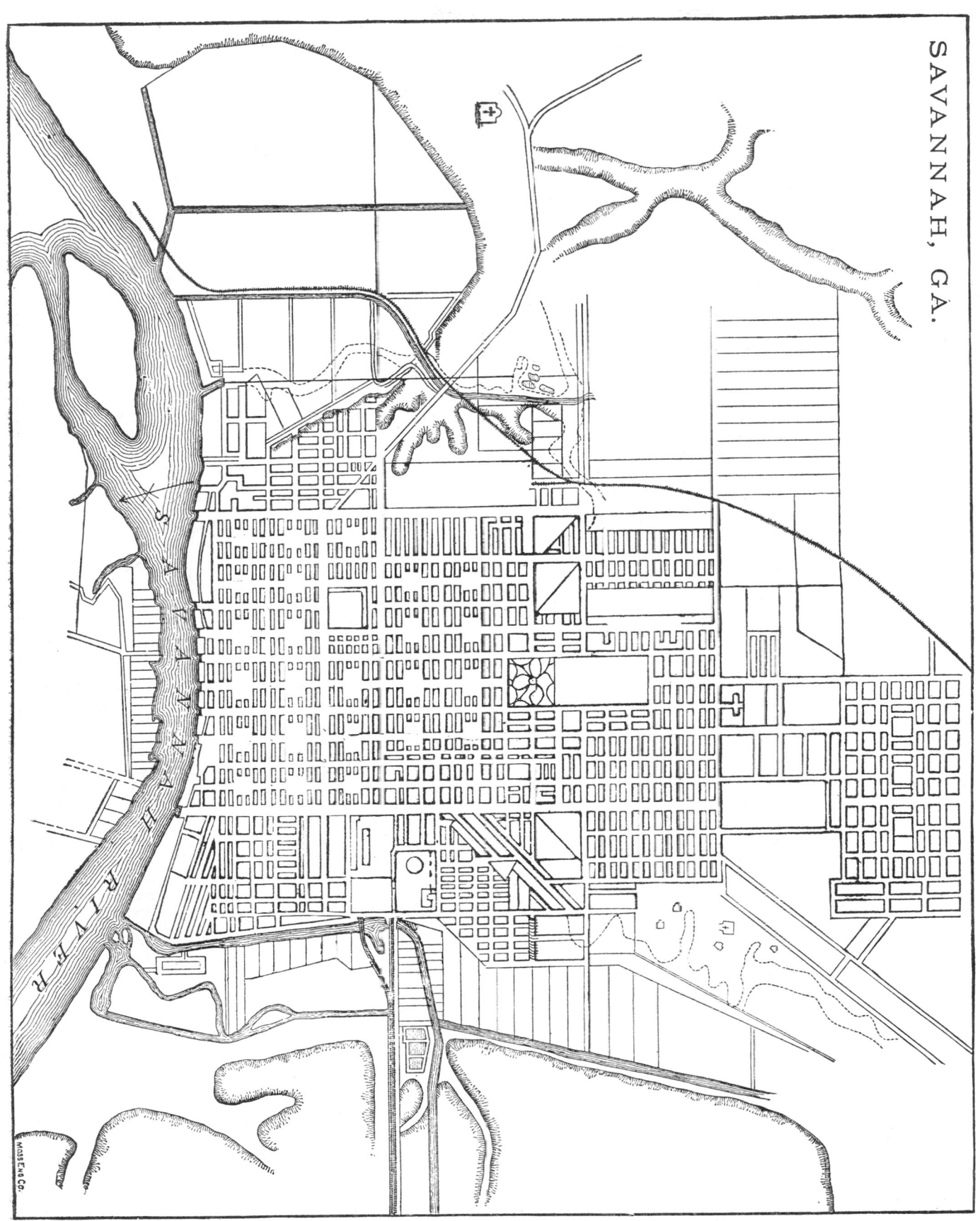

SAVANNAH, GA.

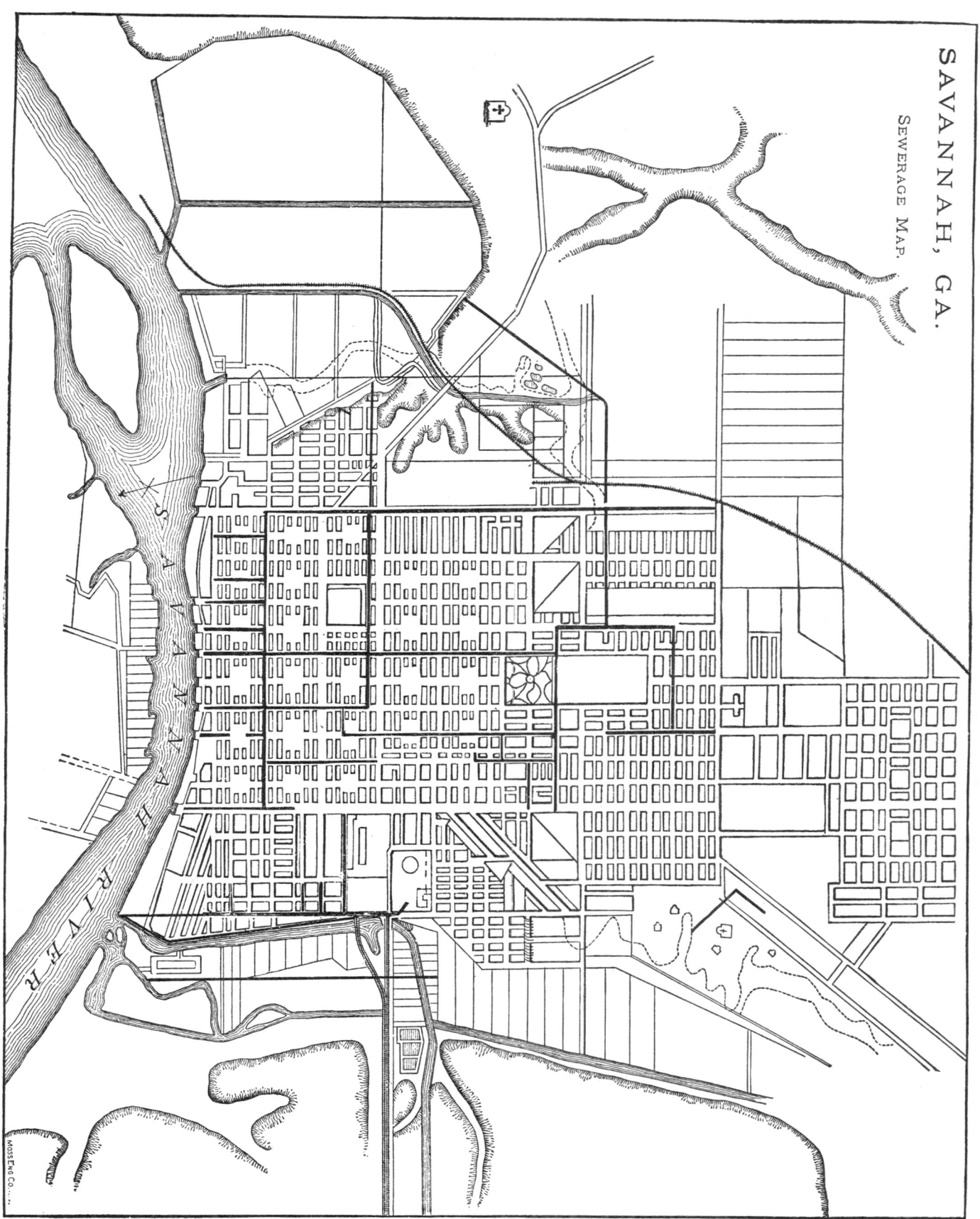

SAVANNAH, GA.

SEWERAGE MAP.

SAVANNAH RIVER

WATER-WORKS.

The total cost of the works for the public water-supply has been $300,000, and they are owned by the city Water is taken from the Savannah river and pumped into four receiving-basins, each capable of holding 1,000,000 gallons. Three Worthington single pumps, with a capacity of 1,000,000 gallons each, were erected in 1854; but since 1875 a Worthington duplex pump of 3,500,000 gallons capacity has been used, although the old ones are still retained. The superitendent of the water-works urges, in his report for 1880, the purchase of a new pump to meet the increased demands for water. The high service is supplied by pumping into a tank 20 feet in diameter and 37 feet high, placed on a brick tower 50 feet high. The pressure in the mains was found by experiment to vary from 42 pounds to the square inch near the reservoir, to only 15 pounds at Duffy and Whitcher streets. There are 22 miles of pipes and mains and 257 fire-hydrants. The average amount pumped daily is 2,000,000 gallons, the greatest amount in any one day being 2,385,000. The yearly cost of maintenance for 1880 is $12,269 72, and the annual income for the same year was $28,198 20, the total receipts from all sources being $42,010 39. No water-meters are used.

GAS.

The city is supplied with gas by the Savannah Gas Light Company, a private corporation. The average daily production is 80,000 cubic feet. The charge per 1,000 feet is $3. The city pays $26 40 a year for each street-lamp, 588 in number.

PUBLIC BUILDINGS.

The buildings owned by the city are valued at $450,000, and include the Exchange building, used for a city hall and offices, a market building, powder magazine, police barracks, 3 fire-engine houses, city dispensary, and stables and pound buildings. The Exchange building was built in 1799 by a joint-stock company in which the city was a stockholder. It came into the city's hands in 1812, and considerable improvements have since been made. Its value to-day is $100,000.

PUBLIC PARKS AND PLEASURE-GROUNDS.

The total area of the parks in Savannah is 60 acres. There are 23 small parks at street intersections, each containing from 1 to 1½ acre; a park of 10 acres; and an extension to the latter containing 20 acres, used as a parade-ground. The cost of laying out the parks was $20,000, and the yearly cost of maintenance for the large one is $2,250, and for the smaller ones $1,000. The parks are controlled by a committee on parks.

PLACES OF AMUSEMENT.

There is 1 theater in the city, with a seating capacity of 800. There are 5 halls, each with a seating capacity of about 500, used for concerts, lectures, etc. Theaters pay a license for each performance. There are 5 concert- and beer-gardens.

DRAINAGE.

The first systematic plan of sewerage was begun in 1869. There are 3 principal lines running parallel with the river. They begin at the outlet with a diameter of 6 feet and gradually diminish in size. At right angles to these are others, 3 feet in diameter, in several of the principal streets. There are also a number of sewers consisting of a single ring of brick, some 24 inches, others 30 inches, in diameter. A few cement-pipe sewers, 12 inches in diameter, have been laid in the lanes for house-drainage; all others are of brick. Most of them are laid with a rate of fall of 3 inches in 100 feet. No deposits are removed by hand. The smaller sewers are occasionally flushed.

The outflow passes through a canal to the river, except in a few instances, where the sewers empty directly into the Savannah river in front of the city. The mouths of the sewers are fully exposed. The only provision for ventilation is through the rain-water leaders of some houses.

In cases where the bottom of the sewers is below the level of ground-water they are built in a wooden cradle, constructed of ribs of 2-inch plank cut to the shape of the outside of the sewer and planked with narrow strips of inch lumber. In such places the bricks at the bottom, for a space of 15 inches or less, according to the size of the sewer, are laid without mortar, and the ground-water is said to force its way up and pass off in a continuous stream.

The entire cost of sewerage works is paid by the city. A charge is made for connections at the following rates: For the connection, $10; for supervision, $3; for permit, $1, making a total charge of $14.

No information is furnished of the extent or cost of sewerage. A map published in 1876, showing sewers, has no scale from which their extent could be ascertained.

CEMETERIES.

There are 3 cemeteries connected with the city, but only 1 is entirely within its limits.

Laurel Grove Cemetery, in the extreme southwestern part of the city, contains 100 acres. Since its opening in 1852 there have been 26,937 burials within this cemetery—11,330 of white and 15,607 of colored persons.

Cathedral Cemetery is situated 1½ mile east of the city. It is controlled by the Catholic church. No information as to its area or the number of interments was furnished.

Bonaventure Cemetery is situated on the Warsaw river, about 4 miles from Savannah, and it is said to be one of the most beautiful resting-places of the dead in the world. No information as to its area, condition, or the number of interments within it was furnished.

Laurel Grove cemetery is controlled by the city, through a keeper. Graves are made from 5 to 6 feet deep. No interment is allowed to be made until the sexton has received a certificate of death signed by a physician, or coroner, or the health officer. Any violation of this rule is punishable by fine or imprisonment.

MARKETS.

A market-building, 150 by 200 feet, was erected in 1871 at a cost of $145,000. A clear space of 50 feet is left all around the building, and market carts and vegetable and huckster wagons are allowed to occupy the portion of this space nearest the market. It has a meat, a vegetable, and a fish department. Meat stalls rent at from $90 to $135 per year; fish stalls at $135; and vegetable stalls at $50. The income from the stalls in 1880 was $3,587 65, and from stores in the basement $2,598 07. The total rental, including collections from venders, was $8,688 70. The market is open every day except Sunday, from 5 to 9 a. m., and on Saturday from 2 to 10 p. m. The gross amount of annual sales was not stated. Nearly all the retail provision-stores obtain their supplies from the market.

SANITARY AUTHORITY—BOARD OF SANITARY COMMISSIONERS.

The chief sanitary authority of the city is vested in a board of sanitary commissioners, consisting of 2 aldermen, 3 citizens appointed by the mayor, and the health officer and the mayor as members *ex officio*. The board thus constituted has no fund at its disposal, and must obtain the consent of the city council to each item of expense. The board was not organized until 1877, and as no epidemic has occurred since then, no statement of its powers to increase its expenditures can be made. It has authority to abate all nuisances within the extended limits of the city, *i. e.*, 1 mile beyond the corporate limits. Its authority in presence of an epidemic has never been tested, but the health officer reports that it would meet any emergency. The board meets regularly once a fortnight, but in practice comes together much oftener. The chief executive officer is the health officer, salary $1,000 a year; his duties are many, but may be summed up in saying he has power to abate nuisances and carry out the orders of the board. An assistant health officer, a physician, is employed as quarantine officer, and stationed at the quarantine station at the mouth of the Savannah river. He has power to make arrests, and reports to the board. Inspections are made during the summer months, by a detail from the police force, once a week, while during the winter they are made but once a month. Three members of the board are physicians.

When nuisances are found or complained of, they are immediately inspected and abated if possible by the person causing them; if not, then by the authorities. Defective privy-vaults, cesspools, and sources of drinking-water are treated as nuisances, and are abated as soon and as well as possible. The sewers and streets are kept as clean as possible. Nothing is done in regard to the pollution of streams. The board compels the removal of garbage daily to some place beyond the extended limits of the city. All sextons are required to obtain a certificate of death signed by an attending physician, the health officer, or a coroner, stating the cause of death, and name, age, sex, etc., of the deceased, before making any interment, under penalty of not more than $100 fine or 30 days' imprisonment. When any death occurs where no physician has attended, the health officer must view the body and furnish the certificate mentioned above, unless the case is one calling for the action of a coroner. No body can be brought within the city unless accompanied by a proper certificate of death; and if death was caused by small-pox, yellow fever, or other pestilential disease, the body can be admitted only by a permit from the board.

INFECTIOUS DISEASES.

Small-pox patients are removed to the hospital grounds, 4 miles from the city, unless they refuse to be moved; in the latter case they are quarantined at home, flags are displayed to warn passers, and other precautions are taken to prevent the spread of the disease. Scarlet fever has not been epidemic since the board began to act, and little attention has been paid to it. Those suffering from the disease are not isolated or quarantined in any way. Should contagious diseases break out in the schools the board would not hesitate to take any action deemed necessary for the public health. Vaccination is not compulsory, but is done free of expense to those wishing it, either at the cost of the city or of charitable physicians. A quarantine station is maintained at the mouth of the river at all times.

The registration of births, diseases, and deaths is very irregularly attended to.

REPORTS.

The board of sanitary commissioners makes no report, although records are carefully kept. A summary is published with the annual reports of the city as a report of the health officer.

MUNICIPAL CLEANSING.

Street-cleaning.—The streets are cleaned by the city scavenger, a contractor paid by the city to remove all offal, dirt, and rubbish from streets and houses. The work is done entirely by hand, and whenever there is need for it. The sweepings are taken 1 mile beyond the city limits and there disposed of. The contractor receives about $15,000 a year for his labor.

Removal of garbage and ashes.—Garbage and ashes are removed by the scavenger. While awaiting removal garbage is generally kept in barrels or boxes placed in the rear of the house-lots adjoining the lanes. It may be kept in the same vessel with ashes. Garbage and ashes are disposed of in the same way as the street-sweepings. The cost of the service is included in the general contract of the scavenger.

Dead animals are removed at the cost of the owner to some point not less than 1 mile beyond the city limits.

Liquid household wastes.—All liquid wastes of the household are disposed of alike. Where sewers exist the wastes run into them, but much the larger portion are thrown broadcast into the lanes, and run into the street-gutters. Less than one-third of the houses are connected with the sewers, and not more than 1 in 20 have cesspools. When cesspools are used they are generally porous and without overflows. When full they are cleaned out by the odorless-excavator process, the city owning the apparatus. As the soil is a fine sand the filtration from cesspools is very rapid, and well-water is perceptibly contaminated from overflow or soakage. The street-gutters are flushed only by the rain, but as the rainfall is large they give no trouble.

Human excreta.—The proportion of the houses in the city which are provided with water-closets is not known; by far the larger proportion depend on privy-vaults. A charge, varying with the size of the vault, from $3 to $7 per annum is levied on all persons using privies, to meet the expense incurred by the city in removing night-soil and in making the vaults water-tight. The contents are removed by the odorless-excavator process. The cost of this service during the past year was $14,659 74. The dry-earth system is not used. Night-soil is removed at least 1 mile beyond the city limits, and there used as manure by the market-gardeners. As the water-supply comes from the Savannah river, it is little affected by the use of night-soil as manure on its banks.

Manufacturing wastes.—With the exception of a paper-mill, there are no factories creating wastes which need to be disposed of. The wastes from the paper-mill pass off through one of the public sewers.

POLICE.

The officers of the police department of Savannah are chosen by the mayor and aldermen; the privates are appointed by the mayor, on recommendation of the chief of police, and the appointments submitted to the council for confirmation. The chief executive officer is the chief of police, salary $1,800 per annum, who has the general charge of his department. The rest of the force consists of 2 lieutenants, salary $1,200 a year each, 4 sergeants, salary $900 a year each, and 50 privates, salary $720 a year each. The uniform is a dark-blue frock coat with brass buttons, dark-blue trousers with white belt, and a cork helmet, United States regulation pattern, covered with black cloth. The city furnishes each man with his uniform. The men are armed with mahogany batons 22 inches long, navy revolvers, and duplex police whistles. They are on duty 6 hours each day and 6 hours each night, and the beats are about 4 miles each. Mounted policemen patrol the remote portions of the city.

During the past year 1,749 arrests were made, the principal causes being drunkenness and disorderly conduct. The number of station-house lodgers for the year was 602, as against 437 in 1879. No meals are given to these lodgers. A detail of 1 sergeant and 8 privates reports for duty to the chief engineer at all fires, and policemen are detailed for duty as sanitary inspectors. Special policemen are appointed by the mayor for the railroad and steamship companies, and these specials are under the command of the chief of police. The total cost of the department for 1880 was $45,000.

FIRE DEPARTMENT.

The fire department is organized on the paid system, and is controlled by the chief engineer and one assistant. The apparatus consists of 4 steam fire-engines, fully equipped, 3 one-horse hose-reels, 1 hook-and-ladder truck, and 4,800 feet of hose. There are 9 horses owned by the department. Two auxiliary hose companies give their assistance. During the past year there were 36 alarms of fire, 4 of them being false. The gross amount of property destroyed was $22,073 37, all but $500 of which was more than covered by insurance. A fire-alarm telegraph is in use. The total cost of the department is stated by the mayor in his annual report for 1880 at $14,194 69.

COMMERCE AND NAVIGATION.

[From the reports of the Bureau of Statistics for the fiscal years ending June 30.]

Customs district of Savannah, Georgia.	1879.	1880.
Total value of imports................	$429,519	$483,802
Total value of exports:		
Domestic	$21,527,235	$23,992,364
Foreign.............................	None.	None.
Total number of immigrants	None.	None.

Customs district of Savannah, Georgia.	1879.		1880.	
	Number.	Tons.	Number.	Tons.
Vessels in foreign trade:				
Entered	245	238,174	265	183,895
Cleared	236	193,014	244	170,092
Vessels in coast trade and fisheries:				
Entered	319	400,048	339	427,293
Cleared	366	431,450	338	443,570
Vessels registered, enrolled, and licensed in district..	71	6,347	72	14,310
Vessels built during the year	3	40	5	67

MANUFACTURES.

The following is a summary of the statistics of the manufactures of Savannah for 1880, being taken from tables prepared for the Tenth Census by B. Frank Gray, special agent:

Mechanical and manufacturing industries.	No. of establishments.	Capital.	AVERAGE NUMBER OF HANDS EMPLOYED.			Total amount paid in wages during the year.	Value of materials.	Value of products.
			Males above 16 years.	Females above 15 years.	Children and youths.			
All industries................................	120	$1,102,970	996	68	66	$447,640	$2,457,606	$3,396,297
Boots and shoes, including custom work and repairing..............	7	1,920	10	....	....	4,738	4,071	12,110
Bread and other bakery products........................	15	71,250	103	....	15	30,342	208,240	272,124
Brick and tile..........................	3	59,500	62	1	2	13,900	11,587	33,900
Carpentering............................	9	12,875	57	....	....	28,335	60,044	107,389
Carriages and wagons (see also Wheelwrighting)..................	3	6,300	17	....	....	7,417	7,000	20,535
Flouring- and grist-mill products..........................	5	121,000	57	....	....	25,096	338,225	405,520
Foundery and machine-shop products	7	64,000	84	3	6	50,197	68,683	176,954
Lumber, sawed	4	43,000	78	....	5	16,904	100,000	135,292
Mineral and soda waters.....................	3	6,300	15	....	....	5,834	4,364	19,248
Painting and paperhanging	8	36,775	54	....	....	31,003	25,343	80,850
Plumbing and gasfitting..........................	6	7,900	20	....	....	8,571	13,874	31,100
Printing and publishing	4	104,800	109	2	14	66,603	52,600	140,500
Saddlery and harness..........................	3	30,500	8	....	....	4,434	4,600	13,050
Tinware, copperware, and sheet-iron ware	6	44,000	19	....	....	9,861	22,700	46,000
Tobacco, cigars and cigarettes	11	8,000	32	1	7	12,311	14,255	34,452
Wheelwrighting (see also Carriages and wagons)	11	22,950	58	....	3	25,156	22,530	65,901
All other industries (a)	15	461,900	213	61	14	106,938	1,499,550	1,801,872

a Embracing blacksmithing; coffins, burial cases, and undertakers' goods; confectionery; cooperage; cotton goods; lumber, planed; marble and stone work; paper; rice cleaning and polishing; stencils and brands; and tar and turpentine.

From the foregoing table it appears that the average capital of all establishments is $9,191 42; that the average wages of all hands employed is $396 14 per annum; that the average outlay in wages, in materials, and in interest (at 6 per cent.) on capital employed is $24,761 87.

FLORIDA.

JACKSONVILLE,
DUVAL COUNTY, FLORIDA.

POPULATION

IN THE

AGGREGATE,

1850-1880.

	Inhab.
1790	......
1800	......
1810	......
1820	......
1830	......
1840	......
1850	1,045
1860	2,118
1870	6,912
1880	7,650

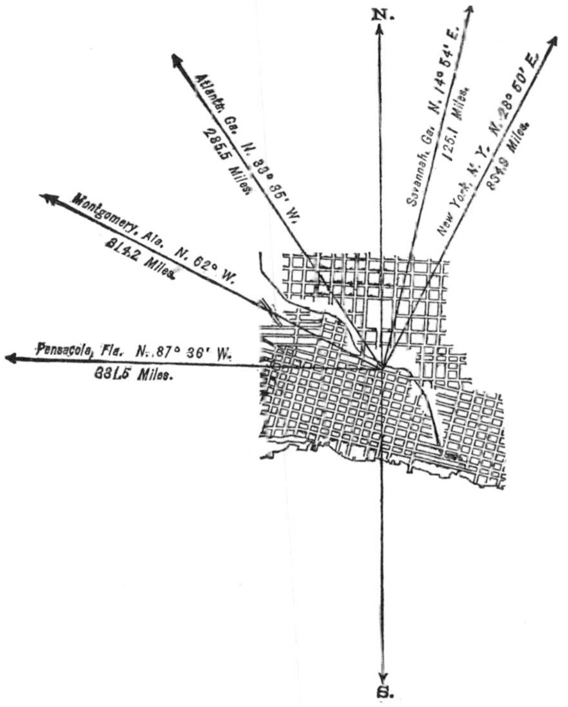

POPULATION

BY

SEX, NATIVITY, AND RACE,

AT

CENSUS OF 1880.

Male	3,758
Female	3,892
Native	6,920
Foreign-born	730
White	3,991
Colored	*3,659

* Including 1 Chinese.

Latitude: 30° 20′ North; Longitude: 81° 39′ (west from Greenwich); Altitude: 1 to 40 feet.

FINANCIAL CONDITION:

Total Valuation: $2,676,990; per capita: $350 00.   Net Indebtedness: $270,916; per capita: $35 41.   Tax per $100: $3 10.

HISTORICAL SKETCH.

Jacksonville, the capital of Duval county, was originally settled about 1828. For the first decade the growth was slow, aggregating only about 800 persons, exclusive of the refugees driven in by the Seminole war. During the next ten years the accession was very gradual, after which, owing to the establishment of numerous lumber-mills in the town and vicinity, the population increased more rapidly, which increase was maintained until the outbreak of the civil war. During the war the place was almost depopulated and destroyed by fire. Previous to this time the business portion of the city had been twice destroyed by fire and rebuilt.

Since the close of the war Jacksonville has seen her best days. Her site has been rebuilt and more than rebuilt. With the late attention that has been paid to the state the situation of the city has been entirely in its favor, and it receives annually large numbers of excursionists and tourists, as well as prospective settlers. A large proportion of the present population of Jacksonville is composed of people of various nationalities and from the North. The cause of the late prosperity is to be found in the fact of its being a port of entry on the most important river of the state, that its railroad facilities are good, and that there is a good prospect of an improvement of its harbor, allowing vessels of a larger class to enter. Its relative importance in a state so sparsely settled as Florida is very great. It is, and from its favorable position will probably long continue to be, the commercial metropolis of the state, the lumber and cigar industries taking the lead.

JACKSONVILLE IN 1880.

The following statistical accounts, collected by the Census Office, indicate the present condition of Jacksonville:

LOCATION.

Jacksonville lies in latitude 30° 20′ north, longitude 81° 39′ west from Greenwich, on the left bank of the Saint John's river, 25 miles from its mouth and 252 miles east of Tallahassee. The altitudes above sea-level are: Average, 38 feet; lowest point, 1 foot; and highest point, 40 feet. Although 25 miles from its mouth, the river is here almost like an inlet of the sea, and affords a fine harbor. The draught of water in front of the city and in the channel averages 50 feet, but, owing to obstructions at the mouth of the river, vessels of large size are prevented from taking advantage of it. The river and its tributaries afford about 600 miles of interior communication with a country which is rapidly settling up with towns and agricultural districts.

RAILROAD COMMUNICATIONS.

Jacksonville is the eastern terminus of the Florida Central railroad, connecting at Lake City with the Jacksonville, Pensacola, and Mobile railroad to Tallahassee, and also, at Baldwin, with the Atlantic, Gulf, and West India Transit railroad, for Cedar Keys on the south and Fernandina on the north.

TRIBUTARY COUNTRY.

The land lying immediately upon the river is devoted largely to the cultivation of fruits—especially those belonging to the citrus family—cotton, rice, sugar-cane, corn, sweet potatoes, and garden vegetables of almost every description, the latter being raised for early export to the North. The products of the forest are yellow pine, cypress, red bay, live-oak, and other useful and ornamental woods. The country tributary to the lower Saint John's is mostly undulating, and in some cases swampy, but when reclaimed forms the most fertile lands.

TOPOGRAPHY.

The surface soil is sandy, mixed with calcareous masses derived from comminuted shells, having a substratum of clay at a depth of from 1 to 10 feet below the surface, and this rests upon a rock of calcareous and Tertiary formation. The rock is ordinarily reached at a depth of from 20 to 30 feet below the surface, and crops out in the river, in front of the city, 28 feet below mean low water. The site is sufficiently rolling to admit of easy drainage. Marshes are interspersed throughout the adjacent country, about half of which is wooded. The soil within a radius of 5 miles does not vary from that of the site described.

CLIMATE.

Highest recorded summer temperature, 104° (1879); highest summer temperature in average years, 97°; mean summer temperature, 81.82°. Lowest recorded winter temperature, 16° (1851); lowest winter temperature in average years, 30°; mean winter temperature, 56.33°. Mean annual temperature (1839 to 1870), 68.98°. The influence of the adjacent waters is to equalize the temperature. The adjacent marshes have, in some localities, a tendency to produce malaria of a mild type, which is generally dispersed by the breezes blowing across the peninsula. The prevailing winds are from the northeast and from the southwest. During the summer the latter come in at one hour or another every day. Very high winds or gales are of very rare occurrence.

STREETS.

Jacksonville has 17 miles 640 feet of streets, none of which are paved. Sidewalks on the business streets are paved with stone or wood, but the greater part are paved with wood. Trees are planted for shade on both sides of the streets, about 10 feet from the fence-line, and from 30 to 40 feet apart. The streets are kept in repair by day work, but the cost is not separated from other street work. There are no horse-railroads or omnibus lines in the city.

JACKSONVILLE

FLA.

SCALE OF FEET.
100 300 600 1000

WATER-WORKS.

The water-works are just being completed by the city at a total cost of $100,000. The system will be direct pumping, with stand-pipe, and the pressure will be for domestic purposes 35 pounds and for fires from 75 to 80 pounds to the square inch. It has been decided to use the Crown water-meters on all services.

GAS.

The gas-works are owned by a private company. The daily average production is 13,000 cubic feet. The charge per 1,000 feet is $3. The city pays $28 per annum for each street-lamp, 79 in number. The yearly income from meter-rates is given as $11,400.

PUBLIC PARKS AND PLEASURE-GROUNDS.

Jacksonville has a single acre of ground, near the center of the city, used as a park.

PLACES OF AMUSEMENT.

There are no theaters in the city, but there are 4 concert-halls, the largest seating 400. As to concert- and beer-gardens, there are stated to be "none worth recording".

DRAINAGE.

No information on this subject was furnished.

CEMETERIES.

Jacksonville has 4 burying-grounds; 2 lie contiguously upon the eastern outskirts of the city, and contain, respectively, 6 and 2 acres; a "new cemetery", of 38 acres, 2½ miles from the city limits; and a recent one, of 6 acres, 1 mile north of the city.

Previous to 1872 the record of interments was very imperfect. For the past eight years the total number of interments has averaged about 15 per month. Before interments can take place the cause of death and the intended place of burial must be reported by the undertaker to the city sexton, who gives a permit. No dead body is allowed to be brought into the city unless accompanied by a certificate from the attending physician, or the health officer, or other competent person of the place whence the body is brought, that death was not caused by any infectious or contagious disease. The new cemetery, just started, belongs to a private corporation. It has a regular keeper, and roads leading to it from the city are now being constructed. The price of lots in the cemetery is from $20 to $50.

MARKETS.

Jacksonville's "City market" is private property, which is leased to the city. It covers about 100 feet square, and has 27 stalls—16 for meat, 8 for vegetables, and 3 for fish. Four outside markets are allowed 1 stall each for meat and 1 for vegetables. The rental of market-stalls averages, each, per month, for meat $12 and for vegetables $8. The market is open from daylight until noon. Nearly all of the retail supply of meats, poultry, fish, and vegetables is obtained at the market, though a few grocery-stores sell certain vegetables. Some also keep and sell poultry at wholesale, receiving it on consignment. In the city are 3 dealers who pack fish in ice for shipment into the interior. All the markets are under strict sanitary rules.

SANITARY AUTHORITY—BOARD OF HEALTH.

The chief health organization of Jacksonville is the board of health, composed of the city council, the mayor, and the city physician, who is also health officer. The only expense incurred is for the salaries of the health officer and 2 inspectors, about $1,500 per year. The health officer is the chief executive officer of the board; he receives a salary of $900 per annum. The board transacts its business at meetings called about once a month by the president. Between May 1 and November 1, 2 assistant inspectors are employed; one is a physician, and both have police powers to the extent of arresting and bringing offenders to trial before the police court. Inspections for the detection of nuisances are made every day, from house to house, as rapidly as the inspectors can get around. Attention is also paid to all special complaints by the health officer, who visits the alleged nuisance in person. This is also the case in the event of defective house-drainage, privy-vaults, cesspools, sources of drinking-water, sewerage, street-cleaning, etc.; and, when necessary, the health officer calls in the city sanitary engineer. The board requires the cremation of all garbage, so far as it can be done. Excrement is not allowed to be thrown into the canal, at one side of the city. The public sewers empty into the Saint John's river.

INFECTIOUS DISEASES.

Small-pox patients are isolated, either in a pest-house or in tents; but scarlet-fever patients are neither isolated nor quarantined at home. In case of the breaking out of contagious diseases in public or private schools the board has power to close the schools. Vaccination is not compulsory.

REPORTS, ETC.

The health officer keeps a record of deaths, and of the causes thereof, and reports the same weekly to the board, which reports weekly to the national board of health. It is contemplated to require, by ordinance, the registry of births. A board of health has been appointed by the governor of the state; but it has never organized, and the old board continues to act.

MUNICIPAL CLEANSING.

Street-cleaning.—The streets are cleaned at the expense of the city and with its own force. The work is done wholly by hand, no sweeping-machines being used. The cleaning is done every day, and is done "as well as it can be done without *sweeping*". This work, including the removal of garbage and ashes, costs the city about $1,500 annually. The street-dirt is taken outside of the city and burned. The present place of deposit will soon have to be abandoned, and another one found farther away.

Removal of garbage and ashes.—Garbage is removed by the city with its own force. By ordinance, the garbage is required to be placed in boxes, barrels, or other suitable receptacles, and then put out on the streets, at the curb-line, on the days designated for removal before the city scavenger comes around. Ashes and garbage may be kept in the same vessels. As far as possible the garbage is burned, and the ashes are used for fertilizer. It is reported that garbage is often kept on the premises too long for health.

Dead animals.—The carcass of any animal dying within the city must be removed by the owner, and buried a mile or two outside the limits. When the owner can not be found the city does the work. The annual cost of this service is included in the cost of street-cleaning. No record is kept of the number of dead animals annually removed.

Liquid household wastes.—Chamber-slops are run into sewers or into cesspools, or are thrown around orange-trees for fertilization. But a small proportion of the wastes find their way into the sewers; none at all are run into the street-gutters, while the larger part are absorbed by porous cesspools, having few, if any, overflows delivering—where they exist—into sewers. These cesspools, however, do not receive the wastes of water-closets. In a very few instances physicians have reported a suspected contamination of drinking-water from wells, by the escape of the contents of privy-vaults, as a cause of some typhoid diseases. Cesspools are cleaned out when it is ordered by the sanitary inspectors.

Human excreta.—About one-third of the houses in the city use privy-vaults, a few have water-closets, while the rest depend mostly on surface- or box-privies. In 1878 the further construction of privy-vaults was forbidden. Those in existence are cleaned out as often as ordered by the sanitary inspector. An ordinance requires that they be emptied at least twice a month, but in practice it is done from once a week to once a month, according to their use. About one-half of the privies use dry earth to a greater or less extent. The ultimate disposal of the night-soil is by converting it into fertilizer. It is not allowed to be used for manuring land within the gathering-ground of the public water-supply.

Manufacturing wastes.—The disposal of liquid and solid manufacturing wastes has never as yet engaged the attention of the authorities, and no regulations concerning the matter exist.

POLICE.

The police force of Jacksonville is appointed and governed by the mayor, with the consent of the city council. The city marshal is the head or chief executive officer of the force, and directly controls it, being responsible to the mayor. He is *ex officio* superintendent of police, serves warrants and legal notices, attends the mayor's court each morning, and opens the same and keeps order, and has charge of the city jail and all prisoners confined therein. The rest of the force consists of 1 captain at a salary of $60 per month, and 9 patrolmen at $45 per month each. The uniform is of navy-blue cloth, dress-coat, vest, and pantaloons, with cap and wreath. In summer a flannel sack-coat and pantaloons, with straw or felt hat, are worn. The men furnish their own uniforms, which cost $40 each. Patrolmen are equipped with club, pistol, whistle, badge, and belt. Their hours of service are, for night men, 14 hours; day men, 10 hours. Each member of the force patrols three-quarters of a mile of streets. The number of arrests made in 1880 was 475, chiefly for drunkenness and disorderly conduct. During the same year property to the value of $550 was reported to the police as lost or stolen, and of this $365 was recovered and restored to the owners. For the same period there were 23 station-house lodgers, as against 39 during 1879. During 1880, 32 free meals were furnished to lodgers, at a cost of $8 to the department. The police force is required to attend fires, to aid in their extinguishment, to protect property, and to preserve order. Special policemen may be appointed by the mayor for special service. Their standing, as compared with the regular force, is secondary. The yearly cost of the police force (1880) is $5,580.

FIRE DEPARTMENT.

The following regarding the fire department of Jacksonville is from the annual report of the chief engineer for the year ending April 17, 1879:

The force of the department consists of 2 hook-and-ladder companies, one of 25 men, and the other not yet complete in its organization; 2 engine companies, of 48 and 30 men, respectively; 1 engine company of 40 men; and 3 hose companies, of 21, 23, and 16 men, respectively. The apparatus in use consists of 2 steam fire-engines, 1 hand-engine, 3 hose-carriages, and 1 hook-and-ladder truck. The hose in the department amounts to 2,600 feet. During the year the department responded to 24 alarms, of which 3 were false. The total value of property destroyed by fire was $110,500, $61,743 of this being covered by insurance.

PENSACOLA,
ESCAMBIA COUNTY, FLORIDA.

POPULATION

IN THE

AGGREGATE,

1850–1880.

	Inhab.
1790	......
1800	......
1810	......
1820	......
1830	......
1840	......
1850	2,164
1860	2,876
1870	3,347
1880	6,845

POPULATION

BY

SEX, NATIVITY, AND RACE,

AT

CENSUS OF 1880.

Male	3,292
Female	3,553
Native	6,304
Foreign-born	541
White	3,554
Colored	3,291

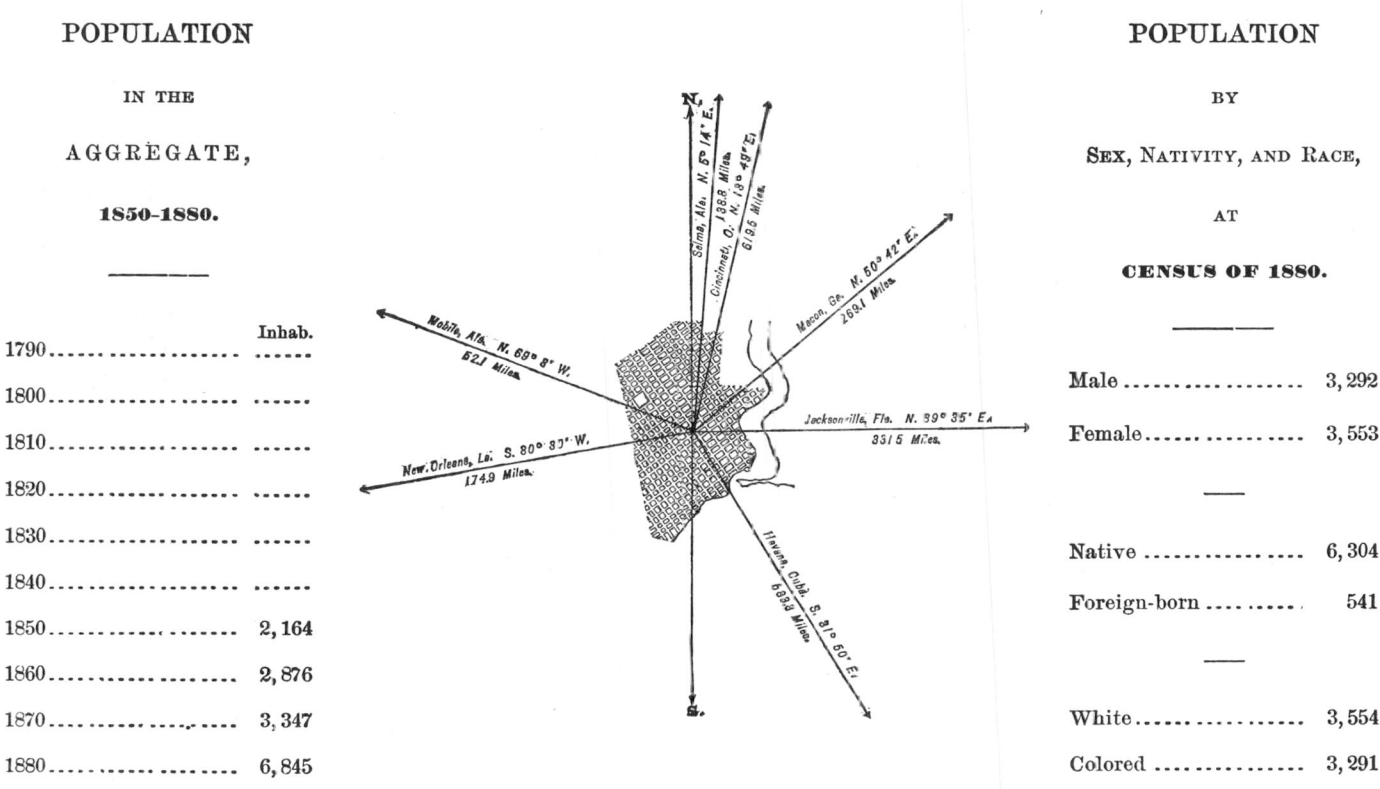

Latitude: 30° 25′ North ; Longitude: 87° 13′ (west from Greenwich); **Altitude: 1 to 60 feet.**

HISTORICAL SKETCH.(a)

The bay now known as Pensacola was first discovered by Pamphile de Narvaes while on an expedition to Florida in 1526, and in 1639 was visited by Diego de Maldonado, a captain of Hernando de Soto, during a search for harborage. From him it received the name of "Port d'Auchusi", a corruption of the Indian name *Ochuse*. De Soto, on the return of Maldonado, sent him to Havana for ships and supplies with which to meet him at Achusi in October of that year—De Soto intending to make Achusi his base of operations. Maldonado returned in October, and afterward visited the bay again and again; but De Soto was then forcing his way through the wilderness toward the Mississippi. Don Tristan de Luna, in 1558, and Don Andre de Pes, in 1693, successively visited Achusi, and by them it was named, first "Santa Maria", then "Santa Maria de Galvez", both of which gave way to "Pensacola". This name is by many supposed to be that of an Indian tribe then inhabiting the shores of the bay; but in a lecture on the subject, Judge R. S. Campbell says: "There is something so Spanish in its sound that I am inclined to the belief that it was derived from *Peniscola*, a village of Spain on the Mediterranean."

---

a Prepared by J. E. Tarble, esq., of Pensacola.

In 1696 Don Andre d'Aricola built a fort and town near what is now Fort Barrancas, on an island formed by two small streams. This he called "Fort Saint Charles", the first Pensacola, and it was probably a penal colony of convicts from Mexico. This settlement was destroyed in 1719, during the first expedition of the French under Bienville. It was at this time that the second Pensacola was founded on Santa Rosa island, somewhat to the east of the present site of fort Pickens. This town was built on the beach, of small one-story houses, save the governor's palace, which was, to judge from a drawing made in 1743, a large and imposing edifice. It also boasted a church, octagonal in shape, and was defended by a small stockaded fort.

This last-mentioned town was destroyed by a storm in or about the year 1754, and the inhabitants moved to the present site of Pensacola. This was ceded to Great Britain in 1763; was then made the seat of government for West Florida, and vigorous steps were taken for its colonization. George Johnston was the first military governor. He was succeeded by Governor Brown; he by Elliot; and in 1772 Peter Chester was appointed. During the years of English rule the town was laid out in regular order, one of the pleasantest features of the plan adopted being the reservation of an immense plot of land reaching along the bay-front for a park. At the time of the Spanish succession in 1783 this was, however, curtailed until nothing remained save two small squares—Seville and Ferdinand VII. Among the legacies in names left the city by the Spanish are Palafox, Saragossa, and Romanna streets. In 1772 the export trade of Pensacola consisted largely in cattle, pelts, and naval stores. The Indian trade was also extensive.

In 1777 Pensacola contained several hundred houses, mostly built of wood, and "the governor's palace was a large pretentious building crowned with a tower". Under English rule this prosperity continued for nearly 20 years, until, war being declared in 1779 between England and Spain, Pensacola was invested by José de Galvez, and on the 9th of May, General Campbell surrendered the post, including the entire province of West Florida. A provision of capitulation required all English subjects to leave the province within eighteen months, they being permitted to dispose of their property in the mean time. This resulted in a general exodus of all life and enterprise, and Pensacola degenerated into a mere garrison town. From 1793 to 1814 nothing of interest seems to have transpired.

In 1814, after the Creeks were defeated by General Jackson, they sought refuge at Pensacola, confident of aid from the Spaniards, and soon after the British fleet, repulsed from fort Bowyer at Mobile, received the protection of the flag of Spain at Pensacola. Jackson, seeing that the point was then to be made a "harbor of refuge" for the enemies of his government, and remonstrances with Governor Manriquez proving futile, determined to seize the place. On November 6 he appeared before the town and demanded its surrender, sending a flag of truce to fort Saint Michael, which was situated on a hill at the head of Palafox street and commanded the city. The flag of truce being fired upon, and after further ineffective efforts to avoid bloodshed, he determined to take possession by force, attacking from the east and so escaping the fire of the fort. Here he was opposed by a battery erected on the beach near Barclay's point. Captain Laval assaulted this battery at the head of 120 men, and took it with small loss, he himself, however, being among the wounded. The army, 3,000 strong, then entered the town, fort Saint Michael surrendered, fort Barrancas was blown up, and the British fleet sailed out of the harbor. In May, 1818, Jackson again captured Pensacola, the Spaniards having again violated their neutrality, and the governor and garrison were transported to Havana at the expense of the United States. Jackson now decided to hold possession until Spain should be able or willing to preserve her neutrality, and to this end he appointed Colonel King military and civil governor, and Captain Gadsden first collector of the port. In 1819, however, on the arrival of 600 Spaniards from Havana, Spain, by permission, again assumed control, and held it until July 18, 1821, when all Florida was formally ceded to the United States, the ceremony of transfer to General Jackson, as governor of Florida, taking place in the square of Ferdinand VII.

Early in the civil war this port was looked upon with longing eyes by the confederates on account of its immense land-locked harbor, its ship-building facilities, its resources in timber and naval stores, its navy-yard, then fully stocked with munitions of war, and its fortifications—forts Pickens, Barrancas, and McRae—which rendered it a point almost impregnable, and hence of the greatest maritime importance. This would be their depot of supplies, and their base of operations in and the key to the control of the gulf. The city proper soon fell into their hands, or rather was already, and also, within a short time, the navy-yard and forts Barrancas and McRae. Fort Pickens, however, being supplied, resisted all attempts to capture it, and the bombardment of the navy-yard and forts rendering them untenable, they were consequently abandoned by the confederates.

After the close of the war new capital and energy began gradually to flow in; business increased, though strangers were, to a great extent, deterred from coming here on account of yellow fever. From this plague the city has been protected since the summer of 1874 by a most stringent quarantine, and by pursuing the same policy in the future the chances of the disease getting a foothold will be reduced to a minimum.

Pensacola has often been visited by destructive fires, but on the morning of December 11, 1880, a fire broke out before which all others fade into insignificance. The fire started from an incendiary origin on Palafox street, between Intendencia and Romanna streets, at about 12.30 a. m. A brisk breeze was blowing from the northeast, and, the buildings being of a most inflammable nature, while the only steam fire-engine was disabled and laid up for repairs, the flames spread rapidly until almost the entire business quarter had been consumed, and the fire was

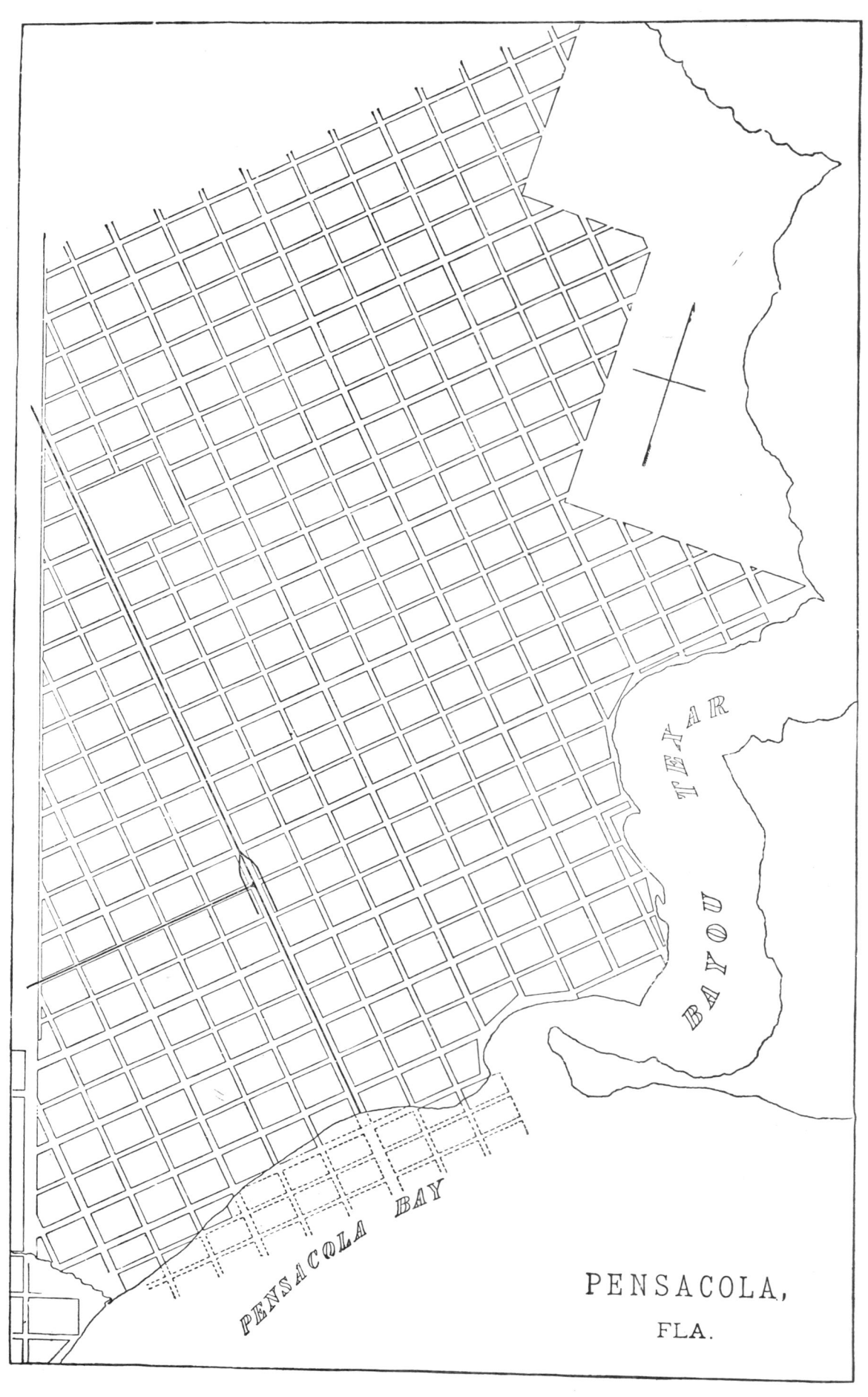

PENSACOLA,

FLA.

checked only for want of materiaL. The inhabitants at once went to work to repair the disaster, and now, within the fire limits, brick buildings are taking the place of those destroyed. The demand for skilled labor far exceeds the supply, and the great fire of 1380 promises to be the beginning of a new era of prosperity for Pensacola.

Though one of the smallest of the cities treated in this report, Pensacola is a rising place. Three newspapers—one tri-weekly, one bi-weekly, and one weekly—are published here. The waters abound in fish, and the forests in game. The trade is quite large in the business season; 200 square-rigged vessels have been seen loading here at one time. There are 10 wharves, aggregating in length over 7 miles and representing an investment of over $275,000. The exports consist chiefly of timber and lumber of all kinds, hides, tallow, wool, cotton, turpentine, and rosin. The fishing interests, both in packing-houses and ice-vessels, are large and flourishing. In the year ending July 1, 1877, 270 foreign, 110 American, and 210 coasting vessels entered the port, while the value of exports for the same period was $2,291,822.

PENSACOLA IN 1880.

The following statistical accounts, collected by the Census Office, indicate the present condition of Pensacola:

LOCATION.

Pensacola lies in latitude 30° 25′ north, longitude 87° 13′ west from Greenwich, on Pensacola bay, 10 miles from the gulf of Mexico. The altitude above sea-level, within a radius of 5 miles, varies from 1 foot to 60 feet, the principal part of the city being from 40 to 50 feet above sea-level. Pensacola enjoys a good, deep, and ample harbor, free from strong tidal currents, and, if the whole bay be considered, is almost land-locked. The draught of water over the bar at the mouth of the bay is 21 feet; inside, the draught of water in the channel ranges from 12 to 30 feet. A number of rivers empty into the bay. The advantages of this harbor were early seen by the Spanish adventurers, who explored and settled at various points on the Florida coast.

RAILROAD COMMUNICATIONS.

Pensacola is touched by two railroads—the Pensacola railroad, terminating at Whiting Junction and connecting there with the Mobile and Montgomery railroad, and the Pensacola and Perdido River railroad, running westerly and terminating, with no connections, at Millview, Florida.

TRIBUTARY COUNTRY.

The country immediately surrounding the city has no agricultural importance, and no industries outside of lumbering, etc., and brick-making; consequently the local trade is very small, the little hamlets in the vicinity purchasing their supplies direct from New Orleans, Mobile, or Montgomery.

TOPOGRAPHY.

The modern city occupies a sandy though fertile plain, gently sloping from the hills—on one of which stood fort Saint Michael—to the bay on the south. On the east and west it is bounded by two fine bayous—Chico and Tarhor. This plain is probably what was called on the old maps "Oyster cove", from which the water has since receded. The soil of the site (and for 40 miles surrounding) is sandy, with very little underlying clay. The surface is rolling, and naturally well drained, abounds in fine springs, and is free from marshes or ponds of consequence. The country around is heavily wooded, and there are within a radius of 10 miles no elevations of more than 160 feet.

CLIMATE.

The highest summer temperature in average years is 93°; lowest winter temperature in average years, 28°. Except in diminishing the extremes of temperature, the adjacent waters exert no marked climatic influence. In summer southerly winds temper the heat, while northerly winds cause a disagreeable dryness. Easterly winds are moist and unpleasant at any season, but there are very few of them.

STREETS.

The total length of streets in Pensacola is 7 miles, all of which are unpaved. Sidewalks are generally paved with brick or wood. The gutters are not paved at all; the soil is so porous that water seldom stands in the streets, and mud is unknown. Shade-trees are planted in the streets 1 foot from the sidewalk. Street-repairing, etc., under direction of the street commissioner, chosen by the aldermen, is done by prisoners who are unable to pay their fines. The streets are lighted by oil-lamps. The city is without horse-railroads or omnibus lines, water- or gas-works. The water-supply is obtained entirely by means of "driven wells", which are simply iron pipes, 1 or 2 inches in diameter, driven into the ground to the depth of 50 or 60 feet, with suction-pumps at the top. The water thus obtained is cool and agreeable.

PUBLIC BUILDINGS.

The city owns and occupies for municipal purposes, wholly or in part, the city hall, jail, and market-house, all together valued at about $10,000.

PUBLIC PARKS AND PLEASURE-GROUNDS.

Pensacola has two small parks or squares, bearing the names of *Seville* and *Ferdinand VII*, lying on the water-front. Public property of this kind is under the control of the street commissioner.

PLACES OF AMUSEMENT.

There is one theater in the city, now in process of construction, which will cost $50,000, and is intended to seat 800. Germania hall, seating 300; Pitt's hall, seating 400; Reache's hall, seating 300; and the hall and reading-room of the Young Men's Christian Association, seating 200, are used for concerts, lectures, etc. There is one beer-garden—Kupfrian's—and two concert-halls—Bay View varieties, built in 1875 at a cost of about $4,000, seating 200, and the Royal Palace varieties, built in 1876, at a cost of $2,000, seating 100.

DRAINAGE.

Pensacola is without sewers. The sewage of the city is carried off by open gutters, and is discharged either into two small streams or directly into the bay. Each spring it is found necessary to open the gutters and remove sediment and vegetable matter. The work is done by hand by prisoners from the police court, under the supervision of the police. After the accumulations are removed the gutters are disinfected with lime. Mr. Tarble says, " The city is greatly in need of some complete plan of sewerage. The grade is very moderate, and, as it is, the gutters being unbricked or otherwise protected, much of the drainage seeps into the soil or remains a black, foul-smelling sediment, which must be removed annually. Were it not for such cleansing and the sandy nature of the soil, the present system would be productive of sickness, but at present the health of the city does not seem to be affected, though, in time, more perfect sewerage will be absolutely necessary."

CEMETERIES.

Pensacola has three cemeteries, as follows:

Saint John's Cemetery and the *Colored Cemetery* lie outside the city, about 1 mile to the northwest; the former contains 4½ and the latter 6 acres.

Saint Michael's Cemetery is situated inside the city, between Chase and Romanna streets.

The record of interments for the different cemeteries was destroyed during the recent fire, and the number of the same can not be given. The matter of issuing burial permits is under the joint control of the board of health and the city, and it is entirely regulated by circumstances. Saint John's cemetery is under the control of the Masonic order, and is laid out in straight roads and walks. A revenue is derived from the lease and sale of lots. Lots owned by private parties are cared for by the owners; but the public portion of the cemetery is kept in order by the Masons. Saint Michael's cemetery belongs to the Catholic church. The lots are owned and cared for by private individuals, subject to corporate and church control, with the exception of public lots for the poor, and a space reserved and dedicated for the use of the convent. Roads and walks are unimproved, and, save in connection with the convent lot, no attempts have been made at landscape-gardening. Mr. Tarble adds: "Much that in most cities is subject to the control of special ordinances is here left to the discretion of the mayor, marshal, sanitary inspector, or board of health, especially all relating to burial permits, limit of time after death, and depth of grave, all being determined according to the particular circumstances. Yet, despite this seeming negligence, such things are sufficiently well regulated to avoid danger therefrom."

MARKETS.

There is one public market and a market-house in the city, but no information regarding them was furnished.

SANITARY AUTHORITY—BOARD OF HEALTH.

The board of health of Pensacola, in whose hands the care of the city's health is placed, is not an independent body, but the board of aldermen, with the mayor and city physician, act as such. The annual expense of the board in ordinary times is about $5,000, expended in maintaining a maritime quarantine. There is no law restricting the expense of the board during an epidemic, and its powers are large in respect to all measures and regulations of a general nature, as well as to enforcing quarantine. It may examine into and endeavor to check all cases of malignant disease. Any member may examine premises on suspicion of nuisances. The president of the board is the chief executive officer; he has power to convene the board; he executes all laws made by it, and he serves without pay. The board transacts its business at regular meetings held twice a month between May and November, and at special meetings held on call of the president. Two assistant sanitary inspectors are employed, both being physicians, and both having police powers for the arrest of such persons as refuse to remove nuisances after notification. Inspections are not made regularly, but only as nuisances are reported.

INFECTIOUS DISEASES.

Small-pox patients are either quarantined at home or removed to the pest-house, situated about 3 miles from the city. Scarlet-fever patients are isolated at home, a red flag is placed on the house, and none but the physician is allowed to enter or leave. Vaccination is not compulsory.

There is no system for the registration of births, diseases, and deaths.

The board of health makes no report.

MUNICIPAL CLEANSING.

Street-cleaning.—The streets are cleaned at the expense of the city and with its own force. The work is done wholly by hand. The streets are cleaned daily in summer, but not so often in winter. It is reported as not very efficiently done. The annual cost is $1,800. The sweepings are deposited on low lands in the suburbs.

Removal of garbage and ashes.—Garbage is removed both by the city, with its own force, and by householders. Ashes and garbage may be kept in the same vessel, and both are disposed of in the same manner as street-sweepings. No nuisance is reported from the improper handling or disposal of garbage.

Dead animals.—The carcass of any animal dying within the city must be removed beyond the limits, and either buried or burned.

Liquid household wastes.—These are all run into the open street-gutters.

POLICE.

The police force is appointed and governed by the mayor, who is at its head. The city marshal is the chief executive officer; he must see that the force does its duty, cause complaint to be made and procure evidence against offenders, attend at the mayor's court and office, and attend at the city prison on the direction of the mayor. He keeps full record of the affairs and operations of the force; his salary is $1,500 per annum. The rest of the force consists of 11 police officers at an annual salary of $1,200 each. The uniform is of blue flannel with brass buttons having the letters C. P. on them, and slouched hat. The men provide their own uniforms. Patrolmen are equipped with belt, club, and revolver. The hours of service are, day force from 7 a. m. to 8 p. m., and night force from 8 p. m. to 7 a. m. The force patrols about 4 miles of streets.

During the past year 1,542 arrests were made, principally for drunkenness, fighting, and using obscene language. During the year but very little property was reported to the police as lost or stolen, all of which, however, was recovered and returned to the owners. During the same time there were 40 station-house lodgers, as against 30 in 1879. The force, when directed, is required to co-operate with the fire and health departments. On extraordinary occasions the mayor appoints special policemen, who for the time have the same standing as the regular force. The yearly cost of the police force (1880) is $15,000.

FIRE DEPARTMENT.

The fire department is under the control of a fire association, and consists of 5 volunteer companies, with a total membership of 189. The full equipment will consist of 2 steam fire-engines, 2 hose-carts, and a hook-and-ladder truck, and will be well organized and rendered thoroughly efficient.

SCHOOLS.

The public schools of Pensacola compare favorably with any in the South in efficiency and organization. There are 2 schools, 1 for white and 1 for colored children. The former is graded from primary to high, and is well patronized by all classes; the latter is well managed and has a large attendance.

The Catholic convent has 4 private schools, 1 each for white and colored boys and white and colored girls. There is an Episcopal school under charge of the rector of the Episcopal church, also several other private schools for the younger children.

CHURCHES.

The following denominations are represented in Pensacola: Roman Catholic, Baptist, Episcopal, Methodist, Presbyterian, and Scandinavian.

COMMERCE AND NAVIGATION.

[From the reports of the Bureau of Statistics for the fiscal years ending June 30.]

Customs district of Pensacola, Florida.	1879.	1870.
Total value of imports	$21,580	$15,149
Total value of exports:		
Domestic	$2,102,423	$1,930,258
Foreign	None.	None.
Total number of immigrants	None.	None.

COMMERCE AND NAVIGATION—continued.

Customs district of Pensacola, Florida.	1879.		1880.	
	Number.	Tons.	Number.	Tons.
Vessels in foreign trade:				
Entered..	313	185, 344	398	256, 327
Cleared	286	176, 981	378	253, 291
Vessels in coast trade and fisheries:				
Entered..	168	42, 062	200	65, 225
Cleared	173	42, 945	219	69, 457
Vessels registered, enrolled, and licensed in district..	103	7, 063	114	12, 289
Vessels built during the year	7	117	2	60

ALABAMA.

MOBILE.

MOBILE COUNTY, ALABAMA.

POPULATION

IN THE

AGGREGATE,

1820-1880.

	Inhab.
1790	......
1800	......
1810	......
1820	1,500
1830	3,194
1840	12,672
1850	20,515
1860	29,258
1870	32,034
1880	29,132

POPULATION

BY

SEX, NATIVITY, AND RACE,

AT

CENSUS OF 1880.

Male	13,189
Female	15,943

Native	26,195
Foreign-born	2,937

White	16,885
Colored	*12,247

* Including 4 Chinese and 3 Indians.

Latitude: 30° 41′ North; Longitude: 88° 2′ (west from Greenwich); Altitude: 15 feet.

FINANCIAL CONDITION:

Total Valuation: $12,991,795; per capita: $446 00.   Net Indebtedness: $2,609,250; per capita: $89 57.   Tax per $100: $2 60.

HISTORICAL SKETCH.

Iberville's settlement (1699), at the eastern extremity of the bay of Biloxi, the nucleus of the French colonization of Louisiana, comprised a small band of adventurers who led a miserable existence during the earlier years of their life in the "land of promise".

The land was low and unhealthful. The settlers, accustomed to the climate of France and of Canada, had suffered during their first winter from excessive cold, against which there was no adequate protection, and the intense heat of summer allowed them to work for only a few hours of the morning. They had neither the strength nor the energy to cultivate their land, but trusted to the arrival of aid from France, many dying of famine and sickness. When relief came (1701) it was accompanied by an order to remove the seat of government to Mobile bay, and a fort, warehouse, and other buildings were erected at the mouth of Dog river. Nine years later this settlement was abandoned, and a new establishment was made at the present site of the city of Mobile.

An official dispatch of April 30, 1704, gives the following account of the colony: "180 capable of bearing arms; 2 French families, with 3 little girls and 7 little boys; 6 young Indian boys (slaves); and officers, whose number is not stated. A little land about the fort had been cultivated, and 80 wooden houses had been erected. For live stock they had 9 oxen, 14 cows, 4 bulls, 6 calves, 100 swine, 3 kids, and 400 hens." In time of famine the colonists were compelled to resort to the sea-coast and live by fishing. On one occasion they were assisted by the Spanish governor of Pensacola, to whom they had previously sent supplies in time of need. In this year a French man-of-war, bringing provisions, brought also 20 girls, to be cared for by Bienville and to be married to such of the soldiers as should be able to support wives. In the following year another ship brought more supplies, soldiers, priests, 4 sisters of charity, 4 families of laborers, and 23 girls, "whom Bienville had orders to marry to Canadians and others able to support them". This year was marked by the outbreak of a fatal epidemic.

During the next four years little progress was made. Bienville, in his dispatches to France, constantly urged the sending of more supplies, as the land under cultivation was not sufficient for the support of the colony. The women positively refused to eat corn-bread, and announced their intention of leaving a place to which they had been decoyed with false promises of luxury and comfort. This was known as the "petticoat insurrection". Fifty men had joined the colony from the upper Mississippi; but, with the scarcity of provisions, this was a drawback rather than an aid, and the colonists wasted in quarrels among themselves the energy that should have been devoted to the cultivation of the land and in resistance to the Indian tribes by which they were surrounded. The life of the governor was harassed by charges of maladministration and incompetence, which made his duty still more difficult. He complained to the French minister that though the land of the Mobile river was fertile, it was too unhealthful during the season of cultivation for white men to work there, and that the efforts of the planters were hindered by want of negroes, horses, and oxen. He found that the Indians were treacherous, and often attacked the French, whom they had learned to despise; that most of the men were too young to be useful as soldiers, and that the Canadians, whom he had retained contrary to orders, were the only persons upon whom he could rely. In 1708 the colony had a total population of 279, including 80 slaves. The live stock comprised 100 horned cattle, 1,400 swine, and 2,000 fowls.

Finding it impossible to persuade the whites to cultivate the fields, and that the Indians, when compelled to do so, would escape to the woods, Bienville requested permission to send Indians to the West Indies, there to exchange them for negro slaves. This the government refused. Eager to increase the population and wealth of the colony, Bienville adopted the short-sighted policy of prohibiting emigration, reducing the whole people practically to a condition of servitude. In 1709 the population was compelled to subsist almost entirely on acorns. A year later the people had to be scattered among the Indians as a dependence for food. In 1711, when the site was removed to the present location of Mobile and a fort was built, only a small garrison was left at the old station on Dog river. The cultivation of tobacco was begun in this year, and at its close further supplies were received from France. The expenses of the colony during this year amounted to 61,504 livres. France itself was at this time suffering from the depletion of the many wars of Louis XIV, and the government hesitated to add to its burden the support of a distant and most unpromising colony. Consequently (September 14, 1712) the king granted to Anthony Crozat the exclusive privilege of trading in Louisiana for fifteen years. He was allowed to send one ship a year to Africa for negroes, and was to possess and work all mines of precious metals which might be discovered, reserving one-fourth of the proceeds for the king. All the lands he cultivated, the buildings he erected, and the manufactories he established were to be his forever. In return he was to send to the colony annually two ship-loads of settlers, and after nine years was to assume all its expenses, including those of the garrison. For the latter he held the nominations of officers. The king undertook to supply for nine years the annual sum of $10,000 toward the expenses of the colony, which was to be governed according to the laws, ordinances, customs, and usages of the prevostship and viscounty of Paris. There was also to be a government entirely similar to the one in San Domingo. At this time the population numbered less than 500, only about 20 of whom were negroes.

In 1713 Cardillac was governor, and Bienville was reduced to the grade of lieutenant-governor. Cardillac thus describes the colony:

The wealth of Dauphin island consists of a score of fig trees, 3 wild pear trees, and 3 apple trees of the same nature, a dwarfish plum tree with 7 bad-looking plums, 30 plants of vines with 9 bunches of half-rotten and half-dried up grapes, 40 stands of French melons, and some pumpkins. This is the terrestrial paradise of which we have heard so much; nothing but fables and lies.

After a more extended exploration, he writes:

This is a very wretched country; good for nothing, and incapable of producing either cattle, wheat, or vegetables, even as high up as Natchez.

June 1, 1714, he says:

The inhabitants are no better than the country. They are the very scum and refuse of Canada; ruffians who have thus far cheated the gibbet of its due; vagabonds who are without subordination to the laws, and without any respect to religion or for the government. The troops are without discipline, and are scattered amongst the Indians, at whose expense they live. * * * The colony is not worth a straw for the moment, but I shall endeavor to make something of it, if God permits me health.

By the end of this year Cardillac had quarrelled with all his subordinates, and the colony was divided between the party of the governor and the the party of the lieutenant-governor.

Cardillac's object in his enterprise was to acquire a large fortune by the discovery and working of mines, and he cared nothing for the slower processes of agriculture. He advised the government to give the colonists as much land as they chose to take, its quality being so bad that there was no occasion to care for the number of acres; so that to give large grants of land would be cheap liberality. He thought it useless to try to encourage commerce, as it was ridiculous to suppose that boats would ever navigate the rivers for purposes of trade, they being "as rapid as the Rhone, and in their crooked course imitated the undulations of a snake". After exasperating the Indian tribes which had formerly been faithful to the French, and causing such ill-feeling in the colony that he feared the result, he retired to Dauphin island. In 1711 he was recalled in disgrace, and Epinay was sent out as governor, with considerable reinforcements. He in his turn immediately quarrelled with Bienville, and the colony was again distracted with disputes.

The change of governor producing no improvement, Crozat, finding his hopes unfounded and his fortunes melting away, requested the king to permit him to resign the charter which had been granted him. On the 13th of August, therefore, the management of Louisiana was formally resumed by the French government; but in less than a month the colony was handed over to the Western Company, or Company of the Indies, under the direction of the notorious John Law. To this company was granted for 25 years the exclusive privilege of carrying on all commerce of Louisiana, and of buying beaver-skins from Canada, the price of the same being regulated by the king. The company was further to be allowed to raise troops, build forts and vessels of war, declare war or make peace with the Indians, and to exercise all of the privileges formerly pertaining to the king, who reserved to himself only the power of appointing the members of the supreme council. The company was bound to build churches and pay the clergy, and to transport to the colony 6,000 whites and 3,000 negroes. The first directors were appointed by the king, with John Law at their head. After this they were to be elected by the votes of the stockholders.

In the prospectus of the company the colony of Louisiana was represented as being the most favored spot on the globe; its climate so healthful that Indians appeared young at the age of 500 or 600 years. They were declared to be so attached to the white race that they voluntarily performed all the arduous duties that were necessary. The fruits of the earth were abundant, and the ground was so fertile that agriculture ceased to be a labor, while the mines of gold and silver were inexhaustible. The shares of the company rose from 500 to 1,000, to 5,000, and to 10,000 livres. Many who owned landed property sold it and invested its value in these shares. Fortunes were rapidly made and lost, and the most unfavorable portions of the territory were actually sold for 30,000 livres a square league.

Additional troops were sent out, and, to the great satisfaction of the inhabitants, Bienville, who had labored among them for 20 years, was appointed governor. His first act was to choose a more suitable place for the seat of government, a decision which led to the settlement of New Orleans. At about this time the importation of African slaves assumed considerable proportions. After the breaking out of the French and Spanish war, 1719, and after the taking and retaking of Pensacola, 2 Spanish brigantines entered the bay of Mobile, and landed 35 men with the intention of burning and plundering one of the establishments on the coast. They were surprised and defeated by a party of Canadians and Indians, and only 6 escaped. Two days later the whole Spanish fleet appeared before Dauphin island, but were unable to effect a landing. Fresh immigrants arrived in Louisiana, but the climate was too unhealthful for European labor, and over 1,000 slaves were imported from Africa, supplies came more rapidly from France, and the colony appeared at last to prosper, though its expenses were still very great. The failure of the Royal Bank of France, and the consequent fall of Law in 1722, caused great distress in the colony. Provisions became so scarce that the garrisons of Mobile and Biloxi were again distributed among the Indians for support, the colonists spreading themselves along the sea-coast to subsist on fish and oysters. In September they were relieved by the arrival of a ship bringing food and ammunition. The people were informed that the management of the colony had been placed by the king in the hands of 3 commissioners, who had given to Bienville the long-desired permission to remove the government to New Orleans. In October of this year the distress was increased by a hurricane which caused great damage. On the 11th of September, 1740, a still more terrible hurricane swept over Mobile, destroying, among other things, the storehouse containing provisions for the garrison; and on the 18th there occurred another, which completed the ruin; so that Mobile had to be dependent on New Orleans for supplies. In 1744 the colony was again at the point of starvation and dependent on the mother country. The population of Mobile, 1745, was reduced to 150 white males, and 200 negroes of both sexes. In 1751 the garrison alone amounted to 475 French and Swiss soldiers.

In 1762, by a secret treaty, the French government, tired of the expenses and annoyances of its Louisiana possessions, ceded so much of them as lay west of the Mississippi river and Orleans island to the king of Spain, who was reluctant and hesitating in his acceptance of the cession. At the same time all that part of the province lying east of the Mississippi river, excepting Orleans island, was ceded to the British, Mobile thereby coming under the British flag. In 1765 British troops arriving from Jamaica brought with them a contagious disease which long left its effect on the settlement.

In 1762 the commerce of Mobile had become considerable; the exports including indigo, Indian corn, raw hides, tallow, pitch, bear's oil, tobacco, tar, myrtle wax, salted wild beef, pecan nuts, sassafras, dried salt fish, oranges, poultry, squared timber, cedar posts and planks, cypress and pine boards, canes, and hogshead shooks. Cotton was at this time cultivated to some extent, but there is no notice of its exportation. In the same year Mobile was again devastated by a storm of such violence that vessels were actually driven into the town, and all vegetation was destroyed by the salt spray.

In 1780, during the war between England and Spain, Galvez, the governor of Louisiana, took possession of the settlement. In the following year he captured Pensacola, with its garrison of 800 men, and the whole of west Florida surrendered to him. In 1783, at the treaty between England and Spain, it was mutually agreed that Mobile should be transferred to the United States, whose independence had been a few months before acknowledged by Great Britain; but the place was not then actually surrendered. In 1813, the United States, being at war with England, determined to seize the port of Mobile, which surrendered, at the demand of General Wilkinson, with a force of 600 men from New Orleans. The following year the British, with a land force of 130 marines and 600 Indians, under Captain Woodbine, assisted by a naval force under Commodore Percy, attacked fort Bowyer, but were repulsed. In June, 1815, the British again surrounded the fort with a large naval force, and landed 5,000 men, Major Lawrence, its commander, surrendering at discretion. A treaty of peace had been made between England and the United States in the previous December, but news of it did not reach Mobile till the middle of March. The British forces withdrew on the 1st of April.

On March 1, 1817, Congress divided the Mississippi territory, which had formerly embraced the whole of the states of Mississippi and Alabama, by the present line dividing these two states, erecting the eastern into another territory and giving it the name of Alabama. In the latter part of the following year the territory received large accessions to its population by immigration from Virginia, the Carolinas, Tennessee, Kentucky, and Georgia, and the country was rapidly settled. In this year Mobile was visited by an intended colony of French refugees, among whom were many men of high social, political, and military station under the Napoleonic *régime*, who were forced to leave France for their adherence to the deposed emperor. After many hardships, and much litigation about their granted lands, they finally settled near the White Bluff, and took their share in the subsequent history of the section. In the fall of this year, 1818, the Bank of Mobile was established, with a capital of $500,000. In 1819 the territory of Alabama had so increased in population that Congress authorized the formation of a state constitution; and, on December 14, 1819, by a joint resolution of Congress, the state of Alabama was admitted into the Union, William W. Bibb being the first governor of the new state, as he had been of the territory.

During the civil war a great amount of trade was carried on, by means of blockade-runners, till August 5, 1864, when Admiral Farragut sailed into the bay, reduced the forts, destroyed the confederate fleet, including the ram "Tennessee", and effectually closed the harbor against blockade-runners, though he failed to capture the city.

MOBILE IN 1880.

The following statistical accounts, collected by the Census Office, indicate the present condition of Mobile:

LOCATION.

Mobile lies in latitude 30° 41' north, longitude 88° 2' west from Greenwich, on the west side of the Mobile river, immediately above its entrance into Mobile bay, and 30 miles from the Gulf of Mexico. The entrance to the harbor is guarded by fort Morgan (formerly fort Bowyer), on Mobile point, and by fort Gaines, on the eastern extremity of Dauphin island, 30 miles below the city. There is also a light-house on Mobile point, the lantern of which is 55 feet above sea-level. In and about the harbor are the remains of several batteries erected during the late war, and on the east side of Tensas river are the ruins of Spanish fort and fort Blakely. Large numbers of sailing-vessels trade between Mobile and New Orleans, the ports on the gulf of Mexico, and the Atlantic coast, while a regular line to Liverpool has been established, and several trips have already been made; but, owing to the shallowness of the harbor, all ships drawing more than 8 or 10 feet of water are obliged to anchor in the bay, 25 miles or more from the city. An appropriation for the deepening of the harbor has been made by the national government, and work will soon begin. Steamboats ply regularly on the rivers that empty into the bay, going for many months in the year as far as Wetumpka, Alabama, on the Coosa; to Aberdeen, Mississippi, on the Little Tombigbee; and to Tuscaloosa, Alabama, on the Black Warrior.

RAILROAD COMMUNICATIONS.

Mobile is touched by the following railroads:

The Mobile and Ohio railroad, to Columbus, Kentucky, and, by connections, with Cincinnati, Saint Louis, and Chicago.

The Mobile and Alabama Grand Trunk railroad, to Bigbee Bridge, Alabama.

The Mobile and Montgomery railroad, to Montgomery, Alabama, and the New Orleans, Mobile, and Texas railroad, to New Orleans, both operated by and included in the system of the Louisville and Nashville railroad.

The Mobile and Spring Hill railroad, to Spring Hill, Alabama.

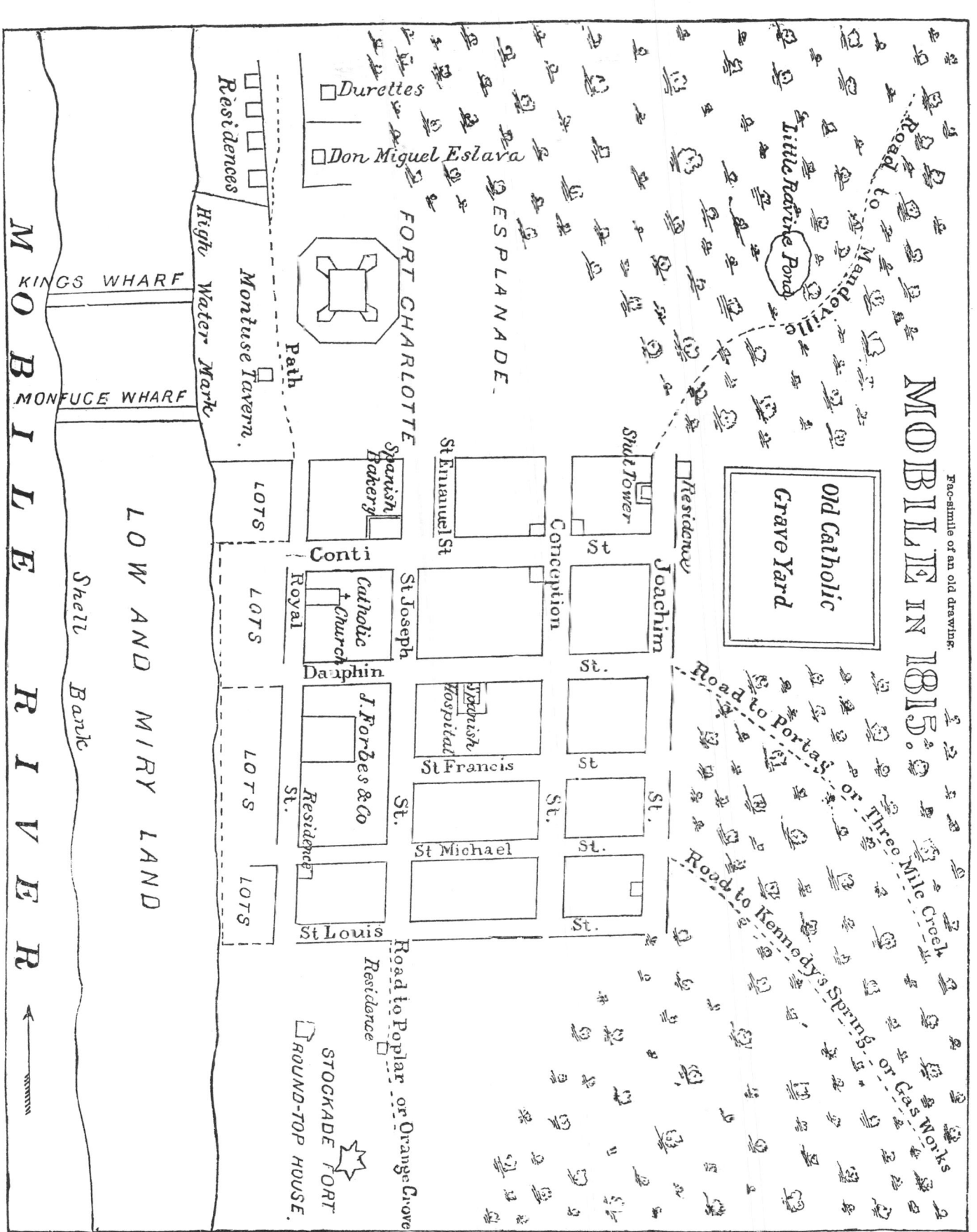

MOBILE IN 1815.

Fac-simile of an old drawing.

Old Catholic Grave Yard

Little Ravine Pond

Road to Mandeville

Road to Portas, or Three Mile Creek

Road to Kennedy's Spring, or Gas Works

Road to Poplar, or Orange Grove

Durettes

Don Miguel Eslava

Residences

ESPLANADE

FORT CHARLOTTE

Spanish Battery

St Emanuel St

Skull Tower

Residence

Joachim

St.

Conception

St.

St.

St Joseph

Catholic Church

Royal

Conti

Dauphin

Spanish Hospital

St Francis

St.

St.

St.

J. Forbes & Co

Residence St.

St Michael

St.

St.

St Louis

St.

Residence

STOCKADE FORT

ROUND-TOP HOUSE.

Road to Poplar, or Orange Grove Residence

Montuse Tavern.

Path

High Water Mark

Residences

KINGS WHARF

MONFUCE WHARF

LOTS

LOTS

LOTS

LOTS

LOTS

Shell Bank

LOW AND MIRY LAND

M O B I L E   R I V E R

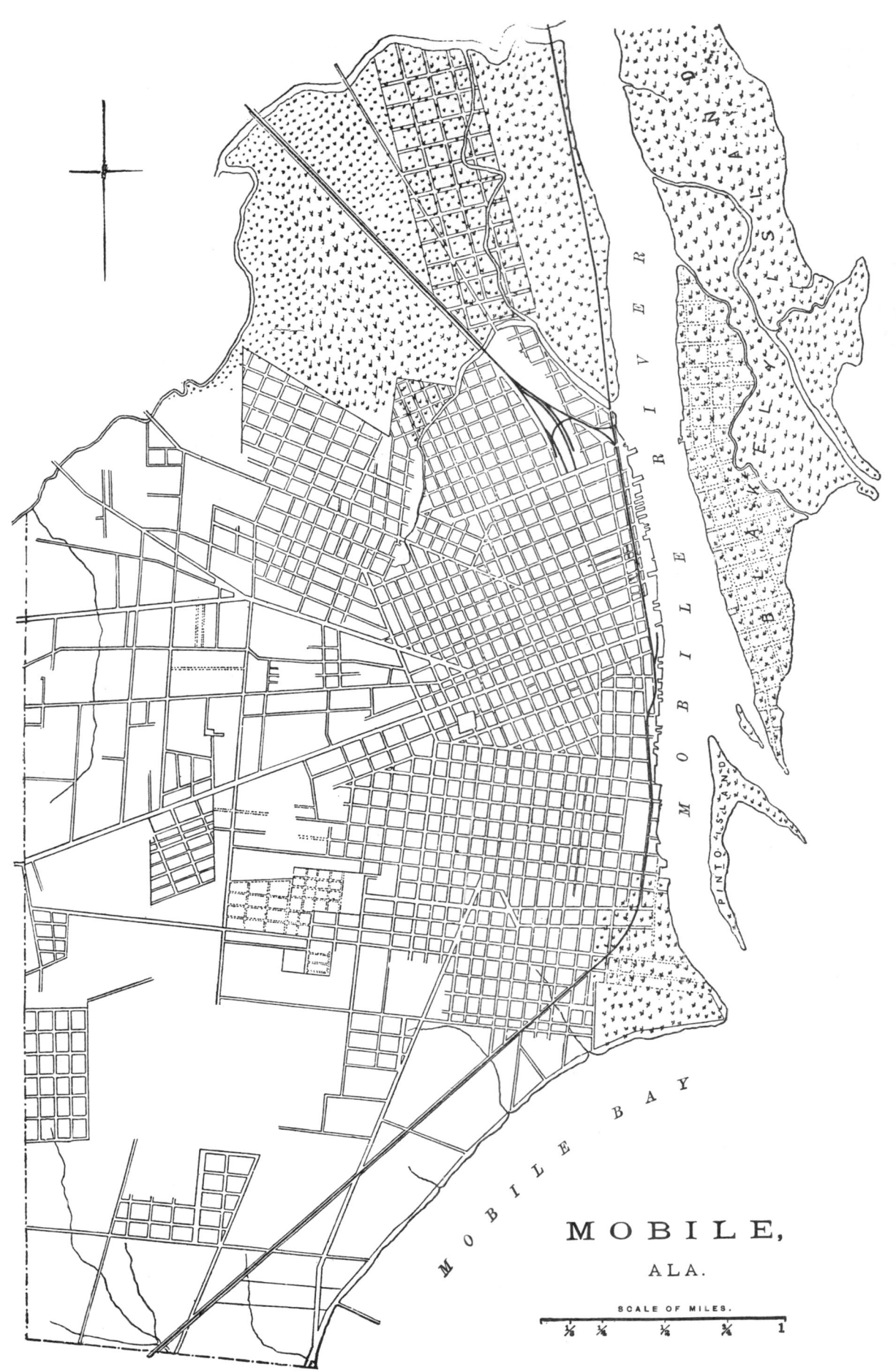

MOBILE,

ALA.

SCALE OF MILES.

TRIBUTARY COUNTRY.

The principal product of the country tributary to the city is cotton, and the receipts and exports of this staple are the most important of the business interests of Mobile. During the year ending September 1, 1880, 358,971 bales of cotton were received here, coming in from the country reached by the several railroad lines or bordering on the rivers that empty into the bay, some 2,000 bales being hauled to the city in wagons. In addition to cotton, vegetables are largely raised and sent here for shipment to the northern cities. Considerable corn and oats are raised along the Alabama, Tombigbee, and Warrior rivers.

TOPOGRAPHY.

The corporate limits of the city extend 6 miles north and south and 2 or 3 miles west from the river. It is built on a sandy plain only slightly elevated above the level of the sea, but sufficiently elevated for fair natural drainage. The soil consists of a coarse loose sand, which absorbs the heaviest rains in a few hours, leaving the streets perfectly dry. The country along the Mobile river, to the north of the city, and also that to the east for a number of miles, is marshy, and at certain seasons of the year malarious; but on the south and southeast there is a broad sweep to the gulf, across which blows the sea-breeze for which Mobile is so noted. The country rises as it recedes from the river, and on the west and northwest are high, sandy pine hills, where pure water is abundant and malaria unknown, affording to the inhabitants of the city delightful summer homes and inexpensive retreats during the hot months.

CLIMATE.

From the tables of the Smithsonian Institution, covering a series of years from 1840 to 1873, the highest recorded summer temperature is given as 98°, and the lowest recorded winter temperature as 19°. The mean summer temperature is 82.45°, and the mean winter temperature 55.05°. The annual rainfall amounts to about 58 inches. The prevailing wind is south, varied by north winds, chiefly in the winter months. The former moderates the temperature to such an extent in summer as to render the city comparatively cool and pleasant, with a temperature below that of many inland cities of higher latitude.

STREETS.

The streets, especially the more modern ones, are generally wide and well laid out, and are shaded by trees, the live-oak, water-oak, magnolia, etc., which give to the city a semi-tropical appearance. Flowers and flower-gardens abound, and the orange tree flourishes and bears fruit. A few of the principal streets are paved for a portion of their distance, but most of these require repairs. There are a few shell roads, some old plank roads, and some are simply defined as dirt-streets. A large amount of work is done annually, but, as it is not permanent, there is no real improvement. The average annual expenditure from 1872 to 1878 is $27,272. There are 6 lines of horse-railroads in the city, and one of these runs to Spring Hill, a pleasant suburban retreat 6 miles from the city.

WATER-WORKS.

The water-supply is brought from Spring Hill and is of unusual purity and excellence.

GAS.

The city is lighted with gas, which to a large extent is manufactured from coal taken from the interior of the state.

PUBLIC PARKS AND PLEASURE-GROUNDS.

Government street, the favorite promenade, is shaded by fine oak trees and bordered by handsome houses, surrounded by luxuriant gardens. Bienville park, between Dauphin and Saint Francis streets, is also a place of much resort. It is improved with live-oak and other shade trees. There is also Washington square, which is kept in good condition. Spring Hill, Frascati Garden, and the grounds of the Agricultural and Mechanical Association of Mobile are among the pleasure-resorts of the citizens.

PLACES OF AMUSEMENT.

There is a theater in the city, and also two halls—Odd Fellows' hall and Temperance hall.

DRAINAGE.

There does not appear to be any system of drainage in the city.

CEMETERIES.

There are 4 cemeteries in the city, as follows:

Magnolia Cemetery, area 60 acres, is situated in the southwestern part of the city.

Jewish Cemetery, area 10 acres, adjoins the above.

Catholic Cemetery, area 65 acres, is situated just outside the northwestern limit of the city.

The *Old Grave-yard*, situated near the center of the city, has an area of 2 acres. The latter is now but seldom used, and then only by the old families, though there is no prohibition against interments being made in it.

MARKETS.

There are three public or corporation markets in Mobile. The Southern market, costing about $50,000, covers about 1¾ acre of land. Prior to an ordinance that reduced the price of stalls to a merely nominal sum, the annual rental of this market was $10,000. The markets are open from 3 to 9 a. m.

SANITARY AUTHORITY—BOARD OF HEALTH.

The chief sanitary authority of the city is vested in a board of health, an independent organization created by state law, but deriving its authority from the city ordinances, and composed of five members, all of whom are physicians. In the absence of any declared epidemic the annual expense of the board is $2,000, incurred in defraying the salaries of health officer and clerk and incidental office expenses. During an epidemic the board has no power to increase expenses; it can only make recommendations, and it remains with the county and city authorities to take action. The board's authority, either in the absence or in the presence of epidemics, is only advisory, except as to abatement of nuisances, etc. The health officer is the chief executive officer of the board; he makes regular inspections and sees that all health ordinances and all regulations of the board are properly enforced. His salary is $100 per month, and he is a physician. One sanitary inspector is employed, who has police powers. The board meets every Monday evening and transacts its business as a distinctive body. One general annual house-to-house inspection is made, and after that a sanitary inspector is employed to attend to all complaints, and to make inspections of the entire city. All nuisances that are considered detrimental to public health are ordered abated, and in case of failure, after due notice, the responsible parties are brought before the recorder. The inspection and correction of all defective house-drainage, privy-vaults, cesspools, sources of drinking-water, etc., are the same as that adopted toward nuisances. Street-cleaning is in charge of the street commissioner. The board exercises no control over the conservation and removal of garbage, except to recommend the manner and time for its removal. Burial permits are issued by the health officer on certificates signed by the attending physician. The board forbids the pollution of streams and harbors, and regulates the removal of excrement.

INFECTIOUS DISEASES.

Small-pox patients are isolated, the well-to-do by being quarantined at their own homes and a yellow flag displayed on the house-front, while the poor are sent to the small-pox hospital, 5 miles southwest from the city limits. Scarlet-fever patients are neither isolated nor quarantined at home. If diseases of a contagious nature should break out in either public or private schools, the board would take action. Vaccination is compulsory for persons living near to localities infected with small-pox, and, if patients are not able to pay, it is done at the public expense. The health officer keeps a full record of all births, diseases, and deaths in the city, and makes weekly returns to the board.

REPORTS.

The board formerly reported to the city authorities, and the reports were published monthly in the official organ of the city as part of the municipal proceedings, and annually at the close of the year. It is not stated how the board reports at present.

MUNICIPAL CLEANSING.

Street-cleaning.—The streets are cleaned at the expense of the city and with its regular force. The work is done wholly by hand. Some of the streets are cleaned every day, some once a week, others once a month, while those in the suburbs receive attention only once a year. There are few complaints as to the efficiency of the work. The annual cost of the work is $20,000, which includes all street-work, and the removal of garbage, etc. The sweepings are dumped in the outskirts of the city.

Removal of garbage and ashes.—All garbage is removed daily at the expense of the city, with its own force. The garbage is kept in suitable vessels, mixed with ashes, and set out on the sidewalks for removal. The garbage and ashes are taken to the "dump" in the same manner as street-sweepings. The system is reported to work well, and there are no complaints.

Dead animals.—The carcasses of all animals are removed to a fertilizing manufactory, 3½ miles from the city, by the contractor, who is paid about 95 cents per head. Owners are required to report all dead animals to the central station. The number of dead animals annually removed is about 800—500 dogs, goats, etc., and 300 horses and cows. The ordinance regulating the system is perfect, but owners fail at times to report promptly.

Liquid household wastes.—The liquid household wastes are generally emptied into the privy-vaults, a very little going into cesspools, and only a small amount into street-gutters. The cesspools are not generally water-tight, are not provided with overflows, in a few instances receive the waste from water-closets, and are cleaned out in the same way as privy-vaults. The street-gutters are occasionally flooded. Offensive drinking-water has been found in wells that were located near privy-vaults.

Human excreta.—There are very few water-closets in the city, some delivering into the sewers and some into cesspools, and nearly all the houses depend on privy-vaults. There are very few of these latter even nominally water-tight. There are no special regulations as to their construction, and they are emptied by regular city scavengers with odorless excavators, the contents being taken outside the city limits and disposed of in such manner as may be prescribed by the board of health. It is allowed to be used for manure, but not on land within the gathering-ground of the public water-supply. It is reported that the regulations for, and the system of, cleaning vaults and cesspools are perfect, but that the careless manner in which the vaults are built tends to interfere with the working of the system and to cause offensive odors. The dry-earth system has increased lately, and about one-fifteenth of the privy-vaults have been abolished.

Manufacturing wastes.—There do not appear to be any special regulations regarding the disposal of either liquid or solid manufacturing wastes.

POLICE.

The police force is appointed by the police board, and its equipment, discipline, control, and management are intrusted to the captain of police, under the control of the recorder, subject to such rules, regulations, and ordinances as may from time to time be made by the corporate authorities. The captain of police is the executive officer, and it is his duty to see that the public peace is preserved. His salary is $112 50 per month. The rest of the force consists of 1 detective at $55 per month; 4 sergeants and 1 clerk at $50 per month each; 1 porter at $33 75 per month; and 2 sentinels and 50 patrolmen at $40 per month each. The uniform is blue, and costs $18 per suit, and each man furnishes his own. The patrols are equipped with clubs, chain twisters, revolvers, and whistles. The hours of service are: Day watch, from 7 a. m. to 7 p. m.; night watch, from 7 p. m. to 6 a. m.; and the total length of streets patrolled by the force is 100 miles.

During the past year 1,434 arrests were made, the principal causes being, for disorderly conduct, 703; drunkenness, 191; larceny, 98; vagrancy, 116, etc. Their final disposition was: Fined, 800; discharged, 425; held for trial, 147; sent to county jail, 52; and turned over to other authorities, 10. The total amount of property lost or stolen and reported to the police during the year was $1,200, and of this, $1,000 was recovered and returned to the owners. During the same period there were 125 station-house lodgers, meals to the value of $20 having been furnished to them. The number of station-house lodgers in 1879 was 150. The force is required to co-operate with the fire department by preserving order and protecting property at all fires, and with the health department by enforcing the health ordinances. Special policemen are not appointed. The yearly cost of the police force is (1880) $28,941 20.

COMMERCE AND NAVIGATION.

[From the reports of the Bureau of Statistics for the fiscal years ending June 30.]

Customs district of Mobile, Alabama.	1879.	1880.
Total value of imports	$544,628	$425,980
Total value of exports:		
Domestic	$6,219,818	$7,187,703
Foreign	None.	1,037
Total number of immigrants	None.	None.

Customs district of Mobile, Alabama.	1879.		1880.	
	Number.	Tons.	Number.	Tons.
Vessels in foreign trade				
Entered	122	59,166	130	61,471
Cleared	131	57,518	156	69,181
Vessels in coast trade and fisheries:				
Entered	84	15,981	74	20,212
Cleared	54	15,652	55	16,787
Vessels registered, enrolled, and licensed in district	109	14,454	121	15,291
Vessels built during the year	3	112	5	141

MANUFACTURES.

The following is a summary of the statistics of the manufactures of Mobile for 1880, being taken from tables prepared for the Tenth Census by Erwin Ledyard, special agent:

Mechanical and manufacturing industries.	No. of establishments.	Capital.	AVERAGE NUMBER OF HANDS EMPLOYED.			Total amount paid in wages during the year.	Value of materials.	Value of products.
			Males above 16 years.	Females above 15 years.	Children and youths.			
All industries......................	91	$525,708	622	37	45	$261,643	$830,961	$1,335,579
Blacksmithing........................	7	900	9	....	....	4,176	1,830	8,000
Boots and shoes, including custom work and repairing...............	6	3,300	10	2	....	6,400	6,700	17,500
Bread and other bakery products......................	9	25,200	25	4	2	9,558	42,470	75,000
Carpentering.........................	9	11,600	117	....	....	37,080	73,500	127,750
Carriages and wagons	4	10,400	26	....	....	12,600	19,500	43,100
Flouring- and grist-mill products......................	6	28,000	49	....	....	18,000	329,500	387,500
Foundery and machine-shop products..................	5	59,808	73	....	5	28,550	19,547	59,900
Furniture...........................	3	3,700	8	1	1	2,400	7,750	13,650
Lumber, sawed	3	147,000	105	....	....	39,500	111,000	185,000
Painting and paperhanging................	3	5,500	14	....	....	4,700	4,500	13,500
Printing and publishing..................	5	37,000	27	....	....	17,740	27,941	58,375
Saddlery and harness....................	3	10,600	7	....	1	3,750	6,200	13,140
Tinware, copperware, and sheet-iron ware	7	12,950	28	....	....	10,600	28,400	52,750
Tobacco, cigars and cigarettes	5	8,300	19	....	2	9,816	7,000	19,000
All other industries (a)	16	161,450	105	30	34	56,773	143,123	261,414

a Embracing bookbinding and blank-book making; brooms and brushes; confectionery; cotton goods; lock- and gun-smithing; lumber, planed; marble and stone work; plumbing and gasfitting; sash, doors, and blinds; scales and balances; shipbuilding; and wheelwrighting.

From the foregoing table it appears that the average capital of all establishments is $5,777 01; that the average wages of all hands employed is $371 65 per annum; that the average outlay in wages, in materials, and in interest (at 6 per cent.) on capital employed is $12,353 26.

MONTGOMERY,

MONTGOMERY COUNTY, ALABAMA.

POPULATION

IN THE

AGGREGATE,

1840-1880.

	Inhab.
1790	......
1800	......
1810	......
1820	......
1830	......
1840	2,179
1850	8,728
1860	8,843
1870	10,588
1880	16,713

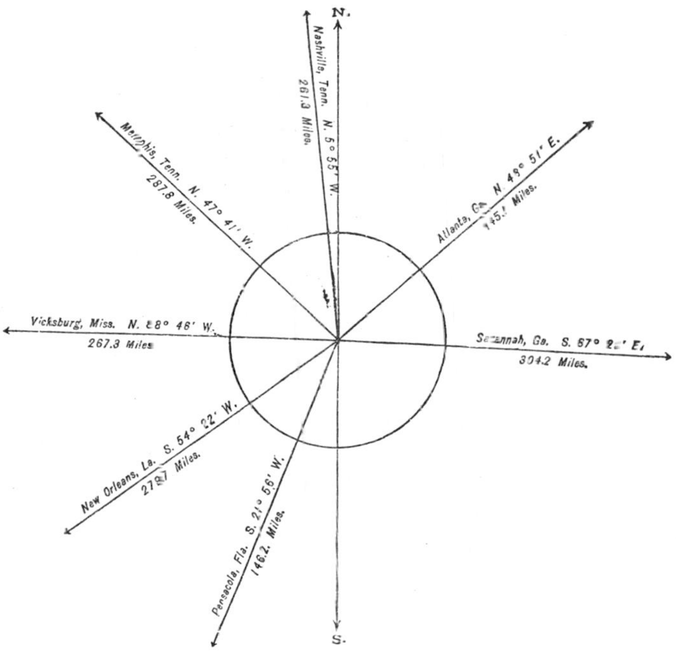

POPULATION

BY

SEX, NATIVITY, AND RACE,

AT

CENSUS OF 1880.

Male	7,591
Female	9,122
Native	16,062
Foreign-born	651
White	6,782
Colored	9,931

Compass rose with distances:
- Nashville, Tenn. N. 5° 55' W. 261.3 Miles.
- Memphis, Tenn. N. 47° 41' W. 287.8 Miles.
- Atlanta, Ga. N. 48° 51' E. 145.2 Miles.
- Vicksburg, Miss. N. 88° 48' W. 267.3 Miles.
- Savannah, Ga. S. 67° 26' E. 304.2 Miles.
- New Orleans, La. S. 54° 22' W. 272.7 Miles.
- Pensacola, Fla. S. 21° 55' W. 146.2 Miles.

Latitude: 32° 23′ North; Longitude: 86° 18′ (west from Greenwich); Altitude: 162 to 413 feet.

FINANCIAL CONDITION:

Total Valuation: $5,506,994; per capita: $330 00.   Net Indebtedness: $567,900; per capita: $33 98.   Tax per $100: $2 41.

HISTORICAL SKETCH.

The town of Montgomery was incorporated in 1819 by the legislature of Alabama, which united the villages of New Philadelphia, East Alabama Town, and Alabama Town to form it. The site is marked by two mounds, about 90 feet square, which show that the spot was known to that mysterious people, the mound-builders. Although it was visited by De Soto in 1540, by Bienville in 1714, and by the English in 1763, no settlement was made until 1817. In that year Andrew Dexter and John Falconer purchased a lot of land about 20 miles below the spot where the Coosa and the Tallapoosa meet to form the Alabama river. Here they founded the village of New Philadelphia, the settlers being chiefly northern men. In the next year, 1818, the villages of Alabama Town and East Alabama Town were settled; and finally, as already stated, the three places were united in 1819 to form the town of Montgomery. Few events of general interest mark its history; the arrival of the "Harriet", the first steamboat, in 1821, the breaking of the ground for the Montgomery railroad in 1836, and the floods in the river recurring at periods of 11 years, being the events of chief interest to the citizens.

Montgomery was made a city in 1837, and in 1846 became the capital of the state in the place of Tuscaloosa. On February 4, 1861, delegates from six southern states met in the city and formed the southern confederacy, and on February 18, Jefferson Davis and Alexander H. Stephens were inaugurated as president and vice-president of the confederacy. Since 1860 the population has nearly doubled. The trade with the surrounding country is important; the annual receipts of cotton average 75,000 bales; and there are several large machine-shops and founderies. Within 60 miles of the city are extensive fields of coal and iron. There are several schools and academies, and about a dozen churches.

MONTGOMERY IN 1880.

The following statistical accounts, collected by the Census Office, indicate the present condition of Montgomery:

LOCATION.

Montgomery is situated in latitude 32° 23' north, longitude 86° 18' west from Greenwich, on the left bank of the Alabama river, 331 miles from Mobile, and about 20 miles below the junction of the Coosa and Tallapoosa rivers. The lowest point is 162 and the highest 413 feet above the level of the sea. The Alabama river from October to April is a stream about half a mile wide, while from April to October the width varies from 34 to 50 feet. The current at low stages runs at the rate of 2 miles per hour; at high stages the rate is 6 miles per hour. Communication by the river is open to steamers to Wetumpka above the city, and to Selma, Claiborne, and Mobile below.

RAILROAD COMMUNICATIONS.

The city is touched by the following-named railroads, all of which are included in the Louisville and Nashville railroad system:

The Western Railroad of Alabama connects Montgomery with West Point, Georgia, and has a branch line to Selma, Alabama.

The Montgomery and Eufala railroad connects these two places.

The Mobile and Montgomery railroad connects the city with the port of Mobile, and a branch line extends to Pensacola.

The South and North Alabama Division of the Louisville and Nashville railroad connects it with Decatur, Alabama.

These railroads furnish easy and rapid communication with all parts of the South and West.

TRIBUTARY COUNTRY.

The country about Montgomery is almost entirely agricultural in character, cotton being the staple product. Farm produce and hay are raised, and the trade in lumber is quite extensive. There is also a considerable trade in bituminous coal from the Alabama coal-fields.

TOPOGRAPHY.

The soil of Montgomery is red clay and alluvium, resting upon underlying limestone. The land slopes gradually to the Alabama river, with a descent of 4 feet per 100. The city is surrounded by high lands, and on the northeast side is shut in by a large swamp, which includes a pond covering about 8 acres. The southwestern shore of the Alabama is subject to biennial overflows, and is therefore rather marshy. To the north, west, and southwest the country is wooded. Within a radius of 5 miles of the city the soil is a heavy clay. The city is situated on a bluff, the character of which is indicated by the Indian name for the spot, "Chunnanuga Chatte"—"high red bluff".

CLIMATE.

The highest recorded summer temperature is 107°, although in average years the thermometer does not go above 100°. The lowest winter temperature in average years is 12°, but a temperature of 8° has been recorded.

STREETS.

The total length of the streets of Montgomery is 73 miles. Of these, 46 miles are paved with broken-stone (pebble) pavement and 26 miles with gravel. No record of the cost of laying or repairing has been kept. The sidewalks are of various materials, grades, and dimensions, but are mainly of gravel. The gutters are of brick and

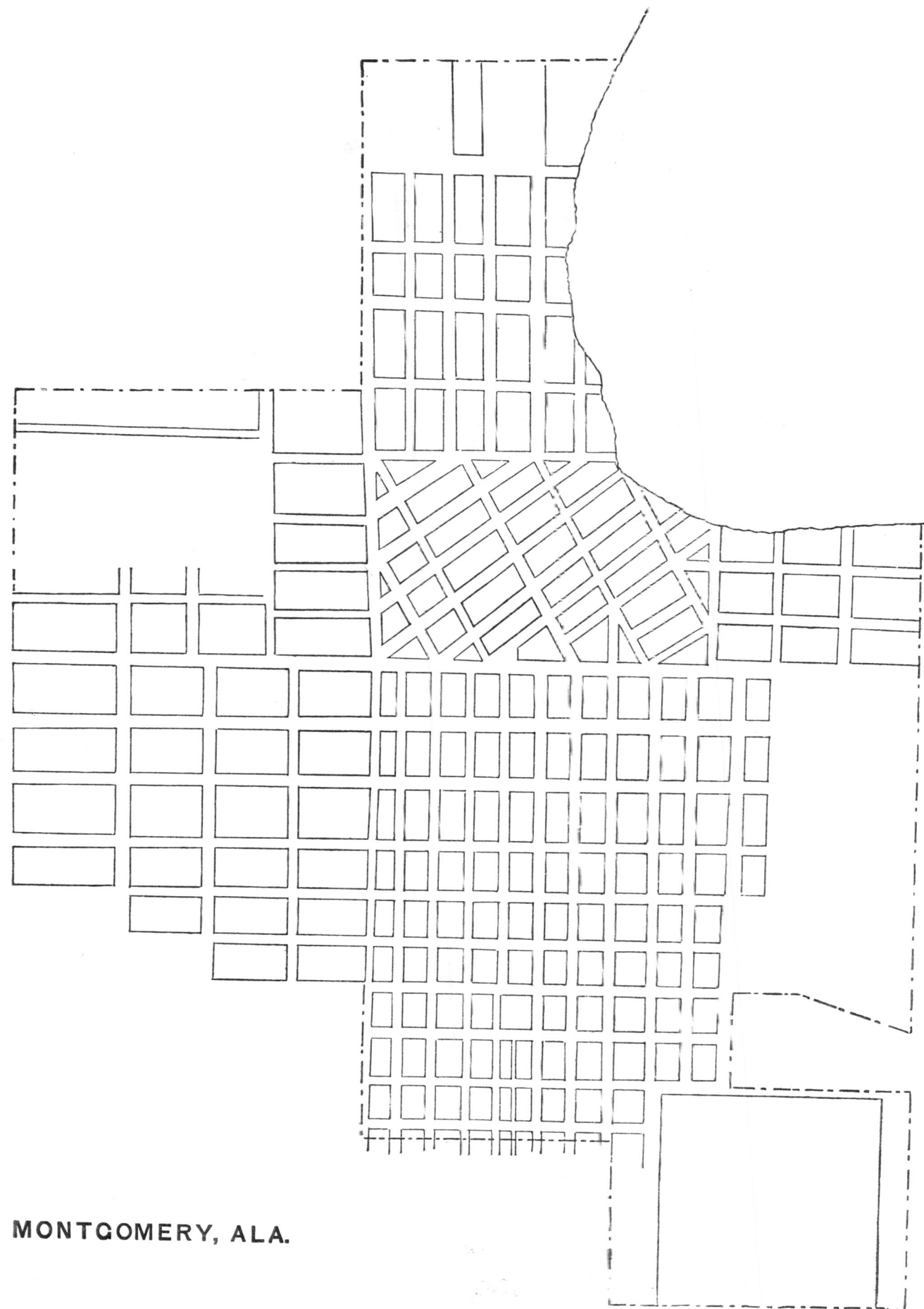

MONTGOMERY, ALA.

ditching, and are chiefly used to carry storm-water into the inlets of the sewers. Many streets have no gutters, while on others the gutters are useless, except for gentle rains. Large wooden sewers serve for subsoil drainage, and when they are open are substituted for gutters. The work of repairing and constructing streets is done by day labor, and in 1880 cost about $140 per week.

There are no horse-railroads. A single omnibus line is maintained. It has 3 vehicles and 6 horses, and employs 4 men. The fare is 5 cents.

WATER-WORKS.

The works for the public water-supply are the property of a private corporation, and were built at a cost of about $130,000. The water is pumped by a Worthington pump to a reservoir, and from there distributed by pipes through the city. About 500,000 gallons are pumped daily. Water-meters are in common use.

GAS.

The city is supplied with gas by a private corporation. The average daily production is about 60,000 cubic feet. The charge per 1,000 feet is $3 50. The city pays $20 per annum for each of its 171 gas street-lamps.

PUBLIC BUILDINGS.

The buildings owned and used by the city include a market building and a city hall combined, a powder magazine, a hospital building, and an engine-house. The total cost of these buildings was $165,000; the city hall and market building cost $130,000.

PUBLIC PARKS AND PLEASURE-GROUNDS.

An effort is being made to create a few public parks. Two spaces have already been set aside as parks, and the city code provides for the election of six park commissioners, to receive and collect subscriptions for the purpose of procuring and beautifying suitable grounds.

PLACES OF AMUSEMENT.

The city has two theaters—McDonald's opera-house, seating 1,000, and Montgomery theater, seating 1,500. Each of these pays an annual license of $200. McDonald's concert-hall, seating 450, is the only concert- and lecture-room. There are no concert- and beer-gardens.

DRAINAGE.

Sewers are built according to the supposed requirements of each case, and not according to any uniform design. They are made of brick, and also to a considerable extent of wood. There are a good many open drains. They are designed only to relieve the city from storm- and surface-water, and are not suitable to receive domestic wastes. The outflow (except from the Common and Goldthwait Streets sewers) is discharged upon low bottom-lands north of the city, overflowed in time of high water. There is no ventilation of sewers, except through inlets and the open mouths. They are said to be flushed at the inlets two or three times a week from the fire hydrants. Men frequently have to be sent in to clear obstructions. For the past few years this kind of work has become so offensive that it is done in the night. The city pays the whole cost of construction. Brick sewers are said to cost, for the brick work, $10 50 per thousand, and for the earth-work and materials, $325 per thousand feet. The wooden drains cost about $590 per thousand feet. The work is done as directed by the street committee, under superintendence of the street overseer. Wooden drains to the extent of 110,000 feet (board measure) have been relaid yearly, and none serve longer than from two and a half to three years.

CEMETERIES.

There is but one cemetery connected with the city. This is situated between Columbus and Ripley streets, and contains a little more than 6 acres. It is controlled by the city government, although the Catholics have purchased a part in the southeast corner, which they manage by themselves, and the Hebrews have also purchased a small portion. The western part of the cemetery is reserved for those unable to pay for burial, while the rest, except the parts owned by the Hebrews and the Catholics, is divided into lots, which are sold at a regular price of $1 per linear foot. Since 1876 there have been 2,952 interments in this cemetery.

No interment is allowed to be made outside the cemetery. The sextons are required to keep a register of burials, and before making any interment must obtain a physician's certificate of death. Graves are generally vaulted and are made 6 or more feet deep, although the city code requires only 5 feet. Burials are ordinarily made within from 18 to 24 hours after death.

MARKETS.

The only market in Montgomery is one situated in the city building and owned and controlled by the city. The cost of the building was $130,000. It contains, in the market portion, 22 butchers' stalls, rental $100 a year; 36 vegetable stalls, $30; 2 stalls used for restaurants, $200; and 2 used by confectioners, $100. The total income from rentals is $4,189 66; from butchers' fees, $1,310 85; and an income from the public sales of $871 25; making a total income of $6,371 76. The market is open daily (Sundays excepted) from April to October between the hours of 4 and 10 a. m., and during the rest of the year between 5 and 11 a. m. In addition, it is open from 2 to 9 p. m. on Saturdays. The gross annual sales are estimated at $250,000. The city compels all dealers in fresh meats, fish, and vegetables in any place other than the market to pay an annual license of $500. No one is allowed to sell articles for sale at the market in any other place during market-hours, except occupants of vegetable stalls, who may make such sales after 8 a. m. Hucksters and peddlers pay an annual license of $50. The clerk of the market collects from each holder of a butcher's stall 25 cents for each head of cattle, and 10 cents for each calf, hog, sheep, lamb, kid, or goat slaughtered or brought to market by him; and from temporary holders of stalls and from dealers on the streets, 25 cents for every quarter of beef offered for sale; 5 cents for every quarter of mutton, lamb, pork, goat, or kid; 10 cents for every sucking pig; 15 cents for every dressed hog under 100 pounds in weight, and 25 cents for every hog dressed of more than 100 pounds. The market is controlled by a committee on the market, and is in charge of a clerk of the market.

SANITARY AUTHORITY—BOARD OF HEALTH.

The board of health of Montgomery is simply a branch of the state board of health, and receives its authority from it. In the absence of an epidemic the board incurs no expense, and its authority is limited to the city and the territory within 1 mile of the city. In time of an epidemic the board can incur any expense, and the limits within its control are extended so as to include the county. It is simply an advisory board to the city council, and exerts no independent authority; it has no regular and stated meetings. The chief executive officer is the health officer of the city, who is also city physician, and *ex officio* registrar of vital statistics; he receives no salary for his duties as health officer. All the members of the board are physicians.

INFECTIOUS DISEASES.

Small-pox patients are isolated at home in most cases. No action is taken in regard to scarlet-fever patients. There is no pest-house, but in case of necessity one is constructed. Vaccination is not compulsory and is not done at the public expense. Physicians and others knowing of cases of infectious, contagious, and malignant diseases in the city are required to report at once to the mayor or chief of police. The city council may at any time establish a quarantine, and any one violating it is liable to a fine of not more than $500.

Since 1870 a careful registration of births, diseases, and deaths has been maintained by the registrar of vital statistics.

REPORTS.

The board reports only to the state board of health.

MUNICIPAL CLEANSING.

Street-cleaning.—The streets are cleaned by the city with its own force and entirely by hand labor. Carts go about the city every day collecting the filth which has been thrown into the streets. The sweepings thus collected are deposited in a ravine on the northern limit of the city. The work is done under the direction of the superintendent of streets and of the health officer.

Removal of garbage and ashes.—Garbage and ashes are removed by the city with its own force. Garbage, while awaiting removal, is kept in boxes, which are placed on the sidewalks at a certain hour, ready for the scavenger on his tour of collection; it may be mixed with ashes. Both garbage and ashes are deposited, like the street-sweepings, in the ravine above mentioned. The cost to the city is about $2,000 a year.

Dead animals are removed by the city, which charges the owner $1 50 for each animal so removed. They are taken to the potter's field, immediately east of the city, and there buried. About 75 animals are removed each year.

Liquid household wastes.—The liquid household wastes run into the sewers where these exist. Where there are no sewers, they pass into the street-gutters or into cesspools, which, while tight on the sides, are dug down until sand is struck and the liquid wastes can thus filter away. The street-gutters are flushed two or three times a week. In some cases cesspools receive the waste of water-closets. No deleterious effects are known to have resulted from the overflow or filtration from cesspools so as to contaminate sources of drinking-water. The cesspools are cleaned under the direction of the superintendent of streets.

Human excreta.—Water-closets are little used outside the business portion of the city, but they are rapidly being introduced into private residences. Most of them deliver into the sewers, some into cesspools. Only about half the privy-vaults are even nominally water-tight. The dry-earth system is not used in the city. Night-soil is removed beyond the city limits and buried.

Manufacturing wastes.—There are no factories giving rise to wastes which need to be disposed of through a sewer system or which are injurious to the public health.

POLICE.

The police force of Montgomery is elected by the city council and governed by the mayor and the chief of police, the latter of whom is the chief executive officer; he has general charge of the department, and receives a salary of $1,500 a year. The rest of the force consists of a captain, salary $90 per month; a sergeant, salary $75 per month; and 16 men, salary $65 per month each. The uniform consists of blue coat and trousers with a black felt hat in winter, while in summer a blue flannel blouse is worn. The men provide their own uniforms, which cost $60 each. They are armed with clubs, are on duty 12 hours each day, and patrol 73 miles of streets. During 1880 the police made 1,964 arrests, the principal cause being drunkenness. The police recovered and returned property to the value of $1,023 which had been lost or stolen. During the year 516 station-house lodgers were accommodated; free meals are furnished to these lodgers, but no record of the cost is kept. The police co-operate with the fire department at fires, and with the health department in reporting unclean premises and unsafe buildings. Special policemen are appointed by the mayor when occasion demands, and these are treated as regular members of the force. The cost of the department in 1880 was $15,546 82.

SELMA,

DALLAS COUNTY, ALABAMA.

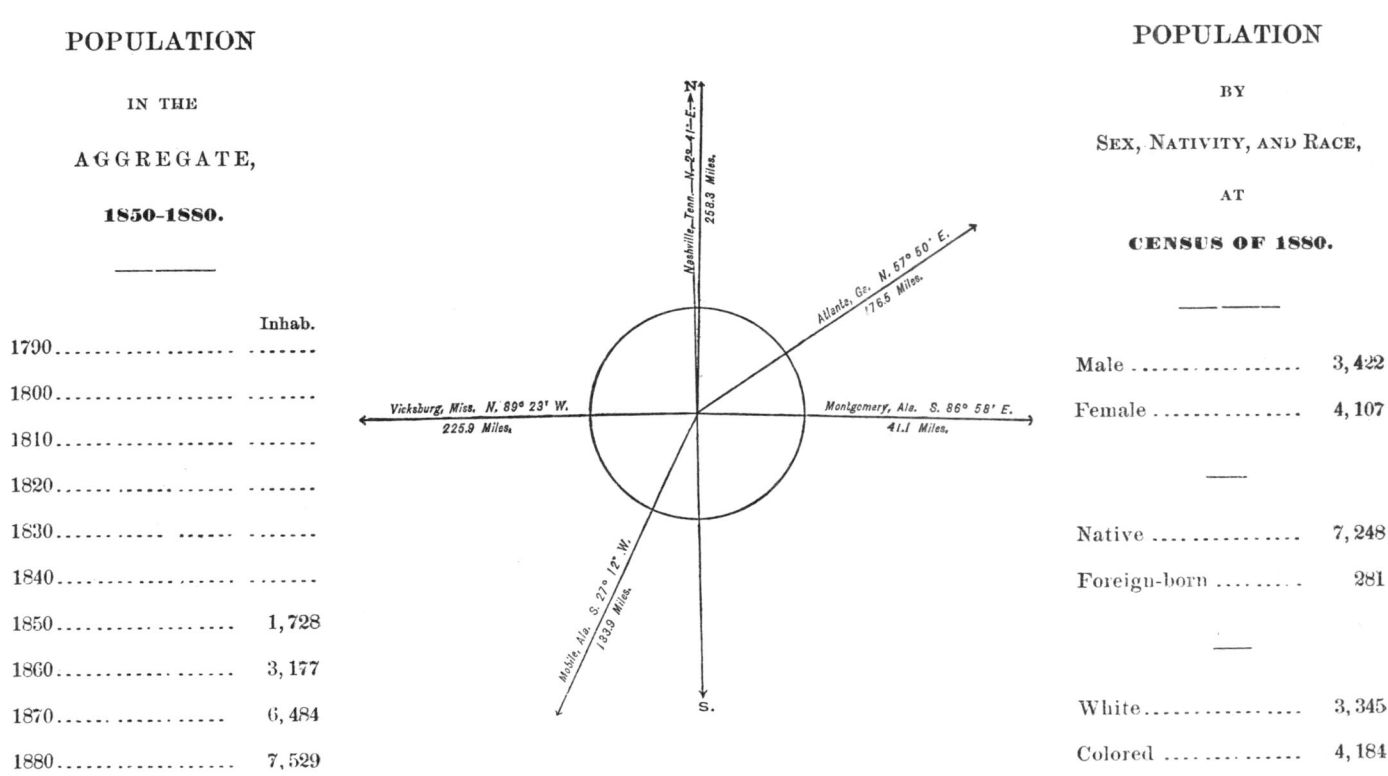

POPULATION

IN THE

AGGREGATE,

1850-1880.

	Inhab.
1790	....
1800	....
1810	....
1820	....
1830	....
1840	....
1850	1,728
1860	3,177
1870	6,484
1880	7,529

POPULATION

BY

SEX, NATIVITY, AND RACE,

AT

CENSUS OF 1880.

Male	3,422
Female	4,107
Native	7,248
Foreign-born	281
White	3,345
Colored	4,184

Latitude: 32° 25' North; Longitude: 87° (west from Greenwich); Altitude: 180 to 240 feet.

FINANCIAL CONDITION:

Total Valuation: $2,500,000; per capita: $332 00.   Net Indebtedness: $323,600; per capita: $42 98.   Tax per $100: $2 65.

HISTORICAL SKETCH.

The first white man to establish himself within what is now the city of Selma, Alabama, was Thomas Moore, who, in 1815, built himself a cabin on what is now known as "High Soapstone bluff". Here he lived alone for nearly a year, but in 1816 a party of settlers established themselves near him and began to cultivate the land. They were, however, unaccustomed to the climate of the region, and rapidly succumbed to malarial disease, so that in 1817 only few were left. In that year the "Selma Town Land Company" was organized for the purpose of dealing in lands. Among other purchases, the company bought the tract on which Moore had settled, and determined to locate a town there. Streets and lots were at once laid out, and the plan of a very pretty village was prepared. Settlers were not slow in coming, and "Moore's Bluff" was soon so flourishing that in 1820 it was incorporated as the town of Selma. The name was taken from the poems of Ossian, in which are sung the praises of Selma, the favorite home of Fingal, and was suggested by Colonel William R. King, a leading member of the land company, who was a devoted admirer of the Scottish bard. Until 1826 the progress of the town was steady, but in that year malarial fever became so prevalent that the population fell off and immigration was almost completely stopped. Energetic measures were taken by the town authorities to improve the health of the town, and with the enforcement of sanitary regulations good health returned, bringing with it increased prosperity. The period from 1830 to 1838 was a time of plenty, but after the crisis of 1837 came hard times, that lasted until the construction of railways— about 1850—again gave an impetus to growth. The population in 1850 was 1,728, but of these inhabitants only 973 were white persons, nearly all the rest being slaves. In 1857 Selma was incorporated as a city, and about that time received quite an addition to its population by the coming of nearly 300 German immigrants.

When the civil war broke out, the city became a very important place for the manufacture of munitions of war. The few iron-clads which disputed with Admiral Farragut the possession of Mobile bay were all built and equipped at Selma. The city was taken by the federal forces, April 2, 1865, and a large extent of the business portion was burned over by the fires which destroyed the confederate supplies and work-shops. Since 1867 the advance of the city has been rapid and encouraging. About 90,000 bales of cotton were shipped from Selma during the past year. There are several machine-shops and founderies, a cotton-mill, an ice factory, a cotton-seed oil press, and other manufacturing establishments. There are twelve churches and many societies. A daily and a weekly newspaper are published in the city. Selma is supplied with gas, it has a good street-railway, and is, in short, a prosperous and pleasant city.

SELMA IN 1880.

The following statistical accounts, collected by the Census Office, indicate the present condition of Selma:

LOCATION.

Selma is situated in latitude 32° 25′ north, and longitude 87° west from Greenwich, on the right bank of the Alabama river, about 70 miles below Montgomery. The highest point is 240 feet and the lowest 180 feet above the level of the gulf of Mexico at Pensacola. The Alabama river is navigable for river steamers from Mobile to Montgomery and Wetumpka, and a large trade is carried on by the city with the places along the river-banks.

RAILROAD COMMUNICATIONS.

The city has excellent railroad communication with the cities of Alabama and the neighboring states, as follows:
The Selma, Rome, and Dalton railroad (the Selma division of the East Tennessee, Virginia and Georgia railroad) connects Selma with Cleveland, Tennessee, by way of Rome and Dalton, Georgia.
The Alabama Central railroad, also controlled by the East Tennessee, Virginia, and Georgia, connects Selma with Meridian, Mississippi.
The Selma and Greensborough railroad extends from Selma to Greensborough, Alabama.
The New Orleans and Selma railroad extends to Martin's station, 21 miles distant.
The Selma and Gulf railroad to Pine Apple, Alabama.
The Western Alabama railroad, a part of the Louisville and Nashville railroad system, to Montgomery, Alabama.

TRIBUTARY COUNTRY.

The country about Selma is strictly agricultural in character, confined almost exclusively to the raising of cotton and corn.

TOPOGRAPHY.

The soil of Selma is a sandy deposit overlying the Cretaceous formation which extends through the state. In boring an artesian well the following strata were found to underlie the city: The drill passed through 37 feet of clay, sand, and gravel, 53 feet of blue rotten limestone, 6 feet of sandstone, 6 feet of gray sand with water, 18 feet of blue clay, 24 feet of blue sticky sand, 17 feet of blue clay, 4 feet of green sand, 42 feet 5 inches of gray sand with water, 11 inches of green sand and sandstone, 3 feet of blue clay, 54 feet 3 inches of gray sand with water, 7 inches of sandstone, and 213 feet 10 inches of blue-grayish sand, crossed occasionally by beds of blue clay from 5 to 10 feet thick. The city is situated on a bluff shut in by the Alabama river on the south, Beech creek on the east, and Valley creek on the west; the natural drainage is into the creeks, and is excellent. There are no lakes in the vicinity. A large swamp lies from 1 to 4 miles distant along Beech creek. The country is well wooded.

CLIMATE.

The mean annual temperature of Selma is about 64.51°, the mean in summer being 79.28° and in winter 49.54°. The adjacent waters tend to produce malarial diseases. The winters are very humid, and are the cause of considerable pulmonary disease. The large swamp along Beech creek may be a cause of ill health, but its effects are not plainly appreciable.

STREETS.

The total length of the streets is estimated by the mayor at 40 miles. None of them are paved. The sidewalks in the business portion of the city are paved with brick; elsewhere they are of dirt. The gutters are of brick and wood. Trees are planted along both sides of the streets throughout nearly the whole city. The work on the streets is done entirely by the day, and costs annually about $5,000.

There is one horse-railroad line. This has $2\frac{1}{8}$ miles of track, 5 cars, and 6 mules; it employs 4 men, and during the year carried about 60,000 passengers; the fare is 5 cents. There are no regular omnibus lines.

WATER-WORKS.

There are no public water-works. The water for general use is obtained largely from artesian wells, which vary in depth from 212 to 620 feet, and yield a copious supply of excellent water. There are 65 of these wells in the city. A kind of well in very common use is made by driving into the ground to the depth of 20 or 30 feet an iron pipe from $1\frac{1}{4}$ inch to 2 inches in diameter and pointed at the end and punctured with small holes.

GAS.

The city is supplied with gas by a private corporation, which began the work of lighting private houses in 1855. The daily average production is 19,500 feet. The charge per 1,000 feet is $3. The city pays $2 75 per month for each gas street-lamp, 100 of which are in use.

PUBLIC BUILDINGS.

The building owned by the city and used for municipal purposes is valued at $10,000, and includes within its walls the city council chamber, the offices of the city marshal and city clerk, a court-room and prison, a market-house, and a hall. Two buildings are leased by the city for the use of fire companies.

PUBLIC PARKS AND PLEASURE-GROUNDS.

Selma has no public parks.

PLACES OF AMUSEMENT.

There is one theater in the city; it has a seating capacity of 1,000. Theaters pay a license of $5 to the city for each performance. A single hall, capable of seating 350, is used as a concert- and lecture-room. There are no concert- and beer-gardens.

DRAINAGE.

No information on this subject was furnished.

CEMETERIES.

The city has 2 public cemeteries and 1 private (Jewish) burial-ground. The area and location of these are not given by the city authorities, nor is the number of interments which have been made within them stated. Timely notice must be given to a sexton before presenting any body to him for burial. The bodies of white and colored people are kept carefully apart. Graves must be at least $4\frac{1}{2}$ feet in depth. Burials are usually made within 24 hours after the death has occurred.

MARKETS.

There is one public market in the city. This contains 24 stalls, classified as follows: 12 butchers' stalls, 7 vegetable stalls, 2 fish stalls, and 3 coffee stalls. The rental of the various stalls is as follows: For meat stalls, from $12 to $15 a month is the minimum price, while some are rented at from $26 to $35 per month; for coffee stalls, $16 per month; for fish and vegetable stalls, $5 per month. The total income from the rental of stalls in 1880 was $1,800. The market is open from 3.30 a. m. to 12 m. between May and October, and during the rest of the year, from 4.30 a. m. until 12 m. Saturdays it is open until 10 p. m. During the year the carcasses of 2,200 cattle, 1,950 sheep, 646 goats, and 550 hogs were sold from the market. No fresh meats are allowed to be sold in any other place than the market, and until after 9 a. m. no fish or vegetables. A space about the market building is reserved for farmers' and hucksters' wagons.

SANITARY AUTHORITY—BOARD OF HEALTH.

The Selma Medical Society is organized as the board of health of the city under an act of the legislature passed in 1865. It has about 20 members, all of them necessarily physicians. The powers of the board are limited to advising the city council, but its acts once approved by the council have the force of ordinances and can be enforced by the board. Its annual expenses are about $325, which includes $180 as salary for the health officer, and the ordinary expenditure for stationery, printing, etc. In time of an epidemic the expenses can be increased to any amount approved by the city council. No epidemic has visited the city since 1853, although small-pox was prevalent in 1866, but when there is reason to expect an epidemic the board is invested by the council with special and extended authority. The board meets regularly once a month, and oftener if necessary. The chief executive officer is a health officer, elected by the board, whose duty is to enforce the health ordinances and to maintain a good sanitary condition of the city by all means in his power. No assistant health officers or inspectors are employed, although one policeman is placed always at the disposal of the health officer, and receives $50 a year for this service.

NUISANCES.

Inspections are made constantly by the health officer in the course of his duty. When nuisances occur they are inspected, and orders are issued for their abatement within a specified time. If these orders are disregarded complaint is made to the mayor, who can take such action as he deems best. No action is taken in regard to the pollution of rivers and streams. Defective house-drainage, cesspools, privy-vaults, sewers, etc., when they become nuisances are treated in the same way as other nuisances. The ordinances prohibit casting of filth, dirt, or offal into the streets and lanes.

GARBAGE.

The board requires that garbage be kept in boxes or barrels convenient for removal, and has charge of the carts which collect it.

BURIAL OF THE DEAD.

Whenever a death occurs, the attending physician is required to give a certificate of death; this is delivered to the sexton, who, before making the interment, must present it to the registrar of vital statistics and obtain from him a burial permit. In cases where there was no attending physician the city physician must view the body and give a certificate of death.

INFECTIOUS DISEASES.

Small-pox patients are isolated in a pest-house owned by the city, and situated just beyond the corporate limits. Scarlet-fever patients are only isolated or quarantined as the attending physician may direct. Should contagious diseases break out in the schools the board of health would take any action that seemed best. Vaccination is neither compulsory nor done at the public expense. The board may, whenever it thinks best, recommend the establishment of a quarantine, and when once declared by the city council this quarantine must be continued until such a time as the board directs.

The registrar of vital statistics keeps a record of births, diseases, and deaths, publishing monthly and annual reports embodying the returns made to him by the physicians of the city.

REPORTS.

The board reports annually to the state board of health, and whenever necessary to the city council. Only the reports of the health officer and the registrar are published by the city.

MUNICIPAL CLEANSING.

Street-cleaning.—The streets are cleaned by the city's force, and entirely by hand labor, no machines being used. The cleaning is done in summer as often as dirt accumulates, but in winter only about once in two weeks. The sweepings are either thrown into the river below the city or dumped on vacant lots beyond the city limits. The annual cost can not be given exactly; it is about $1,200.

Removal of garbage and ashes.—Garbage is removed by carts under the charge of the sanitary policeman. While awaiting removal the garbage is kept in boxes or barrels, which, on the days when collections are made, are placed upon the sidewalks ready for removal. No ordinance prohibits keeping garbage and ashes in the same vessel. Ashes are collected in the same way as garbage, and, like it, are finally disposed of by being dumped on lands outside the city near Valley creek. The annual cost is included in the estimate for cleaning the streets, as the work is done by the same force.

Dead animals.—Under the regulations of the city, the owner of any horse, cow, mule, or any other large animal which may die in the city must remove the carcass beyond the city limits and there bury it. Small animals, such as cats, dogs, rats, poultry, etc., may be buried on the owner's premises. When no owner can be found, removal is made by the city's force.

Liquid household wastes.—The liquid household wastes are either thrown into cesspools and privy-vaults or into surface privies, none being allowed to run into the street-gutters. The cesspools are porous, are not provided with overflows, in some cases receive the wastes from water-closets, and their contents must be rendered inoffensive by the use of deodorizers. Street-gutters are not flushed. No instances of the contamination of wells by the escape of the contents from cesspools and privy-vaults are known.

Human excreta.—A few water-closets are in use, but most of the houses depend on surface privies. Where deep privy-vaults exist, they are required by law to be, and are, water-tight. They must be kept odorless by the use of disinfectants and deodorizers. They may be cleaned only during cold and dry weather between the hours of 10 p. m. and 3 a. m. No vault may be made less than 6 feet distant from the line of any street. The dry-earth system is used to a small extent. Night-soil is finally disposed of by being buried in the ground.

Manufacturing wastes.—No troublesome manufacturing wastes are produced in the city.

POLICE.

The police force of Selma is appointed by the city council. The chief executive officer is the city marshal, whose salary is $1,200 a year, and whose duty is the general supervision of the force. Eight patrolmen, salary $50 per month each, make up the rest of the force. They wear no uniform, their badge of office being a star worn on the outer coat. They are armed with a pistol, a club, and twisters; are on duty 12 hours each day, and patrol about 40 miles of streets. During the past year 623 arrests were made, the principal causes being affrays, assault and battery, disorderly conduct, larceny, and drunkenness. No record is kept of the property reported to the police as lost or stolen, or of the number of station-house lodgers. No free meals are given to these lodgers. The police are required to co-operate with the fire and health departments in all ways. Special police are appointed when circumstances demand it, and while on duty are treated as regular members of the force. The total cost of the department during the past year was $5,200.

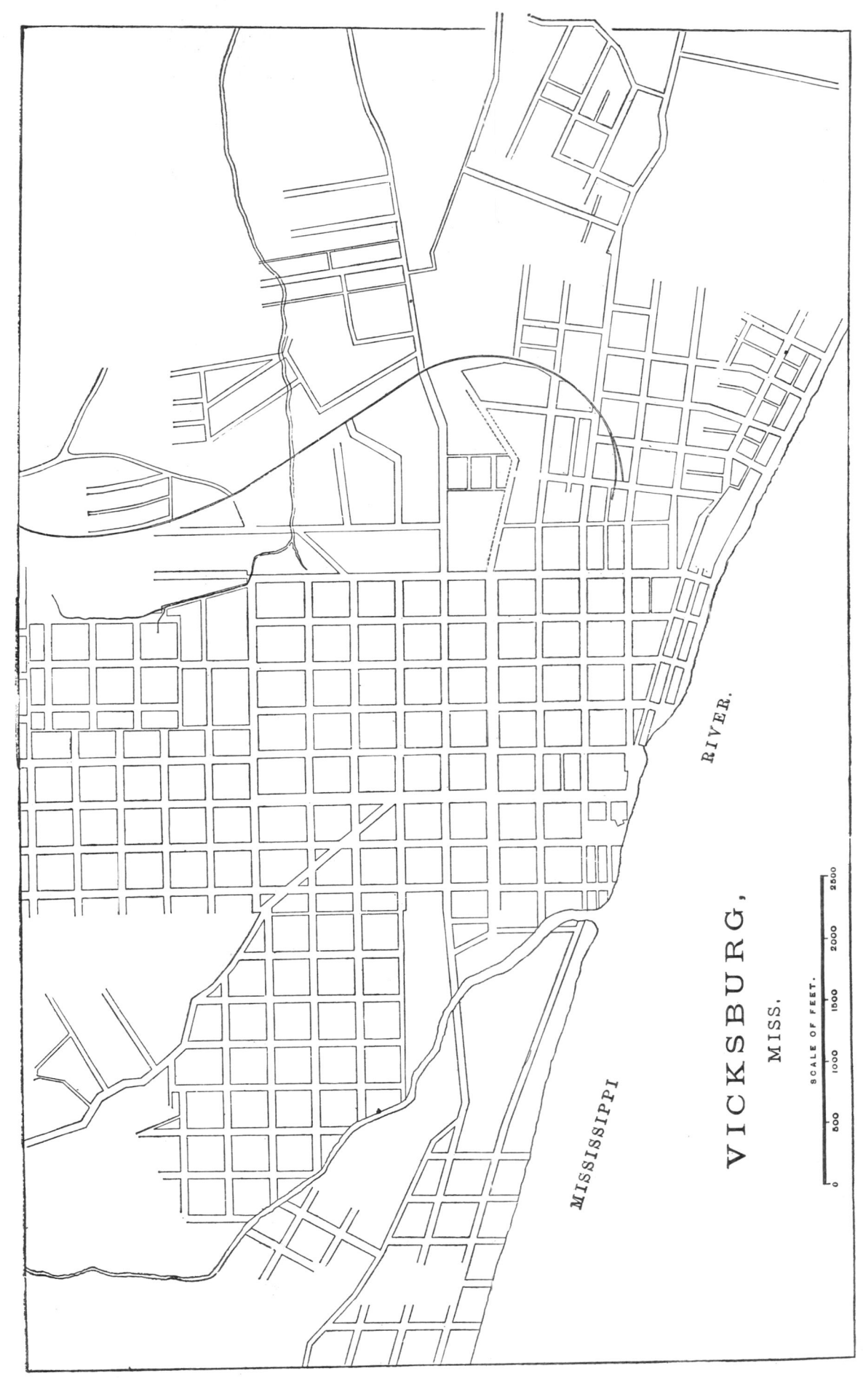

VICKSBURG,

MISS.

SCALE OF FEET.

0   500   1000   1500   2000   2500

MISSISSIPPI

RIVER.

MISSISSIPPI.

VICKSBURG,
WARREN COUNTY, MISSISSIPPI.

POPULATION

IN THE
AGGREGATE,
1840-1880.

	Inhab.
1790	......
1800	......
1810	......
1820	......
1830	......
1840	3,104
1850	3,678
1860	4,591
1870	12,443
1880	11,814

POPULATION

BY
SEX, NATIVITY, AND RACE,
AT
CENSUS OF 1880.

Male	5,575
Female	6,239
Native	10,875
Foreign-born	939
White	5,975
Colored	*5,839

* Including 1 Chinese and 2 Indians.

Latitude: 32° 23′ North; Longitude: 90° 50′ (west from Greenwich); Altitude: 350 feet.

FINANCIAL CONDITION:

Total Valuation: $3,582,000; per capita: $303 00.   Net indebtedness: $373,218; per capita: $31 59.   Tax per $100: $4 45.

VICKSBURG IN 1880.

The following statistical accounts, collected by the Census Office, indicate the present condition of Vicksburg:

LOCATION.

The city lies on the east bank of the Mississippi river, midway between New Orleans and Memphis. It is the capital of Warren county, and is the first city in size and importance in the state. Vicksburg is built on a range of hills that skirt the Mississippi and Yazoo valley from Memphis, and touches the river-bank here. It is therefore the natural outlet for the products of the country near the Mississippi, and the fertile valleys of the Yazoo, Sunflower, and tributary streams. The leading staple is cotton, and the commerce and no small degree of the city's prosperity depend on the success of the cotton crop. Several lines of river steamers have their termini here. Vicksburg has a merchants' and cotton exchange, banks, saw-mills, lumber factories, etc. The Vicksburg and Meridian railroad, from Meridian, terminates here; the Vicksburg, Shreveport, and Pacific railroad has its eastern terminus opposite Vicksburg on the river, and runs to Monroe, Louisiana; and the Mississippi Valley and Ship Island railroad runs from Vicksburg to Goodrum's, Mississippi.

Formerly Vicksburg was situated directly on the east bank of the river, with a long narrow neck of land forming a peninsula opposite the city. During the siege of Vicksburg, in 1863, General Grant attempted to divert the channel of the river through the peninsula, 3 miles below the city, but failed. On the 26th of April, 1876, the peninsula, which had been gradually wearing away for years, had narrowed to 153 feet in width, and, at 2.10 p. m. on that day, the water broke through, forming a cut-off directly opposite the city, so that Vicksburg is now upon a branch of the river with an island in front.

PUBLIC BUILDINGS.

Vicksburg has the usual complement of churches, schools, and municipal accessories.

PLACES OF AMUSEMENT.

Vicksburg has one theater, seating capacity 600, and a concert-hall controlled by a club. Theaters pay a yearly license fee to the city of $50. There are no concert- and beer-gardens.

DRAINAGE.

With the exception of a single brick sewer in Washington street, draining but a limited portion of the city, the sewerage of Vicksburg is entirely by surface gutters, which convey the drainage into the river.

CEMETERIES.

Vicksburg has 2 burial grounds—the *City Cemetery* and the *Jewish Cemetery*. The first lies northeast of the city and contains 50 acres; the latter lies to the east.

The City cemetery is owned and controlled by the city. Lots herein are sold, 20 by 20 feet, at $30 each, and purchasers, it is stated, are not required to exercise any care of their lots or to improve them in any way.

The Jewish cemetery is owned by the Hebrew society. In it interments are made in rows, according to age and sex, there being a row each for male adults, female adults, male infants, and female infants. Lots are not sold as in the City cemetery.

Before burials can be made a certificate of death must be given by the attending physician to the health officer, who then issues a permit. The lawful depth of graves is 5½ feet, but, owing to the wetness of the ground at certain seasons of the year, all graves can not be dug to this depth. There is no regulation concerning the time that may elapse between death and burial. The total number of interments in both cemeteries, from 1852 to 1880, inclusive, is 15,593. This includes many soldiers who died or were killed during the civil war and interred here, all still-born infants, and all who died within the city limits and were afterward sent elsewhere for interment; so in this respect the figures represent the total of a mortuary register rather than a precise record of interment.

MARKETS.

Vicksburg's market-house is located on Munroe street, between Main and Jackson streets. It is 160 by 36 feet in dimensions, and contains 8 meat, 6 fish, and 24 vegetable stalls. Along the sidewalks and around the market is standing-space for at least 50 wagons. Meat stalls rent for $100 a year each, while the total rental for the rest of the stalls is about $900 per annum. The market is open from 4 to 8 p. m., and the building is valued at $4,000. By far the greater amount of the retail supply of meats, poultry, fish, and vegetables of the city is sold at private stores and stands. An ordinance prohibits peddling or hawking during market hours.

POLICE.

The police force of Vicksburg is appointed and governed by the board of mayor and aldermen. Under the supervision of the mayor the chief of police is the commanding and executive officer of the force. He must devote his whole time to the discharge of his duties, which include the enforcement of all laws and ordinances, and he must attend to and endeavor to secure the prosecution and conviction of all offenders. His salary is $125 per month. The rest of the force consists of 16 men, including 2 guards at the prison and 2 guards for the street-gang. The uniform for winter is of heavy blue cloth with black hat, and for summer it is blue flannel with Panama hat. The men pay for their uniforms. Policemen are equipped with pistol, club and belt, and whistle. Patrolmen are divided into day and night forces, each serving 12 hours. During the past year there were 2,136 arrests made, chiefly for drunkenness, disorderly conduct, fighting, gaming, vagrancy, larceny, etc. Property stolen and lost and reported to the police during the year amounted to $22,033, and of this, $19,065 was recovered and returned to the owners. During the same period there were 421 station-house lodgers, as against 511 in 1879. No food of any consequence is furnished to these lodgers. The police force co-operates with the fire department by saving property at fires and preserving it from theft, and by preventing interference with the firemen's work. Special policemen are appointed by the chief, for service at elections and upon holidays; their standing and duties are the same as those of the regular force. The yearly cost of the police force (1880) is about $10,000.

ARKANSAS.

LITTLE ROCK,

PULASKI COUNTY, ARKANSAS.

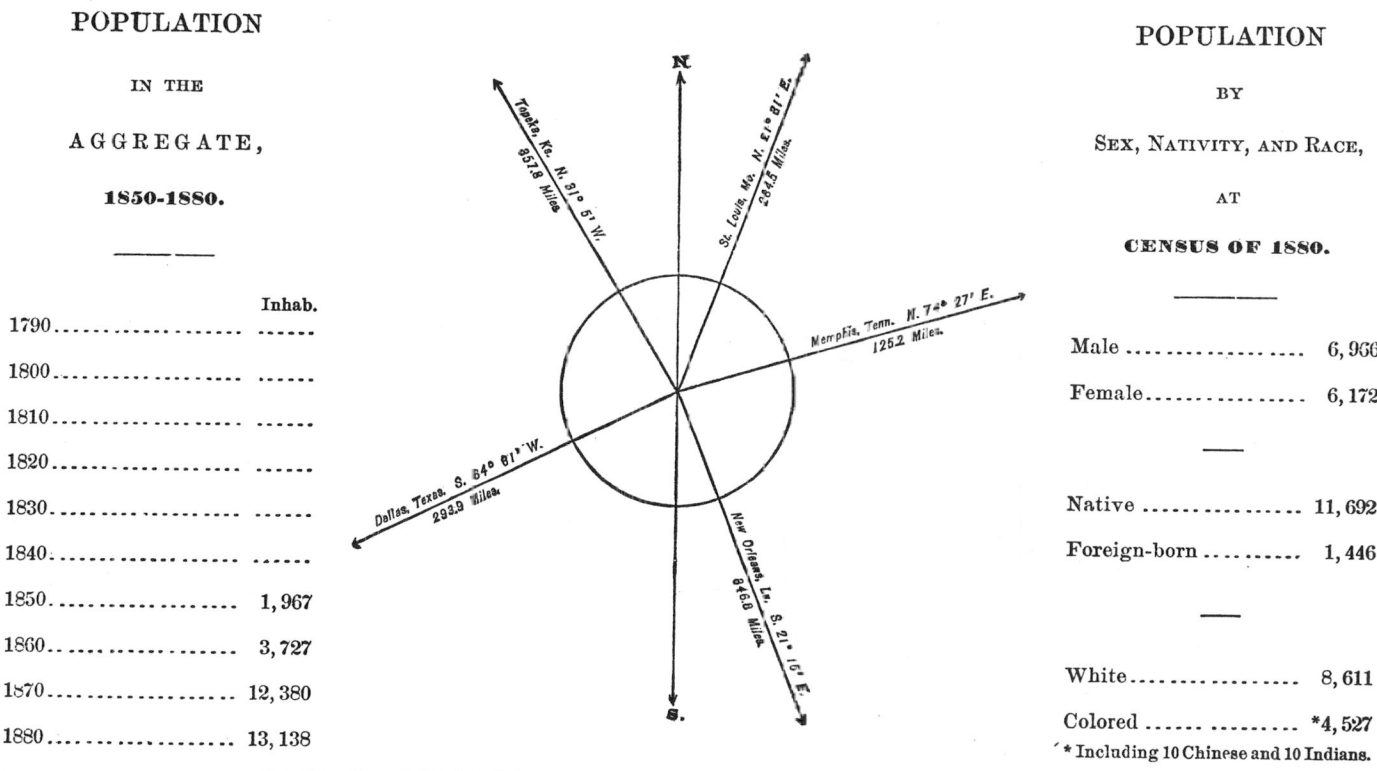

POPULATION

IN THE

AGGREGATE,

1850-1880.

	Inhab.
1790	......
1800	......
1810	......
1820	......
1830	......
1840	......
1850	1,967
1860	3,727
1870	12,380
1880	13,138

POPULATION

BY

SEX, NATIVITY, AND RACE,

AT

CENSUS OF 1880.

Male	6,966
Female	6,172
Native	11,692
Foreign-born	1,446
White	8,611
Colored	*4,527

* Including 10 Chinese and 10 Indians.

Latitude: 34° 40′ North; Longitude: 92° 12′ (west from Greenwich).

FINANCIAL CONDITION:

Total Valuation: $4,465,205; per capita: $340 00.   Net Indebtedness: $335,243; per capita: $25 52.   Tax per $100: $3 85.

LITTLE ROCK.

Little Rock, the capital of the state, was laid out and settled in 1820. It is situated near the center of the state, on the south bank of the Arkansas river, 250 miles above its mouth, where it empties into the Mississippi river. It is built upon the first high land reached in ascending the river, which is here 1,200 feet wide and navigable 8 months in the year for large steamboats, smaller ones plying to Fort Smith, on the border of Indian territory,

300 miles above. The rocky cliff on which the city stands, and from which it takes its name, is not more than 50 feet above the river, while the Big Rock, beginning 2 miles above, is a precipitous range rising abruptly some 500 feet.

RAILROAD COMMUNICATIONS.

Little Rock is touched by the following railroads:

The Little Rock and Fort Smith railroad, to Fort Smith.

The Memphis and Rittle Rock railroad, to Memphis.

The Saint Louis, Iron Mountain, and Southern railroad, from Saint Louis, Missouri, to Texarkana, Texas.

No further information regarding the city was furnished.

LOUISIANA.

NEW ORLEANS.

POPULATION

IN THE

AGGREGATE,

1820-1880.

———

	Inhab.
1790	....
1800	....
1810	17,242
1820	27,176
1830	29,737
1840	102,193
1850	116,375
1860	168,675
1870	191,418
1880	216,090

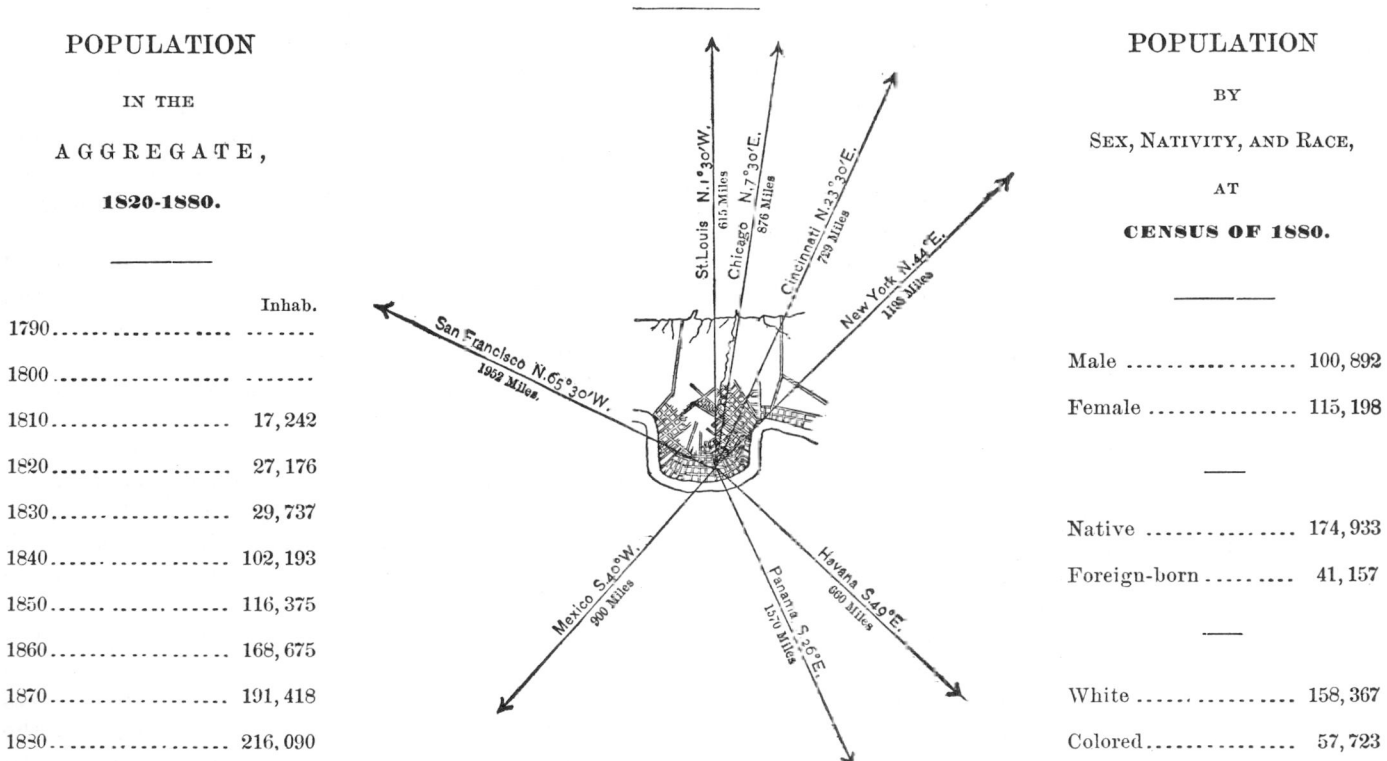

POPULATION

BY

SEX, NATIVITY, AND RACE,

AT

CENSUS OF 1880.

———

Male	100,892
Female	115,198

———

Native	174,933
Foreign-born	41,157

———

White	158,367
Colored	57,723

Latitude: 29° 56′ 59″ North; Longitude: 90° 4′ 9″ (west from Greenwich); Altitude: 0 to 15± feet.

FINANCIAL CONDITION:

Total Valuation: $91,794,350; per capita: $425 00.   Net Indebtedness: $17,736,509; per capita: $82 08.   Tax per $100: $2 63.

HISTORICAL SKETCH.[a]

SITE AND ORIGIN.

The Mississippi river, between the states of Mississippi and Louisiana, flowing at first southward, touches, on its eastern side, at the city of Vicksburg, a line of high, abrupt hills or bluffs, the eastern boundary of its later alluvial basin. The direction of this bluff-line is southwesterly; and the river, turned from its southward course by it, flows in this new direction, occasionally impinging upon the abrupt barrier, as at Grand Gulf, Natchez, and Fort Adams, and presently turns again, with the bluffs, more directly toward the south, striking their base and swinging off from it, at Tunica, at Bayou Sara, and finally at Baton Rouge.

Just beyond this point the bluff-line swerves rapidly to a due eastward course, and declines gradually until in the parish of St. Tammany, in Louisiana, some 30 miles from the eastern boundary of the state, it sinks entirely down into a broad tract of wet prairie and sea-marsh, the mainland coast of various inlets from the Gulf of Mexico. It is the general belief that this line of elevated land, now some 80 or 90 miles due north of the Louisiana coast, was the pre-historic shore-line of the Gulf.

---

a In the preparation of the report on the city of New Orleans, the local assistant, George W. Cable, esq., not only secured and transmitted a very large proportion of the detailed information concerning the present and the past condition of the city, in response to schedules of interrogatories, but to him alone is due the careful and elaborate historical sketch with which the report is introduced.

Close under the Mississippi bluffs, where they make their short turn to the east, the bayou Manchac, once the Iberville river, and a chain of lakes—Maurepas, Pontchartrain, and Borgne—connected by navigable *passes* and *rigolets*, formerly (until the obstruction of bayou Manchac by the military forces of the United States in 1814) united the waters of Mississippi river with those of Mississippi sound. Meanwhile the river itself, turning less abruptly and taking a southeasterly course, cuts off between itself and these lakes a portion of its own delta formation. This fragment of half-made country, comprising something over 1,700 square miles of river shore, swamp and marsh lands, was once widely known as Orleans island.

In outline it is extremely irregular. Its most regular boundary, that of the river bank, is very tortuous, while its width varies, even in its older portions, from 57 miles across the parishes of Plaquemines and St. Bernard, to less than 5 miles from the river at English Turn to the margin of lake Borgne. Another narrow region is seen between the river and lake Pontchartrain, where these two waters approach to within 6 miles of each other.

This occurs at a point almost equally distant from the closed entrance of bayou Manchac, the upper end of Orleans island, and its lower end at the mouth of the Mississippi. In other words, it is 107 miles above the point where the waters of the river finally meet the sea at the outer end of Eads' jetties; in latitude 29° 56′ 59″ and longitude 90° 04′ 09″ west from Greenwich; distant 1,242 miles by river or 700 by rail from St. Louis; 1,760 by sea or 1,377 by rail from New York; 4,800 from Liverpool and 4,800 from Havre. On this spot, in February of the year 1718, was founded the city of New Orleans.

The colony of Louisiana, established nineteen years before at Biloxi, some 85 miles to the east, on the shore of Mississippi sound, had not exceeded at any time the number of a few hundred souls; yet, from the first it had been divided into two factions, one bent on the discovery of gold and silver, the development of pearl fisheries, the opening of a fur trade, and a commerce with South America, and therefore in favor of a sea-coast establishment; the other advocating the importation of French agriculturists and their settlement, in large numbers, on the alluvial banks of the Mississippi.

This wiser design, though faithfully urged by its friends, was for years overruled under the commercial policy and monopoly of the merchant, Anthony Crozat; but when his large but unremunerative privileges fell from his hands into those of John Law, director-general of the famed Mississippi Company, Bienville, governor of the colony, was permitted to found New Orleans, with a view to removing to the banks of the Mississippi the handful of French and Canadians who were struggling against starvation in the irrational search after sudden wealth on the sterile beaches of Mississippi sound and Massacre island.

The site, which Bienville had chosen a year before, offered to a superficial glance but feeble attractions. The land, highest at the river's edge, where it was but 10 feet above sea-level, sank back within the course of a mile to a minimum of a few inches. It was covered, for the most part, with a noisome and almost impenetrable cypress swamp, and was visibly subject to frequent if not annual overflow. One hundred miles and more lay between the spot and the mouth of a river whose current, in the time of its floods, it was maintained no vessel could overcome.

But the sagacity and Canadian pioneer craft of Bienville had seen its advantages. The bayous of St. John and Sauvage, navigable by small sea-going vessels to within a mile of the Mississippi's bank, led by a short course to the open waters of the lakes, and thus to the streams emptying into those lakes on their farther side, to the countries pierced by these streams, and eastward through the same lakes to Mississippi sound and the Gulf of Mexico. On the opposite side of the Mississippi another easy avenue to and from the sea was presented by the bayou Barataria and the net-work of streams and bays of which it forms a part. By the same waters the wide countries of the Atchafalaya, the Attakapas, and the Opelousas were also made accessible; while northward the Mississippi and its great valley stretched beyond known limits.

Here, therefore, M. de Bienville decided to establish the post which later became his capital, and placed a detachment of twenty-five convicts and as many carpenters, who, with some *voyageurs* from the Illinois, made a clearing and erected a few scattered huts along the bank of the river.

POPULATION AND SOCIAL ORDER.

In the following year Bienville advocated the removal of the capital to New Orleans; but while the matter was under discussion, the settlement suffered a total inundation, and the project was for a time abandoned. However, it continued to be a trading post of the Mississippi Company; in January, 1720, it was the final returning point of M. de la Harpe, after his arduous expedition up Red river; in April was put under the military command of M. de Noyan, and in December was again urgently recommended by Bienville, in colonial council, as the proper place for the seat of government. His wishes were still outvoted; but he sent his chief of engineers, Sieur Le Blond de la Tour, a Knight of St. Louis, to the settlement, with orders "to choose a suitable site for a city worthy to become the capital of Louisiana". Stakes were driven, lines drawn, streets marked off, town lots granted, ditched, and palisaded, a rude levee thrown up along the river front, and the scattered settlers of the neighborhood gathered into the form of a town.

In 1721, warehouses had already been erected, and Bienville, in certain governmental regulations, reserved the right to make his residence in the new city. Finally, in June of the following year (1722), the royal commissioners

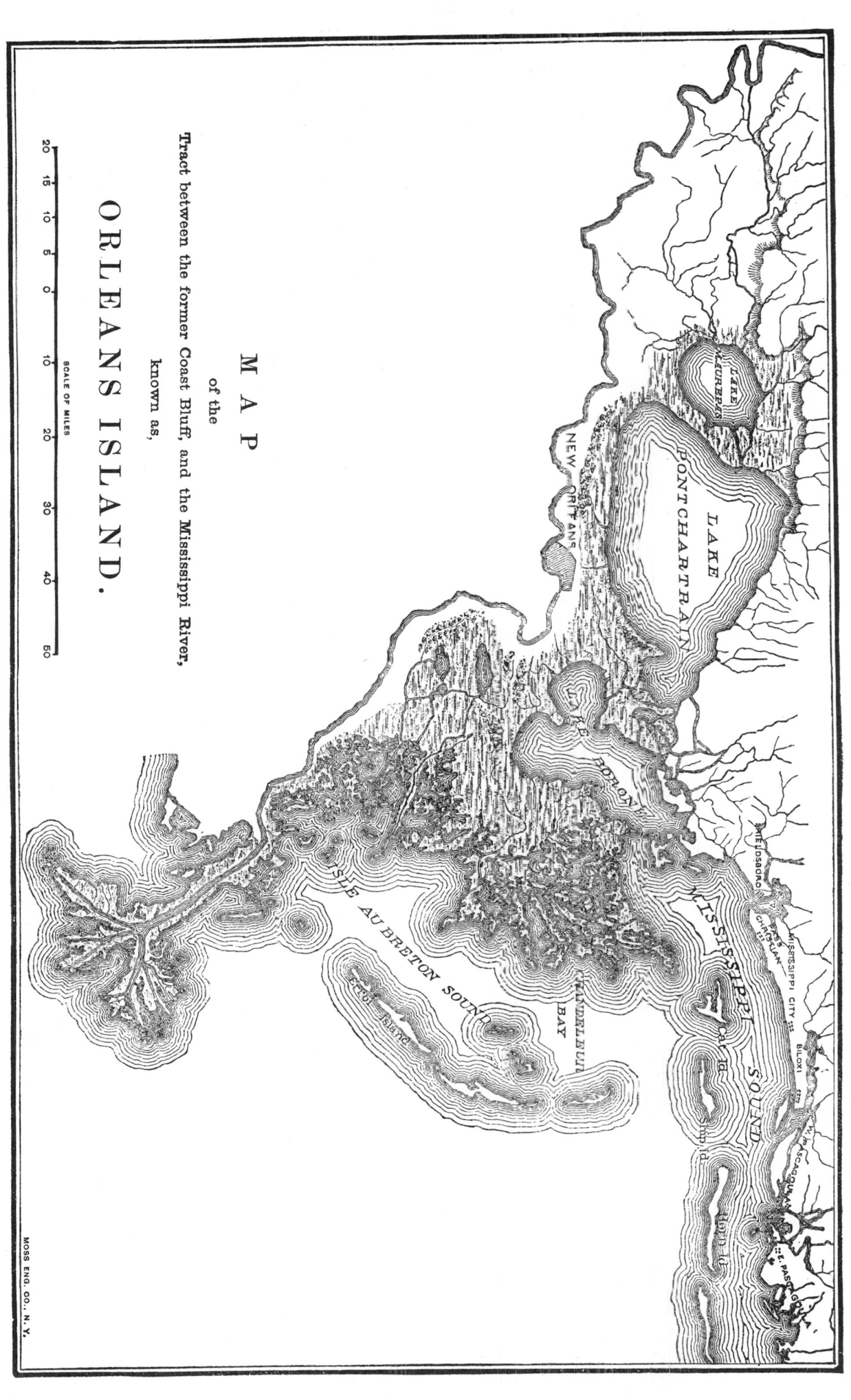

MAP

of the

Tract between the former Coast Bluff, and the Mississippi River,

known as,

ORLEANS ISLAND.

SCALE OF MILES

20 15 10 5 0 10 20 30 40 50

MOSS ENG. CO., N. Y.

having at length given orders to transfer the seat of government, a gradual removal of the company's effects and troops from Biloxi to New Orleans was begun. In August Bienville completed the transfer, by moving thither the gubernatorial headquarters. The place, in January preceding these accessions, already contained 100 houses and 300 inhabitants.

The large proportion of a house to every three persons—if, indeed, the quartering of troops in barracks did not make it still greater—points to the fact that most of these dwellings were not homes in that full significance which includes the family relation. Though a church of some humble sort was not wanting, and a public hospital had been established, and though the presence of a few ships in the river lent one characteristic of a sea-port, yet, in the poverty of its appliances for domestic and for public comfort, in the wildness of the half-cleared ground, in the frailness of its palisade huts, and the rude shelters which took the name of public buildings, and especially in the undue preponderance of adults and males in the population, the place presented more the features of a hunting or a mining camp than of a town.

Its instability had already been brought painfully to view. On the morning of September 11, 1722, a storm fell upon the land with such force that the church, the hospitals, and thirty dwellings were destroyed; crops were prostrated, and the rice, in particular, was rendered worthless.

The next year, 1723, brought no better fortune. The "Mississippi bubble" reached that point in its well-known history, where it was beginning to reveal its embarrassments, and the colonists of Louisiana found themselves participating in the widespread distress which those complications produced.

Resort, even in miniature, to the insane example set them in France, of an absurd system of credits, gave its logical results; the year 1724 brought, for the moment, a satisfactory relation between the suffering planting interest and the company's mercantile representatives in New Orleans; moreover, new industries—notably the raising of indigo and its manufacture—were introduced; debts were paid with paper; and the little city in embryo found herself the metropolis of an agricultural province, the total population of whose far-scattered plantations, missions, and military posts, was approaching 5,000 souls, and giving promise of abundant commercial tribute. When the secondary phase—financial collapse—followed, the colonists were extricated from their mutual obligations by the gross expedient of a scaling process, applied by royal edict and four times repeated; and under this treatment, as under a conflagration, the year 1726 brought in a sounder, though a shorn, prosperity.

But though the population of New Orleans was now approaching the number of 1,600 inhabitants, the restraints of social life continued to be few and weak. A few civil and military officials of high rank had brought their wives from France, and a few Canadians had brought theirs from Canada; but these were rare exceptions, inappreciable in the total population. The male portion of the people, composed principally of soldiers, trappers, miners, galley-slaves, and redemptioners bound for three years' service, was hardly of the disposition spontaneously to assume the responsibilities of citizenship, or to realize the necessity of public order, while the still disproportionately small number of females was almost entirely from the unreformed and forcibly transported inmates of houses of correction, with a few Choctaw squaws and African slave women. Gambling, dueling, and vicious idleness were indulged in to such a degree as to give the authorities grave concern.

But now the company, as required by its charter, addressed its efforts to the improvement of both the architectural and the social features of its provincial capital, and the years 1726 and 1727 are conspicuous for these endeavors. The importation of male vagabonds and criminals had already ceased. Stringent penalties were laid upon gambling, and steps were taken for the promotion of education and religion.

Though the plan of the town comprised a parallelogram of some 4,000 feet river front, by a depth of 1,800, and was divided into regular squares of 300 feet front and depth, yet its appearance was disorderly and squalid. A few board cabins of split cypress, thatched with cypress bark, were scattered confusedly over the swampy ground, surrounded and isolated from each other by willow brakes and reedy ponds and sloughs, bristling with dwarf palmetto and swarming with reptiles.

Midway of the river front two squares, one behind the other, had been reserved, the front one as a parade ground or *Place d'Armes* (now Jackson square), the other for ecclesiastical uses. The middle of this rear square had, from the first, been occupied by a church, and is at present the site of St. Louis Cathedral.

On the left of and adjoining this church was now (1720) erected a convent for a company of Capuchin priests, and the spiritual care of that portion of the province between the mouths of the Mississippi and the Illinois, assigned to them three years before, was given into their charge. A company of Ursuline nuns, commissioned to open a school for girls and to attend the sick in hospital, arrived the year following from France, and was given temporary quarters in a house at the north corner of Bienville and Chartres streets, while the foundations of a large and commodious nunnery were laid for them in the square bounded by the river front, Chartres street, the Rue de l'Arsenal (now Ursulines), and the unnamed street below, afterward called Hospital street—the extreme lower limit of the town as then settled. This building, completed in 1730, was occupied by the order for ninety-four years, vacated by them in 1824 to remove to the larger and more retired convent on the river shore near the present lower limits of the city, where they remain at this day; the older house becoming in 1831 the state-house, and in 1834, as at present, the seat of the archbishop of Louisiana. A soldiers' hospital was built close to the convent in the square next above.

The enlightened aid of the Jesuits was at the same time enlisted in behalf of male education and of agriculture On the 11th of April, 1726, Bienville granted to a company of these a tract of land to which much interest attaches, inasmuch as it afterward became the site of the main "American" commercial quarter of New Orleans. It comprised an area of 20 arpents (3,600 feet) front, by 50 arpents (9,000 feet) depth, within straight lines, and lay within boundaries now indicated by Common, Tchoupitoulas, Annunciation, and Terpsichore streets, and the bayou St John; for at that time this bayou extended far up into the bend of the river in a depression somewhat beyond the present Hagan avenue, and not yet entirely extinct, parallel with the almost south-to-north course of the Mississippi, as it flowed along the front of the described grant. To this was added, January 22, 1728, another grant of 5 arpents front by 50 deep, next above the first. On the 3d of December, 1745, the fathers bought a further tract of 7 arpents front adjoining the second, and thus eventually comprised within their title the whole of the present first district from Felicity to Common streets. The space between Common and Canal streets was reserved by the government as a "terre commune" for fortifications and a public road. On this grant the Jesuits settled in 1727. A house and chapel were built for them, slaves were furnished for their projected fields, and valuable privileges were given them. No educational enterprise seems to have had their immediate attention, but a myrtle orchard (myrtle wax being a colonial staple) was planted on their river front, and much encouragement was given to agriculture by the example of their industry and enterprise. The orange, the fig, the sugar-cane, and probably the indigo plant, were introduced by them into the colony.

It was not Bienville's privilege to effect these and other grateful changes in the aspect of the city he had founded. The schemes of official rivals had procured his displacement, and in the preceding October he had been recalled to France and the office of commandant-general filled by his successor, M. Périer. The new governor was a lieutenant in the French navy, and a man of many excellent qualifications for command, though deserving, far more than the captain-general who filled the same chair fifty years later, the soubriquet of "cruel", which only the latter received.

Under M. Périer improvements progressed rapidly, though several which, in at least one excellent history of the colony, have been enumerated as of this period, must be attributed to later dates. Drainage, however, and protection from flood, received immediate attention. A levee of 18 feet crown was thrown up along the water's edge, exceeding in length the entire front of the town, and was continued, on smaller proportions, 18 miles up, and as many down, the river. But no attempt at fortification was made until three years after. On a well-known official map belonging to the archives of the department of the marine in Paris, the location of every building in New Orleans is shown with undoubted accuracy, as the town presented itself to the eye in 1728. The ancient Place d'Armes, of the same rectangular figure that, as Jackson square, it has to-day, but larger by the width of the present sidewalk, is shown as an open plat of grass crossed by two diagonal paths, and occupying the exact middle of the town front. Behind it stood the parish church, built, like most of the public buildings, of brick, on the site of the present cathedral. On the church's right were a small guard-house and prisons, and on the left was the dwelling of the Capuchins. On the front of the square which flanked the Place d'Armes above, the government-house looked out upon the river. Its ground extended back through the square to Chartres street. In the corresponding square, on the lower side of the Place d'Armes, at the corner of Ste. Anne and Chartres, diagonally opposite the Capuchins, were the quarters of the government employés. The grounds facing the Place d'Armes, in St. Peter and Ste. Anne streets, were still unoccupied, except by cord-wood and intrenching utensils, and a few pieces of parked artillery, on the one side, and a small house for issuing rations, on the other. Just off the river front, in Toulouse street, against the rear grounds of the government-house, were the smithies of the marine, while correspondingly distant on the other hand two long, narrow buildings, lining either side of the street named for the Duc du Maine, and reaching from the river front nearly to Chartres street, were the king's warehouses. The street later known as Ursulines, was called the Street of the Arsenal. On its upper corner, at the river, was the hospital, with its grounds running along the upper side of the street to Chartres, while in the empty square next below, reserved for an arsenal, Charlevoix, in his copy of the map made in 1744, has properly inserted the convent of the Ursulines. The barracks and the company's forges were back in the square bounded by Royal, St. Louis, Bourbon, and Conti streets. In the extreme upper corner of the city, on the river front, at what in late years became the corner of Customhouse and Decatur streets, were the house and grounds of the governor, and in the square immediately behind them the humbler quarters transiently occupied by the Jesuits. At the north corner of Bienville and Chartres was the temporary dwelling of the nuns. No resident had ventured to build beyond Dauphin street, though twenty-two empty squares were free to choose among, nor had any one settled below the street of the Arsenal or above that of Bienville, except Bienville himself and the Jesuit fathers. Orleans street, cutting the little city transversely in half behind the church, seemed a favorite quarter with inconspicuous citizens, while all along the river front, from Bienville to Arsenal street, and also in Chartres and Royal, rose the homes of the official and commercial potentates of the colony—some small, low, and built of cypress wood; others of brick, or half brick, half frame, broad and high; that is, of two or even two-and-a-half stories. Above the Place d'Armes, between the river front and Chartres street, stood those of Delery, Dalby, St. Martin, Dupuy, Rossard, Duval, Beaulieu-Chauvin, D'Ausseville, Perrigaut, Dreux, Mandeville, Tisseraud, Bonnaud, De Blanc, and Dasfeld: below

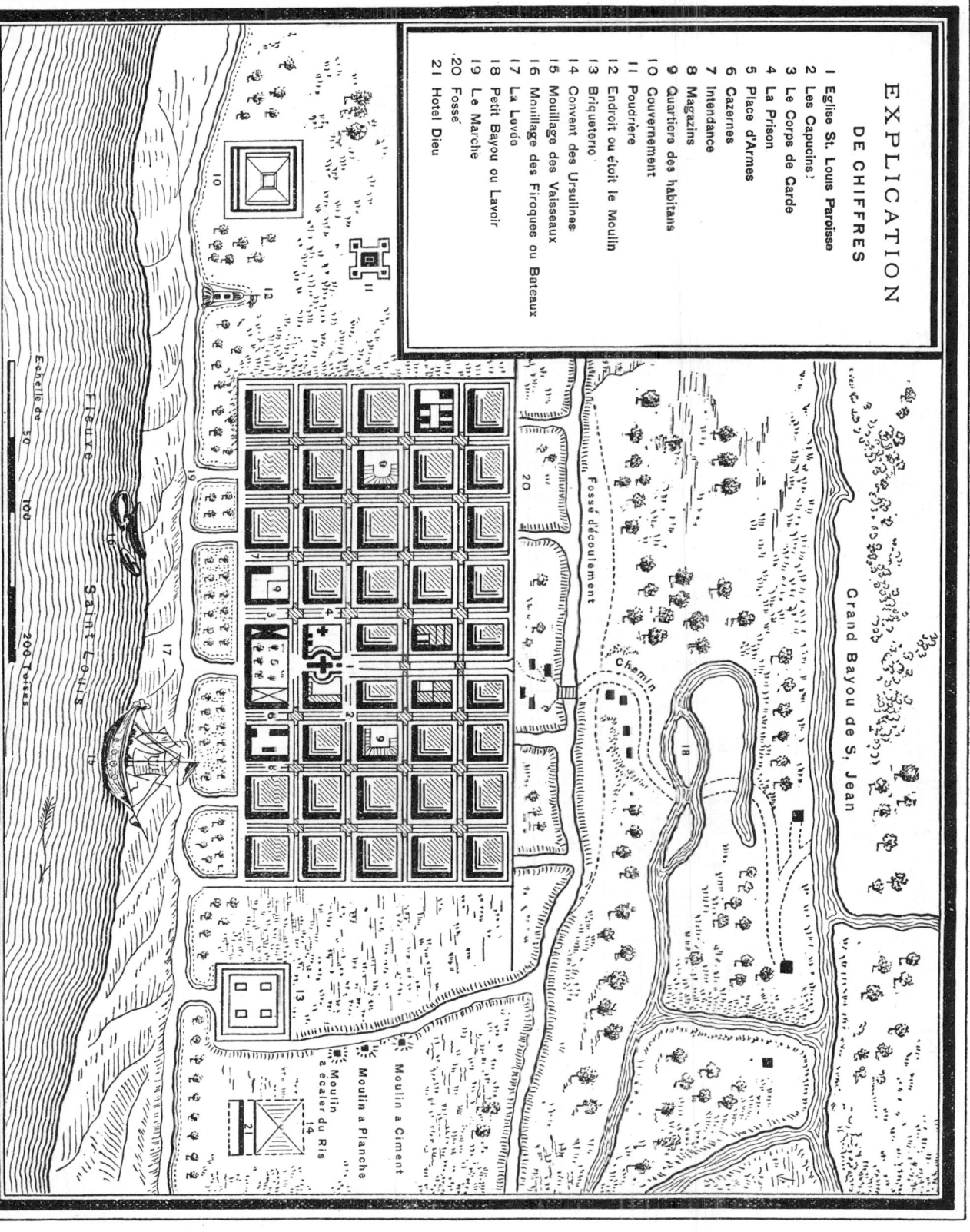

EXPLICATION
DE CHIFFRES

1 Eglise St. Louis Paroisse
2 Les Capucins?
3 Le Corps de Garde
4 La Prison
5 Place d'Armes
6 Cazernes
7 Intendance
8 Magazins
9 Quartiers des habitans
10 Gouvernement
11 Poudrière
12 Endroit ou étoit le Moulin
13 Briquetorio
14 Convent des Ursulines
15 Mouillage des Vaisseaux
16 Mouillage des Piroques ou Bateaux
17 La Lavóa
18 Petit Bayou ou Lavoir
19 Le Marché
20 Fossé
21 Hotel Dieu

Plan de la Nouvelle Orleans Capitale de la Louisiana
1728.

Echelle de 50 100 200 Toises

Fleuve Saint Louis

Fossé découlement

Chemin

Grand Bayou de S. Jean

Moulin a Ciment
Moulin a Planche
Moulin à écaler du Ris

MOSS ENG CO N.Y.

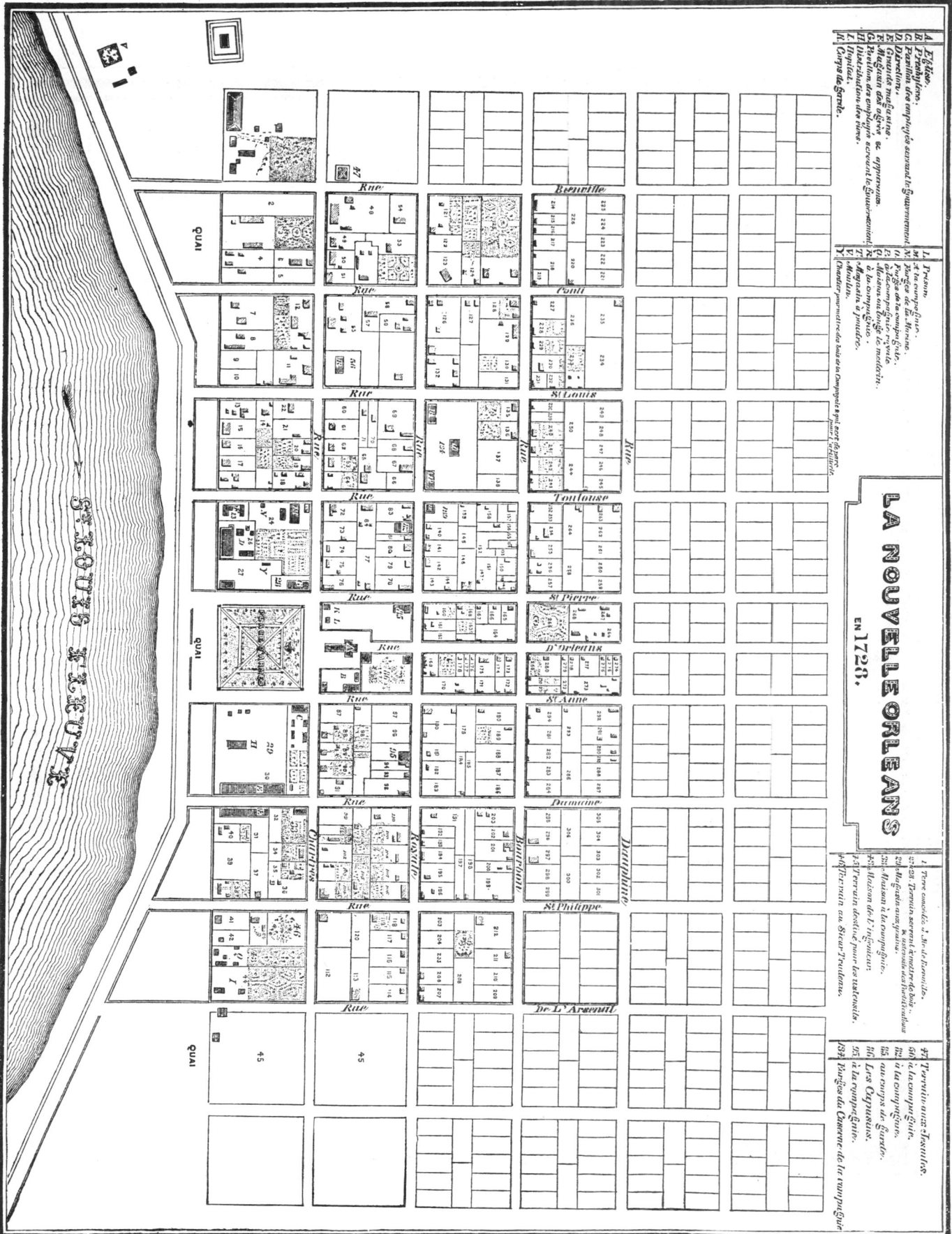

LA NOUVELLE ORLEANS
EN 1728.

the square, Villeur, Provenché, Gauvrit, Pellerin, D'Artaguette, Lazon, Raguet, and others; between Chartres and Royal, De Blanc, Fleurieu, Brulé, Lafrenière, Carrière, Caron, Pascal, and others.

Such was the appearance and condition of New Orleans in 1728, as far as maps could be expected to show them. But the crowning benefit, in this period of innovation, was not to be indicated by charts. In the winter of 1727–'28, there arrived from France the initial consignment of reputable girls, allotted to the care of the Ursulines, to be disposed of, under their discretion, in marriage. They were supplied by the king, on their departure from France, each with a small chest of clothing, and—with similar importations in subsequent years—were long known in the traditions of their colonial descendants, by the honorable distinction of the "*filles à la cassette*"—the girls with trunks, the casket girls.

Thus, as the first decade in the history of New Orleans drew to a close, it became possible to sum up on her account all the true, though roughly outlined, features of a confirmed civilization: the church, the school, courts, hospital, council hall, virtuous homes, a military arm, and a commerce which, though fettered by the monopoly-rights of the Company of the Occident, comprised in its exports rice, indigo, tobacco, timber, furs, wheat, and flour.

INDIAN WARS.

Hardly had the salutary changes just noted been accomplished, when troubles of the gravest sort threatened to arise from the direction of the Chickasaw and Choctaw Indians. Governor Périer called a council of their village chiefs in New Orleans, and the chiefs responding, met and departed with protestations of friendship and loyalty, which persuaded the governor to believe that he had effected a complete pacification. Suddenly, in the winter of 1729–'30, New Orleans was thrown into excitement and consternation by the arrival of a soldier from Fort Rosalie (Natchez), followed in a day or two by a few others, the only survivors escaped to tell of the massacre by the Natchez Indians of over 200 men, and the taking prisoners of 92 women and 155 children. Smaller settlements on the Yazoo river and on Sicily island, in the Washita, had shared a like fate.

The city became at once the base of military operations, and the governor seized the opportunity to effect some improvements of a defensive character. A broad moat was dug around the town, and, by the end of a year, the place was, for the first time, surrounded with a line of fortifications. Meanwhile, every house in New Orleans, and on the neighboring plantations, was supplied with arms and ammunition. From the town and its surroundings, 300 militia and as many regulars were gathered by the governor, and sent, under one of his captains, to the seat of war.

The community which remained behind soon found itself called upon to bear many of the heaviest burdens of war: terror of attack, days of anxious suspense, sudden alarms, false hopes, industrial stagnation, further militia levies, the issue of colonial paper with its natural result—a financial panic—the reception and care of homeless refugees, and an abiding feeling of insecurity, arising from the restiveness of the African slaves in and near the town, where their number equaled or exceeded that of the master race.

The presence of vagrant bands of professedly friendly Indians also became, said Governor Périer, "a subject of terror," and, with a like fear of the blacks, led to the only acts of bloodshed of which New Orleans was the scene in this war. A band of negro slaves, the property of the company, armed and sent for the purpose by Périer himself, fell upon a small party of Chouachas Indians, dwelling peaceably on the town's lower border, and offending in nothing but their proximity, and indiscriminately massacred the entire village. Emboldened by this show of their strength, these negroes conceived the plan of striking for their own freedom, but the plot was discovered, and its leaders executed. Nevertheless, the next year after, the same blacks, incited by fugitive slaves sent among them by the Chickasaws, seemed to have maturely planned an insurrection, and fixed a night for a general destruction of the whites. The unguarded speech of an incensed negress, who had been struck by a soldier, again betrayed them, and eight men and the woman, ringleaders, were put to death, the latter on the gallows, the men on the wheel. The heads of the men were stuck upon posts at the upper and the lower ends of the town front, and at the Tchoupitoulas settlement and at the king's plantation, on the opposite side of the Mississippi.

It affords relief to turn from this record to one which displays human nature in a kindlier aspect. The 250 women and children taken by the Natchez, and retaken from them, were received by the people of New Orleans with every demonstration of compassionate sympathy; they were at first lodged in the public hospital, but the Ursulines, probably just moved into their completed convent, adopted the orphan girls among them; the boys found asylums in well-to-do families, and the whole number of refugees was absorbed into the resident population, many of the widows again becoming wives. Thus this generously accepted burden became a blessing.

By the year 1732, every able-bodied citizen of New Orleans had been called into service. The war lasted three years, and resulted in the total dismemberment of the Natchez people, and the incorporation of its small surviving remnant into the Chickasaw nation. The period of comparative peace that followed, was qualified by the depredations of the Chickasaws, or rather by the people that had found harbor among them—the Natchez and Yazoo Indian refugees.

In 1733, another change of administration restored Bienville to the head of affairs, and the confidence and respect he had always inspired among the Indians may well have raised the hope that the colony and its capital were soon to be extricated from their embarrassments. But no such anticipation was realized. In 1735, the Chickasaw aggressions still continuing, Bienville demanded the surrender of the Natchez and Yazoo refugees, and was refused. Upon this he received instructions from France to make war, and the early spring of 1736 found New Orleans again in the excitement and confusion of marshaling a small army, which by and by, in thirty barges and as many large canoes, embarked on the bayou St. John for a war of extermination against the Chickasaws. In the latter part of June of the same year, Bienville, re-entering the bayou St. John, disembarked the remnant of his forces, sick, wounded, and dispirited, after a short, inglorious, and disastrous campaign.

In September, 1739, another force, consisting of regulars, militia, three companies of marines lately arrived from France, and 1,600 Indians, left New Orleans for the Chickasaw country, this time taking their way up the Mississippi. At a point on the river, near the present site of the city of Memphis, they were joined, according to appointment, by levies from Canada and elsewhere, making a total force of white, red, and black men, numbering upward of 3,600.

Six months passed, the spring of 1740 was at hand, and once more Bienville landed at New Orleans with a sick and starving remnant of the force that had gone out, and with no better result than a discreditable peace. Later, perceiving by the tenor of the French minister's communications to him the severe disfavor with which he was regarded, he wrote to France in January, 1742, asking to be recalled. This was done, and on the arrival of the Marquis de Vaudreuil as his successor, he bade a last farewell to the city which he had founded, and to that Louisiana of which its people fondly called him "the father".

To one who will observe closely the effects of these wars upon the city of New Orleans, in the light of after-events, two main results will come prominently forward, the one moral, the other commercial.

As to the moral, it is enough here to note these two facts: one, that the first generation native to New Orleans sprang up and grew among the harsh influences of a frontier struggle against savage aggression, and for the maintenance of an arbitrary supremacy over two other races; the other, that this struggle was carried on under the deeply corrupted government of Louis XV of France.

The commercial result was one that marked an era in the history of the city. The Company of the Indies, into which the Company of the Occident, or Mississippi Company, had been absorbed, discouraged by the expense and continuance of the Natchez war, and esteeming their privileges on the Guinea coast and in the East Indies more worthy of their attention, had, in January, 1731, tendered, and in April of the same year had effected, the surrender of its western charter to the French government. Thus New Orleans became, for the first time, free from private monopoly rights on its commerce.

In response to the king's establishment, between Louisiana and his subjects elsewhere, of a virtual free trade, a fresh intercourse sprang up with the ports of France and of the West Indies, a moderate but valued immigration set in from these islands and, despite the Chickasaw campaigns and the emission of paper money, increased from year to year, while at the close of these campaigns business still further revived, and the town, as it never had done before, began spontaneously to develop from within outward, by the enterprise of its own people.

THE FIRST CREOLES.

The term Creole is commonly applied in books to the native of a Spanish colony descended from European ancestors, while often the popular acceptation conveys the idea of an origin partly African. In fact, its meaning varies in different times and regions, and in Louisiana alone has, and has had, its broad and its close, its earlier and its later, significance.

For instance, it did not here first belong to the descendants of Spanish, but of French settlers. But such a meaning implied a certain excellence of origin, and so came early to include any native of French or Spanish descent by either parent, whose pure non-mixture with the slave race entitled him to social rank. Much later the term was adopted by, not conceded to, the natives of European-African or Creole-African blood, and is still so used among themselves. At length the spirit of commerce availed itself of the money value of so honored a title, and broadened its meaning to take in any creature or thing, of variety or manufacture peculiar to Louisiana, that might become an object of sale, as Creole ponies, chickens, cows, shoes, eggs, wagons, baskets, cabbages, etc.

And yet the word has its limitations. The Creoles proper will not share their distinction with the native descendants of those worthy Acadian exiles who, in 1756, and later, found refuge in Louisiana. These remain "cadjiens" or "cajuns" in the third person plural, though Creoles by courtesy in the second person singular; and while there are French, Spanish, and even, for convenience, "colored" Creoles, there are no English, Scotch, Irish, Western, or "Yankee" Creoles, these all being included under the distinctive term "Americans".

Neither the subsequent Spanish nor the American domination has given the Creoles any other than the French tongue as a vernacular, and in fine, there seems to be no more serviceable definition of the Creoles of Louisiana or of New Orleans, than to say they are the French-speaking, native, ruling class.

In noticing the origin and development of this people, it does not seem necessary to distinguish narrowly between the upper and lower social ranks of the settlers from whom they sprang. Many lines of descent, it is true, were of such beginnings as are everywhere and always regarded with conventional disfavor, while a few only sprang from progenitors of military rank and social station; yet, in view of the state of society among the French of that day, the misconceptions of civil and personal rights, and the gross oppressions laid upon one rank of society by another, the children of those who held the weapons of tyranny have probably as good reason (but no better) to look with satisfaction upon their origin, as have those whose ancestors suffered the pains and ignominy of strokes that might more justly have fallen on those who inflicted them.

The first forty-six years of the history of New Orleans, between the date of its founding and that of the cession to Spain, divides into two nearly equal periods. The one, 1718 to 1740, includes the origin and struggle for life against neglect, famine, and savages; the other, 1740 to 1764, the formation process of a native community which the first had but brought into existence.

The earlier of these two periods again easily divides into two equal intervals of eleven years each. That from 1718 to the sudden shock of the Natchez outbreak in 1729, was a term of impassive, embryotic accretion in the various parts and functions of the projected town; while the period of Indian wars, beginning in December, 1729, and ending in the peace made with the Chickasaws in 1740, introduced a more active life, evolving as it progressed, a liberation from the trammels of that company to which the city owes its origin, and bringing in, as it drew to a close, the advance-guard of a fresh and native-born generation, and the beginnings of those new sentiments which the succeeding period was to carry to maturity.

The Natchez war and the company's commercial oppressions—if the statement of the officials who, in 1733, assumed direction of affairs is accepted—had reduced New Orleans almost to starvation. While such a statement, even if accurate, is not proof positive of a state of permanent beggary, it does indicate a non-intercourse with sources of supply and a suffocation of commerce. The comparative freedom offered to trade by the royal government brought, as already noted, a gradual improvement in affairs, which rose, after the close of the Chickasaw campaigns in 1740, into positive commercial life and strength.

Thus private enterprise, the true foundation of material prosperity, was already well established. Indigo, rice, and tobacco were moving in considerable quantities to Europe, and lumber to the West Indies; an import trade, especially from St. Domingo, was active, and traffic with the Indians and with the growing white population along the immense length of the Mississippi and its tributaries, was increasing year by year, when, on the 10th day of May, 1743, the Marquis de Vaudreuil landed in New Orleans.

The appointment of the marquis, member of a family of much influence at court, to be governor of Louisiana, inspired in the minds of the colonists bright anticipations of such royal patronage and enterprise as would greatly broaden the prospects of the colony, and, consequently, increase the importance of its capital.

But if the advent of the "Grand Marquis" aroused expectations of municipal adornment and aggrandizement, those expectations were but feebly met. There was an increase in the number of the troops and a great enhancement of military splendor. In 1751 every second man in the population was a soldier in dazzling uniform. But as to material aid or improvement, the very moderate efforts of the government seem to have overreached the town and to have been directed to the encouragement, not to say taxation, of certain agricultural industries, such as the production of tobacco and myrtle wax, the introduction of sugar-cane, and the granting, yearly, to soldiers chosen for good conduct, of tracts of land, and wives from the Casket girls, the last company of which arrived in 1751, honorable source of many of the best Creole families of to-day.

Two exceptional public works were forced upon the superior council, by the stress of events, during the governorship of De Vaudreuil's successor, Kerlerec, a captain in the royal navy, to whom the marquis gave place February 9, 1753. In the fall of 1758, France and England being at war, the French garrison of Fort Duquesne, on the present site of Pittsburgh, evacuated it, and, taking boats, floated down the Ohio and Mississippi to New Orleans. The barracks flanking the Place d'Armes could not accommodate so many additional occupants, and Governor Kerlerec at once began to build another in the lower part of the city front, at a point afterward indicated by the name Barracks street. Two years later the fortifications about the town, which appear to have fallen into complete dilapidation, were renewed; a line of palisades passed from the river bank below entirely around to the river bank above, with salients at the corners, "a banquette within and a very trifling ditch without." The expected British foe, however, never came to the attack.

Beyond these measures the city was still left to its own spontaneous motion. Drainage, sanitation, fire protection, each a long-felt and urgent need, received no official attention; police regulations, little beyond the strict surveillance of the negro-slave element; and the public credit, alone, a detrimental overshare in further inundations of paper money.

Yet despite these and other drawbacks, the presence of pirates in the Gulf of Mexico, and of English privateers sometimes at the very mouth of the Mississippi, the disaffection and insolent encroachments of Indian allies, adverse seasons (one winter, 1748, being so cold as to destroy all the orange trees), and a desperate degree of corruption in the government, there was in New Orleans, notwithstanding, a certain amount of material growth and progress hardly to be looked for in the presence of such embarrassments and distractions. Between the autumn of 1749 and 1752, "forty-five brick houses were erected".

The period was also, as on a more extensive scale in France, one of transmutation. The children of the first settlers, coming more and more to the front, were taking their parents' places, and with the ductility characteristic of the Latin race, had adapted themselves to the novel mold of their immediate surroundings. Their fathers and mothers were passing away, or retiring into the inactivity of advanced life, and the new active element of New Orleans and its adjacent delta country, was now that new variety of French-speaking, but not French, people, which is made the subject of the present chapter.

Its variation from the trans-atlantic original was much the difference between France itself and the Louisiana delta. A soil of unlimited fertility, instead of being an inducement to industry, became, through the institution of slavery, merely a perpetual assurance of plenty, and, with a luxurious and enervating climate, debased even the Gallic love of pleasure to an unambitious apathy and an unrestrained sensuality. The courteous manners of France were largely retained; but the habit of commanding a dull and abject slave class, over which the laws of the colony gave every white man full powers of police, induced a certain fierce imperiousness of will and temper; while that proud love of freedom, so pervasive throughout the American wilderness, rose at times to an attitude of arrogant superiority over all constraint, and became the occasion of harsh comment in reports sent to France by the officers of the king.

To such a people, unrestrained, proud, intrepid, self-reliant, rudely voluptuous, of a highly intellectual order, yet uneducated, unreasoning, impulsive, and inflammable, the royal governors introduced the frivolities and corruptions of the Bourbon camp and palaces.

The Marquis and Marchioness de Vaudreuil held their colonial court with much pomp and dissipation, and it seems fair to impute to their example much of the love of display which, during the twelve years of the "Grand Marquis'" sojourn in Louisiana, began to be developed among the citizens of its humble metropolis.

In the early part of this period of twenty-four years, between 1740 and 1764, New Orleans, itself, contained a comparatively trivial proportion of slaves. In 1744, for example, the census shows but 300 adults of this class, in a total population which, with 800 adult males, "almost all married," could hardly have been less than 3,000. But these 300 slaves were the servants of that better class of society in which controlling popular sentiments originate, and whose intellectual and moral likeness becomes the conventional pattern. The number of slaves, moreover, rapidly increased, while that of the whites, many, it is likely, being the grantees of lands in the interior, diminished; so that the next census, dating even after the close of this period, shows no preceptible increase in total population, yet gives a proportion of two slaves to every three whites; indicating the general exchange from free white to black slave domestic service and manual labor in New Orleans.

The dwellings of the leading class, built at first principally on the immediate front of the town or the first street behind, seem, later, to have drawn back a square or two. They also spread along toward, and out through, a gate in the palisade wall near its north corner. A road, now one of the streets of the city and still known as Bayou road, issued from this gate and continued its northward course to the village and bayou of St. John. Along this suburban way, surrounded by broad grounds deeply shaded by live-oaks, magnolias, and other evergreen forest trees, and often having behind them plantations of indigo or myrtle, rose the broad, red-roofed, but severely plain and simple frame dwellings of the opulent class, commonly of one or one and a half story height, but generally raised on pillars often 15 feet from the ground, and surrounded by wide verandas.

In the lofty halls and spacious drawing-rooms of these homes, frequently in the heart of the town, in houses of almost squalid exterior, their low, single-story, wooden or brick walls rising from a ground but partially drained even of its storm water, infested with reptile life, and in frequent danger of inundation, was beginning to be seen a splendor of dress and personal adornment, hardly in harmony with the rude simplicity of apartments and furniture, and scarcely to be expected in a town of unpaved, unlighted, and often impassable streets, surrounded by swamps and morasses, on one of the wildest of American frontiers.

To the bad example of ostentatious living, the whole number of colonial officials, with possibly an exception here or there, added that of corruption in office. The governors, the royal commissaries, post-commandants, the Marchioness de Vaudreuil conspicuously, and many others of less pretension, stood boldly accusing and accused of the grossest and the pettiest frauds; the retention and sale of merchandise destined for friendly Indians, and of breadstuffs imported for the king's troops; the traffic of all manner of government favors; the distribution of cadets' commissions to infants and young children, and the entry of their names on the commissariat rolls; officers trading, making slaves of their soldiers, and leading idle, dissolute lives.

Doubtless, where all were reciprocally accusers, the degree of corruption was exaggerated; yet the testimony is official, abundant, corroborative, and verified in the ruinous expenses which later drove France to abandon the maintenance and sovereignty of the colony she had misgoverned for sixty-three years.

In the mean time the effect of such widespread official venality on the people was most lamentable. Public morals were debased, idleness and intemperance became general, speculation in the depreciated paper currency which flooded the colony became the principal pursuit, and insolvency the common condition.

The cause of religion and education made little or no headway. Rival ecclesiastical orders quarreled for spiritual dominion. One small chapel, connected with the public hospital, appears to have been the only house of worship founded during the entire period, and finds mention only in connection with the "war of the Jesuits and Capuchins". This strife continued for years, characterized by "acrimonious writings, squibs, pasquinades, and

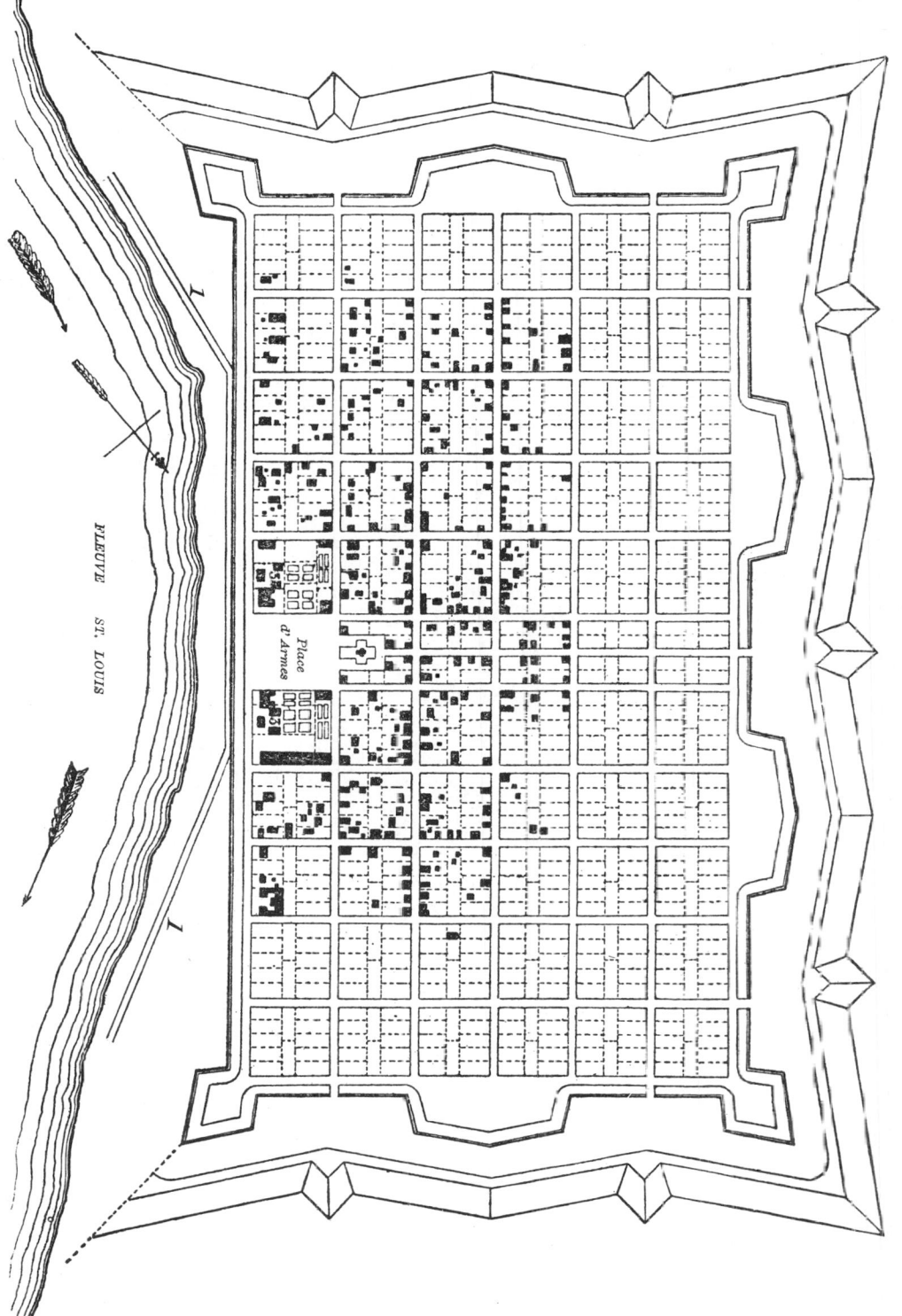

PLAN ET PROJET,
DE LA
NOUVELLE ORLÉANS.
AUGUST 9TH, 1763.
LÉGENDE

1. *Levée de terre pour se garantir des inondations du Fleuve.*
2. *Magasin de la Compagnie.*
3. *Îles de maisons à la Compagnie.*

ECHELLE DE 200 TOISES.

20 40 60 80 100   200 T.

Place d'Armes

FLEUVE ST. LOUIS

satirical songs", the women in particular taking sides with lively zeal. But in July, 1763, the Capuchins were left masters of the field. Agreeably to a decree of the French parliament of the year previous, ordering the expulsion of the Jesuits from the dominions of France, their plantation adjoining the city was confiscated by the superior council. It was sold for a sum equivalent to $180,000, in the latter part of the same year.

The Jesuit fathers, wherever the fault may lie, seem to have put the people of New Orleans, whose male youth they had engaged to educate, very little in their debt, and from the time of their exile this important work was not again regarded as a public interest, until after Louisiana had become an American state.

Thus have been enumerated the origin, surrounding influences, and resulting character and life of the early Creoles of New Orleans. The few events remaining to complete the record of this formative period are of special value, as explaining the sad episode which followed their change of royal masters.

On the 16th of February, 1763, a treaty of peace between England, Spain, and France was signed at Paris. By this treaty the French king ceded to Great Britain "all that he possessed, or had a right to possess, on the left (east) side of the Mississippi", from its source in lake Itasca, by a line through the middle of the stream, to the mouth of Iberville river (bayou Manchac), and so eastward to the sea through the middle of that line of water already indicated as separating Orleans island from the country north of it. "The town of New Orleans and the island on which it stands," therefore, remained to France and to the still immense French province of Louisiana. The navigation of the Mississippi, "including ingress and egress at its mouth," was made absolutely free to the subjects of both empires alike.

The laws governing the French colonies forbade trade with British vessels; yet the wants of the colonists and the mutual advantages offering, soon gave rise to a lively commerce at a point just above the Jesuits' plantation, afterward the river front of the city of Lafayette, and now the fourth district of New Orleans. Here numerous trading vessels, sailing under the British flag, ascending the river and passing the city on the pretext of visiting the new British ports of Manchac and Baton Rouge, landed and carried on their interlope commerce with the merchants from the neighboring city. The corrupt authorities made no attempt to suppress a traffic so advantageous in its pecuniary bearings to the community, though most unfortunate, in accustoming the highest classes and leading minds of the city to justify and practice the getting of honest rights by disingenuous and dishonest courses, and doubly unfortunate in its stimulation of the slave trade. A large business was done at this so-called "Little Manchac" in Guinea negroes, whom the colonists bought of the British, occasioning an increase in the agricultural laboring force of the surrounding country, and the sudden enriching of many of the community.

Meanwhile the English were taking possession of their newly acquired territory. In February, 1764, a Major Loftus, with 400 British troops, came from Mobile to New Orleans, and embarked up the river in ten barges and two canoes for the new British possessions in the Illinois territory. On attempting to land he was fired upon by Indians in ambush, and was finally compelled to return; whereupon he bitterly, and probably unjustly, charged the French colonists with having treacherously instigated the attack. Thus, even extraneous circumstances seemed unhappily tending to create an excited public feeling, at a time when events were impending that called for the most dispassionate consideration. It might be added, that about this time began that assertion of rights and train of events in the thirteen British colonies on the Atlantic coast, which, a few years later, precipitated the American Revolution.

Even before the treaty of Paris, Kerlerec had received orders to return to France and render account of his conduct in office. In March, 1763, the month after the treaty, the king, under the very plausible pretext of retrenchment, ordered the disbanding of all but 300 of his colonial troops. On the 29th of June M. d'Abbadie landed in New Orleans, commissioned to succeed the governor, under the semi-commercial title of director-general, and Kerlerec a little later sailed for France, where he was cast into the Bastile, and "died of grief shortly after his release". The colony was much agitated by the many observable symptoms of some unrevealed design to make a change in their condition, and by and by rumor of what had been secretly transacted came to take the most repellant shape. Yet M. d'Abbadie himself remained as uninformed as the people, and it was only in October, 1764, twenty-three months after the signing of the secret act at Fontaineblean, that the official announcement reached New Orleans of her cession, with that of Orleans island and all Louisiana west of the Mississippi, to the king of Spain.

THE INSURRECTION OF 1768.

"As I was finishing this letter," wrote the director-general, M. d'Abbadie, on the 7th of June, 1764, "the merchants of New Orleans presented me with a petition, a copy of which I have the honor to forward. You will find in it those characteristic features of sedition and insubordination of which I complain."

The object of this petition was to point out a condition of affairs which must have appeared to the New Orleans merchants intolerable, as, in the light of the town's commercial progress, it seems incredible, until it is remembered through what a *débris* of public finances the commerce of a city or country may sometimes make a certain progress.

This despised voice bore, unrecognized by the arbitrary steward who so harshly denounced it to his king's minister, a double prophetic value. There was soon to arise, between the material interests of New Orleans and the heartless oppressions of two corrupt governments, a struggle ending, for her citizens, in ignominy and disaster;

while in the years yet beyond there was a time to come when commerce, not arms, was to rule the destinies, not of a French or Spanish military outpost, but of the great southern seaport of a nation yet to be.

Nothing but the extreme disrelish for such an event could have blinded the people to the fact that the cession was genuine. The king's letter made distinct statement of the fact; the official instructions to M. d'Abbadie, as to the manner of evacuating and surrendering the province, were full and precise; they were, moreover, accompanied by copies of the treaty of cession and the Spanish king's letter of acceptance, and they were ordered to be spread upon the minutes of the superior council at New Orleans, in order that the full text might be publicly and universally accessible.

But to the brave and inflammable Creoles, upon whose character no influence in early life had impressed the habit of calm reasoning, facts were of less value than feelings. Nor can they lightly be criticized for the distemper into which they were thrown. The grievances done their sentiments—of nationality, of justice, even of manhood—need no enumeration; while in their pecuniary interests, unless the transfer was a momentary expedient and a political ruse, the commercial revulsion which it threatened, was likely to leave them no better than bankrupt.

When there was no longer any ground for doubt, a hope was still fostered that a prayer to their king might avert the delayed consummation of the treaty. Early in 1765, therefore, a large meeting was held, of planters from all the nearer parts of the province, and of almost all notable persons in New Orleans, including some of the members of the superior council and other officials. Jean Milhet, the wealthiest merchant in the town, and one of those who had signed the address of the previous June, was sent to France with a petition that the king would arrange with Spain a nullification of the late act. A people much more accustomed than the Creoles to the disappointment of their wishes, might have hoped that a request so consistent with natural rights would not be lightly denied.

Milhet met in Paris Bienville, then in his eighty-sixth year, and in company with him sought the royal audience. This the minister, the Duc de Choiseul—in furtherance of whose policy the transfer had been made—adroitly prevented them from obtaining, and their mission was courteously but early brought to naught.

But a hope that never had real foundations could not be undermined, and the Creoles, though in 1766 they received tidings from Milhet announcing the failure of his undertaking, fed their delusion upon the continued non-arrival of any officer from Spain to take possession of the province, and upon the continued stay of Milhet in France.

It would be strange, too, if this error was not further promoted by the contrast between these delays and the promptness with which the British government was taking possession of that part of Louisiana and the Floridas which had fallen to it by the treaty of Paris. For the acting governor, Aubry—M. d'Abbadie having died on the 4th of February, 1765—was not a little concerned at the perpetual passage through the harbor of New Orleans of English ships of war and troops, while without ships, ammunition, or money, and only a few soldiers, whose term of enlistment was out, he was compelled to await the slow motions of Spain in receiving a gift which she did not covet, and which had been given to her only for fear it might otherwise fall into the hands of Great Britain.

However, in the summer of this year a rumor came to the colonists that Spain had moved a step forward, and not long afterward the superior council received from Havana a letter of the 10th of July, addressed to them by Don Antonio de Ulloa, a commodore in the Spanish navy, a scientific scholar, an author of renown, and at the date of this letter the royally commissioned Spanish governor of Louisiana. The letter announced his expectation soon to arrive in New Orleans in his official capacity.

And yet this event cast another delusive shadow upon the public mind, and was interpreted as a diplomatic maneuver, when month after month passed by, the year closed, January and February, 1766, came and went, and the new governor had not made his appearance. At length, after nearly eight months of suspense, on the 5th of March, 1766, he landed in New Orleans. He was accompanied by but two companies of Spanish infantry, his government having accepted the assurance of France that no necessity would be found for more than this force.

The new governor was received with a cold and haughty bearing, which was silent only for a moment before it became aggressive. On the very day of his arrival his attention was called, by Foucault, the French intendant commissary, to the 7,000,000 livres of paper money left in the colony by the French government, and at that time depreciated to one-fourth its face value. This vital question was promptly and kindly answered: he would recognize it as the circulating medium at its market value, until instructed from Spain as to its retirement. But the people instantly and clamorously took stand for its redemption at par.

A few days after Ulloa's arrival he was waited on by the merchants, with a memorial comprised of a series of formal questions touching their commercial interests, his answers to which they professed to await in order to know how to order their future actions. An address of so startling a tone could only seem to a Spanish official, what Ulloa termed it in a dispatch to his government, imperious, insolent, and menacing.

The first act of the superior council was quite as hostile and injudicious. It consisted in requesting the governor to exhibit his commission. He replied that he would not take possession of the colony until the arrival of additional Spanish troops, which he was expecting; that at any rate the superior council was a subordinate civil body, and that his dealings would be with Governor Aubry.

Thus the populace, the merchants, and the civil government, which, it will be seen, later included the judiciary, ranged themselves at once in hostile attitude before the untried government, sent them by the king who had unwillingly accepted them as subjects. The military was not long in committing the same error. The three or four companies left in Louisiana, under the command of Aubry, refused point blank to pass, as the French government had promised they should, into the Spanish service. In short, Governor Aubry, almost alone, recognized the cession and Ulloa's powers.

Under these circumstances Ulloa thought it best to postpone publishing the commission he had shown only to Aubry, or taking formal possession of the country. Yet he virtually assumed control of affairs, employing his few Spanish soldiers to build and garrison new forts at important points in various quarters of the province, and, in coöperation with Aubry, endeavored to maintain a conciliatory policy, pending the arrival of troops; a policy of doubtful wisdom in dealing with a people who, but partly conscious of their rights, were smarting under a lively knowledge of their wrongs, and whose impatient and intractable temper could brook any other sort of treatment with better dignity and less resentment, than that sort which trifled with their feelings.

Much ill-will began now to be openly expressed against the really mild and liberal Ulloa. An arrangement by which the French troops remained in service, drawing Spanish pay, while continuing under French colors and the command and orders of Aubry, was fiercely denounced by those who had hoped to see the Spanish authority fall into complete contempt.

It seems to have been persistently forced upon Ulloa's recognition, that behind and under all the frivolous criticisms and imperious demands of the New Orleans people, the true object of their most anxious dread and aversion, was the iron tyrannies and extortions of Spanish colonial revenue laws. And for this feeling, notwithstanding the offensive memorial by which it was first made known to him, he appears to have had a kind consideration. As early as the 6th of May, only two months after his arrival, he began a series of commercial concessions, looking to the preservation of that trade with France and the French West Indies which the colonists had believed themselves doomed to lose. Yet neither did these escape the resentment and remonstrance of the citizens, and it clearly shows how supreme the mercantile interest was in this whole movement, that the proposal of Ulloa to fix a schedule of reasonable prices on all imported goods, through the appraisement of a board of disinterested citizens, was the subject of such grievous complaint, even by the mass of consumers whom it was expected to benefit, that the unjust and oppressive, though well-meant, ordinance was verbally revoked.

Quite as active, and not less prevalent, was the influence of those office-holders in the superior council and other civil positions, whom the establishment of a Spanish colonial government might be expected to displace, and it was greatly through the mischievous diligence of these that every incident or mistake, however harmless or trivial, became the subject of vindictive fault-finding against the now incensed and threatening Spaniard, and that even "his manner of living, his tastes, his habits, his conversation, the most trivial occurrences in his household", were construed offensively. The return of Jean Milhet from France in December, 1767, with final word of ill-success, only further increased the hostility of the people.

However, the year passed away and nine months of 1768 followed. Ulloa and Aubry, as between themselves, conducted affairs with almost unbroken harmony, notwithstanding Aubry's poor opinion of the Spanish governor's administrative abilities; and although their repeated innovations in matters of commerce and police, now and then produced painful surprises in the community, yet they were meeting a degree of success which led Aubry to assert, in one of his dispatches to France, and no doubt to believe, that they were "gradually molding Frenchmen to Spanish domination". The Spanish flag had been quietly hoisted over four new military posts, without removing the French ensign from over the older establishments, and the colony was apparently living peacefully under both standards.

But under this superficial disguise, the true condition of the public mind was such as may be inferred from Aubry's own account of the distressing embarrassments that beset the colony; the fate of the 7,000,000 livres of French paper money still remained in doubt; the debts of the colony, assumed by the Spanish government, were unpaid; there were a shrinkage of values amounting to 66 per cent., a specie famine and widespread insolvency, a continued apprehension of disaster to follow the establishment of Spanish power, a governor showing himself daily more and more unable to secure the affections and confidence of the people, and finally, the rumor of a royal decree suppressing the town's commerce with France and the West Indies.

Now it was that a deficiency in habits of mature thought and self-control, and in that study of reciprocal justice and natural rights, which becomes men who would maintain their ground against oppression, became to the people of New Orleans and Louisiana a calamity. With these qualities in them and in their leaders, the insurrection of 1768 might have been a revolution for the overthrow of tyranny, both French and Spanish, and the establishment and maintenance of that right to self-government which belongs to any oppressed people. But the valorous, unreflecting Creoles, though imbued with a certain spirit of freedom, discerned but faintly the profound principles of right which it becomes the duty of revolutionists to assert and to struggle for; they rose merely in passionate revolt against a confused group of real and fancied grievances, sought to be ungoverned rather than self-governed, and, following the lead of a few uneasy office-holders, became a warning in their many-sided shortsightedness, and an example only in their audacious courage.

It was on the 25th of October, 1768, that a secret conspiracy, long and carefully planned, and in which were engaged some of the first officers of the colonial government, and some of the leading merchants of New Orleans, revealed itself in open hostilities. Lafrénière, the attorney-general, was at its head; Foucault, the intendant commissary, was an active spirit; and Jean and Joseph Milhet, brothers, Pierre Caresse, Joseph Petit and Pierre Poupet, prominent merchants, Noyan and Bienville, nephews of the city's founder, Jerome Doucet, a distinguished lawyer, Pierre Marquis, a captain of Swiss troops, and Balthasar de Masan, Hardy de Boisblanc and Joseph Villeré, planters and public men, were leaders in the plot and in its execution.

These men had taken care to create the belief, in the settlement some twenty miles above New Orleans on the Mississippi river, called the German coast, that certain Spanish obligations, some time due the farmers there, would not be paid. On the date mentioned, an agent, intrusted with funds for the payment of these obligations, was arrested by a body of citizens under the orders of Villeré, and deprived of the money.

On the 27th Foucault called a meeting of the superior council for the 28th. "During the night," says the principal historian of this episode, "the guns which were at the Tchoupitoulas gate" (that of the upper river-side corner) "were spiked, and the next morning, on the 28th, the Acadians, headed by Noyan, and the Germans by Villeré, entered the town, armed with fowling-pieces, with muskets, and all sorts of weapons." Other gates were forced, other companies entered, stores and dwellings were closed, heavy bodies of insurgents paraded the streets, and, in the words of Aubry, "all was in a state of combustion." A mass meeting was harangued by Lafrénière, Doucet, and the brothers Milhet, and a petition signed by 600 men was sent to the superior council, then in session, asking the official action which the members of that body were ready and waiting to take. With the help of Aubry, whose whole force numbered only 110 men, Ulloa retired with his family on board the Spanish frigate lying in the river. The council met again on the 29th, and, against the warnings and reproaches of Aubry, adopted, as petitioned by the meeting of the day before, a report enjoining Ulloa to "leave the colony in the frigate in which he came, without delay".

Aubry, requested by the leaders of the conspiracy to resume the government, reproached them with rebellion, and predicted their disastrous end. Ulloa, the wisest and kindest well-wisher of Louisiana that had held the gubernatorial commission since Bienville, sailed on the 31st of October, not in the Spanish frigate, which was detained for repairs, but in a French vessel, enduring at the last moment the songs and jeers of a throng of night roysterers, and the menacing presence of sergeants and bailiffs of the council.

The colonists, as well as Aubry, Ulloa, and Foucault, now hurried forward their messengers, with their various declarations, to the courts of France and Spain. That of Aubry, and that of Ulloa, from Havana, may be passed without comment; that of Foucault, with the remark that it was characterized by the shameless double-dealing, which leaves to the intendant commissary alone, of all the participants in those events, a purely infamous memory.

The memorial of the colonists, with its various accompanying depositions, compels a moment's attention. In the midst of a most absurd confusion of truth and misstatement, of admissions fatal to their pleadings, arrogant announcement of unapplied principles, and enumeration of those real wrongs for which France and Spain, but not Ulloa, were to blame, the banished governor was accused on such charges as having a chapel in his own house, absenting himself from the French churches, fencing in a fourth of the public commons to pasture his private horses, sending to Havana for a wet nurse, ordering the abandonment of a brick-yard near the city on account of its pools of putrid water, removing leprous children from the town to the inhospitable settlement at the mouth of the river, forbidding the public whipping of slaves in town, and thereby compelling masters to go six miles to get their slaves whipped, landing at New Orleans during a thunder and rain storm and under other ill omens, claiming to be king of the colony, offending the people with evidences of "sordid avarice", and (as the text has it) "many others equally just and terrible".

The most unfortunate characteristic of the memorial, however, was the fulsome adulations loaded upon the unworthy king who had betrayed its authors. The chiefs of the insurrection had at first entertained the bold idea of declaring the independence of the colony and establishing a republic. To this end two of their number, Noyan and Bienville, about three months before the outbreak, had gone secretly to Governor Elliot, at Pensacola, to treat for the aid of British troops. In this they failed; and though their lofty resolution, which might, by wiser leaders, have been communicated to the popular will, was not at once abandoned, it was hidden and finally smothered under a disingenuous pretense of the most ancient and servile fealty to the king and government, whose incapacity and perfidy were the prime cause of all their troubles: "Great king, the best of kings, father and protector of your subjects, deign, sire, to receive into your royal and paternal bosom the children who have no other desire than to die your subjects," etc.

Such was the address which Lesassier, St. Lette, and Milhet, the three delegates representing the superior council, the planters, and the merchants, carried to France. The aged Bienville had at length gone to his final rest, and they were compelled to make their appearance before the Duc de Choiseul unsupported. St. Lette, a former intimate of the duke, was cordially received; but the deputation, as such, was met with frowns, and heard only the ominous intelligence that the king of Spain, already informed, had taken all the steps necessary to a permanent occupation. With these tidings Milhet and Lesassier returned, having effected nothing save the issuing of an order for the refunding of the colonial debt, at three-fifths of its nominal value, in 5 per cent. bonds.

In a letter of the 21st of March, 1769, Foucault cautiously and covertly deserted his associate conspirators, and denounced them to the French cabinet.

On the 20th of April the Spanish frigate sailed from New Orleans, first setting the three Spanish officers, Loyola, Gayarre, and Navarro, ashore in the town, where they remained unmolested.

At length the project of forming a republic was revived and given definite shape and advocacy. But the moment of opportunity had passed, and news of the approach of an overwhelming Spanish military and naval force paralyzed the spirit of the people.

Thus have been shown, in outline, the salient causes and events of this bold but misguided uprising against the injustice and oppression of two royal powers at once, by "the first European colony (in America) that entertained the idea of proclaiming her independence". Its results may be still more cursorily stated.

On the 18th of August, 1769, Don Alexandro O'Reilly, accompanied by 3,600 chosen Spanish troops—a force nearly one-half larger than the total number of able-bodied white men in the province—and with fifty pieces of artillery, landed, with unprecedented pomp, at the Place d'Armes, from a fleet of twenty-four vessels.

On the 21st, twelve of the principal movers in the insurrection were arrested. Two days later Foucault was also made a prisoner. One other, Braud, the printer of the seditious documents, was apprehended, and a proclamation announced that no other arrests would be made. Foucault was taken to France, tried by his own government, and thrown into the Bastile. Braud was set at liberty. Villeré died on the day of his arrest. Lafrénière, Noyan, Caresse, Marquis, and Joseph Milhet, were shot, and the remaining six were sentenced to the Moro castle, Havana, where they remained a year, and were then set at liberty. The declaration of the superior council was burned on the Place d'Armes.

On the 25th of November the official machinery of a new colonial and municipal government replaced the old, and by the year 1770 the authority and laws of Spain were everywhere operating in full force. Aubry refused a high commission in the Spanish army, departed for France, and, after having entered the river Garonne, was shipwrecked and lost.

THE SUPERIOR COUNCIL AND THE CABILDO.

The superior council, the administrative body which, in the struggle of 1768, was the bold advocate and champion of those commercial interests whose preservation was the main motive of the uprising, owed its origin to Louis XV.

In 1712 this monarch had granted to Anthony Crozat his monopoly of the colony's commerce. It had been given in contemplation and consideration of Crozat's intention and pledge to settle the country with Europeans, and, there being as yet no officer of justice in the infant colony, it was deemed most convenient to establish, on a sort of probationary tenure of three years, commencing in 1713, a superior council. Jurisdiction was given it in all cases, civil and criminal. It was composed of but two persons at first, the governor and the commissary ordonnateur, or of three, counting its clerk. The system of laws which this body was to administer, was the ancient "custom of Paris", with the laws, edicts, and ordinances of the kingdom of France; it being one of the terms of Crozat's charter that the colony should be so governed.

In the month of September, 1716, the provisional three years being about to expire, a perpetual royal edict re-established the council on a permanent footing. Its dignity was raised in accordance with the increasing importance of the colony, and its organization was enlarged to comprise the governor-general of New France, the intendant of the same province, the governor of Louisiana, a senior counselor, the lieutenant-governor, two puisne counselors, and an attorney-general; also, as before, a clerk. Its powers were those of similar bodies in other French colonies, as St. Domingo and Martinique. It held its sessions monthly, dispensing justice for the entire colony as far as called upon, and administering the civil government of the province. Three of its eight members in civil, and five in criminal, cases formed a quorum. A germ of popular government lay in a provision, that in the event of proper or unavoidable absence of members, a quorum could be made by calling in a corresponding number of notable inhabitants.

A peculiar feature of this tribunal was, that though the governor of New France, and, in his absence, the governor of Louisiana, occupied the first seat in the council, yet the intendant of New France, or, if he were not present, the senior counselor, performed the functions of president, collecting the votes and pronouncing judgment. The principle was found still in full play when, in 1768, Foucault ruled the insurgent council and signed its pronouncements, while the protesting but helpless Aubry filled the seat of honor. In all preliminary proceedings, such as the affixing of seals and inventories, the senior counselor officiated and presided as a judge of the first instance.

Crozat, entirely disappointed in his expectation of opening a trade with Spanish America, in August, 1717, surrendered his charter, and, the province being transferred to the Compagnie d'Occident, or Western Company, its directors solicited certain modifications esteemed necessary in the organization and offices of the superior council.

Consequently, by an edict issued in September, 1719, it was made to consist of such directors of the company as might be in the province, the commandant-general, a senior counselor, the two king's lieutenants or lieutenant-governor, three other counselors, an attorney-general, and a clerk. The quorum, and the arrangements for securing it, remained unchanged; the sessions continued to be monthly; the council was still, as it had been from the first, a court of last resort; but now it was elevated beyond the province of a court of the first instance into a jurisdiction purely appellate, and inferior tribunals were established in various parts of the growing colony.

These lower courts are specially noteworthy, in the fact that they were presided over, not by royal officers, but by agents of the company, one in each, with notables of the neighborhood, two for civil and four for criminal cases. Thus, in various developments, the administration of the colony's civil and judicial affairs was gradually showing more and more the features of a representative rule.

It was this superior council which, in 1722, removed to the new settlement of New Orleans, and thus made it the colony's capital. In 1723 and 1724, it was exercising powers of police, and, in 1726, incurring the searching investigations of the royal commissary, De la Chaise, and the emphatic reprimand of the home government. In 1728, August 10, a decree of the king assigned to the council the supervision of land titles. Special sessions were held once or twice a week as a lower court, by two of its members, chosen, and removable by it, to try causes involving values not exceeding 100 livres ($22).

On surrender of the India Company's charter, in 1732, the superior council was again remodeled. Its membership was increased to twelve and a secretary, beside the governor-general of New France. Two years later, in 1742, the labors of the council were so increased, by litigation arising out of the increase of trade, that four assessors were added, to serve four years, and to sit and rank after the counselors, voting only in cases where the record was referred to them to report on, or where they were needed to complete a quorum, or in the event of a tie vote.

The power over land deeds was, on the 13th of March, 1748, extended, by royal decree, to allow the making of good titles, upon inventories prepared in good faith, and recording them, though unofficial and informal, when such defects were the result of the absence or incompetency of public officers.

Such was the body which, twenty years later, though it could not quite shake off an outward pretense of obeisance to royalty, made bold to demand openly the rights of freemen for the people, of whom it had grown to be a sort of legislature, and to lay plans secretly for free government.

It was through the superior council that, in 1724, was issued that dark enactment which, for so many years, and during three dominations, remained on the statute book—the well-named Black Code. One of its articles forbade the freeing of a slave without reason shown to the council, and by it esteemed good. It was the superior council which, in or about the year 1752, resisted the encroachments of the Jesuits, though these were based on a commission from the bishop of Quebec; and it was this body that, in 1763, anticipated by the space of a year the actual expulsion of the same troublesome order from France, and dispossessed it of its plantations in Louisiana. Rochemore, an intendant commissary sent from France in 1758, found this council, headed by Governor Kerlerec, too strong for him, was rudely jostled by it, and, in 1761, was dismissed from office on its complaint to the king. And it was the superior council which M. d'Abbadie, in a dispatch of the 7th of June, 1764, denounced as a body so filled with what he esteemed the spirit of sedition, that he thought it highly desirable to remove from it the Creole members, and fill their places with imported Frenchmen. It was natural that O'Reilly, invested with special power to establish the civil and military branches of government, in such form as might seem to him best to promote the king's service and the happiness of his subjects, should promptly, and once for all, abolish this exponent of the popular will; and in November, 1769, at his direction, the superior council gave place to the cabildo.

In this passage from French rule to Spanish, the radical nature of the change lay, not in the laws, but in the redistribution of power, the lion's share of which was held in reserve in the hands of the military and ecclesiastical representatives of the crown and the church, while an extremely slender portion was doled out, with much form and pomp, to the cabildo.

This body consisted of ten members, in addition to the governor, who presided at its meetings, and an *escribano*, or minute clerk. Its membership was divided into two main groups, distinguished by the character of their tenure of office: that of the smaller group, of four, being annual and elective, while that of the remaining six was a life tenure acquired by purchase.

The four elected members were chosen on the first of each year, by the whole cabildo, including the votes of those who were about to retire from office. They were required to be householders and residents of the town. Except by a unanimous vote, they could not be re-elected until they had been two years out of office. No officer or attaché of the financial department of the realm, nor any bondsman of such, nor any one under the age of twenty-six, nor any new convert to the Catholic faith, could qualify. Two filled the office of *alcaldes ordinarios*, or common judges, holding each his separate—civil and criminal—daily court in the town hall, and—for causes involving not over $20—an evening court for one hour at his residence, where he rendered unwritten decisions. Their judgments were subject to appeals in all civil cases, and they were without jurisdiction over any who could claim a military or an ecclesiastical connection.

A third elective officer was the *sindico-procurador-general*, or attorney-general-syndic, the official advocate of the people in the deliberations of the cabildo. He was not, as the modern usage of the title might imply, a prosecuting officer, though as the municipal attorney it was his duty to sue for revenues and other debts due the town, and he was present in its interest at all apportionments of lands. The last of the four was the *mayordomo-de-proprios*, the municipal treasurer, who made his disbursements upon the cabildo's warrants, and rendered to it annually, on vacating his office, an account of the year's business.

The seats in the cabildo, acquired by purchase, were bought, primarily, at auction from the government. These could be sold again by those leaving them, to their successors, provided that the royal treasury must receive half the price of the first transfer and one-third the price of subsequent transmissions. In these sat the six *regidors* or administrators—literally, rulers. The first held a merely honorary office under the title of *alferez real*, the royal standard-bearer, and was without official functions, unless the death or absence of one of the alcaldes called him to fill the vacancy to the end of the annual term. The second regidor was the *alcalde mayor provincial*, a magistrate with jurisdiction over crimes and misdemeanors committed beyond town or village limits, and with power to overtake and try persons escaped to such regions. The third was the *alguazil mayor*, a civil and criminal sheriff, superintendent of police and prisons; and the other three, ranking according to the seniority of their commissions, were the *depositario-general*, a keeper and dispenser of the government stores, the *recibidor de penas de camara*, a receiver of fines and penalties, and a sixth, to whom no individual official functions were assigned.

Thus constituted, the cabildo met every Friday in the town hall. It heard appeals from the decisions of the *alcaldes ordinarios*, through two of the regidors, chosen by it to sit with the *alcalde*, who had given judgment; but this was only where judgment had been given for not more than $330, larger cases being assigned by the king to such tribunal as he might select. At its discretion it sold or revoked the meat monopoly, and the many other petty municipal privileges which characterized the Spanish rule. The expenditures of town government were made on the cabildo's warrants, but not without consent of the royal governor, except the most paltry sums; while on the other hand the cabildo was required to exact of the governor, before he entered upon the duties of his office, good and sufficient security for its proper conduct, and his pledge to submit to its investigation any or all of his acts.

Full details of the elaborate machinery of administration, with its laborious forms and pomps, would be unprofitable. The underlying design seems to have been not to confer power, but to scatter and neutralize it in the hands of royal officials and of a cabildo which, loaded with titles, and fettered with minute ministerial duties, was, so to speak, the superior council shorn of its locks; or, if not, a body, at least, whose members recognized their standing as *guardians* of the people and *servants* of the king.

Immediately upon organizing the cabildo, O'Reilly announced the appointment of Don Louis de Unzaga, colonel of the regiment of Havana, as governor of Louisiana, and yielded him the presidential chair. Yet, under his own higher commission of captain-general, he continued for a time to govern. The instructions which he had published established in force the laws of Castile and of the Indies, and the use of the Spanish tongue in the courts and public offices, and so far was this carried, that the notarial records of the day show the baptismal names of property-holders of French and Anglo-Saxon origin, changed to a Spanish orthography, and the indices made upon those instead of upon the surnames. The official use of the French language was tolerated only in the judicial and notarial acts of the military commandants, who ruled everywhere outside of New Orleans.

Thus, in all things save the habits and traditions of the people, the town, and the great territory of which it was the capital, became Spanish. The change in the laws was not a violent one; there was a tone of severity and a feature of arbitrary surveillance in the Spanish, that may have carried an unpleasant contrast, but the principles of both the French and the Spanish systems had a common origin, the one remote, the other almost direct, in the Roman code, and their similarity was specially marked in their bearings upon the all-important points of the marital relation and inheritance. The *recopilaciones* of Castile and the Indies went into force, without other friction than resulted from change of tongue, and under these laws, with the Fuero Viejo, Fuero Juzco, Partidas, Autos Accordados, and Royal Schedules, justice continued to be administered up to and through the recession to France, and until the purchase of the province by the United States. And though in 1808, this system gave place in part to a "digest of the civil laws then in force", arranged after the code of Napoleon, yet from it, and especially from the Partidas, are derived many of the features of the code of practice of Louisiana of to-day. For while, by an act of the Louisiana legislature of March 12, 1828, "all the civil laws in force before the promulgation of the civil code" (of 1825) "were declared abrogated", yet the supreme court has decided that they are still the statute laws of the state, and that the legislature did not intend to abrogate those principles of law which had been established or settled by the decision of courts of justice.

After all is said, it is proper to remark the wide difference between the laws themselves and their administration. Spanish rule in Louisiana was better, at least, than French, which scarce deserved the name of government; while as to its laws, the state of Louisiana, in which by reason of its capital these laws were best known and most applied, "is at this time the only state, of the vast territories acquired from France, Spain, and Mexico, in which the civil law has been retained, and forms a large portion of its jurisprudence."

On the 29th of October, 1770, O'Reilly sailed from New Orleans with the greater part of the troops he had brought with him, thus signifying the completion of his commission in the entire and peaceful establishment of the Spanish powers. The force left by him in the colony amounted to 1,200 men. He had himself made several suggestions to the home government, advantageous to the commercial interests of New Orleans, and his departure was the signal for the commencement of active measures intended to induce, if possible, a change in the sentiments of the people consonant with the political changes forced upon them. Such was the kindlier task of the wise and mild Unzaga.

SPANISH CONCILIATION.

While Spain had been delaying to take possession of Louisiana, and temporizing with the mettlesome citizens of her capital, the commercial adventurers of another nation had been more diligent.

"I found the English," says O'Reilly in a dispatch of October, 1769, "in complete possession of the commerce of the colony. They had in this town their merchants and traders, with open stores and shops, and I can safely assert, that they pocketed nine-tenths of the money spent here. * * * I drove off all the English traders and the other individuals of that nation whom I found in this town, and I shall admit here none of their vessels." Thus pointedly did he set forth the despotic relation which the town and province had been, and still were, forced to accept from their European master, whether he were the French Louis or the Spanish Charles.

That the rule of Spain in Louisiana was grossly oppressive in the letter of its laws and regulations, is a fact, however, merely in keeping with the times in which it existed. Colonies had not yet come to be regarded as having inherent rights, but were looked upon in most cases as commercial ventures, projected in the interest of the sovereign's revenues, and upon which monopolies and like restrictions were laid, or indulgences bestowed, simply as that interest seemed to require.

It was on this principle that Crozat, Law, and Louis XV had, each in turn, conducted affairs in Louisiana. In pursuance of the same course, Charles III, after the momentary concessions of May, 1766, in September of the same year, had established those commercial regulations against which the Creoles so boldly protested. It was not alone against the truly Spanish surveillance placed upon the prices of all imported goods, that this protest had been made; by these regulations commerce with France was reduced to the importation of articles of necessity, and that of St. Domingo and Martinique to the exchange of wine and breadstuffs for lumber and grain, in passported ships, on policed bills of lading, and only until such a time as Spain could take measures to supplant these trades by a commerce exclusively her own. Beyond this the port of New Orleans, with the vast province behind it, was shut out from every market in the world, except certain specified ports of Spain; markets where, her merchants complained, they could neither sell their produce to advantage nor buy the merchandise wanted in the province. They could employ only Spanish bottoms commanded by subjects of Spain. Their vessels could not even put into a Spanish-American port except in distress, and then only under onerous restrictions. The commerce of the port was virtually throttled, merely by an actual application of the principles which had always hung over it, and only by the loose administration of which the colony and town had survived and grown, while Anthony Crozat had become bankrupt, Law's Compagnie d'Occident had been driven to other fields of enterprise, and Louis XV had heaped up a loss of millions more than he could pay.

In fact, the life and growth of the port and of the colony had depended on the double influence of gross disregard of the royal enactments by the officials, and a bold infraction of them by the people. And in 1770 Don Louis de Unzaga, assuming authority, and seeing the extremity to which the people were driven, resumed the accustomed policy, and the same desirable ends began again to be met by the same lamentable expedients. His method, which was also the method of those who came after him, worked in two opposite directions at once, and brought relief to the colony's commerce by procuring, on the one hand, repeated concessions and indulgences from the king, and on the other, by overlooking the evasion by the people of those onerous burdens which the home government still required to be laid on them.

Not that Unzaga began at the beginning. Royal abatements had been made as early as in March, 1768, when an exemption from import duty was decreed on foreign and Spanish merchandise. O'Reilly himself, a year and a half later, had recommended an entirely free trade with Spain and Havana, enumerating the colony's wants—"flour, wine, oil, iron instruments, arms, ammunition, and every sort of manufactured goods for clothing and other domestic purposes"—and its exportable products—"timber, indigo, cotton, furs, and a small quantity of corn and rice", and recommending that vessels owned in the colony be placed on an equality with Spanish vessels. It was probably due to his efforts that, in 1770 or 1771, permission was given, allowing as many as two vessels a year to enter the port of New Orleans from France.

Upon these followed, from year to year, the concessions procured by Unzaga, the equally effective lenity of his administration, and various other events and conditions of kindred influence. The river trade with British vessels increased. Under cover of trading with the British posts on the eastern bank above Orleans island, they supplied New Orleans and the river "coasts", above and below, with goods and with slaves. Anything offered in exchange was acceptable, revenue laws were mentioned only in jest, profits were large, credit was free and long, and business brisk. Under the river-bank where now stands the suburb of Gretna, opposite the present fourth district of New Orleans, two large floating warehouses, fitted up with counters and shelves, and stocked with assorted merchandise, lay moored, when they were not trading up and down the shores of the stream. The sum of this commerce was some $650,000 a year.

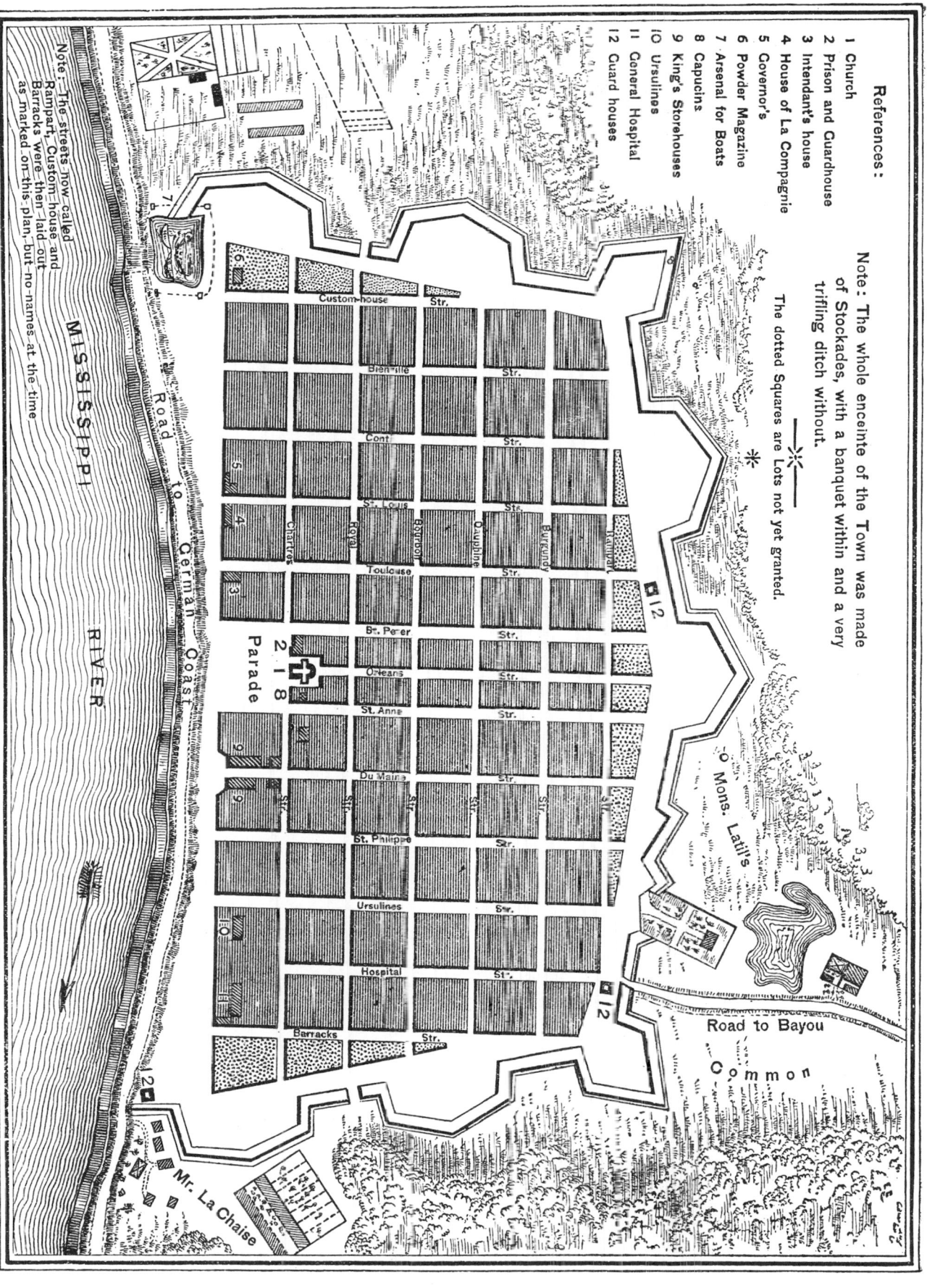

PLAN of New Orleans in 1770, by Capt. Pittman of the British Army.

References:

1 Church
2 Prison and Guardhouse
3 Intendant's house
4 House of La Compagnie
5 Governor's
6 Powder Magazine
7 Arsenal for Boats
8 Capucins
9 King's Storehouses
10 Ursulines
11 General Hospital
12 Guard houses

Note: The whole enceinte of the Town was made of Stockades, with a banquet within and a very trifling ditch without.

The dotted Squares are Lots not yet granted.

Note:—The streets now called Rampart, Custom-house and Barracks were then laid out as marked on this plan, but no names at the time.

MISSISSIPPI RIVER

Road to German Coast

Scale: 600 Feet to an Inch

Custom-house Str.

Bienville Str.

Cont Str.

St. Louis Str.

Toulouse Str.

St. Peter Str.

Orleans Str.

St. Anne Str.

Du Maine Str.

St. Philippe Str.

Ursulines Str.

Hospital Str.

Barracks Str.

Chartres
Royal
Bourbon
Dauphine
Burgundy
Rampart

Parade

Mr. La Chaise

Mons. Latil's

Road to Bayou

Common

The merchants of New Orleans, shut out from participation in this contraband trade, complained loudly but in vain to Unzaga. In 1773, however, when their complaints were turned against their debtors on the plantations, who, waxing prosperous, were buying additional slaves and broadening their lands with money due the New Orleans merchants for crop-advances, the governor's ears were opened, and drawing upon his large reserve of absolute power, he gently but firmly checked and corrected this imposition.

Meanwhile, certain royal concessions, dated August 17, 1772, and made in response to O'Reilly's suggestions, were failing to afford appreciable relief to legitimate commerce, because so narrowed as to be almost neutralized by restrictive provisos. But Unzaga's quiet power worked for the benefit of the people under his rule, not alone in the direction of their commercial relations. While the town was languishing under the infliction of these so-called concessions, his conservative and pacific treatment of a fierce crusade, made by newly imported Spanish Capuchins against their French brethren, and certain customs which these had long permitted to obtain among the laity, averted an exodus of Creoles from New Orleans, which he feared might have even destroyed the colony.

Indeed, the colony had already suffered a grave loss of this character. While O'Reilly was still in the province, so large a proportion of the merchants and mechanics of New Orleans had removed to St. Domingo, that a few days before his own departure he ceased to grant passports. No corresponding influx seems to have offset this depletion, and in 1773 Unzaga wrote to the bishop of Cuba that "there were not in New Orleans and its environs 2,000 souls" (meaning possibly whites) "of all professions and conditions", and that most of these were extremely poor. An imprudent governor might have reduced the town, if not the province also, to a desert. But under Unzaga conciliation soon began to take effect; commissions were eagerly taken in his "regiment of Louisiana" by Creoles—the pay being large and the sword the true symbol of power—while its ranks were filled by soldiers from the late French, as well as from the Spanish troops; and the offices of regidor and alcalde were by and by occupied by the bearers of such ancient Creole names as St. Denis, La Chaise, Fleurieau, Forstall, Duplessis, Bienvenue, Dufossat, Livandais. In 1776 Unzaga was made captain-general of Caracas, and in the following year left in the charge of Don Bernardo de Galvez, then about twenty-one years of age, a people still French in feeling, it is true, yet reconciled, in a measure, to Spanish rule.

At this point a change took place in the Spanish foreign policy, and the French instead of the English merchants commanded the trade of the Mississippi. The British traders found themselves suddenly treated with great rigor, Galvez commencing the new movement by the seizure of eleven of their vessels richly laden, and exceeding the letter of the Franco-Spanish treaty in privileges bestowed upon the French. The prospect for the future of New Orleans brightened rapidly, and the spirit of the people revived.

Under certain restrictions, trade was allowed with Campeachy and the French and Spanish West Indies. The importation of slaves from these islands, because of their spirit of insurrection, had been for a long time forbidden, but the trade in Guinea negroes was now specially encouraged; a little later the prohibition against the former trade was removed. In March, 1777, a 4 per cent. export duty was reduced to 2 per cent. In April, 1778, Galvez, though only governor *ad interim*, by his own proclamation gave the right to trade with any port of France, and a few days later included the ports of the thirteen British colonies then engaged in that struggle for independence, in which the fate of the little captive city at the mouth of the Mississippi was so profoundly though obscurely involved. Furs and peltries shipped to any port of Spain were made free of export duty for ten years. The Spanish government became the buyer of all the tobacco raised in the province, and endeavors were made to induce a French and a French West Indian immigration.

The value of nearly all these privileges was presently reduced to very little, by the issue of British letters of marque against the commerce of Spain, and by the active participation of France in the American revolution. Galvez was looking to his defenses, building gunboats, and awaiting from his king the word which would enable him to try his conscious military talents.

But another trade had sprung up, the direct result of these new conditions. Some eight years before, at the moment when the arrival of 2,600 Spanish troops and the non-appearance of their supply-ships had driven the price of provisions in New Orleans almost to famine rates, one Oliver Pollock entered the port with a brig-load of flour from Baltimore, offered it to O'Reilly on the captain-general's own terms, and finally sold it to him at $15 a barrel, two-thirds the current price. O'Reilly rewarded his liberality with a grant of free trade to Louisiana for his lifetime. Such was the germ of the trade with the United States. In 1776 it appears that Oliver Pollock, at the head of a number of merchants from New York, Philadelphia, and Boston, who had established themselves in New Orleans, had begun, with the countenance of Galvez, to supply, by fleets of large canoes, the agents of the American cause with arms and ammunition delivered at Fort Pitt (Pittsburgh). The same movement was repeated in 1777 and 1778, and Pollock became the avowed agent of the American government.

In this way and in other ways the blockade of the town's West Indian and Transatlantic commerce showed an advantageous side. Immigration became Anglo-Saxon, a valuable increase of population taking place, by an inflow from the Floridas and the United States, of an enterprising element that made its residence in the town itself and took the oath of allegiance. Commercial acquaintance was made with the growing West, as a few years before with Baltimore, Philadelphia, New York, and Boston. To be shut in upon home resources could hardly have been without some lessons of frugality and self-help in the domestic life—the secret of public wealth. This selfsustentation was now practicable; even without the Ohio river. Inside the lines indicated at St. Louis, Natchitoches, New Orleans, and Fort Panmure (Natchez), there was sufficient diversity of products and industries to support an active commercial intercourse; the Attakapas and the Opelousas prairies had been settled by Acadian herdsmen, a long stretch of Mississippi River "coast" by farmers from among the same exiled people; in 1778 immigrants from the Canary islands had founded the settlements of Valenzuela on Lafourche, Galveztown on the Amite, and that of Terre aux Bœufs, just below New Orleans. A paper currency supplied the sometimes urgent call for a circulating medium, and the colonial treasury warrants, or liberanzas, were redeemed by receipts of specie from Vera Cruz sufficiently frequent to keep them in circulation, and at times to give them a moderately fair market value. Such were the sources of a certain prosperity, and to show these is to give the causes of a proportionate degree of public satisfaction.

Whether this feeling had any stronger qualities than that of a passive acquiescence was now to be tested. For in the summer of 1779 Spain had declared war against Great Britain. Galvez discovered that the British were planning the surprise of New Orleans, and under cover of preparations for defense, made haste to take the offensive. Four days before the time he had appointed to move, a hurricane destroyed a large number of houses in the town, and spread ruin to crops and dwellings up and down the "coast", and sunk his gun flotilla. The young commander, nothing dismayed, appeared before the people assembled on the Place d'Armes, and displaying a commission lately received, confirming him as governor of Louisiana, demanded of them to say whether he should appear before the cabildo, as the terms of his commission required, and swear to defend the province from its enemies.

His appeal was responded to with enthusiasm. Repairing his disasters as best he could, and hastening his ostensibly defensive preparations, he marched, on the 22d of August, 1779, against the British forts on the Mississippi. His force, beside the four Spanish officers who ranked in turn below him, consisted of 170 regulars, 330 recruits, 20 carabineers, 60 militiamen, 80 free men of color, 600 men from the coast, "of every condition and color," 160 Indians, 9 American volunteers, and Oliver Pollock.

This little army of 1,434 men was without tents, other military furniture, or a single engineer. The gun fleet followed in the river abreast of their line of march along its shores, carrying one 24-, five 18-, and four 4-pounders. With this force, in the space of about three weeks, Fort Bute on bayou Manchac, Baton Rouge, and Fort Panmure, 8 vessels, 556 regulars, and a number of sailors, militiamen, and free blacks, fell into the hands of the Spaniards. The next year, 1780, re-enforced from Havana, Galvez again left New Orleans by way of the Balize with 2,000 men, regulars, militia, and free blacks, and on the 15th of March took Fort Charlotte on Mobile river.

Galvez next conceived the much larger project of taking Pensacola. Failing to secure re-enforcements from Havana by writing for them, he sailed to that place in October to make his application in person, intending to move with them directly on the enemy. After many delays and disappointments he succeeded, and early in March, 1781, appeared before Pensacola with a ship of the line, two frigates, and transports containing 1,400 soldiers well furnished with artillery and ammunition. Here he was joined by such troops as could be spared from Mobile, and by Don Estevan Mirò from New Orleans, at the head of the Louisiana forces, and on the afternoon of the 16th of March, though practically unsupported by the naval fleet, until dishonor was staring its jealous commanders in the face, moved under hot fire, through a passage of great peril, and took up a besieging position. But an account of this engagement and siege is not essential to the history of New Orleans, and it is only necessary to state, that on the 9th of May, 1781, Pensacola, with a garrison of 800 men, and the whole of West Florida, were surrendered to Galvez. Louisiana had heretofore been included under one domination with Cuba, but now one of the several rewards bestowed upon her governor, was the captain-generalship of Louisiana and West Florida. He sailed from St. Domingo to take part in an expedition against the Bahamas, leaving Colonel Mirò to govern *ad interim*, and never reassumed the governor's chair in Louisiana.

Such is a brief summary of the achievements of the governor and of the people of Louisiana, operating from New Orleans in aid of the war for American independence; and if the motive of Spain was more conspicuously and exclusively selfish than that shown in the co-operation furnished by France, still a greater credit is due than is popularly accorded to the help afforded in the brilliant exploits of Galvez, discouraged by a timid cabildo, but supported initially, finally, and at the first mainly, by the Creoles of New Orleans and the neighboring coasts. The fact is equally true, though overlooked even in New Orleans, that while Andrew Jackson was yet a child, New Orleans had a deliverer from British conquest in Bernardo de Galvez, by whom the way was kept open for the United States to stretch to the Gulf and to the Pacific.

Spain herself, solicited by Galvez, made practical acknowledgment of her colonists' "zeal and fidelity", tried during the last two years not only by war but by storms—one of August 24, 1780, being still more destructive than that of the year before—by inundation, contagion, rainy summer, rigorous winter, and an arrested commerce. Galvez, enlightened as young, had asked for them a free trade with all the ports of Europe and America; but in the words of Judge Gayarre, "neither the court of Madrid nor the spirit of the age was disposed to go so far." By a royal schedule published in New Orleans in the spring of 1782, the privileges granted in October, 1778, which the blockade had made valueless, were revived, enlarged, and extended for ten years, to begin from the prospective peace. The reshipment to any Spanish-American colony of goods received from Spain was allowed, but that of goods from other countries was expressly forbidden. Negroes were allowed to be imported duty-free from the colonies of neutral or allied powers, and might even be paid for in specie. Foreign vessels could be bought without duty and registered as Spanish bottoms. An export duty on staves shipped to Spain was removed. But a final article raised the export and import duty on all merchandise to 6 per cent.

By such measures it was that the Spanish king sought "to secure to his vassals the utmost felicity", and to prove to the Creoles of Louisiana "that a change of government had not diminished their happiness". And such was the condition of affairs when, on the 3d of September, 1783, a treaty of peace between Great Britain, the United States, France, and Spain provided, in its eighth article, that the Mississippi, from its source to its mouth, should ever remain free and open to Great Britain and the United States.

THE CREOLES STILL FRENCH.

The Spanish conquest never became more than a conquest. Those changes of which it originally consisted were almost all that it ever effected. Its customs regulations caused certain transitions in the agriculture of the province and the commerce of the town; and there it stopped—from the beginning to the end a foreign body. The Creole, with a grave and tempered dignity in pathetic contrast with his intemperate fire of 1768, for thirty-five years bore it about in his flesh an unextracted missile, never absorbed, never ejected, but sometimes provocative of slight inflammations that called for wise and gentle handling. The Spanish governors, whatever may be true against them, had the fortunate discretion to treat the people, from first to last, as a wounded and paroled community that might be conciliated, but which it were vain to attempt to proselyte.

It was only by such means that the colony was saved to Spain so long as it was. "The people here," wrote Unzaga in 1772, "will remain quiet as long as they are gently treated; but the use of the rod would produce confusion and ruin. Their dispositions are the result of the happy state of liberty to which they have been accustomed from the cradle, and in which they ought to be maintained, so far as is consistent with the laws of the kingdom."

The changes made in the laws and their administration have already been noticed, with the reserve of power in the royal officers, and its comparative absence in the cabildo. Martin quotes the United States consul at New Orleans as saying, in 1803: "The auditors of war and assessors of government and intendancy, * * * to them only may be attributed the maladministration of justice, as the governor and other judges, who are unacquainted with the law, seldom dare to act contrary to the opinions they give."

The change of agricultural products was felt or seen in New Orleans, only in so far as it called for a different mode of handling the marketed commodities or brought an increase of trade and profits. The transfer to Spanish domination shut out the indigo of Louisiana from the markets in which its producers had found under French domination protection for it, and forced it into the ports of Spain and into ruinous competition with the superior article made in the older and more southern Spanish colonies. When later this burden was much lightened by wiser commercial regulations, a series of new drawbacks arose in continuously unfavorable seasons, and culminated in the appearance of an insect which, by the years 1793–'94, was making such ravages that the planters, despairing of the indigo culture, knew not which way to turn for livelihood.

Cotton had been known in the colony ever since 1713; and as early as 1752 or 1753, M. Debreuil, a wealthy citizen and landholder, and one of the leading minds in the colony, is said to have invented a cotton-gin sufficiently effective to induce a decided increase in the production of an article to which soil and climate were so favorable. Yet the great importance and commercial value of cotton awaited the discovery of some still more advantageous mode of ginning the staple from the seed than any yet known. Those who gave the matter thought had, in 1760, recommended the importation of such apparatus as could be found in India. In 1768, however, with such methods as were known, cotton had already become an article of export from New Orleans, and was mentioned with solicitude in the manifesto of the banishers of Ulloa, as a new and promising source to which they looked for future prosperity.

At the time of the collapse in the indigo culture, the Creoles were still experimenting with it; but the fame of Eli Whitney's newly invented cotton-gin had probably not yet reached them, and the planters—little supposing that in the eighth year from that time the cotton crop of Louisiana and export from New Orleans would be respectively 20,000 and 34,000 300-pound bales—turned their attention in another direction, and renewed their much earlier efforts to produce merchantable sugar.

The sugar-cane, introduced from St. Domingo by the Jesuit fathers in 1751, had been grown in the vicinity of New Orleans ever since. On a portion of the city's wholesale business district, included in the angle of Common and Tchoupitoulas streets, this great staple was first planted in Louisiana. The amount produced, however, was trivial; only in the neighborhood of the town was a limited attention given it. Nothing more than sirup, if even so much, was made from it until M. Debreuil, in 1758, built a sugar mill on his plantation—now that part of the third district adjoining the second on the river front—and endeavored to turn a large crop of cane into sugar.

Accounts of the result vary. It appears, however, that sugar was made, and that for a time the industry grew; but that the sugar was poorly granulated and very wet, and consumed entirely within the province until 1765, when it is said half of the first cargo shipped to France leaked out of the packages before the vessel reached port.

The cession to Spain seems to have quite destroyed this half-developed industry, as might easily have been anticipated, and it was not until the insurrection of the blacks in St. Domingo, in 1791, brought an influx of refugees from that lately prosperous sugar-producing country, that the paralyzed efforts of twenty-five years before came again to life. The connection with Spanish rule may not be as close as would appear, but the coincidence is notable—two Spaniards, Mendez and Solis, erected, the one a distillery and the other a sugar-house, and manufactured rum and sirup.

Thus stood affairs when, in 1794, the people of lower Louisiana despaired of the culture of indigo. At this juncture Étienne de Boré, a Creole of the Illinois district, but a resident of New Orleans, and a son-in-law of Destrehan, an early colonist, who had himself been one of the last to abandon sugar-culture, bought a quantity of canes from Mendez and Solis, planted on the land where the seventh district (late Carrollton) now stands, erected a mill, and, in 1795, electrified the community by making $12,000 worth of superior sugar. This, the absence of those interdictions which had stifled commerce in the earlier days of Spanish rule, enabled him to market advantageously. The agriculture of the Mississippi delta was revolutionized, and by the year 1802 New Orleans was the market for 200,000 gallons of rum, 250,000 gallons of molasses, and 5,000,000 pounds of sugar. The town contained some twelve distilleries, and a sugar refinery which produced about 200,000 pounds of loaf sugar; while, on the other hand, the production of indigo had declined to a total of 3,000 pounds, and soon after ceased.

The frail character of almost all edifices in New Orleans, at the time of its passage from French hands to Spanish, the long neglect of public works, the readiness of the Spanish to supply this omission, the repeated necessity of repairing the ravages of storm and fire, caused the presence of the Spanish authority to have an effect upon the architecture of the town, which remains conspicuously evident in the ancient quarter at this day.

The census ordered by O'Reilly in 1769, showed the place to contain 468 houses. Undoubtedly the more correct term would be premises, embracing the idea of three separate roofs to each entire household, an arrangement common in New Orleans down to a date almost recent, and occasioned by the general use of slave labor. The total population, 3,190 souls, indicated about seven to a residence, which must, therefore, be assumed to have comprised the family dwelling, a kitchen quite apart from it, and a third roof under which the household slaves were quartered. To these the well-to-do added stables and other buildings, slave-service favoring the multiplication of outhouses quite sufficient to offset the confinement of the poor to narrower limits.

In this light it becomes easy to accept the equally authentic statement, that a conflagration, in 1788, nineteen years after—when the increase of the town was but 67 per cent. over the O'Reilly census—destroyed 856 edifices, nearly twice the number in the entire town according to the literal rendering of the previous census. There were probably as many *roofs* burned, out of about 2,300, or about 285 complete domiciles out of about 770.

This conflagration itself had an odd and accidental connection with the presence of Spanish authority. For it was in the private chapel of Don Vincente José Nuñez, the military treasurer, on Chartres street near St. Louis, that on Good Friday, the 21st of March, 1788, at half-past one in the afternoon, a fire broke out that destroyed nearly half the town. The buildings along the immediate river front escaped; but the central portion of the town, including the entire wholesale commercial quarter, the dwellings of the leading inhabitants, the town hall, the arsenal, the jail, the parish church, and the quarters of the Capuchins, were completely consumed.

Six years later, on the 8th of December, 1794, some children playing in a court in Royal street, too near to an adjoining hay store, set fire to it. A strong north wind was blowing, and in three hours 212 dwellings and stores in the heart of the town were destroyed. The cathedral, lately finished on the site of the church burned in 1788, escaped; but the pecuniary losses exceeded those of the previous conflagration, which had been estimated at nearly $2,600,000. Only two stores were left standing; the levee and the Place d'Armes became, as they had been six years before, the camping ground of hundreds of inhabitants, and the destruction of provisions was such as to threaten a famine.

In consequence of these desolating fires, whose ravages were largely attributed to the inflammable building material in general use, the Baron Carondelet, then governor, recommended to his government to offer a premium on roofs covered with tiles, instead of shingles as heretofore; and whether this premium was ever offered or not, from this time the tile roof came into use, and forms to-day one of the most picturesque features of the old French quarter. As the heart of the town filled up again it was with better structures, displaying many Spanish-American features—adobe or brick walls, arcades, inner courts, ponderous doors and windows, balconies, *porte-cochères*, and white and yellow lime-washed stucco. Two-story dwellings took the place of one-story buildings, and the general appearance, as well as the public safety, was improved.

It is noteworthy, that after these fires the record of disasters wrought upon the town itself by hurricanes, becomes unimportant. The conjecture is common, that in the early days of the city's history storms were more frequent and violent than in later days. A much simpler explanation lies in the probability, that at first the saturated state of the undrained soil induced the not too energetic colonist to make shift with very defective foundations, scarcely sunk below the surface of the ground. The structures erected under military direction, with an eye to permanence, did not succumb to the wind. One, the convent of the Ursulines, is still standing.

Public municipal improvements under the Spaniards began with O'Reilly. In an ordinance of the 22d of February, 1770, providing a revenue for the city of New Orleans, he first established petty trade-licenses and

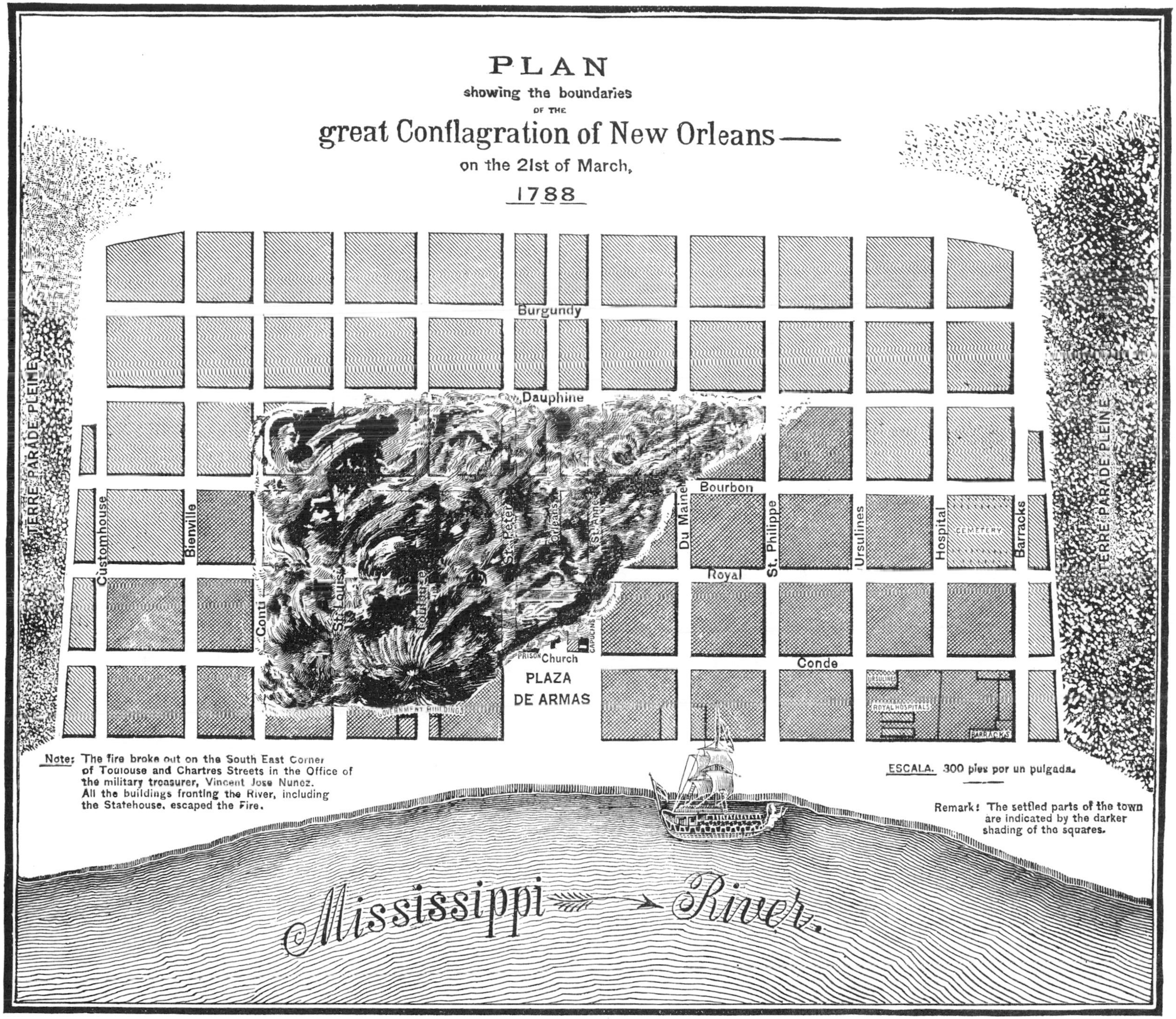

PLAN
showing the boundaries
OF THE
great Conflagration of New Orleans
on the 21st of March,
1788
TERRE PARADE PLEINE
Burgundy
Dauphine
Bourbon
Royal
Customhouse
Bienville
Conti
St. Louis
Toulouse
St. Peter
Orleans
St. Anne
Du Maine
St. Philippe
Ursulines
Hospital
Barracks
CEMETERY
Conde
PRISON
Church
CAPUCINS
PLAZA
DE ARMAS
GOVERNMENT BUILDINGS
URSULINES
ROYAL HOSPITALS
BARRACKS
TERRE PARADE PLEINE
Note: The fire broke out on the South East Corner of Toulouse and Chartres Streets in the Office of the military treasurer, Vincent Jose Nunez. All the buildings fronting the River, including the Statehouse, escaped the Fire.
ESCALA. 300 pies por un pulgada.
Remark: The settled parts of the town are indicated by the darker shading of the squares.
Mississippi River.

port-charges, two unfortunate systems of city revenue, which, unchanged in principle and greatly exaggerated in extent, have been perpetuated to the present day. But in the same ordinance the government reservations of 336 feet front by 84 feet depth, on either side of the Place d'Armes, were granted to the town to become to it a perpetual source of revenue, by ground rents.

At this point there appears in the city's history the name of one of the most enterprising and benevolent citizens it has ever counted among its inhabitants. Don Andres Almonaster y Roxas became the buyer, for a perpetual annual rent, of the grounds granted the town, and early erected upon them two rows of stores, built of brick between wooden posts, of a single story's height, and these became, and for a great many years continued to be, the fashionable retail quarters of the town. In 1787 he built in Ursulines street, adjoining the convent, a small chapel of stuccoed brick, for the nuns. The chapel of the Ursulines is well remembered by persons still young, as a quaint and homely relic of the last century.

The charity hospital founded by the sailor Jean Louis, in 1737, seems to have been removed to a wooden building on the west side of Rampart, between Toulouse and St. Peter streets, at that time just outside the town limits, and to have been destroyed by the hurricane of 1779. In 1784, Almonaster began, and in two years completed, at a cost of $114,000, on the same site, a brick edifice, which he called the Charity Hospital of St. Charles, a name the institution still bears.

In 1792, he began the erection, upon the site of the parish church destroyed by fire in 1788, of a brick church, and in 1794, when Louisiana and the Floridas were made a bishopric separate from Havana, this edifice, completed sufficiently for occupation, became the St. Louis cathedral.

Later still, he filled the void made by the burning of the town hall and the jail—which, until the conflagration of 1788, had stood on the south side of the church facing the Place d'Armes—with the hall of the cabildo, the same that stands there at this time, with the exception of the upper story, added since.

The government itself completed very substantially the barracks begun by the French governor, Kerlerec, on Barracks street. Close by, it built a military hospital and chapel, and near the upper river corner of the town, the square now occupied for the same purpose, but at that time fronting directly on the river, it put up, and then allowed to go into significant dilapidation, a wooden custom-house. The burned jail seems also to have been replaced, likewise the presbytery of the Capuchins. The "old French market", on the river front, just below the Place d'Armes, was erected and known as the Halle de Boucheries.

It was not correct, therefore, for the French colonial prefect, Laussat, sent to take possession of the re-ceded province, in the spring of 1803, to state " that the Spaniards had not made any solid or permanent constructions".

In January, 1792, the same year in which Almonaster founded the cathedral, Governor Carondelet, on succeeding Miró in office, and issuing his *bando de buen gobierno*, or rule of government, divided the town into four wards, placing an *alcalde de barrio*, or commissary of police, over each, with official control of fire-engines, firemen, and axmen, which have no earlier mention. He also recommended the commissioning of night watchmen and the erection of street lamps, the expense of these improvements to be met by a chimney tax of 9 reales ($1 12½) on each chimney. In 1796 he reported to his government that he had commissioned thirteen *serenos*, night watchmen, and established eighty street lamps. The fire of 1794 had so reduced the income from chimney tax, that another levy was either substituted for or added to it, to wit, a tax on wheat-bread and meat.

With the aid of a large force of slaves, contributed gratuitously by residents and neighboring planters, he began, in 1794, and in the following two years finished, the excavation of the "old basin" and of the Carondelet canal, the former comprising almost its present superficial area of some 10,000 square yards, and the latter connecting it, by a navigable depth of water, with the bayou St. John, and thus with lake Ponchartrain and the maritime world.

This work, beyond the rear fortifications of the town, had been undertaken with the double object in view of drainage and navigation. In 1801, as recommended by Carondelet to the cabildo five years before, certain lands contiguous to the basin and canal, which were covered with noisome pools of water, the supposed source of putrid fevers, were divided into garden lots and let out at low ground rents to those who would destroy their insalubrity, by ditching and draining them into the canal.

By such measures as these, which have been described at some length, the government and the laws, the commerce, and the architectural aspect of New Orleans, were made to receive a Spanish impression and acknowledge a Spanish influence. But all that Spain deemed it just or expedient to concede never induced, in the Creole mind, a spontaneous sympathetic response, and not only to the last, but more and more toward the last, their national feeling, their habits of life, their political sentiments, and their language, proclaimed them French Creoles unaltered.

The use of the Spanish tongue, though enforced in the courts and principal public offices, never superseded the French in the mouths of the people, and left but a small proportion of words naturalized in the corrupt French of the negro slaves. *Cocodrie*, from *cocodrilo*, the crocodile, was easier to their African powers of pronunciation than *caiman*, the alligator; the terrors of the famed calaboza, with its chains and whips and branding irons, was condensed into the French trisyllabic *calaboose*, while the pleasant institution of *ñappa*, the petty gratuity added by the retailer to anything bought, grew the pleasanter Gallicized into *lagnappe*. The only newspaper in the town or province, as it was also the first, though published under the auspices of the Baron Carondelet, was *Le Moniteur de la Louisiane*, printed entirely in French. It made its first appearance in 1794. The Spanish Ursulines sent from

Havana to teach their own tongue, found themselves compelled to teach in French, and to content themselves with the feeble achievement of hearing the Spanish catechism from girls who recited it with tears rolling down their cheeks. The public mind followed the progress of thought in France. Many Spaniards cast in their lot with the Creoles; Unzaga married a Maxent; Galvez married her sister; Gayarre took for his wife Constance de Grandpré; the intendant, Odvardo, her sister; Miró wedded a de Macarty. But the Creoles never became Spanish; and in the society balls, when the uncompromising civilian of the one nationality met the equally unyielding military officials of the other, the cotillion was French or Spanish, according to the superior strength of the Creole or Spanish party, more than once decided by actual onset and bloodshed. The best that can be said is, that the Spanish government was least unpopular in New Orleans probably about the year 1791, when the earlier upheavals of the French revolution were being contemplated from a safe distance, and before the Republic had arisen to fire the Creole's long-suppressed enthusiasm.

When war broke out between Spain and Great Britain, a power with whom France was already at war, it was easy enough to rally the Creoles against their hereditary foes under the Spanish banner; but when, in 1793, his Catholic majesty turned his arms against republican France, the Spanish governor, Carondelet, found it necessary to take the same precautions against the people of New Orleans as if he held a town of the enemy. The Marseillaise was wildly called for in the theater, which some French players from St. Domingo, refugees of 1791, had opened, and in the drinking shops was sung defiantly the song "Ça ira—ça ira, les aristocrates à la lanterne". He took the written pledge of the colonists to support the government. He thought it best to make sundry arrests, and, though promising clemency, felt constrained, by later developments, to send the arrested persons to Havana. He rebuilt the fortifications around the city, which had again fallen into ruin, changing their plan and making them stronger than ever. They were finished in 1794, and consisted as follows: at the lower river corner, Fort St. Charles, a small pentagonal fortification, with barracks for 150 men, a parapet 18 feet thick faced with brick, a ditch, and a covered way; at the upper river corner, Fort St. Louis, similar in all regards, but somewhat smaller. The armament of these was some twelve 18- and 12-pounders. Between them, on the river front at the foot of Toulouse street, was a large battery crossing fires with the forts. In the rear of the town, on the line imperfectly indicated by Rampart street, were three lesser forts, one at either corner, and the third a little beyond the straight line, and midway between the other two. They were mere palisaded inclosures, with fraises, large enough for a hundred men each, and armed with eight guns. That which stood at the present corner of Canal and Rampart streets was Fort Burgundy, that on the present Congo square, Fort St. Joseph, and that at what is now the corner of Rampart and Esplanade streets, Fort St. Ferdinand. The wall that passed from fort to fort all around was a parapet of earth 3 feet high, surmounted by a line of 12-foot palisades, and with a moat in front 40 feet wide and 7 feet deep, containing at all times 3 feet of water supplied from Carondelet canal. These fortifications, Carondelet wrote to the Spanish minister, "would not only protect the city against the attack of an enemy, but also keep in check its inhabitants," and added that but for the forts a revolution would have taken place. The enemy looked for from without was the pioneers of Kentucky, Georgia, and so on, instigated by Genet, the French minister to the United States, and headed by one Clark and by Auguste de la Chaise, a Creole of powerful family, who had gone to Kentucky to lead a descent upon New Orleans in the name of liberty.

The letters of Unzaga and of Bishop Peñalvert were written twenty-two years apart, the one in 1773, the other in 1795; but the governor wrote: "I cannot flatter his majesty so much as to say that the people have ceased to be French at heart," and the bishop echoed: "His majesty possesses their bodies and not their souls."

THE AMERICAN GRASP.

The temper of the Creoles was not the only, or even the principal, source of anxiety to the indulgent governors who held them under the paternal despotism of Spain. Commercially and politically, the province had a destiny alien to Spanish dominion, and kindred to that of the new power, which almost from the beginning of Spanish rule in Louisiana, had begun to make its way down the valley of the Mississippi by its own sheer weight. The restless and intrepid American, therefore, even before he had achieved his independence, or poured his thousands of hardy woodsmen into the district of Kentucky, had become, simply by the distinctness of that destiny, the foremost object of distrust and dread to Spain, in regard to her foothold in the Mississippi valley.

Congress had claimed the free passage of the Mississippi, in the negotiations opened with Spain in 1779 for national recognition, and had failed to obtain either. In 1783, by the eighth article of the treaty of peace, the free navigation of the Mississippi was granted to the subjects of Great Britain and the citizens of the United States forever. But so far was this stipulation from being carried out in good faith, that it became the starting point of a series of Spanish intrigues and American menaces, whose confused alternations of oppression, concession, aggression, deception, and corruption, leads the eye of research in hurried review across the whole remaining term of Spanish occupation. Of all these movements, New Orleans, as the gateway of the Mississippi valley, was the foremost objective point. Its commercial greatness, in the early future, had become obvious to all, and while Spain was determined to retain this key of her possessions, the people of the West, and, later, Congress, determined to become the holders of the only seaport west of the Atlantic then accessible to them.

In the autumn, 1785, the state of Georgia sent commissioners to New Orleans, where Miró had lately become governor in the room of Galvez, demanding to be put in possession of the vast territory between her western boundary and the Mississippi, according to her understanding of the treaty of peace. Very properly, the matter was referred to the governments of America and of Spain; but this and similar occurrences aroused the solicitude of the Spaniards, and put them—or probably found them—on their guard. By 1786, if not earlier, the efforts of the settlers on the Ohio and the Cumberland, to find a port for their flat-boat fleets and a market for their breadstuffs and provisions, on the Mississippi, were met with seizure and confiscation.

The instant result of this attitude was excitement, indignation, and open threats on the part of the Kentuckians, presently taking the form of distinct proposals and projects for the capture of New Orleans by force of arms; yet milder counsels presently prevailed, and Congress was first appealed to to treat with Spain for that commercial freedom of which they were resolved to be deprived no longer.

The Spanish officials were in lively and well-grounded alarm, and saw themselves, in their imagination, already overwhelmed. The home government was urged to hasten to their relief with certain proposed measures, if it would save New Orleans, Louisiana, the Floridas, or even Mexico from early conquest. "*No hay que perder tiempo*," wrote the intendant, Navarro. "There is no time to be lost."

Two schemes were projected: the first, so to relax the barriers that had been drawn across the commerce of the river, that the multitudes hovering so threateningly on their northern and northeastern borders might be induced to extend their domains, not as invaders, but as immigrants, ready to yield allegiance to the authority of Spain; the second, to foster and foment the spirit of insurrection, then rife in the West, against what was deemed the negligence of Congress, as to actually bring about the disruption of the West from the East. These schemes were set on foot; a large American immigration did actually set in, and the small town of New Madrid still remains to commemorate the extravagant schemes of western grantees.

A close observer, he had not let the turn of events escape his notice, and in June, 1787, General James Wilkinson, of the United States service, sent and followed to New Orleans a large fleet of flatboats, loaded with the produce of the West, and, working on the political fears of Miró, secured many concessions and made way for a trade which began immediately to inure greatly to the pecuniary benefit of New Orleans, not to say of the Spanish officials.

But an export trade was only half a commerce, either for the West or for New Orleans. Communication with Philadelphia, however, in a measure, supplied the deficiency, though hampered and qualified by a system of false dealings, than which it would be hard to contrive a group of influences more corrupting to a mercantile community. For a while, on one hand, the colonial officials indulged and promoted this trade. Gardoqui, the Spanish minister at Philadelphia, "finding he did not participate in the profits," moved vigorously against it, and those who were engaged in it were able to persevere only by employing and accepting all the subterfuges of contrabandists, not excepting false arrests and false escapes. The conflagration of 1788 was used as a pretext for the liberation of a number whom the intendant, Navarro, had been driven, by fear of royal displeasure, to imprison, and the return to them of their confiscated goods.

The great scarcity of provisions after the conflagration, gave Miró an opportunity to enlarge the trade with Philadelphia, of which he promptly took advantage, and sent three vessels consigned to Gardoqui—whose opposition was now turned into coöperation—for such miscellaneous cargoes as the general ruin called for. The leading item was 3,000 barrels of flour. This exigency met, the trade not only continued but increased, and in August, 1788, Wilkinson received, through his agent in New Orleans, via the Mississippi, a cargo of dry goods and other articles for the Kentucky market, probably the first boat-load of manufactured commodities that ever went up that river to the Ohio.

Others began to follow the example of Wilkinson in matters of commerce, and, under pretense of coming to buy lands and settle, or of returning for their families and property, secured passports and the repeated privilege of buying and selling free of duty. Thus tobacco, flour of a certain poor quality, and the various other crops of the West, were beginning to find a market where they could be profitably exchanged for manufactured goods. As to the communication with Europe, the concessions of 1782 had yielded the transatlantic commerce of New Orleans into the hands of the French traders, and there it still remained. "At this very moment," wrote Miró on the 10th of August, 1790, "France has the real monopoly of the commerce of this colony."

The port of New Orleans, in fact, was neither closed nor open. Commerce was possible, but dangerous, subject to the corrupt caprices of Spanish commandants and customs officers, and full of exasperating uncertainties. While, therefore, Spain was still dealing with Wilkinson and with Dr. O'Fallon, "general agent of the South Carolina Company in Yazoo," the United States government, through its minister at Madrid, was striving to work upon the Spaniards' new fear of Great Britain, and their knowledge of the feebleness of their foothold in America, to press upon them a cession of Orleans island and the Floridas to the United States. But neither the urgent requests of the United States, the possibility of a British invasion from Canada by way of the Mississippi, nor the proposals of the South Carolina Company, to accept which Miró thought equivalent to "taking a foreign state to board with them", were sufficient yet to cause any relaxation of the grasp of Spain upon the key of the greatest agricultural valley in the world.

Still the fears of the officials at New Orleans continued. A spirit was responding within the province itself, to the march of events without, and the interdiction of the slave-trade with revolted St. Domingo, the banishment of clocks branded with the Goddess of Liberty, and Carondelet's fortifications, were but symptoms of it, not cures, and in February, 1793, American encroachment won the valuable concession of an open commerce with Europe and America for citizens of the Spanish colonies. "From this period," says Judge Martin, "a number of merchants in Philadelphia established commercial houses in New Orleans."

Francis Louis Hector, Baron de Carondelet, succeeded to the governorship of Louisiana and West Florida on the 30th of December, 1791, and had therefore been in office something more than a year when this broad concession was made. He had not needed it, however, to indicate to him the waning strength of the Spanish tenure, or the growing supremacy of the people whom Navarro had years before described as "a nation restless, poor, ambitious, and capable of the most daring enterprise". "Since my taking possession of the government," wrote Carondelet in May, 1794, "this province * * * * has not ceased to be threatened by the ambitious designs of the Americans."

To the vigilance and good faith of President Washington, and not to Carondelet's insignificant defenses, his rigid police, or the counterplots which he carried on through Thomas Power and others, Carondelet owed the deliverance of his capital from the schemes of Genet, La Chaise, Clark, and the Jacobins in Philadelphia; and it was that cause, not these, that maintained the safety of Louisiana as a haven for French royalists. It argues more temerity than wisdom on the part of the baron, that the imminence of these dangers was no sooner removed than he began again to hamper and oppress the trade of the Mississippi, in the hope of yet separating the western people from the union of states, to which they had now become devoted.

Nevertheless, the commercial destiny of New Orleans moved on, and while Power was still conveying Carondelet's overtures to Wilkinson, a treaty was signed at Madrid, October 20, 1795, by which the Mississippi was declared free to the people of the United States, and New Orleans became a port of deposit for three years, free of duty or any charge on produce or merchandise, beyond "a fair price for the hire of the stores" where they might be deposited. This privilege was to be renewed at the expiration of the three years, or transferred to some "equivalent establishment" on the river bank, according as the king's interest should require. The American was gradually closing in upon the foremost object of his desire. That this was recognized as the true interest of New Orleans is shown in the fact, that though transit shipments were thus made duty free, the revenues of the custom-house aggregated, in 1795, double those of the preceding year.

Still, Carondelet, under various pretexts, continued to hold the territory conceded to the United States on the east bank of the Mississippi, temporizing with their authorities through the agency of General Gayoso de Lamos, the commissioner for effecting the transfer, spending money freely to procure the treason of unscrupulous Americans, and strengthening his fortifications not only against the federal commanders, but against the western settlers who had filled up the country, and the imminent probability of another threatened invasion from Canada.

Yet, even under so troubled a political sky, the commerce of New Orleans steadily increased. War with France had displaced the foreign trade which Bordeaux, Marseilles, and Nantes had so long monopolized, and had thrown it largely into American ports, although not a little harassed by French privateers infesting the Gulf of Mexico. One of these, in October, 1795, seized, and for eight days held, the post at the mouth of the Mississippi, evacuating and destroying it only on the approach of troops from New Orleans; and after hostilities between France and Spain had ceased, a number of American vessels, seized in the Gulf, were taken to New Orleans, the vessels and their cargoes sold, and the crews maltreated.

At length all schemes against the Union having failed, and every pretext for delay being exhausted, Gayoso, who, in August, 1797, had succeeded Carondelet as governor of Louisiana, yielded to the irresistible pressure of United States officers, acting under the orders of Wilkinson, and in March, 1798, abandoned by stealth, rather than surrendered, the territory so long unjustly retained from the states.

But New Orleans still remained a subject of ill-feeling. While the long delays lately terminated had been taxing the patience of the western people, the three years' term, during which New Orleans might be used as a port of deposit, was drawing toward its close, and before the year 1798 could expire, the exasperated Americans found the city again closed against them by the Spanish intendant, Morales. Not only so, but the plain letter of the late treaty was ignored, and no other point on the river was assigned to take the place of the closed port.

The indignation and resentment aroused in the people of the United States, and in the government as well, was energetic and profound, and secret preparations were at once set on foot by President Adams, for an expedition against New Orleans with an overwhelming force. According to an excellent authority, the West could have sent against it between 20,000 and 30,000 men. The two facts that seem to have arrested the movement, were the contemplated retirement of the President from office at the close of his term, then drawing near, and by and by the disavowal of the intendant's action by his government and its restoration of the suspended privilege.

Meanwhile, another eye was turned covetously upon Louisiana, and in the last year of the century it became the settled, secret policy of both the French republic and the American to acquire that vast, but to Spain unremunerative and indefensible, province. The opportunities and the genius of the first consul enabled him to

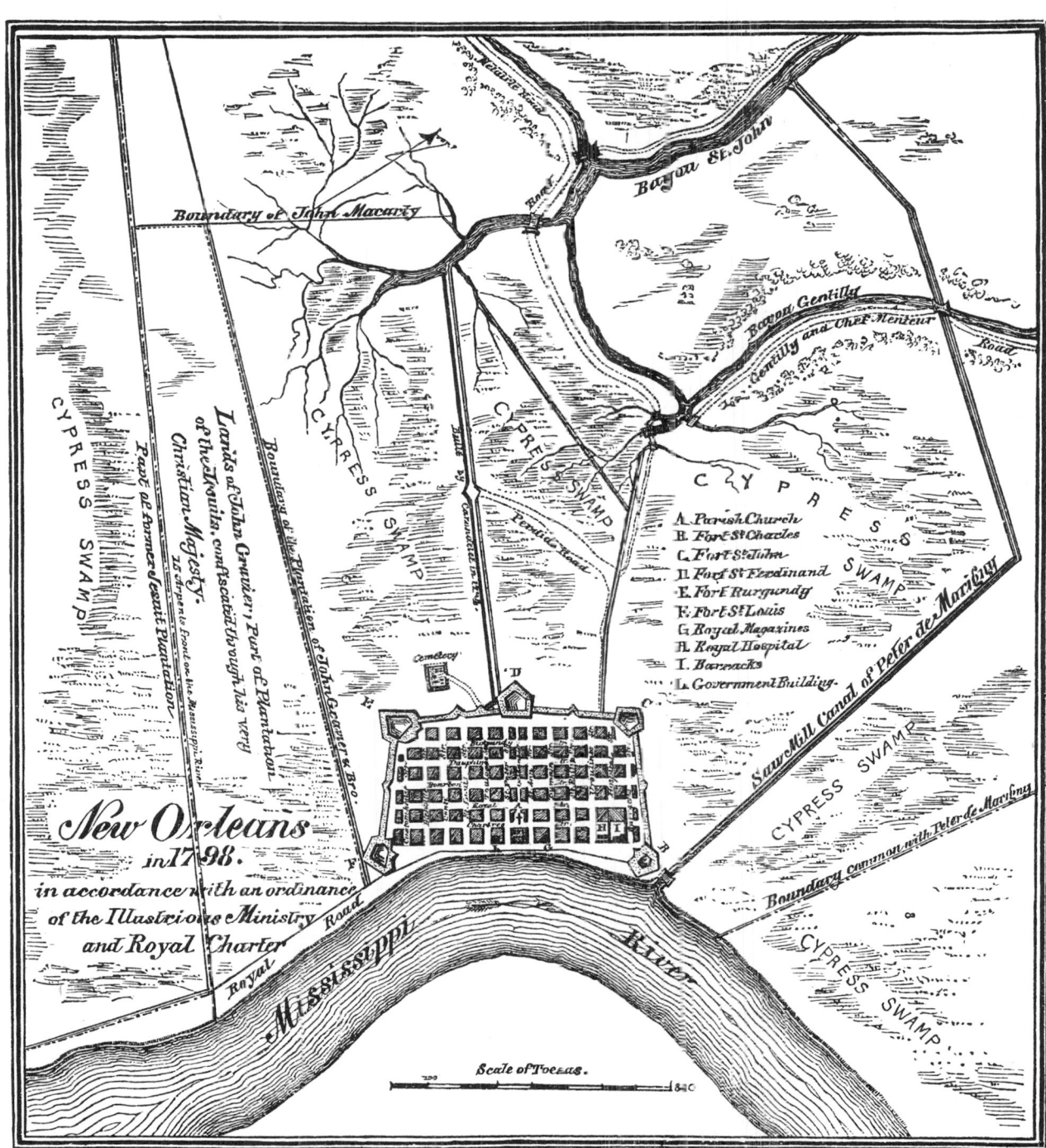

New Orleans
in 1798.

in accordance with an ordinance
of the Illustrious Ministry
and Royal Charter

Boundary of John Macarty

Bayou St. John

Bayou Gentilly

Gentilly and Chef Menteur

CYPRESS SWAMP

CYPRESS SWAMP

CYPRESS SWAMP

CYPRESS SWAMP

CYPRESS SWAMP

CYPRESS SWAMP

C Y P R E S S

Lands of John Gravier, Part of Plantation
of the Louisiana, cultivated through his very
Christian Majesty.

Past at former Jesuit Plantation.

Boundary of the Plantation of John Gravier & Bro.

A. Parish Church
B. Fort St Charles
C. Fort St John
D. Fort St Ferdinand
E. Fort Burgundy
F. Fort St Louis
G. Royal Magazines
H. Royal Hospital
I. Barracks
L. Government Building

Saw Mill Canal of Peter de Marigny

Boundary common with Peter de Marigny

Cemetery

Royal Road

Mississippi River

Scale of Toesas.

move with the superior celerity. On the first of October, 1800, the Spanish king privately entered into certain agreements with the French republic by which, on the 21st of March, 180_, Louisiana passed secretly into the hands of Bonaparte, in exchange for the petty Italian kingdom of Etruria. "France has cut the knot," wrote Minister Livingston to Secretary Madison, when in November, 1802, the secret was no longer unknown.

Yet the Spanish domination continued still beyond this date, and it was not until the 26th of March, 1803, that the French colonial prefect, Laussat, landed in New Orleans, specially commissioned to prepare for the expected arrival of General Victor, in command of a large body of troops destined for the occupation of the province, and to arrange for the establishment of a new form of government.

Governor Gayoso had died of yellow fever in 1799. He had been succeeded by the Marquis of Casa Calvo, and he, in June, 1801, by Don Juan Manuel de Salcedo. The intendant, Morales, had used every measure permitted him to discourage American immigration and hamper American commerce in the river, both of which had become objects of dread. Privileges granted when immigration was desired had been withdrawn. In October, 1802, the overzealous intendant had again suspended the right of deposit, and even cut off all commercial intercourse beyond the mere navigation of the river to and from foreign markets, and, six months after, the king again discountenanced the proceeding.

On the 18th of May, 1803, Casa Calvo—sent from Havana for the purpose—jointly with Governor Salcedo, proclaimed the coming surrender and its contemplated terms, and they held themselves in readiness for the hourly expected arrival of General Victor. Instead of him came a rumor painful to Laussat and incredible to the Creoles, who had so lately received the news of the cession to France with the liveliest delight, and about the last of July, 1803, a vessel from Bordeaux brought the official announcement that, on the 30th of the preceding April, Louisiana had been purchased by the United States.

On the 31st of October, Congress authorized the President to take possession of the ceded territory. On the 30th of November, with troops drawn up in line on the Place d'Armes, and with discharges of artillery, Salcedo, in the hall of the cabildo, delivered to Laussat the keys of New Orleans, and Casa Calvo declared the people of Louisiana absolved from their allegiance to the king of Spain. From a flagstaff in the square the Spanish colors descended, the French took their place, and the domination of Spain in Louisiana was at an end.

On Monday, the 20th of December, 1803, with similar ceremonies, Laussat turned the province and the keys of its port over to Commissioners Claiborne and Wilkinson. The French tricolor, which had floated over the Place d'Armes for the short space of twenty days, gave place to the stars and stripes, and New Orleans was an American town.

A FRANCO-SPANISH AMERICAN CITY.

Within a period of ninety-one years Louisiana had changed hands six times. From the direct authority of Louis XIV it had been handed over, in 1712, to the commercial dominion of Anthony Crozat. From Crozat it passed, in 1717, to the Compagnie de l'Occident; from the company, in 1731, back to the undelegated authority of the government of France; from France, in 1762, to Spain; from Spain, in 1801, back again to France; and at length, in 1803, from France to the United States. Compared with the last of these, the earlier transfers lose even that prominence which is their due, and in the history of the Mississippi valley, the significant transaction which stands at the opening of the present century, indicating the emancipation from the service and bargainings of European masters, needs no other distinctive name than that commonly given it, the Cession.

At the time of this event New Orleans had been under the undisputed sway of Spain for thirty-four years. In the early part of this period its interests had languished, and for many years it had made but indifferent progress. During the first four years, according to the statements of Governor Unzaga, and allowing even for careless understatement, the natural increase of its population had been entirely neutralized by emigration.

With concessions to commerce came a certain advance. In 1785, the sixteenth year of Spanish domination, an official census showed a population within the walls of New Orleans of 4,980 persons, an increase of 56 per cent., and another, three years later, in 1788, of 5,338 souls, or a total increase for the nineteen years of 67 per cent.

This seems to have been principally a natural increase. Certain importations had been made of agriculturists from Malaga, the Canary islands, and Nova Scotia; but except a very few, these remained only momentarily in New Orleans, and then passed on into the rural districts. Even that American immigration, which it later became the policy of Spain to foster, though it peopled the province with thousands of new-comers, added to the population of New Orleans only a few scores of mercantile pioneers, sometimes with families, but oftener without. In 1778 and 1779 Count Galvez required all residents of New Orleans, who had come from the British colonies (United Colonies), to swear allegiance to Spain; and the whole number that did so was but 170.

The British traders whom O'Reilly ejected, in 1769, either returned or were succeeded by others. The freedom given in 1782 to trade with France, brought in some French merchants, and a few years later the French revolution drove many royalists to Louisiana, a few of whom no doubt took refuge in New Orleans, with their families, and goods. Some Germans and Italians seem also to have been received into the growing town, straggling in in the fugitive way common in seaports, and finding place according to the commercial and industrial needs of the port.

The insurrection in St. Domingo, in 1791, caused some refugees from that island to settle in New Orleans, and in this way came the first theatrical troupe that ever played in Louisiana. But the accession was trivial, by reason of a regulation promptly adopted, prohibiting the importation of slaves from the countries where they had revolted. Toward the close of the Spanish tenure, the inflow of Americans became more considerable, and made its way against all royal obstructions, a matter always possible and often easy, through the laxness or the corruption of the colonial officials.

However—and although in 1803 the population of New Orleans, with its suburbs, had reached the number of 10,000 souls—the great majority of the white inhabitants was still Creole. For even in the province at large, where the proportion of aliens was greater than in the city, a contemporary authority states, that the Creoles were three-fourths of the inhabitants. As to the numbers of the Spanish element, it is a singular, but authentic fact, that outside of government circles there were but few.

The city was fast becoming one of the chief seaports of America. In 1802, 158 American, 104 Spanish, and 3 French merchantmen, in all 265, aggregating a total of 31,241 register tons, sailed from her harbor loaded. The tonnage entering port during the first six months of 1803, indicated an increase over the year before of over 37 per cent. The products of the province alone, exported through its metropolis, exceeded $2,000,000 value. Its imports reached the sum of $2,500,000; 34,000 bales of cotton; 4,500 hogsheads of sugar; 800 casks—equivalent to 2,000 barrels—of molasses; rice, peltries, indigo, lumber, and sundries, to the value of $500,000; 50,000 barrels of flour; 3,000 barrels of beef and pork; 2,000 hogsheads of tobacco, and smaller quantities of corn, butter, hams, meal, lard, beans, hides, staves, and cordage passed, in 1802, across the already famous levee.

Under the river bank, just above the corporation limits of the town, "within ten steps of Tchoupitoulas street," where land has since formed and brick stores now cover the spot to several squares depth, the fleets of barges and flatboats from the West moored and unloaded, or retailed their contents at the water's edge. Farther down and immediately abreast of the town, between the upper limits and the Place d'Armes, the shipping lay, to the number of twenty or more vessels of from 100 to 200 tons burthen, hauled close up and made fast to the bank, where they received and discharged "with the same ease as from a wharf". Still farther down, beyond the square and the market, and opposite the government warehouse, was the mooring place of the vessels of war.

The town, at this date, had filled and overflowed its original boundaries. From the masthead of a ship at the levee, one looked down upon a gathering of from 1,200 to 1,400 dwellings, or say 4,000 roofs of all kinds and sizes; those near by, generally two, and often three, stories from the ground, covering substantial brick houses, and themselves covered with half-cylindrical or flat tiles or with slates; those further on, behind the first few streets in front, of two or a single story height, of shingles, broad, outstretched at times over spacious dwellings and environing verandahs, and rendered picturesque with dormer windows and square belvederes. Such houses as these were almost always elevated, on pillars, over open or latticed basements of from 8 to 15 feet height above the ground. The homes of the poor, and of many who were well-to-do, were of the humblest exterior, with apartments on the ground, and were scattered indiscriminately among the rest or hovered on the outskirts. Much greenery brightened the tableaux, whether the season was summer or winter, and a line of watery, grass-entangled ruin, surrounding all, marked the line of fortifications which Carondelet's successors had allowed to tumble to wreck.

Immediately before the eye, a street's width beyond the bottom of the Place d'Armes, stood the occupied but unfinished cathedral, lacking those quaint, white Spanish towers and that central belfry which, in 1814 and 1824, were added to it. At the left of it the old hall of the cabildo rose over its heavy half-Moorish arcade, undisfigured then by the French roof which at present distorts its architecture. On either side of the square were the fashionable retail stores, in two long, unbroken, single-story rows. Other structures remained here and there—the government house, the barracks, the hospital, the convent of the Ursulines—unchanged features of the earlier French town.

The straight and fairly spacious streets were unpaved, ill-drained, and filthy, poorly lighted, and often impassable to vehicles by reason of the mire. The unpaved sidewalks were commonly bordered by wooden ways of 4 or 5 feet width, while a few in the heart of the town had narrow walks of brick.

Along these walks and through these streets, the people moved busily to and fro and in and out, with the activity indicating the life of a commercial port. Toulouse, St. Peter, Conti, St. Louis, Royale, Chartres streets, and the levee, were the scenes of brisk negotiations and the receipts and deliveries of merchandise. The restless American was especially conspicuous, and, with the Englishman and the Irishman, composed the great majority of the commercial class. The Frenchmen, except a small number of cultivated people, had subsided into the retail trade, or the mechanical callings. The Spaniards, beyond the military and civil service, were generally humble Catalans, keepers of shops and of numberless low cabarets, which occupied almost every street corner; while the Creoles sought office and military commission, ruled society, lent money, sometimes at 12 per cent. per annum, and sometimes at 1½ or 2 per cent. per month, and took but a secondary part in that commercial life from which was already springing the future greatness of New Orleans.

Nor can this be regarded as strange, when account is taken of one or two relative facts. Their illiteracy, their non-appreciation of toil—a sentiment which had become traditional—and other disadvantageous characteristics, might easily have given way before the change of circumstances and the allurements of wealth; but the Anglo-Saxon occupation of the Mississippi valley, and the superior ability of England and the Atlantic states over France and Spain, to take the products of that entire valley and to supply its wants, gave such overwhelming advantages to the incoming American, English, or Irish merchants, that the ill-equipped and uncommercial Creole was fortunate to secure even a subordinate mercantile rank in the city of his birth.

As they were the holders of the urban and suburban real estate, they had begun, with the vigorous commercial impulse and immigration of the last decade, to figure as the sellers of lots and as *rentiers*. The Jesuits' plantation of 32 arpents front, confiscated in 1763, had been parceled out into five portions. In 1788 an inheritor of 12 arpents front of this tract, a lady who had been a widow Deslondes, and had been married again to Bertrand Gravier, laid out a line of squares along part of this front on the line of Tchoupitoulas road (street), from the upper boundary of the *Terre Commune*, still recognizable in the name of Common street, to the lower boundary of a tract owned by one Delord, the line of the present Delord street. She called the prospective settlement Villa Gravier. A few years later she died; her husband extended the partition of streets, squares, and lots to the farther side of St. Charles street, and in her memory gave them the name of Faubourg Ste. Marie. The names of its streets still repeat points in its history, Gravier street perpetuating the memory of the faubourg's founder, Delord, Foucher, and others continuing those of his fellow capitalists. Poydras had bought the spot which became the corner of Tchoupitoulas and Poydras; Claude Girod another, that of Tchoupitoulas and Girod; another corner became the property of a free woman of color, Julie Fortier, and the street running back from it, Julia street.

The *Terre Commune* was a government reservation, retained on account of the fortifications along which it lay, and also for a public road running back from the river. Its long triangular form, with the apex on the river front, resulted from the upper boundary of the town and the lower line of the plantation having been drawn perpendicular to the changing directions of the river bank. The same explanation applies to the various other fan-shaped sections added, from time to time, to the growing city. *Calle del Almazen*, otherwise the *rue du Magazin*, rendered in English not severely Storehouse street, but Magazine street, took its title from an immense tobacco warehouse—doubtless the place of deposit of the Kentucky tobacco—upon which the street's lower end abutted, very near the site of the present custom-house. Midway between Poydras and Girod streets, behind Magazine, lay a *campo de negroes*, a slave camp, probably of the cargoes of Guinea slaves. The street that cut through it became, and has ever since continued to be, the *calle de Campo*—Camp street. Next behind it the Spanish sovereign was remembered in St. Charles street; the next, *Briqueterie*, indicating the road to a brick-yard, and another still beyond called Salcedo, were opened and named later than those in front, most probably by Jean Gravier, the son of Bertrand, and before the cession had changed their names to those which they bear to-day, in honor of Carondelet and his wife, the *Baronne*.

Maunsell White relates that in August, 1801, when he first arrived in the port of New Orleans and went ashore in Poydras street, the faubourg Ste. Marie consisted of five houses. The whole space between Common and Poydras, from Magazine to Carondelet street, was appropriated for raising vegetables, and the site of St. Charles hotel was the cottage garden of an "old Mr. Percy".

Other faubourgs were springing up, or about to spring up, beyond the various gates and walls. The high roofs of the aristocratic suburb, St. John, could be seen stretching away among its groves of evergreen alongside the bayou road, and by and by clustering into a village near where a bayou bridge still crosses the stream, some 200 yards below the site of the old one.

Just beyond the parapets of Fort St. Joseph lay the basin and canal Carondelet. They had been allowed to fall into neglect, and had shoaled so that the larger craft had to stop at the village of St. John in the bayou; yet it was still in use by the smaller craft, and in the basin, canal, and bayou together there aggregated, in 1802, 500 arrivals of small half-decked vessels and schooners, of from 8 to 50 tons burden, bringing the cattle and produce of the pine forests from the lake and gulf coasts of East and West Florida.

While the colony's trade was with France—1782, and following—New Orleans Creoles, without fortune, leaned much to mercantile life, for which they considered reading and writing in the French tongue the only education necessary, and toward the end of that time, in 1788, there were eight schools teaching these two rudiments, attended by some 400 children, about one-fourth or one-fifth the number that might have enjoyed these limited benefits. The educational results of Spanish royal patronage were little better than ludicrous. In 1772, there came from Spain Don Andreas Lopez de Armesto, Don Pedro Aragon, Don Manuel Diaz de Lara, and Don Francisco de la Calena, to found a school. "No pupil," writes Governor Mirò, "ever presented himself for the Latin class; a few came to be taught reading and writing only; these never exceeded thirty and frequently dwindled down to six." The fire of 1788 destroyed the school-house and reduced the attendance from 23 to 12, and Don Andreas Almonaster's offer to build another house, at a cost of $6,000, seems never to have been acted on.

The only other schools were the schools of vice, and the only other preventive of moral decadence was, toward the close of the Spanish tenure, a system of police, possessing the questionable merit of indiscriminate severity. Assemblages of more than eight persons were not allowed, and every citizen of New Orleans was required to be and remain indoors by nine o'clock at night, the hour of shutting the gates; quadroon women were forbidden to wear jewelry, and were required to keep their hair bound up in a kerchief. The condition of affairs was none the better, for the fact that this system was sometimes harshly and sometimes feebly administered.

A standard historical writer upon Louisiana, while giving many of the foregoing and similar facts, yet states that "aggravated crimes were rare in Louisiana", and there is a certain way of understanding the remark which may make it applicable to New Orleans. For where so many of the crimes against society went uncondemned and even approved by the popular voice; where the dueling-ground was free to all and accepted by all; where license was almost as broad as the licentiousness that sought it; where the slave and the quadroon castes were practically powerless for offense or defense, and where crimes against them were scarce accounted misdeeds, save on some uncut page of the statute-book—the number of what were set apart in the estimation of society as "aggravated crimes" could hardly be large, and it need not seem surprising if the unfortunate people of a city so afflicted with evil influences and their painful results, were generally unconscious of a reprehensible state of affairs, and preserved their self-respect and a proud belief in their moral excellence.

In outward appearance the Creoles had become the handsome, well-knit race that the freedom of their natural surroundings would have been expected to produce. Of a complexion lacking color, yet free from the sallowness of the Indies, there was a much larger proportion of blondes among them than is commonly supposed. Generally their hair was of a chestnut or but little deeper tint, except that in the city a Spanish tincture now and then asserted itself in black hair and eyes. The women were fair, of symmetrical form, with pleasing features, lively, expressive eyes, well-rounded throats, and superb hair; vivacious, yet decorous in manner, and exceedingly tasteful in dress, adorning themselves with beautiful effect in draperies of muslin enriched with embroideries and much garniture of lace, but with the more moderate display of jewels, which indicated a community of limited wealth. They were much superior to the men in quickness of wit, and excelled them in amiability and in many other good qualities. The more pronounced faults of the men were generally those moral provincialisms which travelers recount with undue impatience; they are said to have been coarse, boastful, vain, and they were, also, deficient in energy and application, and without well-directed ambition, unskillful in handicraft, doubtless entirely through negligence, and totally wanting in that community feeling which begets the study of reciprocal rights and obligations, and reveals the individual's advantage in the promotion of the common interest. Hence, the Creoles were fonder of pleasant fictions regarding the salubrity, beauty, and advantages of their town, than of measures to justify their assumptions. Easily inflamed, they were as easily discouraged, thrown into confusion, and subdued, and they expended the best of their energies in trivial pleasures, especially the masque and the dance; yet they were kind parents, affectionate wives, tractable children, and enthusiastic patriots.

FROM SUBJECTS TO CITIZENS.

It is recorded of the Creoles of New Orleans, that as they stood upon the Place d'Armes and saw the standard of a people whose national existence was a mere twenty years' experiment, taking the place of that tricolor on which perched the glory of a regenerated France, they wept.

Doubtless there were men there not too old to be still in active life, who had even participated in the defiant repudiation of the first cession by force of arms. The difference between the two attitudes is strongly indicative of the difference between the two events. The earlier transfer came to the people loaded with disadvantages and tyrannous exactions; the later came freighted with long-coveted benefits, and with some of the most priceless rights of man. This second transition, therefore, while it might arouse the tenderest regrets in hearts that had just rekindled with their old love of France, and although it forced them into civil and political fellowship with the *Américain*, the object of their special antipathy, could not exasperate and inflame the public mind with the sense of outrage which had been produced by the first.

Nor could they long be entirely blind to the contrast between the two periods; O'Reilly had established a government whose only excellence lay in its strength; Claiborne came to set up a power whose only strength lay in its excellence. His task was difficult, principally because it was to be done among a people distempered by the earlier rule and diligently wrought upon by intriguing Frenchmen and Spanish officials.

To such a community, thus excited, the wisest measures, equally with the most obvious mistakes, were the subjects of wordy resentment. The introduction of the English language, and of a not undue proportion of American appointees into the new courts and the public offices, the suppression of disorder in the public balls at the point of the bayonet, a supposed partiality for Americans in cases at law, the personal character of officials, the governor's ignorance of the French tongue, his large official powers, the alleged bad habits of Wilkinson, the scarcity of money, from the cessation of the annual supply of government funds from Vera Cruz, the formation of American militia companies, and their indiscreet parades in the streets—such were the materials with which was soon kindled a serious degree of excitement.

On the 26th of March, 1804, Congress passed an act dividing the province into two parts on the thirty-third parallel of latitude, the present northern boundary of Louisiana, and establishing for the lower portion a distinct territorial government, under the title of the territory of Orleans. The act was to go into effect in the following

October. One of its provisions was the interdiction of the slave trade. The Creoles heard of it with the liveliest disrelish. Indignation reigned on every side, insurrectionary sentiments were placarded on the corners of the streets, the crowd copied them, and public officers, in attempting to remove them, were driven away.

But at this point, the power of a government which allowed free speech and free opinion to expend itself unmolested, is seen in the fact that unlawful demonstration went no farther. The benevolent and patient Claiborne recognized in these symptoms an insurrection only of the affections, against a forced alienation from that France which had ever been the source of all inspiration, the mutiny of a haughty people's pride against the unfeeling barter of their fealty. Plainly there was not so much a determination of the will that American domination should not continue, as a simple belief of the heart that it would not, and it was not the government, but only some of its measures, that was causing so much heat.

The inference is strong that in this new commercial city, the merchant who, in 1768, had led the people in revolt against legalized ruin, saw plainly that the unwelcome American rule had brought him out of commercial serfdom, and that as a port of the United States, and only as such, his crescent city could enter upon the great future which was hers in virtue of her geographical position.

Indeed, the majority of merchants, as has been shown, were already Americans. As to other influential branches of the community, it was soon plain that they were not entirely blind to the advantages awaiting them under the new domination. For while they still clung to the delusion of a French or Spanish recession, they presently began to make impatient, if not imperious, demand for the rights of American citizens, as pledged to them in the terms of the treaty. The error made thirty-six years before, of appealing to the country that had cast them off, was not repeated; but when in June and July three public meetings were held, called together by some of the most influential private citizens of the territory and city, it was to memorialize the American Congress, not to rescind the treaty of cession, but for the recall of an action which seemed to them likely to delay their admission into the Union. It is highly characteristic of their provincial short-sightedness, that the committee appointed to bear this important, but vain, appeal to Congress, was composed of MM. Derbigny, Sauvé, and Destréhan, two Frenchmen and a Creole.

On the 1st of October the territorial government went into operation. Claiborne was still retained as governor. The division of the province, the establishment of the legislative council by presidential appointment instead of by the votes of the people, the nullification of certain Spanish land-grants and an official reinspection of all titles, were accepted, if not with patience, at least with a certain characteristic grace, which the Creole is wont to assume before the inevitable; but the lessons of the French and the Spanish rule were not to be unlearned in a day, and his respect was not always forthcoming toward laws that could be opposed or evaded. "This city," wrote Claiborne, "requires a strict police; the inhabitants are of various descriptions—many highly respectable, and some of them very degenerate." The attempt of a sheriff and posse to arrest a Spanish officer was prevented by 200 men; swords were drawn, and the resistance ceased only on the appearance of a detachment of United States troops. Above all, the slave trade, which the protesting delegates had represented to Congress as "all-important to the very existence of their country", was diligently persisted in through lakes Borgne, Pontchartrain, and Maurepas, the bayou Barrataria, and many other inlets in the labyrinthian coast-line of the gulf-marshes.

The labors of the legislative council began on the 4th of December. A charter of incorporation was given by it to the city of New Orleans, which constituted "all free white inhabitants of New Orleans a body corporate, by the name of the mayor, aldermen, and inhabitants". There were fourteen aldermen. The city was divided into four wards. The charter went into operation early in March, 1805, and in the election of these aldermen the people of New Orleans, for the first time in her history, exercised the right of suffrage.

The season of amusements was free from the bickerings of the previous winter. The protest of Spain against the cession had long been formally withdrawn, the insinuations and intrigues of her officials, who lingered in Louisiana, were without material effect, and on the last day of the year the governor had reported a gratifying state of order in New Orleans.

The petition to Congress, which had not come before that body until the 4th of January, 1805, was, in the main, as has been intimated, ineffectual. Yet it received some consideration, and on the 2d of March, with many safeguards and limitations unwelcome to the chafing Creoles, the right was accorded them to elect a house of representatives. Thus gradually and guardedly the government began to open before them the wide freedom of American citizenship. The same act empowered them "to form for themselves a constitution and state government as soon as the free population of the territory should reach 60,000 souls, in order to be admitted into the Union".

The course of affairs continued to be marked by a certain feverishness rather than by prominent events. War between Great Britain and Spain, and the opening of Havana to neutral vessels, stimulated the commercial activity of New Orleans; but the pertinacious presence of Casa Calvo, Morales, and other Spaniards (whom Claiborne was finally compelled to force away in February, 1806), the rumors which they kept alive, the apprehension of war with Spain, the doubt as to the resultant attitude of the Creole and European population, the malignant enmity of sundry American malcontents led by the younger Daniel Clark, and a fierce quarrel in the church, between the vicar-general and the pastor of the cathedral, with their respective parties, kept the public mind in a perpetual ferment.

Still, in all this restiveness and discord, there was an absence of revolutionary design. The community, whose planting, springing, and gradual development have been so studiously and minutely followed in the foregoing pages, had at length undergone its last transplanting, and taken root in American privileges and principles. From this point its interesting history, replete with the incidents of war, fire, pestilence, blood, commercial aggrandizement and decay, as it will be shown to be, may often be treated with comparative cursoriness, which could not be indulged in while studying the causes of its existence and the origin and growth of its peculiar people.

Of this people Claiborne, in November, 1806, was able to write, alluding to the seditious plot which is next to be considered: "Were it not for the calumnies of some Frenchmen who are among us, and the intrigues of a few ambitious, unprincipled men, whose native language is English, I do believe that the Louisianians would be very soon the most zealous and faithful members of our republic."

BURR'S CONSPIRACY.

On the 26th day of June, 1805, there arrived in the port of New Orleans from the West "an elegant barge", equipped with "sails, colors, and ten oars", manned by "a sergeant and ten able, faithful hands", and carrying a single passenger. He was the bearer of letters from General Wilkinson, introducing him in the city, and one, specially, to Daniel Clark, stating that "this great and honorable man would communicate to him many things improper to letter, and which he would not say to any other". Governor Claiborne wrote to Secretary Madison, "Colonel Burr arrived in this city on this evening." He remained in New Orleans ten or twelve days, receiving much social attention, and then left for St. Louis, expressing his intention to return in the following October.

During the winter of 1805–'06 the seeming imminence of war with Spain induced the governor to make such diligent preparations for defense as his meager resources allowed, and he naturally thought it strange that at such a juncture General Wilkinson should, from only 220 serviceable troops in the city, remove to Mississippi territory an entire company, but, forced to look to his Creole militia as a source of reliance, he was pleased to see them throw off, momentarily, their habitual apathy, and to hear from them expressions of patriotic ardor. The city banks contained at that time some $2,000,000, and with good reason he feared that it would attract the cupidity and arouse the enterprise of its enemies. The real danger, however, lurked where it was little suspected, for as yet he probably knew nothing of the dark plot for the plunder of New Orleans and the conquest of Mexico, growing in the mind of the man in whose honor he had himself, a few months before, spread a public banquet.

The expulsion of Casa Calvo and Morales, on the 1st and 15th of February, 1806, increased the ill-feeling between the United States and Spain. On the 15th of March the Spanish governor on the east of the territory forbade the future transmission of United States mails through his province, and on the western border, at the river Sabine, the Spanish-American officials began a show of armed muster and aggression. The upright young patriot who governed at New Orleans, passed the spring and summer in sad perplexity, beset by dangers both outward and manifest and internal and hidden. The encroachments of the Spaniards, the fierce enmity of certain influential American residents, the mortifying supineness of the Creoles, for which he was continually making excuses, the too hastily suspected sedition of Père Antoine, the pastor of the cathedral, were not to him more serious cause of alarm and mortification, than the inactivity of the United States forces under the orders of Wilkinson.

"My present impression is," he wrote to the acting governor of Mississippi territory, "that *all is not right*. I know not whom to censure, but it seems to me that there is wrong somewhere."

Even the brighter hopes now and then inspired by the more generous freaks of an unstable and whimsical public sentiment, betrayed a touch of pathos. On the 17th of October he wrote to the Secretary of War: "I hasten to announce to you the patriotism of the citizens of New Orleans and its vicinity. At a muster this morning of the first, second, and fourth regiments of militia, every officer, non-commissioned officer, and private present made a voluntary tender of their services for the defense of the territory generally, and more particularly for the defense of the city. This display of patriotism affords me much satisfaction, and has rendered this [day?] among the happiest of my life." Within three months he wrote: "Their enthusiasm has in a great measure passed away, and the society here is now generally engaged in what seems to be a primary object, the acquisition of wealth."

But unknown equally to the preoccupied money-getters of New Orleans, and to their anxious governor, the principal danger had passed. Late in the previous September Wilkinson had arrived at Natchitoches, and had taken chief command of the troops there confronting the Spanish forces. On the 8th of October Samuel Swartwout, an adherent of the bad cause, brought him a confidential letter from Aaron Burr. He was received with much attention, remained eight days, and departed for New Orleans. On the 21st of October Wilkinson dispatched a messenger to the President of the United States, bearing a letter, in which the nefarious schemes believed to be cherished by Aaron Burr were exposed.

Eight days later he effected an arrangement with the Spaniards for the withdrawal of the troops of both governments from the contested boundary, leaving the question of its final location to be settled by their respective governments, and, dispatching Major Porter in advance of him with a force of artificers and a company of 100 soldiers, hastened to New Orleans.

The arrival of these in the city in November, their early re-enforcement, the hurried repairing, mounting, and equipping of every siege gun and field piece in the town, the preparation of shell, grape, and canister, of buckshot cartridges and of harness, the manning of the redoubts, the issue of contracts for palisades and other appointments of defense, and the prevalence of many rumors, threw the city into a state of panic.

Wilkinson demanded of Claiborne the proclamation of martial law: "The dangers which impend over the city and menace the laws and government of the United States, from an unauthorized and formidable association, must be successfully opposed at this point, or the fair fabric of our independence, purchased by the best blood of our country, will be prostrated, and the Goddess of Liberty will take her flight from this globe forever."

To this request the law-honoring Claiborne declined to accede; but the chamber of commerce of the city was called together, the plot laid before them, and the resources and needs of land and naval defense explained. The members at once subscribed several thousand dollars, and recommended a transient embargo of the port for the purpose of procuring sailors. But Wilkinson presently decided to act without Claiborne's co-operation. If Claiborne did not distrust his motives, it was not from want of advice from one who did. The acting governor of Mississippi territory wrote to him in December:

Should he [Burr] pass us, your fate will depend on the general [Wilkinson], not on the colonel. If I stop Burr, this may hold the general in his allegiance to the United States. But if Burr passes this territory with 2,000 men, I have no doubt but the general will be your worst enemy. Be on your guard against the wily general. He is not much better than Catiline. Consider him a traitor, and act as if certain thereof. You may save yourself by it.

Wilkinson, on his part, wrote: "I believe I have been betrayed, and therefore shall abandon the idea of temporizing or concealment the moment after I have secured two persons now in this city." On Sunday, the 14th of December, Dr. Erick Bollman was arrested by order of Wilkinson. On the 16th, when a writ of *habeas corpus* was obtained from the courts in favor of Bollman and of two others, Swartwout and Ogden, who had been arrested at Fort Adams and were then confined on board a United States bomb-ketch in the river, opposite the city, Bollman was not to be found; no boat could be hired to carry the officer of the court to the bomb-ketch, and on the following day, when one was procured, Swartwout had been removed. Ogden was set free, but only to be rearrested with one Alexander, and held despite writs of *habeas corpus*, a powerless writ of attachment against Wilkinson, and the vain application of the court to the governor to sustain it with force. The judge resigned, and the power of Wilkinson became supreme.

On the 14th of January, 1807, General Adair, the intimate of Burr, arrived in New Orleans unannounced, stating that Colonel Burr, unattended save by a servant, would be in the city in three days. The same afternoon his hotel was surrounded by 120 regulars, commanded by one of Wilkinson's aids, by whom he was arrested at the dinner table. He was put in confinement and presently sent away. The troops beat to arms, a force of regulars and militia paraded the streets of the terrified city, and Judge Workman, the issuer of the late writs, and two others, Kerr and Bradford, were thrown into confinement. Bradford was at once released, however, and Workman and Kerr were set at liberty the next day on writs from the United States district court. At this inopportune moment a Spanish force of 400 men, from Pensacola, arrived at the mouth of bayou St. John, a few miles from the city, on their way to Baton Rouge. Their commander asked of Claiborne, for himself and suite, the privilege of passing through New Orleans. They were promptly refused.

On the 22d of January the legislative council, which had convened ten days before, addressed the governor, disclaiming for the Creoles all participation and sympathy in the treason which threatened their peace and safety, but boldly expressing their intention to investigate the "extraordinary measures" of Wilkinson "and the motives which had induced them, and to represent the same to the Congress of the United States".

On the 28th of January news was received that Burr, having arrived at a point near Natchez with fourteen boats and 80 or 100 men, had been met by a large detachment of Mississippi militia, arrested, taken to Natchez, and released on bond to appear for trial at the next term of the territorial court. He left the territory, however; the governor of Mississippi offered a reward of $2,000 for his apprehension, and on the 3d of March word came to New Orleans announcing his rearrest at Fort Stoddart, Alabama.

About the middle of May Wilkinson sailed from New Orleans to Virginia, to testify in that noted trial which, though it did not eventuate in the conviction of Aaron Burr, made final wreck of the treasonable designs attributed to him, and restored public tranquillity.

THE WEST INDIAN IMMIGRATION.

The fact, that in the period between the cession and the taking of the United States census of 1810, the city more than doubled its population, has given color to the erroneous impression, that there occurred as early as this a large influx of Americans. This was not the case.

In 1806, the third year after the cession, the whole number of white inhabitants in New Orleans whose language was not French or Spanish, comprised but 350 men capable of bearing arms. If allowance is made for the fact that many of these were most likely newcomers and unmarried, the whole number of souls represented by these 350 able-bodied men can hardly be estimated to have exceeded 1,400. In 1803 the population of New Orleans was over one-fourth that of the whole population of those portions which became the territory of Orleans. A like proportion in the census of 1806, would show a population in the city not less than 12,000, of which about three-fifths, or 7,500, were white. There were, therefore, only about 14 Americans in each 75 white—18½ per cent., or 12 per cent. of the whole population.

Between 1806 and 1809, the total American immigration to the whole territory was scarcely 2,400 persons, and the American population within the city most likely did not rise above a total of 3,100. Yet the United States census, taken in the following year, showed an entire population in New Orleans and its precincts of 24,552. The American element, therefore, was a very inconsiderable part of the whole, at least as to numerical value, and the source of increase must be looked for in an opposite direction.

The wars of Napoleon had provoked the descent of hostile expeditions upon various islands of the French West Indies, and brought much distress upon their inhabitants. In Cuba large numbers of white and mulatto refugees, who, on the occasion of the insurrection in St. Domingo, had escaped across to Cuba with their slaves, were now, by the state of war between France and Spain, forced again to become exiles. Within sixty days, between the 19th of May and the 18th of July, 1809, 34 vessels from Cuba brought to New Orleans over 1,800 whites, nearly as many free persons of color, and about 2,000 slaves; in all, 5,797 souls. Others followed later from Cuba, Guadeloupe, and other islands, until they amounted in total to 10,000. There is no record of any considerable number having returned home after the termination of these wars, or of their leaving New Orleans to settle elsewhere.

The ties of a common religion, a common tongue, and a common political sentiment, with what probably seemed to many a similarity of misfortunes, naturally made the Creoles of the West Indies welcome to the Creoles of Louisiana. To these they came somewhat in the character of re-enforcements, at a moment when the power of the *"Américains"*, few in numbers but potent in energy and in advantages, was looked upon with hot jealousy.

On the other hand, the Americans quite as naturally looked upon these unprofitable raisers of the price of bread and of rent with fierce disfavor. They had themselves done little to improve the state of morals or of order. Some had come to the region to make their permanent residence there; many more had no such intention; both sorts were, alike, simply and only seeking wealth.

In fact the city was ill prepared to receive a large and sudden accession to its population, unless the increase was to come from some superior source. To re-enforce and fortify the indolent and unyielding Creoles, inflamed and exasperated by the new and untempered national pride and aggressive energies of the Americans, was to postpone the common harmony which it was so desirable to hasten. And yet the native Creole element was one of the best in the community. The Spaniards were very few, being in all probability less in number than in 1806, when the mayor of New Orleans reported their total at 230. But few as they were, fewer would have been better. "They are generally of that description," wrote Secretary Graham to Madison, "who would be ready to seize any moment of disturbance to commit the vilest depredations, and, whether in peace or in war, they are a nuisance to the country." Even the mild Claiborne mentioned them as "for the most part composed of characters well suited for mischievous and wicked enterprises".

The free people of color were an unaspiring, corrupted, and feeble class, of which little was feared and nothing hoped. In numbers they were on the increase, and from an official report of those among them able to bear arms in 1806, their whole number in 1809 must be estimated at not under 2,000. The German and Irish elements had begun to come in, but were inappreciable. The floating population was extremely bad. Sailors from all parts of the world took sides, according to the hostile nations from which they came, in bloody street riots and night brawls, and bargemen, flatboatmen, and raftsmen from the wild regions, not then entirely wrested from the Indians, along the banks of the Ohio, Tennessee, and Cumberland rivers, abandoned themselves, at the end of their journey, to the most shameful and reckless excesses.

A spirit of strife seemed to pervade the whole mass. A newspaper article reflecting upon Napoleon, in 1806, gave rise to a storm of indignation that had almost ended in a riot, and that led the governor to suspect the French consul of intriguing with the Creoles. Plays were put upon the theater boards which caused the Ursulines to appeal to the governor for protection against public derision. Even the humble Père Antoine, the pastor of the cathedral, was momentarily under suspicion of exercising a seditious influence among the people of color. In 1807 a public uprising was hardly prevented, as the consequence of the action of three young officers of the navy forcibly releasing a slave girl who was being punished by her master.

In September of the same year occurred the "batture riots", a fierce contest between the public and some private claimants, represented by the noted jurist, Edward Livingston, for the ownership of the sandy deposits made by the Mississippi river in front of the faubourg Ste. Marie. Two distinct outbreaks occurred. In the second, which took place on the 15th of September, 1807, the Creoles, ignoring the decision of the Supreme Court, rallied by thousands to the *batture* (as the new deposits of alluvium outside the levee are called), led by the beat of a drum, and were only quieted and dispersed by the patient appeals of Governor Claiborne, addressed to them on the spot, and by the recommittal of the contest to the United States courts, in whose annals it is so well known a cause. The month of August, 1808, was rendered conspicuous by collisions between American and European sailors, who met each other in battle array and actual skirmish on the levee. The condition of the city became alarming, and Claiborne wrote to the commander of the United States troops in Mississippi for a re-enforcement of regulars.

At this time the United States government was preparing for the war which threatened with transatlantic powers. Claiborne, though anxious to speak well of his people, was forced to confess some lack of confidence in the ardor of a populace that—always ripe for disturbance—furnished no volunteers for war. "You are not uninformed," he wrote in 1809, "of the very heterogeneous mass of which the society of New Orleans is composed. England has her partisans; Ferdinand the Seventh some faithful subjects; Bonaparte his admirers; and there is a fourth description of men, commonly called Burrites, who would join any standard which would promise rapine and plunder." A paper was published, devoted to the interests of this faction, and known as *La Lanterne Magique*, whose "libelous publications against the government and its officers" gave the executive much anxiety, issued among a people "still for the most part strangers to our government, laws, and language".

Such was the city into which, suddenly—despite the loud hostility of Americans, English, and Spanish, the laws against the importation of slaves, the appeal of Claiborne to the American consuls at Havana and Santiago de Cuba to impede the movement, the point-blank order to the free people of color to depart from the territory, and the actual effort to put it into execution—there began to pour these thousands of West Indian exiles; Creoles, free mulattoes, and slaves, some with goods and chattels, others in absolute destitution, and "many * * * of doubtful character and desperate fortune", until their numbers about equaled the original population upon whose hospitality they were thrown, and the cost of living daily increased the numbers of distressed poor.

The readiness with which the three different classes of this immigration dissolved into the corresponding parts of the New Orleans community, is indicated in the fact, that they never appeared again in the city's history in anything like a separate capacity. And yet it might be much easier to underestimate than to exaggerate the silent results of an event that gave the French-speaking classes twice the numerical power with which they had begun to wage their long battle against American absorption.

But it was not by the force of mere numbers that the American was either to assert his value or to be more than momentarily checked in his peaceful onset. He confronted the Creole with the power of capital and of an active, enterprising, practical mind, a vigorous offshoot of the greatest commercial nation on the earth; with new aims, a new tongue, new modes of thought, new conceptions of the future destiny of New Orleans, and with an ill-disguised contempt for the more dignified sentiments and customs of the ancient Louisianians, he came unasked, proposing to accomplish a commercial conquest of their city and territory.

The year 1811, therefore, may be set forward to mark a turning point in the history of New Orleans. The Creole, attained to the climax of comparative numerical strength, and armed with all the privileges and advantages with which a free government could invest him, stood forth to give to American civilization the only prolonged conflict that has ever been maintained against it by a small and isolated community. The course of events now turned to the advantage of the new New Orleans and its prospective new master. On the 4th of November, 1811, a convention, elected by the people of Orleans territory, met in New Orleans, and on the 28th of the following January adopted a state constitution; and on the 30th of April, 1812, "Louisiana" was admitted into the Union.

In the meantime an incident had occurred of even greater significance. "On the 10th of January, 1812, the inhabitants of New Orleans witnessed the approach of the first vessel propelled by steam" that navigated the Mississippi, the "Orleans" from Pittsburgh.

THE WAR OF 1812–'15.

A magnificent future seemed now to await only a clearer political sky on and across the Atlantic, to lift and bear New Orleans forward to an imperial position among the great commercial cities of the world. The Spanish-American colonies encircling the Gulf of Mexico, were asserting their independence; the triumphs of inventive genius were making cotton one of the world's great staples; steam navigation promised a secured and a mightier freedom of the Mississippi; and the boundless valley of which New Orleans seemed the only gateway for commerce, was bidding fair to become the provision-house of the world, and the consumer of an untold wealth of European manufactures. But even the partial realization of these expectations was destined to be forerun by a season in which the very existence of the city was threatened. On the 18th of June, 1812, Congress declared war against Great Britain.

The persistent effort to make Canada the seat of hostilities, left New Orleans virtually undefended, though surrounded and infested with dangers. Congress, it is true, authorized the President to hold and occupy that part of Florida west of the Perdido river. In 1813, Wilkinson marched to the Mobile, drove the Spaniards out of Fort Charlotte on the 13th of April, and established a small fortification, Fort Bowyer, on a point of land commanding the entrance to Mobile bay, thus removing as far as Pensacola a neighbor only less objectionable than the British. But, this done, he was ordered to the seat of operations on the Canada line, and even a part of the small force of regulars which was in Louisiana was withdrawn in the same direction.

The English were already in the Gulf of Mexico; the Creek Indians were growing offensive; in July, 700 of them crossed the Perdido, and, on the 13th of September, 350 whites—men, women, and children—were massacred at Fort Mimms, in Mississippi, and the Creek war set in. Within New Orleans the elements of danger were almost equally great. Bands of drunken Choctaws—a people who, it was constantly feared, would take up the hatchet and join the Creeks—roamed through the streets. Lafitte and his men, a numerous band of piratical smugglers, made their rendezvous in the neighboring waters of Barataria bay, and appeared daily in the city's public resorts. A crevasse overflowed a portion of the town, and incendiary fires became so common as to produce a profound sense of unsafety through this cause alone. In the midst of these excitements and alarms, the batture trouble again sprang up, and for a time agitated the public mind.

Under this condition of affairs, Claiborne, in July and September, ordered the state militia to hold itself ready to take the field at a moment's notice, and was much encouraged by the alacrity with which this easy preliminary of a sterner duty was performed. As the autumn wore on the rumors of invasion multiplied, relief continued still to be unfurnished, and the commander of United States forces in Mississippi and Louisiana (the seventh military district), not only assured Governor Claiborne that he could muster at most only 700 regulars, but, under order of the President, made requisition upon the state of Louisiana for 1,000 militia, to be mustered into the service of the general government for six months.

On the 25th of December, 1813, Claiborne ordered the mustering of this quota. Certain rural parishes at once responded; but New Orleans as promptly displayed that perfectly sincere insubordination of the individual's liberty and opinion to the common welfare or the common conviction. Three or four companies only of the city militia answered the call. The rest firmly refused either to volunteer or to be drafted, some at the same time expressing their entire readiness to do service within the state, while others were ready for duty inside the limits of the city and its suburbs, but only by companies, under their own officers, and in such a way as to be relieved at short intervals.

In February, 1814, 400 militia from the rural districts having reported in a body at the Magazine barracks, opposite New Orleans, the governor renewed his order of the previous December, and directed that delinquents be dealt with according to law and military usage. It was met with clamorous denunciation and refusal to obey. The country militia declined to be mustered in without the city militia, and volunteered their services to enforce obedience; this tender came to the knowledge of the city companies, and only the discreet refusal of Claiborne to lean upon any support but the law, averted the mortifying disaster of a battle without an enemy. As it was, the rural military, already melting away by desertion, was disbanded, and the governor, unsupported by the legislature and denounced on all sides as a tyrant, was compelled to report a failure, amiably apologizing for the community at the last, as being emphatically ready to "turn out in case of actual invasion". Fortunately, that actual invasion for which the strangely but conscientiously lethargic city was willing to prepare, whenever it should be obviously too late, did not come that spring, nor until the events of the Creek war had brought to view the genius of Andrew Jackson.

Meantime affairs in New Orleans grew rather worse than better. In March it became necessary for the governor to suppress a projected filibustering expedition to Texas. In April, although the national government, too late for the act to afford relief, had raised the embargo, the New Orleans banks suspended payment. The same month brought word of the fall of Paris and of the abdication of Napoleon, and of the consequent ability of England to throw new vigor into the war with America, and to spare troops for the conquest of Louisiana. The knowledge became painfully distinct, too, that while the majority of the people were lamenting at once the disasters of France and the fresh dangers of British invasion, there were those in the city, Spaniards and Englishmen, to whom the new face of affairs was entirely welcome.

However, the issue was fast approaching. In July the Creeks sued for peace, and a treaty was made with them on the 9th of August. About the same time a number of British officers arrived at Apalachicola, in Florida, forerunners of an expected military force. They brought with them several pieces of artillery. To these some still disaffected tribes of the Creek nation joined themselves, and were by them armed and drilled.

But the point had at length been reached, when the United States government—of which too little could hardly have been expected since it had not yet protected its own capital—began to take active measures for the preservation of its territory and the defense of its citizens in the southwest. General Jackson was appointed to the work, and in August was expected soon to arrive in New Orleans to take command. Commodore Paterson received instructions from Washington to take the schooner Carolina, ordered to New Orleans for the purpose, and with the coöperation of Colonel Ross, of the forty fourth regiment, to make a descent on the Baratarians.

The requisition for the state's quota of 1,000 militia was now made again, coming, this time, direct from the President, and Claiborne received the assurances of the officers of the city militia, including a corps of free men of color, that they would be ready when called upon to obey orders. Yet, certainly less ill-disposed than in the previous year, their attitude was still characterized by an entire lack of zeal. On the 15th of August Jackson wrote directing, through Claiborne, that they be ready to march to any point at a moment's warning; but the experienced governor did not issue his order calling them to rendezvous at New Orleans until the 5th of September, when Jackson had repaired to Mobile, where the invasion was about to take place.

A little after the landing of the British officers at Apalachicola, some companies of British infantry had arrived at Pensacola, in the sloops of war Hermes and Caron, coming from Bermuda via Havana, under command of Colonel Nichols. He had landed and established his headquarters, unopposed by the nominally neutral Spanish authorities, and had soon been joined by the officers from Apalachicola, at the head of a considerable body of Indians. Toward the close of August he had issued a proclamation, appealing to native Louisianians to aid in liberating their paternal soil, and restoring it to its rightful Spanish master; and to Spaniards, Frenchmen, Italians, and Britons to lend their strength to abolish American usurpation; Kentuckians were promised money for supplies, and an open Mississippi in exchange for neutrality.

Claiborne applied to the governor of Kentucky to hasten forward the troops expected from that state. In a general order he warned his own people against the pretensions of the enemy, and exhorted them to an exercise of that spirit of zealous and united effort, the want of which was their greatest and most perilous deficiency.

The moment was certainly critical. The enemy was treating with the Baratarians, and endeavoring, by offers of commissions and rewards in the British service, to seduce them from their love of country. One of the brothers Lafitte, who were the leaders of the band, had sent the British letter and laid it before Claiborne, with the offer of his services and that of his men in the American cause, on condition that their proscription be annulled. The governor called a council, comprising, with others, Commodore Paterson and Colonel Ross. The patriotism of the smugglers, displayed only when an expedition had been ordered and was almost ready to move for their destruction, was not highly esteemed. It was decided to have no communication with the pirates, and preparations were hurried forward to bring them to justice.

Under such portentous clouds as these the people could not but awake, at last, to the necessity of united effort, and, at a public meeting on the 15th of September, passed patriotic resolutions, and appointed six Creoles and three Americans a committee of safety. How soon afterward another was formed, with conflicting views and plans, is not plainly stated, but it is certain that on the very same day that the first public meeting was held, 700 British troops, 600 Indians, and 4 vessels of war, with 92 pieces of heavy artillery, attacked Fort Bowyer, the small but important fortification erected by Wilkinson to command the entrance to Mobile bay and Mississippi sound. The garrison of 130 men, with 20 guns, repulsed the attack, and the enemy retired again to Pensacola with the loss of 162 men killed and as many wounded; the sloop-of-war Hermes, which, having grounded, they were compelled, themselves, to burn.

Three days later the expedition of Paterson and Ross attacked and destroyed the piratical rendezvous at Barataria, taking vessels and some prisoners, and scattering those who succeeded in escaping. The brothers Lafitte fled up the Lafourche to the "German coast", a part of the Mississippi shore whence the Lafourche starts to empty into Barataria bay. Others by and by gathered upon Last island, at the mouth of the Lafourche, and others found asylum in New Orleans, where they increased the fear of internal disorders.

The British, meanwhile, awaiting the arrival of troops that had sailed from Ireland early in September, to the number of 12,000 or more, were, with or without the consent of the Spaniards, occupying Pensacola, and even garrisoning its forts. General Jackson gathered 4,000 men on the Alabama river, regulars, Tennesseeans, and Mississippi dragoons, and on the 6th of November encamped within three miles of Pensacola and demanded of the Spanish governor that American garrisons be received into the forts until Spaniards could be supplied. On the 7th, this proposition having been rejected, he entered the town and attacked and took the two forts, St. Michael and St. Charles. The British, with some Indians, retreated to the shipping in the bay and sailed away; the remainder of the Indians fled across the country, and Jackson returned to Mobile, and soon after called upon Claiborne to prepare the whole body of the Louisiana militia for service.

On the 10th Claiborne convened the legislature, and on the 15th, with great fear that that body "would not act with the promptitude and energy which the crisis demanded", laid General Jackson's letter before it.

The condition of affairs was indeed deserving of anxiety. The absence of a master spirit to command the confidence of a people accustomed to act only upon individual convictions and interests, caused a general state of discord, apprehension, and despondency. The two committees of safety were engaged in miserable disputes. Credit was destroyed. Money could be borrowed only at 3 or 4 per cent. per month. In the legislature, where time and means were being wasted in idle formalities, the Creole himself finally raised the voice of a noble impatience, and Louaillier, a member from Opelousas, asked: "Shall we always confine ourselves to addresses and proclamations?" It may be he distributed the blame more evenly than the governor had done: "Are we," continues his spirited report, "always to witness the several departments intrusted with our defense languishing in a state of inactivity, hardly to be excused even in the most peaceful times? No other evidence of patriotism is to be found, than a disposition to avoid every expense, every fatigue. Nothing, as yet, has been performed." For the defense of 600 miles of coast there were but one sloop-of-war and six gunboats, the feeble Fort St. Philip on the Mississippi, and the unfinished and but half defensible Fort Petites Coquilles on the Rigolets. The supply of ammunition, especially that for artillery, was totally inadequate, and the marching force in New Orleans numbered but 700 regulars, the 1,000 militia which it had required three imperative calls to bring into the field, and 150 sailors and marines. At Tchefuncta, on the farther side of lake Pontchartrain, lay a half-finished, flat-bottomed frigate, destined to carry 42 guns, work on which had been suspended and so remained, despite the appeals of Commodore Paterson and Governor Claiborne to the general government. "Our situation," says La Carrière Latour, in his invaluable memoir, "seemed desperate."

Suddenly confidence returned; enthusiasm sprang up; all, in a moment, was changed by the arrival, on the 1st of December, of General Jackson. On the day of his arrival he reviewed the uniformed city militia, a small, but well drilled and thoroughly equipped body of Creoles and French. The next day he went down the Mississippi, inspected Fort St. Philip, ordered its wooden barracks demolished and additional cannon mounted, a new battery of 24-pounders constructed opposite the fort, and another erected half a mile above St. Philip on the same bank. Returning to New Orleans, he visited the country northward and eastward behind the city, ordering the erection of a battery at the confluence of bayous Sauvage and Chef Menteur, and sending instructions to Governor Claiborne to obstruct all bayous on Orleans island leading to the Gulf; which instructions it was supposed by all in authority, until too late to repair the oversight, had been thoroughly carried out. The energy and activity of Jackson were imitated on all sides. Soon every able-bodied man in New Orleans and its environs was ready for the field, and the whole militia of the state was organizing and preparing to march.

But the new leader's example was not the only spring of this tardy alacrity. The enemy had hove in sight off Pensacola, a British fleet of 80 sail, under the dreaded Cochrane, so lately the ravager of the Atlantic coast and capturer of Washington city, and was bearing down toward Ship island; and when the legislature, on the 13th, appropriated some $30,000 for purposes of defense, a force of 45 barges, carrying 43 guns and 1,200 men, was at that moment eagerly endeavoring to join battle with the retiring American flotilla of five gunboats and a schooner, near the narrow passes of lake Borgne.

On the night of the 13th this little fleet took a defensive stand across the western passage of Malheureux island, and on the 14th, retreat being impossible by reason of a calm and a strong outward current, it fell, after a gallant resistance, into the hands of an enemy almost ten times its strength. The British were thus in complete possession of lake Borgne and its shores. Had this occurred before the arrival of Jackson in New Orleans, the British army would almost certainly have marched into the city without another battle.

On the next day Claiborne informed the legislature of the disaster, and on the 16th advised its adjournment. The matter was debated, and the legislature decided to remain in session, whereupon Jackson, displeased, took another step, which the same body had pronounced inexpedient, and himself proclaimed martial law, closing with the ringing announcement that, "the safety of the district intrusted to the protection of the general must and will be maintained with the best blood of the country; and he is confident * * * that unanimity will pervade the country generally; but should the general be disappointed in the expectation, he will separate our enemies from our friends. Those who are not for us are against us, and will be dealt with accordingly."

Measures of defense received a further acceleration. At the previous suggestion of the legislature slaves were furnished, by the planters of the neighboring parishes, for work on fortifications, in greater number than could be employed. Major Lacoste, with the battalion of free men of color, the Feliciana dragoons, and two pieces of artillery, was sent to the junction of bayous Sauvage and Chef Menteur, to erect and occupy a redoubt surrounded by a fosse. The garrison of the little post at the mouth of bayou St. John was re-enforced by a company of light artillery. Measures were taken to protect the unfinished frigate at Tchefuncta, and a passport system was established on lake Pontchartrain. The commander of Fort Petites Coquilles was ordered to defend it to the last extremity, and if not able to hold out, to spike his guns and fall back upon the post at Chef Menteur. Word was dispatched to the troops coming from the west to hasten their march. The commander at Mobile was warned to be on the alert against attempts of the enemy to disembark there. A second battalion of free men of color was raised, and the two bodies were put under Colonel Fortier, an opulent white Creole merchant. A Captain Juzon was ordered to collect the Choctaw Indians about the city's outskirts and on the shores of lake Pontchartrain into companies. The inmates of the prisons were taken out of confinement and placed in the ranks. John Lafitte, upon action of the legislature and governor, intended to encourage the movement, again offered the services of himself and his men, bearing his overtures to Jackson in person. They were accepted, some of his band were sent to the forts Petites Coquilles, St. John and St. Philip. Others under Dominique and Beluche, private captains, were enrolled in a body as artillery, and all judicial proceedings against them were suspended.

On the 18th Jackson reviewed and addressed his troops. Edward Livingston appeared as one of his aids. The same day Major Plauché was put in command at bayou St. John, with his battalion. The commanders of outposts and pickets received minute instructions. A guard consisting of firemen and men beyond military age, under General Labatut, policed the city, which was put under the strictest military rule. On the 19th General Carroll arrived at the head of 2,500 Tennesseans, and on the 20th General Coffee came in with 1,200 riflemen from the same state.

The army of Jackson was thus increased to the number of about 6,000 men. Confidence, animation, concord, and even gaiety filled the hearts of the people. "The citizens," says Latour, "were preparing for battle as cheerfully as for a party of pleasure. The streets resounded with Yankee Doodle, *La Marseillaise, Le chant du Départ,* and other martial airs. The fair sex presented themselves at the windows and balconies to applaud the troops going through their evolutions, and to encourage their husbands, sons, fathers, and brothers to protect them from their enemies."

That enemy numbered 14,450 men and a powerful fleet. Sir Edward Packenham commanded the land forces, with Gibbs, Lambert, and Kane for generals of divisions. The fleet was under Admirals Cochrane, Codrington, and Malcolm.

The British, reconnoitering on lake Borgne, soon found at its extreme western end the mouth of a navigable stream, the bayou Bienvenue. It flowed into the lake directly from the west, the direction of New Orleans. There were six feet of water on the bar at the mouth, and more inside. It was more than a hundred yards wide. A mile and a half up the stream they found a village of Spanish and Italian fishermen, who used the bayou as a daily water route to the city market. These men were readily bribed, and under their guidance the whole surrounding country was soon explored. The bayou was found to rise close behind the lower suburb of New Orleans, whence it flowed eastward through a vast cypress swamp lying between bayou Sauvage on the north and the Mississippi river on the south, emerging by and by upon the broad quaking prairies bordering lake Borgne, and emptying into that water. Various plantation draining-canals ran back from the cultivated borders of the Mississippi, and, connecting with the bayou, were found to afford on their margins firm standing ground and a fair highway to the open plains of the Mississippi river shore, immediately below New Orleans. By some oversight, which has never been explained, this easy route to the city's very outskirt had been left entirely unobstructed. On the 21st of December American scouts, penetrating to the mouth of the bayou, saw no enemy, and established themselves as a picket in the fishermen's village, which they had found deserted save by one man.

Meanwhile the enemy had been for some days disembarking on the *Isle aux Pois* (Pea island), at the mouth of Pearl river. On the morning of the 22d General Keane's division embarked from this point in barges, pushed up the lake, and some time before dawn of the following day surprised and overpowered the picket at the fishermen's village, passed on in their boats by way of bayou Bienvenue through the trembling prairie and into and through the swamp forest, disembarked at canal Villeré, and at half past eleven in the morning, the 23d, emerged, at the rear of General Villeré's plantation, upon the open plain, without a foot of fortification confronting them between their camping ground and New Orleans. Here, greatly fatigued, they halted until they should be joined by other divisions.

But General Jackson resolved to attack them without delay. At seven o'clock in the evening, the night being very dark, the American schooner Carolina dropped down the river to a point opposite the British camp, and anchoring close ashore suddenly opened her broadsides and a hot musketry fire at short range. At the same moment General Jackson, who, at the head of 1,200 men and two pieces of artillery, had marched upon the enemy from the direction of New Orleans, and had found them drawn up in echelons half a mile along the river bank, with their right wing extended toward the woods at right angles of the plain, fell upon them first with his right, close to the river shore, and was presently engaged with them along his whole line. The British right, unaware of the approach of General Coffee from the direction of the woods, with 600 men, under cover of the darkness, and attempting to flank Jackson's left, only escaped capture by an unfortunate order of the American colonel in command, restraining the Creoles, as they were about charging with the bayonet. The enemy gave way and succeeded in withdrawing under cover of the night, a rising fog, and the smoke, which was blown toward the American line. The engagement continued for a time with much energy on both sides, but with little system or order. On Jackson's right the British attempted the capture of the two guns, but their charge was repulsed. Companies and battalions on both sides, from time to time, got lost in the darkness and fog, sometimes firing into friendly lines, and sometimes meeting hostile opponents in hand to hand encounters. At the same time the second division of British troops were arriving at the fishermen's village, and hearing the firing, pushed forward in haste, some of them arriving on the field shortly before the state of the elements put a stop to the contest.

At four o'clock on the morning of the 24th Jackson fell back about two miles nearer to the city, and, behind a canal running from the river to and into the wooded swamp, and known as Rodriguez's canal, took up and began to fortify his permanent line, choosing this ground on account of the narrowness of the plain. This was only some four miles from the lower limits of the city.

Here from day to day the preparations for defense went rapidly on, while the British were diligently gathering their forces and laboriously, through much inclement weather and over miry ground, bringing up their heavy artillery. Skirmishing was frequent and of great value to Jackson's raw levies. On the 27th and 28th a brisk cannonade was interchanged from newly erected batteries on either side, resulting in the destruction of the Carolina with red-hot shot, leaving but a single American vessel, the Louisiana, in the river, but ending, on the other hand in the demolition of the British batteries. On the 1st day of January, 1815, the enemy opened suddenly from three formidable batteries, driving Jackson from his headquarters, and riddling it with shot and shell. The Americans replied with vigor, opposing 10 guns to 28, and succeeded in dismounting several of the enemy's pieces. A few bales of cotton, forming part of the American fortifications, were scattered in all directions and set on fire. No further use was made of this material during the campaign. This artillery contest ceased at three in the afternoon, and during the night the British dismantled their batteries, abandoning five pieces of cannon.

Thus they were, day by day, training their inexperienced foe, and while being augmented by the steady arrival of troops from their fleet in the Gulf, were allowing Jackson, also, to be materially re-enforced. Three hundred Acadians had joined him on the 30th of December. On the 1st of January 500 men arrived from Baton Rouge.

and on the 4th the expected Kentuckians, poorly clad and worse armed, but 2,250 in number, gave Jackson, after he had manned all strategic points, an effective force on his main line of 3,200 men. This line was half a mile of rude and extremely uneven earthworks, lying along the inner edge of Rodriguez's canal, across the plain, from the river bank to a point within the swamp forest on the left, and dwindling down after it entered the wood to a double row of logs laid over one another, with a space of two feet between the two rows filled with earth. The artillery defending this half mile of breastwork and ditch consisted of twelve pieces.

Winter rains had greatly impeded the British movements, but Lambert's division at length joined the others, and preparations were made for the decisive battle. On the 6th and 7th they were busy making ready to storm the American works, preparing fascines for filling the ditch and ladders for mounting the breastworks, and also getting boats through from Villeré's canal into the river, in order to cross and throw a force against Commodore Paterson's very effective marine battery on the farther side of the river, and some against extremely slender defenses beyond.

A little before daybreak on the 8th, the enemy moved out of their camp, and by daylight were plainly seen spread out upon the plain across two-thirds of its breadth, seemingly about 6,000 strong. The British plan was, at a given signal, to make four simultaneous demonstrations upon the American line, one to be made on the farther and three on the nearer side of the river.

About half past eight o'clock a rocket went up on the British side, near the woods, the Americans replied by a single cannon shot, and the attack began. On the American extreme left, inside the cypress forest, some black troops of the British force made a feeble onset—an evident feint—and were easily repulsed by Coffee's brigade. On the right, near the river, the enemy charged in solid column with impetuous vigor, and with such suddenness, that before the American battery stationed at that point could fire the third shot, the British were within the redoubt and had overpowered its occupants; but, in attempting to scale the breastworks behind, their leader, Colonel Rennie, was killed, and the Americans presently retook the redoubt.

On the opposite side of the river, a column of the enemy had been expected to engage the Americans defending that quarter, and thus save the other attacking columns from the enfilading fire of the battery on that side. But this force had not been able to move with the celerity expected of it, and though it later reached its intended field of action, it easily driving the Americans, some 600 in number, from their indefensible line, and compelling the abandonment of the marine battery, this partial success was achieved only after the British had, everywhere else, lost the day.

The main attack was, meantime, made against that part of the American line in the plain, but near the edge of the swamp. At a ditch, some 400 yards in front of the American works, the main force of the enemy formed in close column of about 60 men front, and, burdened not only with heavy fascines made of ripe sugar-canes and with ladders, but with their weighty knapsacks also, they advanced, giving three cheers, literally led to the slaughter. Preceded by a shower of Congreve rockets, they moved forward in perfect order, covered for a time by a thick fog, but soon entirely exposed not only to the full storm of artillery and musketry from the American breastworks, but, upon their extended flank, to the more distant fire of Paterson's marine battery, not yet diverted by the forces sent against it, and manned by the trained gunners of the United States navy. The American fire was delivered with terrible precision, that of Flaugeac's battery, against which the onset was principally directed, tearing out whole files of men. Yet, with intrepid gallantry, their brave enemy came on, still moving firmly and measuredly, and a few platoons had even reached the canal, when the column faltered, gave way, and fled precipitately back to the ditch where it had first formed. Here the troops rallied, laid aside their cumbersome knapsacks, were reinforced, and advanced again in the same fatal columnar form, though now at a more rapid gait and with less order. But the same deadly storm met them as before. The part of the line directly attacked was manned by Tennessee and Kentucky riflemen—Indian-fighters, accustomed to firing only upon selected victims. This fact, with the unfortunate slowness of onset in the first attacking column, is probably the true explanation for the well-nigh unaccountable defeat of so fine an army by so ill-equipped a foe. First Sir Edward Packenham, then General Gibbs, then General Keane, the first two mortally and the last severely wounded, with many others of prominent rank, were borne from the field, the column again recoiled, and, falling back to its starting point, could not be induced to make a third attack. The British batteries, which had opened vigorously at the outset, continued to fire until two in the afternoon, and the British troops remained drawn up in their ditches to repel an American attack, if such should be made; but, from the first signal of the morning to the abandonment of all effort to storm the line was but one hour, and the battle of New Orleans was over at half-past nine.

On the 9th, two bomb-vessels, a sloop, a brig, and a schooner, a part of the British fleet, appeared in sight of Fort St. Philip, on the Mississippi, and, anchoring two and a quarter miles away, began a bombardment which continued until the 18th without result, whereupon they withdrew; and the same night General Lambert stealthily evacuated the British camp. On the 27th the last of his forces embarked from the shores of lake Borgne.

Even in the recital of history the scenes of triumphant rejoicing, the hastily erected arches, the symbolical impersonations, the myriads of banners and pennons, the columns of victorious troops, the crowded balconies, the rain of flowers, the huzzahs of the thronging populace, the salvos of artillery, the garland-crowned victor, and the ceremonies of thanksgiving in the solemn cathedral, form a part that may be left to the imagination. In New

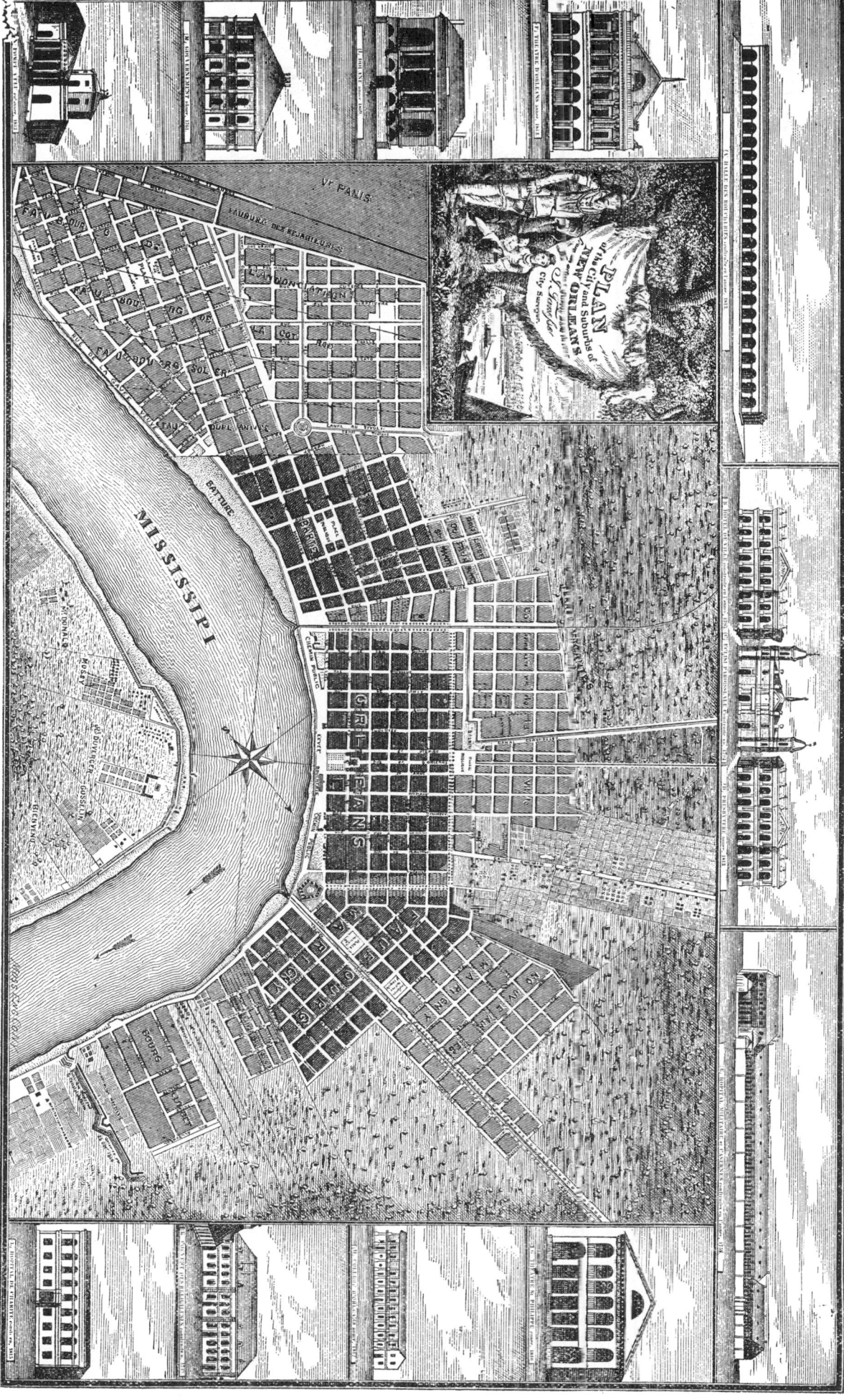

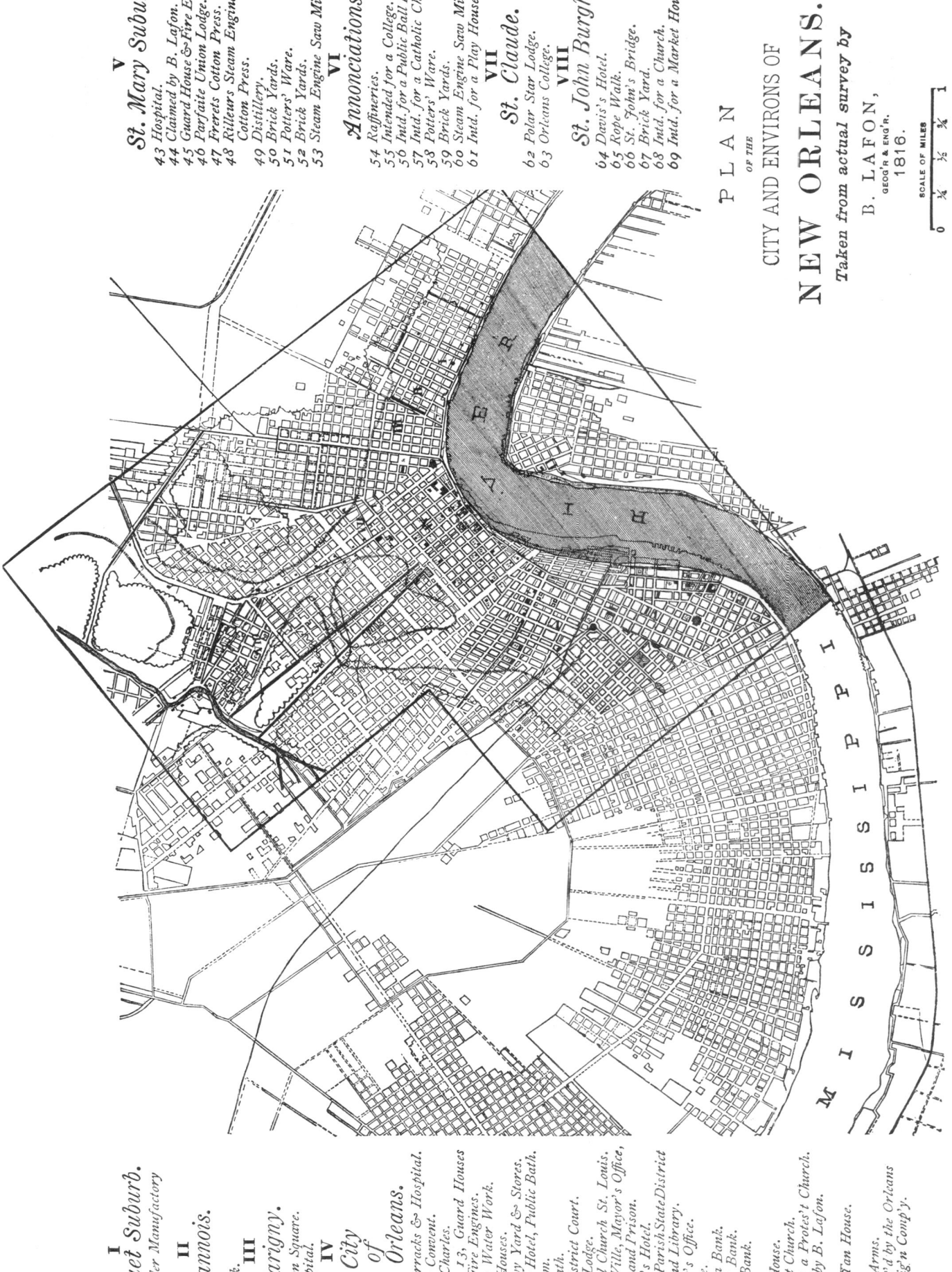

V

St. Mary Suburb.

43 Hospital.
44 Claimed by B. Lafon.
45 Guard House & Fire Engine.
46 Parfaite Union Lodge.
47 Frerets Cotton Press.
48 Rilleur's Steam Engine
   Cotton Press.
49 Distillery.
50 Brick Yards.
51 Potters' Ware.
52 Brick Yards.
53 Steam Engine Saw Mill.

VI

Annonciations.

54 Raffineries.
55 Intended for a College.
56 Intd. for a Public Ball Room.
57 Intd. for a Catholic Church.
58 Potters' Ware.
59 Brick Yards.
60 Steam Engine Saw Mill.
61 Intd. for a Play House.

VII

St. Claude.

62 Polar Star Lodge.
63 Orleans College.

VIII

St. John Burgh.

64 Davis's Hotel.
65 Rope Walk.
66 St. John's Bridge.
67 Brick Yard.
68 Intd. for a Church.
69 Intd. for a Market House.

PLAN

OF THE

CITY AND ENVIRONS OF

NEW ORLEANS.

Taken from actual survey by

B. LAFON,

GEOG'R & ENG'R.

1816.

SCALE OF MILES

0   ¼   ½   ¾   1

I

Declouet Suburb.

1 Gun Powder Manufactory
2 Distillery.

II

Dannois.

3 Distillery.
4 Rope Walk.

III

Marigny.

5 Washington Square.
6 Navy Hospital.

IV

City of New Orleans.

7 U. S. Barracks & Hospital.
8 Ursulines Convent.
9 Fort St. Charles.
10, 11, 12, 13, Guard Houses
   and Fire Engines.
14 Latrobe's Water Work.
15 Market Houses.
16, 17, Navy Yard & Stores.
18 Turpin's Hotel, Public Bath.
19 Ball Room.
20 Public Bath.
21 U. S. District Court.
22 Charity Lodge.
23 Cathedral Church St. Louis.
24 Hotel de Ville, Mayor's Office.
25 Goal and Prison.
26 Tremolet's Hotel.
27 Superior Parish State District
   Court and Library.
28 Governor's Office.
29 Exchange.
30 Louisiana Bank.
31 Planters' Bank.
32 Orleans Bank.
33 Hotel.
34 Custom House.
35 Methodist Church.
36 Int'd for a Protes't Church.
37 Claimed by B. Lafon.
38 Lioteau.
39 Furcas Tan House.
40 Paton.
41 Place of Arms.
42 Canal int'd by the Orleans
   Navig'n Comp'y.

Orleans there was little of sorrow mingled with the joy of deliverance. Six of her defenders alone had fallen, and but seven were wounded. The office of healing was exercised principally on the discomfited enemy, whose dead and wounded were numbered by thousands.

On the 13th of February, Admiral Cochrane wrote to General Jackson: "I have exceeding satisfaction in sending to you a copy of a bulletin that I have this moment received from Jamaica, proclaiming that a treaty of peace was signed between our respective plenipotentiaries at Ghent, on the 24th of December, 1814, upon which I beg leave to offer you my sincere congratulations." It was not until the 17th of March that the American commander received official information of the same fact. On the day previous, Claiborne had written to Mr. Monroe, Secretary of War: "Our harbor is again whitening with canvas; the levee is crowded with cotton, tobacco, and other articles for exportation. The merchant seems delighted with the prospect before him, and the agriculturist finds in the high price for his products new excitements to industry."

COMMERCIAL EXPANSION—1815 to 1840.

Now, at length, that era of great prosperity, so freely predicted, actually opened upon New Orleans. The whole Mississippi valley began to increase in population with wonderful rapidity. Its numbers in 1815 cannot be given with exactness, but the United States census shows the growth to have been from 1,078,000 in 1810, to 3,363,000 in 1830. These broadly scattered multitudes, applying themselves for a time almost solely to the development of their new country's vast agricultural resources, accepted for the fruits of their toil those broad avenues to the world's markets which nature afforded in the Mississippi and its immense tributaries; they used either the most primitive modes of transportation or only those improvements upon them furnished by distant enterprise.

Steam navigation, which it has been seen made its first descent of the Mississippi in 1812, began in 1816, after a four years' struggle, successfully to ascend the powerful current of that stream. In 1817 the produce of the great valley came to New Orleans in 1,500 flatboats and 500 barges. In 1821 the arrivals of laden river craft at the levee numbered 287 of steamboats, 174 of barges, and 441 of flatboats.

This new and immeasurably superior mode of transportation was accepted, unquestioned, by the agricultural West. Not yet recognized as the stepping-stone from the old system of commerce by natural highways, to the new system by direct and artificial lines, it held out to the merchants of New Orleans, and the newcomers that daily poured into the town, not only present wealth, but the delusion of absolute and unlimited commercial empire inalienably bestowed by the laws of gravitation. It was hardly possible, but it would have been invaluable, to New Orleans to have discovered, thus early, the real truth unconsciously let slip by one of her citizens of that day, when, sharing, and intending to express, the popular conviction, he wrote: "No such position for the accumulation and perpetuity of wealth and power ever existed."

But for a long series of years nothing transpired to force upon the notice of her merchants the change which lay, as yet, undeveloped in the future, and each year saw her expanding commerce choking her streets and landings, and her harbor front more and more crowded with river and ocean fleets. Her exports rose and sank on the wave of financial inflation and collapse that swept the country in 1815–'19, and, with the clearing away of the wreck in 1820, showed a net increase from five million to seven and a half million dollars.

Population pressed in "from all the states in the Union and from almost every kingdom in Europe. The people numbered 33,000 in 1815 and 41,000 in 1820. New energies asserted themselves in every direction. The ancient parallelogram of ditch and palisades that had so long marked the city's ultimate bounds had disappeared in 1803, and the town was spreading far beyond it on every side. The hands of architect and builder were busy in the narrow streets of the old town, as well as in the broader ones of the suburbs; and halls, churches and schools, stores, warehouses, banks, hotels, and theaters went up in rapid succession. The old Charity hospital was built in Canal street in 1815.

In the faubourg Ste. Marie the development outstripped that in all other quarters. The change in the nature of the city's commerce caused her trade to fall largely into new hands. The French and Creole merchants, looking to the West Indies, to France, and to Spain for a continuance of the old interchange of products and of merchandise, were forced to witness the growth of New Orleans outside the former boundaries and abreast the landing-place of the western and southern produce fleet. This landing-place, convenient to the flatboats because of its slack water, was the contested *batture*, large areas of which were, from 1817 to 1820, reclaimed and soon became the sites of well-compacted store buildings for the accommodation of the commercial Americans. Coffee, indigo, sugar, rice, foreign fruits, and wines the older town managed to retain; but cotton, tobacco, pork, beef, corn, flour, and northern and British fabrics—in short, the lion's share, was intercepted in its descent of the river, or in ascending, was carried above and received at the faubourg Ste. Marie and fell into the hands of the swarming Americans, whose boastful anticipations of the city's future began to leave the Creole out of the account. These newcomers, still numerically in the minority, were seen on every side, looking about with the eye of the invading capitalist; but the faubourg Ste. Marie became distinctively the American quarters.

Here in 1817, in the face of much skepticism on account of the yielding nature of the soil, on Gravier street, between Tchoupitoulas and Magazine, the first square of cobblestone pavement was laid. In 1820 the wooden sidewalks and curbs on the main thoroughfares gave place to others of brick and stone, and in 1822 a general paving of the principal commercial streets, both in the old and the newer towns, was begun.

It cannot seem strange, that among the Louisiana Creoles—a people not prepared by anything in their earlier career to welcome and appropriate the benefits of such a torrent of immigration—the feeling should have been hostile to it, or that they sought no farther in accounting for the lamentable condition of public order and morals. In December, 1816, Claiborne gave place in the gubernatorial office to General Villeré, a Creole, who, in a special message of March, 1818, called for by the "scandalous practices almost at every instant taking place in New Orleans and its suburbs", said, "indeed we should be cautious in receiving all foreigners."

Yet steam navigation, and the enormous fruitfulness of the Mississippi valley, brought a prosperity wide enough to take in all, and the same governor, in the following year, not only congratulated the community on the suppression of disorder, through the establishment of an effective criminal court and the subsidence of party spirit and "idle prejudice", but persevered in an attitude of loyal affection to the American Union which had inspired him even earlier to say: "The Louisianian who retraces the condition of his country under the government of kings, can never cease to bless the day when the great American confederation received him into its bosom."

In 1825 the exports of New Orleans were twelve and a half and her imports four and a half million dollars. The earlier and extraordinary development, between 1810 and 1820, of a simple export and import trade to four times its original size, had caused the population of the city during that time, in the face of annual pestilence, repeated inundation, local disorders, a low state of morals, strangeness of manners and customs, and remoteness from the world's center, almost to double its numbers.

Yet these very figures, indicating an increase of trade twice as large as that of population, should have demonstrated to her citizens the insufficiency of mere commerce, without the aid of manufactures, to enhance the population or the wealth of their city in a proportion at all parallel to the growth of its opportunities. Between 1820 and 1830, the disproportion became still more evident. With an increase of 75 per cent. in the volume of its trade, the numbers of the population advanced from 41,351 only to 49,826, an increase of but 20 per cent. In truth, the influx of population in this period, seems to have consisted of only such limited numbers as the allurements of sudden fortune tempted to take the chances of a short sojourn amid many dangers and discomforts, with little idea of permanent residence. In the same period the population of Baltimore increased 25 per cent., that of Philadelphia 39 per cent., and that of New York 67 per cent.

Not only did the increase of numbers in New Orleans fall so far below its increase of trade and the growth of population in the Atlantic cities, but it failed to keep pace with the numerical and commercial growth of that great valley of which it was supposed to be the sole entrepot. Between 1820 and 1830 the population of this immense region advanced 61 per cent., or three times as rapidly as that of New Orleans. As countries fill up with people, the proportion of those who dwell in towns and cities steadily enlarges; but while New Orleans increased 20 per cent. the states of Louisiana, Arkansas, and Mississippi, entirely tributary to it, without developing any considerable town-life elsewhere, increased in population 57 per cent.

The states farther up the Mississippi did not wait on New Orleans. Other towns and cities rose into importance and grew with astonishing speed. Cincinnati increased from 32,000 to 52,000; Pittsburgh became "in the extent of its manufactures the only rival of Cincinnati in the West"; the embryo city of St. Louis added 41 per cent. to its single 10,000; while smaller, yet not exceeded in its significance by any, the town of Buffalo quadrupled its 2,100 inhabitants as the gateway of a new freight route to northern Atlantic tide-water, many hundreds of leagues more direct than the long journey down the Mississippi to New Orleans and around the dangerous peninsula of Florida. For in 1825 the new principle of commercial transportation began to appear in the opening of the Erie canal. In the same year the Ohio canal was begun, and in 1832 connected the waters of the Ohio river with those of lake Erie, and in 1835 the state of Ohio alone sent through Buffalo to Atlantic ports 86,000 barrels of flour, 98,000 bushels of wheat, and 2,500,000 staves.

Thus early, while New Orleans was rejoicing yearly in an increase of population, commerce, and wealth, its comparative commercial importance was actually decreasing, and that sun of illimitable empire which had promised to shine forever upon her, was beginning to rise upon other cities and to send its rays eastward and even northward, away from and across those natural highways which had been fondly regarded as the only available outlets to the marts of the world. Even steam navigation, which had seemed at first the very pledge of supremacy to New Orleans, began on the great lakes to demonstrate that the golden tolls of the Mississippi were not all to be collected at one or even at two gates.

The ability of New Orleans to arrest these escapes of a commerce that had promised at the opening of the century to be all her own, has been much overrated, as well by lethargic believers in the greatness of her destiny, as by ungenerous critics, dazzled with the success of rival cities. The moment East and West recognized the practicability of taking straighter courses in the direction of the great commercial continent of Europe, the direct became the natural route, and the circuitous the unnatural. New Orleans might, it is true, have delayed the application of the new system by increasing the efficiency of the old, and thus have pushed forward into a more distant future facts which could never be pushed aside; but upon the establishment of east-and-west trade lines New Orleans stood at once and of necessity in a subordinate relation to the commerce of both continents, save in so far as she could continue to remain the most convenient port of the lower Mississippi valley, and until the growth of countries behind her in the Southwest should bring her upon the line of their commerce on its direct way to and across the Atlantic.

Moreover, the drawbacks that beset the city were many and great. Most of them have frequently been mentioned in these pages. Between 1810 and 1837 there were fifteen epidemics of yellow fever. Small-pox was a frequent and deadly visitor, and, in 1832, while the city was still suffering from an epidemic of yellow fever, it was stricken with cholera, which alone destroyed one-sixth of the entire population. So great was the distress, that many of the dead were buried on the spot where they died, and many were thrown into the river.

The danger of navigation on the Ohio and the Mississippi was another serious disadvantage. The losses of property on these two rivers alone, in the five years ending in 1827, were one and a third million dollars, or nearly 2 per cent. of the city's entire export and import trade. Through the offices of the federal government these losses, during the next five years to 1832, were greatly reduced, but in a third term, ending with 1837, the improvement was less obvious, and during a long subsequent period the ill-fame of steam navigation on the Mississippi was part of the count against New Orleans. In 1837 300 lives were lost on the Mississippi by the sinking of a single steamer, and 130 by the burning of another. In 1838 an explosion on the same river destroyed 130 lives, and another on the Ohio, 120 lives. The cost of running a steamboat on these waters was six times as great as on the northern lakes.

The low state of morals and of order continued to give the city an unfortunate character in the esteem of distant communities. In 1823 the legislature, seconded by the governor, who pronounced it "wonderful to have escaped for so long a time from serious internal commotion", urged that the number of United States troops in and near the city be not diminished. The strife between American and Creole continued to call forth the exhortations of governors against jealousies and party spirit, with reference to the accidental circumstances of language or birthplace, and in 1836 it culminated in the division of the city into three separate municipalities, under distinct governments and independent powers, with a mayor and a general council over the whole city. The old town formed the first, the faubourg Ste. Marie the second, and the faubourg Marigny the third municipality. A "native American" party sprang up in 1837, founded on the fear, real or assumed, of the results to be apprehended from immense European immigration. Accounts of travelers ascribed to the St. Domingan element a bad influence on the city's morals, in carrying the love of pleasure to licentiousness, giving themselves passionately to gambling, and resorting with great frequency to the field of honor. This latter practice was carried on in society to a fearful extent. During a visit of General Lafayette to New Orleans, which he made in 1825, a serious feud between officers of the militia, who were engaged in the ceremonies of his enthusiastic reception, was prevented from ending in a duel between the leaders only by Lafayette's personal intervention. When, many years later, it was decided to disfranchise all persons engaging in affairs of honor and to disqualify them from holding office, a Mr. Garcia exclaimed, in the legislature: "It seems to me that there is a conspiracy against the chivalric portion of our population." The legislature continued to make New Orleans the state capital throughout this period, except that from 1830 to 1832 it sat at Donaldsonville. Whether this body and the managers of financial corporations were really open to the charges of bribery and corruption, so fiercely brought against them by a rampant city press, or not, the very recklessness of the accusations indicate a lowness of pitch in the public moral sentiment; and this is still more plainly evidenced in the long tolerance of such scenes as those open-air Sunday afternoon African dances, carousals, and debaucheries in the rear of the first municipality, which have left their monument in the name of "Congo" square. The city was a favorite rendezvous for filibusters. The year 1819 is marked by "General" Long's naval expedition from New Orleans to Galveston bay, with men and supplies. In 1822 an expedition was fitted out to aid Bolivar in his struggle against Spanish power in South America. One hundred and fifty men sailed in a sloop of war, the Eureka, for Porto Cabello in Venezuela, and joined in the naval demonstration to which the place, after a siege, surrendered. The war of independence in Texas, in 1835 and later, produced much excitement in New Orleans, and many hastened to the standard of revolution there, though at that date it was totally discountenanced by both the state and the general government.

Such are some of the impediments that partially obstructed this city's aggrandizement and progress. It may seem that the most of them might have been removed, but another existed which riveted these shackles upon every part: an invincible provincialism pervaded the entire mass of the heterogeneous population. Intensified by Creole influence, by remoteness from civilization, by a "peculiar institution" which doubled that remoteness, and by an enervating climate, it early asserted itself in the commercial and financial creeds of the New Orleans merchant, and in the general conduct of municipal affairs. From this radical misfortune resulted that apathetic disregard of obstacles, that surrender of advantages which need not have been parted with, at least for generations, and that long, boastful oblivion to the fact, that with all her increase in wealth and population, the true status of New Orleans was really slipping back upon the comparative scale of American cities.

The impulse toward municipal improvement that sprang up in 1822 soon subsided. Paving stones could be had in that alluvial region only by being brought from distant shores as ship's ballast, and up to 1835, although there had been another movement in the same direction in 1832–'34, only two streets in New Orleans had been paved in any considerable part of their length, notwithstanding pavements were found as useful and serviceable as elsewhere, and without them even carriages, in bad weather, sank to the axle in the mire. But gas was brought into use for lighting the streets in 1834, and a supply of Mississippi water was furnished through mains under the principal thoroughfares in 1836.

In the matter of sanitation, which so painfully called for attention, measures were well nigh as scarce as appropriations for their performance. Between 1825 and 1838 a natural drain in the rear of the second municipality was broadened and deepened into Melpomene canal. In 1836 a municipal draining company began operations with a draining machine on bayou St. John; but such partial means were totally inadequate to effect a tithe of what the most urgent sanitary necessities of the city actually demanded. In 1821 a quarantine was established, continued until 1825, and then abandoned. For the one item of generous and gratuitous care of the plague-stricken stranger, both in and out of its justly famed charity hospital, the city earned much well-deserved credit. (This institution left its buildings on Canal street, to occupy its present quarters on Common street, in 1832. The old buildings became the state house.) Beyond these efforts no notice was given the subject, except to make the perpetual assertion of the salubrity of the town, unsupported either by statistics or by the effort to obtain them.

The bar at the mouth of the Mississippi remained untouched until 1835, when an appropriation of $250,000 by the general government was so nearly exhausted upon a survey and the preparation of dredging apparatus, that nothing more was done for several years. "Northeast pass," then the deepest mouth of the river, gave 12 feet of water, a depth whose inadequacy for the commercial needs of a near future was overlooked. At that time new vessels, built expressly for the carrying trade between New York and New Orleans, did not exceed 500 tons register. The steamboats on the Mississippi seem to have been about the same capacity, but in 1834 they numbered, on this river and its tributaries, 234.

Indeed, when all is recounted to explain the partly unnecessary and partly inevitable failure of New Orleans to secure the unrivaled supremacy which had been too confidently waited for, it is nevertheless true that the city, in the less immeasurable sphere to which the improvements of the age had consigned her, increased rapidly in commerce and in wealth, and, in the decade between 1830 and 1840, more than doubled her population. The conviction forces its way, that could the people of New Orleans, as a whole, have been inspired with the enthusiasm and enterprise which their merchants expended upon the mere marketing of crops, and have turned those impulses to the removal of obstacles and the placing of their city in an advantageous light before the intelligent world, it would have been then, and for a long time might have remained, the boldest competitor of New York in population, wealth, and imports, as it already was in exports. In 1831 her total exports and imports were $26,000,000. In 1832 they were somewhat less. In 1833 they reached $28,500,000; in 1834 they rose suddenly to over $40,000,000, and in 1835 to $53,750,000.

This sudden expansion is largely accounted for in the extraordinary rise in prices, which became in the whole country the leading feature of these two years. But there was beside, over and above the commerce indicated by these figures, another and a separate source of wealth to New Orleans. The enormous agricultural resources of Arkansas, Mississippi, and Louisiana, and especially the world's ever-increasing demand for cotton, offered the most tempting returns for the investment of even borrowed money. The credit system became universal among the planters of cotton, sugar, and tobacco in these regions, and New Orleans became not only the lender of millions in money at high rates of interest, but the depot of all manner of supplies, which it advanced in large quantities to the planters throughout that immense region. The whole agricultural community became, in a manner, the commercial slaves of the New Orleans factors, unable either to buy or sell save through these mortgagees. A common recklessness in borrower and lender kept the planters constantly immersed in debt, and the city drained of its capital almost the whole year round, to supply the extravagant wants of the planters and the needs of their armies of slaves. Much the larger portion of all the varied products of the West received in New Orleans was exported, not to sea, but to the plantations of the interior, often returning, along the same route, half the distance they had originally come. In this way not only was much of the capital of New Orleans diverted from channels which would have yielded ultimate results incalculably better, but it was converted into planters' paper, based on the value of slaves and the lands they tilled, a species of wealth unexchangeable in the great world of commerce, and, when measured by its results, as utterly fictitious as paper money itself, while even more illusory. But like the paper money which was then inundating the country, this system produced an immense volume of business, which, in turn, called in great numbers of immigrants to swell the ranks of manual labor. New Orleans once more surpassed Cincinnati in population. From 1830 to 1840 no other leading American city increased in such a ratio.

And yet among all causes, there was probably none more potent in suppressing that industrial development, outside of mere commerce, which might so properly have taken place in New Orleans at this stage of her growth, than the all-prevailing blight which fell upon labor, and especially upon intelligent, trained labor, through this institution of African slavery, which seemed to assure untold wealth alike to town and country. A large share of capital was bound up in the labor itself, and that labor, from the necessities of the case, of a very inferior and really unremunerative sort. Hence, the city, though beset with opportunities and filling up daily with immigrants from the British isles and from Europe, failed either to evolve or to attract from abroad those classes of adepts in the mechanical and productive arts which most rapidly augment the common wealth. The gross increase in population between 1830 and 1840 was from 49,826, at the opening of the decade, to 102,193 at its close. One-third of this increase was composed of slaves and free persons of color, classes of population which, under the laws and conventionalities of the time and place, were to the higher orders of the community far more a burden than an advantage. The remaining two-thirds, less so much as is to be accounted to natural increase, was an immense inpouring of Irish and Germans of the poorest classes. The state of society, notwithstanding these re-enforcements, which might so soon, in other regions, have yielded great numbers of the most valuable operatives, remained unattractive, repelled the prospecting manufacturer and his capital, and diverted them to newer towns where labor was uncontemned and skill and technical knowledge sprang forward at the call of enlightened enterprise.

The year 1837 will long be memorable in the history of the United States as the date of the calamitous crisis which followed the mad speculation in lands and the downfall of the United States Bank. In those parts of the Union, especially, where large results had intoxicated enterprise, banks without number and often without foundation, strewed their notes among an infatuated people. In New Orleans, where enterprise had shown but little spirit of adventure outside the factorage of the staple crop, the number of banks was comparatively small, but the spirit of the day was evident in the fictitious character of much that pretended to be banking capital. In 1835-'36 the banks of Louisiana (which may be read New Orleans), with but little over $2,500,000 specie in their vaults, and a circulation of $7,000,000, purported to have an aggregate capital of $34,000,000. One account, of the following year, gives them at the time of their suspension $60,000,000 capital, $4,000,000 deposits, $1,200,000 specie, $1,800,000 real estate, and $72,000,000 receivables, mostly protested.

The condition of affairs was described at that time as a "whirlwind of ruin which had prostrated the greater portion of the city". So-called shinplasters became the currency of the day, driving out everything of intrinsic value. So great was the feeling against the banks and all banking schemes, and so general the ignorance of their true province, that a constitutional convention, sitting at the time, provided that no banking corporation should be established in the state, thus unwittingly turning a banking monopoly into the hands of the few institutions that weathered the long financial stress, and that in 1843, having abandoned to shipwreck the weaker concerns, finally resumed the payment of specie with $4,500,000 in their vaults, and their circulation reduced to $1,250,000.

The foreign commerce of New Orleans, at the date of this change, was $34,750,000, and for the first time in the city's history her exports of cotton exceeded 1,000,000 bales.

POSITIVE GROWTH WITH COMPARATIVE DECLINE.

The great inventions for the facilitation of commerce were each, as they came into the field, attended by a fresh discovery of the pecuniary value of time, which made the adoption of these facilities imperative on every city that sought to press its own aggrandizement or even to retain its commercial station. But even so, to seize these new advantages was practicable only to those cities that lay somewhere on right lines between the great centers of supply and demand, and it was the fate, not the fault, of New Orleans, that she was not found at either end or anywhere along the course of such a line. The case was more fortunate with St. Louis, Louisville, Cincinnati, Pittsburgh, Boston, New York, Philadelphia, Baltimore, while some cities owe their existence entirely to the requirements of these new conditions, as Cleveland, Buffalo, and Chicago.

The successful introduction of the locomotive engine into the United States as a commercial power, about the opening of the century's fourth decade, distinctly ordered what the projection and partial construction of great canals had previously threatened, the division of the commercial domain claimed by New Orleans in halves, and the apportionment of the best part of the commerce and trade beyond the mouth of the Ohio among her rivals.

It was pre-eminently the decade of development, of which the inflation of 1835, the collapse of 1836-'37, and the prostration of 1838-'40, with which it closed, were but symptoms, and when these had passed, the southern regions of the Mississippi valley had thrown their entire fortunes and energies into the "plantation idea". The more northern had at the same time filled up with farmers, towns had sprung up without number, and railroads and canals had started out eastward and westward from all the fortunately located cities, bearing immense burdens of freight and travel, and changing the measurement of distance from the scale of miles to that of hours.

Boston and New York had made what seemed, then, enormous outlays with an intrepidity sufficient in itself to assure the future, and had newly emphasized their union with the states along the northern banks of the Ohio by lines of direct transit. Pennsylvania had connected Philadelphia directly with the southern shore of the same river, laying out a larger capital in railroads and canals than any other state in the Union. Baltimore had pushed her Chesapeake and Ohio canal and railway well out toward the region of mines, with the resolution of ultimately piercing the great western valley. Ohio and Indiana had spent millions for canals by which to grasp hands with the East.

It was while these rail and water ways were being constructed, and were only gradually and one by one reaching profitable stages of completion, that New Orleans, as already noticed, more than doubled the number of its inhabitants. At the close of the decade she was the fourth city of the United States in population, being exceeded only by New York, Philadelphia, and Baltimore. Boston was nearly as large, but beside these there was no American city of half its numbers.

Truly unfortunate was it for New Orleans, that this result had been rather thrust upon her than achieved by her enterprise, and so, instead of becoming a spur to future efforts, it bred nothing better than an overweening confidence in the ability of the city to become speedily and without exertion the metropolis of America, if not eventually of the world.

That New Orleans was growing—that it was growing as the delta sands on which it stands had grown—by the compulsory tribute of the Mississippi, was the shining but illusory fact under whose beams the city entered, in 1841, upon the fifth decade of the century. Before that decade had advanced far the more reflective portion of the community began to perceive the less obtrusive though more important truth, that the rapid growth of the city was seriously slackening speed, and that the vast increase of production taking place in the upper and central parts of the Mississippi basin was being in great part poured into the laps of other cities.

The leading advantage lost being that of speedy transportation, the inroads upon the city's commerce were not yet seriously felt in the movement of those raw crops and milled breadstuffs, whose great bulk still demanded the cheapest rate of freights. The receipts of the great staples from the valley above kept steady pace with the immense increase in production, or seemed to do so. In 1842 these receipts from the interior amounted in value to more than $45,700,000; in 1843, to over $53,750,000; in 1844, to $60,000,000; in 1846, to more than $77,000,000; in 1847, to $90,000,000; and in 1850 they reached nearly the sum of $97,000,000.

In 1840 the total production of corn in the eight states of Ohio, Indiana, Illinois, Missouri, Kentucky, Arkansas, Tennessee, and Louisiana was something over 210,500,000 bushels. In 1850 it was more than 350,000,000, an increase of over 66 per cent. In the same period the receipts of corn at New Orleans rose correspondingly from some 268,000 sacks and 168,000 barrels, to over 1,000,000 sacks and 42,000 barrels.

In the same period the production of tobacco in these states diminished in those south, and more than correspondingly increased in those north, of the Ohio, yet the receipts in New Orleans rose in full proportion.

As a palpable result the city expanded. Each year large numbers of new buildings were erected, while at the same time "rents continually rose". In 1845, in the second municipality alone—the American quarter—295 houses and stores were built, more than half the number being of brick and granite. It should be noted, however, that their average cost did not reach $3,500. Thus, if the proportions of home consumption and marketable surplus in the agricultural movement of these states had remained the same, the relative importance of New Orleans would at least not have been retrograding, and her merchants might have repelled the charge brought by one, that they "sold the skin for a groat and bought the tail for a shilling". But improved transportation, denser population, and labor-saving machinery had almost indefinitely increased the individual producing power of the western man, and truly to have kept pace with it New Orleans should have been the receiver and exporter of a rapidly and steadily increasing fraction—in place of merely an increasing quantity—of the agricultural products of the country. Not perceiving, or unable to meet this necessity, she abandoned this magnificent surplus to the growing cities of the West and East.

Still more New Orleans failed to maintain a leading position in relation to the immense growth of western manufactures. It was the subject of much pardonable boasting that her commerce was so rapidly increasing, and during the decade it did expand in gross receipts, in exports, and, on a much lower scale, in imports, almost or quite 100 per cent. But meantime, and almost unnoticed by New Orleans, absorbed as she was in moving the crude products of the fields and supplying the wants of the producers, the manufactures of the eight states mentioned increased in value from about $50,000,000 to a little less than $164,000,000.

Nor was any adequate compensation found in the city's import trade. In 1835 this had reached the amount of $17,000,000; but in the crash that followed it had shrunk to $8,000,000 in 1842, and in 1845 had risen only to $9,750,000. In 1847–'48, while the city actually exceeded New York in exports of domestic produce, and in the total of exports was surpassed only by that city, her imports were less than a tenth of those of New York and not quite a third those of Boston. Coffee, iron, hardware, salt, and French fancy goods formed the chief items of this commerce.

At the close of the decade that ended with 1850, New Orleans had fallen back from the fourth place to the fifth in the list of American cities. Boston had surpassed her in numbers, Brooklyn was four-fifths her size and St. Louis seven-eighths, Cincinnati lacked but one twenty-fifth of her numbers, and Louisville, Chicago, Buffalo, and Pittsburgh had populations ranging from 40,000 to 50,000.

One or two considerations, however, somewhat modify the unfavorableness of these comparisons. During this time large numbers of Transatlantic immigrants made New Orleans their first landing-place on their way to the great West. Between 1845 and 1850 they numbered on an average 30,000 a year. Many stopped in the city and settled. As early as 1842 the population was reported "largely mixed with Germans". Before this sort of competition slave service gave ground, and the number of slaves in New Orleans was actually 5,330 less in 1850 than it had been in 1840.

Again, no other part of the population in New Orleans was held in such total disesteem as the free mulatto class. This unenterprising, despised, and persecuted people had grown from an inconsiderable fraction of the whole in earlier years, to be in 1840 nearly one-third as numerous as the whites. The feeling which had always existed against them grew in intensity as the agitation concerning the abolition of slavery rose and increased.

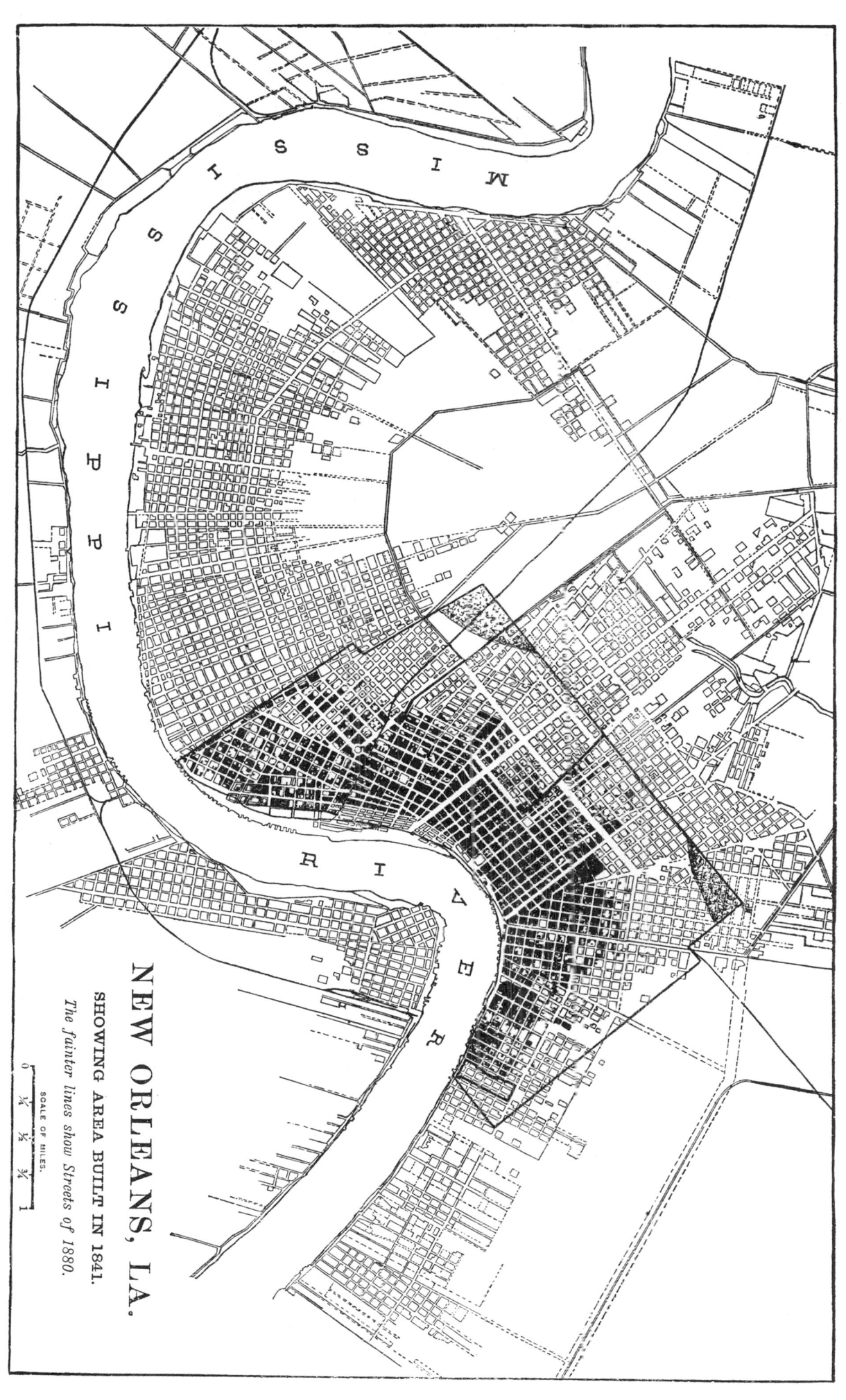

NEW ORLEANS, LA.

SHOWING AREA BUILT IN 1841.

The fainter lines show Streets of 1880.

SCALE OF MILES.

0   ¼   ½   ¾   1

They were looked upon as fit subjects of general suspicion, became the objects of grossly restrictive, unjust, and intolerant state legislation, and between 1840 and 1850 made such an exodus from the city that their numbers fell from over 19,000 to less than 10,000 souls. Allowing for natural increase, not less than 11,000 or 12,000 free persons must have left the city during this period, nor is there any evidence that they ever returned.

Under correct social conditions, such a loss of population could not rightly be counted a gain. If under all the circumstances there was in it an element of real advantage, it lay in the fact that the proportion was increased of that master class, whose strong hand and will ruled the fortunes of the community.

Furthermore, another town had sprung up immediately against the city's upper boundary. In 1833 three sparsely peopled suburbs, to wit, Lafayette, Livaudais, and Réligieuses, the last occupying lands that had belonged to and been bought from the Ursuline nuns, were consolidated into one and made a body politic, under the name of the City of Lafayette. In what was then considered the rear of this town many of the wealthy citizens of New Orleans began about 1840 to settle down in "large, commodious, one-story houses, full of windows on all sides, and surrounded by broad and shady gardens". Nearer the river front the immigrant Germans and Irish of the laboring class poured in abundantly, and by 1850 Lafayette, virtually a part of New Orleans, comprised a population of 12,319 white and 1,871 colored inhabitants.

By these two movements of slave and mulatto exodus and European immigration, the proportion of whites to the whole population rose from 58 to 78 per cent., and the whole number of the one community which formed New Orleans and Lafayette was 133,650.

But now New Orleans began to take note of facts which ought long before to have been anticipated as possibilities. Her people began to perceive the losses she was sustaining, and to inquire with alarm into their causes. At one moment with admissions and the next with boastful denials of this or that unfavorable condition or relation, the progress of other cities at her expense was anxiously noted; much was remembered of those earlier times when New Orleans was the commercial queen of her great valley, and merchants and property-holders exhorted each other to throw off their lethargy and establish their city in that universal supremacy for which her citizens were still confident that nature—that is, their river and their wish—had destined her.

The city's curable ailments found many physicians and few nurses; while those difficulties of the situation which were really insuperable remained unmentioned by the more politic few, or were charged by sanguine commercial writers as the inexcusable sins of unprogressive financiers. It was confessed that New Orleans had depended too entirely upon the mere movement of crops; that there had long been a false pride among the cultivated classes of the South generally opposed to mercantile pursuits; that the sanitary condition of the city had been entirely overlooked; that no attempt had been made to cheapen the city's notorious port charges or to facilitate the safe and expeditious handling of freight. It was even boldly and ingeniously asserted by one, that the institution of slavery had much to do with the non-progressive attitude of New Orleans and her surrounding country; that that part of the community which mainly felt the inconvenience of antiquated methods was the voiceless slave class, and that the liberty which the northern workingman enjoyed, of thinking, speaking, and acting in his own interests, gave that section an immense preponderance through its multitude of practical thinkers. The absurd municipality system of city government, which virtually divided the city into three corporate communities beside that of Lafayette, was rightly blamed as the source of much confusion and non-progression.

Such were some of the verdicts of those who spoke or wrote. Doubtless the quieter financiers and capitalists, who carefully studied the city's relative position and possible development, found other facts confronting them. The absence of railroads was not attributable only to the neglect to build them. Those laws of nature, upon which so much reliance was misplaced, included the nature and wants of mankind, and such observers could not but see that then, and for some time to come, capital—that winged and inexorable fate—could not swing out a railroad from New Orleans in any direction that had not better be stretched across from some point near the center of supply in the West, to some other point within the bounds of the manufacturing and consuming East. Or, to come to an underlying, fundamental fact, the peculiar and unfortunate labor system of the South had handed over the rich prize of European and New England immigration to the unmonopolized West, and the purely fortune-hunting canal-boat and locomotive pushed aside the slave and his owner and followed the free immigrant. In truth, it was not until some years later, when the outstretched iron arms of northern enterprise began to grasp at the products of the Southwest itself, that New Orleans capitalists, with more misgiving than enthusiasm, thrust out their first railroad worthy of the name through the great plantation state of Mississippi.

A lack of banking capital was attributed as a cause of decadence. But New Orleans bankers knew that New York, with a banking capital not three times as large as that of New Orleans, carried on a commerce three and a half times as great as hers, beside a large manufacturing interest.

The absence of thousands of residents during the summer season was given as another drawback; but this, also, was true of the other great cities, of New York especially.

The want of common sentiment and impulse in a community made up from individuals of so many nationalities was much emphasized. This deficiency did not result merely—as often stated—from the large proportion of foreigners. When, by the census of 1860, this proportion came to be known, it was found to be but 44½ per cent. of the whole white population in New Orleans, against 42 in Cincinnati, 48 in New York, and 52 in St. Louis. But in these cities American thought prevailed and more or less inspired the foreign elements as they came in; hence a comparative unity of motive. In New Orleans, on the other hand, American thought was itself not only foreign, but unwelcome, disparaged by the unaspiring and satirical Creole, and often apologized for by the American, who found himself a minority in a combination of social forces, far more frequently in sympathy with European ideas than with the moral energies and the enthusiastic and venturesome enterprise of the New World. Added to this there were, in New Orleans, 28,000 persons—9 of whom out of every 14 were enslaved, and the other 5 practically expatriated—hampering, as by sheer dead weight, the progress of the community.

The languishing of the import trade was attributed to simple neglect to cultivate it. But among the vast plantations of the southern valley, where town life was comparatively unknown, where masters were few and spent the proceeds of their exports with their own hands in foreign cities, where the wants of slaves and of indigent whites were only the most primitive, and where a stupid and slovenly, unpaid laboring class made the introduction of labor-saving machines a farce, no stimulus to a large import trade could be hoped for. And as to the West, it was idle to think of competing with direct routes for the transportation of commodities which, unlike the bulkier articles of the export trade, could well afford to subordinate cheap freight rates to prompt delivery.

Much reproach was heaped upon the moneyed class for the non-development of manufactures; but nothing ought to have been plainer than the total irreconcilability of the whole southern industrial system with such establishments; a system employing one of the most unintelligent and uneconomical classes of laborers in the world, upon which it was useless to attempt to graft the higher-spirited operatives of other countries.

These conditions, then, recognized at that day only in their superficial aspect and assumed to be easily removable, were the causes of non-progression. Summed up in one, and this stripped of its disguise, it was a triumph of machinery over slave labor, unrecognized, however, or unconfessed, because if reparable at all, only so through a social revolution so great and apparently so ruinous that the mention of it kindled a white heat of public exasperation.

And yet, after this is said, something must still be allowed to a luxurious, enervating climate, under which all energies, Anglo-Saxon, Gallic, Celtic, Teutonic, in greater or less degree, surrendered; something to remoteness from competing cities; and something to the influence of that original people, a study of whose history and its resultant traits forms so much of the present work. For the Creoles, retaining much power as well by their natural force as by their extensive ownership of real estate and their easy coalition with foreign elements of like faith, caring little to understand and less to be understood, divided and paralyzed when they could no longer rule public sentiment, and often met the most imperative necessities for innovations with the most inflexible conservatism. Such causes kept the city comparatively unimproved, its municipal government in confusion, its harbor approaches and landings much neglected, and its morals and its health unestimated by careful statistics and a by-word in all lands.

Most of the improvements that had arisen during this long term of purely commercial development dated well back toward that era of inflation of which the crisis of 1837 has become the index, and were mainly confined to the American quarter. The parish prison, the same antique and gloomy pile of stuccoed brick that still stands on Orleans street just beyond Congo square, was built in 1830 at a cost of $200,000. Several market-houses were completed about this time, the French vegetable market in 1830, St. Mary's and Washington in 1836, and Poydras in 1837. In 1834–'35 the United States government, having six years before sold the old Spanish barracks in the heart of the French quarter, built the present Jackson barracks, then three miles below the city, now on its lower boundary. In 1832–'34 the old Charity hospital in Canal street had become the state-house, and the present hospital was erected in Common street at an expense of $150,000. In 1832 and 1835 two extensive cotton-presses and warehouses had added an important feature to the commercial city. The Levee cotton-press cost $500,000, and the Orleans, in the lower part of the city, over $758,000. In 1835 the water-works, and in 1837 the gas-works, had come into operation. In the earlier year, also, the New Canal, some seven miles in length, begun in 1832, had been finished. It brought the waters of lake Pontchartrain into an artificial basin deep enough for coasting schooners, situated immediately behind Rampart (then Hercules) street, between Julia and Delord. In this year, too, the branch United States mint of New Orleans was founded on the small square bounded by Esplanade, Barracks, Decatur, and Peters streets, which had been the site of Fort St. Charles, and after the destruction of that fortification had been known as Jackson Square, a name afterward transferred to the ancient Place d'Armes. In 1833 had appeared that unique and still well-remembered structure, Banks' Arcade, a glass-roofed mercantile court in the midst of a large hotel in Magazine street, now long known as the St. James. In 1836 the Merchants' Exchange, just below Canal street, and extending through from Royal to Exchange alley, had been completed and had become the post-office. The first St. Charles hotel, called then the Exchange hotel, begun in 1835, had been completed three years later, at a cost of $600,000. The same year saw the completion, diagonally opposite on Common street, of the old Verandah hotel, with an outlay of $300,000. In 1834 the (second) First Presbyterian church, on Lafayette square, had been built. In 1837 the Carondelet Methodist church, on the corner of that street and Poydras, had followed, and in the same year the old Christ's church, on the corner of Bourbon and Canal streets, had replaced the small octagonal predecessor, erected in 1809, and which the town wits had nicknamed "The Cockpit". In 1835 the St. Charles theater had been built, at a cost of $350,000. Between 1833 and 1839 several bank buildings of more or less pretensions had arisen; the Commercial, the Atchafalaya, the Orleans (later occupied by the Bank of America), the Canal, at the corner of Magazine and Gravier, the City, in Camp street near Canal, and that extremely picturesque ruin in Toulouse street of Grecian architecture, built for the Citizens' Bank and afterward occupied by the Consolidated. Many charitable associations and establishments—Poydras orphan asylum, the Female orphan asylum, the asylum for destitute boys, the Catholic male orphan asylum, the Fireman's charitable association, the Howard association, Stone's hospital, the Circus Street infirmary, and many others had their beginnings at various dates between 1830 and 1840.

Such a list as this, extending over more than a decade, is probably doubtful evidence of that degree of progress which should have characterized a growing American city, or even of that degree of effort which would have excused some features of her decadence. Orphan asylums were indifferent substitutes for sanitation, and short-lived banks for improved harbor approaches. "Had a tithe of the exertion," writes one in New Orleans, in 1847, "been made to retain it, that has distinguished the efforts of the North to draw it off, we should not now be called to look with astonishment at beholding one-half in bulk and value of western produce seeking a market at the northern Atlantic cities, where twenty years ago not a dollar was sent through the channels now bearing it away from New Orleans."

Yet it would have been unreasonable and unjust to assume that all deficiencies were due to lack of enterprise; and the fact that in the list of local movements and schemes, scarcely more than one or two bore any likeness to that bold outward reach which was making rival cities, through their more fortunate location, daily greater, should rather be taken as proof that the capitalists of New Orleans discerned and silently acknowledged the immovability of some of the fundamental difficulties that beset their town and port.

Two railroad enterprises alone, in this period, ventured to project their lines beyond the boundaries of Orleans island; but the "New Orleans and Nashville" scheme, ripening prematurely, fell to the ground, and the "Mexican Gulf" road, which it was hoped would develop the deep waters of Cat island into a harbor of easy access to large vessels, and greatly shorten the journey between New Orleans and New York, never got beyond the farther bounds of the adjoining parish, and is long since extinct.

About the year 1840 or '41, there seems to have arisen in the room of that sort of public spirit, enterprising yet near-sighted, which had characterized the previous decade, a sentiment of more urgency, which began to contemplate relations beyond the boundaries of parish and state, and to realize the value and the necessity of public measures, addressed to higher and less strictly material wants, than could be supplied by gas- or water-works, banks, mints, or cotton-presses. An obvious subsidence of the tide of improvement which had made New Orleans at least a brisk laggard, united with this new feeling of exigency to produce inquiry, exhortation, and a general exchange of both deserved and undeserved reproach. Actual efforts presently followed, and steps were taken in the direction of popular education, culture, and social order, which, had they been taken when first proposed by a wise few in executive office, 25 or 30 years before, would have made New Orleans by that time, in fact and in spirit, as well as in name, an American, instead of a Franco-American city.

But the end contemplated in the earlier suggestions, wanted something of that popular and general benefit which has made the more modern idea of public education acceptable throughout America, not excepting Louisiana.

On the earnest recommendation of Governor Claiborne, in 1804, an act had been passed in April of the following year, by the legislative council, "to establish a university in the territory of Orleans". A primary object of this act had been the institution of the "College of New Orleans". Fifty thousand dollars were appropriated to carry out the provisions of the act; but the amount was to be raised by two lotteries. In 1811 nothing had yet been effected. Thirty-nine thousand dollars were then appropriated for state educational purposes, $15,000 of which were for the institution of a college in New Orleans, where, in addition to those who paid for their tuition, 50 children, selected from the poorest classes, were to be admitted without charge. Under this stimulus New Orleans college was built and put in operation in 1812, at the corner of Bayou road and St. Claude street. Ten years later it was the only educational institution in New Orleans, of a public character, though some private or church schools accommodated a few charity scholars.

In March, 1826, another legislative act established one central and two primary public schools in New Orleans. Ten thousand dollars a year were set apart for their support; they were duly established—the central and one primary in the old Ursuline convent, and the other primary in Tchoupitoulas near St. Joseph street—and "all the branches of a polite education" were taught. "Harby's public school," in the third municipality, finds mention in 1838, but New Orleans college seems to have disappeared.

At length, a convention called to frame a new state constitution, meeting in New Orleans, in January–April, 1845, again decreed the establishment of the University of Louisiana. It was intended to consist of four faculties, one each for law, medicine, natural science, and letters. The department of medicine was already in existence as the medical school of Louisiana, and this branch, and that of law, were in full operation in 1847, with 162 students in the former and 31 in the latter, and they have ever since continued to be a source of honor and pride to the city and the state.

But the mass of educable youth had not been reached—had scarcely been sought—in these schemes. Another sentiment was lacking, a feeling of common interest in a common elevation. This feeling once aroused, men of public spirit were not wanting to give it guidance, and the names of such pioneers as Samuel J. Peters, Glendy Burke, Judah Touro, Martin, Dimitry, De Bow, Forstall, Gayarre, and others, are gratefully remembered by a later generation for their labors in the cause of intellectual advancement. The year 1841 dates the establishment in New Orleans of the modern system of free public schools; for although they were not begun within the city's corporate limits until in the following year, when a single school was opened in the second municipality, "with some dozen scholars of both sexes", yet the adjoining city of Lafayette, always virtually a part of New Orleans, had founded the system in the earlier year.

In the beginning of the year 1842 there were in the American quarter 300 children in private schools and 2,000 destitute of school advantages. By the end of that year there were 238 pupils in the public schools of Lafayette, and 800 in those of the American quarter of New Orleans proper. In the next year the total attendance in the public schools of both sections was 1,314. In 1844 it was 1,798.

Meanwhile there was a movement in the interest of adults. In 1842 Mr. B. F. French, having bought a collection of books known as the "Commercial Library", threw it open to the public. In 1846 it occupied two rooms in the Merchants' Exchange, on Royal street, and comprised almost 7,500 volumes. About the same time the state library was formed with about 3,000 volumes, but was intended for the use of the legislature rather than for the general public. In this year, too, the New Orleans city library came into existence through the efforts of Samuel J. Peters and others, as an adjunct of the public-school enterprise in the second municipality. It numbered at first some 3,000 volumes, and in 1848 had been increased to over 7,500. It required, however, a yearly subscription of $5 to gain free access to this library. It was placed in the newly founded and unfinished municipal hall, the same whose classic Grecian architecture now adorns Lafayette square. The Young Men's Free Library Association, a body of commercial citizens, threw open a collection of some 2,000 well-selected volumes at the corner of Customhouse street and Exchange place.

In 1846 a course of public lectures by leading citizens was attended by a body of hearers which taxed the capacity of the city's largest hall. In the same year an historical society, originally founded in 1838, was revived, with Judge Martin, the historian of Louisiana, as president. During a few years following, this body caused valuable researches to be made in the archives of the French and Spanish governments, in Paris and in Madrid, through its zealous secretary, Mr. John Perkins, jr., and even began the transcription of important documents. In 1847 Judge Charles Gayarre delivered before the Library and Lyceum Association the four lectures which afterward constituted the first four chapters of his history of Louisiana; and in the winter of 1848 J. D. B. De Bow delivered the initial lecture of a projected series on public economy, commerce, and statistics; but a terrible epidemic of cholera cut them short.

About the latter date Alvarez Fisk, a merchant, bought Mr. French's library, and in order to carry out the designs of a deceased brother for the establishment of a public library in New Orleans, which should be free to strangers, offered the entire collection, then containing some 6,000 volumes, to the city, with a "building on Customhouse street for their reception". But the late public enthusiasm had subsided. No adequate provision was made by the city council or public for the acceptance of this gift, although under the generous zeal of Mr. French, its custodian, it grew considerably in extent. As late as 1854 it had not been put into efficient operation, and the city was still without a single entirely free library.

A line or two may be proper here to afford a comparative view of library facilities in New Orleans and elsewhere at the time spoken of. In 1850 the public libraries of Louisiana numbered five and contained 9,800 volumes, and her school libraries two, with 12,000 volumes. Much the greater part of these were, doubtless, in New Orleans. However, taking the state at large, there was one school, Sunday school, or public library to each 73,966 persons, or 100 volumes to each 2,310 persons. In Delaware there were 100 volumes to each 707 persons; in Rhode Island there were 100 volumes to every 206 persons; in Massachusetts there were 100 volumes to each 188 persons. This disproportionate dearth of books in Louisiana might appear less by eliminating the numbers of the slave element; but even after thus omitting from the count what could not be omitted from the community, there would still appear but 100 volumes to each 1,218 free persons, while that could hardly be called a more favorable exhibit, which pointed out the fact of nearly 245,000 persons in the established population being without books, and legally incapacitated to receive them. In Michigan, a pioneer state without any large city, there were 100 volumes to every 397 persons. Probably of the 22,400 volumes in Louisiana, all of those in public and half of those in school libraries, or 15,800, were in New Orleans, which would give 100 volumes to every 642 free persons in the city.

Nothing else seems to have taken such hold upon the estimation of the whole body of citizens in New Orleans, as did the public schools. These continued to grow rapidly in numbers and in efficiency, and it is pleasant to turn from the contrast just indicated, and find New Orleans in 1850 ranking well up among American cities in the advantages offered her youth, and received by them, in free schools maintained at the public charge. The pupils in the public schools of Boston numbered 16 per cent. of the whole population; in Philadelphia they were 11¾, and in New Orleans 7⅓ per cent. The character of the reports of New York, in the pages from which these facts are taken, makes the percentage there doubtful, but it seems not to have been greatly superior to New Orleans; St. Louis was slightly so; but those of Baltimore, Cincinnati, Charleston, and other towns, were more or less

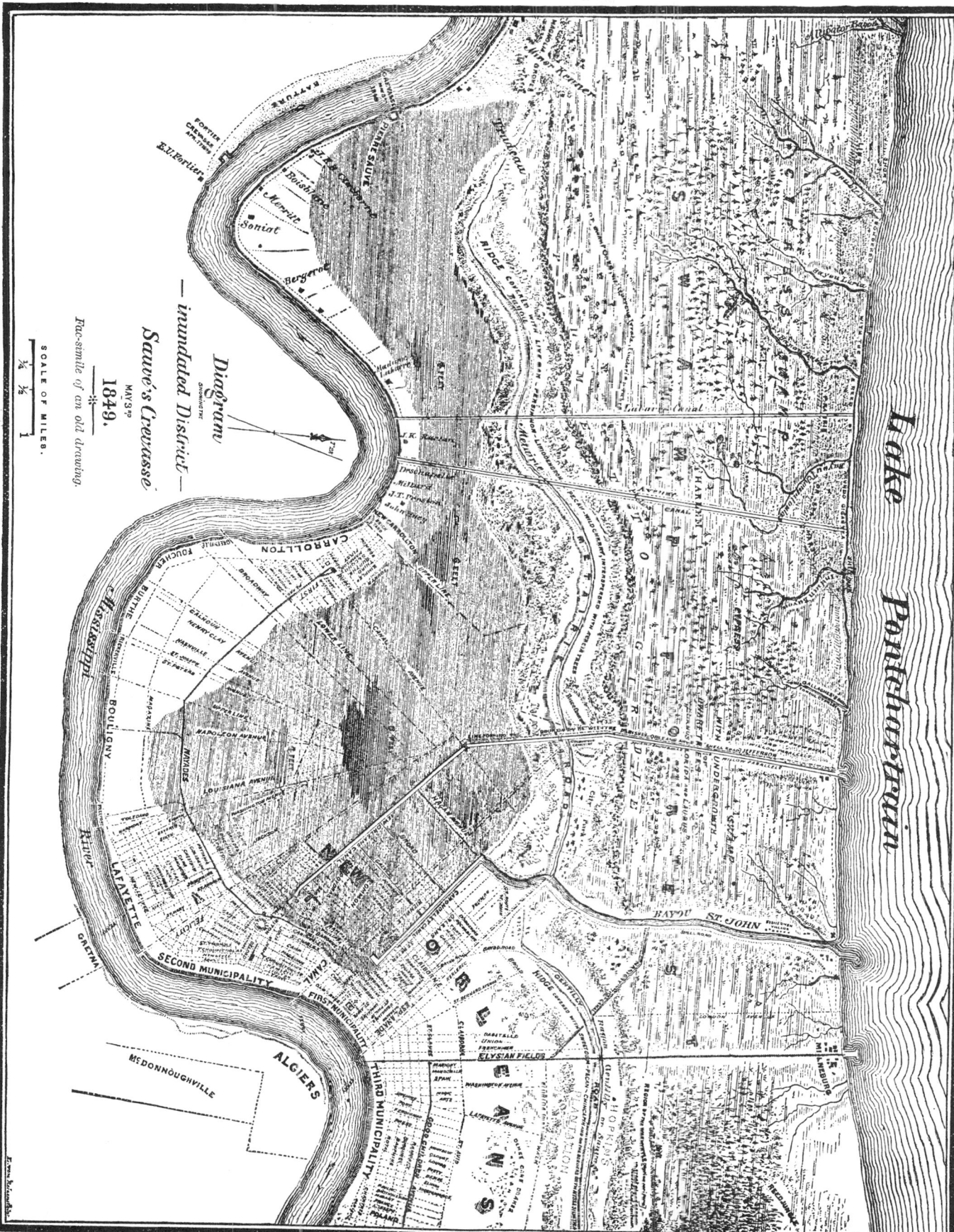

Diagram
SHOWING THE
— inundated District —
Sauve's Crevasse.
MAY 3RD
1849.

Fac-simile of an old drawing.

SCALE OF MILES.

Lake Pontchartrain

Mississippi River

inferior. The total number of educable youth in New Orleans and Lafayette was over fourteen thousand, of which 6,700 attended public schools. In 1858 these numbers had increased to 16,392.

Few conspicuous improvements in real property, either public or private, appeared to view in this term. In the second municipality the massive and beautiful tower of St. Patrick's arose, and the city hall was pushed on toward completion. The first municipality ceded to the United States government the site of the present custom-house, and for many years the huge and lofty scaffolding of this still uncompleted pile of granite was one of the most prominent objects in a bird's-eye view of the city. The United States marine hospital, on the opposite side of the river, facing the second municipality, which had been commenced in 1834, but was unfinished and half in ruins, was taken under contract for its completion by James N. Caldwell, founder of theaters and gas-works, projector of the Nashville rail route, and, in short, the personal exponent of the material advance and enterprise of those times. This hospital, turned into a powder-house during the late war, met its end one day by being blown to atoms.

Yet the city was growing from year to year with greater or less rapidity, and in every direction. For some years the swamp lands in the rear had been in process of clearing and draining; and streets and houses appeared in the place of forest or marshy fields. Algiers, a suburb on the point of land opposite the river front of the old city, began to grow into notice through its marine workshops, though still but feeble in population. Lafayette, almost unknown to the "down-town Creole", reached, as has been seen, a population of 14,000 and upward, while the third municipality, almost as completely unobserved by the American as was Lafayette by the Creole, spread in unpretentious cottages down toward the near edge of Jackson's field of renown.

This growth was effected in the face of many obstacles, chief among which was the still frequent mishap of inundation. This event in New Orleans must occur either by a crevasse—a giving way of the levee during a time of high water in the river—or by the rise of backwater from lake Pontchartrain, when long-prevailing southeast winds obstruct the outflow of the lake's waters through the narrow passes by which they commonly reach the Gulf of Mexico, or when a violent storm from the north more suddenly produces the same result. Against both these contingencies much vigilance has to be exercised at certain seasons.

The effects of these inundations, however, are easily overestimated. Property within the boundary of their probable encroachment is desirable only to those who must seek the very fewest advantages of location, and they have been a prime cause for the inconvenient lengthening out of the city along the higher grounds down, and especially up, the river shore. But the city is not engulfed by the waters, life is not endangered, the business districts and those occupied by highly improved houses are rarely or never invaded, and the extent of the disaster is mainly confined to a distressing interruption in the daily affairs of the humbler classes, the destruction of their market gardens and poultry, the damage of household goods, and the injury to such public property as street bridges and the like. The sickness which might be supposed to follow the subsidence of the waters has not been such, at least, as to make inundations a subject of alarm on this account, and probably no actual feature of these overflows does New Orleans as much material injury as is done by their exaggerated bad fame.

Their frequency, also, is easily overrated. In the early history of the town they occurred at first almost yearly, and for a long time extremely often; but later they grew much more infrequent. The moat and palisaded embankment which surrounded the Spanish town seems not to have protected it from this enemy. A serious overflow took place in 1780, another in 1785, another in 1791, another in 1799. All these resulted from crevasses in the river levee above the town. The last of these occurred in the month of May, in the "Macarty levee", near the site of the later town of Carrollton, now part of New Orleans. Subsequently putrid fevers were ascribed to it, but the statement is made without proper investigation of the facts.

Another inundation in 1813 was caused by a crevasse in the levee of Kenner's plantation, a mile or two only above Macarty's.

Next followed the noted overflow of 1816. On the 6th of May, of that year, Macarty's levee, being undermined by the powerful current which there strikes the river bank, again broke, and on the fourth day after, the rear parts of suburbs Montague, La Course, St. Mary, and Marigny, and the whole of the suburbs behind them—Gravier, Trémé, and St. John—were under water to the depth of from 3 to 5 feet. One could travel in a skiff from the corner of Chartres and Canal streets to Dauphin, down Dauphin to Bienville, down Bienville to Burgundy, thus to St. Louis street, from St. Louis to Rampart, and so throughout the rear suburbs. The waters found vent by way of Fisherman's and St. John's bayous to lake Pontchartrain, and in 25 days had subsided. The ensuing summer is stated, on the highest medical authority, to have been remarkably healthy.

In 1831 the waters of an inundation reached the line of Dauphin street, the fifth from the river front—the result of a violent storm on lake Pontchartrain. A similar event occurred in October, 1837. In 1844 a storm backed the lake waters up to Burgundy street, sixth from the river front, and a similar disaster happened again in 1846.

But probably the most serious overflow the city of New Orleans ever suffered was that of 1849. On the afternoon of the 3d of May, in that year, the waters of the Mississippi, being then at a higher stage than had been witnessed before for twenty-one years, broke through the levee in front of Sauvé's plantation, some 17 miles above New Orleans by the river's course, and at once defied all restraints. It was at first thought that they would not reach New Orleans, but would find their way into lake Pontchartrain by some route nearer at hand. But the swamp rapidly filled up behind the city, the opportunity for throwing up a levee along the rear of the town was let slip, and by the 15th of May Rampart street was under water.

The residents of the first municipality (French quarter) strengthened the small levee of Canal Carondelet on its lower side, and thus entirely shut out the advancing flood from the district beyond that canal; but the rears of Lafayette and of the second municipality were completely exposed. The water reached its highest stage on the 30th of May. Its line ran along behind Bacchus (Baronne) street, sometimes reaching to Carondelet, from the upper limits of Lafayette to Canal street, crossed that street between Carondelet and St. Charles streets, and thence stretched downward and backward to the old basin. "About 220 inhabited squares were flooded, more than 2,000 tenements surrounded by water, and a population of near 12,000 souls either driven from their homes or living an aquatic life of much privation and suffering."

All efforts to close the crevasse utterly failed until, on the 3d of June, Messrs. Dunbar and Surgi, engineers, being allowed entire liberty as to ways and means, began work, and in seventeen days stopped the breach. On the 22d of June the water had virtually disappeared, heavy rains washed away its filthy deposits, and the people were able to begin the repair of their disasters. Public property, too, had suffered; pavements and gutters were much damaged and street bridges had been washed away. The second municipality in the following year (1850) levied $400,000 to cover "actual expenditures on streets, wharves, and crevasses", and built a levee in the rear of the municipality from the point where Claiborne street crosses the new canal up to Felicity road (street) and along this street to its intersection with Apollo (now Carondelet) street.

Time showed these provisions to be entirely inadequate. The city continued at intervals to suffer from the same cause, the last occasion being no longer ago than February of the present year (1881). At such times the pecuniary and personal aid of her citizens is generously poured out to the unfortunate; but these admirable deeds are the fruits of emotional impulses, and, the distress passed, precautions against future calamity are omitted or soon fall into neglect. The last overflow simply overran the top of a neglected and decayed protection levee. The uneconomical habits of the South have not passed suddenly away with the change of its labor system. Private extravagance still makes public parsimony; public burdens are but feebly recognized, and New Orleans is not yet entirely protected from these pitiful disasters to her hard-working poor.

A number of other events require to be briefly summarized as making notable a short period between 1849 and 1852. It was in the first of these years that New Orleans ceased to be the capital, and the small Mississippi river town of Baton Rouge became the capital of the state. Nor was this loss restored to New Orleans until after the destruction of the state-house in Baton Rouge by fire, and the occupation of New Orleans by United States forces, during the late war. In 1880 the seat of government was again removed to Baton Rouge, and the legislature, at its next regular session, will meet there.

As late as 1846 New Orleans was without telegraphic communication, but in 1847, and later, certain lines were taken under contract, and by 1850 the city was in telegraphic connection with St. Louis and other points.

The first street pavement with square granite blocks was made in 1850.

The project of a railroad across the isthmus of Tehuantepec received its first decided impulse in 1850, on the transfer by one Hargous to Judah P. Benjamin, J. M. Lapeyre, Samuel J. Peters, and others, of extensive grants and privileges conveyed to him by José Garay, the original grantee of the Mexican government. Surveys were begun by United States engineers, and by 1852 one route had been surveyed; but the Mexican government put a stop to the work, and the project, thus crippled, dragged feebly along. In 1853 a rival grantee, Mr. Thomas Sloo, appeared, and the state of Louisiana gave a charter to a new company, formed with $10,000,000 capital, of which Mr. Sloo was to receive half. To have realized so great a project would have redeemed New Orleans from the reproaches so freely bestowed upon her by her sister cities; but against the state of affairs existing in Mexico no headway could be made, though much effort was exhausted by the capitalists of the city, and the last year before the absorbing political campaign which preceded the outbreak of civil war, found their chamber of commerce recommending the enterprise with bare resolutions. Meantime two other enterprises of more moderate scope, but of even greater urgency, met a better fate. In 1851 those two great works of internal improvement, which have proved, as they were intended to be, the commercial salvation of New Orleans, were set on foot, to wit, the two railroads that now respectively unite the city with the great central railroad system of the Union in the Mississippi valley, and with the vast southwest, still comprised within the outstretched boundaries of the state of Texas. The first of these roads was to stretch due north toward Jackson, the capital of Mississippi; the other was to strike westward toward the town of Opelousas, in Louisiana. Both received state aid, and the first by the year 1855, the second by 1857, had reached a distance of over 80 miles from New Orleans, and on the northern road work was progressing rapidly in the direction of Jackson.

Hardly of less importance to the city's future, was the consolidation of Lafayette and the three municipalities into one city government, on the 12th of April, 1852. Sixteen years of subdivision had demonstrated to Creole, to American, and to European immigrant the value of unity. Yet it was probably essential, that during just that term the progressive and the conservative elements of the city should have lived and worked apart, and thus their adverse ideas, operating side by side, be practically compared, and the superiority of the American principles of growth be plainly proven.

The first great step after the cession toward the *Americanization* of New Orleans, was the arbitrary establishment of the English tongue. The second was that enforced one of its military defense against conquest in 1814–'15. The third, a stage rather than a step, was the shifting of the port's commerce from the French and Spanish Americas on the south to the great valley on the north, and its consequent transfer into American hands and an American quarter. The division of the municipalities, in 1836, is of uncertain value; the next undoubtedly effective step was the establishment of the American public school system throughout the municipalities, a greater advance than its most sanguine advocates probably supposed could have been made at one stride. The fifth step was the consolidation. By this movement the second municipality, the American quarter, became the acknowledged center and core of the whole city. Its municipality hall became the municipal hall; its public grounds became the chosen rendezvous of all popular assemblies; its streets became the place of business domicile for all the main branches of trade; the rotunda of its palatial St. Charles, at whose memorable burning in 1850 the people wept, restored in 1852–'53, usurped the early pre-eminence of the St. Louis *Bourse*, and became the unofficial guild-hall of all the more active elements—merchants, politicians, strangers from every quarter, and Cuban and Nicaraguan filibusters; and banks, whose charters still prevented their moving across the "neutral ground" of Canal street, moved close up toward it to catch a share of the financial breezes that blew so favorably upon its farther side.

The consolidation did not come before a stern necessity called for it. The report of the "commissioners of the consolidated debt of New Orleans" in 1855, says:

"The commissioners * * * found the city without credit, confusion in most of its branches of government, and the people disheartened. To-day (January, 1855) its credit is above par." "The spirit of the people," they farther added, "has been awakened * * * and a brighter future is before us."

At the passage of the act of consolidation, the debts of Lafayette and the three municipalities aggregated $7,700,000, of which $2,000,000 were past due. Through the improved credit of the consolidated city, $5,000,000 of these debts were early extinguished, and the total debt of the city on the 1st of April, 1853, the greatest commercial year that thus far had ever risen upon New Orleans, was but little over $3,000,000.

A small steel-engraved picture of New Orleans, made just before this period, is obviously the inspiration of the commercial and self-important American. The ancient plaza, the cathedral of St. Louis, the old hall of the cabildo, the calaboza, the remnant of Spanish barracks, the emptied convent of the Ursulines, the antiquated and decayed rue Toulouse—all that was time-honored and venerable are pushed out of view, and the lately humble faubourg Ste. Marie, grown to be the center of wealth and activity, fills the picture almost from side to side, with long ranks of huge Mississippi steamers smoking at the levee, and the majestic dome of the first St. Charles and the stately tower of St. Patrick's, rise high above the deep and solid phalanxes of brick and stone, in the midst of which they stood queen and bishop of the board.

A little later a worse fate befell the group of ancient landmarks, than being left out of a picture. Renovation came in. In 1850 the cathedral was torn down to its foundations, and began to rise again with all its Spanish picturesqueness lost, and little or nothing gained in beauty. On its right and on its left absurd French roofs were clapped upon the cabildo and the court-house. The Baroness Pontalba, daughter of the benevolent Almonaster, replaced the plain, old-fashioned stone buildings on either side the square, with large, new rows of red brick. The city government laid off the Place d'Armes in blinding white shell-walks and dusty flower-beds, and later —in 1855—placed in its center the bronze equestrian figure of the deliverer of New Orleans, and called the classic spot Jackson square. Yet even so it remains to the present, the last lurking-place of the romance of early New Orleans.

The commerce of the city waxed greater. That "forest of masts" of which she was so pardonably boastful, grew yearly longer and darker upon her splendid harbor front. In 1851 the receipts of cotton were greater than had ever before been handled: The total value of products from the interior was nearly $107,000,000. The mint coined $10,000,000 in silver and gold, the most of which had come from the new-found treasure-fields of California, whither large numbers of the more adventurous spirits of New Orleans had hastened. The tobacco trade, which for some years had languished, revived.

The year 1853 brought still greater increase. The receipts of cotton alone reached the value of $68,250,000. The sugar crop was, by many tens of thousands of hogsheads, the largest ever known in Louisiana, and the total value of produce from the interior exceeded $134,000,000. Over 10 per cent. of all the arrivals from sea were steamships.

But just here a symptom of decay, long overlooked, began to force itself upon public notice. The increase in size of sea-going vessels had been steady and rapid, and had not received the attention, in the port of New Orleans, which its importance merited, until the larger vessels had begun to shun the bars and mud-lumps of the Balize. In 1852 there had been, within a period of a few weeks, nearly 40 ships aground on the bar at the mouth of the Mississippi, suffering detentions ranging from two days to eight weeks. Some had been compelled to throw part of their cargoes overboard, and others to discharge into lighters, over 100 miles from their wharves in New Orleans.

There had not been a total neglect, even in earlier years, to call the attention of government to the defects of this all-important entrance to the continent. Government, too, had responded; surveys and reports had been made as far back as 1829 and continuing through 1837, 1839, 1847, and 1851. Shortly after certain expensive surveys in 1837, Northeast pass, then the chosen channel, shoaled up; but Southwest pass was presently found to serve present purposes, being only less convenient of approach, and continued to be used with tolerable facility until about 1850. Then the increasing draught of ships brought a new difficulty, and "owing to pressing memorials of the citizens of New Orleans, Congress ordered an exploration of the region, and appropriated a large sum for the deepening of the channels of the river". Neglect to pursue the matter to the point of consummating some permanent remedy, seems not more blamable upon government than upon the port itself. While various measures and half measures were timidly recommended in the reports of engineers—dredging, harrowing, jettying, the cutting of a canal to gulf waters several miles above the passes—vessels of less than 1,000 tons were grounding on the bar, and a committee of the New Orleans chamber of commerce, in petitioning Congress for the establishment of a navy-yard at New Orleans, was stating in its address that "formerly the bar at the mouth of the Mississippi presented a difficulty which is now obviated, for modern skill has applied to naval architecture the happy combination of increased capacity of hull, with diminution of draft", and so on. Naturally the Balize remained unimproved, and in 1853 vessels were again grounding on the bar and remaining, with valuable cargoes, for weeks, and even for months.

But the year 1853 will always be more famed in the history of New Orleans for another calamity, so painful in its purely human aspect, that its commercial results, considerable as they were, are entirely obscured by its dark shadow. The yellow fever of that year gave New Orleans, for all time, a sad eminence in the list of plague-stricken towns, and must long continue to be a standard of comparison, for all pestilential visitations preceding or following it, in the annals of American cities.

From the beginning nothing could have been more obvious to the most superficial glance, than the insalubrity of the site chosen for New Orleans. But the almost total neglect of government and people to attempt its improvement, was hardly less so. Governor Perier, in 1726, did himself the credit to urge, in his dispatches, the necessity of sanitary measures, and the Baron Carondelet, toward the close of the last century, stood conspicuously apart from the long line of royal governors, in the attention he gave to the matter of public health, and for certain limited works, prosecuted with a view to decreasing the prevalence of malarial and putrid fevers.

Some beneficial changes came about gradually, without any intended reference to public sanitation. A certain defective surface-drainage, some paving, improved house-building, wiser domestic life, removal of much noxious forest and undergrowth, a better circulation of air, probably a slight reduction of temperature, and probably, too, what was more important, a reduction in humidity. But it was long before a system of public scavenging was adopted, and when it came it was only better than none. Later still open canals, intended for drainage, began to multiply, but they were ill-placed, poorly constructed, and entirely neglected.

Many features in the system of municipal cleansing were so far from being true sanitary measures, that a studied effort to make matters as bad as possible could hardly have been more vicious. Most of these, however, need no mention, being easily found in the contemporaneous history of almost any city. A singular effect of their combination in New Orleans, more amusing now than then, was that for a term of years—notably between 1837 and 1840—*rats* became a common and intolerable pest that defied extermination.

The undrained state of the soil was the main source of many evils. Prominent among them was the custom of sepulture in tombs above ground, and the almost total interdiction of burial in the earth. A grave in the ground was lower than the water level. For a long time the tombs, later composed only of brick or stone, included wood in parts of their structure, and fell into decay so early as often to expose the bones of the dead. As the town grew in age and in density of population it daily, and as unconcernedly as other towns, made the ground beneath it more and more poisonous, and spreading out upon the low grounds behind it, actually began to occupy a district which had been used as a dumping-ground for its night-soil.

Meanwhile the town, expanding into a brisk commercial port, was yearly multiplying its communications with the West Indies, and a horrid and fatal disease began to make itself conspicuous, which in earlier days had visited the colony rarely if at all, and had been but vaguely recognized. In 1796, for the first time, a fatal epidemic disease was distinctly and popularly identified as the yellow fever. From that date its appearance was frequent, if not annual, and the medical records of the city enumerate, between that date and the present writing, 13 violent and 24 lighter epidemics of this dread visitant. It was present in 1799, in 1800, 1801, 1804, 1809, 1811, and 1812; was violent in 1817 and 1822, and from this time until the blockade of New Orleans by the United States fleet, in 1861, it made its appearance, sometimes in epidemics and sometimes only in sporadic form, every summer.

In 1832, when the first great cholera wave swept across the Atlantic, New Orleans suffered fearfully from its presence. It "made its appearance about the 25th of October, in the midst of an epidemic of yellow fever, and in * * * 20 days * * * killed about 6,000 people". The mortality amounted in some days to as high as 500, in a population which was estimated to have been reduced, by the flight of many, to at most 35,000.

In 1839 over 1,300 persons died in New Orleans of yellow fever. In 1841 there were 1,800 victims. Between 1837 and 1843 some 5,500 deaths were from this cause. In the summer and fall of 1847 over 2,800 perished. In the second half of 1848, 872 died. It had barely disappeared when the cholera, which had again been ravaging Europe and the British isles, appeared and raged for eight months, carrying off 4,100 victims. A month later, August, 1849, the yellow fever returned, and by the end of November had destroyed 744 persons. In this month the cholera again revived, and by the end of the year 1850 had added 1,851 to the long roll.

It would seem, at first glance, that a city under such calamities would have been aroused to grapple with the facts of its condition, and at any cost to effect a sanitary revolution that would have presented to its own people and to the outer world the well-authenticated figures of a low death-rate. But sanitation could scarcely make its way, where insalubrity was flatly denied or disbelieved; and it probably requires a residence among a lethargic and intensely provincial people, to understand with what honesty of conviction such communities can assert and maintain the non-existence of the most dreadful evils. " New Orleans, disguise the fact as we may," writes De Bow in 1846, " has had abroad the reputation of being a great charnel house. * * * We meet this *libel* with facts;" and thereupon, though a professional statistician, he presents assertions, but no figures. In January, 1851, at the close of the frightful ills just recounted, the mayor officially pronounced the city to have been " perfectly healthy during the past year and free from all epidemic". The fact was omitted that the mortality had been 62 per 1,000 of the population, and in the previous three years respectively, 77, 66, and 84. The press was not behind the public officials in a stout non-statement of facts, of which so purely commercial a people supposed they had a right to require the withholding; and its persistent reiteration of the city's salubrity and of the longevity of the native population, was oddly interwoven with the assertion that the unacclimated absented themselves on the approach of every summer by thousands.

A few medical men, alone—Barton, Symonds, Fenner, Axson—about the year 1849, had begun to extricate from oblivion and bring to light the city's vital statistics, and boldly and intelligently to publish truths which should have alarmed any community. But the disclosures that the mortality of New Orleans in 1849, even after deducting the deaths by cholera, had been about twice the common average of Boston, New York, Philadelphia, or Charleston, fell upon insensible ears. Doctor Barton's recommendation of underground sewerage, urged in 1850, was received in silence and soon forgotten, to be revived and adopted in improved form thirty years afterward. A quarantine had been established in 1821, continued through 1824, withdrawn as useless in 1825, and has never been re-established. Improved police measures were alluded to in general terms as being in force, but it is not clear what they could have been intended to compass; a plan for daily flushing the open street gutters, which are universal in New Orleans, was proposed to the city council and rejected, and the gutters left to present " a most disgusting aspect". Stagnant water stood under houses and in vacant lots. The streets were proverbially muddy and filthy. A large portion of the dead were buried in thickly settled regions of the city.

As the year 1853 drew near, all these unfortunate conditions seemed to approach a climax, under a contract scavenging system, and the "foul and nauseous steams arising from the street gutters and other depositories of decayed animal and vegetable matter" became the subject of public outcry.

In the report of the board of health for the week ending the 28th of May, 1853, a death by yellow fever was announced, an exceptionally early commencement. The daily papers left it unpublished. Other reports in June were received in the same way. On the 2d of July, 25 deaths from yellow fever were reported for the closing week. A season of daily rains set in. At the end of the next week 59 deaths were reported. This was equivalent to not less than 300 cases, and the newspapers slowly and one by one began to admit the presence of danger.

The disease now suddenly broke out like the flames of a conflagration. For the week ending July 16, 204 deaths were reported. The Howard Association began active service. During the following week the admissions to the Charity hospital alone were from 60 to 100 a day, and its floors were covered with the sick. From the 16th to the 23d of July the deaths from the fever averaged 61 per day. Yet it was only in the preceding week that a city journal had professed its ignorance of the presence in New Orleans of any prevalent diseases, and in this week Dr. McFarlane, a noted physician of New Orleans, " supported by many others," advanced the theory that the accumulation of filth and offal in the yards, alleys, and streets of the city was calculated to retard the formation of a yellow-fever atmosphere. " It was ridiculed," says a medical writer in De Bow and an eye-witness of the great epidemic, " throughout the world outside of New Orleans." In that city some denounced the doctrine and others denied the filthiness of the streets. On the 25th of July the city council established a quarantine at Slaughter-house point, opposite the city.

The interments of fever victims for the week ending July 30, averaged 79 a day. The rains continued and the weather became unseasonably cool. The usual summer custom of the municipal authorities of ordering the poisoning of vagrant dogs, had not been suspended, and their bloated carcasses lay in abundance, exposed in the streets and floated by dozens in the eddies among the wharves. Gormley's basin, a small artificial harbor at the intersection of Dryades walk and Felicity road, for the accommodation of cord-wood and shingle cutters, was termed " a pestilential muck-and-mire pool of dead animals and filth of every kind". The fever raged with special violence in the fourth district (Lafayette), where German immigrants abounded.

The month of August set in. The weekly report of the 6th showed 187 deaths from other diseases, an enormous death-rate, to which was added 947 victims of the fever. The deaths throughout the week, in the Charity hospital solely, had averaged night and day 1 every half hour. As the 7th of August drew to a close, 71 bodies, in a single cemetery in an inhabited district, were left unburied, " piled on the ground, swollen and bursting their coffins, and enveloped in swarms of flies." In the twenty-four hours of the 8th of August the deaths were 228. Of these deaths 198 were reported as the result of yellow fever; but such an appalling mortality, as this would leave to be attributed to other diseases, is incredible, and the true explanation must be found in the infatuation with which many professional men will at such times cling to theories concerning the name of a prevailing pestilence.

Such a state of affairs now existed, that the city was well described as a "theater of horrors", and the results of the plague were turned into fresh causes. "Alas," cried the editor of one of the daily papers, giving utterance to a literal fact, "we have not even grave-diggers." Sufficient numbers of these could not be hired at five dollars an hour. While some of the dead were buried with pomp and martial honors, the drivers of dead-carts went knocking from door to door, asking at each if there were any dead to be buried. Long rows of coffins were laid in furrows of scarce two feet depth and hastily covered with a few shovelfuls of earth, which the heavy rains falling daily washed away, and the whole mass was left "filling the air far and near with the most intolerable pestilential odors". In the neighborhood of the graveyards funeral trains jostled each other and quarreled for place, in an air reeking with the effluvia of the earlier dead. Many "fell to work and buried their own dead". Many sick died in carriages and carts on their way to the hospitals. Many were found dead in their beds, in stores, in the streets, and in other places. The lengthened police reports indicated one of the natural results of a common mortal jeopardy. But heroism, too, was witnessed on every hand. The "Howards" won a fame as wide and lasting as the unhappy renown of their city, while hundreds of others displayed an equal, though often unrecorded, self-abnegation. Forty-five distant cities and towns sent pecuniary relief.

On the 11th of August 203 persons died of the fever, and in the week ending two days later, the total deaths were 1,494. Rain fell every day for two months, and it became almost impossible for the hearses to reach some of the cemeteries. On the 20th of August the week's mortality was 1,534. On the 18th 400 discharges of cannon were made and large quantities of tar burned, in the forlorn hope of purifying the air. The noise of the cannon threw many sick into convulsions, and was promptly discontinued. In the little town of Algiers, on the river shore opposite the city, there died in this week one thirty-sixth part of the whole population. On the 21st, in New Orleans, there were 269 deaths.

At last, on the 22d day of August, the maximum was reached when death struck a fresh victim every five minutes, and 283 deaths summed up the confessedly incomplete official record of the day. The next day there were 25 less. The next there was a further reduction of 36. Each day following the number diminished, and by the 1st of September was reduced to 119. By the 10th it was 80, by the 20th 49, and by the 30th 16. The total interments in the cemeteries of New Orleans, between the 1st of June and the 1st of October, was but a few short of 11,000.

But this number does not include the many buried without certificate, nor the hundreds who perished in their flight from the city, nor those who fell victims to the fever brought into their towns by refugees. On the 7th of September the mail-bill was returned to New Orleans from the little town of Thibodeauxville, with the indorsement, "Stores closed; town abandoned; 151 cases of fever; 22 deaths; postmaster absent; clerks all down with the fever." It raged in these interior towns with the most terrible virulence until the middle of October.

In New Orleans it lingered through the autumn, and disappeared only in December. In the next two summers, 1854 and 1855, it returned and destroyed more than 5,000 persons; to which number cholera added 1,750. The rate of mortality for these two years exceeded, respectively, 72 and 73 per 1,000. That of 1853 was 111, or one-ninth of the whole population.

Thus closed the darkest period in the history of New Orleans. In three years more than 35,000 people had died, in a population reduced by flight to about 145,000.

In the twenty-eight years since, only one mild and three severe epidemics of yellow fever have fallen upon the city. In 1858 the total deaths from all causes was 11,720; in 1867 they were 10,096; in 1873 they were a few less than 8,000, and in 1878 a few over 10,700. The epidemic of 1878 is the last in the city's history, and the only severe one in fourteen years.

The rate of mortality since the "great epidemic" of 1853, has been steadily and greatly reduced. That visitation awakened New Orleans to the necessity of measures heretofore neglected, and even while the fever was still epidemic, a sanitary commission was formed with comprehensive instructions and powers to investigate the nature of the disease, to pronounce upon the adaptability of a sewerage system to the needs of New Orleans, to inquire into the real value of quarantine, and to recommend rules of general sanitation.

Of the sewerage scheme nothing came; but in March, 1855, the legislature re-established quarantine, and the efficiency of that branch of sanitation and the enforcement of health laws have ever since, with little or no interruption, improved. The average annual death rate, which in the five years ending with 1855 was 70, fell in the next five to 45; in the next to 40; in the next to 39; in the next to 34½, and in that which closed with 1880, notwithstanding the terrible epidemic of 1878, the rate sank to 33½. The mortality of 1879 was under 24, and that of 1880 under 25 per 1,000.

It has already been intimated that the effect of the great epidemic upon the commerce of New Orleans was great. It may be too much to say that the whole reduction in its volume, which so promptly followed that calamity, was due to it alone; yet a careful search among contemporaneous authorities fails to reveal any other cause, and the coincidence, otherwise, remains unexplained.

In 1853 the aggregate value of exports, imports, and domestic receipts in New Orleans, exceeded $236,000,000. In 1854 it fell below $213,500,000. In 1855 it slightly recovered, and in 1856 the lost ground was much more than retaken.

This year marked the beginning of another era of inflation, and the numbers which are being used in these pages to indicate the amount of the city's business—but which, it will be noticed, do not include the immense, unascertained amounts of shipments *into* the interior—rose to the unprecedented total of $271,750,000. Yet the movement of 1857 cast this in the shade and reached an aggregate of $302,000,000.

In this year, nevertheless, came the crash, a crisis grievously felt throughout the entire country. In New Orleans 58 mercantile houses were wrecked before the opening of the next year, and in 1858, 45 others followed. This result, bad as it was, compared most favorably with that in other cities, New York chronicling 1,321 and Boston 376 failures. In 1858 another epidemic of fever visited New Orleans, but it was undoubtedly the effect of the crisis, not of the epidemic—whose commercial results would not be seen until the following year—that the year's total of exports and imports declined in value more than $36,000,000.

The year 1860 must close this record. Much, even, that belongs to earlier years has already been passed by almost or quite unmentioned,—the city's political attitude toward, and relations with, American and Central American states, and her internal agitations, the growth and the decline of filibustering schemes which divided the public attention with the Know-nothing disorders in 1853–'58, the history of her slave system and of her free people of color, the gradual though still partial amalgamation of Creole, American, and immigrant, the story of her world-renowned carnival, and the development of the fierce "abolition" question. This question in its growth, stifled for a time that love of the American union which had come to be, and is again to-day, a characteristic of all classes of her people. In that year New Orleans rose to the proudest commercial exaltation she has ever enjoyed, and at its close began that sudden and swift descent, which is not the least pathetic episode of our unfortunate civil war, whose events do not as yet bear cold discussion. In 1860 the city that one hundred and forty years before had consisted of one hundred palmetto-thatched huts in a noisome swamp, counted as the fraction of its commerce, comprised in its exports, imports, and domestic receipts, the value of $324,000,000.

NEW ORLEANS IN 1880.

LOCATION.

New Orleans lies on both banks of the Mississippi river, its principal part being on the left bank, 107 miles from the outer end of the jetties at the mouth of the South pass. Its site is of the formation peculiar to river deltas. Its greatest natural elevation is 10 feet 8 inches above the sea-level, but this is artificially increased by the levee on the river bank to 15 feet. Half a mile back from the left bank of the river the elevation is but little above the sea-level, so that, especially during high stages of the river, a large part of the city is below the natural water line, and depends for its safety on the high river bank and on the protection levees at the upper and lower sides and along lake Pontchartrain, which lies a few miles back from the river. More than half the distance between the river and the lake is an almost unreclaimed swamp, through which runs Metairie ridge, which reaches an elevation of only 3 feet and 2 inches, and a few other minor elevations of considerable relative importance. The margin of lake Pontchartrain (natural surface) is about 3 feet and 4 inches above the swamp.

Lake Pontchartrain is 30 miles long and 24 miles wide. It receives a considerable influx from the Mississippi river through old crevasses, and has several tortuous navigable outlets to lake Borgne and Mississippi sound, and thence to the Gulf of Mexico. A small lake, Maurepas, lies to the west of Pontchartrain in the course of the crevasse channels. There are indications that the course of the Mississippi river, at no very distant period, followed the course of these present crevasses, and that lake Maurepas bore the same relation to the Gulf of Mexico that Mississippi sound now does, the various divisions between the present lakes being the result of a formation of bars similar to what has more recently occurred in front of the several passes of the present river.

During the prevalence of high water in the Mississippi, or of continuous northerly winds backing up the waters of lake Pontchartrain, or of strong north winds which pile these waters up against the south shore, the swamp lands between the lake and the settled portions of the city are often covered with water. At times these overflows, one of which occurred in the winter of 1880–'81, cause serious inundations to occupied portions of the city. A settled district between Hagan avenue and Broad street is only 3 feet above sea-level. The land on the right bank (Algiers) is lower than that on the left, its minimum elevation above sea-level being only 12 inches. The elevation of the water of the river, as it passes through the city, is from 0.79 of a foot below the mean level of the Gulf of Mexico (low water of 1871) to 14.65 feet above that level,(a) so that the conditions obtaining in the rear portions of the city, on both sides of the river, are quite similar to those of Holland, and the city depends for its drainage on a rude form of pumping machinery similar to the older works of that country.

THE HARBOR.

The harbor of New Orleans comprises several turnings of the stream, and its shores are subject to certain changes, owing to the action of the great current. At points the slackening of the current produces heavy deposits of the alluvium with which its waters are charged, producing at these points a constant extension known as the "batture". This formation has created a considerable extension of the river front, amounting since the first settlement of the city to nearly 1,500 feet at the greatest width, near the foot of Delord street, and extending from near the foot of Felicity street, to about the Place d'Armes, at the center of the old French town. At other points the current, deflected with great force along the shore, produces a constant tendency of the bank to yield and "cave", thus shifting the bed of the river gradually in the direction of the yielding bank, without materially altering the width of the stream. This tendency produces on each side of the harbor two sorts of shore: first, the abrupt banks, where at all stages there is a sufficient depth of water to accommodate the largest vessels at the wharves; and, second, the batture, which has been followed up by the annual extension of the wharves at that

---

a Thus the Mississippi river, 107 miles from its mouth, has been more than 9 inches lower than the nominal levels of the gulf at its mouth. This condition would be possible during the prevalence of long-continued strong north winds.

locality by moving them forward and filling behind them with earth to the level of the levee, so as to retain a minimum depth during the lowest stages of the water of 10 feet at the wharves of the river-going craft, and of 20 feet at those of sea-going vessels. The width of the river (the harbor) varies from 1,500 to 3,000 feet. The length of harbor in actual use for steamers and shipping, is about 7 miles on either shore.

On the left bank, where the greater part of the active commerce is carried on, there are 66 wharves capable of accommodating large steamers two abreast, or sail-vessels four abreast, and a wharf for river and coasting steamers and barges of nearly 1½ mile front.

The shipping wharves have a length of from 80 to 140 feet. Large steamers, loading grain in bulk from floating elevators, sometimes receive their cargoes while at anchor in the stream. The bottom affords good anchorage throughout, being of tenacious clay, but of very irregular depth, the variations within a short distance being as much as 100 feet. The channel occupies the entire width of the river, its depth varying from 60 feet to 208 feet.

During high water the current reaches a speed of 5 miles an hour, while at low water it becomes extremely sluggish, sometimes less than 1 mile an hour. In August, 1846, there was no perceptible current. At extreme low water there is a tidal variation of a few inches.

Beside the river harbor two navigable canals pierce the city from lake Pontchartrain to within about one mile of the river, where they end in artificial basins. These are frequented by a large fleet of schooners and a few light-draught steamers, doing business with the northern shore of the lake and of Mississippi sound, with Mobile, Pensacola, the Pearl and the Amite rivers, and the sand and shell yielding coast east of the mouths of the Mississippi. "The Old Basin" is 400 feet long by 225 feet wide at the head of the navigable canal which runs to lake Pontchartrain through the bayou St. John. "The New Basin" is a large excavation with a head frontage of 250 feet. The total frontage of this basin and the sides of the canal, available for wharfage, is about seven-eighths of a mile. This canal runs directly to the lake.

WATER COMMUNICATION.

Not only is New Orleans within easy and safe communication with all points along the northern shore of the Gulf of Mexico to the east, and by the Mississippi river with the great northwestern basin, but it has recently, by the successful carrying out of the jetty enterprise, been brought into uninterrupted communication with the whole world, having now a safe entrance for the largest shipping, whereas a few years since vessels drawing 10 feet of water were often subject to detention in channels maintained by artificial dredging. Even the Great Eastern could now steam directly and at all times from the Gulf to the city's front.

So far as present experience and future probabilities warrant the formation of an opinion, it seems clear that a new departure has been taken in the commerce of New Orleans, and of the great district for which the Mississippi river and the lines of railway leading to New Orleans furnish a natural outlet.

THE JETTIES.

The vast burden of silt brought down by the Mississippi river and discharged at its several mouths, is carried seaward so long as the current maintains enough of its initial velocity to move it. When the current becomes so retarded by the waters of the Gulf as to lose its carrying power, the silt is deposited, forming bars which rise until their reduction of the depth of the stream secures a surface velocity adequate to its movement. The extension of the bar seaward seems to be prevented by the action of a littoral current moving mainly from east to west.

The bar thus formed in front of the South pass had its crest distant about 2 miles from the mouth of the pass, and carried a depth of only about 8 feet of water. The former navigation channel was maintained by mechanical means through the bar in front of the Southwest pass. It was shifting and uncertain, and rarely of adequate depth. The delays that it caused to navigation were a serious drawback to the commercial prosperity of the city and of the Mississippi valley.

Projects for the improvement of the navigation have always been entertained. The first of which record has been preserved is described, in the *Journal Historique de l'Establissement des Français à la Louisanne*, by Bernard La Harpe, one of the king's officers and a standard authority on every subject of which he treated. He reports the observations made in April, 1721, of M. de Pauger, a knight of St. Louis, and an engineer, who arrived from France in November, 1720, being commissioned (under De La Tour) to fix a permanent site for the capital of the colony. He says:

Le 17, M. de Pauger se rendit à l'embouchure du fleuve; après l'avoir bien sondée et examinée, il trouva que la barre était un dépôt de vase de cinq cents à neuf cents toises de largeur, au-dedans de l'entrée du fleuve, formé par la rencontre du flux de la mer et de l'affaiblissement du courant de la rivière, qui se deborde en plusieurs branches et canaux; que, dans ses débordemens, il est bourbeux, et dépose en s'abaissant une vase sur les terres et îles qu'il inonde, et sur les embarras d'arbres échoués dont elles paraissent avoir été formées. Comme le fleuve charriait alors une grande quantité de ces bois, dont partie sont échoués de côté et d'autre du canal de cette embouchure, il lui sembla qu'il serait aisé d'en placer d'avance, et d'en former des digues ou stacades, ainsi que d'en boucher quelques passes en les arrêtant à de vieux vaisseaux coulés à fond, ce qui augmenterait le courant sur la barre, la ferait couler, et l'emporterait, puisque la nature avait fait en partie d'elle-même cette opération depuis l'année passée; qu'il n'y avait trouvé que onze à douze pieds d'eau, et au bout de huit mois treize à quatorze pieds; cette barre s'étant élargie jusqu'auprès de l'île à la Balise, où les ingénieurs se proposaient d'établir une batterie et une place maritime devant laquelle plusieurs vaisseaux tirant seize à dix-huit pieds d'eau, pourraient mouiller en sûreté.(a)

The conditions described by La Harpe had been considerably modified before Captain Eads, in 1874, "made a formal proposition to Congress to open the mouth of the Mississippi river, by making and maintaining a channel 28 feet deep between the Southwest pass and the Gulf of Mexico." The procedure adopted by him in opening a channel through the bar, in front of the Southwest pass, was substantially that suggested by De Pauger, modified to meet the changed conditions.

Captain Eads' proposition met with very strenuous opposition, especially on the part of the United States Engineer Corps, and his undertaking was embarrassed from the outset nearly to its completion, by political and financial obstacles of the most serious character. He pursued his project with indomitable pertinacity, and is entitled to almost as much credit for the perseverance with which he overcame these collateral obstacles, as for the complete success which attended the final execution of the work.

Important improvements were made at the head of the South pass and in its course, and two jetties were extended for a distance of about 12,000 feet beyond the most advanced bank, that on the west side. The jetties were located about 1,000 feet apart, but the channel was afterward narrowed by the construction of wing-dams to a width of from 600 to 800 feet. By the original proposition, which was accepted by the government, Captain Eads was to receive $500,000 on the securing of a continuous channel from the river to the Gulf with a least depth of 20 feet, and a width of channel of 200 feet. For each 2 feet additional depth he was to receive an additional payment of $500,000. The total compensation for the securing of a channel 350 feet wide, with a minimum depth of 30 feet, was to be $5,250,000. One million dollars of the amount to be paid is to be retained by the government for ten years. If at the end of that time the channel is still maintained in good condition, one-half of the money withheld is to be paid, and the same condition being maintained for 20 years, the whole remaining sum is to be paid.

The work was practically completed in the month of July, 1879, though minor modifications and a re-enforcement of the ends of the jetties, by loading them with blocks of béton, have been continued since that date.

Opinions vary still as to the future of this work. The ultimate relation between the projected live current and the diverted littoral current to result from it will influence the future deposit of silt in a manner which can now be only a matter of conjecture. All that it is safe now to say is, that thus far the success of the enterprise is complete, and that there is no reason to apprehend insuperable difficulties, should it become necessary to extend the jetties still farther. The effect of this improvement on the prosperity of New Orleans cannot be a matter of conjecture, and its importance is hardly less to the whole Mississippi valley, and to that portion of the southwest connected with New Orleans by railway.

RAILROADS.

In 1880 New Orleans had the following railway communications:

New Orleans and Pacific railway—not completed.

Chicago, St. Louis, and New Orleans railroad to Cairo, Illinois.

New Orleans and Mobile railroad to Mobile, and thence by Montgomery or Columbus, Kentucky, to the east and north.

Morgan's Texas railway to Morgan City, thence by steamers to Galveston, and by rail to Houston and central Texas.

New Orleans and Texas railroad to Donaldsonville, Louisiana.

TRIBUTARY COUNTRY.

In one sense, and in the most important sense, the country tributary to New Orleans is the whole central basin of the United States, from the Alleghanies to the Rocky mountains. When we consider the district immediately contiguous and dependent upon this city for supplies as well as for the outlet of its products, we find that its industries are almost exclusively agricultural, devoted mainly to the production of sugar and cotton. The low pine and cypress lands along the northern shores of lake Pontchartràin, and for a distance of from 60 to 80 miles northward, send large quantities of pine and cypress lumber for local consumption and for export. Bricks are

---

a The 17th, M. de Pauger went to the mouth of the river; after having sounded it well and examined it, he found that the bar was a deposit of mud from 500 to 900 yards wide within the mouth of the river, formed by the meeting of the incoming tide of the sea and the weakening of the current of the river, which overflows in several branches and channels; that in its overflows it is muddy, and as the water falls deposits silt on the lands and islands that it inundates, and on the multitude of fallen trees, of which these seem to have been formed. As the river carries a great quantity of this wood, part of which is deposited on one side or the other of the channel of this mouth, it seemed to him that it would be easy to place some of them in advance and to form of them dikes or stockades; also, to close some of the passes by sinking old vessels in them, which would augment the current on the bar, cause it to flow and carry it away, since nature itself has partially performed this operation since last year; that he had found only 11 or 12 feet of water, and at the end of 8 months 13 or 14 feet; this bar had extended itself as far as the island of Balise, where the engineers proposed to establish a battery and a harbor, before which several vessels, drawing from 16 to 18 feet, could ride in safety.

largely manufactured for domestic use and for export, those made along the shores of the lake being universally preferred for pavements and for foundations. A softer sort of red building brick is made on the right bank of the river near the city. There are in the region turpentine orchards and charcoal districts of importance. The hill country lying beyond these wooded lands, and within easy reach of transportation by rail, produces large quantities of fruits and early vegetables for southern and even for remote northern and eastern towns. These industries are, however, all unimportant as compared with the production of the two great staples of the region, sugar and cotton. The waters along the coast and about the low pine-covered sand keys are rich in fish of the choicest kinds. Some of these islands also furnish inexhaustible supplies of building sand of the best quality, and of small fossil shells useful in road-making. Along the banks of the river above and below the city, the soil, a sandy alluvium of great fertility, is covered by an almost unbroken series of large plantations devoted to the production of sugar and rice. Sugar culture predominates, but on many of the lower lands the facility for irrigation and the occasional presence of a stiff black soil, are especially favorable for rice culture. Indian corn is largely raised, but only for plantation use. The well-known Perique tobacco is produced with the greatest success in the parish of St. James, about 60 miles from New Orleans, and some 3 or 4 miles back from the river, on a tract of slightly elevated country. The lands immediately about the city, where tolerably drained, are principally devoted to market gardening. Fine groves of orange trees in the "coast" country—as the river plantations are termed—both above and below the city, furnish the market with an abundant supply of fruit of the very best quality. The successful production of this fruit extends for a distance of 80 miles below the city. As a rule, the plantations line the banks of the Mississippi and of the several rivers or bayous entering the Gulf, these banks being higher than the lands farther back, which are mostly swamps covered with forests. The cultivation of onions and garlics is an important item of the industry of the parish of St. Bernard, immediately below the city—an old Spanish colony.

Of late efforts have begun to be made to reclaim and appropriate for the cultivation of rice, certain tracts of the marsh lands back of the plantations forming so large a proportion of the territory of lower Louisiana, and of the quaking prairies, whose soil is a vegetable mold resting on a stratum of clay of variable thickness, and often apparently underlaid by quicksands. It is from the mouths of small bays and bayous piercing these immense marshes that New Orleans is supplied with oysters, and from other innumerable lagoons that she obtains her abundant supply of wild duck and other water-fowl. The timbered swamps supply timber and Spanish moss as articles of commerce.

THE SITE.

New Orleans occupies a tract of land lying 12 miles along the left bank and across the convexity of a bend on the right bank of the Mississippi. Its width varies from $4\frac{3}{4}$ to $7\frac{1}{4}$ miles as to corporate limits, and from $\frac{3}{4}$ of a mile to 2 miles as to actual settlement. The natural drainage is away from the banks of the river, and generally toward neighboring waters, communicating with the Gulf or with the lakes to the north. The surrounding country, for a radius of about 5 miles, was formerly densely wooded, but now has been almost completely cleared. The soil, whether the sand of the river banks and slight elevations, or the dark stiff earth of the swamp lands, is of great fertility. The alluvial deposit is generally but 2 or 3 feet in thickness, resting on a substratum of uniform and tenacious blue clay. The sinking of an artesian well, begun in 1854, in the heart of the city, pierced this clay to a depth of 15 feet, and then struck another stratum of clay mixed with woody matter of less than 4 feet thickness. Beneath this lay a mixture of sand and clay 10 feet thick, resembling the annual deposits of the river. Below these was a continual though irregular alternation of these strata of clay, varying in thickness from less than 12 inches to more than 60 feet, with layers of sand and shell and of mixtures of these with the clay. At a depth of 335 feet a uniform stratum of 145 feet was struck. The well was abandoned at a depth of 630 feet. No masses of rock were found, only a few water-worn pebbles and some contorted and perforated stones. At a depth of 582 feet there was encountered a stratum of hard pan. No other investigations seem ever to have been made of the geological character of the site of the city or of the country immediately surrounding it.

THE CLIMATE.

The climate of New Orleans is of the character known as "insular", the city being almost completely surrounded by open bodies of water and swamps and marshes. The winds from all quarters become charged with moisture, and thus modify the extremes of heat and cold. The highest recorded summer temperature since 1819 is 100° Fahr. This point has been reached but three times in this period. The highest summer temperature in average years is 94.7° Fahr. The lowest recorded winter temperature, reached but once, is 16° Fahr. The lowest winter temperature in average years is 27.4° Fahr. The cold and dry northeasterly winds, noticeable to the northwest and southwest of New Orleans, lose their reputed evaporating power, and by the time they have reached the city have become tempered by the marshes and bodies of water over which they have passed. The prevailing winds are from the southeast, bringing much vapor gathered in their passage over the marshes skirting the Gulf of Mexico. The air is therefore always in a condition of high humidity. The heat rays are absorbed and the direct solar heat made much less intense than it would be were the climate more dry. There are no elevations of land sufficiently near to affect the air-currents reaching the city from any direction. The influence of the immense sea marshes, which lie a few miles away on several sides, is probably confined to the dampening of the atmosphere already noted. The swamp lands, either now or formerly covered with forests, still undrained and surrounding the immediate suburbs of the city, are the cause of much malarial fever. No record of "sick rate" has been kept, except in a very fragmentary form; but the general verdict of the best-informed physicians of New Orleans, attributes fully one-third of all the sickness (not of the mortality) to malarial fevers, resulting from the proximity of these wet lands and from the deficient drainage of the city itself, notably the latter. It is also maintained by the same authorities, that other diseases, almost without exception, are subject to malarial complications. This malarial influence is not of a severe type, save in districts nearest the swamps, particularly the lower part of the city, where the swamp approaches very near to the river, and in that part lately joined to it on the right bank of the Mississippi. The river, by its great width and rapid movement, seems to act as a barrier to the malarious influence of the swamps beyond it, and malarial fevers are rarer and generally milder in proportion as they occur in those parts of the city near the river bank. The high humidity of the atmosphere of New Orleans seems to tend to a reduction of the natural powers of resistance to this influence, inducing lassitude, affections of the alimentary canal, and general depletion during the warmer seasons, and affections of the respiratory organs, rheumatism, and kidney derangements during winter. On the other hand, the resulting moderate range of temperature, both daily and annual, gives a climate favorable to young children, an effect further heightened by the free ventilation and the full exposure of the generally low houses to sunlight and air.

STREETS.

The total length of the streets of New Orleans is 566.29 miles, of which 472.34 miles are unpaved. Total length paved with each of the following materials:

	Miles.
Cobble-stones	32.94
Stone blocks	22.06
Nicholson	1.66
Broken stone	8.87
Plank road	4.88
Shell	23.54

The estimated cost of each is as follows:

Cobble-stone, per square yard	$2 25
Stone blocks, per square yard	4 75
Nicholson, per square yard	3 40
Broken stone, per running foot of 20 feet width	2 25
Plank road, per M feet, board measure	18 50
Shell, per running foot of 20 feet width	2 25

The cost of repairs cannot be exactly determined. There is an undivided appropriation of $300,000 for the expense of keeping streets in repair, keeping them clean, and removing garbage.

The estimated annual cost of repairs, per square yard, is as follows: Cobble-stones, 10 cents per annum; stone blocks, 10 cents per annum; broken stone or shell, 25 cents per annum.

Concerning the relative facility with which each is kept clean, the report says: "Stone blocks are far the easiest kept clean; cobble-stones much easier than wood (plank), broken stone, or shell."

Concerning economy, stone blocks are found to be beyond comparison the best and cheapest for streets of heavy traffic, where alone they are used. Cobble-stones are cheaper than wood, broken stone, or shell. These latter are more expensive than unpaved streets. Shell roads, made of oyster-shells pulverized and rolled, make fine carriage drives, but they wear rapidly, and easily fall into bad repair, so that their maintenance is difficult and costly.

The great length of unpaved streets is one of the serious drawbacks of the city. The natural soil is of such a character, that, under the action of heavy rains it becomes an almost impassable mire, and during drought is extremely dusty. At times, on such streets, traffic is almost restricted to the lines of the street railroads, which are either planked or paved between the tracks, and to the sidewalks.

SIDEWALKS.

The sidewalks, called "banquettes", are generally from 10 to 12 feet wide, and paved for the whole width. In streets occupied by the better class of residents, they are often much wider and paved with German flags, or with an artificial stone called Schillinger pavement, which is excellent. In most of the business parts of the city, the sidewalks are covered with North River blue-stone flags; but the common sidewalk pavement, of the closely settled but poorer districts, is almost exclusively of brick. In the newer quarters, especially in those recently included within the extended corporate limits, sidewalks are generally of plank only, and narrow.

Each property owner is required to keep in repair the sidewalk in front of his premises; hence no report of the total amount of sidewalk, or of the extent of walks of different materials, has ever been made.

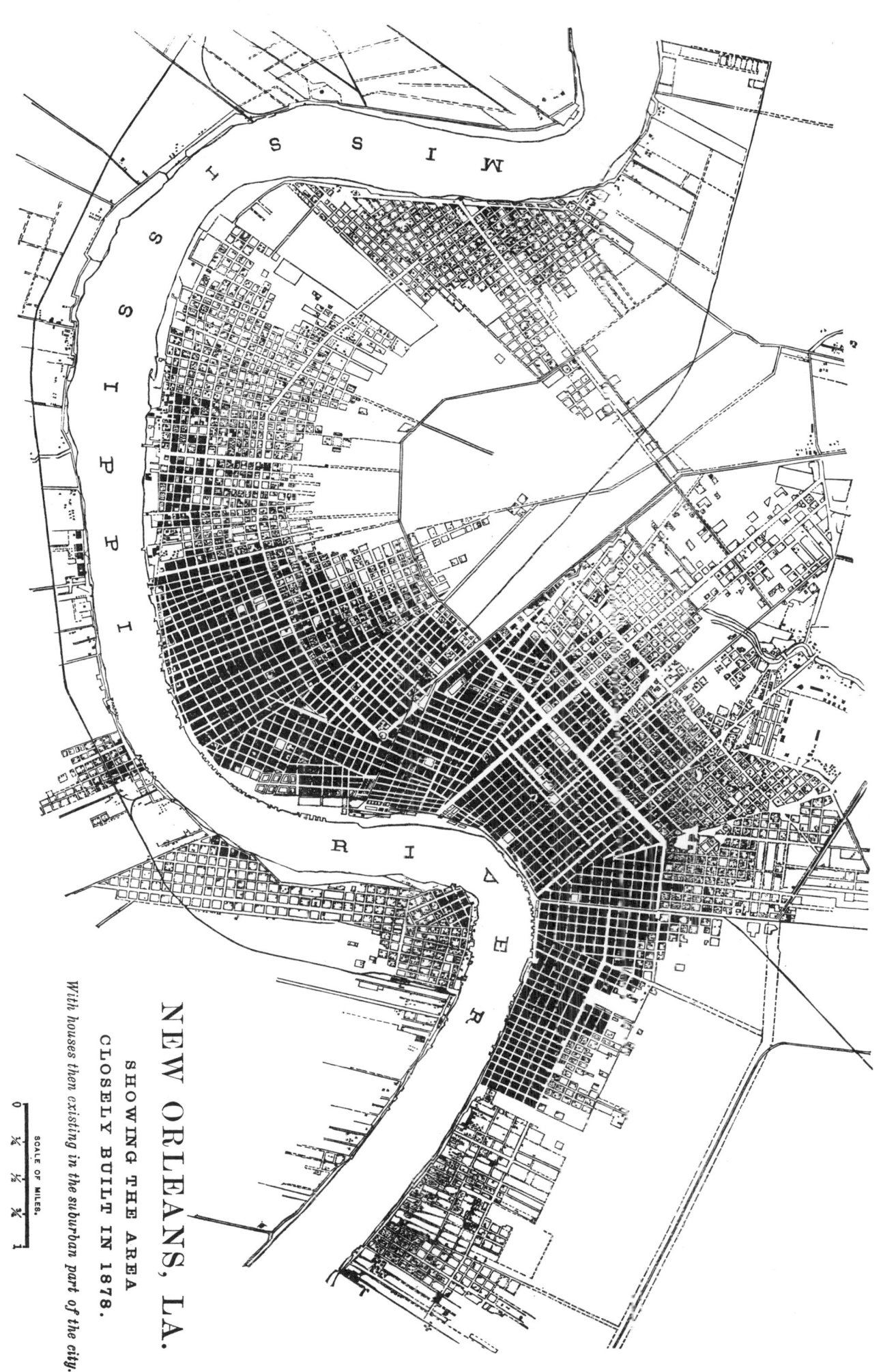

NEW ORLEANS, LA.

SHOWING THE AREA
CLOSELY BUILT IN 1878.

With houses then existing in the suburban part of the city.

SCALE OF MILES.

0   ¼   ½   ¾   1

GUTTERS.

On the paved streets the gutter is bounded by a curb of North River blue-stone or of Boston granite, and the stone pavement of the arched street extends to this in paved streets. In those paved with wood, shell, or broken stone, the gutters have a bottom of heavy plank, and these are often separated from the sidewalks by wooden curbs.

On many of the streets running back from the river the gutters are deep channels from 2 to 3 feet wide, curbed on both sides with stone or wood, and capable of carrying large bodies of water, the excessive rainfall of tropical storms often exceeding the capacity of these gutters and of the drainage canals beyond, and flooding the whole width of the street at a distance of about half a mile back from the levee, where the flatter grade begins.

TREE PLANTING AND GRASSED PLACES.

Trees are very extensively planted throughout the entire city, outside of the more active business districts, both on private grounds and on the outer edges of sidewalks. Some streets are almost completely over-arched with forest trees. Formerly, in the French quarter, trees were planted on the street side of the gutter, but this practice no longer exists.

Several of the wider streets have two distinct roadways, separated by broad grassed places known as "neutral grounds", for the reason that most of them were originally the boundaries of distinct *faubourgs*, or municipalities. These are planted with forest trees, sometimes with three continuous rows forming a double avenue. These avenues have quite generally been appropriated for street-car routes, with the effect of relieving the roadways of the inconvenience of car tracks, and preventing the wear and tear of the track by ordinary street traffic.

There are 13 of these neutral grounds, several of which are traversed in the whole or a part of their length by open draining canals.

A late report of the city surveyor shows the number of trees in these places and in the public squares to be 5,027, which is but a small fraction of the trees in the city, the vast majority of which are planted and maintained by private owners.

Street construction work is generally done by contract, and repairing by the day, all new work being given out by contract under careful specifications, the payment of the contractor being dependent on a proper execution of the work. For repairing and cleaning streets and bridges and removing garbage the system of day's work is preferred, owing to the difficulty of holding contractors to its proper execution. Both plans have been tried, and the contract system proved an utter failure.

STREET RAILROADS.

In the following statement there are included two lines of road, using steam dummies exclusively, running to different points on lake Pontchartrain, and one line using steam dummies on a part of the road to Carrollton.

All termini are within the city limits. The total length of all roads is equal to 140 miles of single track. Total number of cars, 373; of which 313 are horse cars, and 60 small passenger coaches; total number of horses (mules), 1,641; total number of steam engines, 20; total number of men employed, 671; total number of passengers carried during the year (number of fares taken), 23,716,327.

The rate of fare on horse cars is 5 cents, and on the steam trains to the lake 15 cents to go and return.

There are no omnibus lines on fixed routes, only one small line for the accommodation of railroad and steamer passengers, which employs 7 omnibuses, 5 wagons, 14 men, and 25 horses. The total number of persons carried during the year is about 6,000, and the rate of fare 50 cents.

WATER-WORKS.

The water-works were originally built by the Commercial Bank of New Orleans, in 1836. They were purchased in 1869 by the city, and bonds were issued in payment therefor. In 1878 a charter was granted by the legislature, incorporating the New Orleans Water Works Company, and April 10, 1878, the entire property was deeded by the city to this company.

The total cost is given as $1,250,000. The water is taken from the Mississippi river in the upper part of the city, and is pumped into the mains and stand-pipe, under an extreme head of 150 feet, the usual head being from 80 to 90 feet.

The distribution is through 71 miles, mainly of cast-iron pipe, varying from 36 inches to 3 inches in diameter.

The average amount pumped daily is 8,000,000 gallons; the greatest, 11,000,000 gallons; the least, 7,000,000 gallons. The average cost of raising 1,000,000 gallons 1 foot high is 11 cents. The yearly cost of maintenance, aside from the cost of pumping, is $20,000. The yearly income from water-rates is $91,000. No water-meters are used.

There has been as yet no provision made for the settling or filtration of the water, and the deposit of sediment in the pipes during the six months of high water, frequently prevents the free working of the smaller mains.

WATER-WORKS COMPANY.

The following is taken from the annual report of the New Orleans Water Works Company, April 10, 1880:

The New Orleans Water Works Company, as reorganized, has a capital stock of $2,000,000, and has issued bonds to the amount of $182,500. Its capital is invested in the works, which were purchased from the city. Its improvements have cost, up to April 9, 1880, $185,256 52. Its receipts for the year ending April 9, 1880, for water-rates, were $91,339 63. It expended for improvements in the works during the year ending April 9, 1880, $178,744 63, and for ordinary running expenses, $20,987 68.

The amount of water pumped (from the Mississippi river) during the year ending April 9, 1880, was 3,054,762,000 gallons. The coal consumed in this service was 31,734 barrels. Prior to the improvements the service-pipes throughout the city were not only too small for the efficient distribution of water, but they had become so filled with silt deposited by the muddy river-water that their original efficiency was very much reduced, and in some instances entirely destroyed. Some of this obstructing deposit has, since the improvement of the pumping-works, been forced out by flushing under a strong head, so that pipes in the lower part of the city, formerly nearly or quite useless, have been restored to their full efficiency.

The pipes laid in the course of the improvement to April 9, 1880, are:

	Feet.
36-inch	2,325.5
30-inch	9,052.3
20-inch	2,168.5
12-inch	3,751.0
8-inch	13,454.6
6-inch	7,686.5
Total (7.28 miles)	38,438.4

Since the date of the report the pumping-works and stand-pipe have been completed, the service is much improved, and the use of the water is rapidly extending.

The most important remaining need of these works is an arrangement for the supply of water clarified by settling in basins. It is thought that the demand and the financial condition of the company will not at present justify this work. When the improvement shall have been made it is proposed, in order to flush the gutters of the perpendicular streets, to set aside for that purpose pipes not needed for the general distribution, and to send through them water pumped directly from the river without settling.

Experience with the New Orleans water-works indicates the advisability of removing cement and iron pipes, where these were originally laid, and substituting pipes of cast iron.

GAS.

The gas-works are owned by a private corporation. Daily average production, 598,000 feet. Rate, where consumption is less than 500 feet per month, $3 per thousand; where 500 feet or more, $2 70 per thousand feet.

The city pays $13 88 per annum each for street lamps, of which there are 3,600.

The income from rates is $505,825 79.

PUBLIC BUILDINGS.

The buildings owned or occupied by the city for municipal uses are the city hall and court-house, opposite Lafayette square; court-house opposite Jackson square; court-house in the fifth district; court-house in the sixth district; second judicial court, Carrollton; house of the aged and infirm; boys' house of refuge; mortgage office; workhouse; parish prison, and insane asylum.

The total cost of the municipal buildings belonging to the city is about $500,000.

The original contract price of the city hall was $120,000.

Mr. Cable appends the following note to his report: "No printed list of the municipal buildings, giving their original cost, is known to be extant, and the imperfect condition of the city archives, consequent upon various periods of disorder and neglect, especially that of the late war, make it improbable that any search among them would yield a list of undoubted accuracy."

PUBLIC PARKS AND PLEASURE-GROUNDS.

The total area of the public squares inclosed and within inhabited limits is 659.42 acres.

On Metairie ridge, in the rear of the second district, between Ursuline and St. Louis streets, a tract of 175 acres has been for many years set apart as a public park. It is covered with a natural growth of majestic live-oaks. It remains, thus far, very much in a state of nature. The question of its further adornment and utilization for

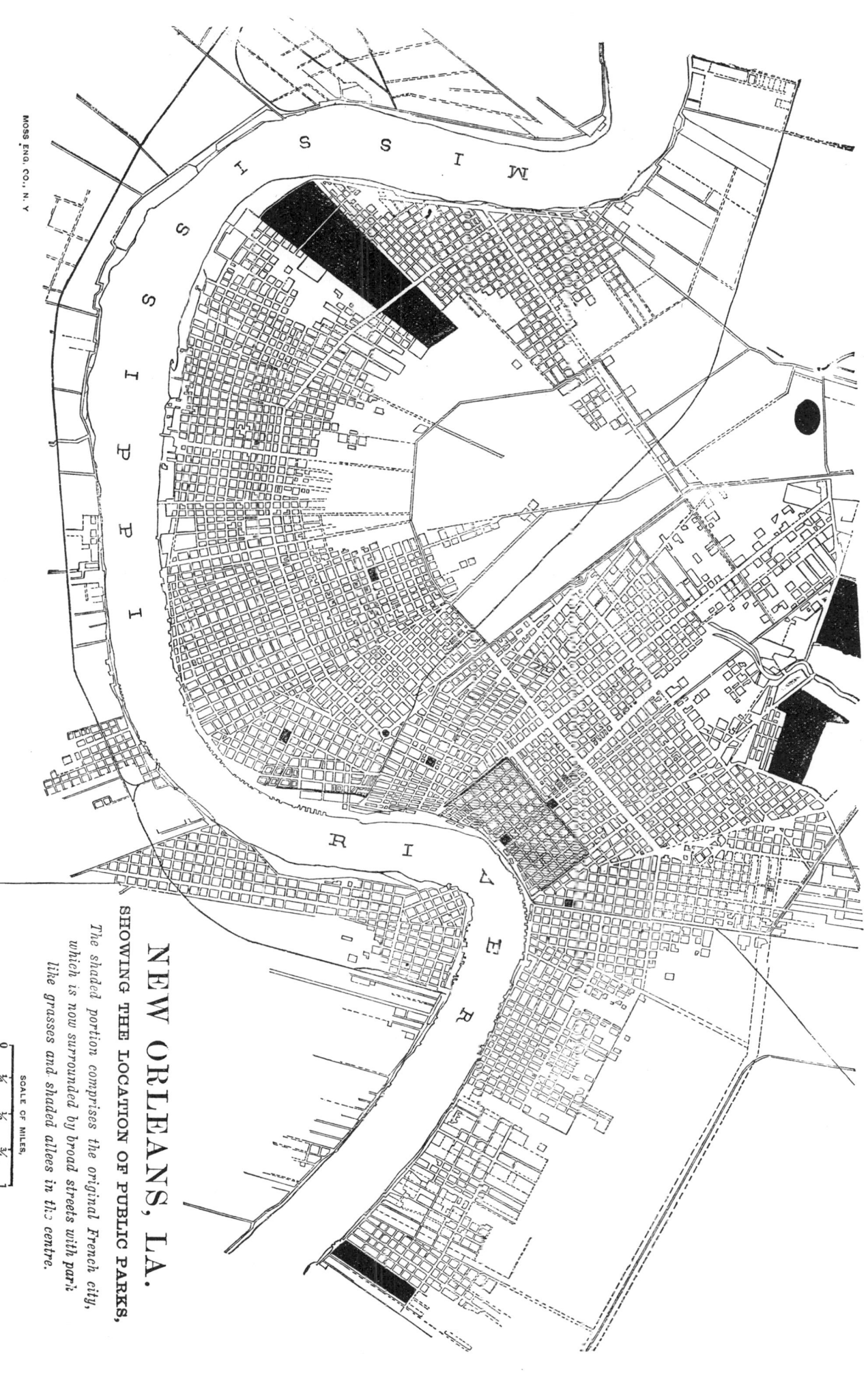

MOSS. ENG. CO., N. Y.

MISSISSIPPI

RIVER

NEW ORLEANS, LA.

SHOWING THE LOCATION OF PUBLIC PARKS,

The shaded portion comprises the original French city,
which is now surrounded by broad streets with park-
like grasses and shaded allees in the centre.

SCALE OF MILES.

0   ¼   ½   ¾   1

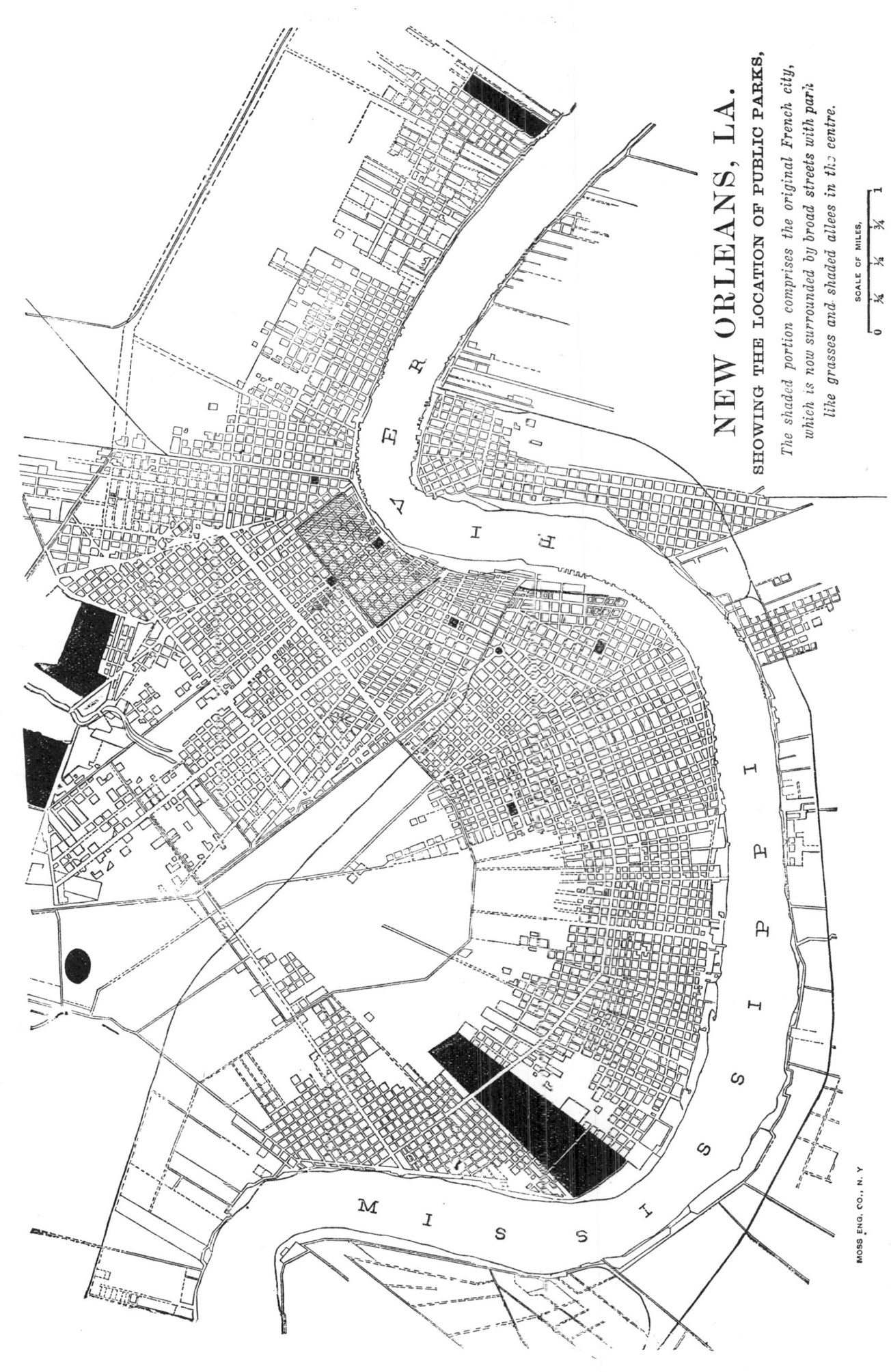

NEW ORLEANS, LA.

SHOWING THE LOCATION OF PUBLIC PARKS,

The shaded portion comprises the original French city,
which is now surrounded by broad streets with park
like grasses and shaded allees in the centre.

SCALE OF MILES,

0   ¼   ½   ¾   1

MOSS ENG. CO., N. Y

R I V E R

M I S S I S S I P P I

pleasure purposes would involve an arrangement for the drainage of the area and its neighborhood such as no administration of the city government has ever felt justified in undertaking. It is roughly fenced in, and is in charge of an unpaid keeper, "who finds his remuneration in using it as a cow-pasture."

In 1871 there was acquired, through the action of a commission appointed to purchase land suitable for a city park and for the site of a state-house, a tract of 250 acres of unimproved land, with a frontage of 2,423 feet on the left bank of the river, 5½ miles above Canal street by the course of the river, and extending to St. Charles avenue, with an average depth of 5,580 feet, about 4 miles above Canal street by that road, and with a frontage on that avenue of 1,621 feet. It has a uniform fall from the river bank of about 8 feet to the mile. Excepting a very fine avenue of live-oaks, near the river, it is destitute of trees, and in its present condition is simply an expanse of inclosed common.

The cost of this city park, now being paid, was $800,000. No appropriation has ever been made for its improvement.

The total cost of the public parks cannot be ascertained. With few exceptions, the smaller public squares were laid off by the persons who owned the surrounding land and divided it into town lots; these have generally become public property by donation.

The lower city park, on Metairie ridge, was expropriated at a valuation of $40,880 from the estate of John McDonough, the cities of New Orleans and Baltimore being equal heirs to the greater part of that estate, which included this tract. Baltimore abandoned its undivided half to New Orleans in payment of taxes.

No outlay is made for the maintaining of the larger parks; the smaller public squares receive, however, a certain amount of attention. All are nominally under the control of the administrator of police.

Jackson square, in front of the Cathedral, the old Place d'Armes, is well kept and much frequented, and, with its wealth of orange trees and other sub-tropical vegetation, is extremely attractive. It is closed at night, and has a day and a night watchman and a gardener.

There are no ordinances relating to the control of the parks.

PLACES OF AMUSEMENT.

New Orleans has five theaters:

	Seating capacity.
Grand opera-house, Canal street	1,800
French opera-house, Bourbon street	2,000
National theater, Perdido street	1,600
St. Charles theater, St. Charles street	3,000
Academy of Music, St. Charles street	2,200

Theaters pay to the city a license fee of $250, and to the state of $500. In addition to this they pay to the charity hospital, in accordance with a stipulated provision, as follows:

SECTION 397. For every public ball or concert, the sum of ten dollars shall be paid to the treasurer of the hospital; and annually, for each theater, one hundred dollars; for each circus, one hundred and fifty dollars; for every menagerie, fifty dollars; for every show, twenty-five dollars. And it shall be the duty of the mayor of the city of New Orleans, in authorizing any of these exhibitions, previously to require the receipt of the treasurer of the hospital for the payment of the said sums respectively, and in case he should issue any license without such receipt the city of New Orleans shall be liable therefor.

Grunewald hall, in Baronne street, occupies the upper portion of a large building erected in 1874. It has a seating capacity of 1,000, and is provided with the conveniences and appurtenances of a concert hall of the better class, including a stairway at each of the four corners for escape to the ground in case of fire.

Odd Fellows' hall, on Lafayette square, is a well-appointed music hall, with a seating capacity of 1,000.

Masonic hall, in St. Charles street, at the corner of Perdido street, has a seating capacity of 1,200.

There are no concert or beer gardens properly so-called or paying license as such. The two steam railways leading from Canal street to lake Pontchartrain and terminating, one at West End, at the mouth of the New Canal, and the other at Spanish Fort, at the mouth of the bayou St. John, have been made favorite places of resort.

At West End a promenade and a shell-paved carriage-drive have been made on the ground of the protection levee for a length of about half a mile. The ground has been neatly dressed, about 1,000 trees have been planted, and pagodas have been built. The establishment includes a hotel and restaurant. There is an open-air instrumental concert every evening except in winter. The rowing club and the yacht club have erected convenient houses at the end of the canal, and hold their regattas in the mouth of the canal or on the lake. This resort is also approached by the shell roads of Canal street, Carrollton avenue, and the New Canal, which are favorite carriage routes. The improvements are now substantially completed, and have cost about $75,000.

At Spanish Fort the improvements are of much the same character, but somewhat more elaborate. A garden has been laid out, where beer is served, and there is a display of fireworks on Saturday nights. These improvements, which are but partially completed, have cost thus far about $55,000.

During eight months of the year, omitting the winter months, both Spanish Fort and the West End are nightly patronized by thousands, including those of all classes of society and of both sexes. Each occupies an area of about eight acres.

DRAINAGE.

The drainage of New Orleans is of the most ineffective and simple character, adapted solely to the removal of surface-water from the streets and house-lots. The whole vast area of the city, except the elevation along the bank of the river and its inland slope and a few trifling elevations like Metairie ridge, is naturally a marsh so far as its frequent submersion is concerned, though not bearing a vegetable soil of great depth. It has been made substantially dry by a rude adoption of the Polder system of Holland; that is to say, it is inclosed by protection levees or dikes at the upper and lower boundaries and along the lake and the canals, the river front being protected by an artificial elevation of the natural shore. The floods against which it has to be protected are of three sources: first, the rise of the river to such a height as to overflow the levee in part of the city, and this even now requires at times vigilant attention; second, the flood occasionally caused by crevasses in the levees above the city, and assailing the upper protection levee; and third, the piling up of the waters of lake Pontchartrain from the long continuance of strong north or northeast winds, forcing the water into the canals and overflowing their banks or the protection levee on the lake shore.

During floods the water of the river rises to a height of 10 or 12 feet above the general level of the back lands of the city. The same cause, acting through a crevasse of the levee above the city, would produce a flood of varying height, according to the capacity of the opening and the level of the river. The level of lake Pontchartrain is substantially the level of the sea, but the accumulation of its waters along the south shore and in the canals sometimes reaches, owing to the influence of protracted winds, several feet above that level.

Without artificial aid the great level plain of New Orleans would be flooded by the rains falling upon it and running to it from the river slope, and by the large volume of the artificial water-supply of the city, none of which has any other means of discharge. The artificial aid is given by the use of three "draining-machines" situated at the rear of the city, one at Dublin avenue, one at the beginning of bayou St. John, and one at London avenue. These are the old Dutch paddle-wheel pumps, revolving vertically and forcing the water from the canal behind them to the higher level of the canal beyond them. They are driven by steam, and as their capacity is considerably beyond the dry-weather needs they work only intermittently and moderately, except during storms, when their full force is not adequate to the complete removal of the torrent. The water is led to these machines by open draining canals, which penetrate the city at different points, and which accumulate the flow of the intermediate territory by cross canals. The rapid removal of storm water from the river slope is facilitated by wide and deep gutters which, during the almost tropical downpour that occasionally takes place, deliver such volumes as to overflow the whole territory at the foot of the slope a half mile, more or less, back from the levee.

The gutters of New Orleans are the receptacles of nearly all of the liquid wastes of houses, and become, especially during the summer time, extremely foul. They receive also more or less garbage and rubbish, and, especially the deeper gutters of the streets running back from the river, are subject to very foul accumulations. To remedy this condition the Auxiliary Sanitary Association, during the years 1879 and 1880, established a system of flushing by water taken from public hydrants, and by water lifted directly from the river by a powerful steam-pump erected for the purpose. This has been, so far as these perpendicular streets are concerned, quite effective, but has also had the effect of adding materially to the amount of water to be discharged by the draining-machines.

Up to the present time this constitutes the entire drainage of the city of New Orleans. The soil is saturated almost to its surface, and saturated very largely with the oozings of foul privy-vaults and the infiltration of accumulations on the surface of the streets and in the rear of houses.

Rightly or wrongly, to this condition of saturation and filth the notorious insalubrity of the city, in winter as well as in summer, is mainly ascribed. The charge gains presumptive force if we accept Dr. Bowditch's theory as to the relations between soil-moisture and consumption. A careful sanitary survey of the city, made by the Auxiliary Sanitary Association in 1879, gives the following classification of the causes of mortality during that year—a year when yellow fever was prevented from becoming epidemic only by the most strenuous efforts of the association to secure the careful policing of the ground and the general disinfection of the city:

Causes of death in 1879.

Yellow fever	19
Malarial fevers	209
All diarrheal diseases	376
Trismus nascentium and tetanus	236
Diphtheria	61
Scarlet fever	1
Consumption	824
All other diseases	3,396

This city has been peculiarly subject to epidemics of yellow fever, cholera, and dengue (break-bone fever), all of which are believed to be especially virulent in such a climate, under the influence of a foul and moist condition of the ground.

A discussion of the question of the drainage of New Orleans would not be complete without a description of the present project for its improvement, so far as that project has received the indorsement of legislation and has been made at least a potential fact.

As the financial burdens of the city are already a great embarrassment, and, to a certain extent, a bar to its prosperity, it was deemed unwise to propose any scheme which would call for the expenditure of public money, and the hope was expressed that the work of sewerage and drainage might be accomplished by private enterprise. With this view the legislature of Louisiana authorized the incorporation of associations for sewerage and drainage, to be chartered for a period of 99 years; it authorized municipalities to consent to the construction of works of drainage, sewerage, and land reclamation through the streets of any incorporated city or town; "and such council giving such consent to any corporation formed for the purposes of drainage, sewerage, and land reclamation may, in the interest of public health and cleanliness, pass all needful ordinances and bills and regulations to make effective the plan of sewerage and drainage it may so adopt with reference to all houses and lands within the municipal limits." The further provision was also made that "any corporation established for drainage and sewerage and land reclamation may, by contract with the owner of real property, duly recorded, have a privilege on said property for the price and value of work done and facilities furnished".

Under these provisions the "New Orleans Drainage and Sewerage Company" was organized early in 1880. On the 12th of April, 1881, the council adopted an ordinance providing for a contract between the city and the company, of which the following is the text:

AN ORDINANCE to provide for a contract between the city of New Orleans and the New Orleans Drainage and Sewerage Company, to provide for the effective operation of the plan so adopted, to establish certain police regulations in regard to drainage and sewerage, and to define and punish violations of such regulations.

SECTION 1. *Be it ordained by the city council of New Orleans,* That the mayor be, and he is hereby, authorized and directed to enter into a notarial contract with "The New Orleans Drainage and Sewerage Company", a company organized under the laws of Louisiana, and domiciled in New Orleans, and whose charter was established by act before N. B. Trist, notary public, passed March 17, 1880, which contract shall embrace the following stipulations, and such others as may be necessary and proper to carry them into effect:

1. Giving the said company the right during the term of its said charter to lay and maintain sewers and drains in the streets and through the public places of the city of New Orleans, and other places hereinafter named, at a depth in said streets of not less than four feet; the house branches to be nowhere less than two feet below the surface, and proper house branches to be furnished in connection with each main sewer pipe in any street to the inside banquette line of each inhabited house, or through alley-ways or other passages to the rear lines of property, and also to a point within premises where a house now exists, and connections may be made as hereinafter provided. The sewer pipes so laid to be water-tight and adapted to receive the fœcal matter, household wastes, slops, drainage from bath-tubs and the like, but not storm water, which is intended to pass off, as now, by gutters and canals; and each sewer is to be furnished at the head with an automatic flush-tank. The system to be substantially that which has been adopted and put into operation during the last year in Memphis, Tennessee, except so far as modified by mutual consent. The said company shall be bound to keep its street sewer-pipes in good order and free from obstructions. The said company shall be bound to restore the streets and banquettes, after laying pipes, to their previous condition within a reasonable time; and its neglect or refusal to do so, after notice from the department of improvements, shall subject it to a penalty of $25 for each day and place, after notice given, to be recovered before a competent court. If said work of restoration be not commenced within 24 hours after notification from the department of improvements, the said work may be done by the said department of improvements at the expense of the company.

2. Authorizing and requiring said company to lay, in connection with said system of water-tight sewer-pipes, a system of porous draining tile-pipes, such as are used for agricultural underdraining, for the purpose of underdraining the soil of streets and other places where they may be laid and removing therefrom subsoil water.

3. Providing that said sewerage pipes and subsoil drainage tiles shall terminate, at some point or points to be agreed upon, into a receptacle or receptacles, in such a way as to give the same facilities of discharge as would exist if they discharged into a natural low outlet, the same to be pumped into the Mississippi river below low-water mark; but the subsoil waters from the drainage tiles may be received into a separate receptacle and pumped into the city draining canals, at the option of the company. Said receptacle or receptacles to be kept pumped down to a proper low level.

4. Providing that said company shall receive into its said sewerage pipes, free of charge to the city, the sewerage matter from all public buildings of the city, from all the public-school buildings owned by the city, and all charitable institutions that are not self-sustaining: *Provided,* That said buildings are situated on the streets in which the said sewerage pipes shall be laid in accordance with the provisions hereinafter set forth and proper service-pipes furnished by the city or other owners of such property.

5. Providing that the said company shall begin its operations in the territory bounded by Louisiana avenue on the upper side, by Enghien street on the lower side, by Rampart street to Washington avenue and thence by Carondelet street on the west side, and by the Mississippi river on the east side; shall commence its surveys within six months after the execution of said contract, and shall complete at least one-fifth of its work in said territory in each year thereafter for five years: *Provided,* That no period during which said company shall be prevented from carrying on its operations by injunction, overflow, order of the board of health, or epidemic, shall be calculated as a portion of said period.

6. Providing that in consideration of the laying of said porous draining tiles and the extending of sewerage facilities free of charge to said public buildings, and in consideration of the public health and convenience, and the great expense which will be incurred and risks taken in the building of said system, and in consideration of the right vested by this agreement in the city to purchase the said works, the city of New Orleans will not adopt any other system of sewerage during the term of (25) twenty-five years after the execution of the work under said contract in the territory within named; and the city will at all times, by a proper exercise of its police powers and other powers, protect the pipes and other property of the company from obstruction and injury, and will by every lawful means promote and enforce the adoption and proper use of the system herein provided, and will at all times during the term of said contract provide and enforce the provisions and prohibitions contained in the second section of this ordinance, or their equivalent, with diligence and in good faith.

7. The said company shall, after the completion of its works in said territory, extend the same at the same annual ratio in the other parts of the city, on the left bank of the river, wherever the inhabited houses are not more than fifty feet apart, but it shall not be compelled to pass an interval of more than fifty feet on either side of the street to drain a closely built area beyond; and the company may, at its option, extend its lines anywhere within the present limits of the city. It shall not be compelled to accept or to furnish an outlet for any drain or sewer not of its own construction, nor unless the fixtures used in the house shall have been approved by it (its

approval or refusal to approve being subject to the sanction of the state board of health, whose decision shall be final) as of safe and proper construction; nor to accept any connection with any property until its owner shall have executed the contract contemplated by section second of act No. 125 of 1880, providing for securing the proper compensation to the company by privilege and servitude.

8. Providing that the said company shall not charge for the facilities furnished to any house for sewerage and drainage in excess of the following sums:

For dwelling-houses not exceeding 4 rooms, for all connections, per month, 85 cents.

For dwelling-houses having 5 or more rooms, but not exceeding 8 rooms, for all connections, per month, $1 20.

For dwelling-houses having 9 or more rooms, but not exceeding 13 rooms, for all connections, per month, $1 60.

For dwelling-houses having 14 or more rooms, but not exceeding 16 rooms, for all connections, per month, $1 85.

For dwelling-houses having 17 or more rooms, but not exceeding 20 rooms, per month, $2.

For store and office buildings of 4 or more stories, for all water-closet connections, per month, $1.

For each additional connection, 30 cents.

For store and office buildings of 3 stories, for all water-closet connections, per month, 85 cents.

For each additional connection, 30 cents.

For store and office buildings of 2 stories, for all water-closet connections, per month, 70 cents.

For each additional connection, 30 cents.

For store and office buildings of 1 story, for all water-closet connections, per month, 50 cents.

Stores not exceeding 2 stories in height, occupied by the family of the dealer, may be considered as dwelling-houses.

Stores and office buildings having more than 30 feet front or more than 120 feet depth may be charged sums proportionately greater.

Houses exceeding 20 rooms, hotels, factories, stables, warehouses, cotton-presses, and similar buildings to be charged pro rata rates to be fixed by agreement, and in case of dispute by arbitration.

These rates to be due and payable in advance for each calendar month.

If payment thereof be made on or before the last day of the month for which so due, the company to grant a discount, or rebate, of not less than 20 per cent., and for the balance give a receipt in full. If the dues are paid annually in advance, the discount shall be 30 per cent.

Wherever the said company shall lay its sewer pipes and tile drains at its expense from the inside banquette line to the place within the premises where the house connections are received, the proprietor may pay for the same the actual cost, either at once or in such installments as may be agreed on, or, in lieu of such payment, 8 per cent. per annum on the cost of such pipes and drains may be added by the company to the charges for furnishing sewerage and drainage facilities to the building as hereinbefore and hereinafter fixed.

The said company shall further agree in the said contract to make an annual rate of dwelling-houses which, if paid strictly in advance at the office of the company, shall not exceed, exclusive of such charges or installments, or percentage for service-pipe and subsoil drains, the following sums:

For dwelling-houses not exceeding 4 rooms, for all connections of every kind, per annum in advance, $6.

For dwelling-houses having 5 or more, but not exceeding 8 rooms, for all connections of every kind, per annum in advance, $9.

For dwelling-houses having 9 or more, but not exceeding 13 rooms, for all connections of every kind, per annum in advance, $13.

For dwelling-houses having 14 or more, but not exceeding 16 rooms, for all connections of every kind, per annum in advance, $16.

For dwelling-houses having 17 or more, but not exceeding 20 rooms, for all connections per annum in advance, $17.

But said company shall not be required to receive into its pipes or drains any storm water or surface water.

Said rates shall be payable in all cases by the owner of the property in absence of agreement to the contrary.

9. The city to have the privilege at any time after 20 years to buy the company's works for cash or its equivalent, at an appraised value to be fixed by 4 appraisers, 2 to be appointed by the city, and 2 by the company, and in case of disagreement, a majority of said appraisers shall call in a fifth person.

10. The said company, on the execution of said notarial contract, shall give its bond in the penal sum of $50,000, conditioned as the law directs, for the faithful performance of the work called for by the contract.

SECTION 2. *Be it further ordained, &c.,* That the following police regulations for the purpose of promoting the health, comfort, and convenience of the inhabitants of New Orleans with respect to the works of the New Orleans Drainage and Sewerage Company and the system of sewerage to be constructed by it, which is hereby adopted, and to protect and enforce said system, are hereby enacted and established:

1. It shall be unlawful for any person to obstruct or injure the pipes, drains, works, or machinery of the said company.

2. It shall be unlawful for any person to drop or throw into any sink, water-closet, bath-tub, vessel, or drain connected with the pipes of said company, any substance which may obstruct or injure the same, or to use the said pipes to carry off storm water or any natural surface drainage.

3. Whenever, in any street or part of a street of said city, the said company shall have laid its sewer-pipes and shall be ready to receive therein sewerage matter from the houses and buildings in said street or part of a street, and to remove the same according to the system provided in this ordinance, and notice thereof shall have been given to the occupant of said building, or by advertisement in the official journal of the city, then, and from thenceforth, it shall be unlawful for any privy, water-closet, slop-sink, slop-drain, urinal, or any other similar receptacle for sewerage matter or slops of any kind, to be maintained on said premises, except in connection with said sewerage pipes of the said system of sewerage hereby adopted, during its said term of twenty-five years. Such connections shall be made without delay; and all vaults, sinks, cesspools, drains, and similar receptacles theretofore existing shall be properly emptied, disinfected, and filled with dry earth, river sand, or similar substance, in such manner as the public health may require.

And when in any street said sewerage and drainage facilities shall have been provided as aforesaid by said company, it shall be unlawful from thenceforth to build any privy-vault on any property abutting on such street, or to have, let, or occupy any house on said street without proper water-closet and slop-sink arrangements for connection with said sewers; or to build on said street any house or building without proper water-closet and slop-sink arrangements, and service-pipes and tile-drains for connection with such sewers and subsoil drains, during the term for which said system is hereby adopted.

And any person committing any offense or violating any of the provisions of this section, whether owner, agent of absent owner, lessee, or other person, shall be fined in a sum not less than five nor more than twenty-five dollars, and if the said fine be not paid, shall be imprisoned for not less than five nor more than thirty days.

And each persistence in the violation of the third paragraph of this section, for the space of twenty-four hours after notice, shall constitute a separate offense and violation of this ordinance, and shall be punished by another similar fine and imprisonment; and no punishment for one violation of this ordinance shall bar or prevent prosecution for another violation as herein defined.

Adopted April 12, 1881.

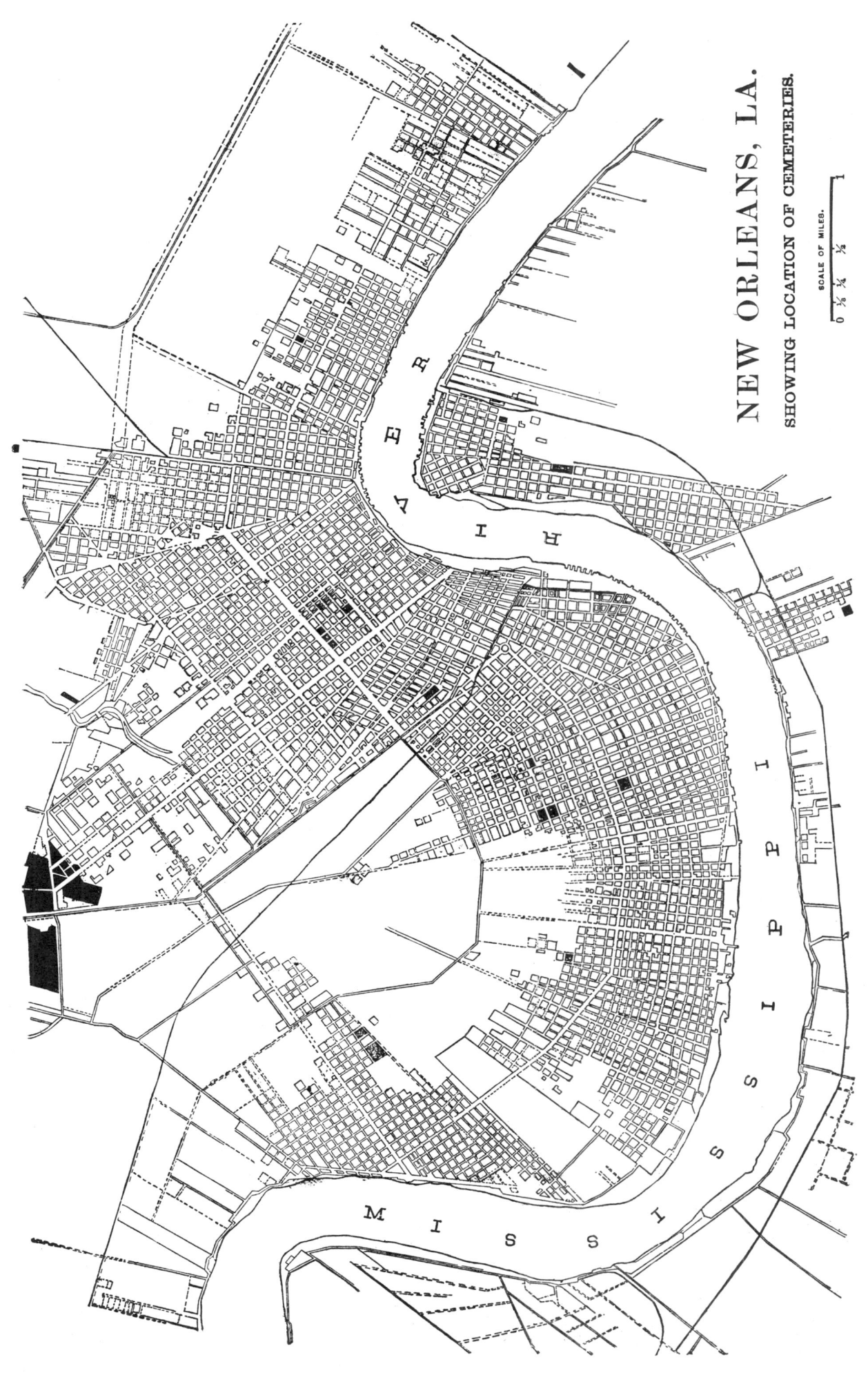

NEW ORLEANS, LA.

SHOWING LOCATION OF CEMETERIES.

SCALE OF MILES.

0 ½ ¾ ½ 1

It is proposed under this contract to construct a main sewer 6 feet in diameter along Rampart street, from Esplanade street as far as Washington avenue, having a very slight fall, and being, generally, at a depth of 13 feet below the surface of the street. This will give a total fall, from the surface of the levee to the center line of the main sewer, of about 23 feet. Into this main, sewers adapted for the removal of household and manufacturing wastes only, and subsoil drainage-pipes for the removal of soil water, will deliver. At the lower end of the main at about the corner of Esplanade and Rampart streets, there will be located a pumping station with a capacity of 30,000,000 gallons per diem, to deliver the entire flow through an iron force-main laid under Esplanade street, entering the Mississippi river below low-water mark. This arrangement will have practically the effect of raising the city at least 10 feet above its present level, so far as sewerage and subsoil drainage are concerned.

The scheme also contemplates a considerable re-enforcement of the protection levees at the north and south city lines and along the lake and canals; the deepening of the drainage canals, and the constant pumping of the natural drainage, so as to reduce the water-level from 6 to 10 feet below the surface of the whole swamp between the city and the lake.

CEMETERIES.

There are in the city 31 public and private cemeteries and burial grounds, as follows:

St. Louis Cemetery No. 1.—North Basin, North Liberty, Conti, and St. Louis streets.

St. Louis Cemetery No. 2.—Bounded by Customhouse, St. Louis, Claiborne, and Robertson streets.

American Cemetery, or St. Louis Cemetery No. 3.—Located in second district, size 1 square, bounded by North Basin, St. Louis, Conti, and North Liberty streets.

Lafayette Cemetery No. 1.—Located in fourth district, size 1 square, bounded by Washington avenue, Prytania, Coliseum, and Sixth streets.

Lafayette Cemetery No. 2.—Located in fourth district, size 1 square, bounded by Washington avenue, Sixth, South Basin, and St. David streets, 350 feet front on each street.

Valence Street Cemetery.—Located in sixth district, size 1 square, bounded by Valence, Bordeaux, Rampart, and Dryades streets.

Carrollton Cemetery.—Located in seventh district, size 4 squares, bounded by Adams and Lower Line, Seventh, and Eighth streets.

St. Joseph Cemetery.—Located in fourth district, size 2 squares, bounded by Washington avenue, St. David, South Liberty, and Sixth streets.

St. Vincent Cemetery.—Located in sixth district, size 3 squares, bounded by St. David, Green, and St. Patrick streets.

Locust Grove Cemeteries Nos. 1 and 2.—Located in fourth district, size 1 square each, bounded by Locust, Freret, Sixth, and Seventh streets. Sometimes called "Potter's Field".

St. Vincent de Paul Cemetery.—Located in third district, size 1 square, bounded by Louisa, Piety, Urquhart, and Villeré streets.

Girod Cemetery.—Located in first district, size 250 feet wide and 400 feet deep, bounded by South Liberty, Perillat, Cypress, and Magnolia streets.

Holt's Cemetery.—Located in first district, size 5 to 6 acres.

Hebrew Cemetery.—Located on Elysian Fields, near Gentilly road, size 1 square.

Hebrew Cemetery, "Dispersed of Judah."—Located on Canal street, between Anthony street and Metairie ridge, size 250 feet square.

The Polish Hebrew Cemetery.—Located on Canal street, opposite the one last named. Sometimes called "Jewish Rest".

Hebrew Cemetery.—Located in sixth district, on Joseph street, known as "Hebrew Place of Prayer", size 1 square.

German Hungarian Lutheran Cemetery.—Located on Canal street, between Anthony and Bernadotte streets, size 1 square; 4 lots only made for burial, rest cultivated.

Odd Fellows' Cemetery.—Located on Canal street and Metairie road, size 360 feet square.

Charity Hospital Cemetery No. 1.—Located on Canal street, between Anthony street and Metairie road. Exclusively for burials from Charity Hospital; size 200 feet wide, and 1,600 feet long.

Charity Hospital Cemetery No. 2.—Located on Metairie road, between Bienville and Canal streets, size 1 square.

Masonic Cemetery.—Located on Bienville street, between Metairie ridge and Anthony streets, size 3 squares.

St. Patrick Cemetery No. 1.—Located on Canal, between Anthony street and Metairie ridge, size 400 feet wide, 1,500 feet long.

St. Patrick Cemetery No. 2.—Located on Canal, between Anthony and Metairie road, opposite No. 1, size 1 square.

St. Patrick Cemetery No. 3.—Opens from No. 2. Located on Metairie road between Canal and Bienville streets, size 2 squares.

The Freeman's Cemeteries.—Known as Cypress Grove Nos. 1 and 2, and Greenwood. Located on Metairie ridge and Canal street.

Metairie Ridge Cemetery.—Located on Metairie ridge and the New Canal, size 108 acres.

Chalmette National Cemetery.—One mile below barracks, on river. For burial of Union soldiers.

Olivier Cemetery.—Located in sixth district, corner of Verret and Market streets.

St. Bartholomew Cemetery.—Located in fifth district, bounded by De Armas, Lasseyrusse, Franklin, and Hancock streets.

William Tell Cemetery.—Located in Gretna, Tenth street, between Lavoisier and Nerota streets.

There is no interment in church-yards.

The Hebrew Cemetery, belonging to the Hebrew Association, opened in 1828, was closed to interments in 1866. The following are the annual interments for a period of 14 years:

Year 1867 (yellow-fever epidemic)	9,456	Year 1874	6,798
1868	4,338	1875	6,117
1869	6,001	1876	6,257
1870	7,391	1877	6,708
1871	6,059	1878 (yellow-fever epidemic)	10,318
1872	6,122	1879	5,122
1873	7,505	1880	5,623

The following is the practice concerning interments: In most of the cemeteries lots are sold to private purchasers wherein to build tombs or to dig graves. These are the private property of the purchaser and his heirs. The fees for interment, which are appropriated to the cost of maintaining the cemetery, are, for each opening and closing of a tomb or vault, from $3 to $5. Burials usually take place within 24 hours after death, but this time may be extended when circumstances require it. Except the destitute, buried at public expense, only Israelites are interred under ground. Graves are dug from 3 to 4 feet deep, except at the cemeteries on Metairie ridge, where, the ground being higher than in other parts of the city, it is possible to dig to a depth of 7 feet. All other interments are made in vaults of brick, stone, or iron, which are built on the surface of the ground. In some of the cemeteries the removal of bodies is not allowed until one year or more after interment.

A certificate, signed by the medical attendant or the coroner, stating the cause of death, with other particulars, is required by law as a pre-requisite to interment; these must be registered with the state board of health. The board also grants permits to bring bodies into or to remove them from the city, and to open tombs.

In "St. Joseph's Cemetery" benefit of interment is bestowed upon "St. Joseph's Orphan Asylum", and ordinary burials must be paid for every 5 years at the risk of losing the right of burial. In the Hebrew Cemetery, "Dispersed of Judah," as in the other Hebrew cemeteries, all interments are made in graves, since this sect never disturbs the dead, nor buries two persons on the same spot. A certain portion of this cemetery is reserved for suicides.

In the Masonic Cemetery the sexton's fees are devoted to improvement and embellishment. The sale of lots is here restricted to Masons—though their heirs may retain ownership even if not Masons. The grounds in this and most of the other cemeteries are planted with trees, shrubs, and flowers, and are well kept.

In St. Patrick's Cemetery No. 1 permission for interment must be obtained from the Catholic priests, and the burials are mostly limited to poor Roman Catholics.

The Cypress Grove cemeteries belong to the Firemen's Charitable Association. Here no tombs, vaults, or graves are to be opened for interment or removal except on the written order of the treasurer of the association. All building materials must be removed within a specified time after the completion of work. A portion of each cemetery is set apart for colored persons. These cemeteries are laid out in regular walks and avenues, and are well planted and kept.

Greenwood Cemetery contains the monument to the Confederate dead.

Metairie Ridge Cemetery, belonging to the Metairie Ridge Association, was bought at a cost of $175,000, and $171,000 were expended in improvements, such as broad shell walks, carriage roads, artificial lakes, rustic bridges, flower-beds, and shrubs. The whole grounds are inclosed in a hedge of Cherokee rose. A revenue is derived from the sale of lots and from sexton's fees. The capital stock of the association is $500,000.

MARKETS.

There are 17 public markets in New Orleans, as follows:

Pilie Market.—First district, Poydras, between Rampart and South Basin streets, contains 100 stalls.

Poydras Market.—First district, Poydras, between Baronne and South Rampart streets, contains 320 stalls.

St. Mary's Market.—First district, New Levee and Tchoupitoulas streets, contains 375 stalls.

Dryades Market.—First district, Dryades street, extending from Terpsichore to Thalia streets, spanning Melpomene street, contains 325 stalls.

French (Beef, Fruit, and Bazaar) Markets.—Second district, on North St. Peter and Decatur, extending from St. Ann to Ursuline streets, contain 550 stalls.

Washington Market.—Second district, Chartres, corner of Louisa streets, contains 36 stalls.

Port Market.—Third district, North Peter, between Marigny and Elysian Fields, contains 120 stalls.

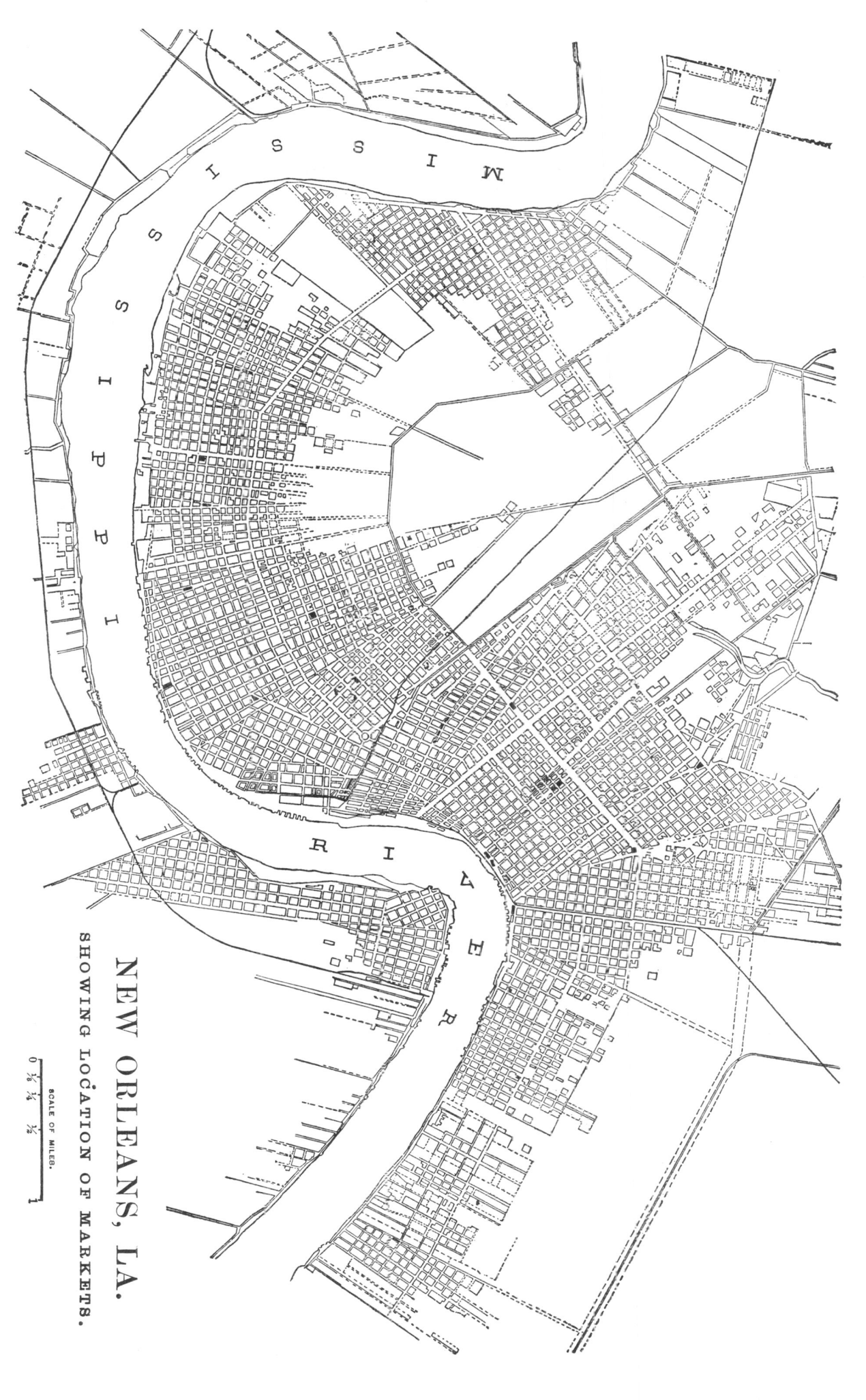

NEW ORLEANS, LA.

SHOWING LOCATION OF MARKETS.

SCALE OF MILES.

0   ⅛   ¼   ½   1

St. Bernard Market.—Third district, St. Bernard, corner of North and Claiborne streets, contains 59 stalls.

Claiborne Market.—Third district, Claiborne, between Common and Gasquet streets, contains 66 stalls.

Trémé Market.—Third district, Orleans, between Marias and North Robertson streets, contains 91 stalls.

Second Street Market.—Fourth district, corner Second and Dryades streets, contains 48 stalls.

Keller Market.—Fourth district, Felicity, St. Andrew, Locust, and Magnolia streets, contains 90 stalls.

Soraparu Market.—Fourth district, Soraparu, between Tchoupitoulas and Rousseau streets, contains 72 stalls.

Magazine Market.—Fourth district, between Camp, Magazine, St. Andrew, and St. Mary streets, contains 155 stalls.

Ninth Street Market.—Fourth district, Magazine, between Ninth and Harmony streets, contains 56 stalls.

Jefferson Market.—Sixth district, between Napoleon and Berlin, on Magazine street, contains 30 stalls.

Carrollton Market.—Seventh district, corner Dublin and Second streets, contains 96 stalls.

Around each market there is standing room for from 15 to 25 wagons.

The confused condition of the city archives and early records make it impossible to ascertain the original cost of these markets.

The markets are all let by contract to one person for about $170,000 per annum; $8,000 is appropriated for repairs. The gross proceeds of the annual sale of stalls for 1879 amounted to $280,000.

The stalls are let by the day at the following rates:

	Cents.
Butcher's stall and block	50
Each corner table additional	5
Each additional foot	5
Fish, game, and vegetable stalls	15
Coffee stands	75
Each additional foot	2

The markets are open from 3 a. m. to 12 m.

The public markets are mostly well arranged sheds in streets and public squares. The old French market in the second district is very extensive, and is the most important in the city. On Sunday mornings it displays, better than anything else in New Orleans, the mixed and picturesque character of the population.

Much the larger proportion of the retail supply of meats, poultry, fish, and vegetables is from the public markets, sales from private stores and stands being comparatively unimportant, although there are the following private markets which pay license to the city:

First district	21
Second district	18
Third district	18
Fourth district	20
Sixth district	8
Total	85

The ordinances relating to markets specify the amounts which the contractor, lessee, or "farmer" may charge for various animals sold within the markets, as follows: For every head of horned cattle, 90 cents; every head of veal, mutton, or venison, 25 cents; every head of pork weighing less than 100 pounds, 25 cents; over 100 pounds, 50 cents. They also prohibit the sale of fish or vegetables at the beef market of the second district. Each vendor is required to have his or her name conspicuously placed over stall or stand, under penalty of $10. All stalls, tables, and stands are to be kept "in the highest state of cleanliness", by daily cleansing, under a penalty of $5 for each offense. No person can lease more than two stalls, nor sub-lease any stall or stand, under $50 fine.

Article 606 (10) provides:

If any person shall sell or expose for sale within markets any imperfect or unwholesome provisions, or meat of any animal that died of disease, such provisions shall be seized by the commissary and shall be thrown into the nuisance boat, and the offender shall be fined from $10 to $50 for the first offense, and for the second he shall be deprived of vending in any market or of hiring any stall. It shall be the duty of the commissaries of the markets to make daily inspection of meat and all articles exposed for sale, and to enforce strict observance of this regulation.

The sale of intoxicating liquors is forbidden within or on footways surrounding the markets under a penalty of $10.

All refuse from markets is to be conserved and disposed of as other offal.

SANITARY ORGANIZATION.

The chief health authority having control of the sanitary affairs of the city is the board of health of the state of Louisiana. This is an independent board of 9 members, all of whom may be physicians. At least 1 of the state members and 2 of the city members must be physicians.

The annual expense of the board, when there is no declared epidemic, is $40,000. Out of this sum the 3 quarantines, viz, that of the Mississippi, that of the Rigolets, and that of the Atchafalaya, have to be sustained; as also all of the official sanitary work of the city, including the registration of vital statistics, the inspection of coal oils, and the expense of maintaining the central office.

During epidemics the amount to be expended may be increased by the city authorities to whatever is required.

In the absence of epidemics the board is charged with the administration of the state quarantine, and has a large discretion in controlling the policy of the state for protection against the importation of pestilential diseases from abroad. It has also the power, concurrently with the city council, to enact sanitary ordinances for defining and abating nuisances within the city.

During epidemics the legal powers of the board are not enlarged, but are exercised with increased vigor and latitude.

The chief executive officer of the board is its president. His salary is $2,400 per annum. He presides at meetings of the board, and when the board is not actually in session he is clothed with its authority as director and superintendent of the sanitary service. He is also *ex officio* registrar of births, marriages, and deaths, and has 2 clerks for this service.

The office of the board is at the corner of Royal and St. Louis streets, a central and convenient situation, and is open daily during business hours. The board has a secretary and treasurer, who is not necessarily a member of the board, and a clerk and messenger.

The auxiliary officers of the board are a resident physician at each of the quarantine stations, each with a non-medical assistant, a boatman, a watchman, hospital nurses, etc. In the sanitary service of the city there are employed 6 medical inspectors, and 10 to 25 non-medical inspecting officers. The inspecting officers are commissioned as policemen, with power to make arrests and to bring charges for violation of sanitary ordinances.

A regular house-to-house inspection is made annually, at which time a large number of observations are made and noted. Bad localities are inspected more frequently, and complaints receive attention at all times. The character of this service is indicated by the following tables:

HOUSE-TO-HOUSE INSPECTION.

FIRST DISTRICT.

Number of premises inspected	11,188
used as dwellings only	7,613
stores and manufactories only	1,658
stores and dwellings	1,582
vacant	335
with cisterns only	7,346
hydrants only	1,216
hydrants and cisterns	2,122
wells	287
without water supply	217
Number of houses built of wood	7,090
brick	4,097
iron	1
in good condition	10,562
bad condition	626
rooms in dwellings	48,997
Persons occupying dwellings:	
White	39,764
Colored	12,580
Condition of privies:	
Good	3,180
Foul	6,880
Defective	995
Number of horses on above premises	1,137
mules on above premises	1,059
cows on above premises	258
hogs on above premises	79
vacant lots inspected	318
not filled to grade	21

Miscellaneous.

Total number of inspections	27,277
reinspections	9,377
Nuisances requiring abatement	9,377
abated	9,284
Notices served to empty privy vaults	7,025
rebuild privy vaults	208

Notices served to repair privy vaults	794
disinfect privy vaults	175
clean premises	779
construct gutters	66
repair gutters	77
supply water	32
repair cisterns	9
remove hogs	27
construct ventilators to vaults	110
fill low lots	13
rebuild cow stables	3
clean alleys	64
close pipes connecting privy vaults with street gutters	3
Number of dangerous buildings reported	3
premises disinfected	7
fumigated	7
ships fumigated	3
warehouses fumigated	6
building permits issued	18
persons prosecuted for non-compliance	24
parents notified to record births	813
complaints attended to	667

SECOND DISTRICT.

Premises	8,013
Premises with hydrants only	1,661
cisterns only	3,343
cisterns and hydrants	2,819
wells	836
without water supply	190
Houses built of wood	5,050
brick	2,963
used as dwellings only	5,880
stores and manufactories only	521
stores and dwellings	1,284
vacant	364
Rooms in dwelling houses	33,243

Persons occupying premises:

White	29,050
Colored	11,335
Natives of China	46

Children registered 1879:

Males	406
Females	377

Condition of floor:

Good	7,975
Bad	38

Condition of roof:

Good	7,978
Bad	35

Condition of privy:

Good	5,481
Foul	3,250
Defective	233
Vacant lots	242
Lots not filled to grade	4
Application for building permits	4
Private complaints attended to	273

Miscellaneous.

Inspections made	19,057
Reinspections made	3,231
Nuisances requiring abatement	3,520
abated	3,459
Notices to empty privy vaults	3,159
rebuild privy vaults	36
repair privy vaults	117
disinfect privy vaults	3,205
clean premises	70
repair houses	3
fill lots	10
supply water	10
construct gutters	34
repair gutters	26
remove hogs	6
Dangerous buildings reported	3
Premises disinfected	8,013
fumigated (rooms 28, vessels 1)	29

Persons vaccinated:

White	22
Colored	2
Cases of yellow fever	3
Persons reported for non-compliance	7

THIRD DISTRICT.

Number of premises	6,269
dwellings	5,810
manufactories	54
stores and dwellings	405
vacant houses	196
rooms in dwelling-houses	28,172

Persons occupying premises:

White	25,220
Colored	8,567
Number of premises with cisterns	5,661
cisterns and hydrants	205
hydrants	143
wells	2,792
without water supply	48
houses built of wood	5,703
brick	566
premises in good condition	6,091
bad condition	178
privies in good condition	4,308
foul condition	1,812
defective condition	1,188

Children born in 1879:

White	943
Colored	378

Number of children registered, 1879:

Male	420
Female	429
Number of horses kept on premises	453
mules kept on premises	525
cows kept on premises	1,185
hogs kept on premises	276
vacant lots	397
lots not filled to grade	20

Miscellaneous.

Number of inspections made	6,358
reinspections made	1,254
nuisances requiring abatement	1,085
abated	660
notices served to empty privy vaults	1,681
rebuild privy vaults	45
repair privy vaults	50
disinfect privy vaults	1,426
clean premises	25
fill lots	6
construct gutters	2
repair gutters	2
remove hogs	21
premises disinfected and fumigated	14
cases of yellow fever	1
small-pox	1
diphtheria	23
complaints attended to	125
notices served to supply water	7
applications for building permits	22

FOURTH DISTRICT.

Premises	7,387
Premises, with cisterns only	7,281
cisterns and hydrants	92
wells	1,153
without water supply	14
Houses built of wood	6,861
brick	526
used as dwellings only	6,129
stores and manufactories only	191
stores and dwellings	1,067
vacant	316
Rooms in dwelling-houses	37,761

Persons occupying premises:

White	27,175
Colored	6,056

Children born and registered in 1879:

White	534
Colored	62
Children born but not registered in 1879	341

Condition of premises:

Good	7,201
Bad	186

Condition of floor:

Good	7,380
Bad	7

Condition of roof:

Good	7,379
Bad	8

Condition of privy:

Good	3,127
Foul	4,260
Defective	2,267
Premises with (549) horses, (953) mules, (522) cows, and (264) hogs	653
Vacant lots	5,346
Lots not filled to grade	375
Applications for building permits	23
Private complaints attended to	392

Miscellaneous.

Inspections made	11,203
Reinspections made, regular	4,198
Auxiliary Sanitary Association	11,094
National Board of Health	10,238
Nuisances requiring abatement	244
abated	3,959
Notices to empty privy vaults	3,708
rebuild privy vaults	45
repair privy vaults	95
disinfect privy vaults	373
clean premises	186
fill lots	19
supply water	8
construct gutters	76
repair gutters	50
remove hogs	47
register births of children	341
Dangerous buildings reported	1
Building permits issued	23
Certificates of vaccination issued	50
Premises disinfected altogether	21,360
fumigated	21
Rooms fumigated and disinfected	68
Cases of small-pox	1
Persons vaccinated, white	21
Cases of yellow fever	34
Persons reported for non-compliance with health ordinances	25

FIFTH DISTRICT.

Inspections made	1,331
Number square blocks inspected	105
running blocks inspected	426
vaults disinfected	1,331
squares around which lime was distributed	109
cart-loads of garbage removed	24
Drainage gutters cleaned	7
Trees whitewashed	750
Number feet of fences whitewashed	875
Premises sprinkled with lime	61
Number barrels of lime used	120
copperas used	5

SIXTH DISTRICT.

Premises	3,586
Premises with hydrants only	1,009
cisterns	2,746
wells	840
Houses built of wood	3,495
brick	91
used as dwellings only	3,110
stores and manufactories only	65
stores and dwellings	190
vacant	221
Rooms in dwelling-houses	11,561
Persons occupying premises:	
White	11,236
Colored	4,105
Children born in 1878:	
White	286
Colored	102
Children registered:	
Male	127
Female	92
Children born but not registered:	
Male	68
Female	101
Condition of floor:	
Good	3,586

Condition of roof:	
Good	3,586
Condition of privy:	
Good	2,422
Foul	1,164
Defective	11
Premises with (391) horses, (337) mules, (1,195) cows, and (368) hogs	441
Vacant lots	8,434
Applications for building permits	31
Private complaints attended to	207

Miscellaneous.

Special inspections made	261
Regular inspections made	8,418
Reinspections made, regular	3,231
Nuisances requiring abatement	2,493
abated	2,470
Notices to empty privy vaults	1,164
rebuild privy vaults	10
disinfect privy vaults	139
repair privy vaults	14
clean premises	837
repair houses	6
fill lots	3
Water supply in gallons	4,624,400
Number of dairies inspected weekly	91
Notices to construct gutters	19
repair gutters	53
remove hogs	18
Dangerous buildings reported	6
Premises disinfected altogether	1
fumigated	1
Persons vaccinated:	
White	24
Colored	33
Cases of yellow fever	1
Persons reported for non-compliance with health ordinances	2
Revaccinations:	
White	11
Colored	5
Births reported by midwives	146

SEVENTH DISTRICT.

Number of premises inspected	1,327
with cistern only	1,318
wells	353
no water supply	10
Number of houses built of wood	1,325
brick	2
used as dwellings only	1,161
stores and manufactories only	31
vacant	79
rooms in dwelling-houses	4,346
Persons occupying premises:	
White	2,476
Colored	2,503
Children born in 1878:	
White	73
Colored	15
Children registered:	
Males	38
Females	55
Number of floors in good condition	1,327
roofs in good condition	1,327
privies in good condition	1,144
foul condition	184
premises with (100) horses, (12) mules, (241) cows, and (83) hogs	129

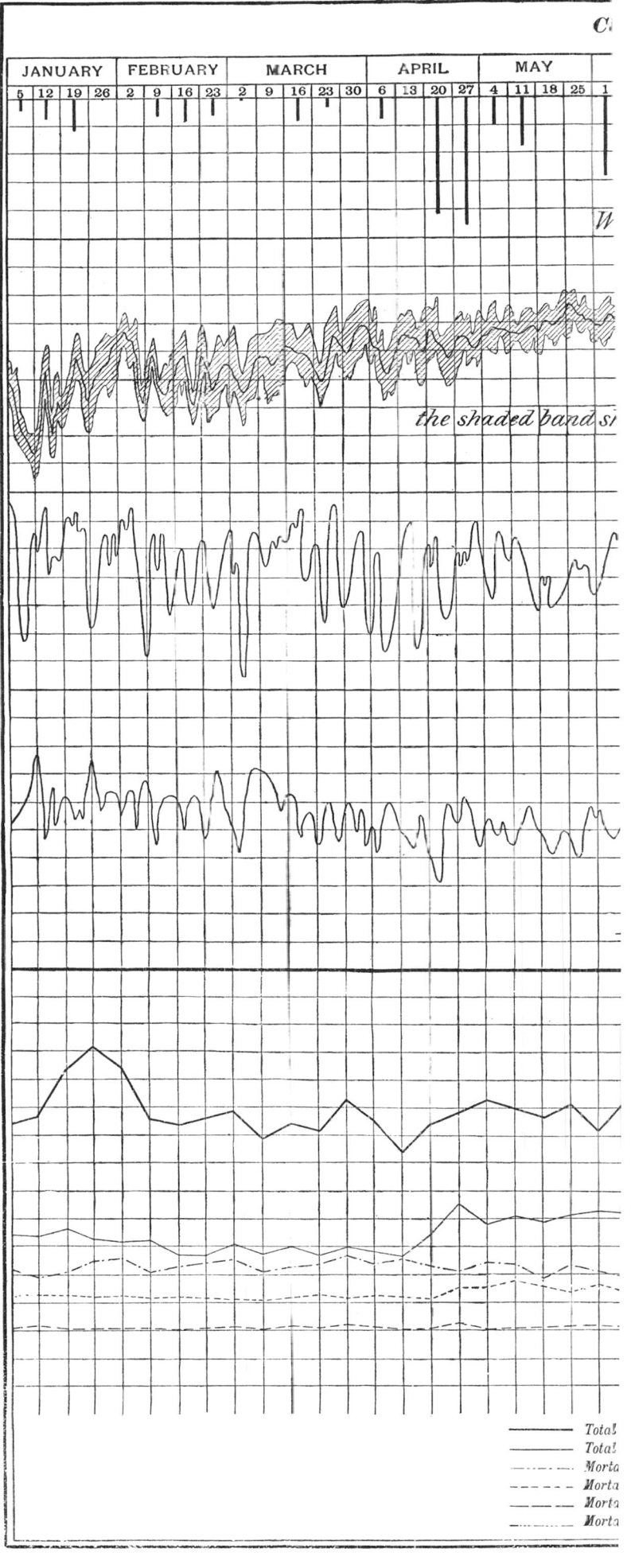

	JANUARY				FEBRUARY				MARCH					APRIL			MAY			
5	12	19	26	2	9	16	23	2	9	16	23	30	6	13	20	27	4	11	18	25	1

W

the shaded band s

Total

Total

Morta

Morta

Morta

Morta

called by the negroes " dandy-fever ", and commonly known as " break-bone fever ". This disease seems to have found its way to America from the western coast of Africa, via Havana, though its history is by no means accurately traced. Neither are the means of its causation and communication well defined, nor yet the circumstances and conditions which lead to its assuming an epidemic form. It seems to confine itself chiefly to cities and towns, spreading little, if at all, into the country. This would lead to the possible inference that the foul accumulations of the denser communities constitute a favoring circumstance. The disease has some features in common with yellow fever, but, while extremely painful and debilitating, it is very rarely fatal. One attack affords no protection against a second one, and its spread is more general than that of any other disease when once it assumes an epidemic form.

Dengue is discussed with considerable minuteness in papers published in the sixth volume of the Reports of the American Public Health Association, written by Dr. J. G. Thomas, of Savannah, Dr. Henry B. Horlbeck, of Charleston, and Dr. D. C. Holliday, of New Orleans, to which papers those interested in the subject are referred.

Yellow Fever.—New Orleans has suffered more extensively than any other city in the Union from serious epidemics of yellow fever. Excepting the epidemic of 1853, by which over 7,800 persons died, that of 1878 was the most serious of all, not only in its extent and fatality, but also in its influence on the industries and on the public sentiment of the communities of the lower Mississippi valley. It is estimated by those competent to judge that the well-marked cases of this year reached the enormous total of 25,000, and that no less than 4,500 died from the disease. The official reports place the total number of deaths at 4,046; but it is believed that many of the deaths ascribed to malarial fevers were really from yellow fever, these so-called malarial fevers appearing in the records of this year as the cause of a very unusual number of deaths.

The first case of the year was that of Clark, the purser of the steamship Emily B. Souder, who came ashore sick on the morning of May 23d, and died on the night of the 24th. His death was followed by that of Elliott, the engineer of the steamer, who died on the night of the 29th. There is some dispute whether the infection thus brought into the city was continued, but the continuance seems to be well established. The first death resulting from this infection took place early in July, in which month 26 deaths were recorded; in August there were 1,025; in September 1,780; in October 1,065; in November 147, and in December 3. Of the total deaths recorded, 3,863 were of whites and 183 of colored persons, the colored population being about one-fourth of the whole.

The contagion spread and became epidemic as far up as Hickman, on the Mississippi river, and at various other cities and towns, some quite remote from the river and apparently fully protected by their isolation. "Shot-gun quarantine" was established throughout the whole lower Mississippi valley, and commerce and all intercourse were practically suspended. So great were the suffering and loss and excitement resulting from these epidemics, that a new and vigorous impulse was given to the sanitary movement throughout the whole country. The establishment of the national board of health, of the sanitary council of the Mississippi valley, and the auxiliary sanitary association of New Orleans, all owe their origin and their great efficiency to the terrors of this terrible year.

There was another invasion (or a revival) of yellow fever in New Orleans in 1879, but so active were the measures taken for its suppression, and so efficient were the services of the auxiliary sanitary association, that it reached a total of only 19 deaths. In Memphis, where the means of immediate protection were much less, there were about 500 deaths.

The late Dr. Samuel Choppin, president of the state board of health of Louisiana, in his report dated January 10, 1880, says:

Great as are its natural advantages as a mart of trade—and they are unsurpassed by any city of the earth—its growth in population, business, and wealth, has hitherto been inconceivably retarded by these visitations of yellow fever. Were these natural advantages less than they are, its utter destruction would have been inevitable. But for this one great drawback to its progress, I think I am warranted in the belief that New Orleans, at this hour, might aspire to be considered the first commercial city of the Union. This is not the language of exaggeration. It is the natural deduction of facts. During the last 84 years (from the first introduction of yellow fever into New Orleans in 1796) not less than one hundred thousand of the flower and strength of the land have fallen victims of yellow fever within the limits of the city. And if we add to this the numbers that have died of the disease in neighboring towns and the country, the total mortality from this dread scourge brought here would range between *fifty* and *seventy-five thousand more*. The people who have died here of yellow fever would have built up a state.

THE AUXILIARY SANITARY ASSOCIATION.

As a direct outgrowth of the epidemic of 1878, and as a result of the interest in the subject displayed during the succeeding winter, there was organized on the 31st of March, 1879, an association of citizens known as "The Auxiliary Sanitary Association of New Orleans", which has been of the utmost value to the sanitary interests of the city. Mr. Edward Fenner, vice-president of the association, in his annual address in 1880, says:

The ready disposition of neighboring communities to blockade this city by barbarous shot-gun quarantines, which effectually paralyzed business and rendered inter-state communication almost impossible, showed but too plainly that, while the geographical position of New Orleans is most favorable to its increase in population, manufactures, commerce, and wealth, if its good health and good name can be established, it is the reverse of favorable, should public neglect subject it to the ravages of yellow fever.

The gentlemen chiefly instrumental in giving form and motion to this association were actuated by the most patriotic motives—the *rehabilitation of this city*.

They realized the fact that the time had come when the people could be appealed to with success to give countenance and material aid in support of any well-devised plans of sanitary improvement, to be undertaken by a committee of citizens and paid for by voluntary subscriptions.

The experience of the past had taught them that political corporations cannot be depended upon for that prompt and sustained action which enables men trained in the severe school of business affairs to execute large undertakings with economy and dispatch.

*   *   *   *   *   *   *   *   *

The task assumed by this association was surrounded with innumerable and apparently almost insurmountable difficulties. The movement was novel and the projectors untried; money was needed and the contributors must necessarily be numerous. The success attending your efforts to create a sustaining public opinion in favor of the radical reform proposed in your address to the people, issued the 6th of April, 1879, is evinced by the large number of your subscribers and the amount placed at your disposal.

*   *   *   *   *   *   *   *   *

The views of this association may be fitly illustrated by a quotation from the reply made by Lord Palmerston to the presbytery of Edinburgh, when they wrote to him to ask whether a national fast ought not to be appointed in consequence of the appearance of cholera.

His lordship gravely admonished the presbytery that the Maker of the universe had appointed certain laws of nature for the planet on which we live, and that the weal or woe of mankind depends on the observance of those laws—one of them connecting health with the absence of those noxious exhalations which proceed from overcrowded human beings, or from decomposing substances, whether animal or vegetable. He, therefore, recommended that the purification of towns and cities should be more strenuously carried on, and remarked that the causes and sources of contagion, if allowed to remain, will infallibly breed pestilence and be fruitful in death, in spite of all the prayers and fastings of a united but inactive people.

The enormous loss of life and values inflicted upon the country by the epidemic of 1878, not to speak of the boundless charity bestowed to alleviate local distress, has created an unwonted interest throughout the United States in measures of prevention.

The discussion of the American Public Health Association, composed of representative men from every state in the Union, on city sanitation and practical questions connected with the management of an actual or threatened outbreak of yellow fever, should be accepted by the people of New Orleans as conclusive evidence that our neighbors, near and far, will not permit us to remain indifferent to their wise suggestions.

Self-protection, and a very natural desire to avoid a repetition of the loss to the country caused by the epidemic of 1878, which has been estimated by good authority at not less than $175,000,000, gives them the right to demand a corresponding interest and an unflinching determination on the part of our citizens to foster and promote the work plotted out by this association.

Dr. Choppin, in the report above referred to, says:

Undoubtedly the most impressive lesson of the great epidemic of 1878, to the people of this city, was the importance of improving its sanitary condition. It was apparent that the $10,000 appropriated by the city authorities for the board of health would fall far short of the requirements of the case, and, as the legislature had afforded no aid, the only recourse was to raise means by voluntary contributions. The outcome of the necessities of the case was the organization of the auxiliary sanitary association and the contribution of about $30,000 by the citizens. Although most of its funds were expended in works under the immediate control of the association, material aid was afforded to the board of health in the house-to-house inspection by ten efficient sanitary policemen placed at its disposal by the association for about four months.

*   *   *   *   *   *   *   *   *

On the whole, then, it may safely be affirmed that the sanitary condition of New Orleans in 1879, though far short of what is both desirable and possible, has been more satisfactory than at any other time in its history, unless we except a portion of the time when it was under martial law during the late war; and the propriety of this exception is doubtful.

The association has directed its attention to a reformation of the present privy system of the city; to the filling and draining of lots occupied by dwellings or in the vicinity of habitations, with a proper adjustment of the grade; to an improvement and extension of the water supply; to the reformation of the drainage canals by which the surface water of the city is removed in a very inefficient manner; to the establishment of public bath-houses and wash-houses; to the organization of an efficient system of garbage boats whereby the garbage of the entire city is removed daily to a point in the middle of the river below the city line and there thrown to the fishes which swarm in enormous numbers to feed upon it; and to the establishment of quite extensive and efficient means for flushing the gutters of the streets perpendicular to the river with water pumped directly from the Mississippi.

MUNICIPAL CLEANSING.

Street-cleaning.—The streets of New Orleans are cleaned by the city and the sidewalks by the property-holders at their own expense. In the work of street-cleaning the city administration receives material aid and co-operation from the auxiliary sanitary association.

Street-cleaning work is done by the city's own force, not by contract. There are two sweeping-machines employed, but most of the work is done by hand, the machines being used only at night and on the square-block pavements in the business part of the city. These pavements are gone over every second or third night when the weather permits. Cobblestone and other pavements are swept at longer intervals, according to the force of laborers which the funds at the disposal of the department allow to be employed, preference in frequency being given to the more thickly settled streets.

On the square-block pavements the cleansing is done with a fair degree of efficiency. On other pavements, those which are hand-swept, the efficiency is considerably less, and on the unpaved streets it is very imperfectly done, the difficulties being much greater and the limited working force being inadequate.

The cost of this work in 1879 was $105,821 32. The expenditures of the auxiliary sanitary association for this work, during 1879, exceeded $7,500.

The sweepings are deposited in the back portions of the city for the purpose of raising the grade on low streets.

The system as organized, if carried on by a sufficiently large working force, might be made very satisfactory, except in the matter of disposal; but the lack of a sufficient force, of both men and machines, has caused it to be much less than satisfactory. The use of the sweepings and scrapings of the streets for filling low places is quoted as being "decidedly advantageous". This opinion must of course be taken to relate to the benefit of raising the grades of streets rather than to the effect of depositing street filth in such proximity to habitations.

The street-cleaning ordinance is as follows:

ARTICLE 1116. It shall be the duty of the street cleaners to clean the gutters (with hoes or scrapers) of all filth, and put the same in piles, and have it carried away the same day to such places as the street commissioners may designate; and after the gutters shall have been scraped with hoes or scrapers, the water may be let in the gutters from the fire-plugs, and while it is running the street cleaners shall use brooms and sweep the gutters; always using hose to convey water from the fire-plugs to the gutters: for any violation of this ordinance the offender shall be liable to a fine of ten dollars for every offense, recoverable before any magistrate, one-half of the fine to go to the informer.

Garbage and ashes.—Garbage is removed by the city's force only. All such refuse matters are required to be set upon the sidewalk in some suitable receptacle between the hours of 3 a. m. and 8 a. m., and the receptacles are required to be removed by 10 a. m., before which time they are emptied by the drivers of the offal carts.

Ashes and garbage may be deposited in the same vessel. All is carried daily to the garbage boats, towed below the lower limits of the city and dumped in the middle of the river.

The annual cost to the city of the removal of ashes and garbage is about $30,000, householders being subjected to no further cost or trouble than that of depositing these matters as above stated.

The whole question of municipal cleansing is at present receiving active attention, and popular sentiment in favor of sanitary reformations, especially such as relate to an improved condition of the streets, sidewalks, and gutters, "is daily growing and daily showing new results."

Mr. Cable expresses the opinion that generally there is no such improper keeping of garbage on premises, infrequent removal, improper handling, or improper final disposal of garbage, as to occasion nuisance or injury to health, except in certain remote portions of the city, such as the region of the dairies on Metairie ridge, and a similar region in the lower part of the city. In these sections the ordinances bearing on such matters are grossly violated, serious nuisance and probable injury to health resulting. This defective condition is the more important from the fact that a great proportion of the city's milk-supply comes from these two sections.

The system of garbage removal and disposal has the special merit of great simplicity, demanding neither elaborate apparatus nor skilled labor. Its defects lie in the difficulty of its execution on the unpaved streets in continued bad weather, when the roadways often remain for a long time practically impassable to loaded vehicles. This defect is the more serious since a great majority of the city's streets are unpaved. Also, the garbage boxes, during the hours of the morning when they are necessarily left standing on the sidewalks, are in themselves a nuisance. The defect in this regard, however, is not greater than in other cities where, according to the usual custom, refuse matters are set out by the householders, except in so far as the climate of New Orleans increases the resulting offensiveness. The gutters of the streets parallel to the river are generally in a most unclean condition.

Dead animals.—The ordinance concerning the removing of dead animals is as follows:

SECTION 30, Ordinance 6022.—Whenever any horse, mule, cow, or other animal shall die within the limits under the control of the board of health, the owner or keeper thereof shall have it forthwith removed to properly located and authorized factories, to be disposed of for useful purposes under proper regulations; or bury such animals beyond the inhabited portion of the city limits, or cast the same into one of the boats moored to the nuisance wharves.

Carcasses of the larger animals are taken by manufacturers of fertilizers and are removed to their factories at their own cost; those of smaller animals and fowls are deposited along with the ashes and garbage. This service entails no additional cost upon the city except in so far as it increases the amount of garbage to be removed. No record is kept of the number of dead animals of different kinds annually removed.

The chief defect of the system relates to the removal of the smaller carcasses, especially of animals without owners; this is often neglected and is a subject of frequent annoyance and complaint. The demand for the larger animals leads to their immediate removal, and the factories where they are disposed of are so situated as to create no noticeable public annoyance.

Liquid household wastes.—Chamber slops (the waste water from sleeping chambers) are, theoretically, generally thrown into the privy vaults; but to obviate the necessity for the costly emptying of vaults, such liquids are often surreptitiously discharged along with the laundry and kitchen wastes, which, according to universal custom, are carried by superficial or shallow drains to the street gutter.

Cesspools are prohibited by law, and violations of the law in this respect are probably infrequent, the open-gutter system affording at least the cheapest and least troublesome means for getting rid of such wastes.

In the more thickly settled parts of the city, including the district occupied by the residences of at least two-thirds of the total population, the gutters of the streets running back from the river are flushed daily, as are also such of the parallel streets as have stone pavements. It is noticeable, however, that the cleansing of the gutters on those streets parallel with the river is very much less perfect, and that the accumulations of the solid matters carried to them by house drains are frequent and often offensive.

The contamination of drinking water.—Owing to the necessarily foul condition of the soil of the occupied portions of the city, no use—certainly no considerable use—is made of well-water. This is employed to some extent for watering animals; but it is generally conceded to be unfit for any manner of domestic use. The entire supply is by the public water-works, which furnish river water on premises and at street hydrants, and, very largely, by rain water caught and held in wooden tanks or cisterns above ground. Frequently these cisterns are placed one above the other, so as to furnish water to each floor of the house. They are of course entirely protected against contamination by the foulness of the soil, though they are obviously subject to considerable accumulations of dust containing much organic matter of foul origin, which, lodging on roofs and in gutters, is washed into the cisterns in considerable quantity, often accumulating to such a degree, and undergoing such decomposition, as to render the water decidedly unpleasant in taste, and not free from suspicion on sanitary grounds. The more careful householders adopt devices for discharging upon the ground the earlier portion of the rainfall, an automatic device being provided for diverting the flow from the cistern until after the roofs and gutters shall have become thoroughly cleansed.

The comparative immunity of New Orleans from typhoid fever is believed by many observers to result from the entire disconnection of the stored water from sources of contamination to which it would be subject if kept in underground cisterns.

In reply to the questions as to the merits and defects of the system in use, Mr. Cable says:

By the system of removal of more household waste above ground the danger of the accumulation of sewer gases is avoided, and emanations from such waste are rapidly carried into the air. One defect of the system is the emptying of chamber slops into privy vaults, which, in many of them, are liable to overflow, even from other abuses [misuses]. Another defect is the fouling and stagnation of the street gutters, especially in unpaved streets, where it is difficult to flush them properly, and the consequent generation of noxious gases and offensive odors.

The ordinance now in force concerning garbage, refuse, and corrupt or putrid water, is as follows:

SECTION 1. *Be it ordained by the council of the city of New Orleans,* That from and after December 12, 1878, it shall be unlawful for any person or persons to keep or deposit any offal, ashes, cinders, filth, foul or offensive matter, corrupt or putrid water, or any shells, hay, straw, kitchen stuff, paper, vegetable matter, or any substances of any kind, that may be offensive to smell, or injurious to health, or liable to become so, in any yard, lot, space, or building, or to throw the same on any sidewalk, or in any gutter, street, drain, or canal, or to cause the same to be done, or to permit or suffer any servant, employé, or member of the family to do so. That upon being notified by the administrator of improvements, or by any of his assistants or foremen, or by any member of the Crescent City police, it shall be the duty of the occupants or owners of the dwellings, stores, offices, buildings, or lots before which or in which the said stuff may be found, to immediately remove the same.

SEC. 2. *Be it further ordained, etc.,* That it shall be the duty of the ward superintendents or foremen employed under the direction of the administrator of improvements, and of all members of the Crescent City police, to make against any person or persons violating the foregoing section an affidavit before the recorder of the district within whose jurisdiction the offense is committed, and upon conviction the offender shall be fined not more than $25 nor less than $10, and, in default of payment of fine, be imprisoned for a period of time not exceeding 30 days nor less than 5 days.

SEC. 3. *Be it further ordained, etc.,* That it shall be the duty of the occupants of all dwellings, offices, stores, or buildings of every character to put, or cause to be put, the ordinary refuse, sweepings, ashes, cinders, and kitchen offal, and all other substances mentioned in section 1, coming from said buildings or premises, into tubs, boxes, barrels, or other suitable receptacles, to have the same placed on the outside of the banquettes, immediately in front of their dwellings, offices, or stores, convenient to be taken off by the offal carts, and hereafter such deposits shall not be made earlier than 3 a. m. nor later than 8 a. m., and the receptacles, as above, shall not be left by said persons on the banquettes later than 10 a. m. All persons violating this section shall be liable to a fine not exceeding $25 nor less than $5, and in default of payment of said fine, to imprisonment for a period of time not exceeding 30 days nor less than 5 days, said fine or imprisonment to be imposed by the recorder of the district within whose jurisdiction the offense is committed.

SEC. 4. *Be it further ordained, etc.,* That it shall be the duty of all the members of the Crescent City police to enforce all the sections of this ordinance, to make affidavits before the recorder having jurisdiction against any and all persons violating any of the sections of this ordinance, and to arrest immediately any and all persons caught violating the same.

SEC. 5. *Be it further ordained, etc.,* That all ordinances or parts of ordinances conflicting herewith be and the same are hereby repealed.

Human excreta.—There being no public sewers, and all delivery of excretal matters into the street gutters being prohibited, the city is supplied, almost without exception, with privy vaults.

By ordinance, all privy vaults must be water-tight; as a matter of fact, owing largely to the saturated condition of the soil, few if any of them are so. Almost the only exception to the vault system relates to the use of about 800 earth closets in the whole city.

The disposal of the night soil is by the emptying of vaults by "vidangeurs". It is carried to the river in close carts and is transferred to nuisance boats by which it is dumped into the middle of the river below the city limits. It is not permitted to use human excreta for the manuring of land.

Manufacturing waste.—The water of the gas-works is delivered into the draining canals, and constitutes a serious source of nuisance. The water of sugar-refineries, which is comparatively inoffensive, is delivered into street gutters. Water from ice-works and elevators is used with advantage for flushing the street gutters. Slaughter-house waste is made into fertilizers on the spot—near the lower limits of the city. The waste of cotton-seed oil factories is burned under the boilers. Rice chaff, tin cuttings, and other solid wastes are dumped by the garbage boats along with the domestic refuse.

Concerning the merits and defects of this system, Mr. Cable says:

The discharge of sugar-refining water into the gutters, and so into the canals, must produce more or less alcoholic and acetic fermentation. The city authorities assert that the gas water is the principal cause of the corrupt condition of the waters in the canals, which are extremely offensive, dark, and foul.

NOTE.—It is proper to repeat that the system of municipal cleansing is now enjoying the benefit of a revolution in public sentiment in New Orleans.

PUBLIC SCHOOLS.

The last report of the superintendent of public schools, that has been received, is that of 1879. This shows that the total number of pupils on the register is 24,150. Of these 17,294 are white and 6,856 are colored.

The following is the budget of expenditures submitted by the finance committee of the board and adopted:

Salaries of teachers	$231,288 00
Wages of porteresses	17,544 00
Rents	17,256 00
Superintendent's office, clerk and messengers	1,200 00
Treasurer	1,200 00
Secretary	3,000 00
Supplies, brooms, etc., for porteresses	2,200 00
Stationery for schools	2,500 00
Fuel	3,150 00
Sanitary company contract	850 00
School furniture	12,000 00
Repair to school-houses	11,500 00
Total expenditures	303,688 00

The actual receipts for the year 1878 have been $179,721 06, derived as follows:

Receipts from city tax	$159,045 66
From state tax	20,675 40

The actual disbursements were $171,459.

The report of the superintendent indicates an insufficient appropriation of funds for the securing of the best results, and especially a low scale of salaries for teachers; these ranging between $324 and $1,620 per annum. Only 25 of the teachers are males, and 407 are females, averaging one teacher to about 55 registered pupils.

Concerning the school accommodations the following statements are made:

Notwithstanding the erection of 9 McDonough school-houses, 2 of which have been completed during the current year, and the fact that two additional school-houses are rapidly approaching completion under the direction of the commissioners of this fund, our school accommodations are entirely inadequate to meet the wants of the city. We require additional accommodations for 2,000 children residing in the older and more thickly settled portions of the city.

* * * * * * * * * *

The condition of the school buildings has been greatly improved during the current year. The want of means prevented as extensive repairs as were necessary and desirable, but the limited resources were judiciously expended, and many of the buildings present a marked contrast to their previous appearance. The action of the city government in requiring the school board to make all necessary repairs upon the school-houses imposes a burden greater than the means at the disposal of the board can sustain. The buildings are too numerous; many of them too far gone in decay to be placed in good condition without larger expenditures than are warranted by the appropriation for the support of the schools.

STATISTICS OF EDUCATIONAL AND RELIGIOUS INSTITUTIONS.

The enumeration of 1880 furnishes the following statistics of the religious and educational institutions of New Orleans:

Public schools	39	Methodist Episcopal	22
Actual attendance on schools	15,316	Methodist, South	11
Private elementary schools	106	Presbyterian	13
Private high schools	42	Protestant Episcopal	11
Colleges	3	Swedish Lutheran	5
Business colleges	5	Roman Catholic	32
Professional schools	4	Greek	1
Baptist churches	35	Unitarian	1
Congregational churches	7	Christian	1
Jewish churches	6		

There are in the city 16 libraries, having together 111,644 volumes.

CHARITABLE INSTITUTIONS.

[Contributed by Rev. Fred. H. Wines, special agent.]

No account of the city of New Orleans would be complete without mention of its many institutions of beneficence, for the care of the infirm and the destitute, of which there are nearly 40. Nearly half of them are under the direction of some one or another of the religious orders connected with the Roman Catholic church. The city authorities maintain a home for the aged and infirm, a house of refuge for boys, and an insane asylum. In addition to the Charity hospital (which is widely known on account of its connection with the Louisiana State Lottery, and is a splendid establishment), there are three other smaller hospitals, beside the Louisiana retreat for the insane (a private asylum). One of these bears the honored name of the Touro Infirmary. The Hebrews also maintain a home for Jewish widows and orphans. The number of asylums for orphaned and friendless children is about twenty.

The following list of institutions in the city is believed to be accurate and complete. It exhibits not only the title and location of each, together with the name and title of the officer in charge, but also the reported capacity and the number of inmates returned as actually present June 1, 1880, the day of taking the census. The Roman Catholic institutions are distinguished by a † prefixed:

Name.	Capacity.	Number of inmates June 1, 1880.	Name of chief executive officer in charge.	Official title.	Location.
† Asile de la Ste. Famille (for colored children)	....	5	Sister Charles Josephine	Superior	
Asylum for Destitute Orphan Boys	150	50	George Burns	Superintendent	Saint Charles.
Asylum of the Société Française de Bienfaisance	100	5	J. Schneetzer	President	Saint Ann, near Roman.
† Charity Hospital	1,000	514	Sister Agnes	Superior	Common.
Children's Home (P. E.)	50	40	Sister Roberta	Superior	Jackson, corner Saint Thomas.
City Insane Asylum	160	161	John C. Pooley	Superintendent	Common, corner White.
Fink Asylum (for Prot. widows and their children)	40	39	Mrs. S. M. Packard	Matron	Camp, corner Amelia.
German Protestant Orphan Asylum	130	102	Gustave Pixberg	Superintendent	State, corner Camp.
† Home for the Aged Poor (Little Sisters)	215	221	Mother Joseph Theresa	Superior	North Johnson, corner Laharpe.
Home for Aged and Destitute Women		21	Miss J. P. Moore		Magnolia, corner Lafayette.
Home for the Aged and Infirm (city charity)	60	57	Mrs. E. B. Stokes	Matron	Annunciation, corner Calliope.
† Hôpital de la Ste. Famille (for old colored people)	....	22	Sister Theresa	Directress	49 Saint Bernard avenue.
† Hôtel Dieu (infirmary)	50	15	Sister Mary Carroll	Superior	Common.
† House of the Good Shepherd	300	209	Sister Mary Rose	Superior	Bienville, corner Magazine.
House of Refuge (boys)	600	242	Thomas Brennan	Superintendent	Metairie road.
† House of Refuge (destitute colored girls)	350	42	Sister Mary Rose	Superior	Annunciation.
Jewish Widows' and Orphans' Home	170	101	N. J. Bunzel	Superintendent	Jackson, corner Chippewa.
† Louisiana Retreat for the Insane	160	95	Sister Mary Jane	Superior	Henry Clay avenue.
Luzenberg Hospital (for contagious diseases)	50	....	S. S. Hayes, M. D.	Proprietor and super't	431 Elysian Fields.
† Mount Carmel Female Orphan Asylum	100	85	Sister Justine	Superior	53 Piety.
† New Orleans Female Orphan Asylum	130	135	Sister Eustolia	Superior	Clio, corner Camp.
Newsboys' Lodging House	....	....	Charles R. Roos	Superintendent	167 Franklin.
Orleans Infirmary	40	....	Dr. Beard	Superintendent	142 Canal.
† Orphan Girls' Asylum, Immaculate Conception	125	95	Sister Mary	Superior	871 North Rampart.
Poydras Female Orphan Asylum	250	85	Mrs. Carrie M. Sutherland	Matron	Magazine, corner Peters avenue.
Protestant Orphans' Home	150	140	Ann Walker	Matron	Seventh, corner Constance.
Providence Asylum for Female Colored Children	....	40			Hospital, corner North Tonti.
† Saint Alphonsus' Orphan Asylum	130	104	Mother M. Joseph Devereux	Superior	Fourth, corner Saint Patrick.
Saint Anna's Asylum (P. E.)	100	85	Mrs. E. E. Kip	Matron	Prytania, corner Saint Mary.
† St. Elizabeth's House of Industry (orphan girls)	150	133	Sister Angelica	Superior	Napoleon, corner Prytania.
† Saint Isidore's Institute (industrial farm school)	100	....	Rev. Father Fourmond	Provincial	North Peters, corner Reynes.
† Saint Joseph's German Orphan Asylum	200	182	Sister Mary Jacobina	Superior	Laurel, corner Josephine.
† Saint Mary's Catholic Orphan Boys' Asylum	350	343	Sister Mary of the Desert	Superior	Chartres, corner Mazant.
† Saint Vincent's Half Orphan Asylum (for girls)	80	15	Sister Ernestine	Superior	Cambronne, corner Third.
† Saint Vincent's Home for Destitute Boys	50	31	Father O'Brien	Director	371 Bienville.
† Saint Vincent's Infant Orphan Asylum	200	189	Sister Mary Agnes	Superior	Magazine, corner Race.
Touro Infirmary	40	15	F. Loeber, M. D.	Surgeon	South Peters, corner Calliope
United States Marine Hospital	....	....	Not in use.		
Widows' Home	40	41	C. Barjac		352 Esplanade.
Total	5,820	3,660			

The jail of Orleans parish, with 59 cells and a reported capacity of 350, contained, June 1, 1880, 189 persons.

POLICE.

System.—Strictly municipal. Under control of a board of commissioners composed of the mayor of the city and the administrator of police, both *ex officio* members, and four members appointed by the mayor, of whom the term of one expires each year.

Jurisdiction.—Only within the boundaries of the parish of Orleans; that is, from the upper line of the seventh district, late the town of Carrollton, to Poland street, the city's lower boundary; and from the rear limits of the fifth district, late Algiers, on the west bank of the Mississippi, to the southern shore of lake Pontchartrain.

Area of territory.—One hundred and fifty square miles, including that part of the Mississippi river forming the harbor of New Orleans.

Force (numbers).—Officers: 1 chief of police, 1 chief of aids, 6 aids patrolmen. On special detail as follows:

Sanitary officers under orders of the board of health	4
Patrolmen in the recorders' courts	6
In police stations	22
In the public squares	8
In the market-houses	7
On regular active duty in public streets:	
Day	64
Night	124
On regular active duty on harbor-front:	
Day	20
Night	10
On regular active duty, as mounted suburban police	3
Total force of patrolmen	268

Mode of appointment.—Appointed by the mayor and confirmed by the council.

Term of tenure.—During good behavior.

Mode of removal.—Only for cause, and only by the board of police commissioners.

Duties.—General only to enforce city ordinances and make all arrests for criminal offenses.

Uniform.—Winter: captains and sergeants, double-breasted frock coat of navy-blue cloth, with double row of brass buttons. Corporals and patrolmen, single-breasted coat of same, with one row of silver buttons. Summer: captains and sergeants, double-breasted sack of navy-blue flannel, with brass buttons; corporals and patrolmen, single-breasted blouse of same, with silver buttons.

Equipment.—Policeman's club and whistle.

Arms.—None. The law against carrying concealed weapons applies in full force to policemen. But this law is not enforced as against the police.

Pay.—Chief of police, $290 per month; chief of aids, $150; aids, $100; patrolmen, $50. Uniform and whistle at expense of individual; club furnished by the city.

Houses of detention.—Lock-ups, 11; workhouse, 1; boys' house of refuge, 1; county jail (called parish prison), 1.

How kept.—Lock-ups by regular police; workhouse and boys' house of refuge by administrator of police; and parish prison by the criminal sheriff of the parish of Orleans.

Police courts.—Four in number; sit daily; presided over by magistrates known as "recorders", who hold office by popular election.

Efficiency.—The police of New Orleans is well officered; but the entire force is ill-paid, and at times not paid; it is therefore deficient in *morale*, and is totally inadequate in point of numbers.

There is also a body of police under the management of a private company, and known as the

HARBOR PROTECTION POLICE.

Duties.—It is a thoroughly organized and equipped body, whose duty it is, under contracts made with owners or custodians, to police ships, wharves, and the like, and to receive and watch cargoes, for which the company becomes, for the time being, responsible. And also to co-operate with the regular city police, and to assist them at all times when they can do so without jeopardizing the property over which they are specially in charge.

Working force.—Its numbers vary according to the amount of commercial movement in the port; from about 120 in winter to some 70 in summer.

Appointment.—The appointment of the force is made by the company, based on the recommendation, in each case, of three good citizens, who become bondsmen for the appointee. The patrolmen are commissioned by the mayor of the city, under the provisions of the following city ordinance:

No. 6715 Administration series.

AN ORDINANCE relative to M. J. Farrell's Harbor Protection Police.

Be it ordained by the mayor and administrators of the city of New Orleans, in common council convened, That the mayor of the city of New Orleans be and is hereby authorized, at his discretion, to commission as a patrolman, with police powers, each person employed as a member of "M. J. Farrell's harbor protection police".

Be it further ordained, etc., That the persons commissioned by the mayor in conformity with the provisions hereof, shall not be required to furnish the bond to be executed by patrolmen under ordinance No. 3914, A. S.; nor shall such person receive or be entitled to any salary or compensation of any kind from the city of New Orleans. Adopted by the council of the city of New Orleans, November 9, 1880.

Uniform.—Their uniform, which they are required to wear at all times, is a suit of blue flannel and a stiff hat of black felt, to which is added, when on duty, a patent-leather band bearing the initials of the organization in bright metal on the front.

Equipment.—They are equipped with an English police-whistle and club.

Pay.—Each policeman is paid $55 per month. The officers are 1 superintendent, 1 captain, 1 sergeant, and 2 corporals. The company charges for the services of each man for each twelve hours, $2 50. Vessels often employ as many as three men from this force, assigning one to the ship's deck, one to the freight on the wharf, and a third to the water approaches around and beneath the wharf. The company, formed on account of the great frequency of incendiary fires on shipboard, reports its total gross losses, in the 11 months in which it has existed, at $18, after having watched nearly 500 vessels and cargoes. This organization comprises also a branch agency known as the

CITY PROTECTION PATROL.

This body consists of some 18 men, and undertakes the night-watching of stores, factories, warehouses, and offices in the streets of the city. Each patrolman moves on a beat, reporting every few minutes throughout the night to a central office by means of a series of ordinary American district telegraph signal-boxes encased in iron, under lock and key. Subscribers pay from $5 to $15 per month, according to the magnitude or importance of their establishments, and are furnished with a regular and minute morning report, in writing, from the central office.

There has also been in operation another body of men holding special police powers, under the management and in the employment of the New Orleans Cotton Exchange. Their duty is thoroughly to police the handling of the immense cotton receipts and shipments of the port, from the moment of arrival until its final stowing in the vessel's hold for export. This body of ununiformed police holds commissions from the mayor of the city, but is appointed by the New Orleans Cotton Exchange and retained entirely under its control. It is divided into 25 supervisors acting in the cotton-presses and yards, and 7 inspectors in railroad yards, on steamboat-landings, and on ship-wharves. Their pay is $100 per month. The operation of this force is known to have put a stop to a general pilfering of cotton, which amounted in value to as much as half a million dollars a year.

COMMERCIAL STATISTICS.

During the fiscal year ending June 30, 1880, the value of the exports of merchandise from the port of New Orleans amounted to an aggregate of $90,238,503. In this amount, the following items are included:

Cotton (1,428,996 bales)	$75,553,195
Wheat	4,697,726
Corn	4,120,511
Cotton-seed	2,487,103
Oil-cake	1,687,158

During the same fiscal year the imports of merchandise into this port amounted to $10,611,353, including—

Coffee	$4,010,166
Iron	1,357,808
Sugar	647,377
Molasses	142,813

Beside this, merchandise was imported and passed through to other cities to the amount of $425,809.

The number of emigrants arriving from foreign ports was about 3,000.

The number of vessels entered was 852, with a tonnage of 760,910 tons.

The number of vessels cleared was 915, with a tonnage of 858,765 tons.

The number of vessels owned in New Orleans is: Ocean steamers, 21; tonnage, 27,920. River steamers, 163; tonnage, 29,042. Sailing vessels, 353; tonnage, 16,134.

COMMERCE AND NAVIGATION.

[From the reports of the Bureau of Statistics for the fiscal years ending June 30.]

Customs district of New Orleans, Louisiana.	1879.	1880.
Total value of imports	$7,250,597	$10,842,254
Total value of exports:		
Domestic	$63,794,426	$90,249,874
Foreign	$187,187	$203,516
Total number of immigrants	1,834	2,663

Customs district of New Orleans, Louisiana.	1879.		1880.	
	Number.	Tons.	Number.	Tons.
Vessels in foreign trade:				
Entered	734	652,739	852	760,910
Cleared	724	666,037	915	858,765
Vessels in coast trade and fisheries:				
Entered	298	274,233	442	438,828
Cleared	373	279,920	382	360,394
Vessels registered, enrolled, and licensed in district	387	54,302	396	57,848
Vessels built during the year	10	362	16	202

MANUFACTURES.

The following is a summary of the statistics of the manufactures of New Orleans for 1880, being taken from tables prepared for the Tenth Census by E. A. Deslonde, chief special agent:

Mechanical and manufacturing industries.	No. of establishments.	Capital.	Average number of hands employed. Males above 16 years.	Females above 15 years.	Children and youths.	Total amount paid in wages during the year.	Value of materials.	Value of products.
All industries	915	$8,565,303	7,666	1,286	552	$3,717,557	$10,771,892	$18,808,096
Blacksmithing (see also Wheelwrighting)	64	31,020	147	1	8	71,965	53,975	185,673
Bookbinding and blank-book making	6	11,000	16	....	3	10,211	5,520	24,369
Boot and shoe findings................	9	57,200	40	2	6	20,270	98,932	171,080
Boots and shoes, including custom work and repairing	64	43,200	269	....	6	116,809	174,745	367,531
Boxes, fancy and paper	4	14,600	41	12	46	29,483	59,400	125,928
Boxes, wooden packing................	4	15,200	15	12	6	7,572	10,220	25,200
Bread and other bakery products	99	109,020	317	8	17	120,766	540,450	981,160
Brooms and brushes	6	11,750	63	....	3	22,614	89,381	134,619
Carpentering	22	58,600	262	....	4	138,595	226,400	439,850
Carriages and wagons (see also Wheelwrighting)................	8	38,700	92	....	6	51,196	46,500	135,600
Clothing, men's................	33	190,300	276	628	30	175,971	743,407	1,078,559
Clothing, women's	6	83,000	2	273	....	43,875	113,353	189,278
Coffee and spices, roasted and ground	3	1,300	3	....	1	1,524	9,510	11,876
Coffins, burial cases, and undertakers' goods	7	2,900	9	....	....	2,911	4,122	13,866
Confectionery	21	132,800	86	11	17	33,754	274,571	393,040
Cooperage	53	53,650	256	....	....	109,839	105,704	276,618
Cordials and sirups	4	48,000	30	....	....	11,966	43,000	82,000
Cotton compressing................	19	2,135,000	560	....	....	399,780	105,788	747,500
Dentistry, mechanical	3	9,200	6	....	3	5,350	8,250	20,150
Drugs and chemicals................	7	16,700	13	....	....	4,190	8,850	22,750
Dyeing and cleaning................	12	6,925	13	3	1	5,080	3,890	22,850
Flouring- and grist-mill products	4	69,600	31	....	....	13,823	248,480	317,000
Food preparations................	4	16,000	12	1	3	5,328	19,600	47,880
Foundery and machine-shop products (see also Iron work, architectural and ornamental).	20	738,375	748	....	9	405,745	596,800	1,228,300
Furniture (see also Mattresses and spring beds; Upholstering)......	33	32,976	62	1	6	30,281	35,429	104,593
Galvanizing	3	700	1	....	....	360	700	3,005
Hairwork................	6	6,100	6	6	....	3,592	6,900	17,600
Instruments, professional and scientific	3	1,600	3	....	....	1,260	1,700	5,460
Iron work, architectural and ornamental (see also Foundery and machine-shop products).	3	1,800	10	....	....	3,477	4,200	14,500
Liquors, malt................	8	157,613	113	....	....	54,992	295,353	457,744
Lithographing (see also Printing and publishing)................	3	2,000	8	....	....	4,500	3,250	13,500
Lock- and gun-smithing................	12	2,600	11	....	....	2,700	1,980	11,670
Looking-glass and picture frames................	5	7,050	6	....	1	2,892	8,575	16,559
Lumber, planed (see also Sash, doors, and blinds; Wood, turned and carved).	7	78,500	98	....	4	44,873	162,610	267,280
Lumber, sawed	6	152,200	53	....	....	17,595	180,985	234,340
Marble and stone work	11	62,550	65	....	....	32,575	61,208	134,490
Masonry, brick and stone................	16	17,500	85	....	15	36,500	30,700	90,500
Mattresses and spring beds (see also Furniture)................	3	3,450	8	1	....	2,712	25,500	39,200
Mineral and soda waters................	7	29,100	37	....	....	18,312	24,350	75,900
Oil, cottonseed and cake................	7	785,500	836	15	65	275,165	1,630,150	2,751,150
Painting and paperhanging................	12	10,425	98	....	....	30,412	33,800	86,000
Photographing................	12	39,100	37	6	2	27,390	19,399	79,765
Plumbing and gasfitting	9	16,300	31	....	....	17,441	40,500	71,600
Printing and publishing (see also Lithographing)................	25	303,050	503	4	17	407,946	226,600	764,036
Rice cleaning and polishing................	6	225,000	162	....	....	56,040	1,328,387	1,573,281
Saddlery and harness	23	169,500	144	1	15	74,674	204,750	370,505
Sash, doors, and blinds (see also Lumber, planed; Wood, turned and carved).	4	285,000	159	....	....	81,800	246,000	432,000
Shipbuilding................	17	145,200	194	....	....	99,366	101,965	263,050
Soap and candles	12	118,450	45	....	6	19,790	89,990	142,495
Sugar and molasses, refined................	4	385,000	190	....	....	50,000	1,340,000	1,483,000

Mechanical and manufacturing industries.	No. of estab-lish-ments.	Capital.	AVERAGE NUMBER OF HANDS EMPLOYED.			Total amount paid in wages during the year.	Value of materials.	Value of products.
			Males above 16 years.	Females above 15 years.	Children and youths.			
Surgical appliances	3	$1,550	5	....	....	$2,070	$1,675	$6,000
Tinware, copperware, and sheet-iron ware.................	34	94,300	110	....	3	51,271	105,890	199,559
Tobacco, chewing, smoking, and snuff (see also Tobacco, cigars and cigarettes).	8	248,000	127	6	88	70,540	242,100	424,085
Tobacco, cigars and cigarettes (see also Tobacco, chewing, smoking and snuff).	47	175,674	680	187	87	179,999	152,156	506,612
Upholstering (see also Furniture).......................	12	8,325	15	....	....	3,335	9,575	20,640
Upholstering materials	3	30,000	21	41	2	19,530	100,000	153,000
Watch and clock repairing	13	11,600	23	....	....	14,795	8,346	32,379
Wheelwrighting (see also Blacksmithing; Carriages and wagons) ...	10	13,900	25	....	1	7,708	7,825	25,112
Wood, turned and carved (see also Lumber, planed; Sash, doors, and blinds).	3	5,400	11	....	....	6,225	21,542	39,404
All other industries (a)	43	944,250	377	67	71	156,822	426,954	855,360

a Embracing bags, other than paper; baskets, rattan and willow ware; brick and tile; brass castings; cars, railroad, street, and repairs; cordage and twine; cork cutting; cotton goods; cutlery and edge tools; fertilizers; flags and banners; fruits and vegetables canned and preserved; gold and silver, reduced and refined; hammocks; hardware; ice, artificial; japanning; leather, curried; leather, tanned; liquors, distilled; mirrors; patent medicines and compounds; perfumery and cosmetics; plated and britannia ware; pumps; stencils and brands; stone- and earthen-ware; trunks and valises; umbrellas and canes; and vinegar.

From the foregoing table it appears that the average capital of all establishments is $9,360 99; that the average wages of all hands employed is $391 16 per annum; that the average outlay in wages, in materials, and in interest (at 6 per cent.) on capital employed is $16,397 12.

SHREVEPORT,

CADDO COUNTY, LOUISIANA.

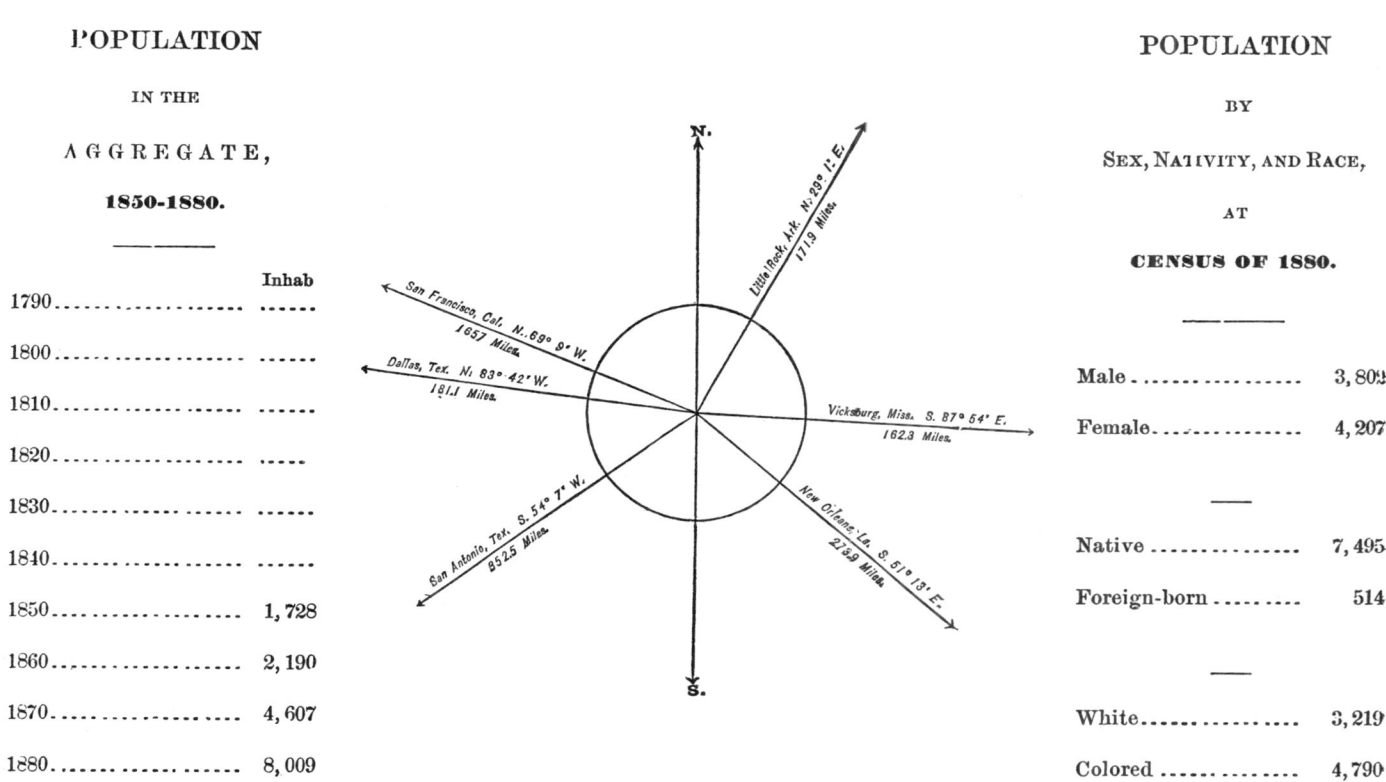

POPULATION

IN THE

AGGREGATE,

1850-1880.

	Inhab
1790	......
1800	......
1810	......
1820	......
1830	......
1840	......
1850	1,728
1860	2,190
1870	4,607
1880	8,009

POPULATION

BY

SEX, NATIVITY, AND RACE,

AT

CENSUS OF 1880.

Male	3,802
Female	4,207
Native	7,495
Foreign-born	514
White	3,219
Colored	4,790

Latitude: 32° 30' North; Longitude: 93° 45' (west from Greenwich); Altitude: 260 to 355 feet.

FINANCIAL CONDITION:

Total Valuation: $1,956,100; per capita: $244 00.   Net Indebtedness: $457,144; per capita: $57 08.   Tax per $100: $3 10.

HISTORICAL SKETCH.(a)

The original area and town site of Shreveport is a section of land (640 acres) reserved by the Caddo Indians, the original proprietors, and donated to Larkin Edwards, a friendly white man, who had lived among them for several years, and to whom they were very much attached and indebted for services rendered them in their intercourse with the frontier people of Louisiana, Texas, and Arkansas, also with governmental authorities. The treaty granting their lands to the government was entered into before the year 1835, although they were still roaming the forest; and one of its articles seems to have stipulated that Edwards was given the privilege of locating

a Hon. A. Currie, mayor of Shreveport, not only secured and transmitted nearly all the detailed information regarding the present condition of the city, but furnished the historical sketch with which this report is introduced.

his claim at any point of the lands vacated. He selected what was then known as Cane and Bennett's bluff. A substantial log house decorated the site, which was then very probably a trading-post. A few additional log dwellings were erected in 1835. The selection made by Edwards crossed different sections, townships, and range lines. When the United States surveyor traversed the claim and marked out its boundaries in May, 1836, it was designated on the township maps as section 37, township 18, range 14 west, in the northwestern district of Louisiana, containing 634 acres and a portion of an acre. On January 24, 1835, Edwards sold his floating claim to Angus McNeil for the sum of $5,000. In July, 1835, Jehial Brooks, acting for the government, formally ratified the claim, and his act was subsequently confirmed by a decree of the Supreme Court of the United States. The act of conveyance was soon afterward completed, acknowledged, and accepted.

By an act dated May 27, 1836, Captain Henry M. Shreve, of Kentucky, James B. Pickett, of South Carolina, Thomas T. Williamson, of Arkansas, Sturgis Sprague, of Mississippi, Bushrod Jenkins, and the commercial firm of Cane & Bennett, of Natchitoches, Louisiana, became associated with McNeil in the Edwards claim, " share and share alike", for the sum of $4,136 66⅔, the members binding themselves to select a lot and build a dwelling on the same. These gentlemen soon formed an organization called the "Shreve Town Company", naming the place after Captain Shreve. Angus McNeil, the original proprietor, was chosen president. That portion of the site extending from the river to the highlands, bounded in the southwest by Common street, was subdivided into blocks, streets, and alleys, regularly numbered, named, and mapped out. The principal thoroughfare was named Texas street, after the neighboring republic of Texas, and its extension, as the town grew into a city, was called Texas avenue.

In March, 1836, about the time the Shreve Town Company was organized, the state legislature chartered the Lake Providence and Red River Railroad Company. The line was drawn to run from the Mississippi river, near Lake Providence, in Carroll parish, via Monroe, on the Ouachita river, to an indefinite point on Red river, between the great raft and Rigolet Bon Dilu, in Natchitoches point. Caddo point was then a portion of Natchitoches, and continued so until January, 1838, when, by an act of the legislature, it was organized, and the house of Thomas L. Wallace made the seat of justice, in case no public place was provided. The above road would doubtless have terminated at Shreve Town if it had been built, as the site of the town was almost midway between the great raft and Rigolet Bon Dieu. Stock-books were opened at Lake Providence, Vicksburg, Monroe, Natchitoches, and Philadelphia, by special commissioners. The state was also authorized by the act to take stock and aid its construction.

On the 7th of February, 1837, by a public act of the Shreve Town Company, to which all the members or their agents subscribed, full power and authority was lodged in their president to convey and transfer to all persons desiring to purchase the same any of the subdivisions of their land. A number of sales were immediately made, and the town began to grow populous. On the 20th of March, 1839, the legislature of Louisiana granted a charter to the inhabitants, named the place "Shreveport", and made it the seat of justice for Caddo parish. The first election was held in May of the same year, five trustees being chosen, and they elected one of their number mayor, as required by the charter. A full corps of other officials, as designated in the charter, was selected by the trustees, clothed with authority, and installed in office. The power of taxation was given, but the gross amount to be collected was limited to $1,000. The charter of 1839 was never entirely superseded until the charter of 1878 was granted, but was altered, amended, and greatly extended from time to time by act of the legislature. The powers of the trustees and the number of the members was increased; also the power of taxation, etc.; and in 1852 the revenues of the ferry were divided with the parish of Bossier. The ferry then was merely a cumbersome flat-boat, bearing no comparison to the magnificent steam-ferry now in use and making trips every 10 minutes.

The country adjacent was rapidly settled by thrifty and experienced planters from the older states, who brought a large number of slaves with them. The city itself, being at the head of low-water navigation on Red river, became the *entrepôt* of the inhabitants, not alone of northwest Louisiana, but also of southwest Arkansas and of eastern Texas. Through judicial proceedings instituted against McNeil, the original town company was dissolved, and the unsold lots and lands were appraised or valued, and partitioned out among the members on the 10th of May, 1843.

In 1853 a very malignant type of yellow fever spread from New Orleans up the Red River valley and seized upon Shreveport, which had the effect of checking the rapidity of its growth for a short time. In a few years, however, all traces of its effect disappeared.

In 1858 the Vicksburg, Shreveport, and Texas railroad began operations at Shreveport, and before the breaking out of the war, in 1861, had completed about 20 miles of its road and was operating the same westward into Texas. The same company had also constructed about 90 miles of road from the banks of the Mississippi river, opposite Vicksburg, to Monroe, on the east bank of the Ouachita river, and had bridged the last-named stream. The war stopped operations at both ends. The gap between Shreveport and Monroe, 90 miles east, is still unclosed, owing to complications in title, which have been finally settled by the United States Supreme Court. The old bondholders were given possession. They reorganized the company, changed its name to the Vicksburg, Shreveport, and Pacific, and are moving with a view of completing the road to this point at an early day, to connect with the Texas and Pacific road, which already has its terminus here.

During the late civil war quite a trade sprang up between Shreveport and Mexico, cotton being sent there in wagons and exchanged for medicines, coffee, and other needed supplies. The round trip lasted about 3 months, and trains, numbering as high as 50 wagons, went and came. On December 24, 1861, Shreveport was created the state capital, and in the spring of the following year the records, archives, offices, etc., were moved hither.

In the summer of 1867 the yellow fever again invaded the Red River valley from New Orleans, and broke out in Shreveport in a mild form. It was chiefly noted for the long period it continued to manifest its presence; some citizens returning to their homes long after heavy frost and cold weather had set in became infected.

Some time previous to this, the Southern Pacific Railroad Company leased for a term of 20 years that portion of the Vicksburg, Shreveport, and Texas road running from Shreveport to the Texas line, and completed the same to Marshall, Texas, 4 miles west of Shreveport, and in 1869 began building toward Longview, Texas, 65 miles west of Shreveport, toward which the International and Great Northern, coming north from Houston, was aiming. Its name was changed to the "Texas and Pacific", and in 1873 it was pushed to Dallas, Texas, 185 miles west from Shreveport, and in a short time extended from Marshall north to Texarkana, connecting there with the Iron Mountain railroad to Saint Louis. The years 1870, '71, '72, '73 marked the beginning and end of a lively era in Shreveport. A line of boats was inaugurated to run from Saint Louis direct to the city, boats also began running direct from Cincinnati, and the fleets from New Orleans began to increase. This, together with the advance of the Texas and Pacific railroad into a country that immediately sought a market at Shreveport, quadrupled its commerce and doubled its population in a short period.

In 1873 the population was variously estimated at between 8,000 and 10,000. Yellow fever again appeared this year about the middle of August, and, owing to the miserable sanitary condition of the city, which seems to have been totally neglected, the disease assumed a very malignant type and carried off about 800 people, among whom was an unusual proportion of the most prominent merchants. Two bankrupt menageries were camped in the heart of the city; one of them, reported to have come from Mexico, added to the filth, and at the same time a steamboat-load of cattle sank on a bar opposite the city. The carcasses of some of the drowned animals floated to the shore, where they festered in the sun, adding their stench to the prevailing pestilence, and probably augmenting its virulence. The existing authorities seemed paralyzed or incapable of appreciating the situation. A Howard association was speedily organized by men of experience and nerve, who were soon reinforced by the Howards of New Orleans in the person of the then president, followed by a skillful and capable corps of male and female nurses and several of the most distinguished and expert physicians. Lieutenant Woodruff, in charge of the United States engineer corps engaged above Shreveport in removing the great Red River raft, left the scene of his labors, lent efficient aid, and established a hospital in Tally's opera-house. His noble efforts exposed him to the disease, and, with many others, he sacrificed his life to the cause of humanity. The epidemic of 1873 was a serious blow to Shreveport, caused a loss of fully one-half its then existing wealth and population, and nearly destroyed its commercial relations with that portion of eastern Texas bordering on the Texas and Pacific railroad. The connection of the latter with the Iron Mountain railroad to Saint Louis, however, probably was the greatest cause of its loss. At present the effect has disappeared, and public confidence is now in a great measure restored. The population is rapidly increasing, and the disasters and disorders of the past are thought of only to guard against their recurrence.

With the exception of a cottonseed-oil mill, recently destroyed by fire and in progress of reconstruction on a larger scale, there are no extensive manufacturing industries in Shreveport. There are 2 large cotton compresses, capable of turning out 1,600 bales per day, and 7 large brick warehouses, with a capacity of 20,000 bales. During the past cotton year, ending September, 1880, the factors of Shreveport handled 120,000 bales of cotton.

SHREVEPORT IN 1880.

The following statistical accounts collected by the Census Office indicate the present condition of Shreveport:

LOCATION.

Shreveport is situated midway of the eastern boundary-line of Caddo parish, Louisiana, on Red river, 500 miles above its mouth, and in latitude 32° 30' north, longitude 93° 45' west from Greenwich. It is 60 miles below the point where the great Red River raft, removed finally in 1876, was located, and is 740 miles by water from New Orleans. Its mean height above sea-level is 307½ feet, the lowest point, at edge of low water in the river, being 260 feet and the highest 355 feet above sea-level. The draught of water in the river varies from 35 feet during the highest stage to 2 feet at the lowest. The harbor capacity is 1 mile of water-front. The current in the river is 3 miles per hour. Water communication is open up the river to Fulton, Arkansas, and below with the Mississippi river and its navigable tributaries.

RAILROAD COMMUNICATIONS.

The city is on the Shreveport division of the Texas Pacific railroad, between Texarkana, Arkansas, and Eastland, Texas, with connections to all railroad points. The New Orleans Pacific and the Vicksburg, Shreveport, and Pacific, are now under construction toward this point, and the Memphis and Shreveport railroad has been chartered.

TRIBUTARY COUNTRY.

The country within a radius of 75 miles, including several small towns, is an agricultural district and is tributary to the city. Cotton, corn, all kinds of herbaceous plants, and fruits are grown. The soil in the river-bottom is very rich, while that in the hill-lands is generally poorer.

TOPOGRAPHY.

The soil under the site of the city is alluvial, ferruginous, clay, and sand. The variations in level are 100 feet, and there is good natural drainage into Red river and the adjoining lakes. The elevation of the surrounding country is 50 feet higher than the city. The marshes and ponds are gradually disappearing since the removal of the great raft. The lakes dry up in summer, as the river feeding them lowers its stage of water. The country, which was formerly well wooded, is now open. It is reported that a good many petrefactions are found in the surface of the soil.

CLIMATE.

Highest recorded summer temperature, 102°; highest summer temperature in average years, 98°. Lowest recorded winter temperature, 6°; lowest winter temperature in average years, 16°. The influence of the adjacent waters at low stages, and the marshes, tend to create malaria. The prevailing winds are from the south and are healthful.

STREETS.

There are 16 miles of streets in the city, 1½ mile of which is paved with broken stone, and 1½ mile with wood. The broken stone costs $4 25 per cubic yard, laid down. The broken stone is preferred, but as good oak, well drained, lasts some time, and as rock is scarce, the wood pavement will finally supplant the other. The sidewalks are principally brick. In the main business streets, gutters are of stone, and in the balance of the streets they are simply ditches. No trees are planted, except by private individuals in front of their houses. The annual appropriation for streets is $5,000, which includes repairs, construction, gutters, crossings, and removal of garbage. Day work is preferred when the same is in charge of an honest and capable street commissioner. There is one street-railroad, with a length of 1 mile, using 4 cars and 8 horses, and employing about 6 men. During the year 100,000 passengers are carried, and the rate of fare is 5 cents.

WATER-WORKS.

Shreveport has no water-works.

GAS.

The gas-works are owned by a private company. The daily average production is 200,000 feet. The charge per 1,000 feet is from $3 50 to $4. The city pays $40 per annum for each street-lamp, 44 in number.

PUBLIC BUILDINGS.

The city occupies, for municipal purposes, the upper story of the market. The city hall and market-house, owned by the city, originally cost $30,000. The county buildings in the city are owned and occupied by the parish authorities.

PUBLIC PARKS AND PLEASURE-GROUNDS.

There are 30 acres of parks in the city. Part of this area is occupied by private parks, used for picnics and like entertainments, and the remainder belongs to the city, but is not improved. The city paid some $25,000 for the land. No appropriation is made for maintenance.

PLACES OF AMUSEMENT.

There is one theater in Shreveport—Tally's opera-house—with a seating capacity of 400. There are also 2 halls, seating 250 each. All exhibitions pay a license to the city, and the annual revenue from this source aggregates $500. There is one beer-garden, seating 100 people, size 60 by 70 feet, open only in summer, and patronized exclusively by men. There is no singing or music in this garden.

DRAINAGE; CEMETERIES; MARKETS.

No information on the above subjects was furnished.

SANITARY AUTHORITY—BOARD OF HEALTH.

The chief sanitary authority of Shreveport is the board of health, an independent organization, composed of 5 members—2 physicians and 1 citizen being appointed by the governor and 1 physician and 1 citizen being appointed by the mayor by and with the advice and consent of the city council. The annual expense of the board in ordinary times is about $2,000, for salaries of health officer and sanitary policeman, and for day scavenger-carts. In case of an epidemic the expense can be increased to any amount deemed necessary to meet the emergency, the board and city council in joint session making the assessment. In absence of epidemics the board has authority to execute all sanitary measures. During epidemics the law requires the concurrence of the city council in order to establish quarantine, after which the board has full power. The chief executive officer is the health officer, with an annual salary of $500. His duties are to carry into effect the provisions of the act creating the board, to see that all health ordinances are carried out, and to execute all orders of the board; he is also secretary. One sanitary policeman is employed, who acts under the direction of the health officer. The board transacts its business as a deliberative body. Inspections are made regularly from house to house throughout the city. A complaint-book is also kept open at the health office, in which any and all nuisances can be entered, and such entries receive prompt attention. When nuisances are discovered or reported, the health officer, or sanitary policeman under his direction, immediately notifies the owner or tenant of the premises to abate the same, and refusal or neglect to do so within the time designated subjects the offender to fine in the mayor's court. So far the board has done little or nothing concerning the inspection and correction of defective house-drainage. There are neither privy-vaults nor cesspools nor sewers in the city. The board exercises sufficient control over the conservation and removal of garbage to prevent it becoming a nuisance. No body can be buried in or removed from the city without a permit from the health officer showing that all requirements have been complied with. The board has no regulations concerning the pollution of streams, but it controls the removal of excrement.

INFECTIOUS DISEASES.

Small-pox patients are isolated by being sent to the pest-house, situated 1 mile below the city, on the river-bank, in a very unfrequented place. Scarlet-fever patients are neither quarantined at home nor isolated, nor does the board take cognizance of the breaking out of contagious diseases in either public or private schools. Vaccination is not compulsory; it is done by the health officer gratuitously, on application.

All births, marriages, and deaths are required to be reported to the board for registry in books kept for that purpose.

REPORTS.

The board makes no reports, except a weekly mortality report to the secretary of the National Board of Health.

MUNICIPAL CLEANSING.

Street-cleaning.—The streets are cleaned at the expense of the city with its regular force. The work is done wholly by hand. The cleaning is confined almost exclusively to gutters, and is thoroughly done daily in the main streets and alleys. The annual cost of the work is $1,800, and the sweepings are dumped into the river. It is reported that the system is the only practical one for a city of this size, and that the river is an advantageous place for final deposit.

Removal of garbage and ashes.—Garbage is removed both by the city and by householders. Pending removal it is required to be kept in suitable vessels, and is taken at night by the *vidangeurs*. Ashes may be kept in the same vessel, and both garbage and ashes are disposed of in the same way, by being dumped into the river. The annual cost to the city is about $900; the cost to householders is not given. In spite of sanitary ordinances the garbage is often thrown into open lots, streets, and gutters, where it is tramped into the soil. The mayor reports that the defect of the system is "the impossibility of a human all-seeing eye to prevent careless, thoughtless, and filthy people from violating the sanitary laws".

Dead animals.—The carcasses of all animals dying in the city are thrown into the Red river, the matter being under supervision of the police and the health officer. The cost of this service is included in the general street-work. It is remarked that the carcasses should be buried deep in the soil as a better means of disposal.

Liquid household wastes and human excreta.—Chamber-slops are thrown into privy receptacles, while laundry wastes and kitchen-slops are run into the gutters and ditches. These privy receptacles are either half-barrels, or else boxes 2 feet square and 18 inches deep. When full they are removed by regular licensed *vidangeurs*, who act under rules and regulations of the board of health, and the contents are dumped into the Red river. It is reported that these receptacles are poor, fall to pieces, and often deliver their contents into the streets and alleys. The dry-earth system is used only to a very limited extent.

Manufacturing wastes.—There is only one manufacturing establishment in Shreveport, and it delivers its waste into the river. Being situated above the city, the waste passes its front.

POLICE.

No information on this subject was furnished.

TEXAS.

AUSTIN,
TRAVIS COUNTY, TEXAS.

POPULATION

IN THE

AGGREGATE,

1840-1880.

	Inhab.
1790	......
1800	......
1810	......
1820	......
1830	......
1840	806
1850	*629
1860	3,494
1870	4,428
1880	11,013

* Exclusive of slaves.

POPULATION

BY

SEX, NATIVITY, AND RACE,

AT

CENSUS OF 1880.

Male	5,473
Female	5,540
Native	9,628
Foreign-born	1,385
White	7,407
Colored	3,606

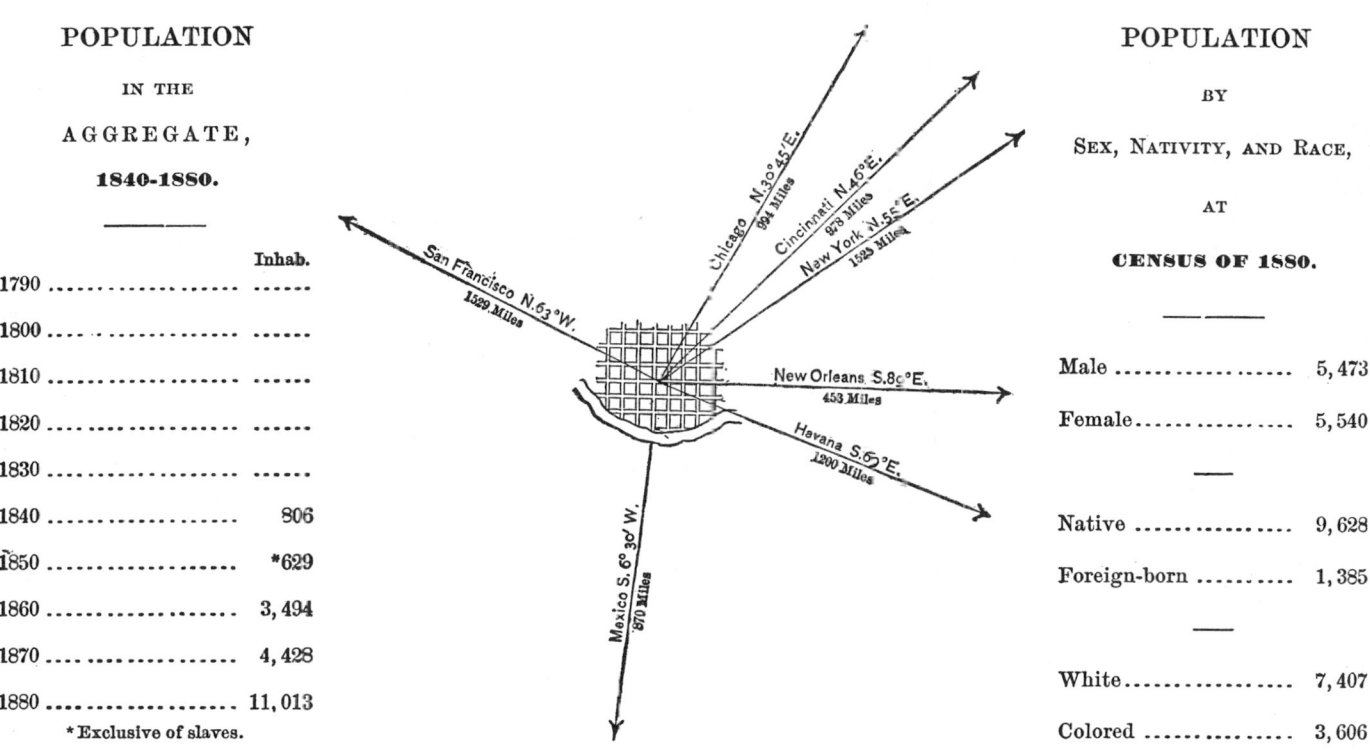

Latitude: 30° 6′ 25″ North; Longitude: 97° 43′ (from Greenwich); Altitude: 376 to 718 feet.

FINANCIAL CONDITION:

Total Valuation: $4,949,534; per capita: $449 00.   Net Indebtedness: $106,744; per capita: $9 69.   Tax per $100: $1 90.

HISTORICAL SKETCH.

The declaration of independence of Texas having been made March 2, 1836, Houston was made the temporary capital.   On the 14th of January, 1837, by act of congress, commissioners were appointed to select a proper site for the permanent capital.   The conditions imposed were that the tract should lie between the Colorado and the Trinity rivers, and above the old San Antonio road; that it should be taken from public lands, by purchase or by donation, and that it should contain not more than four leagues and not less than one league of land; the price not to exceed three dollars per acre.   The act provided for the appointment of an agent to lay out in town lots one square mile of the tract so selected, retaining a sufficient number of the most desirable lots for public buildings, and selling not more than half the remainder at public sale.   The act provided that the capital should be called the City of Austin, in commemoration of Moses Austin, a former resident of Missouri, who inaugurated the first scheme for the settlement of Texas by colonization from the western part of the United States; a scheme which, after his death, was carried into effect by his son, Stephen F. Austin.   After weighing the claims of different localities, the commissioners decided in favor of a hamlet containing then but two families, and called Waterloo, on the east bank of the Colorado river, where they purchased the land and made a report to the president, describing the same and its advantages. This report closed with the following:

The commissioners confidently anticipate the time when a great thoroughfare shall be established from Santa Fé to our seaports, and another from Red river to Matamoros, which two routes must almost of necessity intersect each other at this point. They look forward to the time when this city shall be the emporium of not only the productions of the rich soil of the San Saba, Pendernales, Hero, and Pecan bayou, but of all the Colorado and Brazos, as also of the produce of the rich mining country known to exist on those streams. They are satisfied that a truly national city could, at no other point within the limits assigned them, be reared up; not that other sections of the country are not equally fertile, but that no other combined so many and such varied advantages and beauties as the one in question. The imagination of even the romantic will not be disappointed on viewing the valley of the Colorado and the fertile and gracefully undulating woodlands and luxuriant prairies at a distance from it. The most skeptical will not doubt its healthiness, and the citizen's bosom must swell with honest pride when, standing in the portico of the capitol of his country, he looks abroad upon a region worthy only of being the home of the brave and the free. Standing on the juncture of the routes of Santa Fé and the sea-coast, of Red river and Matamoros, looking with the same glance upon the green, romantic mountains and the fertile and widely extended plains of his country, can a feeling of nationality fail to arise in his bosom, or could the fire of patriotism lie dormant under such circumstances?

A land agent was immediately appointed for laying out the land, and on the 1st day of August, 1839, the first sale of lots took place, the sales amounting to $182,588. During the month of October the city grew rapidly; public as well as private building was energetically pushed to completion. On the 17th of this month the president, accompanied by a portion of his cabinet, arrived at Austin. General A. Sidney Johnson, secretary of war, and General Burleson, followed by a procession of citizens, met the president a few miles out of the city. The usual address of welcome was delivered, and festivities followed.

There had been erected for the use of the government a frame building, inclosed by a stockade, as capitol (on the present site of the city market), and on the opposite side of the hill another frame building, which served as an executive mansion, log cabins being built for the accommodation of the heads of departments.

The arrival of these officers gave a new impetus to the city; emigration poured in, and improvements progressed more rapidly than before.

During this same month the *Austin City Gazette* was started, and was followed soon after by *The Sentinel*. A reading-room was opened, and on the 11th of November, 1839, the first session of the fourth congress met at the capitol. A proposition was made agitating a change of the seat of government. A bill calling for a vote of the people to settle the matter was introduced, supported among others by General Houston, a congressman from the St. Augustine country. It was, however, voted down, and the question for a time remained at rest.

On the 13th of January, congress having incorporated the city of Austin, an election was held for city officers; and on the same day the first meeting of the supreme court of Texas was here held, the session occupying 13 days. The duties of the mayor of the city were not complicated, but consisted largely in keeping the community in a state of intelligent defense against occasional Indian raids, which were apprehended with reason, but which were never of a very serious character.

In the spring of 1840 a census of the city was taken, showing a total population of 806, of whom 550 were adult men and 150 were blacks. They were a heterogeneous assemblage, including representatives of almost every nation and profession.

During the year 1841 Austin continued to increase. The independence of Texas had been acknowledged by the United States, France, Great Britain, and Belgium. M. de Saligny, the French minister, with a scientific corps, had already arrived, and had built for himself the finest house then in Texas. His relations with the government were, however, of short duration. It appears that one of his servants had killed some pigs that annoyed him, which belonged to Mr. Bullock. Mr. Bullock whipped the servant, and thereby enraged the minister, who called upon Mr. Bullock and was ordered off the premises. The minister, conceiving that the honor of France had been compromised, demanded of the president that he rebuke Mr. Bullock. The president refused to interfere in a personal quarrel, and referred him to the civil authorities. The subsequent behavior of M. de Saligny was such that the president asked of the French government that he be recalled, which request was promptly granted. This petty quarrel became a matter of public interest, inasmuch as it led to the breaking off of negotiations for a loan about to be made by the French government to the government of Texas.

An election for president was held on the first Monday in September, 1841. Three names were prominent among the nominations: those of General Sam. Houston, David G. Burnet, and Governor Welsh. The latter promised, if elected, to serve for a salary of $500 per annum, to pay his own expenses, and to do the public blacksmithing free of charge. General Houston was elected; and on the second Monday of December was inaugurated president of the Republic of Texas. He established many reforms, and enforced rigid economy. But, notwithstanding this fact, owing to loose regulations for the collection of customs (most of the goods consumed in the eastern part of the state being smuggled across the Sabine river), the public credit and the currency gradually improved.

Early in the spring of 1842 General Vasquez, at the head of 1,200 Mexican regulars, invaded Texas, sacking San Antonio on the 6th of March. A citizen escaping at sunrise reached Austin about dusk with the astounding news. Great energy was shown, and by the morning of the 8th Austin had mustered from 1,500 to 2,000 citizen soldiers. The president became greatly alarmed, and issued an order forbidding any soldiers to leave the city. He ordered the archives removed to Houston. In spite of his orders, however, many soldiers did leave for the front the same night. Meanwhile the government officers were rapidly preparing to leave the town, burying many of the less important archives which they could not well carry away. The next morning the executive department and other officials departed for the lower country. The Austin soldiers, returning after Vasquez had been driven beyond the Nueces river, disbanded and returned to their homes, where they beheld a discouraging sight. The flourishing young city which they had left a month before, was now a straggling "deserted village". Four or five families and about 25 men only had remained. These, with the few who had previously returned from San Antonio, had organized for their own safety and for the security of the remaining government archives. A consideration of the position of affairs caused great exasperation. Over half a million dollars had been expended for land alone, and the value of their property was threatened, if not destroyed. In spite of the most earnest solicitation the president refused to return, and soon afterward issued a proclamation convening congress in extra session at Houston on the 21st of March. These measures decided the people of Austin to take the affairs of the city into their own hands. During the removal of the officials, the papers of the general land office had been left behind; these, the citizens determined to retain. The president sent a commissioner to remove these archives. He was sent back, with the information that the people of Austin considered that city the seat of government, and would not allow their removal. An archive committee and a vigilance committee were formed. And although the commissioner of the general land office retained charge of the archives, and was in sympathy with the government, he did not dare attempt their removal. So jealously were these archives guarded, that at times the baggage of persons leaving the city was examined. Late in September the president made several attempts to induce the people of Austin to allow the archives to be removed; but they persistently refused to do so. Dependent at this time, as they were, mainly on their rifles as a means of subsistence, their ammunition became exhausted. They applied to the officer in charge of the arsenal for ammunition for their actual needs. This being refused in the absence of a requisition, and the refusal being persisted in, they surrounded his house, got possession of the keys of the arsenal, helped themselves to what they required, and removed a howitzer, with its caisson and ammunition, placing them under guard in the shed near the corner of Congress avenue and Pecan street, intending to use the same as a means of defense and as the signal for the assemblage of the population.

In September of this year Mexico sent out a still more formidable invading army, under General Woll, who, at daybreak on the morning of the 14th, at the head of about 2,000 troops, entered San Antonio, meeting with little or no resistance. The district court was in session at the time, and so complete was the surprise that he captured the presiding judge and other officers of the court. The citizens of Gonzalez, receiving notice on the same day of the capture of San Antonio, mustered to the number of 80 and marched to meet the enemy. Others joined them on the road, augmenting their number to 220. Woll was drawn out from San Antonio by a skirmishing party, which he followed to the position of the Texans, on the Salado, about seven miles east of San Antonio, where, being decidedly worsted, he withdrew, having lost heavily. This action is supposed to have changed Woll's plans, and instead of advancing to Austin he continued his retreat to Mexico. Until the end of the year the peace of Austin was broken only by occasional Indian raids. On the morning of the 29th December, 1842, without warning of their approach, an armed force of 35 men had entered Austin, had reached the government buildings and loaded three wagons with the land-office archives before they were discovered. The citizens remonstrated, but the party announced their determination to take the archives to Houston, stating that they had an ample force outside of the town to carry out their purpose in spite of any opposition. They were informed that the people of Austin were as firmly determined to retain the archives; and some show of resistance was made, including a discharge of the captured howitzer; which, while ineffective as against the marauding party, assembled on the ground all within hearing of its report. The removing party started their teams for Bushy creek, pursued by a body of citizens whose progress was retarded by the attempt to carry the howitzer with them; so that they were not overtaken until nightfall, at their camp in the Bushy valley. On being overtaken, Captain Smith, who headed the party removing the archives, endeavored to effect a compromise. He was informed that nothing short of the return of the archives would be listened to. This he refused. However, the next morning he again visited the camp and became satisfied from their tone and numbers that it was useless to resist them; he proposed to turn the documents over to them. It was insisted that he should carry them back himself to Austin, which he finally agreed to do. As both parties were on their way back, Captain Smith's men, being mounted, left the road under pretense of watering their horses, and did not return. On the arrival of the citizens with the recovered archives there was great rejoicing. This is substantially all of what is known in Texas as the "Archive war", an episode which, while trifling in itself, doubtless determined the permanent maintenance of the capital at Austin, no further efforts having been made to get control of these most important papers. During the summer of 1843 the Indians increased their hostility and activity. Provisions became very scarce; shoes and clothing were mostly of home manufacture and of the rudest character, and there was great suffering on all hands. The status did not improve during the subsequent year. In 1844 there was a new election of president. The great question now agitating the whole of Texas related to its annexation to the United States. In 1836 that government had declined to take Texas, doubting its ability to maintain its independence. The sentiment in its favor, however, had been growing in the meantime, and the Congress which met in 1844 adopted measures looking to the accomplishment of the purpose. The question was introduced into the United States Senate by Mr. Calhoun, in April, 1844, but was defeated. In the presidential election of this year, the annexation of Texas became a leading issue; and on this issue Mr. Polk was elected.

On the 1st of March, 1845, a joint resolution of Congress to admit Texas into the Union was passed, and received the signature of President Tyler. The Texan congress assembled at Austin on the 4th of July, 1845, and on the first day of its session the annexation bill was passed, and Austin was recognized as the seat of government until 1850. The first state legislature assembled in Austin, and on the 19th of February, 1846, President Jones handed over the executive authority to J. Pinckney Henderson, the first governor of the new state of Texas. Immediately after the annexation a considerable influx of settlers was noticeable. Most of them were without means, and added little to the immediate material wealth of Austin. The old settlers had unshaken faith in the future of the city, and continued to make such improvements as their small means permitted. Lots increased in value, new surveys and subdivisions were made, and the city gradually extended its limits. In accordance with the provisions of the state constitution, an election was held in 1850 to determine the location of the capital for twenty years, resulting in favor of Austin. About the beginning of 1851 the necessity for providing churches and school-houses had become manifest, and several of these edifices were erected. At about the same time a number of business men were attracted to Austin, and several substantial brick and stone buildings were constructed. An attempt was made to establish steam navigation on the river, but the difficulty of navigation and the limited demand for such service soon caused regular trips to be abandoned. Communication with distant points was established, and the surrounding country gradually became settled. The prosperity of Austin continued to increase steadily until 1861, when the breaking out of the war of the Rebellion checked all improvement and had a very depressing effect on trade, which thenceforth for some years was confined mainly to traffic with Mexico.

During the war Austin contributed largely in men and means to the confederate army. The close of the war found all of its interests and industries very greatly depressed, and no material progress was made thereafter until it became certain that a projected railroad would make Austin its terminal point. This gave an impetus to the growth of the city, such as it had not known before. After the building of the Houston and Texas Central railroad, in 1871, the place began to develop into a city. Prosperity appeared on every hand, and the population increased to about ten thousand, more than double that of the year before.

In 1877 Austin had grown to a population popularly estimated at 16,000, and had become a regularly laid-out city, with blocks of buildings of considerable pretensions. "Hundreds of costly residences greet the eye on every side; a dozen church spires point aloft to the clouds; institutions of learning to prepare the youthful mind for the duties of maturer years are numerous. The daily papers carry the news from all quarters of the globe to their thousands of readers, while the hum of the mill-wheel, the ring of the anvil, and the scream of the steam-whistle attest the already developing manufacturing interests of the city." The city directory of that year gives account of 13 churches, 10 educational establishments of considerable pretension, beside 11 private schools, Masonic lodges, Odd Fellows' lodges, Hebrew associations, and other secret and benevolent societies, water-works, gas-works, a city railway, two ice companies, shooting clubs, theaters, halls, and four newspapers.

AUSTIN IN 1880.

The following statistical accounts, collected by the Census Office, indicate the present condition of Austin:

LOCATION.

Austin lies in latitude 30° 6' 25'' north; in longitude 97° 43' west. Its elevation above the sea-level is at an average of about 550 feet. The Colorado river, on which the city lies, is not navigable. The low-water level of the river at the foot of Congress avenue is 376 feet above mean coast-tide. The summit of Mount Bonnell, three miles back, is 718 feet.

RAILROAD COMMUNICATIONS.

Austin is touched by the following railroads: The Houston and Texas Central railroad, terminus at Sherman, Texas; the International and Great Northern, termini at Longview and San Antonio. The latter is being fast pushed beyond San Antonio to the Rio Grande, and northward to connect with the main western railway system.

TRIBUTARY COUNTRY.

The country immediately tributary to Austin is mainly agricultural. The soil on the rivers and stream margins is alluvial. On the table lands it is argillaceous, and rich with vegetable matter. Both of these soils are of great fertility. Within a radius of about five miles nearly one-half the country is considerably wooded. The underlying rock is cretaceous limestone, especially adapted for building purposes. The region is very undulating, the average in the district immediately about the city being about 500 feet.

TOPOGRAPHY.

The following statement concerning the topography of Austin is condensed from notes furnished by John W. Glenn, C. E., Austin, Texas:

The city is situated on the Colorado river. The floor of the railroad bridge crossing the river is 451 feet above mean tide. The principal part of the city is about 150 feet higher than this. The natural drainage of the city is perfect in all parts. Johnson's creek, Shoal creek, and Waller creek give a rapid discharge for the drainage of an area of about ten square miles, which passes through the city limits. Congress avenue, West creek, Raymond's creek, and Pease creek are important auxiliary channels. The Colorado river is a rapid, clear stream, especially adapted to receive and carry away rapidly any sewage that may flow to it from the city. On the other side of the river there is a series of large springs, which are sufficient to supply a city of half a million with excellent water. The country to the northwest is broken; some of the summits, locally called "mountains", reaching an elevation of over 300 feet above the highest point of the city. To the northeast, south, and southwest the country is more level and extremely fertile. There are no marshes, ponds, or lakes in the vicinity. The agricultural character of this district is indicated by the fact that in the average of years it produces three-quarters of a bale of cotton, 30 bushels of corn, 20 bushels of wheat, or 75 bushels of oats per acre. Hay from the sweet bottom-grass is yielded at a rate of from three to four tons per acre. The usual garden products are abundantly produced, and pears, peaches, plums, raspberries, and melons thrive.

CLIMATE.

The highest recorded summer temperature is 106°. The highest summer temperature in average years, 88°. The lowest recorded winter temperature, 6°. Lowest winter temperature in average years, 46°.

During the summer season the city is subject to the tropical trade-winds.

STREETS.

Total length, 72.63 miles. None of the streets are paved, but about three-quarters of a mile of Congress avenue is finished with broken stone.

The city is hilly, the surface-drainage is active, and the soil is mostly gravel, so that the streets are maintained in a fair condition at very little cost. The amount expended during the fiscal year ending November 2, 1879, for grading and repairing streets and building bridges, was $12,505 59.

The streets become muddy under heavy rains, but a few days of sun and wind restore them to good condition. On Congress avenue and Pecan street the sidewalks are paved with limestone slabs. These are the only finished sidewalks of any considerable extent. On these two streets the gutters are made with cobble-stones, and are set with limestone curbs, 6 inches thick and 18 inches deep. The city has very few trees in the streets, and no grassed places. By the city ordinances all street work amounting to over $100 must be done by contract, and this system is considered advantageous. There is a horse railroad one and one-half mile in length, with 6 cars, 14 horses, and 9 employés. The total number of passengers carried during the year was 20,000, and the rate of fare is 5 cents. There are no regular omnibus lines. The works for water-supply are the property of a private corporation. The reservoir is 2½ miles from the pumping station, and has a capacity of 2,500,000 gallons. The pressure in the street mains is from 65 to 85 pounds. The water is elevated by 2 Blake steam-pumps, the average pumping being 450,000 gallons per diem. The gas-works are owned by a private corporation. The average daily production is 15,000 cubic feet. The charge per thousand is $4. The city pays $40 per annum for each street-lamp, 100 in number. The income from private meters and from street-lamps is given as $18,000 per annum.

PUBLIC BUILDINGS.

The city owns and occupies for municipal uses, wholly or in part, 2 engine-houses, 1 hook-and-ladder house, and 1 combined market-house and city hall, which cost $13,616 29. The total cost of the municipal buildings belonging to the city is $17,117 29.

The state and county buildings are separate from those occupied by the city.

PUBLIC PARKS AND PLEASURE-GROUNDS.

The total area of the public parks is 29.8 acres. There are 4 small parks, as yet without names, located in different parts of the city proper, each containing 1.7 acre. *Pease Park*, in the northwest quarter of the city, contains 23 acres. These parks are as yet entirely unimproved. The land was donated to the city; the single appropriation of $500 for their improvement has not yet been expended.

PLACES OF AMUSEMENT.

Millett's opera-house has a seating capacity of 1,400. Smith's opera-house has a seating capacity of 700.

Jones' commercial library, in which weekly concerts are given, has a seating capacity of 500.

Tip's hall, the meeting room of the Austin Mænnerchor, has a seating capacity of 700.

Theaters pay a license when an admission fee is charged. The revenue from this source is $250 per annum.

Scholz's hall and beer garden have a seating capacity of 300 in the hall and 250 in the garden. This hall is held by the Germania society and is well patronized, though no statistics on this point are furnished. The cost of its construction is not given.

The Turner hall and beer garden, constructed in 1872 at a cost of about $20,000, including land purchased, has a seating capacity of 400 in the hall and about 4,000 in the garden.

CEMETERY.

Austin has a public cemetery which is the property of the city and under the charge of the public sexton, an officer appointed by the mayor, who is required to give bonds of $1,000 per annum for the faithful performance of his duty. Ground in the cemetery is sold to private persons, the price for a single grave being five dollars, with increasing rates up to a full block at $50; the deed of sale is made by the mayor.

By ordinance—

The sexton shall keep a map or plat of the portions of the cemetery not divided into blocks or lots, and also a record-book of the same; and, whenever any burial of any stranger, pauper, or other person shall have been made in such portion, shall make a record of the same, giving a description of the spot, the name of the person so buried, if known, and mark the same upon his map to show that the interment has there been made, and report the same to the city clerk.

The sexton shall receive within the cemetery no corpse unless the bearer or bearers thereof shall deliver to him the certificate of a licensed physician, or of the mayor, or some magistrate or coroner, containing a statement of the place from whence taken, the cause of death, sex, color, and the name of each, if known. And if the bearer or bearers, as aforesaid, shall refuse to give the certificate as above, or if the body be borne to another place for burial, after application as above to the sexton, the sexton shall notify the mayor of the fact at once in order that he may proceed to inquire if any crime has been committed.

* * * * * * * * * * * *

The sexton shall faithfully inter in their appropriate places the dead bodies of all persons properly presented to him for interment; he shall prepare the ground for their reception in a proper manner as promptly as possible, taking care that no grave shall be less than four feet in depth; he shall superintend the depositing of the body and refill and properly finish the grave after the body has been buried, and preserve order and quiet while the same is being done, and for his services shall be entitled to the following fees:

For digging grave and for the interment of persons buried at the cost of the city	$2 50
For digging grave and interment of other persons, to be paid by the person contracting therefor	5 00
For superintending the work of interment where the work is done by others	2 00
For disinterment, removal, and reinterment of a body, for the whole work	15 00

which shall in all cases include the cost of removing the dirt and cleaning up the streets.

* * * * * * * * * * *

It shall not be lawful for any person to have a grave dug or a body buried in the city cemetery without the knowledge and approval of the sexton, nor upon any ground therein, without the written consent of the person owning or controlling the same; and if a grave be so dug or a dead body so buried in places not purchased by the person so digging and burying, or by those under whose authority he acts, the sexton shall cause the grave to be closed or the body to be disinterred and buried in that portion of the cemetery set aside for the interment of strangers. And the sexton's fees therefor shall be collected as other costs against the person or persons so offending.

It shall not be lawful for any person to disinter, or remove from any grave or vault in the city cemetery, any dead body, or any of the articles thereto belonging, except upon the written consent of the nearest friends of the deceased, the written order of the mayor, and under the superintendence of the sexton.

* * * * * * * * * * *

The mayor may, using a sound discretion, order the burial in the city cemetery of the dead body of any pauper or person thrown upon the care of the city, without friends, at the cost of the city.

* * * * * * * * * * *

The ordinances also make the usual provisions for the protection and care of the cemetery.

MARKETS.

A considerable tract of land in Austin was set apart by the legislature of the state of Texas in 1856, to be used exclusively and permanently as a city market. Its regulation is in the hands of the city council.

Concerning the leasing of the stalls there is this somewhat unusual provision:

The lessee or lessees shall pay in cash at the time of renting said stall or stalls one-half of the amount bid for the same, and shall at once execute his or their promissory notes, with at least two good and solvent securities to be approved by the mayor, for the payment of the remaining one-half of the amount on the 31st day of August, or the 28th day of February, as they may have rented for the six months beginning March 1 or September 1; said notes shall bear interest at the rate of ten per cent. per annum from date until paid.

The ordinance contains the following provisions:

All fresh meats, fish, or vegetables intended for the people of the city shall be brought to the city market, or to some other market established by the city council, as hereinafter provided, to be sold or disposed of during market hours: *Provided,* That any person shall have the right to sell butcher's meat in quantities not less than the whole animal, or any produce of his own soil, or game killed by him, or fish caught by him, anywhere in the city, after market hours: *And provided further,* That any licensed butcher may deliver butcher's meat to his regular customers anywhere within the city at all times, provided the same shall first be exposed in the market for the inspection of the market-master.

* * * * * * * * * * *

It shall not be lawful for any person to establish any slaughter-house in this city, or to slaughter any animal for butcher's meat within the limits of the said city, except for the use of the person so slaughtering.

* * * * * * * * * * *

Immediately and within one-half hour after the closing of the city market on each day, each lessee shall scrape, wash, sweep, and thoroughly cleanse every part of the stall or stand occupied by him or her, and to the middle of the hall or pass-way in front thereof, and shall keep the same in the highest state of cleanliness. And they shall within the same time remove their tubs and barrels containing refuse matter, and shall thoroughly cleanse the same before returning them to the stall. Said lessee or lessees shall be neat and clean in their personal appearance while in attendance at the stalls; butchers shall not be permitted to wear bloody, greasy or soiled clothes, or such as they may have worn while butchering.

* * * * * * * * * * *

No person shall be permitted to hawk, peddle, or sell any kind of goods, wares, or merchandise in said city market, or on the sidewalks and footways surrounding the same, except as herein provided.

Within one-half hour of the closing of the market on each day, all meats, poultry, vegetables, fish, and other articles left over and not sold shall be removed from said market, and the same shall not be returned thereto until the hour provided for.

*   *   *   *   *   *   *   *

The other provisions of the ordinances relate to the usual rules and precautions of city markets in warm climates.

SANITARY AUTHORITY—BOARD OF HEALTH.

The chief health organization of Austin is a board of health appointed by the mayor, consisting exclusively of physicians. There are 5 members who work without compensation. The president receives a salary of $600, but as city physician, not as president of the board. So far as any increase of expense during an epidemic is concerned, the board can act only to the extent of making recommendations to the board of aldermen. In the absence of epidemics it has authority to abate nuisances, and take charge of contagious or infectious diseases. Its authority, by law absolute, is really greatly limited by the fact that it is dependent on the city council for funds with which to carry out its enactments. During epidemics, with the possible restriction above mentioned, its power is absolute.

HEALTH ORDINANCES.

ARTICLE 271 (2). It shall be the duty of the health physician to see that all the provisions of the ordinances of the city relative to health are strictly complied with; and to this end he shall have power, concurrent with the city marshal, to see that the health inspectors and policemen perform their duty faithfully in ascertaining and making complaint against the authors of all nuisances. He shall superintend the city hospitals, visit the city work-house and jail, and take charge of and attend all cases of disease or accident certified to him by the mayor as demanding medical attention.

ART. 272 (3). It shall be the duty of the health physician, whenever, in his opinion, any thing, or state of things, in this city is or may become a nuisance, or dangerous to the health of the city, to certify the same to the mayor, who shall, if necessary, order the city marshal to cause the same to be removed, corrected, abated, or destroyed; and thereupon it shall be the duty of the city marshal to notify the author of said nuisance, or the person owning or controlling the property or thing which is or may be liable to become a nuisance, to remove, correct, or abate the same; and in case of the refusal or failure of said person to comply with such notice, it shall be his duty to cause the same to be done, calling such assistance as may be necessary therefor, and all costs attending such action shall be charged to the author of said nuisance, or to the person owning or controlling the property on which the same exists, and said costs shall be collected as other costs: *Provided*, That nothing herein contained shall be so construed as to prevent a proceeding against the same party or parties for any misdemeanor of which they may have been guilty in the premises.

ART. 273 (4). It shall be the duty of the health physician to keep himself advised of the existence of any pestilential, contagious, or infectious diseases at all ports or other places within the state; and if at any time there may, in his opinion, be danger of such disease being introduced into this city, he may require the owner, driver, conductor, or person or persons in charge of any railway car, engine, or train, stage coach or wagon, carriage, or other vehicle, or any person or persons whatever, to remain in quarantine at such place or places and for such period as the city council may direct.

ART. 274 (5). It shall be the duty of the health physician, whenever he is informed of the existence of any pestilential, contagious, or infectious disease within this city, to cause the person or persons so diseased to be taken to such place as he may designate, away from all probable danger of communication, for treatment; and such place shall become a pest-house, and shall be under exclusive control of the health physician, who shall issue such orders as will, if possible, prevent the spread of such disease.

ART. 275 (6). It shall be the duty of every physician, hotel-keeper, or other person in this city to report at once to the health physician any case of pestilential, contagious, or infectious disease which may in any manner come to their knowledge.

ART. 276 (7). It shall not be lawful for the owner, driver, conductor, or person in charge of any engine, car, train, stage, carriage, or other vehicle whatever, to bring to or transport within this city any person afflicted with any pestilential, contagious, or infectious disease, or any property whatever infected with the same.

ART. 277 (8). The health physician may establish such sanitary regulations for the government of places under his charge as he may deem necessary, with the consent of the city council, and it shall not be lawful for any person to violate such regulations when so established, nor at any time to interfere with or hinder the health physician in the discharge of his duty.

ART. 278 (9). Whenever it becomes necessary, for the preservation of health or the prevention of disease, to use any disinfectant, or to use any other precaution therefor, the mayor may, by consent of the council, order the same to be done, and it shall be deemed a misdemeanor for any person in this city to fail or refuse to obey such order.

*   *   *   *   *   *   *   *

ART. 280 (11). The mayor may, by and with the advice and consent of the board of aldermen, whenever it is deemed necessary, appoint health inspectors for the city, to the number of one for each ward, who may be removed at any time by the mayor or the city council, and whose compensation shall be the same as that of policemen.

ART. 281 (12). It shall be the duty of the health inspectors to ascertain every nuisance which may exist in this city, or in the ward or wards to which they may be assigned, and forthwith have the same corrected, or abated, or reported to the proper officer. And in the discharge of their duties they may enter upon any premises or into any house in this city where they may have reason to believe any nuisance may exist, may examine into the condition and cleanliness of any premises, inspect vaults, privies, stables, and other outbuildings, and shall execute all orders of the council, mayor, or health physician.

ART. 282 (13). The word "nuisance", as used in this connection shall be understood to mean anything whatever that may be liable, or about to become liable, to affect the health or comfort of the people of the city of Austin; and it shall be the duty of the health inspectors to report, as such, all premises, houses, vaults, privies, sinks, stables, smoke-houses, lumber-rooms, undrained grounds, stagnant water, hog-pens, barn-yards, cemeteries, slaughter-houses, hotels, boarding-houses, restaurants, market-houses or stalls, streets, alleys, sidewalks, or other grounds, houses, or premises, and all pestilential, contagious, or infectious diseases in man or animal, or whatever may, in their opinion, be liable to affect the health of the city.

ART. 283 (14). Any person or persons violating any of the provisions of the preceding articles relative to health regulations shall be deemed guilty of a misdemeanor, and on conviction shall be punished by fine, or otherwise, as in other cases of misdemeanor.

SANITARY INSPECTOR.

The board is assisted in its work by one inspector who acts as market-master and health-inspector. He has police powers not only in sanitary matters, but in all respects the same as the regular police. His duties include the inspection of all parts of the town and the abatement of nuisances. He has full power to prosecute for the enforcement of the penalties of fine and imprisonment.

HOUSE-DRAINAGE.

There is no law or custom concerning the inspection and correction of defective house-drainage, privy vaults, cesspools, sources of drinking water, etc. But the inspector has power, and it is his duty, to look after cesspools and privies, and to order them emptied when necessary. He has also the general supervision of streets.

GARBAGE.

The board exercises no control concerning the conservation and removal of garbage, further than to prevent its being scattered or deposited in the public streets.

BURIAL OF THE DEAD.

No interment is permitted unless the certificate of the attendant physician is delivered to the sexton. He makes monthly returns of these certificates to the president of the board of health.

INFECTIOUS DISEASES.

Small-pox patients are removed to the pest-house, outside the city limits. Scarlet-fever has never been an epidemic in Austin, and there is no custom relating to the isolation or home quarantine of patients.

The board takes no cognizance of the breaking out of contagious diseases in public and private schools.

Vaccination is not compulsory, but at certain seasons it is done at the public expense on application of the city physician.

There is no system of registration of diseases, births, and deaths beyond the recording of the physician's certificate for burial.

REPORTS OF THE BOARD OF HEALTH.

The board reports to the board of aldermen at each of its meetings, which occur as occasion requires.

In seeking for information concerning the board of health, indications were found that it may be much hampered in its action by the dissent of the city council, and of physicians who are not members of the board. Nominally the power of the board is all that is necessary; but virtually the co-operation of the mayor and council is necessary for its best efficiency.

MUNICIPAL CLEANSING.

Street-cleaning.—The streets are cleaned at the expense of the city, and by its own regular force. The work is done by hand, no sweeping-machines being used. The work is performed every day or as required; and in connection with the natural cleansing due to the rapid slope, and thorough washing of the streets by storms, it is efficient. The cost of the work is about $1,250 per annum. Matters removed from the streets are deposited outside the city limits.

Removal of garbage and ashes.—Garbage is removed by householders, and ashes by the city's own force. The regulation concerning the conservancy of garbage requires that it be kept in barrels, and that these be emptied, and the garbage removed within twelve hours. It is permitted to keep ashes and garbage in the same vessel, though ashes are often used in the disinfection of privy vaults. The cost of removal, so far as it is done by the city, is included in the cost of street-cleaning. It is thought that no injury to the public health results from the improper keeping of garbage on premises, from infrequent removal, from improper handling, or from improper final disposal.

Dead animals.—The owner is required to remove the carcass of any animal dying, to a point at least one thousand yards beyond the city limits, immediately after its death. Failure in this respect subjects the offender to a heavy penalty. If the owner is not known, the carcass is removed by the city's force. There is no record of the cost of this service, and the number of animals removed, irrespective of dogs (of which about 600 die annually), is about 50.

Liquid household wastes.—There are no sewers in Austin. Laundry and kitchen wastes may be run into the street gutters; chamber-slops being usually deposited in privy vaults. Dry wells or cesspools other than privy vaults are not used. The gutters are flushed as occasion requires; at some seasons as often as two or three times each week, and at others not more than once a month. Drinking-water is stored in tight cisterns; and in so far as these are actually tight, no contamination arises.

Human excreta.—There are few if any water-closets in Austin, the use of vaults being universal. In the more thickly settled parts of the city it is stated that these vaults are tight boxes. The only regulations concerning the construction and emptying of privy vaults relate to their depth and location.

Privy vaults are under the direct supervision of the health inspector, who, when occasion requires, orders them emptied by the licensed scavenger, between the hours of 12 midnight and 4 a. m. The matters removed must be deposited like garbage at least one thousand yards outside the city limits. There is no law concerning the use of night-soil as a manure; but such use is at least very rare. There is no manufacturing in the city of such a nature as to require regulations concerning the disposal of its wastes.

POLICE.

The police force of Austin is under the charge and command of the city marshal, and the service is administered in accordance with ordinances making the usual provisions. The only one of these ordinances which seems peculiar to Austin is as follows:

Every policeman of this city shall, and any citizen may, have a police-whistle; and it shall be the duty of any policeman hearing any such whistle blown to go to the relief of any person blowing the same. But it shall not be lawful for any policeman or other person to blow any such whistle for any trivial cause, nor unless the presence of the policeman is actually necessary for the performance of some duty herein required.

The annual report of the city marshal for 1879 is as follows:

The police force of the city of Austin consists of nine men, and are distributed as follows: One officer on duty at the police office; one mounted officer patrolling the city at night; one officer guarding and working the city prisoners, the balance being on patrol duty at night in different parts of the city.

There have been arrested by the police force from the 20th of October, 1878, to the 19th October, 1879, 1,114 persons; of which 851 were fined, 205 dismissed, and 13 appealed to the county court, 40 were transferred to justices' courts, and 5 to the United States court.

The fines for the above year amounted to $6,280; amount of cash collected, $3,865 80; amount of fines worked out, $2,414 20. Value of stolen and missing property reported at police headquarters, $5,472, of which $3,307 were recovered by the police and returned to the owners.

CHARITABLE INSTITUTIONS.

[Information furnished by Rev. Fred. H. Wines, special agent.]

The city of Austin is the seat of three of the state charitable institutions of the state of Texas, namely, the State lunatic asylum, the Texas deaf and dumb asylum, and the Texas institution of learning for the blind.

The State lunatic asylum was opened in the year 1861. It is governed by a board of 5 managers appointed by the governor. It can accommodate 350 patients comfortably; but the number present June 1, 1880, was 373. The lands, buildings, and improvements, including furniture, cost about $300,000, and the annual cost of maintenance is $60,000 or $65,000, which is principally met from the state treasury. The amount of land owned by the institution is 106 acres. Dr. W. E. Saunders is the medical superintendent.

The deaf and dumb asylum received its first pupil in 1857. The legislature, in 1856, made a grant of 100,000 acres to this institution, of which about 15,000 acres were sold, under an act of 1874, for $22,440. The remainder is estimated to be worth from $125,000 to $150,000, and constitutes, with the proceeds of the former sale, a permanent endowment fund. The legislature also makes annual appropriation for the support of the establishment, which costs for maintenance $12,000 or $15,000 a year. The number of pupils in attendance June 1, 1880, was 61; but the institution is of sufficient capacity to receive 100. The buildings and grounds cost about $40,000. Mr. John S. Ford is the superintendent, and under his direction the pupils are instructed not only in the elements of an English education, but in several handicrafts, such as printing and shoemaking.

FINANCIAL STATEMENT.

The following is taken from the annual report of the mayor for 1879:

Amount of warrants outstanding October 20, 1879	$14,805 76
Cash in city treasury October 20, 1879	5,881 61
Bonded indebtedness of the city October 20, 1879	91,900 00
Ad valorem tax collected of 1877 to October 20, 1879	752 28
Ad valorem taxes collected of 1876	231 25
Back taxes collected to October 20, 1879	698 38
Ad valorem taxes collected for the year 1878 to October 20, 1879	47,689 48
Ad valorem taxes collected for the year 1879 to October 20, 1879	752 17
Ad valorem taxes uncollected for the year 1879, now due	43,793 63
License collected to October 20, 1879	10,217 00
Income from market-house to October 20, 1879	1,417 05
Income from cemetery to October 20, 1879	882 50
Fines from mayor's court to October 20, 1879	2,595 80
Income from ground rent to October 20, 1879	190 00
Income from dog-tax to October 20, 1879	5 75
Income, miscellaneous, to October 20, 1879	108 29
Cash on hand October 20, 1878	7,560 15

Expenses of the city for the year ending October 20, 1879.

Fire department	$7,504 39
Streets and bridges	12,505 59
Miscellaneous	1,127 42
Market-house	941 55
Printing, postage, and stationery	1,025 63
Charity	2,132 73
Police	8,814 17
Sanitary	1,465 10
Salaries of city officers	6,493 31
Commissions of city assessor, collector, and city attorney	1,384 98
City cemetery	563 57
Street lamps	6,415 20
Water rents	5,647 94
Interest	10,429 85

DALLAS,

DALLAS COUNTY, TEXAS.

POPULATION

IN THE

AGGREGATE,

1880.

	Inhab.
1790	......
1800	......
1810	......
1820	......
1830	......
1840	......
1850	......
1860	......
1870	......
1880	10,358

POPULATION

BY

SEX, NATIVITY, AND RACE,

AT

CENSUS OF 1880.

Male	5,462
Female	4,896
Native	9,035
Foreign-born	1,323
White	8,431
Colored	*1,927

* Including 6 Chinese.

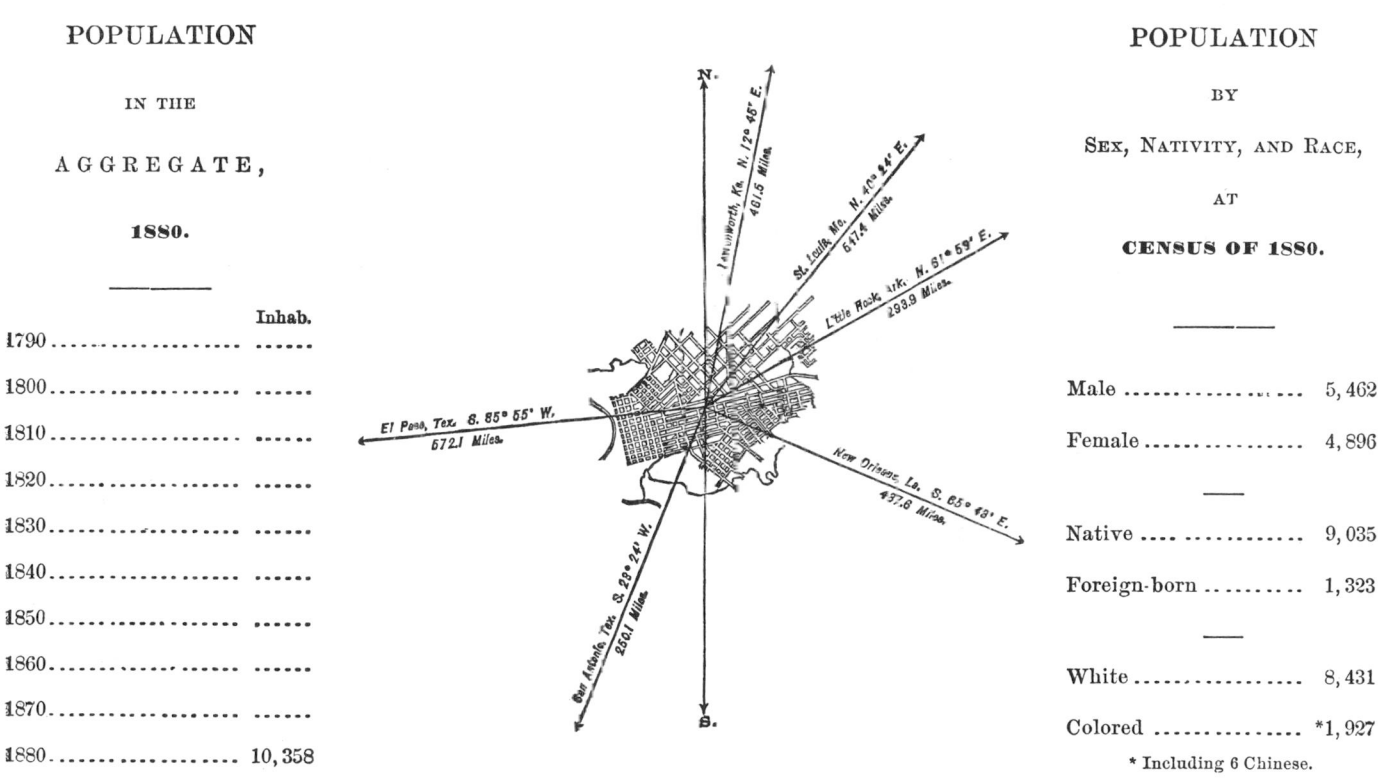

Latitude: 32° 45' North; Longitude: 96° 46' (west from Greenwich); Altitude: 510 to 600 feet.

FINANCIAL CONDITION:

Total Valuation: $3,585,379; per capita: $346 00.   Net Indebtedness: $304,354; per capita: $29 38.   Tax per $100 00: $3 00.

HISTORICAL SKETCH.

Eight years ago the present prosperous city of Dallas was a little village of perhaps 1,500 inhabitants, contented and well-to-do, who little expected that their city, which had been thirty years in reaching the point at which they saw it, would in less than ten years increase over six times in population, while in importance it would pass from a quiet village to a thriving city.

Dallas was founded in 1841 by John Neely Bryan, but settlers did not come in any numbers until 1844, when many emigrants from Virginia, Kentucky, Illinois, and Missouri established themselves there and built up around themselves a quiet town. Dallas county was organized in 1846, and the little town of Dallas, which was almost exactly in the center of the county, was made the shire town. Such importance as this fact gave it was the only distinction the town could boast. In 1860 a large part of the town was destroyed by fire. After the close of the war Dallas again assumed its quiet way, repaired its losses, and laid the foundation for the rapid growth which began in 1872 with the completion of the Houston and Texas Central railroad to Dallas, when the city sprang at once into importance. In little more than a year the population had increased from 1,500 to 7,063. Manufactures were established and trade was extended. Increased importance was given by the extension of the Texas and Pacific railroad to Dallas. The city now has a population of 10,358. There are 6 large flour-mills, an extensive cottonseed-oil factory, 2 iron founderies, 3 planing-mills, several broom factories, and other flourishing manufacturing establishments. Dallas is lighted by gas and supplied with water; it has 3 daily and 7 weekly newspapers. There are 20 churches—14 attended by white and 6 by colored congregations.

DALLAS IN 1880.

The following statistical accounts, collected by the Census Office, indicate the present condition of Dallas:

LOCATION.

The city of Dallas is situated in latitude 32° 45′ north, longitude 96° 46′ west from Greenwich, on the east bank of the Trinity river, 3 miles below the mouth of Elm Fork. The average level of the city is 520 feet above the level of the sea, the lowest point being 510 feet, the highest 600 feet above the sea-level. The Trinity river is not navigable at this point.

RAILROAD COMMUNICATIONS.

Three railroads enter Dallas, as follows:
The Houston and Texas Central railroad, termini Houston and Denison.
The Texas and Pacific railroad, termini Texarkana and Eastland.
The Dallas and Wichita railroad, termini Dallas and Denton.
Other railroads are fast being extended toward the city.

TRIBUTARY COUNTRY.

Dallas is situated in the midst of the richest agricultural district of the state. The soil is what is known as "black waxy loam", and is very fertile. The city is the wholesale depot for the whole of northern Texas.

TOPOGRAPHY.

The city is built on a sloping prairie, ranging from 60 to 150 feet above the Trinity river. The soil is of black loam, or sand, underlaid by limestone, which lies from 3 to 10 feet below the surface. The natural drainage is excellent. The surrounding country is generally higher than the city. There are no marshes or lakes in the vicinity. Except on the east, the country is wooded.

CLIMATE.

The highest recorded summer temperature is 102°; the highest summer temperature in average years is 96°. The lowest recorded winter temperature is 28°; the lowest winter temperature in average years is 38°. The elevated lands about the city protect it from the severe winter winds, while breezes from the gulf of Mexico temper the summer heat and make the climate pleasant during the hot season.

STREETS.

Dallas has in all about 90 miles of streets, 6 miles of which are paved with gravel and 1 mile with broken stone. The cost of the broken-stone paving per square yard was about $2; of the gravel, 50 cents. The total cost of repairs on the streets is $15,000 annually. The sidewalks are of all kinds of material—gravel, plank, brick, concrete, stone flags, asphalt, and artificial stone. The street-gutters are of either plank, stone, or cast iron. Shade-trees are planted along many of the streets, and the municipal authorities encourage the planting by offering a bounty of $2 for each tree so set out after it has reached two years' growth. Work on the streets is done by the day, no contracts having been made for several years.

There are 4 horse-railroad lines. The total length of track is 9¼ miles. The lines use 22 cars and about 90 mules, and employ about 40 men. The fare is 5 cents. An omnibus line has 6 vehicles and about 30 horses, and employs 10 men. The fare is 25 cents per mile.

WATER-WORKS.

The works for the public water-supply are the property of a private corporation, the Dallas Water Supply Company, and were erected at a cost of $100,000. The water is pumped from springs into a stand-pipe, and thence distributed through a part of the city. About 1,500,000 gallons are pumped daily, the largest amount pumped in any one day being 2,200,000 gallons, the least, 1,000,000 gallons. No estimate of the expenses or income of the company could be obtained.

GAS.

The Dallas City Gas Light Company, a private corporation, supplies the city with gas. The charge per 1,000 feet is $3 90. The city pays $35 a year for each gas street-lamp, of which 150 are in use. The average daily production and the annual income were not stated.

PUBLIC BUILDINGS.

The buildings owned and used by the city are valued at $40,000, and include a city hall, a market-house, 2 engine-houses, and a city prison. The city hall was built at a cost of $28,000.

PUBLIC PARKS AND PLEASURE-GROUNDS.

The total area of the parks and pleasure-grounds connected with Dallas is about 100 acres. There is a park of about 45 acres situated about 1½ mile from the city to the north, which includes a large pond shaded by oak groves. To the east of the city is a large pleasure-ground of about 40 acres; here there is a fine race-track. South of Dallas there is another park containing 14 acres, which is used as a picnic- and pleasure-ground. The last of the pleasure-grounds is a small park of about 3 acres, situated northeast of the city. They are controlled partly by the city, partly by private corporations. The original cost of the various grounds is estimated at $100,000, and probably about $40,000 has been spent in improvements, while additions are being made constantly.

PLACES OF AMUSEMENT.

Thompson's theater, seating capacity 500, and Craddock's theater, seating capacity 600, are the only theaters in Dallas. Theaters pay a license of $250 per annum, or $2 50 for each performance. The following halls are used as concert- and lecture-rooms: Turner's, seating 400; Loeb's, 250; Forshin's, 150; and Gruetly hall, 150. The city has the following concert- and beer-gardens: Apollo hall, built 1876, seating 300; Tivoli hall, built 1874, seating 150; Musterhaus, built 1874, seating 400, a Sunday place of amusement; and Shady View park, built in 1876, including about 2 acres of land, which is used as a picnic-ground.

DRAINAGE.

The natural drainage of Dallas is good, and it is stated that the necessity for sewerage has become imperative only in the business centers. The natural water-ways were first boxed in with plank, and afterward walled with stone, but they are now being gradually taken into brick sewers. No information is given of the extent of sewerage works, but it is stated that only a small amount of work has been done. The outflow of sewers is carried to the river, 1 mile below the city. During the summer months sewers are flushed every two days. Some cleaning is done by hand, but no data are given of the extent or cost of this work. The city pays one-third of the cost of building sewers, the remaining two-thirds is assessed upon abutting property on the basis of frontage. A brick sewer built in 1880, egg-shaped, 5 feet 10 inches by 3 feet 6 inches, cost $6 per foot; a 12-inch pipe sewer, $1 50 per foot.

CEMETERIES; MARKETS.

No information was furnished on these subjects.

SANITARY AUTHORITY—BOARD OF HEALTH.

A board of health for Dallas was organized during the present year. It consists of the health officer, 3 physicians, and 4 citizens, all appointed by the city council, and is a simple advisory board without any authority apart from the council. Up to the present time it has incurred no expense, and has exerted only a little of its slight authority. Its powers are alike in the absence of and during an epidemic. It has no stated meetings—in fact has not met for some months. The chief executive officer is the health officer, who has charge of the maintenance of the public health. His duties are quite extensive, and he has authority to order nuisances abated, and to complain to the mayor if his orders are disregarded. Thorough inspections of the city are made but once a year. Nuisances are generally inspected only when reported, and the health ordinances are only poorly enforced. When a nuisance is found to exist, the owner of the premises is requested to remove or abate it, and if he refuses he is brought before the mayor and tried. There is no custom in regard to the inspection and correction of defective house-drainage, privy-vaults, cesspools, and sources of drinking-water. The city engineer has charge of sewers and streets, and does what he can to remedy defects in the former and inefficient cleansing of the latter. The board has no control over the conservation and removal of garbage. The health officer is given power to make such regulations regarding the burial of the dead as he may think best, but as yet no health officer has exercised this authority.

INFECTIOUS DISEASES.

Small-pox has not visited Dallas for years, and scarlet fever has so far been unknown, so no action has ever been taken in regard to the treatment of those suffering from these diseases. The board has assumed no control over the schools on the appearance of contagious diseases among the pupils—indeed during the present winter measles have been epidemic, and the children, as the health officer states, "were permitted to take it *ad libitum*". There is no pest-house. Vaccination is not compulsory, nor is it done at the public expense.

The city council can establish a quarantine at any time it thinks such action necessary. There is no system of registration of births, diseases, and deaths.

MUNICIPAL CLEANSING.

Street-cleaning.—The streets are cleaned by the city's force, under the superintendence of the city engineer, and entirely by hand. The streets in the business portion are cleaned daily, accumulations of filth being removed, while in the residence portion this work is done once a week. The same force collects garbage from the houses of those who wish it. The total annual cost is about $8,000. The sweepings are deposited on land owned by the city, and 2 miles beyond the corporate limits.

Removal of garbage and ashes.—Garbage is removed both by the city and by the householders. In cases where the latter choose to collect their garbage and place it convenient for removal by the city's cart, the city will make the removal. The ordinances require garbage to be kept in covered boxes or barrels, but do not demand that it be kept separate from ashes. The matter collected is dumped outside the city limits. No particular attention is paid to the removal of ashes. The city engineer reports, as the chief defect of the system, that the householders do not exercise sufficient care in collecting their garbage and placing it ready for removal.

Dead animals.—The owner of any animal dying within the city must remove the carcass to the city dumping-ground and there bury it. About 100 horses and 1,500 smaller animals are disposed of in this way every year.

Liquid household wastes.—There is no established system for the disposal of liquid household wastes. In the present unfinished state of the sewers no wastes are allowed to enter them; accordingly most is run into cesspools, but some pass into the street-gutters in spite of the city ordinances, which forbid such a disposition of the wastes. The cesspools are in some cases porous, in some water-tight, and generally receive the wastes of water-closets where these are used. The street-gutters are flushed every day during the summer months. Many wells in the business portion of the city have been abandoned, owing to the contamination of the water by the overflow or soakage from cesspools. The cesspools are cleansed at night by licensed scavengers.

Human excreta.—Much the larger portion of the houses depend on privy-vaults, only a few on water-closets. About one-third of the privy-vaults are nominally water-tight. By an ordinance passed late in the present year, the dry earth system of privies has been introduced, and persons using privy-vaults in the past are directed to discontinue them within six months, and, if they exceed 4 feet in depth, to discontinue their use immediately. The night-soil is disposed of by carting it to the city dumping-ground. The further disposal of it is not stated by the city authorities. None is used as manure on lands within the gathering-ground of the public water-supply.

Manufacturing wastes.—No system for the disposal of manufacturing wastes has been elaborated, as none has been needed.

POLICE.

The police force of Dallas is appointed and governed by the board of police, which consists of the mayor, and 2 aldermen chosen by the city council. The chief executive officer is the city marshal, who has the general supervision and charge of the department. His salary is $100 per month. The rest of the force consists of a deputy marshal, salary $75 per month; 2 mounted policemen, salary $65 per month each; and 10 patrolmen, salary $55 per month each. The uniform is of navy-blue cloth, and costs $26 50, each man furnishing his own. The men are armed with Colt's revolvers and clubs. They are on duty 12 hours each day, and patrol all the city's territory. The principal causes of arrest are drunkenness, vagrancy, and fighting. No records of arrests or of any recoveries of property could be obtained. Special policemen may be appointed by the board of police whenever it thinks necessary, and are, while on duty, subject to the orders of the city marshal.

GALVESTON,
GALVESTON COUNTY, TEXAS.

POPULATION

IN THE

AGGREGATE,

1850-1880.

POPULATION

BY

SEX, NATIVITY, AND RACE,

AT

CENSUS OF 1880.

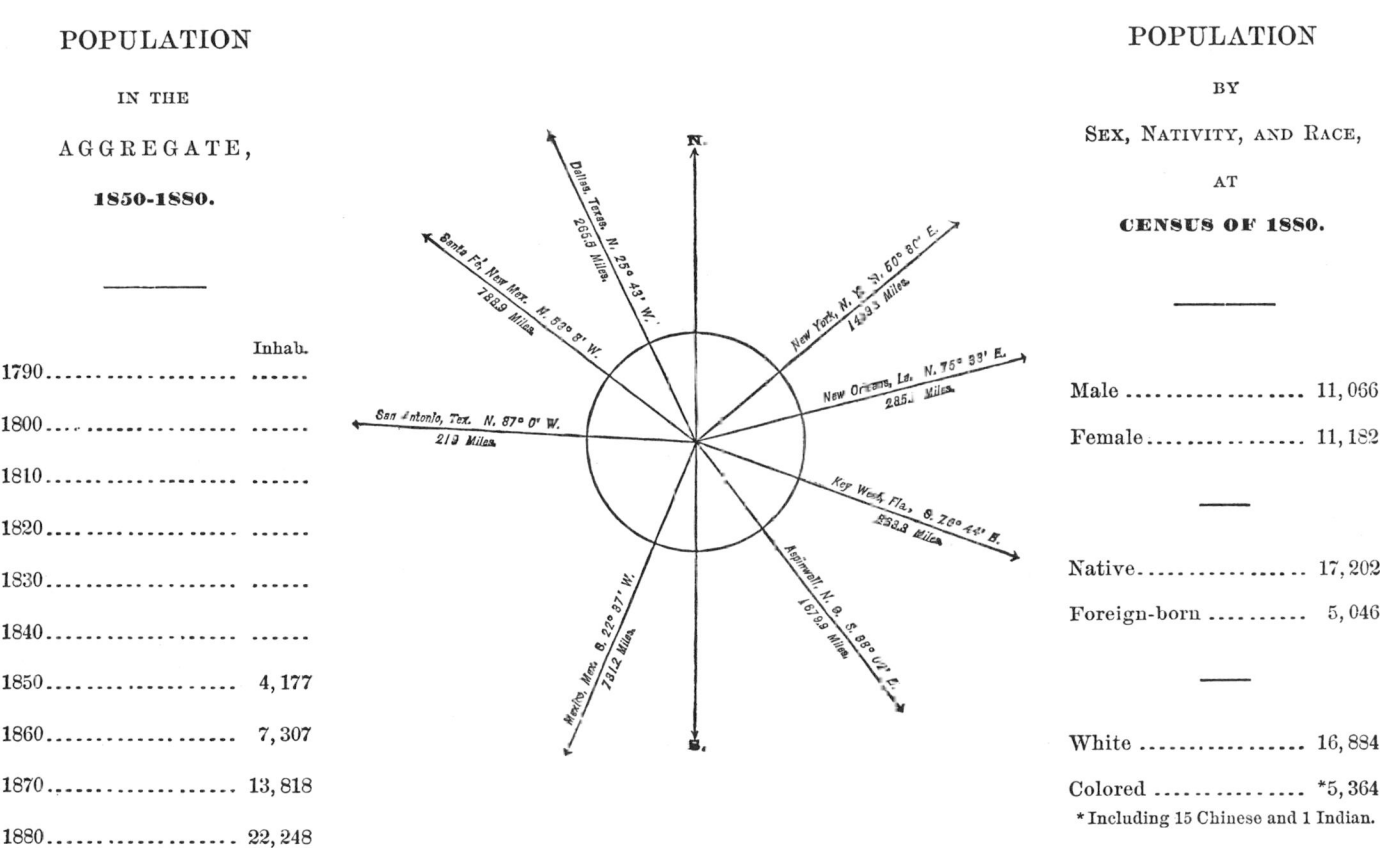

	Inhab.
1790	......
1800	......
1810	......
1820	......
1830	......
1840	......
1850	4,177
1860	7,307
1870	*13,818
1880	22,248

Male	11,066
Female	11,182
Native	17,202
Foreign-born	5,046
White	16,884
Colored	*5,364

*Including 15 Chinese and 1 Indian.

Latitude: 29° 17′ North; Longitude: 94° 50′ (west from Greenwich); Altitude: 3 to 9.5 feet.

FINANCIAL CONDITION:

Total Valuation: $14,904,856; per capita: $670 00.   Net Indebtedness: $1,023,249; per capita: $45 99.   Tax per $100: $2 70.

HISTORICAL SKETCH.

Galveston island was first known to the Spanish about the year 1526.   But the illiberal policy of Spain toward her colonies prevented the establishment of settlements upon many of the advantageous spots on the Texan coast, and the island remained uninhabited, except by roving bands of Indians, for almost three centuries.   In 1816 Don Manuel Herrera was sent by the Mexican patriot congress to the United States as a commissioner to represent the interests of the Mexicans, who were then trying to throw off the yoke of Spain.   Herrera endeavored to secure the co-operation of the independent cruisers of the Gulf, and became in this manner apprised of the great advantages of the island as a base of operations against Spain; he accordingly decided to make it his rendezvous for this purpose, having especially an eye to the rich commerce of the mother country. Herrera secured the co-operation of Don Luis Aury, a distinguished naval commander then in command of the fleets of the republics of Venezuela, La Plata, and New Granada, all armed enemies of Spain and engaged in preying upon her commerce. Herrera had blank commissions to issue to those who would take the oath of allegiance to the patriot government of Mexico.

On the 1st of September, 1816, Herrera and Aury, with a squadron of 12 or 15 vessels and 300 or 400 men, sailed for Galveston island. On the 12th a meeting was held, in accordance with previous arrangement, and a government was organized. Aury was appointed by Herrera civil and military governor of Texas and Galveston island, and took the oath of fidelity to the republic of Mexico; the national flag was raised, and Galveston island was declared a part of the Mexican republic. This island had received its name some years previously, being called after Don José Galvez, who, when Spain declared war against England in 1779—he being then governor of Louisiana—engaged in active hostilities and received a few recruits from Texas. After the close of the war, in 1783, Galvez continued to figure prominently in the negotiations between Spain and the United States relating to the navigation of the Mississippi.

Aury's fleet at once began operations against the commerce of Spain; and so active and daring was it, that in a short time the Gulf was swept clean of Spanish merchantmen. Toward the end of the year (1816) the land force was increased to about 700 men by the arrival of 300 men under the immediate command of General Xavier Mina and Colonel Perry. The many valuable prizes captured by the fleet supported the government handsomely. Numbers of slaves were often captured with the prizes, sold to speculators, and resold to the planters of Louisiana. While affairs were in this prosperous condition, Commodore Aury learned that the town of Soto La Marino, situated on the Santander river, about 60 miles from its mouth, was in a defenseless state. Whereupon, taking his entire land and naval force, he sailed from Galveston island and captured the place without opposition. In the mean time dissensions had arisen between the three commanders. Colonel Perry "disdained" the authority of Aury, and placed himself under command of Mina. Aury realized that without harmony of action the expedition would be a failure, and, after landing his recalcitrant leaders, returned to the coast of Texas about May 10, 1817, and proceeded to explore Matagorda bay, with the ostensible purpose, if this afforded equal facilities to his fleet for offense and defense against the Spanish, of removing his seat of government here and fixing it at some point on the mainland. After spending some days in his investigation of the harbor, etc., Aury set sail for Galveston, and, upon arriving there, was surprised to find the renowned buccaneer, Jean Lafitte, in possession of the island. In vain did Commodore Aury protest against this usurpation; Lafitte paid no attention to him, but proceeded to organize a government, somewhat similar to that of Aury's, to rebuild the houses and cabins he had destroyed, and generally to settle himself upon the island. At the close of 1817 Lafitte's followers numbered more than 1,000 men. Probably a more motley assembly was never before seen; there were representatives of all nations and al conditions; refugees from justice and from injustice; adventurers of all classes, and what not, who, hearing of the highly romantic and prosperous state of things under Lafitte's sway, had been glad to join his service.

Meanwhile, to exonerate himself and to define his position, Commodore Aury, in a letter dated July 21, 1817, addressed to Commissioner Herrera, had denounced Lafitte and his men as pirates, informing him that for the present he had determined to abandon Galveston island; that he had taken the collector, Rouselin, with him, and that all proceedings there after the 31st of July would be without his consent. On the 28th of the same month he addressed a similar letter to the collector of the port of New Orleans. Within five days after Aury's departure the redoubtable Lafitte had taken complete possession of the island, and thus and then began a *régime*, supported by the shadowy authority of letters of marque from the Mexican republican government, of romantic, daring exploits against the Spanish commerce of the Gulf, which lasted five years and inflicted a blow upon the trade of Spain from which it never recovered.

Complaints of Lafitte's despoliations were frequently made to the United States authorities at Washington, and the government would have taken vigorous measures to break up his nest but for the interposition of the Spanish minister, whose government feared that if the United States should disperse the buccaneers from their haunt, it would afterward hold the same for its own possession; so the business of the buccaneers prospered. Soon after the departure of Aury, Lafitte located a town on the ruins of his predecessor's village, built himself a house at the foot of Fifteenth street, and threw up a fort around it, upon which he mounted guns commanding the entrance of the harbor. Other houses were erected, and soon the title "Campeachy" was borne by a busy village of from 1,500 to 2,000 inhabitants. Such of Lafitte's adherents as had wives or mistresses brought them here, and thus the society of Campeachy, without being any way strained as to its *morale*, soon possessed all the elements of permanency. New Orleans furnished a lucrative market for that which their efforts produced, and these farmers of the sea reaped no bad crop. Gambling-houses and sporting establishments flourished. Among other conveniences were an arsenal and a dock-yard for the overhauling and repairing of their vessels.

In 1819 Lafitte took the oath of allegiance to the Mexican republican government and received the appointment of governor of Galveston. He soon after became involved in trouble with the United States through the reckless conduct of one of his leaders—a Captain Brown—a ferocious character who knew no law but that of might; and in

1820, depredations were again committed by Lafitte's cruisers against American commerce, which finally decided the powers at Washington to break up the buccaneer's rendezvous. Early in 1821 the brig "Enterprise" sailed for Galveston with this end in view. Notification was given that the island was to be abandoned, and sufficient time was given the buccaneers to remove such property as they desired. General Long (mentioned later), who was encamped at Bolivar point, urged Lafitte not to destroy the buildings which had been erected, as he intended now to change his base of operations from the point to the island. But Lafitte was inexorable in his purpose to remove the last vestige of habitation from the island. However, he informed General Long that what buildings he could remove before his departure he might have, but what then remained would be committed to the flames. After settling with his adherents and supplying them with money and abundant supplies, the chief of the buccaneers issued orders for their dispersion, and, when their last sail was hull down, ordered the torch applied to what was left of his town of Campeachy; "and, when the last vestige of a habitat had succumbed to the flames, he piped all hands aboard of his own favorite vessel, the 'Pride', and stood out to sea, a wanderer on its broad bosom."

General Long, who had conceived a plan of establishing an empire west of the Sabine, occupied Galveston and Bolivar peninsula for a few months, as a rendezvous for his daring followers; then, after having been the home of the last and greatest of the buccaneers of the Gulf for about five years, Galveston island again became a lonely, desolate waste, whose solitude was broken only by occasional parties organized to search for supposed treasures left buried by Lafitte.

The peculiar advantages of Galveston had been observed by Stephen F. Austin, who was convinced that it would early become the commercial metropolis of the Southwest. In pursuance of a colonization scheme of his own he applied, in 1824, to the Mexican government for a grant to him of the island, with authority to lay out and establish a town on its eastern extremity; but his application was refused. A similar attempt was also made by others, but it was not until the Texan republic was established that a title was received and perfected to "a league and labor" of the coveted land, by Colonel Juan N. Seguin. This "league and labor", embraced in the site of the city, was conveyed by a decree of Veramendis, governor of Coahuila and Texas, dated Monclova, April 27, 1833, "with order to whomsoever it might concern to put him (Seguin) in possession". Colonel Michael B. Menard, attorney for Colonel Seguin, purchased the head right, and, after the republic of Texas was established, applied to the first congress for a quitclaim deed to perfect the title, under the new dispensation, to the "league and labor" secured through Seguin. Congress granted the application on condition of $50,000 being paid to the republic. Menard complied with this condition, formed a company in 1837, and laid out the town of Galveston in 1838, the first sale of lots taking place at public outcry on April 20. During the year, 700 lots were sold, at an average price of $400 each, $3,100 being paid for the first one.

The "Columbia", the pioneer of the Morgan line, was the first steamship to enter the harbor of Galveston, from New Orleans, in 1837. The first issue of the first newspaper, the *Commercial Intelligencer*, appeared in July, 1838. It was short-lived, and was followed by the *Civilian* in October following. The first hotel and the first wharf were erected in 1838, and the first election to the republican congress was held in August of the same year. Religious worship was first held in a building at the corner of Twenty-first and Market streets, and resulted in a church organization and the erection of a house, which afterward became the property of the Presbyterians, the first distinct religious body formed in the place. The collector of the port was Gail Borden, who had his office and the custom-house in the old brig "Perseverance", stranded during a storm in the fall of 1837. The city received its charter in the spring of 1839, organizing a city government with John M. Allen as mayor. In the following fall Galveston county was organized. The *Galvestonian* and *Times* newspapers were begun. The first exportation to Liverpool direct was made in the latter part of 1839, and in the next year an English ship brought over a small hydraulic press to compress cotton for exportation. The population at the close of 1839 was fully 1,200, and it rapidly increased. Some of the merchants of Quintana, Velasco, and other rival towns along the coast, recognizing Galveston's superior advantages, removed hither and largely assisted the increasing ascendency of the place, which quickly grew into commercial importance, until the merchantmen of nearly all maritime nations entered and cleared from the port. When Texas was annexed to the United States in 1845, Galveston was in a highly prosperous condition. After annexation foreign shipping ceased, in a measure, to come here, the commerce of the port being monopolized by American vessels, and the growth of the city became slower. But commercial relations, however, were fully established with foreign ports in 1857, '58, '59, '60. Regular lines of packets to foreign and domestic ports were established; large cotton-compresses were put up; many manufacturing enterprises were started; and, in 1860, the future had an especially bright forecast.

Then came the civil war, and brought Galveston to the verge of ruin. Out of a population of 7,307 in 1860, there were left in 1865 but 3,500 souls. "With their beautifully embowered homes dilapidated and in ruins, broken in fortune, their trade gone, her citizens did not lose faith," but began at once to retrieve their fortunes. Galveston received considerable aid in her work of recuperation from her share of the emigration to the South which followed the close of the war. As Texas had suffered less than any other southern state, so her recovery was more rapid. In five years Galveston had regained her lost population, together with an increase of 6,511. For the next five years her growth was marvelous, in both population and wealth, and her commercial and maritime progress has been no less remarkable. Prior to the war, Galveston made no pretensions as a cotton market; but since the war she has become the third cotton and the fourth coffee market of the United States. While cotton has been and still is the staple of Galveston's exports, other articles are coming, for this purpose, into importance—such as wool, hides, cottonseed oil, and oil-cake. The manufactures of Galveston are already quite extensive. Outside of the cotton business are, a foundery and machine-shop, a sash-and-blind factory, an ice manufactory, 2 large flouring-mills, an oil factory, a street-car manufactory, and numerous smaller establishments.

GALVESTON IN 1880.

The following statistical accounts, collected by the Census Office, indicate the present condition of Galveston:

LOCATION.

Galveston lies in latitude 29° 17′ north, longitude 94° 50′ west from Greenwich, on an island of the same name, lying just off and parallel with the eastern coast of Texas, with the gulf of Mexico on the south and the bay of Galveston on the north. The island is about 25 miles long and from 1½ to 2½ miles wide. The city occupies the northeast portion of it. Navigable water surrounds it on all sides. The harbor is well protected on the north side of the island, and consists of a channel about 8 miles long and from 200 to 5,000 feet wide. The channel has an average depth of 20 feet, and on the bar, at the entrance, of 14 feet. There is wharfage for about 100 large vessels and a large number of small craft. Water communication is maintained with all Gulf and Atlantic ports, and inland on the Trinity river with Houston and points up for about 400 miles.

RAILROAD COMMUNICATIONS.

The city is touched by the following railroads: Galveston, Houston, and Henderson railroad, connecting at Houston with six lines centering at that place; and the Gulf, Colorado, and Santa Fé railroad, connecting at Rosenberg's Junction with the San Antonio railroad.

TRIBUTARY COUNTRY.

The peculiar situation of Galveston gives it but little variety in the character of the adjacent country, and only a very limited local trade with the sparsely settled island and a few small places along the bay.

TOPOGRAPHY, ETC.

The island upon which the city is situated is low and almost level. The soil is fine sand, underlaid by quicksand, beneath which, at a depth of from 50 to 100 feet below the surface, is clay. The drainage is good, as the island is highest in the middle, and the slopes each way, though not great, are sufficient for the carrying off of water. Excepting a few small salt marshes west of the city, and a few salt-water bayous of small area, there are neither marshes nor ponds in the vicinity. Within 5 miles of the city the country is formed only of sandy prairies, with small farms.

CLIMATE.

Highest recorded summer temperature, 98½°; highest summer temperature in average years, 95°. Lowest recorded winter temperature, 21°; lowest winter temperature in average years, 28°. The waters of the bay and Gulf, to the influence of which the city is peculiarly open, tend at all seasons to equalize the temperature. Even the "norther" (wind) does not blow so cold here as at points inland to the west. The slight marshes to the west of the city are not thought to exert any climatic influences. The prevailing winds are from the southeast and south, and this latter wind (from the Gulf) is the main cause of Galveston's mild and delightful climate, which, as the maximum figures show, is less warm in summer than that of many other cities of the United States.

STREETS. (a)

The city has 200 miles of streets, of which 100 miles are paved with broken stone and 1½ mile with wood, which latter costs, per square yard, from $3 to $4, and for yearly repairs about 1 per cent. on the cost. It is also considered here the best kind of pavement for quality and permanent economy. The sidewalks are laid with wood, asphalt, tile, and cement, while the gutters are paved with wood. Trees are planted 2 feet inside the curb on most of the streets. Avenue J has, besides the usual sidewalks, an esplanade 20 feet wide in the center, with trees on each side. The paving of streets is done by contract, but the repairing is done by the city. Under good supervision, contract work is preferred. There are two horse-railroads in the city, but no statistics regarding them were furnished.

---

a It is to be regretted that so little information on this subject was furnished by the city authorities.

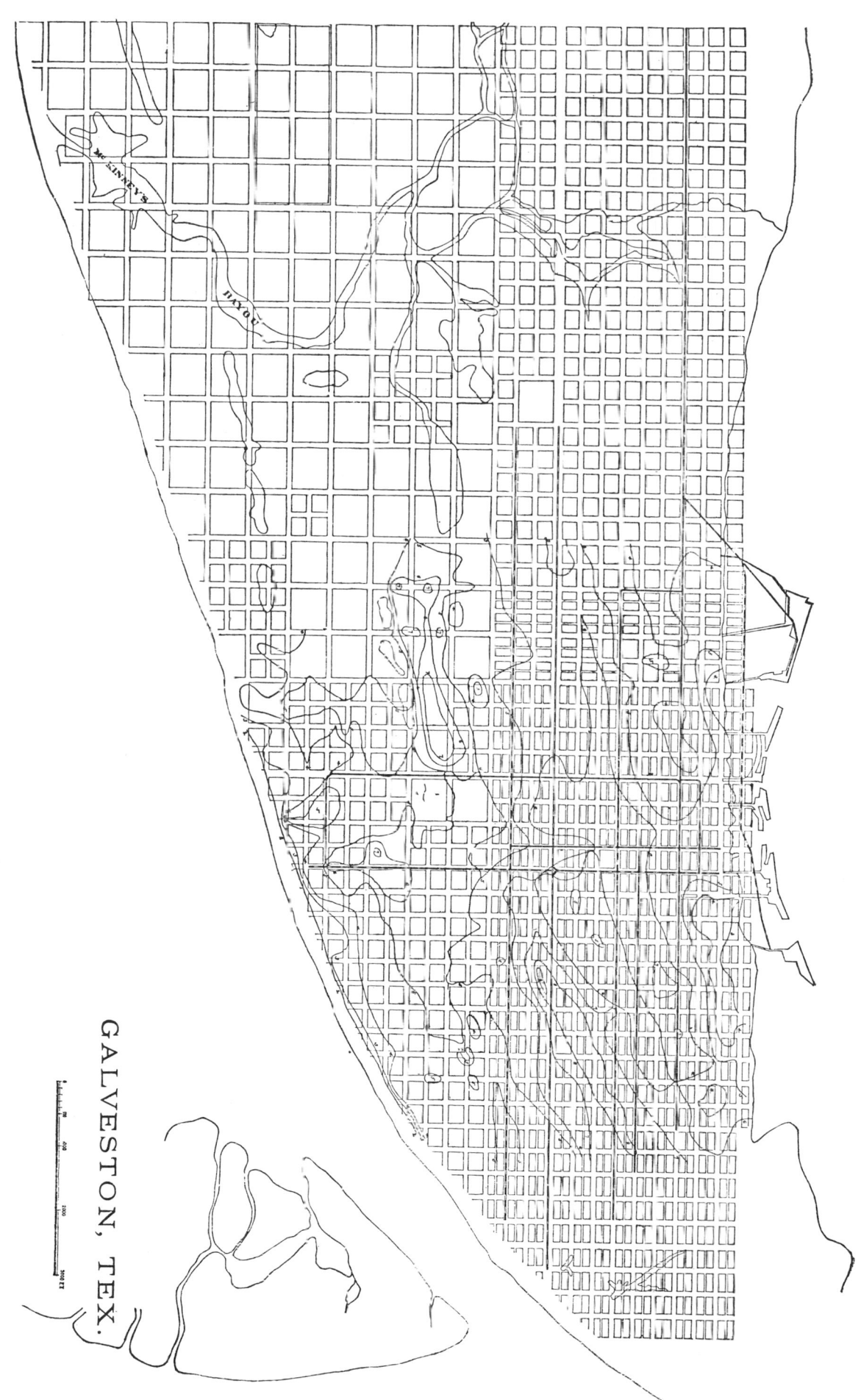

GALVESTON, TEX.

McKINNEY'S

BAYOU

WATER-WORKS.

No information as to the water-supply of Galveston was given.

GAS.

The gas-works are owned by private persons. The charge per 1,000 feet of gas was not stated. There are 179 street-lamps, and the city pays annually nearly $11,000 for lighting.

PUBLIC BUILDINGS.

The city owns and occupies for municipal purposes, wholly or in part, 1 city hall, 2 market-houses, 1 hospital, and 4 engine-houses. Their total cost was not given.

PUBLIC PARKS AND PLEASURE-GROUNDS.

The total area of these is 15 acres, and they consist of blocks of about 2 acres each, situated in various parts of the city. Outside of the city limits is a park called the "Winter Palace", but no information regarding it was furnished. The parks are controlled by a committee of 3 aldermen, called the "committee on public squares and esplanades".

PLACES OF AMUSEMENT.

Galveston has 2 theaters: Tremont opera-house, with a seating capacity of 1,200, and the New London Novelty theater, seating capacity 700. These theaters pay an annual license each of $250 to the city. In addition there are Artillery hall, Turner hall, and Casino hall—the last two being provided with stage and scenery—used for concerts, etc. There are no beer-gardens, properly so called, in the city.

DRAINAGE.

Galveston has no system of sewerage.

CEMETERIES.

There are 5 cemeteries in the city—1 public and 4 private—and all adjoining. Combined, these cemeteries occupy 6 blocks of 300 by 260 feet each, and the streets between, 80 feet in width. The city cemetery occupies 2 blocks and the others 1 block each. Their location is about 2 miles west of the center of the city, on both sides of Avenue K, between Fortieth and Forty-third streets. A part of the City cemetery, which was used for the interment of yellow-fever victims during the epidemic of 1867, is no longer used, and is known as the "Yellow-fever cemetery". The total number of interments in all of the burial-grounds from 1866 to 1880, including the epidemic years of 1867, 1870, and 1880, is 9,167. The limit of time between death and burial is 24 hours. Graves are dug only 3 feet deep, on account of the underlying quicksand. The Catholic and Episcopal cemeteries each employ a sexton, who has charge of the grounds. The other cemeteries are all under the control of a sexton who is elected by the city council. Lots are sold in all the cemeteries, though a part of the City cemetery is set aside for the burial of paupers. The usual charge for a single grave is $5. A full-sized lot, 16 feet square, is sold for $40. The following statement is made in this connection by the city clerk: "There is no revenue from the cemetery to the city any more, as almost all the lots belonging to the city are (already) sold, and only private cemeteries are being used now for burying."

MARKETS.

Galveston has two public markets. The main market consists of 2 buildings, situated in the center of the business portion of the city, one building being devoted to the sale of meat and the other to the sale of fish and vegetables. The former contains 44 and the latter 24 stalls—8 for fish and 16 for vegetables. These 2 buildings cover an area 390 feet in length by 43 feet in width, and are little more than long roofs resting on brick columns. The spaces between the columns are closed by "blinds". The stalls are situated along the sides, with a space of 18 feet between, and are 10 by 10 feet in area. The floor is made of cement, which is cleaned with scrapers and streams of water from a force-pump. Behind the vegetable market is an open space of 130 by 43 feet, for wagons to stand. The other, and smaller, market is situated in the 1st ward, and contains but 8 stalls. The public markets are open from 3 to 9 a. m. in summer and from 4 to 10 a. m. in winter, sales being held every morning. It is estimated that from one-half to three-fifths of the retail supply of meats, poultry, fish, and vegetables is sold in the public markets, as compared with two-fifths to one-half sold by private stores and stands. In the main market the city receives for such meat stalls as are used an annual rental of $75 each, and for fish and vegetable stalls $50 each per annum; for the First Ward market, $50 per annum for each stall rented; and for each of the 31 private stores or stands of the city, $50 per annum; making a total yearly rental of $6,300, divided as follows: Main market, $4,500; First Ward market, $150; and the stores, $1,650. Concerning the wholesale distribution of the foods mentioned above, the city clerk says: "There is hardly any wholesale trade in meat; every butcher buys direct from the stock-yards, and sells his meat either in his own or the public markets. The wholesale trade in vegetables is also insignificant; most gardeners have their vegetable stands in the market, or sell their vegetables to peddlers, who peddle from wagons and from house to house.

SANITARY AUTHORITY—BOARD OF HEALTH.

The Galveston board of health is the chief sanitary organization of the municipality. The board consists of 9 members, 3 of whom are physicians, appointed by the mayor and confirmed by the city council. Owing to the large amount of work undertaken by the board, its annual expenses in ordinary times appear large. The city allows the board the use of certain drays and men, for sanitary street-cleaning, etc., and charges it with the amount so expended ($6,527 87 in 1880), although this sum is deducted from the street appropriation. The expenses of the board, at all times, are regulated by the appropriations made by the city council. In the absence of epidemics the board has, in addition to its control over the cleaning of streets, supervision over yards, privies, etc., and can compel the cleansing of the same at its discretion. During epidemics the board, by charter, has power to isolate cases of contagious diseases, and to use all necessary means to prevent the spread of an epidemic, with absolute power of quarantine. The board has a chief executive officer in the person of its secretary, who is also the health officer, and in this capacity draws a salary of $1,500 per annum. Ordinarily one inspector is employed. He is a police officer detailed for the purpose; and, in case of necessity, other policemen are detailed for this duty by the city council. Their police powers, during their service as inspectors, remain full and complete. The board holds regular meetings twice a month, at which business is transacted in the usual manner. Inspections are made regularly by the inspector, and also when nuisances are reported. When nuisances are found to exist they are ordered to be abated, and if this is neglected the responsible parties are fined. The scope of the inspector's work includes the noting for correction of defective house-drainage, privy-vaults, cesspools, and street-cleaning. Fortunately drinking-water needs no supervision, as cisterns, either above ground or else tightly cemented, are relied upon. The board has control over the conservation and removal of garbage. Deceased persons may be interred only in regular cemeteries, and then only upon the presentation to the sexton of a certificate signed by the attending physician, or, in the absence of a physician, by two citizens, setting forth the cause of death, age, and other particulars concerning the deceased. Privies are emptied and excrement is removed by scavengers, who receive a permit to engage in the business from the city physician.

INFECTIOUS DISEASES.

Small-pox patients are isolated either at their homes or by being sent to the quarantine station at the extreme eastern end of the island. Scarlet-fever patients (of which disease there is very little here) are quarantined at home. Vaccination is neither compulsory nor is it done at the public expense.

REGISTRATION AND REPORTS.

Although provided for in the city charter, there exists no system of the registration of births and diseases. Interments are returned by the city sexton to the health officer. The board of health reports annually to the city council, but its reports are not published.

MUNICIPAL CLEANSING.

Street-cleaning.—The city's force cleans the streets by hand. A gang of men is kept constantly at work, so that the principal streets are cleaned about 3 times a week, and the work is said to be well done. Its annual cost to the city is about $4,500, but whether or not this sum is included in the amount expended by the board of health for the same purpose is not stated. Unobjectionable portions of the sweepings are used in the city for filling, while the rest is buried on the beach or bay shore.

Removal of garbage and ashes.—Most of the garbage is removed by the city; a small portion is removed by butchers, in licensed carts, outside the city limits. What the city removes is taken by its own force two or three times a week. The garbage while awaiting removal must be kept in tight vessels, but there is no law requiring it to be kept separate from the ashes. Such garbage as is taken by the city is buried remotely. Ashes are not removed from premises, but are used there for filling low places, for fertilizing purposes, etc. The cost of the service is included in that given for street-cleaning.

Dead animals.—If the owners of dead animals can be found, they are required to remove them; otherwise the city is forced to do it, taking the carcasses beyond the corporate limits. The cost of this work is also included in the street-cleaning.

Liquid household wastes.—Offensive wastes, such as chamber-slops, etc., are thrown into cesspools, while laundry wastes are allowed to run into the gutters of alleys, but not of streets. As Galveston is without water-works, the gutters can not be artificially flushed. About 90 per cent. of the cesspools are porous, the rest are nominally water-tight, while none have overflows. When the inspector reports to the health officer that a privy or cesspool needs cleaning, the latter orders this done by a licensed scavenger.

Human excreta.—Less than 5 per cent. of the houses of the city have water-closets, and these deliver into cesspools. Of privy-vaults, not more than 10 per cent. are water-tight. Since 1877 all privy-vaults are required by law to be made of brick or stone, with the sides and bottom cemented, and the edges rising above the level of the ground; but the statement is made that, though they are so constructed, they are apt soon to fall into decay and become no longer tight. The dry-earth system is not in use to any extent. The night-soil is dumped into the bay, at either the eastern or the western extremities of the city.

Manufacturing wastes.—Galveston has no manufactories of such nature as to require the regulations by law of the disposal of their wastes, either liquid or solid.

POLICE.

The police force is appointed and governed by the chief of police, subject to the approval of the mayor and the city council. The duties and powers of the chief of police are rather larger than ordinarily attach to this office, and include attendance at the recorder's court and the execution of its warrants and processes; the general supervision of the discipline of the force, including the investigation into charges against policemen; the promulgation of orders to the police, and the keeping of numerous books and records relating to the business of the department. His salary is $1,700 per annum. The rest of the force is as follows: 2 sergeants and 1 clerk at $1,080 each per annum; and 35 patrolmen at $900 each per annum. The uniform is of navy-blue, indigo-dyed, all-wool cloth coat and trousers, with brass buttons, and cap, the difference in rank being shown on the cap. The men provide their own uniform, at a cost of $35. Patrolmen are equipped with clubs, revolvers, nippers, and whistles. They are divided into day and night force, and go on duty at 7 p. m. and 7 a. m., respectively. About 12 miles of streets are regularly patrolled, and occasionally this is extended so as to cover 20 miles.

During the past year there were 2,002 arrests made by the force, the principal causes being, for drunk and disorderly, 305; disorderly, 290; assault and battery, 244; fighting, 182; abusing and insulting, 162; drunk, 117; vagrancy, 110; violating sanitary regulations, 97; theft, 82; assault with intent to murder, 42; carrying concealed weapons, 37; burglary, 8; and miscellaneous, embracing 46 different offenses, 46. Out of these there were 1,280 convictions, while the remainder were discharged. During the same time, property to the estimated value of $2,400 was reported to the police as either lost or stolen, and of this, $2,010 worth was recovered and returned to the owners. In the same period it is estimated that 1,000 night-lodgers were accommodated, and free meals valued at from $250 to $300 furnished. The police force is required to co-operate with the fire and health departments in a general way, by helping to execute the regulative ordinances. Special policemen are appointed by the mayor or chief of police to attend places of amusement, balls, etc., and also as night-watchmen for private property, at the owner's expense. The yearly cost of the police force (1880) is $32,766 76.

FIRE DEPARTMENT.

Galveston's fire department consists of a manual force of 1 chief and 3 assistant engineers, and 7 companies, with 6 engineers, 7 drivers, and 1 tillerman. The apparatus consists of 6 steamers, 2 hook-and-ladder trucks, and 6 hose-carriages. There are 19 horses. The cost of the department in 1879 was $18,430.

COMMERCE AND NAVIGATION.

[From the reports of the Bureau of Statistics for the fiscal years ending June 30.]

Customs district of Galveston, Texas.	1879.	1880.
Total value of imports	$871,938	$1,107,241
Total value of exports:		
Domestic	$16,393,877	$16,712,861
Foreign	$58,184	$37,028
Total number of immigrants	18	7

Customs district of Galveston, Texas.	1879.		1880.	
	Number.	Tons.	Number.	Tons.
Vessels in foreign trade:				
Entered	215	135,500	195	117,974
Cleared	203	128,399	173	99,007
Vessels in coast trade and fisheries:				
Entered	371	384,326	455	472,165
Cleared	286	250,603	539	282,546
Vessels registered, enrolled and licensed in district..	200	11,526	184	9,780
Vessels built during the year	8	242	7	87

MANUFACTURES.

The following is a summary of the statistics of the manufactures of Galveston for 1880, being taken from tables prepared for the Tenth Census by Edward J. Byrne, special agent:

Mechanical and manufacturing industries.	No. of establishments.	Capital.	AVERAGE NUMBER OF HANDS EMPLOYED.			Total amount paid in wages during the year.	Value of materials.	Value of products.
			Males above 16 years.	Females above 15 years.	Children and youths.			
All industries	170	$871,350	633	15	36	$499,785	$1,283,246	$2,375,965
Blacksmithing...	14	32,700	20	....	2	14,975	18,880	52,525
Boots and shoes, including custom work and repairing	21	6,800	19	....	....	14,050	34,875	78,050
Bread and other bakery products.....................................	8	15,200	19	....	....	13,511	59,300	96,300
Carpentering	8	14,800	38	....	....	28,500	48,750	101,600
Confectionery..	3	61,500	18	....	3	15,300	86,000	146,600
Cooperage	8	18,300	42	....	....	35,850	81,000	147,000
Flouring- and grist-mill products....................................	4	97,000	22	....	....	15,290	257,168	313,340
Foundery and machine-shop products.	4	76,000	57	....	....	32,336	51,500	103,000
Furniture	11	7,450	8	....	3	5,425	4,225	23,600
Painting and paperhanging...	10	24,450	33	....	....	29,050	30,300	81,500
Patent medicines and compounds.....................................	3	9,000	6	....	....	5,250	16,500	35,500
Photographing	4	7,300	4	3	....	5,100	2,950	20,200
Plumbing and gasfitting...	3	21,500	18	....	2	17,050	24,400	52,900
Printing and publishing	5	287,000	107	6	21	112,593	52,738	230,500
Saddlery and harness	5	19,900	13	....	....	9,525	24,600	42,850
Shipbuilding...	4	1,300	1	....	....	1,430	4,060	6,000
Tinware, copperware, and sheet-iron ware	9	51,000	32	....	....	29,000	84,500	150,000
Tobacco, cigars and cigarettes	18	15,700	56	....	....	43,950	53,200	178,850
All other industries (a)	28	104,450	120	6	5	71,600	348,300	515,050

a Embracing bags, other than paper; boxes, fancy and paper; carriages and wagons; coffins, burial cases, and undertakers' goods; clothing, men's; drain and sewer pipe; hand-stamps; hats and caps, not including wool hats; looking-glass and picture frames; marble and stone work; mattresses and spring beds; mineral and soda waters; musical instruments, pianos and materials; perfumery and cosmetics; pickles, preserves, and sauces; safes, doors, and vaults, fire-proof; sash, doors, and blinds; shirts; show-cases; stencils and brands; and umbrellas and canes.

From the foregoing table it appears that the average capital of all establishments is $5,125 59; that the average wages of all hands employed is $730 68 per annum; and that the average outlay, in wages, in materials, and in interest (at 6 per cent.) on capital employed is $10,795 95.

HOUSTON,

HARRIS COUNTY, TEXAS.

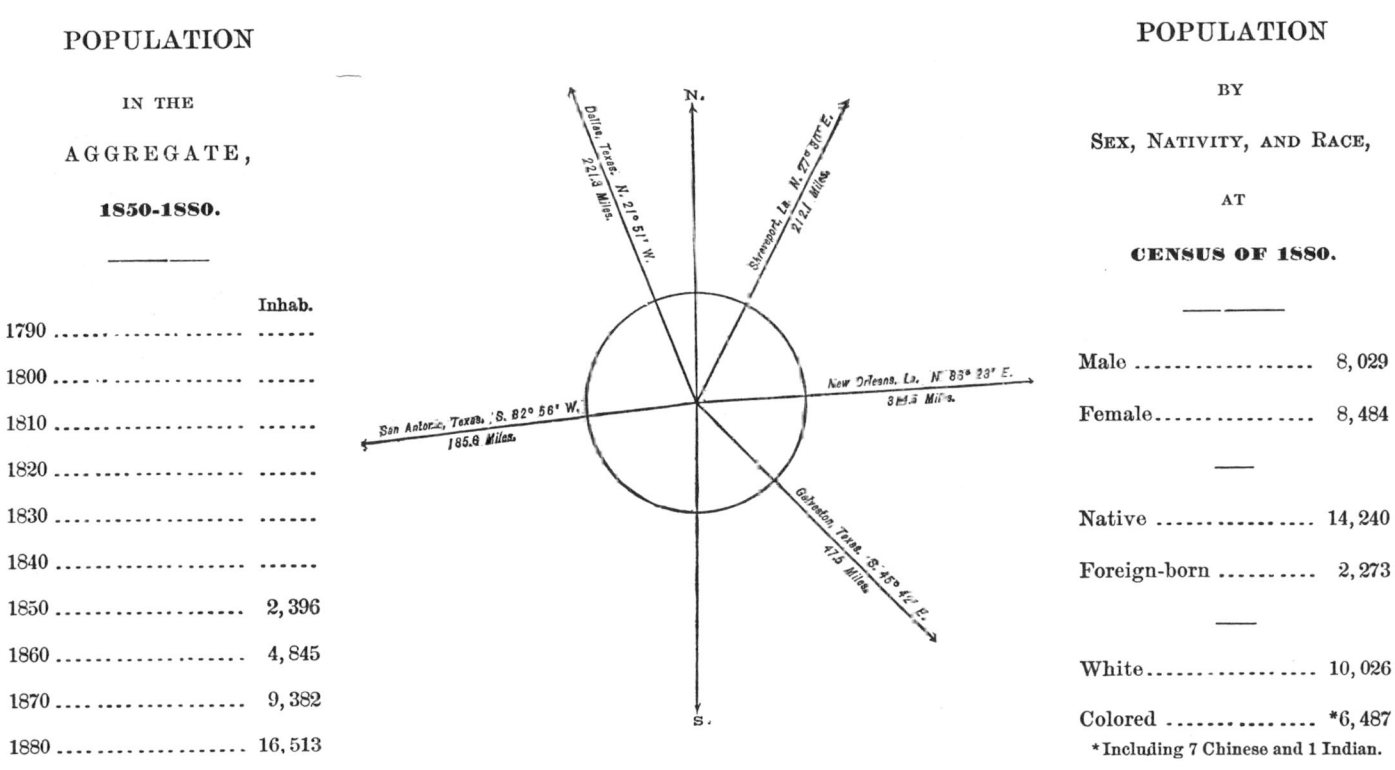

POPULATION

IN THE

AGGREGATE,

1850-1880.

	Inhab.
1790	......
1800	......
1810	......
1820	......
1830	......
1840	......
1850	2,396
1860	4,845
1870	9,382
1880	16,513

POPULATION

BY

SEX, NATIVITY, AND RACE,

AT

CENSUS OF 1880.

Male	8,029
Female	8,484
Native	14,240
Foreign-born	2,273
White	10,026
Colored	*6,487

*Including 7 Chinese and 1 Indian.

Latitude: 29° 47' North; Longitude: 95° 21' (west from Greenwich); Altitude: 35 to 45 feet.

FINANCIAL CONDITION:

Total Valuation: $5,352,314; per capita: $324 00.   Net Indebtedness: $1,501,592; per capita: $90 93.   Tax per $100: $2 70.

HISTORICAL SKETCH.

The site of the city of Houston was chosen by John K. Allen in the year 1836, not long after the decisive battle of San Jacinto (April 21, 1836) had established the independence of Texas; and its name was given in honor to the man to whom, more than to any other, Texas owed her freedom—General Samuel Houston, the victor of San Jacinto. It was immediately laid out in streets and lots, and in August the "town lots" were offered for sale on the market. The advantages of the site were soon apparent. The city was at the head of navigation, and was an excellent point from which to ship the productions of the central part of the state, which could easily be gathered there, and the founder foresaw that at this point the future railroad system of the state would find its center. It is said that he pointed to one street, to which he had given the name "Railroad street", and predicted that along it would run the great railroad of Texas. His prediction has come true; the street is still called "Railroad street", and through it pass continually the trains of the Houston and Texas Central railroad. In May, 1837, the Texas congress met in

Houston, holding its sessions in a capitol which had been erected by the city at a cost of $36,000 and presented to the state; but in a few years the new city of Austin was made the capital, and Houston was thus deprived of some of her importance. With the annexation of Texas to the United States the growth of the city became more rapid, capital was attracted to it, and immigrants came in considerable numbers. In 1849 or 1850 the design of a railroad from Harrisburg to Austin was conceived, and the projector, General Sidney Sherman, took active measures to make his plan a success. New England capitalists were induced to take an interest in the road, a charter was obtained from the legislature containing a proviso empowering the city of Houston to tap the road at some convenient point, and the enterprise was pushed with energy. The citizens of Houston thenceforth interested themselves in railroad construction, and obtained charters for three roads to center in their city—the Galveston, Houston and Red River, now the Houston and Texas Central railroad, the Houston Tap and Brazoria, and the Texas and New Orleans. The Texas legislature made liberal grants to the several lines, and by 1861 there were 357 miles of railways centering in Houston. All progress stopped with the outbreak of the civil war. Houston was just entering upon a period of great prosperity and of rapid advance, but was now suddenly checked in her career. Although trade seemed active during the war, it was carried on upon too precarious a foundation to be a permanent advantage to the city. The citizens of Galveston, alarmed by the blockade, took refuge in Houston, and entered heartily into the work of advancing the interests of their asylum, but little real progress was made until the close of the war. With the advent of peace Houston began rapidly to advance toward the goal which the war had moved five years into the future, and is now an important railroad center of Texas, and a city of 16,513 inhabitants, surpassed in numbers only by Galveston and San Antonio, while in trade it is fully the equal of any in the state. The shipments of cotton during the past year amounted to 459,697 bales; while during the same period the receipts of hides were over 2,000,000 pounds; of wool, 250,000 pounds; of sugar, 8,000 hogsheads; of molasses, 18,600 barrels; and of sirup, 24,000 barrels. The first fire company was organized in 1836 or 1837, and from this beginning has grown an excellent department. The city has never been swept by any one great fire, yet her losses from this cause at various times have been large, and since 1874, when the fire department was organized and a record of losses began, amount to more than $2,000,000.

Gas was introduced in 1866–'67, and water within a few years. The city has 22 churches and 23 public and private schools, while her secret, literary, and social societies are very numerous. There are 4 banks and 2 private banking-houses, and 3 daily and 4 weekly newspapers.

HOUSTON IN 1880.

The following statistical accounts, collected by the Census Office, indicate the present condition of Houston:

LOCATION.

Houston is situated in latitude 29° 47' north, longitude 95° 21' west from Greenwich, on both sides of the Buffalo bayou, about 45 miles from the gulf of Mexico, and 50 from the city of Galveston. The lowest point is 35 feet, the highest 45 feet above the sea-level, the average altitude of the city being about 40 feet above the level of the gulf of Mexico. The Buffalo bayou empties into Galveston bay, and is navigable as far as Houston, although vessels drawing 12 feet of water are compelled to stop 3 miles below the city. The tide comes up as far as Houston.

RAILROAD COMMUNICATIONS.

The following railroads center in Houston, and connect it with their terminal points:

The Houston and Texas Central, termini Houston and Sherman.

The International and Great Northern, termini San Antonio and Longview.

The Galveston, Harrisburg, and San Antonio, termini Houston and San Antonio.

The Galveston, Houston, and Henderson, termini Galveston and Houston.

The Texas and New Orleans, termini Houston and Orange.

The Houston, East and West Texas (narrow gauge), termini Houston and Goodrich.

The Texas Western Narrow Gauge, termini Houston and Pattison.

The Gulf, Colorado, and Santa Fé, termini Galveston and Cameron; this road does not enter Houston on its own tracks.

The Texas Transportation Company, termini Houston and Clinton.

TRIBUTARY COUNTRY.

The surrounding country is almost exclusively devoted to agriculture, cotton, sugar, and vegetables being the leading products.

TOPOGRAPHY.

The site of Houston is of recent geological formation, belonging to the Tertiary (Miocene) period, and borings have never been made of sufficient depth to ascertain what is the underlying rock. The city is on a level plain, extending for miles, and free of trees except along the river-banks, which are well wooded. The natural drainage is not good. The soil is generally alluvial, in some places quite sandy. There are a few marshes within a radius of 5 miles, but no ponds or lakes.

CLIMATE.

The highest summer temperature is about 102°, but in average years the temperature does not exceed 97°; the lowest temperature ever known in winter is 18°, while it is rare for the thermometer in average years to fall below 27°. The climate does not seem to be influenced by adjacent waters or by the marshes.

STREETS.

None of the streets are paved. The question of paving them is now being agitated, and a committee has been appointed to ascertain the relative cost and advantages of the different paving materials. In the main part of the city the sidewalks are of brick or asphalt in almost equal proportions, while in the suburbs plank sidewalks are generally used. There are a few cement sidewalks in the business portion. The street-gutters in the compact portion of the city are of brick laid in cement, with brick curbs topped with cypress wood as a protection; in the more scattered parts there are frequently no gutters at all, and the curbs are sometimes of wood. The custom of the abutters to plant shade-trees along the streets in front of their premises is becoming more common every year. The city does not undertake to regulate the planting, but leaves the matter entirely to individual taste. The work of construction and repairs of streets is done by the day, and at an annual cost of $20,000, which, however, includes also the expense of cleaning the streets, and of removing the garbage, etc.

HORSE-RAILROADS.

There is a horse-railroad which has a little more than 3 miles of track, owns 16 cars, 2 horses, and from 50 to 55 mules, and employs 37 men. The fare is 5 cents. There are no omnibus lines.

WATER-WORKS.

Beyond the fact that the city is supplied with water by a private company, which has in use about 12 miles of pipes and mains for distributing the water, which it takes from the Buffalo bayou, nothing could be learned in regard to the water-works.

GAS.

The city is supplied with gas by the Houston Gas Light Company, a private corporation. No further information was furnished.

PUBLIC BUILDINGS.

The city owns and uses for its municipal purposes a market-house (in which are also located the city offices and the city hall), a station-house, 11 school-houses, a powder-house, and a pest-house. The last two buildings are situated outside the city. The market-house cost $100,000, while the other buildings are valued at about $50,000.

PUBLIC PARKS AND PLEASURE-GROUNDS.

The Texas State Fair Grounds, area 70 acres, although private property, are open to the public for walking or driving free of expense. The total cost of these grounds was over $80,000, and $2,500 is annually expended in maintaining them.

PLACES OF AMUSEMENT.

Gray's opera-house, seating 800, and Pillot's opera-house, seating 700, are used by traveling companies for theatrical performances, but have no regular stock companies attached to them. Theaters pay a license of $2 50 for each performance, or of $62 50 per quarter. Lyceum hall, situated in the market-house, is used regularly by the Lyceum association, a literary society, and lectures are occasionally given there. The city has no concert- and beer-gardens.

SEWERAGE AND DRAINAGE; CEMETERIES; MARKETS.

No information on these subjects was furnished.

SANITARY AUTHORITY—BOARD OF HEALTH.

The chief sanitary authority is the board of health, consisting of 5 members of the board of aldermen, appointed by the city government, and the health officer. The expenses of the board in ordinary times are only for salaries. Such members as do not receive salaries in other capacities are paid $5 for each meeting. The board is controlled by the city council, especially in matters of expenditures. Its authority in sanitary matters is absolute; the whole city is under its supervision, and an inspector is kept constantly employed in investigating and suppressing nuisances. The chief executive officer is the health officer, who receives a salary of $1,000 per year. The board meets only for the transaction of necessary business, but during the prevalence of an epidemic it comes together once a week, or oftener if summoned by the president. One inspector is employed; he has power to enter premises for sanitary purposes at any hour between 6 a. m. and 6 p. m. Inspections are made regularly in all parts of the city.

NUISANCES.

When nuisances are found to exist they are abated at once. The inspector at all times supervises house-drainage, privy-vaults, and cesspools. The drinking-water of most of the inhabitants is obtained from cisterns, and is therefore not exposed to contamination; accordingly it is rarely inspected. The streets are cleaned by men employed under the supervision of the president of the board and licensed for this purpose. No others are allowed to do this work. No regulations prohibit the pollution of the streams.

GARBAGE.

The board compels all garbage to be kept in tight vessels, and placed convenient for removal by the city scavenger.

BURIAL OF THE DEAD.

A physician's certificate of death must be presented to the graveyard sexton before an interment is allowed. The sextons make weekly reports to the health officer.

INFECTIOUS DISEASES.

Small-pox patients are isolated in a pest-house situated just outside the city limits on a farm of 17 acres closely fenced in. No attention is paid to scarlet fever. If contagious diseases break out in the schools, the board has authority to take any action it thinks advisable. Any one knowing of the existence of any contagious disease must report it to the health officers, under penalty of $100 fine for neglect. Vaccination is not compulsory, but is done at the public expense for those wishing it.

A record of births, diseases, and deaths is kept by the health officer.

MUNICIPAL CLEANSING.

Street-cleaning.—The streets are cleaned by a force paid by the city and employed solely for this work, for which a license is issued by the board of health. The cleaning is done under the supervision of the president of the board of health, and as often as is necessary; sometimes as often as once a day, especially in the sickly season. The sweepings are used for filling up low places in the suburbs.

Removal of garbage and ashes.—In the heart of the city garbage is removed by the city scavenger-cart, but in the thickly settled parts it is disposed of by the householders. In the first case the collection is made by the city's force, each householder placing the barrels or zinc-lined boxes containing his garbage on the sidewalks ready for the collector, who makes his rounds between 9 a. m. and 1 p. m. Garbage and ashes may be placed in the same vessel. The garbage is removed beyond the city limits. Ashes are used for filling, and often for disinfecting-purposes, in privies.

Dead animals.—The city requires the owner of any animal dying within the city to remove the carcass beyond the corporate limits.

Liquid household wastes.—Chamber-slops are disposed of in the same way as kitchen and laundry wastes. There are only 5 sewers in the city, and where it is practicable the houses are connected with them; but in general the wastes are thrown into cesspools. These are in all cases porous, the custom being to dig down to quicksand and thus provide a means for the liquid to soak away; no overflows are provided. No wastes are allowed to run into the street-gutters. During the hot weather the gutters are flushed daily, at other times occasionally during the week. No cases of contamination of sources of drinking-water are known to have occurred, as the cisterns in which such water is caught and stored are not exposed to the soakage from cesspools. The wastes from water-closets very often run into cesspools. When these pools are full, or when the health inspector, after an examination, thinks it necessary, he orders them emptied. A record is kept of date, and after a certain period the inspector orders another cleaning, the record showing about when the pool should be full again.

Human excreta.—Less than 5 per cent. of the houses have water-closets, and of these only few deliver their wastes into the public sewers, much the larger part going into cesspools. Privy-vaults are thus in general use. No regulations govern their construction, but in nearly all cases they are water-tight boxes. They are emptied, like cesspools, in accordance with the schedule of dates kept by the health officer, the work being done by licensed scavengers. The dry-earth system is very little used. The night-soil is taken beyond the city limits, and is generally used by farmers for manure. None is allowed, however, on the gathering-ground of the public water-supply.

Manufacturing wastes.—There are no manufactures creating wastes liable to be a cause of nuisance.

SAN ANTONIO,

BEXAR COUNTY, TEXAS.

POPULATION

IN THE

AGGREGATE,

1850-1880.

	Inhab.
1790	......
1800	......
1810	......
1820	......
1830	......
1840	......
1850	3,488
1860	8,235
1870	12,256
1880	20,550

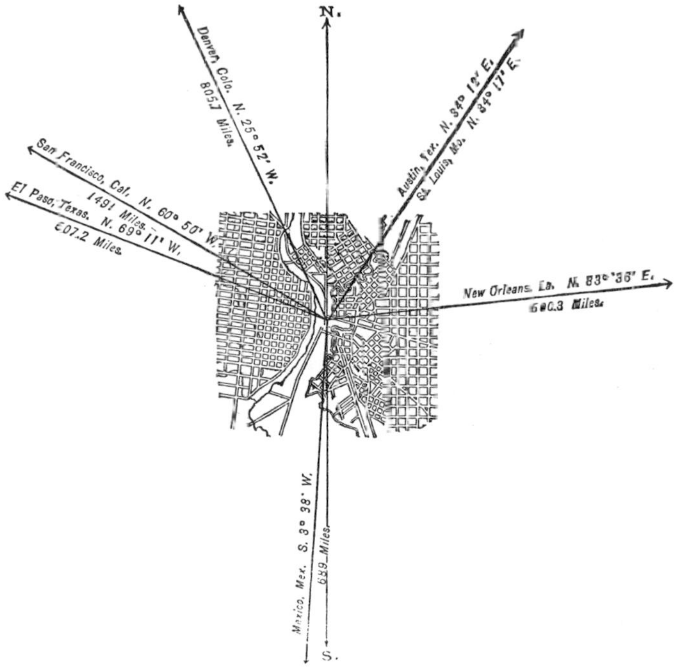

POPULATION

BY

SEX, NATIVITY, AND RACE,

AT

CENSUS OF 1880.

Male	10,673
Female	9,877
Native	14,952
Foreign-born	5,598
White	17,514
Colored	3,036

Latitude: 29° 25′ North ; Longitude: 98° 25′ (west from Greenwich) ; Altitude: 676 feet.

FINANCIAL CONDITION:

Total Valuation: $8,296,252; per capita: $404 00.   Net Indebtedness: $155,266; per capita: $7 56.   Tax per $100: $2 35.

HISTORICAL SKETCH.

As early as 1595, Spanish settlements were made along the Rio Grande, and the records of the early settlers show that there was then an Indian town where now stands the city of San Antonio. No record of its early Indian history remains, but the spear- and arrow-heads and the stone implements which are found buried deep in the earth around the city tell mutely of Indian battles as fierce and sanguinary as any which have since reddened the streets of a city whose history is so inseparably united with that of Texas that it can not be understood if told by itself.

The Spanish began to make settlements in Texas during the last decade of the seventeenth century, and in 1692 a little village was founded near the head of the San Antonio river. This place, which was known as San Fernandes, was the germ of the present San Antonio. In the year 1714, St. Denis, sent by Cardillac, then governor of Louisiana, on a trading expedition to Mexico, built the "old San Antonio road", which became the great thoroughfare through Texas. The little San Fernandes was greatly benefited by this road, and received added importance from the removal thither in 1718 of the mission of San Antonio de Valero, which had been established in 1703 upon the Rio Grande; the *Alamo*, destined to eternal remembrance in Texan hearts, was built as the chapel of this mission.

Already, in 1716, the place had received its baptism of blood, for a French force under St. Denis and La Harpe was defeated there by the Spanish. The first determined effort at a settlement was made in 1718 under De Alarcoune. An effort was made to obtain settlers from the best of Spanish families, and, in 1730, 16 families were brought thither from the Canaries at the royal expense. The Indians were determined in their hostilities to the new-comers, and from 1729 until 1806 the town, which was made the presidio of San Antonio de Bexar on November 28, 1730, was engaged in a continual struggle with the Indians for its very existence.

Americans seem never to have visited the town prior to 1801, but the news of the wonderful fertility of the land of Texas began to attract attention about that time, and when the Louisiana purchase transferred to the United States the title to the French possessions in America, an old claim of France to the possession of Texas, based on the landing of La Salle in 1585 at Matagorda bay, was revived. This claim came very near becoming a cause of war, when coupled with the harsh treatment to which all Americans were subjected by the Mexican authorities, and only an agreement of the opposing Mexican and American commanders prevented actual hostilities. By this agreement a narrow strip of land between the Sabine river and the Arroyo Hando was declared neutral territory. Upon this a band of outlaws established themselves for the purpose of robbing the trains of merchandise which crossed it on their way from Mexico and Texas to the Red river; and they became so annoying that, in spite of the fact that they were upon Texan territory, the Secretary of War gave orders for an expedition to be sent against them. The expedition was commanded by Lieutenant Magee, and proved successful, but it had consequences which had not been foreseen.

Mexico was then, 1812, divided between the royalist and the republican factions; and Magee was so much moved by the representations of Don Bernardo Guticorez, a Mexican sent to the United States to obtain recruits for the republican cause, that he resigned his commission in the United States army, collected a force called the "republican army of the north"—ostensibly under Guticorez' command, but really under his own—and by a series of brilliant movements soon made himself master of Nacogdoches and La Bahia. He was besieged in the latter place by the Mexicans, and, becoming disheartened, determined to surrender; but his men refused to yield, and after a hard contest defeated the enemy. Magee perished by his own hand, and his place was taken by Major Kemper, who, after defeating the Mexicans at Rosalie, received the capitulation of San Antonio, the chief city of Texas. The glory of this victory was dimmed by an act for which, however, the Americans were in no way responsible. One of the captains in the Mexican contingent of the "republican army of the north", eager to revenge the death of his father at the hands of the royalists, secretly obtained the consent of the Mexican commander to the murder of the captured officers. The American officers were so grieved and enraged at this outrageous act that they threw up their commissions and returned to the United States. The army, released from the strict discipline they had maintained, soon became demoralized, and barely escaped defeat at the battle of the Alazan, June 4, 1813, while it was completely routed in August at the battle of the Medina. The royalists took ample vengeance for the murder at San Antonio, and after shooting their prisoners, marched into San Antonio, where they committed the wildest excesses.

The royalist rulers, now firmly established, opposed American influences by all means in their power; but, in spite of opposition, Moses Austin obtained a grant of land from the Mexican government in 1820, and established upon it an American colony in Texas. The war between the two parties in Mexico had by no means ended with the defeat of the republicans in Texas. It was continued until (in 1824) the triumph of the republican party was complete and Mexico was made a republic. Under the constitution of 1824 Texas was united with Coahuila to form one of the states of the republic, and the rights of the American colonists were recognized and guaranteed. The seat of government was removed from San Antonio. This was a severe blow to its prosperity, and its effects were not lessened by attacks from the Indians, who for the next ten years sought every opportunity of annoying the citizens. But in spite of these disadvantages, many Americans established themselves in San Antonio, and engaged in trade in and around it.

With the growing success of the party of Santa Anna in the republic, the position of the American colonists became worse and worse. They were gradually deprived of their rights, and finally ordered to leave the country. This was too much. Organizing rapidly, the colonists determined to compel the fulfillment of the constitution of 1824 by force of arms. Convinced that their only hope of safety and success lay in the capture of San Antonio, which was held by a force under General Cos, the little army, under command of Stephen T. Austin, advanced October 20, 1835, to within a few miles of the city. Twice the Mexican forces were defeated in the open field, and finally they shut themselves up in the city to await the result of the siege which General Austin now began. Austin was, however, called away by an appointment as commissioner to the United States on behalf of the provisional government of Texas, and his place was taken by General Burleson, who continued to prosecute the siege vigorously. The colonists had left their homes at a moment's warning; they received no pay for their services, and their families were sadly in need of their presence. The siege operations were, of course, slow, and dissatisfaction grew and spread, till it seemed as if the army would give up the attempt to take the city and disperse. Accordingly it was decided to try and storm the place, and on December 6, 1835, a column under Colonel Milam advanced to the assault. Forcing its way into the city, and fighting from house to house, the storming party, after three days of battle, on the second of which its leader was killed, was successful, and San Antonio surrendered.

SAN ANTONIO,
TEXAS.

SCALE OF FEET

0   500   1000 1500 2000

In the mean time Santa Anna had been extending his power over Mexico, and now Texas alone stood out against him. He therefore determined to undertake its reduction, and on February 22, 1836, appeared before San Antonio, which was defended by a small force of 145 men under Colonel Travis. The defenders posted themselves within the Alamo, the mission of San Antonio de Valero, which was admirably calculated for defense; and here Colonel Travis held out for 11 days against the whole army of Santa Anna. On Sunday, March 6, 1836, the twelfth day of the siege, the Mexican bugles sounded the charge and the column under Santa Anna's best leaders sprang forward, their bugles now sounding the order "No quarter!" The Texans, nerved to the struggle by this sound, twice repulsed the attacking parties, but were unable to beat back the third charge, and withdrew to the chambers of the Alamo, where they sold their lives as dearly as they could. Not a man of the defenders is known to have escaped; the orders of Santa Anna to spare not were obeyed to the letter. Forty-six days later, "Remember the Alamo!" was the cry which spurred on Houston's men at San Jacinto, and with the defeat and capture of Santa Anna, San Antonio became Texan, the leading city of the new republic.

Until 1842 San Antonio was not again troubled by the Mexicans, but a continual warfare with the Indians kept the citizens always on the alert. In 1840 several Camanche chiefs asked for peace. They were told to come to San Antonio and bring with them their captives. They came bringing only one, although it was known that others were in their power. A dispute arising on this subject, the chiefs were told they would be detained as hostages until all the captives had been returned. Seizing their weapons the Indians fought until all were killed; thus adding another to the bitter contests which have taken place within the city.

Although Texas had been recognized as an independent nation, Mexico still refused to acknowledge her independence, and, in 1842, sent a force to seize San Antonio. The unsuspecting city fell at once into the invaders' hands, but no harm was inflicted. The government was remodeled, Mexican alcaldes put in the places of magistrates, and, after a stay of two days, the unwelcome visitors departed. This performance was repeated in September of the same year, a Mexican force under General Woll suddenly seizing the city. Many citizens were imprisoned, among them several who had come to San Antonio to attend the courts, which were then sitting there. Tired of these infringements of their rights, the Texans got together a small body of men, defeated the Mexicans, and drove them from the city, which has never since been in Mexican hands. In 1846 Texas was annexed to the United States, and San Antonio was made the military headquarters of the department of Texas. During the civil war the trade with Mexico was still maintained, and San Antonio was perhaps the most prosperous city in confederate hands. In 1865 the United States troops were again established in the city, and from that time its growth has been constant.

But while constant, the growth was not rapid until 1877, when the Galveston, Harrisburg, and San Antonio railroad reached the city. Change followed change with wonderful rapidity, and the old Spanish and Mexican town was soon transformed into an American city. San Antonio has become the principal wool market of western Texas. The San Pedro and San Antonio rivers offer a good water-power. The city is also the leading market for hides, and is an important distributing point for cotton, large amounts of which are sent to Mexico. The trade with Mexico is already large, but it is capable of being greatly extended. The city is an anomaly. Old houses, whose fort-like appearance speaks of a time when Indian wars were a constant source of apprehension, stand side by side with the wooden warehouses. The old mission buildings of the pious Catholic priests look out upon the railroad station, and gas-pipes run through streets still intersected by the irrigation ditches of the early Spanish settlers. It is full of interest to the tourist, but to the sons of Texas it is almost a shrine; for in its streets has flowed again and again the blood of heroes, fighting for home, for liberty, and for independence.

SAN ANTONIO IN 1880.

The following statistical accounts, collected by the Census Office, indicate the present condition of San Antonio:

LOCATION.

San Antonio is situated in latitude 29° 25' north, longitude 98° 25' west from Greenwich, and about 216 miles by railroad from Houston. The altitude of the city, at the office of the Signal Service, is 676 feet above the sea-level. The San Pedro and San Antonio rivers flow through the city, offering a considerable water-power, which has not, however, been utilized. Neither is navigable.

RAILROAD COMMUNICATIONS.

Until 1877 no railroad entered the city, but since that date the Galveston, Harrisburg, and San Antonio railroad, termini Houston and San Antonio, and the International and Great Northern railroad, termini San Antonio and Longview, have been completed to this point. The two companies enter the city over the same road-bed, the trains of the International and Great Northern using the Galveston, Houston, and San Antonio tracks.

TRIBUTARY COUNTRY.

The country immediately tributary to San Antonio is devoted almost entirely to agriculture, although there are a few wool-washing establishments on the river below the city.

TOPOGRAPHY.

San Antonio is situated in the midst of a level plain, crossed by two little rivers—the San Pedro and the San Antonio—and shut in on the west by the heights of Alazan, a mile distant from the city. The soil is a fertile black loam from 2 to 6 feet in depth and resting upon a gravelly clay. The contour is admirably adapted for surface-drainage. The heights of the Alazan furnish a soft magnesian limestone, which has been extensively used in building.

CLIMATE.

The highest summer temperature in average years is 103°, but a temperature of 108° was recorded in 1877. The lowest recorded winter temperature is 10°, but in average years the thermometer rarely falls below 17°.

STREETS.

There is no record of the total length of the streets. From 15 to 20 miles are paved with gravel resting upon a soft limestone bed; no other streets are paved. The cost of the gravel paving is about 75 cents per square yard. The sidewalks are mostly of sandstone, but new ones are generally made of cement, which gives great satisfaction, and will undoubtedly become the favorite and prevailing material. No street-gutters are made, the roadway being extended clear to the curbstones, which are generally of limestone or cement, the latter predominating, though in thinly settled portions they are sometimes of wood. The householders have planted shade-trees quite generally along the residence streets, consulting their own tastes as to the methods of planting and the species of trees, which are mostly China trees, mulberry, and hackberry; the city exercises no supervision. Construction of streets is generally done by contract, repairing by day labor, both under supervision of the street commissioner. About $10,000 is annually expended in building, repairing, and cleaning the streets. The city owns a steam stone-crusher, but does not use it, as the sifted flint gravel is considered quite as good as broken stone and much cheaper. No steam-roller is used.

HORSE-RAILROADS.

There is one horse-railroad. This has about 6 miles of track, owns 14 cars and 50 mules, employs 23 men, and during the past year carried 507,243 passengers at fares of 5 cents.

WATER-WORKS.

The city is supplied with water by a private corporation which completed its works in 1878. Water is pumped from the San Antonio river by 2 Worthington duplex pumps driven by 2 large double turbine water-wheels, and is raised to a reservoir 150 feet above the Main plaza; from there it is distributed through more than 15 miles of pipes and mains.

GAS.

Gas has been introduced into all parts of the city, and nearly all the streets are lighted by it. The works are owned by a private corporation.

PUBLIC BUILDINGS.

The public buildings of San Antonio are valued at $40,000, and include a two-story building used as the recorder's court and the police headquarters, a two-story engine-house, and 5 other buildings. The city hires a portion of the "French building" for municipal offices, and a building for the high school. There is no city hall.

PUBLIC PARKS AND PLEASURE-GROUNDS.

The total area of the public parks is about 61 acres, of which *San Pedro Park*, situated at the northern end of the city, has 50 acres; *Travis Park*, on the east side of the San Antonio river, not far from the center of the city, has about 4 acres; and *Madison Square*, on the west side of the San Antonio, has 7 acres. With the exception of Madison square, which was a gift, the land upon which all the parks are situated belonged to the city, and little or nothing has ever been paid for construction and repairs. The ground on which San Pedro park, the only one of any importance, now stands was originally leased to a private person, the consideration being that he should construct the park in its present form, and during the lease, which is still running, keep it in good repair at his own expense. The yearly cost of maintenance of the parks to the city is less than $500.

PLACES OF AMUSEMENT.

There are 3 theaters in the city: The Turner opera-house, seating capacity 1,126; Casino hall, seating capacity 600; and the Vaudeville theater, seating capacity about 800. The last-named place of amusement is closely akin to a concert- and beer-garden, as liquors are sold during the performances. Theaters pay a license of $10 for each performance, of which $5 goes to the state, $2 50 to the county, and $2 50 to the city. There are no concert-halls and lecture-rooms. The San Pedro park is rather a place of amusement than a public park as at present managed.

DRAINAGE; CEMETERIES; MARKETS.

No information on these subjects was furnished.

SANITARY AUTHORITY.

The chief sanitary officer of the city is the city physician, but the mayor and aldermen act as a board of health when necessary, their authority as the latter organization being, of course, co-extensive with their power in the former capacity. The city physician receives a salary of $75 a month, and has charge of the maintenance of the public health. During the months of July and August, one policeman in each ward is assigned to the duty of inspecting all premises, and a number of cartmen are employed to carry away all filth, dirt, and rubbish every morning. The city physician reports to the city council all nuisances coming under his notice.

NUISANCES.

The city ordinances state at length the various acts and conditions which are declared nuisances. When a nuisance comes under the notice of the city physician, or of the street commissioner or city marshal, orders are given to the person causing it to abate it at once, and if this order is neglected he becomes liable to a fine. Nuisances rarely arise from defective sewerage or poor street-cleaning. Garbage is removed beyond the city proper and burned.

BURIAL OF THE DEAD.

No burial is allowed within 1 mile of the court-house, without a permit from the city council, under penalty of a fine of not less than $50 nor more than $100. The city sextons are forbidden to make any interment within the limits of the city without a certificate from the city physician, and they are required to keep a record of these certificates and interments, and to make a report every Saturday to the city physician and to the mayor of all persons deceased and interred during the past week.

INFECTIOUS DISEASES.

Small-pox patients are isolated in tents or in a pest-house situated in the western part of the city, the place being conspicuously marked with a small-pox flag to warn passers of their danger. Scarlet fever is rather unusual in San Antonio, but when a case occurs the patient is quarantined at home. When contagious diseases occur in schools, those exposed to contagion are removed, and those suffering from the disease are isolated at home. Vaccination is not compulsory, and is done at the public expense only for the poor. Any person who knows of the existence of contagious, infectious, or malignant diseases in the city must notify the mayor at once.

A correct register (weekly, monthly, and yearly) is kept at the mayor's office of deaths, and one of diseases when in epidemic form. No record of births is kept.

REPORTS.

The board of health makes no reports as a board to the city council. The city physician makes regular reports in regard to the performance of his duty.

MUNICIPAL CLEANSING.

Street-cleaning.—The streets are cleaned by a force hired especially for the purpose by the city, the work being done entirely by hand. After every rain the force is set to work to scrape and clean the paved streets, and every day a scavenger force is kept busy removing filth and rubbish from them. No cleaning is done on the unpaved streets. The sweepings are taken outside the city proper, but not outside its limits, and there burned. The cost of this work is included in the $10,000 annually expended on the streets.

Removal of garbage and ashes.—Household rubbish is removed by the city, but offal is removed by individuals. Ashes, rubbish and garbage may be kept in the same vessel. They are disposed of in the same way as street-sweepings. The cost of this service is about $2,200, and is included in the street appropriation.

Dead animals.—The owner of any animal dying within the city is required to remove the carcass to the soft-rock quarries at Powder-house hill, and there bury it not less than 4 feet deep.

Liquid household wastes.—The liquid household wastes are run into cesspools, only very little passing into the two small sewers that have been built. The cesspools are in all cases porous, most, if not all, of them being simple pits, not even bricked on the sides, and they have no overflows, the contents escaping through the soil. The street-gutters are not flushed, as no wastes run into them. It seems probable that wells have been contaminated by the overflowing or underground escape of the contents of vaults and cesspools, but such cases are uncommon.

Human excreta.—About 1 per cent. of the houses are provided with water-closets, all the rest depending on privy-vaults, which are nearly always simple holes dug in the ground and used until they are full, when some dirt is thrown over them, the privy placed over a new hole, and the process repeated. The dry-earth system is rarely used.

Manufacturing wastes.—The city requires that wool-washing, if done in or near the river, shall be done at some point below San Antonio. There are no other wastes likely to be a cause of nuisance.

POLICE.

The police force of San Antonio is appointed and governed by the mayor and city council. The chief executive officer is the city marshal, who receives a salary of $125 a month, and has general charge of his department, subject to the orders of the mayor. He is assisted by 2 assistant marshals, the first receiving $125 and the second $100 per month. The number of patrolmen is limited by the city ordinances to 13, each of whom receives $70 per month. An allowance of $40, payable semi-annually in instalments of $20 each, is made to each man for a uniform. No details as to the number and causes of arrests, or the cost of the department during the past year, could be obtained. Special policemen can be appointed at any time by the mayor when he thinks it necessary, and while on duty they receive a salary of $2 per day, and are treated as members of the regular force.

MANUFACTURES.

The following is a summary of the statistics of the manufactures of San Antonio for 1880, being taken from tables prepared for the Tenth Census by Max Neuendorff, special agent:

Mechanical and manufacturing industries.	No. of estab-lish-ments.	Capital.	AVERAGE NUMBER OF HANDS EMPLOYED.			Total amount paid in wages during the year.	Value of materials.	Value of products.
			Males above 16 years.	Females above 15 years.	Children and youths.			
All industries	71	$310,050	300	13	48	$137,781	$328,476	$642,412
Blacksmithing	10	15,450	29	3	10	10,850	9,440	28,750
Boots and shoes, including custom work and repairing	7	8,600	20	....	....	5,750	7,800	31,300
Carpentering	3	3,500	23	....	....	10,200	16,000	33,300
Carriages and wagons	3	12,000	12	....	3	6,064	7,000	20,980
Flouring- and grist-mill products	3	40,000	19	....	....	10,100	162,600	205,000
Mineral and soda waters	4	7,600	2	8	....	1,860	1,850	6,400
Painting and paperhanging	4	4,200	24	....	....	6,875	3,900	14,000
Printing and publishing	4	27,700	46	2	26	29,520	16,500	71,000
Saddlery and harness	6	30,300	26	....	4	11,650	19,300	44,700
Tinware, copperware, and sheet-iron ware	3	4,400	10	....	1	2,100	3,500	7,250
All other industries (a)	24	156,300	89	5	4	42,812	80,086	179,732

a Embracing brick and tile; cement; confectionery; cooperage; foundery and machine-shop products; ice, artificial; jewelry; leather, curried; leather, tanned; lime; liquors, malt; lumber, sawed; soap and candles; stone- and earthen-ware; tobacco, cigars and cigarettes; and wheelwrighting.

From the foregoing table it appears that the average capital of all establishments is $4,366 90; that the average wages of all hands employed is $381 66 per annum; and that the average outlay in wages, in materials, and in interest (at 6 per cent.) on capital employed is $6,820 01.

THE WESTERN STATES.

OHIO.

AKRON,   CLEVELAND,   PORTSMOUTH,   TOLEDO,
CANTON,   COLUMBUS,   SANDUSKY,   YOUNGSTOWN,
CHILLICOTHE,   DAYTON,   SPRINGFIELD,   ZANESVILLE.
CINCINNATI,   HAMILTON,   STEUBENVILLE,

INDIANA.

EVANSVILLE,   INDIANAPOLIS,   NEW ALBANY,   SOUTH BEND,
FORT WAYNE,   LA FAYETTE,   RICHMOND,   TERRE HAUTE.

ILLINOIS.

AURORA,   CHICAGO,   JOLIET,   ROCKFORD,
BELLEVILLE,   GALESBURG,   PEORIA,   ROCK ISLAND,
BLOOMINGTON.   JACKSONVILLE,   QUINCY.   SPRINGFIELD.

MISSOURI.

HANNIBAL,   KANSAS CITY,   SAINT JOSEPH,   SAINT LOUIS.

MICHIGAN.

BAY CITY,   EAST SAGINAW,   JACKSON,   MUSKEGON
DETROIT,   GRAND RAPIDS,   KALAMAZOO,

WISCONSIN.

BELOIT,   FOND DU LAC,   MADISON,   OSHKOSH,
EAU CLAIRE.   LA CROSSE,   MILWAUKEE,   RACINE.

MINNESOTA.

MINNEAPOLIS,   SAINT PAUL,   WINONA.

IOWA.

BURLINGTON,   COUNCIL BLUFFS,   DES MOINES,   KEOKUK.
CEDAR RAPIDS,   DAVENPORT,   DUBUQUE,

NEBRASKA.

LINCOLN,   OMAHA.

KANSAS.

ATCHISON,   LAWRENCE,   LEAVENWORTH,   TOPEKA.

COLORADO.

DENVER,   LEADVILLE.

CALIFORNIA.

LOS ANGELES,   OAKLAND,   SAN FRANCISCO,   STOCKTON.
                SACRAMENTO,   SAN JOSÉ,

OREGON.

PORTLAND.

UTAH TERRITORY.

SALT LAKE CITY.

OHIO.

AKRON,

SUMMIT COUNTY, OHIO.

POPULATION

IN THE

AGGREGATE,

1850-1880.

	Inhab.
1790	......
1800	......
1810	......
1820	......
1830	......
1840	......
1850	3,266
1860	3,477
1870	10,006
1880	16,512

POPULATION

BY

SEX, NATIVITY, AND RACE,

AT

CENSUS OF 1880.

Male	8,228
Female	8,284
Native	12,901
Foreign-born	3,611
White	16,231
Colored	*281

* Including 3 Chinese.

Latitude: 41° 5′ North; Longitude: 81° 32′ (west from Greenwich); Altitude: 793 to 1,123 feet.

FINANCIAL CONDITION:

Total Valuation: $7,316,182; per capita: $443 00.   Net Indebtedness: $17,619; per capita: $107 00.   Tax per $100: $2 25.

HISTORICAL SKETCH.

In the year 1825, as soon as the Ohio canal was located, General Simon Perkins and Paul Williams laid out a town in Portage, Portage county, Ohio, at the highest point along the line of the canal between the Ohio river and lake Erie, to which they gave the appropriate name of "Akron," from the Greek word meaning "summit." This was the beginning of Akron proper; but the present city contains parts settled before 1825, as Middlebury, now the sixth ward, was founded in 1818, and settlers were located on some of the territory now included in Akron as early as 1802. The work of building the Ohio canal was begun at Licking Summit on July 4, 1825, and in September

335

following ground was broken at Akron. The canal was completed to Akron in 1827, and a boat cleared from there for Cleveland July 4; but the entire work was not finished until 1832. In that year the Pennsylvania and Ohio canal was extended to Akron, and, connecting there with the Ohio canal, linked the canal systems of Ohio and western Pennsylvania. These two inland water-ways gave the town its first importance; but it was the enterprise of Eliakim Crosby, one of the citizens, which placed at its command the means of future eminence. In 1831 Crosby conceived and executed the design of bringing the Little Cuyahoga river from Middlebury to Akron, and thus supplied the town with the fine water-power to which its present manufacturing prosperity is almost entirely due.

Akron was incorporated as a town in 1836, and five years later was made the county seat of Summit county, which had been organized by the legislature in 1840. The county is rich in deposits of coal, and contains large beds of clay suitable for all kinds of coarse pottery and fire-brick. Akron was soon busily engaged in working these clays, and laid the foundation for the present extensive manufactures of stoneware and fire-brick which have made the name of Akron familiar throughout America.

The Atlantic and Great Western railway reached the town in 1852, and gave a great impetus to its manufactures. Its natural and acquired advantages became at once apparent with the increased facilities of transportation, and in the following ten years many new industries were introduced, which have proved valuable additions to its wealth. The town early earned an enviable reputation for its manufactures of flour; but this fame is now entirely overshadowed by the renown of its establishments for the manufacture of agricultural implements, as well as of sewer-pipe and all kinds of stoneware, and of oatmeal. A capital of $6,127,250 is invested in manufactures, which, during the past year, furnished employment to 4,163 workmen and produced finished goods valued at $9,313,451. The manufacturing interests of Akron have not claimed all the energies of the citizens. The schools, churches, and societies have received their share of attention. In 1867 a few gentlemen organized a library association and started a library, which, after a few years of successful operation, they presented to the city, on condition that it be made free and not less than $3,000 be spent annually in its maintenance and improvement. The gift was accepted, and Akron now has a library of over 7,000 volumes, open freely to all who choose to use it. In 1870 the Ohio Universalist convention determined to found a college, and offered to locate it in Akron if the sum of $60,000 should be raised and presented to the convention. Steps were taken to raise the necessary amount, and in 1871 work was begun on the college building. The public schools of the city are in a flourishing condition, and it has 16 churches, many of which have beautiful edifices. Akron, which was incorporated as a city in 1865, has had more than its share of misfortunes, large fires in 1848, 1849, 1851, 1854, 1855, 1856, 1857, 1872, and 1878 sweeping over it and destroying large amounts of property; but after each calamity the city has sprung up to an increased prosperity.

AKRON IN 1880.

The following statistical accounts, collected by the Census Office, indicate the present condition of Akron:

LOCATION.

Akron is situated in latitude 41° 5′ north, and longitude 81° 32′ west from Greenwich, in nearly the center of Summit county, Ohio, about 36 miles south of Cleveland, and 110 northeast of Columbus. The highest point is 1,123 feet, and the lowest 793 feet above the sea-level. The Ohio canal, extending from Portsmouth, on the Ohio river, to Cleveland, on lake Erie, passes through the city, within the immediate vicinity of which it has 21 locks. This canal still does a large business in carrying lumber, coal, stone, and other heavy freight.

RAILROAD COMMUNICATIONS.

Akron is touched by the following-named railroads:

The New York, Pennsylvania, and Ohio railroad (formerly the Atlantic and Great Western), termini, Salamanca, New York, and Dayton, Ohio.

The Cleveland, Mount Vernon, and Columbus railroad, termini, Hudson and Columbus.

The Valley railroad, termini, Cleveland and Canton.

These railroads pass through the city, and connect it closely with the cities of Ohio and the mineral deposits of the surrounding country.

TRIBUTARY COUNTRY.

The country tributary to Akron is rich and varied in its productions. On all sides farming is general; wheat, fruit, dairy products, and stock-raising claiming most of the farmers' attention. To the south are large coal-fields, which are extensively mined, and to the east large deposits of clay, from which stoneware, sewer-pipe, and coarse pottery are manufactured. The city owes much of its prosperity to the richness of the country tributary to it.

A K R O N,

OHIO.

TOPOGRAPHY.

The city is situated at the highest point along the line of the Ohio canal, and is about 500 feet above the level of lake Erie. The surface is very much diversified, variations in level of 330 feet occurring within the corporate limits. The soil is a sandy loam, with occasional small areas of clay, underlaid with sandstone, shale, fine and coarse sand, and clays of various kinds. A portion of the city is underlaid by thick beds of stratified sand and gravel, containing angular blocks of conglomerate and many fragments of coal. There are many lakes in the vicinity. Summit lake, a body of water a mile long and half as wide, lies about $1\frac{1}{2}$ mile south of the city, and furnishes a considerable water-power. There are also a few small marshes. The natural drainage is excellent, as the city stands on the water-shed between the Ohio river and lake Erie, one stream from Summit lake flowing to the former and one to the latter. The forests once covering the region have been largely cut off, but considerable timber still stands upon some of the farms. The soil within a radius of 5 miles is generally a rich sandy loam, with occasional small beds of clay.

CLIMATE.

The variations in temperature are large, the highest recorded temperature being 100° and the lowest —33°; but the average years show a range between $97\frac{2}{8}$° in summer and —$13\frac{5}{8}$° in winter. The winds from lake Erie tend to keep the climate much warmer than it otherwise would be. The country for miles around is not much different in its elevation from that of the city, and affords it no protection from the chilling winds.

STREETS.

The total length of the streets is about 75 miles. Only little more than 2 miles are paved; of these, 750 feet are paved with stone blocks, 900 feet with broken stones, 9,600 feet with Nicholson pavement, and 1,900 feet with gravel. The cost of each of these per square yard is as follows: Stone blocks, $1 60; broken stone, 70 cents; wood, $2 25; and gravel, 35 cents. The Nicholson pavement is worn out and must soon be replaced, and the streets are in general badly kept. The sidewalks are of plank, brick, or stone; the gutters mostly of cobble-stones. Trees are planted by the property-owners along the streets in front of their lots, or the lawns between the walks and the curbing. The work of the construction of streets is done by contract; repairing by day labor. The mayor reports that there are no available data of the annual cost of street work. Both a steam-crusher and a roller are used on the streets with excellent results. There are no horse-railroads and no omnibus lines.

WATER-WORKS.

Works for a public water-supply are being built by a private company at a cost of $220,000. Water is taken from a well and pumped into a reservoir 220 feet above the average level of the city, and the mains will be supplied partly from the reservoir and partly from direct pumping into the pipes. The pressure will be about 86 pounds to the square inch. The pumps are of the Worthington manufacture, and pump, on the average, 200,000 gallons daily.

GAS.

The city is supplied with gas by a private corporation, which charges private persons $2 50 per 1,000 feet. Owing to an alleged violation of its contract with the gas company, the city uses no gas street-lamps, but lights its streets with coal-oil.

PUBLIC BUILDINGS.

The public buildings are valued at about $30,000, and include a city building, which cost $17,000, and contains the various municipal offices, an armory, a city prison, and an engine-house for the fire department.

PUBLIC PARKS AND PLEASURE-GROUNDS.

The total area of the parks of Akron, which are seven in number and vary in size from 1 to 10 acres, is 25 acres. They are finely laid out in walks and drives, and shaded by trees which were growing there when the town was laid out. The parks were donated by the original proprietors of the town, and have cost only a small sum for improvements. About $500 is annually expended in their maintenance. *Fountain Park*, a picturesque tract of about 50 acres, mostly within the limits of the city, belongs to the Summit County Agricultural Society, but is largely used by the people of Akron as a pleasure-ground. The parks are controlled by the city council through a board of park commissioners.

PLACES OF AMUSEMENT.

Akron has only one theater, the Academy of Music, which has a seating capacity of 850. Phœnix hall, seating 450; Kaiser's hall, seating 400; and Music hall, seating 350, are used as concert- and lecture-rooms. The city ordinances require a license of $3 for all theatrical performances, except minstrel shows, which pay $5.

DRAINAGE.

In March, 1880, plans were adopted for a regular system of sewerage to embrace the entire city. Prior to that time only a few drains had been laid, and they were only for storm-water. The principal outfall is to the Little Cuyahoga river. The mouth of the main sewer is above water, and fully exposed; but the plan contemplates a small outlet for the ordinary flow, and proposes to close the mouth of the large storm-sewer by a hinged flap. The ventilation of the main sewer is described as being through manholes, but communication with the outside air is only through a box filled with charcoal, placed in a chamber built for the purpose between the manhole and the sewer. The cost of the sewers is assessed upon the abutting property, on the basis of benefits. In the case of the larger and more expensive works such assessments are laid in the same manner to an amount not exceeding $2 per foot front, and the remaining cost, above the amount so realized, is assessed upon the whole area to be drained by the main sewer.

No information is furnished of the cost and extent of sewers, except that the average cost of each inlet-basin is $50 and of each manhole $80. The average depth is 13 feet.

CEMETERIES.

Akron has five cemeteries, as follows:

Akron Rural Cemetery, 53 acres, is situated in the northwestern part of the city, and was founded in 1839. It is managed by a private corporation, consisting of the owners of lots, and is beautifully laid out. Among its ornaments is a fine chapel, dedicated May 30, 1876, as a memorial to the citizens of Akron who lost their lives during the civil war. There have been 3,518 interments in this cemetery.

German Catholic Cemetery, area 4 acres, joins the Rural cemetery. It was opened in 1866.

Irish Catholic Cemetery, area 4½ acres, is situated in the extreme northwest corner of the city, and has been in use only a few years.

German Reformed Cemetery is located beyond the city limits, to the north, and was opened during the present year. It contains about 10 acres.

Sixth Ward Cemetery, area 8 acres, is situated in the southeastern part of the city, and was opened in 1853.

All these cemeteries are managed by private corporations or by churches. There are no ordinances regarding the burial of the dead; each of the cemeteries has its own rules. All of them require graves to be made at least 5 feet deep. The use of vaults is discountenanced, owing to the close proximity of the cemeteries to the inhabited districts, and there is but one public vault in the city.

MARKETS.

There are no public or corporation markets in Akron.

SANITARY AUTHORITY—BOARD OF HEALTH.

The city has no board of health, and up to the present time has made no ordinances regarding sanitary matters. The advisability of creating a board of health is now under consideration, and it is probable that one will soon be organized, and given ample authority for the preservation of the public health.

MUNICIPAL CLEANSING.

Street-cleaning.—The citizens are expected to sweep the streets in front of their premises and place the dirt and rubbish in piles, ready for removal by the city teams, which are expected to remove the accumulations once a week in the business portion of the city, and as occasion may require on the other streets, and carry the sweepings to the various ravines which need to be raised to the city grade. The mayor thinks the work, which is done entirely by hand, is fairly well done. No separate account of the cost of the work to the city is kept.

Removal of garbage and ashes.—Garbage and ashes are removed by the householders, no special regulations governing the matter. Garbage is usually buried, while ashes are deposited in places that need to be filled up.

Dead animals.—In case any animal dies within the city, the owner, if known, is compelled to remove the carcass and bury it; if the owner is not known the work is done by the city marshal at the expense of the city.

Liquid household wastes.—The liquid household wastes are either run into cesspools, or simply thrown upon the surface of the ground, only very little running into the public sewers, which are in an unfinished condition. The cesspools are porous, being simply holes dug in the ground to hold the wastes until they can be absorbed. There are no rules regulating their construction or the manner in which they shall be cleansed.

Human excreta.—Almost all of the houses depend on privy-vaults, only a few of which are water-tight. No regulations govern their construction or cleansing. The dry-earth system is used to a slight extent. The night-soil is generally disposed of by either burying it in deep trenches, or throwing it into the Cuyahoga river outside the city limits. It is used to a slight extent as manure, sometimes, though not often, on the gathering-ground of the public water-supply.

Manufacturing wastes.—There is no system for the disposal of manufacturing wastes.

POLICE.

The police force is appointed by the mayor and confirmed by the city council. The chief executive officer is the city marshal, salary $700 per annum, who has the general supervision of the force and the execution of the orders of the city council. The rest of the force consists of 10 patrolmen, at $600 per annum each. The uniform is a blue cloth suit, stiff, round-crown, felt hat, with wreath and number on the front, and a police badge. The men furnish their own uniforms. The patrolmen are equipped with a club, revolver, chain twisters, and police whistle, and are on duty 12 hours daily, alternately day and night.

During the past year there were 804 arrests made, the principal causes being for drunkenness and disorderly conduct. During the year 43 station-house lodgers were accommodated, as against 143 in 1879. Free meals are furnished to these lodgers at an annual cost of about $20. Special policemen are appointed by the mayor when he thinks necessary, and while on duty they receive the same pay and are treated in the same manner as members of the regular force. In a general way the police are required to co-operate with the other departments of the city government. The cost of the police force in 1880 was about $7,000.

CANTON,

STARK COUNTY, OHIO.

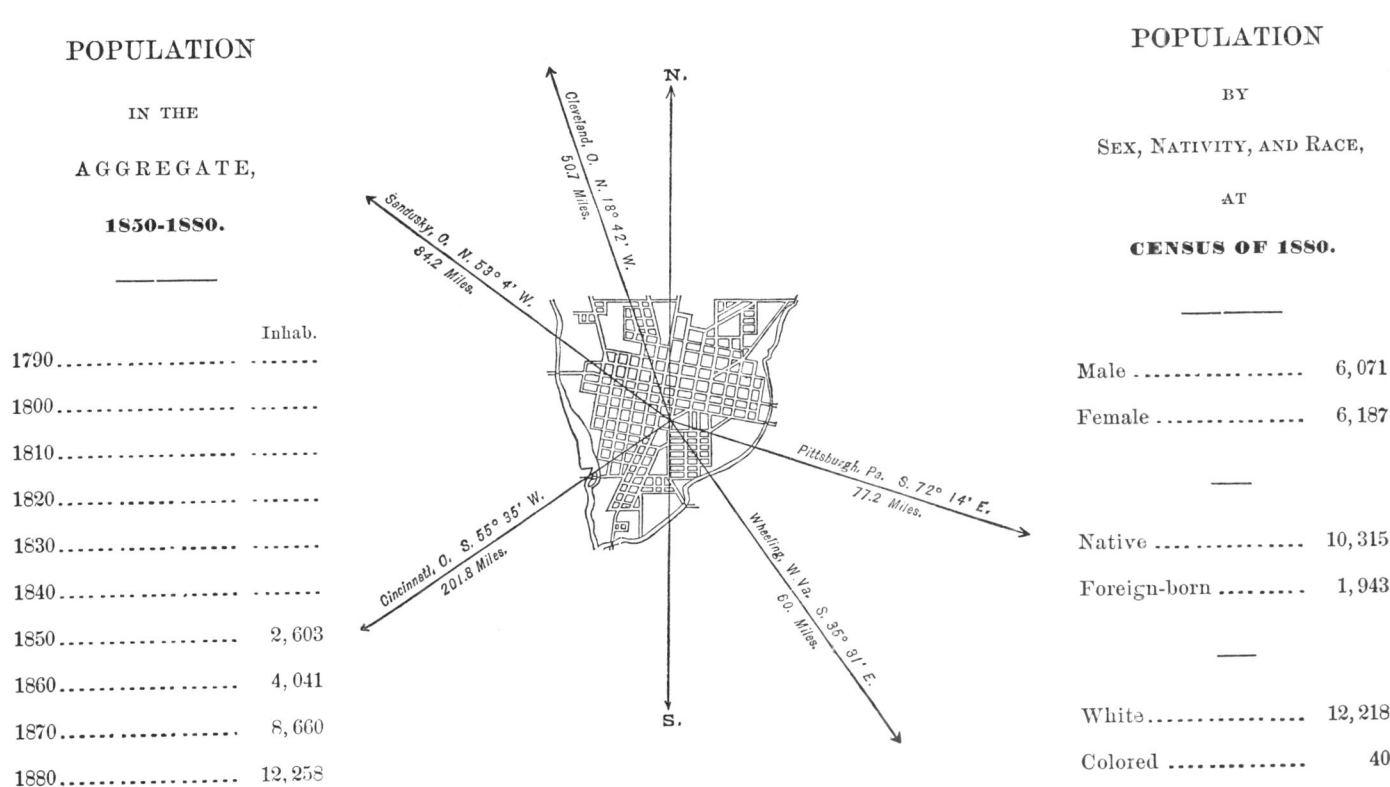

POPULATION

IN THE

AGGREGATE,

1850-1880.

	Inhab.
1790	....
1800	....
1810	....
1820	....
1830	....
1840	....
1850	2,603
1860	4,041
1870	8,660
1880	12,258

POPULATION

BY

SEX, NATIVITY, AND RACE,

AT

CENSUS OF 1880.

Male	6,071
Female	6,187
Native	10,315
Foreign-born	1,943
White	12,218
Colored	40

Latitude: 40° 48′ North; Longitude: 81° 23′ (west from Greenwich).

FINANCIAL CONDITION:

Total Valuation: $5,056,070; per capita: $412 00.   Net Indebtedness: $180,657; per capita: $14 74.   Tax per $100: $2 14.

CANTON.

NOTE.—Canton, the capital of Stark county, Ohio, is situated at the confluence of the east and west branches of Nimishillen creek, and is on the line of the Pittsburgh, Fort Wayne, and Chicago railroad. The Connotton Valley railroad, from Dell Roy, Ohio, terminates here. Coal is abundant in the vicinity, and the city derives its prosperity chiefly from its manufactures, especially the manufacture of agricultural implements. The surrounding country is very rich agriculturally. The city is supplied with water from a lake 3 miles northwest of the place by means of a Holly engine. No detailed information or statistics of any kind were furnished, and therefore no report on the present condition of the city can be made.

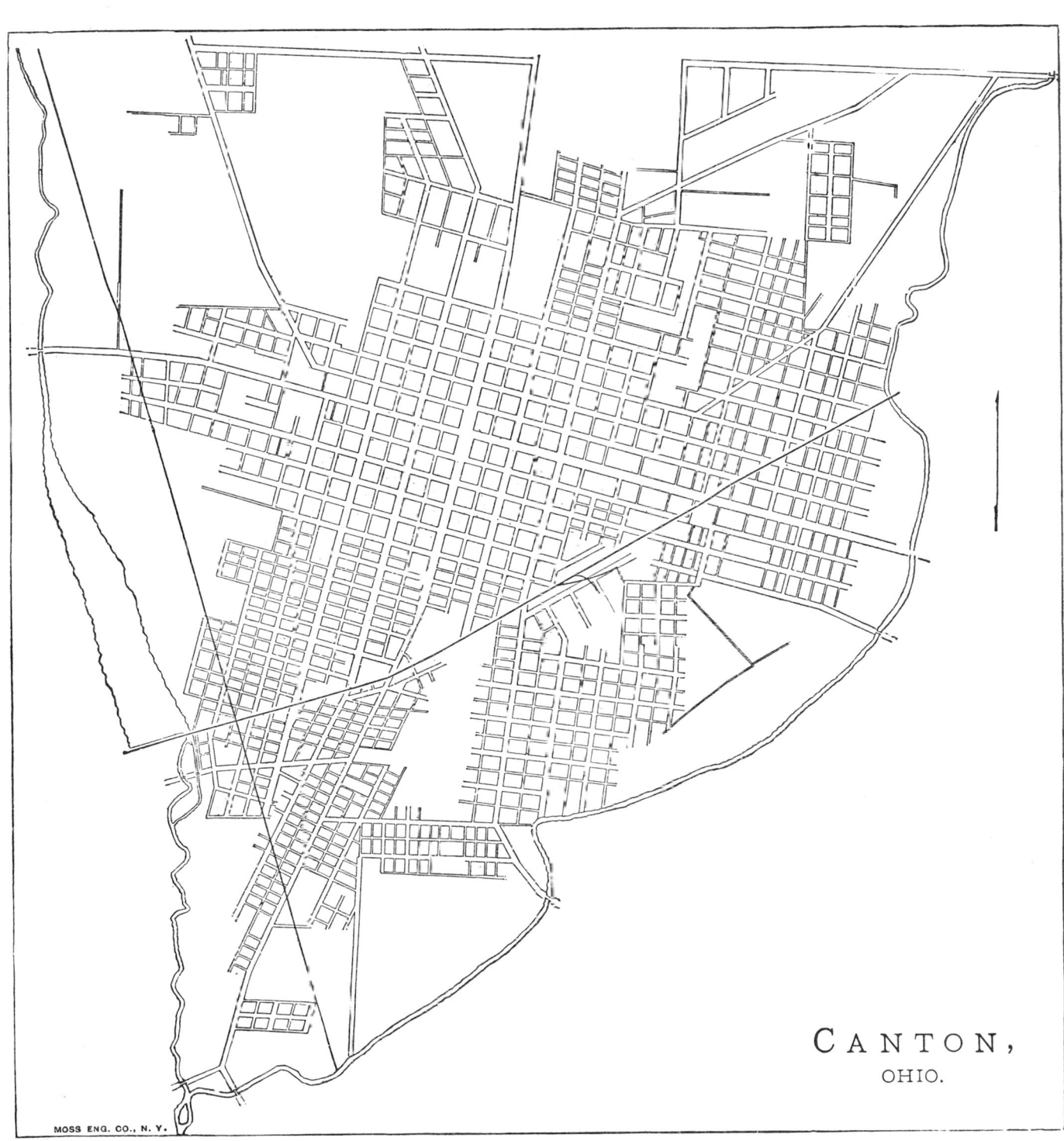

CANTON,
OHIO.

CHILLICOTHE,

ROSS COUNTY, OHIO.

POPULATION

IN THE

AGGREGATE,

1850-1880.

	Inhab.
1790	......
1800	......
1810	......
1820	......
1830	......
1840	......
1850	7,100
1860	7,626
1870	8,920
1880	10,938

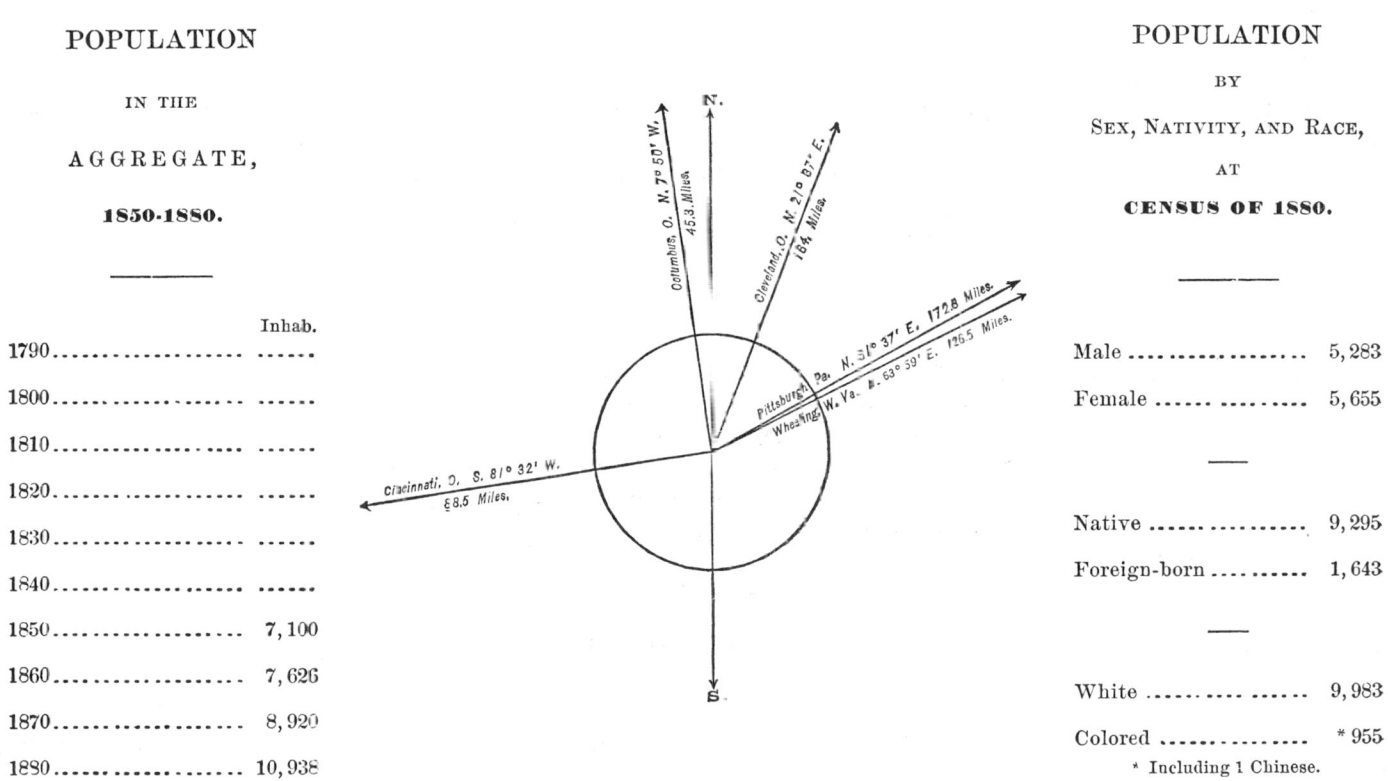

POPULATION

BY

SEX, NATIVITY, AND RACE,

AT

CENSUS OF 1880.

Male	5,283
Female	5,655
Native	9,295
Foreign-born	1,643
White	9,983
Colored	* 955

* Including 1 Chinese.

Latitude: 39° 18′ North; Longitude: 82° 52 (west from Greenwich).

FINANCIAL CONDITION:

Total Valuation: $4,732,745; per capita: $433 00.   Tax per $100: $1 89.

HISTORICAL SKETCH.

Chillicothe, the capital of Ross county, Ohio, was founded in 1796 by emigrants from Virginia and Kentucky, and in 1800 it became the seat of the state government.   The convention which formed the constitution of Ohio met here in November, 1802, and the sessions of the state legislature were held in Chillicothe until 1810, when the seat of government was moved to Zanesville.

CHILLICOTHE IN 1880.

The following statistical accounts, collected by the Census Office, indicate the present condition of Chillicothe:

LOCATION.

Chillicothe is situated on the right bank of the Scioto river, about 45 miles below Columbus and the same distance above Portsmouth, the Scioto at the latter place entering the Ohio river. The river at this point is not navigable. The city is situated on a plain, partly inclosed by verdant and cultivated hills 500 feet high. Paint creek flows along the south side of the city and enters the river 3 miles below. The Ohio canal, from Portsmouth to Cleveland, Ohio, passes through the place. Chillicothe is the center of trade in the populous valley of the Scioto—one of the best farming regions in the country.

RAILROAD COMMUNICATION.

Chillicothe is touched by the following-named railroads:

The Dayton and Southeastern railroad, from Dayton to Wellston, Ohio, and by connecting roads with all points east and west.

The Marietta and Cincinnati railroad, between the points named, included in the Baltimore and Ohio Railroad system.

The Scioto Valley railroad, from Columbus to Portsmouth.

STREETS.

There are 22 miles of streets in the city, all of which are paved with gravel. The sidewalks are principally of brick, but many are laid with sandstone, from 8 to 15 feet wide. Some sidewalks are laid in brick, 4 feet wide, with a grass plat on either side of the same width. All the gutters are of cobble-stones, 8 inches deep and 5 feet wide. Tree-planting in the streets is universal, they being set only at the curb-line; one street, however, has four rows of trees. The construction and repair of streets are done by day work. There are 2 miles of horse-railroads in the city, using 7 cars and 14 horses, and carrying passengers at 5 cents for each fare. The omnibus lines have 6 vehicles and 12 horses, and give employment to 8 men. The rate of fare is 25 cents, and during the year 21,900 passengers were carried.

WATER-WORKS.

The works for the water-supply are now in process of construction by the city.

GAS.

The gas-works are owned by a private company. The charge to consumers is $2 40 per 1,000 feet. The city pays for 139 street-lamps.

PUBLIC BUILDINGS.

The total cost of municipal buildings belonging to the city is $25,000.

PUBLIC PARKS AND PLEASURE-GROUNDS.

With the exception that the parks have a total area of 50 acres, and cost $10,000, no information on this subject was furnished.

PLACES OF AMUSEMENT; DRAINAGE.

No information on these subjects was furnished.

CEMETERIES.

Chillicothe Cemetery, area 50 acres; *Township Cemetery*, area 4 acres; *Roman Catholic Cemetery* (Irish), area 2 acres; and *Roman Catholic Cemetery* (German), area 2 acres, are used for interments. There are also 1 Methodist grave-yard, but little used, and 1 Catholic grave-yard, in which burials are no longer made. No permits are required for interments. Chillicothe cemetery is the only one of the above that is public.

MARKETS.

There are no public or corporation markets in the city.

SANITARY AUTHORITY.

There is no board of health in Chillicothe. The city council attends to the sanitary needs of the city, and can make such rules and expend such sums as may appear necessary. When nuisances are reported they are abated by the city marshal. There is no pest-house. Vaccination is not compulsory, but it is done at the public expense when deemed necessary.

MUNICIPAL CLEANSING.

Street-cleaning.—The streets are cleaned by the city, at its own expense and with its own force. The work is done wholly by hand. The streets are cleaned twice a year, and the work is reported as being well done. The annual cost is about $2,500, and the sweepings are carted off.

Removal of garbage and ashes.—The householders remove their own garbage and ashes. There are no regulations as to the conservancy of garbage while awaiting removal, and it, as well as the ashes, is carted out of the city. The cost of the service is not given. It is stated that no injury to health results from either the manner of removal or disposal of the garbage.

Dead animals.—The carcasses of all animals dying within the city are removed by the city marshal, if the owners do not do it.

Liquid household wastes and human excreta.—Most of the liquid household wastes in the city are thrown into vaults and cesspools, but little going into the public sewers, and only a small portion into the street-gutters. The cesspools are nominally water-tight, have no overflows, and receive the wastes from the few water-closets there are in the city. Nearly all the houses in the city depend on privy-vaults. These must be not less than 6 feet nor more than 12 feet deep, and none of them are reported as even nominally water-tight. The manner of cleansing them or the final disposition of the night-soil was not stated.

Manufacturing wastes are run either into the river or the creek.

POLICE.

The police force of Chillicothe is appointed by the mayor, subject to the confirmation of the city council, and is governed by the mayor. The executive officer is the chief of police, salary $730 per annum, and he has command of the force, under direction of the mayor. The remainder of the force consists of 8 regular policeman, salary $1 75 per day each, and 4 reserve policemen at $1 25 per day each. The latter are called on duty only occasionally. The uniform is of dark-blue cloth, and each man provides his own, at a cost of $23 per annum. The policemen are equipped with clubs only; their hours of duty are from 6 p. m. to 6 a. m., and they patrol 20 miles of streets. During the past year 350 arrests were made by the force, and the cause of four-fifths of these arrests was intoxication. The cases were disposed of either by fines of from $1 to $50, or by imprisonment of from 5 to 30 days. The force is required to co-operate with the fire department only in a general way. Special policemen are appointed by the mayor for temporary service. The yearly cost of the police force is about $6,000.

CINCINNATI,

HAMILTON COUNTY, OHIO.

POPULATION

IN THE

AGGREGATE,

1810-1880.

	Inhab.
1790	......
1800	......
1810	2,540
1820	9,642
1830	24,831
1840	46,338
1850	115,435
1860	161,044
1870	216,239
1880	255,139

POPULATION

BY

SEX, NATIVITY, AND RACE,

AT

CENSUS OF 1880.

Male	125,492
Female	129,647
Native	183,480
Foreign-born	71,659
White	246,912
Colored	*8,227

*Including 38 Chinese and 10 Indians.

Latitude: 39° 6 North; Longitude: 84° 30′ (west from Greenwich); Altitude: 440 to 904 feet.

FINANCIAL CONDITION:

Total Valuation: $169,305,635; per capita: $664 00.   Net Indebtedness: $21,992,500; per capita: $86 20.   Tax per $100: $2 91.

HISTORICAL SKETCH.(a)

At the close of the Revolutionary war it was found that but six of the thirteen American states had well-defined boundaries. The rest laid claim to lands running west to the Pacific ocean, and in many cases the same territory was covered by two or more of the charters on which these claims were based. To complicate the question, the states that had none of these unappropriated lands denied the exclusive right of their sister states to them, maintaining that their claim was unjust and inequitable. They contended that as the war had been sustained and the independence of the country acquired by the blood and treasure of all the states, whatever had

a Prepared by Robert Luce, esq.

been conquered from the crown belonged to them in common as a matter of right, and should be held for their joint and equal benefit. So great an excitement sprang up over this subject that propositions were made in the public prints of the day urging the destitute states to seize on portions of these lands for their own benefit. To allay the ferment, Congress made strong appeals to the sense of justice and the patriotism of the states holding the claims to make liberal cession, which they were generous enough to do.

The territory now embraced in the state of Ohio was covered by the claims of four states—Massachusetts, Connecticut, New York, and Virginia. Massachusetts and New York ceded their rights unconditionally. Connecticut ceded jurisdiction but retained the title in that district on lake Erie known as the "Western Reserve of Connecticut". In the cession made by Virginia, March, 1784, the lands north of the Ohio river, between the Scioto and the Little Miami, were reserved for satisfying legal bounties to their troops in case certain lands to the south of the Ohio should be insufficient.

There yet remained other titles to be extinguished—those of the real owners of the land, the Indians. During the late war the Indians had generally sided against the colonists, and after its termination they seemed disposed to continue hostilities. Various expeditions were sent against them, and they were brought into some degree of subjection. On the 21st of January, 1785, by a treaty concluded at fort McIntosh, they ceded to the United States the lands watered by the Muskingum, Scioto, Little Miami, and Great Miami rivers. By this treaty, and by other treaties, the Indian title to a large part of the territory within the present state of Ohio was extinguished.

Congress at once made the necessary preparations for the survey and sale of these lands, and a new impulse was given to the emigration to the West which has since continued so constantly, and which has assumed such mammoth proportions.

After the Revolutionary war, General Washington, in parting with the Revolutionary officers, received from General Rufus Putnam a petition from 243 officers of the army, mostly those of New England, asking his influence with Congress to secure to them lands between the Ohio river and lake Erie. Putnam was clear-sighted enough to prophesy that this region "would be filled with inhabitants, and thereby free the Western territory from falling under the dominion of a foreign power". After Congress had finally got control of this country, General Putnam had the honor of leading the first band of settlers that penetrated it. This company, known as the New England Ohio Company, reached the mouth of the Muskingum river in the spring of 1788, and began the settlement of their purchase at Marietta.

The ordinance of the 13th of July, 1787, authorizing the board of treasury to contract with any applicants for lands in the territory northwest of the Ohio river, was accepted in that same year by the Ohio company just mentioned, and by another body composed of such as could be enlisted for this sort of enterprise from among the inhabitants of the country immediately west of New England, principally citizens of New Jersey, foremost among whom was John C. Symmes. This gentleman, who had been a delegate to Congress from New Jersey, was then holding a conspicuous judicial position in that state, and was subsequently appointed one of the three judges of the Northwest territory.

The latter of these associations aimed at the acquisition of the next eligible tract to that chosen by the first-mentioned one. It was farther down on the Ohio river, and was separated from the other mainly by what was known as the Virginia military district or reservation, which it bounded on the west. It was thought to be a tract unsurpassed in its inviting character.

Judge Symmes petitioned Congress, August 29, 1787, that there be sold to him the tract of land fronting on the Ohio, bounded on the east and west, respectively, by the Little Miami and Great Miami rivers, and running back to a certain line, which Symmes thought would give him about 2,000,000 acres. Subsequent measurements reduced this figure to 600,000. But though the negotiation for the portion of territory upon which those joining in this interest had fixed their aim was begun, and some sales of shares and of warrants for locations within its expected limits were made in 1787, it was not until late in 1788, and after the preliminary steps had been taken for entering into possession by the first companies of colonists, that there was any formal execution of an agreement with the commissioners of the treasury, or a conclusion as to the boundaries to be stated in the conveyance. The commissioners, indeed, manifested a strong disposition utterly to repudiate the claim of Judge Symmes to any contract whatever with them, even after he had gone on his way to the promised land, like Abraham, with a cumbrous train. This he had done in the latter part of July, 1788, setting out from New Jersey with a retinue of fourteen four-horse wagons and sixty persons. His route was by way of Pittsburgh and Wheeling, the journey from the latter place being made by water. The Miami country was reached September 22, 1788.

Meanwhile Congress had heard of this expedition; and as no agreement had yet been concluded, that body feared that Symmes meant to seize and hold this land without more ado. Under this impression Congress came near repudiating all that they had done, when some of the company who were in Washington heard of it and barely succeeded in preventing such action by entering into a contract in Symmes' name, dated October 15, 1788, by which the price paid for the land was two-thirds of a dollar per acre, one-seventh of which was payable in United States military land warrants.

By the plan adopted by Symmes in 1787, he set apart for his own use and benefit the entire township lying farthest down in the point formed by the Ohio and Great Miami rivers, together with the three fractional townships lying northwest and south, between it and those rivers, estimated to contain 40,000 acres. He engaged with his associates to pay for that land himself, and they consented that he should hold and dispose of it for his own benefit. They had the privilege of selecting as much of the residue of the purchase as they saw proper, and the community at large were invited to become associates and to locate as much of the land as they desired at the contract price. To induce them to do so without loss of time, it was stated that after the 1st of May then next, the price of the land would be $1 per acre, and that it would be still further increased as the settlement of the country should justify. It was, however, expressly stipulated that all the money received above the congressional price should be laid out in opening roads and erecting bridges for the benefit of all the purchasers.

Judge Symmes, we have seen, reached his purchase in the latter part of September, 1788. After an unsatisfactory attempt to explore it he returned to Limestone, and here he made his headquarters for the next few months, sending down as opportunities offered detachments of surveyors and others to prepare his way. With the corps of surveyors sent out November 25 ventured Benjamin Stites, to the place where his flag was to fly, at the mouth of the Little Miami. He had been the first to make and was the first to enter upon a purchase. He immediately erected two or three block-houses on the low grounds, and conferred upon it the name of Columbia. Under this name the place, or rather an extension of it back on higher grounds, continued to exist as a small village, with nothing particularly noteworthy to mark its fortunes until it was merged in the outgrowth from the second point on the purchase to be settled, the present city of Cincinnati, the process of absorption having been consummated within the last decade.

The second point to be settled on the purchase was on the bank of the Ohio opposite the mouth of the Licking. Of this spot Matthias Denman, of Springfield, New Jersey, had either secured the refusal or made purchase, it does not clearly appear which, some time shortly after Symmes formed his company. In the summer of 1788 he came out to see the lands he had bought and to examine the country. At Limestone he met Colonel Robert Patterson and one John Filson, each of whom he induced to take a third interest in his land. To this last-named gentleman was due the wonderful name that was given to the town they intended to found—"Losantiville", compounded of "os", Latin for mouth, "anti", Greek for opposite, "ville", French for city, and the initial "l", which stood for Licking—the whole meaning "city opposite mouth of Licking".

Filson's death caused the surviving partners to postpone for a while their plans of starting a town on their land, and they returned to Limestone with Symmes after his first visit to the Miami country. It was while returning to the Ohio from Symmes' exploring party that Filson met his death. At Limestone another man, Israel Ludlow, was found to take Filson's place, and the rest of the fall was spent in making a new plat of the proposed town and in making the necessary preparations for settling it.

On the 24th of December Patterson and Ludlow, with 24 others, left Limestone for their new homes. They were greatly incommoded by the floating ice that filled the Ohio from shore to shore, and the exact date of reaching their destination is unknown. It has generally been supposed that it was December 28, 1788, and therefore that day has usually been celebrated as the date of the founding of Cincinnati. Three or four log cabins were at once erected, the first of which was located on Front street, east of and near Main street. In the course of the following January were completed the survey and laying off of the town, then covered with sycamore and sugar trees on the first or lower table, and beach and oak on the upper or second table. Through this dense forest the streets were laid out, their corners being marked upon the trees. This survey extended from Eastern row, now Broadway, to Western row, and from the river as far as Northern row, now Seventh street. The population of the place not long afterward was said to consist of 11 families, besides 24 unmarried men, dwelling in about 20 cabins, mostly adjacent to the present landing.

On the 29th of January the third branch of the original company left Limestone for the mouth of the Great Miami, led by Judge Symmes himself, accompanied by his family and a portion of a company of troops. On the 2d of February he disembarked at North Bend, about 6 miles above his destination, the waters being too high to warrant his going farther down the point. Here he founded what he intended to be the capital of the purchase and the metropolis of the surrounding country.

At this period an abundant supply of game and fish made good the failure of the provisions brought by the settlers. Although the Indians were unfriendly, Losantiville at least did not then suffer from their hostilities or depredations. They were, however, often seen hovering about the settlements, and began to annoy many of the settlers by stealing their horses and destroying their cattle. They killed, during the spring, several of a surveying party and five or six soldiers at North Bend. This hostile spirit of their savage neighbors so alarmed the settlers that they strengthened their little garrison, and resorted to every means of security in their power.

About the 1st of June, 1789, Major Doughty arrived at Losantiville with 140 men from fort Harmar on the Muskingum, and built four block-houses nearly opposite the mouth of the Licking. When these were finished he laid off a lot of 15 acres east of Broadway, extending from the brow of the upper bank to the river, as a lot on which to erect fort Washington. The fort was immediately begun, and was finished by November. It was a simple fortification of logs hewed and squared, of a square form, each side about 180 feet in length, formed into barracks two stories high. Extending along its whole front was a fine esplanade about 80 feet wide, and inclosed with a handsome paling on the brow of the bank, the descent from which to the lower bottom sloped about 30 feet. General Harmar arrived with 300 men and took possession of it on the 29th of December.

The three principal settlements of the Miami country were begun in the manner above described. Although they had one general object, as Burnet says in his notes, and were threatened by one common danger, yet there existed a warm spirit of rivalry between them which exerted a strong influence over the feelings of the pioneers of the different villages, and produced an *esprit du corps* scarcely to be expected under circumstances so critical and dangerous as those which threatened them. For some time it was a matter of doubt whether Columbia, Losantiville, or North Bend would eventually become the chief seat of business. At first Columbia took the lead both in the number of its inhabitants and in the convenience and appearance of its dwellings. The settlers there were greatly aided in the first year by being able to raise considerable quantities of corn from fields that had formerly been tilled by the Indians. But this lead in the race was soon lost, the advantages conferred on Losantiville by the building of the fort enabling it to go to the front before the close of the year 1790.

Losantiville then became the military headquarters of the region and the depot of the army. In addition to this, in January, 1790, it was made the county-seat of Hamilton county. This was the second county in the territory. At this time Governor St. Clair gave to the place the name of "Cincinnata", which was changed by common usage within a few years to Cincinnati. The name "Losantiville" soon disappeared.

The growth of the town in 1790 was considerable. The increase in families numbered about 40, and nearly as many cabins were erected. Judge Symmes, writing from here November 4, 1790, makes the following report of its progress:

The advantage is prodigious which this town is gaining over North Bend ; upwards of forty framed and hewed-log two-story houses have been and are building since last spring. One builder sets an example for another, and the place already assumes the appearance of a town of some respectability. The inhabitants have doubled here within nine months past.

Some fifteen or twenty of the inhabitants were killed by the Indians this year. About 20 acres in different parts of the town were planted with corn. The men worked in companies and kept a guard on the lookout for the savages. The corn when ripe was ground in hand-mills. Flour, bacon, and other provisions this year, as for a number of the years following, were chiefly imported. Provisions of all sorts were very scarce and dear. A barrel of flour brought $10 and a bushel of salt $8. Game, on the other hand, was so plentiful as to give a most bountiful supply of meat. It formed the principal support of the army at fort Washington. Turkeys were so plentiful that their breasts were salted down, smoked, and chipped for the table as dried beef has been in later days.

Some of the inhabitants brought with them a few light articles of household furniture, but many were nearly destitute of any thing of the kind. Tables were made of planks, and the want of chairs was supplied with blocks of wood; the dishes were wooden bowls and trenchers. The men wore hunting-shirts of linen and linsey-woolsey, and round these a belt, in which were inserted a scalping-knife and a tomahawk. Their moccasins, leggings, and pantaloons were made of deer-skins. The women wore linsey-woolsey manufactured by themselves; and all this was only ninety years ago in the place now called the "Paris of America"!

The Indians were very unpleasant neighbors for the settlers scattered over their vast wilderness. They were continually prowling about the various clearings, "insomuch that those who ventured beyond sight of the forts were in imminent danger, and often fell victims to savage ferocity." To be sure they had ceded their lands to the white man by the treaty of Fort McIntosh, and had renewed and confirmed the cession two years later, in January, 1787, at fort Harmar, but the favorable results anticipated therefrom did not follow. Their lands they would cede, but their good-will could not be bought or forced from them.

Negotiations proving unavailing, General Harmar was finally directed to attack their towns. In pursuance of his instructions he marched from Cincinnati in September, 1790, with 1,300 men, of whom less than one-fourth were regulars. Although he succeeded in burning the Indian villages and destroying their standing corn, yet this was more than counterbalanced by the heavy loss sustained in an ambuscade and in a hard-fought battle. Dispirited by these severe misfortunes, Harmar very shortly returned to Cincinnati. The object of the expedition in intimidating the Indians was entirely unsuccessful.

As the savages continued hostile, a new army, superior to the former, was assembled at Cincinnati, under the command of Governor St. Clair. The regular force amounted to 2,300 men; the militia numbered about 600. Various delays occurred, and it was the middle of September, 1791, before the expedition was fairly started. Misfortune attended it almost from the beginning. Two forts, Hamilton and Jefferson, were established and garrisoned on the route, about 40 miles from each other. On the 14th of October the army, consisting now of only 1,700 non-commissioned officers and privates fit for duty, left fort Jefferson with not more than three days' supply of flour. Many of the horses died for want of forage, and on the 31st, 60 of the Kentucky militia deserted in a body. The first regiment was ordered to pursue them and to secure the advancing convoys of provisions, which it was feared they designed to plunder. Thus weakened by desertion and division, St. Clair approached the Indian villages. November 3 he halted, intending to await the return of the absent regiment. On the following morning, however, about half an hour before sunrise, the American army was attacked with great fury, as there is good reason to believe, by the whole disposable force of the northwest tribes. On November 4 the Americans were totally defeated. General Butler and upward of 600 men were killed. General St. Clair at once returned to Cincinnati, gave Major Ziegler the command of fort Washington, and returned to Philadelphia.

This year Cincinnati had little increase in population. About one-half of the inhabitants were attached to the army, and many of them were killed. The unfortunate event of the campaign not only alarmed the citizens for their safety, but so discouraged several of them that they removed to Kentucky. No new manufactures were established, except a horse-mill for grinding corn. Indian outrages of every kind multiplied after St. Clair's defeat, and immigration was almost entirely suspended. In 1792, however, 40 or 50 settlers came to Cincinnati. Several cabins and 3 or 4 houses were built in that year.

President Washington now urged forward the vigorous prosecution of the war for the protection of the Northwest territory, but various obstacles retarded the enlistment and organization of a new army. In April, 1792, General St. Clair resigned his command, and Anthony Wayne, a bold, energetic, and experienced officer of the Revolution, was appointed by President Washington to succeed him.

The troops that had been recruited for Wayne's army assembled at Pittsburgh during the summer and autumn of 1792, and encamped for the winter on the Ohio, about 20 miles below that place. In the next spring they descended the river under the command of General Wayne, and landed at Cincinnati. Here the general made an encampment, where he remained for two or three months, and then marched to the spot where he established fort Greenville. The army remained at this fort during the winter and until July following (1794). Thence Wayne led his force, consisting of about 2,000 regular troops and 1,500 mounted volunteers from Kentucky, against the enemy. On the 20th of August he encountered them, and after a short and deadly conflict the Indians fled in the greatest confusion.

This great victory did not reduce the savages to submission. Their corn-fields and villages were destroyed, their country was laid waste, and forts were erected in the heart of their territory before they could be entirely subdued. At length, however, they became thoroughly convinced of their inability to resist American arms, and sued for peace. On the 3d of August, 1795, General Wayne made a treaty with them at fort Greenville, which put an end to their hostilities and made possible a peaceful and rapid settlement of the Northwest territory.

The return of peace gave the settlers new ambition and new hopes. They removed from their forts into the adjacent country, selected farms, built cabins, and began to subdue the forest. As soon as the news of peace reached the states emigrants began to flock across the mountains in great numbers. The natural result of the security afforded them by the treaty was that they passed by the villages and penetrated the heart of the wilderness, preferring to spread themselves over a newer country, where land could be obtained more cheaply. Thus, although the population of the territory increased very rapidly, that of the towns increased but slowly for a few years. For instance, Cincinnati in 1795 contained 94 cabins, 10 frame houses, and about 500 inhabitants. In 1800 the population was estimated at 750, and in 1805 at 960 only. This period of ten years shows, comparatively speaking, less growth than any equal period since. To be sure, in that time the population was almost doubled, but that is by no means a rare occurrence in frontier towns, and indicates far less real progress than a much smaller percentage of increase would show in later years.

During the time of the Indian war, or, for that matter, during the years immediately following, few incidents worthy of note occurred in Cincinnati. The encampment here of Wayne's army was in one sense a benefit, inasmuch as it made business lively. It was followed, however, by a disaster that more than counterbalanced the gain that had been made. In the fall of 1794, after the army left town, the small-pox broke out among the soldiers in fort Washington, and spread through the town with such malignity that nearly one-third of the soldiers and citizens fell victims to its ravages.

Soon after the conclusion of the war the fort was put under the command of William H. Harrison, afterward President of the United States, who had been aide-de-camp of Wayne, and who was now given a commission as captain. Captain Harrison held this place until his resignation from the army in 1798. He then became secretary of the Northwest territory, and in 1799 was chosen to represent it in Congress. In 1801 he became governor of the new territory of Indiana. Some forty years later he was elected President of the United States. It was while he was in command of fort Washington that he married the daughter of Judge Symmes, the proprietor of the purchase.

It was said that Captain Harrison resigned his commission because the idleness and dissipation of a garrison life comported neither with his taste nor with his active temper. However that may have been, it is certain that he was one of the few officers that lived in fort Washington who were not addicted to idleness, drinking, and gambling. These habits prevailed to a greater extent in the army at that time than they ever have since. As Cincinnati, like all the western settlements during this period, contained but few individuals and still fewer families that had been accustomed to mingle in the circle of polite society, the military had it in their power to give character to the manners and customs of the people. But the example they set at fort Washington was by no means calculated to have the most favorable effect on the morals and society of any community.

A very large proportion of the officers under General Wayne, and subsequently under General Wilkinson, were hard drinkers. Gambling was also a common practice at the garrison. As a natural consequence the citizens indulged in the same practices. As proof of this may be instanced Judge Burnet's statement that when he came to the bar in Cincinnati there were nine resident lawyers in the town: all but one of them became confirmed sots and descended to premature graves. This was the fate of almost all the lawyers throughout the territory.

To the presence of the soldiers was also due, in all probability, the remarkable amount of unpleasantness that existed in conjugal relations. The newspapers of the time are conspicuously full of complaints of husbands against wives in various forms, and of notices not to trust the wife on the husband's account.

But it must not be supposed that the inhabitants of early Cincinnati were altogether immoral and vicious. On the contrary, a considerable number of them were drawn up on the side of law and morality, and honesty and virtue early made themselves felt by establishing in the community those institutions that enable the right to triumph and civilization to progress—the church and the school.

In laying out the plat of Cincinnati the square between Walnut, Main, Fourth, and Fifth streets was dedicated for the use of a meeting-house, a graveyard, and a school. At first the sabbath devotions were in camp-meeting style, under the native forest trees of this consecrated spot. Such was the state of society then that, by the law of the territory, male adult attendants at these meetings were required to be armed with loaded guns. On the 16th of October, 1790, Rev. David Rice, of Virginia, the pioneer Presbyterian minister in Kentucky, came here in the course of his missionary circuit, gathered together 8 devout persons and formed the first Presbyterian society. In October of the following year the little flock agreed to raise $700, and from the timber growing on the spot to build a meeting-house. Until it was furnished services were held in a horse-mill on Vine street, used for grinding corn. A frame building was under cover by October, 1792, but it had only an earth floor and log seats then; later a floor was laid of boat-plank resting on wooden blocks. The building was not really completed till 1799. Judge Burnet says that at the time of the treaty of Greenville, "on the north side of Fourth street, opposite where St. Paul's church now stands, there stood a frame school-house, inclosed, but unfinished, in which the children of the village were instructed". On the other hand, Drake, in his *Picture of Cincinnati*, published in 1815, says:

The proprietors of the town * * * made no donation for the support of education, not even a site for a school-house. [In this, at least, he was mistaken, for the square on which the meeting-house stood was also to be used for a school-house.] The business of tuition was therefore generally conducted by strangers and transient teachers in rented rooms till the year 1811, when ten or twelve individuals purchased a small lot, erected a couple of school-houses, and employed two or three teachers; but notwithstanding their laudable exertions this academy has not flourished.

So it seems that schools were early established here, but that in the first years of the town's existence little attention was paid to the advancement of learning.

At the beginning of the present century the entire surface of cleared lands at Cincinnati did not begin to equal that which is now built over by a solid mass of houses. West of Western row there was a forest, with here and there a small cabin, connected with the village by a narrow winding road; in fact, where the best part of the city now is, was then but a mere clearing, with here and there a field and a few cabins. At the intersection of Main and Fifth streets there was a pond of water, full of alder bushes, to pass which a wooden causeway had to be constructed. The men of wealth and business were chiefly located on Front street, which even had a few patches of sidewalk pavement. Near the hotel, which was on the corner of Front and Sycamore streets, was a small wooden market-house built over a cove, into which barges and other craft, when the river was high, were poled or paddled, to be tied there to the rude columns. From Fourth street to the river was the military reserve around fort Washington. In 1803 the fort was evacuated, and soon after the grounds were divided and sold. The post-office was kept on the eastern side of this military common, near the corner of Lawrence and Congress streets, where the great eastern mail generally arrived as often as once a week; but frequently, when the traveling was bad, the town would not hear from the East for two weeks or more.

In those early times the sparse population, as well as the rude state of the arts, required the duties of several professions to be performed by one person. The physician was at once surgeon, physician, dentist, and apothecary; and the merchant was a sort of universal purveyor to society, whose store was an *omnium gatherum* of all needed wares. Something of this we see in the country towns now, but not to the same extent. The difficulties of locomotion made a great difference in relative prices. Merchandise brought from a distance was very dear, while the personal services of a professional man were very cheap. A doctor would ride five, eight, or ten miles of a dark night to visit a patient, and receive without complaint the regular price of a visit—feed for his horse and a cut quarter in cash.

"Cut quarters" were quite common as currency in early times. The peculiarity of "cut money" was that a dollar by the cutting process yielded five quarters. Everybody seems to have taken them, and so nobody was injured by the operation, except those who held them when they ceased to be acceptable coins. Their use originated in the scarcity of cash, of which article the Miami purchase, like most new countries, could keep very little till the settlers ceased to make their purchases in the East. This state of affairs necessitated a great deal of barter. Debts were often contracted payable in trade. A due-bill of a farmer, dated 1793, to one of the first lawyers in Cincinnati for professional services, reads, "For a cow and a calf, payable next spring." Another due-bill, of the same date, is for $30, payable in pork, the debt having been incurred on the same score. Flour was extensively exchanged with the bakers for bread, pound for pound, the baker making a very fair profit in the operation. In store dealings change was made by giving a row or two of pins or a few needles.

In 1799 the legislative power of the governor and judges was superseded by that of a general assembly, composed of a house of representatives, elected by the people, and a legislative council, appointed by Congress.

The first assembly was appointed to convene at Cincinnati on the 16th of September, 1799. It was this assembly that sent Harrison to Congress. After the close of the first session a law was passed by Congress removing the seat of government to Chillicothe, and there it remained from 1800 to 1810. After that the sessions of the assembly were held for two years at Zanesville, and then at Chillicothe again until 1816, when Columbus became the permanent capital of the state.

A division of the territory was made and the boundaries of Ohio were determined in 1802, when Congress passed a law enabling the people of the state to form a constitution; and in 1803 the state government went into operation.

January 2, 1802, the territorial legislature incorporated the town of Cincinnati. The officers appointed were a president, a recorder, 7 trustees, an assessor, a collector, and a town marshal.

Josiah Espy, in his journal of a *Tour in Ohio, Kentucky, and Indiana Territories*, made in 1805, wrote: "Cincinnati is a remarkably sprightly, thriving town, containing, from appearance, about 200 dwelling-houses, many of these elegant brick buildings."

About this time Cincinnati took a decided start. In 1810 its population had increased to 2,540. In that year, according to the "*Topographical Description of Ohio, Indiana Territory, and Louisiana*, by a late officer of the army," published at Boston in 1812, this place contained "about 400 dwellings, an elegant court-house, jail, 3 market-houses, a land office for the sale of Congress lands, 2 printing-offices issuing weekly gazettes, and 30 mercantile stores".

According to another authority there were then in Cincinnati 397 houses, divided as follows: Frame houses, 242; log, 55; brick, 86; and stone, 14. The number of looms in town was 31; of spinning-wheels, 230; the amount of woolen cloth made in the previous year was 755 yards; of cotton cloth, 2,967 yards; of linen cloth, 2,098 yards; of "mixt" cloth, 685 yards. The writer of the *Topographical Description* says in this connection: "The various branches of mechanism are carried on with spirit. Industry of every kind being duly encouraged by the citizens, it is likely to become a considerable manufacturing place."

The houses were located generally on the lower level, below what is now Third street. The principal street was Main street, and it was pretty well built upon as high as Sixth or Seventh streets, the latter being yet the northern boundary of the village. It had its Presbyterian meeting-house, grave-yard, court-house, jail, and public whipping-post, all on the same square. Upon this same ground, between the court-house and the meeting-house, bands of friendly Indians would occasionally have war-dances, much to the amusement of the villagers, after which the hat would be handed round.

When fires occurred, every one able to labor was required to be on hand with his long leathern fire-bucket, and to form a line to the river to pass water to the burning house. Every householder was required to keep one of these buckets hung up, marked and ready for instant use.

The streets were for a large portion of the year covered with dust six inches deep, and at other times with mud much deeper. Causeways of logs, generally a foot in diameter, were laid in various parts of Main street from Front to Lower Market; this street, then many feet below its present grade, had boat gunwales laid as footways a part of the distance. In very muddy weather the citizens walked upon the rails of the post-and-rail fences that inclosed the lots along the street.

The year 1811 was remarkable for two things—the building of the first steamboat to navigate the western waters, and the great earthquake. The history of Ohio steamboating will be taken up later.

In the morning of the 16th of December, 1811, the inhabitants of the Miami country, and especially of Cincinnati and its neighborhood, were awakened at about 3 o'clock by a shaking of their houses and by rumbling noises that seemed like distant thunder. The most intelligent persons soon discovered it to be an earthquake; but this by no means allayed the alarm, and even after the shocks had continued throughout the winter and the people had got quite used to them, they were none the less dreaded. The original seat of this shaking of the earth seems to have been near New Madrid, on the Mississippi, a point 400 miles in a direct line from Cincinnati. There the convulsion was terrific. Boats on the river were thrown into a boiling whirlpool, and many were engulfed in its vortex. The banks of the river were rent, the earth was opened, the waters rushing in formed lakes for miles where the land was dry before. Explosions from beneath took place, and fossils, buried in the alluvium of ages, were forced to the surface. The movements, as of a lever, of this central force were felt throughout North America, diminishing in intensity in the inverse ratio of the distance. The power of the original cause may be estimated from the effects at Cincinnati, where the shocks threw down the tops of chimneys, made fissures in the walls, and produced vertigo and nausea in many instances.

In the war of 1812 that part of Ohio and the neighboring states about lake Erie was the scene of active military operations. The British, however, never penetrated into the southern part of the state, and at no time in the war was Cincinnati in any way conspicuous. Yet the war was not without a most powerful influence on the place. By paralyzing the enterprise of the Atlantic states, the war sent out vast numbers to the West, and was thereby the means, to a great extent, of filling the country with population, of causing an extraordinary development of its natural resources, and of giving an artificial stimulus to commerce and business of all sorts.

CINCINNATI, OHIO,

IN 1815.

By producing an almost complete exclusion of European goods, the war of 1812 caused new manufactures to spring up throughout the country and gave new life to the old ones. Cincinnati shared in the apparent prosperity. Everybody gave and took credit, and nearly everybody engaged in some sort of commercial business. Physicians became merchants, clergymen bankers, and lawyers manufacturers. Farmers and mechanics, not tempted to become tradesmen and bankers, turned their attention to town-making, always an attractive occupation in new countries. Within 100 miles of Cincinnati hundreds of new towns were laid out, all of which were guaranteed by their proprietors to have unrivaled advantages, and the sure prospect of becoming a Rome or a Venice.

Here as elsewhere throughout the land raged a great fever for banking. In addition to the Miami Exporting Company, which had been incorporated in 1803, and had begun banking operations in 1807, there now sprang up the Farmers and Mechanics' Bank, incorporated in 1812, with a capital of $500,000; the bank of Cincinnati, incorporated 1816, with a capital of $600,000; the United States Branch Bank, which began operations in 1817; and in the same year John H. Piatt & Co.'s Bank. The Cincinnati Insurance Company was incorporated in 1819, with a capital of $500,000. Five banks and an insurance company seems a rather large allowance for a town of less than 10,000 inhabitants.

The close of the war broke down all the barriers against the importation of foreign goods. The country was at once flooded with English and French merchandise, and American manufactures went to the wall. Prices came tumbling down, and continued importations brought them still lower. For a while business stood the storm bravely, but to pay for the imports the country was drained of coin, and it began to be difficult to get money to pay debts. The trouble was aggravated by the paper issues of the great number of local banks that had been established. When the crash came credits were destroyed, and men and banks failed in large numbers. Thus began the desolating storm that swept the entire country from east to west, and continued from 1817 to 1823.

For a few years it seemed as if the town would have to go into liquidation. The credit of its merchants with the East sank lower than ever before or since. Cincinnati's want of credit was proverbial throughout the eastern states and cities. It was not until 1825 that the town fairly recovered from the shock and business resumed its wonted activity.

The condition of Cincinnati in 1815 is well portrayed in Drake's *Picture of Cincinnati*, published in that year. Among other things the price of lots receives mention:

For several years after the settlement of this place the lots along the principal streets were sold for less than $100 each. They gradually increased in price until the year 1805, when, from a sudden influx of population, they rose for a short time with great rapidity. Their advancement was then slower till 1811, since which the rate of increase has been so high that for a year past the lots on Main, from Fourth to Third streets, have sold at $200 per foot, measuring on the front line; from thence to Sixth street, at $100; in Broadway, Front, and Market streets, from $80 to $120; and on the others from $50 to $40, according to local advantages.

Drake furthermore says that on the plat of Cincinnati there were, in July, 1815, nearly 1,100 houses, exclusive of kitchens, smoke-houses, and stables. Of these, more than 20 were of stone, 250 of brick, and the rest of wood; 660 contained families; the remainder were public buildings, shops, warehouses, and offices. The dwelling-houses were generally two stories high, and built in a neat and simple style, with sloping shingled roofs and Tuscan or Corinthian cornices. Very few of the frame houses were painted. There were 3 market-houses, one of them being upward of 330 feet in length, the others smaller.

A large proportion of the water used was drawn up from the Ohio in barrels. It was often impure and required time to settle, but for most domestic purposes it was preferred to well-water. Cisterns were common. Wood was the chief article of fuel—beech, ash, hickory, sugar-tree, oak, red maple, honey-locust, and buckeye being the varieties most in use. Little coal was as yet consumed here except by manufacturers. It was brought from Pittsburgh, and sold on the river-shore at 10 or 15 cents per bushel.

There was as yet no iron foundery, but a manufactory of cotton and woolen machinery had been in operation for six years. Among other manufacturing establishments were a steam saw-mill, 4 cotton-spinning factories, 2 breweries, and a mustard factory.

A public library was opened in 1814, and in 1815 had 800 volumes.

Drake gives a very *naïve* description of the state of society at the time:

Wealth is pretty equally distributed, and the prohibition of slavery diffuses labor, while the disproportionate immigration of young men, with the facility of obtaining sustenance, leads to frequent and hasty marriages, and places many females in the situation of matrons who would of necessity be servants in older countries. The rich, being thus compelled to labor, find but little time for indulgence in luxury and extravagance, their ostentation is restricted, and industry is made to become a characteristic virtue.

It need scarcely be added that we have as yet no epidemic amusements among us. Cards were fashionable in town for several years after the Indian war that succeeded its settlement; but it seems they have since been banished from the genteeler circles, and are harbored only in the vulgar grog-shop or the nocturnal gaming-room. Dancing is not infrequent among the wealthier classes, but is never carried to excess. Theatrical exhibitions, both by amateurs and itinerants, have occurred at intervals for a dozen years, and a society of young townsmen has lately erected a temporary wooden play-house, in which they have themselves performed. Sailing for pleasure on the Ohio is but seldom practiced; and riding out of town for recreation, on horseback or in carriages, is rather uncommon, for want of better roads. Evening walks are more habitual, in which the river-bank and adjacent hills (the Columbian garden) and the mound, at the west end, are the principal resorts.

A comparison of Drake's statements with the following, taken from the *Cincinnati Directory* for 1819–'20, will show well the progress that Cincinnati made in these four years just following the war, before the town had yet felt the full effects of the commercial crisis, and while prosperity yet appeared, at least, to prevail:

It is the opinion of several well-informed mechanics that not less than 300 buildings were erected in 1818; and, notwithstanding the depression of commercial business, probably not less than two-thirds that number will be built in 1819. The buildings, however, which are occupied as dwellings are insufficient to contain the inhabitants with any tolerable convenience. * * * The actual number of dwelling-houses being 1,003, the average number in each family, allowing 1 family to each house, is more than 9 persons. Most of the houses that have been built within the last five or six years have been constructed of brick, and by far the greater portion of them are 2 or 3 stories in height. One prevailing trait displayed in almost all the houses in town is a want of architectural taste and skill.

According to the best estimate we can make, the length of pavement in the several streets is between 8,000 and 9,000 feet; that of the sidewalks is vastly greater. The streets in width are between 60 and 120 feet.

Within two or three years, two bridges have been built within the limits of the city, one at the confluence of Deer creek with the Ohio, and the other a few squares north of it on the same stream, the first 340 feet in length. Another has also, within the same period, been erected over the mouth of Mill creek, near the western extremity of the city, by Ethan Stone. This is a toll-bridge, and, with the exception of two or three, is probably the finest in the state.

In 1819 a charter was obtained from the state legislature, by which Cincinnati was incorporated as a city. This charter, since repeatedly amended and altered, forms the basis of its present municipal authority. By the act of 1819, the legislative power of the corporation was vested in a city council, composed of a president, a recorder, and 9 trustees. The usual powers were given them. The judicial power was vested in a city court, consisting of a mayor and 3 aldermen, appointed by the city council from among the citizens. This court was to hold its sessions once every two months. It had original jurisdiction over all crimes and misdemeanors committed within the city, the punishment of which did not amount to confinement within the penitentiary, appellate jurisdiction from the decisions of the mayor in all cases, and concurrent jurisdiction with the court of common pleas in all civil cases where the defendant resided within the corporation, and where the title to real estate might not be called in question.

Cincinnati owed her birth as a mart of business to the Ohio river; to it was due her wonderful growth. The canal, and still later the railroad, contributed much to her wealth, but it was principally to the river that Cincinnati owed her prominence.

The early navigation of the Ohio was carried on by means of keel- and flat-boats, barges, and pirogues or large canoes. The first regular packet line on the river was formed between Pittsburgh and Cincinnati in January, 1794, consisting of 4 keel-boats of 20 tons each. In 1810, a journey from New York to Cincinnati, going by vessel to Philadelphia, by Conestoga wagon to Pittsburgh, and then by keel-boat down the Ohio, took sixty days. From Cincinnati to New Orleans by barge, keel-boat, or broadhom, and return on horseback through the Indian country, took from three to four months.

In those days Cincinnati's imports were principally brought, at great expense, across the mountains from Philadelphia, Baltimore, and New York. The exports, necessarily, followed the channel of the Ohio and the Mississippi to New Orleans. But as the boats which took the produce to market were principally flats, which never returned, and the rest keels and barges, which were brought back with immense labor, delay, and expense, the export trade, as was to be expected, was languid and dull. The steamboat revolutionized all this.

The pioneer steamboat on the western rivers was the "New Orleans", built by Robert Fulton, at Pittsburgh, in 1811, at a cost of $40,000. She was provided with a stern-wheel and sails, and was between 300 and 400 tons burden. In October, 1812, she made the trip from Pittsburgh to Louisville in 70 hours. She then made several trips to Cincinnati, and in December went to New Orleans, and was there put into the trade between that city and Natchez. She was wrecked on a snag in 1814.

None of the first boats built were able to ascend the Mississippi. They went downstream well enough, but never came back. The ascent was not accomplished till 1815, when the "Enterprise", a small boat of only 70 tons burden, with a single wheel at the stern, for the first time made the voyage up river from New Orleans to Cincinnati, arriving there in 28 days.

The first steamboat built at Cincinnati was the "Vesta", launched in 1816. It was not, however, until the next year that steamboating was actively and extensively pursued in the West. Boats then began to be built in large numbers, and trade was opened with every part of the Mississippi valley. Cincinnati became the mart of a vast commerce, and the center of an immense transit. The voyage to distant places was made in as many days as it had taken weeks, and suddenly 30,000 miles of river coast opened to her a commerce and traffic as extensive as if she had been placed on the shores of the Mediterranean or the Pacific. She became the point for the receipt, distribution, and transhipment of the immense surplus products of the great regions of which she was a center. These exports were paid for by vast quantities of imports from all quarters of the world. The increase in business which immediately followed may be judged from the statistics of imports in the years in question. The publisher of the directory for 1819–'20, estimating from the best data he could obtain, put the imports from places east and south of Cincinnati in the four preceding years as follows:

1815	$534,680
1816	691,075
1817	1,442,266
1818	1,619,030

In 1819 he thought that, owing to temporary reasons, the imports would not be over $500,000, but estimated the exports at $1,554,080. At that time about 75 steamboats were navigating the western waters, occasionally plying between Pittsburgh, Saint Louis, and New Orleans. Of these, nearly a quarter had been built in the vicinity of Cincinnati within two years.

Of the 143 steamboats running on western waters in 1826, 48 were built in Cincinnati, 35 at Pittsburgh, 10 at New Albany, and the rest at different places along the rivers. In 1841 there were 437 steamboats in the West, of which 88 belonged to the district of Cincinnati. The following are the steamboating statistics of Cincinnati in 1857: Boats built, 33, tonnage, 9,500; separate steamers arrived, 357, tonnage, 87,453; arrivals, 3,600; departures, 3,500. The average capacity of these boats was 250 tons.

The legitimate offspring of the steamboat was the canal. The enterprising citizens of Cincinnati quickly saw that something more than mere mud roads was necessary to transmit the cargoes of the steamboats over the country, and to bring the products of the land to the steamboat-landing.

The first canal enterprise in which the citizens of Cincinnati took an active share was one to facilitate the movements of the steamboat. The aim was to construct a canal around the falls of the Ohio at Louisville, or rather at Jeffersonville, on the opposite shore. The Jeffersonville and Ohio Canal Company was chartered by the legislature of Indiana in 1818, with a capital of $1,000,000. Most of the stock was taken up by the citizens of Jeffersonville and Cincinnati. As the steamboats built in later years were mostly able to ascend the rapids, this canal was not needed, as was anticipated, to prevent Louisville from being "the head of navigation during the greater part of the year".

An inspection of the map of southern Ohio and Indiana will show that there are four valleys which are of importance to Cincinnati. The first is the small valley of Mill creek, which is about 20 miles in length and terminates at the city. This is the only opening through which a road can reach the city without passing over hills and descending steep declivities. In consequence of this natural formation of the ground, the "Hamilton" road, as it is called, was for many years almost the only avenue by which business was transacted with the back country.

Then come the valleys of the Little and the Great Miami rivers, and lastly the valley of the Whitewater river, which joins the Great Miami very near its mouth. The whole of this last-named valley lies in Indiana, but trades with Cincinnati.

Through the most important of these valleys, that of the Great Miami, in connection with the Mill Creek valley, was constructed the earliest of the great works of internal improvement immediately connected with Cincinnati. The Miami canal was begun in 1825. Governor De Witt Clinton came from New York to dig the first spadeful of earth, this ceremony being performed at Middletown. The work was finished in 1828 to the mouth of Mad river, where Dayton now stands, a distance of about 67 miles. Later it was extended to Defiance, 178 miles from Cincinnati, where it met the Wabash and Erie canal. The cost was $8,750,000. The whole distance to lake Erie is 265 miles.

One of the subsidiary benefits conferred on Cincinnati by this canal was the water-power which it brought to the aid of her manufacturing industries. The original estimate of its amount was 3,000 cubic feet per minute. Most of this power was quickly employed within the corporate limits of the city. The opening of this canal gave the city a new start, infusing fresh life into its veins. So beneficent were its effects that the people at once began looking round for new fields to conquer in the same way. The Whitewater valley met their eye, and the Cincinnati and Whitewater canal was forthwith projected. The plan was to build a canal 25 miles in length, from Cincinnati to Harrison (on the state line), and there to connect with the Whitewater canal, an enterprise of the state of Indiana.

The city made an effort greater than she ever made for any other single improvement when she voted $400,000 toward this new project, and again when later she loaned the canal company the further sum of $30,000. This canal was unfortunate. Unforeseen accidents befell it; unusual floods came and swept away its embankments. One disappointment succeeded another, till heavy debt weighed down its prospects. The difficulties of construction and the cost were far greater than had been anticipated; and the Whitewater canal in Indiana, upon which it depended for success, was found much out of repair, which disappointed the hopes of the city from that source. It was finally abandoned seventeen years ago. A railroad now occupies its bed, and the Central Avenue freight depot is on its basin.

Prior to the opening of the Miami canal the city depended altogether upon the river and the mud roads for its daily provisions. Occasionally during a mild and open winter the mud roads would become impassable for wagons, and the people would be subjected to short allowances. The canal partially remedied this, but not enough to preclude the immediate necessity of better roads. The first macadam road or turnpike was built in 1831, and was soon followed by others. Most of the turnpikes were built, or at least started, within the next ten years. In 1841 there were five leading directly out from Cincinnati, and nine more branching out from the main lines or subsidiary to them. Some of these were finished, and most of the others were nearly so.

Cincinnati's first railroad was the Little Miami. This road was 85 miles in length, running from Cincinnati up the valley of the Little Miami river to Xenia, and thence to Springfield. Long and severe was the struggle by which its construction was accomplished. It was chartered in 1836, and was not finished until 1846. Its capital stock was chiefly subscribed by public corporations. The state, the city, and the counties along the line took $400,000 in stock, and the city loaned $100,000 besides; while the utmost that was received in individual subscriptions before the road was finished and in successful operation was $132,000.

The second railroad leading out of Cincinnati, the Cincinnati, Hamilton, and Dayton, was built without the aid of county or town subscriptions. Such was the faith at home in the enterprise that within a month a cash subscription of three-quarters of a million was made by the citizens. New York capitalists took the remaining stock and the first issue of bonds at par.

This was in 1848, just at the beginning of the period in which the mania for building railroads reached such a height, and which culminated in the financial crisis of 1857. During these years Cincinnati had her share of the craze, and at the end of that time was bountifully supplied with roads. Cist, in *Cincinnati in 1859*, gives a list of those that then radiated from the city and connected her with the rest of the country, by which it appears that there were 12 such lines, with an aggregate of 2,275 miles of finished road, and 5 sets of auxiliary lines, with a like aggregate of 957 miles, making a total of 3,232 miles; besides this there were 4,789 miles of other roads, more than one-half of which were completed and in use.

It is, then, to the river and the canal, the turnpike and the railroad, that Cincinnati principally owes her wonderful career; but it must be recognized that her success is not wholly due to her commercial relations. Her commerce has been seconded, and well seconded, by her manufactures.

As is usual in any new town, a few manufactures were early carried on in Cincinnati; but, as has been previously said, they did not assume any prominence until after the war of 1812 had begun. The chief manufacturing establishments of the town in 1815 have been mentioned. In 1819 there was a steam-mill, for making flour, and also for carding and dressing cloth, a steam saw-mill and an ox saw-mill, a woolen- and a glass-factory, a sugar refinery, an oil mill, and 2 founderies. In all the other manufacturing industries of the city 1,238 hands were employed, and the annual products amounted to $1,059,459.

The industrial development in Cincinnati from 1826 to 1858 is shown by the estimate made in the following table:

Year.	Number of establishments.	Number of hands.	Value of products.
1826	400	2,950	$1,850,000
1840	1,594	10,608	17,328,051
1850	3,850	33,098	52,109,374
1858	5,000	58,000	100,000,000

Among the manufacturing establishments during these years the most conspicuous are those for the curing of meats, the manufacture of clothing, of furniture, and of iron. In the curing of meats (especially the products of the hog), and the minor products made from them, Cincinnati has long been famous. Pork began to be a great staple about 1820. The business increased wonderfully, making the city the greatest in the world for this article, both as to quantity and quality, up to 1874–'75, when a sister city of the West surpassed it. The brewing of beer, begun in 1812, formed another great branch of manufacture and export, and for the last 15 years it has reached enormous proportions. About 1850 the manufacture of steam fire-engines became a distinctive feature. The same can be said of the manufacture of fire- and burglar-proof safes. Large stove-works, and also carriage and buggy manufactories, have been important factors of the business interests of Cincinnati. Ready-made clothing is manufactured in large quantities, giving employment to a great many people. The boot and shoe trade is also very extensive. Cotton and woolen manufactories have never been successful, and but one of each remains at the present time. Furniture-making of every description has added greatly to the manufacturing importance of the city.

Taking up the thread of history of the city again, little is met that is noteworthy. In 1825 and 1826 the city was undergoing the severe ordeal of paying off "old debts". Through the branch established here by the United States Bank in 1817, during the years of inflation and extravagance that followed, most of the large real-estate owners had become hopelessly in debt, and large portions of their property had been taken by the United States Bank and subsequently sold at an advance. Some few obtained the right of redemption, and, by borrowing money in New York and Philadelphia, succeeded in saving their estates; but many, if not a majority of debtors, went under. Interest ranged from 10 to 36 per cent. per annum, and there was no legal limit. At this period the valuation of property listed for taxation was $6,848,433.

The opening of the Miami canal in 1828 gave new life to all business. Real estate again advanced, and those who had money to invest reaped a harvest.

It has been said that Cincinnati never went backward. This is true as regards population, but not as to the value of real estate. Once, and once only, has her real estate decidedly receded in its market or salable value. That was during the ten years preceding the opening of the Miami canal. For instance, 740 feet front by 100 on Seventh street sold at public sale in 1817 for $4,000; at private sale in 1827 for $2,100, *i. e.*, about $3 per front foot; now worth $300 per front foot.

The revenue of Cincinnati in 1826 was as follows:

Direct tax, 3 mills on the grand-levy	$9,472 17
Licenses to taverns, coffee-houses, and pork-houses	4,445 00
Wharfage (about)	2,200 00
Rent of market-stalls	1,400 00
Tax on animals	975 05
Licenses for plays, exhibitions, etc. (about)	500 00
Fines and miscellaneous items (about)	800 00
Total	19,792 22

In 1826 the health department expended $1,200 for vaccinating, at the public expense, 2,300 persons, in consequence of an alarm occasioned by the appearance of a few cases of small-pox in the city and its prevalence on the river below.

In the winter of 1829-'30 what are known as the great fires of the city in its early history took place. One of these burnt the buildings on half a square on Main street above Third, causing a loss of about $300,000. The other was the burning of the pumping-house and machinery of the water-works. This was not intrinsically a heavy loss, but in its results was the most disastrous the city ever felt. It happened in midwinter, when the river was very low and was frozen over so that engines were taken on the ice and worked to extinguish the fire. There were few cisterns or wells, and the stoppage of the water-works involved great discomfort as well as positive loss. Nearly all the manufacturing establishments using steam were compelled to close up. Those that did not, obtained water by hauling at great expense. For instance, one firm that obtained its supply from the water-works at $75 a year brought suit against the company to recover $700, paid for hauling water during two months. Besides this source of loss the city was compelled to go to the expense of employing five hundred police to watch the city, to guard against incendiarism.

The year 1832 was a disastrous one for Cincinnati. In February occurred the great freshet, when the water rose 63 feet above low-water mark, which is supposed to be about 5 feet higher than it reached in 1792 or in 1815. This flood was of the most distressing character, turning hundreds of families houseless upon the community, and destroying thousands of dollars' worth of property. The water extended over thirty-five squares, floated away many houses, undermined and overturned others, and carried off the large bridge over the mouth of Mill creek. Business of almost every description was stopped. Since the greater proportion of the flour and other provisions in the city had been kept below high-water mark, provisions became scarce, and a partial famine ensued.

No sooner had the city recovered from this calamity than it was afflicted by another, far more terrible and disastrous. In October came the Asiatic cholera. The reports of the board of health, as published in the city papers, beginning on the 10th of that month, and ending on the 3d of November, showed the number of deaths from the plague to be 351, which was probably much less than the real number. The greatest number of deaths in any one day was on the 21st of October, when 42 persons died.

The city was also visited by this scourge in the two subsequent years. Three successive seasons of the cholera is what has seldom fallen to the lot of any place in the United States. In the year 1833, as Dr. Drake remarked in the *Medical Journal*, the deaths per day were far less than they had been in the autumn of 1832, but, on the other hand, the disease remained four times as long. It began about the middle of April and continued till September. In 1834 it was perhaps still less violent than in 1833, but it was prevalent during the whole season of warm weather, and cast its fear and shadow upon all things.

When, however, in 1835 it became evident that the dreaded plague had left the country, a season of extraordinary activity ensued. In the East began that series of enormous speculations whose center was at New York, and which, in some respects, has never been surpassed in this country. It spread to the West, but prevailed comparatively little at Cincinnati. The speculations here were on a small scale, and it is doubtful whether they did more than give a necessary and healthy excitement to the business community, which had been so long in a dull quiescent state. The year 1836 was marked by the destruction of the *Philanthropist* newspaper printing-office by a mob on the 30th of July. The paper was printed for the Anti-Slavery Society of Ohio, and had been running for about three months, under the editorship of James G. Birney.

In September, 1841, the *Philanthropist* office was again sacked by a mob, and for a day and a half the city was the scene of various riotous demonstrations. Several rioters were killed and 20 or 30 wounded. The negroes in the city suffered seriously in these disturbances.

On the 11th of January, 1842, the Miami Exporting Company's Bank assigned its effects, and on the next morning the Bank of Cincinnati closed its doors. A mob assaulted their offices, destroyed all their movable property, and for a while had undisputed possession of the city. After destroying another bank and an exchange office, they were dispersed.

The most terrible accident that ever happened in Cincinnati was the explosion of the boilers of the new and elegant steamboat "Moselle", which left the wharf in Cincinnati April 26, 1838, loaded down with passengers for Louisville and Saint Louis. She first went up the river to take a family on board at Fulton, and while there held all possible steam, that she might come down at racing speed and overtake and pass another boat that had just left for Louisville. The wheels had scarcely made the first revolution when the boilers exploded, utterly wrecking the boat; over 200 persons perished.

There may well be introduced here some facts regarding old streets, boundaries, and incidents taken from notes by George W. Jones, published in King's *Handbook*. It appears that at the time of the flood of 1831 a large number of the original citizens lived near the river; and it was not until the "miserable Yankees" came and made a fuss about fever and ague, "and such aboriginal invigorators", that people who were "anybody" lived on the hill, say Fourth street. Front street, from Walnut to Elm, was lined with beautiful houses. The wharf was the meeting-place, especially on Sunday mornings. Here the townsmen exchanged the news, took a quiet "nip" at the "Orleans Coffee-House", situated just east of Main street, on the public wharf, and surrounded by a large open garden, and thence went to church. The chief business streets were Main and Lower Market, now East Pearl street. Pearl street was opened in 1832, and at what is now its intersection with Main street stood a large tavern, with a large wagon-yard into which teamsters drove. West of Walnut, Pearl street was opened in 1844. Fifth street, except from Main to Vine, was occupied by cheap residences, and a wooden market-house filled the space now occupied by the esplanade. About 1833, Broadway and East Fourth street began to be pretentious as desirable residence streets. Prior to 1841, Fourth street, west of Walnut, as far as Plum street, was a beautiful street.

In 1841 improvements were made west of Plum street, and in due time reached the "fence", which ended the street at what is now Wood street. In 1832 Columbia, now Second street, was merely a dirty creek, crossed by wooden bridges at all intersections west of Walnut street. No business of importance was done west of Main street. The wharfage was between Main street and Broadway, and even as late as 1846 the wharf space was a great mudhole, sprinkled with coarse gravel.

In 1840, streets beyond the canal were simply unmacadamized roadways. Central avenue was then Western row, which north of Court street ran through pastures. Nearly every family kept a cow, and the cows were driven to the pastures in the morning, and were turned loose to wander home at night to be milked in the alleys and side yards.

The great characteristics of a city were not to be seen in Cincinnati until about 1848, when a "hog law" drove those "first scavengers" from the streets. Ash-piles were condemned, and the city was supplied with water and gas. Most of the houses were cheaply built, and but few people kept carriages. There were only a few schools worthy of note. The merchants often entertained customers at their homes, and the general habits of pioneer simplicity prevailed. Turnpikes from the city were built between 1834 and 1840, and many of the citizens of to-day remember the mud roads to Walnut hills. Prior to 1840 Clifton was unknown. Cumminsville, now the 25th ward, and Camp Washington, now the 24th ward, were all farms. The "sports" gathered at a mile race-track south of the old Brighton House, where the John Street horse-car stables now are. The principal drives were up the river-bank to "Corbin's", or down to old Joe Harrison's place. Only occasional pleasure-parties ascended the hills, and then chiefly toward Cleves. A few elegant homes, some yet in good condition, lined the hill-side of the road which was approached by Front street, and by a road, the Sixth street of the present time. West of Western row Sixth street was not improved much earlier than 1840. A great orchard stood on a high bank west of Park street; milk-yards and brick-kilns generally occupied that locality.

The great Barr estate was north of Sixth street, and was subdivided after 1843, and the Hunt or Pendleton estate, at the head of Broadway, about 1846. In that neighborhood few houses were seen. The pork-houses were on Sycamore and Canal streets, the wholesale dry-goods houses on Pearl and Main streets, and the large grocery houses on Main, Front, and Pearl streets. Such is a faint outline of what the great city of Cincinnati was only 40 years ago.

The flood of 1847 was another serious blow to the business interests of the people, but in a short time energetic business men were again on a fair footing. The greatest prosperity was then enjoyed, and the growth of the city was remarkable—increasing 150 per cent. from 1840 to 1850—until 1857, in which year the failure of the Ohio Life and Trust Company caused serious local disaster. Cincinnati suffered less than any other city of importance in the country, only a few business houses failing. Still, business lost its vigor, and not until 1860 did it recover. Trade generally was paralyzed at the beginning of the war, but during its progress the immense purchases of the government made here gave an impetus to trade such as had never before been known.

Martial law was declared in Cincinnati September 5, 1862. The ten days ensuing will be forever memorable in the annals of the city. A pontoon bridge across the Ohio river was completed between sundown and sundown. In three days there were 10 miles of intrenchments lining the hills, making a semicircle from the river above the city to the banks of the river below, and they were thickly manned from end to end. Luckily, they were never needed.

The area of Cincinnati previous to 1870, when the first annexation was made, was 4,480 acres, or 7 square miles. The territory annexed in 1870 amounted to 8,085 acres, or 12.75 square miles. The last annexation, in 1873, brought in 2,695 acres, or 4.25 square miles. Total number of acres, 15,260; total square miles, 24. The Ohio River frontage of the city, from Columbia on the east to Riverside on the west, is 11 miles.

The year 1873, which brought disaster to the whole country, brought it also to Cincinnati, but from its effects the city has now almost wholly recovered.

The history of the water-works of Cincinnati dates back to 1817, when the town council granted by ordinance to the Cincinnati Manufacturing Company the exclusive privilege of supplying the city with water for the term of 99 years, upon the condition of their paying annually to the corporation $100, and furnishing in all cases of fire the necessary supplies of water. To accomplish this they were bound to place a fire-plug on each block along which water should be introduced, and to fill, free of expense, all such cisterns and reservoirs as might be constructed in future by the corporation, the water from them to be used only in case of fire. This company in 1820 transferred to Samuel W. Davies this privilege, he refunding to the company all its expenses incurred since the beginning of the work. July 1, 1820, the water was introduced into the upper and lower plains of the city, as was required by the ordinance. Subsequently to this the proprietor made repeated efforts to engage the citizens in the undertaking, and with scarcely a hope of being able to complete it, he offered the whole establishment to the council at a price stated to be below the actual cost. The proposition was submitted to the voters of the city, who decided against the purchase of a privilege which ought never to have been granted away. As a last resort the proprietor obtained during the winter of 1825–'26 an act incorporating the Cincinnati Water Company. Stock was immediately taken by a few individuals of the city to an extent sufficient to make all the improvements and additions necessary for completing the establishment.

Cincinnati claims the distinction of having given to the world the steam fire-engine. Until 1852 the putting out of fires was left to a volunteer fire department. Companies of 100 were formed, who worked for nothing, but asked subscriptions from citizens to buy engines, etc., and appropriations from the city to build engine-houses. This plan worked well enough when the city was small, but as it grew and its population became more mixed, it was found that the volunteer fire companies became nests of corruption, if not of crime. Men joined them for the purpose of pilfering from burning buildings. At last the evil became so great that incendiary fires were started in the interest of the evil-disposed of the volunteer fire department, and, notwithstanding the fact that many excellent citizens were members of the volunteer companies, the bad element predominated, and the city council resolved to buy the engines and establish a paid fire department. It was then that Mr. George Graham, still living, who was at that time chairman of the finance committee of the council, advanced $400 of his private means to A. B. Lotta, a machinist, in whom he had implicit confidence, to make the experiment of building a steam fire-engine. The first trial showed that in six minutes' time steam could be raised and water thrown 100 feet high. This was the first practical steam fire-engine. Lotta had an order to build a large one, and, insisting on making them self-propellers, built the "Joe Ross", at a cost of $14,000. Since then the self-propelling engines have been discarded.

Cincinnati's claims to immunity from fire rest on several grounds. Chief, in the estimation of the people, is her excellent fire department and her effective fire-engines, the product of municipal enterprise. Next is the material used in buildings, which are mainly of brick and stone. Another point in which Cincinnati is peculiar is that her engines do not depend on fire-plugs connected with water-pipes for a supply of water to the engines, but upon fire-cisterns, which are located at the corners of all the principal streets. Into them supply-pipes of half a dozen engines can be dropped at once, and the cistern itself can be kept full by opening a valve leading from the main supply-pipe in the street. By this arrangement there is never a lack of water, even when the whole fire department is called out.

Another cause that operates to prevent disastrous fires in Cincinnati is the absence of high winds. It is only on rare occasions, and then only for a short time, that any thing like a gale is blowing, since the hills on the valley of the Ohio river are so situated as in a great degree to break the force of winds coming from any direction.

Within recent years the most notable fires were the burning of Pike's opera-house in March, 1866, and the burning of the freight depot of the Marietta and Cincinnati railroad and the adjoining buildings in 1874. The burning of Pike's opera-house involved a loss of between $400,000 and $500,000. The fire of 1874 made a loss of three-quarters of a million.

As to the history of the schools of Cincinnati, only a few disjointed facts can be given. The ordinary schools of the early years of the city have already been mentioned. Of the higher schools, Lancaster seminary was the earliest. This institution went into complete operation in 1815 with 420 pupils. Four years later it was incorporated as the Cincinnati college.

About $40,000 had been subscribed for the foundation of a college and the erection of a college building, but, by reason of bank troubles, much of that subscription was never paid. Although part of the building was completed and the college was opened, yet in 1826 instruction was suspended for want of funds. It was reopened in 1836, and continued for two years, when it was again closed, and remained closed until 1841. The building was burned in 1845, and shortly afterward rebuilt. In 1869, after the building was again damaged by fire, it was remodeled into its present shape. The college holds a very liberal charter, containing a restriction only against the teaching of denominational theology. The value of its property is about $200,000. The income is about $10,000, and is used chiefly to support the Cincinnati law school and its library.

In 1830 the average number of teachers required in the public schools of Cincinnati was 22, at a cost of $5,190 per annum. In 1855, exclusive of expenditures for real estate and buildings, the actual maintenance of the schools cost the city $120,787 29 for an average attendance of 10,537 pupils, being at the rate of $11 47 per pupil. In this is included the support of the high school, which cost $13,047 77 for an average attendance of 251 pupils, which was at the rate of $51 98 per pupil.

In 1860 there were 46 parochial and private schools and seminaries in Cincinnati, of which 27 were Roman Catholic, containing 9,600 pupils.

The first settlers of Cincinnati were emigrants from New Jersey and Pennsylvania. Then followed people from Virginia, Maryland, and New York. The New Englanders came later. These all supplied native American residents. The English and Scotch were the first foreigners; then came the hosts of Germans, who, in 1841, constituted one-third of the adult population. The Irish and Welsh also came early in the history of the city. But never has the original native population been supplanted by other nationalities. At the present time nearly one-third of the population is foreign-born. The proportion of the German element to the whole population at a few different periods is here given:

	Per cent.
Citizens of German birth in 1830 (estimated)	5
Citizens of German birth in 1840 (estimated)	28
Citizens of German birth in 1850	27
Citizens of German birth in 1860	30

Since 1860 the proportion of nationalities has changed but little.

Such is the history of Cincinnati. It covers but a single lifetime, for the first white child born in the place (William Moody, March 17, 1790) has just died (in 1879), yet it is a history in which is typified the growth of the West.

Many years ago Cincinnati began to be called the "Queen City". This name was given in recognition of the fine situation, the lovely surroundings, the excellent climate, the fertile soil of the neighborhood, and the bright prospects for the future greatness of the city, and also in appreciation of the early development of enterprise, culture, refinement, and prosperity among the citizens.

CINCINNATI IN 1880.

The following statistical accounts, collected and forwarded by Major W. H. Chamberlin, indicate the present condition of Cincinnati:

LOCATION.

Cincinnati lies on the north bank of the Ohio river, directly opposite to the mouth of the Licking river, and in the center of a large valley which is about 12 miles in circumference, its geographical position being north latitude 39° 6', and longitude 84° 30' west from Greenwich. It is nearly under the meridian of Lexington and Detroit, and about on the same parallel as Baltimore and Saint Louis.

The semicircular tract of alluvial or bottom land on which Cincinnati stands, rises in a series of terraces as it recedes from the Ohio river. The first terrace rises to a height of about 55 feet above low-water mark. The second is 100 feet above the first, and varies in width from 1 mile in the central part of the city to 5 miles up Mill Creek valley, narrowing suddenly to a few hundred feet from Sedamsville to the lower portion of the city limits. The principal portion is built on the second terrace, which terminates on the north at the base of steep hills rising 800 and 900 feet above tide-water, or from 400 to 500 feet above low water in the Ohio. These uplands have an undulating surface, generally receding as they reach northward, while on and beyond them are built Mount Auburn and Mount Adams, Walnut Hills, Corryville and Price's Hill, within the city, with Clifton and Avondale just outside. Some of the finest residences in the city are built here, as this section contains all the advantages of both city and country.

The Ohio river is here navigable, the public wharf extending from Broadway to Main street, a distance of 1,035 feet; but nearly the entire water-front of the city is available as a landing. The depth of water in the channel varies from 2 feet at extreme low water, to 62 feet during the floods, the average depth in 1879 having been 17 feet. Occasionally the river is obstructed by ice, or navigation is suspended on account of a low stage of water, but usually there is water communication with all points on the Ohio, Mississippi, and Missouri rivers, and their navigable tributaries. Regular lines of steamboats ply between Cincinnati and Pittsburgh, Wheeling, Louisville, Cairo, Saint Louis, Memphis, Vicksburg, and New Orleans.

RAILROAD COMMUNICATIONS.

Cincinnati has the following railroad facilities:

The Little Miami railroad, to Columbus, Ohio, 120 miles, is now leased by the Pennsylvania railroad, and forms part of the Pittsburgh, Cincinnati, and Saint Louis line.

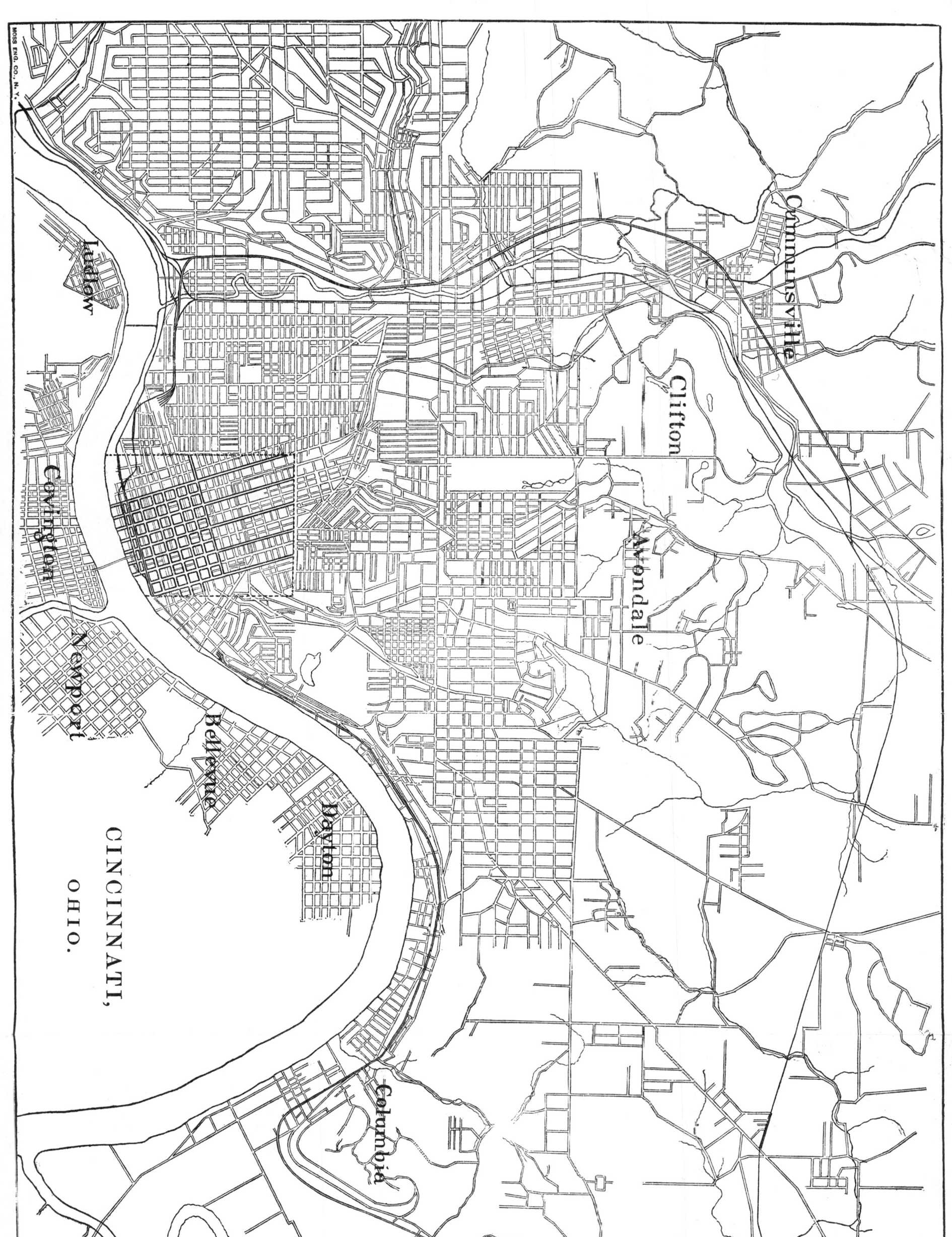

CINCINNATI,
OHIO.

The Marietta and Cincinnati railroad, to Parkersburg, West Virginia, 200 miles, is now leased by the Baltimore and Ohio railroad.

The Cincinnati and Baltimore railroad, to Ludlow Grove, 7 miles, connecting there with the Marietta and Cincinnati, and the Cleveland, Columbus, Cincinnati, and Indianapolis railroad.

The Cincinnati and Springfield railroad, to Springfield, Ohio, 80 miles, is leased by the Cincinnati, Cleveland, and Indianapolis line.

The Cincinnati, Hamilton, and Dayton railroad, to Dayton, Ohio, 60 miles, connects with roads to Toledo, New York, Indianapolis, Chicago, etc.

The Cincinnati, Indianapolis, Saint Louis, and Chicago railroad, between the points named.

The Ohio and Mississippi railroad, to Saint Louis, 338 miles, with branch to Louisville.

The Cincinnati Southern railroad, to Chattanooga, Tennessee, 335 miles.

The Kentucky Central railroad, to Lexington, Kentucky, 99 miles.

The Louisville, Cincinnati, and Lexington railroad, between the points named.

In addition to the above, the following-named narrow-gauge roads are in operation:

The Cincinnati and Eastern railroad, to Sardinia, Ohio, 66 miles.

The Cincinnati and Portsmouth railroad, to Bethel, Ohio, 36 miles.

The College Hill railroad, to Mount Pleasant, 10 miles.

The Cincinnati and Westwood railroad, between the points named, 8 miles.

The Miami Valley Narrow Gauge railroad will soon be completed to Waynesville, 40 miles.

TRIBUTARY COUNTRY.

The city is in the center of an agricultural district of great fertility, and covering a wide range of products. What is known as the bottom-lands along the streams in Ohio and Indiana are "self-fertilizing", and are among the most productive in the world. On the higher lands, in western and central Ohio and Indiana, the soil varies from reclaimed marshes to gravel and clay, adapted to grain, fruit, and grass. In Kentucky the surface of the country next the Ohio river is hilly, but at from 30 to 100 miles in the interior it is more even, and the soil is of that peculiar fertility pertaining to warm limestone formations, which gives it the name of the "bluegrass region". Within the range of 150 miles from Cincinnati can be found territory adapted to all classes of fruits pertaining to this climate, and to the successful production of wheat, corn, oats, barley, buckwheat, hemp, flax, clover, timothy, tobacco, and all the vegetables. It also includes, in Ohio and Indiana, a considerable portion of coal and iron lands, which are in process of development.

The industrial character of the country is mainly agricultural, stock-raising forming a feature of the Kentucky bluegrass region, as well as of the interior of Ohio. Coal-mining and iron furnaces form the chief industry in the district referred to, while the fine water-power along the Miami and Erie canal has offered opportunities for manufactures that have not been neglected. The paper-mills tributary to Cincinnati produce nearly 50,000,000 pounds of paper annually, and this, with all the products of the region already mentioned, finds a market in the city.

TOPOGRAPHY, ETC.

The following description of the geological and topographical characteristics of the site of the city is condensed from a paper kindly prepared by Mr. Florian Gianque, at the request of Major Chamberlin:

Geological.—One of the great folds of the earth's crust, much lower yet much older than the Alleghany mountains, passes through Ohio and Kentucky parallel with these mountains; and an area, composed of Hamilton and some other adjacent counties in these two states, is situated upon what was once its highest part. When this fold began, nearly all of North America was at the bottom of a rather shallow ocean, in which corals, shell-fish, and other forms of animal life were existing. Their secretion of limy matter, which became their skeletons and shells, being at or falling to the bottom of the ocean, and some of them becoming broken or ground up by the action of the waves, gradually formed, with others not thus broken, the materials which, by further upheaval of the kind described, have been lifted above the level of the sea, and which now compose the limestone rock of our hills.

The limestones and the intervening shales in the hills about Cincinnati constitute what the geologists call the "Cincinnati group of the old Silurian system". The area mentioned above was lifted out of the water and became an island, still surrounded by this ocean, in which animal life of various forms and kinds continued to live and die. and in which in many hundred, and in many places many thousand, feet of other rocks, containing animal remains of kinds differing from those of the old Silurian rocks, were deposited and formed. In course of time the folds of the Alleghanies, and later those of the Rocky mountains, and in time the entire region between these mountain systems, were lifted out of the water. Parts of these regions rose and fell slowly at different periods, being, possibly, more than once again sunk below and lifted out of the ocean. When out of the water, agencies of another kind began to operate. All that region embraced in the counties designated was then a level plain, without hills and valleys; but the rain that fell had to flow off, and as it did so it gradually began to form channels, the streams uniting to form larger ones, till the valleys, much as we now see them, through which flow the Ohio, the Miamis, and the creeks, brooks, and rivulets which feed them, were outlined, and in the course of ages were finally widened and deepened to their present condition.

It was not the waters alone that excavated the valleys. The climate for a long epoch became and continued to be like that of the Frigid zone, and all the region north of this became a vast field of ice, forming glaciers of enormous thickness. Ice in the form of glaciers flows somewhat as pitch does on a warm day, possibly less than 1 inch a day; but owing to its great mass and weight it moves with tremendous force. In parts of Ohio it crushed and ground to gravel and to powder (or mud), and pushed before it, thousands of feet of solid rock. It deepened the valleys, lowered the hills, and, in places, filled up the old channels of rivers and cut new ones. These ice-fields never reached much, if any, farther south than the present site of Cincinnati, but a branch, at least, once filled and helped to plow out the valley of Mill creek.

This part of Ohio was then higher than it is now, and the channel of the Ohio, of the Miamis, and the main valley of Mill creek were at least 100 feet deeper than they are now. But as the land sunk and the ice melted, vast quantities of water, laden with sand, gravel, mud, and other *débris*, flowed down the valleys and assorted and deposited this gravel, sand, etc., filling them up in time to their present levels. These loose materials vary in character, depending upon the kind of rock from which they were ground up and formed. For instance, the gravel in the valleys of Mill creek, of the Miamis, and about Cincinnati generally, is of the limestones north of the city, while the blue clay, so called, of these valleys is composed of the shale which was interstratified with the more solid limestone rocks. The sand and yellow clays come from still farther north.

But in addition to the twigs and branches of trees found in the blue clay, there are well-defined layers of leaves, logs, stumps in position, and other evidences of forest growth and decay deep down below the glacial deposits; and these are found to be very widespread, as deep wells can be dug in few places in these valleys without striking them. Of late years a number of artesian wells have been sunk in Cincinnati, from which, at a depth of about 2,400 feet, there is an abundant and strong flow of water, highly impregnated with mineral and gaseous matter.

Topographical.—A person on the Kentucky highlands south of Cincinnati, viewing that city, would see before him an almost circular and amphitheater-like valley, somewhat more than 3 miles in diameter, surrounded by steeply sloping hills. To the east he would see a narrow opening through which the Ohio river flows into this valley, crossing it through a channel in the form of a bow, with its concave side toward the north, and flowing out through a similar opening in the hills to the west. To the right would be another entrance into this amphitheater from the south, from which the Licking river flows into the Ohio, and to the left he would see the valley of Mill creek opening from the north into the extreme western part of the circular area. To the right, north of the Ohio, and on the extreme east of this amphitheater, he would see a large ravine, cut into, but not through, the hills, and reaching the river, known as Deer creek. Between Mill creek and Deer creek, and perhaps a quarter of a mile north of the river, and extending to the foot of the hills, he would see a terrace comparatively level, yet with slope enough for good drainage everywhere, and whose average height above the low water in the river is about 110 feet. The tops of the surrounding hills are about 400 feet above the river, the highest point being 465 feet, or a little over 900 feet above sea-level.

Within this circular valley, south of the Ohio, are the Kentucky cities of Covington and Newport, and outside of it, stretching along the river, are the towns of Dayton, Fairview, Ludlow, etc., while north of the Ohio one would see Cincinnati, built compactly from the river's edge to the foot-hills, clinging to the steep hillsides and stretching over the hilltops, in that part designated as East and West Walnut Hills, Mount Auburn, Mount Adams, Corryville, and the contiguous but separate corporations of Avondale, Clifton, and others. East and west, between the river and the hills, and at the hillsides, would be seen the city extending for several miles each way, with important villages and towns thickly built along the lines of railroads entering the city through each of these openings.

But in Mill Creek valley are seen some low unoccupied grounds, subject to overflow during high water, across which, however, streets are graded and railroad embankments are built, and which is being steadily filled up and occupied. The fills must be made from 3 to 25 feet in height.

The terrace above mentioned, upon which the most important part of the city is built, is composed entirely of beds of sand and gravel, as is also the low ground between it and the river, thus giving excellent foundations and dry cellars, as well as healthful locations for residences and business houses. Advantage is taken of this by the latter class of structures, many of which have cellars and subcellars, in which goods are kept perfectly dry, though far under ground.

CLIMATE.

Highest recorded summer temperature, 103°; highest summer temperature in average years, 96°. Lowest recorded winter temperature, −10°; lowest winter temperature in average years, −1°. The influence of the adjacent waters is hardly perceptible, though malaria is supposed to arise from stagnant water left by overflows in Mill Creek valley. There are no marshes within the city limits, while the few small ones adjacent are not sufficient to exert more than a local influence. The elevated lands tend to temper the extremes of temperature in the lower portions of the city. Winds from the southeast, south, and southwest bring rain, while those from the northwest, north, and northeast are usually followed by colder, clear weather.

STREETS.

There are 402 miles of streets in Cincinnati, 209 being improved and 193 unimproved. Of the improved streets 100 miles are paved with cobble-stones, 7 miles with stone blocks, 95 miles with broken stone (macadam), and 7 miles with wood. About 3 squares have been laid with asphalt block as an experiment. The accounts relating to the cost of the several classes of pavement are all kept by the front foot of each side of the street, and average as follows:

		Per square yard.
For cobble-stone pavement	$4 26, or about..	$5 75
For broken-stone pavement	2 12, or about..	2 80
For wood pavement	about..	5 00
For stone-block pavement	about..	7 25

No separate account is kept of the repairs. The cobble-stone or bowlder pavement is much easier to keep clean than either broken stone or stone blocks, but not so easy as the wood. This latter, however, becomes troublesome when it begins to need repairs, so that decided preference is given to bowlders. Nearly all the broken-stone pavements are in the suburbs, where the traffic is light "Bowlder pavement finds almost universal favor. When well laid it is the best and cheapest. Experiments with asphalt blocks and limestone blocks have been made, but never to the disadvantage of a first-class bowlder pavement." The city engineer, however, differs decidedly from the above in regard to the stability of the bowlder pavement, and while he acknowledges that it possesses some qualities that render it desirable where a cheap pavement is necessary, he claims that it is not a good pavement for Cincinnati, the difficulty of securing good surface drainage and keeping it in repair being among his chief objections.

The principal material used for the sidewalks is brick, though there are many wooden sidewalks in the suburbs, and long stretches of freestone flagging in the business portion, with here and there samples of concrete. The latter, of improved quality, laid in diamond-shaped blocks of light and dark shades, is growing in favor. The city engineer says: "A serious defect in the construction of brick walks in clay soil is the scanty foundation, the general impression being that only enough sand is required for bedding the bricks, regardless of subdrainage. There should at least be 4 inches of clean sand under the bricks, and in some localities more sand or gravel should be used to insure perfect drainage."

Gutters in the older and broader streets are paved with the same material, but on all streets made or repaired during the past 10 years, the gutters are formed by a limestone curb and a flat limestone bottom. As thus constructed they are much more easily kept clean.

Tree-planting is not encouraged in the business parts of the city. In residence portions and in suburbs, trees are planted along the center line of the sidewalk, which is generally 12 feet in width. There are no grassed places in any of the streets. Streets are repaired by contract, each ward being a street-repairing district, and contracts are let to the lowest bidder for the year. The cost was, in 1878, $180,000; 1879, $179,404 31; and for the first half of 1880, about $90,000. "Contract work has been proved to be much more economical. Under the day-work system gross abuses arose, by reason of efforts to make political capital out of this branch of municipal work. The city is too large for one man, or even four, as was the plan before the contract system was adopted, to oversee the work to advantage. Contractors are paid so much per month, and it becomes their interest not to do unnecessary work, as was done under the former system, but to keep all streets promptly repaired."

A steam-roller has been used on many streets for several years, with uniformly satisfactory results. It is used first to roll the earth before it receives any part of the paving. In case of "bowldered" streets it has been used with excellent effect to fasten and smooth the bowlders, but its greatest efficiency has been shown in making macadamized road-beds. It reduces the surface to a hard, smooth condition, especially when a layer of gravel is first spread over the broken stone, and the wear on the streets is thus made much more uniform. Streets made in this way are said to keep in better condition, with half the cost for repairs.

HORSE-RAILROADS.

There are 76¾ miles of street-railways in Cincinnati that traverse the city in all directions. They have 264 cars, use 1,722 horses or mules, and give employment to 699 men. During the past year there were 18,593,787 passengers carried, the rates of fare being 5 cents cash, or 25 tickets for $1, except on one line that charges but 4 cents for cash fare, with 25 tickets for 90 cents. There are 4 inclined planes, connecting with the horse-railroads, and operated by steam, that lift passengers from the lower to the upper levels of the city. These inclines have an aggregate length of about 4,000 feet, have each 2 cars, except one, which has 4, and each employs 12 men. During the year 4,690,000 passengers were carried on the inclines, at a uniform rate of fare of 5 cents.

OMNIBUSES, ETC.

With the exception of the omnibuses running between the several railroad stations and the hotels, and two small suburban lines, there are no regular omnibus lines in the city. Street-cars are so abundant that they are sufficient "for all practical purposes".

WATER-WORKS.

Water was first introduced in 1826 by a private corporation, but in 1839 the works were purchased by the city. Their total cost has been $6,500,000. Water is taken from the Ohio river nearly opposite the center of the city, and about 5 miles below the upper city limits. There are two inlet-conduits of masonry 134 feet long, one being 10 by 21 and the other 19 by 20 feet. There are also two pipes, 40 inches in diameter, resting on the river-bottom, and extending to the channel. All the conduits have to be cleaned once a year to remove the river silt. Owing to the great rise and fall of the river, the pumps work in a pit 60 feet below the floor of the house, upon which the engines rest.

There are two reservoirs, the low-service one, on Third street, having a capacity of 6,000,000 gallons when 24 feet deep, and being 165 feet above the pumping works. The Eden Park reservoir is formed by a retaining-wall built of masonry across a ravine. The high-service consists of one duplex, non-condensing, horizontal engine, and one vertical compound engine. They take their water from the supply-mains of the Eden reservoir, under a head of 60 feet, and pump to two tanks on Mount Auburn, under a head of 340 feet.

The average amount of water pumped per diem is 17,000,000 gallons, the maximum being 24,000,000 and the least 11,000,000 gallons. During 1879 the average cost of raising 1,000,000 gallons 1 foot high was $6\frac{1}{4}$ cents; the yearly cost of maintenance, $178,175 42, being net expenses $72,445 36, interest $105,730 06; and the yearly income from water-rates, $442,378 47. There are 190 miles of distributing-pipe, varying in size from 3 to 5 inches, 789 hydrants, and 23,000 water-takers. There are about 500 water-meters in use, and, though they are not enough to affect the consumption of water, are found to be economical to the consumers.

GAS.

The gas-works are owned by private companies. Their daily average production is 1,232,876.7 cubic feet. The charge per 1,000 feet is $1 70 to private consumers, with 10 per cent. off for prompt payment, and $1 50 to public buildings. The city pays annually $29 each for street-lamps, 6,180 in number, which includes the cost of lighting, cleaning, and repairs. It is reported that the income from meter-rates during 1879, when the charge was $2 20 per thousand, was $700,000.

PUBLIC BUILDINGS.

The city owns and occupies for municipal purposes, wholly or in part, the city hall, house of refuge, city hospital, workhouse, city infirmary, public library, Hughes high school, Woodward high school, McMicken university, 36 school-houses, 9 police-stations, 21 fire-engine houses, and an observatory. The total cost of the above is stated to be $6,460,000. The city hall is owned and occupied entirely by the city, and cost, including land, $150,000, the building proper costing about $50,000.

In addition to the above, there is the United States government building, containing the post office and custom-house, situated in the center of the city, at the corner of Fourth and Vine streets. It is built in the Roman-Corinthian style, of sawed freestone, and has a porch with six columns. A new building is now being erected to contain the post-office, custom-house, and court-rooms. It will be 354 feet long by 164 feet, and four stories high, of granite, and in the renaissance style. It is on the square bounded by Main and Walnut, Fifth and Sixth streets. The county court-house, on Main street, is a large and handsome building, of Dayton stone, in the Roman-Corinthian style, and has a porch with six columns. The Chamber of Commerce, on Fourth between Main and Walnut streets, has a hall that will hold 25,000 people. The county jail is in the rear of the county court-house. The Masonic Temple, corner of Third and Walnut streets, is built of freestone in the Byzantine style. It is 195 by 100 feet, with two towers 140 and a spire 180 feet high. The interior is handsomely decorated. The Exhibition buildings, on Elm street, opposite Washington park, cover 3½ acres of ground, and have 7 acres of space for exhibiting.

PUBLIC PARKS AND PLEASURE-GROUNDS.

Cincinnati possesses a total area of 388 acres devoted to public parks. The largest, *Eden Park*, area 206 acres, is situated on high, broken ground to the northeast of Fountain square. It was originally a vineyard, but it has been set with shade trees, and laid out with roads, including a line on which cars run. The large reservoir belonging to the city water-works, and previously described, is so well arranged that it has the appearance of a natural lake. From this park visitors have a magnificent view of the city, the valley of the Ohio, and the surrounding country.

Burnet Woods Park, area 164 acres, is the second in size, and is situated on a hill-top, 2 miles north of the lower portion of the city. There are 50 acres covered by a natural forest growth, and the park is improved with drives and a lake. Free concerts are given here every week in summer, the expense of which is defrayed from a fund of $50,000, donated by the Hon. W. S. Groesbeck, for the purpose.

Lincoln Park, situated in the western part of the city, contains only 18 acres of land, but it has well-shaded walks and a lake.

The cost of each of the above parks, including land purchase and construction, was: Eden park, $1,500,000; Burnet Woods park, $1,000,000, and Lincoln park $300,000. The annual cost of maintenance for all parks is $11,900, and they are under the care of a board of public works, composed of 5 members. The designer of the larger parks was Mr. A. Strauch.

Washington Park, in the city, and *Hopkins Park*, on Mount Auburn, are two small pleasure resorts.

One of the chief works of art in the city is the Tyler Dairdson fountain, given to the city in 1871 by Henry Probasco, as a memorial of his brother-in-law, Tyler Dairdson. It stands in the center of the esplanade in Fountain square. The base and basin are of porphyry, quarried and polished in Europe. The fountain itself is of bronze, and weighs 24 tons. It is made of condemned cannon obtained from the Danish government. It was designed by August von Kuling, of Nuremberg, and cast by Ferdinand von Muller, director of the Royal Bronze Foundery of Bavaria. The cost of the fountain was $105,000 (in gold), and the total cost, including the esplanade, was over $200,000. The diameter of the basin is 43 feet, and the weight of the porphyry 85 tons. The height of the fountain above the esplanade is 38 feet.

PLACES OF AMUSEMENT.

The city contains the following theaters: Pike's opera-house, on Fourth street between Walnut and Vine streets, with a seating capacity of 2,000; Grand opera-house, on Vine and Langworth streets, which can accommodate 2,300 persons; Robinson's opera-house, on Ninth and Plum streets, which also seats 2,300 people; National theater, on Sycamore below Fourth street, which holds 2,500 people; Heuck's opera-house, with a seating capacity of 1,500, is situated on Vine and Thirteenth streets; Vine Street opera-house, on Vine and Canal streets, with a seating capacity of 1,200; Volks theater, seating 1,100, at No. 522 Vine street; the Coliseum, on Vine, near Twelfth street, seats 1,000; and Lookout opera-house, at Mount Auburn, with a seating capacity of 1,500. These theaters pay an annual license to the city of $50 each.

There are also the following concert-halls and lecture-rooms, not including those connected with churches: Music hall seats 4,428, and is on Elm and Fourteenth streets. It was built from funds given by Reuben R. Springer and other citizens for the use of the general public, at a rental only sufficient to cover the expense of its care. Dexter hall, seating 400, is in the same building; College hall, seating 400, is on Walnut between Fourth and Fifth streets; Melodeon hall, seating 500, is on Sixth and Vine streets; Hibernia hall, corner of Ninth and Plum streets, seats 500; Jefferson hall, corner of Twelfth and Main streets, seats 600; Turner hall, seating capacity 1,600, is on Walnut above Allison street; Arbeiter hall, on Vine above Allison street, seats 700; Apollo hall, seating 300, corner of Sixth and Walnut streets; Eureka hall, corner of Ninth and Walnut streets, seats 500; and Mozart hall, in the Grand Opera-house building, seats 500.

Ten years ago there were numerous beer-gardens in what is commonly called the "Over-the-Rhine" district, north of the Miami and Erie canal, which is occupied almost exclusively by Germans. The gardens were situated in the back yards of the different premises, and were fitted up with tables sheltered from the sun, where the customers drank beer and smoked while listening to bands of music. There was usually no charge for admission, the profits being made out of the beer, cigars, etc., sold. The beer-gardens are now much reduced in number, as the hill-top resorts become more attractive and popular. The chief town beer-gardens still remaining are, one on Vine street, which is handsomely fitted up, with accommodations for about 800 people; and the Atlantic garden, on Vine street, and reaching as far as College street.

Among the hill-top resorts may be mentioned the following: The Lookout house, built 8 years ago at the head of the inclined-plane railway from Main street, is a large building which cost about $20,000. It is open on all sides and has a large garden attached. There is no charge for admittance. Pierce's Hill pavilion, opened in 1875, is at the head of the inclined railway leading from Eighth street. It was formerly used for picnics, no spirituous liquors being sold, but it has lately been turned into a beer-garden. The pavilion can be opened or closed, according to the weather, and there is a large garden attached, with an esplanade overlooking the city. There are seats inside for 1,800 people, and its cost was about $20,000. The Bellevue house, farther west, and at the head of the inclined railway from Elm street, was erected in 1876 at a cost of from $25,000 to $30,000. It is a wooden building with long verandahs and a large esplanade overlooking the city, and has accommodations for 10,000, with seats for 600 inside, and a large dancing-floor. The Highland house, in the eastern part of the city, adjoining Eden park, contains a theater, dancing-hall, indoor beer-hall, and large, handsome esplanade. It seats 10,000 people inside, and was built in 1877 at a cost of $40,000.

The customers of the old beer-gardens were principally Germans, while the frequenters of the hill-top resorts are almost entirely Americans, either residents of or visitors to Cincinnati. The entertainments are often of a high order, and are attended by the better class of citizens. Though the use of beer is almost universal among the patrons of these resorts, drunkenness is rare. In the place set apart for entertainment at the Highland house no beer is served. These are the most respectable of the beer-gardens; but there are also many smaller places where beer is sold and where the entertainments and the visitors are of a low and objectionable character. In addition to the above-named public places of amusement, the wealthier citizens of Cincinnati have many clubs and places of resort, such as archery clubs, athletic clubs, gymnasiums, turn-verein, etching clubs, literary clubs, historical and horticultural societies, etc.

DRAINAGE.

The accompanying sketch, showing a cross-section of this portion of the valley of the Ohio, is copied from a sketch in the possession of Dr. T. C. Minor, of Cincinnati. It serves to illustrate the division of the city into its old parts—"the bottom," a plateau near the river, and about 40 feet above low-water mark, and "the hill" about 100 feet above low water, with the abrupt elevations on both sides of the river, reaching to an elevation of more than 400 feet. The recently incorporated suburbs, such as Walnut Hills and Mount Auburn, lie on this much higher land. Extreme floods of the Ohio cover the low district known as the "the bottom".

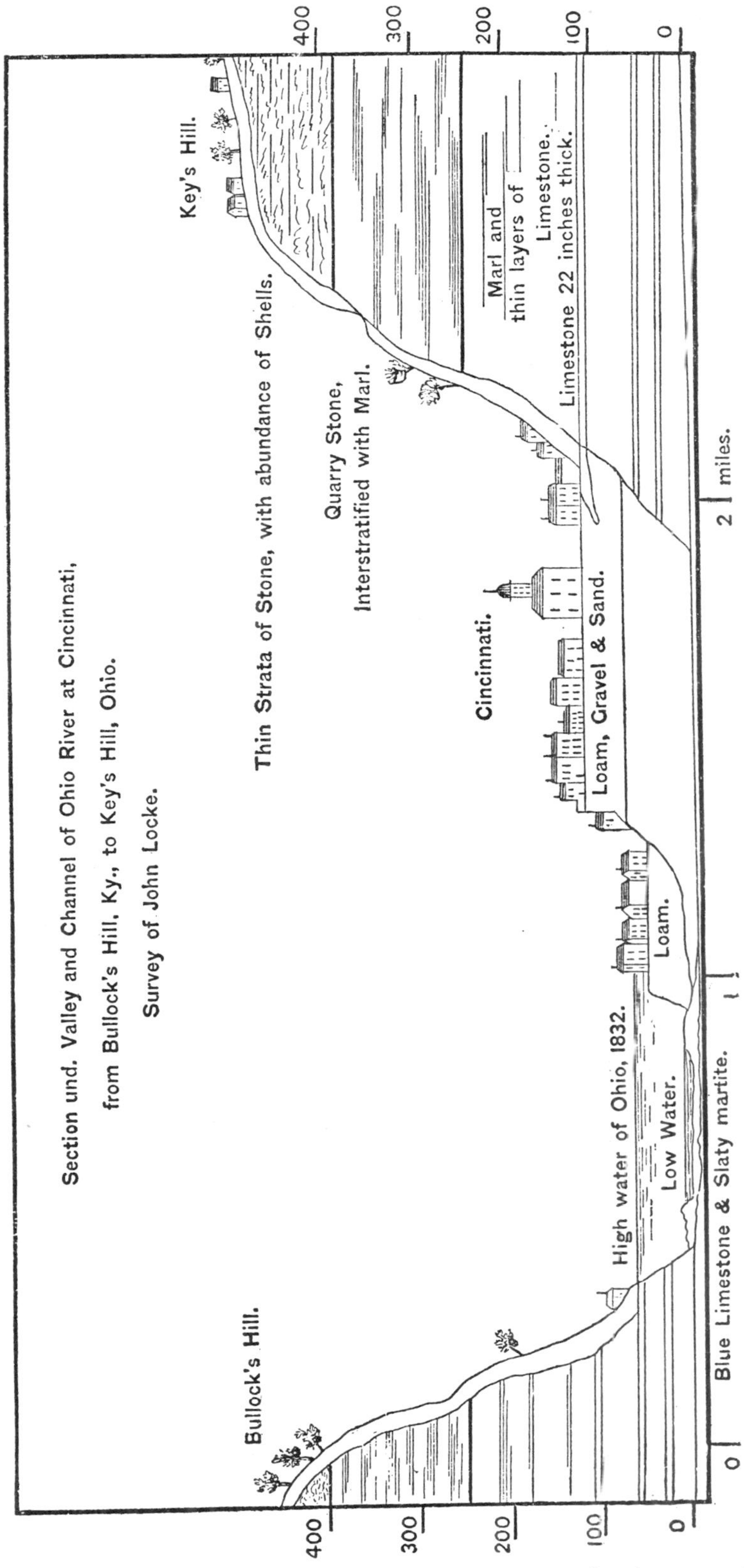

The district belongs to the great limestone region, and at Cincinnati we find horizontal layers of Silurian limestone of coarser texture and of varying degrees of hardness, the strata being 6 or 8 inches in thickness, sometimes more, with intermediate deposits of soft rock, clay, earth, slate, and shale, of all degrees of consistency, the softest material sometimes lying next the hardest rock. The proportion of rock to softer material is about as 1 to 10; hence a layer of rock may usually be found about every two or three, or perhaps five, feet. The valleys of the rivers have been cut through this bed of rock to a depth of from 400 to 500 feet. As the lower portions are less stable than the upper, the tendency has been to undermine the bottom, allowing the harder formation to fall or slide, leaving the banks steep and precipitous and exposing plainly to view the stratified structure of the bluffs. Such bare and precipitous hill-sides form a conspicuous feature in the scenery about Cincinnati, as seen from the river or from the opposite shore, whence the horizontal portions of the rock, with intermediate softer material, may be traced for an indefinite distance along the irregular bank. Most of the broad and deep valleys formed by the process above described now contain deposits of sand and gravel, together with rounded pebbles and bowlders brought down from the upper waters of the rivers, forming a drift extending to the original river-bottom, and reaching a height far above the highest floods of the present day. It is upon the elevated terrace thus formed (gravel and sand) that that part of Cincinnati originally known as "the Hill" is built. It is bounded approximately by Pike, Third, and Bay Miller streets. Its surface inclines slightly backward toward the bluffs. It is a notable feature of the upper terrace along the Ohio that streams coming down from the upland do not cross them directly, but follow along the foot of the bluff for greater or less distances. This upper terrace affords a deep dry subsoil for building, where cellars may be dug to any desired depth

and remain always dry and wholesome. In the business parts of the city advantage is sometimes taken of this characteristic to construct two or three drains below the level of the street. This work is facilitated by the fact

Section und. Valley and Channel of Ohio River at Cincinnati, from Bullock's Hill, Ky., to Key's Hill, Ohio.

Survey of John Locke.

Key's Hill.

Quarry Stone, Interstratified with Marl.

Thin Strata of Stone, with abundance of Shells.

Marl and thin layers of Limestone.

Limestone 22 inches thick.

Cincinnati.

Loam, Gravel & Sand.

Loam.

High water of Ohio, 1832.

Low Water.

Blue Limestone & Slaty martite.

Bullock's Hill.

2 miles.

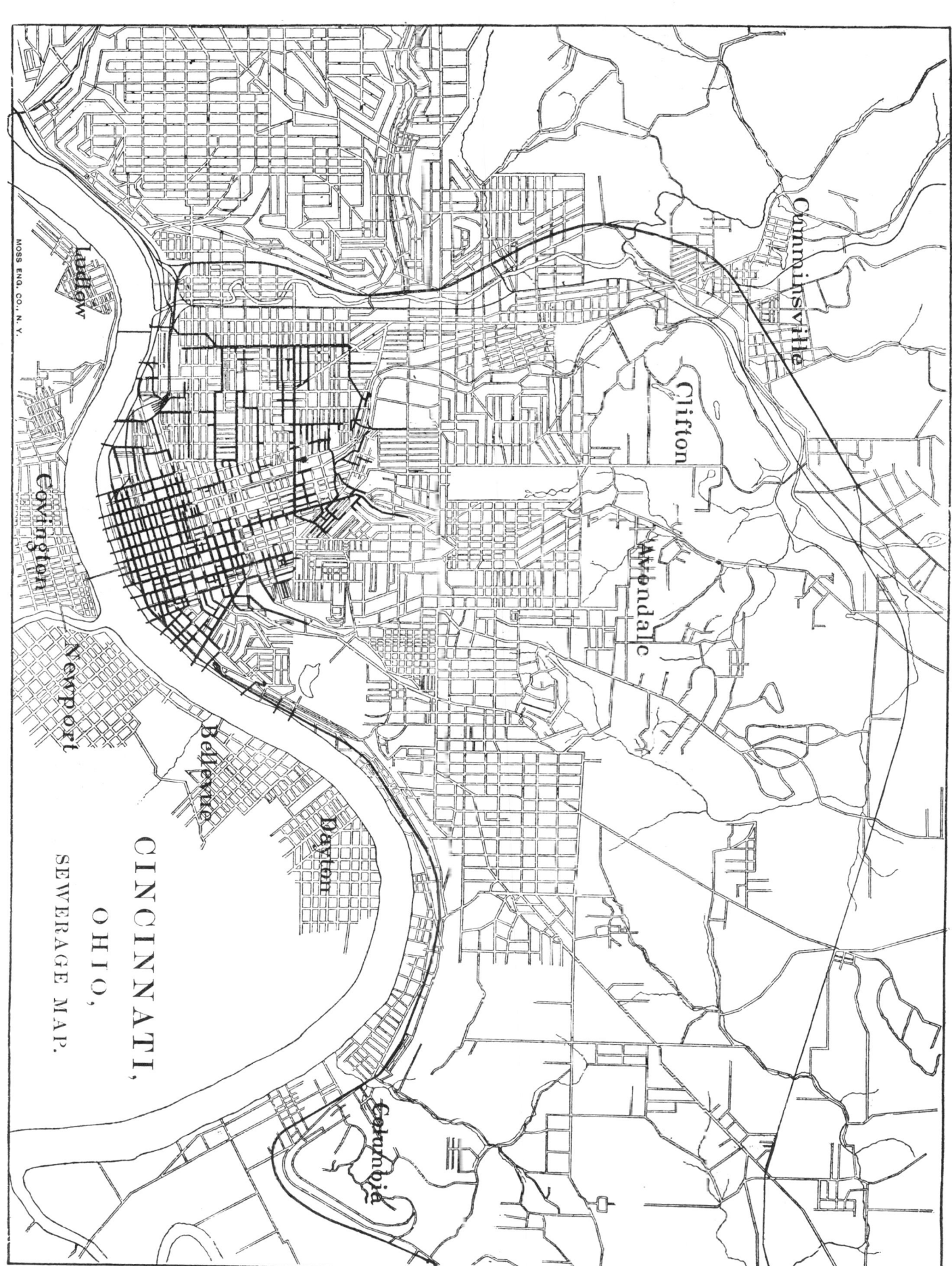

Cumminsville

Ludlow

MOSS ENG. CO., N. Y.

Covington

Clifton

Avondale

Newport

Bellevue

Dayton

CINCINNATI,

OHIO,

SEWERAGE MAP.

Columbia

that excavations can be made in this material to a great depth without danger of sliding or caving before the cellar walls can be built, while the proportion of binding clay and loam mixed with the sand is not enough to prevent free drainage, the surface of the water-bearing stratum being 60 or more feet below the surface of the streets.

The lower level, "the bottom," is built on a very different formation. The deposit contains more clay, loam, mud, and sand, conforming more nearly to the alluvial deposits left by high floods at the present day. Cellars dug in this soil are damp, and when the river is high they are at times filled with water. In fact, large areas of this district are sometimes submerged for weeks together, especially along the valley of Mill creek, in the western part of the city. The descent from the upper to the lower terrace is steep and abrupt, while that from the surrounding hills, Walnut hills, etc., is still steeper and the difference of elevation much greater, transit from one level to the other being effected by inclined planes or elevators, operated by powerful stationary engines. Only by the courses of ravines and valleys in a few places can the suburbs of the city be reached by the ordinary horse-railways.

The accompanying map, showing the contour lines, indicates roughly the boundary of the original terraces, showing a greater area of bottom and terrace land in the valley of Mill creek than along the Ohio river. The bottom lands along the Little Miami extend around in the rear of the city until they meet those of Mill creek, so that the high bluffs slope and drain not only toward the Ohio, but back to the rear valley. This map also shows very clearly the precipitous nature of the slopes in some parts of the city, and the direction of the natural drainage. The original surface has in some places been somewhat modified by removing the crest of the ridge along Third street, and filling in adjacent low grounds to regulate the grade of the streets leading to the river. Near the foot of the bluffs the earth and clay from the hill-sides has been graded or washed down until the gravel has in some cases been buried beneath the reach of ordinary cellars, the flow from the higher land keeping the soil more damp and less perfectly drained. Much of the low ground adjacent to Mill creek on the west side of the city has been filled in to form streets and building lots, the material used being sometimes earth and rock from the hill-sides, from excavated cellars, and from streets the grade of which has been lowered. A considerable portion, however, consists of ashes, street dirt, and the ordinary waste of a city. Many of the minor streams and ravines have been obliterated by grading. Some of these ravines in the valley of Mill creek once contained running streams—notably one which was known as Bloody run, flowing through the 14th and 23d wards, in the vicinity of York and Linn streets, and receiving the waste from slaughter- and packing-houses.

As the flow of the natural streams became obstructed by the filling of lots and streets, and as their waters became polluted, they were converted into large stone drains, constructed of limestone, and not suitable for use as sewers. Some of them have been cut off and their flow has been diverted into modern sewers of better construction. Some have been abandoned and their location has been lost. Others are still doing duty as drains and as sewers. In the filling of ravines and low places the provision of underdrainage has often been neglected, and much of the lower part of the city, once submerged during high stages of the river, has been intersected by elevated streets and railroad embankments, forming reservoirs to collect rain and surface water. The water thus ponded becomes stagnant and filthy, and the adjacent filling of ashes and other loose material becomes saturated, causing damp and flooded cellars. As the water subsides by evaporation, or by the falling of the river, a residuum of mud and filth is left.

One instance may be noted of the disappearance of a considerable stream in the valley of Deer creek, in the easterly part of the city. The stream was taken into a large sewer in Eggleston avenue, and its valley has been filled, so that the branch has entirely disappeared, and is said to have been covered to a depth, in places, of 50 feet. The main branch of Deer creek now flows through a deep valley between Eden park and Mount Auburn. It is still visible in places as an open stream, finding its channel in other parts of its course, through old stone drains, across streets and lots many feet below the surface. The old drains form no part of the sewerage system of the city, and they are rapidly falling in pieces.

Some culverts have been built by the Narrow Gauge Railroad Company where their embankment crosses branches of the stream. There are also culverts under streets, and private owners construct stone drains under their lots as they fill them in. All this work is done without system as to size or level, and can not be made useful as a part of the sewerage of the city. Deer creek is, ordinarily, a small stream, and it receives waste from tanneries and slaughter-houses, as well as much sewage and yard-wash from houses at Mount Auburn, which have no other drainage. Its flow is about as foul as that of most sewers.

SEWERAGE.

The sewerage of Cincinnati comprises 47½ miles of sewers of all kinds, as indicated by the map. There are 8.4 miles of large sewers, exceeding 4 feet in diameter, 14.5 miles of circular brick or stone sewers, from 2 to 4 feet in diameter, and 24.4 miles of vitrified pipe. The sewer area is about 2,000 acres in extent, with a population of about 160,000.

About 18 miles of the work had been constructed up to 1871, and about 29 miles have been constructed during the past 10 years, over 7 miles in 1880. The number of catch-basins and manholes could not be ascertained. This comparatively small area, lying mainly below the bluff and east of Mill creek, is occupied by about two-thirds of the population of the entire city.

There are three principal drainage districts. The first embraces those sewers which flow from their summits in straight lines direct to the Ohio river, occupying 16 streets. Their sizes vary from 2 feet to 5½ feet in diameter at the outlet. Second, sewers in the valley of Deer creek and its tributaries, discharging through the great stone sewer, 12 by 14 feet, in Eggleston avenue, just below the pumping-station of the water-works. This system now comprises 3¾ miles of brick or stone sewers, and 5½ miles of pipe sewers. The third, and most extensive system, drains a large area in the western part of the city, the natural discharge of which is to Mill creek.

The main sewers of the first system are short and large, draining small areas, their laterals extending only half a block each way. Their fall is very irregular, but usually very steep, the flow being rapid and strong. The descent from the summit at Sixth or Ninth street is comparatively gentle as far as Fourth street, whence there is a sudden descent of from 4 to 6 feet per hundred as far as Pearl or Second street, thence the descent is more gentle for two or three squares, until they plunge down the steep river-bank, entering the river near low-water mark. Their greatest length does not exceed three-quarters of a mile. Their current is rapid, and there seems to be no deposit of organic matter. Sewers in many parts of the city are effectively flushed by the discharge from hydraulic elevators.

A curious condition was found in the main sewer in Sycamore street, the flow of which is not rapid. The water was not excessively foul, but the whole interior of the sewer and manholes was coated with a thick gelatinous substance of a yellow color, hanging from the top and sides in strings and festoons, adhering tenaciously to every thing it touched. It somewhat resembled the slimy deposits caused by soil-water leaking through the wall, but was much more abundant. The sewer had no ventilation, the manholes being close, with tight covers, and the outlets being submerged. The same condition is said to exist in other unventilated sewers of the city. It is thought to be a fungous growth due largely to the condition of the atmosphere of the sewer.

The main sewer in Eggleston avenue is well built of large blocks of dressed limestone, neatly finished inside; its cross-section is that of two semicircles with 6 feet radius, connected by vertical walls 2 feet high, making it 12 feet wide by 14 feet high. Some of the branch sewers discharging into this main deliver by a fall at manholes, and others discharge over a flight of stone steps; the work seems all to have been done in the best manner. The sewer in Deer Creek road is of stone for a short distance from the Eggleston Avenue main; above that it is of brick. The bottom of this sewer is covered 2 or 3 feet deep in places with gravel and large stones. Its arch is badly damaged by the uneven pressure caused by a heavy embankment on one side. Cracks have opened in the crown of the arch, and the injury seems to be increasing. This sewer is intended to remove the future sewage of Walnut hills and Mount Auburn, now entirely without sewerage, though thickly built over and having a large population.

The sewer in Sycamore street presents some interesting features of construction. Below Abigail street it was tunneled through sand and gravel under the canal and around a curve into Court street, and thence to the Eggleston Avenue main, near Broadway. It is a circular sewer 8 feet in diameter, with walls and three concentric rings of brick. The tunnel was driven with a wrought-iron shield, supporting the sand until the masonry was laid, but within it. The shield was then advanced 2 feet by means of hydraulic jacks, and 2 feet more of brick-work was laid within it as before, the sections being connected by toothing. The face of the cut was maintained in a vertical position by shelves in the shield, allowing the sand at the head of the tunnel to be worked out between the shelves. The work is not very true to line, and presents some rather abrupt changes of grade, but it has apparently maintained its shape, and shows no signs of weakness. The western district (the third) lies principally north of Eighth street and west of Vine street, and extends to the foot of the bluffs. Some of the old rough-stone circular drains, constructed to take the water of former brooks, now receive a considerable amount of sewage. They are usually made to discharge into sewers of the new system, in which a large collecting sewer has been laid under McLean avenue. Its sectional area is about equal to a circle 12 feet in diameter, and its fall is rapid. As it approaches the river it is changed to a sewer 7 feet high and 24 feet wide. At the time of the examination it was full of back-water for nearly a mile from its outlet. When in this condition it is subject to much deposit.

Another sewer of this district, in Liberty street, of brick, is 9½ feet in diameter.

W. H. Baldwin, esq., who made the examination of the sewerage of Cincinnati, submits the following general considerations:

The situation of the city is remarkably favorable for good surface drainage, being sufficiently elevated to afford any desirable rate of fall into its main sewers. The streets running toward the river are steep, and at intervals almost precipitous, while those running parallel to the river are nearly level, and drainage is secured by giving them a rise in the middle of the square, with a considerable fall toward the streets on either side, giving an undulating or wave-like appearance, favorable for drainage, but not conducive to good appearance, especially when there are large buildings in the block. The arrangement of the main sewer in each street, with laterals right and left to the middle of the block, is favorable for sewerage, as it gives a short and direct run to the river, allowing the sewage no time to remain at rest and stagnant, and but little time to stay beneath the surface of the street before it is shot out into the river.

That part of the city which inclines back from the river toward the foot of the bluffs is intended to be drained in substantially the same manner, but the main sewer in each street below Vine usually pitches toward the west, being intended to receive laterals from each side in the cross streets and to discharge into the McLean Avenue collecting sewer. Very few laterals have yet been laid in this part of the city, the water now flowing along the street-gutters and carrying with it the house-slops poured into the gutters along the way, discharging eventually into the basins in streets having main sewers.

Main sewers in the back part of the city usually have a longer run and a less pitch than those on the river front, but they are washed out by large quantities of water from breweries, many of which have artesian wells, and use much more water than if they had to pay for it at usual water-rate prices. Most of the larger mains in the back part of the city are also washed out by water from natural water-courses, coming down from the bluffs.

So far as can be observed, the sewers are well built, of good material, substantially put together, and only in a few instances have signs of settlement or giving way been observed. Foundations are usually good, though occasionally beds of quicksand have been encountered, and in some places sewers have been built on made ground. The interior of the sewer is generally free from deposits of organic or decomposed matter, and the top and sides are, with few exceptions, clean and dry. * * * The steep pitch of most sewers in Cincinnati has demonstrated the unsuitableness of brick for their water-way, however hard or well burnt, and all sewers now constructed of more than 2 feet diameter have the inverts made of stone. Many sewers have been provided with stone inverts after a few years of use. Few, if any, of the sewers have less inclination than 1 to 200; they are usually made substantially parallel to the surface of the street.

The ventilation of main sewers is by perforated manhole covers. The excessive rise of the river sometimes keeps the outlets closed for many weeks at a time and interferes with their ventilation. Some sewers, built many years ago, have tight manhole covers, and are badly ventilated.

The cleaning of sewers, basins, and streets is all under one management, and no information can be given as to the cost of each part of the work. * * * Dead ends of some sewers, having but little street water to wash them out, sometimes require to be flushed. This is usually done by hose from a convenient street hydrant. * * * The deposits in pipes usually consist of street mud, sand, and gravel washed in through the inlet-basins. Obstructions in larger sewers usually consist in paving- and building-stones, macadam, gravel, and quarry-waste washed in from the hillsides. These are removed with shovel and bucket, or wheelbarrows. While the sewers extend over an area of about 3 square miles (2,000 acres), there are districts within this area, sometimes embracing many squares, which are entirely unsewered, and such undrained districts are in the most densely populated parts of the city. The district lying between Fifth and Liberty streets, from Bay Miller street to Eggleston avenue and Sycamore street, including about 600 acres, which contained, in 1879, an aggregate of 1,618 tenement houses, with 31,493 inmates, had only 125 houses drained by sewers, 1,515 being furnished with ordinary back-yard vaults. The soil of this district is gravel and sand, and vaults are purposely constructed so that most of the liquid contents soak into the ground. The laundry, kitchen, and other liquid waste is thrown into alleys and street-gutters, whence it is presumed to find its way to sewers, but most of it evaporates or soaks into the ground. The effect of these combined influences, together with that of a similar condition among the remaining 50,000 population of this district, not living in tenement houses, but similarly situated as regards drainage, is extremely bad. The sewers of Cincinnati in the district drained are good, but there are not enough of them.

All of that part of the city lying outside of the boundaries of the 2,000 acres above described is practically without sewerage works, and is undrained except by the street-gutters. All the lower part of the city west of McLean avenue is without sewerage, and much of it is densely populated.

The valley of Mill creek, west of McLean avenue, and all north of Harrison avenue is without sewerage, and in this valley are the stock-yards and packing-houses where hundreds of thousands of animals are slaughtered annually. Most of the waste from these establishments is utilized, but a vast amount is thrown away and washed directly into Mill creek, making it an open sewer. Besides the manufacturing industries, there is a large population along this valley.

A considerable population lives in the upper part of the city above Eggleston avenue. Its whole drainage is delivered into the Ohio river above the intake of the water-works.

Dr. T. C. Minor, health officer, in his report for 1879 gives a minute description of this part of the city. He says that house-drainage and slops are discharged into privies and cesspools in the back yards; that these are overflowed and the contents washed out by heavy rains, leaving them filled with water, which becomes foul and offensive before it has time to soak away; that streets and back yards are washed into the river, and all combine to pollute the water supply.

Mr. W. H. Chamberlin, who collected much statistical information concerning Cincinnati, says with regard to sewerage:

From time to time, as occasion required, small stone sewers were built, and finally a sewerage committee was appointed by the city council and the work of sewerage was fairly begun. This committee in 1869 had made many contracts, and had entered upon the work of building the great sewer in Eggleston avenue, which was to carry the water of the Miami and Erie canal underground to the Ohio river.

The legislature then created a board of sewer commissioners, who were to have at their disposal the sewerage fund, and were to employ an engineer and to prepare plans for the entire sewerage of the city. This board organized in 1870, and from that date begins the systematic work of sewering Cincinnati. The subsequent five years were busy ones in building sewers. The property-holders were anxious to have these necessary improvements, and petitions were presented to the commission for the improvement of different localities. The city had to pay the excess of cost above $2 per linear foot, and for a time the property-holder imagined that his assessment of $2 per front foot was all he had to pay. But in time the taxes began to be burdensome, and the large sums paid out by the sewerage commission, which in 1874 reached the sum of $256,000, called attention to that source of expenditure, and by legislative action the sewerage commission was abolished and its work assigned to the board of public works. The sewerage levy, however, was summarily stopped, and for several years no progress was made. In time, however, the levy was made available again, and regular sewerage work was resumed.

The total length of sewers constructed in Cincinnati to December 31, 1880, is 47,384 miles. The number of available sewer connections is 20,800. The number of connections made to date is 2,980. From this it appears that property-owners are slow to avail themselves of the opportunity of using the sewers, there being an average of only 63 connections to the mile, or, counting both sides of the street, one connection for every 167 feet. Even where connections are made there is a failure to make them complete, so that surface-drainage still runs across the sidewalks in covered or open ditches to the gutters.

Mr. Chamberlin gives the cost of each inlet-basin and its connection with the sewer as $66, and the cost of each manhole of average depth as $42.

The mouths of the sewers are exposed during low stages of the Ohio river, into which all the sewage of the city ultimately flows.

The cost of the work is assessed upon abutting property to the amount of $2 per front foot; all excess of that assessment is paid by the city.

The following table gives the contract prices for sewers built in 1880:

	Cost per linear foot.
2 feet, brick, complete	$3 00
2½ feet, brick, complete	3 50
3 feet, brick, complete	4 00
3½ feet, brick, complete	5 00
4 feet, brick, complete	6 50
4½ feet, brick, complete	7 00
5 feet, brick, complete	8 00
5½ feet, brick, complete	9 00
6 feet, brick, complete	10 00
12-inch pipe, complete	1 50
15-inch pipe, complete	1 75
18-inch pipe, complete	2 00
21-inch pipe, complete	2 50
24-inch pipe, complete	3 00
For each branch on 12-inch pipe	80
For each branch on 15-inch pipe	1 00
For each branch on 18-inch pipe	1 50
For each branch on 21-inch pipe	2 00
For each branch on 24-inch pipe	2 50

For each 6-inch slant in brick sewer, 50 cents.

For each 12-inch slant in brick sewer, $1 25.

Colonel A. L. Anderson, civil engineer, has expressed the opinion concerning the sewerage of Cincinnati that the plan is fairly well made and the workmanship has been good, but that it was a mistake to construct such a large proportion of main sewers at the outset, throwing a heavy assessment on abutters for expensive works of which the cost should be charged over the whole district drained. Also that the sanitary effect of the sewers is much of it lost by the failure of property-owners to make the necessary house-connections.

The consequence is that fecal matter is collected in vaults, whence it often permeates the soil, and so vitiates cisterns as well as the atmosphere. Besides this, the drainage from roofs, and the house and kitchen slops run over the sidewalks into the gutters, where, in hot weather, mixed with the natural filth from the streets, it fills the air with unwholesome exhalations.

In Colonel Anderson's judgment, the worst feature of the system is its inlet-basins, which become receptacles of the dirt and whatever loose substances may get into the gutters, and soon become " a stench in the nostrils of all who pass". Then this decaying mass of filth must be taken out by hand—an expensive operation—and one which during its progress further vitiates the air in the vicinity. A much more effective plan, and of much greater sanitary value, is to have direct openings into the sewers, which will admit every thing that comes from the gutters, and allow it to pass off immediately through the sewer. This plan assumes that the streets shall be kept reasonably clean, and that no objects shall be permitted to clog the sewer-inlets. It also assumes that a thorough system of sewer ventilation shall be established, either by perforated manholes at the street intersections, or, better still, at all the house-connections by pipes running to the top of the roof.

CEMETERIES.

There are 48 cemeteries and burial-grounds connected with Cincinnati, 31 being within the corporate limits (23 of which are no longer used for interments) and 17 in the suburbs. The following are now used:

Spring Grove Cemetery, area 600 acres, is situated in the Mill Creek valley to the north of the city, and was founded in 1844. The size of lots varies from 200 to 10,000 square feet, and the cost of the same is 30, 40, and 50 cents per square foot. The cost of single interments ranges from $6 to $10, and the annual cost of maintenance averages $50,000. It is estimated that 35,000 burials have been made here.

Saint Mary's Cemetery (Roman Catholic), area 60 acres, is situated outside the city and north of Avondale. It was founded in 1877, and the number of interments to date is said to be about 2,000. Lots are from 200 to 2,000 square feet in size, and cost from 25 to 30 cents per square foot. Single interments range from $3 50 to $6.

Reformed German Protestant Cemetery, area 31¼ acres, is located between the towns of Clifton and Avondale, north of the city. It was founded in 1844, and the number of burials made here is 18,000. Lots contain 256 square feet, and cost from 50 to 80 cents per square foot. The cost of single interments ranges from $4 30 to $7 30, the depth of graves being from 4 to 6 feet.

Saint John's Cemetery (German Catholic), area 22 acres, is situated outside the city, near Saint Mary's Cemetery. It was founded in 1844, and contains about 35,000 graves. Lots are 16 feet square, and cost $75 each. Single interments cost from $3 50 to $6.

German Cemetery, area 6 acres, is located in Avondale, and is not much used. There have been about 3,000 interments made here.

United Jewish Cemetery, area 13 acres, situated north of Woodburn, on Rural avenue, was founded in 1857, and is used by two congregations, about 1,200 burials having been made here. Lots range in size from 260 to 700 square feet. Single interments to members of the church are from $50 to $100, but the Jewish poor are buried free of charge. All the dead in the cemetery are buried with their feet to the east.

Calvary Cemetery (German), adjoining the above, has an area of 12 acres, and contains the remains of about 15,000 persons. Lots are 16 feet square, and cost 20 cents per square foot; the price of single interments is from $3 50 to $7.

German Protestant Cemetery, between Billings and Lincoln streets, in the city, was founded in 1843, and contains 38 acres. Lots are 16 feet square, and vary in price from 20 to 35 cents per square foot, the price of single interments being from $5 30 to $8 30.

Wesleyan Cemetery (Methodist Episcopal), situated on the west fork of Mill creek, has an area of 25 acres, and was founded in 1843. Lots are 16 feet square, and cost from 20 to 25 cents per square foot; single interments, $5 to $7; number of interments estimated at 24,000.

Friends' Cemetery, area 5 acres, is situated on the west fork of Mill creek, just below the preceding one. It is but little used now.

New Joseph Cemetery is situated outside the city, and 3 miles due west of the Old Saint Joseph, and was founded in 1858. It has an area of 65 acres, and so far about 17,000 interments have been made therein. Lots cost 25 cents per square foot, single graves $5, and burials $1 to $3.

Jewish Cemetery, in Delhi township, west of the city, contains three separate burial-places, viz: (*a*) Judah Touro, founded in 1856, has an area of 7 acres, and contains 313 interments. Lots are 200 feet square, and cost 10 cents per square foot. Burials are free to members or their families, while strangers or non-members are charged from $3 to $5 for a single grave, with interment. (*b*) K K. Adeth Israel was founded in 1856, and so far there have been 406 burials. There are no lot-owners, burials being almost always made in rotation, in the order of their occurrence, and the expense is defrayed by the congregation. (*c*) Adeth Israel, area 1½ acre, was founded in 1856, and is similar to (*a*). In this triple cemetery a guard is hired to watch by night, for from ten days to two weeks after each interment, to prevent grave-robbing.

Colored Baptist Cemetery, situated 2 miles west of the city, contains 16 acres of land, divided into 528 lots. Total number of interments, about 700. Price of single graves, $2 50 to $8.

Colored American Benevolent Association Cemetery, situated in Avondale, contains about 6 acres and 3,000 interments.

Saint Joseph and Saint John's Cemetery (Roman Catholic), area 20 acres, is situated about 4 miles north of the city, and is not now used.

Saint Joseph Cemetery (German), in the western part of the city, near Price's hill, has an area of 33⅓ acres, and was founded in 1843. Total interments, about 25,000.

Saint Matthew's Cemetery (German) is situated on the New Baltimore pike, in the northwestern part of the city.

Presbyterian Cemetery, Old Fulton Cemetery, and *Baptist Cemetery* are the first cemeteries that were established in the Northwest territory, and they are still used by the descendents of the early settlers. They are all together, in the southeastern part of the city, near the river.

Potter's Field, in Delhi township, is used by the city for the burial of its pauper dead.

Saint Jacob Catholic Cemetery, area 3 acres, is situated in Green township, northwest of the city.

Fulton Cemetery, area 4 acres, is situated on the Madison pike, just outside the city. It was founded in 1820, and is now but little used.

Baptist Cemetery, area 3 acres, is situated northeast of the city, on Deer creek. It is well kept up as a country church-yard and is sometimes used by the city.

Mount Washington Cemetery, 3½ miles east of the city, is sometimes used by the inhabitants of the 1st ward. In the Jewish cemeteries the depth of the graves is always 6 feet. In all the others the depth is 5 feet for a child and 6 feet for an adult, very few reporting a less depth than 5 feet. In all well-regulated cemeteries, which includes all these now in use, permits are first required of the secretary. In the Roman Catholic cemeteries the secretary must first obtain a permit from the priest. In the Jewish cemeteries the sexton must first obtain a permit from the board of health before making an interment.

In the following cemeteries (all but one being within the corporate limits) interments are no longer permitted:

Name of cemetery.	Area.	Interments remaining.	Location.	Founded.	Abandoned.	Removals to other cemeteries (estimated).	Remarks.
	Acres.						
Old Saint Joseph (Irish)	14	1,600 (record)	Cemetery road, Price's hill	1844	1864		
Friends'	1	None	Poplar, corner of Freeman street			500	
Saint Peters	15	7,000 (accurate)	Lick Run pike, near Vanhart street	1830	1848	7,000	
Potter's Field	10	Very many	Freeman street	1840	1852		Near Lincoln park.
Catholic	3	Very few	Between Mound and Cutter streets	1829	1849	(?)3,500	
Methodist Episcopal	3	None	Between Mound and Cutter streets	1829	1851	(?)2,500	
Baptist	3	None	Between Mound and Cutter streets	1829	1851	2,000	
Jewish	0⅛	200 (estimate)	Central avenue and Chestnut street	1838	1849	80	
Potter's Field	3¾	Very few	Fourteenth street and the canal		1836	(?)1,000	Built over.
Presbyterian and Episcopal	7	None	Fourteenth street and the canal	1829	1843	5,000	Washington park.
Friends'	0½	Very few	Corner of John and Fifth streets			400	
Catholic	1	Very few	Vine, corner of Liberty street			800	
Presbyterian, First Church	2	Very few	Fourth, corner of Main street	1798	1824	2,000	
Methodist Episcopal	0½	Very few	Fifth street and Boundary	1807	1829	400	
Old Family	0⅛	None	Fifth street and Boundary	(a)		12	Piatt family.
Methodist Protestant	10½	2,400	Burnet avenue and Sycamore street	1833	1873	600	4 acres sold.
(Nameless)	0¼	Very few	Morton street, near water-works	(b)			
Ruddle Family	2	Very few	Between Burns street and the canal	1810	1860	125	
Presbyterian	1¾	Very few	McMillan, Lane, and Jones streets	1829	1860	800	
Old Family	0 1/20	70	Linwood road, near toll-house	(b)			
Methodist	0½	Very few	Grandin road, near Edward's road	1810	1861	300	Sold for street taxes.
Potter's Field	7	Few	Near eastern limits of the city	(l)			Now a pasture.
Jewish	2½	1,000	In Clifton, outside city limits				

a Very early. b Very old.

A summary of the several cemeteries in Cincinnati shows that there are 8 cemeteries within the city limits having an aggregate area of 112⅔ acres, with a total interment of 82,500; 17 cemeteries without the city limits having an aggregate area of 898⅚ acres, with a total interment of 148,900, all now in use, and 23 cemeteries, all but one within the city limits, having an aggregate area of 88½ acres, with a total interment of 30,000.

MARKETS.

The following table shows the principal markets in the city:

Name.	Location.	Ground area.	DIMENSIONS AND COST OF BUILDING.				No. of stalls.	No. of benches.
			Width.	Length.	Height.	Cost.		
		Feet.	*Feet.*	*Feet.*	*Feet.*			
Pearl Street market	On Pearl street, between Main street and Broadway	42 by 400	42	390	20	$7,000	60	62
Sixth Street market	Between Sixth, Main, Mound, and Clark streets	40 by 350	32	340	18	8,000	48	52
Court Street market	On Court, from Main to John streets	40 by 400	28	400	18	7,000	44	48
Findlay Street market	Between Findlay, Vine, Elm, and Race streets	40 by 360	40	360	30	12,000	48	52
Wade Street market	Between Wade, John, Cutter, and Liberty streets	32 by 160	28	160	20	5,000	26	20

The buildings all stand in the center of Market space, with room on each side for wagons. Pearl Street market has 40 feet on either side, the whole length of the building. Sixth Street market has the same, and also an open space 120 by 400 feet on the adjoining square. Court Street market has the same, with an open space in adjoining square 126 by 190 feet. Findlay market has a space 113 by 332 feet, while Wade Street market has a space 140 by 250. In addition to the above, space in all the streets adjoining the markets is set apart by ordinance for the use of wagons.

The annual rental of stalls and benches in the different markets is as follows: Pearl Street and Sixth Street markets—stalls $150, benches $30; Court Street market—stalls $75, benches $15; Findlay Street market—stalls $50, benches $15; Wade Street market—stalls $25, benches $5. No separate accounts are kept of the rentals of the different markets, but the total receipts from this source during 1880 amounted to $14,205.75. The market hours are: From October 1 to April, from daylight till noon, and during the remainder of the year from daylight till 10 a. m. every day in the week except Sunday. Findlay Street and Sixth Street markets are open from 3 to 10 p. m. on Saturdays.

The public markets are long sheds supported by brick columns, well roofed, and the ceilings plastered. On a line with the brick columns, which stand about 8 feet within the eaves of the roof, there is a partition which forms the back of the inner stalls, passage-ways being left at convenient distances. The inner stalls, which are used solely by butchers, are about 10 feet in length, and have each a bench in front for cutting meat. The outer stalls are designed for the sale of vegetables; but many of them are occupied as lunch counters, as the vegetable dealers prefer to take position along the sidewalks.

In closing his report on the subject under this head, Major Chamberlin says:

The public markets in Cincinnati are in a state of decadence. They could be entirely abolished with very little inconvenience to any one. The original theory that the market-houses should provide an inexpensive exchange between the producer and the consumer has been abandoned in practice, for during the greater portion of the year the market is used by hucksters, or middlemen, who buy of producers. Besides, the location of the markets is such as to render them practically inaccessible to a large, if not the greater, portion of the population. Consequently "daily markets", as they are called, are abundant all over the city, where every thing needed in families in the way of meats and vegetables, as well as groceries, is kept for sale. These *green-grocers* buy in the public markets and deliver their goods to their customers. There are no statistics upon which to base an estimate of the proportion of the retail supply of meats, poultry, fish, and vegetables by the public markets compared with private markets, but taking the above facts into consideration it seems fair to say that about one-tenth of the supply is from the public markets. This perhaps should be modified during the later summer months and early fall, when wagons from the country line the streets for miles on market-days. But even then the consumers do not form the larger portion of the purchasers. All the green-grocers, all over the city, go to the market daily for their supplies, and their profits in many cases simply amount to a fair payment for drayage and delivery. At the time of the year referred to the supply of this market is not excelled anywhere. The adjacent country is largely devoted to raising fruits and vegetables for Cincinnati, and in quantity and quality the supply can hardly be excelled.

As a whole, the city of Cincinnati is abundantly supplied with the best quality of meats, fruits, and vegetables, and generally at most reasonable prices. Its location makes it easily accessible from the South and the North, and it becomes a distributing center for the products of the different sections of the country. Its railroad connection with the South brings southern products here in good time and at low rates, and its close connections with the lakes gives it always a bountiful supply of fish.

SANITARY AUTHORITY—BOARD OF HEALTH.

The chief sanitary authority of Cincinnati is vested in a board of health, an independent body composed of 6 members, appointed annually by the common council, with the mayor as member *ex officio*. The act providing for a board of health does not fix the number of physicians to be included in the membership, that matter being left to the council; for the present year, however, there is one physician in the board. The ordinary annual expenses of the board, when there is no declared epidemic, amount to $15,526 55 (for 1879) and $24,918 59 (for 1880), being for salaries, medicine, and care of indigent sick, surgical appliances, advertising, printing, stationery, etc. During an epidemic the board can increase its expenses practically to an unlimited amount, it being the duty of the city council to make all necessary appropriations to meet such expenses. During 1879, when yellow fever prevailed in some of the Southern states, the board exceeded its regular appropriation by nearly $5,000, in order to establish a sufficient quarantine, etc. The authority of the board, in the absence of any epidemic, extends to the abatement of all nuisances and the treatment of all indigent sick. It has also the power to make and pass all such rules and regulations as it may deem necessary for the preservation of the public health and the prevention of disease, such rules having all the force of ordinances when they have received the approval of the city council. During an epidemic the board has authority to do any thing that may be thought best for the suppression of the disease.

The health officer, salary $2,400 per annum, is the chief executive officer of the board, and he is a physician. It is his duty to enforce all existing laws which have for their object the preservation of life, the prevention of disease, and the abatement of nuisances. He has supervision over all the inspectors and assistants, and has general care over the books and records of the office and all the property of the department. There are 3 meat inspectors and 1 milk inspector, whose duties are sufficiently explained by their titles. In addition to the above there are 13 sanitary policemen, one for each of the health districts into which the city is divided, and 27 district physicians, who are required to act as assistant health officers in their respective districts. All the above have police powers sufficient to enable them to enter premises, and to cause the arrest of persons who interfere with them in the execution of their duties.

NUISANCES, ETC.

Inspections are made daily in all parts of the city. When nuisances are reported the parties offending or responsible are ordered to abate the same within two days, and the sanitary police see that the orders are carried out. Questions of house-drainage and sewer connections, beyond such cases where pronounced nuisances exist, are wholly in the hands of the city commissioners and city engineer. The control and management of all cesspools and privy-vaults, outside of the immediate construction of the same, is in the hands of the board. The cleaning of streets and the removal of garbage and ashes are in the hands of the city commissioners, but the board is required to have a general sanitary supervision over the streets. The burial of the dead is under control of the board, and permits for interments are issued by the health officer, on death certificates signed by a physician.

INFECTIOUS DISEASES.

Small-pox patients are either quarantined at home or sent to the pest-house, which is situated in the western part of the city, the whole matter being at the discretion of the board. Nothing is done regarding scarlet fever, except when the disease appears in tenement houses or becomes epidemic. When diseases of a contagious nature appear in public schools the board recommends certain action to the board of education, which is generally adopted. Vaccination is not compulsory, neither is it done at the public expense, the furnishing by the health department of virus for schools being the only exception.

REGISTRATION AND REPORTS.

Full records of all diseases, births, and deaths are kept in the health department, the classification of such being the same as that adopted by the National Board of Health.

The board reports annually to the city council, and the report is published with the other city documents.

MUNICIPAL CLEANSING.

Street-cleaning.—The streets are cleaned at the expense of the city and by its regular force. The work is done almost wholly by hand, there being but one sweeping-machine in the city, which is employed only to a limited extent by private persons. The cleaning is not done regularly, the business streets being attended to once every two or three weeks, while in more remote localities the intervals are greater. There is constant complaint of filthy gutters. Heavy rains do much more efficient work than the street-cleaners. The annual cost to the city is from $50,000 to $80,000, and the sweepings are either sold to persons who use them as fertilizers, or are deposited on new streets that require to be brought up to grade. Regarding this work, Major Chamberlin says:

> The chief merit of the system consists of its being kept under control of the city. Its defects are that it naturally becomes the prey of the political party in power, and its management is oftener in the interest of the party than of the public. Then there is great expense connected with keeping up stables and the care of necessary horses and wagons. It is thought that the contract system, with the city divided into districts, would be much cheaper and better, but though authority exists for such contracts the city council has not exercised it. There is universal complaint by physicians of the unhealthfulness of depositing street-cleanings on public streets or building lots.

Removal of garbage and ashes.—The removal of all garbage and ashes is done at the expense of the city by the street-cleaning department. While awaiting removal the garbage is required to be kept in water-tight vessels, and unmixed with ashes, shells, or other rubbish. It is reported that this requirement is not fully enforced. The garbage is either dumped into the river or carried to a fertilizing factory, while the ashes generally go upon streets that require filling. The city pays a contractor $15,000 per annum for removing all dead animals and all garbage, etc., that may be delivered to him by the street-cleaning department. The only complaint made regarding the system is from mixing garbage and ashes, and using the same for street-filling. The stench therefrom affects the neighborhood to a greater or less extent.

Dead animals.—The contractor for the removal of garbage has, as part consideration, the exclusive right to the removal and ownership of all dead animals found in the city. The officers of the board of health promptly notify the contractor when any dead animals are discovered, and, as the carcasses are of more or less value, he removes them without delay. During 1879 the following dead animals were removed: Hogs, 9,393; cattle, 398; sheep and goats, 790; horses, 1,200; and dogs, 1,000.

Liquid household wastes.—There are no special regulations on this subject, but the custom is to put chamber slops into privy-vaults, when the house is not connected with the sewer. The greater portion of laundry wastes and kitchen slops are run into the street-gutters, some being thrown into vaults. Cesspools are almost unknown in the city, and, where they do exist, are constructed in the same manner as vaults. Wells are very rarely used, the water for drinking purposes being taken from the city water-works.

Human excreta.—Major Chamberlin reports that there is no way of determining the exact number of water-closets in the city, but it is estimated that about one house in seven is so furnished, with probably a greater proportion in the central parts of the city. About three-fourths of the water-closets deliver into the public sewers, the remainder delivering into privy-vaults. The privy-vaults are required to be water-tight, but it is reported that very few of them are so. They must be 20 feet deep, walled with stone, and not nearer than 6 feet to any street or 2 feet to any party-line. No vaults are allowed to be built when a sewer-connection can be made. The vaults are cleaned by licensed cleaners, who must obtain a permit from the health officer before opening any vault, and who receive from $1 to $2 for each load. Two plans of cleaning are in common use—the pumping and the bucket system, the latter not being permitted during the warm summer months. The night-soil is carried to a *sullage*-boat, moored at the foot of Wood street, on the Ohio river, and when this boat becomes full it is dropped downstream, into the current of the river, and its contents are discharged into the channel. The boat is then thoroughly washed and returned to her station.

Manufacturing wastes.—According to Major Chamberlin, no provision is made for manufacturing wastes except that for the removal of ashes and street sweepings.

POLICE.

The police force of Cincinnati is appointed by the mayor, who has full power to make all rules and regulations for its government. The superintendent of police, salary $2,500 per annum ($800 of which is paid by the county), is the chief executive officer of the force. He is required to devote his whole time to the duties of his office, has authority to give orders to the force for its guidance, and can issue warrants for arrests, prosecute offenders, etc. The remainder of the force, in the several grades, and the salaries of each, are as follows: 1 inspector at $1,500 per annum; 17 lieutenants at $900 a year each; 295 patrolmen at $800 a year each; 5 police-court officers at $800 a year each; 20 station-house keepers at $600 a year each; 1 clerk at $1,500 per annum; and 3 assistant clerks at $1,000 a year each. The uniform consists of a navy-blue cloth suit, frock coat with brass buttons, overcoat of the same material, and flannel blouse for summer, and a stiff black hat with gold cord and acorn tips. The men pay for their own uniforms, the average cost of each suit complete being $67 60, but are required to buy the cloth at one place, to secure uniformity in color and quality. The men are equipped with wooden maces made of maple, and revolver, the latter being their own property. They also wear ebony batons in a belt when on parade, and all the men are required to wear badges with numbers. The day patrolmen are on duty 12½ hours at a time, and the night patrolmen 10 hours, nearly 300 miles of streets being covered by the force.

During 1880 there were 14,592 arrests made—9,474 being for offenses, and 5,118 for safe-keeping. The latter were discharged without trial before court. The principal offenses were: Drunkenness, 2,374; disorderly conduct, 1,786; on suspicion, 1,284; assault and battery, 894; vagrancy, 674; larceny, 611; abusing family, 178; suspicious characters, 169; and carrying concealed weapons, 147. In the final dispositions of the arrests 3,012 were sent to the work-house and 172 before the grand jury.

No record is kept of the amount of property lost and stolen during the year and reported to the police. The number of station-house lodgers during 1880 aggregated 40,046 (males, 36,694; females, 3,352) as against 47,658, (males, 44,818; females, 2,840) in 1879. No free meals are given to these station-house lodgers, but during the past year 6,182 free meals were furnished to indigent prisoners, at a cost of $906 60.

The police force is required to co-operate with the fire department by promptly giving alarm and aiding in the preservation of order and property at fires, and with the department of public works by reporting all street obstructions, dangerous buildings, excavations, etc.

About 8 or 10 patrolmen, called specials, are detailed for duty at the most crowded street-crossings and to form a reserve at the central station. The mayor appoints private watchmen, who have the same powers as the regular force, but are not paid by the city. During the past year 5 policemen died (2 of these being killed while performing their duty), 20 resigned, and 219 were dismissed. The cost of the force for 1880 was $279,473 76. Major Chamberlin closes his information on the subject of police as follows:

The police force of Cincinnati has for a number of years borne a good name for general efficiency, but in the past eight years it has been sorely tried by reason of legislation concerning it with a view to political advantage. As the legislature has been under the control of one or another party the laws governing the police force have been changed. At one time the mayor was deprived of all power over the police, and even did not possess a clear right to call upon them to suppress a riot. This was the condition in 1877, when the railroad riots were causing apprehension everywhere. Happily there was no serious outbreak here, and disaster was averted. Only in 1880 was the mayor given power to appoint and control the police. That power had been vested in a board of commissioners; and the personnel of that board was more than once changed by the legislature, to place the control of the police in the hands of one party or the other. One effect of this tossing about has been to create a public opinion which is opposed to all political use of the police, and considerable progress has been made toward keeping the police out of politics. They are now specifically prohibited from an active participation in political work beyond casting their votes.

The method of patrolling the streets at night is for two men to go together over the same beat. In day-time the patrolmen go about singly. The hours of service of the night patrolmen are so fixed that one of two "partners" goes on duty an hour earlier than the other, and goes off an hour earlier. This leaves no gap between the hours of day and night men, and keeps up an unbroken watch.

FIRE DEPARTMENT.

The fire department of Cincinnati is well equipped and efficient, and was organized as a paid department in 1853. It is managed by a board of fire commissioners, composed of 5 members, appointed by the mayor with the approval of the common council, who hold office for five years, without compensation. The term of one member expires each year. The force of the department consists of a chief engineer, with assistants, a telegraph corps, and 143 firemen. The apparatus now in use consists of 18 steam fire-engines, 1 hand-engine, 1 chemical engine, 5 hook-and-ladder trucks with life-saving apparatus attached, and 35 one-horse hose-reels, all in active service. There are 95 horses and 34,250 feet of hose in use. The steam-engines are all made in the city, and are, for the most part, of the class known as Lotta engines. The members of the department are always on duty, having one night off in each week. The engine-houses are well constructed, the sleeping-apartments being well lighted, ventilated, and fitted up, and, owing to this care of details, the health of the force is generally very good. There is no insurance patrol.

What is known as the Gamwell system of fire-alarm telegraph is in use, with which are connected 213 alarm-boxes. To supply water for extinguishing fires, 289 large, self-emptying cisterns and 753 fire-hydrants are always in readiness. The annual cost of the department is about $175,000.

MANUFACTURES.

The following is a summary of the statistics of manufactures of Cincinnati for 1880, being taken from tables prepared for the Tenth Census by Henry Cole, chief special agent:

Mechanical and manufacturing industries.	No. of establishments.	Capital.	AVERAGE NUMBER OF HANDS EMPLOYED.			Total amount paid in wages during the year.	Value of materials.	Value of products.
			Males above 16 years.	Females above 15 years.	Children and youths.			
All industries	3,276	$50,533,100	38,993	10,483	5,041	$19,553,629	$62,376,710	$105,259,165
Artificial limbs (see also Surgical appliances)	3	3,350	11	....	1	4,904	3,155	12,225
Awnings and tents	9	7,450	19	30	....	11,492	34,095	64,750
Bags, paper	3	85,000	42	41	2	26,377	376,072	472,808
Baking and yeast powders (see also Drugs and chemicals)	6	28,000	19	....	4	8,560	54,347	119,700
Baskets, rattan and willow ware	9	9,000	13	....	2	4,175	10,595	24,060
Belting and hose, leather	3	57,000	26	....	....	15,429	73,107	104,554
Blacksmithing (see also Wheelwrighting)	128	115,745	328	....	5	161,816	123,530	437,019
Bookbinding and blank-book making	18	157,910	122	148	22	116,534	116,377	387,640
Boot and shoe findings	5	28,000	9	2	....	4,366	63,200	91,000
Boot and shoe uppers	3	5,400	13	9	3	9,000	14,900	29,900
Boots and shoes, including custom work and repairing	333	1,066,656	2,352	579	283	1,088,248	2,305,219	4,132,637
Boxes, cigar	8	23,750	47	44	23	32,090	60,185	118,740
Boxes, fancy and paper	7	38,550	27	35	7	26,726	32,012	72,809
Boxes, wooden packing	5	43,100	75	8	11	30,469	71,900	125,612
Brass castings	14	220,777	226	....	33	109,249	306,962	551,696
Bread and other bakery products	232	391,860	551	66	82	246,344	1,159,917	1,827,216
Brick and tile	35	90,360	249	....	41	79,155	59,950	215,035
Brooms and brushes	18	101,237	108	13	13	41,438	64,835	148,050
Carpentering	119	290,305	875	....	13	386,095	745,720	1,515,097
Carpets, rag	21	4,775	32	3	6	11,425	15,899	41,822
Carriage and wagon materials	5	368,440	178	2	20	92,318	160,089	430,636
Carriages and wagons (see also Wheelwrighting)	50	1,252,131	2,694	81	522	1,207,319	3,061,264	5,287,113
Clothing, men's	237	6,279,783	3,731	4,898	646	2,670,130	8,628,133	13,878,903
Clothing, women's	19	194,802	31	898	8	222,380	608,002	1,036,454
Coffee and spices, roasted and ground	10	86,400	65	4	3	32,542	258,170	410,100
Coffins, burial cases, and undertakers' goods	8	636,500	464	98	96	258,446	462,675	1,002,866
Coke	3	14,000	13	....	....	4,012	17,206	42,887
Confectionery	20	177,075	148	60	23	83,595	467,820	660,260
Cooperage	58	359,950	531	....	11	205,559	258,428	587,083
Coppersmithing (see also Tinware, copperware, and sheet-iron ware)	5	34,000	50	....	2	25,054	57,740	102,536
Corsets	3	2,900	....	5	1	1,395	3,800	10,000
Cotton goods (see also Hosiery and knit goods)	3	715,000	97	275	26	99,147	298,465	684,158
Cutlery and edge tools (see also Hardware; Tools)	12	40,100	31	....	4	16,452	13,500	48,900
Dentistry, mechanical	24	18,550	14	1	1	9,763	12,179	72,495
Drugs and chemicals (see also Baking and yeast powders; Patent medicines and compounds).	8	102,200	49	....	....	16,844	159,225	225,025
Dyeing and cleaning	12	47,050	24	16	3	18,731	10,080	52,475
Dyeing and finishing textiles	7	58,300	27	13	3	20,401	78,400	144,295
Electrical apparatus and supplies	5	83,500	31	8	6	15,260	80,700	173,580
Electroplating	7	33,160	88	2	5	30,637	23,065	83,440
Engraving and die-sinking	12	11,050	26	8	10	16,838	6,894	38,021
Engraving, steel	3	1,300	3	....	....	1,600	1,100	5,600
Engraving, wood	3	2,100	8	....	....	4,150	825	9,500
Fancy articles	3	4,500	5	8	5	2,502	4,048	9,600
Flavoring extracts	4	10,800	10	1	2	3,980	9,300	17,800
Flouring- and grist-mill products	14	210,500	101	....	....	36,913	544,226	634,964
Food preparations	3	6,300	6	4	....	2,000	5,860	13,910
Foundery and machine-shop products (see also Iron work, architectural and ornamental).	90	4,088,475	3,503	6	126	1,749,584	2,592,096	5,723,508
Fruits and vegetables, canned and preserved	4	221,380	179	577	150	79,173	565,234	743,928
Furniture (see also Mattresses and spring beds; Upholstering)	119	2,642,711	2,853	138	470	1,335,213	1,641,141	4,372,339
Furniture, chairs	16	71,850	167	17	14	73,775	50,222	208,635
Gas machines and meters	6	121,000	76	....	1	41,998	77,100	139,670
Glass, cut, stained, and ornamented	3	5,650	14	....	....	8,700	3,525	23,600
Gloves and mittens (see also Hosiery and knit goods)	3	1,100	4	1	....	1,400	3,500	7,000
Glue	3	189,000	46	....	26	21,180	34,700	143,000
Grease and tallow	7	44,550	34	....	1	18,486	187,200	229,600

Mechanical and manufacturing industries.	No. of establishments.	Capital.	AVERAGE NUMBER OF HANDS EMPLOYED.			Total amount paid in wages during the year.	Value of materials.	Value of products.
			Males above 16 years.	Females above 15 years.	Children and youths.			
Hairwork	14	$32,050	11	31	....	$9,988	$16,090	$42,680
Hardware (see also Cutlery and edge tools; Tools)	18	959,309	671	3	48	249,533	507,852	1,051,193
Hats and caps, not including wool hats	9	9,350	25	19	3	14,205	37,870	66,770
Hosiery and knit goods (see also Cotton goods; Gloves and mittens)	9	76,400	32	213	76	55,425	147,300	235,825
Ink	3	41,200	13	....	2	7,360	45,200	78,800
Instruments, professional and scientific	8	33,200	37	1	2	17,557	11,998	47,549
Iron and steel	4	610,689	305		8	163,590	338,479	596,160
Iron railing, wrought	5	18,150	58	....	4	22,183	32,969	69,386
Iron work, architectural and ornamental (see also Foundry and machine-shop products).	8	50,250	84			39,025	152,124	255,847
Jewelry	9	152,600	179	25	49	131,886	142,385	418,900
Leather, curried	21	379,000	184			86,175	1,425,505	1,700,426
Leather, tanned	29	918,600	341		5	168,393	1,594,137	2,090,672
Lightning rods	3	40,000	13			6,950	96,000	144,500
Liquors, distilled	10	3,143,500	750		....	312,500	3,604,120	5,293,466
Liquors, malt	19	4,139,968	1,373			595,363	2,566,000	4,580,579
Lithographing (see also Printing and publishing)	9	322,400	286	20	39	185,063	283,517	633,744
Lock- and gun-smithing	13	6,095	9		4	4,328	3,035	14,410
Looking-glass and picture frames	9	404,350	462	....	44	187,120	249,500	524,000
Lumber, planed (see also Sash, doors, and blinds; Wood, turned and carved).	11	247,676	541	1	1	168,000	400,959	656,824
Lumber, sawed	9	502,000	295		20	110,979	974,097	1,247,191
Malt	14	839,000	107	....	....	57,316	736,613	884,310
Mantels, slate, marble, and marbleized	5	235,000	199	....	17	93,362	136,540	304,330
Marble and stone work	44	468,650	623	5	38	262,647	287,562	856,863
Masonry, brick and stone	18	23,050	133	....	5	58,591	85,628	183,509
Mattresses and spring beds (see also Furniture)	13	37,940	48	14	15	22,239	74,150	135,350
Millinery and lace goods	22	81,450	25	259	11	77,486	162,852	320,091
Mineral and soda waters	11	34,600	50	....	5	18,192	29,991	82,742
Models and patterns	13	8,350	26	8	4	10,243	6,140	29,346
Musical instruments and materials (not specified)	7	12,300	17	....	....	6,875	4,925	19,625
Oil, lard	5	220,000	55			14,272	357,916	395,145
Oil, lubricating	4	104,775	29	....	1	18,404	169,100	238,000
Painting and paperhanging	87	95,711	368	....	5	133,939	148,174	414,469
Patent medicines and compounds (see also Drugs and chemicals)	41	505,750	102	11	11	56,360	361,163	540,120
Photographing	30	34,700	66	13	3	37,434	33,780	122,747
Pickles, preserves, and sauces	3	35,000	56	12	....	16,800	95,000	130,000
Plumbing and gasfitting	59	200,488	235	....	22	95,767	237,101	423,113
Printing and publishing (see also Lithographing)	89	2,527,791	1,910	349	830	1,168,592	1,397,880	4,006,450
Refrigerators	4	44,100	41	....	2	11,303	13,425	42,040
Regalia and society banners and emblems	5	46,200	17	76	7	18,550	45,800	80,500
Roofing and roofing materials	25	230,520	234	1	3	91,764	409,244	612,491
Saddlery and harness	51	413,955	543	14	35	236,473	511,749	1,155,564
Safes, doors, and vaults, fire-proof	4	784,000	865	....	10	502,428	425,000	1,335,000
Sash, doors, and blinds (see also Lumber, planed; Wood, turned and carved).	9	410,600	391	....	12	137,949	355,400	735,200
Saws	5	112,750	96	....	....	37,518	66,410	145,550
Sewing machines and attachments	6	14,700	13	1	2	8,035	152,104	168,800
Shipbuilding	8	131,000	231			134,995	395,100	566,700
Shirts	21	188,400	69	418	2	107,271	253,325	416,627
Show-cases	4	26,200	92	....	3	41,616	53,019	116,637
Silk and silk goods	5	21,700	19	68	39	10,700	18,355	46,140
Slaughtering and meat-packing, not including retail butchering	49	4,074,682	1,107	....	36	338,302	10,454,991	11,614,810
Spectacles and eyeglasses	3	1,125	2	....	....	460	500	2,500
Stencils and brands	4	9,450	19	....	7	12,924	3,450	22,620
Stereotyping and electrotyping	3	19,600	20	....	2	13,495	7,600	28,348
Stone- and earthen-ware	12	287,100	275	41	75	139,508	93,730	356,900
Surgical appliances (see also Artificial limbs)	4	16,300	8	2	....	6,452	8,060	26,000
Tinware, copperware, and sheet-iron ware (see also Coppersmithing)	107	344,333	390	3	19	138,933	406,303	780,333
Tobacco, chewing, smoking, and snuff (see also Tobacco, cigars and cigarettes)	13	490,645	431	85	60	161,986	1,138,489	1,508,486
Tobacco, cigars and cigarettes (see also Tobacco, chewing, smoking, and snuff).	250	746,935	2,009	372	384	901,628	1,043,066	2,767,401
Tools (see also Cutlery and edge tools; Hardware)	3	17,800	28	....	1	13,100	14,700	45,800
Trunks and valises	11	93,700	199	20	14	61,200	100,935	226,706

Mechanical and manufacturing industries.	No. of estab- lish- ments.	Capital.	AVERAGE NUMBER OF HANDS EMPLOYED.			Total amount paid in wages during the year.	Value of materials.	Value of products.
			Males above 16 years.	Females above 15 years.	Children and youths.			
Umbrellas and canes	7	$20,250	12	11	3	$9,800	$31,525	$55,600
Upholstering (see also Furniture)	11	152,850	113	16	45	48,883	168,495	265,825
Varnish	4	94,500	23	....	....	14,355	131,958	186,090
Vinegar	8	92,750	49	....	....	16,848	79,600	167,728
Watch and clock repairing	36	84,520	68	4	8	33,686	15,040	106,151
Wheelwrighting (see also Blacksmithing; Carriages and wagons)	45	122,012	206	....	4	84,345	55,945	218,304
Window blinds and shades	6	17,100	17	4	1	9,484	61,000	100,424
Wirework	6	82,600	170	....	36	36,157	97,200	198,600
Wood, turned and carved (see also Lumber, planed; Sash, doors, and blinds).	17	27,070	60	4	2	26,979	23,965	104,160
Wooden ware	3	83,064	70	....	42	50,850	77,291	173,684
All other industries (a)	74	2,783,615	1,144	260	184	547,141	2,632,395	4,310,063

a Embracing agricultural implements; axle-grease; bags, other than paper; billiard tables and materials; blacking; calcium lights; carriages and sleds, children's; cars, railroad, street and repairs; cement; cigar molds; cleansing and polishing preparations; cloth finishing; combs; cordage and twine; drain and sewer pipe; enameled goods; envelopes; explosives and fireworks; fertilizers; files; flags and banners; foundery supplies; furnishing goods, men's; furs, dressed; gas and lamp fixtures; gold and silver leaf and foil; hand-knit goods; hand-stamps; housefurnishing goods; lamps and reflectors; lapidary work; lasts; lead, bar, pipe, sheet, and shot; lime; millstones; mirrors; mixed textiles; oleomargarine; oil, cottonseed and cake; oil, illuminating; oil, linseed; paints; pens, gold; pocket-books; printing materials; scales and balances; smelting and refining; soap and candles; springs, steel, car, and carriage; starch; steam fittings and heating apparatus; taxidermy; type founding; veneering; washing-machines and clothes-wringers; and woolen goods.

From the foregoing table it appears that the average capital of all establishments is $15,425 24; that the average wages of all hands employed is $358 67 per annum; and that the average outlay in wages, in materials, and in interest (at 6 per cent.) on capital employed is $25,934 78.

CLEVELAND,

CUYAHOGA COUNTY, OHIO.

POPULATION

IN THE

AGGREGATE,

1820–1880.

	Inhab.
1790	......
1800	......
1810	......
1820	606
1830	1,876
1840	6,071
1850	17,034
1860	43,417
1870	92,829
1880	160,146

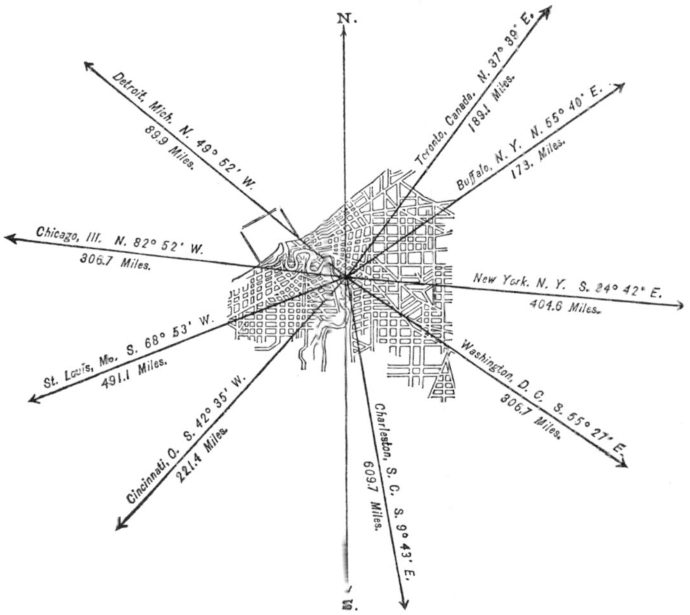

POPULATION

BY

SEX, NATIVITY, AND RACE,

AT

CENSUS OF 1880.

Male	80,174
Female	79,972
Native	100,737
Foreign-born	59,409
White	158,084
Colored	*2,062

* Including 23 Chinese and 1 Indian.

Latitude: 41° 30' North; Longitude: 81° 42' (west from Greenwich); Altitude: 570 to 813 feet.

FINANCIAL CONDITION:

Total Valuation: $70,548,104; per capita: $441 00.   Net Indebtedness: $6,467,046; per capita: $40 38.   Tax per $100: $3 04.

HISTORICAL SKETCH.

The site of Cleveland, where the Cuyahoga river empties into lake Erie, was known to the Indians long before the coming of the white man, and the river was for many years a part of the boundary that separated the lands of the "Six Nations" from the "Wyandot Confederacy". Early in the eighteenth century trading-posts were established in this vicinity, and in 1752 Benjamin Franklin called attention to the place by recommending that a "fort and town for trade" should be erected at the mouth "of the *Tioga* [Cuyahoga] south of lake Erie". Even after the Revolutionary war the British refused to yield the country west of the river, and occupied it until 1790.

Cleveland was settled in 1796, at the time of the first survey of the Western reserve by the proprietors in Connecticut. General Cleaveland, who was in charge of the survey, was directed to lay out at this point "one capital town", and it was laid out, so far as it was then done, substantially as it now exists. The settlement was first called "Euclid", but this was soon changed to "Cleveland". Progress was very slow for many years, several inland towns surpassing it in population and wealth. The prevalence of fever and ague in the vicinity, probably, had much to do with the slow growth. Its harbor proved to be of little value, as the mouth of the Cuyahoga river was obstructed by sand-bars that reduced the draught of water to 10 inches. In 1802 the price of lots, formerly sold at $50 each, fell off to $25, and even this was not promptly paid. In 1805 the customs district of Erie was formed, and the mouth of the Cuyahoga was made a port of entry. Even yet vessels could seldom get into the river without discharging their cargoes into lighters. In 1808 boat-building began, the "Zephyr", a schooner of 30 tons, being launched. In 1810 Cuyahoga county was organized, with Cleveland as the county-seat. During the war of 1812 a depot of supplies was established at this point, and troops destined for operations farther west were collected here. A small stockade was built on the lake shore, where now is the foot of Seneca street, and a permanent garrison occupied it. Though the ships of the enemy made several appearances off the mouth of the river, the little settlement was not disturbed during the war. In the latter part of 1814 Cleveland was incorporated as a village, the first election taking place in June of the following year, when 12 votes were cast. In 1818 the first newspaper, the Cleveland *Gazette and Commercial Advertiser*, was issued.

In 1825, the Ohio and Erie canal, connecting the waters of lake Erie with those of the Ohio river, was begun, the work being finished in 1832, with the northern terminus at this point. Steps were at once taken to improve the harbor. Piers were built out into the lake, the bar at the mouth of the river was cut through, and when the canal was opened Cleveland had a harbor all ready for the increased shipping that would be drawn to the port. The completion of these works begins a new era in Cleveland's history. The population of the village in 1830 was but little over 1,000. In *Life on the Lakes* the following description of Cleveland, in August, 1835, is given:

> The town is growing with a rapidity absolutely magical, has doubled its population in three years, and quadrupled its business in the same time. The buildings are either frame, clapboarded and very neatly painted, or brick, faced with a blue-gray stone which is found in great abundance about 3 miles from here up the creek, and which is an excellent material for building. There has lately been a very destructive fire, but they are already busied in preparing the site for larger buildings. The whole place is noise, bustle, and confusion. The inhabitants are very sanguine of the future onward progress of the place, and anticipate a great increase of business on the completion of the railroad which is to terminate here. From the amazing advance in the price of real estate here, and the number of speculators from all parts of the country who make Cleveland the theater of their operations, confidence in its future prosperity must be very generally felt among the knowing ones.

In 1836 Cleveland was granted a city charter, and the same year Ohio City, situated on the west bank of the river directly opposite Cleveland, was also incorporated as a city. There was more or less rivalry between the two cities until 1854, when Cleveland absorbed its neighbor on the west bank.

In 1837, the speculation in land, which had been running high since 1834, was brought to a stop by the general commercial revulsion of that year. Some improvements were planned and begun during this period, and there was still a steady advance, especially in the building of vessels for the lakes. These latter included many steamers for passenger traffic, as the bulk of emigration to the newer states was by water transportation. In 1841 a breakwater of piles and stone was built along a part of the city front from Ontario street to Seneca street, it having been found that the waters of the lake had encroached upon the site of the city about 200 feet since 1796. About 1850 the first railroad to this point was completed, and in a short time two or three others were projected. Improvements of all kinds were apparent; buildings of a better class were erected; the paving (with planks) of some of the streets was begun, and the completed railroads began rapidly to increase the population and business. The progression was hardly checked by the financial disturbance in 1857, though many individuals suffered.

The tremendous activities of the war period were in a measure favorable to the profitable employment of existing industries and caused the development of many new enterprises. The discovery of petroleum about this time and its introduction into general use was a great benefit to the city, much of the crude oil coming here for refining and shipment. Many large fortunes were made, and, as a rule, the lucky possessors remained in Cleveland to enjoy their wealth. During this period building was brisk everywhere. Many small homesteads were purchased, and, under the influence of speculation, the prices of land were rapidly carried up. Many public works and improvements were completed, and though these increased the debt of the city to some extent, they were of benefit to the citizens generally.

No very severe or sweeping fires have ever visited the city, though there have been several of considerable magnitude. Oil refineries and lumber mills and yards have frequently been burned, but these establishments are generally isolated in their situation.

The original settlers of Cleveland came from Connecticut, but immigrants soon came from the other New England states and from New York. About 1830, foreigners began to come in, and of these the Germans were soon, numerically speaking, the strongest.

CLEVELAND,

OHIO.

SCALE OF FEET.

HARBOR

of it is used locally in various manufactures, but the greater portion comes here, either for domestic use or for shipment. Iron ore is found in nearly the same localities as the coal, and much of it, after being smelted, comes here for general distribution. The refining of crude petroleum is largely carried on here, while the lumber region of Northern Michigan uses Cleveland as a shipping center for its products.

TOPOGRAPHY.

The city of Cleveland is located on a plain of stratified drift, sand, clay, and gravel, from 70 to 100 feet above the surface of the lake, the natural drainage being of the best possible kind. There is no rock visible in this plain, but at a depth of 80 to 100 feet below lake-level there is a Devonian shale, with bands of fine-grained sandstone, which is from 500 to 600 feet thick, with limestone underneath. The surrounding country is open, cultivated, and free from marshes or ponds. What are known as the "Lake ridges", near lake Erie, are usually of sand or a sandy loam.

CLIMATE.

Highest recorded summer temperature, 96°; highest summer temperature in average years, 92°. Lowest recorded winter temperature, −17°; lowest winter temperature in average years, −12°. The adjacent waters of lake Erie not only influence the direction of the winds to a considerable extent, but greatly ameliorate the severity of the climate. As the winds bring with them the temperature of the regions they have traversed, a southerly wind is a warm current and a northerly wind a cold one; but since the temperature of the lake is more uniform than that of the land, winds passing over it do not cause such variations of temperature during the year as winds passing over the land. As an atmosphere loaded with vapor obstructs the terrestrial radiation, moist winds blowing from the lake are accompanied by a milder temperature in winter (when not frozen) and a cool temperature in summer.

In summer, when there is no atmospheric disturbance to overcome the influence, the difference in temperature between the land and the lake produces northerly winds during the day and southerly winds during the night, thus rendering calms, or a stagnant condition of the atmosphere, very infrequent.

STREETS.

Cleveland includes within her city limits 17,165 square acres, or within a fraction of 27 square miles. The streets, paved and unpaved, would make a continuous highway 369.7 miles long, and, if the alleys were added, 424.7 miles. There are over 60 miles of paved streets, 26.5 miles of curbed streets, and 104 miles of graded streets. The paved streets are laid with the following materials: Stone blocks, 17.64 miles; asphalt, 2.20 miles; asphalt and stone combined, 1.20 miles; broken stone, 5.90 miles; wood, 10.10 miles; wood and stone combined, 14.02 miles; and gravel, 9.60 miles. The cost per square yard of each, as nearly as it may be estimated, and the cost of keeping each in good repair during the past two years, is as follows:

Material.	Cost of construction per square yard.	Cost of repairs per mile.
Stone blocks	$1 71	$425 00
Asphalt	2 30	2,315 00
Asphalt and stone	2 30	1,676 00
Wood	2 30	1,081 00
Wood and stone	2 30	611 00
Broken stone	1 40	425 00
Gravel	Not stated.	Not stated.

The relative facility with which each is kept clean is said to be in the following order: Concrete, stone blocks, wood, broken stone, and gravel. In regard to the quality and permanent economy of each, the city engineer says:

The concrete used (Abbott's) has not been first-class, but is more easily repaired. Wood pavements, if made of good well-seasoned lumber, are good for from seven to ten years. Coal-tar, Thilmeny, and the Seeley and Pelton processes have been tried. The tar is considered to preserve the thin bed-boards, but to hasten decay in the thick blocks. The Thilmeny process has not proved successful, and in some instances the pavements treated with it have been the first to decay. One street only has the pavement treated with the Seeley and Pelton process; after seven years' use it appears to be in good condition. All stone pavements in the city are laid with Medina (New York) sandstone, and are by far the most economical, as far as the cost of actual pavement is concerned, but the indirect expense in the wear and tear of horses and vehicles is fully two or three times as great. Macadam or broken stone pavements are not a success here, for want of proper material, the native stone being too soft. Graveled streets are successful, but require constant care to prevent them from rutting.

The sidewalks are mostly laid with stone flags, either sawed, crandled, or split, 6 feet wide, and cost from 12 to 16 cents per square foot, put down. In some cases the sidewalks are laid with hard-burned brick, costing from 8 to 10 cents per square foot, put down, while in the suburban districts walks are sometimes made with cinders, which have not been found to answer very well. Gutters upon all paved streets are of the same material as the roadway, while on the dirt streets, except where the grades are heavy, they are usually open ditches. On the steep grades the gutters were formerly made of plank, costing from 25 to 30 cents per linear foot, but now they are being replaced with stone gutters, 5 feet wide, and costing from 2½ to 3¾ cents per square foot, which prove to be very successful.

All tree-planting, except in one street, has been left to the abutters, and, as a general thing, every street has been well planted. The trees are mostly maples and elms, and are set between the curb-line and the flagging, while nearly every residence street has a grass plat between the curb and the flagging, which is cared for by the property-owners.

All street improvements, such as construction and general or systematic repairing, are done by contract, the work being let to the lowest bidder, while all small jobs are done by the city with its regular street force. The city engineer expresses a preference for contract work, as it is much cheaper. A steam stone-crusher has been used, but, as it was found to be too powerful for the class of stones here, all crushing is now done by hand. A steam-roller is used on the macadam and concrete streets, and the authorities "would not think of doing without it".

HORSE-RAILROADS, ETC.

The horse-railroads in the city have an aggregate length of 36 miles, with 90 cars, 750 horses or mules, and 250 men. The rates of fare are 5 cents (22 tickets for $1) or all roads but one, where the fare is 6 cents for each passenger.

There are no regular omnibus lines in the city, but about 50 vehicles carry passengers from the several railroad stations to all parts of the city, at fares varying from 50 cents to $2, according to the distance traveled.

WATER-WORKS.

The water-works are owned by the city, and their total cost has been $2,529,301 44. Water is taken from lake Erie, and is pumped into a reservoir, 150 feet high and 6,000,000 gallons capacity, the pressure varying from 10 to 65 pounds to the square inch in the pipes. In order to improve the water-supply, in 1874 a crib was made out into the lake, with a tunnel leading to it. The crib is constructed of timber, filled with stone, and the outside is protected with a riprap of stone, being covered with iron plates to protect it from the ice. The tunnel is $5\frac{1}{6}$ by 5 feet in diameter, 6,661 feet long, and connects with the crib through a vertical shaft 8 feet in diameter, extending 90 feet below the surface of the lake. A similar shaft at the shore end is $67\frac{1}{2}$ feet deep. The construction of this work was peculiarly difficult, and occupied five years. The lower portion of the shaft, at the lake end, for a distance of 46 feet is lined with cast iron 2 inches thick, and the remainder with boiler iron $\frac{3}{8}$-inch thick, the top of the shaft being 9 feet below the lake surface. The new pumping machinery was put in in 1874, and consists of three pairs of pumping engines of 5,000,000 gallons capacity each.

The greatest amount pumped per diem is 16,000,000 and the least 8,000,000 gallons, the daily average consumption being 10,179,461 gallons. The average cost of raising 1,000,000 gallons 1 foot high is 5 cents; the yearly cost of maintenance, aside from the cost of pumping, is $28,212 58, and the yearly income from water-rates is $182,000. There are 402 water-meters in use, and it is found that, where set, they tend to prevent waste, as well as to increase the revenues. There are 125.6 miles of mains, 10,800 service-pipes, 2,205 stop-gates, and 998 fire-hydrants.

GAS.

The gas-works are owned by private corporations. The daily average production is about 440,000 cubic feet. The charge per 1,000 feet is, to consumers, $2; to the city, $1 25. The city pays about $16 per annum each for street-lamps, 2,595 in number.

PUBLIC BUILDINGS.

The city owns and occupies for municipal purposes, wholly or in part, 1 work-house, 1 infirmary, 4 market-houses, 2 armory buildings, 6 police stations, 13 fire-engine houses, and 44 school buildings, the approximate cost of all being $850,000. The city hall, costing $600,000, is owned by the "Case School of Applied Sciences", being the gift of the late Leonard Case, and is rented by the city for municipal purposes.

The viaduct, which stretches from Superior street to Pearl street, is 3,211 feet long, 64 feet in extreme width, with a roadway 42 feet between the curbs, and two sidewalks 11 feet wide. The draw-bridge is 332 feet long and 46 feet wide, with a roadway of 32 feet, and 7-foot sidewalks. The part west of the river is solid arched masonry, the piers being built upon pile foundations. All of the remainder of the viaduct is of iron, except 150 feet next to Superior street, which is of stone. The roadway is 60 feet above the surface of the river. The work of construction began in 1874, and was completed in 1878, at a cost of $2,164,578 17.

PUBLIC PARKS AND PLEASURE-GROUNDS.

There are 6 public parks in the city, with an aggregate area of 29.411 acres, as follows:

Monumental Park comprises an area, as originally laid out, of 10 acres, "the center of the park being the exact junction of Superior and Ontario streets." In 1836 the streets around the park were laid out, and the park proper, the four quarters, now contains 4.44 acres.

Lake View Park comprises all of the territory lying north and including 25 feet of the north side of Summit street to the tracks of the Cleveland and Pittsburgh railroad, west of the east line of Erie street, and east of a line drawn through the center of Seneca street, and contains 10.415 acres. By ordinance passed June 29, 1875, the park commissioners were authorized to take charge of all the lands fronting the park, lying north of lands owned by the railroad companies, for bathing and boating purposes.

Franklin Circle is located at the junction of Franklin avenue, York, Fulton, and Hanover streets, and contains, including the streets surrounding and passing through it, 1.414 acre.

Clinton Park contains 1.981 acre, which includes 12 feet of the streets surrounding it. It is located at the northern extremity of Dodge street, lying between Davenport street on the north and Lake street on the south.

Miles Park contains 2.450 acres; the streets surrounding it being included, it comprises the square bounded by Woodland Hills avenue on the east, Sawyer street on the west, and Park street on the north and south.

South Side Park contains an area of 9.116 acres, and lies east of Jennings avenue, with Starkweather avenue on the south, Merchant avenue on the east, and Kellogg avenue on the south.

The original cost of Lake View park was $235,000, and of South Side park $50,000. The following table shows the receipts and expenditures, for all park purposes, since 1872:

Year.	Receipts.	Disbursements.
1872	$45,152 50	$43,873 19
1873	240,437 50	242,316 47
1874	64,004 17	10,858 46
1875	17,895 08	60,643 14
1876	14,484 30	21,102 92
1877	19,109 47	9,190 24
1878	3,709 93	6,678 19
1879	209 50	7,338 75
1880	10,357 44	10,877 20
Total	415,359 89	412,878,56

The disbursements for 1880 represent a fair average of the present yearly cost of maintenance for all the parks. The parks are managed and controlled by a board of park commissioners, composed of three members, who are appointed by the mayor and confirmed by the city council.

PLACES OF AMUSEMENT.

There are four theaters in Cleveland, as follows: The Opera-house, with a seating capacity of 1,280 persons; the Globe theater, seating 900; the Academy of Music, with a seating capacity of 1,100; and the Theatre Comique, seating 950. These theaters pay an annual license of $50 each to the city.

Of the concert-halls and lecture-rooms, not including those connected with churches, may be mentioned Ease hall, seating 1,240; People's tabernacle, with a seating capacity of 3,400 persons; the East Cleveland tabernacle, seating 900; and Reeves' opera-house, seating 600.

DRAINAGE.

In 1860 the central portion of the city was divided into five sewerage districts, plans for main drainage being prepared for each district and some main sewers built. Since that time other main lines have been added and new districts provided for as needed. As a rule the public works have preceded any private attempts at sewerage or drainage. Water-courses used as a receptacle for sewerage generally run in open channels. The final disposition of the outfall of sewers is lake Erie, the mouths of the sewers being above the surface of the water and fully exposed.

It is stated that no provision is made for the ventilation of sewers in public streets, and, though ventilation from closets and traps inside of houses is required, the ordinance is not always complied with.

The smaller sewers, consisting of 9- and 12-inch pipes, have to be flushed occasionally. There are about 1,900 catch-basins, constructed with traps with sand-boxes beneath, to retain street deposits and prevent solid matters from entering the sewers. The cost of cleaning the catch-basins is about $1 25 each per year.

The cost of sewers is paid entirely by the owners of the property within the district drained, an assessment, not exceeding $2 per front foot, being laid upon the abutting property; and if this does not afford sufficient means to pay for the work, the deficiency is levied on the whole sewerage district on the basis of valuation of property.

No sewers were built during 1880, nor was any information furnished regarding the extent or cost of the present system of sewerage or of the details of construction. The cost of each catch-basin is from $35 to $40, and of its connection with the sewer from $18 to $20; manholes cost from $35 to $40 each.

City ordinances place all house-sewer connections, inside the line of public streets or places, under the control of the board of improvements, while those beyond the street lines are under control of the board of health. No person is allowed to do any work of construction, alteration, or repairs, in connection with house-drains or sewers, without a license from the board of improvements, licenses being granted for only one year. No construction or alteration of waste- or soil-pipes, in plumbing work, may be done except by a person licensed by the water-works board. No person is allowed to lay any drain or build any cesspool, vault, or catch-basin for house-drainage without first obtaining a permit from the proper department of the city, no matter whether the work is intended to be connected with a public sewer or not. All sewers or drains, before entering a house, cellar, or basement, are required to be connected with a suitable ventilating-shaft, extending at least 8 feet above the main roof of the house, and all soil-pipes are required to be extended above the roof.

In his annual report for the year ending December 31, 1880, the city engineer has the following regarding the sewerage of Cleveland:

The sewers in the lower or older part of the city, especially in the 3d ward, are in bad shape. They were constructed, very many of them, a long time ago, and are now too small and too near the surface. They should be repaired, with new ones, especially the one in Bank street, before the street is paved.

There should be a main intercepting sewer run along the vicinity of Canal street and the tracks of the Cleveland, Columbus, Cincinnati, and Indianapolis railroad, from Commercial street to lake Erie, to take up the sewers that now empty into the river in that part of the city; but before any more main sewers are built due consideration should be taken as to the probable future growth of the city. If Cleveland should become a very large city it might become necessary to run an intercepting sewer along the lake shore as far as Willson avenue, to take up sewers that now run into the lake in front of the city, provided that the future growth and needs of the city should require it. The intercepting sewer referred to above, on the east side of the river, could be connected by proper appliances with Wolworth Run sewer, when built, and then extended by trenching under Lake and other streets as far as Willson avenue, and then empty into the lake; or the tunnel could be carried out under the lake a proper distance from shore, so that the discharge of sewage matter would not be detrimental to property in that vicinity.

In his annual message to the city council, Mayor Herrick comments on the recommendations of the city engineer, as follows:

The necessity for some such sewers, especially the one just east of the river, is obvious. Under the present system of sewering the city we have what is equivalent to two large open sewers, one, the Cuyahoga river, traversing the city from north to south its entire length; the other, Wolworth run, from east to west, through the westerly half of the city. Into these pours all the house and surface drainage of a large portion of the city—the filth from the slaughtering-houses, oil-refineries, and manufactories which line their banks. Their waters become impregnated with the foul mixtures, and when exposed to the summer's sun can not but exhale a noisome and unhealthful odor. Some of the filthy substances which find their way into the river settle to the bottom, and there remain until brought to the surface by the action of the wheels of some passing steamer, when they give forth a disease-breeding stench and sink back to await the next opportunity to rise.

Another ill-effect of the deposit of so much nastiness in the river was seen in the condition of our drinking-water from the lake at the time of the ice gorge at the mouth of the river this winter. The ice in the lake prevented the egress of that in the river, so that when the latter broke away it was forced by the current under the lake-ice until it reached such a depth as to plow up the concentrated filth at the bottom of the river and in the lake just at its mouth. This was carried out toward the water-works crib, and a considerable quantity found its way into the water-pipes and was distributed throughout the city. * * * Much, too, of the offal that is thrown into the river and Wolworth run is carried by the current into the lake, and is then washed landward and deposited along the shore and there left to putrefy and decay, emitting in the mean time noxious odors and rendering the neighborhood disagreeable both to sight and smell.

CEMETERIES.

Of the several cemeteries used by the people of Cleveland for the burial of their dead, the following belong to the city:

Woodlawn Cemetery, area 60½ acres, was organized in 1853, and is situated on Woodland avenue, between Quincy, Giddings, and Cemetery streets. Total number of interments to date, 14,675.

Erie Street Cemetery, area 30 acres, is situated between Erie, Dale, Brownell, and Sumner streets, and was organized in 1827. Total number of interments to date, about 15,000.

Monroe Street Cemetery is located between Monroe street and the Cleveland, Columbus, Cincinnati, and Indianapolis railroad, contains about 60 acres of ground, and was organized in 1850. Total number of interments to the present time, 7,407.

Harvard Grove Cemetery, situated on Harvard street, near the southeastern limits of the city, contains about 20 acres, and has just been organized. The remains of about 2,000 persons, that were formerly interred in the old Axtel Street cemetery, will be removed here.

The cemeteries owned by private corporations, societies, etc., are as follows:

Saint John and Saint Joseph Cemeteries, on Woodland avenue, just south of Woodland cemetery, have an aggregate area of 23 acres, and were organized in 1842. Total number of interments in the two cemeteries to the present time, 25,200.

The Jewish cemeteries of Tiffret Israel and Auchie Cleried are located together, at the corner of Monroe and Millet streets, and have a combined area of 3½ acres. They were organized in 1850, and so far there have been 860 interments made in them. They belong to the Huron and Eagle Street congregations, lots being sold to members only, at prices ranging from $25 to $150. The lots are 9 by 20 feet.

The Hungarian, Austia Emeth, and Russian Jewish cemeteries occupy about 2½ acres of land, and are used by the several congregations named.

North Brooklyn Cemetery, located on Scranton avenue, in the 12th ward, area 2½ acres, was organized as early as 1788. There have been nearly 2,000 interments made here, and, as the cemetery is nearly full, it is not much used now.

Riverside Cemetery, area 102½ acres, is situated just outside the city limits, on the Brooklyn road, and was organized October 21, 1875. Total number of interments to date, 1,015.

Lake View Cemetery, area 350 acres, is situated outside the western limits of the city, and was organized in 1870. The cemetery is well laid out, with macadamized roads, artificial lakes, etc. Lots are sold at prices ranging from 30 to 70 cents per front foot. Total number of interments to date, about 1,300.

The *Infirmary City Cemetery* is attached to the infirmary, on Scranton street, and is used for the burial of the poor who die in that institution. It occupies 1 acre of ground, and so far 750 interments have been made here.

Before any interment can be made a permit must be obtained from the health officer. These permits are granted on death certificates signed by the attending physician.

MARKETS.

There are four public markets in Cleveland, owned by the city, as follows:

Name of markets.	Location.	Area of ground.	Length of curb space.	STALLS. Number.	STALLS. Yearly rent.	BENCHES. Number.	BENCHES. Yearly rent.	CURB STANDS. Number.	CURB STANDS. Yearly rent.
		Square feet.	*Feet.*						
Central	Woodland avenue and Bolivar street	24,700	5,670	68	$100	68	$40	88	$30
Pearl Street	Corner of Pearl and Lorain streets	12,500	4,607	29	75	26	20	32	20
Eighteenth Ward	Broadway, corner of Canton street	6,000	600	11	40	8	20	19	20
Fifth Ward	Corner of Oregon and Oliver streets	6,000	1,850	20	40	24	20	32	20

The total annual rental for all the markets amount to $18,395, and to this should be added the sum of $15,000, which is realized every year as premiums on the stalls, benches, and curbs, as they are disposed of.

The market buildings are all of wood, three of them having been built ten or fifteen years ago and one two years ago, and their estimated value at the present time is $40,000, exclusive of land, which is valued at $100,000.

The markets are open daily from 6 a. m. to 1 p. m., also on Saturdays from 6 to 10 p. m.

SANITARY AUTHORITY—BOARD OF HEALTH.

The chief sanitary authority in Cleveland is the board of health, an independent organization, composed of five physicians and one civil engineer, appointed by the city council, to hold office for a term of three years, with the mayor a member *ex officio*. The ordinary annual expenses of the board vary from $12,000 to $15,000, for salaries, small-pox hospitals, printing, postage, vaccine virus, etc. During epidemics the expenses of the board are practically unlimited, as the state laws require the council to furnish all necessary funds. In the absence of any declared epidemic the authority of the board extends over the sanitary area of the city and the general health of the inhabitants, while during epidemics it has full power to do all things necessary to check and control the disease. The board meets the first and third Thursdays in each month, and transacts its business as a legislative body.

The health officer, salary $1,500 per annum, is the chief executive officer of the board, and has authority to carry out all the orders of the board and to see that the health ordinances are enforced. He is a physician. He has as assistants 1 inspector of sewers at $780 a year, and 6 sanitary policemen at $720 a year each. These assistants have full police powers. There are also 18 district physicians, one for each of the sanitary districts into which the city is divided, who have general supervision of the condition and health of their respective districts.

NUISANCES, ETC.

Inspections are made daily in all parts of the city, and the sanitary policemen report twice a week at the health office to receive complaints that may be made there. When a nuisance is reported or discovered the health officer or one of his assistants examines the place, and if the nuisance is found to exist it is ordered abated. From the annual report of the sanitary police it appears that 18,125 nuisances or defects were abated or corrected during the past year. The board of health exercises full control over the conservation and removal of garbage and the removal of excrement.

BURIAL OF THE DEAD.

No interments are allowed, except on permits issued by the board of health.

INFECTIOUS DISEASES.

When possible, all small-pox patients are removed to the pest-house (or small-pox hospital), which is situated on a farm of 30 acres, 6 miles outside the city. If patients can not be removed they are quarantined at home, a notice being posted on the door and police supervision invoked to keep up the isolation. In scarlet-fever cases the house is disinfected and guarded as much as possible. The board takes cognizance of the breaking out of contagious diseases in public or private schools only so far as vaccination is concerned and where sickness exists in the family of a pupil. Vaccination is compulsory, but it is done at the public expense only when persons are unable to pay.

REGISTRATION AND REPORTS.

All births and deaths are registered at the health office, in records prepared for the purpose, and all physicians are required by law to make full returns. The board reports annually to the city council, and its report is published with the regular city documents.

MUNICIPAL CLEANSING.

Street-cleaning.—The streets are cleaned at the expense of the city by contract, the work being done wholly by hand. The cleaning is done as often as necessary, the streets being usually in good condition. The cost of this work in 1879 was $11,321 54. The sweepings are deposited on low grounds or used on gardens as a fertilizer.

Removal of garbage and ashes.—All garbage is removed, under direction of the board of health, to a boat and then taken down the lake; swill is removed by a contractor, while the ashes must be disposed of at the expense of the householders. Ashes and garbage are not allowed to be kept in the same vessel, and regulations for the proper conservancy of garbage while awaiting removal are now under discussion. The cost of the service to the city is $100 per month for the removal of garbage, and nothing for swill; while the householders pay 50 cents per cubic yard for the removal of the ashes.

Dead animals.—The carcasses of animals dying within the city limits are removed by a contractor, who makes two collection trips each day. The service is a source of revenue to the city, the contractor paying for the privilege. During 1879, 1,150 carcasses were removed.

Liquid household wastes.—A large portion of the household wastes of the city are run into sewers, about 25 per cent. going into cesspools and but very little into street-gutters. The cesspools have tight sides but porous bottoms, are not provided with overflows, do not receive the wastes from water-closets, and are cleaned out when ordered by the health officer.

Human excreta.—It is stated that all water-closets in the city deliver into the public sewers. About 1 per cent. of the privy-vaults are reported as being nominally water-tight. They are required to be 10 feet deep, at least 40 feet from any dwelling or spring, and may be built only under permits from the board of health. All vaults are emptied by regular contractors, some of the night-soil being made into a fertilizer and some being sold to farmers.

Manufacturing wastes.—The greater portion of the manufacturing wastes of Cleveland find their way either into the river or into Wolworth run.

POLICE.

The police force of Cleveland is appointed and governed by the police commissioners, a body composed of four members elected by the people, with the mayor *ex officio* as president. The chief executive officer is the superintendent of police, salary $2,000 per annum, who has full control of the force, and administers it in accordance with the rules and regulations making the usual provisions. The remainder of the force, with their annual salaries, is as follows: Three captains at $1,296 each; 10 lieutenants and 8 detectives at $950 each; 8 sergeants at $875 each; 1 superintendent's clerk at $900; 1 telegraph operator and 2 doormen at $600 each; 2 janitors at $720 and $700; 1 fireman at $480; 123 patrolmen at $756 each; and 6 patrolmen on special duty. The uniform is of navy-blue cloth, made after the New York style, and costs complete about $110. Each man provides his own uniform.

The city is divided into eight police precincts. The first precinct includes the territroy bounded between the lake on the north, the river on the west, and a line running along Tracy street, the New York, Pennsylvania, and Ohio railroad tracks, Cross and Erie streets. The second precinct embraces the territory north of Euclid avenue between Erie street and Willson avenue. The third precinct takes in the 4th and 6th wards. The fourth precinct is co-extensive with the West Side. The fifth precinct is the South Side. The sixth precinct embraces the 14th and 15th wards. The seventh precinct comprises the 16th and 17th wards (East End); the eighth precinct, the 18th ward (South Cleveland).

The patrolmen are distributed among the precincts as follows: First, 41; second, 13; third and sixth, 20; fourth, 25; fifth, 8; seventh, 8; eighth, 8. About two-thirds of the policeman are on duty at night. The average extent of a day-beat is $9\frac{1}{5}$ miles; of a night-beat, $6\frac{1}{16}$ miles. The average of policemen is 5.8 to the square mile.

During the past year there were 7,432 arrests made by the police, the principal causes being: For assault, 373; larceny, 355; disorderly conduct, 528; disturbance, 567; intoxication, 2,973; suspicious character, 209; vagrancy, 174; and violating minor city ordinances, 905. The final disposition of the cases were either by fines and costs, committed, discharged, or held for trial. The total amount of property lost or stolen during the year and reported to the police was $28,780, and of this, $24,913 was recovered and returned to the owners. The number of station-house lodgers for 1880 was 1,237.

A detail from the force attends all fires to preserve order and protect property. Special policemen are appointed by the commissioners and are known as "merchant police". They receive no pay from the city, but are subject to the regular police rules. The total expense of the police force for 1880 was $132,802 61.

FIRE DEPARTMENT.

The full control and management of the fire department of Cleveland is vested in the board of fire commissioners, a body composed of five members, four being elected by the citizens for terms of four years each, and the chairman of the committee on fire and water of the city council, *ex officio*. The force is composed of 143 men, as follows: 1 chief engineer at $2,000 per annum; 1 assistant engineer at $1,700, 1 at $1,600, and 1 at $1,500 a year; 13 engineers and 4 captains of hook-and-ladder companies at $960 a year each; 13 stokers, 13 leading hosemen, and 4 tillermen, at $744 a year each; and 1 harness-maker, 1 line-repairer, 3 telegraph-operators, 3 supply-drivers, and 83 firemen, at $720 a year each. The apparatus consists of 15 steamers, of which 5 are first-sized rotaries, 4 second-sized rotaries, and 2 third-sized rotaries, Silsby manufacture; 2 are second-size piston, Amoskeag pattern, and 2 third-size piston; 4 hook-and-ladder trucks, provided with fire-extinguishers, ladders, buckets, etc.; 4 four-wheeled hose-carriages, 18 two-wheeled hose-carts, 11 heaters, 1 aerial ladder, 1 patrol-wagon, 3 heavy open buggies, 3 fuel-wagons, 1 telegraph-wagon, and 6 exercise-wagons. There are 67 horses and 18,000 feet of hose in the department. The total amount disbursed on account of the fire department during the year was $148,426 60.

During the year 1880 there were 337 alarms. The total losses by fire amounted to $268,799 58, and the total insurance involved was $700,320. The following table shows the losses by fire in the city since April 1, 1864:

Date.	Number of fires.	Amount of losses.
To April 1, 1865	68	$261,341 48
To April 1, 1866	56	173,990 62
To April 1, 1867	111	206,942 82
To April 1, 1868	144	300,441 76
To April 1, 1869	149	196,984 19
To April 1, 1870	143	378,635 61
To April 1, 1871	149	300,453 71
To April 1, 1872	195	153,193 53
To December 31, 1872	144	309,725 72
To December 31, 1873	157	348,410 64
To December 31, 1874	285	641,506 35
To December 31, 1875	284	137,122 63
To December 31, 1876	274	253,558 73
To December 31, 1877	320	25,910 50
To December 31, 1878	266	206,835 95
To December 31, 1879	294	215,357 96
To December 31, 1880	305	268,799 58

The following table shows the comparative expenses of the department during the past seven years:

Year.	Number of firemen.	Number of engine-houses.	Running expenses.	Total disbursements.
1874	118	10	$138,267 39	$161,991 64
1875	152	11	140,705 71	170,976 59
1876	143	11	136,153 87	149,894 72
1877	143	13	147,340 00	156,019 12
1878	133	13	144,034 56	159,970 44
1879	142	13	146,721 15	151,972 99
1880	142	13	143,918 05	148,426 60

The estimated value of the fire department property is $394,176, divided as follows: Engine-houses and lots, $205,000; apparatus, $67,600; reservoirs, $48,000; telegraph line, $33,000; and miscellaneous articles, $40,516.

PUBLIC SCHOOLS.

The value of school property belonging to the city is to-day not far from $1,500,000, and accommodations are provided for not far from 20,000 pupils, for whom about 400 rooms are set apart. Since 1859, members of the board of education have been elected by the people, and since 1868 that board has been independent of the council, except in the matter of purchasing sites and building, which restraint was removed in 1875, when the power to levy tax was placed in the hands of the board.

The real estate owned by the city and purchased for school purposes aggregates within a fraction of 33 acres.

The following table is interesting as showing the progress and present condition of the public schools of the city:

Year.	Number of teachers.	Number of enrolled pupils.	Number of children of school age.	Average daily attendance.
1836	3	229	....	....
1837	8	490	2,132	240
1840	10	990	....	....
1845	....	....	3,177	....
1846	15	1,500	3,455	9,956
1850	25	2,081	5,042	1,440
1855	60	4,701	12,947	3,061
1860	83	5,110	14,399	3,930
1865	115	8,315	18,607	5,333
1866	123	9,643	20,775	5,387
1867	131	10,154	25,823	6,623
1869	144	11,151	27,824	7,222
1870	177	12,257	32,157	7,765
1879	389	22,741	....	15,634

COMMERCE AND NAVIGATION.

[From the reports of the Bureau of Statistics for the fiscal years ending June 30.]

Customs district of Cuyahoga (a), Ohio.	1879.	1880.
Total value of imports	$39,259	$237,442
Total value of exports:		
Domestic	$711,901	$417,976
Foreign	$22	$221
Number of immigrants	238	54

Customs district of Cuyahoga (a), Ohio.	1879.		1880.	
	Number.	Tons.	Number.	Tons.
Vessels in foreign trade:				
Entered	380	105,063	321	75,100
Cleared	423	114,566	339	73,480
Vessels in lake trade and fisheries:				
Entered	2,594	1,155,282	3,264	1,485,910
Cleared	2,610	1,161,326	3,313	1,502,798
Vessels registered, enrolled, and licensed in district	193	64,973	175	64,287
Vessels built during the year	5	270	9	3,311

a Cleveland.

MANUFACTURES.

The following is a summary of the statistics of the manufactures of Cleveland for 1880, being taken from tables prepared for the Tenth Census by M. M. Hobart, chief special agent:

Mechanical and manufacturing industries.	No. of establishments.	Capital.	Males above 16 years.	Females above 15 years.	Children and youths.	Total amount paid in wages during the year.	Value of materials.	Value of products.
All industries	1,055	$19,430,989	18,018	2,286	1,420	$8,502,935	$31,629,737	$18,604,050
Agricultural implements	5	101,200	39	....	8	16,606	53,930	85,420
Blacksmithing (see also Wheelwrighting)	28	31,650	72	....	4	31,249	29,030	84,770
Bookbinding and blank-book making	12	116,000	115	71	10	66,705	114,112	210,200
Boot and shoe uppers	3	19,000	16	15	1	8,488	27,450	42,920
Boots and shoes, including custom work and repairing	103	227,045	320	44	2	121,238	242,879	455,536
Boxes, cigar	3	6,900	11	12	8	8,500	24,000	44,000
Brass castings	6	37,500	81	....	2	35,200	60,000	118,140
Bread and other bakery products	45	110,303	131	16	7	63,163	290,515	452,823
Brick and tile	21	89,100	256	....	22	74,914	37,169	159,450
Bridges	4	347,000	573	....	4	180,122	504,348	925,063

Mechanical and manufacturing industries.	No. of establishments.	Capital.	AVERAGE NUMBER OF HANDS EMPLOYED.			Total amount paid in wages during the year.	Value of materials.	Value of products
			Males above 16 years.	Females above 15 years.	Children and youths.			
Brooms and brushes	6	$22,000	210	64	101	$54,675	$57,725	$141,666
Carpentering	13	36,550	120		2	56,240	104,000	185,150
Carpets, rag	9	760	5			1,050	2,372	9,815
Carriages and wagons (see also Wheelwrighting)	25	165,400	283		2	126,388	122,480	335,684
Cars, railroad, street, and repairs	4	144,500	216			103,925	461,000	661,000
Clothing, men's	73	1,086,600	824	1,172	61	634,319	1,488,780	2,687,409
Coffee and spices, roasted and ground	4	138,000	62	1	6	43,440	199,000	300,000
Coffins, burial cases, and undertakers' goods	3	198,000	144	39	10	70,012	103,780	265,150
Confectionery	5	61,500	47	25	9	23,300	111,500	161,550
Cooperage	11	42,575	194			88,625	334,315	474,050
Cutlery and edge tools (see also Hardware)	3	97,000	116			47,531	54,326	123,000
Dentistry, mechanical	3	9,000	7	1		4,918	6,050	19,450
Drugs and chemicals (see also Patent medicines and compounds)	6	563,000	202	4	1	63,400	323,875	557,500
Engraving, wood	3	1,200	7		1	3,000	800	10,000
Flouring- and grist-mill products	6	120,000	71			34,200	988,659	1,105,768
Foundery and machine-shop products (see also Iron work, architectural and ornamental).	53	1,961,038	2,426	3	108	946,877	1,786,420	3,820,685
Furniture (see also Upholstering)	28	326,600	392	12	23	167,251	183,199	470,835
Hairwork	10	14,740	5	19		4,335	10,230	21,140
Hardware (see also Cutlery and edge tools)	8	49,000	69		11	28,550	59,875	142,500
Hats and caps, not including wool hats	3	2,000	12	5	1	6,200	4,100	17,800
Hosiery and knit goods	5	27,000	4	192	2	21,960	42,100	97,550
Iron and steel	10	2,839,042	2,788		211	1,960,237	6,491,506	9,435,432
Iron bolts, nuts, washers, and rivets	5	307,500	364			153,923	482,926	860,711
Iron forgings	3	305,000	206			86,500	323,000	523,000
Iron railing, wrought	4	28,200	25		8	8,885	23,800	45,500
Iron work, architectural and ornamental (see also Foundery and machine-shop products).	3	11,500	37			18,844	47,274	84,354
Jewelry	4	5,900	26			10,500	11,600	30,000
Leather, curried	4	47,000	19			8,200	159,608	178,500
Leather, tanned	4	68,000	32			14,850	143,700	181,800
Lime	4	44,600	45		4	19,100	35,750	63,500
Liquors, malt	23	1,286,200	328	1	1	162,345	699,666	1,249,502
Lithographing (see also Printing and publishing)	4	100,700	136	16	5	70,600	124,100	223,000
Looking-glass and picture frames	8	41,650	24	1	3	11,200	40,050	61,850
Malt	4	260,000	40		2	20,603	259,673	333,452
Marble and stone work	11	168,600	161		36	100,290	219,364	412,850
Masonry, brick and stone	5	20,700	168		2	63,000	93,750	187,000
Mineral and soda waters	4	21,500	25		4	9,230	12,955	43,000
Models and patterns	4	2,800	11			6,800	1,500	12,200
Oil, lubricating	5	655,850	122		6	56,123	850,102	1,163,714
Painting and paperhanging	24	47,420	139			58,267	59,590	160,366
Paints (see also Varnish)	10	423,500	207	12	15	113,214	801,334	1,202,480
Patent medicines and compounds (see also Drugs and chemicals)	3	6,700	5		1	2,400	9,006	14,311
Photographing	14	31,450	33	7	6	18,471	18,411	68,400
Plumbing and gasfitting	17	22,850	85		2	34,061	60,600	142,411
Printing and publishing (see also Lithographing)	11	693,300	392	18	16	258,590	236,947	666,509
Pumps, not including steam pumps	3	9,500	10			4,300	7,900	15,200
Roofing and roofing materials	4	61,000	41			19,292	113,000	169,000
Saddlery and harness	35	36,031	77		2	28,951	60,900	118,300
Sash, doors, and blinds (see also Wood, turned and carved)	15	406,314	489		11	202,703	533,035	857,687
Sewing-machine cases	5	36,000	275		22	108,600	126,000	255,600
Shipbuilding	12	167,100	282			144,200	301,250	510,550
Shirts	7	20,300	7	48		14,589	51,812	87,295
Slaughtering and meat-packing, not including retail butchering	12	447,000	388		28	192,892	4,886,771	5,427,938
Soap and candles	5	55,000	20		2	8,420	47,715	68,700
Stencils and brands	3	1,200	6			2,825	2,100	9,300
Stereotyping and electrotyping	3	4,150	6		1	3,400	1,900	8,500
Tinware, copperware, and sheet-iron ware	60	140,650	215	1	25	100,080	227,019	447,811
Tobacco, cigars, and cigarettes	68	106,950	299	36	11	119,315	166,320	366,412
Trunks and valises	6	28,700	35	3	5	12,200	29,100	49,600
Umbrellas and canes	3	3,300	2	1	2	550	3,045	7,500

The following table is interesting as showing the progress and present condition of the public schools of the city:

Year.	Number of teachers.	Number of enrolled pupils.	Number of children of school age.	Average daily attendance.
1836	3	229		
1837	8	490	2,132	240
1840	10	990		
1845			3,177	
1846	15	1,500	3,455	9,936
1850	25	2,081	5,042	1,440
1855	60	4,701	12,947	3,061
1860	83	5,110	14,309	3,930
1865	115	8,315	18,607	5,333
1866	123	9,643	20,775	5,837
1867	161	10,154	25,823	6,623
1869	164	11,151	27,824	7,222
1870	177	12,257	32,157	7,765
1879	389	22,741		15,694

COMMERCE AND NAVIGATION.

[From the reports of the Bureau of Statistics for the fiscal years ending June 30.]

Customs district of Cuyahoga (a), Ohio.	1879.	1880.
Total value of imports	$39,259	$237,442
Total value of exports:		
Domestic	$711,901	$417,973
Foreign	$22	$221
Number of immigrants	238	54

	1879.		1880.	
Customs district of Cuyahoga (a), Ohio.	Number.	Tons.	Number.	Tons.
Vessels in foreign trade:				
Entered	380	105,063	324	75,100
Cleared	423	114,566	339	76,430
Vessels in lake trade and fisheries:				
Entered	2,594	1,155,282	3,264	1,485,910
Cleared	2,610	1,161,326	3,313	1,502,798
Vessels registered, enrolled, and licensed in district	193	64,973	175	64,237
Vessels built during the year	5	270	9	3,311

a Cleveland.

MANUFACTURES.

The following is a summary of the statistics of the manufactures of Cleveland for 1880, being taken from tables prepared for the Tenth Census by M. M. Hobart, chief special agent:

Mechanical and manufacturing industries.	No. of establishments.	Capital.	Males above 16 years.	Females above 15 years.	Children and youths.	Total amount paid in wages during the year.	Value of materials.	Value of products.
All industries	1,055	$13,430,989	18,018	2,286	1,420	$8,502,935	$31,629,737	$48,604,050
Agricultural implements	5	101,200	39		8	16,006	53,930	85,420
Blacksmithing (see also Wheelwrighting)	28	31,650	72		4	31,249	29,030	84,770
Bookbinding and blank-book making	12	16,000	115	71	10	66,705	114,112	210,200
Boot and shoe uppers	3	19,000	16	15	1	8,488	27,450	42,920
Boots and shoes, including custom work and repairing	103	227,045	320	44	1	121,238	242,879	455,536
Boxes, cigar	3	6,900	11	12	8	8,500	24,000	44,000
Brass castings	6	37,500	81		2	35,200	60,000	118,140
Bread and other bakery products	45	110,303	131	16	7	63,163	290,515	452,823
Brick and tile	21	89,100	256		22	74,914	37,169	159,450
Bridges	4	347,000	573		4	180,122	504,348	925,063

Mechanical and manufacturing industries.	No. of establishments.	Capital.	AVERAGE NUMBER OF HANDS EMPLOYED.			Total amount paid in wages during the year.	Value of materials.	Value of products
			Males above 16 years.	Females above 15 years.	Children and youths.			
Brooms and brushes....................................	6	$22,000	210	64	101	$54,675	$57,725	$141,666
Carpentering................................	13	36,550	120	....	2	56,240	104,000	185,150
Carpets, rag................................	9	760	5	....	....	1,050	2,372	9,815
Carriages and wagons (see also Wheelwrighting)............	25	165,400	283	....	2	126,388	122,480	335,684
Cars, railroad, street, and repairs............	4	141,500	216	....	....	103,925	461,000	661,000
Clothing, men's........................	73	1,086,600	824	1,172	61	634,319	1,488,780	2,687,409
Coffee and spices, roasted and ground	4	138,000	62	1	6	43,440	199,000	300,000
Coffins, burial cases, and undertakers' goods	3	198,000	144	39	10	70,012	103,780	265,150
Confectionery	5	61,500	47	25	9	23,300	111,500	161,550
Cooperage	11	42,575	194	....	....	88,625	334,315	474,050
Cutlery and edge tools (see also Hardware)............	3	97,000	116	....	....	47,531	54,326	123,000
Dentistry, mechanical	3	9,000	7	1	....	4,918	6,050	19,450
Drugs and chemicals (see also Patent medicines and compounds)...	6	563,000	202	4	1	63,400	323,875	557,500
Engraving, wood	3	1,200	7	....	1	3,000	800	10,000
Flouring- and grist-mill products	6	120,000	71	....	....	34,200	988,659	1,105,768
Foundery and machine-shop products (see also Iron work, architectural and ornamental).	53	1,961,038	2,426	3	108	946,877	1,786,420	3,820,685
Furniture (see also Upholstering)............	28	326,600	392	12	23	167,251	183,199	470,835
Hairwork........................	10	14,740	5	19	....	4,335	10,230	21,140
Hardware (see also Cutlery and edge tools)............	8	49,000	69	....	11	28,550	59,875	142,500
Hats and caps, not including wool hats	3	2,000	12	5	1	6,200	4,100	17,800
Hosiery and knit goods........................	5	27,000	4	192	2	21,960	42,100	97,550
Iron and steel	10	2,839,042	2,788	....	211	1,960,237	6,491,506	9,435,432
Iron bolts, nuts, washers, and rivets............	5	307,500	364	....	....	153,923	482,926	860,711
Iron forgings	3	305,000	206	....	....	86,500	323,000	523,000
Iron railing, wrought........................	4	28,200	25	....	8	8,885	23,800	45,500
Iron work, architectural and ornamental (see also Foundery and machine-shop products).	3	11,500	37	....	....	18,844	47,274	84,354
Jewelry	4	5,900	26	....	....	10,500	11,600	30,000
Leather, curried	4	47,000	19	....	....	8,200	159,608	178,500
Leather, tanned	4	68,000	32	....	....	14,850	143,700	181,800
Lime	4	44,600	45	....	4	19,100	35,750	63,500
Liquors, malt........................	23	1,286,200	328	1	1	162,345	699,666	1,249,502
Lithographing (see also Printing and publishing)............	4	100,700	136	16	5	70,600	124,100	223,000
Looking-glass and picture frames............	8	41,650	24	1	3	11,200	40,050	61,850
Malt........................	4	260,000	40	....	2	20,603	259,673	333,452
Marble and stone work	11	168,600	161	....	36	100,290	219,364	412,850
Masonry, brick and stone	5	20,700	168	....	2	63,000	93,750	187,000
Mineral and soda waters........................	4	21,500	25	....	4	9,230	12,950	43,000
Models and patterns........................	4	2,800	11	....	....	6,800	1,500	12,200
Oil, lubricating........................	5	655,850	122	....	6	56,123	850,102	1,163,714
Painting and paperhanging........................	24	47,420	139	....	....	58,267	59,590	160,366
Paints (see also Varnish)	10	423,500	207	12	15	113,214	801,334	1,202,480
Patent medicines and compounds (see also Drugs and chemicals)....	3	6,700	5	....	1	2,400	9,006	14,311
Photographing........................	14	31,450	33	7	6	18,471	18,411	68,400
Plumbing and gasfitting........................	17	22,850	85	....	2	34,061	60,600	142,411
Printing and publishing (see also Lithographing)............	11	693,300	392	18	16	258,590	236,947	666,569
Pumps, not including steam pumps........................	3	9,500	10	....	....	4,300	7,900	15,200
Roofing and roofing materials........................	4	61,000	41	....	....	19,292	113,000	169,000
Saddlery and harness........................	35	36,631	77	....	2	28,951	60,900	118,300
Sash, doors, and blinds (see also Wood, turned and carved)..........	15	406,314	489	....	11	202,703	533,035	857,687
Sewing-machine cases	5	36,000	275	....	22	108,300	126,000	255,600
Shipbuilding........................	12	167,100	282	....	....	144,200	301,250	510,550
Shirts........................	7	20,300	7	48	....	14,589	51,812	87,295
Slaughtering and meat-packing, not including retail butchering....	12	447,000	388	....	28	192,892	4,886,771	5,427,938
Soap and candles	5	55,000	20	....	2	8,420	47,715	68,700
Stencils and brands	3	1,200	6	....	....	2,825	2,100	9,300
Stereotyping and electrotyping........................	3	4,150	6	....	1	3,400	1,900	8,500
Tinware, copperware, and sheet-iron ware........................	60	140,650	215	1	25	100,080	227,019	447,811
Tobacco, cigars, and cigarettes........................	68	106,950	299	36	11	119,315	166,320	366,412
Trunks and valises	6	28,700	35	3	5	12,200	29,100	49,600
Umbrellas and canes	3	3,300	2	1	2	550	3,045	7,500

Mechanical and manufacturing industries.	No. of establishments.	Capital.	AVERAGE NUMBER OF HANDS EMPLOYED.			Total amount paid in wages during the year.	Value of materials.	Value of products.
			Males above 16 years.	Females above 15 years.	Children and youth.			
Upholstering (see also Furniture)	8	$4,300	16	6	2	$5,820	$21,500	$33,350
Varnish (see also Paints)	4	432,500	53	....	....	32,695	562,939	691,245
Watch and clock repairing	3	12,800	10	1	2	3,450	5,600	12,500
Wheelwrighting (see also Blacksmithing; Carriages and wagons)	19	10,900	39	....	....	16,235	15,800	48,600
Wirework	4	118,500	78	2	25	3,175	200,500	287,000
Wood, turned and carved (see also Sash, doors, and blinds)	3	17,250	30	....	9	17,000	20,895	53,489
Wooden ware	3	108,500	140	10	58	52,550	158,000	232,500
All other industries (a)	73	3,609,921	3,052	428	488	1,007,679	5,052,410	7,316,707

a Embracing artificial limbs; awnings and tents; bags, other than paper; baking and yeast powders; baskets, rattan and willow ware; belting and hose, leather; belting and hose, rubber; billiard tables and materials; boxes, fancy and paper; carriage and wagon materials; clothing, women's; cordage and twine; dyeing and cleaning; electric lights; electroplating; fancy articles; fertilizers; files; foundery supplies; fruits and vegetables, canned and preserved; furs, dressed; gas and lamp fixtures; hand-stamps; ink; instruments, professional and scientific; iron nails and spikes, cut and wrought; iron pipe, wrought; lamps and reflectors; lead, bar, pipe, sheet, and shot; leather, dressed skins; liquors, distilled; lumber, planed; lumber, sawed; mantels, slate, marble, and marbleized; mattresses and spring beds; millstones; musical instruments, organs, and materials; oil, lard; oil, linseed; paper; rubber and elastic goods; rules, ivory and wood; saws; screws; sewing-machines and attachments; shoddy; show-cases; silk and silk goods; springs, steel, car, and carriage; surgical appliances; taxidermy; telegraph and telephone apparatus; tobacco, chewing, smoking, and snuff; tools; vinegar; wheelbarrows; wire; and woolen goods.

From the foregoing table it appears that the average capital of all establishments is $18,418; that the average wages of all hands employed is $391 41 per annum; and that the average outlay in wages, in materials, and in interest (at 6 per cent.) on capital employed is $39,145 53.

COLUMBUS,

FRANKLIN COUNTY, OHIO.

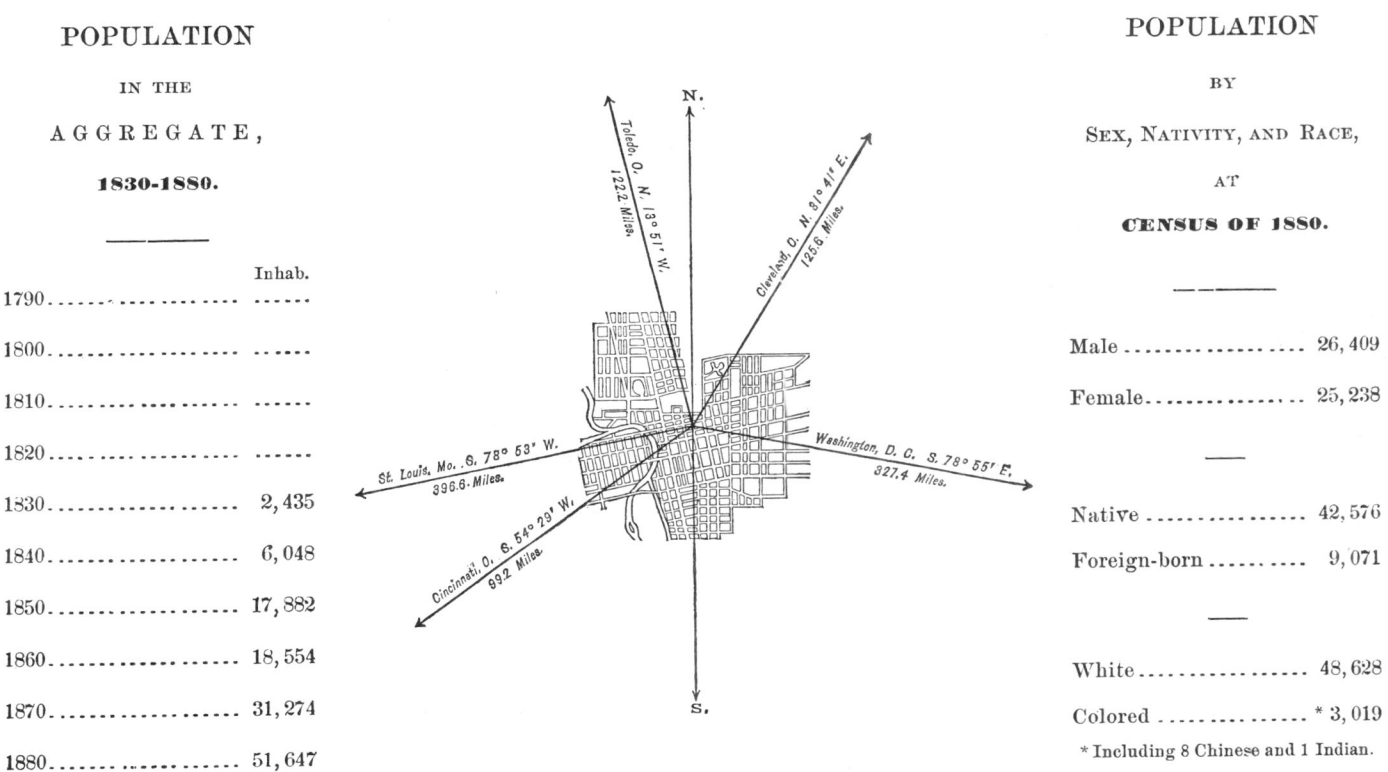

POPULATION

IN THE

AGGREGATE,

1830-1880.

	Inhab.
1790	......
1800	......
1810	......
1820	......
1830	2,435
1840	6,048
1850	17,882
1860	18,554
1870	31,274
1880	51,647

POPULATION

BY

SEX, NATIVITY, AND RACE,

AT

CENSUS OF 1880.

Male	26,409
Female	25,238
Native	42,576
Foreign-born	9,071
White	48,628
Colored	* 3,019

* Including 8 Chinese and 1 Indian.

Latitude: 39° 57' North; Longitude: 82° 59 (west from Greenwich); **Altitude: 834 feet.**

FINANCIAL CONDITION:

Total Valuation: $27,439,382; per capita: $531 00.   Net Indebtedness: $1,259,162; per capita: $24 38.   Tax per $100: $2 12.

HISTORICAL SKETCH.

In 1812, as it was desired to have the capital as near the center of the state as possible, the present site of Columbus was selected for the purpose. Chillicothe was originally the seat of government. In February, 1810, the legislature appointed five commissioners to examine and select the most eligible site. In their report to the legislature, dated September 12 of the same year, they recommended a site 12 miles below Franklinton, now a part of Columbus (made so by annexation in 1872). At the session in 1812 a company, composed of Lyne Starling, John Kerr, Alexander McLaughlin, and James Johnston, proposed that the legislature establish the seat of the state government on the high bank east of the Scioto river, nearly opposite Franklinton. This same company made proposals for the erection of a state-house, penitentiary, and other public buildings, the same to be completed in 1817. An act was passed February 14, 1812, accepting the proposals and the bond of the company, and permanently establishing the seat of government on the lands named therein, the legislature to begin its sessions there on the first Monday of December, 1817, and there continue to May, 1840, and thenceforth until otherwise provided by law.

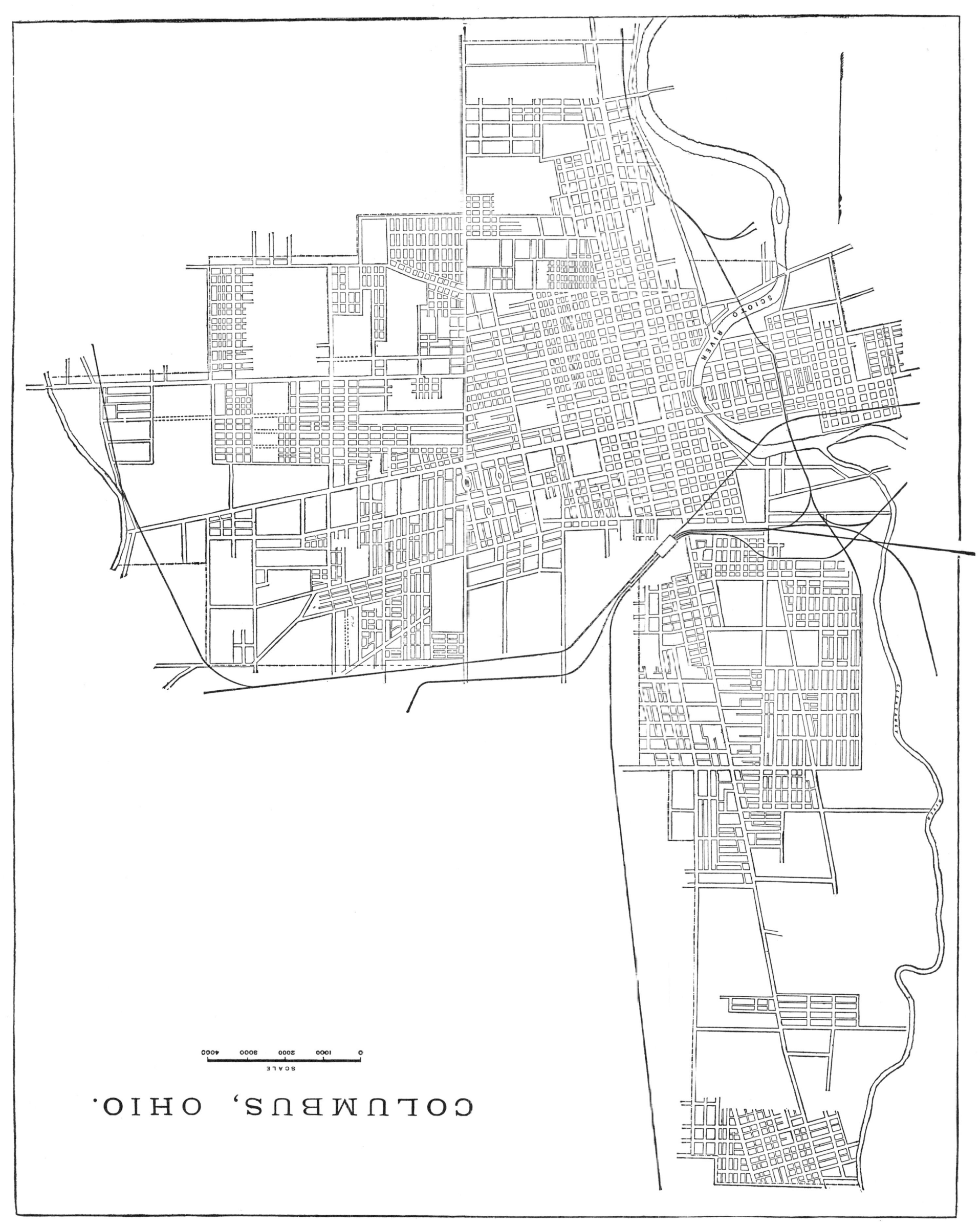

SCIOTO RIVER

COLUMBUS, OHIO.

SCALE

0   1000   2000   3000   4000

The "refugee lands", upon which the town was located, comprised a narrow tract of 4 miles wide from north to south, and extended 48 miles eastwardly from the Scioto river. On the 18th of June, 1812, on the same day that the United States declared war against Great Britain, the first public sale of lots took place. At this time the site was an almost unbroken forest, with no residents within its limits. In 1814 the *Western Intelligencer* was removed from Worthington to this place and the title was changed. The first saw-mill, the first tavern, and the first bridge over the Scioto river were built in 1813; the first school and the first market-house were built in 1814, and two churches were erected the same year; and in 1815 the first census was taken, showing a population of 700 souls. The town was incorporated February 10, 1816, and a United States court was erected in 1820. The town increased rapidly in population, and on March 3, 1834, was granted a city charter.

COLUMBUS IN 1880.

The following statistical accounts, collected by the Census Office, indicate the present condition of Columbus:

LOCATION.

Columbus lies in latitude 39° 57′ north, longitude 82° 59′ west from Greenwich, on both sides of the Scioto river, but principally on the east side, about 90 miles above its junction with the Ohio river. Its altitude above sea-level, as given in the reports of the Smithsonian Institution, is 834 feet. The river is not navigable here. The whole area of the city contains 6,752 acres, and it is well surrounded on all sides by an almost unlimited extent of level land. The Ohio canal passes 11 miles south of this point, and is connected with the Scioto river at Columbus by a feeder.

RAILROAD COMMUNICATIONS.

Columbus is touched by the following railroads:
The Baltimore and Ohio railroad, from Baltimore to Chicago.
The Cleveland, Columbus, Cincinnati, and Indianapolis railroad, between the points named.
The Cleveland, Mount Vernon, and Columbus railroad, from Cleveland to Columbus.
The Cincinnati, Sandusky, and Cleveland railroad, from Cincinnati to Sandusky.
The Columbus and Hocking Valley railroad, from Columbus to Athens.
The Columbus and Toledo railroad, between the points named.
The Ohio Central railroad, from Toledo to Corning.
The Pittsburgh, Cincinnati, and Saint Louis railroad (Pan Handle route), from Pittsburgh to Saint Louis.
The Scioto Valley railroad, from Columbus to Portsmouth, Ohio.

STREETS.

The streets are wide, and are laid out with great neatness and uniformity. Broad street, 120 feet wide, extends from east to west, and is crossed by High street, 100 feet wide, on which the principal business is transacted. At the intersection of these is a public square of 10 acres. There are 141¾ miles of streets in the corporate limits of the city, 72½ miles of which are unimproved. Of the improved streets, 55.60 miles are paved with gravel, 7.07 miles with macadam, 6 miles with asphalt or concrete, 0.41 mile with bowlders, and 0.17 mile with wooden blocks. The gravel streets are not all fully improved, portions of them being without curb, gutter, or sidewalk, and nearly all of them are in bad condition and need repairs. The asphalt or concrete pavement has cost from $7 83 to $2 26 per foot front, and the wooden blocks have cost from $10 88 to $4 50 per foot front, the latter including the curb. There are 4 horse-railroads, with an aggregate length of 11¾ miles.

WATER-WORKS.

The water-works are owned by the city, and cost to March 31, 1880, $700,358 50. The water is taken from the Scioto river through a filtering-basin over a mile long, and pumped directly into the mains. The daily average of water pumped during the year was over 2,000,000 gallons. The average cost of raising 1,000,000 gallons one foot high is 8 cents. The actual running expense, including repairs, for the year was $19,044 92, and the receipts from water rents were $44,572 57. There are 50½ miles of pipe, 319 fire-hydrants, and 534 water-meters.

GAS.

The gas-works are owned by a private corporation.

PUBLIC BUILDINGS.

The state-house, costing $1,359,121; the deaf and dumb asylum, costing $625,000; the new insane asylum, costing over $1,000,000; the penitentiary, and many others, are owned by the state. Among the buildings owned by the city and occupied for municipal purposes is the city hall, costing $210,000.

PUBLIC PARKS AND PLEASURE-GROUNDS.

There are 2 well-located public parks of good size in Columbus.

PLACES OF AMUSEMENT.

Comstock's opera-house, seating 2,000, and the Grand opera-house, seating 1,500, are the two theaters in the city. They pay an annual license of $100 each. In addition to the theaters there are about 20 small halls used for all kinds of entertainments: There are 3 concert- and beer-gardens, the largest containing an acre of ground, inclosed, and seating 2,000 persons. It is largely patronized by Germans.

DRAINAGE.

In his annual report for the past year, the city engineer states that the 12½ miles of main trunk sewers in use, which have cost the city $302,000, are all working in a satisfactory manner. The sewage is discharged into the Scioto river, one sewer delivering opposite the thickly populated part of the city.

SANITARY AUTHORITY.

The police board of Columbus is vested with the powers of a board of health, but has never organized as such. In case of an epidemic the board would probably take all necessary measures, and the city would pay the expense. A sanitary policeman is employed, who makes inspections as nuisances are reported, and uses all necessary means to have the same abated. Small-pox patients are sent to the pest-house, situated outside the city limits. Vaccination is made compulsory when small-pox breaks out, and is done at the public expense. The registration of all diseases, births, and deaths is kept by the infirmary director.

MUNICIPAL CLEANSING.

Street-cleaning.—The streets are cleaned at the expense of the city and with its regular force. Sweeping-machines are used on the asphalt and concrete pavements only, the work on the others being done by hand. The concrete pavements are cleaned every night, and the macadamized and cobble stone pavements are cleaned as necessity demands. The cleaning, while not entirely satisfactory, is fully in accord with the amount appropriated by the city council for the work—$11,200 annually. In addition to the cost to the city, private persons pay $2,300 annually. The sweepings are deposited in low portions of the city.

Removal of garbage and ashes.—These are removed by the householder under private contract. There are no rules as to the conservancy of garbage while awaiting removal, but it is not kept in the same vessel with ashes. The garbage is taken off by gatherers, while the ashes are dumped into low lots. The probable cost to householders for the service is $5,000 annually. No complaints are reported from the system.

Dead animals are removed by the owners when they are able; if not, then by the city. The annual cost of removal to the city is $400, and the system is reported to answer all purposes.

Liquid household wastes nearly all run into the sewers, a small portion only into cesspools, and none at all into street-gutters. The cesspools are porous, have no overflows, and receive the wastes from water-closets. There are no regulations concerning the cleaning out of cesspools, and considerable complaint is made of the stench from them.

Human excreta.—One-third of the houses in the city are provided with water-closets, nearly all of which deliver into the sewers, and the remainder depend on privy-vaults. Probably one-half the vaults are nominally water-tight. They are required to be 15 feet deep for business houses and 10 feet deep for dwellings, at least 5 feet from any party-line, and must be walled up with either brick or stone. They are cleaned out when offensive, this cleaning in the summer months being done at night, and the contents removed in covered carts. The night-soil is taken outside the city and buried, none being used for manuring land within the gathering-ground of the public water-supply.

POLICE.

The police force of Columbus is appointed and governed by the board of police commissioners, which consists of five members, with the mayor as president. The superintendent of police, salary $1,200 per annum, is the chief executive officer, and has general charge of the force, under the orders of the board. The remainder of the force consists of 2 sergeants at $840 each per annum; 2 roundsmen at $780 each per annum; and 36 patrolmen at $720 each per annum. The uniform is of dark-blue navy-cloth, and each man provides his own. The patrolmen are equipped with revolver and mace, they are on duty twelve hours at a time, and all the streets in the city (141¾ miles) are patrolled by the force.

During the past year 3,218 arrests were made, 315 for state offenses and 2,787 for city offenses. They were disposed of by fines or commitment, or held for trial, turned over to institutions, etc., or discharged. The value of property lost or stolen during the year was $13,832 52, and of this, $11,036 87 was recovered and returned to the owners. There were 164 station-house lodgers during the year. The force is required to co-operate with the fire department by preserving order and protecting property at fires. Special policemen are appointed by the commissioners, on the request of persons or corporations. They are paid by the parties for whose benefit they are appointed, but are under the orders of the superintendent of police. The cost of the police force for the past year was $34,878 27.

FIRE DEPARTMENT.

The manual force of the department consists of 1 chief engineer, 1 superintendent of fire-alarm telegraph, 8 captains, and 21 firemen—a total of 31 officers and men. The apparatus consists of 3 four-wheel two-horse hose-carriages, 3 two-wheel one-horse hose-carts, 1 two-tank chemical-engine (160 gallons capacity), and one hook-and-ladder truck. There are 15 horses and 7,800 feet of hose. The fire-alarm telegraph has 44 street signal-boxes. During the past year there were 79 box alarms and 3 still alarms, involving a loss by fire of $30,024 57, being $9,174 58 on buildings and $20,849 99 on personal property. The total insurance involved was $257,434. The total disbursements on account of the department for the year were $27,042 77.

MANUFACTURES.

The following is a summary of the statistics of the manufactures of Columbus for 1880, being taken from tables prepared for the Tenth Census, by Isaac W. Tucker, special agent:

Mechanical and manufacturing industries.	No. of establishments.	Capital.	AVERAGE NUMBER OF HANDS EMPLOYED.			Total amount paid in wages during the year.	Value of materials.	Value of products.
			Males above 16 years.	Females above 15 years.	Children and youths.			
All industries	316	$5,379,401	4,935	289	266	$1,961,394	$5,534,496	$9,646,679
Blacksmithing (see also Wheelwrighting)	20	5,855	20			6,515	8,455	26,675
Bookbinding and blank-book making	3	41,200	26	20	8	27,800	66,200	153,600
Boots and shoes, including custom work and repairing	25	61,250	102	17		51,383	77,105	159,637
Brass castings	3	13,200	31			13,420	54,250	115,000
Bread and other bakery products	10	49,653	51	5		25,241	142,193	198,395
Brick and tile	7	187,036	174		4	53,113	96,941	232,630
Brooms and brushes	8	31,500	45	4	6	20,714	60,004	99,572
Carpentering	12	25,650	83			36,784	98,676	191,747
Carriage and wagon materials	5	221,000	158			49,481	81,625	222,999
Carriages and wagons (see also Wheelwrighting)	10	393,000	555	2	40	248,722	598,376	1,008,179
Clothing, men's	3	23,000	80	20		11,560	56,053	86,458
Confectionery	4	6,400	4	3	3	4,430	20,447	33,800
Dentistry, mechanical	5	4,350	2			600	3,450	16,000
Flouring- and grist-mill products	3	15,000	2			804	27,429	31,161
Foundery and machine-shop products	16	376,500	376		6	142,965	233,231	446,350
Furniture	3	197,000	187	8	12	79,883	62,000	208,500
Iron and steel	3	800,000	504		26	177,008	734,794	1,149,525
Liquors, malt	4	510,000	149			67,459	290,895	519,529
Lumber, planed	9	213,100	119		15	56,940	317,245	445,500
Marble and stone work	11	34,750	59			19,954	28,500	70,925
Painting and paperhanging	14	4,625	39		1	19,000	16,043	55,818
Photographing	6	16,100	12	2		7,391	8,100	27,900
Printing and publishing	10	167,100	199	8	11	129,271	110,900	272,358
Pumps, not including steam pumps	4	3,800	8			3,050	2,750	10,786
Saddlery and harness	9	24,900	24			10,783	18,300	57,243
Shirts	3	7,400		18		4,400	13,900	25,500
Tinware, copperware, and sheet-iron ware	22	39,300	103			40,012	75,875	161,975
Tobacco, cigars and cigarettes	19	46,645	131	6	18	43,831	79,766	188,039
Vinegar	3	4,300	3			2,750	7,888	18,100
Wheelwrighting (see also Blacksmithing; Carriages and wagons)	6	7,250	8			2,801	2,050	8,499
All other industries (a)	56	1,798,537	1,681	176	116	603,329	2,140,965	3,404,249

a Embracing agricultural implements; baskets, rattan and willow ware; boxes, fancy and paper; carriages and sleds, children's; cars, railroad, street, and repairs; coffee and spices, roasted and ground; cooperage; cordage and twine; cutlery and edge tools; enameled goods; engraving and die-sinking; files; furniture, chairs; glass; hairwork; handles, wooden; hardware, saddlery; hosiery and knit goods; iron bolts, nuts, washers, and rivets; iron railing, wrought; iron work, architectural and ornamental; jewelry; leather, curried; leather, tanned; lime; lock- and gun-smithing; looking-glass and picture-frames; masonry, brick and stone; mattresses and spring beds; mineral and soda waters; oil, lard; paper; paving materials; regalia and society banners and emblems; sash, doors, and blinds; saws; soap and candles; trunks and valises; watch and clock repairing; watches; window blinds and shades; wire; and wirework.

From the foregoing table it appears that the average capital of all establishments is $17,023 42; that the average wages of all hands employed is $357 27 per annum; and that the average outlay in wages, in materials, and in interest (at 6 per cent.) on capital employed is $24,742 58.

DAYTON,

MONTGOMERY COUNTY, OHIO.

POPULATION

IN THE

AGGREGATE,

1810-1880.

	Inhab
1790	......
1800	......
1810	383
1820	1,000
1830	2,950
1840	6,067
1850	10,977
1860	20,081
1870	30,473
1880	38,678

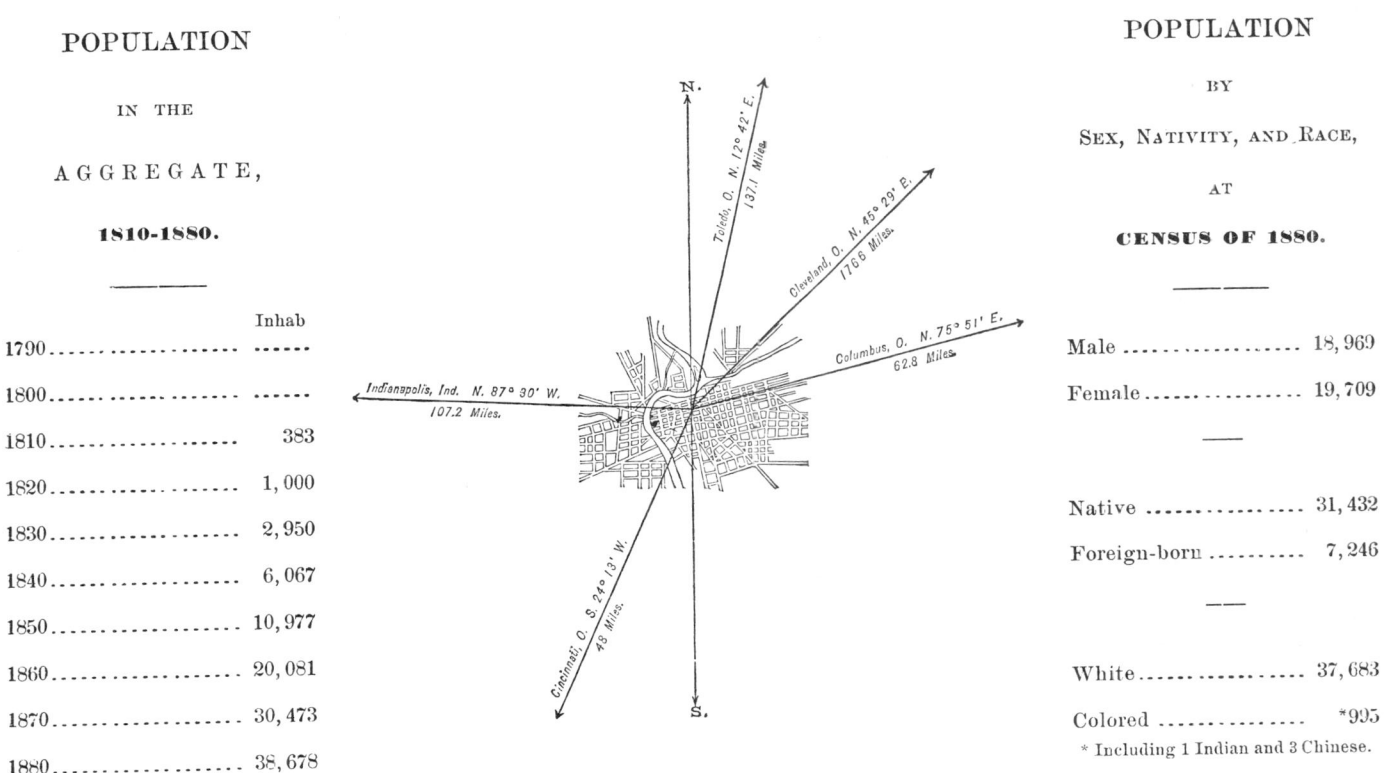

POPULATION

BY

SEX, NATIVITY, AND RACE,

AT

CENSUS OF 1880.

Male	18,969
Female	19,709
Native	31,432
Foreign-born	7,246
White	37,683
Colored	*995

* Including 1 Indian and 3 Chinese.

Latitude: 39° 44' North; Longitude: 84° 8' (west from Greenwich); Altitude: 775 to 950 feet.

FINANCIAL CONDITION:

Total Valuation: $18,888,270; per capita: $488 00.   Net Indebtedness: $1,101,521; per capita: $28 48.   Tax per $100: $2 23.

HISTORICAL SKETCH.(a)

A sketch of the history of Dayton may not be considered as properly incepted which does not contain a reference to that mysterious prehistoric race which, while it has left in the Miami valley and elsewhere abundant proofs of its existence, has left nothing more, not even a name. The name given them indicates about all that is known of them; they were "mound builders"; but why and when, no man knows. In the vicinity of Dayton are several of their make. At Miamisburg, on the east side of the Miami river, is one of the largest mounds in the West. It is symmetrical in form, 68 feet high, and 800 feet in cicumference at base, and was formerly covered with trees. Some archæologists suppose it to have been the sepulcher of a ruler. Two miles north of the mound is an earthwork, perhaps for military purposes, circular in form, and formerly connected with the river by parallel embankments. But the connection of this people with the locality is a matter of curiosity rather than of importance, and may be thus dismissed.

---

a Taken from a paper written for this report by Ashley Brower, esq.

The territory lying between the Miami rivers (Big and Little) north from the Ohio, to Mad river, had not been occupied by Indians, except as common hunting grounds for the tribes to the northward, since the year 1700, and until the whites came it was a vast forest, unbroken except by small prairies and scattered areas of wet land. With the organization of the Northwestern territory came governmental protection for the pioneers of the West, and troops were stationed at fort Harmer, at the mouth of the Muskingum, and afterward at fort Washington, opposite the mouth of the Licking river. The Miami valley was explored as far north as Mad river, and in June, 1789, a bargain was made with Judge Symmes for the purchase of the seventh range of townships, which included the lands at the mouth of Mad river. A settlement was to be made, a town platted to be called "Venice", and a road cut through the woods from Columbia, at the mouth of the Little Miami. Mad river was to have been named "the Tiber". Indian hostilities defeated this enterprise. On August 3, 1795, General Wayne concluded a treaty of peace with the Indians, and on the 20th of that month Governor St. Clair, Jonathan Dayton, of New Jersey. General James Wilkinson, and Colonel Israel Ludlow, of Cincinnati, contracted with Judge Symmes for the purchase of the seventh and eighth ranges between Mad river and the Little Miami. On the following 21st of September two parties of surveyors left Cincinnati to run the boundaries of the purchase and locate a road. November 1 came Colonel Ludlow with a party to lay out the town. This he completed on the 4th, and named the place in honor of the proprietors, "Dayton". The next day, on the spot, those present, for themselves or for others who desired to settle with the colony, drew for donation lots, each man being allowed one in-lot and one out-lot, with the privilege of purchasing 160 acres of land at the rate of a French crown per acre. The whole party then returned to Cincinnati, where, during the winter, a colony was organized, though but nineteen persons fulfilled their engagement when in the following spring (1796) the time for emigration arrived. The little colony moved in three parties, the first arrival at the site being on the 1st of April. The survey had been made on the site located on the south bank of the Miami, just below the mouth of Mad river. The plot was laid out in 280 in-lots, each 100 by 200 feet, and 54 out-lots of 10 acres each. There were also reservations for markets, schools, churches, and burial-grounds. Some of the settlers were induced to locate along the river-front on Water street, in the belief that the most desirable property would be near the landing from which in future years must be shipped the surplus products of the country; but the majority preferred to settle on the farming lands around. Over the plat were a number of small prairies, thickets, and clumps of timber. Cabins were at once constructed, and all timber within rifle range was felled, while a guard to prevent surprise from the Indians was maintained day and night. During the winter of 1796–'97 two or three families joined the colony, though the majority of newcomers took land away from the settlement. April 1, 1799, three years after the settlement of Dayton, the spot had nine cabins, but at the close of the winter of 1802–'03 about one-half of them were vacant. The probable cause of this was the discontent of the settlers and the hostility of the Indians. Fearing an attack, the settlers down the Miami had built a block-house opposite the mouth of Bear creek. Settlers above Dayton, on Mad river, and near, had on one or two occasions abandoned their cabins, but it was not until 1799 that the inhabitants of the section deemed it necessary to take special precautions. Block-houses were built in that year in all of the settlements. A large one was erected on the river-bank at the head of Dayton's main street. The men were organized and armed for defense, and made ready with their families to assemble at the block-house at the first alarm; but for a time the danger passed. In 1806 there were again fears of an Indian outbreak. The country to the north and west was thoroughly patrolled. Hunting and trading parties of Indians were constantly roaming through the forests to the west of the Miami. Often upon such expeditions large camps of them would locate opposite Dayton, but few at a time crossing over to the village to barter furs, venison, or wild honey for provisions, clothing, and ammunition. There was never serious trouble in keeping them under control.

On March 24, 1803, Montgomery county was formed, the act to take effect May 1, and Dayton was designated as the county-seat. The little hamlet in the woods possessed but few points to recommend it for such distinction. One-half the cabins were empty; except on Water street the whole plot was covered with bushes, vines, scrub-oaks, and plum thickets; wild game was abundant; wolves howled through the forest, and panthers were occasionally killed. There was not a store in the place. But now, as if under the impetus of this recognition, the village began at once to improve; streets were cleaned up and graded; and in 1804 a store was opened and a post-office was established. On the 12th of February the town was incorporated, the expense for running the same for the first year being $72. This year also saw the erection of the first brick building, "McCollom's tavern". Brick store-rooms were put up the next year, and in 1808 the first brick residence was erected, while roads were being opened to neighboring settlements. In 1810 the population of Dayton was 383. On the 12th of April, 1812, Dayton was designated as the rendezvous for the Ohio militia which had been called into governmental service in the war of that year against Great Britain, and for two years the town was filled with the business and excitement of a military camp. Men with capital came to engage in business, new stores were started, and every branch of trade prospered; real-estate speculation ran high and the place greatly improved.

At first the route from cabin to cabin was marked by blazed trees; thus bridle-paths were worn which were finally widened for sleds, and the one most used became the "big road" that led to Dayton. In this way roads to surrounding settlements were located. They were narrow, with but a single track, marked by deep ruts cut by loaded wagons, and were not much improved until 1839 After the invention of macadam, turnpike companies were chartered and good toll pikes were built out from the town in all directions. Grain, pork, flour, whisky, and pelts were shipped by flat-boats to Cincinnati and New Orleans; and trade in this way increased until the canal was opened in 1829. The trip to the Ohio took nearly a week's time, and from six to ten weeks were required to reach New Orleans. Whatever of supplies were brought to the town were transported overland on pack horses, or up the river in dugouts and pirogues. It was nearly a week's trip from Cincinnati by pack-horse, and ten days by river. Boating up the river was continued until the canal to Piqua was opened in 1837. Teaming could be carried on only in dry seasons, or when the roads were frozen.

As early as September 1, 1799, in the block-house at the head of Main street, Benjamin Van Cleve, as master, opened a school. Vacation was had through corn gathering, after which the term was continued until spring work began. In the fall of 1804 Cornelius Westfall opened a school on the east side of Main street, south of First street, where he taught a year, being succeeded in 1805 by Swansey Whiting, who was followed by John Little, who arranged for the purpose and taught school in the Presbyterian cabin meeting-house, which stood in the burying-ground on Main and Third streets. In 1807 the Dayton Academy was incorporated, a two-story brick school-house was built on Saint Clair street, north of Third street, and instruction was given until, in 1833, the property was sold and a new building was erected at the southeast corner of Fourth and Wilkinson streets. The first Ohio school law was passed in 1821, and simply authorized a vote in the townships upon the question of an organization of school districts. The law of 1825 authorized a general tax for school purposes, but "subscription schools" were continued in Dayton until 1831, when the public schools were first regularly organized. The first district school was organized December 5, 1831, on Jefferson street, between First and Water streets. The number of schools was increased as necessity required. The limits of the corporation of Dayton were made one school district in 1836, and $808 40 school-tax was collected and added to $500 received from the state fund. From these rude elements has grown the present admirable school system of Dayton.

Religious services were first held in the block-house at the head of Main street. During the next year the men of the village, aided by several from the neighborhood around, put up a log-cabin meeting-house for the Presbyterians on their lot at the northeast corner of Third and Main streets, where services were held until, in 1805, this denomination, by loaning the county $412, secured the right to use the court-room for church purposes, which right was exercised until the building of their brick church in 1817. The Methodists first held meetings at Hamer's hill, 2 miles up Mad river, where, in 1797, a class was formed. Services were occasionally held there and in Dayton until, in 1807, a class was formed in the village, which in 1811 had 24 members. In 1813 this sect built a church on Third street, opposite the old burying-ground. But few Baptists had settled in Dayton up to the year 1820, although in neighboring settlements there were flourishing churches. In May, 1824, a council assembled in Dayton, and a Baptist church was organized. The Episcopalians first held services in 1817, and two years later the parish was organized, but after a few years ceased to exist. A second effort was made in 1830, and in 1832 the church was built on Jefferson street. The Roman Catholics were a feeble colony until the arrival of several families of that faith in 1832, when frequent meetings were held in a room on Saint Clair street, and occasionally in the court-house. Their number steadily increased, and in 1837 Emmanuel church was built on Franklin street. The Lutherans formed a society in 1839, and in 1841 erected their building at the southwest corner of Fourth and Jefferson streets. The first German Reformed church was organized in 1833, and built a church edifice on Ludlow street in 1837. The First United Brethren church perfected an organization in 1850, and built a church on Sixth street, east of the canal, in 1852. All of these denominations, except the Episcopal, from time to time built branch churches in different parts of the city. Later other denominations and sects, including Dunkards and Jews, established themselves in the place.

The pioneer burying-ground was at the northeast corner of Main and Third streets, which point was deemed to be far enough from the settlement to remain undisturbed for many years. This proved not to be the fact; but the same mistake was made in 1805 in locating the new graveyard on Fifth street, west of Ludlow; in 1841, in locating the beautiful Woodland cemetery; in 1844, in fixing the site of Saint Henry's cemetery; and ten years later, in establishing the Jewish cemetery. Dayton entirely underestimated its own probable growth, and the question of discontinuing interments in several of the cemeteries has now become a serious one.

The dissemination of news early became one of the enterprises of Dayton. The first paper was started in 1806, but did not continue long. It was followed by the Dayton *Repository*, from September, 1808, to January, 1810; the *Ohio Sentinel*, from May 3, 1810, to 1813; the *Ohio Republican*, from October, 1814, to 1816; the *Ohio Watchman*, from 1816, with several changes of name, to 1826; the *Miami Republican and Dayton Advertiser*, started in 1823, to 1826, when this and the last-named journal were consolidated, and in 1846 issued as the Dayton *Daily Journal*, which still continues; the Dayton *Republican* was started in 1830, and after various changes settled down as the *Herald and Empire*, being consolidated in 1876 with the Dayton *Democrat*, and called the Dayton *Daily Democrat*. In addition to these, several German papers were started, both daily and weekly. Two weekly religious papers are also published here, and besides those referred to above many others have been begun here, served their purpose, and ceased to exist.

The town charter was amended by the legislature in the winter of 1828-'29. By this act no person was entitled to vote at town elections except "free white male freeholders or householders over twenty-one years of age, who

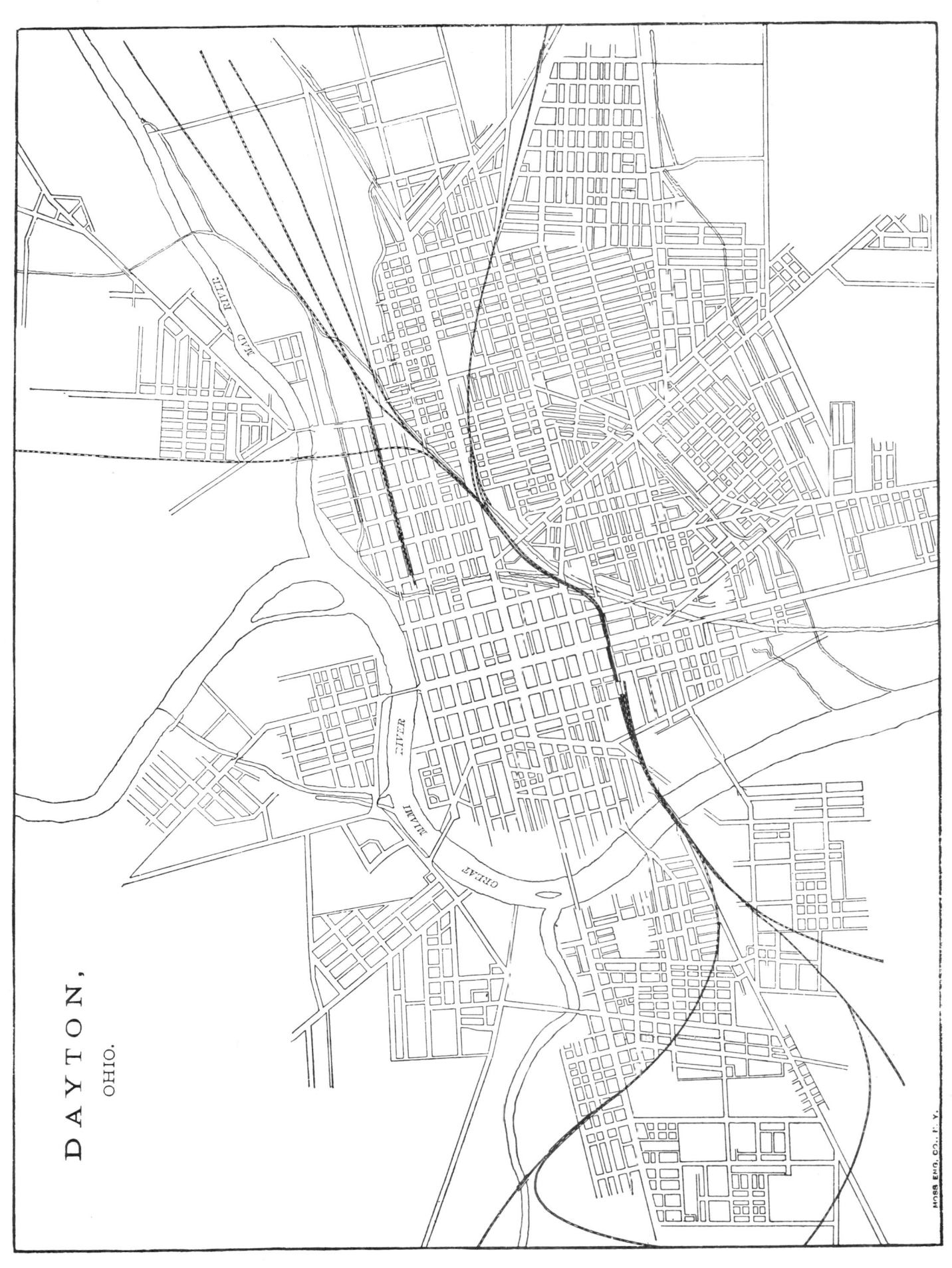

DAYTON,
OHIO.

have resided within the corporation one year next preceding the election". A city charter was granted March 8, 1841, subject to a vote of the people. The question was voted upon May 3, when 382 ballots were cast in favor of the charter and 378 against it; thus Dayton became a city by the small majority of 4 votes.

From a bend in Mad river at the northeast corner of the town damage by flood had often threatened the destruction of property, and several times in the history of the city the whole flat had been inundated. In 1840 surveys were made for straightening the channel of the river from the canal aqueduct west to the Miami river. Excavations were begun the next year and completed in the fall of 1842. During the winter water was turned into the new channel. After this change the canal was extended from First street up to the junction near the aqueduct.

Subscription books for a railroad, to be called the "Mad River and Lake Erie railroad", were opened March 8, 1847. The city subscribed $25,000, individuals as much more, and the next year the amount was increased to $150,000, of which $115,000 was collected. But the work was delayed until in February the city subscribed again for $25,000. Contracts were let, and the last rail was laid on Saturday, January 25, 1851, and on the 27th the first train came through from Springfield. The name of the road was subsequently lost in the "Cincinnati, Sandusky, and Cleveland railroad". Dayton's next road, the Cincinnati, Hamilton, and Dayton, was put under contract between Dayton and Hamilton in August, 1850, and was opened September 18, 1851; two train-loads of Dayton people going to Hamilton, where they were met by two trains of Cincinnati people, and the whole party returned to Dayton, where a great dinner was given. In June, 1848, the city subscribed $25,000 to aid the construction of the Dayton and Western railroad from Dayton to New Paris. In May, 1849, the city voted to loan the road $50,000. During the year the road was built 15 miles, out to Dodson. The Dayton, Xenia, and Belpré railroad was chartered February 19, 1851. Dayton township voted $15,000 to the road, and a large force was put to work between Dayton and Xenia. On May 17, 1854, this part of the road was opened, but it was never built farther.

From the first the water-power of the three streams that unite at or near the city limits, and flow through the city, has been a prominent feature. There is an abundance of water-power at this place, which supplies 100 of the larger mills and manufactories. The water-power frequently fails in dry seasons, so that all of the establishments have steam-power to fall back upon. The aggregate value, $12,000,000 of annual manufactures, is made up of work turned out by the car-shops, machine-shops, and founderies, in water-wheels, mill-machinery, engines, boilers, bridges, all kinds of heavy castings and machinery, stoves, malleable iron, and brass-work; and of the product of the extensive agricultural-implement shops, wood-working establishments and furniture factories, flour, oil, planing- and paper-mills, printing offices, breweries, and other large enterprises.

This tracing of the growth of the thriving subject of this sketch must close with a short notice of an institution that has contributed not a little to its fame.

THE SOLDIERS' HOME.

The National Home for Disabled Volunteer Soldiers was located on the hills 4 miles west of Dayton, in the year 1867, and now in the handsome buildings on the 600 acres of land are comfortably quartered 4,000 disabled veterans. The fine buildings include headquarters, the church, hospital, barracks, hotel, memorial hall, officers' residences, farm buildings, etc. In the cemetery lie buried the remains of 2,100 heroes, and near by is the beautiful monument of white marble erected to their memories by surviving comrades. Among the attractions of the home are the libraries, lake, conservatories, beautiful avenues and lawns, war relics, zoological garden, and the great siege guns and batteries with their pyramids of shot and shell.

DAYTON IN 1880.

The following statistical accounts, collected by the Census Office, indicate the present condition of Dayton:

LOCATION.

Dayton lies on the south bank of the Great Miami river, and a little below the mouth of Mad river, 60 miles north-northeast of Cincinnati, 67 miles west by south of Columbus, and in latitude 39° 44' north, longitude 84° 08' west from Greenwich. The altitudes above sea-level are, average 800 feet, lowest point 775, and highest 950 feet. Its streams are not navigable, but water communication is afforded for canal-boats by the passage through the city of the Miami canal, connecting the Ohio river with lake Erie. It lies in the central eastern part of Montgomery county, of which it is the capital.

RAILROAD COMMUNICATIONS.

Dayton is admirably situated as to railroad communications, being upon the following lines:
The Cincinnati, Sandusky, and Cleveland railroad, termini Cincinnati and Cleveland.
The Cincinnati, Hamilton, and Dayton railroad, from Cincinnati to Toledo.

The Dayton and Western railroad, from Dayton to Richmond, Indiana.

The Dayton and Union railroad, between the points named

The Dayton and Xenia railroad, between the points named

The Dayton and Michigan railroad, termini Dayton and Toledo.

The New York, Pennsylvania, and Ohio railroad, between Dayton and Salamanca, New York.

The Columbus, Cleveland, Cincinnati, and Indianapolis railroad, from Cleveland to Indianapolis, with branches to Cincinnati and Columbus.

The Dayton and Southeastern railroad, from Dayton to Wellston, Ohio.

TRIBUTARY COUNTRY.

A few miles above Dayton the Great Miami receives the Stillwater river, and just above the city the Mad river. The valleys of these three rivers are unsurpassed in fertility, producing the most bountiful crops of corn, wheat, and tobacco. The water power furnished by these streams (now largely supplemented by steam-power) is used in very extensive and varied manufactures in wood, iron, paper, grain, etc. The excellent limestone which underlies all this region forms a most important item of wealth. In some of the quarries nearest to Dayton the stone sells in the ground at $17 50 per rod, or $2,800 per acre, the title to the land not being alienated. This stone is readily converted into lime of excellent quality.

TOPOGRAPHY.

The soil of the site is gravel, which furnishes excellent cellarage. The country is rolling and higher than some portions of the city. The river affords natural drainage. Originally the whole region was densely wooded, but a large part has been cut off, and only occasional groves remain.

CLIMATE.

Highest recorded summer temperature, 100°. Lowest recorded winter temperature, —22°. The mean annual temperature, taken during a period of 5 years, is 51.4°. There are no marshes of sufficient size in the neighborhood to influence the climate. The prevailing winds are from the southwest.

STREETS.

Dayton has 100 miles of streets, and these, excepting about one-quarter of a mile of cobble-stones, are laid in gravel. The cost of the graveling is about 10 cents per square yard, the material being obtained freely at the river. Gravel is considered more economical than the cobble-stones. Of sidewalks, it is estimated that 80 per cent. are of gravel, 15 per cent. of stone flagging, and 5 per cent. of brick. Concrete, which was formerly used, is now prohibited. Gutters are paved with bowlders. The streets have rows of shade-trees along the outer edge of the sidewalks. The construction of streets—grading and graveling—is done by contract. All curbing, guttering, and the making of sidewalks, which is not done by the abutters in the time allotted for the work, is also let out by contract. Street repairs are made by day-work, under superintendence of the street commissioners. The cost of repairs for the year ending March 1, 1879, was $13,981 18. For all street-work a preference is expressed for the contract system. No steam-roller or stone-crusher is used.

There are 14¼ miles of horse-railroads, with 55 cars and 157 horses, and giving employment to 60 men. During the year 1,251,500 passengers were carried, at a uniform rate of fare of 5 cents, or 25 tickets for $1. The omnibus lines have 5 vehicles and 8 horses, employ 4 men, and carry annually 5,475 passengers, at 25 cents for each fare.

WATER-WORKS.

The water-works are owned by the city, and their total cost was $492,592 89. The Holly system is used, the pressure per square inch being, for ordinary purposes, 50 pounds, and for fires, 120 pounds. The average daily amount pumped during 1879 was 1,019,539 gallons. The cost of pumping 1,000,000 gallons is $26 25. Yearly cost of maintenance, aside from cost of pumping, $6,376 27, and the yearly income from water-rents, $18,640. Water-meters are used to a certain extent, and are found to result, where placed, in a marked reduction of consumption.

GAS.

The gas-works are not owned by the city. The charge per 1,000 feet is, for the city, $1 60, and for individuals, $1 75. The city pays annually $24 30 each for street-lamps, 884 in number.

PUBLIC BUILDINGS.

The city owns and occupies for municipal uses, wholly or in part, 1 city hall and market-house, 6 engine houses, 2 police stations, 1 work-house, and 1 armory. The total cost of these buildings is given as $110,000. The cost of the city hall was $65,000.

PUBLIC PARKS AND PLEASURE-GROUNDS.

Dayton has but one park, dedicated to the city in the early part of its existence, a small one, with dimensions of 400 by 400 feet. It is called city park or public square, and is situated in the central part of the city. It costs annually to maintain from $800 to $1,000, which includes the salary of the superintendent, $40 per month. The park is controlled by a committee appointed by the city council.

PLACES OF AMUSEMENT.

The city contains 2 theaters: Music hall, seating capacity 1,400, and Gebhart's opera-house, seating capacity 1,300. Theaters pay a yearly license fee to the city of $50. There are also Reed's variety hall, seating 150, and Association hall (Y. M. C. A.), seating 600, mostly used for meetings, lectures, and sacred concerts. The Tivoli concert- and beer-hall, with garden attached, is the first and only institution of the kind in Dayton. It was constructed in May, 1875, is 75 by 100 feet in size, and cost $5,000. Its seating capacity is 1,500 in the hall and 600 in the garden.

DRAINAGE.

Dayton is without sewers. There are some private drains, of which no public record is kept. Much of the wastes are run into sinks and hauled beyond the city limits at intervals.

CEMETERIES.

There are connected with the city 5 cemeteries and burying-grounds:

Woodland Cemetery, containing 90 acres.
Calvary Cemetery, Roman Catholic, containing 81 acres.
City Cemetery (potter's field), containing 7 acres.
Saint Henry's Cemetery, Roman Catholic, containing 6 acres.
Hebrew Cemetery, containing 2 acres.

Interments are still made in all of these grounds. From the old City cemetery the remains have been removed and the spot has been built over. The total number of interments in Woodland cemetery is 10,608, the first having been made July 1, 1843; in Calvary cemetery 899, the first having been made July 1, 1875; and in Saint Henry's cemetery 4,000, where but few interments are now made, with a probability that its use will soon be forbidden by ordinance. Until recently records of interments in the City cemetery were not kept. Woodland cemetery is within the city limits, in the extreme southeast corner. It is located on a spur of ground of considerable elevation above the city. From this fact it is not likely to be encroached upon, nor is its nearness to the city objectionable. Calvary cemetery is situated 2½ miles from the city. The city burial-ground adjoins Woodland cemetery, and has been placed under the charge of that association. But few interments are now made in it. Woodland cemetery and Calvary cemetery belong to associations. The matter of interments is in the hands of the board of health, whose clerk, upon the return of the physician's certificate as to details of death, and the undertaker's as to the proposed interment, duly signed, issues a burial permit. Graves are dug 5 feet deep.

MARKETS.

Dayton has two markets. The Central market, owned by the city, cost $65,000, and contains 48 butchers' stalls and 40 side benches. In the public streets surrounding the market are 2,400 feet of standing space for farmers and hucksters. Wayne Street market-house, owned by a stock company but governed by city ordinances, is 300 feet long by 40 feet wide and contains 16 butcher stalls with 20 side benches. There is also about 50 feet of standing space for farmers and hucksters. In the Central market the butcher stalls and side benches are rented every five years, and bring $200 and $50, respectively. In the Wayne Street market-house the butcher stalls rent for $25 and the side benches from $8 to $30 per annum, according to location. The total annual rental is, for Central market $11,600, and for Wayne Street market $800. Central market is open from 3 to 10 a. m. daily; Wayne Street market (on Mondays and Wednesdays only) from 5 to 10 a. m., and on Saturdays from 1 to 6 p. m. No record is kept of the annual sales from the markets, but it is thought that at these markets is sold about one-half of the city's retail supply of meats, poultry, fish, and vegetables, the rest being supplied by retail stores and stands.

SANITARY AUTHORITY—BOARD OF HEALTH.

The chief sanitary organization of Dayton is the board of health, composed of 6 members, appointed by the city council—2 each year to serve three years—1 of whom is a physician, with the mayor as president *ex officio*. It is an independent body, and its action is controlled only by laws and ordinances. The annual expense of the board when there is no declared epidemic is about $2,400, for printing and for salaries. During an epidemic there is no limit to the amount of expense the board may incur. The board has full care of the health of the city. Its authority enables it to suppress nuisances, to regulate the emptying of privy-vaults and the sale of diseased or decayed meats and vegetables, to prevent the pollution of streams, etc., and during epidemics to take measures for the checking of disease, establishing a quarantine, etc. The health officer is the chief executive of the board, carrying out its orders, and seeing that all health ordinances are enforced; his salary is $600 per annum. There are 2 sanitary policemen employed, salary $660 per annum each, who serve notices and have full police powers, and 2 river patrolmen are employed, to prevent the pollution of the stream above the water-works when the river is drawn on for supply. The board meets every two weeks, and transacts its business as a deliberative body. Regular house-to-house inspections are made over the entire city, special complaints, which form the basis of daily reports to the health officer, being attended to. These reports, on blanks made for the purpose, give the name of owner, kind of house, location, number and size of rooms, occupants, condition of yard and cellar, distance of vaults and sinks from wells, whether or not births or deaths have occurred since last visit, and whether or not reported to the clerk, and any other facts deemed of importance. When nuisances are reported a verbal order is given to abate; if this is not done, the fact is reported to the board, whose resolution is then secured, giving the offending party a specified time in which to comply, after which, if the nuisance still remains, it is abated by the board and the cost is assessed on the property. The regular inspections of the board include the noting and correcting of defective house-drainage, privy-vaults, cesspools, and sources of drinking water; but in cases of defective sewerage, street-cleaning, etc., it passes a resolution calling the attention of the city council, in whose charge these matters lie, to the defect, and here the board's obligation ceases. Over the conservation and removal of garbage the board exercises no authority, unless a nuisance is created. The board regulates the burial of the dead, and issues burial permits on receipt of the physician's and undertaker's certificate. The 2 sanitary policemen are in summer kept continually on duty to prevent the pollution of the river; and all excrement must be thoroughly disinfected before being removed.

INFECTIOUS DISEASES.

Small-pox patients are isolated at their residences, upon which are placed yellow flags; but cases of scarlet fever are not quarantined in any way. The board takes cognizance of the breaking out of contagious diseases in public and private schools, and removes the patient, closing the schools if necessary. The public pest-house is situated just within the city limits, remote from dwellings. Vaccination is compulsory only upon children attending schools, and is done at the public expense.

No record is kept of diseases, but births and deaths are reported by the attendant, or, if there be none, by the sanitary police, to the clerk of the board, who keeps a register of the same, which the health officer reports each week in condensed form, and publishes in the daily newspapers.

MUNICIPAL CLEANSING.

Street-cleaning.—The streets are cleaned at the expense of the city and with its own force. The work is done wholly by hand. The principal streets are cleaned about once a month, and the others about twice a year. The service is as efficient as it can be for the money expended for it, which, including the removal of garbage and ashes, is about $12,000 annually. The least offensive part of the sweepings is deposited on the low lots for filling, while the rest is cast on the river-banks. Complaint is made that not enough money is expended on the work, as the city covers much territory, and that the place of final deposit is too distant.

Removal of garbage and ashes.—Garbage is removed by the city with its own force. There appear to be no rules as to the conservancy of garbage while awaiting removal, except that it must be kept unmixed with ashes. It is cast into the alleys and streets previous to removal, and is finally thrown into the river, where also most of the ashes are deposited. The annual cost of the removal of these matters is $3,000. It is thought that no nuisance or injury to health results from improper handling or final deposit of garbage, but that occasionally improper keeping on premises may affect unfavorably the public health, and of this the board of health sometimes complains. In reply to the request, "Specify the merits and the defects of the system or of its execution," Mayor Hosier writes: "Cattle of all kinds running at large, upsetting vessels containing ashes, etc., is a serious detriment to cleanliness, etc."

Dead animals.—Animals dying within the city are removed beyond the limits by scavengers, who utilize their fat, etc., and receive nothing for the service. About 700 or 800 are annually removed, including cats and dogs. The defect of the system is that such small animals as it does not pay to render are frequently left in the streets and alleys.

Liquid household wastes.—The liquid household wastes, of whatever kind, are run indifferently into sinks and gutters. About four-fifths of it is run into the street-gutters, which receive very little flushing, and the rest into "sinks" or cesspools. Most of these latter are porous and without overflows, though a few have overflows delivering into the canal. When cesspools are used they often receive the wastes from water-closets. Cesspools are cleaned out in the same manner as vaults.

Human excreta.—The city of Dayton contains about 7,500 houses, of which about 500, or 6⅔ per cent., have water-closets, while the balance depend on privy-vaults, very few of which, if any, are water-tight. The dry-earth system is not used. The board of health requires that its permit be first obtained before the removal of the contents of any vault, sink, or cesspool; also that all such before removal, and privy-vaults after emptying, shall, from May 1 to October 1 of every year, be disinfected and rendered inoffensive. Night-soil is taken beyond the city limits and disposed of to gardeners, but its use as manure on lands within the gathering-ground of the public water-supply is not allowed.

Manufacturing wastes.—Most of the liquid and solid manufacturing wastes of Dayton runs into the river below the water-works supply, the rest runs into the canal. It is stated that this manner of disposal is not considered injurious to the public health.

POLICE.

The police force of Dayton is appointed and governed by the board of police commissioners. The chief executive officer is the captain and acting superintendent. His duties are a general supervision of the force and the making of "daily reports of such facts as may be imparted to him by the patrolmen". His salary is $1,200 per annum. The rest of the force, with their salaries, is as follows: 2 sergeants and 2 detectives at $810 per annum each; 3 roundsmen at $765 per annum each; 25 patrolmen at $720 per annum each; and 2 turnkeys at $600 per annum each. The uniform is of dark-blue cloth, made in the usual manner; costs about $40 per suit, and each man provides his own. The patrolmen are equipped with "fatigue clubs" or maces and belts, night clubs, double-acting revolvers, and whistles. The tours of duty are 11½ hours each, and all the streets in the city are patrolled by the force. During the past year 2,928 arrests were made, chiefly for the following causes: Drunkenness, 1,296; disturbing the peace, 313; assault and battery, 129; abusive language, 118; for safe-keeping, 117; suspicious characters, 100; and larceny, 97. The disposition of the prisoners was as follows: Fined and discharged, 752; committed to city prison, 641; and to work-house, 477; discharged, 372; dismissed, 213; bound over, 79; and miscellaneous, 394. During the year property to the value of $6,546 12 was reported to the police as stolen within the city, while the amount of property stolen both within and without and recovered by the police was $3,610 55, all of which was returned to the owners. At the station-house during the year 2,484 lodgers were accommodated, and meals to the value of $219 09 were furnished them. During 1879 there were 2,640 lodgers. The police force is required to co-operate with the fire department by responding to all alarms and affording protection to life and property. Upon the application of merchants and manufacturers for night-watchmen for their establishments, special policemen, in addition to the regular force and governed by the same rules, are appointed by the board of commissioners. During the past year one patrolman was murdered while in the discharge of his duty. The yearly cost of the police force (1880) is $27,597 32.

One of the features of the police system of Dayton is the holding by the board of a fund called the "police life and health insurance fund". By law no member of the board or of the police force is allowed to retain any fee, present, or emolument for public service other than the regular salary, except by the unanimous consent of the board; but all such fees, gifts, rewards, etc., and all moneys received from the sale of unreclaimed property is turned in to the board and constitutes this fund; "and whenever any member of the police force, in actual performance of his duty, shall become bodily disabled, his necessary expenses during the time of his disability may be paid from the above fund at the discretion of the board." The balance in this fund at the close of the present year (1880) is $871 07.

FIRE DEPARTMENT.

The Dayton fire department consists of a manual force of 28 officers and men, with the following apparatus: 3 steam fire-engines, 2 being held in reserve; 1 chemical extinguisher; 1 two-horse hook-and-ladder truck, and 1 one-horse hook-and-ladder truck held in reserve; 6 hose-reels; 3 wagons; and 9,500 feet of 2½-inch hose. There are also 14 horses used by the department. During the past year the department has responded to 42 alarms in which fire occurred, involving a loss of $3,535. The amount of insurance involved was $17,200, and the total value of property jeopardized was $788,555. The Gamewell automatic system of fire-alarm telegraph is in use, and includes 30 miles of wire, divided into 4 circuits, to which 40 street signal-boxes are attached. The engine-houses, hose-houses, and the residence of the chief engineer are in communication by telephone.

PUBLIC SCHOOLS.

Dayton's school system includes 1 high school, with 8 rooms; 1 normal school, with 1 room; 1 intermediate school, using 4 rooms; and 10 district schools, using 105 rooms. This leaves 7 school-rooms not in use. The seatings number 6,149. The number of school-children between the ages of 6 and 16 years is 8,693. They are taught by 125 teachers (including 1 teacher in normal school)—21 males and 104 females—as follows: High school, 3; normal school, 1; intermediate school, 5; district schools, 109; and 1 music and 1 writing teacher. The enrollment for the year, is 6,114.

MANUFACTURES.

The following is a summary of the statistics of the manufactures of Dayton for 1880, being taken from tables prepared for the Tenth Census by J. H. Thomas, special agent:

Mechanical and manufacturing industries.	No. of establishments.	Capital.	AVERAGE NUMBER OF HANDS EMPLOYED.			Total amount paid in wages during the year.	Value of materials.	Value of products.
			Males above 16 years.	Females above 15 years.	Children and youths.			
All industries	495	$6,063,334	5,071	513	441	$2,293,630	$6,434,225	$11,985,483
Agricultural implements	12	914,000	577	....	20	212,613	468,536	1,187,204
Blacksmithing (see also Wheelwrighting)	15	12,100	36	....	....	15,780	9,400	47,330
Bookbinding and blank-book making	3	22,000	11	11	3	10,700	21,500	54,000
Boots and shoes, including custom work and repairing	52	11,975	72	5	2	35,108	30,663	95,208
Bread and other bakery products	20	101,025	64	2	6	26,975	163,349	229,110
Carpentering	37	139,050	240	....	4	120,701	300,222	642,591
Carpets, rag	4	925	4	....	....	1,250	1,650	3,750
Carriages and wagons (see also Wheelwrighting)	12	78,000	146	....	7	56,930	81,750	212,000
Clothing, men's	19	115,700	226	119	2	122,155	202,900	426,900
Coffee and spices, roasted and ground	4	18,700	18	4	....	10,495	86,300	112,675
Confectionery	10	17,100	29	22	....	10,343	78,190	114,500
Cooperage	9	26,450	51	....	1	17,670	46,447	81,151
Flouring- and grist-mill products	8	314,000	64	....	....	29,705	1,134,529	1,341,558
Foundery and machine-shop products (see also Iron work, architectural and ornamental).	16	785,000	697	....	36	299,739	484,852	1,062,887
Furniture (see also Upholstering)	14	151,850	136	3	12	55,490	89,150	217,554
Iron work, architectural and ornamental (see also Foundery and machine-shop products).	3	33,000	61	....	....	11,800	57,200	104,600
Iron railing, wrought	3	23,400	13	....	1	5,060	14,400	30,000
Leather, curried	4	31,000	13	....	....	6,340	75,030	96,275
Leather, tanned	4	19,500	8	....	....	3,740	49,434	63,925
Liquors, malt	8	133,428	49	....	....	25,139	108,690	194,021
Lock- and gun-smithing	3	1,300	6	....	....	2,500	1,750	5,600
Looking-glass and picture frames	4	34,200	5	1	....	2,676	13,800	26,000
Marble and stone work	6	21,300	32	....	....	13,280	17,100	45,100
Masonry, brick and stone	33	35,125	287	....	7	121,070	162,225	379,900
Oil, linseed	3	102,500	30	....	....	11,500	255,000	315,000
Painting and paperhanging	12	4,250	46	....	....	16,785	10,525	41,570
Paper	4	676,000	199	35	20	89,975	143,769	476,104
Patent medicines and compounds	4	3,700	3	1	2	1,145	7,700	23,750
Plumbing and gasfitting	6	38,300	47	....	....	23,118	61,211	105,612
Printing and publishing	10	244,600	133	55	22	97,885	126,018	332,624
Pumps, not including steam pumps	4	1,200	5	....	1	1,850	2,200	8,000
Saddlery and harness	11	41,350	72	....	5	31,500	63,050	133,460
Slaughtering and meat-packing, not including retail butchering....	5	56,500	27	....	2	20,980	178,136	236,318
Tinware, copperware, and sheet-iron ware ...	18	27,600	70	....	2	31,525	37,350	93,625
Tobacco, cigars and cigarettes	28	71,900	144	57	25	74,387	91,060	296,976
Upholstering (see also Furniture)	4	17,300	8	....	2	4,460	15,700	29,300
Watch and clock repairing	8	5,525	16	....	1	9,330	5,235	22,370
Wheelwrighting (see also Blacksmithing; Carriages and wagons) ..	6	5,900	17	....	....	5,780	5,950	19,610
Window blinds and shades	4	3,900	5	2	....	2,800	7,200	12,950
All other industries (a)	65	1,728,181	1,404	196	258	653,351	1,725,054	3,064,375

a Embracing awnings and tents; bagging, flax, hemp, and jute; bags, paper; baskets, rattan and willow-ware; boxes, cigar; boxes, fancy and paper; brass castings; bridges; brooms and brushes; cars, railroad, street, and repairs; carriage and wagon materials; clothing, women's; cotton goods; cutlery and edge tools; drain and sewer pipe; dyeing and cleaning; electroplating; fancy articles; files; flax, dressed; hairwork; hardware; hats and caps; hosiery and knit goods; ink; kaolin and ground earths; lasts; liquors, distilled; lumber, sawed; malt; mineral and soda waters; models and patterns; musical instruments, organs and materials; oil, lard; paints; refrigerators; roofing and roofing materials; sash, doors, and blinds; saws; shirts; soap and candles; stationery goods; steam fittings and heating apparatus; stencils and brands; stone- and earthen-ware; tobacco, chewing, smoking, and snuff; toys and games; trunks and valises; umbrellas and canes; varnish; and woolen goods.

From the foregoing table it appears that the average capital of all establishments is $12,249 16; that the average wages of all hands employed is $380 69 per annum; and that the average outlay in wages, in materials, and in interest (at 6 per cent.) on capital employed is $18,366 98.

HAMILTON,

BUTLER COUNTY, OHIO.

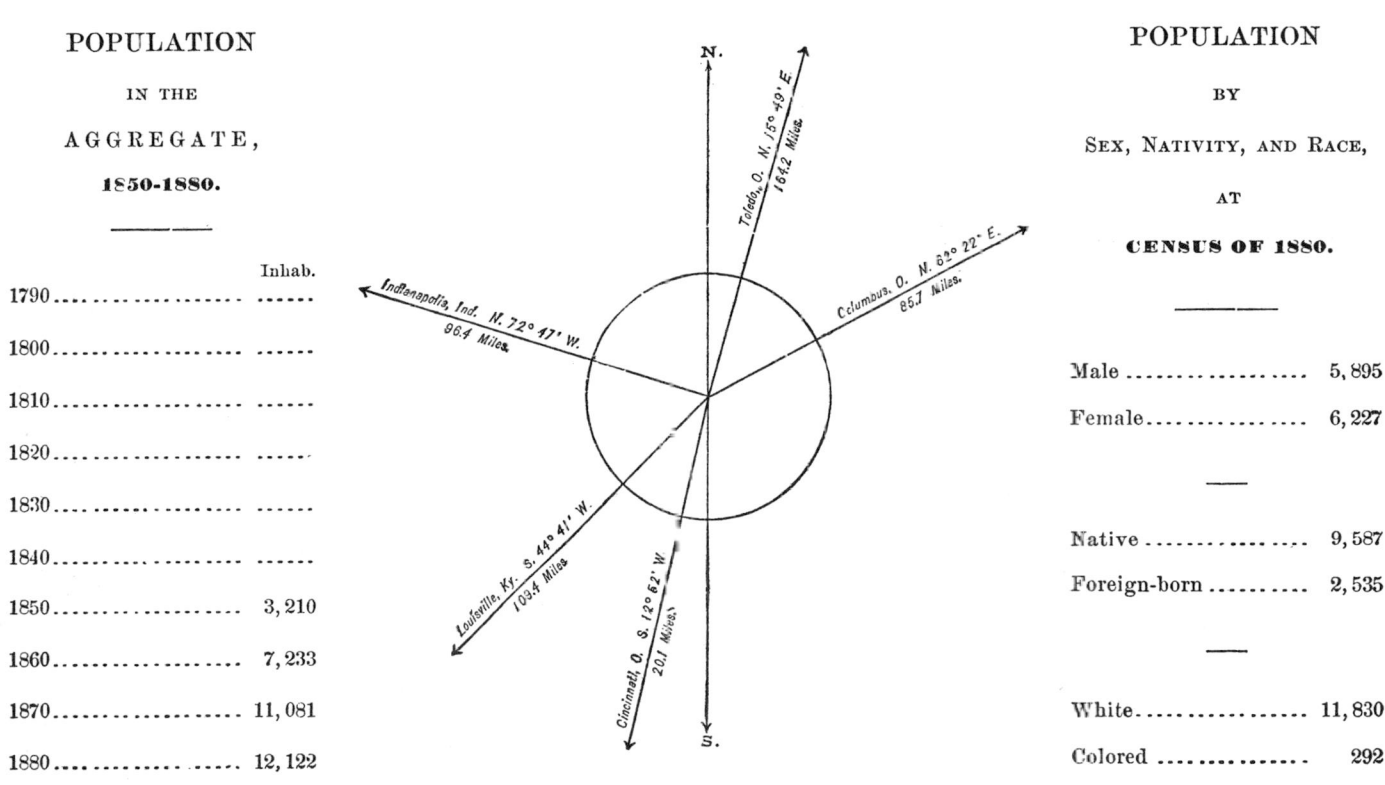

POPULATION		POPULATION
IN THE		BY
AGGREGATE,		SEX, NATIVITY, AND RACE,
1850-1880.		AT
		CENSUS OF 1880.

POPULATION IN THE AGGREGATE, 1850-1880.

	Inhab.
1790	......
1800	......
1810	......
1820	......
1830	......
1840	......
1850	3,210
1860	7,233
1870	11,081
1880	12,122

POPULATION BY SEX, NATIVITY, AND RACE, AT CENSUS OF 1880.

Male	5,895
Female	6,227
Native	9,587
Foreign-born	2,535
White	11,830
Colored	292

Latitude: 39° 23' North ; Longitude: 84° 25' (west from Greenwich).

FINANCIAL CONDITION:

Total Valuation: $6,194,460; per capita: $511 00.   Net Indebtedness: $53,067; per capita: $4 38.   Tax per $100: $2 30.

HAMILTON.

Hamilton, the capital of Butler county, is situated on either bank of the Great Miami river, about 25 miles north of Cincinnati. The Cincinnati, Hamilton, and Dayton railroad, from Cincinnati to Toledo; the Cincinnati, Richmond, and Chicago railroad, from Cincinnati to Richmond, Ohio; the Cincinnati, Hamilton, and Indianapolis railroad, between the points named; and the New York, Pennsylvania, and Ohio railroad, from Salamanca, New York, to Cincinnati, pass through the city. The Miami and Erie canal also passes through Hamilton. The city has quite extensive manufacturing industries, the canal and river affording united water-power.

No further information regarding the city was furnished.

PORTSMOUTH,

SCIOTO COUNTY, OHIO.

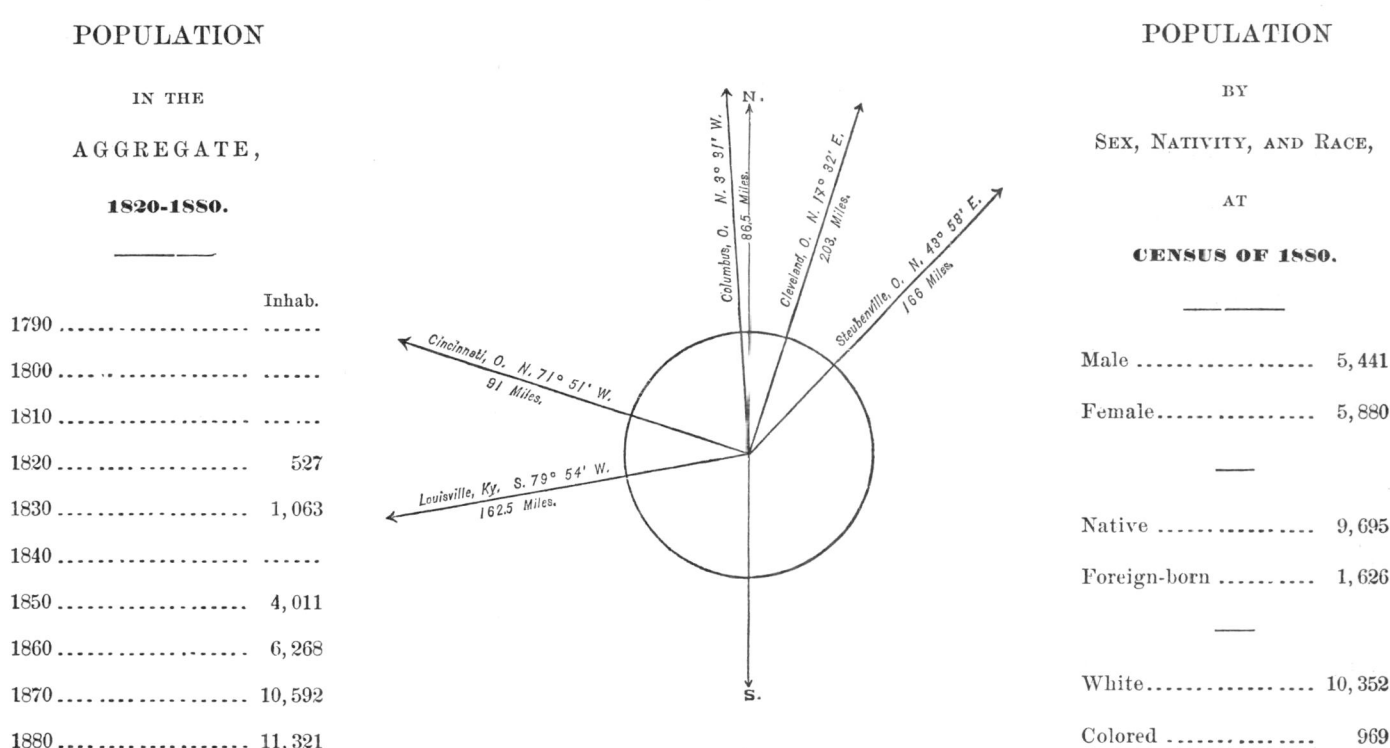

POPULATION

IN THE

AGGREGATE,

1820-1880.

	Inhab.
1790	......
1800	......
1810	......
1820	527
1830	1,063
1840	......
1850	4,011
1860	6,268
1870	10,592
1880	11,321

POPULATION

BY

SEX, NATIVITY, AND RACE,

AT

CENSUS OF 1880.

Male	5,441
Female	5,880
Native	9,695
Foreign-born	1,626
White	10,352
Colored	969

Latitude: 38° 42′ North; Longitude: 82° 53′ (west from Greenwich); Altitude: 520 to 537 feet.

FINANCIAL CONDITION:

Total Valuation: $4,694,617; per capita: $415 00.   Net Indebtedness: $317,809; per capita: $28 07.   Tax per $100: $2 86.

HISTORICAL SKETCH.

The commercial importance of the mouth of the Scioto river was early recognized by the French pioneers in America, and a trading-post was established on the western shore of the river, some time, it is claimed, before fort Duquesne was founded. The site thus chosen was again selected for the location of a town in 1790, when Alexander Parker founded the town of Alexandria near where the French post had stood; but the place was only 50 feet above the low-water mark in the Ohio, while floods often rose 50 and 60 feet above that point, and after being inundated several times the settlement was abandoned in 1808. Five years previously, however, Henry Massey purchased several sections of land on the east bank of the Scioto, and here, on a bluff high above the highest floods, he founded the town of Portsmouth. The first decided impetus was given the town in 1832, when the Ohio canal, which entered the Ohio river at Portsmouth, was completed. This canal connected the waters of lake Erie with those of the Ohio, and by its means a large internal commerce was carried on, from which Portsmouth derived great advantage. The decade from 1830 to 1840 was one of very rapid advance in wealth and population. The years since 1840 have seen a steady advance in the prosperity of the town, now city, which has been checked only by causes which affected also the whole country. It is the distributing point for the mineral and agricultural productions of southern Ohio and northeastern Kentucky, carrying on a wholesale trade to the amount of over $7,000,000 in 1876, at a time, too, when all business was dull; for Portsmouth, after sharing the great prosperity of the years from 1868 to 1873, shared also in the period of depression which followed. It has several rolling-mills, founderies, and other manufacturing establishments. It has numerous schools, churches, and societies.

PORTSMOUTH IN 1880.

The present condition of the city may be seen from the following statistical accounts, mainly furnished by Hon. George W. Crawford, mayor:

LOCATION.

Portsmouth is situated in latitude 38° 42' north, longitude 82° 53' west from Greenwich, on the east bank of the Scioto river at its junction with the Ohio river, about 116 miles above Cincinnati and 90 miles south of Columbus. The lowest point is 520 feet and the highest 537 feet above the sea-level, while the average altitude of the city is about 530 feet. The city is at the head of navigation on the Ohio during the season of low water; it has an excellent river front, said to be with one exception the finest on the river. The Scioto is navigable for only 7 miles above Portsmouth. The city is the southern terminus of the Ohio canal, through which it has water communication with lake Erie at Cleveland.

RAILROAD COMMUNICATIONS.

The city is connected with Cincinnati and Marietta by a branch of the Marietta and Cincinnati railroad, and with Columbus by the Scioto Valley railroad.

TRIBUTARY COUNTRY.

The valleys of the Scioto and Ohio rivers are rich agriculturally, and send a large part of their products to market by way of Portsmouth. The city is on the edge of a fine iron region, in which there are a number of iron furnaces and mills; but in general the tributary country is devoted to agriculture rather than to manufacturing.

TOPOGRAPHY.

The city is situated on a bluff extending some miles eastward from the Scioto river. The soil of the surrounding valley is very fertile; the country within a radius of 5 miles is not covered with wood, though there is a considerable growth of underbrush.

CLIMATE.

The highest recorded summer temperature is 106°, the highest in average years, 98°. The lowest recorded winter temperature is —12°, and the lowest in average years —2°. The Ohio river tends to moderate the cold of winter, and from September 1 to December 1 and in spring causes much fog. There are no marshes, but the low rich land holds much decaying vegetation and is a cause of considerable malaria. Elevated lands in the vicinity protect the city from winds and render the latter very changeable.

STREETS; WATER-WORKS; GAS; PUBLIC BUILDINGS.

No information on these subjects was furnished by the city authorities.

PUBLIC PARKS AND PLEASURE-GROUNDS.

Tracy Park, a tract of land containing about 3 acres, and situated between Chillicothe, Gray, Ninth, and Tenth streets, was presented to the city by Mr. Samuel Tracy, and is the only public park in Portsmouth. The cost of maintenance is nothing to the city, as the park is leased to a florist who keeps it in order in return for its use. It is under the supervision of the committee on parks, one of the committees of the common council.

PLACES OF AMUSEMENT.

Wilhelm's opera-house, seating capacity 850, is the only theater. It pays an annual license of $50. There are a number of small halls, seating from 100 to 300, which are used chiefly as ball-rooms. There are 3 beer-gardens, all well patronized.

DRAINAGE.

Sewerage works are built according to the supposed requirements of each case, or extended as the city is able to make the expenditure. There is no official map of existing sewers, nor plan fixing the future work to be done. A large number of sewers are reported to have been built, but there is no authentic record of their extent or cost. The outfall of sewers is to the Scioto or to the Ohio river. Mouths of sewers are above water and fully exposed, except a few, which are exposed only at low water. Ventilation is through cast-iron gratings in the stone-covering of inlets.

The cost of construction is paid by the city. Inlets cost, at the average rate, $25 to $35 each; manholes, $22 to $28 each.

CEMETERIES.

Portsmouth has 2 cemeteries: *Green Lawn Cemetery*, situated on a hill a mile east of the city, and containing 25 acres; and *Catholic Cemetery*, situated about 2 miles east of Portsmouth, and containing 12 acres. Both are managed by private corporations, the latter by the Catholic church. No burial is allowed until a permit has been granted by the board of health. Graves are made 4 feet deep. The control of the board of health has been exercised only during the past two years, and hence no record of the number of interments is obtainable.

MARKETS.

The city has 2 market-houses, but no information in regard to their business and income was furnished by the city authorities.

SANITARY AUTHORITY—BOARD OF HEALTH.

The chief sanitary authority is vested in a board of health, consisting of the mayor *ex officio* and 5 members, 1 a physician, appointed by the city council. The board is an independent body, and meets once a month, or when summoned by the mayor, who is president *ex officio*. The annual expenses in the absence of an epidemic are about $800, for salaries of the sanitary policeman, market-master, and clerk, for medicines, and for the abatement of nuisances. There is no limit, except the discretion of the board, during the prevalence of an epidemic. Its authority both in the presence and in the absence of an epidemic is sufficient to prevent the introduction of disease, to maintain a good sanitary condition of the city, and, if necessary, to care for the sick. One assistant, the sanitary policeman, is employed; he has the same police powers as any policeman.

NUISANCES.

Inspections are made by the committees of the board of health, and when nuisances are found they are abated at once, either by the owner of the premises on which they occur or by the sanitary policeman, who is also expected to make inspections. Defective house-drainage, privy-vaults, cesspools, and sources of drinking-water are inspected and treated as nuisances. Defective sewerage and street-cleaning are rectified by the street commissioner when his attention is called to them by the sanitary policeman or by the board of health.

BURIAL OF THE DEAD.

A permit must be obtained from the clerk of the board of health before any interment will be allowed. This states the name of the deceased, with birthplace, date of birth, date of death, date of interment, disease, occupation, and the name of the undertaker in charge, and is given to the sexton of the cemetery in which the burial is to be made.

INFECTIOUS DISEASES.

Small-pox patients are isolated in a pest-house not far from the city; scarlet-fever patients are quarantined at home. When contagious diseases break out in the public schools they are closed by the school board, the sufferers from the disease coming under the control of the board of health. Vaccination is not compulsory, but is done at the expense of the city for those who wish it.

REPORTS.

The board makes an annual report to the city council, which is published with the other city reports.
Births are recorded by the probate judge; deaths by the clerk of the board of health.

MUNICIPAL CLEANSING.

Street-cleaning.—At present the streets are cleaned by a contractor, but the system fails to give satisfaction.
Removal of garbage and ashes.—The householders are required by the city ordinances to place their accumulations of house-offal, rubbish, and ashes in the alleys back of their residences, so that it can readily be collected by a contractor paid by the city for this service.

Dead animals.—The carcasses of dead animals are removed by the sanitary policeman and buried. About 25 are removed each year, at a cost to the city of about $50.

Liquid household wastes.—Only a small part of the kitchen and laundry wastes flow into the public sewers, nearly all running into the street-gutters, which are flushed only by the rain. Chamber-slops are thrown into privy-vaults. Cesspools are not in use.

Human excreta.—Nearly all the houses of the city depend on privy-vaults, which in all cases are pits 40 or 50 feet deep dug down until sand or gravel is reached. The liquid matter from these filters away through the earth, the solid matter remains, and when the pit is full it is covered with earth and the privy removed and placed over a new pit. The liquid wastes find their way into the Scioto and Ohio rivers, the water in the river sensibly affecting the contents of the pits. Only a few water-closets are in use, while earth-closets are unknown.

Mannfacturing wastes.—No system of disposing of manufacturing wastes has been elaborated.

POLICE.

The police force of Portsmouth is appointed by the mayor, and is under the command of the city marshal, who has general charge of the department, and receives a salary of $650 from the city, $100 from the state, and constable fees in all cases. The rest of the force consists of 6 night-watchmen, salary $50 per month; 1 day-policeman, salary $40 per month; and 1 turnkey, salary $30 per month. The uniform consists of a blue-cloth suit with brass buttons, and a helmet hat in summer, a police cap in winter. The men purchase their suits, but the hats and caps are furnished by the city. They are armed with a revolver and a short club; the night-watchmen are on duty from one hour after sunset until daylight. During the past year they made 385 arrests, the principal cause being drunkenness. There is no record of the station-house lodgers. Special police are appointed by the mayor for duty at railway depots, steamboat-landings, factories, etc.; they are under the general control of the marshal, but are not paid by the city.

The police are not expected to assist the other departments of the city government except when the city ordinances and laws are being broken. The annual cost of the force is nothing besides the salaries of the men.

SANDUSKY,

ERIE COUNTY, OHIO.

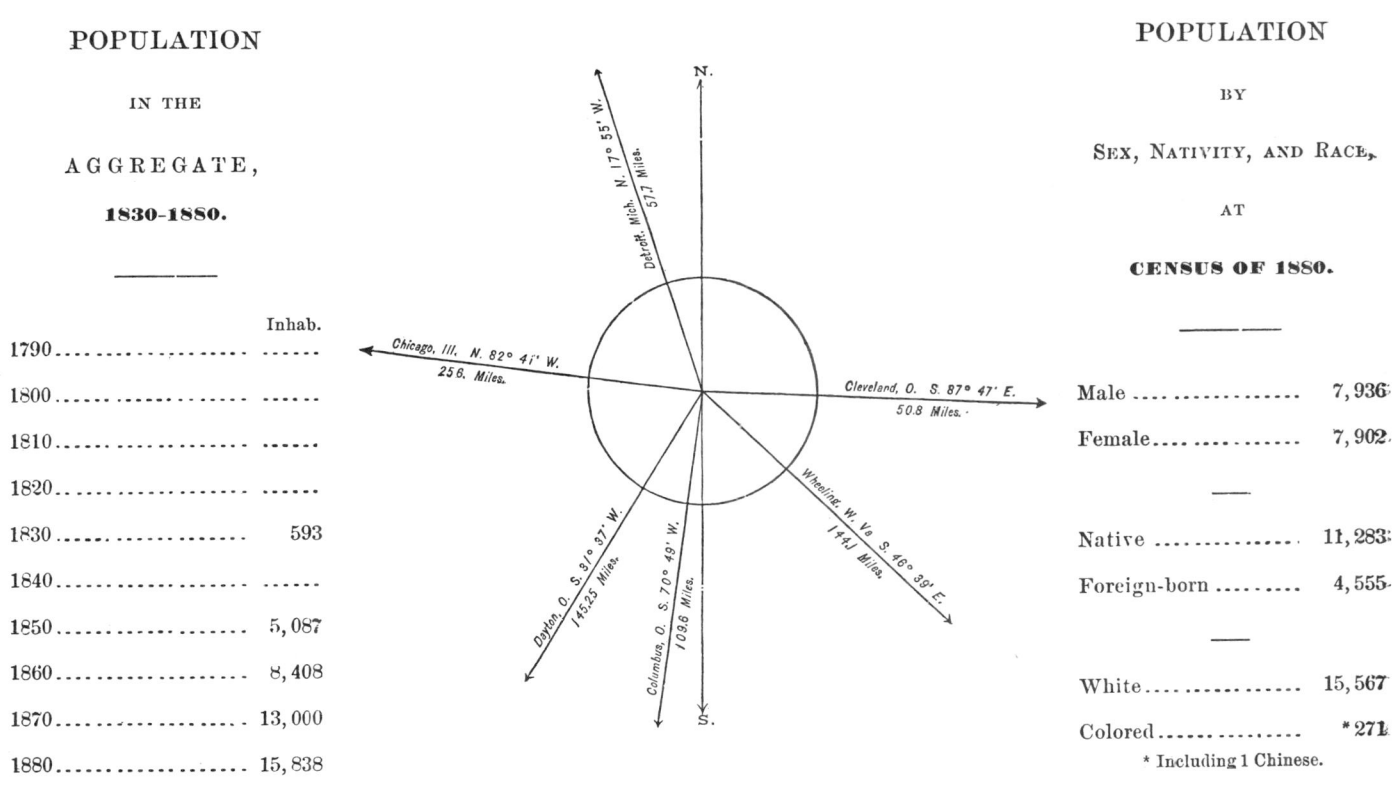

POPULATION

IN THE

AGGREGATE,

1830-1880.

	Inhab.
1790	......
1800	......
1810	......
1820	......
1830	593
1840	......
1850	5,087
1860	8,408
1870	13,000
1880	15,838

POPULATION

BY

SEX, NATIVITY, AND RACE,

AT

CENSUS OF 1880.

Male	7,936
Female	7,902
Native	11,283
Foreign-born	4,555
White	15,567
Colored	*271

* Including 1 Chinese.

Latitude: 41° 32′ North; Longitude: 82° 42′ (west from Greenwich).

FINANCIAL CONDITION:

Total Valuation: $4,041,913; per capita: $255 00.   Net Indebtedness: $381,215; per capita: $24 07.   Tax per $100: $3 80.

SANDUSKY.

Sandusky is situated about 50 miles west, in an air-line, from Cleveland, and 100 miles north by east from Columbus, on land rising gently from the shore of Sandusky bay, an arm of lake Erie, about 15 miles long and 4 miles wide, and was laid out in 1817 by Zalman Wildman and Isaac Hill. It early became an important point, as its harbor is one of the finest on the lake, and engaged largely in ship-building and fisheries, both of which are still leading industries. It was among the first places in Ohio to engage in railroad construction, and was largely instrumental in building the Sandusky, Dayton, and Cincinnati railroad, which was completed about 1847, and immediately verified the expectations of the merchants of Sandusky by the additions it made to the trade of the town. Within easy reach of large coal- and iron-fields, it has availed itself of its advantages, and is now quite important as a manufacturing city. Its schools are among the best in the state, and many of the buildings are fine specimens of architecture. The city is underlaid by rock near the surface, in which are fine quarries of excellent building-stone, which has been largely used in its buildings. It is supplied with both gas and water. The Baltimore and Ohio, the Cincinnati, Sandusky, and Cleveland, and the Lake Shore and Michigan Southern railroads enter the city and connect it with all the important eastern and western cities, while lines of steamers run regularly to Detroit, Toledo, Cleveland, and the islands of lake Erie. Its location is a beautiful one, and the health of the city is so good that until recently no attention has been paid to sanitary matters, which are, however, now beginning to attract attention. The streets of the city, while well laid out, have not been carefully kept; the household accumulations of garbage and ashes are left to private persons to care for; two-thirds of the household wastes are run into the street-gutters, as there is no system of sewers; and not 2 per cent. of the houses are provided with water-closets. Sandusky has 2 theaters and 2 public halls. There are about 30 churches.

No other information was furnished.

SPRINGFIELD,

CLARKE COUNTY, OHIO.

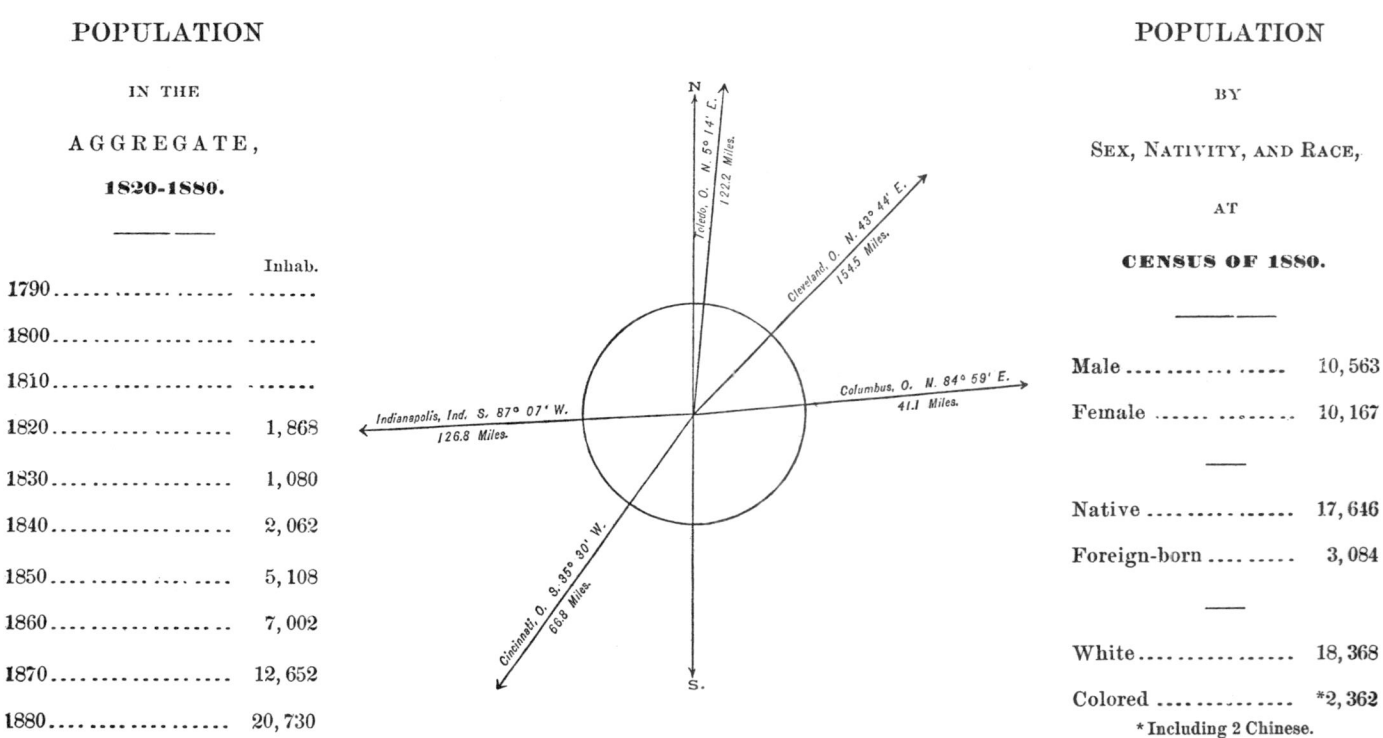

POPULATION

IN THE

AGGREGATE,

1820-1880.

	Inhab.
1790	....
1800	....
1810	....
1820	1,868
1830	1,080
1840	2,062
1850	5,108
1860	7,002
1870	12,652
1880	20,730

POPULATION

BY

SEX, NATIVITY, AND RACE,

AT

CENSUS OF 1880.

Male	10,563
Female	10,167
Native	17,646
Foreign-born	3,084
White	18,368
Colored	*2,362

* Including 2 Chinese.

Latitude: 39° 54′ North; Longitude: 83° 46′ (west from Greenwich).

FINANCIAL CONDITION:

Total Valuation: $9,682,759; per capita: $467 00.   Net Indebtedness: $58,627; per capita: $2 83.   Tax per $100: $1 90.

HISTORICAL SKETCH.

In the year 1803 a settlement was made in the rich farming lands near the junction of Lagonda creek with the Mad river, and from this insignificant hamlet has grown the city of Springfield. The town was found to rest upon valuable quarries from which limestone in almost inexhaustible quantities could be obtained. The layers near the surface produce lime of so fine a quality that Springfield lime is the standard in the markets of Cincinnati and the West; while the deeper layers yield a stone admirably adapted to building purposes. The Mad river rushes along near at hand, furnishing a water-power which the people were not slow in utilizing. The old national road and the road from Cincinnati to Sandusky passed through the town and greatly aided its growth. With the construction of railways the progress became more rapid; and the result of a fine location, excellent natural advantages, and good means of transportation in the possession of an energetic people is seen in the Springfield of to-day—a city of 20,730 inhabitants busily engaged in trade and manufactures, principally of iron goods, proud of their fine public schools, and mindful of the claims of their many churches; the seat of Wittenberg college; and, in rank, the fifth city of Ohio.

SPRINGFIELD IN 1880.

The following statistical accounts, collected by the Census Office, indicate the present condition of Springfield:

LOCATION.

Springfield is situated in latitude 39° 54' north, longitude 83° 46' west from Greenwich, in the center of Clarke county, Ohio, about 45 miles west from Columbus, 60 miles north-northeast from Cincinnati, and 150 miles southwest from Cleveland. It is not on navigable water.

RAILROAD COMMUNICATIONS.

The New York, Pennsylvania, and Ohio railroad, termini Salamanca, N. Y., and Cincinnati, passes through the city; the Cincinnati, Sandusky, and Cleveland; the Columbus, Springfield, and Cleveland; and the Cleveland, Columbus, Cincinnati, and Indianapolis railroad connect it with the cities mentioned in the names of the lines. The city is on the Springfield branch of the little Miami division of the Pittsburgh, Cincinnati, and Saint Louis railroad, and is the northern terminus of the Springfield Southern railroad, which connects it with Jackson, Ohio.

TRIBUTARY COUNTRY.

The land surrounding the city is largely devoted to agriculture, yet much manufacturing is carried on in the vicinity; and there are many quarries from which are obtained valuable building stone, and a limestone, yielding, when burned, lime of an excellent quality.

TOPOGRAPHY.

The soil of Springfield is a drift deposit of great fertility, overlying limestone rocks belonging to the Niagara group. The variations in level are considerable, and the natural drainage through Lagonda creek and Mad river is excellent. There are no lakes in the immediate vicinity; and the demand for wood created by the lime-kilns has stripped the country of most of its forests.

CLIMATE; STREETS; WATER-WORKS; GAS; PUBLIC BUILDINGS; PUBLIC PARKS AND PLEASURE-GROUNDS.

No information on these subjects was furnished.

PLACES OF AMUSEMENT.

Black's opera-house, seating about 1,500, and the Grand opera-house, seating 1,200, are the theaters of Springfield. Each pays an annual license of $50 to the city. The city hall, seating capacity 800, and Duquesne armory, seating capacity 500, are used as public halls, as is also the Wigwam, a hall with room for 2,000 seats. There are no concert- and beer-gardens.

SEWERAGE AND DRAINAGE.

Springfield has no system of sewers. The only public sewer is Mill Run creek, which has been covered over for one-third of a mile, and receives the contents of drains. It is ventilated at the gutter-openings. Several private sewers empty below the surface into Buck creek, and others into several ditches which traverse the city. The Mill Run sewer and one underground drain in the eastern part of the city were built at the public expense. The cost of the private drains is met by an assessment upon those who use them, based upon the front foot and the amount of actual use. Plans and specifications for the construction of an adequate system of sewers are now under consideration.

CEMETERIES.

No information on this subject was furnished.

MARKETS.

The space on Market street, from High to Washington streets, except 40 feet in the center of the street, is divided into stands, and with the market-house, a small two-story brick building, constitutes the market of Springfield. There is no classification either of stalls or of stands, and they are let to the highest bidder, provided that no individual has more than one. The annual income is about $1,300. The market is under the supervision of the market clerk, salary $200 a year, and is open on Tuesdays, Thursdays, and Saturdays, from 5 to 9.30 a. m., and on Saturday afternoons from 5 to 9.30. About one-half of the retail supply of meats for the city is obtained at the market, and one-quarter of the vegetables. No estimate of the gross amount of the annual sales could be made. The second story of the market-building is used as a city hall.

SANITARY AUTHORITY—BOARD OF HEALTH.

In the year 1876 the city council passed an ordinance creating a board of health for the city, to consist of the mayor *ex officio*, and 6 members to be appointed by the city council, which should have power, both in the presence and absence of any epidemic, to care for the public health, and to remove and abate all nuisances, charging the expense upon the offending estate. This board has been appointed only when the council wished, and its authority has practically been nothing. The members serve without compensation, and the annual expenses in the absence of an epidemic amount to very little. By an ordinance passed in September of the present year two sanitary marshals are created, whose duty is to see that all sanitary ordinances are obeyed; to serve such notices as the council may direct, and, in general, to assist in maintaining a good sanitary condition of the city. The marshals receive $1,200 a year each, and are not under the control of the board of health.

NUISANCES.

The sanitary marshals are supposed to make an inspection of all parts of their districts once each month. When nuisances are found they are at once abated, and the expense is charged upon the estate at fault; the assessment is then certified to the county auditor, becomes a lien on the estate, and is collected according to law.

BURIAL OF THE DEAD.

No interment can be made until a permit has been obtained from the city clerk, or, in his absence, from one of the committee on cemeteries.

INFECTIOUS DISEASES.

Small-pox patients are isolated in a pest-house on the northern confines of the city; scarlet-fever patients are quarantined at home, and no members of the family are allowed to attend the public schools. Should contagious diseases break out in the public schools the board of education has full authority to take any action it deems best. Vaccination is neither compulsory nor done at the public expense.

There is no system of registration of births, diseases, and deaths.

MUNICIPAL CLEANSING.

Street-cleaning.—The streets are cleaned by the abutters, and the piles of dirt thus made are removed by the city's force. On business streets this is done once a week, on other streets occasionally. The system gives no satisfaction, though it costs the city from $2,000 to $4,000 a year. The sweepings are used in filling up low lands.

Removal of garbage and ashes.—Garbage is removed by the householders in such ways as they see fit; ashes are removed by the city's force. No ordinance prohibits keeping garbage and ashes in the same vessel. The ashes are used for filling in low places. The cost of the service to the city is about $1,000 a year. Nuisances arise from the improper handling and keeping of garbage, and the present system causes much dissatisfaction owing to its incompleteness.

Dead animals.—The carcasses of dead animals are in general removed by teams sent from a rendering establishment not far from the city; sometimes by the street commissioner. The city ordinances forbid any owner of a dead animal to allow the carcass to remain in the city, or to throw it into any stream within the city limits.

Liquid household wastes.—Fully one-half of the kitchen and laundry wastes are run into the street-gutters, one-fourth goes into cesspools, and the rest into the few public and private sewers. Chamber-slops are thrown into privy-vaults. The cesspools are porous and unprovided with overflows, and in a few cases receive the wastes from water-closets. Many wells have been contaminated by the leakage from cesspools and privy-vaults. The street-gutters are flushed only by the rain.

Human excreta.—Little more than 1 per cent. of the houses are provided with water-closets, the rest depending on privy-vaults, as the dry-earth system is not in use. Perhaps 15 per cent. of the water-closets deliver into the public and private sewers, the rest delivering into cesspools and privy-vaults. Very few of these vaults are water-tight. The city ordinances require the owners to prevent the vaults becoming nuisances. Night-soil is disposed of by dumping it into either Buck creek or Mad river, below the city. It is not used as manure.

Manufacturing wastes.—There are no wastes needing ordinances to regulate their disposal.

POLICE.

The police force is appointed by the mayor and confirmed by the city council. It is governed by the mayor and the chief of police, the latter of whom is the chief executive officer, who is expected to enforce the laws and ordinances and to superintend his department; his salary is $75 per month. The rest of the force consists of 11 patrolmen, each of whom receives $60 per month. The uniforms are of blue cloth, and are furnished by the men at an average cost of $60. The men are armed with revolver, hand cuffs, twisters, and a police club; they are on duty 10 hours for day men, 9 hours for night men, and patrol 50 miles of streets. During the past year 2,360 arrests were made, drunkenness and disorderly conduct being the principal causes. No record is kept of property lost and recovered, or of the number of station-house lodgers. The force is expected to co-operate with the fire department. Five reserve policemen are appointed by the mayor and confirmed by the council, from whom all vacancies in the regular force are filled. The annual expense of the department is about $10,000.

MANUFACTURES.

The following is a summary of the statistics of the manufactures of Springfield for 1880, being taken from tables prepared for the Tenth Census by J. Milton Benson, special agent:

Mechanical and manufacturing industries.	No. of estab-lish-ments.	Capital.	AVERAGE NUMBER OF HANDS EMPLOYED.			Total amount paid in wages during the year.	Value of materials.	Value of products.
			Males above 15 years.	Females above 15 years.	Children and youths.			
All industries	170	$7,255,953	3,741	47	182	$1,637,212	$4,550,569	$8,462,443
Agricultural implements	13	5,773,000	2,284	....	95	1,050,725	3,083,490	5,738,382
Blacksmithing (see also Wheelwrighting)	13	9,485	30	....	....	11,789	8,906	29,410
Boots and shoes, including custom work and repairing	8	14,300	26	2	1	14,000	10,937	33,850
Bread and other bakery products	9	24,250	38	5	1	17,268	48,453	84,100
Brick and tile	7	87,200	135	....	17	28,021	12,027	65,445
Carpentering	22	22,800	106	....	....	49,369	105,574	177,957
Clothing, men's	7	33,500	38	26	....	29,000	57,488	110,000
Flouring- and grist-mill products	9	171,000	33	....	....	13,762	331,894	368,662
Foundery and machine-shop products	8	172,100	251	....	20	77,616	155,376	431,730
Lime	5	75,500	62	....	....	22,935	24,225	70,180
Marble and stone work	3	9,000	7	....	....	5,300	5,900	14,000
Painting and paperhanging	6	6,000	21	....	....	9,760	11,690	30,381
Photographing	6	6,400	12	2	....	6,400	3,200	13,710
Printing and publishing	5	137,200	79	6	3	43,800	77,400	166,852
Pumps, not including steam pumps	3	1,600	6	....	....	2,950	3,000	8,500
Saddlery and harness	3	7,400	17	....	1	8,100	11,200	26,500
Tinware, copperware, and sheet iron ware	7	18,500	19	....	1	8,510	23,731	44,100
Wheelwrighting (see also Blacksmithing)	6	21,950	31	....	7	12,980	10,690	27,383
All other industries (a)	30	564,768	546	6	36	224,927	565,988	1,021,301

a Embracing baking and yeast powders; bookbinding and blank-book making; carriages and wagons; coffins, burial cases, and undertakers' goods; cooperage; drain and sewer pipe; electroplating; files; furniture; leather, tanned; liquors, distilled; liquors, malt; lumber, planed; lumber, sawed; masonry, brick and stone; mattresses and spring beds; oil, linseed; paper; sash, doors, and blinds; sewing machines and attachments; stencils and brands; and washing-machines and clothes-wringers.

From the foregoing table it appears that the average capital of all establishments is $42,682 08; that the average wages of all hands employed is $412 40 per annum; and that the average outlay in wages, in materials, and in interest (at 6 per cent.) on capital employed is $38,959 64.

STEUBENVILLE,

JEFFERSON COUNTY, OHIO.

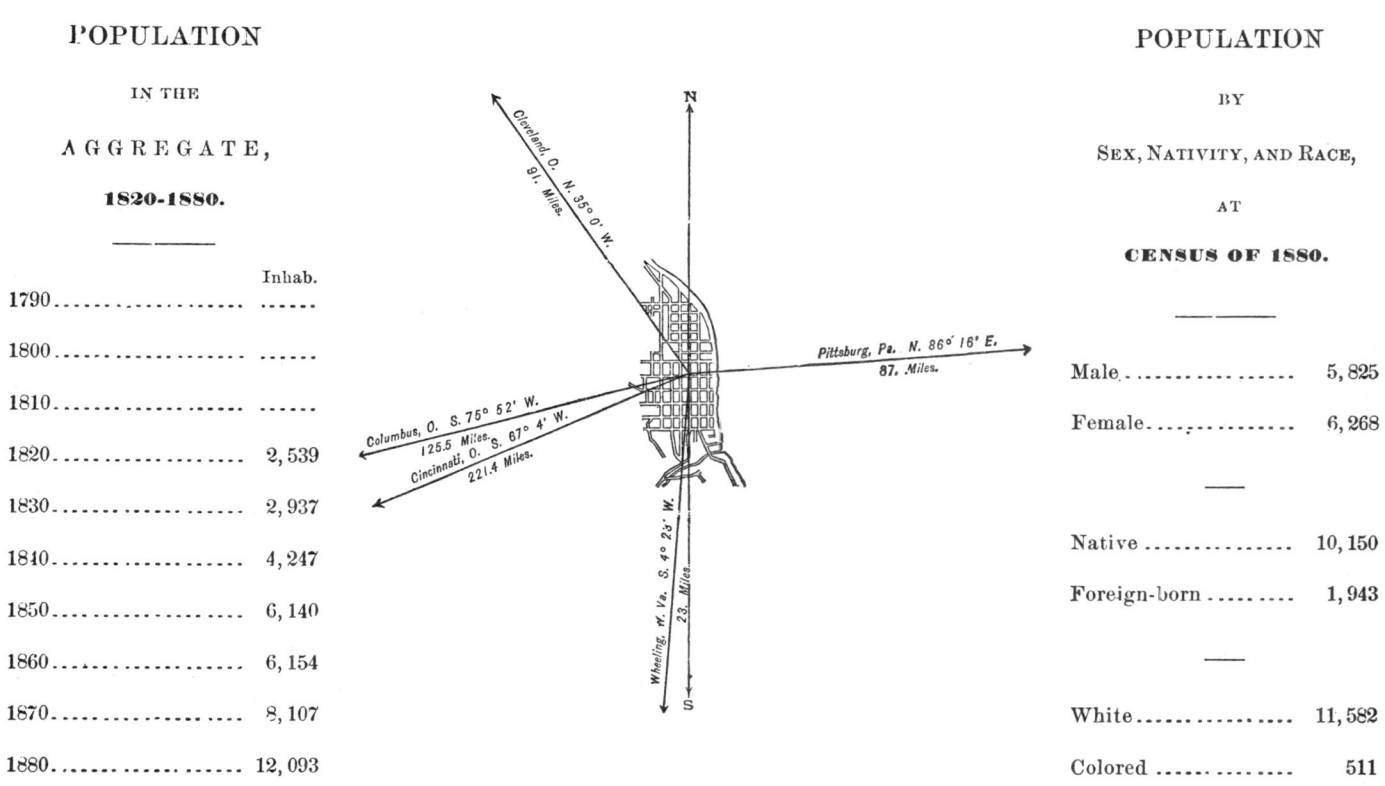

POPULATION

IN THE

AGGREGATE,

1820-1880.

	Inhab.
1790	......
1800	......
1810	......
1820	2,539
1830	2,937
1840	4,247
1850	6,140
1860	6,154
1870	8,107
1880	12,093

POPULATION

BY

SEX, NATIVITY, AND RACE,

AT

CENSUS OF 1880.

Male	5,825
Female	6,268
Native	10,150
Foreign-born	1,943
White	11,582
Colored	511

Latitude: 40° 25′ North; Longitude: 80° 41′ (west from Greenwich); **Altitude: 677 to 1,100 feet.**

FINANCIAL CONDITION:

Total Valuation: $5,173,520; per capita: $428 00.   Total Indebtedness: $30,190; per capita: $2 50.   Tax per $100: $1 66.

HISTORICAL SKETCH.(a)

Late in 1785, or early in 1786, Captain Hamtramck built a block-house on the site of Steubenville, as a protection for the government surveyors. This was replaced in 1787 by a fort, which was called fort Steuben, in honor of Baron Steuben; but after a few months this fortification was evacuated. Its destruction by fire occurred in 1790.

In 1797 Bezaleel Wells, a native of Baltimore county, Maryland, and James Ross, of Pittsburgh, purchased sections 29, 30, 35, and 36, in fractional township 2, range 1, now Steubenville township, and on sections 29 and 30 laid out a town, which they called Steubenville. The first lot was sold February 13, 1798. As early as November, 1797, a territorial court was held in the settlement; the sittings were held in private houses until, in August, 1798, a tract of land in the center of the village was purchased and a court-house was built upon it. This building, a

---

a The material for the sketch, as well as nearly all the statistical information under the head of "Steubenville in 1880", was collected and furnished by Joseph B. Doyle, esq., of Steubenville.

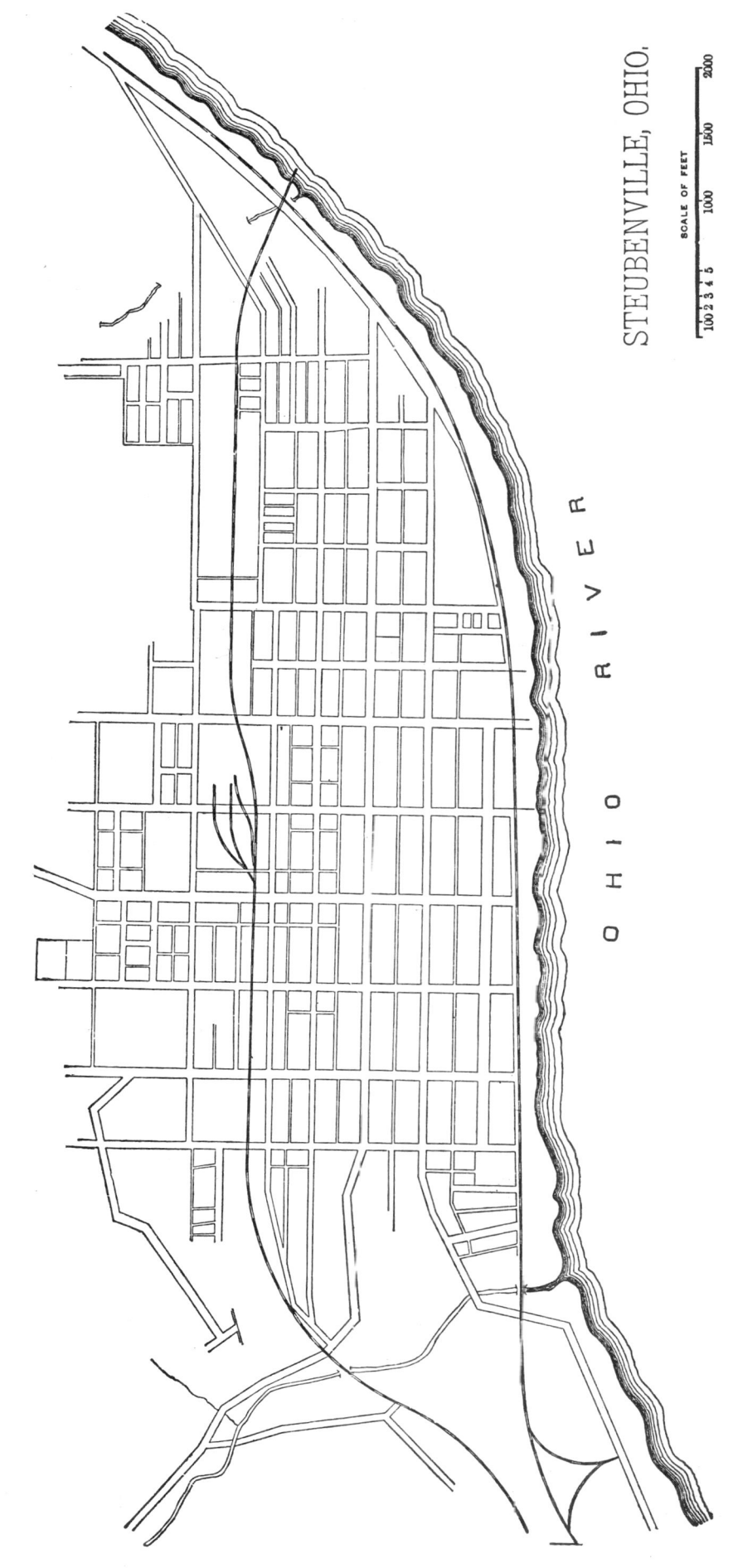

STEUBENVILLE, OHIO.

SCALE OF FEET

100 2 3 4 5   1000   1500   2000

OHIO RIVER

rude log structure of two stories—the jail in the lower story, the court-room in the upper—was used until 1809, when it was torn down to make room for a brick court-house, which stood until 1870, and then gave way to the present building. The first settlers brought with them from their Maryland and Pennsylvania homes habits of thrift. The government land-office was located there, and the town, which was incorporated February 14, 1805, was made the county-seat of a county extending from lake Erie to the Ohio river. The year after the incorporation of the town the *Western Herald*, the first newspaper, was started; and four years later the first attempt was made to obtain a public water-supply. Water was brought in pipes made of hollow logs from springs at the western end of the town, and the supply was increased in 1821 by the extension of the pipes to other springs; but the decay of the wooden mains made the supply unreliable, and a good supply was not obtained until 1835, when water was taken from the Ohio river and pumped to a reservoir three-fourths of a mile distant and 192 feet above the pumping-station. These works were rebuilt in 1864, a new reservoir was added, $80,000 was spent in improvements and extension, and the wants of the community were fully supplied.

In 1809 a stage line to Wheeling was started, and other lines to various points were soon established. Later many steamers, owned in whole or part at Steubenville, were found on the Ohio and Mississippi rivers. The building of steamboats was begun in the town about 1819, and many fine ones were constructed there.

The Steubenville and Indiana railroad was incorporated in 1848, and opened for business in 1853; a few years later the Pittsburgh and Steubenville railroad was begun, but it was not completed until 1865, while 9 years previously the Cleveland and Pittsburgh railroad reached the city. These roads, with the Pittsburgh, Wheeling, and Kentucky, now a part of the Pan Handle route, offer easy means of transportation for the product of the city's manufactories.

Steubenville early became a manufacturing town. A tannery was started in 1798 or 1799; a saw- and grist-mill in 1802; a nail factory in 1811; a paper-mill and a steam flouring-mill in 1813; and in 1814 the pioneer woolen-mill of the region was established here. Men were brought from the East to run the machines, and merino sheep were imported from Spain to increase and improve the supply of wool. This importation laid the foundation of the present vast industry of wool-growing in eastern Ohio and western Pennsylvania. Other woolen-mills were started, and the growth of the town rapidly increased. The Pioneer mill failed in 1830, and the crises of 1837 stopped the others. One by one the woolen-mills have passed away, until only one now stands, deserted and idle. A similar fate befel the cotton industry. The first mill was started in 1824–'25, and others began soon after. They did a large business for many years, but cotton manufacturing is now abandoned.

In 1846 glass-making was introduced, and is now one of the leading manufactures, the making of tumblers being especially prominent.

In 1851 Steubenville was incorporated as a city. In the early days all coal at this point was obtained from seams lying near the top of the hills, but in 1857 the first effort was made to reach the lower coal-beds, and the success of the venture has given to Steubenville an abundant supply of excellent coal, which is used in the iron founderies which have grown up since 1859. Free clay lies in veins under some of the coal-layers, and within a few years the manufacture of pottery has assumed importance.

The territory of the city was largely increased in 1871, and the effect is seen in the increased population in 1880. The schools of the city are excellent, the first board of education having been elected in 1838, and continual progress having since been made in the management of the schools. There are 17 churches and 27 societies, literary, social, and secret. The city has 2 daily, 4 weekly, and 1 monthly newspapers, and 3 banks, with 1 private banking-house.

STEUBENVILLE IN 1880.

The following statistical accounts, collected by the Census Office, indicate the present condition of Steubenville:

LOCATION.

Steubenville is situated in latitude 40° 25' north, longitude 80° 41' west from Greenwich, on the Ohio river, 68 miles by river from Pittsburgh, and 398½ miles above Cincinnati. The highest point is 1,100 feet, the lowest 677 feet above the sea-level. The Ohio river is here about 1,000 feet wide at average stages of the water. During high water there are 40 feet over all bars below the city, but during low stages the depth is only about 12 inches. The harbor is a pool about a mile long and as wide as the river, and has an average depth at low water of 7 feet. The current flows at the rate of 8 miles an hour during high stages, and 3 miles an hour during low stages.

RAILROAD COMMUNICATIONS.

Steubenville is touched by the following-named railroads:

The Pittsburgh, Cincinnati, and Saint Louis railroad, termini Pittsburgh and Saint Louis.

The Cleveland and Pittsburgh railroad, termini Pittsburgh, Bellaire, and Cleveland.

The Pittsburgh, Wheeling, and Kentucky railroad, termini Steubenville, and Wheeling, West Virginia.

TRIBUTARY COUNTRY.

The city is the center of a great wool-growing district, the spring returns of the present year showing that within a radius of 50 miles there were 1,431,479 sheep. Large numbers of blooded cattle are raised in the vicinity. The tributary district is also rich in manufactures.

TOPOGRAPHY.

The larger portion of Steubenville is situated in an amphitheater fronting for 3 miles on the Ohio river, and extending back half a mile at the center to the hills, which shut in the city while they form at the same time part of its territory. A short distance from either end a valley of considerable size opens back into the country. There are two well-defined river-benches of the alluvial period, the lower being at an average height of 39 feet, the other of 37 feet above low-water mark, the latter following a slope of varying regularity to the part of the hills 77.98 feet higher. The front of the hills is precipitous, but not sufficiently so to prevent cultivation or building. In the northern part of the town the benches are of gravel, but elsewhere of sand and small bowlders. The underlying rocks are the sandstones and limestones of the Lower Barren Measures of the Carboniferous series. The hills rise to a height of 400 and 500 feet above the river. The natural drainage is excellent, and there are no marshes, ponds, or lakes in the vicinity. The surrounding country was once thickly wooded, but has now been almost entirely stripped of its forests. The soil is light and loamy and well adapted to the cultivation of corn and small grains.

CLIMATE.

The highest recorded summer temperature is 100°, the highest in average years rarely exceeding 98°. The lowest recorded winter temperature is −12°, while in average years about −5° marks the lowest descent of the mercury. The Ohio river has a marked effect in moderating the cold of winter, the thermometer in Steubenville never falling so low as in the country remote from the river, while in the spring vegetables are from a week to ten days in advance of those in the inland country. The hills protect the city from the wind and tend to equalize the temperature.

STREETS.

Steubenville has about 17½ miles of streets, 3,175 feet of which are paved with cobble-stones laid on a gravel foundation, and 603 feet on a foundation of furnace-cinders and gravel; 3,900 feet are paved with furnace-cinders; 603 feet with locust-wood blocks; while quite a number of streets are naturally of gravel. The cost of the cobble-stone paving with gravel foundation is about $1 25 per square yard; with cinder foundation, about $1 50; and of the wood paving, $2 85. The streets are about 35 feet wide between the curb-stones. Very little repairing has been done on the paved streets, and no account of the cost has been kept. The wooden pavement was laid in 1872, and has needed no repairs as yet. The sidewalks are almost entirely of brick, and from 9 to 15 feet in width; the gutters are of sandstone or cobble-stone, and are made large, as the surface-drainage is considerable. Trees are planted along the edges of the sidewalks inside the curbing. Repairs on the streets are made by day-labor under the direction of the city commissioners, and will cost for the present fiscal year about $10,000.

There are no horse-railroads and no omnibus lines.

WATER-WORKS.

The water-works are owned by the city, and have grown from a small beginning in 1810 to the present works, capable of meeting a daily consumption of 2,480,000 gallons. The total cost can not be given. The daily average consumption is 1,280,000 gallons. There are about 15 miles of pipes and mains, varying in diameter from 20 inches to 2 inches.

GAS.

The city is supplied with gas by a private corporation. The daily average production is 24,000 cubic feet, for which the charge is $1 90 per 1,000 feet. The city pays $20 a year for each of the 159 gas street-lamps in use.

PUBLIC BUILDINGS.

The buildings owned by the city and used for municipal purposes are valued at $10,000, and include three houses of the fire department, in one of which are the offices of the mayor and the city lockup. There is no city hall.

PUBLIC PARKS AND PLEASURE-GROUNDS.

A park of about 15 acres is being formed about the public landing by the accumulation of *débris,* and another of similar size is being formed at the north end of the city by private persons. These parks have caused no expense, except for the planting of a few trees.

PLACES OF AMUSEMENT.

The city has no theaters. Three halls, seating, respectively, 800, 600, and 400, are used for entertainments of all kinds. Each entertainment pays a license fee to the city. There are no concert- and beer-gardens.

DRAINAGE.

The city has no system of sewers. Storm-water and most of the liquid household wastes pass off through the street-gutters and find their way to the Ohio river.

CEMETERIES.

There are 2 cemeteries connected with the city, as follows:

Union Cemetery, area 125 acres, situated in the southwestern part of the city, was opened in 1855, and contains 4,576 bodies, 383 of which have been moved from the church-yards and burial-grounds that have been abandoned as population pressed around them.

Roman Catholic Cemetery, area between 2 and 3 acres, is situated in the western part of the city, and was opened in 1853. About 500 interments have been made within its limits.

Union cemetery is in the hands of a private corporation; the other is managed by the Catholic church. No interments are allowed to be made in any place other than these two cemeteries. Graves are made 5 feet deep. There were once several other burial-grounds and church-yards, but all of them are now closed.

MARKETS.

Steubenville has no public or corporation markets.

SANITARY AUTHORITY.

The city has no board of health, though under the laws of the state the city council has power to create one and give it very extended powers. The ordinances of the city prohibit all things likely to be a cause of injury to the public health, and those who break the ordinances are tried before the mayor and dealt with like other offenders. The pollution of the streams and harbors by casting any dead or decaying animal or vegetable substances into them in such a way that they will not at once be carried off is forbidden by the ordinances.

INFECTIOUS DISEASES.

Small-pox and scarlet-fever patients are not quarantined or isolated, the city marshal simply marking the house in which a case of either disease exists. There is no pest-house. Vaccination is not compulsory, nor is it done at the public expense. There is no system of registration of births, diseases, and deaths.

MUNICIPAL CLEANSING.

Street cleaning.—The streets are cleaned by the city's force, and the expense is charged to the property-holders. The work is done entirely by hand, and with tolerable efficiency. There is a general cleaning up of the streets in spring, but during the rest of the year they are cleaned only when it is necessary. The sweepings are deposited on the river-bank. The cost of the work is about $500.

Removal of garbage and ashes.—Garbage and ashes are removed by the householders, in whatever way they see fit. There are no regulations governing the conservancy of garbage while awaiting removal, provided it does not become a nuisance; it may be kept in the same vessel with ashes. Few nuisances arise.

Dead animals.—The city makes a contract with a scavenger to remove the carcasses of dead animals at a schedule rate fixed by the city. The price is collected by the scavenger, if possible, from the owner of the animal; but if he is unable to obtain it he is paid by the city. The service cost $291 95 to the city during the past year, when 2 horses, 1 cow, 957 cats, 1,754 rats, 848 chickens, 185 hogs, and 247 dogs were removed.

Liquid household wastes.—Chamber slops and kitchen and laundry wastes are generally disposed of alike, by running them into the street-gutters. None goes into sewers, but about one-tenth passes into cesspools, which are porous, unprovided with overflows, and in some cases receive the wastes from water-closets. No regulations govern their construction or cleansing. The street-gutters are flushed at irregular intervals.

Human excreta.—About 5 per cent. of the houses are provided with water-closets; the rest depend upon privy-vaults, none of which are water-tight. The water closets all deliver into cesspools. No privy is allowed to be built within 2 feet of the line of any alley or any adjoining premises, or within 20 feet of any street. The vaults must not be allowed to become a nuisance. The dry-earth system is not used. Night-soil is taken beyond the city limits and dumped into the river or elsewhere.

Manufacturing wastes.—These usually drain to the river, like other liquid wastes, and often cause much annoyance.

POLICE.

The police, with the exception of the marshal, are appointed by the mayor and confirmed by the city council; the marshal is elected by the people. The force is subject to the general orders and supervision of the mayor, but the general charge of the department is intrusted to the marshal, who is *ex officio* superintendent of police, and receives a salary of $750. There are 7 policemen, each of whom is paid $1 75 a day. Their uniform is of blue cloth, with brass buttons, and a metal star; each man provides his own, the average cost being $17. The men are armed with revolvers and heavy maces, and are on duty from 6 p. m. to 6 a. m., but have no regular beats. During the past year they made 850 arrests, chiefly for drunkenness and disorderly conduct. Most of those arrested were released on payment of fines. There is no record of the amount of property lost or stolen and reported to the police, or of the amount recovered and returned. The force co-operates with the fire department. The mayor, with the consent of the council, may appoint 5 reserve police in each ward, who may be called on for service when necessary. These, while on duty, receive the same pay and have the same powers as regular members of the force. The expense of the department in 1880 was $6,972 50.

FIRE DEPARTMENT.

The fire department is organized on the volunteer system, although small salaries are paid to the chief fire director and the engineers of the steamers, and the men receive $10 a year and a few privileges. The force consists of 1 chief and 2 assistant fire directors; 2 engine and hose companies and 1 hook-and-ladder company, each of 22 men. The apparatus includes 2 steam fire-engines, 2 hose-carriages, 3 hose-trucks, 1 hook-and-ladder truck with equipments, and 3,250 feet of hose. Alarms are given by the bells on the engine-houses, and by a fire-alarm attached to the court-house bell. The force is efficient, and losses by fire are consequently small.

TOLEDO
LUCAS COUNTY, OHIO.

POPULATION

IN THE

AGGREGATE,

1840-1880.

	Inhab.
1790	......
1800	......
1810	......
1820	......
1830	......
1840	1,224
1850	3,829
1860	13,768
1870	31,584
1880	50,137

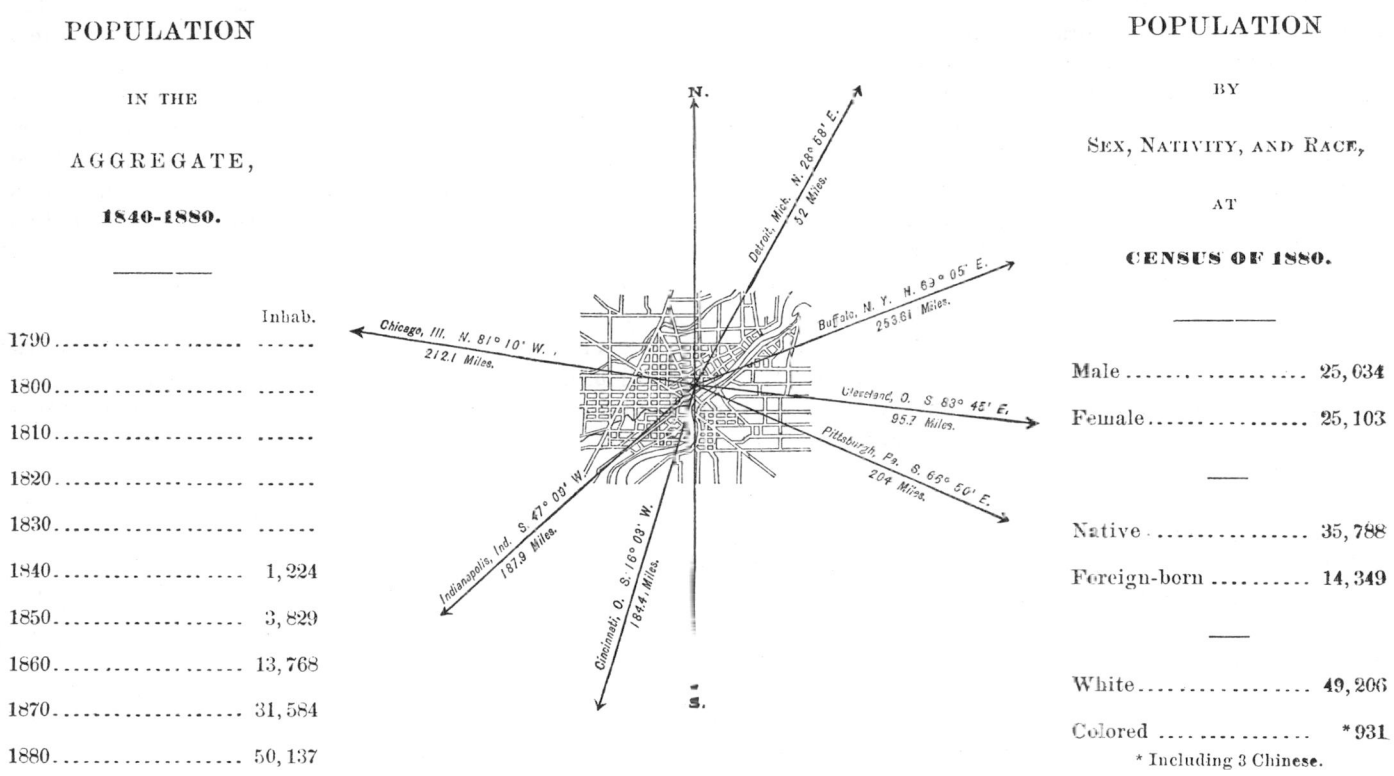

POPULATION

BY

SEX, NATIVITY, AND RACE,

AT

CENSUS OF 1880.

Male	25,634
Female	25,103
Native	35,788
Foreign-born	14,349
White	49,206
Colored	*931

* Including 3 Chinese.

Latitude: 41° 40′ North; Longitude: 83° 33′ (west from Greenwich); **Altitude: 604 feet.**

FINANCIAL CONDITION:

Total Valuation: $18,687,955; per capita: $373 00.   Total Indebtedness: $3,224,660; per capita: $64 32.   Tax per $100: $4 45.

HISTORICAL SKETCH. (a)

The Maumee valley, 8 miles up the Maumee river, at fort Meigs (Perrysburg), and directly on the opposite bank at Maumee City, now South Toledo, was settled from the close of the war of 1812; but what is now Toledo was settled by not more than 4 white families prior to January, 1832, and these a mile or more apart.   The settlement of Port Lawrence, laid out on the northwest corner of the 12 miles square reservation, at the foot of the rapids of the Miami of lake Erie, and on the westerly bank of the Maumee, and the settlement of Vistula, adjoining and below Port Lawrence, became the nucleus about which the present city was formed.   During the winter of 1831–'32 arrangements had been perfected to erect warehouses and a few buildings upon the breaking up of the ice, on the

---

a Prepared by H. A Chamberlin, esq., of Toledo.

westerly bank of the river, by the proprietors of the land—one at the mouth of Swan creek (Port Lawrence), the other a mile below (Vistula). Quite a number of buildings, perhaps half a dozen rude structures at each point, were erected during the year 1832.

During the summer of 1833 it became apparent to the proprietors of the two settlements, as well as to the new settlers and tradesmen, that common cause should be made of the interests of the two points, and upon meeting to discuss their joint interests, as neither party was willing to yield the name of one settlement to the other party, a compromise was effected by giving the two places the name of "Toledo", which, it was argued at the time, was a name not given to any town in the new world, and a name made historic in Spain. From that time to the present, Port Lawrence and Vistula have had no existence, save as describing two important divisions of land planted under these names and in the very heart of the Toledo of to-day.

The area of the present city of Toledo, exclusive of the area of the navigable waters of the corporation, is a trifle over 20 square miles. Toledo was a mere settlement, a part of a township in its government, until 1837, in the spring of which year, after being incorporated, the first mayor was elected. Until 1835 all mail matter for the new settlement on the river was received at Tremoinsville, on the Monroe and Maumee pike, which "ville", since the enlargement of the corporate limits of Toledo in 1874, is a part of the city. From the spring of 1835 until June, 1836, every thing, so far as governmental regulations were concerned, was unsettled. The questions growing out of the disputed boundary line between Ohio and the then territory of Michigan, known as "the Toledo war", was indeed unfortunate for a growing community. The cause of the trouble was the disagreement as to the northern boundary of Ohio. Michigan claimed to the "Fulton line" on the south, being a line due east from the southern extremity of lake Michigan intersecting lake Erie; and Ohio claimed to the "Harris line" on the north, which was a line from the southern extremity of lake Michigan to the most northerly cape of the Maumee bay. These two respective lines left in dispute all the territory now in the city of Toledo, being a strip of land at the eastern end (Toledo), 8 miles in width, and at the Indiana line 5 miles in width, including all the Maumee bay and Toledo harbors, and the outlet of the contemplated Miami and Erie canal.

In 1835, by direction of the general assembly of Ohio, a commission was appointed to re-mark the northern boundary (Harris line) of the state. Governor Mason, of Michigan, directed General Brown, in charge of the Michigan troops, to intercept the commission and prevent the marking of this line. Governor Lucas, of Ohio, upon learning of the decision of the Michigan authorities, at once directed a portion of the Ohio militia, some 600 strong, to protect the commission in the discharge of the duty imposed upon it. Finally, with varying changes of fortune, and through the aid of peace commissioners on the part of Governor Lucas, of Ohio, and President Jackson on the part of the United States, in behalf of the territory of Michigan, a statu quo was effected until the close of the session of Congress in 1836. In June, 1836, Michigan was admitted as a state of the union, with her southern boundary the northern, or "Harris", line. After this time all jurisdictional questions which had been unsettled for some eighteen months were readily adjusted, the functions of local government assumed a regular order, and taxes, which had been uncollected on account of the conflict of authority, were regularly assessed and collected. Aside from a few wounded, when making or resisting arrests under Michigan authority, and the animosities engendered by confining some of the settlers in the jails of Lenawee and Monroe counties, Michigan, for non-compliance with the Michigan laws in the disputed territory, no material loss arose through the unsettled state of society and government and the consequent cloud upon business in this new settlement.

Maumee City (now South Toledo), 8 miles up the river, was the county-seat of Lucas county until the year 1852, when Toledo was made the county-seat. In 1872 the city purchased the property and franchise of the Cherry Street Bridge Company, which controlled the toll-bridge; since the purchase, the bridge, over 2,000 feet in length, and connecting the easterly and westerly parts of the city, divided by the Maumee, has been rebuilt and maintained as a free bridge. The travel over this is very large, it being no uncommon occurrence for 2,000 teams to pass in a single day, with a constant flow of pedestrians in addition. In 1874 the limits of the city were materially enlarged. The chief suburb thus brought within Toledo was Manhattan, a settlement near the mouth of the Maumee, and at the northern terminus of the Miami and Erie canal. In 1835 and 1836 Manhattan had a very rapid growth; warehouses, shops, and docks were built, or in process of construction, on a large scale; but after the panic of 1837 the business of the place was transferred to Toledo. Quite a number of dwellings erected before 1837 are still occupied, interspersed among the more modern buildings; the early warehouses and docks are known only by their foundations.

The settlement of Toledo, where speculation had been rife for some four years, and paper money, under the old state-bank system, had been abundant, was left almost lifeless after the crisis of 1837, and did not fully recuperate from this blight until the completion of the Miami and Erie canal, extending from Toledo to the Ohio river at Cincinnati, in 1843. The depression after the crisis of 1873–'74 did not really take effect until the latter half of 1875, from which time until the summer of 1880 the hitherto rapid development and increase in population and wealth of the city were practically at a standstill. Now the former enterprise and improvement of the city has asserted itself, and vast undertakings, by railroads and other corporations and by individuals, are going forward on all sides. Toledo has never been visited by any devastating conflagrations. The original settlers, mainly from

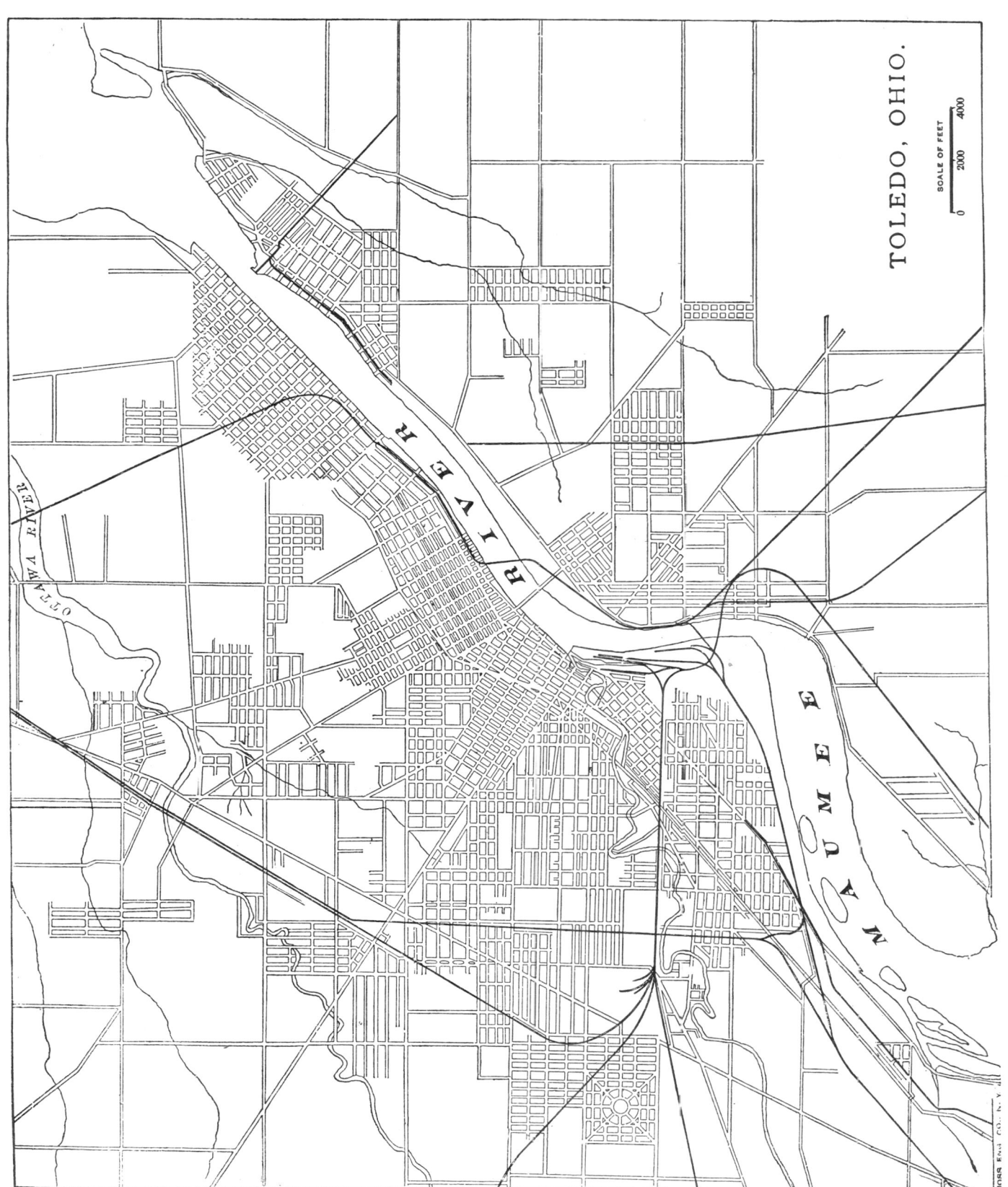

TOLEDO, OHIO.

SCALE OF FEET

0   2000   4000

New York and the New England states, were largely supplemented by Irish in 1840, drawn hither by the construction of the Miami and Erie canal. Since that time many Germans have come in, and to-day this element ranks next to the native-born.

TOLEDO IN 1880.

The following statistical accounts, indicating the present condition of Toledo, were furnished by the mayor, Hon. Jacob Romeis:

LOCATION.

Toledo lies in latitude 41° 40′ north, longitude 83° 33′ west from Greenwich, on both sides of the Maumee river, 1 mile from Maumee bay, and 5 miles from lake Erie, just south of the Michigan state line. The Ottawa river, parallel to the Maumee and to the north of it, also empties into Maumee bay, and the greater part of the city is on the peninsula formed by the two rivers. The area of the city includes 21.5 square miles, 15.3 square miles being on the northwest side and 6.2 square miles on the southeast side of the Maumee river, not less than nine-tenths of the population, however, living on the northerly side. The altitude of the city, as given in the reports of the Smithsonian Institution, is 604 feet above mean sea-level, or about 29 feet above the surface of lake Erie.

HARBOR AND WATER-COURSES.

The harbor, as known to sailors and shippers, includes the extreme southwestern part of lake Erie, the Maumee bay, and the river to the central part of the city. The bay has an area of about 15 square miles. The average width of the river, within the city limits, is more than 1,800 feet, with a good spacious channel of not less than 20 feet depth. The harbor is easily made by sail- and steam-craft upon the western part of lake Erie, and no winds can get sweep enough to injure shipping within it. The anchoring-ground is good, neither the bottom nor banks being rocky. The shallow water, which originally impeded navigation in the bay, near the lake, has been deepened at the expense of the United States government, so that the vessels of all the chain of great lakes have ready access to the warehouses and elevators. Water communication is open with the Atlantic sea-board either via the Welland canal, lake Ontario, and the river Saint Lawrence, or by the Erie canal and Hudson river. The Maumee river is navigable to Fort Wayne, Indiana. The city has also water communication, via the Miami and Erie canal, with Cincinnati.

RAILROAD COMMUNICATIONS.

Toledo is touched by 16 different railroad lines; 7 of these are included in the management of the New York Central and Hudson River Railroad system, and the other 9 are as follows:

The Wabash, Saint Louis, and Pacific railroad, to Saint Louis.
The Cincinnati, Hamilton, and Dayton railroad, to Cincinnati.
The Flint and Pere Marquette railroad, to Ludington, on the east shore of lake Michigan.
The Canada Southern railroad, to Buffalo, New York.
The Ohio Central railroad, to Pomeroy, on the Ohio river.
The Pennsylvania railroad, to Pittsburgh, via Mansfield.
The Columbus and Toledo railroad, to the former place.
The Toledo and Ann Arbor railroad, to Ann Arbor, Michigan.
The Toledo, Delphos, and Burlington railroad, to the Mississippi river. This last is a narrow-gauge road.
In addition to the above the Wheeling and Lake Erie railroad, from Toledo to Wheeling, with an iron bridge 2,000 feet long over the Maumee river, is now in process of construction.

TRIBUTARY COUNTRY.

The country immediately surrounding Toledo is an agricultural one. There are also several outlying towns and many market-gardens near the city. By the aid of the Maumee river, the canal, and the many railroads, Toledo has close commercial relations not only with the thickly settled country that surrounds her on three sides, but with the country west to the banks of the Mississippi.

TOPOGRAPHY.

The natural soil of the city on the eastern side of the river, and a strip on the opposite bank, is clay underlaid with blue-clay hard pan; westerly of this line, which extends back from the river an average distance of 1,500 feet, the soil is a sandy loam. To the south and east of the river the soil is a rich and productive black muck, underlaid with clay. It was originally covered with forests of oak, cottonwood, and varieties of timber adapted to such soil, but is now largely cleared and tilled, producing wheat, corn, hay, vegetables, etc. Northwesterly from the river is a belt of sandy loam, varying in width from 4 to 8 miles, and extending to the middle of Monroe county, Michigan, well adapted for gardening and small vegetables. Beyond this belt the surface is slightly undulating, with the soil a gravelly clay, very productive, and well adapted to grazing or cereal growth. The underlying rock is limestone and shale. The surrounding country for a radius of 30 miles partakes of the same characteristics, and there are no elevations exceeding 80 feet above lake Erie. The Maumee river drains a comparatively level section of country, originally very heavily timbered, nearly all of which is susceptible of proper drainage. There is but very little actual marsh, and there are no ponds or lakes within a radius of 5 miles.

CLIMATE.

Highest recorded summer temperature, 100°; mean summer temperature in average years, 70.20°. Lowest recorded winter temperature, —16°; mean winter temperature in average years, 28.88°. The influence of the waters of lake Erie tend greatly to modify the extremes of heat and cold. The prevailing wind is southwesterly, and generally raises the temperature.

STREETS.

The total length of the streets of Toledo is 271 miles, paved as follows: 3.62 miles with cobble-stones; 7.51 miles with stone blocks, Medina sandstone, and limestone; 3.86 miles with broken stone; and 30.64 miles with wood, cedar blocks, Nicholson, and plank. The cost per square yard of each, as nearly as it may be estimated, is, for cobble-stones, $1 10; stone blocks, Medina, $2; limestone, $1 50; broken stone, $1 20; wood (cedar), 75 cents to $1 50; Nicholson, $2 25; and plank, 67 cents. The relative facility with which each is kept clean is, first, plank, then cedar blocks, stone blocks, cobble-stones, and broken stone, in the order named. The stone blocks of Medina sandstone are reported to give the best satisfaction. The sidewalks are mostly plank, except on the principal streets, where stone flagging is used. An ordinance, however, now requires sidewalks, on all graded streets, to be either stone, brick, or asphalt. The curb and pavement form the gutters, and the unpaved streets have no gutters, other than those made by the grade of the street. Though there is no tree-planting by public authority, property-owners are permitted to plant trees on the street lines. The work of repairs of streets is done by the day, and is so connected with other work that the separate cost of each per annum can not be ascertained. The work on construction of streets is done wholly by contract, as the municipal code requires that all improvements shall be let to the lowest responsible bidder. There are 15 miles of horse-railroads in the city, with 44 cars and 139 horses, and giving employment to 62 men. The total number of passengers carried during the year is 1,500,000, and the rate of fare, for all distances, is 5 cents. There are no regular omnibus lines, but several omnibuses and hacks run to and from the railroad stations and also to all parts of the city. About 25,000 passengers are annually carried by these vehicles, the "bus" fare being 25 cents, and the hack fare 50 cents and upward, according to the distance.

WATER-WORKS.

The water-works are owned by the city, and cost, in round numbers, $1,000,000. The system is pumping into stand-pipe, the daily capacity of the pumps being from 12,000,000 to 14,000,000 gallons, and the pressure in the mains varies from 60 to 108 pounds to the square inch. The least amount pumped per diem is 2,670,720 gallons, and the greatest, 3,890,560 gallons. The average cost of raising 1,000,000 gallons 1 foot high is 5.61 cents. The yearly cost of maintenance, aside from the cost of pumping, is $13,000, and the annual income from water rents is $24,000. The city pays nothing for the water used, and the secretary estimates the income from this source, provided the city paid fair rates, at over $40,000 a year. A few water-meters are used, but they do not appear to give satisfaction.

GAS.

The gas-works are owned by the city. The daily average production is 166,700 cubic feet. The charge per 1,000 feet is $2 25. The city pays $37 36 per annum each for street-lamps, 1,026 in number.

PUBLIC BUILDINGS.

The city owns and occupies for municipal uses, wholly or in part, buildings valued at $175,000, viz: Council room, police station, 7 engine-houses, city workhouse, and house of refuge and correction. There is no city hall, but the city and county contemplate the erection of a building, to be used in common, for court-house and city-hall purposes.

PUBLIC PARKS AND PLEASURE-GROUNDS.

There are 3 parks in Toledo, with a total area of 41 acres, as follows: The largest one has an area of 20 acres, and is situated on the banks of the Maumee river; *Court Park*, area 6 acres, is situated in the heart of the city; and *City Park*, area 15 acres, is situated on a sandy knoll 1 mile from the center of the city. The total cost of the parks was $125,000. Aside from beautifying the City park, little money has been expended, save in sodding and tree-planting, beyond first cost. The yearly cost of maintenance for all the parks has not exceeded $1 000 per annum for the last four years. The estimated number of visitors annually to the large parks is, on foot, 90,000; in carriages, 10,000. The parks are controlled by a board of park commissioners, appointed by the mayor and confirmed by the council.

PLACES OF AMUSEMENT.

There are 4 theaters in the city: Wheeler's opera-house, seating capacity, 2,200; Adelphi theater, seating capacity, 1,200; Theater Comique, seating capacity, 600; and Academy of Music, seating 500. These theaters pay an annual license of $50 each to the city. White's hall, Odeon hall, Walbridge hall, etc., seating capacity from 800 to 1,500 each, are used for concerts, lectures, etc. Schützen park and beer-garden, built and arranged in 1878, is on the bank of and overlooking the Maumee river; it contains 15 acres, has a large 2-story hall, with a capacity for 2,000 persons, and the total cost of the improvements was $25,000.

DRAINAGE.

In preparing the general plan for the sewerage of Toledo, it was necessary to place the main sewers at such a depth that all the water-courses and sink-holes could be drained. This was accomplished without giving any rates of fall less than 1 in 400. All sewerage works are now made in accordance with the plan regulating location, depth, and grade. The disposal of sewage is to the Maumee river. Mouths of sewers are being changed so as to deliver below the surface of the water. Within the past few years some sewers have required both flushing and cleansing by hand. This is done by the street commissioner, and there are no correct data of the amount or cost of such work done. Storm-water is admitted through brick catch-basins, 4 feet in diameter and $5\frac{1}{2}$ feet deep below the water-surface, trapped with a 6-inch seal, and connected with the sewer by a 12-inch pipe; covers of basins are circular, 4 feet 8 inches in diameter, and made of three thicknesses of 3-inch plank bolted together; a hole in the center, 2 feet 6 inches square, is covered with a movable lid, also of wood. Provision for ventilation is made by erecting a stand-pipe of galvanized iron, 10 inches in diameter, 40 feet high above the surface of the ground, supported on a stick of timber set in the ground for the purpose and connected with the sewer by a pipe 12 inches in diameter. Such a ventilator is placed at the head of each sewer, and the mouth of the sewer is trapped with a stench-trap. The cost of sewers was formerly paid one-half by the city and one-half by assessment on the abutting property, but in recent years the whole cost has been assessed upon the property. The basis of assessments is according to supposed benefits, the property most remote being assessed at the highest rate. Sewers 2 feet in diameter, built in 1880, cost from $1 46 to $1 52 per foot; manholes, $10; catch-basins, $30 each.

CEMETERIES.

There are 5 cemeteries connected with Toledo, all situated on the westerly boundary of the city, and not surrounded with dwellings. They are as follows:

Forest Cemetery, area 25 acres; *Woodlawn Cemetery*, area 160 acres; and *Collingwood Cemetery*, area 20 acres, are Protestant; and *German Cemetery*, area 40 acres, and *Saint Patrick's Cemetery*, area 22 acres, are Catholic.

There are no church-yards or private burial-grounds where interments are no longer permitted.

All the above-named cemeteries are in use, and all, save Woodlawn, have been for more than twenty years. The average death-rate for about ten years past has been about 16 in 1,000, taking the average population for the last decade as 42,000. The board of health has unlimited power over interments. Burial permits are granted by the city clerk, on the certificate of the attending physician. In case of death from any contagious disease the funeral must be private, and direct from the house or hospital. Woodlawn cemetery is the only one owned by a private corporation, and is governed by practically the same regulations.

MARKETS.

There are no public market buildings in Toledo. In two places, originally plotted for market-houses, the city has designated certain hours when market-stuff may be sold, under certain regulations, and during these hours no huckstering is allowed upon the streets.

SANITARY AUTHORITY—BOARD OF HEALTH.

The board of police commissioners, composed of 4 members, appointed first by the governor and afterward elected by the people, with the mayor a member *ex officio*, is vested with the full power of a board of health. At present there is no physician on the board. The annual expenses of the board in ordinary times are about $4,000, for salaries, printing, advertising, etc. During an epidemic there is no limit to the amount of expenditures. In absence of an epidemic the board has full power over the general sanitary condition of the city, and during epidemics has authority to take such steps as may be necessary to check and control the spread of disease. The chief executive officer of the board is the health officer, salary $900 per annum. He is a physician, has general supervision of the affairs of the board, carries out its orders, and reports to it at each meeting. Two policemen are detailed from the police force to carry out the orders of the health officer. The board meets bi-monthly, and transacts its business as a deliberative body. All orders entered upon the journal have all the force and effect of city ordinances, so far as the public health and the prevention of diseases are concerned.

Nuisances are attended to as reported, and general inspections are made to some extent. The latter are made not so fully as they should be, owing to the small number of inspectors. When a nuisance is found or reported it is inspected by either the sanitary policemen or the health officer, and notice is served to abate. If the order is not complied with the board either proceeds by criminal prosecution or has the work done by contract at the expense of the owner of the property on which the nuisance exists. During the past year 4,942 nuisances were found, and of these 3,639 were abated. All cases of defective house-drainage, privy-vaults, cesspools, sources of drinking-water, etc., if found to be dangerous to health, are declared nuisances and ordered abated, either by the health officer or, in some cases, by direct notice from the board. Defective sewerage, street-cleaning, etc., is reported to the common council, with a request to have the same corrected. The board orders the removal and burial or destruction of garbage, and, during the summer months, employs a collector. The board exercises full control over the burial of the dead. City ordinances prohibit the pollution of streams and regulate the removal of excrement. The board reports annually to the common council, and its reports are published with the regular city documents.

INFECTIOUS DISEASES.

Small-pox patients are removed to the pest-house, which is situated in a remote suburb. Scarlet-fever cases are quarantined at home, and public notice of the existence of the case, with the locality, is given. In case of the breaking out of a contagious disease in either public or private schools, the board has power to close the schools. Vaccination is compulsory, when ordered by the board, and, in cases of persons who are unable to pay, is done at the public expense. Diseases are not registered. The registration of births is imperfect, while the record of deaths is complete or nearly so.

MUNICIPAL CLEANSING.

Street-cleaning.—All general accumulations of dirt and filth are removed by the city at the public expense. The work is done by the city's own force and by hand. All paved streets are cleaned at least twice each month, and all the others from twice to four times each season. The work gives satisfaction. The annual cost of the work to the city is $35,000, and to private persons perhaps $10,000. The sweepings are deposited on lands removed from the settled parts of the city. One of the merits of the system is stated to be that many of the street hands, if not employed by the city, would have to be wholly supported by the infirmary.

Removal of garbage and ashes.—Garbage and ashes are removed both by the city and by householders under contract. The garbage must be kept wholly covered, removed every twenty-four hours, and the surroundings disinfected. Garbage and ashes are not allowed to be kept in the same vessel. The former is buried in arable land, while the latter is generally spread on land. The cost of the service is about $6,000, but how much is paid by the city and how much by the householders is not stated. The board of health, for the past few years, by prompt attention, has well managed this department, and the excellent health of the city proves that no ill effects are noticeable.

Dead animals.—The carcasses of all animals are removed by contract, at so much per head, according to size, and disposed of to glue- and bone-factories beyond the city limits. The annual cost of this service is $3,000, and the system is reported as satisfactory.

Liquid household wastes.—All the liquid household wastes in the city go into the public sewers; none is allowed to run into the street-gutters, and there are no cesspools or dry wells. The sewers are frequently flushed or flooded to their full capacity. It has been claimed in times past that water has been contaminated from defective sewers and from vaults; now, however, aside from the water-works, drinking-water is obtained from artesian wells.

Human excreta.—All the houses in the thickly settled districts have water-closets, all of which deliver into the sewers, and where privy-vaults are used they must be connected with the sewers by "goose-necks". The privy-vaults are required to be water-tight and to be cleaned by the odorless-excavator process under orders of the board of health. The night-soil is buried in arable land beyond the corporate limits, and not within 5 miles of the gathering-ground of the public water-supply.

Manufacturing wastes, when not suitable for the filling of wharves and the like, are hauled to the arable lands outside the city.

POLICE.

The police force of Toledo is appointed and governed by the board of police commissioners, composed of 4 members, with the mayor also a member *ex officio*. The chief executive officer is the captain and acting superintendent, salary $1,500 per annum, who has the active charge of the entire force. The remainder of the force consists of 1 lieutenant, salary $900 a year; 4 sergeants at $720 a year each; 3 detectives at $720 a year each; and 45 patrolmen at $600 a year each. The uniform is of dark-blue cloth, with white-metal buttons. Each man provides his own uniform, at a cost of $60 per annum. The patrolmen are equipped with batons and revolvers. They are on duty ten hours in each twenty-four, and patrol 185 miles of streets.

During the past year 3,403 arrests were made, the principal causes being for assault and battery, disturbance, drunkenness, larceny, and suspicious appearance. The cases were disposed of by fines and costs, sent to jail or work-house, bound over to higher court, sentence suspended, etc. Of the total number of those arrested 2,838 were males and 565 were females; 2,115 were natives of the United States; 3,026 could read and write; 115 could read only; and 262 could neither read nor write. The amount of property lost or stolen during the year and reported to the police was $4,835, all of which was recovered and nearly all returned to owners. During the same time there were 2,807 station-house lodgers, 2,724 males and 80 females, as against 4,785 in 1879. Meals, to a certain extent, are furnished the station-house lodgers, but no record is kept of the cost. The members of the force assist at fires and report every thing of an unhealthy nature to the health officer, removing and abating the latter when practicable. During the past year there were 15 complaints made against policemen, all of which were examined by the board of police commissioners with the following results: Dismissed from the force, 6; suspended, 2; and complaint not sustained, 7. Special policemen are appointed by the board, at the request of citizens, to guard private property, and they are accountable to the board for their conduct. The yearly cost of the police, 1880, is $26,791 93.

FIRE DEPARTMENT.

The annual report of the chief engineer for the year ending December 31, 1880, shows the following regarding the fire department: The force consists of 1 chief and 1 assistant engineer, 1 superintendent of telegraph, 1 batteryman, 23 full-pay and 27 half-pay men—a total of 54. The apparatus consists of 3 steam fire engines, 7 hose-carts, and 1 hook-and-ladder truck in active service, and 3 engines and 2 hose-carts in reserve. There are 5,500 feet of serviceable hose, which, with 2,000 feet ordered, will make 7,500 feet available for the coming year. During the year the department answered 144 alarms, 5 of which were false. Two persons were killed and 5 injured at the fires, and 3 persons had their lives saved by the firemen. The cost of the department during the year was $26,745 24. The fire-alarm telegraph has 95 miles of wire and 47 street signal-boxes.

MANUFACTURES.

The following is a summary of the statistics of the manufactures of Toledo for 1880, being taken from tables prepared for the Tenth Census by John W. Hiett, special agent:

Mechanical and manufacturing industries.	No. of establishments.	Capital.	AVERAGE NUMBER OF HANDS EMPLOYED.			Total amount paid in wages during the year.	Value of materials.	Value of products.
			Males above 16 years.	Females above 15 years.	Children and youths.			
All industries	440	$5,534,285	5,028	1,020	690	$2,260,456	$6,355,399	$10,600,074
Blacksmithing (see also Wheelwrighting)	30	33,565	65	....	....	30,375	24,295	69,045
Boots and shoes, including custom work and repairing	26	44,750	103	20	1	57,203	94,672	181,488
Bread and other bakery products	19	100,300	96	19	14	43,980	182,274	277,960
Brick and tile	3	29,000	95	....	17	24,000	12,950	47,000
Brooms and brushes	3	26,100	34	70	102	14,050	14,740	36,000
Carpentering	32	99,800	243	10	10	90,005	227,520	356,770
Clothing, men's	16	205,200	156	210	1	99,260	248,690	409,580
Clothing, women's	3	51,000	19	240	40	48,150	143,000	225,000
Coffee and spices, roasted and ground	3	68,000	33	9	....	17,475	201,000	240,000
Cooperage	8	72,700	93	....	49	42,045	65,695	139,731
Drugs and chemicals	4	43,000	26	....	6	7,550	71,925	101,069
Flouring- and grist-mill products	6	129,500	50	....	....	23,000	562,500	619,720
Foundery and machine-shop products	13	267,000	257	....	15	104,667	227,036	447,750
Furniture (see also Upholstering)	9	153,020	141	6	....	45,490	77,450	152,100
Hats and caps, not including wool hats	3	17,000	7	117	....	14,920	11,006	33,740
Liquors, malt	4	456,400	245	....	....	107,351	463,200	827,164
Looking-glass and picture frames	6	104,900	88	....	22	34,419	82,143	138,189
Lumber, planed (see also Sash, doors, and blinds)	3	18,500	20	....	....	7,295	16,550	32,500
Lumber, sawed	5	428,000	229	....	20	83,900	457,000	622,150
Marble and stone work	9	52,750	67	....	....	26,920	38,330	86,500
Masonry, brick, and stone	9	26,640	66	....	....	20,500	26,500	55,160
Mineral and soda waters	4	30,000	34	....	3	8,354	15,010	31,800
Painting and paperhanging	17	17,260	80	....	2	31,635	27,470	72,375
Photographing	8	14,100	24	7	1	11,373	5,780	29,810
Plumbing and gasfitting	5	24,800	37	....	1	16,014	40,350	66,325

Mechanical and manufacturing industries.	No. of establishments.	Capital.	AVERAGE NUMBER OF HANDS EMPLOYED.			Total amount paid in wages during the year.	Value of materials.	Value of products.
			Males above 16 years.	Females above 15 years.	Children and youths.			
Printing and publishing	16	$353,700	241	39	50	$141,322	$180,169	$401,616
Roofing and roofing materials........................	4	9,000	19	....	....	7,725	9,300	20,000
Saddlery and harness	11	25,250	51	....	....	23,055	42,375	77,275
Sash, doors, and blinds (see also Lumber, planed).....	7	336,300	439	....	100	178,549	344,000	621,519
Shipbuilding	6	53,050	79	....	....	43,850	46,450	100,300
Slaughtering and meat-packing, not including retail butchering.....	3	86,000	46	....	....	17,200	278,393	333,600
Tinware, copperware, and sheet-iron ware	20	58,400	75	6	38	40,255	95,780	171,270
Tobacco, chewing, smoking, and snuff (see also Tobacco, cigars and cigarettes).	3	240,000	51	114	86	118,942	384,383	751,000
Tobacco, cigars and cigarettes (see also Tobacco, chewing, smoking, and snuff).	22	41,950	123	24	24	59,417	61,195	196,223
Upholstering (see also Furniture)....................	4	8,200	17	2	4	7,450	28,400	41,141
Watch and clock repairing	8	6,200	18	....	....	8,975	5,650	20,700
Wheelwrighting (see also Blacksmithing)	7	14,600	26	....	1	10,300	7,650	22,050
Wirework	3	7,600	23	1	1	8,200	10,000	22,200
All other industries (a)	78	1,780,250	1,507	126	82	583,805	1,524,598	2,519,254

a Embracing agricultural implements; awnings and tents; bookbinding and blank-book making; boxes, cigar; boxes, fancy and paper; boxes, wooden packing; brass castings; bridges; carpets, rag; carpets, wood; carriage and wagon materials; carriages and sleds, children's; carriages and wagons; corsets; cutlery and edge tools; dentistry, mechanical; dentists' materials; electroplating; fertilizers; fruits and vegetables, canned and preserved; furnishing goods, men's; hairwork; housefurnishing goods; instruments, professional and scientific; iron and steel; iron railing, wrought; iron work, architectural and ornamental; kindling wood; leather, curried; leather, tanned; lime; models and patterns; oil, castor; oil, linseed; paints; perfumery and cosmetics; pumps; refrigerators; saws; sewing machines and attachments; show-cases; soap and candles; stencils and brands; stereotyping and electrotyping; stone- and earthen-ware; surgical appliances; trunks and valises; umbrellas and canes; varnish; vinegar; wheelbarrows; window blinds and shades; wooden ware; woolen goods.

From the foregoing table it appears that the average capital of all establishments is $12,577 92; that the average wages of all hands employed is $335 48 per annum; and that the average outlay in wages, in materials, and in interest (at 6 per cent.) on capital employed is $20,336 16.

YOUNGSTOWN,

MAHONING COUNTY, OHIO.

POPULATION

IN THE

AGGREGATE,

1850-1880.

	Inhab.
1790	
1800	
1810	
1820	
1830	
1840	
1850	2,802
1860	2,759
1870	8,075
1880	15,435

POPULATION

BY

SEX, NATIVITY, AND RACE,

AT

CENSUS OF 1880.

Male	7,963
Female	7,472
Native	10,678
Foreign-born	4,757
White	15,112
Colored	*323

* Including 3 Chinese.

Latitude: 41° 7' North; Longitude: 80° 38' (west from Greenwich).

FINANCIAL CONDITION:

Total Valuation: $4,459,340; per capita: $289 00.   Net Indebtedness: $193,407; per capita: $12 53.   Tax per $100: $2 54.

HISTORICAL SKETCH.(a)

   Youngstown, Ohio, is situated on the Mahoning river, whose waters ultimately reach the Ohio river. It is nearly on the direct line from Cleveland to Pittsburgh, and about 70 miles distant from each city. It was one of the first townships of the Western Reserve to be settled, the first settlement occurring in 1797. The township received its name from John Young, who in that year purchased it from the Connecticut Land Company, and immediately began a settlement. The town plat, which was the nucleus of the present city, was then laid out, but was not formally recorded until 1802. The first settlers were largely from Connecticut and Pennsylvania, but many of the pioneers were from other eastern states, as far south as Maryland. The population has been increased by immigrants from the eastern and southern states, and from different European countries.

a The following sketch of Youngstown was prepared by Mr. John M. Edwards.

Bituminous coal of an excellent quality was found in the township at an early period, and to supply the demand in the township and vicinity it was mined to a considerable extent. On the opening of the Pennsylvania and Ohio canal, about 1840, David Tod sent from his coal-mine at Brier hill, north of the present city, a few boat-loads of coal to Cleveland. It was on trial found to be excellent as a fuel for making steam on the boats navigating the lakes, and also in manufactories. This was the beginning of the coal trade from the region, and this trade is now very large. By experiment it was found that the Brier Hill coal, or "block coal", as it is technically termed, could be successfully used, in its raw state, in making pig-iron from the ore. A blast-furnace for making iron with raw coal was constructed at Lowellville, about 8 miles southeast of Youngstown, in 1845. In 1846 the second furnace for using mineral coal was built in Youngstown. In the same year a rolling mill was erected in the city by the Youngstown Iron Company. This mill has received numerous additions, and is now one of the largest iron-manufacturing works in the United States. Other furnaces and rolling-mills have been built in the city and township from time to time, and five extensive rolling-mills, in which are made all the various kinds of merchant-iron, hoop-iron, nails, spikes, etc.

Other manufacturing works have also been erected, and are now in operation. Among these are mower- and reaper-works, two foundery- and machine-shops, a nut and washer factory, bridge-works, stove-works, carriage and wagon manufactories, scale-works, pump factory, flouring-mills, etc., while still other industrial enterprises are being contemplated. The iron-mills, furnaces, and other works, up to 1856, depended upon the canal for means of transportation, but in that year the Cleveland and Mahoning railroad was built and went into operation. This afforded facilities then much needed for additional transportation, and gave a stimulus to additional manufacturing business. The road only connected Youngstown with Cleveland, but by later roads the city is connected with all the railroads running to the Atlantic and Pacific coasts.

The advantages of Youngstown as a manufacturing city are marked. It has coal in abundance; it has a river draining a large extent of country, always maintaining a good flow of water, supplying the city with all that is needed for domestic use and for extinguishing fires, and for use in manufacturing. This is in addition to the water of excellent quality for drinking purposes easily obtained by sinking a well a few feet into the ground. The surrounding country is fertile, capable of supplying food for a large population, and is now to a great extent under cultivation. Within a short distance there are inexhaustible deposits of limestone, and in the hills bordering the river sandstone is found of the best known varieties and qualities for building and for making glass. Clay, for building and fire-brick, is near at hand, and wood used in manufacturing tools and implements can be obtained from the portions of the native forests yet left standing. The city is lighted by gas, has good schools, and churches of all the leading denominations, and has a healthy climate.

The first newspaper was published in 1843 and was called the *Olive Branch*. There are now seven, of which two are daily and five weekly papers. Four banks and one private banking-house meet the needs of the business men of the city.

Mahoning county was organized in 1846 from parts of Trumbull and Columbiana counties, with its shire town at Confield. By a vote of nearly two-thirds of the legal voters, taken in 1874, in pursuance of an act of the legislature, the county-seat was removed to Youngstown in 1876 on the completion of the county buildings, erected by the citizens at a cost of over $100,000.

YOUNGSTOWN IN 1880

The following statistical accounts, collected by the Census Office, indicate the present condition of Youngstown:

LOCATION.

Almost exactly half way between Cleveland and Pittsburgh stands the city of Youngstown, in latitude 41° 7′ north, longitude 80° 38′ west from Greenwich. The altitude of the city has never been exactly ascertained. It is situated on the Mahoning river, a stream navigable only for small boats.

RAILROAD COMMUNICATIONS.

Youngstown is touched by the following named railroads:

The Mahoning division of the New York, Pennsylvania, and Ohio railroad, termini Cleveland, Youngstown, and Chenango, Pa.

The Pittsburgh and Lake Erie railroad, termini Youngstown and Pittsburgh.

A branch of the Lake Shore and Michigan Southern railroad, termini Youngstown and Andover.

The Painesville and Youngstown railroad, termini Youngstown and Fairport.

TRIBUTARY COUNTRY.

The city is the commercial, manufacturing, and business center for a rich agricultural district extending for many miles. Coal-mining is an important industry throughout this district.

YOUNGSTOWN,

OHIO.

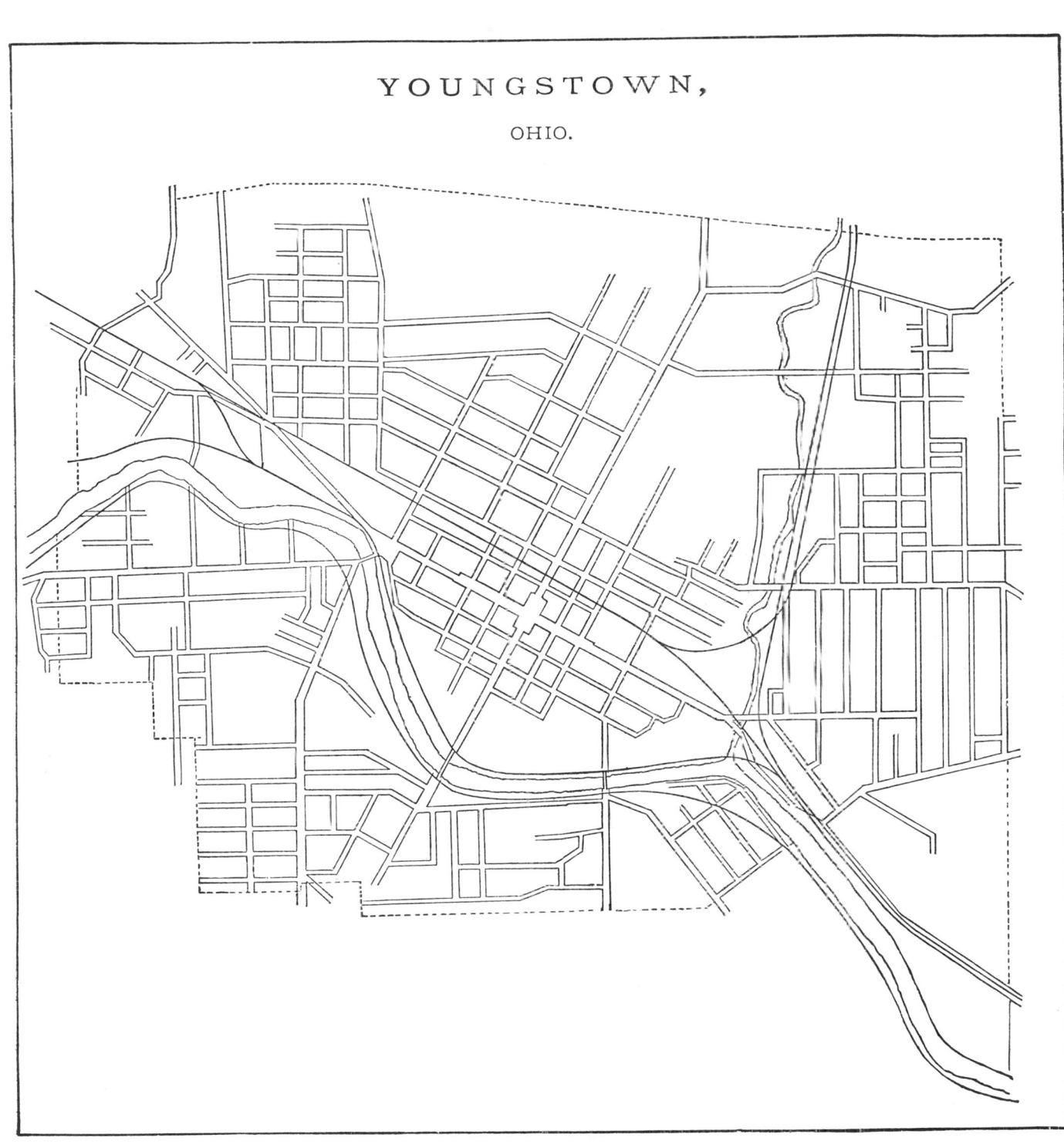

TOPOGRAPHY.

Youngstown stands on both sides of the Mahoning river, which here flows through a channel 300 feet below the tops of the neighboring hills. The surface is very irregular, the district standing on the divide between lake Erie and the Ohio river, forming the southern rim of the drainage basin of lake Erie. The soil is in some places sandy loam, in others clayey, and rests upon underlying rock of the Carboniferous age, the sandstone and limestone of the Ohio Coal Measures, rich veins of bituminous coal lying beneath the city and in its vicinity. The natural drainage to the Mahoning is good. There are no marshes, lakes, or ponds in the vicinity, and within a radius of 5 miles the country in general is open, although here and there a few traces of the original forests still remain.

CLIMATE.

The highest recorded summer temperature is 96°, and the lowest recorded winter temperature is —23°.

STREETS.

The total length of the streets is 39.7 miles, about 25 miles of which are of gravel; no other paving has ever been laid. The cost of the gravel streets is 20 cents per square yard, exclusive of the cost of grading. The sidewalks are principally of stone, either natural flags or blocks cut to a desired size; a few plank sidewalks are in use. The street-gutters are paved with cobble-stones. Trees are planted along the streets, being placed in a grassed plat between the curbstone and the sidewalk, not nearer than 2 feet to the curb, and sometimes as much as 5 feet distant.

There is one horse-railroad line. This has 2 miles of tracks, 4 cars, and 20 horses; it employs 9 men, and charges fares of 5 cents. There are no omnibus lines.

WATER-WORKS.

The works for the public water-supply are owned by the city, and have been erected at a cost of $160,000. A pressure of 75 pounds to the square inch is maintained by a system of pumping directly into the mains. The pump in use is of Worthington manufacture, and pumps daily from 750,000 to 1,500,000 gallons. The cost of maintenance, aside from the cost of pumping, was $2,261 06 during the past year, and the income from water rates was $10,157 59. Water-meters are used at manufactories, either of Worthington, Eagle, Rotary, or Union Water-meter Company patterns. They generally effect an increase of revenue.

GAS.

The city is supplied with gas by a private company. The average daily production is 30,000 cubic feet, for which a charge of $2 per 1,000 feet is made. There are 194 gas street-lamps, for each of which the city pays $1 75 per month.

PUBLIC BUILDINGS.

The city owns and uses for municipal purposes the following buildings, which together are valued at $12,000: The marshal's residence, the mayor's office, the fire-department building, and a hospital. It pays a rent of $300 per annum for rooms in the court-house, which it uses for a council-chamber, the engineer's office, and the office of the water-works.

PUBLIC PARKS AND PLEASURE-GROUNDS.

There are no public parks.

PLACES OF AMUSEMENT.

The city has a fine theater in the opera-house, a building seating 1,500 people. An annual license of $50 is required from all theaters. Excelsior hall, seating 900, is used as a concert- and lecture-room. A concert- and beer-garden, erected in 1876, and capable of seating 500, is situated beyond the city limits, but draws a large attendance on Sundays from the city's population.

DRAINAGE.

Sewerage works are being constructed in accordance with a comprehensive plan. Subsoil drainage is done by agricultural tiles discharging into catch-basins or conducted to the surface gutters of streets on a lower level. The main outlet for the ordinary flow of sewage is submerged at all times of the year. Ventilation is by perforated manhole covers and by house-drains extended to the roofs of houses without any intervening trap. Only one sewer has required cleansing by hand, and this is reported to be on account of bad construction. It was built in 1873, and about 800 feet had to be cleaned in 1880 at an expense of about $100. All other sewers are reported to be self-cleansing, not even requiring to be flushed.

The cost of main-trunk sewers is paid by the districts to be drained by them, that of laterals is assessed upon the abutting property on the basis of frontage across the shortest end of the lot. The cost of a main sewer built in 1881, from 60 to 84 inches in diameter, was: for trenching, $2 95 per foot; brick-work, $14 95 per thousand. Pipe-sewer cost from 75 cents to $2 50, according to size and depth of cutting. The average cost was nearly $1 per foot, including manholes, lamp-holes, and basins.

CEMETERIES.

There are 4 cemeteries connected with the city, as follows:

Oak Hill Cemetery is the property of the Mahoning Cemetery Association, and contains 10½ acres.

Rose Hill Cemetery, area 2 acres, is owned by the Catholic church.

The other two cemeteries are quite small.

No record of interments in any of these grounds except Oak Hill has been kept, and the record of that cemetery extends back only to 1879. The rules of the Mahoning Cemetery Association require all graves not to be less than 3 feet nor more than 7 feet deep; and provide that before any interment can be made a permit must be obtained of the secretary, who must be informed of the name of the deceased, his place of birth, date of birth, of decease, and of interment, cause of death, names of parents, name of undertaker, and name of person applying for the permit. Landscape gardening has been practiced in the arrangement of the cemetery.

MARKETS.

The city has no public or corporation markets.

SANITARY AUTHORITY—BOARD OF HEALTH.

The chief sanitary organization of Youngstown is a board of health, consisting of 6 members, appointed by the city council. Five members of the present board are physicians; the board meets once a month. In the absence of an epidemic its expenses are small—during the past year $655; but in case of an epidemic it has power to increase its expenses to any amount deemed necessary. Its authority when no epidemic exists is confined chiefly to the abatement of nuisances and the general maintenance of a good sanitary condition of the city; during an epidemic its authority is without limit. The chief executive officer is a health-officer, who serves without pay; one assistant, the sanitary policeman, is employed; he has full police powers. Inspections are made regularly in all parts of the city, and especially when nuisances are reported.

NUISANCES.

The board has authority to pass and enforce regulations defining and placing a penalty on nuisances. When a nuisance is found to exist orders are at once issued for its abatement, and if these orders are disregarded the offender is arrested and brought before the mayor for trial. Defective house-drainage, privy-vaults, cesspools, sources of drinking-water, sewerage, and street-cleaning are all treated as nuisances. In case nuisances arise from the improper conservation and removal of garbage, the board has authority to enforce proper methods.

BURIAL OF THE DEAD.

Persons dying of small-pox must be buried within 24 hours after death; those dying from diphtheria or scarlet-fever, within 48 hours. In no case of death from the above diseases must the burial be made from a church, or more than four persons, besides the undertaker and two assistants, be present at the burial.

INFECTIOUS DISEASES.

Small-pox patients are removed to a pest-house situated 2 miles distant from the city. Scarlet-fever patients are quarantined at home. In cases where the board of health for any reason allows a person suffering from the small-pox to be quarantined at home, the house is placarded, and a heavy penalty is incurred by any one who removes this card without the permission of the board. Should contagious diseases break out in the schools, the board has full authority to take any action it may deem best. Vaccination is compulsory and is done partly at public expense. Every one knowing of the existence of any infectious, contagious, or pestilential disease must at once notify the board. The regulations to prevent contagion and infection are very strict.

The registration of deaths is in the hands of the board of health; that of births is included in the assessor's yearly returns, while diseases are registered only in contagious or infectious cases.

Weekly reports are made to the secretary of the national board of health.

MUNICIPAL CLEANSING.

Street-cleaning.—The streets are cleaned by the city's force and entirely by hand. The work is done daily, and reasonably well. The sweepings are deposited on a dump below the city. The cost for the year ending March 31 was $2,708 22.

Removal of garbage and ashes.—Garbage and ashes are removed at the expense of the householders. The regulations of the board of health prohibit keeping garbage more than 24 hours before removal, but allow it to be kept in the same vessel with ashes. Both are disposed of by taking them to the dump below the city. The system is considered good enough.

Dead animals.—The carcasses of dead animals must be removed within 24 hours after death, at the expense of the owner. They are taken to what is known as the "bone-yard". During the past year the service cost $125; 40 horses, 6 hogs, 80 dogs, and 7 cows being removed.

Liquid household wastes.—About one-third of the liquid household wastes run into the public sewers, the rest going into porous cesspools. None are allowed to pass into the street-gutters. The cesspools are cleaned once a year. No cases of contamination of drinking-water by the soakage from cesspools are known to have taken place.

Human excreta.—Only few water-closets are in use, most of the houses depending on privy-vaults. These are water-tight, and are cleaned from to time when necessary to prevent their becoming nuisances. Only a very limited use is made of the dry-earth system. The night-soil is disposed of by dumping it into the river below the city.

Manufacturing wastes.—No system of disposing of manufacturing wastes has yet been elaborated, though one is greatly needed.

POLICE.

The police force is appointed by the mayor, and is governed by him, with the assistance of the marshal, who is the chief executive officer of the force, and receives an annual salary of $600. The rest of the force consist of 3 day and 6 night policemen, each of whom receives a salary of $55 a month. The uniform is of blue cloth, with brass buttons. Each man furnishes his own, at a cost for the entire suit of $65. The men are armed with batons, handcuffs, and revolvers. The night police are on duty from 6 p. m. to 5 a. m. from May 1 to November 1, and until 6 a. m. during the rest of the year. During 1880 the force made 678 arrests, principally for intoxication and disorderly conduct. The force is not expected to co-operate with the fire department of the city government.

Special police are sometimes appointed. The total cost of the department in 1880 was $3,500. The force has been increased since the fiscal year 1880 expired, and in the future the expense will be greater.

ZANESVILLE,

MUSKINGUM COUNTY, OHIO.

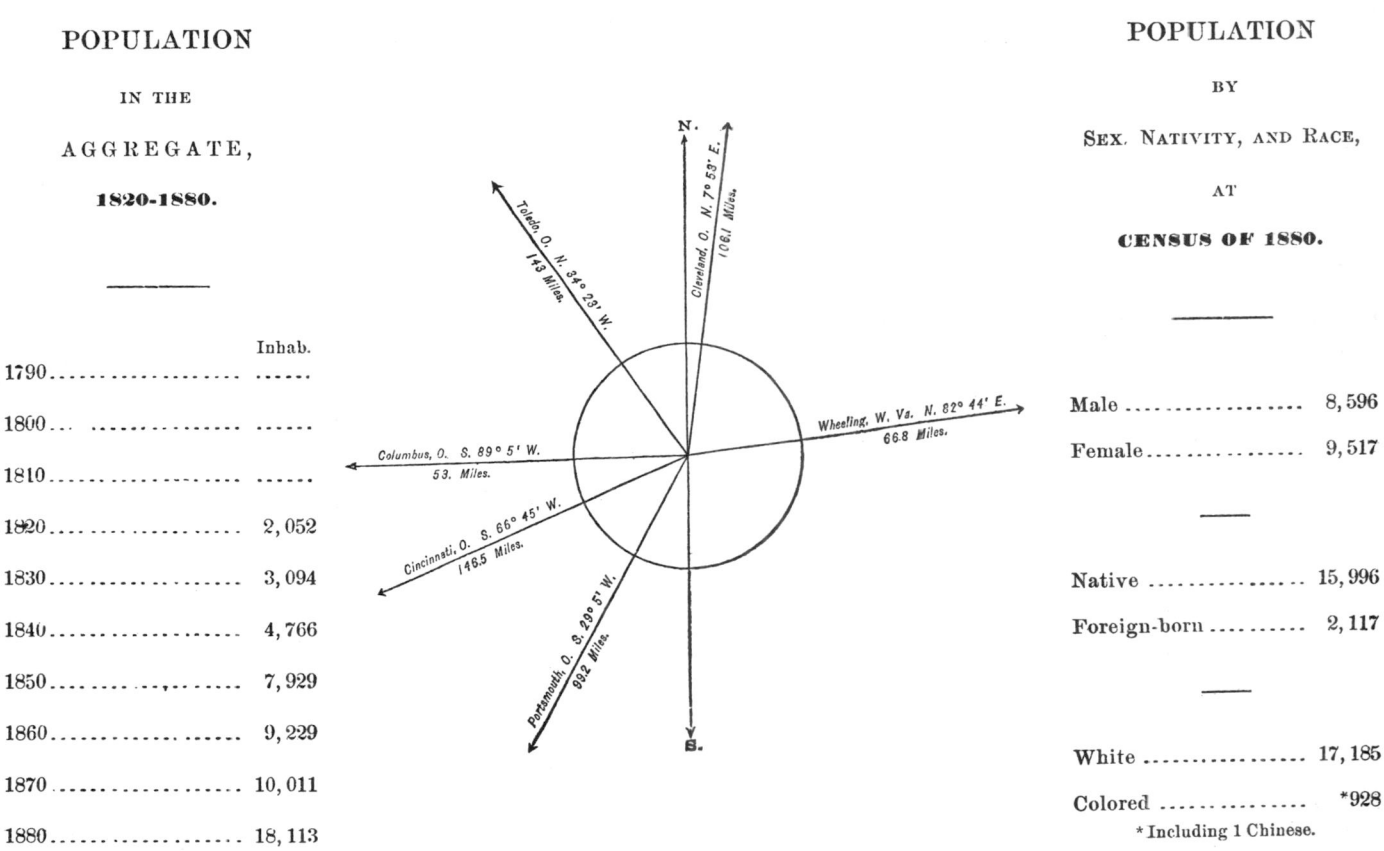

POPULATION

IN THE

AGGREGATE,

1820-1880.

	Inhab.
1790	......
1800	......
1810	......
1820	2,052
1830	3,094
1840	4,766
1850	7,929
1860	9,229
1870	10,011
1880	18,113

POPULATION

BY

SEX, NATIVITY, AND RACE,

AT

CENSUS OF 1880.

Male	8,596
Female	9,517
Native	15,996
Foreign-born	2,117
White	17,185
Colored	*928

* Including 1 Chinese.

Latitude: 39° 58′ North; Longitude: 81° 59′ (west from Greenwich); Altitude: 700 feet. (a)

FINANCIAL CONDITION:

Total Valuation: $7,122,850; per capita: $393 00.   Net Indebtedness: $529,097; per capita: $29 21.   Tax per $100: $2 35.

HISTORICAL SKETCH.

In May, 1796, an act was passed by Congress authorizing and directing Ebenezer Zane, of Wheeling, Virginia, to survey and construct a road from Wheeling to Limestone, now Maysville, Kentucky. The work was begun in the following year by Zane, with the assistance of his brother, Jeremiah, and his son-in-law, John McIntire. It had at first been intended to cross the Muskingum river at what is now Duncan's Falls; but, led by the finer water-power offered by the river at the confluence of the Licking, the surveyors determined to cross at the present site of

a At station of Smithsonian Institution.

Zanesville. In consideration for surveying and building the road three sections of land were granted by Congress, one of them at the crossing of the Muskingum, and here in 1799 Zane and McIntire laid out a town which they called Westbourn. A post-office called Zanesville was soon after established there, and its name was assumed by the village, that of Westbourn passing out of use. In 1804 the commissioners appointed to choose a county-seat for the new county of Muskingum selected Zanesville. In the year 1810 the legislature of Ohio, which had up to that time held its sessions in Chillicothe, voted to meet at Zanesville, but after two sessions the capital was removed to Columbus, the present seat of the state government.

The Maysville road, as it was called, brought many immigrants to Zanesville, but the extension of internal improvements to other parts of the state soon diverted immigration to other places, and the town lost much of its importance. The site has great advantages for manufacturing. Coal and iron in abundance are close at hand; the Muskingum offers good water-power, but the cheapness of coal has led to the almost exclusive use of steam for supplying motive power; clay for fire-brick and kaolin for pottery are found in the country not far distant; and limestone for use as a flux in the blast-furnaces, and sandstone for the manufacture of glass, are obtained in abundance from the neighboring hills. Few cities are so admirably situated in relation to the places from which the raw materials of their manufactures must come. The Muskingum is navigable for small steamers to a point 15 miles beyond Zanesville, and connects with the Ohio canal, through which the products of its manufactories find their way to lake Erie. The completion of railroads to Zanesville, which was incorporated as a city in 1855, led to a decided advance in its interests. The increase in population between 1860 and 1870 was small; but during the last decade it has been rapid, in spite of the business depression which has so generally prevailed.

A public water-supply was obtained in 1842, water being taken from the Muskingum and pumped to a reservoir 185 feet above the river, from which it was distributed through the town. Gas was introduced in 1848–'49. The public schools are partly maintained by a fund left by John McIntire, one of the founders, for the education of poor children. There are 22 churches and 2 charitable institutions. One daily and several weekly newspapers are published. Among the manufacturing establishments are large rolling-mills, machine-shops, glass-works, a cotton-mill and several woolen-mills, a file factory, a foundery, and other industrial enterprises.

ZANESVILLE IN 1880.

The following statistical information in regard to the present condition of the city has been obtained by the Census Office:

LOCATION.

Zanesville is situated in latitude 39° 58' north, and longitude 81° 59' west from Greenwich, on both banks of the Muskingum river, at its confluence with the Licking, 170 miles by railroad northeast from Cincinnati, 137 miles southwest from Cleveland, and 59 miles east from Columbus. The Muskingum is navigable here for small steamers.

RAILROAD COMMUNICATIONS.

Zanesville is touched by the following-named railroads:
The Central Ohio division of the Baltimore and Ohio railroad, termini Newark and Wheeling.
The Cincinnati and Muskingum Valley division of the Pittsburgh, Cincinnati, and Saint Louis railroad, termini Cincinnati and Dresden.

TRIBUTARY COUNTRY.

The city is surrounded by a thickly populated district, devoted largely to agriculture, although coal and iron mining are extensively carried on. In the immediate vicinity of the city the land is chiefly devoted to market-gardening, but farther away, stock-raising and farming on a larger scale are followed. Muskingum county is one of the largest sheep-growing counties in the state.

TOPOGRAPHY.

Zanesville is placed on almost level ground along the Muskingum and Licking rivers, shut in by hills, and its natural drainage to these rivers is excellent; there are no marshes, ponds, or lakes in the vicinity. The underlying rocks are the shales, sandstones, and limestones of the Ohio Coal Measures. Coal lies in veins under the city. The whole country was once densely wooded, but the forests have now largely been cut away. The soil along the river is a rich alluvial deposit; on the hills the disintegration of the limestone rocks has formed a fertile soil, and in some places a clayey soil is found, from which, with care, excellent crops have been raised.

CLIMATE.

The tables of temperatures published by the Smithsonian Institution show that in the forty years from 1819 to 1859 the mean annual temperature was 53.76°. The summer mean is 74.20°; the winter mean, 33.21°.

STREETS.

The total length of the streets is about 64 miles. Stone-block paving, of limestone blocks, is laid for a distance of 500 feet; broken-stone pavement, a distance of 22.7 miles, and gravel pavement, 41.7 miles. The cost of the broken-stone pavement per square yard was 36 cents, the gravel 25 cents, and the stone blocks $1 80. The sidewalks are of brick, with 5-inch limestone curbings; and the street-gutters are paved with limestone. The work of paving and curbing the streets is done by contract, repairing by day-labor. The annual cost of repairs could not be ascertained. Neither a steam stone-crusher nor roller is in use on the streets.

The total length of the horse-railroad tracks is 4½ miles. There are 11 cars in use, and 55 horses and mules; 15 men are employed, and during the past year about 255,000 passengers were carried, at fares of 5 cents. There are no regular omnibus lines.

WATER-WORKS.

The water-works are owned by the city, and have cost in all $600,000. The water is pumped from the Muskingum to 2 reservoirs 185 feet above the river. These reservoirs are each about 100 by 200 feet in dimensions, and are built of brick and stone. The pumps are of Worthington make, and have a capacity of 2,000,000 and 3,000,000 gallons. To supply the higher portions of the city a Knowles pump is used, pumping into a stand-pipe 75 feet high. There are 33.81 miles of cast-iron pipe, varying from 30 to 2 inches in diameter. The average number of gallons pumped daily is 2,282,131; the daily consumption is 1,947,000 gallons. The cost of raising 1,000,000 gallons 1 foot high is 10 cents. The yearly cost of maintenance, aside from the cost of pumping, is $2,000; the yearly income from water rates is $24,000. A few Worthington and Crown meters are in use, and effect quite a saving of water.

GAS.

The gas-works are owned by private persons, and produce on the average 56,000 cubic feet a day. The charge per 1,000 feet is $2. The city has 391 gas street-lamps, for each of which it pays $23 a year.

PUBLIC BUILDINGS.

The city owns a market-house, in the second story of which are the city offices; several hose-houses, and a station-house.

PUBLIC PARKS AND PLEASURE-GROUNDS.

No information in regard to the parks of the city was furnished.

PLACES OF AMUSEMENT.

Schultz & Co.'s opera-house and Black's music-hall, the former seating 1,200, the latter 800, are the only theaters in Zanesville. They pay a license of $50 and $25, respectively, per annum, or $5 for each entertainment. There are 3 halls used for concerts and lectures. Two beer-gardens have been built just outside the city limits.

DRAINAGE.

No information on this subject was furnished.

CEMETERIES.

Four cemeteries are connected with the city:

The *City Cemetery*, bordering on the eastern side of the city, contains about 100 acres.

The *Irish Catholic Cemetery*, also on the east side of Zanesville, contains 25 acres.

The *German Catholic Cemetery*, near the two others, has an area of 10 acres.

The *Woodlawn Cemetery*, situated at the western extremity of the city, has an area of 58 acres.

No record of the number of interments within these cemeteries has been kept. McIntire burying-ground and Putnam burying-ground, the former in the eastern, the latter in the western part of the city, contain about 1 acre each, but are now disused and closed, no burials within them being permitted.

MARKETS; SANITARY AUTHORITY.

No information on these subjects was furnished.

MUNICIPAL CLEANSING.

Street-cleaning.—The streets are cleaned both by the householders and by the city scavengers. The work is done without the aid of machines, and about twice a month. The cost to the city is about $1,500 a year. The sweepings are deposited on the river-bank.

Removal of garbage and ashes.—The householders dispose of their garbage and ashes as best they can. When garbage is taken away it is generally dumped on the river-bank and carried away by any rise in the waters. Ashes are used on newly made streets and walks. No estimate of the cost of removal can be made. No regulations govern the conservation and removal of garbage, but apparently no nuisances or injuries to the public health result.

Dead animals.—The carcasses of large animals are removed by the teams of a glue manufacturer, who uses them in his industry; about 50 are removed annually.

Liquid household wastes.—Nearly all the liquid household wastes run into the public sewers, very little going into the street-gutters, while cesspools are almost entirely abandoned. Such as exist are porous and without overflows; no regulations govern their construction and cleansing.

Human excreta.—Two-thirds of the houses of the city depend upon privy-vaults, the rest upon water-closets, all of which deliver into the public sewers. There are no regulations in regard to the construction and emptying of privy-vaults. Night-soil is removed beyond the city limits, but no regulations govern its ultimate disposal.

POLICE.

The police force is appointed and governed by the mayor, the appointment being subject to confirmation by the city council. The chief executive officer is the marshal, whose salary is $600 a year and fees. The rest of the force consists of 9 men, each of whom receives a salary of $50 per month. The uniform is of blue cloth, with brass buttons, each man supplying his own, at a cost of about $35. The men are armed with a billy and a revolver, and are on duty at night from 6 p. m. to 6 a. m. Between 400 and 500 arrests were made during the past year, drunkenness being the principal cause. No record of the amount of property reported to the police as lost or stolen has been kept, nor of the number of station-house lodgers. The force is not expected to co-operate with the fire or other departments of the city government. Special police can be appointed by the mayor when necessary. The annual cost of the department is about $10,000.

INDIANA.

EVANSVILLE,

VANDERBURGH COUNTY, INDIANA.

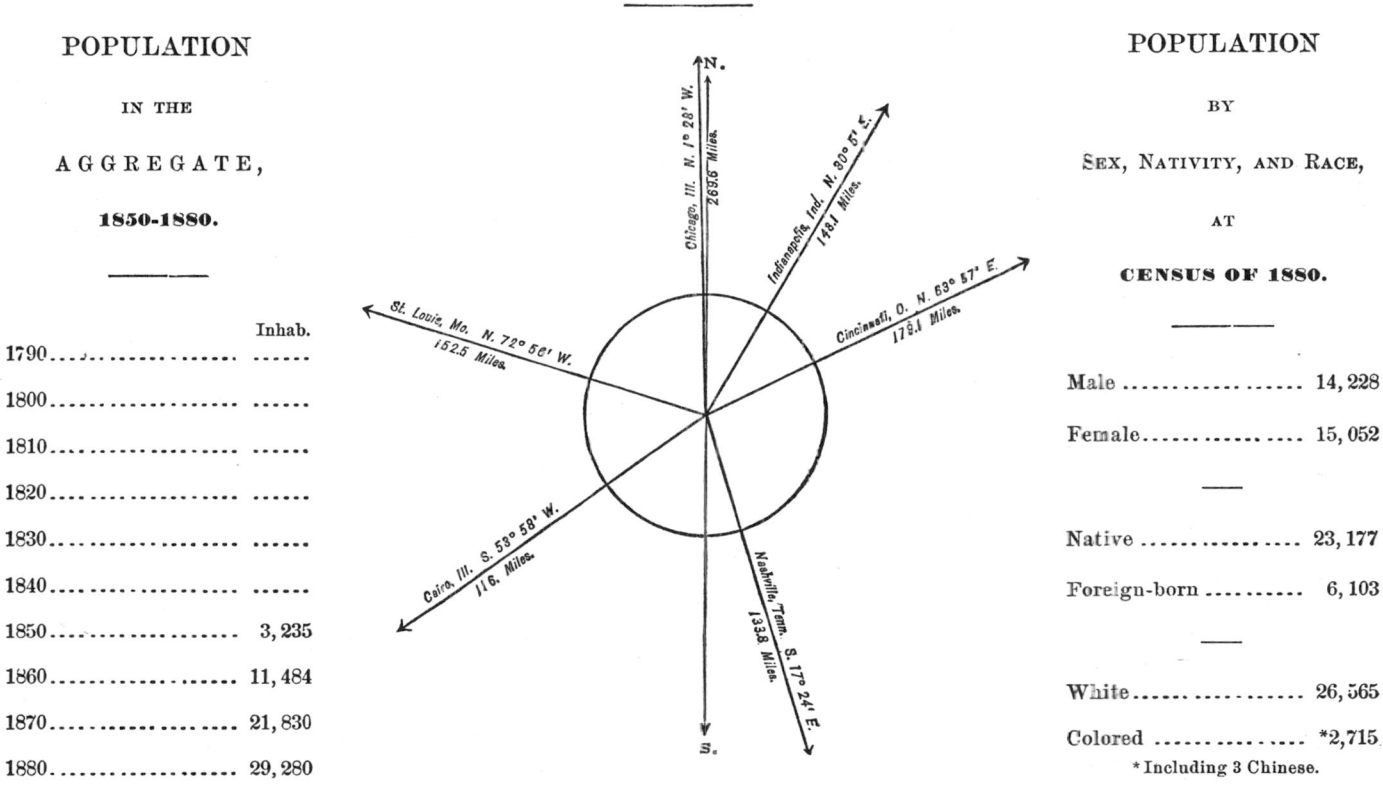

POPULATION IN THE AGGREGATE, 1850-1880.	
	Inhab.
1790	......
1800	......
1810	......
1820	......
1830	......
1840	......
1850	3,235
1860	11,484
1870	21,830
1880	29,280

POPULATION BY SEX, NATIVITY, AND RACE, AT CENSUS OF 1880.	
Male	14,228
Female	15,052
Native	23,177
Foreign-born	6,103
White	26,565
Colored	*2,715

* Including 3 Chinese.

Latitude: 38° North; Longitude: 87° 30′ (west from Greenwich); **Average altitude: 370 feet.**

FINANCIAL CONDITION:

Total Valuation: $17,307,725; per capita: $591 00.   Net Indebtedness: $1,984,000; per capita: $67 76.   Tax per $100: $3 22.

HISTORICAL SKETCH.(a)

Several years prior to the erection of the county of Warrick (1813), Colonel Hugh McGary emigrated from Kentucky and settled upon a part of the fractional section 30, township 6 south, range 10 west of the second principal meridian, where he built a rude log cabin, and in the month of June, 1814, laid out the first plan of the town of Evansville. He donated a tract of land to the new county of Warrick upon condition that Evansville should be

---

a The following is taken from a sketch of the history of Evansville furnished by the mayor, Hon. John J. Kleiner.

made the seat of justice. The donation was accepted. But the creation of the counties of Posey and Perry from the territory of Warrick so changed its shape that Evansville was left in the extreme southwestern corner, and the legislature accordingly ordered the removal of the county-seat to Darlington, 12 miles northeast of Evansville, and appointed an agent to reconvey to Colonel McGary the land he had deeded for county purposes. About this time he made a conveyance of part of his real estate to James W. Jones and General Robert M. Evans, and he then abandoned the original plan of Evansville (which had up to this time been known as McGaryton, or McGary's Landing), and made a new survey and plan of the town, which was officially recorded in the spring of 1817. The town so laid out fronted 2,160 feet on the Ohio river, and ran back from it 1,126 feet, so that it included about 56 acres, and was the original plan of the present Evansville, which has been formed by successive additions.

In 1818, about two years after the admission of Indiana as a state of the Union, the general assembly passed an act creating the counties of Vanderburgh and Spencer from the territory of Warrick, and appointed a commission to locate the seat of justice for the new county of Vanderburgh. The commissioners met at the house of Colonel McGary, in Evansville, where they received a communication from the proprietors of the town-site, offering to deed 100 acres of land in the center of their town, about the spot reserved on the plan for a public square, to the county for the erection of county buildings, and, on behalf of John Gwathmey, of Louisville, to give the sum of $500 toward the cost of these buildings, if Evansville should be chosen as the county-seat. This offer was accepted by the commissioners, and, on their recommendation, the seat of justice of Vanderburgh county was formally established at Evansville.

The organization of a town government took place March 20, 1819, Colonel McGary being chosen president of the board of trustees. At this time the village contained a hotel or tavern and a store, and had about 100 inhabitants. The taxes assessed that year were $191 28, a larger sum than the average annual assessment of the succeeding years until 1835, when they reached the sum of $417 67. The town government continued until 1846, by which time the valuation of real estate had become $547,476, and of personal estate $270,595, while the tax-levy was $3,386 89. A city charter was granted to Evansville by the legislature January 27, 1847, and was drafted by James Jones, esq., a son of one of the original proprietors. This charter, though frequently amended, has been retained to the present time. The first election under it took place on the first Monday of April, 1847, and the city government went into operation on the 12th of April following. By this charter the city officers consist of a mayor and common council, a clerk, marshal, recorder or city police judge, treasurer, and scavenger, all elected by the people, the mayor and recorder for a term of three years, the members of the common council, two for each ward for a term of two years, one from each ward going out each year, and the others for a term of one year. The common council has almost absolute control of the city's affairs; by a simple order entered on the minutes of the clerk, money can be voted for almost any purpose and direction given for the execution of many kinds of public works. The mayor has no veto, and, although presiding at the meetings of the council, has a vote only in case of a tie. The council is divided into seventeen committees, which have large discretionary powers in regard to the subjects under their control, and can decide finally many questions referred to them without making any report to the council as a whole. The various administrative officers, with the exception of the auditor, who is appointed by the mayor and confirmed by the council, are elected by the latter body. The mayor receives a salary fixed by the council (at present $2,500), and is the executive head of the city government.

This charter also granted liberal powers regarding schools, so that the free-school movement, which took form here in 1853, has grown without the interruption caused generally in Indiana, first, by a decision of the supreme court in the fall of 1854 declaring unconstitutional the 130th section of the general school law, which authorized local taxation for the support of free schools; (a) and, secondly, by a supreme court decision, promulgated in January, 1858, declaring unconstitutional the first section of an act of 1855 for supporting, by local taxation, free schools in incorporated cities and towns. (a)

The schools are noted for their efficiency and for the neatness of the property occupied.

The streets of the city are numbered on what is known as "the decimal plan"; starting at a fixed point with the number 1, the houses are numbered in regular order, odd on one side, even on the other, until a cross-street is reached; beginning again with 100, the numbers follow regularly until a second cross-street is met; the numbers then begin with 200; and so on, each cross-street beginning the appropriate hundred. Gas is supplied to the citizens for private consumption and to the city for street purposes by a private corporation, which was originally chartered for fifty years. Whenever the property-holders upon a particular street wish gas-mains extended through it they subscribe the cost of laying the mains, and the company is then compelled by its charter to lay them. The price is regulated by a special contract between the city and the gas company, and is now $2 for 1,000 feet for both public and private consumption. A very extensive system of sewerage has been constructed, and the drainage of the city is excellent.

At the time the charter was granted, the city included in all about 280 acres. In 1837 John Law, William H. Law, James B. MacColl, and Louis H. Scott, owners of a considerable tract of land in the immediate vicinity of Evansville, laid out a new town upon it, which they called "Lamasco". The name was formed by taking the first

---

a Report of the Superintendent of Public Instruction of Indiana, 1878, pp. 344, 345.

two letters of Law, the first two of MacColl, and the first three of Scott, and combining them in La-ma-sco. Their town included about 735 acres, and improved rapidly, so that about the time Evansville was made a city Lamasco was made a town. The two municipalities continued separate until March 2, 1857. Since their union it has been the policy of the city to annex all suburban property as fast as the owners see fit to lay it out in streets and blocks. By an amendment of the city charter the common council can, by means of an application of the board of commissioners of Vanderburgh county, add to the corporate limits territory which has not been subdivided for town purposes. This method is occasionally resorted to when the streets or sewers have to be extended through parcels of ground not plotted into town lots.

Evansville has been particularly fortunate in escaping the ravages of destructive fires. While damage has occasionally been done by the burning of valuable property, fires have not been frequent or of great extent. A fire in 1843 destroyed a whole block in the center of the city. Another fire in 1845 destroyed the adjoining block. A short time afterward two volunteer fire-companies were organized, and small hand-engines were purchased. Cisterns were excavated in appropriate parts of the city to furnish a supply of water in case of a fire; and in process of time additional companies were organized until five were in operation. In the summer of 1859 the first steam fire-engine was purchased. The introduction of steamers led the volunteer companies to disband; the hand-engines were sold, and two steamers were purchased to take their places.

In 1871 a contract with the Holly company was made, and in 1872 the water-works were completed and accepted. Additional machinery has since been found necessary to supply the demand for purposes of domestic use and in case of fire, but the system has proved a success. The use of steam fire-engines has been abandoned, and well-regulated hose-companies, with fire-hydrants placed at convenient distances throughout the city, have furnished ample protection against fire during the last eight years.

While the trade and commerce of Evansville have been subject to the same vicissitudes that have attended the business of the whole country during seasons of financial depression, her business interests on the whole have prospered. The financial disturbances of 1857, and the business panic of 1873, for a time retarded the business of her tradesmen and manufacturers, but they have recovered with remarkable alacrity, and are now in an unusually flourishing condition. Perhaps the severest blow to the commerce of the city was the civil war in 1861. Located on the border of the insurrectionary states, and chiefly dependent upon the South for customers, the suspension of business relations had the effect, in a great measure, of closing the doors of her merchants and putting out the fires in the furnaces of her manufactories. The resumption of amicable relations with the South has been productive of a healthy revival of southern trade, which is now far in excess of any former business period.

The early settlers were chiefly of southern birth, most of them coming from Kentucky; but between 1840 and 1850 occurred a large immigration of foreigners, Germans predominating.

EVANSVILLE IN 1880.

The following statistical accounts, collected by the Census Office, indicate the present condition of Evansville:

LOCATION.

Evansville is situated in latitude 38° north, longitude 87° 30′ west from Greenwich, on the right bank of the Ohio river, 8 miles below the mouth of Green river, 185 miles below Louisville and 192 miles above Cairo. The mean altitude of the city above the sea-level is 370 feet. It is located upon an almost level plain, the variation in level between the highest and the lowest point not exceeding 17 feet. The Ohio river at this point is open for navigation at all periods of the year. During the lowest stages the water at Evansville is 2.5 feet deep, during the highest 46.7 feet. Extreme low water is reached almost every year; but extreme high water only at intervals of several years, the ordinary high-water mark being 7 or 8 feet below the highest. The current at low water is about 2 miles per hour; at high water it is 4 miles per hour, and in some places even more. Water communication is at all times open to all points on the Ohio and Mississippi rivers; also with all points on Green river (in Kentucky) as far as Bowling Green, 225 miles; on the Tennessee river as far as Eastport, Mississippi; on the Cumberland river as far as Nashville, Tennessee; and, for about ten months, on the Wabash, during the winter and spring months as far as a point 150 miles from its confluence with the Ohio.

RAILROAD COMMUNICATIONS.

The Evansville and Terre Haute railroad connects these two cities, distant 109 miles.

The Lake Erie, Evansville, and Southwestern railroad connects Evansville with Boonville, Indiana, 17 miles distant.

The Louisville and Nashville railroad, through its two links, the Saint Louis and Southeastern and the Evansville, Henderson, and Nashville, which meet at Evansville, connects it with Saint Louis, Missouri, 161 miles away, and with Nashville, Tennessee, 155 miles distant.

TRIBUTARY COUNTRY.

The tributary country is devoted to raising wheat, corn, grass, and live stock, for all of which Evansville is the distributing point.

TOPOGRAPHY.

The city is on a level plain along the Ohio river, while on the east, west, and north it is shut in by a range of hills about 115 feet above the city level, which extends completely around the city within a radius of 2 miles. The soil is a moderately productive alluvion, overlying strata of yellow clay, fine sand, sandstone, shale, and coal deposits. The surrounding hills are filled with gray limestone. The drainage by means of small streams and rivulets running to the Ohio river is good. There are no marshes. Within a radius of 5 miles the country was originally heavily wooded with several varieties of oak, and of hickory, walnut, poplar, and ash timber, but the forests have for the most part been cleared away, and the land is cultivated.

CLIMATE.

The highest recorded summer temperature is 110°, the highest in average years being 95°. The winters are cold, a temperature of 22° below zero having been recorded, while in average years the thermometer touches —20°. The adjacent waters are not thought to influence either the health or the climate of the city. There are no winds that can be said to prevail.

STREETS.

The total length of the streets is 100 miles 870 feet. Of these, 15,120 feet are paved with cobble-stones (bowlders), and 32,400 feet with gravel; the rest are unpaved. The cost per square yard of the bowlder pavement averages $2 94; of the gravel, $1 32. The cost of repairing the former per year is 2½ cents; of repairing the latter, one-half cent. The gravel streets are generally preferred. The sidewalks are of brick; the gutters are made of limestone laid in courses, or of hard-burned brick laid edgewise. Shade-trees are planted along the streets just inside the curb-stones. Repairing is done under the direction of the street commissioners, there being one for each of the two districts, who keep a force of from 10 to 15 men at work constantly, at wages of from $1 25 to $1 50 per day. The construction of streets has been done largely by contract work, but it has been found more expensive than construction by day labor, under the supervision of the city officers. There is no stone-crusher or road-roller in use.

There are 6 miles of horse-railroad tracks. The roads make use of 12 cars, and 50 horses and mules. They employ 22 men, and during the past year carried 400,000 passengers. The fare is 5 cents. Two omnibuses and 2 baggage-wagons ply between the depots, landings, and hotels. They use 8 horses, employ 7 men, and carried 14,925 passengers during the past year. The fare is 25 cents, with an additional 25 cents for baggage.

WATER-WORKS.

The works for the public water-supply are owned by the city, and have cost in all $500,000. They are arranged on the Holly system, and give a pressure of 30.4 pounds per square inch. The average amount pumped per diem is 3,000,000 gallons. The yearly cost of maintenance, including the cost of pumping, is $12,925; the yearly income from water-rates is $18,900. No water-meters are in use.

GAS.

The works for the gas supply of Evansville are the property of a private company, and the city authorities were unable to obtain any detailed information in regard to the daily average production, income, etc.

PUBLIC BUILDINGS.

The buildings owned by the city and used for municipal purposes are valued at $5,000. The city hall cost $3,500.

PUBLIC PARKS AND PLEASURE-GROUNDS.

The total area of the public parks and pleasure-grounds is 399,000 square feet. There are 4 parks, all small; 2 have an area of 62,500 square feet each, the third has an area of 100,000 square feet, and the fourth an area of 174,000 square feet. The last is situated along the Ohio; the others are in the interior of the city. All the parks were donations from the original proprietors; the largest from Hugh McGary, James W. Jones, and Robert M. Evans; the others from John Law, William H. Law, Louis H. Scott, and James MacColl. The only expense incurred in maintenance has been for setting out trees, a merely nominal sum. The parks are not laid out for carriage drives. They are under the direct control of the city council.

PLACES OF AMUSEMENT.

The places of amusement in Evansville are Evans hall, seating capacity, 2,200; Opera-house, 1,266; Apollo theater, 1,150; Turner hall, 600; and Cahn's vaudeville theater, 100. Evans hall is a fine brick edifice with a large auditorium and a single capacious gallery; it is used mainly for lectures, public meetings, and conventions, and was erected in 1879 by the friends of temperance. It is provided with four separate committee rooms, vestibule, kitchen, and dining-room for the accommodation of festivals, and cost $30,000. The opera-house, used for operas and the drama, was built in the usual style of theaters, by a stock company, in 1866; it has double galleries, and cost $65,000. Apollo theater, a substantial frame building, is used for vaudevilles. It is private property, and was built in 1872, and rebuilt during the present year at a cost of $5,000. Turner hall, a brick building, is used for the exercises of the Turnverein and for theatrical purposes; it is private property and is valued at $7,000; built built in 1876. Cahn's theater is a small building built in 1879 for the accommodation of patrons of a beer and wine hall.

Theaters pay no annual license. The city council can, if it wishes, require the payment of a license for every performance, but it has never used this power. There are two or three small summer beer-gardens whose seating capacity is 200 or 300 each; they are not of expensive construction. The Crescent City Springs is a fine property used as a summer beer-garden, for pleasure parties, picnic-grounds, etc. It embraces 16 acres of ground, with several buildings, a dwelling-house, dancing-hall, billiard and ten-pin alley room, and a fine grove with carriage drives. It is owned by a stock company and is worth $100,000. There are saline waters upon it, a well having been bored there 577 feet deep.

DRAINAGE.

Evansville has an extensive system of sewers, but no information in regard to it was furnished.

CEMETERIES.

There are 4 cemeteries—2 public and 2 private—connected with the city, all located beyond the corporation limits. *Oak Hill Cemetery*, area 60 acres, situated 1 mile east of the city limits, and *Locust Hill Cemetery*, area 75 acres, located about 1½ mile north of the city limits, are managed by boards of trustees appointed by the city council, one for each cemetery. *Rose Hill Cemetery*, area 4 acres, situated about 1 mile east of Locust Hill and about equally distant from the city, belongs to the Jewish congregation. *Saint Joseph's Cemetery*, area 72 acres, is located about 1½ mile northwest from the city limits, and is controlled by the Catholic church. There are two small parcels of ground formerly used by the Jewish and Catholic congregations, but they have now been vacated, and many of the bodies buried in them have been removed to Rose Hill and Saint Joseph's cemeteries. These were within the city limits. The number of interments within the various cemeteries is as follows: Oak Hill, 10,053, which includes about 500 who were soldiers in the civil war; Locust Hill, 2,037; Saint Joseph's, 2,034, of which 610 are removals; and Rose Hill, 75, of which 36 are removals. Lots in these cemeteries vary in price from $15 to $150; all are carefully maintained. No burial is permitted within either Oak Hill or Locust Hill cemetery until a certificate of death, showing its cause, is presented to the sexton. This must be signed by the attending physician or in his default by a member of the board of health, or by a coroner if a coroner's jury investigated the matter. If through any cause it is impossible to obtain the signature of any of these, the mayor may make out a certificate stating the facts of the case, and this will justify the sexton in making the interment.

MARKETS.

There is no market building in Evansville, but a street 120 feet wide and 600 feet long is used as a market-place and divided into 120 stands, and an area of 1,000 feet adjacent is used by farmers' and hucksters' wagons. The annual income of the city from this market space is about $2,000. The market hours are from 4 to 9 a. m. on Tuesdays, Thursdays, and Saturdays, and from 5 to 9 p. m. on Saturdays. The market is under the charge of a market-master appointed by the city council.

SANITARY AUTHORITY—BOARD OF HEALTH.

The chief sanitary authority of Evansville is a board of health, consisting of the mayor *ex officio*, and 5 physicians appointed by the city council. The term of office of the members is five years, and one retires each year. The annual expenses of the board, when there is no declared epidemic, are about $900—for the salary of the health officer $300, and the expense of maintaining a city dispensary, the city council being required by the ordinance establishing the board of health to appropriate $50 each month for this purpose. In case of an epidemic the expenses may be increased to any amount deemed necessary by the board, as no limit is set by the city ordinances. The board has authority in the absence of an epidemic to maintain a good sanitary condition of the city and to compel the removal of nuisances, while during an epidemic it may establish a quarantine or take any other measures it may deem proper to arrest the spread of disease. The board meets weekly, and the city ordinances provide that if any member is absent without good cause, in the opinion of the board, for three consecutive meetings, he shall be dismissed and another appointed. The chief executive officer is the health officer, who is appointed by the city council. He is assisted by 2 sanitary policemen, who have full police powers.

NUISANCES.

Inspections are made regularly in all parts of the city by the health officer and his assistants, and specially when requested. When a nuisance is found to exist the owner of the premises in fault is ordered to remove it; if this order is disobeyed he is prosecuted in the city courts. Defective house-drainage, privy-vaults, cesspools, and sources of drinking-water are treated in the same way as nuisances; and the same is true in case of the pollution of the streams and river if it causes a nuisance.

INFECTIOUS DISEASES.

The board has authority to prevent the introduction and spread of contagious and infectious diseases. Small-pox patients are generally removed to a small-pox hospital, situated about one-half mile beyond the city limits; but if they are allowed to remain at home they are quarantined, and the house is marked with a yellow flag. Scarlet-fever patients are isolated at home, and the children from families where the disease exists are excluded from the schools. If contagious diseases break out in the public or private schools the board of health has full authority to take any action it thinks wisest. Vaccination is compulsory only for children in the public schools; it is done at public expense only when so ordered by the board.

There is no system of registration of births; but burial certificates are preserved and form a record.

REPORTS.

The board of health reports regularly to the city council, but these reports have not been published.

MUNICIPAL CLEANSING.

Street-cleaning.—The city's force cleans the streets from time to time as their condition requires it, with moderate efficiency. No sweeping-machines are used. The annual cost to the city is $15,000.

Removal of garbage and ashes.—Garbage is removed by a contractor paid by the city, who takes it to the country and disposes of it. He receives $1,000 per annum for this service. Complaint has been made that, through infrequent removal of the garbage, injuries have resulted to the public health. Garbage must not be kept in the same vessel with ashes. The householders provide for the removal of ashes as best they may, generally using them as filling.

Dead animals.—The carcasses of animals are removed by a contractor, paid by the city, on receiving notice from the owner of the dead animal. This notice is left at any of the engine-houses of the fire department and received by the contractor, who makes a daily round. He receives $180 per annum. No account of the number of animals removed has been kept.

Liquid household wastes.—All the liquid household wastes are generally disposed of in the same way. A part goes into the public sewers, very little into the street gutters, and considerable into porous cesspools, which do not receive the wastes, however, from water-closets. The board of health controls the cleansing of cesspools.

Human excreta.—A large proportion of the houses depend on privy-vaults. Where water-closets are in use they nearly all deliver into the public sewers, none into cesspools. The ordinances of the city require that privy-vaults shall be at least 20 feet deep and walled with brick or stone 9 inches in thickness, unless they are circular in form, in which case the walls need be only 4 inches thick. Hardly any of them are water-tight. The dry-earth system is not in use. The night-soil is taken into the country and there disposed of. None is allowed to be used in manuring lands within the gathering-ground of the public water-supply.

Manufacturing wastes.—Nearly all the factories of the city connect with the public sewers and dispose of their wastes through them.

POLICE.

The police force is appointed and governed by the city council. The chief executive officer is the chief of police, who has the command of the force and general charge of it. His salary is $19.25 per week. The rest of the force consists of a first lieutenant, salary $15.75 per week; a second lieutenant, 2 sanitary policemen, 27 patrolmen, and 1 man attached to the city prison, each of whom receives $14 per week. The city contracts for uniforms for the whole force, and retains the cost from the policemen's salaries. The men are armed with revolver, mace, and police whistle, and each man carries a fire-alarm box key. They are on duty 9 and 10 hours alternately. During the past year 856 arrests were made, the principal causes being drunkenness, disorderly conduct, vagrancy, prostitution, and associating with prostitutes. The cases are generally disposed of by fines, and in default of payment the offender is compelled to break stone for macadamizing purposes. No record was kept of property lost or stolen and reported to the police, or of the amount recovered and returned. During 1880 the number of station-house lodgers accommodated was 1,146, as against 1,225 in 1879. An allowance of $172 was made to the lockup keeper to provide meals for these lodgers. The force co-operates with the fire, health, and building departments when so ordered by the chief. Special policemen are appointed by the council at the request of one or more citizens; their services are chiefly for the protection of private property and as watchmen for individuals. They are not paid by the city, and while they have the same powers as members of the regular police force, they are entirely distinct from that force. The total cost of the department in 1880 was $17,493.

MANUFACTURES.

The following is a summary of the statistics of the manufactures of Evansville for 1880, being taken from tables prepared for the Tenth Census by Charles H. McCarer, special agent:

Mechanical and manufacturing industries.	No. of establishments.	Capital.	AVERAGE NUMBER OF HANDS EMPLOYED.			Total amount paid in wages during the year.	Value of materials.	Value of products.
			Males above 16 years.	Females above 15 years.	Children and youths.			
All industries...........	313	$4,733,815	2,945	337	387	$1,365,006	$4,972,690	$8,091,914
Agricultural implements	5	266,414	111	....	7	53,516	103,481	233,929
Blacksmithing (see also Wheelwrighting)	18	17,250	27	....	....	8,501	9,960	32,130
Boots and shoes, including custom work and repairing.............	35	26,050	72	11	2	37,314	61,331	137,260
Bread and other bakery products	16	30,300	26	1	6	10,107	58,056	86,731
Brick and tile.............	4	43,000	45	....	8	14,250	8,100	30,100
Brooms and brushes.............	3	7,000	21	2	5	7,670	18,900	37,000
Carpentering	5	6,850	20	....	....	8,803	10,382	25,438
Carriages and wagons (see also Wheelwrighting)	6	67,500	46	....	1	20,900	35,550	79,300
Confectionery	4	6,150	5	3	5	4,052	25,850	33,680
Cooperage	12	102,500	167	....	7	69,421	76,150	198,310
Flouring- and grist-mill products	12	337,800	91	....	....	48,342	1,167,400	1,348,215
Foundery and machine-shop products	12	823,253	330	....	8	166,440	349,418	734,458
Furniture (see also Mattresses and spring beds).............	5	303,000	292	1	99	151,714	223,609	467,000
Furniture, chairs.............	4	119,200	117	24	42	46,120	38,952	113,496
Leather, curried.............	4	82,001	23	....	....	13,344	170,455	214,950
Leather, tanned.............	4	63,999	28	....	....	11,965	137,622	168,000
Lumber, planed.............	5	104,521	127	....	3	60,774	190,520	338,178
Lumber, sawed.............	10	580,350	376	....	25	134,048	633,050	958,405
Marble and stone work.............	7	35,827	85	....	4	27,317	35,803	82,573
Mattresses and spring beds (see also Furniture).............	3	13,000	8	5	....	3,000	5,550	14,300
Painting and paperhanging.............	11	6,300	34	....	....	13,443	14,450	46,400
Patent medicines and compounds.............	3	11,500	3	1	1	1,700	11,500	25,000
Printing and publishing.............	6	125,500	127	5	21	75,290	32,901	146,735
Saddlery and harness.............	17	134,400	122	....	13	55,028	178,400	287,260
Shipbuilding.............	8	16,650	28	....	....	15,770	40,070	60,955
Slaughtering and meat-packing, not including retail butchering.....	4	199,000	75	....	....	11,600	324,623	346,278
Stone- and earthen-ware.............	3	13,300	14	....	1	5,800	2,850	14,000
Tinware, copperware, and sheet-iron ware.............	16	120,550	123	....	13	62,224	105,766	254,131
Tobacco, cigars and cigarettes.............	16	26,400	60	....	9	24,253	29,462	79,043
Wheelwrighting (see also Blacksmithing; Carriages and wagons)...	11	15,150	14	....	2	4,948	5,450	17,700
All other industries (a)	44	1,029,100	343	284	103	197,352	867,079	1,480,959

a Embracing bags, other than paper; baking and yeast powders; bookbinding and blank-book making; boxes, cigar; brass castings; clothing, men's; coffins, burial cases, and undertakers' goods; cotton goods; drain and sewer pipe; files; hats and caps; iron and steel; liquors, malt; liquors, vinous; lock- and gun-smithing; malt; mantels, slate, marble, and marbleized; mineral and soda waters; mixed textiles; models and patterns; musical instruments, organs and materials; paper; plumbing and gasfitting, pumps; safes, doors, and vaults, fire-proof; shirts; stencils and brands; tobacco, chewing, smoking, and snuff; trunks and valises; umbrellas and canes; vinegar; watch and clock repairing; wooden ware; and woolen goods.

From the foregoing table it appears that the average capital of all establishments is $15,124 01; that the average wages of all hands employed is $372 04 per annum; and that the average outlay in wages, in materials, and in interest (at 6 per cent.) on capital employed is $21,155 67.

FORT WAYNE,

ALLEN COUNTY, INDIANA.

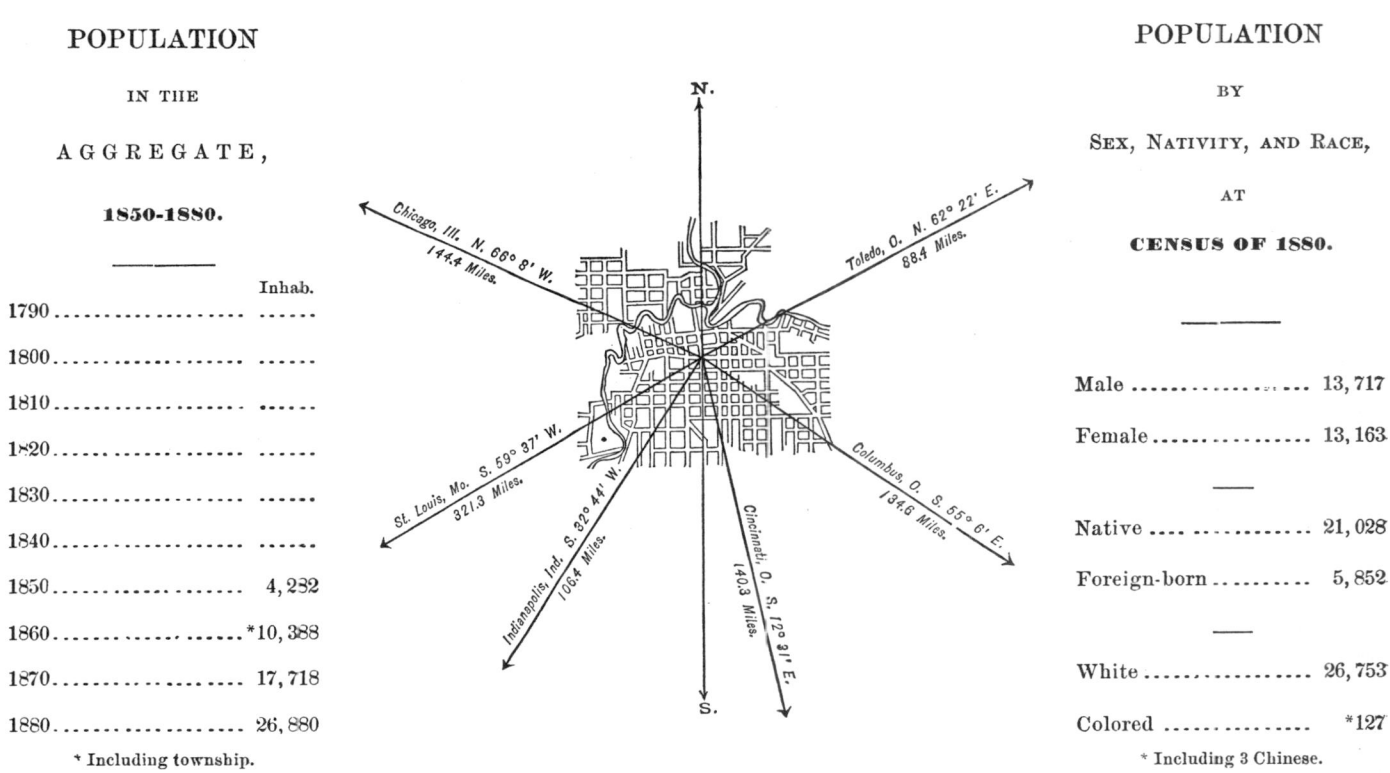

POPULATION

IN THE

AGGREGATE,

1850-1880.

	Inhab.
1790	......
1800	......
1810	......
1820	......
1830	......
1840	......
1850	4,232
1860	*10,388
1870	17,718
1880	26,880

* Including township.

POPULATION

BY

SEX, NATIVITY, AND RACE,

AT

CENSUS OF 1880.

Male	13,717
Female	13,163
Native	21,028
Foreign-born	5,852
White	26,753
Colored	*127

* Including 3 Chinese.

Latitude: 41° 5' North; Longitude: 85° 4' (west from Greenwich).

FINANCIAL CONDITION:

Total Valuation: $13,450,075; per capita: $500 00.   Net Indebtedness: $856,900; per capita: $31 88.   Tax per $100 00: $2 58.

HISTORICAL SKETCH.

The Indian village of Twightwee once stood where now stands the city of Fort Wayne; but in 1794 General Wayne, during his expedition against the Maumee Indians, ordered a fort to be built on the spot, and a garrison was stationed there until 1819. It was natural that settlers should cluster about the fort, and, in time, the settlement became a flourishing town. The country about it was fertile, several plank-roads led from it to various places in Ohio and Indiana, and the Wabash and Erie canal, which passed through it, added greatly to its importance. In 1840 it was made a city, and in 1850 was a place of 4,282 inhabitants. Shortly afterward the construction of railways through the city gave it an impetus which led to a rapid advance in population and importance. In ten years the population had doubled, in twenty had quadrupled, while the Census of 1880 shows that Fort Wayne is six times as large as it was in 1850. Here are located the great workshops of the Pittsburgh, Fort Wayne, and Chicago and the Wabash railroads. There are many churches. The schools of Fort Wayne began

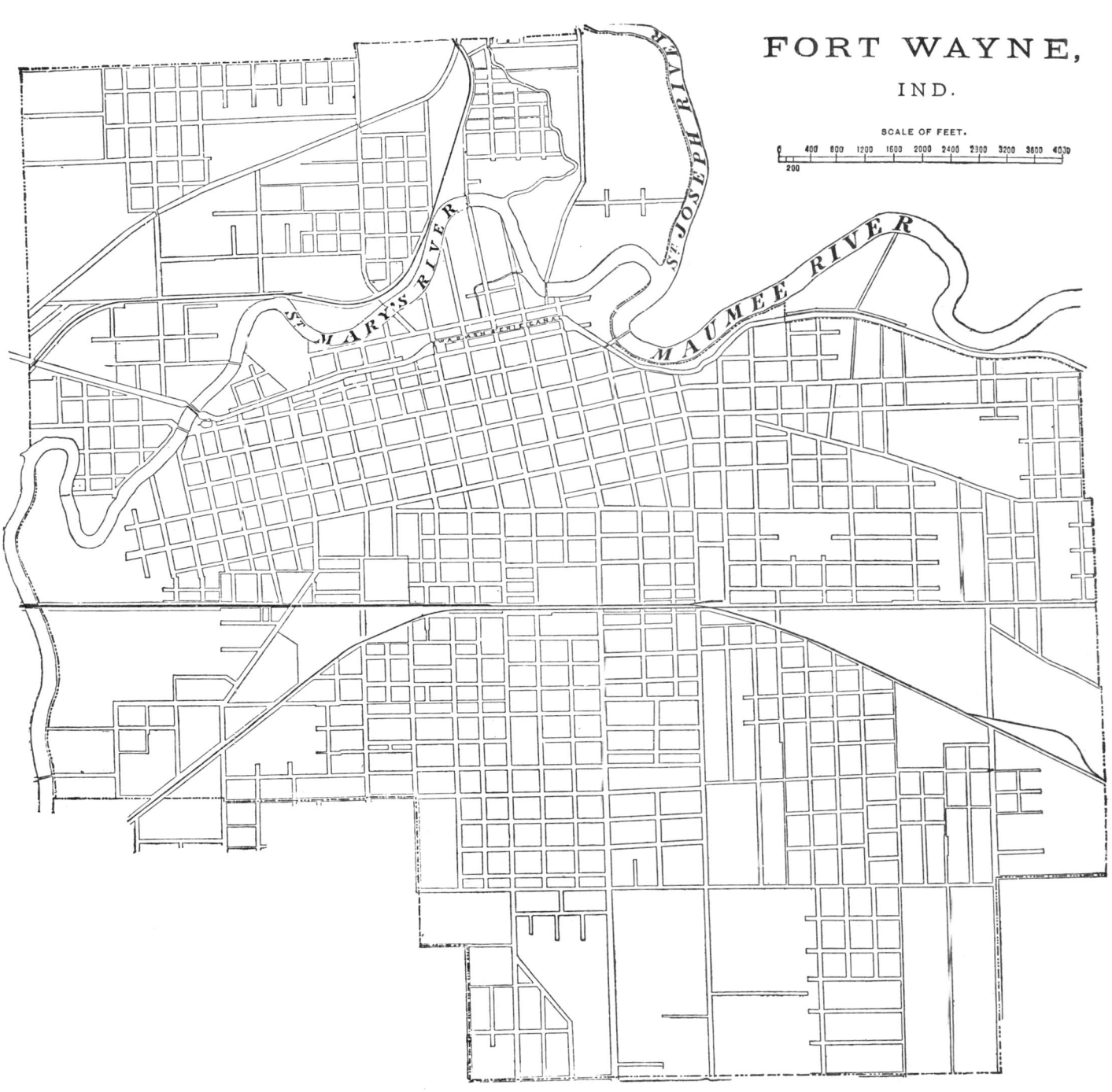

FORT WAYNE,

IND.

SCALE OF FEET.

St. MARY'S RIVER

St. JOSEPH RIVER

MAUMEE RIVER

WABASH ERIE CANAL

in 1852, with little available means, but had secured a good standing when an adverse decision of the supreme court checked them. From the reorganization, in 1873, the schools have had a good repute. In 1878 the board dropped the name of high school, not intending, however, to lower the standard of their work. The streets are lighted with gas, and the principal ones are traversed by horse-cars; while the houses are supplied with water from public water-works. The city's trade is large, extending over Michigan, northern Ohio, and northern Indiana. A few years ago there were nearly 150 manufacturing establishments and 1,600 stores. Few cities of Indiana surpass Fort Wayne in importance, and only Indianapolis and Evansville exceed it in population.

FORT WAYNE IN 1880.

The following statistical accounts, collected by the Census Office, indicate the present condition of Fort Wayne:

LOCATION.

Fort Wayne is located in latitude 41° 5' north, longitude 85° 4' west from Greenwich, at the point where the Saint Joseph's and Saint Mary's rivers join to form the Maumee, about 145 miles in a direct line east-southeast from Chicago, 115 miles northeast from La Fayette, and 106 miles east-northeast from Indianapolis. The Maumee is not navigable at this point, the only means of water communication being the Wabash and Erie canal, which extends from Toledo, on lake Erie, to Evansville, on the Ohio river.

RAILROAD COMMUNICATIONS.

The city is an important railroad center, and is touched by the following-named railroads:

The Pittsburgh, Fort Wayne, and Chicago railroad connects Fort Wayne with Chicago, 148 miles, and Pittsburgh, 320 miles distant.

The Fort Wayne and Jackson railroad connects it with Jackson, Michigan, 100 miles distant.

The Grand Rapids and Indiana railroad, which operates the Cincinnati, Richmond, and Fort Wayne railroad also, connects it with Richmond, Indiana, 92 miles, and Petoskey, Michigan, 332 miles distant.

The Fort Wayne, Muncie, and Cincinnati railroad connects it with Connersville, Indiana, 108 miles distant, there connecting with the Cincinnati, Hamilton, and Indianapolis railroad for Cincinnati.

The Wabash, Saint Louis, and Pacific railroad connects the city with its numerous terminal points—with Toledo, 94 miles; with Saint Louis, 342 miles; with Quincy, Illinois, 360 miles; with Burlington, Iowa, 366 miles; and with the other cities touched by the members of this vast railroad system.

TRIBUTARY COUNTRY.

The country in the vicinity of Fort Wayne is devoted chiefly to agriculture.

TOPOGRAPHY; CLIMATE.

No information on these subjects was furnished.

STREETS.

The city has in all about 82 miles of streets, 1 mile of which is paved with broken stone, 6 miles with wood, and 12 miles with gravel. The cost of paving per square yard has varied from 80 cents to $1. No separate account is kept of the cost of repairs. In the central parts of the city the sidewalks are of brick and flagstone, but in the less thickly settled sections they are of wood. The street gutters are of wood on streets paved with wood; elsewhere they are of cobble-stone. It is customary to have a grass plot about 4 feet wide between the curbstones and the walks, and in this space trees have been quite generally planted by the property-holders. New streets are generally built by contract labor, while repairing is done by day laborers under the supervision of the street commissioners. Neither a steam stone-crusher nor a steam road-roller is in use.

There are 7 miles of horse-railroad tracks in the city. Ten cars and 32 horses are in use, 21 men employed, and during the year 1880, 420,000 passengers were carried. The fare is 5 cents. Omnibuses ply between the hotels, railroad stations, etc. There are 16 vehicles, using 30 horses and furnishing employment to 16 men. The fare is 25 cents, and during the past year 42,000 persons made use of these vehicles.

WATER-WORKS.

The total cost of the public water-works has been thus far $300,000; the works are owned by the city. At present water is pumped directly into the pipes, yielding a pressure of 50 pounds to the square inch; but when the reservoir which is now building is completed, the distribution through the pipes will be by gravity, pumps being used only in keeping the reservoir full, and the pressure is expected to be 40 pounds to the square inch. The engines are of Holly manufacture, and pump from 575,000 to 1,000,000 gallons daily, the consumption increasing steadily. The yearly cost of maintenance, aside from the cost of pumping, is $3,500; and the yearly income $6,500. A few Worthington and Crown water-meters are in use, but sufficient time has not yet elapsed to show whether or not they effect a saving.

GAS.

The gas-works are the property of a private corporation. They produce 40,000 cubic feet of gas daily, for which $2 50 per 1,000 feet is charged. The city pays $27 50 per annum for each of its 245 gas street-lamps.

PUBLIC BUILDINGS.

The public buildings owned by the city and used for municipal purposes are valued at $55,000, and include a city hall, which cost about $20,000, a market-house, the houses of the fire department, and the city prison.

PUBLIC PARKS AND PLEASURE-GROUNDS.

There are no public parks or pleasure-grounds in the city.

PLACES OF AMUSEMENT.

The Academy of Music, seating 1,200, is the only theater in Fort Wayne. It pays an annual license of $100 to the city. There are 2 halls used for lectures and concerts, and 4 concert- and beer-gardens, each seating from 300 to 500.

DRAINAGE.

No information on this subject was furnished.

CEMETERIES.

There are 4 cemeteries connected with the city: 1 Lutheran, 1 Catholic, and 1 Jewish, and *Lindenwood Cemetery*. The first three are small, and no information could be obtained in regard to them. Lindenwood cemetery is located on Huntington road, one-half mile west of the city limits, and contains 170 acres. It was opened in 1860, since which time there have been 2,880 interments within its limits. It is finely laid out and carefully kept. Previous to its opening a small burial-ground, not far from the city limits as they existed prior to 1850, had been in use; but it was becoming rapidly filled up, and the city was extending around and beyond it, so that it was finally abandoned, and the bodies it contained were removed, mostly to Lindenwood cemetery.

MARKETS.

The market-house of Fort Wayne is located on Barr street, between Berry and Washington streets, and cost $12,000. It contains 12 stalls, 4 of which rent at $25 per year, the others at $35 per year. A space about the market building is reserved for farmers' and hucksters' wagons. From May 1 to November 1 the market is open from 4 a. m. to 10 a. m.; the days of the week on which it is open are not stated. The amount of business done in the market is very small compared with that done by private stores. No wholesale dealing is carried on there.

SANITARY AUTHORITY—BOARD OF HEALTH.

A board of health, consisting of 3 members, all physicians, is appointed by the city council, upon which the board relies for its authority. Each member receives a salary of $75 per year. The expenses of the board in the absence of an epidemic are very small; no epidemic has occurred to test its powers as to increasing its expenses. It has authority to abate nuisances and to command any police officer or councilman to assist in abating them. The city ordinances give it authority to order the street commissioners to remove nuisances, but it has been found difficult to enforce this. The board meets regularly twice a year, oftener if the public health demands it. The only assistants employed are the police officers, who are commanded to serve notices.

NUISANCES.

Inspections are made only when nuisances are reported. When a nuisance is found to exist an order issued by the board directing the removal of the nuisance is served by a policeman on the owner or occupant of the premises at fault. An interval of from one hour to five days is allowed within which to make the removal; if the owner refuses to obey the notice he is prosecuted. The board makes inspections of defective house-drainage and privy-vaults when requested; an inspection of drinking-water is made on complaint. It compels the cleansing of privy-vaults and cesspools when they cause nuisances or are overflowing. When defects are found in the city sewerage, the matter is referred by the city council to the committee on sewers, which investigates the trouble and has it rectified as soon as possible. When complaint is made that garbage is causing a nuisance, the board can compel its removal.

BURIAL OF THE DEAD.

The board requires that a permit, giving the name, age, nativity, condition (single, married, or widowed), and cause of death of the deceased, shall be obtained before a burial can be made.

INFECTIOUS DISEASES.

Small-pox patients are generally removed to a pest-house located about 2 miles from the city. Scarlet-fever patients are cared for at home. The board obtains no special control of the schools in case contagious diseases break out in them. Vaccination is compulsory only when specially ordered by the city council, and is not done at the public expense.

There is no system for the registration of births or diseases, deaths alone being recorded.

REPORTS.

The board reports annually to the city council, and specially when it has measures to recommend.

MUNICIPAL CLEANSING.

Street-cleaning.—The streets are cleaned by the city's force under direction of the street commissioner, and the work is done wholly by hand-labor. The paved streets are cleaned whenever they need it, at an average annual cost to the city of $600; the dirt streets are cleaned only once a year, the cleansing consisting in removing the accumulations from the gutters. Part of the cost of the latter work is met by a special tax, called the "road-labor tax". The total annual cost to the city is about $1,800. The sweepings are deposited upon Clinton street, north of the city.

Removal of garbage and ashes.—The householders remove the garbage and ashes which collect upon their premises, being compelled to remove garbage before it becomes offensive. Garbage must be kept apart from ashes; it is finally disposed of by being removed beyond the city limits, and ashes are disposed of in a similar manner.

Dead animals.—The carcasses of animals dying within the city are removed at the city's expense, about $50 being spent annually in paying for this service.

Liquid household wastes.—All the liquid household wastes are disposed of alike, nine-tenths of them passing into the public sewers. None are allowed to run into the street-gutters. About one-tenth goes into cesspools; these are porous, but do not receive the wastes from water-closets. They must be kept clean. No cases of contamination of drinking-water are known by the street commissioner to have occurred.

Human excreta.—Ten per cent. of the houses are provided with water-closets; the rest depend upon privy-vaults. About one-half of the water-closets deliver into the public sewers, the rest into privy-vaults. They must be at least 8 feet deep and walled with brick or stone. They are cleaned by the odorless-excavator process, and the night-soil is removed beyond the city limits. None is used as a fertilizer on lands within the gathering-ground of the public water-supply.

Manufacturing wastes.—Industries which produce wastes likely to be a source of nuisance or injury to the public health are not allowed within the city.

POLICE.

The police force is appointed by the city council and governed by the chief of police, who is the chief executive officer, and receives a salary of $900 and fees per year. The rest of the force consists of a lieutenant, salary $800 per year; 20 patrolmen, $730 per year each; a marshal, salary $900 per year; and 3 deputy marshals, salary $730 per year each. The uniform is a blue-cloth suit and a stiff felt hat, with shield and number; each man provides his own. The men are equipped with revolver, billy, twisters, whistle, and dark lantern; they are on duty 10 hours, patrolling the entire city. They made 1,123 arrests during the past year, chiefly for intoxication and disorderly conduct. Property to the value of $3,741 was reported to the police as lost or stolen, and of this, $1,904 was recovered and $1,836 returned to the owners. No account is kept of the number of station-house lodgers accommodated, but there are about 500 annually; free meals are not given. The force must co-operate with the fire department at all fires, and must serve the notices of the board of health. Special police are appointed by the chief of police in case of emergency, and while on duty are treated as members of the regular force. The annual cost of the department for 1880 was $19,886.

MANUFACTURES.

The following is a summary of the statistics of the manufactures of Fort Wayne, Indiana, for 1880, being taken from tables prepared for the Tenth Census by Martin A. Nolle, special agent:

Mechanical and manufacturing industries.	No. of establishments.	Capital.	AVERAGE NUMBER OF HANDS EMPLOYED.			Total amount paid in wages during the year.	Value of materials.	Value of products.
			Males above 16 years.	Females above 15 years.	Children and youths.			
All industries	114	$2,252,101	2,426	164	145	$1,020,793	$4,007,955	$5,816,924
Blacksmithing (see also Wheelwrighting)	6	8,750	10	....	....	5,540	3,850	15,800
Boots and shoes, including custom work and repairing	11	5,400	29	....	1	12,812	13,625	37,000
Bread and other bakery products	4	34,000	27	2	....	11,232	83,906	109,385
Carpentering	3	13,500	72	....	....	24,600	43,250	83,000
Carriages and wagons (see also Wheelwrighting)	4	25,000	46	....	1	18,000	27,000	56,600
Cooperage	3	10,900	12	....	4	4,980	5,950	17,000
Flouring- and grist-mill products	5	105,000	33	....	....	17,440	473,150	532,265
Foundery and machine-shop products	5	785,000	900	....	45	387,000	1,941,400	2,529,000
Furniture	5	71,000	35	....	1	17,515	33,100	70,300
Liquors, malt	3	95,000	23	....	....	10,710	46,240	85,438
Lumber, sawed	5	295,000	282	....	30	93,100	285,300	458,300
Marble and stone work	3	15,000	17	....	....	10,550	9,500	29,500
Printing and publishing	5	68,500	88	1	43	45,780	70,700	157,000
Saddlery and harness	11	29,200	38	....	....	16,725	53,400	90,500
Tinware, copperware, and sheet-iron ware	4	9,800	15	....	....	7,750	14,200	27,500
Wheelwrighting (see also Blacksmithing; Carriages and wagons)	9	16,650	35	....	1	17,700	14,750	44,700
All other industries (a)	28	764,401	764	161	19	319,359	888,634	1,473,636

a Embracing agricultural implements; bookbinding and blank-book making; brooms and brushes; carriage and wagon materials; clothing, men's; coffee and spices, roasted and ground; confectionery; files; handles, wooden; iron work, architectural and ornamental; leather, curried; leather, tanned; lumber, planed; masonry, brick and stone; oil, linseed; painting and paperhanging; patent medicines and compounds; plumbing and gasfitting; pumps; sash, doors, and blinds; shirts; trunks and valises; upholstering; and woolen goods.

From the foregoing table it appears that the average capital of all establishments is $20,632 46; that the average wages of all hands employed is $373 23 per annum; and that the average outlay in wages, in materials, and in interest (at 6 per cent.) on capital employed is $45,349 77.

INDIANAPOLIS,

MARION COUNTY, INDIANA.

POPULATION

IN THE

AGGREGATE,

1840-1880.

	Inhab.
1790	.....
1800	.....
1810	.....
1820	.....
1830	.....
1840	2,692
1850	8,091
1860	18,611
1870	48,244
1880	75,056

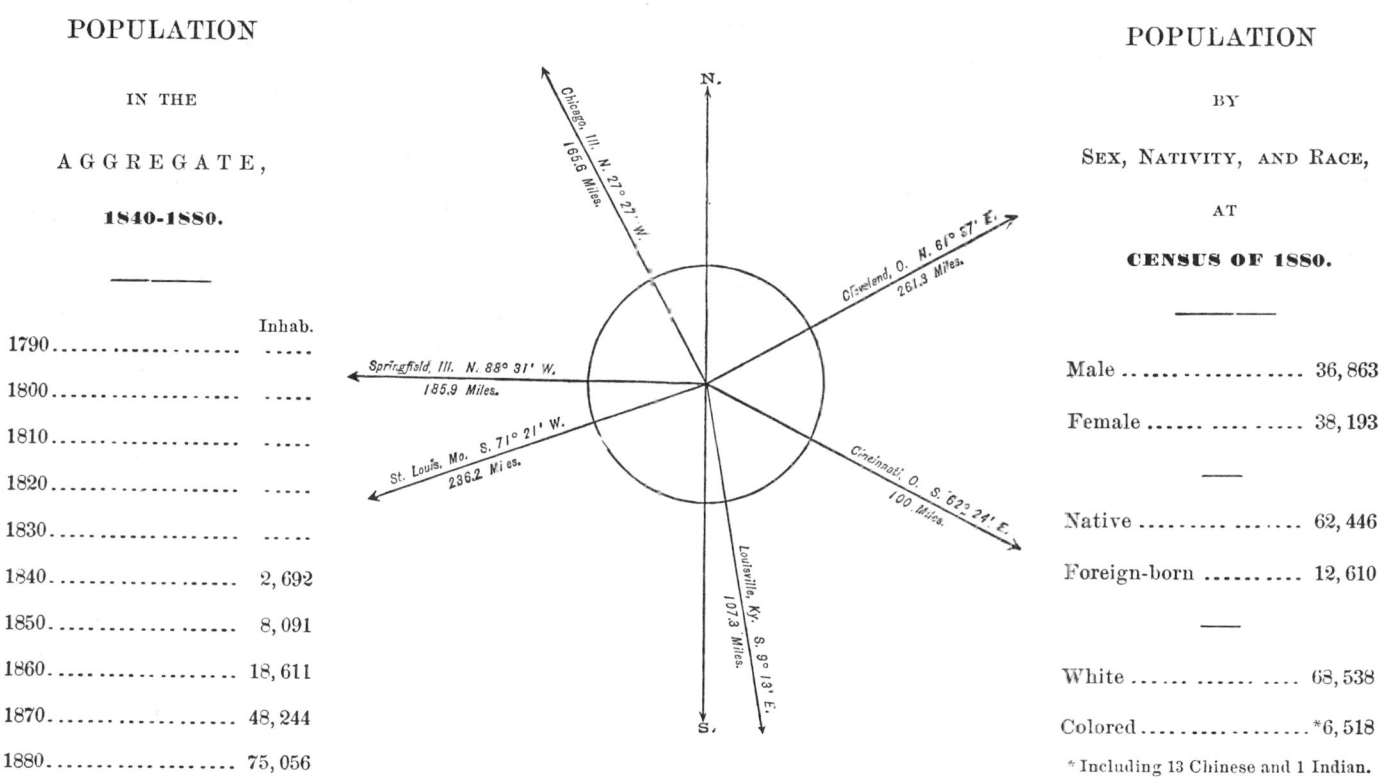

POPULATION

BY

SEX, NATIVITY, AND RACE,

AT

CENSUS OF 1880.

Male	36,863
Female	38,193
Native	62,446
Foreign-born	12,610
White	68,538
Colored	*6,518

* Including 13 Chinese and 1 Indian.

Latitude: 39° 47′ North; Longitude: 86° 9′ (west from Greenwich); Altitude: 691 to 753 feet.

FINANCIAL CONDITION:

Total Valuation: $48,099,940; per capita: $641 00.   Net Indebtedness: $1,914,500; per capita: $25 51.   Tax per $100: $1 60.

HISTORICAL SKETCH.

Sixty years ago the site of the present great city of Indianapolis was a wilderness. For 40 miles on all sides stretched an unbroken forest. Whether or not a settlement was made here in 1819 is a matter in dispute, but it is certain that several families established themselves on the spot in 1820. In the same year the United States government gave to the new state of Indiana, which had been admitted to the Union in 1816, four sections of land at this place as a site for its capital. The land was surveyed, and a town was laid out early in 1821. The original plat was 1 mile square, and was divided into regular 40-acre squares, each to contain twelve lots. They were divided through the middle by alleys, those running east and west 30 feet wide, and those running north and south 15 feet wide. The streets in general were made 90 feet wide, while Washington street, the central street of the city, was made 120 feet wide, partly because through it passed the great "National road". A circular plot in the center of the city was reserved for the mansion of the governor and was surrounded by a street 30 feet wide. The state offices were removed from Corydon in 1824, and in January, 1825, the legislature met for the first time in Indianapolis. The first settlers were from the Whitewater valley, in the eastern part of the state, but soon others came from Kentucky, Tennessee, and North Carolina.

Until 1847 the growth of the town was very slow. Far from civilization, surrounded by swamps, which extended for miles, and across which only corduroy roads had been built, that were absolutely impassable for wheeled vehicles, and on which even horsemen sometimes spent a week or ten days in ... ching the river towns, there was little inducement to immigration. To remedy the lack of easy communication the legislature planned a vast state system of railroads and canals. Large amounts of money were borrowed, and the building of the various roads was pressed with all possible rapidity. But the crisis of 1837 ruined the credit of the state, and it was forced to leave the roads unfinished. By the plan which the legislature had elaborated, the various railway lines had centered in Indianapolis, and this feature was preserved in the system of railroads that finally grew up. In 1847 the Madison and Indianapolis railroad was completed, and from this moment the increase of Indianapolis began and its future was assured. The population was then only about 4,000, but in 1850, not four years later, it had increased to 8,091. Other lines were fast completed, the La Fayette and Indianapolis, the Peru and Indianapolis, the Terre Haute and Richmond, the Indianapolis and Bellefontaine, and the Indiana Central, all radiating from Indianapolis and bringing to it trade and population. The crisis of 1857 checked the advance of the city, and the opening of the civil war also delayed its progress; but the United States government made it a great depot for ordnance and supplies for the southern and western armies. Most of Indiana's contingent were assembled here before being sent to the front. Manufacturing in the city dates from the beginning of the civil war. Fields of coal and iron within easy reach were then first utilized, and the discovery of the so-called "block" coal in the region tributary to the city, about the year 1870, greatly assisted the iron industry. The location of the city near the great corn-belt made it an important point for the distribution of this cereal, and elevators and flouring-mills have sprung up, while pork-packing became an important industry.

Many of the charitable institutions of the state are located here, the state asylum for the blind, the deaf and dumb, and the insane. Just a little beyond the city limits there is a United States arsenal, surrounded by beautiful grounds, including in all about 78 acres. At the beginning of last year there were 79 churches, with a membership of 26,000 and owning property valued at $1,577,000. There were 5 daily newspapers, 16 weeklies, and 10 monthly publications. In addition to the public schools, Indianapolis has 24 educational institutions.

INDIANAPOLIS IN 1880.

The following statistical accounts, collected by the Census Office, indicate the present condition of Indianapolis:

LOCATION.

Indianapolis, the capital of Indiana and the seat of justice for Marion county, lies in latitude 39° 47' north, longitude 86° 9' west from Greenwich, near the center of the state, and on the east bank of the White river, which is not navigable. The altitudes above mean sea-level are—lowest point, 691 feet; track at the Union depot, 721 feet; and highest point, 753 feet.

RAILROAD COMMUNICATIONS.

The city is touched by the following-named railroads:

The Indianapolis division of the Cleveland, Columbus, Cincinnati, and Indianapolis railroad, from Indianapolis to Galion, Ohio, 203 miles.

The first division of the Pittsburgh, Cincinnati, and Saint Louis railroad, from Indianapolis to Columbus, 187 miles.

The Cincinnati, Hamilton, and Dayton railroad, to Hamilton, Ohio, 90 miles.

The Indianapolis, Saint Louis, and Chicago railroad, to Kankakee, Illinois, 250 miles.

The Jeffersonville, Madison, and Indianapolis railroad, between the points named.

The Indianapolis and Vincennes railroad, to the latter place.

The Saint Louis, Vandalia, and Terre Haute railroad, to Saint Louis.

The Indianapolis and Saint Louis railroad, also to Saint Louis.

The Indianapolis, Decatur, and Springfield railroad, to Decatur, Illinois.

The Indiana, Bloomington, and Western railroad, to Peoria, Illinois.

The Indianapolis, Peru, and Chicago railroad, to Michigan City.

The Union Railway transfer, extending around the city, 12 miles in length, and connecting the numerous lines.

Besides the completed roads, there are partially finished and organized the Indianapolis and Evansville, and the Indianapolis, Delphi, and Chicago railroads.

INDIANAPOLIS,

IND.

TRIBUTARY COUNTRY.

The neighboring country is devoted almost entirely to agriculture, having, however, some industrial establishments, principally connected with the working of the soil, such as saw- and grist-mills, and brick and pipe kilns.

TOPOGRAPHY.

Indianapolis lies in the midst of a gentle depression, 12 miles long and 5 miles wide, which is covered to an average depth of 80 feet with glacial drift. The average difference in level between this depression and the surrounding uplands is about 50 feet. Under the east half of the county lies Carboniferous limestone, the western edge of the "Flat rock" formation. In the center is found Marcellus shale, and on the western limit Marshal limestone, which crops out in the bluffs of White river south of the city. The soil is a sandy loam, changing into clay at the eastern and western limits. The drainage is by and into White river, which runs almost through the center of the county from north to south, all the streams of the county being tributary to it. There are now no near considerable marshes, and with one slight exception no lakes or ponds. Originally the country around Indianapolis was heavily timbered, but now only occasional woodlands remain.

CLIMATE.

Highest recorded summer temperature, 97°; highest summer temperature in average years, 89°. Lowest recorded winter temperature, −22°; lowest winter temperature in average year, −10°. Ordinarily the city is not in a position to be climatically influenced by bodies of water; but in winter, when the wind blows from the north so as to pass over lakes Superior and Michigan, the temperature is modified about 10°. There are no marshes or elevated lands sufficient to influence the climate. Southerly and westerly winds prevail, and their immediate effect is to produce rain.

STREETS.

The streets measure about 211 miles, paved as follows: Cobble-stones, 45 miles; broken stone, about 1 mile; and wood, 5 miles; the remainder being of gravel or bowlders. The cost per square yard of each, as nearly as may be estimated, is, cobble-stones, 53 cents; broken stone, 58 cents; wood, $1 65; and gravel, 30 cents. The relative facility with which each is kept clean is, first, the wooden blocks, then the broken stone, and, lastly, cobble-stones and gravel. As to the quality and permanent economy of each, the street commissioners think broken stone is the best and cheapest in the long run; next are preferred cobble-stones for the business part of the town, and raked river gravel for the less-used streets, while the wooden pavement has not been satisfactory. A few of the sidewalks are paved with stone, also a little paving with cement and artificial stone was done several years ago; but the majority of the walks are laid with brick and gravel. Gutters are frequently of earth only. Where the street has cobble-stone or macadam pavement the gutters are of the same material, while in the wooden streets they are laid with wood blocks. Trees are very generally planted for shade at the outer edge of the sidewalks. In some instances narrow lawns are prepared for them, but this is optional with the property-owners. Most of the tree-planting is done under ordinance, and this feature is quite general—so general that Indianapolis is said to have the reputation of having more shade-trees than any other city of its size in the country. Streets are constructed by contract. The cost is assessed upon the abutting property, the city paying only for the intersections. Street repairs are made by the city, and the estimate of the cost of this work, which includes their cleaning and the care of sewers and bridges, for the year ending May 30, 1880, was $35,000. For construction of streets contract work is preferred, while day-labor for repairs and cleaning is considered best. Some years ago the city bought a road-roller, but it was found to be too heavy for the graveled streets. It was tried on a broken-stone pavement and worked tolerably well, but its use has long since been discontinued. There are 19 miles of horse-railroads (single track) in the city, including 4 miles in the suburbs, using 59 cars and 300 mules, and giving employment to 125 men. On an average, 2,250,000 passengers are carried annually, at rates of fare of 5 cents in the city, and 10 cents on the suburban lines. In addition to a short line, operated by one of the street-car companies, a single line of omnibuses, with 18 vehicles, 35 horses, and 25 employés, carries passengers to all parts of the city for the uniform fare of 50 cents, and 25 cents for baggage.

WATER-WORKS.

The water-works are the property of a private corporation, and cost about $750,000. The Holly system of pumping is used, affording a pressure to the square inch of 45 pounds for domestic and 110 pounds for fire uses. The yearly cost of maintenance, aside from the cost of pumping, is $16,000, and the yearly income from water-rates is $66,256. Water-meters are used, but the water company is taking them out as fast as possible, and does not recommend them.

GAS.

The gas-works are not owned by the city. The daily average production of the Indianapolis Gas Company is 363,259 cubic feet. The charge per 1,000 feet is $2. The city pays this company $25 per annum each for 2,400 street-lamps. The Citizens' Gas Company produces 5,000 feet of gas per day, for which the charge to customers is $2 per 1,000 feet.

PUBLIC BUILDINGS.

The city owns one fire-engine house. A property, assessed at $75,000, has been left by J. T. Tomlinson, the proceeds to be used in erecting a city hall, but nothing has yet been done toward realizing the bequest. The municipal offices are now located in the county court-house, being rented from the county at an annual cost of $3,000.

PUBLIC PARKS AND PLEASURE-GROUNDS.

The public parks of Indianapolis comprise about 150 acres of land. *Southern Park* is located south of the city, on Pleasant run, and covers 90 acres of woodland and pasture. A strip of land 100 feet wide and 4 miles long, on both sides of Fall creek, north of the city, has been set aside by the property-owners for a pleasure-drive, but it has never been improved. In the city are 2 open squares, owned by the state, one called *Military Park*, and covering 16 acres of land, and the other, *University Square*, with an area of 4 acres. These latter were donated by the state government, and set aside for the purpose by the commissioners who laid out the city. They have been improved by the city and are under its police supervision, but the title to the land is irrevocably in the commonwealth. The total cost of the parks is $109,500, which is the price paid for Southern park, none of the others having cost any thing. The annual appropriation for the maintenance of the parks is $1,200, which includes the cost of police attendance in summer. The parks are controlled by the committee on public property, appointed by the council and the board of aldermen.

PLACES OF AMUSEMENT.

There are 2 theaters in the city—Grand opera-house, seating 1,608, and Park theater, seating 1,200. There are also, under the control of singing societies and used mostly for amateur performances, Germania theater, seating 600, and Männerchor hall, seating 500. The two first mentioned pay a yearly license fee of $100 each. Of concert-halls, etc., having no stage appliances, there are Masonic hall, a large room in Masonic temple, seating capacity 800; Mozart hall, situated on the third floor of a business house, seating 500; Washington hall, on the third floor of a business block, capacity 600; and Ryan's hall, also on a third floor, capacity 400. Among the pleasure resorts are the following concert- and beer-gardens: Come's garden and theater, which superseded a garden attached to a saloon, is roofed over, has a permanent stage, a capacity of from 800 to 1,000, and is open the year round; and Gilmore's Zoölogical garden, with a saloon attached, in which music is furnished. These two places pay an annual license to the city. In addition there are many saloons that have music and give variety performances, but they can hardly be classed as concert- and beer-gardens.

DRAINAGE.

No sewers, either public or private, were built until the year 1870. At that time a general plan was adopted providing for the sewerage of the whole city, and the work of building was begun. Since then all sewers constructed have been made to conform to this general plan. Most of the city is built on a formation of sand and gravel, from 30 to 40 feet deep, into which there have been sunk about 1,500 wells, for water-supply, and about 30,000 cesspools and privy-vaults now in use, besides an equal or a greater number of old ones that have been abandoned and filled in.

Beneath the surface-sand were alternate layers of clay, sand, hard pan, and gravel, to a depth of 90 feet or more before reaching the limestone bed-rock. In the southern part of the city the clay comes to the surface, and there damp or wet cellars are often found. The elevation of the city is 40 feet or more above the water of White river. The surface drainage flows generally to a small stream flowing through the city. From the porous character of its soil a large proportion of rain-water is immediately absorbed. The system of sewerage adopted provides for the drainage of the southern part of the city, about 280 acres, to the sewer in Ray street; the western district, 340 acres, to the sewer in Bright street; and the principal part of the city to a main-trunk sewer, 8 feet in diameter at the outfall and 7 feet in diameter at its upper end, which is intended to remove the drainage of 1,600 acres within the city limits and of 1,500 acres without the city limits. All sewers thus far built are of brick, and discharge into White river, the mouths of the outfalls being fully exposed at low water. No provision has been made for ventilation. No necessity for the removal of deposits by hand or by artificial flushing has yet been developed. The grades are reported to be sufficient to insure cleansing by the action of storm-water.

The cost of construction is assessed upon abutting property to the amount of $1 50 per linear foot of the frontage on each side of the street, the excess of cost above this amount being paid by the city.

The prices paid for sewer construction in 1880 were: For sewers 2 feet in diameter, per foot, $1 75 and $2 25; for sewers 2½ feet in diameter, per foot, $1 65; for sewers 7½ feet in diameter, per foot, $11.

The average cost of inlet-basins is $80; of manholes, $40.

CEMETERIES.

Indianapolis uses the following cemeteries and burial-grounds:

Green Lawn Cemetery lies in the western part of the corporation, and contains about 25 acres. The first interment therein was made about the year 1822.

Crown Hill Cemetery lies about 4 miles northwest of the city and 50 feet above its highest part, and contains 385 acres of land.

Catholic Cemetery lies one-half mile south of the city, and contains 18 acres.

Lutheran Cemetery, area 3 acres, also lies south of the city, distant three-quarters of a mile.

Jewish Cemetery is situated near the last two, and has an area of 2 acres.

The three last named are near White river, and below the level of the city. All of the cemeteries drain to the westward and away from the city. There are no cemeteries or burial-grounds in which interments are no longer permitted. The number of interments in the different cemeteries of those only who died within the city limits, from 1872 to 1880, inclusive, is as follows:

Green Lawn cemetery, 4,480; Crown Hill cemetery, 3,243; Catholic cemetery, 1,578; Lutheran cemetery, 331; Jewish cemetery, 64; total, 9,696.

Indianapolis has a society whose object is to induce the adoption of a system of cremation instead of ordinary burial. It is as yet without a furnace; but a member of the society dying about a year ago, his remains were taken to a crematory in Pennsylvania and there cremated.

SANITARY AUTHORITY—BOARD OF HEALTH.

The chief sanitary organization of Indianapolis is the board of health, composed of 3 physicians, elected by the common council and the board of aldermen in joint convention. The annual expense of the board does not exceed $1,000, and is incurred for salaries, pay of sanitary policemen, etc. At no time may the board increase its expenses except by order of the city council, and its authority is at all times very limited. The executive officer of the board is the secretary, who receives $200 a year, while the president and the other member receive $100 each per annum. The board meets regularly. Until the 1st of June, 1880, 2 sanitary policemen were detailed from the police force to act as inspectors; since June 1 the number has been increased to 4. In this capacity they retain their police powers. An attempt is made to inspect all parts of the city regularly, but on account of the inadequacy of the number of sanitary policemen there is practically no inspection except as nuisances are reported. Under the liability to a fine of not more than $25 for refusal, the parties maintaining a nuisance, when such are reported, are notified to abate the same within 10 days. There is no regular system for the inspection and correction of defective sewerage, street-cleaning, house-drainage, privy-vaults, cesspools, and sources of drinking-water. The board maintains no control over the handling of garbage unless it becomes a nuisance. Previous to interments a permit must be obtained from the board.

INFECTIOUS DISEASES.

Small-pox patients are isolated at home, and a flag is placed on the house. Scarlet-fever cases are neither quarantined nor isolated. The board has no control over the public or private schools in the case of the breaking out therein of contagious diseases. The public pest-house is situated northwest of the city, in the hollow between Fall creek and White river. Vaccination is not compulsory, nor is it done at the public expense.

REGISTRATION, REPORTS, ETC.

The registration of births, diseases, and deaths is conducted by the state board of health, which furnishes blanks for the purpose, to be filled up and returned by physicians, midwives, and householders. The board reports to the common council and the board of aldermen.

During last year a city dispensary was organized, with 3 physicians to do the work, and a staff of 21 physicians who render voluntary service in consultations, etc. This is doing a good work.

MUNICIPAL CLEANSING.

Street-cleaning.—The streets are cleaned at the expense of the city and with its regular force. The work is done wholly by hand. There are no stated times for street-cleaning; the board of public improvements orders the street commissioner, upon motion of the city council, and when, in its judgment, it is necessary. When done at all the work is well done; but it is not sufficiently general to be of much advantage from a sanitary point of view. The sweepings are deposited on low lots and in the river. The cost of the work is included in the sum appropriated for streets.

Removal of garbage and ashes.—Garbage is removed only by the householders. Its conservancy and hauling are not regulated, except that it must not be left in the streets or allowed to become a nuisance; it is disposed of variously as each householder may arrange. Ashes are generally used for filling low grounds. The annual cost of the removal of these matters is not given. The manner of keeping, handling, and disposing of the garbage is, in the opinion of the board of health, injurious to health.

Dead animals.—The question of the disposition of animals dying within the city is satisfactorily disposed of by means of a contract between the city and a fertilizing company for the removal of all such carcasses, the company paying the city $100 annually for the privilege. No record of the number annually removed is kept.

Liquid household wastes.—Where there are sewers, all household wastes are run into them; where sewers do not exist, chamber-slops are generally thrown into vaults, while laundry wastes and kitchen-slops go into sinks or cesspools; but in some cases all the wastes are thrown into vaults. The amount going into the sewers is small, while a good deal is thrown into alleys and gutters, which are never artificially flushed. The cesspools are porous, being dug in the loose earth with which the city is underlaid, allowing the contents to soak away into the ground, and are unprovided with overflows. The cesspools receive the wastes from water-closets. Concerning the pollution of drinking-water by the underground escape of the contents of privy-vaults and cesspools, it is stated that out of 100 wells in the city, the water of which was analyzed, only 10 proved to be good.

Human excreta.—Not over 10 per cent. of the houses of the city have water-closets. Of these half deliver into the sewers and half into cesspools; the remaining houses depend on privy-vaults. Very few of the vaults are even nominally water-tight, as an ordinance providing that the sides shall be tightly lined says nothing regarding the bottoms. These and cesspools may be ordered cleaned by the board of health. The night-soil is dumped into the river at a place designated by the city, none of it being allowed for manuring land within the gathering-ground of the public water-supply.

Manufacturing wastes.—There are no regulations as to the disposal of either liquid or solid manufacturing wastes.

POLICE.

The police force of Indianapolis is appointed and governed by a police board consisting of 3 councilmen. The chief of police is the executive officer; he has a general superintendence of the force, and receives a salary of $1,200 per annum. The rest of the force consists of 4 captains at $2 50 per day each, and 2 turnkeys and 57 patrolmen at $2 per day each. The uniform is a double-breasted frock, buttoned up to the chin, with two rows of brass buttons, and a helmet hat; the men provide their own uniforms. The patrolmen carry a 14-inch mace. The hours of duty are twelve for day men and ten for night men. The arrests made in 1880 numbered 4,151, the chief cause for which was drunkenness. Stolen and lost property to the value of $12,313 96 was recovered by the police during the year.

FIRE DEPARTMENT.

The manual force of the department consists of 1 chief, 6 engineers, 13 foremen, and 56 men. The apparatus consists of 6 fire-engines, 5 hose-carriages, and 2 hook-and-ladder trucks, with 1 engine and 1 hose reel in reserve. There are 9,000 feet of hose and 36 horses in service. During the year ending June 1, 1880, the department attended 155 alarms of fire. The buildings, with their stock, in which these fires occurred were covered by an insurance of $558,506, and 10⅞ per cent. of this amount was lost. There were 41 fires where no insurance was involved, on which the loss was $2,913 75. A fire-alarm telegraph is in use, and in addition to this the several engine- and hose-houses as well as the residence of the chief have telephone connections, the telephone company granting the department the use of the instruments in return for the privilege of using the poles of the fire-alarm telegraph for their lines. In addition to 599 hydrants, there are, for fire purposes, 144 cisterns, distributed throughout the city, and having a capacity of 120,838 barrels.

PUBLIC SCHOOLS.

The public schools of Indianapolis represented an irregular effort of the community to 1856, when a general system of public schools was inaugurated. This was cut short by the decisions of the supreme court that the laws authorizing taxation for school purposes were unconstitutional. After an entire stoppage for some years, followed by short terms in other years, the school organization was renewed in 1863, and has expanded with the growth of the city.

Of all taxes in 1879, 24½ per cent. was for educational purposes.

MANUFACTURES.

The following is a summary of the statistics of manufactures of Indianapolis, Indiana, for 1880, being taken from tables prepared for the Tenth Census by J. M. Ridenour, chief special agent:

Mechanical and manufacturing industries.	No. of establishments.	Capital.	AVERAGE NUMBER OF HANDS EMPLOYED.			Total amount paid in wages during the year.	Value of materials.	Value of products.
			Males above 16 years.	Females above 15 years.	Children and youths.			
All industries	638	$10,049,500	8,671	830	499	$3,917,114	$19,198,102	$27,453,089
Agricultural implements	3	41,000	55	....	....	11,400	31,200	55,500
Baking and yeast powders (see also Drugs and chemicals)	3	5,500	10	2	....	6,620	35,000	56,500
Baskets, rattan and willow ware	3	850	5	....	....	790	1,150	4,720
Blacksmithing (see also Wheelwrighting)	22	14,600	44	....	1	19,623	24,994	70,112
Boots and shoes, including custom work and repairing	79	24,495	114	4	1	47,398	65,804	176,973
Boxes, wooden packing	3	37,300	52	....	....	29,020	43,200	118,200
Bread and other bakery products	25	95,900	142	27	6	75,821	234,110	423,071
Brick and tile	8	86,300	117	....	10	38,950	34,118	101,000
Brooms and brushes	5	13,900	38	8	17	10,892	27,604	55,350
Carpentering	23	60,575	235	....	29	89,225	221,484	384,460
Carpets, rag	7	6,550	5	7	2	4,347	12,350	21,850
Carriages and wagons (see also Wheelwrighting)	14	248,500	260	....	3	78,400	115,620	250,420
Clothing, men's	27	172,410	219	127	1	165,235	375,410	658,960
Coffee and spices, roasted and ground	4	63,000	24	4	....	10,130	197,450	230,100
Coffins, burial-cases, and undertakers' goods	5	67,000	31	....	....	28,464	43,800	99,140
Confectionery	12	90,750	54	24	6	29,568	181,835	273,200
Cooperage	13	277,700	520	....	75	153,100	812,475	1,107,582
Dentistry, mechanical	16	10,780	9	6	1	5,212	8,670	38,921
Drugs and chemicals (see also Baking and yeast powders)	6	62,700	55	26	....	22,450	56,000	113,000
Dyeing and cleaning	6	4,850	16	24	....	12,350	9,900	32,900
Dyeing and finishing textiles	5	4,400	15	24	....	12,100	9,850	32,000
Electrotyping	3	1,400	3	....	....	1,218	1,150	4,550
Fertilizers	5	103,000	94	....	....	41,424	714,000	920,000
Flouring- and grist-mill products	12	462,000	110	....	....	56,654	1,511,885	1,655,517
Foundery and machine-shop products (see also Iron work, architectural and ornamental).	15	1,188,000	1,275	4	34	534,090	742,000	1,736,000
Furniture (see also Mattresses and spring beds; Upholstering)	17	357,900	483	7	57	197,083	582,212	917,600
Hardware	4	3,295	3	....	....	1,500	3,575	8,500
Hats and caps, not including wool hats	3	2,725	5	3	....	3,500	7,800	15,420
Iron work, architectural and ornamental (see also Foundery and machine-shop products).	3	103,000	126	....	....	41,600	79,191	136,592
Liquors, malt	3	400,000	148	....	....	66,036	280,558	508,740
Looking-glass and picture frames	8	36,050	37	1	6	21,830	51,800	90,500
Lumber, sawed	6	255,500	116	....	10	44,400	348,600	497,200
Marble and stone work	11	46,050	91	....	5	47,700	112,985	237,265
Masonry, brick and stone	4	22,000	104	....	1	67,625	108,300	200,000
Mattresses and spring beds (see also Furniture)	4	10,700	25	1	1	11,300	26,440	53,900
Millinery and lace goods	6	37,000	....	69	....	12,100	78,000	132,000
Painting and paperhanging	16	38,800	111	39	1	70,929	179,350	301,050
Photographing	19	20,000	20	8	1	10,185	11,650	45,800
Plumbing and gasfitting	9	19,400	52	....	....	22,635	38,960	76,300
Printing and publishing	24	446,320	541	75	21	322,302	301,652	811,377
Pumps, not including steam pumps	4	20,650	44	....	1	17,289	35,000	71,500
Roofing and roofing materials	4	13,200	13	....	....	5,288	41,500	71,500
Saddlery and harness	19	42,500	85	....	3	30,509	104,600	193,300
Sash, doors, and blinds (see also Wood, turned and carved)	8	306,500	178	1	24	87,945	261,000	442,000
Saws	3	112,000	64	....	....	56,050	161,000	291,000
Shirts	4	12,300	11	45	6	21,260	24,800	59,600
Slaughtering and meat packing, not including retail butchering	7	1,618,000	892	....	....	345,236	7,890,203	9,014,422
Soap and candles	3	12,500	21	....	....	6,600	33,000	47,500
Stencils and brands	3	1,800	10	....	2	5,400	5,200	18,000
Tinware, copperware, and sheet-iron ware	28	62,760	117	2	13	50,562	124,305	240,461

Mechanical and manufacturing industries.	No. of establishments.	Capital.	AVERAGE NUMBER OF HANDS EMPLOYED.			Total amount paid in wages during the year.	Value of materials.	Value of products.
			Males above 16 years.	Females above 15 years.	Children and youths.			
Tobacco, cigars and cigarettes.............................	43	$52,025	189	9	34	$83,776	$121,482	$298,950
Trunks and valises	6	20,600	47	....	1	18,012	26,600	60,500
Upholstering (see also Furniture)	6	13,425	24	2	1	12,800	46,000	72,500
Watch and clock repairing	12	11,850	14	1	3	10,192	5,770	30,400
Wheelwrighting (see also Blacksmithing; Carriages and wagons)...	24	33,365	64	....	3	21,769	29,815	77,579
Window blinds and shades	3	22,000	28	1	....	10,900	22,000	59,000
Wood, turned and carved (see also Sash, doors, and blinds)	3	15,000	44	....	1	20,127	43,155	93,500
Wooden ware	3	124,000	107	32	37	55,250	59,000	158,000
All other industries (a)..................................	45	2,612,825	1,334	247	81	632,933	2,431,535	3,501,107

a Embracing awnings and tents; belting and hose, leather; boxes, paper; carriage and wagon materials; cheese and butter (factory); clothing, women's; cotton goods; engraving, wood; fruits and vegetables, canned and preserved; furniture, chairs; glue; grease and tallow; hairwork; hosiery and knit goods; iron and steel; liquors, distilled; lock- and gun-smithing; mineral and soda waters; oil, lard; oil, linseed; paper; patent medicines and compounds; regalia and society banners and emblems; starch; surgical apparatus; telegraph and telephone apparatus; varnish; and woolen goods.

From the foregoing table it appears that the average capital of all establishments is $14,606 83; that the average wages of all hands employed is $391 71 per annum; and that the average outlay in wages, in materials, and in interest (at 6 per cent.) on capital employed is $34,474 11.

LA FAYETTE,

TIPPECANOE COUNTY, INDIANA.

POPULATION

IN THE

AGGREGATE,

1840-1880.

	Inhab.
1790	......
1800	......
1810	......
1820	......
1830	......
1840	1,570
1850	6,129
1860	9,387
1870	13,506
1880	14,860

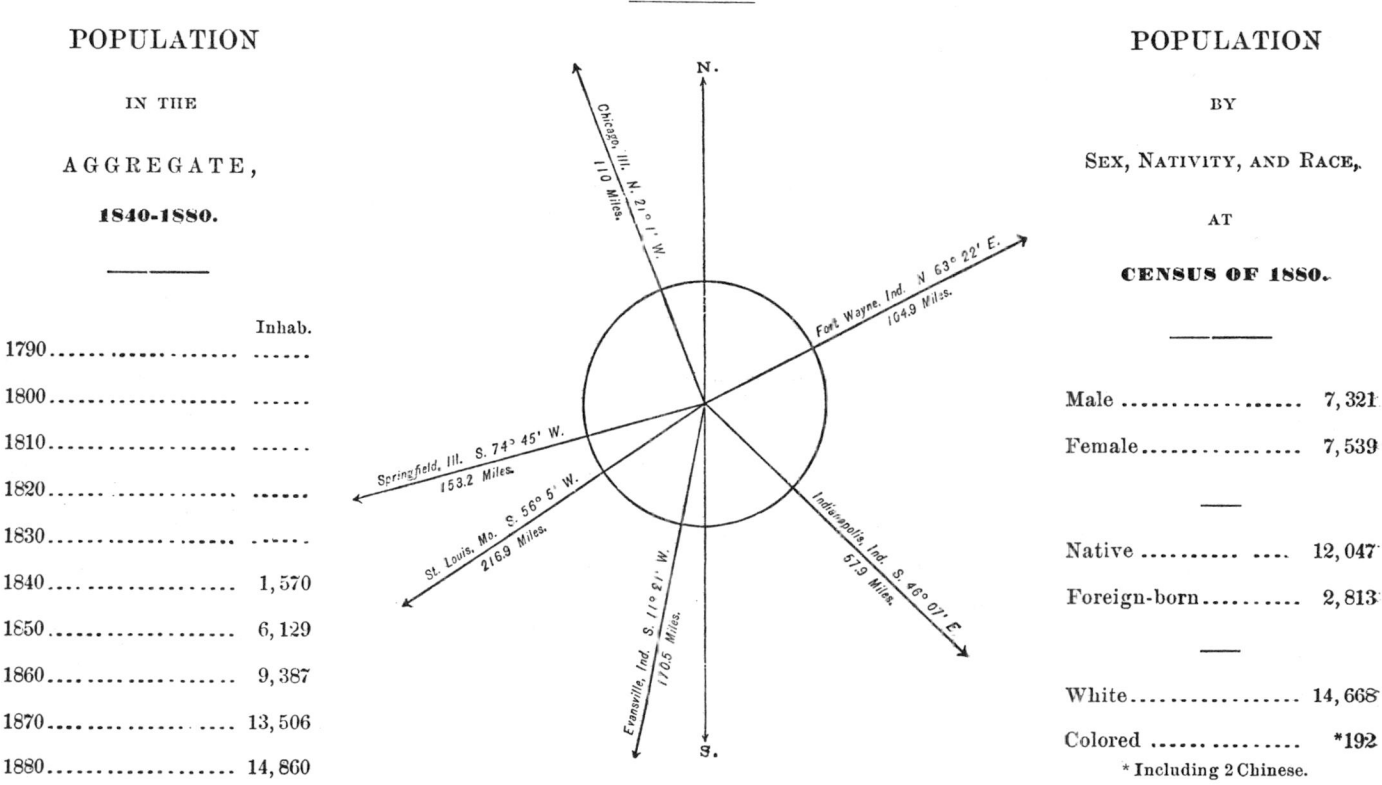

POPULATION

BY

SEX, NATIVITY, AND RACE,

AT

CENSUS OF 1880.

Male	7,321
Female	7,539
Native	12,047
Foreign-born	2,813
White	14,668
Colored	*192

* Including 2 Chinese.

Latitude: 40° 25′ North; Longitude: 86° 52′ (west from Greenwich); Altitude: 506 to 682 feet.

FINANCIAL CONDITION:

Total Valuation: $9,263,490; per capita: $623 00.   Net Indebtedness: $300,000; per capita: $20 19.   Tax per $100: $1 87.

HISTORICAL SKETCH.

Soon after the visit of La Fayette to America, in 1824, the public lands of Tippecanoe county became subject to entry. On the 25th of May, 1825, the town of La Fayette was laid out by William Digby, and in 1826 it was made the county-seat of Tippecanoe county. Prior to the completion of the Ohio and Erie canal in 1840 trade was carried on mainly by means of steamboats and smaller craft traversing the waters of the Wabash. Now, however, the railroads do most of the transportation. Free schools were first instituted in 1854, but were seriously interrupted for several years by the adverse decisions of the supreme court. The high school, established in 1864, is the pride of the city. The property of the public schools now consists of five buildings, which, with their furniture and apparatus, are valued at fully $150,000. A fitting climax to the free educational facilities of La

Fayette was supplied by the donations and bequests of the Hon. John Purdue, one of her public-spirited citizens. By means of them Purdue University was founded and put into successful operation, and its total assets to-day amount to near $600,000. No serious conflagrations have ever visited the city; and with an admirable system of water-works in operation, and an efficient fire department, the probabilities of large fires occurring are reduced to a minimum. The business depression which swept over the country in 1873 did not reach La Fayette until two or three years later, and its effect passed sooner than in most other cities. Only one bank suspended payment, and but few failures in business occurred, and of these none were leading houses. In its people La Fayette is cosmopolitan, all the leading nations of Europe and some of Asia being represented. Of Europeans the great majority are Irish and Germans. Of immigrants from sister states, Ohio, Pennsylvania, and New York have contributed the greater part.

LA FAYETTE IN 1880.

The following statistical accounts, collected for the Census Office by W. H. Caulkins, esq., indicate the present condition of La Fayette:

LOCATION.

La Fayette lies in latitude 40° 25′ north, longitude 86° 52′ west from Greenwich, on the left bank of the Wabash river, at the head of steamboat navigation, and on the Wabash and Erie canal, no longer in use, about 66 miles northwest from Indianapolis. The average altitude above sea-level is 600 feet. The lowest portion of the city, lying along the line of the canal, is 506 feet above sea-level, 26 feet above the level of the river at low water, and 67 feet below the level of lake Erie. The highest point has an elevation of 682 feet above sea-level, 227 feet above low water in the river, and 109 feet above the level of lake Erie. The Wabash river is navigable about eight months in the year for boats drawing 3 feet of water, and by means of its communication is open to all points upon the Ohio and Mississippi rivers and their navigable tributaries.

RAILROAD COMMUNICATIONS.

La Fayette is touched by the following-named railroads:
The Cincinnati, Indianapolis, Saint Louis, and Chicago railroad, from Cincinnati to Chicago, Louisville.
The New Albany and Chicago railroad, from Michigan City to New Albany.
The Peoria division of the Wabash, Saint Louis, and Pacific railroad, from Toledo to Burlington.
The Lake Erie and Western railroad, from Fremont to Bloomington.

TRIBUTARY COUNTRY.

The country tributary to La Fayette is mainly agricultural, the staple crops being wheat and corn. To the west and northwest the country is well adapted to grazing, and thousands of cattle, sheep, and hogs are annually fattened for both home and foreign consumption. Much attention is paid to the improvement of stock. As a result the county has secured an enviable reputation for the amount and variety of its imported breeds of horses, cattle, sheep, and hogs. To the south and southeast extends the fertile *Wild Cat* prairie, while to the southwest lies the far-famed *Wea plain*, very fruitful, and the site of ancient Oiatenon, founded by the French *voyageurs*, contemporary with La Salle. Farther to the southwest, at a distance of 30 miles from the city, the northern extension of the coal and iron belt of the state is reached. This produces iron-ore of good quality and inexhaustible supplies of coking and block coal, the latter being the typical coal for the manufacture of iron and steel.

TOPOGRAPHY.

Geologically speaking, the district of country about La Fayette is thickly covered with glacial drift, consisting of clay, sand, gravel, and bowlders. This rests upon the upper series of the Subcarboniferous formation, the Genesee bituminous black shale appearing in the northeast corner of the county and the Carboniferous conglomerate in the southwest corner. The site of the city is partly in the trough of the Wabash valley and partly upon the sides and top of the high bluffs which form its rim. The lower town stands upon a bed of drift and rounded gravel, 170 feet thick, as shown by the *débris* from the bore of an artesian well which pierces it. The upper town is built upon a heavy deposit of bowlder clay, resting upon strata of sand and gravel, that are, in places, consolidated by percolations of iron-charged water. The best possible drainage is secured to the city by the rapid slope of its site and the porous nature of its underlying beds. From the top of the bluffs, back, the country is level or gently undulating, and is entirely free from marshes or ponds. For a radius of 5 miles the country is equally divided between timber and prairie, but at a greater distance it expands into wide reaches of country. The soil is generally a rich black or brown loam, from 1 to 4 feet thick, with a subsoil of clay, sand, or gravel.

CLIMATE.

Highest recorded summer temperature, 104°; highest summer temperature in average years, 99°. Lowest recorded winter temperature, —20°; lowest winter temperature in average years, —10°. These figures are taken from observations extending over 16 years. The prevailing winds are from the south and southwest, and tend to increase the humidity of the atmosphere, as well as to modify the extremes of heat and cold.

STREETS.

Total length, 69½ miles, of which one-half mile is paved with cobble-stones, 2½ miles with broken stone, 1 mile with wood, and 30 miles with gravel. The cost per square yard of each, as nearly as may be estimated, is: Broken stone, 75 cents; wood, $2 45; and gravel, 20 cents. Of sidewalks there are 30 miles of brick and 30 miles of gravel, with stone curbs; 1¼ mile of plank, and three-quarters of a mile of flag and concrete. There are 60 miles of gutters paved with bowlders. The principal residence streets are planted throughout their whole length with a continuous line of shade-trees on either side. The work of construction for many years past has been done by contract, and the repairs by day labor. The annual cost of the latter ranges from $10,000 to $12,000. There are 4 omnibuses in the city, with 16 horses and 6 men, carrying annually 75,000 passengers.

WATER-WORKS.

The water-works are owned by the city, and their total cost was $400,000. The water is taken from the Wabash river and pumped into a distributing reservoir, the pressure being 45 pounds to the square inch. The average amount pumped per diem is 900,000 gallons, the least being 800,000 and the greatest 1,000,000 gallons. The average cost of raising 1,000,000 gallons 1 foot high is $6\frac{1}{28}$ cents. The yearly cost of maintenance, aside from the cost of pumping, is $4,000, and the yearly income from water-rates is $9,000. There are a few water-meters in use, and they have been found to diminish the consumption of water.

GAS.

The gas-works are owned by a private company. The daily average production is 48,000 cubic feet. The charge per 1,000 feet is $2 75. The city pays $37 yearly for each street-lamp, 342 in number.

PUBLIC BUILDINGS.

The only municipal buildings are 2 engine-houses, valued at $4,000 each.

PUBLIC PARKS AND PLEASURE-GROUNDS.

There are 3 parks in the city, with a total area of 83 acres. *Fairground Park*, area 70 acres, lies in the high table-land south of the city, and cost $20,000. It contains a spring of never-failing water, has a number of picturesque drives, and is covered with a fine growth of young timber. About 8,000 people visit this park annually— 5,000 on foot, 1,000 in carriages, and 2,000 on horseback. *Summit Park* cost $4,000, and *Reservoir Park* $6,000. These two last named are controlled by the city council, and the larger one by the city council conjointly with the association owning it.

PLACES OF AMUSEMENT.

There is one theater in the city, the opera-house, built in 1872, at a cost of $75,000, and having a seating capacity of 2,500. It pays an annual license to the city of $50. In addition to this there are 2 halls, used for lectures, concerts, entertainments, etc.

No further information was furnished.

NEW ALBANY,

FLOYD COUNTY, INDIANA.

POPULATION

IN THE

AGGREGATE,

1830-1880.

	Inhab
1790	...
1800	.....
1810	.....
1820	.....
1830	2,079
1840	4,226
1850	8,181
1860	12,647
1870	15,396
1880	16,423

POPULATION

BY

SEX, NATIVITY, AND RACE,

AT

CENSUS OF 1880.

Male	7,833
Female	8,590
Native	14,011
Foreign-born	2,412
White	15,080
Colored	*1,343

* Including 6 Indians.

Latitude: 38° 19′ North; Longitude: 85° 51′ (west from Greenwich); Altitude: 375 to 930 feet.

FINANCIAL CONDITION:

Total Valuation: $3,725,390; per capita: $227 00.   Net Indebtedness: $358,482; per capita: $21 83.   Tax per 100: $2 20.

HISTORICAL SKETCH.

The present site of New Albany was first settled November 12, 1814, and the place was incorporated as a town by act of assembly January 1, 1817. The early settlers were from the New England states and New York state, with some from England and Germany. Until 1830 the growth of the town was slow. New Albany became a city in 1839. The "general act of incorporation" was adopted by the city March 7, 1853. Boat-building was a very prominent industry, and some gunboats were built here during the civil war. Recently the English element of the population has rapidly increased, owing to the establishment of many large manufactories here employing English operatives. Glass-works of large capacity are among the present industries. No great fires have occurred to impede the onward march of the city. The trade and commerce are large, and the manufactories, driven by water-power afforded by the falls of the Ohio, are very extensive. New Albany is the capital of Floyd county.

The first school was opened in 1823. The liberal donation of a private individual, combined with public effort, had established a good system of public schools, but the adverse decisions of the supreme court made them irregular and finally closed them.

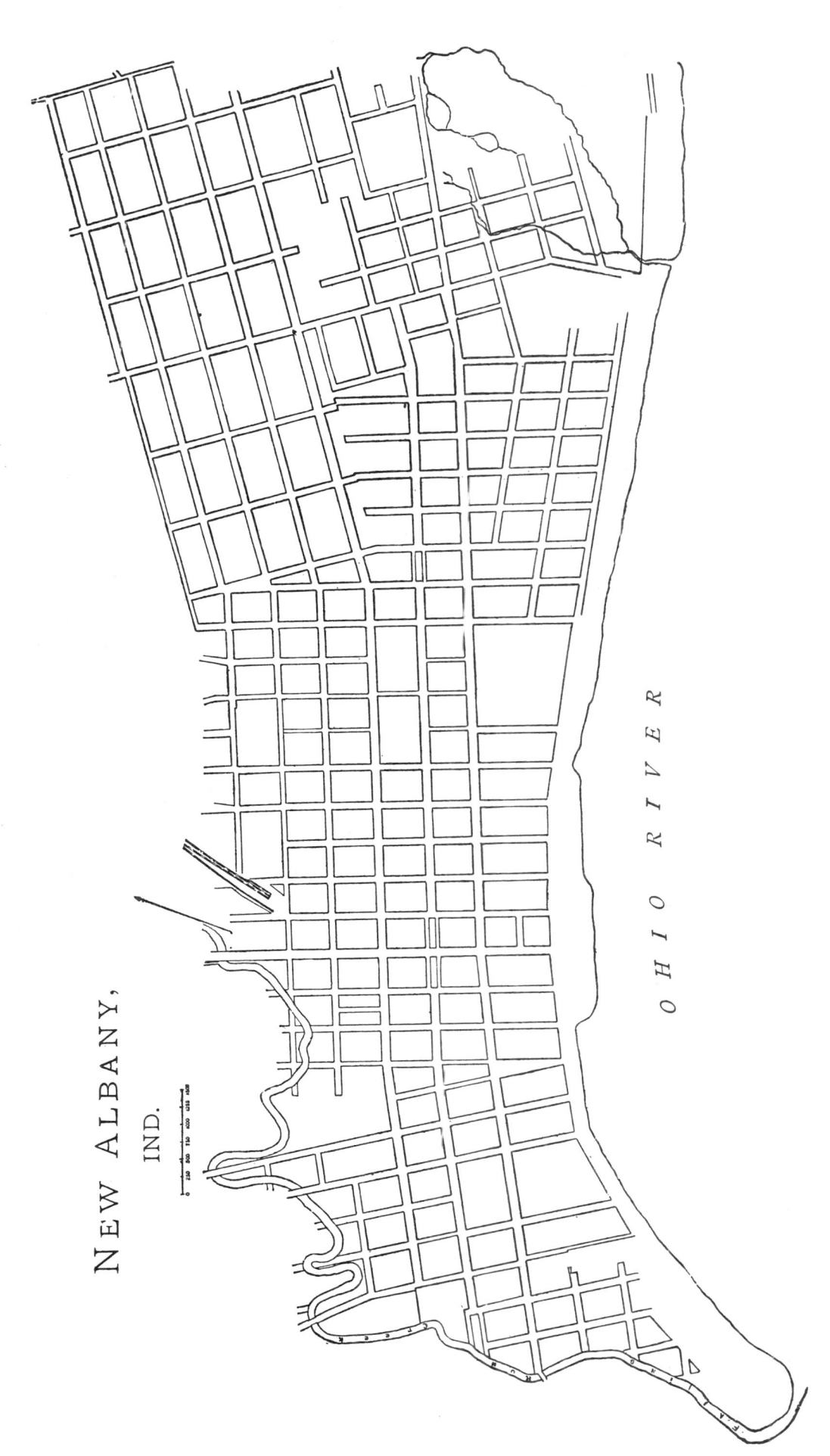

NEW ALBANY,
IND.

OHIO RIVER

For over a year, 1862–'63, the United States government leased some of the school-houses for hospital purposes, but in September, 1864, the law having been remodeled and the buildings refitted, the schools were reopened.

NEW ALBANY IN 1880.

The following statistical accounts, collected by the Census Office, indicate the present condition of New Albany:

LOCATION.

New Albany lies in latitude 38° 19′ north, longitude 85° 51′ west from Greenwich, on the right (north) bank of the Ohio river, opposite the lower end of Louisville, Kentucky, and about 2 miles below the foot of the falls of the Ohio. The altitudes of the city above mean sea-level are: At railroad station, 436 feet; at court-house, 448 feet; low-water mark in the Ohio river, 375 feet; and the "knob", northeast of the city, 930 feet. The draft of water in the Ohio river here averages 6 feet, the channel being half a mile wide and the current running 5 miles per hour. The harbor has a capacity for 40 steamboats and 100 barges.

RAILROAD COMMUNICATIONS.

New Albany is touched by the following-named railroad lines:
The Louisville, New Albany, and Chicago railroad, from Louisville to Chicago.
The Jeffersonville, Madison, and Indianapolis railroad, from New Albany to Indianapolis.
The Louisville, New Albany, and Saint Louis railroad, between Saint Louis and Louisville.
The Ohio and Mississippi railroad, from Cincinnati to Saint Louis.

TRIBUTARY COUNTRY.

The soil of the river-bottoms is a rich black loam, which is very productive. The upland soil is good, producing all the cereals and good fruits, of which latter quite a specialty is made. The adjoining country is thickly settled and highly cultivated, and abounds in mechanical industries, such as tanneries, flour-mills, smithies, agricultural-implement factories, and woolen-mills.

TOPOGRAPHY.

The surface of the site is generally level or gently rolling, with a range of hills on the west and north of from 500 to 550 feet above the city. Underlying the soil is a rock formation, part drift and part with underlying freestone. There are no near lakes or ponds. The natural drainage is good. About three-quarters of the adjoining territory has been cleared of its woods; the remainder is in isolated woodlands.

CLIMATE.

Highest recorded summer temperature, 106°; highest summer temperature in average years, 92°. Lowest recorded winter temperature, —10°; lowest winter temperature in average years, 20°. The hills near the city prove a shelter from the winds coming from the north and west, and are believed to cause a higher temperature. East winds are damp and south winds are considered healthful, while the winds from the west and northwest are pleasant in summer but cold in winter.

STREETS.

There are 66 miles of streets in the city, of which 27.3 miles are paved with Telford pavement, the cost of which was $6 per square yard, 1 mile being partially improved with sidewalks and gutters. The sidewalks are paved with brick laid in sand, under which are placed 2 inches of fine cinders. The gutters are made from 4 to 5 feet wide, having a limestone center 1 foot wide and 9 inches deep; the rest of the gutter is laid with limestone blocks on about 5 inches of clean gravel. Streets are constructed by contract, but repairs are made by day-labor. The annual cost of such work is between $7,000 and $8,000. A preference is expressed for day-work, as it is better, though more expensive. No steam stone-crusher or roller is used. There are 5 miles of horse-railroads, using 14 cars and 32 horses, and giving employment to 12 men. The rate of fare is 5 cents.

WATER-WORKS.

The water-works are owned by a private company, and cost $200,000. The pumping system is used, the pressure in the pipes being 85 pounds to the square inch. The average amount of water pumped per diem is 500,000 gallons, the greatest being 700,000 and the least 370,000 gallons. The average cost of raising 1,000,000 gallons 1 foot high is 4.53 cents. The annual cost of maintenance, aside from the cost of pumping, is $5,000, and the yearly income from water-rates is $10,000. A few water-meters are used, generally in manufacturing establishments, and are found to be in favor.

GAS.

The gas-works are not owned by the city. The daily average production is 30,000 cubic feet. The charge per 1,000 feet is $2 50. The city pays $18 per annum for each street-lamp, 431 in number.

PUBLIC BUILDINGS.

The city owns and occupies for municipal purposes the city hall, which covers the council-chamber, police court, and the offices of the city officials.

PUBLIC PARK.

The city had given it by the founders a spot of ground covering 2 acres. This has not been greatly improved, and is now a mere inclosure set with shade-trees and controlled by the city.

PLACES OF AMUSEMENT.

New Albany has one theater, the Opera-house, with a seating capacity of 1,200. It pays an annual license-fee to the city of $125. In addition, there is Turner's hall, size 50 by 120 feet, which is used for concerts, lectures, etc. There are no concert- and beer-gardens.

DRAINAGE.

The city has but one sewer, and this is about half a mile in length, and built of brick and stone. Only a few private drains enter it, most of the city's drainage running off through the street-gutters into Falling Run creek and then into the Ohio river. The only inlet-basin in connection with the work cost $250. The average cost of the manholes is $50. It is thought that the gutter-drainage (open) is better than sewers, owing to the topographical conformation. The fall is such as to move water rapidly, leaving but little *débris* or deposit.

CEMETERIES.

New Albany has connected with it 5 cemeteries, 2 public and 2 private, and the *National Soldiers' Cemetery*. The public cemeteries are as follows:

Northern Burying Ground (white), containing 40 acres of land, is laid out in regular system, handsomely decorated with trees and shrubbery, and has a lake or fish-pond.

Colored Cemetery, containing 6 acres.

The private cemeteries are: *German Catholic Cemetery*, containing 20 acres, and laid out in squares; and *Irish Catholic Cemetery*, of the same area, and also laid out in squares.

All these are either within or near the city limits. Aside from the National cemetery, which contains 3,200 bodies, the aggregate number of interments in these burial-grounds made during the past 30 years is 6,000, showing an average interment of 200 per year.

The city has complete control over the public cemeteries, but none over the private or church cemeteries. In the latter, lots are sold only to members of the church, who are required to conform to certain rules governing the grounds. No regular plan of ornamentation is followed, but the drives are excellent. Lots 12 by 12 feet sell at an average price of $10 each. The National cemetery is under the care of a superintendent, who is appointed by the Secretary of War. Of the total number of interments in this cemetery 1,000 are colored. By ordinance no burial is allowed to take place unless a permit is first obtained from the city clerk. Bodies may be placed in the vaults of the city cemeteries to remain for a period not exceeding three months.

MARKETS.

There are 2 public markets in the city, "Lower" and "Middle" market-houses. The two buildings are situated on adjoining squares, on Market, between Upper and Lower First streets. Each cost $10,000, and has 80 stalls for butchers inside, and the same number on the porches outside for hucksters. Each building is 250 feet long and 30 feet wide, with porches on either side, and each has a market-space 20 feet wide on both sides for farmers' and hucksters' wagons. The stalls rent for from $5 to $25 a year, according to position, etc. The markets are open from 4 a. m. to 12 noon, and on Saturdays from 6 to 10 p. m. in addition. It is estimated that the gross annual sales from the markets will amount to $1,000,000 per annum, about nine-tenths of the city's retail supply of meats, poultry, fish, and vegetables being sold from these markets.

SANITARY AUTHORITY—BOARD OF HEALTH.

The city council appoints the board of health, which consists of 3 physicians, and, except in time of an epidemic, controls it entirely. The members of the board receive no fixed salary, but are paid out of an appropriation made for the purpose, according to the service rendered. During an epidemic the board may incur any expense and adopt any measures it may deem necessary, usually acting in conjunction with the mayor and council, by whom its actions, before they can become binding, must be approved. The president of the board is its chief executive officer. He may act without the whole board in time of emergency. The business of the board is transacted at meetings held irregularly. No assistant health officers or inspectors are employed. Inspections are made ordinarily only as nuisances are reported, but in case of epidemics more vigorous measures may be employed. When a nuisance is reported and declared such by the board, the city marshal gives official notice to the party concerned to abate the same. In cases of defective house-drainage, privy-vaults, cesspools, and sources of drinking-water, the city takes the matter in hand and issues notices through the city clerk, which are served by the marshal, for the correction of all defects. Failure to obey this notice subjects offenders to a heavy penalty. Defective sewerage and street-cleaning are treated as nuisances. The board exercises no control over the conservation and removal of garbage or the pollution of streams, except the same become nuisances.

INFECTIOUS DISEASES.

As a rule, small-pox patients are isolated, an "eruptive hospital" being provided for them some 3 miles from the city on the grounds of the county poor asylum. Sometimes, but not generally, scarlet-fever patients are isolated or quarantined at their homes. The board takes cognizance of the breaking out of contagious diseases in public and private schools, and may dismiss the same. Vaccination is compulsory, and, for the indigent only, is done at the public expense.

REGISTRATION AND REPORTS.

A register is kept of births and deaths, but not of diseases. Whenever called upon, the board reports to the city council, and its reports, together with the proceedings of the council, are published in the newspapers. The medical profession of New Albany cordially co-operate with the board.

MUNICIPAL CLEANSING.

Street-cleaning.—The work of street-cleaning is done by the city's force and entirely by hand. As far as possible the principal streets are cleaned once in every two weeks, and, as a rule, the work is done efficiently. The annual cost to the city is $8,000. The sweepings are used for filling.

Removal of garbage and ashes.—Garbage is removed both by the city and by householders. If the city removes it, it does so, when the quantity is great, at the expense of the householder. When ready for removal it is placed on the street or alley, and the street commissioner is notified. Ashes and garbage may be kept in the same vessel, and both are disposed of in the same manner as street-sweepings. The cost to the city for the service is included in the cost of street-cleaning. In a few cases it is thought that a nuisance or probable injury to health may result from the improper keeping or handling or disposal of the garbage; but, as a rule, the system is reported to work fairly and to be as good as could be had with the city's ability to pay.

Dead animals.—An officer is appointed by the city council whose duty it is to remove the carcasses of animals dying within the city. If available, the carcasses are used by the fertilizing factories; otherwise they are buried. About 300 animals are annually removed, at a cost of $300. The system is reported to be defective in that carcasses are frequently allowed to remain too long before removal.

Liquid household wastes.—As a rule, all liquid household wastes are disposed of together, being thrown into privy-vaults or cesspools, but very little going into the one sewer of the city and very little into the street-gutters. The cesspools are nominally water-tight, but there are no special regulations as to their cleansing. The street-gutters are frequently flushed. The opinion is expressed that wells of drinking-water in the thickly settled parts of the city are doubtless somewhat contaminated by the escape of the contents of vaults and cesspools.

Human excreta.—About 10 per cent. of the houses of the city have water-closets, one-third of which deliver into the sewer. The remaining houses depend on privy-vaults. Very few of these latter are nominally water-tight. All are dug down to sand or gravel, and lined, except on the bottom, with brick or stone. The average depth is 18 feet, and the contents are not allowed to come nearer the top than 4 feet. The dry-earth system is used only to a limited extent. Night-soil is disposed of to the fertilizing factories, which convert it into "bromophyte". It is not allowed to be used for manuring land within the gathering-ground of the public water-supply.

Manufacturing wastes.—The wastes from manufactories are run off by the sewer or by gutters to the streams. Sometimes, during long heated terms, the liquid wastes become noxious and unhealthful.

POLICE.

The police force of New Albany is appointed by the council, and governed by the police commissioners, consisting of the mayor and police committee of the council. The chief of police is the executive officer, being at the head of the force and responsible for its discharge of duty; his salary is $2 per day. The rest of the force consists of 12 patrolmen, 2 for each ward. The chief and 2 men comprise the day force, and the rest the night force.

The patrolmen also receive $2 per day each. The uniform is of blue cloth, the frock coat being trimmed with brass buttons. The men provide their own uniforms. The patrolmen are equipped with mace and revolver. Their hours of duty are from 6 a. m. to 7 p. m. and from 7 p. m. to 6 a. m., and 31 miles of street are patrolled.

During the past year 218 arrests were made, the principal causes for which were drunkenness and disorderly conduct. During the same time property to the value of $700 was reported to the police as either lost or stolen, and of this amount $400 was recovered and returned to the owners. During the year there were 121 station-house lodgers, to whom 40 free meals were furnished, as against 136 in 1879. The police force is required to co-operate with the fire department in keeping the streets clear and guarding property at fires, and it may also enforce the orders of the board of health. Special policemen are appointed by the mayor for elections, etc. The yearly cost of the police force (1880) is $8,760.

RICHMOND,

WAYNE COUNTY, INDIANA.

	Inhab.
1790	......
1800	......
1810	......
1820	......
1830	......
1840	2,070
1850	1,443
1860	6,603
1870	9,445
1880	12,742

POPULATION

BY

SEX, NATIVITY, AND RACE,

AT

CENSUS OF 1880.

Male	6,217
Female	6,525
Native	10,956
Foreign-born	1,786
White	12,104
Colored	*638

* Including 2 Chinese.

Latitude: 39° 41' North; Longitude: 84° 51' (west from Greenwich); Altitude: 580 to 707 feet.

FINANCIAL CONDITION:

Total Valuation: $7,785,350; per capita: $611 00.   Net Indebtedness: $167,000; per capita: $13 11.   Tax per $100: $1 84.

HISTORICAL SKETCH.

The land on which the city of Richmond now stands was originally included in the lands belonging to John Smith and Jeremiah Cox, and though it was settled as early as 1803 the place had no corporate existence until 1818. Wayne county was organized in 1810, and in 1816 Smith laid out into town lots the land along Front and Pearl streets, south of Main, the lots being "5 poles wide and 8 poles back". An acre, called the "Public Square", was reserved by Smith for such public uses as he should think proper. Agreeably to an act of the legislature, the citizens met September 1, 1818, and unanimously declared themselves in favor of the incorporation of the town, 24 votes being polled. The town was located on the National road, furnishing an outlet for its products and for direct intercourse with other towns. The Wayne County turnpike was incorporated in 1850, and several others were completed during the next few years. Railroad communication was opened with Cincinnati, via Dayton, in 1853, and later in the same year via Eaton. Richmond has been noted for its manufactures, from its foundation to the present time, the principal industries being the making of caskets and burial-cases, thrashing-machines, engines, saw-mills, mill machinery, school- and church-furniture, cigars, galvanized iron, etc. The early settlers were mostly from North Carolina and Virginia, and belonged to the society of Friends, a Quaker meeting-house having been erected as early as 1807. The progress has been uniform and steady, and the city has never suffered much from financial depression.

RICHMOND IN 1880.

The following statistical accounts, collected by the Census Office, indicate the present condition of Richmond:

LOCATION.

Richmond lies in latitude 39° 41' north, longitude 84° 51' west from Greenwich, on the left bank of the Whitewater river, which is not here navigable, 4 miles from the eastern border of the state, and about 68 miles east of Indianapolis. The altitudes above mean sea-level are, average, 625 feet, lowest point 580 and highest point 707 feet.

RAILROAD COMMUNICATIONS.

Richmond is touched by the following-named railroads:
The Grand Rapids and Indianapolis railroad, to Petoskey, Michigan.
The Cincinnati, Richmond, and Chicago railroad, to Hamilton, and from there to Cincinnati and Chicago.
The Pittsburgh, Cincinnati, and Saint Louis railroad, between the points named.

TRIBUTARY COUNTRY.

The country immediately tributary to the city is agricultural, producing wheat, corn, oats, rye, barley, flax, potatoes, tobacco, hay, orchard- and small-fruits, etc. Horses, cattle, mules, sheep, hogs, etc., are raised to a considerable extent, and the amount of dairy products is large.

TOPOGRAPHY.

The underlying rock is the Lower Silurian limestone, cropping out on the west and north of the city, overlaid with gravel and clay. The surface soil is not deep within the city limits. The Whitewater river has here cut for itself a regular cañon, the banks being composed of from 100 to 110 feet of Hudson River rocks, that in places form almost vertical mural shores to the stream. The Pan Handle Railroad bridge spans this stream across a narrow part of its cañon. The differences in level in various parts of the city are considerable, and the natural drainage is good. The site of the city is 60 feet below the surrounding country, which is open, with a few wooded spaces remaining uncleared. The soil of the surrounding country is a sandy loam and clay.

CLIMATE.

Highest recorded summer temperature, 106°; highest summer temperature in average years, 98°. The lowest recorded winter temperature is not stated, but the lowest winter temperature in average years is said to be about —20°. The prevailing winds are from the west, northeast, and southwest, according to the season of the year.

STREETS.

Total length, 39.6 miles, paved as follows: One-quarter of a mile with cobble-stones, 22¼ miles with gravel, and the remainder unpaved. The cost per square yard of each, as nearly as it may be estimated, is, for cobble-stones, including the necessary grading and gravel-bed, 50 cents, and for gravel, about 35 cents. The former are kept in repair at the cost of 2 mills per square yard annually, and the latter at 4¼ mills per square yard annually. The facility with which each is kept clean is about the same, but the cobble-stones are preferred for quality and permanent economy. The sidewalks are principally of hard-burnt bricks, laid flat on a bed of gravel and sand 8 inches deep; some few are of flagstones, laid in the same way; and the remainder are of gravel, 10 inches in depth. The gutters are paved to a width of 6 feet with good smooth cobble-stones; in some instances three or four bricks are laid on edge next the curb. Each individual owner of property is permitted to plant shade-trees on sidewalks, near the curb-line. There is usually about 2 feet left for a grass-plot in a 12-foot walk, and the trees are planted in the center of the plot. The construction of streets is done by contract, and for the past four years about $4,000 have been expended annually.

HORSE-RAILROADS, ETC.

There are 3 miles of horse-railroads in the city, with 7 cars and 19 horses, and giving employment to 7 men. The rate of fare within the city limits is 5 cents. One omnibus, with 4 horses and employing 2 men, annually carries about 9,000 passengers, at the uniform rate of fare of 25 cents. There are no water-works.

RICHMOND,
IND.

GAS.

The gas-works are owned by a private company. The daily average production is 35,000 cubic feet. The charge per 1,000 feet is $2 50. The city pays $25 68 per annum each for street-lamps, 196 in number.

PUBLIC BUILDINGS.

The city owns and occupies for municipal purposes one building containing the city offices and the city prison. Its total cost was $10,000. There is no city hall.

PUBLIC PARKS AND PLEASURE-GROUNDS.

There are none in the city.

PLACES OF AMUSEMENT.

There are two theaters in the city, with an aggregate seating capacity of 1,200. They pay no license, but all exhibitions pay a license of $5 per day to the city. In addition to the theaters there are four halls used for lectures, concerts, etc. There are no concert- and beer-gardens.

DRAINAGE.

There are no sewers in Richmond.

CEMETERIES.

There are 7 cemeteries in and connected with the city, as follows:
Maple Grove Cemetery, area 20 acres, situated in the easterly part of the city between Main and North D streets.
Earlham Cemetery, area 50 acres, is situated outside the city limits, one-half mile west of the river.
Lutheran Cemetery, area 10 acres, is 1 mile south of the city.
Saint Andrew's Cemetery, Catholic, area 3 acres, is one-quarter of a mile south of the city.
Old Catholic Cemetery, area one-eighth of an acre, is situated on South Fifth street near Liberty avenue.
City Cemetery, area one-quarter of an acre, is situated on South Seventh street, corner of South E street.
Quaker Cemetery, area 16 acres, on North Tenth street between F and H streets.
Burials are made on permits issued by the board of health on physicians' certificates of death.

MARKETS.

There are no public or corporation markets in the city.

SANITARY AUTHORITY—BOARD OF HEALTH.

The chief sanitary authority of Richmond is the board of health, an independent organization, composed of three members, two of whom are physicians, appointed annually by the city council. The salaries of the members are designated by the council, being at present $100 per annum for the president, and $50 per annum for each of the members. In ordinary times the expenses are $200 for salaries, but the board can employ inspectors if necessary. In case of an epidemic there is no limit to the expenses the board may incur. In absence of any declared epidemic the board has authority to exercise general supervision over the health of the city. After proclamation by the mayor that an epidemic exists the board has power to take all steps and use all measures necessary to avoid suffering, or to mitigate such disease, supplying such officers and agents and providing such hospitals as it may deem fit. The president is the chief executive officer, and is *ex officio* the health officer of the city. Meetings of the board are held only when business of importance is to be transacted. Complaints to any member of the board are referred to the president, and a record is kept of the action taken. Inspections are made in all parts of the city at least once a year, or oftener if ordered by the city council, and special inspections are made on complaints. When nuisances are found to exist, the city marshal is directed to abate them. All defective house-drainage, privy-vaults, cesspools, or sources of drinking-water are inspected and corrected. In case of defective street-cleaning, recommendations for correction are made to the city council, this being the mode of procedure prescribed by law; but during an epidemic, the board having unlimited authority, orders for correction are given. By custom (not by law) the board has entire control over the conservation and removal of garbage. Physicians are required to report all deaths to the board, and, when the reports are satisfactory, permits for burial are issued, the undertakers being required to report all interments. No body is allowed to be removed from the city except by permission of the board. There are no regulations regarding the pollution of streams.

INFECTIOUS DISEASES.

Small-pox patients are either isolated at home, the house being strictly quarantined, or removed to the pest-house, which is situated about 1½ mile outside the city limits. Scarlet-fever patients are quarantined at home in some cases, the board having full discretion in the matter. The board has full authority in the case of the breaking out of a contagious disease in either public or private schools, and can exclude pupils or close the schools, as it may deem necessary. Vaccination is compulsory only when ordered by the board, and at such times is done at the public expense.

REGISTRATION.

All births, diseases, and deaths must be reported to the board, and a complete record of the same is kept. In case of births, the date, sex, age, residence, color, and nativity of parents are required; and, in case of death, a statement is required giving residence, age, sex, nativity, duration of disease, cause of death, and name of physician or other attendant.

REPORTS.

The board reports annually to the city council, and its report is published with the regular city documents in pamphlet form.

MUNICIPAL CLEANSING.

Street-cleaning.—The streets are cleaned at the expense of the city and with its regular force. The work is done wholly by hand. There is one general cleaning in the spring, and after that as often as it becomes necessary. The work is reported as well done. The annual cost to the city averages $1,500, and the sweepings are either sold or spread on low lots.

Removal of ashes and garbage.—During the summer months the garbage is removed by the city, and during the remainder of the year it is removed by the householders. It is required to be kept in tight covered vessels, unmixed with ashes, and in a place convenient for removal by the gatherers, who must collect the same at least once in three days. It is hauled outside the city and fed to hogs. The ashes are gathered by the city and disposed of in the same way as street-sweepings. The annual cost to the city for this service is $150 for garbage and $200 for ashes. The cost to private parties was not stated. The removal of garbage being superintended by the board of health, no nuisance or injury to health is reported to occur.

Dead animals.—The carcass of any animal dying within the city limits is required to be taken outside and buried on the city farm. This work is done by the owners of the animals.

Liquid household wastes.—The majority of the liquid household wastes are run into the street-gutters, a portion only being thrown into vaults or cesspools. The latter are porous, have no overflow, do not receive the wastes from water-closets, and are cleaned in the same manner as vaults. The gutters depend on rain for flushing, but, as the grades are good, the accumulated filth is carried into the river. The board of health, in its annual report for the past year, says that the water used for domestic purposes is "seriously contaminated", and supports its statement by analysis.

Human excreta.—The hotels are provided with water-closets that empty into vaults, but nearly all the houses in the city depend on privy-vaults. The vaults are required by ordinance to be water-tight, but very few really are so. They are emptied by regular licensed scavengers, one odorless excavator and three carts with buckets being used for the purpose. The "excavator" gives general satisfaction, but the use of the bucket-and-cart process is very objectionable. The night-soil is either used as manure on farms, 3 miles from the city, or buried in pits dug for the purpose on the city farm.

POLICE.

The police force is appointed and governed by the police board, consisting of the mayor and 2 councilmen. The chief of police is the executive officer, has full charge of the force, and governs it in accordance with rules and regulations making the usual provisions; his salary is $65 per month. The remainder of the force consists of 8 police officers, all of equal grade, at $60 per month each. The uniform consists of a dark-blue frock-coat with police buttons, dark-blue trousers, and blue police cap with metal wreath and number in front. Overcoats are of dark-blue cloth, double-breasted. The men provide their own uniforms. The patrolmen are equipped with maces and revolvers. Their hours of duty are from 6 a. m. to 6 p. m. and from 6 p. m. to 6 a. m., and they patrol all the streets of the city. During the past year 694 arrests were made, the principal causes being, assault and battery, 63; disorderly, 51; drunk, 324; drunk and disorderly, 20; larceny, 25; selling liquors unlawfully, 24; vagrancy, 76, etc. Most of these were fined, and those who could not pay their fines worked them out on the streets. The number of station-house lodgers during the same time was 142, as against 320 in 1879. No free meals were furnished to the lodgers. The police force is required to co-operate with the fire department when ordered by the chief of police, the chief engineer, or the mayor. Special policemen are appointed by the board to guard private property. They are under the orders of the chief of police, but receive no pay from the city. During the year one policeman was crippled for life, by a rowdy, while in discharge of his duty. The yearly cost of the police force (1880) is $6,566.

FIRE DEPARTMENT.

The force of the Richmond fire department consists of 22 men, viz, 9 who are permanently employed, 12 minute-men, and 1 chief engineer. The apparatus consists of 2 steam fire-engines, 1 hook-and-ladder truck, 3 two-wheeled hose-carts, and 2,800 feet of hose, 1,000 feet of which, though not reliable, can be used in case of necessity. There are 8 horses belonging to the department, 7 of which are in service. There is a fire-alarm telegraph, with 27 street signal-boxes. Water for fire purposes is taken from 50 wells and cisterns, some of them being small. During the year there were 27 alarms, 4 of which were false, 18 not requiring the throwing of water, and 9 were for fires needing the engines to work. The value of the property exposed was $231,000; property destroyed, $550, on which there was paid $525 insurance; property destroyed on which there was no insurance, $25; and the total amount on the property exposed was $68,775.

SOUTH BEND,

SAINT JOSEPH COUNTY, INDIANA.

POPULATION

IN THE

AGGREGATE,

1850-1880.

	Inhab.
1790	......
1800	......
1810	......
1820	......
1830	......
1840	......
1850	1,652
1860	3,803
1870	7,206
1880	13,280

POPULATION

BY

SEX, NATIVITY, AND RACE

AT

CENSUS OF 1880.

Male	6,825
Female	6,455
Native	9,854
Foreign-born	3,426
White	13,066
Colored	214

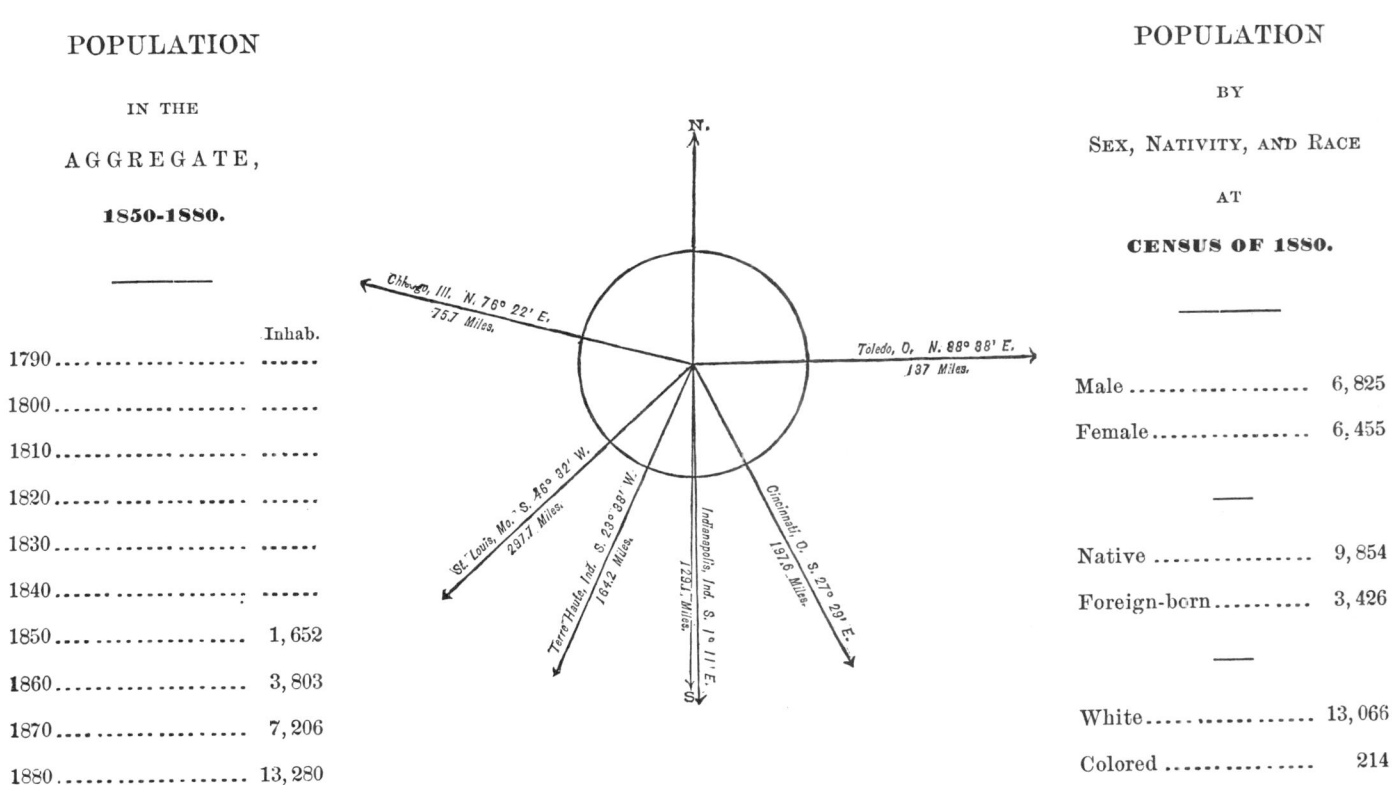

Latitude: 41° 39′ North; Longitude: 86° 12′ (west form Greenwich); Altitude: 729 feet.

FINANCIAL CONDITION:

Total Valuation: $4,809,005; per capita: $362 00.   Net Indebtedness: $316,975; per capita: $23 87.   Tax per $100: $1 89.

SOUTH BEND.

South Bend is situated in Saint Joseph county, in the extreme northerly part of the state, not far from the Michigan state line. The river Saint Joseph, on which the city lies, was at one time navigable for steamboats and barges from its mouth, on lake Michigan, to South Bend, but since 1867 several dams have been built across the river, and navigation has been suspended. The altitude of the city, taken at the track of the Michigan Central railroad, is 156 feet above lake Erie, or 729 feet above mean sea-level. South Bend is touched by the following railroads: The Chicago and Grand Trunk railroad, from Chicago to Port Huron; the Lake Shore and Michigan Southern railroad, from Chicago to Buffalo; and the Niles branch of the Michigan Central railroad, between Chicago and Detroit. The great Kankakee swamp begins about 1½ mile southwest of the city, and covers several square miles of territory. The rest of the country tributary to the city is remarkable for its fertility, beauty, and wealth.

South Bend is a manufacturing place, producing largely and giving employment to many operatives. Some of the larger industries are the making of sewing-machines, 3 wagon-factories, 2 paper-mills, 2 woolen factories, 2 plow factories, 1 clover-huller factory, flouring-mills, etc.

The first white settler at South Bend was Alexis Coquillard, who came in the spring of 1824, and he was followed by Lathrop M. Taylor, who came in September, 1827. Both these men were Indian traders, and together they laid out the town. The original population was composed mostly of immigrants from New England, New York, Pennsylvania, and Virginia, and, though of late years many Poles and Germans have settled here, their descendants still form the major-part of the population.

It is to be regretted that no information was furnished from which a report of the "present condition" of South Bend could be prepared.

TERRE HAUTE,

VIGO COUNTY, INDIANA.

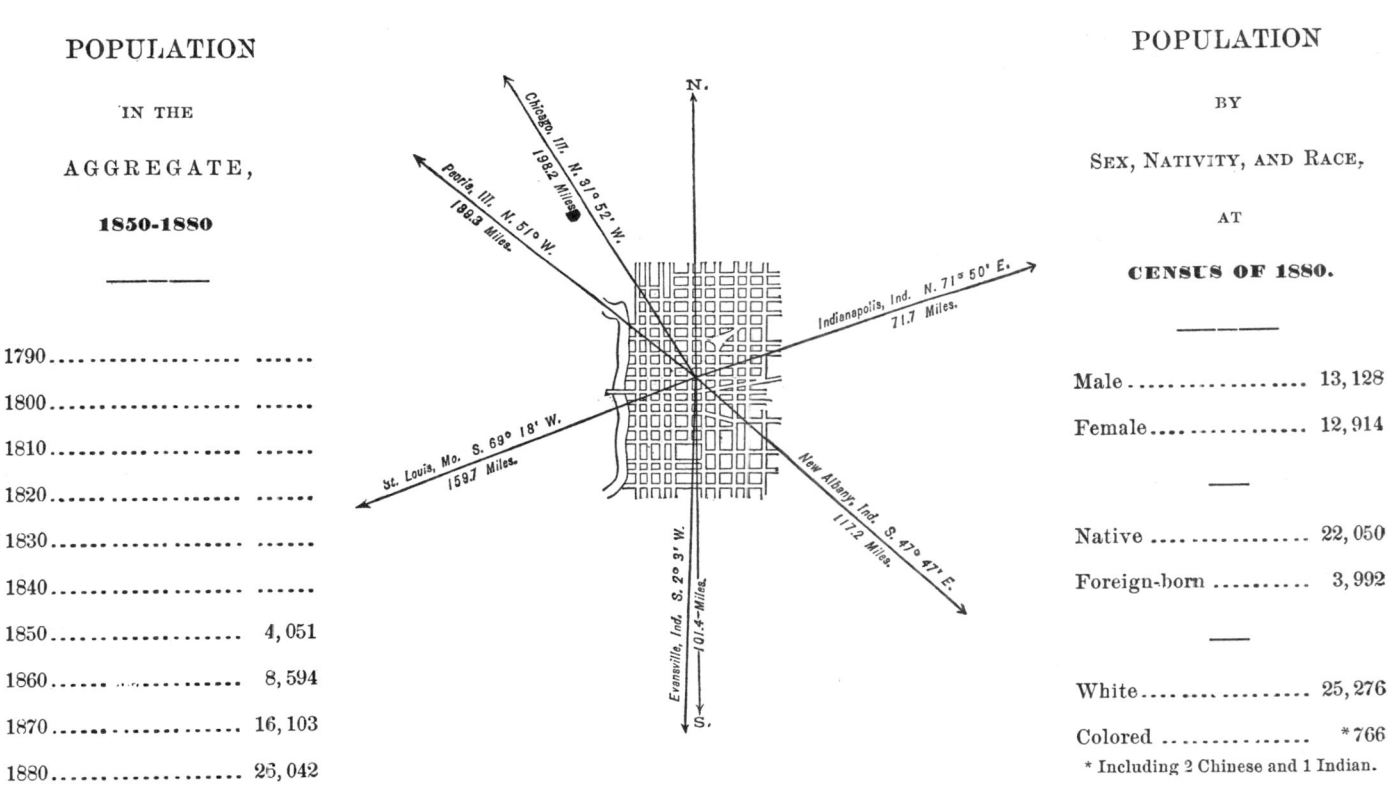

POPULATION IN THE AGGREGATE, 1850-1880	
1790	......
1800	......
1810	......
1820	......
1830	......
1840	......
1850	4,051
1860	8,594
1870	16,103
1880	26,042

POPULATION BY SEX, NATIVITY, AND RACE, AT CENSUS OF 1880.	
Male	13,128
Female	12,914
Native	22,050
Foreign-born	3,992
White	25,276
Colored	*766

* Including 2 Chinese and 1 Indian.

Latitude: 39° 28′ North; Longitude: 87° 26′ (west from Greenwich); Altitude: 647 feet.

FINANCIAL CONDITION:

Total Valuation: $13,562,625; per capita: $521 00.   Net Indebtedness: $267,224; per capita: $10 26.   Tax per $100: $1 81.

TERRE HAUTE IN 1880

Terre Haute, capital of Vigo county, is situated on the west border of Harrison prairie, a long, narrow area of gently rolling prairie land in the western portion of the state, and on the east bank of the Wabash river, in latitude 39° 28′ north, longitude 87° 26′ west from Greenwich, about 70 miles southwest of Indianapolis. The bank on which the city is built is 60 feet above the river, and the altitude above mean sea-level, as taken on the railroad-track at the station of the Vandalia line, is 647 feet. The Wabash river is navigable here during the high stage of water, while the Wabash and Erie canal gives water communication with lake Erie. The plan of the city is rectangular, and the streets are wide and bordered with numerous shade-trees. In Vigo and the adjoining counties a good quality of block-coal is found, which has stimulated manufactures of different kinds in Terre Haute. The city is also a center of trade for the surrounding country, and is one of the most important shipping points of the Wabash and Erie canal. Terre Haute has gas- and water-works, and all the metropolitan conveniences. The

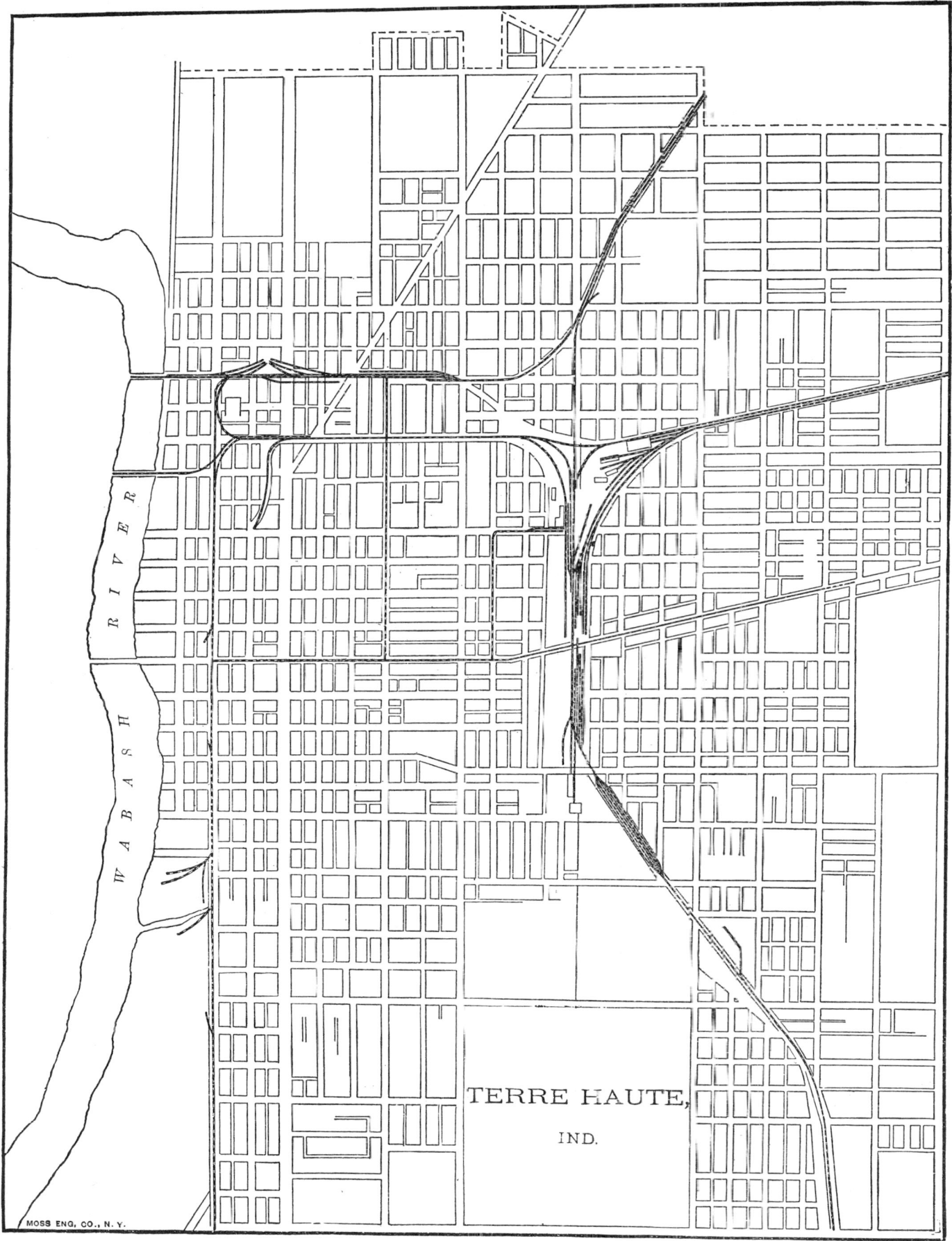

TERRE HAUTE,

IND.

RIVER

WABASH

Chicago and East Illinois, the Evansville and Terre Haute, the Illinois Midland, the Indianapolis and Saint Louis, the Terre Haute and Southeastern, and the Vandalia Line railroads pass through the city, and, with their several connections, afford ample communication with all railroad points in the country.

Public schools were opened in Terre Haute in 1853, but in 1854 they were interrupted for want of funds until a reorganization, dating from 1860. The schools now have a good degree of general efficiency.

The collection of social statistics for Terre Haute has been attended with but indifferent success, but what has been obtained is given below, that the city may not be wholly unrepresented.

DRAINAGE.

Formerly the drainage of the city was almost entirely surface, a few short drains near the river aiding the gutters to dispose of the surface water. Now sewers are built according to a regular plan, and the short drains are either taken up or incorporated with the system. The average cost of each inlet basin and its connection with the sewers is $80, and the average cost of each manhole, the average depth being 15 feet, is $30. Sewers are ventilated at the manholes only. Inverted blocks for subsoil drainage are not used. The sewers deliver into the Wabash river, the mouths being fully exposed; but their bottoms are built on a line with the low-water mark of the river. The sewers are reported as self-cleansing, the removal of deposits by hand or artificial flushing not being required. The cost of the main lines is paid by the city from the general tax fund, while the cost of lateral sewers is paid by abutters, the assessment being made by the front foot. All work on the sewers, making connections, etc., is under the supervision of the civil engineer, and a city ordinance provides that all houses connected with the sewers must have good fixtures. An ordinance also forbids the introduction of any substance into the sewers that would tend to obstruct the same. The contract price for work on sewers during the past year was from $3 60 to $4 per foot.

CEMETERIES.

Terre Haute has a public cemetery, area 80 acres, which is the property of the city, and under the charge of the public sexton, an officer appointed by the city council. About 5,000 interments have been made in this cemetery. The sexton has charge of all interments and keeps a record of the same. Graves are dug 4 feet deep for persons under ten years of age, and 5 feet for persons over ten years. Lots are sold by the city clerk, the prices ranging from $2 50 upward, according to size and location. No burials are allowed anywhere in the city except in this cemetery.

MARKETS.

There are 2 public markets in the city—one costing $8,000, which is no longer used, and the other, corner of Fourth and Ohio streets, costing $30,000. This latter has an area of 60 by 100 feet, with a street area for wagons of 120 by 300 feet, and has 20 stalls. The stalls rent for $4 and $8 per month, about half at each rate, and the total rentals amount to $400. The market is open on Tuesdays, Thursdays, and Saturdays, the hours being from 4 to 9 a. m. from April to October, and from 5 to 9 a. m. from October to April. The gross annual sales from the stalls are estimated at $30,000. The private stores in the city sell ten times as much as is sold at the market. The market is under charge of a market-master, appointed by the city council, who gives bonds for the proper performance of his duties.

SANITARY AUTHORITY—BOARD OF HEALTH.

The chief health organization of Terre Haute is vested in a board of health, composed of three members, all of whom are physicians, appointed and controlled by the city council. In ordinary times the annual expense of the board is $1,250, for examining the city, declaring nuisances, issuing orders, etc. During an epidemic the expenses are governed by the city council. In absence of an epidemic the authority of the board is confined simply to defining nuisances, while during epidemics it makes proper regulations to check and control the disease. Each member of the board acts as health officer for one month at a time. There are 2 sanitary policemen, who have police powers. The board meets monthly, or oftener if necessary. Inspections are made in all parts of the city regularly, and also as nuisances are reported. When a nuisance is discovered or reported it is ordered abated within a certain time, and if the order is not complied with the parties who are responsible are prosecuted before the mayor. All defective house-drainage, privy-vaults, cesspools, and sources of drinking-water are corrected. The board exercises full control over the conservation and removal of garbage. Small-pox patients are either quarantined at home or removed to the city hospital, situated on the northwest part of the city. Scarlet-fever patients are generally isolated at home. The board takes cognizance of the breaking out of diseases of a contagious nature in either public or private schools, and, if possible, controls the same. Vaccination is neither compulsory nor is it done at the public expense. There is no system of registration of births, diseases, or deaths. The board reports monthly to the common council.

MUNICIPAL CLEANSING.

Street-cleaning.—The streets are cleaned at the expense of the city and with its own force, wholly by hand. The cleaning is done quarterly, and is reported as thoroughly done. The annual cost is $4,000, and the sweepings are deposited outside the city limits.

Removal of garbage and ashes.—Ashes and garbage are removed by the city, under contract, at an annual cost of $5,000. Garbage is required to be removed, in water-tight barrels or boxes, to a place outside the city limits, designated by the board of health. Ashes are not allowed to be kept in the same vessel with the garbage, and they are hauled outside the city.

Dead animals.—Dead animals are removed by contractors, who take the hide and render the balance of the carcass.

Liquid household wastes.—A small portion of the liquid household wastes are run into the public sewers, while the majority are thrown into vaults and cesspools. No wastes are allowed to run into the street-gutters. The cesspools are generally porous, have no overflows, sometimes receive the wastes from water-closets, and are cleaned out in the same manner as privy-vaults.

Human excreta.—About 10 per cent. of the houses have water-closets, nearly all of which deliver into the sewers, while the remainder depend on privy-vaults. The vaults are required to be 10 feet deep, and walled with either brick or stone. None of them are even nominally water-tight. They are emptied by the odorless-excavator process, under direction of the board of health, and the night-soil is dumped into the river below the city limits, none of it being used as manure within the gathering-ground of the public water-supply. Manufacturing wastes are disposed of in the same manner.

POLICE.

The police force of Terre Haute is appointed and governed by the police board, an organization of which the mayor is chairman. The chief of police, salary $950 per annum, is the executive officer, and has direct command of the force. The remainder of the force consists of 1 captain at $2 20 per day, and 30 patrolmen at $2 per day each. The uniform is a dark-blue sack coat with brass buttons, and the men provide their own, at a cost of $35 each. The patrolmen are equipped with common wooden clubs covered with leather. The night hours of duty are from 7 p. m. to 6.30 a. m., and the beats are so arranged as to give 71 squares to every 2 patrolmen. During the past year there were 1,521 arrests made, the principal causes being drunkenness, disorderly conduct, larceny, suspicious, etc. They were disposed of either by fines or by imprisonment in the penitentiary. The total amount of property lost or stolen in the year was $1,987 75, and of this, $1,224 10 was recovered and $1,200 returned to the owners. There were 172 station-house lodgers during the year, and meals, costing from 12½ to 15 cents each, were furnished them. The force is required to assist the fire department at all fires. Special policemen, to act as watchmen over private property, are appointed, but they have no connection with the regular force. The yearly cost of the police force (1880) is $9,785.

MANUFACTURES.

The following is a summary of the statistics of the manufactures of Terre Haute for 1880, being taken from tables prepared for the Tenth Census by Joseph R. Gaddes, special agent:

Mechanical and manufacturing industries.	No. of establishments.	Capital.	AVERAGE NUMBER OF HANDS EMPLOYED.			Total amount paid in wages during the year.	Value of materials.	Value of products.
			Males above 16 years.	Females above 15 years.	Children and youths.			
All industries	224	$2,566,750	3,090	144	142	$1,406,352	$6,743,719	$9,185,246
Blacksmithing (see also Wheelwrighting)	10	9,900	30		1	9,110	13,183	35,805
Boots and shoes, including custom work and repairing	30	17,725	41		1	13,675	23,045	59,127
Brick and tile	9	35,200	116		6	21,100	21,125	51,975
Carpentering	25	45,000	132		1	52,245	133,005	235,400
Carriages and wagons (see also Wheelwrighting)	4	40,000	65		1	30,250	58,500	105,000
Confectionery	3	14,000	26		6	9,400	36,950	52,700
Cooperage	8	35,800	195			65,760	146,150	230,000
Flouring- and grist-mill products	9	583,500	172			70,152	2,708,395	2,908,557
Foundery and machine-shop products	6	122,000	141		14	66,863	109,100	210,500
Iron and steel	3	355,000	495		50	337,925	788,390	1,221,968
Lumber, sawed	5	181,000	146		13	50,500	187,800	290,320
Marble and stone work	6	19,500	42			12,584	21,775	52,570
Masonry, brick and stone	5	4,800	56			19,040	29,700	56,550
Painting and paperhanging	9	4,025	41			9,370	15,500	35,658
Plumbing and gasfitting	4	13,600	6			4,450	9,500	23,020

Mechanical and manufacturing industries.	No. of establishments.	Capital.	AVERAGE NUMBER OF HANDS EMPLOYED.			Total amount paid in wages during the year.	Value of materials.	Value of products.
			Males above 16 years.	Females above 15 years.	Children and youths.			
Printing and publishing	8	$37,000	75	6	21	$42,380	$23,620	$86,700
Pumps, not including steam pumps	4	7,200	16	....	1	5,000	6,880	18,500
Saddlery and harness	8	30,900	40	....	1	17,052	40,541	69,340
Tinware, copperware, and sheet-iron ware	10	66,100	65	....	....	24,300	108,000	171,700
Tobacco, cigars and cigarettes	14	29,000	103	....	5	40,500	38,640	106,597
Watch and clock repairing	5	12,700	13	....	1	6,200	3,900	19,000
Wheelwrighting (see also Blacksmithing; Carriages and wagons)	3	400	....	....	....	....	615	2,065
All other industries (a)	36	902,400	1,074	138	20	498,496	2,219,405	3,142,394

a Embracing boxes, cigar; brass castings; brooms and brushes; carpets, rag; carriage and wagon materials; cars, railroad, street, and repairs; clothing, men's; coffee and spices, roasted and ground; coppersmithing; files; furniture; hones and whetstones; iron rails and spikes, cut and wrought; liquors, distilled; liquors, malt; lock- and gun-smithing; looking-glass and picture frames; lumber, planed; mattresses and spring beds; mineral and soda waters; musical instruments and materials (not specified); scales and balances; shirts; slaughtering and meat-packing; stencils and brands; and woolen goods.

From the foregoing table it appears that the average capital of all establishments is $11,458 71; that the average wages of all hands employed is $416 73 per annum; and that the average outlay in wages, in materials, and in interest (at 6 per cent.) on capital employed is $37,071 77.

ILLINOIS.

AURORA,

KANE COUNTY, ILLINOIS.

POPULATION

IN THE

AGGREGATE,

1850-1880.

	Inhab.
1790	......
1800	......
1810	......
1820	......
1830	......
1840	......
1850	1,895
1860	6,011
1870	11,162
1880	11,873

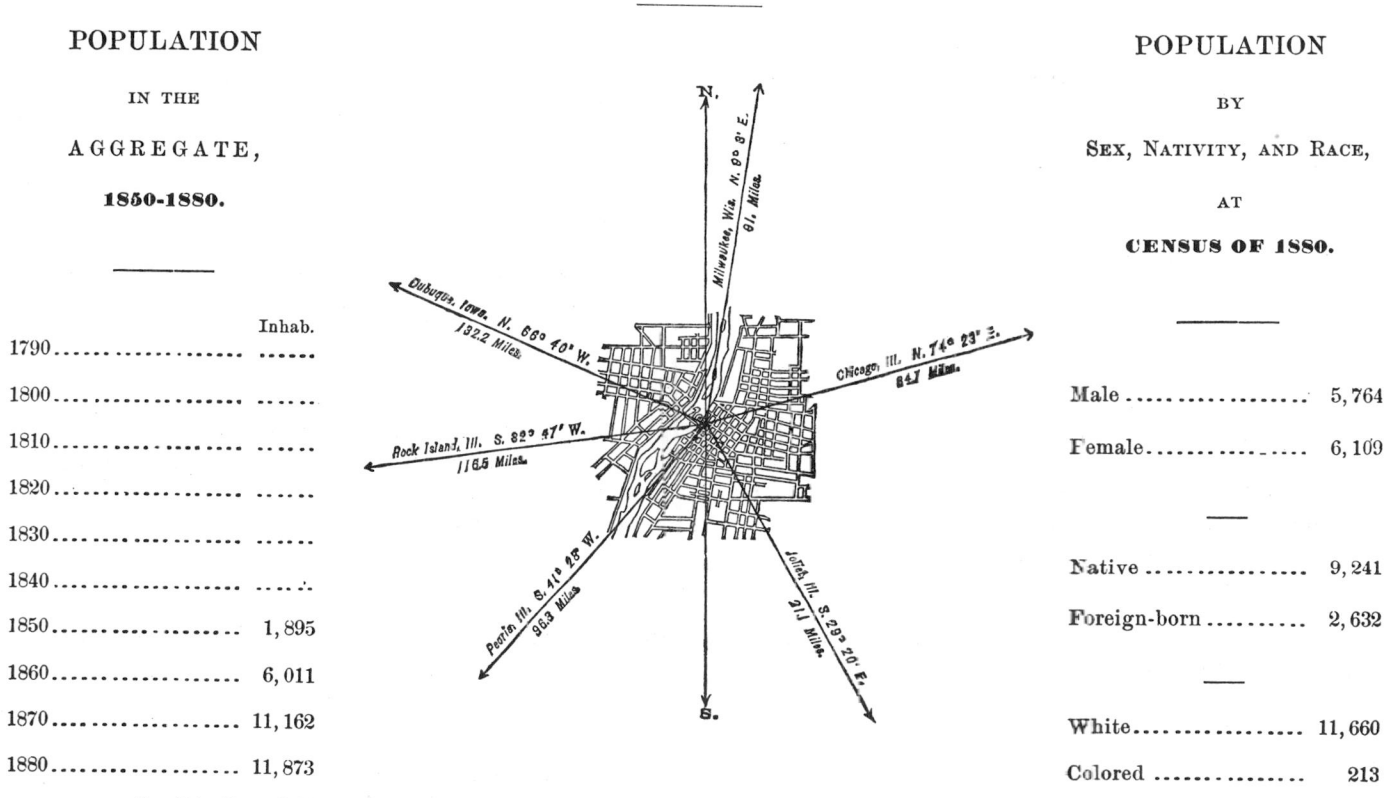

POPULATION

BY

SEX, NATIVITY, AND RACE,

AT

CENSUS OF 1880.

Male	5,764
Female	6,109
Native	9,241
Foreign-born	2,632
White	11,660
Colored	213

Latitude: 41° 46 North; Longitude: 88° 17′ (west from Greenwich); **Altitude: 670 feet.**

FINANCIAL CONDITION:

Total Valuation: $2,882,900; per capita: $243 00.   Net Indebtedness: $25,506; per capita: $2 15.   Tax per $100: $3 24.

HISTORICAL SKETCH.

Aurora was first settled in 1834. Saw-mills and flouring-mills were erected and manufactures on a small scale were first carried on. After the Chicago, Burlington, and Quincy railroad was built through the town, manufactures rapidly increased. The railroad company have built large shops here, employing about 1,200 men, while a number of the trainmen have their homes in the city. The principal industries now are the making of wood-working machinery and agricultural implements, silver-plating, woolen factories, and flouring-mills. Aurora has had superior public schools for many years. They are controlled by district officers under the general state law, and not by city ordinances.

With the exception of the burning, in 1872, of some of the machine-shops belonging to the railroad—the loss being quickly repaired by the erection of better buildings—there have been no serious fires in Aurora. During the past ten years the city has not advanced much, but the present year has brought about a change; a large amount of building is going on and manufactures are increasing. The original settlers were from the eastern states, New York being largely represented, and, though many Germans have come in of late years, the population now is largely native-born.

AURORA IN 1880.

The following statistical accounts, collected by the Census Office, indicate the present condition of Aurora:

LOCATION.

Aurora lies in latitude 41° 46′ north, longitude 88° 17′ west from Greenwich, on both sides of the Fox river, and about 39 miles, by railroad, south of west from Chicago. The river is not navigable. The altitude above mean sea-level, taken at the track of the Chicago, Burlington, and Quincy railroad, is 670 feet.

RAILROAD COMMUNICATIONS.

Aurora is touched by the following-named railroads:

The Chicago, Burlington, and Quincy railroad, from Chicago to Council Bluffs, and with branches to Geneva and Streator.

The Chicago and Iowa railroad, to Forreston and Rockford, Illinois.

TRIBUTARY COUNTRY.

The country immediately tributary to the city is agricultural, corn and hogs being the chief products. Butter and cheese are produced quite largely, and are rapidly increasing, being largely made in factories constructed for the purpose.

TOPOGRAPHY, ETC.

The soil is alluvial, and, within the city limits, there is gravel near the surface which crops out in places. The underlying rock is Upper Silurian of the Niagara and the Lower Helderberg periods. The surface is slightly rolling, and the natural drainage is by small streams and, mainly, the Fox river, passing through the city. The surrounding country is about the same as the city, there being but little elevated land. There are no lakes, but marshes and ponds are somewhat abundant.

CLIMATE.

Highest recorded summer temperature, 98°; highest summer temperature in average years, 90°. Lowest recorded winter temperature −18°; lowest winter temperature in average years −6°.

STREETS; WATER-WORKS; GAS.

But little information was obtained under these heads. No statement was furnished as to the total length of streets, number of miles paved and unpaved, different classes of pavement, and cost of same, gutters, or tree-planting. The sidewalks are reported as being of plank, stone, and gravel. From the annual report of the street commissioners it does not appear that any of the streets are paved with other material than gravel. The city has water-works on the Holly system. The gas-works are owned by a private company. The charge per 1,000 feet is $3. The city pays $42 per annum each for street-lamps, 128 in number.

PUBLIC BUILDINGS.

The city owns and occupies for municipal purposes, wholly or in part, 1 city hall, and 4 houses for the fire department. The total cost of the municipal buildings is $89,500, the cost of the city hall being $80,000.

PUBLIC PARKS AND PLEASURE-GROUNDS.

No public parks or pleasure-grounds were reported.

PLACES OF AMUSEMENT.

There is 1 theater, Colter's opera-house, with a seating capacity of 820, and the following halls: Brady's hall, seating 400; Hoyt hall, seating 300; and Driving's hall, seating 550; these halls are sometimes used for theatrical exhibitions. The buildings pay no license, but each performance pays $8 to the city.

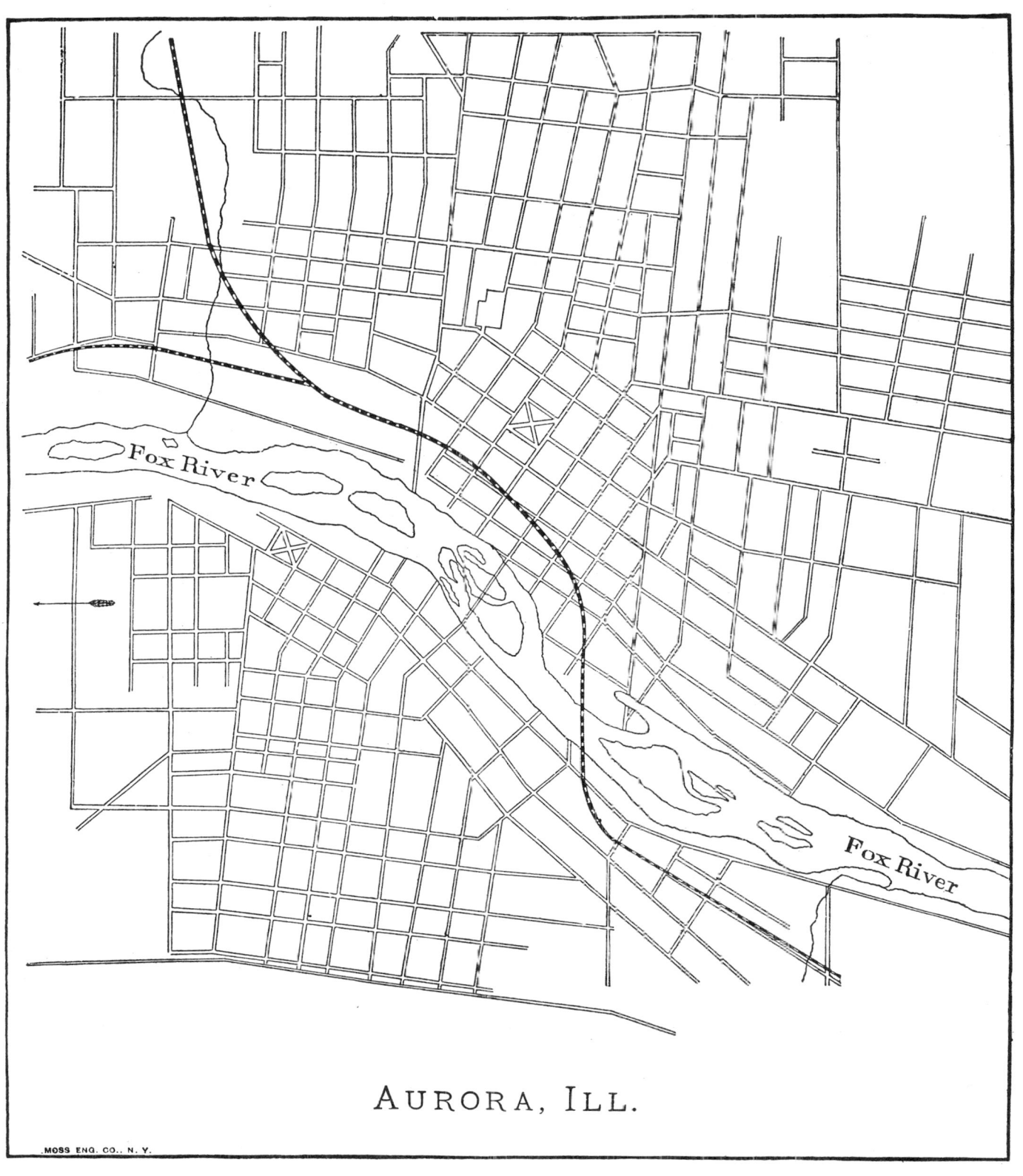

Fox River

Fox River

AURORA, ILL.

MOSS ENG. CO., N.Y.

DRAINAGE.

There are no sewers in Aurora.

CEMETERIES.

There are 5 cemeteries within the city, viz:

Spring Lake Cemetery, belonging to a private corporation, on Lincoln avenue, near Fox river, in the extreme southwestern part of the city.

German Catholic Cemetery, area 4 acres, on Ohio street, near the eastern limits.

Irish Catholic Cemetery, area 5 acres, on Fox river, adjoining the northern boundary of the city.

West Aurora Cemetery, area 12 acres, between Cemetery and Illinois avenues; and a small cemetery of 2 acres in the 8th ward, on Fulton street.

The only information regarding interments was that 64 had been made in Spring Lake cemetery for the year ending March 1, 1880.

MARKETS.

There are no public or corporation markets in the city.

SANITARY AUTHORITY—BOARD OF HEALTH.

The chief sanitary organization of Aurora is the board of health, appointed by the city council, which exercises general control over its action, and is composed of 3 members, one of whom is a physician. In ordinary times the annual expense is $100 for salary, and this sum may not be increased in case of epidemics except by authority of the city council. In absence of epidemics the board has authority to do what it deems best for the preservation of the health of the city, but if to carry out its plans any expense is proposed the matter must be submitted to the common council for its action. In case of an epidemic the board has power to do all that it deems best to limit or control the disease. The president of the board is *ex officio* health officer, with a salary of $100 per annum. His duties are to carry out the orders of the board, to make such inspections as he may deem necessary, and to take such action, with the advice of the board, as may seem to be best. He has full police power. No assistant health officers or inspectors are employed, but the police are required to assist the health officer when he calls on them. The board meets monthly, or specially when necessary, and acts on business presented by the president. The ordinances provide for inspections only as nuisances are reported, but it has been the custom to make an occasional one of a more or less general character. When a nuisance is reported, the party on whose premises the same exists is notified to remove the same within a given time, usually from 2 to 5 days, and if this is not done proceedings against the offender are instituted. In the case of a non-resident the board abates the nuisance and charges the cost against the property. Defective privy-vaults and cesspools are treated as nuisances when offensive, but the powers of the board are advisory only so far as the disposal of sewage, street-cleaning, etc., are concerned. The board exercises no control over the conservation and removal of garbage, except to see that it does not become offensive or injurious to the public health. Burial permits are issued by the clerk of the board on certificates of death signed by the attending physician. The pollution of Fox river is prohibited, and the board regulates the removal of excrement.

INFECTIOUS DISEASES.

Small-pox patients are quarantined at home or removed to the pest-house, about a mile beyond the city limits. The ordinances do not provide for the isolation of scarlet-fever cases, but attention is given to them so that possible epidemics may be prevented. In case of the breaking out of a contagious disease in either public or private schools the board sees that no pupils from infected families attend. Vaccination is compulsory for all those who may be exposed to contagion, and in cases where persons are unable to pay it is done at the public expense.

There is no system of registration of diseases, except when they terminate fatally. A complete record of all births and deaths is kept by the city clerk, who is *ex officio* clerk of the board.

REPORTS.

The board reports to the common council monthly and annually; the annual reports are published with the regular city documents.

MUNICIPAL CLEANSING.

Street cleaning.—The streets are cleaned at the expense of the city and with its regular force. The work is done wholly by hand. There are no stated times for cleaning, it being done when necessary, and as well as can be by shovels and teams. No separate account is kept of the cost, and the sweepings are used about the suburbs where grading is necessary.

Removal of garbage and ashes.—The garbage and ashes are removed both by the city and by householders. So much as is done by the city is under charge of the street commissioner. While awaiting removal the garbage is kept in boxes and barrels, and garbage and ashes are allowed to be kept in the same vessel. The garbage is deposited outside the city limits, while the ashes are used for grading purposes. The annual cost to the city for this service is $100, the balance of the expense being borne by the householders. No nuisance or probable injury to health is reported to result from either the manner of keeping or of removing garbage.

Dead animals.—The carcass of any animal dying within the city is ordered to be removed by the board of health, and the annual cost of this service is $50.

Liquid household wastes and human excreta.—All the liquid household wastes are either thrown into cesspools or into privy-vaults. The cesspools are porous, have no overflows, and there are no ordinances regarding their cleansing. The houses in the city, with but few exceptions, depend on privy-vaults. None of them are reported as even nominally water-tight. They are cleaned by a licensed scavenger, between the hours of 10 p. m. and 6 a. m., and the contents are removed in water-tight carts, either outside the city limits or buried at least 3 feet deep.

POLICE.

The police force of Aurora, with the exception of the city marshal, is appointed and governed by the common council. The city marshal is elected by the people, and acts as chief of police; his salary is $800 per annum. The regular force is composed of 4 policemen, with salaries varying from $720 to $96 per annum each, according to the duty performed. The uniform is of navy-blue cloth, and each man provides his own. The patrolmen are equipped with clubs and revolvers; they are on duty all night, and the business part of the city is patrolled by the force. During the past year there were 253 arrests made, the principal causes being for drunkenness, disorderly conduct, vagrancy, assault and battery, etc. Station-house lodgers are cared for by the county. The police force is not required to co-operate with the fire department. Special policemen are appointed by the council, but receive no pay from the city. The yearly cost of the police force (1880) exclusive of the salary of the city marshal, is $1,953 50.

FIRE DEPARTMENT.

The manual force of the fire department of Aurora consists of 1 chief and 1 assistant engineer and 84 men. The apparatus consists of 2 steam fire-engines with 2 two-wheeled hose-carts, 1 Holly hose-cart, and 1 hook-and-ladder truck complete. In addition, the city has the use of a company of 26 men, with 1 engine and 1 hose-cart, located at the Chicago, Burlington, and Quincy Railroad shops. The railroad company keeps this engine and hose-cart in repair, and the apparatus is brought to fires when specially called. Water, for fire purposes, is obtained from 16 hydrants and 8 cisterns, the latter having an aggregate capacity of 3,950 barrels. A fire-alarm telegraph is also in use. During the past year there were 14 fires. The total loss was $4,865 and the amount of insurance paid was $3,355, making the loss not insured $1,510. The cost of the department for the past year was $3,423 54.

BELLEVILLE,
SAINT CLAIR COUNTY, ILLINOIS.

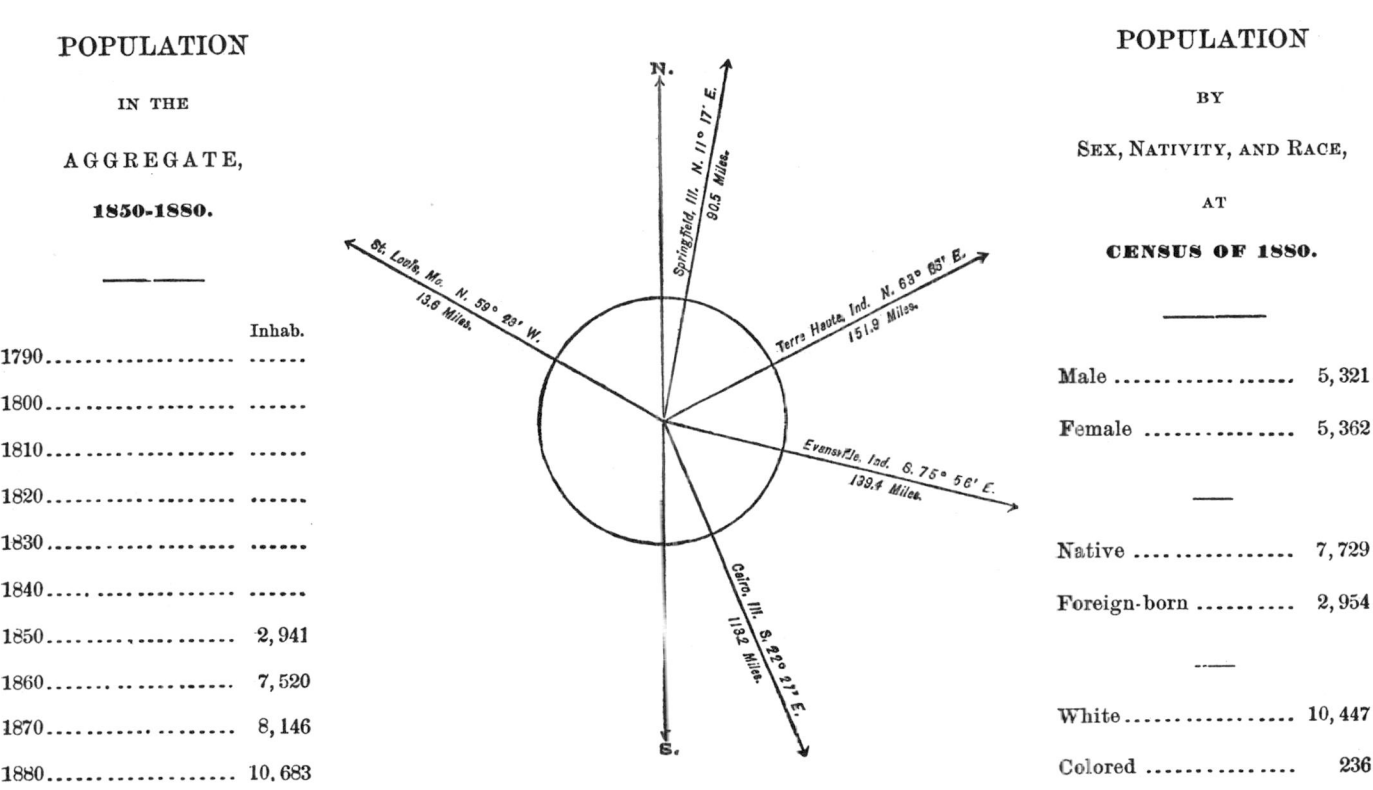

POPULATION

IN THE

AGGREGATE,

1850-1880.

	Inhab.
1790	......
1800	......
1810	......
1820	......
1830	......
1840	......
1850	2,941
1860	7,520
1870	8,146
1880	10,683

POPULATION

BY

SEX, NATIVITY, AND RACE,

AT

CENSUS OF 1880.

Male	5,321
Female	5,362
Native	7,729
Foreign-born	2,954
White	10,447
Colored	236

Latitude: 38° 29 North; Longitude: 89° 58' (west from Greenwich); Altitude: 600 feet.

FINANCIAL CONDITION:

Total Valuation: $1,592,557; per capita: $149 00.   Net Indebtedness: $217,712; per capita: $20 38.   Tax per $100: $4 71.

HISTORICAL SKETCH.

In 1813 the citizens of Saint Clair county, Illinois, determined to remove the county-seat from the old French settlement of Cahokia to a more eligible point, and, with this end in view, the court of common pleas appointed commissioners to decide on some convenient place. The commissioners recommended a site on the high, rolling ground between the Mississippi and Kaskaskia rivers, about 14 miles from each, and near what was then known as Compton Hill. This site was accepted, the county-seat was laid out and called Belleville, and the records were moved hither. In 1814 the first court-house was built and a hotel was opened. In 1819 Belleville was incorporated as a town. Up to this time the settlers were from the eastern states, and still continued so until 1829, when a steady influx of Germans set in, attracted by the fertility of the soil and the proximity of Saint Louis as a market.

They spread over the whole county, and by their industry and thrift soon developed its resources. In 1850 Belleville was incorporated as a city. No serious fires have occurred, and there have been no serious periods of depression. Though the coal industry in Saint Clair county is quite extensive, the steady growth of the city must be attributed to agriculture, the returns of 1880 showing that this county alone produced over 2,000,000 bushels of corn and nearly 3,000,000 bushels of wheat.

BELLEVILLE IN 1880.

The following statistical accounts, collected by the Census Office, indicate the present condition of Belleville:

LOCATION.

Belleville, the capital of Saint Clair county, Illinois, lies in latitude 38° 29' north, longitude 89° 58' west from Greenwich, in the southwestern part of the state, midway between the Mississippi and Kaskaskia rivers, and about 14 miles southeast of Saint Louis. The average elevation of the city above mean sea-level is 600 feet. It is not situated on navigable water.

RAILROAD COMMUNICATIONS.

The city is touched by the following-named lines of railroad:
The Cairo Short line, from Saint Louis to Du Quoin.
The Louisvile and Nashville railroad, from Saint Louis to Nashville.
The Illinois and Saint Louis railroad, between Saint Louis and Belleville.

TRIBUTARY COUNTRY.

The country immediately tributary to Belleville is devoted to agriculture, wheat and corn being the chief product.

CLIMATE.

Highest recorded summer temperature, 107°; highest summer temperature in average years, 100°. Lowest recorded winter temperature, −22°; lowest winter temperature in average years, −12°. Southwest winds are considered more or less unhealthful.

STREETS.

Total length, 25 miles, of which 13 miles are paved with broken stone, at a cost of 90 cents per square yard. The cost of keeping this class of pavement in repair is about 15 cents per yard per year, and it lasts about 7 years.

Sidewalks are mostly laid in brick, while the gutters are laid with stone. Day work upon streets is preferred, the work being done by the city, except the building of stone gutters and bridges, which is done by contract work. In the breaking of stone for street paving no steam stone-crusher or roller is used, it being done by hand. The usual price paid for this is $2 per square rod. There are 3 miles of horse-railroads in the city, using 5 cars and 10 horses, and giving employment to from 8 to 10 men; the rate of fare is 5 cents. There are two lines of omnibuses, with 4 vehicles and 16 horses, employing 4 men; the rate of fare is 15 cents.

WATER-WORKS.

There are no water-works, but the city has large public cisterns.

GAS.

The gas-works are owned by private parties. The charge per 1,000 feet of gas is $2 50. The city pays $23 per annum for each of its 204 street-lamps.

PUBLIC BUILDINGS.

The city owns and occupies for municipal purposes, wholly or in part, the city hall, three engine-houses, and one market-house. The total cost of these buildings is about $18,000. The city hall cost $6,000, and is owned entirely by the city.

PUBLIC PARKS AND PLEASURE-GROUNDS.

There are no public parks or pleasure-grounds in Belleville.

BELLEVILLE,
ILL.

SCALE OF FEET.

0   1000

PLACES OF AMUSEMENT.

The following places in the city are used for theatrical exhibitions, concerts, lectures, etc.: Academy of Music, with a seating capacity of 1,000; City Park hall, with a seating capacity of 1,000; and Turner hall, seating capacity, 550. Theaters pay to the city a yearly license of $25 each. There are 2 concert- and beer-gardens—City Park garden, 200 by 300 feet, which has been opened about 20 years; and King's garden, which has been in operation about the same length of time. Both are patronized during the summer months, and largely by Germans. Each can seat about 1,200 persons.

DRAINAGE.

There is no general system of sewerage in Belleville. Some small stone pipes, 6 inches in diameter, are laid only through a few streets in the lower part of the city to drain cellars. These drains all empty into the creek and branches, but as they carry only surface-water, no nuisance is created. They are built and paid for by persons living along the line. Permission must be granted by ordinance before drains are allowed to be laid.

CEMETERIES.

There are 4 cemeteries connected with the city, as follows:
Green Mount Cemetery, area 40 acres, is situated 2 miles southeast of the city.
Walnut Cemetery, area 25 acres, adjoins the southeast limits.
Harrison Cemetery, area 1 acre, is situated in the eastern part of the city.
Catholic Cemetery, area 300 feet square, is in the south part of the city.
In the last-named cemetery no interments have been made for 30 years, while in Harrison cemetery no interments have been made for 10 years. It is stated that the burial permits issued to persons not owning lots in the cemeteries average 90 every six months, permits being issued simply to give a right of burial to those not owning lots. The depth of graves varies from 4 to 4½ feet. Concerning the care and management of cemeteries the following note is added by the mayor: "The private cemeteries are kept up by owners thereof, who have gardeners residing thereon. A city sexton is kept at Walnut Hill cemetery, who has charge of city property therein. Lots 20 by 20 feet are sold; prices range from 5 to 15 cents per square foot in private cemeteries. The city also sells lots in their portion of Walnut Hill at $20 per lot."

MARKETS.

The market-house is in Market square, adjoining Public square on the north. The building is 125 feet long. There are also sheds 300 feet in length, containing tables used by hucksters. Butchers' stalls rent for $40 per annum, while 2-horse wagons pay 15 cents and 1-horse wagons 10 cents per day. The total rental of the market is about $900 per annum. The market is open from daylight till 9 a. m.

SANITARY AUTHORITY—BOARD OF HEALTH.

The sanitary interests of the city are in the hands of a board of health, which is composed of 7 members of the city council. The board has no expense as a board, all expenditures being regulated by the city council. The chairman of the board is the chief executive officer. Inspections are made as nuisances are reported, and referred to the mayor. In the case of defective house-drainage, privy-vaults, cesspools, and sources of drinking water the board visits the locality and inspects as a committee. The board has no control over defective sewerage or street-cleaning. In the conservation and removal of garbage the board, if it thinks necessary, recommends measures and actions. In case of small-pox or scarlet-fever, the house containing the patient is placarded. If disease of a contagious nature should break out either in the public or in the private schools, the board would recommend the closing of the schools. Vaccination is not compulsory, nor is it done at the public expense. A record of diseases, births, and deaths is kept by the county clerk, reports being made to him by physicians. The board reports to the city council as often as it may be expedient.

MUNICIPAL CLEANSING.

Street-cleaning.—The streets are cleaned by the city and by private abutters. All work done by the city is done by hand. The streets are swept and scraped after a continued wet season. The annual cost of the service is included in the regular street appropriation. The sweepings are deposited on low grounds adjoining the city.
Removal of garbage and ashes.—Garbage is removed by householders. An ordinance provides that when it is placed upon the streets it must be immediately removed. Ashes may be kept in the same vessel, and both are used as filling for low lands. The expense attending this service is slight.
Dead animals.—The carcasses of animals dying within the city are removed outside its limits by the city scavenger, at the cost of the owner, and are usually converted into soap or grease. About 75 carcasses are annually removed, and the system is reported as being satisfactory.

Liquid household wastes and human excreta.—All of the liquid household wastes of the city are thrown either into cesspools or privy-vaults. Regulations require the cleaning out of vaults and cesspools before they become nuisances. It is reported that there are no water-closets in the city, all the houses being dependent on privy-vaults. Probably about one-third of them are nominally water-tight. The opinion is expressed that privy-vaults affect the water in wells that are located within 20 feet of them.

Manufacturing wastes of all kinds are emptied into the creeks and streams.

POLICE.

The police force of Belleville is appointed by the mayor, subject to confirmation by the city council, and is governed by the mayor. The superintendent of police, salary $800 per annum, is the chief executive officer, and has general charge of the force, which consists of 1 captain and 5 patrolmen. The captain receives a salary of $60 per month, and the patrolmen $50 per month each. The uniform is of blue cloth; in winter a frock coat is worn, and in summer a sack coat, and each man provides his own. Patrolmen are equipped with club and revolver; their hours of duty are from 8 p. m. to 5 a. m., and all the streets in the city are patrolled. The arrests made during the past year were mostly for disturbances of the peace. The amount of property lost or stolen during the year did not exceed $200, and about one-third of this was recovered and returned to the owners. The number of station-house lodgers in 1880 was 200, as against 300 in 1879. Bread, meat, and coffee, at a cost of 15 cents per meal, are given to such of these lodgers as are destitute or crippled. When ordered by the mayor, the police force co-operates with the fire and health departments. Special policemen, as exigency may require, are appointed by the mayor, and while on duty have the same powers as members of the regular force. The annual cost of the police force in 1880 was $5,000.

BLOOMINGTON,

McLEAN. COUNTY, ILLINOIS.

POPULATION

IN THE

AGGREGATE,

1850-1880.

	Inhab.
1790	......
1800	......
1810	......
1820	......
1830	......
1840	......
1850	1,594
1860	7,075
1870	14,590
1880	17,180

POPULATION

BY

SEX, NATIVITY, AND RACE,

AT

CENSUS OF 1880.

Male	8,443
Female	8,737
Native	13,689
Foreign-born	3,491
White	16,775
Colored	*405

* Including 4 Chinese.

Latitude: 40° 30′ North; Longitude: 89° (west from Greenwich); **Altitude: 796 feet** (average).

FINANCIAL CONDITION:

Total Valuation: $3,431,134; per capita: $200 00.   Net Indebtedness: $221,463; per capita: $12 89.   Tax per $100: $3 89.

HISTORICAL SKETCH.

At the first settlement of the region a great prairie extended over all this part of the state, broken by belts of timber along the larger streams and by isolated groves. One of the largest and finest of these isolated groves was called Blooming grove. It consisted of a miscellaneous growth of forest trees, some of them of remarkable size. The grove occupied between 40 and 50 square miles, being some 8 miles long north and south, and some 6 miles wide east and west. The prairie near it was of unusual elevation, and the locality was naturally very attractive as soon as settlers pushed back from the vicinity of navigable water.

The first settlement in the vicinity was made in 1822, and the town of Bloomington was laid out July 4, 1831, partly in the north edge of Blooming grove. Some twenty years later railroads were opened through the place and large machine-shops were established. Paper bags, boots, shoes, and plows are made to a considerable extent, as well as drain-tile and coarse pottery. Bloomington has been visited by several severe conflagrations, one in October, 1855, loss $120,000; one in September, 1856, loss $50,000; one in October, 1867, when the railroad machine-shops were burned, loss $100,000; and one in 1871, loss $60,000. The damages occasioned by these fires were quickly repaired, and the buildings burned were replaced with others of brick or stone. The original population was from Kentucky and Ohio, but now people from all the states east and south are represented. Irish and Germans predominate among foreigners.

BLOOMINGTON IN 1880.

The following statistical accounts, collected by the Census Office, indicate, in part, the present condition of Bloomington:

LOCATION.

Bloomington lies in latitude 40° 30' north, longitude 89° west from Greenwich, near the center of the state, and about 130 miles southwest from Chicago. It is the capital of McLean county, and is not on any navigable water. The average altitude above mean sea-level is 796 feet, with a difference of 80 feet between the highest and lowest points in the city.

RAILROAD COMMUNICATIONS.

Bloomington is touched by the following-named railroads:
The Chicago and Alton railroad, from Chicago, Illinois, to Saint Louis and Kansas City, Missouri.
The Illinois Central railroad, from Chicago to Cairo, Illinois.
The Indiana, Bloomington and Western railroad, from Peoria, Illinois, to Indianapolis, Indiana.
The Lake Erie and Western railroad, from Bloomington, Illinois, to Sandusky, Ohio.

TRIBUTARY COUNTRY.

The adjacent country is wholly agricultural. Corn is the staple grain, and many of the farmers are stock-raisers on an extensive scale.

TOPOGRAPHY.

The city is built on a rolling prairie, the difference between the highest and lowest elevations being 80 feet. The drainage is by small streams from the northeast and southeast, joining in the western portion of the city and running west. The street grades vary from 10 inches to 5 feet in 100 feet. The soil is a black loam, underlying which is blue clay, yellow clay and quicksand. There is but little difference in elevation of surrounding country, and there are no marshes, ponds, or lakes. The country within a radius of 5 miles is mainly a rolling prairie, with planted groves, in addition to the original Blooming grove, and the soil is a black loam, from 1 to 3 feet deep.

CLIMATE.

Highest recorded summer temperature, 102°; highest summer temperature in average years, 85° to 90°. Lowest recorded winter temperature, —30°; lowest winter temperature in average years, about 0°. The only characteristic of the climate reported is that it is "changeable".

STREETS.

Total length of streets 86 miles, of which 4,174 feet are laid with stone blocks, 9,186 feet with broken stone, 4,000 feet with wood (which is to be taken up and laid with stone), and 300 feet with brick. The cost per square yard of each, as nearly as may be estimated, is, stone blocks, $1 15 to $1 40; broken stone, $1 50; wood, $1 75 to $2 25; brick, $1 13. The cost of keeping each in good repair is, for stone blocks one-half cent, and for broken stone 5 cents per square yard per annum. The brick pavement is the easiest to keep clean. The stone block, or merchant pavement, is constructed of stone and sand or cinders. The drainage is thrown toward the center of the street. The pavement is made by laying down 4 lines of flagging, the stones being 18 inches wide, not less than 6 inches thick, and from 3 to 8 feet in length. These stones form two continuous tracks for vehicles, and are laid 6 inches lower than the pavement. At the curb-lines, between the lines of flagging, and between the outside lines of flagging and the curb-lines, is a filling of stone blocks laid in a bed of from 4 to 6 inches of coal-cinders or sand. All interstices are filled with dry sand well brushed in, and the surface is thoroughly rammed. This street will clean itself on a grade of 1 in 100. The sidewalks are mostly wood, with some brick, and, in the business portion, some stone. The building of wooden sidewalks has, however, been prohibited by ordinance that took effect May 1, 1880. Gutters are paved only on paved streets, and are mostly of rubble-stone, but there is a mile of flat-stone gutters with rubble sides. Nearly every street in the city has a line of trees on the outside of the sidewalks, soft and hard

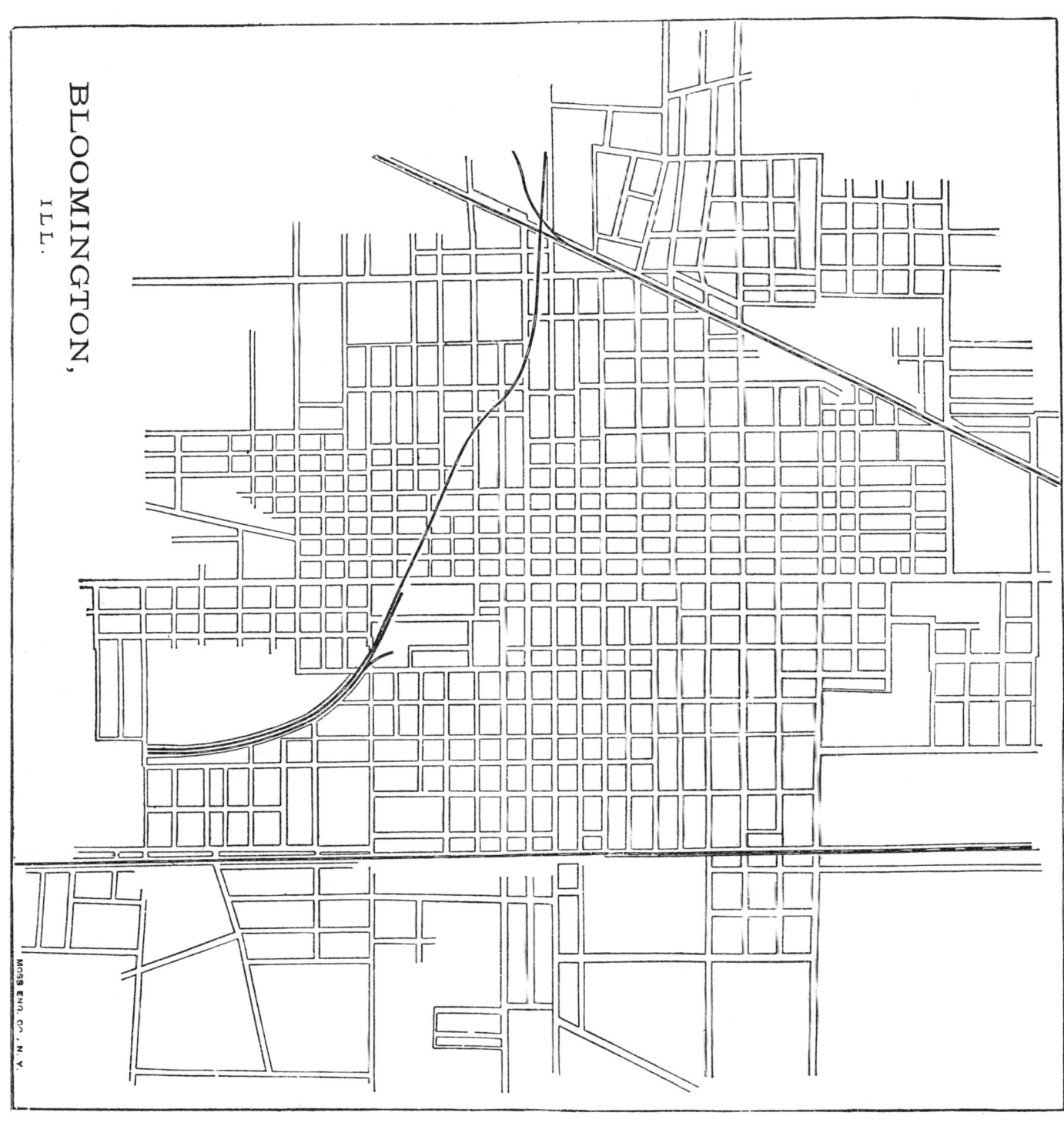

BLOOMINGTON,
ILL.

maple and elm. The construction of streets is done by contract, while repairs are done by the day, and the annual expenditure for both ranges from $5,000 to $25,000. The city officials report a preference for contract work, as, when the city builds, the class of laborers employed is usually of the poorest kind.

HORSE-RAILROADS.

There are 3 miles of horse-railroads, with 6 cars and 32 mules, and giving employment to 6 men. The rates of fare are 5 and 10 cents. There are no regular omnibus lines, but 4 carriages, 2 omnibuses, and 2 baggage-wagons, with 26 horses, and employing 15 men, transfer passengers from the railroad station at rates of fare of 25 cents for each trip.

WATER-WORKS.

The water-works are owned by the city, and cost $100,000. The system is by pumping into a stand-pipe from a well sunk into a vein of sand, and the pressure is 75 pounds to the square inch in the highest part of the city. The average amount pumped per diem is 300,000 gallons, the greatest being 450,000 and the least 150,000 gallons. The total yearly cost of running the works, including salaries, is $3,670, and the yearly income from water-rates is $6,000. Water-meters are not used.

GAS.

The gas-works are owned by a private individual, and the daily average production was not stated. The charge per 1,000 feet is $2 for the city and $2 50 to private parties. The city has 521 street-lamps.

PUBLIC BUILDINGS.

The city owns and occupies wholly for municipal purposes one city hall that cost $12,000. The city and county buildings are not in common. The county court-house is a commodious edifice occupying the interior of a square whose outer sides are composed of business blocks, facing the streets that separate them from the court-house.

PUBLIC PARKS AND PLEASURE-GROUNDS.

There is but one park in the city, and this, as yet, is only a public ground with no improvements. Its area is 4.47 acres, and the land was donated. No money is spent on it for maintenance. It is controlled by the city council.

PLACES OF AMUSEMENT.

There are no regular theaters in Bloomington, but Durley hall, seating 1,500, and Schroeder's opera-house, with a seating-capacity of 1,000, are used by traveling theatrical companies. These halls pay no license, but all exhibitions pay $10 per night, or $15 for two performances. In addition to these there are Phœnix hall, seating 600, and Washington hall, seating 500, used for balls, political meetings, etc. There are no concert- and beer-gardens.

DRAINAGE.

Though there are sewers in Bloomington, no report on the system was made by the city authorities, and therefore this subject has to be omitted.

CEMETERIES.

There are 3 cemeteries connected with Bloomington, two of them being outside the city limits. One inside the city limits, with an area of 40 acres, is laid out in Blooming grove, with drives and walks, and is kept with care. Its slopes drain into a brook that runs through the city.

MARKETS.

There are no public or corporation markets in the city.

SANITARY AUTHORITY—BOARD OF HEALTH.

The chief sanitary authority of Bloomington is a committee of the city council, composed of 3 aldermen, with the mayor as chairman, and styled the board of health. There are no physicians on the board, and in ordinary times no expenses are incurred. In case of an epidemic the sum to be expended depends on the vote of the council. The board is controlled by the council, and its authority, either in presence or absence of an epidemic, is dependent on that body. The chief executive officer of the board is the health officer, salary $40 per month, who has police powers granted by the council to abate nuisances. No assistant health officers or inspectors are employed. The board meets once a week, and reports its action to the council. The health officer uses his best judgment regarding inspections, and is supposed to make them regularly all over the city. When nuisances are reported the council orders the health officer to abate them. The board has no custom regarding the inspection and correction of defective house-drainage, privy-vaults, cesspools, sources of drinking-water, sewerage, street-cleaning, etc., nor are there any regulations regarding the burial of the dead or the pollution of streams. The health officer attends to the conservation and removal of garbage, while city ordinances regulate the removal of excrement. Small-pox patients are sent to the pest-house, which is situated in an isolated position, nearly a mile from the resident portion of the city. Scarlet-fever patients are not isolated, and the board does not take cognizance of the breaking out of contagious diseases either in public or in private schools. Vaccination is not compulsory, nor is it done at public expense. The registration of births, diseases, and deaths is kept by the county clerk, physicians reporting to him. The board reports to the city council, but its reports are not published.

MUNICIPAL CLEANSING.

Street-cleaning.—The mayor reports that as there are only about 3 miles of paving, there is no system of street-cleaning.

Removal of garbage and ashes.—Merchants place ashes and garbage in boxes on the edge of sidewalks, and the city cart removes the same, replacing the boxes. Garbage is carted outside the city limits, while the ashes are used on roads and to fill low places. This service, which seems to comprise only the business portions of the city, costs about $2 50 per day.

Dead animals.—Carcasses not taken by parties who render the same are buried outside the city limits. The cost of this service is trifling, not exceeding $50 per annum.

Liquid household wastes and human excreta.—In the thickly settled portion of the city most of the houses are connected with the sewers, and the liquid wastes are run into them; but as most of the houses in the rest of the city are built on large lots, the wastes are thrown on the ground, none going into the street-gutters, and only a small portion being deposited in vaults. The number of houses provided with water-closets is small, a large majority depending on privy-vaults. None of the vaults are even nominally water-tight, and they are required to be cleaned only when the health officer orders it. The night-soil is carted outside the city.

POLICE.

No information on this subject was obtained.

PUBLIC SCHOOLS.

The public schools are organized under a special charter. The school board consists of 7 members elected by the people. The municipal authorities act simply in a ministerial capacity to assess and collect the tax reported by the board as necessary to supplement the funds derived from other sources, and the whole of the revenues are under the direct control of the board. The superintendent of the schools, the principal of the high school, and all the remaining teachers are women.

CHICAGO,

COOK COUNTY, ILLINOIS.

POPULATION

IN THE

AGGREGATE,

1840-1880.

	Inhab.
1790	......
1800	......
1810	......
1820	......
1830	......
1840	4,470
1850	29,963
1860	112,172
1870	298,977
1880	503,185

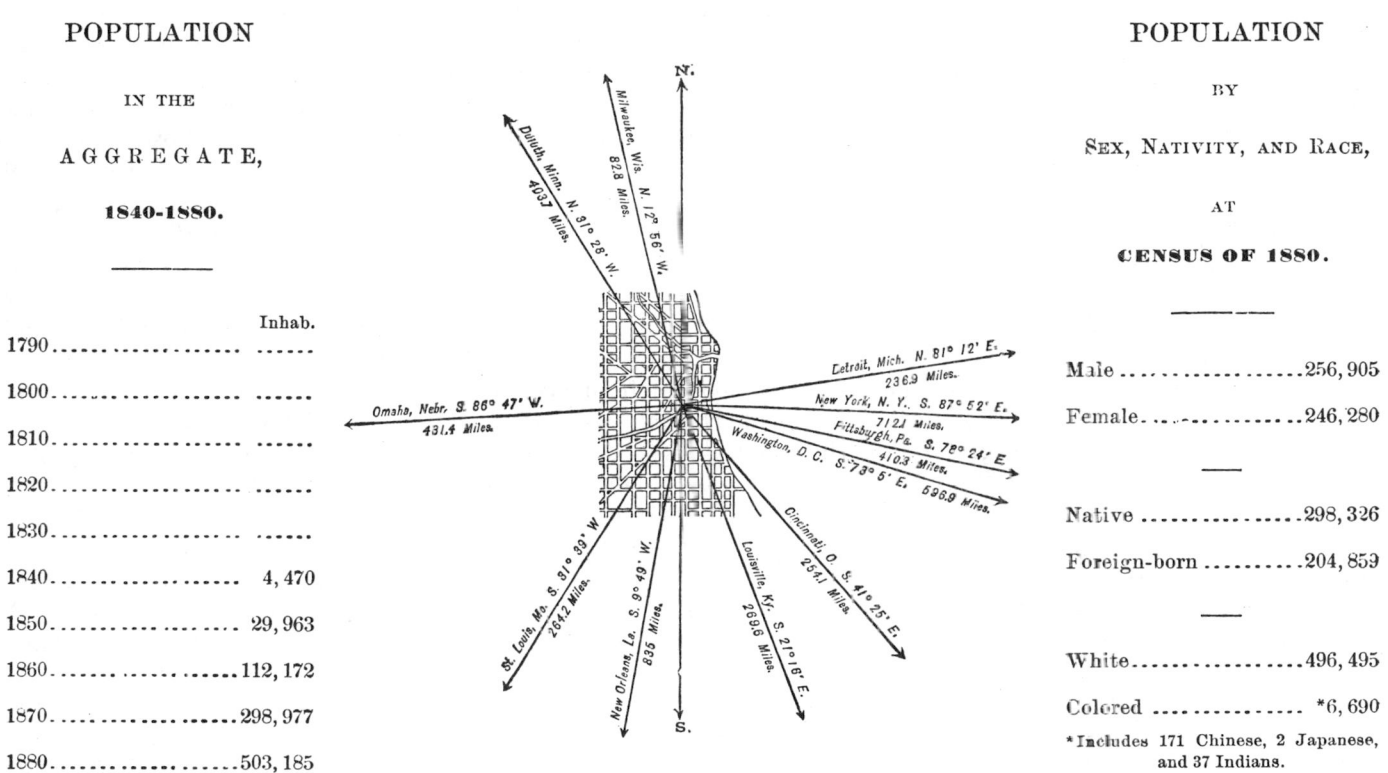

POPULATION

BY

SEX, NATIVITY, AND RACE,

AT

CENSUS OF 1880.

Male	256,905
Female	246,280
Native	298,326
Foreign-born	204,859
White	496,495
Colored	*6,690

*Includes 171 Chinese, 2 Japanese, and 37 Indians.

Latitude: 41° 54′ North ; Longitude: 87° 38′ (west from Greenwich,; **Altitude: 58 ? to 600 feet.**

FINANCIAL CONDITION :

Total Valuation : $117,970,035 ; per capita : $234 00.   Net Indebtedness : $12,794,271 ; per capita : $25 43.   Tax per $100 : $4 34.

HISTORICAL SKETCH.(a)

Less than fifty years ago the site of the city of Chicago was a low prairie lying on the shore of lake Michigan, intersected by a sluggish stream known as the Chicago river. Fort Dearborn, a trading-house for the exchange of merchandise for skins and furs with the Indians, and a few scattered houses constituted all there was in the way of improvement.

The Chicago river, the main branch of which rises in Mud lake, west of the city and very near the Des Plaines river, is a deep stream, and up this river from lake Michigan, and across the short portage to the Des Plaines river, and through the latter to the Illinois river, and thence to the Mississippi, has, with the exception of the short portage from Mud lake to the Des Plaines, always been a water-way from lake Michigan to the Mississippi. As such it was used by the Indians, then by the French, and then by the French and English.

---

a Hon. I. N. Arnold, of Chicago, secured much of the detailed information regarding the city, and prepared the historical sketch with which this report is introduced.

In 1803 orders were issued by the War Department for the construction of a fort at the mouth of the Chicago river. These orders were executed by the construction of a stockade fort on the shore of lake Michigan, on the south side of the river, consisting of two block-houses, built of hewn timber, with a parade-ground and quarters inclosed by palisades. Chicago, Detroit, and Mackinaw were then the extreme outposts of the United States in the extreme Northwest.

John Kinzie settled at Chicago in 1804, and was engaged in the fur trade with the Indians, and they gave him the name of *Shaw-nee-an-kee*—the silversmith—probably because he paid them for their peltries in silver. The fort was named "Fort Dearborn", in honor of a gallant soldier of the Revolution, afterward Secretary of War.

Early in the war of 1812 fears were felt for the safety of fort Dearborn and its small garrison, so far from settlements and succor, and General Hull, in command at Detroit, sent orders to Captain Nathan Heald to evacuate the fort. On the 5th of August, 1812, the garrison of about 60 men, with a few settlers, including John Kinzie, left the fort and started on their march around the head of the lake. The family of John Kinzie, in a Mackinaw boat, set off at the same time by water for Saint Joseph, Michigan. The Indians, in ambush, attacked the party from the garrison, when about 2 miles south of the fort, near where Eighteenth and Twenty-second streets now terminate on the banks of lake Michigan. The Indians, 400 or 500 in number, most of them Pottawattamies, hiding behind the sand-hills until the party had entered the trap set for them, killed, with little resistance, most of the officers and soldiers. Mrs. Helm, Mrs. Holt, and Mrs. Heald were saved by Black Partridge, Waubansia, and other friendly chiefs. The fort was dismantled, and was burnt the next day. It was rebuilt in 1816.

That an important town would be built up at Chicago seems to have been anticipated from its very earliest settlement. The importance of connecting the great lakes with the Illinois and Mississippi rivers, and the facility with which it could be accomplished by a canal from the Chicago river, were obvious to the early explorers and first settlers of the country.

In 1814 President Madison recommended a ship-canal from lake Michigan to the Illinois river. The first government survey of the land into sections was made in 1821. In 1822, four years after Illinois was admitted into the Union as a state, Congress granted the right of way over the public lands for a canal from lake Michigan to the Illinois river. In 1827 the United States granted to Illinois each alternate section of land for a distance of 5 miles on either side of the contemplated canal, to aid in its construction.

On the 4th of August, 1830, canal commissioners, appointed by the state, laid out and platted the original town of Chicago. In 1831 the county of Cook, in which Chicago is situated, was organized. In the spring of that year Congress made the first appropriation for improving the harbor. The total tax at that time was $149 29. In 1836 the state authorized a loan of $500,000 for the opening of the canal, and on July 4 of that year ground was broken for its construction.

On the 10th of August, 1833, the people of Chicago organized as a town, under the laws of the state, and elected five trustees, there being at that time 28 voters.

On the 26th of September, 1833, a treaty was concluded between the United States and the Pottawattamie, Ottawa, and Chippewa Indians, by which 20,000,000 acres of land in northern Illinois and southern Wisconsin were ceded to the United States. On the same day the *Chicago Democrat*, the first newspaper published in Chicago, was issued. Only one mail per week was received at Chicago until late in 1834. In 1836 the first census was taken, and gave an aggregate population of 3,265. On March 4, 1837, Chicago received a city charter. The first election for city officers was held in May, 1837, and William B. Ogden was elected mayor, receiving 469 votes, against 237 cast for John H. Kinzie, a son of John Kinzie, the first settler.

From 1837 to 1842 was a period of great financial depression and depreciation in the value of property. In 1842 work upon the canal was abandoned; the state was largely in debt for money expended on the canal and other unfinished and unproductive works of internal improvement, and for a time suspended payment of interest on her obligations. In 1842 a proposition was made by the holders of canal bonds, which had been issued by the state and others interested, to advance the sum of $1,600,000, the amount then estimated as necessary to complete the canal. This money was to be advanced on condition that the state, as security for such advance, would place the canal lands and lots in the hands of trustees, who should proceed to finish the canal, and who, from the tolls and revenues and the proceeds of the canal lands and lots to be sold, should pay, "first, the amount so advanced; second, the canal debt," etc. This proposition was accepted by the state, laws were enacted under which it was executed, trustees were appointed, the money was advanced, and the canal was completed. In 1848 it was opened, and went into successful operation. From that time the growth of Chicago in population, wealth, and prosperity has been most rapid. The canal debt has been entirely paid, and the canal has reverted to the state.

The United States government from 1831 has, from time to time, made appropriations for the construction and improvement of the harbor at Chicago, and it has thus been made one of the most safe and convenient on the lakes. To secure appropriations for Chicago and other harbors on the great lakes, and also aid for the improvement of the navigation of the western rivers, there was held at Chicago, in July, 1847, a great harbor and river convention. Edward Bates, of Missouri, was president, with vice-presidents from 17 states. Letters in favor of appropriations by the national government for the improvement of rivers and harbors, written by Daniel Webster, Silas Wright, Henry Clay, Thomas H. Benton, and many others, were read, and resolutions in favor of such appropriations were adopted.

The various railways centering in Chicago have contributed very largely to its prosperity and rapid growth. The territory west of lake Michigan and south of lake Superior, and extending west to the Rocky mountains, has been intersected by a network of railroads centering at this point. They always kept pace with, and often extended beyond, the line of settlement. The first railroad built from the city, northwest, was the Galena and Chicago Union railroad, incorporated in 1836, but nothing of importance was done toward its construction until 1847, when a few miles of strap rail was laid. In 1850 it reached Elgin, on the Fox river, 42 miles from Chicago. The Michigan Southern and the Michigan Central were the first to enter the city from the east, both reaching it in 1852. The Illinois Central was opened in 1852. From that time until the present the number of railroads terminating in Chicago has been constantly and rapidly increasing, so that now the city is one of the greatest railroad centers of the world.

The Illinois and Michigan canal, under a plan known as the "deep cut", was originally designed to be a ship canal from lake Michigan to the Mississippi. This plan the state was compelled to abandon on account of its great cost, and it was finished on what was known as the "shallow cut", and supplied with water from the Des Plaines and Fox rivers and water pumped from the Chicago river. In 1865–'70 the canal was deepened by the city of Chicago, at an expense of $3,251,621, the highest level of 26 feet being cut down to $8\frac{1}{2}$ feet below the ordinary level of lake Michigan. This greatly improved the navigation, and for a time carried off the sewage of the city to the Illinois river. After the great fire of 1871 the state refunded to the city the money expended in deepening the canal. This enlargement was not sufficient for the primary purpose of a ship-canal, nor has it created a sufficient current to dispose of the sewage of the city. But the great project of a ship-canal of a capacity to take steamboats and vessels from Saint Paul, Saint Louis, and New Orleans to the lakes, and which would enable gunboats to pass to and from the Mississippi and the lakes, has never been abandoned. President Lincoln, in December, 1861, in his annual message, called attention to the subject, and so much of his message as related to it was referred to a select committee of Congress, which reported unanimously in its favor. Francis P. Blair, jr., chairman of the committee of military affairs, at the same session of Congress, reported a bill which provided for a ship-canal for the passage of armed naval vessels from the Mississippi to lake Michigan.

In June, 1863, in pursuance of a call issued by Edward Bates, then Attorney General of the United States, and 80 senators and members of Congress, a canal convention was held at Chicago to aid the project. The convention passed resolutions in its favor, and a memorial to Congress was prepared and adopted, which, in December, 1863, was communicated to Congress by President Lincoln. The committee on roads and canals reported a bill which appropriated $5,000,000 of United States bonds to aid Illinois in the work. It provided for the enlargement and deepening of the channel so as to be navigable for ships and gunboats, and provided that, in consideration of such aid, the arms, gunboats, and all materials of war, also soldiers, should pass through such canal free. This bill passed the House of Representatives, but failed in the Senate.

On Sunday night of October 8, 1871, began the most destructive fire of modern times. The city had been rapidly built, and, to a very large extent, of pine lumber, so that there were miles of buildings and sidewalks of thoroughly seasoned pine.(a) For a long time there had been no rain, and when to this is added a violent southwest wind, conditions existed as favorable as can be conceived for a conflagration. The fire began in what is called the West division, near the South branch of the river, in the midst of pine shanties and lumber-yards. Crossing the river, it progressed with such rapidity that very shortly resistance was utterly powerless. Its fury, the rapidity of its progress, its appalling character, seemed to create a universal panic. The wind increased, and the fire rushed forward, east and west, sweeping all before it. Raging all Sunday night, and Monday and Monday night, it had not burnt out the material which it fed on until Tuesday afternoon. It destroyed every thing in its course from where it crossed the South branch of the Chicago river, south of Polk street and east to lake Michigan, and all between the lake and the river to its mouth; thence, crossing the main river, it laid in ashes all of north Chicago east of Market street, and north to Lincoln park, leaving only a solitary house standing in its path.

The area burnt was $3\frac{1}{3}$ square miles, and the fire laid in utter ruin the entire business center and a very large proportion of all the residences in the city. The aggregate number of buildings destroyed was more than 18,000, and it left homeless more than 100,000 people. All the principal hotels, and all the public buildings, national, state, city, and county, were consumed. The vast warehouses, grain-elevators, steamboats, vessels in the river, bridges, railway stations, etc., were burnt. The total loss has been carefully estimated at $200,000,000, and 57 insurance companies were made insolvent by their losses in this fire. No adequate idea of the ruin and suffering caused by this fire can be conveyed; but as soon as knowledge of this overwhelming calamity was communicated, all the world hastened to furnish relief. Food, clothing, money, material for rebuilding, every thing needed, were generously and lavishly furnished from every part of America, from Europe, Asia, Africa, and the islands of the

---

a The fire department was exhausted by a fire on the preceding night, which had burnt over some 20 acres west of the river. The blank space thus caused served to protect the west side in the great fire of the following days.

sea. In money alone the sum of $4,996,782 74 was sent to the Relief and Aid Society for distribution. While therefore, this was the greatest and most destructive fire of modern times, there has never been before, in the history of the world, such an exhibition of generous liberality.

The energy, activity, pluck, and enterprise of the people in rebuilding the city are also without a parallel Chicago was rebuilt far better, safer, with better material, greater convenience, and far greater magnificence than before—so much so that there can be found among its citizens those who insist that the great fire was to the city a blessing.

The financial crash of 1836-'37 was a sad blow to Chicago. Most of her citizens were forced into bankruptcy, and the value of property sank to merely nominal figures. Recovery and the increase of population were gradual until the completion of the Illinois and Michigan canal, in 1848, caused it to grow rapidly. The opening of railroads, in 1852-'58, greatly accelerated its progress in wealth and population, when the financial crash of 1857-'58 again brought its prosperity to a halt. But the stimulus of the war of the rebellion, 1861-'65, gave the city a tremendous impetus onward, as Chicago furnished the government with most of the food and other supplies for the army. On July 14, 1874, another great fire burnt over many acres on State street and Wabash avenue, destroying at least $2,000,000 of property. This loss made the financial crash of 1873 very disastrous. The depression in business and the value of property reached bottom in 1877. Since then business has been slowly but surely reviving, and Chicago is now marching steadily onward to her "manifest destiny"—to become (as her citizens fondly hope) the largest city upon the American continent.

The population of Chicago is composed of people from all the states east of the Mississippi, and from all the nations of Europe. No one nationality has supplanted another, but all are mixed up, as it is believed, to form one of the most energetic and powerful communities to be found on the surface of the globe.

CHICAGO IN 1880.

The following statistical accounts, mainly collected and forwarded through the kindness of Hon. I. N. Arnold, indicate the present condition of Chicago:

LOCATION.

Chicago lies in latitude 41° 54' north, longitude 87° 38' west from Greenwich, on the west side of lake Michigan, near its southern end, and in the northeastern part of the state of Illinois. The mean water-surface of the lake is 581.92 feet above sea-level. The city is in a nearly level plain, only a few feet above the lake, the elevations being, lowest point, surface of the lake; highest, 18 feet above. The city, being on the shore of lake Michigan, is on navigable water. The Chicago river, together with its branches, is already navigable for 12 miles, and is capable of being made so for 5 miles more, within the present limits of the city. Besides the river and branches, there exist already about 5 miles of docks on the lake and at the mouth of the river, thus affording a total wharf frontage of more than 40 miles for vessels. The depth of the navigable portion of the river varies from 16 to 11 feet, according to the force and direction of the wind, the height of the surface of the lake, due to the season or the period, and the condition of the channel itself, which in many places must be dredged to preserve the proper depth. Ordinarily vessels drawing 13½ feet of water have no difficulty in entering the river and going up 2 miles or more. Except when caused by heavy rains or strong winds, the currents of the river are very slight. The lunar tide is less than 2 inches.

The United States government has constructed a breakwater in front of the city. This is not quite completed, but will eventually form an outer harbor capable of furnishing 5 miles or more of wharf front for the largest class of lake vessels.

Chicago is connected by navigation with all of the great lakes, and, through the Welland canal and Saint Lawrence river, with Europe; but the small class of vessels capable of passing through the canal and the Saint Clair flats makes direct trade with Europe unprofitable. Westward the city is connected by the Illinois and Michigan canal and the Illinois river with the navigable waters of the Mississippi river and its tributaries.

RAILROAD COMMUNICATIONS.

The following railroads center in the city:

The Chicago and Northwestern, to Omaha, Nebraska, and Fort Pierre, Dakota, on the west, and to Milwaukee and lake Superior on the north.

The Michigan Central, to Detroit, Michigan, and, via connecting lines, to Buffalo and the East.

The Lake Shore and Michigan Southern, to Buffalo, New York, with branches to Detroit and Grand Haven, Michigan.

The Illinois Central, to Cairo, Illinois, connecting there with the New Orleans line, and to Keokuk and Sioux City on the west. A branch also runs to Saint Louis.

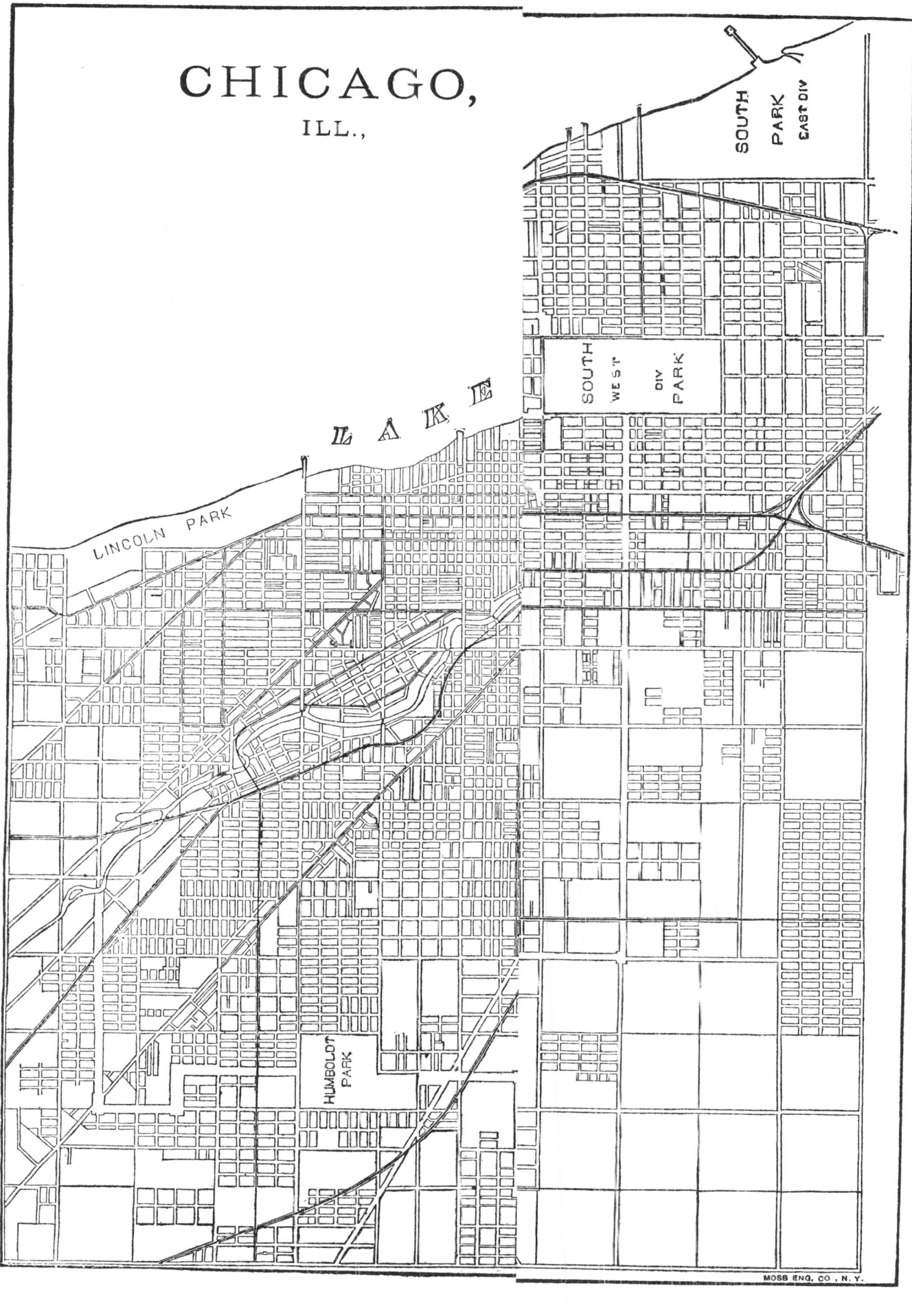

CHICAGO,
ILL.,

LAKE

LINCOLN PARK

SOUTH PARK EAST DIV

SOUTH WEST DIV PARK

HUMBOLDT PARK

MOSS ENG, CO , N. Y.

The geological structure of the region embracing Chicago and the surrounding country is exceedingly simple. The underlying rock is the Niagara limestone, which has a general dip north-northeast, and consequently sinks deeper as traced lakeward. Upon this floor was originally deposited a mass of blue clay not less than 100 feet in thickness, but as traced toward the former rim of the lake it rapidly thins out. This rim is clearly defined in one or more terraces which are traceable from the head of the lake far into Indiana. To the west of the city, however, 8½ miles distant, at Oak Park, they constitute the "divide" between the waters of lake Michigan and those of the Mississippi.

While the lake has receded far below its former level, it has left behind a series of land ridges, the intervals between which were occupied by ponds, which, by reason of the sluggish flow of the water and their sheltered position, have proved favorable to the growth of the peat-producing plants, from whose decay have resulted large accumulations of humus, or vegetable matter. It is upon this ancient lake-bed that Chicago was founded.

In the vicinity of the lake, and generally parallel with its shores, are beds of sand and gravel that alternate with clay. Near the lake the sand predominates and forms a sandy soil. At the western and southwestern limits of the city the rock approaches near the surface and is quarried and used for quicklime or building stone. In sinking to the depth of 50 feet in the lake, and running thence by tunnel to the old water-works, no rock was reached. In extending the 6-mile tunnel on shore at a depth of 70 feet, the rock was first struck about 4 miles southwest of the crib.

Artesian wells are made by boring through this rock and the two groups next below—the Cincinnati and Trenton—into the Saint Peter's sandstone and Lower Magnesian limestone. Water is reached near the western limits of the city at a depth of about 700 feet. Farther east it is found at a depth varying from 1,000 to 1,500 feet.

CLIMATE.

Highest recorded summer temperature, 99°; highest summer temperature in average years, 93°. Lowest recorded winter temperature, −20°; lowest winter temperature in average years, −16°.

Dr. John H. Rauch, secretary of the Illinois state board of health, states the following regarding the influence of the lake and the winds on the climate here:

Of all the local conditions that obtain at Chicago, none exercise a greater influence on the climate than lake Michigan. It moderates the extreme cold of winter and the oppressive heat of summer, increases the humidity of the atmosphere and the quantity of rain that falls, and causes local currents of air, thus partially changing the prevailing winds of this latitude, producing necessarily local changes of temperature. These local undulations are most marked in the spring, owing to the fact that the specific heat of the land is only one-quarter that of the water, and is both absorbed and given out more rapidly, while water, on the other hand, absorbs it more slowly, owing, no doubt, to the difference in their conducting and radiating properties. It is mainly due to this fact that our springs are so cold, raw, and long-continued; that is, the water is not as soon heated as the land, thus giving rise to local changes of temperature and of winds. In the autumn the heat of the water is less readily abstracted than that of the land, thus causing the temperature in the immediate vicinity of the lake to be milder than even at localities farther south and west. The mean temperature of the lake is no doubt the same as that of the land for the year, differing only in the absorbing and parting powers of heat, as is evidenced by the fact that the freezing point obtains only a short distance from the shore. It will therefore be seen how for eight months of the year, and sometimes even for nine, the lake exercises a wholesome influence upon health, counteracting the great and sudden changes incident to our open and level topography, while, during the remaining months, it is injurious to health on account of the cold and chilling effect it has, in addition to causing sudden changes. Its agency in purifying the atmosphere by absorption it is hardly necessary to dilate upon in this connection.

The north wind, which is less frequent than any other, generally exercises a beneficial influence, and in the winter is the mildest, with the exception of the southeast and east winds. The northwest wind of March, April, and May is cold and moist, but during the summer months, when the heat is extreme, or in winter, when very cold, it is beneficial and salutary. The east wind, with the exception of the north, is the least frequent, and is more common in the spring than in any other season of the year. The lake exercises a marked influence on this wind and that from the northeast. Of all winds none is so depressing and enervating as the southeast wind. The south wind is more common than either the east or north wind, and exercises a beneficial influence in moderating the extreme cold of the westerly winds. The prevailing wind, not alone of Chicago but of the greater portion of the Mississippi valley, is the southwest wind. This wind, sweeping over a greater expanse than any other, necessarily exercises a great influence on health. There are years in which this is the hottest, and again it is the coldest. The west wind is the most frequent in winter, when it is the coldest and driest, while the northwest wind is cold, keen, and penetrating in winter; cold and bleak in spring; and in summer cool and refreshing.

STREETS.

Chicago covers an area of nearly 36 square miles, or 23,040 acres. There are 789 acres in the public parks; 355 acres in the river, its branches, the slips, and the Illinois and Michigan canal; and 5,200 acres in the streets, which have a total length of 651 miles, and are known by 907 names. Of the streets, 139 miles are paved with the following materials: Stone blocks, 1 mile; cinders, 9 miles; broken stone, 6 miles; wood, 115 miles, and gravel, 8 miles. The cost per square yard of each, as nearly as may be estimated, is: For stone blocks, $2 50; cinders, 15 inches deep, 60 cents; broken stone, 15 inches deep, $1; wooden blocks (average), $1 25; and gravel, 15 inches deep, 90 cents.

In all contracts awarded by the city the contractor is required to keep the pavement in repair for two years, free of cost. After that time the repairing is done by the city; but from the fact that the repair of all streets, whether improved or not, is paid for from one general appropriation, it is impossible to separate the different items so as to give even an approximate estimate of the cost of keeping each kind of improved streets in repair. The wooden-block pavement, for from three to five years, is more easily cleaned than any of the other kinds of pavement in use, but after the expiration of that time there is little difference between it and the other classes of pavement, so far as cleaning is concerned. The stone-block pavement for streets subjected to heavy traffic seems to be the most economical. For streets with a moderate traffic, the cedar-block pavement, laid upon a foundation of 2 inch plank, the interstices filled with lake-shore gravel and paving composition, has proved very satisfactory; while for streets used for light driving, macadam of about 15 inches in depth with a top-layer of clean gravel or broken granite is, without much doubt, the most economical as well as the most satisfactory pavement that has been used here.

There are 756 miles of sidewalks. In the business portion of the city the sidewalks are principally of flagstones, while in the residence portion they are of flagstone, cement, concrete, and plank, the last-named predominating. The commissioner of public works, in his annual report for the year ending December 31, 1880, has the following regarding the sidewalks:

Our sidewalks, like our streets, being generally constructed of wood, are in a like dilapidated and unsatisfactory condition. * * * Our present sidewalk system is very imperfect and unsatisfactory; the delays in having new sidewalks built, or old ones repaired, are so great that we have continually many places in the city where the sidewalks are not only unpleasant but unsafe to walk upon. I submitted a statement to the city council in November last, showing that it was costing the city an average of over $1,000 per month for damages because of injuries incurred through defective sidewalks. As with the streets so with the sidewalks, we should discard *wood* as rapidly as possible.

The gutters in all the wooden-block, stone, and cindered streets are composed of the same material as the roadway. On graveled and macadamized streets they are, in nearly every case, composed of cobble-stones. Tree-planting is entirely a private enterprise, the trees being always set along the sides of the streets. The construction on all improved streets is done almost exclusively by contract. All street improvements are made by special assessments on the property benefited, and the annual cost varies in accordance with the number of improvements ordered by the council. For the year 1877 the cost was $124,000; for 1878, $284,000; and for 1879, $642,000. The repair of streets is done by the city at an annual cost of about $50,000. Regarding the difference between contract and day work, Mr. H. J. Jones, superintendent of the special assessment department, says:

In all specific work, such as paving and cleaning improved streets, when the exact amount to be done can be ascertained before the work is commenced, in my opinion the contract system is preferable, from the fact that a full and free competition will, in nearly every instance, bring the price as low, if not lower, than it could be done by any other method; while in such work as the repair of streets, where the amount to be done can never be correctly estimated in advance, it would be almost impossible to do it economically in any other manner than by the day.

A 16-ton steam-roller has recently been purchased for use on the streets.

HORSE-RAILROADS, ETC.

The horse-railroads in the city have a total length of 126 miles, use 675 cars and 4,007 horses or mules, and give employment to 2,450 men. The total number of passengers carried during the year is 48,776,790, and the average rate of fare is about 4¾ cents. There are no regular omnibus lines, but 50 transfer coaches, with 185 horses and employing 145 men, run between the railroad stations and the several hotels. The average number of passengers carried annually is 240,000, and the rate of fare is 50 cents, which includes the transfer of baggage.

TUNNELS.

The Chicago river, and its North and South branches, divide the city into three distinct parts—the north, west, and south divisions. To pass from the north to the south side one must cross the main river; from the north to the west side, the North branch must be crossed; and from the south to the west side, the South branch must be crossed. The travel between these different parts of the city, up to a recent time, had been by swing-bridges, which were constantly opened for the passage of vessels, thus causing more or less inconvenience to the public. This inconvenience was greatly lessened by the construction of a tunnel, consisting of a double-track roadway for vehicles and sidewalk for foot-passengers at Washington street. It is an arched tunnel, 920 feet long, and gives an unobstructed passage between the south and west divisions of the city. This proved so successful that another tunnel has been built at La Salle street, under the main river, by which communication can at all times be had between the north and south divisions.

In addition to the tunnels there are thirty-two bridges within the city limits, that cost on an average about $25,000 each.

WATER-WORKS.

Chicago has always been supplied with water from lake Michigan. In its days of village and town life, before it was organized as a city, water was obtained near the shore of the lake by dipping it into barrels and thus distributing it in carts drawn by horses. A chartered company began supplying the city with water in 1840. Its reservoir was on the corner of Lake street and Michigan avenue, with an iron pipe extending about 150 feet into the lake, through which water was pumped into the reservoir and distributed through large conduits, with a bore of 5 inches in diameter for the mains and 3 inches for the subordinate connections.

In 1851 a board of water commissioners was created by the state legislature with authority to construct water-works to supply the city with pure water. Under this act the city was supplied with water-works until its growth, and the question of sewage disposal, in 1862–'63, compelled the authorities to consider in what way an adequate supply of pure water could be obtained, to be drawn so far from the mouth of the Chicago river, into which the sewage of the city was discharged, as would furnish it without impurity. On February 13, 1863, the legislature conferred upon the city full power to extend "aqueducts or water-pipes into Lake Michigan far enough to be beyond river and shore impurities, so as to insure a full supply of pure water". Congress, on January 16, 1864, sanctioned this act, and the city, having obtained all necessary authority, finally adopted the plan, now in operation, for supplying water. Work was begun March, 1864, and the crib was launched July, 1865. The works on land were erected on the shore north of the east end of Chicago avenue, and consisted of the engine, the pumping apparatus, and the water tower. An iron shaft, 9 feet in diameter, was sunk near the shore to a sufficient depth below the level of the lake, and from this shaft a tunnel was excavated, at right angles with the shore, a little north of east, for 2 miles out under the surface of the lake, 5 feet wide by 5 feet 2 inches high, with top and bottom arched. The bottom of the inside of the tunnel, at its east end, is 66 feet below water-level, and has a slope toward the shore of 2 feet per mile. At the east end of the tunnel is a crib, constructed of logs 1 foot square, within which is fixed the iron cylinder, 9 feet in diameter, sunk to communicate with the tunnel from the shore, and is 64 feet below the surface of the water and 31 feet below the bottom of the lake at this point. The crib is 12 feet below the water-line, and over and upon it is built a house for those in charge. Thoroughly braced and strengthened, it has withstood without injury all storms. A water-tower 154 feet high was built west of the pumping-works, within which is a wrought-iron stand-pipe, 36 inches in diameter and 138 feet high, to the top of which water is raised. On March 25, 1867, water was let in and the works were inaugurated.

The supply was ample until 1870, when the rapid increase of the city demanded a greater quantity of water than could be supplied by one tunnel. Arrangements were accordingly made for a second tunnel, that should extend to a point in the southwestern part of the city, 31,490 feet distant from the crib. On July 12, 1872, the work was begun from the shore end, and on October 2 from the crib end, and was completed July 7, 1874, at a cost of $956,510. This tunnel is 7 feet in diameter and is lined with brick. It is parallel with the first tunnel and about 50 feet from it, and is connected with it by a cross-tunnel at the crib. After connecting with the pump-well at the shore end it is extended across the city and under the river 4 miles to the west-side pumping station. The cost of the new tunnel and the pumping works was $1,638,249 92. The total cost of the works for the water-supply of Chicago is $8,550,000. The system is by pumping direct into the mains or into a stand-pipe, the average pressure in the mains being 40 pounds to the square inch. The average amount of water pumped per diem is 57,384,337 gallons, the largest amount supplied in a single day being 73,000,000, and the smallest, 45,872,500 gallons. The average cost of raising 1,000,000 gallons 1 foot high is $5\frac{42}{100}$ cents. The total receipts from all sources for 1880 were $920,785 16, and the total expenditure, including interest on bonds, was $1,050,958 01. The excess of expenditures over receipts is caused by the retirement of $291,000 bonds, payable July 1, 1880. But for this large extra expenditure the receipts would be $160,827 15 over expenditures. There are 2,113 meters in use, and, where set, a considerable reduction in the consumption of water has been found to be the invariable rule. There are $455\frac{1}{2}$ miles of pipe and 3,361 hydrants connected with the works.

GAS.

Gas is supplied to Chicago by private corporations, the charge being $2 25 per 1,000 feet. There are 11,080 street-lamps. The city does not pay by the lamp, but by the number of feet burned, as ascertained by test-meters, being $1 65 per 1,000 feet for the north and south divisions, and $2 per 1,000 for the west side. This makes each lamp cost on the average about $17 32 a year—$13 for the gas, and $4 32 for lighting, repairs, etc.

PUBLIC BUILDINGS.

The buildings owned or occupied by the city for municipal purposes, wholly or in part, include the city hall, city hospital, small-pox hospital, house of correction, and the buildings owned by the fire, police, and school departments. The total cost of all buildings belonging to the city, exclusive of those connected with the water-works, is $2,117,985. The cost of the present city hall was $78,330, but a structure combining city hall and court-house, to cost $1,500,000, is now in process of construction by the city and county, and already $446,000 has been expended on it.

PUBLIC PARKS AND PLEASURE-GROUNDS.

The public parks of Chicago contain nearly 2,000 acres, of which 1,870 acres are in 6 large parks, and the remainder in 12 public squares and similar places. In addition to this a park scheme provides for more than 20 miles of parkways, locally termed "boulevards", of which 10 miles are 200 feet wide, and 10 miles 250 feet in width. The 6 parks are all on the outskirts of the city, and are well distributed north, west, and south. The boulevards are so located as to form a continuous chain, linking each park to the others. Besides these there are in the heart of the city 7 miles of streets of the ordinary width, which form part of the park system, being under the same management, specially constructed to fit them for park travel, and all general traffic thereon prohibited. Street-car routes, on broad avenues, also extend in direct lines to the main entrances to each park, and easy access to the parks for all classes, from all parts of the city, is thus provided. There are 3 park districts, corresponding to the divisions of the city, and the cost of the construction and maintenance of each park or boulevard is borne by the district in which it is located; but the general plan of park improvement in each district has been designed with special reference to the others, so that all combine to form one harmonious public pleasure-ground for the whole city. The 6 larger parks are as follows:

Lincoln Park, area 250 acres, is situated on the shore of the lake, about 2 miles north of the harbor entrance, and extends northward until a little beyond the city limits. Out to its south border the city is quite compactly built up, and, as there is a large population in the immediate vicinity, this park is much frequented at all seasons, and occasionally crowded during fine days in summer. There are 7 miles of driveways (2 miles being along the lake shore) and 9 miles of walks, while near the middle of the park there is a pleasure-pond, covering 12 acres, which is fed by 2 artesian wells. A long pier, well shaded by a canvas canopy, stretches out into the lake, and in summer this is used as a health resort, chiefly for sickly and weak children. Only a small portion of this park remains to be improved, but the construction of a permanent breakwater to protect the shore line and adjoining drive from damage by storms will be costly. The total cost of the land was $1,000,000, and so far $1,200,000 has been expended on improvements and annual maintenance. The park is controlled and managed by the board of commissioners of Lincoln park, composed of 5 members.

In the west district there are 3 parks, all inside the city limits, and about 5 miles back from the lake. They are situated about 1½ mile apart, on an irregular line from north to south. *Humboldt Park*, area 200 acres, is the most northerly; *Central Park*, area 185 acres, comes next, to the south; and *Douglas Park*, area 180 acres, is the most southerly. The plan and method of improvement have been, in their general features, quite similar in each park, and the water-supply in each is from artesian wells. The parks are all connected by boulevards that extend north and south to the limits of the district, while Washington street forms a parkway from the center of population to the main entrance of Central park. The total cost for land and improvements was $1,876,965 36, for all the parks, and $18,000 is expended each year for their maintenance. The names of the designers of these parks are Messrs. Jenney, Schermerhorn, and Bogart, and Mr. Oscar F. Dubois. The parks of the west side are managed and controlled by a board of commissioners, composed of 7 members, appointed by the governor of the state.

The lower division, or *Lagoon Park*, has an area of 593 acres. It is situated on the shore of lake Michigan, 6¼ miles south of the court-house and outside the city limits. The upper division, or the *West Park*, has an area of 372 acres, and is situated north of Lagoon park, about 1¼ mile from the lake. These 2 parks are connected by a pleasure-way, called the "Midway Plaisance", 726 feet wide, and having an area of 90 acres. Three boulevards extend from the parks to the city limits, and the one to the west will be continued so as to be connected with the park system in that district. These parks were designed by Messrs. Olmstead, Vaux, & Company, and are now in process of construction. The total cost to date has been, for land $2,964,754 97 (with 250 acres more to be bought), and for construction, $2,222,763 65. The cost of boulevards for these parks, as well as for those connected with the other systems, is included in the above sums. The south-side parks are controlled by a board of 5 commissioners, appointed by the judges of the circuit court of Cook county. They hold office for five years, one being elected each spring. The following-named parks are controlled by the department of public works:

Lake Park embraces 41 acres, and is bounded by Randolph street, Lake Park place (Park row), Michigan avenue, and the Illinois Central Railroad lands. That part south of Madison street was dedicated as "public grounds" by the canal commissioners on their plat of fractional section 15, recorded July 20, 1836, while the northern portion is shown on the record of Fort Dearborn addition, made by the United States government in 1839.

Union Park was acquired by purchase in December, 1853, and February, 1854. It contains 14.8 acres, and is bounded by West Lake street, Bryan place, Ogden avenue, Warren avenue, and Ashland avenue.

Jefferson Park was purchased in 1850, contains about 5½ acres, and is located between Loomis and Throop, and West Monroe and West Adams streets.

Wicker Park is a triangular piece of ground, bounded by North Robey street, Fowler street, and Park street (or Wicker court), and covers an area of 4 acres.

Vernon Park, donated to the city by Henry D. Gilpin, October 17, 1859, embraces very nearly 4 acres, and is bounded by Macalester place, Gilpin place, Sibley street, and Lytle street.

Ellis Park was dedicated to the city by Samuel Ellis, March 21, 1855; contains 3⅜ acres, and lies between Vincennes and Cottage Grove avenues and north of Thirty-seventh street.

Washington Square, with an area of about 2¼ acres, was donated by O. Bushnell and others, September 14, 1842, and is bounded by La Fayette place on the north, Washington place on the south, North Clark street on the west, and Dearborn avenue on the east side.

Dearborn Park, lying east of Dearborn place, west of Michigan avenue, south of Randolph street, and north of Washington street, is shown on the recorded plat of Fort Dearborn addition as "public ground".

Congress Park was dedicated by F. W. and James L. Campbell in their subdivision of lots 13 to 24 of block 4, Rockwell's addition to Chicago, recorded April 8, 1873. It has an area of seven-tenths of an acre, and is situated between West Van Buren and West Harrison streets, about 200 feet west of Rockwell street.

Union Square was donated by H. O. Stone in his subdivision of Astor's addition, contains about one-half acre, and forms the northwest quarter of a block bounded by Goethe, Scott, Astor, and Stone streets.

Campbell Park, containing about one-half acre, is located between Woodbine place and Evergreen place, and extends from Leavitt street to Oakley avenue. It was dedicated July 28, 1871, as a public park by F. W. and James L. Campbell.

Aldine Square is situated in the north half of block 3, of Ellis' west addition, about 300 feet south of Thirty-seventh street, extending from Vincennes avenue west a distance of 330 feet. It was made a public park by the owner, and recorded as such April 26, 1875.

PLACES OF AMUSEMENT.

The following are the principal theaters in the city:

McVicker's, with a seating capacity of 2,180; Haverly's theater, seating 2,080; Hooley's theater, with a seating capacity of 1,400; and Hamlin's theater, with a seating capacity of 1,000. There are also Olympic theater, on Clark street, between Lake and Randolph, seating 1,100; Academy of Music, on Halsted, near Madison, with a seating capacity of 1,500—this latter is devoted to variety and melodrama, and has the most brilliantly finished interior in the city, said to be one of the finest theaters of its class in the world; Halsted Street opera-house, corner of Halsted and Harrison streets, known as a "dime theater", seats 1,100; Lyceum theater, melodrama, on Des Plaines street, near Madison, seats 900; National theater, dime, on Clybourn avenue, seats 1,000; Müller's opera-house, dime, is situated on North avenue, and seats 800; the Stock Yards theater, at the stock-yards, has a seating capacity of 700, and charges a dime for admission; and the Twenty-second Street theater, dime, that seats 800, but is not open continuously. All theaters pay an annual license of $300 to the city. Of the concert-rooms and lecture-halls, not including those connected with churches, there are, Central music-hall, corner of State and Randolph streets, having 1,789 numbered seats and a total capacity of 3,100 persons; Fairbank hall, in the same building, with a seating capacity of 900; McCormick hall, Clark and Kinzie streets, seats 2,200; Farwell hall, on Madison street, seats 2,000; Brand's hall, Clark and Erie streets, seats 800; Turner hall, Clark and Chestnut streets; and Aurora Turner-hall, on Milwaukee avenue, seat 1,000 each; Twelfth Street Turner-hall has about the same seating capacity; Central hall, Wabash avenue and Twenty-second street, seats 800; and Standard hall, Michigan avenue and Thirteenth streets, seats 600. Of the above halls, Brand's, all the Turners', and the Standard are provided with stages and scenery.

The principal concert- and beer-gardens are, Baum's pavilion-garden, seating 800; Fisher's garden, with stage and music-stand, seating 1,000; Lincoln's Park pavilion, seating 1,000; Eagle garden, seating 1,500; Wabash Avenue pavilion, seating 1,200; and "a score of small affairs not worth mentioning".

DRAINAGE.

The ground on which Chicago is built is a level plain, once a prairie, lying only a few feet above the surface of lake Michigan. The soil is naturally a rich black loam. Along the shore of the lake it is underlaid with sand and gravel, but in parts of the city more remote from the shore the subsoil is stiff hard clay, almost impervious to water. In wet weather the level surface of the ground is saturated with water; the roads in the suburban and rural districts soon become a soft, black, bottomless quagmire, almost impassable, especially as travel is concentrated upon them near the city. But within the city limits streets and avenues made of such materials are useless at such times unless protected by pavement or other artificial means. Hence the amount and character of the pavements in a city like Chicago is of more than usual interest.

Much of the older part of the city along the shores of the Chicago river was built upon ground even lower than the adjacent prairie, some of the land being reclaimed from the river and filled to a height of only a few feet above its surface. In after years, as the city limits extended and it became necessary to provide for the drainage of more remote districts, it was discovered that there was not room enough beneath the pavement of the streets for the necessary sewerage works. In fact, houses and ground near the river could not be properly drained. The city at this time was rapidly growing. Miles of streets were already lined with lofty and expensive houses, all built from 3 to 6 or more feet too low, while every year the matter was becoming more serious and complicated. Not only the business part of the city, but even more remote districts devoted to residences, would have to be rebuilt on a higher level, or else all the houses would have to be raised and the streets and sidewalks graded up. The latter course was adopted. The work of raising the city extended over a period of several years. Those who lived in or visited Chicago while the work was going on remember how vast storehouses, hotels, business houses, and residences were lifted from 4 to 6 and sometimes 10 feet without serious interruption to the business carried on within them, and how streets, sidewalks, horse-car tracks, lamp-posts, hydrants, and sometimes shade-trees, were raised to conform with the new grade-lines.

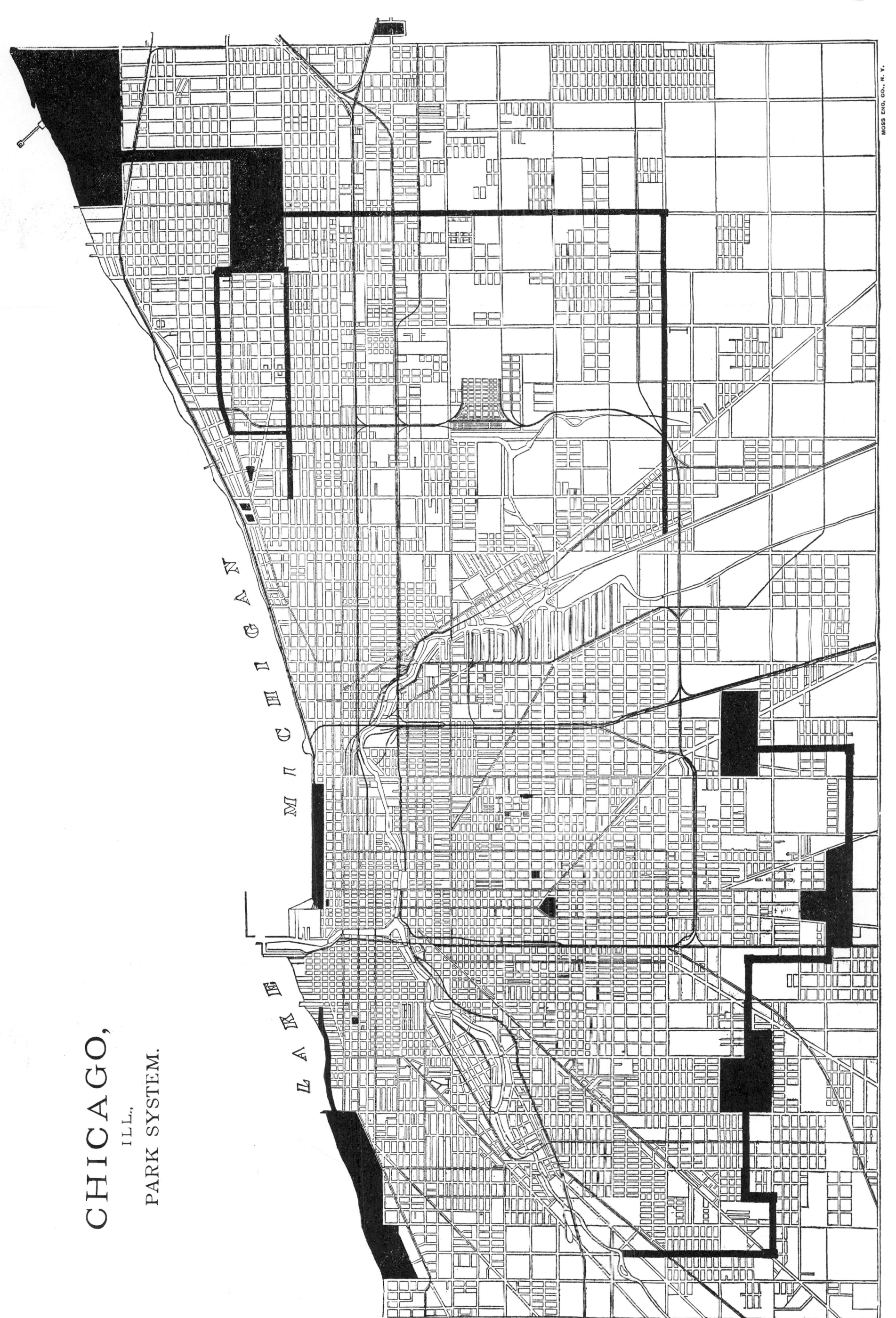

CHICAGO,
ILL.,
PARK SYSTEM.

The accompanying map shows in black shade the part of the city so raised. The district lies principally between State and Halsted streets, and extends from Twelfth street to Chicago avenue, covering an area of about 4 square miles.

Besides this, many other streets laid out and improved from year to year are in some places raised several feet above the level of the adjacent lots, as, for instance, Blue Island avenue, portions of Clybourne and Fullerton avenues, some of the streets above Humboldt park, and other places.

The process of grading up streets, undertaken by the city, may be described as follows: A stone wall is built on the curb-line, between the sidewalk and the gutters, to support the curb-stones at the required grade; the space between the curb-walls is filled in by the city with ashes, street-dirt, building-waste, and earth to support the pavement and gutters; the sidewalks are bridged over with plank, leaving the space beneath open to be used as vaults for storage of coal, etc., in front of the cellars or basements of houses; but when there are no houses the space is in open communication with the vacant lots adjacent. Streets treated in this way are said to be "improved", and the same term is applied whether they are graded up or simply paved upon the natural surface of the ground.

Of course, when streets are filled in to a depth of several feet and immediately paved, the pavements settle out of shape and have to be relaid. Sometimes this has to be done several times before the ground beneath is fairly settled. There are many miles of pavements in the city which are still passing through the transformation stage. If not promptly repaired, when they begin to fail they soon break up and disappear in a shapeless mass of wood, mud, and water.

PAVEMENTS.

The material used for street pavements is almost exclusively wood, as will be seen by the following:

Table showing extent of improved streets in Chicago January 1, 1880, from annual report of the department of public works, 1879.

Materials.	Miles.	Remarks.
Wooden blocks	$114\frac{4447}{5280}$	82 per cent.
Cinders	$9\frac{1322}{5280}$	
Gravel	$8\frac{794}{5280}$	
Macadam	$6\frac{42}{5280}$	
Stone pavement	$0\frac{5175}{5280}$	$\frac{7}{10}$ of 1 per cent.
Three-inch plank	$0\frac{2167}{5280}$	
Total number of miles	$139\frac{3374}{5280}$	

That wooden pavements are not a thing of the past, and are not going out of use, will be apparent from the two following tables, taken from the same source, showing street improvements made during the years 1879 and 1880, where it appears that fully 80 per cent. of all the street improvements during that time consist of wooden pavements, and in the year 1879 that fully 70 per cent. of all the work done—estimated in miles of streets—consisted in relaying pavements already laid before, or, as the report says, "old improved" was "reimproved".

Table showing street improvements during the year 1879.

Materials.	Miles.
Wooden blocks	$5\frac{3312}{5280}$
Medina stone	$0\frac{1695}{5280}$
Cobble-stone	$0\frac{300}{5280}$
Macadam	$0\frac{665}{5280}$
Cinders	$0\frac{2843}{5280}$
Three-inch oak planking	$0\frac{2167}{5280}$
Total number of miles	$6\frac{4410}{5280}$

Of the above, $4\frac{3372}{5280}$ miles of old improved was reimproved.

Table showing street improvements during the year 1880.

Materials.	Miles.
Wooden blocks	$13\frac{3594}{5280}$
Macadam	$2\frac{5503}{5280}$
Stone	$0\frac{1039}{5280}$
Graveling	$0\frac{1738}{5280}$
Oak planking	$0\frac{1635}{5280}$
Curb wall and filling	$1\frac{5541}{5280}$
Curbstone and filling	$0\frac{793}{5280}$
Total number of miles	$18\frac{1918}{5280}$

The method of laying wooden pavements now in practice is to lay a plank floor 2 inches thick (sometimes on ground sills of heavier timber), forming the shape of the roadway and gutters. On this floor round blocks of cedar, formed by sawing off the logs in uniform lengths of from 6 to 8 inches, are placed standing on end; the spaces between the circular blocks are then filled with screened lake gravel, the pebbles being about as large as hazel-nuts or filberts; and over all is poured a composition of coal-tar boiling hot, and the whole *is covered with* fine lake-shore gravel, the pebbles about as large as grains of corn or coffee. Such a pavement when new is neat, pleasant, and beautiful, and is suitable for both light and heavy traffic, as carriages pass over it easily and noiselessly. In fact, one of the first things noticed in coming to Chicago from another city is the remarkable quiet of its busy streets, and the conspicuous absence of that increasing clang and din incident to cities where stone pavements are used.

The drainage of paved streets is accomplished by making the gutters descend toward the sewer-inlets, so that, while the center of the streets and the top of the curbstones and sidewalks maintain level lines, the bottom of the gutters gets deeper and deeper until it is not unusual to see it 18 inches or more below the sidewalk at the catch-basins.

Wooden pavements when new appear to give good drainage, but when they become worn and the surface becomes uneven they absorb water and filth until they are saturated, and soon decay and go to pieces. There are about 25 miles of wooden pavement in Chicago which may be classified as new and affording good drainage. There are fully 90 miles that are in various stages of dilapidation and do not afford good drainage.

If we could safely assume that pavements as now being laid would last eight years, it would be necessary to rebuild each year not less than 14 miles in order to maintain the present existing streets, aside from the paving of new ones. By reference to the tabular statements given above, it will be seen that in 1879 only 5½ miles were laid, and in 1880, 13½, but of these a large share was in new streets. At this rate the whole system of wooden pavements in Chicago will go to pieces in a few years. But there are still 500 miles of streets not paved at all. On this subject the commissioner of public works, in his annual report for 1879, says:

The cheap and short-lived wooden pavements of the city are a species of shoddy that should not be encouraged. Cheap only in the first payment, in the long run, when aggregated, they are, in my opinion, the dearest and most unsatisfactory pavement the city has ever used.

And in his annual report for 1880 (page 17) he says:

Surely the wretched condition of our streets to-day furnishes an unanswerable argument against continuing the system of laying wooden blocks. Millions of dollars have been expended in paving the city, and yet we are but little nearer the goal of well-paved streets now than at the commencement. A few of the latest paved streets with wooden blocks are temporarily good, but these must all be removed under a permanent system. With 651 miles of streets now, and the city rapidly growing, what possible hope can we have, under the present system of short-lived wooden pavements, ever to see our city well and universally paved? * * * If we use such material as will speedily decay and will necessitate being done again over every few years, can we ever hope to get through or to see our streets in much better condition than they are at present?

SEWERAGE.

The sewerage of Chicago appears to have been developed under one general plan, and is uniform in its design and execution throughout the city. There are no broad drainage areas from which the drainage is gradually concentrated to one great outlet, but rather numerous small subdistricts draining each to its own separate outfall. Nor are there any very long lines of sewers, as the streets are only 10 feet above the lake, and sewers of great length, with a reasonable descent, could not be kept below the pavement.

The general principle on which the system is based appears to be to lay a main sewer in each alternate street leading toward the river, and to drain the intermediate and cross-streets to these by short laterals on both sides. For instance, a main sewer in West Madison street begins at the Chicago river and extends in a straight line for a distance of 2¾ miles, receiving laterals from cross-streets, which drain also part of Washington street on one side and Munroe street on the other. A main sewer in West Adams street extends in a straight line from the river to Western avenue, about 2½ miles, and receives short laterals in the same manner as above, beginning on Munroe street on one side and Jackson street on the other, and discharging through each of the cross-streets.

The same may be said of Van Buren, Harrison, Polk, Tyler, and other streets on both sides of the Chicago river, and Clark street and others on the north side. In some instances two or more sewers, when they come near the river, are united and discharge at a single outfall, as, for instance, Rush and State streets, which are connected through Kinzie and discharge at Rush; Market and Wells, which are brought through Michigan street one square and discharged through Franklin street, on the north side. But these form the exceptions, and do not interfere with the general uniformity of design. The drainage into lake Michigan is arranged on the same plan, but the sewers are brought together and form systems of considerable extent, having in all only three outfalls, viz, at Twelfth street, at Twenty-second street, and at Douglas avenue.

Although the sewers of Chicago are not combined in comprehensive systems of mains and branches winding about through various streets, still it is not unusual for one outfall to drain a considerable extent of territory, through a good many miles of lateral sewers. For instance, in Harrison street a sewer 2.4 miles long in a straight line drains 300 acres of territory through a total length of 7.4 miles of sewers to an outfall 5 feet in diameter, the

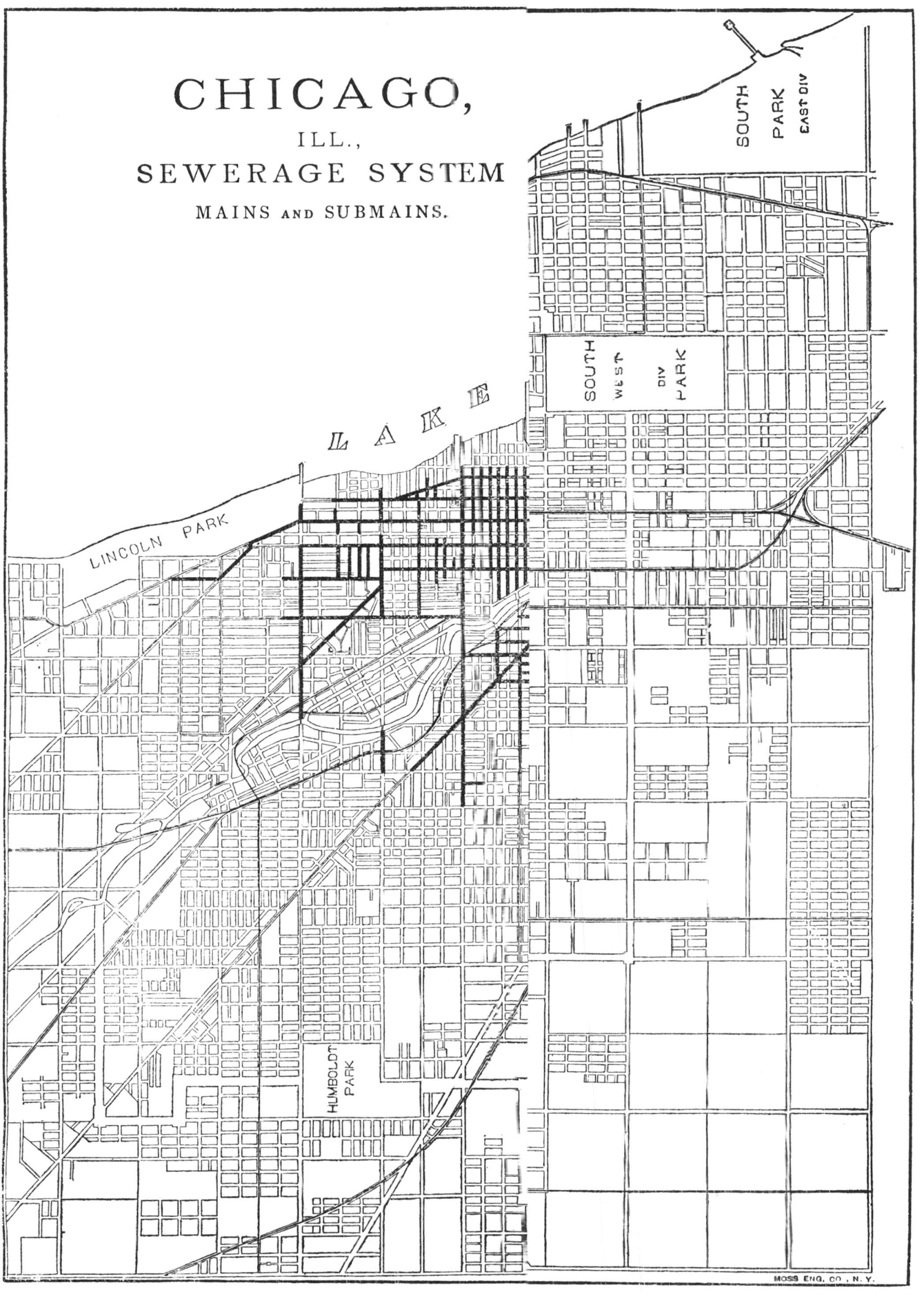

CHICAGO,
ILL.,
SEWERAGE SYSTEM
MAINS AND SUBMAINS.

LAKE

LINCOLN PARK

SOUTH PARK EAST DIV

SOUTH WEST DIV PARK

HUMBOLDT PARK

MOSS ENG. CO., N. Y.

The following table shows length of sewers of each size, December 31, 1880:

Size.	BUILT IN 1880.		TOTAL.	
	Feet.	Miles.	Feet.	Miles.
9 feet, brick	1,559	....	1,559	0.29
6½ feet, brick	....	....	1,330	0.26
6 feet, brick	1,972	....	12,512	2.37
5½ feet, brick	....	....	5,460	1.03
5 feet, brick	2,614	....	72,889	13.80
4½ feet, brick	668	....	73,917	14.00
4 feet, brick	995	....	89,471	17.00
3½ feet, brick	....	....	29,552	5.60
3¼ feet, brick	....	....	665	0.12
3 feet, brick	2,113	....	74,700	14.14
2½ feet, brick	4,905	....	124,808	23.63
2¼ feet, brick	....	....	6,359	1.20
2 feet, brick	13,882	2.6	542,050	102.66
20-inch pipe	1,625	....	1,625	0.30
18-inch pipe	10,886	2.06	10,886	2.06
15-inch pipe	13,446	2.5	81,287	15.39
12-inch pipe	24,463	4.6	651,571	123.40
Total	79,128	15.00	1,780,689	337.25
House-drains laid from sewer to curb line	138,691	26.3	1,841,362	348.74
Manholes	554		11,953	
Catch-basins	271		10,062	

Rates of fall of sewers.—The datum plane to which all elevations are referred is low water in the lake, which is 582 feet above tide-level.

Most of the sewers discharge at the level of the city datum. Some of those discharging into the Chicago river at a considerable distance from its mouth have their outlet a little higher, as, for instance, Ashland avenue, which is 5 feet, and Harrison street, 1 foot above datum.

Most of the large mains are built on the uniform grades of 1 foot in 2,500. As the size of the sewers diminishes, the rates of fall are increased, the descent of 2-foot sewers (which include about one-third of all the sewers in the city) is 1 in 1,000, except in localities where they can be made steeper near their summits and in high ground. The usual rate of fall for pipe sewers, except where they can be made steeper, is 1 in 500.

The question is, of course, naturally suggested whether or not sewers on such slight grades will keep themselves free from deposits, especially where they are built with circular cross-sections, as they all are in this city.

Flushing and cleaning out sewers.—The most troublesome thing encountered in the way of deposits is sand and fine gravel. Almost every thing else can be flushed out, but these form so solid a mass that water takes little effect upon them, and if once loosened and washed away they subside again as soon as the velocity of the flush is over. In some of the larger sewers deposits of this kind become so solid that they have to be removed with pick and shovel. Not many sewers collect sand, however, as it comes in principally from newly laid pavements or macadam roads, finding its way through the catch-basins or perforated manhole covers. Other deposits, such as organic matter or soft clay and street-dirt, readily yield to the appliances used in cleaning the sewers.

The interior condition of the sewers is well known, as they are constantly inspected, and are cleaned and kept in repair by a force of men regularly employed by the city, some of whom have been engaged in this work for many years.

Sewers less than 3 feet in diameter, and hence too small to be entered, are flushed by apparatus designed especially for the purpose. There are two of these flush-tanks belonging to the city, one holding 1,800 and the other 2,100 gallons of water. A tank is filled from the nearest fire-hydrant and hauled by four horses to the manhole, and the contents are discharged in from 40 to 60 seconds, filling the sewer completely and sometimes the manhole also, and in its rush clearing out all lighter deposits and washing the sewer clean. During the year 1880 there were 82 miles cleaned in this way. The force employed was a 4-horse team, 1 foreman and 3 men, and the time about 265 days. In 1879 there were 120 miles flushed at an expense of $7,000, and in 1877, 83 miles were flushed at a cost of $8,000. In other years, about the same. Deposits that will not yield to the action of water are removed from small sewers by the "derrick and chain machine". Manholes are about 75 feet apart; a chain is first passed through the sewer and around sheaves and up through the manholes. This chain, which carries an iron scraper, is operated by a derrick at each end by which it can be drawn either forward or backward. By this means the sand and gravel, or other obstructions, are brought to the manholes and thence passed up in buckets to the surface.

Sewers 3 feet or more in diameter are cleaned by men who go through them with scrapers and other suitable tools and buckets, the pick and shovel being used when necessary. The usual manner of cleaning the large mains is by a scraper shaped to fit the bottom of the sewer, and drawn by a dozen or more men by means of a drag-rope. The action of the feet of so many men loosens the sediment and mixes it with the water so that it readily yields to the scraper, which is guided and controlled by one of the men. Those who do this work are regularly employed in the sewerage department of the city, and are usually occupied in cleansing out catch-basins and other work. They are employed with the understanding that they are to do this work when required. It is usually done in the winter when the lake is low, and occupies only a few days in each year.

The amount of work done and the money expended in keeping the sewers cleaned for the past twenty years is shown in the following table. It does not include cost of cleaning catch-basins. Other information on this subject may be found in the annual report of the department of public works for the year 1879, and in other reports. From these sources of information it appears that about 46 per cent. of the entire length of the sewers has to be cleaned each year, supposing that the work reported does not include cleaning the same sewer more than once in each year.

The superintendent states that when a sewer is once thoroughly cleaned it requires no more attention for four or five years.

	FOR EACH YEAR.				For 19 years ending December 31, 1879.
	1877.	1878.	1879.	1880.	
Total cost of cleaning sewers	$17,576 16	....	$12,352 69	....	$267,891 64
Annual cost per mile, based on the miles of sewers in use at beginning of year	66 00	....	42 00	....	94 69
Total number of miles of sewers in use at beginning of year	265 75	$278 05	294 73	$322 27	2,829 20
Number of miles cleaned during the year	122 10	....	136 60	106 31	1,370 60
	Per cent.	Per cent.	Per cent.	Per cent.	Per cent.
Percentage of sewers cleaned to the total number of miles in use at the beginning of the year.	46	....	46	33	48½

EXAMINATION OF THE INTERIOR OF SEWERS.

A careful examination has been made of the interior of sewers, selecting for the purpose those in all parts of the city, examining some by looking or going down into the manholes, and others by walking through the sewers.

The greatest possible courtesy has been shown by the superintendent in this matter, and every facility offered for a careful and complete examination. All necessary appliances for comfort and convenience were provided, and men who have been for many years in the department appeared to take pride in exhibiting the result of their care and attention.

East Twelfth Street sewer, from Michigan avenue to the lake. This sewer, 5 feet in diameter, is the outlet of three sewers, each 3 feet in diameter, forming a three-way junction, which is a fine piece of brick masonry. One of the 3-foot sewers contained about 5 inches of soft sand, the other two were clear. The 5-foot main was clear most of the way and the bottom was smooth and slippery. The water was about 10 inches deep at the junction, and increased to 2 feet at the outlet, as the lake was a little higher than usual on the day when the inspection was made.

East Twenty-second Street sewer, from Cottage Grove avenue to the lake, was examined. The outlet of this sewer in former years was often obstructed by sand and gravel washed in from the lake. To prevent this, a cut-stone chamber has been built around it, with a temporary 36-inch iron-pipe outlet extending beyond the breakwater. The top of the chamber is covered with a wooden hood, and the sewer outfall is further protected from back-action of waves by a wrought iron trap covering the outlet. This structure appears to be effective in protecting the outfall from sand and gravel, but it interferes with the ventilation of the sewer, and appears also to retard the outflow, causing a deposit of from 3 to 5 inches of soft matter on the bottom of the sewer. This sewer is evidently laid in wet ground, as there is a considerable drip from the top, while the arch and sides are considerably incrusted with hard crystalline matter. The water is 18 inches deep, and the flow is apparently about 1 mile per hour. There is a more noticeable odor in this sewer, probably because the outlet is closed. It drains an area of a little more than 600 acres, lying between Sixteenth street, State street, Thirtieth street, and lake Michigan, and has a combined length of sewers of 19 miles. Some of the manhole-covers are perforated and some catch-basins are not trapped. There is very little, if any, circulation of air.

Douglas Avenue sewer is laid very deep in a sandy soil saturated with water. The depth of the sewer at Cottage Grove avenue is about 20 feet. The flow of water is from 12 to 14 inches deep, and quite rapid. In one or two places a slight deposit of not more than 2 or 3 inches was noticed, but most of the way the bottom was clean and smooth. This sewer has been built about seventeen years, and is in a good state of preservation; the grade is true and the alignment is good. The brick-work is smooth and even and well finished, and there seems to be no good reason why it should not last as long as it will be wanted.

Examinations have also been made in the west and north divisions of the city. A sewer in Leavitt street was entered and examined. This has recently been built, and affords a good example of brick masonry, is true to line and grade, smooth, and well finished, and has some fine junctions, especially at Blue Island avenue. The storm-overflow into it from the 9-foot sewer in Twenty-second street, recently built, is well constructed. There is but little water in this sewer, and it flows over a deposit of mud about 8 inches deep. The mud is very soft, and the foot readily sinks through it and finds a firm footing on the bottom of the sewer. The deposit is not sticky, and when disturbed it does not give off bubbles of gas as if it contained organic matter, but only the sulphurous smell characteristic of fresh-water meadow-muck. It has probably been washed in from the river at high water.

As a fair example of the sewers in the more densely populated part of the city, the one in Fulton street was selected and examined. On throwing off the manhole cover some steam escaped, and steam was also noticed in the catch-basin at the corner of Union street. There was very little deposit in this sewer, and that only at intervals. Several gas-pipes pass through it (crosswise), and these were heavily festooned with paper, rags, etc.; in one place a piece of plank was found which appeared to have been used by the workmen when cleaning out the sewer. It was loosened by one of the men and floated away with the current. The atmosphere of this sewer was stifling, which some of the workmen said was caused by fumes from the lead-works which drain into it.

On the north side the Market Street sewer was selected as a fair example of those in that vicinity. The long curve from Market street into Michigan street was noted, and shows a fine piece of brick-work, true to line, with an even, regular curve, and a smooth bottom. The brick-work is evenly laid, and presents a smooth surface. The air of this sewer was not particularly oppressive, although it drains a large area and the manhole covers had to be dug up from beneath a mass of street mud. There was very little deposit of mud in this sewer, and that only at intervals, and but 2 or 3 inches deep anywhere. The diameter of the sewer is 5 feet in Market street and 4 feet in Wells street. The two unite after flowing through Michigan street, and discharge through Franklin street in a sewer 6 feet in diameter.

One thing was noticeable throughout the inspection, and that was the readiness shown by the men to throw off the covers and go directly into any of the sewers without any apparent fear of danger from bad air or from explosion of gas. Only one instance of explosion appears to be known, and that was occasioned by a defective street gas-pipe. This conduct on the part of the men leads one to think that the atmospheric condition of the sewers is not dangerous, and the appearance of the men who have worked for many years inspecting and cleaning sewers indicates strength and health, and they make no complaint of any ill-effects of the work.

A very noticeable feature of all sewers examined was the excellent quality of masonry, the great care bestowed upon the alignment and grades, and especially the skill and attention bestowed upon building the junctions where laterals were brought into the mains, or where sewers of nearly equal size were brought together. The amount of deposits found in the mains was not large, while that in the laterals was evidently kept down by the constant use of flushing and other apparatus.

The sewers of Chicago are not self-cleaning, but they are kept in good condition by constant supervision and continual labor, the amount of which can best be judged from the amount of money expended, and by the apparatus and appliances invented for the purpose, described and noted above.

Manholes and catch-basins.—The only thing peculiar about the manholes which has been noticed is their wooden covers and frames. These are made of 3-inch plank in three thicknesses, the upper course of oak, forming a frame 9 inches thick and about 4 feet in diameter. The cover itself is of oak, and is usually perforated with five holes, 2 inches in diameter. These covers cost about $6 each, will last a good many years, are comfortable to drive over, and are regarded by the authorities as economical, although in many streets permanently improved, iron frames and covers have been put in. Catch-basins are built beneath the gutters at the street corners or at other convenient places, and are covered with wooden frames and covers precisely like those of manholes described above. Catch-basins now being constructed are not trapped, but open directly to the sewers.

HOUSE-DRAINS.

Private drains are from 6 to 9 inches in diameter, and are brought into the sewers at an angle of about 40 degrees. Connections with brick sewers already built are made by means of an oblique junction-piece of vitrified pipe, the sewer around being carefully rebuilt and pointed upon the inside and all rubbish and bats removed. Drain-pipes are carefully laid, under the supervision of the city, to true lines and grades, with a descent not less than 1 in 200, and a record of their location is kept in the office of the sewerage department. Sewers now being built are provided with branches extending to the curb-line of the sidewalk. In streets, also, where macadam or pavements are to be laid, such branches are also laid, so that connections can be made in future without disturbing the streets or gutters. Many miles of such drains have been laid within the past few years, and their total length is now greater than that of the public sewers, amounting, January 1, 1881, to 348.74 miles, while the length of the public sewers at the same time was 337.25 miles.

The city ordinances of Chicago forbid the discharge of kitchen or laundry slops directly to the sewers, but require a grease-trap to be constructed to receive such water, like a tight cesspool, with an overflow to the sewer. Thus the most troublesome fouling mentioned is kept out of the sewers and accumulated nearer to the houses.

The sewers of Chicago have been built by the city by general tax and appropriation, and are regarded as the exclusive property of the city, under the care and control of its proper officers. Private parties may use the sewers for their legitimate purposes by conforming to the prescribed regulations. Persons who are not willing to use the city property reasonably, but persist in turning in any thing likely to obstruct or destroy the sewers, or to prevent their proper inspection and care (as, for instance, steam or hot water), may have their drainage cut off.

SEWAGE DISPOSAL.

That part of the city provided with sewers is shown on the accompanying map. The part draining directly into lake Michigan covers about 1,200 acres, on the south side, below Van Buren street and east of Clark street. The remainder of the city drains into the Chicago river

This was originally a small stream running in a direction nearly parallel with the lake shore, except for the last mile or less of its course, where the united branches turned to the lake through a changeable channel. The North branch is about 30 miles long and the South branch 5 miles long. There are no correct topographical maps by which the water-shed of this stream can be determined, but from an inspection of the ordinary maps it seems to drain an area of about 300 square miles. Its flow was always sluggish, and the last mile afforded the harbor for the commerce of early Chicago. This river, within the city limits, has been widened and deepened by dredging, and numerous slips and basins have been made along its line, until now there are 29 miles of river-frontage and 12 miles of slip and basin frontage, making 41 miles of water-frontage in the inner harbor. This broad water-surface has no daily tide from the lake to supply it with clean water, and receives but little from the stream draining so small an area. What water it does receive from this source is more or less contaminated before it reaches the city. The inner harbor is estimated to contain about 54,000,000 cubic feet of water. The city water-works supply about 7,000,000 cubic feet daily, which is used by half a million people and discharged in the form of sewage. At this rate this long and narrow basin of slack-water receives daily about 13 per cent. of its volume of sewage, besides other and perhaps greater sources of contamination from the distilleries, packing-houses, and manufacturing establishments along its shores. To rid itself of the nuisance thus created has been the great sanitary problem of Chicago for many years.

For the relief of the North branch of the river a tunnel 12 feet in diameter was built beneath Fullerton avenue and extended into lake Michigan. Water is forced through this tunnel by means of two propeller screws, capable, at the ordinary rate of speed at which they are run, of forcing 15,000,000 cubic feet of water daily either from the river into the lake, or, by reversing the action of the machinery, from the lake into the river. These works have been in operation since January, 1880. They are intended to draw off the foul water, assuming that its place would be supplied by a current of clean water coming in from the lake through the river, and up the stream in a direction contrary to the natural flow. In order to reverse the current of the water in this way it is necessary first to pump out all the water coming down the stream from its source, together with the discharge from the sewers along the shore between the pumping station and the mouth of the river. The excess of water pumped out above that furnished from these two sources, would then be supplied, either from the lake or from the South branch of the river. As a matter of fact, some of the foul water does flow in from the South branch, but still it is claimed, by those who have observed the effect of the pumping-works, that the condition of the river is considerably benefited by them at times of low water, when their action is most needed.

For the relief of the South branch of the river many suggestions have been made. The most important thing yet accomplished was the cutting down of the summit of the Illinois and Michigan canal to secure a constant current of water out of the South branch through the canal to the Des Plaines river at Joliet, and thence ultimately to the Mississippi river. By this means the canal and the small streams and mill-ponds below it have been made the receptacles of the filth and waste of Chicago.

The cutting down of the canal did not, however, afford the desired relief, and, as the city increases, the nuisance of its inland basin of foul water increases with it. A discussion of this subject may be found in a paper read by Dr. John H. Rauch for the Illinois state board of health, 1880, entitled "The Sanitary Problems of Chicago".

The state board of health, in view of the pollution of the canal and small streams below it, advised that the city provide pumping machinery to lift a large quantity of water into the canal, and so, by increasing the flow of water, dilute the sewage of the city until the present nuisance shall be remedied.

In accordance with this recommendation the city has entered into contract for machinery capable of pumping 60,000 cubic feet per minute or 86,000,000 cubic feet per day into the canal.

The "Citizens' Association" also appointed a committee of its members, known as the "Main Drainage Committee", which examined various means for abating the nuisance of the inner basin of the Chicago river, which, in its present condition, is little better than a sewage reservoir. It was concluded that the Illinois and Michigan canal, or, in fact, a ship-canal, if constructed, would not be able to carry the amount of water necessary to dilute the sewage, if discharged in that way, without having so rapid a current as to impede navigation, and the committee recommended a main sewer to be constructed from Chicago to Joliet, 31 miles, in the form of an open conduit, 20 feet wide at one end and 49 at the other, at a total cost of about $12,000,000. The sewage conduit proposed by them has not yet been begun. Its capacity, according to the engineer who made the plans, is but one-half that of the pumping machinery provided by the city to pump into the Illinois and Michigan canal. Most of those who have made a study of the drainage of Chicago appear to agree that the foul water from the Chicago river can not be forced into lake Michigan without polluting the whole city lake-front, and at the same time endangering the water-supply, and that the only alternative left will be to pump it into the Des Plaines river and let it flow thence away toward the Mississippi river and the gulf of Mexico, and to send along with it a sufficient quantity of pure water from the lake to prevent the pollution of the streams along its course. This amounts practically to making an artificial river to receive the sewage of Chicago, using lake Michigan as a reservoir of supply, and pumping the water to a height of about 10 feet. This river must of course be large enough to receive all the sewage of the city and enough clean water to dilute it to such an extent that it will not become a nuisance or destroy the usefulness of the streams along its course, which are used as a water-supply for the cities on their banks.

CEMETERIES.

No information on this subject was furnished.

MARKETS.

There are no public or corporation markets in the city, all supplies being obtained from private shops or stores.

SANITARY AUTHORITY—COMMISSIONER OF HEALTH.

In 1876 the board of health of Chicago was abolished, and all the powers and duties of that body were relegated to one officer, called the commissioner of health, who is appointed by the mayor, subject to the confirmation of the common council, for a term of two years, or until his successor is appointed. He appoints and removes all the employés of the health department, and receives an annual salary of $3,000. He is a physician. In ordinary times the annual expenses of the department are about $80,000, being, according to the estimate of the commissioner for 1880, for salaries, medicines, supplies, disinfectants, printing, stationery, incidentals, and scavenger-work. This last item aggregates $39,000, or nearly half the annual expenditures. During epidemics this amount can be increased to any extent, as the ordinances direct that all expenses incurred by the commissioner in case of pestilence or epidemic disease must be met by the mayor and common council. Where there is no declared epidemic the commissioner of health has authority to do, or cause to be done, all things which promote or preserve the health, safety, and sanitary condition of the city, that are not inconsistent with the constitution or laws of the state. In case of an epidemic he has power to adopt such measures as he may from time to time deem necessary to prevent the spread of the disease; can disinfect houses or premises, or close the same; can isolate persons; can prescribe the time and mode of abating nuisances, etc. The commissioner is on duty all the time, the health office being open every day.

ASSISTANTS.

The force of the department consists of 1 secretary at $1,000 a year; 1 registrar at $1,500 a year; 1 clerk at $1,000 a year; 3 medical inspectors at $500 a year each; 6 special inspectors at $800 a year each; and 5 meat inspectors and 20 sanitary policemen at $800 a year each. Four of the above are physicians, while the meat inspectors and sanitary policemen are invested with full police powers. The city is divided into sections, and certain officers are placed in charge of each. These officers make daily reports to the commissioner—coming to the health office at 4 p. m. in winter and 5 p. m. in summer for the purpose—of work done during the day, and receive instructions for the next day.

NUISANCES.

Inspections are made regularly in all parts of the city, and all complaints received at the office are promptly attended to. When a nuisance is either reported or described, the officer of the section in which the nuisance is said to be, examines the same within twenty-four hours, and if he finds the complaint is well founded he orders the nuisance abated within a reasonable time. If this is not done, suit against the owner of the property is brought in the police courts, or the commissioner can have the work done, and the cost assessed against the property. This latter plan is resorted to when no owner, agent, or occupant of the property where the nuisance exists can be found.

Defective house-drainage, privy-vaults, cesspools, etc., are treated as nuisances and corrected accordingly. Defective sewerage is treated as a nuisance, while street-cleaning is under the direction of the department of public works. The commissioner exercises full control over the conservation and removal of garbage and the removal of excrement.

BURIAL OF THE DEAD.

No removal or interment of any dead body can take place in the city without a permit from the commissioner of health. These permits are granted after a certificate, setting forth cause of death, etc., and signed by a physician, has been filed with the registrar at the health office.

INFECTIOUS DISEASES.

All cases of small-pox found before the suppurating stage are removed to the pest-house, which is situated near the western limits of the city, in grounds having an area of 12 acres, and surrounded by a high and strong board fence. If found after the suppurating stage, the patient remains in his domicile, with a police officer always present to insure quarantine. When the patient is removed or has recovered, the premises, clothing, furniture, etc., are fumigated with sulphurous acid gas.

Scarlet-fever patients are neither isolated nor quarantined at home, but a large red card, with the words "scarlet fever here", is placed on the door of the house where a case exists, and this card must remain there for from 20 to 30 days after convalescence has begun.

The commissioner of health takes cognizance of the breaking out of contagious diseases either in public or in private schools, and no child living in a house where a case of contagious disease exists is permitted to attend school until all danger of infection is passed, or until permission is granted by the commissioner.

Vaccination is made compulsory when small-pox is threatening, and for those who are unable to pay it is done at the public expense.

REGISTRATION AND REPORTS.

A record of all births and deaths is kept by the registrar of vital statistics. Physicians or professional advisers are required to report each death, stating name, residence, color, sex, nativity, with date, hour, and cause of death; and every physician, midwife, or other person who may assist at a birth must report the same to the health officer.

The commissioner of health reports annually to the common council, and publishes his report with funds provided for the purpose, and included in the annual appropriation.

MUNICIPAL CLEANSING.

Street-cleaning.—The streets are cleaned at the expense of the city, the work being done both by contract and by the city's own force. The improved streets are cleaned by contract, sweeping-machines being used, while the unimproved streets are cleaned by the city's force, wholly by hand. Of the improved streets, those in the business portion are cleaned twice a week, and those outside once a week, while the unimproved streets are cleaned when ordered by the commissioner of public works. The cleaning is reported to have been well done during 1879 and 1880. During the past year 1,683 miles of streets were cleaned by contract, at the rate of $26 50 per mile, making the cost $44,599 50, and 385 miles of unimproved streets were cleaned, graded, and otherwise worked upon, at a cost of $113,223 77, the cost of cleaning the unimproved streets not being kept separate. The sweepings are used for filling low places, being generally mixed with ashes and sand.

Removal of garbage and ashes.—This service is performed both by the city and by householders. So much as is done by the former is done with its own force under supervision of the commissioner of health, forty-two 2-horse teams being constantly employed. Those householders, generally in the suburbs, who attend to the removal themselves, employ scavengers. While awaiting removal the garbage must be kept in suitable vessels unmixed with ashes, and placed either in the alley or on the sidewalk in front of the house. Such garbage as is not suitable for feeding swine is taken outside the city limits and buried. The ashes are used for filling, unless mixed with garbage; in the latter case they are disposed of in the same manner as garbage that is not used for feed. The annual cost of this service is about $37,000. No nuisance or probable injury to health is reported to result from either the keeping or handling of the garbage, nor are any ill-effects perceived from the manner of its final disposal. Regarding the defects of the system, Dr. De Wolf says: "Garbage and ashes oftentimes mixed; garbage not promptly removed. It would require $100,000 at least to properly (promptly) remove garbage from every house."

Dead animals.—By city ordinances all dead animals must be removed at least 4 miles beyond the city limits. The contractor for the present year (1880) promptly gathers the carcasses of all dead animals, with such materials from the markets as ordered by the commissioner of health, and removes them by railroad, twice a day, to a rendering establishment 26 miles from the city. The annual cost of this service is $3,500 to the city. During the past year the following carcasses, which does not include the dead animals taken from the stock-yards, were removed: 1,500 horses, 400 cattle, and between 8,000 and 12,000 dogs. Though the system is reported as being excellent, so far as Chicago is concerned, complaints are made by those who live in the neighborhood of the rendering establishment.

Liquid household wastes.—Chamber and kitchen slops and laundry wastes are all disposed of in the same way; i. e., in all sewered streets they go into the public sewers, and, where the sewers do not extend, into the street-gutters. Cesspools or dry wells are not often found in the city. The street-gutters are flushed two or three times a week during the hot months, except in localities so much below grade that the water will not run off. Referring to the contamination of drinking-water by the overflowing or underground escape of the contents of privy-vaults, etc., Dr. De Wolf says:

Not a well in use within the city limits. Lake water is taken to every domicile. This water, drawn from the lake 2 miles from shore, is very perfect. Twice in the four years past it has been contaminated by sewage being carried out from the mouth of the river to the "crib". This accident can only occur when water is so high in the river as to change the direction of the flow. It can be prevented in future by keeping all sewage out of the river, or by extending the tunnel 2 miles further from shore. The result of this contamination was extensive diarrheal troubles for a few days in April, 1877, and April, 1880.

Human excreta.—It is estimated that nearly half the houses in the city are provided with water-closets, and, as there are very few cesspools, nearly all these deliver into the sewers. About one-half of the privy-vaults are said to be nominally water-tight. They must be constructed under the direction of the health department, and must be emptied by licensed scavengers when so ordered by the commissioner of health. The night-soil is taken outside the city limits and buried in trenches, the whole matter being controlled by the commissioner of health.

Manufacturing wastes.—There do not appear to be any rules governing the disposal of either liquid or solid manufacturing wastes, as there is " very little of it within the city limits".

POLICE.

The police force of Chicago is appointed and governed by the general superintendent of police, who is appointed by the mayor, with the concurrence of the city council, for a term of two years ; he directly controls the force, sees that the laws and ordinances of the city are executed, preserves the peace, order, and cleanliness of the city, and sees that the rights of persons, property, etc., are respected ; his salary is $3,780 per annum. The number of the force in the several grades, with the salaries of each, is as follows: 1 secretary at $2,625 per annum, 1 custodian at $1,260 per annum, 3 clerks at from $1,000 to $1,500 per annum each, 6 captains at $1,785 per annum each, 19 lieutenants at $1,365 per annum each, 15 sergeants at $1,050 per annum each, 20 detectives at $1,155 per annum each, 31 station-keepers at $970 per annum each, 390 patrolmen at $945 per annum each. The uniform is in the metropolitan style, made of blue-black police cloth, and each man furnishes his own, the cost of the suit complete, including overcoat, being $75 50. Each patrolman is equipped with a baton, pistol, nippers, star, and belt. Their hours of active service average twelve per day, but they are always considered on duty, and they patrol 600 miles of streets.

During the past year 28,480 arrests were made by the force, the principal causes being—

Assault (various)	1,235	Burglary	629
Carrying concealed weapons	443	Drunk	2,113
Drunk and disorderly	2,229	Disorderly	9,952
Inmates of houses of ill-fame	1,237	Inmates of disorderly houses	1,081
Inmates of gaming-houses	352	Larceny	2,313
Robbery	382	Violating city ordinances	3,850

In the final disposition of the persons arrested, 12,868 were fined in the police courts, 1,406 were sent to the house of correction, 2,135 were held for trial, 10,253 were discharged, etc. During the year, property to the value of $142,599 41 was reported to the police as either lost or stolen, and of this, $123,509 35 was recovered and returned to the owners. The number of station-house lodgers during 1880 was 13,172, as against 8,629 in 1879. During the year 30,672 meals were furnished to prisoners and lodgers, at a cost of $1,840. The police force is required to co-operate with all the city departments and to attend all fires. Its chief duties at fires are to guard the limits set by the fire marshal, to protect persons and property, to preserve order, to prevent crowds from obstructing the firemen, etc. Special policemen are appointed by the general superintendent, upon the application of any person showing the necessity thereof, for duty at any fixed place within the city. They are subject to the rules of the force, but are paid by the persons at whose request they are appointed. During the past year there were 2 deaths in the force, and 29 policemen were more or less injured while in discharge of their duty. The yearly cost of the police (1880) is $493,672 38.

The police telephone and signal system has recently been introduced, and is now in operation in what is known as the Twelfth Street district, and may be briefly described as follows: The district connected with a station is divided into any number of posts or beats. On each of the beats there is erected a box or house, similar to a sentry-box, octagonal in shape, 2 feet 5 inches in diameter and about 7 feet high, painted a bright color, and having a sign on the door—" Police-alarm No. —." The doors of the boxes are secured by a patent trap lock that retains the key, and as none but police officers are in possession of the release key, the person opening any of them must await the arrival of an officer or lose his key ; and as each of the keys is numbered and a record kept of the name and residence of the person holding it, any one giving a false alarm can easily be detected. Inside the house or sentry-box described there is a box, about the size of a fire-alarm box, and through an opening in the end of this box projects a lever; inside the box there is a telephone with the usual mechanical contrivance for transmitting the arbitrary call. None but officers are in possession of keys for the inside boxes. All the inside boxes are connected with the station in the same manner as the fire-alarm, and the signal is registered on the same kind of a register in use in all electric fire-alarm systems. A person desiring the services of a policeman opens the outside door and pulls down the lever at the side of the box; the signal is immediately registered in the station, where there is a detail of 3 men with a horse and wagon, who are furnished with all facilities for quick hitching, and who immediately respond to all calls. The officer on post is required to report by telephone once an hour at night and once every half-hour during the day-time. He can also receive information of crime committed in any other part of the city, and is required to report all that comes to his notice of any importance, at any time during the day or night, without leaving his post. In cases of emergency he can use the arbitrary call, which will bring the patrol-wagon to any box, or he can use the telephone, and have assistance at any place that he may designate.

FIRE DEPARTMENT.

The manual force of the fire department of Chicago consists of 1 fire marshal and chief of brigade, 9 assistant fire marshals—1 as inspector, 1 as secretary, and 7 as chiefs of battalion—2 clerks, 1 veterinary surgeon, and 357 men, divided into 43 companies. The apparatus now in active service consists of 31 steam fire-engines, 31 hose-carts, 9 hook-and-ladder trucks complete, and 3 chemical engines. There are 178 horses and 41,485 feet of hose in the department.

The following comparative statement shows the expenses of the department since 1870:

Year.	Number of companies.	Total.
1870	26	$366,700 66
1871 a	28	182,023 15
1872	35	423,057 34
1873	41	586,618 96
1874	43	624,795 22
1875	43	411,245 12
1876	41	478,340 22
1877	42	507,001 12
1878	42	389,692 36
1879	41	420,308 82
1880	43	454,304 18

a Six months.

The following table shows the number of fires, and the losses and insurance, during the past seventeen years:

Years.	Number of fires.	Number of false alarms.	Amount of loss.	Amount of insurance.	Loss for each fire.
1863–'64	186	16	$355,660	$272,500	$1,912
1864–'65	193	32	651,798	585,300	3,408
1865–'66	243	21	1,216,466	941,602	5,006
1866–'67	315	26	2,487,973	1,643,445	7,898
1867–'68	315	57	4,315,332	3,417,288	8,135
1868–'69	405	67	560,169	463,248	1,333
1869–'70	600	45	871,905	600,061	1,453
1870–'71	667	35	2,447,845	2,133,498	3,658
1871–'72 a	489	44	972,800	745,000	1,989
1872–'73	441	44	680,099	3,763,275	1,542
1873–'74	466	68	1,013,246	3,641,735	2,174
1874–'75 b	473	83	2,345,684	6,789,300	4,959
1875 c	332	67	127,014	2,323,150	383
1876	477	123	387,951	3,780,060	811
1877	445	132	1,044,997	6,173,575	2,340
1878	473	88	306,317	3,327,348	641
1879	638	135	572,082	5,112,631	896
1880	804	154	1,135,816	5,409,480	1,411

a The great fire not included.   b The large fire included.
c Nine months ending December 31, 1875.

The fire-alarm telegraph is in charge of 1 superintendent, with a force of 4 operators, 5 repairers, 1 batteryman, and 2 linemen. The system includes 3,176 poles, 498 miles of wire (28 miles being underground, in cables), and 501 alarm-boxes.

PUBLIC SCHOOLS.

The earliest records of the public schools to be found among the official documents of the city begin with the incorporation of Chicago as a city in 1837, and it is stated in the reports for the quarter ending November 1 of that year that there were 400 pupils enrolled in five out of the seven districts.

The following table shows the growth of the public-school system from 1837 to 1879:

For year ending—	Total population of the city.	Number under 21 years of age.	Total enrollment in the public schools.	Average daily membership.	Number of teachers.	Total amount paid for tuition.	Total amount paid for all current expenses.
1837	4,170						
1840	4,470	2,109	317				
1841			410		5	$1,889 82	$2,676 75
1842			531		7	2,289 88	3,225 99
1843	7,580	2,694	808		7	2,379 38	3,099 97
1844			915		8	2,363 32	3,106 22
1845	12,088		1,051		9	2,277 53	5,413 45
1846	14,169		1,107		13		5,635 87
1847	16,859	7,603	1,317		18		4,248 76
1848	20,023		1,517		18		5,790 82
1849	23,047		1,794		18	5,195 50	
1850	29,963		1,919	1,224	21		6,037 97
1851		12,021	2,287	1,409	25	6,921 17	7,398 97
1852			2,404	1,521	29	9,107 64	10,704 04
1853	59,130	17,404	3,086	1,795	34	10,829 58	12,129 59
December 31, 1854			3,500		35	13,316 79	14,254 72
December 31, 1855	80,000	31,235	6,826		42	15,826 73	16,546 13
December 31, 1856	84,113		8,577	3,688		23,365 00	29,720 00
February 1, 1858			10,786	4,464	81	36,079 00	45,701 00
February 1, 1859			12,873	5,516	101	43,009 89	58,686 80
February 1, 1860	109,206	52,861	14,199	6,649	123	49,612 43	69,630 53
December 31, 1861			16,547	7,582	139	60,994 46	81,533 75
December 31, 1862			16,441	8,217	160	68,607 97	86,755 32
December 31, 1863	138,186	58,955	17,521	8,962	187	75,326 18	92,378 86
August 31, 1864			21,188	10,820	212	88,111 56	113,305 24
August 31, 1865 a	178,492	82,996	29,080	12,688	240	131,034 91	176,003 73
August 31, 1866	200,418	89,150	24,851	14,609	265	162,383 79	219,198 66
July 1, 1867			27,260	16,392	319	227,524 97	296,672 89
July 1, 1868	242,373		29,954	18,322	401	278,133 06	352,001 80
July 1, 1869	252,054	209,583	34,740	22,838	481	350,515 43	446,786 50
July 1, 1870	306,605	136,333	38,939	25,755	537	414,655 70	527,741 60
July 1, 1871			40,832	28,174	572	444,634 53	547,461 74
July 1, 1872 b	367,396	152,470	38,035	24,539	476	378,670 55	479,444 44
July 1, 1873			44,091	28,832	564	430,462 64	524,702 09
July 1, 1874			47,963	32,777	640	492,893 17	588,643 11
July 1, 1875	395,408	175,549	49,121	34,983	700	552,327 37	662,093 47
July 1, 1876 c	407,661	184,499	51,128	38,081	762	588,721 41	710,628 19
July 1, 1877			53,529	39,495	730	450,252 46	551,621 17
July 1, 1878	436,731	200,473	55,109	41,569	797	490,462 64	579,508 68
July 1, 1879 d			56,587	43,741	851	529,164 45	630,711 17

a Embraces one year and a half.

b The falling off in enrollment, membership, etc., was occasioned by the great fire of October 8 and 9, 1871.

c Extra teachers were dispensed with this year.

d A general reduction of about 25 per cent. in salaries was made during this year.

The school fund is now estimated in value at over $3,000,000. In addition to the pupils in the public schools there are about 15,000 pupils in the fifty Roman Catholic schools, and the twelve large schools under the supervision of the German Lutherans.

COMMERCE AND NAVIGATION.

[From the reports of the Bureau of Statistics for the fiscal years ending June 30.]

Customs district of Chicago, Illinois.	1879.	1880.
Total value of imports	$272,766	$847,935
Total value of exports:		
Domestic	$2,829,582	$3,438,671
Foreign	$6,980	$6,708
Total number of immigrants	59	388

Customs district of Chicago, Illinois.	1879.		1880.	
	Number.	Tons.	Number.	Tons.
Vessels in foreign trade:				
Entered	214	72,169	349	127,189
Cleared	286	94,972	418	145,943
Vessels in lake trade and fisheries:				
Entered	10,678	3,547,185	12,457	4,207,204
Cleared	10,613	3,506,706	12,495	4,193,302
Vessels owned in district	390	78,219	384	76,478
Vessels built during the year	5	180	1	37

MANUFACTURES.

The following is a summary of the statistics of the manufactures of Chicago for 1880, being taken from tables prepared for the Tenth Census by Charles Randolph, chief special agent:

Mechanical and manufacturing industries.	No. of establishments.	Capital.	AVERAGE NUMBER OF HANDS EMPLOYED.			Total amount paid in wages during the year.	Value of materials.	Value of products.
			Males above 16 years.	Females above 15 years.	Children and youths.			
All industries............................	3,519	$36,836,885	62,431	12,185	4,793	$34,653,462	$179,209,610	$249,022,948
Agricultural implements	3	3,110,000	981	....	49	559,532	1,642,748	2,699,480
Awnings and tents	8	10,350	20	24	1	13,540	46,872	72,031
Baking and yeast powders (see also Drugs and chemicals)............	3	135,000	75	37	1	44,134	485,000	635,000
Baskets, rattan and willow ware.......................	11	107,750	119	....	14	48,750	54,225	120,400
Billiard tables and materials................	4	263,200	310	....	....	137,225	283,900	665,400
Blacksmithing (see also Wheelwrighting)	146	110,375	325	....	11	199,689	123,609	482,029
Bookbinding and blank-book making................	26	176,100	268	163	39	165,102	203,725	481,131
Boots and shoes, including custom work and repairing	133	997,475	1,387	358	66	770,191	1,355,208	2,479,805
Boxes, cigar	6	54,800	40	43	22	36,263	114,090	179,411
Boxes, fancy and paper................	12	66,200	63	178	32	81,550	116,400	254,792
Boxes, wooden packing	14	225,000	895	....	95	414,953	1,271,682	1,883,073
Brass castings	11	442,500	515	....	....	232,125	361,700	737,500
Bread and other bakery products	118	553,200	680	159	37	398,081	1,817,078	2,613,186
Brick and tile (see also Terra-cotta ware)...........	35	313,800	1,176	13	61	454,557	128,573	800,400
Bridges	3	318,000	642	....	....	311,763	1,473,000	1,974,000
Brooms and brushes	41	73,200	255	106	46	132,830	271,337	517,324
Carpentering	171	62,050	1,733	1	53	893,642	1,337,890	2,598,508
Carpets, rag	5	1,275	3	1	....	1,700	2,843	6,450
Carriages and wagons (see also Wheelwrighting)	40	1,351,080	1,152	35	123	590,166	702,532	1,809,759
Cars, railroad, street, and repairs................	5	421,500	562	....	20	286,742	675,291	1,043,682
Clothing, men's........................	102	6,449,650	4,101	4,001	374	3,539,169	11,631,764	17,342,207
Clothing, women's....................	19	254,500	72	1,488	23	334,885	1,017,720	1,585,990
Coffee and spices, roasted and ground	10	177,900	185	40	45	137,496	2,342,021	2,808,879
Coffins, burial cases, and undertakers' goods	5	73,650	107	12	2	67,020	164,500	290,600
Confectionery........................	24	275,200	310	163	132	211,604	1,424,830	1,953,558
Cooperage	65	325,560	686	....	20	313,977	644,380	1,137,694
Coppersmithing (see also Tinware, copperware, and sheet-iron ware).	3	3,100	10	....	....	4,460	4,820	14,200
Cork cutting........................	3	45,800	24	15	17	22,103	125,038	217,220
Cutlery and edge tools (see also Hardware; Tools)	12	113,700	135	8	27	69,581	49,670	177,000
Dentistry, mechanical	48	37,000	28	2	2	14,000	25,000	144,000
Dentists' materials..................	3	21,000	18	5	....	11,300	12,000	46,000
Drugs and chemicals (see also Baking and yeast powders; Patent medicines and compounds).	14	408,500	165	45	11	93,440	617,800	959,850
Dyeing and cleaning.................	16	73,450	74	13	7	47,023	46,815	140,461
Dyeing and finishing textiles	11	69,450	72	13	7	46,519	45,565	135,521
Electrical apparatus and supplies........	3	271,500	127	25	....	100,603	143,587	543,000
Electroplating.......................	9	24,800	31	2	6	18,645	9,820	59,000
Engraving and die-sinking	5	18,100	22	3	....	17,397	13,550	49,000
Engraving, wood....................	16	35,325	66	3	8	51,785	12,970	116,775
Flavoring extracts	4	71,290	65	40	5	36,730	334,500	461,500
Flouring- and grist-mill products	12	652,140	176	....	....	103,542	1,939,709	2,217,564
Food preparations	5	89,600	27	12	8	15,940	58,500	119,000
Foundery and machine-shop products (see also Iron work, architectural and ornamental; Steam fittings and heating apparatus).	133	4,455,457	4,736	6	145	2,371,361	5,088,619	8,934,629
Fruits and vegetables, canned and preserved	5	90,000	113	40	27	58,700	417,415	587,223
Furnishing goods, men's................	13	586,140	144	1,119	47	392,700	1,143,275	1,835,597
Furniture (see also Mattresses and spring beds; Upholstering)	149	2,443,175	4,160	57	347	2,028,371	2,996,088	6,177,114
Furniture, chairs....................	6	216,500	278	....	57	121,200	139,440	334,072
Furs, dressed	10	160,500	49	88	2	51,058	227,000	370,000
Gas and lamp fixtures	3	17,300	46	1	2	18,600	41,225	96,600
Gas machines and meters.............	3	45,500	42	....	....	19,723	28,884	64,800
Glass, cut, stained, and ornamented	6	39,600	76	1	3	47,345	38,564	113,612

Mechanical and manufacturing industries.	No. of establishments.	Capital.	Males above 16 years.	Females above 15 years.	Children and youths.	Total amount paid in wages during the year.	Value of materials.	Value of products.
Gloves and mittens (see also Hosiery and knit goods)	7	$50,200	36	109	5	$40,075	$110,150	$170,800
Gold and silver leaf and foil	3	22,000	34	45	2	25,750	41,000	85,000
Grease and tallow	6	117,000	111			64,044	1,123,025	1,327,000
Hairwork	15	48,650	8	110		26,782	65,300	135,915
Hand-knit goods	7	14,900	4	106	9	14,065	43,470	64,072
Handles, wooden	3	2,850	4		2	1,950	4,485	9,000
Hand-stamps	4	5,500	11	1	1	7,140	11,600	26,050
Hardware (see also Cutlery and edge tools; Tools)	13	134,870	136		31	70,293	89,395	244,018
Hardware, saddlery	3	30,100	32	1	20	18,200	48,200	87,000
Hats and caps, not including wool hats	11	18,950	34	27	7	28,226	36,500	88,200
Hosiery and knit goods (see also Gloves and mittens)	7	57,800	121	341	63	66,966	184,831	300,577
Ink	3	33,750	18	2	12	11,450	15,000	61,000
Iron and steel	11	3,875,000	2,871		-125	1,477,563	8,006,970	10,441,891
Iron doors and shutters	3	7,500	18			11,720	19,800	40,560
Iron forgings	4	135,800	115			56,130	349,337	485,581
Iron railings, wrought	5	10,000	27			15,590	17,400	42,881
Iron work, architectural and ornamental (see also Foundery and machine-shop products).	11	64,000	133		12	63,294	170,900	203,900
Japanning	3	9,100	26		1	6,300	5,000	17,100
Jewelry	11	48,600	67		5	45,396	73,380	192,004
Lamps and reflectors	4	453,500	345	25	55	159,250	648,408	1,051,346
Lasts	3	16,500	34		2	19,988	34,075	61,700
Leather, curried	9	481,002	225			129,196	1,762,756	2,146,500
Leather, tanned	19	1,932,998	981	99	29	541,184	3,790,522	4,914,550
Liquors, distilled	7	1,175,000	750			330,000	2,961,281	4,387,545
Liquors, malt	18	3,395,500	892			445,891	1,886,165	3,429,375
Lithographing (see also Printing and publishing)	13	494,150	307	12	11	220,955	263,549	698,387
Lock- and gun-smithing	14	10,400	20		1	10,481	7,155	34,094
Looking-glass and picture frames	52	338,675	787	31	156	357,625	600,540	1,268,855
Lumber, planed (see also Sash, doors, and blinds; Wood, turned and carved).	15	471,008	686		56	297,730	3,441,100	4,080,900
Malt	16	870,200	230		1	108,709	1,583,019	1,960,780
Marble and stone work	43	491,150	891		14	456,014	583,915	1,275,355
Masonry, brick and stone	59	241,250	1,613		10	759,843	1,616,845	2,623,137
Mattresses and spring beds (see also Furniture)	24	216,950	281	63	48	131,286	333,900	739,938
Millinery and lace goods	12	108,100	48	289	65	85,280	244,060	430,900
Mineral and soda waters	13	120,150	196		6	84,380	182,810	406,900
Models and patterns	16	11,400	57		1	31,380	8,251	64,572
Musical instruments, organs and materials	9	81,500	177		22	105,307	195,028	376,650
Musical instruments, pianos and materials	5	20,300	27			16,902	11,800	37,615
Oil, lard	3	190,000	82		3	42,600	928,000	1,107,000
Oil, linseed	5	655,000	143	4	9	85,005	1,590,500	1,967,000
Oleomargarine	3	208,800	63		7	21,310	328,500	437,800
Painting and paperhanging	134	280,207	963	1	33	519,973	549,015	1,403,026
Paints (see also Varnish)	12	785,500	251	18	7	153,128	2,110,845	2,796,000
Patent medicines and compounds (see also Drugs and chemicals)	12	176,050	94	32	2	45,878	516,500	674,280
Paving materials	3	58,500	81			36,787	244,500	307,000
Photographing	47	181,625	115	57	7	100,738	81,885	325,978
Pickles, preserves, and sauces	6	27,000	49	5	2	25,400	216,470	288,200
Pipes, tobacco	5	6,700	4		1	3,050	3,025	14,200
Plumbing and gasfitting	86	108,201	302	2	54	190,114	253,938	563,012
Pocket-books	3	22,300	61	28		31,890	95,840	150,599
Printing and publishing (see also Lithographing)	135	2,886,400	2,750	453	316	1,930,881	2,451,360	5,959,295
Printing materials	4	20,200	24		7	17,452	26,300	61,000
Roofing and roofing materials	15	192,521	221			82,331	422,827	593,431
Rubber and elastic goods	3	10,500	8	10		4,540	25,750	35,600
Saddlery and harness	82	219,250	329	100	62	179,574	403,625	746,247

Mechanical and manufacturing industries.	No. of establishments.	Capital.	Males above 16 years.	Females above 15 years.	Children and youths.	Total amount paid in wages during the year.	Value of materials.	Value of products.
Sash, doors, and blinds (see also Lumber, planed; Wood, turned and carved).	27	$1,213,538	1,793	16	190	$805,233	$1,649,555	$2,961,508
Saws	6	40,300	26	....	....	18,283	12,300	43,500
Scales and balances	4	51,450	74	....	....	40,500	111,250	217,600
Sewing-machine cases	6	70,800	139	....	26	106,706	79,615	262,355
Sewing-machines and attachments	11	91,300	147	4	6	59,906	130,800	259,513
Shirts	28	156,150	111	417	7	132,020	420,677	721,167
Shipbuilding	21	355,000	347	....	....	181,675	358,820	659,133
Show-cases	11	55,100	107	....	8	59,976	111,500	227,000
Silk and silk goods	5	82,000	37	135	57	72,195	125,895	244,150
Slaughtering and meat-packing, not including retail butchering	70	8,455,200	7,120	....	298	3,392,748	74,546,319	85,324,371
Soap and candles	16	1,230,800	402	33	79	199,292	3,135,047	3,627,310
Springs, steel, car, and carriage	5	45,500	64	....	1	36,740	151,000	222,500
Stationery goods	3	5,600	3	4	3	4,100	17,050	25,500
Steam-fittings and heating apparatus (see also Foundery and machine-shop products).	11	99,700	220	....	6	115,590	411,780	580,530
Stereotyping and electrotyping (see also Type founding)	3	25,000	45	....	12	23,672	18,300	65,554
Straw goods	8	114,000	85	335	19	119,514	297,744	484,609
Surgical appliances	4	20,500	16	12	....	10,700	17,200	48,800
Terra-cotta ware (see also Brick and tile)	3	28,000	81	....	13	26,500	22,576	68,000
Tinware, copperware, and sheet-iron ware (see also Coppersmithing).	106	647,875	919	198	154	513,329	1,157,831	2,164,496
Tobacco, chewing, smoking and snuff (see also Tobacco, cigars and cigarettes).	4	287,500	142	97	15	77,060	1,206,187	1,387,598
Tobacco, cigars and cigarettes (see also Tobacco, chewing, smoking, and snuff).	287	538,350	1,489	134	101	701,573	1,058,916	2,315,174
Tools (see also Cutlery and edge tools; Hardware)	5	15,300	15	....	....	6,200	4,850	19,224
Trunks and valises	12	155,000	212	....	10	102,170	295,700	508,300
Type founding (see also Stereotyping and electrotyping)	4	290,000	127	95	96	109,300	86,000	314,000
Umbrellas and canes	6	2,775	8	....	2	2,516	2,100	7,600
Upholstering (see also Furniture)	19	43,900	110	21	9	51,383	121,691	226,195
Varnish (see also Paints)	4	207,000	32	....	1	24,646	302,600	389,000
Vinegar	13	106,300	63	....	4	36,189	179,900	328,338
Watch and clock repairing	28	26,950	49	1	1	31,174	8,537	63,194
Wheelwrighting (see also Blacksmithing; Carriages and wagons)	118	184,205	426	....	21	213,500	165,049	532,734
Whips	4	2,400	8	3	1	3,325	3,950	11,369
Window blinds and shades	4	11,500	12	8	9	6,550	32,600	51,250
Wirework	24	21,122	213	....	39	108,294	753,786	1,065,860
Wood, turned and carved (see also Lumber, planed; Sash, doors, and blinds).	14	86,010	106	10	21	54,767	79,587	181,840
All other industries (a)	74	4,114,271	2,207	461	318	1,258,133	8,060,254	10,787,109

a Embracing axle-grease; bags, other than paper; bags, paper; belting and hose, leather; cleansing and polishing preparations; cordage and twine; corsets, cotton goods; envelopes; explosives and fireworks; fancy articles; files; fire extinguishers, chemical; glass; glue; gold and silver, reduced and refined; iron bolts, nuts, washers, and rivets; iron nails and spikes, cut and wrought; iron pipe, wrought; ivory and bone work; jewelry and instrument cases; labels and tags; lapidary work; lard, refined; lead, bar, pipe, sheet, and shot; lightning rods; lime; mantels, slate, marble, and marbleized; matches; mixed textiles; musical instruments and materials (not specified); oil, essential; perfumery and cosmetics; photographic apparatus; pumps; refrigerators; regalia and society banners and emblems; safes, doors, and vaults, fire-proof; screws; shoddy; soda-water apparatus; stencils and brands; stone- and earthen-ware; stamped ware; telegraph and telephone apparatus and supplies; toys and games; vault-lights; washing-machines and clothes-wringers; watch cases; and wooden ware.

From the foregoing table it appears that the average capital of all establishments is $19,561 49; that the average wages of all hands employed is $436 36 per annum; and that the average outlay in wages, in materials, and in interest (at 6 per cent.) on capital employed is $61,947 51.

GALESBURG,

KNOX COUNTY, ILLINOIS.

POPULATION

IN THE

AGGREGATE,

1850-1880.

	Inhab.
1790	......
1800	......
1810	......
1820	......
1830	......
1840	......
1850	882
1860	4,953
1870	10,158
1880	11,437

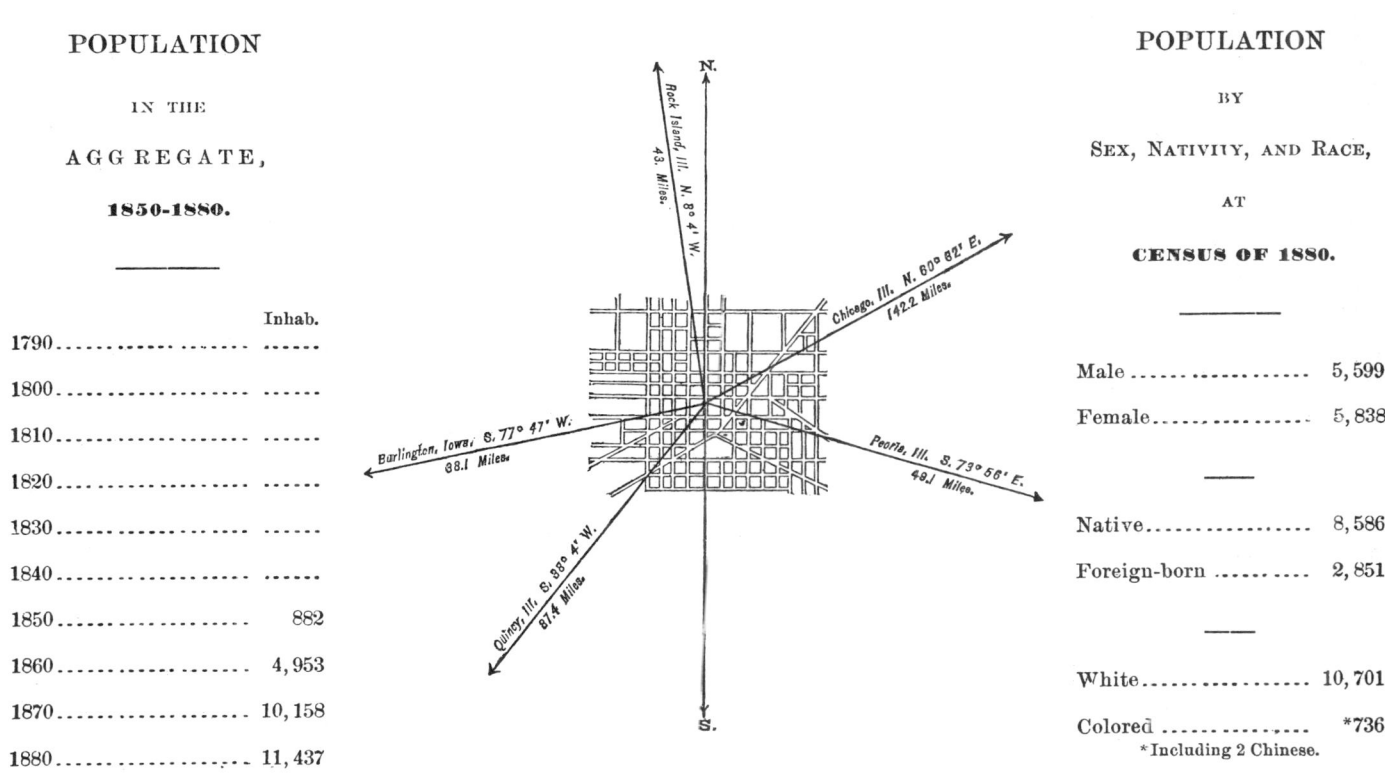

POPULATION

BY

SEX, NATIVITY, AND RACE,

AT

CENSUS OF 1880.

Male	5,599
Female	5,838
Native	8,586
Foreign-born	2,851
White	10,701
Colored	*736

*Including 2 Chinese.

Latitude: 40° 55′ North; Longitude: 90° 24′ (west from Greenwich); Altitude: 755 to 810 feet.

FINANCIAL CONDITION:

Total Valuation: $3,022,493; per capita: $264 00.   Net Indebtedness: $53,250; per capita: $4 66.   Tax per $100: $2 54.

HISTORICAL SKETCH.

Galesburg was first settled by a colony of "Christian" people from central New York and northern Vermont, with the intention of building up a "Christian" college and other schools. In 1836, 11,000 acres of land were bought at the government price, and, when properly laid out, resold to the settlers at such an advance as to form an endowment for the college. In 1837 the settlement began, and the enterprise was marked by a steady progress, changed only as the great tides of business depression or revival swept over the country. In 1854 the first railroad was built from Chicago to Galesburg, attended with the usual rapid growth of a temporary terminus. Extensive railroad shops and the junction of five branches of a great railway give the city a very large business. No very

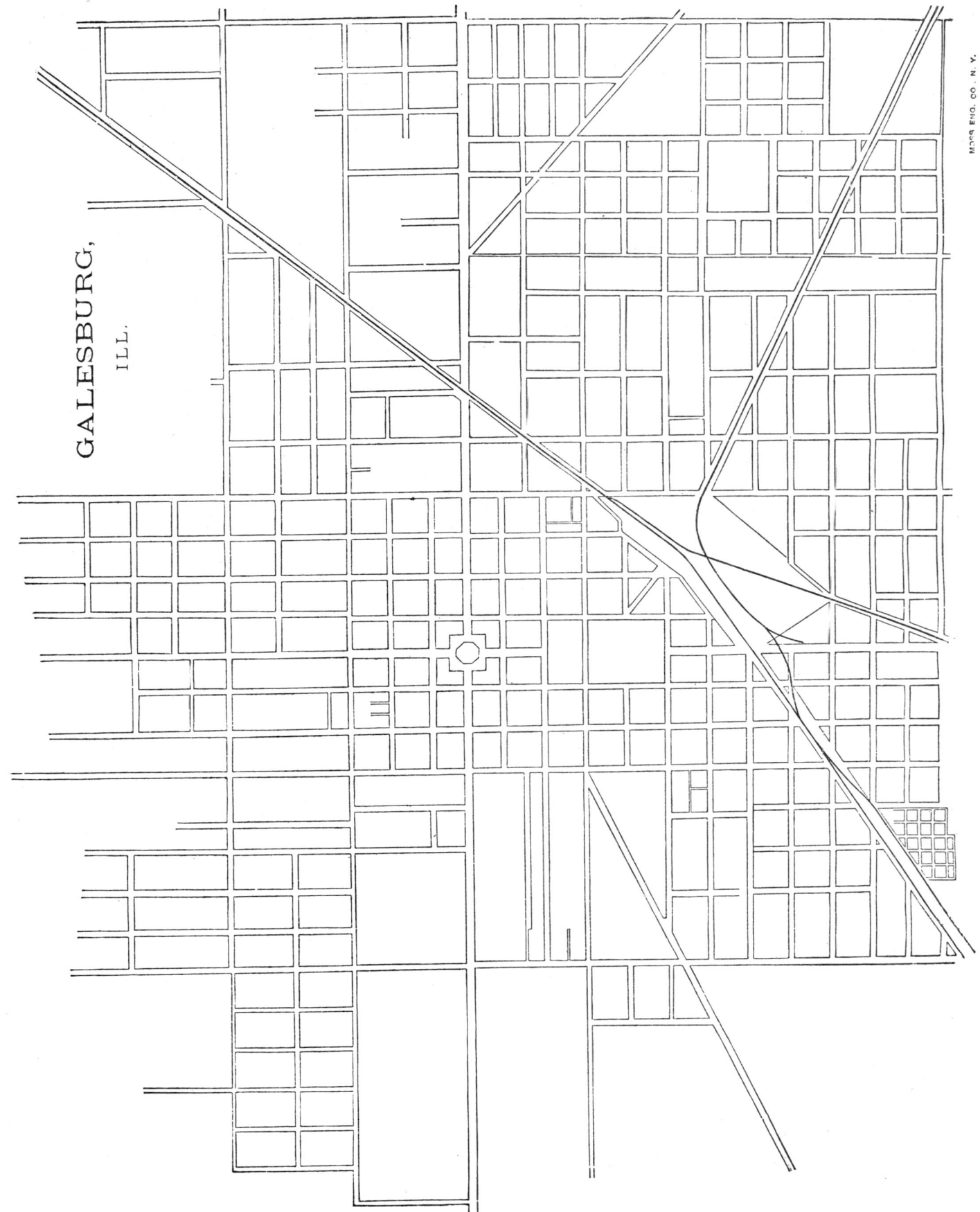

GALESBURG, ILL.

destructive fires have occurred. At present there is a steady and constant improvement, more, however, in the way of betterments than in actual new building. The people are still mostly of New York and New England antecedents, with the usual sprinkling of all foreign nationalities. Among these, Swedes predominate largely, and they are considered as being among the most esteemed and valuable citizens. They acquire wealth rapidly, and are fast buying out the smaller native farmers, who go farther west and secure larger farms.

GALESBURG IN 1880

The following statistical accounts, collected by the Census Office, indicate the present condition of Galesburg:

LOCATION.

Galesburg lies in latitude 40° 55′ north, longitude 90° 24′ west from Greenwich, on the water-shed between the Illinois and Mississippi rivers, 163 miles southwest from Chicago and 100 miles northeast by north from Quincy The elevations of the city above sea-level are, average at the railroad station, 799 feet; lowest point, 755; and highest point, 810 feet. The city is not on navigable water.

RAILROAD COMMUNICATIONS.

The city is touched by the following railroad line: Chicago, Burlington, and Quincy railroad, from Chicago to Council Bluffs, with branches to Quincy, Peoria, Saint Louis, and Kansas City. This line, with its numerous connections, gives Galesburg railroad communication with all points in the country.

TRIBUTARY COUNTRY.

The character of the surrounding country is essentially agricultural, with much stock-raising. The principa crops are corn, oats, broom-corn, rye, and a very small amount of wheat. It is noted for its fine hogs and cattle, and, latterly, for dairy products. The industries are such as naturally pertain to an agricultural district, and the commerce is of the same character.

TOPOGRAPHY.

The soil is a rich black loam from 3 to 5 feet deep, resting on a stratum of yellow clay from 8 to 12 feet thick, and that upon sand or gravel, followed by a hard blue clay. The rocks lie deep, and are generally limestone, with some soft sandstone. Bituminous coal is mined in the vicinity. The surface is quite level, though most of it is sufficiently undulating to afford good drainage, part of the rainfall going east to the Illinois river, and part west to the Mississippi. There are no ponds, lakes, or marshes, and the country within a radius of 5 miles is about the same as that portion occupied by the site of the city. The country was originally a prairie, with heavy forests bordering the small water-courses, but now the prairies have artificial groves scattered over them, while much of the original forest has been cleared off.

CLIMATE.

Highest recorded summer temperature, 99°; highest summer temperature in average years, 96°. Lowest recorded winter temperature, −22°; lowest winter temperature in average years, −7°. None of the winds seem to be of a more healthful character than others. Southwest winds prevail in summer. and northwest winds in winter, the former being warm and dry, and the latter cold and dry. Southeast winds usually bring rain, while those from the northeast are generally accompanied by a cold drizzling rain.

STREETS.

Total length, 75 miles, and, with the exception of 3,500 feet laid in gravel, none of these are paved. The graveled streets cost $1 15 per square yard, but as it is yet only an experiment, its permanent economy is said to be an open question. Sidewalks are generally of wood, some are of concrete, and a few are of stone. The graveled streets have stone gutters in part, while the remainder of the streets are simply ditched. There is an abundance of trees planted along the sides of the streets. General repair on streets is done by the day, but the permanent work is done by contract. This latter class of work is preferred by the city authorities, although there are cases of emergency when day work is thought to be better. Street expenses amount annually to about $7,000. There are no horse-railroads. Three omnibuses carry passengers to all parts of the city, at the uniform rate of fare of 25 cents.

WATER WORKS.

The works for the water-supply cost $16,000, but, with the exception of the statement that the water-pipes are connected with two manufacturing establishments that furnish the pumping-power when necessary, no other information regarding them was given.

GAS.

The gas-works are owned by private parties. The charge to consumers per 1,000 feet is $2 70. The city pays $18 25 per annum each for gas street-lamps, 149 in number. There are also 90 gasoline street-lamps, cared for by the city, and their cost, including lighting, is $12 per annum each.

PUBLIC BUILDINGS.

The city owns and occupies for municipal uses, wholly or in part, 1 building for city offices and 2 fire-engine houses. The estimated cost of these buildings is $9,000. The cost of the buildings used for city offices is $5,000.

PUBLIC PARKS AND PLEASURE-GROUNDS.

There is but one park proper in Galesburg, area 7 acres, though there is a small piece of ground in the center of the public square that is fenced off for park purposes in a sixteen-sided figure. The cost of the park proper, including land purchase and construction, was $21,000. The yearly cost of maintenance is $500. The park was designed by the board of commissioners, and that body controls it.

PLACES OF AMUSEMENT.

There are two theaters in the city—the Opera-house, with a seating capacity of 1,500, and the Academy of Music, seating 1,000. They pay a license to the city of $5 per day when performances are had. In addition to the theaters there are several small halls which can be used for various purposes, but seldom for concerts, etc. There are no concert- and beer-gardens in the city.

DRAINAGE.

A small water-course, running through the city in open channel, receives the surface drainage from both sides and the discharge from sewers and drains. The bed of this stream is about 28 feet below the general surface of the city, and it affords a good fall for sewers extending as far back as they have yet been built. The first public sewerage work was begun about the year 1870, consisting of a brick sewer, 36 inches in diameter and 1,266 feet long, running northerly into the stream. Since that time four other streets, running north and south, have been furnished with sewers, viz, one 2,600 feet long and 24 inches in diameter, of brick; one 1,500 feet long is of 18-inch pipe; and two, having a combined length of 5,000 feet, of 15-inch pipe. Streets crossing these in an east-and-west direction are provided with 12-inch pipe sewers. Many streets are so level as to be difficult to provide with good surface drainage. Within a few years porous drain-tiles have been laid beneath the gutters, on each side, and have done good service. Some of these are laid with a fall of only 1 inch in 100 feet.

The mouths of sewers are exposed, except in time of floods. Ventilation is provided for, in some instances, by grated manhole covers, while in others no provision for ventilation is made. No trouble has yet been caused by deposit of solid matter, the wash of storm-water having been sufficient to remove all obstructions. No water-closets are allowed to drain into any public sewer, but the outfalls are beginning to cause some inconvenience and complaints, and the disposal of sewage is receiving the attention of the people and of the council.

The cost of sewerage-works is paid, one-third by the city and two-thirds by owners of abutting property. Assessments are sometimes based on the value of the lots and buildings to be drained, but those based on the frontage of lots appear to have given the best satisfaction.

No information is furnished of the cost of sewers. That of catch-basins is given at $25, and for connecting the drain with the sewer from $15 to $20 each.

CEMETERIES.

There are 4 cemeteries in and connected with the city: *Hope Cemetery*, area 12 acres, is situated between Main and Academy streets, while *Catholic Cemetery*, area 15 acres; *Linwood Cemetery*, area 30 acres; and *Jewish Cemetery*, area three-fourths of an acre, are all outside the city limits. There are no church-yards or private burial-grounds in which interments are no longer permitted. It is impossible even to approximate the number of interments that have been made in the above cemeteries. Burials have been going on for the past thirty years, sometimes one on top of another, and many without record. No statement could be made that would be better than a random guess. Burial permits are issued by the city clerk, upon the filing of a certificate of death. Persons dying of contagious or infectious diseases are required to be buried privately and without delay.

MARKETS.

There are no public or corporation markets in the city. A lot 156 by 104 feet is set apart for standing-ground for loads of corn and wood offered for sale.

SANITARY AUTHORITY—BOARD OF HEALTH.

The chief sanitary authority of Galesburg is the board of health, composed of the mayor, with the marshal, overseer of the poor, and a physician appointed by the council. The action of the board is determined by the action of the council in the passage of ordinances. In ordinary times the annual expenses of the board are $260, for salaries and stationery, and during epidemics any increase of expense depends on the amount appropriated by the council. Either in the absence of or during epidemics the extent of the authority of the board is limited to a general supervision over health matters. The mayor is presiding officer, but by tacit consent the physician of the board is allowed to have control and to exercise his judgment; his salary is $150 a year. The board meets only in extraordinary cases, and then transacts business as a deliberative body. Last year there were 5 inspectors employed during the summer months to make a house-to-house inspection; but this year only one has been appointed, and he co-operates with the physician. Three inspectors are usually detailed from the police force. At intervals general inspections are made. The practice this year is confined to acting on the nuisances that may be reported, and to such matters as incidentally come to the knowledge of the board. When a nuisance is reported the inspector visits and examines the premises; if the complaint is well founded, notice to abate within a certain time is served, and if this is disregarded, suit is begun. No regular inspection of drainage or of drinking-water is had. When cases come to the knowledge of the board such action is taken as will remedy the evils. The same is also applicable regarding defective privy-vaults and cesspools. The board exercises complete control over the conservation and removal of garbage. There are no special regulations regarding the burial of the dead. The board reports annually, and from time to time, to the city council, but the reports are not formally published.

The record of diseases, births, and deaths is kept by the city clerk at his office, all physicians reporting to him.

INFECTIOUS DISEASES.

Small-pox patients are isolated, a temporary pest-house being erected in the suburbs for the purpose. Scarlet-fever patiets are quarantined, as much as possible, at home; communication is cut off from the family, cards are posted on houses, rooms are required to be disinfected, and every precaution is taken to prevent the spread of the disease. The board prohibits the attendance of pupils either in public or in private schools coming from houses in which contagious diseases exist. Vaccination is not compulsory and is not done at the public expense.

MUNICIPAL CLEANSING.

Street-cleaning.—The streets are cleaned at the expense of the city and with its regular force. The work is done wholly by hand, no sweeping-machines being used. The graveled streets are cleaned about every two weeks, and the others are cleaned as required. The droppings and garbage are removed, loose matter is swept into pails and carried off, and the gutters are cleaned. The annual cost of the service is estimated at $200. The sweepings are either used for grading or are taken as a fertilizer.

Removal of garbage and ashes.—All garbage is removed by the city scavenger at the expense of the city. There are no special regulations as to the conservancy of garbage while awaiting removal, the matter being under the supervision of the board of health. It is used by the scavenger to feed hogs. The ashes are used for gardening purposes. The annual cost of the service is $108, being the salary of the scavenger. The board of health is diligent in causing the garbage to be removed promptly. The system is reported to work well, the only difficulty being to get the people to appreciate the necessity of having the garbage ready for removal at stated intervals.

Dead animals.—The city marshal is required to see that all dead animals are disposed of. They are usually hauled off and buried on the commons in the suburbs, the cost of the service being generally paid by the owner. No record is kept of the number of different animals annually removed.

Liquid household wastes.—A comparatively small portion of the houses in the city are connected with the public sewers, so that nearly all of the liquid wastes are thrown into cesspools and privy-vaults, none being allowed to pass into the street-gutters. The cesspools are generally tight, do not receive the wastes from water-closets, and are cleaned out when they are complained of. The board-of-health physician has in several cases analyzed the well-water on premises of diphtheria patients, and has expressed his opinion that the impurity of the water, owing to its proximity to privy-vaults, was probably the cause of the disease.

Human excreta.—Nearly if not quite all the dwelling-houses in the city depend on privy-vaults; hotels have water-closets, delivering into the sewers. Very few of the privy-vaults are water-tight, they being mostly boarded up. Vaults are required to be a certain distance from wells, and are emptied at night in covered water-tight boxes. The board of health has totally prohibited the digging of vaults, and has endeavored to bring into use the dry-earth system. The board is meeting with some success, as well as violent opposition in some quarters, and a few dry-earth closets are now in use, with their number gradually increasing. The night-soil is used as manure by farmers a few miles from the city, but it is thought that none is so used on the gathering-ground of the public water-supply.

POLICE.

The police force is appointed by the mayor, subject to the approval of the city council, and is governed by the city marshal, who, in addition to police supervision, performs police duty, and is *ex officio* a constable; his salary is $800 per annum. The remainder of the force consists of 4 regular policemen at $600 per year each. The uniform consists of a blue suit, costing complete about $30, and when required to be worn each man furnishes his own. The policemen are armed with club, revolver, and nippers. Each policeman is on duty twelve hours at a time, and patrols 3 miles of streets. During the past year 393 arrests were made, including 144 tramps for vagrancy, the principal causes being, intoxication 148; assault, theft, robbery, disorderly conduct, etc. The majority of these paid or worked out their fines, and some were turned over to the county. The force is not required to co-operate with the other city departments except when it is in the line of police duty. Special policemen are appointed by the mayor for the time required, and the appointments are reported to the city council. These specials are under the direction of the marshal, unless appointed for the board of health or something not connected with the regular force. The yearly cost of the police force (1880) is $4,000.

JACKSONVILLE,

MORGAN COUNTY, ILLINOIS.

POPULATION

IN THE

AGGREGATE,

1850-1880.

	Inhab.
1790	......
1800	......
1810	......
1820	......
1830	......
1840	......
1850	2,745
1860	5,512
1870	9,203
1880	10,927

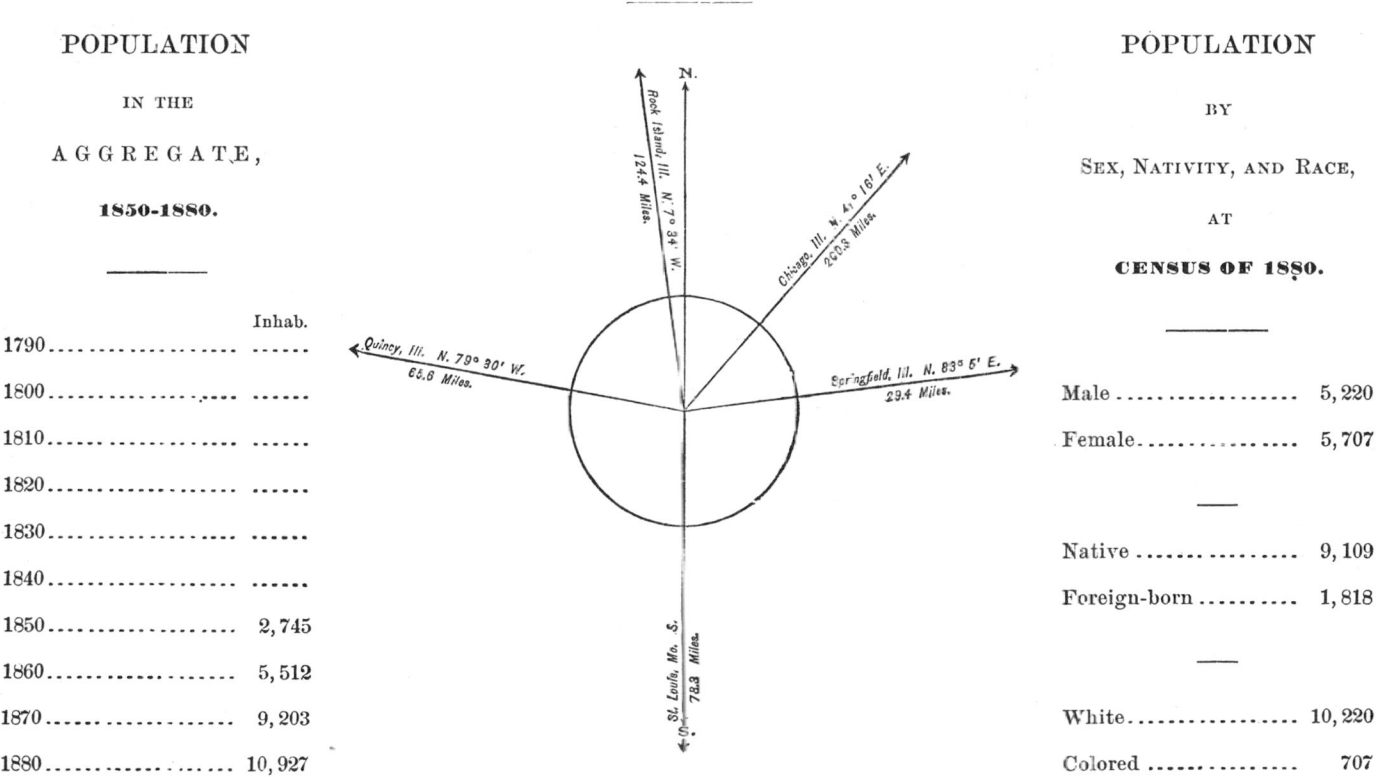

POPULATION

BY

SEX, NATIVITY, AND RACE,

AT

CENSUS OF 1880.

Male	5,220
Female	5,707
Native	9,109
Foreign-born	1,818
White	10,220
Colored	707

Latitude: 30° 45′ North; Longitude: 90° 12′ (west from Greenwich); Altitude: 676 feet.

FINANCIAL CONDITION:

Total Valuation: $2,000,000; per capita: $183 00.   Net Indebtedness: $273,336; per capita: $25 01.   Tax per $100: $5 03.

JACKSONVILLE.

The site of Jacksonville, the county-seat of Morgan county, was one of the most beautiful spots on the native prairies. To the east and to the north, about a mile from the spot where the court-house was built, a line of heavy timber marked the changing course of the Mauraisterre creek on its way to the Illinois river, about 20 miles to the west. To the south, some 4 miles away, a line of timber marked the western course of Big Sandy creek. About a mile west was a magnificent prairie grove of large timber, through which the prairie ridge gradually rose to culminate in what is locally called the Mound, 3 miles away. South of this grove on another swell of the prairie was a second similar grove, within a mile, and later known as Diamond Grove.

The town was platted on the well-drained prairie ridge in 1825, in which year there were 20 families there. (a) The site for Illinois college was early selected in the shade of the prairie grove west of the settlement, and in 1829 a school was opened as its beginning. This institution, the focal point of the work of a band of graduates of Yale college, was the first of a group of educational and benevolent institutions now clustered at Jacksonville. Next after the college came the Jacksonville Female academy. The state put here its institution for the deaf and dumb, its first insane asylum, the institution for the blind, and temporarily the school for the feeble-minded, at intervals of some years. Other public and private institutions swell the present number.

The streets are adorned with shade-trees. Horse-cars run on the principal avenues. The city is provided with gas, a complete system of water-works, and sewerage.

No details were furnished as to the present condition of various departments of city and social organization.

RAILROADS.

In 1837–'38 the state progressed far enough with its system of internal improvements to put a locomotive on a track of strap-rails through Jacksonville from Meredosio, on the Illinois river, to Springfield. When the locomotive was no longer capable of use, mules were used for a time to draw freight on the track, which fell into entire disuse in time. The franchise of the road was sold, and in 1848 a modern track was laid from the Illinois river to Jacksonville as a part of what is now the Wabash, Saint Louis, and Pacific railroad. Besides this track, Jacksonville has connections by the Peoria, Pekin, and Jacksonville division of the same road, by the Jacksonville and Southeastern railroad, and by the Jacksonville division of the Chicago and Alton railroad.

JOLIET,

WILL COUNTY, ILLINOIS.

POPULATION

IN THE

AGGREGATE,

1850-1880.

	Inhab.
1790	......
1800	......
1810	......
1820	......
1830	......
1840	......
1850	2,659
1860	7,104
1870	7,263
1880	11,657

POPULATION

BY

SEX, NATIVITY, AND RACE,

AT

CENSUS OF 1880.

Male	5,875
Female	5,782
Native	8,509
Foreign-born	3,148
White	11,559
Colored	98

N.

Chicago, Ill. N. 39° 53' E. 36.1 Miles.

Rock Island, Ill. N. 88° 9' W. 126 Miles.

Peoria, Ill. S. 54° 12' W. 91.5 Miles.

Bloomington, Ill. S. 34° 59' W. 84. Miles.

La Fayette, Ind. C. 40° 42' E. 98.2 Miles.

S.

Latitude: 41° 30' North; Longitude: 88° 5' (west from Greenwich); Altitude: 543 to 550 feet.

FINANCIAL CONDITION:

Total Valuation: $3,293,363; per capita: $283 00.   Net Indebtedness: $54,000; per capita: $4 63.   Tax per $100: $2 64.

HISTORICAL SKETCH.

In 1837 the village of *Juliet* was incorporated by an act of the legislature, and was known under that name until 1853, when the legislature changed its name to Joliet and incorporated it as a city. It early became a distributing point for the produce of the surrounding country, and this fact, together with the establishment of many industries here and the opening of several lines of railroads gave the city an impetus that has not since declined. The state penitentiary, a large building, said to be one of the model institutions of the kind in the country, is situated near Joliet. It was built of limestone quarried in the vicinity, and cost about $1,000,000. The city has never been seriously ravaged by fire, and the only marked period of depression was between 1873 and 1878, when Joliet suffered in common with the other cities of the country. No population of one nationality or state has supplanted others previously established, but several nationalities have held a very even representation since the first settlement of the place.

JOLIET IN 1880.

The following statistical accounts, collected by the Census Office, indicate the present condition of the city:

LOCATION.

Joliet lies in latitude 41° 30′ north, longitude 88° 5′ west from Greenwich, on both sides of the Aux des Plaines river, about 37 miles southwest of Chicago. The surface of the river at the city is 543 feet, and the track at the railroad station is 550 feet above mean sea-level. The river on which the city lies is not navigable, but the Illinois and Michigan canal, from Chicago to La Salle, Illinois, passes this point.

RAILROAD COMMUNICATIONS.

Joliet is touched by the following railroads:
The Chicago, Pekin, and Southwestern railroad, to Peoria, Illinois.
The Chicago and Alton railroad.
The Chicago, Rock Island, and Pacific railroad.
The Joliet division of the Michigan Central railroad.

TRIBUTARY COUNTRY.

The city is the reshipping point for a very large amount of grain of all kinds for the eastern markets. The several industries comprise the Joliet iron and steel mills, with blast-furnaces; 7 large barbed-wire fence factories, 1 flouring-mill, 2 agricultural-implement factories, and 1 paper-mill. There are also 5 large limestone quarries and extensive gravel-beds near the city, while cement and fire-clay are largely obtained in the vicinity.

TOPOGRAPHY.

The city is situated mainly in the river valley, but part of it is on bluffs, situated on either side, and rising to an altitude of 50 feet above the surface of the water. The soil of the city and vicinity is a rich black prairie soil, underlying which is a fine stratified limestone 200 feet thick. There are no marshes, ponds, or lakes within a radius of 5 miles, and the surrounding country is open. The natural drainage is good.

CLIMATE.

Highest recorded summer temperature, 96°, while the highest summer temperature in average years is said to be the same. Lowest recorded winter temperature, —25°; lowest winter temperature in average years, —15°. There are no adjacent waters that exert any climatic influence.

STREETS.

There are about 60 miles of streets in the city, and of these, 45 miles are paved, having a foundation of broken stone with gravel on the top. The cost of this pavement is 50 cents per square yard, and, owing to the fact that the materials are obtainable here, is considered the most economical for the section of country. The sidewalks are of stone flagging and planks, about half of each. The gutters are laid with cobble-stones. Trees are planted along the sides of the streets. The construction of new streets is done by contract; repairs are done by day labor, and cost $3,000 annually. The city authorities express a preference for grading new streets, etc., by contract and doing all repairs by the day. There are 5 miles of horse-railroads in the city, with 14 cars and 25 horses, and giving employment to 10 men. Passengers are carried at the uniform rate of fare of 5 cents.

WATER-WORKS.

At present there are no water-works in the city, but a private company has been formed, and works for the water-supply have just been begun.

GAS.

The gas-works are not owned by the city. The daily average production is 18,000 cubic feet. The charge per 1,000 feet is $2 50. The city pays $25 per annum for each gas street-lamp, 124 in number. In addition there are 60 gasoline street-lamps, which are maintained by the city at a cost of $20 each per annum.

PUBLIC BUILDINGS.

The city owns and occupies for municipal purposes, wholly or in part, 1 city hall, 2 engine-houses, 8 school-houses, and 1 bridewell. The cost of the municipal buildings is $70,700. The city hall was built by and belongs to the city; its total cost was $7,500.

JOLIET,
ILL.

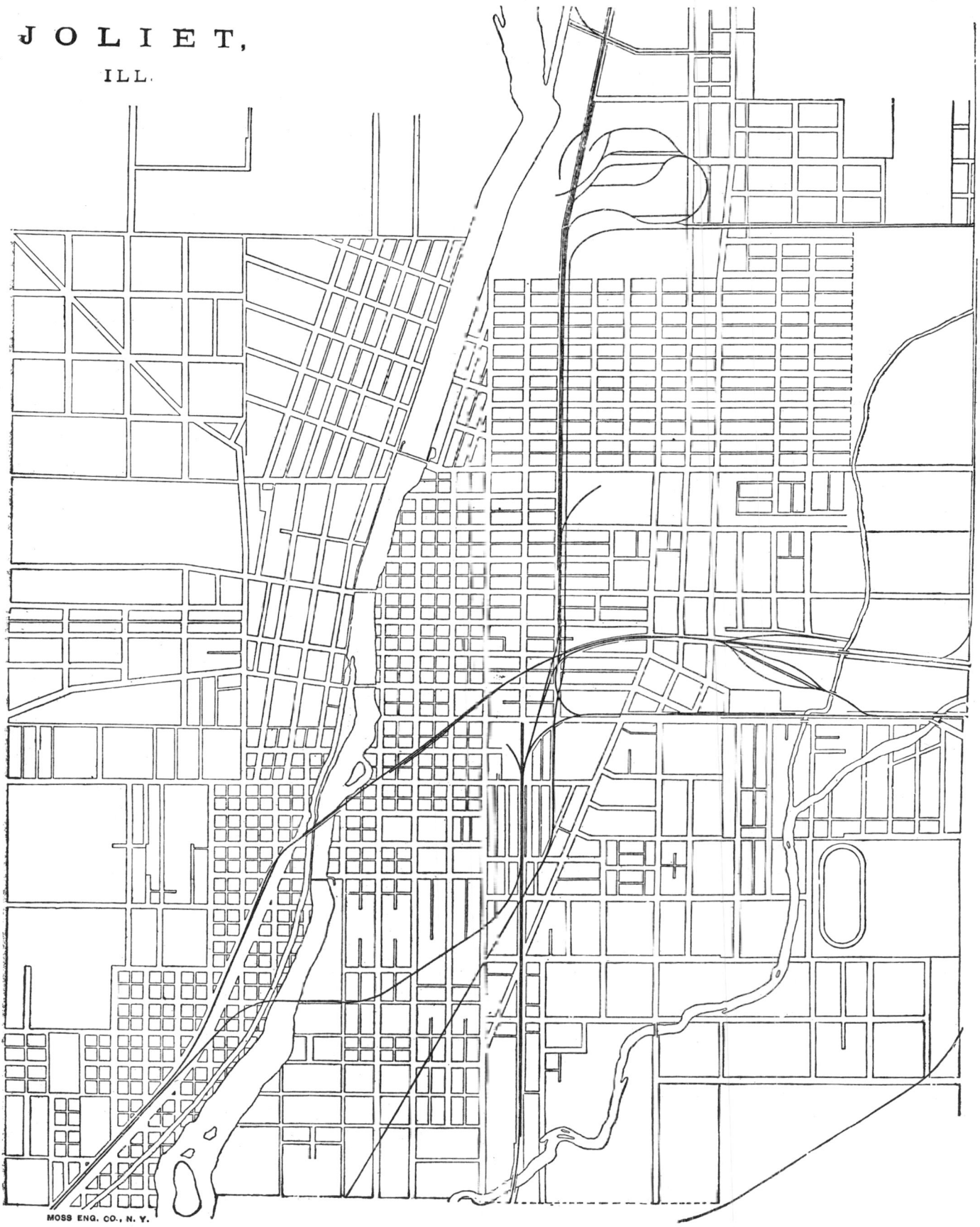

PUBLIC PARKS AND PLEASURE-GROUNDS.

There are no parks in Joliet. "Court-house square", the title of which is in the name of the county, is about 500 feet square, and is maintained at the expense of the county.

PLACES OF AMUSEMENT.

The following buildings are used for theatrical exhibitions, lectures, concerts, balls, etc.: Opera-house, with a seating capacity of 800; Werner's hall, seating 400; Munroe's hall, seating 400; Walsh's hall, seating 300; and Theiler's hall, seating 300. Exhibitions pay a license to the city, and the total amount received from this source, through the above halls, during a year is about $125.

DRAINAGE.

The city has never adopted any regular system of sewerage. It is situated in the valley of the Aux des Plaines river, which runs south, dividing the city into east and west sides, with natural drainage. There are but three sewers of any importance, one of which passes under the center of two of the central business streets. This latter one is three-quarters of a mile in length, 6 feet wide, and 4 feet high, and is built of stone, with a stone arch, at an average depth of 3 feet from the road-bed to the top of the arch; it empties into the river. The other two sewers are open. One is about half a mile east of the river, runs parallel with the same through the city for nearly 2 miles, and is always well supplied with running water. The other is intended for and carries off surface water; it is about 1 mile in length. The sewers are paid for wholly by the abutters, the cost being assessed by the front foot.

CEMETERIES.

There are 6 cemeteries in or connected with the city, as follows:

Oakwood Cemetery, area 35 acres, situated 1 mile east of the city limits.
Irish Catholic Cemetery, area 25 acres, situated in the western part of the city.
German Catholic Cemetery, situated just outside the northern limits of the city.
Lutheran Cemetery, area 20 acres, 1 mile from the city.
Zorley's Cemetery (private), also about 1 mile from the city.
Potter's Field, area 10 acres, half a mile from the city.

There is also one private burial-ground 1½ mile from the city, and outside the limits, in which burials are no longer made. In Oakwood cemetery there have been about 2,000 interments. Of the other burial-grounds above mentioned there are no statistics available from which the number of interments can be given. The mayor of the city reports that there are no ordinances regulating burial permits, limit of time after death for burial, depth of graves, etc.

MARKETS.

There are no public or corporation markets in the city, all meats, poultry, fish, and vegetables being sold at private markets and stores.

SANITARY AUTHORITY—BOARD OF HEALTH.

The chief sanitary organization of Joliet is the board of health, an independent body, composed of one citizen from each ward of the city, appointed by the mayor and subject to confirmation by the city council. Generally at least one member is a physician. The expenses of the board, either in the absence of or during epidemics, are regulated by the city council, and its authority is at all times sufficient to cover all cases affecting the general health of the city. When there is no declared epidemic a health officer is appointed by the mayor, and confirmed by the council, at a salary of $100 per annum. He is the executive officer of the board, and has full power to act; he also has police powers. Inspections are generally made as nuisances are reported. When reported nuisances are found to be such they are abated at once by the proper officer.

INFECTIOUS DISEASES.

Small-pox patients are taken to the public pest-house, which is situated outside the city limits. Scarlet-fever patients are quarantined at home. In the case of the breaking out of contagious diseases either in public or in private schools the board can cause the same to be closed. Vaccination is not compulsory nor is it done at the public expense.

REGISTRATION AND REPORTS.

By law all births are registered by the county clerk. The board reports to the city council.

MUNICIPAL CLEANSING.

Street-cleaning.—The streets are cleaned at the expense of the city, with its own force, and entirely by hand. The streets are cleaned as often as necessary, and the work is reported as well done. The annual cost of the service is included in the regular street appropriation, no separate account being kept. The manner of disposing of the street-sweepings is not stated.

Removal of garbage and ashes.—Garbage is removed both by the city and by householders, the city doing its part with its own force. There are no special regulations as to the conservancy of garbage while awaiting removal, but it and ashes are not allowed to be placed in the same vessel. The garbage is finally disposed of by being dumped outside the city limits, while the ashes are used for filling holes. No nuisance or probable injury to health is said to result from the manner of handling and disposing of the garbage, and the system is reported to be satisfactory.

Dead animals.—These are removed outside the city limits and buried, but by whom this service is performed is not stated. The carcasses of 75 dogs, 15 horses, and 15 cattle are annually buried at a total cost of $100.

Liquid household wastes and human excreta.—Most of the liquid household wastes of the city are thrown into privy-vaults, probably about one-third being run into sewers and none into the street-gutters. There are no cesspools. The city is largely supplied with water from artesian wells, which are, on an average, 460 feet in depth, and not affected in any way by the contents of vaults. A large proportion of the houses depend on privy-vaults, there being but few water-closets, one-fourth of which deliver into the sewers. Very few of the privy-vaults are even nominally water-tight. They are cleaned during the night by scavengers, under permits from the board of health, and their contents must be disinfected before removal. The night-soil is taken outside the city limits.

Manufacturing wastes.—There are no regulations regarding the disposal of either solid or liquid manufacturing wastes.

POLICE.

The police force of Joliet is appointed by the mayor, subject to confirmation by the city council, and is governed and controlled by the mayor. The executive officer is the chief of police, salary $780 per annum, who has general supervision over the force. The remainder of the force consists of 10 patrolmen at $50 a month each. The uniform is of blue cloth, with brass buttons, and each man provides his own. The patrolmen are equipped with pistols and clubs. They are on duty twelve hours at a time, and patrol 8 miles of streets. The number of arrests for the past year was not stated, but the principal offenses for the same were larceny, burglary, drunkenness, etc. Most of those arrested were fined, and in default of payment sent to "bridewell". The police force is required to co-operate with the fire and health departments only in a general way. Special policemen are appointed by the mayor only for special occasions, their duties and powers being the same as those of the regular force during the time they serve. The yearly cost of the police force (1880) is $7,000.

PEORIA,

PEORIA COUNTY, ILLINOIS.

POPULATION

IN THE

AGGREGATE,

1850-1880.

	Inhab.
1790	......
1800	......
1810	......
1820	......
1830	......
1840	......
1850	5,095
1860	14,045
1870	22,849
1880	29,259

POPULATION

BY

SEX, NATIVITY, AND RACE,

AT

CENSUS OF 1880.

Male	14,567
Female	14,692
Native	22,134
Foreign-born	7,125
White	28,765
Colored	*494

* Including 12 Chinese.

Latitude: 40° 43′ North; Longitude: 89° 30′ (west from Greenwich); Altitude: 433 to 518 feet.

FINANCIAL CONDITION:

Total Valuation: $6,763,320; per capita: $231 00. Net Indebtedness: $716,500; per capita: $24 49. Tax per $100: $4 27.

HISTORICAL SKETCH.

Though the site of the present city of Peoria was visited by La Salle in 1680, during his famous search for the mouth of the Mississippi, it was not until 1819 that the permanent settlement of the place may be said to have begun. In spite of its advantageous position, the growth of the town was slow, and in 1845, when it was incorporated as a city, the population numbered less than 2,000. In 1847 a canal from lake Michigan to the headwaters of the Illinois river was opened, and Peoria sprang into new life. The canal afforded a more convenient access to markets than had previously existed, and a very considerable trade sprang up with Chicago. The river business increased rapidly, and in 1850 there were no less than 60 steamboats engaged at Peoria. Owing to the opposition of the steamboatmen the contemplated running of the Illinois railroad through the city was defeated, and it was not until 1854, when a line was constructed to connect with the Chicago and Rock Island railroad, that Peoria enjoyed railroad communication. Other lines soon followed, and it was not long before the city was well connected with the whole railroad system of the state. Their effect was marked, and the increase in wealth and population of Peoria went steadily forward.

Among the industries of Peoria may be mentioned the distilleries. The first enterprise of the kind was started in 1845, and the business has grown to such an extent that now more proof-gallons of spirits are produced here than in any other city in the country. It is estimated that three-sevenths of all the alcohol exported from the United States is manufactured here. As a natural outcome of the distilleries, the stock-yards have become a necessity, as a way of disposing of the swill, and in 1879 there were 300,000 hogs and 50,000 cattle handled here. The flouring interest has also developed largely, the exports rising from 34,000 barrels in 1850 to 573,500 in 1870.

PEORIA IN 1880.

The following statistical accounts, collected by the Census Office, partially indicate the present condition of Peoria:

LOCATION.

Peoria lies in latitude 40° 43′ north, longitude 89° 30′ west from Greenwich, on the west bank of the Peoria river, at the head of Peoria lake (formed by the widening of the river), and about 160 miles southwest of Chicago. The altitudes above mean sea-level in the city are, surface of the river 433 feet, and highest point about 518 feet. The river is navigable for steamboats at all stages of water, and communication, by this means, is had with all points on the Ohio and Mississippi rivers and their tributaries.

RAILROAD COMMUNICATIONS.

The city is touched by the following railroad lines:

The Chicago, Burlington, and Quincy railroad, between the points named, and to Omaha, Nebraska, and Kansas City, Missouri.

The Chicago, Pekin, and Southwestern railroad, to Joliet, Illinois.

The Chicago, Rock Island, and Pacific railroad, from Chicago to Omaha, with branches to Atchison, Kansas, and Kansas City, Missouri.

The Illinois Midland railroad, to Terre Haute, Indiana.

The Indiana, Bloomington, and Western railroad, to Indianapolis, Indiana.

The Peoria, Decatur, and Evansville railroad. to Packenburg, Illinois.

The Peoria, Pekin, and Jacksonville railroad, between the points named.

The Rock Island and Peoria railroad, to Rock Island, Illinois.

The Wabash, Saint Louis, and Pacific, from Toledo to Saint Louis, Kansas City, and Omaha.

TRIBUTARY COUNTRY.

Peoria is situated in one of the richest corn-producing districts of Illinois, and the handling of this cereal, as well as the numerous industries connected with it, forms the principal business of the city.

TOPOGRAPHY.

The city is located upon a plateau which rises from the lake to an average elevation of about 85 feet above the water, extending 4 miles along the river and lake, and varying in width from one-half to 1½ mile. Back of this plateau are the "bluffs", which rise from 100 to 125 feet higher. Lake Peoria, formed by the expansion of the river, is 1 mile wide by 20 miles long, and is a beautiful sheet of water. Many residences are built on the bluffs that overlook the river, lake, and surrounding country.

CLIMATE.

No report on this subject was received. The mean annual temperature, taken from the reports of the Smithsonian Institution, covering a period of over fourteen years, is 51.36°.

STREETS.

The city is laid out in rectangular blocks, and the streets are wide and well graded. No detailed information regarding them was received.

WATER-WORKS.

The water-works are owned by the city, and their total cost was $450,000. Water is taken from the Illinois river and pumped directly into the mains. The pressure in the pipes is from 60 to 140 pounds per square inch. The average daily consumption is 2,000,000 gallons. The annual cost for maintenance and repairs (1880) is $18,989, and the yearly income from water-rates, $24,800. There are 43 miles of pipe and 267 fire-hydrants.

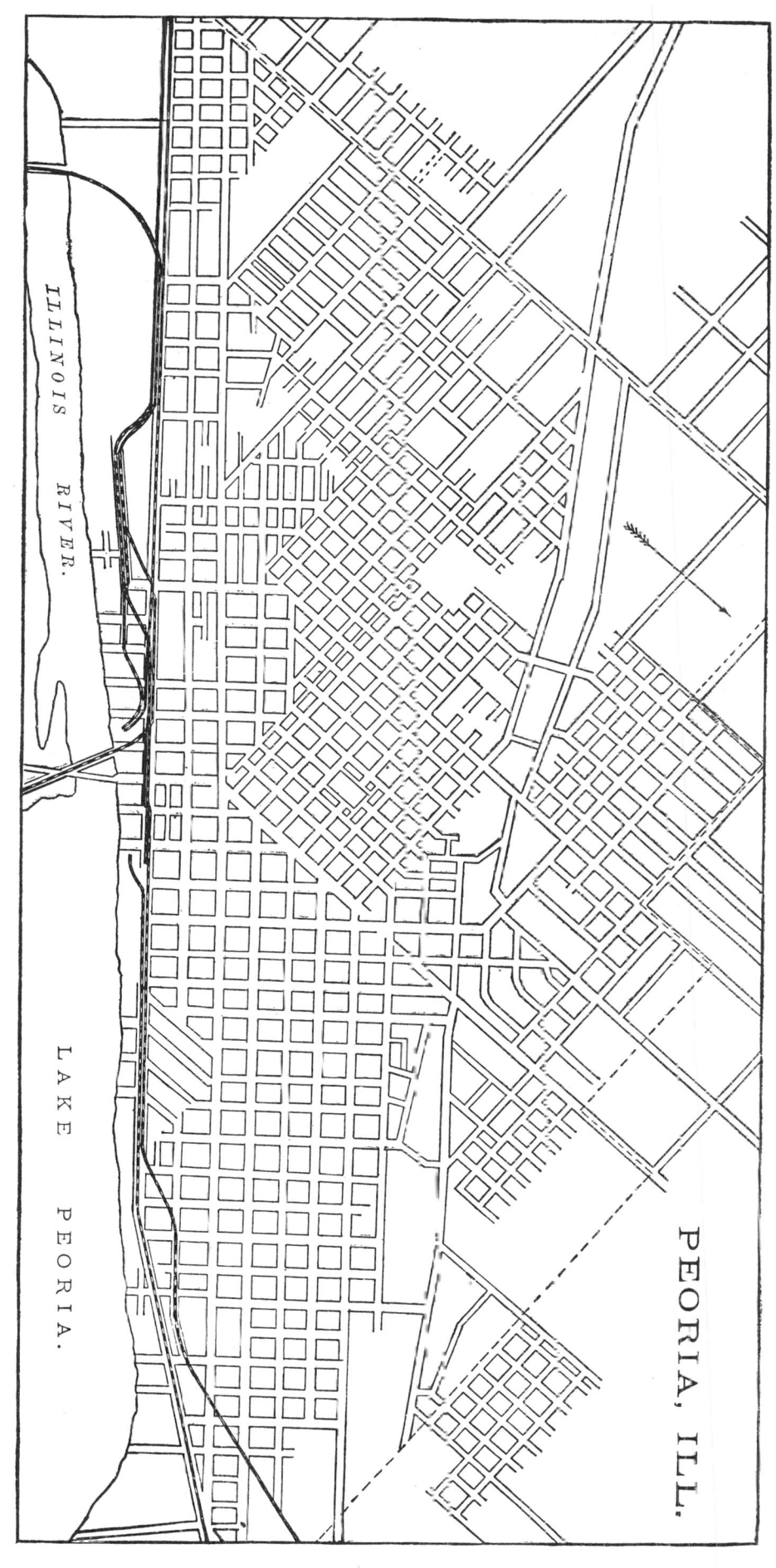

ILLINOIS RIVER.

LAKE PEORIA.

PEORIA, ILL.

GAS.

The city is lighted by gas, but no statistics on the subject are given.

PUBLIC BUILDINGS.

No information regarding the municipal buildings was furnished.

PUBLIC PARKS AND PLEASURE-GROUNDS.

There is 1 park, area 40 acres, that has just been donated to the city. There are also 2 small squares, each 360 feet square, located in the city. In addition to these there are several parks and pleasure-grounds, owned by private parties, outside the city limits.

PLACES OF AMUSEMENT.

There are 2 halls, each with a seating capacity of about 1,000, called opera-houses, and used for theatrical exhibitions, concerts, lectures, etc. Exhibitions, etc., pay a license to the city, and the annual revenue from this source is $1,374. There is 1 concert- and beer-garden, with an area of 7 acres, that is well patronized on pleasant Sundays.

DRAINAGE.

No information on this subject was given by the city authorities.

CEMETERIES.

There are 5 cemeteries connected with the city, as follows: *Springdale Cemetery*, area 220 acres; *Saint Mary's Cemetery* (Catholic), area 10 acres; and *Saint Joseph's Cemetery* (Catholic), area 8 acres—all situated about 2 miles from the center of the city; *Hebrew Cemetery*, area 3 acres, 3 miles out; and *Moffai's Cemetery*, area 7 acres, 2½ miles out. There are no church-yards or private burial-grounds in which burials are no longer allowed. Nothing further regarding the cemeteries of Peoria or the manner of interments, etc., could be learned.

MARKETS.

There is one public market—Central market—located on the corner of South Madison and Fulton streets. Its dimensions are 144 x 140 feet, and it cost $9,000. There are 35 stalls, and the streets around the market are used for standing-places. The stalls rent for from $75 to $150 per annum; only part of them are rented, as the rental value of the market amounts but to $2,200. The market is open every day until 11 o'clock a. m., and about one-quarter of the retail supply of meats, poultry, fish, and vegetables for the city is sold here.

SANITARY AUTHORITY—BOARD OF HEALTH.

The chief sanitary organization of Peoria is the board of health, composed of three members, one of whom is a physician, appointed and controlled by the board of aldermen. The annual expenses of the board of health are $500, and no provision seems to be made for an increase in case of an epidemic. The board has authority to abate nuisances, to remove infected persons to the pest-house, and to prevent boats and cars from bringing infected persons into the city. The president, salary $200 per annum, is the chief executive officer of the board. No assistant health officers or inspectors are employed. Inspections are made only as nuisances are reported, and when a nuisance is found to exist it is ordered abated under penalty. The board inspects and corrects defective house-drainage, privy-vaults, cesspools, sources of drinking-water, etc., when it is necessary. The board exercises no control over the conservation and removal of garbage. Burial permits are issued by the president of the board. Excrement must be removed outside the city and buried.

INFECTIOUS DISEASES.

Small-pox patients are removed to the public pest-house, situated in the suburbs. Scarlet-fever patients are quarantined at home and a notice is placed on the door. The board has had no experience in regard to the breaking out of a contagious disease either in public or in private schools. Vaccination is not compulsory, but it has been done at the public expense.

REPORTS.

Every physician, midwife, etc., is required to report all births and deaths to the county clerk, and, by ordinance, to the physician of the board of health.

The board reports annually to the city council, and the report is published.

MUNICIPAL CLEANSING.

Street-cleaning.—There is no regular system of street-cleaning in Peoria. The streets are cleaned by the city as often as required, at an annual cost of $2,500 per annum.

Removal of garbage and ashes.—Garbage is removed by the householders. There are no rules or regulations governing the matter, but householders are required to keep their premises, and all alleys in the rear of the same, clean. The final disposal of garbage is not stated. Ashes are taken out of the city.

Dead animals.—The carcass of any animal dying within the city is removed outside the limits and buried. It is not stated by whom this service is performed, but the annual cost is said to be $500.

Liquid household wastes and human excreta.—Most of the liquid wastes of the city go into cesspools, which are porous. When they are filled new ones are dug. About 10 per cent. of the houses are provided with water-closets, a few of which empty into the sewers, while the remainder depend on privy-vaults. The vaults are required to be dug 10 feet deep, and none of them are even nominally water-tight. The water-supply is taken from the Illinois river, above the city, and is not contaminated here; but a fear is expressed that, owing to the pumping of the sewage of Chicago into the headwaters of the Illinois and Michigan canal, whence it flows into the Illinois river, it will be before long. When vaults are cleaned the night-soil is taken outside the city and buried.

Manufacturing wastes, both liquid and solid, are run into the river below the city.

POLICE.

The police force of Peoria is appointed by the mayor, subject to the confirmation of the city council, and is governed by that official. The superintendent of police, salary $1,000 per annum, is the chief executive officer, and has general supervision over the force, which consists of 1 captain and 28 patrolmen. The captain has a salary of $900, and the patrolmen receive $720 each a year. The uniform is blue "Metropolitan", and the men provide their own. Patrolmen are equipped with clubs and revolvers and are on duty twelve hours at a time. During the past year 1,397 arrests were made by the force, the principal causes being, drunk and disorderly, assault and battery, inmates of houses of ill-fame, etc. Of these, 343 were committed to the work-house, 77 were sent to jail, and the remainder were fined. During the year there were 343 station-house lodgers, as against 557 in 1879. Special policemen are appointed, and, when on duty, have the same powers as the regular force. The yearly cost of the police (1880) is $23,000.

MANUFACTURES.

The following is a summary of the statistics of the manufactures of Peoria for 1880, being taken from tables prepared for the Tenth Census by Henry C. Bestor, special agent:

Mechanical and manufacturing industries.	No. of establishments.	Capital.	AVERAGE NUMBER OF HANDS EMPLOYED.			Total amount paid in wages during the year.	Value of materials.	Value of products.
			Males above 16 years.	Females above 15 years.	Children and youths.			
All industries	296	$4,160,707	3,619	313	135	$1,507,666	$9,556,476	$14,228,134
Agricultural implements	5	250,000	241	....	4	87,500	217,000	438,000
Baking and yeast powders	3	9,200	9	7	....	5,675	27,150	43,500
Blacksmithing (see also Wheelwrighting)	15	11,950	34	....	....	13,986	15,490	44,370
Boots and shoes, including custom work and repairing	26	8,025	29	....	....	11,007	16,750	45,225
Carpentering	22	97,400	265	....	....	96,827	265,400	429,550
Carpets, rag	3	1,700	5	1	....	2,555	4,100	9,450
Carriages and wagons (see also Wheelwrighting)	6	66,000	52	....	10	26,200	62,000	110,232
Coffins, burial cases, and undertakers' goods	5	18,500	4	....	....	1,550	11,000	23,725
Clothing, men's	15	160,750	97	179	....	64,045	422,853	603,865
Cooperage	15	43,300	216	....	4	96,460	193,391	330,650
Flouring- and grist-mill products	3	80,000	29	....	....	16,500	263,250	309,500
Foundery and machine-shop products	7	142,100	210	....	....	97,932	124,100	268,750
Furniture (see also Upholstering)	6	41,700	47	....	....	25,596	41,735	90,625
Furs, dressed	3	4,400	7	14	....	4,600	8,300	16,750
Hairwork	3	800	....	4	....	560	1,800	4,000
Liquors, distilled	14	1,679,000	1,076	....	....	480,000	5,735,000	8,196,000
Liquors, malt	3	153,000	44	....	....	16,685	81,528	127,667
Lock- and gun-smithing	5	3,700	12	....	....	3,752	3,429	12,300
Lumber, planed	4	109,000	74	....	3	36,615	56,000	120,500
Marble and stone work	8	17,300	32	....	....	16,650	25,500	57,650
Mineral and soda waters	3	23,500	12	....	2	3,046	6,400	15,300
Painting and paperhanging	17	11,840	50	....	1	15,970	24,950	58,400
Plumbing and gasfitting	6	62,500	74	1	10	34,448	103,500	176,000
Printing and publishing	12	100,750	121	21	37	82,069	52,575	186,215
Saddlery and harness	6	22,470	37	....	....	16,715	47,612	94,518

Mechanical and manufacturing industries.	No. of estab-lish-ments.	Capital.	AVERAGE NUMBER OF HANDS EMPLOYED.			Total amount paid in wages during the year.	Value of materials.	Value of products
			Males above 16 years.	Females above 15 years.	Children and youths.			
Slaughtering and meat-packing, not including retail butchering.....	3	$205,000	174	....	19	$15,900	$713,881	$756,033
Tinware, copperware, and sheet-iron ware.............................	16	81,775	62	....	1	31,506	89,800	150,650
Tobacco, cigars and cigarettes.......................................	10	24,525	53	....	21	30,509	43,092	95,430
Upholstering (see also Furniture)	3	1,200	4	....	....	1,790	1,800	6,300
Wheelwrighting (see also Blacksmithing; Carriages and wagons) ...	5	3,400	12	....	....	5,272	7,200	15,700
All other industries (a)	44	725,922	537	86	23	165,736	889,890	1,391,279

a Embracing awnings and tents; baskets, rattan and willow ware; bookbinding and blank-book making; boxes, cigar; boxes, fancy and paper; bread and other bakery products; brick and tile; brooms and brushes; buttons; coffee and spices, roasted and ground; confectionery; cordage and twine; corsets; drugs and chemicals; electroplating; engraving and die-sinking; files; glucose; grease and tallow; hats and caps; housefurnishing goods; iron work, architectural and ornamental; lime; looking-glass and picture frames; lumber, sawed; pumps; roofing and roofing materials; safes, doors, and vaults, fire-proof; saws; shipbuilding; shirts; show-cases; soap and candles; starch; stone- and earthen-ware; trunks and valises; and wire.

From the foregoing table it appears that the average capital of all establishments is $14,056 44; that the average wages of all hands employed is $370 70 per annum; and that the average outlay in wages, in materials, and in interest (at 6 per cent.) on capital employed is $38,222 24.

VOL 19——34

QUINCY,

ADAMS COUNTY, ILLINOIS.

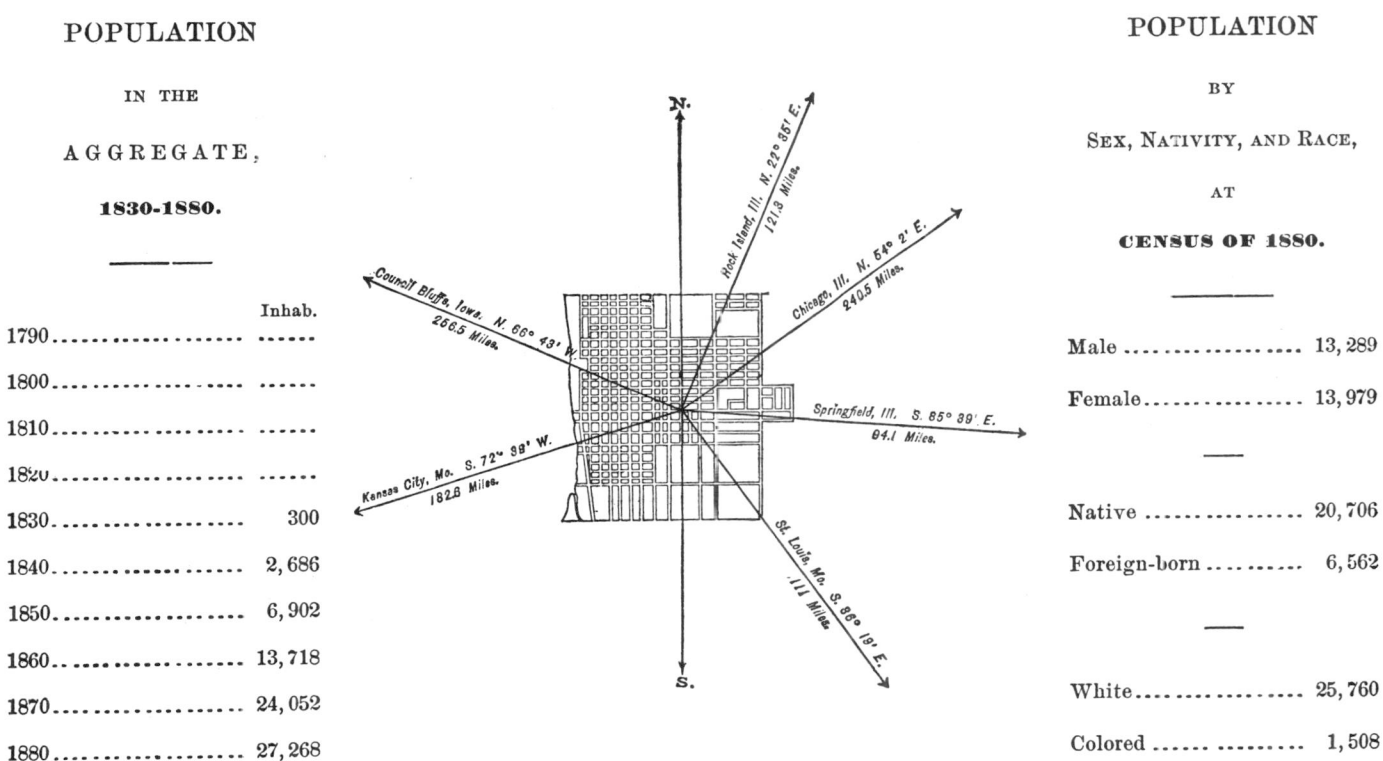

<table>
<tr><td colspan="2">POPULATION</td></tr>
<tr><td colspan="2">IN THE</td></tr>
<tr><td colspan="2">AGGREGATE,</td></tr>
<tr><td colspan="2">1830-1880.</td></tr>
<tr><td></td><td>Inhab.</td></tr>
<tr><td>1790 ....</td><td>......</td></tr>
<tr><td>1800 ....</td><td>......</td></tr>
<tr><td>1810 ....</td><td>......</td></tr>
<tr><td>1820 ....</td><td>......</td></tr>
<tr><td>1830 ....</td><td>300</td></tr>
<tr><td>1840 ....</td><td>2,686</td></tr>
<tr><td>1850 ....</td><td>6,902</td></tr>
<tr><td>1860 ....</td><td>13,718</td></tr>
<tr><td>1870 ....</td><td>24,052</td></tr>
<tr><td>1880 ....</td><td>27,268</td></tr>
</table>

POPULATION

BY

SEX, NATIVITY, AND RACE,

AT

CENSUS OF 1880.

Male 13,289

Female 13,979

Native 20,706

Foreign-born 6,562

White 25,760

Colored 1,508

Latitude: 39° 55′ North; Longitude: 91° 25′ (west from Greenwich); **Altitude: 423 to 628 feet.**

FINANCIAL CONDITION:

Total Valuation: $6,487,997; per capita: $238 00.   Net Indebtedness: $1,917,888; per capita: $70 33.   Tax per $100: $0 89.

HISTORICAL SKETCH.

The site upon which Quincy is built was known in the early part of the century as "The Bluffs", or "Old Sauk Village", from the fact that in 1812 a body of Illinois and Missouri troops passed the place on their march from the lower end of the territory of Peoria and found here a deserted village, lately occupied by the Sauk tribe of Indians. But it was not until 1822, when the first log cabin was erected, that the permanent settlement of the town can be said to have taken place. In January, 1825, the legislature provided for the organization of Adams county, fixing its boundaries as they now exist, and appointed commissioners to locate the county-seat. The commissioners decided on the "Bluffs" as the place best calculated for the future convenience and accommodation of the people, and, in honor of the President, christened the embryo town "Quincy". In November of the same year, the town was surveyed and laid off, and on the 13th of December the first sale of lots took place. For ten years the growth of Quincy was not rapid, owing, in a great measure, to her distance from other settlements. In

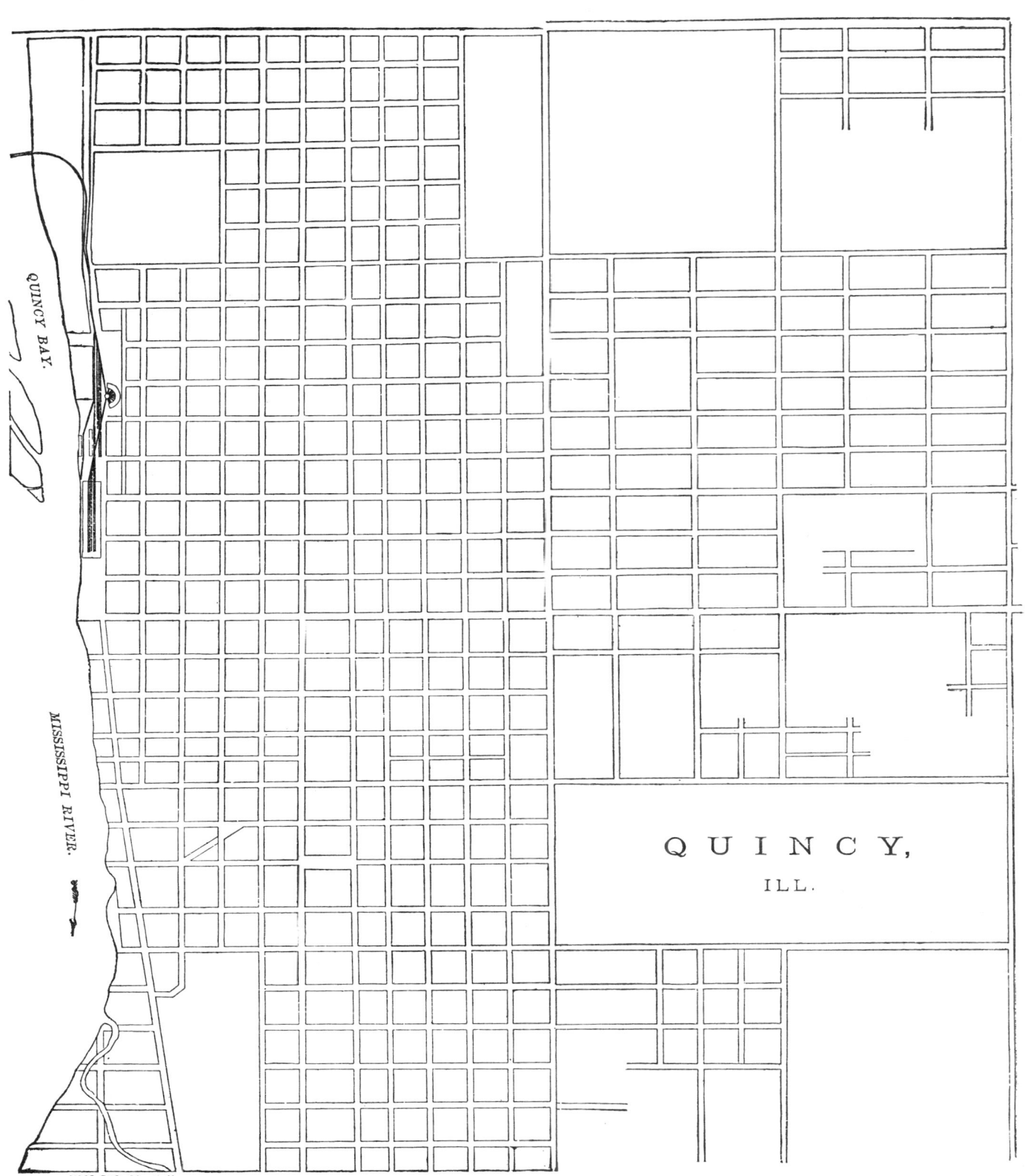

QUINCY BAY.

MISSISSIPPI RIVER.

QUINCY,
ILL.

1830 the first regular church was organized. In 1832 the Black Hawk war broke out, but it had no appreciable effect on Quincy, except somewhat to increase the number of military titles previously held by the citizens. In 1833 an epidemic of cholera broke out, and, though no record was kept of the number of deaths, 43 cases were reported for July 7, out of a population of about 400. In 1834 the town was incorporated and trustees were elected. In 1837 the first hotel was built, and in 1840 a city charter was granted.

The position of Quincy, on the immediate bank of the river, at the head of the great *Sny Cartee*—a bayou which cuts off access with the river for a long distance below—soon made her the market for a fertile and productive country, now being rapidly settled; while the opening of railroads and the developing of coal-mines in the vicinity insured her subsequent growth and prosperity. The city rapidly increased both in wealth and population, a decided impetus being given during the latter part of the late war, and for a year or two after its close, through influences connected with her location on the borders of Missouri. Considerable capital and some large manufacturing interests (notably of tobacco) were transferred during this period from the neighboring districts of Missouri, not only from considerations of safety, but probably from better prospects for business, while the disturbed condition of the country west of here tended largely to increase the general business of the city.

Quincy has never had any serious conflagration. The greatest loss from any one fire was $125,000. No local influences have produced periods of depression specially affecting the city, those of 1837, 1857, and 1873 having been felt here in common with the rest of the country. Of the 300 inhabitants in 1830 a considerable majority were from Kentucky, Virginia, and the southern states, though most of the eastern states were partially represented. About 1834 New England people began to arrive, some 50 or more reaching here in the fall of that year. From this period immigration from the New England and middle states far exceeded that from the southern states, and such has continued to be the tendency since. The causes for this change are due to the facts that when the first settlement began the states bordering on the Ohio river had the facilities afforded by water communication, while people from the New England states were obliged to take a long and tedious journey overland by wagon, through a sparsely settled country. It is also stated that the slavery agitation between 1840 and 1850 retarded and finally almost stopped emigration from the slave to the free states. After the opening of railroad communication with the East— about 1852-'54—the tide of eastern comers increased rapidly. Foreign immigration reached here in considerable numbers at an early day, and the increase of population from this source from 1845 to 1860 was specially noticeable. At present the Germans form the bulk of the foreign-born population, the Irish coming next. The percentage of English, French, and other nationalities is small, the increase of the foreign population being chiefly from German immigration.

QUINCY IN 1880.

The following statistical accounts, the materials for which were furnished by J. G. Rowland, esq., and Albert Demaree, esq., the late and the present comptroller, indicate the present condition of Quincy:

LOCATION.

Quincy lies in latitude 39° 55' north, longitude 91° 25' west from Greenwich, on the east bank of the Mississippi river, 160 miles above Saint Louis, and about 110 miles west of Springfield, the seat of government of Illinois. The average altitude of the city is 553 feet above sea-level—the lowest point, on the river-bank, being 423 feet, and the highest point 628 feet above sea-level. The draught of water in the Mississippi here varies with the height of the river, from $2\frac{1}{2}$ to 14 feet usually. The harbor is on the city front open to the river, the levee, or paved landing for steamboats, etc., being 1,600 feet in length. Boats can, however, land at any point on the city front ($2\frac{1}{2}$ miles in extent) except in portions of the bay, in the northern part of the city. This bay is a natural harbor, $3\frac{1}{2}$ miles long by 500 feet average width, and when deepened and improved, by dredging or otherwise (a work now being carried on by the United States government), will afford a secure harbor for all the shipping of the upper Mississippi. Extremes of very low water and the highest floods would present minima and maxima of the water-depth beyond the figures given above, but they can be taken as a fair average of variation. Probably the draught in the channel opposite Quincy will average about 6 feet. Average width of channel in front of city 650 feet; average area of cross-section 3,900 feet. The current is about 3 miles per hour, and the channel-flow per second is 15,600 cubic feet. The entire width of the river here is about 3,600 feet. Water communication is open to all points on the Mississippi river and its tributaries.

RAILROAD COMMUNICATIONS.

The following railroads either pass through or terminate in the city:

The Chicago, Burlington, and Quincy railroad, between the points named, and to Omaha and Saint Louis.

The Wabash, Saint Louis, and Pacific railroad, terminal connections at Chicago, Toledo, Saint Louis, and Keokuk.

The Saint Louis, Keokuk, and Northwestern railroad, from Saint Louis to Keokuk.

The Hannibal and Saint Joseph railroad, between the points named, with lines to Quincy and Kansas City. The Quincy, Missouri, and Pacific railroad, to Milan, Missouri.

TRIBUTARY COUNTRY.

The country adjacent to Quincy was originally mixed prairie and wooded uplands, with timber on the bottom or low lands near the Mississippi river. It is now so generally cultivated that the greater part of this timber, both in the uplands and bottoms, has been removed. The farms and farming implements are excellent, while the yield of the staple grains is above the average. The soil is well adapted to wheat, corn, oats, and hay, the production increasing per acre as better agricultural appliances are introduced and better modes of cultivation are adopted. Hogs, cattle, the cereals above named, hay, dairy products, and fire-wood form the bulk of the trade from the farming district that is tributary to the city.

TOPOGRAPHY.

The site of the city is of the limestone formation, the stone cropping out at all points along the river-bluffs, and yielding an excellent building rock. The overlying soil is about as follows: First 3 or 4 feet, black loam; below that, 6 to 15 feet of clay (good brick-clay); then a mixed clay-and-sand formation, with streaks of sand, for a depth of 60 or 75 feet; and below that the first stratum of limestone. The geological formation may be described as a narrow neck (15 miles wide) of Carboniferous limestone lying between the bituminous coal-basin of Illinois and that of Missouri; the rock conglomerate and compact limestone. The surface of the country is varied by gentle undulations, and broken by water-courses and ravines running to the river through the bluffs. The variations of level cover about 200 feet, but the general plane of the city is about 150 feet above the river. The topography of the surrounding country is the same, with elevations 2, 4, or 6 miles from the city rising from 230 to 260 feet above the river. The highest elevation within the corporate limits is 225 feet above the river. In the bottom-lands adjacent to the Mississippi there are many lakes, ponds, and sloughs that connect with the river at high flood-water. For a radius of 5 miles on the bluffs or uplands 70 per cent. is open, while on bottom-lands timber covers about 60 per cent. of the area. Within this radius one-fourth of the area has a rich black loamy bottom soil, very productive, while the remainder has a good tillable soil, part loam, part clay, some of it, however, beginning to need fertilization.

CLIMATE.

Highest recorded summer temperature, 105°; highest summer temperature in average years, 100.8°. Lowest recorded winter temperature, −22°; lowest winter temperature in average years, −3.75°. Northerly and northwesterly winds bring lower temperature and clear weather. Northeasterly, easterly, and southeasterly winds usually accompany protracted rains. Westerly winds bring cooler and clearing weather. Winds from the south and southwest raise the temperature. Thunder-storms generally come from the south or west.

STREETS.

There are 88 miles of streets in the city, 7 miles being paved with broken stones (macadam) and 8 with gravel. The cost per square yard of each, as nearly as may be estimated, is, for broken stone 36 and for gravel 20 cents. The cost of keeping each in good repair per mile annually is, for broken stone $542 and for gravel $121. The gravel road is said to be the easiest to keep clean, and to be better and cheaper than the broken stone. The sidewalks are of brick and stone curbing, the average width being from 12 to 15 feet. The gutters are laid with limestone rock, and are from 5 to 10 feet wide. With the exception of the business portion of the city, trees are planted, as a rule, on all improved blocks, being set 2 feet inside the curbing. Work on the streets is done both by the day and by contract, the former being preferred for repairs and the latter for new work. The annual cost of street repairs is $8,000. A roller drawn by horses has been used on the streets, and it is reported that not much benefit was realized from it.

HORSE RAILROADS, ETC.

The horse-railroads in the city have a length of 4¼ miles. They use 15 cars and 65 mules, and give employment to 14 men. The rate of fare is 5 cents. Three omnibuses, with 8 horses and 6 men, carry annually 25,000 passengers to all parts of the city at the uniform rate of fare of 25 cents.

WATER-WORKS.

The works for the water-supply are in process of construction, and are owned by a private corporation. The total cost so far is $114,478 85. The system at present is pumping, the pressure being 90 pounds to the square inch; but a reservoir is to be built with an elevation of 230 feet above the city datum line. The average amount of water pumped per diem is 171,397 gallons, the greatest amount being 435,000 and the least 38,000 gallons. During 1879 the total cost of maintenance was $6,860 01, and the total income from all sources was $15,714 26. Only 3 water-meters are in use.

GAS.

The gas-works are not owned by the city. The daily average production is 87,100 feet. The charge per 1,000 feet is $2 25. The city pays $30 annually, which includes the lighting, cleaning, and keeping in repair, for each street-lamp, 700 in number.

PUBLIC BUILDINGS.

The city owns and occupies for municipal uses, wholly or in part, 7 engine-houses, 3 market-houses, 8 public-school buildings, 1 hospital, 1 house of correction, and 1 police station. The total cost of these buildings is given at $300,000. There is no city hall proper, the city offices being located over one of the engine-houses.

PUBLIC PARKS AND PLEASURE-GROUNDS.

The total area of the public parks in Quincy is 30 acres. They are 5 in number, and, except one of 15 acres, which is projected but not yet improved, are too small for driving purposes. They are scattered over the city, 2 being suburban and 3 centrally located. The latter are well improved, and are resorted to largely by the people. The land for these parks was donated to the city, and the cost of improvements has been $10,000. The parks are controlled by the usual police regulations.

PLACES OF AMUSEMENT.

There are two theaters in the city—the Opera-house, seating capacity 1,500, and a small variety theater, with a seating capacity of 300. The Academy of Music, recently burnt, was also used as a theater. Each exhibition or performance pays a license to the city of $5. There are 3 halls used for concerts and social entertainments, and 6 minor halls used for lodge-rooms and sometimes for lectures. There are 5 concert- and beer-gardens in or near the city. Of these, 2 are in the suburbs, 1 occupying several acres, established in 1860, costing $8,000, and seating 2,000 persons, and the other, rather smaller, established in 1870, and cost $6,000, and 3 in the city, having an aggregate seating capacity of 600, costing $4,500, and built about fifteen years ago. All these gardens are largely patronized during the summer months.

DRAINAGE.

There are no sewers in Quincy at present, but there soon will be, as work on a system of sewerage has been begun.

CEMETERIES.

Quincy has 5 cemeteries now in use, as follows:

Woodland Cemetery, area 38 acres, owned by the city, is situated on the bluff overlooking the river, and at an average elevation of 80 feet above low-water mark. A very large proportion of the lots are 20 feet square, and originally sold for $10 each; they now sell for $100 each, and most of the available ones have been disposed of. The cemetery has been in use about thirty years, and was named in honor of Hon. John Wood, the first white settler in the city.

Saint Boniface Cemetery, area 6 acres, owned by the German Catholic churches, is situated on State street, 175 feet above low-water mark. Lots are 15 by 15 feet, sell for $25 each, and most of them have been disposed of. The cemetery has been in use 22 years.

Saint Peter's Cemetery, area 11 acres, owned by the Irish Catholic church, is situated just outside the city limits, and 169 feet above low-water mark in the river. It has been in use six years. It is laid off regularly in blocks 33 feet square, divided into four lots each, with a 5-foot avenue between the blocks. The lots sell for $33 each.

Hebrew Cemetery, area 6 acres, situated near Saint Peter's, and 200 feet above low-water mark, is owned by the Jewish congregations in the city, and has been in use six years. Lots are regularly laid off 20 feet square, and sell for $25 each.

Green Mount Cemetery, area 13½ acres, outside the city limits and 90 feet above low-water mark, is owned by the Salem German Protestant church, and has been in use 7 years. The lots are 20 feet square, and sell for $20 each.

In addition to these there are 4 old cemeteries in which burials are no longer made, and from which most of the bodies have been removed, as follows: Old Hebrew cemetery, Old Saint Boniface cemetery, Old Public cemetery, and an old burial-ground near where the court-house now stands.

The record of interments is very imperfect, none having been kept previous to 1877, and none during 1878–'79. During 1880 the interments were Woodland, 251; Saint Boniface, 133; Saint Peter's, 40; Green Mount, 41; and Hebrew, 2. Burial permits are granted, on certificates of death signed by the attending physicians, by the board of health, which also issues permits for the removal of any body from the city. No body can remain in the vault of Woodland cemetery for a period longer than four weeks, unless by special consent of the mayor.

MARKETS.

In reply to the schedule of interrogatories asking for information on this subject, Comptroller Demaree says:

The city of Quincy, Illinois, owns 3 market-houses, but for the past three years the use of them for the ordinary purposes of market-houses has been abandoned. They are rented by the year to private individuals. One of them is used as a wholesale hat and fur store, and the other two as butcher-shops. Fresh meat, fish, and vegetables are sold in any part of the city, vegetables in nearly all grocery stores and from the garden-wagons. Fresh meat is sold in butchers' shops in various parts of the city, 28 in number, paying to the city an annual license of $25 each. There are also 5 stands or stores for the sale of fresh fish, each of which pays an annual city license of $5. There is no time fixed by ordinance for the opening or closing of butcher-shops, and the ordinances in force for the protection of the public against unwholesome meat and decayed vegetables are practically a dead letter, and no effort is made by the health department to enforce the law. Every purchaser must be the judge as to the wholesomeness or otherwise of meat or vegetables purchased.

SANITARY AUTHORITY—BOARD OF HEALTH.

The chief sanitary authority of Quincy is the board of health, composed of the mayor and 2 aldermen, with 4 citizens and 1 health officer appointed annually by the city council. This year 5 of the members of the board are physicians. In ordinary times the annual expenses of the board are $800 for scavenger work, for removing and burying dead animals, and for salary of health officer, but at no time must the board increase its expenses beyond the amount appropriated, unless by special permission of the council. The board has power by ordinance to do all things necessary to promote the health and general cleanliness of the city, to abate nuisances, and to use any measures it may deem fit to prevent the introduction of any disease of an infectious or contagious nature. The health officer, salary $200 per annum, is the chief executive officer of the board, and sees that its regulations, as well as the health ordinances of the city, are enforced; he is secretary of the board, and keeps a complete record of its proceedings. No assistant health officers or inspectors are employed, but the city marshal is required to act as a sanitary policeman, and for this service receives an extra compensation of $240 per annum. No regular inspections are made, nuisances being inspected when reported, or as they may come under the observation of the sanitary policeman. When nuisances are found to exist, the owner of the property is served with a written notice from the health officer to abate the same. The board meets regularly once a month and transacts its business as a deliberative body; the board does nothing regarding the inspection and correction of defective house-drainage, privy-vaults, cesspools, and sources of drinking-water unless complaints are made. The board has full control over the conservation and removal of garbage. The board, through the health officer, issues burial permits on certificate of attending physician stating cause of death, etc.

INFECTIOUS DISEASES.

Small-pox patients are quarantined at home, and a placard is placed on the house to warn the public. Physicians are requested to report all cases of small-pox or other infectious or contagious disease to the health officer within 12 hours after the same comes to their notice. Vaccination is compulsory only to children attending the public schools, but it is not done at public expense.

REPORTS.

The board is required to keep complete mortuary records. The board reports to the city council once a year, and the report is published with the annual reports of the city officials.

MUNICIPAL CLEANSING.

Street-cleaning.—The streets are cleaned at the expense of the city and with its regular force. The work is done wholly by hand, no sweeping-machines being used. The cleaning is done whenever it is deemed necessary, and its efficiency is stated to be "just passable". The annual appropriation for the work is $10,000, and the sweepings are used to fill lots.

Removal of garbage and ashes.—Garbage is removed by the city under contract. While awaiting removal it is required to be kept in tight barrels or tubs, in a place convenient for removal and unmixed with any ashes, soot, or house-dirt. It is taken out of the city and fed to pigs. It is removed twice a week. The ashes are also removed by the city and used for fillings. The cost for the service during the past year was $490. It is stated that neither nuisances nor probable injury to health, to any great extent, result from the manner of handling or disposing of the garbage, and if the contract is faithfully executed the system is considered a good one.

Dead animals.—The carcass of any animal dying within the limits of the city is required to be removed by the owner. When the owner can not be found the work is done by the board of health, the carcass being generally thrown into the river. The cost of the service annually is very small, and no record is kept of the number of dead animals so disposed of.

Liquid household wastes.—Nearly all the liquid household wastes in the city are either thrown into cesspools or run into the street-gutters. The cesspools are stated to be nominally tight; they are not provided with overflows; generally receive the wastes from water-closets, and their cleaning is left to the judgment of the householders. The gutters are very seldom flushed, but they are cleaned by the street force.

Human excreta.—A large majority of the houses depend on privy-vaults, there being but few water-closets, which nearly all deliver into cesspools. Very few of the vaults are even nominally water-tight. They are cleaned out under contract, and the night-soil is deposited in the river. The dry-earth system is not used at all.

Manufacturing wastes, both liquid and solid, eventually find their way into the river.

POLICE.

The chief of police, sergeants, and detectives are appointed annually by the city council, the patrolmen are appointed by the chief with the concurrence of the council, and the force is governed by the mayor and chief of police, under the ordinances. The chief of police, salary $900 per annum, is the commanding officer of the force, and his duties are to see that the laws and ordinances are enforced by the men under his command. The rest of the force and the salaries of each grade are as follows: 2 detectives, $60 per month; 2 sergeants, $54 per month; 9 patrolmen, $45 per month; and 1 turnkey, $30 per month. The uniform consists of a dark-blue coat, vest, and pantaloons, with brass buttons, and a black soft felt hat; it costs, complete, including overcoat, $45, and the men provide their own, the city furnishing the buttons. The patrolmen are equipped with revolvers and clubs, and their hours of duty are from 8 p. m. to 5 a. m.

During the past year 1,249 arrests were made by the force, the principal causes being: Disturbing the peace, 285; drunkenness, 252; inmates of houses of ill-fame, 142; larceny, 48; vagrancy, 206, etc. Of these, 426 were fined, 326 committed, 394 discharged on probation, and the remainder variously disposed of. There were 161 station-house lodgers during the year, as against 891 in 1879. The force is required to assist the fire department when occasion requires. Special policemen are appointed by the mayor or chief whenever their services may be required. Private watchmen in the employ of railroads, manufacturers, etc., are appointed special policemen, but have nothing to do with the regular force. The yearly cost of the police force (1880) is $9,187 15.

FIRE DEPARTMENT.

The following, regarding the fire department of Quincy, is taken from the last annual report of the chief engineer:

The manual force of the department consists of 1 chief engineer, 9 permanent firemen, and 19 minute-men. The apparatus consists of 3 steam fire-engines, 4 hose-reels, and 1 chemical engine. In addition there are 2 volunteer hand-engine companies. During the past year there were 42 alarms of fire, 7 of which were false. The loss by fire and water was $90,411, more than one-half this amount having been caused by one fire, and a loss of $22,000 at another. The total expenditure on account of the department for the year was $15,734 08.

MANUFACTURES.

The following is a summary of the statistics of the manufactures of Quincy for 1880, being taken from tables prepared for the Tenth Census by A. L. Langdon, special agent:

Mechanical and manufacturing industries.	No. of establishments.	Capital.	AVERAGE NUMBER OF HANDS EMPLOYED.			Total amount paid in wages during the year.	Value of materials.	Value of products.
			Males above 16 years.	Females above 15 years.	Children and youths			
All industries	318	$4,073,200	2,866	151	309	$1,271,995	$5,089,880	$8,103,277
Agricultural implements	5	160,000	137			52,326	66,019	174,000
Blacksmithing (see also Wheelwrighting)	10	3,150	16			4,274	4,975	13,050
Boots and shoes, including custom work and repairing	18	5,075	25		2	8,063	8,435	23,130
Boxes, wooden packing	3	16,500	28	8		10,000	15,550	26,240
Bread and other bakery products	19	56,850	93	17		33,875	134,505	189,785
Brick and tile	10	25,400	68		2	15,180	7,660	29,250
Carpentering	15	20,550	69		1	26,550	42,325	95,175
Carriages and wagons (see also Wheelwrighting)	5	277,000	193		20	86,355	150,639	351,300
Clothing, men's	12	30,500	58	1	1	23,250	45,000	93,500
Cooperage	39	23,200	139		2	82,725	60,460	128,975
Drugs and chemicals	8	33,000	29	2	2	12,690	18,700	49,500
Flouring- and grist-mill products	9	289,000	99			60,725	1,555,921	1,723,365
Foundery and machine-shop products	11	869,900	425		15	213,319	300,826	954,484
Furniture	7	139,300	197	10	12	87,750	59,500	194,700
Lime	5	51,500	93			35,505	70,832	140,675
Liquors, malt	7	406,650	88			89,970	171,871	306,980
Looking-glass and picture frames	3	4,300	5		1	1,470	5,500	11,000
Lumber, planed	4	62,000	126		4	39,000	69,000	187,000
Marble and stone work	4	9,700	61			16,000	24,200	42,200
Painting and paperhanging	8	5,950	49			14,040	11,690	31,584

Mechanical and manufacturing industries.	No. of estab-lish-ments.	Capital.	AVERAGE NUMBER OF HANDS EMPLOYED.			Total amount paid in wages during the year.	Value of materials.	Value of products.
			Males above 16 years.	Females above 15 years.	Children and youths.			
Photographing..	5	$13, 500	10	3	....	$4, 796	$4, 335	$17, 950
Printing and publishing......................................	4	54, 000	80	4	17	56, 820	67, 500	135, 900
Saddlery and harness..	12	49, 650	63	....	....	24, 211	53, 776	95, 300
Slaughtering and meat-packing, not including retail butchering	4	180, 000	100	....	1	18, 500	836, 000	967, 650
Tinware, copperware, and sheet-iron ware.....................	16	32, 750	42	....	4	15, 674	36, 550	78, 300
Tobacco, chewing, smoking, and snuff (see also Tobacco, cigars and cigarettes).	4	740, 250	161	75	178	151, 075	822, 335	1, 176, 070
Tobacco, cigars and cigarettes (see also Tobacco, chewing, smoking, and snuff).	25	34, 625	85	....	10	31, 839	38, 602	102, 200
Wheelwrighting (see also Blacksmithing; Carriages and wagons) ...	9	9, 600	26	....	1	10, 250	10, 100	26, 550
All other industries (a)	37	414, 300	301	31	36	145, 763	397, 074	737, 464

a Embracing awnings and tents; bone-, ivory-, and lamp-black; bookbinding and blank-book making; brass castings; brooms and brushes; coffee and spices roasted and ground; coffins, burial cases, and undertakers' goods; dyeing and cleaning; files; hairwork; hats and caps; lead, bar, pipe, sheet, and shot; lumber, sawed; mattresses and spring beds; mineral and soda waters; musical instruments, organs and materials; paper; saws; shirts; show-cases; soap and candles; steam fittings and heating apparatus; stencils and brands; stone- and earthen-ware; trunks and valises; vinegar; windmills; and wooden ware.

From the foregoing table it appears that the average capital of all establishments is $12,824 52; that the average wages of all hands employed is $382 43 per annum; and that the average outlay in wages, in materials, and in interest (at 6 per cent.) on capital employed is $20,775 36.

ROCKFORD,

WINNEBAGO COUNTY, ILLINOIS.

POPULATION

IN THE

AGGREGATE,

1850-1880.

	Inhab.
1790	......
1800	......
1810	......
1820	......
1830	......
1840	......
1850	2,093
1860	6,979
1870	11,049
1880	13,129

POPULATION

BY

SEX, NATIVITY, AND RACE,

AT

CENSUS OF 1880.

Male	6,263
Female	6,866
Native	9,857
Foreign-born	3,272
White	13,030
Colored	99

N.

Madison, Wis. N. 65° 14' W. 170.9 Miles.
Dubuque, Iowa. N. 77° 24' W. 82.7 Miles.
Chicago, Ill. S. 72° 28' E. 76.2 Miles.
Rock Island, Ill. S. 56° 36' W. 88.8 Miles.
Quincy, Ill. S. 37° 47' W. 202 Miles.
Springfield, Ill. S. 10° 5' W. 171.9 Miles.

S.

Latitude: 42° 15' North ; Longitude: 89° 5' (west from Greenwich); Altitude: 707 feet.

FINANCIAL CONDITION.

Total Valuation: $3,508,647; per capita: $267 00.   Net Indebtedness: $178,090; per capita: $13 56.   Tax per $100: $2 94.

HISTORICAL SKETCH.

In 1834 two white men, with their families, took up land on Rock river, and in the following year a family crossed the river, taking a farm on the opposite side. In this latter year about 20 settlers arrived, and the nucleus for the future city of Rockford was formed. In 1844 the Rockford Hydraulic Company was organized, and a dam 800 feet long was built across the river. This improvement insured the manufacturing interests of the place, and when the Chicago and Northwestern railroad reached here the future prosperity of Rockford was assured. Prior to the advance of white settlers, a large area of land on Rock river had been reserved for "Polanders", but there being no emigration the termination expired, and northern Illinois became occupied by men of industry, enterprise, and capacity. The chief industry is the making of agricultural implements, but there are also furniture factories, a watch manufactory, cotton- and woolen-mills, and several flour-mills.

ROCKFORD IN 1880.

The following statistical accounts, collected by the Census Office, indicate the present condition of the city:

LOCATION.

Rockford lies in latitude 42° 15′ north, longitude 89° 5′ west from Greenwich, on both sides of the Rock river, in the northern part of the state of Illinois, and about 90 miles by rail west of Chicago. The elevation of the city above sea-level, as given in the reports of the Smithsonian Institution, is 707 feet. The navigation of the river, on which the city lies, is interrupted by draws, but should a steamboat require to pass the draw at Rockford the expense of getting her from the water below to that above would have to be paid by the owners of the draw. The Rock river empties into the Mississippi about 2 miles below Rock Island.

RAILROAD COMMUNICATIONS.

The city is touched by the following railroad lines:

The Chicago and Northwestern railroad—one division, to Freeport, Illinois, connecting with the Illinois Central for Dubuque, Iowa, and the other division to Kenosha, Wisconsin.

The Chicago and Iowa railroad, to Forreston, Illinois.

The Chicago, Milwaukee, and Saint Paul railroad has extended its line from Milwaukee to Rockford, thereby competing with the Northwestern road.

TRIBUTARY COUNTRY.

In addition to the manufacturing interests of Rockford, which have developed to a marvellous extent, the country immediately tributary to the city is an agricultural one. The production of wheat, barley, rye, and oats has decreased from 40 bushels to 10 and 12 bushels per acre. This decrease has been in the last twenty years, and is said to be owing to the fact that farmers have neglected the fertilization of their land and so have impoverished the soil. The exportation of hogs, cattle, butter, and poultry to markets varying from New England to California has enriched the agriculturists of the surrounding country and made them satisfied. Though the soil has decreased in fertility, yet the corn crop holds its own.

TOPOGRAPHY.

Winnebago county, of which Rockford is the capital, consists of prairies bounded by elevated ridges of land. The underlying rock is of limestone formation. Acres of woodland in the adjacent townships are covered with forest timber. The hill-slopes and broad prairies are now no longer flooded, and all farm lands have natural drainage. The old marshes and swampy lands have dried up, and are now productive.

CLIMATE.

Highest recorded summer temperature, 106°; highest summer temperature in average years, 95°. Lowest recorded winter temperature, —27°; lowest winter temperature in average years, —18°. In the early settlement of the country the winds were very strong, but the spread of timber, by planting and cultivation, has diminished the force of the aerial currents, and now tornadoes are not frequent.

STREETS.

There are 125 miles of streets in the city, and of these, 25 miles are paved with broken stone and 5 miles with gravel. The cost per square yard of each, as nearly as may be estimated, is, for broken stone $1 and for gravel 50 cents. The cost of keeping broken stone in good repair is 5 cents per yard, and gravel 3 cents per yard. Broken stone is reported as being much the easier to keep clean, while in point of quality and permanent economy it is said to be far superior to gravel. The sidewalks are of wood and stone, and the gutters are of stone. Trees are planted along the sides of the streets, being set 8 feet from the street line. All street work is done by day labor, and the annual cost is about $10,000. Day work is preferred, as it is considered that more satisfactory results are obtained for the money expended. All stone-breaking is done by hand. There are no horse-railroads in the city. An omnibus line, with 14 vehicles and 40 horses, and giving employment to 10 men, annually carries about 18,000 passengers at a rate of fare of 25 cents.

WATER-WORKS.

The water-works are owned by the city, and their total cost was $260,000. Water is taken from springs, though a supply-main runs to the river in case of failure of the regular supply. The water is pumped directly into the pipes, on the Holly system. The pressure is ordinarily 60 pounds to the square inch, but in case of fire this can be raised from 120 to 150 pounds to the square inch. The number of gallons pumped per diem is 1,500,000, the least being 1,000,000 and the greatest 2,250,000. The average cost of raising 1,000,000 gallons one foot high is $14\frac{94}{100}$ cents. The yearly cost of maintenance, aside from the cost of pumping, is $300, and the yearly income from water-rates is $8,000. Water-meters are not used.

GAS.

The gas-works are owned by a private person. The daily average production is nearly 28,000 cubic feet. The charge per 1,000 feet is $2 70 net, but in case of large consumers only $2 50 is charged. The city pays $27 60 per year, which includes every thing—as repairs, lighting, etc.—for each street-lamp, 300 in number.

PUBLIC BUILDINGS.

The city owns and occupies 3 engine-houses and 8 school-houses, the total cost of these being $125,000. There is no city hall. The city rents for its offices rooms in the county court-house, which is a large stone edifice occupying, with its surrounding grass plat, an entire block, except the space at the corner occupied by the county jail.

PUBLIC PARKS AND PLEASURE-GROUNDS.

There are 2 public parks in Rockford, area about 2 acres each, and centrally located, one on each side of Rock river. The land covered by these parks was deeded to the city by the former owners. A board of commissioners has just been appointed to control the parks, with a view to improving them. The court-house square serves some of the purposes of a park, and there are some small plats at the intersections of diagonal streets that have been improved.

PLACES OF AMUSEMENT.

There are 2 public halls in the city, with a seating capacity of 700 each, used for theatrical exhibitions, concerts, lectures, etc. They pay no license to the city. There are no concert- and beer-gardens.

DRAINAGE.

There are no public sewers of any importance, except one draining the county buildings, with which adjacent owners have been permitted to make connections. Water is conveyed to the river mainly by surface gutters.

CEMETERIES.

There are 2 cemeteries of considerable extent on either side of the river, just above the city, and much taste has been displayed in their adornment. There is also a Catholic cemetery contiguous to the West cemetery. No information regarding the size of the cemeteries or the number of interments made was furnished.

The company controlling the West cemetery sets apart from the sale of lots a fund to furnish an income after the sale of lots cease, that the grounds may be perpetually well kept.

MARKETS.

There are no public or corporation markets in the city.

SANITARY AUTHORITY.

The sanitary needs of Rockford are looked after by the police marshal, who receives a special salary of $200 per annum for his services as health officer. He is appointed by the mayor, with the consent of the council. He makes frequent inspections, and when nuisances are reported or discovered they are removed. In the case of defective house-drainage, privy-vaults, cesspools, or sources of drinking-water, the health officer orders the same to be corrected by the owner, and if it is not done then, the health officer has the correction made, and the expense is assessed on the property. The health officer exercises control over the conservation and removal of garbage only when it becomes a nuisance or endangers public health. Physicians report all cases of contagious diseases to the health officer, who makes any necessary arrangement. The system of registration of births, diseases, and deaths is attended to by the county officers.

MUNICIPAL CLEANSING.

Street-cleaning.—The streets of the city are cleaned with its own force, and entirely by hand. The cleaning is done when it is required, and the expense, which is small, is included in the general street appropriation.

Garbage and ashes are removed by the householders, but when complaints are made the health officer causes it to be done.

Dead animals.—A piece of ground is rented by the city, in which is buried the carcass of any animal dying within the city. The health officer causes the carcasses to be removed, and the total cost of the service for the year 1879–'80 was $54 50.

Liquid household wastes, etc.—With the exceptions of the statements that but very little of the liquid household wastes deliver into sewers and that there are but few water-closets, no information regarding the disposal of liquid household wastes, human excreta, or manufacturing wastes was furnished. The principal manufactures have no wastes, except fragments of wood or metal, and these are utilized. The small amount of liquid wastes goes off into the river, with no perceptible effect.

POLICE.

The police force of Rockford is appointed by the mayor and confirmed by the council. The chief executive officer is the city marshal, salary $800 per annum, who has general supervision of all police business. The remainder of the force consists of 7 assistant marshals at $600 a year each. The uniform is of dark-blue-cloth with a great many brass buttons. The cost of the uniform is $59, and is furnished by the city. The men are equipped with pistols and clubs. They are on duty 10 hours out of the 24, and patrol about 3 miles of streets. During the past year 250 arrests were made, the principal causes being drunkenness, disorderly conduct, and violating liquor ordinances. These cases were finally disposed of either by fines or by imprisonment. During the same time there were 300 station-house lodgers, as against 450 in 1879. Free meals to the value of $20 were furnished to station-house lodgers during 1880. The police assist the fire department by guarding property at all fires, and as the marshal has been health officer for many years, he has the force to assist him. Special policemen are appointed in the same manner as the regular force and have the same powers. The yearly cost of the police force under the old system was $2,854 43, but the cost under the present system is not given.

FIRE DEPARTMENT.

The manual force of the department consists of 1 chief and 2 assistant engineers, 24 company officers, and 162 men—a total of 189. The apparatus consists of 1 hand-engine, 9 hose-carts, and 1 hook-and-ladder truck. The public water-supply is by the Holly system, by which a fire-pressure is communicated to the hydrants. There are 4,300 feet of hose in use. There were nine alarms of fire during the year ending May 5, 1879, and the loss by fire was $1,600. The total cost of the department during the same time was $2,038 25.

ROCK ISLAND,

ROCK ISLAND COUNTY, ILLINOIS.

POPULATION

IN THE

AGGREGATE,

1850-1880.

	Inhab.
1790	......
1800	......
1810	......
1820	......
1830	......
1840	......
1850	1,711
1860	5,130
1870	7,890
1880	11,659

POPULATION

BY

SEX, NATIVITY, AND RACE,

AT

CENSUS OF 1880.

Male	5,874
Female	5,785
Native	8,308
Foreign-born	3,351
White	11,475
Colored	*184

* Including 2 Chinese and 2 Indians.

Latitude: 41° 32′ North; Longitude: 90° 31′ (west from Greenwich); Altitude: 546 to 734 feet.

FINANCIAL CONDITION:

Total Valuation: $2,462,702; per capita: $211 00.   Net Indebtedness: $289 050; per capita: $24 79.   Tax per $100: $3 95.

HISTORICAL SKETCH.

The city of Rock Island takes its name from an island in the Mississippi river nearly 3 miles long and averaging half a mile in width.   Here was the chosen camping-ground of the Sac and Fox Indian tribes, and it was not until the year 1832, at the close of the Black Hawk war, that they departed for a region west of the Mississippi.   The island was first occupied by the whites in 1816, during which year fort Armstrong, consisting of a series of block-houses, was erected on the lower end, directly opposite to the place where the city of Rock Island now stands. It no longer exists, but during the Black Hawk war it was a special place of interest and security, where the early pioneers used to rendezvous when the signal of alarm was given.   Originally the island was a military and trading post, but in 1825 the government made it a military reservation, and in 1839 it was surveyed and a report was filed in the War Department recommending it as a suitable place for a United States armory.   No definite action was taken till 1861 or 1862, when it was selected and designated by act of Congress as the site for a western arsenal out of six strong and urgent competitors within the limits of Illinois. The civil war being in progress at this time, the island was selected by the War Department as a military prison, and no less than 14,000 confederate prisoners were held there at different times during the war.

The first house within the present city limits of Rock Island was erected in 1826 by George Davenport and Russell Farnham, Indian traders, the location being known as Farnhamburg. The vicinity was gradually settled by the early pioneers, who came there in order to be within the protection of fort Armstrong. In 1835 the commissioners of Rock Island county, under authority from the state legislature, entered at the Galena land-office a fractional quarter-section of land in what is now the central part of the city, and laid out a town called Stephenson, which was made the county-seat. An act of the state legislature passed in March, 1841, changed the name to Rock Island, and incorporated it as a town, under a board of 9 trustees; in 1849 it was incorporated as a city. The present city government, adopted in March, 1880, is under the general incorporation act of the state.

The main channel of the Mississippi is on the west side of Rock island. The east channel has been dammed so as to produce an immense water-power and to form a good harbor below. These improvements were made in the most durable manner at government expense, and the right was thus acquired by the United States to three-fourths of the power. The availability of this power, together with the central location of Rock island, the abundance of fuel and building materials, and the fact that Rock Island city is a central-market for iron, steel, copper, lead, wood, and leather, the principal materials used in the manufacture of arms and accouterments, induced the government to enter upon the construction on Rock island of the most extensive armory and arsenal in the country. The bridges establishing communication with Rock Island city on the Illinois shore and Davenport on the Iowa shore have already been built. They are of iron, with a passage for railway trains above and for vehicles below. The cost of these bridges was over $1,000,000, a portion of which was borne by the Chicago, Rock Island, and Pacific railroad; they are among the finest in the country. Besides this the government has laid out streets and avenues, so that the island, which is well wooded, is quite a pleasure resort. In all there are ten extensive shops on the island, built of Joliet stone roughly dressed.

The advantages furnished by this immense water-power have been utilized by Rock Island and Moline (a thriving manufacturing city east of and adjoining Rock Island) to such an extent that they, with Milan (formerly Camden), which lies southwest of Rock Island, make this one grand center of business and manufactures. The communication afforded with all markets east, north, south, and west by the Mississippi river and the railroads passing through the city of Rock Island, combined with its natural resources, sufficiently explain its past and present prosperity, and indicate a prosperous future. The first railroad, the Chicago and Rock Island, came into the city in 1856; up to that time the city had made slow progress as to wealth and population, but since then it has had a steady and rapid growth.

The city has suffered from no fires of any magnitude. There have been only two serious depressions in business—one from 1837 to 1840, and the other from 1857 to 1862, during which time Rock Island suffered in common with the whole country. The depression of 1873 was of short duration there. The early settlers represented all parts of the United States, the New England element being in the majority; at present a good share of the population is foreign-born, coming mainly from Germany, Ireland, and Sweden.

ROCK ISLAND IN 1880.

The present condition of Rock Island is indicated by the following statistical accounts collected by the Census Office:

LOCATION.

Rock Island lies in latitude 41° 32' north, longitude 90° 31' west from Greenwich, on the left bank of the Mississippi river, and 180 miles west of Chicago. The average altitude above sea-level is 556 feet, the lowest point being 546 feet and the highest (the general level of the bluffs) 734 feet above sea-level. The river here is navigable, the draught of water varying from 4 feet at extreme low water to 16 feet at high water. The harbor capacity is one-half mile of river levee; opposite the city the river is 3,800 feet wide and navigable from shore to shore. The current averages, for all stages of water, about 1½ mile per hour. The city has water communication with all points on the Mississippi river and its tributaries.

RAILROAD COMMUNICATIONS.

The city is touched by the following railroad lines:

The Chicago, Rock Island, and Pacific railroad passes through Rock Island, connecting the city with Chicago on the east and with Council Bluffs on the west.

The South Western division of the Chicago, Milwaukee, and Saint Paul railroad, which terminates in Rock Island, connects it with the North and the Northwest.

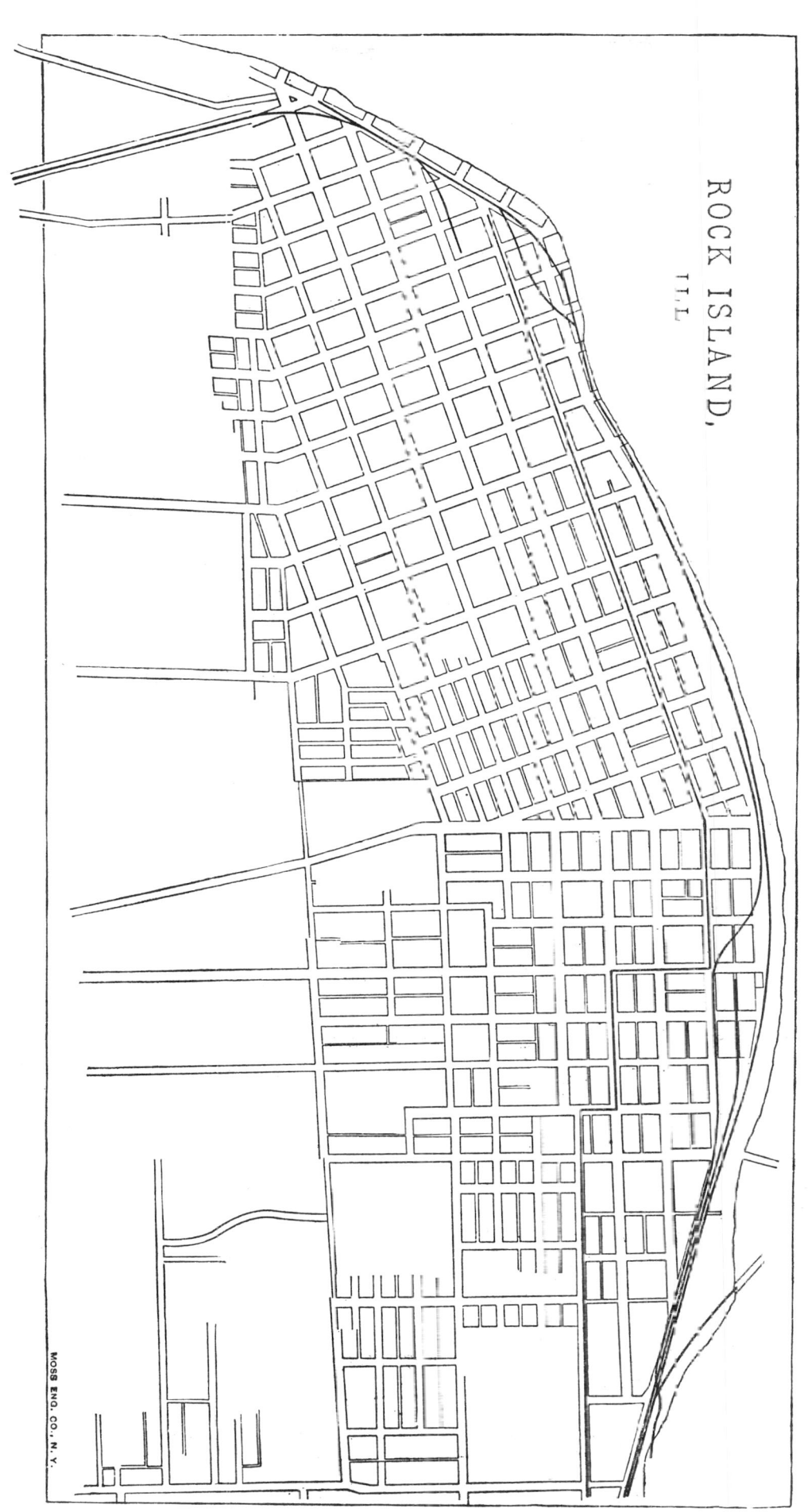

ROCK ISLAND, ILL.

The Saint Louis and Rock Island division of the Chicago, Burlington, and Quincy railroad gives a third line to Chicago, and makes direct connection with Saint Louis and the South.

The Rock Island and Peoria railroad runs to Peoria.

The Rock Island and Mercer County railroad runs through Mercer county.

TRIBUTARY COUNTRY.

Rock Island county is 13 miles long, lying upon the east bank of the Mississippi river; the city of Rock Island is nearly in the center of it. The county is thickly settled with farms, and contains, besides the cities of Rock Island and Moline, some 20 towns, with from 300 to 1,500 inhabitants each, most of the trade of which comes to Rock Island; besides this, much trade comes from the places through which run the railroads centering in Rock Island. The farms in the surrounding country are mostly in a high state of cultivation. There are five or six wholesale houses in the city, three national banks, having a capital of $3,000,000, and one bank of deposit.

TOPOGRAPHY.

The city stands on a nearly level plateau, which is for the most part from 10 to 25 feet above the high-water mark of the river, and from one-half to 1 mile wide from the river to the foot of the bluffs. The variation from a level plain gives ample drainage; the bluffs generally rise 200 feet above high water. The soil is a rich loam, with occasionally deposits of clay, sand, and gravel, and has an underlying bed of magnesian limestone, generally from 3 to 10 feet below the surface of the ground. For a radius of 5 miles the country is wooded, the soil is excellent, and there are no marshes, ponds, lakes, etc.

CLIMATE.

Highest recorded summer temperature, 104°; highest summer temperature in average years, 98°. Lowest recorded winter temperature, −38°; lowest winter temperature in average years, −18°. The influence of adjacent waters and elevated lands on the climate is unimportant. The north winds are cold and the south winds are hot; all winds cause a dry atmosphere.

STREETS.

The total length of the streets is about 45 miles. No data could be obtained as to the length paved with various materials or as to cost, etc. The sidewalks are generally of wood, some of stone, and some of brick. The gutters are paved with curbed stone or with broken stone. Construction and repairs are done by the city itself, and the annual cost is about $12,000. Day work is preferred to contract work. Neither a steam stone-crusher nor a roller is used. There are 4½ miles of horse-railroads in Rock Island and Moline together, having 10 cars and 33 horses, and employing 11 men. The rates of fare are 10 cents for the whole and 5 cents for half the distance. There are no omnibus lines.

WATER-WORKS.

The water-works are owned by the city; their total cost was $165,000. Direct pumping (the Holly system) is is employed, the average head of water under ordinary pressure being 140 feet, the ordinary pressure being 50 pounds to the square inch; under fire pressure (125 pounds to the square inch) the head is 320 feet. The average amount pumped per day is 1,400,000 gallons; the least amount, 880,000, the greatest, 1,987,000 gallons. The average cost of raising 1,000,000 gallons 1 foot high is 7½ cents. The yearly cost of maintenance, aside from the cost of pumping, is $3,300. No water-meters are used.

GAS.

The gas-works are not owned by the city. The daily average production is 45,000 feet, and the charge per 1,000 feet is $3. The city pays $34 for each street-lamp, and there are 101 of them in all.

PUBLIC BUILDINGS.

No buildings are owned by the city excepting small hose-houses.

PUBLIC PARKS AND PLEASURE-GROUNDS.

There are no improved parks in the city.

PLACES OF AMUSEMENT.

Harper's opera-house has a seating capacity of 1,000. Besides this there are Darl's hall, Central theater, and Turner hall. There are no concert- or beer-gardens in the city.

DRAINAGE.

No information on this subject was furnished by the city authorities.

CEMETERIES.

There are 3 cemeteries connected with the city, as follows:

The *Chippiannoch Cemetery*, area 60 acres.

The *Lutheran Cemetery*, area 1 acre.

The *Catholic Cemetery*, area 6 acres.

These are all situated south of the city, in the same neighborhood, about a mile from the city limits. The Catholic cemetery was organized in 1854. The total number of interments up to the present time, including those from Rock Island, Moline, and the country for 20 miles around, is 600. The Lutheran cemetery was organized in 1870. The interments have been as follows: 1870, 5; 1871, 10; 1872, 14; 1873, 23; 1874, 21; 1875, 18; 1876, 16; 1877, 20; 1878, 24; 1879, 23; 1880, 24; total, 198. The Chippiannock cemetery was organized in 1855. The interments, which embraced many from different parts of the country and some removals from abroad, as well as interments from the city of Rock Island, have been as follows: 1855, 6; 1856, 74; 1857, 78; 1859, 66; 1860, 38; 1861, 58; 1862, 62; 1863, 69; 1864, 188; 1865, 119; 1866, 97; 1867, 92; 1868, 98; 1869, 128; 1870, 148; 1871, 103; 1872, 155; 1873, 161; 1874, 158; 1875, 139; 1876, 173; 1877, 169; 1878, 170; 1879, 183; 1880, 152; total, 2,780. Total for the three cemeteries, 3,578. The regulations regarding interments require permits from the city clerk, and the Catholic cemetery also requires permits from the pastor of Saint Joseph's church. There are no special limits as to time. The depth of graves for children is 5 feet, for adults 6 feet.

MARKETS.

There are no public or corporation markets in the city.

SANITARY AUTHORITY—BOARD OF HEALTH.

The chief sanitary authority of Rock Island is the board of health, composed of the mayor, the city clerk, and 4 commissioners. The ordinance establishing this board and prescribing general sanitary regulations was passed in 1857, but this is the first year that the city has really had an active board. At present 3 of the 4 commissioners are physicians. The ordinary annual expenses are about $300, but this year $500 more was expended in a struggle with small-pox. A member of the board reports that he does not know the limit to which the board might increase its expenses during an epidemic, but thinks it would have the full power of the city if it were necessary to exercise it. The ordinance says that the board has full power to use all measures to promote the health of the city. It also has power to do whatever may be necessary to prevent the spread of disease. The members of the board all receive the same pay, $2 for each meeting. The commissioners shall serve all precepts and notices issued by the board, which are signed by the mayor and by the clerk, in the districts assigned to them. Last year the city marshal was one of the commissioners, and the board executed its orders through him. There are no assistant health officers or inspectors, the physicians and the marshal acting as such. About once or twice a month tours of inspection are made, there being no regularity about the work. If nuisances are reported, some of the commissioners examine into the matter, and if the nuisances really exist they have the clerk write an order for their abatement, which is given to the marshal. The commissioners are appointed by the mayor and confirmed by the city council. The expenses of the members are submitted to the board for approval, and by them to the council. The board is careful to contract no bills which the council would not pay. Stated meetings are held once a month, and special meetings at such times as in their opinion the public welfare may require. As regards defective house-drainage, privy-vaults, cesspools, and sources of drinking-water, last year, the board being in its infancy as a practical body, contented itself with exercising moral suasion. It examined into any thing tending to produce disease, including the above subjects, and used its influence, generally supported by the press, with tolerably good results. As yet there are but few sewers in the city, but the city and private parties are building some each year. The ordinance gives the board power over the streets, but it is reported that the board does nothing with them. It exercises very little control over the conservation and removal of garbage, but hopes before long to see the adoption of a thorough system of scavengering. No dead body may be removed from the city without a burial permit from the board. There are no regulations concerning the removal of excrement, except that it must be taken so far away below the city as to create no nuisance.

INFECTIOUS DISEASES.

Small-pox patients are isolated by placing a guard outside the premises and allowing nobody to pass out, unless permitted by the board. Scarlet-fever patients are not isolated or quarantined at home, but no person is permitted to attend school from a house containing scarlet fever. Dangerous contagious or infectious diseases are reported forthwith by the attending physician to the clerk of the board of health, who, on the same night, notifies the superintendent of schools. The latter allows no person to attend school from the house where the patient is, without a permit from the board of health. There is no public pest-house. Vaccination is not compulsory, and is not done at the public expense.

REPORTS.

All births and deaths are registered, under the same requirements as those of the Illinois state board. The board reports to the council simply as matters arise to which it wishes to call the attention of the council, and such reports are published only with the usual council proceedings. The board has, among other things, persistently pressed the necessity of a public abattoir, and this year received a small appropriation for the purpose.

MUNICIPAL CLEANSING

Street-cleaning.—The streets are cleaned by the city, the work being done by the city's own force, and wholly by hand. Streets are cleaned monthly, alleys in the spring and fall. It is reported to be done fairly well. The annual cost to the city is $1,600. The sweepings are mostly deposited in slough lots.

Removal of garbage and ashes.—Garbage is removed by the city at the time of the alley-cleaning, the work being done by the city's own force. If complaints are made as to the conservancy of garbage while awaiting removal, the owner is notified to abate the nuisance. Garbage and ashes are finally disposed of in filling up slough lots, the cost of removal being charged to the street- and alley-cleaning account. Nuisances and injury to health often result from infrequent removal and from improper final disposal.

Dead animals.—Under the regulations of the police department dead animals are dragged off and buried outside the city limits. The annual cost of this service is about $20, from 20 to 30 dogs, with occasional cows and horses, being removed annually.

Liquid household wastes.—Chamber slops are disposed of in the same way as laundry waste and kitchen slops, nearly all the liquid household waste of the city being delivered into the public sewers where the sewers exist. The city has water-works, and very few wells are used for drinking purposes. The only regulations concerning the cleaning out of cesspools are those for abating nuisances if complaints are made.

Human excreta.—About half the houses of the city have water-closets, and the other half depend on privy-vaults. About one-third of the water-closets deliver into public sewers and about two-thirds into cesspools. None of the privy-vaults are nominally water-tight, and there are no regulations concerning their construction and emptying. The dry-earth system is not used to any extent. Night-soil is ultimately hauled outside the city limits and buried. None of it is allowed to be used for manuring land within the gathering-ground of the public water-supply.

Manufacturing wastes.—There are no regulations concerning the disposal of liquid and solid manufacturing wastes.

POLICE.

The police force is appointed by the mayor, subject to the approval of the city council, and is governed by the mayor. The chief executive officer is the city marshal, with a salary of $900 per year, besides whom there is a deputy with a salary of $700, and two patrolmen with salaries of $600 per year each. Their uniform is of the regulation style, being of dark blue throughout, with brass buttons and shield. Men provide their own uniforms, except winter overcoats, and are allowed $75 each for clothing. Each man is provided with a revolver, nippers, a duplex whistle, and a 22-inch locust baton. They serve twelve hours per day and patrol a territory three-quarters of a mile long and one-half mile wide. In 1880 there were 433 arrests, mainly for larceny, assaults, and drunkenness; 30 were sentenced to the state prison, 102 to the county jail, and there were 301 city cases. About $900 worth of property, stolen or lost, was reported to the police, of which about $500 was recovered and returned to the owners. There were 261 station-house lodgers during the year 1880, against 512 in 1879. Meals were given them by the overseers of the poor at the county expense.

The police force is required to co-operate with the health department by reporting nuisances, etc.

Special police officers are appointed by the mayor for the same service as regular policemen, and their standing, while on duty, is the same. The cost of the police force for the year 1880 was $8,600.

SPRINGFIELD,
SANGAMON COUNTY, ILLINOIS.

POPULATION

IN THE

AGGREGATE,

1840–1880.

	Inhab.
1790	......
1800	......
1810	......
1820	......
1830	......
1840	2,579
1850	4,433
1860	9,320
1870	17,364
1880	19,743

POPULATION

BY

SEX, NATIVITY, AND RACE,

AT

CENSUS OF 1880.

Male	9,805
Female	9,938
Native	15,459
Foreign-born	4,284
White	18,414
Colored	* 1,329

* Including 1 Chinese.

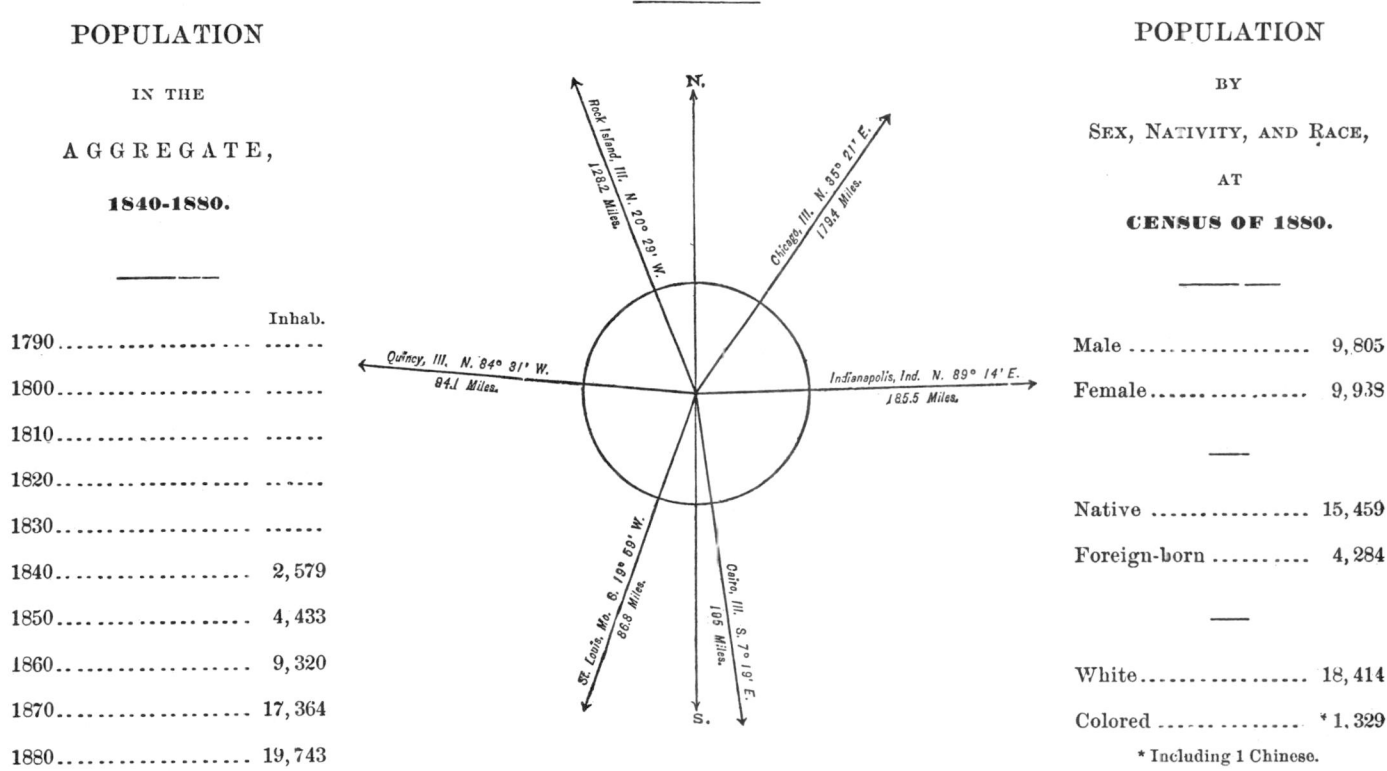

Latitude: 39° 48′ North; Longitude: 89° 39′ (west from Greenwich); Altitude: 550 feet.

FINANCIAL CONDITION:

Total Valuation: $4,226,575; per capita: $214 00.   Net Indebtedness: $778,780; per capita: $39 45.   Tax per $100: $2 74.

SPRINGFIELD IN 1880.

Springfield, the capital of the state of Illinois, is situated on the edge of a rich prairie, about 3 miles south of the Sangamon river, near the center of the state, and about 180 miles southwest of Chicago by rail. It was laid out in 1822 on a regular plan, with a public square in the center, and with wide streets crossing each other at right angles. At first its growth was slow, but after the establishment of the state government here in 1850 it rapidly advanced in manufactures, commerce, and population. The Chicago and Alton, the Illinois Central, the Ohio and Mississippi, the Springfield and Northwestern, and the Wabash, Saint Louis, and Pacific railroads pass through the city, affording ample railroad facilities. There are two horse-railroads, gas-works, a paid fire department, and adequate water-works. There are six coal-shafts on the verge of the city, where superior coal in inexhaustible quantities is mined. Springfield was the home of Abraham Lincoln, President of the United States, and his remains now rest in Oak Ridge cemetery, adjoining the city, marked by a handsome monument.

SANITARY AUTHORITY—BOARD OF HEALTH.

The chief sanitary organization of Springfield is the board of health, composed of 6 members, 1 from each ward of the city, appointed by the mayor and confirmed by the city council, with the mayor *ex officio* president, and the city clerk *ex officio* clerk of the board. For the present year the 6 members appointed are all physicians. The annual expense of the board in the absence of any declared epidemic is $300, and in case of epidemics this sum may be increased to any amount deemed necessary by the council. The board has authority over the general health and cleanliness of the city; can cause all nuisances to be abated or removed, can erect temporary hospitals, and destroy infected clothing, bedding, etc., and generally do all things that may be necessary to prevent the introduction or spread of contagious diseases. The board meets once a month, or oftener at the call of the president, and transacts its business as a deliberative body, a majority forming a quorum. After the orders of the board have been certified by the clerk, the mayor causes them to be executed by the supervisor, by the marshal, or by a policeman. There are 4 inspectors employed, and all have police powers. One general inspection is made annually. When nuisances are reported they are ordered abated within 24 hours. The same mode of procedure is observed toward defective house-drainage, privy-vaults, cesspools, sources of drinking-water, etc. Small-pox patients are removed to the public pest-house, situated outside the city limits. Scarlet-fever patients are neither isolated nor quarantined at home. The board has power to disband public schools or public meetings of any kind in case of contagious diseases. Vaccination is compulsory, and is done at the public expense when persons are unable to pay.. All births and deaths are required to be reported at the office of the county clerk as soon as practicable.

MUNICIPAL CLEANSING

Street-cleaning.—The streets are cleaned at the expense of the city, with its own force, and entirely by hand. The streets are cleaned when they need it, and the work is reported as but poorly done. The annual cost is $3,500.

Ashes and garbage are removed by the city with its own force. Garbage and ashes are allowed to be kept in the same vessel.

Dead animals are removed under contract to a rendering establishment, at an annual cost of $150.

Human excreta.—About one-third of the houses in the city are provided with water-closets, all of which deliver into the sewers, and the remainder depend on privy-vaults. None of the vaults are even nominally water-tight, and they must be cleaned when the health inspector gives notice. It is reported that in the center of the city the well-water is very bad, from the effects of old privy-vaults that were in use before the sewers were built. Night-soil is not allowed to be used for manuring land within the gathering-ground of the public water-supply.

Liquid household wastes.—Although the city is well sewered, only about one-half of the liquid household wastes are run into the public sewers. Gutters are never flushed.

Manufacturing wastes.—All manufacturing wastes are run into the sewers.

MANUFACTURES.

The following is a summary of the statistics of the manufactures of Springfield for 1880, being taken from tables prepared for the Tenth Census by J. O. Humphrey, special agent:

Mechanical and manufacturing industries.	No. of establishments.	Capital.	AVERAGE NUMBER OF HANDS EMPLOYED.			Total amount paid in wages during the year.	Value of materials.	Value of products.
			Males above 16 years.	Females above 15 years.	Children and youths.			
All industries..................................	116	$1,709,775	1,391	75	232	$656,253	$3,156,279	$4,123,883
Blacksmithing..................................	6	4,400	10	....	....	5,800	4,540	17,340
Boots and shoes, including custom work and repairing	13	7,930	12	....	1	5,400	6,177	17,688
Bread and other bakery products...............	8	16,700	15	4	3	7,140	23,800	39,000
Carriages and wagons..........................	4	67,500	52	....	....	27,200	37,000	93,000
Confectionery..................................	3	14,500	12	3	6	7,000	24,500	38,000
Flouring- and grist-mill products.............	5	140,000	40	....	....	16,800	268,550	336,495
Foundery and machine-shop products...........	6	107,500	121	....	3	62,665	131,297	240,626
Furniture (see also Upholstering).............	3	1,600	7	....	....	4,200	3,300	8,700
Printing and publishing.......................	6	50,300	123	3	44	49,050	22,150	105,300
Saddlery and harness..........................	8	9,300	35	2	....	13,764	26,400	61,106
Tinware, copperware, and sheet-iron ware......	5	12,000	18	....	1	9,540	17,400	34,090
Tobacco, cigars and cigarettes................	9	17,400	30	....	11	10,216	13,808	36,650
Upholstering (see also Furniture).............	3	3,200	6	....	2	2,660	4,300	8,700
All other industries (a)......................	37	1,247,145	910	63	161	434,818	2,573,057	3,067,188

a Embracing agricultural implements; bags, paper; baking and yeast powders; bookbinding and blank-book making; brooms and brushes; clothing, men's; coffee and spices, roasted and ground; coffins, burial cases, and undertakers' goods; cooperage; files; iron and steel; liquors, malt; lock- and gun-smithing; looking-glass and picture frames; lumber, planed; marble and stone work; mineral and soda waters; paper; patent medicines and compounds; roofing and roofing materials; sash, doors, and blinds; shoddy; slaughtering and meat-packing; stereotyping and electrotyping; trunks and valises; wheelwrighting; wirework; wood, turned and carved; and woolen goods.

From the foregoing table it appears that the average capital of all establishments is $14,739 44; that the average wages of all hands employed is $386 48 per annum; and that the average outlay in wages, in materials, and in interest (at 6 per cent.) on capital employed is $33,751 02.

MISSOURI.

HANNIBAL,

MARION COUNTY, MISSOURI.

POPULATION

IN THE

AGGREGATE,

1850-1880.

	Inhab.
1790	......
1800	......
1810	......
1820	......
1830	......
1840	......
1850	2,012
1860	6,505
1870	10,125
1880	11,074

POPULATION

BY

SEX, NATIVITY, AND RACE,

AT

CENSUS OF 1880.

Male	5,542
Female	5,532
Native	9,809
Foreign-born	1,265
White	9,232
Colored	*1,842

*Including 1 Chinese and 3 Indians.

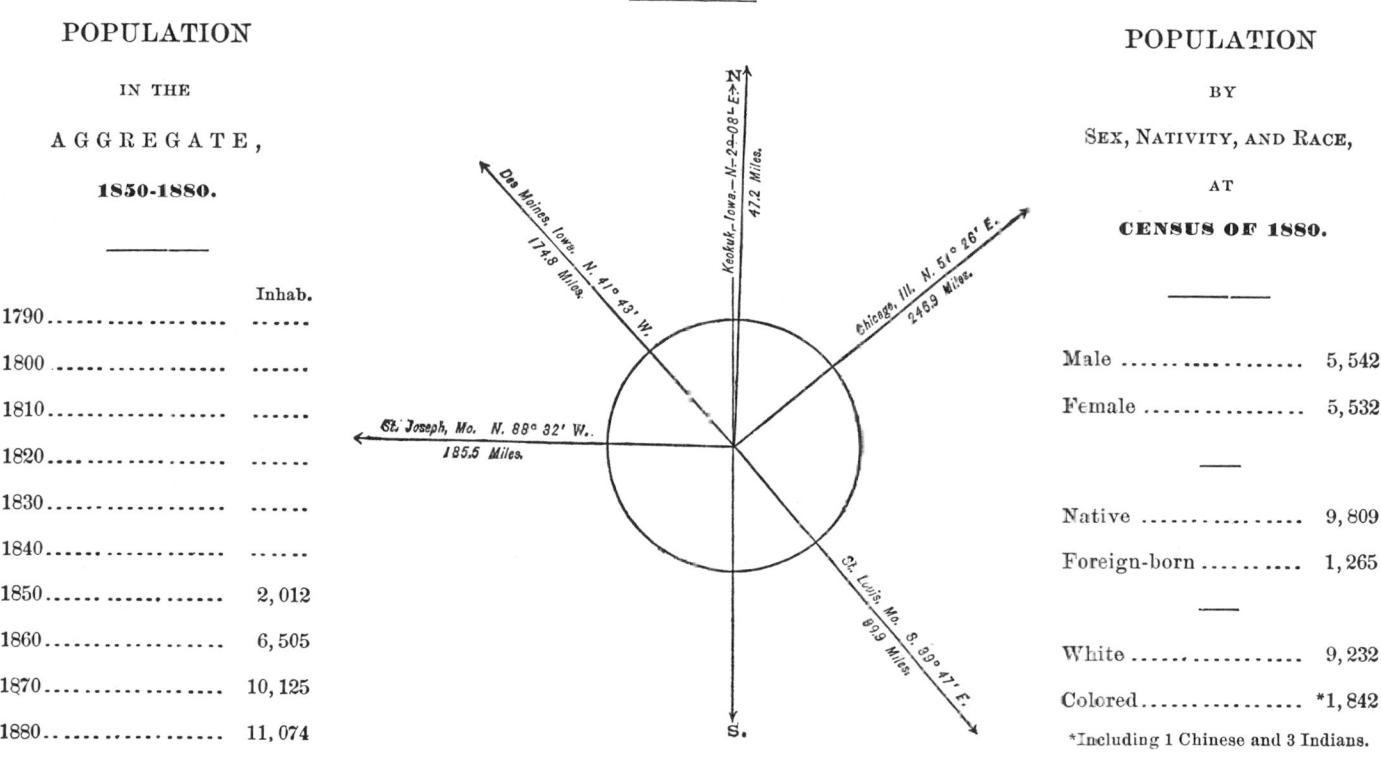

Latitude: 39° 44' North; Longitude: 91° 23' (west from Greenwich); Altitude: 486 feet.

FINANCIAL CONDITION:

Total Valuation: $2,300,460; per capita: $253 00.   Net Indebtedness: $190,173; per capita: $17 17.   Tax per $100: $2 95.

HISTORICAL SKETCH.

The site of the present city of Hannibal was first settled in the year 1819, but the growth of the place was very slow, and it was not until 1836 that the town was regularly laid out. In 1845 it was incorporated as a city, and in the same year the Keokuk and Saint Louis Packet Company was established. In 1847 the Hannibal and Saint Joseph railroad was chartered, but it was not built before 1859. It extended directly across the state, tapping the Missouri river at Saint Joseph, and its completion infused new life into the quiet city of Hannibal. The western terminus of the road became the starting point for the overland traffic to California, and Hannibal profited greatly by the tide of travel passing through her limits. Her growth for a few years was exceedingly rapid, and, but for the civil war, might have continued. From 1861 to 1865 Hannibal was at a standstill, and suffered a business prostration in common with the rest of the state. After the close of the war, however, the city began once more to advance, and steadily increased in population and material wealth. The extension of the several railroads touching the city was another source of profit, and quite an extensive trade in lumber sprang up with Missouri, Kansas, and Texas. The extensive machine-shops and general offices of the Hannibal and Saint Joseph railroad are located here, and contribute largely to the general business of the place. Until within fifteen years the city has suffered greatly by fires, the business portion having been nearly destroyed in 1857, and again in 1859. The principal periods of depression were in 1857 and 1863. The original settlers were mostly from the southern states, but during the past twenty years the population has changed considerably. The cause of the change was largely due to the opening of the railroads to this point, thereby furnishing increased facilities for eastern emigration.

HANNIBAL IN 1880.

The following statistical accounts, mainly collected by the Census Office, indicate the present condition of Hannibal:

LOCATION.

Hannibal lies in latitude 39° 44' north, longitude 91° 23' west from Greenwich, on the west bank of the Mississippi river, 144 miles from Saint Louis by river and 285 miles from Chicago by rail. The city of Quincy, Illinois, is a short distance above Hannibal, on the opposite bank. The altitude of the city above sea-level is 486 feet. The draught of water in the Mississippi at this point varies from 3 to 12 feet, and from the spring to July or to September boats drawing 8 feet of water can come to the city. After that, however, it is navigable here only for boats drawing from 2 to 4 feet. Water communication is open to all points on the Mississippi and Missouri rivers and their navigable tributaries. The current of the river here is stated to be 4 miles per hour.

RAILROAD COMMUNICATIONS.

Hannibal has the advantages afforded by the following railroad lines:
The Chicago, Burlington, and Quincy railroad, to Chicago.
The Hannibal and Saint Joseph railroad, between the points named.
The Kansas and Texas division of the Missouri Pacific railway, to Denison, Texas.
The Saint Louis, Hannibal, and Keokuk railroad, now completed to Bowling Green, Missouri.
The Saint Louis, Keokuk, and Northwestern railroad, from Saint Louis to Keokuk.
The Wabash, Saint Louis, and Pacific railroad, an air-line to Toledo, Ohio, with good eastern connections.

TRIBUTARY COUNTRY.

The country immediately tributary to the city is agricultural, wheat, hemp, and tobacco being largely raised. The local trade, aside from manufacturing interests, etc., is altogether from the farming community, a large part of Marion, Pike, Monroe, and Ralls counties, in Missouri, as well as the counties of Pike and Adams, in Illinois, adding largely to the trade of the city.

TOPOGRAPHY.

The vicinity of the river on the Missouri side from the Iowa state line to a point near Hannibal is alluvial. A range of high bluffs closely skirts the river's bank for many miles below Hannibal. A point of the bluffs also joins the river above, forming by the detour a natural amphitheater, about a mile across along the river, open toward the river and inclosed on the other three sides. Hannibal is situated in this recess, the ground rising gradually from the river's edge toward the west. The bluffs are mostly of limestone of a good quality, probably similar in formation to those on which the city of Quincy, Illinois, is located, and described in the report of that city. The country within a radius of from 5 to 10 miles is wooded, while the soil outside the city limits is a deep rich loam.

CLIMATE.

No daily record of temperature has been kept.

STREETS.

There are 75 miles of streets in the city, paved as follows: Stone blocks, 1 mile; broken stone, 10 miles; and gravel, 15 miles. The cost per square yard of each, as nearly as may be estimated, is, for stone blocks, $1 10;

HANNIBAL,

MO.

for broken stone, $1; and for gravel, 40 cents. The annual cost of keeping the paved streets in repair is $1,500. The stone blocks are said to be the cheapest and most permanent in the end. The sidewalks are of stone, wood, and brick, while the gutters are laid with stone. Tree-planting is quite general, and altogether on the outside of the pavements. The work of construction and repair of streets is done under the supervision of the street commissioner, with the advice of the committee on streets and alleys, and the annual amount expended varies from $3,000 to $5,000.

HORSE-RAILROADS.

The horse-railroads in the city have a total length of 1¾ mile, have 3 cars and 14 horses, and give employment to 6 men. There are 96,000 passengers carried annually, the rate of fare being 5 cents. There are no omnibus lines in the city.

WATER-WORKS.

The works for the water-supply have just been begun, and so far their cost has been $100,000. The system is to be pumping into a reservoir, with an elevation of 230 feet.

GAS.

The gas-works are owned by a private corporation. The daily average production is 20,000 cubic feet. The charge per 1,000 feet is $3. The city pays $18 per annum for each street-lamp in use, 133 in number.

PUBLIC BUILDINGS.

The city owns and occupies for municipal purposes, wholly or in part, the city hall, market-house, engine-house, and city prison. The total cost of the buildings belonging to the city is $19,500. The city hall is owned entirely by the city, and cost $6,000.

PUBLIC PARKS AND PLEASURE-GROUNDS.

With the exception of one square with an area of 5 acres, which is public, there are no parks or pleasure-grounds in Hannibal.

PLACES OF AMUSEMENT.

There are 2 halls in the city used for concerts, lectures, theatrical performances, etc.: Mozart hall, with a seating capacity of 600, and the Academy of Music, seating 1,000. The city charges a license for each exhibition given. There are no concert- and beer-gardens.

DRAINAGE.

There is no system of public sewers in Hannibal, and there are no private sewers deserving mention. The matter of public sewers, it is reported, will come before the council this winter.

CEMETERIES.

There are 4 cemeteries now in use, 2 within and 2 outside the city limits:
Riverside Cemetery, overlooking the river inside the southern limits, has an area of 15 acres.
Mount Olivet Cemetery, area 22 acres, is situated just outside the southern limits.
Baptist Cemetery, in the northern part of the city, has an area of 2 acres.
Catholic Cemetery, one-quarter of a mile northwest of the city, has an area of 5 acres. There is also one Catholic cemetery, area 3 acres, located south of the city, now no longer used for burial purposes.

As no records of interments were kept prior to January 22, 1880, the number of burials in all or any of the cemeteries can not be given. Burial permits are issued by the city clerk, and must be presented to the officers of the cemeteries before interments are allowed to be made. All of the above cemeteries except the Baptist are new, and there has not been much done in the direction of landscape-gardening, etc.

MARKETS.

There is one public market, situated near the center of the city. The lot is 132 by 132 feet, and the building, which is of brick, is 80 by 120 feet; the cost, including the land, was $8,000. There are 10 meat-stalls, renting for $8 a month each, and 14 vegetable- and 4 fish-stalls, renting for $1 a week each; the total rental from the market is about $125 per month. The market-houses are open from 4 to 10 a. m. and from 4 to 8 p. m., and on Saturdays until 10 p. m. About one-half of the retail supply of meats, poultry, fish, vegetables, etc., of the city is sold at the public market. There are no statistics available from which to show the amount of annual sales from within the market. The market-building is reported as in good repair.

SANITARY AUTHORITY—BOARD OF HEALTH.

The chief sanitary organization of Hannibal is a board of health, composed of the city clerk and the city physician, with 3 members of the board of aldermen, who are appointed annually by the mayor and confirmed by the city council. The annual expense of the board, when there is no declared epidemic, is merely nominal, and no provision by law has been made for any increase in case of epidemics. The extent of the authority of the board in ordinary times is, a general supervision over the health and cleanliness of the city, with special authority during epidemics. The board organizes by electing one of its members chairman and one clerk. The city physician receives a salary of $300 per annum. All cases requiring action are reported to him, and he presents them to the board. The street commissioner acts as messenger of the board; he attends all meetings, serves all notices that have been attested by the secretary and makes due return of same, and reports to the board all matters pertaining to public health which in his opinion require attention. No regular inspectors are employed, but one or all of the police officers may be detailed for the duty. The members of the board have authority to enter premises. The board meets regularly once a month, and also on call of the chairman. Inspections are in general made regularly once a year, and afterward as nuisances are reported. When a nuisance is found to exist, the party responsible is notified to remove or abate the same within a specified time. The board has no custom regarding the inspection of defective house-drainage, privy-vaults, cesspools, or sources of drinking-water unless the same becomes a nuisance, and then property-owners are notified to correct. The board exercises no control over the conservation or removal of garbage. The carcasses of dead animals and the contents of vaults are not allowed to be cast into any other stream than the Mississippi river.

INFECTIOUS DISEASES.

Small-pox patients are isolated by being removed to a house provided for that purpose for the time being. Scarlet-fever patients are quarantined at home, but there is no law on the subject. So far no occasion has arisen for the board to take action on the breaking out of contagious diseases either in public or in private schools, but should the contingency occur the board would act. Vaccination is neither compulsory nor is it done at public expense.

REPORTS.

Death certificates are filed with the city clerk, and it is presumed that he keeps some record. The board does not make any reports, but the city physician reports quarterly to the council.

MUNICIPAL CLEANSING.

Street-cleaning.—The streets are cleaned at the expense of the city and with its regular force. The work is done wholly by hand, no sweeping-machine being used. The streets are cleaned at irregular intervals, according to their condition, and the work is said to be done in a satisfactory manner. The cost of the service is included in the general street appropriation. The sweepings are used for filling streets and lots, and it is reported that the only advantage in this mode of disposal is that it helps to bring the streets up to grade.

Removal of garbage and ashes.—All garbage is removed by the householders. It is kept in barrels and removed daily by persons who use it as feed for hogs. Ashes and garbage are allowed to be kept in the same vessel, but, as a rule, this is not done. Ashes are thrown into the alleys, and are removed when the alleys are cleaned by the householders. The annual cost of removal to each person varies from 25 cents to $5, according to the amount. It is thought that no nuisance or probable injury to health occurs from infrequent removal of garbage, improper handling, etc.; but the defect in the system is that parties are apt to be governed by their own convenience instead of promptly complying with the ordinances.

Dead animals.—The carcass of any animal dying within the city is removed and thrown into the Mississippi river. This work is performed by the owners, but when they are not known it is done by the street commissioners. The cost of the service is very little, the number of dead animals removed annually being between 50 and 100. It is reported that the system works well for a city of this size.

Liquid household wastes.—Chamber-slops, laundry wastes, and kitchen-slops are generally disposed of in the same manner, and, as there is but one sewer, they are generally thrown into vaults and cesspools. The cesspools are nominally water-tight, are not provided with overflows, receive the wastes from water-closets, and are cleaned out at night, the contents being taken outside the city. Contamination of drinking-water, owing to the escape of the contents of vaults and cesspools, is thought to have occurred in the low lands and bottoms, producing a mild form of cholera and typhoid fever.

Human excreta.—Nearly all the houses in the city depend on privy-vaults. There are some water-closets, and nearly all of them deliver into cesspools, but very few delivering into the sewer. All the privy-vaults on the high land are nominally water-tight. Vaults are required to be 10 feet deep and to be walled up either with brick or with stone. They are emptied at night as often as required, and the night-soil is taken below the city and dumped into the river, none of it being allowed to be used for manuring land within the gathering-ground of the public water-supply.

Manufacturing wastes.—There are no regulations regarding the disposal either of liquid or of solid manufacturing wastes.

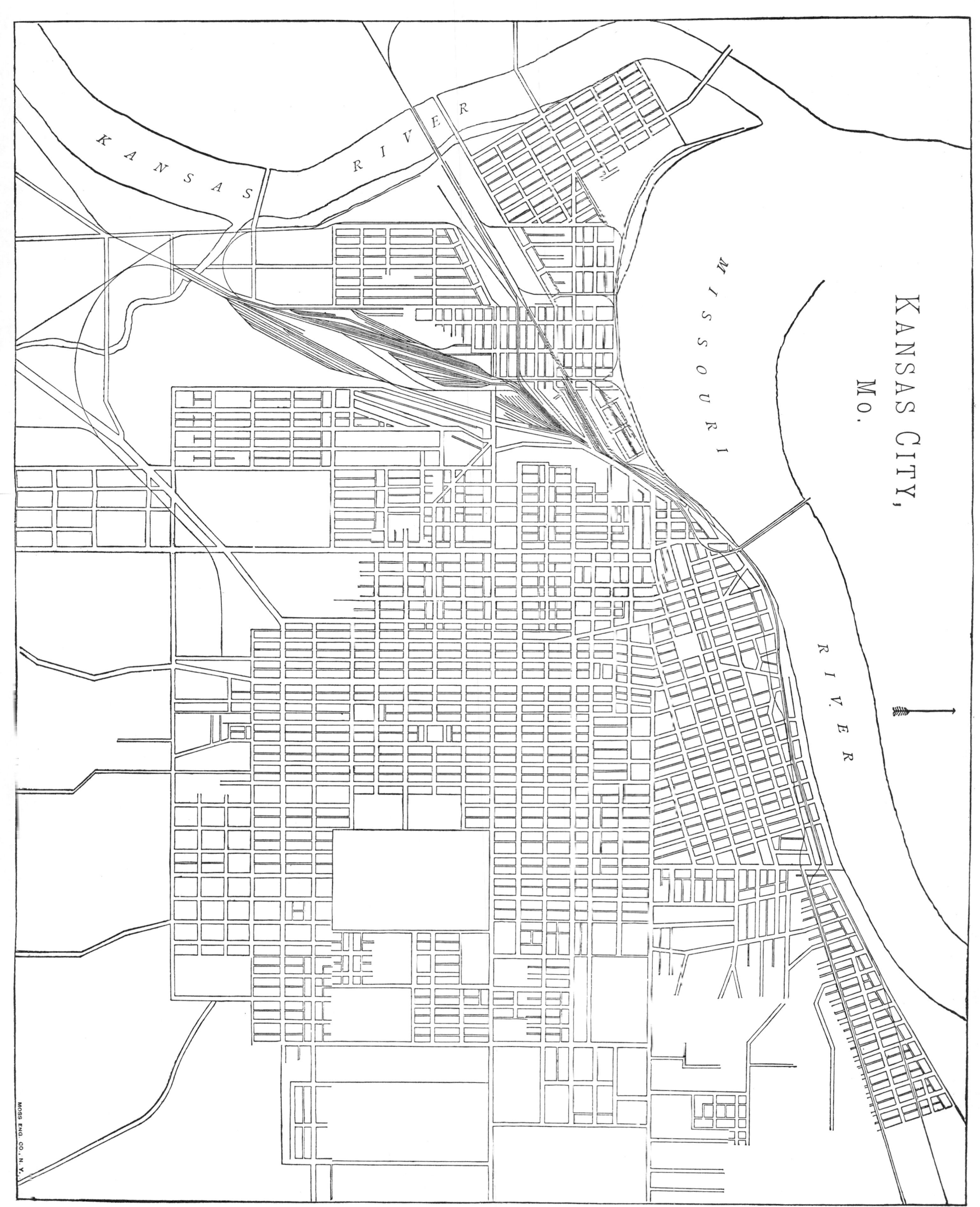

KANSAS CITY,
Mo.

KANSAS CITY,

JACKSON COUNTY, MISSOURI.

POPULATION

IN THE

AGGREGATE,

1860-1880.

	Inhab.
1790	......
1800	......
1810	......
1820	......
1830	......
1840	......
1850	......
1860	4,418
1870	32,260
1880	55,785

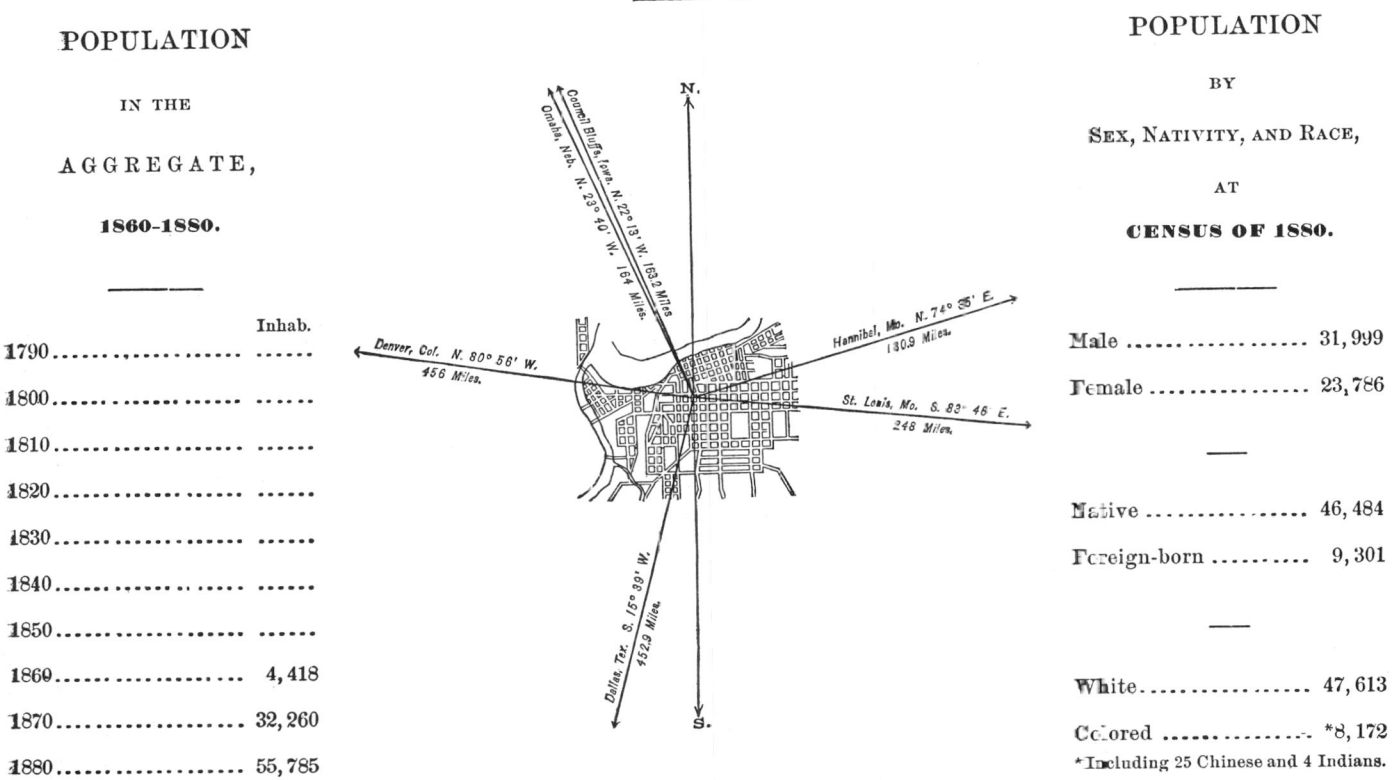

POPULATION

BY

SEX, NATIVITY, AND RACE,

AT

CENSUS OF 1880.

Male	31,999
Female	23,786
Native	46,484
Foreign-born	9,301
White	47,613
Colored	*8,172

*Including 25 Chinese and 4 Indians.

Latitude: 39° 5′ North; Longitude: 94° 40′ (west from Greenwich); Altitude: 647 to 860 feet.

FINANCIAL CONDITION:

Total Valuation: $10,577,260; per capita: $190 50.   Net Indebtedness: $1,339,224; per capita: $24 00.   Tax per $100: $4 55.

HISTORICAL SKETCH.

The country around the site of Kansas City was well settled thirty years ago, and some of the settlers even came as far back as 1825. The city itself dates back to 1846, although a few families were here before the great flood in 1844. Little progress was made till 1856-'57, at which time settlers began to pour into the territory of Kansas in great numbers. Kansas City profited by this, and flourished greatly until 1861; but during the civil war, being on the border, she suffered very much. The first railroad reached the city in 1865, and from that time to 1873 she gained largely in population and wealth. From 1873 to 1879 there was continual depression—worst in 1874 and 1875, when the Rocky Mountain locust or grasshopper covered the North and West both spring and fall, destroying every thing that was green. The plague extended but a few miles east of here. The city has been singularly free from great fires. The chief importance of Kansas City consists in its being a distributing point for

POLICE.

The police force of Hannibal is appointed by the mayor, subject to the approval of the city council, and is governed by the mayor. The city marshal, salary $720 per annum, is the chief executive officer, and has direct supervision over the police. The rest of the force consists of 6 patrolmen at $540 a year each. The uniform is of navy-blue cloth, with silver-plated buttons, and each man provides his own. The patrolmen are equipped with "Bean's patent flexible police club", are on duty 10 hours at a time, and each one patrols about 12 blocks. The total number of arrests during the past year was 425; the principal causes being for disturbing the peace, drunkenness, burglary, larceny, etc. In their final disposition 215 paid fines and 210 were sent to work breaking stone. There were 93 station-house lodgers during 1880. The force is required to co-operate with the fire and health departments under the instruction of the mayor and the marshal. Special policemen are appointed for elections, circus days, etc., and work with the regular force. The yearly cost of the department (1880) is $3,287 50.

the live-stock traffic of the Southwest, a business which has enormously increased since the completion of the Missouri, Kansas, and Texas railroad connecting this city through the Indian territory with the great stock-raising regions of Texas. The pork-packing business has also assumed considerable importance. Manufacturing industry is as yet small.

The original settlers were French Canadians and half-breed Indians. Next came emigrants from the slave states, principally from Kentucky. It is reported that it is impossible to give any intelligent opinion as to changes in population. At present the representation of nationalities and states in the city is decidedly varied.

KANSAS CITY IN 1880.

The present condition of Kansas City is shown by the following statistical account, mainly gathered by the Census Office:

LOCATION.

Kansas City lies in latitude 39° 5' north, longitude 94° 40' west from Greenwich, on the right bank of the Missouri river, half a mile below the mouth of Kansas river, 1 mile from the boundary line between Kansas and Missouri, and 235 miles west of Saint Louis. Its lowest altitude above the level of the sea is 647 feet, and its highest 860 feet. The city is located at the great southern bend of the Missouri river, where it finally turns to the east. The river is navigable, having an average width of 1,300 feet, and a depth of main channel varying at this point from 19 to 39 feet, the greatest variation recorded being 37 feet in 1844. The main channel is close to the south shore for two thirds of the city's frontage on the river.

RAILROAD COMMUNICATIONS.

The Kansas City, Saint Joseph, and Council Bluffs railroad runs from Kansas City to Council Bluffs.
The Hannibal and Saint Joseph railroad runs to Hannibal.
The Southwestern division of the Chicago, Rock Island, and Pacific railroad connects Kansas City with Chicago via Davenport, Iowa.
The Wabash, Saint Louis, and Pacific railroad makes nearly a straight line from Kansas City to Toledo, Ohio.
The Chicago and Alton railroad runs from Kansas City to Saint Louis and Chicago.
The Missouri Pacific railroad gives another line to Saint Louis.
The Kansas City and Eastern railroad (narrow-gauge) runs to Lexington.
The Kansas City, Fort Scott, and Gulf railroad has Kansas City and Joplin as its terminals.
The Kansas City, Lawrence, and Southern railroad has Kansas City and Harper as its terminals.
The Atchison, Topeka, and Santa Fé railroad runs to Santa Fé and Denver.
The Kansas division of the Union Pacific railroad runs from Kansas City to Denver.

TRIBUTARY COUNTRY.

Surrounding the city lie fine lands for grazing and agriculture, well suited for the growth of any of the cereals and other products of the western states. The lands in the adjoining counties of Kansas are thickly settled, and are about the best in the state; the Missouri counties near the city are of superior fertility, and were settled before those of Kansas.

TOPOGRAPHY.

The site of the city was originally very rough and uneven, part of the city being on a bluff and part on bottom-lands. All the rocks above the level of the river are limestone, and for a depth of 250 feet below that level there is nothing but limestone, clays, and shales; below that depth lie bowlders. Above the limestone are heavy deposits of soil, clay, etc., very little land being unfit for tillage. There are no lakes, ponds, or marshes near by. On the river-bottom there are a few ancient channels partly filled up. The country to the north and east of the city is (or was) heavily timbered; to the south and west it is mostly prairie, beginning about 5 miles from the city.

CLIMATE.

The highest recorded summer temperature is 113°; the highest in average years, about 100°. The lowest recorded winter temperature is —19°. The winters have been very variable, that of 1878–'79 being the hardest in thirty years, while in the preceding and succeeding winters there was but little ice. Parties living on the river-bottoms are subject to ague, malaria, etc. On account of the malarial exhalations of the lowlands, the uplands are the more sought after, and more populous. In summer the prevailing winds are from the south, and are always cool and pleasant. In the spring and winter they are from the north and west, blistering, cold, and disagreeable East winds bring rain or snow.

STREETS.

The total length of streets is 89 miles, 1,500 linear feet of which are paved with stone blocks and 16.4 miles with broken stone. The cost per square yard of sandstone blocks, as nearly as it can be estimated, was $3 50, and of broken stone 60 cents. The sandstone, having just been laid, has so far needed no repairs; the annual cost of repairing the broken-stone pavement is about 10 cents per square yard. It is impossible to keep the broken stone clean; for each wetting a new coat of mud appears on the surface. The broken limestone of this locality is stated to be unfit for the wear and tear of streets. Sandstone and granite are too costly, on account of the long distances from which they must be brought. Pine planks are principally used for sidewalks; brick, limestone, flags, and cement are occasionally used. The gutters are principally made of limestone blocks. Trees are planted at the curb-lines, and tree-planting has been very generally done on improved residence property. Maple and elm are the most used. The construction of streets is done by contract. Repairs are done by day labor, and the annual cost, including the clearing of stone-paved streets, is about $20,000. The contract system is given the preference.

HORSE-RAILROADS.

There are 17.25 miles of horse-railroads in the city, with 61 cars (small ones for heavy grades) and 360 mules, employing 90 men. The rate of fare is 5 cents.

WATER-WORKS.

For the water-supply pumping is employed, the pressure for ordinary supply being 85 pounds for the lower town, 135 for the upper, which is increased from 50 to 75 pounds in case of fire. The Holly system is used in connection with a reservoir. The average amount pumped is about 3,000,000 gallons per day—the greatest 5,000,000, the least 2,000,000. Water-meters are used, and are found very effective in stopping waste. The water-works are owned by a private company.

GAS.

The gas-works are not owned by the city. Their daily average production is 200,000 cubic feet, and the charge per 1,000 feet is $2 50. The city pays $22 per year for each street-lamp, there being 605 of them.

PUBLIC BUILDINGS.

The city owns a city hall, 4 engine-houses, a work-house, and a hospital. The total cost of the municipal buildings belonging to the city was about $20,000. The city hall was built 25 years ago, for city and county use, at a cost of about $16,000. It is now used entirely by the city.

PUBLIC PARKS AND PLEASURE-GROUNDS.

The city has one small park or block of ground, containing 2.11 acres, used originally for a cemetery, of which it retains possession from the fact of its still containing the remains of persons buried therein. There is no attempt at maintenance except mowing the grass.

PLACES OF AMUSEMENT.

The theaters of the city, with their seating capacities, are as follows: Coats' opera-house, 2,000; Theater Comique, 6,000; Coliseum theater, 800; Casino, 400. Jillis' opera-house, at present under construction, will probably have a seating capacity of 2,200. Theaters pay a license of $50 per year. There are 2 halls—the Board of Trade and the Turner. There are 3 small open-air gardens for concerts and refreshments. The attendance varies from 50 to 200 persons.

DRAINAGE.

The foundation of the sewerage-works of this city is a number of natural water-courses running in ravines, which were inclosed in stone conduits laid with lime and mortar. These channels were of various sizes and shapes, and are ill-adapted to the removal of foul sewage, but they are still used as main outlet-sewers. No plan has been made for the sewerage of the whole city, each case being provided for according to the ideas of the city authorities as to what is required. A distinction is made between what are called public sewers, which are paid for by the city, and district sewers, which are paid for by assessments on the drainage districts within which they lie.

The city is naturally divided into three drainage areas. What is known as West Kansas, above the railroad, is low and sandy, and, though quite densely peopled, is poorly provided with sewers. It has a stone sewer, about three-quarters of a mile long, discharging into the Missouri river, and a few pipe-sewers extending only one or two blocks. That portion of the city which faces the Missouri river rises to a high ridge at a distance of about 4,000 feet from the bank. This was originally cut by deep ravines, making a very uneven surface, and requiring expensive grading. Its principal drainage is to a sewer begun in 1860, laid along the bed of a water-course crossing streets and lots, and discharging into the river just below the public landing. It is of all shapes and sizes, and in both material and workmanship is so bad as to require constant outlay to restore portions which fall in. For a considerable portion of its length it has been buried to a depth of 40 feet or more. In 1878 a portion of this sewer, covered to a depth of 60 feet, caved in and had to be repaired at considerable expense. It forms the only outlet for the drainage of the most thickly settled portion of the city, from the river to Eleventh and Twelfth streets, and from Locust to Wyandotte street. This district contains about 3 miles of sewers, though only a small proportion of the length of streets within it was sewered.

Another outlet-sewer, 4 feet in diameter, discharges at the foot of Broadway, near the railroad bridge; another about 3,000 feet farther down the stream. A very large part of the city, and one most difficult to drain, lies on the southerly slope beyond the dividing ridge along Ninth and Eleventh streets. This drains naturally away from the river into a small stream about a mile and a half from the Missouri, running in an opposite direction to the Kansas river, and entering it about 2 miles from its mouth. This small stream is quite insufficient to carry away the sewage from the large area naturally draining to it. About 3½ miles of the sewers constructed in 1880 discharge into it at least 2 miles from the Kansas and 4 miles from the Missouri. It has been proposed to provide this district with an outlet-sewer, carried around by the water-works and through West Kansas, a distance of nearly 3 miles, to the Missouri river, which it would meet with a sharp bend above the city, rendering it probable that its extension along the front of the city, discharging into the river below, would become necessary.

The rates of fall in Kansas City are usually very rapid, and there has been no trouble from deposits requiring removal by hand. The sewers discharge below high-water mark, but are exposed during the greater part of the year. The only provision for ventilation is by perforations in the covers of manholes, save when the imperfectly constructed inlet-basins furnish an additional outlet. Many of these are being rebuilt. The sewers are circular and mostly of brick, but few pipes having thus far been used.

For purposes of assessment the city is divided into drainage districts, each of which pays for its own sewer, a system which has failed of popularity because of the difficulty of so arranging the districts as to equalize the tax. The low-lying districts along the river and the water-courses have the least value, but require the most expensive sewerage works, while the more valuable property, which is better able to pay taxes, lies in the higher portions, which are easily drained and require less expensive sewers. In some districts the tax has not exceeded 63 cents per hundred square feet of lot area, while in others it has reached $4 50.

The cost of sewers built in 1880 was as follows:

A sewer having an average depth of 14 feet, with much rock excavation, and being of brick, 3 feet in diameter, cost $7 per foot.

A sewer 2 feet in diameter, under the same conditions, cost $5 50 per foot, and 13-inch pipe, $4 50 per foot.

A sewer in good clay, with an average depth of 14 feet and a diameter of 3 feet (brick), cost $4 20 per foot.

A sewer in made ground, average depth 16 feet, diameter 3 feet (brick), cost $4 90 per foot.

A sewer partly in made ground, partly in good clay, and partly in solid rock, average depth 14 feet, 3 feet diameter (brick), cost $4 65 per foot; 2 feet diameter (brick), $3 10; 18-inch pipe, $3 50.

All of the above prices include manholes and inlet-basins. The average cost of each inlet-basin and its connection with the sewer is $50. The cost of each manhole is $30. The total amount of sewerage completed in 1880 amounted to over 7 miles.

CEMETERIES.

The city has 4 cemeteries, as follows:

Union Cemetery, situated three-fourths of a mile south of the city, containing 49 acres, in which there have been 4,819 interments.

Elmwood Cemetery, 2½ miles east of the city, containing 51 acres, in which the number of interments has been about 2,000.

Saint Paul's Cemetery, one-half mile south of the city, containing 14 acres, in which there have been 150 interments.

Saint Mary's Cemetery, 2½ miles northeast of the city, containing 45 acres; interments not ascertainable.

Union and Elmwood cemeteries are owned by stock companies, and the lots in them are sold according to location; each has macadamized roads. The other two are church burying-grounds.

MARKETS.

There is one market-house in the city, built on the north side of the public square. It cost about $8,000, and covers an area, including the platform around the building, of 65 by 150 feet. There are 16 stalls inside, 32 stands outside, and places for 32 wagons to back up against the walk. The market-house itself is a one-story brick building, built about twenty-five years ago. The greater part of the public square is also a part of the market-place. The rent of the butchers' stalls within averages $10 per month, and the stands rent for 25 cents each per day. The total revenue from this market in 1880 was $7,500. It is open from daylight till 11 a. m., and on Wednesdays and Saturdays from 3 to 9 p. m. also. Not over two-thirds of the farm produce brought to the city comes to the regular market. The fish and poultry business is almost entirely confined to the market-house, and the market butchers retail about one-fifth of the meat retailed in the city. The great packing-houses do most of the wholesale business.

SANITARY AUTHORITY—BOARD OF HEALTH.

The chief sanitary authority is the board of health, composed of the mayor, the chief of the fire department, the chief of police, the city physician (who is sanitary superintendent), and two other persons annually elected by the common council, one of whom shall be assistant sanitary superintendent, and the other the clerk of the board. The expenses of the board have so far been very small. The ordinance establishing it does not specifically define its powers in the presence or absence of epidemics, but gives general authority to abate nuisances and care for the public health. There are but two salaried officers—the assistant sanitary superintendent, with a salary of $75 per month, and the clerk, with a salary of $100 per year. The board has stated meetings monthly. The ordinance makes inspection duty devolve upon each officer of the police force as well as upon the assistant sanitary superintendent. Inspections are made continuously throughout the city, and attention is given to all complaints made to the board. When nuisances are reported a notice is served that said nuisance must be abated, and upon failure to do so within a given time the matter is put into the hands of the city attorney for prosecution. In regard to defective house-drainage, etc., the board has power to order the defects remedied, but upon failure to do so has no resort save power to prosecute for failure. The board has no fund with which to do this, but taxes the parties for the same. The ordinance specifies that garbage shall be collected by each household in receptacles, and the same shall be removed by the city authorities, but this summer the board of aldermen made no provision for such a purpose, each family providing for its own garbage.

INFECTIOUS DISEASES.

Small-pox patients are isolated in the pest-house, which is situated on an island in the Missouri river a mile below the city. Scarlet-fever patients are quarantined at home as well as can be done, and the building is placarded. Children from infected families are not permitted to attend school until given permission by the proper parties. The treatment and selection of a physician is left unrestrained. Vaccination is neither compulsory nor done at the public expense.

REPORTS.

The board, by its clerk, keeps a record of all marriages, births, and deaths in the city. It reports annually, or oftener if required, to the common council as to its proceedings, receipts, and expenditures, and the general sanitary condition of the city. It is stated that the board bears no special relation to the medical profession, and is in many respects yet in a crude state, but efforts are being made to make it more efficient.

MUNICIPAL CLEANSING.

Street-cleaning.—Street-cleaning is done by the city by its own force, and by hand, only those streets being cleaned which are closely built upon and heavily traveled. It is reported that it is done whenever it is needed; the city usually waits until three inches or more of mud accumulates, and that it is not well done. The expense to the city is about $2,500 annually. The sweepings are usually deposited along the river-bank or in some deep ravine, without any system.

Garbage and ashes.—Garbage is removed by householders, and is generally dumped into the river. Ashes are not usually removed. No complaints are made of the final disposition of garbage. The defect in the system lies in the lack of sufficient regulations and the non-enforcement of what regulations do exist.

Dead animals.—The city annually contracts with some private party for the removal of dead animals. There are no regulations on the subject. Such as are suitable are tanked, and the rest are buried and thrown into the river. The annual cost is about $400. The service in this respect is very irregular.

Liquid household wastes.—Chamber and kitchen slops are disposed of in the same way. About one-tenth of the liquid household waste of the city goes into the sewers, the rest into vaults, cesspools, or gutters. But a small portion goes into dry wells, cesspools, or gutters. The cesspools have few overflows, since the soil is porous clay. Such as there are usually empty into alleys or gutters. Street-gutters are cleaned and flushed when the streets are cleaned, and oftener if needed in case of continuous dry weather. Where cesspools or dry wells are used they receive the waste of water-closets. Previous to the construction of the water-works nothing but cisterns were used. A large part of the city now uses water from the water company, and wells are scarce, such as there are being looked upon with suspicion.

Human excreta.—About one-twentieth of the houses of the city have water-closets, the remainder depending upon privy-vaults. About one-third of the water-closets deliver into the public sewers, and the rest into cesspools. None of the privy-vaults are nominally water-tight. There are no regulations regarding their construction. While there are certain rules laid down as to emptying them, there is no system and no attempt at regulating such matters. The dry-earth system is used very little. Night-soil is taken to the river.

Manufacturing wastes.—There are no regulations governing the disposal of manufacturing wastes.

POLICE.

The police force of the city is appointed by the mayor and two commissioners, the former of whom is elected annually, and the latter are appointed by the governor of the state for a term of three years. All orders are issued by the chief of police, who is the chief executive officer. He has general supervision of the entire department, and his salary is $2,000 per annum. The rest of the force, with their salaries, are as follows: 1 captain, $1,140; 1 clerk, $900; 2 sergeants, $930; 2 roundsmen and 2 detectives, $780 each; 1 officer for special duty, 2 jailers, 2 mounted police, and 25 patrolmen, $750 each. Their uniform is blue, with brass buttons, and each man furnishes his own at a cost of $75. They also furnish their own side-arms and equipments. They carry Colt's revolvers, 14-inch clubs, and nippers. The department has an armory consisting of a Gatling gun, 60 Springfield rifles, and 60 revolvers. The tours of duty are 12 hours per day, and the men patrol 89 miles of streets. Last year there were 3,877 arrests, principally for intoxication. About $8,000 worth of stolen property was recovered and returned to the owners. There were about 2,000 station-house lodgers during 1880, about the same as in 1879. A very few meals were furnished, at a cost of 12 cents per meal. The police force is required to co-operate with the fire department in removing goods and guarding property; with the health department in serving notices, inspecting alleys, vaults, etc., and with the building department in noting dangerous places in the streets and sidewalks, and violations of building ordinances. Special policemen are appointed by the commissioners to act as railroad and merchant police and as night watchmen. They are under the control of the chief, and assist the regular force when called upon. Specials wear a gray uniform. The yearly cost of the police force is $38,000. Since 1874 the police department has been operated upon the metropolitan system, which has been found very satisfactory; officers and patrolmen are appointed for three years, and are removed only for cause after trial and examination. On the reorganization preference is given to those in the service. The standard height is 5 feet 10 inches; standard weight, 185 pounds; average age, 33 years.

FIRE DEPARTMENT.

The city ordinances provide, among other things, that the more thickly settled portion of the city shall be divided into two fire districts, and that within their limits both outside and party-walls of new buildings shall be built of brick, stone, or some other incombustible material; outer walls shall be not less than 1 foot thick, and in case of buildings more than two stories in height the walls of basement and first story shall be at least 16 inches thick; walls of 3 inches less thickness will be allowed in dwellings; party-walls must extend 12 inches above the roof; roofs and chimneys must be made of some incombustible material; smoke-pipes must enter flues at least 12 inches from the ceiling; there must be 2 inches space between wood-work and flues filled in with mortar; the openings of theaters and public halls are to be not less than 5 feet in width and not less than 18 inches for every 100 seating capacity, and doors of all public places must swing outward. The fire department is composed of a chief engineer, with a salary of $1,200 per year, 3 hose companies of 5 men each, 1 hose company of 3 men, and a hook-and-ladder company of 2 men. The monthly pay-roll of the department, exclusive of the salary of the chief, is $958 33. In the current year the expenses of the department were $16,253 85; 118 calls were answered, and property valued at $342,310 was destroyed, on which there was $296,400 insurance. The alarm in 98 cases out of 118 was given by telephone. The principal causes of the fires were defective flues, 23 being due to them. The loss from the largest fire was $40,000 on building and $340,000 on stock, the insurance being $264,500.

MANUFACTURES.

The following is a summary of the statistics of the manufactures of Kansas City for 1880, being taken from tables prepared for the Tenth Census by E. J. Nickerson, special agent:

Mechanical and manufacturing industries.	No. of establishments.	Capital.	Males above 16 years.	Females above 15 years.	Children and youths.	Total amount paid in wages during the year.	Value of materials.	Value of products.
All industries	224	$2,147,305	2,127	233	188	$1,420,713	$3,723,916	$6,382,681
Blacksmithing (see also Wheelwrighting)	17	12,850	47	....	1	29,800	18,000	73,200
Boots and shoes, including custom work and repairing	18	7,575	42	....	2	24,600	21,225	63,281
Bread and other bakery products	8	82,700	76	20	5	56,350	284,600	366,300
Brick and tile	15	75,000	315	....	87	163,020	51,392	369,900
Brooms and brushes	3	1,700	12	....	2	5,300	5,725	17,000
Carpentering	26	45,150	279	....	....	202,300	447,050	775,500
Carriages and wagons (see also Wheelwrighting)	5	29,000	44	....	....	25,800	41,900	105,000
Clothing, men's	5	41,344	71	4	....	48,334	96,120	165,436
Confectionery	5	6,200	10	4	6	8,250	14,800	27,000
Flouring- and grist-mill products	4	71,500	56	....	....	27,300	581,400	683,450

Mechanical and manufacturing industries.	No. of establishments.	Capital.	AVERAGE NUMBER OF HANDS EMPLOYED.			Total amount paid in wages during the year.	Value of materials.	Value of products.
			Males above 16 years.	Females above 15 years.	Children and youths.			
Foundery and machine-shop products..........................	8	$221,500	207	....	8	$129,770	$243,500	$471,000
Furniture...	7	2,825	13	....	....	8,050	14,200	30,000
Lumber, planed...	4	46,000	71	....	....	43,800	92,000	206,000
Marble and stone work......................................	4	16,200	29	....	2	15,300	26,100	54,000
Painting and paperhanging..................................	5	4,100	28	....	....	18,920	22,570	55,500
Paints..	3	120,000	41	....	....	20,000	180,000	255,000
Photographing..	3	6,750	9	2	....	6,400	4,350	18,600
Printing and publishing....................................	4	255,000	159	49	12	152,800	130,000	432,000
Saddlery and harness.......................................	8	23,400	35	1	....	19,156	46,580	85,500
Slaughtering and meat-packing, not including retail butchering.....	3	437,500	253	....	35	166,500	739,071	965,000
Tinware, copperware, and sheet-iron ware.....................	4	11,400	18	....	....	8,550	20,450	37,000
Tobacco, cigars and cigarettes..............................	13	70,200	75	....	9	50,860	109,050	210,600
Wheelwrighting (see also Blacksmithing; Carriages and wagons)...	4	6,500	12	....	....	5,800	4,400	14,100
All other industries (a)....................................	48	551,911	225	153	21	183,753	529,433	902,314

a Embracing awnings and tents; bags, other than paper; baking and yeast powders; bookbinding and blank-book making; boxes, wooden packing; carpets, rag; cement; cheese and butter (factory); clothing, women's; drain and sewer pipe; engraving and die-sinking; furniture, chairs, hand-stamps; hats and caps; iron work, architectural and ornamental; liquors, distilled; liquors, malt; looking-glass and picture frames; mattresses and spring beds; mineral and soda waters; models and patterns; patent medicines and compounds; refrigerators; roofing and roofing materials; shipbuilding; shirts; show-cases; soap and candles; tools; trunks and valises; upholstering; vinegar; watch and clock repairing; and wire.

From the foregoing table it appears that the average capital of all establishments is $9,586 18; that the average wages of all hands employed is $557 58 per annum; and that the average outlay in wages, in materials, and in interest (at 6 per cent.) on capital employed is $23,542 26.

SAINT JOSEPH,

BUCHANAN COUNTY, MISSOURI.

POPULATION

IN THE

AGGREGATE,

1860-1880.

	Inhab.
1790	......
1800	......
1810	......
1820	......
1830	......
1840	......
1850	......
1860	8,932
1870	19,565
1880	32,431

POPULATION

BY

SEX, NATIVITY, AND RACE,

AT

CENSUS OF 1880.

Male	17,832
Female	14,599
Native	26,775
Foreign-born	5,656
White	29,201
Colored	*3,230

*Including 2 Chinese and 1 Indian.

Latitude: 39° 45' North; Longitude: 94° 53' (west from Greenwich); **Altitude: 837 to 1,021 feet.**

FINANCIAL CONDITION:

Total Valuation: $8,508,529; per capita: $265 00.   Net Indebtedness: $1,843,662; per capita: $56 85.   Tax per $100: $2 00.

HISTORICAL SKETCH.(a)

Saint Joseph was founded by Joseph Robidoux, a French Roman Catholic, who was born in Saint Louis in 1784, and who was one of the most noted pioneers of the West. About the time when the general government incorporated the territory of Louisiana (1803) Robidoux left Saint Louis for the then wild country of the west to trade with the Indians. Selecting a beautiful spot among the hills on the bank of the Missouri, 545 miles from its mouth, he built a hut and began trafficking with the red men, by whom the country round about was thickly inhabited. In 1840 the rich country surrounding this trading point, known as the "Platte Purchase", was opened to settlement by treaty with the Indians. The fertile land was rapidly taken up, and the settlement immediately became the principal frontier town west of the Mississippi. In June, 1843, the original town was laid out by Mr. Robidoux

---

a For the greater part of the information concerning Saint Joseph the Census Office is under obligations to General R. C. Bradshaw, late city register and assessor.

and named Saint Joseph. Two years later the county-seat was removed from Sparta to Saint Joseph, and most of the buildings and people of the former place moved with it. In 1849 the town became the great outfitting point for emigrants and gold-seekers leaving the states for California, it lying directly on the great highway across the plains. In February, 1851, with a population of about 4,000, it became a city, having been incorporated as a town in February, 1845. In February, 1859, the Hannibal and Saint Joseph railroad, the first road to penetrate so far west, was completed to this city, and from that time on Saint Joseph made rapid strides in wealth and population. In the following year the famous "pony express", designed to transmit quickly a limited mail from the states to San Francisco, was started from the city. The war period was a gloomy one. The government occupied and fortified the city, and it became a point for the centralization and distribution of troops. The population had dwindled to about 7,000 in 1865, but the return of peace brought prosperity again, an immense trade flowed in, and the city grew rapidly. On May 31, 1873, it celebrated the completion of a magnificent iron railway bridge across the Missouri river, costing $1,500,000. The first church was built in 1845; there are now 28 in the city. The first school was opened in 1846; the city now claims to have some of the best public schools in the West. The only period of depression in the history of the city was the war period. Since the war many people have removed to the city from the southern states.

SAINT JOSEPH IN 1880.

The following statistical accounts, mainly gathered by the Census Office, indicate the present condition of the city:

LOCATION.

Saint Joseph, the capital of Buchanan county, Missouri, lies in latitude 39° 45' north, longitude 94° 53' west from Greenwich, on the left (east) bank of the Missouri river, 340 miles above Jefferson City, and 496 miles by water from Saint Louis. The altitude of its lowest point, for which was taken the high-water mark reached by the river in 1844, is 837 feet above the level of the sea; the highest point in the city is 1,021 feet above sea-level. The Missouri is navigable, but the channel at this point is constantly changing both in position and in depth.

RAILROAD COMMUNICATIONS.

The city is well supplied with railroad communications. Her five railroads are as follows:
The Saint Joseph and Western division of the Union Pacific, running from Saint Joseph to the main line at Grand Island.
The Hannibal and Saint Joseph, connecting the two cities named.
The Saint Joseph division of the Wabash, Saint Louis, and Pacific, connecting at Lexington junction with the Kansas City line, which gives a road to Saint Louis and the East.
The Kansas City, Saint Joseph, and Council Bluffs railroad, connecting the places named.
The Saint Joseph and Des Moines railroad, reaching at present only to Albany, but with Des Moines as its objective point.

TRIBUTARY COUNTRY.

The region around Saint Joseph is very fertile, and its inhabitants are wholly devoted to agriculture. The soil is very rich, chiefly alluvial. Buchanan county is intersected by the Little Platte river, which flows southward, and is drained also by Castile and Livingston creeks.

TOPOGRAPHY.

The soil of the city is known to geologists as "loess", which is a name given to the "bluff formation" of the rivers of the West. The loess is simply a river-silt, just such as now renders the waters of the Missouri so remarkably turbid, and is merely a facing to the rocky bluffs which form the true walls of the river valleys. The country on the Missouri bluffs at Saint Joseph is rolling and well timbered; that in the bottoms is entirely at the mercy of the river; in the present year, for example, the entire country being inundated from bluff to bluff, an average distance of 4.5 miles. The underlying rock is limestone. For a radius of 5 miles about the country is well cultivated, with alternating wood and open land. The former channel of the river has left a few small lakes and ponds.

CLIMATE.

No definite data is given as to the temperature of the city, but it varies from about —20° in winter to 105° in summer. The influence of the marshes is malarial. The air is generally very dry in the summer time, this being especially noticeable this summer (1880), when, notwithstanding the intense and long-continued heat, only two cases of sunstroke were reported.

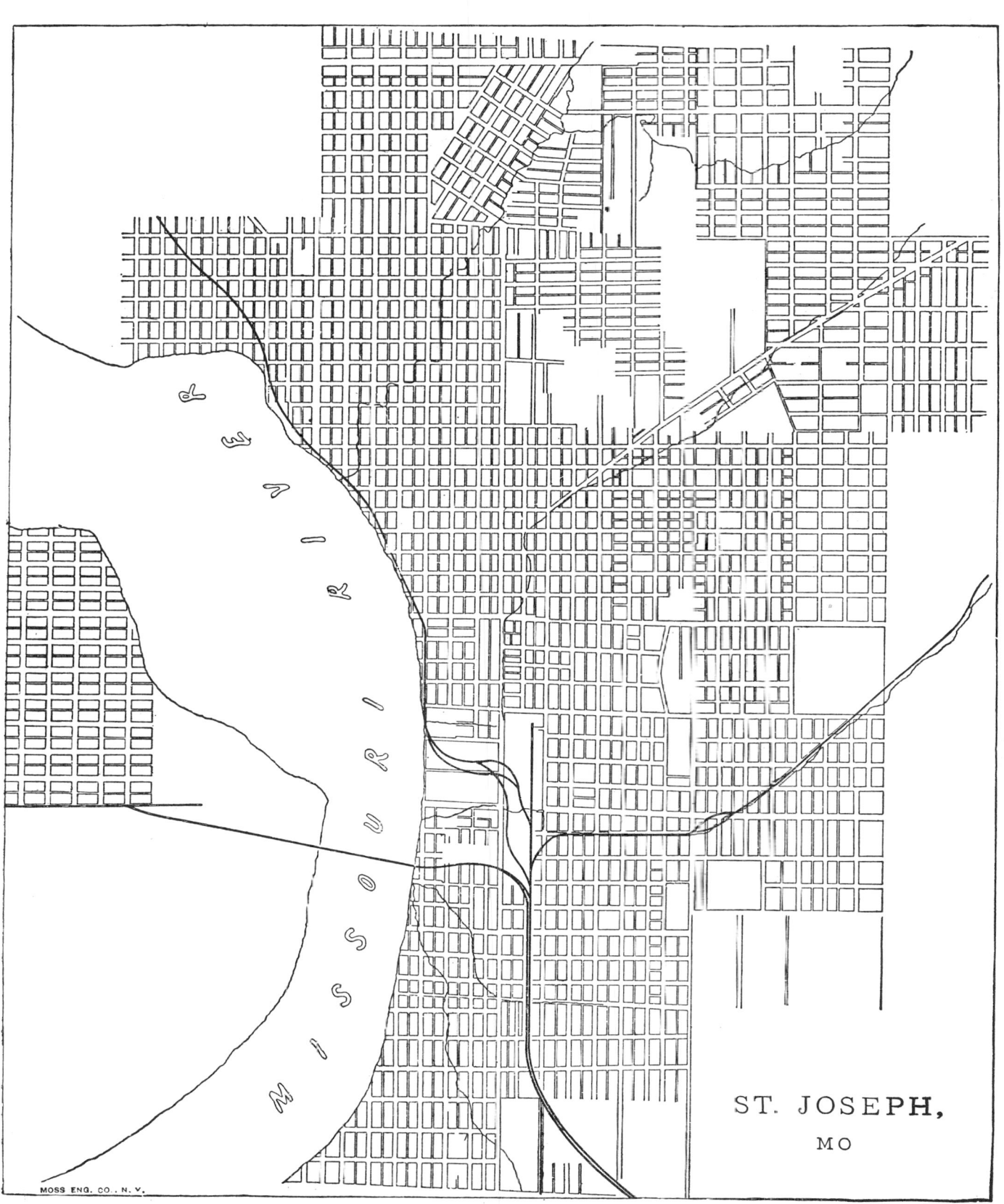

ST. JOSEPH,
MO

STREETS.

Total length, 112 miles, of which 24 are paved with cobble-stones, the original cost being 60 cents per square yard. This paving is kept in repair at the cost of the adjacent property-owners. The quality of the stone used is frequently very inferior. The sidewalks in the business portion of the city are made of brick and sawed sandstone, and, in the portion devoted to residences, of brick. From two fifths to one-half the streets occupied by residences are provided with shade-trees, set just inside the curb-line. The construction and repair of streets is done by contract, at so much per square, at the expense of the adjacent property-owners, who have the right to contract for the same when the city council orders it done; but in case of their failure to do the work themselves or make contracts for its performance the city makes the contracts and assesses them. It is reported that the preference is decidedly in favor of the contract system. A steam stone-crusher is partially used in crushing rock, but no roller of any kind is employed.

HORSE-RAILROADS.

The city has three horse-railroads, with a total length of 6 miles of track, 32 cars, about 110 horses, and employing about 30 men. The rate of fare is 5 cents.

WATER-WORKS.

The total cost of the works for water-supply was $700,000. Water is pumped, under the Worthington system, from the Missouri river, north of the city, to reservoirs at a distance of 1,000 feet, and with an elevation of 320 feet, giving an effective head in the city of from 50 to 135 feet, according to location. The greatest amount pumped in one day was 5,000,000 gallons; the least 2,000,000. The average cost of raising 1,000,000 gallons 1 foot high is 9 cents. The yearly income from water-rates is estimated at about $124,000.

GAS.

The gas-works are not owned by the city. The daily average production is 30,000 feet, and the charge per 1,000 feet is $2 50. The city pays $25 per annum each for street-lamps, there being 430 of them.

PUBLIC BUILDINGS

The city owns and occupies for municipal purposes, wholly or in part, the city hall, costing $50,000; the city work-house, costing $5,000; hospital, $2,000; and markets, $5,000.

PUBLIC PARKS AND PLEASURE-GROUNDS.

There are 3 parks with an area of 2 acres each; one is thickly set with forest trees, but there are no improvements on the others. They were donated, the city having spent only a few hundred dollars in fencing them.

PLACES OF AMUSEMENT.

There is 1 theater, Tootle's opera house, with a seating capacity of 1,500, paying no license; there are 2 halls, Turner hall and Red-Ribbon hall, seating about 300 each. There are 3 beer-gardens, but the buildings were not built for such a purpose, and are cheap and inferior.

DRAINAGE.

The sewerage-works of this city consist principally of main sewers built of brick, located in ravines or other convenient lines for main drainage. About 4 miles of such sewers have been built, of about equal proportions, being 10 feet, 6 feet, and 5 feet in diameter. The sewage is delivered into the Missouri river, the outfalls being open and fully exposed for about ten months of the year, and submerged during high stages of the river. Lateral sewers are built according to the requirements of each case—sometimes of brick and sometimes of vitrified pipes. Storm-water is admitted through inlet-basins, which are usually left open for the ventilation of the sewers. Flushing is done during the summer season with water supplied from the water company's mains without charge, the labor being furnished by the fire department. There is no map showing any general plan of sewerage. It is reported that the need of such a plan is apparent, large sewers having in some cases already been made to discharge into those of smaller size. Main sewers are paid for by the city, and about $200,000 has been expended on these works. Lateral sewers are built under an act of the Missouri legislature, "authorizing cities acting under special charters, and containing more than 30,000 and less than 50,000 inhabitants, to establish a system of sewerage, and to construct, establish, and keep in repair sewers, culverts, and drains". By the provision of this act the cost of lateral sewers is assessed upon abutting property, the assessment bills being given to the contractor for collection. Assessments are based on the frontage of lots, and the amount expended in this way has been about $18,000.

The cost of constructing sewers is as follows: For sewers 6 feet in diameter, 2 rings of brick, the contractor furnishing all labor and materials, average depth to bottom of invert 10 to 16 feet, soil alluvial, digging very good, no rock, contract price $5 70 per foot. Sewers 5 feet in diameter, under the above conditions, $4 80 per foot. Fifteen-inch pipe sewers, 14 feet deep, digging less favorable, in some cases very bad, no rock, some quicksand, a Y-branch for house-connection every 20 feet, the contractors repairing pavement and road-beds, contract price $3 73 per linear foot. Eighteen-inch pipe, under the same conditions, $3 93 per foot. The average cost of inlet-basins is $28, and of manholes $18.

CEMETERIES.

There are 8 cemeteries, as follows: 2 Catholic, 1 Baptist, 1 Lutheran, 1 Jewish, 1 City, 1 Freemason, and Mount Mora. The last-named is 10 acres in extent, while the others are small. They are all outside the city. There is no limit of time imposed as to burials, it being generally twenty-four to thirty hours after death. The depth of grave is from 4½ to 6 feet, according to age of deceased and location of ground. The Jewish cemetery is exclusively for Jews; the Catholic, for Catholics; the Freemason, for Freemasons; the City, for paupers. In the others lots are sold to whoever will buy. Mount Mora cemetery is handsomely laid out. There is a vault in it, but at present it is not fit for use. One of the Catholic cemeteries, known as the Carby grave-yard, about 2 miles north of the city, contains a mortuary chapel, built at a cost of some $30,000.

MARKETS.

The ground floor of the city hall is used as the central market. There are 10 butchers' stalls around the walls, and in the center there are long tables for vegetable markets and florists' stands; also, there are tables outside the walls for summer use. The market is open from 5 a. m. to 11 a. m., and in summer on Saturdays from 3 p. m. to 7 p. m. also. Most of the butchers buy their animals direct from drovers or farmers. There are two cattle- and hog-yards, one owned by the city and the other by railroad men, where cattle are always found for sale. Hucksters have to be licensed, marketmen and retailers of fresh provisions generally being included under that head. Peddlers also must be licensed.

SANITARY AUTHORITY—BOARD OF HEALTH.

The chief health organization is a board of health, consisting of one councilman from each ward (5), and the health officer, the hospital steward acting as clerk. Although it is composed of members of the council, its acts are independent. When there is no epidemic its annual expenses are from $3,000 to $4,000. In any case it is limited to the appropriations made by the city council. Its duties are to see that all laws and ordinances relating to the sanitary well-being of the city are properly enforced, to visit the city hospital and see that patients are properly cared for, to employ nurses and inspectors, to order the abatement of nuisances, and to direct the payment of bills contracted by the board. During epidemics its duties are to establish quarantine stations, and to do and perform all things necessary to abate the epidemic. The chief executive officer of the board is the health officer, whose salary is $500 per year. A hospital steward and from one to three nuisance-inspectors are employed. Only the health officer is a physician, and none of them have police powers. Inspectors report any person violating the health ordinances to the city attorney, and then the attorney files a complaint before the city recorder, who issues his warrant for arrest. Then the accused is brought before the court, and if found guilty is fined. During the summer months tours of inspection are supposed to be regularly made to all parts of the city; in cool weather they are made only upon reports of nuisances. The board is appointed annually by the mayor; it is dependent upon the city council for appropriations to pay its bills; it meets monthly, but may adjourn from day to day. Defective house-drainage, etc., is treated like any other nuisance, no action being taken except in case of complaint. The street commissioner is required to keep the streets clean, and to report to the city recorder any person who may deposit in any street, avenue, or alley any garbage, filth, ashes, etc.; said officer is also required to keep the sewers free and in good condition. The board has full power to require the removal, at the expense of the householder, of the garbage, offal, etc. The only regulation concerning the burial of the dead seems to be that the sexton shall be furnished with a certificate from the attending physician, stating age, sex, and cause of death. The city ordinances prohibit the pollution of the water in the two creeks running through the city, and impose a fine for any violation thereof.

INFECTIOUS DISEASES.

In case of small-pox, public patients are isolated in the pest-house; the families of private patients are quarantined. There is no law concerning scarlet-fever patients. There have never been any cases of serious contagious diseases in the schools, but the board has power to act as it may see fit should the emergency arise. There is a public pest house, situated on a high bluff of the river and isolated. Vaccination is compulsory, but the law has never been enforced; in cases of indigent persons it is done at the expense of the city.

REGISTRATION AND REPORTS.

The system of registration of diseases and births and deaths is very defective. The people have not yet learned the benefits of statistics, and look upon laws requiring statistical information as an invasion of individual rights.

No reports are required of the board; the health officer reports annually to the mayor, but his reports are not published. There are two medical colleges in the city. Saint Joseph has been blessed with uniform good health since its incorporation.

MUNICIPAL CLEANSING.

Street cleaning.—The streets are cleaned by the city's own force under the management of the street commissioner, and wholly by hand. In the business part of the city it is done about every two weeks, and done very poorly. The annual cost to the city is about $10,000. Sweepings are deposited in the river, the place being well selected. As a whole the system is very defective, but the class benefited by it, together with the force of habit, are powerful enough to continue it.

Removal of garbage and ashes.—The ordinances require that householders shall remove garbage before it becomes offensive, but the law is poorly enforced. Part of the work is done, however, by the city's force. What they do not take scavengers gather up, and use what they can of it for feeding hogs, the rest being thrown into the river. There is probably some injury to health in a few cases from improper treatment of garbage, but this is rare. The system is poor and is indifferently executed.

Dead animals.—Dead animals are removed by the owner if known; if not, then by the street commissioner, who disposes of them to a glue factory south of the city, or deposits them in the Missouri.

Liquid household wastes.—Chamber slops, laundry waste, and kitchen-slops are all disposed of in the same way, a small part only going into the public sewers because the sewer system is not yet complete. Perhaps one-half goes into cesspools or dry wells on the premises. These are generally porous, and no provision is made for overflows; they do not receive the waste of water-closets. In the past the rain has done all the flushing of street-gutters, the water-works being just in process of completion. The overflow and underground escape of cesspools and privy-vaults has been very injurious to drinking-water and to health in the old or business portion of the city; in the residence portion the people have relied on cisterns built with brick and cemented. Ordinances require the cleaning out of cesspools, but the law is not enforced.

Human excreta.—The entire population has depended on privy-vaults except a very small portion residing near the main sewers. None of these vaults are nominally water-tight. The ordinances require that they shall be sunk to a depth of not less than 8 feet, and must be emptied or cleaned when they become offensive to neighbors or to passers-by, but as a rule they have not been enforced. The dry-earth system is very little used. Night-soil is generally deposited in the river between the hours of 10 p. m. and 4 a. m.; it is not allowed to be used for manuring land within the gathering-ground of the public water-supply.

Manufacturing wastes.—Liquid manufacturing wastes are conducted by sewer to the river; the solid wastes from wood manufactories are consumed as fuel; those of iron-, tin-, copper-, bone-, and horn-works are collected and shipped east.

POLICE.

The police force is appointed by the mayor and city council, who have general supervision over it and the right to dismiss any of its members for cause. The chief executive officer is the marshal, who has the general management of the force, and whose salary is $50 per month. There are 20 patrolmen and 2 special policemen. Their uniform, which they provide themselves, is dark navy blue; clubs are furnished by the city, but the men provide their own revolvers. Their hours of service are from 7 p. m. to 7 a. m., and they patrol about 20 miles of streets. In 1880 there were 1,712 arrests, intoxication being the chief cause; of these, 1,013 were dismissed on payment of fine, 686 were sent to the work-house, and 13 were discharged. Free meals were given to station-house lodgers, but as to the number of lodgers, or meals, or cost of meals no record was kept. The police force is required to co-operate with the fire department to the extent of preserving order and preventing theft at fires, and with the health department in reporting violations of the sanitary laws of the city to the city recorder. Two special policemen are appointed by the mayor, and are subject to his orders and those of the city marshal; they are separate from the patrolmen. The cost of the police force for 1880 was $12,572.

SCHOOLS.

The following details concerning the schools of the city were taken from the report of the superintendent for the year ending September 1, 1879: The total number of children of school age for the year was 7,658. The city occupied 19 school-houses, of which 10 were rented; the value of the school property owned by the city January 1, 1880, was $122,560. There was 1 high school, with 5 teachers and an attendance of 177; 15 district schools, with 47 teachers and an attendance of 3,087; 2 colored schools, with 4 teachers and an attendance of 427. The total attendance was 3,691, but the average daily attendance was only 2,521. One of the schools is a German-English school, in which 450 pupils were enrolled last year. The total expenditures for the year were $52,263 50, and this was $8,575 73 more than the receipts. The bonded indebtedness of the school board is $50,000. There is great need of more school-houses. Besides the public schools there are numerous private institutions of learning in the city, among them being the College of Saint Joseph, with an attendance of 160 students. Saint Patrick's parochial school, with 100 students; the Convent of the Sacred Heart, with 68 boarders and 40 day pupils, with which is connected a parochial school with 100 pupils; and the school of the Immaculate Conception, with about 200 pupils—all of which are Catholic institutions; Saint Joseph Female College, a flourishing school; the Young Ladies' Institute, with 83 scholars, and other smaller Protestant and non-sectarian institutions.

MANUFACTURES.

The following is a summary of the statistics of the manufactures of Saint Joseph for 1880, being taken from tables prepared for the Tenth Census by Willis M. Sherwood, special agent:

Mechanical and manufacturing industries.	No. of establishments.	Capital.	AVERAGE NUMBER OF HANDS EMPLOYED.			Total amount paid in wages during the year.	Value of materials.	Value of products.
			Males above 16 years.	Females above 15 years.	Children and youths.			
All industries..........................	238	$1,423,650	2,040	94	124	$896,762	$3,210,080	$5,143,585
Blacksmithing..........................	19	18,650	29	....	2	14,145	18,710	51,000
Boots and shoes, including custom work and repairing	15	55,100	65	10	....	40,686	88,030	156,400
Brick and tile.........................	10	31,860	208	....	57	71,235	41,050	146,055
Carpentering	30	31,450	316	....	....	141,356	229,264	453,950
Carriages and wagons	9	22,800	52	....	3	26,716	25,500	67,850
Clothing, men's........................	14	17,350	39	14	....	19,350	46,000	88,150
Cooperage	8	12,150	49	....	4	20,312	28,300	57,200
Drugs and chemicals...................	3	22,850	9	5	2	5,190	11,625	46,500
Flouring- and grist-mill products	4	108,000	38	....	....	14,400	292,924	338,056
Furniture..............................	4	75,350	106	....	3	49,300	23,100	96,750
Liquors, malt..........................	5	200,000	44	....	....	21,492	92,582	165,325
Lock- and gun-smithing................	3	4,400	4	....	....	2,180	4,200	9,200
Marble and stone work	4	68,000	77	....	1	35,600	35,500	87,500
Masonry, brick and stone..............	5	10,750	71	....	....	32,390	44,200	93,500
Painting and paperhanging	14	10,150	51	....	....	18,887	20,750	55,900
Photographing.........................	5	4,700	7	2	....	4,408	6,550	21,000
Printing and publishing	8	129,500	112	....	11	85,040	69,708	194,250
Saddlery and harness	8	81,400	84	....	5	52,096	164,485	275,800
Slaughtering and meat-packing, not including retail butchering.....	5	134,500	190	....	14	37,290	1,224,208	1,439,843
Tinware, copperware, and sheet-iron ware...........................	10	37,700	63	....	....	30,925	83,200	139,700
Tobacco, cigars and cigarettes.........	12	20,950	53	5	5	27,397	60,291	118,340
All other industries (a)	43	326,040	373	58	17	146,367	599,903	1,041,316

a Embracing baking and yeast powders; bluing; bookbinding and blank-book making; boxes, wooden packing; bread and other bakery products; bridges; brooms and brushes; coffee and spices, roasted and ground; coffins, burial cases, and undertakers' goods; confectionery; coppersmithing; electroplating; foundery and machine-shop products; fruits and vegetables, canned and preserved; grease and tallow; hosiery and knit goods; looking-glass and picture frames; lumber, planed; mattresses and spring beds; mineral and soda waters; patent medicines and compounds; plumbing and gasfitting; pumps; roofing and roofing materials shirts; show-cases; stone- and earthen-ware; trunks and valises; upholstering; vinegar; wheelwrighting; whips; and woolen goods.

From the foregoing table it appears that the average capital of all establishments is $5,981 72; that the average wages of all hands employed is $397 14 per annum; and that the average outlay in wages, in materials, and in interest (at 6 per cent.) on capital employed is $17,614 54.

SAINT LOUIS,

SAINT LOUIS COUNTY, MISSOURI.

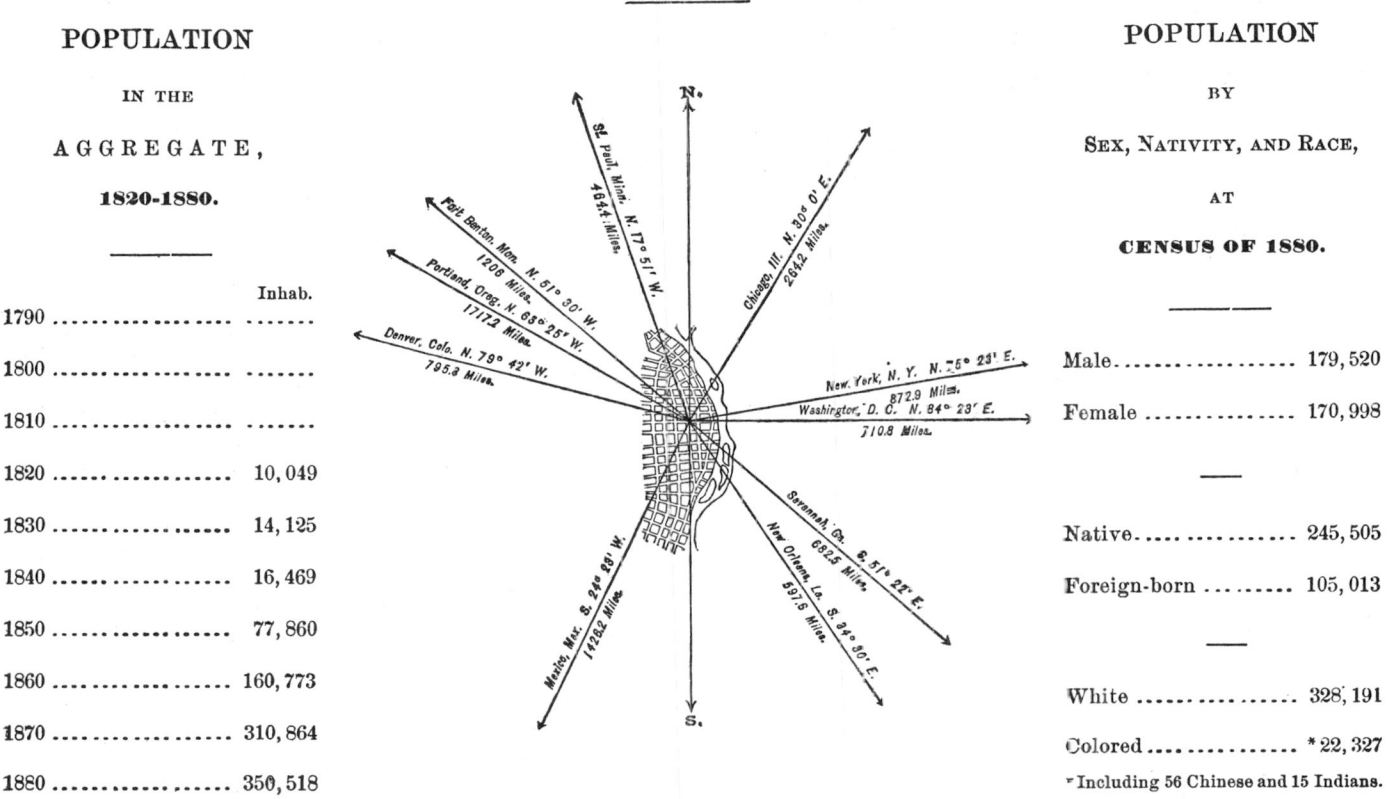

POPULATION

IN THE

AGGREGATE,

1820-1880.

	Inhab.
1790	....
1800	....
1810	....
1820	10,049
1830	14,125
1840	16,469
1850	77,860
1860	160,773
1870	310,864
1880	350,518

POPULATION

BY

SEX, NATIVITY, AND RACE,

AT

CENSUS OF 1880.

Male	179,520
Female	170,998
Native	245,505
Foreign-born	105,013
White	328,191
Colored	*22,327

*Including 56 Chinese and 15 Indians.

Latitude: 38° 37′ North; Longitude: 90° 12′ (west from Greenwich); Altitude: 374 to 610 feet.

FINANCIAL CONDITION:

Total Valuation: $165,288,400; per capita: $472 00.   Net Indebtedness: $22,847,761; per capita: $65 18.   Tax per $100: $2 23.

HISTORICAL SKETCH.(a)

EARLY SETTLEMENT.

It was nearly two centuries and a quarter after the brilliant but unfortunate expedition of De Soto, eighty years after the last exploration of La Salle, and forty years after the founding of New Orleans, before the vast resources

---

a Professor S. Waterhouse, of Washington University, Saint Louis, not only secured many of the statistics and much of the detailed information regarding the present condition of the city, but to him alone is due the careful and valuable historical sketch, from the settlement to the incorporation of Saint Louis, with which this report is introduced. But the necessity of shortening a sketch too long for the allotted space has required the omission of a large amount of subject-matter, together with copious notes and citations of authorities; and the readjustments of connection in a narrative interrupted by this abridgment have compelled frequent departures from the exact words of the author.

of the valley of the upper Mississippi began to attract the attention of commercial enterprise. In 1762 the firm of Maxent, Laclede, & Company obtained from the governor-general of Louisiana an exclusive control of the fur-trade with the Missouri and other tribes of Indians, as far north as the river Saint Peter, and the company immediately took steps to avail itself of the valuable privilege of its charter. Laclede, the junior member of the firm, was directed to select a site for a trading-post in upper Louisiana, and under the royal license and the instructions of his firm, he at once began active preparations for his expedition. In the cumbersome boats of that period, heavily laden with goods for the Indian trade, and manned by a hardy band of pioneers, Laclede left New Orleans on August 5, 1763. There were but few villages at that time even along the banks of the lower Mississippi, but for 700 miles from Natchez stretched an unbroken wilderness, which was peopled only by savages. After months of weary toil, the expedition reached Sainte Genevieve, the only French settlement on the west side of the river. There is legal evidence of its existence in 1754. Its origin is assigned by tradition to about 1735. Not finding there the accommodations he desired for his goods, he continued his trip to fort De Chartres, the commandant of that post, M. de Villiers, having offered him the necessary shelter. The expedition was just three months in making the voyage from New Orleans to fort De Chartres.

Leaving his merchandise and some of his men at the fort, Laclede, with a few companions, set out to accomplish the object of his mission. He ascended the stream to the mouth of the Missouri, and, after carefully observing all the natural advantages of situation as well as the merits of several locations, chose the spot on which Saint Louis now stands as the site for his trading-post, being about 50 miles above fort De Chartres. Its local superiority relieved him of the embarrassment of a doubtful choice. High, salubrious, and central, the situation possessed the twofold excellence of fitness for healthful residence and of matchless facilities for commercial exchange. Indeed, so favorably did the advantages of the place strike Laclede, that on his return to fort de Chartres he told M. de Villiers that "he had found a situation where he intended to establish a settlement which might become hereafter one of the finest cities of America". The winter months were spent in active preparations for the future settlement, and an open spring permitted an early resumption of the work of colonization. Before leaving the site of his trading-post Laclede had marked the trees so as to indicate the spot, and early in the following year he sent Auguste Chouteau, with a party of about 30 men, to clear the site and to put up temporary shelters. Chouteau reached the spot February 14, 1764, and on the following day began the humble labors which subsequent events have rendered memorable. His party cleared a space in the primeval forest, sheltered themselves with temporary scaffoldings, and then built a tool-shed and a few log huts. These buildings, the rude beginning of a metropolitan greatness, were erected on the block, as now laid out, where Barnum's hotel stands. Laclede selected a site for his own residence and laid out a plan for the future village.

Saint Louis owes its title to a mingled sentiment of piety and patriotism. Under the illusion that the vast domain lying west of the Mississippi was still a French possession, Laclede named the newly founded post "Saint Louis", after the patron saint of Louis XV. According to tradition, the companions of Laclede wished to name the place after their leader, but the founder declined the deserved distinction.

The expected arrival of the English troops at fort De Chartres induced Laclede to hurry the removal of his merchandise to Saint Louis; but the sudden arrival, on October 10, 1764, of 100 Missouri warriors, with several hundred women and children, delayed his movement. There were no Indian villages in the immediate vicinity of the new post, and though the Illinois Indians claimed to be owners of the ground on which Saint Louis stands, they did not disturb the French settlers, and demanded no remuneration for the occupancy of the land. Still, the sudden appearance of such a large body of savages caused some uneasiness. The ostensible object of the visit was to procure a supply of provisions, but the food given for the purpose of conciliating the visitors proved a dangerous gift. The Indians were so delighted with the hospitality of their reception that they expressed a determination never to leave their generous entertainers. This was more than the French had bargained for, and, after trying various pacific measures to rid himself of his troublesome guests, Laclede finally threatened to bring over the French troops from fort De Chartres and expel the savages by force of arms. This had the desired effect, and the Indians reluctantly withdrew. This left Laclede free to carry out his intentions regarding the removal of his goods. The desire to insure the safety of his goods was not his only motive in making the transfer. Laclede disliked the English, and this feeling, shared by all the French in upper Louisiana, did much to foster the growth of the infant colony. The Seven Years' war in Europe had recently closed, and the Peace of Paris changed the bounds of empire in America as well as in Europe. The French residents of eastern Louisiana bitterly resented the transfer, and while many of them went to New Orleans, a number of others, entertaining the erroneous belief that the country west of the Mississippi was still a part of France, came to Saint Louis. Many of the latter recrossed to the east side when the Missouri Indians made their visit, but, after seeing that there was no danger, they returned. The Indians, also sharing the dislike of the French to the English, withdrew a large part of the fur trade from fort De Chartres, Kaskaskia, and Cahokia, and transferred it to Saint Louis. This combination of circumstances so materially increased the population and business of Saint Louis that the village became in the first year of its life one of the most important places in upper Louisiana, and the settlements of Carondelet, Saint Charles, Bon Homme, Florisant, and Portage des Sioux sprang from this strong young colony. The information, officially proclaimed to the people of Louisiana in October, 1764, that all the territory on the west side of the Mississippi had been transferred to the king of Spain, aroused here the same antagonism among the French people that was so violently expressed in New Orleans, and which is so fully described in the report on that city.

At first no organized form of civil government existed in Saint Louis. The few mechanics and hunters who accompanied Laclede were bound to each other by the ties of personal friendship and of common interests. The restraints of law were not needed to preserve public order. The imperial charter doubtless vested in Laclede discretionary powers of government; but, as if unwilling to transcend the express privilege of his royal license, he preferred to devote his attention exclusively to mercantile interests. However, it was necessary that the settlers should have a title to the ground on which they built their cabins, and therefore Laclede granted allotments of land, with the right of use, until the inchoate claim was confirmed by an authority competent to confer a full title. But the accession of immigrants was gradually changing the conditions of the young settlement, and after the transfer of fort De Chartres to the English, in October, 1765, Saint Ange de Bellerive, with some 40 soldiers, came to Saint Louis. The presence of an indolent soldiery did not improve the morals or the tranquillity of the colony, and the need of an organized government, to repress the growing tendencies to disorder and to punish violations of the law, became urgent. In view of these facts, and without awaiting the sanction of the Spanish authority, the people unanimously vested in M. de Bellerive the power of civil government, which he was to exercise until the arrival of his legally appointed successor, it being presumed that Spain would imitate the example of England in promptly taking possession of its newly acquired territory. As after events showed, Spain took its time.

Associated with Saint Ange de Bellerive were Judge Lefebvre (a) and Joseph Labuscière (the latter a notary public), both of whom had come from fort De Chartres; and while M. de Bellerive attended to the maintenance of public order, to the concessions of land and to the direction of the military, the latter performed the purely civil functions of the government. The system of registered land grants was begun in April, 1766, the first concessions bearing the signature of M. de Bellerive as acting governor, and Lefebvre as former judge. Lefebvre died in August of this year, and after his death all legal documents were executed by Labuscière and kept in his custody. When the Spanish authorities took possession of Saint Louis, in 1770, Labuscière delivered to Governor Piernas 194 legal documents. It is a singular incident in the history of Saint Louis that its first form of government, though instituted during a period of rigorous imperialism, was distinctly republican in its character. The king of France could not legally appoint the lieutenant-governor of a province that had ceased to be a part of the French empire, neither could the vice-regent in New Orleans do an act which his sovereign was not empowered to perform. But though the governor-general could not confirm the action of the Saint Louis colonists with full official sanction, he yet sustained the popular choice by his personal approval. The appointment of officers whose purely ministerial functions did not involve the grant of lands was vested in the director-general of Louisiana until Spain assumed control of her possessions, and in the exercise of this right Governor Aubri completed the organization of the civil government of Saint Louis by the appointment of two judges, an attorney-general, and a notary.

Several events, interesting from the novelty of first occurrence in the little colony, took place in 1766. The first marriage recorded in the archives was celebrated on the 20th of April; the first baptism was administered in May, the ceremony being performed in a tent; the first recorded mortgage was executed on September 29, and the first grist-mills were built during this year.

In the summer of 1767 news reached Saint Louis that Spain had appointed officers to take charge of Louisiana, and Rios, the Spanish officer sent to take possession of upper Louisiana, arrived at Saint Louis August 11, 1768. The Spanish officer quickly saw that any attempt on his part to exercise his authority would, in all probability, lead to bloodshed; and though he went through the formality of taking military possession of upper Louisiana, he did not exercise any civil functions, the government being administered by M. de Bellerive during the time Rios remained in Saint Louis. On July 17, 1769, the Spanish forces retired from Saint Louis, to the great joy of the colonists.

The inclemency of the winter of 1768–'69 was extraordinary. It was so cold that fruit trees were killed on the borders of the Gulf, and ice was formed on the banks of the lower Mississippi. The famous Indian chief Pontiac visited Saint Louis during 1769 as the guest of M. de Bellerive. While on a visit to Cahokia, across the river, Pontiac was murdered by a Kaskaskia Indian, and the body was brought to Saint Louis and buried with military honors. It was during this time that Saint Louis, made up mostly of hunters and traders, received the name of "Pain Court" from the citizens of Carondelet, who were mainly farmers, a name given to it on account of its inadequate supply of grain.

SPANISH DOMINION.

Shortly after Don Alexander O'Reilly had occupied New Orleans and fully asserted the authority of Spain in Louisiana, Don Pedro Piernas was sent with a body of troops to take possession of upper Louisiana. The date of his arrival in Saint Louis is not definitely known, but it was probably early in the spring of 1770. The colonists, probably overawed by the stern measures taken by O'Reilly, received the lieutenant-governor in sullen silence,

---

a His full name was Joseph Lefebvre d'Inglebert Desbruisseau.

while he, not entering at once on the discharge of his duties, lived quietly in the house of Laclede and spent some months in cultivating friendly relations with those over whom he was placed, and in learning the resources of his department. The result of his observations was highly gratifying to the Spanish magistrate. He found his province blessed with every bounty of nature. The beauty of scenery, richness of soil, and facilities for commerce, excited well-grounded expectations of rapid development. Saint Louis, enriched by the wealth of an extensive Indian trade, was actively prosperous, and had already grown from a small trading-post to a village of about 700 inhabitants.

On the 20th of May, 1770, Piernas took formal possession of upper Louisiana and assumed the functions of government. One of his first acts was the erection of a church on a plot of land which had been reserved for religious purposes by Laclede when the village was first laid out. The church stood on the west side of Second street, between Market and Walnut streets, as now named, and was built of upright logs, the crevices being plastered with clay. This church was dedicated June 24, 1770. The administration of the new governor was popular and conciliatory. Piernas was married to a French lady, and this fact, together with the filling of many of the minor civil offices with Frenchmen, contributed in no small degree to his success. The original settlers were much alarmed over the tenure by which they held their lands; but Piernas quietly relieved this anxiety by publicly confirming all the land titles which M. de Bellerive had granted. When the settlers asked that the bounds of all lands should be properly defined, the governor appointed a Frenchman as official surveyor. The Spanish military force then in Saint Louis numbered 6 officers and 20 men.

During the administration of Piernas nothing of special interest occurred in Saint Louis. On the 27th of December, 1774, M. de Bellerive died, and his remains were interred in the grave-yard adjoining the Catholic church. At this time the duties levied by Spain on all English imports were almost prohibitory, and many of the Saint Louis dealers evaded the laws by systematic smuggling.

In May, 1775, Piernas was superseded by Don Francisco Cruzat, an officer who continued the conciliatory policy of his predecessor. The Atlantic colonies were now agitated by the commotion that attended the outbreak of the Revolution, and though no ripple as yet disturbed the serenity of the little village on the banks of the Mississippi, it began to be rumored that after war was declared England might instigate Indian attacks on the Spanish settlements west of the river. It was supposed that Saint Louis would offer a favorable point of attack for hostile parties from Canada, and Cruzat began to mature a system of fortifications. Before much could be done he was removed from office, and was succeeded, in 1778, by Don Fernando de Leyba. Shortly after this change the father of the colony died.

Pierre Laclede Liguest came to New Orleans from Bion, in southern France. His personal appearance was striking. An erect figure, somewhat above the ordinary stature of Frenchmen, a dark olive complexion, a broad forehead, a prominent nose, and penetrating black eyes were the physical traits of the founder of Saint Louis. Endued with a restless nature, Laclede could not be content with the uneventful life of an obscure French province. A longing for a career of adventure and an ambition to found a French colony in the domain of Louisiana were the supreme motives that impelled Laclede to seek his fortunes in the new world. At his solicitation a number of his countrymen accompanied him to America for the express purpose of establishing a new settlement, and history records few examples of a more complete realization of ambitious hopes. Reared at the foot of the Pyrenees, he could scarcely have grown to manhood without acquiring a familiarity with the Spanish language, and in Louisiana, under Spanish rule, this accomplishment was of practical service to Laclede in the conduct of his business. Laclede occupies but little space in the political history of the colony which he founded. He devoted himself exclusively to commercial pursuits. His charter guaranteed to him a monopoly of the Indian trade for eight years. Smitten with a fatal illness while coming up from New Orleans, he was carried to the military post near the mouth of the Arkansas, where he died June 20, 1778, at the age of 54. His remains were buried in the wilderness, on the south bank of the Arkansas river. In a few years every vestige of the grave was obliterated; and now the city which would gratefully erect a monument in honor of its founder will search in vain for the place of his burial.

During the remainder of the time that Saint Louis was under the Spanish rule but little of interest transpired, though there were several governors. On the 26th of May, 1780, Indians surprised some farmers at work, and before they could get to shelter five were killed. The Indians withdrew without making any attempt to attack the village. This event admonished the colonists of the insecurity of their village, and a system of fortifications was at once begun. In June, 1785, a great flood swept down the Mississippi. The water at Saint Louis rose 20 feet above all then known water marks, and the inhabitants prepared to leave their houses, and had already begun to remove some of their property to the highlands in rear of the village, when the subsidence of the water allayed their anxiety. With the exception of the high water of 1844 this is said to have been the heaviest flood that ever inundated the valley. In 1787 a band of pirates that had for many years infested the Mississippi and seriously interfered with commerce was broken up. About this time numerous small parties of Indians hung about Saint Louis and made the surrounding country very unsafe for the settlers. In 1792 the first honey bees came to Saint Louis, causing much curious interest and satisfaction. In the following year the governor, becoming impressed with the economic importance of immigration, offered generous grants of lands to all who would come in and settle. This had a good effect, and not only did many immigrants take advantage of the offer, but many merchants came to the growing settlement to avail themselves of its superior facilities for trade. Business became more active, new buildings were more spacious and elegant, and in every branch of industry the indications of increasing prosperity were distinctly visible. In 1799 the total number of people in upper Louisiana was 6,028, and of these 925 lived in Saint Louis. The winter of 1799–1800 was the coldest known, the temperature falling as low as —32°. In 1801 the small-pox broke out in Saint Louis, and it is noted as the first appearance of this dread disease in upper Louisiana.

Though the purchase of Louisiana was ratified by Congress in October, 1803, it was not until the 9th of March, 1804, that Governor Delassus transferred upper Louisiana to Captain Amos Stoddard, of the United States army, who, by virtue of a commission from the first consul, took possession of it in the name of France, and on the following day delivered it to the United States authorities. For forty years the province had been under the sway of France and Spain, but now another race, filled with the energies of liberty and progress, assumed control.

AMERICAN JURISDICTION.

In 1804 Saint Louis was still a small village, containing 180 houses and nearly 1,100 inhabitants, with only two American families in the place. The accompanying map indicates the extent of the settlement and the location of the buildings. Most of the people lived on the present Main and Second streets. There was no street fronting on the river, but the rear yards of the first line of buildings extended to the edge of the bluffs. There were only two pathways up from the water, one of these leading up through Market street and the other through the present Morgan street. There was no post office, and for the transmission of their letters the villagers were forced to rely on the courtesy of travelers, years sometimes elapsing before an opportunity presented itself of sending a letter to a distant friend. There was no ferry across the Mississippi, the only one theretofore established having been discontinued for want of patronage. There were only three small inns, and even these seemed unnecessary, as the stranger was welcome to the free hospitality of every home. At the time of the cession one of these inns had just been opened; the other two, situated on the corners of the present Main and Second streets, had been in existence several years. The only place of worship was the little log church already mentioned. In their respective vocations, one physician, one baker, and three blacksmiths supplied the wants of the village. Most of the dwellings were low-studded, one-story buildings, and in exceptional cases, where two stories occurred, the family ordinarily lived up stairs, while the first floor was the little shop which courtesy dignified by the name of store. The merchants generally kept their goods in boxes, and frequently the trader's whole stock of merchandise was contained in a single chest.

At the time of its transfer to the United States the luxury of an indolent life was deemed preferable to the attractions of wealth or the gratifications of ambition. The people had an aversion to any systematic industry.

Within a few months after the cession the boundaries of the province were defined, and all that portion north of the 33d parallel was called the "district of Louisiana", Captain Amos Stoddard being appointed the first governor, with headquarters at Saint Louis. The civil and military control of the district was intrusted to the territorial government of Indiana, and in the fall of this year General Harrison, the governor, and several officers from Indiana, came to Saint Louis to discharge their new duties. Laws were formed and regulations were enacted for the guidance of the new acquisition. Toward the close of the year the first session of the court of common pleas was held in the old fort, where now is the corner of Fourth and Walnut streets, and the supreme court was organized shortly afterward. The government also provided postal facilities, and appointed a postmaster at Saint Louis. On March 3, 1805, the district was transformed into the "territory of Louisiana", with a full territorial government, General James Wilkinson being appointed governor. In July of this year Aaron Burr visited Saint Louis and was entertained by the governor. In 1806 Lewis and Clarke returned from an expedition which had been inaugurated in 1803. They had left Saint Louis in 1804 to cross the continent. They had explored the Missouri river to its source, had crossed the Rocky mountains, and had descended the Columbia river to the Pacific ocean. The expedition had developed many valuable facts, and in recognition of the service performed, Clarke was appointed governor in place of Governor Wilkinson, who had been ordered to New Orleans.

The increasing demand for transportation across the Mississippi river led to the establishment of two ferries. The flat-boats used in this service were at first impelled by oars, then by horse-power, and it is said that the number of immigrants so greatly exceeded the capacity of the ferries that persons were sometimes detained on the eastern bank for days before their turn, in the order of arrival, permitted them to cross the river. Merchants with increased capital came in, while larger stores and better buildings were erected. On July 12, 1808, the *Missouri Gazette*, the first newspaper printed on the west bank of the river, was established. The first issue of the *Gazette* was on paper only 12½ by 16 inches, but the lapse of time has developed this little sheet into the ample pages of the *Missouri Republican*. On September 16 of the same year, a young man was hung for murder, this being the first execution of a white man in the territory of Louisiana. In this year the Saint Louis Fur Company, with a capital of $40,000, was organized. The company established a trading-post on the Columbia river, and in 1812 was reorganized as the Missouri Fur Company, with a capital of $50,000, but it seems that its influence upon the commercial development of Saint Louis was greater than its own success. On October 11, 1809, Governor Lewis died by his own hand, and was succeeded by Governor Howard. On the 9th of November the district court of common pleas incorporated Saint Louis as a town.

A board of trustees was appointed and ordinances were passed for the better protection of the new town. Fire companies were organized; every householder was required to keep two buckets in readiness for use, and to have his chimneys swept once a month; while the occurrence of a fire created a presumption of negligence, and subjected the tenant to a fine of $10 unless he could prove that he had complied with the terms of the ordinance. The supervision of roads and bridges was lodged in the hands of an overseer, and whenever there was need of repairs, assessors levied a tax, payable in manual labor, on the abutting property-owners. In 1810 six or seven buildings were erected, but the supply was still unequal to the demand. In January, 1811, a market-house was built on the square now bounded by Market and Walnut streets, Main street and the river, the square being subsequently occupied by the old Merchants' Exchange. Though small, it was for a number of years the only market-house.

At this time the population of Saint Louis was estimated at 1,400, and there were twelve stores, two schools, and one printing-office in the place. The estimated value of the stock of merchandise was $250,000. Trade was still largely carried on by barter; peltries, lead, and whisky forming the common medium of exchange. Business, which had been languishing for a while, began to improve, and, though many new buildings were erected, there was not a house to rent in the town. During this year the trustees passed an ordinance regulating the assessment and collection of taxes. On December 17, 1811, the great earthquake, so destructive at New Madrid, caused much alarm at Saint Louis, but inflicted no damage there.

In 1812, when the state of Louisiana was admitted into the Union, the name of the territory of Louisiana was changed to the "territory of Missouri". Up to this time the people had no voice in the administration of public affairs, the government of the territory being vested in the hands of officers appointed by the President. But the act of Congress which altered the name of the territory also granted to the people a liberal measure of republican power, and in all subordinate matters the inhabitants were entitled to vote. Town meetings were held and a house of representatives was elected, one of whose duties was to nominate to the President the members of an executive council. The governor, council, and house of representatives constituted the territorial legislature. The first sessions were held in Saint Louis during the winter of 1812.

During 1812 trade was active, wages were high, and money was abundant, while real estate rose to unnatural values. Business was carried on by means of borrowed capital, and land and merchandise were largely purchased for speculative purposes. High prices and long credits controlled trade.

The breaking out of the war of 1812 caused great depreciation of prices, and temporarily suspended the trade carried on with Mackinaw. But peace soon relieved business of its depression and allowed the full tide of trade to flow in its wonted channels. In 1813 William Clark was appointed governor, and about this time the first brick house was erected. Even so late as 1814 there was not a public hall in the town, all entertainments being given in barns or stable-lofts. The want of better facilities for the transaction of business had long been felt, and the merchants determined to remedy the defect. The Bank of Saint Louis was chartered August 21, 1816, and this was soon followed by other banks. On the 2d of August, 1817, the first steamboat reached the wharf at Saint Louis. This inaugurated a new era of commercial development.

In the same year a duel was fought on Bloody island, between Thomas H. Benton and Charles Lucas, the United States attorney for the territory, in which the latter was wounded. On September 27 they met again, and Mr. Lucas was killed.

During the fiscal year 1817 the revenue from the whole county of Saint Louis did not much exceed $2,000, and the expenses for the same period were but little more than $1,000. In this year the legislature granted license to lottery companies.

In 1818 the sidewalk on Market street, between Main street and the river, was laid with stone blocks set on edge. This was the first pavement in Saint Louis. The same year the little log church was torn down and a brick cathedral was built in its place. Though the edifice was never wholly finished, yet it was occupied for some time as a place of worship. The same year the Saint Louis college was built, and the excellence of the institution soon attracted students from other parts of the country, notably from Kentucky and Louisiana. Up to this time the only church belonged to the Roman Catholics, but now the Baptists erected a place of worship at the corner of Market and Third streets. Though never completed, it was used not only as a church but as a court of justice.

In 1818 the application of Missouri for admittance to the Union gave rise to the exciting political discussion terminated by the famous "Missouri Compromise". The territory was permitted to determine the character of its institutions. A pro-slavery constitution was adopted, every member of the constitutional convention of 1820 being pledged to advocate slavery.

During 1819-'20, in addition to the ordinary expenses of sustaining public worship, $18,000 was raised for the erection of churches. In 1820 Alexander McNair was elected governor of Missouri, being the first governor elected under the state laws.

About this time the derangement of currency, incident to the failure of the banks, seriously affected the business interests of Saint Louis. To relieve the financial wants of the community the legislature created a loan office, but this not proving effectual, the courts were authorized to grant an arrest of execution in judgment for a period of two and a half years. This latter, though affording some measure of relief, wrecked the fortunes of many merchants, who, dependent on the collection of moneys due to meet their own liabilities, were forced into bankruptcy. It was several years before Saint Louis recovered from this financial depression.

In 1821 a brick sidewalk was laid in front of block 52, the first pavement of this class put down in Saint Louis. In the same year the first Methodist church was erected. The first directory of Saint Louis was published during this year, and, as many of the streets bore no distinctive names, the compiler supplied names, using the letters of the alphabet to a considerable extent for streets running north-and-south. The names thus given remained in use for some time, being finally superseded by the present system. The introduction of many new industries was a gratifying indication of public progress, and agriculture, which had been neglected from the first settlement of the province, began to receive greater attention. At a meeting held in Saint Louis in 1822 a society for the encouragement of agriculture was formed, and for several years did good work in actively promoting the interest of agriculture in the state.

On the 9th of December, 1822, the legislature granted to the town of Saint Louis a city charter, and on the first Monday of April, 1823, the city government was inaugurated by the election of a mayor and nine aldermen. The area comprised within the corporate limits was 385 acres, and the population of Saint Louis at that time was about 5,000.

CIVIC GROWTH. (a)

Immediately after the organization of the new city government the city engineer was instructed to submit a plan for grading and paving the streets. He recommended a grade for Main street, from near where the Iron Mountain depot now stands to the intersection of Green street, which was adopted by ordinance; and the grading and paving between Market and Walnut streets was completed in the autumn of 1823. The grading was done at the cost of the city, but the paving and curbing were done at the cost of the owners of lots fronting on the streets paved. As a result many of the owners of large lots found it desirable to divide and sell them, and thus an opportunity was afforded for the improvement of the city in its central parts, where it had long been disfigured by rustic and nearly useless inclosures.

In consequence of this and similar changes many old French families, who were fond of a rural life, retired into the country in the course of this decade. As the facilities for their obtaining a subsistence in the city were daily diminished, hunters, trappers, bargemen, and voyageurs also gradually disappeared, and their places of residence were occupied by newcomers of other occupations, so that, although the population of the city increased only about 600 from 1820 to 1828, there was yet much real growth. In the latter part of the decade the influx of population from Illinois was important.

In 1824 the first Presbyterian church was erected, and in 1825 the first Episcopal church. Both of these structures disappeared long ago. Two years later, in 1827, the old court-house was built. The market-house, on the north end of Place d'Armes, the only one in the city, was found to be too small, and from the proceeds of a loan a new one was built, which, by having a town-house above and stores below, seemed for a short time to satisfy the needs of the growing town. The erection of this building induced many owners of lots in the immediate vicinity to improve them—a procedure which soon gave this part of the city a more animated and commercial appearance, and obliterated most of the old landmarks, except the streets themselves.

Improvements seemed not to be confined to this locality only; they extended to all parts of the city. At the same time new brick-yards were established, new lumber-yards and quarries were opened in the suburbs, and sites for new dwellings were selected and improved. An ordinance was passed for paving Olive and Chestnut streets from Fourth street to the river, and Green street from Main street to the river. The new buildings differed so far in materials and symmetry from what had been in use in former years that all imitation of former style was abandoned, and the monuments of French and Spanish architecture rapidly gave place to the new order of improvement. But even yet half the families residing in the city spoke the French language, and in all Saint Louis there were less than half a dozen German families.

In 1829 the progress of the city became still more marked. The new buildings of any former year were doubled. The United States Bank, then in the zenith of its financial glory, established a branch here—an act which at this crisis was fraught with advantage to every kind of business, inasmuch as this institution had no competitor and was guided by persons identified with every local interest. One of its results was the substitution of United States notes and half-dollars for the heterogeneous currency then in use. For many years silver coin had been the circulating medium of the country, and the vast influx of foreigners from many parts of the world had put the coins of nearly all the enlightened nations into circulation among the people of Missouri, so that more than half the currency was foreign coin, chiefly Mexican dollars, 5-franc French or Italian pieces, and Prussian or German thalers.

---

a By Robert Luce, A. M.

In 1830 the number of brick buildings in the city increased considerably. The frame or one-story cottage houses, with their piazzas and large yards, significant of the French and Spanish time, were fast disappearing. Most of the extensive gardens, frequently occupying a whole square, in which grew delicious fruit, and in which were raised abundance of vegetables, had now either lost their original owners by death, and so the property had become divided, or had risen to such value that the price offered was a temptation to part with it.

Many of the old French families, after the advent of the Americans, still preserved their simple mode of life, nor seemed sensible of the changing circumstances around them. They gathered the fruit from their trees and raised their vegetables until taxes and other demands so accumulated that they were forced every few years to lop off a slice from their grants, and their simplicity and unbusiness-like habits were often taken advantage of by the enterprising race that had settled among them.

A writer in one of the public journals of 1831 thus speaks of Saint Louis: "Our city is improving with great rapidity. Many good houses are building in a style worthy the most flourishing seaport towns. The arts and useful manufactures are multiplying and improving. Mills, breweries, mechanical establishments, all seem to be advancing successfully for the good of the country, and we hope for the great profit of our industrious and enterprising fellow-citizens. The trade and navigation of this port are becoming immense." During the year 1831, according to the wharfmaster's report, 60 different steamboats visited the harbor, making 532 entries, with an aggregate tonnage of 7,769 tons. The city derived a revenue from wharfage amounting to $2,167.

In common with other cities of the Union, Saint Louis was visited by the cholera in 1832. In spite of all the precautions that had been taken, two well-defined cases were discovered September 25. The disease spread rapidly, and in the five weeks of its continuance about 4 per cent. of the population perished. It reappeared in the next year in a milder form, but as it continued several months longer, it was on the whole as detrimental to the city's mercantile interests as in 1832. It put a marked check on immigration and enterprise.

In April, 1835, a destructive fire occurred in the heart of the city, by which the large unfinished brick cathedral and many other buildings were destroyed, together with about 50 houses, and much other valuable property.

At this time the Mississippi river passed the city in two streams of about equal size, being divided by Bloody island, now a part of East Saint Louis. The current on the eastern side of the island was daily increasing, and threatening to leave no channel on the west side. The departure of so large a portion of the river from its western shore slackened the velocity of the current and allowed the muddy water from the Missouri to deposit the heavy material it held in suspension near the shore in front of the lower part of the city, where the stream in 1800 was 70 feet deep, until it formed a bar on which vast quantities of flood-wood lodged and defended the accumulations until, assisted by a growth of willows, cottonwood, and sycamores, it had become in one lifetime an apparently permanent island. Its presence in the former deep channel of the river quite ruined the navigation along the bank as far as it extended, and its rapid growth up stream gave signs that it would eventually thrust itself, like a wedge, between Bloody island and the city, and thus destroy the port entirely. It had progressed so far northward that no steamboat could land below Market street, and some boats had grounded directly in front of the Merchants' Exchange before those most interested could be brought to contemplate their danger. Congress was then induced to make an appropriation of $15,000 for a preliminary survey and examination of the river and harbor, and subsequently to appropriate additional funds to finish the work. By the system finally adopted, Bloody island, the scene of many tragic encounters in the days of the code of honor, became a part of East Saint Louis, then familiarly called Illinoistown, and the pile of *débris*, known as Duncan's island, was largely washed away.

Meanwhile the commerce of Saint Louis was taking giant strides, and was fast bringing the city into national prominence as a business center. In 1835, 121 different steamboats visited this harbor, against 60 in 1831. After another period of four years, in 1839, the total steamboat arrivals were 2,095, while the entries in 1831 had numbered only 532. By September, 1836, the place had reached such prominence that the Post-Office Department granted it a daily mail to and from the East. In that year a new hotel, a new church, and a theater were completed, and a city directory was published.

The theater was the old Saint Louis theater, which stood on the site later occupied by the custom-house, on the corner of Third and Olive streets. The lot on which it stood was 60 feet front by 160 feet deep, and cost the trifling sum of $3,000, an amount then considered enormous. The theater cost $60,000.

We learn from a *Gazetteer of Missouri*, published in 1837, that even then many of those manufactures were carried on that are auxiliary to commerce and agriculture, including flouring-mills, saw-mills, which fell far short of furnishing supplies of lumber sufficient for building purposes, and founderies and engine-shops, operating on a large scale.

At that time the wholesale and retail dry-goods houses were generally located in First street, which had been widened for the convenience of business operations, wherever it could be done, by the removal of balconies and houses of little value. In streets farther back from the river were located the tradesmen and artisans. From the river to the high ground, a distance of about 600 yards, the streets were generally graded and paved.

Two years later (1839) the city proper extended westward only as far as Seventh street. Beyond that line there were some scattered residences, ditches, and prairie. In the neighborhood of Washington avenue, west of the boundary of Seventh street, there were more buildings than in any other quarter in that direction, as the Saint

Louis college was located there. On the north the city extended to Middle street, and on the south to a point just below the convent of the Sacred Heart. Beyond these limits the residences were scattering and the population was inconsiderable.

It was the early custom here, as well as throughout the state, for mechanics and laborers to work for their employers from sunrise to sunset, taking a recess of one hour from 6 to 7 a. m. for breakfast, and another hour from 12 m. to 1 p. m. to dine. In May, 1840, the bricklayers of the city demanded a fixed number of hours for a day's labor, and uniformity throughout the year. Being refused, they quit work. The movement being joined by workmen of many other occupations, a general change was effected, and ultimately the ten-hour system was adopted.

Early in 1841 the city limits were extended considerably on the southwest and north, so as to begin on the river east of the southeastern corner of the suburb of Saint George, and thence to run due west to Second Carondelet avenue; thence north to Chouteau avenue; thence in a direct line to the mouth of Stony creek, and thence east to the river—so that the city now embraced 2,630 acres.

Charles Dickens, who visited Saint Louis in 1842, has left us in his *American Notes* a brief account of the place as he saw it. As one of the very few pen pictures of the Saint Louis of the first half of this century, it is well worth quoting here:

In the old French portion of the town the thoroughfares are narrow and crooked, and some of the houses are very quaint and picturesque—being built of wood, with tumble-down galleries before the windows, approachable by stairs, or rather ladders, from the street. There are queer little barbers' shops; and abundance of crazy old tenements with blinking casements, such as may be seen in Flanders. Some of these habitations, with high garret gable windows peeking into the roofs, have a kind of French shrug about them; and being lop-sided with age, appear to hold their heads askew, besides, as if they were grimacing at the American improvements.

It is hardly necessary to say that these consist of wharves and warehouses, and new buildings in all directions, and of a great many vast plans which are still progressing. Already, however, some very good houses, broad streets, and marble-fronted shops have gone so far ahead as to be in a state of completion; and the town bids fair in a few years to improve considerably, though it is not likely ever to vie in point of elegance or beauty with Cincinnati.

Saint Louis was now beginning to make improvements, and so to raise its taxes and debt to an extent disproportioned to its rate of growth. In the first year of its existence as a city, 1823, the amount of tax raised by assessment was $4,050 23. The next year it rose to $5,665 85; but after that it fell considerably, and did not exceed this amount for ten years, varying in that time between $1,970 41, the lowest figure, in 1825, and $4,765 98, the highest, in 1829. Then in 1835 it went up to $8,332 08, and in 1836 to $26,615 41. After that the rise was steady, and in 1842 it had reached $47,780. In 1843 the whole taxable property of the city was assessed at $11,721,425, and the tax levied was 1 per cent. of that amount.

About this time the commerce of Saint Louis with the Missouri and the upper Mississippi, which has since contributed so much to the growth of the city, began to assume immense proportions. The steamboat arrivals at this port from the upper Mississippi for the five years ending with 1845 were: 1841, 143; 1842, 195; 1843, 244; 1844, 647; 1845, 663. In the last-named year the steam tonnage enrolled here amounted to 22,425.92 tons. In 1854 this had increased to 48,557.51.

The first steamboat, with all her engines, tackle, and machinery, built in Saint Louis was launched in April, 1842.

In June, 1844, about the 8th or 10th of the month, the waters of the river began rising. The levee was soon covered, and by the 16th the curbstones of Front street were under water, and the danger to property and business became quite alarming. Illinoistown and Brooklyn were nearly submerged, the occupants of the houses being driven to the upper stories. The American bottom was a turbid sea. On the 24th the river reached its greatest height, when it was 7 feet 7 inches above the city directrix. This surpassed the great flood of 1785, known as "*l'année des grandes eaux*", and also those of 1811 and 1826. The misfortunes that it brought in its train were heavy, but notwithstanding them the year was one of general prosperity. One of the signs of this was the erection of 1,146 new buildings.

That the social progress of the community was not neglected during these years was shown by the formation, in 1846, of the Mercantile Library Association. It opened rooms in April, 1847. This association prospered and grew rapidly, so that in a short time a joint-stock company was formed, with the erection of a suitable library building as its main object. In 1851 a lot was secured, and a building was put up at a total cost of $95,500.

Saint Louis was lighted with gas for the first time on the evening of November 4, 1847.

On the 20th of December of the same year the telegraph lines connecting with the East reached Illinoistown, now East Saint Louis. On the 28th of the same month an important meeting of the citizens took place to consider the advisability of a city's subscription of $500,000 toward the construction of the Ohio and Mississippi railroad. The measure was supported by a general vote of the people. In March, 1850, the Missouri Pacific railroad was chartered. Ground for this road was broken on the following 4th of July, with suitable ceremonies. The first locomotive was put on the track in November, 1852, and the first division of the line was opened in July, 1853.

On the 18th of May, 1848, a fire broke out on a steamer lying at one of the wharves, and soon spread to other boats and then to the shore. In a few hours nearly all the buildings from Locust to Market street, and between Second street and the river, were destroyed or badly injured. The progress of the flames was arrested only by blowing up buildings with gunpowder. The whole value of property destroyed reached over $3,000,000; of this amount,

$440,000 was the value set upon 23 steamboats, 3 barges, and 1 canal-boat that were burnt. This was a serious blow to the city; but the citizens displayed great activity in repairing the ravages of the flames, and the evidences of desolation and ruin soon disappeared; new buildings were erected of a more substantial character than the old, and Main street was considerably widened.

Far more terrible than the fire of 1848 was the cholera of 1849. The coming of this contagion had been heralded in the fall of the previous year, and, in spite of the precautions taken, it appeared in a violent epidemic form in June, and spread rapidly. Most of the alleys were unpaved, and had long been used as repositories for all kinds of filth thrown from the dwellings and stores. This had been blended with the soil for a foot or two below the surface, and as only the surface was scraped when the alleys were cleansed, the rest was left to exhale its poisonous particles. In many parts of the city the cellars contained water, which, becoming stagnant, infected the atmosphere. There were no sewers in the city.

When the terrific malady was raging in all its virulence and nothing seemed able to stay its progress, the columns of the daily journals were teeming with speculative theories on the cause of the disease and the proper measure to effect its cure. A board of the most respectable physicians in the city, after careful consultation, gave it as their opinion that a vegetable diet was highly injurious, and a meat diet less liable to objection than any other. In accordance with this decision the city council issued an ordinance prohibiting the sale of vegetables. This was serious to the market-gardeners of the vicinity, but the butchers reaped a golden harvest; for the approval of meat as an article of diet was construed by some as a remedy for the disease, and meat was consumed in quantities unknown before in domestic annals. In spite, however, of the meat diet, the cleansing and purifying of streets and alleys, and all the various applications of disinfectant agents, day by day the pestilence still spread. The ordinance prohibitory of vegetables was repealed. At last the plague wore itself out.

Saint Louis had been grievously smitten. Out of a population of less than 64,000 it had lost 5,989 in the short time between April 30 and August 16, and of these 4,060 had been the victims of the cholera. The greatest mortality had occurred between June 25 and July 15, in which period the number of deaths from the contagion reached as high as 160 per day.

The calamities of 1848 and 1849 were serious blows to the prosperity of Saint Louis, but with wonderful elasticity the city sprang up again, and 1850 found her prospects more cheerful than ever before. The census of that year showed that her population numbered 77,860, of which 37,436 were born in America, 23,774 in Germany, 11,257 in Ireland, 2,933 in England, and 2,460 in other countries. It is to be noticed that Germany had contributed over a quarter of the city's inhabitants, a proportion which has since remained tolerably constant.

According to the census returns of 1850 the total value of the yearly manufactures of the city amounted to over $15,000,000, which shows that manufactures had now got a firm hold in the city. As for the condition of commerce at this time, it is enough to say that in 1850 the tonnage enrolled at Saint Louis was 24,995 tons; in 1851, 34,065 tons; and in 1852, 45,441 tons.

In 1853, Front, Main, and Second streets contained the principal wholesale stores. Second street was occupied by heavy grocery, iron, receiving and shipping houses. Fourth street, then the fashionable promenade, contained the finest retail stores.

A United States gazetteer for 1853 says: "It may be doubted whether any city of the Union has improved more rapidly than this in the style of its public buildings. * * * Saint Louis is handsomely built, especially the new portion of the city; the principal material is brick, although limestone is employed to some extent." At that time, in the "new city", as the later-settled portion was called, the private dwellings were mostly surrounded by garden plots and ornamental shrubbery.

This period, down to the breaking out of the civil war, was the most prosperous in the history of Saint Louis. To be sure, in 1853 her population was seventeen times and her wealth nineteen times what they had been twenty years before, but now in a period of six years she was to increase her population by almost one-half. In the seven years from 1852 to 1859 the population of Saint Louis nearly doubled, it having 94,000 inhabitants at the former and 185,000 at the later date. In the last three of these years, from 1856 to 1859, the city grew from 125,200 inhabitants to 185,587.

Perhaps the rapidity of the growth of Saint Louis in the decade immediately preceding the war can be better appreciated by considering the rise in the value of real and personal estate. In 1825 this amounted to but $1,013,167; in 1840, to $8,682,506; in 1850, to $29,676,649; and in 1859, to $104,621,361. Even better than these overwhelming totals will be some concrete instances of the astonishing rise in real-estate prices.

In 1822 the trustees of the First Presbyterian Church purchased a lot fronting 150 feet on Fourth street and 90 feet on Washington avenue and Charles street for $300. In April, 1853, the ground was leased for a term of fifty years at the rate of $4,000 per annum. The lot on the corner of Third and Chestnut streets, extending 120 feet on the former and 150 feet along the latter, was sold in 1826 for $400; in 1853 it was valued at $30,000, exclusive of improvements. A block situated between Fourth, Fifth, Locust, and Saint Charles streets, which in 1833 was sold for $6,000, was said to be worth in 1853 $182,000. Lots on Second street, which in 1848 could be bought for $100 or $150 per front foot, sold in 1853 for $500 per front foot. In 1845 a lot on Second street, between Lombard

WESTERN STATES: SAINT LOUIS, MO.

and Hazel street, running to the river, was bought for $800. In 1855 one-third of it was sold for $42,000, and the rest was held for $100,000. Hundreds of similar instances might be given, but from these the reader can see how marvelous the growth of Saint Louis has been.

As is not unusual in times of great prosperity, few occurrences worth chronicling are met with in the course of these years. History treats of breaks in the current of affairs rather than of the smooth-running current itself, and breaks are rare at this period of the history of Saint Louis; but, on the other hand, history must measure this current occasionally.

A paid fire department was established in 1857. The history of the volunteer department, which was superseded at this time, dates back to 1832, when the organization of the Central Fire Company gave a nucleus around which the department was formed. By 1854 there had come to be 10 organized companies in the city, with 805 enrolled active members. These had built their own houses and had supplied all their engines, hose, etc.; but at this time the city was paying them $1,000 each per annum toward meeting their heavy expenses. The companies had fallen into debt, and the city had paid up their debts and taken liens on their property. This made it much easier for the city to effect the change to a paid department in 1857, a change rendered imperative by the increased growth of the city and the consequent need of more systematic and effective protection against fire. At the time of the change there was but one steam fire-engine in the city, but others were soon added. The fire-alarm telegraph was put in operation in 1858, there being at the close of that year 63 boxes.

In 1858 the Saint Louis and Iron Mountain railroad was opened for business to Pilot Knob, a distance of 85 miles. Up to 1859 the omnibus was the only public means of local transportation in Saint Louis. It had made its appearance in 1843, and several lines were now used. In 1859 came the street railway, three lines being opened within a short period. In subsequent years a number of other lines were built.

In 1861 came the civil war, with its terrible train of disasters. Saint Louis, being on the border, in a doubtful state, suffered severely, though never the scene of actual warfare. The business of the city was reduced to about one-third its former amount, and yet refugees from the seat of war sought safety and sustenance in the impoverished city. During the last two years of the conflict the prodigious expenditures of the government in the Southwest enriched many citizens of Saint Louis, and gave employment to some thousands of them.

The condition of things in the early part of the war can be judged from the following remarks in a book of travel in America, by Anthony Trollope, who visited this country in 1861. In speaking of Saint Louis, he says:

I cannot say that I found it an attractive place, but then I did not visit it at an attractive time. The war had disturbed everything, giving a special color of its own to men's thoughts and words, and destroyed all interest except that which might proceed from itself. The town is well built, with good shops, straight streets, never-ending rows of excellent houses, and every sign of commercial wealth and domestic comfort—of commercial wealth and domestic comfort in the past; for there was no present appearance either of comfort or wealth . . . Up to the time at which I was at Saint Louis martial law had chiefly been used in closing grog-shops and administering the oath of allegiance to suspected secessionists. Something also had been done in the way of raising money by selling the property of suspected secessionists.

In July, 1862, the court-house was finished. Its site—the block bounded by Chestnut, Market, Fourth, and Fifth streets—was given to the city at an early day by Judge J. B. C. Lucas and Colonel Auguste Chouteau. Work was begun on the building in 1839, but progress on it was very slow and tedious. The form of the Greek cross was adopted, and the Doric style of architecture was employed. The total cost of the building was $1,199,817 91.

After the war prosperity quickly returned to Saint Louis, and railroads were greatly extended. In 1866 the city did more business than ever before. In 1860 there was a little less than 4,250,000 bushels of corn received and disposed of in this and previous years. The increase may be seen by comparing the amounts of corn received and 1,500,000, in 1865 less than 3,000,000, and in 1866, 7,233,671.

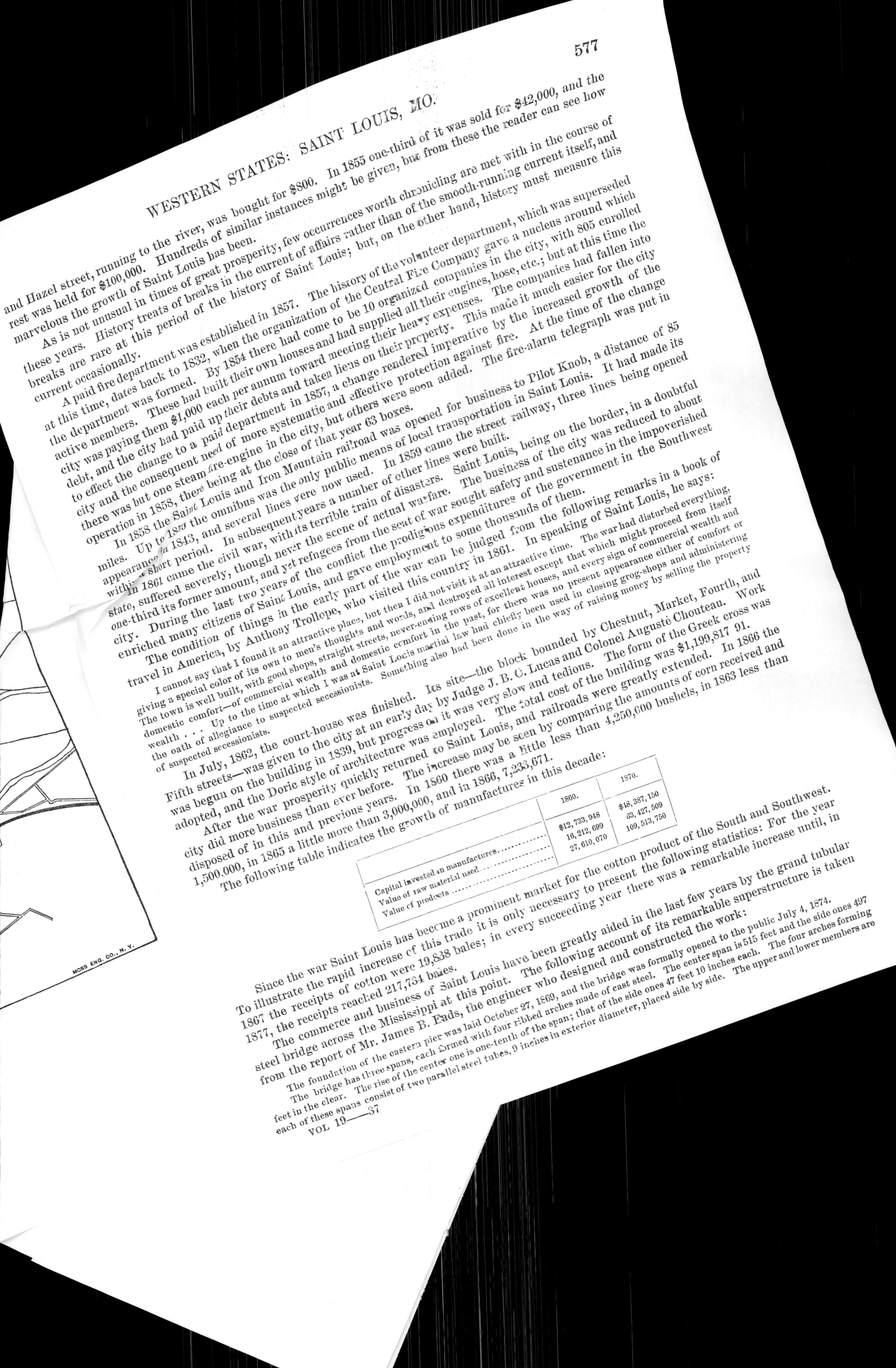

The following table indicates the growth of manufactures in this decade:

	1860.	1870.
Capital invested in manufacture	$12,733,948	$48,387,150
Value of raw material used	16,212,699	53,427,509
Value of products	27,610,070	109,513,750

Since the war Saint Louis has become a prominent market for the cotton product of the South and Southwest. To illustrate the rapid increase of this trade it is only necessary to present the following statistics: For the year 1867 the receipts of cotton were 19,838 bales; in every succeeding year there was a remarkable increase until, in 1877, the receipts reached 217,734 bales.

The commerce and business of Saint Louis have been greatly aided in the last few years by the grand tubular steel bridge across the Mississippi at this point. The following account of its remarkable superstructure is taken from the report of Mr. James B. Eads, the engineer who designed and constructed the work:

The foundation of the eastern pier was laid October 27, 1869, and the bridge was formally opened to the public July 4, 1874. The bridge has three spans, each formed with four ribbed arches made of cast steel. The center span is 515 feet and the side ones 497 feet in the clear. The rise of the center one is one-tenth of the span; that of the side ones 47 feet 10 inches each. The four arches forming each of these spans consist of two parallel steel tubes, 9 inches in exterior diameter, placed side by side. The upper and lower members are

MOSS ENG. CO., N. Y.

12 feet apart, measured from the center of the upper to the center of the lower tubes. At regular intervals of about 9 feet these members are braced from each other by a vertical system of cast-steel bracing on each side of them. These braces are secured at each end to cast-steel plates, formed something like the voussoirs of a stone arch, and against which the tubes are abutted and secured every 9 feet, to about the arches. A horizontal system of bracing extends from pier to pier between the four upper curved members, and a similar one between the four lower ones, for the purpose of securing the four arches in their relative distances from the latter by three systems lateral pressure.

The two center arches of each span are 13 feet 9¼ inches apart. The outside arches are each 15 feet 1¼ inches from the two center arches. horizontal bracing just described, a system of diagonal bracing, securing the upper members of one arch to those of the next arch, and the two other members in like manner. The outside arches are each 15 feet 1¼ inches from the two center arches. of the middle arches extend only from the piers to those described as between the two center arches. The latter are the latter by three systems of bracing similar to those described as between the two center arches. The latter are two inner arches near their crown, the outside arches being supported in this interval against lateral

The roadways are formed by transverse iron beams 12 inches in depth, supported by iron both the upper and the lower roadways. Between the iron beams forming the iron roadways for arches at the points where the vertical bracing of the latter is secured. That portion of arches at the points where the vertical bracing of the latter is secured, and serving to maintain the iron beams are introduced, extending from pier to pier, and serving to maintain the iron beams carriage-way rest in one roadway and the flanges of the beams, and are there secu 9 feet long, and their ends rest upon the flanges of the beams, and are there secu system of diagonal horizontal bracing serves to bind the whole together, an railings. The railway passages, below the carriage-way, are each 13 fe openings of equal size in the abutments and in piers. The latter are

The upper roadway is 34 feet between the foot-walks. The whole together, foundations in it very difficult. The rock underlying the rive being only 13 feet below extreme low water, while at the e the body of the stream are alike, except that the easterly through the shifting sand down to the bed rock of the

In April, 1871, went into operation th city limits it brought Carondelet into S

The growth of the city in the 1 following statistics, compiled in 1 the total length of street pav wharf (11½ miles river front) $1,948,000.

In 1812 Congress includes Saint Lou act vesting in a of Congress a support of sc and in 1831 fu was organized, handed over to t pupils; were erecte had been levied. In from leases, etc., amoun was under the charge of the by 72 teachers.

Since that time the growth the school funds by the state auth been free. The feature of German-A learning to read was introduced in t Froebel, system of education was introd well, and has since become an important br

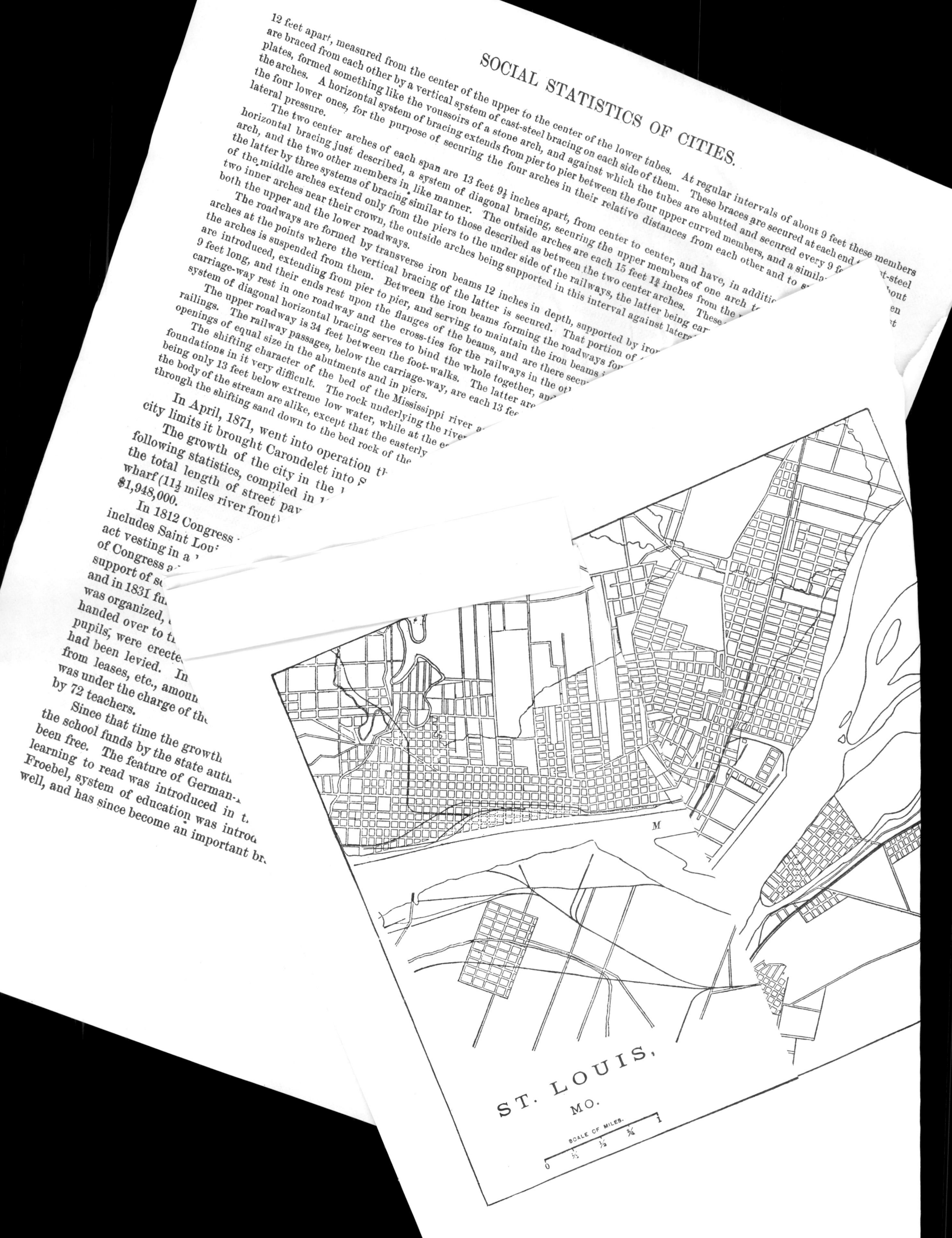

ST. LOUIS,
MO.

SCALE OF MILES.

SAINT LOUIS IN 1880.

LOCATION.

Saint Louis lies in latitude 38° 37′ north, longitude 90° 12′ west from Greenwich, on the right bank of the Mississippi river, 18 miles below the mouth of the Missouri, and about 1,240 miles by river above New Orleans. The city datum line has been established at 408.55 feet above the level of the sea; the lowest point is the Mississippi river, 34 feet below the datum line, or 374 above sea-level; while the highest point in the city is 610 feet above the sea-level, or 201½ feet above the city datum line. The Mississippi river forms the eastern boundary of the city for a distance of 19 miles. The entire length of the water front is called the wharf, or *levee*, and of this the harbor proper occupies 3.31 miles, of which 1.53 mile is paved with granite blocks, and 1.78 mile with riprap and macadam. The total annual expense of the harbor and wharf proper is about $55,000, and the receipts are about $60,000. The average depth of water here is 20 feet; the velocity of the current varies from 2 to 7 feet per second, according to the stage of water in the river; and the average quantity of water carried past the city is 225,000 cubic feet per second, the maximum quantity being 750,000 cubic feet per second. The waters of the Missouri and the Mississippi (the former muddy and the latter clear) do not mingle freely as the point where the two rivers meet, and in low stages of water the distinction is quite marked at Saint Louis, the discolored waters of the Missouri keeping near the right bank, while the clearer water of the Mississippi hugs the Illinois shore. Water communication is had with all parts of the Mississippi Valley that border on the navigable affluents of the Mississippi river.

RAILROAD COMMUNICATIONS.

The following railroads center in the city:

The Chicago, Alton, and Saint Louis railroad, between the points named and Kansas City, Missouri.

The Chicago, Burlington, and Quincy railroad, to Chicago, via Quincy, Illinois, and to Omaha, Nebraska.

The Cairo Short Line, to Cairo, Illinois, connecting there with the southern roads.

The Saint Louis, Alton, and Terre Haute railroad, main line to Terre Haute, Indiana, and Vandalia line, to Indianapolis, connecting there with eastern roads.

The Illinois and Saint Louis railroad, to Belleville, Illinois.

The Indianapolis and Saint Louis railroad, between the points named.

The Missouri Pacific railroad, to Kansas City, Missouri.

The Ohio and Mississippi railroad, to Cincinnati, Ohio.

The Wabash, Saint Louis, and Pacific railroad—Eastern division, to Toledo, Ohio, and Western division, to Kansas City and Omaha.

The Saint Louis, Iron Mountain, and Southern railroad, to Texarkana, Texas, with branches to Cairo, Illinois, and Belmont, Missouri.

The Saint Louis and San Francisco railroad, to Vinita, Indian territory, with branches to Wichita, Kansas, and Fayetteville, Arkansas.

The Louisville and Nashville railroad, to Louisville, Kentucky.

The Cairo and Saint Louis railroad, to Cairo, Illinois.

The West End Narrow Gauge railroad, to Florisant, Missouri, 16 miles.

The Union Railway Transit Company, to East Saint Louis, Illinois.

All these roads, excepting the Saint Louis, Iron Mountain, and Southern, the Wabash, Saint Louis, and Pacific, and the West End Narrow Gauge, use the Union depot, situated near the business center of the city, and connected by a tunnel with the bridge over the Mississippi. This arrangement gives excellent facilities for the management of the railroad traffic.

TRIBUTARY COUNTRY.

The country immediately surrounding the city is agricultural, but the situation of Saint Louis has given it a very large local trade of an immense territory of which it is the legitimate capital. It is a distributing and supply point for the country south, west, and north, and naturally represents the wants and production of the population of that region. It is the market for a large proportion of the cotton, grain, live stock, etc., of the range of country penetrated by the many railroads radiating from the city, or touched by the navigable tributaries of the Mississippi. This is more especially true of the West and Southwest; and as this large region becomes settled, railroads are extended, and the merchants of Saint Louis draw its trade to their doors.

TOPOGRAPHY.

The site of Saint Louis has a gradual rise from the river toward the west, and is intersected by a number of small creeks, which empty into the Mississippi river and which have formed valleys of denudation. The most important of these valleys is that formed by Mill creek, through which the railroads from the west enter the city.

The soil consists of clay, underlaid with limestone rock, often penetrated by sinkholes, the thickness of the stratum of clay varying from a few feet to 70 feet. The extreme northern part of the city alone is subject to overflow during very high water, as the general elevation of the bottom-land here is about 7 feet below the high-water mark of 1844. This bottom is now overflowed about once in 12 years. The natural drainage of the rest of the city is very good.

The country around Saint Louis consists mainly of cultivated lands, interspersed with groves of fine timber. The land is very fertile. There are no marshes in the immediate vicinity.

CLIMATE.

Highest recorded summer temperature, 104°; highest summer temperature in average years, 98°. Lowest recorded winter temperature, —30°; lowest winter temperature in average years, —10°.

The Mississippi river probably influences the temperature of that portion of the city only which is located close to the bank of the river. The southerly winds are the warmest, those from the southwest generally bringing storms; northwest winds produce the greatest fall in temperature, while the winds from the east are generally accompanied by rain.

STREETS.

The estimated total length of the streets and alleys in Saint Louis is 450 miles, of which 354¼ miles are paved with the following materials: Stone blocks (granite), 1 mile; alleys (limestone blocks), 51 miles; asphalt blocks, ⅛ of a mile; broken stone, 292 miles; and wood, 10 miles. Gravel is used only as a top-dressing by the Telford and macadamized streets. The cost per square yard of each, as nearly as may be estimated, is: Wood, $1 40; granite blocks, $3; limestone blocks, $1 20; asphalt blocks, $3; broken stone (Telford), 70 cents; and broken stone, 45 cents.

The annual cost of keeping each in good repair per square yard, including cost of removal when worn out, is: For granite blocks, 10 cents; limestone blocks, 15 cents; asphalt blocks, about 75 cents; wood, 21 cents; and broken stone, 5 cents. These figures refer to streets with an average traffic. On streets with very light traffic the repairs of asphalt blocks would probably not exceed 20 cents, wood about the same, and broken stone 2 cents per square yard; while the cost of repairing stone blocks on such streets would not differ greatly from the figures given above. On streets with a very heavy traffic, on the other hand, the repair of broken stone pavements has sometimes cost the city from 40 to 45 cents per square yard. The data in regard to the asphalt blocks are based on a very short experience, and on estimates rather than results.

The relative facility with which each class of pavement is kept clean, taking the asphalt blocks at 100, may be graded as follows: Stone blocks (granite), 90; limestone, 80; wood, new, 90; old, 70; and broken stone, 20.

Regarding the quality and permanent economy of each class of the Saint Louis pavements, it is said that the granite blocks furnish the most durable pavements, and, for streets subjected to heavy traffic, the most economical; but it produces great wear on vehicles and horses, and, on account of the noise which the traffic over it causes, is not recommended for residence streets. Its great cost also makes it ineligible for streets with moderate traffic.

Limestone blocks, when of the best quality of stone obtainable here, make a very fair pavement; but it is much less durable than the granite, as it wears more rapidly and is apt to crack under very heavy loads as well as under the influence of frost. It is principally used on alleys, and is open to the same objection as granite so far as noise is concerned. Asphaltum blocks, if they could be made to stand the wear, would make the best possible pavement here, as it is easily cleaned, does not absorb any moisture, is noiseless, free from dust, and easy on horses and vehicles. The asphaltum blocks also seem to give a better foothold to horses than the ordinary asphalt pavement. In the residence streets, where heavily loaded teams but rarely use it, this pavement appears to be the best; but according to the experience here the blocks laid on streets with tolerably heavy traffic have worn nearly one inch during one year, so that the life of this pavement on streets of this character would probably not exceed 4 or 5 years.

Wooden-block pavement has some of the good points of the asphaltum, and exceeds it somewhat in durability and greatly in cheapness. For streets with medium traffic it is probably the best and most economical here. Its life is from 6 to 7 years, but by impregnating it with antiseptics it can probably be made to last twice as long, provided the wood itself has sufficient power of resistance against abrasure and crushing. As an experiment, impregnated blocks of gum and elm have been used during the past year in reconstructing some of the wooden pavements, and if it proves to be as durable as expected it will be the most economical. The impregnation increases the cost 60 cents per square yard.

The broken-stone pavement is the worst, both as to quality and as to permanent economy, if used on streets subject to heavy traffic. It is impossible to keep it clean, and its surface alternates between dust and mud. With a top-dressing of gravel it makes a fair pavement for streets subject to very light traffic, and in sparsely populated districts the cost of the pavements would be too great a burden on the property-owners, who, in Saint Louis, have to pay for all street improvements by a special tax.

The sidewalks in the city have by ordinance the following widths: On streets 50 feet wide the sidewalks are 10 feet wide; on streets 60 feet wide the sidewalks are 12 feet wide; on streets 80 feet wide the sidewalks are 16 feet wide; on streets 100 feet wide the sidewalks are 20 feet wide. They are mostly paved with hard-burned brick laid in a bed of sharp sand. In some of the principal business streets stone flagging is used.

The gutters are all 3 feet 6 inches wide and 6 inches deep. On the streets paved with blocks of stone or wood the gutters are laid with the same materials, while on the broken-stone streets the gutters are made with blocks of limestone. Between the gutter and the sidewalk a line of curbstone is placed, consisting of dressed limestone, 4 inches thick and 22 inches in depth. Many streets are planted with trees, which are set on the sidewalks close to the curbstones.

The construction of streets is all done under contract, a special contract being entered into for each particular improvement authorized by ordinance. Repairs of streets are made under annual contracts, under direction of the board of public improvements, and are paid for by the city. Repairs of alleys and sidewalks are also made under annual contracts and paid for by the abutting property-owners. The cost of repairs of the streets, alleys, etc., in the city during the fiscal year ending April 12, 1880, was as follows:

For streets paved with stone and wood blocks	$25,566 63	
For streets paved with broken stone	154,215 99	
For miscellaneous expenses	44,528 69	
For salaries	19,741 48	
		$244,052 79
For repairs of alleys	5,586 61	
For repairs of sidewalks	2,072 91	
For repairs of street bridges and culverts	12,361 37	
		20,020 89
Total		264,073 68

The city charter provides that all public work on streets and alleys shall be done under contract, except in case of necessary repairs requiring prompt attention. The city has no need of a steam stone-crusher, but uses steam and horse rollers for repair of macadam streets. The contractors use both stone-crushers and steam-rollers, and their use has greatly improved the macadamized streets.

TRANSPORTATION.

The horse-railroads in the city have a total length of 119.6 miles. There are 496 cars, with 2,280 horses in use, and employment is given to 1,010 men. The total number of passengers carried annually is 19,600,000, and the rates of fare are 5 and 7 cents, tickets on all the roads, however, being sold 5 for 25 cents.

There are no omnibus lines in operation here.

WATER-WORKS.

Water from the Mississippi river was first introduced in 1830, but in 1867–'72 new works were constructed that have almost entirely superseded the old plans. The water-works are owned by the city, and their total cost has been $7,200,000. Water is taken from the Mississippi at a point opposite the northerly limit of the city, a cast-iron tower being built in the river, resting on bed-rock, and extending a little above the highest known water-mark. Gates for the admission of water are placed at various elevations, to be used according to the stage of water in the river. An iron pipe 5 feet 6 inches in diameter and 200 feet long connects the tower with the pumping-well, where there are 3 engines, with a combined capacity of 60,000,000 gallons every 24 hours, that pump the water through 3 force-mains, each 36 inches in diameter, and 365 feet long to the settling-basins, the "lift" being from 15 to 50 feet, according to the stage of the river. There are four of these settling-basins, each 600 by 270 by 19 feet, 2 being used at a time for subsiding tanks, while one is being filled and the other emptied.

After settling, the water is taken to the high-service station, where 3 engines, with a combined capacity of 57,000,000 gallons per diem, force it to the storage reservoir of Compton Hill. This reservoir has a capacity of 60,000,000 gallons. Midway between the high-service pumps and the reservoir is a stand-pipe, 160 feet high and 48 inches in diameter. It has 1 inlet and 2 outlets, one of the latter going to the city and the other to the reservoir; and as the force-main is connected with the distribution system, only the surface-water goes into the reservoir.

The average amount pumped per diem is 25,000,000 gallons, the greatest being 35,000,000 and the least 21,000,000 gallons. The average cost of raising 1,000,000 gallons one foot high is, for the low service 11½ cents, and for the high service $4\frac{7}{10}$ cents. The yearly cost of maintenance, aside from the cost of pumping, is $96,000. The total expenses of the department for the year were $225,000, and the total revenue collected is $660,000. Water-meters are used in manufactories, breweries, hotels, livery-stables, etc., and are found to prevent waste. There are 212 miles of supply mains, varying in size from 3 to 36 inches in diameter; 1,606 gates and 1,696 fire-plugs.

GAS.

Gas is supplied by 3 private companies, their combined daily production being 1,800,000 cubic feet. The charge per 1,000 feet is $2 50. The city pays $27 per annum each for 7,278 street lamps.

PUBLIC BUILDINGS.

The city owns and occupies for municipal uses, wholly or in part, a city-hall, a court-house, 4 court-buildings, insane asylum, house of refuge, work-house, poor-house, city hospital, female hospital, morgue, quarantine, 20 engine-houses, and 6 market-houses. The total cost of the municipal buildings belonging to the city is $4,000,000. The cost of the city hall is $100,000, and it is owned and occupied entirely by the city.

PUBLIC PARKS AND PLEASURE-GROUNDS.

There are 18 parks in the city, with an aggregate area of 2,107 acres, as follows:

Benton Park, area 14.30 acres, is situated at Jefferson avenue and Arsenal street, and was acquired by the city in 1866. It is tastefully laid out and improved to the highest degree.

Carondelet Park, Old, area 3.17 acres, and *Carondelet Park, New*, area 180 acres, are situated at Kansas street and Loughborough avenue, in the extreme southern portion of the city. The former was acquired by the city in 1812, and the latter was purchased in 1875. This park has a lake for boating, skating, etc., and about 6 miles of good drive-ways.

Carr Square, area 2.36 acres, situated at the corner of Washington and Sixteenth streets, was acquired by the city in 1842, and is largely used as a play-ground.

Exchange Square, area 12.86 acres, situated at Market street and the levee, was acquired by the city in 1816.

Forest Park, 1,371.94 acres, was acquired by the city in 1875. It is situated in the extreme western part of the city, midway between the northern and southern limits. So far about 20 miles of excellent drives and several large lawns have been completed, and the work of improvement is being rapidly pushed. The river Des Peres flows through the park, and it is capable of indefinite ornamentation.

Gamble Place, corner of Garrison avenue and Dayton street, was acquired by the city in 1874, and has an area of 1.15 acre.

Gravoir Park, area 8.26 acres, is situated at Louisiana avenue and Potomac street, and was acquired by the city in 1812. It is handsomely ornamented and contains a number of beautiful trees.

Hyde Park, located on Salisbury street and Bremen avenue, has an area of 11.84 acres, and was acquired by the city in 1854. It is tastefully laid out and well kept.

Jackson Place, corner of Eleventh and North Market streets, was acquired by the city in 1829, and contains 1.62 acre.

Laclede Park, area 3.17 acres, was acquired by the city in 1812, and is situated on Iowa and Gasconade avenues.

Lafayette Park, area 29.94 acres, was acquired by the city in 1844, and is situated in the heart of the city. It is beautifully laid out, and is considered one of the handsomest parks in the country.

Lyon Park, corner of Carondelet and Arsenal streets, contains 10.62 acres, and was acquired by the city in 1872. It is well improved.

Missouri Park, area 3.92 acres, was acquired by the city in 1854, and is located on Thirteenth and Olive streets. It is well cared for, and contains a handsome fountain and trees.

O'Fallon Park, at Bellefontaine road and O'Fallon avenue, contains 158.32 acres, and was acquired by the city in 1875. It is well improved with trees and lawns, and has 4 miles of good drives.

Saint Louis Place, area 10.80 acres, was acquired by the city in 1850, and is situated at the corner of Benton and North Seventeenth streets. It was selected as the place for the propagation of German carp by the state fish commission.

Tower Grove Park, area 276.76 acres, is well improved in the old French style, and is the most popular park in the city. In 1869 it was donated to the city on consideration that $25,000 in gold should be expended on its improvement. It is beautifully laid out, and contains 8 miles of drives.

Washington Square, area 6 acres, is situated at the corner of Market and Twelfth streets, and was acquired by the city in 1840. It is handsomely improved, and is much used by the children of the neighborhood as a playground.

The following table shows the cost, with the total amount paid for maintenance and improvements, for all the parks:

Names.	Area in acres.	How acquired.	COST.		
			Purchase.	Improvements and maintenance.	Total.
Benton park	14.30	City commons		$53,926 83	$53,926 83
Carondelet park (old)	3.17	......do		3,011 86	3,011 86
Carondelet park (new)	180.00	Purchase	$140,570 10	105,530 85	246,100 95
Carr square	2.36	Donation		37,657 09	37,657 09
Exchange square	12.86	......do		15,445 72	15,445 72
Forest park	1,371.94	Purchase	849,058 61	596,813 16	1,445,871 77
Gamble place	1.15	From city		5,985 65	5,985 65
Gravois park	8.26	City commons		19,573 28	19,573 28
Hyde park	11.84	Purchase	36,250 00	72,635 34	108,885 34
Jackson place	1.62	Donation		20,459 59	20,459 59
Laclede park	3.17	City commons		11,992 05	11,992 05
Lafayette park	29.94	......do		333,214 28	333,214 28
Lyon park	10.62	United States donation		15,893 67	15,893 67
Missouri park	3.92	Purchase and donation	95,500 00	44,222 25	139,722 25
O'Fallon park	158.32	Purchase	259,065 35	112,000 99	371,067 34
Saint Louis place	10.80	Donation		76,639 51	76,639 51
Tower Grove park	276.76	Conditional donation		565,390 06	565,390 06
Washington square	6.00	Purchase	25,000 00	63,198 01	88,198 00
Totals	2,107.03		1,405,444 06	2,150,591 19	3,556,035 24

At present the annual cost of maintenance for Tower Grove park is $25,000, and for Lafayette park about $20,000, while $30,000 is appropriated for the care of all the others. No record is kept of the number of persons visiting the parks. The designers of the larger parks were: Max G. Kern, for Forest park; Francis Tunica, for O'Fallon park; F. Soloman and Max G. Kern, for Carondelet park; Henry Shaw, for Tower Grove, and Krausevick and Kern, for Lafayette park.

Tower Grove and Lafayette parks are controlled and managed by the special boards appointed from among the citizens residing in the vicinity, while all the other parks are controlled by the park commissioner, who is a member of the board of public improvements.

During the summer a band plays in Lafayette park every Thursday afternoon, and in Tower Grove park every Sunday afternoon.

PLACES OF AMUSEMENT.

Saint Louis has the following theaters: Olympic theater, seating capacity 1,700; De Bar's opera-house, seating 1,700; Pape's theater, seating 2,000; Globe theater, 700; Canterbury, with a seating capacity for 1,000; Crystal Palace; Alhambra, seating 400; Lafayette Park theater, seating 200; and the Pickwick, seating 500. Theaters pay an annual license of $100 each to the city.

Of concert halls and lecture rooms, not including those connected with churches, there are: Mercantile Library, seating 1,600; Armory hall; Liederkränz hall, seating 600; Germania hall, seating 800; Druid's hall, Masonic hall, Harmonia hall, Merchants' Exchange hall, Saint George's hall, and Stolle's hall.

There are 10 or 12 large concert- and beer-gardens in the city. They pay no license, other than the ordinary dram-shop license, and no information as to their size, cost, or attendance was furnished.

DRAINAGE.

The sewerage system of Saint Louis dates from the passage by the general assembly of the state of an act (approved March 12, 1849) "To provide a general system of sewerage in the city of Saint Louis." Prior to this a number of short box drains had been built across the public landing to the river, nearly or quite all being built by private parties for the drainage of their own property. In the ordinances authorizing these sewers it was customary to provide that they should not be used for the drainage of privies. In March, 1850, the first public sewer was begun. This was a sewer 12 feet in diameter, known as the *Biddle Street sewer*. This sewer was built to drain a large pond, formed by the closing of sink-holes or openings in the rock, which were the natural outlets for a large basin centering in the vicinity of Ninth and Biddle streets. Other sewers for similar purposes soon followed.

Benton Street sewer was made from the river to Fifteenth street, thence along Fifteenth street to Howard street, draining a smaller basin adjoining the Biddle Street basin on the south and the southwestern sewer on Lesperance street, and Emmet street was made about the same time to drain the southern part of the city; while smaller sewers in the central part of the city were built on each street from the river westerly to the summit of the grades near Sixth street.

The above-mentioned main sewers, with branches, embraced nearly all the sewers built up to 1859, making a total length in round numbers of about 30 miles. On March 14, 1859, the general assembly passed an act establishing the present sewer system. One of the first sewers begun under this system was the Mill Creek sewer, which was begun in August, 1860. This sewer is 20 feet wide by 15 feet high, and is now 3 miles long. The Mill Creek valley, through which it is located, divides the southern part of the city from the central, and is the entrance into the city of all the railroad lines west of the Mississippi, except the Iron Mountain road. Several large tributaries to Mill Creek sewer have been constructed in the valleys, branching to the north and south, and the western portion will require considerable extension.

Among the main sewers may be mentioned Arsenal Street sewer, with its branches, draining an area of 700 acres west of the United States arsenal; the southern sewer, on Chippewa street, draining an area of 1,000 acres; the Stein Street sewer, in South Saint Louis, and the Trudeau Street, Carroll Street, Rutger Street, Rocky Branch, Louisa Street, Barton Street, Miller Street, Chambers Street, Bremen Avenue, and Ferry Street sewers, making a total length of 45.23 miles. To this add 157.15 miles as the total length of the district sewers, which makes a total length of sewers in Saint Louis of 202.38 miles, draining an area of 4,215 acres.

The following table shows the construction of sewers from 1861 to 1880:

| Date. | BUILT DURING THE YEAR. | | | Total length. |
	Public.	District.	Total.	
	Miles.	Miles.	Miles.	Miles.
Up to April, 1861	10 63	20.89	31.52	31.52
Year ending April, 1862	0 74	....	0.74	32.26
Year ending April, 1863	0 63	0.54	1.17	33.43
Year ending April, 1864	0.26	1.70	1.96	35.39
Year ending April, 1865	0 60	2.65	3.25	38.64
Year ending April, 1866	1.36	8.10	9.46	48.10
Year ending April, 1867	1 56	17.24	18.80	66.90
Year ending April, 1868	2.52	15.88	18.40	85.30
Year ending April, 1869	2 20	14.60	16.80	102.10
Year ending April, 1870	2 10	6.93	9.03	111.13
Year ending April, 1871	2 14	3.89	6.03	117.16
Year ending April, 1872	1 28	10.81	12.09	129.25
Year ending April, 1873	2 21	9.54	11.75	141.00
Year ending April, 1874	1 21	7.79	9.00	150.00
Year ending April, 1875	2 64	10.75	13.39	163.39
Year ending April, 1876	1 58	7.03	8.61	172.00
Year ending April, 1877	1 23	4.30	5.53	177.53
Year ending April, 1878	1 29	0.45	1.74	179.27
Year ending April, 1879	3 67	5.32	8.99	188.26
Year ending April, 1880	3 86	4.23	8.09	196.35
Total	43.71	152.64	193.35	

The following table shows the cost of sewers from 1862 to 1880, by years ending April:

| Date. | COST OF CONSTRUCTION DURING THE YEAR. | | | Total cost of sewers. |
	Public.	District.	Total.	
1862	$666,215 79	$309,970 97	$976,186 76	$976,186 76
1863	28,209 73	8,859 13	37,068 86	1,013,255 62
1864	30,678 57	10,582 61	41,261 18	1,054,516 80
1865	42,690 58	27,236 34	69,926 92	1,124,443 72
1866	80,767 56	129,256 44	210,024 00	1,334,467 72
1867	131,083 90	409,728 97	540,812 87	1,875,280 59
1868	126,246 96	441,838 86	568,085 82	2,443,366 41
1869	240,846 59	329,368 22	570,214 81	3,013,581 22
1870	219,748 58	112,217 13	331,965 71	3,345,546 93
1871	286,653 53	52,551 24	339,204 77	3,684,751 70
1872	255,300 91	123,334 75	378,635 66	4,063,387 86
1873	304,111 06	131,695 81	435,806 87	4,499,194 23
1874	214,858 67	164,616 93	379,475 60	4,878,669 83
1875	182,445 74	179,111 82	361,567 56	5,240,237 39
1876	132,792 14	115,274 00	248,066 14	5,488,303 53
1877	78,400 41	55,386 52	133,786 93	5,622,090 46
1878	88,626 56	4,547 64	93,171 20	5,715,261 66
1879	141,178 07	63,260 86	204,438 93	5,919,700 59
1880	146,307 10	43,058 38	189,365 48	6,109,066 07
Total	3,397,169 45	2,711,896 62	6,109,066 07	

As a guide to the present cost of the work, the following tables show the work done during the past year on the public sewers, not including cost of inlets, manhole connections, and other appurtenances:

Public sewers.

Name.	Size.	Average depth.	Length.	Cost per linear foot.
	Feet.	Feet.	Feet.	
O'Fallon Street sewer	4 by 5	19	1,790	$3 73
Wyoming Street sewer	2 by 3	18.2	1,332	2 56
Grand Avenue sewer	2 by 3	19.7	530	2 54
Cherokee Street sewer	3½ diam.	16.7	1,360	3 00
Do	2½ by 3½	16	635	2 51
Potomac Street sewer	3 diam.	13½	495	2 41
Do	2 by 3	16	517	2 31
Rocky Branch sewer	10½ diam.	23	200	16 00
Ohio Avenue sewer	7 diam.	31	187	13 05
Utah Street sewer	3½ diam.	13	822	3 50
Total	....	....	7,868	

District sewers.

District.	Size.	Length.	Cost per linear foot.	INLETS. Number.	INLETS. Cost.	MANHOLES. Number.	MANHOLES. Cost.	Cost of lumber, etc.	Total cost.
		Feet.							
No. 10.... {	2 by 3 feet, brick..............	155	$2 21	2	$84 68	4	$180 10	$63 27	} $1,475 90
	12 inches, pipe	947	85						
No. 2.......	12 inches, pipe	937	70	3	139 38	5	270 21	48 60	1,114 09
No. 34.... {	15 inches, pipe	1,432	80	8	492 90	7	254 09	62 00	} 2,079 19
	12 inches, pipe	178	70						
No. 4.......	12 inches, pipe	692	1 40	3	140 88	3	164 83	23 50	1,298 01
No. 6.......	12 inches, pipe	518	70	1	45 03	3	149 06	22 88	579 62
No. 33.... {	15 inches, pipe	570	1 35	2	96 29	3	150 86	44 10	} 1,088 19
	12 inches, pipe	28	98						
No. 1...... {	2½ by 3½ feet, brick...........	742	2 39	17	668 18	12	419 82	268 65	} 9,584 65
	2 by 3 feet, brick..............	1,632	2 14			13	531 90		
	15 inches, pipe	1,606	1 00						
	12 inches, pipe	910	90						
No. 35.... {	2 by 3 feet, brick..............	172	1 80	6	247 28	..	30 98	48 50	} 1,645 12
	15 inches, pipe	452	68			5	201 15		
	12 inches, pipe	666	75						
No. 17.... {	15 inches, pipe	582	75	3	116 78	4	165 41	38 70	} 863 09
	12 inches, pipe	151	70						
No. 4..... {	15 inches, pipe	244	1 10	2	89 56	3	147 85	40 61	} 772 02
	12 inches, pipe	240	94						
No. 13.... {	15 inches, pipe	728	97	3	139 62	4	191 12	62 07	} 1,238 47
	12 inches, pipe	186	75						
No. 11.... {	2 by 3 feet, brick..............	113	4 00	27	1,292 11	7	324 30	339 77	} 13,358 19
	2½ feet diameter, brick...........	510	2 80			15	841 06		
	2 by 3 feet, brick..............	1,380	2 70						
	18 inches, pipe	840	1 40						
	15 inches, pipe	1,068	1 15						
	12 inches, pipe	2,533	1 00						
No. 1..... {	15 inches, pipe	490	1 00	3	122 64	6	272 62	106 83	} 1,389 89
	12 inches, pipe	442	90						
No. 20.... {	2 by 3 feet, brick..............	760	2 21	5	196 47	3	99 89	58 25	} 2,563 50
	15 inches, pipe	492	80			2	86 46		
	12 inches, pipe	64	70						
No. 15.... {	2 by 3 feet, brick..............	370	2 00	11	412 30	2	73 87	89 63	} 4,158 96
	15 inches, pipe	849	84			14	620 41		
	12 inches, pipe	1,902	77						
No. 12......	12 inches, pipe	368	68	1	44 88	2	100 28	19 00	414 40
	Total	25,949	....	97	4,359 03	118	5,286 27	1,336 36	43,623 29

The following table shows the total length of all the sewers in the city, classified by diameters:

Diameter.	Length in feet.	Diameter.	Length in feet.
15 by 20 feet, stone and brick	15,892	3¼ feet, brick	951
15 feet, stone and brick	1,297	3 feet, brick	150,353
12 feet, stone and brick	7,366	2½ feet, brick	424,212
10½ feet, stone and brick	9,905	2¼ feet, brick	39,735
9 feet, brick..........................	2,905	2 feet, brick	51,931
8½ feet, brick.........................	1,036	21 inches, brick	12,613
8 feet, brick..........................	6,454	18 inches, brick	4,383
7½ feet, brick	6,854	24 inches, cement pipe	618
7¼ feet, brick	2,565	18 inches, cement pipe	15,610
7 feet, brick..........................	2,767	15 inches, cement pipe	22,323
6½ feet, brick	2,924	12 inches, cement pipe	1,300
6 feet, brick..........................	10,824	18 inches, clay pipe	12,080
5½ feet, brick	13,511	15 inches, clay pipe	91,086
5 feet, brick..........................	7,071	12 inches, clay pipe	32,478
4¾ feet, brick	9,487	Total	1,068,000
4½ feet, brick	41,846	Or 202.38 miles.	
4 feet, brick..........................	27,369		
3½ feet, brick	38,794		

The average cost of inlet basins is $49 32 each, and the average cost of manholes $40 69 each.

Each sewer or sewer district is regulated according to the requirements, as it comes up, but it is made to conform to the existing systems. Though perforated manhole covers are placed on some of the sewers, as a rule the greater portion of the sewers are not ventilated. Hollow invert blocks for subsoil drainage are not used.

The mouths of the smaller sewers deliver below the surface of the river, except at low water, while the upper portions of the larger sewers are above the surface during the ordinary boating stage. The outflow of all the sewers is carried off by the Mississippi.

There are 6 men regularly employed for draining catch-basins, removing deposits, and examining and flushing sewers. They receive $60 per month each, and their time is mostly occupied in cleaning catch-basins. No deposits have been removed by hand during the past year, and but very little was removed the previous year. It has, however, been necessary in times past to remove deposits caused by slaughter-houses, dairies, and, in a few cases, street detritus; but in most cases it can be successfully done by flushing, which amounts to the labor of two of the aforesaid men for about three months in the year, at a cost of $360.

Public sewers, which are the main channels of drainage, are paid for out of the general revenue of the city, while district sewers are paid for by the property-owners within the district in proportion to the grand area.

HOUSE-DRAINAGE.

During the past year an ordinance was passed by the municipal assembly regulating the construction of house-drains, which provides that every house-drain, connecting with any sewer, hereafter to be built or extended, must be provided with a trap, so constructed as to bar the passage of air from beyond the trap into the house by at least one inch in depth of water. Between this trap and the foot of the soil-pipe an inlet-pipe for fresh air must be placed, and the soil-pipe must be continued above the roof of the house and left open.

Whenever any person desires to construct a house-drain, intended to be connected with the public or district sewer, he must first file with the sewer commissioner a full plan of the proposed work, which shall not only show the whole course of the drain, but all fixtures that are to be connected with it. If the plan conforms to all requirements, the commissioner issues a permit for the work, it being forbidden to build any drain connecting with the sewers until this permit has been obtained.

In addition, the ordinance provides that the sewer commissioner, or his authorized assistants, can at any time enter any houses that have filed plans for drains, and inspect the same to see that all requirements have been complied with.

SEWER GAUGINGS.

During the spring of 1880 Sewer Commissioner Moore made a series of observations, as a part of an investigation undertaken by George E. Waring, jr., for the National Board of Health, for the purpose of determining the relative size of sewers required to carry off the house-drainage, exclusive of the surface-drainage or storm-water. Two sewers were selected as offering the greatest facilities for observation.

The *Compton Avenue sewer* is $7\frac{1}{4}$ feet in diameter, and the area drained by it is 445 acres. The area considered in connection with these observations is 240 acres within the lot lines, and having 1,370 houses with sewer-connections, the population being about 8,000. It is almost entirely a residence district, hardly any factories, and but a very small proportion of stores, being found in it.

The observations were taken by sending men into the sewer and constructing a small dam, with a section of 12-inch pipe running through the dam on the bottom of the sewer. In this manner all the flow in the sewer was made to pass through the small pipe, and it was found that in the middle of the day—when the flow is the highest, as a rule—the water was only $6\frac{1}{2}$ inches deep in the small pipe. In other words, the ordinary house-drainage from a district containing 1,370 houses only a little more than half filled a 12-inch pipe. While the quantity of the flow shown seems remarkably small, it nevertheless indicates a consumption equal to over 80 gallons of water per day for every man, woman, and child in the area drained by the Compton Street sewer.

The *Ohio Avenue district* has an entire area of 570 acres, the diameter of the sewer being 7 feet. The district under consideration has an area of 44 acres within lot lines; 120 buildings, with a population of 760, are connected with the sewer, and 94, with a population of 590, are connected with both the sewer and the water systems.

Observations were made here in the same manner as in the Compton Avenue sewer, except that a 6-inch instead of a 12-inch pipe was used, and at the time of greatest flow the depth of water in the pipe was only $1\frac{1}{2}$ inch.

The following table shows the measurements and gaugings in detail:

Gaugings of the dry-weather flow in Compton Avenue sewer, Saint Louis, Missouri, 1880.

Date of observations.	DATA.				DEDUCTIONS.				
	Greatest discharge in cubic feet per minute.	Greatest depth in feet.	Least discharge in cubic feet per minute.	Least depth in feet.	Average discharge in cubic feet per minute.	Average depth in feet.	Velocity in feet per second.		
							Greatest.	Least.	Average.
March 15, 16	154.25	0.5833	74.67	0.3751	92.39	0.4356	5.41	4.54	4.69
March 19	144.69	0.5341	77.64	0.3985	114.30	0.4389	5.65	4.43	5.27
March 20	132.34	0.5144	69.06	0.3751	102.18	0.4519	5.41	4.16	4.94
March 21	133.79	0.5177	68.58	0.3568	96.49	0.4298	5.86	4.27	4.98
March 22	128.57	0.4961	69.54	0.3802	101.78	0.4452	5.54	4.23	5.02
March 23	118.79	0.4701	73.95	0.3725	79.74	0.3940	5.46	4.47	4.62
Typical day, or average of March 20, 21, 22					100.22	0.4420	5.86	4.16	4.99

Gaugings of the dry-weather flow in Ohio Avenue sewer, Saint Louis, Missouri, 1880.

Date of observations.	Greatest discharge	Greatest depth	Least discharge	Least depth	Average discharge	Average depth	Greatest	Least	Average
April 5, 6	5.96	0.1198	2.327	0.0755	3.58	0.0954	2.86	1.83	2.28
April 6, 7	6.29	0.1263	2.478	0.0690	3.70	0.0891	3.07	2.16	2.60
Typical day, or average of above days					3.65	0.0923	3.07	1.83	2.44

CEMETERIES.

There are 28 cemeteries connected with Saint Louis, 15 being within the city and 13 outside, varying in distance from 1 to 6 miles from the city limits. Those within the city are as follows:

Potter's Field, in the 27th ward.

Gravois-Saxon, area 12 acres, in the 26th ward.

Saint Paul's, area 9 acres, in the 25th ward.

Saint Mark's, area 27½ acres, in the same ward.

Saint Peter and Saint Paul's, area 21½ acres; also in the same ward.

New Pickers, area 9 acres; also in the same ward.

Old Pickers, or *Holy Ghost*, area 20 acres, in the 21st ward.

Rock Spring, area 8 acres, in the 27th ward.

West Lutheran, or *Papin-Saxon*, area 15 acres, in the 15th ward.

Friedensgemeinde, area 12 acres, situated partly in the 23d ward and partly outside the city.

Bellefontaine, area 333 acres, in the 23d ward.

Calvary, area 240 acres, situated near the former, in the same ward.

Holy Trinity, in the 23d ward.

Saint Matthew's, area 12 acres, in the 25th ward.

Bremen-Saxon, in the 23d ward.

Those outside the city are:

Mount Sinai, ¼ mile from the limits, on the Gravois road.

New Wesleyan, 8 miles from the court-house, on the Olive Street road.

Mount Olive, 1 mile farther out, on the same road.

Mount Shereth Israel, 8 miles out, on the Olive Street road.

Bethania, 7 miles out, on the Saint Charles Rock road.

Greenwood, 7 miles out, on the Hunt road.

Salem, the same distance out, on the Natural Bridge road.

Saint John's, 8 miles out, on the Saint Cyr road.

Mount Olive, on Lamé Ferry road, 3 miles south of city limits.

Evangelical Lutheran, 1 mile farther south, on the same road.

Oakdale, 3 miles outside of limits, on the same road.

Saint Ann's, 8 miles from city.

From the annual report of the board of health for the year ending April 1, 1879, the number of interments in each of the following cemeteries was: Bellefontaine, 665; Bethania, 142; Bremen-Saxon, 108; Calvary, 1,444; Friedensgemeinde, 131; Greenwood, 261; Holy Trinity, 580; Evangelical Lutheran, 37; Mount Olive (Lamé Ferry road), 101; Mount Olive (Olive Street road), 30; Mount Sinai, 50; Mount Shereth Israel, 2; New (or Gravois) Saxon, 66; New Pickers, 170; Saint Peter and Saint Paul's, 501; Saint Peter's, 402; Saint Paul's, 104; Saint Mark's, 236; Saint John's, 99; Saint Ann's, 6; Saint Matthew's, 25; Salem 31; Rock Spring, 30; West Lutheran, or Papin-Saxon, 59; Wesleyan, 57; Old Pickers, or Holy Ghost, 387; Oakdale 33; Potter's Field, 704. Total number of interments, 6,742.

All graves must be at least 6 feet in depth from the surface of the ground. No interment may be made unless a permit is first granted by the health department.

MARKETS.

The people of Saint Louis depend greatly on the public markets for the purchase of their daily food supplies, and there are several markets located for the convenience of different sections, some of which are remarkable for the display of their general supplies. The German market-gardeners have from early years supplied fresh vegetables; the local fish supply is considerable, and some of the fresh fruits are of remarkable quality.

Detailed statistics of the markets were not furnished.

SANITARY AUTHORITY—BOARD OF HEALTH.

The entire sanitary interests of Saint Louis, and of all medical and strictly eleemosynary institutions, are in charge of the health department, composed of a board of health and the health commissioner. The board of health consists of the mayor, the presiding officer of the assembly, a commissioner of police, to be designated by the mayor, and 2 regular practicing physicians, who are appointed by the mayor and confirmed by the assembly. The members of the board hold office for four years, or until their successors are appointed, and the two last named receive a salary of $500 each per annum. The health commissioner, who is a member of the board, and, in the absence of the mayor, the presiding officer, is appointed by the mayor and confirmed by the assembly. He holds office for four years, and his salary is $3,000 per annum.

The health commissioner is the executive officer of the board, and has general supervision over the public health of the city. He sees that all health laws and ordinances are enforced, and for that purpose he is authorized to make such rules and regulations, with the approval of the board of health, as will tend to preserve and promote the health of the city; with the approval of the board he appoints all employés that may be necessary for the execution of his orders; he can call on the police force for assistance; he can enter and inspect premises; and can declare and abate nuisances, if his action is approved by the board. He provides for the registration of all vital statistics. He has charge of all city hospitals, quarantine, insane asylum, morgue, and city dispensary, and, with the advice and consent of the board, makes all necessary rules for their government. His office is in the city hall, and is open every day. The board is required to meet twice each week during the year, and can meet at any time in special session.

The annual expenses of the department, based on estimates for the year ending April, 1880, are $270,000, as follows: Board of health, for salaries, printing, stationery, vaccine virus, disinfectants, etc., $17,000; city dispensary, $15,000; quarantine and small-pox hospital, $9,500; city hospital, $15,000; female hospital, $38,000; insane asylum, $66,500; poor-house, $51,000; and for abating nuisances and also for general sanitary measures, $10,000. During an epidemic the expenses must not exceed the amount appropriated by the assembly.

NUISANCES, ETC.

It is made the duty of all police officers to observe the sanitary condition of their districts, and promptly report to the health commissioner any nuisance or accumulated filth found to exist in any part of the city. When a nuisance has been reported to the board, and by it declared to exist, the health commissioner notifies the parties responsible to abate the same. If this is not done, or if the owners or agents of the property on which the nuisance exists can not be found, the health commissioner has the work performed and charges the cost against the property. Defective house-drainage, sewerage, and street-cleaning are controlled by the board of public improvements. When any nuisance exists on any street or alley, or public place, the board of public improvements abates the same in the manner recommended by the board of health.

The removal of garbage is under the direction of the board of health, as is also its final disposition.

BURIAL OF THE DEAD.

The board of health designates such cemeteries as shall be used for burials, and forbids interments anywhere else in the city, except under special permission from the health commissioner. All cemeteries are in charge of either a sexton or an overseer, who must be certified to and recorded in the office of the health commissioner by the person or corporation owning the cemetery. The health commissioner grants burial permits only on the certificate of a physician, given at the place of death, or the certificate of the coroner of Saint Louis.

INFECTIOUS DISEASES.

Whenever a case of any infectious, malignant, or contagious disease is found to exist, the patient is removed to the hospital provided by the city for the treatment of all such cases. If, however, it is impracticable to remove the patient, the house is quarantined and steps are taken to make the quarantine effective, a printed placard stating the nature of the disease being displayed on the premises.

Every physician having cognizance of any case of malignant, infectious, or contagious disease, either within the city or within a radius of ten miles outside, must report the same within twelve hours, either to the health commissioner or to the nearest police station. All keepers of hotels or boarding-houses, owners of tenement houses or private residences, etc., must promptly report all cases of infectious diseases to the office of the health commissioner. Children from a family in which any contagious disease exists are prohibited from attending school, and principals or teachers either in public or in private schools are required to see that no child from any family so infected shall attend.

The health commissioner, with the approval of the board, has authority to establish and enforce special or general quarantine regulations within the limits of Saint Louis, whenever in his judgment the sanitary interests of the city demand it. Last year over 4,000 persons were vaccinated at the public expense, the work being performed under the direction of the health commissioner.

REGISTRATION AND REPORTS.

A full record of all births, marriages, and deaths is kept by the health commissioner. All births are required to be reported at his office by the physician or midwife in attendance, or by the parents. Marriages are required to be reported within ten days by the persons performing the ceremony. Deaths are reported by physicians or by the coroner in weekly reports, in addition to the certificate of death which is given and on which permits are issued.

The health commissioner reports annually to the mayor, and the report is published with the regular city documents.

MUNICIPAL CLEANSING.

Street-cleaning.—The streets are cleaned at the expense of the city and with its own force. The work is done wholly by hand, no sweeping-machines being used. As a large proportion of the paved streets are macadamized, no regular time can be set for cleaning, neither can a regular force be employed. The street commissioner has to use his own judgment as to where, when, and with what force the cleaning is to be done. The nature of the pavement does not permit very effective cleaning at any time, and during certain seasons the whole force of street-cleaners, which is frequently increased to several hundred men, can not even keep the street-crossings in a passable condition. This is more particularly the case in spring-time, when the frost is coming out of the ground. The streets paved with block pavement, as well as the gutters all through the city, are very efficiently cleaned.

During the past year there were 64,160 cubic yards of dirt removed from the streets, at a cost of $68,993 13, or $1 07 per cubic yard, the cost of the day labor being $63,593 13, and for supervision $5,400. The sweepings are used for grading public streets and alleys, filling ponds, etc. The street commissioner strongly recommended the placing of barges along the levee to be used as dumps, and thus reduce the cost of the work. At present the average number of trips a cart makes during the day is ten, and this number could be nearly doubled by having the distance to the dumps reduced. It is reported that the present system in use is the only one that can be recommended, since the time of cleaning and the force to be employed depend entirely upon the weather. In some seasons the amount of cleaning required may be small, while in others it is much greater. Contractors would have to bid high enough to leave a large margin for contingencies, and then the city would have to pay more than at present; while if a contract was made at too low a figure it would be difficult to enforce thorough cleaning, as no definite provisions as to time and force to be employed could be fixed by contract.

Removal of garbage and ashes.—All garbage is removed at the expense of the city, under contract, while ashes are removed at the expense of the householders. The garbage, which includes all house offal or waste, except ashes, must be kept in iron or tight wooden vessels, set in a convenient place in either the street or alley, where it can be moved by the contractor as he makes his rounds. Alleys are universally used as a place for the vessels containing the garbage. Ashes and garbage are not allowed to be kept in the same vessel. All garbage is hauled to the scavenger dumps, established by the city, and discharged into the Mississippi river. Ashes are disposed of by the householders, and are generally used for filling lots. The city pays $12,000 annually for the removal of garbage, while the removal of ashes costs each householder about 10 cents per week, on an average.

The whole matter of the removal of garbage (or slops) is under the direction of the board of health, which makes the contract. It is said that no nuisance or injury to health results from the manner of collecting or handling the garbage, and that the system gives general satisfaction; no complaint has been made in regard to the execution of the contract.

Dead animals.—The city has made a contract with a rendering company, which provides that the carcasses of all animals dying within the limits of the city must be promptly removed. As the company is granted the exclusive privilege of taking all carcasses, the city pays nothing for the removal. The company is required to remove every dead animal within six hours after a report has been made to it, either by the police or by an agent of the board of health, that a carcass requires removal. No record is kept of the number of dead animals removed annually. It is reported that the system is good and that it is well carried out.

Liquid household wastes.—The city is provided with over 200 miles of sewers, and wherever they extend all liquid household wastes are run into them. Where there are no sewers the wastes are run into cesspools, not more than 1 per cent. of the houses in the city delivering their liquid wastes into the gutters. The cesspools are built and cleaned in the same manner as privy-vaults, and receive the wastes from water-closets. They rarely have overflows, except into the sewers. It is said that they are tight when built in solid clay, but that when they are constructed in "made ground" they generally are only nominally tight.

The water from many wells, dug in the made ground, was subjected to a chemical analysis, and chlorine was generally found to such an extent that its presence could be accounted for only on the theory of the infiltration of the contents of the vaults and cesspools in the neighborhood. In many instances ammonia was largely represented.

Human excreta.—It is estimated that out of the 43,000 dwelling-houses in the city 15 per cent. are provided with water-closets, the remaining 85 per cent. depending on privy-vaults. With the exception of 300 or 400, all the water-closets deliver into the public sewers; those that deliver into the cesspools soon create a nuisance, and the construction of sewers becomes an urgent necessity.

Privy-vaults are required to be 10 feet deep, walled up with either brick or stone, and not nearer than 2 feet to any street, alley, or party line. In his annual report of 1879 the health commissioner says:

The common privy-vault exists in numerous portions of the city, and is a nuisance wherever found. As a factor in the defiling of well-water it is equaled by no other agency. They are often of the rudest construction, but in the remoter parts of the city they can not be well regulated in this respect. When these vaults are emptied the existing nuisance is often aggravated tenfold by the means adopted to clean them—a common method being by bucket and cart.

Privy-vaults are not allowed to be emptied between the 15th day of May and the 15th day of October, except by special permission of the health commissioner, and they must be cleaned between the hours of 12 p. m. and 3 a. m. The night-soil is almost entirely thrown into the river, none of it being used as manure within the city limits nor in the country adjacent.

Earth-closets are not used at all.

Manufacturing wastes.—Both liquid and solid manufacturing wastes are disposed of in the same manner as household wastes.

POLICE.

The police force of Saint Louis is appointed and governed by the board of police commissioners, which is composed of 4 members, who are appointed for a term of 4 years each, with the mayor a member *ex officio*. The executive officer is the chief of police, salary $3,500 a year, who exercises general supervision over the force and administers it in accordance with rules and regulations making the usual provisions. The remainder of the force in the several grades and the annual salaries of each member are as follows: 6 captains at $1,800; 40 sergeants at $1,200; 10 detectives at $1,200; 401 patrolmen at $900; 1 armorer at $900; 1 carpenter at $900; 13 turnkeys at $720; 11 hostlers at $650; 5 janitors at $600.

The winter uniform consists of a navy-blue cloth overcoat, dress coat, and pantaloons, in army style, with a blue flannel blouse for summer wear. The men provide their own uniforms. The patrolmen are armed with clubs (or batons) and pistols, and are divided into 10 divisions or platoons, the first platoon serving from 11 p. m. to 11 a. m., and the second platoon the other 12 hours. The platoons alternate their hours of duty every three months. The city is divided into 6 police districts, aggregating 62½ square miles of police territory, all of which is patrolled by the force.

The total number of arrests made by the force during the past year was 15,443, the principal causes for which were as follows:

Assault	243	Inhabiting bawdy-house	418
Careless driving	212	Larceny	1,037
Carrying concealed weapons	291	Street-walking	298
Disturbing the peace	1,715	Using profane or obscene language	2,604
Drunkenness	4,623	Vagrancy	1,213
Gambling	466	Violating city ordinance	355

In the final disposition of the persons arrested it is stated that 2,326 were sent to the workhouse. During the past year the total amount of property lost or stolen that was reported to the police amounted to $245,501 55, and of this $176,178 75 was recovered and returned to the owners.

The police co-operate with the fire, health, and building departments by reporting all cases belonging to their jurisdiction. Among the miscellaneous duties performed by the force may be noted the following: Nuisances found, 15,439, 13,927 of which were abated by verbal notice; nuisances reported to the health officer, 622; lost children returned to their parents, 550; doors, stores, etc., found open and secured, 896; number of dead animals reported, 2,308; dangerous walls, buildings, holes, and depressions reported, 862; broken and stopped-up sewers and inlets reported, 865; and broken sidewalks reported, 1,078.

There are on an average 189 watchmen employed throughout the city at the sole expense of the employers, who are, however, sworn in by the board of police commissioners, and required to give earnest and prompt assistance to the regular force as it may be required. They are furnished with a badge of authority by the department, and are required to report to the officer in charge of the district in which they serve, being borne on the police-rolls of such district.

During the year an officer, while in the performance of his duty, was shot and killed by a thief.

The total cost of the police force during the past year was $489,998 42.

In addition to the regular force there is a voluntary auxiliary organization, known as the "police reserves", numbering about 500 men, which was called into existence during the riots of 1877, and has been perpetuated in the interests of law and social order.

FIRE DEPARTMENT.

The manual force of the department consists of 7 officers and 199 men. The fire apparatus consists of 19 steam fire-engines, 19 hose-carriages, 4 hook-and-ladder trucks, 1 large chemical engine, 5 fuel wagons, about 20,000 feet of 2½-inch rubber and cotton hose, all in good condition, and 127 horses, all in active service, with one steam fire-engine and 1 hose-carriage held in reserve.

In his report for 1879 the chief engineer states that there were 291 alarms, only 8 of which were false. The loss of property by fire was $606,925, and the amount of loss to the insurance companies was $558,025, leaving a loss to owners of property not insured of $49,260.

A fire-alarm telegraph is in operation, by which immediate notice of fire can be sent to the engine-houses from the most distant residence districts. The cost of supporting the department is about $270,000 per annum, including the alarm system.

The value of property in charge of the department is $339,000, as follows: Engine-houses, $168,000; fire-engines, hose-carriages, etc., $137,000; and horses, harness, furniture, wagons, etc., $34,000.

CITY GOVERNMENT.

The present plan of the municipal government presents some peculiar features. The existing charter was prepared under authority granted by the state constitution in a special provision relating to Saint Louis. Formerly the city was embraced in the county of Saint Louis, and a county and a city government were both administered within the municipal limits. The new constitution authorized a separation of the city from the county, and the work of preparing the scheme of separation and a charter for the city was intrusted to a board of thirteen freeholders, elected by the people for that purpose. The scheme and the charter when completed were submitted to the people at a special election held in 1876, and were adopted. They went into operation the ensuing year, and a reorganization took place under the new law. The city became wholly independent of county control. It levies and collects its own revenue and the state revenue within its limits, and manages and conducts its own affairs, except so far as the constitution admits of action by the legislature. The constant changes in the charter in past years exercised a detrimental effect on the welfare of the city, and it was partly to prevent this evil that the new plan was devised. The present charter can be amended at intervals of two years by proposals therefor submitted by the law-making authorities of the city to the qualified voters at a general or at a special election. The legislature may amend the charter, but only under the restrictions respecting special legislation.

The legislative power of the city is vested in a council and a house of delegates, styled the municipal assembly. The council is composed of 13 members, chosen on a general ticket by the voters of the city, and the house of delegates consists of one member from each of the 28 wards, elected by the voters in said ward. The mayor and heads of departments, including the president of the board of public improvements, are elected by the people for a term of four years, and the rest of the more important officers are appointed by the mayor, with the approval of the council.

It is claimed that under the operation of this charter a better execution of public work and a more economical system of expenditures have been secured.

MANUFACTURES.

The following is a summary of the statistics of the manufactures of Saint Louis for 1880, being taken from tables prepared for the Tenth Census by David B. Gould, chief special agent:

Mechanical and manufacturing industries.	No. of establishments.	Capital.	Males above 16 years.	Females above 15 years.	Children and youths.	Total amount paid in wages during the year.	Value of materials.	Value of products.
All industries	2,924	$50,832,885	33,980	4,761	3,084	$17,743,532	$75,379,867	$114,333,375
Agricultural implements	7	434,000	443	....	5	190,179	478,140	856,430
Artificial feathers and flowers	3	33,000	9	54	15	25,450	66,000	147,250
Awnings and tents	9	127,200	47	165	5	54,850	249,185	388,940
Bagging, flax, hemp, and jute	3	370,000	149	16	76	150,216	545,900	867,395
Bags, paper	4	88,250	12	30	42	29,700	174,800	231,500
Baking and yeast powders (see also Drugs and chemicals)	8	111,700	48	26	10	39,714	182,900	323,500
Baskets, rattan and willow ware	7	9,015	13	....	....	6,140	3,960	18,020
Blacksmithing (see also Wheelwrighting)	168	224,745	343	....	6	188,954	201,598	616,909
Bookbinding and blank-book making	10	132,500	143	56	7	80,700	105,600	257,087
Boot and shoe uppers	3	12,000	13	....	....	7,052	17,400	29,200

Mechanical and manufacturing industries.	No. of establishments.	Capital.	Average number of hands employed.			Total amount paid in wages during the year.	Value of materials.	Value of products.
			Males above 16 years.	Females above 15 years.	Children and youths.			
Boots and shoes, including custom work and repairing	184	$679,630	658	217	197	$425,664	$874,842	$1,634,594
Boxes, cigar	6	57,550	51	22	11	34,100	47,700	105,600
Boxes, fancy and paper	6	21,590	27	44	19	23,300	45,800	91,200
Boxes, wooden packing	11	40,690	80	....	2	33,601	75,430	140,400
Brass castings	14	186,100	149	....	8	70,087	395,275	570,450
Bread and other bakery products	195	719,070	614	57	68	312,913	1,672,843	2,575,350
Brick and tile	45	727,250	787	....	153	307,581	197,588	701,032
Brooms and brushes	25	95,175	117	2	110	83,349	149,770	281,280
Carpentering	185	361,840	1,108	....	9	667,900	1,585,094	3,005,411
Carpets, rag	2	350	2	....	....	450	900	5,100
Carriage and wagon materials	3	126,000	189	....	3	91,638	134,440	264,600
Carriages and wagons (see also Wheelwrighting)	39	740,050	1,012	8	51	447,831	811,865	1,614,236
Cars, railroad, street, and repairs	7	314,200	601	....	....	293,384	732,460	1,100,809
Clothing, men's	100	1,351,355	1,191	1,652	12	779,908	1,895,342	3,425,167
Clothing, women's	13	140,800	75	451	30	119,775	238,700	483,000
Coffee and spices, roasted and ground	6	230,000	90	2	4	41,840	391,500	568,000
Coffins, burial cases, and undertakers' goods	5	30,500	23	4	....	12,530	109,200	157,396
Confectionery	31	307,560	207	185	21	159,649	774,790	1,158,185
Cooperage	78	493,295	860	....	88	377,056	798,262	1,431,405
Coppersmithing (see also Tinware, copperware, and sheet-iron ware)	3	3,500	9	....	1	6,200	12,000	24,000
Cordage and twine	14	12,375	37	....	40	16,423	33,250	67,664
Corsets	3	720	2	3	....	1,450	2,410	6,460
Cotton goods	3	825,500	106	171	163	86,325	335,381	453,295
Cutlery and edge tools (see also Hardware)	4	4,000	20	....	....	9,596	8,450	24,400
Dentistry, mechanical	8	6,700	5	3	1	4,184	6,400	32,400
Drugs and chemicals (see also Baking and yeast powders; Patent medicines and compounds).	15	696,000	216	57	28	123,940	665,365	1,166,743
Dyeing and cleaning	5	16,450	17	6	1	6,950	2,650	23,900
Dyeing and finishing textiles	3	16,000	14	5	4	7,500	5,500	22,200
Electroplating	8	17,600	29	1	2	12,725	9,420	43,200
Engraving and die-sinking	7	9,675	14	....	1	7,165	10,750	30,000
Engraving, steel	10	72,100	47	2	3	25,050	62,500	120,900
Engraving, wood	3	12,200	22	....	2	11,350	1,370	21,070
Files	6	38,900	35	....	....	17,142	7,870	34,300
Flouring- and grist-mill products	24	2,067,500	668	....	....	488,879	12,031,364	13,783,178
Food preparations	4	17,100	13	....	....	4,800	11,375	30,840
Foundery and machine-shop products (see also Iron work, architectural and ornamental).	62	3,605,713	3,433	....	33	1,854,046	2,700,844	5,952,770
Fruits and vegetables, canned and preserved	3	31,500	38	8	1	11,614	54,902	123,250
Furniture (see also Mattresses and spring beds; Upholstering)	54	920,702	1,044	11	68	511,915	1,082,825	1,979,683
Glass	5	280,000	395	....	220	261,098	238,946	597,277
Glass, cut, stained, and ornamented	3	11,000	16	....	....	9,450	7,100	27,600
Gloves and mittens	3	13,000	29	35	4	18,000	19,000	46,000
Glue	5	36,350	24	....	4	13,220	41,575	73,800
Grease and tallow	6	43,250	20	....	....	9,150	66,220	107,300
Hairwork	8	17,600	6	23	....	7,375	19,350	40,700
Hardware (see also Cutlery and edge tools)	10	210,150	111	....	1	51,321	102,256	188,862
Hats and caps, not including wool hats	9	60,400	49	82	4	42,865	77,740	177,531
Ink	3	3,600	8	....	....	3,568	7,200	16,234
Instruments, professional and scientific	4	54,660	22	....	....	12,700	35,725	81,450
Iron and steel	10	5,960,600	2,158	....	110	616,575	2,823,058	3,950,530
Iron bolts, nuts, washers, and rivets	4	235,000	123	....	14	60,498	301,937	493,550
Iron railing, wrought	6	23,400	34	....	5	20,760	25,360	63,400
Iron work, architectural and ornamental (see also Foundery and machine-shop products).	4	34,000	44	....	....	17,850	31,860	67,610
Jewelry	8	52,000	55	....	7	37,600	98,000	189,500
Labels and tags	3	10,300	12	....	....	7,868	10,910	25,500
Lamps and reflectors	7	261,600	139	....	20	74,139	376,540	519,300
Leather, curried	7	59,250	40	....	....	16,595	240,797	282,417
Leather, tanned	17	123,450	82	3	7	39,191	299,926	399,063
Lightning-rods	3	54,000	16	....	....	7,250	14,491	39,292
Lime	4	64,500	33	....	....	13,800	32,925	63,200
Liquors, malt	23	4,184,600	1,230	....	105	634,988	2,565,074	4,535,630

Mechanical and manufacturing industries.	No. of establishments.	Capital.	Average number of hands employed.			Total amount paid in wages during the year.	Value of materials.	Value of products.
			Males above 16 years.	Females above 15 years.	Children and youths.			
Liquors, vinous	3	$380,000	30			818,830	$52,000	$131,000
Lithographing (see also Printing and publishing)	5	71,500	94	6	17	51,265	83,344	214,989
Lock- and gun-smithing	17	5,325	18			8,514	4,970	24,714
Looking-glass and picture frames	19	323,900	129	1	22	80,251	102,825	268,682
Lumber, planed (see also Sash, doors, and blinds; Wood, turned and carved).	9	272,350	335	2	22	152,609	502,742	756,936
Lumber, sawed	3	620,000	119			72,086	251,600	412,000
Marble and stone work	56	237,825	473		18	237,207	245,707	707,721
Mattresses and spring beds (see also Furniture)	8	21,750	50	19	10	24,934	75,436	135,300
Masonry, brick and stone	68	82,375	386			206,389	216,321	575,700
Mineral and soda waters	11	112,100	97	5	27	45,846	58,090	193,000
Models and patterns	3	11,700	10			6,400	1,420	16,400
Musical instruments and materials (not specified)	8	60,000	10	1	1	5,350	8,775	28,250
Musical instruments, organs and materials	3	10,600	9			6,000	5,200	16,600
Musical instruments, pianos and materials	7	21,350	19			10,398	8,060	27,500
Oil, lard	3	96,000	25			13,050	505,750	539,000
Paints (see also Varnish)	13	1,688,350	522	10	4	250,532	2,006,480	2,570,860
Painting and paperhanging	119	369,945	863	15	18	393,932	549,654	1,255,552
Patent medicines and compounds (see also Drugs and chemicals)	24	1,383,200	198	87	13	134,696	482,235	1,145,090
Photographing	25	86,050	59	18	6	43,130	48,950	170,094
Pickles, preserves, and sauces	3	48,200	58	25	25	41,999	134,200	211,200
Plumbing and gasfitting	61	115,775	239		7	126,099	214,958	494,683
Printing and publishing (see also Lithographing)	101	2,480,060	1,978	175	117	1,239,299	1,249,094	3,668,287
Pumps, not including steam-pumps	9	529,850	109		2	65,900	701,570	926,750
Refrigerators	3	28,700	86		15	42,950	183,300	309,500
Roofing and roofing materials	5	53,700	75			48,000	81,900	177,800
Saddlery and harness	92	1,370,350	1,143	4	72	533,442	1,382,074	2,364,858
Sash, doors, and blinds (see also Lumber, planed; Wood, turned and carved).	12	586,195	661		43	275,321	669,871	1,191,670
Shipbuilding	7	243,000	279			187,380	265,592	506,712
Shirts	17	122,100	52	274		84,416	127,100	278,700
Show-cases	4	23,000	74	4	1	28,499	11,750	89,100
Slaughtering and meat packing, not including retail butchering	32	1,243,000	564		20	289,763	7,085,909	8,424,064
Soap and candles	15	718,927	253	2	2	95,501	1,262,701	1,607,545
Stencils and brands	6	4,750	11		2	5,925	5,565	21,425
Stone- and earthen-ware	5	34,500	31		10	16,090	19,985	46,430
Tinware, copperware, and sheet-iron ware (see also Coppersmithing).	120	418,325	508	13	62	227,546	553,208	1,095,959
Tobacco, chewing, smoking, and snuff (see also Tobacco, cigars and cigarettes).	21	1,146,200	763	143	325	402,959	3,950,956	4,813,769
Tobacco, cigars and cigarettes (see also Tobacco, chewing, smoking, and snuff).	201	272,925	576	6	72	265,967	312,725	888,993
Trunks and valises	14	105,500	156		8	73,125	205,775	340,560
Umbrellas and canes	4	1,400	3			1,020	1,150	4,370
Upholstering (see also Furniture)	18	209,025	48	4	6	20,850	62,100	148,727
Varnish (see also Paints)	3	26,500	10			8,962	35,000	54,600
Vinegar	14	249,650	115	12	4	69,520	296,000	572,400
Watch and clock repairing	17	36,250	19		1	9,367	13,175	39,740
Wheelwrighting (see also Blacksmithing; Carriages and wagons)	52	51,950	110		3	47,598	42,632	140,121
Whips	4	1,260	12			4,639	8,960	17,414
Wirework	8	153,700	134	4	38	60,890	112,620	371,600
Wood, turned and carved (see also Lumber, planed; Sash, doors, and blinds).	18	28,725	42		2	19,183	19,945	84,207
All other industries (a)	85	6,300,388	2,944	381	288	1,471,217	13,722,533	17,276,752

a Embracing artificial limbs; babbitt metal and solder; bags, other than paper; belting and hose, leather; billiard tables and materials; bluing; bone-, ivory-, and lamp-black; bridges; carriages and sleds, children's; cordials and sirups; cork cutting; dentists' materials; explosives and fireworks; fertilizers; flavoring extracts; furniture, chairs; furs, dressed; gold and silver, reduced and refined; hosiery and knit goods; ice, artificial; iron forgings; jewelry and instrument cases; lard, refined; lead, bar, pipe, sheet, and shot; liquors, distilled; malt; mantels, slate, marble, and marbleized; oil, castor; oil, cottonseed and cake; oil, lubricating; oil, neat's-foot; paving-materials; perfumery and cosmetics; photographic apparatus; plated and britannia ware; regalia and society banners and emblems; safes, doors, and vaults, fire-proof; saws; silk and silk goods; silversmithing; sporting goods; stamped ware; stationery goods; steam fittings and heating apparatus; stereotyping and electrotyping; sugar and molasses, refined; surgical appliances; tar and turpentine; telegraph and telephone apparatus; terra-cotta ware; toys and games; type founding; upholstering materials; washing-machines and clothes-wringers; watch cases; window blinds and shades; wire; and wooden ware.

From the foregoing table it appears that the average capital of all establishments is $17,384 70; that the average wages of all hands employed is $424 23 per annum; and that the average outlay in wages, in materials, and in interest (at 6 per cent.) on capital employed is $32,891 03.

MICHIGAN.

BAY CITY,

BAY COUNTY, MICHIGAN.

POPULATION

IN THE

AGGREGATE,

1860-1880.

	Inhab.
1790	......
1800	......
1810	......
1820	......
1830	......
1840	......
1850	......
1860	1,583
1870	7,064
1880	20,693

POPULATION

BY

SEX, NATIVITY, AND RACE,

AT

CENSUS OF 1880.

Male	11,318
Female	9,375
Native	11,389
Foreign-born	9,304
White	20,541
Colored	*152

* Including 1 Chinese.

Sault de St. Marie, Mich. N. 6° 08' W. 200.6 Miles.

Pierre Marquette, Mich. N. 40° 24' W. 271.7 Miles.

Grand Rapids, Mich. S. 66° 13' W. 100.3 Miles.

Lansing, Mich. S. 32° 20' W. 68. Miles.

Detroit, Mich. S. 26° E. 97.2 Miles.

Latitude: 43° 36′ North; Longitude: 83° 53′ (west from Greenwich).

FINANCIAL CONDITION:

Total Valuation: $7,651,130; per capita: $370 00.   Net Indebtedness: $438,470; per capita: $21 19.   Tax per $100: $1 86.

NOTE.—Bay City, the capital of Bay county, Michigan, is situated on the right (east) bank of the Saginaw river, 4 miles from its mouth and at the head of navigation. It was incorporated as a city in 1865. The principal trade of the city is in lumber and salt, immense quantities of which are produced. It is said to have excellent school facilities, a number of banks, two parks, the Holly water-works, and a street railway.

Three railroads run out of the city: The Detroit, Saginaw, and Bay City railroad to Detroit; a short branch connecting with the Flint and Père Marquette railroad, which has Toledo and Ludington as its terminals; and the Mackinaw division of the Michigan Central railroad, giving a line to Chicago. Several lines of steamers connect it with all lake points.

Bay county, of which Bay City is the capital, is drained by the Saginaw, Rifle, and Saganing rivers. The surface is nearly level, and is mostly covered with forests. The soil is fertile.

BAY CITY IN 1880.

The following is all the information that was furnished regarding the present condition of Bay City:

SANITARY AUTHORITY—BOARD OF HEALTH.

The board of aldermen of Bay City acts as a board of health. There are 14 aldermen, none of whom are physicians. The only annual expense of the board is for a health officer, whom it appoints, with a salary of $400 a year. In the absence of epidemics the board has power to order nuisances abated; in their presence, to do any thing which in its judgment is necessary to stop the spread of disease. The chief executive officer of the board is the mayor, who has no salary. The health officer has power to make complaints to the police, who make the arrests; he makes all inspections, and in general looks after all such matters. Defective sewerage, street-cleaning, etc., are looked after principally by the street commissioner. Garbage is treated like any other nuisance when it becomes a nuisance. There is an ordinance against polluting streams and rivers, also one for the removal of excrement by an odorless machine.

INFECTIOUS DISEASES.

Small-pox patients are taken to the city pest-house, situated in an isolated spot near the city limits. There has been very little scarlet fever in Bay City, and the patients were not isolated or quarantined at home. In case of the breaking out of contagious diseases in a school it would be closed for a while. Vaccination is neither compulsory nor is it done at the public expense. Once a year the supervisors of each ward canvass their ward and report all births and deaths to the county clerk, receiving 10 cents for each birth or death so reported. The city is very healthy. Ague is not uncommon.

MUNICIPAL CLEANSING.

Street-cleaning.—The streets are cleaned by the city's force by hand once a week, and it is reported to be well done. The annual cost to the city is about $500. The sweepings are deposited in the low places in the streets, or used for making docks, or for manure.

Removal of garbage and ashes.—Garbage is generally removed by householders, being placed in vessels and removed at intervals. While awaiting removal it must be covered up in barrels. Most of it is removed by those who wish it for swine, cows, or manure. Ashes are taken by soap or potash manufacturers.

Dead animals.—Dead animals found in the street are buried by order of the city marshal at the city's expense, provided the owner can not be found. The cost of this service is perhaps $50 a year.

Liquid household wastes.—Chamber-slops, laundry waste, and kitchen-slops are either run into the sewers, or into privy-vaults, or are thrown on the gardens. Cesspools are porous and have no overflows. Street-gutters are flushed only by the rain. No contamination of drinking-water ever occurs, since almost all the water used in the city comes from Saginaw bay through the system of the Holly water-works. As the city grows older better sewerage is expected. There are several brick 4-foot sewers now under way.

Human excreta.—Almost all the houses of the city have privy-vaults, the business portion alone depending on water-closets. Very few privy-vaults are even nominally water-tight. The ordinance about them provides that they shall be walled up with 2-inch plank, or with brick or stone, and be sunk at least 4 feet below the level of the earth; if there be a public sewer within 100 feet the vault must be drained into it.

Manufacturing wastes.—There are no manufacturing establishments in Bay City which have any wastes to amount to any thing. The saw-mills burn all their sawdust and slabs.

MANUFACTURES.

The following is a summary of the statistics of the manufactures of Bay City for 1880, being taken from tables prepared for the Tenth Census:

Mechanical and manufacturing industries.	No. of establishments.	Capital.	AVERAGE NUMBER OF HANDS EMPLOYED.			Total amount paid in wages during the year.	Value of materials.	Value of products.
			Males above 16 years.	Females above 15 years.	Children and youths.			
All industries	80	$4,235,500	2,066	21	151	$802,488	$3,851,553	$5,533,621
Cooperage	6	10,200	39	....	4	19,220	30,100	60,450
Foundery and machine-shop products	9	278,000	322	....	5	126,583	176,200	340,695
Lumber, sawed	22	3,042,000	1,079	....	95	351,500	2,831,608	3,702,298
Salt	20	673,000	405	....	21	191,642	296,297	707,741
All other industries (a)	23	232,300	221	21	26	113,543	517,348	722,437

a Embracing blacksmithing; boots and shoes; carriages and wagons; clothing, men's; flouring- and grist-mill products; liquors, malt; lumber, planed; mineral and soda waters; models and patterns; needles and pins; sash, doors, and blinds; slaughtering and meat-packing; tinware, copperware, and sheet-iron ware; tobacco, cigars and cigarettes; and wooden ware.

From the foregoing table it appears that the average capital of all establishments is $52,943 75; that the average wages of all hands employed is $358 90 per annum; and that the average outlay in wages, in materials, and in interest (at 6 per cent.) on capital employed is $61,352 13.

DETROIT,

WAYNE COUNTY, MICHIGAN.

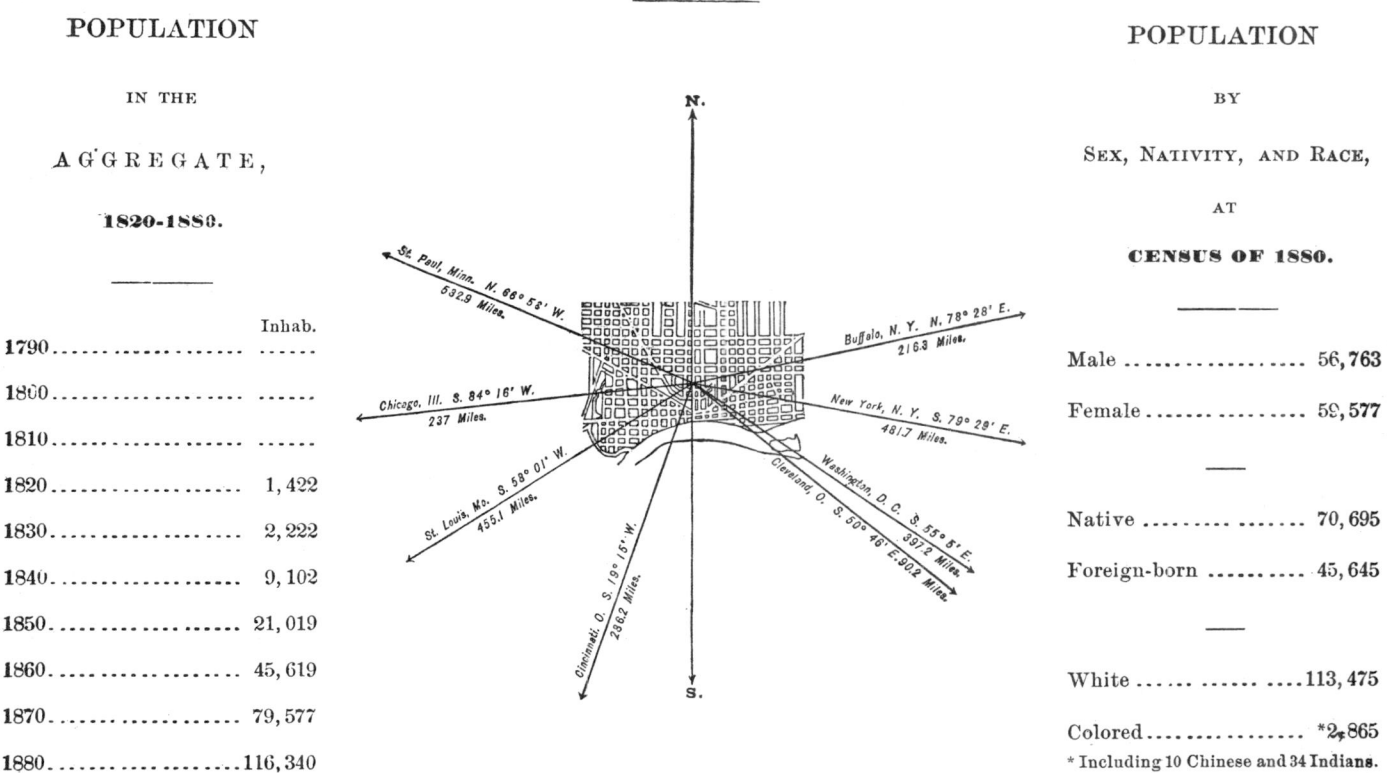

POPULATION IN THE AGGREGATE, 1820-1880.	
	Inhab.
1790	......
1800	......
1810	......
1820	1,422
1830	2,222
1840	9,102
1850	21,019
1860	45,619
1870	79,577
1880	116,340

POPULATION BY SEX, NATIVITY, AND RACE, AT CENSUS OF 1880.

Male	56,763
Female	59,577
Native	70,695
Foreign-born	45,645
White	113,475
Colored	*2,865

* Including 10 Chinese and 34 Indians.

Latitude: 42° 20′ North; Longitude: 83° 3′ (west from Greenwich); Altitude: 580 to 635 feet.

FINANCIAL CONDITION:

Total Valuation: $83,198,040; per capita: $715 00.   Net Indebtedness: $2,282,772; per capita: $19 62.   Tax per $100: $1 46.

HISTORICAL SKETCH.(a)

Near the outlet of lake Erie, on the northern shore, a trading post was established, to which was given the name "Fort Frontenac", in honor of the governor-general of New France.

In 1678 La Salle returned to France and obtained royal letters authorizing him to spend five years in exploring, with liberty to build forts where he should deem it necessary, and hold them with the same privileges as at Fort Frontenac. On his return from France he traversed the length of lake Ontario, ascending the Niagara river to the falls, where he made the portage, and in the winter of 1678-'79 he began building a vessel of 60 tons burden a few miles above the falls. This vessel was called the "Griffin", and on the 7th of August, 1679, she set sail on the

---

a J. C. Holmes, esq., of Detroit, not only collected and forwarded nearly all the statistical information regarding the city, but also much of the information contained in the historical sketch with which this report is introduced.

first voyage which had ever been made by Europeans on lake Erie. La Salle was the commander, and the crew consisted of fur-traders belonging to Canadian colonies. The wind being favorable, she made a quick passage over lake Erie and anchored at the mouth of the Detroit river on the evening of the 10th of August. On the 11th of August, 1679, the Griffin weighed anchor and entered the river, and it is recorded that on ascending it the explorers found along its banks several Indian villages. A large village of the Hurons, called "Teuchsa Gromdie", stood on the present site of Detroit. The Griffin proceeded on her way, and soon after reached Mackinac in safety.

La Motte Cadillac was the founder of Detroit. In 1701 he planted the little military colony which time has transmuted into a thriving American city. At an earlier date some feeble efforts had been made to secure possession of this important pass, and when La Houtan visited the lakes, a small post, called fort Saint Joseph, was standing near the present site of fort Gratiot. At about this time the wandering Jesuits made frequent sojourns upon the borders of the Detroit river, and baptized the savage children whom they found there.

Fort Saint Joseph was abandoned in the year 1688. La Motte Cadillac's enterprise was destined to a better fate. In 1699 he first proposed to the French government to make a settlement for habitation at Detroit, but finding he was not likely to succeed in his scheme by correspondence, he went to France and laid his plans before Pontchartrain, the prime minister of Louis XIV. The result was that he was informed by the minister that he should have 200 men of different trades and 6 companies of soldiers.

On his return from France he reached Quebec on the 8th of March, 1701. He left for his new post on the 5th of June with 50 soldiers and 50 artisans and tradesmen. They reached the site of Detroit on the 24th of July and began to build a fort, which was called fort Pontchartrain, after the friendly minister who had favored it. This fort was about 200 feet square, encircled with cedar pickets, with wooden bastions at each angle. Within this inclosure Cadillac caused a few log huts to be erected, the roofs of which were thatched with grass.

Detroit soon rose to distinguished importance among the western outposts of Canada. In December, 1750, the late Governor De la Gallissonière prepared an elaborate memoir on the French colonies, in which he said:

Detroit demands now the greatest attention. Did it once contain a farming population of 1,000, it would feed and defend all the rest. Throughout the whole interior of Canada it is best adapted for a town where all the trade of the lakes would concentrate; were it provided with a good garrison and surrounded by a goodly number of settlements it would be enabled to overcome almost all the Indians of the continent. It is sufficient to see its position on the map to understand its utility.

In pursuance of these suggestions, in 1751 emigrants were sent out from France and advances were made to them by the government until they were able to take care of themselves. At the close of the French war, as Major Rogers tells us, the place contained 2,500 inhabitants. The center of the settlement was the fortified town, currently called "the fort". Above and below, both sides of the stream were lined with small Canadian dwellings, extending at various intervals for nearly 8 miles. Each had its garden and its orchard, and each was inclosed by a fence of rounded pickets. The farms attached to them were long and narrow, fronting on the stream. The titles to these were generally derived from the governor-general, but permits to occupy were sometimes granted gratuitously by the French commandants. These grants and rights to occupancy were later confirmed by the British, and in the early part of this century by the United States government, through a commission.

The whole lake region, from its discovery until 1760, was under the dominion of France. On the 18th of September, 1759, Quebec passed from the hands of the French. On the 8th of September, 1760, Montreal and all its dependencies were surrendered to the British crown. This capitulation included Detroit, Mackinac, and all other portions of Canada yet in possession of the French.

On the 12th of September, 1760, Major Robert Rogers received orders from General Amherst to advance with sufficient force and take possession of Detroit, Mackinac, and indeed all the Northwest, and to administer the oath of allegiance to the inhabitants. No resistance was offered on the part either of French or of Indians, and on the 29th of November Detroit fell quietly into the hands of the English. The garrison were sent as prisoners down the lake, but the Canadian inhabitants were allowed to retain their farms and houses on condition of swearing allegiance to the British crown. The fort was at once garrisoned with British troops.

At this time, within the limits of the settlement were three Indian villages. On the western shore, a little below the fort, were the lodges of Pottawattamies; nearly opposite, on the eastern side, was the village of the Wyandots; and on the same side, 2 miles higher up, Pontiac's band had fixed their abode. The settlers had always maintained the best terms with their savage neighbors. In truth, there was much congeniality between the red man and the Canadian. Their harmony was seldom broken, and among the woods and wilds of the northern lakes roamed many a lawless half-breed, the mongrel offspring of intermarriage between the colonists of Detroit and the Indian squaws. "The king and lord of all this country," as Rogers called him, was Pontiac—brave, cunning, ambitious, treacherous—whose friendship the English could never win. Actuated by dreams of power, and goaded on by the scheming French, he plotted a most dangerous uprising against the British dominion. Of this bloody and cruel war Detroit was the center. It was besieged by the Indians under their sagacious leader on the 9th of May, 1763, and was not relieved till late in the fall of that year. Of all the small posts scattered at wide intervals through the wilderness to the westward of Niagara and fort Pitt, this one alone was able to maintain itself.

Throughout the winter of 1763-'64 the settlement was left in comparative quiet, but with the opening of spring the Indians resumed their hostilities; not, however, with the same activity and vigor as during the preceding summer. In August an expedition, which had been sent into this part of the country under General Bradstreet, relieved the long-imprisoned garrison. Early in September a peace was concluded, and thenceforth Detroit ceased to figure in the struggle which Pontiac kept up into the next year.

The official census made in 1768 showed but 572 souls at Detroit. In 1778 there were about 70 houses in the town, most of them one story, and the rest a story and a half high, there not being a two-story house in the place. They were all built of logs, some of which were hewed and some round. The population is said to have been 60 families, comprising about 200 males and 100 females, but probably this did not include the whole settlement, but only the part within the inclosure. About 500 troops were stationed here.

The old town of Detroit was in the form of an oblong square, covering about 3 acres. It was surrounded by a palisade of oak and cedar pickets, 25 feet high, in which there were four gates—east, west, north, and south. Over three of these gates were block-houses, containing four 6-pound guns each. Between the palisade and the houses of the time was a wide passage-way, known as the *Chemin de ronde*. Besides this, there were four streets running parallel to the river, intersected at right angles by two other streets and two alleys, all exceedingly narrow. The only public buildings were a council-house and a rude little church.

Under British rule there was a constant improvement in the appearance of this town, but more especially in the military appointments.

The success of the American arms at Vincennes in 1778, and the prospect that the victorious troops would continue their course onward to Detroit, induced Major Le Noult, the commanding officer, to erect a fort on the rising ground, or "second terrace," outside of the palisades and back of the town. This large and efficient fortification was called fort Le Noult until after the war of 1812, when it was named fort Shelby, in honor of the governor of Kentucky. It was located at the intersection of the present Fort and Shelby streets, and was removed in 1827.

In addition to this, new barracks for officers and soldiers were built, and a handsome esplanade and two or three military gardens were laid out between the fort and the town.

The people all lived like one family. Social forms were, however, carefully observed. Assemblies were held once a fortnight, sometimes once a week, and ladies went to them in their silks. Dining-parties were frequent, and they drank their wine freely.

In social life, the French characteristics predominated. During the summer the days were devoted to business, and the evenings were spent by the older portion of the inhabitants in social visiting, and in the younger in dancing, promenading, and moonlight sailing on the beautiful river. Barbecues were occasionally held in a grove near by. In the winter the denizens of the fort and the town gave themselves up to unrestrained pleasure-seeking, and the summer's earnings scarce sufficed for the winter's waste.

The citizens depended principally for eatables on the Indians, who supplied them plentifully with game. A milch-cow was worth $100, and a pair of steers would sell for $250. The circulating medium in the country consisted chiefly of paper money, issued by the merchants, in denominations ranging from 6 pence to 20 shillings; it purported to be payable to bearer. The troops brought considerable money into town. In those days the river Savoyard ran across the site of the future city, crossing what is now Woodward avenue somewhere near the line of Congress street. It was sufficiently large to float canoes, but was always an insignificant stream, and was in later years filled in. The line of Detroit did not then at all correspond to the present line of the river. The southern edge of the present city is all made ground, and in 1796 the river washed up as far as the present block between Atwater and Woodbridge streets, and Woodbridge street prolonged to the west would have ended in the water before Cass street was reached. The bulk of the business of the town was near the river, and between Griswold and Wayne streets as they exist now.

In the year 1787 the whole region claimed by the Americans, lying northwest of the Ohio river and reaching to the great lakes, though still partly occupied by the British, was organized by Congress into a Northwest territory, and General Arthur Saint Clair was appointed governor. By the stipulations of the treaty of Greenville, made by General Wayne with the Indian tribes, and signed August 3, 1795, it was conceded that as far as they were concerned Detroit and all the region of the Northwest should become the property of the United States. In July, 1796, under the provisions of Jay's treaty, Captain Porter, with a detachment of troops from General Wayne's army, took possession of Detroit, and flung out to the breeze the first American banner that ever floated over the Peninsular state. Thereupon the ordinance of 1787 was extended over the peninsula of Michigan, and it became part of the Northwest territory. On the 11th of August following, Winthrop Sargent, acting governor of the territory, set apart the new county of Wayne, and designated Detroit as the county-seat. The county included all of Michigan, northern Ohio, and Indiana, and a part of Illinois and Wisconsin. It elected delegates to the first territorial legislature, which met at Cincinnati September 16, 1799. By an act of Congress of April 30, 1802, the Northwestern territory ceased to exist, the state of Ohio was organized, and the territory of Indiana was formed, of which Michigan formed a part.

On January 11, 1805, Congress enacted "That from and after the 30th day of June next, all that part of Indiana territory which lies north of a line drawn east from the southerly bend or extreme of lake Michigan, until it shall intersect lake Erie, and east of a line drawn from the said southerly bend through the middle of said lake to its northern extremity, and thence due north to the northern boundary of the United States, shall, for the purpose of temporary government, constitute a separate territory, and be called Michigan."

William Hull was appointed governor, and Augustus Brevoort Woodward, Frederick Bates, and John Griffin, were created judges. Detroit was made the seat of government. Governor Hull reached here on the 1st of July, 1805, and on the next day he administered the oath of office to the other officers, and the territory of Michigan began its existence. Its boundaries remained as they were until 1818, when, at the time of the admission of Illinois as a state, all of what is now Wisconsin was added to Michigan. In 1839 Iowa and Minnesota were added for the purpose of temporary government.

During the British domination the large grants of land offered to actual settlers, with rations from the fort for a specified time after their arrival, had induced a few Scotch and English families to immigrate and settle along the banks of the Detroit and Saint Clair rivers. The French inhabitants, many of whom had intermarried with the Indians, had been permitted to retain and enjoy their farms above and below the town, and were now in a prosperous condition.

Soon after the stars and stripes began to wave above the fort, a number of emigrants from France, who had spent some years in the colonies, removed to Detroit, and about the same time a few Americans also ventured farther. From 1796 to 1805 there was a constant gradual accession to the number of inhabitants in the town and surrounding country.

Within the town all was bustle and business. Some of the French traders still remained, and they and the British merchants had full possession until 1799. All kinds of merchandise brought good prices and met with ready sales. Coffee sold for 38 cents a pound, tea for $2, calico was 75 cents a yard, and all articles of wearing apparel were in like proportion.

Colonel Stephen Mack was the first American merchant in Detroit. He came in 1799, and at once built a shanty in the very center of the town, where he spread out his goods to the admiring gaze of thronging customers. At that time the narrow streets and alleys were constantly thronged with savages hastening to the trading-houses to exchange their peltries for goods, or reeling about under the influence of the baneful "fire-water". At the wharves vessels were busy discharging their freights of merchandise and receiving return cargoes of fur from the well-filled storehouses. The prevailing style of the dwellings was as yet that of one-story block-houses with dormer windows, a few of them being covered with clapboards.

Americans now began to come in, and soon outnumbered the French population. The town grew apace, and all was prosperous, until on the 11th of June, 1805, sudden and dire disaster befell it, and for a while at least put an end to progress. On that day, just five months after Governor Hull's appointment, a fire broke out at noon, and at nightfall it was a scene of smoldering ruins, and the population was homeless. Within the limits of the stockade one small French-built dwelling-house on Saint Anne street, and a large brick storehouse near the river, were all that remained of the thriving town. The next day the government and territorial officers arrived. A sad spectacle presented itself to their astonished gaze. Instead of a flourishing town or settlement, growing rich by a lucrative traffic with the Indians, they found only a widespread waste of still smoking ruins. The inhabitants, suddenly impoverished and greatly disheartened, were gathered on the common within range of the guns of the fort, with no other abiding place than cloth tents, or rude huts hastily erected. It was a hard blow, but the people felt that this, the seat of the government of the territory, was sure to be an important place, and again inspired with hope, went to work to build new homes. Numerous dwellings were soon completed, and the town began to assume a less desolate appearance. Yet there was much suffering among those of the inhabitants whose whole available property had been destroyed. In October an official statement of the destruction of the town and the consequent deplorable condition of the inhabitants was made to the Secretary of State of the United States by Governor Hull and his associates. At the next session of Congress it was accordingly enacted for the relief of the sufferers, and to encourage an increased immigration, that the governor and judges of the territory should be authorized to lay out a new town, including the whole of the old town of Detroit and 10,000 acres adjacent, and to any person who, "not owning or professing allegiance to any foreign power, and being above the age of 17 years", owned or inhabited a house in Detroit at the time it was burnt, they were authorized to grant a lot not exceeding 5,000 square feet, and they were ordered to sell what land should be left, and to apply the proceeds toward building a court-house and jail.

The plan of the new town of Detroit, said to be similar to that of Byzantium, was on a magnificent scale, and, if fully carried out, would have far surpassed the present city. Jefferson and Woodward avenues and some of the streets near the river were immediately surveyed, and the adjudication of claims went on as rapidly as possible. Early in 1807 the whole survey was completed. The triangle around the fort was the military reservation, and was not divided into lots until about 1826. The governor and judges who laid out the new town seemed to anticipate the future importance of the city, and to their foresight, good taste, and judgment is it indebted for the numerous parks and the wide avenues for which the city is famed.

In 1806 the celebrated chief Tecumseh and his brother devised a plan quite similar to the famous project of Pontiac, to effect the destruction of Detroit and the other American settlements in the territory. The disaffection soon manifested by the Wyandots and other Indians in the vicinity of Detroit caused the governor early in 1807 to order the inclosure of the inhabited part of the new town by a strong palisade. During the year 1807 a treaty was effected with some of the tribe, yet the threatening movements of the Shawanese, and the little reliance that could be placed on Indian fidelity, had its influence in retarding the growth of Detroit. Still there was constant progress. Many of those who have since given character and influence to this city were young, enterprising immigrants to Detroit between 1807 and 1812.

In June, 1812, Congress declared war against Great Britain. The first shock fell upon Michigan. Mackinac was early obliged to surrender. On the 14th of August, General Brock arrived at fort Malden with a reinforcement; on the 15th he appeared at Sandwich and summoned General Hull to surrender. General Hull refused, and a cannonade upon Detroit was immediately begun, which was returned with effect. On the 16th General Brock crossed the river with his army 3 miles below the town, without opposition, and at once marched up to the fort without meeting resistance. A negotiation soon began between the two commanders, which ended with the surrender of the army and the territory of Michigan to the British general, to the mortification and bitter indignation of the American troops, who were impatiently waiting for orders to attack the enemy. General Brock's forces are said to have been only 1,400, while those of General Hull amounted to 1,800. This ignominious and cowardly capitulation met with universal reprobation throughout the Union. An army was at once raised to retrieve the disgrace, and started off for Michigan under General William H. Harrison in the ensuing winter. Not much was effected until after Perry's glorious victory of the 10th of September, on lake Erie. General Harrison was soon after joined by General Shelby, and with their forces united they sailed for fort Malden, which they occupied September 8, General Brock having evacuated it in anticipation of this movement. Detroit was vacated on the 29th.

On the 14th of October, 1813, General Harrison appointed General Lewis Cass provisional governor of Michigan territory; he was subsequently made permanent governor. He made Detroit his home for the remainder of his life, and was not only a most successful governor, but also a much respected and honored citizen.

Detroit quickly recovered from the losses incident to the disasters of war, and by 1815 was in such a prosperous condition that on the 24th of October, 1815, the governor and judges passed an act incorporating it as a city. Its government was vested in 5 trustees, and they chose one of their number as president.

At that time no road led out of Detroit, except the one up and down the river. The mail was brought around the lake, through Ohio, on horseback, and when the road was very bad a man carried it on his shoulders through the black swamps. The first line of wheel carriage between Detroit and Ohio was established in 1827. A "public" vessel, the brig Hunter, was the ordinary means of communication between Detroit and Buffalo. The road around the lake was not practicable for wheels one-third of the distance, and for four months of the year was scarcely passable for a horse.

The collection district of Detroit had been defined in 1799, and a collector of the port of Detroit was appointed in June of that year. Although the importations at that early day were comparatively large, no statistics have been found regarding them. As late as 1815, not a vessel that then navigated the lakes was owned in Detroit. In fact, there were but three or four on lake Erie, and they mostly belonged to the British. There was then but one wharf here. It was called the "public wharf", and consisted merely of a pier, formed by a crib of logs, filled in with stone or gravel, and about 150 feet from the shore, with which it was connected by a bridge or plank-way. The rest of the water-front of the place was nearly in a state of nature.

Shortly after this boats began to be built and owned at this port. Up to 1830 the vessels on the lake were almost all small sloops and schooners, rarely reaching 100 tons, and generally under 60. They were mostly built at Huron, Ohio, and at Buffalo.

The steamboat "Walk-in-the-Water" was the first to navigate lake Erie (see *History of Buffalo*). Her first arrival at Detroit was chronicled May 20, 1819.

The first steamer enrolled as belonging to the port of Detroit was the Argo, and she was called a steam-sloop. She was built here in 1830, was 42 feet long, and had a capacity of 9 tons. She was used as a ferry-boat, and occasionally ran up the river Rouge to Dearborn. Another boat was built here in 1832, and a number more in 1833 and 1834. From that time on steamboat-building became an important factor in Detroit industries.

In 1818 the amount of tonnage on lake Erie was estimated at about 1,000 tons. In 1836 it was 24,045 tons, of which it was said the Detroit district had 6,703 tons. In this district were enrolled, in 1836, 17 steamboats, 3 brigs, 43 schooners, and 37 sloops. In 1855 there were here enrolled 83 steamboats (of which 23 were propellers), with a tonnage of 34,285 tons; 5 barks, 9 brigs, 123 schooners, 15 scow schooners, 17 scows, 44 sloops—total 213 with a tonnage of 35,653 tons. Total number of vessels, 296; total amount of tonnage, 69,938.

As late as 1827 Detroit was little else than a military and fur-trading post. The buildings were mostly constructed of wood, one or two stories high, with steep roofs and dormer windows. The banks of the river within view of the city were studded with wind grist-mills, and flour was brought to the city and sold only in sacks.

The earth of fort Shelby, which was removed in 1827–'28, was used in filling up the embankments then being constructed along the whole water-front of the city, which had been bad for a year or two previous. This was done as a sanitary measure, and the health of the city was very much improved.

Water-works were begun by individual enterprise in 1825, and in 1827 the citizens were first supplied with water from them. Two years later a company was organized, which continued to extend the works until 1836, when they were bought by the city. The city projected the present works, and the construction began in 1837.

The project of a railroad across the peninsula of Michigan was agitated as early as 1830. Two years later the Detroit and Saint Joseph Railroad Company was incorporated. This company did not begin the construction of its road till 1836, when it proceeded to grade about 10 miles in detached parts between Detroit and Ypsilanti. Michigan was admitted into the Union as a state on the 26th of January, 1837. Soon after, the legislature adopted a grand scheme of internal improvements, and effected a loan of $5,000,000 for the purpose of constructing public works—railroads and canals. This had the effect of checking individual enterprise, and the Detroit and Saint Joseph Company transferred its interest to the state at once. The state completed and opened the road to Ypsilanti in 1838, to Ann Arbor in 1839, to Jackson in 1842, and to Kalamazoo in 1843. In 1846 it sold out the road to New York and New England capitalists for $2,000,000, and they were incorporated as the Michigan Central Railroad Company.

To the railroad enterprise of the following years Detroit owed much of her growth.

It may here be mentioned that the city secured a new charter in 1824. In 1832 and in 1834 the cholera produced great mortality.

The first great fire—that of 1805—has been referred to. The second destructive fire broke out at about 10 o'clock a. m., May 1, 1837, on the east side of Woodward avenue, near the river, and burnt over a district extending from the river to Woodbridge street and from Woodward avenue to Baker street. Fifty-six buildings were burnt; the individual sufferers were 37, and the entire loss was estimated at $130,000, of which but a small portion was covered by insurance.

On the night of January 1, 1842, a fire broke out in an old wooden hotel, situated on the west side of Woodward avenue, midway between Jefferson avenue and Woodbridge street, that destroyed every building in the square bounded on the north by Jefferson avenue, south by Woodbridge street, west by Griswold street, and east by Woodward avenue. The loss was estimated at $200,000.

A very disastrous fire occurred at 10 o'clock on the morning of May 9, 1848. Sparks from the smoke-stack of a propeller lying at a wharf set fire to an old wooden warehouse, and in spite of the efforts of all the people the fire progressed with great rapidity. It destroyed the buildings south of Atwater street, crossed that street, consumed all the buildings east of the alley between Bates and Randolph streets eastward to Brush street, excepting a building on the southeast corner of Atwater and Brush streets. Crossing Woodbridge street it continued to Jefferson avenue; then turning eastwardly it extended nearly to Beaubien street, where its course was stayed at 4 o'clock in the afternoon. Nearly 250 buildings were consumed, 107 of which were dwellings, rendering 300 families houseless. Among other buildings that were burnt was the Wales hotel. This was a brick building erected by General William Hull in 1807 as his residence, and the first brick dwelling built in Detroit. It was his headquarters at the time of his surrender of Detroit to the British in August, 1812. About 10 acres of territory were burnt over, and the loss was over $250,000.

After each of the large fires the ground burnt over was soon covered with better and more substantial buildings.

Since the advent of steam fire-engines and paid firemen here no extensive fires have occurred.

Detroit was the capital of the state for 10 years after Michigan was admitted into the Union.

"Common schools were first established in 1842. Previous to that time but little interest had been manifested in the cause of general education. A report made to the common council in 1841 showed that there were 27 English schools, 1 French, and 1 German school in the city, and that the whole number of pupils in them was about 700, while there were upward of 2,000 children of the proper school age in the city. In 1842 an act was passed by the legislature incorporating the schools into one district under the style of the 'board of education of the city of Detroit'. The board is composed of 2 school inspectors from each ward, one of whom is annually elected for a term of 2 years.

"The first house for public worship erected at Detroit was built by the Roman Catholics in the year 1723. The cathedral of Saint Ann was begun in 1817. The first Protestant society was organized by the Methodists in 1812. The first Episcopal society was organized in 1824, the first Presbyterian in 1825. In 1855 there were 28 church edifices in the city.

"In 1855 there were 7 plank roads leading from the city into the country, aggregating 300 miles in length." (a)

From tables of population it appears that the period of the greatest increase have been the decades between 1844 and 1854, and between 1864 and 1874, about 29,000 inhabitants having been added in the former and 47,000 in the latter. The apparently disproportionate increase at certain times has been partly due to extensions in the city's limits. Occasional extensions have been made to the east and north into the township of Hamtrank, and on the west into the township of Springwells. Within a few years the car building and repair shops of the Michigan Central railroad, the Detroit car-works, and some other extensive manufacturing establishments, have been removed a short distance outside of the city limits into the adjoining townships, taking several hundred employés, who have erected dwellings for themselves in the vicinity of their work. Had these establishments remained in the city limits the increase of population from 1874 to 1880 would have shown quite differently.

At the present time the population of Detroit consists of Americans, French, Germans, Irish, English, and Africans, with a good sprinkling of people of almost all other nationalities.

---

a Detroit in 1855.

DETROIT IN 1880. [a]

LOCATION.

"The river or strait of Detroit, which connects lakes Saint Clair and Erie, has a general course north or south, but at one point it turns northeasterly and southwesterly. At this point it is the boundary between Michigan and Ontario, and here, on the north shore, the city of Detroit stands, 18 miles northeast of lake Erie and 7 miles southwest of lake Saint Clair, in latitude 42° 20' north and longitude 83° 3' west." [b]

The river is 580 feet above the sea-level; the lowest point of the city is at the shore, from which it rises gradually to the northwest for about 2¼ miles, until Frederick street is reached, where it attains an altitude of 55 feet above the ordinary river-level.

The river opposite the city is half a mile wide, and nearly the whole width forms the channel, and is navigable. The harbor may be said to extend the whole width of the river and along the entire front of the city. The draught of water is not less than 30 feet. The velocity of the current is about 1½ mile an hour. There is water communication open to lakes Superior, Michigan, Huron, Saint Clair, Erie, and Ontario, and through the river Saint Lawrence to the Atlantic ocean.

RAILROADS

Detroit has the following lines of railroad:

The Michigan Central railroad extends from Detroit to Chicago. It connects at Chicago with roads running to all points of the compass, and at Detroit with the Great Western, which runs through Canada to Suspension Bridge. This line also connects with and operates the Grand River Valley railroad, running from Jackson to Grand Rapids; the Michigan Air Line railroad, from Jackson to South Bend; the Joliet and Northern Indiana railroad, from Lake Erie to Joliet; the Jackson, Lansing, and Saginaw railroad, from Jackson to Gaylord; and the Kalamazoo and South Haven railroad, between the two points named.

The Detroit and Grand Haven railroad, connecting Detroit with Grand Haven, where connection is made with steamers for Milwaukee.

The Detroit, Hillsdale, and Southwestern railroad runs from Detroit on the Michigan Central's track 30 miles to Ypsilanti; then on its own track, by way of Hillsdale, to Bankers, Michigan, distant from Detroit 94 miles, where it connects with the Fort Wayne, Jackson, and Saginaw railroad.

The Detroit, Lansing, and Northern railroad extends from Detroit through Lansing to Howard City.

The Lake Shore and Michigan Southern railroad runs from Detroit via Toledo to Chicago.

The Grand Trunk railroad runs from Detroit through Canada to Portland, Maine

The Chicago and Canada Southern railroad runs westward to Fayette, Ohio, and eastward to Buffalo and Niagara.

The Detroit and Bay City railroad extends from Detroit to East Saginaw.

TRIBUTARY COUNTRY.

Nearly the whole state of Michigan is tributary to her chief city, either by railroad, wagon-road, or water communication. The state is divided by the straits of Mackinac into the upper and lower, or the northern and southern peninsulas. The latter, in which is Detroit, is celebrated for its agricultural products, particularly its winter wheat and other grains. The raising of superior breeds of horses, cattle, sheep, and swine is made a specialty by some of the farmers. One of the leading industries of the state is its horticultural products, such as apples, pears, peaches, plums, grapes, and other small fruits, some parts of the lower peninsula being particularly adapted to their growth.

In this section also a very important branch of business is the manufacture of lumber and staves, this part of the state being rich in pine and hard-wood timber. Salt is produced in large quantities from the salt wells in the Saginaw valley, while lime and gypsum are abundant in some parts of the state. Nearly all kinds of lumber being plentiful, the manufacture of cabinet-ware, vehicles of all kinds, pails and all other wooden-ware, is extensively carried on in Detroit and a number of the interior towns.

Iron and copper ores of superior quality are found in inexhaustible quantities in the upper peninsula, and the inhabitants of that part of the state are largely dependent upon the mining interest for their support, while the many extensive founderies and machine-shops of Detroit look there for their supply of the raw material.

TOPOGRAPHY, ETC.

"In the year 1829 a company was organized for the purpose of erecting water-works. In furtherance of this object the company bored a 4-inch hole to the depth of 260 feet, at a point 30 feet above the level of the river, and

---

a The detailed information concerning the present condition of Detroit was collected and forwarded by J. C. Holmes, esq., of that city.　　　　b Detroit in 1855.

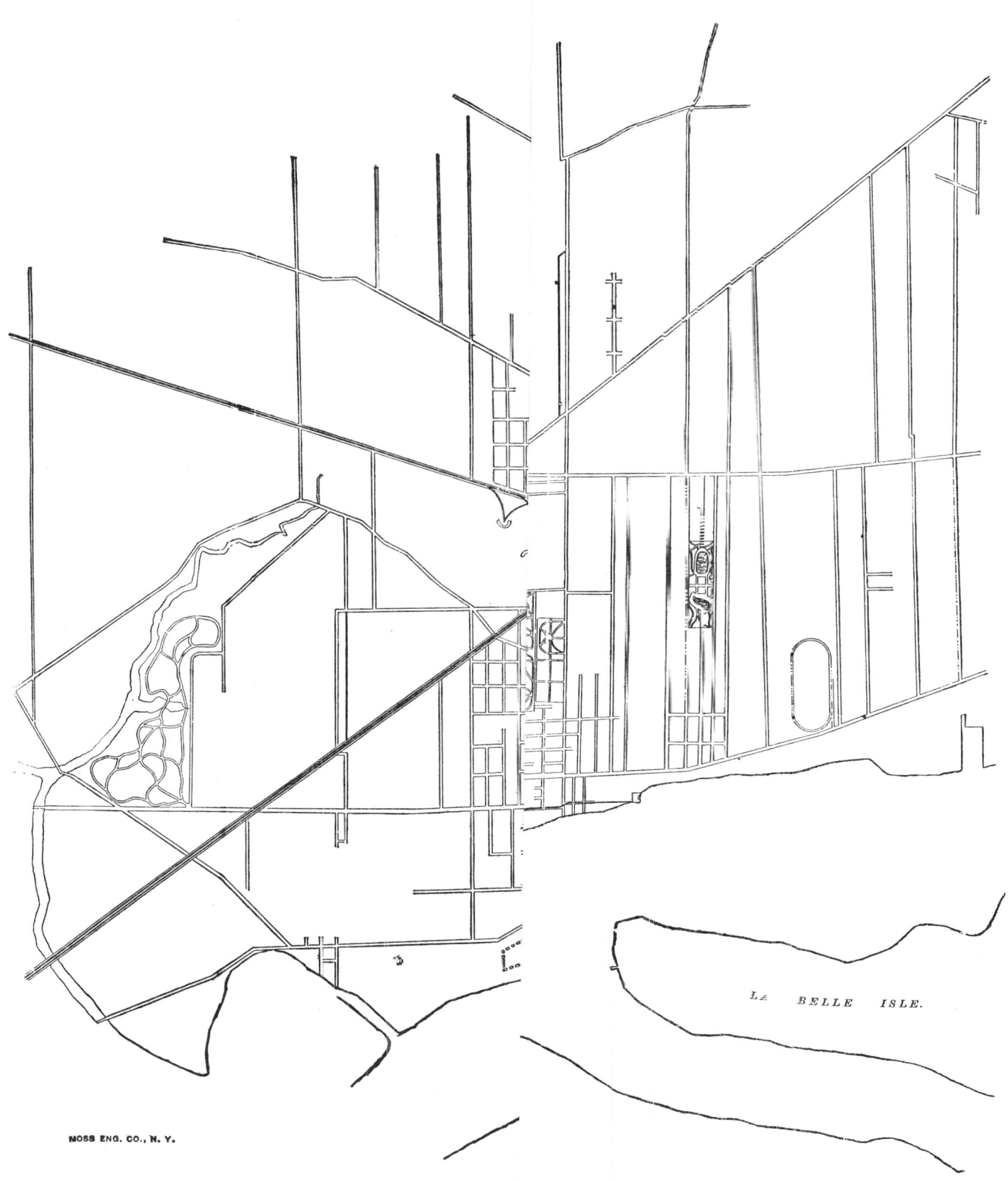

LE BELLE ISLE.

at the corner of Fort and Wayne streets. First, 10 feet of alluvial earth was passed through; next a stratum of tenacious marly clay, with veins of quicksand, for 115 feet; 2 feet of beach sand with pebble stones succeeded, and then rock was struck. This consisted of a stratum of geodiferous lime rock, 60 feet in depth. The auger then penetrated 65 feet into lias, in the course of which it fell into a cavity 2¼ inches in depth. A stratum of carbonate of lime impregnated with salt in a rather friable and yielding form succeeded, which was considered a subordinate bed in the lias, for the latter was again found below it. The boring was continued but 8 feet further, where, no water being obtained, the project was abandoned." (a)

The natural drainage of Detroit is not very good, and is by no means depended on for the drainage of the city In the vicinity of Detroit the land rises gradually toward the west. At Birmingham, 18 miles northwest of the city, an altitude of 300 feet above the river is attained; but in a western line the ascent is much less. There are some extensive marshes in the vicinity of Detroit; but, the principal ones having been drained by open ditches leading to the river, they are now mostly (excepting on the border of the river) under cultivation.

Formerly a large part of the country within a radius of 5 miles from the city was heavily wooded, but cultivated farms, nurseries, gardens for the production of small fruits and culinary vegetables, and extensive brickyards, have taken the place of the forests. The character of the soil within this radius is variable, but principally clay, with strips of sand and gravel resting on a clay subsoil.

CLIMATE.

Records extending from 1835 to 1879, inclusive, show the highest temperature to have been 98°, and the highest summer temperature in average years to be about 94°; the lowest temperature to be −18°, and the lowest winter temperature in average years to be about −10°.

The influence of the great lakes surrounding the state of Michigan appears, (1) in a modification of extremes, the mean of summer being several degrees lower and that of winter several degrees higher near the lake borders than farther inland; (2) in a prolongation of spring and autumn—in other words, a more gradual extension into summer and winter temperatures; (3) in a modification of *single* extremes, both of heat and cold. Within the last 40 years the thermometer has fallen to −34° and risen to 100° within 100 miles east and west of the lake borders.

While the wet lands of Michigan are cold and frosty, no observations appear to have been taken showing any peculiar influence of theirs upon the climate of the uplands. Lower Michigan has no mountains. The interior rises 500 feet, and at points in the westerly central parts to 800 feet, above lake Erie; and here again it is not known that any observations have been made to show the climatic influence of the highlands as distinct from that of the lakes. It may be noted that snow falls deeper and lasts longer on the elevated tracts.

The amount of rainfall varies but little throughout the peninsula, falling off slightly in amount toward the western extremity, and increasing 2 or 3 inches in the interior and west more than at Detroit. During about two-thirds of the year the winds are from the west, southwest and northwest winds prevail—seldom east. In spring, east and northeast; in summer, southwest and west; in autumn west—seldom north or east. These winds render the winters and springs variable, the summers warm and the autumns prolonged. Passing over such large water surfaces the westerly winds temper the extremes both of heat and of cold. The summer storms and the most severe and destructive gales are from the west, but the long rains and snow-storms come with easterly winds.

STREETS.

The total length of streets in Detroit is 236.50 miles, of which 150.75 miles are unpaved, and 85.75 miles are paved with the following materials: Wood, 68.68 miles; cobble-stones, 6.36 miles; Sandusky limestone blocks, 9.15 miles; Medina stone, 1.06 mile; asphalt, 0.50 mile.

There are also 10.495 miles of paved alleys laid with cobble-stones.

The cost per square yard of each, as nearly as it could be estimated in 1879, was: Wood, 60 cents; cobble-stones, 75 cents; Sandusky limestone blocks, $1; Medina stone blocks, $1 75; asphalt, $1 50.

During 1880, 70,840 square yards of wood pavement were repaired, the whole cost of which was $15,110 66, or an average of 21⅓ cents per square yard, and 22,046 square yards of stone pavement were repaired, costing $4,009 46, or an average of about 18⅕ cents per square yard, making the total for repairs $19,120 12, and an average cost of keeping the paved streets of the city in repair about $223 per mile. There were "worked, graded, and repaired" during the same year 72,189 square rods of unpaved streets at a cost of $17,009 02, an average of about 23.56 cents per square rod.

During 1880, 9 streets were repaved, measuring 4.301 miles in length, and 12 streets were graded and paved, measuring 4.251 miles, making 8.552 miles of streets paved, or 168,464.29 square yards, of which 149,327.14 square yards were cedar blocks (24,311.18 linear feet being wood entire, and 20,845.79 linear feet being wood centers with stone gutters) and 19,137.15 square yards were cobble-stone pavement. The whole cost of this pavement was $188,595 13, or an average of about $1 12 per square yard. The total length of streets in the city paved and repaved is 107.24 miles, costing $3,422,053 38, or an average of about $6 04½ per linear foot.

a Detroit in 1855.

For the same period (1880) 5 alleys were paved with cobble-stones, containing 3,778.77 square yards (1,847.02 linear feet), costing $4,770 90, or an average of about $1 26¼ per square yard. The total length of paved alleys—10.498 miles—cost $178,346 43, or an average of about $3 31⅕ per linear foot.

The following table shows the length of streets and alleys paved each year from 1849 to 1880, inclusive, and the cost of the same:

Year.	STREETS. Length in feet.	Cost.	Year.	ALLEYS. Length in feet.	Cost.	Year.	STREETS. Length in feet.	Cost.	Year.	ALLEYS. Length in feet.	Cost.
1849	4,728.60	$10,156 00	1849	420	$420 00	1867	14,209	$186,511 59	1867	1,159	$5,856 65
1850	3,192.41	14,597 55	1850	652	1,229 39	1868	10,644	160,157 34	1868	744	3,351 99
1851	3,861	21,130 48	1851	180	427 85	1869	12,853	139,361 10	1869	1,727	8,501 01
1852	1,962.98	15,287 03	1852	412	913 86	1870	24,777	19,888 45	1870	1,756	6,528 06
1853	10,323	57,576 99	1853	3,130	....	1871	77,547	62,095 91	1871	5,411	22,575 18
1854	13,026	62,971 65	1854	3,716	8,565 10	1872	10,170	71,569 89	1872	2,437	8,114 26
1855	9,392	60,460 14	1855	1,754	9,357 79	1873	37,407	235,114 64	1873	4,739	18,595 81
1856	12,905.42	75,679 90	1856	1,754	4,674 14	1874	28,705.76	197,950 88	1874	5,475	20,057 89
1857	8,143	47,275 35	1857	200	369 75	1875	43,683.18	267,172 25	1875	993	3,469 45
1858	....	....	1858	360	908 71	1876	42,055.58	160,170 65	1876	2,902	9,333 82
1859	8,771	49,568 11	1859	....	....	1877	33,223.71	102,086 87	1877	936.09	1,365 07
1860	9,922	38,565 60	1860	479	974 12	1878	47,140.23	177,273 14	1878	8,568.53	18,633 78
1861	1,955	8,746 04	1861	....	....	1879	38,327.46	130,229 81	1879	3,269.71	6,829 20
1863	1,166	2,250 50	1863	350	1,237 46	1880	45,156.97	188,595 13	1880	1,847.02	4,770 90
1864	343	4,246 59	1864	1,083	6,714 84	Total..	566,233.30	2,685,054 38		57,262.35	178,346 43
1865	2,944	37,922 67	1865	528	3,087 83						
1866	7,698	80,443 13	1866	280	1,482 52						

In his report for 1880 to the board of public works the city engineer says:

Considerable complaint is made because of the necessity for repaving and renewing so frequently the street pavements of the city. There is no question but what this necessity is due in a large extent to the wearing and cutting of the pavements by the use thereon of narrow tires on the many vehicles in daily use for the purpose of heavy trucking.

I believe the cause of complaint can be substantially removed and the life of our pavements lengthened by the passage and enforcement of a stringent ordinance regulating and prescribing the width of tires to be used on vehicles for hauling freight and all bulky articles. This matter is very important, and I submit it for your serious consideration.

Sidewalks are paved with flagging, plank, or asphalt. Gutters are ordinarily of wood, though in many cases of wood-paved streets the gutters are laid with stone.

Shade trees are numerous, and are planted, according to the pleasure of lot owners, on the side of the streets between the curb and the sidewalk.

Street-work experience in Detroit indicates a preference for day work as far as labor is concerned, but the charter of the city requires that the materials shall be furnished by contract.

HORSE-RAILROADS.

There are 8 lines of horse-railroads in Detroit, viz:

The Woodward Avenue road, 3½ miles long, having 13 cars, 85 horses, and employing 46 men.

The Jefferson Avenue line, 2¾ miles long, having 12 cars, 80 horses, and employing 45 men.

The Michigan Avenue line, 3¼ miles long, having 12 cars, 63 horses, and employing 45 men.

The Gratiot Street line, 2 miles long, having 5 cars, 30 horses, and employing 9 men.

The Cass Avenue line, 3¼ miles long, having 9 cars, 54 horses, and employing 25 men.

The Congress and Baker streets line, 2¾ miles long, having 6 cars, 60 horses, and employing 20 men.

These 6 lines are operated by one company. The regular fare is 5 cents over either of these lines; tickets, 50 cents per dozen; tickets for school children, 8 dozen for $3.

The Fort Wayne and Elmwood railway, which extends from Fort Wayne, in Springwells township, to Elmwood Cemetery, in the eastern part of Detroit, is 5½ miles long, has 21 cars, 132 horses, and employs 65 men. The fare within the city limits is 5 cents; outside of them it is 8 cents.

The Grand River Avenue line is 2¾ miles long, and has 5 cars, 50 horses, and employs 18 men; the rate of fare is 5 cents.

It will be seen by the above statements that the total length of the horse-railroads in Detroit is 25¾ miles; the total number of cars run on these roads is 84; the total number of horses is 554; and the total number of men employed is 273.

OMNIBUS LINES.

There are no regular omnibus lines in Detroit; but 6 omnibuses and 4 wagons carry passengers and baggage from the railroad stations, etc., to all parts of the city. These employ 15 men and 19 horses. Without baggage, passengers are charged 25 cents.

WATER-WORKS.

Water was first introduced in 1827, by a private individual; the works were purchased by the city in 1836 and abandoned, and a new site was selected. Works were then built by the city, taking water from the Detroit river nearly opposite the heart of the city. Two pumping-engines of 18,000,000 gallons capacity were built.

In 1877, owing to the contamination of the water, new works were built, taking their supply from the river 4 miles above the city. The inlet is a cast-iron pipe 60 inches in diameter, 1,100 feet long, supported at the river end on a crib of timber filled with stone, and taking water 22 feet below the surface. The shore end connects with a settling basin 200 feet from the river, 17 feet deep, and trapezoidal in shape, the sides being 800 and 750 feet, and the ends 365 and 370 feet in dimensions. Water is pumped by two compound condensing beam engines of 12,000,000 gallons capacity each. One was built in 1877, the other in 1880. A 42-inch force-main extends from the works 15,240 feet to the reservoir, 77 feet above the river. A 30-inch branch from the force-main connects with a stand-pipe near the works, 132 feet high, 60 inches in diameter at the bottom, and 30 inches at the top, made of wrought iron and inclosed in a brick tower 17½ feet in diameter at the bottom and 12 feet at the top.

The reservoir is 15,240 feet from the new pumping-works and 4,500 feet from the old; it is 77 feet above the river, and is in two compartments, each 200 feet square and 26 feet deep. Its capacity is 7,592,000 gallons. It was built in 1858.

There are 210 miles of distributing pipes from 30 to 3 inches in diameter, of which 86 miles are wooden bored logs and the remainder cast iron. The life of wooden pipes is found to be about 16 or 20 years, and they cost only one-fourth as much as cast iron. Some have been laid in sparsely settled portions of the city as late as 1880. It was found that by the time they are worn out they have paid for themselves, and pipes of larger size are required. There are 25,000 water-takers.

Most of the pumping is done from the new works, but the old ones are still more or less used. But 15 meters are in use.

The cost of the works thus far (June 1, 1880) is $2,560,000; when completed according to the plan proposed they will have cost $2,915,000.

The average quantity of water pumped daily in 1879 was 14,053,696 gallons; the greatest quantity pumped per day was 17,892,060 gallons, and the least 9,599,460 gallons. The cost of pumping 1,000,000 gallons 1 foot high is 5 cents, and the yearly cost of maintenance, aside from cost of pumping, is $20,292 82 (exclusive of interest on the bonded debt, which is $1,451,000).

The income from water rates (1879) was $218,110 13, and the total cost of operating was $40,809 63.

The following table shows the number of gallons of water distributed in the several years from 1852 to 1879, inclusive, and its cost:

Year.	Gallons of water pumped.	Cost of fuel consumed.	Average daily delivered.	Gallons of water for one cent cost of fuel.
1852	235, 840, 271		646, 411	
1853	303, 531, 743	$2, 129 37	931, 594	1, 425. 45
1854	376, 265, 126	2, 271 34	1, 030, 866	1, 656. 57
1855	542, 807, 364	3, 325 81	1, 487, 143	1, 632. 10
1856	692, 124, 305	4, 017 44	1, 896, 231	1, 722. 79
1857	697, 190, 523	3, 993 20	1, 909, 837	1, 745. 94
1858	718, 091, 207	3, 655 20	1, 967, 373	1, 964. 57
1859	782, 112, 587	3, 194 15	2, 142, 774	2, 448. 57
1860	870, 036, 451	4, 196 21	2, 383, 580	2, 070. 90
1861	895, 129, 423	4, 414 07	2, 452, 409	2, 027. 00
1862	994, 945, 329	3, 150 95	2, 725, 878	3, 157. 60
1863	1, 035, 798, 043	4, 670 86	2, 837, 803	2, 217. 57
1864	1, 018, 390, 256	7, 647 62	2, 839, 978	1, 331. 64
1865	1, 049, 514, 887	7, 372 89	2, 875, 383	1, 423. 47
1866	1, 196, 317, 922	9, 349 16	3, 277, 583	1, 279. 59
1867	1, 425, 535, 230	10, 121 82	3, 905, 576	1, 408. 37
1868	1, 666, 545, 125	11, 379 23	4, 507, 248	1, 464. 55
1869	1, 646, 810, 325	11, 247 92	4, 511, 809	1, 464. 10
1870	1, 866, 060, 068	12, 713 78	5, 112, 493	1, 467. 74
1871	2, 300, 150, 605	14, 681 05	6, 301, 732	1, 567. 42
1872	2, 782, 292, 578	17, 736 86	7, 601, 892	1, 453. 64
1873	3, 198, 393, 948	20, 233 30	8, 762, 723	1, 580. 76
1874	3, 289, 872, 635	20, 431 71	9, 013, 350	1, 610. 18
1875	4, 207, 454, 260	21, 393 98	11, 527, 272	1, 966. 73
1876	4, 065, 334, 470	19, 832 89	11, 107, 499	2, 049. 79
1877	4, 213, 239, 790	17, 433 72	11, 543, 123	2, 416. 72
1878	4, 345, 743, 330	10, 943 82	11, 906, 146	3, 976. 95
1879	5, 129, 599, 110	11, 219 51	14, 053, 696	4, 572. 03

In obedience to the instructions of the board of water commissioners a thorough and careful analysis of the water at the source of supply was made in August and September, 1879, by Mr. Frederick Stearns, chemist, of this city. A summary of his report gives these conclusions:

The water in the settling-basin is as pure as that in the American mid-channel; the water in the American channel is as pure as that in the Canada channel; the water in the settling-basin gives no evidence of infiltration of poisonous marsh-water; the river below the city is distinctly less pure than that above the city; the water in Detroit river is as healthful as the best of that supplied in Boston.

GAS.

The city owns no gas-works. There are here 1 naphtha and 2 gas companies. The Detroit Gaslight Company supplies gas to the western district (the line dividing the city into two districts running through the center of Woodward avenue). Its daily average production for 1879 was 218,000 cubic feet. It charges $2 25 per 1,000 feet. This company furnishes gas to 909 street lamps, the city paying $1 50 per 1,000 feet, with no charge for meters.

The Mutual Gas Company's works are situated in the eastern district of the city, which it furnishes with gas at the same rate. Its daily average production for the same year was 205,000 cubic feet. Its charge is the same to private consumers and to the city lamps as the other company, and it supplies gas to 893 street lamps in its district.

Consumers using less than 500 feet of gas per month pay 25 cents per month meter rent; to those using more than this no rent is charged.

The Naphtha Company furnishes naphtha to lamps in the newer parts of the city where gas-pipes are not yet laid. There are 940 naphtha street-lamps. For the naphtha consumed by these the city pays for each lamp per year $13 95, the city attending to their lighting and care.

The 1,802 gas street-lamps burn an average of 4 feet each per hour.

PUBLIC BUILDINGS.

The city owns and occupies the following buildings: City hall, cost $600,000; Central market (part in course of erection), $60,000; Cass market, $1,000 (cost of both markets exclusive of land).

The city also owns a house of correction, 31 public-school buildings, a public library, the buildings for which cost $125,000; also, appropriate buildings for the accommodation of the water, fire, and police departments.

PUBLIC PARKS AND PLEASURE-GROUNDS.

The total area of the public parks owned by the city is 714.05 acres. These are 12 in number, of which 9 are very small, hardly attaining the dignity of the name "park". Their locations and areas are:

Adelaide Campan Park, between Clinton and Millet streets, at the intersection of Campan avenue, area 0.61 acre; *Clinton Park*, between Paton, Antoine, and Clinton streets, and Gratiot avenue, area 1.48 acre; *Crawford Park*, at the intersection of Fifth and High streets, area 0.60 acre; *Center Park*, between Center, Grand River, and Randolph streets, area, 0.22 acre; *East Park*, between Turner, Bates, and Randolph streets, area 0.27 acre; *Elton Park*, at the intersection of Fifth and Orchard streets, area 0.60 acre; *Macomb Park*, between Seventeenth and Eighteenth streets, at the intersection of Rose street, area 0.53 acre; *Stanton Park*, between Seventeenth and Eighteenth streets, at the intersection of Marquette street, area 0.61 acre; *West Park*, between State and Grand River streets, and Park place and West Park place, area 0.52 acre; *Cass Park*, between Ledyard and Bagg streets, at the intersection of Second street, area 3.99 acres; *Grand Circus Park, East*, between Woodward, Williams, and Adams avenues, area 2.31 acres; and *Grand Circus Park, West*, between Woodward, Park, and Adams avenues, area also 2.31 acres—total 4.62 acres.

Detroit's one large park is *Belle Isle*, situated in the Detroit river, about 3 miles above the center of the city, and containing 700 acres.

Four or five of the parks enumerated above, including the East and West Grand Circus parks, were reserved as such by the governor and judges when they laid out the town in 1806. The other small parks were donated to the city by the owners of the land when their farms were laid out into city lots.

With the exception of Belle Isle, all of these parks have been ornamented with shade-trees; in some of them fountains have been erected, walks laid out, and seats placed in them.

The only cost of maintaining these small parks is the planting of trees, keeping the walks and fountains in order, and cutting the grass. Cass park is the only one of them surrounded by a fence.

Belle Isle park is a beautiful island of 700 acres, situated in the Detroit river, about 3 miles above the foot of Woodward avenue and at the entrance to lake Saint Clair. It was bought by the city from the heirs of the late Barnabas Campan, in September, 1879, for $200,000. Portions of the island have been under cultivation for several years, and the remainder is well covered with a great variety of forest trees in their natural state.

In the early part of the season of 1880 the board of public works, under the direction of the common council, expended $1,297 05 in cutting and removing underbrush and such dead timber as was found to have fallen to the ground, also in repairing the docks.

During the summer months steamboats run regularly from the foot of Woodward avenue to the island, frequently carrying at each trip several hundred passengers. Here picnics and parties are held and games and other amusements are enjoyed. The fare by steamboat to Belle Isle for the round trip is but 10 cents, and its value to the city as a playground is almost incalculable.

PLACES OF AMUSEMENT.

Detroit's theaters are: Detroit opera-house, seating capacity 1,700; Whitney's opera-house, seating 1,500; the Coliseum, seating capacity 1,200; the Theater Comique, a small place, lately closed; and Long's place of amusement, also small.

The two first named pay an annual license fee each of $200; the others pay a license of $50 each.

In addition to the foregoing, the following are occupied at times as lecture and concert rooms, etc.: Harmonic hall, Merrill hall, Saint Andrew's hall, Abstract hall, Reform hall, Arbeiter hall, Weber hall, Young Men's Society hall, Kanter's hall, Phœnix hall, and Lafayette hall. A company lately organized is erecting a music hall, which will have a seating capacity of 5,000.

A few years since there were three or four beer-gardens in Detroit, but, in consequence of a state law passed in 1879 prohibiting the sale of beer or intoxicating drinks on Sunday, the gardens were closed and abandoned.

DRAINAGE.

The surface of the ground rises gradually to a height of 35 feet in the northwest and 50 feet at the northeast corner, except at Jefferson avenue, where the rise is a little more abrupt, to a height of about 20 feet. The soil and subsoil are generally an impervious clay, interspersed with pockets of quicksand.

The area of the city is 13 square miles, of which about 6 square miles are drained quite completely by means of public and private sewers.

There are 75½ miles of public sewers, ranging from 12 inches to 8 feet in diameter, usually of oval cross-section and built of brick. Their depth below the ground is from 6 to 42 feet, and their rates of fall are from 1 inch to 36 inches per hundred feet. There are 93.8 miles of lateral sewers, averaging 9 feet deep, with grades generally 1 in 200. They are built of brick, are oval in cross-section, and are usually 20 inches high by 15 inches wide. The total length of sewers at the close of the year 1880 was 169.339 miles. Some sewers built as long ago as 1836 are still in use. A report with a plan of sewerage was made in 1861 proposing main sewers in ten of the principal streets, discharging into an intercepting sewer to carry the ordinary flow, each main to be extended to the river for a storm overflow. The main feature of this proposal does not seem to have been applied. In 1871 another system was recommended by the sewer commissioners, proposing 2 principal main sewers to be built in Eighteenth street and McDougal avenue to a line about 2 miles from the river, and then approach each other along Fremont street. This cuts out a square about 2 by 3 miles in the heart of the city, and intercepts all drainage coming from beyond. The intercepting sewer was begun in 1873 and completed in 1877, having a total length of 6 miles.

The rectangular space within these lines is drained by numerous main sewers extending directly to the river. At the time when the older sewers were built in the lower district no general or comprehensive plan was adopted in their construction. Each sewer was built to drain some particular locality, without regard to the probable increase of growth of the city. The consequence is that some sewers are deficient in capacity, in others the grades are defective, while a few were so shallow that cellars of ordinary depth could not drain into them. Many of these had to be rebuilt, and many others are in bad condition and much out of shape. Sewers are built or extended as the present demand requires.

The final disposal of the outflow of sewers is to the Detroit river. Mouths of sewers are either fully or partially submerged; for instance, outlets 6 or 8 feet in diameter have from 1 to 2 feet of their section above water. This allows the sewage to set back from 200 to 3,000 feet, according to the rates of fall, and causes deposits of silt to be formed in the slack-water to a sufficient extent to become a serious obstruction to the outflow of storm-water. The city engineer, in his report of 1877, states that the efficiency of sewers along the water-front would have been greatly increased had the grades of streets near the river been established from 2 to 4 feet higher, thus affording an opportunity for building an intercepting sewer along the river. No inconsiderable amount is expended from year to year in repairing and rebuilding the wooden outlets through which the sewers in the lower districts discharge into the river.

It is stated by the harbor-master that "some of the outlets extend far enough out for the current to take the flow from the sewers". He then gives a list of streets where the outfall is "from 90 to several hundred feet from the current". Soundings made opposite the mouths of sewers in 1878, 1879, and 1880, indicate a rapid shoaling of the water in the slips and docks, plainly indicating that the sewers ought to be extended to the pier-heads and discharged into deep water.

Lateral sewers are made of uniform size and shape. They have no manholes, lamp-holes, or provision for inspection or ventilation. They connect with main sewers, usually at right angles and at convenient places, sometimes level with the bottom, at other times through the top, and in a number of instances through a well-hole or manhole by a perpendicular drop of from 3 to 25 feet or more. The supply of water in most laterals is too small to keep them clean. Storm-water is admitted through open gratings, and brings a large amount of rubbish and silt.

Catch-basins were formerly built with open connections, but in later years, owing to complaints of offensive odors coming from the sewers, most of the basins in the business part of the city have been trapped. The number of basins in 1880 is not stated, but in 1877 there were 2,307 storm-basins with water-traps, 781 untrapped receivers, 21 receivers provided with patent traps. In streets not paved, the receivers for storm-water are made by simply carrying the pipe from the sewer to the surface of the ground and covering it with an iron grate, no trap being used except in the thickly settled localities. Receiving-basins are cleaned once in winter, but, because of nuisance created by disturbing them in hot weather, they are not cleaned in the summer.

There is no provision for ventilation of sewers. No flushing is done except in a few instances. Three men are employed to make house-drain connections, and it is their duty to dig down and open lateral sewers when clogged or obstructed. No other supervision is employed.

The cost of public main sewers and of all manholes and catch-basins is paid by the city. Laterals usually built in the alleys and back streets are paid for by the abutting property. Assessments are laid on the basis of the area of abutting lots.

Sewers constructed in 1880 cost as follows: A brick sewer, 36 by 48 inches, 20 feet deep, cost $2 85 per foot; one, 39 by 52 inches, 21 feet deep, cost $2 95 per foot; one, 48 by 72 inches, 20 feet deep, cost $4 05 per foot; another sewer, to be 78 inches in diameter, was contracted for at $7 40 per foot. Laterals averaging from 9 to 10 feet deep, consisting of a single ring of brick laid in oval sections, 15 by 20 inches, cost in 1880 from $0 53 to $1 08 per foot; 17,763 feet cost $12,315, an average of about 70 cents per foot; 21,886 feet built in 1877 cost $11,856, an average of 54 cents per foot. Manholes average $50 each; catch-basins, $45. Brick-work is laid in mortar, composed of sand and water-lime; 4,346 barrels of water-lime in 1880 cost 85 cents per barrel.

CEMETERIES.

There are at present in use in Detroit 7 cemeteries, viz: 2 Protestant, *Elmwood* and *Woodmere;* 1 Catholic, *Mount Elliott;* 1 Lutheran, and 3 Jewish.

Elmwood cemetery, with an area of about 80 acres, is located on Elmwood avenue, in the eastern part of the city. Woodmere cemetery, with an area of 202 acres, is located at Springwells, 4¾ miles west of the center of the city.

Mount Elliott cemetery, with an area of about 60 acres, is located on Mount Elliott avenue, and adjoins Elmwood cemetery on the east. The Lutheran (German) cemetery, containing 10 acres, is situated on Mount Elliott avenue, about 3 miles north of the city hall. The Beth El (Jewish) congregation has a cemetery containing 1 acre on Elmwood avenue, south of and adjoining Elmwood cemetery; it has also about 3 acres in the north part of Woodmere cemetery. The association of the "Sons of Israel" (Jewish) has a cemetery containing 1¼ acre, situated at the corner of Mount Elliott avenue and Mack road. The Jewish cemetery, Shaary Zedeck, is situated about 3½ miles northwest of the center of the city.

The city of Detroit does not own a cemetery, but has privileges in the three principal ones named above— Elmwood, Woodmere, and Mount Elliott.

A number of the earlier burial-grounds have been abandoned as such, but in every case the remains have been removed therefrom, and in some instances the former grounds are now covered with buildings.

There are but few interments in any of the Jewish cemeteries, except in the 3 acres in Woodmere belonging to the Beth El congregation, where the interments average 4 or 5 in number per year. In the statistics given herein of the interments in Woodmere the Jewish burials are included.

The following table gives the yearly number of interments in the 4 principal cemeteries. The early records of Elmwood cemetery from October, 1846, to November, 1852, were stolen, and the number of interments for this period is estimated from other data at 1,000, while the interments during the rest of 1852 were 18:

Year.	Total.	Year.	Total.
Previous to 1853	1,018	1867	1,207
1853	261	1868	1,346
1854	476	1869	1,713
1855	361	1870	2,089
1856	329	1871	1,845
1857	328	1872	2,421
1858	306	1873	2,501
1859	352	1874	2,266
1860	304	1875	2,245
1861	336	1876	2,286
1862	442	1877	2,144
1863	462	1878	2,028
1864	646	1879	2,215
1865	1,115	1880	1,871
1866	1,261		

The city ordinance, as revised in 1871, declared 3 principal cemeteries to be public burial-ground, "and no person or persons, societies or congregations, shall establish or locate any other burying-ground within the limits of the city of Detroit."

The grave for an adult is required to be at least 6 feet deep, and for a child at least 5 feet deep. The common council designates suitable lots in the city cemetery for the interment of deceased strangers and poor persons. The following is the ordinance relative to the interments within the public cemeteries:

It shall be the duty of every undertaker, or other person acting as such, having in charge the interment of any deceased person, to deposit with the city sexton, or sextons, or superintendent of the cemetery wherein said interment is to take place, a certificate from the attending physician of the deceased; or, in case no physician was in attendance, from one of the city physicians called by said undertaker to make examination into the case, stating all the particulars as to the name, age, sex, nativity, social condition, manner of death, character of disease of the deceased person, which said certificate in blank shall be furnished to any undertaker or other person applying therefor to the city clerk; and it shall be the duty of the city sexton or sextons and superintendents of cemeteries in the city of Detroit to keep a register, to be provided by said city, of all persons buried in each of said cemeteries, giving in alphabetical order the name of the deceased, the number of the lot in which the body was buried, together with a transcript of the certificate furnished in the case, which said register shall be kept in the office of the city clerk.

It shall further be the duty of the sextons or superintendents aforesaid, at least once in each month, to record in the register herein provided for, and in the manner herein set forth, the burials which have been made since their last report, and also to file in the office of the city clerk all certificates in their possession: *Provided*, That in all cases of persons dying in the city of Detroit, where interments are to be made in cemeteries beyond the limits of the said city, the certificate hereinbefore mentioned shall be served by the undertaker in charge on the city sexton, and shall be by him recorded and filed as in other cases provided.

The following extracts are taken from the ninth report to the lot-owners of the trustees of Elmwood cemetery, embracing the period from January 1, 1878, to January 1, 1880:

In 1846 a few gentlemen purchased 42 acres of ground on Bloody run, laid the same out for a cemetery, and caused it to be conveyed to trustees, with power to fill vacancies in their body, and with a stipulation that all revenues for the sale of lots should constitute a fund for the care and improvement of the grounds. Several purchases were afterwards made, so as to increase the quantity within the inclosure to 78 acres. There are also 3.37 acres which were thrown out by the opening of German street. The service of the trustees have been entirely gratuitous for the whole period.

Every lot-owner is a member of the corporation, and is in duty bound to co-operate with the trustees in beautifying and protecting the grounds, because it is simply impossible for the trustees with their limited force to do so without the help of those for whose interests they are devoting valuable time. This point is again urgently pressed upon lot-owners. Elmwood is far behind many other rural cemeteries in respect to embellishment, for want of this co-operation of lot-owners.

The number of lots sold is 2,944, and of lots unsold 379.

The total amount received for lots sold and from all other sources, except interest on investments, from October, 1846, to January, 1880, 33 years and 3 months, is $262,895 83; for interest on loans and investments, $31,102 39; total, $293,998 22.

The total amount expended for purchase of land is $19,500; all other expenses, $216,899 50; total, $236,399 50; securities and money in treasury, $57,598 72—making a grand total of $293,998 22.

The efforts of the trustees to create a fund, from whose income the cemetery may be kept in order after all the lots are sold, have been partially successful, so that by the end of this year [1880] there will be about $60,000; but the income of this will be quite inadequate to the necessary expenses. It will be prudent to avoid any disbursement for mere ornamentation at present, and carefully to add to the principal as opportunity offers. Much of the expenditure of past years has been for grading and filling and making available lots, and the future expenses will grow less as the grounds approach completion; but the trustees do not lose sight of the fact that our revenues from lots sold will soon cease, and then our dependence must be chiefly upon the interest of the accumulated fund.

In the early summer of 1867 several gentlemen organized an association for a new rural cemetery, now known under the name of Woodmere cemetery.

On the 30th of July a code of by-laws was adopted, providing, among other things, for an organization as a corporation by the same name whenever the holders of two-thirds of the scrip should so vote. The trustees at the same time reported that they had already completed the purchase of 195.68 acres of land.

Another purchase was afterward made increasing the amount to over 200 acres.

During the fall of 1867 and the winter of 1867–'68, a very careful, minute, and accurate topographical survey of the grounds was prepared, and in the course of the summer and fall of 1868 considerable progress was made in the preparation of the grounds.

The formal opening of the cemetery took place on Wednesday, the 14th day of July, 1869.

MARKETS.

Detroit has 3 public markets, viz: the Central meat market, which cost $50,000, has a ground area of 8,000 square feet and 16 stalls; a building with two departments, called the vegetable and fish markets, which cost $20,000, has a ground area of 12,000 square feet and but 1 stall.

Wagons of hucksters and farmers are allowed to stand in the space between the meat and vegetable markets—about 8,000 square feet—in the adjacent streets, and in the hay and wood markets.

The rates of rental for a stall in the different markets are as follows: the Central meat market, $420 to $540 per year; the vegetable market, $47 to $112 50 per year; the fish market, $47 to $63 50 per year; Cass market, $75 per year.

The total yearly rental of each market is: the Central meat market, $7,476 per year; the vegetable and fish markets, $6,650 per year; Cass market, $75 per year—total $14,201.

The Central market is open from 4 a. m. to 12 m. daily, and on Saturdays also from 3 p. m. to 10 p. m.; the vegetable market is open from 4 a. m. to 3 p. m., daily, and on Saturdays it is kept open until 10 p. m.; and the fish market is opened from 4 a. m. to 12 m.

The following is from the market ordinance, and prescribes the method for the collection of wagon fees:

In addition to the duties already prescribed, the market clerk, pound-masters, and every other officer in charge of any market, shall collect a fee of 10 cents from every owner, driver, or other person in charge of any team or vehicle standing upon or occupying, for market purposes, the public market grounds of the city, which fee shall be additional to any license fee paid by any person occupying such grounds, streets, or spaces. For every fee so collected the said clerk, or pound-master, or other officer, shall deliver to the person from whom he collected the same a ticket receipt, furnished such clerks and pound-masters, or other officer, by the city controller, as hereinafter mentioned.

The controller shall cause to be prepared a sufficient number of suitable ticket-receipts for the purpose of the preceding section, with the name of the market clerk and date stamped thereon, which said ticket-receipts shall be delivered daily to said clerk, pound-masters, or other officers, by the controller, in such quantities as shall be deemed necessary for use during the day, which said ticket-receipts when so delivered shall be charged to said clerk, pound-master, or other officer, in a suitable book, prepared for such purpose.

The controller shall likewise deliver daily to an officer of the metropolitan police force, to be designated by the superintendent of police, a like number of ticket-receipts, to be of the same form as those delivered to the market clerk, but of different color, having the word "Police" stamped thereon; and it shall be the duty of said police officer to demand of each owner, driver, or other person in charge of any team or vehicle standing upon or occupying for market purposes the public market-grounds of the city, the ticket-receipts previously given to the owner, driver, or other person in charge of such team or vehicle, as aforesaid, by the clerk of the market, giving in exchange for such ticket-receipts the ticket-receipts of different color with the word "Police" stamped thereon, as aforesaid. The said police officer shall report daily at or before the hour of 4 o'clock in the afternoon, to the controller, surrendering the ticket-receipts of the market clerk collected by him as aforesaid, which ticket-receipts, together with the unused ticket-receipts issued to him, shall equal the number of the same issued to said officer.

The following are extracts from the same ordinance:

No person shall slaughter, sell, offer, or expose for sale, or barter, or trade, the meat of any calf less than four weeks old.

No person shall burn, sear, or cut the inner part of, or confine the mouth of any calf by rope, twine, or any kind of muzzle. And no person shall in any manner tie or confine by rope, twine, or otherwise, the feet of any calf, sheep, lamb, or swine, or poultry, which may be brought to or exposed in the city for sale.

There are also for the sale of hay, etc., two spaces called the Eastern hay market and the Western hay market.

SANITARY AUTHORITY.

The city charter provides for the appointment of a city board of health, but the city authorities have discontinued such appointments, and there is no special health organization except as provided in the general laws of the state, which makes the mayor and aldermen of each incorporated city a board of health, and requires them to "perform all the duties of a board of health" in cities where, as in this case, no board is actually organized under the city charter. The common council has full authority to pass laws, with severe penalties for their infraction, providing for the cleanliness and general sanitation of the city. The laws are enforced by the police department through a municipal tribunal known as the recorder's court.

The executive officers of the board are 1 sergeant of police and 8 patrolmen, one of whom is designated as "inspector of meats and provisions". There is no health officer. The sanitary policemen (the 9 referred to above) make regular inspection in all parts of the city, and also whenever and wherever nuisances are reported. In cases of an ascertained nuisance the responsible party is notified to abate the same forthwith; if the order is not obeyed the offender is prosecuted in the recorder's court.

The city ordinance provides for the proper draining and care of houses, privies, cesspools, etc. The matters of sewerage and street-cleaning are in charge of the board of public works.

Each householder is required by ordinance to provide a suitable and tight vessel for the reception of garbage, and to cause the contents of the same to be removed twice in each week from the 1st of May to the 1st of November, and once in each week during the remainder of the year, to some place without the limits of the city.

One person in each ward, called a ward officer, is appointed by the common council to see that this law is enforced. He may enter and inspect any premises between the hours of 8 a. m. and 4 p. m., and if he finds garbage unlawfully remaining may remove the same, being in such case entitled to receive of the householder for every such entry and removal the sum of 3 cents.

Sextons are required to report all burials to the city clerk, but the board requires neither burial nor removal permits.

The pollution of the water of the river is prohibited under heavy penalties. Excrement is required to be removed from vaults by an odorless apparatus.

Small-pox patients are either removed to the pest-house or are isolated at their residences, upon the front of which is placed a card with the words "small-pox" thereon in large letters. Scarlet-fever patients are not the subject of municipal regulations. Under the following provision of a state law passed in 1879 vaccination may be made compulsory and at the public expense:

The people of the state of Michigan enact that the board of health in each city, village, and township, may at any time direct its health officer or health physician to offer vaccination with bovine vaccine virus to every child not previously vaccinated, and to all other persons who have not been vaccinated within the preceding five years, without cost to the persons [person] vaccinated, but at the expense of each city, village, or township, as the case may be.

Concerning the registration of diseases and health matters generally in Detroit the secretary of the state board of health thus writes:

There is no city registration of diseases. Though the state laws require the report and record of every case of disease dangerous to the public health, these laws are disregarded in Detroit. Births and deaths are not registered as they occur, but such facts required by the state law, as can be ascertained after so long delay, are collected by persons appointed by the city council in the spring following the year in which the births and deaths occur. The statistics relative to births and deaths are thus reported to the county clerk, who makes a report for the county to the secretary of state.

The state law requires reports (by the board of health) to be made to the state board of health. No report is made.

The medical profession in Detroit stands high in the respect of the people of the city and of the state. It seems to be well supported, but it has no relation to a public-health service of the city, for the reason that no systematic public-health service exists.

Detroit appears to the casual observer, and is claimed by its citizens, to be an exceptionally healthful city. There seems to be no attempt by the city authorities to ascertain the truth of such an assumption, by means of reports of communicable diseases and by reliable vital statistics. The city is not now officially represented in the annual reports of the state board of health, or in the weekly bulletin of the national board of health, among the cities which secure reliable mortality statistics.

As a kind of branch health organization, a city ordinance provides for the appointment by the common council annually of 6 physicians, to be called "city physicians". To each of these is assigned one of the 6 "city physician districts" into which the city is divided. When required by the common council or board of health they examine in their several districts into all sources of danger to the public health, and, from time to time, make such recommendation to the common council concerning the sanitary condition of the city as seems necessary. They also, when directed by the mayor and aldermen, or director of the poor, attend any sick, disabled, or infirm person who may be a charge upon the city, and render such medical assistance as may be necessary; also, when any person is taken to the pest-house, the physician from the district from which the patient is taken attends on such person. In their several districts they also vaccinate without charge any inhabitant of the city of Detroit not previously vaccinated, who may apply to them for that purpose, giving certificate of vaccination to such children as may have been vaccinated by them.

They furnish at their own expense all medicines which may be necessary in the proper treatment of such sick or disabled persons as may be a charge upon the city, and also such vaccine matter as may be required in their vaccinating as above. Each city physician is entitled, at the end of each quarter during his term of office, upon his affidavit that he has vaccinated, free of charge, all inhabitants of the city of Detroit who have called upon him for that purpose, to receive from the city treasury the sum of $12 50, in addition to the salary of his office.

MUNICIPAL CLEANSING.

Street-cleaning.—In 1880, as theretofore, paved streets were cleaned by the city's own force by hand and by day labor. They were cleaned from five to twelve times each during the season; and, approximating the distance from the number of times cleaned, the measurement is ascertained to be 382.49 miles, or 5,609,875 square yards, and the cost $17,485 28, or an average of about $45 71 per mile. The service is performed chiefly by old and indigent men, who would otherwise have difficulty in obtaining employment, and is well done. The sweepings are deposited principally in low grounds.

Removal of garbage and ashes.—Garbage and ashes are removed exclusively by householders, except in case of failure to remove promptly, when it may be done (in the case of garbage) by the ward officer at an expense to the householder of 3 cents for each removal. Ashes and garbage may be kept in the same vessel. Wood ashes are usually disposed of to soap-makers, while coal ashes are used for filling. While the system of removal is somewhat imperfect, it is not thought to work any special injury to the public health.

Dead animals.—The carcasses of animals dying in the city are removed by contract, being carried at least 3 miles beyond the city limits and buried. The cost of the service is about $500 per annum, about 2,500 animals of all kinds being removed.

Liquid household wastes.—Where sewers exist they receive all the liquid waste of the house; where they do not exist the said waste is run into privy-vaults, which, where practicable, drain into sewers. They are unprovided with overflows, and are cleaned out at least twice in each year, and oftener if it is needful.

Human excreta.—About two-thirds of the houses of the city have water-closets and connection with sewers, and one-third depend on privy-vaults. About two-thirds of the number of the latter are nominally water-tight. They are emptied by an odorless excavating apparatus, and are ordinarily constructed about 5 feet deep, 3 feet long, and 3 feet wide. The dry-earth system is not at all in use. Night-soil is removed out of the city, and to some extent utilized in manufacturing fertilizer. It is not allowed to be used in manuring land within the gathering-ground of the public water-supply.

Manufacturing wastes.—Manufacturing wastes are discharged into the sewers. No inconvenience has as yet arisen from this practice. The discharge of sewers in the Detroit river is several miles below the water-works, and as the current here is 2 miles per hour, no contamination of the water-supply is apparently to be apprehended.

POLICE.

The police force of Detroit is appointed by 4 police commissioners, who are appointed by the governor of the state and confirmed by the senate. The chief executive officer of the force is the superintendent. He has full charge of the department, subject to the orders of the police commission, and his salary is $2,000 per year.

The rest of the force consists of 3 captains at a salary of $1,100 each, 8 sergeants at $900 each, 9 roundsmen at $800 each, and 106 patrolmen on actual patrol duty and 18 detailed on special duty. They are divided into two classes, the members of one receiving $600 each and those of the other $700 each.

The men furnish their own uniforms, which cost, including the dress and overcoats, about $80 each.

The patrolmen are armed with batons, revolvers, and handcuffs. Their hours of service are 8 hours for night and 9 hours for day duty. The area patrolled by the force comprises 13 square miles.

The number of arrests made in 1880 was 4,284. During this year property was stolen and reported to the police to the amount of $63,928 34, of which $43,959 21 was recovered and returned to the owners. The station-house lodgers numbered 8,810, as against 8,774 in 1879. No free meals are given to these lodgers, except in case of sickness.

At the request of individuals or corporations, and at their expense, special police are appointed by the police commissioners.

The cost of the force for 1880 was $135,000.

FIRE DEPARTMENT.

The following is taken from the mayor's annual message relating to the year 1878:

The fire department needs no commendation at my hands, or, in fact, from any quarter. The department speaks for itself. Its economy, discipline, and equipments, with its complete system of electric fire-alarm telegraph, are unsurpassed by any department of its size in the country. The valuation of the department property is $865,190 50, with no debt of any kind.

The department consists of 117 officers and men, uniformed, drilled, and disciplined. The territory of this department comprises 13.44 square miles, to protect which it has 8 engines, 2 chemical engines, 2 hook-and-ladder companies, besides 2 extra engines, with hose carts, equipped as a reserve. The commission commend very highly the office of fire marshal, lately created, and say at no time in the history of the city have the ordinances governing fire prevention been so well enforced, and regard it as an indispensable economy.

SCHOOLS.

The following statistics for the school year ending August 31, 1879, are obtained from the report of the board of education for that year. The whole number of school-houses, not including two new ones (the Norvell and the John Owen schools), not quite completed, is 28:

Number of persons between 5 and 20 years, shown by school census	37,684
Cost of superintendence and instruction	$143,221 87
Cost of incidentals, including repairs and all current expenses	$38,295 86
Number enrolled in the schools from each 100 persons counted in school census	39.4
Average number of weeks of attendance of each person enrolled	28.75
Whole number of different names enrolled in all the schools	14,837
Average daily attendance for the whole year	10,665
Number of men teachers at the close of school year, including one special teacher of music and the superintendent	10
Number of women teachers at the close of school year	234
Average number of pupils to each teacher (excluding special), based on average membership	47.1
Total cost of education per capita, including all expenses except interest on money invested in school property	$16 04

The percentage of attendance of membership of the schools is as follows: For the primary department, 93.9; for the grammar department, 94.7; for the high-school department, 97.1; for all departments, 94.4.

Number of pupils in membership, December 31, 1879, in each department of the schools: Number belonging in high school, 583; number belonging in grammar schools, 3,039; number belonging in primary schools, 6,722; total, 10,344.

The course of study is divided into 12 parts, corresponding to grades or years. The primary department comprises the first four grades; the 5th, 6th, 7th, and 8th grades constitute the grammar department; and the 9th, 10th, 11th, and 12th, the high-school department.

The free public library, in connection with and under the control of the board of education of this city, now containing over 40,000 volumes, is an institution highly appreciated and valued by the citizens, and adds greatly to the many attractive features of the city. The average number of books daily drawn from the library is over 600, and numbers of citizens daily visit it to consult books of reference that are not for circulation. About 10,000 names of citizens entitled to draw books are now on the register.

COMMERCE AND NAVIGATION.

[From the reports of the Bureau of Statistics for the fiscal years ending June 30.]

Customs district of Detroit, Michigan.	1879.	1880.
Total value of imports	$1,342,600	$1,703,838
Total value of exports:		
Domestic	$2,475,386	$2,326,831
Foreign	$62,346	$77,572
Total number of immigrants	1,913	4,921

Customs district of Detroit, Michigan.	1879.		1880.	
	Number.	Tons.	Number.	Tons.
Vessels in foreign trade:				
Entered	2,949	236,339	3,595	294,782
Cleared	2,852	231,739	3,657	307,298
Vessels in coast trade and fisheries:				
Entered	2,449	773,460	2,760	938,575
Cleared	2,539	788,249	2,948	968,609
Vessels registered, enrolled, and licensed in district	308	64,462	313	70,815
Vessels built during the year	11	2,491	21	7,502

MANUFACTURES.

The following is a summary of the statistics of the manufactures of Detroit for 1880, being taken from tables prepared for the Tenth Census by James E. Tryon, chief special agent:

Mechanical and manufacturing industries.	No. of establishments.	Capital.	AVERAGE NUMBER OF HANDS EMPLOYED.			Total amount paid in wages during the year.	Value of materials.	Value of products.
			Males above 16 years.	Females above 15 years.	Children and youths.			
All industries	919	$15,594,479	12,477	2,430	1,203	$6,306,460	$18,150,995	$30,181,416
Baking and yeast powders	6	38,000	33	10	3	17,596	84,800	141,600
Baskets, rattan and willow ware	6	11,100	18	9	7	12,570	9,325	29,900
Blacksmithing (see also Wheelwrighting)	39	43,575	80		3	37,064	33,300	109,350
Boot and shoe uppers	3	7,300	22	12	2	12,150	20,500	42,200
Boots and shoes, including custom work and repairing	69	331,700	529	54	29	317,100	605,450	1,066,025
Boxes, cigar	4	41,000	30	25	29	23,450	58,000	103,000
Boxes, fancy and paper	3	5,900	6	30	1	10,160	34,500	58,000
Boxes, wooden packing	6	32,600	149		17	54,600	145,500	226,800
Bread and other bakery products	47	225,400	229	12	35	146,580	656,389	930,157
Brooms and brushes	10	39,400	55	19	44	32,409	72,009	127,538
Carpentering	30	272,000	669		3	254,236	580,495	955,195
Carriages and wagons (see also Wheelwrighting)	23	209,000	285	2	8	127,945	174,000	400,220
Clothing, men's	31	363,500	273	767		389,926	1,364,016	2,056,182
Clothing, women's	3	12,800		44		9,280	8,300	24,100
Coffee and spices, roasted and ground	3	55,000	27	6	1	16,950	100,000	145,000
Confectionery	8	207,200	93	72	5	63,800	467,400	584,200
Cooperage	20	118,300	183		13	69,500	146,650	266,400
Corsets	4	6,800	20	115	16	41,450	111,100	208,500
Cutlery and edge tools (see also Hardware)	4	9,000	14		2	7,920	5,270	20,500
Dentistry, mechanical	5	9,000	7	2	1	4,700	11,000	27,500
Dyeing and cleaning	6	16,200	10	14		9,228	5,700	22,100
Flouring- and grist-mill products	14	467,000	123			62,795	1,438,752	1,649,627
Foundery and machine-shop products	24	1,262,050	960		64	431,065	915,955	1,808,355
Furniture (see also Upholstering)	32	248,800	264	18	78	119,620	229,002	438,801
Hairwork	4	3,200		19		5,120	5,000	15,800
Hardware (see also Cutlery and edge tools)	3	27,000	55		7	18,142	20,300	49,000
Hats and caps, not including wool hats	6	298,000	100	133	1	73,069	129,400	293,500
Instruments, professional and scientific	3	12,500	10			4,880	4,470	14,540
Iron and steel	7	1,547,386	1,088		7	436,986	1,872,407	2,498,634
Jewelry	9	84,302	56		4	40,490	58,251	135,600

Mechanical and manufacturing industries.	No. of estab-lish-ments.	Capital.	AVERAGE NUMBER OF HANDS EMPLOYED.			Total amount paid in wages during the year.	Value of materials.	Value of products.
			Males above 16 years.	Females above 15 years.	Children and youths.			
Leather, curried....................................	7	$104,336	34	....	....	$16,088	$233,975	$284,118
Leather, tanned................................	10	498,634	139	2	....	56,493	465,526	629,696
Lime..	4	95,500	30	....	....	10,440	18,733	37,555
Liquors, malt.......................................	28	1,205,120	299	4	1	149,677	640,768	1,143,601
Lock- and gun-smithing	6	4,500	10	....	....	4,200	1,850	13,300
Looking-glass and picture frames	13	252,650	266	74	60	126,472	217,797	462,669
Marble and stone work	16	110,100	173	....	9	109,446	160,300	348,200
Models and patterns...............................	3	3,800	4	....	1	2,130	1,475	6,400
Painting and paperhanging.........................	23	88,500	315	....	10	130,235	194,229	384,930
Patent medicines and compounds..................	5	48,000	23	36	6	16,920	25,000	87,000
Perfumery and cosmetics	4	25,500	20	9	5	12,900	42,000	94,000
Photographing	16	40,550	35	11	3	19,892	24,860	74,600
Plumbing and gasfitting............................	16	136,200	183	....	3	93,861	173,897	359,954
Printing and publishing	39	866,050	677	78	57	373,262	301,359	986,098
Roofing and roofing materials......................	5	30,000	65	....	4	25,700	60,500	108,200
Saddlery and harness	28	39,100	70	1	6	33,415	51,100	120,700
Sash, doors, and blinds (see also Wood, turned and carved)..........	15	261,000	338	....	68	148,525	278,850	553,000
Shipbuilding.......................................	16	187,200	756	....	....	310,605	364,262	738,975
Shirts...	5	4,700	18	30	1	12,866	15,800	36,420
Slaughtering and meat-packing, not including retail butchering.....	7	485,000	137	....	10	79,067	1,413,426	1,721,231
Spectacles and eyeglasses........................	3	45,000	53	5	19	23,400	24,500	71,000
Stencils and brands	6	9,200	18	....	....	10,750	10,500	34,100
Tinware, copperware, and sheet-iron ware	47	108,650	142	....	24	68,781	100,725	232,700
Tobacco, chewing, smoking, and snuff (see also Tobacco, cigars and cigarettes).	5	495,000	138	125	80	100,725	719,554	1,212,146
Tobacco, cigars and cigarettes (see also Tobacco, chewing, smoking, and snuff).	58	453,700	723	102	74	310,828	572,080	1,196,870
Trunks and valises	3	35,500	78	....	12	44,142	82,758	145,900
Upholstering (see also Furniture)	5	52,200	67	5	9	28,115	112,400	172,400
Wheelwrighting (see also Blacksmithing; Carriages and wagons) ..	15	12,300	32	....	3	13,670	10,150	36,300
Wirework	4	87,000	135	10	22	69,900	97,500	192,500
Wood, turned and carved (see also Sash, doors, and blinds)..........	11	15,550	31	....	3	14,306	13,850	49,849
Wooden ware	5	273,000	243	25	6	67,680	131,500	226,950
All other industries (a)	59	2,842,496	1,837	550	327	971,185	2,222,470	3,971,730

a Embracing artificial limbs; billiard tables and materials; boot and shoe findings; brass castings; brick and tile; bridges; carpets, rag; carriages and sleds, children's; cars, railroad, street and repairs; combs; drugs and chemicals; files; fruits and vegetables, canned and preserved; furniture, chairs; furs, dressed; gas machines and meters; gloves and mittens; hosiery and knit goods; ink; lasts; lumber sawed; masonry, brick and stone; matches; musical instruments, organs and materials; musical instruments, pianos and materials; needles and pins; oil, lubricating; pens, gold; pickles, preserves, and sauces; pipes, tobacco; refrigerators; regalia and society banners and emblems; safes, doors, and vaults, fire-proof; saws; scales and balances; show-cases; stone- and earthen-ware; telegraph and telephone apparatus; umbrellas and canes; varnish; whips; and window blinds and shades.

From the foregoing table it appears that the average capital of all establishments is $16,968 96; that the average wages of all hands employed is $391 46 per annum; and that the average outlay in wages, in materials, and in interest (at 6 per cent.) on capital employed is $27,631 25.

EAST SAGINAW.

SAGINAW COUNTY, MICHIGAN.

POPULATION

IN THE

AGGREGATE,

1860-1880.

———

	Inhab.
1790	......
1800	......
1810	......
1820	......
1830	......
1840	......
1850	......
1860	3,001
1870	11,350
1880	19,016

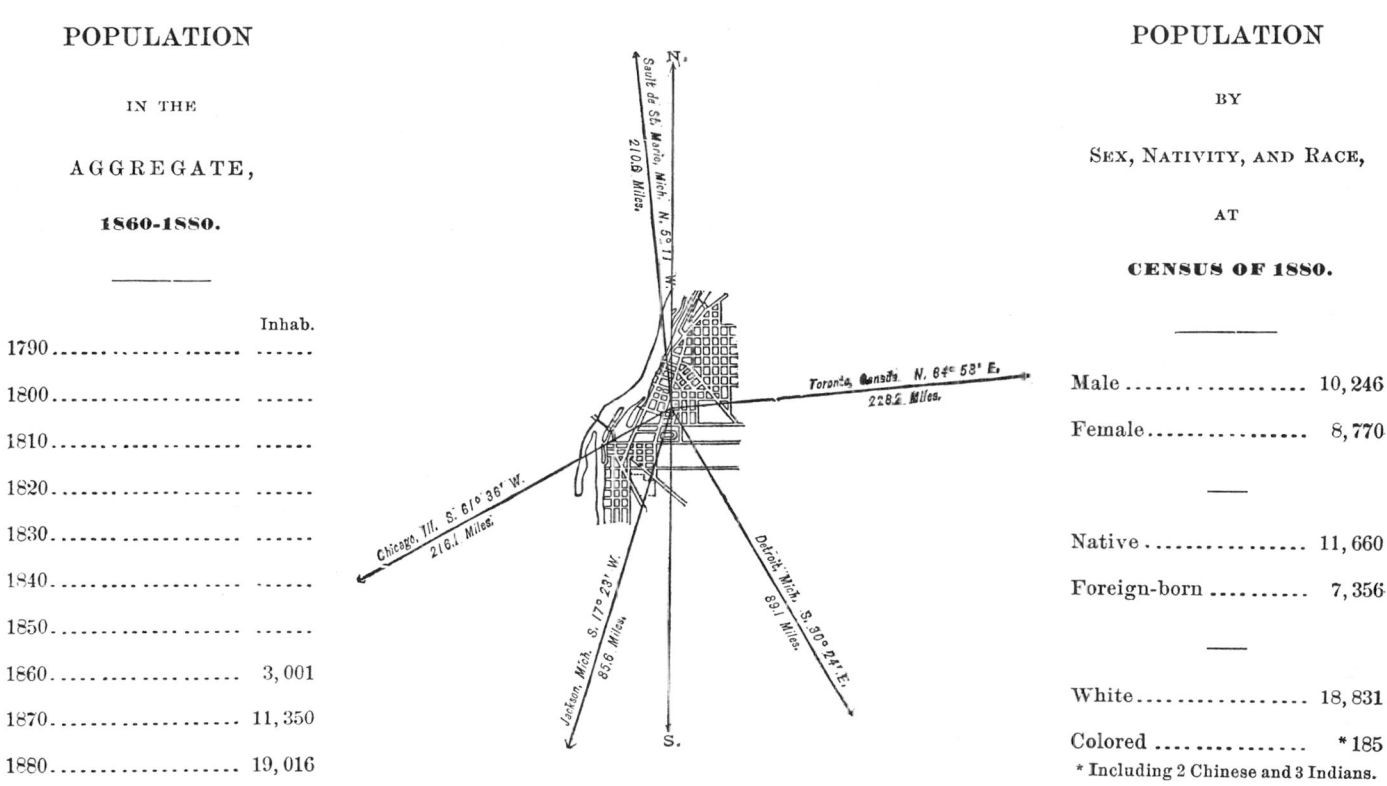

POPULATION

BY

SEX, NATIVITY, AND RACE,

AT

CENSUS OF 1880.

———

Male	10,246
Female	8,770
—	
Native	11,660
Foreign-born	7,356
—	
White	18,831
Colored	*185

* Including 2 Chinese and 3 Indians.

Latitude: 43° 27′ North; Longitude: 83° 56′ (west from Greenwich); **Altitude: 596.6 to 615 feet.**

FINANCIAL CONDITION:

Total Valuation: $7,539,090; per capita: $396 00.   Total Indebtedness: $610,475; per capita: $32 10.   Tax per $100: $2 58.

HISTORICAL SKETCH.(a)

The land upon which a good portion of the city of East Saginaw now stands was originally entered by Dr. Charles Little in 1836, and in 1849 it was purchased by Hoyt and Company, of New York. In 1847 there were not more than half a dozen people in the place; but in 1850 the village of East Saginaw was plotted, and the first township election was held in that year. The commercial and manufacturing advantages were early recognized, and a steady stream of immigration followed. The city was incorporated in 1859. The first railroad reached this point in the same year, and since that time the growth of the city has been rapid and of a substantial and enduring character.

The city has been singularly free from great fires. In common with towns in a wooded country, where inflammable materials enter largely into its construction, more or less destruction from fire occurs, but there have

a Ferd. A. Ashley, esq., city clerk of East Saginaw, secured and forwarded the detailed information, in response to schedules of interrogatories from this office, and furnished the data for the historical sketch with which this report is introduced.

been no sweeping conflagrations that have caused marked changes. The business portion of the city is compactly built of brick and stone, many of the public buildings equaling in solidity of construction and architectural beauty those of larger cities. Brick is now entering largely into the construction of private residences, although the greater number at present are of wood. The materials used in rebuilding, in nearly all cases, are of brick and stone. The city has experienced no exceptional depression in its history, beyond that induced by the panic of 1873. Its growth and business have steadily increased from year to year, and the disasters incident to the panic were few and of limited character compared with those of most manufacturing and commercial cities.

East Saginaw has undergone little or no change as regards the various sources of population. From the first settlement they have been principally from Germany, Canada, and the eastern states of the Union. The Canadian population is, in some respects, to quite an extent transient, the element locating here being chiefly the laboring class, who came in pursuit of employment at better wages than can be found in their own country, and many return after a few months. The various elements are pretty evenly distributed through the various occupations incidental to a city where the chief pursuits are connected with lumber and salt, and no one element has supplanted any other to any marked extent, the prosperity that attends one being equally the boon of all. During the last ten years agriculture has attracted more attention than it did in the early history of the city, and the German element is chiefly prominent in this pursuit.

The manufactures of East Saginaw consist of lumber, salt, shingles, furniture, mill and salt block machinery, sash, doors, blinds, etc. There are also numerous small manufactures, in the aggregate employing many operatives and doing a large business. The manufactures of lumber form one of the chief industries, and were first begun in 1837, but it was not until ten years later that the product had assumed proportions sufficient to enable the shipment of the first cargo. The second mill was erected in 1850, and in 1855 the flow of capital and the importance of the industry began to be recognized; since which time rapid progress has been made. In 1873 there were within the corporate limits of East Saginaw 18 lumber manufactories, with an invested capital of $750,000. This has been increased to over $1,000,000 at the present time. The making of sash, doors, blinds, and kindred articles furnishes employment to a large number of men throughout the entire year. The manufacture of rough lumber affords employment to operatives during only about $8\frac{1}{2}$ months of the year. The manufacture of salt in Michigan was first begun in East Saginaw in 1859, and in 1860 the product was 4,000 barrels. In 1862 the product had reached 243,000 barrels, and the increase has been rapid from that date. The product of the state last year (1879) was 2,000,000 barrels, of which East Saginaw contributed nearly one-half. The blocks are operated in connection with saw-mills, the refuse from the logs being used as fuel and in the making of laths. The brine is pumped from wells, sunk to an average depth of 900 feet, and the supply seems to be unlimited. The manufacture of dairy salt was first begun here in 1878, and the product now amounts to 25,000 barrels annually.

These are the principal industries of East Saginaw, though the making of agricultural implements is rapidly advancing.

EAST SAGINAW IN 1880.

LOCATION, ETC.

East Saginaw lies in latitude 43° 27' north, longitude 83° 56' west from Greenwich, in the northwestern part of Saginaw county, on the east bank of the Saginaw river, 16 miles from its outlet into Saginaw bay and 2 miles below Saginaw city, which is located on the opposite bank. The city extends along the river from north to south a distance of 4 miles, and has an average depth of one mile, covering an area of 3,904.82 acres, according to the government survey. The altitudes above sea-level are: Lowest point, 596.6, and the highest point 615 feet. The Saginaw river, which, with its tributaries, is the second largest river in the state, has an average width here of 400 feet, and is navigable for vessels drawing 10 feet of water at average low stage. There is very little current here during ordinary stage of water. The banks from the city to the mouth of the river are very low, and are bordered on either side by low prairie land and marshes for an average width of 1 mile, after which the land rises gradually and is well adapted for gardening purposes. The city has water communication with the entire lake system, and regular lines of steamers ply during the season of navigation between this point and the principal lake ports.

RAILROAD COMMUNICATIONS.

The city is touched by the following railroad lines:

The Flint and Père Marquette railroad, from Toledo to Ludington, Michigan, with a branch line to Bay City, connecting at various points with the Chicago and Grand Trunk railroad.

The Detroit, Grand Haven, and Milwaukee railroad.

The Detroit, Lansing, and Northern railroad.

The Lake Shore and Michigan Southern railroad.

The Detroit and Bay City division of the Michigan Central railroad, to Detroit.

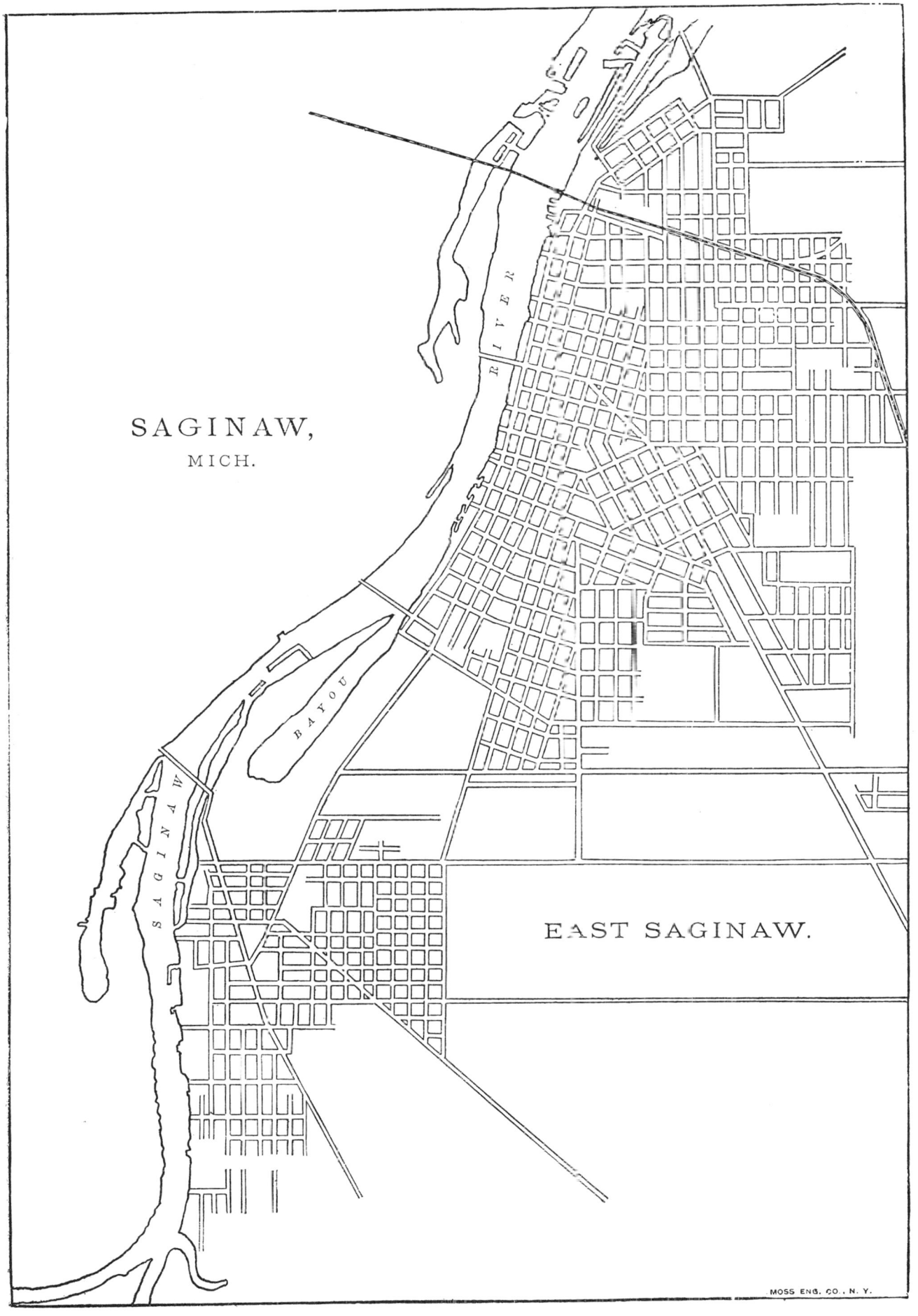

SAGINAW,
MICH.

RIVER

SAGINAW

BAYOU

EAST SAGINAW.

TRIBUTARY COUNTRY.

The country immediately surrounding East Saginaw is one of the richest farming sections in the state, being well adapted to the raising of winter wheat, while all cereals do well. The lowlands afford a rich pasturage and an abundance of hay. In addition to the manufacturing interests the city is the base of supplies for the lumbering region of northeastern Michigan, furnishing the necessaries to an army of from 6,000 to 10,000 men during the winter months. The five streams that unite near the southern limits of the city to form the Saginaw give a combined length of river navigation of over 1,500 miles, and the vast amount of lumber floated down them materially swells the volume of the city's trade.

TOPOGRAPHY, ETC.

The immediate surface is generally a black loam or clay, resting on a stiff blue clay, which is underlaid with a thin stratum of bowlders and gravel intermixed with quicksand; this immediately overlies the rock, and affords an abundant supply of good water. The first rocks are sandstone, about 90 feet thick, while the depth from the surface soil to rock averages 100 feet. There is good natural drainage north and south, but east and west there is little or no fall. The elevation of the surrounding country is from 28 to 34 feet above the level of the river.

CLIMATE.

Highest recorded summer temperature, 98°; summer temperature in average years, 71°. Lowest recorded winter temperature, —22°. The highest summer and the lowest winter temperature in average years was not given.

STREETS.

Total length, 100 miles, of which 7.5 miles are laid with plank, 1.2 mile with wood blocks, and 2 miles with gravel. The cost per square yard of each, as nearly as may be estimated, is, for plank, 35 cents; wood blocks, $1 75; and gravel, $1. The cost of keeping each in good repair is, wood blocks, 17 cents; plank, 5 cents, and gravel, 10 cents, per square yard per annum. The wood blocks cost 35 cents, and the plank 20 cents, per linear foot a year to keep clean. Mr. Ashley says:

The cedar block pavements have been laid but a short time, but are evidently the best pavements we have for durability and healthfulness. The planked streets are costly, having to be removed every two or three years. The gravel streets are comparatively an experiment with us, but we like them very much, and deem them successful when properly constructed.

The sidewalks are of 2-inch pine plank, laid lengthwise of streets, supported by 4 by 4 and 4 by 6 stringers, laid 4 feet apart, and spiked with 40-penny spikes, two in each bearing. The gutters, except on the paved and gravel streets, are open ditches, ranging from 2½ to 3 feet wide at bottom, with side slopes of ½ to 1 foot. They are constructed with great care, all grades being set by the city surveyor. All tree-planting is done by the property-owners, at the sides of the streets. The city has an ordinance in force, passed last year (1879), that makes an allowance of 50 cents for each tree planted by the abutters in front of their premises, provided the same is in a thrifty condition one year after being set out, and this sum is deducted from the amount of the highway tax levied on the parties interested.

Trees must be set in regular rows, not less than 12 nor more than 20 feet apart; and on streets 99 feet in width 15 feet from the line of lots, and on streets 66 feet in width 11 feet from the line of lots. The trees must be properly set out and protected by a stake or guard, and must be not less than 1½ inch in diameter 1 foot above the ground, the lower limbs to be not less than 8 feet above the ground. The advantages offered by the ordinance have been very generally sought, and it is estimated that some 1,500 trees have been set out since its adoption, although many property-owners do not ask for the credit. After the trees have been set out, accepted by the city, and the allowance for their planting made, they can not be disturbed unless with the permission of the street commissioner.

The construction and repairs of streets are done by contract, the system having been in practice here for years, and being deemed the most satisfactory. During the past 5 years there has been expended on streets $79,260 97, or an average annual expenditure of $15,852 19.

The street railroad of East Saginaw, to Saginaw, has a total length of 2½ miles, and its equipment consists of 8 cars and 30 horses. Twelve men are constantly employed, and sometimes more. The average number of passengers carried daily is about 800.

WATER-WORKS.

The works for the public water-supply are owned by the City. They were constructed in 1873 at a total cost of $350,000. The Holly system, or direct pumping, is used, the power being furnished by two pairs of double-cylinder condensing steam-engines and 1 Holly rotary steam-engine. The ordinary pressure in the mains is 40 pounds to the square inch, and the fire pressure 85 pounds. The average amount of water pumped per diem is 1,245,895 gallons, the least being 915,840 and the greatest 1,708,000 gallons. The average cost of raising 1,000,000 gallons one foot high is 18.37 cents. The yearly cost of maintenance, aside from the cost of pumping, is $3,000, and the yearly income from water rates is $19,218 50. A few water-meters are used. The total length of pipes of all kinds is nearly 22 miles. There are 157 hydrants, 136 stops and flushing valves, and 736 consumers. The daily pumping capacity of the works is 3,000,000 gallons.

GAS.

The gas-works are owned by a corporation, the capital stock being $150,000. There are 10½ miles of pipes; a brick building, 30 by 120 feet, containing 8 benches, with 5 retorts on a bench; and a coal-shed, with a capacity of 5,000 tons. The total cost of the works, including pipeage, was $160,000. There are 485 consumers. The daily average production is 200,000 cubic feet. The charge per 1,000 feet is $3. The city pays annually $24 for each street-lamp, 110 in number.

PUBLIC BUILDINGS.

The city owns and occupies for municipal purposes, wholly or in part, a hospital for contagious diseases, costing $4,000; city prison, $1,000; 2 engine-houses, brick, $4,200; 4 frame hose-houses, $300; city pound buildings, $300; and the school buildings, $175,388 60—making a total cost for the municipal buildings belonging to the city of $185,188 The buildings used for city hall, city offices, recorder's court, etc., are rented, and are not owned by the city.

PUBLIC PARKS AND PLEASURE-GROUNDS.

There are no public parks or pleasure-grounds in East Saginaw.

PLACES OF AMUSEMENT.

There is one theater in the city, seating capacity 1,000, used for theatrical exhibitions; also one variety theater, seating 500. Theaters pay no license to the city. There are in addition to these 4 public halls, each with a seating capacity varying from 400 to 500, used for concerts, lectures, etc. The Germania institute, with a seating capacity of 1,000, has a beer-garden connected with it, and is well patronized. There are also several small beer-gardens, open a portion of the time.

DRAINAGE.

Sewerage works were begun here in 1866. The city was divided into districts, and sewerage plans were made and adopted for each district. All work done since 1867 has been done in accordance with these plans, under the direction of the board of sewer commissioners. The natural drainage of the city is very defective, and was made much worse by the raising of the grade at the streets, which increased the number of stagnant pools and wet places in various parts of the city. The engineer of the board of sewer commissioners states that there are still many ponded places in grades of streets, rendering it difficult to get rid of surface-water. These low spots are being drained as fast as the required sewers can be built.

The sewers discharge into the Saginaw river at the level of one foot below ordinary low water. This leaves the mouths of the outfalls exposed except for about one month during spring freshets. The first outlet sewer built was of brick and 60 inches in diameter. For a number of years the supply of water was not sufficient to keep it clean, and it was further obstructed by logs and rubbish floated in from the river at high water, until the outlet was protected by an iron grating. After the supply of sewage was increased by extending the number of lateral sewers there was no further difficulty from deposits. Since the introduction of a public water-supply, sewers have been flushed from the street hydrants for the purpose of cleansing, although deposits are not formed in sufficient amount to obstruct the flow. No repairs of consequence have been required since the beginning of the work in 1866. Regular inspections are made during the winter season, and the interior condition is found to be sound and good. No special provision is made for the ventilation, but in a few cases private drains have been connected with open rain-water leaders. It is only within the past few years that pressure of sewer air has ever been great enough to overcome the ordinary water-traps.

Sewers of 12, 15, and 18 inches diameter are of vitrified pipe; larger sizes are built with two rings of brick laid in cement. All materials are purchased by the city and kept in store. The work of trenching and laying is done by contract. Much difficulty was at first experienced in getting brick of suitable quality for sewers. A large quantity had to be purchased and stored, and even then but a poor selection could be secured. In later years better bricks have been made. One of the principal faults has been the presence in the clay of lumps of lime which slack and burst the brick on exposure to water.

The cost of sewers is assessed upon the abutting property to an amount equal to the cost of an ordinary lateral sewer with the usual number of basins and manholes. The additional cost above such an average rate is paid by the city. The average price of a 12-inch pipe sewer of ordinary depth is from $1 50 to $2 10 per foot, including basins and manholes. The cost of catch-basins is $75 to $80 each, and of manholes for brick sewers $33 to $90. Manholes for pipe sewers, $12 to $20 each, according to depth. The cost of cast-iron manhole covers is $18 each in addition to the above.

Statistics of sewers in East Saginaw, Michigan, for 1880.

Brick sewers—

60-inch brick, including 30 feet wood trunk	feet..	770
54-inch brick, including 40 feet wood trunk	feet..	2,866
48-inch brick, including 113 feet wood trunk	feet..	897
42-inch brick, including 88 feet wood trunk	feet..	5,426
36-inch brick, including 69 feet wood trunk	feet..	2,930
30-inch brick	feet..	430
24-inch brick	feet..	6,067

Pipe sewers—

18-inch stone ware and cement	feet..	5,485
15-inch stone-ware and cement	feet..	4,187
12-inch stone-ware and cement	feet..	12,544
Total feet	feet..	41,602
Total miles		7.88
Total number of inlet basins		208
Total number of manholes		323
Percentage of pipe sewers		0.53
Percentage of sewers 24 inches or less		0.68
Total cost		$188,657
Total cost per mile		$23,941
Total cost per foot		$4 53

CEMETERIES.

There are 3 cemeteries in East Saginaw, as follows: *Brady Hill Cemetery*, area 20 acres, is on Brewster, between Salina and Jefferson streets, in the 5th ward, and is owned by the city; new cemetery (not yet named), on Maple street, adjoining the southern corporation line, has an area of 97½ acres, and is also owned by the city; and *Roman Catholic Cemetery*, area 5⅔ acres, is situated a little south of Brady Hill cemetery, and belongs to the Roman Catholic church.

The total number of interments made in Brady Hill cemetery from the time it was first used until the close of the present year is 4,010; but a portion of these are from the adjoining townships, and a large number are from Saginaw city, so that it is impossible to give the number of the city dead buried here.

No interments have so far been made in the new cemetery, but as Brady Hill cemetery is now nearly full, burials will soon have to be made here.

The number of interments in the Catholic cemetery is not reported.

There is no limit of time as to burial, except that it shall be within a reasonable time after death. In all interments in the city cemeteries a certificate from the attending physician is required, showing name of deceased, date and cause of death, place of birth, age, sex, and occupation, with name of attending physician.

MARKETS.

There are no public or corporation markets in the city.

SANITARY AUTHORITY—BOARD OF HEALTH.

The chief sanitary organization of the city is vested in the board of health, which is composed of the mayor and aldermen, with one health officer, who is always a practicing physician. The annual expenses of the board in ordinary times are about $600, for salaries, and in case of an epidemic this can be increased to any amount deemed necessary. In absence of epidemics the board has a general control over the health and cleanliness of the city, with power to abate nuisances, etc.; while during an epidemic it can take all measures necessary to check and control the disease. The health officer—salary $400 per annum—is not only the executive officer of the board, but has full power to act in nearly all cases, the board convening only when something of extra importance comes up. The mayor and alderman receive $1 each for every meeting of the board. The meetings average one or two per month.

The police force is required to assist the health officer when called upon, and its members are required to report nuisances when they find them. Inspections are made as often as deemed necessary, and also as nuisances are reported. When nuisances are found to exist, the persons responsible are notified to abate the same, and if they fail to comply they are prosecuted. When defective house-drainage, privy-vaults, cesspools, or sources of drinking-water are found they are ordered to be corrected.

The board exercises full control over the conservation and removal of such garbage as is removed by the scavenger. The board requires that all burials, in cases of death from any contagious disease, shall be private. No one is allowed to pollute the river, and the removal of excrement is by the odorless excavator process.

INFECTIOUS DISEASES.

Small-pox patients are removed to the public pest-house, just outside of the city limits. Scarlet-fever patients are isolated at home as much as possible, no visitors being allowed. In case of the breaking out of contagious diseases either in public or in private schools, such as scarlatina, measles, diphtheria, small-pox, cholera, whooping-cough, and typhoid fever, the board closes the schools. Referring to this subject, the health officer says: "Last winter [1879–'80] we had an epidemic of diphtheria; then the board closed the schools for six weeks, but can not say that there was much benefit derived from the same." Vaccination is not compulsory and is not done at the public expense.

All births, diseases, and deaths are registered. Sextons report all burials quarterly to the common council and weekly to the health officer.

MUNICIPAL CLEANSING.

Street-cleaning.—The streets are cleaned both by the city and by private abutters, the city carting off the dirt at its own expense. The work is done wholly by hand, no sweeping-machines being used. The principal streets are cleaned every Saturday morning, and the work is reported as well done. The sweepings are deposited in low places. The cost of the service was not stated.

Removal of garbage and ashes.—Garbage is removed both by the city and by the householders, but the greater part is taken by persons who use it as feed for hogs. Garbage and ashes are not allowed to be kept in the same vessel. The wood ashes are used to make potash. It is possible that some nuisances detrimental to health may arise from the improper keeping of garbage on premises, from infrequent removal, from improper handling, or from improper final disposal, although the whole matter is closely watched by the health officer and the police.

Dead animals.—The carcass of any animal dying within the city is generally removed by the bone-man, at his own expense, outside of the city limits. No record is kept of the number of animals removed annually.

Liquid household wastes; human excreta.—Most of the liquid household wastes in the central part of the city go into the public sewers, while in other parts of the city they are thrown into vaults, none being allowed to run into the street-gutters or ditches. About 25 per cent. of the houses in the city have water-closets, all of which deliver into the sewers, while the remainder depend on privy-vaults. The vaults are mostly lined with brick or wood, and probably one-third of them are nominally water-tight. They are emptied by the odorless excavator process, and the night-soil is deposited on farms outside of the city. It is allowed to be used for manuring land within the gathering-ground of the public water-supply—Saginaw river.

Manufacturing wastes are run either into the sewers or directly into the river.

POLICE.

The police force of East Saginaw is appointed and governed by a board of police commissioners, consisting of the mayor, and two citizens appointed by the common council. The chief of police, salary $1,000 per annum, is the chief executive officer, and has direct control of the department. The remainder of the force consists of 1 captain at $900 a year, 1 sergeant at $725 a year, and 11 patrolmen at $675 a year each, with 1 special, who is paid only for actual duty performed. The men wear the "ordinary police uniform, sack overcoats", and each one furnishes his own. The patrolmen are equipped with clubs, handcuffs, and whistles, the night men usually carrying revolvers. The patrolmen are on duty 12 hours at a time, but the number of miles patrolled by the force was not stated.

During the past year 701 arrests were made, the principal causes being—assault and battery, 50; disorderly conduct, 88; intoxication, 336; murder, 4; larceny, 39; and vagrancy, 64. Of these cases, 48 were discharged, 41 discontinued on payment of costs, and the remainder were convicted. During the same time property to the value of $1,600 was reported to the police as either lost or stolen, and of this, $1,000 was recovered and returned to the owners.

During 1880 there were 316 station-house lodgers, as against 402 in 1879. Free meals to the number of 481, at 16 cents each, were furnished to the lodgers during the year.

The force is required to co-operate with the fire department in preserving order and protecting property at fires, and with the health department in reporting nuisances, etc. Special policemen are appointed by the board of police commissioners when their services are required. The yearly cost of the police force (1880) is $9,605 88.

FIRE DEPARTMENT.

Mr. Ashley writes as follows in regard to the fire department of East Saginaw:

The city being provided with the Holly-system of water-works, through which an ordinary pressure is kept up of 40 pounds, and which can be increased upon the sounding of an alarm to 80 or 100 pounds, no engines are required, the hose being attached directly to the fire-hydrants, from which streams can be thrown over the highest buildings when under fire pressure. Of these fire-hydrants there are now in use in the city 157. For outlying property, however, the city has one Silsby fire-engine, always ready for work. The hose carriages are as follows: One two-horse four-wheeled cart, 2 one-horse two-wheeled carts, and 5 two-wheeled hand hose-carts. The department consists of 1 chief and 8 men at the Central hose-house, and 5 firemen and 32 men at the five outside houses.

GRAND RAPIDS,

KENT COUNTY, MICHIGAN.

POPULATION

IN THE

AGGREGATE,

1850-1880.

	Inhab.
1790	......
1800	......
1810	......
1820	......
1830	......
1840	......
1850	2,686
1860	8,085
1870	16,507
1880	32,016

POPULATION

BY

SEX, NATIVITY, AND RACE,

AT

CENSUS OF 1880.

Male	16,183
Female	15,833
Native	22,016
Foreign-born	10,000
White	31,584
Colored	*432

*Including 2 Chinese and 1 Indian.

Latitude: 43° North; Longitude: 84° 42′ (west from Greenwich); **Altitude: 780 feet.**

FINANCIAL CONDITION:

Total Valuation: $8,692,571; per capita: $272 00.   Net Indebtedness: $471,000; per capita: $14 71.   Tax per $100: $4 58.

HISTORICAL SKETCH.

In March, 1831, the legislative council of the territory of Michigan set off certain townships in the western part of the territory with a separate county, named Kent county, after Chancellor Kent, the celebrated jurist. The county was settled slowly until after the lands granted by Congress for internal improvements were put into the market by the state in the summer of 1843. The nominal price was the same as the government lands, $1 25 per acre; but the obligations called warrants, taken in payment for these lands, could be purchased for 40 cents on the dollar, which made the cost of lands only 50 cents per acre. This low cost attracted the attention of immigrants then passing through Michigan to what were thought better lands farther west, who, on looking at these lands, were so well satisfied that they concluded to go no farther. Grand Rapids was made the county-seat, and as the country around became more thickly settled it grew proportionally in size and wealth. On April 2, 1850, it was incorporated as a city. Its progress since then has been steady and rapid. It has an immense water-power, the finest in the state, and one of the finest in the country. This is brought into use by means of two canals, one on each side of the river. The east canal is half a mile long, 140 feet wide at the guard-gates, and 30 at the lower end; best head of water, 12 feet; height of dam, 6½ feet. It is completely lined with factories from one end to the other. The west-side canal, completed by W. T. Powers in 1869, is 3,300 feet long, 100 feet wide at the upper end and 50 at the lower; amount of fall, 15 feet; height of dam, 6½ feet. The chief industry in the city is the manufacture of furniture and wooden-ware in general. Immediately in or near the city are fine plaster or gypsum quarries, which furnish an almost inexhaustible supply of the finest land and calcined plaster. Large quantities of choice brick clay are also found here, and from 15,000,000 to 20,000,000 of brick for home and foreign use are annually manufactured. A good quality of lime is also made from stone taken from the bed of the river.

GRAND RAPIDS IN 1880.

The attempts of the Census Office to secure information concerning the present condition of the city were only partially successful, and the following statistical accounts are consequently not as complete as could have been wished:

LOCATION.

Grand Rapids lies in latitude 43° north, and longitude 84° 42′ west from Greenwich, on the rapids of the Grand river, 40 miles from its mouth, and 60 miles west-northwest of Lansing. The Grand river gives it water communication with lake Michigan most of the year for boats of from 100 to 150 tons burden, and small boats ascend about 50 miles above the rapids. These rapids are caused by a stratum of limestone rock, which extends about 2 miles along the channel with a descent of 17 feet, affording extensive water-power. The river here is some 800 feet wide, and the bluffs are from 2 to 3 miles apart. The city is built on both banks of the river and on the bluffs, which at their highest point rise from 150 to 200 feet above the river. The corporation limits are 3½ miles long by 3 miles wide, with a small addition, irregular in form, extending down the east bank of the river, making its total area about 11 square miles.

RAILROAD COMMUNICATIONS.

Grand Rapids has the following railroads:
The Grand Rapids and Indiana railroad, the terminals being Petoskey, Michigan, and Richmond, Indiana.
The Detroit, Grand Haven, and Milwaukee railroad, passing through the city from Detroit to Grand Haven, where it connects by regular lines of steamers with Milwaukee and Chicago.
The Chicago and West Michigan railroad, connecting the city with Chicago, Muskegon, and Pentwater.
The Grand River Valley division of the Michigan Central railroad, connecting with the main line at Jackson.
The Kalamazoo division of the Lake Shore and Michigan Southern railway, connecting with the main line at White Pigeon.
The Grand Rapids, Newaygo, and Lake Shore railroad, extending from Grand Rapids to Morgan.

TRIBUTARY COUNTRY.

The city is in the midst of an excellent agricultural and fruit-growing region, of which it is the business center. Kent county has a great diversity of soil and surface. It lies at an elevation of from 10 to 400 feet above lake Michigan. At the usual stage of the water in the lake the foot of the rapids at Grand Rapids is not more than 10 feet above lake Michigan. The country is rolling and well timbered. Scattered through it are swamps, ponds, and lakes.

TOPOGRAPHY, ETC.

Grand Rapids is for the most part much elevated above the river. The townships immediately around the city are made up of hills, plains, swamps, and lakes; the soil is fair, though in the northeast quarter are some poor, sandy hills. About 2 miles east of the city lies Reed's lake—a body of water about 2 miles long—a delightful summer resort. About a mile from the river on the west rise abrupt bluffs, beyond which is a rolling open country, and in the northern part some timbered land—all a good soil. Below the city are some extended bottom-lands along the river, and also below and near the river are plaster quarries and mills. Plaster rock was struck under the lime rock at all the borings for salt at and above the city. Salt was manufactured, but the brine did not prove of sufficient strength to warrant its continuance. The surface of the bluffs is sandy and gravelly, as has been mentioned. Brick clay has been found in considerable quantities.

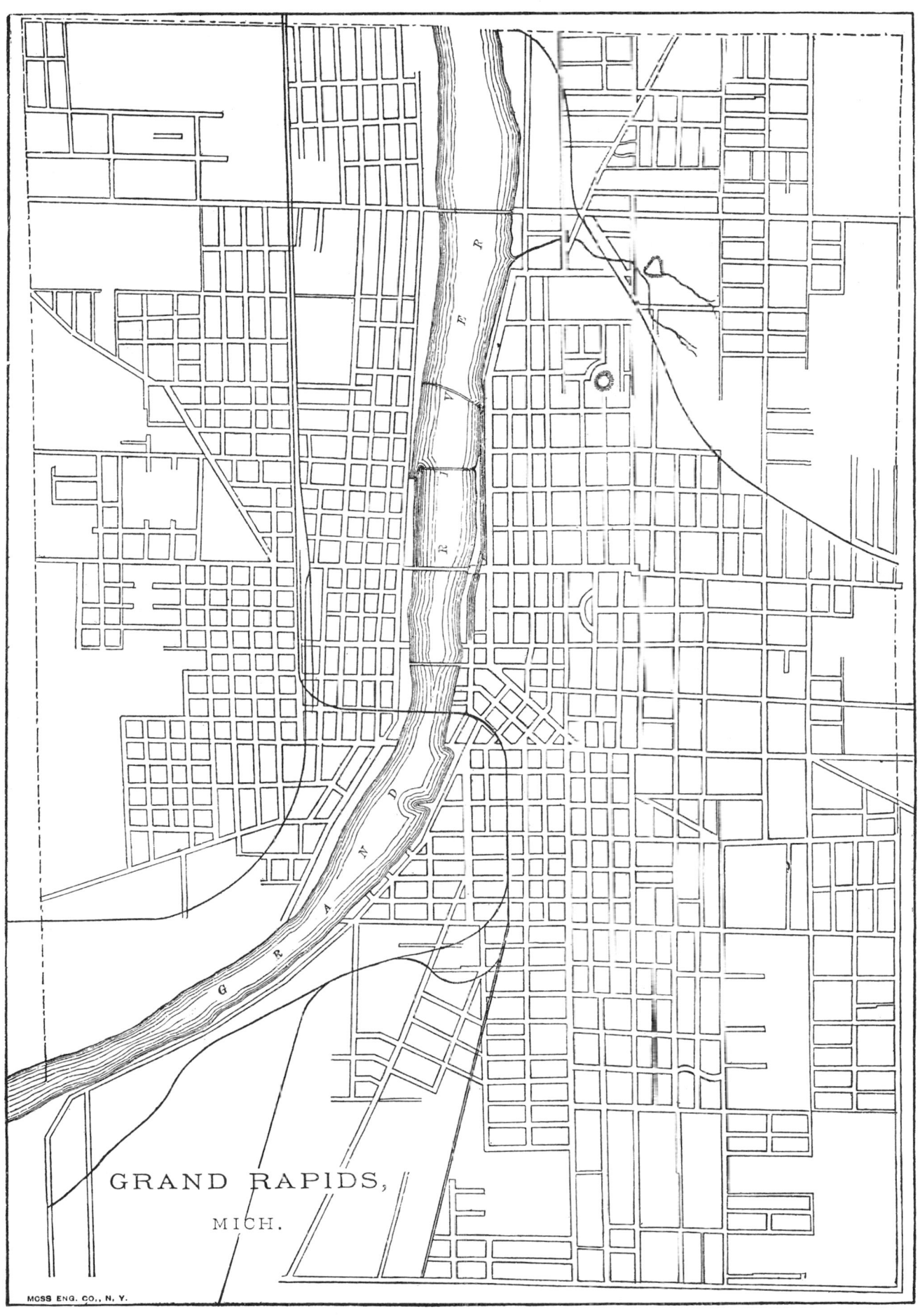

GRAND RAPIDS,
MICH.

CLIMATE.

From the publications of the Smithsonian Institution it is learned that the mean annual temperature of Grand Rapids is 46.90°, the mean winter temperature 24.62°, the mean summer temperature 69.75. The average annual rainfall is 35.55 inches.

STREETS.

The total length of streets is 132.16 miles, of which 1.55 mile is paved with cobble-stones, 0.07 mile with wood, 3.97 miles with wood and stone together (*i. e.*, the side wings or gutters of cobble stones and the central part of wood), and 53.53 miles with gravel. Cobble-stone pavement costs from 30 to 50 cents per square yard, wood from 50 to 75 cents, gravel from 15 to 25 cents. The sidewalks throughout the city, with the exception of a few hundred feet in the business portion, are nearly all of pine planks, and are from 6 to 12 feet wide. There are a few asphalt and tar concrete sidewalks. About 28.4 miles of streets have their gutters paved with cobble-stones. The sidewalks are usually graded from 14 to 16 feet wide, and the plank-walks 6 or 8 feet in width laid next to the property line; the rest of the walk is sodded for a lawn and planted with trees, the hard or sugar maple being generally used. The construction of streets is done by contract under a board of public works. Repairs are done by '. labor under the supervision of a highway commissioner, directed by the common council.

HORSE-RAILROADS.

The total length of horse-railroad track in the city is 8⅞ miles; total number of cars, 19; of horses, 60; of men employed, 29. During the year 664,000 passengers were carried. The rate of fare is 5 cents, commutation tickets a little less.

WATER-WORKS.

The total cost of the works for the water-supply was $401,589 50. The water is pumped into a distributing reservoir about 150 feet above the lower portion of the city. In the year ending May 1, 1879, the pumps were worked for 342 days an average of 8.13 hours per day, and an average of 117,740 gallons per hour was pumped. The average cost of raising 1,000,000 gallons 1 foot high was 8.96 cents. The yearly cost of maintenance, aside from cost of pumping, was $2,223 81; the yearly income from water-rates, $13,016 74. Ninety-four water-meters are used.

GAS.

The gas-works are not owned by the city. The daily average production is about 100,000 cubic feet. The charge per 1,000 feet is $2 for the city; from $2 25 to $2 40 for private persons. The city pays $11 25 each for gas street-lamps, 176 lamps in number.

PUBLIC BUILDINGS.

The city owns 6 engine-houses, which cost about $48,000. There is no city hall, the municipal offices being located in rented apartments. The city owns school-houses valued at $352,000.

PUBLIC PARKS AND PLEASURE GROUNDS.

There are 3 public parks, with a total area of 19 acres, as follows: *Lincoln Park*, 12.5 acres, unimproved; *Highland Park*, 5 acres, unimproved; *Fulton Park*, 1.5 acre, which has some gravel walks, band-stand, and trees, and is kept in decent order. The total cost of these was $12,200, Lincoln park alone costing $11,000. The parks are controlled directly by the common council.

PLACES OF AMUSEMENT.

The city has 3 theaters, viz: Power's opera-house, seating about 1,200; Pruith's opera-house, seating about 500; and Luce's hall, seating about 500. Theaters pay an annual license of $300. Besides these large halls there are the Young Men's Christian Association hall, used for lectures, etc.; the Harmonia Singing Society's hall, for concerts and as a beer-garden, and the Herman hall, for amusements. There are 4 concert- and beer-gardens.

DRAINAGE; CEMETERIES.

No information on these subjects was furnished by the city authorities.

MARKETS.

The city has no public market. Private meat-markets pay a city license of $1 per annum; meat-peddlers pay a city license of $20 per annum.

SANITARY AUTHORITY—BOARD OF HEALTH.

The chief health organization is the board of health, consisting of 3 members, nominated by the mayor and confirmed by the city council, and the city physician *ex officio*. When there is no declared epidemic its annual expenses are about $2,000, incurred for salaries of members, cost of abating nuisances, etc. In case of an epidemic the board may increase its expenses to any extent which the judgment of the majority of the members may deem necessary. Its authority is unlimited so far as pertains to the abatement of any nuisance, or any thing detrimental to the public health. During epidemics its authority is almost unlimited; it can close up or put under quarantine any building, public or private; forbid any railroad train, steamboat, stage-coach, or other public conveyance from entering the city, if it is suspected that a case of contagious disease is on board, etc. This board after its appointment is entirely let alone by the city government. It holds regular meetings every two weeks. Each member devotes one day in every week to inspections. When nuisances are reported from any neighborhood a visit is paid and the whole neighborhood inspected; in case the nuisance exists, a notice to abate within a specified time is served on the owner or occupant. In cases of defective house-drainage, privy-vaults, or cesspools, the board orders the defects remedied, and if they are not, then the officer has the repairs done, and the owner is assessed for the amount spent. Drinking-water is analyzed by a chemist, and if found impure the wells are filled up. The board has no control over city sewers or streets. It can and does order the removal of garbage; it furnishes a ground for burning it, and keeps a man there at times to do this. It exercises no control as to the burial of the dead, except that in the case of death from a contagious disease it can order a private funeral. The depositing of filth or garbage in the streams is forbidden.

INFECTIOUS DISEASES.

Small-pox patients are isolated at home, since there is no pest-house, but the board is urging the council to build one. Scarlet-fever patients are quarantined at home by a notice posted on the house. Under the ordinances, in case of the breaking out of contagious diseases in the public schools, the board would have full control, but the emergency has not yet arisen. Vaccination is not compulsory, nor is it done at the public expense.

REPORTS.

There is no registration of births or deaths, or of diseases, except contagious ones, which are reported to the city clerk. The board reports to the common council at the end of the year, but this action is not compulsory.

MUNICIPAL CLEANSING.

Street-cleaning.—Streets are cleaned both by the city and by private abutters. That which the city does is done by its own force and wholly by hand. The main street is cleaned about once a week, sometimes only once in two weeks, and other streets as often as they may need. The special defect of the system is that the city has provided no special place where the sweepings may be deposited, as should be done.

Removal of garbage and ashes.—Garbage is removed by householders, except in cases where the owner can not be found, and then the city removes it. While awaiting removal it must be kept in a tight box or vessel, and must be removed twice a week between the first day of May and the first day of November, and once a week during the rest of the year. If this is neglected it is the duty of the city scavenger to see that it is done. Garbage must either be buried to such a depth that it is not a nuisance, or else must be taken outside the city limits. As to ashes, the householders in a certain specified district of the city must put them three times each week in a metallic vessel on the outer edge of the sidewalk, whence they are removed by the city scavenger, that officer receiving 25 cents per month from the householders for each vessel so emptied by him. The city should own a few acres of land outside the city limits where garbage and ashes should be deposited.

The ordinances are very explicit as to scavengers, and deserve notice. Scavengers must be licensed and file bonds. Under the direction of the mayor, marshal, or a member of the board of health, they have the power to enter any premises in the daytime and examine any vault, sink, privy, or private drain. In case of a householder's failure to clean, alter, relay, or repair any of these on notice given by any of the authorized city officials, it is the scavenger's duty to do it. It is also his duty to clean or empty any vault, drain, or privy, and remove any and all nuisances when requested, and he may demand and receive his fees in advance.

Dead animals.—Dead animals are removed by the marshal or scavenger, as the case may be, and are disposed of by burial. As in the case of ashes and garbage, there should be one place set apart by the city for burial.

Liquid household wastes.—Nearly all of the liquid household waste of the city is delivered into the public sewers; none of it is allowed to run into the street gutters. What few cesspools are used are porous. Sometimes they or "dry wells" are found to be used to receive the waste of water-closets, but such cases are prosecuted. Cesspools are cleaned out by the city scavenger.

Human excreta.—A very large proportion of the houses depend on privy-vaults. Most water-closets deliver into the public sewers. The contents of privy-vaults are removed between the hours of 12 and 2 at night by the scavenger, who receives from the person requiring his services 20 cents for each cubic foot so removed. Between the first day of May and the first day of November no privy shall be cleaned except upon written order or permission of the board of health in such special cases as in the opinion of said board the health and safety of the public may require. The contents of privy-vaults must in no case be used to manure ground within the city limits, and they must be carried outside those limits by the scavenger.

Manufacturing wastes.—No information could be secured under this head. The city ordinances are silent concerning the subject.

MANUFACTURES.

The following is a summary of the statistics of the manufactures of Grand Rapids for 1880, being taken from tables prepared for the Tenth Census by George W. Gage, special agent:

Mechanical and manufacturing industries.	No. of establishments.	Capital.	AVERAGE NUMBER OF HANDS EMPLOYED.			Total amount paid in wages during the year.	Value of materials.	Value of products.
			Males above 16 years.	Females above 15 years.	Children and youths.			
All industries	355	$4,864,298	4,509	295	368	$1,895,072	$3,956,663	$7,405,007
Agricultural implements	7	259,525	197	3	15	72,978	163,166	303,029
Blacksmithing (see also Wheelwrighting)	18	9,425	19			10,200	11,520	32,974
Boots and shoes, including custom work and repairing	18	28,310	45	3		27,270	53,130	101,292
Bread and other bakery products	14	80,750	57	4	8	31,420	195,050	253,500
Carpentering	14	21,100	98	5		46,385	89,863	162,492
Carriages and wagons (see also Wheelwrighting)	9	88,500	92		1	41,790	75,930	138,822
Clothing, men's	9	118,920	106	89		62,150	165,329	323,742
Coffins, burial cases, and undertakers' goods	3	71,300	86		1	37,048	33,929	119,308
Confectionery	4	53,075	72	18	5	28,774	124,650	165,000
Cooperage	9	27,050	49			17,503	48,451	75,058
Drugs and chemicals (see also Patent medicines and compounds)	3	65,500	35	1	—	11,590	34,536	78,427
Files	3	3,200	18			8,900	10,700	22,000
Flouring- and grist-mill products	5	129,500	33			17,550	356,775	398,988
Foundery and machine-shop products	13	267,971	276		—	133,499	188,451	384,611
Furniture	11	1,313,156	1,702	6	99	647,587	823,086	1,831,172
Liquors, malt	7	278,000	65			29,883	128,553	229,526
Looking-glass and picture frames	4	10,600	9	5		5,950	14,650	30,518
Lumber, sawed	8	1,014,685	252			79,059	457,259	755,476
Marble and stone work	4	8,500	11			4,644	9,300	20,800
Masonry, brick and stone	8	17,300	89			25,533	49,055	83,320
Painting and paperhanging	11	8,500	41			15,270	24,940	54,475
Patent medicines and compounds (see also Drugs and chemicals)	4	3,100	3			1,490	3,600	9,132
Photographing	10	13,850	11	6		7,974	6,180	26,423
Plumbing and gasfitting	4	16,350	16			9,194	27,322	46,630
Printing and publishing	20	93,450	151	8	57	79,250	46,662	168,324
Saddlery and harness	10	15,150	40		1	16,628	36,100	62,156
Sash, doors, and blinds	6	66,500	96		1	38,489	93,396	160,043
Tinware, copperware, and sheet-iron ware	10	26,600	53			28,274	48,775	93,740
Tobacco, cigars and cigarettes	18	39,800	63	5	8	26,145	74,655	124,463
Upholstering materials	3	13,500	7		4	4,200	7,806	18,425
Watch and clock repairing	12	4,650	15			9,776	5,375	23,972
Wirework	3	1,100	1			700	1,900	4,124
Wheelwrighting (see also Blacksmithing; Carriages and wagons)	13	8,400	26		4	11,790	13,250	35,448
All other industries (a)	60	686,381	675	147	168	301,974	533,319	1,067,597

a Embracing awnings and tents; baking and yeast powders; baskets, rattan and willow ware; belting and hose, leather; bookbinding and blank-book making; boxes, cigar; boxes, wooden packing; brick and tile; brooms and brushes; carriages and sleds, children's; carriage and wagon materials; corsets; cutlery and edge tools; electroplating; engraving and die-sinking; fertilizers; flavoring extracts; furs, dressed; gloves and mittens; hats and caps; housefurnishing goods; instruments, professional and scientific; iron work, architectural and ornamental; lime; lock- and gun-smithing; lumber, planed; mattresses and spring beds; mineral and soda waters; musical instruments, organs and materials; pumps; roofing and roofing materials; saws; sewing machines and attachments; shirts; soap and candles; sporting goods; steam fittings and heating apparatus; stencils and brands; stone- and earthen-ware; surgical appliances; toys and games; upholstering; wood, turned and carved; wooden ware; and woolen goods.

From the foregoing table it appears that the average capital of all establishments is $13,702 24; that the average wages of all hands employed is $366 41 per annum; and that the average outlay in wages, in materials, and in interest (at 6 per cent.) on capital employed is $17,305 89.

JACKSON,

JACKSON COUNTY, MICHIGAN.

POPULATION

IN THE

AGGREGATE,

1850-1880.

	Inhab.
1790	......
1800	......
1810	......
1820	......
1830	......
1840	......
1850	2,363
1860	4,799
1870	11,447
1880	16,105

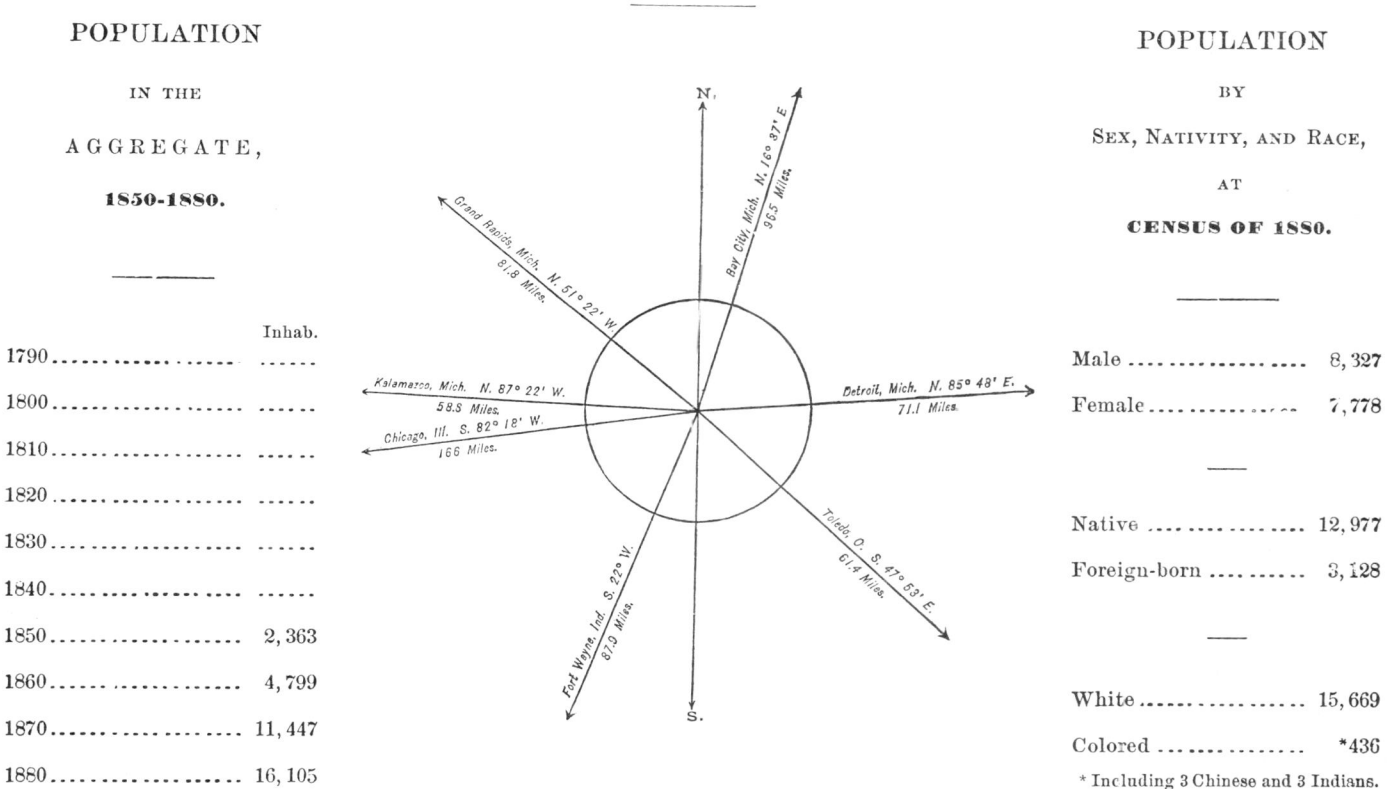

POPULATION

BY

SEX, NATIVITY, AND RACE,

AT

CENSUS OF 1880.

Male	8,327
Female	7,778
Native	12,977
Foreign-born	3,128
White	15,669
Colored	*436

* Including 3 Chinese and 3 Indians.

Latitude: 42° 16′ North; Longitude: 84° 26′ (west from Greenwich); **Altitude: 931 feet.**

FINANCIAL CONDITION:

Total Valuation: $2,142,350; per capita: $133 00.   Net Indebtedness: $184,000; per capita: $11 43.   Tax per $100: $5 14.

HISTORICAL SKETCH.

The first settlement by white people on the site of what is now the city of Jackson was made in 1829. A portion of the ground had long previously been occupied and cultivated by the Indians, for whom this had been a favorite camping-ground, and a central point for their trails leading to all parts of the Indian territory. Some nine or more of these trails diverged from this place, among them the great Washtenaw, the Saint Joseph, and the Chicago trails, the marks of some of which are yet visible, and which a few years since could be distinctly traced for some distance east and west of the city. It was a forbidding site for a village or city. The low ground was a swamp, the high land a succession of sand knolls or hills of a very uneven character, interspersed with springs and bog-holes. The river bottom was heavily timbered, very low and wet, and so difficult to improve that it was thirty years after the town was started before there was a good, well-established street passing through it. In making improvements to-day, such as laying water-pipes or building sewers, the old log causeways several feet below the surface of the ground are often found.

JACKSON.

MICH.

SCALE OF FEET

0   500   1000 1500

MILL POND

In 1829, Mr. Horace Blackman, a young man from Tioga county, New York, went through this country on a tour of inspection, and finally "located" a piece of land where now is the heart of the city of Jackson; and in the fall of this year, with the assistance of his brother, he erected a log cabin on his land, preparatory to his occupation of it in the spring. In October of this year the legislative council of the territory of Michigan created the region round about here into Jackson county. In 1830, the commissioners who were locating the territorial road, together with a party of Ann Arbor citizens, stayed a couple of days and nights in Blackman's empty cabin, and after much festivity christened the place Jacksonburg. The first actual settlement was made in the spring of 1830 by a number of Ann Arbor people, some of whom proceeded at once to build a dam, race, and saw-mill, and soon afterward the village was laid out and platted. In the fall of the same year a post-office was established, called Jacksonopolis.

Settlers now began to come in rapidly, and the village grew in proportion. In 1837 a court-house and county clerk's office was built. On December 29, 1841, the Michigan Central railroad was completed to Jackson; and as it was nearly three years before it was completed to Albion—an interval of time in which Jackson was the terminus of the road and commanded the business of the country north and west—undoubtedly laid the foundation not only of the future prosperity of the city, but also that of most of its successful business men. In 1838 the state penitentiary was located at Jackson, and has been in progress of erection ever since, or rather additions have always been in progress. The system of letting the labor of the convicts to work for contractors has been the policy pursued by the state, and the manufactures thus carried on have grown.

The city of Jackson was incorporated in 1857. The general progress of the city has been quite regular, with no great depressions at any time. It held its own very well during the late hard times. It has had no extensive fires.

JACKSON IN 1880.

The following statistical accounts, mainly collected by the Census Office, indicate the present condition of Jackson:

LOCATION.

Jackson, the capital of Jackson county, Michigan, is situated on the Grand river near its source, 76 miles west of Detroit and 38 miles south by east of Lansing, at an altitude of about 930 feet above the level of the sea. The highest elevation of the city is reported to be about 100 feet above its lowest point. It is not situated on navigable water.

RAILROAD COMMUNICATIONS.

Its railroads with their terminal connections are as follows:

The Michigan Central railroad, from Detroit to Chicago, passes through the city, the air-line division of which leaves the main road here, joining it again at Niles.

The Fort Wayne and Jackson railroad connects Jackson with Fort Wayne, Indiana, and with the many roads diverging from there.

The Jackson branch of the Lake Shore and Michigan Southern railroad (running from Chicago to Buffalo) connects with other divisions at Adrian, and so with the main line at Toledo.

The Saginaw division of the Michigan Central railroad runs to Bay City.

The Grand Rapids division of the same road runs to Grand Rapids.

TRIBUTARY COUNTRY.

The surrounding country is principally a farming country, with wheat, wool, and live stock as its most important products. There are a number of flour-mills scattered over it. There are quite important coal mines in the immediate vicinity, and even within the city limits. A considerable trade, both wholesale and retail, comes from along the railroads running into the heavily timbered lands from 20 to 25 miles north, south, and southwest.

TOPOGRAPHY.

The country in the immediate vicinity is generally level, but originally it was mostly oak openings with much marshy land, which is now nearly all improved in farms.

CLIMATE.

The highest recorded temperature is 104°; highest in average years, between 98° and 100°. Lowest winter temperature in average years, about 20°. It is reported that spring and fall are of short duration—that, in other words, the changes from summer to winter and from winter to summer are quite abrupt. The influence of adjacent waters, marshes, and elevated lands is insignificant. The prevailing winds are southerly and southwesterly.

STREETS.

About 0.5 mile of streets is paved with cobble-stone, 0.5 mile with wood, and about 10 miles with gravel; the cobble-stone pavement cost about 60 cents per square yard, the wood 50 cents. The sidewalks are mostly made of planks, except a small portion of the business quarter, where they are of stone; recently the tendency has been toward brick and concrete, and perhaps a mile of them has been laid during the past year in place of plank. Gutters are generally paved like the street. Nearly all the streets have one row of trees on the outer edge of the sidewalk, and many have a second row some 10 or 12 feet out into the street, with a grass-plot between. The work of construction and repair of streets is done by the day, the cost being from $10,000 to $15,000 a year. So far as economy is concerned, the preference is for contract work. But little street work, however, has been done by contract. The city covers 9 square miles, and ordinary grading and repairs are so scattered that the authorities say it can not well be done by contract, and they say, besides, that if done by the day it would give more employment to a class of poor laborers that might otherwise be obliged to call on the city poor-fund for help.

WATER-WORKS.

In 1870 the city constructed water-works on the Holly plan. The average amount pumped per day is 1,000,000 gallons; the greatest amount, 1,300,000; the least, 800,000. The yearly income from water rates is $8,500.

GAS.

The gas-works are not owned by the city. The charge per 1,000 cubic feet is, to individuals, $3; to the city, $2 50. There are 121 street lamps.

PUBLIC BUILDINGS.

The city owns no municipal buildings.

PUBLIC PARKS AND PLEASURE-GROUNDS.

There are 2 small parks in the city of a total area of 2 acres. The County Agricultural Society owns 28 acres within the city limits, which it uses for fairs, races, etc.; by agreement this is kept for public uses.

PLACES OF AMUSEMENT.

There are no regular theaters in the city, but there are two theater buildings for the use of traveling companies, which seat from 2,600 to 2,800 persons, and pay an annual license of $75 each. The Young Men's Library Association has a hall seating 800; the German Harmonic Society, one seating 500; the Young Men's Christian Association, one seating 700; and the Reform Club, one seating 500. There are no public concert- and beer-gardens.

DRAINAGE.

There are in Jackson about 2 miles of brick sewers from 20 to 30 inches in diameter—usually 24 inches—and 1 mile of pipe sewers from 9 to 16 inches in diameter. They are laid within the lines of streets, and do not follow the natural water-courses, though some small streams have been taken into the sewers. There is no regular system for the whole city. Each sewer is regulated according to the supposed requirements of the case as it comes up. The outflow of sewers is discharged into Grand river. The mouths of outfalls are on a level with the ordinary stages of the river, and are submerged only in times of high water. No provision is made for ventilation, and there has been no artificial flushing or cleansing by hand. It is reported that the waste water from houses and the surface-water from storms keep the sewers clean. The city pays two-thirds of the cost of building sewers, and the other third is assessed upon property benefited, whether abutting or not. Assessments are laid on the basis of benefits, and are apportioned by a board of 3 assessors, subject to the approval of the common council. Brick sewers 24 inches in diameter are reported to cost on the average $1 10 per linear foot. Differences in cost depend more on the cost of trenching under different circumstances than on the size of the sewers.

CEMETERIES.

The city has 5 cemeteries, including one which has been laid out but in which there are as yet only a few interments. The information furnished on this head, as on all the rest, was very meager.

MARKETS.

There are no public markets. There is very little wholesale business done in the city, the retailers getting meat and produce directly from the farmers.

SANITARY AUTHORITY—BOARD OF HEALTH.

The chief health organization is the board of health, an independent board with three members, one of whom is a physician. None of them have police powers. It makes reports to the chief of police and to the city council. It is appointed by the mayor, and its action is subject to the control of the city government. Inspections are made in the spring and fall, and when nuisances are reported; in the latter case the matter is looked up, and if after three days the nuisance has not been abated a warrant is issued. Scarlet-fever patients are quarantined at home and the house is placarded. The city owns a pest-house situated out in the country. The reports of the board are published only in the city papers.

MUNICIPAL CLEANSING.

Street-cleaning.—Streets are cleaned by the city's own force and by hand, except in the spring and fall, when a machine is used. The business streets are cleaned each week; alleys adjacent thereto each month; other streets and alleys once a year. It is reported to be done thoroughly. The sweepings are either deposited on the river bank or used in filling up low streets. The system seems satisfactory, except in respect to the place of deposit.

Removal of garbage and ashes.—Garbage is removed both by householders and by the city. Part of it is used to feed swine outside the city, and a very large portion of the rest is thrown into the river. Ashes are either used for filling in streets or dumped into the river. The cost to the city is included in the cleaning of alleys. Nuisances and injury to health are not uncommon.

Dead animals.—The removal of dead animals is under the charge of the chief of police. They are said to be promptly cared for by the proper authorities. The smaller ones and part of the larger ones are buried in the southwestern portion of the city, half a mile distant from the inhabited portion; the rest are used in the manufacture of soap. Small animals are occasionally thrown into the river. The annual cost of this service is $50. The only defect in the system reported is the place of burial. It is reported that it would be better if this were changed to the northern or eastern portion of the city.

Liquid household wastes.—Waste water from sleeping-rooms is disposed of in the same way as laundry waste and kitchen slops. It is delivered into the public sewers where they exist. Very little if any runs into either gutters, cesspools, or dry wells. What cesspools and dry wells exist are porous and are not provided with overflows. When these are used they do not receive the waste of water-closets. There are no regulations as to the cleaning out of cesspools, except when they become nuisances, and then the board of health sees to it.

Human excreta.—Three-fourths of the business portion of the city has water-closets, and perhaps also 5 per cent. of the dwellings have them; the rest depend on privy-vaults. The small percentage of dwellings having water-closets is mainly due to the recent construction of sewers. Nearly all the water-closets deliver into the public sewers, and only a small portion into cesspools. Privy-vaults must not be located within 20 feet of the street. The board of health has the general supervision of their emptying, which is carefully looked after. The dry-earth system is not used to any extent. Night-soil is ultimately removed outside the city, and it is not allowed to be used for manuring land within the gathering-ground of the public water-supply.

Manufacturing waste.—Manufacturing waste is deposited near or in the river below the city.

POLICE.

The police force is appointed by the mayor and confirmed by the common council; it is governed by the chief of police, who receives a salary of $1,000 per year. There are 7 patrolmen, with salaries of $700 per year each. Their uniforms are blue, with brass buttons, each man furnishing his own and the city furnishing the buttons. The city also furnishes belts, batons, and handcuffs; the men buy their own revolvers if they wish to carry them. They serve 12 hours each day, being changed at noon and at midnight. Last year there were 496 arrests, the principal cause being drunkenness. During 1880 there were about 700 station-house lodgers; in 1879, 856. The department furnished them no free meals. The police are required to co-operate with the fire department merely to the extent of guarding property and keeping order at fires. Special policemen are appointed like the regular force. The yearly cost of the police force (1880) is $7,900.

KALAMAZOO,

KALAMAZOO COUNTY, MICHIGAN.

POPULATION

IN THE

AGGREGATE,

1850-1880.

	Inhab.
1790	......
1800	......
1810	......
1820	......
1830	......
1840	......
1850	2,507
1860	6,070
1870	9,181
1880	11,937

POPULATION

BY

SEX, NATIVITY, AND RACE,

AT

CENSUS OF 1880.

Male	5,670
Female	6,267
Native	9,203
Foreign-born	2,734
White	11,475
Colored	462

Latitude: 42° 18′ North; Longitude: 85° 35′ (west from Greenwich); Altitude: 663 to 901 feet.

FINANCIAL CONDITION:

Total Valuation: $5,478,360; per capita: $404 00.   Net Indebtedness: $25,000; per capita: $1 84.   Tax per $100: $1 48.

HISTORICAL SKETCH.(a)

The site of the village of Kalamazoo was formerly occupied by Indian trading-posts that were established here in 1823; but the first regular settlement was not made until 1829–'30. The county of Kalamazoo was organized in 1830, and the county-seat was located here in the January following. The village organization was made in 1843, and that form of municipal government is still retained. A fine water-power is afforded by the river at this point. There have been no serious ravages by fire. Commercial and financial depression first occurred in 1837, and subsequently at dates corresponding with those affecting the "Northwest" or the entire country. The population came originally and mainly from New England and western New York, and this element with its descendants still predominates. The foreign-born population comprises Hollanders, Irish, and German, the former class being the most numerous.

---

a Dr. Foster Pratt, of Kalamazoo, collected and forwarded to this office the information on which this report is based.

KALAMAZOO IN 1880.

LOCATION.

Kalamazoo lies in latitude 42° 18' north, and longitude 85° 35' west from Greenwich, on the left bank of the Kalamazoo river, about 65 miles above the point where it enters lake Michigan, and in the southwestern part of the state. The average elevation of the village above mean sea-level is 693 feet, or 120 feet above the surface of lake Michigan, the lowest point being 663 feet and the highest 901 feet above sea-level. The river on which the village is situated is navigable for vessels of 50 tons from its mouth to Allegan, Michigan, 25 miles below Kalamazoo.

RAILROAD COMMUNICATIONS.

The village is touched by the following railroads:

The Michigan Central railroad, from Detroit to Chicago.

The Kalamazoo and South Haven railroad (now operated by the Michigan Central), to South Haven, on lake Michigan.

The Grand Rapids and Indiana railroad, between Richmond, Indiana, and Mackinac, Michigan.

The Kalamazoo division of the Lake Shore and Michigan Southern railway, between White Pigeon and Grand Rapids, Michigan.

TRIBUTARY COUNTRY.

The country immediately tributary to Kalamazoo is principally agricultural, the main products being those of a "mixed agriculture"—that is, wheat, corn, oats, barley, potatoes, hogs, cattle, milk, butter, hay, apples, peaches, pears, quinces, grapes, berries, etc. Also timber products, consisting of pine, and various kinds of hard wood suitable for manufacturing purposes.

TOPOGRAPHY, ETC.

The site of the village is supposed to lie over the "Waverly group", but no stratified rock has been found in the county, one boring having been made to the depth of 150 feet. The surface is rolling, the average variations of level being about 200 feet. The entire valley is drained by the Kalamazoo river and its tributaries. The soil is a sandy and gravelly loam, the gravel consisting largely of carbonate of lime. There is a large amount of "lake surface" in the county, of which 200 acres are close to the village. Some marshy formations on the borders of streams are now nearly all drained and cultivated. The surrounding country, originally wooded, is now open, and the character of the soil is as stated above. The entire surface is gently rolling.

CLIMATE.

Highest recorded summer temperature, 99°; highest summer temperature in average years, 92°. Lowest recorded winter temperature, —32°; lowest winter temperature in average years, —15°. The prevailing winds are from the west, blowing over lake Michigan, and tend to delay spring, to mitigate the summer heat, and to prolong the autumn weather. Vegetation is delayed here from ten days to two weeks, as compared with points in the same latitude 100 miles east.

STREETS.

Total length of streets in the village, about 80 miles; of these, 1.06 mile is paved with wood (Nicholson), and 12 miles with gravel. The cost per square yard for the Nicholson pavement varies from $1 50 to $2 25; the cost of the gravel pavement can not be accurately given, as gravel-beds are found in the hills near the village, while the excavating, hauling, and spreading are done partly by day's work and partly by private subscription. It is said that the natural soil, except in the fall and spring, makes good roads. The quality and the permanent economy of each class of pavement can not be stated, as the wood is laid on the business streets and the gravel on residence streets, the wear and tear therefore greatly differing. The sidewalks are of plank or Portland cement, varying in width from 4 to 14 feet; and of all kinds there are 150 miles in length. Gutters, when paved at all, are laid in cobble-stones. The soil is very porous, and on gravel streets gutters are but partially paved. But little tree-planting is done by the municipality. The village is situated on what was originally a burr-oak plain, or "opening", the natural growth having been carefully preserved, and allowed to be cut only when necessary to accommodate dwellings, to open streets, etc. Dr. Pratt says: "Maple and elms have been put into spaces by private enterprise. Ours is the 'burr-oak village', and has so much *rus in urbe* that little needs to be done in this direction. Indeed, in some localities, shade has become so dense as to require cutting out." On nearly all the streets grass-plots border the driveways. Nearly all street work is done by the day. For a large amount of definite work or material for construction, contracts are preferred. The annual cost of street work was not stated.

There are no horse-railroads or regular omnibus lines in the village. There are, however, 21 licensed hacks and omnibuses, with 60 horses and employing 97 men, which carry passengers to all parts of the village at rates of fare of from 25 to 50 cents, according to distance.

WATER-WORKS.

The works for the public water-supply are owned by the village, and their first cost was $158,000. The Holly system, or direct pumping, is used, the pressure in the mains varying from 40 pounds for domestic to 150 pounds for fire purposes to the square inch. The average amount of water pumped per diem during the year was 776,635 gallons. Yearly cost of maintenance, aside from the cost of pumping, $3,233 72, and yearly income from water-rates, $5,131 69. A few water-meters are used, only for the purpose of testing the average amount used by large consumers. In reply to the question concerning the cost of raising 1,000,000 gallons one foot high, Dr. Pratt says:

An answer to this can be based only on uncertain data. We use pine slabs largely for fuel, with some hard wood and some coal. Annual cost of pumping, $2,450 37, delivering 776,000 gallons to consumers daily, under 45 pounds average pressure. During the fiscal year ending March 31, 1880, 287,535,600 gallons of water were delivered, under a pressure of 45 pounds, to about 500 consumers; and for fire purposes, cost of pumping was $2,450 37; other cost, $3,233 72; total cost, $5,684 09. Total revenue, $5,131 69; deficit, $552 40 (charged to fire department); add $5,817 64, other cost of fire department, makes total cost of the department $6,370 04 The water-works take the place of fire-engines in our fire department, and a financial exhibit of their expenses and revenues should recognize their twofold purpose.

GAS.

The gas-works are not owned by the village. The daily average production was not given. The charge per 1,000 feet is from $2 20 to $2 25. The village pays $15 annually for each gas street-lamp, 120 in number. There are also 50 oil street-lamps, making a total of 170. The meter rent is 25 cents per quarter.

PUBLIC BUILDINGS

The village owns and occupies for municipal purposes, wholly or in part, a corporation hall, used for village offices, library, school-board, and central fire station; and 2 hose-houses. The village has no joint ownership or occupancy with the county in any building. The corporation hall and the hose-houses cost to build $20,000; the land on which they stand, which is now very valuable, cost originally but little.

PUBLIC PARKS AND PLEASURE-GROUNDS.

Total area, 6½ acres. *Bronson Park*, the donation of the first settlers and land-owners, has an area of 5 acres, which with contiguous open grounds makes an area of 6½ acres. It is situated in the center of the village. The ground cost the municipality nothing, and so far $3,000 has been expended for improvements—grading, turfing, trees, fountain, cement walks, etc. The park was designed by Adam Oliver, esq., and is controlled by the village board.

PLACES OF AMUSEMENT.

One hall, with a seating capacity of about 1,000, is used for theatrical purposes. There are 2 other halls, with a seating capacity of 300 each, that are not, properly speaking, theaters. Each performance pays a license tax, which amounts in the aggregate to $150 annually. The hall first mentioned is in the second story, over five stores, and has a front and a rear entrance. The other halls are in the third stories, one of them having reception rooms, parlors, kitchen, dining-room, etc., used for balls, parties, etc. There are no concert- and beer-gardens in the city.

CEMETERIES.

There are 2 cemeteries now used by the village. *Mountain Home Cemetery*, lying on the western limits of the village and north of Main street, fronting thereon, has an area of 20 acres; and *Riverside Cemetery*, outside the corporate limits, just north of the northeastern line, extends down nearly to Kalamazoo river, and contains 30 acres of land. There is also an old burial ground, between Park and West streets and north of Axtele creek, containing 2 acres of land, in which no interments have been made since 1857. Prior to 1873 no proper records were kept in the several cemeteries; since that time there have been 1,213 interments in Riverside and Mountain Home cemeteries, or an average of about 151 interments each year. This number, however, includes a few from outside the village; just how many can not be accurately stated. There are no municipal regulations concerning interments.

Mountain Home Cemetery association deeds lots at stipulated prices, but subject to restrictions in certain matters by the general regulations of the association. The ground is naturally rolling, soil sand and gravel, landscape-gardening well designed and executed, and the roads are graded, graveled, well laid out, and well kept. The minimum charges of the sexton are, for digging graves, $5, and for care of lots, $3. The accumulated fund amounts to $17,000; last year's income from the fund was $1,800, all expended in improvements. Riverside cemetery, excepting the fund, is equally applicable to it.

Dr. Pratt closes his report on cemeteries as follows:

In a sanitary sense Mountain Home cemetery, lying on the hills west of the village may seem to be badly located; but the soil beneath us for more than 100 feet (how much more we do not know) is sand and gravel, which admits of the percolation, directly downward, of all dangerous liquids. Riverside cemetery, northwest of the village, is on the river, sloping rapidly down to it, and on the opposite side from the village, and below it, as the water runs. The "old burying-ground", of 2 acres in the southwest part of the village, abandoned in 1857 as a burial place, is now nearly empty, most of the bodies buried there having been removed by their friends to other grounds; but the ground is well kept and cared for. This, like Riverside, is the property of the township. Our statistics do not admit of showing progressive changes and existing conditions, except in the general way herein indicated.

MARKETS.

There are no public markets in the village. The meat-markets are wholly owned and controlled by private individuals. There are 5 slaughter-houses, three inside and two outside the village, from which dealers draw their supplies. Fresh fish is brought daily from lake Michigan by rail and distributed to private dealers. Poultry is bought from farmers and sold at meat and grocery stores. Vegetable gardens are abundant, so too are all kinds of large and small fruit gardens and orchards, the products being sold at groceries or peddled from door to door by hucksters.

SANITARY AUTHORITY—BOARD OF HEALTH.

The municipal board of Kalamazoo, composed of the president and trustees, acts as a board of health. The annual expenses of the board are not large, being, in the absence of any declared epidemic, $50 as salary of health officer. In time of an epidemic no limit by law is placed on the amount to which the expenses can be increased. By charter the board has authority to visit and inspect all premises, and, if nuisances exist, to direct or cause their removal. By general statutes it has the same powers as are conferred on townships. No extraordinary powers are granted the board in view of possible epidemics, the powers conferred by the statutes being deemed sufficient. The chief executive officer is the health officer, salary $50 per annum. His powers are such as the village board may from time to time confer, while his duties are mainly discretionary, all action or suggestion by him requiring the approval of the board. The board holds regular meetings monthly, or oftener if necessary. Petitions or complaints concerning nuisances or questions of health are presented to the president or trustees, and by the board referred to its committee on health, or, if necessary, to the health officer. The committee or health officer then makes an inspection and reports, and the board takes such action as it deems best. Inspections are, as a rule, made only when nuisances are reported; but, should an epidemic occur, inspections may be ordered. Nothing is done concerning defective house-drainage, privy-vaults, cesspools, and sources of drinking-water, and during the prevalence of epidemics the matter would be governed wholly by circumstances. The board exercises no control over the conservation and removal of garbage, except to forbid its being deposited within the village limits. The board has no regulations for the burial of the dead, other than that all interments must be made in a legally established cemetery. The board has chartered powers to prevent the pollution of streams. Excrement is removed at night.

INFECTIOUS DISEASES.

Small-pox patients, if poor, or strangers without means, are removed to an isolated house. If residents, or with means to provide for their wants, the case is left where the disease originated, and a complete quarantine is established on the house and its inmates. Scarlet-fever patients are treated in the same manner. The board takes cognizance of the breaking out of contagious diseases in either public or private schools, by closing the schools and isolating the sick. Vaccination is compulsory only on school-children, and at times and in part is done at the public expense.

REPORTS.

There is no system of registration of births, diseases, and deaths, except under state laws. There are no reports made, except a brief *résumé*, made by the health officer at the close of the municipal year. Dr. Pratt adds:

Being a village, under our state constitution, we are a part of a township and governed in the main, as are all townships, by the general laws of the state in all matters of health. But our township health authorities never interfere with village action. The health officer is always a physician.

MUNICIPAL CLEANSING.

Street-cleaning.—The streets are cleaned both by the village and by private abutters, the latter collecting the dirt into piles and the former taking it away. The work is done wholly by hand, no sweeping-machines being used, and the village does its share with its own force. The paved streets are cleaned once a week, and the others when required. It is said that the work when done is well done. The cost of the service is not given. The sweepings are deposited in such places as may be designated by the village board or the committee on streets. The system is reported to be sufficient for the wants of the village, and deposits are seldom complained of.

Removal of garbage and ashes.—All garbage is removed by the householders, and, with the exception that it must be carried out of the village, no regulations whatever govern the matter. Some of it is fed to hogs, while some is buried on the premises. The removal of ashes is not regulated. The improper keeping and infrequent removal of garbage is undoubtedly injurious to health. Dr. Pratt says: "Practically no system; but our people, as a rule, are careful and intelligent in handling such matters, and there is little to criticise in these respects."

Dead animals.—When dead animals are reported, the village marshal removes or otherwise properly disposes of the carcass. Neither the number of dead animals removed nor the cost of the service was given. "Whatever is needed in this respect is well done, but without system."

Liquid household wastes; human excreta.—The liquid household wastes are thrown either into cesspools or into privy-vaults, none being allowed to pass into the street gutters. The cesspools are porous, are not provided with overflows, sometimes receive the wastes from water-closets, and when full are cleaned out or new wells dug. In case of epidemics an order to clean may follow inspection. "The well-water of the village, formerly excellent, is now so contaminated by the percolation from privies and cesspools that it is unfit for use and generally abandoned." There are but few water-closets, and, with the exception of those in the hotels that deliver into a running stream, all waste runs into cesspools. Privy-vaults are the rule, and but very few of them are even nominally water-tight. There are no regulations as to their construction, and they are emptied at night by the old plan, or by day with the odorless excavator. The night-soil is carried outside the village, and either used as manure by gardeners or else buried. The night-soil is not used as manure on land within the gathering-ground of the public water-supply.

The disposal of *manufacturing wastes* is not governed by any regulations.

POLICE.

The marshal, who by the village charter is chief of police, is appointed by the president and trustees; and all members of the force, paid or unpaid, are nominated by the chief and confirmed by the village board, the whole force being governed by the chief or marshal, subject to the orders of the board. The marshal or chief of police receives a salary of $1,000 per annum; 2 regular policemen are paid $600 a year each, and this constitutes the regular uniformed force. In addition there are 3 special policemen, paid by private parties to do police duty, and 40 unpaid policemen, at hotels, stations, theaters, etc., who have power to make arrests. These also are under the orders of the marshal. The uniform is navy-blue frock coat, pantaloons, and vest, with police buttons, and each man provides his own. The regular policemen carry a club or cane, are on duty from dark to daylight, and patrol 2 miles of streets. During the past year 230 arrests were made, the principal causes being, for disorderly conduct 143, prostitution 35, assault and battery 9, vagrancy 6, etc. Of these, 125 were committed and 99 fined. The department is required to be present at all fires, to preserve order, and to assist the board of health by serving notices, executing orders, etc. During the year one policeman was stabbed, but has since recovered. The yearly cost of the police force (1880) is $2,701 29. Crimes and misdemeanors come under the cognizance of the township and county officers. Village officials make no arrests except for disorderly conduct, etc., under village ordinances.

FIRE DEPARTMENT.

The manual force of the Kalamazoo fire department consists of 1 chief engineer, 1 assistant chief, and 50 men. The apparatus consists of 2 hose-carts drawn by horses and 4 drawn by hand, 1 hook-and-ladder truck, and 1 hand engine. The total number of feet of hose in use is 3,150. During the year there were 27 alarms of fire. The total amount of loss was $10,336 47; total insurance paid, $6,176 47; total net loss, $4,160. There is a fire-alarm telegraph, with 6 miles of wire and 12 street signal-boxes. The cost of the department for the year was previously stated under the head of "water-works".

MUSKEGON,

MUSKEGON COUNTY, MICHIGAN.

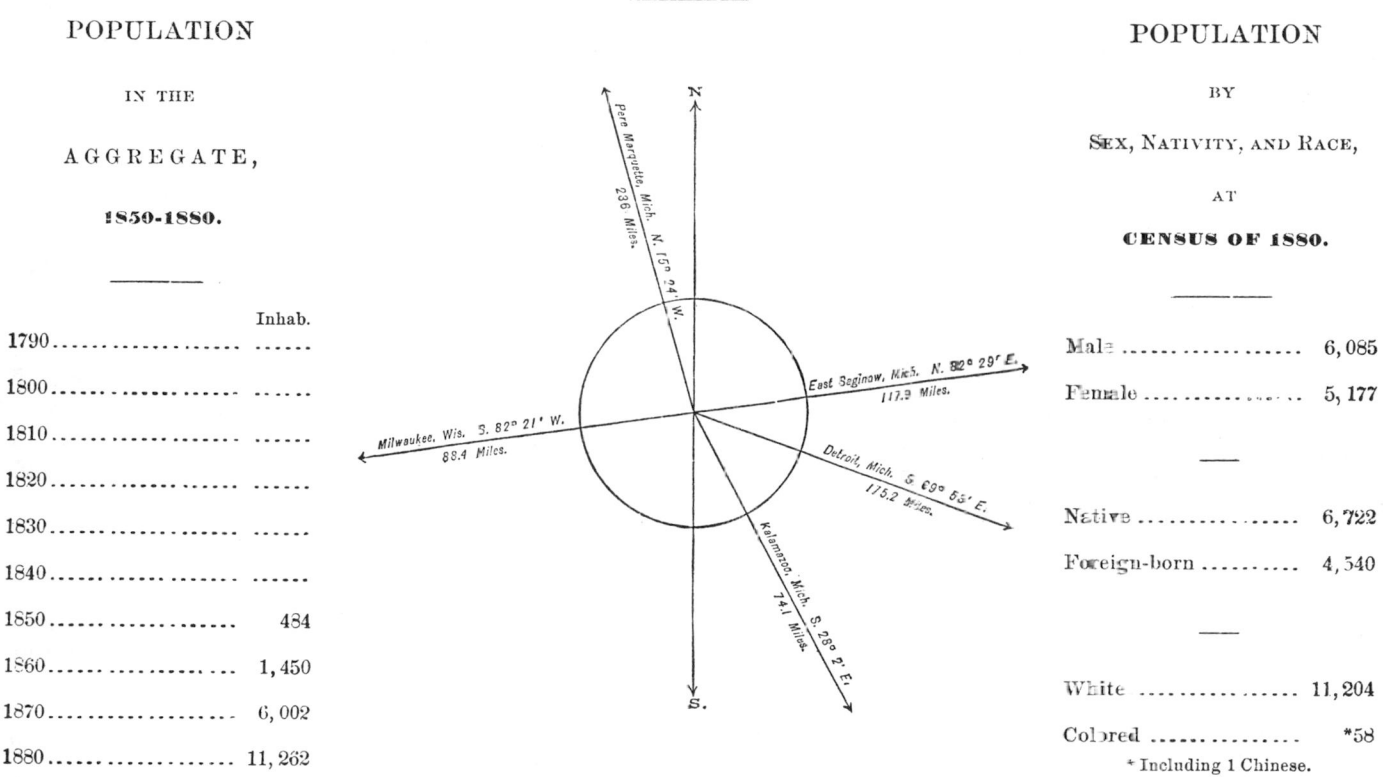

<table>
<tr><td colspan="2">

POPULATION

IN THE

AGGREGATE,

1850-1880.
</td></tr>
<tr><td></td><td>Inhab.</td></tr>
<tr><td>1790.....................</td><td>......</td></tr>
<tr><td>1800.....................</td><td>......</td></tr>
<tr><td>1810.....................</td><td>......</td></tr>
<tr><td>1820.....................</td><td>......</td></tr>
<tr><td>1830.....................</td><td>......</td></tr>
<tr><td>1840.....................</td><td>......</td></tr>
<tr><td>1850.....................</td><td>484</td></tr>
<tr><td>1860.....................</td><td>1,450</td></tr>
<tr><td>1870.....................</td><td>6,002</td></tr>
<tr><td>1880.....................</td><td>11,262</td></tr>
</table>

POPULATION

BY

SEX, NATIVITY, AND RACE,

AT

CENSUS OF 1880.

Male 6,085

Female 5,177

Native 6,722

Foreign-born 4,540

White 11,204

Colored *58

* Including 1 Chinese.

Latitude: 43° 15′ North ; Longitude: 86° 16′ (west from Greenwich).

FINANCIAL CONDITION:

Total Valuation: $1,332,323 ; per capita: $118 00.   Net Indebtedness: $180,000 ; per capita: $15 98.   Tax per $100: $4 85.

HISTORICAL SKETCH.

The history of Muskegon has its origin in 1812, when John Baptiste Recollect began to occupy a trading-post at the mouth of Bear lake, within the present city limits. Other trading-posts were built in the vicinity from time to time, and in 1837, at the first session of the legislature after the state was admitted into the Union, the country round about was organized into the township of *Muskego*. The next year it was reorganized under the name of *Muskegon*, and in 1848 a post-office of that name was established. The land in this part of the state was only brought into the market in 1839, and none of it on the site of the present city was platted till 1849. Nothing of any account was done for several years toward opening the streets, and the hill was so steep where Western avenue and Pine street now are that a man could not ride up on horseback. The first road into the surrounding country was not cut until 1846. From time to time saw-mills had been built, and in 1850 six were on the lake; in the next ten years 10 more were built, and in 1876 there were 26 of them. The first school-house was built in 1849, the first church in 1857, and the first newspaper was established the same year.

The harbor at the mouth of Muskegon river and lake remained in its natural condition until 1863, when the work of improving it was begun. Up to this time, at the best stage of water, there was scarcely ever more than 6 feet on the bar—oftener not more than 4 or 5 feet, and at times the sand would be drifted in so that men could wade across. In 1863 the Muskegon Harbor Company was organized, and built a slab pier on each side of the channel, the south pier being 1,500 feet long, and the north pier 500 feet. To make a channel, the somewhat novel expedient was resorted to of having a propeller force her way backward from lake Michigan into Muskegon lake. The revolutions of the wheel cleared away the sand, and the attempt was successful. Congress soon after made appropriations for the same purpose; the result of all which is that this harbor is now one of the best on lake Michigan, there being about 14 feet of water on the bar. The current is so strong that the channel never freezes over.

Muskegon is the capital of Muskegon county, which was organized in the winter of 1859. The village of Muskegon was incorporated in 1861 and the city in 1869. It has grown more in the last three years than in any other three of its existence. There was a very large fire here in 1874, which destroyed a number of acres of buildings. The burnt area has been mostly rebuilt with a better class of structures. American nationality prevails, although there is a large percentage of foreigners, particularly Hollanders, Germans, Swedes, and Norwegians.

MUSKEGON IN 1880.

The following statistical accounts, mainly furnished by Henry H. Holt, esq., in part indicate the present condition of Muskegon:

LOCATION.

Muskegon lies on the south shore of Muskegon lake (which is an expansion of the river of the same name), 5 miles north of lake Michigan, 15 miles north of Grand Haven, and 112 miles by water northeast of Chicago, in latitude 43° 15' north, and longitude 86° 16' west from Greenwich. As has been stated, it has a good harbor, with 14 feet draft of water in the main channel. It thus has direct water communication with Chicago, Milwaukee, and all other points on the great lakes.

RAILROAD COMMUNICATIONS.

Muskegon railroad facilities are as follows:

The Chicago and West Michigan railroad runs from Pentwater down the shore of the lake, through Muskegon, to New Buffalo, where it connects with the Michigan Central, thus giving communication with Chicago and Detroit at Muskegon.

The Big Rapids branch of the same road.

The Grand Haven railroad runs from Muskegon to Allegan, where it connects with the Kalamazoo division of the Lake Shore and Michigan Southern railroad, the terminals of which are Buffalo and Chicago.

TRIBUTARY COUNTRY.

The surrounding country is tolerably well adapted to grain-growing, but is more suited to fruit-raising, and particularly to the growth of peaches, plums, and grapes, the latter succeeding very finely here. The principal trade of the city is lumber, amounting to 400,000,000 feet and over per year. This lumber is sent mostly to Chicago in vessels. Muskegon is one of the largest lumber-manufacturing cities in the country.

TOPOGRAPHY.

The soil in the immediate vicinity is mostly sandy. The country is open. The land is high above Muskegon lake, giving natural drainage to it.

CLIMATE.

Highest recorded summer temperature, 92°; highest summer temperature in average years, 90°. Lowest winter temperature in average years, −10°. Lake Michigan has a very marked influence on the climate, as shown by the success met with in fruit-raising. What marshes there are have no particular effect. The prevailing winds, being from the west, and off Lake Michigan, tend to moderate the temperature.

STREETS.

The total length of streets is not stated. Two miles are paved with wood, pine planks being used. The planks are laid like the roadway of a bridge, covering the entire surface of the street between the sidewalks; they are 3 inches thick, and cost about 25 cents per square yard. This class of pavement lasts about 5 years. Meantime it costs but little to keep in repair, since if laid with good plank it gives out nearly all at the same time, and when worn out it can not be repaired to much advantage. All the business streets are so paved. Sidewalks are of pine planks, laid 8 feet wide. There are no gutters, with the exception of a slight depression at the edge of the sidewalks. Maple and elm trees have been very generally planted along the streets, and on many of the best streets grass-plots are kept at the edge of the sidewalks. It is reported that the experience of the city authorities shows that work done under carefully made contracts is more satisfactory than day work.

There are no horse-railroads in the city. An omnibus line, with 4 vehicles and 10 horses, and employing 4 men, carries annually 20,000 passengers, at a regular rate of fare of 25 cents each.

WATER-WORKS.

The water-works are owned by the city, and their first cost was $160,000. Water is taken from springs and pumped directly into the mains, the pressure varying from 40 pounds for domestic to 80 pounds for fire purposes. The least amount of water pumped per diem is 350,000 gallons, and the greatest 1,500,000 gallons. The yearly cost of maintenance and repair is $4,900, and the annual income from water rents is $5,200. Water meters are used, but to how great an extent is not stated. There are 15 miles of pipes and 184 hydrants.

GAS.

The gas-works are owned by a private company. The daily average production is 12,000 cubic feet. The charge per 1,000 feet is $3. The city pays $25 per annum for each street-lamp, 44 in number. The yearly income from meter rates is reported as $9,500.

PUBLIC BUILDINGS.

The city owns no public buildings for municipal purposes, but hires a hall and offices for the city government at an annual cost of $200.

PUBLIC PARKS AND PLEASURE-GROUNDS.

The city has no public parks or pleasure-grounds.

PLACES OF AMUSEMENT.

There is an opera-house, capable of seating 1,500 persons, and paying a license of $50 per annum. In addition there are Masons' hall, with a seating capacity of 300, and Banks' hall, Gustins' hall, Rippenberg's hall, and Workingmen's hall, which will seat about 200 each. There are no concert- and beer-gardens in the city.

DRAINAGE; CEMETERIES; MARKETS.

No information on the above subjects was furnished.

SANITARY AUTHORITY—BOARD OF HEALTH.

The mayor and aldermen, together with the city physician, the latter being nominated by the mayor and confirmed by the city council, act as a board of health, and the only expense incurred is the salary of the city physician, which is $500 a year. There is no limit to its authority in the matter of expense or in any other respect, either in the absence of or during epidemics. An ordinance passed in December, 1879, designates, among other of its powers, that of taking "immediate possession of any dwelling-house, hotel, factory, or other building, premises, or grounds, any steamboat, vessel, or other craft, or any railroad cars, in or upon which" there exists, in the judgment of the board, any nuisance prejudicial to the public health; and provides that if the owner or occupant refuses to abate it the board shall proceed to do so. And the ordinance further provides that "it shall be the duty of the board of health, the marshal, and all police constables of the city to use all the force necessary to enforce the provisions of this ordinance and to prevent a violation of the same". There is no specific rule about making inspections, these being made when the board deems it necessary.

INFECTIOUS DISEASES.

In case of death from any of the dangerous infectious diseases, the funeral shall not be public, and the body must be at once placed in a hermetical coffin or burial case, which shall be immediately sealed and not opened again. No person is allowed to be present at the burial service whose presence, in the opinion of the board, is liable to endanger the health of others, and all persons who take part in the funeral must use disinfectants before communicating with others. These and other very stringent rules in connection with the subject of infectious diseases were passed because of the prevalence of diphtheria, 320 cases of which have been reported since the disease first made its appearance in July, 1879; and at present, early in 1880, 2 cases a day are reported. Small-pox patients are isolated in the pest-house, a small building in the suburbs of the city, while scarlet-fever cases are kept at home as much as possible. Vaccination is not compulsory, nor is it done at the public expense.

There is no system for the registration of births, diseases, or deaths, except as provided by the general laws of the state. The board reports to the city council, but not regularly.

MUNICIPAL CLEANSING.

Street-cleaning.—The streets are swept by the abutting property-owners, and the rubbish is removed by the city's force. The sweeping is all done by hand, once a week. It is reported as being done efficiently, the cost to the city being very slight and to private persons "none to speak of".

Removal of garbage and ashes.—The garbage is removed mostly by the householders. Such part of this work as the city does is done by its own force. No further information on the subject was given.

Dead animals.—The carcasses of animals dying within the city limits are removed by the city authorities, and it is reported that not more than 10 are removed annually.

Liquid household wastes; human excreta.—There being no sewers in Muskegon, the house wastes are run into cesspools or vaults. The cesspools are nominally water-tight, are not provided with overflows, and are not governed by regulations as to their cleansing, etc. It is said that nothing has been heard of the contamination of wells by the escape of the contents either of vaults or of cesspools. Very few of the houses—not 1 in 100—are provided with water-closets, nearly all depending on privy-vaults. Usually when a vault is full it is covered with earth, a new hole is dug, and the privy-house is moved over it. In some cases the vault is cleaned out and the night-soil is removed.

Manufacturing wastes.—There are none here of any account.

WISCONSIN.

BELOIT,

ROCK COUNTY, WISCONSIN.

POPULATION

IN THE

AGGREGATE,

1850-1880.

	Inhab.
1790	......
1800	......
1810	......
1820	......
1830	......
1840	......
1850	2,732
1860	4,098
1870	4,396
1880	4,790

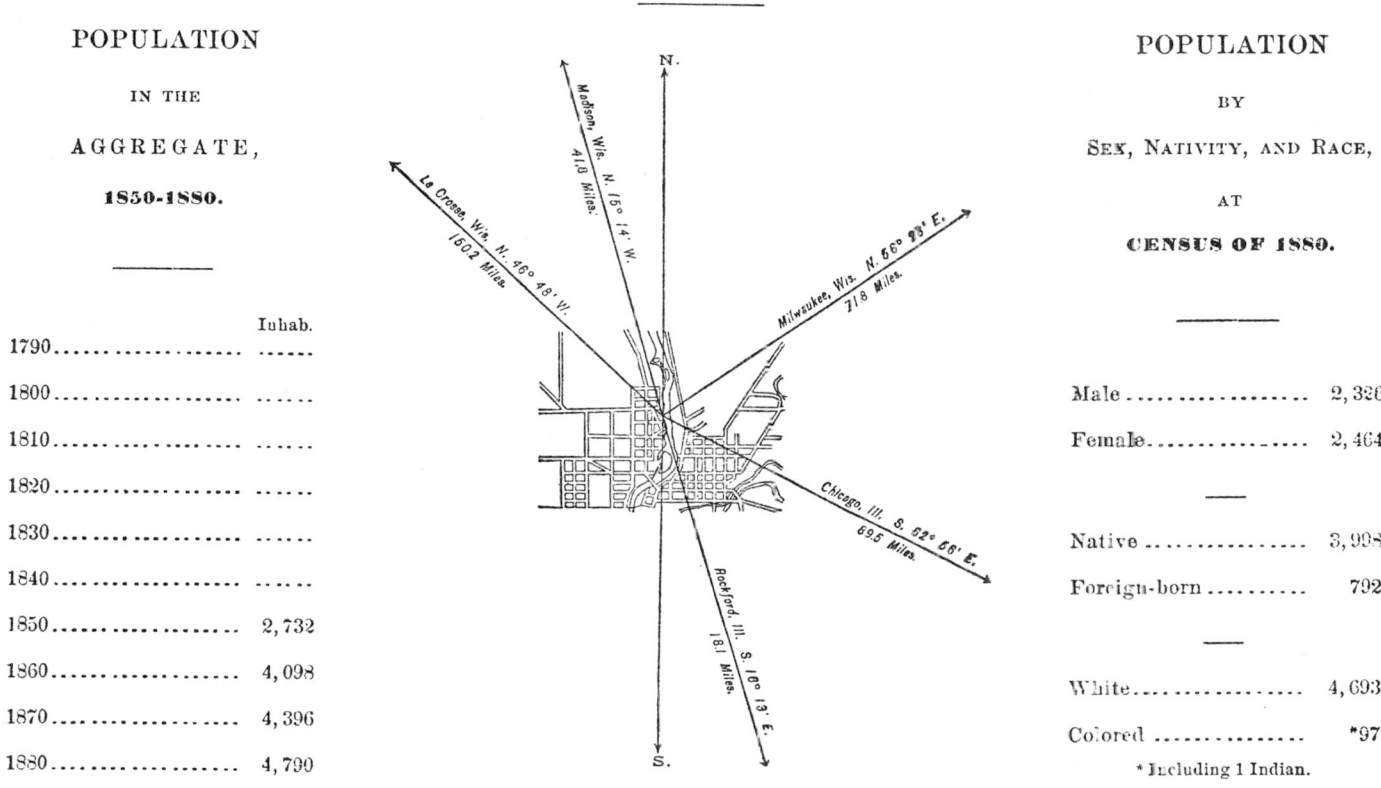

POPULATION

BY

SEX, NATIVITY, AND RACE,

AT

CENSUS OF 1880.

Male	2,326
Female	2,464
Native	3,998
Foreign-born	792
White	4,693
Colored	*97

* Including 1 Indian.

Latitude: 42° 30′ North; Longitude: 89° 11′ (west from Greenwich); Altitude: 730 to 800 feet.

HISTORICAL SKETCH.

In 1823 or 1824 a settlement was made in or near the present site of Beloit, but it was not permanent. The first permanent settlement was made in 1835, and for some years after that time its growth was quite rapid. In 1845 there were 3 churches, 3 schools, and a male and female seminary in the place. In that year a convention of ministers and laymen of the Congregational and Presbyterian churches in Wisconsin and northern Illinois decided to establish a college for young men at Beloit. The next year a charter was secured, and in June, 1847, the corner-stone of the first building was laid. Since then over 2,000 young men have received instruction at the institution, about one-eighth of that number having completed the full course. The city of Beloit was incorporated in 1856. There have been two important fires in the city, both in February, 1871, only four days apart. The buildings then destroyed were quickly replaced. The early settlers were largely from New York, many also coming from New England. There are a number of Norwegians in the city and a considerable percentage of colored people.

BELOIT IN 1880.

The following statistical information, collected by the Census Office, indicates the present condition of Beloit:

LOCATION.

Beloit is situated in Rock county, Wisconsin, on Rock river, at the mouth of Turtle creek, on the southern state line, 47 miles south-southeast from Madison, and 91 miles northwest from Chicago. The altitude of the lowest point of the city is 730 feet above the level of the sea; of the lower plain, 745 feet; of the upper plain, 780 feet; and of the highest point, 800 feet. Rock river is nominally navigable below Beloit, but practically not so, being interrupted by dams at frequent intervals.

RAILROAD COMMUNICATIONS.

Beloit is situated on the Madison division of the Chicago and Northwestern railway, which gives direct communication with Chicago, Minneapolis, and all other points on this great road; and also on the Racine and Southwestern division of the Chicago, Milwaukee, and Saint Paul railway, which division runs from Racine to Rock Island.

TRIBUTARY COUNTRY.

The soil of the adjacent region is in part a marly clay and in part a slightly sandy loam. Both kinds are excellently adapted to agriculture. The growing of grain which formerly prevailed has recently given place on the best farms to stock-raising; cattle, horses, hogs, sheep, and poultry being raised with excellent returns. Rock county, in which Beloit is situated, is traversed from north to south by Rock river, into which flow several large streams. The surface is undulating. Rock prairie, the largest in the state, occupies nearly half of the county, extending from the river eastward. The most abundant rock of the county is the blue limestone. Rock river is a fine stream, flowing through a valley remarkable for beauty and fertility, and affording extensive water-power.

TOPOGRAPHY.

The Trenton limestone, immediately underlaid by the Saint Peter's sandstone, forms a rocky substratum, overlaid by a deep deposit of glacial gravel, the upper portion of which has disintegrated into a loamy, occasionally clayey, soil of moderate depth. The city rests in part upon the flood plain of Rock river (10 to 75 feet above it), and upon an elevated plateau, both kept dry by the porous subsoil. Drainage is excellent. Marshes are very rare. The country is mainly open, and immediately surrounding the city is moderately elevated, dry, and undulatory.

CLIMATE.

The highest recorded summer temperature is 100.5°; the highest summer temperature in average years, 94°. Lowest recorded winter temperature, −36°; lowest in average years, −20°. Occasional winds from lake Michigan are felt, but with this exception the climate is free from the influence of adjacent waters. The influence of marshes and elevated lands is very slight. There are no local peculiarities so far as the winds are concerned, except the occasional lake-winds mentioned, and chilly northeast winds in the spring, when there are large deposits of snow in the northern forests.

STREETS.

Total length of streets, about 30 miles, all of which are of gravel rounded up. Sidewalks are usually made of plank. At present the city is experimenting with a composition of Portland and Louisville cements, and it is thought to be a success; 500 square yards of it have lately been laid at a cost of 80 cents per yard. Gutters are unpaved except in the business portion of the city, where the ordinary limestone is used for paving them. In the residence portion of the city the streets are well lined with trees—elm, hard and soft maple, and locust, being the predominating varieties. In some of the main streets the earth is filled in between the sidewalks and gutters, and is grassed over to a width varying from 4 to 8 feet. The city gives permission to the property-owners to do this, and each one has it done as he chooses.

WATER-WORKS.

The city has no water-works.

GAS.

The gas-works are owned by a private company.

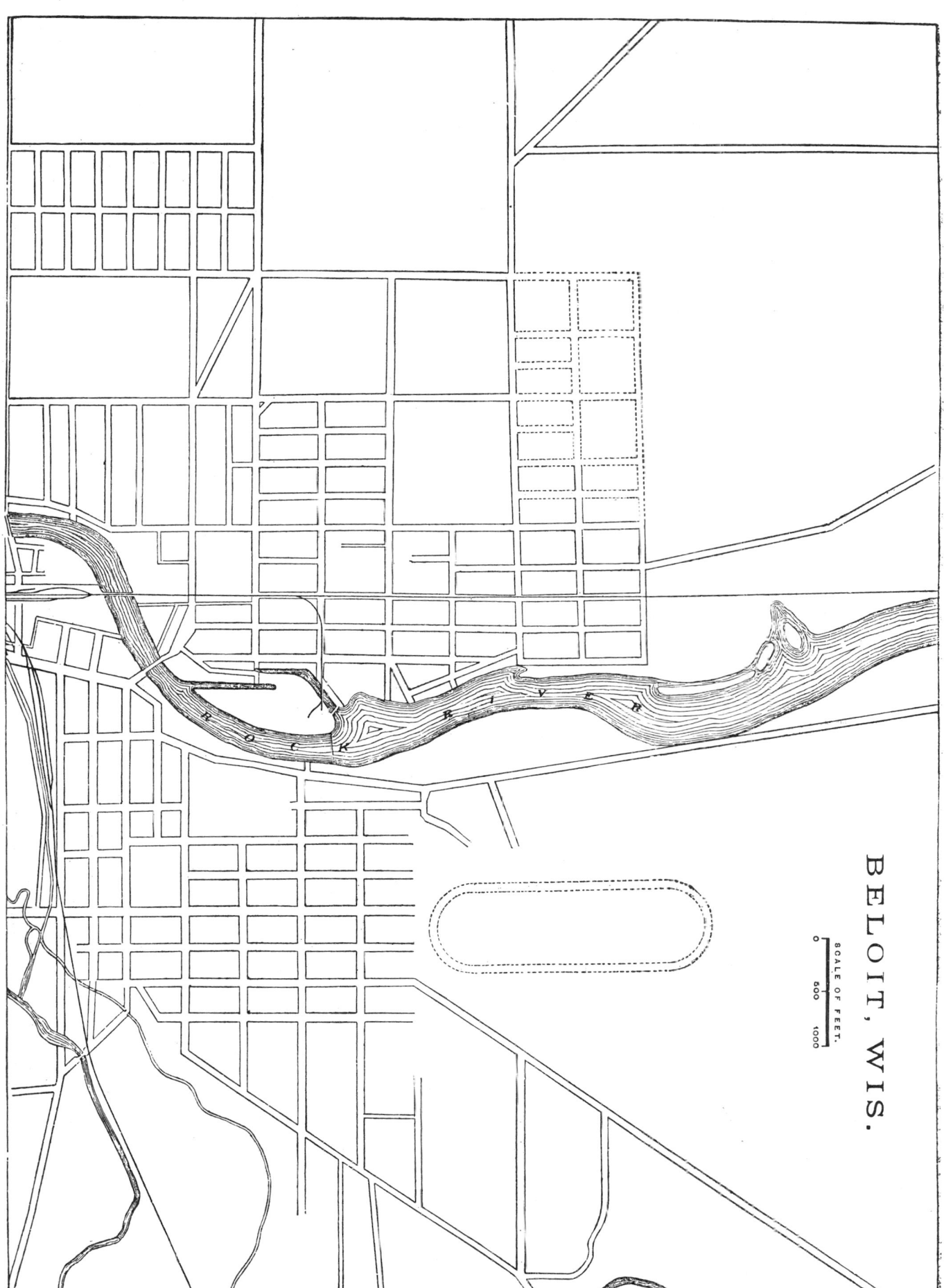

BELOIT, WIS.

SCALE OF FEET.

0   500   1000

PUBLIC BUILDINGS.

There are no buildings owned by the city of Beloit for municipal uses.

PUBLIC PARKS AND PLEASURE-GROUNDS.

There is one park with an area of 9.58 acres, centrally located. It was donated to the city, and its yearly cost of maintenance is $50. It is controlled by the city council.

PLACES OF AMUSEMENT.

There is an opera-house in the city, but no details were received concerning it, other than the fact that it pays an annual license amounting to $25 in money, besides free tickets.

DRAINAGE.

It was reported that no accurate or approximately accurate information could be furnished on this subject, as the city is without any system of sewerage, and depends almost wholly on surface drainage.

CEMETERIES.

There are 2 cemeteries, both within the city limits—a Protestant cemetery, containing 15 acres, in which there have been about 3,000 interments, situated 1 mile north of the center of the city; and a Roman Catholic cemetery, containing 6 acres, situated 1.25 mile from the center of the city. The graves in them must be 5 feet in depth. The title to the lots is absolute in the owners, and the city sexton has the general care of them. There is no attempt at landscape-gardening. The large number of interments is due to the fact that the dead from the entire vicinity are brought here. There is no separate record kept of the inhabitants of Beloit buried in these cemeteries.

MARKETS.

There are no public or corporation markets. The city council usually designates a place in the city where hay and wood may be sold, and their ordinance is to a greater or less extent observed.

SANITARY AUTHORITY—HEALTH COMMITTEE.

The chief health organization of Beloit is the committee on health, a regular standing committee of the common council, appointed annually by the mayor. It usually consists of 3 aldermen, none of whom are at present physicians. During epidemics this committee would be authorized to incur any proper expense for the sanitary regulation of the city. At any time the city marshal, under the direction of the committee, may abate any nuisance which jeopardizes the public health. The members of the committee themselves have no police powers. Inspections are made only as occasion requires. When nuisances are reported, the ordinances provide that the marshal shall investigate, and if in his opinion they exist, he shall order their abatement, and the penalty for neglect or refusal to abate shall be $5 for every 24 hours the party concerned shall so neglect or refuse. This committee is subject to the control of the city government. The city council has power to provide hospitals for those infected with small-pox and other contagious diseases, and to order and regulate their removal from the city whenever it is deemed necessary. There is no public pest-house, and vaccination is not compulsory, nor is it done at the public expense. The reports of the committee are published in the official paper of the city as a part of the minutes of the city council.

MUNICIPAL CLEANSING.

Street-cleaning.—The streets are cleaned by the city's own force, wholly by hand. The city gathers up the dirt, and it is usually spread upon the higher and less fertile parts of the public grounds. The main streets are cleaned as often as seems necessary. The annual cost of this work is about $600.

Removal of garbage and ashes.—Garbage and ashes are removed by householders. There are no regulations on this head except the general regulations regarding nuisances.

Dead animals.—The removal of dead animals is in charge of the marshal. There are no regulations on this head.

Liquid household wastes.—Waste water from sleeping-rooms, laundry waste, and kitchen slops are all disposed of in the same way. There are no sewers in the city, and probably cesspools are used, but nothing was reported on this point.

Human excreta; manufacturing wastes.—There are no ordinances on these subjects, and no reports were made.

EAU CLAIRE,

EAU CLAIRE COUNTY, WISCONSIN.

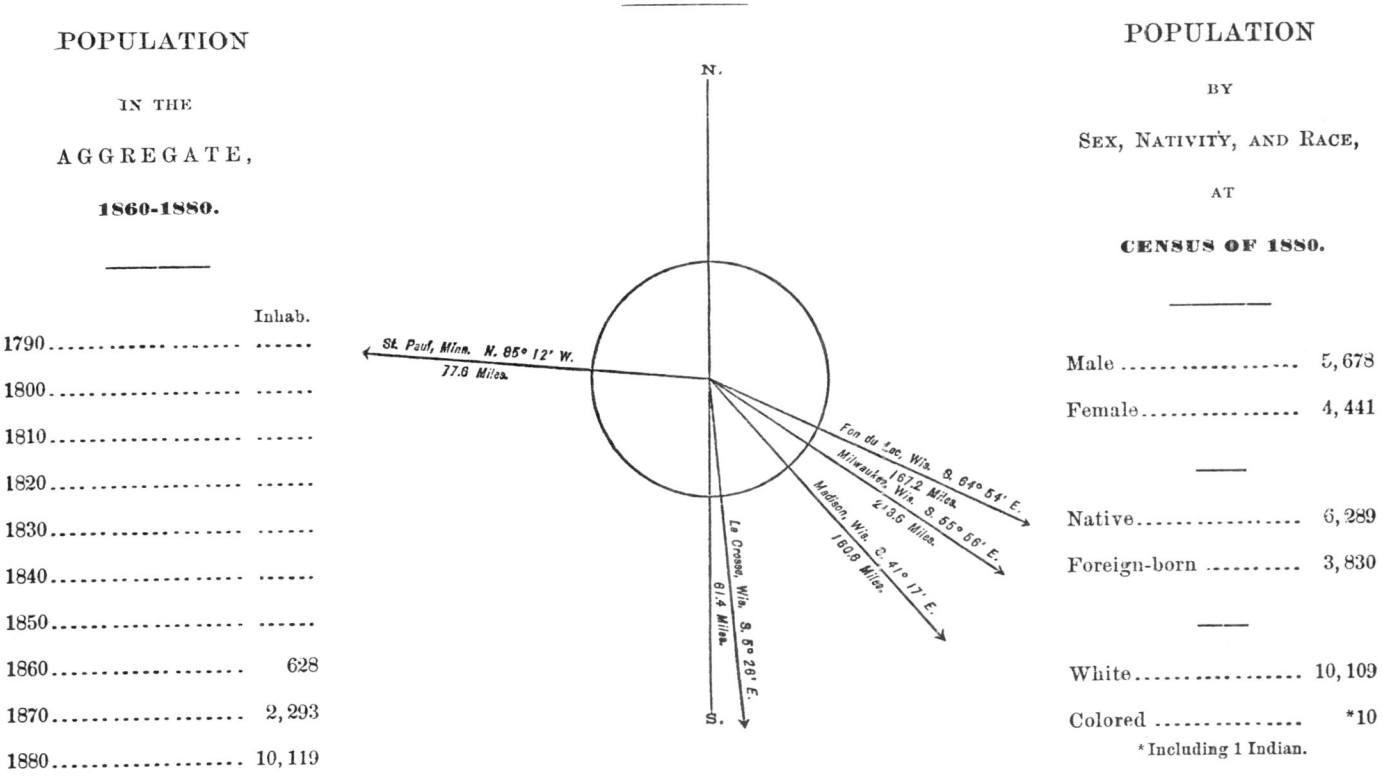

POPULATION

IN THE

AGGREGATE,

1860-1880.

	Inhab.
1790	......
1800	......
1810	......
1820	......
1830	......
1840	......
1850	......
1860	628
1870	2,293
1880	10,119

POPULATION

BY

SEX, NATIVITY, AND RACE,

AT

CENSUS OF 1880.

Male	5,678
Female	4,441
Native	6,289
Foreign-born	3,830
White	10,109
Colored	*10

* Including 1 Indian.

Latitude: 44° 51' North; Longitude: 91° 30' (west from Greenwich).

FINANCIAL CONDITION:

Total Valuation: $3,541,686; per capita: $350 00.   Net Indebtedness: $101,000; per capita: $9 98.   Tax per $100: $1 96.

NOTE.—Eau Claire, the capital of Eau Claire county, Wisconsin, is situated at the junction of Eau Claire and Chippewa rivers, at the head of navigation on the Chippewa. The principal business is lumbering, over 150,000,000 feet being manufactured in the vicinity yearly. It is the chief commercial city of northwestern Wisconsin. The surface of the surrounding country is uneven and the soil is productive. Eau Claire is connected by a short branch with the Wisconsin Central railroad, whose terminals are Ashland on Lake Superior, and Chicago; it is also on the main line of the Chicago, Saint Paul, Minneapolis, and Omaha railway, which connects the cities named in its title.

FOND DU LAC,

FOND DU LAC COUNTY, WISCONSIN.

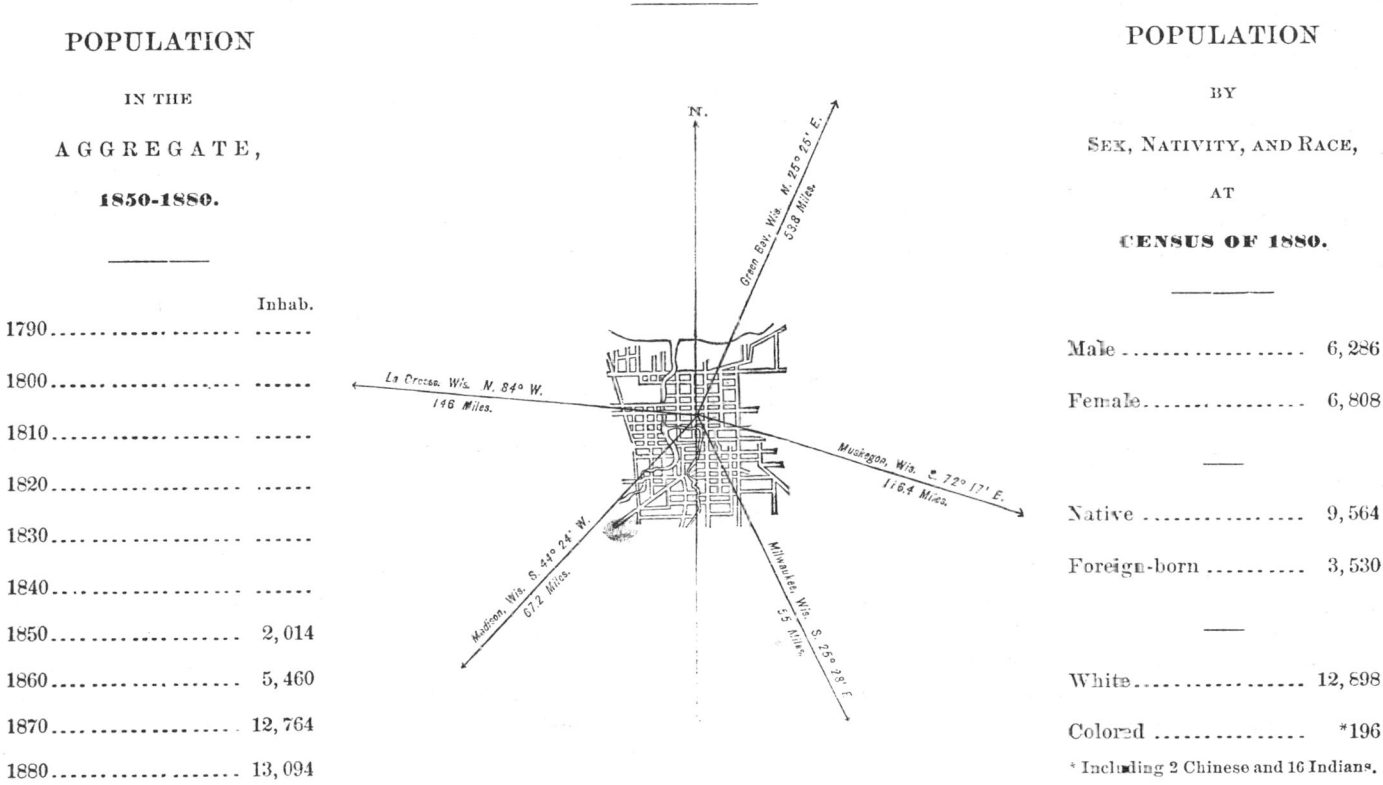

POPULATION

BY

SEX, NATIVITY, AND RACE,

AT

CENSUS OF 1880.

Male	6,286
Female	6,808
Native	9,564
Foreign-born	3,530
White	12,898
Colored	*196

* Including 2 Chinese and 16 Indians.

Latitude: 43° 47′ North; Longitude: 88° 28′ (west from Greenwich); **Altitude: 751 feet.**

FINANCIAL CONDITION:

Total Valuation: $3,417,175; per capita: $261 00.   Net Indebtedness: $165,000; per capita: $12 60.   Tax per $100: $3 50.

HISTORICAL SKETCH.

In the latter part of the last century and the early part of the present century, from time to time different Indian traders settled transiently in different parts of what is now Fond du Lac county, but the land was not even surveyed by the government till 1834–'35. In 1835 a number of citizens of Green Bay formed a stock company for purchasing lands somewhere near the head of lake Winnebago, and by January 1, 1836, they had secured a tract of 1,375 acres. In the preceding November, a survey having been made, a village was at once laid out on paper. This part of the country had been called by the French Canadian traders "Fond du Lac", which literally signifies "bottom of the lake", but to them meant "farthest point of the lake". This name was given to the "paper village", and the lands were at once put in the market. The first actual settler, Colwert Pier, in June, 1836, took possession of a log house which had been built there by the company in the preceding year. In December, 1836, Fond du Lac county and town were established, although there was then but one house within its limits. In 1838 another family came, and from that time on settlers began to arrive in large numbers. In 1843 the first steamer was put on the lake, in 1846 a court-house was built, and in 1847 a village charter was adopted. At that time Fond du Lac had 400 inhabitants, who had chiefly come from New England and western New York. It grew very fast, and in 1852 was incorporated as a city. The first railroad brought into use in the county was the Rock River Valley Union railroad, which was completed in 1853 from Fond du Lac through Oakfield to near Waupun, some 20 miles only. In 1851 the first work on the Chicago and Northwestern railway line proper was done in Fond du Lac, so this city is really the birthplace of that mighty fan of railway lines. The line was not completed to Janesville till 1860. Since she has had railway communication with the world her growth has been steady and rapid.

Lake Winnebago, on which Fond du Lac is situated, is 30 miles long, north and south, and from 8 to 15 miles wide, east and west, and at no point is more than 120 feet deep. In the early days of Fond du Lac the steamboat navigation of this lake was an important consideration. In 1851–'52 steamboating became almost a mania with the people, and much money was lost. As the railroads extended their lines, what steamboat business there was fell off, and now Fond du Lac is neither the proprietor of any boats, save lumber-tugs, nor in the enjoyment of regular trips from boats owned elsewhere, although large quantities of wood, logs, and lumber are brought each season by Oshkosh steamer.

The city has never suffered much by fire, the largest having been a $100,000 fire in 1871, when 22 buildings were destroyed. The most noticeable depression in business was from 1875 to 1879, the lumbering and iron industries suffering the most. The rich agricultural district round the city buoyed up the trades that during this period suffered so much in other cities. In 1879 and 1880 the mills and factories were run to their utmost capacity. The business population of the city is mostly American. In the industrial class Germans and French form important elements. One ward of the city contains a settlement of colored people brought from the South during the war.

FOND DU LAC IN 1880.

The following statistical accounts, gathered mainly by the Census Office, indicate the present condition of Fond du Lac:

LOCATION.

Fond du Lac is situated at the south end of lake Winnebago, at the mouth of Fond du Lac river, 72 miles north-northwest of Milwaukee and 90 miles northeast of Madison. The surface of the lake is 162 feet above lake Michigan and 751 feet above the level of the sea. The harbor is not excellent, but is a fair one, and both harbor and channel are deep enough for all the craft plying on the lake. The Fox river, which empties into the lake at Oshkosh, has been connected by a canal with the Wisconsin; and the Fox river, connecting the lake with Green bay, has been improved so that boats from Fond du Lac can enter either the Mississippi or lake Michigan.

RAILROAD COMMUNICATIONS.

Fond du Lac lies on the Milwaukee, Green Bay, and Marquette line of the Chicago and Northwestern railway, which connects Chicago with lake Superior at Marquette, via Milwaukee, on the Green Bay and Lake Superior line of the same road, which connects Chicago with Green Bay via Janesville; and on the Sheboygan and Western railroad. The Fond du Lac, Amboy, and Peoria (narrow-gauge) railroad connects with the Chicago, Milwaukee, and Saint Paul at Iron Ridge, thus giving another line to Milwaukee and Chicago and to the Northwest.

TRIBUTARY COUNTRY.

The surrounding country is mostly rich prairie, and is a wheat-raising district. Fond du Lac is a great wheat and wool market. Dairying is carried on to a considerable extent in the vicinity. The business of breeding thoroughbred stock of all kinds has also got a strong foothold. Recently some of the farmers have turned their attention to raising sugar-cane, and the contracted crop for 1880 was a large one.

TOPOGRAPHY, ETC.

The city lies on an almost level plain but a few feet above lake Winnebago. The surrounding country is equally level except to the east, where, some 2 miles distant, extends a ledge 100 feet high. This ledge, which is the elevated edge of a thick layer of limestone, well broken and thoroughly marked by the erosion of the glacial period, is remarkable for the thousands of clear, cold springs which gush from its cleft face from base to summit. Elsewhere in the county the water from this limestone layer which here crops to the surface is secured by means of artesian wells. The term artesian wells is here confined to flowing wells without regard to depth. Flowing wells depend on these requisite conditions: There should be an impervious stratum to prevent the escape of water below, a

FOND DU LAC,
WIS.

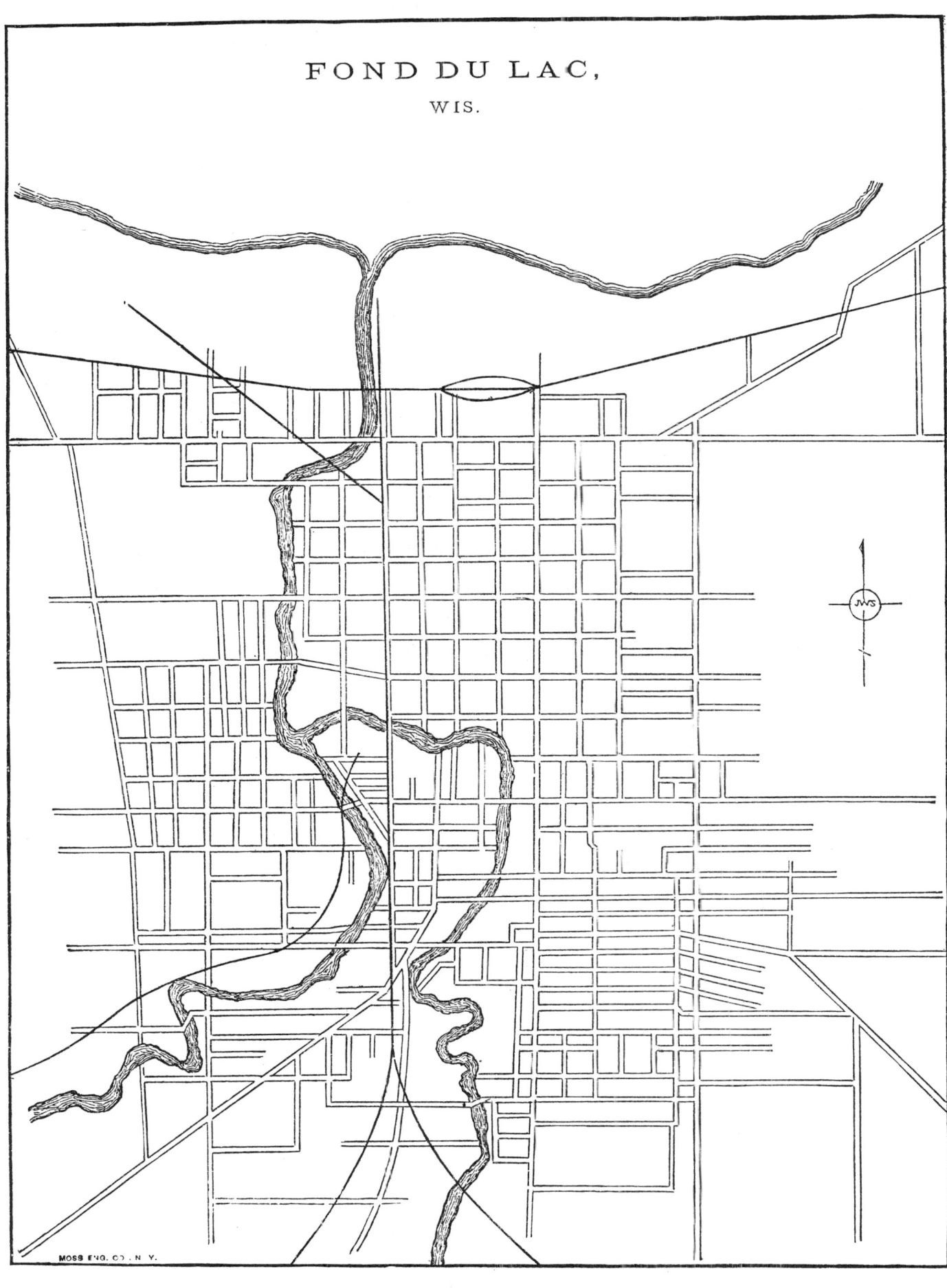

water-bearing stratum on this to furnish the flow of water, and a second impervious layer upon this to prevent the escape of the water above, it being under pressure from the fountain-head. These must dip, and there must be no adequate outlet for the water at a lower level than the well. All these conditions are met with in Fond du Lac county. The wells of the county derive their flow either entirely from the drift, from the junction of the drift with the indurated rocks below, from the Galena and Trenton limestone, or from the Saint Peter's sandstone.

In the city of Fond du Lac the vast majority of wells are comparatively shallow, deriving their flow from within 20 feet of the surface of the Galena limestone rock, either above or below it, it being from 100 to 200 feet beneath the soil. One well, the fountain on First street, belonging to B. Wild and Company, may be taken as an example. It is 326 feet deep, and passes entirely through the Galena and Trenton limestone, reaching the Saint Peter's sandstone below, whence it derives a flow of 48 gallons per minute. The stream has been carried by pipes 53 feet above the surface. It flows with such force that, with a hose and quarter-inch nozzle attached, it projects a stream from 30 to 35 feet high, and 48 feet horizontally. The water of this, like that of all the other wells, has strong mineral properties, the analysis showing the presence of various substances as follows (the figures are the thousandths of 1 per cent.): Lime, 63; magnesia, 40; soda, 61; silica, 61; sulphuric acid, 49; chlorine, 45; carbonic acid, 90. The following is the section of the well on the high-school grounds:

	Feet.
Drift, red and blue clay	95
Magnesium limestone (Trenton and Galena)	195
Saint Peter's sandstone	135
Total	425

The soil of the vicinity is a rich, productive loam, with a very few gravel knolls and occasional patches of sandy soil remarkable for its warmth and fertility. As to marshes, using the word as meaning low, wet land, unfit for cultivation or use, the county contains none; but there are certain low lands overflowed in spring and fall, which are used in the summer as pastures or meadows. There is one such west of Fond du Lac city. The county contains 3,000 acres of peat marsh. There are no forests near the city, except a small patch about 3 miles to the southeast.

CLIMATE.

Highest recorded summer temperature, 112°; lowest recorded winter temperature, −36°. From the publications of the Smithsonian Institution it is learned that the mean summer temperature is 67.5°, and the mean winter temperature 22°. The presence of lake Winnebago has the effect of cooling the air in summer, of delaying frosts in the fall, and of prolonging the cold winds in spring.

STREETS.

Total length 100 miles, of which 25 miles are paved with stone blocks covered with gravel, 4 miles with broken stone, 3 miles with wood. The cost of the wood per square yard varied from 75 cents to $1 25, according to the process used; the cost of the other kinds was not reported. The stone blocks covered with gravel are said to be almost indestructible. The wood laid without the Nicholson process decays in 4 or 5 years; laid with that process it has to be renewed once in 10 years. The sidewalks on the business streets are generally made of limestone slabs from 6 to 12 feet wide; those on residence streets of pine plank. All the streets of the residence portion of the city are shaded by trees which have been transplanted, soft maple, poplar, and rock maple predominating in the order named. The work of paving, repairing, etc., is done by contract.

WATER-WORKS.

As has been stated, the water-supply comes from hundreds of artesian wells scattered throughout the city. Water-works for fire purposes cost only $10,000, and are owned by the city, being supplied by waste water from private fountains.

GAS.

The gas-works are not owned by the city. The charge per 1,000 feet is $3. There are 183 street-lamps, for which the city pays $26 each per year.

PUBLIC BUILDINGS.

The city owns no city hall, but has a public building, built in 1878–'79, at a cost of $2,300, and also owns 3 brick engine-houses—one of which is one of the finest in the state—worth $40,000.

PUBLIC PARKS AND PLEASURE-GROUNDS.

There are no grounds that can properly be called parks. The original plat of the city left a strip of land 8 rods deep on each side of the blocks, but they have generally been confiscated by private parties, and no public use is made of them.

PLACES OF AMUSEMENT.

Armory hall seats 1,500; Opera hall seats 800; Music hall, 600. There are a number of smaller halls in the place, used mostly for balls, parties, etc. None of these halls pay licenses as theaters, but traveling theater companies pay a license of $25 each before playing, as also do circuses and all traveling shows. Besides the above there is the Turner hall, owned and used by the Turnverein of Fond du Lac. There are no concert- or beer-gardens in the city.

DRAINAGE.

The city has no regular sewerage system, but it has underground drains on various streets, emptying into the river. There is a system of reservoirs for fire purposes, connected by pipes and supplied from artesian wells, the surplus water from which is carried into drains and thence to rivers.

CEMETERIES.

The principal cemetery of Fond du Lac is known as *Rienzi Cemetery*. It now contains 32.5 acres, composed of beautiful hills and valleys, covered with oaks. It is situated 2.5 miles southeast of the city, and lies nearly half a mile in from the street, being approached by a smooth carriage-way shaded by trees. The "old grounds" in the cemetery contain a "potter's field", a lot belonging to the Freemasons, and one owned by the Odd Fellows.

MARKETS.

There are no public or corporation markets in the city. All the surplus meat and poultry raised in the vicinity is bought from the producers and shipped by local butchers and dealers to dealers in the mining regions in northern Wisconsin and Michigan. These regions offer a ready market for all the surplus products of this section of the state.

SANITARY AUTHORITY—HEALTH OFFICER.

The health of the city is in charge of the health officer, who is appointed annually by the city council, and who receives a salary of $150 per year. His action is subject to the control of the city government only to the extent of consulting with the health committee of the council. The health ordinance of 1880 provides that, after taking and filing the oath of office, he shall have and exercise all the powers for the preservation of the public health, and perform all the duties conferred by the charter and this ordinance within the limits of the city of Fond du Lac, and take such measures and make such rules and regulations as may be deemed most effectual for the preservation of the public health, and see that all ordinances and regulations in relation to the health of the city be observed and enforced. He shall have authority to enter into and examine, or cause the same to be done, at any time, all buildings, lots, and places of all descriptions within the city, for the purpose of examining and ascertaining the condition thereof as far as the public health may be affected thereby. He shall order all nuisances abated, and if this is not done he shall proceed to have it done at the expense of the delinquent.

The ordinance further provides that the common council shall, in making their annual estimates and levy for the expenses of the city government, estimate and provide such sum as may be necessary for the compensation of the health officer and for all other necessary expenses incurred by him in the performance of his duties, and such expenses shall be audited and allowed and paid as other city expenses are allowed and paid.

The health officer is given power to appoint or employ such persons as may be necessary to assist in the discharge of his duties, by and with the advice and consent of the mayor and common council, and the expense of services so authorized is to be certified to the common council, and audited and paid as other accounts against the city.

He exercises control over the conservation and removal of garbage only when it comes under the head of nuisances. As to the burial of the dead, the provisions are that the attending physician must furnish the undertaker with a certificate as to name, age, and sex of deceased, and date, place, and cause of death. The undertaker must get a permit for burial from the health officer, or, in his absence, from the city clerk, and the permit shall not be given till the above-mentioned certificate is presented. In case of death when no physician was in attendance, the health officer, or in his absence the city clerk, is empowered to issue a burial permit after investigation.

The health officer has control of persons infected with small-pox, scarlet fever, and other contagious diseases, and may quarantine or isolate if he chooses. There is no pest-house, but the health officer may hire one if he sees fit. He also keeps record of deaths, and every year reports to the city council their number and cause, together with such information and recommendations as he sees fit. These reports are published in the official newspaper of the city.

MUNICIPAL CLEANSING.

Street-cleaning.—Streets are cleaned either by the city, by the wards, or by private individuals, as the case may be. That which is done by the wards is done by contract. On the business streets of the city a sweeping-machine is used, and the annual cost to the business men is from $5 to $10; these streets are cleaned twice a week, and the others only when it is ordered by the health officer. The work is said to be done quite efficiently, and the system, which has been employed for a number of years, gives satisfaction. The sweepings are generally deposited in low places, a small part being used for fertilizing purposes.

Removal of garbage and ashes.—Garbage is removed by householders. That on the city's own property is removed by contract; each householder has it removed as he sees fit. The only regulation concerning its conservancy while awaiting removal is the general ordinance about nuisances, that no person shall "allow an offensive matter to be or remain on his premises, or in any outhouse, stable, privy, or other place owned or occupied by him, or in any street or alley in front of such premises, or in any pen, yard, or other place within the city". Garbage is removed from the inhabited part of the city and buried. Ashes are usually sold to soap-manufacturers; coal ashes are used for filling. No nuisances of more than very brief duration are reported as resulting from the improper treatment of garbage, and the system is said to be working efficiently.

Dead animals.—Dead animals found on private property are to be removed by the owner or occupant thereof; if it is not done at once the health officer proceeds to do it, and issues a tax certificate against the property for the entire cost. Dead animals found in the streets are removed at the expense of the city, the annual cost varying from $25 to $50, the number removed being from 50 to 100. They are all buried.

Liquid household wastes.—Waste water from sleeping-rooms is generally thrown into privy-vaults, kitchen and laundry slops into the back yard. In localities where sewers exist, nearly all liquid waste is conducted into them. Very little runs into street-gutters, it being strictly prohibited, and also very little runs into cesspools or "dry wells". Privy-vaults are practically tight, owing to the nature of the soil, and few are provided with overflows. Drinking-water is not subject to contamination by the escape of the contents of cesspools or privy-vaults, owing to this impervious subsoil, and to the fact that the wells in use are seldom less than 60 feet deep and are mostly flowing fountains. The matter of cleaning out privies and cesspools is under the direction of the health officer, and on his efficiency a great deal depends.

Human excreta.—Nearly all the houses of the city depend upon privy-vaults. The school board is adopting the dry-earth system for the public schools, so far with good success; otherwise this system is little used. Very few water-closets deliver into public sewers or cesspools, most of them delivering into vaults. Night-soil is either sold to persons outside the city for fertilizing purposes, or buried in some out-of-the-way place.

Manufacturing wastes.—Liquid manufacturing wastes must be caught in water-tight vessels or cisterns, and removed every 24 hours when of an offensive character.

POLICE.

The police force is appointed by the city council and governed by the mayor. The chief executive officer is the chief of police, who controls and directs the subordinate officers of the force, and receives a salary of $600 a year. In 1880 there were 5 policemen under him, one of whom was a captain, who was on duty in the daytime, and the rest of whom were night patrolmen, at salaries of $480 per year each. Their uniform is of navy-blue cloth, with brass buttons; they furnish their own suits, the city supplying buttons. Each man uses a revolver, a billy, a pair of handcuffs, and a pair of nippers. They patrol about 3 miles of streets. There were 273 arrests in 1880, the principal causes being drunkenness and vagrancy; 70 paid fines and costs, 56 were committed to the county jail, 9 had sentence suspended, 110 were discharged, and the rest were variously disposed of. There were 101 station-house lodgers in 1880, to whom free meals were given evening and morning. The police are required to co-operate with the fire and health departments at the request of the chief fire marshal or city health officer, respectively. Special police are appointed by the mayor for any service performed by the regular force; while on duty their standing is the same as that of the regular policemen. The pay-roll for 1880 was, for regular salaries, $2,727 25; for special police, $279 75.

FIRE DEPARTMENT.

The volunteer system was continued in the fire department of Fond du Lac up to August 7, 1878, when the city council disbanded the old companies and reorganized the entire department. Its members are now appointed by the city council after recommendation by the chief fire marshal. The department now consists of 3 engine companies and 1 hook-and-ladder company. The chief fire marshal receives $250 per year; assistant fire marshal, $100; engineers, $54 25 per month; drivers, $32 50 per month; stokers, $27 50; cart drivers, $25, and pipemen, $8 per month. The average total cost of the fire department is about $10,000 per year. The engine-houses are all of brick, well furnished with beds and accommodations for those who always remain with the engines.

PUBLIC SCHOOLS.

The city now contains, in addition to the high-school building, 18 public school-houses, which with their sites are owned by the corporation. They contain 40 main rooms, will accommodate 2,800 pupils, and have a cash value of $98,700. The sites are valued at $22,000. Nearly every school-house is provided with a fountain. In 1879 there were 5,900 children in the city of lawful age for school attendance, of whom 2,484 were enrolled as pupils in the public schools; there were 47 teachers, with an annual pay-roll of $18,136 25. The whole cost of the schools was $30,215 64; the average salary paid to teachers per year was $385 87. The present high-school building was erected in 1873 at a cost of $45,000, exclusive of the foundation.

LA CROSSE,

LA CROSSE COUNTY, WISCONSIN.

POPULATION

IN THE

AGGREGATE,

1860-1880.

	Inhab.
1790	......
1800	......
1810	......
1820	......
1830	......
1840	......
1850	......
1860	3, 860
1870	7, 785
1880	14, 505

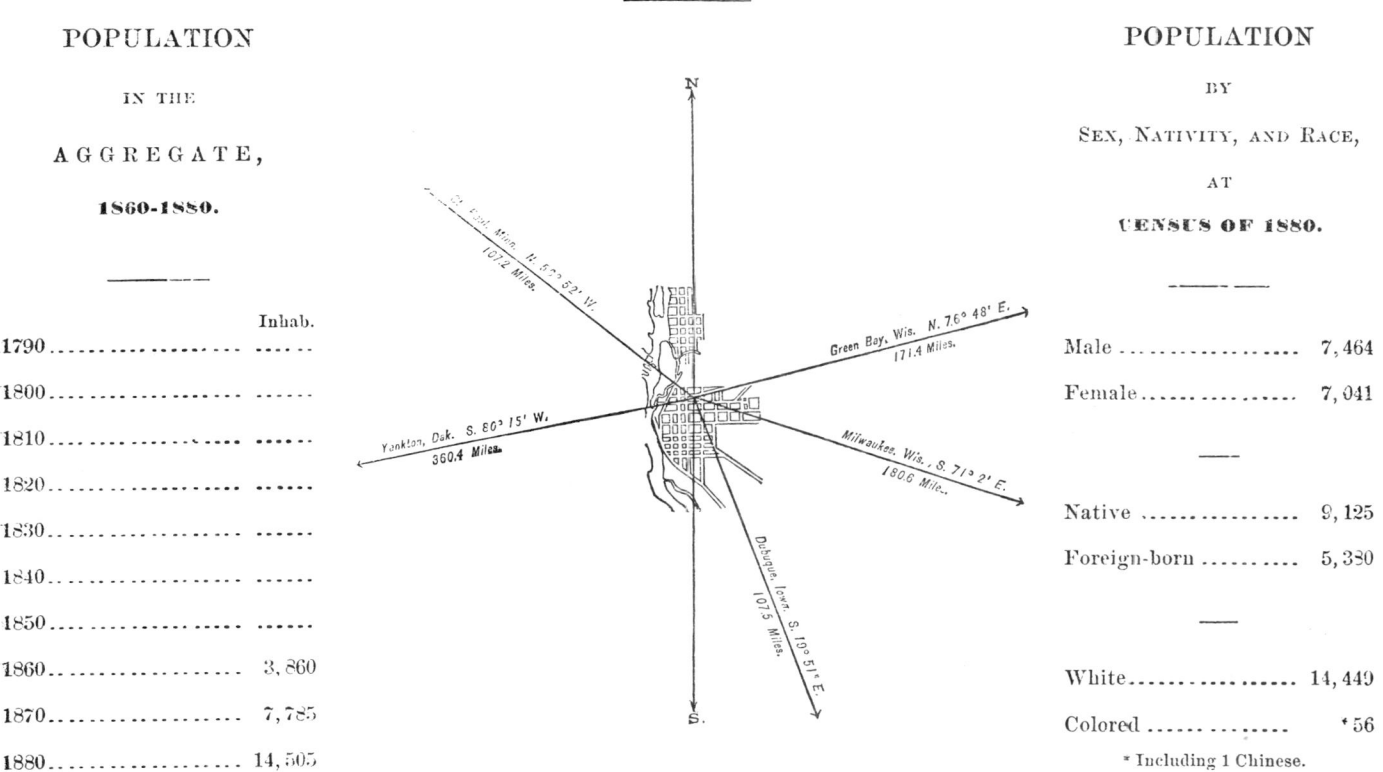

POPULATION

BY

SEX, NATIVITY, AND RACE,

AT

CENSUS OF 1880.

Male	7, 464
Female	7, 041
Native	9, 125
Foreign-born	5, 380
White	14, 449
Colored	*56

* Including 1 Chinese.

Latitude: 43 58 North; Longitude: 91 23 (west from Greenwich); **Altitude: 700 feet.**

FINANCIAL CONDITION:

Total Valuation: $3,125,686; per capita: $215 00.   Net Indebtedness: $135,000; per capita: $9 31.   Tax per $100: $3 20.

LA CROSSE IN 1880.

The name of the city is derived from the ball games which, up to dates considerably later than the white settlement, were played on the plains by the Indian tribes.

No history of La Crosse could be obtained, and the following statistical accounts, being all that could be collected by the Census Office, indicate in part the present condition of the city:

LOCATION.

The city lies in latitude 43° 58′ north, longitude 91° 23′ west from Greenwich, on the east bank of the Mississippi river, at the mouth of the Black river, from the north, and the La Crosse river, from the east. The place was first settled in 1850, and its growth from that time has been rapid. There have been no serious fires, while the financial troubles of 1857 and 1873 were quickly recovered from. The population is represented by people from every land and clime, no one nationality or state having supplanted others previously established. The average altitude of

650

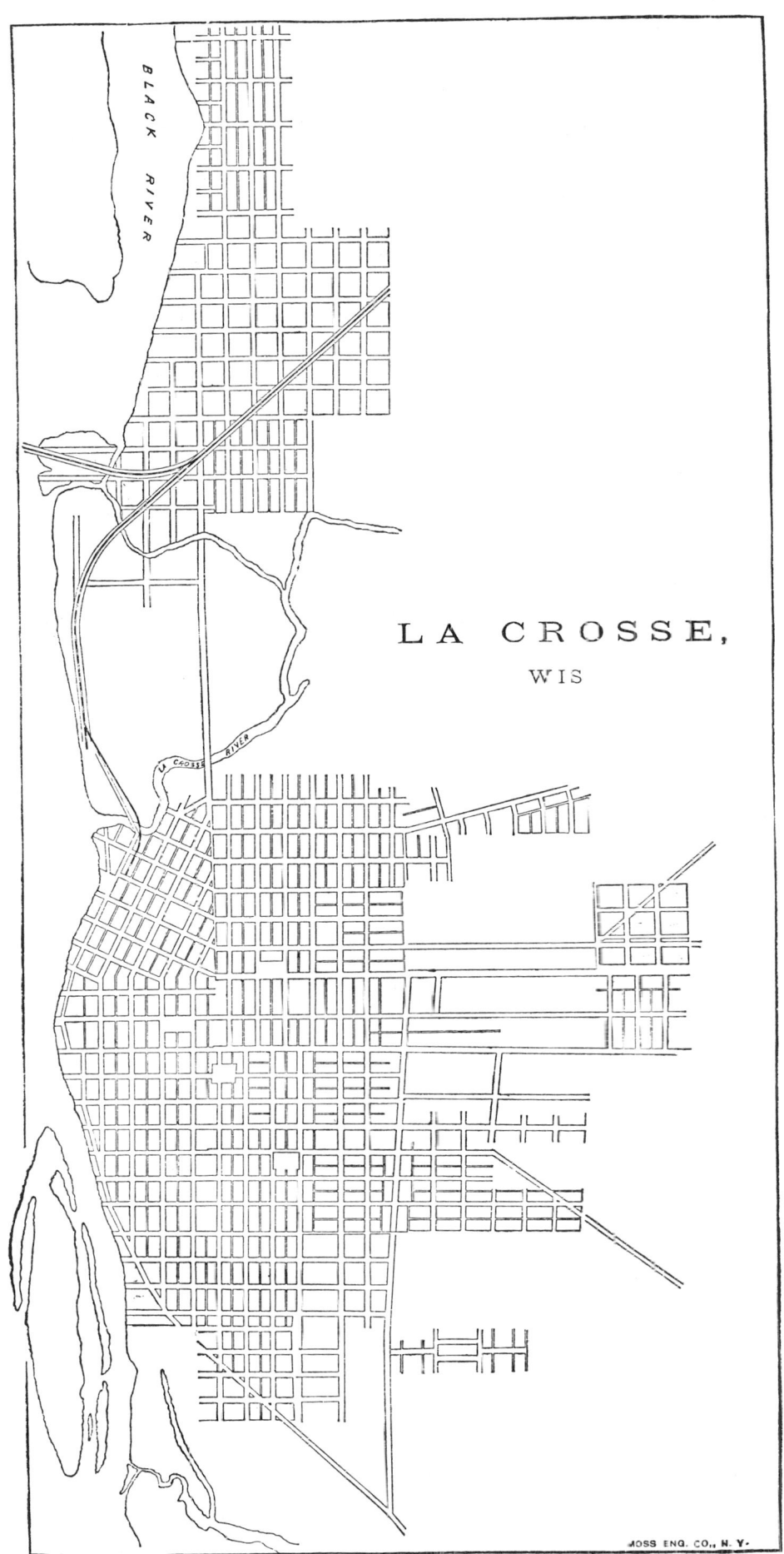

LA CROSSE,

WIS

BLACK RIVER

LA CROSSE RIVER

MOSS ENG. CO., N. Y.

the city is 700 feet above sea-level, the differences being about 40 feet either above or below this. The Mississippi river has here a depth of from 3 to 6 feet, with an average current of 3 miles per hour. Water communication is had from Saint Paul to New Orleans, as well as with all points on the navigable tributaries of the Mississippi.

RAILROAD COMMUNICATIONS.

La Crosse has ample railroad facilities, afforded by the following lines:

The Chicago, Milwaukee, and Saint Paul railroad, between the points named, with the Dubuque division, from here to Clinton, Iowa, and the Southern Minnesota division, from here to Flandreau, Minnesota; the Minnesota division of the Chicago and Northwestern railroad, from Chicago to Watertown, Minnesota; and the Green Bay and Minnesota railroad, from La Crosse to Green Bay, Wisconsin.

TRIBUTARY COUNTRY.

The country immediately tributary to the city is agricultural, wheat and barley being the staple products. The La Crosse river drains one of the finest farming valleys of the state, while opposite, in Minnesota, is the Root River valley, a large and rich agricultural section. In addition the Black river has an annual lumber product of over 250,000,000 feet, and the numerous industries that this gives rise to, materially swells the volume of the city's trade.

TOPOGRAPHY, ETC.

The site of the city is a level sandy prairie, the bluffs on the Mississippi and the Black river rising to a height of from 400 to 500 feet above the water. The soil is sandy, with underlying sand rock. There are 600 acres of marsh land near the city, and this is covered at high stages of water in the river. There is but little wood in the surrounding country, and the soil, like that under the city, is sandy.

CLIMATE.

Highest recorded summer temperature, 108°; highest summer temperature in average years, 96°. Lowest recorded winter temperature, —40°; lowest winter temperature in average years, —20°. Neither the adjacent waters and marsh, nor the prevailing winds, appear to have any marked climatic influence.

STREETS.

There are 35 miles of streets in the city, 8 miles of which are paved with broken stone, the cost being, as nearly as it may be estimated, 65 cents per square yard. The annual cost of keeping the pavement in repair is $1,200, and the broken stone is preferred on streets in this section. The sidewalks are of plank. On the paved streets gutters are laid with stone. Trees are planted at the sides of the streets by the abutting property-owners. The construction of streets is done by contract, repairs by the day, and the annual cost of both is from $10,000 to $20,000. The mayor expresses a preference for contract work.

HORSE-RAILROADS.

The horse-railroads have a total length of 2 miles. There are 5 cars and 13 horses in use, while employment is given to 7 men. There were 100,000 passengers carried during the year, the rate of fare being 5 cents. There are no regular omnibus lines, but 3 vehicles with 12 horses, and employing 7 men, carry passengers to all parts of the city at rates of fare of from 25 to 50 cents.

WATER-WORKS.

The water-works are owned by the city, and their total cost was $120,000. The system used is the direct pumping into the mains, the ordinary pressure being 40 pounds to the square inch. The greatest amount pumped per diem is 2,500,000 gallons, and the least 500,000 gallons, the average amount pumped per diem not being given. The annual cost of maintenance, aside from the cost of pumping, is $1,200, and the yearly income from water-rates is $4,500. Water-meters are not used.

GAS.

The gas-works are not owned by the city. The charge per 1,000 feet is $3. The city pays $40 per annum for each street-lamp, 61 in number.

PUBLIC BUILDINGS.

The city owns and occupies for municipal purposes wholly or in part 1 city hall and 2 engine-houses, their total cost being given as $21,000. The city hall is said to have cost $1,500; but whether it is owned in common with the county, and this sum is the city's portion, or whether it is the total cost of the building, was not stated.

PUBLIC PARKS AND PLEASURE-GROUNDS.

There are two small parks of one-half block each, with shade-trees and grass sod

PLACES OF AMUSEMENT.

The Opera House, with a seating capacity of 1,000, and Germania hall, seating about 700, are used for theatrical exhibitions. Theaters pay a license to the city amounting to about $10 annually. There are no halls used for concerts, lectures, etc. There is one concert- and beer-garden, 150 by 300 feet, built in 1878 at a cost of $5,000, that is patronized by Germans on Sunday, but which the mayor thinks "not worth mentioning".

DRAINAGE.

Only one street is sewered, and its sewer extends but four blocks, discharging into the river below the surface of the water. This sewer is new and has not required any flushing or cleansing. It was paid for by the city. The length and size are not stated, but the cost is reported at $1 57½ per linear foot. Cost of manholes, $25; cost of catch basins, $25 each. There is no plan for the future sewerage.

CEMETERIES.

There are 3 cemeteries connected with La Crosse. The Protestant cemetery, area 60 acres, is situated 1 mile northeast of the city, and the Catholic and Jewish cemeteries are 1 mile southeast of the city. Each of the last two has an area of 5 acres. There are no churchyards or private burial-grounds in which interments are no longer permitted. The total number of interments in the 3 cemeteries aggregates 1,862. There are no ordinances regulating interments, and there is no limit of time after death for burial. Graves are dug 5 feet deep. Owners pay $3 each to have their lots cared for, while the management of the cemetery is vested in a committee which attends to the gardening, flower-beds, sodding, grading, etc.

MARKETS.

There are no corporation markets in the city.

SANITARY AUTHORITY—BOARD OF HEALTH.

The sanitary needs of La Crosse are in the hands of a board of health, composed of one alderman from each ward in the city, 6 in all, appointed annually by the mayor and controlled by the city council. With the exception of the salary of the nuisance-inspector, the board incurs no expense in ordinary times, but, in case of an epidemic, expense may be incurred to any sum necessary. In absence of epidemics the board has authority to see to the sanitary condition of the city, with powers to correct. In presence of an epidemic it can enforce quarantine and do all things necessary for the suppression of the disease. The board has no stated time for meeting and no specified system of transacting business. The executive officer of the board is the nuisance-inspector, who is always a physician. He has a general supervision over each ward in the city, and reports all sanitary defects to the board. He, as well as all the members of the board, has sufficient police powers to enforce the health regulations. Inspections are made in all parts of the city during the summer months. When nuisances are reported they are ordered to be abated, and if this is not done the responsible parties are prosecuted and the abatement is enforced. Defective house-drainage, privy-vaults, cesspools, and sources of drinking-water are treated the same as nuisances when complained of. The board has entire control over the conservation and removal of garbage. The board has no regulations concerning the burial of the dead, the pollution of streams, or the removal of excrement.

INFECTIOUS DISEASES.

Small-pox patients are sent to a pest-house, prepared for the purpose, situated about 3 miles from the city. Scarlet-fever patients are isolated at home. The board takes cognizance of the breaking out of contagious diseases in either public or private schools, and closes the same if necessary. Vaccination is not compulsory, nor is it done at the public expense.

REPORTS.

The record of births, diseases, and deaths is attended to by the county register of deeds. The board reports annually to the council, and its reports are published in the local press.

MUNICIPAL CLEANSING.

Street-cleaning.—The streets are cleaned both by the city and by private abutters, the city doing its portion with its own force. The work is done wholly by hand, no sweeping-machines being used. The business streets are cleaned once a week and the others "as often as expedient", all being said to be "kept clean". The annual cost of this service to the city is $200, and very little to private persons. The sweepings are used, when needed, for filling-purposes.

Garbage and ashes are removed by the householders at their own expense. There are no special regulations governing the conservation of garbage while awaiting removal, except that it must not be thrown into the streets or alleys, or kept long enough on the premises to create a nuisance. Both it and the ashes may be kept in the same vessel, and their final disposition is the same, *i. e.*, used for filling. The cost of the service is very little, and it is said that no nuisance or probable injury to health results from the working of the system.

Dead animals.—The carcass of any animal dying within the city limits is removed by order of the police if necessary. Who performs the service, or where the carcasses are disposed of, was not stated. About 75 dead animals are removed annually at a cost of $50.

Liquid household wastes.—A limited part of the house wastes goes into the sewers, none into the street gutters, a small proportion into cesspools, and the larger part into vaults. The cesspools are porous, are not provided with overflows, in some cases receive the wastes from water-closets, and are not governed by any regulations as to cleaning, etc.

Human excreta.—About 1 per cent. of the houses in the city are provided with water-closets, half delivering into sewers, half into cesspools, and 99 per cent. depend on privy vaults. None of the vaults are even nominally water-tight, and there are no regulations concerning their construction, or prescribing the manner of emptying them. As a rule, when full they are covered with sand, a new vault is dug and the privy moved over it. Night-soil is not allowed to be used for manuring land within the gathering-ground of the public water-supply.

POLICE.

The chief of police is appointed by the mayor, and he appoints the members of the force, the department being governed by the mayor and council. The chief of police, salary $1,200 per annum, has direct control of the force, and administers it in accordance with rules and ordinances making the usual provisions. The remainder of the force consists of 6 patrolmen at $60 a month each. The force is not uniformed. Patrolmen are equipped with revolvers and clubs; they are on duty 12 hours at a time and patrol 5 miles of streets. During the past year 893 arrests were made; the principal cause was for drunkenness, and the cases were disposed of by fines or imprisonment, or by the offenders being ordered out of the city. There was very little lost or stolen property reported to the police, but 30 per cent. of what was lost or stolen was recovered and returned to the owners. During the year there were 420 station-house lodgers, as against 470 in 1879. Free meals are not furnished to these lodgers. The force is required to co-operate with the fire, health, and building departments "in all ways in which services can be rendered". Special policemen are appointed by the chief when necessary, but have no standing with the regular force. The yearly cost of the department (1880) is $6,240.

MADISON,

DANE COUNTY, WISCONSIN.

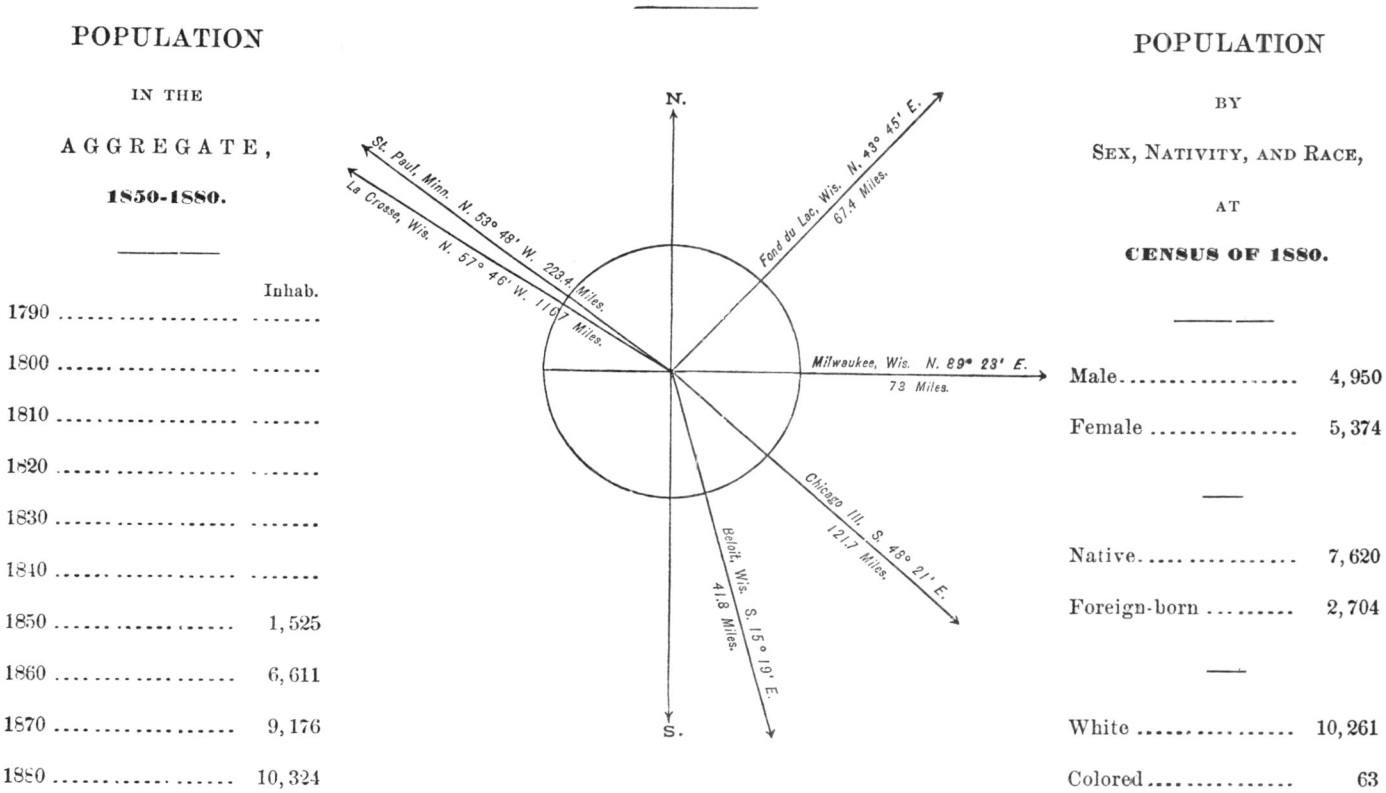

POPULATION

IN THE

AGGREGATE,

1850-1880.

	Inhab.
1790	....
1800	....
1810	....
1820	....
1830	....
1840	....
1850	1,525
1860	6,611
1870	9,176
1880	10,324

POPULATION

BY

SEX, NATIVITY, AND RACE,

AT

CENSUS OF 1880.

Male	4,950
Female	5,374
Native	7,620
Foreign-born	2,704
White	10,261
Colored	63

Latitude: 43° 5′ North; Longitude: 89° 24′ (west from Greenwich); Altitude: 848 to 949 feet.

FINANCIAL CONDITION:

Total Valuation: $4,560,234; per capita: $442 00.   Net Indebtedness: $136,769; per capita: $13 25.   Tax per $100: $1 96.

HISTORICAL SKETCH.(a)

The first settlement in the county of Dane was in 1827–'28, by Ebenezer Brigham, who died in this city, at the age of 72 years, in 1861. Shortly after the Black Hawk war, and on the 15th of October, 1832, an encampment was made on the present site of Madison by Captain Low, James Halpine, and Archibald Crisman. The public surveys were extended over the *Four Lake Country*, embracing this section, and were completed in 1834, and the lands were purchased by James Duane Doty, governor of the territory of Wisconsin, and Stevens T. Mason, governor of the territory of Michigan. In 1836 the territorial legislature selected the Four Lake Country as the site for

---

a B. J. Stevens, esq., of Madison, secured and transmitted the detailed information concerning the past and present condition of the city, in response to schedules of interrogatories sent to him from this office, and to him is due the careful historical sketch with which this report is introduced.

the capital, but decided to hold session at Burlington (now in Iowa) until March 4, 1839, unless the government buildings should be earlier completed. The commissioners chosen to construct the buildings were Augustus A. Bird, James Duane Doty, and John F. O'Neill.

The first legislative assembly of the territory of Wisconsin convened October 25, 1836, at Belmont, in what is now La Fayette county, Wisconsin, and on the 28th of November the bill fixing the capital at the Four Lake Country passed to a third reading; the legislature shortly thereafter adjourning to meet again at Burlington, as stated above. On the 6th of November, 1837, the second session of the first legislature convened at Burlington, and continued in session until January 20, 1838, when it adjourned again to meet on the second Monday of June following. The June session was held at Burlington, lasting nearly two weeks, and on the 25th the first assembly adjourned without date, provision having been made, however, for the meeting of the next legislative assembly at Madison. The survey and plot of the city was made under the direction of James Duane Doty, with the capitol square in the center, with a succession of streets parallel to the square. These were crossed diagonally by streets running from the corners of the square, and all were crossed by avenues at right angles to the sides of the square. The Capitol square, or park, consisting of 14.4 acres, was surveyed and staked out by Moses M. Strong, in February, 1837.

Mr. Eben Peck and wife, in the spring of 1837, built the first house in Madison which was used as a residence. Although John Catlin erected a log-house earlier in the same spring, the interior was destroyed by fire before it could be occupied. On Saturday night, April 15, 1837, Mrs. Peck was awakened from her slumbers in a tent, 3 miles from the site of Madison, by the howling of wolves, and pushed on through a violent snow-storm to the site of her more substantial dwelling, subsequently built, where she sat in her wagon under a tree the remainder of the night—25 miles from the nearest white resident, at Blue Mounds, and nearly 100 miles from the settlement at Milwaukee. In June, 1837, there were 36 men engaged in work upon the grounds of the capitol building. On the 4th of July in the same year, the corner-stone was laid, and in November, 1838, the senate and assembly chambers were finished. The first meeting of the legislative assembly in Madison was held in the American hotel, before the completion of the capitol, on February 26, 1838. Soon after March 1 of the same year, the legislature moved into the capitol building, and before it was completed. The American hotel had been completed in January, 1838; it was destroyed by fire in 1868. The Madison hotel was built in 1838, and in June of that year the territorial supreme court held its first session therein. The first newspaper published in Madison was conducted by Josiah A. Noonan, and appeared in 1839.

As early as January, 1838, the territorial legislature prepared to incorporate what afterward became the State university. On the 12th of June, 1838, Congress made an endowment of public lands "for a seminary in Wisconsin, amounting to 46,080 acres". The first quorum of the board of visitors (regents) stands on record as having met pursuant to adjournment December 1, 1838, when Mr. Henry L. Dodge was chosen treasurer and John Catlin secretary. Immediately on the admission of Wisconsin as a state into the Union, in 1848, the university was formally incorporated. The present site (in the city of Madison) was purchased from Mr. Aaron Vanderpoll, of New York, on the 17th of October, 1848. A preparatory department was opened in February, 1849. John H. Lathrop, LL. D., was elected chancellor, at a salary of $2,000 per annum, and the formal inauguration took place January 16, 1850. The north dormitory was completed in 1851, and the south dormitory in 1854. The university has continued on in prosperity, and fine buildings and extensive grounds have been added. The number of the faculty consists of 34 members, and there are 450 students, and the yearly income of the university exceeds $80,000.

The state law library dates from the earliest existence of the territorial government. The first purchase of books was in 1837, from an appropriation made by Congress in the act creating the territory of Wisconsin, and later purchases were made from appropriations by the state. The library now contains the English, Irish, and Scotch reports complete, and only two volumes of the regular series of reports of the American courts are lacking.

The state historical society, located in Madison, began its course in October, 1846. The first annual meeting was held in January, 1847, and Morgan L. Martin was chosen president. The second annual meeting was held in January, 1848, and William R. Smith was chosen president. On January 30, 1849, a new organization was effected, at which Nelson Dusey was made, ex officio, president, and I. A. Lapham, corresponding secretary; Mr. Dusey was then governor of the state. In 1852, when Leonard J. Farwell, as governor, became president, he ordered a full set of the territorial and state laws and journals to be placed in the society's library. These, together with complete volumes of proceedings of the American Ethnological Society, presented by Frank Hudson, comprised the total works in the library when the present secretary, Lyman C. Draper, arrived in 1852. The society was again reorganized in January, 1854, under a charter obtained from the legislature in March, 1853, when William R. Smith was chosen president. In 1855 Daniel L. Durrie was chosen librarian, who, since 1858, has given to the society his constant and continuous service. To these two, Messrs. Draper and Durrie, is largely due the credit of building up the library and the interest in the society. In January, 1866, the library contained 21,000 books and documents, increased in 1879 to over 80,000 volumes—books and documents and pamphlets—besides newspaper files, maps, pictures, etc. Especial pains have been taken to collect from other states documents bearing upon topics of legislative and humane institutions, to aid legislative committees, boards of charities and reform, railroad commissioners, and members of geological surveys. In these departments the records are very full and valuable. The collection of prehistoric relics, especially copper and stone tools, is remarkable.

The growth of the city was rapid at first, culminating in 1856, but since then has been steady and slow, without marked periods of depression and without serious ravages by fire. Its early rapid growth was owing to the fact that it was the capital of a great territory, first being opened up to occupancy and cultivation, and to the natural beauty of the location. The foreign population or the foreign-born is about 26 per cent. of the total population, corresponding in that respect with the total population of the county of Dane.

MADISON IN 1880.

LOCATION.

Madison lies in latitude 43° 5′ north, longitude 89° 24′ west from Greenwich, in the southern central portion of the state, and 82 miles by rail west of Milwaukee. The city is pleasantly situated on an isthmus between lake Mendota and lake Monona, and is surrounded by heights from which it can be seen at a distance of several miles. The altitudes above sea-level are, average, 900 feet; lowest point, surface of lake Monona, 848 feet; and highest point, University hill, 949 feet. It has been judicially determined that one at least of the lakes near Madison is "navigable", but they are not connected with each other or with other water by navigable channels. Monona, or Third lake, is 4 miles in length by from $1\frac{1}{4}$ to 2 miles in width; Mendota, or Fourth lake, is 6 miles in length by from $1\frac{1}{4}$ to 4 miles in width, and at places from 50 to 100 feet deep. There are four connecting lakes and one disconnected, between three of which Madison is situated.

RAILROAD COMMUNICATIONS.

The Chicago, Milwaukee, and Saint Paul railroad, extending from Chicago, via Milwaukee, Madison, and Prairie du Chien, to the West, and another line from Milwaukee via Portage (at which place a branch from Madison connects), La Crosse, Saint Paul, etc., to the Northwest; and the Chicago and Northwestern railroad, extending from Chicago via Madison; to Winona, Minn., and thence to the West, and from Elroy, over the track of the Chicago, Saint Paul, and Minneapolis railroad, to Saint Paul and the Northwest.

TRIBUTARY COUNTRY.

The character of the tributary or surrounding country is agricultural. There is less of the land under cultivation for 2 or 3 miles out than farther; but, as a rule, all the land is taken into farms, leaving no unsold government lands, and but little held by non-resident owners. Very nearly all the land in Dane county is occupied by parties owning the same, the percentage in the occupation of tenants being very small, probably less than 5 per cent. Every variety of crop and farm product peculiar to the climate is to some extent raised. Wheat, corn, and stock are the chief products, the chief varieties of stock being horned cattle, sheep, and hogs. Garden vegetables, small fruits, and, to some extent, hops are raised near the city in considerable quantities. Butter and cheese are also made in considerable quantities for shipment.

TOPOGRAPHY, ETC.

The soil is clay loam, with small tracts of gravelly sand. The underlying rock is Lower Magnesian limestone. The variations in level are slight, seldom being more than 75 feet, and the surface of the ground is sufficiently undulating for good drainage. Immediately adjoining the city on the northwest is lake Mendota, with an area of about 15 square miles. Lake Monona adjoins upon the southeast and is about 6 square miles in extent, while 1 mile south of the city lake Winger occupies an area of about 2 square miles. The remainder of the country for a radius of 5 miles is mostly open, with limited tracts of small timber scattered about.

CLIMATE.

Highest recorded summer temperature, 98°; highest summer temperature in average years, 86°. Lowest recorded winter temperature −28°; lowest winter temperature in average years, −10°. The lakes adjoining are small and their influence is merely local, tending, however, to moderate the fall winds and to chill those of spring. The prevailing winds are from the west, southwest, and northwest, and tend to make the climate a dry one, thus increasing the extremes of heat and cold.

STREETS.

There are about 40 miles of streets in Madison, of which 3 miles are paved with broken stone and 7 miles with gravel. There was at one time about one-half mile of wood pavement, but it has been removed. The cost per square yard of the present pavements, as near as may be estimated, is, broken stone, 75 cents, and gravel, 25 cents. The cost of keeping each in repair is slight. Heavy accumulations from country teams are most easily removed from

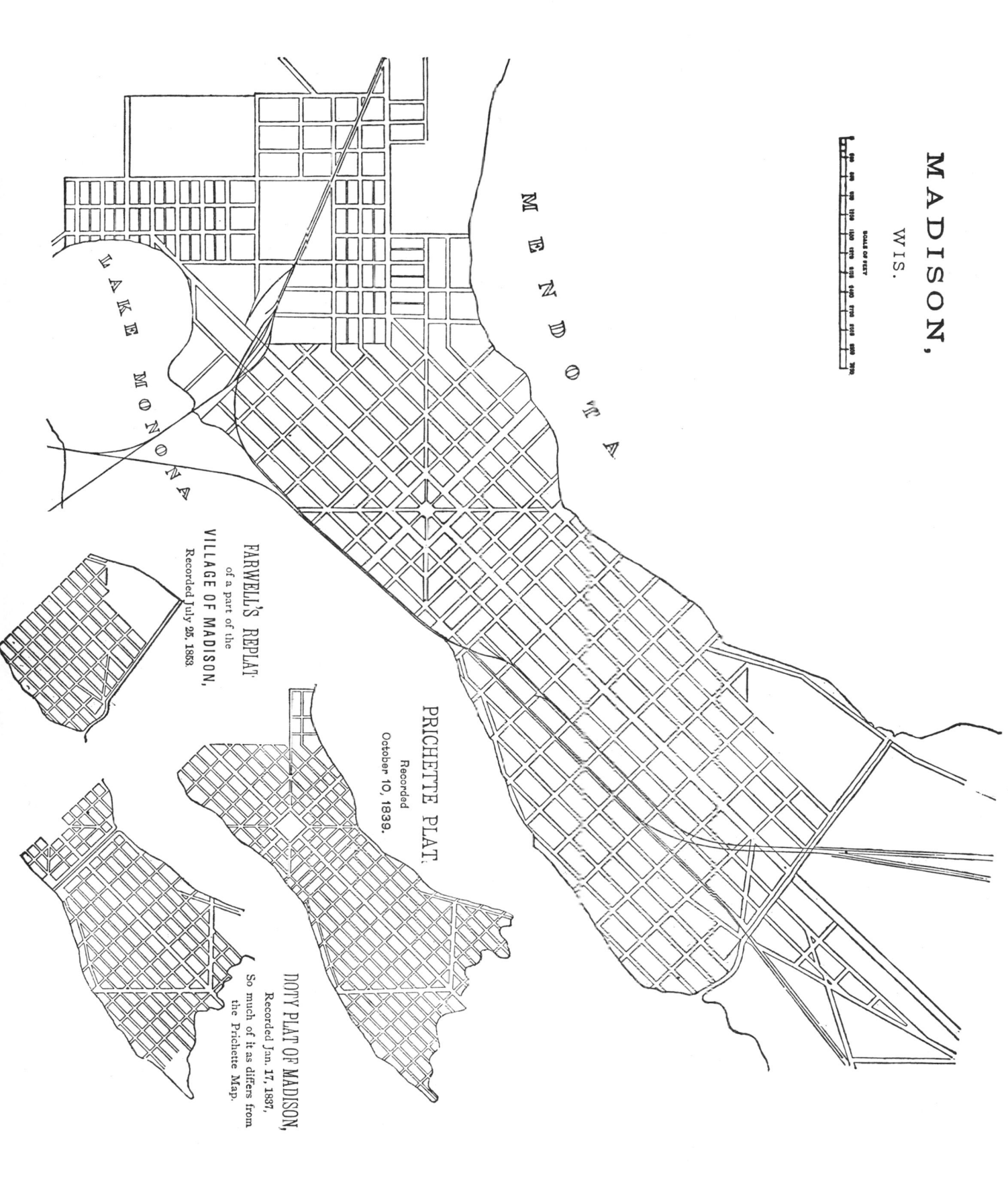

MADISON,
WIS.

SCALE OF FEET

LAKE MONONA

MENDOTA

FARWELL'S REPLAT
of a part of the
VILLAGE OF MADISON,
Recorded July 25, 1853

PRICHETTE PLAT.
Recorded
October 10, 1839.

DOTY PLAT OF MADISON,
Recorded Jan. 17, 1837,
So much of it as differs from
the Prichette Map.

the broken stone, this class of pavement being preferred here for quality and permanent economy. The sidewalks are of all kinds, boards, plank, stone, brick, and asphalt being used. Brick sidewalks, laid on a good foundation, are considered best. Gutters are paved with cobble and broken quarried stone, which is effective and durable, and requires cleaning only after heavy rainfalls. The gutters have an average fall of 4 inches in one rod. There has been little or no organized tree-planting along the streets, each abutter placing upon his own land, or opposite streets, such trees as he may select. The construction and repair of streets are done both by contract and by the day. The former, under proper guidance, is preferred. An iron roller weighing 5,600 pounds is used, but is useless for the gravel streets unless a surface of screenings is put on, in which case the road after rolling is left in a finished condition.

HORSE-RAILROADS, ETC.

There are no horse-railroads in the city. Two lines of omnibuses, with 9 vehicles, 18 horses, and employing 9 men, annually carry 36,000 passengers to various parts of the city at the uniform rate of fare of 25 cents, not including baggage.

WATER-WORKS.

There are no water-works, but the city intends to construct a complete system at an early day.

GAS.

The gas-works are owned by private parties. The daily average production of gas is 25,934 cubic feet. The charge per 1,000 feet is $4 50, with a discount of $1 for prompt payment. The city pays $3 per 1,000 feet for gas, and this makes each street-lamp cost annually, including lighting, extinguishing, and care, about $20. There are 91 street-lamps.

PUBLIC BUILDINGS.

The total cost of the municipal buildings belonging to the city is $38,400, and includes the city hall, engine-houses, and hook-and-ladder house. The cost of the city hall is $32,000, and is not owned in common with the county.

PUBLIC PARKS AND PLEASURE-GROUNDS.

The only park in the city of Madison is the inclosure in which the state capitol stands, its area being 14.4 acres to the center of the streets surrounding it. It is in form nearly square, and is inclosed by an iron fence. The total cost of the park, including land, improvements, etc., is $72,807 97. The yearly cost of maintenance has averaged $3,659 29 for the past 10 years. The present plan of the park, with reference to walks, trees, etc., was designed by Messrs. Cleveland and French, of Chicago, and was approved by Governor Washburne. Its control is vested in the superintendent of public property, subject to the approval of the governor.

PLACES OF AMUSEMENT.

There is 1 theater in the city, known as the Opera House, with a seating capacity of 600, and the following halls used for concerts, lectures, etc.: Turner's hall, seating 600; City hall, seating 650; and University chapel, seating 1,000. No license is required on any theater building, but, by ordinance, all exhibitions are required to pay a license of not less than $1 nor more than $20. The Shutzen park, area 20 acres, is situated just outside the city limits, and cost $7,000. It pays an annual license to the state of about $15, is fairly patronized, and was first established in June, 1871. In the present year it was consolidated with Der Madison Turnverein, an association incorporated in 1859, and whose hall cost $10,000.

DRAINAGE.

There are no public sewers in Madison, only a few private sewers, one of which was built by the state, running from the capitol to the Third lake. A few laterals from hotels and residences discharge into this. The other private sewers discharge mostly into Fourth lake. The mouths of the sewers are below the surface of the lake, usually in 6 feet of water, or at a depth sufficient to prevent causing a nuisance, and the conditions relating to discharge are generally mentioned in the permit granted by the city council. Persons desiring to construct sewers do so at their own expense, after obtaining permission from the city council.

CEMETERIES.

There is one public cemetery in Madison—*Forest Hill*—owned by the city, and divided into two parts, one used by the Protestants and the other by the Roman Catholics. It contains 80 acres of land, according to the government survey, and is crossed diagonally by a highway that cuts off about 20 acres. This latter is the Roman Catholic cemetery, the remainder being used by the Protestants. It is situated 2½ miles southwest of the capitol, which stands in the center of the city. A cemetery, now no longer used, and from which all bodies are thought to have been removed, is located in the eastern part of the city, and contains about four blocks of ordinary size. There are no private burial-grounds known as such, though one or two graves lie on one of the lots bordering on Fourth lake; and there have never been any churchyard cemeteries. Reliable records of interments have not been kept for long periods of time. From what are supposed to be approximately reliable records there were 100 interments in 1879 and 121 in 1880. No burial is allowed to be made in the cemetery until the party applying shall furnish the sexton with the name, age, sex, nativity, and cause and date of death of the deceased. The sexton keeps a record of such reports, and after noting interment gives them to the superintendent, who files the same with the city clerk. The depth of graves is 4 feet for children and 5 feet for adults. The sale of lots in Forest Hill cemetery is attended to by the superintendent, all conveyances being executed by the mayor and the city clerk, and no burial is permitted in any lot until the same is paid for.

MARKETS.

There are no public markets in the city. Hitching-posts or railings, for the convenience of farmers wishing to hitch teams, have been erected, by lease of the council and by the city, in a portion of one of the avenues but little used. This is the nearest approach to a city market.

SANITARY AUTHORITY—BOARD OF HEALTH.

The chief sanitary organization of Madison is the board of health, composed of 5 aldermen—one from each ward in the city—appointed by the mayor and under control of the mayor and council. There is no requirement that the members of the board be physicians, but at present two are such. In ordinary times the expenses of the board, including the removal of nuisances from the streets, are from $150 to $200, and during an epidemic there is no limit to the amount expended, the bills being audited by the council. In absence of an epidemic the board has no authority beyond what may be granted by the council from time to time, excepting the power given by the charter to employ a physician at $5 per day when acting, to abate nuisances, to order the cleaning of cesspools, etc., and also to employ officers at $2 per day to see that the health ordinances are enforced. During epidemics the authority of the board does not appear to be extended, but the practice is to do what seems to be for the best and trust to the council to ratify what is done. The chairman of the board is the executive officer; he receives no salary, and his duties are to see that the health ordinances are enforced. A health officer—a physician—is employed when necessary, and the chief of police and street commissioner also act with the board. The board has no formal mode of transacting business, no rules, and no regular or fixed times for meeting. Inspections are made regularly once a year, between April 15 and July 1, and afterward as reports are made. When a nuisance is reported the health officer is sent to examine, with directions, at his discretion, to order abatement, and if this is not done the parties offending are prosecuted for violation of ordinance. Defective house-drainage, privy-vaults, cesspools, sources of drinking-water, and sewerage are treated in the same manner, when either found at the annual inspection or reported afterward. The board has no control over the conservation and removal of garbage unless it becomes a nuisance. There are no regulations concerning the burial of the dead, other than what have been noted under the head of "Cemeteries", and the board has no regulations in regard to the pollution of streams, etc.

INFECTIOUS DISEASES.

Whenever small-pox appears and there are several cases, a pest-house is improvised, there being no permanent one. When the cases are few they are treated where found, but intercourse with them is prohibited, and largely prevented. Scarlet-fever patients are quarantined at home in such manner as the health officer, or some member of the board, may direct. The board takes cognizance of the breaking out of contagious diseases in either public or private schools, and, when thought best, close the same. Vaccination is not compulsory, nor is it done at the public expense.

Practically there is no registry of either births, diseases, or deaths. At times a registry of deaths is more or less reliably kept. The statutes direct that the register of deeds of each county shall keep a record of marriages, births, and deaths, and it is made the duty of attending ministers and physicians to report, with penalty of $25 for neglect.

REPORTS.

The board reports to the council from time to time, and annually a report is made to the state board of health. Reports to the council are published as part of its proceedings in the daily papers, and the report to the state board, in whole or in abstract, is published in the proceedings of the board in book form by the state. The medical profession are required by the ordinances to report to the board of health all cases of contagious disease, under the penalties therein stated. So little of sickness obtains of a contagious nature that the regulations are not so completely observed as otherwise they would be.

MUNICIPAL CLEANSING.

Street cleaning.—The streets are cleaned both by the city and by the abutters, the city doing its share with its own force. The work is done wholly by hand, no sweeping-machines being used. The cleaning by the city is done chiefly in the spring and fall, and is apparently thoroughly done. The cost to the city is between $200 and $300 per annum, but the cost to private persons was not ascertainable. The sweepings are deposited on low lots in remote parts of the city, the present system being "probably as good as could be applied here at present. Deposits improve the low lots".

Removal of garbage and ashes.—All garbage and ashes, excepting the refuse from the public buildings, are removed by the householders, but frequently, on request, the city wagon will take such garbage and ashes as may be placed on the street for removal. Garbage must not be kept long enough to create a nuisance, and must not be thrown on the ground or into the lakes. Some of it is taken by persons as food for swine. but the majority of it is disposed of in the same way as street-sweepings. So far as is known, no ill-effects have arisen from the manner of handling or disposing of garbage, and the system is reported as satisfactory.

Dead animals.—The carcasses of all dead animals are removed by the city and buried outside its limits. The annual cost of the service is about $15 or $20.

Liquid household wastes.—With the exception of a small portion disposed of by private sewers and drains, the greater part of the liquid household wastes is run into cesspools and privy-vaults, a little being thrown on the surface of the ground, and a little at times reaching the street-gutters. The cesspools, as a rule, are not closed at the bottom, and sometimes are not walled up. They are not provided with overflows, do not usually receive the wastes, and are cleaned out in the same manner as privy-vaults. An analysis from 300 wells was made by a student of chemistry at the university, under order of the city council, and he reports that there is considerable contamination of wells by sewage, not more than 10 per cent. being entirely free from organic matter, while about 10 per cent. were regarded by him as being unfit for use. It is proper to say that this report is not approved by certain of the citizens who claim to have given study to these subjects, but have not made general experiments. In only one case to date (1880) has typhoid fever been traced, by a report of the attendant physician, to contaminated well-water.

Human excreta.—Not more than 5 per cent. of the houses in the city are provided with water-closets, 3 per cent. of which deliver into the private sewers, while the remainder depend entirely on vaults. There do not appear to be any regulations concerning the construction of privy-vaults, and probably less than 5 per cent. of them are even nominally water-tight. They are not allowed to be cleaned out in the daytime between June 1 and November 1, and the contents must be thoroughly disinfected before being taken out. The dry-earth system is used but little. The night-soil is taken outside the city, and is in some cases used for farming lands.

Manufacturing wastes.—The liquid and solid manufacturing wastes, chiefly from breweries, are discharged into the lakes.

POLICE.

The police force of Madison is appointed by the mayor, subject to confirmation by the city council, and is governed by the mayor. The chief of police, salary $4 per day, is the executive officer, and has direct charge of the force, which consists of 4 policemen at $1 a day each. The men wear no uniform, only a star on the breast of the coat, and are equipped with clubs and revolvers, the former being furnished by the city. The policemen do no patrol duty, but remain at the station-house, subject to call, all night. A private watchman, who is paid by certain citizens, patrols a portion of the city. No account of arrests was kept for 1880, but the principal causes of arrests during the year were drunkenness and vagrancy. The offenders were taken before the municipal courts and sentenced either to hard labor or to pay fines. During the year property to the value of $300 was reported to the police as either lost or stolen, and of this about one-half was recovered and returned to the owners. There are no station-house lodgers here. The force is not especially required to co-operate with either the health or fire department, but it generally does so. Special policemen are appointed by the mayor, and while on duty are under the orders of the chief and receive the same pay as members of the regular force. The annual cost of the police force is $2,000.

MILWAUKEE,

MILWAUKEE COUNTY, WISCONSIN.

POPULATION

IN THE

AGGREGATE,

1840-1880.

	Inhab.
1790	......
1800	......
1810	......
1820	......
1830	......
1840	1,712
1850	20,061
1860	45,246
1870	71,440
1880	115,587

POPULATION

BY

SEX, NATIVITY, AND RACE,

AT

CENSUS OF 1880.

Male	57,475
Female	58,112
Native	69,514
Foreign-born	46,073
White	115,280
Colored	* 307

* Including 6 Chinese.

Latitude: 43° 4′ North; Longitude: 88° (west from Greenwich); Altitude: 580 to 755 feet.

FINANCIAL CONDITION:

Total Valuation: $55,875,969; per capita: $483 00.   Net Indebtedness: $2,160,289; per capita: $18 69.   Tax per $100: $2 04.

HISTORICAL SKETCH.(a)

Those who have been reaping, and those who may continue to reap, benefits from the admirable location of Milwaukee as a commercial and manufacturing center, must render thanks to the Indians for choosing the site. The first civilized or semi-civilized people who visited Wisconsin for any but missionary purposes came solely to trade with the aborigines. They therefore sought no particular location; were not influenced in any degree by eligibility, soil, or prospective commercial advantages. They went wherever the Indians, with whom it was desired to establish commercial relations, had built their straw-like villages, no matter whether in desert or swamp. These nomadic traffickers were not in search of the best foundation for a city, site for a capital, or tract for an empire; their sole object and thought was to find the Indians. They found them at the mouth of the Mahn-ah-wauhee river, and there tarried. Hence came "Milwaukee."

a Prepared by Robert Luce, esq.

The natural attractions of the place in those days were not easily discernible. The streams that emptied into the bay at this point were sluggish, their mouths obstructed by wide sand-bars, their shores rank with obnoxious weeds; and the whole Menomonee valley was an uninviting swamp, alternately covered with water and weeds, and a little farther back with a tamarack forest. Therefore men prospecting for desirable locations would in all likelihood have passed this by for one of a half-dozen places on the lake shore, which would apparently more nearly answer their purpose; but the Indians were there.

These Indians were the remnants of several tribes, viz., the Pottawatomies, Winnebagoes, Chippewas, Menomonees, and a few Ottawas. The early traders knew them under the collective name of the "Milwachy Indians". It is settled, however, that this and the modern "Milwaukee" are corruptions of the old Pottawatomie term "Mahn-ah-wauh", which meant universal or common council grounds.

It is known that as early as 1757 at least, traders came to Milwaukee, as we may for convenience call the point, though not a house stood there, and that they sold rum, trinkets, beads, hatchets, powder, and firearms, taking pay in skins and furs. Later in the century this became more prominent as a trading-post; and for the first twelve or fifteen years in the present century there were a number of families residing here, and the place contained from 8 to 20 houses and trading-posts. Each trader had a number of hired men, who were generally unmarried, and spent much of their time in remote portions of the country collecting furs. At certain portions of the year, generally during the fall and winter, they were all at home. As Indian trading began to diminish in volume and profit the traders removed farther west or returned home to enjoy their wealth.

It is doubtful whether the honor of being the first white man to come here to settle—to found a home—belongs to Jean Baptiste Mirandeau or to Solomon Juneau. The latter, however, is generally credited as the first settler. The date of his coming was September 14, 1818; but not for some years after this was there any thing like a settlement here. In fact, no settlement was possible till the Indian title to the land was extinguished.

The Menomonees ceded to the United States their rights in the land north and east of the Milwaukee river, February 8, 1831, and after that date all this land was open to pre-emption or private entry. The land south of the river was claimed by the Pottawatomies, and the treaty of cession was not ratified until February 21, 1835. They had reserved the right to occupy the land three years longer. At Chicago, Mackinac, and Detroit, adventurers were waiting for these treaties to be concluded and the lands at Milwaukee to be opened to settlement. The first four of these pioneers arrived at the tamarack residence of Solomon Juneau on the 18th of November, 1833, and to them belongs the honor of being the founders of the first Anglo-Saxon settlement at Milwaukee. As soon as the next spring opened a comparatively large number of travelers, land-seekers, adventurers, and traders visited this place, but only about a dozen came to stay. The year 1835 witnessed a large influx of this class of people, and in 1836 still more of them came.

Milwaukee contained 7 structures built by Indian traders before the Anglo-Saxon began building in 1834; in that year 5 structures were completed. One of these, put up by Mr. Juneau, was the first frame building erected here. It stood on what a few years later became the corner of East Water and Wisconsin streets; and although its dimensions did not exceed 12 by 16 feet, it was used successively as a school room, a justice's office, a recorder's office, a jail, a barber's shop, and then for several years as a gunsmith's shop.

In 1835 building began in earnest. A mill that had been put up in the previous summer began sawing oak and basswood lumber early in March. In this summer 16 structures were finished and 3 were got under way. In the summer of 1836 Milwaukee claimed over 500 inhabitants; about 60 frame buildings were completed, and 50 more were under contract. A lime-kiln and a brick-kiln were in active operation, and 3 saw-mills were sawing lumber for builders within 3 miles of the village. A land office was opened, a newspaper was started, the court-house was built, streets were laid out and graded, and money was plenty.

Then the financial crisis of 1837, that naturally resulted from the enormous speculations of the preceding years, spread ruin all over the land, and the Milwaukee speculators were not the least among the countless sufferers. Many a lot for which the owner had paid $500 or even $1,000 in 1836 was in 1837 or 1838 given in exchange for a barrel of pork or flour, or a suit of clothes. Many of the richest and most enterprising of the citizens, fearing if they remained longer they would lose every thing, left; those who remained were largely such as were too poor to do otherwise.

A considerable portion of what then constituted the village of Milwaukee had been bid off at the land sale at Green Bay in 1835 by Byron Kilbourn, George H. Walker, and Solomon Juneau. Walker purchased land in the vicinity of what is now Walker's Point; Kilbourn located his on the west side of the river, where his possessions were known as Kilbourntown; and Juneau purchased on the east side of the river, his possessions including the present court-house, park, and many acres of surrounding lots. At once there sprang into existence the two rival villages of Kilbourntown and Milwaukee.

At this time there were four roads leading away from this point—two diverging from the south side, one of which led to Chicago, the other to Fox river; one leading from the west side to Green Bay, and one proceeding up the peninsula to Port Washington. They very nearly followed the four principal Indian trails which the first Anglo-Saxon visitors found centering here, and had been chosen because these were seen to be the best routes. To get a road from Chicago to the west side, Kilbourn now built a bridge across the Menomonee and tapped the

Chicago road on the south side, about half a mile before it reached Walker's Point, where it crossed the Milwaukee by means of a ferry and terminated in Juneau's embryo city. The construction of this bridge greatly incensed the east-siders, since it gave easier access to the rival village than to the older site. The two villages were now formally organized, and the independence thereby declared aggravated the animosity already developed. One result of this jealousy will be seen as long as the city stands. Kilbourn made his survey in such manner as to prevent the streets upon the two sides from matching each other, always insisting that the west side did not want any communication with the east side, except by boats.

The east and west sides were consolidated by act of legislature approved March 11, 1839. Then for the first time the town of Milwaukee had a corporate existence.

A post-office had been established in Milwaukee in 1835, Juneau being the first postmaster. A two-horse mail coach between Milwaukee and Chicago began running, once a week, in March, 1836. The first vessel launched here was the schooner "Solomon Juneau", in the summer of 1836. The first newspaper issued here was the *Milwaukee Advertiser*, a six-column, large imperial sheet, which made its appearance July 14, 1836.

Two years passed before the town showed any signs of recovery from the blow, but when the great land sale for Milwaukee and the surrounding country began here, February 16, 1839, it became clear that prosperity and progress had received merely a temporary check. On the first day of this sale, although there was some delay in getting things into working order, over $50,000 was received for lands sold before sundown. At the end of seven days lands to the value of $260,000 had been disposed of, and March 19 the sales amounted to $600,000. The commissioner of public lands at Washington declared this to be the largest and most remarkable sale known to the department. Nine-tenths of the land at least was purchased by actual settlers; not a single speculator got an acre of claimed lands at this sale. The settlers united against the speculators, or "land-sharks", as they were called, with such effect that, though the land was offered to the highest bidder, not over half a section brought more than the minimum price set by the government, $1 25 per acre. Any "shark" who attempted to outbid a settler was treated to a cold-water bath until he agreed to desist.

In 1840, 132 of the citizens of the busy portion of the town were engaged in farming, 38 in navigation, 277 in commerce and trade, and 46 in professional occupations. The amount of maple sugar manufactured during the year ending June 1, 1840, was 13,900 pounds, and 6,625 cords of wood were sold.

Building was now resumed with almost as much energy as had been displayed before the panic. In 1841 and 1842 over 250 buildings were erected, and in the latter year there were 800 buildings standing in Milwaukee. Many of these, it is true, were temporary one-story frames, but there were many substantial buildings of neat workmanship. It was said that houses put up at that time brought from 40 to 50 per cent. on the cost, including the cost of the lot, as annual rent, such was the demand for shelter and homes. There were then 50 stores in the place, 8 large forwarding houses, 12 regular inns, 30 groceries, 1 furnace, 2 printing establishments, 30 attorneys, 8 physicians, and 8 ministers. The imports of the town had increased from $588,950 in 1835, to $1,805,277 in 1841; and the exports in the same time from $26,145 to $286,777.

Several grain warehouses had been erected in and previous to 1840. The first wheat sent from Milwaukee was shipped July 8, 1841, on the schooner "Illinois", and consisted of a cargo of 4,000 bushels. It took three days to load it; that amount can now be loaded in about fifteen minutes. The construction of the Red warehouse some years later was considered a great advance, for in it a single horse did the elevating; and still more of an advance was the Blue warehouse, where two horses were used. In the fall of 1848 the first steam elevator was completed.

Milwaukee had no natural water-power. The Milwaukee and Rock River canal was a scheme for connecting the waters of lake Michigan and Rock river. In 1838 Congress granted all the odd-numbered sections along the proposed route; this land the territory was to sell, devoting the proceeds to building the canal. Notwithstanding conflicting legislation and interests, contracts were let and considerable work was done. During the summer of 1842 a dam was constructed across the Milwaukee river, above the present Racine Street, or Humboldt Avenue, bridge. In December of that year this dam was closed up, and water was turned into the canal, which had been dug from near the present Chestnut Street bridge, in the second ward, to the dam. This gave a good water-power, and public attention was drawn from the canal to the water-power. Business at once became very brisk along this mile of canal. The next year saw-mills and factories were opened along it, and the completion of the rest of the canal was little thought of. Finally the time for completing it, ten years from June 18, 1838, elapsed, and all rights and privileges were thus forfeited; and afterward, by act of Congress, all unsold canal lands were given to the state of Wisconsin for educational purposes, after paying certain small debts from the proceeds of their sale. Thus the city and the state profited, the former getting a good dam and water-power, the latter many thousand acres of land, while the two counties through which the canal was to pass were the losers, since their settlement and development were greatly hindered by the failure of the enterprise.

The dam built was 480 feet long, 18 feet high, and 85 feet wide. It was a very solid and substantial piece of work. Lots on the canal sold at from $10 to $25 per linear foot, while water-privileges were to bring a perpetual rental of $75 per year for 100 cubic feet of water per minute. In 1849 there were 5 flouring-mills propelled by water. A steam flour-mill, the first in Milwaukee, had been built in 1847, with 17 run of stone, each run capable of turning out 80 to 100 barrels of flour per day, and consuming 7,000 bushels of wheat; many others have since been built.

The pioneer brewery in Milwaukee was erected in 1840 on the lake front at the foot of Huron street. The first firm soon built up a trade extending throughout the territory, and even reaching as far southward as Chicago. In the same year a brewery was started on the south side; others followed, and within a few years the brewery interests of Milwaukee assumed vast proportions. To-day the brewing of liquors is an industry of great importance.

The first settlement here was established about 2½ miles from the mouth of the river, although but one-half mile from the lake shore. There was a bar at the mouth of the river, but it was narrow, and there was but a small amount of drifting sand which might accumulate here by any agitation of the water. The water within the river was very deep, and the shores were bold; outside the bar the lake deepened, in the distance of 6 or 8 rods, to 10 or 12 feet of water, and then went off with a bold descent, with clay bottom, having no tendency to wash, drift, or change its position. For this reason it was thought that a harbor could easily be made.

In 1836 two lieutenants of the United States topographical engineer corps were ordered to make a survey here. They reported in favor of the "straight-cut" scheme, i. e., of cutting through the narrow point that for some distance separates the river from the lake, and making a new mouth for the river, which would greatly shorten the distance from the village to the lake.

Meantime the commerce of the little town was rapidly growing. In 1835 but 2 steamers and 80 other vessels arrived here, while in 1836 there were 314 arrivals. In this latter year $45,000 was subscribed for the purpose of having a steamboat built to ply between this place and Chicago. She arrived in June, 1837, but was lost in the following November. In 1837 a steamboat was built here; it was a cheap scow of 50 tons burden, furnished with an engine of small power, and fit only for river work. It was the third craft of any kind constructed here, a schooner and a sloop having been built in the previous year.

The steamboat arrivals in 1839 were said to number 182, and in 1840, 174. The citizens were complaining loudly because the fine river front was practically unavailable on account of its inaccessibility. Communication with the lower lake ports in 1841 was so irregular that great inconvenience was experienced. The weary fight for federal help drove the merchants and vessel-owners to a more self-reliant course of action, and in 1843 the first pier at Milwaukee was constructed. It was placed at the foot of Huron street.

In the harbor appropriation bill passed in the spring of 1843, $30,000 was appropriated for Milwaukee. When the news reached the town the joy showed itself in a procession, a dinner, and a ball; but it did not last long, because it was soon clear that this appropriation had no reference to the survey of 1836, and that a new survey was necessary. The engineer who took charge reported against the "straight cut" and in favor of piers at the mouth of the river. The people, however, were unanimous for the straight cut, and a corporation loan of $15,000 was voted in April, 1844, for improving the straight cut.

Meantime government work had proceeded on the public improvement at the mouth of the river in the summer of 1843; piers were extended out nearly 1,000 feet. By the close of navigation in the fall of that year, vessels of 6 feet draft were able to enter the river safely. In May, 1844, the brig "Virginia", drawing 7 feet of water, came up the river without meeting obstruction; and the harbor presented a busy scene, with numerous craft lying at the several docks. In this year the piers were extended out farther.

From time to time Congress appropriated comparatively small sums of money for the improvement of the old harbor, but in 1852 that body appropriated $15,000 for the improvement of the straight cut. Local energy once more took up the case, and the state legislature was induced to empower the city authorities to levy a direct tax upon the property of the citizens, this sum to be applied to improving the cut. Much time was necessarily lost in this proceeding, and it was 1855 before this sum was available. The whole was superintended by the United States engineer assigned here. The work was begun and prosecuted vigorously in 1856. Its total cost to the city from 1855 to 1870, inclusive, was $238,355.79. Piers were built 1,120 feet in length, and the channel was dredged for its full length and width to the depth of 12 feet. No further steps for this improvement were taken by the United States government till 1866, when $48,283.17 was appropriated. In 1870, $40,000 more, and in 1871, $38,000 more were given by Congress. Other smaller sums have been expended here from time to time. Since these improvements Milwaukee has had a superior harbor.

As Milwaukee gradually developed, better land as well as lake communication with the older settlements was necessary. Mails were sent overland. The early roads were but openings through timber or over prairie, with logs laid across swamps and marshes, or rudely thrown over small and unfordable streams. The early files of Milwaukee newspapers contain weekly complaints of the non-arrival on time of through stages; but these stages were always loaded.

The first plank-road company was chartered in 1846; in the next few years a number of roads were built. In 1854 there were seven of them tributary to Milwaukee, with a total length finished of 139 miles. On the building of railroads, plank-roads, except for local purposes, ceased to be in demand. The first railroad company was chartered in 1847. Under the name of the "Milwaukee and Mississippi Railroad Company" it ran its first train in February, 1851, from Milwaukee to Waukesha. This was the first piece of railway built in Wisconsin. The advent of the railroad gave even greater prosperity to Milwaukee.

Resuming the thread of current events in Milwaukee, we find that in the spring of 1843 the small-pox in an alarming form made its appearance here. So rapidly did it spread that a pest-house was established. Three years later, in the fall of 1846, the pest-house was again called into requisition, and as the disease continued its virulence in the spring of 1847, the common council passed an ordinance rendering vaccination imperative. A committee was also appointed to make house-to-house inspections. By these means the spread of the disease was checked.

The jealousy between the east and west sides, already mentioned, found its vent in a quarrel over the means of communication between the two. They disputed over the building of bridges, and after these had been built the division of the cost of the maintenance furnished a pretext for continuing the quarrel. It finally culminated in a riot, which took place May 8, 1845, when the west-siders tore down the west end of the Chestnut Street bridge, and rendered the Oneida Street bridge impassable. This party desired a change in the location of the bridges, and the east-ward people had merely opposed this; but now the latter conceived a violent hatred of all bridges. This resulted, May 28, in another riot, in which the east-siders destroyed the draw of the Springfield Street bridge and tore down the bridge over the Menomonee.

The bridge matter being relegated to separate action, a city charter was passed by the legislature, which the village ratified. This act was approved on the 31st of January, 1846.

The new municipality was divided into 5 wards, a number which remained constant for the next six years, there being in that time no substantial changes in the corporate limits of the city. But after 1852, up to 1856, there seemed to be a general outward movement of the young city, and it threw out its arms so vigorously that it boasted 8 wards. In 1857 three of the wards increased in size toward the west, and the west side added another ward. The next ward created was in 1872. In 1873 two more were added, and in 1874 another and the last accession was made.

The elective officers of the new city were mayor, treasurer, marshal, and police justice for the city, and 3 aldermen, 1 assessor, 1 constable, and 1 justice of the peace for each ward. All other officers were chosen by the common council. In 1852 the office of city attorney was made elective, and in the same year that of city controller came into existence. The office of city marshal was abolished and that of chief of police was created in 1858. In the next year a municipal court, with a judge elected for six years, was substituted for the police justice. In 1858 the common council was divided into two distinct bodies—the board of councillors, consisting of two persons from each ward, and the board of aldermen, one from each ward. During 1859 the first superintendent of city schools went into office. It was not until 1869 that the city work, surveying, engineering, and street-inspecting were fairly concentrated. In that year a city engineer was first appointed, in conjunction with the board of public works. Up to 1878 the mayor appointed a board of health, consisting of 5 aldermen, to take charge of the sanitary condition of the city. This was the nucleus in 1878 for a separate department of the city government, whose head is the health commissioner.

The first record of any sanitary action taken by the city authorities was an ordinance passed by the common council, June 29, 1846, whereby 5 physicians were appointed, being one for each ward, to attend the poor of their respective districts. The board of health was established in August of that year.

In consequence of the defeat of the republican element in Germany in 1848, the number of emigrants from that source to Milwaukee was very large; and the failure of the potato crop in Ireland in 1847, and the penal measures adopted by the British government in that and succeeding years, caused a great influx of immigrants.

For many months previous to the spring of 1849, before the epidemic reached Milwaukee, cholera appeared in San Antonio, New Orleans, Saint Louis, and Cincinnati, gradually coming north. The public thoroughfares were ordered to be cleansed of impurities. The city authorities took the greatest precautions against the spread of the epidemic, both before it broke out and after its first appearance. It broke out in all portions of the city and in the country adjacent at nearly the same period in July. On the 31st of August, when the scourge had passed by, the board of health reported that out of the 209 cases, 104 had proved fatal.

The cholera appeared at almost the same date the next year, and was at its height about the first of September. The effects were even more serious than in the previous summer. Finally 300 deaths were reported.

Milwaukee escaped the cholera in 1851, and had but few cases in the two following years. In 1854 the epidemic was severe, but not so fatal or so general as in 1849 or 1850.

The city was not again visited by any epidemic until 1868, when small-pox appeared. From December 1, 1868, to April 1, 1869, there were 500 cases of this disease reported to the health office, and this was not more than two-thirds of the whole number of cases in the city. From that time on it gradually decreased until October, in which month only one case was reported. In 1871, 774 cases of small-pox were reported, 263 of which proved fatal. In 1872 the number of cases was 616, of which 217 proved fatal. During the year 5,000 persons were vaccinated at the expense of the city. In 1873 there were 114 deaths from small-pox, since which time the city has been comparatively free from the ravages of this disease.

When Milwaukee became a city her population was 9,450; in 1847 it was 14,061; in 1848, 15,598. In the last-named year the division by nationality was: American, 6,969; German, 5,708; Irish, 2,487; and the proportion has not greatly changed since.

Gas was introduced into the city in 1852.

The first street pavements were laid in 1854, cobble-stones being the material used.

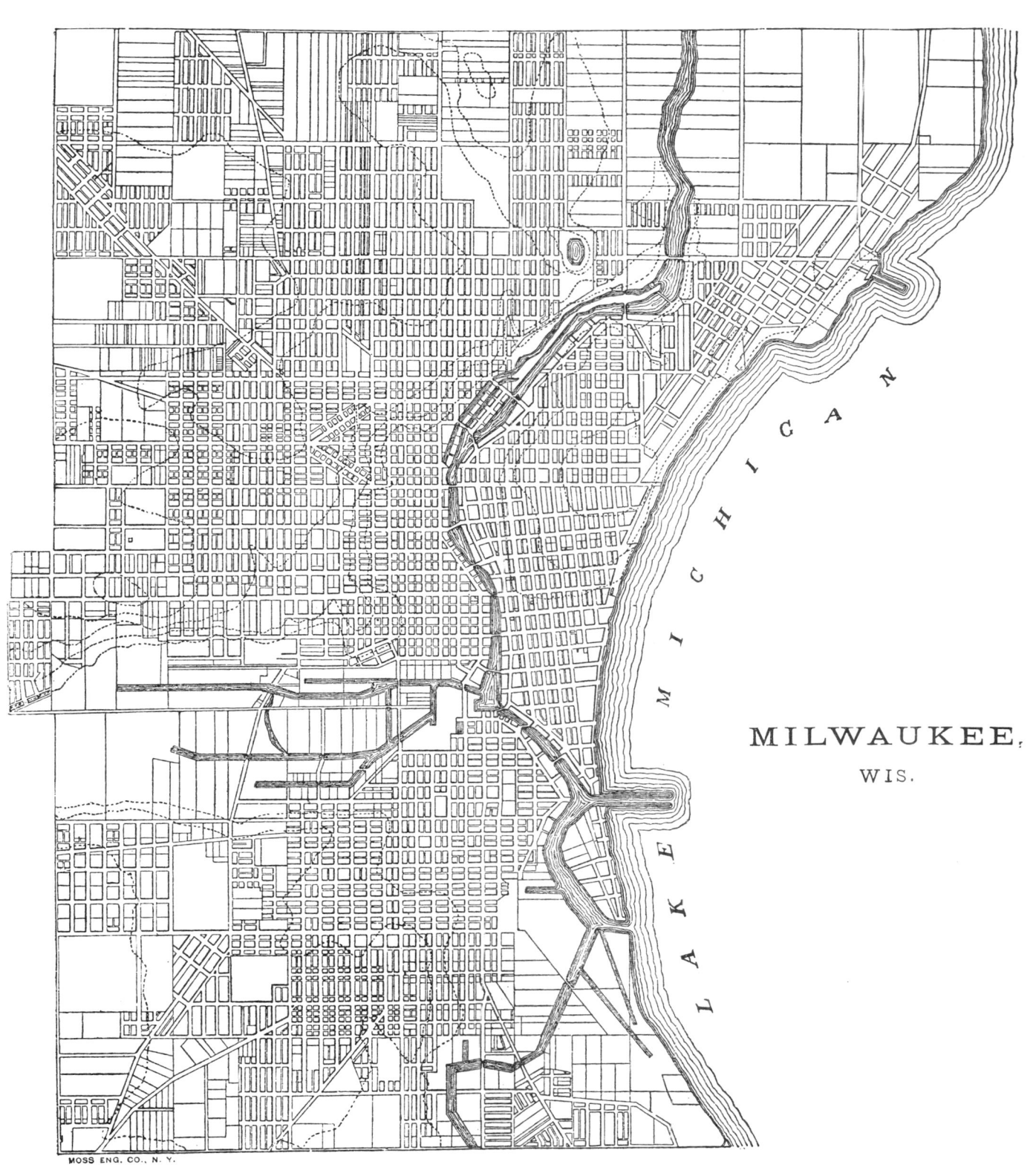

MILWAUKEE,
WIS.

MOSS ENG. CO., N. Y.

The only very disastrous fire that has ever visited the city broke out August 24, 1854. The total loss was $381,900, and insurance, $233,050.

The first steam fire-engine here was purchased in 1861. A paid fire department was substituted for the old volunteer department in 1866.

The panic of 1857 seriously affected Milwaukee. Its most serious cause of embarrassment was the delinquency of the railroads in meeting the interest due on their bonds. The floating debt of the city was in bad shape, and trouble followed; but by 1868 the city's finances were in much better condition.

The first street railway was opened to travel in May, 1860.

Saturday, September 8, 1860, will ever be recognized as the saddest day in the city's history. On the previous Thursday evening a band of 400 excursionists, comprising some of the most prominent Irish citizens and many members of the city military companies, left Milwaukee on a steamboat for Chicago. On the return trip on Saturday morning, when only 16 miles from Chicago and 4 or 5 miles from land, the boat ran into a schooner, and soon sank. A storm had just come up, and the scenes which followed were horrible. To make the sad story short, 225 lives were lost, all of persons who were either residents of Milwaukee or who had friends there.

On the 4th of April, 1866, the dam of the Rock River Canal Company gave way, carrying off two bridges and damaging others, flooding mills, and entailing a loss of $130,000.

The present water-works system was planned about ten years ago. Water was first pumped into the reservoir October 24, 1873, the length of pipe then laid being about 55 miles.

The most expensive improvement ever undertaken here was the work generally known as the Menomonee Improvements, which consisted in converting an extensive tract of morass, principally on the south side, to commercial use. It was begun in 1869. The cost was about $200,000, and 13,700 linear feet of dockage was by it rendered available for shippers.

The present court-house, the headquarters of the city and county governments, was begun in 1870 and finished in 1873.

The public library was established by legislative act, February 7, 1878.

MILWAUKEE IN 1880.

The following statistical accounts, nearly all of which were collected and forwarded by John Johnston, esq., of Milwaukee, indicate the present condition of the city:

LOCATION, ETC.

Milwaukee, the commercial metropolis of the state of Wisconsin, lies in latitude 43° 4' north, longitude 88° west from Greenwich, on the west shore of lake Michigan, about 100 miles north of the southern end of the lake. The bluffs along the lake in the northeasterly part of the city rise to a height of 109 feet above the lake surface, while in the northwesterly part of the city the ground rises 175 feet above the lake. The lowest point, the beach on the lake shore, is 500 feet above sea-level.

The city lies on Milwaukee bay, a semicircular indentation of lake Michigan, which is 6 miles across and 3 miles deep, the north and south capes affording an excellent protection to shipping. No trade is handled now as formerly from piers run into the bay, but all commerce is carried on along the docks of the Milwaukee, Menomonee, and Keinnickinnic rivers, whose united streams fall into the lake soon after their confluence. The channel of the united streams is 230 feet wide, with an average depth of 14 feet. The Milwaukee river, which is the main river, has the above depth and width for 2 miles, through the heart of the city. The Menomonee river was originally an extensive marsh, but is now being dredged into canals and slips, properly docked, and affording suitable sites for coal and lumber yards and all factories, having railroad as well as canal accommodations. The same is true of the Keinnickinnic river. There are over 10 miles navigable within the city limits.

RAILROAD COMMUNICATIONS.

Milwaukee has the following railroad facilities:

The Chicago, Milwaukee, and Saint Paul railroad, to Chicago; to Running Water, on the Missouri river, opposite the mouth of the Nebraska, via Prairie du Chien, on the Mississippi, through Northern Iowa and Southern Dakota, with branches to Sioux Falls in Dakota, and Sioux City in Iowa; to Saint Paul and Minneapolis via La Croix, with branches to Ortonville, Mankato, and Flandreau, in Minnesota; to Oshkosh, Winneconne, and Berlin, Wisconsin; and Davenport and Fort Atkinson, Iowa, in Rock Island, Illinois—making a total of 3,009 miles.

The Chicago and Northwestern railroad, to Chicago, to Ishpeming, Michigan, via Menomonee branch, to Saint Paul, Minnesota; to Watertown, Dakota, etc.—making a total of 1,509 miles.

The Wisconsin Central railroad, to Green Bay, Ashland, and Eau Claire, Wisconsin—making a total of 444 miles.

The Milwaukee, Lake Shore, and Western railroad, to Wausau, Wisconsin, via Appleton, with branch to Oshkosh—making a total of 220 miles.

All the above roads, except the Chicago and Northwestern, have their headquarters here, and the total number of miles of railway centering in the city is 5,182.

TRIBUTARY COUNTRY.

The country immediately tributary to Milwaukee, and with which it has a local trade, is an agricultural one, studded with flourishing towns and villages. The crops raised are such as are common in the Northwest, and in some localities tobacco and hops are cultivated. The region is well watered, and the numerous water-powers on the several streams are utilized for grist and other mills. Though this is, strictly speaking, the country with which the city has a *local* trade, Milwaukee has intimate commercial relations with all that large expanse of territory touched by the several lines of railroads diverging from this point.

TOPOGRAPHY.

The city of Milwaukee is situated on three great promontories, separated by the valleys of the Milwaukee and Menomonee rivers, and the Keimickinnic creek, which join each other and lake Michigan in the south central part of the city. The suburb, Bay View, occupies a fourth prominence. In recent geological times the whole site of the city was a gently undulating plain, continuous with that which now slopes easily upward for many miles westward. Into this the Milwaukee river, flowing from the north, nearly parallel to the lake, the Menomonee from the west, and the Keimickinnic from the southwest, have cut their valleys to an average depth of about 100 feet, carving into relief the existing prominences.

The outline of the lake here curves deeply landward, forming a beautiful open bay. Except in the vicinity of the harbor proper, which lies within the mouths of the three streams, the lake frontage is formed of bold bluffs from 40 to 50 feet in height. From the nearly level crest of these bluffs the surface slopes by easy gradient westward to the Milwaukee river. On the opposite side, after passing a moderately level flood-plain, the surface rises to a plateau, almost 100 feet above the river, which stretches backward into the general plain of the surrounding country. On the south side, between the Menomonee and the Keimickinnic, is a similar river from flood-plain to plateau. The slopes, therefore, afford an efficient natural drainage, except near the mouths of the Menomonee and the Keimickinnic, where there is some low land, which is being filled artificially.

The subsoil is in the main a marly clay, freely pervious to water or gases. Beneath this in portions of the city there lie beds of sand and gravel, which in turn repose on strong clay. The rock is deeply concealed in general, but appears in the 4th ward, at the base of the bluffs facing the Menomonee, and at one point in the south suburb. Both outcrops are Niagara limestone. It is quite possible that the Hamilton cement rock may underlie the northern portion of the city, as a valuable quarry has been opened here, from which is taken a rock which makes a good hydraulic cement.

The country within a radius of 5 miles from the city is open, with probably 20 per cent. of timber on it, and there are no large ponds or marshes. The soil is diversified, but the greater part is a dark loam resting on clay subsoil, with occasional small areas of sand, and larger areas of brown sandy loam lying upon a gravelly subsoil. There are also occasional ridges of stiff clay that extend over limited areas. The elevations within this area are about the same as those of the city, though 20 miles back the land rises to a height of from 300 to 400 feet above the lake.

CLIMATE.

Highest recorded summer temperature, 98°; highest summer temperature in average year, 93°. Lowest recorded winter temperature, —25°; lowest winter temperature in average year, —20°. The average coldest mean temperature during 20 years is 22.76°, and the warmest, 70.21°—the average mean for the year being 46.18°.

The most important local climatic influence arises from lake Michigan, its waters very markedly subduing the severity of winter and the heat of summer. During the latter season lake breezes are prevalent, and they frequently reach back 20, 30, and occasionally 60 miles into the interior. The temporary influence of the lake is manifest in the native vegetation, and extends on the one hand and limits on the other the available cultivated varieties. The influence of the lake gives a frequency, if not predominance, to easterly winds, that are unusual in this general region of prevalent westerly winds.

Neither marshes nor elevated lands exert a sensible climatic influence. The former prevalence of forest added to the moisture derived from the lake, but this has been very essentially modified by clearing and cultivation.

STREETS.

The total length of streets in the city is 231.83 miles. There are 9 stationary bridges—4 of iron, 5 of wood; 17 swing bridges—9 of iron, 8 of wood; and 1 combination float bridge. Of the streets, one-quarter of a mile is paved with broken stone, 25⅘ miles with wood, and 150 miles with gravel. The cost per square yard for each, as nearly as it can be estimated, is, for gravel, 35 cents; common wood pavement, 80 cents; wood blocks, Thilmany process, $1 30; and broken stone, $1 25. Of the wood streets, 1½ mile is paved with blocks of wood, prepared by the Thilmany process, and it is found that when this pavement is properly laid it will require but little repair during the first eight years. On ordinary wood pavement the average annual cost of repairs, after the first three years, is about 20 per cent. of the original cost.

The greater portion of the sidewalks are constructed of pine planks; a few walks are laid with flagstones, and in a few small sections cement is used. On all the graveled streets gutters are paved with cobble-stones, while on the other streets they are of the same material as the roadway.

Nearly all of the residence streets have rows of trees planted parallel to the curb. This work is done by the abutting property-owners at their own expense, and persons planting trees are required by ordinance to place the same in line two feet inside the curb. About 6 miles of streets have grass-plots on both sides.

The work of constructing streets is done by contract. Last year there were 13¼ miles of streets improved and paved at a total cost of $191,849 98. In the repair of streets most of the material needed is purchased by contract, and put into the work by laborers employed by the city. The work is under charge of the board of public works, and the annual cost of repairs is about $40,000. It is stated that formerly the street repairs were done under contract, but the present method seems to give the best results.

HORSE-RAILROADS, ETC.

There are 30 miles of horse-railroads in the city, using 101 cars and 541 horses, and giving employment to 174 men. Single fares are 5 cents each, but a package of 100 tickets is sold for $4. There were 4,014,765 passengers carried during the year.

There is 1 omnibus line, with 9 vehicles and 18 horses, and employing 15 men, that carries passengers at rates varying from 25 to 50 cents.

WATER-WORKS.

The water-works are owned by the city, and their total cost is $2,149,000. Water is taken from lake Michigan, through a conduit 200 feet long and 36 inches in diameter, and pumped into a distributing reservoir of 21,000,000 gallons capacity, about 150 feet above the lake level. The inlet and outlet to the reservoir are connected by mains in the bottom, so that direct pumping can be resorted to in case of necessity. In addition there is a stand-pipe for the high-service, 4 feet in diameter, 130 feet high, and inclosed in a stone tower. The average pressure in the mains varies from 36 to 60 pounds to the square inch.

The amount of water pumped per diem ranges from 10,000,000 to 14,000,000 gallons, the average being 12,269,000 per day. The average cost of raising 1,000,000 gallons one foot high is 20 cents.

The total expenditure during the year past was $83,768 39, of which $62,510 30 was for maintenance, and $21,258 09 for construction; and the total receipts were $161,993 54, the amount received from water-rates being $131,634 04. A few water-meters are used, but they have not been set long enough to show what effect they have on the consumption of water. There are nearly 91 miles of distribution mains, 7,524 taps, and 718 hydrants.

GAS.

The gas-works are owned by a private corporation. The daily average production is 275,000 cubic feet. The charge per 1,000 feet is, to small consumers, $2 25; to large consumers who pay promptly, $2; and to the city, $1 75. The city pays annually $35 ($31 for gas and $4 for rent of post) for each street-lamp, 1,368 in number.

PUBLIC BUILDINGS.

The city owns and occupies for municipal purposes, wholly or in part, the city hall, one-half of the county court-house, 24 school buildings, 3 police stations, and 8 fire-engine houses. The total cost of the municipal buildings (exclusive of the court-house) belonging to the city is $976,000. The old city hall cost $25,000. The court-house, owned by the city and county, is built of Lake Superior sandstone, and cost over $600,000. All the municipal offices are in this building.

Among the public buildings may be mentioned the United States custom-house, which contains the post-office, United States courts, etc. It is built of stone quarried at Athens, Illinois, and stands at the corner of Wisconsin and Milwaukee streets. The new county court-house, the Academy of Music, the Opera House, Mitchell's bank, etc., are all fine buildings and architectural ornaments to the city.

PUBLIC PARKS AND PLEASURE-GROUNDS.

The municipality owns no public park of any size. Six of the wards in the city have small parks of 2 or 3 acres each, and the 7th ward has a beautiful slope of some 7 acres, on the shore of the lake. There are also several very handsome parks belonging to private persons on the shore of lake Michigan, and on the banks of the Milwaukee and Menomonee rivers, that are open to the public.

The grounds of the "Northwestern Branch, National Home for Disabled Volunteer Soldiers," are situated about a mile southwest of the city limits. They embrace some 400 acres, and are largely used by the people of Milwaukee as a place of recreation and pleasure. The women of Wisconsin had raised the sum of $100,000 for the establishment at Milwaukee of a home for all disabled Wisconsin volunteers; but when Congress, in 1865, established the National Asylum, with 3 branches, this sum was used for the purchase of land so as to insure the location of one of the branches here. With the exception of 250 acres that are reserved for farming purposes, the whole tract has been laid out as a park. The buildings and grounds are managed by a commandant appointed by the United States government, and all expenses, about $125,000 per annum, are provided for by congressional appropriation. No account is kept of the number of persons visiting the grounds, but it is estimated that about 100,000 of the citizens of Milwaukee visit the park during the year.

PLACES OF AMUSEMENT.

There are 3 theaters in the city, as follows: Academy of Music, with a seating capacity of 1,400; Opera House, seating 1,000; and the German theater, seating 600. The amount of the license for theatrical performances is left to the option of the mayor, and is usually nominal, being large only when some very objectionable performance calls for discouragement. The buildings or halls used for theatrical purposes pay no license as such.

Of concert-halls or lecture-rooms, not connected with churches, some of which are used at times for theatrical performances, there are: Second Ward Rink hall, seating 2,500; North Side Turner hall, seating 1,000; South and West Side Turner hall, seating 700; Turner hall, on the east side, seating 500; Bouaccord hall, seating 500; Progress hall, seating 800; Saint Andrew's hall, seating 400; Burman's hall, Liffe hall, and Concordia hall, of the same seating capacity (400); Semi hall, seating 500; and Dickinson's hall, seating 300.

Among the concert- and beer-gardens, Schlitz Brewing Company park is situated in the thickly settled part of the city, and has an area of 7 acres. It has a capacity for and can entertain 20,000 persons at one time. The concert-hall in the grounds has a capacity for 5,000 persons. The Milwaukee gardens, also in the thickly peopled part of the city, has an area of 2 acres, and a concert-hall, with a seating capacity of 400. In the suburbs there are Lueddemann's, on the lake, with an area of 20 acres, but no improvements; Mineral Spring park, area 33 acres, on the Milwaukee river; Miller's garden, area 6 acres; Greenfield's park, area 18 acres; and Ferny Brae, on the lake, area 6 acres. This last has a good house for entertainment. No record is kept of the patronage of any of these resorts.

DRAINAGE.

Milwaukee is now very largely sewered, in accordance with a systematic plan as shown by the accompanying map.

Before the adoption of this system the surface drainage of the city was effected with the aid of paved stone gutters from 5 to 6 feet wide, carrying the flow in some cases to natural water-courses or ravines, and in others to the river. The lower part of the city was drained through the alleys by means of wooden box-sewers, 4 feet across, save that brick sewers were laid in or across a few of the principal streets.

The present sewers are built very largely of vitrified earthenware or cement pipes, the choice between these materials being left to the contractor.

The sewers are ventilated only by means of perforated manhole covers and through ventilation pipes built in with the catch-basins, as shown in the accompanying illustration. It is difficult to see what better purpose is effected by this arrangement than would be received by carrying the 12-inch pipe directly into the catch basin at the water-line. The grade of the sewers at the outlets of the river is generally from 6 inches to 1 foot below low-water mark, so that they are sometimes submerged as much as 3 feet. All sewage flows directly or indirectly into one of the rivers intersecting the town. The need for removing deposits by hand is confined chiefly to the lower parts of the city, where the grade is slight, and to the catch-basins. This cleansing is ordinarily done once a year, in autumn or winter. In the upper parts of the city the sewers have sometimes to be cleansed by flushing.

The cost of minor sewers is assessed upon the abutting property to the amount of $1 60 or less per linear foot, one-half the actual cost being charged on each side of the street. Street and alley crossings are paid for out of the general sewer fund, as is the cost of main and other sewers in excess of $1 60 per foot, the cost of which is so assessed on the property. The contractor receives certificates of the board of public works, being a lien against such property, entered upon the tax-list and collected at the close of the year with the general city and other taxes.

Assessment is made on the basis of frontage, not of area or valuation.

The contract prices for sewers in 1880, including manholes, is as follows: Pipe sewers—12-inch, $1 14 per linear foot; 15-inch, $1 48 per linear foot; 18-inch, $1 66 per linear foot. Brick sewers—24-inch, $1 71; 30-inch, $2 68; 36-inch, $3 45; 42-inch, $3 56; 72-inch, $8 75. Catch-basins, $45 each.

Based on specific authority contained in the city charter, the following ordinance, regulating the construction and use of public and private drains, was enacted by the council in October, 1874:

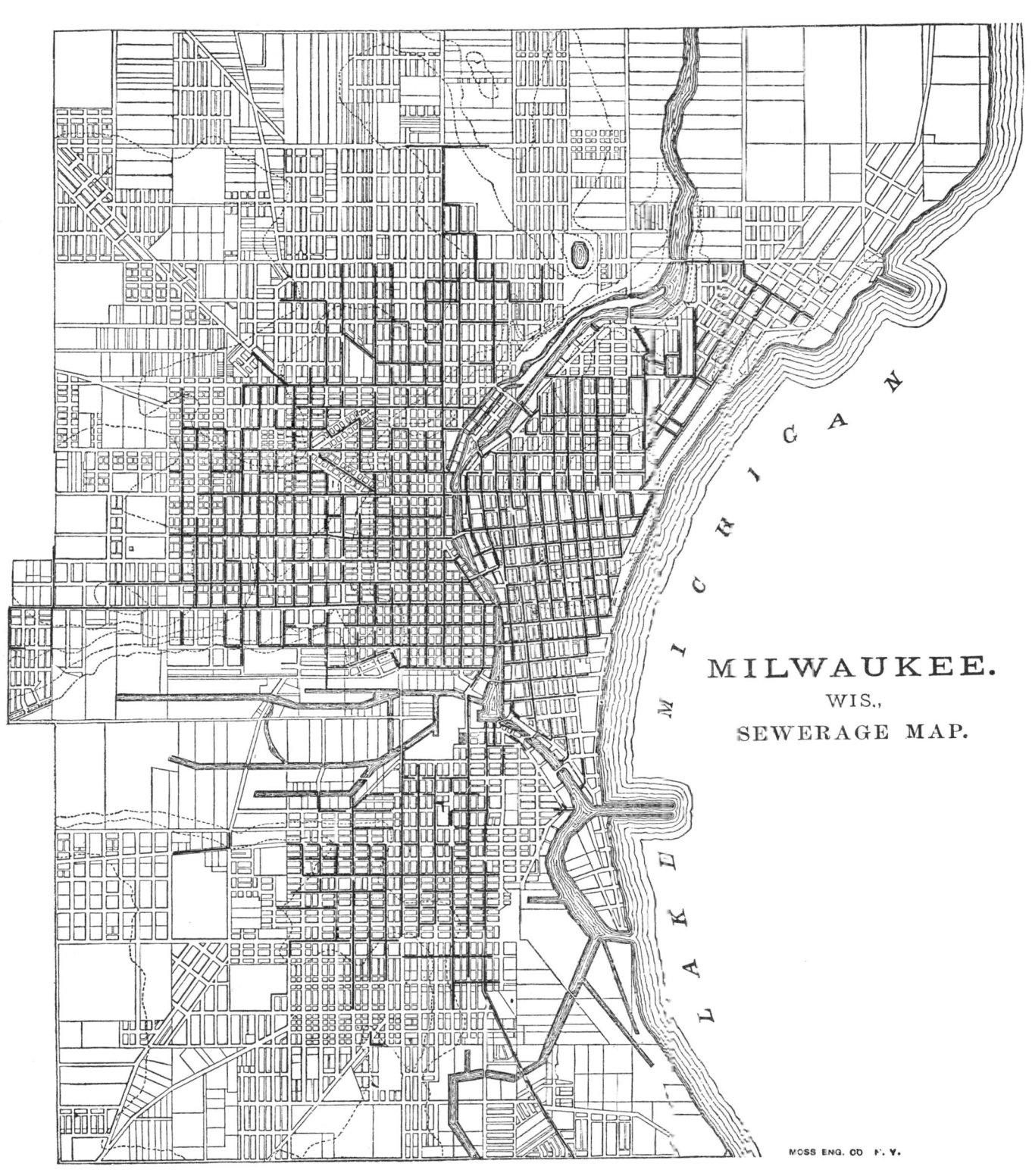

MILWAUKEE.
WIS.,
SEWERAGE MAP.

LAKE MICHIGAN

An ordinance to regulate the construction and use of public sewers and private drains.

The mayor and common council of the city of Milwaukee do ordain as follows:

SECTION 1. Any person who shall uncover or excavate under or around the brick or pipe sewers laid in this city for any purpose whatever, without the written consent of the board of public works, shall be subject to a fine of not more than five hundred dollars ($500); the person or persons by whom the work is done and their employers shall be deemed guilty of a violation of this section.

SEC. 2. Any person who shall make any connection with or opening into the brick or pipe sewers laid in this city, without having first obtained a written permit in each case from said board, shall be subject to a fine of not more than five hundred dollars for each offense, which fine shall be recoverable against the owners of the property in which such drain is made, or against the person or persons making it the same or causing it to be made, or their employers.

SEC. 3. The board of public works shall grant licenses to such persons as they may deem qualified to lay, alter, or repair any parts of house drain or drains, catch-basins, or strainer of said drain or drains, cesspool or water-closet connected with any brick or pipe sewer belonging to this city; and any person who shall do such work without being duly licensed to perform the same by said board, shall be subject to a fine not exceeding five hundred dollars for each offense.

SEC. 4. It shall be the duty of any person or persons using or constructing any private drain, sewer, cesspool, water-closet pipe, or any other pipe connecting with or emptying into any brick or pipe drain or sewer belonging to the city, to construct the same with proper traps when they enter houses, and otherwise construct and use the same strictly in conformity with the directions of the board of public works. Any person who shall use or construct any drain or sewer in a different manner from that directed by the board of public works or in violation of the order of said board, shall be subject to a fine of not more than five hundred dollars, which shall be recoverable against any person or persons constructing said sewers or their employers; and the owner of the lot or lots, or premises in which said work is constructed or used, shall be considered as authorizing such construction or use and liable to such penalty. The license of any person found constructing private sewers or drains in a manner different from the rules of said board shall be taken away from him.

SEC. 5. Any owner or occupant of premises who shall deposit or cause to be deposited any substance such as garbage, grease, rags, sand, earth, or such other substances as the said board may find it necessary to exclude from said sewers, pipes, house drains, or catch-basins connected with said sewers, or allow any substance to flow into the same in such a manner as to obstruct the same, shall be liable to a penalty of not more than five hundred dollars for each offense, and shall be liable for the cost of removing said obstructions.

SEC. 6. Said board and their authorized agents shall have free and unobstructed access to any part of the premises where house drains, cesspools, or water-closets connected with or draining into said sewers are laid, for the purpose of examining the construction, condition, and usage of the same, and making necessary alterations or repairs at any time of the day between the hours of 7 o'clock a. m. and 6 o'clock p. m., and any owner, occupant, or other person, on refusing to allow any officer or agent of said board access to any premises for such purposes, shall be liable to a fine of not more than five hundred dollars.

SEC. 7. Any person who shall willfully or maliciously injure or obstruct any sewers, house drain, cesspool, catch-basin, or any pipe laid or connected under the supervision or direction of said board, shall be liable to a penalty of not more than five hundred dollars, and to pay all expenses incurred on account of repairs and damages arising from the same.

Passed October 19, 1874.

In pursuance of the above ordinance the board of public works has issued specific rules for the laying of private drains, from which the following extracts are made:

APPLICATION FOR DRAINS.

*   *   *   *   *   *   *   *

No drain pipe can be extended from work previously done and accepted, or new connections of any kind be made with such work, unless previous notice of at least twenty-four hours is given to board of public works.

No work of laying drains can be commenced or continued without [*sic*] the permit is on the ground, in the hands of the drain-layer or one employed by him.

RULES FOR LAYING DRAINS.

*   *   *   *   *   *   *   *   *

No pipes or other materials for the drains can be used until they have been examined and approved by the city engineer, or by one of his assistants, or by a duly authorized inspector, and all pipes used from the connection with the sewer to the line of the lots to be of hydraulic cement or vitrified stone.

The least inclination that can be allowed for the water-closet, kitchen, or other drains of not over 6 inches in diameter, liable to receive solid substances, is one-half an inch in two feet, and for cellar and other drains to receive water only, one-quarter of an inch in two feet. All drains to be laid at a grade of not over one-half an inch in two feet between the sewer and the sidewalks.

*   *   *   *   *   *   *   *   *

The inside of every drain after it is laid must be left perfectly clean and smooth through the entire length.

In case it shall be necessary to connect a drain pipe with a public sewer where no junction is left in the public sewer, the new connection with public sewer can only be made either by one of the employés of the board or when the officer of the board as named in regulation third is present to see the whole work done.

*   *   *   *   *   *   *   *   *

In case a water- or gas-pipe should come in the way of a drain, the question of passing over or under the water- or gas-pipe, or of raising or lowering it, must be determined by one of the officers named in regulation third. In no case can the pipe-layer be allowed to decide the question himself.

No exhaust from steam-engines can be connected with private or public drains, and no blow-off from steam-boilers can be connected without special permission from the board or its engineers.

*   *   *   *   *   *   *   *   *

Such information as the board has with regard to the position and junctions will be furnished to the drain-layer, but at their risk as to the accuracy of the same.

When any change of direction is made in the pipe, either in horizontal or vertical direction, curves must be used. No pipe can be clipped in any case.

Milwaukee has been confronted by a very serious problem in connection with the disposal of its sewage and of the foul waste of packing-houses and other establishments along the banks of the Menomonee river. The rivers discharge together mainly through, an artificial channel, and there is at times of low water little perceptible current in any of them. The Menomonee river, owing to the large amount of slaughtering, etc., carried on along its banks, is especially foul.

Some of its foulness is doubtless swept by the winds into Milwaukee river, and the sewage and surface wash of the city are an important element in the general contribution of filth.

Prior to 1880 various projects for the improvement of the rivers as well as of the general sanitary condition of the city were much discussed, and in November, 1879, a commission of engineers consisting of E. S. Chesbrough, Moses Lane, and G. E. Waring, jr., was employed to consider the whole subject and to recommend measures of relief.

The report of this commission was as follows:

CHICAGO, Illinois, *January* 12, 1880.

Messrs. HILBERT, BLODGETT, CASGRAIN, and ABERT, commissioners of public works, and Dr. O. W. WIGHT, commissioner of health, Milwaukee, Wisconsin.

GENTLEMEN: In your communication of December 2, 1879, you submit to us the following problems:

1. The best means of abating the river nuisance, the case being stated as follows: The best method of abating the so-called river nuisance of this city, and to report a definite plan on the same. It is expected of you to recommend through us to the legislative department of the municipal government the best means of abating the nuisance aforesaid. Any required changes in the sewer system of the city may be pointed out in a general and comprehensive way without entering into elaborate and detailed plans.

2. Possible needed alterations in the water-works, stated as follows: If the plan reported by you shall leave the water-supply of the city still liable to pollution from sewage or other deleterious matter, you will then be expected to recommend such changes in the water-works as necessity may require, designating the point where the water shall be taken.

3. The advisability of adopting the plan of your city engineer for a system of intercepting sewers.

After careful consideration of the whole subject we herewith submit the following report: The foulness of the rivers is due, of course, to the fact that they receive the outflow of all the sewers of the city, and the organic waste of the slaughter-houses and packing-houses in the Menomonee valley, while during the dry seasons their current is insufficient to carry these foul matters forward into the lake. There are no means by which these foreign substances can be purified and made inoffensive after being once delivered into the rivers. Their production is a necessary and constant accompaniment of the life and business of the city. The question is simply how to dispose of them otherwise and in such a manner as not to create a nuisance elsewhere. This question is here, as always, one of the gravest connected with municipal administration.

The tendency of the best practice of the world is more and more in the direction of the purification of sewage by application to the land—what is known as irrigation disposal. There are exceptional cases where these matters may, without injury, be delivered into water-courses or great bodies of water. These exceptions, however, are rare. The extent to which a delivery into lake Michigan would be safe with reference to the cleanliness of the shore and the purity of the water-supply can be determined only by actual experience.

In our judgment, while an outlet into the lake may answer a good temporary purpose, and while it may continue for a long time to be satisfactory during the winter and spring, it would not be safe to rely on this alone. The time must come, sooner or later, when at least during the summer and autumn such delivery would create a nuisance. We have, therefore, given much attention to the matter of irrigation disposal. This method is very extensively applied in Great Britain and on the continent of Europe. Its introduction has been greatly favored by the hope that it would result in a profitable return from the agricultural operations connected with it. This hope has in almost every instance been disappointed. Instances of profit have been very rare, and there is no sort of probability that the cost of construction and the considerable pumping charges necessary in the case of Milwaukee would meet with an adequate return from any agricultural result that could be obtained. It would nevertheless be reasonable to expect that the agricultural return would constitute a considerable relief in meeting these charges. This should not, however, be seriously taken into the account. The arguments in favor of irrigation disposal in your case are chiefly of a sanitary character, and they are sufficient. Such disposal would unquestionably secure under a proper adjustment of area of land to amount of sewage a well-purified effluent, so that the drainage from the irrigation farm would enter your streams as pure water. The certainty of this result and the uncertainty as to the permanent result of an outlet into the lake make it important that preliminary steps looking to ultimate irrigation disposal be taken at an early day.

Land well adapted for the purpose south of the Menomonee valley may be found in several quarters, and it can probably be purchased more cheaply now than later. The economical arrangement of the work would require considerable study, and probably the cost would be less and the efficiency greater if ample time were taken for such preliminary preparation. We therefore recommend, in view of the advisability of a resort to irrigation at no distant day, the purchase of about 500 acres of land if to be obtained at a fair price.

In the suggestions given below the work has all been regulated with reference to the addition to the general scheme of the irrigation feature with the least additional cost. So, too, the scheme suggested for immediate adoption is, so far as it goes, precisely what we should advise were irrigation to be undertaken immediately, for in any case it would be necessary to have an alternate arrangement for delivery into the lake during any necessary temporary stoppage of the irrigation works.

We recommend as being less costly, and as requiring less time in construction (but with the limitations indicated above), a temporary delivery of the whole dry-weather flow of the sewers, together with the necessary flushing water and the foul waste of all business establishments, into the lake at a point 1 mile south of the present harbor entrance, and 1,000 feet from the shore.

To select a point of outlet north of the present mouth of the river would increase the liability of offense to the city, and would very greatly increase the danger of contaminating the water-supply. Probably with an outlet at that point a new intake would be absolutely necessary. Sewage matter delivered at the point which we have indicated (1 mile south of the present harbor entrance) would reduce to a minimum the chance of nuisance, and as the lake water contaminated at that point would have the outflow of the river between it and the present crib, the probability is very strong that it would not, except under extraordinary circumstances, reach the water-supply, and even then so diluted as to be inappreciable by the senses.

The sewage of the city can be delivered into the lake only by the aid of pumping, and in order to secure a well-flushed condition of the intercepting sewers, pumping from a depth of 12 or 15 feet will be necessary

We recommend that the pumping works be located in the Kinnickinnic valley, not farther north than the old harbor entrance, and that they be built to scale capable of discharging into the lake, at the point indicated above, the whole dry-weather outflow of the city, together with the necessary flushing water, allowance being made for probable increase of population. The intercepting sewers needed to carry the sewage to this point should, so far as practicable, be laid low enough to admit of their being flushed by the rivers. The interception of the whole east side may be by means of a single sewer lying east of the Milwaukee river. In like manner the whole of the west side and of the south side may be intercepted at one level. The intercepting sewers should accommodate all sections of the city, and should be properly connected and carried across the rivers at suitable points, all delivering at the pumping station. The intercepting sewers should in all cases be connected with the present sewers at points higher than the highest high-water mark, so that during high stages of the lake the river water may not flow back into the intercepting sewers. This arrangement will require that portions of the city lying on low levels, and now connecting with the sewers at points below the high-water mark, should have new connections directly with the intercepting sewers, or with the present sewers at points above where their inverts are at high-water level.

It is our idea that during dry weather, when only foul sewage is flowing in the sewers, the whole of it should be conveyed to the pumping station and sent into the lake, but that during rains, when the flow would be too great for the capacity of the pumps, pumping should cease entirely, allowing the intercepting sewers to fill, and the whole outflow to pass out at the present mouths of the sewers into the rivers. The foul matter discharged at such times would be much diluted, and the rainfall would give a current to the rivers which would render such temporary delivery into them unimportant. After the storm-water has ceased running in the street gutters, pumping can be resumed.

It is proper here to refer to the well-studied plan of intercepting sewers prepared by your city engineer and submitted to our notice. We have deviated from his suggestions so far as to dispense with his middle and high level sewers, for the reason that for the dry-weather flow these would be unnecessary, and that the cost of pumping they would save would not equal the interest on their extra cost. As stated above, the foul ingredients of the whole storm-flow will be so much diluted that it will be safe to discharge it directly into the rivers at a time when their current is increased by rain.

The commissioner of health has submitted to us a suggestion that in addition to the present sewers a separate set of small pipe sewers be laid throughout the city to receive and carry to the pumping station all domestic and manufacturing waste, leaving the present sewers to serve only the purpose of discharging storm-water, street-wash, and subsoil drainage. While we fully appreciate the advantages of a separate set of sewers for house-drainage, we have considered it our duty to take the existing conditions of the city as we find them, and to turn its existing works to the best use in seeking the end desired. If the present sewers are not in good condition they can be made so for much less than the cost of a new system of sewers. Being in good order, it is only necessary to secure their proper flushing to enable them to work with full effect as an aid to the abatement of the river nuisance. We therefore recommend:

1. That all sewers in the city be thoroughly and minutely inspected, a record being made of every imperfection, and that systematic repair or reconstruction be undertaken at once.

2. That at the heads of the sewers there be constructed suitable self-acting flush-tanks to secure the through daily cleansing not only of the dead ends of the sewers where the discharge of the solid matters from house-drains is sometimes too great for the liquid discharge of the houses to carry forward, but also in connection with flushing apparatus advisable to other points, sufficient to remove any deposit of road detritus, etc., which, owing to the inclination, the form, or the roughness of the sewer, may be found to collect. To secure the full flushing effect of the discharge of the flush-tanks and apparatus, and of the natural flow, and to prevent contamination of the soil by sewage matters, the sewers should be made, if they are not so already, as nearly water-tight as possible, especially to the height of their usual flow-line.

3. The establishment of a system of frequent periodic inspection, to be continued until it shall have been demonstrated that the adjustment of the flushing arrangements is effective in every part of the sewers.

These recommendations being carried out, there will be secured the important condition suggested by the commissioner of health: that all foul matters be delivered at the outlet before decomposition has set in, such decomposition now taking place in the sewers, or in the rivers, being probably the most serious factor in the present foul condition of the latter. The evils to be apprehended from the delivery of sewage into the lake will be greatly less serious when the discharge of all organic matter in a fresh condition shall have been secured.

As we are in doubt as to what the future may develop in regard to the necessity for a new point of intake for the water-works, it seems unadvisable now to suggest further expenditure in that direction, which may not be required for a long time if the sewage is delivered in a fresh condition into the lake south of the river outlet, and which surely will not be required after the system of irrigation-disposal is adopted.

At the same time, as such a scheme has been considered, and as its execution may still become expedient, we recommend that the requisite preliminary details upon which to base future calculations as to such work be obtained.

We believe that the complete carrying out of the foregoing suggestions will result in a permanent abatement of what is known as the river nuisance.

Very respectfully,

E. S. CHESBROUGH.
MOSES LANE.
GEO. E. WARING, Jr.

The following is taken from the report for 1880 of the board of public works:

The general influence of the report given above was to induce further investigation and strengthen the friends of interception, and the subject continued to command public attention until the legislature of 1880 took up the subject and passed the bill introduced by Senator Paul, entitled "An act to preserve and promote the public health of the city of Milwaukee," approved March 11, 1880, when public opinion soon concurred upon the execution of the works specified and required by that act as a substitute or a modification of all preceding plans for interception. The general features of this act are: (1) Prohibiting the deposit of any obnoxious or unhealthful matter from any slaughter-house or factory in any of the rivers of our city after July 1, 1880. (2) Making it the duty of the board of public works to provide for the disposal of all filth, refuse offal, obnoxious and unhealthful matters emanating from any such establishment, and to convey the same beyond the limits of the city by shortest and most practical route. (3) Giving authority to purchase property, pay for damage done in the performance of such duty, and necessary for such disposal, assessing the establishments named and benefited for a just part of the expense of construction, and specifying other powers for the construction and maintenance of the necessary improvements, with limitations upon municipal expenditures therefor. The tenor of this act and its provisions evidently coincides with the before-cited conclusion: That the slaughter-houses and manufacturing establishments in the Menomonee valley are the principal source of the pollution of that river, and that the other rivers were also seriously affected thereby, the act thus recognizing and including the discharge of all ordinary sewage into the river as a secondary evil to be relieved. The general plan adopted for the whole city under this act contemplates the interception and removal by gravitation, to one or more pumping stations, of all sewage and liquid refuse from an area of 8,700 acres, included within the limits of the city, together with one-fourth of an inch rainfall in twenty-four hours from the same area. The capacity of the works embraced in this plan is calculated for a prospective population of 280,000 inhabitants within the present area of the city, 150 gallons of sewage daily for each inhabitant being safely regarded as a maximum estimate, or 42,000,000 gallons of sewage every twenty-four hours, and 59,000,000 gallons rainfall. In order to discharge this aggregate amount of 101,000,000 gallons daily, it is designed that the sewers shall flow only three-quarters full, and at the minimum velocity of 2¼ feet per second. The works in the Menomonee valley are designed to prevent the polution of the Menomonee river and its canals, thus affording the largest relief at the least expense, in the shortest time, by making an outlet to the lake for the liquid refuse of manufacturing establishments there located, and by intercepting sewage from the south sewage district as far as Mineral and Virginia streets and National avenue. The capacity of the proposed intercepting sewer is 25,000,000 gallons daily, but the amount of sewage tributary thereto at the present time does not exceed 4,000,000 gallons daily. This excess of capacity in the sewer may be employed in removing impure water from the west end of Burnham's canal and from the Menomonee, Muskego road, or from any other point adjacent to the line of the intercepting sewer that may be deemed advisable until other connections are made. The pumping-works are located south of the present harbor entrance, such central location being considered also practicable for delivering the sewage any distance out into the lake or wherever it will be most harmless; or by force-mains to any location where it may be wanted for irrigation in the future. The board of public works approved the plan, and in a communication to the common council, July 19, 1880, recommended the execution of it. A letter from the health commissioner was also sent to the council, which says: "In regard to your plan submitted to me several days ago for my opinion as to its sanitary value, and to be recommended by you to the common council, for the removal of all foul liquids from the city without allowing it to enter the rivers, I have carefully considered the plan, and give it my hearty indorsement." The common council in due time authorized the execution of the same as recommended.

CEMETERIES.

With the exception of one cemetery, area 7 acres, in which 24 bodies still remain, there are no cemeteries or burial grounds within the corporate limits of Milwaukee. The following burial places adjoining the city are used by the citizens for the burial of their dead:

Forest Home Cemetery, area 188 acres, is situated 4 miles from the post-office. Lots are sold for burial purposes only, and their improvement, etc., must be in accordance with the rules of the cemetery association. There has been a total of 6,459 interments made here since 1871, 748 having been made during the past year. Graves must be at least 6 feet deep and 12 inches within the line of the lot.

Greenwood Cemetery (Hebrew), area 10 acres, is situated 5 miles from the post-office and directly south of Forest Home cemetery. Lots are conveyed to purchasers in fee, subject to the rules of the cemetery. The restrictions are simply the use of the cemetery for Israelites and their families; the rules simply provide that there shall be no monuments, designs, or inscriptions of an improper kind, or contrary to the Jewish faith. The first interment made here was in 1872, and, up to the close of 1880, 154 burials have been made. Graves are dug 6 feet in depth.

Calvary Cemetery (Roman Catholic), area 70 acres, is situated 3½ miles from the post-office, at the corner of Spring avenue and Spring Hill road, in the town of Wauwatosa. Lots are sold at prices varying from $10 to $50, and the money received from this source is used for the improvement of the grounds. Up to November 1, 1880, there were 10,307 interments made in this cemetery, which was consecrated November 2, 1857, 709 of them being for the 10 months of 1880. The cemetery is governed in accordance with the rules of the Catholic church, and all graves must be from 3 to 6 feet in depth, according to the age or size of the deceased.

Union Cemetery, area 85 acres, is situated 4 miles from the post-office, and is used chiefly by the Lutheran church. The total number of interments is not stated, but during 1879 571 burials were made here.

Pilgrim's Rest Cemetery, area 20 acres, is situated 3½ miles from post-office, and is owned by the Saint Stephen Evangelical Lutheran church. The price of lots varies from 10 to 25 cents per square foot. The cemetery was opened the present year, the first interment having been made August 9, 1880. Graves must be dug at least 12 inches within the lot line, and at least 6 feet deep.

The location of Spring Hill and Trinity cemeteries was not stated.

In addition to the above there is a cemetery attached to the National home, in which are interred only the officials and inmates of the home, their wives and children, and soldiers dying in the vicinity of the home who have at times been inmates thereof. There is also a cemetery, with an area of 2 acres, attached to the county almshouse, situated 6 miles from the post-office. It is used for the deceased poor from the city and county, as well as for those dying either in the almshouse or in the county hospital. The limit of time after death for interment is from 24 to 48 hours, and the depth of graves is 4½ feet.

MARKETS.

There is no public or corporation market in the city. There is a joint-stock market of small dimensions, belonging to an association of gardeners.

SANITARY AUTHORITY—HEALTH COMMISSIONER.

The sole sanitary authority of Milwaukee is vested in an officer called the health commissioner, appointed by the mayor, subject to the confirmation of the common council, who holds office for the term of 2 years. The office was created by a state law, which vests in the health commissioner all power formerly belonging to the board of health. The city government has no control over the commissioner except power of removal. The duties of the health commissioner are to examine into and consider all measures necessary for the preservation of the public health of the city, and to see that all regulations in relation thereto are enforced. He has authority, subject to the confirmation of the common council, to appoint such clerks, agents, assistants, laborers, etc., as he deems necessary for the proper discharge of his duties, and can call on the police force of the city for any assistance needed. He has authority to enter into and inspect any premises or buildings in the city; to order the removal or destruction of any articles deemed prejudicial to health; to regulate or remove any manufactory that creates a nuisance or carries on a business that is considered detrimental to the public health; and in fact to do all things necessary for the sanitary care of the city. During epidemics the commissioner has authority to take possession of and occupy as temporary hospitals any building in the city, the common council being required to pay a just compensation for the use of the same, and to do all things needful to check and control the spread of the disease. His salary is $2,500 per annum.

The annual expenses of the commissioner are from $6,000 to $8,000, being for salaries, printing, and incidental expenses. The removal of garbage is paid out of the general city fund, the removal of night-soil by the persons owning the vaults, and the abating of nuisances by the parties responsible. During epidemics the commissioner has power to increase expenses, limited only by its reasonable exercise.

ASSISTANTS.

At present the commissioner has 7 assistants, as follows: 2 physicians, 1 secretary, 1 meat inspector, 2 general inspectors, and 1 disinfector; none of these have police power, but, as has been stated, the commissioner has power to make requisition on the police force, even to call out a *posse comitatus*, and all his orders are served by policemen.

NUISANCES.

Inspections are made regularly in all parts of the city, and also as nuisances are reported. When a nuisance of any kind is proved to exist, an order is at once issued to abate or remove the same within a given time, and if this is not done the party responsible is liable to arrest and summary trial for the offense. If the commissioner deems it necessary to have any nuisance removed at once, or if the nuisance exists on property the owner of which is not known, he can have the nuisance abated at the expense of the city, and the sum expended for the work becomes a lien on the property in the same manner as any tax upon real estate.

Defective house-drainage, privy-vaults, cesspools, and sources of drinking-water are inspected, and, if found to exist, orders are issued by the commissioner to attend to house-drainage, to clean vaults or cesspools, and to fill up all polluted wells. In the case of defective sewerage, street-cleaning, etc., an order for correction of the same is sent by the commissioner either to the board of public works or to the ward foreman.

GARBAGE.

The health commissioner makes the contract for the removal of garbage, subject to the confirmation of the common council, and also makes rules and regulations, which he can enforce, for the conservation of the garbage and the proper manner of removal. The removal of excrement is controlled by the commissioner. The pollution of streams and harbor is now the dominant sanitary question of the city.

BURIAL OF THE DEAD.

All interments are made outside the city limits, but before a burial is allowed the death must be reported to the health commissioner, and a permit for interment obtained from the secretary. The undertaker must take this permit to the cemetery.

INFECTIOUS DISEASES.

Small-pox patients are either quarantined at home (all communication with the house, except by physician or nurse, being stopped) or sent to the public pest-house, situated in the southwestern suburbs of the city, 60 rods from any habitation. Scarlet-fever patients are quarantined at home, and a notice is placed on the house. Schools, both public or private, are notified of all cases of contagious diseases, and are required to reject children from infected houses. When a disease of a contagious nature appears in a boarding-school the house is placarded, which practically closes the school.

Vaccination is not compulsory, but it is frequently done at the public expense. All diseases of a contagious or infectious nature must be reported within 24 hours to the health commissioner either by the attending physician or by persons having cognizance of the same, and a penalty is imposed for non-compliance.

REGISTRATION AND REPORTS.

All deaths, with the diseases causing the same, are recorded by the health commissioner. The record of births is kept by the register of deeds. The health commissioner reports monthly and annually to the common council, and his reports are published. This annual report covers all the work done by his department during the year, together with such recommendations for future action as he deems advisable.

MUNICIPAL CLEANSING.

Street-cleaning.—The streets of Milwaukee are cleaned at the expense of the city and with its regular force. The work is done wholly by hand. The paved streets are cleaned about once a week, and the other streets about once a month, or as often as is deemed necessary. The work is under the direction of the board of public works, and is only tolerably well done. The annual cost of the service is between $53,000 and $54,000. The sweepings are used for filling low lots. The service has no particular merit, and is more costly than it should be. The principal defect is the manner of disposing of the sweepings, the practice of using them as filling being objectionable. The health commissioner in his annual report for 1879 says:

One thing is certain, the sweepings of streets should not be used for filling low places and vacant lots. Such places usually contain an abundance of moisture, and an accumulation of wet street-sweepings is but little, if any, better than a rotting manure-heap. Houses built upon such made ground are especially unhealthy. The ground air comes up freighted with poisonous gases from the decaying organic matter below, filling the habitations of unsuspecting people, intensifying, if not producing, many diseases that flourish in the midst of filth.

Removal of garbage and ashes.—All garbage is removed under contract at the expense of the city, the matter being under the direct supervision of the health commissioner. While awaiting removal the garbage must be kept in tight-covered wooden vessels, not exceeding one bushel each in capacity, unmixed with ashes, and must be placed at a point on the premises most accessible for the collector. From April 20 to October 20 the garbage is removed daily, and during the remainder of the year twice a week. The garbage-collectors are required to drive through alleys in preference to streets, where alleys exist and are passable. The garbage is taken outside the city limits. Ashes are collected by the board of public works, and are generally used for filling. The annual cost to the city for the collection and removal of garbage is $10,000. It is reported that nuisances and probable injury to health sometimes result from the improper keeping of garbage on premises, from infrequent removal, from improper handling, and from improper final disposal.

Dead animals.—The removal of the carcasses of all animals dying within the limits of the city is included in the contract for removing garbage. The contractor makes his rounds and collects the carcasses in the same manner as he collects garbage. All dead animals are taken outside the city and disposed of to glue factories, etc. During the past year 850 dead animals were removed. It is said that the system works well, and that the carcasses, being of more or less value, are promptly removed.

Liquid household wastes.—In those portions of the city where the public sewers extend, the liquid wastes from houses are run into them, and where there are no sewers the wastes are thrown into cesspools or privy-vaults. Here and there cases occur where the house wastes are run or thrown into the street-gutters, but, as the commissioner of health is making a vigorous war on the practice, it is being discontinued. From 5 to 10 per cent. of the premises in the city are provided with cesspools or dry wells. These are usually porous, a few overflow into the sewers, in some places they receive the waste from water-closets, and when they receive excreta they are treated in the same manner as privy-vaults in regard to cleansing. The street-gutters are not flushed. Touching the contamination of drinking-water by the overflowing or the underground escape of the contents of cesspools and privy-vaults, the health commissioner in his annual report of 1879 says:

The waters of *shallow wells*, or of wells in the drift formation, are regarded as the most dangerous of all. * * * In our city the shallow wells are very diverse. The waters of some are exceedingly bad, of others fairly good. The geological structure of the drift and topographical features determine their character. If we penetrate the earth as in sinking a well, we first find soil and loose dirt of varying thickness, then we strike the "upper red clay" in most places. After passing through this we enter a beach deposit of sand and gravel. Going down we next find the "lower red clay". Beneath this is another beach deposit of sand and gravel. Under that lies a sheet of "blue bowlder clay". There are six layers—three of clay and three of looser, more porous, material. The three sheets of clay intercept the water which percolates freely through the earth, sand, and gravel beds that lie upon them at different levels. Some of our shallow wells only reach down to the upper red clay. The waters of these are very bad. Other wells penetrate deeper, to the lower red clay. The waters of these are not good, but by no means so bad as the first. Many wells go down fifty feet or more, to the blue bowlder clay. The waters of these are very good where surface drainage does not run into them from the top of the ground. The first class of shallow wells, or those which only reach to the uppermost layer of clay, are little better than cesspools. They receive the surface water which is impregnated with slops, offal, stable manure, and the contents of privies. The second class, or those which descend to the gravel bed between the upper and lower sheets of red clay, are very much better. They receive water that has been partially filtered, yet in most cases the surface water drips down into them, poisoning them more or less, according to the conditions of the locality in which they are found. The third class, or those that descend to the sand and gravel beds between the lower red clay and the blue bowlder clay, reach water that has been more thoroughly filtered, and may be regarded as fair in quality; but they are liable to contamination in the same way as the second class. The number of these shallow wells, somewhat technically so called, runs into the thousands. Many of our people are still dependent upon them for water. All of them are dangerous, some of them extremely so. * * * In the low lands, along the rivers, where the process of denudation has gone on cutting through the regular formation of the drift, some shallow wells have been sunk in the alluvial deposit, which are little more than receptacles of surface-water in which every description of filth has been steeped.

Human excreta.—It is estimated that less than 4,000 of the 18,748 dwellings in the city are provided with water-closets, the remainder depending on privy-vaults. The majority of the water-closets deliver into the sewer, very few delivering into cesspools. There are no ordinances regulating the construction of privy-vaults. They are cleansed by regular licensed scavengers, who must use air-tight carts for this purpose, and the work must be performed between the hours of 11 p. m. and 4 a. m.   The night-soil is taken outside the city limits and used for manure, and though it is used on land within the gathering-ground of the public water-supply, it has no appreciable effect on the water, as lake Michigan is a large reservoir.

Manufacturing wastes.—Liquid manufacturing wastes are, as a rule, run into the river, while the solids are hauled outside the city limits.   In some cases the latter have been thrown into privy-vaults, but this practice is not allowed.

POLICE.

The chief of police is appointed by the mayor, subject to confirmation of the city council; and the members of the force are appointed by the chief, subject to the approval of the mayor.   The chief of police, salary $3,000 per annum, has direct command of the force, and is held responsible for its efficiency, general good conduct, etc.   It is his duty to see that the public peace is preserved, and that all the laws and ordinances are enforced.   The remainder of the force in the several grades and the annual salaries are as follows: One first lieutenant at $1,500; 1 second lieutenant at $1,200; 4 detectives at $1,000 each; 2 sergeants at $900 each; 3 roundsmen at $850 each; 6 station-keepers at $800 each; and 69 patrolmen at $800 each.   The uniform consists of dark-blue suit, with brass buttons, and a cap, hats being worn part of the year.   The men furnish their own uniforms, the average cost being for each suit $30, for each overcoat $25, and for head-gear $2 75 per man.   The patrolmen are equipped with pistols and clubs, which are carried concealed.   The hours of duty are for day men from 7 a. m. to 8 p. m., and the night men from 8 p. m. to 5 a. m., and the streets in the city are patrolled by policemen.

During the past year (1880) there were 2,564 arrests made by the police, the principal causes for which were: drunk and disorderly 668, drunk 557, disorderly 566, assault and battery 101, and larceny 160.   In the majority of the cases disposed of the prisoners were either fined or sent to the house of correction.   During the year property to the value of $23,928 97 was reported to the police as lost or stolen, and of this, $14,480 50 was recovered and returned to the owners.

There were 3,167 station-house lodgers during 1880, as against 3,445 in 1879.

The force is required to co-operate with the fire department by rendering all the assistance it can, and with the health department and board of public works by serving notices and executing orders.   Special policemen are appointed by the chief and approved by the mayor.   They are hired by private persons to protect property, and though appointed as policemen, so as to give them a legal status, they receive no pay from the city.

The annual cost of the police force is about $76,000.

FIRE DEPARTMENT.

The following is taken from the annual report of the chief engineer for the year ending December 31, 1880:

The manual force of the department consists of 1 chief engineer, who is also superintendent of the fire-alarm telegraph, 1 assistant chief engineer, 1 assistant superintendent of fire-alarm telegraph, 1 veterinary surgeon, and 95 officers and men, divided into 13 companies.   The apparatus consists of 7 steam fire-engines in service and one old one in reserve; 1 chemical engine, 6 two-wheel hose-carts, 3 four-wheel hose-carriages, 3 hook-and-ladder trucks, and 1 fire-escape.   There are 14,050 feet of hose and 43 horses in use.

The department responded to 257 alarms during the year.   There were 167 fires, by which property to the amount of $95,284 was destroyed, the total amount of insurance involved being $1,036,050.

The total expenses of the department for the year were $104,267 11.

COMMERCE AND NAVIGATION.

[From the reports of the Bureau of Statistics for the fiscal years ending June 30.]

Customs district of Milwaukee, Wisconsin.	1879.	1880.
Total value of imports	$75,220	$102,151
Total value of exports:		
Domestic	$1,346,852	$1,395,806
Foreign		
Total number of immigrants		27

Customs district of Milwaukee, Wisconsin.	1879.		1880.	
	Number.	Tons.	Number.	Tons.
Vessels in foreign trade:				
Entered	65	24,008	127	54,932
Cleared	55	19,679	59	22,011
Vessels in lake trade and fisheries:				
Entered	8,458	3,749,692	9,338	3,911,878
Cleared	8,606	3,755,541	9,584	4,016,670
Vessels registered, enrolled, and licensed in district.	361	73,330	348	67,855
Vessels built during the year	5	231	16	2,627

MANUFACTURES.

The following is a summary of the statistics of the manufactures of Milwaukee for 1880, being taken from tables prepared for the Tenth Census by A. A. Loper, chief special agent:

Mechanical and manufacturing industries.	No. of establishments.	Capital.	Males above 16 years.	Females above 15 years.	Children and youths.	Total amount paid in wages during the year.	Value of materials.	Value of products.
All industries...............................	844	$18,766,914	16,015	3,922	949	$6,946,105	$28,975,872	$43,473,812
Baskets, rattan and willow ware.............	4	90,600	108	15	161	46,660	38,825	114,300
Blacksmithing (see also Wheelwrighting)......	34	54,850	103	....	....	52,264	31,410	122,540
Bookbinding and blank-book making...........	7	21,700	56	47	18	31,505	26,681	78,713
Boots and shoes, including custom work and repairing	59	296,275	462	55	9	162,263	380,074	665,183
Brass castings...............................	6	108,300	140	2	2	51,112	76,436	167,114
Bread and other bakery products..............	96	61,350	102	16	29	37,254	255,449	358,866
Brick and tile..............................	5	328,500	346	....	43	89,720	77,276	225,808
Brooms and brushes.........................	4	13,000	50	5	....	15,240	16,720	47,620
Carpentering...............................	47	149,780	745	....	....	311,581	543,315	986,685
Carpets, rag................................	5	5,100	19	25	....	4,900	12,550	22,350
Carriages and wagons (see also Wheelwrighting)	11	97,000	148	....	2	62,265	76,500	184,000
Clothing, men's.............................	52	1,895,128	1,902	2,350	50	912,657	2,243,365	3,763,987
Clothing, women's...........................	4	64,000	34	163	....	29,900	109,000	147,160
Coffee and spices, roasted and ground.......	9	257,621	125	19	15	89,550	693,042	931,640
Confectionery...............................	4	144,054	110	30	20	43,542	378,370	474,922
Cooperage..................................	39	142,250	526	....	35	234,115	337,880	680,445
Coppersmithing (see also Tinware, copperware, and sheet-iron ware).	3	41,500	20	....	....	10,692	22,370	44,392
Cordage and twine..........................	3	5,000	9	....	....	3,200	10,000	16,600
Dentistry, mechanical.......................	5	8,000	10	1	2	4,500	10,500	30,000
Drugs and chemicals........................	6	40,872	15	12	....	9,386	55,179	85,393
Flouring- and grist-mill products............	11	1,066,000	265	....	....	136,266	3,795,289	4,204,708
Foundery and machine-shop products.........	30	1,286,445	1,437	....	30	673,392	1,173,907	2,252,784
Furnishing goods, men's.....................	3	7,000	7	9	1	1,890	17,000	28,850
Furniture (see also Mattresses and spring beds; Upholstering)	16	329,800	497	14	15	212,501	223,301	568,268
Furs, dressed...............................	3	61,000	14	38	5	25,000	89,500	136,000
Hairwork...................................	3	8,500	....	11	....	2,800	6,050	13,200
Hand-knit goods............................	5	26,000	2	538	52	14,500	45,500	83,000
Hardware..................................	5	11,700	19	....	10	8,600	14,900	32,160
Hats and caps, not including wool hats.......	3	26,000	8	14	....	7,500	17,928	34,000
Jewelry....................................	4	15,000	18	....	....	8,316	31,000	47,000
Leather, curried............................	17	800,425	375	....	....	160,441	1,874,595	2,219,978
Leather, dressed skins......................	5	71,500	46	....	....	20,900	67,925	104,581
Leather, tanned............................	17	1,008,525	407	....	....	173,861	1,612,400	2,101,195
Lithographing (see also Printing and publishing)	4	69,125	116	2	13	57,751	79,640	166,860
Liquors, distilled...........................	2	142,000	20	....	....	9,180	95,425	145,650
Liquors, malt..............................	13	4,732,900	1,040	....	....	525,573	2,259,345	4,034,319
Looking-glass and picture frames............	4	12,975	10	....	....	7,222	19,900	35,470
Lumber, planed (see also Sash, doors, and blinds)	3	70,000	115	4	11	35,000	50,000	117,000
Marble and stone work......................	11	95,000	167	....	2	73,256	106,450	220,396
Masonry, brick and stone....................	4	8,500	27	....	2	12,000	14,000	34,750
Mattresses and spring beds (see also Furniture)	4	3,800	8	5	2	2,550	12,000	17,500
Mineral and soda waters.....................	6	34,200	44	5	5	14,208	31,450	62,950
Painting and paperhanging..................	31	53,950	204	....	2	68,105	95,607	206,546
Plumbing and gasfitting.....................	8	47,600	95	....	1	43,600	71,700	138,400
Printing and publishing (see also Lithographing)	24	434,700	518	43	48	268,270	200,486	675,087
Pumps, not including steam pumps...........	4	4,075	9	....	....	3,150	4,622	11,500
Saddlery and harness.......................	20	73,300	107	....	38	44,451	112,620	199,525
Sash, doors, and blinds (see also Lumber, planed)	7	261,000	512	....	18	139,100	303,000	557,000
Shipbuilding...............................	8	136,500	227	....	....	110,413	133,963	301,705
Shirts.....................................	3	2,100	4	17	....	4,990	5,790	17,050

Mechanical and manufacturing industries.	No. of establishments.	Capital.	AVERAGE NUMBER OF HANDS EMPLOYED.			Total amount paid in wages during the year.	Value of materials.	Value of products.
			Males above 16 years.	Females above 15 years.	Children and youths.			
Slaughtering and meat-packing, not including retail butchering	7	$789,000	928	....	25	$187,596	$5,529,618	$6,099,486
Soap and candles	5	120,000	50	4	11	24,620	204,100	280,090
Stone- and earthen-ware	8	69,700	67	....	....	17,511	21,755	66,600
Tinware, copperware, and sheet-iron ware (see also Coppersmithing)	29	95,950	150	....	4	56,687	106,994	215,544
Tobacco, chewing, smoking, and snuff (see also Tobacco, cigars and cigarettes).	3	331,000	200	3	20	78,500	786,645	978,281
Tobacco, cigars and cigarettes (see also Tobacco, chewing, smoking, and snuff).	56	238,375	733	4	77	301,934	344,939	835,506
Trunks and valises	4	183,000	218	....	45	76,720	115,800	244,600
Upholstering (see also Furniture)	6	11,900	46	....	....	22,800	97,500	146,500
Vinegar	5	62,000	32	....	....	18,415	42,000	149,000
Watch and clock repairing	4	4,100	8	....	1	3,780	4,800	12,675
Wheelwrighting (see also Blacksmithing; Carriages and wagons)	13	47,500	67	....	.....	27,870	29,800	80,950
Wirework	5	4,750	8	....	....	3,140	3,185	10,885
All other industries (a)	69	2,084,830	2,160	468	125	1,059,440	3,728,001	6,437,945

a Embracing agricultural implements; artificial feathers and flowers; artificial limbs; bags, paper; baking and yeast powders; boot and shoe uppers; boxes, cigar; boxes, fancy and paper; boxes, wooden packing; bridges; carriages and sleds, children's; carriage and wagon materials; drain and sewer pipe; dyeing and cleaning; electroplating; engraving and die-sinking; engraving, wood; fertilizers; files; food preparations; furniture, chairs; galvanizing; gloves and mittens; ink; iron and steel; lightning rods; lumber, sawed; mixed textiles; models and patterns; musical instruments, organs and materials; musical instruments, pianos and materials; oil, linseed; paints; patent medicines and compounds; pickles, preserves, and sauces; refrigerators; roofing and roofing materials; safes, doors, and vaults, fire-proof; scales and balances; show-cases; starch; steam fittings and heating apparatus; stencils and brands; stereotyping and electrotyping; straw goods; tools; toys and games; type founding; wood preserving; wood, turned and carved; and woolen goods.

From the foregoing table it appears that the average capital of all establishments is $22,235 68; that the average wages of all hands employed is $332 57 per annum; and that the average outlay in wages, in materials, and in interest (at 6 per cent.) on capital employed is $43,895 72.

OSHKOSH,

WINNEBAGO COUNTY, WISCONSIN.

POPULATION

IN THE

AGGREGATE

1860-1880.

	Inhab.
1790	......
1800	......
1810	......
1820	......
1830	......
1840	......
1850	......
1860	6,086
1870	12,663
1880	15,748

POPULATION

BY

SEX, NATIVITY, AND RACE,

AT

CENSUS OF 1880.

Male	7,733
Female	8,015
Native	11,094
Foreign-born	4,654
White	15,661
Colored	* 87

* Including 2 Chinese and 8 Indians.

Latitude: 44° 1' North; Longitude: 88° 32' (west from Greenwich); Altitude: 758 feet.

FINANCIAL CONDITION:

Total Valuation: $4,444,000; per capita: $282 00.   Net Indebtedness: $148,500; per capita: $9 43.   Tax per $100: $2 26.

HISTORICAL SKETCH.

A so-called French trading-post was established on the upper Fox river, 10 miles above the present site of Oshkosh, in the year 1818, but no Americans settled in the vicinity until more than fifteen years later, when a few adventurous pioneers came into the wilderness around lake Winnebago and began to build huts and saw-mills and to make farms.   In 1836 one of these hardy adventurers removed from the village of Neenah, where he had been at work on the mill, to the south side of Fox river, at what is now known as Algoma, and bought out a ferry, a poor affair, which he began to run.   At that time the land south of the river was owned by the government, and that mouth of the river where Oshkosh now stands was still held by the Indian tribe, the Menominees.   In August, 1836, Governor Dodge effected a treaty at Grand rapids for the purchase of the land north of the river.   Learning of this, Stanley and one Chester Gallup moved across the river, took up land, and built houses.   Other people came, and a settlement gradually sprang up to which they gave the somewhat inappropriate name of Athens.   In the spring of

OSHKOSH.
WIS.

FOX RIVER

1840 the English, French, and Halfbreeds, or Canadians, in the vicinity, met and voted that this should be changed to the less euphonious but more suggestive name of Os-kosh, the name of the chief of the Menominees. In some inexplicable way an "h" has been added, making it Oshkosh. In 1846 the first village plot was made, the settlement having gained considerable size meanwhile. In 1858 it was organized as a city. Oshkosh has been peculiarly unfortunate in having had no less than six extensive conflagrations, besides a number of smaller ones, within the last twenty-one years. On May 9, 1859, the entire business portion of the city was destroyed, 170 buildings being burnt; on May 24, 1861, the whole side of a street on the south side of the river was destroyed, including many stores and 2 hotels; on May 1, 1866, half the business portion of the city was burnt; on May 9, 1874, 28 residences, 6 barns, and much lumber were destroyed; on July 14, 1875, 600 dwellings were destroyed, the loss being estimated at from $600,000 to $800,000; on April 28, 1875, 500 residences, 69 stores, and numerous public buildings, manufactories, etc., were destroyed, with a total loss estimated at from $2,500,000 to $3,000,000. After every fire better buildings were erected than those burnt.

Oshkosh is in the remarkable diagonal valley occupied by Green bay and the Fox and Wisconsin rivers, which traverses the state obliquely like a great groove, and cuts down the central elevation half its height. A line passing across the surface from lake Michigan to the Mississippi at any other point would arch upward from above 400 to 1,000 feet, according to location, while along the trough of this valley it would reach an elevation barely exceeding 200 feet. This elevation is reached near Portage, at a point where the Fox and Wisconsin rivers are separated only by a flat, sandy plain, which during high water the Wisconsin overflows. A canal 12,400 feet in length has been dug across here, and the United States government has from time to time expended much money in improving the courses of the Wisconsin and Upper Fox and Lower Fox rivers, with a view to establishing communication for boats of large size between the Mississippi and lake Michigan. Small boats have often passed through, and boats and barges for the Mississippi have been built at Oshkosh. When the government improvements are finally completed, Oshkosh will be greatly benefited by the traffic which will follow. The distance from Oshkosh to the Mississippi by this route is very nearly 225 miles.

About one-third of the population of Oshkosh is of German origin; the majority of the rest is of American origin.

OSHKOSH IN 1880.

The following statistical accounts, collected by the Census Office, indicate the present condition of Oshkosh:

LOCATION.

Oshkosh, the capital of Winnebago county, is situated on both sides of the Fox river, at its entrance into lake Winnebago, at an average altitude of 758 feet above the surface of the sea; the altitude of lake Winnebago is 751 feet above sea-level. The Fox river is 500 feet wide at Oshkosh, and its mouth is very deep; the channel has upward of 20 feet of water, which continues along the whole river front of the city, thence to lake Butte des Morts, just above the city, and through that lake there is a depth of over 12 feet of water; the river is broad and deep, with no perceptible current. Over the 15.5 miles of lake navigation between the Upper and Lower Fox rivers, there is a depth of over 20 feet. The level of the lake does not reach more than 3.5 feet above the ordinary level maintained by the dams at the outlets, but it is occasionally drawn by the water-power mills nearly 2.5 feet below this level. About 10 miles above Oshkosh the Fox river is joined by the Wolf river, a stream of nearly its own size. This river is navigable for small boats for 50 miles.

RAILROAD COMMUNICATIONS.

Oshkosh communicates with the world by means of 3 railroads:

The Milwaukee, Green Bay, and Marquette line of the Chicago and Northwestern railroad, which connects the places named.

The northern division of the Chicago, Milwaukee, and Saint Paul railroad, the branch of which terminating at Oshkosh connects with the main line at Horicon Junction, and so with Chicago and the Northwest.

The Milwaukee, Lake Shore, and Western railroad, whose terminals are Wausau and Milwaukee, Oshkosh being on a branch that joins the main line at Hortonville Junction.

TRIBUTARY COUNTRY.

Oshkosh is situated near the somewhat uncertain line dividing the timber-lands on the north from the prairies on the south. The country around the city is mostly prairie land, the soil being a rich loam. The Wolf river, which has been mentioned as emptying into the Fox above Oshkosh, penetrates the lumber regions in the northern part of the state, and a great quantity of logs and sawed lumber is floated down the river to Oshkosh, which naturally becomes the entrépot of the whole valley.

TOPOGRAPHY.

The site of Oshkosh is nearly level. The soil is calcareous and very fertile, with a substratum of limestone. There is good natural drainage, the surface being sufficiently undulatory. Numerous gravel-beds are found in the county, furnishing material for road-making. These have been largely utilized, and excellent roads prevail. Good drinking-water is abundant, flowing wells being common. On the south side of the river, between the settled district and Algoma, a large portion of the territory is low and marshy, with water setting back into the land at certain seasons, but being removed from the business and residence portions of the city it is of little consequence. What other bays and marshy spots there were along the river have been gradually filled up. There are 3 carriage bridges and 2 railroad bridges across the river. The total area of the city is about 8 square miles.

CLIMATE.

Highest recorded summer temperature, in 1879, 97°; lowest recorded winter temperature, in 1879, —26°. The temperature charts published by the Smithsonian Institution show that the mean summer temperature is 68°, mean winter temperature 21°. Owing to the proximity of so much water, the heats of summer are tempered, the nights being particularly cool and pleasant.

STREETS.

Total length of streets 45 miles, of which 0.75 mile is paved with the Nicholson wooden pavement, and 25 miles are well graveled. The latter are cheaply constructed and easily kept in good repair. Sidewalks are for the most part made of 2-inch pine plank. A large number of trees have been transplanted and set out along the streets, the varieties most common being hard and silver-leaf maple and poplar, with some linden and elm.

WATER-WORKS.

There are no water-works.

GAS.

The gas-works are not owned by the city. The amount paid by the city for each street-lamp is $25.

PUBLIC BUILDINGS.

The city owns 3 fire-engine houses, 5 brick school buildings, and 2 wooden buildings, of which the total cost was about $90,000. There is no city hall.

PUBLIC PARKS AND PLEASURE-GROUNDS.

There are no public parks and pleasure-grounds.

PLACES OF AMUSEMENT.

The city contains 2 halls used for theatrical purposes, seating, respectively, 700 and 600, and 6 smaller halls used for concerts, dances, etc., with seating capacities varying from 300 to 500. There are no concert- or beer-gardens. Theater companies pay a license of $5 per night.

DRAINAGE.

The city has no system of sewerage.

CEMETERIES.

There are 2 cemeteries connected with the city—one managed by the city authorities, located within the city limits on the north bank of the river, at the mouth of lake Butte des Morts, just opposite Algoma; and the other controlled by the Roman Catholics, location not given. The former contains about 20 acres, and the latter 5 acres. There being no records kept of interments, and no regulations concerning them, no information on these heads can be given.

MARKETS.

The reports state that there are "no public markets except one for hay and one for wood, and no market buildings".

SANITARY AUTHORITY.

The chief health organization of Oshkosh is the board of health, an independent board, with 5 members, 3 of whom are physicians. Its expenses are generally very light, since the members receive no pay, and the only expenditures are for printing and police duty. During an epidemic its expenses might be increased to an unlimited extent. It may cause nuisances to be abated, issue burial permits, and perform all the usual duties of such a board. The president of the board has general superintendence of the sanitary condition of the city. There are no assistant health officers or inspectors employed. The board is appointed by the common council, and meets once a month, or oftener if called together. As to the conservation and removal of garbage the board is reported to exercise absolute control. Small-pox patients are isolated in a pest-house, but scarlet-fever patients are not isolated. Attendance at school is forbidden to children from any house where contagious diseases exist. There is no public pest-house. Vaccination is not compulsory. Births, diseases, and deaths are registered under the state law. The board reports every year to the common council, and no separate report is published.

MUNICIPAL CLEANSING.

Street-cleaning.—The streets are cleaned both by the city and by private abutters, the city's work being done by the city's own force by hand. Main street is cleaned every week, and the others when necessary. The work is said to be well done, the annual cost being $150. The sweepings are deposited in the marsh.

Removal of garbage and ashes.—Garbage is removed by housholders, being finally buried or burned. Wood ashes are used in making soap.

Dead animals.—Dead animals are buried, the annual cost being very slight.

Liquid household wastes.—Chamber slops, laundry waste, and kitchen slops are all disposed of in the same way, but in what way is not reported, except that none of it goes into sewers, because there are none. The overflow from cesspools and privy-vaults is thought to contaminate water more or less.

Human excreta.—The dry-earth sytem is very little used. Night-soil is buried.

POLICE.

The police force is appointed by the common council and governed by the mayor. The chief of police has a salary of $750 per year, and the 8 patrolmen, $450 each per year. They wear blue uniforms, which they provide themselves. The patrolmen serve 10 hours per day each, and patrol 4 miles of streets. There were 640 arrests last year, the principal causes being drunkenness and disorder, burglary, and assault and battery. There were 14 station-house lodgers in 1880, against 24 in 1879; 28 free meals were furnished at a cost of 25 cents per meal. Special policemen are appointed by the mayor and common council. The yearly cost of the police force (1880) is $5,070.

PUBLIC SCHOOLS.

The school government of the city is provided for by a board of education consisting of a superintendent appointed by the city council, and six commissioners, one from each ward, elected biennially by the people. There are 7 school buildings, one for the high school and each of the 6 ward schools. At present 51 teachers are employed, 7 males and 44 females, with a salary list of $20,800 per year. The expenditure for all school purposes from April 1, 1880, to April 1, 1881, was $31,623 40. In September, 1880, there were 5,874 children of school age in the city; of these, 988 were in attendance at private and denominational schools in the city, and about 125 at a state normal school located here.

RACINE,
RACINE COUNTY, WISCONSIN.

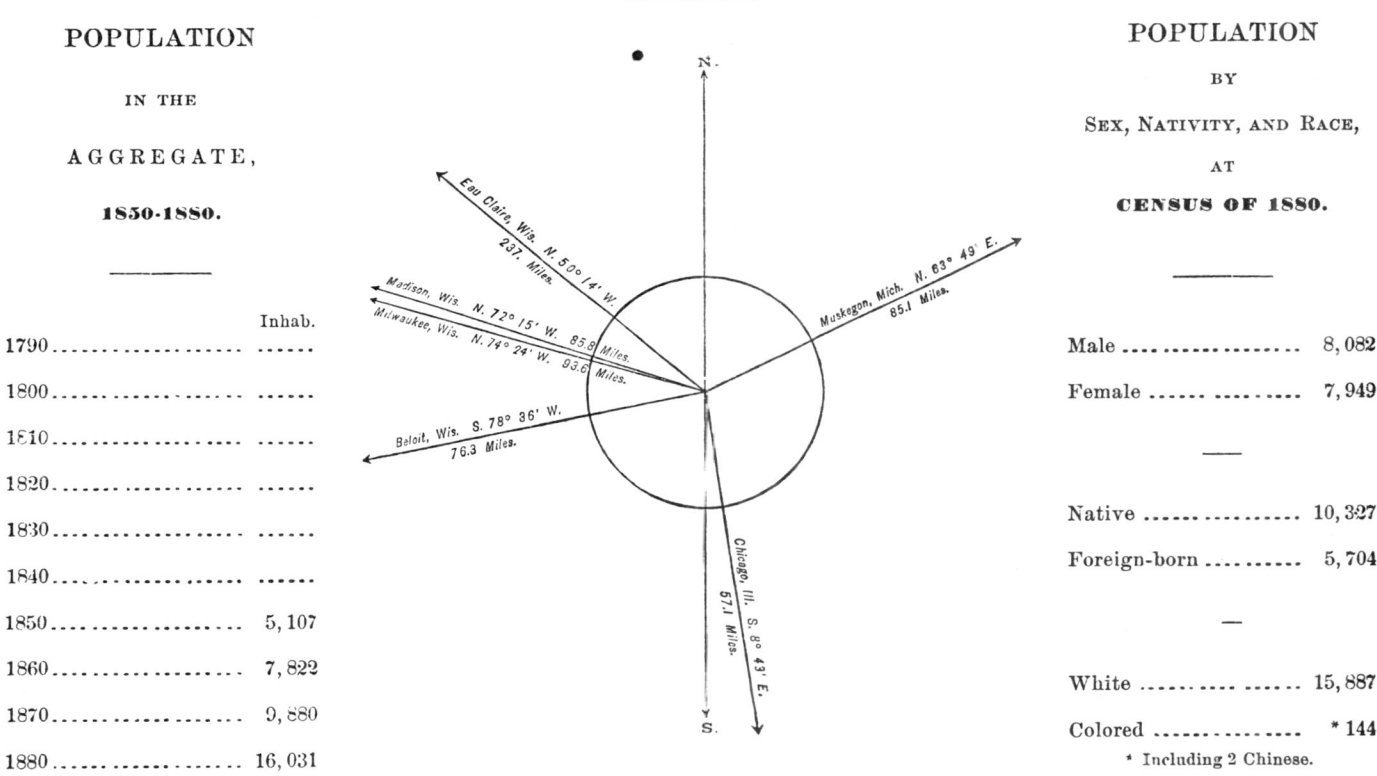

POPULATION

IN THE

AGGREGATE,

1850-1880.

	Inhab.
1790	......
1800	......
1810	......
1820	......
1830	......
1840	......
1850	5,107
1860	7,822
1870	9,880
1880	16,031

POPULATION

BY

SEX, NATIVITY, AND RACE,

AT

CENSUS OF 1880.

Male	8,082
Female	7,949
Native	10,327
Foreign-born	5,704
White	15,887
Colored	* 144

* Including 2 Chinese.

Latitude: 42° 43' North; Longitude: 87° 47' (west from Greenwich); Altitude: 589 to 639 feet.

FINANCIAL CONDITION.

Total Valuation: $7,692,669; per capita: $480 00.   Net Indebtedness: $218,512; per capita: $13 63.   Tax per $100: $1 32.

HISTORICAL SKETCH. (a)

The first settlement made on the present site of Racine was in 1834, Captain Gilbert Knapp, of the United States Navy, making a claim on all the land now covered by the principal part of the city. Early in 1835 a large immigration set in. The first store, the first hotel, and the first school were opened in 1836. The first election of county officers was held in 1837. The first newspaper (Racine *Argus*) was issued February 14, 1838. The village was chartered in 1841; the harbor was completed so as to admit the first steamboat in 1844; and the city was incorporated in 1848.

A fire occurred January 14, 1861, in which valuable records were lost by the burning of the probate judge's office. January 14, 1866, there was a very large fire, destroying real and personal property to the value of $200,000,

---

a The following sketch, as well as a good deal of the statistical information under the head of "Racine in 1880", was prepared and forwarded by a committee appointed by the city authorities for this purpose.

including the first business block in the city, one hotel, one church, and several valuable buildings. There have been but three churches burnt, and these were speedily replaced by better buildings. In two instances only have fires occurred in manufacturing establishments. The city has not been exempt from the depressions in value incident to the general financial crises of the country; but, with the exception of these temporary set-backs, there has been a gradual, steady, and solid improvement; and since the adjustment of its bonded indebtedness and the beginning of its manufacturing industries, the growth of the city in population and the increase in the value of its real estate have been constant.

The country adjacent to the present city of Racine being farming land, and the harbor of Racine being one of the best on the lake, forming a convenient shipping point, this vicinity was early settled by emigrants from the farming communities of the eastern states. The direct and comparatively quick communication by water with the state of New York had a great deal to do in forming the character of the early settlements, as by far the larger number of settlers came from that state. These farmers required supplies, and we find in the earlier history of the city that the only occupations of the residents were store-keeping and the avocations incident to the moving, handling, and selling of goods. There were two mills on the river to grind the home grists of the farmers. Soon, however, more grain was raised than could be consumed at home, and more warehouses and docks were built along the natural harbor afforded by the river. Thus began a shipping interest which in time assumed no small dimensions, and finally a line of steamers, owned in the city, was exclusively engaged in carrying away grain and bringing merchandise. Plank roads were built, reaching into the country 60 miles, and the streets were filled with wagons, bringing grain to the warehouses for shipment and taking goods back into the interior. The residents of the early city were Americans; the foreign element was small, comprising one or two Jewish merchants and quite a colony of Irish, the latter engaged in the labor of loading and unloading vessels. Their homes were naturally in sight of the river, and there they have remained. The natural advantages of the city as a shipping point were increased by the building of a railroad running west to the Mississippi, and the ready access to the timber of northern Wisconsin and Michigan led one and another to begin the making of some tool or implement.

The proximity to Milwaukee and Chicago, with their large stocks of goods and greater capital, offering better advantages to the farmer, soon led him to take his grain to those markets where he could obtain more for his money, and as the trade of those cities increased, the farming and grain trade was diverted from Racine, the warehouses and elevators became useless and were torn down, until there was left only one elevator, solely used to store grain when those in Milwaukee were full; the wheat vessels were exchanged for smaller craft suitable to the local trade, and the line of steamers owned here were either sold, or, when wrecked, the loss was not replaced. Racine ceased to be a trading-point, but the natural advantages for manufacturing remained and were improved upon, one shop succeeding another, while the number of stores increases only as there are more workmen to supply. Americans who at first worked in the small shops of Racine left to start shops of their own, or in search of farms over which they might have exclusive control, and their places were soon filled with the patient, steady-going, skilled workmen from the manufactories of Europe. English and Scotch machinists and wood-workers soon became predominant, and when the small wagon and thrashing-machine shops grew to larger dimensions they were filled with mechanics, nine-tenths of whom are found to be of foreign birth, quietly working year after year with no ambition to take the place of the American foreman.

RACINE IN 1880.

The following statistical accounts, collected by the Census Office, indicate the present condition of Racine:

LOCATION.

Racine lies in latitude 42° 43' north, longitude 87° 47' west from Greenwich, at the mouth of Root river, on the west shore of Lake Michigan, 62 miles north of Chicago and 23 miles south of Milwaukee by rail. The city is situated on a promontory extending into the lake, the principal portion being on a plateau 50 feet above the water of the lake. The altitudes above sea-level vary from 589 feet, surface of lake Michigan, to 639 feet. The river on which the city lies affords a good harbor, admitting vessels drawing 14 feet of water, and allowing wharfage room for 100 vessels at a time. The channel is here 200 feet wide and the current is very slight.

RAILROAD COMMUNICATIONS.

The city is touched by the following trunk lines:

The Milwaukee division of the Chicago and Northwestern railroad, from Chicago to Milwaukee.

The Racine and Southwestern division of the Chicago, Milwaukee, and Saint Paul railroad, from Racine to Cedar Rapids, Iowa.

TRIBUTARY COUNTRY.

The country immediately tributary to Racine is purely agricultural, much attention being given to stock-raising. Aside from the manufacturing interests the city can not be said to have much trade with the surrounding country.

TOPOGRAPHY, ETC.

The site of the city is a level plateau, about 50 feet above the level of the lake, with Root river flowing through it. The soil at the surface is a sandy loam for the east half of the city and clay on the west, with a thick stratum of clay about 10 feet below the surface and limestone underlying this. There is a gentle inclination toward the river, thus affording good natural drainage. The country back lies in swells or ridges running north and south. The top of the first one, 3 miles west of the city, is 150 feet above lake Michigan. Directly north and south of the city the soil is sandy, with patches of sand underlaid with gravel, while to the west the "prairie" soil prevails, underlaid with clay. There are no marshes, ponds, or small lakes in the vicinity. Within a radius of 5 miles there was formerly considerable timber, but it is now nearly all removed.

CLIMATE.

Highest recorded summer temperature, 104°; highest summer temperature in average years, 95°. Lowest recorded winter temperature, —25°; lowest winter temperature in average years, —15°. The proximity of the lake tends to moderate the extremes of temperature, while the northeast winds make the summer very pleasant.

STREETS.

There are 43 miles of streets in the city, and, with the exception of about three-quarters of a mile of broken stone laid on one street, none of them are paved. From the manner and time in which the work was done it is not possible to make any estimate on the cost of the broken stone. It is stated that "the nature of the soil does not render paving imperative". Sidewalks are made of 2-inch plank, and a legal sidewalk is 6 feet wide. In the principal streets the gutters are of plank. In all the residence parts of the city trees are planted along the sides of the streets at the outer edge of the sidewalks. Each ward raises a fund by taxation for street repairs, etc., and the same is expended under the supervision of the alderman from the ward. From $5,000 to $8,000 is used each year, mostly in filling in broken stone and gravel into the lowest parts of the streets. Contract work is preferred when practicable. There are no horse railroads in the city. An omnibus line with 3 vehicles and 6 horses, and employing 6 men, carries passengers at the uniform rate of fare of 5 cents.

WATER-WORKS.

There are no water-works, but an artesian well, owned and managed by a private corporation, supplies about one-quarter of the territory of the city with water sufficient for drinking and sprinkling purposes only. Two other artesian wells were sunk by private parties, and so far used by themselves only, the water from which is excellent, being suitable for all purposes.

GAS.

The gas-works are not owned by the city. The daily average production is 50,000 cubic feet. The charge per 1,000 feet is $2 50 net. The city pays $24 per annum for each street-lamp, 54 in number.

PUBLIC BUILDINGS.

The only buildings owned by the city are 8 school buildings and 3 engine-houses. They are built of cream-colored brick made in the vicinity, and their total cost was $60,000. The city owns no city hall and uses no part of the county buildings, which latter are owned and occupied wholly by the county. A large room, containing the council chamber and offices of city clerk and treasurer, is rented by the city for municipal purposes.

PUBLIC PARKS AND PLEASURE-GROUNDS.

There are no pleasure-grounds, strictly speaking, in the city. There are 3 public parks and 1 square, two being 240 by 280 feet, one 230 by 285, and one 160 by 100. They are simply vacant squares planted with trees, except one, which has been improved with a fountain, seats, etc., erected and maintained by private enterprise. The land included in these parks was deeded to the city by the original owner, and their annual cost for maintenance is merely nominal. They are controlled by the city council in the same manner as the streets.

PLACES OF AMUSEMENT.

The Opera House, seating capacity 600, and 3 halls, with a seating capacity of 400 each, are used for theatrical purposes, etc. There is one lecture hall used for concerts, with a seating capacity of 300. All traveling companies pay a license to the city of $3 for the first exhibition, and $1 50 for each succeeding night. There are "no regularly organized concert- and beer-gardens, as such institutions are ordinarily managed. There are 3 beer-halls in or near the city, at which dances are occasionally held during the summer, and beer sold and which have beer-gardens for dancing attached".

DRAINAGE.

Racine has no system of sewerage, and, with the exception of a few private drains, there are no sewers.

CEMETERIES.

There are 3 cemeteries connected with Racine, as follows: *Mound Cemetery*, area 120 acres, and *Roman Catholic Cemetery*, area 10 acres, are situated 2 miles west of the city, and *Evergreen Cemetery*, area 10 acres, is situated 2 miles south of the city. Burials in this latter cemetery are no longer permitted. The total number of interments in all the cemeteries is reported as 4,125, and it said that about 400 people die annually. Graves for adults are required to be 6 feet deep, and for children under 10 years of age 4½ feet deep. Mound cemetery is owned and controlled by the city. Lots are sold by the common council, and a portion of the cemetery is set apart for the use of non-residents.

MARKETS.

The city has no public market-houses, all meat, vegetables, etc., being sold by private parties at their places of business.

SANITARY AUTHORITY—BOARD OF HEALTH.

The chief sanitary organization of Racine is the board of health, an independent body composed of 3 members, 2 of whom are physicians, appointed annually by the mayor. Including the small salary paid to the health officer, the annual expenses of the board, in absence of any declared epidemic, are $150, and this sum can be increased only by appropriations from the city council. There is no fund set apart for the use of the board, so that unless there is a special necessity its work is limited and somewhat superficial. Its authority extends to a general cleaning of the city, with sufficient power during epidemics to meet all emergencies, "but it needs money to carry them out." The health officer, salary $100 per annum, makes inspections, etc. He has sufficient powers to arrest for non-compliance with health orders. The members of the board receive no pay, and the president (or chairman) does most of the work. The board meets about once a month and reports all necessary work done and the sanitary improvements needed to the city council for final action or appropriations of money. Regular inspections are not made. When nuisances are reported the localities are visited by the health officer; if it is a doubtful case the board inspects, and its decision is final. So far the work of the board has not been extended to the inspection and correction of defective house-drainage, sources of drinking-water, etc. The board does not appear to exercise any control over the conservation and removal of garbage, nor has it published any regulations concerning the pollution of streams. Burial permits are issued by the board on certificates of the attending physicians.

INFECTIOUS DISEASES.

There have not been 6 cases of small-pox in the city during the past fifteen years. Scarlet-fever patients are quarantined at home, so far as it can be done. If diseases of a contagious nature should break out, either in public or private schools, the board would take cognizance of the fact. "Whooping-cough and measles are not noted particularly, as in fact the result with these diseases is not worth the expense and inconvenience. Keeping children from school when the diseases are in the family does not prevent the spread of them." There is no pest-house. Vaccination is not compulsory, and is not done at the public expense.

REPORTS.

The record of all births and deaths is kept by the board, the former being reported within 30 days, and the latter within 24 hours, while the registration is governed somewhat by a state law. The board reports annually to the mayor and council, and the reports are published with the proceedings of the council.

MUNICIPAL CLEANSING.

Street-cleaning.—The streets are cleaned at the expense of the city, with its own force, and wholly by hand. The cleaning is done about twice a year, and is reported as being done efficiently. The annual cost of the service is not much, as it is done mostly by tramps, and the sweepings are taken out of the city. The defect of the system is said to be that the streets are not cleaned often enough.

Removal of garbage and ashes.—The garbage is removed both by the city and by householders. A few persons have it removed daily, or every other day; "but too often it is thrown out upon the ground, scattered about, removed only as it is raked together in heaps and carted off." Garbage is taken anywhere it can be disposed of, while ashes are deposited on the streets. It is reported that nuisances and probable injury to health occur from keeping garbage on the ground on premises, and that the system has all the defects that belong to "no system".

Dead animals.—The carcasses of all animals dying within the city are at once removed, and either buried or turned over to a soap factory. The annual cost of the service is from $30 to $40, and from 25 to 30 dead animals are removed annually.

Liquid household wastes.—The larger portion of the liquid wastes from the houses in the city are thrown out on the ground about the yards, one-fourth of this entering the gutters, and of the remainder, not over 25 per cent., goes into cesspools. The cesspools are porous, are not provided with overflows, in some instances receive the wastes from water-closets, and are not governed by any regulations as to construction or cleansing. The entire system is "wholly defective". Dr. J. G. Meacham, jr., chairman of the board of health, analyzed the waters from 144 wells used for drinking purposes in the 1st ward of the city, and reported only 47 good at time of examination; "all others contaminated by a soil saturated with filth-matters, sewage, etc." This examination was conducted in but one ward, and regarding other parts of the city Dr. Mecham says: "Incidentally with this investigation several specimens of water from other wards have been sent me, and from their condition I am aware that in some parts of the 2d and 3d wards the water is at present unwholesome. The supply is from the same source (wells) as in the 3d ward, and as the soil becomes more and more impure the unwholesomeness of the water will increase."

Human excreta.—Nearly all the houses in the city depend on privy-vaults. There are perhaps about 40 water-closets all told, and these deliver into cesspools. Very few of the privy-vaults are water tight, and there are no regulations as to their construction or cleansing. They are occasionally cleaned, but "generally covered over and filled with earth and a new vault made". In not over half-a-dozen cases is the dry-earth system used.

Manufacturing wastes, both liquid and solid, flow into the river and thence into lake Michigan.

POLICE.

The chief of police is appointed annually by the mayor, subject to confirmation by the city council, while the other members of the force are appointed by and may be removed by the mayor. The chief of police, salary $600 per annum, is the executive officer, and has general supervision over the force, which consists of 6 patrolmen at $600 a year each. The uniform is blue, with brass buttons, and the men provide their own at a cost of $35 per suit. The patrolmen are equipped with clubs and revolvers; they are on duty from 7 p. m. to 5 a. m., and patrol 6 miles of streets. During the past year 275 arrests were made, the principal causes being for drunkenness, disorderly conduct, vagrancy, and violating city ordinances. Their final disposition was either by fines or imprisonment. During 1880 property to the value of $3,000 was reported to the police as either lost or stolen, and of this $1,200 was recovered and returned to the owners. The county jail being used by the city for a lockup, there are no station-house lodgers. The force is required to co-operate with the fire department by protecting property at fires, with the health department by using all measures to prevent the spread of contagious diseases, and with the building department by seeing that all houses are erected in accordance with the city ordinances. Special policemen are appointed by the mayor to preserve order on special occasions. The yearly cost of the police force (1880) is $4,200.

FIRE DEPARTMENT.

The following regarding the fire department of Racine is all that was mentioned on the subject in the report on the city, made by the special committee. "The fire department consists of 2 steamers, 1 chemical engine, and a hook-and-ladder apparatus, operated by paid men, and doing good and effective service."

SCHOOLS.

The public schools consist of the high school and the grammar and primary department, using 8 buildings, costing $57,000, and employing 44 teachers. The public schools are under the immediate supervision of a city superintendent, acting under and by authority of a board of commissioners, who are appointed by the mayor subject to the approval of the city council. The schools are supported by direct taxation on the city, and are also entitled to a portion of the revenue from the sale of school lands by the state. The curriculum includes geometry and trigonometry, but no higher mathematics; the elementary principles of science, mental, social, and physical, and Latin. No provision is made for the modern languages.

Of private schools there are Racine college, McMyren's academy, Saint Catherine academy, Home school, Passuer business college, and two schools attached to the Roman Catholic church. These institutions are reported as being in a flourishing condition.

MINNESOTA.

MINNEAPOLIS,

HENNEPIN COUNTY, MINNESOTA.

POPULATION

IN THE

AGGREGATE,

1860-1880.

	Inhab.
1790	......
1800	......
1810	......
1820	......
1830	......
1840	......
1850	......
1860	2,564
1870	13,066
1880	46,887

POPULATION

BY

SEX, NATIVITY, AND RACE,

AT

CENSUS OF 1880.

Male	25,291
Female	21,596
Native	31,874
Foreign-born	15,013
White	46,509
Colored	*378

* Including 2 Chinese and 14 Indians.

Latitude: 44° 58′ North; Longitude: 93° 15′ (west from Greenwich); Altitude: 838.5 feet.

FINANCIAL CONDITION:

Total Valuation: $23,415,733; per capita: $499 00. Net Indebtedness: $1,137,467; per capita: $24 26. Tax per $100: $1 46.

HISTORICAL SKETCH.

The honor of the discovery of the falls of Saint Anthony in 1680 is claimed by historians for two men, Accault, a French *voyageur* and explorer, and Louis Hennepin, a Catholic priest who accompanied Accault in his upper Mississippi explorations as companion, clerical assistant, and missionary. Hennepin claims the discovery for himself, and history has generally acknowledged his claim. For nearly 140 years after this time the falls remained in obscurity, being visited only by adventurous travelers like Carver or Pike. The establishment of a military post at Fort Snelling (as it was subsequently called) in 1819 attracted renewed attention to the spot. In 1822 the water-power was first utilized by a small saw-mill built by the quartermaster of the fort in order to get lumber with which to finish the buildings at the fort; a grist-mill was subsequently added. No permanent settlement, however, was made until 1838. The previous year a treaty had been made by Governor Dodge, of Wisconsin, with the Sioux and Chippewas, by which the latter agreed to cede all their lands between the Mississippi and Saint Croix rivers, thus throwing a large tract open to settlement by white men. The instant that the news of the ratification of this treaty by the Senate reached the fort, which was not until June, 1838, claims were staked out around the falls and shortly a settlement was under way. In 1847, Mr. W. A. Cheever purchased for Boston parties a large share in the water-power, and steps were at once taken to improve it and to erect mills. In the summer of 1848 a dam was completed across the east channel of the river from Hennepin island to the main shore. By September, two saws were got in operation. With a good supply of lumber the prospects of the falls brightened wonderfully. The land had been sold at government sale this summer and bought by the parties holding the claims. The Saint Anthony town site was surveyed in the spring of 1849. Minnesota territory was organized during the winter of 1848–'49, and this gave a further impetus to the place.

At this time the territory west of the river, being an Indian tract, was not open to settlers, and the military reservation of Fort Snelling extended over most of the present site of Minneapolis. In 1849 Hon. Robert Smith, then a member of Congress from Illinois, and John H. Stevens secured permits from the government to occupy 160 acres each on the reservation. In the fall of that year Colonel Stevens began the erection of a house, the first one in what is now Minneapolis west. By the close of 1853 there were a dozen houses or more. The difficulty of obtaining a title to the land was a great hinderance to the growth of the village, and it was not until 1855 that the right of pre-emption, the same as on other government lands, was secured to the settlers by an act of Congress. Disputes among the settlers as to the real ownership of claims were not rare, but they were generally submitted to arbitration, and in the end, it is believed, the rights of all *bona fide* claimants were secured to them. From this time dates a more prosperous era for the struggling village.

Hennepin county was organized on October 21, 1852, only 73 votes being polled from what is now Minneapolis and vicinity. This territory was for a short time known as West Saint Anthony. At a claim association meeting in 1851, at which a number of settlers were present, "Lowell" was adopted, but this did not suit, and later on it was changed to "Albion". Finally the editor of the Saint Anthony *Express* printed an article proposing the name Minneapolis, a compound of the Sioux *minne*, water, and the Greek πόλις, city. This did not at first sound well, but the editor adhered to the use of the word, and in a few weeks its sound became familiar, and was then adopted by all.

In 1854 John H. Stevens had his claim surveyed and laid out into a town plot. The Smith claim also was soon surveyed into blocks and lots. At the close of 1854 it was estimated that the town contained 100 buildings and about 1,000 inhabitants. In that year the first flouring-mill (not a permanent one), and also the first bridge, were built. During the earliest days of the village there had been great difficulty in getting back and forth across the river, teams having to ford it, which was possible only during low water. In 1851 Franklin Steele secured a ferry charter from the legislature, a bridge was built across the east channel to the island, and a ferry-boat soon plied on the west channel. In 1854 the "Minneapolis Bridge Company" was organized, and a fine wire suspension bridge was erected, the first bridge ever thrown across the Father of Waters. It was dedicated in January, 1855, with a great celebration. In March it was almost destroyed and had to be chiefly rebuilt. After that it did good service till 1877, when the present magnificent structure was erected in its place.

Minneapolis was first organized into a town government in 1858. The town organization lasted only until 1862, when, the discouragements and drawbacks resulting from the civil war leading many to think a more economical form of government could be adopted, the charter was repealed, and a simple township organization was substituted. After the close of the war the rapid growth in wealth and population necessitated some more effective form of government, and in 1867 a city charter was secured from the legislature. Saint Anthony had obtained a city charter in 1855. In 1873, by an act of the legislature, the two cities were consolidated under the name of Minneapolis, which by that time had become the more populous of the two.

In 1878 an explosion and fire in the milling district destroyed 6 of the largest flouring-mills, diminishing the flour-producing capacity of the city one-half. These were all rebuilt during the next two years with increased capacity. In June, 1880, the total capacity for the city was 25,000 barrels per day. No periods of depression worthy of note have occurred in the history of the city except that during the war time. The population of Minneapolis is largely made up of hardy, thrifty, intelligent New Englanders. There have been large accessions from the middle and other states of native-born people, and there is also a strong admixture of foreign population, the Scandinavian, German, Irish, and French predominating.

The growth and prosperity of Minneapolis have been almost wholly due to the natural advantages of its site. The power of the falls of Saint Anthony is enormous. The river, passing through the strata of rock on its bed of solid limestone, precipitates, even at a low stage, 450,000 cubic feet of water per minute down a declivity of 80 feet in a distance of less than a mile. Scientific computations have established the fact that the force represented is equal to 120,000 theoretical or 100,000 actual horse-power. The shores are of such a character as to allow

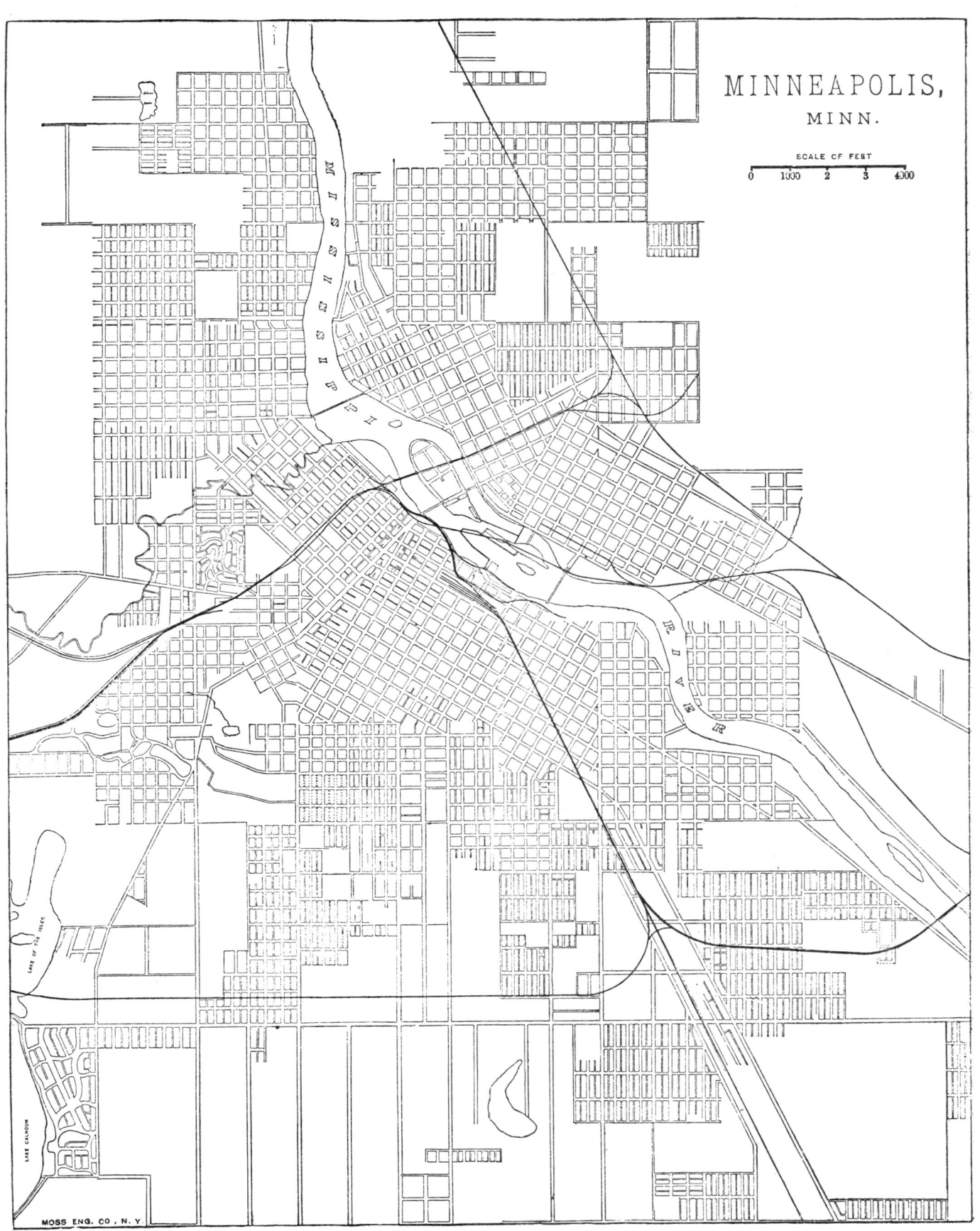

MINNEAPOLIS,
MINN.

SCALE OF FEET

0   1000   2   3   4000

MOSS ENG. CO , N. Y

canals to be excavated parallel with the stream to any desired extent, with the best of rock for their bottoms and sides; and the water can easily be led from the river into these canals. Another excellence, which adds to the availability of the power and the security of investments in it, is the superior foundation afforded by the hard limestone rock for dams and mills. These have never been swept away from their foundations, and the present dams, built almost a quarter of a century ago, remain perfectly intact and unimpaired. The rise of the river here is always gradual; destructive freshets do not occur. This is due to the level nature of the country at the sources of the stream, which is but one vast chain of lake reservoirs and sluggish streams, covering hundreds of square miles. The heaviest rainfalls are thus distributed over a vast area of country and drain into the main stream gradually.

The only drawback in connection with the water-power furnished by these falls is the danger that in time they will wear away. When the water is low the greater portion of it is very often drawn through the sluices, leaving the limestone ledge nearly bare, and subject to rapid disintegration by the action of frost. The precipitation of such a volume of water so constantly upon the underlying friable sandstone at the foot of the falls slowly undermined the overhanging ledge, large sections gave way from time to time, and the recession of the falls began to be looked upon with alarm. In 1868 a long tunnel was started lengthwise under the river with the intention of mitigating the evil, but the attempt was a failure and increased rather than lessened the danger. The survey of the falls in 1869 by Major General G. K. Warren, United States Army, drew the attention of the government to the necessity of arresting their destruction. An appropriation of $50,000 was accordingly made in 1870 and expended, but the results were not so satisfactory as to afford a sense of entire security. In 1872, and again in 1874, a board of engineers recommended the construction of a wall in the bed of sandstone beneath the ledge, 4 feet thick and 38 feet in height, the whole distance across the river, which would effectually prevent any further leakage. The plan was carried out, and a wall was constructed which has thus far sustained the ledge and prevented the ingress of water. In 1878 the apron was remodeled and rebuilt in its preset shape. In 1879 a sluiceway was built by the government at the west end of the apron, for the passage of logs down the river without damage to the apron. This sluice is 6 feet wide and 346 feet long. The falls of Saint Anthony being now in the hands of the government for preservation, there is an annual expenditure for repairs only.

MINNEAPOLIS IN 1880.

The following statistical accounts, mainly collected by the Census Office, indicate the present condition of Minneapolis:

LOCATION.

Minneapolis, the capital of Hennepin county, is situated on both banks of the Mississippi river, at the falls of Saint Anthony, in latitude 44° 58′ north, and longitude 93° 15′ west from Greenwich, 8 miles northwest of Saint Paul, at an average altitude of 838.5 feet above the level of the sea. Above the falls the river is navigable 80 miles for light-draft boats, there being 2 feet of water at its lowest stage. Below, it is navigable 8 months in the year, and with proper improvements would have 5 feet of water in the channel at all times.

RAILROAD COMMUNICATIONS.

Minneapolis is touched by the following railroads:

The main line of the Chicago, Milwaukee, and Saint Paul railroad runs from Minneapolis to Chicago via Saint Paul and Milwaukee.

The Breckenridge division of the Saint Paul, Minneapolis, and Manitoba railway runs from Saint Paul to Saint Vincent via Minneapolis, giving connection with Winnipeg.

The Minneapolis and Saint Louis railway connects at Albert Lea with the Burlington, Cedar Rapids, and Northern railroad, giving lines to Saint Louis and the South.

The Chicago, Saint Paul, and Minneapolis line of the Chicago, Saint Paul, Minneapolis, and Omaha railroad gives a line to Chicago via Madison, and to Sioux City via Saint Paul.

The Minneapolis, Lyndale, and Lake Calhoun railroad, a short road, runs to lake Harriet. These roads, with their various connections, reach every important point, east, north, west, and south.

TRIBUTARY COUNTRY.

The country in the immediate vicinity is divided between grain- and stock-raising. Minneapolis is the chief manufacturing and distributing point for the timber lands of the whole upper Mississippi valley. More than half of the surplus wheat produced in Minnesota is manufactured into flour at Minneapolis.

TOPOGRAPHY.

The soil is a sandy loam, underneath which there is a layer of gravel resting on limestone, and that on a soft sandstone. The official examinations made by the engineering department of the government shows the composition of the bed of the river at the falls as follows: first, 15 feet drift, containing beds of marl, sand, clay, gravel, and bowlders; second, 13 feet buff-colored sandstone; third, 13 feet best blue limestone, hard, disintegrating slowly on exposure to the air; fourth, 1.5 foot ash-colored, crystal limestone; fifth, 5 feet marlite, containing sand, and clay of blue, green, and yellow color, interstratified; sixth, 5 feet white sandstone, 5 feet above the water level. The dip of these strata is to the south.

The site of the city is gently undulating, and nearly level for from 1 to 2 miles back from each side of the river, at which distance rise chains of wooded bluffs of moderate height, on which there are many residences. The natural drainage is good, and there are no marshes.

CLIMATE.

The highest recorded summer temperature is 101°; the highest in average years, 94°; the mean summer temperature, 67°. The lowest recorded winter temperature, −40°; the lowest in average years, −30°; mean winter temperature, 12.5°. There are no adjacent waters, marshes, or elevated lands to produce a sensible effect on the climate. The only influence of the prevailing winds is to make the atmosphere dry.

STREETS.

Total length of streets about 200 miles, none of which are paved. The city engineer, in his report to the city council for the year ending April 1, 1880, said:

I would here call attention to the necessity of adopting some more durable material for the construction of our roadways, sidewalks, and crossings than the ordinary dirt or mud roadway and wooden side- and cross-walks, especially for the business portion of our city. * * * To undertake the work of street-paving would, as a matter of course, necessitate the expenditure of considerable money, and owing to the great width of our streets the property-holders are very reluctant about commencing such an improvement. * * * I have returned to your honorable body during the past year special sidewalk assessments to the amount of $10,086 10. All of the above sidewalks were ordered constructed of pine lumber. Our sidewalks having been laid at different times are consequently in different conditions, some good, others fair, and a great many in very bad condition. * * * Resurveys and establishment of street lines by planting iron monuments have been carried out as far as possible the past working season with the regular force in the office.

It appears from the same report that during the year, $2,760 37 was spent in street-grading, of which $2,554 63 was spent on contract, and the rest on day work, and that the cost of street work, as done by the street commissioners during the year, was $17,669 66. Nearly all the sidewalks of the city are made of pine lumber. A few blocks have cobble-stone gutters, the rest being of earth. As fast as improvements are made shade-trees are set out. All streets outside the business section have about one-fourth of their width devoted to grass-plats, with foot-walks varying from 6 to 8 feet in width, running in the middle of the portion allotted on each side of the street. The trees are planted about 30 feet apart in the middle of the grass-plats, so as to alternate and make the distance between the trees about 17 feet (i. e., a line connecting the trees would zigzag across the sidewalk). There is a decided preference for contract work for grading. Repairing is done by day work. The bridges owned by the city are as follows:

Table of bridges.

Kind of bridge.	Number of spans.	Length of bridge.	Length of span.
		Feet.	*Feet.*
Suspension, wire	1	675. 0	
Arch, stone	5	383. 5	
Pratt truss, iron	6	1,080. 0	
Howe truss, wood	10	1,560. 0	
Bent and braced truss, wood	9	354. 0	
Arched culvert, stone	1	22. 0	22
Do	1	25. 0	25
Queen truss, wood	1		25
Bent, wood		160. 0	
Queen truss, wood	1		25
Pile, wood		330. 0	
Queen truss, wood			40
Howe truss, wood	1	70. 0	
Queen truss, wood	1	40. 0	
Bent, wood		40. 0	

The total length of horse-railroad track in the city is 9 miles; total number of cars, 21; of horses, 90; of men employed, 35; of passengers carried during the year, 987,267. The rate of fare is 5 cents.

WATER-WORKS.

The water-works are owned by the city. The Holly system of direct pumping is used, and an average pressure of 53 pounds is maintained. The annual report of the superintendent of water-works for the year ending March 31, 1880, shows the following facts: The total pumping capacity is 7,500,000 gallons per day; the expenditures of the water-works, exclusive of interest and current expenses to March 31, 1880, were $396,298 83. In 1879, 14,018.5 feet of water-mains were laid, at an expense of $10,188 14; previous to 1879, 34,483 feet had been laid, making the total pipe laid (exclusive of hydrant pipe) 18 miles 3,461 feet. The receipts from water-rates, penalties, etc., for the year were $16,008 72; an average of 2,628,569 gallons was pumped per day; and the total cost of maintenance, aside from the actual cost of pumping, was $5,615 51; the cost of pumping (including salaries, repairs, oil, and other supplies pertaining to the pumping-machinery) was $4,343 11.

GAS.

The gas-works are not owned by the city; their daily average production is 60,000 cubic feet, and the cost per 1,000 feet varies from $2 50 to $2 80. The city pays $2 50 per month each for 300 street-lamps.

PUBLIC BUILDINGS.

The city owns a city hall valued at $50,000, a city prison valued at $5,000, a pest-house valued at $3,000, and a number of engine-houses valued at about $75,000.

PUBLIC PARKS AND PLEASURE-GROUNDS.

There are no artificial parks, but in the suburbs there are small lakes, groves, etc., which supply their place. Within 3.5 miles of the city there are 4 lakes, each about 1.5 mile in length and the same in breadth; in them the water is clear and cool, and there are plenty of fish. The celebrated falls of Minnehaha are but 3 miles distant.

PLACES OF AMUSEMENT.

The city has 2 theaters, seating, respectively, 1,500 and 1,100, and a large lecture hall seating about 1,600. The theaters pay no license. There are no concert- or beer-gardens within the jurisdiction of the city.

DRAINAGE.

No reports as to the drainage of the city were received from the city officials. From the city engineer's report for the year ending April 1, 1879, it appears that previous to that time 12,069.5 feet of sewers had been laid, and from the report for the following year it does not appear that any have since been laid.

CEMETERIES.

There are 5 cemeteries connected with the city, as follows: *Lakewood*, containing 153 acres, situated 3.5 miles south from the city center; *Layman's*, 20 acres, 2 miles southeast from the city center; *Maple Hill*, 10 acres, 1.5 mile northeast from the city center; a Catholic cemetery and a Hebrew cemetery. The total number of interments in Lakewood cemetery from 1872 to 1880, inclusive, was 715. Within 30 hours after death the attending physician must issue a certificate as to cause of death, etc.; this is delivered to the health officer, who thereupon issues a burial permit; this in turn is given to the cemetery superintendent, who issues an order for burial. Graves must be from 5 to 6 feet in depth. In Lakewood cemetery the price of lots varies from $25 to $200; the cost of grading and sodding is $10 per lot; of the annual care of lot, $5 to $7 50; burial fees are $4 and $5, and the annual revenue is from $5,000 to $7,000. Every lot-owner is a proprietor under the general statute of the state, and all moneys received must be expended for the purchase and improvement of the grounds.

SANITARY AUTHORITY.

A city ordinance passed in 1873 provides that "The city council shall elect annually a physician who shall be a graduate of some college of medicine in good standing with his profession, and fitted by capacity and experience for the performance of the duties of the office to be health officer. Such health officer, together with two aldermen and two private citizens, to be appointed by the city council, shall be constituted a board of health, whose duty it shall be faithfully to execute all laws of the state relating to public health, and perform such other duties as shall be assigned to them by the city ordinance." At present the two "private citizens" are physicians, making in all 3 physicians on the board. The expenses of the board are mainly incurred for printing, disinfectants, burial of carcasses found, the salary of the health officer ($400) and that of the health inspector ($720), in all about $1,200 per year. The total expenditure on account of the health department last year was $1,834 06, which included quite a large expenditure for "dumping-ground". The board has no authority to expend money except by the permission of the city council granted from time to time, and it has no more authority during epidemics than at other times. The health officer is *ex officio* president of the board. It is his duty "to make regular monthly sanitary inspections of the city as to all matters affecting the health of its citizens, and to make written reports of these inspections at each regular meeting of the board"; at the end of the year he makes to the city council a detailed statement of his operations during the year. The board meets monthly unless called oftener, and transacts its business in the usual way. One inspector is employed who expends his whole time in making inspections and seeing that nuisances are abated; he has police powers like any city policeman. When any nuisance, source of filth, or cause of sickness is found on private property, the board must order its removal within 24 hours by the owner or occupant; if this is not done in that time the board proceeds to have it done and charges the expense to the owner or occupant. If any person prevents the board from entering any building for the purpose of examining into and destroying, removing, or preventing any nuisance, etc., he may be punished, if convicted in the municipal court, by a fine not exceeding $50 and costs, and, in default of payment, imprisoned not more than 60 days, and the court may issue a warrant to the chief of police requiring him to accompany the board of health and aid it in the suppression of any nuisance, etc., that may be found. As to defective house-drainage, privy-vaults, cesspools, and sources of drinking-water, the inspector inspects as far as he is able to without complaint from citizens—always where complaint is made; as to defective sewerage, street-cleaning, etc., reports are made to the street commissioners, but the board has no authority over them. As to the conservation and removal of garbage, the board can take action only in case of nuisances arising. In case of death the attendant physician or, if there was none, the owner or occupant of the building, or nearest relative, must make a register of the cause of death, with the name, nativity, residence, sex, occupation, date, hour, place, and street of such death, and this register must be presented to the board of health within 30 hours after death; no interment shall be made without a permit from the health officer. Excrement must be removed in tight boxes and at night.

INFECTIOUS DISEASES.

Small-pox and scarlet-fever patients are isolated by stopping communications with the outside world from all persons occupying houses where the disease exists; the ordinances provide that if the patient can be removed to a separate house without danger it shall be done; if not, the persons in the neighborhood may be removed if thought necessary. The board takes no cognizance of the breaking out of contagious diseases in public and private schools, except to the extent of isolating the patients. There is no public pest-house. Vaccination is compulsory only for those attending school; it is not done at the public expense.

REPORTS.

The system of registration in case of deaths has been mentioned; that in case of births is similar; except that the items to be entered are the time, ward, and street of such birth, the sex and color of the child born, and the name and residence of each of the parents, and that 5 days are allowed for the presentation of the register. It is reported that the authority of the board is very limited.

In the annual report of the health officer, Dr. A. H. Salisbury, presented to the city council April 1, 1880, he says:

That Minneapolis has thus far been able to maintain a good reputation for health is due to the natural healthfulness of the place, and not to the existence of any active and watchful health department. The department has not kept pace with the other branches of the city government in the improvements of the last few years. * * * It consists now (as in 1874) of a health officer, whose small salary only permits him to devote a part of his time to the duties of his office, and a health inspector, whose duties are so varied and numerous that he is unable to make a systematic sanitary inspection of any part of the city. * * * The three great requisites of health—pure air, pure water, and pure soil—were found here by the early settlers in absolute perfection. * * * The old inhabitants who knew the place in its primitive purity can hardly realize that it is no longer a sanitarium. They call it slander when told that their beloved city is no longer possessed of pure air, pure water, and pure earth, and is in danger of becoming notorious as an unhealthy city. At present our death rate is not above the average of cities of this size; but we are neglecting those sanitary measures which a little bitter experience has taught other communities to take. We have thus far escaped any extensive epidemic, but the fact that a very large percentage of the total mortality is from zymotic diseases, which alone form the real guide to the sanitary condition, renders our situation alarming. We are almost totally exempt from malarial diseases, a large relative proportion die from accident, while many deaths from tuberculous diseases are among the transient population. * * * The school buildings of this city, while not perfect from a sanitary standpoint, are perhaps as nearly so as public school buildings usually are. Some of them did lack proper ventilation, but that defect has been overcome. * * * If any reliance can be placed on the table of deaths presented with the report—and it is undoubtedly approximately correct—there has been a steady and alarming increase of the death rate during the past three years—9, 11, 14. At this rate, in three more years our death rate will equal that of the most unhealthy city of the Union. * * * Last year I caused an inspection of some houses where deaths had occurred to be made. The tabulated results go far to prove that these diseases, which cause almost one-third (31.54 per cent.) of our total mortality, are the result of impure air and water, and are therefore preventable. I feel positively sure that were the water from a few miles up the river distributed throughout the city, and every well filled up or pulled up, the use of cesspools and vaults prohibited, and sewers constructed wherever needed, the death rate from zymotic diseases, which is now $4\frac{1}{2}$ per 1,000, would be reduced to 1 per 1,000, or even less. This would have saved during the last year 182 lives, or, at the usual computation, of a life at a $1,000, $182,000. * * * The total number of deaths last year was 744.

MUNICIPAL CLEANSING.

Street-cleaning.—The streets are cleaned by the city's own force by hand, under the direction of the street commissioners. The mayor reports that it is "well done", which differs somewhat from the intimation of the health officer on the same subject. The latter says in his annual report:

The [health] department having no means under its own control of cleaning alleys, gutters, etc., had to depend upon the oftentimes slow movements of the street commissioners. But by considerable persistence on the part of Inspector Rich the streets and alleys were kept in a respectable condition until winter. Toward the spring the use of the dumping-ground was discontinued; considerable stable and other refuse was suffered to accumulate. New grounds having been procured, it s now being rapidly removed. Under the present plan the health department is held responsible for the sanitary condition of the streets, and yet has no means of keeping them in order, except to request the street commissioners, and then patiently await their slow pleasure.

Removal of garbage and ashes.—Scavengers remove all garbage. While awaiting removal it is kept in boxes or barrels, and it is allowable to keep ashes in the same vessel. The cost of removal is $1 per load. The health officer, in his report above mentioned, said:

I discover that it has not been the custom to remove these substances [*i. e.*, refuse matter] from the city limits, at least only such portions as the farmers removed to be used as fertilizers. The scavengers and others employed in this business were in the habit of dumping their savory loads in any secluded spot they could find. Hoag's lake was being rapidly filled up with a most abominable variety of filth. I peremptorily discontinued the use of this vicinity as the city dumping-ground, * * * and succeeded in securing a spot near Chicago avenue, about 2 miles from the city; * * * during the summer and fall hardly any material of this kind was deposited elsewhere.

Three scavenger's licenses were taken out last year, bringing $21 65 into the city treasury.

Dead animals.—The mayor reports that scavengers deliver dead animals to bone-burners, receiving $1 each for removal, and that about 1,000 are annually removed. As the controller's report shows that the health department last year paid $33 25 to scavengers for removing dead animals, there would seem to be a discrepancy here unless the owners were found for the other 966.75 animals, which seems hardly probable.

Liquid household wastes.—The mayor further reports that waste water from sleeping-rooms, laundry waste, and kitchen slops are all disposed of in the same way, *i. e.*, emptied into cesspools and sewers, about two-thirds, in his opinion, going into cesspools or "dry wells", and one-third into sewers; where the former are used they receive the waste of water-closets; cesspools are cleaned out at midnight by city scavengers, emptied at the dumping-ground, and covered with lime. He says: "We are introducing on lines of street-mains public spigots, and filling up wells." In this connection the health officer's report says:

In this city, as long as the soil remained unpolluted, the water from the * * * wells and springs was of the best quality, and, being easily obtained, was universally used. But gradually, as the population increased, the soil was made the depository for all the filth accompanying a high state of civilization, * * * and it is doubtful if there is now a well within the limits of the city, the water of which is as healthful as that of the Mississippi. * * * To determine * * * the comparative purity of the drinking-water taken from a variety of sources within the city, * * * the water from 7 wells was analyzed. There had been more or less sickness among those using the water from these wells, but in no case were they selected on account of the proximity of filth, and in this respect are no worse than the majority of wells in the city. * * * The analysis showed that 5 of the wells were absolutely unfit for use. These wells were all driven wells, so that impurities could only reach them after being filtered through the soil. * * * The result * * * establishes these facts: The well-water is generally impure, unwholesome, poisonous, and is becoming more so each year. * * * In order to ascertain, if possible, what effect bad hygienic surroundings had in causing or propagating zymotic diseases, I caused an inspection of some houses where deaths had occurred to be made. The houses inspected were not selected for the purpose of establishing any theory, but were taken from the reports of deaths as they occurred. * * * Of the 13 houses, occupied by at least 30 families, only 2 used hydrant water. All the others used well-water, or water taken from the river where it must necessarily be contaminated with sewage. * * * The wells were all shallow, being from 12 to 20 feet deep, and privies usually about 20 feet distant.

In an earlier part of this report Dr. Salisbury says:

We have buried in our light, porous soil all manner of filth. Only within the last year or two has any thing been removed from the city. Privy-vaults and cesspools, whenever they become full, have been covered with a few inches of earth and new ones dug. The filth from stables and yards has been deposited in large masses as filling for low places. The filth from sewers and gutters has been used for the same purpose. Is it any wonder then that the water has become contaminated?

Human excreta.—About one-third of the houses of the city have water-closets; of these about one-half deliver into the public sewers, and one-half into cesspools. The dry-earth system is used by very few. Night-soil is removed at night to the dumping-ground, where it is covered with lime. It is not allowed to be used for manuring land within the gathering-ground of the public water-supply.

Manufacturing wastes.—Milling and wood-work make little offensive waste to require special care.

POLICE.

The police force is appointed by the mayor, confirmed by the city council, and governed by the mayor. The chief executive officer is the chief of police, with a salary of $1,500 per year; he has general supervision of the force, and is its responsible head and director. The rest of the force, with their salaries per year, are as follows: Captain, $1,100; sergeant, $1,000; detective, $1,100; 26 patrolmen, $840 each; jailor, $700; man stationed at stone pile, $840. Their uniform is of blue cloth with brass buttons, and they provide their own, the city furnishing only hats and caps. The patrolmen serve 10 hours a day, being divided into three reliefs; the first roll-call is at 7.30 a. m., the second at 6 p. m., and the third at 9 p. m. They regularly patrol about 50 miles of streets. In 1880 there were 2,607 arrests. In the fiscal year ending April 1, 1880, there were 1,956 arrests, of which 416 were for intoxication, 258 for vagrancy, 238 for being found in houses of ill-fame, 138 for larceny, 108 for assault and battery, 78 for grand larceny, 58 for selling liquor to minors, 56 for keeping saloon open on Sunday, 50 for violating city ordinances, 47 for keeping house of ill-fame, and the rest for miscellaneous offenses; of these, 598 were fined in the municipal court, 576 discharged, 347 committed to the county jail, 105 sent out of the city, 98 dismissed, 57 had sentence suspended, 56 were remanded to authorities abroad, 65 bound over to await the action of the grand jury, and the rest bound over to keep the peace, or sent to the house of correction, the reform school, etc. In 1880 there were 1,157 station-house lodgers, against 731 in 1879. No free meals were given them. Special policemen are appointed by the mayor and confirmed by the council, because they are night watchmen, janitors, etc., or for special occasions when the regular force is insufficient. The cost of the police force for 1880 was $27,378 87.

PUBLIC SCHOOLS.

The government of the schools is vested by legislative charter in a board of education of 7 members, elected triennially by the people, on one general ticket, 1 from each ward and 1 at large, who serve without compensation, and who are chosen as non-partisans. The money necessary for the maintenance of the public-school system is derived partly from the general school fund of the state (a princely endowment of public lands), the residue from direct taxation. The amount of money necessary to be raised by taxation is recommended by the board of education and included in the general tax-levy for other purposes.

The Census of 1880 shows that there are 14,037 children between the ages of 5 and 21 in the city; the whole number enrolled last year was 6,142, with an average daily attendance of 4,248. The total cost of maintaining the schools for the year was $76,259 99, the per capita cost of the pupils enrolled being $12 42; of pupils, based on the average attendance, $17 95.

The financial statement of the board accompanying the report for 1880, covering 1879, from which also the above facts are quoted, shows the total receipts of moneys from all sources to be $117,015 90; disbursements, $105,644 54, including $13,946 23 for redemption of bonds and interest, and $3,263 26 for permanent improvements.

The property in possession of the board of education includes 14 school buildings, valued at $359,362, and unoccupied real estate worth $5,400. The high-school building, completed last year, cost $86,427. All this school property is by law exempt from taxation.

The university of Minnesota, the state university, is located here. At present it has 17 instructors, 159 college students, and 149 preparatory students. There are no tuition fees and no dormitories. The endowment is made up of public lands granted by Congress (1) to the territory, 46,000 acres; (2) to the state, 46,000; (3) to the College of Agriculture and the Mechanic Arts, 120,000; from which is to be deducted 10,000 not located, leaving a balance of 202,000 acres. The value of the grounds and buildings is estimated at $220,000.

Besides the above, there are several institutions of a private character, supported as denominational schools, and for various technical purposes, which have a reasonably good attendance.

FIRE DEPARTMENT.

The annual report of the chief engineer of the fire department for the year ending April 1, 1880, shows the following: The manual force of the present department numbers 59 men. This force took the place of 304 volunteers disbanded. The following apparatus is in actual service: 2 steam fire-engines, 5 two-horse hose-carriages, 1 one-horse hose-cart, 1 two-horse hook-and-ladder truck. The department has in service 20 horses, 12 of which the city owns. It has in service 10,000 feet of rubber hose, 2,000 of which may be considered second-class. The city has a fire-alarm telegraph which gives good satisfaction. There are 221 hydrants in the city. During the year the department responded to 130 alarms, an increase of 32 over the previous year. The companies averaged about 80 hours each on fire duty. As near as could be ascertained, the total loss by fire during the year was $56,945; insurance paid, $46,845; total insurance on property involved, $418,025. The total expenses of the department last year amounted to $41,136 10, of which $11,249 37 was for property purchased, and $29,886 73 for salaries and other expenses. The principal causes of fires and alarms were: supposed incendiary, 18; carelessness, 16; unknown, 15; defective chimneys, 14; sparks from locomotives, chimneys, etc., 10; chimney fires, 10.

MANUFACTURES.

The following is a summary of the statistics of the manufactures of Minneapolis for 1880, being taken from tables prepared for the Tenth Census:

Mechanical and manufacturing industries.	No. of establishments.	Capital.	AVERAGE NUMBER OF HANDS EMPLOYED.			Total amount paid in wages during the year.	Value of materials.	Value of products.
			Males above 16 years.	Females above 15 years.	Children and youths.			
All industries..............................	401	$9,002,650	4,702	457	185	$2,582,253	$24,274,623	$29,973,476
Blacksmithing (see also Wheelwrighting)	29	30,250	68	....	....	39,695	43,313	132,200
Boots and shoes, including custom work and repairing	34	153,050	100	4	....	63,500	123,280	240,265
Boxes, fancy and paper......................................	3	1,600	3	4	5	2,085	1,900	6,800
Bread and other bakery products	7	38,300	44	10	1	19,250	139,960	185,355
Brick and tile..	6	21,000	108	....	....	37,350	11,200	65,600
Carpentering	13	36,700	164	....	....	88,500	188,800	343,000
Carriages and wagons (see also Wheelwrighting)	13	40,100	102	....	....	56,930	78,300	174,700
Clothing, men's..............................	25	105,675	190	40	5	118,150	197,750	386,700
Cooperage	11	68,000	282	....	35	148,914	235,514	447,152
Flouring- and grist-mill products........................	29	3,820,500	721	....	....	555,669	19,011,239	20,502,305
Foundery and machine-shop products	15	474,700	380	....	....	200,500	451,640	807,783
Furniture (see also Mattresses and spring beds).....................	14	126,300	190	2	1	88,450	125,000	273,000
Furs, dressed	4	7,700	3	16	....	3,960	15,200	25,800
Liquors, malt..............................	3	180,000	58	1	....	25,083	106,870	190,678
Lock- and gun-smithing.....................................	4	2,200	7	....	....	3,950	2,200	10,700
Lumber, planed (see also Sash, doors, and blinds)	6	66,500	81	....	....	32,742	49,950	131,577
Lumber, sawed.....................................	16	2,405,000	877	13	30	374,500	1,649,430	2,740,848
Marble and stone work	5	16,300	40	....	....	17,050	22,300	53,000
Mattresses and spring beds (see also Furniture).....................	3	9,000	17	3	....	7,000	17,500	37,000
Mineral and soda waters.....................................	5	10,600	14	....	....	5,400	12,300	23,200
Photographing	6	25,500	12	4	....	7,880	5,100	23,376
Plumbing and gasfitting.....................................	3	26,500	35	....	....	17,100	49,300	79,000
Printing and publishing.....................................	14	142,000	196	10	13	123,900	104,000	321,500
Pumps, not including steam pumps.....................	3	5,500	17	....	....	7,500	12,000	24,500
Saddlery and harness	14	36,950	71	....	....	33,560	55,100	118,400
Sash, doors, and blinds (see also Lumber, planed)	5	201,000	246	....	35	112,746	374,000	601,193
Slaughtering and meat-packing, not including retail butchering.....	4	39,000	37	....	1	14,300	197,990	270,600
Tinware, copperware, and sheet-iron ware	21	37,200	88	....	....	42,870	87,175	174,300
Tobacco, cigars and cigarettes.........................	5	12,650	28	....	....	16,250	19,400	52,700
Watch and clock repairing	14	7,475	22	....	1	11,300	7,480	30,400
Wheelwrighting (see also Blacksmithing; Carriages and wagons)...	9	8,600	29	....	....	14,541	12,761	36,377
All other industries (a)	58	846,800	472	350	58	291,528	866,671	1,463,467

a Embracing agricultural implements; awnings and tents; bags, other than paper; bookbinding and blank-book making; boxes, wooden packing; brass castings; brooms and brushes; carpets, rag; coffee and spices, roasted and ground; confectionery; corsets; cotton goods; cutlery and edge tools; drain and sewer pipe; dyeing and cleaning; electroplating; files; flavoring extracts; furnishing goods, men's; glass, cut, stained, and ornamented; gloves and mittens; hosiery and knit goods; iron work, architectural and ornamental; leather, dressed skins; looking-glass and picture frames; masonry, brick and stone; models and patterns; musical instruments, organs and materials; oil, linseed; oil, lubricating; painting and paperhanging; paper; pickles, preserves, and sauces; saws; shirts; show-cases; soap and candles; steam fittings and heating apparatus; stencils and brands; tools; trunks and valises; washing-machines and clothes-wringers; wirework; wood, turned and carved; and woolen goods.

From the foregoing table it appears that the average capital of all establishments is $22,450 40; that the average wages of all hands employed is $483 20 per annum; and that the average outlay in wages, in materials, and in interest (at 6 per cent.) on capital employed is $68,321 78.

SAINT PAUL,

RAMSEY COUNTY, MINNESOTA.

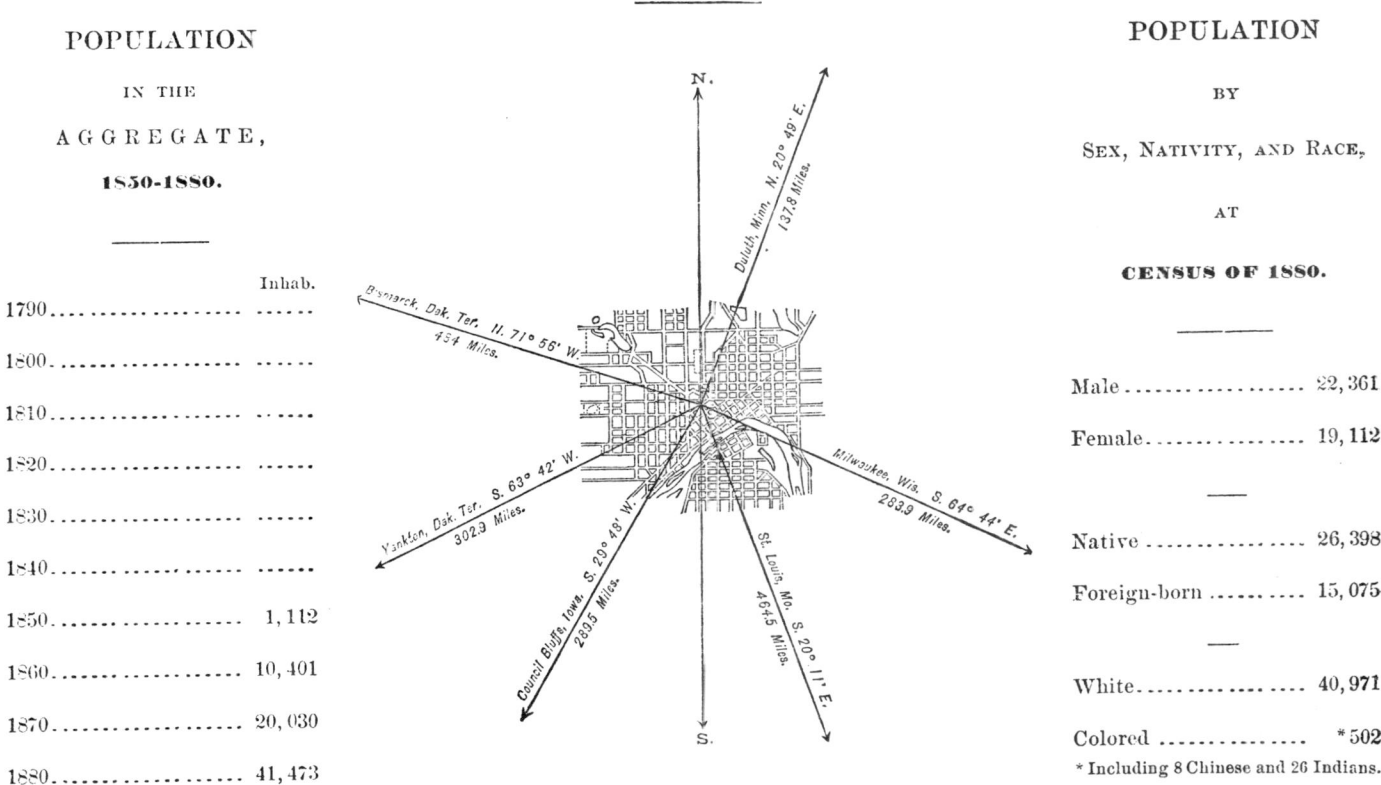

POPULATION

IN THE

AGGREGATE,

1850-1880.

	Inhab.
1790	......
1800	......
1810	......
1820	......
1830	......
1840	......
1850	1,112
1860	10,401
1870	*20,030
1880	41,473

POPULATION

BY

SEX, NATIVITY, AND RACE,

AT

CENSUS OF 1880.

Male	22,361
Female	19,112
Native	26,398
Foreign-born	15,075
White	40,971
Colored	*502

* Including 8 Chinese and 26 Indians.

Latitude: 44° 56' North; Longitude: 93° 5' (west from Greenwich); Altitude: 800 feet.

FINANCIAL CONDITION:

Total Valuation: $24,000,000; per capita: $579 00.   Net Indebtedness: $1,526,715; per capita: $36 81.   Tax per $100: $1 40.

HISTORICAL SKETCH.(a)

The first human habitation on the present site of Saint Paul was built in 1838. It was a mere hovel, built by a squatter named Pierre Parrant, whose object was to get just outside the lines of the Fort Snelling reservation, where he could sell whisky to the soldiers and Indians in a secret way.

At about the same time, Congress ratified the treaty with the Sioux, which threw open the lands east of the Mississippi to settlement, and a few squatters, principally refugees from the Red River settlement who had been driven away from there by calamity, settled on the lands now included in the limits of the city. In 1841 a small log chapel was built by a Roman Catholic priest from Dubuque, named Lucien Gaultier. It was named by him the "chapel of Saint Paul", and thus gave its name to the little village.

a By J. F. Williams, esq., secretary of the State Historical Society.

In 1847 the proprietors of the lands now in the central part of the city caused a tract of land of about 80 acres to be surveyed into lots, and the plat was filed for record under the name "town of Saint Paul". It was then included in the boundaries of Wisconsin territory. On May 29, 1848, Wisconsin was admitted as a state, and that portion of the former territory on which Saint Paul stood was left outside the new state boundary, and without any government whatever. Its inabitants at once took active measures to secure a territorial government, and Congress passed an act organizing the territory of Minnesota, with Saint Paul as its capital. This act was approved March 3, 1849.

At this time there were only 30 buildings in the town and not over 200 inhabitants, but the organization of the territory and location of the seat of government attracted crowds of settlers, and the town grew very rapidly. Within 3 or 4 years it had become a populous and thriving point. A town charter was granted it by the first legislature in 1849, and a city charter by the legislature of 1854. By a census taken in 1855 there was a population of 4,716.

The rapid growth of Saint Paul and of the territory produced one of the most remarkable periods of speculation and inflation, especially in real estate, ever known in American history. It began to be marked in 1854 or 1855; grew intense in 1856, and in 1857 the wild speculative frenzy had grown to be a perfect madness, which appeared to affect all classes. In August of that year it met with a sudden check by the financial panic which began in New York city. The revolution affected Saint Paul with extreme severity, and a trying period of depression set in. There were at that time little capital, limited trade, but few industries, and no accumulated wealth. The population of the city decreased, empty dwellings and vacant stores by the score attested to the severity of the times, and it was three years before perceptible recovery began. During this period there were scarcely any new buildings erected, and the tax duplicate shows a remarkable falling off in the assessed valuation. Real estate was utterly unsalable.

Some improvement began to be noticed in 1860, but was of transient duration, as the secession movement soon produced another period of depression, and the years 1861 and 1862 were years of extreme distress. The Indian massacre in August, 1862, which depopulated all the western part of the state, farther intensified it. The issue, about this time, of "greenbacks" by the government soon produced another period of inflation and great ease in the money market. The expenditure of large sums by the War Department, the building of railroads, etc., gave a considerable revival to business.

From 1865 to the fall of 1873 was one of the busy and prosperous periods of the city. Numerous fine and costly public buildings, business blocks, dwellings, schools, churches, etc., and works of improvement were constructed. Real estate became almost as inflated as during the "kiting" days of 1857. But the financial revulsion in the fall of 1873 again utterly prostrated every thing. A period of depression ensued, not so severe and disastrous as that from 1857 to 1862, but very trying and gloomy. It lasted, with more or less stagnation, until 1879, when business recuperated and real estate again became active and buoyant. Since 1879 the growth of the city has been remarkable. Its increase of population, business, capital, etc., has been unprecedented. The number of buildings erected, their size and costliness, etc., have been a subject of remark.

Saint Paul has never been visited by any widespread, devastating conflagrations, but in its early days it suffered frequently from fires very damaging and depressing in their consequences. In early days the buildings were mostly "balloon" frames, and there being no effective fire department, when a fire occurred whole blocks would be swept away by the flames. In 1856, '57, '58, '59, and '60—indeed almost every year from 1855 to 1865— were considerable fires. Old settlers have seen Third street, the principal business street of Saint Paul, leveled from one end to the other, a distance of more than a mile, both sides. Yet all these burnt spaces were soon covered with fine substantial blocks of stone or brick.

The early population of Saint Paul (1838–'47) was largely composed of French Canadians and "Red River French", the latter being refugees from Switzerland. They intermarried to a considerable extent with the native races, and a heterogeneous class of half-breeds sprang from these unions. In Saint Paul, prior to 1849, more than half of the population was Indian, full and half blood. The old *voyageurs* who were employed by the fur companies had large families of these mixed bloods. They nearly all spoke three languages—English, French, and their own mother tongue, Sioux, Ojibwa, Cree, Kooberias, etc.

With the opening of immigration in 1849 the population rapidly changed. There was a strong influx of New England people. Ohio and Pennsylvania also contributed largely to the new town. But for several years French Canadians were quite a large element of the population. A knowledge of the French tongue was almost indispensable for a tradesman then. But gradually the French-speaking population to a considerable extent gave way to other races; its importance, politically, declined.

On the census of 1850 there were so few German names as to attract the notice of those studying such statistics. But by the year 1855 there began to be a strong German element in the population. In 1857 a very considerable proportion of the names were German. The census of 1860 showed a still larger proportion. Fully one-third of the foreign-born population then were Germans.

From 1856 to the close of the war the Irish population was considerable. It was perhaps greatest in 1867, when there was occasion for a large body of laborers in the city for public improvements. It has been thought recently by those studying the subject that the percentage of Irish population is not so great now as it was 15 or 18 years ago. They furnished the bulk of the laborers at that time: now it is noticed that Swedes are the laborers most usually employed. Laborers' boarding-houses and other strongholds of the Irish population at that time are observed to have passed into the hands of the Scandinavians; still there is a large Irish population.

During the last ten or twelve years there has come in a considerable population of Poles and Bohemians.

SAINT PAUL IN 1880.

The following statistical accounts, collected by the Census Office, indicate the present condition of Saint Paul:

LOCATION.

Saint Paul lies on the left bank of the Mississippi river, 2,082 miles from its mouth. A recent extension of its corporate limits includes a considerable area on the west side of the river, the two sections being connected by a free bridge. Its latitude is 44° 56′ north, and its longitude 93° 5′ west from Greenwich. The altitude has a range of 360 feet between highest and lowest points above sea-level, the station of the Smithsonian Institution here being 800 feet above sea-level. The draft of water in the river is from 12 to 15 feet, with a naturally good levee front, and deep water extending about 2 miles. The current here flows from 3 to 4 miles per hour.

RAILROAD COMMUNICATIONS.

Saint Paul has the benefit of the following railroads:

The Chicago, Milwaukee, and Saint Paul railroad, between the first- and last-named cities.

The Chicago, Saint Paul, Minneapolis, and Omaha railroad, running from Saint Paul to Sioux City on the southwest, and to Chicago on the southeast.

The Minneapolis and Saint Louis railroad, from Saint Paul, connecting at Albert Lea with the Burlington, Cedar Rapids, and Northern railroad, giving lines to Saint Louis, etc.

The Northern Pacific railroad (Saint Paul division), from Saint Paul to Brainerd.

The Saint Paul and Duluth railroad, running between the two cities named.

The Saint Paul, Minneapolis, and Manitoba railroad, running from Saint Paul to Winnipeg, with numerous connections and divisions. These roads represent over 4,000 miles of track, and have added in no small degree to the importance of the place.

TOPOGRAPHY.

The site of Saint Paul is rolling, owing not to an upheaval of the rocks, but to the present position of the drift materials. The rocks lie practically horizontal, but have been numerously eroded by streams. The soil is mostly loam, underlaid by a clay drift. The rock formations at Saint Paul are numerous and variable. Within the county (Ramsey) the following substances are found: Saint Peter's sandstone, Lower Trenton limestone, Green shales, Upper Trenton, drift, and loess loam. Natural drainage is toward the Mississippi on the south.

CLIMATE.

The highest recorded summer temperature (1874) is 99°; highest summer temperature in average years, 95°. Lowest recorded winter temperature (1879), −39°; lowest winter temperature in average years, −27°.

The prevailing winter winds are from the northwest, and lower the temperature; the summer winds are from the southeast, and increase the heat.

STREETS.

Saint Paul contains 325 miles of streets, of which about 2 miles are paved with broken stone and about 1 mile with wood. The city engineer, L. W. Rundlet, esq., says: "We have no well-graveled streets, on account of the difficulty of obtaining good material." The wooden pavement is the easier kept clean; some of this has been laid 8 years, and during the last 2 years has needed constant repairs.

Some sidewalks are laid with asphalt and flags, but the majority are constructed of wood, being of 2-inch plank, 8 inches wide, laid crosswise and spiked to stringers, the outer stringers of 8- and 10-feet walks being 3-inch planks 16 inches deep.

Gutters are paved with stones laid in courses, with a limestone curb set on edge. The best gutters have a curbstone 6 inches wide and 18 inches deep on the edge nearest the property. Shade-trees are usually set inside the lot line, in streets where there are no grassed places on the outside edge of the sidewalk; but when a space is left for grass, they are planted just outside of the sidewalk line. The streets are from 60 to 66 feet wide and are without grassed centers. Street repairs are made by the day, which practice has always prevailed. No steam stone-crusher or roller is used at present, though the purchase of one is contemplated.

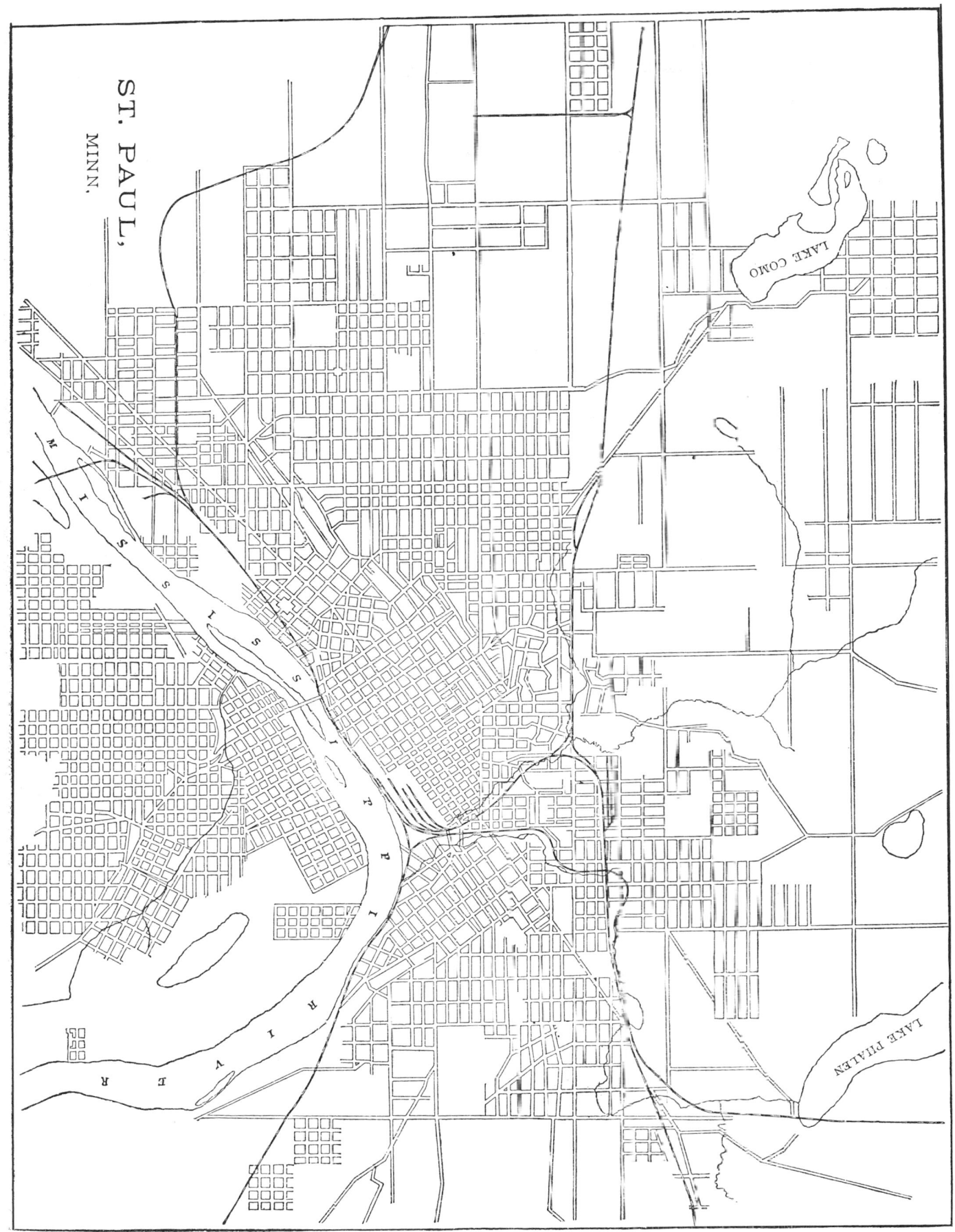

ST. PAUL,
MINN.

The city has 11 miles of horse-railroads; 26 cars and 150 horses are used; 55 men are employed; and during the census year 975,102 passengers were conveyed, the rate of fare being 5 cents.

The omnibus lines of Saint Paul run 46 vehicles, use 44 horses, employ 25 men, and carry 100,000 passengers per annum, at fares of 25 cents.

WATER-WORKS.

The total cost of the works for water-supply was $500,000, and they are the property of a private corporation. The water is brought in by gravity from lakes in the rear of the city, and has a head of 174 feet above low water of the river. The water is furnished through 24 miles of pipe. About 120 water-meters, of the Ball and Fitts pattern, are used; all work well.

GAS.

The gas-works are also owned privately. The daily average product of gas is from 60,000 to 70,000 feet. The net charge per 1,000 feet is $3 40. The city pays $30 per annum for each of the 250 street-lamps. The income from meter-rates is from $1,500 to $1,600.

PUBLIC BUILDINGS.

The city owns and occupies the city hall and the market-house, costing, respectively, $30,000 and $80,000; the former, notwithstanding its cost, is said to be a poor building.

PUBLIC PARKS AND PLEASURE-GROUNDS.

Saint Paul's one large park is situated in the northwest part of the city, borders on the west side of lake Como, and covers 240 acres. It is as yet in a state of nature; the land is rolling, and is covered with trees and underbrush. Its total cost was $100,000. The Saint Paul rifle park is situated in the eastern part of the city, and the state-fair ground and Saint Paul driving-park are in the western part. There are also 3 small parks, of about 3 acres each, which have been donated to the city, and are more or less improved. The parks are under the control of the council, except one of the three small parks (Rice), which by an ordinance is placed under the control of the mayor.

PLACES OF AMUSEMENT.

Saint Paul supports one opera-house, seating 1,100; the Atheneum, or German theater, seating 800; a concert-hall, seating 800; and the Varieties, seating about 400. The opera-house and Varieties only pay a license to the city, the former $75 and the latter $50 per year. There is also a beer-garden, with perhaps 25 tables.

DRAINAGE.

The sewerage works are carried out in accordance with a general plan, so far as main lines are concerned, but lateral sewers have to be adapted somewhat to local requirements. Owing to the peculiar geological formation, a good many sewers are tunneled through the soft sandstone at less trouble and expense than if made in open cut. Such tunnels are driven to the requisite width, are 6 feet high and lined with brick. No information is furnished of the extent or details of construction. The outfall is to the Mississippi river. The mouths of the sewers are all exposed except during high water. Ventilation is provided for by holes in the manhole covers. The only deposits that have been troublesome are gravel and sand washed into the sewers by heavy rains. The sewers are flushed with water from the fire-hydrants. No account is kept of the removal of heavy deposits, but the cost is estimated by the city engineer not to exceed $200 per year.

Main sewers are partially paid for out of a sewerage-bond fund. The whole cost of lateral sewers is assessed on the abutting property without regard to size or cost of the sewers. Assessments are laid on the basis of frontage.

The average depth of sewers is from 12 to 15 feet, and their cost per foot has been as follows: For brick sewers in open cut, 20 inches in diameter, $3; 24 inches, $3 25; 30 inches, $4; 36 inches, $5; 60 inches, $10 50. For sewers tunneled in sand rock, the bottom lined with brick 4 inches thick, tunnel 6 feet high by 2½ feet wide, $1 05 to $2 25 per foot. Sewers of vitrified-clay or cement pipe, 9 inches, $1 50 to $2 25; 12 inches, $1 75 to $2 50; 15 inches, $2 to $2 75 per foot. Catch-basins of brick, 8 to 12 inches thick, with cut-stone covers, $90 to $125 each. Manholes of brick, 8-inch walls, with iron covers, $70 to $80 each. Catch-basins quarried out of soft sand-rock, $150 to $175 each. Manholes, $130 to $150.

HOUSE-DRAINAGE.

The city ordinances require a plan to be filed with the city engineer before house-drainage work is begun. This must show the whole course of the proposed drain from its connection with the sewer to its terminus within the house, with the location of all branches, traps, and fixtures to be connected with it. Unless the proposed plan conforms in every respect to the city ordinances no permit is given to connect with the public sewers. Every private drain is required to have a trap with at least one inch water-seal, with a fresh-air inlet between the trap and the soil-pipe. The soil-pipe within the house must be continued above the roof and left open. The city engineer or his agents are authorized to enter all premises drained to the public sewers, to ascertain whether the provisions of the ordinances are complied with. If a private drain connected with the public sewers becomes clogged, obstructed, broken, or out of order, or detrimental to the use of the sewer, or unfit for the purposes of drainage, and the owner or occupant of the property neglects or refuses to make suitable repairs, they may be made by the board of public works at the expense of the owner of the property. The board of health may compel sewer connections to be made from any house or lot whenever in its opinion such connection shall be necessary. No one but a licensed drain-layer is allowed to lay any part of a private drain connected or intended to be connected with a public sewer.

CEMETERIES.

There are in Saint Paul 2 cemeteries proper: *Oakland*, containing 80 acres, and *Calvary* (Catholic), containing 40 acres. There are also 6 graveyards, small in size, belonging chiefly to German or Scandinavian Lutheran or Jewish churches. Oakland cemetery, situated in the northern part of the town, was organized under the original act for the "Formation and Regulation of Cemetery Associations", in 1858. It is vested in and controlled by a rotating board of trustees, elected annually by the lot-owners. No profits or dividends accrue to any one. No interment is allowed to take place without a permit from the health officer. Graves of adults are required to be 5 feet deep, and but one body may be buried in the same grave. No vaults are permitted above or even partly above the surface of the ground. The receiving-tomb is seldom used between April 1 and December 1, and even then bodies are kept here but a day or two; but from December 1 to April 1 bodies may remain, and ordinarily do remain, till the advent of warm weather before interment. The perpetual care of all lots sold is included in the price paid for them, and the system embraces minute and continued improvements of the whole grounds. The method employed is closely modeled upon that of Spring Grove cemetery, Cincinnati. No lots are owned in fee simple, but virtually in partnership with the entire list of lot-owners. No transfer of any lot is allowed without the consent of the trustees, and every lot-owner must conform to the rules and by-laws of the association. A sinking fund is in process of accumulation for the perpetual care of the cemetery after all other sources of revenue shall have ceased. In the Catholic cemetery and the small graveyards the system is not so strict.

MARKETS.

In 1880 Saint Paul built a fine market-house, costing about $80,000, neatly fitted with stalls, and having a stand for wagons with sheds separate from the building. On account of the burning of the state capitol, the market-house has been used for the accommodation of the state officers. The public market has heretofore been held on a square with temporary sheds for the accommodation of hucksters, all under the control of a market-master.

Wagons from the country pay a rental of 10 cents per day for the privilege of standing at the market, or 50 cents per week. In the old market, butchers paid from $100 to $150 for their stalls for the season. The total rental of the market for 1880 was $1,200. The market is ordinarily open from 4 a. m. to 12 m.

The wholesale trade of the city in meat, poultry, fish, etc., is done by commission merchants. In the case of fish, the retail merchants have their orders filled directly from the East and lake Superior in refrigerator cars.

SANITARY AUTHORITY—BOARD OF HEALTH.

The board of health has charge of the sanitary interests of the city. It is an independent body, composed of the city physician, 4 aldermen, and the city engineer. The physician of the board is elected by the city council, the 4 aldermen are appointed by the president of the council, the engineer is elected by the council and board of public works, and the inspectors are appointed by the council and the physician. The annual expenses of the board are $500 for the salary of the city physician and $840 each for 2 inspectors. With the consent of the common council the board may during an epidemic increase its expenditures to any extent demanded by the exigencies of the occasion. In the absence of epidemics the board has power to remove nuisances and to purify dwellings and premises; may require the police to execute its orders; may require reports as to the condition of all public buildings; may also require clergymen to report marriages, physicians deaths, and coroners their verdicts; and has jurisdiction over cemeteries, over the removal of dead animals, etc. During epidemics, in the words of the ordinance:

And in the presence of great and imminent peril to the public health in said city by reason of impending pestilence, it shall be the duty of said board to take such measures, and to do and order and cause to be done such acts, though not herein elsewhere or otherwise authorized, and make such expenditure (having first for said expenditures obtained the consent of the common council of the city of Saint Paul) as it may in good faith declare the public safety and health demand. And such peril shall not be deemed to exist except when and for such period of time as the mayor of the city of Saint Paul, together with said board, shall declare by proclamation the same to continue or exist.

The executive officer of the board is chief sanitary superintendent. He presides over the meetings, directs the inspectors, and attends to the duties of city physician. The board meets once a month, or on call of the president. The 2 inspectors employed are not physicians, but have police powers. Inspections are made regularly. In the spring a general cleaning up is required, and it is the duty of the inspectors to look up and abate all nuisances. When nuisances are reported they are investigated, and, if found to require it, are ordered to be abated. If this is not done the delinquent parties are arrested and fined. The inspectors have charge of the inspection and correction of defective house-drainage and sources of drinking-water, and especially of privy-vaults and cesspools.

But little has been done in regard to defective sewerage. House connections are inspected when laid, and arrangements for ventilation are required. Street-cleaning is done by the city's own force under charge of the street-inspectors. None is needed and no care is ordinarily taken by the board as to the handling of garbage. When, however, it does become a nuisance, the inspectors order its removal. As to the dead, no body is allowed to be buried, removed, received, or passed through the city without a written permit. There has not been any trouble concerning the pollution of streams, except some small ones by slaughter-houses, which the board of health compelled the owners to remove.

Small-pox patients are removed to the pest-house, but scarlet-fever patients are not isolated. In one or two instances schools have, on the breaking out in them of contagious diseases, been suspended for short periods. The pest-house is situated near the poor-farm, about 3 miles northwest of the center of the city. Vaccination is compulsory on all children attending the public schools. The board reports to the council, and these reports are published in the official proceedings.

The city engineer adds the following note to the foregoing information:

The medical profession are taking a great interest in the subject [public-health authority] at the present time on account of prevalence of typhoid fever and kindred diseases, and I think the board of health will be reorganized on a firmer basis, having more physicians, etc.

MUNICIPAL CLEANSING.

Street-cleaning.—Streets are cleaned by the city with its own force, wholly by hand. Wooden-paved streets are cleaned on an average once in ten days. On other streets the gutters are cleaned out and the ruts filled whenever it is absolutely necessary, depending somewhat on the amount of travel on the particular street. "Most of our streets have not been properly graded or macadamized, and we only try to keep them passable; in dry weather they are pretty good; in wet weather, muddy." About $18,000 per year is expended in this work. The street-sweepings are deposited on low streets, below grade, where there is not much travel, and on low bottom-land near the river.

Removal of garbage and ashes.—Garbage is removed by scavengers, who make this their business, employed by householders for the purpose. It is mostly fed to cattle and swine. Ashes also are removed by householders. Soap factories take the wood ashes, while coal ashes are used for filling. The statement is made that the system has worked as well as could be expected, but, as the city is rapidly increasing in size and population, the ordinances in the future will undoubtedly be more strictly enforced than at the present time.

Dead animals are removed by the scavengers, who are allowed by ordinances a price for each animal, as $1 for a horse, 50 cents for a cow, hog, dog, etc. The carcasses are generally taken to rendering establishments outside the city limits. The service is said to be very well performed, and to be quite satisfactory.

Liquid household wastes.—Only a small part of Saint Paul is sewered, but where sewers exist they are very generally used. Where there are no sewers, dry wells, cesspools, and privy-vaults are used. The cesspools are generally porous, and, in the few cases where they are provided with overflows, these deliver generally into water-courses, and do not, as a rule, receive the wastes of water-closets. No household waste is allowed to run into the street-gutters. The opinion is expressed that there is more or less contamination of drinking-water by imperfect drainage.

Human excreta.—The proportion of houses having water-closets is small, but most of the recently erected houses have closets. About one-third of the water-closets deliver into the public sewers. There are no regulations as to the construction of privy-vaults, and it is said that not one in a hundred is water-tight. When the sanitary inspector orders the emptying of a privy-vault it must be done. The scavengers performing this work must use tight carts. The dry-earth system is used only to a very slight extent. Night-soil is dumped into the Mississippi, not being used for manure.

Manufacturing waste.—One soap factory and one brewery connect with the sewer near its outlet, but have given no trouble, and few manufactures produce liquid and solid wastes.

POLICE.

Saint Paul's police force is appointed and governed by the mayor. The chief executive officer is the chief of police. He has general supervision over the whole department, and his salary is $1,500 per annum. The rest of the force comprises 1 captain at $1,200, 2 sergeants at $1,000 each, 2 detectives at $1,000 each, 2 court officers, 1 jailer, and 27 patrolmen at $840 each. The uniform is the same as that worn by the New York metropolitan police force, and is provided by the men themselves. Patrolmen serve 10 hours per day, and patrol all of the city's streets. During 1880, 2,441 arrests were made, chiefly for assault and battery, disorderly conduct, drunkenness, and vagrancy. For the same period property to the amount of $5,329 was stolen and reported to the police, of which $4,184 was recovered and returned to the owners. During the same year there were 2,710 station-house lodgers, against 1,983 for the preceding year. No free meals were given them. The force co-operates with the fire department to the extent of its ability, and with the health department by reporting all nuisances, etc., to the health officers. Special policemen are appointed only in case of emergency. The cost of the force for 1880 was $42,000.

MANUFACTURES.

The following is a summary of the statistics of the manufactures of Saint Paul for 1880, being taken from tables prepared for the Tenth Census:

Mechanical and manufacturing industries.	No. of establishments.	Capital.	AVERAGE NUMBER OF HANDS EMPLOYED.			Total amount paid in wages during the year.	Value of materials.	Value of products.
			Males above 16 years.	Females above 15 years.	Children and youths.			
All industries...........................	593	$3,738,791	3,930	1,092	208	$2,254,340	$5,719,067	$10,286,363
Awnings and tents......................	3	11,750	8	19	4	7,760	96,000	129,900
Blacksmithing (see also Wheelwrighting)	18	7,500	31	....	....	15,427	16,450	53,700
Bookbinding and blank-book making	4	43,500	32	17	8	25,541	17,769	68,941
Boots and shoes, including custom work and repairing	41	275,150	286	18	21	158,162	421,198	716,733
Boxes, cigars	3	4,500	6	3	....	2,602	4,750	9,500
Bread and other bakery products...............	20	64,200	52	1	4	28,095	171,990	246,800
Brick and tile........................	5	13,000	74	....	2	15,322	8,027	32,200
Brooms and brushes	4	6,500	12	1	....	7,100	13,600	29,600
Carpentering	58	127,475	622	....	....	268,516	568,865	960,642
Carpets, rag	3	210	....	....	1	150	800	1,850
Carriages and wagons (see also Wheelwrighting)	6	103,000	105	....	....	57,760	82,500	200,000
Clothing, men's	22	264,500	154	485	3	210,490	553,050	974,200
Clothing, women's...................	9	31,200	1	80	....	24,100	93,350	147,900
Coffee and spices, roasted and ground	4	106,500	11	6	9	11,350	107,750	153,500
Confectionery.......................	9	63,000	41	5	1	23,010	108,450	156,950
Cooperage	4	2,400	10	....	....	5,080	2,100	11,300
Dentistry, mechanical	14	14,050	7	....	1	3,670	7,260	40,530
Drugs and chemicals (see also Patent medicines and compounds)....	5	13,050	9	....	....	3,800	16,500	35,300
Dyeing and cleaning..................	3	1,650	1	1	....	550	750	3,050
Flouring- and grist-mill products.............	7	143,500	40	....	....	17,464	461,048	540,927
Foundery and machine-shop products	9	104,650	213	....	....	119,750	239,700	416,500
Furniture (see also Upholstering).............	13	75,050	54	....	....	30,000	60,775	132,150
Furs, dressed	5	120,600	27	50	2	36,810	163,550	344,000
Housefurnishing goods	5	108,000	44	25	1	35,740	321,467	510,270
Liquors, malt	11	371,500	95	4	2	38,960	167,542	298,972
Lithographing (see also Printing and publishing).........	3	14,000	14	1	1	9,785	19,657	37,525
Lock- and gun-smithing................	4	4,400	7	....	....	3,750	3,850	13,500
Looking-glass and picture frames...........	3	11,750	3	....	....	1,400	13,000	19,200
Lumber, planed	4	48,000	44	....	....	24,150	80,000	128,500
Malt	4	30,500	18	....	....	9,485	49,300	74,000
Marble and stone work	12	37,500	67	....	....	39,100	32,555	90,975
Masonry, brick and stone	58	126,250	780	....	....	271,687	274,150	642,668
Millinery and lace goods	3	13,500	....	34	....	9,500	33,000	60,500
Mineral and soda waters...............	3	7,000	12	....	....	4,436	7,500	22,000
Painting and paperhanging..............	24	20,650	84	....	....	37,620	67,210	147,500
Patent medicines and compounds (see also Drugs and chemicals)	5	14,900	6	5	2	3,038	6,000	24,000
Photographing.......................	9	14,625	13	2	....	6,150	4,640	28,200
Plumbing and gasfitting................	9	33,350	47	....	....	23,831	67,800	115,850
Printing and publishing (see also Lithographing)...........	19	502,000	261	13	82	222,384	146,959	527,764
Saddlery and harness	11	31,193	54	....	2	28,783	83,760	147,191
Shirts.............................	4	4,700	4	32	....	10,800	4,700	22,500
Slaughtering and meat-packing, not including retail butchering.....	5	165,000	31	....	2	17,100	371,050	429,747
Tinware, copperware, and sheet-iron ware.............	20	30,356	62	....	4	36,820	91,464	165,593
Tobacco, cigars and cigarettes	27	79,212	116	2	32	84,778	147,600	388,674
Upholstering (see also Furniture)...........	4	2,150	5	....	....	1,600	3,350	9,500
Watch and clock repairing..............	14	13,000	22	....	....	13,970	5,150	36,700
Wheelwrighting (see also Blacksmithing; Carriages and wagons)...	15	43,750	47	....	....	23,610	28,000	71,400
All other industries (a)	48	414,400	298	288	24	223,258	473,131	867,461

a Embracing agricultural implements; baking and yeast powders; boot and shoe uppers; boxes, fancy and paper; brass castings; buttons; coffins, burial cases, and undertakers' goods; corsets; cutlery and edge tools; drain and sewer pipe; engraving and die-sinking; engraving, wood; explosives and fireworks; furnishing goods, men's; hairwork; hats and caps; instruments, professional and scientific; iron work, architectural and ornamental; ivory and bone work; kindling wood; liquors, distilled; lumber, sawed; models and patterns; musical instruments and materials (not specified); musical instruments, organs and materials; pumps; regalia and society banners and emblems; safes, doors, and vaults, fire-proof; sash, doors, and blinds; scales and balances; show-cases; soap and candles; steam fittings and heating apparatus; stereotyping and electrotyping; trunks and valises; type founding; vinegar; wirework; and wood, turned and carved.

From the foregoing table it appears that the average capital of all establishments is $6,304 87; that the average wages of all hands employed is $431 04 per annum; and that the average outlay in wages, in materials, and in interest (at 6 per cent.) on capital employed is $13,824 17.

WINONA,

WINONA COUNTY, MINNESOTA.

POPULATION

IN THE

AGGREGATE,

1860-1880.

	Inhab.
1790	......
1800	......
1810	......
1820	......
1830	......
1840	......
1850	......
1860	2,464
1870	7,192
1880	10,208

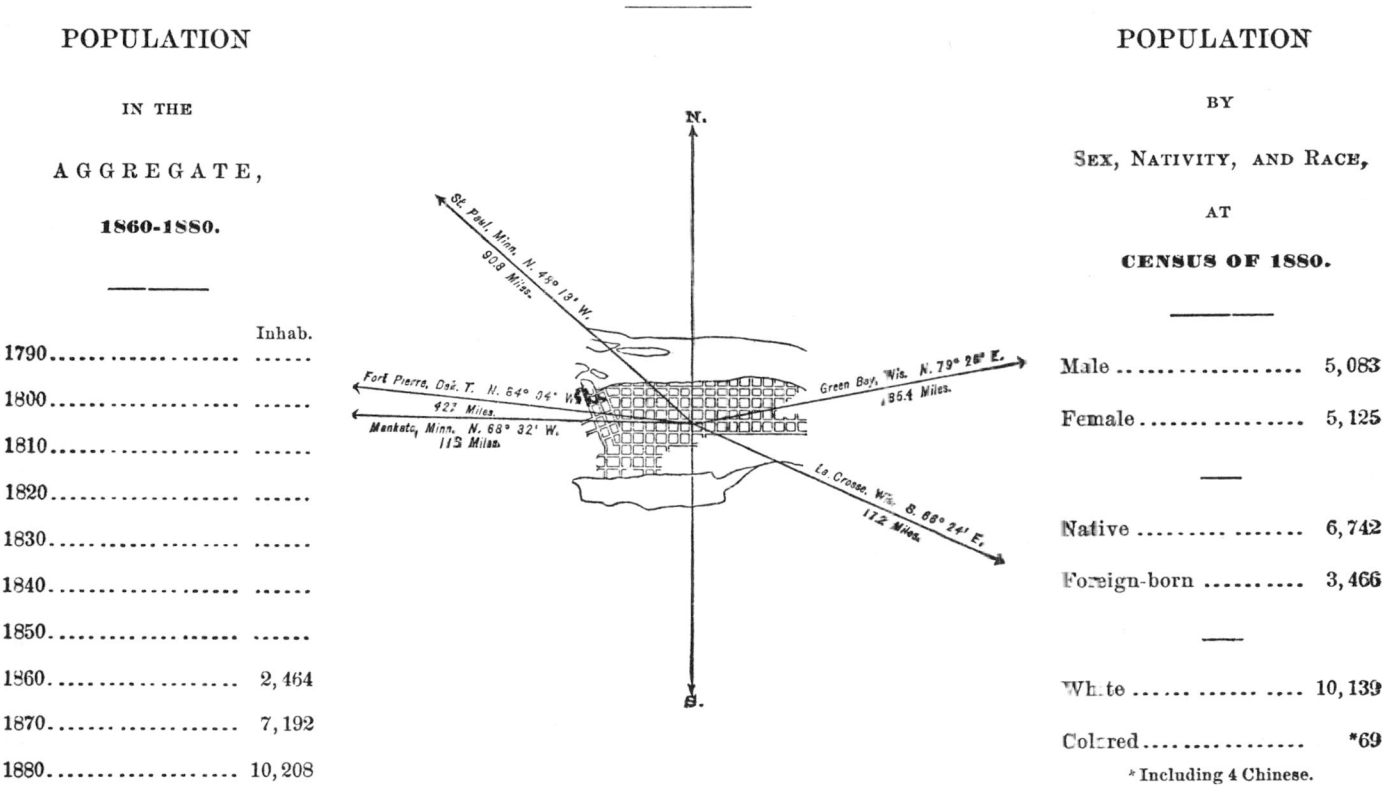

POPULATION

BY

SEX, NATIVITY, AND RACE,

AT

CENSUS OF 1880.

Male	5,083
Female	5,125
Native	6,742
Foreign-born	3,466
White	10,139
Colored	*69

* Including 4 Chinese.

Latitude: 44° 4′ North; Longitude: 91° 42′ (west from Greenwich); Altitude: 616 feet.

FINANCIAL CONDITION:

Total Valuation: $3,780,698; per capita: $370 00.   Net Indebtedness: $183,000; per capita: $17 93.   Tax per $100: $1 50.

HISTORICAL SKETCH.

The first white settler came to Winona in 1851. In June, 1852, the original plat of the city was surveyed. By 1853 a population of 60 had gathered together, and, two years later, when the public lands were first offered for sale, the number rose to 800. In 1857 the city government was organized. A great fire swept away a large part of the city on the 4th of July, 1861. At that time the buildings were nearly all of wood, there being only two of brick on the town site; since then their character has greatly improved, both in point of material and in style of architecture, brick or stone having been used for all business blocks, churches, houses, and principal public buildings. In the early years of the town the settlers came mostly from New England and the middle states, and the American element still predominates, although many emigrants have come here from Germany, Scandinavia, Ireland, Poland, Bohemia, etc.

WINONA IN 1880.

The following statistical accounts have been compiled from very full reports furnished the Census Office by Messrs. William P. Phelps, secretary of the Winona board of trade, and L. F. von Wimpffen, city and county engineer:

LOCATION.

Winona is situated on the west bank of the Mississippi river, about 100 miles below the head of navigation, and 700 miles above its junction with the Missouri. The river here has a depth of water of from 12 to 20 feet in the channel, which is 1,000 feet wide, and has a current of from 3 to 3.5 miles per hour. By means of this river, water communication is open with Saint Paul on the north, and La Crosse, Dubuque, Davenport, Keokuk, Saint Louis, Memphis, New Orleans, and all ports on the Ohio and Missouri, on the south.

RAILROAD COMMUNICATIONS.

Winona is a center of three railway lines. The Chicago and Northwestern and the Chicago, Milwaukee, and Saint Paul systems intersect at this point. Winona is also the present western terminus of the Green Bay and Minnesota railway. The Winona and Saint Peter division of the Chicago and Northwestern is completed westward from Winona to the Missouri river at Fort Pierre. Through the Chicago, Milwaukee, and Saint Paul railway the city has direct connection with the Northern Pacific system, and with the great lines of the West and North. Winona is connected with the great lakes at four different points.

TRIBUTARY COUNTRY.

Winona is located on the eastern margin of the remarkable wheat belt that extends through Minnesota and Dakota, for a great part of which it is the base of supplies. The agricultural region immediately surrounding the city is composed of rich valleys skirting the small streams emptying into the Mississippi, and of prairie land terminated by the bluffs which line the great basin of the river. The chief productions of this region are wheat, rye, oats, barley, Indian corn, flax, potatoes, and turnips, all of which grow in great profusion. Grapes, especially the Delaware and other hardy varieties, are produced in considerable quantities, and the cultivation of amber sugar-cane is receiving much attention. The immense lumber districts of the Chippewa river and other streams are more or less tributary to the city.

TOPOGRAPHY.

The city is built upon an ancient river-bed, which makes a terrace, the highest point of which has an elevation of about 25 feet above the low-water mark of the Mississippi. The soil is composed of gravel, sand, and loam. The range of bluffs bordering this terrace rises abruptly to a height varying from 450 to 595 feet. The rocks in them are the Potsdam sandstone and the Upper Magnesian limestone. The distance from bluff to bluff across the river varies from 5 to 7 miles. The natural boundaries of the city are: on the south, the lake of Winona and the bluffs mentioned, rising almost directly from the shores of the lake; on the north, the Mississippi; on the east, swamp and meadow land; on the west, swamp and meadow land and sandy prairie. The city limits inclose an area of about 3,233 acres. The natural drainage is good, running partly to the lake and partly to the Mississippi, with an inclination of not less than 9 inches in 300 feet. The country for a radius of 5 miles is considerably wooded, especially on the bluffs and in the valleys. The soil is like that of the city, except that on the prairie it is a rich clayey loam.

CLIMATE.

Highest recorded summer temperature, 100°; highest in average years, 95°; lowest recorded winter temperature, −40°; lowest in average years, −25°; average summer temperature (according to Smithsonian Institution charts), 67.5°; average winter temperature, 16.5°. The current of the Mississippi being rapid, no deleterious influence on the climate has been noticed; through its broad, deep basin cooling winds have a free passage. There are not marshes enough in the vicinity to affect seriously the sanitary condition of the city. The south winds descending in summer from the high bluffs have a considerable influence in mitigating the summer heat; the west winds are very cold in winter, and at all times lower the temperature; these are the prevailing winds. Occasionally in the winter east winds coming from the great lakes are very chilly; they usually bring snow.

STREETS.

Total length of streets, a little over 49.5 miles, of which 1 mile is paved with broken stone. Though 30 miles are reported paved with gravel, it is practically a natural roadway made through gravel, as the soil is a gravelly loam; hence the cost is merely nominal. The sidewalks are of stone on the principal business streets and of plank on the rest. In a few cases the gutters are of stone, but generally are ditches at the roadside. Tree-planting has been very general along the margin of the sidewalks. The repair of streets is done by day work, under the

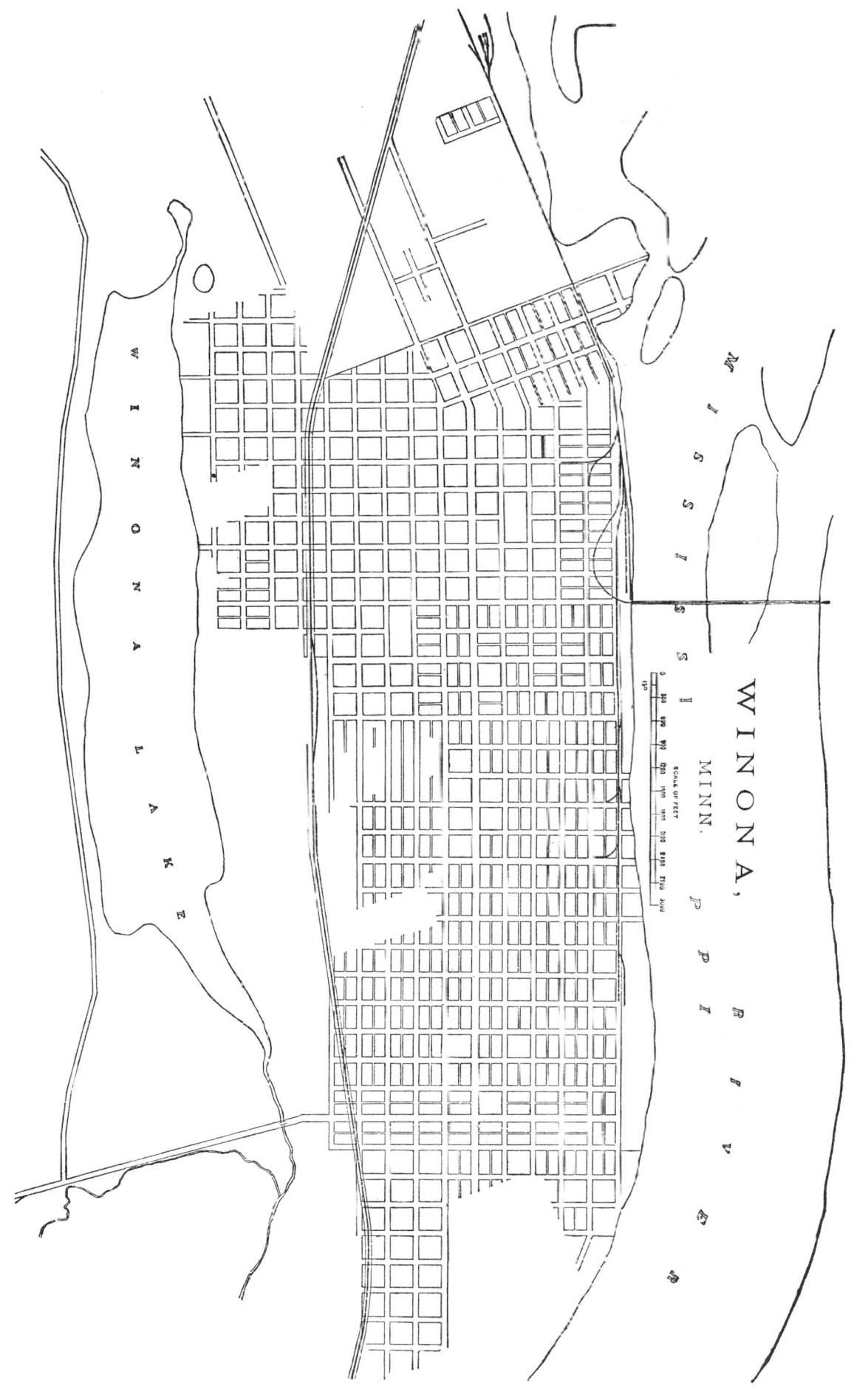

WINONA, MINN.

SCALE OF FEET

WINONA LAKE

MISSISSIPPI RIVER

direction of the street commissioner, the annual cost being from $2,000 to $2,500. In the past year $8,087 02 was expended on roads and streets (including construction and repair of sidewalks), and $1,471 75 on State roads and bridges. There is a preference for day work, but no experience has been had with contract work. There are 2 wooden bridges within the city limits, with a total length of 563 feet. The city expended $3,272 in the past year for the maintenance of the ferry across the Mississippi, and received $3,217 68. No horse-railroads have yet been constructed, but a charter has been granted for one, and work is to be begun shortly.

WATER-WORKS.

The total cost of the water-works up to the present time has been $40,000. The Holly system of direct pumping is used, and a pressure of from 50 to 80 pounds is maintained. Between 500,000 and 1,500,000 gallons per day are pumped. The yearly cost of maintenance, aside from the cost of pumping, is reported to be $526 75. The annual income report of the finance committee of the city council shows that for the past year the income from water-rents was $1,632 61; the expenditure on the water-works, including operation, repairs, and 3,730 feet extension, were $12,822 95. Previous to February 10, 1880, 42,510 feet of water-pipe had been laid, as follows: Six-inch pipe, 24,650 feet; 7-inch, 12,480; 8-inch, 5,380. The steam-power of two mills is used for pumping.

GAS.

The gas-works are not owned by the city. The annual consumption of gas is 700,000 cubic feet; in 1879, to produce this, 678 tons of coal were used. The charge per 1,000 feet is $3 50. The city pays $25 per month for each street-lamp using gas, and there are 77 such, and 27 that burn oil. The gas company has laid 44,194 feet of pipe.

PUBLIC BUILDINGS.

There is a "city building" used wholly for municipal purposes, which cost $10,000. The county court-house cost about $7,500.

PUBLIC PARKS AND PLEASURE-GROUNDS.

There are 3 public parks, containing 90,000 square feet, and occupying one square each. They are laid out in irregular plats and ornamented with evergreens and other trees. Two of them were given to the city; the third cost $6,000. The improvements have mostly been made by private effort, there having been no public expenditures on them.

PLACES OF AMUSEMENT.

There are 2 halls adapted to theatrical purposes—Philharmonic hall, seating from 600 to 700, and Ely hall, seating from 400 to 500; both these halls are sometimes used for concerts and lectures, but not often. In the year ending March 31, 1881, $228 was received for license for "shows", as the report of the finance committee puts it. The Normal hall, in the third story of the state normal-school building, seats 1,000, is well lighted, heated, and ventilated, and is very popular for public purposes. There are no concert- or beer-gardens within the city limits; several have been started from time to time, but none have been successful.

DRAINAGE.

There is no system of sewerage in the city.

CEMETERIES.

The city has 2 cemeteries, one Protestant, known as *Woodlawn*, and one Roman Catholic. Woodlawn cemetery embraces 40 acres, and is about 1½ mile from the city, due south on the opposite side of lake Winona. It lies in a valley formed by two bluffs, 596 feet high, their summits being about 800 feet apart. In the inclosure there are 3 comparatively level plateaus. The more abrupt ground is made available by terracing. The soil is clayey. Graves are dug 4 feet deep for children and 5 feet for adults. Lots are sold at 25 cents per square foot. The revenue amounts to $150 per year. The total number of interments up to December 31, 1880, was 2,068.

MARKETS.

There are no public or corporation markets in the city. No hucksters' wagons are accustomed to stand in the streets, except those containing wood and hay, and these are confined to one street a hundred feet wide for a distance of a block (300 feet). Peddlers of any thing except wood, hay, and agricultural produce have to obtain a license and pay $10 per month for it..

SANITARY AUTHORITY—BOARD OF HEALTH.

The chief health organization of the city is the board of health, consisting of 5 aldermen, one from each ward, appointed by the mayor. A city physician annually elected by the city council attends the meetings of this board, and is its chief executive officer. The expenses of the board itself are merely nominal; the members receive no pay, but the city physician receives $300 per year. The board can order, and enforce through the police, the abatement of nuisances of all kinds; the members themselves have no police power. Inspections are made regularly, and on reports of nuisances. The board meets weekly in summer. The burial of the dead within the corporate limits of the city is forbidden. Small-pox patients are isolated in the public pest-house, situated on the open prairie remote from the city. Scarlet-fever patients are merely isolated at home. The board may take cognizance of the breaking out of contagious diseases in schools, but no occasion has ever yet been presented for summary measures. It is one of the duties of the city physician to see that all persons, so far as possible, are properly vaccinated, especially those in the vicinity of any persons attacked by the small-pox. There is no registration of births; deaths are registered only so far as burials are registered by the superintendent of cemeteries. The board reports to the city council not oftener than once a year.

The report of the state board of health for 1878 says that Winona has never known an epidemic of diphtheria. The number of deaths from sporadic cases of this disease from January, 1870, to December, 1878, was 32, and the total of deaths from all causes, 1,367.

MUNICIPAL CLEANSING.

Street-cleaning.—Streets are cleaned both by the city and by private abutters, the city's work being done by its own force and entirely by hand. There is no regularity about the work, but it is reported that the streets are generally in good condition. The annual cost of the work to the city is about $1,500. Sweepings are deposited on low grounds at a distance from the city. The city ordinances provide that " the owner or owners, occupant or occupants, of any tenement or lot in this city shall keep or cause to be kept such tenement or lot, and so much of the streets and alleys adjacent thereto as lie between such tenements or lots and the center of such streets or alleys, free from all dirt, filth, rubbish, or any offensive or unwholesome substance or matter". If they fail of doing this the city marshal or any member of the board of health shall cause it to be done, and the expense shall be recovered from the delinquent party by a civil action before any justice of the peace in the city. The special defect of the whole system of street-cleaning is reported to be the lack of uniformity in the time and manner of doing the work.

Removal of garbage and ashes.—Garbage is removed wholly at the expense of householders. While awaiting removal it must be kept in suitable vessels. It is generally used to feed swine. Ashes are used on soil and for soap-making.

Dead animals.—Dead animals are hauled to a considerable distance, and allowed to decay on unoccupied ground.

Liquid household wastes.—Chamber-slops are deposited in privy-vaults. None of the liquid household waste of the city is delivered into public sewers; perhaps one-fourth of it goes into dry wells or cesspools, and these are very porous. Investigations indicate a gradual deterioration of the well-water of the city, but the use of water from the city water-works is increasing. The cleaning out of cesspools is done entirely according to private necessity. As the city is small, the defects of the system are not so noticeable as they will be shortly when the soil is more thoroughly saturated with filth. A thorough system of sewerage will soon be indispensable.

Human excreta.—Probably not more than a dozen houses have water-closets, nearly all depending upon ordinary privy-vaults; all water-closets deliver into cesspools. The only regulation as to the removal of human excreta is that it must be done between the hours of 11 p. m. and 4 a. m. The dry-earth system is not at all used.

Manufacturing waste.—It is reported that there are no deleterious manufacturing wastes from any establishment in the city.

POLICE.

The police force is appointed by the city council. Its chief executive officer is the city marshal, who receives a salary of $600 per year and fees. The rest of the force consists of a deputy marshal and 6 patrolmen, with salaries of $50 per month each. Their uniforms are navy blue in color, and each man furnishes his own. They serve 12 hours per day each, and patrol from 6 to 8 miles of streets in all. In 1880 there were 333 arrests, the principal causes being drunkenness and disorder. There were 150 tramps lodged in the station-house, against 300 in 1879. The police department co-operates with the fire department in times of fire to prevent theft, etc., and with the health department in seeing that nuisances are abated, streets cleaned, etc. Special policemen are appointed by the city marshal; their standing while on duty is the same as that of the regular officers. The expenditures on account of the police department for the year ending March 31, 1881, were $4,289 54.

FIRE DEPARTMENT.

The annual report of the chief engineer of the fire department shows that the apparatus in use consists of 1 second-class Silsby steam-engine, 4 hose-carts—3 two-wheeled and 1 four-wheeled—and 1 hook-and-ladder truck, with 3,700 feet of hose on hand. The fire department consists of 4 hose companies and 1 hook-and-ladder company, with a total number of 111 active firemen. The total number of fires last year was 18; of alarms, 23; total amount of property destroyed, $6,850, upon which insurance was paid to the amount of $5,150. The city has now 92 hydrants.

IOWA.

BURLINGTON,

DES MOINES COUNTY, IOWA.

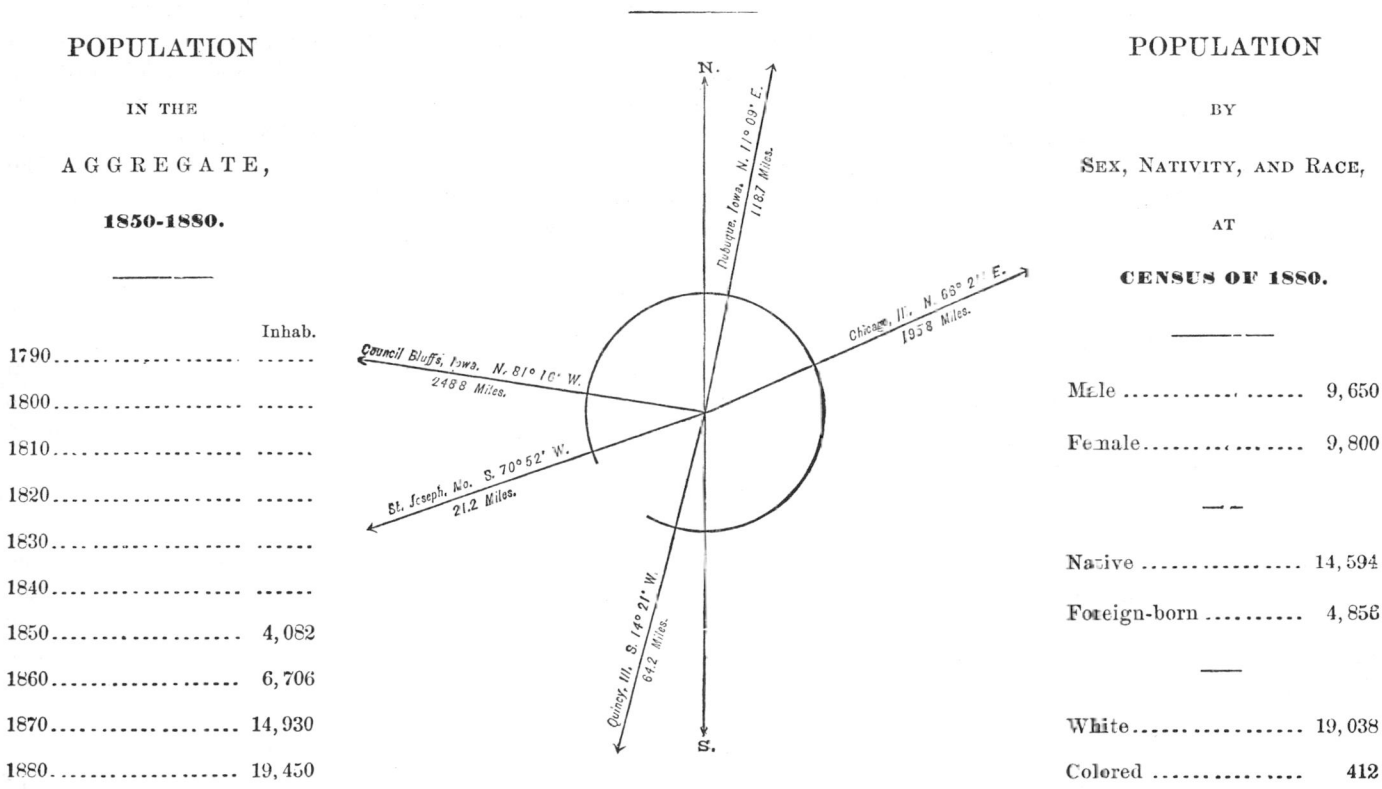

POPULATION

IN THE

AGGREGATE,

1850–1880.

	Inhab.
1790	......
1800	......
1810	......
1820	......
1830	......
1840	......
1850	4,082
1860	6,706
1870	14,930
1880	19,450

POPULATION

BY

SEX, NATIVITY, AND RACE,

AT

CENSUS OF 1880.

Male	9,650
Female	9,800
Native	14,594
Foreign-born	4,856
White	19,038
Colored	412

Latitude: 40° 49 North; Longitude: 91° 7′ (west from Greenwich); **Altitude: 600 feet.**

FINANCIAL CONDITION:

Total Valuation: $4,001,982; per capita: $206 00.   Net Indebtedness: $128,061; per capita: $6 58.   Tax per $100: $5 12.

HISTORICAL SKETCH.

In 1836, Wisconsin territory was organized, and Iowa made a district of it, with the seat of government for the whole territory fixed at Burlington. In 1838 Iowa territory was organized, and in 1839 the capital of the territory was removed from Burlington to Iowa City. In 1846 the territory became a state.

A few Frenchmen had settled at Montrose and Dubuque before the close of the last century, and some French pioneers and American hunters had long lived among the Indians, but the first settlements of whites permitted by the United States government within the present limits of Iowa were made in 1833–'34 at Fort Madison, Burlington, and Dubuque. Notwithstanding the removal of the seat of government, the growth of Burlington has been steady and healthy. It is the seat of Burlington university.

BURLINGTON IN 1880.

The following statistical accounts, collected by the Census Office, indicate the present condition of Burlington:

LOCATION.

Burlington, Iowa, is situated on the west bank of the Mississippi river, 45 miles above Keokuk; 207 miles west southwest of Chicago, 250 miles by water above Saint Louis, and 296 miles by railroad east of Omaha, at an average altitude of 600 feet above the level of the sea. The river is here a broad, deep, and beautiful stream, and gives direct communication with Keokuk, Saint Louis, Cincinnati, New Orleans, Saint Paul, and all other points on the great rivers.

RAILROAD COMMUNICATIONS.

The main line of the Chicago, Burlington, and Quincy railroad runs through Burlington from Chicago to Council Bluffs and Omaha, giving Burlington connections with these places and with Saint Joseph, Kansas City, and Indianola, the most western point yet reached by this road; the Carthage branch of this line connects Burlington with Quincy. The Toledo, Peoria, and Burlington short line of the Wabash, Saint Louis, and Pacific railroad connects Burlington with all the places named in the titles, as well as with Ottumwa and Van Wort to the west, Keokuk and Warsaw to the south, and Chicago. The Burlington, Cedar Rapids, and Northern connects at Albert Lea with the Minneapolis and Saint Louis, thus giving Burlington a direct line to the North and Northwest. The Burlington and Southwestern connects at Laclede with the Hannibal and Saint Joseph, and the Burlington and Northwestern connects at Washington, Iowa, with the Chicago, Rock Island, and Pacific.

TRIBUTARY COUNTRY.

Burlington is the capital of Des Moines county, and is naturally its center of business. The surface of this county is agreeably diversified, and is divided between prairies and woodlands in convenient proportions; the soil is excellent, and is extensively cultivated. The Mississippi forms its boundary on the east and southeast; it is drained also by Flint creek. Cattle, grain, wool, hay, and dairy products are extensively raised. Of manufactories those of wagons are most numerous. Coal and limestone are abundant.

TOPOGRAPHY.

The city is regularly laid out, and is partly situated on the high bluffs which border the valley. Like all the cities along the Mississippi, it lies mainly along the terrace between the present bed of the river and the bluffs. Burlington limestone, a variety of sub-carboniferous magnesian limestone, derives its name from the city, the typical locality where it was first studied. It is a valuable building stone, and is peculiarly interesting to naturalists. The upper bed is of a light gray color, and is nearly pure carbonate of lime. The lower bed contains more magnesia.

CLIMATE.

The temperature tables published by the Smithsonian Institution show that the mean annual temperature of Burlington is 51.28°; the average winter temperature is 26.93°.

STREETS.

Total length of streets, 100 miles; 9.5 miles have been paved with broken stone (macadam), which is the only paving used, at a cost of about $2 50 per square yard. Plank, brick, stone, and composition are the principal materials used for sidewalks. Trees are planted along most of the streets, except the business thoroughfares. The construction of streets is done by contract work, the repairs by day work. The annual expenditures of the street department amount to about $10,000. There are 9 miles of horse-railroad tracks. The total number of cars is 19; of horses, 100; of men employed, 35. The rate of fare is 5 cents.

WATER-WORKS.

The works for water-supply cost $230,000. The Holly system of direct pumping is used; a pressure of 90 pounds is maintained under ordinary circumstances, which is increased to 175 in cases of fire. The greatest amount pumped per day is 1,600,000 gallons; the least, 550,000. The yearly cost of maintenance, aside from cost of pumping, is $300, (?) and the yearly income from water-rates is $12,000. Water-meters are used, and it is reported that they save at least 50 per cent. of waste, and bring the price of water to an average of 18 cents per 1,000 gallons. The mayor's message to the city council for the year ending March 17, 1879, said in regard to the water-works:

"The city practically owns the works, and the company operates them. The city is interested in the receipts of the water company in precisely the same way as though it absolutely owned and controlled the works. After the payment of the 12 per cent. interest upon the amount of money actually invested by the stockholders, all profit will go toward liquidating the corporate indebtedness."

GAS.

The gas-works are not owned by the city. The daily average production is about 35,000 feet, and the charge per 1,000 feet is $3 50.

PUBLIC BUILDINGS.

The city uses one building wholly for municipal purposes. Its cost was $15,762.

PUBLIC PARKS AND PLEASURE-GROUNDS.

There is one park, given to the city by the United States government. Its yearly cost of maintenance is $100.

PLACES OF AMUSEMENT.

The city has 2 theaters, viz: The Opera House, with a seating capacity of 1,800, and Grimes' opera-house, with a seating capacity of 1,500. A license of $5 must be paid for each theatrical performance. There are 3 halls used for concerts, lectures, dances, etc., viz: Mozart hall, seating 1,200; Turner hall, seating 800; and Marion hall. There are 2 beer-gardens patronized by the German population, but used only on Sundays and legal holidays.

DRAINAGE.

No report on this subject was received from the city authorities.

CEMETERIES.

There are 4 cemeteries connected with the city, viz:

Aspen Grove Cemetery, containing 53 acres, being 2 miles from the center of the city, in the northwest corner of the town.

Catholic Cemetery, 2½ acres, 1 mile northeast of the center.

Hebrew Cemetery, 1 acre, 2 miles west of the center.

Cemetery of the Bleeding Heart of Mary and Jesus, 15 acres, south of the town.

Up to December 23, 1881, there had been 289 interments in Aspen Grove, 35 in the Catholic cemetery, 3 in the Hebrew cemetery, and 37 in the Cemetery of the Bleeding Heart of Mary and Jesus. There has been no attempt at landscape-gardening in Aspen Grove, but personal taste is unrestricted as to the improvement and decoration of lots.

MARKETS.

The market building has been converted into offices for the city officials, and a council-chamber. The street around the square in which it is situated is occupied by wagons of farmers and hucksters, who pay from $3 to $4 per season for a space 6 feet wide. The revenue from this source for the year ending April 1, 1879, was $246 75. Business is done between 4 and 8 a. m. on Tuesdays, Thursdays, and Saturdays. The city ordinances provide that no person shall be allowed to sell fresh meats or fish at retail without first obtaining a written permit therefor from the city council. A market-master is annually elected by the city council, but now that the market building has been closed, his duties are light. He reports the receipts from the city scales (of which he has charge) for the year ending April 1, 1879, to have been $951.

SANITARY AUTHORITY—BOARD OF HEALTH.

The following sections of chapter 151 of the acts of the 18th general assembly of the state of Iowa are now in force, and are given in full as applying to all the cities and towns of the state:

The mayor and aldermen of each incorporated city, the mayor and council of any incorporated town or village in the state, or the trustees of any township, shall have and exercise all the powers and perform all the duties of a board of health within the limits of the cities, towns, and townships of which they are officers.

Every local board of health shall appoint a competent physician to the board, who shall be the health officer within its jurisdiction, and shall hold his office during the pleasure of the board. The clerks of the townships and the clerks and recorders of cities and towns shall be clerks of the local boards. The local board shall also regulate all fees and charges of persons employed by them in the execution of the health laws and of their own regulations.

It shall be the duty of the health physician of every incorporated town, and also of the clerk of the local board of health in each city or incorporated town or village in the state, at least once a year to report to the state board of health their proceedings, and such other facts required, on blanks and in accordance with instructions received from said state board. They shall also make special reports whenever required to do so by the state board of health.

Local boards of health shall meet for the transaction of business on the first Monday of May and the first Monday in November of each year, and at any other time that the necessities of the health of their respective jurisdictions may demand; and the clerk of each board shall transmit his annual report to the secretary of the state board of health within two weeks after the November meeting. Said report shall embrace a history of any epidemic disease which may have prevailed within his district. The failure of the clerk of the board to prepare, or caused to be prepared, and forward such report, as above specified, shall be considered a misdemeanor, for which he shall be subject to a fine of not more than twenty-five dollars ($25).

It will be seen that the legislature has provided who shall constitute the local boards of health. They have only, therefore, to organize and adopt the necessary regulations concerning nuisances, sources of filth, causes of sickness, etc., and at once proceed to enforce them. The law provides ample penalties for violations, which penalties may be used to defray the expenses of the local board.

In Burlington no distinct account has been kept of the expense of sanitary measures. Except in the case of an epidemic many years ago, it has been merely nominal. Inasmuch as the city council is the board of health, its authority in regard to expenditures and all sanitary measures is limited only by the authority vested in the city council. The business of the board is transacted at regular meetings of the council. Its chief executive officer is the city marshal, and only through him does it exercise police powers. Inspections are made only as nuisances are reported, there being no regular system about it. In case of a nuisance reported, the board of health directs the marshal to notify the delinquent to abate, and, if not done, it is abated by the city at the expense of the owner of the property. As to defective house-drainage, privy-vaults, sources of drinking-water, defective sewerage, etc., the practice is the same, i. e., to inspect only on complaint.

BURIAL OF THE DEAD.

No dead body is allowed to be buried without a permit issued by the clerk of the board (the city clerk).

INFECTIOUS DISEASES.

There has been but one case of small-pox for a number of years, and that was isolated by establishing quarantine with a police guard. Very little attention is publicly paid to scarlet fever unless it becomes prevalent, and no quarantine has yet been required. There is no public pest-house; one was established temporarily for small-pox in 1874. Vaccination is not compulsory, nor is it done at the public expense.

REPORTS.

The city ordinances provide that the board, through its clerk, shall keep a complete record of births and deaths within the city, but the record has never been complete. The city clerk writes that recent statutes, requiring reports to be made to the county clerk, have made it more difficult to secure reports under the city ordinances.

MUNICIPAL CLEANSING.

Street-cleaning.—The city ordinances provide that between April 1 and November 1 in every year abutters within the limits of the macadamized streets and paved alleys of the city shall, on every Saturday morning before 8 o'clock, sweep and clean from the curbing of the street or wall or alley to the center of street or alley, as the case may be, and put the dirt into convenient heaps for removal. Neglect to do this subjects the abutter to a fine. The street commissioner, with his teams and laborers, removes the dirt without expense to abutters, except in case of alleys. There is no separate account kept of the cost of the work to the city. There is no definite place for depositing the sweepings; they are used, wherever needed, to correct the grade of streets, and this is reported to be the only defect of the system, as sweepings are not suitable for street-making.

Removal of garbage and ashes.—Householders remove garbage and ashes. There are no regulations on the subject except the general ordinances about nuisances. It is reported that only the general habits of cleanliness of the people prevent serious results from the lack of system.

Dead animals.—The removal of dead animals is in charge of the city marshal. The annual cost of this service is $200.

Liquid household wastes.—Laundry waste and kitchen-slops are usually drained into surface gutters or sinks; chamber-slops into privy-vaults. Very little of the liquid household waste of the city is delivered into public sewers, that from 2 hotels being all that is known certainly so to drain; probably 80 per cent. of it is run into the street-gutters, and nearly all the rest into dry wells or cesspools on the premises. Street-gutters are not flushed except when it is incidentally done by the water company in flushing their mains.

Human excreta.—Not more than 15 per cent. of the houses of the city have water-closets, the remainder depending on privy-vaults. All water-closets deliver into public or private sewers. The ordinances provide that privy-vaults must be at least 10 feet deep and sufficiently walled up, and that every person owning a privy-vault must deposit in the vault 10 pounds of copperas in July, August, and September each. The dry-earth system is not at all used. Night-soil is deposited in the channel of the Mississippi river below the city.

Manufacturing waste.—There are no regulations on this head. Surface drains are relied upon to remove liquid waste of this sort.

POLICE.

The police force is appointed by the mayor and confirmed by the city council. The mayor has exclusive charge and control of the force, and governs it through a chief of police. The chief receives $800 per year, and there are 9 patrolmen receiving $50 per month each. The men furnish their own uniforms. They serve 12 hours per day each, and patrol in all about 6 miles of streets. In the year ending March 31, 1881, there were 809 arrests, of which 296 were for intoxication, 156 for misdemeanor, 80 for disturbing the peace, 60 for assault and battery, 44 for vagrancy, and the rest for minor offenses. The mayor may appoint special policemen, "who shall be authorized to make arrests when called upon, or when crime has been committed in their sight". They have the same standing and pay while on duty as the regular force. The cost of the police for 1880 was $7,655 50.

FIRE DEPARTMENT.

On March 1, 1879, the fire department consisted of 18 men, including the chief and assistant engineers, 8 of whom were station-men regularly employed, and 8 minute-men. The apparatus consisted of 4 hose-carriages and 1 hook-and-ladder truck, with 5 horses. The actual running expenses for the previous year was $6,863 22. The telephone fire-alarm was used; the department was called out 65 times during the year. The total loss from fire was $29,845 50, on which there was insurance to the amount of $28,908 50.

CEDAR RAPIDS,

LINN COUNTY, IOWA.

POPULATION

IN THE

AGGREGATE,

1860-1880.

	Inhab.
1790	......
1800	......
1810	......
1820	......
1830	......
1840	......
1850	......
1860	1,830
1870	5,940
1880	10,104

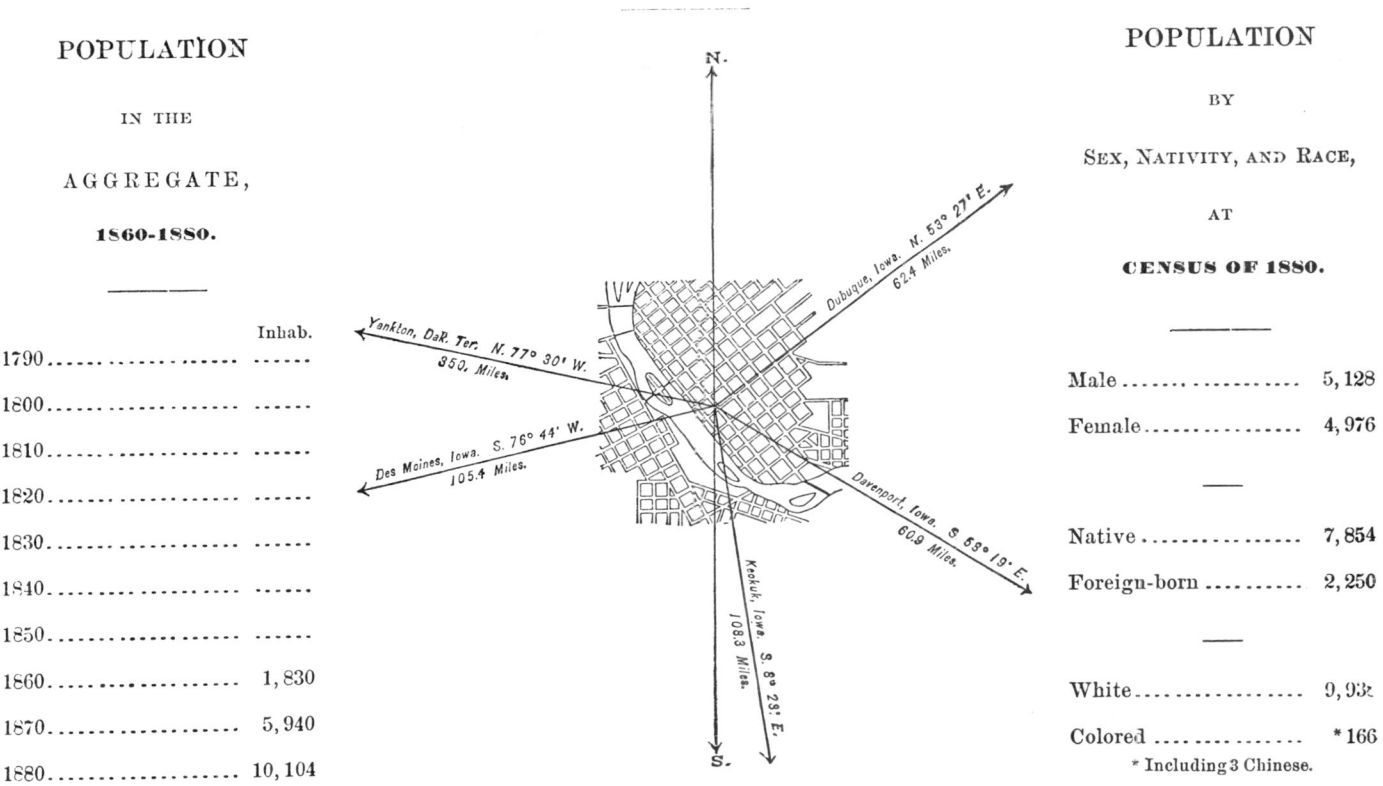

POPULATION

BY

SEX, NATIVITY, AND RACE,

AT

CENSUS OF 1880.

Male	5,128
Female	4,976
Native	7,854
Foreign-born	2,250
White	9,93.
Colored	*166

* Including 3 Chinese.

Latitude: 41° 58' North; Longitude: 91° 31' (west from Greenwich).

FINANCIAL CONDITION:

Total Valuation: $1,674,250; per capita: $166 00.   Net Indebtedness: $40,867; per capita: $4 04.   Tax per $100: $3 73.

CEDAR RAPIDS IN 1880.

The following statistical accounts, collected by the Census Office, indicate the present condition of Cedar Rapids:

LOCATION.

Cedar Rapids is situated in Linn county, Iowa, on the Cedar (or Red Cedar) river, 219 miles west of Chicago, 265 miles south of Saint Paul, and about 60 miles west-southwest of Dubuque.

RAILROAD COMMUNICATIONS.

The Burlington, Cedar Rapids, and Northern railway runs from Burlington through Cedar Rapids to Albert Lea, where it connects with the Minneapolis and Saint Louis railroad for the North and Northwest. The Council Bluffs, Denver, and California line of the Chicago and Northwestern railroad passes through Cedar Rapids, connecting

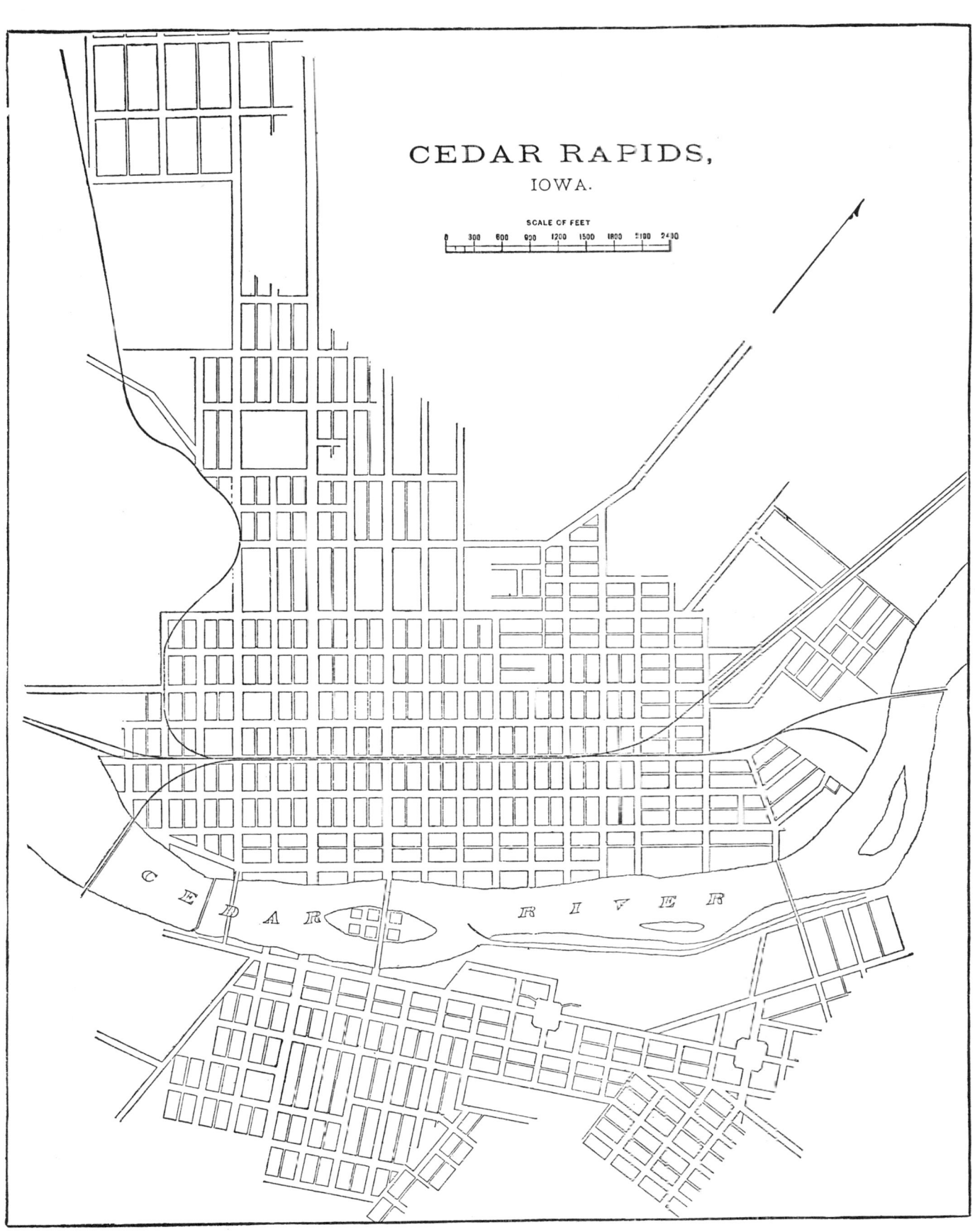

CEDAR RAPIDS,
IOWA.

SCALE OF FEET

0 300 600 900 1200 1500 1800 2100 2400

CEDAR RIVER

it with Chicago and Council Bluffs. The Cedar Rapids line of the Chicago, Milwaukee, and Saint Pau connects at Sabula, giving an almost straight road to Chicago; the Dubuque branch of the same road gives a line to Dubuque via Monticello.

TRIBUTARY COUNTRY.

The character of Linn county, in which Cedar Rapids is situated, may be taken to illustrate the country tributary to the city. This county is intersected by Cedar and Wapsipinicon rivers, which flow in a southeasterly direction, affording abundant water-power. It is also drained by two creeks. The surface is agreeably diversified, and is said to be well timbered. The soil is excellent and the water good. The wholesale trade of the city with this and the surrounding country is important.

TOPOGRAPHY.

Devonian and magnesian limestone are abundant along the banks of the Cedar river, and, no doubt, occur at Cedar Rapids. The river here furnishes a good water-power.

CLIMATE.

From the temperature charts published by the Smithsonian Institution it appears that the mean summer temperature of Cedar Rapids is about 70.5°, and the mean winter temperature about 21°.

STREETS.

The construction and repair of streets is done by day work at an annual cost of $4,000. Wood, stone, and brick are all used in the construction of sidewalks. There is a street railroad with 5 miles of track and 6 cars, the motive power being furnished by a steam motor; the rate of fare within the limits of the corporation is 5 cents.

WATER-WORKS.

The water-works are owned by a private corporation, and their first cost was $119,245. The supply is taken from Cedar river and pumped directly into the mains, the pressure on the pumps being 60 pounds to the square inch. The average daily consumption is estimated at 600,000 gallons. There are $7\frac{1}{2}$ miles of mains and 330 water-takers.

GAS.

The gas-works are owned by a private corporation. The charge per 1,000 feet is $4. The city pays $30 for each street-lamp, 147 in number.

PUBLIC BUILDINGS.

The city owns a city hall and a city jail. Their total cost was $15,000.

PUBLIC PARKS AND PLEASURE-GROUNDS.

There is 1 park, situated in the central part of the city, 300 feet square. It was given to the city. A committee of the city council controls it, and $100 is annually spent in its maintenance.

PLACES OF AMUSEMENT.

The theater of the city is Greene's opera-house, which has a seating capacity of 2,000. It pays an annual license of $75. There are no concert- or beer-gardens.

DRAINAGE.

Sewerage-works are constructed according to the requirements of each case as it comes up. There is no comprehensive plan. The outfall of sewage is to the Cedar river. Mouths of sewers are open and exposed, except at high water, when they are submerged. It is reported that there are no deposits in sewers requiring artificial flushing or removal by hand. The work of constructing sewers is done by the day under the direction of the city. One-half the cost is paid by the city. The other half is levied upon abutting property. Assessments are paid on the basis of frontage.

CEMETERIES.

There are 3 cemeteries connected with Cedar Rapids, viz:
Oak Hill, $\frac{1}{2}$ mile east of the city limits, comprising about 80 acres.
A cemetery 1 mile south of the city, 20 acres.
Catholic Cemetery, $2\frac{1}{2}$ miles southeast of the city, 10 acres.

MARKETS.

There are no public or corporation markets here.

SANITARY AUTHORITY—BOARD OF HEALTH.

As provided by the state law (quoted under "Burlington, Iowa", at page 709), the board of aldermen acts as a board of health. The annual expenses of the board are about $500. Inspections are made only as nuisances are reported. In such cases, if the nuisances exist, the city marshal serves written notices to owners or occupants to abate them. As the statutes provide, the board of health holds 2 regular meetings each year. Small-pox patients are isolated by a public quarantine of the house. Scarlet-fever patients are not isolated. There is no public pest-house. Vaccination is not compulsory. The board reports semi-annually to the state board of health.

MUNICIPAL CLEANSING.

Street-cleaning.—The streets are cleaned by the city's force by hand. Sweepings are generally deposited in the river.

Removal of garbage and ashes.—Garbage is removed by householders. Garbage and ashes are allowed to be kept in the same vessel.

Liquid household wastes.—No information was furnished on this head.

Human excreta.—Probably not more than 10 per cent. of the houses have water-closets.

Manufacturing wastes.—Manufacturing wastes are dumped into the Cedar river, which soon disposes of it, as the current here is about 5 miles per hour.

POLICE.

The police force is appointed by the mayor and confirmed by the city council; it is governed by the mayor and the city marshal. The city marshal is elected by the people, and receives a salary of $60 per month; the deputy marshal receives $50 per month, and 6 patrolmen are paid $40 per month each. Their uniforms are of blue cloth with brass buttons, and each man furnishes his own. They serve 12 hours per day each, and patrol from 3 to 5 miles of streets in all. In 1880 there were 385 arrests, the principal causes being drunkenness and disturbance of the peace. There were 200 station-house lodgers in 1880, against 300 in 1879. Free meals were given at a cost to the city of 12½ cents per meal. Special policemen are appointed by the mayor; their standing while on duty is the same as that of the regular force. The cost of the police force in 1880 was $3,450 58.

COUNCIL BLUFFS,

POTTAWATTAMIE COUNTY, IOWA.

POPULATION

IN THE

AGGREGATE,

1860-1880.

	Inhab.
1790	......
1800	......
1810	......
1820	......
1830	......
1840	......
1850	......
1860	2,011
1870	10,020
1880	18,063

POPULATION

BY

SEX, NATIVITY, AND RACE,

AT

CENSUS OF 1880.

Male	10,191
Female	7,872
Native	14,496
Foreign-born	3,567
White	17,511
Colored	*552

* Including 3 Chinese and 2 Indians.

Latitude: 41° 16' North; Longitude: 95° 51' (west from Greenwich); Altitude: 1,000 feet.

FINANCIAL CONDITION:

Total Valuation: $2,606,400; per capita: $144 00.   Net Indebtedness, $138,400; per capita: $7 66.   Tax per $100: $3 30.

HISTORICAL SKETCH.

Council Bluffs derived its name from a council held here on the bluffs with the Indians by Lewis and Clark in 1804. No settlement, however, was made until the fall of 1845, when a party of Mormons, composed mostly of English emigrants on their journey westward, started a village on the bluffs. The next year others came, and the little place slowly grew. In 1852-'53 part of these Mormons left for the West, but their places were quickly filled by settlers mostly from Missouri, Illinois, and Indiana. On January 19, 1853, an act was passed by the general assembly of Iowa to change the name of the town, theretofore called Kanesville, to Council Bluffs, and on the 24th of the same month an act was passed incorporating it as a city; in the following April the first city government was elected. In 1857 and 1864 the city suffered from periods of depression, but since the close of the war its growth in wealth and population has been steady and rapid. The only great fire from which it has suffered took place in the winter of 1854-'55, when the upper part of the city was almost entirely destroyed.

COUNCIL BLUFFS IN 1880.

The information concerning the condition of Council Bluffs in 1880, contained in the statistical accounts given below, was secured by the Census Office mainly through the mayor of the city, Hon. W. R. Vaughan:

LOCATION.

Council Bluffs is situated on the east side of the Missouri river, opposite Omaha, about 412 miles above Saint Louis and 135 miles west of Des Moines, at an average altitude of 1,000 feet above the surface of the sea. The Missouri is navigable, and gives water communication with all river ports on the Missouri, Mississippi, and Ohio rivers.

RAILROAD COMMUNICATIONS.

The city has become a great railroad center, mainly from the fact that it is practically the eastern terminus of the Union Pacific, the pioneer line across the Rocky mountains, which gives the East connection with San Francisco over the Central Pacific from Ogden. At Council Bluffs center 5 other roads, which connect with the Union Pacific at the Union depot, viz:

The Chicago, Rock Island, and Pacific runs to Chicago via Rock Island.

The Chicago, Burlington, and Quincy runs to Chicago via Burlington.

The Council Bluffs, Denver, and California line of the Chicago and Northwestern runs to Chicago via Cedar Rapids.

The Saint Louis and Omaha line of the Wabash, Saint Louis, and Pacific runs to Saint Louis, connecting at Moberly with the main line for Toledo via Hannibal and Wabash.

The Kansas City, Saint Joseph, and Council Bluffs runs to Kansas City via Saint Joseph.

TRIBUTARY COUNTRY.

The city has a large wholesale trade, and is the outlet for the vast grain region of Pottawattamie county, of which it is the capital. This county contains 700 square miles, is diversified with fine scenery, and presents a fair proportion of timber and prairie. The soil is fertile, adapted to grain and grass. It is well populated and has large commercial interests.

TOPOGRAPHY.

The city is built principally upon a plain at the base of the high bluffs from which it derives part of its name, although not a few of the finest residences are to be found in the numerous " glens" which intersect the bluff in every direction. The soil is of light yellow clay, which is very fine but packs hard. The bluffs are generally covered with a layer of black earth, the balance of the bluff being the bright yellow clay. There is no rock immediately underlying the surface. There are several lakes in the vicinity.

CLIMATE.

From the Smithsonian publications it appears that the mean summer temperature is 75.48°, the mean winter temperature 22.06°, and the mean annual temperature 49.96°.

STREETS.

The cost of keeping the paving of the city in repair is about $6,000 per year. Some of the sidewalks are of brick with stone or oak curbing, and the rest are of pine plank laid on oak stringers, varying from 4 to 15 feet in width. Trees are sometimes planted inside and sometimes outside the curbing. The repair of streets is done partly by contract work and partly by day work, at a total annual expense of from $10,000 to $12,000. The gutters are wholly of earth. The preference of the city authorities is for contract work for large jobs, and day work for general repairs. There is a horse-railroad with 0.5 mile of track, 3 cars, and 16 horses, employing 7 men; 57,400 passengers were carried during the year; the rate of fare is 15 cents. There is a herdic line with 14 coaches and 30 horses, employing 20 men, the fare being 5 cents.

WATER-WORKS.

Water-works are now in process of construction by the Council Bluffs City Water Works company, and are expected to be completed and in operation by September 1, 1882. The source of supply is to be the Missouri river.

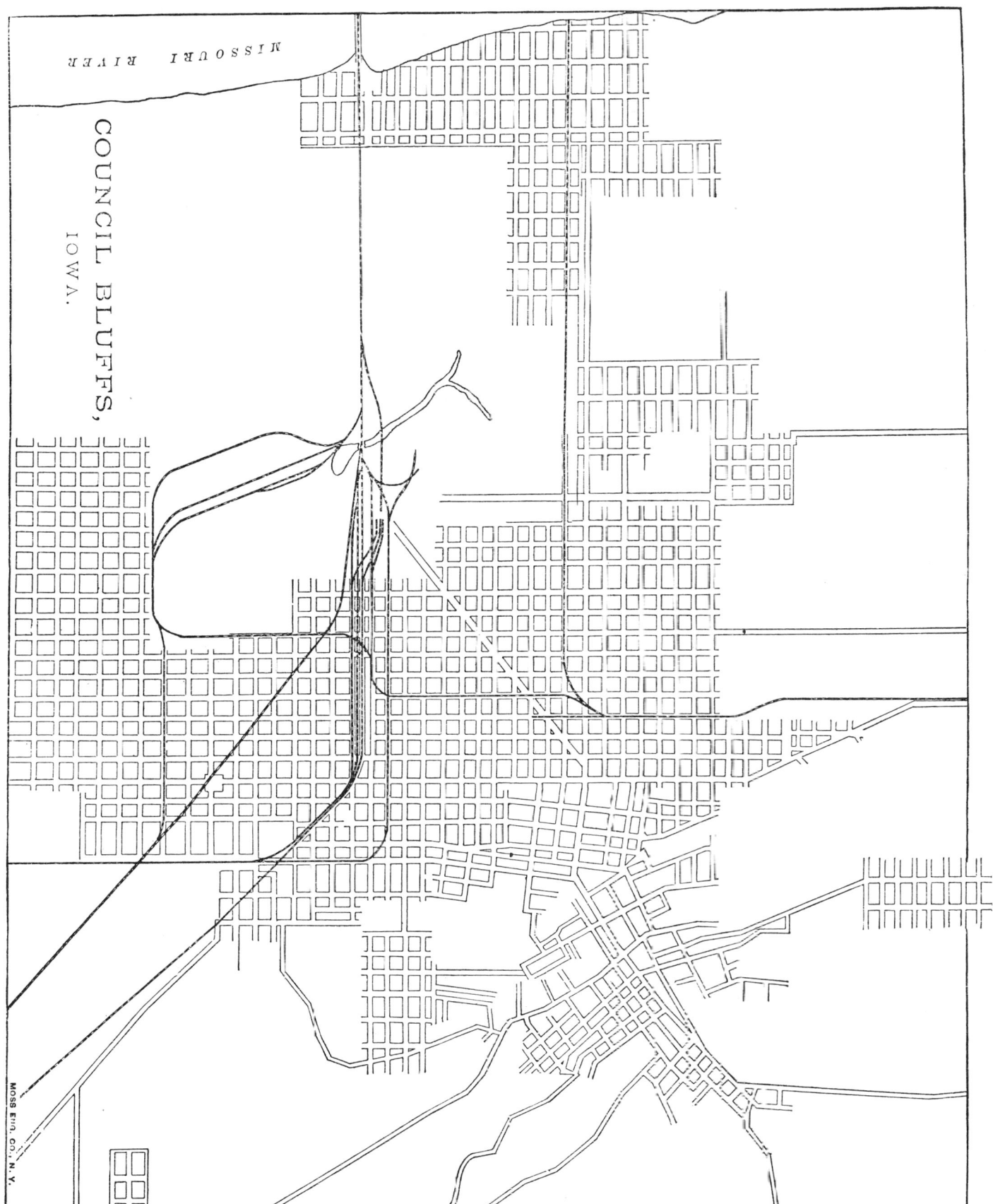

COUNCIL BLUFFS,
IOWA.

MISSOURI RIVER

MOSS Eng. CO., N.Y.

GAS.

The city has been lighted with gas for the past 10 years by a private company. The daily average production is 30,000 feet, and the charge per 1,000 feet is $4 50. The city pays $30 per year each for 175 street-lamps. There are about 15 miles of gas-mains.

PUBLIC BUILDINGS.

There is a city building owned by the city, which cost $10,000, and the city owns 2 engine-houses. The total cost of municipal buildings belonging to the city is given as $25,000.

PUBLIC PARKS AND PLEASURE-GROUNDS.

The city has 4 parks, viz: *Spring Park*, in the western part of the city, with an area (including Spring lake) of 600 acres; *Carr Lake*, south of the city, 106 acres; *Fairmount Park*, in the center of the city, 90 acres; *Bayliss Park*, in the business portion of the city, 4 acres. All but Fairmount park were given to the city. The total cost is said to be $20,000, and the yearly cost of maintenance (including improvements) is $1.000. They are controlled by the park committee of the board of aldermen.

PLACES OF AMUSEMENT.

There are 5 halls used for theater purposes, concerts, and lectures, as follows: Dohaney's hall, seating 1,000; Bloom and Wilson's hall, 600. There are 8 or 10 smaller halls used for various purposes. Theaters pay an annual license of $100. There are 2 concert- and beer-gardens: Brock's garden, 4 acres in extent, which cost $1,000 and has seats for 800, and Hom's park, 1 acre, which cost $4,000 and has seats for 600. Both are well patronized at all times.

DRAINAGE.

No system of sewers has yet been adopted. There are now in the city about 600 linear feet of 3-foot circular brick sewer, and 1,000 linear feet of wooden sewers from 2 to 4 feet square. These empty into sloughs along the Mississippi.

CEMETERIES.

There are 3 cemeteries, viz:
Fairview Cemetery, containing 30 acres.
Walnut Cemetery, 15 acres.
Catholic Cemetery, 40 acres.
No record has been kept of interments, but the total is estimated at 7,000. The first two cemeteries belong to private corporations; the last, to a church. The price of lots ranges from $10 to $25.

MARKETS.

There are no public markets in the city, except a locality designated by the city council for standing-room for wagons loaded with hay and wood offered for sale. There are no market revenues except the weighmaster's fees, 10 per cent. of which goes to the city. There are 4 or 5 wholesale private markets for the sale of fish, game, vegetables, etc.

SANITARY AUTHORITY—BOARD OF HEALTH.

In accordance with the state law (*vide* "Burlington, Iowa", at page 709), the board of aldermen acts as a board of health. Their powers are, of course, identical with those given the city council by the city charter, and their duties are the usual ones of such a board, *i. e.*, to take all measures necessary for the good of the public health, and especially to abate nuisances and to prevent the spread of infectious diseases. Except in case of infection, inspectors and assistant health officers are not employed. Inspections are ordinarily made only as nuisances are reported, and if the nuisances really exist it is ordered that they shall be abated immediately. The health committee of the board is appointed by its presiding officer, the mayor. Small-pox patients are sent to the pest-house, which is situated about 3 miles from the city. Scarlet-fever patients are quarantined at home. At times when small-pox is prevalent, vaccination is compulsory, and is done at the public expense. The registration of births, diseases, and deaths is performed under the state law.

MUNICIPAL CLEANSING.

Street-cleaning.—The streets are cleaned by the city's own force. No further information on this head was received.
Removal of garbage and ashes.—Garbage is removed by private parties.
Dead animals.—Dead animals are generally removed by parties engaged in the manufacture of glue and fertilizer. In case they become nuisances, the owner of land on which they are found is obliged to bury them. About 200 animals of different kinds are annually removed.

Liquid household wastes.—The dry-wells and cesspools of the city are very porous. It is reported that there has been no complaint of the contamination of drinking-water from this source. None of the waste runs into street-gutters.

Human excreta.—The houses of the city depend entirely on privy-vaults.

POLICE.

The regular police force is appointed by the city council, and is governed by the mayor and council.

The executive officer is the chief of police; he receives a salary of $1,080 per year. There are 6 patrolmen, receiving $840 per year each. They wear the common blue uniform, which they themselves provide. They serve 10 hours per day each, and patrol 10 miles of streets in all. In 1880 there were 1,300 arrests, the principal causes being intoxication, disturbance of the peace, and violation of the city ordinances. The amount of property stolen during the year was $1,500, of which $1,200 was recovered; 500 free meals were given to station-house lodgers, at a cost of $100. The police force co-operates with the fire department to the extent of guarding property in case of fire, and with the health department in enforcing its orders. Special policemen are appointed by the mayor to serve on legal holidays, etc.; they are under the orders of the regular force. There was one casualty in the force in 1880, caused by the accidental discharge of a revolver. The cost of the force for 1880 was $5,400 53.

DAVENPORT,

SCOTT COUNTY, IOWA.

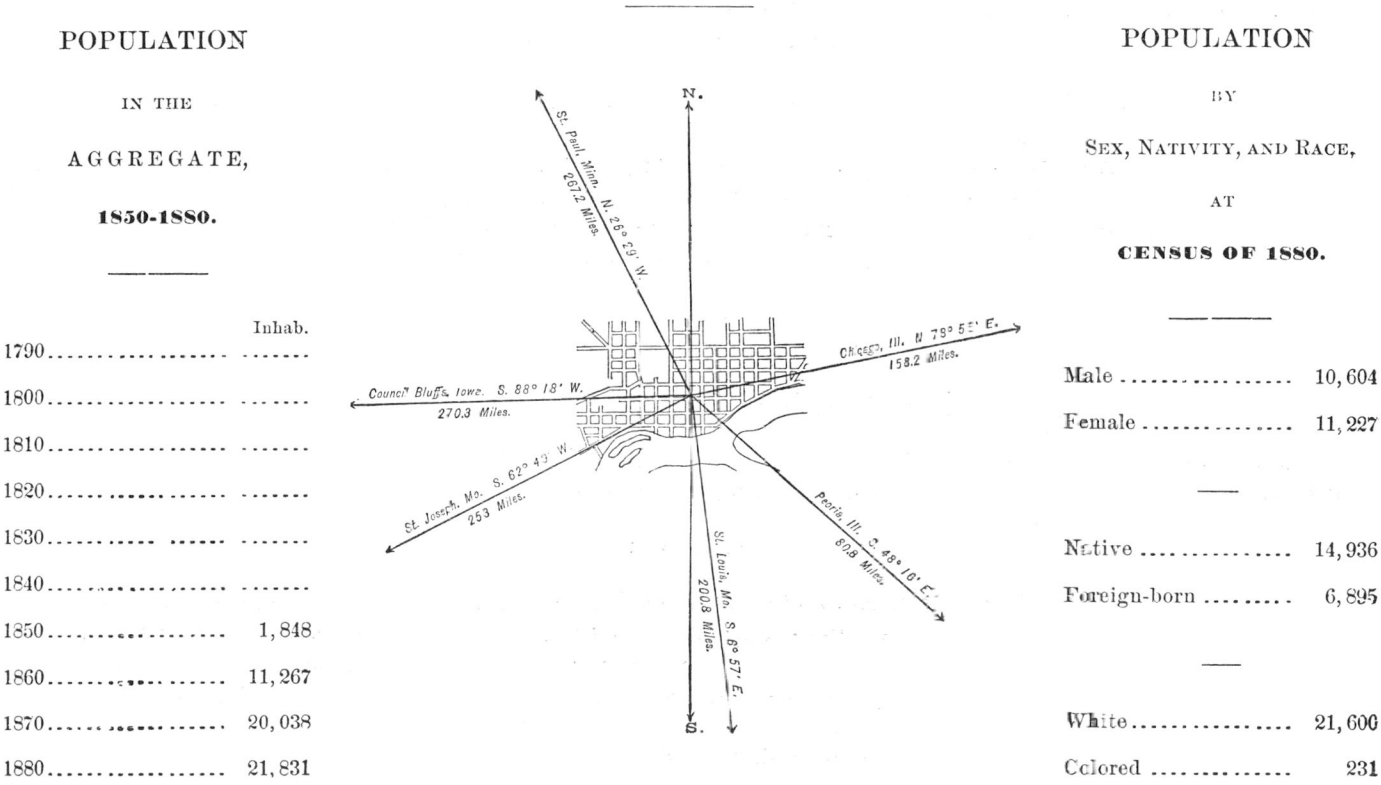

POPULATION IN THE AGGREGATE, 1850-1880.		POPULATION BY SEX, NATIVITY, AND RACE, AT CENSUS OF 1880.	
	Inhab.		
1790	....	Male	10,604
1800	....	Female	11,227
1810	....		
1820	....		
1830	....	Native	14,936
1840	....	Foreign-born	6,895
1850	1,848		
1860	11,267		
1870	20,038	White	21,600
1880	21,831	Colored	231

Latitude : 41° 30′ North ; Longitude : 90° 39′ (west from Greenwich) ; **Altitude : 534 to 714 feet.**

FINANCIAL CONDITION :

Total Valuation : $6,693,413 ; per capita : $307 00.   Net Indebtedness : $290,675 ; per capita : $13 31.   Tax per $100 : $2 69.

HISTORICAL SKETCH.

The treaty with the Sac and Fox Indians in 1832 opened up a wide and fertile country for settlement, and in 1833 there were one or two claims made upon the lands now covered by the lower part of the present city of Davenport. In the fall of 1835 a company was formed to purchase and lay out a town site, and after due deliberation the land now included in the area bounded on the east by Harrison street, north by Seventh, west by Warren, and south by the river, was selected. The cost of the entire site was $2,000, divided into 8 shares of $250 each. The necessity of a town between the upper and lower rapids, the unexampled fertility of the surrounding country, the beauty of the location and its apparent freedom from malaria-breeding marshes, the facilities for good drainage, and the nearness of an immense water-power, had much to do with the choice of the company.

In the spring of the following year the site was surveyed and laid out, and in May the lots were offered for sale by auction, a steamboat coming up from Saint Louis laden with passengers to attend the sale. The sale, however, was not a success, probably owing to the fact that the titles conveyed were simply such as were included in a squatter's claim, and only 50 or 60 lots were sold, the remaining lots being divided among the members of the company.

In 1836 Wisconsin was organized, and by an act of the legislature the "Black Hawk purchase" was divided into 2 districts, one of which included Davenport. In 1838 Iowa was set apart as a territory, and Scott county was formed with Davenport, incorporated as a town in 1839, finally settled on as the county-seat in 1840. The early growth of the town was slow; but when it is considered that at the time the site was purchased the whole country was staggering under the effects of the crisis of 1837, this is not to be wondered at. Though the pioneers of Wisconsin sent plenty of lumber down the broad bosom of the natural highway flowing past Davenport, provisions were high, and immigration, owing to the lack of transportation facilities, was slow.

The year 1850 began a new era, and the prospect of soon being connected with the eastern cities by rail gave an impetus to Davenport. In 1851 a city charter was obtained. In 1853 ground was broken for a railroad from this point westward to the Missouri river. In 1854 the first train came into Rock Island from Chicago, and the same year saw the corner-stone laid for a bridge over the Mississippi, connecting Davenport with Rock Island, Illinois. Immigration, which had begun a few years previously, increased, new industries sprang up, and business rapidly increased. From this time forward the progress of the city has been steady, with at times a growth that has been particularly marked.

Davenport has never suffered from any destructive conflagrations, and, with the exception of the financial crises of 1857 and 1873, from no marked periods of depression. The original population was native-born, with a few French; but since 1848 a large German element has been added, so that now the Germans, with their descendants, form a considerable portion of the inhabitants and have their own quarter of the city.

DAVENPORT IN 1880.

The following statistical accounts, much of which was furnished to the Census Office by Dr. R. J. Farquharson and E. H. Schmidt, esq., indicate the present condition of Davenport:

LOCATION.

Davenport lies in latitude 41° 30' north, and longitude 90° 39' west, from Greenwich, on the west bank of the Mississippi river, at the foot of the upper rapids, opposite the city of Rock Island, Illinois, and 330 miles by river above Saint Louis. The altitudes above sea-level are: lowest point, low-water mark on the government bridge, 534 feet; average level of the top of the curbstone in front of the United States signal office, 559 feet; and highest point, 714 feet. The river here is navigable for steamers drawing 3 feet of water at all times. The harbor capacity is unlimited. The channel in the Rock Island rapids, 3 miles above Davenport, has been improved so as to give a depth of 4 feet at low water and a width of 200 feet. The current here is from 1½ to 2 miles per hour, while in the rapids above it is sometimes 6 miles an hour. Davenport is in communication with all places on the Mississippi and its navigable tributaries.

RAILROAD COMMUNICATIONS.

The city is touched by the following railroads:

Chicago, Rock Island, and Pacific Railroad, main line, from Chicago to Council Bluffs.

The Davenport division of the Chicago, Milwaukee, and Saint Paul railroad, from this point to Calmar, on the Iowa and Minnesota division of the same road.

TRIBUTARY COUNTRY.

The local trade of Davenport is almost exclusively confined to the supply of Scott county, which is entirely devoted to farming.

TOPOGRAPHY.

Davenport is divided by an escarpment into 2 plateaus, the lower being on an average 30 feet above low-water mark, and is composed of alluvial soil overlying Hamilton limestone (Niagara group, Devonian system), which rock in some places crops out and in others is buried many feet. The upper plateau is composed of drift exclusively, no rock being found in it except bowlders. It has an average elevation of 160 feet above low-water mark (of 1864). On the upper level the drainage of the plateau is by means of numerous ravines, which widen as they approach the river; these afford excellent conduits for the passage of the surplus water, and also for the sewerage of the city wherever they have been preserved. There are no lakes, ponds, or marshes near the city. The country in the vicinity is open, no forest trees being found, except on the banks of the Mississippi, and to a less degree along

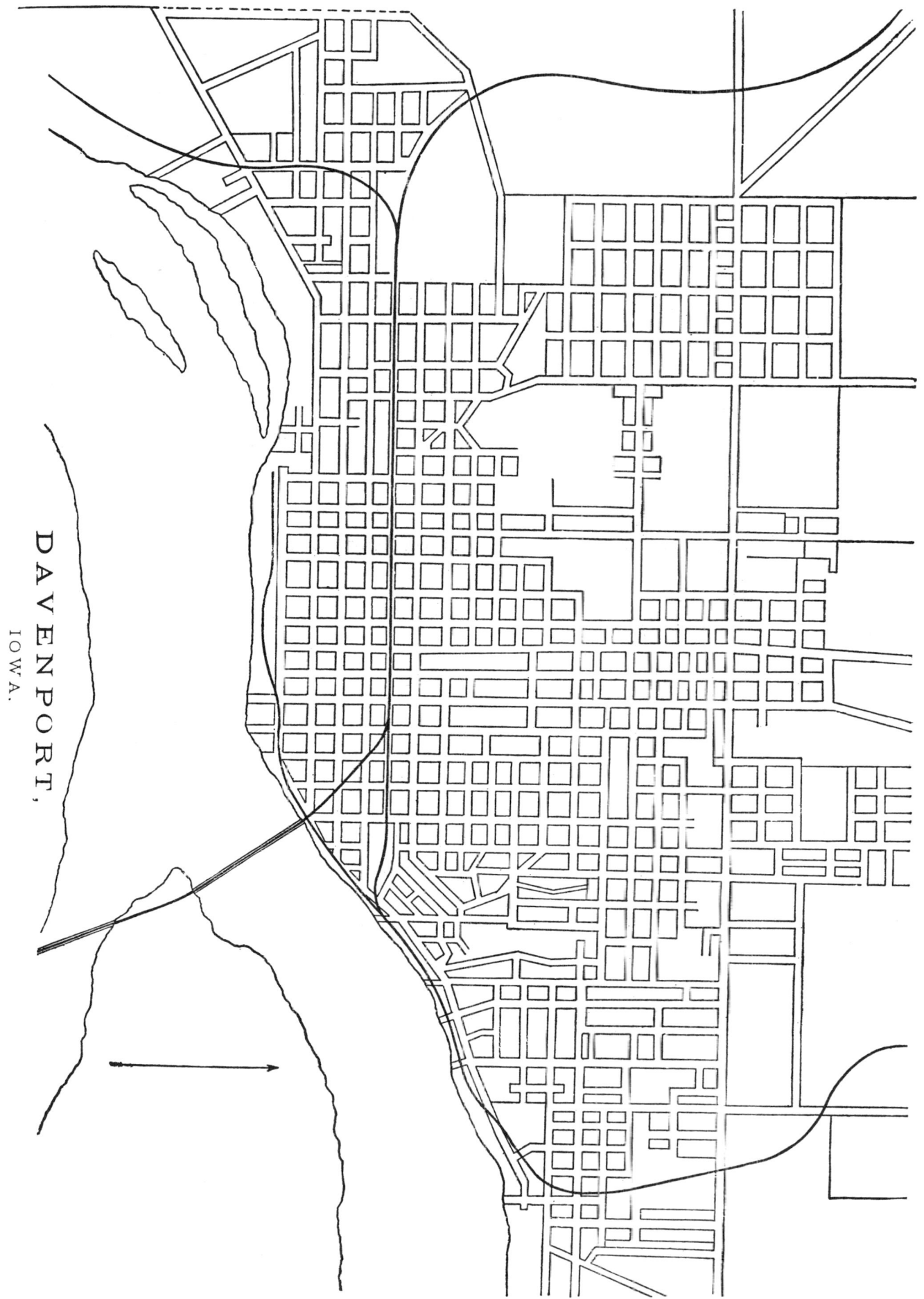

DAVENPORT,
IOWA.

its small tributaries. The soil near Davenport is a dirt loam, of exceeding fertility, producing large crops of the cereals, especially Indian corn; of most of the fruits of the temperate zone, especially grapes; and also of roots, especially of Irish potatoes and onions. Indeed, for the production of the latter bulb, the soil of Scott county is so well adapted, and the growth so enormous, as to exceed that of any other county in the United States, and to make of Davenport another *Wethersfield* (Connecticut), indeed, much to surpass that famous town as an "onion mart".

CLIMATE.

During observations extending over 9 years the highest recorded summer temperature was 98°; highest summer temperature in average years, 93°. Lowest recorded winter temperature, −22°; and lowest winter temperature in average years, −15°. The prevailing winds are southwesterly in summer and northwesterly in winter, tending to increase the extremes of temperature more than the latitude and elevation would lead one to expect. Any decided change of wind in direction from the points named has a moderating influence.

STREETS.

The total length of streets is about 135 miles, of which 35 miles are paved with broken stone. The cost of this pavement per square yard, as nearly as it may be estimated, is $1 50; this does not include the gutters, which cost $1 25 per running foot. The sidewalks are chiefly of wood, a few being of stone or brick. Gutters are laid with flat stones. An ordinance lately passed fixes the width of streets north of Fifth street at 40 feet and the width of sidewalks at 20 feet, with 14 feet of the latter reserved for grass-plots and trees; but "so far this is only on paper." About $20,000 is annually expended for the repairs of streets, including the unpaved ones. The city authorities express a preference for contract work for large jobs, and day work for repairs. There is no stone-crusher, but a roller, weighing 5,000 pounds and drawn by horses, is used. There are 12½ miles of horse-railroads in the city, using 35 cars, with 96 horses and mules, and giving employment to 30 men. The number of passengers carried during the year was not stated. The rate of fare is 5 cents. There are no regular omnibus lines, but the hotels have omnibuses running to and from the railroad stations.

WATER-WORKS.

The water-works are owned by a private corporation, and their first cost was $500,000. The water is taken from the Mississippi river and pumped directly into the mains on the Holly system, the average pressure being about 80 pounds to the square inch. The estimated daily consumption is about 3,000,000 gallons. The average annual cost of maintenance and repairs is about $26,000. There are 22 miles of distributing mains and 242 hydrants. Dr. Farquharson says, regarding the water supply: "As the water supply of Davenport is drawn from the rapids, it is very highly aerated, so much so as to be of a milky color, and like soda-water when first drawn from the hydrants. This large admixture of atmospheric oxygen must have an important influence in destroying any organic matters, and hence add much to the wholesomeness of the water as a drink."

GAS.

The gas-works are not owned by the city. The charge per 1,000 feet is $2 50. The city pays $36 per annum for each street-lamp, 223 in number.

PUBLIC BUILDINGS.

The city owns and occupies for municipal purposes, wholly or in part, 1 city hall, costing $7,500; 1 police station and grounds, costing $15,000; and 1 pest-house and 5 engine-houses, costing $35,000; making total cost of all municipal buildings belonging to the city, $57,500. None of the buildings are owned in common with the county, which has a court-house of its own, costing $50,000, and proposes to erect a new one next year at a cost of $100,000.

PUBLIC PARKS AND PLEASURE-GROUNDS.

There are 3 parks, aggregating 7½ acres: *Court House Square*, 2¼ acres; *Washington Park*, 3 acres; with another of 2¼ acres. In addition to these, there is *Shooting Park*, area 25 acres. The former are owned by the city and the latter by a private company; it is, however, open to the public at all times, and, being situated on a high point overlooking the river, with many shade trees, is much resorted to. Washington park cost $5,000. The annual cost of maintenance for the 3 parks belonging to the city is $700, and they are controlled by a committee of the city council.

PLACES OF AMUSEMENT.

There are 2 theaters in Davenport: Burtis opera-house, seating capacity 2,000, is used by traveling companies, and the German theater, in Turner hall, seating 800, and in which performances are given every Sunday evening. The theaters pay an annual license of $75 each. Library hall, with stage, and Forest hall, seating 1,000 each,

Temperance hall, with a seating capacity of 600, and Metropolitan hall, seating 800, are used for concerts, lectures, etc. Among the concert- and beer-gardens are Washington gardens, area 4 acres, rebuilt in 1870 and lately sold for $5,000, and having an average attendance on Sundays during the summer of 1,000 persons; and P. N. Jacobs' summer garden, with an average attendance of about 500. The most prominent resorts of this class are situated outside the city limits.

DRAINAGE.

Until 1876 the entire drainage of the city was by surface gutters, with exception of a few private sewers. The system now adopted and partially built contemplates a sewer in each street running north and south, with laterals extending to the middle of the block on each side. Sewage is discharged into the Mississippi river. The mouths of sewers are submerged. Rates of fall are considerable, and no artificial flushing or cleaning is done. The cost of construction is assessed upon the abutting property on the basis of square feet of area extending to the middle of the block. The prices paid for building sewers in 1880 were as follows: Pipe sewer, 18 inches in diameter, 14 feet deep, length, 5,000 feet, $1 95 per foot, including manholes and basins; a 36-inch brick sewer, 14 feet deep, 3,500 feet long, $2 80 per foot; a pipe sewer 18 inches in diameter, 13 feet deep, 2,000 feet long, $1 80 per foot. The average cost of each inlet-basin is $35, and of each manhole $25.

CEMETERIES.

There are 5 cemeteries in Davenport, one owned by the city and the rest belonging to private institutions. There are no church-yard or private burial grounds in which interments are no longer permitted. The number of interments in all the cemeteries, so far as past records show, is: *City Cemetery*, during 18 years, 4,532; *Oakdale Cemetery*, during 8 years, estimated at 700; *Pine Hill Cemetery*, during 9 years, estimated at 380; *Saint Mary's Cemetery*, during 18 years, estimated at 2,400; and *Jewish Cemetery*, estimated at 200. The City cemetery is under charge of a sexton, appointed annually by the city council, and who has police powers. He sees that all graves are dug 5 feet deep, and is required to keep a record of all burials. Mr. Schmidt reports that, owing to the defective records of the private cemeteries, he can not communicate much information regarding them.

MARKETS.

There are no public or corporation markets in the city. Some time ago 2 buildings were erected for this purpose, but, as persons could not be induced to attend them, one was torn down and the other is now occupied as a store-room by various firms.

SANITARY AUTHORITY—BOARD OF HEALTH.

The chief sanitary organization of Davenport is the board of health, composed of the mayor, 3 aldermen, 2 citizens, one of whom is a physician, and the city clerk, *ex-officio* clerk of the board. The board is appointed annually by the mayor, subject to the confirmation of the city council. The expenses of the board last year were $700, which was expended for removing nuisances, and during epidemics this sum can be increased to any amount deemed necessary by the council. In the absence of epidemics the board has full power over the general health and sanitary condition of the city, while during epidemics it has power to meet the emergency in any way necessary. The mayor is chairman of the board and also executive officer, with sufficient powers to cause all orders and regulations to be complied with. The board meets once a week in summer and once a month in winter, and conducts its business as a deliberative body. The city marshal acts as health-inspector, and can arrest persons for creating a nuisance or otherwise endangering the public health. Inspections are made regularly in all parts of the city. When nuisances are reported they are ordered to be abated or removed within 12 hours, and if this order is not complied with the board has the work done and the cost assessed on the property where the nuisance exists. The same mode of procedure is observed toward defective house-drainage, cesspools, privy-vaults, sources of drinking-water, etc. The board has full power over the conservation and removal of garbage. Burial permits are issued by the city clerk on certificates of death signed by the attending physician.

INFECTIOUS DISEASES.

Small-pox patients are taken to the public pest-house, situated north of the city limits, or quarantined at home. Scarlet-fever cases are quarantined at home. Physicians are required promptly to report to the board of health any case of contagious disease to which they may be called to attend, and all clothing, bedding, etc., exposed to contagion must be fully disinfected before being removed. Vaccination is not compulsory, nor is it done at the public expense. The board recommends that every child should be vaccinated before 2 years of age, and all persons should be revaccinated as often as once in every 5 years.

REPORTS.

By a new state law all births and deaths must be reported to the city clerk by the attending physician, or other persons, and a record is kept of them. The board reports to the state board of health presumably once a year.

MUNICIPAL CLEANSING.

Street-cleaning.—The streets are cleaned at the expense of the city, with its own force and wholly by hand. The macadamized streets are cleaned perhaps about twice a year, but none of the streets are ever swept. The estimated cost of the work is $500 per year, and the street dirt removed is used to fill other streets. Concerning the merits and defects of the system, Mr. Schmidt says: "Not enough street-cleaning done to answer the above."

Removal of garbage and ashes.—All garbage and ashes are removed by the city under contract. They are required to be kept in tight receptacles and placed in the rear of residences, convenient for removal. Ashes and garbage may be kept in the same vessel, and they are both disposed of by being dumped into the river. The annual cost is $500. No nuisance or probable injury to health results from the manner of keeping, handling, or disposing of the garbage.

Dead animals.—The carcass of any animal dying within the limits of the city must be removed by the owner, and if he is not known, then the city has the carcass removed and disposed of, generally sending it to a rendering establishment. The cost of the service is nothing, and the number of dead animals removed annually is not known.

Liquid household wastes.—Where sewers exist the liquid wastes from the houses run into them; where there are no sewers the wastes go into cesspools and vaults, none being allowed to pass into the paved gutters. The cesspools are mostly porous, are not provided with overflows, receive the wastes from water-closets, and are cleaned out in the same manner as privy-vaults.

Human excreta.—Nearly all the houses in the city depend on privy-vaults; not more 2½ per cent. have water-closets, nearly all of which deliver into the sewers. Very few of the privy-vaults are water-tight. The only regulations concerning the construction of vaults is that they must be at least 20 feet from any well or spring the water from which is used for drinking purposes. The vaults are cleaned out at least once a year by regular night scavengers, with covered water-tight carts; and between May 1 and November 1 the contents must be disinfected before being removed. The night-soil is deposited on a scow and dumped into the Mississippi river 2 miles below the city. The dry-earth system is used only to a limited extent, probably not more than 10 cases.

Manufacturing wastes.—Liquid wastes, when not injurious to health, are not regulated; injurious wastes are disposed of as ordered by the board of health.

POLICE.

The police force of Davenport is appointed and governed by the police committee, composed of the mayor and 3 aldermen. The chief of police, salary $900 a year, is the executive officer, and has direction and supervision over the department. The remainder of the force consists of 1 captain at $60 a month, and 14 patrolmen at $50 a month each. The uniform is what is known as the "New York regulation", and the city gives each man $5 a month for his uniform and a chain "come-along". The men are on duty 12 hours at a time and patrol 15 miles of streets. During 1880 there were 842 arrests, principally for disturbing the peace, and the cases were finally disposed of by fines or work on the city stone-yard. During the past year property to the value of $716 15 was reported to the police as lost or stolen, and the amount rescued and returned to the owners during the same time was $813 70. There were 750 station-house lodgers in 1880, as against 1,178 in 1879. No free meals are furnished to lodgers. The police are not required to co-operate with the health or building department, as the city marshal and his deputies attend to this. Special policemen, or watchmen for private property, and also to assist the regular force, are appointed by the mayor. The yearly cost of the police force (1880) is $10,920.

MANUFACTURES.

The following is a summary of the statistics of the manufactures of Davenport for 1880, being taken from tables prepared for the Tenth Census by James R. Graham, special agent:

Mechanical and manufacturing industries.	No. of establishments.	Capital.	AVERAGE NUMBER OF HANDS EMPLOYED.			Total amount paid in wages during the year.	Value of materials.	Value of products.
			Males above 16 years.	Females above 15 years.	Children and youths.			
All industries	188	$2,806,222	1,473	82	150	$685,469	$2,960,668	$4,468,978
Agricultural implements	3	325,000	137			68,558	167,615	344,900
Blacksmithing (see also Wheelwrighting)	16	16,952	16		1	8,447	9,650	30,555
Boots and shoes, including custom work and repairing	14	41,440	33	1	3	15,894	18,580	52,230
Bread and other bakery products	7	97,700	39	2	1	17,105	95,610	132,015
Brick and tile	6	30,500	53		9	12,804	6,350	25,750
Carpentering	10	50,400	51		9	29,805	92,755	147,600
Carriages and wagons (see also Wheelwrighting)	4	35,870	35		1	23,400	26,383	65,500
Clothing, men's	13	110,900	82	30	1	62,068	109,759	209,378
Confectionery	3	19,650	7	5	1	4,320	55,800	78,000
Cooperage	4	16,700	33			12,060	29,590	47,642

Mechanical and manufacturing industries.	No. of estab- lish- ments.	Capital.	AVERAGE NUMBER OF HANDS EMPLOYED.			Total amount paid in wages during the year.	Value of materials.	Value of products.
			Males above 16 years.	Females above 15 years.	Children and youths.			
Flouring- and grist-mill products	5	$123,000	36	....	....	$19,458	$569,585	$644,699
Foundery and machine-shop products	3	76,500	51	....	3	26,950	50,300	99,250
Furniture	5	110,500	91	1	2	40,212	61,732	124,650
Liquors, malt	4	205,000	62	....	....	24,135	103,590	178,370
Lumber, sawed	5	655,000	240	....	64	101,800	576,350	828,080
Marble and stone work	4	20,500	19	....	1	9,865	13,816	31,931
Printing and publishing	4	79,500	45	9	3	29,213	53,986	108,123
Saddlery and harness	9	16,200	21	....	2	8,645	19,317	38,585
Sash, doors, and blinds	3	135,000	83	....	25	40,240	252,182	333,475
Slaughtering and meat-packing, not including retail butchering	3	285,000	49	....	....	7,310	266,559	273,634
Tinware, copperware, and sheet-iron ware	14	49,100	36	....	....	15,907	29,365	64,202
Tobacco, cigars and cigarettes	15	70,380	73	22	7	45,178	82,162	184,609
Wheelwrighting (see also Blacksmithing; Carriages and wagons)	4	4,780	6	....	1	2,192	3,810	8,438
All other industries (a)	30	230,650	125	12	16	59,903	265,822	417,362

a Embracing bookbinding and blank-book making; boxes, wooden packing; brass castings; brooms and brushes; coffee and spices, roasted and ground; coffins, burial cases, and undertakers' goods; cordage and twine; engraving, wood; hairwork; leather, curried; leather, tanned; lock- and gun-smithing; looking-glass and picture frames; malt; mineral and soda waters; models and patterns; painting and paperhanging; paints; paving materials; photographing; roofing and roofing materials; shirts; soap and candles; trunks and valises; vinegar; and window blinds and shades.

From the foregoing table it appears that the average capital of all establishments is $14,926 71; that the average wages of all hands employed is $402 03 per annum; and that the average outlay in wages, in materials, and in interest (at 6 per cent.) on capital employed is $20,289 94.

DES MOINES,

POLK COUNTY, IOWA.

POPULATION

IN THE

AGGREGATE,

1850-1880.

	Inhab.
1790	.....
1800	.....
1810	.....
1820	.....
1830	.....
1840	.....
1850	502
1860	3,965
1870	12,035
1880	22,408

POPULATION

BY

SEX, NATIVITY, AND RACE,

AT

CENSUS OF 1880.

Male	11,531
Female	10,877
Native	18,205
Foreign-born	4,203
White	21,787
Colored	*621

* Including 9 Chinese.

Latitude: 41° 36′ North; Longitude: 93° 88′ (west from Greenwich); Altitude: 780 feet.

FINANCIAL CONDITION:

Total Valuation: $4,361,090 ; per capita: $195 00.   Net indebtedness: $578,000 ; per capita: $25 79.   Tax per $100: $5 18.

HISTORICAL SKETCH.(a)

The present site of the city was originally a part of the Sac and Fox Indian reservation. On the 11th of October, 1842, the government purchased the reservation from the Indians, and, for the better protection of the settlers against depredations from the Pottawattomies and Sioux, on May 9, 1843, a detachment of troops reached this point, landing where Court Avenue bridge now stands. Barracks were immediately erected and the post was named "Fort Des Moines", taking its name from the river flowing past it. The county of Polk was organized by the legislature in 1846, and a board of commissioners, appointed for the purpose, fixed upon Fort Des Moines as the county-seat. The first survey of the town was made July 8, 1846. On September 22, 1851, the citizens voted to have it incorporated as a town, articles of incorporation being adopted by the people October 18, and the first election occurring 2 days after. This was ratified by the legislature in 1853, and in 1854 an act was passed by

---

a The following sketch was furnished by J. P. Bushnell, esq., secretary of the board of trade.

which Fort Des Moines became the capital of the state. In 1857 the archives of the state were removed from Iowa City and deposited in the new state-house, and in the same year *Des Moines* was incorporated as a city without the prefix "Fort".

Des Moines has rapidly yet substantially grown into prominence as one of the leading cities of the West. Her progress of late has been most marked in the direction of wholesale trade and manufactures, all of which are in a prosperous condition. Pork-packing has become a prominent industry, the packers having paid out over $1,000,000 for hogs during 1879. The amount of capital employed in coal-mining is between $350,000 and $400,000, and the products of the mines in 1879 amounted to 125,000 tons. The proximity of coal, and an inexhaustible water-power, serve to stimulate the increasing manufacturing industries of the city. The immense trade that centers here is supported by the country for hundreds of miles in extent, reaching into the territories beyond.

The growth of the city has been very rapid since the opening of the railroads, which center here from every part of the state and make this place a convenient market for a large number of flourishing towns and villages.

Des Moines has never been visited by any disastrous conflagrations, neither have there been any serious business depressions, other than those affecting the country at large. The population comprises many nationalities, none of which have supplanted others previously established.

DES MOINES IN 1880.

The following statistical accounts, collected by the Census Office, indicate the present condition of Des Moines:

LOCATION.

Des Moines lies near the center of the state, in latitude 41° 36′ north, and longitude 93° 88′ west from Greenwich, on the Des Moines river, at the junction of the Raccoon river, 154 miles west of Davenport, and 138 miles east of Omaha by rail. The altitude of the city, as given for the observatory of the Smithsonian Institution, is 780 feet above sea-level. The rivers on which the city lies are not navigable, but it is thought that the Des Moines river can be improved so that steamboats can ascend from its mouth, the Mississippi at Keokuk, to this point.

RAILROAD COMMUNICATIONS.

The city is touched by the following railroads:
The Chicago, Rock Island, and Pacific railroad, main line, from Chicago to Omaha.
The Chicago, Burlington, and Quincy railroad, Des Moines line to Burlington, Iowa.
The Des Moines division of the Chicago and Northwestern railroad between the points named, connecting at Waukee with the Des Moines and Northwestern railroad to Panora, Iowa.

TRIBUTARY COUNTRY.

The country immediately tributary to Des Moines is strictly agricultural, cereals and live stock, principally hogs, being the chief products. The retail trade of the city extends to a distance of 30 miles in all directions, while the wholesale trade embraces northwestern, western, and southwestern Iowa, and reaches into Nebraska, Kansas, and Dakota.

TOPOGRAPHY.

The city is situated at the confluence of two rivers, the Des Moines and the Raccoon, which are spanned by 8 handsome and substantial bridges, with a plateau on either side skirted by bluffs, rising in gentle acclivities and forming fine residence sites. The level portion is large enough to accommodate all the business of the city. The total area of the city included in the corporate limits, and all suitable for building purposes, is about 12 square miles. The soil is alluvial, underlaid with limestone of a poor quality and soft coal. The natural drainage is into the rivers, and is good. The surrounding country is high and rolling, with no marshes, ponds, or lakes, and, with the exception of along the numerous streams that intersect it in every direction, is open prairie without timber. The soil within a radius of 5 miles is the same as that on which the city is built.

CLIMATE.

Highest recorded summer temperature, 106°; highest summer temperature in average years, 96°. Lowest recorded winter temperature, —25°; lowest winter temperature in average years, 15°. The south winds are warm and damp, while those from the west and northwest are dry and cool.

STREETS.

The length of the streets in the city is about 200 miles, and, with the exception of 2 blocks on Fourth street laid in gravel, none of them are paved. In his annual report for 1880 the mayor says: "It is a subject for congratulation that the council realizes the necessity of immediate action in the direction of street improvements, and that preliminary steps have been taken for the adoption of a general plan of street-pavement." The

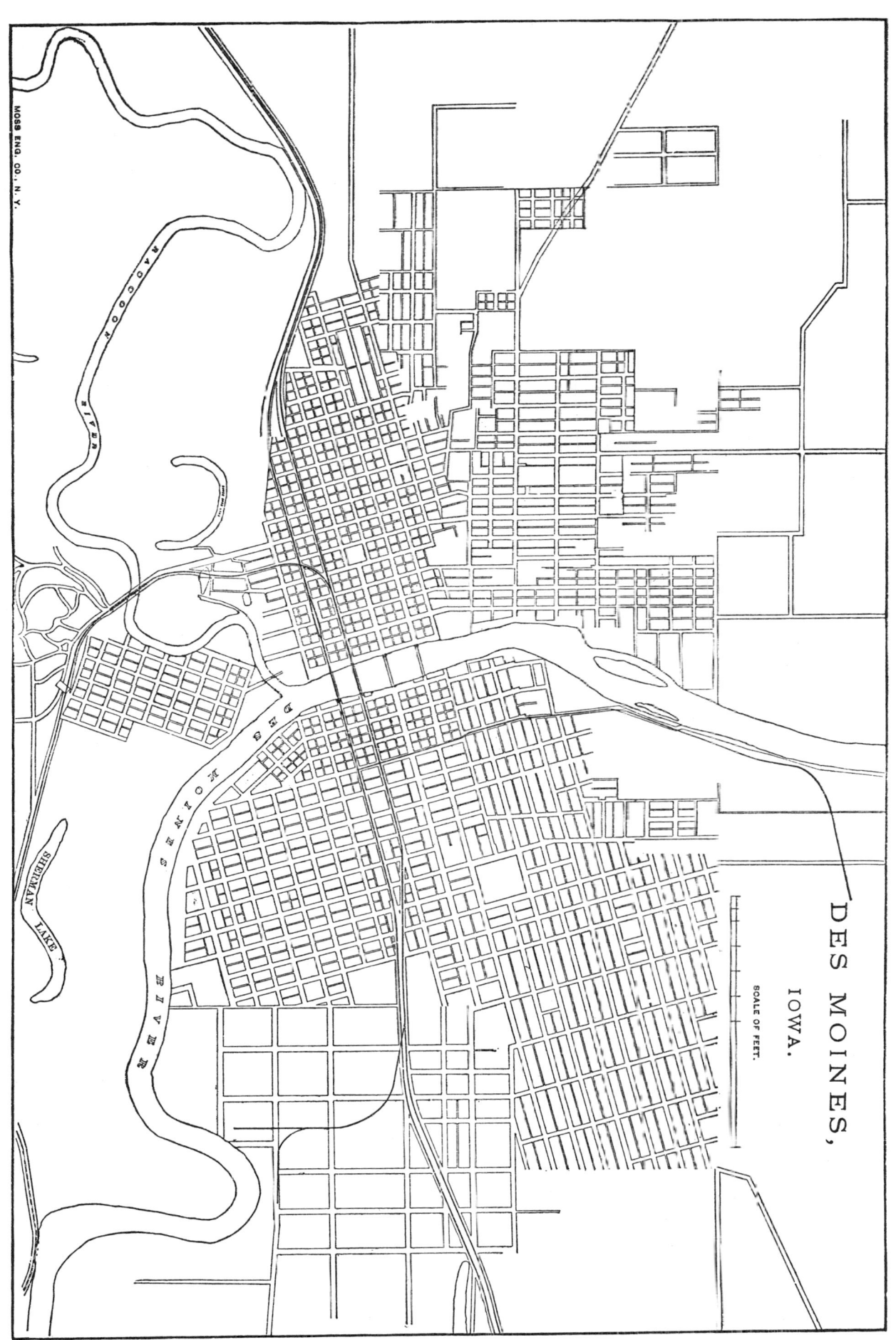

DES MOINES,
IOWA.

SCALE OF FEET.

MOSS ENG. CO. N. Y.

RACCOON RIVER

DES MOINES

SHERMAN LAKE

MAIN RIVER

sidewalks are of brick flag-stones and wood, and the gutters are paved with stone. Trees are planted along the sides of streets just inside the gutters. Streets are improved by day labor under the direction of the street commissioner, the annual cost being $20,000. It is said that the street repairs are of such a character that they can not be done by contract.

HORSE-RAILROADS.

There are 3½ miles of horse-railroads in the city, using 6 cars and 24 horses, and giving employment to 10 men. The number of passengers carried during the year was not stated. The rate of fare is 5 cents. There are no regular omnibus lines, but 3 omnibuses run between the railroad stations and hotels, carrying passengers at rates of 25 and 50 cents.

WATER-WORKS.

The water-works are owned by a private corporation, and their first cost was $350,000. Water is taken from the Raccoon river and pumped directly into the mains on the Holly system, the pressure being from 80 to 150 pounds to the square inch. The estimated consumption is about 2,000,000 gallons per diem. The yearly cost of maintenance is not stated. The annual receipts from water-rates is said to be $35,000. Water-meters are used. There are 20 miles of distributing mains and 187 hydrants.

GAS.

The gas-works are not owned by the city. The daily average production is 60,000 cubic feet. The city pays $2 25 per month for each street-lamp, 452 in number.

PUBLIC BUILDINGS.

The city owns municipal buildings costing $2,500, including 2 hose-houses, 1 pest-house, and a house at the cemetery. There is no city hall, the council room, etc., being rented, and no buildings are owned in common with the county. In addition to the city buildings, there are the state-house, costing $3,500,000; the United States court-house and post-office, costing $200,000, and the county court-house.

PUBLIC PARKS AND PLEASURE-GROUNDS.

The mayor reports one park in the city, area 2 acres, but gives no statistics concerning it. The county court-house is surrounded by fine grounds, which are ornamented with a fountain and shrubbery, and much resorted to.

PLACES OF AMUSEMENT.

There are three theaters in Des Moines—two opera-houses, seating 1,000 and 800, respectively, and the Academy of Music, seating 800. These theaters pay an annual license of $40, $60, and $100 respectively. In addition to these, there are several halls that are occasionally used.

DRAINAGE.

There are in Des Moines a few private drains, but neither these nor the water-courses are included in the regular sewerage system. Nothing has been done with water-courses except to put culverts or bridges at points where they cross streets. A regular plan of sewerage has been adopted, and all sewers have been built in accordance therewith. Sewage is discharged into the rivers below the city, and is conducted to the outfalls by intercepting sewers. The mouths of outfalls are exposed, but their dry-weather flow is delivered by iron pipes under the surface of the river. There is no provision for ventilation, but the plan provides that, when streets shall be paved, perforated iron manhole covers shall be substituted for the wooden ones now used. In very dry weather it is sometimes necessary to flush the intercepting sewers. Stationary iron flood-gates are built for the purpose. All the cost of constructing sewers is assessed upon abutting property, except when the contract price exceeds $3 per linear foot. All excess above $3 per foot is paid by the city, and in streets where there are lots on only one side the excess above $1 50 per foot is paid by the city. Assessments are laid by area of all property within 150 feet of the street on which a sewer is built, except when a regularly laid-out alley intervenes; in such cases the assessment goes only to the alley.

Sewers in 1880 cost as follows: One 30 inches diameter, 12 feet deep, $3 10 per foot; one 60 inches diameter, 14 feet deep, $6 20 per foot; one 48 inches diameter, 12 feet deep, $5 13 per foot, including manholes and catch-basins. The city ordinances require all sewers not exceeding 20 inches in diameter to be built of sewer pipe, while those exceeding 20 inches may be built of one ring of best quality of hard-burned or vitrified sewer brick. All sewers shall be laid by contract, and persons proposing for the work must deposit with the city engineer a sample of the pipe or brick they propose to use. No information is given of the extent or total cost of work.

CEMETERIES.

There are five cemeteries, one of 65 acres, one of 20 acres, one of 10 acres, one of 5 acres, and one of 2 acres, all within the corporate limits of the city. There are no church-yards or private burial grounds in which interments are no longer permitted. The records of the several cemeteries not having been regularly kept, it is impossible to give any statistics concerning the number of interments made in them. In the city cemetery, on the east and west sides of the river, burial permits are required from the mayor; there is no limit of time after death for interments, and the depth of graves is 4 feet. In the other cemeteries these matters are arranged either by the church or by the order to which the cemetery may belong. Lots are deeded to individuals with no special restrictions in regard to the care of them. The grounds in the cemeteries are laid out with avenues and walks, and ornamented with trees, shrubbery, and flowers. The average price of lots is 10 cents per square foot.

MARKETS.

There are no public or corporation markets, but the mayor in his annual message strongly advocates that the city erect a building for this purpose at an early day.

SANITARY AUTHORITY—BOARD OF HEALTH.

The chief sanitary organization of Des Moines is vested in the board of health, composed of the full city council, with the mayor as president. By statute the board has authority to make regulations in regard to public health and to carry the same into effect. The expenses of the board are limited only as other expenses of the several departments are, and its authority, either in absence of or during epidemics, is absolute. The mayor, as president, is the chief executive officer, and has sufficient police powers to cause the removal of nuisances, etc. The board transacts its business as a deliberative body. Inspections are not made regularly. When nuisances are reported, resolutions are offered to abate them. The board has no custom concerning the inspection and correction of defective house-drainage, privy-vaults, cesspools, sources of drinking-water, etc. Defective sewerage and street-cleaning are under the direction of the marshal. The board has no control over the conservation and removal of garbage, and has made no regulations concerning the burial of the dead, the pollution of streams, or the removal of excrement. Small-pox patients are taken to the public pest-house, situated outside the city, while cases of scarlet fever are neither isolated nor quarantined at home. No measures against the breaking out of contagious diseases either in public or in private schools have been taken. Vaccination is compulsory, and is done at the public expense.

The record of births, diseases, and deaths is kept by the county clerk. The board reports to the state board of health once a year.

MUNICIPAL CLEANSING.

Street-cleaning.—The streets are cleaned at the expense of the city, with its own force, and wholly by hand. The business streets are cleaned about every 30 days, and the other streets when they need it. The work is reported as being well done. The annual cost is $500, and the sweepings are deposited on vacant ground and used for filling-up purposes. "The system is not good, as it is mostly done by prisoners who don't like to work;" "place of deposit good enough, as it reclaims waste land."

Removal of garbage and ashes.—Garbage is removed both by the city and by householders, the former doing its share with its own force. While awaiting removal, the garbage is kept in vessels and must not be mixed with ashes. Garbage is finally disposed of by being buried, while ashes are thrown on waste lands. The annual cost of the service was not stated. The system is said to be not so good as it will be. The mayor says: "The ordinance prohibiting people from depositing ashes, *débris*, and filth in the streets and alleys is entirely ignored, rendering it almost impossible at times to get through them with a loaded wagon, and seriously endangering the health of the citizens on the approach of warm weather."

Dead animals.—The carcass of any animal dying within the city limits is removed and buried by the marshal, if the owner is not known. The annual cost of the service is nominal, and no record of the number of dead animals of different kinds removed is kept.

Liquid household wastes; human excreta.—Where sewers exist the liquid household wastes are run into them, none being allowed to pass into street-gutters or into cesspools. What cesspools there are are porous and are cleaned out in the same manner as vaults. The larger part of the houses depend on privy vaults, none of which are even nominally water-tight. They are required to be cleaned by regular licensed scavengers, and, except where the odorless excavator process is used, this cleaning must be done between the hours of 11 p. m. and 4 a. m. The night-soil is thrown into the river.

Manufacturing wastes.—The liquid manufacturing wastes are run into the ground, but in a short time will be carried off by the sewers.

POLICE.

The police force of Des Moines is appointed by the mayor, and is under his exclusive control, the city council merely fixing the number of men and the wards they shall be taken from. The force is composed of 1 chief of police, who is the executive officer, salary $55 a month, and 1 captain and 8 patrolmen at $50 a month each. In addition there are 1 marshal at $800 per annum; 2 deputy marshals at $50 a month each, and 2 specials from each of the seven wards, who are subject to call, and when on duty rank the same as the regular force. The uniform is of blue navy or army cloth, and is made after that worn by officers of United States infantry. Each suit complete costs about $35, and the men provide their own.   Patrolmen are equipped with revolvers, clubs, and duplex whistles; the hours of duty are from 6 a. m. to 6 p. m., and each beat covers about 2 miles.   During the past year 1,037 arrests were made, the principal causes being for drunkenness, assault and battery, larceny, keeping or frequenting houses of ill-fame, and disturbing the peace.   The final disposition of these cases was not stated.   During the year property to the value of $1,489 was reported to the police as lost or stolen, and of this, $805 was recovered and returned to the owners.   There were 298 station-house lodgers in 1880, as against 249 in 1879.   The police force co-operates with the fire department by protecting property at fires, and, if necessary, by enforcing necessary regulations for fire protection; and with the health department by abating nuisances and seeing that streets and alleys are kept clean.   The yearly cost of the police force (1880) is $9,900.

His Honor, William H. Merritt, mayor, who furnished the foregoing information concerning police, closes the report as follows:

My observation teaches that cities are best governed where there is but one police department.   In cities of the first class in Iowa the law provides for marshal and deputies, whose duty it is to see that the ordinances are executed, streets and alleys cleaned, nuisances abated, order preserved during sittings of the council, and mandates of police court executed.   This could all be done by the regular force at less cost and avoid unprofitable jealousy and rivalry between two departments.

FIRE DEPARTMENT.

The last annual report of the chief engineer shows the manual force of the department to consist of 1 chief and 2 assistant engineers, 3 drivers, and 20 men, making a total of 26.   The apparatus consists of 1 steam fire-engine, 2 hook-and-ladder trucks, 6 hose-carriages, and 3,850 feet of hose.   There are 13 horses owned by the department.   During the past year there were 36 fires and 1 false alarm.   The losses from fire aggregated $6,398 65, and the total amount of insurance involved was $21,580 60.   The cost of the fire department for the year was $6,162 62.

MANUFACTURES.

The following is a summary of the statistics of the manufactures of Des Moines for 1880, being taken from tables prepared for the Tenth Census by J. P. Bushnell, special agent:

Mechanical and manufacturing industries.	No. of establishments.	Capital.	AVERAGE NUMBER OF HANDS EMPLOYED.			Total amount paid in wages during the year.	Value of materials.	Value of products.
			Males above 16 years.	Females above 15 years.	Children and youths.			
All industries....................................	155	$1,463,250	1,211	71	96	$667,699	$2,810,396	$4,220,709
Agricultural implements	3	55,000	18	....	....	8,000	14,200	46,200
Blacksmithing (see also Wheelwrighting)	5	3,300	8	1	....	4,700	5,100	14,500
Boots and shoes, including custom work and repairing	5	7,500	16	....	....	7,350	8,240	22,195
Bread and other bakery products	6	14,050	31	1	....	13,995	41,000	64,362
Brick and tile....................................	3	12,700	80	....	2	21,000	12,375	42,000
Carpentering	5	17,000	52	....	....	28,900	94,500	142,750
Carriages and wagons (see also Wheelwrighting) ...	4	22,500	27	....	....	13,750	27,000	53,000
Clothing, men's.................................	13	60,700	43	13	....	39,050	70,300	134,600
Cooperage	3	3,000	17	....	....	9,100	21,100	32,300
Flouring- and grist-mill products	7	142,500	40	....	....	13,105	204,380	239,235
Foundery and machine-shop products	8	94,000	75	....	4	46,702	50,823	151,848
Furniture.......................................	4	47,500	29	....	3	17,600	45,500	80,000
Liquors, malt...................................	5	84,000	25	....	....	10,605	35,610	81,295
Marble and stone work	5	43,000	36	1	....	20,100	21,600	68,700
Painting and paperhanging	3	4,800	14	....	....	8,580	21,000	36,700
Paving materials	3	4,100	14	....	....	5,900	6,300	16,000
Printing and publishing	13	320,500	148	21	14	136,102	174,850	399,438
Saddlery and harness	4	5,100	16	....	1	6,200	24,000	39,000
Tinware, copperware, and sheet-iron ware........	8	32,000	35	....	....	18,442	47,200	109,400
Tobacco, cigars and cigarettes....	5	17,700	32	4	4	20,700	36,050	74,500
Wheelwrighting (see also Blacksmithing; Carriages and wagons) ...	6	8,500	11	....	....	5,300	5,150	14,074
All other industries (a)	37	463,800	444	30	53	212,513	1,844,118	1,358,612

a Embracing bookbinding and blank-book making; boxes, cigar; brass castings; brooms and brushes; coffee and spices, roasted and ground; confectionery; corsets; engraving and die-sinking; files; glucose; hairwork; hardware; liquors, distilled; lithographing; looking-glass and picture frames; lumber, planed; lumber, sawed; oil, linseed; pumps; roofing and roofing materials; scales and balances; shirts; slaughtering and meat-packing; soap and candles; steam fittings and heating apparatus; stereotyping and electrotyping; stone- and earthen-ware; vinegar; wirework; and woolen goods.

From the foregoing table it appears that the average capital of all establishments is $9,440 32; that the average wages of all hands employed is $484 54 per annum; and that the average outlay in wages, in materials, and in interest (at 6 per cent.) on capital employed is $23,005 73.

DUBUQUE,

DUBUQUE COUNTY IOWA.

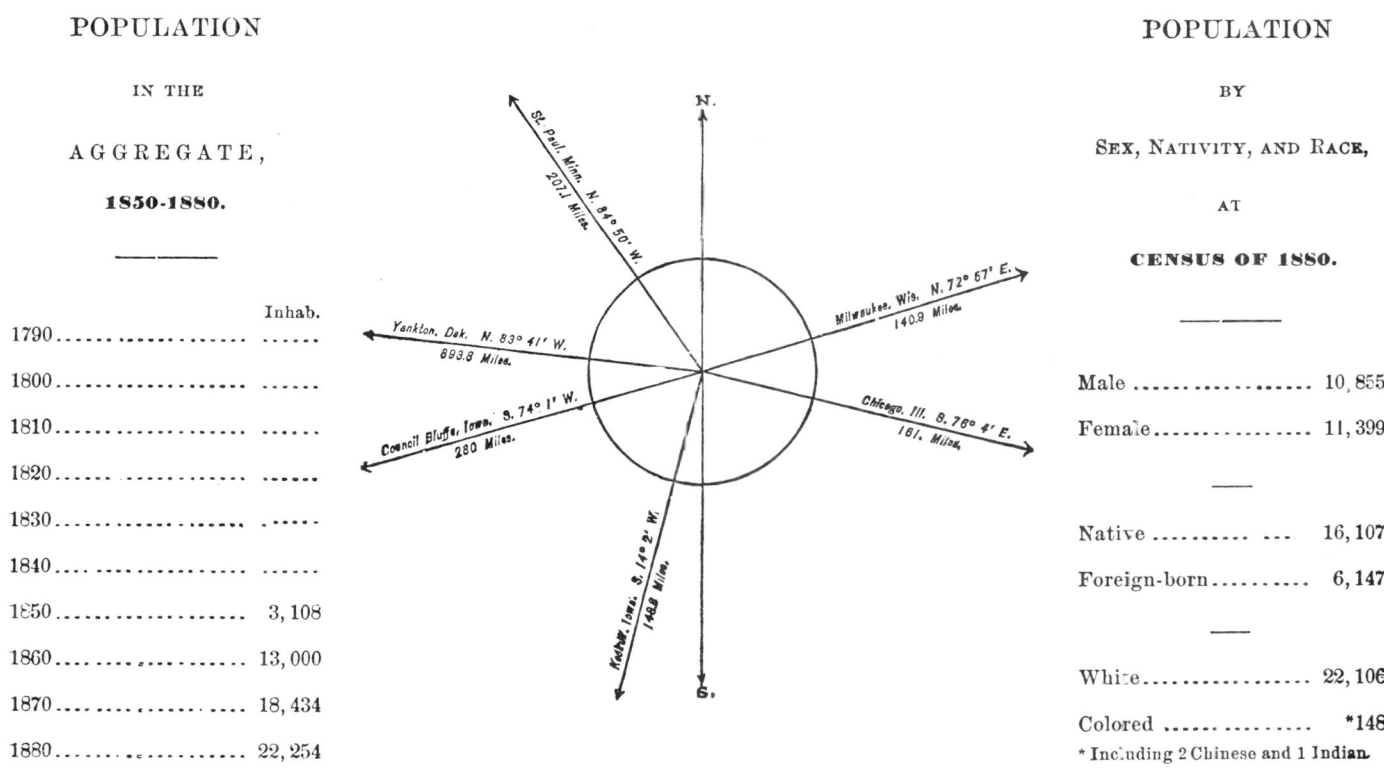

POPULATION

IN THE

AGGREGATE,

1850-1880.

	Inhab.
1790	......
1800	......
1810	......
1820	......
1830	......
1840	......
1850	3,108
1860	13,000
1870	18,434
1880	22,254

POPULATION

BY

SEX, NATIVITY, AND RACE,

AT

CENSUS OF 1880.

Male	10,855
Female	11,399
Native	16,107
Foreign-born	6,147
White	22,106
Colored	*148

* Including 2 Chinese and 1 Indian.

Latitude: 42° 30′ North; Longitude: 90° 40′ (west from Greenwich); **Altitude: 588.05 to 908.25 feet.**

FINANCIAL CONDITION:

Total Valuation: $13,000,000; per capita: $584 00.   Net Indebtedness: $804,611; per capita; $36 16.   Tax per $100: $2 00.

HISTORICAL SKETCH.

From 1788 to 1810 Julien Dubuque, a Frenchman, obtained from the Indians permission to work the lead mines in this vicinity. His associates and followers continued the same business until the year 1830. In the summer of 1832 the Black Hawk war closed, and the Indian title to the eastern part of Iowa was extinguished. In the fall of the same year a few permanent settlers began to mine. In 1836 the mines were incorporated in the territory of Wisconsin. Iowa became a separate territory. Dubuque became an incorporated village in 1837 and a city in 1841. The Illinois Central railroad reached the river in 1855. No great ravages of fire have occurred. In 1857 a financial crash ended the speculation fever, which raged beyond all reason. Since 1869 the city has begun to recover, and has nearly doubled its population and business. Manufactures increased from $3,194,000 in 1870 to $5,000,000 in 1878. Population has been made up from all sources and nationalities. Americans were the principal early settlers.

DUBUQUE IN 1880.

The following statistical accounts, collected by the Census Office, indicate the present condition of Dubuque:

LOCATION.

Dubuque, capital of the county of Dubuque, is situated on the right bank of the Mississippi river, 470 miles north of Saint Louis, 200 miles south of Saint Paul, and 199 miles west of Chicago. It is opposite the point where the line between Wisconsin and Illinois reaches the river, and is in one of the richest lead regions known. It is the chief depot of the lead region of Iowa, Illinois, and Wisconsin. It is the center of a large and ever-widening trade, and during the season of navigation has several lines of steamers to Saint Louis and Saint Paul. It has large and increasing manufactures of shot, steam-engines, farming implements, machinery, brick, white lead, leather, wooden ware, etc. In railroad facilities, in schools, churches, societies, both secular and religious, and all the institutions usually accompanying a thriving American city of its size, Dubuque is amply endowed. The city is connected with Dunleith (Illinois) by an iron railway bridge.

The average depth of water in the river at low water is 7.6 feet, the variation of level between high and low water is 21.8 feet, the average width of the river here is 2,300 feet, the harbor capacity is 20 acres, and the current flows from $1\frac{1}{2}$ to 2 miles per hour.

RAILROAD COMMUNICATIONS.

Dubuque has the following railroads:

The Chicago, Dubuque, and Minnesota railroad, running to La Crosse, Wisconsin.
The Chicago, Clinton, and Dubuque railroad, running to Clinton, Iowa.
The Illinois Central railroad, running to Cairo.
The Iowa division of the Illinois Central railroad, running to Sioux City.

TRIBUTARY COUNTRY.

The country surrounding Dubuque is devoted to agriculture and lead mining and smelting.

TOPOGRAPHY.

The business portion of the city is built on a sandy and gravelly soil, reaching from the surrounding bluffs to the river, with natural drainage toward the river and a gradual descent of 50 feet. Encircling the above site are bluffs averaging in height 200 feet above the river, separated by ravines, through which the elevated residence portion of the city is reached. These bluffs are formed of Galena limestone and are covered with a clay soil. Several miles north of the city is a small lake surrounded by low meadow land. There are some unfilled sloughs between the city and the river. The surrounding country for a radius of from 5 to 15 miles is about half covered with wood, chiefly oak, of recent growth.

CLIMATE.

Highest recorded summer temperature, 99°; highest summer temperature in average years, 97.33°. Lowest recorded winter temperature, —20°; lowest winter temperature in average years, —12°. The elevated lands near are a protection against wind. Few severe hurricanes have visited the city, while to the eastward they have often occurred. Northwest winds are cold and clear, and easterly winds moist and raw.

STREETS.

Dubuque's improved streets and alleys measure 29.07 miles in length, of which 0.234 mile is paved with stone blocks, while there are of broken stone 16.39 miles curbed and guttered, 8.11 miles of streets and 3.84 miles of alleys only macadamized. Stone-block pavement costs $1 25 and broken stone 30 cents per square yard. The stone-block pavement is by far the easier to keep clean. On the principal streets the sidewalks are chiefly brick or stone; elsewhere they are mostly plank. Gutters are from 4 to 6 feet in width and are laid with stone. Trees are planted along the curb-line, 2 feet from the edge of the curbstone. No grass places in the streets exist. The construction of streets is done by contract, repairing by the day. The average annual cost of improvements to streets, alleys, and sewers for the past 3 years has been $38,702 74, and the average expense per year of repairs and street-cleaning, $11,397 36. The average cost of grading streets by contract in 1878 was 14.5 cents per cubic yard; that done by the city, employing men needing work, some of whom are old and feeble, cost per cubic yard 17.7 cents. The cost of macadamizing per cubic yard by contract was 79.3 cents; by day's work, $1 049. A steam stone-crusher has been used by a contractor. There is also used a road roller, drawn by horses, the weight of which is not sufficient to make it very effective. There is a short steam-railroad of a total length of 1.7 mile running in the streets of the city. It ascends 260 feet, its steepest grade is 443 feet to a mile, uses 3 cars and 2 motors, employs 6 men, and carries annually 120,000 passengers at a fare of 5 cents.

The horse-railroads are 3 miles in length, run 14 cars, use 24 horses, employ 11 men, and, at a fare of 5 cents, annually carry 240,000 passengers.

WATER-WORKS.

The water-works are owned by a private corporation, and their total cost was $155,000. Water is received in two reservoirs—one of 1,500,000, and one of 250,000 gallons capacity—that are situated at the mouth of a valley which drains an extensive area of lead mines, and from there is taken to a distributing reservoir of 1,220,000 gallons, being supplied to the city by gravity. The water is pure, with carbonate of lime in solution. The yearly cost of maintenance is $4,000, and the income from water-rates is $12,000.

GAS.

The gas-works are owned privately. The daily average production is 50,000 cubic feet, for which the charge per 1,000 feet is $3 50. The city pays annually $30 for each of its 276 street-lamps, 100 of these being supplied with gasoline.

PUBLIC BUILDINGS.

The city owns and occupies for municipal purposes a city hall, four buildings for fire purposes, a sexton building, and a city hospital. The total cost of municipal buildings belonging to the city is $53,000, the city hall alone costing $50,000.

PUBLIC PARKS AND PLEASURE-GROUNDS.

The only public parks in the city are the two squares laid out by the government for this use, called *Washington Park* and *Jackson Park*. They are laid out with walks, planted with shade trees, and furnished with a pagoda or music stand. Their total cost was $3,000, and the yearly cost of maintaining them is about $500. They are controlled by a "committee on public grounds and buildings" of the city council.

PLACES OF AMUSEMENT.

Dubuque has one theater, the Opera House, seating 850. Theaters pay a yearly license to the city of $100. Of amusement halls there are Kistler's hall and Rush's hall, used for lectures, dances, and concerts; Turner's hall, used for concerts and dances, and Tabernacle hall, used for lectures, concerts, and meetings. Of concert- and beer-gardens, there are the Pagoda, at the Western brewery, built in 1878; dimensions of building, 100 by 25 feet; cost $2,500, and seats 200 persons; there are pleasure-grounds adjoining, and it is in summer well patronized; and Centennial beer-gardens, built in 1876; dimensions of building, 60 by 30 feet; cost $1,000; has grounds attached 110 by 600 feet in dimensions, and costing $3,000; seats 500 persons, and is tolerably well patronized. Formerly an adjoining tract of ground was used as a garden, and styled the Tivoli; also the Northern brewery park, or beer-garden, 100 by 400 feet in dimensions, costing $2,000.

The foregoing is all that was furnished concerning the present condition of Dubuque.

MANUFACTURES.

The following is a summary of the statistics of the manufactures of Dubuque for 1880, being taken from tables prepared for the Tenth Census by Abram S. Bunting, special agent:

Mechanical and manufacturing industries.	No. of establishments.	Capital.	AVERAGE NUMBER OF HANDS EMPLOYED.			Total amount paid in wages during the year.	Value of materials.	Value of products.
			Males above 16 years.	Females above 15 years.	Children and youths.			
All industries	346	$3,446,866	2,619	292	92	$1,339,730	$3,837,846	$6,328,889
Blacksmithing (see also Wheelwrighting)	8	6,750	24	....	....	12,250	4,525	23,880
Bookbinding and blank-book making	4	17,750	15	3	6	9,100	8,600	24,300
Boots and shoes, including custom work and repairing	34	41,475	80	4	1	38,900	64,825	128,100
Bread and other bakery products	15	55,135	51	9	3	26,558	92,107	149,664
Brick and tile	8	12,600	84	....	....	16,900	9,562	35,300
Carpentering	26	28,200	389	....	....	161,277	149,100	355,550
Carpets, rag	7	480	8	1	....	3,700	4,450	14,000
Carriages and wagons (see also Wheelwrighting)	9	532,900	283	....	....	150,050	324,250	627,000
Clothing, men's	18	241,150	71	188	1	66,500	254,875	403,000
Cooperage	10	58,150	109	....	3	55,750	70,630	168,655

Mechanical and manufacturing industries.	No. of establishments.	Capital.	AVERAGE NUMBER OF HANDS EMPLOYED.			Total amount paid in wages during the year.	Value of materials.	Value of products.
			Males above 16 years.	Females above 15 years.	Children and youths.			
Dentistry, mechanical	6	$5,900	10			$9,300	$2,675	$16,430
Flouring- and grist-mill products	4	30,000	14			5,030	69,740	83,257
Foundery and machine-shop products (see also Steam fittings and heating apparatus).	4	157,500	109			57,500	86,960	181,320
Furniture	6	87,500	159		1	70,250	100,600	219,000
Hairwork	3	3,700	2	9	2	3,100	6,750	12,300
Liquors, malt	6	265,000	63			26,975	110,132	211,125
Lock- and gun-smithing	6	2,500	5			2,900	650	6,204
Looking-glass and picture frames	4	4,000	10			4,750	7,000	17,500
Lumber, sawed	4	295,000	160		23	53,000	212,200	345,000
Marble and stone work	7	7,650	28			15,450	13,200	37,058
Masonry, brick and stone	19	3,396	107			43,210	52,775	121,450
Painting and paperhanging	11	6,950	47		2	24,250	15,150	50,900
Photographing	7	5,500	12	7	1	9,490	2,045	17,100
Printing and publishing	8	111,800	74	8	9	56,252	38,300	137,475
Saddlery and harness	7	63,300	36			18,124	42,500	78,227
Sash, doors, and blinds	3	114,000	71		15	50,000	191,000	284,000
Slaughtering and meat packing, not including retail butchering	5	183,000	133		1	86,500	1,237,400	1,379,000
Steam fittings and heating apparatus (see also Foundery and machine-shop products).	3	50,400	61			27,000	36,000	90,800
Tinware, copperware, and sheet-iron ware	16	21,850	44			22,250	28,250	74,100
Tobacco, cigars and cigarettes	10	9,600	34		1	14,822	18,275	45,750
Vinegar	3	53,000	24			12,350	35,535	89,650
Watch and clock repairing	10	6,050	18			11,900	2,770	24,300
Wheelwrighting (see also Blacksmithing; Carriages and wagons)	10	5,600	29			12,500	9,450	34,100
All other industries (a)	45	959,080	305	63	23	151,842	535,565	813,396

a Embracing agricultural implements; awnings and tents; bags, paper; baskets, rattan and willow-ware; bellows; boxes, paper; brass ware; bridges; brooms and brushes; carriage and wagon materials; clothing, women's; coffee and spices, roasted and ground; coffins, burial cases, and undertakers' goods; confectionery; dyeing and cleaning; files; furs, dressed; hats and caps; iron work, architectural and ornamental; lead, bar, pipe, sheet, and shot; lightning rods; lime; liquors, vinous; mattresses and spring beds; mineral and soda waters; models and patterns; roofing and roofing materials; shipbuilding; shirts; show-cases; soap and candles; tobacco, chewing, smoking, and snuff; trunks and valises; upholstering; wirework; and wooden ware.

From the foregoing table it appears that the average capital of all establishments is $9,962 04; that the average wages of all hands employed is $446 13 per annum; and that the average outlay in wages, in materials, and in interest (at 6 per cent.) on capital employed is $15,561 81.

KEOKUK,

LEE COUNTY, IOWA.

POPULATION

IN THE

AGGREGATE,

1850-1880.

	Inhab.
1790	......
1800	......
1810	......
1820	......
1830	......
1840	......
1850	2,478
1860	8,136
1870	12,766
1880	12,117

POPULATION

BY

SEX, NATIVITY, AND RACE,

AT

CENSUS OF 1880.

Male	5,813
Female	6,304
Native	9,850
Foreign-born	2,267
White	11,034
Colored	*1,083

*Including 1 Chinese and 1 Indian.

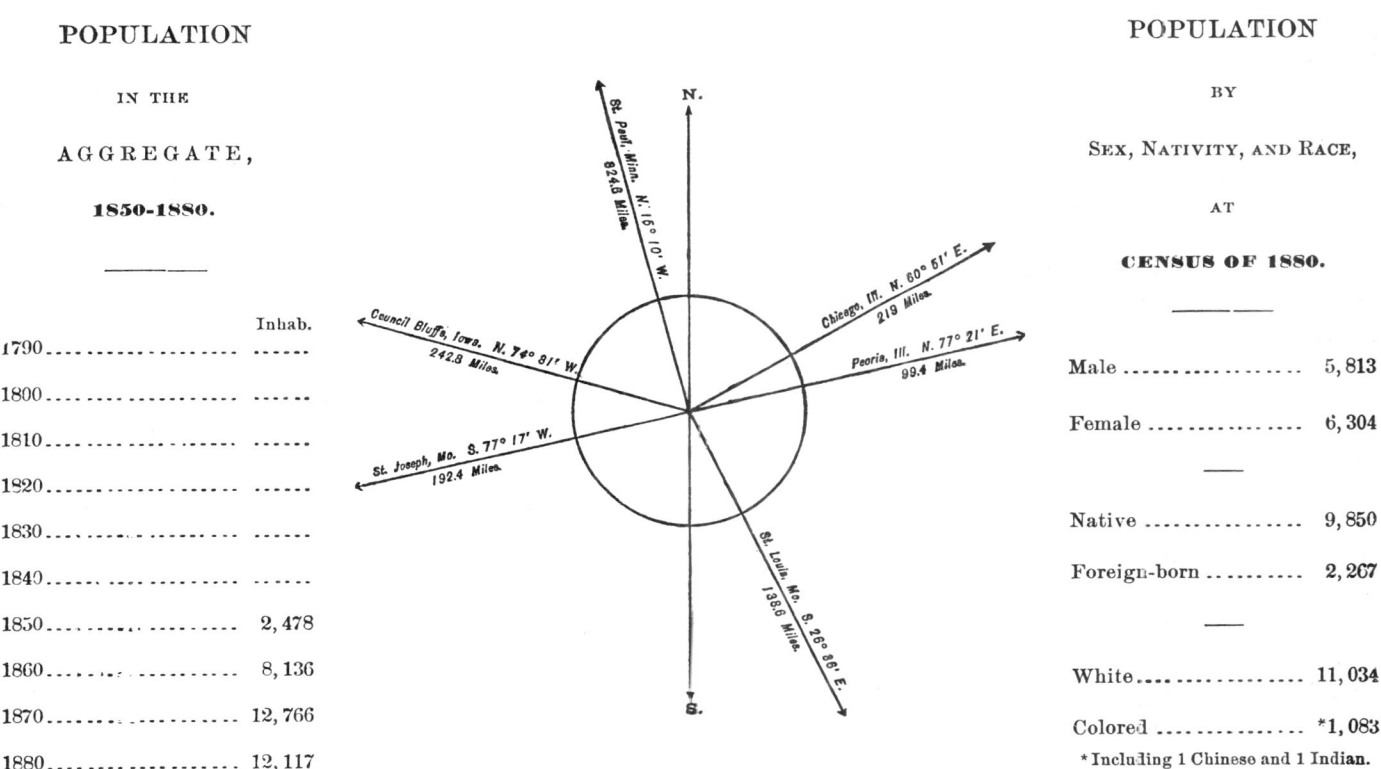

Latitude: 40° 25' North; Longitude: 91° 21' (west from Greenwich); Altitude: 495 to 658 feet.

FINANCIAL CONDITION:

Total Valuation: $4,104,155; per capita: $339 00.   Net Indebtedness, $372,375; per capita: $30 73.   Tax per $100: $3 60.

HISTORICAL SKETCH.

The first cabin built on the site of the present city of Keokuk was erected by Dr. S. C. Muir, a graduate from the university of Edinburgh, in the year 1827. In 1831 the first white child was born here. There have been but few ravages by fire that have not been speedily obliterated. In 1856 there was a period of great excitement; lots were sold for fabulous prices; grand buildings were erected, and speculation ran mad. Then followed the financial depression of 1857, and Keokuk suffered. The city is now recovering from it, after a steady growth in wealth and prosperity for 24 years. The substantial wealth, indicated by buildings, improvements in living, bank deposits, and exchanges, libraries, churches, trade and manufactures, is as marked here as in any town of the same size in the state. The population was generally from Pennsylvania and Ohio, with representations from nearly all nations and states.

KEOKUK IN 1880.

The following statistical accounts, collected by the Census Office, which are, owing to the paucity of information sent by the city authorities, not so full as could be wished, indicate to some extent the present condition of Keokuk:

LOCATION.

Keokuk lies in the extreme southeast corner of the state, in latitude 40° 25′ north, and longitude, 91° 21′ west from Greenwich, on the west bank of the Mississippi river, near its confluence with the Des Moines river, at the foot of what are known as the "lower rapids", and 200 miles by river above Saint Louis. The altitudes above sea-level are: lowest point, the city datum line between high and low water marks, 495 feet; average, corner of High and Second streets, 648 feet; and highest, corner of Grand avenue and Thirteenth street, 658 feet. In Reid's addition, adjoining the city, grades have been run at an elevation of 667 feet above sea-level. Keokuk was formerly at the head of low-water navigation above Saint Louis, but the completion of the government canal around the rapids now makes navigation above uninterrupted. Draft at low water, 5 feet; maximum velocity at low water, 3 miles an hour; range of river between high- and low-water mark, 22 feet. The river has a width of 2,600 feet at low water, and 5,500 feet at high water. The slope of the river-bed over the rapids averages 2 feet 2 inches to the mile. Water communication is open to all points on the Mississippi and its navigable tributaries.

RAILROAD COMMUNICATIONS.

The city is touched by the following trunk lines:

The Keokuk and Des Moines division of the Chicago, Rock Island, and Pacific railroad, to Des Moines, and connecting there with the main line.

The Saint Louis, Keokuk, and Northwestern railroad, to Saint Louis.

The Iowa division of the Wabash, Saint Louis, and Pacific railroad, to Chicago, Illinois.

The Keokuk branch of the Chicago, Burlington, and Quincy railroad, to Burlington, Iowa.

TRIBUTARY COUNTRY.

The region which gives Keokuk a local trade embraces 3 counties: Lee, in Iowa; Clark, in Missouri; and Hancock, in Illinois. This region is agricultural, producing the principal varieties of grains and grasses common to this latitude, as well as fruits, apples, pears, peaches, and berries, the latter growing very profusely. The farm stock, principally cattle and hogs, are of improved breeds, and much of the grasses and corn is marketed by means of fat cattle and hogs. The country roads leading from the city are laid out after the western plan, and "are as good as the general run". A bridge over the Mississippi river, and another over the Des Moines river, greatly facilitate the bringing of farm produce to the city, while the several railroads radiating from this point further extend the trade of Keokuk. In addition to the agriculture of the surrounding country, there are several manufacturing industries in the city, notably pork-packing, the making of shoes, beer, stoves, engines, plows, etc. Much money has been invested in vineyards and the appliances necessary to make wine.

TOPOGRAPHY.

Keokuk is in the center of the "Geode" bed. The limestone belongs to the Keokuk formation, and bears with it fine specimens of the Crinoids. It is used for building, macadamizing, and the manufacture of lime. There are sandstones of the coal measure; also the Saint Louis, Warsaw, and Keokuk groups. The magnesia limestone crops out at the medium elevation. There are no lakes. The "ponds" are made by the overflow of the Mississippi. The country, for a radius of 5 miles, is open. Originally the site of the village was covered with a heavy growth of timber, which has since been cut off. The islands in the river, the high banks on the Illinois side, and the banks of the small streams are, however, still well covered with trees. As a general rule, the soil is alluvial, from 4 to 6 feet deep, with occasional clay surfaces, and places where the limestone crops out. Within a radius of 4 miles there are several springs, more or less valuable, not noted, however, for any special medicinal quality.

CLIMATE.

Highest recorded summer temperature, 102°; highest summer temperature in average years, 98°. Lowest recorded winter temperature, —26°; lowest winter temperature in average years, —15°. The record from which these figures are taken extends over a period of 7 years. It is stated that "the Mississippi river in moderate stages never affects the general health; after high water, vegetable decomposition favors development of periodical fevers, neuralgia, fluxes, etc." The marshes "conduce somewhat to malarial fevers varied in type", while the northwest winds "generate acute lung diseases and precipitate development of tuberculosis in those predisposed to it".

STREETS.

Total length, 90 miles, of which 12 miles are paved with broken stone and 4 miles with gravel. The cost per square yard of each, as nearly as it may be estimated, is, for broken stone 32 cents, and for gravel 16⅔ cents. "Macadam broken from limestone is an improvement over mud, but has the serious defect of being dusty in dry weather and muddy in wet. Gravel is being abandoned as both expensive and defective in every particular." The sidewalks are of plank and brick, usually good, and the gutters are of cobble-stones. Trees are not planted in the streets. The construction and repair of streets are paid for out of the general fund, the amount being expended by the supervisor, who keeps no itemized accounts. The city engineer expresses a preference for contract work instead of day work for the construction and repair of streets, "as contractors can be made reponsible; while if left in the hands of the city by day work there might be as many heads as there are aldermen".

There are no horse-railroads in the city. An omnibus line, with 7 vehicles and 20 horses, and employing 9 men, carries about 28,500 passengers annually at 25 cents each, including one piece of baggage.

WATER-WORKS.

The water-works are owned by a private corporation, and their first cost was $100,000. Water is taken from the Mississippi and pumped directly into the mains on what is known as the Holly system, the available head being from 35 to 75 pounds. The estimated daily consumption is about 70 gallons per head of the population. The annual cost for maintenance and repairs is $5,000, and the yearly income from water-rents is $11,500. Water-meters are used in a few cases, and when used are found materially to reduce the consumption of water.

GAS.

The gas-works are not owned by the city. The daily average production is 30,000 cubic feet. The charge per 1,000 is $3 50. The city pays $32 per annum for each street-lamp, 140 in number, which includes lighting, repairs, etc.

PUBLIC BUILDINGS.

The city owns and occupies for municipal purposes 1 "calaboose" and 2 engine-houses, the actual cost of which was $8,000; also a pest-house, costing $1,800. There is no city hall, a floor being rented for city offices, etc., in the Odd Fellows' building, corner of Seventh and Main streets.

PUBLIC PARKS AND PLEASURE-GROUNDS.

There are several parks in Keokuk, with a total area of 18 acres and costing $5,000, which have been set aside in the various additions to the city. None of them have been improved.

PLACES OF AMUSEMENT; DRAINAGE; CEMETERIES; MARKETS.

No information on these subjects was furnished by the city authorities.

SANITARY AUTHORITY—BOARD OF HEALTH.

The chief sanitary organization of Keokuk is the board of health, composed of the mayor *ex officio*, 2 aldermen, and 1 physician. The board is appointed by the city council, and may be said to be subject to its control. In ordinary times the annual expenses of the board are $150, for salary and incidentals, and during epidemics this amount is not limited by ordinance. The board has a general supervision over the health of the city, the cleanliness of streets, alleys, public places, lots, yards, etc., and may enter at any time during daylight to examine the same; can cause all nuisances to be abated; has power to remove all persons infected with contagious diseases, to provide for and compel vaccination; and can enforce any reasonable sanitary regulations necessary to protect the city against Asiatic cholera and other epidemics. The mayor, *ex officio* president of the board, with a salary of $100 per annum, is the executive officer, and sees that the health ordinances and regulations of the board are properly enforced. He has power to command what assistance may be needed from the marshal. No assistant health officers or inspectors are employed. Inspections are made only as nuisances are reported or "carelessly discovered". When a nuisance is found to exist, the property-owner or tenant is ordered to abate it, and if this is not done the president of the board is required to file an information and abate the nuisance, the expense being charged against the property. The board exercises no control over the conservation and removal of garbage, other than to see that it does not become a nuisance. There are no special regulations concerning the burial of the dead.

INFECTIOUS DISEASES.

Small-pox patients are isolated by being removed to the public pest-house, situated 2 miles north of the city, on high bluffs overlooking the river. Scarlet-fever patients are neither isolated nor quarantined at home, "except by public sentiment, or rather fear". The board can, if it deems it necessary, close all schools in the case of the breaking out of diseases of a contagious nature. As to vaccination, it is either compulsory or it is not, as "the ordinance may be interpreted either way". It is done at the public expense only when persons are too poor to pay.

REPORTS.

Deaths, with the diseases causing them, are registered. "Births too numerous to keep track of, and no ordinances compelling registration." The board reports once a year to the council, and the reports are only published by courtesy of the daily papers.

MUNICIPAL CLEANSING.

Street-cleaning.—The streets are cleaned at the expense of the city, wholly by hand and whenever needed. No account is kept of the service, and the sweepings are deposited anywhere that is convenient. There is no system, the work being done very imperfectly and not as often as it should be.

Removal of garbage and ashes.—Garbage and ashes are removed by the householders, and "everybody do as they please".

Dead animals.—The carcasses of dead animals are disposed of under the direction of the city marshal, horses, etc., going to the glue factory.

Liquid household wastes.—Part of the liquid household wastes are run into sewers and the rest into cesspools and vaults. There are no regulations as to the disposal of either liquid or solid manufacturing wastes. The gutters are not artificially flushed.

Human excreta.—All the houses in the city are said to depend on privy-vaults. The night-soil is dumped into the river below the city.

The city engineer, in returning the schedules on the above subject, says: "No one pays attention to these things here, and I haven't time on the present pay to investigate this as you ask."

POLICE.

No information on this subject was communicated.

NEBRASKA.

LINCOLN,

LANCASTER COUNTY, NEBRASKA.

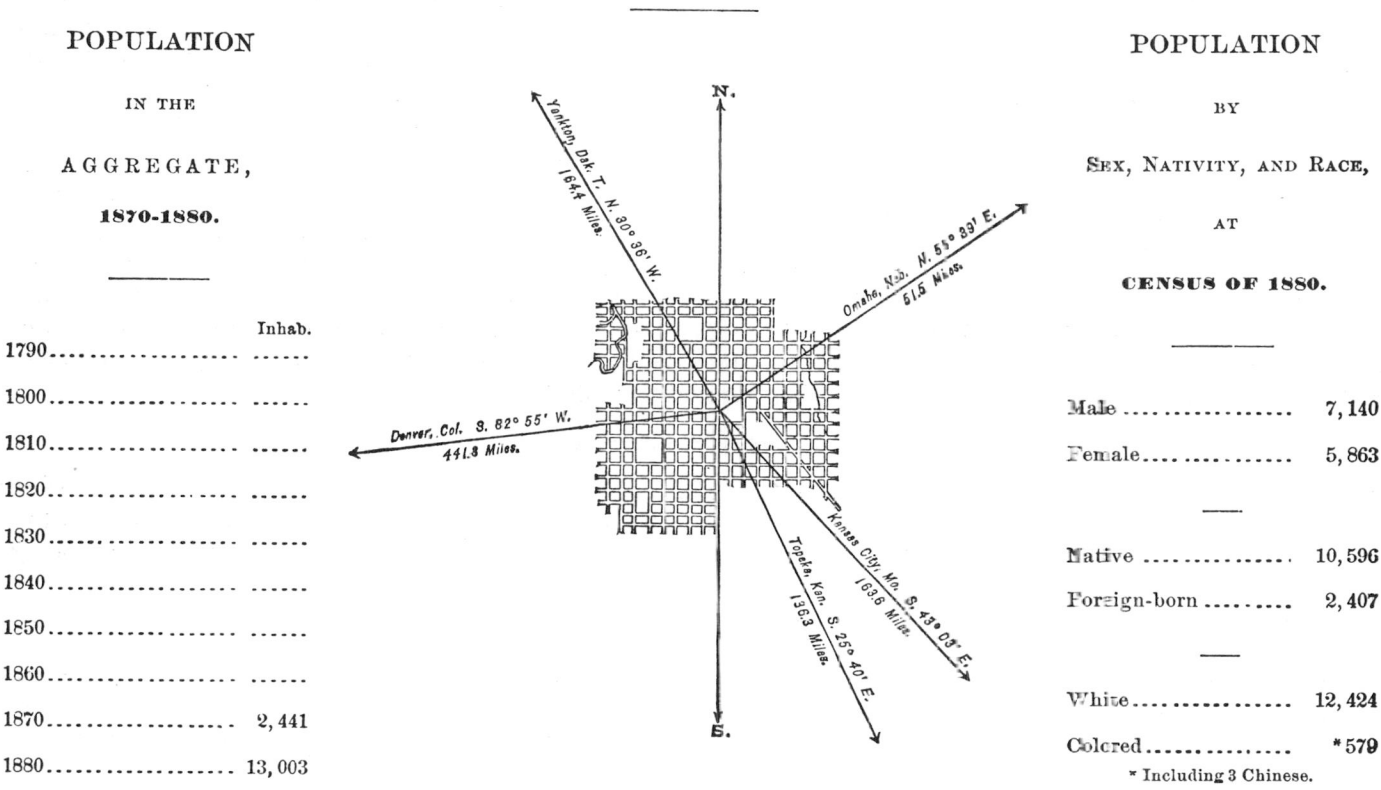

POPULATION IN THE AGGREGATE, 1870-1880.		POPULATION BY SEX, NATIVITY, AND RACE, AT CENSUS OF 1880.	
	Inhab.		
1790	......		
1800	......		
1810	......	Male	7,140
1820	......	Female	5,863
1830	......		
1840	......	Native	10,596
1850	......	Foreign-born	2,407
1860	......		
1870	2,441	White	12,424
1880	13,003	Colored	*579

* Including 3 Chinese.

Latitude: 40° 50 North; Longitude: 96° 45 (west from Greenwich); Altitude: 1,647 feet.

FINANCIAL CONDITION:

Total Valuation: $1,133,389; per capita: $87 00.   Net Indebtedness: $199,615; per capita: $15 35.   Tax per $100: $6 75.

HISTORICAL SKETCH.

Nebraska was a part of the Louisiana territory ceded to the United States by France in 1803. It was visited by Lewis and Clark in 1804–'05, and they are believed to have been the first white explorers to pass through it from east to west. In 1854 it was formed into a separate territory, and in February, 1867, Nebraska was admitted into the Union. Previous to this time there had been but one house on the present site of Lincoln, but, it having been selected as the location for the state capital, buildings began to spring up on every side. It was laid out by 3 state commissioners, and in the following January the legislature met there for the first time. In 1868 the erection of a state penitentiary was begun, and since then additions costing $200,000 have been made. In 1870 the state university was built here at a cost of $150,000, the money being the proceeds of the sale of lots. This institution opened in 1871 with 70 students, and now has 300. The state insane asylum was built here in 1870, and was burnt down and rebuilt in 1872. A large opera-house built in 1873 was burnt down, but was rebuilt the next year. The United States court-house and post-office cost $160,000. Two sessions of the United States court are held each year. A new capitol is in process of erection, to cost, when completed, $450,000; one wing has already been finished at a cost of $100,000.

LINCOLN IN 1880.

The following statistical accounts, mainly gathered by the Census Office, indicate the present condition of Lincoln:

LOCATION.

Lincoln, the capital of the county of Lancaster and of the state of Nebraska, is situated in the eastern part of the state, southwest of Omaha, and directly west of Nebraska City. In the Smithsonian publications its altitude is given as 1,647 feet above sea-level, but the reports forwarded by Professor Samuel Aughey, of the state university, gives its lowest altitude at 1,164, and its highest at 1,208 feet. Salt creek, a stream from 40 to 60 feet in width, runs through the city and empties into the Platte river some 25 miles to the northeast. Oak and Middle creeks empty into Salt creek on the northwest side, and Antelope creek flows along the east side of the city. None of these streams are navigable.

RAILROAD COMMUNICATIONS.

Lincoln lies on the Omaha and Republican Valley branch of the Union Pacific railway, the branch connecting with the main line at Valley, 58 miles from Lincoln and 35 miles from Omaha. It is also on the Burlington and Missouri River Railroad in Nebraska, several divisions of which intersect here. The Burlington and Missouri River division of this line runs from Kearney junction through Lincoln to Plattsmouth, where it connects with the Chicago, Burlington, and Quincy for Chicago and the East; a branch runs from Oreapolis, on this division, up to Omaha; the Nebraska Railway division runs from Nebraska City through Lincoln to Central City; the Atchison and Nebraska division runs from Atchison, Kansas, through Lincoln to Columbus.

TRIBUTARY COUNTRY.

The country surrounding Lincoln is gently rolling and is intersected by many small streams. The soil is rich, and about half of it is under cultivation. The great majority of the people are engaged in farming; corn is the leading product; next comes wheat, and then the other cereals. There is much stock-raising, cattle and hogs being most extensively raised. The general business of the city is with the farmers of the vicinity.

TOPOGRAPHY.

Lincoln is largely built on slopes running down to Salt creek on the north and west, and to Antelope creek on the east. The higher elevations toward the south have some fine residences. The surface soil is loess; underneath this there is a drift material, and underneath that in turn is dark-brown sandstone of the Dakota group of the Cretaceous; this in turn is underlaid by the Permian rocks. The surface drainage is into Salt and Antelope creeks. Taken as a whole, the site would be called gently rolling. Its highest portions are on a level with the highest portions of the surrounding country, but the terrace on which the main part of the city is built averages a few feet below the general level. The country for a radius of five miles is generally open. Two miles north of the city there is a salt marsh covering about 600 acres, on which at the present time water stands.

CLIMATE.

The highest recorded summer temperature is 113°; the highest in average years, 96°. The lowest recorded winter temperature is —30°; the lowest in average years, —15°. The numerous streams in the vicinity give Lincoln a moister atmosphere than is usually found in this longitude. There are no marshes or elevated lands near enough to affect the climate. The most prevalent winds are those from the southwest. If such a wind changes suddenly to the northeast, rain or snow is sure to follow. Occasionally in summer this southwest wind is nearly suffocating, and in rare cases it even burns vegetation. Next to these, the north and northeast winds are most common. The latter in winter are cold and piercing.

STREETS.

There are no pavements in the city. The streets are generally repaired by day labor, under the direction of the overseer of streets, the annual cost being about $6,000. The city authorities report that they find it much cheaper to use contract work for large and day work for small jobs. Trees are planted in rows four feet from the lines of the lots, along the sides of the streets. The work is all done and the expenses are met by the lot-owners.

LINCOLN, NEBR.

There are no horse-railroads, but a herdic line has recently been established, on which the fare is 5 cents.

WATER-WORKS.

The city is preparing to build water-works.

GAS.

The gas-works are not owned by the city. The charge for gas is $4 per 1,000 feet.

PUBLIC BUILDINGS.

The city occupies one building for municipal purposes. It cost $4,500. The public buildings here owned by the state have been mentioned in the historical sketch.

PUBLIC PARKS AND PLEASURE-GROUNDS.

There is a city park, with an area of 10 acres, but it can hardly be called a pleasure-ground, for its improvement has received little attention. The land was set apart for park purposes by the state commissioners when the city was located in 1867, and cost the city nothing. The city expends very little on it, not over $50 to $100 per year. It is controlled by the mayor and city council.

PLACES OF AMUSEMENT.

There is one theater, with a seating capacity of 1,200. It pays an annual license to the city of $100. There is a city hall, with a seating capacity of 1,000, used for all sorts of public purposes, and besides this, there are one or two minor halls. There are no concert- or beer-gardens.

DRAINAGE.

There is no system of sewerage in Lincoln. Storm-water and surface drainage flow through natural channels into the ravines, which have been straightened in some places, but which are still open ditches. A storm-water sewer has been laid near the surface in the business portion of the city. It begins with a wooden box 4 by 6 feet, and enlarges to 6 by 8. For most of its length it consists of a stone-paved bottom with sides of plank, and is covered sometimes with plank and sometimes with an arch of two feet rise. It is not more than half a mile long, and discharges into an open ditch about half a mile from Salt creek. A number of drains from cellars, markets, and other places discharge into this storm drain, but not from any vaults or cesspools. A 12-inch-pipe sewer from the post-office, Arlington hotel, and *State Journal* block extends about three-quarters of a mile to Salt creek. It takes also the overflow of mineral water from an artesian well and the drainage from the baths supplied by it. All other sewage goes into vaults or cesspools.

CEMETERIES.

There are 2 cemeteries connected with the city, one Protestant and the other Catholic. They are located 1½ mile east of the city. The former contains 80 acres and the latter 10 acres. There are no complete records of interments. There is no limit of time of burial after death. The depth of grave is 5 feet. The revenue from the sale of lots in *Wyuka*, the Protestant cemetery, is used exclusively for beautifying and improving the grounds, walks, fences, etc. This cemetery has been surrounded with a substantial fence, has been laid out with walks, parks, drives, etc., and a good sexton's house has been built, all from the proceeds of the sale of lots. The ground for it was donated by the state legislature in February, 1869, for a state cemetery, to be called "Wyuka cemetery", with a provision that the city of Lincoln should elect 3 trustees to have the control and management of it.

MARKETS.

There are no public or corporation markets in the city. Pedlers or hawkers carrying articles for sale in a cart must pay a license of $10 per annum, but this rule does not apply to retail venders of vegetables, eggs, butter, and produce raised by themselves in their own farm or garden.

SANITARY AUTHORITY—BOARD OF HEALTH.

The mayor, the chairman of the committee of the city council on fire, police, and health, and the city marshal constitute the board of health of the city. None of these officials are necessarily physicians. When there is no epidemic the expenses of the board are merely nominal. In case of an epidemic its authority is unlimited. At any time it may call to its assistance such medical aid and advice as it may deem necessary. It has general supervision of the health of the city, and has power to take all necessary steps to promote cleanliness and the sanitary condition of the city, to abate nuisances, and to enforce any and all lawful measures necessary to prevent the spread of contagion. All the orders, rules, and regulations of the board are made known to the public by the proclamation of the mayor. Inspections are made only when nuisances are reported, but the chief of police is supposed to have general charge of such matters. If a nuisance is not abated within a reasonable time after the board orders it, the delinquent is arrested and fined. The board meets only when called together by the mayor. It has never exercised any control over the removal of garbage, or its conservancy while awaiting removal. The only regulation concerning the burial of the dead seems to be that they must be buried outside the city limits. The removal of excrement generally comes under the charge of the chief of police rather than the board of health.

INFECTIOUS DISEASES.

There is no practice about small-pox, as there have been no cases of this disease in the city. The board has never had scarlet-fever patients isolated, nor has it treated this differently from ordinary diseases. The city has had no cases of serious contagious diseases breaking out in the public schools. There is no public pest-house. Vaccination is not compulsory, nor is it done at the public expense.

REPORTS.

There is no system of registration of births, diseases, or deaths. The board has never made a report, except in one year, when it was constituted differently from what it is now. It was then composed of physicians appointed by the mayor and council, but it was so arbitrary that it did not give satisfaction.

MUNICIPAL CLEANSING.

Street-cleaning.—The streets are cleaned by the city's own force by hand, and the work is said not to be done very efficiently. The sweepings are deposited outside the city limits.

Removal of garbage and ashes.—Garbage is removed both by the city and by householders. The part done by the city is done by its own force. The only regulation as to the conservancy of garbage while awaiting removal is that it shall not become so offensive as to create a nuisance. Ashes and garbage are never kept in the same vessel. Garbage and ashes are removed outside the city limits. No nuisance or injury to health from improper treatment of garbage has been noticed.

Dead animals.—By a city ordinance, dead animals must be removed outside the corporation limits and buried by their owners. When the owners can not be found the police take charge. The annual cost of this service to the city is about $100.

Liquid household wastes.—Laundry- and kitchen-slops are generally thrown on the ground; chamber-slops into cesspools. Only a small part of the waste goes into the public sewers, and none of it into gutters. Cesspools and dry wells are very porous, and therefore are not provided with overflows. There are few water-closets, and such as there are empty into sewers. In the center of the city the contamination of drinking-water by the escape of the contents of cesspools is becoming very great, and the question of water-works is being agitated. The ordinances require that cesspools should be kept clean and not allowed to become offensive.

Human excreta.—Nearly all the private dwellings in the city depend on privy-vaults; the hotels have water-closets which empty into the sewers. As has been said, all water-closets empty into sewers and none into cesspools. The dry-earth system is very little used. Privy-vaults, if within 20 feet of a street, dwelling, shop, or well, must be 8 feet deep and made tight, according to the city ordinances, and all privy-vaults must be cleansed by using lime or some other disinfectant once in each week between June 15 and September 15 in each year. During that time no vault may be emptied without permission of the health officers, and it must be done between 11 p. m. and 4. a. m.

Manufacturing wastes.—The city has very few manufactories, and they are compelled to bury all substances which would be injurious to health or offensive if not removed.

POLICE.

The police force is appointed by the mayor, confirmed by the city council, and governed by the mayor and council. The chief executive officer is the chief of police, who has general superintendence of the force, and receives a salary of $720 per year and certain fees. There are 6 patrolmen, receiving $600 per year each. Their uniform is navy blue in color, and they wear helmet caps, shield badges, and belts, and carry rosewood batons. They furnish their own clothing, but hats, badges, belts, and batons are supplied by the city at a cost of about $10 per man per year. Besides their batons they carry revolvers, nippers, and whistles. The night men are on duty from 7 p. m. to 5 a. m., and the day men from 7 a. m. to 6 p. m. They patrol about 7 miles of streets in all. In 1880 there were 264 arrests, of which 121 were for being drunk and disorderly, 95 for prostitution, 16 for larceny and assault, 9 for vagrancy, 8 for felony, and the rest for minor offenses. Of these, 48 were dismissed, 7 were bound over to the district court, and the rest were fined or committed to jail. About $1,000 worth of property was stolen, and about a quarter of it was recovered and returned to the owners. There were very few, possibly 20, station-house lodgers during the year, and a few meals were given them. The police notify and prosecute offenders against the health ordinances. The chief of police has the supervision of building permits. Special policemen are appointed by the mayor on occasions of circuses, fairs, etc., to serve as special patrolmen; they take orders from the regular police, who for the time being act as sergeants of special police districts. The cost of the force for 1880 was $4,420.

OMAHA,

DOUGLAS COUNTY, NEBRASKA.

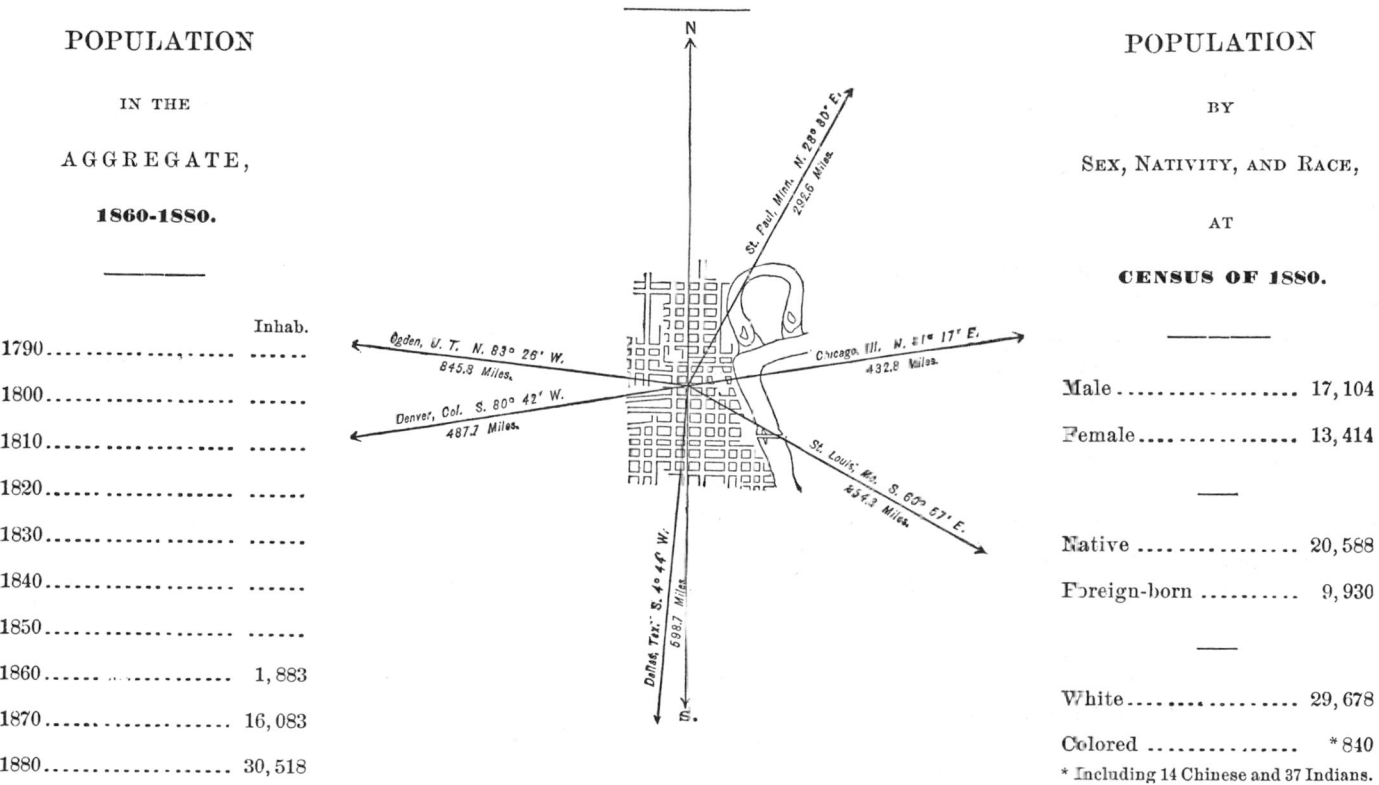

POPULATION			POPULATION
IN THE			BY
AGGREGATE,			SEX, NATIVITY, AND RACE,
1860-1880.			AT
			CENSUS OF 1880.

	Inhab.		
1790	......	Male	17,104
1800	......	Female	13,414
1810	......		
1820	......		
1830	......	Native	20,588
1840	......	Foreign-born	9,930
1850	......		
1860	1,883		
1870	16,083	White	29,678
1880	30,518	Colored	*840

* Including 14 Chinese and 37 Indians.

Latitude: 41° 15′ North; Longitude: 95° 56′ (west from Greenwich); **Altitude: 947 to 1,094 feet.**

FINANCIAL CONDITION:

Total Valuation: $7,512,683; per capita: $246 00.   Net Indebtedness: $227,578; per capita: $7 46.   Tax per $100: $4 65.

HISTORICAL SKETCH.(a)

The spot on which Omaha is situated was visited as early as the year 1804 by Lewis and Clarke during their memorable expedition to explore the Louisiana purchase.   Prior to that time it had been the site of an Indian village inhabited by the Otoes, whose descendants are now to be found on a little reservation in the southern part of the state.   For nearly half a century after that date it was uninhabited except by Indians and an occasional trader or trapper; but soon after the discovery of gold in California, and the subsequent immigration across the plains to that land of promise, its attractive situation drew the attention of settlers on the left bank of the Missouri at the spot now called Council Bluffs, who waited with ill-concealed impatience until the Indian title to its productive acres should be extinguished.

---

a Hon. James W. Savage, judge of the supreme court of Nebraska, not only furnished nearly all the detailed information concerning the present condition of Omaha, but wrote the historical sketch of the city with which this report is introduced.

Early in 1854 negotiations with the Omahas and Otoes resulted in the signing of a treaty by which the aboriginal title to the land was extinguished and the way was opened for the establishment of the territory of Nebraska.

The bill organizing the territories of Kansas and Nebraska was the leading and most absorbing topic of the Thirty-third Congress. Its repeal of what is known as the Missouri Compromise gave it a national importance which it would not have possessed without such a clause, and the opposition to it was violent and bitter. After a prolonged controversy, however, the bill passed the Senate on the 4th of March, 1854, and the House on the 23d of May in the same year, and from that period the region about Omaha was, although unsurveyed, regarded as subject to pre-emption.

A few months prior to the passage of the organic act a steam-ferry company had been organized by residents of Council Bluffs under the name of the "Council Bluffs and Nebraska Ferry Company", for the purpose of establishing and maintaining a ferry across the Missouri river at Omaha. Immediately after the close of the fierce struggle, this company took steps to lay out a town at the western landing of their ferry, and the survey was completed in July, 1854. The town was laid out in 322 blocks, each block being 264 feet square and containing eight lots 66 feet in width by 132 in depth. The streets were given a width of 100 feet. To this prospective city was given the name of an Indian tribe, once the most powerful and wealthy in the region, whose lands adjoined those of the Otoes and reached the northern boundary of the city.

Francis H. Burt, of South Carolina, had been appointed by President Pierce the first governor of the new territory of Nebraska, and arrived at Bellevue, some 12 miles below Omaha, with his secretary, Thomas B. Cuming, of Iowa, on the 6th of October, 1854. Being taken ill, however, immediately on his arrival, he rapidly grew worse, until on the morning of Wednesday, October 18, 1854, he died at the old Presbyterian mission house at Bellevue. By virtue of his office, Secretary Cuming became governor, and at once entered upon the duties of his office.

Various points on the right bank of the river had by this time become clamorous for the territorial capital which it was the duty of the governor, in the first instance, to name. Governor Burt was supposed to have favored Bellevue; but Governor Cuming, in spite of determined and vigorous opposition, designated Omaha as the spot for the holding of the first legislature, and that place remained the capital until the territory became a state.

The growth of Omaha during 1856 and the earlier portion of 1857 was rapid. The spirit of speculation abroad over the whole country was speedily developed in that city. Money was made easily; corner lots commanded absurdly inflated prices; "wild-cat" banks, established without authority of law, and having no substantial basis of capital, were numerous; city scrip assisted in increasing an already abundant currency, and the future of the place looked very bright to the owners of real estate within its limits. In February of the last-mentioned year, the town, having reached a population of about 1,500, received from the legislature of the territory a charter of incorporation as a city.

With the financial depression, however, of that year, which began with the suspension of the Ohio Life and Trust Company in New York city and rapidly spread over the entire country, a reverse overtook Omaha, which was far more severe in its consequences than any which could have befallen established towns in the East. Nearly every bank in the territory closed its doors, real estate was absolutely unsalable, business dragged heavily, and population actually decreased. Fortunately the discovery of gold in Colorado and the settlement of Denver in that state attracted general attention to that region; and Omaha, being on the line of travel, became an important outfitting point, obtaining a share of the trade which gave once more a cheerful and hopeful look to its affairs.

During all this time the title to the land on which the city was situated was still vested in the general government. Under the municipal act of Congress of 1844, the land covered by the site of Omaha was granted in two patents, one to John McCormick, as trustee, dated May 1, 1860, and the other to Jesse Lowe, mayor, dated October 1, 1860. These patents were in trust for the owners and occupants of the lots patented, and were by the trustees, from time to time, conveyed to such persons.

In 1862 Congress passed an act for the construction of a railroad to the Pacific ocean, and the initial point was fixed by the President on the western boundary of the state of Iowa, at a point opposite Omaha. Work on this road began December 8, 1863, and it was finished in about five years. Its construction gave an impulse to trade and business of all kinds in Omaha, which showed itself in a steady increase in population and a revival of speculation rivaling that of 1857. The census of 1870 showed a population of over 16,000.

The completion of the road, however, was followed by another fall in prices and a period of considerable depression. The expenditures necessary for the rapid pushing of the road had almost entirely ceased, and the city was found to have outgrown the demands of the still sparsely settled surrounding country. The financial difficulties which began in New York in 1873, moreover, were not long in reaching Omaha, and its population in 1875 was probably not much in excess of that of 1870. In the last-named year, however, the rapid increase of population in the state brought with it a demand for more commercial facilities, and Omaha began once more a vigorous growth, which has continued to the present time without material obstacle. Its population now exceeds 30,000.

The great width of the streets, while it has rendered their improvement expensive and slow, has in more than one instance prevented the spread of what might have become serious conflagrations. Though in the business portions of the city the houses were, until recently, mostly of wood, and though fires are not infrequent, they have never in a single instance spread beyond the block in which they had their origin.

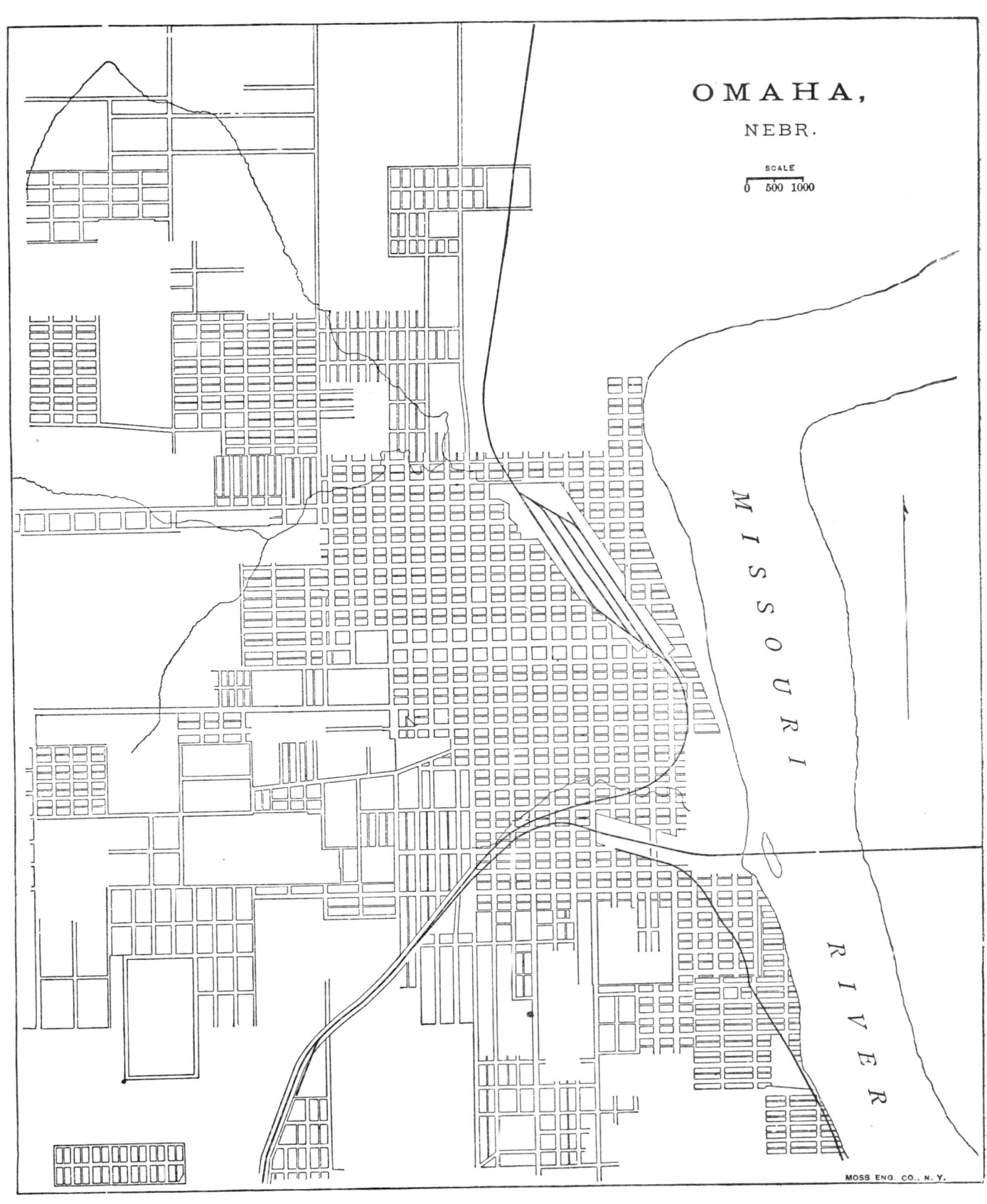

OMAHA,

NEBR.

SCALE
0   500 1000

MISSOURI

RIVER

MOSS ENG. CO., N. Y.

The only serious fire which demands mention in a sketch of the city was the burning of the Grand Central hotel, a commodious and elegant edifice which, during the progress of repairs to the building in September, 1878, took fire and was burnt to the ground, occasioning a loss of perhaps $200,000.

Omaha is governed by virtue of a general law of the state of Nebraska incorporating all cities of more than 15,000 inhabitants as cities of the first class. It has 6 wards, and the common council consists of 2 members from each ward. The city officers consist of a mayor, treasurer, city clerk, marshal, and police judge, who hold their respective offices for 2 years. The city election takes place annually on the first Tuesday in April, and the terms of office of the councilmen have been so arranged that one from each ward is elected in each year.

The population of Omaha, besides Americans, comprises in a noticeable degree Germans, Scandinavians, Irish, and Bohemians.

OMAHA IN 1880.

The following statistical accounts give a clear idea of the present condition of the city:

LOCATION.

Omaha, the capital of Douglas county, Nebraska, is situated on the west bank of the Missouri river, opposite Council Bluffs, 18 miles by land above the mouth of the Platte, 125 miles west by south of Des Moines, and 150 miles by land, or about 250 by river, above Saint Joseph, Missouri. Judge Savage in his report gives the altitude of the lowest point of the city as 947 feet above sea-level; of the highest point, 1,094; of the court-house, 1,034. The track of the Union Pacific railroad on the high bridge across the Missouri, 52 feet above high water, has an altitude of 1,036 feet. There is a draft of water in the Missouri immediately in front of the city of about 30 feet. The banks frequently change, as well as the depth of water. Water communication is open with all river ports on the Missouri, Mississippi, and Ohio rivers.

RAILROAD COMMUNICATIONS.

The main line of the Union Pacific runs through Omaha on its way from Council Bluffs, just across the river, to Ogden, where it connects with the Central Pacific for San Francisco and the whole Pacific slope. At Council Bluffs this road connects with 5 others, viz, the Chicago and Northwestern, the Chicago, Rock Island, and Pacific, the Chicago, Burlington, and Quincy, the Wabash, Saint Louis, and Pacific, and the Kansas City, Saint Joseph, and Council Bluffs, which give Omaha the best of connections with all points to the East.

Omaha is the most northeastern point of the network of lines covering the southeastern part of the state, known as the Burlington and Missouri River Railroad in Nebraska. The branch of the road on which Omaha is situated connects with the trunk line of Oreapolis, giving communication with Lincoln, and so by various branches with Columbus, Central City, Kearney Junction, Indianola, Atchison, and Nebraska City. Omaha is the most southwestern point of the lines controlled by the Chicago, Saint Paul, Minneapolis, and Omaha company, the Omaha division of one of which lines, the Saint Paul and Sioux City, runs from Omaha to Blair and the North.

TRIBUTARY COUNTRY.

In so new a country as Nebraska it is not always easy to calculate exactly the region destined ultimately, when routes of trade and travel have been finally established, to become tributary to any given city. At present Omaha seems to be the natural outlet for an extensive region comprising most of the northwest portion of the state. But in a more restricted sense the country tributary to the city may be called Sarpy, Douglas, and the southern portion of Washington counties, comprising an area of about 25 miles in width from east to west, and 50 miles in length from north to south. This country consists of a gently rolling prairie, timbered along the streams, and nearly every acre of it susceptible of cultivation. It is well adapted to the growth of corn, hay, spring wheat, and small fruits. For 10 miles north, south, and west of the city the country is not so well settled as further west, the speculations of 1866 having withdrawn large areas from the market, which have been so long held that the wave of emigration has overleaped them and passed on to more easily purchased tracts.

Douglas county has an area of 215,000 acres, of which 40,000 and upward are under cultivation. The Platte river is its western boundary line, while the Missouri lies on its eastern borders. The Papillion and Elkhorn rivers run through the center; and numerous tributaries of these four rivers furnish a good supply of water. It has upward of 20,000 fruit trees, 30,000 acres of native and cultivated forests, and an abundance of lime and sandstone suitable for building material. At Waterloo, a thriving town in the western portion of the county, the Elkhorn river affords one of the best water-powers in the state. Sarpy county contains 142,258 acres of land, 43,531 acres of which are under cultivation. There are 50,000 fruit-trees in the county in good condition. It is well watered, and the west and southwest portions are supplied with extensive quarries of fine building stone, strips of timber, and fine springs of pure water.

TOPOGRAPHY.

Omaha, as has been said, is situated on the right bank of the Missouri river. Immediately on the shore is a strip of bottom-land, on which have been placed the machine-shops of the Union Pacific railroad, the smelting-works, and such other establishments as require large space or isolation. Some 1,200 feet back from the river the land rises abruptly about 60 feet, and there spreads out into a table, upon which is situated the principal business portion of the city. Half a mile further west the surface again rises, though more gradually, about 75 feet higher, and upon this elevation nearly all of the dwelling-houses have been erected. Here is met the gently undulating ground which extends over the greater portion of the city, and which, resembling the billows of the ocean, has been called a "rolling prairie".

The country rises toward the west and the north. The surface of each terrace, however, descends as it recedes from the river, until it reaches the foot of the next bluff. The natural drainage is therefore away from the river for some distance, and then both north and south until it reaches creeks which respectively bound the city on those sides, and which empty into the Missouri.

The soil of Omaha consists mainly of loess. This, at a distance varying from 25 to 75 feet, is underlaid by loosely compacted drift materials. Geologically speaking, the region has but recently emerged from the waters of the Loess age, and still exhibits as a whole many of the phenomena of a recently drained lake bed. Analysis of this loess gives the following results: Insoluble silicious matter, 81.28 per cent.; ferric oxide, 3.86; alumina, 0.75; lime, carbonate, 6.06; phosphate, 3.59; magnesia, carbonate, 1.28; potassa, 0.27; soda, 0.15; organic matter, 1.07; moisture, 1.09; loss in analysis, 0.59. It is said to absorb excessive rainfall like a sponge.

To the west of the city the rolling prairie is open; to the north and east along the banks of the river it is considerably wooded.

CLIMATE.

The highest recorded summer temperature is 105°; the highest in average years, 97.5°. The lowest recorded winter temperature is −22°; the lowest in average years, −13.5°. The mean summer temperature is 74.26°; the mean winter temperature, 23.36°; the mean annual temperature, 40.28°. The influence of such adjacent waters, marshes, and elevated lands as there are is imperceptible. The prevailing wind in summer is from the south, and in winter from the northwest. These winds, passing over a great expanse of level territory, doubtless increase the heat of summer and the cold of winter.

STREETS.

Total length of streets, 118 miles. None of them are paved except 0.4 mile, which has been paved with broken stone at a cost of $1 67 per square yard. The sidewalks are of wood of varying thickness, width, and condition, like those of most new western cities. There are only 2 miles of guttering, and this consists of irregular limestone blocks set on edge. "Generally the water wanders round at its own sweet will." By a city ordinance, owners of lots abutting on streets not occupied for business purposes have the right to inclose 14 feet of street, upon condition of planting trees in the space so inclosed. Lot-owners have almost universally availed themselves of this privilege. The streets devoted to residences are therefore generally bordered with shade-trees, usually the box elder, soft maple, or some species of rapid growth. Streets are constructed and repaired by contract. The annual cost of such work is about $11,500. The city's work has usually been done by contract, but the data are reported not sufficient to warrant any expression of opinion as to the relative merits of the contract and day systems. Neither steam stone-crusher nor roller is used.

The total length of horse-railroad track in the city is 5 miles; total number of cars, 10; of horses, 70; of men employed, 20; of passengers carried during the year, 495,000; the rate of fare is 5 cents for any distance.

WATER-WORKS.

A contract for water-works has just been concluded and work has been begun; hitherto the only sources of supply have been cisterns and wells.

GAS.

The gas-works are not owned by the city; the daily average production of gas is 30,000 feet; the charge per 1,000 feet is $3 50; there are 160 street lamps, and the city pays $27 50 per year for each.

PUBLIC BUILDINGS.

The building used for city-hall purposes, meetings of city council, mayor's office, etc., is not owned by the city. There are, belonging to the city, only 3 wooden engine-houses, of trifling value, perhaps $2,000.

PUBLIC PARKS AND PLEASURE-GROUNDS.

There are three public parks, with a total area of 85.5 acres: *Hanscom Park*, containing 73 acres, is situated in the southwestern part of the city, about a mile from the center of business, is heavily rolling, and is covered with a good growth of natural trees. It was presented to the city on condition that the city should spend $5,000 per year for five years on it. Its designer was George Smith, esq. The two smaller parks have cost nothing, having been reserved at the laying out of the city. The parks are controlled by the city council. The city ordinance in regard to Hanscom park provides, among other things, that huckstering and the sale of alcoholic liquors shall not be allowed in it.

PLACES OF AMUSEMENT.

There are three theaters, seating, respectively, 900, 650, and 250. They pay an annual license to the city of $100. There are five or six concert-halls and lecture-rooms of various sizes. There are three concert- and beer-gardens, viz, Bohemia hall, with a seating capacity of 450, built in 1870; Metz garden, seating 750, constructed in 1875; and Bauman's garden, seating 1,000, constructed in 1872. They cost $5,000 each.

CEMETERIES.

No report on this subject was received.

MARKETS.

There are no public or corporation markets, and no standing-ground is used by farmers' and hucksters' wagons, except by those of the venders of hay and wood. Certain portions of wide streets in the center of the city are set apart by a city ordinance for market-stands, but farmers generally dispose of their produce, except hay and wood, to green-grocers who keep retail shops. The city marshal is made the conservator of the market. Any person occupying any of this space set apart must make his stand in the center of the street, in such manner as not to interfere with public travel, and a space at least 20 feet wide must be kept free and unobstructed on each side of the street and contiguous to the sidewalk.

SANITARY AUTHORITY—BOARD OF HEALTH.

The chief health organization of Omaha is the board of health, consisting of the mayor, the president of the city council, and the city marshal. The mayor is president of the board. Its duties consist in having charge of the sanitary condition of the city, adopting such regulations as are consistent with the lawful exercise of its powers concerning the public health, nuisances, sources of filth, and causes of sickness, and taking prompt and efficient measures to prevent the introduction or spread of contagious diseases. Its annual expenses are about $240, incurred for current expenditures and the salary of a secretary. The ordinance makes no provision as to its expenditures either in the presence or the absence of epidemics. It is the duty of the city physician to take charge of all persons suffering from infectious, contagious, malignant, or epidemic diseases, to examine into all nuisances, sources of filth, and causes of sickness within the city, and to report the same weekly, or oftener if required by the board, together with the number and character of cases of diseases, contagious, malignant, etc., that may come under his treatment. In case of epidemics the board may establish such temporary hospitals or pest-houses as the emergency may require. The city does not own a pest-house. None of the board have police powers, except the president in his capacity as mayor and magistrate. Particular inspections are made only as nuisances are reported. If the nuisance really exists the city marshal orders it abated. The board meets monthly at the call of the president. There is no special practice concerning the inspection and correction of defective house-drainage, privy-vaults, cesspools, sources of drinking-water, defective sewerage, etc. These things and the conservation and removal of garbage the board takes cognizance of only as nuisances are apparent or are reported. No dead body is allowed to be buried without a permit from the secretary of the board.

INFECTIOUS DISEASES.

Small-pox patients are isolated in a pest-house; scarlet-fever patients, when the disease is of the malignant type, are quarantined at home. Except in case of these two diseases the board takes no cognizance of the breaking out of contagious diseases in the public schools. Vaccination is not compulsory, nor is it done at the public expense.

REPORTS.

The ordinances provide that the secretary of the board shall register all births and deaths, but no registry of diseases is kept, further than that of contagious diseases mentioned under the city physician's duties. The board reports to the city council as often as necessary, and at least once a year. Their reports are not published. The general health of the city is said to be remarkably good.

MUNICIPAL CLEANSING.

Street-cleaning.—The streets are improved—never cleaned—by the city, and but rarely by private abutters. It is reported that the city has found it impracticable to do this. When it has been done at all it has been by hand.

The sweepings are deposited on the river-bottom, whence they are washed into the river by rain and overflows. Efforts are being made for the construction of pavements, and these, with the water from the new water-works, are expected to produce a speedy improvement in this matter of street-cleaning.

Removal of garbage and ashes.—Garbage is removed by householders. It is finally disposed of in the Missouri river. Ashes are disposed of in the easiest way possible, there being no uniform practice on the subject. Doubtless the carelessness in the treatment of garbage is injurious to health, but it is probably less so than in most cities, on account of the dryness of the climate. Judge Savage says: "All these things will be speedily changed. Thus far the city has grown too fast for public improvements to keep up."

Dead animals.—A city scavenger removes dead animals to phosphate works, where they are disposed of. No complaints have been made of the system. The animals are removed as soon as discovered, and the rendering works are far enough from the city to prevent any unpleasant effects from the processes.

Liquid household wastes.—Chamber, laundry, and kitchen slops are all disposed of in the same way. As sewers have not yet been constructed to any extent, very little of the liquid household wastes goes into them. Most of it goes into dry wells or cesspools on the premises, which are mostly porous and are not provided with overflows. They seldom receive the waste of water-closets.

Human excreta.—Houses built prior to 1880 depend on privy-vaults. Few, if any, of these vaults are nominally water-tight. Scavengers must at no time cleanse out any cesspool or vault without first procuring an order or license from the board of health specifying the manner, means, and time for such cleansing.

Manufacturing waste.—There is neither practice nor regulation on this head.

POLICE.

The police force is appointed by the mayor, with the consent of the city council. The chief executive officer is the city marshal. He receives a salary of $1,200 per annum. He has the direction and control of the police force while on duty. The rest of the force consists of a deputy marshal and 8 patrolmen, who receive $840 per annum each. Their uniform consists of a double-breasted frock coat of blue cloth and a blue cap. The men provide their own uniforms. Each man carries a billy, a revolver, and Philip's patent police nippers. Each serves 12 hours a day and patrols four blocks, about 400 feet square. In 1880 there were 867 arrests, the principal causes being drunkenness, larceny, assault and battery, disorderly conduct, and prostitution; $3,000 worth of property was stolen, of which $1,500 was recovered and returned to the owners; there were 100 station-house lodgers, against 130 in 1879; a few free meals were given them, at a total cost of $14. Special policemen are appointed by the mayor and council at the request of any firm or corporation, to do service in or about the business or premises of such firm or corporation. They have the powers of regular police in the discharge of their duties. In 1880 the force cost about $10,000. The mayor in his annual report, presented April 13, 1880, said: "It is a remarkable fact that during the past year no case of the commission of a capital crime has occurred in the city, nor has there been scarcely a case of street robbery or garroting." Of the present quarters in the city prison, the same document says: "They are unfit to be the recipient of the vilest prisoner. * * * To keep prisoners confined in their present rooms during the summer would be an act of inhumanity."

FIRE DEPARTMENT.

The Omaha fire department has 14 paid men, 12 horses, 4 engines, 2 houses. In the year ending April, 1880, there were 43 alarms. By far the most disastrous fire was that of Boyd's packing-house, the loss in that instance being $137,000. The total loss by fire was $175,340; of this, $145,890 was covered by insurance. The expenses for the year were as follows: Salary of the chief, $1,200; expenses of three engine companies, $13,252 56; hook and ladder, $1,585 52; fire alarm, $108 22; general expenses, $456 40; new engine, $4,400; lot of land, $676. Total, $21,678 70.

The value of the total amount of property in charge of this department is estimated at $70,201.

SCHOOLS.

The management of the city public schools is, under a state law creating a board of education, composed of 12 members, 2 from each ward, elected by the people for a term of 2 years. The course of instruction is thoroughly graded, offering to the children of the city a course of free instruction covering a period of 12 years. To supervise and manage the detail working in the schools, the board of education annually elects a superintendent. The principals of the several schools and teachers of the various grades are elected annually. Liberal salaries are paid to all, and excellent services are required.

The high-school building occupies the most prominent position in the city. It has a beautiful campus of ten acres, which is well known as "Capitol hill". The building is 4 stories high, containing 17 school-rooms, with an average seating capacity of 55 pupils to each room. There are also in this building 4 large recitation-rooms, an office room, library, and apparatus rooms connected with the high school. This building was erected in 1872 at a cost of $200,000. It is heated throughout by furnaces and hot-water coils of pipe, and is ventilated by the Rattan system. Of the 9 other buildings, 5 are of brick and the rest of wood.

The entire school population of the city between the ages of 5 and 21 years is 7,285, an increase in one year of nearly 900 children. The entire enrollment in the public schools for the year 1879–'80 was 3,517, an increase of 600 in one year. The average daily attendance was 2,477. The cost of maintaining the public schools for the year ending August 30, 1880, for supervision, teachers' salaries, incidentals, janitors, fuel, and repairs, was $69,573 05.

Of the private institutions, the most noticeable is Creighton college, conducted under Catholic auspices. The building is a large and beautiful brick structure, occupying a commanding position. It has a frontage of 50 feet, and is 125 feet deep. The present building was completed in January, 1879, at a cost of $63,000. It is well furnished throughout, and is arranged with an eye to comfort and convenience. The estimated cost of the building when completed according to the plans, by the addition of two wings, will be about $200,000. The college was opened for the reception of pupils in September, 1878. There were 140 pupils reported on the rolls, and this number has steadily increased, until now there are nearly 200 in attendance. Although it is a free Catholic institution, students of other religions are not excluded, and hence among the pupils there are found quite a number of Protestants.

There are other Catholic schools, with a total attendance of about 450. Brownell hall, a seminary of the Protestant Episcopal church for young ladies, has an attendance of about 100 students. Saint Barnabas school has an attendance of about 60.

MANUFACTURES.

The following is a summary of the statistics of the manufactures of Omaha for 1880, being taken from tables prepared for the Tenth Census by Philip Andres, special agent:

Mechanical and manufacturing industries.	No. of establishments.	Capital.	AVERAGE NUMBER OF HANDS EMPLOYED.			Total amount paid in wages during the year.	Value of materials.	Value of products.
			Males above 16 years.	Females above 15 years.	Children and youths.			
All industries	154	$1,835,800	1,466	64	158	$726,918	$2,527,476	$4,280,866
Blacksmithing (see also Wheelwrighting)	7	14,550	11			6,240	6,225	20,575
Boots and shoes, including custom work and repairing	9	22,650	29			15,930	12,550	38,760
Bread and other bakery products	5	24,800	36	3	4	17,050	61,300	103,400
Brick and tile	8	35,100	76		45	42,960	30,736	101,771
Carpentering	10	12,500	77			46,900	57,780	109,760
Clothing, men's	4	26,400	28		1	21,918	26,950	55,268
Cooperage	5	23,000	41			25,500	48,387	78,603
Foundery and machine-shop products	4	43,000	77			39,543	26,748	80,000
Furniture	3	8,650	5	2		2,700	10,350	17,800
Jewelry	3	49,000	25		2	14,500	105,000	210,000
Liquors, malt	4	285,000	93			37,595	133,117	259,460
Marble and stone work	3	4,400	7			2,100	3,800	11,100
Masonry, brick and stone	6	25,500	140		12	40,200	65,036	129,000
Painting and paperhanging	7	30,750	64		5	25,515	34,239	88,000
Printing and publishing	9	145,750	127	22	51	112,380	112,300	284,461
Saddlery and harness	3	68,950	21		1	11,713	33,900	50,400
Slaughtering and meat-packing, not including retail butchering	5	249,200	147		1	49,420	790,256	991,790
Tinware, copperware, and sheet-iron ware	7	32,000	51			22,250	49,300	94,000
Tobacco, cigars and cigarettes	8	35,450	43	2	14	28,267	51,200	113,194
Wheelwrighting (see also Blacksmithing)	4	5,700	7			4,772	3,830	14,572
All other industries (a)	40	693,450	361	35	22	175,535	864,478	1,428,955

a Embracing billiard tables and materials; boxes, wooden packing; brass castings; brooms and brushes; carpets, rag; carriages and wagons; clothing, women's; coffee and spices, roasted and ground; drugs and chemicals; dyeing and cleaning; fertilizers; flouring- and grist-mill products; furs, dressed; iron and steel; liquors, distilled; looking-glass and picture frames; lumber, sawed; mineral and soda waters; oil, linseed; paints; patent medicines and compounds; photographing; plumbing and gasfitting; rubber and elastic goods; safes, doors, and vaults, fire-proof; shirts; show-cases; upholstering; vinegar; watch and clock repairing; and wirework.

From the foregoing table it appears that the average capital of all establishments is $11,920 77; that the average wages of all hands employed is $430 63 per annum; and that the average outlay in wages, in materials, and in interest (at 6 per cent.) on capital employed is $21,847 67.

KANSAS.

ATCHISON,

ATCHISON COUNTY, KANSAS.

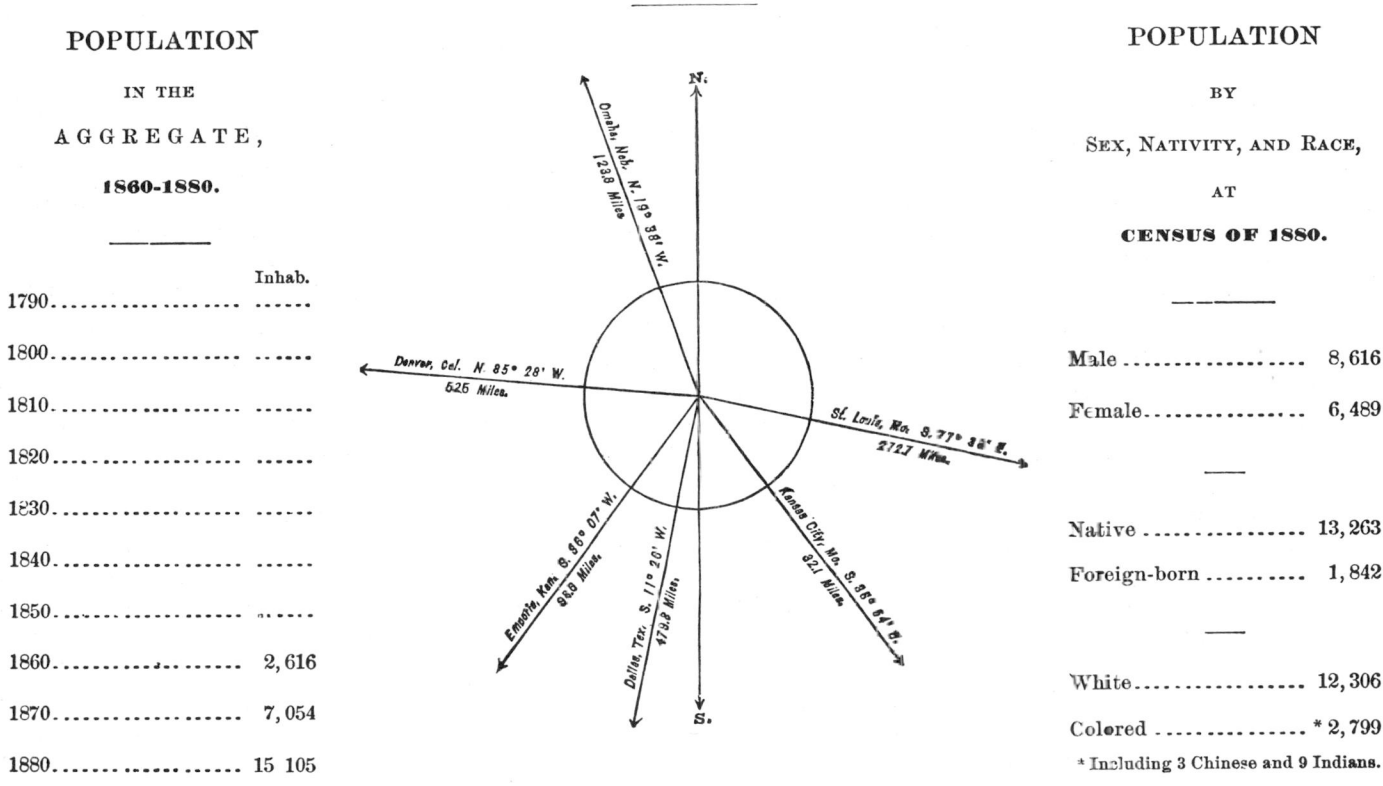

POPULATION

IN THE

AGGREGATE,

1860-1880.

	Inhab.
1790	......
1800	......
1810	......
1820	......
1830	......
1840	......
1850	......
1860	2,616
1870	7,054
1880	15 105

POPULATION

BY

SEX, NATIVITY, AND RACE,

AT

CENSUS OF 1880.

Male	8,616
Female	6,489
Native	13,263
Foreign-born	1,842
White	12,306
Colored	* 2,799

* Including 3 Chinese and 9 Indians.

Latitude: 39° 34' North; Longitude: 95° 8' (west from Greenwich); Altitude: 1,000 feet.

FINANCIAL CONDITION:

Total Valuation: $1,809,830; per capita: $120 00.   Net Indebtedness: $449,687; per capita: $29 77.   Tax per $100: $4 28.

HISTORICAL SKETCH.

Colonel David R. Atchison, for whom this city was named, was a United States Senator from Missouri from 1843 to 1855. His name appears among those of seventeen persons, all from Platte county, Missouri, except two who were already residents of what is now Atchison county, who on July 27, 1854, in a grove at what is now the foot of Atchison street, organized the "Atchison Town Company". A survey of 480 acres was made for a town site, and on the 21st of the following September the first sale of lots took place, 400 being sold to actual settlers.

Probably political motives connected with the struggle then in progress for the control of the territory of Kansas, between the pro-slavery and anti-slavery parties, had much to do with establishing this settlement; but just why this spot was chosen is a mystery. "The peculiar configuration of the earth was not favorable for the easy building of a metropolis on the site of Atchison. Abrupt bluffs stood up from the banks of the river, rift only to allow an unromantic stream, with unstable banks, to empty its feeble current into the uncontrollable Missouri. It was an uninviting spot for the purposes to which it was dedicated, but not devoid of the picturesque." There is one fact, however, that redeems the choice of the first settlers, viz, its location on the Missouri. The Missouri river here makes a great curve to the westward, and Atchison makes the center of the bow, nearest the mountains. Others saw the point, and Doniphan, 5 miles up the river, and Sumner, 3 miles below, were established in harmony with this idea of being on the Missouri, and yet as near the mountains as possible in order to secure the commerce of the West and Southwest. Atchison has far outrivaled her two competitors, and has won a success due in large part to her location.

Even early in 1855 the village attracted the attention of those interested in such matters, and became the Missouri River outfitting and starting point for a number of Salt Lake and other overland freighters, thus securing its first claim for recognition as a business center within twelve months from its inception. In February of that year the first newspaper was started, and in April the first postmaster was appointed. On February 22, 1858, it was incorporated as a city by the territorial legislature. During all these years "border warfare" had been continually waging over the territory, but Atchison, though founded by a party of pro-slavery men from Missouri, seems almost wholly to have escaped the turmoil and lawlessness from which Lawrence, Leavenworth, and other places suffered so much.

The first railroad between Kansas and the East was secured by the labors of the citizens of Atchison. In 1854 a charter was obtained from the Missouri legislature for the Atchison and Saint Joseph railroad, but it was not pushed to completion until February, 1860. Hitherto all communication with the outside world had been by the Missouri river or overland, but now an all-rail route was open to the Atlantic seaboard. The next year Kansas, although not yet rested from the struggle within her own borders, sent 21,806 men to the Union army, her total voting population being only 21,835.

For nearly four years Atchison, with the rest of Kansas, waited till the war should be over. This finished, her sons went to work at home, and since then the city, in common with the state, has flourished greatly. The financial crisis of 1873, and the general depression of the subsequent years, of course affected its growth more or less, and the visitation of grasshoppers or locusts, which so severely tried this region, destroying two-thirds of the growing crop of Indian corn and reducing the settlers of sixteen or eighteen of the new counties to destitution, redounded to the loss of Atchison, as well as of every commercial mart in the state. It did not fully recover from the depression of business till 1879, a year which marks a new era in its business history. "The general revival of trade, lending courage to capital and stimulating all branches of commerce, has been demonstrated by an extraordinary activity in building, in manufactures, in the carrying traffic, in jobbing, and in every department of business. Nearly 700 houses were erected during the year, and at this time an overteeming population cry out for more." As a mark of growth of the railroad business in Atchison may be instanced the erection of an elegant and commodious union depot within the last year, at a cost of $120,000. It is the most costly structure ever built in the city and the largest depot in the state.

There is a very fine bridge across the Missouri here, of which Atchison is justly proud. It was constructed in 1874–'75 by the American Bridge Company, of Chicago, Major O. B. Green being chief engineer and Captain H. L. Marvin first assistant. "It is built of wrought iron, and rests upon stone piers; its length is 1,182 feet and the approaches aggregate 2,000 feet, 500 on the west and 1,500 feet on the east side. Its width is 19 feet 6 inches, and it has 5-feet sidewalks on each side. The bridge consists of a draw-span on the western side, swinging on a circular pier sunk to the bed-rock, and 3 fixed spans, the former 382 feet long, giving 160 feet clear water-way on either side; the fixed spans each 260 feet long. The bottom chord of the bridge is 10 feet above the high-water mark of 1844, that being the greatest rise of the Missouri on record. The foundations consist of 4 stone piers and 2 stone abutments, with a pneumatic iron pier on the west side. All of the piers and both of the abutments are sunk to bed-rock. They are all constructed of stone from the Cottonwood quarries in this state. The bridge is floored, so as to be used for highway as well as for railroad traffic."

ATCHISON IN 1880.

The following statistical accounts, collected by the Census Office, with the assistance of H. R. Bostwick, esq., city clerk, furnish an idea of the present condition of the city:

LOCATION.

Atchison lies on the right bank of the Missouri river, about 25 miles by land above Leavenworth, Kansas, and 20 miles by road southeast of Saint Joseph, at an elevation of 1,000 feet above the level of the sea, in latitude

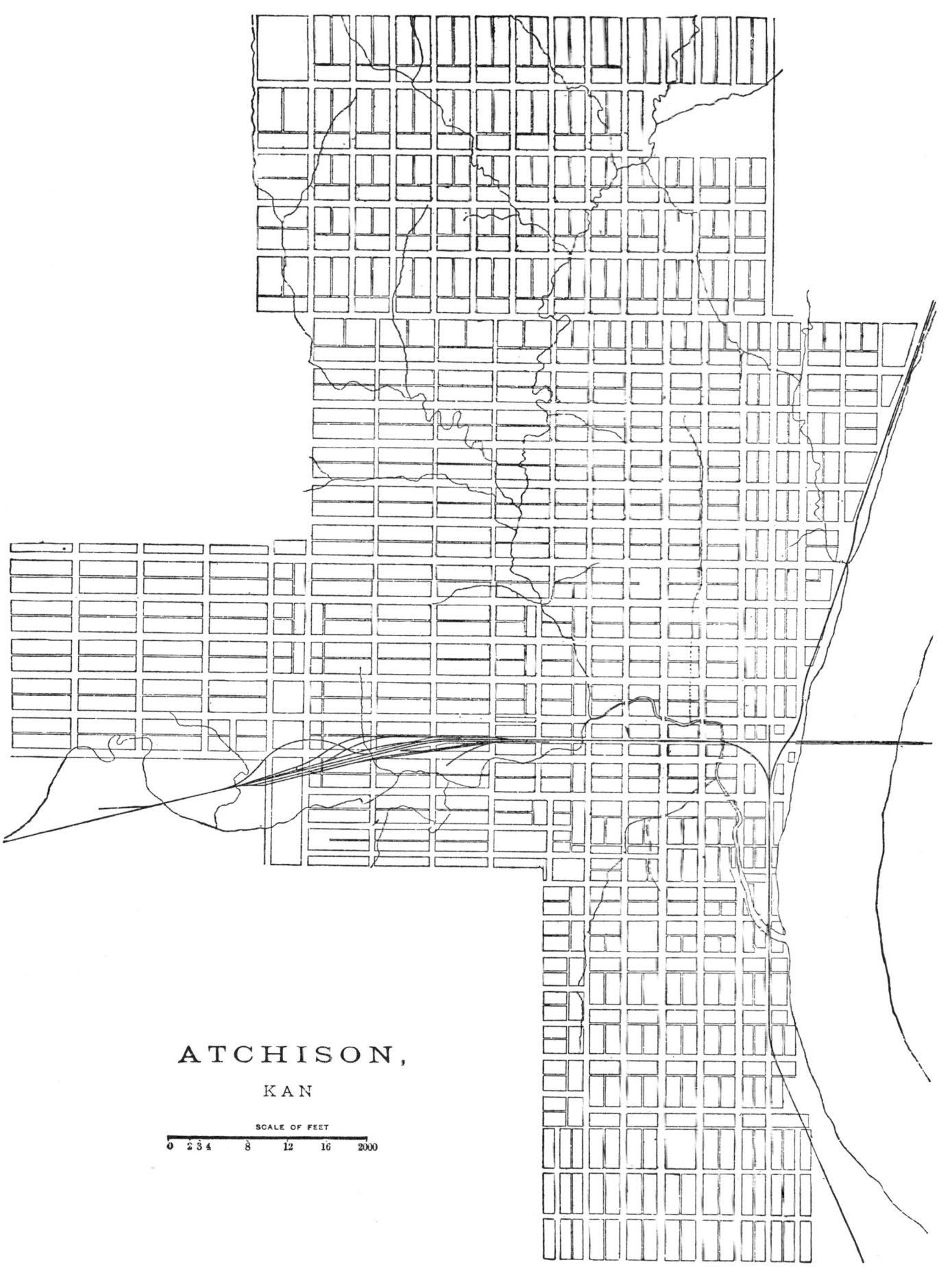

ATCHISON,

KAN

SCALE OF FEET

0 2 3 4   8   12   16   2000

39° 34' north, and longitude 95° 8' west from Greenwich. The Missouri river gives water communication with all points between Fort Benton, Montana, and Saint Louis, as well as with all points on the Mississippi and Ohio rivers. It has here a draft of water of 18 feet, a channel capacity of 200 feet, and a current of about 4 miles per hour

RAILROAD COMMUNICATIONS.

Atchison, like all the flourishing western cities, is a great railroad center. Its 6 railroads, with the points to which they give immediate communication, are as follows:

The Atchison, Topeka, and Santa Fé railroad runs from Atchison via Topeka and Denver to Santa Fé. This road at present terminates at San Marcial, but is shortly to be finished to Guaymas.

The Atchison and Nebraska division of the Burlington and Missouri River railroad runs to Lincoln, where it connects with the other division, intersecting all southeastern Nebraska.

The southwestern division of the Chicago, Rock Island, and Pacific railroad, which terminates at Atchison, gives nearly straight lines to Chicago and Milwaukee via Rock Island.

The Kansas City, Saint Joseph, and Council Bluffs railroad, to the points named, is connected with Atchison by a short branch at Winthrop junction.

The Missouri Pacific railroad runs from Saint Louis, through Atchison, to Logan, its present western terminus; it is shortly to be completed to Denver. The Texas line of this road runs to Galveston.

TRIBUTARY COUNTRY.

The country immediately tributary to Atchison is mainly comprised in Atchison county, of which the city is the capital. This county has an area of 424 square miles, is bounded on the east by the Missouri river, and is drained by two creeks. The soil is pleasantly diversified and very fertile. The streams are bordered with forest trees. Almost the sole occupation of its inhabitants is farming, the most important products being wheat, corn, oats, dairy products, hay, and potatoes. In this county, as in the whole region of which Atchison is the center, hogs are very extensively raised. Last year, of 1,264,499 head of swine over 6 months old owned in the 113 counties of Kansas, 140,801 were owned in Atchison and the four surrounding counties. The country just east of the city, in Missouri, is also an important hog-raising district. The grain trade is of the greatest importance to Atchison. Less than four years ago this trade was confined to the purchase of farmers' deliveries from the country within a circle of about 25 miles. To-day the city is the center of the grain trade of Kansas, to accommodate which 4 large elevators and 5 extensive and thoroughly equipped flouring-mills are taxed to their utmost.

TOPOGRAPHY.

Atchison is surrounded on all save the river side by a semicircle, or rather horseshoe, of hills. The business part of the city, near the river, is 38 feet above low water. Half a mile to the west the ground is 60 feet above low water. The White Clay creek, running through the town from west to east, has a valley with an average width of one-quarter of a mile, and this forms the division between north and south Atchison. The ground rises to the north and south of this to an elevation of 180 feet, each side, in three-fourths of a mile. The continuous effort of Atchison engineering has been to reduce the grades of the streets running north and south, and to raise the level and increase the width, originally inconsiderable, of the White Clay valley. This process never ceases, and has so far progressed that the streets are now of gentle ascent, and ample room is afforded for the constant growth of the business portion, on Commercial and Main streets, Kansas avenue, and the intersecting streets in the valley. White Clay creek is the great natural sewer of the city, carrying off the waste water and refuse into the Missouri. There are no ponds or collections of stagnant water anywhere in or about the city. The soil is a rich black loam, and the rock is principally blue limestone. Of the hills surrounding the city some are covered by the natural forest, others form the eastern boundary of the rolling prairie which stretches away to the great plains. Beyond the former the country for three or four miles is generally wooded and gently undulating, then opening out into rich prairie.

CLIMATE.

According to the Smithsonian publications the average mean summer temperature of Atchison is 74.86°; average mean winter temperature, 27.06°; highest recorded summer temperature, 101°; lowest recorded winter temperature, —14°; and mean annual temperature, 51.35°.

STREETS.

Total length of streets, 52.25 miles, 3 miles of which have been paved with broken stone at a cost of $1 85 per cubic yard. This kind of pavement here will last 8 years without repairs. The sidewalks are of wood, and many of the gutters are paved. Mr. Bostwick, in his report, says that there is no tree-planting along the sides of the streets, but Atchison is very fortunate in the possession of many natural forest trees. In Topeka, now a reasonably well shaded town, every tree has been planted; but in Atchison there are hundreds and thousands of oaks, the original trees or their descendants. Last year the street expenditures, including sidewalks, gutters, and bridges, was over $11,000. The city authorities prefer contract work on the streets, as they think it cheaper. A horse-roller is used. There are no horse-railroads or omnibus lines in the city, but 4 miles of track for a street-railway are now being laid.

WATER-WORKS.

The water-works are owned by a private corporation, and so far have cost $150,000. The supply is taken from the Missouri river, and is lifted, by pumping, 224 feet into a settling reservoir 50x145 feet at bottom, and 106x185 feet at surface, and 13 feet deep. When the river is frozen the water is clear enough to use without settling; but at other times it is allowed to settle from 8 to 12 hours, and is then drawn into distributing reservoirs adjoining. Distribution is by gravity, through 4,000 feet of 12-inch cast-iron mains and 8 miles of pipe from 4 to 12 inches in diameter. There are 54 fire-hydrants, and the city pays $6,000 annually for them. The average daily consumption is not stated, the operation of the works having only begun this year (1880).

GAS.

With the exception of the statement that the gas-works are not owned by the city, no information on this subject was furnished.

PUBLIC BUILDINGS.

The city owns and occupies for municipal purposes a city hall, which cost $5,000.

PUBLIC PARKS AND PLEASURE-GROUNDS.

There are no public parks or pleasure-grounds in the city.

PLACES OF AMUSEMENT.

There are 2 theaters: Corinthian hall, with a seating capacity of 600, and the Coliseum theater, with a seating capacity of 300. A license fee of $5 for each performance is paid to the city, the total annual receipts from this source being over $500. There are no concert- and beer-gardens.

DRAINAGE.

The city has no system of sewers as yet. It is now being divided into districts, preparatory to introducing a system for which the city engineer is preparing plans, but it is stated that nothing will be done before the early part of 1882.

CEMETERIES.

There are 3 cemeteries, all owned by private corporations, as follows:
Oak Hill Cemetery, area 8 acres, adjoining the city limits.
Mount Vernon Cemetery, area 20 acres, situated 2 miles from the city limits.
Saint Benedict Cemetery, area 5 acres, 1 mile from the city limits.
During the past year there were 86 interments in Mount Vernon, 62 in Oak Hill, and 43 in Saint Benedict; a total of 191. Graves are required to be 6 feet deep. In Mount Vernon, lots 10 by 20 feet sell for $25; in Oak Hill, lots 20 by 20 feet sell for from $25 to $50; and in Saint Benedict, lots 10 by 20 feet sell for $20. All of the above cemeteries are finely laid out and beautifully located, the grounds being rolling and well timbered with native trees, besides being planted with many ornamental trees and shrubs. The revenue last year from the sale of lots was: Mount Vernon, $855; Oak Hill, $425; and Saint Benedict, $103 50; making a total of $1,383 50.

MARKETS.

There is no market building proper in Atchison, but a public market stand is provided, where tables are placed on one side and teams stand on the other, with a shed roof over all, for the sale of garden products. The charges are, for basket-men 5 cents and for teams 10 cents per day. All persons, teams, etc., bringing vegetables to market are required to stand at the market-place during market hours. The net proceeds to the city from this source in 1880, after paying all expenses except the market-master's salary of $176, were $623 80. The market is open daily from 4 to 10 a. m. The annual sales of vegetables in the market amount to $22,000, being about 75 per cent. of the gross sales of vegetables in the city. There are no wholesale meat-markets; all meat- and fish-markets are retail, and occupy private buildings. The city ordinances provide that all country produce, except grain and meats, brought to the city shall not be sold except in the market place during market hours; but during the remainder of the day persons may dispose of them as they see proper.

SANITARY AUTHORITY—BOARD OF HEALTH.

The chief sanitary organization of Atchison is the board of health, consisting of the mayor and 1 councilman from each ward, 4 in all, annually appointed by the mayor and council. When there is no declared epidemic the expenses of the board are merely nominal; during an epidemic they may be increased to any amount authorized by the city council. The board exercises general supervision over the health of the city, has power to take all steps necessary to promote its cleanliness and salubrity, to abate all nuisances, to do what may be deemed advisable to prevent the introduction or spread of contagious diseases, and to establish hospitals. The ordinances provide that the city marshal shall attend the meetings of the board, and shall serve all orders and precepts on persons when directed so to do by the board. The board meets at the call of the mayor. None of the members are physicians and none of them have police powers. Inspections are made only as nuisances are reported. When nuisances are found to exist the marshal serves a notice to abate within 24 hours. The board takes cognizance of defective house-drainage, privy-vaults, cesspools, etc., only when they come under the head of nuisances, and the same is true of the conservation and removal of garbage and the removal of excrement. There are no regulations governing the burial of the dead.

INFECTIOUS DISEASES.

Small-pox patients are isolated in a pest-house owned by the city and situated near the city limits. Scarlet-fever patients are neither isolated nor quarantined at home. The board of education has full control of the city schools, and can close them at will in case of the breaking out of contagious diseases in them. Vaccination is not compulsory, nor is it done at the public expense.

REGISTRATION AND REPORTS.

There is no system of registration of births, diseases, and deaths. The board reports to the city council as often as the council requires it; these reports are not published. The board has power to employ one or more physicians, at the expense of the city, in case of the breaking out of an epidemic.

MUNICIPAL CLEANSING.

Street-cleaning.—The cleaning of the streets of the city is under charge of the street commissioner. The work is done by the city's own force, wholly by hand, and once a week. Private abutters must clean the adjacent gutters once a week and leave the dirt in piles for removal by the street-commissioner's force. The sweepings are hauled off and deposited on low lands.

Removal of garbage and ashes.—All garbage and ashes are removed by the householders and deposited on low lands. There are no city regulations on the subject. No nuisance or probable injury to health is reported to result from the improper treatment of garbage.

Dead animals.—The carcasses of all animals dying within the city limits are hauled away by the owner and buried, at no cost to the city.

Liquid household wastes; human excreta.—No liquid household waste runs into the street-gutters. Most of it goes into cesspools on the premises, which are deep, are not provided with overflows, receive the wastes from water-closets, and are not governed by regulations as to cleansing. The greater proportion of houses in the city rely on privy-vaults. Hotels have water-closets delivering into private sewers leading to the river, but nearly all the few other water-closets in the city empty into cesspools. Privy-vaults within 20 feet of any street, shop, or business house must be not less than 6 feet deep and water-tight. There are no regulations concerning the emptying of privy-vaults. The dry-earth system is little, if any, used. In answer to the question as to the contamination of well-water by the escape of the contents of cesspools and privy-vaults, Mr. Bostwick says: "Our city has but few wells, rain-water collected in cisterns being generally used for drinking and household use, especially outside the limit reached by the water-works."

Manufacturing wastes.—There are no regulations on this head, and no report was made as to practice.

POLICE.

The police force of Atchison is appointed by the mayor, subject to the confirmation of the city council, and is governed by the mayor. The chief executive officer is the city marshal, who has general supervision of the force, under the direction of the mayor, and receives a salary of $1,200 per year. The rest of the force consists of 10 officers, receiving $600 a year each. They wear a blue uniform, with regulation cap, etc., which they themselves provide, and are each equipped with a club, whistle, navy revolver, and dark lantern. They are on duty 12 hours at a time, and patrol about 3 miles of streets each. In 1880 there were about 780 arrests, the principal causes being "disturbing the peace, drunk and disorderly, visiting houses of ill-fame, carrying concealed weapons", etc. Most of the persons arrested were fined from $1 to $25, and if unable to pay were put to work on the streets. About 850 free meals were furnished during the year, at a cost of 10 cents for each meal. The force co-operates with the fire department merely to the extent of maintaining order and guarding property at fires. Special policemen are appointed by the mayor for the same service and with the same standing as the regular force. The only casualty during 1880 in the force was the shooting and killing of a policeman by a drunken negro. The annual cost of the department is about $7,000.

FIRE DEPARTMENT.

On January 1, 1880, the old volunteer fire department was superseded by the present combined paid and volunteer department, the change having been made with entire harmony. The chief of the fire department, who entered upon his duties at that time, says in his report for the year:

On assuming this * * * position * * * I was much embarrassed on account of the deficiency in apparatus to work with, a lack of a sufficient water-supply (for the first year at least), and the bad and unserviceable condition we found the hose in, and with an inconvenient way to transport them to fires. During this time no provisions were made for fire alarms; consequently too much time was often consumed in finding out the locality of the fire. Some of these embarrassments have in part been overcome, such as a sufficient supply of water, the purchase of new hose, hose-carriage, etc., but yet enough remain to prevent the organization of a good and efficient department, such as a city of the proportions and pretensions of Atchison demand.

The paid force of the present department consists of 1 chief and 1 assistant chief engineer, fireman, driver, pipeman, and night-watchman, with an annual pay-roll of $2,940. The apparatus consists of a second-class steam fire-engine, a two-horse hose-carriage, a two-wheel hand hose-cart, a two-horse hook-and-ladder truck, 6 fire-extinguishers, and 1,500 feet of serviceable hose.

SCHOOLS.

There are 5 public-school buildings in the city, and, during the first term of 1880, 858 boys and 985 girls, a total of 1,843, were enrolled as scholars. There are 29 teachers, receiving an average salary of about $54 per month. Saint Benedict's college, an institution conducted by the Benedictine fathers, has two commodious brick buildings. The number of students now in attendance is 95. The Atchison institute, claiming chiefly to fit its pupils for business and teaching, has between 200 and 300 students. Saint Scholastica's academy, under the care and management of the sisters of the Benedictine order, was completed in 1874 at a cost of $60,000. The school now has 113 students. A Catholic parochial school, also under the charge of the Benedictine sisters, has about 200 pupils.

LAWRENCE,
DOUGLAS COUNTY, KANSAS.

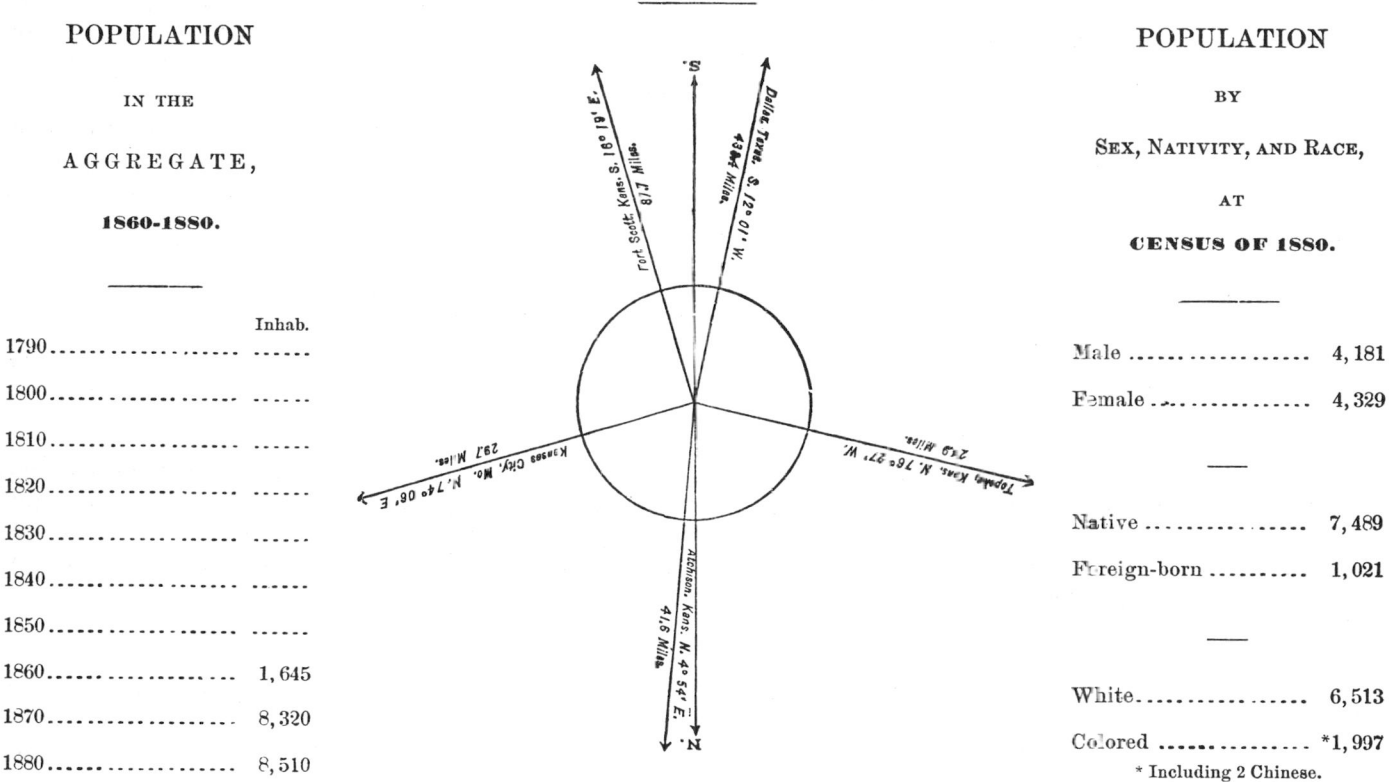

POPULATION
IN THE
AGGREGATE,
1860-1880.

	Inhab.
1790	......
1800	......
1810	......
1820	......
1830	......
1840	......
1850	......
1860	1,645
1870	8,320
1880	8,510

POPULATION
BY
SEX, NATIVITY, AND RACE,
AT
CENSUS OF 1880.

Male	4,181
Female	4,329
Native	7,489
Foreign-born	1,021
White	6,513
Colored	*1,997

* Including 2 Chinese.

Latitude: 38° 58′ North; Longitude: 95° 12′ (west from Greenwich); Altitude: 846 to 1,050 feet.

FINANCIAL CONDITION:

Total Valuation: $1,848,640; per capita: $217 00.   Net Indebtedness: $654,115; per capita: $76 86.   Tax per $100: $4 75.

HISTORICAL SKETCH.

In the years immediately following the Mexican war, settlers began to cross the Missouri and seek for homes along the eastern borders of what was then known as the vast wilderness of Nebraska. It soon became evident that the fertile lands in the southeastern corner of this region, now eastern Kansas, were to be the object of contention between the friends and the opponents of slavery. Both sides were terribly in earnest. In Massachusetts and Connecticut emigrants' aid societies were chartered in the spring of 1854, to assist emigrants to remove to Kansas, and to furnish them with weapons of defense. In May, Congress passed the Kansas-Nebraska bill, organizing the two territories, and expressly declaring the Missouri compromise to be inoperative in regard to them. The emigrants forwarded by the emigrants' aid societies entered the territory in very considerable numbers in the spring and summer. One of the companies sent out left Massachusetts on July 17, and, with a few other persons from states outside of New England who had joined it on the way, arrived on August 1 at the place where Lawrence now stands. Two weeks later a second company arrived, numbering 60 or 70 persons, which was soon followed by a third and a fourth party. At first the place was known by the name of New Boston, but on October 1 of this year (1854) the name Lawrence was adopted in honor of Amos A. Lawrence, of Boston, who afterward gave $10,000 to the town for educational purposes.

During the struggle for a free state which followed the Kansas-Nebraska bill, Lawrence took a very prominent part on the anti-slavery side, being the headquarters of John Brown, Lane, Robinson, and Conway, and other noted leaders. In common with nearly all the settlements in the state, it suffered severely in the turmoil of these years, being twice besieged and burnt. In spite of all its disasters the place flourished, and at the breaking out of the civil war was in a most prosperous condition.

Lawrence was checked in its growth by the absence of many of her citizens on the battle-field, but she was more unfortunate than the rest in being subject to the terrible calamity of sack and pillage.

On the morning of the 21st of August, 1863, the town was surprised by a party of Confederate raiders under Quantrell, who killed about 180 persons, among whom, it is said, there were a number of Union soldiers sick in hospital, and burnt some 75 dwellings and nearly as many other buildings owned as stores, workshops, etc., being nearly the entire business portion of the city. It is estimated that $2,000,000 worth of property was destroyed. Rebuilding began actively in the spring of 1864, and in 18 months the burnt portions were nearly all restored, and its growth for the next 6 years was steady and prosperous. It has received accessions to its population from all the northern states. The character of its population has remained substantially the same from its first settlement.

LAWRENCE IN 1880.

The following statistical accounts, which have been compiled by the Census Office, will give a clear idea of the present condition of Lawrence:

LOCATION.

Lawrence is situated in Douglas county, in the eastern part of Kansas, on the Kansas river, 32 miles south-southwest of Leavenworth and 25 miles east by south of Topeka, at an average height of 875 feet above the level of the sea. Its lowest point has an altitude of 846 and its highest of 1,050 feet. Steamboats have traversed the whole course of the Kansas river at high water, but its navigation is not of any practical value, being obstructed by sand-bars and frequent changes in the channel.

RAILROAD COMMUNICATIONS.

The Kansas division of the Union Pacific railroad runs through Lawrence on its way from Kansas City to Denver, and the Leavenworth branch of this road runs from Lawrence to Leavenworth. One branch of the Atchison, Topeka, and Santa Fé starts from Atchison and one from Kansas City, meeting at Topeka, the latter coming via Lawrence; from Topeka the road runs to Denver, to Santa Fé, and at present to San Marcial, but it is shortly to be put through to Guaymas. One branch of the Kansas City, Lawrence, and Southern railroad starts from Kansas City and one from Lawrence; they meet at Ottawa, and thence the road runs down through southeastern Kansas as far as Harper.

TRIBUTARY COUNTRY.

The character of Douglas county, of which Lawrence is the capital, may be taken to illustrate that of all the country immediately tributary to Lawrence. This county has an area of about 500 square miles. It is partly bounded on the north by the Kansas river and is intersected by the Wakarusa river. The surface is pleasantly diversified and the soil is highly productive. Limestone is abundant. Groves of timber grow along the streams, and large prairies are numerous. Cattle, grain, tobacco, wool, hay, and dairy products are the principal articles produced, and agriculture is almost the sole occupation of the inhabitants.

TOPOGRAPHY.

Geologically, Lawrence is situated at the extreme upper portion of the true coal measures (carboniferous formation). That portion of the city lying south of the Kansas river has at the surface an average of from $1\frac{1}{2}$ to 2 feet of alluvial soil, underlaid by compact clay from 10 to 25 feet in thickness; below the clay is limestone rock. The city is chiefly located in the broad valley of the Kansas river at its junction with the valley of the Wakarusa. Mount Oread, within the city limits, is the termination of the "high prairie" level between these two valleys. It is 175 feet above the general level of the city. The natural drainage is good. There are no ponds or marshes. The country for a radius of 5 miles is wooded along the two rivers, otherwise open. The soil is of the richest quality.

CLIMATE.

The highest recorded summer temperature is 108°; the highest in average years, 100°. The lowest recorded winter temperature, —26°; the lowest in average years, —10°. Local rains often follow the valleys of the two rivers, but fogs resting over them rarely extend over the city. The prevailing winds in summer are from the south-southwest; in winter, from the northwest. The former are often hot and dry, but bring from the gulf of Mexico the moisture which produces rain the latter are cold and uniformly dry.

STREETS.

Total length of streets, 58 miles, of which ½ mile is paved with broken stone, ¼ mile with wood, and the rest are unpaved. The broken-stone pavement cost 35 cents, and the wooden $2 75, per square yard. The broken stone was laid but a few years ago to replace worn-out wooden paving, and very little repairing has since been needed. The city clerk reports that the wooden pavement wears out faster than it can be repaired, and goes on to say that experience shows that its cost is very high and that it will last only about 6 years. The city paid $70,000 for ⅝ mile of wooden pavement laid in 1871 and 1872; the ¼ mile yet left is worn out and will soon be taken up; the rest has been replaced by macadam. The sidewalks on the main streets are nearly all of wood, stone, or brick, varying from 4 to 5½ feet in width. Gutters on the main streets are of stone, elsewhere of earth. There are no trees or grass plots in the center of the streets. Sidewalks are 1 foot and trees 9 feet from the fences, there being a single row of the latter on each side of the streets. Some of the work on the streets, such as macadamizing and the building of culverts, is let by contract, but most of the work is done by the day. The annual expenditures for all street work will average $7,000 per year. Neither steam stone-crusher nor roller is used. There are no horse-railroads in the city, nor are there any water-works.

GAS.

The gas-works are not owned by the city. The daily average production of gas is 15,000 feet and the charge per 1,000 feet is $3 25. The city pays $22 per year for each street-lamp, of which there are 116.

PUBLIC BUILDINGS.

The city owns a city hall, 2 jails, and another building, not now occupied, for municipal purposes. The total cost of municipal buildings belonging to the city is $35,000; of the city hall separately, $32,000. The county rents rooms from the city.

PUBLIC PARKS AND PLEASURE-GROUNDS.

The total area of the parks in the city is 73.68 acres, divided as follows: *New University grounds*, 41.54 acres; *Old University grounds*, 8.27 acres; *South Park*, 12.86 acres; *Central Park*, 6.88 acres; *Clinton Park*, 4.13 acres. They were obtained by dedication, not by purchase, and very little has been done as yet toward their development.

PLACES OF AMUSEMENT.

There are neither theaters nor concert- and beer-gardens in this city. There are 2 halls used for concerts, lectures, etc., viz: Liberty hall, with a seating capacity of 800, and Fraser's hall, with a seating capacity of 500.

DRAINAGE.

No report on this head was received.

CEMETERIES.

There are 4 cemeteries connected with the city, as follows:
Oak Hill, 40 acres, ½ mile east of the city limits, 2 miles from center.
Maple Grove, 20 acres, 1 mile north of city limits, ½ mile from center.
Roman Catholic, 10 acres, 1½ mile southeast of city limits, 4½ miles from center.
Old City Cemetery, 1 mile west of city limits, 3½ miles from center.
Oak Hill cemetery since 1865 has had about 2,000 interments; Maple Grove, since 1869, about 500. Nothing could be learned in regard to the others. There is no limit as to time of burial after death. Graves are dug not less than 5 feet in depth. Permits for burials in Oak Hill and Maple Grove cemeteries are obtained from the city clerk, and a full record is kept. The city clerk reports that the Roman Catholic cemetery is the only private one near the city; that it has been surveyed into lots and has been used for a number of years, but that there is no record either of burials or of ownership of lots, and, as far as he can learn, every Catholic does about as he pleases in selecting ground and making burials, without any regard to payment or surveyed lines. Oak Hill and Maple Grove are owned by the city. Lots are sold to individuals. There is no attempt in them at more than simple landscape gardening. All moneys received from the sale of lots and groves and from work done is kept in a separate fund for the use of cemeteries alone. This fund now amounts to $6,400. The Old City cemetery was the original burying ground of the settlement; many bodies have been removed from it to Oak Hill.

MARKETS.

There are no public or corporation markets in the city.

SANITARY AUTHORITY.

There is no board of health, and there has been none for ten years. The city clerk says that the city has not needed any. Nuisances are punishable like any other offense against the city ordinances, the delinquent being brought into the police court on complaint and there tried. There are no regulations concerning the burial of the dead. There have been no small-pox patients in the city since 1871; there were a few then and they were isolated. Scarlet fever has been rare. Vaccination is not compulsory, nor is it done at the public expense. There is no system of registration of births, diseases, or deaths. The city has had no epidemic since 1864. The mayor and marshal have the right to order nuisances to be abated whenever found.

MUNICIPAL CLEANSING.

Street-cleaning.—On the paved portions of the main streets the dirt is scraped up by private persons and removed by the city's own force. No other street-cleaning is attempted. This paved portion is cleaned once a week, and is said to be done very fairly. No separate account of the cost to the city is kept. The sweepings are used in filling up low places in back streets.

Removal of garbage and ashes.—The city clerk reports:

Our ordinances require all this matter to be taken care of by householders, under penalty of fine if they permit a nuisance to exist or create one. Offensive matter when removed is generally buried in a sand-bar on the banks of the river below the city. * * * No injury from the improper treatment of garbage has been made apparent here yet. The system is good, but fails somewhat in execution, by reason of laxity of individuals in entering complaint.

Dead animals.—When the owner of a dead animal is known he is compelled to remove the carcass outside the city limits within 24 hours; if he is not known, the carcass is buried at the city's expense in the sand-bar on the banks of the river below the city.

Liquid household wastes.—The city has no sewers, no water-works, and no water-closets, and the drainage is all surface drainage. No contamination of drinking-water from the escape of the contents of cesspools or privy-vaults has as yet been discovered.

Human excreta.—The city relies wholly on privy-vaults or water-tight boxes, the ordinances providing that every house must have a privy with a vault not less than 6 feet deep, or a portable water-tight box not less than $1\frac{1}{2}$ foot deep, or a patent earth-closet. Earth-closets are very rare. Privies must be emptied between 10 o'clock p. m. and 4 o'clock a. m. Night soil is buried near running water away from the city, most often on the sand-bars in the Kansas river.

Manufacturing wastes.—The city has very little solid or manufacturing waste.

POLICE.

The police force is appointed by the mayor and council. Its chief executive officer is the city marshal; his duties consist in enforcing the city ordinances, and his salary is $700 per year. There are 6 policemen, receiving $600 per year each. They were not uniformed previous to 1881. They serve 12 hours a day each, and have no regular beats. In 1880 there were about 350 arrests, the principal causes being drunkenness and disturbance of the peace. Free meals were given to station-house lodgers (of whose number no record was kept) at a cost of 14 cents per meal. Special policeman are appointed by the mayor as occasion may require, and during their time of service they become part of the regular force. For the year ending June 15, 1881, the cost of the force was about $4,700.

LEAVENWORTH,
LEAVENWORTH COUNTY, KANSAS.

POPULATION

IN THE

AGGREGATE,

1860-1880.

	Inhab.
1790	......
1800	......
1810	......
1820	......
1830	......
1840	......
1850	......
1860	7,429
1870	17,873
1880	16,546

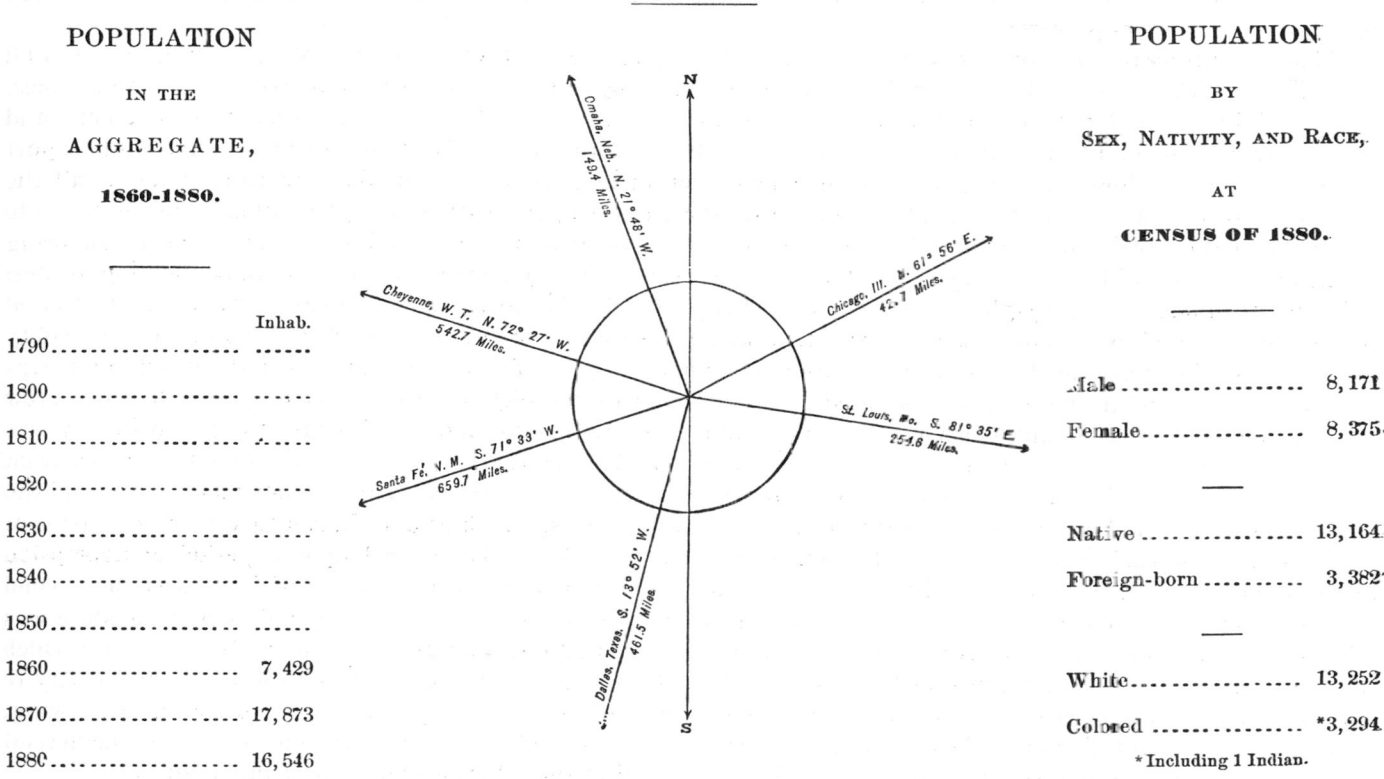

POPULATION

BY

SEX, NATIVITY, AND RACE,

AT

CENSUS OF 1880.

Male	8,171
Female	8,375
Native	13,164
Foreign-born	3,382
White	13,252
Colored	*3,294

* Including 1 Indian.

Latitude: 39° 15' North; Longitude: 94° 44' (west from Greenwich); Altitude: 890 feet.

FINANCIAL CONDITION:

Total Valuation: $2,995,838; per capita: $181 00.   Net Indebtedness: $396,573; per capita: $23 97.   Tax per $100: $2 95.

HISTORICAL SKETCH(a).

The city of Leavenworth takes its name from the United States fort and reservation located at this point, which was originally known as Cantonment Leavenworth, established by Colonel Leavenworth, of the Third United States Infantry, in May, 1827. The first settlement was made by a company of 32 persons from Weston, Missouri, who "claimed" the town site on June 9, 1854, thus making this the first town settlement in the territory. The town site was located on the "Delaware trust lands", as they were called, being a portion of the lands ceded to the United States by treaty with the Delaware tribe of Indians. It contained 320 acres, lying between the

---

a This sketch was abridged from a "History of Leavenworth" by W. S. Burke and J. L. Rock, published under the supervision of the Leavenworth board of trade in 1880.

military reservation of Fort Leavenworth on the north and Three-Mile creek on the south, and extending west from the Missouri. The association which had been formed expended about $4,500 during the summer of 1854 in cutting the timber and brush with which the site was thickly covered. A number of buildings were erected during the summer and fall, the first dwelling-house being completed about October 1. The first sale of lots took place on October 9 and 10, and netted $12,000. The credit of naming the streets after the Indian tribes should be given to Major E. A. Ogden, one of the first trustees of the town association, as he suggested to the company as eminently proper that the Indian names should be preserved, and that they were out of the usual style of street names and especially euphonious.

The next spring the town progressed very rapidly; a city soon sprang into being as if by magic. The first newspaper printed in the territory, the *Kansas Herald*, was started here on September 15, 1854. The next one in this town was the *Kansas Territorial Register*, established July 1, 1855. The *Herald* was a pro-slavery organ, but the *Register* was a free-state paper, and was very independent and outspoken. Like most of its successors in Leavenworth, the *Register* was shortlived, and was thrown into the Missouri river, type, presses, and all, by a mob on the night of December 22, 1855. A city charter was granted by the first territorial legislature in 1855, and by the close of the year the United States court and the territorial, city, and county organizations were in full operation.

The growth of Leavenworth was rapid. The beginning of the civil war found the place a city in fact as well as in name, with streets and walks graded and paved, with fine churches, fine school-houses, elegant residences, with solid blocks of large and substantial business houses, and with a levee crowded with river steamers, and presenting a scene of life and animation such as is to be witnessed now only at the docks of important seaport towns. The war, which then began to bring demoralization and hard times or absolute ruin to nearly all the "border" towns and cities of the country, had the opposite effect upon Leavenworth, and stimulated the place to a new and more wonderful growth. The horrors of war drove away people and business from the neighboring towns of Missouri, which were subject to alternate raids from roving bands of soldiers of both contending armies, being pillaged one day by "jayhawkers" and sacked the next by "bushwhackers". Leavenworth, being situated immediately adjoining the government reservation, and protected by the guns of the fort, gave shelter and safety to hundreds of people who had been driven from their homes by the fortunes of war. The thousands of troops who were at the fort in those days stimulated the retail trade of the city to a wonderful extent. The town grew rapidly, money was abundant, everybody was busy and prosperous; but much of this growth and prosperity was artificial, and when the war ended the bubble quickly burst. The number of troops at the fort was reduced from many thousands to a few hundreds, cutting off nearly half the trade upon which the retail shops had lived; and the restoration of law and order gave security to the neighboring towns, which at once began to repair the wastes of war and recover their lost business at Leavenworth's expense. The city entered upon a period of depression extending over several years. It had been built to a large extent upon an inflated and fictitious basis, far beyond the demands of the country surrounding it; indeed, at that time one-fifth of the entire population of the state was within the corporate limits of Leavenworth. The town had grown to be a great city in the midst of a state which was yet comparatively without business and without people, and it was now compelled to wait for the country to grow up to it. This caused improvements to stop and business to languish, and soon gave the once growing, rushing city the reputation of a "dead town". Hitherto the sole dependence of the place had been upon commercial interests, mere buying and selling; now the people were forced to turn their attention to manufactures.

During the ten years following the close of the war a large number of manufacturing enterprises were engaged in, small at first, but all meeting with success from the start, and growing rapidly in magnitude and profitableness. In 1868 a mining company, which had been organized in 1863, was reorganized, and after about a year's work, coal was found of excellent quality and in abundance. This gave a fresh impetus to the rapidly growing manufacturing industries of the place.

As a money center, and the base of supplies for the vast West and Southwest, the financial importance of Leavenworth during the war, and for many years thereafter, excelled that of most cities of five times its population. Up to 1873 there were eight institutions doing a banking business, but the panic of that year, and the subsequent depression, coupled with a season of drought and failure of crops in Kansas, shortly followed by the terrible grasshopper scourge on her prairie, was too much for most of them, and only three survived. For the past few years the city has been growing at a very steady rate in population, wealth, and business. The population traces its origin to nearly every state in the Union, but mainly to New England and the middle states. There is a considerable portion of foreign-born residents, mainly from Ireland and Germany. No radical changes have occurred in the character of the population.

LEAVENWORTH IN 1880.

The following statistical accounts of the present condition of Leavenworth have been compiled mainly from information furnished by the Hon. W. M. Fortescue, mayor of the city :

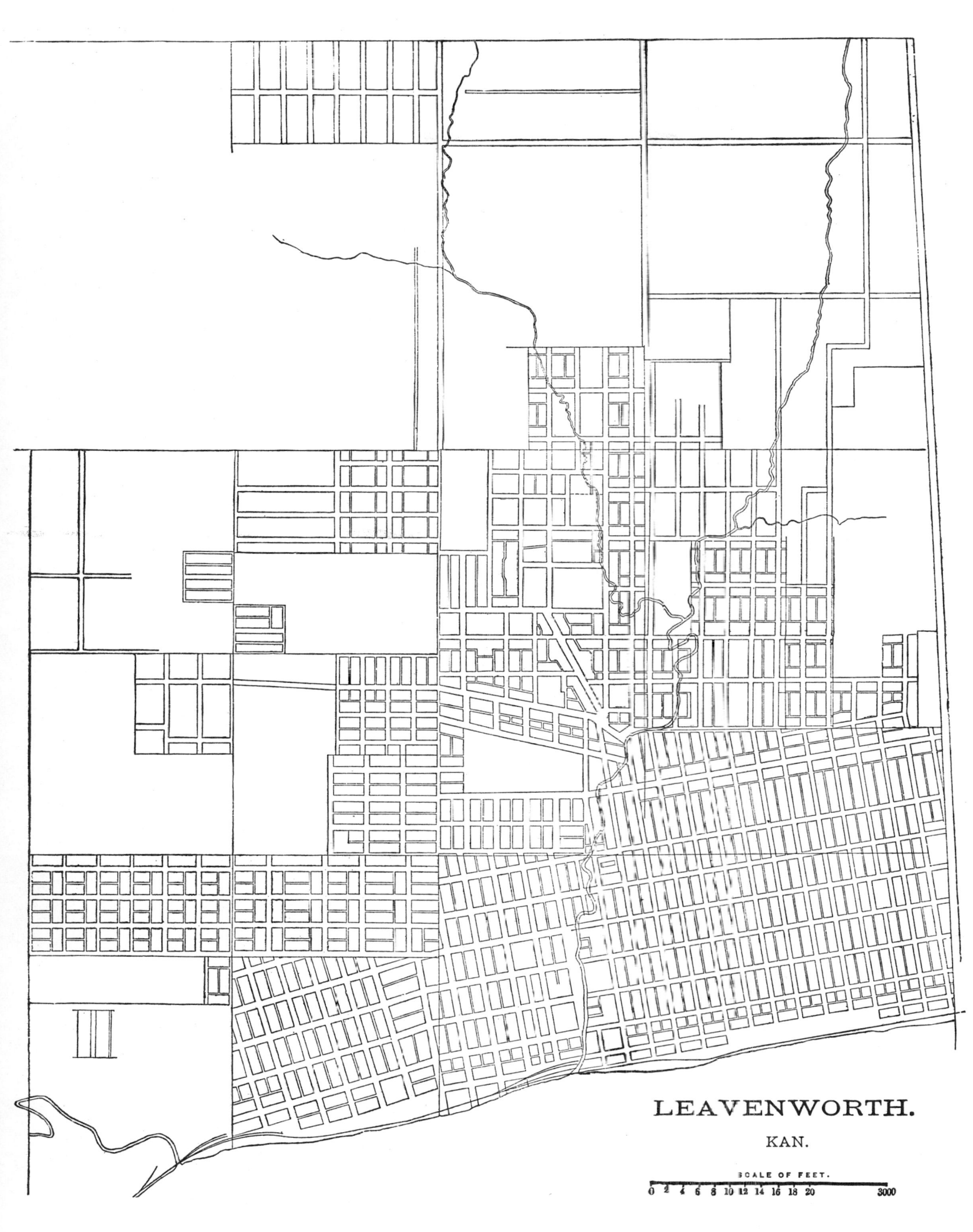

LEAVENWORTH.

KAN.

SCALE OF FEET.

0 2 4 6 8 10 12 14 16 18 20   3000

LOCATION.

Leavenworth is situated upon a high plateau on the west bank of the Missouri river, 2 miles south of fort Leavenworth, about 30 miles in a direct line south of Saint Joseph, and 40 miles east-northeast of Topeka, at an average of 890 feet above the level of the sea. The highest point has an altitude of 970 and the lowest of 729 feet. The Missouri is navigable for the larger classes of inland steamers nine months in the year. In front of the city there is a current of 3 miles per hour. There is a good levee, paved with round stone. The river affords water communication with all ports on the Missouri, Mississippi, and Ohio rivers. The "The History of Leavenworth" says:

The town site is rolling, and furnishes a perfect natural system of drainage; the inclinations are not sharp enough to cause any steep grades, or to interfere with the use or beauty of the streets, but sufficient to carry water from all points to the river. * * * It is surrounded on three sides by a range of hills, at an average distance of 2.5 miles. * * * Forming a crescent, which incloses the city upon the north, south, and west, [they] completely protect it from the force of the prevailing storms, which nearly always set from one of these three points. * * * There is nothing in the location or surroundings of the city to generate or aggravate disease—no swamps, no malarial places, no stagnant water, no imperfect drainage.

RAILROAD COMMUNICATIONS.

The southwestern division of the Chicago, Rock Island, and Pacific railroad runs from Leavenworth to Edgerton junction, where the line from Atchison joins it, and thence via Rock Island to Chicago and Milwaukee. The main line of the Missouri Pacific runs from Saint Louis via Kansas City through Leavenworth to Atchison, where it splits into lines going to Saint Joseph and Logan. At Sedalia, Missouri, this is crossed by the Texas line of the same road, running from Hannibal to Galveston, Texas. The Kansas City, Saint Joseph, and Council Bluffs railroad, connecting the places named in its title, passes through East Leavenworth, just across the river. The Leavenworth branch of the Kansas division of the Union Pacific connects with the main line at Leavenworth junction. The termini of this division are Kansas City and Denver. The Kansas Central railroad runs from Leavenworth to Garrison.

TRIBUTARY COUNTRY.

Leavenworth is surrounded on all sides by a very rich agricultural country, peculiarly adapted to growing wheat, rye, corn, and fruit, including apples, pears, peaches, apricots, plums, and all the varieties of small fruits grown in a temperate latitude.

Leavenworth county, of which the city is the capital and business center, has an area of about 450 square miles. It is bounded on the east by the Missouri river, and is intersected by Stranger creek. The surface is undulating, with a number of prairies, and well supplied with timber. Cattle, grain, and wool are the staple products. Tobacco, clothing, and carriages are the most important articles of manufacture. The principal occupation of the inhabitants of this, as of all the counties with which Leavenworth has trade, is agriculture, though the discovery of valuable deposits of coal at many points within a radius of 150 miles is rapidly developing manufacturing interests.

TOPOGRAPHY.

The soil of Leavenworth is what is commonly known as "black sandy loam", and is from 2 to 4 feet in depth. The subsoil is porous silicious marl. The underlying rock is sandy shale, and at the highest and lowest points limestone, all having a slight uniform dip toward the northwest. A workable vein of coal is found at a depth of 700 feet.

CLIMATE.

The highest recorded summer temperature is 110°; the highest in average years, 96°; the lowest recorded winter temperature, −21°; the mean summer temperature, 74.24°; the mean winter temperature, 28.69°. The prevailing winds are from the south and southwest. When they begin to blow they are mild and dry, but steadily increase in velocity and humidity until about the third day, in summer, thunder-storms occur. If the storm is extensive the maximum rainfall does not occur till the wind veers to the northwest. Occasionally the southeast wind will produce similar effects, but not in the same degree. The northerly winds are next in frequency, but are nearly always accompanied by lower temperature and less humidity. Easterly winds are always of moderate force and short duration, rarely bringing rain. Occasionally a protracted blow from the northeast in winter will bring rain or snow.

STREETS.

Total length of streets, 50 miles, of which 20 miles are paved with broken stone, and the rest are unpaved. The first of the paving with broken stone was done by contract during the war, and cost about $1 35 per yard; the rest was done at a later period by day work, and cost about 70 cents per yard. The cost of keeping it in good repair is said to be "about one-half of 1 per cent. of average cost per annum". The sidewalks are of brick and stone. Gutters are paved with stone blocks. About 80 per cent. of the streets have trees planted on both sides.

The work of construction and repair of streets is done by the day, under the supervision of the street commissioner, and costs the city about $6,000 per year. The experience of the city authorities indicates a decided preference for day work, for they think they procure better work at much less expense.

There are no horse-railroads.

WATER-WORKS.

A private company is preparing to construct water-works.

GAS.

The gas-works are not owned by the city. The daily average production of gas is 30,000 feet, and the charge per 1,000 feet is $3. The city pays $25 per year for each street-lamp, of which there are 60. The yearly income from water-rates is $22,000.

PUBLIC BUILDINGS.

There is a market-house, with accommodations in it for the city council and city officers and the fire department, which cost $30,000. The total cost of municipal buildings belonging to the city is given as $80,000.

PUBLIC PARKS AND PLEASURE-GROUNDS.

The following statement in regard to this subject was forwarded by Mayor Fortescue:

The absence of parks and pleasure-grounds maintained by the city of Leavenworth is accounted for by the fact that the city is joined on the north by the United States reservation at Fort Leavenworth, a magnificent tract of 6,000 acres, kept in a high state of improvement by the general government. It is provided with graded and paved public ways, with romantic drives, with smooth grass plots, and shady and cleanly kept grounds. It is a much finer, better, and far more extensive park and pleasure-ground than the municipality could afford to maintain, and being within 15 minutes' walk of the center of the city, it completely supplies the demand for public pleasure-grounds, and obviates the necessity of such a place maintained by the city. It reaches from the Missouri river to and beyond the high range of inner hills, 2½ miles to the west, and includes every variety of surface and scenery. With its natural beauties and its elegant improvements it is unsurpassed in beauty and attractions by any public grounds in the United States.

PLACES OF AMUSEMENT.

For theaters, the city has the New opera house, finished in the most modern and approved style, with a seating capacity of 900, and the Delaware Street opera-house, lately repaired, seating about 800. Shows pay a license varying from $5 to $15 per night. There are 7 concert-halls and lecture-rooms of various sizes. There are 5 concert- and beer-gardens, situated in the suburbs, visited mainly as Sunday resorts, having seats and accommodations for 4,000 persons. On Sundays, in pleasant weather, they are generally all crowded.

DRAINAGE.

An 18-inch pipe sewer extends the length of Fourth street, discharging into the Missouri river. The cost was assessed upon the abutting property on the basis of frontage. A new charter adopted by the city in 1880 authorizes the construction of sewers, drains, and other public works. No information is given of the extent or cost of sewers to the present time, except that catch-basins cost $125 each, and there are no manholes.

CEMETERIES.

There are 4 cemeteries connected with the city, viz:

Mount Muncil Cemetery, 2½ miles southeast from the city limits, containing 160 acres.

Mount Saint Mary Cemetery, 2½ miles south, 160 acres.

Greenwood Cemetery, 1½ mile southwest, 60 acres.

Mount Calvary Cemetery was opened June 1, 1869, and in no year since then have there been more than 88 nor less than 80 burial permits issued.

In Mount Muncil, from its opening, on July 21, 1866, to January 1, 1881, there were 3,181 interments; and in Greenwood, from 1867 to 1880, inclusive, there were 1,151. Mount Muncil cemetery is owned by a private corporation, and is handsomely laid out, being shaded by many natural trees and having gravel walks and drives; the price of lots ranges from $30 to $300; the ground is rolling and the landscape-gardening is good.

MARKETS.

Farmers' and hucksters' wagons occupy the sidewalk and half of the roadway of Shawnee, Fourth, and Fifth streets. A charge of 10 cents per week is made in order to pay the market-master. The market is open from 10 a. m. to 9 p. m. on Wednesdays and Saturdays. The rest of the trade of the city in provisions is carried on in private shops.

SANITARY AUTHORITY—BOARD OF HEALTH.

The chief health organization of Leavenworth is the board of health, an independent body, with 4 members, all of whom are physicians, acting with the city physician. They receive no compensation except during epidemics. The board may increase its power during epidemics to "what becomes necessary", and in the absence of epidemics it "has full power over the city". None of the members have police powers. Inspections are regularly made, and results reported to the mayor and council. If nuisances are not abated upon order so to do, the police authorities proceed to abate, and the delinquent is punished by fine or imprisonment. The board is appointed by the mayor, and is under the direction of the mayor and city council. It meets at the call of the chairman. Defective house-drainage, privy-vaults, cesspools, sources of drinking-water, sewerage, street-cleaning, etc., are reported to the mayor and council, and the street commissioner is ordered to rectify the same. The board exercises no control over the conservation and removal of garbage. There are no regulations concerning the burial of the dead, the pollution of streams and harbors, or the removal of excrement. The last two are under the control of the street commissioner. Small-pox patients are sent to the public pest-house, situated 3 miles from the city. Scarlet-fever patients are isolated at home. Vaccination is not compulsory, and is done at the public expense only to the poor. The board reports to the mayor and council when necessary.

MUNICIPAL CLEANSING.

Street-cleaning.—Streets are cleaned by the city's force by hand, under the direction of the street commissioner, twice a week, and oftener when necessary. It is reported to be very well done. The annual cost is about $3,500. Sweepings are deposited in the outskirts of the city. The place of deposit is the weak point in the system, as the results from the exposure of the sweepings to the weather are more or less deleterious to the health of the inhabitants.

Removal of garbage and ashes.—Garbage and ashes are removed by the city's own force to the outskirts of the city, the annual cost being about $1,000, and, as in the case of street-sweepings, it is probable that injury to health arises from the place of final deposit. As to this system the report says: "It can be much improved by adopting systems executed in the larger eastern cities. All methods are defective in this vicinity, but are greatly improved of late years."

Dead animals.—Upon notification the proper persons at once remove dead animals and render them for grease. This service costs the city nothing, and is very good.

Liquid household wastes.—Nearly all the liquid household waste of the city is delivered into the public sewers. What dry wells or cesspools are used are nominally tight; they are all cleaned out at night.

Human excreta.—The dry-earth system is very little used. Night-soil is carried to the outskirts of the city and deposited near creeks.

Manufacturing wastes.—Manufacturing wastes run into the Missouri river.

POLICE.

The police force is appointed by the mayor. The chief executive officer is the city marshal, whose salary is $1,000 per year. He is under the orders of the mayor, and has general supervision of the department. The rest of the force consists of a deputy marshal, receiving $65 per month; a jailor, a guard, 2 specials, and 8 regular policemen, receiving $50 per month each. They wear metropolitan uniforms, which are furnished by the city, and carry revolvers and clubs. They serve 12 hours per day each, and patrol the whole city. In 1880 there were 1,442 arrests. The station-house lodgers averaged 2 per night, against 3 per night in 1879. Free meals were given almost daily during the winter, at a cost of 8¼ cents per meal. Whenever necessary the members of the force are compelled to co-operate with the fire and health departments; they are instructed to report to the latter "at once any disease in their respective wards". Special policemen are appointed by the mayor for enforcing the collection of the dog-tax and impounding animals. In 1880 the only casualty in the force was a death caused by being thrown from a wagon. The cost of the force for the year was nearly $11,000. There are between 15 and 20 special policemen besides those just mentioned, who act as night watchmen for wholesale and manufacturing firms, and who serve without pay from the city. The street commissioner and other city officers are made special policemen, and it is found that it greatly increases their ability to carry out their instructions, as their word is regarded as law.

TOPEKA,

SHAWNEE COUNTY, KANSAS.

POPULATION

IN THE

AGGREGATE,

1860-1880.

	Inhab.
1790	
1800	
1810	
1820	
1830	
1840	
1850	
1860	759
1870	5,790
1880	15,452

POPULATION

BY

SEX. NATIVITY, AND RACE,

AT

CENSUS OF 1880.

Male	8,140
Female	7,312
Native	13,590
Foreign-born	1,862
White	11,799
Colored	*3,653

* Including 5 Chinese.

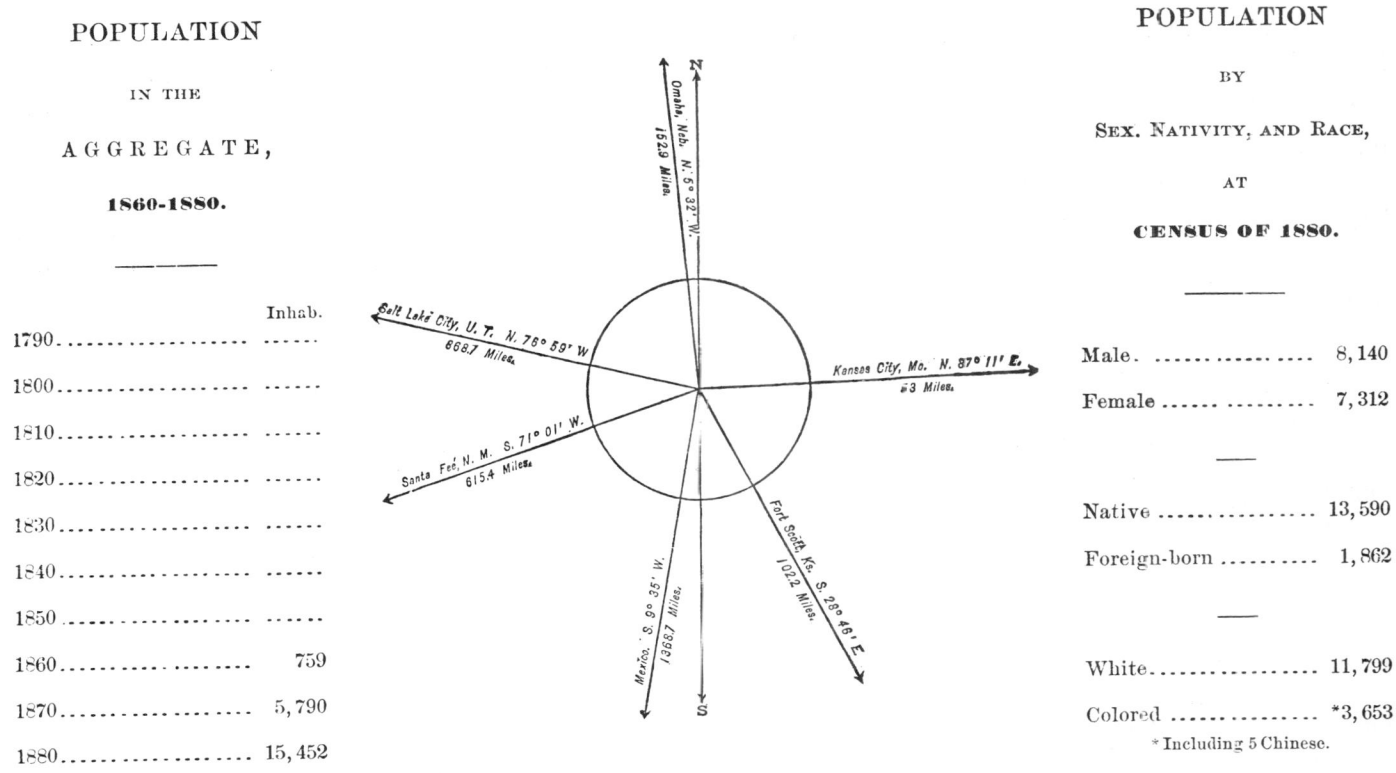

Latitude: 39° 3' North; Longitude: 95° 39' (west from Greenwich); Altitude: 904 feet.

FINANCIAL CONDITION:

Total Valuation: $2,341,480; per capita: $152 00.   Net Indebtedness: $333,249; per capita: $21 57.   Tax per $100: $4 36.

TOPEKA IN 1880.

The following statistical accounts, collected by the Census Office, indicate the present condition of Topeka:

LOCATION, ETC.

Topeka, the capital of the state of Kansas, is situated on the Kansas river, about 70 miles above its confluence with the Missouri river, 68 miles west of the Missouri state line, in latitude 39° 3' north, and longitude 95° 39' west from Greenwich. The observation station of the Smithsonian Institution at this point is 904 feet above sea-level. The river on which the city lies has been traversed nearly its whole course by steamboats during the high stage of water, but its navigation has very little, if any, practical value. The site of the city is upon high ground, commanding a fine view of some of the most charming prairie-landscape scenery of the West.

RAILROADS.

The Kansas division of the Union Pacific railroad, from Kansas City to Denver, and the Atchison, Topeka, and Santa Fé railroad, now completed from Kansas City to San Marcial, New Mexico, intersect here.

PLACES OF AMUSEMENT.

There is one opera-house, with a seating capacity of 600, and one temporary hall used for theatrical exhibitions, lectures, etc., with the same seating capacity. The theaters pay a license to the city of $10 per night each. In addition there are four halls, used for various purposes.

SANITARY AUTHORITY.

There is no regular board of health, the sanitary needs of the city being cared for by the committee on health, consisting of 3 members, of the city council. The authority to expend money, either in absence or presence of epidemics, rests entirely with the council, and the members of the committee receive no pay for this service. In absence of epidemics the power of the committee is confined to looking after the general cleanliness of the city, while during epidemics it is governed by orders coming from the mayor and council. All matters pertaining to the public health are referred to the committee, and it reports back to the council such action as it may deem best to be taken. Though the ordinances provide for regular inspections during the summer months, it is reported that inspections are made only when nuisances are reported. When a nuisance is found to exist the person responsible for the same is ordered to abate it, and if this is not done, then the council directs the committee to do the work, assessing the cost upon the property. The conservation and removal of garbage are controlled by ordinances. There are no regulations concerning the burial of the dead. Small-pox patients are removed to a separate building on the poor-farm, outside of the city. Scarlet-fever patients are quarantined at home. The record of deaths is kept by the superintendent of the cemetery.

MUNICIPAL CLEANSING.

Street-cleaning.—The streets are cleaned by the city with its own force, and wholly by hand. The work is done as often as the street commissioner deems necessary, and is as efficient as circumstances will permit. The sweepings are deposited outside the city limits.

Removal of garbage and ashes.—All garbage and ashes are removed by the householders. They are required to be kept in covered vessels, and removed at least twice a week in summer and when directed at other times, to some place designated by the city council. The garbage must not be thrown out in the streets or alleys. It is stated that nuisance and probable injury to health sometimes result when the ordinances governing the system are not strictly enforced.

Dead animals.—These are removed by the city and buried outside its limits, under a contract with the owner of the ground. The annual cost of this service is from $75 to $100, and from 75 to 100 dead animals are annually removed.

Liquid household wastes.—These are run into either street-gutters, sewers, or cesspools, probably one-half going into the former, which are not artificially flushed. The cesspools are nominally water-tight, receive the wastes from water-closets, and are cleaned out regularly. It is stated that in some localities drinking-water may be affected by the escape of the contents of vaults and cesspools, but no particulars were cited. The city is at present constructing some sewers.

Human excreta.—The water-closets in the city deliver half into the sewers and half into cesspools. The construction and emptying of vaults are regulated by ordinances. The night-soil is removed during certain hours of the night, in close-covered wagons, outside the city limits, and is allowed to be used for manuring land.

Manufacturing wastes.—Solid manufacturing wastes are sold to farmers, and liquids pass into cesspools.

POLICE.

The police force of Topeka is appointed by the mayor, subject to the approval of the city council, and is governed by the mayor. The chief of police, salary $1,200 per annum, is the executive officer, and has direct supervision of the department. The remainder of the force consists of 9 patrolmen at $625 a year each. The uniform is of navy-blue—coat, pantaloons, and vest—with a regulation hat, and each man furnishes his own, the city allowing $25 to each man for this purpose. The patrolmen are furnished with regular police equipments. The hours of duty are from 6 a. m. to 6 p. m. During the past year the number of arrests was between 700 and 800; the principal causes being drunkenness, disturbing the peace, larceny, and violation of city ordinances. They were finally disposed of by either fines or imprisonment. From $2,500 to $4,500 was reported to the police as lost or stolen during the year, and of this about one-half was recovered and returned to the owners. The force is required to keep order at fires and to serve health orders. In case of necessity special policemen are appointed by the mayor to serve for short periods, and perform the same duties as the regular force. During the past year the cost of the police force was about $7,000

COLORADO.

DENVER,

ARAPAHOE COUNTY, COLORADO.

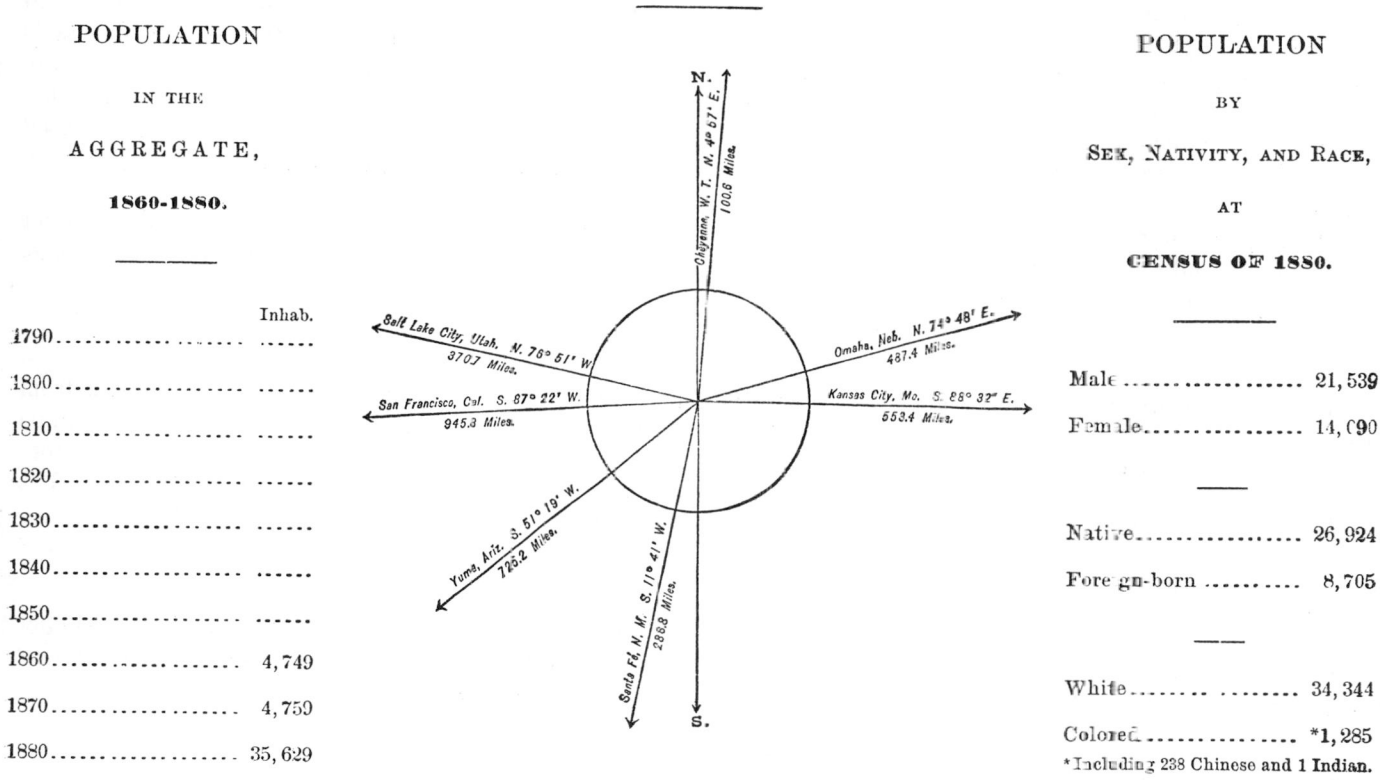

<table>
<tr><td colspan="2">POPULATION
IN THE
AGGREGATE,
1860-1880.</td></tr>
<tr><td></td><td>Inhab.</td></tr>
<tr><td>1790</td><td></td></tr>
<tr><td>1800</td><td></td></tr>
<tr><td>1810</td><td></td></tr>
<tr><td>1820</td><td></td></tr>
<tr><td>1830</td><td></td></tr>
<tr><td>1840</td><td></td></tr>
<tr><td>1850</td><td></td></tr>
<tr><td>1860</td><td>4,749</td></tr>
<tr><td>1870</td><td>4,759</td></tr>
<tr><td>1880</td><td>35,629</td></tr>
</table>

POPULATION BY SEX, NATIVITY, AND RACE, AT CENSUS OF 1880.

Male	21,539
Female	14,090
Native	26,924
Foreign-born	8,705
White	34,344
Colored	*1,285

*Including 238 Chinese and 1 Indian.

Latitude: 39° 45' North; Longitude: 105° (west from Greenwich); Altitude: 5,250 feet.

FINANCIAL CONDITION:

Total Valuation: $16,194,091; per capita: $455 00.   Net Indebtedness: $20,000; per capita: $0 56.   Tax per $100: $3 75.

DENVER IN 1880.

The following statistical accounts, collected by the Census Office, indicate in part the present condition of Denver.

LOCATION

Denver, the commercial center of Colorado, and its most populous city, lies 15 miles east of the base of the Rocky mountains, on the South Platte river, in latitude 39° 45' north, and longitude 105° west from Greenwich.

The city occupies a series of plateaus, rising, as they recede from the river, by gentle ascents, the altitudes above sea-level varying from 5,250 to 5,375 feet. The river on which the city is situated is not navigable. Denver was first settled in 1858, and during the past decade its growth has been very rapid.

RAILROAD COMMUNICATIONS.

The following railroad lines touch this point:

The Colorado division of the Union Pacific railroad to Cheyenne, Wyoming territory, with branches to Central City and Georgetown, Colorado, and the Kansas division of the same road from Denver to Kansas City, Missouri.

The Denver and Rio Grande railroad to Espanola, New Mexico, with branches to Leadville and Durango, Colorado.

The Denver, South Park, and Pacific railroad to Leadville, Colorado.

CLIMATE.

The temperature tables of the Smithsonian Institution give for Denver a mean annual temperature of 48.13°; the warmest month being July, with a mean of 72.86°, and the coldest, January, with a mean of 26.57°.

STREETS.

There are 200 miles of streets in the city, none of which are paved. The sidewalks are of wood, cement, and stone, while the gutters are of cobble-stones or else the natural soil. Tree-planting along the sides of streets is almost universal, and is done entirely by the owners of the abutting property. The trees, to a large extent, are set at the outer edge of the sidewalks. The annual cost for construction and repair of streets is $20,000, and day work is entirely used, the city hiring, at so much a day, what teams and wagons may be necessary. It is stated that the city gave up owning teams about four years ago, and since then no disposition has been shown to return to the old plan.

There are 8 miles of horse-railroads, with 20 cars and 50 horses, furnishing employment to 25 men. The number of passengers carried annually was not stated. The rate of fare is 5 cents. There are no regular omnibus lines, but 7 vehicles carry passengers for 50 cents each to any part of the city.

WATER-WORKS.

The water-works are owned by a private corporation, and their first cost was $600,000. Water is taken from the South Platte river and pumped directly into the mains on the Holly system. The pressure on the pumps varies from 50 pounds for domestic purposes to 135 pounds for fire. The amount pumped per diem varies from 1,250,000 to 4,000,000 gallons, the consumption being 75 gallons per day for each head of the population. The annual cost of maintenance and repairs is $25,000. The yearly income from water-rates was not given.

GAS.

The gas-works are not owned by the city. The charge per 1,000 feet is $3. The city has been paying $40 per annum for each street lamp, 343 in number, but has now made a contract with an electric-light company, under which the whole area within the corporate limits will be lighted by electric light.

PUBLIC BUILDINGS.

The only municipal buildings owned by the city are 6 fire-engine houses, costing $25,000. A city hall and jail, to cost $100,000, is to be erected shortly.

PUBLIC PARKS AND PLEASURE-GROUNDS.

There are 2 parks in Denver, with an area of 4 acres each. The land was given to the city, and so far nothing seems to have been done toward improving them. The parks are controlled by the city council.

PLACES OF AMUSEMENT.

There are 2 theaters in the city, one seating 300 and the other 500, and 2 halls that are occasionally used for theatrical performances, concerts, dances, etc. The theaters pay a license to the city amounting to $100 annually. There are also 4 beer-gardens, with a seating capacity of 2,000, that are tolerably well patronized in summer.

CEMETERIES.

There are 4 cemeteries, all situated about 2½ miles from the center of the city, viz:

The *City Cemetery*, area 120 acres.

The *Hebrew* and *Catholic Cemeteries*, each 20 acres.

The *Riverside Cemetery*, size not given.

The *Masonic Cemetery*, area 40 acres, situated 1½ mile from the center of the city, has been abandoned, and is now no longer used for interments.

It is estimated that the total number of interments in all the cemeteries is about 5,000, but it is stated that it is impracticable to obtain the number at different periods. There are no ordinances regulating interments. Riverside cemetery has been improved and tastefully laid out. It is owned by a private corporation, and nine-tenths of the interments are now made here.

SANITARY AUTHORITY—BOARD OF HEALTH.

The chief sanitary organization of Denver is the board of health, composed of the mayor, 3 aldermen, and the city physician, with 3 citizens appointed by the common council, and the city clerk, *ex officio* clerk of the board. At present 3 members are physicians. In ordinary times the annual expenses are $1,500 for street-cleaning, sprinkling, and general sanitary measures. No provision has been made for the increase of expenses during epidemics. The authority of the board is almost unlimited in matters pertaining to health in absence of epidemics, while during epidemics its authority is unlimited. The city physician (salary $1,200 per annum) acts as the executive officer, and has police powers on all matters concerning health. The board has regular monthly meetings and transacts its business as a deliberative body. Inspections are made regularly in all parts of the city. When a nuisance is reported a record is made and the proper officer is sent to examine and abate. Defective house-drainage, privy-vaults, cesspools, and sources of drinking-water are constantly inspected, and corrected when required. The board has entire control over the conservation and removal of garbage.

INFECTIOUS DISEASES.

There have been no cases of small-pox since the destruction of the pest-house, and nothing was said respecting the treatment of possible cases. Scarlet-fever patients are generally quarantined at home, and a flag is displayed. The board takes cognizance of the breaking out of contagious diseases in either public or private schools "to such extent as it may deem proper". Vaccination is compulsory, but it is not done at the public expense.

REPORTS.

Physicians are required to report monthly to the health officer (city physician) all cases of births and deaths, giving in the latter case the cause and when and where contracted. The board makes no regular reports.

MUNICIPAL CLEANSING.

Street-cleaning.—The streets are cleaned at the expense of the city, the teams being hired, and the manual work being done by prisoners. No sweeping-machines are used. The work is done fairly well, at an annual cost of $3,000, and the sweepings are deposited 1 mile outside the city.

Removal of garbage and ashes.—All garbage is removed by the city, under contract. While awaiting removal it is required to be kept in barrels, and it is not allowed to keep ashes in the same vessel. It is finally disposed of by being taken outside the city and fed to swine. The annual cost to the city for this service is $2,000. Ashes are removed by the householders, and are finally deposited in the bed of the creek. It costs each householder about $2 a year for this work. It is reported that no complaints have been made concerning the keeping, handling, or removal of garbage.

Dead animals.—The carcasses of all animals dying within the city are removed under contract and buried. The cost of the service was not stated; the number of dead animals removed annually aggregating 1,000.

Liquid household wastes; human excreta.—There being no public sewers, the liquid wastes from houses pass into cesspools or privy-vaults. The cesspools are nominally water-tight, are not provided with overflows, receive the wastes from water-closets, and are cleaned out as often as required, under the direction of the scavenger or police. One-fifth of the houses have water-closets, all delivering into cesspools, and the remainder depend on privy-vaults. All the vaults are required by ordinance to be water-tight, and they are emptied at night in close-covered carts. The ultimate disposal of the night-soil is not stated, but none of it is allowed to be used for manuring land within the gathering-ground of the public water-supply.

MANUFACTURES.

The following is a summary of the statistics of the manufactures of Denver for 1880, being taken from tables prepared for the Tenth Census by William Odenheimer, special agent:

Mechanical and manufacturing industries.	No. of establishments.	Capital.	Males above 16 years.	Females above 15 years.	Children and youths.	Total amount paid in wages during the year.	Value of materials.	Value of products.
All industries..	259	$2,301,850	2,550	264	130	$1,574,438	$5,715,215	$9,367,749
Blacksmithing..	14	31,400	66	....	5	37,400	31,600	98,900
Boots and shoes, including custom work and repairing	13	8,700	45	....	2	22,178	23,200	66,725
Bread and other bakery products	16	97,200	100	6	11	82,800	355,900	574,552
Brick and tile..	24	104,800	441	....	24	118,710	92,808	286,028
Carpentering	26	80,800	227	....	1	210,220	546,600	964,600
Carriages and wagons	9	261,000	123	....	2	102,000	194,000	435,000
Clothing, men's..	6	3,350	5	16	....	13,225	27,350	52,350
Clothing, women's..	3	18,300	....	130	5	60,200	92,150	176,500
Confectionery	6	7,900	23	1	4	17,250	20,700	49,550
Flouring- and grist-mill products	7	162,000	85	....	....	44,486	926,112	1,124,442
Foundery and machine-shop products	10	176,500	249	....	10	157,420	426,130	771,522
Furniture	7	68,400	42	3	2	33,300	43,000	138,850
Hairwork	3	3,300	....	10	....	4,125	6,600	15,200
Leather, curried..	3	16,700	13	1	....	8,500	53,250	90,550
Leather, tanned	3	16,700	13	1	....	9,000	38,300	55,800
Liquors, malt..	6	281,500	70	....	....	22,065	119,470	217,710
Lock- and gun-smithing	3	2,600	11	....	....	3,700	2,200	10,500
Marble and stone work..	5	19,500	62	....	....	23,600	21,750	61,500
Mineral and soda waters	3	6,100	9	....	....	6,500	14,750	32,675
Printing and publishing	4	181,000	156	12	19	135,050	95,300	305,500
Saddlery and harness	9	91,250	61	2	12	47,050	94,600	207,350
Slaughtering and meat-packing, not including retail butchering.....	4	49,000	35	....	5	15,920	536,920	590,945
Tinware, copperware, and sheet-iron ware.............	12	25,250	47	....	10	26,650	60,900	128,100
Tobacco, cigars and cigarettes.............	9	14,150	23	3	....	16,578	33,500	77,025
Vinegar	3	13,000	10	....	3	4,300	13,000	24,500
Watch and clock repairing	10	25,500	13	....	1	11,130	18,800	50,880
All other industries (a)	41	535,900	621	79	14	331,011	1,826,325	2,760,495

a Embracing awnings and tents; baking and yeast powders; brass castings; brooms and brushes; coffee and spices, roasted and ground; cutlery and edge tools; drugs and chemicals; dyeing and cleaning; flavoring extracts; fruits and vegetables, canned and preserved; furs, dressed; gloves and mittens; iron and steel; iron work, architectural and ornamental; jewelry and instrument cases; leather, dressed skins; lithographing; looking-glass and picture frames; lumber, planed; masonry, brick and stone; mattresses and spring beds; patent medicines and compounds; pickles, preserves, and sauces; plumbing and gasfitting; roofing and roofing materials; sash, doors, and blinds; soap and candles; stencils and brands; stereotyping and electrotyping; trunks and valises; upholstering; wheelwrighting; and whips.

From the foregoing table it appears that the average capital of all establishments is $8,837 45; that the average wages of all hands employed is $534 79 per annum; and that the average outlay in wages in materials, and in interest (at 6 per cent.) on capital employed is $28,678 62.

LEADVILLE,

LAKE COUNTY, COLORADO.

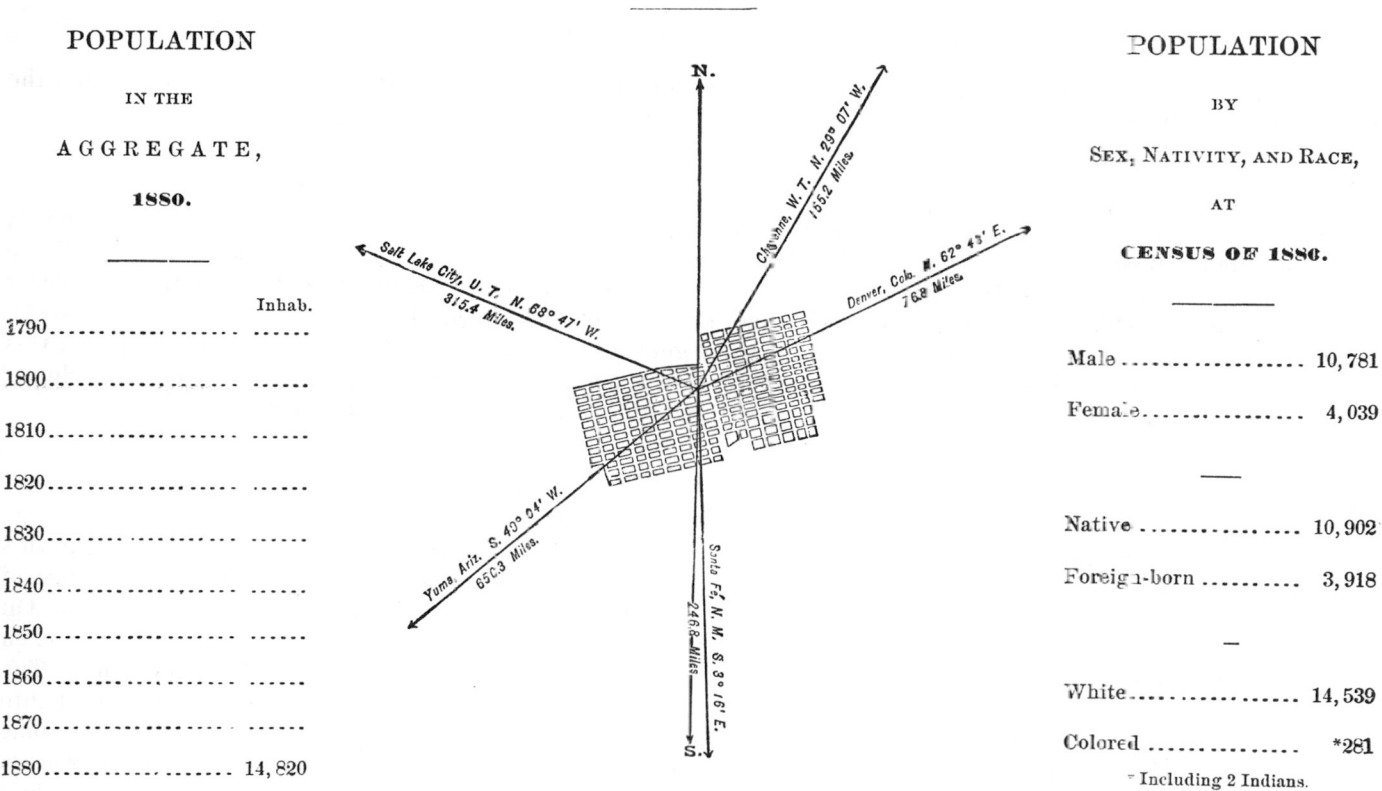

POPULATION

BY

SEX, NATIVITY, AND RACE,

AT

CENSUS OF 1880.

Male	10,781
Female	4,039
Native	10,902
Foreign-born	3,918
White	14,539
Colored	*281

* Including 2 Indians.

Latitude: 39° 15′ North; Longitude: 106° 17′ (west from Greenwich); Altitude: 9,950 to 10,300 feet.

FINANCIAL CONDITION:

Total Valuation: $2,433,327; per capita: $164 00.   Net Indebtedness: $112,000; per capita: $7 56.   Tax per $100: $5 97.

HISTORICAL SKETCH.

The first white settlers came into California gulch at the time of the Pike's Peak gold excitement in 1859. A small town named "Oro" quickly grew up, and in 1860 for a short time the population numbered nearly 5,000. As the gulch was gradually worked out this number was reduced to a few hundred. In 1876 the carbonate veins were discovered, and the region again attracted the attention of the mining world. In the next year miners began to come into the place in large numbers, and the first reduction works were built. Mines were quickly developed and opened, and their extensive operation rapidly increased. In the summer of 1880 40 furnaces were in blast, 36 of which have kept in constant operation; also 3 stamp-mills for treating low-grade ores. Most of the houses of Leadville are built of wood, but many brick buildings were erected on the main business street in 1880. Several times fire has threatened to destroy the town, but the excellently organized fire companies have succeeded in preventing any serious conflagrations.

LEADVILLE IN 1880.

The following statistical accounts of the present condition of Leadville have been compiled by the Census Office:

LOCATION.

Leadville is situated in northwestern central Colorado, in the heart of the Rocky mountains. Its lowest point has an altitude of 9,950 and its highest of 10,300 feet. It lies at the mouth of California gulch. The stream flowing through the gulch empties into the Arkansas river about 3 miles west of the city and about 10 miles south of the springs whence it takes its origin, and is, of course, not navigable.

RAILROAD COMMUNICATIONS.

Leadville communicates with the outer world by means of two railroads, the Denver and Rio Grande and the Denver and South Park, both running from Leadville to Denver.

TRIBUTARY COUNTRY.

Leadville is the center of a mining district directly dependent upon it, having a radius of from 15 to 20 miles, and including the west slope of Park range, the east slope of the Continental range, and the mining camps of Eagle valley, Gold park, Twin lakes, Independence, and others. Ores extracted from the veins worked at these places are shipped to Leadville for treatment and reduction; and in exchange Leadville furnishes them with food, tools, and other necessaries. In former years gulch-mining for gold was actively carried on in California gulch, but this branch of mining has now become of minor importance. In some gulches within 10 miles of the city new fields of gold-bearing gravel-beds have been found, and renewed activity in gulch-mining is not improbable.

TOPOGRAPHY.

The valley of the Arkansas is limited by the Sawatch range, rising to a height of about 13,500 feet on the west, and by the Park or Mosquito range, rising to about 13,000 feet on the east. It is about 6 miles wide in this portion, and has an altitude of about 9,500 feet. The bottom of the valley consists of a terraced alluvial plain of gravel and sand of considerable thickness. It slopes up gently toward the foot of the range on either side. On this alluvial plain at the foot of Park range is built up the city of Leadville, protected on the east by the range, on the north by a prominent foothill, and looking out on the south over the flat open ground of the valley. The valley was originally covered with sage-bush, but by irrigation the greater portion of it has been converted into grass-land. The sloping sides of the valley between the bottom and the foothills were densely covered with pine until within a year or two, but it has been cut for mining, smelting (charcoal-burning), and building purposes. These forests ran up the mountain side to an altitude of from 11,500 to 12,000 feet, the timber line; but at least half of them have now been cut. A great portion of the woods was destroyed by forest fires. The soil of these forest lands is fertile and favorable to new growth.

The surface rock of the foothills east and north of the city is a felspathic porphyry of eruptive origin. This porphyry is invariably underlaid by a silurian limestone, the limestone by other sedimentary beds, and these by granite. In the different terraces formed by the foothills at the point of contact between the porphyry and the limestone are found mineral veins, consisting chiefly of iron and lead ores, which contain silver in varying quantities. These veins extend under a surface of about 5 square miles, and are opened and developed by many extensive mines, comprising many miles of shafts, tunnels, and drifts. The general character of the contact veins is the same throughout. Their course is the same as that of the Park range, being north and south, and their dip is to the east, varying from 10 to 15 degrees below the horizontal. The thickness varies from that of a thin seam to 50 feet. Large portions are filled with gangue which does not carry enough silver to pay for mining. The paying ore usually occurs in the gangue, or replaces it in the form of well-defined chutes of considerable length and of several hundred feet width, generally having a southeasterly direction. They are separated by portions of the vein, which the miners call barren, either because it is too thin to be mined or because the gangue is poor. Frequently the ore is found in pocket form in the gangue or in veins and caves of the limestones which are in connection with the contact vein. From these veins in the last three years immense quantities of lead and silver have been taken, and to this fact alone are due the existence and growth of Leadville. "The mining developments prove that for a series of years these veins will keep such an existence."

In the gravel beds of California gulch pure water is found at a depth of from 10 to 50 feet. A small stream of water flows through the gulch all winter; in spring and summer the quantity increases, so that it can be used for gulch-mining and for watering purposes.

LEADVILLE, COLO.

CLIMATE.

From November, 1878, to December, 1879, Mr. Huber made a series of observations in order to establish the general features of the climate of the city. The observations were made at or about sunrise, 1 o'clock p. m., and after or about sunset.

The following table gives the result of these observations:

Temperature.

Month.	Maximum.	Minimum.	Maximum daily changes.
1878. December	43° F.	10° F.	32° F.
1879. January	41	11	28
February	42	13	28
March	56	14	28
April	58	10	29
May	66	27	33
June	72	30	34
July	77	41	36
August	76	28	35
September	69	30	36
October	66	18	37
November	46		33

The regular observations were discontinued after November, 1879, but exceptionally high and low temperatures were noticed. The lowest temperature recorded was in December, 1880, when the mercury fell to — 28°, and the highest in August, 1881, when it rose to 84°. Both extremes were of but short duration, and were exceptional. In general the winters and summers have shown the same features as those of 1879. The great uniformity of the temperature in the winter months is remarkable, the mean daily changes in none of them exceeding 12°. During the winter the weather is usually much calmer than in any other season. The cold in the calm, sunny days, even if intense, is not felt so much as in lower latitudes, at less altitude, and movement in the open air is agreeable and refreshing. In March, April, October, and November the morning and evening temperature remains below the freezing point, but at noon rises above it. In March, April, and November snow-storms often occur, but those of November are never severe. Those that last some days usually come from between northwest and southwest. October is pleasant and clear. In May and September the days are generally warm and agreeable, but the nights are cold and frosty; the morning temperature is seldom above the freezing point. Short, light snow-falls are not unusual in both months. June, July, and August being very moderate summer weather, it is exceptional when the mercury reaches 80°, and in June and August, at night, it sometimes goes down to the neighborhood of freezing. July is the only month that for the 3 years following December, 1878, had no frost. About the beginning of August the rainy season sets in, and always lasts from 4 to 6 weeks. During this period it rains almost daily. In the morning the air is usually calm and the sky clear; toward noon it becomes cloudy, and during the afternoon it rains in showers. These showers are generally accompanied by electric storms. The prevailing winds at Leadville come from the northwest; less often from the southwest and south; and very rarely from the southeast. The most violent storms occur in spring. During the summer and early autumn there is a regular daily air current from the northwest, beginning gradually about 10 a. m. and increasing in force till 3 or 4 p. m.; near sunset it abates again and the air remains calm all night. This current often increases to a storm-wind of great velocity.

STREETS.

Total length of streets, 88,000 feet, of which 3,500 feet are paved with slag, 12,000 with gravel, and the rest unpaved. The gravel costs 25 cents per square yard. No cleaning has been done on the paved streets. Sidewalks with but a few exceptions are of plank. There are about 1,000 feet of cobble-stone gutters, and about 20,000 feet of gutters excavated between the sidewalk and the road-bed, but not paved. Grass does not exist in this city, and there is no tree-planting. Ordinary repairs are done by day work, the chain-gang being employed. Street improvements are done by contract.

The total length of horse-railroad track in the city is 5,000 feet; total number of cars, 4; of men employed, 8; 10 mules are used. The road runs only 3 months in the year. The rate of fare is 10 cent.

WATER-WORKS.

The water-works are owned by a private company. They employ the gravity system, and pumping to a distributing reservoir. The total cost of the works was $175,000. The available head of water will average 165 feet. The yearly cost of maintenance is $12,000. The yearly income from water-rates is stated to be $50,000. The daily consumption of water is estimated at 100,000 gallons. Water-meters are not used.

GAS.

The gas-works are not owned by the city. The daily average production of gas is 75,000 cubic feet, and the charge per 1,000 feet is $4 05 net. The city pays $5 per month for each street-lamp, 100 in number.

PUBLIC BUILDINGS.

The city owns no public buildings except the jail, which cost $2,000; it is provided with rooms for the police court. A hall is rented for the city council and rooms for the city offices.

PUBLIC PARKS AND PLEASURE-GROUNDS.

The city has neither public parks nor pleasure-grounds.

PLACES OF AMUSEMENT.

The following list of theaters, with their respective seating capacities, is reported: Tabor opera-house, 700; Grand Central theater, 400; Gaieties, 400; Theater Comique, 300; Carbonate-beer hall, 400; Academy of Music, 700. Theaters pay an annual license of $300. There are 2 concert-halls and lecture-rooms, seating capacities not given. The report says there are no concert- and beer-gardens in the city, but probably some of the places enumerated as theaters are of this description.

DRAINAGE.

There are no sewers in the city.

CEMETERIES.

There are 2 cemeteries connected with the city, viz:
Old City Cemetery, containing about 3 acres, one-half mile due west from the center of the town.
Evergreen Cemetery, containing 120 acres, about 1 mile northwest of the center.
Interments are no longer made in the former. Evergreen cemetery is controlled by a private corporation. In the Old City cemetery, from the time of its opening in 1878 to its closing in November, 1879, there were 286 interments; since then there have been about 40 removals. In Evergreen cemetery from November, 1879, to November, 1881, there were 736 interments, including burials from the whole county and a number from Summit county. Graves therein must be 5 feet deep for children and 6 feet deep for adults. The stock company which owns it has invested some $4,000 in surveying, fencing, and laying out the grounds. Every lot on the ground is either on a 15-, 20-, or 30-foot drive. The lots are sold for from $10 to $30 each. The income, after paying all wages, averages $120 per month, which is put into a fund for the continual improvement of the grounds.

MARKETS.

There are no public or corporation markets in the city.

SANITARY AUTHORITY—BOARD OF HEALTH.

The chief health organization of Leadville is the board of health, consisting of the mayor and 2 aldermen, and 1 citizen annually selected by the city council. This board may appoint a physician to be the health officer of the city, to be known as the city physician. As to their power in respect to expenses, the ordinance establishing the board provides that "said board shall have full power to incur such indebtedness as shall be necessary for the proper execution of the powers herein conferred, and all debts lawfully contracted by said board shall be allowed and paid by the city council in the same manner that other claims and demands against the city are allowed and paid". The mayor is *ex officio* chairman of the board. His salary as mayor is $3,000 per year. The board meets regularly once a month, and the mayor or any two members may call a special meeting at any time. The duties of the board are to "exercise a general supervision over the health of the city, with full power to take all measures to promote the cleanliness and salubrity thereof; to abate nuisances on every description of public or private property, and to prevent the introduction or spread of contagious diseases". They may appoint one or more persons to aid them in the discharge of their duties, such persons to be subject to the orders of the board or any member thereof, and, in carrying into effect the provisions of the health ordinance, to possess full police power. In the prosecution of their duties the board, or any of its members, agents, or employés, may enter any premises between 6 o'clock a. m. and 6 o'clock p. m., and cause the abatement of all nuisances therein by serving a notice to abate within 24 hours. Through the city scavenger the board exercises complete control over the conservation and removal of garbage.

INFECTIOUS DISEASES.

As to small-pox, the mayor reports that the altitude is too high for the disease to exist, but the city ordinance makes full provision for it, stating that any physician who does not report to the clerk of the board within 12 hours the existence of any case of small-pox or other contagious disease he may be called to attend shall pay a fine of $25 to the city; and, further, that any person who shall go about the city after the small-pox or varioloid eruption has made its appearance on him shall forfeit and pay to the city a sum not less than $50 nor more than $200. In case of any malignant, contagious, or infectious disease, the patient must be at once removed to the hospital or pest-house, if it can be done without danger; if not, "the board shall then take such measures as may be deemed necessary to prevent the spread of the contagion or infection". As yet there is no public pest-house. Vaccination is not compulsory, and is done at the public expense only in case of the poor.

REPORTS.

The board reports to the city council monthly, and its reports are published, but how is not stated. Aside from rare attacks of erysipelas, mountain fever, and, more frequently, pneumonia, which last is occasioned mostly by drinking and exposure, and occurs usually among the miners, the public health is excellent, and is gradually getting even better as the place improves and rains are more frequent.

MUNICIPAL CLEANSING.

Street cleaning.—The streets are cleaned by the city scavenger by contract, wholly by hand. He employs 4 ms and 12 men daily. There is no cost to the city. Sweepings are dumped two miles away from the city. The system is said to work well.

Removal of garbage and ashes.—Garbage is removed by the scavenger at the expense of the householders. Garbage is carried to the dumping-grounds. No nuisance or probable injury to health is thought to arise from the ill-treatment of garbage. Ashes are treated in the same way.

Dead animals.—Dead animals are hauled to the dumping-ground, and burned when they accumulate. About 240 are annually so disposed of. The city scavenger is allowed to receive $4 for each large and $1 for each small animal removed.

Liquid household wastes.—Chamber, laundry, and kitchen slops are all disposed of in the same way, but in what way is not stated. No further information on this head was supplied.

Human excreta.—Of the houses of the city less than 1 per cent. depend on privy-vaults and the rest on water-closets. All the latter empty into cesspools. Night-soil is taken to the dumping-ground by the city scavenger's force.

Manufacturing wastes.—All liquid and solid manufacturing wastes go to the dumping-ground.

Many of the ordinances are published without date, and the time when they went into force can not be ascertained. As an example of this uncertainty the cost of this department may be instanced. The mayor, in his report to the Census Office dated August, 1880, says that the annual cost to householders of street-cleaning, the removal of garbage and ashes, and the burial of dead animals combined, is about $1,000 a month, and to the city nothing. On the other hand, a copy of the city ordinance, forwarded on January 15, 1881, provides that the "taking and removing of all swill, slops, and offal from premises within the city limits" shall be let out by contract. Again, the revised ordinances of August, 1881, provide that the city scavenger shall do this work, receiving no compensation from the city beyond his salary of $100 per month, and being allowed to receive no extra remuneration from outside beyond the fees for removing dead animals.

POLICE.

The members of the police force are elected annually by the city council. The force is governed by the mayor, and its chief executive officer is the city marshal. The marshal has control and supervision, under the direction of the mayor, of the whole force and of all officers of the city on whom may be conferred police powers, and he receives a salary of $180 per month. The rest of the force consists of a captain, with a salary of $125 per month, 2 sergeants and 18 patrolmen, with salaries of $100 per month each. They wear navy-blue uniforms with brass buttons, and each provides his own. They carry clubs and navy revolvers. They serve 8 hours per day each in winter and 12 in summer, and patrol about 6 blocks. In 1880 there were 4,320 arrests, the principal causes being intoxication and disturbance of the peace. The mayor may appoint as special policemen without pay any persons of suitable character who may be in the employment of the city in other departments, or, upon the application of any five responsible citizens showing the necessity thereof, any number of additional patrolmen or watchmen. All such policemen possess the same powers as policemen on the regular force, and are subject to the orders of the city marshal and the rules and regulations of the police department. The yearly cost of the force is about $30,000.

CALIFORNIA.

LOS ANGELES,

LOS ANGELES COUNTY, CALIFORNIA.

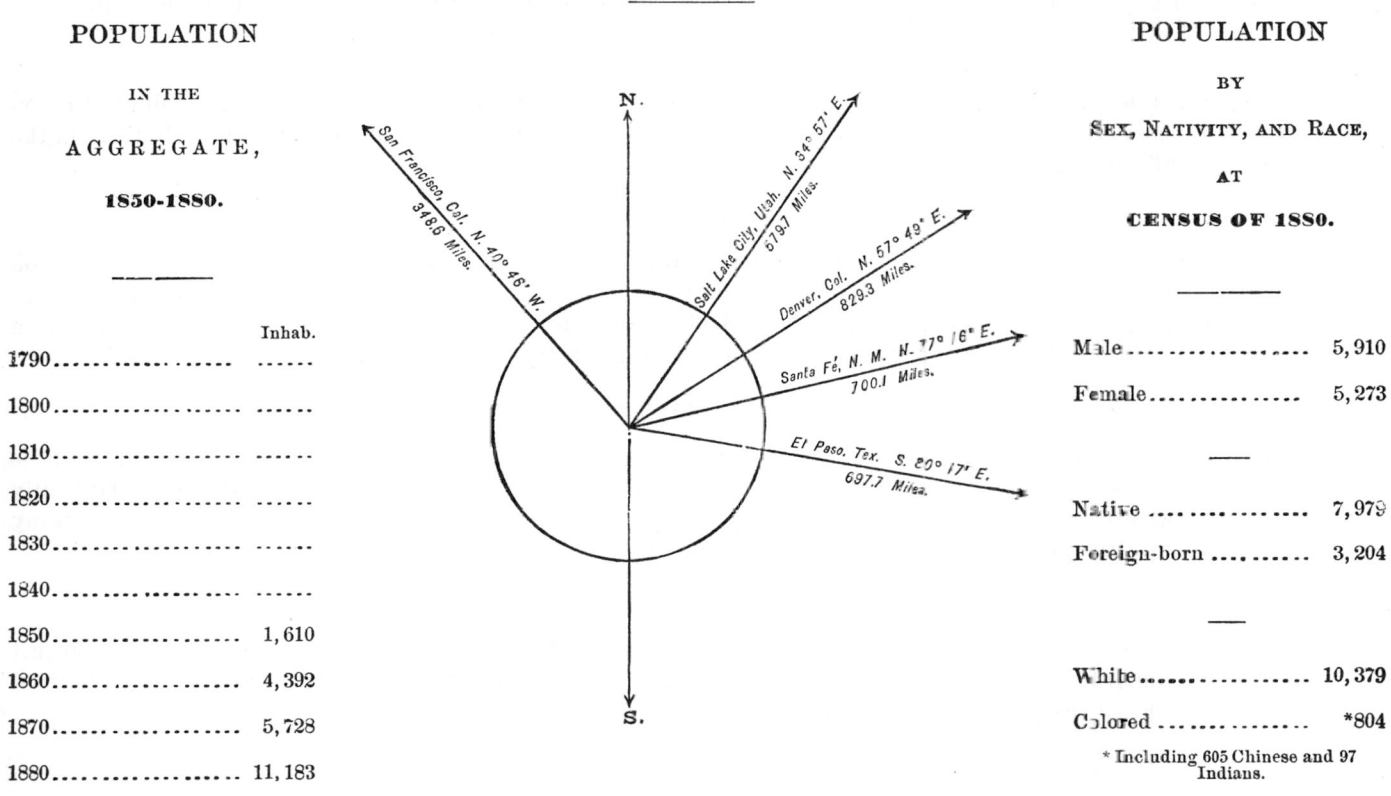

POPULATION

IN THE

AGGREGATE,

1850-1880.

	Inhab.
1790	......
1800	......
1810	......
1820	......
1830	......
1840	......
1850	1,610
1860	4,392
1870	5,728
1880	11,183

POPULATION

BY

SEX, NATIVITY, AND RACE,

AT

CENSUS OF 1880.

Male	5,910
Female	5,273
Native	7,979
Foreign-born	3,204
White	10,379
Colored	*804

* Including 605 Chinese and 97 Indians.

Latitude: 34° 3′ North ; Longitude: 118° 14′ (west from Greenwich); Altitude: 457 feet.

FINANCIAL CONDITION:

Total Valuation: $5,814,141 ; per capita : $520 00.   Net Indebtedness : $310,177 ; per capita : $27 74.   Tax per $100 : $2 90.

HISTORICAL SKETCH.

Pueblo de la Reina de los Angeles (town of the queen of the angels) was founded in September, 1781, by discharged soldiers who had been serving at the neighboring mission of San Gabriel. It was made a city and the capital of California by the Mexican congress in 1836, and was the seat of the last government, 1844–'46. It was captured by the American forces during 1846, after the battles of San Gabriel and La Masa.

Los Angeles remained a Mexican town in character for many years, but since 1868 the change has been great, and a new city has sprung up, the beauty of the situation, the equable climate, the fertility of the soil when subjected to irrigation, and the opening of railroads to this point having much to do with its later growth. There have been no large fires, and, except during 1878–'80, no periods of serious financial depression. Americans now predominate, and to their energy and perseverance the prosperity of the place is due.

LOS ANGELES IN 1880.

The following statistical accounts, mainly furnished to the Census Office by Hon. J. R. Toberman, mayor, indicate the present condition of the city:

LOCATION.

Los Angeles is situated in the center of the region known as " semi-tropical California", about 14 miles east of the Pacific ocean, in latitude 34° 3' north, and longitude 118° 14' west from Greenwich, on the west bank of the Los Angeles river, 30 miles above its mouth, and about 350 miles southeast of San Francisco. The altitude above sea-level at the Smithsonian Institution station is 457 feet. The river on which the city lies is not navigable, but a short railroad line to a seaport on the Pacific connects with coast-line steamers to San Francisco and other points.

RAILROAD COMMUNICATIONS.

The Southern Pacific railroad from San Francisco to Yuma, with a branch from here south to Wilmington, on the Pacific, 23 miles, and the Los Angeles and Independence railroad west to the harbor of Santa Monica, on the Pacific, 18 miles, afford ample railroad communications.

TRIBUTARY COUNTRY.

The country immediately tributary to the city is agricultural, and is said to be capable of sustaining a population of 1,000,000. Dairy products, barley, wheat, oats, orchard fruits, grapes, oranges, lemons, and limes are largely raised. The last three, at 14 years old, produce from $200 to $600 net per acre, while the vineyards produce from $40 to $200 per acre in raisins and brandy. Irrigation is carried on to a considerable extent.

TOPOGRAPHY.

The area of the city covers 6 square miles, two-thirds of which is in valley and one-third in hills. The soil is sandy, gravelly, " adobe", and red clay. The surrounding country, with the exception of a few places artificially planted, is open, with no marshes or overflowed lands, and the soil is the same as that underlying the city. Many of the hills have an altitude of from 200 to 400 feet and more above the sea-level.

CLIMATE.

Highest recorded summer temperature, 98°; highest summer temperature in average years, 80°. Lowest recorded winter temperature, 33°; lowest winter temperature in average years, 52°. The southwest trade-wind prevails for 9 months in the year and is cool and moist.

STREETS.

There are 200 miles of streets in the city, 20 miles of which are paved with broken stone, at a cost, as near as it may be estimated, of 10 cents per square yard. The sidewalks are of brick, asphalt, wood, cement, and gravel, and the gutters are laid with cobble-stones. There is no system of tree-planting along the sides of the streets. In street work all grading is done by contract, while repairs are done by day labor. A roller is used with good effect. There are 11 miles of horse-railroads in the city, using 10 cars and 40 horses, and giving employment to 15 men. The rate of fare is 5 cents.

WATER-WORKS.

The water-works are owned by a private corporation, and the total cost to date is $500,000. Water is taken from the Los Angeles river and distributed by gravity, the available head being from 20 to 120 feet. The average daily consumption is estimated at 125 gallons for each head of the population, but the supply is at times deficient. There are 23 miles of pipe and 60 hydrants. The annual cost of maintenance and repairs is $6,000 and the yearly income from water-rates $20,000. Water-meters are not used.

GAS.

The gas-works are not owned by the city. The charge per 1,000 feet is $4 50. The city pays $51 12 for each street-lamp, 140 in number.

PUBLIC BUILDINGS.

The city owns and occupies for municipal uses, wholly or in part, the jail, clerk's office, police office, and jailer's dwelling, the total cost of which is stated to be $5,000. There is no city hall, and the city owns no buildings in common with the county.

PUBLIC PARKS AND PLEASURE-GROUNDS.

There are 6 acres of parks in the city, that cost $800, and in which are spent $900 annually for care and maintenance. Mayor Toberman says: "Our city is 6 miles square, contains 10,000 acres of orchards and vineyards, which answer for public parks."

PLACES OF AMUSEMENT.

There are 2 theaters, with a seating capacity of about 600 each, and they pay a license to the city of $5 per night. There are also 6 halls used for concerts, lectures, etc. There are one or two concert- and beer-gardens, that succeed but indifferently.

DRAINAGE.

There are 4 miles of main sewers and 6 miles of laterals in the city. These have been built according to the requirements of each case as it came up. Main sewers are of brick, and laterals are of burnt clay and cement pipes. Frequent flushings are required. The removal of deposits is done by day's work, but the amount and cost are not stated. The question, "What final disposition is made of the outflow of the sewers?" is answered: "Manuring gardens, vineyards, and orchards." The cost of sewers is paid one-third by the city and two-thirds by the owners of the abutting property. Assessments are laid on the basis of frontage. The price paid for a brick sewer 2 by 4 feet, 12 feet deep, built in 1880, is stated at $12 per foot. The average cost of manholes is $3 each, and it is reported that there are no inlet-basins. No further information on this subject was obtained.

CEMETERIES.

There are 4 cemeteries connected with the city: 1 public, containing 18 acres, and 3 private, containing 130, 15, and 5 acres, respectively. There are no church-yards or private burial grounds in which interments are no longer permitted. The number of interments was not stated, and the mayor reported that, as the city was small and "statistics meager", not much information could be furnished. The public or city cemetery is under charge of a sexton, who is appointed by the mayor and confirmed by the city council.

MARKETS.

There are no public or corporation markets in the city, the distribution of meats, poultry, fish, vegetables, etc., being effected through about 30 wholesale and retail meat-markets, 20 vegetable- and fish-markets, and 60 huckster wagons, 50 of the latter being owned by the Chinese.

SANITARY AUTHORITY—BOARD OF HEALTH.

The board of health of the city of Los Angeles is composed of the mayor and president of the common council ex officio, and 3 members of the common council. In ordinary times the annual expenses of the board are $1,500 for salaries, and during an epidemic the board can increase its expenses. The authority of the board, either in absence of or during epidemics, is by ordinances full and complete so far as the sanitary needs of the city are concerned. The mayor is president of the board and general manager; he receives no salary for this duty. The executive officer is the health officer, salary $840 per annum, appointed by the board by and with the consent of the council; he has full police powers. One assistant health officer, or "steward", at $600 per annum, is also employed. In addition, the policemen are ex officio assistants to the health officer, and report all nuisances or violations of the health ordinances to him. The board meets weekly, and transacts its business as a deliberative body. General inspections are made semi-annually and special ones when ordered by the mayor. When nuisances are reported, the health officer is instructed to order the same abated within 3 days, and if this is not done the delinquent parties are prosecuted and fined from $5 to $50. In cases of defective house-drainage, privy-vaults, cesspools, sources of drinking-water, sewerage, or street-cleaning, special instructions are given to the health officer. The control exercised by the board over the conservation and removal of garbage is to see that no nuisances occur. Burial permits are issued by the health officer on death certificate, which must be signed by the attending physician, the sextons of the several cemeteries reporting back all interments made.

INFECTIOUS DISEASES.

Small-pox cases are removed to the pest-house, situated northeast of the city, while scarlet-fever patients are quarantined at home. In case of an epidemic the board orders the schools closed. Vaccination is compulsory, and is done at the public expense, the health officer having an office for the purpose.

The record of all births, diseases, and deaths is kept by the health officer, who reports them weekly to the council and to the National Board of Health. The board, as a rule, makes no reports that are published, but the health officer reports once a year to the city council, and his report is published with the other city documents.

MUNICIPAL CLEANSING.

Street-cleaning.—The streets are cleaned at the expense of the city, with its own force, and wholly by hand. The work is done once a week, and is said to be efficient. The annual cost of the service is $6,000, and the sweepings are deposited in the river-bed below the city, the trade-winds carrying the smell away, and no deleterious effects being perceptible.

Removal of garbage and ashes.—Garbage is removed both by the city and by householders, the city doing its portion with its own force. It is required to be kept in back yards, from which it is taken twice a week. Ashes and garbage may be kept in the same vessel, and they are both disposed of in the same manner as the street-sweepings. The cost to the city is included in the sum expended for street-cleaning, while that to the householders is not given. Mayor Toberman reports that the system is crude, but, owing to the peculiar conditions of the climate, effective, and no nuisance or probable injury to health arises from the manner of handling or disposing of the garbage.

Dead animals.—The carcasses of all dead animals are taken to the river-bed south of the city and there buried in the sand. The cost of this service, which is borne by the city, is included in the street-cleaning appropriation. Probably about 50 animals are so disposed of annually.

Liquid household wastes.—The principal portion of the liquid household wastes of the city are run into the public sewers, some going into cesspools, some being spread upon the ground in the rear of houses, and scarcely any going into the street gutters. The cesspools are usually porous, are not provided with overflows, sometimes receive the wastes from water-closets, and when full are abandoned and covered with earth. There are no particular regulations concerning their cleansing, but the health officer sees that they do not develop any nuisances. As the water-supply is from a distance, there is said to be no contamination from the escape of the contents of vaults and cesspools.

Human excreta.—About 20 per cent. of the houses have water-closets—90 per cent. of these delivering into the sewers and 10 per cent. into cesspools—while the remainder depend on privy-vaults. None of the latter are water-tight, and they are cleaned out when it is ordered by the health officer. The night-soil is used as manure on vineyards and orchards. It is reported that none is so used within the gathering-ground of the public water-supply; but as the Los Angeles river has a water-shed of about 180 square miles, it is more than likely that it is so used. About 2 per cent. of the houses in the city use the dry-earth system.

Manufacturing wastes.—The solid wastes are taken to the river-bed below the city, while the liquid wastes are run either into sewers or cesspools.

POLICE.

The police force of Los Angeles is appointed and governed by the police commissioners, consisting of the mayor, president of the council, and chief of police. The latter, with a salary of $125 per month, is the executive officer and has general superintendence of the force, which is composed of 10 patrolmen, at $75 a month each. The uniform is a military blue-dress coat with brass buttons, and each man provides his own. The patrolmen are equipped with revolvers and clubs, and are on duty 8 hours, with 8 hours off. The center of the city is patrolled by 8 men, while 2 policemen, mounted, patrol the suburbs. During the year 1880 930 arrests were made, the principal causes being, drunkenness, 346; disturbing the peace, 47; vagrancy, 86; larceny, 65; fighting, 58; disorderly and drunk and disorderly, 46, etc. Of these, 261 were fined, 257 discharged, 90 sent to the justice courts, 15 to San Francisco, etc. During the same time 50 station-house lodgers were accommodated, but no free meals were furnished them. The police co-operate with the fire, health, and building departments. Special policemen are appointed by the commissioners when they deem it necessary, generally for elections, holidays, etc. The yearly cost of the police force is about $13,000.

OAKLAND,
ALAMEDA COUNTY, CALIFORNIA.

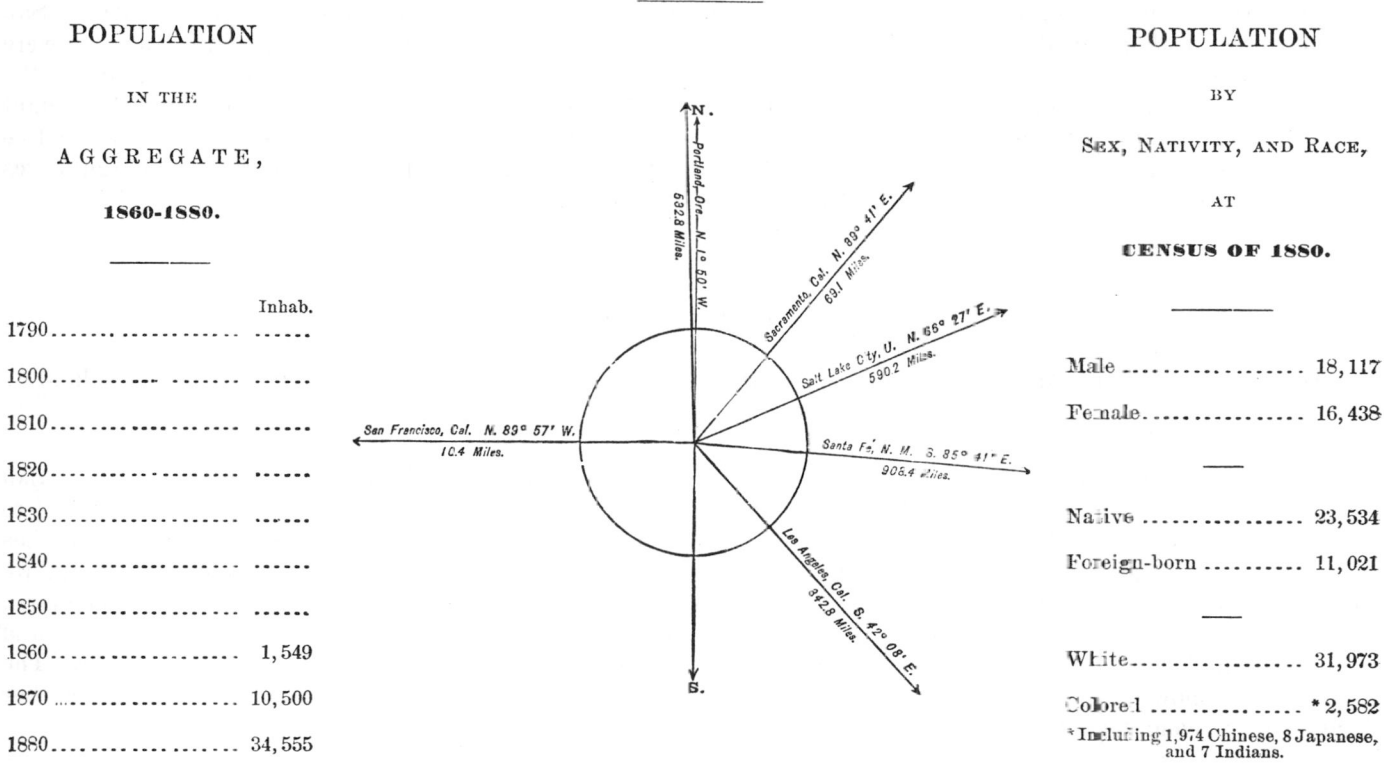

POPULATION	
IN THE	
AGGREGATE,	
1860-1880.	

	Inhab.
1790	......
1800	......
1810	......
1820	......
1830	......
1840	......
1850	......
1860	1,549
1870	10,500
1880	34,555

POPULATION

BY

SEX, NATIVITY, AND RACE,

AT

CENSUS OF 1880.

Male	18,117
Female	16,438
Native	23,534
Foreign-born	11,021
White	31,973
Colored	*2,582

*Including 1,974 Chinese, 8 Japanese, and 7 Indians.

Latitude: 37° 48′ North; Longitude: 122° 15′ (west from Greenwich); Altitude: 3.25 to 119 feet.

FINANCIAL CONDITION:

Total Valuation: $28,348,778; per capita: $320 00.   Net Indebtedness: $669,126; per capita: $19 36.   Tax per $100: $2 14.

HISTORICAL SKETCH.

The Contra Costa hills, just back of the present city of Oakland, were first visited in 1769 by some of the people belonging to Portala's land expedition. In 1820 Don Luis Peralta, a Spanish soldier of 40 years' service, applied to his government for a land grant and asked for a portion of the Contra Costa hills. His petition was granted, and a plot containing four or five leagues of land was assigned to him in this locality. The grant was called the "Rancho San Antonio", and it touched the lands belonging to the *Mission of San Francisco*. In 1842 Peralta divided his land among his sons, and that portion which is now embraced within the corporate limits of Oakland fell to Vincente Peralta. In 1850 the first actual settlement of Oakland was made. Part of the land was leased from the original owners and part of it was occupied by *squatters*, the latter being under the impression that the property belonged to the government. The proprietorship of this land, including the whole water-front, was, owing to conflicting claims, long in dispute; and though the titles were partially settled in 1868, many cases are even now before the courts for final adjudication.

In 1852 the town of Oakland was incorporated, and on March 25, 1854, a city charter was granted. For the next twelve years the growth of the young city was slow. The school facilities were very inferior; only three or four churches were built; none of the streets were paved; land-title disputes were interminable, and occupied much of the time of the courts; fraudulent claims multiplied, the city was run into debt, and the future of Oakland looked gloomy. However, the opening of the creek and the construction of an opposition line of steamers to San Francisco, the completion of the local railroad, and the prospect of the terminus of the trans-continental railroad being located here revived interest in the city, and in 1866 business, as well as the prices of real estate, began to grow better. In 1868 a partial settlement of the "water-front question" was reached, and on November 8, 1869, the first through passenger train for the East left Oakland on the Central Pacific railroad, the first overland train from the East arriving here on the afternoon of the same day.

From that time on the growth of Oakland has been rapid. In 1873 the adjoining town of Brooklyn was annexed, thus adding over 3,000 to the population of the city, and in 1874 the county buildings were ordered to be located here. Municipal improvements were many; the harbor was enlarged, and the bar at the mouth of San Antonio creek was dredged; railroads branched out, and the means of communication with San Francisco were further increased, while the fact that the city was the terminus of the great overland trunk-line added much to the general prosperity. Oakland has never suffered from any serious conflagrations, and has been singularly exempt from either disastrous floods or severe earthquakes. The early settlers were from the eastern states, but of late years the tide of immigration has set strongly in this direction, and the population now contains representatives not only from every state in the Union, but from nearly every nationality on the globe.

OAKLAND IN 1880.

The following statistical accounts, collected by the Census Office, indicate the present condition of Oakland:

LOCATION.

Oakland lies in latitude 37° 48′ north, and longitude 122° 15′ west from Greenwich, on the east shore of San Francisco bay and about 7 miles from the city of the same name. The altitudes above sea-level range from $3\frac{1}{4}$ to 119 feet. The frontage of Oakland on the bay is over a gently sloping beach, that reaches out more than two miles into the water before affording sufficient depth for commercial purposes. The estuary of San Antonio, opening into the bay opposite the city of San Francisco, extends inland for over two miles on the southern boundary of Oakland, and affords the opportunity for an artificial harbor. This creek has been so far improved as to give a depth of water of from 15 to 17 feet, with a channel width of 800 or 1,000 feet, and about one mile of shipping harbor. The improvements now in progress will widen and deepen the channel, as well as give four miles of additional harbor front. Water communication is now had with all points on the bay and the Pacific coast.

RAILROAD COMMUNICATIONS.

Oakland is the western terminus of the Central Pacific railroad, the main line running to Ogden, Utah, and numerous branches touching the northern and southern parts of the state, a short line of the same road running from here to San José and Tracy.

TRIBUTARY COUNTRY.

The country immediately tributary to the city is agricultural, many farms raising vegetables for the San-Francisco market.

TOPOGRAPHY, ETC.

The soil in and about Oakland is mostly a black sandy loam, well adapted for farming and gardening purposes. The country for 10 or 12 miles each way, up and down the bay, is open, the city having many oak trees, and from these it took its name. The land slopes up from the bay, San Antonio creek affording good natural drainage for most of the area covered by the city. Back from Oakland, at a distance of from three to five miles, rises the range known as the Contra Costa hills.

CLIMATE.

From the annual report of the health officer for 1880, from observations extending over a period of five years, the mean temperature of the warmest day is said to be 75.33°; mean temperature of the coldest day, 33.66°; maximum temperature for the year (1876), 97°; and minimum temperature for the year (1876–'77), 30°. The greatest monthly range of temperature is 49° and the least 19°.

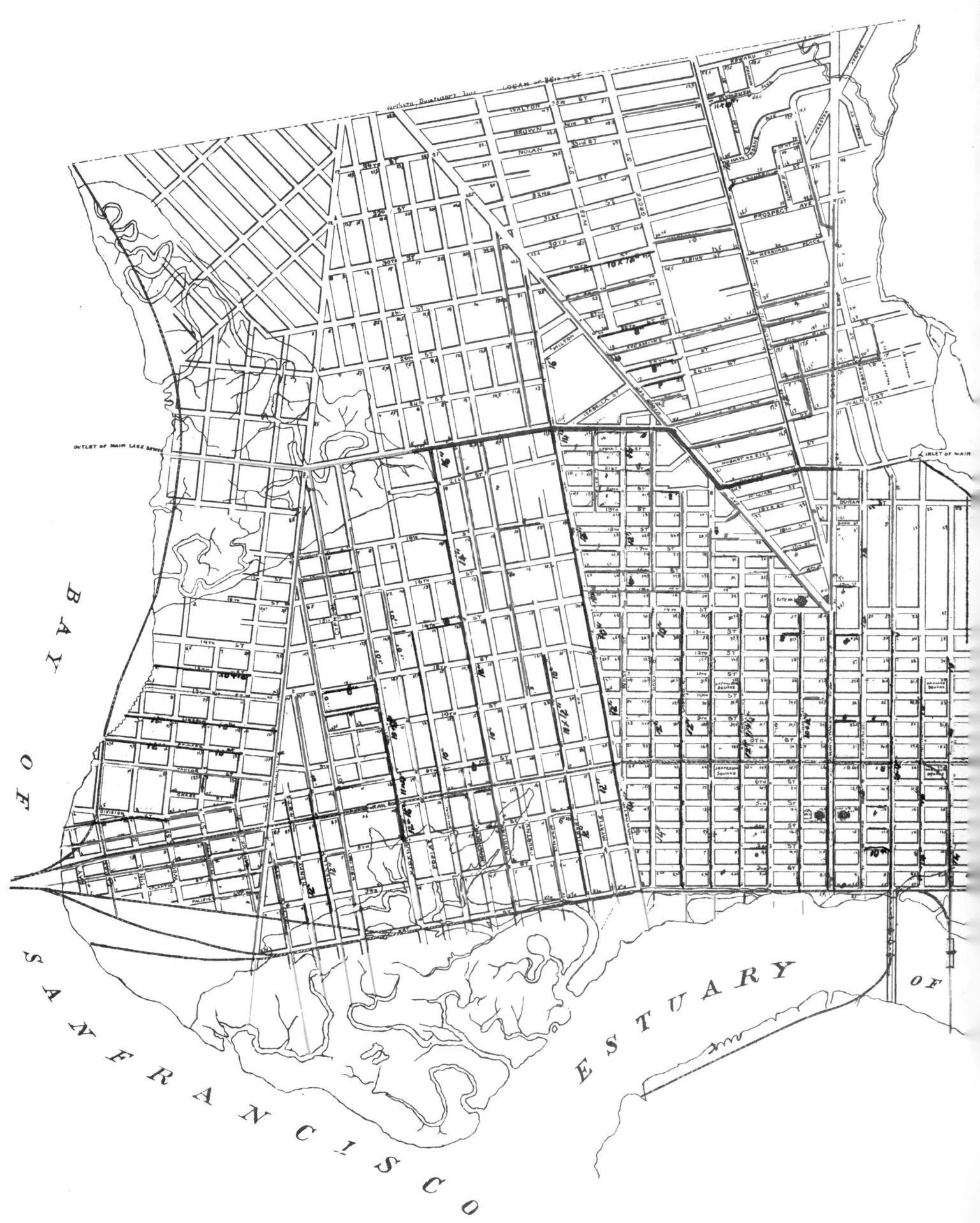

SEWER MAP
of the
CITY OF OAKLAND
Showing the different kinds of sewers.
their sizes and depths. also the grades of streets

Brick Sewer
Cement pipe Sewer
Iron stone pipe Sewer
Wooden box Sewer

Size of sewers in numerals of corresponding colors
Depth of bottom of sewers below street grade in Roman numbers
Elevations of Street grades above high tide in black numerals

BELL BROS., PHOTO-LITHOGRAPHERS, WASHINGTON, D. C.

water on one side and to the lake sewer, which passes along a low place on the line of Twenty-second street. Sewers are laid at a depth of 8 or 9 feet, where such depths can be secured, but near their outlet they come within 4 or 6 feet of the street surface. The mouths of outlets are open and above water at ordinary tides. Ventilation is provided for by perforated covers in manholes built at intervals of 300 feet. It is reported that only those sewers in the west end of the city need flushing to a great extent. This is done from street hydrants, at a cost of from $100 to $150 per year. The main lake sewer was cleaned in 1880 by boat, buckets, and windlass, at a cost of $750. It had not been cleaned before in two years.

The cost of building sewers is assessed upon the abutting property. Assessments are laid on the basis of frontage. The ordinary price paid for trenching, laying, and back-filling was from 25 to 75 cents per foot, according to depth. Brick manholes, with covers, cost from $22 50 to $40 each. Brick catch-basins, with cast-iron grating and granite curb, $83; with iron curb and pipe-trap, $62. Catch-basins made of 18- and 12-inch pipe and cast-iron collar, $27. Lamp-holes of 6-inch pipe and iron cover, $10 each. Pipes were used of three classes. The vitrified pipe, from 8 to 18 inches diameter, costs from 40 cents to $1 25; Portland-cement pipes, circular, from 8 to 16 inches diameter, cost from 30 cents to $1 10 per foot; egg-shaped cement pipes, from 10 to 12 inches, cost from 50 cents to $1 25 per foot.

No sewerage work has been done since the new constitution of California came into effect in 1879, as it repealed the laws under which such work was done, and there has been no legislative action to provide funds for carrying on the work.

CEMETERIES.

There are 3 cemeteries connected with the city; all have been in existence for about sixteen years, and they are all situated together near the northern terminus of Webster street, at a distance of 2½ miles from the city hall:

The *Mount View Cemetery*, area 200 acres, is owned by a private corporation, that was organized under the provisions of an act approved April 18, 1859, and has a total of 4,000 interments.

Saint Mary's Cemetery, area 40 acres, is owned by the Saint Mary's Cemetery association (Roman Catholic), and has a total of 1,500 interments.

Hebrew Cemetery, area 4 acres, has a total of about 50 interments.

There are no church-yards or private burial-grounds in which interments are no longer permitted. No burial is allowed to be made without a permit from the health officer. There is no special time after death for interment. For adults, graves are 6 feet deep, and for children, from 4½ to 5 feet deep. These figures apply to all cemeteries. The use of lots in the several cemeteries is solely for burial. The Saint Mary's Cemetery association guarantees to the lot-owners and their heirs possession of lots up to the year A. D. 2200, and the improvements and care are at each lot-owner's option, provided that the rights of others are not infringed. The construction of roads and other permanent works is at the expense of the cemeteries. The price of lots varies from 25 to 50 cents per foot, according to location. The revenue of Mount View cemetery for the year 1880 was about $18,000; that of the other cemeteries was not stated.

MARKETS.

There are no public or corporation markets in the city. The markets are all in private buildings, with the exception of one that has 15 stalls, each renting for from $10 to $20 per month. None of them have more than one occupant. These markets are open from 6 a. m. to 6 p. m., and on Saturdays until 9 p. m. Each morning meat is brought from the slaughter-houses, which are about 5 miles from the city, and distributed to the markets.

SANITARY AUTHORITY—BOARD OF HEALTH.

The chief sanitary organization of Oakland is the board of health, an independent body, composed of 3 physicians, appointed by the city council, with the mayor, president of the council, and the city engineer, members *ex officio*, and the city physician, who as health officer is a member. The annual expense of the board in ordinary times is $2,100, for salaries; the health officer receives $100 per month, the 3 active members (physicians) receive $25 a month each, while the *ex officio* members serve without pay. The matter of increasing the expenses rests with the city council, except during a small-pox epidemic, when, by ordinances, the board can do what is necessary irrespective of the cost. The powers of the board, except as stated, are at all times only such as are defined by the ordinances of the city council, "of which it is the creature". The mayor presides at all meetings, appoints the committees, etc. The health officer is the executive officer of the board, and as such has general supervision of the sanitary needs of the city. In ordinary times he has the services of one health inspector, and in times of epidemics all the assistants that may be needed. The health inspector and assistants have police powers sufficient to enable them to enter premises, make arrests, etc. The board meets once a month and transacts its business as a deliberative body. There are three standing committees—one on sewerage, garbage, etc.; one on prevailing diseases and their causes; and one on air, water, and food. Each committee has a physician as chairman. Inspections are made as nuisances are reported, and, if any time can be spared, systematically, in the neighborhood of the complaints. When a reported nuisance is found to be such, notice is served to abate. Defective house-drainage, privy-vaults, cesspools, and sources of drinking-water are ordered to be corrected. The board does not at present do much toward the correction of defective sewage, and all street-cleaning is under direction of the city marshal. The report of the sanitary inspector for the year 1880 shows: Number of premises inspected during the year, 3,497; number of premises reinspected during the year, 1,566; number of private complaints attended to during the year, 474; number of privy-vaults connected with sewers during the year, 1,145; number of premises found connected with sewers, 1,698; number of premises supplied with city water, 2,796; number of premises supplied with well water, 559; number of inspected premises occupied by owners, 1,565; number of inspected premises occupied by tenants, 1,908; number of permits for sewer connections granted by marshal, 367. At present the board practically has no control over the conservation of garbage, but may cause arrest for non-removal; ordinances regulating the whole subject are now being prepared. All burial permits are issued by the health officer on certificates of death signed by a graduate in medicine or by the coroner. These certificates, which are filed at the health office, must state, in addition to the usual information as to cause of death, date and place, by whom treated, age, sex, nativity, etc., "location of residence"—whether on wet or dry land; "sewerage of residence"—whether connected with city sewer, cesspool, surface drainage, or no sewerage; "circumstances in life"—affluence, medium, poor; and "primary cause of disease". The board has no specific regulations as to the pollution of streams and harbors or the removal of excrement, only exercising a general supervision.

INFECTIOUS DISEASES.

As before stated, the authority of the board over diseases of an infectious or contagious nature is confined to small-pox, and at present (close of 1880) an epidemic of that disease has prevailed on the Pacific coast since last July. Patients who have no homes are removed to a pest-house, a tent being used for this purpose, while others are quarantined at home, a yellow flag is displayed, and the house guarded by special policemen. The ordinances forbid any child to attend the public schools from a house in which a case of contagious disease exists. Vaccination is compulsory, and is done by the health officer at the public expense. From the appearance of the first case of small-pox in Oakland, July 27, until the close of the year 1880, there were 21 cases, 4 of which were fatal. The health officer reports the number of vaccinations, either at his office or by his direction, as 4,740, and the number of revaccinations as 517.

REPORTS.

All births and deaths are recorded by the health officer in books kept for the purpose. No record of diseases is kept other than the cause of death, but the public-schools department reports to the health officer the relative proportion of sickness in the different sections. The board makes no report as a board, but the health officer is required to report monthly to the common council all births and deaths, as well as the number of persons treated by him. The health officer also makes an extended report as to the sanitary condition of the city, which, as well as his monthly report, is published in pamphlet form.

MUNICIPAL CLEANSING.

Street-cleaning.—The streets are cleaned at the expense of the city, with its regular force, and wholly by hand. The cleaning is done "as often as finances will allow", a force of from 16 to 20 men being employed 8 or 10 months during each year. The work, when done at all, is done thoroughly. The annual cost is from $15,000 to $18,000, and the sweepings are deposited either in the bay or on low ground. It is said that the former is the best place for final disposal, as the water carries off the *débris.*

Removal of garbage and ashes.—All garbage and ashes are removed by the householders at their own expense. There are no regulations as to the conservancy of garbage while awaiting removal, but it is not allowed to be kept in the same vessel with ashes. The garbage is finally dumped into San Antonio creek or into the bay, and the ashes are deposited in low lots. The cost to householders is from 50 cents to $1 a month each. It is reported that complaints are seldom made of the manner of keeping or disposing of the garbage.

Dead animals.—The carcasses of all animals dying within the corporate limits are removed and buried by the pound-master at the expense of the city. The annual cost of this service is $1,187, and during the past year 59 horses, 11 cows, 41 sheep, 14 goats, 95 hogs, and 69 calves were buried.

Liquid household wastes; human excreta.—The principal portion of the liquid household wastes is run into the sewers, some going into vaults and cesspools, and none being allowed to reach the street gutters. The cesspools are being rapidly done away with. Those that now exist are generally porous, are sometimes provided with overflows that enter the sewers, receive the waste from water-closets, and are cleaned out when necessary. These, as well as the privy-vaults, are required by ordinances to be connected with the sewers, provided they are within 150 feet of any street in which a sewer is laid. Owing to the efforts of the health officer and his assistants these connections are being rapidly made. The health officer, in his last annual report, mentions several cases of well water that were more or less impure, the impurity being due to surface pollution or the escape of the contents of vaults and cesspools.

POLICE.

The police force of Oakland is appointed by the city council, and governed by the captain of police, who receives a salary of $150 per month. The force consists of 25 patrolmen, with 2 sergeants, at $100 per month each. The uniform is dark-blue beaver cloth with brass buttons, a dress coat, with a straight vest, each man providing his own. The patrolmen are equipped with clubs and pistols; they are on duty 10 hours out of the 24; the length of streets patrolled by them varies. During the past year 2,141 arrests were made, the principal causes being for larceny, misdemeanor, drunkenness, assault and battery, and violation of city ordinances. The majority of these were convicted. The total value of property lost or stolen during the year and reported to the police was $15,687 45, and of this $8,431 60 was recovered and returned to the owners. During 1880 there were 1,177 station-house lodgers, and a few meals, costing 5 cents each, were given to them. The force is required to co-operate with the fire department at all fires. Special policemen are appointed by the city council, and, though paid by private parties, are under the control of the captain of police. The yearly cost of the police force was not stated.

MANUFACTURES.

The following is a summary of the statistics of the manufactures of Oakland for 1880, being taken from tables prepared for the Tenth Census by James R. Hardenberg, chief special agent:

Mechanical and manufacturing industries.	No. of establishments.	Capital.	AVERAGE NUMBER OF HANDS EMPLOYED.			Total amount paid in wages during the year.	Value of materials.	Value of products.
			Males above 16 years.	Females above 15 years.	Children and youths.			
All industries	72	$1,371,457	1,369	13	5	$759,917	$2,012,695	$3,181,066
Boots and shoes, including custom work and repairing	4	37,000	19	2	....	8,257	9,760	23,802
Bread and other bakery products........................	6	10,400	22	1	....	14,790	54,900	88,000
Carriages and wagons	4	20,872	31	1	....	20,830	29,500	75,800
Flouring- and grist-mill products	3	240,000	44	....	....	24,974	710,000	800,510
Foundery and machine-shop products	4	21,500	22	....	....	11,440	15,200	38,500
Liquors, malt........................	3	105,000	67	....	....	28,235	102,327	183,500
Lumber, planed	3	169,535	108	....	....	77,538	72,000	178,000
Marble and stone work	3	4,500	12	....	....	7,550	7,400	18,970
Plumbing and gasfitting................	5	67,000	41	....	2	23,810	44,780	79,000
Saddlery and harness	6	17,050	19	....	....	9,638	15,560	37,688
Shipbuilding	3	120,300	166	....	....	187,911	432,268	686,296
Tobacco, cigars and cigarettes..........	6	7,800	17	....	1	4,850	11,650	26,000
All other industries (a)	22	550,500	801	9	2	340,214	457,350	947,000

a Embracing bags, other than paper; blacksmithing; boxes, wooden packing; brooms and brushes; carpentering; confectionery; furniture; hats and caps; ice, artificial; iron railing, wrought; leather, tanned; painting and paperhanging; stone- and earthen-ware; terra-cotta ware; tinware, copperware, and sheet-iron ware; upholstering and upholstering materials.

From the foregoing table it appears that the average capital of all establishments is $19,048 01; that the average wages of all hands employed is $547 per annum; and that the average outlay in wages, in materials, and in interest (at 6 per cent.) on capital employed is $39,651 38.

SACRAMENTO,

SACRAMENTO COUNTY, CALIFORNIA.

POPULATION

IN THE

AGGREGATE,

1850-1880.

	Inhab.
1790	......
1800	......
1810	......
1820	......
1830	......
1840	......
1850	6,820
1860	13,785
1870	16,283
1880	21,420

POPULATION

BY

SEX, NATIVITY, AND RACE,

AT

CENSUS OF 1880.

Male	12,271
Female	9,149
Native	14,372
Foreign-born	7,048
White	19,180
Colored	*2,240

* Including 1,781 Chinese and 4 Indians.

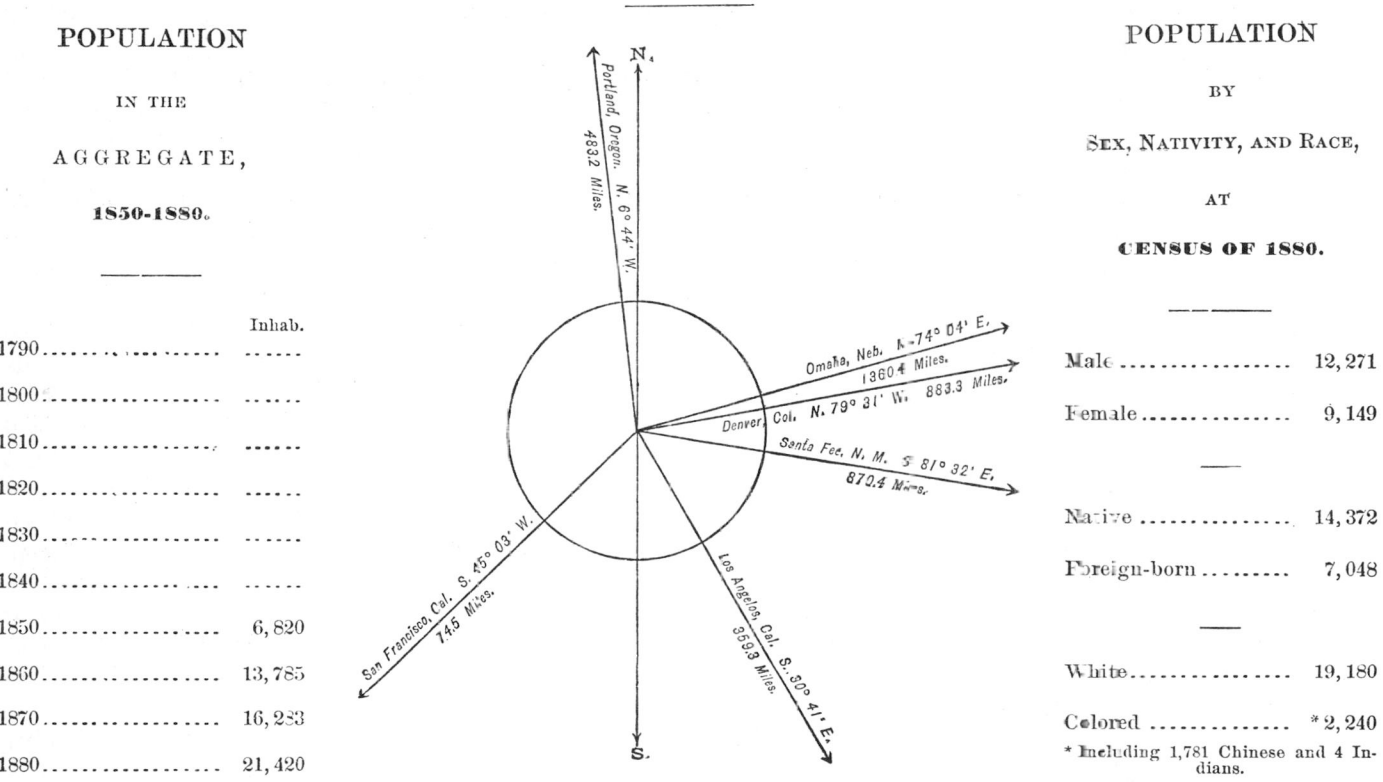

Latitude: 38° 34' North; Longitude: 121° 26' (west from Greenwich); Altitude: 52 to 85 feet.

FINANCIAL CONDITION:

Total Valuation: $10,504,225; per capita: $490 00.   Net Indebtedness: $861,000; per capita: $40 20.   Tax per $100: $4 00.

HISTORICAL SKETCH. (a)

In 1769 occurred the real discovery of the bay of San Francisco. In this year some fathers of the Franciscan order, accompanied by a military force, entered upper California and made the first white settlements. The military governor who came with them, in the course of an exploring expedition, discovered the bay of San Francisco, and in 1776 the Mission of San Francisco de los Dolores was founded on its western shore. This was one of a number of missions scattered along the coast, each one of which was the center of a large plantation, worked by the Indians whom the fathers had converted, and who lived in a condition of semi-slavery, but yet infinitely better than the barbarous state in which they had been found. For half a century these missions were very prosperous; but in 1826 the Mexican government passed an act for the liberation of the mission Indians, and the

---

a History of Sacramento County, Thomson and West, 1880.

demoralization and dispersion of the people soon ensued. The downfall of the missions quickly followed, being hastened by the wretched government of the Mexicans; and in 1845 the fathers were formally deprived of all their lands and wealth.

In the mean time a few white settlers had made their way over the mountains from the east, and now took advantage of the troubles between Mexico and the United States to claim this rich territory for their own country. The details of the "American-conquest", as it is called, do not belong in such a sketch as this, and it must suffice to give the leading facts. In 1846 the American settlers in California raised the standard of revolt and declared it an independent state. On the 7th of July of that year Commodore Sloat hoisted the American flag over Monterey, the capital of upper California, and issued a proclamation declaring the province henceforth a portion of the United States; and on the 10th the revolutionists pulled down the bear flag and hoisted the stars and stripes in its stead. Commodore Stockton, who succeeded Sloat, having received official notice of existing war between the United States and Mexico, proclaimed California a territory of the United States and organized a temporary government. After the war was closed a territorial government was established.

One of the small number of foreign settlers who had entered California was General John A. Sutter, a native of Baden, but of Swiss education and citizenship. He came to America in 1834, and after many adventures found himself, in July, 1839, in the bay of San Francisco. He had heard glowing accounts of upper California, and especially of the valley of the Sacramento river, and, on expressing a desire to settle there, procured from the Mexican government, without difficulty, the grant of a large tract of land. To find the Sacramento was not so easy; but at length he succeeded, and after some exploration selected his land at the mouth of the American river, where he afterward erected fort Sutter, and where Sacramento now stands. He named this place "New Helvetia". The fort was soon built, and quickly became the chief trading post of that part of the country. The settlement around it grew, and General Sutter's property fast accumulated, until the latter part of January, 1848, when a sad change took place in the affairs of the old pioneer. Then came the discovery of gold—a discovery which made California what it is, which brought wealth and prosperity to thousands of men, but which ruined the man who was so unfortunate as to be one of the chief instruments in making it. At this time General Sutter had completed his establishmen at the fort; had performed all the conditions of his grants of land; had, at an expense of at least $25,000, cut a race of nearly three miles in length, and had nearly completed a flouring-mill near the present town of Brighton; had expended toward the erection of a saw-mill near the town of Coloma about $10,000; and had got under way a large farm. But his mills were deserted by his workmen and became a dead loss; his laborers and mechanics, from his cook to his clerk, were taken with the gold fever; reckless immigrants from the East robbed him of his flocks, his herds, and finally of his lands; his possessions and his hopes were soon scattered and destroyed.

From the first discovery of California by the Spaniards the impression prevailed that the country was rich in silver, gold, and precious stones; but there is no reliable account of the finding of any of these till 1802, when it is said that silver was found in Alizal, in Monterey county, but the mine never produced any thing of consequence. The first mine to produce any noticeable amount of precious metal was the gold placers in the cañon of the San Francisquito creek, 45 miles northwest of Los Angeles. It was discovered about 1838 and was worked continuously for 10 years, when it was deserted for the richer discoveries in the Sacramento basin. Its total yield was probably not over $60,000. Prior to the Mexican war it was known that gold-bearing rock was to be found in the country, and some gold-washing was done by the natives. It was reserved, however, for James W. Marshall to make the discovery on the 19th of January, 1848, at Sutter's saw-mill, on the south fork of the American river, near the present town of Coloma, in El Dorado county, 54 miles west of Sacramento. In the previous summer Marshall had formed a copartnership with General Sutter to build and run a saw-mill near the place, and about Christmas work was begun on it. In January a narrow ditch for a race was begun. On the 19th of that month Marshall discovered the gold near the lower end of the ditch. He immediately went down to the fort and showed some of the metal to General Sutter, who quickly proved that it was gold. The next day they went to Coloma and prospected about the place together with encouraging results. In spite of General Sutter's earnest request that the discovery be kept secret till his mills were finished the news leaked out, and soon all his employés, as well as everybody else in the vicinity, were hunting for gold. Then in the spring the people came rushing up from San Francisco and other parts of California. In San Francisco only five men were left to take care of the women and children. The single men locked their doors and left for "Sutter's fort", and thence went to the El Dorado. Large companies of men, women, and children could be seen on every road leading to the mines, their wagons loaded down with tools, provisions, etc. By the middle of August 4,000 persons were engaged in gold-mining. A month later the number was set at 6,000, and the average find per day for each person was put at one ounce. During the first 8 weeks of the golden times the receipts of gold-dust at San Francisco amounted to $250,000, and during the 8 weeks ending September 23 they were $600,000. Instances were known where one person collected from $1,500 to $1,800 in one day, and when a man with his pan or basket did not easily gather from $30 to $40 in a day he moved to another place.

Shortly after the great discovery at Sutter's mill there were a number of stores located at the fort, and an immense business was at once created at that point. A village quickly grew up, and in December the first plat of Sacramento was made. During the winter the roads to the mines were nearly impassable. Freight from the fort to Coloma was $1 per pound—$2,000 per ton.   Even at that price it was impossible to transport the necessaries rapidly enough to prevent serious apprehensions of famine in the remoter mining districts.   At the blacksmith-shop at the fort $64 was charged for shoeing a horse all round, $16 for a single shoe.   The upper part of the building in the fort was used as a boarding establishment, the cost of board being $40 per week.   The front room below was used for drinking and gambling purposes, the price of a drink being 50 cents.   In those times hardly any one ever drank alone.   Trading yielded an enormous profit.   Fifty per cent. covered the expense of transportation from San Francisco, yet the Sacramento sales averaged 200 per cent. profit above the cost of goods in San Francisco.   The political and social condition was anomalous; there was no law or system of government, and yet there was little actual disorder or discord.   Miners came to town freighted with bags of gold, which they stored away as indifferently as they did their bags of tools, and the gold was seldom touched.

On the 1st of April, 1849, the number of inhabitants at the fort and in the city did not exceed 150.   From February until June there was a steady course of improvement, the immigration coming by sea, and as yet in not very large numbers.   In June immigrants by water began to arrive in thousands on their way to the mines. Sacramento, being the starting-point for all the northern mines, became the scene of unexampled activity.   The several branches of the American, Bear, Yuba, and Feather rivers were the great points of attraction, and Sacramento was the fitting-out place for all of them.   In June an overwhelming business was in progress, without a particle of method and in utter confusion and recklessness of manner.   On the 26th of June the city numbered 100 houses, including the city hotel, which was 35 by 55 feet and 3 stories high, and had been framed for a saw- and grist-mill for General Sutter.   Every sort of material that could be used in the construction of tents, houses, and stores rose to enormous value.   Muslin, calico, canvas, old sails, logs, boards, zinc, tin, and old boxes became almost priceless commodities.   Immigrants were coming in by hundreds, with no places to stay, and no shelter from the night air or the noonday sun except the shade of trees, and even this had been appropriated by earlier comers.

As was common anywhere at that early day, public gambling became a leading and absorbing feature of life in the city.   While merchants, bankers, and corporations would hazard nothing in architectural ornament, gamesters were erecting magnificent saloons at enormous cost.   A few poles stuck in the ground and covered with a wind-sail constituted the first gaming rendezvous.   In the summer the famous "Round Tent" was put up, where every species of gambling was carried on in its most seductive aspect.   "The toilers of the country," says Dr. John F. Morse in a history of Sacramento, "including traders, mechanics, and speculators, lawyers, doctors, and some apostate ministers, concentrated at this gambling focus like insects around a lighted candle at night." The gambling of this time was often upon a stupendous scale.   Every saloon was crowded and every table blockaded by an eager crowd of gamesters.   Not one person in ten, either by his absence or his condemnation, attempted to discountenance the mania.   After the popularity of the Round Tent decreased, a great number of smaller and meaner establishments were started.   Such was the ascendency of gambling then, that the leaders of the craft were men of great influence, and for a while almost controlled the policy of the city.   But while gambling was allowed a temporary ascendency, there was another powerful influence approaching—that of the church—which at length effected a moral revolution in public sentiment.   The first sermon was preached in April, 1849, and in the summer regular services were established.   Against this influence gambling could make no more headway, and its votaries soon came to be viewed in their true relations.

In July a movement was made to organize a city government, and an election of councilmen was held.   On the 20th of September a city charter, which had been prepared by the council, was voted upon, and was rejected, chiefly through the influence of gamblers, who preferred the lawless state of society which had hitherto existed. In a new election the law-and-order men turned out and adopted an amended charter.   This one was not entirely satisfactory, and finally two new ones were submitted to the legislature, which combined them in a way that suited everybody.   The city government, thus established out of chaos, encountered very serious difficulties, growing out of the prevailing sickness and destitution among the immigrants.   Nine-tenths of the adventurers arriving in San Francisco made their way to Sacramento as soon as possible, where they arrived, many of them sick, debilitated, and almost penniless.   The scurvy-stricken subjects of the ocean, and another more terrible train of scorbutic sufferers coming from the overland roads, began to concentrate here.   Sacramento became a perfect lazar-house of disease, suffering, and death long before an effective city government was organized.   Such was the difficulty of procuring attendance for the sick, that even invalids who had money could not obtain attention. An informal association of Odd Fellows went to work to relieve the prevailing misery, but all they could do was not sufficient to dissipate it.   Men continued to sicken and die without attention, and were buried without even the formality of being sewed up in a blanket.   On the 23d of September the first rains came, and the bleak weather of fall and winter followed all too quickly, increasing the miseries of the sick and destitute to an almost incredible extent.   Every one who could, began to erect more substantial buildings, and, notwithstanding the enormous prices of building material, stores and hotels were run up like magic.   Hospitals, too, were secured, and the horrors of the situation were somewhat mitigated.

In January, 1850, a violent southeast storm swelled the waters of the Sacramento to such an extent that the whole city for a mile from the embarcadero was submerged, and but few houses escaped having their lower floors covered with water. Business and merchandise were greatly damaged, a great quantity of goods and provisions being swept away. Invalids and the inmates of the hospitals suffered severely, and Dr. Morse says "many died in consequence of the terrible exposure to which they were subjected." The water quickly subsided and business was resumed. In March the city came near being flooded again, but active exertion saved the town from a second inundation. In the spring tents and canvas houses gave place to large and commodious stores and dwellings. Business began to assume something like system. Stage lines were established, threading every valley which led to the mines. The seasons in which this state of business was developed were remarkably exempt from disease, and the almost innumerable physicians of the former period of maladies were compelled to take to the less congenial business of mining. As a result the city rapidly grew both in numbers and in prosperity. But while every thing seemed so harmonious and prosperous, trouble was brewing beneath the surface, which was soon to throw the whole neighborhood into turmoil and confusion. This trouble culminated in the "squatter riots", as they are called. Nearly all this trouble came from the fact that the titles to land in California were principally held by the grantees of the Mexican government, who were protected in their rights by treaty. The settler from the East, not being conversant with this state of affairs, nor aware of the great elasticity of the lines of a Mexican grant, would frequently find his home claimed by some one, till then known only as a large land-owner, living often ten or more miles away. Others hoped to get tracts of land by taking advantage of defects in title; and a third class proposed to help themselves, and let the owner get them off if he could. In 1849, less than a year after the beginning of immigration into Sacramento, we find that trouble had arisen on this vexed question of titles. General Sutter claimed the land embraced within the city limits, through grants from the Mexican government and the guarantees of the treaty of peace between the United States and Mexico. His claim was sustained by adjacent settlements, by costly and valuable improvements, and by occasional occupation of the site of the city. He also had a survey and a map made of the land in question, and upon this claim conveyed the whole to his son, John A. Sutter, jr., who sold it in detail to citizens of Sacramento, all of whom were therefore interested in the maintenance of the Sutter title. On the other hand, the squatters, as the other party was called, maintained that the town plat was not in the grant from the Mexican government; that Sutter had overstepped the boundaries of his rightful possessions, and that the site was public land of the United States, and therefore subject to pre-emption, occupation, and improvement.

During the flood of January, 1850, among the only portions of the city not submerged was the ground immediately upon the edge of the river, which was at once occupied by tents and shanties. After the subsidence of the water the occupants refused to leave, and room for the levee, for the transaction of shipping business and the landing of merchandise, became scanty. At that time no one paid the slighest respect to a land title where it conflicted in any way with his own interest, and to resort to the processes of law would have caused ruinous delay in those rushing days. Thereupon the merchants and bankers took the matter into their own hands and proceeded to remove these obstructions by force, which they did with little opposition. This increased the bitter feeling between the squatters and the holders of Sutter titles. The squatters began to demonstrate their principles by settling upon lots in various parts of the town. Contentions ensued and multiplied, and removals were from time to time effected. On the 10th of May, 1850, a suit was begun against one John T. Madden, to secure his ejection from a lot which he had settled upon and claimed. The suit was decided against Madden, who then appealed his case to the county court, and on August 8 it came up for hearing. On the next day the judge rendered a decision sustaining that of the recorder. During this trial both parties became excited to the utmost degree, and on the 14th a party of some forty or fifty settlers, officered, mounted, and well drilled, reinstated Madden in the lot of which he had been dispossessed. The mayor, sheriff, and some citizens met them, and shots were interchanged, resulting in the death of three squatters and one of the citizens' party and the wounding of four citizens and a squatter. The city was at once put under martial law, and by evening order was effectually restored. The next day the sheriff, who had proceeded to Brighton with a party of citizens to make arrests, was killed and one of his party was wounded. In this fight two squatters were killed and two were wounded. This brought a summary end to the squatter party, and serious quarrels over land titles were heard of no more.

On the 20th of October the cholera made its appearance in Sacramento; on the 24th, 7 cases were reported, 5 of which were fatal; on the 27th, 6 cases were reported; on the 29th, 12; on the 30th, 19; and so the list goes on. On the 14th of November the daily mortality had decreased to 12, and on the 17th the plague was reported as having entirely disappeared. The precise number of deaths from this contagion can never be known, as many were returned as having died of dysentery, fevers, etc., for the purpose of quieting public apprehension. Of the physicians not a single educated one turned his back upon the city in its distress and threatened destruction, and 17 of them perished at the post of duty. In the week ending November 4 the deaths, so far as known, were 188, and at that date the daily mortality was about 60. What with the deaths and the consequent migration from the city the population soon diminished to not more than one-fifth of its ordinary standard, and when the disease finally disappeared the city was nearly depopulated, and there were not a few who thought it dead beyond the possibility of resurrection. Those who had survived the calamity, however, quickly returned, confidence in the health of the city was almost immediately restored, and business communications with the mines were reopened. In a few weeks, such was the elastic energy of the people, nearly all traces of the great calamity had disappeared, and the city was once more prosperous.

From this time Sacramento began to assume more the appearance, character, and habits of a well-regulated city, and consequently its subsequent history is almost entirely devoid of the charm and interest associated with the beginnings, however rude they may be, of a mushroom mining town. After 1850 the place sank into a dignified tranquillity, disturbed only by floods and fires, and such unromantic incidents as the entrance of the first railroad or the establishment of the state capital.

Sacramento has suffered from many floods. The first two, those of January and March, 1850, have been described. On March 7, 1852, the levee near the mouth of the American river caved in, and within five hours the city was almost entirely submerged. The flood lasted four days, but the damage to the city does not seem to have been extensive. January 1, 1853, it was again completely flooded, but the damage was slight. From 1853 to 1861 there was an intermission, but on December 9 of the latter year the levee upon the eastern boundary of the city gave way, and the waters of the American poured in on the city with the speed of a hurricane. Many lives were lost, but the number could never be ascertained. The loss of property was estimated at about $1,500,000. On January 9, 1862, in consequence of incessant rains and the melting of snow upon the mountains, came another flood, in which it is believed that the Sacramento reached a height of 23 feet above low-water mark, or 5 inches higher than any previously recorded flood. While it lasted, four deaths from drowning were reported and the destruction of property was considerable. On January 22 and February 24 of the same year other floods and breaks in the levees occurred, but by comparison they were of minor consequence. No other flood worthy of note occurred till February, 1878. On the 20th of this month the river rose to 25 feet 10 inches above low-water mark, the highest yet known, but the levee system had been so perfected that the damage was slight.

The first general conflagration in the history of Sacramento occurred on November 2, 1852, at which time fully seven-eighths of the city was destroyed, the loss aggregating between $5,000,000 and $6,000,000. In July, 1854, another serious fire occurred, 200 frame buildings being destroyed, the total loss amounting to nearly $500,000. Since then there have been a number of conflagrations, in which the loss was between $40,000 and $100,000, but none over the latter amount.

The first legislature under the constitution of 1849 met in that year at San José. In 1850 the people selected Vallejo as the state capital, but when the legislature assembled there on January 5, 1852, it was found that the place was too small, and on the 12th it was voted to adjourn to the new court-house at Sacramento, the free use of which had been offered to that body. The session was finished at Sacramento, but Vallejo was still considered the seat of government. In 1853 Benicia was chosen for the capital, and in 1854 the legislature met there. On February 25 a bill fixing the permanent seat of government at Sacramento became a law, and the state officers and legislature moved to that city at once, and the government has since remained there. The capitol building was not finished till December, 1869.

The first shovelful of dirt thrown in the construction of the Central Pacific railroad was in Sacramento on February 22, 1863. The history of the completion of this mammoth enterprise does not belong here. Suffice it to say that Sacramento claims a great part of the praise for the successful execution of the idea of connecting the Atlantic and the Pacific. The first railroad in California, the Sacramento Valley, was built in 1855–'56 from Sacramento to Folsom, the first train being placed on the track August 14, 1855.

SACRAMENTO IN 1880.

The following statistical accounts, mainly compiled by the Census Office, indicate the present condition of Sacramento:

LOCATION.

Sacramento, the capital of California and the county-seat of Sacramento county, is situated nearly in the middle of the state, on the left bank of the Sacramento river, at its junction with the American river. It is about 75 miles northeast of San Francisco in a direct line, 120 miles distant by water and 135 by rail. It varies in altitude from 52 to 85 feet above the level of the sea. The Sacramento river is navigable to this point for large boats, and light-draft boats can go 108 miles above the city. This gives it water communication with an immense grain country, but with no very important points above, and with San Francisco and all points on the bay below. During the high-water stage of the river in the season of 1878–'79 its greatest discharge past the city was 69,400 cubic feet per second. The cross-sectional area of the water-way at the foot of K street was 16,360 square feet; the mean velocity per second was therefore 4.24 feet, or 15,264 feet per hour. The least discharge in 1878 was 6,400 cubic feet per second; the corresponding cross-sectional area was 4,400 square feet; and the mean velocity therefore was 1.45 foot per second, or 5,320 feet per hour. As was remarked in the historical sketch of the city, it has suffered from many floods, and these have been invariably due to the rise in the waters of the American, not the Sacramento, river. In a report by Messrs. Goddard and Leet, engineers, made soon after the flood of December, 1861, we read:

Descending from the summit of the Sierra Nevada mountains, with a fall of from 500 to 50 feet per mile, confined by cañons from 2,000 to 600 feet in height, gathering in its course the accumulated waters of the gulch, stream, and cataract, the American river pours the drainage of more than 1,300 square miles of mountain area through the cañon at Folsom into the Sacramento valley with a torrent velocity, due to the fall, of 6,000 feet in 75 miles, in the form of a crushing, roaring wave, carrying destruction to everything movable in its course.

The many resulant inundations forced the city to build a system of strong levees. At no point is the Front Street levee along the Sacramento lower than 28 feet above the low-water mark. From this levee at G street going northerly and easterly is the "north levee", intended to protect the city directly from the waters of the American. This is the line on which all the breaks of former years, with one exception, have occurred. The danger of a break here has been reduced to a minimum by turning the course of the American river, thus avoiding the constant attrition and occasional heavy strains to which the levee was formerly subjected by the current and the sudden rises of the inconstant stream. By means of a canal the American has been made to empty into the Sacramento about a mile north of its old mouth. The north levee up to the American River bridge, a distance of about 2 miles, is from 0.5 to 1.5 mile east of the river channel, is strong and broad, and is deemed secure against breaking. Above the bridge it runs perhaps 3 miles, is 14 feet through at the top, and on the lowest ground 100 feet wide at the bottom. Throughout on both slopes it is grown with salt and alkali grasses, and has on the outside a strong turf. Below the bridge, in the space between the levee and the river, willows have grown up, and a great amount of sand and *débris* is thrown up every year. This *débris*, which is sent down from the mountains, is caused by hydraulic mining, and is rapidly filling up the channels of the American and the Sacramento. The "*débris* question" is one of the political and legislative questions of the day, but as yet little has been done about it.

RAILROAD COMMUNICATIONS.

With the exception of the Sacramento and Placerville railroad—a line running 49 miles to Shingle Springs—all the roads running out of Sacramento are controlled by the Central Pacific. The main line of this immense road runs from San Francisco to Sacramento in two divisions—one via Stockton and one via Benicia—and thence runs straight to Ogden, Utah, where it connects with the Union Pacific for the East. The California Pacific, now controlled by the Central Pacific, runs from San Francisco to Sacramento via Napa Junction. The Oregon division of the Central Pacific runs from Sacramento to Redding, in northern California.

TRIBUTARY COUNTRY.

Part of the country tributary to Sacramento is devoted to agriculture and part to mining. The character of Sacramento county may be taken as typical of the agricultural portion. The character of the soil in this county is varied; the river-bottoms are rich black soil when not covered with mining *débris*, which, as a whole, has done little injury to the lands of Sacramento county, except by causing more danger of overflow during the rainy season. The lands lying along the water-courses are very prolific; back from them the soil is generally of good quality, raises fair crops of wheat, and seems particularly well adapted to small fruits and vineyards. Along the margin of streams and on the prairie land live and white oak, with some sycamore trees, constitute the principal timber, affording to a considerable extent an article of export for fuel. Toward the east, in the mountainous region, pine and fir trees abound. Some black-walnut trees are found. The staple product is wheat, much of which is safely and profitably exported from the state. It stands the long sea voyage so well because it is so dry. In this, as in all the grain-producing valleys of the state, there is rarely ever any rain from April to October, and the heat for a large portion of the time is intense. From April to June the kernel is standing in the ear ripening and drying; when thrashed, it is placed where the sun or hot dry air has free access, and the drying process is completed. Thus nature does for California what in the eastern states is accomplished by artificial means. Sacramento county is fast becoming a large grape-growing district, being now the fifth in the state in the amount of acreage, which is increasing each year. In 1879, according to the surveyor-general's report, 3,640 acres were devoted to grape-growing in this county. The principal vineyards lie to the southeast, in close proximity to the city. In 1863 Mr. Wilson Flint, writing on grape culture, divided California into four districts, differing widely in isothermal and meteorological conditions as well as in variety of soil. He places the great plains and rolling slopes of Tulare, San Joaquin, and Sacramento valleys in the third, and the foothills of the Sierra Nevada, as well as the eastern slopes of the coast range west of the Sacramento valley, in the fourth; giving the warm and dry valleys preference over the first and second divisions—which lie west of the San Joaquin valley and south of Monterey county—for the uniform and perfect bunches, both in size and equal quality of cured raisins. To the fourth, or mountainous district, he gives the preference for the most valuable wines, because of its elevation and unevenness of surface, as well as favorable soil ingredients.

Besides Sacramento county the whole valley of the river is more or less tributary to the city. The small boats plying above Sacramento bring vast quantities of grain and other agricultural products to the city, where they are transhipped to other parts of the state, and indeed of the world.

Placer mining has almost entirely disappeared around Sacramento, having been superseded by hydraulic and quartz mining. In the immediate vicinity of the city the mining industry has shrunk to small proportions, but in regions more remote, but still to a certain extent tributary to Sacramento, it continues to be profitable and prosperous. Gold and silver are the metals mined.

TOPOGRAPHY.

The soil on the immediate site of Sacramento and for a large area round about consists of sedimentary deposits of a sandy character mixed with decomposed vegetable matter. This is from 40 to 60 feet in depth, and is underlaid by coarse gravel, in which there are large bowlders. In one of the numerous unsuccessful attempts to secure water by means of artesian wells a stratum of loose bowlders was reached at a depth of 860 feet. In this attempt the borer was sent down 2,147 feet without striking a spring. These trials have shown that the bank of the Sacramento river is impervious to its waters. The annual floods which have been spoken of overflow some of the low land of the county, and the water is apt to remain and form stagnant swampy pools after the river has receded; but this is much less the case than formerly, owing to the system of levees which has been constructed over the county. There are a number of sloughs round the city, but most of them have been filled in. On the west bank of the river there are tule marshes. The country for a radius of 5 miles is open. On the east there are plains gradually rising toward the foothills of the mountains which range along the east of the county.

CLIMATE.

The highest recorded summer temperature is 108°; the highest summer temperature in average years, 96°. The lowest recorded winter temperature is 16°; the lowest winter temperature in average years, 27°. The mean summer temperature is 71°; the mean winter temperature, 48°; the mean annual temperature, 60°. Adjacent waters have very little influence on the climate. The marshes produce fever and ague, and bilious and other malarial fevers. A south wind from October to May generally brings rain. In the winter the north wind is dry and cold; in the summer it is very disagreeable and hot. Notwithstanding the rich soil, warm days, and luxuriant vegetation, the nights are always cool, as a breeze from the ocean reaches the city about 4 o'clock of each day during summer. The greatest rainfall in any year between 1849 and 1879, inclusive, was 36.36 inches in 1852–'53; the least was 4.71 inches in 1850–'51. During that time in only 2 years was there any rain in August; in only 5 years was there any rain in July; in only 7 years was there rain in September. In 1850–'51 rain fell in only 5 months (from January to May, inclusive), and in 1866–'67 in only 6 months (November to April, inclusive). The general rainy season begins from the first to the latter part of November and ends from the first to the middle of May. December 3, 1878, snow fell to the depth of one foot in the valley. Light snow had fallen in 1851, 1853, 1858, 1868, and some other years, but in no year as heavy as this. It is the boast of the inhabitants that "Sacramento has more pleasant days in the year than any other place yet known".

STREETS.

The total length of streets is not reported. They are 80 feet wide, with the exception of M street, which is 100 feet wide. The total length paved with cobble-stones is 12,430 feet; stone blocks, 1,200 feet; asphalt, none; broken slag from smelting works, 3,640 feet; wood, 1,000 feet; gravel, 14,320 feet. The cobble-stone pavements cost $1 25 per square yard; the gravel, $0 75; the slag, $0 65 to $0 75; stone blocks, $2 50 to $3. The cost of keeping in good repair, including sprinkling and cleaning, is $30,000 per year. The sidewalks, 8 feet wide, are mainly of plank, with a space of 6 feet outside, which is faced with a 12-inch curbing and sowed with grass. The gutters are of cobble-stone. The manner of construction of sidewalks in the most thickly settled portion of the city is minutely regulated by a city ordinance. Trees have been planted on nearly all save the principal business streets of the city. They are set 12 feet from the fence-line. The work of tree-planting and grass-platting is all done by the property-owners at their own expense. The construction of streets is all done by contract; repairs by the day. There is a decided preference for this system. There are 6 miles of horse-railroad track, and the fare is 5 cents.

WATER-WORKS.

Water was introduced into the city in 1854. The works then built were superseded in 1873 by works using the Holly system, which are still in operation. They are owned by the city. Up to January 1, 1880, the water-works cost, exclusive of repairs and interest, $514,492. The total cost of maintenance for the past year was $42,242 60; the income from water-rates, $39,127 86. The supply of water is obtained from the Sacramento river. The pressure in the mains for domestic use is 40 pounds; for fire purposes, 60 pounds. There are 25 miles of mains and 3,900 taps. The greatest amount pumped per diem is 3,000,000 gallons, and the least 1,000,000 gallons.

GAS.

The gas-works are not owned by the city. The charge per 1,000 feet is $3 50. The daily average production is 110,000 cubic feet. The city pays $4 10 per month for each street-lamp, 259 in number.

PUBLIC BUILDINGS.

There is no city hall, properly speaking. The city offices are situated in the water-works building.

PUBLIC PARKS AND PLEASURE-GROUNDS.

There are 2 public parks, with a total area of 32.5 acres. *Capitol Park*, on which is situated the state capitol, contains 30 acres, and is beautified with terraced lawns, shrubbery, patent-stone walks, and drives. It is bounded by L and N, Tenth and Fifteenth streets, and was deeded to the state by the supervisors in April, 1860, for capitol purposes. It is controlled by the secretary of state. The *City Park* contains 2.5 acres, cost $50,000, and is highly improved with walks, fountains, lawns, and shade trees. It is controlled by a board of trustees. The Agricultural park, owned by the state agricultural society, and controlled by its board of directors, has a mile race-track, which is watered and kept open for driving when not in use for racing.

PLACES OF AMUSEMENT.

The city has 1 theater, the Metropolitan, with a seating capacity of 1,500. There are 4 concert-halls and lecture-rooms, seating capacity not reported, but none large. The mayor writes that there is no really good hall in the place. Theaters pay a license fee to the city of $5 for each performance. There is no place which could properly be called a beer-garden, except a small grove in which picnics are held, principally Sundays, by military and other societies, and at such times beer and other intoxicants are sold there.

DRAINAGE.

The part of the city supplied with sewers covers an area of about 500 acres. A main sewer is laid in each alternate street. Laterals are in each of the alleys at right angles. The total length of sewers is 10½ miles, of which 1¼ mile is made of wood, 1½ mile is of brick, egg-shaped, 3 feet by 5, and 6¾ miles are of clay and cement pipes. Those in the streets are 16 and 18 inches in diameter, and have a fall of from 5 to 10 inches in a block of 400 feet. Those in the alleys are 8 and 10 inches in diameter, and have a fall of from 6 inches to 3 feet in a block of the same length. The brick sewers discharge into the 16- and 18-inch pipes, and the outlet for the whole system is a cement-pipe sewer 30 inches in diameter and 1,800 feet long.

Sewers are flushed about once a month, and deposits are removed by hand through the manholes twice a month. Two men are constantly employed at this work. The cost is $1,000 per year. The mouth of the outlet sewer is above water, and exposed for nine months of the year. Ventilation is provided for by manholes and open catch-basins. In two instances pipes for ventilation purposes are extended to the tops of houses. Water-closets are not allowed to discharge into sewers except by overflows from vaults. It is stated that the soil in many parts of the city is completely saturated with cesspool oozings.

The cost of main sewers and of all branches at street crossings is paid by the city. Branch sewers in alleys are paid for by the owners of abutting property. Assessments are laid on the basis of valuations of land. The prices paid in 1880 are stated to be for 18-inch pipes, 84 cents per foot; 10-inch pipes, 34 cents; 6-inch, 25 cents per foot; manholes, $35 each; catch-basins, $30 each; 6-inch house branches, 29 cents each.

The main sewer at its outlet is 20 feet below high water and about level with low water in the Sacramento river. It discharges into an open canal, made for the purpose, 10 feet wide on the bottom, and having a rate of 1 in 2,000 for about 1 mile. Here it joins another drainage canal coming from the easterly part of the city, and is enlarged to 15 feet on the bottom, and the grade is reduced to 1 in 3,840 for 1 mile farther, where it flows into a lake or slough, and thence by a series of lakes and canals 20 miles to tide-water. The total fall of the canal and lakes is about 10 feet to mean tide-water in San Francisco bay.

The sewerage system is described in the schedule furnished as "rather incomplete and very unsatisfactory", owing to the low-lying position of the outlet, and also to the flat surface of the city. The highest street in the city is but 25 feet above low water in the river, and the ordinary level of street is about 13 to 15 feet. Most of the streets are from 8 to 10 feet higher than the lots, and the sewers, in some places remote from the outfall, are above the level of the adjacent lots. The rates of fall are so slight that deposits are constantly forming. It is reported that the extension of sewerage works to the eastern and more distant parts of the city has been discontinued on account of the condition of the sewers already laid. The beds of the Sacramento and American rivers are rapidly filling with *débris* from the mountains, caused by hydraulic mining. The city is surrounded by dikes to protect it from the higher floods. Pumping machinery has recently been set up to relieve the city from sewage and surface water in time of back water in the drainage canals.

CEMETERIES.

There are 5 cemeteries connected with the city, as follows:

City Cemetery, 33 acres, 10,238 interments.
New Helvetia Cemetery, 20 acres, 4,134 interments.
Saint Joseph's Cemetery, 20 acres, 1,015 interments.
Sunset Hill Cemetery, 5 acres, 827 interments.
Jewish Cemetery, 2½ acres, 171 interments.

The Helvetia cemetery contains within its limits the original burial plot of Sutter's fort. This was a public burying-ground until 1853, when the adjacent grounds were sold to private parties, who maintained the whole as a private cemetery until 1877. In that year the city trustees purchased it and incorporated it as a city cemetery, and since then the interments in it have more than doubled. The grounds are laid out into wide avenues and alleys, and are tastefully planted with trees and shrubs. There is a public reception vault within the grounds, and 3 large reservoirs supply plenty of water to keep the grass plots green.

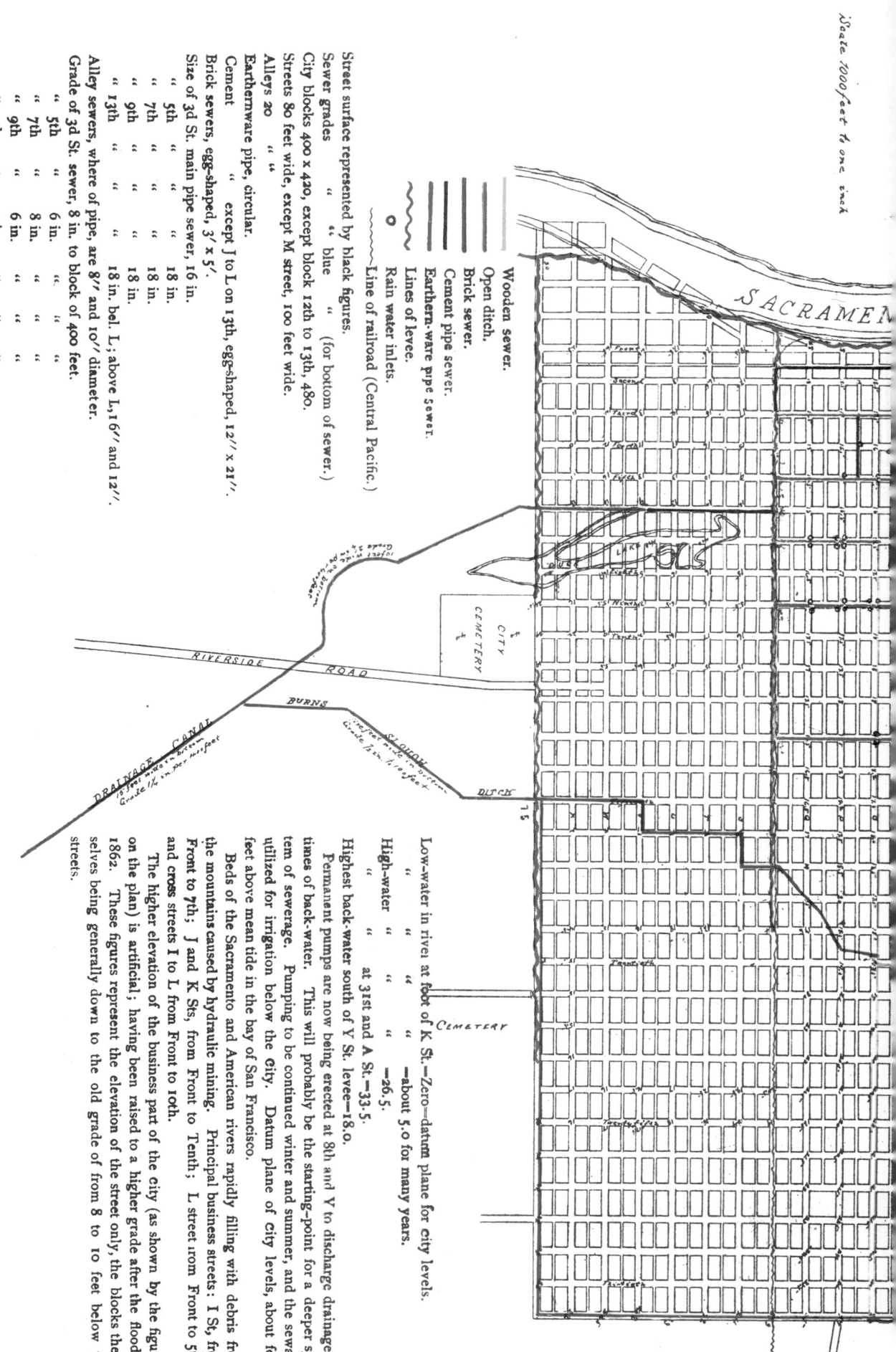

Scale 1000 feet to one inch

Wooden sewer.
Open ditch.
Brick sewer.
Cement sewer.
Cement pipe sewer.
Earthen-ware pipe sewer.
Lines of levee.
Rain water inlets.
Line of railroad (Central Pacific.)

Street surface represented by black figures.
Sewer grades   "   blue   "   (for bottom of sewer.)
City blocks 400 x 420, except block 12th to 13th, 480.
Streets 80 feet wide, except M street, 100 feet wide.
Alleys 20   "   "
Earthenware pipe, circular.
Cement   "   circular.
Cement   "   except J to L on 13th, egg-shaped, 12''x 21''.
Brick sewers, egg-shaped, 3' x 5'.
Size of 3d St. main pipe sewer, 16 in.

"   5th   "   "   "   "   18 in.
"   7th   "   "   "   "   18 in.
"   9th   "   "   "   "   18 in.
"   13th   "   "   "   "   18 in. bel. L; above L,16'' and 12''.

Alley sewers, where of pipe, are 8'' and 10'' diameter.
Grade of 3d St. sewer, 8 in. to block of 400 feet.

"   5th   "   6 in.   "   "   "   "
"   7th   "   8 in.   "   "   "   "
"   9th   "   6 in.   "   "   "   "
"   13th   "   6 in.   "   "   "   "
"   13th   "   5 in.   "   "   "   "

Alley sewers varies from 6 in. to 3 ft. per block.
Cement pipe sewer in 6th St. from R to V, 30 in. diameter.

Low-water in river at foot of K St.—Zero=datum plane for city levels.
"   "   "   "   at 31st and A St.—33.5.
High-water   "   "   —about 5.0 for many years.
"   "   "   —26.5.
Highest back-water south of Y St. levee=18.0.

Permanent pumps are now being erected at 8th and V to discharge drainage in times of back-water. This will probably be the starting-point for a deeper system of sewerage. Pumping to be continued winter and summer, and the sewage utilized for irrigation below the City. Datum plane of city levels, about four feet above mean tide in the bay of San Francisco.

Beds of the Sacramento and American rivers rapidly filling with debris from the mountains caused by hydraulic mining. Principal business streets: I St, from Front to 7th; J and K Sts, from Front to Tenth; L street from Front to 5th; and cross streets I to L from Front to 10th.

The higher elevation of the business part of the city (as shown by the figures on the plan) is artificial; having been raised to a higher grade after the flood of 1862. These figures represent the elevation of the street only, the blocks themselves being generally down to the old grade of from 8 to 10 feet below the streets.

PLAN OF THE SEWERAGE SYSTEM

— OF —

SACRAMENTO.

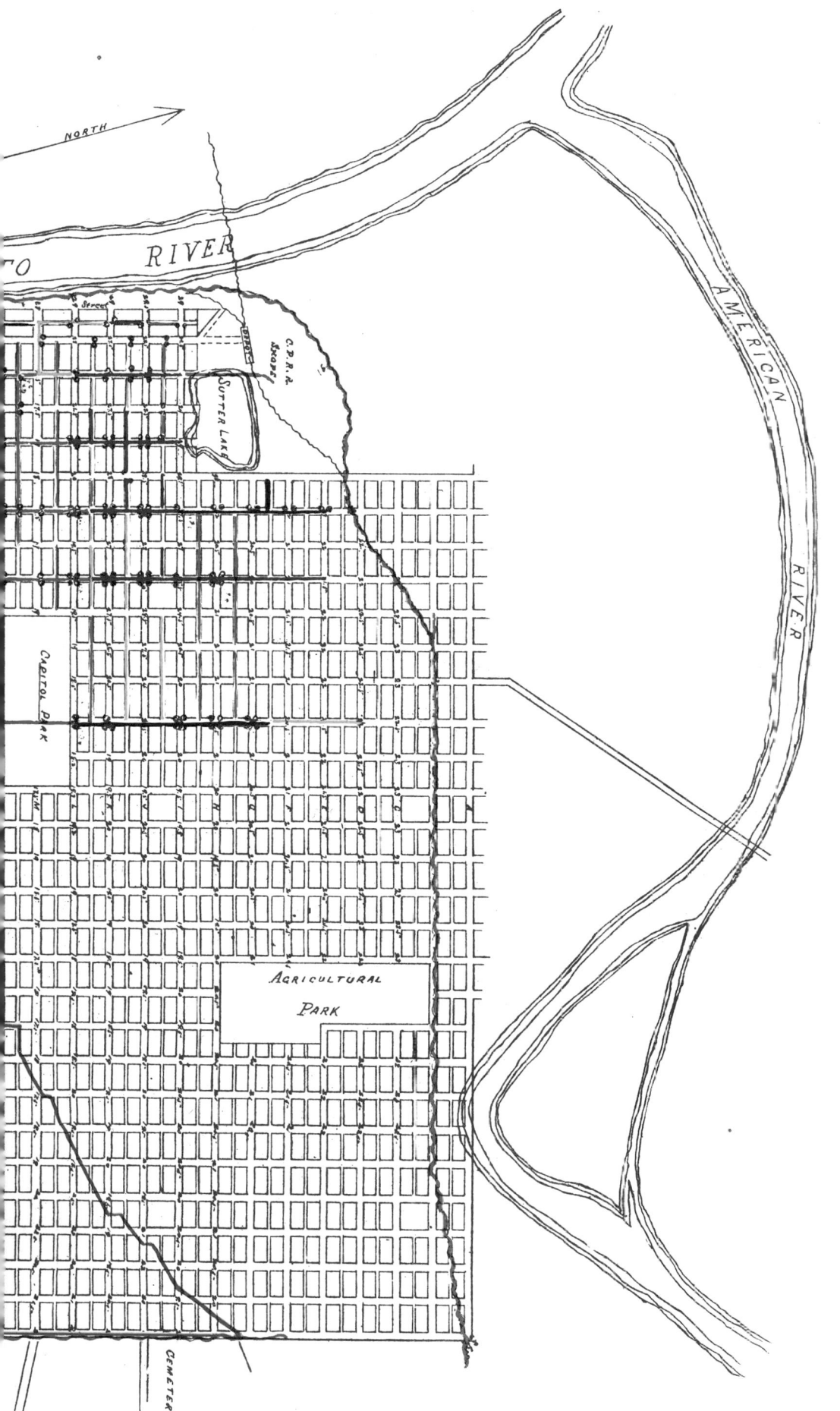

connected with the county hospital, about 3 miles from the city. The city owns no pest-house. Vaccination is supposed to be compulsory, but the law is not strictly enforced. Only the poor are vaccinated at public expense.

REPORTS.

The board publishes no regular reports. It sometimes sends a communication to the board of trustees, and reports monthly to the state board of health the number of births and deaths. The mayor states that in April, 1879, two homeopathic physicians were elected on the board, and that the rest of the board, who were allopathic, at once resigned. At present the board is composed entirely of homeopathic physicians. The mayor further reports that the people of the city are quite willing to conform to sanitary laws and the simple municipal regulations, and that the system works very well.

MUNICIPAL CLEANSING.

Street-cleaning.—Streets are cleaned both by the city and by private abutters. It is done partly by contract and partly by the city's own force. In the business portion of the town it is done every day, and is said to be done very well. The annual cost to the city goes in with street repairs, and so was not reported separately. In the report of the board of trustees we find that last year the disbursements for sprinkling streets amounted to $8,738 50; for water for sprinkling streets, $1,597 25; for labor and cleaning streets, $3,655 38. The sweepings are carted to low lots and covered with earth.

Removal of garbage and ashes.—Garbage is removed both by the city and by householders. This summer a chain-gang is being used to do the work. The garbage is mostly taken off by swill-gatherers; ashes are carted off to low places and then covered with dry earth. The frequent inspections of the health officer, by preventing the accumulation of garbage, lessens the danger of nuisances or probable injury to health. The city ordinances provide that garbage shall not be thrown into the streets, and that if placed on the edge of the sidewalk in boxes or barrels it shall be removed within two hours.

Dead animals.—Dead animals are removed and buried outside the city limits at the owner's expense. If the owner can not be found, they are removed and buried at the city's expense. The annual cost of this service is inconsiderable.

Liquid household wastes.—Chamber, laundry, and kitchen slops are all disposed of in the same way. The city is full of cesspools. Wherever it is possible they are connected with the sewers to prevent overflows. Some house drains, but not many, are connected with the alley sewers. None of the liquid household waste runs into the gutters. The mayor says that "our subsoil is to a very great extent highly charged with sewage".

Human excreta.—It can not be definitely stated what proportion of the houses have water-closets, but it is certain that privy-vaults are largely in the excess. It is reported that none of the water-closets deliver into public sewers, but all into cesspools. Few, if any, of the privy-vaults are nominally water-tight. There are no regulations as to their construction and emptying. The dry-earth system is not used to any extent.

Manufacturing waste.—There are no establishments in Sacramento that produce any manufacturing wastes of consequence.

POLICE.

The police force is appointed by a board of police commissioners, consisting of the mayor, the police judge, and the chief of police, the last-named receiving a salary of $1,800 per year. The board of police commissioners makes such rules as it may judge necessary for the appointment, employment, uniforming, disciplining, trial, and government of the members of the department. The force is composed of 11 regular and 6 local or special policemen. The regular officers receive $1,200 per year each, and the local officers are paid by subscription. The uniform is of blue, with a black Alpine hat with gold band. The men provide their own uniforms. Each man carries a revolver, handcuffs, and a club. The day-watch serves 14 and the night-watch 7 hours. The force patrols 109 miles of streets. All local officers must report for duty at the police office at 8 o'clock p. m. and report off at 5 o'clock a. m., and all must answer the call of the chief or captain. The only peculiar section in the police regulations is this:

All local and special officers are directed to make monthly reports in writing to the police commissioners of all sums paid to them for services as such officers and by whom paid; also to make special reports in writing within 24 hours after the receipt of any money or other property coming to their possession as a present or reward for official services rendered or to be rendered; such reports shall give the amount of money and description of property received and the circumstances of its reception, with the name and address of the donor.

In 1880 there were 2,592 arrests, the principal cause being, as is concisely reported by the chief, "whisky". During the year there were 752 station-house lodgers. Free meals were given at a cost of 10 cents per meal. The force is required to co-operate with the fire department to the extent of rendering all the assistance possible and of preserving order at fires. Special policemen are appointed by the police commissioners, are under the direction of the chief of police, and are required to assist the regular officers. The only casualty in the force in 1880 was the breaking of an officer's wrist. The total cost of the department for the year was $17,663 19.

MANUFACTURES.

The following is a summary of the statistics of the manufactures of Sacramento for 1880, being taken from tables prepared for the Tenth Census by James R. Hardenberg, chief special agent:

Mechanical and manufacturing industries.	No. of establishments.	Capital.	AVERAGE NUMBER OF HANDS EMPLOYED.			Total amount paid in wages during the year.	Value of materials.	Value of products.
			Males above 16 years.	Females above 15 years.	Children and youths.			
All industries............................	160	$1,672,400	868	10	46	$547,692	$2,911,889	$4,093,934
Agricultural implements.............	3	14,000	6	....	....	3,840	18,050	31,125
Blacksmithing (see also Wheelwrighting)	8	23,600	27	1	2	19,990	14,700	43,300
Boots and shoes, including custom work and repairing	12	7,000	16	....	....	12,860	14,531	39,041
Bread and other bakery products.................	9	50,400	28	....	2	19,881	81,241	127,338
Carriages and wagons (see also Wheelwrighting)	4	69,000	42	....	....	24,477	26,600	74,445
Coffee and spices, roasted and ground	5	17,650	7	....	....	3,300	32,300	43,660
Confectionery.............................	5	34,050	16	....	....	15,028	63,315	112,200
Cooperage	3	35,000	25	....	15	16,000	25,000	59,500
Foundery and machine-shop products	5	120,000	65	....	4	41,600	50,600	114,700
Furniture (see also Upholstering)	7	76,000	83	....	4	40,441	97,000	158,600
Liquors, malt.............................	6	105,000	51	....	....	23,975	92,310	165,600
Lock- and gun-smithing	3	3,200	5	....	1	3,400	1,900	8,500
Marble and stone work	9	45,700	38	....	....	27,508	27,900	77,700
Plumbing and gasfitting..............	5	8,200	17	....	1	12,350	21,580	39,850
Saddlery and harness.................	11	50,200	57	....	....	37,144	78,725	138,324
Slaughtering and meat-packing, not including retail butchering.....	3	65,000	19	....	....	8,860	120,550	138,500
Tinware, copperware, and sheet-iron ware	7	12,100	19	....	2	17,360	21,500	52,400
Tobacco, cigars and cigarettes..........	8	14,600	25	....	2	9,232	68,680	102,100
Upholstering (see also Furniture)	3	9,600	9	....	....	3,480	9,400	20,750
Wheelwrighting (see also Blacksmithing; Carriages and wagons)...	4	4,500	11	....	....	2,588	3,600	18,500
All other industries (a)	40	907,600	302	9	13	194,698	2,040,407	2,527,801

a Embracing awnings and tents; baskets, rattan and willow ware; boxes, wooden packing; brass castings; brick and tile; brooms and brushes; carpentering; carriage and wagon materials; clothing, men's; coffins, burial cases, and undertakers' goods; electrical apparatus and supplies; flavoring extracts; flouring- and grist-mill products; gloves and mittens; glue; grease and tallow; leather, dressed skins; leather, tanned; liquors, distilled; lumber, planed; malt; mineral and soda waters; patent medicines and compounds; pickles, preserves, and sauces; printing and publishing; roofing and roofing materials; sash, doors, and blinds; shirts; soap and candles; stone- and earthen-ware; umbrellas and canes; watch and clock repairing; wood, turned and carved; and woolen goods.

From the foregoing table it appears that the average capital of all establishments is $10,452 50; that the average wages of all hands employed is $592 74 per annum; and that the average outlay in wages, in materials, and in interest (at 6 per cent.) on capital employed is $22,249 53.

SAN FRANCISCO,
SAN FRANCISCO COUNTY, CALIFORNIA.

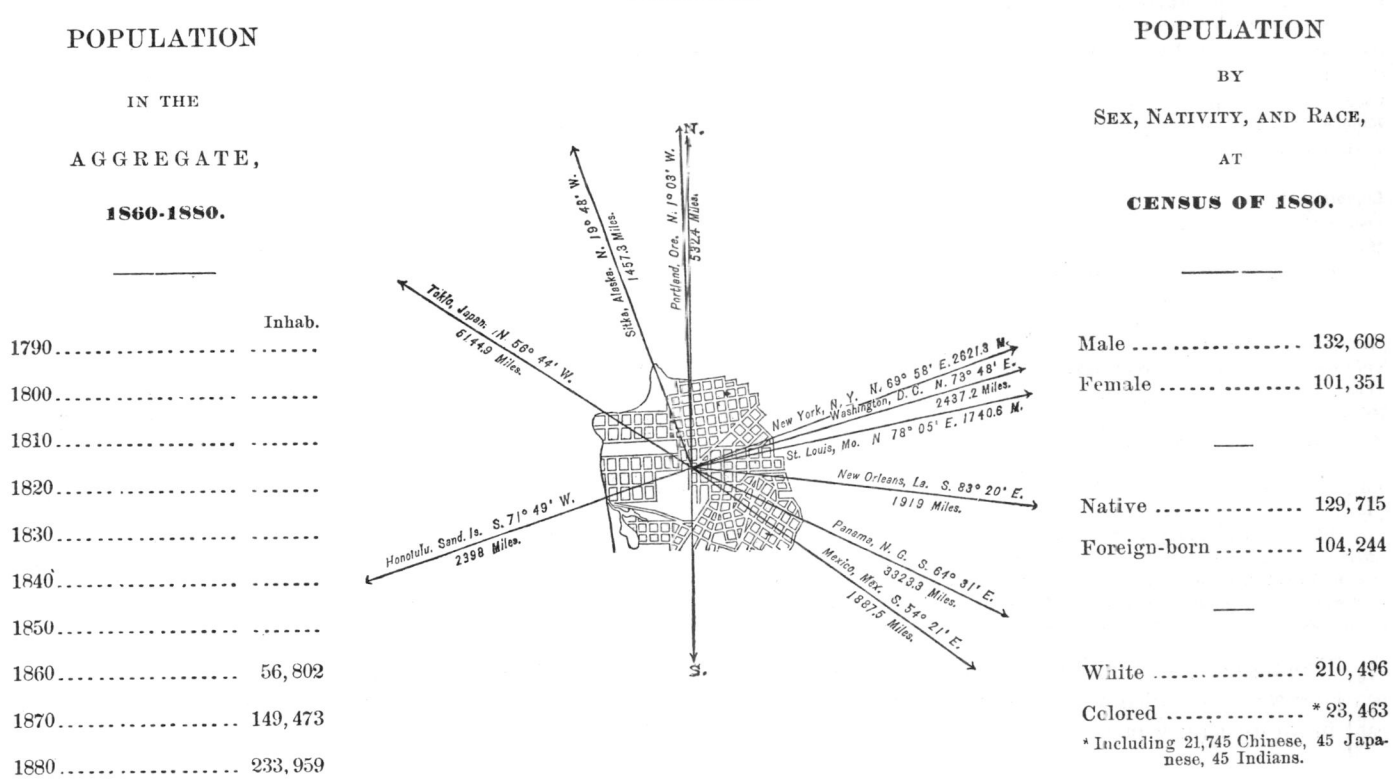

POPULATION

IN THE

AGGREGATE,

1860-1880.

	Inhab.
1790	....
1800	....
1810	....
1820	....
1830	....
1840	....
1850	....
1860	56,802
1870	149,473
1880	233,959

POPULATION

BY

SEX, NATIVITY, AND RACE,

AT

CENSUS OF 1880.

Male	132,608
Female	101,351
Native	129,715
Foreign-born	104,244
White	210,496
Colored	* 23,463

* Including 21,745 Chinese, 45 Japanese, 45 Indians.

Latitude: 37° 48 North; Longitude: 122° 24' (west from Greenwich); Altitude: 0 to 400 feet.

FINANCIAL CONDITION.

Total Valuation: $244,477,360; per capita: $1,045 00. Net Indebtedness: $3,059,285; per capita: $13 08. Tax per $100: $2 24.

HISTORICAL SKETCH.(a)

The first settlement within the limits now occupied by the city was made in 1776 by some Franciscan monks, who established a mission and presidio near the bay, to which they had given the name of their patron saint. September 17, 1776, the soldiers who were placed under the orders of the monks to afford them protection in case of need, took possession of the presidio, or military post, in the name of the king of Spain. The mission, which was named the "Mission Dolores", was situated about one mile from the northern extremity of the peninsula on which the

a Nearly all the information and statistical accounts concerning San Francisco, including the historical sketch, were furnished by his honor Mayor M. C. Blake and A. Ballam, esq., city and county assessor.

present city is built, and about two miles from the bay. The mission had been founded for the purpose of spreading the doctrines of christianity among the Indians, and for more than half a century the population of the peninsula remained almost without change.

In 1831 the population, including Indians, was as follows: Mission, 237; presidio, 371. But at about this time there was a considerable increase in the population of the surrounding country from trappers, whalers, and adventurers of various kinds, who began to settle at various points. There began to be a considerable trade in hides and tallow, and the Mexican governor determined to establish a port of entry on the bay of San Francisco, and selected the shore of Yerba Buena cove for its site. He appointed Captain W. A. Richardson harbor-master, and in the latter part of 1835 that official erected the first structure, about which the modern city has grown.

In July of the next year Jacob P. Leese erected a building adjoining that of Captain Richardson, and the town of Yerba Buena was thus founded. In 1846 it had increased to a town boasting 200 inhabitants and 50 houses. On July 8 of that year, news of the war between Mexico and the United States having reached the Pacific coast, Commander Montgomery, of the United States sloop-of-war Portsmouth, acting under orders from Commodore Sloat, took possession of the town on the shore of Yerba Buena cove and raised the American flag on the plaza. The town was retained by the Americans until the close of the hostilities in 1848, when California was ceded to the United States by the treaty of Guadalupe Hidalgo. January 30, 1847, the name of the town had been changed to "San Francisco" by order of Washington A. Bartlett, the alcalde.

In April, 1848, San Francisco had 135 dwelling-houses, 10 unfinished houses, 12 stores and warehouses, and 35 shanties, while its population was about 1,000. At about this time the discovery of gold at Coloma, 60 miles from Sacramento, where it had been found the preceding January, became generally known. The first effect of this discovery upon San Francisco was to cause a rush of the greater portion of its inhabitants to the gold fields. But as soon as the discovery of precious metal became known in the eastern states immigration to California began, and in July, 1849, San Francisco had fully 5,000 inhabitants. At the close of the following year the number of inhabitants had increased to 34,776; and during the next 10 years over 22,000 people were added to the population. The discovery of the rich mineral lodes in Nevada at a time when the placer mines had been nearly worked out gave another impetus to the growth of the city, which was still further aided by the conviction that California was to be one of the great wheat-producing states.

After the cession of California to the United States the old Mexican form of the town government was retained by the inhabitants of San Francisco until May, 1850, when a charter was granted by the legislature, then in session, and San Francisco became an incorporated city. This charter, with an amendment that was made during the next year, remained in force until 1855, when the city was reincorporated. April 19, 1855, however, a radical change was made in the city government. By an act of the legislature, known as the "consolidation act", the city and county of San Francisco were consolidated. The old municipal government by two boards of aldermen was abolished, and in its stead was established a board of supervisors, consisting of one person elected from each of the 12 wards into which the city was divided, presided over by a president, who was the chief executive officer of the municipality. The president had all the powers of a mayor, and in a short time that title was by act of legislature attached to the office. The consolidation act was adopted by the new constitution as a part of its framework, so far as it related to the city of San Francisco, and is still in force.

During the years immediately following the discovery of gold the town rapidly spread over all that area bordering Yerba Buena cove that was available for building purposes, and the work of filling in the cove itself, which was very shallow, was begun soon after immigration commenced. The immigration was so great that it was with great difficulty that even the meanest accommodation could be provided. In consequence of the extraordinary growth of the town in population the structures that were erected were for the most part of the cheapest description and of the most inflammable character. Tents and houses built of canvas and boards existed everywhere, and the city was thus exposed to great danger from fire.

The first great fire occurred December 24, 1849, and in a few hours burnt to the ground nearly all the buildings in a block in the busiest portion of the city. The loss was estimated at $1,000,000, but before the ashes were cold the work of rebuilding was begun, and in a short time new structures had taken the place of those destroyed. But on the morning of May 4, 1850, another conflagration started upon almost the spot where the fire of the previous December had begun. In a few hours three entire blocks had been cleared of their buildings, and property amounting to $4,000,000 had been destroyed. Within ten days, however, more than half of the area desolated by fire had been covered with new buildings. June 14 another great fire began, and property valued at $5,000,000 was burnt; but, as in former instances, the work of rebuilding was at once begun, and in a few weeks the burnt district was again covered with hastily erected and inflammable structures. September 17 of the same year another fire entailed a loss of about $300,000; and December 14 a more serious conflagration destroyed $1,000,000 worth of property.

But the most destructive fire that has ever visited the city broke out May 4, 1851. In less than twelve hours the entire business portion of the city, over twenty blocks in area, was burnt to the ground. Fully 1,500 buildings of different kinds were burnt and property valued at $10,000,000 or $12,000,000 was destroyed. But another fire was yet to come, and on June 22 the buildings covering ten blocks in another portion of the city were burnt, at a loss of $3,000,000.

This was the last great fire that visited San Francisco in its early days. The erection of more substantial buildings and the organization of an efficient fire department protected the city from other great conflagrations. The next large fire occurred August 28, 1876, when 142 buildings were destroyed and property valued at $703,734 was burnt.

One of the last fires of any consequence occurred in 1877, when 62 buildings were burnt. The total loss at this fire was $264,000.

During the first years of the gold excitement, when a constant stream of precious metal was pouring into San Francisco, business was flourishing and large fortunes were easily and rapidly made. But by the beginning of 1854 the glut of the market by speculators; the lack of water in the interior for mining purposes, and the consequent falling off in the production of gold; the effects of building which had gone on far in excess of the needs of the city; the difficulty experienced by banks in obtaining coin; the corrupt character of the municipal government, all contributed to bring on a financial crisis, which was precipitated by the failure of Page, Bacon, and Company's bank. Many other banks in the city and several in the country also suspended payment. But a winter followed during which there was rain enough for the mines, and gold was produced in abundance. The surplus stock of goods had been got rid of, much being left on the docks to spoil. Immigration continued, and confidence was restored.

But hard times followed again in the course of a few years. There were fears that as the placer mines became exhausted, which must eventually happen, San Francisco must decline; and these forebodings as to the future of the city were intensified by the breaking out of the Frazer River gold excitement in the latter part of 1857. The discovery of gold on the banks of that river would, it was feared, build up a powerful rival to San Francisco.

At the beginning of 1858 it became impossible to sell real estate or any other kind of property, and an exodus from the city began which threatened to depopulate it. A financial panic prevailed, during which there was a wholesale foreclosure of mortgages. But in December the fears as to the future of the city were somewhat calmed, and business began to revive. There was a steady improvement in business up to 1859–'60, when a new impulse was given to the prosperity of the whole coast, and to that of San Francisco in particular, by the discovery of rich gold and silver deposits in that great mineral-bearing ledge known as the Comstock lode. The excitement caused by the discovery of several rich bodies of ore increased steadily until 1864, when there began to be felt much doubt as to the future of the Comstock. The building of the Central Pacific railroad, which was begun in 1864, helped to tide over the depression, but eventually led to another period of depression in 1869. The benefits to be derived from the completion of the transcontinental road had been discounted, and when the road was opened for traffic in 1869, and it was seen how extravagant had been the expectations based upon it, a reaction took place and prices began to decline, and a period of depression ensued, from which, however, the city gradually recovered.

In August, 1875, the failure of the Bank of California produced another financial panic. The day after the failure of this bank the National Gold Bank and Trust Company closed its doors, but resumed business in a few days. For some days it was almost impossible to obtain money anywhere. In consequence of the panic the Merchants' Exchange Bank withdrew from business, and financial troubles growing out of the failure of the Bank of California were the prime cause of much financial distress. The energetic action of the directors of the Bank of California, aided by the good-will of the people, who did not wish to see an institution of which they were so proud utterly ruined, put the Bank of California upon its feet again in a few days, and the crisis, which was sharp while it lasted, was soon passed.

The last period of depression occurred during the years 1878–'79. The quasi-socialistic agitation, which was begun in 1877, led to a period of great depression during the next two years. Confidence in the security of property was weakened, business was depressed, and considerable capital left the city. But after the agitation had died out confidence slowly returned, and the year 1880 closes with a bright prospect for future prosperity.

The discovery of gold in California caused to flock to the Pacific coast adventurers and desperate men from every part of the world. The roughs from eastern cities, the criminals from England and Australia, and dangerous characters from almost every civilized nation came in great numbers to San Francisco, and they became so numerous that they bade defiance to the law, and began to roam through the city in gangs, assaulting, robbing, and murdering. It became necessary for peaceable citizens, early in the history of the gold excitement, to take some measures for the protection of their lives and property, and to relieve the city of the tyranny to which it was subjected. Accordingly a call was made for a meeting of citizens on the plaza July 16, 1849, and an organization was there effected. A body of armed men was formed, and the arrest of notorious criminals was begun. Many were tried before a court formed of some of the best citizens and were promptly convicted, but in no cases did the punishment inflicted extend to the taking of the life of the prisoner. The action of the organization, however, had a wholesome influence, and, many of the most desperate characters having been driven from the city, there succeeded a period of comparative quiet. But there still remained many criminals who chafed at the restraints put upon them, and who still continued to commit many crimes. Many of the large fires which swept over the city were believed to be set by them. In two years there were over 100 murders, for which not one criminal was hung. In 1851 affairs had

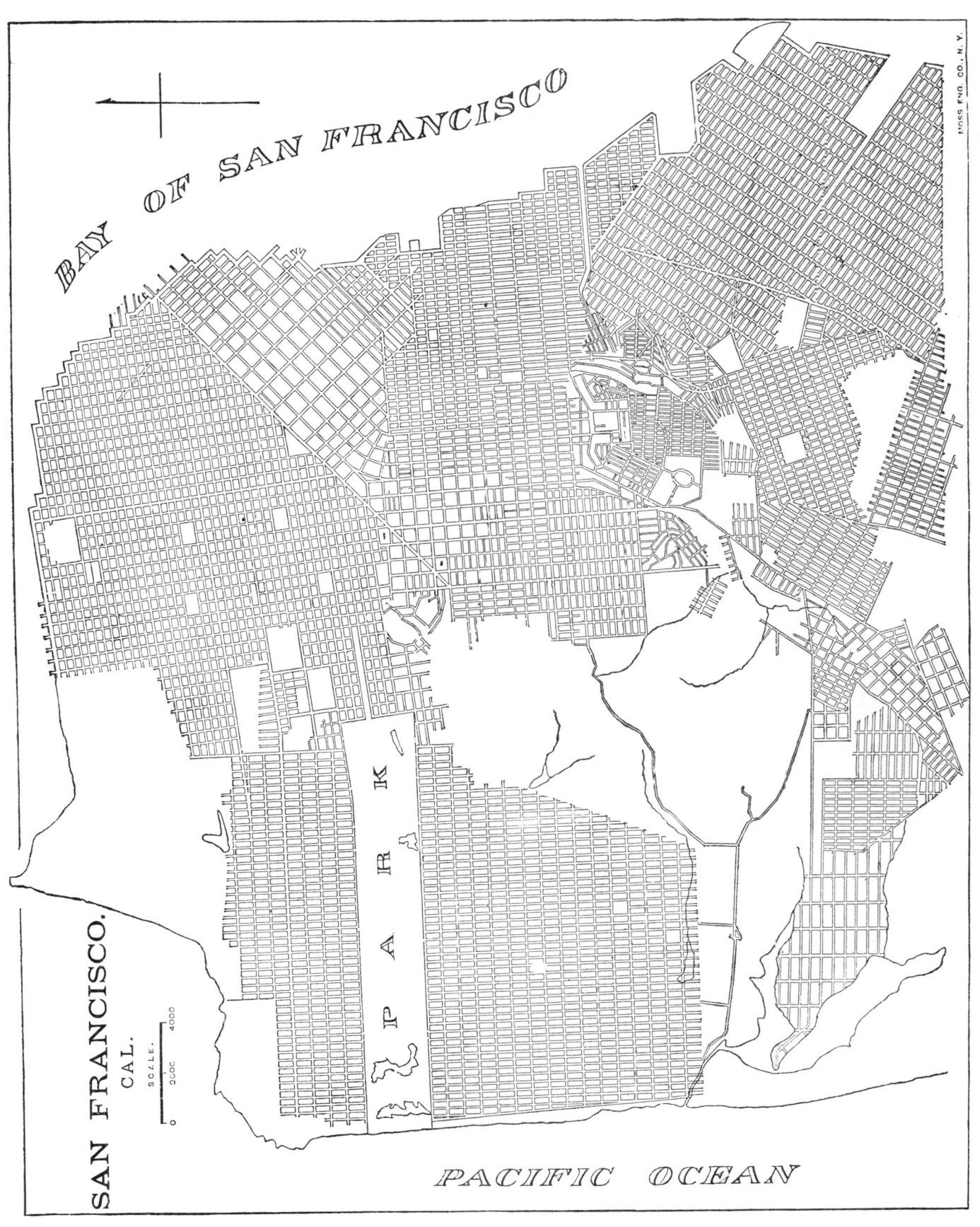

BAY OF SAN FRANCISCO

SAN FRANCISCO.
CAL.

SCALE.

0   2000   4000

PARK

PACIFIC OCEAN

MOSS ENG. CO., N. Y.

become so bad that in June of that year it was determined to organize a vigilance committee. Such a committee was formed, having written articles of association, and including many of the most influential citizens. Several murderers were arrested, tried, and executed, and many more were driven away. Crime was to a great extent suppressed, although many criminals yet remained. Municipal government was corrupt and many men of unsavory character held municipal offices. The war against this corruption begun by James King, editor of the *Evening Bulletin*, gave rise to the second vigilance committee, which was organized in 1856. King was shot May 14 by James P. Casey, whom he had charged with stuffing ballot-boxes, and whose imprisonment in Sing Sing, New York, on a charge of felony, he had published. Casey had placed himself in the hands of the sheriff after the shooting, and was conducted to the county jail, where he was believed to be among friends. On the night following the shooting a large number of citizens met and organized a vigilance committee. By the end of the week several thousands of citizens had been enrolled. They were organized into companies of 100 each, electing their own officers. Each company also elected three members to represent it in the executive committee, which acted with the vigilance committee, and without whose concurrence no condemned prisoner could be executed. The companies were regularly drilled, and the whole force was placed under the command of a leader of military experience.

On Sunday, May 18, several thousands of the committeemen marched to the county jail, and, having planted a cannon in front of its door, demanded that Casey, and a criminal named Cova, charged with having murdered Major Richardson, be delivered up to them. Their demands were complied with, and several days were spent in the examination of the prisoners, who were sentenced to death. King died May 20, and the committee's prisoners were hanged from the windows of the committee's headquarters on the day of his funeral. The vigorous action of the committee struck terror in the hearts of the criminal classes, and a better state of affairs began. Crime was crushed out to a great extent, and politics were purified. The vigilance committee gradually became less and less a military organization, and was at last known as the People's party, the beneficial effects of whose influence were felt in politics for years after the committee ceased to exist.

The riots of 1877, when considerable property was destroyed by incendiaries, caused the organization of what was known as the safety committee, which was joined by many thousands of the best citizens. Its influence was healthful, and the danger of a serious riot was soon averted. Again, in 1879, the danger that was feared from those engaged in the quasi-socialistic movement gave rise to another organization for the protection of the city, and the fear which the ignorance respecting it inspired doubtless did much to quell the excitement and to bring about that peace and quiet which now exist.

The condition of affairs in San Francisco at the present time is gratifying. Much encouragement has been given to manufactures, and a determined effort is being made to procure the immigration to California of good settlers to assist in developing the resources of the state. All of the buildings erected within the past twelve months and in process of erection at the present time are far superior in design, quality of material, and care in construction, to most of the buildings erected prior to 1880.

SAN FRANCISCO IN 1880.

The following statistical accounts, collected by the Census Office, indicate the present condition of the city:

LOCATION.

San Francisco, the chief city of California and the commercial metropolis of the Pacific coast, lies in latitude 37° 48′ north, and longitude 122° 24′ west from Greenwich, at the northern extremity of a peninsula which separates the bay of San Francisco from the Pacific ocean. The city stands on the inner side of the peninsula, which is 30 miles long and 6 miles across at this point, and at the base of high hills. The average altitude above sea-level is 183 feet; the lowest point being tide-level, and the highest 376 feet in settled portions, rising to 400 feet above sea-level in the northwestern portion of the city.

HARBOR.

The entrance to the bay of San Francisco is through a narrow, deep channel, called the Golden Gate, formed by the extension of the peninsula on which the city is built, which here approaches close to the coast on the northern side of the bay. There is, however, several miles off shore, a bar composed of loose sand which has a channel depth of 23 feet of water at low tide. Inside the bar the channel is much deeper, the average depth of water in the harbor proper being 42 feet. The land-locked water, to which the Golden Gate gives entrance from the ocean, has an area of 400 square miles, more than 200 square miles of which have a depth of over 6 fathoms. The harbor is protected on the ocean side by high hills, which, toward the north, rise to the dignity of mountains.

This inland sea is composed of three bodies of water connected with each other by comparatively narrow but very deep channels. The most southern of these divisions is San Francisco bay proper; connected with it on the north is San Pablo bay; and connected with the latter on the east is Suisun bay, into which flow the Sacramento and San Joaquin rivers, draining 53,000 square miles of territory in the interior of the state. The average rise and fall of the tides at the wharves in the city is 3½ feet, the largest tide being 9½ feet amplitude. The current along the city front at ebb spring tide is about 5 knots per hour, and the ebb at neap tide about 3½ knots.

There are five ferries from the city to the several towns along the shores of the bay. The principal ones are those between San Francisco and Oakland and San Francisco and Alameda, two lines running to the former place. The rate of fare is 15 cents each way, a considerable reduction being made when monthly tickets are purchased. These three ferries carry about 6,000,000 passengers during the year. There is one ferry between San Francisco and Saucelito, distance 6 miles, and one between the former city and San Rafael, distance 15 miles. The fare over the former ferry is 25 cents, and over the latter 50 cents, each way.

RAILROAD COMMUNICATIONS.

The city has the following railroad facilities:

The Central Pacific railroad, main line to Ogden, Utah, connecting with the Union Pacific to the East, the northern division to Callstoga and Willows, the Oregon division to Redding, and the southern division to Tulare and Yuma, Arizona.

The North Pacific Coast railroad, to Duncan Mills, 80 miles.

The San Francisco and North Pacific railroad, to Cloverdale, 83 miles.

The South Pacific Coast railroad, to Vera Cruz.

The Southern Pacific Railroad of California, to Soledad, 143 miles.

The termini of the Central Pacific and main line of the Southern Pacific roads are on the Oakland side of the bay, but freight-cars are transported to this city on large boats, making San Francisco the practical terminus. The same is true of the South Pacific Coast road, which transfers its passengers and freight at Alameda across the bay.

TRIBUTARY COUNTRY.

The country in the immediate vicinity of the city is devoted principally to dairy farms, chicken ranches, and vegetable gardens. Oakland and Alameda, on the opposite side of the bay, are largely used as places of residence by persons doing business in San Francisco.

In addition to the local trade with this country, San Francisco may be said to control the trade of the Pacific coast as far north as Alaska and south to Panama. The whaling fleet in the Pacific draws most of its supplies from this point. In fact, all the country touched by the many railroads centering here may be said to be tributary to the city, and a large proportion of the wheat crops of the state come to San Francisco to be shipped.

TOPOGRAPHY.

The area of the city and county of San Francisco is 42 square miles, and includes, besides the entire end of the peninsula across to the ocean, Goat island, with an area of 141 acres, 2 miles east; Alcatraz island, with 30 acres, 1 mile north; and the Farallones islands, 24 miles off shore in the ocean. These latter are, strictly speaking, merely a collection of rocky islets. The surface of the extremity of the peninsula is very irregular. The southern half of the city is only a little above tide-water, while the northern part varies from 20 to 376 feet above tide, one point stretching up 24 feet higher. This forms a sort of amphitheater about a comparatively small tract of level land, the houses spreading over many of the hills to the north and west.

In 1846 the hills were steep and cut up by numerous gullies, and the low ground at their base was narrow, save in what is now the south part of the city, where there was a succession of ridges or dunes of loose barren sand, almost impassable for loaded wagons. The sand ridges have been leveled, the gullies and hollows filled up, and the hills cut down, and where large ships rode at anchor in 1849 there are now paved streets. Not less than 300 acres of the bay have been filled in, and the total expense of grading has been over $30,000,000.

The underlying rock is calcareous sandstone, and its disintegration has produced the sand of which the peninsula is composed. There is no soil, the underlying rock being covered only with sand. In the southern part of the city there is an area which was once swamp land, and through which a creek now winds. The drainage of the city is bad, the waters from the hills coming down with great force into sewers that have little, if any, grade, and filling them with sand and *débris*. In the western part of the city, near the ocean, there is a lake of fresh water, of considerable size, called lake Merced. The peninsula is destitute of trees.

CLIMATE.

The climate of San Francisco is very equable, owing partly to the influence of the surrounding water, but principally to the steady westerly winds of summer, which reduce the temperature so that it ranges little above that of winter. The lowest recorded temperature is 25°, in January, 1854, and the highest temperature—97° and 98°—was on September 10 and 11, 1852. The average highest summer temperature is 82.6°, and the average lowest winter temperature 40.2°. In 30 years the mercury has stood above 90° only 12 times. September is the warmest month and October the next warmest. Only twice has snow fallen in the city; once on December 29, 1856, when 3 inches fell, and again on January 12, 1868, when 2 inches fell. The mean annual amount of precipitation, in rain and melted snow, is 26.55 inches. The constant temperature of the ocean current which bathes the shore is 54°.

It is reported that the marshy ground in the southern part of the city exercises a harmful influence upon the health of that section.

STREETS.

The approximate length of the streets in San Francisco is 500 miles. Of these, 25 miles are paved with cobble-stones, 20 miles with stone blocks, 5 miles with asphalt or other composition, 57 miles with broken stone, and 31 miles with wood, 27 miles of this latter being plank and 4 miles blocks. The cost per square foot of each, as nearly as it may be estimated, is, for cobble-stones, 20 cents; stone blocks, 28 cents; asphalt, 27 cents; macadam, 12 cents; wood blocks, 28 cents; and planks, 10 cents. The cost of keeping each class of pavements in repair is not known, the accounts for this class of work not being kept separately. Stone blocks are said to be the easiest to keep clean, and are considered preferable as to quality and permanent economy. The sidewalks are of plank and asphaltum, laid on either wood or brick, the former largely predominating. In some parts of the city the sidewalks are laid with patent stone. Very few of the streets have gutterways, only the length of a few blocks being laid with gutters. There are but few trees planted in the streets. The climate here is such that sunshine is preferable to shade, and, owing to the strong and continuous winds from the ocean, it is difficult to keep growing trees in an upright position.

All streets are graded, paved, and sewered by contract, the cost being assessed on the abutting property-owners. When accepted by the city, it keeps them in repair by day labor.

The laws governing the city authorities in regard to the manner of accepting streets have been changed several times. Formerly, when any street or portion of a street had been constructed to the satisfaction of the committee on streets, wharves, grades, and public buildings, it was accepted whether the same had been paid for or not, and thereafter kept in repair at the public expense; but in 1878 this was changed, and a law was passed which provided for the acceptance of any portion of a street, and suspended from the benefits of acceptance those portions fronting properties whose owners had failed to pay the improvement assessments, which form the basis of acceptance. The accepted streets are now classified as follows:

1. Streets accepted to October 9, 1871, by resolutions under which the roadways and sidewalks are accepted.

2. Streets accepted from October 9, 1871, by resolutions under which the roadway only is accepted.

3. Streets accepted partially from April 4, 1870; that is, where no sewer is constructed, property remaining chargeable therewith when the sewer is deemed necessary; roadway only accepted.

4. Streets accepted partially from April 1, 1878; those portions of streets only being accepted in front of property the owners of which have paid the assessment for the work done.

The following table shows the annual sum disbursed on account of street work during the past 24 years:

Year.	Amount.	Year.	Amount.	Year.	Amount.
1856–'57	$47,441 00	1864–'65	$1,157,052 00	1872–'73	$506,498 00
1857–'58	42,793 00	1865–'66	1,089,558 00	1873–'74	667,488 00
1858–'59	46,259 00	1866–'67	1,003,083 00	1874–'75	603,492 00
1859–'60	204,304 00	1867–'68	1,511,481 00	1875–'76	1,037,026 00
1860–'61	308,168 00	1868–'69	1,565,612 00	1876–'77	1,862,134 00
1861–'62	381,144 00	1869–'70	1,246,125 00	1877–'78	912,270 00
1862–'63	487,165 00	1870–'71	843,415 00	1878–'79	699,793 00
1863–'64	662,423 00	1871–'72	380,698 00	1879–'80	624,858 57

STREET TRANSPORTATION.

There are 10 lines of horse-railroads in the city, with an aggregate length of 45 miles, and 4 cable roads, with an aggregate length of 10 miles, but as most of the roads here have a double track there are over 100 miles of rails laid in the streets. Including the cable roads, these lines have 275 cars and 1,800 horses in use, and furnish employment to 650 men. The number of passengers carried annually is about 35,000,000, and the rate of fare on all roads is 5 cents. After the horse-cars had been in operation for some time, and were even being extended, it was found that the many high, steep hills in the northern and western portions of the city necessitated the adoption of other means of transportation at these points. A rise of from 50 to 80 feet in a block of 412 feet in length made horse-cars an impossibility, and the cable roads were the resort. On these lines a trench 3 feet deep is dug between each line of rails from one end of the road to the other, and a permanent channel, either of wood or iron, constructed therein. This channel is connected with the street above by a slot from ⅞ of an inch to 1 inch wide. In the channel is stretched a wire rope running on sheaves, and driven by an engine placed at some convenient point. The passenger cars are attached to a "dummy", which also has seats for passengers, with which is connected the "grip", that drops down through the slot in the roadway and grasps the moving cable. The cars are thus easily hauled up the steep grades. When it is desired to stop a car the grip in the cable is unloosed and the cable is allowed to run through it, while the dummy is at rest. Of the roads now in operation one passes over a hill 325 feet high, another over one hill 300 feet high, and another 280 feet high, while the highest point reached by the other two roads is 200 feet. When the roads were first constructed it was thought that they must all be laid on straight streets without any curves; but a road is now in course of construction which will have a curve of about 60°, and around this the cars will be allowed to run by force of gravity, the grip upon the cable to be relaxed just before the curve is reached. When one cable road crosses the other at right angles the cars pass over the point of intersection by force of gravity. In this case the grip, having been loosed and raised, passes above the intersecting cable and grasps it again on the other side.

These roads, which are peculiar to San Francisco, have not only solved the problem of rapid and cheap transportation of passengers over very steep grades, but have proved so economical in point of running expenses that not only are new lines being continually projected, but some of the horse-car lines are to be converted to cable roads.

WATER-WORKS.

The works for the water-supply for San Francisco are owned by a private corporation, the Spring Valley Water Works Company, and are estimated to have cost between $8,000,000 and $15,000,000. Water is brought to the city from 3 storage reservoirs, with a combined capacity of over 24,000,000,000 gallons, and is distributed by gravity, only 2,000,000 gallons a day being pumped. The average pressure in the mains in the city is 50 pounds to the square inch, the extremes being 10 and 100 pounds. The average consumption of water per diem is 16,000,000 gallons. The average cost of raising 1,000,000 gallons 1 foot high (coal duty) is $7\frac{1}{2}$ cents. The income of the company for the year ending June 1, 1879, was $1,258,000. This sum was almost entirely expended as follows: Operating expenses, $300,000; interest on debt of about $4,000,000, $287,000; dividend on capital stock ($8,000,000) at 8 per cent. per annum, $640,000: a total of $1,227,000. There are 5,460 water-meters in use, and they are found to reduce waste. Families consume, almost invariably, less than their rates when they use meters, and from 2 to 100 times more water without meters.

GAS.

The gas-works are owned by a private corporation. The daily average production of gas is 1,000,000 cubic feet. The charge to consumers is $3 for 1,000 feet. The city pays $14\frac{1}{2}$ cents per night for each street-lamp, 3,500 in number.

PUBLIC BUILDINGS.

The city owns and occupies for municipal purposes a building known as the old city hall, which was bought for $100,000. A new city hall is now in course of erection, and so far about $4,000,000 has been spent on it. No further information was furnished concerning the municipal buildings belonging to the city.

PUBLIC PARKS AND PLEASURE-GROUNDS.

The 3 principal parks of San Francisco are: *Golden Gate Park*, area 1,050 acres; *Buena Vista Park*, area 36.22 acres; and *Mountain Lake Park*, area 20 acres. There are also 18 small squares located in different parts of the city. Golden Gate park is some 3 miles long and $\frac{1}{2}$ mile wide, and extends to the ocean. Owing to disputes in regard to the titles to the land, the state purchased the property now comprised in this park and presented it to the city. There are 48,682 feet of macadamized roads and 4 miles of footwalks in this park. The total cost of improvement for the 3 larger parks is $450,715 13, and the yearly cost of maintenance is about $50,000. During the past year the number of visitors to Golden Gate park was as follows: On foot, 826,000; in carriages, 748,000; and on horseback, 35,134; the number of carriages being given as over 260,000. The larger parks are controlled by 3 park commissioners, 2 of whom are appointed by the governor, and the third chosen by these two.

PLACES OF AMUSEMENT.

There are 12 buildings in the city used for theatrical exhibitions, as follows: Grand opera-house, with a seating capacity of 2,000; California theater, seating 1,500; Baldwin theater, seating 1,000; Bush Street theater, seating 900; the Standard, seating 800; the Bella Union, seating 600; the Adelphi, seating 400; Tivoli garden, seating 1,000; Winter garden, seating 700; Woodworth pavilion, seating 4,000; Chinese Royal theater, seating 1,000, and the Chinese Grand theater, seating 1,000.

The above theaters pay a license to the city, based on their respective seating capacities, according to measurement, each seat being considered at 22 inches. They are divided into two classes, all over 975 seats being ranked as first class, paying $101 per quarter or $301 per annum, and all under 975 being ranked as second class, paying $76 per quarter or $201 per year. The total amount received from this source during the past year was $3,770.

There are about twenty small concert- and beer-halls in the city, with an average seating capacity of about 500.

DRAINAGE.

The total length of sewers constructed up to the census year is about 126 miles. Of these, about 75 miles had been constructed at the time of the preparation of a complete plan of sewerage (1876) by William P. Humphreys, city and county surveyor. Mr. Humphreys thus describes the condition of the sewers existing at that time:

The greater portion of these sewers are of brick, but their cost has been excessive, because, amongst other reasons, they have been unnecessarily large. The general size of the sewers is 3 feet by 5 feet. The brick sewers are egg-shaped, as they should be, with the smaller end down. Most of the streets in the older portion of the city have brick sewers, which extend up the hillsides to irregular distances. Where these sewers approach the lower portions of the city, where the foundation is not sufficiently solid to sustain a brick sewer without a resort to piling, the sewers are of wood, and are generally level, or nearly level. Being down, or nearly down, to low water, the tide rises and falls in them, so checking their outflow that most of them are to-day nothing more than elongated cesspools badly choked with offensive sewage matter. This evil must go on increasing from year to year until some change is effected and some remedy applied.

In fact, the existing sewers in the city have been built without regard to a system of any kind which looks to the general drainage of the city. Each sewer appears to have been built independent of all others and without regard to the duty it has to perform. Some of the alleys and short streets in the city, for instance, where there are only a few houses, have sewers of the same size as those in the larger streets, whereas a foot earthenware pipe, at one-fifth the cost of the great brick sewer, would have afforded much more efficient drainage for all such alleys and short streets.

Concerning the outfall of the sewers, he says:

The bay of San Francisco, being of great size, with strong tidal currents, affords great facilities for getting rid of the sewage matter of the city; but to make it available the sewers must be carried out to points where there are strong currents. If they stop short, the lower parts of the city must always remain in an offensive and unhealthy condition.

Along the busy water-front of the city some of the sewers do not extend out into the bay, but stop short, terminating inside of the rubble-stone bulkhead, where the offensive solid matter is deposited, and the liquid matter allowed to escape as best it can, rendering the slips between the wharves at times offensive to the last degree of endurance. All of these sewers should be carried out to the ends of the wharves, discharging their contents through a bent-hood, leading from the outer end of the sewer down below the level of low water. Discharging at such points, the tide will speedily remove the sewage matter away from the city, and there will be no offensive smell about the wharves.

In the construction of new wharves along the water-front, preparations should be made for continuing the sewers under them out to their ends, and also for the protection of the outer ends of the sewers at these points.

The system of sewers furnished by Mr. Humphreys is on what is known as the "combined" system, provision being made for the removal in the same channel of both storm-water and foul sewage. Most of the system is provided with an outflow by gravitation. One portion of the city, especially that east of Montgomery street, between Eastern and Pine streets, the heart of the business center of the city, is described as having very defective drainage, and the scheme for its improvement includes provision for steam-pumping, a 2-foot brick sewer being built along Front street, starting at Pine street and terminating in a large masonry tank near the water-front.

This sewer would run beneath all the present sewers, water- and gas-pipes. Its bottom on the inside, at Pine street, would be at a level of about 11 feet below the city grade, and falling about 1 foot to each block it would enter the tank at about 20 or 22 feet below the city grade, according to the position of the tank.

One-foot pipe-sewers laid at the proper grade below the present sewers would then convey all house sewerage within this district to the Front Street sewer, these small sewers leading from Montgomery street to Front street, and also from the city front to that street.

The present sewers in this district are to remain undisturbed, in order to carry the surface water of rains and the sewage west of Montgomery street, as far as these sewers extend, into the bay. But all house-sewers and drains within the pumping district are to be disconnected from them and be discharged into the lower or pumping system. In this way deep and dry cellars may be obtained throughout this important part of the city.

It is supposed that this new system will be self-cleansing; but if any difficulty in this respect should ever occur it will be a simple matter to flush them with salt water without pumping the water, for it will be seen that all these sewers are down to or below the level of low tide. An 8-inch pipe may therefore be laid at the level of half-tide or lower, beginning, say, at the foot of Davis street, extending southward along the water-front to the foot of Market street, thence up Market to Pine street, thence up Pine to Montgomery street, thence along Montgomery to Jackson street, the said pipe to have valves, worked from the street-level, and so arranged as to discharge the full capacity of the pipe into the head or the highest point of every sewer. By this arrangement the entire system of sewers may be completely flushed every day, or as often as may be found necessary.

The tank into which these sewers discharge must then be pumped out every day, its contents being discharged through an iron pipe into the strong tidal currents at the foot of Front street, or any other convenient place. For the better draining of some portions of the city a change of street grade is recommended, even in cases where the district is more or less occupied by buildings.

The only provision made for the ventilation of the sewers is by the perforation of manhole covers.

In his report for the year 1879–'80 the health officer of the city and county, J. L. Meares, M. D., says:

The most inexpensive and, in my opinion, the most practical and effective way of ventilating sewers is to have perforated instead of solid manhole covers, or, what would be better still, open grates.

In my report three years ago, where the subject is more fully discussed, I stated that the experience of other cities demonstrated that if these manholes are placed at proper distances, admitting a free circulation of atmospheric air, the foul and noxious vapors are so entirely diluted as to render them not only inodorous but comparatively harmless. The sewers of London are ventilated by gratings placed at intervals of 100 feet. The sewers of Paris, being under the sidewalks, are ventilated through the gutters. The reduction of the death rate of London in a few years, from 37½ in 1,000 population to about 23, is probably more due to the thorough ventilation of its sewers than all other causes combined. In further verification of these views I desire to call your attention to the construction of the Geary Street cable railroad.

The engineer under whose supervision this road was constructed found it necessary for purposes of drainage to connect the tubes through which the cable runs with the sewer in the street by cement pipes 4 inches in diameter. The pipes are placed at intervals of 40 feet, and so thorough does the ventilation seem to be that no complaint has been made of any offensive odors from this sewer since the construction of this road. Speaking from a sanitary standpoint, I believe Geary street to be the most desirable thoroughfare to live on in the city.

The report pays much attention to the question of flushing and cleansing, it being recommended that the heads of the sewers be connected with the water-supply in such manner that by the mere opening of stop-cocks flushing streams may be introduced. Mr. Humphreys thus discusses the system of flushing by damming up the sewage in the sewers and liberating it suddenly:

This requires an elaborate system of special flushing-gates or sluices fixed in the sewers to act first as dam to the sewage and then as a gate giving it free passage. These gates are of various descriptions and are fully described in some of the works on sewerage. They are expensive in construction, and require constant care and attention to render them effective. I apprehend that the latter would be the chief objection to their introduction into the sewers of this city. If we have not yet learned to take care of and keep clean the simple catch-basins alongside of our sidewalks, it is fruitless to hope that we will be able to keep in order and operate successfully an elaborate system of sluice-gates fixed in the sewers where they can not be seen or worked except by an expert.

After careful examination of all the authorities on this subject within my reach I can not recommend this system of flushing sewers in San Francisco at the present time. At best, supposing it to be carried out as perfectly as possible, it is only a poor expedient for cleansing the sewers.

He estimated the cost of flushing, by the system recommended, as that of the wages of three efficient men, costing $4,000. This, it was thought, would be sufficient to secure thorough cleansing, whereas the city now pays $15,000 a year for this purpose, and the sewers are not half cleansed.

The length and cost of the sewers constructed for the fiscal year 1879–'80 were as follows:

	Feet.	Cost.
Brick sewers	9,464.6	$49,552 39
Pipe sewers	8,694.6	20,462 35
Redwood sewers	1,550.0	3,097 65
Cement sewers	2,208.9	4,690 98
Total	21,918.0	77,803 37

The following details are taken from the responses to the schedule of interrogatories furnished by the Census Office:

Brick sewers, with few exceptions, are egg-shaped, 3 feet wide by 5 feet high, built of two courses of brick. Cement and stone-ware pipes are round, from 12 to 18 inches in diameter. The redwood sewers are 3 by 5 feet in size. The mouths of the sewers are all exposed at low water. The final disposition of all sewage is into tide-water. About one-third of the deposits of the sewers is removed by hand, the remainder by flushing. Flushing is accomplished to a great extent by winter rains, owing to the contour of the city. The cost of the sewers is assessed on abutting property by the front foot.

USE-DRAINAGE.

In his report (1876) Mr. Humphreys says:

The construction of house-drains in this city depends at present upon the property-holders, each one building his own drains as he thinks best. House-drains are therefore private property; but, in a sanitary point of view, what concerns one citizen concerns all. I can not, therefore, be considered as touching on private rights by devoting a few words to this subject.

*　　　*　　　*　　　*　　　*　　　*　　　*

The material to be used in the construction of house-drains should have as smooth a surface as possible. It will then cause the least amount of friction, and consequently the least impediment to the progressive motion of its contents. The internal projections and the many impediments to the flow of sewage which are unavoidable in a brick drain, force upon us the necessity to look for a material which will guarantee a smoother surface, and which will also afford the assurance of impermeability without being subject to the frequent patchwork to which the numerous interstices of a brick sewer always render it liable. Glazed earthenware pipes of 6 inches diameter for a house of ordinary size are recommended as capable of obviating all these difficulties. For factories, hotels, and other large buildings the size should be increased.

*　　　*　　　*　　　*　　　*　　　*　　　*

The civic authorities should exercise a surveillance over the mode of laying house-drains and connecting them with the sewers by licensing a competent officer to discharge these duties, and exacting bonds as a guarantee for the faithful performance of the work, permits for that purpose being made always necessary when a connection is to be made.

CEMETERIES.

There are 11 cemeteries connected with San Francisco, but no information concerning them was furnished. There is 1 cemetery in the city which is no longer used for burial purposes. The total number of interments in all the cemeteries from June 30, 1867, to June 30, 1880, was 55,235. The number of interments for the year ending June 30, 1879, was 5,154, and for the year ending June 30, 1880, 4,992. It is estimated that the total interments made in all the cemeteries aggregate about 85,000.

A burial permit is granted by the health officer on presentation of a physician's certificate as to cause of death. The depth of graves is, for adults 6 feet and for children 5 feet.

MARKETS.

There are no corporation or public markets in the city.

SANITARY AUTHORITY.

The chief health organization of San Francisco is the "board of health for the city and county of San Francisco". It consists of the mayor, who is *ex officio* president, and 4 physicians of good standing, appointed by the governor of the state, and holding office for five years. The annual expenses of the board, when there is no declared epidemic, are $30,000, expended for the maintenance of quarantine, for the record of vital statistics, and for salaries. It has also the management of hospitals, almshouses, cemeteries, city physicians, etc.

During an epidemic the board may increase its expenses to any amount. In the absence of epidemics its authority enables it to abate nuisances, to examine markets and the articles sold therein, condemning such of the latter as are unfit for food, and to take a certain part in the management of public institutions. Section 3,012 of the "health and quarantine laws" of the city and county is as follows:

The board of health have general supervision of all matters appertaining to the sanitary condition of the city and county, including the city and county hospital, the county jail, almshouse, industrial school, and all public health-institutions provided by the city and county of San Francisco, and may adopt such orders and regulations, and appoint or discharge such medical attendants and employés, as to them seem best to promote the public welfare, and may appoint as many health inspectors as they deem necessary in time of epidemics.

The health officer is elected by the board of health, and holds office at its pleasure. He must be a graduate of some medical college in good standing, and must reside within the city limits of San Francisco. He is the executive officer of the health department, and may, in his discretion, cause the removal to a hospital of any and all persons within the limits of the city and county of San Francisco infected with variola.

The board of health appoints 1 quarantine officer, who shall be a physician in good standing, 1 secretary, 1 assistant secretary, 6 health inspectors, 1 market inspector, and 1 messenger, whose duties must be fixed by the board of health. It also appoints 1 superintendent physician, 1 resident physician, 1 steward, 1 matron, 1 apothecary, 2 visiting physicians, 2 visiting surgeons, as officers of the city and county hospital in and for the city and county of San Francisco, one each of said visiting physicians and surgeons to be nominated by the faculty of the medical department of the University of California, and one each of said visiting physicians and surgeons to be nominated by the Medical College of the Pacific. The board may also appoint 1 engineer for the city and county hospital. It may also appoint 1 superintendent, 1 resident physician, 1 matron, and such other employés as are now authorized by law, to be employed in and for the almshouse of said city and county. It also has power to appoint and prescribe the duties of 1 city physician and 1 assistant city physician, who shall be designated as police surgeons, and whose duty it shall be to make all autopsies required of them by the coroner of said city and county; and said board is also empowered to appoint such employés and such medical attendants as it may deem necessary in the health department and in all the various institutions which are by law placed under its supervision, and the compensation of such attendants and employés is to be fixed by the board of health. The appointing power aforesaid is vested solely in said board of health, and said board has power to prescribe the duties of said appointees, and may not remove the same without just cause. The heads of departments appointed by the board of health, to wit, the health officer, resident physician of city and county hospital, and superintendent of almshouse, can not be removed except by the concurrence of four members of said board of health.

The following annual salaries are allowed to the officers of the health department and such other officers and employés as are mentioned in the preceding section, viz: Health officer, $3,000; quarantine officer, $1,800; secretary, $2,100; assistant secretary, $1,200; health inspectors, $1,200 each; market inspector, $1,200; messenger, $900; city physician, $1,800; assistant city physician, $1,200. All of said salaries, together with the salaries of such other employés of the health department as may be appointed by the board of health, must be paid in equal monthly installments out of the general fund of the city and county of San Francisco in the same manner as the salaries of the other officers of said city and county are paid.

The 8 inspectors employed have the same police powers as regular officers.

In the Chinese quarter regular house-to-house inspections are made. In other parts of the city inspections are made only as nuisances are reported. In the latter case an inspector examines the place, and, if the report is found to be true, serves upon the responsible person a notice to abate the nuisance, giving a reasonable length of time, varying according to the nature of the evil, to abate it. If his order is not obeyed, he issues another notice, when if this is not complied with within 48 hours he arrests the offender.

The inspection and correction of defective house-drainage, privy-vaults, cesspools, sources of drinking-water, sewerage, and street-cleaning is carried on in the same manner as that of any other nuisance. This is true also of improperly kept or removed garbage. The determination of what constitutes a nuisance is vested entirely in the board, as per the following extract from the health and quarantine laws:

The board of health is hereby vested with power to act upon, define, determine, and adjudge what shall constitute a nuisance in said city and county, and to require the same to be abated in a summary manner. Any person who maintains, permits, or allows a nuisance to exist upon his or her property or premises after the same has been determined by said board to be a nuisance, and after notice to remove the same has been served upon such person, is guilty of a misdemeanor and shall be punished accordingly, and each day of existence after notice shall be deemed a separate and distinct offense; and it is the duty of the health officer to prosecute all persons guilty of violating this law by continuous prosecutions until the same is abated and removed.

The following are the regulations concerning the burial of the dead:

No person shall deposit in any cemetery or inter in the city and county of San Francisco any human body without first having obtained and filed with the health officer a certificate signed by a physician or midwife, or a coroner, setting forth, as near as possible, the name, age, color, sex, place of birth, occupation, date, locality, and cause of death of the deceased, and obtain from such health officer a permit; nor shall any human body be removed or disinterred without the permit of the health officer or by order of the coroner. Physicians, when deaths occur in their practice, must give the certificate herein mentioned.

* * * * * * * * *

It shall be the duty of the health officer to see that the dead body of a human being is not allowed to remain in any public receiving vault for a longer period than five days. At the expiration of that time he shall cause the body to be placed in a vault or niche constructed of brick, stone, or iron, and hermetically sealed. It shall also be his duty to require all persons having in charge the digging of graves and burial of the dead to see that the body of no human being who had reached ten years of age shall be interred in a grave less than 6 feet deep, or if under ten years of age the grave to be not less than 5 feet deep.

Superintendents of cemeteries within the boundaries of the city and county of San Francisco must return to the health officer, on each Monday, the names of all persons interred or deposited within their respective cemeteries for the preceding week.

No superintendent of a cemetery can remove or cause to be removed, disinter or caused to be disinterred, any corpse that has been deposited in the cemetery without a permit from the health officer, or by order of the coroner.

A general order of the board of supervisors covering the pollution of streams and harbor is:

No butcher's offal, garbage, or any dead animal, nor any putrid or stinking animal or vegetable matter shall be allowed to remain on the premises of any person, or to be thrown into any street or alley, place, or receiving basin, or in any standing water or excavation, or upon the grounds or premises of any person; nor shall any dead animal be buried or thrown into any of the tide-waters, lakes, streams, or reservoirs within the limits of the city and county.

Another regulation concerning the removal of excrement and night-soil is:

No person shall remove the deposits from any privy-vault or cesspool, or use any night-cart, without first having obtained from the superintendent of public streets, highways, and squares a permit authorizing the removal of such deposit, and designating a place where the same may be discharged, or the use of such night-cart, designating the location where such cart may be loaded or discharged.

Every such permit shall be carried, if for a vault or cesspool, at the work, if for a night-cart, with the cart, and exhibited on demand of any police officer, and be returned within thirty days from issue to the said superintendent.

No person shall load or discharge any night-cart at a different place from that designated in said permit, or alter any permit granted under this section.

All night-carts shall be under the control of the superintendent of public streets, highways, and squares, and the said superintendent may, for good cause, revoke any permit granted by him.

Small-pox patients are either taken to the hospital outside of the city or are isolated at their residences, upon which is placed a yellow or quarantine flag, or a placard is posted upon the doorway setting forth the fact that there is small-pox there. If the health officer deems it best, it is compulsory upon the patient to go to the hospital. Scarlet-fever patients are quarantined at home, and a flag is placed upon the premises.

The board of health requires that no child may attend the public schools without a certificate of vaccination. Should scarlatina break out in a school, the patient must be isolated.

Vaccination is not compulsory by law, but a public sentiment, made intelligently apprehensive by several severe visitations of small-pox, has made it well-nigh universal.

The health officer is required to keep a record of all births, deaths, and interments occurring in the city and county of San Francisco. Such records, when filled, are deposited in the office of the county recorder, and produced when required for public inspection.

Physicians and midwives are required on or before the fourth day of each month to make a return to the health officer of all births, deaths occurring in their practice, and of the number of still-born children during the preceding month. In the absence of such attendants the parents must make such report within thirty days after the birth of the child. Such returns must be made in accordance with rules adopted and upon blanks furnished by the board of health. Superintendents of cemeteries are required to make to the health officer weekly returns of all interments in their respective cemeteries. Except where they terminate fatally, no record is kept of diseases.

The health officer reports to the board of health once a month, and once a year to the board of supervisors. In his report for the year 1879–'80 he (J. L. Meares, M. D.) says, concerning the sanitary aspects of the Chinese population:

Estimating our population at 233,700, the annual ratio of deaths per 1000 is 18.50. Estimating the Chinese population (U. S. census) at 22,000, the annual ratio of deaths per 1000 is 21.22. Estimating the population of all other nationalities at 211,700 (U. S. census), the annual ratio of deaths per 1000 is 18.29; thus showing that there are nearly three deaths in a thousand more among the Chinese than other nationalities, notwithstanding the Chinese population is composed almost entirely of adults, while more than one-third of the deaths in other nationalities are under five years of age.

Considering the miserable condition of our sewers and the presence in the very heart of our city of more than 20,000 Chinese, who live for the most part in underground habitations without any proper ventilation, breathing an atmosphere so contaminating as to be absolutely nauseating to those unaccustomed to it, we have much to be thankful for in estimating our ratio of mortality. Protected, as we are, by the presence of our trade-winds and the general salubrity of our climate, it is to be feared that only a repetition of virulent epidemics will awaken our people to the necessity of removing these constantly menacing causes of disease.

I have over and over again urged the enforcement of the cubic-air law as the only possible means of correcting the sanitary evils of the Chinese quarter.

By constant vigilance many nuisances are abated, and a great deal of money [is] expended to make this portion of the city even tolerable; but so long as these people are permitted to live as at present in overcrowded dens, socially, morally, and in a sanitary point of view they are a curse to San Francisco. The daily enforcement of the cubic-air law would compel many of these people to leave the city or to live in less-crowded quarters.

MUNICIPAL CLEANSING.

The city undertakes to clean the public streets, having the work done by contract. Sweeping-machines are used in all streets except those having steep grades (i. e., hilly). The streets of the city are graded into classes according to the amount of their use. The principal streets are cleaned once a week, those of the second class once in two weeks, those of the third class once in four weeks, and those of the fourth class once in two months. This service is said to be performed very efficiently. The contract price is $47 per mile per year. The sweepings are deposited on the swamps lying around the bay.

Removal of garbage and ashes.—Garbage is removed by householders. It is forbidden to throw it into streets or waters or allow it to become a nuisance, but it must be kept in iron or tin vessels and removed at least once a week. Garbage and ashes may be kept in the same vessel, and both, like the sweepings of the streets, are disposed of by being used for filling in marshes and swamp lands. The cost of removal of these two substances is about 50 cents per month to each householder. It is stated that the only probable injury to health resulting from the handling of garbage in the manner stated arises from the fact that it is sometimes retained too long on the premises where it is produced.

Dead animals.—The carcasses of animals dying within the city are removed by contract made with the city. Horses and cows are removed at no expense to the city, but the removal of cats, dogs, etc., costs the city $75 a month. The system is said to be a good one and the contracts to be well fulfilled.

Liquid household wastes.—All the liquid household wastes are run into sewers where sewers exist. In the suburbs of the city, where they do not exist, cesspools and privy-vaults are used instead, no liquid wastes being allowed to run into street-gutters. As no well-water is used in San Francisco, the question of the possible pollution of drinking-water by the escape of the contents of privies, cesspools, etc., does not come up. Vaults, cesspools, etc., may be cleaned out only upon a permit therefor obtained from the health officer, which permit must accompany the vehicle in which the contents are to be conveyed, and must be exhibited upon the demand of any police officer.

Human excreta.—About three-quarters of the houses of the city have water-closets, while the rest depend upon privy-vaults. All of the water-closets deliver into public sewers. All privy-vaults are nominally water-tight, the law for their construction reading thus:

No person shall construct, without consent in writing of the health officer, any privy-vault on premises belonging to him or under his control, unless the walls and bottom of such vault be of stone or brick, laid in cement, and at least 8 inches in thickness.

No person shall construct or maintain, or suffer to be or remain upon his or her premises, or premises under his or her control, any privy or privy-vault, cesspool, sink, or drain, without connecting the same, by means of a cement, iron-stone, or iron pipe, with the street sewer in such a manner that it shall be effectually drained and purified, if there be a sewer in the street on which said premises may be situated with which the same can be connected. Every drain or branch sewer which shall connect with a dwelling-house or building, with any privy or privy-vault or cesspool, shall be constructed of cement, iron-stone, or iron, with a trap or apparatus which will effectually prevent the escape of gases from the sewer into such dwelling-house, building, privy, privy-vault, or cesspool.

Having obtained a permit for the emptying of a vault from the superintendent of streets, the regulations declare that no person shall—

use or drive any of the vehicles commonly known as "night-carts" in any portion of the city and county lying east of Van Ness avenue, south of Market street, and north of Seventeenth street, except between the hours of 12 o'clock midnight and 5 o'clock in the morning; use any night-cart or swill-cart at any time, unless the same be perfectly staunch, tight, and closely covered, so as to wholly prevent leakage or smell.

Night-soil is taken in boats out to sea and there dumped.

Manufacturing wastes.—The wastes of manufacturing establishments are disposed of, the liquid parts by running them into the sewers, and the solids as in the case of street dirt or garbage.

POLICE.

The police force of the city and county of San Francisco is appointed and governed by a board of three police commissioners, appointed by the judges of the superior court. The head executive officer of the force is the chief of police. He has immediate control of the force, and is responsible for its general conduct and efficiency. His salary is $4,000 per annum. The rest of the force, with their respective yearly salaries, are as follows: Five captains at $1,800 each, 1 clerk to chief at $1,800, 1 property clerk at $1,800, 12 detectives at $1,500 each, 25 sergeants at $1,500 each, 12 corporals at $1,380 each, 337 patrolmen at $1,200 each. The uniform is of dark-blue cloth, and is furnished by the men themselves. Patrolmen are armed with clubs and revolvers. Their time of service averages 9 hours per day, and 43 square miles of territory are patrolled. For the year ending June 30, 1880, there were 21,063 arrests made by the force, the principal causes being as follows: Assault, 2,353; burglary, 345; disturbing the peace, 331; drunk, 9,127; gambling-tools in possession, 372; soliciting for house of ill-fame, 547; using obscene language, 1,037; larceny, 1,088; misdemeanor, 1,745; and obstructing streets, 526. The value of the property reported to the police during the year as either lost or stolen was $104,302 80, and of this amount $43,708 was recovered and returned to the owners. There were 2,030 station-house lodgers for the year ending June 30, 1880, as against 1,920 during the year ending June 30, 1879. Meals are freely furnished to the lodgers.

The police force is required to co-operate with the fire, health, and building departments in every way that may be conducive to the public interest. Special policemen are appointed at the request and at the expense of persons who desire their services. The total cost of the force for the year last mentioned is $512,000.

FIRE DEPARTMENT.

The total force of the fire department of San Francisco numbers 303 men, apportioned as follows: One chief engineer, 1 assistant chief engineer, 4 assistant engineers, 1 clerk to commissioners, 1 janitor and messenger, 25 foremen of companies, 12 engineers of steam fire-engines, 12 stokers of steam fire-engines, 12 drivers of steam fire-engines, 9 drivers of hose-carriages, 9 stewards of hose-carriages, 4 drivers of trucks, 4 tillermen of trucks, 150 hosemen, 48 hook-and-ladder men, 1 superintendent of steam fire-engines, 1 assistant superintendent of steam fire-engines, 1 clerk of corporation yard, 1 sub-engineer and machinist, 1 veterinary surgeon, 2 hydrant-men, 1 carpenter, 1 corporation-yard watchman, 1 corporation-yard drayman. The apparatus consists of 17 steam fire-engines (5 being held in reserve), 18 two-wheel tenders (6 in reserve), 6 four-wheel hose-carriages (1 in reserve), and 5 hook-and-ladder trucks (1 in reserve). There are 72 horses and 24,150 feet of hose in use with the apparatus. In addition to the above, there are 1 hand-engine, 5 hose-reels, and 17,000 feet of hose stationed at various points over the city and used for the protection of property in the immediate vicinity. There are 1,352 fire-hydrants, located in different parts of the city, 43 of which are private, and 55 cisterns, with a total capacity of 2,011,856 gallons, for the use of the department.

The fire-alarm telegraph has 120 miles of wire, with 150 signal-boxes, and employs a force consisting of 1 superintendent, 3 operators, and 3 repairers. During the year ending June 30, 1880, there were 245 alarms given through the telegraph, 207 being for fire, 2 for second alarms, 11 duplicate alarms, 6 false alarms, 18 for chimney fires, and 1 for a bonfire.

The annual cost of the fire department for the fiscal year, including $24,779 95 for materials purchased, is $266,348 74, and the annual cost of the fire-alarm telegraph, including $9,975 35 for extensions and repairs, $18,075 35.

COMMERCE AND NAVIGATION.

[From the reports of the Bureau of Statistics for the fiscal years ending June 30.]

Customs district of San Francisco, California.	1879.	1880.
Total value of imports	$35,046,879	$41,265,317
Total value of exports:		
Domestic	$35,548,417	$37,213,443
Foreign	$4,117,816	$513,217
Total number of immigrants	9,253	7,153

Customs district of San Francisco, California.	1879.		1880.	
	Number.	Tons.	Number.	Tons.
Vessels in foreign trade:				
Entered	567	639,536	619	704,054
Cleared	667	748,119	672	777,595
Vessels in coast trade and fisheries.				
Entered	260	320,285	208	269,132
Cleared	346	374,626	323	332,826
Vessels registered, enrolled, and licensed in district	901	199,310	867	201,139
Vessels built during the year	30	3,860	18	5,795

MANUFACTURES.

The following is a summary of the statistics of the manufactures of San Francisco for 1880, being taken from tables prepared for the Tenth Census by Henry G. Langley, chief special agent:

Mechanical and manufacturing industries.	No. of establishments.	Capital.	AVERAGE NUMBER OF HANDS EMPLOYED.			Total amount paid in wages during the year.	Value of materials.	Value of products.
			Males above 16 years.	Females above 15 years.	Children and youths.			
All industries	2,971	$35,368,139	23,662	3,588	1,192	$14,928,534	$47,978,072	$77,824,299
Artificial feathers and flowers (see also Millinery and lace goods)	4	2,550	2			962	2,700	5,850
Awnings and tents	4	26,100	5	5	3	6,675	15,850	29,602
Bags, other than paper	3	275,000	55	50	14	51,300	1,410,000	1,565,000
Baking and yeast powders (see also Drugs and chemicals)	4	48,000	24	5		16,575	97,490	142,345
Baskets, rattan and willow ware	8	8,575	20	5	3	6,560	4,165	19,400
Belting and hose, leather	4	85,000	31			18,565	73,100	117,780
Billiard tables and materials	5	102,000	39			24,632	45,618	98,360
Blacking	3	3,500	3			1,809	2,250	7,400
Blacksmithing (see also Wheelwrighting)	106	59,973	155		7	104,653	102,410	364,886
Bookbinding and blank-book making	13	108,300	118	55	32	110,766	172,890	382,440
Boot and shoe findings	4	10,700	11	1		8,080	20,800	44,750
Boot and shoe uppers	5	6,700	9	1		5,536	15,030	31,980
Boots and shoes, including custom work and repairing	310	1,090,772	2,464	184	96	1,199,730	2,187,811	4,141,547
Boxes, cigar	6	130,635	149	35	10	72,940	75,165	206,200
Boxes, fancy and paper	4	24,500	18	42	9	20,165	20,450	50,550
Boxes, wooden packing	7	154,750	232	30	30	108,400	216,300	460,500
Brass castings	8	142,200	184	2	6	117,940	232,570	374,350
Bread and other bakery products	119	428,860	431	14	45	315,082	1,403,001	2,070,384
Brick and tile	3	8,800	79			22,050	12,025	46,700
Bridges	8	99,000	344			172,970	374,000	694,000
Brooms and brushes	15	70,800	96		3	37,049	69,600	132,200
Carpentering	181	431,690	1,190	1	1	907,331	1,690,833	3,121,851
Carriages and wagons (see also Wheelwrighting)	52	338,071	373		1	230,849	284,814	714,098
Clothing, men's	110	1,126,164	1,087	610	18	908,559	2,204,148	3,782,963
Clothing, women's	27	424,250	31	532	7	220,688	659,152	1,150,207
Coffee and spices, roasted and ground	20	445,450	160	6	10	99,132	1,057,628	1,336,718
Coffins, burial cases, and undertakers' goods	13	72,150	46			33,753	54,425	142,060
Confectionery	29	166,150	88	29	14	54,622	345,826	507,026
Cooperage	28	424,350	254		5	181,311	304,620	605,704
Cordage and twine	3	500,700	145		18	57,215	402,115	545,230
Cordials and sirups	9	72,200	44			28,610	134,590	208,000
Corsets	4	4,300		9	1	3,000	3,550	12,200
Cutlery and edge tools (see also Tools)	11	104,500	54		1	39,653	37,150	119,339
Dentistry, mechanical	28	10,480	15			7,320	9,010	39,525
Drugs and chemicals (see also Baking and yeast powders; Patent medicines and compounds).	27	357,925	118	2	3	76,899	273,801	571,691
Dyeing and cleaning	9	27,225	21	9	1	16,331	14,269	46,466
Electroplating	10	21,500	11	3	1	6,542	13,523	34,375
Engraving and die-sinking	13	4,320	5			3,288	2,430	20,340
Engraving, wood	8	995	2			425	3,340	17,100
Fertilizers	3	145,000	35			21,583	66,600	106,160
Flags and banners	3	16,000	5	11	2	7,000	13,200	35,600
Flavoring extracts	6	17,500	13	6	1	7,164	36,100	54,500
Flouring- and grist-mill products	9	635,600	142			103,992	1,991,609	2,275,360
Food preparations	7	53,400	35	1	4	22,348	80,892	164,025
Foundery and machine-shop products	58	2,391,739	1,888		33	1,243,234	2,017,267	3,889,503
Fruits and vegetables, canned and preserved	6	926,000	226	340	80	207,000	609,000	978,000
Furnishing goods, men's	12	362,350	121	189		126,265	509,540	744,245
Furniture (see also Mattresses and spring beds; Upholstering)	41	918,975	556	20	12	352,583	683,895	1,280,210
Furniture, chairs	3	2,300	10			5,820	3,750	13,300
Furs, dressed	6	102,250	17	101		81,429	158,600	224,400

Mechanical and manufacturing industries.	No. of establishments.	Capital.	AVERAGE NUMBER OF HANDS EMPLOYED.			Total amount paid in wages during the year.	Value of materials.	Value of products.
			Males above 16 years.	Females above 15 years.	Children and youths.			
Glass, cut, stained, and ornamented	5	$77,450	36	....	....	$22,100	$66,900	$103,000
Gloves and mittens	6	74,500	49	137	....	49,700	101,805	191,520
Glue	3	21,200	23	....	2	11,800	21,940	49,800
Hairwork	11	14,550	10	19	....	12,167	16,000	46,284
Hand-stamps	5	13,000	16	....	....	14,830	13,532	51,430
Hats and caps, not including wool hats	16	35,925	20	39	....	29,032	38,717	83,678
High explosives	6	934,000	172	....	....	76,786	680,416	1,565,868
Ink	3	31,000	15	....	....	9,450	59,000	97,500
Instruments, professional and scientific	8	18,050	17	....	1	9,948	17,088	44,712
Iron forgings	4	42,000	40	....	1	27,702	47,081	91,310
Jewelry	12	283,500	128	....	11	100,597	159,753	315,115
Lapidary work	7	4,425	9	1	3	11,035	16,670	39,120
Leather, curried	41	225,700	111	....	2	72,256	941,120	1,102,475
Leather, tanned	47	1,161,800	261	....	7	166,754	1,530,298	2,014,345
Liquors, distilled	5	199,000	36	....	1	20,250	170,075	258,200
Liquors, malt	38	1,666,520	813	....	....	404,830	1,507,284	2,722,270
Liquors, vinous (see also Liquors, distilled)	6	120,000	49	....	....	16,236	51,445	83,521
Lithographing (see also Printing and publishing)	7	122,000	84	....	9	63,391	77,200	193,712
Lock- and gun-smithing	30	24,750	20	....	....	13,234	14,546	57,163
Looking-glass and picture frames	21	229,600	78	2	11	58,406	135,975	281,900
Marble and stone work	32	229,150	219	....	....	155,767	223,554	469,646
Masonry, brick and stone	24	75,650	191	....	1	135,827	182,633	391,734
Matches	3	30,600	53	....	5	21,500	156,800	198,600
Mattresses and spring beds (see also Furniture)	8	123,200	59	2	2	35,143	94,215	159,737
Millinery and lace goods (see also Artificial feathers and flowers)	19	137,600	13	198	2	78,932	305,900	456,300
Mineral and soda waters	8	40,300	27	....	1	18,365	31,160	80,175
Models and patterns	7	8,900	15	....	1	9,532	3,856	23,966
Musical instruments and materials (not specified)	4	2,550	7	....	....	3,660	1,150	8,400
Musical instruments, pianos and materials	5	49,500	27	....	....	18,425	41,250	87,700
Paints	3	318,000	89	1	....	40,720	298,552	402,670
Painting and paperhanging	117	87,485	409	1	16	260,907	197,839	639,503
Patent medicines and compounds (see also Drugs and chemicals)	15	52,800	45	6	....	16,732	71,820	156,000
Perfumery and cosmetics	3	13,000	11	11	16	12,400	27,300	61,900
Photographing	33	127,950	105	27	3	100,900	80,833	293,960
Pickles, preserves, and sauces	3	5,000	3	....	2	1,524	6,475	13,200
Plumbing and gasfitting	94	175,050	265	1	23	179,565	332,244	671,735
Printing and publishing (see also Lithographing)	152	1,744,755	1,326	98	103	1,217,349	1,015,305	2,987,576
Roofing and roofing materials	16	69,450	150	....	....	91,021	120,920	271,875
Saddlery and harness	58	285,650	234	12	17	121,977	198,199	400,715
Safes, doors, and vaults, fire-proof	3	36,500	14	....	....	8,590	13,808	32,835
Sash, doors, and blinds (see also Wood, turned and carved)	16	555,000	431	....	30	272,213	360,081	769,030
Saws	6	87,185	29	....	4	22,348	40,390	83,026
Shipbuilding	56	1,681,523	349	....	....	393,283	463,069	1,087,843
Shirts	25	88,100	181	173	1	85,188	153,940	303,050
Show-cases	6	4,320	8	....	....	5,088	10,875	23,800
Silk and silk goods	4	159,300	19	104	25	40,700	78,625	155,705
Silverware	3	116,000	24	....	6	20,550	37,500	87,000
Slaughtering and meat-packing, not including retail butchering	24	1,586,200	295	....	14	239,868	4,511,721	6,013,602
Soap and candles	19	458,650	150	14	5	86,855	676,489	886,293
Stencils and brands	5	6,125	10	1	....	5,894	2,860	16,792
Straw goods	8	33,500	33	72	3	38,600	26,450	85,200
Surgical appliances	5	4,925	2	....	....	1,976	2,400	11,672
Tinware, copperware, and sheet-iron ware	69	428,975	341	....	64	226,978	542,041	949,499
Tobacco, cigars and cigarettes	147	1,687,603	3,110	110	198	911,988	1,929,357	3,720,813
Tools (see also Cutlery and edge tools)	4	13,100	11	....	....	9,365	17,300	38,150
Trunks and valises	7	106,631	43	....	4	29,312	84,500	166,508
Umbrellas and canes	4	20,850	5	11	....	9,616	26,600	53,950
Upholstering (see also Furniture)	50	164,350	108	7	1	72,297	208,032	360,332
Upholstering materials	4	47,250	28	10	4	16,885	32,550	62,050
Watch and clock repairing	93	91,235	75	2	4	62,013	54,119	223,215

Mechanical and manufacturing industries.	No. of estab-lish-ments.	Capital.	AVERAGE NUMBER OF HANDS EMPLOYED.			Total amount paid in wages during the year.	Value of materials.	Value of products.
			Males above 16 years.	Females above 15 years.	Children and youths.			
Wheelwrighting (see also Blacksmithing; Carriages and wagons)...	20	$20,875	34	....	1	$23,142	$23,350	$74,712
Windmills	4	11,500	8	....	....	7,100	13,200	27,500
Window blinds and shades	10	92,100	43	2	....	23,909	74,200	141,840
Wirework	6	273,308	70	....	7	40,665	176,910	273,776
Wood, turned and carved (see also Sash, doors, and blinds)	16	15,125	30	....	3	21,006	28,390	72,776
All other industries (a)	88	5,682,100	1,815	128	107	1,121,786	9,103,563	11,203,095

a Embracing agricultural implements; axle-grease; babbitt metal and solder; bags, paper; bells; boot and shoe cut stock; calcium lights; cement; drain and sewer pipe; electric lights; electrical apparatus; explosives and fireworks; fancy articles; files; foundery supplies; galvanizing; glass; gold and silver, reduced and refined; grease and tallow; housefurnishing goods; iron and steel; iron bolts, nuts, washers, and rivets; iron pipe, wrought; iron railing, wrought; ivory and bone work; jewelry and instrument cases; kindling wood; lamps and reflectors; lasts; lead, bar, pipe, sheet, and shot; leather dressed skins; lumber, planed; malt; mantels, slate, marble, and marbleized; millstones, mirrors; mixed textiles; musical instruments, organs and materials; oil, essential; oil, linseed; photographic apparatus; pipes, tobacco; pumps; regalia and society banners and emblems; rubber and elastic goods; salt, ground; spectacles and eyeglasses; springs, steel, car, and carriage; stamped ware; stationery goods; steam fittings and heating apparatus; stereotyping and electrotyping; stone and earthen-ware; sugar and molasses, refined; taxidermy; tobacco, chewing, smoking, and snuff; toys and games; type founding; varnish; vinegar; whips; wooden ware; woolen goods; and zinc.

From the foregoing table it appears that the average capital of all establishments is $11,904 45; that the average wages of all hands employed is $524 87 per annum; and that the average outlay in wages, in materials, and in interest (at 6 per cent.) on capital employed is $21,887 81.

SAN JOSÉ,

SANTA CLARA COUNTY, CALIFORNIA.

POPULATION

IN THE

AGGREGATE,

1860-1880.

	Inhab.
1790	......
1800	......
1810	......
1820	......
1830	......
1840	......
1850	......
1860	4,579
1870	9,089
1880	12,567

POPULATION

BY

SEX, NATIVITY, AND RACE,

AT

CENSUS OF 1880.

Male	6,553
Female	6,014
Native	8,733
Foreign-born	3,834
White	11,834
Colored	* 733

* Including 634 Chinese and 8 Indians.

N.

San Francisco, Cal. N. 41° 7' W. 42.9 Miles.

Sacramento, Cal. N. 15° 55' E. 88.7 Miles.

Stockton, Cal. N. 38° 56' E. 54.9 Miles.

Los Angeles, Cal. S. 43° 10' E. 305.5 Miles.

Santa Barbara, Cal. S. 81° 33' E. 236.1 Miles.

S.

Latitude: 37° 20' North; Longitude: 121° 53' (west from Greenwich).

FIANCIAL CONDITION:

Total Valuation: $9,005,658; per capita: $717 00.   Tax per $100: $2 18.

NOTE.—San José, the capital of Santa Clara county, California, is pleasantly situated near the center of the beautiful Santa Clara valley, about 50 miles southeast of San Francisco, and 30 miles from the Pacific ocean. It was settled early in the present century, and the first legislature of California, under the constitution of 1849, met here. A branch of the Central Pacific, the Southern Pacific, and the South Pacific Coast railroads, respectively, pass through the city.

No information concerning this city was furnished by its officials.

STOCKTON,
SAN JOAQUIN COUNTY, CALIFORNIA.

POPULATION

IN THE

AGGREGATE,

1860-1880.

	Inhab.
1790	....
1800	....
1810	....
1820	....
1830	....
1840	....
1850	....
1860	3,679
1870	10,066
1880	10,282

POPULATION

BY

SEX, NATIVITY, AND RACE,

AT

CENSUS OF 1880.

Male	5,870
Female	4,412
Native	6,852
Foreign-born	3,430
White	9,392
Colored	*890

* Including 687 Chinese and 4 Indians.

Latitude: 37° 57' North; Longitude: 121° 15' (west from Greenwich); Altitude: 25 feet (about).

FINANCIAL CONDITION:

Total Valuation: $6,011,098; per capita: $585 00.   Net Indebtedness: $385,615; per capita: $37 50.   Tax per $100: $2 70.

HISTORICAL SKETCH.

The site of Stockton is part of a large Mexican grant called the Rancho Campo de los Francises, owned by Captain Charles M. Weber. Here, at the head of a slough of the same name, navigable and connecting with the San Joaquin river 3 miles distant, in 1843 and 1844 settlements were made, but were very soon abandoned through fear of the Indians. Another attempt was made in 1846, but was again abandoned upon the breaking out of the war between the United States and Mexico. However, in 1847 a permanent lodgment was effected. "Being at the head of navigation and a convenient point of departure for the gold-mining regions of Calaveras, Tuolumne, and Mariposa counties, it soon became a place of considerable business importance, and commanded the trade of those prosperous counties." The most important change that has occurred in the history of the place (and it is generally conceded to have occurred about 1860) was when the grain-growing and agricultural interests succeeded the mining industry, or, as it has been called, the "transition from the gold period to the wheat period".

In December, 1848, a large portion of the cloth tents and houses which then constituted the town was destroyed by fire, causing an estimated loss of $200,000. July 23, 1850, the town received a city charter. Again in May, 1851, nearly 7 acres of wooden and cloth houses were burnt, at an estimated loss of $1,500,000. All kinds of merchandise and material at that time commanded a high price. The fires which occurred in February and July of 1855, and in 1858 and 1865, while destructive, burnt a cheap and temporary class of buildings, whose loss was not seriously felt. In fact, these fires increased rather than depressed business, as in many cases the material for the new buildings was being prepared before the fire was dead.

The population was cosmopolitan in its character, with a preponderance of Americans, and it has been thus since the discovery of gold.

STOCKTON IN 1880.

The following statistical accounts, collected by the Census Office, indicate the present condition of Stockton:

LOCATION.

Stockton is located in latitude 37° 57′ north, and longitude 121° 15′ west from Greenwich. Its altitude above the San Joaquin river varies from 10 feet at its western boundary to 23 feet at its eastern side. Stockton slough, at whose head, 3 miles from the San Joaquin river, the city is located, is navigable, 1 mile and 900 feet of navigable water being within the city limits. Mormon slough, a branch of the Stockton slough, is navigable for 1 mile 1,640 feet within the city; and Fremont slough, another branch of the same, is navigable for 1,900 feet within the city; making a water front of $5\frac{3}{5}$ miles available for wharves. Wharves have already been built upon $1\frac{1}{6}$ mile of this distance. Stockton slough has a width of from 150 to 375 feet and a depth at low water of from 8 to 10 feet. Mormon slough has an average width of about 150 feet and a depth of from 4 to 10 feet. In Stockton slough the tide at low water rises and falls 2 feet. Below its mouth the San Joaquin river has a minimum width of 100 feet and a depth at low water of 7 feet. A daily line of passenger steamers of 400 and 500 tons plies between Stockton and San Francisco the year round, and for from 6 to 10 weeks in the spring and summer the San Joaquin river is navigable for small steamers from 200 to 250 miles above Stockton.

RAILROAD COMMUNICATIONS.

The western division of the Central Pacific, from San Francisco to Sacramento, passes through the city, and at Lathrop, 10 miles distant, connects with the southern division and the Southern Pacific, the present terminus being Tucson, Arizona. The Stockton and Copperopolis railroad terminates at Milton, 30 miles distant. The Stockton and Visalia railroad terminates at Oakdale, distant 34 miles.

TRIBUTARY COUNTRY.

Stockton is the chief depot for supplies for the grain-growing country of the San Joaquin valley, and for the wool-growing and mining country of the Sierra Nevada mountains, lying to the eastward of the valley.

TOPOGRAPHY.

The site of the city is at the foot or outlet of the San Joaquin valley, on level land, gradually rising toward the northeast at the rate of about 6 feet per mile, the nearest hill being about 15 miles distant, and the foothills of the Sierra Nevada about 35 miles. There are no forests in the valley, and only in some places scattering oak trees. The geological character of this part of the valley is gravel drift of great depth, borings of 1,200 feet having failed to find any rock basis. It consists of alternate strata of gravel and sand and clay, with a rich surface soil of from 4 to 6 feet in depth. The natural slope of the valley gives it good surface drainage by means of the water-courses through the valley. To the west of the city is a large scope of flat lowland, subject to periodical overflow, known as swamp and overflowed land, and originally covered with a dense growth of "tules". A great portion of this land is now reclaimed by banks and levees, and is in a high state of cultivation.

CLIMATE.

Highest recorded summer temperature, 110°; highest summer temperature in average years, 100°. Lowest recorded winter temperature, 20°; lowest winter temperature in average years, 27°. Mean annual temperature for 10 years, 61.35°.(a)

STREETS.

Stockton's total length of streets is 99 miles, of which 1 mile is paved with broken stone, and $10\frac{1}{2}$ miles with gravel. Broken stone costs $32\frac{1}{2}$ cents and gravel 28 cents per square yard. The streets are kept in repair at an

---

a These figures cover a period of 10 years.

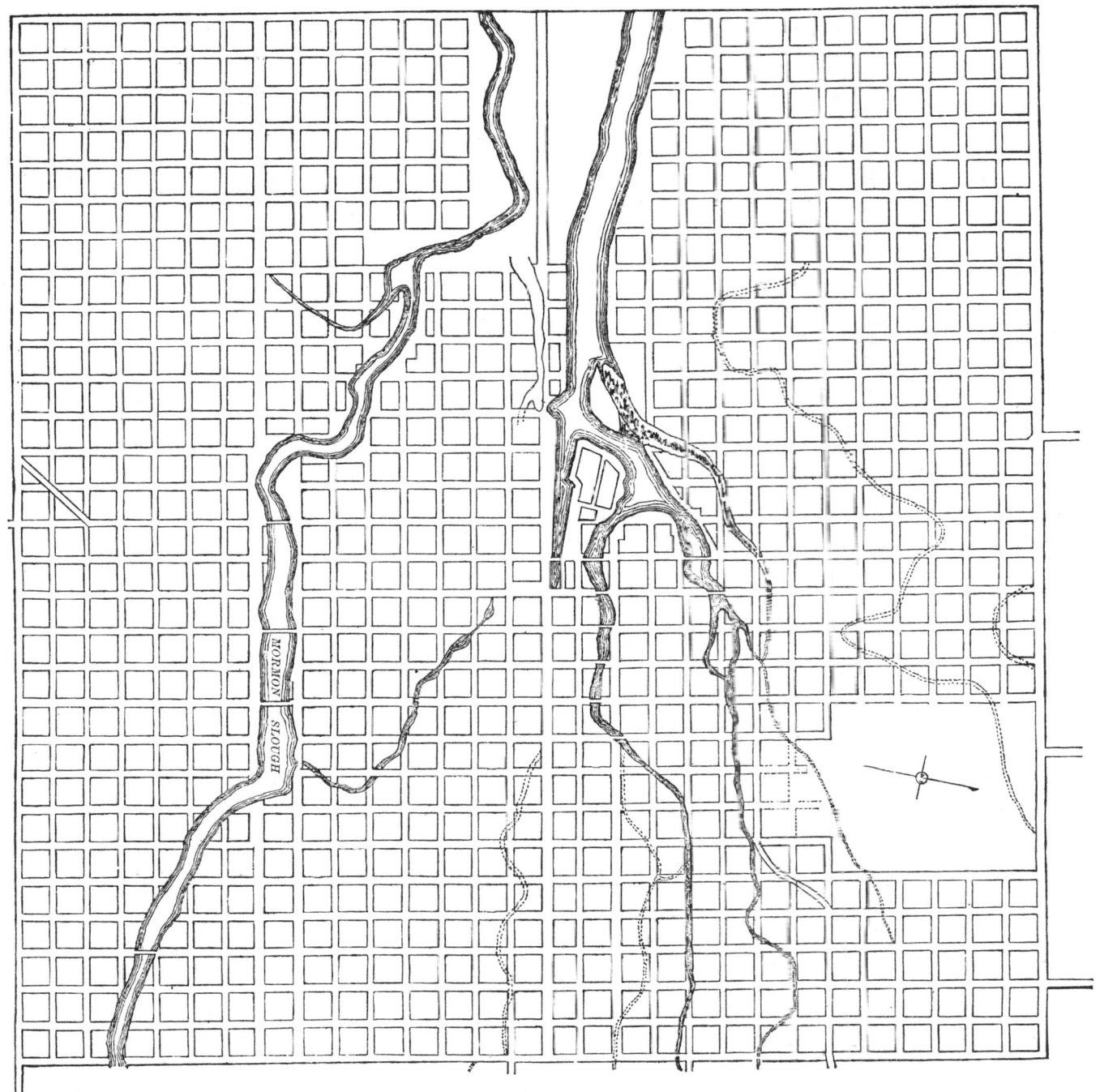

MORMON SLOUGH

STOCKTON, CAL.

SCALE OF FEET

0   500   1000

annual cost of about $2,500. A few of the sidewalks are of asphaltum, but they are mostly of plank. The gutters are laid with redwood plank. The planting of shade-trees in front of private residences is almost universally practiced. These trees are chiefly cork elms, and are planted by the owners of the property abutting, being placed between the street and the sidewalk. There is annually expended on streets for construction, repairs, etc., about $15,000. This work has always been done by contract.

There are 2 miles and 1,236 feet of horse-railroads in the city, the property of the Stockton Street Railroad Company, employing 5 men, 13 horses, and 4 cars, and carrying annually nearly 100,000 passengers at fares of 5 cents each.

The city is without omnibus lines.

WATER-WORKS.

The works for the water-supply belong to a private corporation. The water is pumped from 5 driven wells by 1 Cameron and 2 Blake direct-acting pumps into a tank and stand-pipe. The amount per day varies from 700,000 to 250,000 gallons. The company leases one of the flowing wells from the county and city, and furnishes free of charge water for public buildings and grounds and for fire purposes; the other wells belong to the company. There are about 8 miles of cast-iron pipe laid. Hydrants for fire purposes are not used, as the water is derived for this use from cisterns.

GAS.

The gas-works also are the property of a private company. The daily average production is 51,000 feet. The charge per 1,000 feet is $3 75. The gas company furnishes street-lamps, to the number of 140, for $3 57½ each per month.

PUBLIC BUILDINGS.

The city and county own and occupy jointly the court-house and city hall and the county and city jail. The city owns 9 school-houses and the 3 fire-engine houses. The city hall and court-house cost $80,000, of which the city paid one-half; the jail cost $11,000, of which the city paid one-fourth; the school-houses cost $85,569, and the fire-engine houses cost $12,500.

PUBLIC PARKS AND PLEASURE-GROUNDS.

Stockton has 7 small unimproved public parks, each of them being 300 feet square. These were given to the city by Captain C. M. Weber, the original owner of the land on which the city was laid out.

PLACES OF AMUSEMENT.

There is but one theater in the city, called the Stockton theater. Its seating capacity is 450. Entertainments pay a license fee of $5 for the first day's performance and $3 for each succeeding performance. There are also used for concert-halls and lecture-rooms, National hall (unfurnished), seating capacity about 500; Mozart hall, with a seating capacity of about 300; and Turn Verein hall, having a seating capacity of about 200.

DRAINAGE.

Concerning this subject the city clerk writes as follows:

There is no system of sewerage adopted by the city of Stockton. At the same time I doubt if there is a city in the United States more in need of one. Stockton is almost level, there being a fall from east to west of an average of about 6 feet in 335 feet. The streets are laid out nearly north and south and east and west. Two sloughs flow entirely through the city from east to west—one near the southern boundary (Mormon slough) and one near the center (Miner slough). In the winter or rainy season these sloughs are full of water, but both are dry in the summer or dry months, except the western portion of them, where they are affected by the tides. Another slough (Stockton channel) is a navigable stream as far as El Dorado street, about the center of the city. Miner channel is used by many persons to drain their kitchen wastes into. But the drains from kitchens and business-houses and water-closets are led into cesspools dug in the yards in nearly all instances. In fact, that is about the only means of drainage there is, except for a few who live near enough to the sloughs to drain into them.

Of course the result is that the yards are honeycombed with foul cesspools, which must eventually produce a fatal result on the health of the city.

Some 6 or 8 years ago the city council advertised for plans for sewerage. Several plans were presented, but none have been adopted. The subject is getting to be a very important one, and I hope that within a year or so some positive action will be taken whereby a general system may be adopted.

CEMETERIES.

On this subject no information was furnished by the city authorities, except that the principal cemetery, *Stockton Rural Cemetery*, is about 2 miles north of the city.

MARKETS.

There are no public markets in the city, all supplies of meat, poultry, fish, etc., being obtained at private stores.

SANITARY AUTHORITY—BOARD OF HEALTH.

The sanitation of the city is in the hands of the board of health, which board consists of 5 physicians elected annually by the city council. In the absence of epidemics the board incurs no expense; but in case of an epidemic, present or feared, any measures (and presumably any expense) deemed necessary may be taken. In addition to the duty of recommending to the city council such sanitary measures as may appear advisable—

The board of health shall have power to adopt such measures as will in their judgment best promote the health of the city and prevent the spread of disease; and they, or either of them, shall have authority to enter into and examine, or cause to be entered into and examined, in the day time all the vessels in port, buildings, lots, and plans in the city; to forbid or prevent communication with infected families or houses, and by and with the consent and control of the city council establish a pest-house or hospital and provide the necessary supplies therefor; direct and enforce the cleansing and purifying of all vessels, buildings, lots, vaults, and other places; to supply infected persons or families with provisions when communication with such persons or families has been prohibited; and generally to exercise a supervision over hospitals, prisons, school-houses, and public buildings, in so far as in their judgment the promotion of health requires, and to have the medical care of any pest-house or hospital that may be established under the provisions of this ordinance.

The board elects its own president and secretary, meeting as often as occasion requires; and, by the ordinance quoted from above, the chief of police is made the executive officer of the board, whose duty it is to carry into execution all of its orders and directions, both general and special. No assistant health officers or inspectors are employed, but the chief of police receives for his services in this connection a monthly salary fixed by the city council.

Inspections are made only as nuisances are reported, when, if they are found to be such, they are ordered to be abated. All defects in house-drainage, privy-vaults, cesspools, sources of drinking-water, sewerage, street-cleaning, etc., are noticed and acted upon only on complaint. The city attends to the removal of garbage. The pollution or filling up of streams is forbidden by ordinance.

INFECTIOUS DISEASES.

Small-pox patients are usually removed to the pest-house, which is situated about $\frac{1}{4}$ mile east of the city limits. But little attention is paid to the quarantining of scarlet-fever patients. The board requires the exclusion from schools of children from families suffering from contagious diseases. Vaccination is not done at the public expense, and is compulsory only on children attending school.

A register of diseases and deaths is kept by the board of health; one of births is kept by the county recorder. The board "reports to the state board of health, if required; no compulsion by statute".

MUNICIPAL CLEANSING.

Concerning this topic the city clerk writes:

Properly speaking, there is no such thing as municipal cleansing (as I think you understand it). The city employs a man with his horse and cart every Saturday, at $2 50 per day, to go around the principal streets and pick up the dirt and sweepings from stores and cart them away; and that's all there is to it.

POLICE.

The chief of police is elected annually in May. The rest of the force is elected by the police commissioners, who are the mayor, police judge, and chief of police. The last-named is the chief executive officer of the force. He serves warrants from the police court, makes arrests for violation of ordinances, attends police court, and supervises and directs the police force. Salaries are as follows: Chief of police, $1,200 per annum; 7 patrolmen at $75 each per month; and 1 special policeman at $30 per month. The force is not uniformed, and it is stated that they carry no arms or equipments. During the year ending April 30, 1881, 1,163 arrests were made, the principal causes for which were: Drunkenness, 523; disturbance of the peace, 182; battery, 82; vagrancy, 81; petit larceny, 67. The force co-operates with and executes the orders of the board of health in regard to nuisances. But 1 special policeman (included in the enumeration of the force) is appointed by the police commissioners with the consent of the city council. He is stationed at the railroad depot and receives $30 per month. The cost of the police force for 1880 was $10,977 10.

FIRE DEPARTMENT.

Stockton has 3 engine companies and 1 hook-and-ladder company. The following is furnished by the city authorities on this head:

The fire department is voluntary, and consists of a chief engineer and first and second assistant engineers, who are elected annually, on the first Monday in August, by the active members of the department; a board of delegates, consisting of 4 members of each company, who are elected annually and have power to make laws for the government of the fire department, [to] issue certificates of election, membership, and exemption, and to try any officer or member for any violation of the laws of the department. This board also annually elects a president, secretary, and treasurer of the fire department. There are 4 companies, of a maximum of 65 men each, possessing their own apparatus, as follows: 1 second-class Amoskeag steam-engine, 1 second-class Jeffries steam-engine, 1 second-class Babcock chemical engine, and 1 hook-and-ladder truck.

The city owns a Neafy and Levy engine, second class, which is kept as a relief engine. It also owns the engine-houses, hose-carts used with the company engines, hose, etc. Water for the supply of the department is furnished by 24 dug cisterns of a depth of about 23 feet, which ordinarily furnish sufficient water, but in the business portion of the city 8 of these cisterns are connected by 3-inch pipes with the mains of the water-works.

The chief engineer's report for the year ending September 1, 1879, gives 18 alarms, and estimated damage to property $4,000. The engines, truck, and hose-carts are drawn by horses, which are the property of the several companies. The city furnishes supplies to the department and keeps the apparatus and houses in repair, under the supervision of the fire and water committee of the city council. The chief engineer receives a salary of $20 per month; each steam-engine company is paid by the city $220 per month, the Babcock engine company $110 per month, and the hook-and-ladder company $90 per month, for services of stewards, drivers, engineers, and horses. The total expenditures for the fire department for the year ending May 5, 1881, was $10,438 94.

PUBLIC SCHOOLS.

The school department is under the management of the board of education, which is charged also with the disbursement of the public-school fund. The annual report of the board for the year 1879 gives the following statistics: Number of school-houses, 9; number of schools, 26; number of teachers, 33; number of children under 17 years, 3,167; number of children between 5 and 17 years, 2,300; number of children enrolled, 1,926; average number belonging, 1,288; current expenses for school department, $38,903 64; total expenses for school department, $39,469 15.

mouth by Lewis and Clarke by order of our government in 1804-'05; and the treaty of limits concluded between Spain and the United States in 1819, by which all the territory north of the 42d degree of north latitude was expressly declared to belong to us, constituted our title to this region. In 1832 the first settlers from the East arrived.

In 1834 Jason Lee, with other Methodist missionaries, entered Oregon. Messrs. Parker and Marcus Whitman were sent by the American Board of Commissioners for Foreign Missions to the Snake region in 1835. Dr. Whitman returned to the states, and in 1836 again went to Oregon, accompanied by Rev. Mr. Spaulding. Their wives, who accompanied them, were the first white women who had crossed the plains, and their children were the first white children born in Oregon. Others followed soon after, and in 1842 the immigration was large. Two of these pioneers—A. L. Lovejoy and a gentleman named Overton—whilst en route for Vancouver to Oregon City, stepped ashore from their canoe at the point where Portland now stands, and, having examined the topography of the surrounding country, concluded at once that it was a most eligible position for a town site. At some time during the ensuing winter they returned, and began at once to clear off the land and to make preparations for the erection of a log cabin. Before they had carried out this scheme Overton disposed of his interest in the claim to J. W. Pettygrove, who, in conjunction with Lovejoy, had the claim surveyed and occupied by an employé during the next winter. In the summer of 1845 a more accurate survey was made, and the ground was laid off into streets and blocks. D. H. Lownsdale bought Pettygrove's rights, a part of which he sold to Colonel U. W. Chapman and St———— in 1849. These men finally got patents from the United States. Until then titles of lots were insecure.

Meanwhile the affairs of this region had been in a somewhat unsettled condition. Engla—— The dispute was not settled till 1846, when a treaty was concluded between the 49th parallel in 1843. In the previous year it had been———— between the United States and British America on the 49th parallel. Oregon was formally—— what is now Washington territory, but the first governor did not arrive till March, government had been formed for the inhabitants till 1849. In December, 1850, it reached the—— territory as far south as the Columbia river and even below, and finally offered to compromise the——

The newspaper—the Weekly Oregonian—sprung into existence within a incredibly short space of time. The buildings were sprung into existence within as favorably with the general dingy appearance of the city since 1850.

Few details have been found concerning the history of the city since 1850. The growth of Portland was de—— increased so rapidly that in 1857 a convention was called, and though for some years admission as a state. This was granted in 1859, and the discovery of gold in the ea—— opening of railroads in the Willamette valley. The growth of Portland has been mo—— its growth has been much more rapid. The burnt district has since been re—— large part of the city in 1851. The only serious The burnt district has suffered occur——

as a city in 1851. The city was destroyed of Europeans and Mongolians. Education is guided by—— American, with a large mixture of Great Britain and Germany. The New England element has had a marked influen—— and middle states, Great Britain and Germany. Business—— northern states. The New England element has had a marked in——

Statistical accounts of the present condition of Portland, Oregon, m—— swers from Hon. D. T. Thompson,—— county, Oregon,—— —— umbia, 50 mile—— ies:

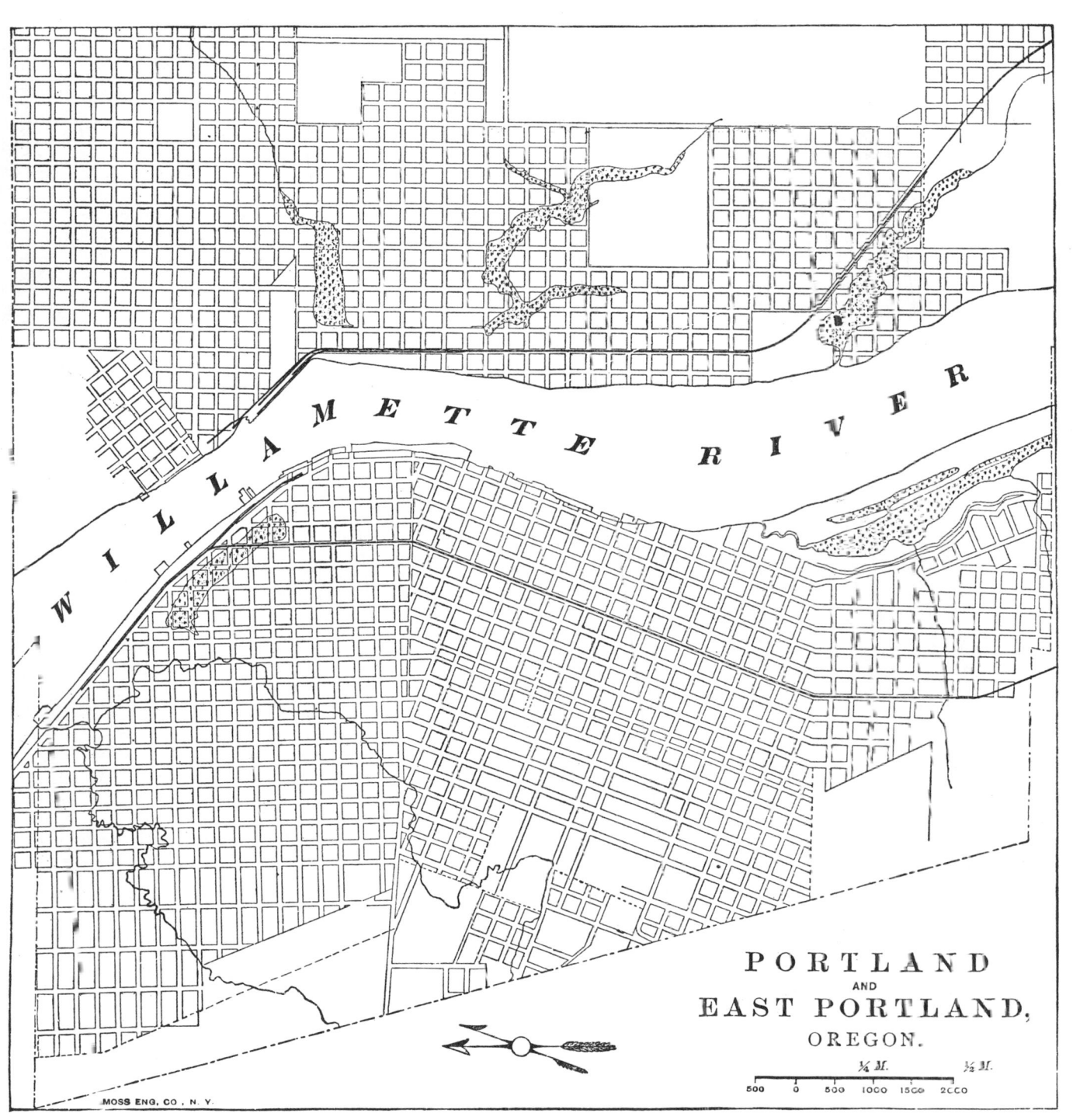

PORTLAND
AND
EAST PORTLAND,
OREGON.

¼ M.   ½ M.

500   0   500   1000   1500   2000

MOSS ENG. CO., N.Y.

WILLAMETTE RIVER

and Columbia, Portland is in daily connection with the southern terminus of the Pacific division of the Northern Pacific railroad at Wallula, Washington territory, and there is frequent communication with British Columbia and San Francisco.

RAILROAD COMMUNICATIONS.

Although numerous railroads are projected, and some under way, to give to Portland connection with different parts of Oregon and the whole Northwest, at present only two roads run out of the city—the Oregon and California, to Roseburg, and the Western Oregon, to Corvallis.

TRIBUTARY COUNTRY.

The Columbia basin has at present but one commercial center—the city of Portland. The Willamette valley, of which Portland is more especially the metropolis, is nearly as large as Maryland. It is 155 miles long and from 40 to 50 miles wide. The land is chiefly prairie. The mayor of Portland claims that is the finest valley in the United States, and that with good cultivation it will produce a larger quantity of wheat or other cereals to the acre than any other land in the country. It contains 6,000,000 acres, of which a little over 1,000,000 are now under cultivation. Droughts, high winds, and severe hail-storms are very rare. The most important towns and fully two-thirds of the population of western Oregon are in this valley. Lint, or fiber flax, from here carried off the first prize at the centennial exposition in 1876, where it was in competition with samples from Ireland, Holland, Russia, and Australia. The cultivation of flax is becoming an important factor in the agriculture of the state.

The Umpqua valley, a little farther south, is a first-class sheep-raising valley, 75 miles long and 40 broad. The soil is fertile. Still farther south lies the Rogue River valley, hilly and often mountainous, of about the same size as the Umpqua. In both of them coal, gold, and other minerals exist, and mining is carried on with profit. The Rogue River valley is especially adapted to fruit-raising, grapes and peaches being the predominant varieties. There are vast reserves of timber-lands scattered through the state, which affect largely its commercial interests. The large rivers are bountifully stocked with salmon, in fishing for which a large class finds profitable employment. Multnomah county, in which Portland is situated, is about 50 miles long and will average 10 miles in width. It is pretty generally covered with fir timber; there are also pine (but of a poor quality) and some oak and ash. Comparatively speaking, there is little good tillable land, a great portion of it being rough and mountainous. Along the northern line, on the Columbia river, may be found some of the grandest scenery in the world.

TOPOGRAPHY.

The city is located on a plateau, which gradually increases in height as it recedes from the river until it forms a range of hills at the western extremity of the city, whose greatest altitude is about 200 feet above the surface of the river. From this hill there is a beautiful view, embracing the meanderings of the Columbia and the Willamette, the Cascade range of mountains, and the snow-capped summits of mounts Hood, Saint Helen's, and Jefferson. At the low-water line the soil is alluvial, overlying gravel. The hills are of basalt rock, covered with soil and considerable timber. North of the city there is a lake covering 250 acres, which connects with the Willamette at high stages of the river. The country for a radius of 5 miles is wooded.

CLIMATE.

The highest recorded summer temperature is 99°; the highest in average years, 93°. The lowest recorded winter temperature is 3°; the lowest in average years, 17°. The mean summer temperature is 68°; the mean winter temperature, 40°. The Pacific ocean has much influence on the climate. The miasmatic influences exerted by the marshes are inconsiderable. The Cascade range of mountains on the east condenses the moist air of the Pacific, causing considerable rain. West and north winds are dry, south winds are wet. The chief rainfall occurs from November to March, inclusive, during which months the mean amount of precipitation in rain and melted snow is 35.88 inches, against 11.32 inches in the other seven months of the year. During July, August, and September this amount is only 1.79 inch.

STREETS.

The total length of streets is about 160 miles, of which 1.5 mile is paved with stone blocks, 15 miles with broken stone, 12 miles with plank, 1.5 mile with Nicholson pavement, and 4 miles with gravel. The stone-block pavement costs $2 per square yard, the broken stone and gravel 50 cents, the plank 45 cents, the Nicholson $2 12. Repairs are made by the abutting property-owners, and the cost can not be given. It is reported that stone blocks are the most easily cleaned, and the Nicholson, plank, gravel, and broken stone in the order mentioned. In the annual report for the year 1879 the mayor says that during the year—

there was expended for street improvements the sum of $140,884 61. A large amount of this portion was paid for macadam. The past year has demonstrated the fact that this character of street will not answer where there is a large amount of heavy travel. Say east of Fourth street and between G and Jefferson streets, one year wears out the best macadam that has been made here, and something more durable must be devised. Either return to the Nicholson pavement (which will last about 4 years), which makes a fine street and is not expensive, or adopt the Belgian-block pavement. * * * I think it safe to assume that there will not be less than $175,000 expended in street improvements in 1880.

In his report to the Census Office, in speaking of the permanent economy of these different kinds of pavement, the mayor says that the question is still undecided, but that for the main business streets stone block is growing in favor, and probably after this comes broken stone. The subject is under the immediate control of a street commissioner, receiving a salary of $1,500 per year. The sidewalks are of wood, asphalt, or stone, and vary in width from 12 to 15 feet. Gutters are of wood, in box form, or of stone blocks. Trees are very generally planted on the residence streets, maple, locust, and elm being the principal varieties. Back of Fourth street about 6 feet of the width of the sidewalk, in the center, is used for the path, and the space on each side is devoted to grass-plots. The construction of streets is done by contract. The mayor writes that contract work is much the cheaper and day work much the better. Two steam stone-crushers are used. Much of the crushing is done by hand with heavy sledge-hammers after the stone is deposited on the street, but steam-crushed stone is preferred.

There is 1½ mile of horse-railroad track. One-horse cars are used, and there are 5 of them. The total number of horses is 25, and of men employed 9. During the past year 218,000 passengers were carried. A single fare is 10 cents; four tickets are sold for 25 cents.

WATER-WORKS; GAS.

The water-works and gas-works are private. No information concerning them was furnished.

PUBLIC BUILDINGS.

The city owns a police building, in which are located the court-room and jail. The offices of the auditor and clerk, surveyor, superintendent of streets, and assessor are in a rented building; and the city attorney, city treasurer, and mayor have no offices whatever provided for them. There are 7 buildings belonging to the fire department. The total cost of municipal buildings belonging to the city is reported as having been $90,000.

PUBLIC PARKS AND PLEASURE-GROUNDS.

The total area of public parks and pleasure-grounds is 49 acres. The *City Park*, containing 40 acres, is situated ½ mile west of the city boundary, on high rolling hills covered with scattering fir and dogwood trees. It was purchased seven years ago at an expense of $32,000, and still remains unimproved. The mayor reports that in round numbers there are annually 20,000 visitors to it on foot, 10,000 in carriages, and 5,000 on horseback. In the city there are 2 squares, of an acre each, which were given to the city by the owners of the town-plot. Parks are controlled by the common council and the superintendent of streets.

PLACES OF AMUSEMENT.

There are 2 theaters, viz, the New Market theater and the Turn-Verein, with seating capacities, respectively, of 900 and 450. Theaters pay an annual license of $200 to the city. The only concert-hall and lecture-room is in the Masonic temple, which was constructed in 1873 at a cost of $54,000; it will seat 350 persons. There are 2 beer-gardens, embracing about 4 acres each, with seats among the shade-trees. Each will accommodate about 400 persons. They are exceedingly well patronized, much more so than the theaters and lecture-rooms.

DRAINAGE.

The city is built on the west bank of the Willamette river, and the surface slopes gently toward the river, so that sewers from all parts of the city reach the river with a good rate of fall. All sewers are made of clay pipe from 8 to 20 inches in diameter. Outfalls are extended to the bottom of the river, and the mouths of outlets are submerged. Sewage is swept away by the rapid current of the river. The fall of the sewers is usually 1 in 12, and any deposits forming are easily swept away by flushing. Such work is done by the superintendent of streets with men employed regularly by the city for all kinds of work, and no record of cost is made. There is no provision for ventilation except through the inlet-basins located at each corner. The cost of sewers is paid by assessment on the abutting property. The blocks of the city are 200 feet square and the streets are 60 feet wide. The cost of each sewer is assessed upon the adjacent property on both sides as far as the middle of the block. The price paid for building sewers in 1880 was, for 12-inch pipe, 16 feet deep, $1 80 per foot; for 10-inch pipe, 12 feet deep, $1 25; for 8-inch pipe, 10 feet deep, 90 cents; for 6-inch pipe, 10 feet deep, 75 cents per foot; catch-basins, $32 50 each. Manholes every 200 feet are included in the price of the sewer. The amount expended in 1880 was $26,000. There is no record of the length or cost of the location of sewers built in former years.

CEMETERIES.

There are 3 cemeteries, and all are private. *Lone Fir Cemetery* is 1½ mile east of the city, the *Jewish Cemetery* 1½ mile south of the city, and the third, name not given, 3 miles south of the city. In the early days of the city, small plots within the present city limits were used for burial purposes, but by ordinance of the city council all bodies interred in these places have been removed to the cemeteries mentioned. No dead body is allowed to remain unburied more than 48 hours without permission from the chief of police. Graves must be not less than 4 feet in depth. The lots in the cemeteries are sold to individuals, in plots of 20 by 30 feet. They then become the private property of the purchasers, but can be used only for burial purposes. The roads are built and kept up by the corporation that lays out the grounds. Each individual improves the lot belonging to him as he pleases.

MARKETS.

There are no public or corporation markets in the city. The city ordinances require that all places used as markets shall be kept clean, and impose heavy penalties on the proprietors for violations of the rule.

SANITARY AUTHORITY—BOARD OF HEALTH.

The board of health of the city consists of the mayor, the chairman of the standing committee of the common council on health and police, and the chief of police, who is *ex officio* health officer; and every regular and special police officer having a regular beat is *ex officio* a health inspector, but they receive no extra pay therefor. Whenever it is deemed necessary the board may employ a physician to visit and examine persons sick with any contagious or infectious disease, and to advise the board in any matter relating to the health of the city. He receives such compensation as the board considers reasonable, subject to the approval of the common council. A city ordinance authorizes the board to make such expenditures as may be necessary for work and materials in and about the small-pox hospital and for furnishing and maintaining it, and for the suppression of contagious or infectious diseases, provided that the aggregate of such expenditure shall at no time exceed the amount of any appropriation applicable to its payment. The mayor reports that the board has power to adopt rules and regulations for the preservation of the health of the city in the absence of epidemics, subject to approval by a majority of the common council. The only regulation as to inspections is that, should a police officer observe that any building, premises, or street on his beat is in a condition offensive to the public health, he shall immediately report the same to the health officer. As to the appointment of the board, it is reported that the mayor is elected by the people, the chairman of the standing committee of the council on health and police is appointed by the mayor, and the chief of police is appointed by a board of police commissioners. The board meets when called together by the mayor. The inspection and correction of defective house-drainage, privy-vaults, cesspools, and sources of drinking-water are under charge of the police officers, acting as inspectors. It is within the power of the board to have the evil corrected at the expense of the property-owner. Defective sewerage, street-cleaning, etc., are under charge of the street commissioner, whose duty it is to correct all defective sewerage and see that the streets are kept clean. The expense is borne by the abutting property-owners. The board can direct the removal of garbage at the expense of the owner of the property from which it is removed; and the same statement applies to excrement.

INFECTIOUS DISEASES.

Small-pox patients may be isolated. Scarlet-fever patients are not isolated, but the occupant of the house where a case exists must display a red flag at the entrance. The school board may close the schools during the prevalence of disease. There is no public pest-house, but one is established, when necessary, in the outskirts of the city. Vaccination is not compulsory, nor is it done at the public expense.

REPORTS.

There is no system of registration of births, diseases, or deaths. The board makes no regular reports. The mayor writes:

We have been very fortunate in having but little business for the board of health to perform. There has been no necessity for the employment of a physician for three years past.

The following city ordinance deserves note:

For the purpose of preventing disease and preserving health, it shall be unlawful for any person or persons to use any tenement-house or other building used as a sleeping-apartment within the city of Portland which contains less than 550 cubic feet of air or space for each and every person lodging in such house or apartment.

The punishment for violating the above ordinance is a fine of not less than $5 nor more than $50 for each offense, or imprisonment in the city jail not exceeding 10 days.

MUNICIPAL CLEANSING.

Street-cleaning.—The streets are cleaned by private abutters at their own expense. The work is done by contract and by hand. The city ordinances provide that when the streets have been paved, macadamized, or planked they shall be swept or scraped clean every Friday afternoon. The streets are said to be kept clean. The sweepings are deposited in the suburbs, at a place designated by the street commissioner.

Removal of garbage and ashes.—Garbage is removed by householders. The work must be done between 4 and 6 o'clock a. m. Garbage is hauled outside the city. Ashes are used to fill up hollows in empty lots. The system works well.

Dead animals.—Dead animals are removed outside the limits of the city and buried at the cost of the owner when found; otherwise at the cost of the city. The police have charge of the matter.

Liquid household wastes.—Nearly all the household waste of the city runs into the public sewers. None of it goes into street gutters, and only a very little into cesspools, which exist only in the outskirts, where sewers have not been constructed. The cesspools are usually so porous as not to need overflows. When cesspools are used they receive the wastes of water-closets. The water used in the city is taken from the Willamette river some distance above the city, and there is no possible chance of contamination at present. Cesspools are noticed by the city authorities only when they come under the head of nuisances.

Human excreta.—A very small proportion of the houses of the city depend on privy-vaults, almost every one being connected with a sewer and having water-closets. Few water-closets empty into cesspool. None of the privy-vaults are nominally water-tight. In case a vault is allowed to become a nuisance and the nuisance is not abated within 24 hours after the chief of police orders it, the delinquent is subject to a fine of not more than $50 nor less than $20, and must pay the cost of abating the nuisance. No privy or cesspool is allowed to be built under the sidewalk. The dry-earth system is not used to any extent. Night-soil is used to manure land outside the city, but not within the gathering-ground of the public water-supply.

Manufacturing waste.—Manufacturing waste runs into the sewers.

POLICE.

The police force is appointed by the mayor with the consent of the city council, and is governed by the mayor together with the committee on health and police. The general supervision of the force is under the charge of the chief of police, whose duty it is to see that all the ordinances of the city and criminal laws of the state are enforced within the city limits. He must give bonds in the sum of $15,000, and receives a salary of $2,400 per year. Captains receive $1,200 and policemen 1,080 per year.

The force consists of 12 men, exclusive of the chief of police, 2 captains, 1 detective, and 1 clerk. Twelve men are thus left for patrol duty. These 12 men are divided into 3 watches, each of which does day and night duty. Their hours of service are so arranged that between the hours of 10 o'clock p. m. and 3 o'clock a. m. there are always two watches on duty, the usual number of men on patrol in the daytime being doubled at the most dangerous season of the night.

The watches are divided to do duty as follows: Watch A consists of 4 men who report and go on duty at 8 a. m. and remain until 12 o'clock noon, and again at 7 p. m. and remain until 12 midnight; watch B is composed of 4 men who report and go on duty at 12 noon and remain until 4 o'clock p. m., and again at 10 p. m. and remain until 3 a. m.; watch C is composed of 4 men who report and go on duty at 4 o'clock p. m. and remain until 7 p. m., and again at 12 o'clock midnight and remain until 6 o clock a. m.

The members of the force wear a uniform of blue beaver with brass buttons, stiff round-top felt hats with cords, and overcoats like the rest of the suit. The uniform complete costs about $110. The men furnish their own, but the city furnishes buttons, star, club, and belt. Each patrolman carries a short billy and a pistol. The cloth for the uniforms is purchased at wholesale by the chief of police. The force patrols 75 miles of streets. During the past year there were 529 arrests in state cases and 2,049 in city cases, a total of 2,578. Of these, 1,466 were for being drunk and disorderly, 182 for assault and battery, 131 for disorderly conduct, 129 for being disorderly by fighting, 126 for larceny, and the rest for minor offenses; 1,917 were fined, 889 were committed to jail for non-payment of part or whole of fine, 194 were dismissed by the court, 104 were held to answer, and the rest were disposed of in various ways. In 1880 there were 187 station-house lodgers, as against 124 in 1879. About 100 were furnished with free meals at a cost of 15 cents each. The amount of property reported lost or stolen was $8,874; the amount recovered was $7,339, all of which was returned to the owners. There were 6 special policemen appointed by the mayor in 1880 at the request of their employers, receiving no pay from the city. These policemen are governed by the rules and regulations of the police department, possess the same powers as the regular police force, are furnished with a star and belt and club, and have procured for themselves new full "regulation" uniforms. In cases of emergency the specials render assistance to the regular force. The salaries paid to members of the force in 1880 amounted to $18,846; the board of prisoners cost $1,321 20; the expenses of the police building were $750; the salaries of the police commissioners amounted to $387. The receipts from 1,257 days' work done by prisoners, at 50 cents per day, were $628 50; the amount received for fines was $7,067 40.

Among the arrests in 1879 there were 27 for keeping an opium-house and 64 for visiting one; among those in 1880 were 8 for keeping such a house and 23 for visiting one. In his annual report for 1879 the chief of police says:

Another evil, and a rapidly growing one, is the habit of opium-smoking, which is ruining the health and destroying the minds of many of our young men and girls. There are a large number of these dens, kept principally by Chinese, where men and women, young men and girls—some not over 13 years of age—congregate and indulge in this vile and filthy habit, and sleep off the stupor, subject to the insults and indignities that may be committed upon them by those not under the influence and by the Chinese themselves. Some of the females who frequent these places are married and have families, and young girls of the most respectable class of society. Could their names be published society would stand amazed.

It is almost impossible for the police to find out these places, as they are generally in rooms to reach which it is necessary to pass through dark, winding passages and doors fastened and guarded, sometimes requiring a guide; and when the den is reached all is dark, the inmates having escaped over roofs and by underground passages. Some more stringent and severe measures should be taken to break up these dens of infamy. No wonder that so many of our young girls fall from virtue. From the best evidence I have, there are about 500 to 600 white males and females who visit these dens in this city.

In his report for 1880 the chief recommends the adoption of a most stringent ordinance, making opium-smoking in any way or shape whatever a misdemeanor, punishable by a fine of not less than $100 nor more than $300, or imprisonment of not less than 90 days in jail.

UTAH TERRITORY.

SALT LAKE CITY,
SALT LAKE COUNTY, UTAH TERRITORY.

POPULATION

IN THE

AGGREGATE,

1850-1880.

	Inhab.
1790	......
1800	......
1810	......
1820	......
1830	......
1840	......
1850	6,157
1860	8,236
1870	12,854
1880	20,768

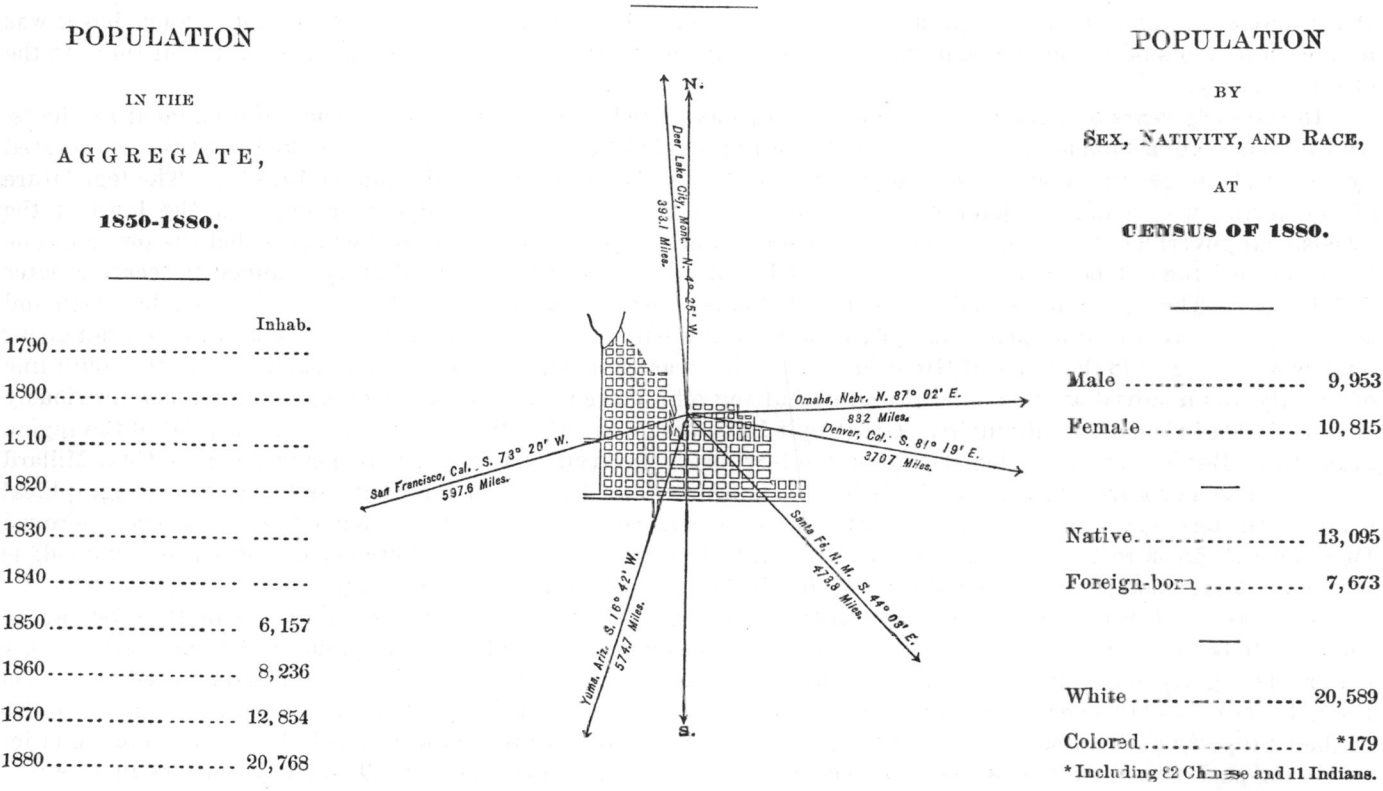

POPULATION

BY

SEX, NATIVITY, AND RACE,

AT

CENSUS OF 1880.

Male	9,953
Female	10,815
Native	13,095
Foreign-born	7,673
White	20,589
Colored	*179

* Including 82 Chinese and 11 Indians.

Latitude: 40° 46′ North; Longitude: 111° 54′ (west from Greenwich); Altitude: 4,350 feet.

FINANCIAL CONDITION:

Total Valuation: $7,364,325; per capita: $352. Net Indebtedness: $67,000; per capita: $3 23. Tax per $100: $1 70.

HISTORICAL SKETCH.(a)

Salt Lake City, the capital of Utah territory, was settled by a company of "Latter Day Saints", or *Mormons*, under the leadership of Brigham Young. This company is known in local history as the "*Pioneers*", or Mormon *Pioneers*, and was the advance-guard of the large body of Mormon people who were expatriated from Nauvoo, Hancock county, Illinois, in the year 1846. The pioneers left their winter quarters on the banks of the Missouri river (now Florence, Nebraska) April 7, 1847, numbering 143 persons, with 73 wagons, and were joined by about a dozen others on the journey. Orson Pratt and Erastus Snow, of the pioneers, entered the valley of the Great

---

a John T. Caine, esq., recorder, collected and forwarded to this office all the statistical information concerning the city of Salt Lake here presented. John Jaques, esq., prepared the historical sketch with which this report is introduced.

Salt lake through Emigration cañon, about 5 miles southeast of the city, on July 21 of the same year, Mr. Pratt being the first to set foot on the site of Salt Lake City, as his companion remained three or four miles behind. In the evening the two returned to their camp, 1½ mile up the cañon. The next day the main body of the pioneers entered the valley and encamped two or three miles south of the site of the city, moving northward on the 23d and camping near where Washington square is now located. On the 24th Brigham Young, who was sick with mountain fever, and the rear of the pioneers entered the valley. July 24 has ever since been recognized as "Pioneer day", and has generally been observed as a holiday. On the 29th about 150 members of the Mormon battalion, consisting of detachments of sick who had wintered at Pueblo, on the Arkansas river, arrived, accompanied by a party of Mormon emigrants, numbering about 50, who had started from Mississippi in 1846 and had also wintered at Pueblo. The battalion party was under the direction of Captains James Brown and Nelson Higgins and Lieutenant Wesley Willis. A fort, constructed of logs and adobes, was soon built on a 10-acre block now known as Pioneer square, in the 2d municipal ward, and within a few months the fort was increased to more than three times its original size. During the same fall about 1,500 Mormon emigrants, mostly from winter quarters, followed the pioneers and settled with them.

In 1847 a survey was made for the city. It was laid off in blocks of 10 acres each, or 40 rods square, with streets crossing each other at right angles, 8 rods wide, and including sidewalks of 20 feet. Each block was divided into 8 lots of 1¼ acre each, or 20 by 10 rods. Several additions have been made at different times to the original survey.

In the early years of settlement the government was vested in an ecclesiastical council of prominent residents, who assumed provisional municipal powers with the approval of the people. Great Salt Lake City was incorporated by an act of the general assembly of the provisional state of Deseret, approved January 19, 1851. The legislature of the territory of Utah, by joint resolution, approved October 4, 1851, adopted or legalized the laws of the provisional government of Deseret. The incorporation act, approved January 20, 1860, repealed the previous one but confirmed the old boundaries, except the north and east lines, which were slightly changed to secure greater definiteness. The corporation limits were about 8 miles east and west, and rather more than 6 miles north and south. An act approved January 18, 1867, removed the western boundary line from the bank of the Jordan about 2 miles west. In 1868 the name of Great Salt Lake City was changed to Salt Lake City, and in 1872 the south line of the city was removed about a mile north, thus cutting off a large portion of the farming lands that had previously been included in the corporate limits. Great Salt Lake City was naturally, from the first, the capital of the region around it. But an act of the legislature of the territory, approved October 4, 1851, made Fillmore City, Millard county, the seat of government, that city being 150 miles south of Great Salt Lake City and nearer the geographical center of the territory, and one wing of a state-house was subsequently built there. An act of legislature, approved December 15, 1856, removed the seat of government to Great Salt Lake City, where it has ever since remained, as by far the larger portion of the population resides in the northern part of the territory.

The passage through the city of many thousands of gold-seeking emigrants to California in 1848–'50 caused business to be very good, helped as it was also by the occasional arrival of gold dust from the Pacific coast. These emigrants eagerly engaged in barter, furnishing many articles of which the settler stood in great need. Some of the gold-seekers were so eager to reach the end of their journey that they not only abandoned or destroyed much of their property on the road, but on arriving at this point disposed of teams, wagons, clothing, oxen, etc., in order to obtain pack-horses or mules and thus continue on their way more rapidly. The early settlers in this way got possession of many animals, carts, wagons, carriages, and other useful articles, at a price that was below cost in the Atlantic states. In the early summer of 1850 provisions became very high, flour selling for $1 a pound, and even bringing $25 per 100 pounds after harvest time. There were 5 mills busy all the time making flour, while numbers of emigrants stood around each begging for enough to carry them to the new El Dorado. The gathering of several thousand soldiers at camp Floyd (afterward fort Crittenden), about 40 miles southwest of the city, in 1858–'61, and the consequent demand for supplies, with the forced sale of large amounts of provisions, clothing, wagons, harness, implements, military stores, equipments, etc., when the encampment was broken up, made business exceedingly lively. In 1863 and several following years the development of the gold mines in Montana and Idaho caused much business and high prices in the city and vicinity, wheat being sold for $5 or $6 a bushel, flour from $12 to $25 a hundred pounds, and other things in proportion. In 1869 the construction and opening of the Union and Central Pacific railroads, followed closely by the discovery and development of valuable silver and lead mines in the territory, induced a most notable era of prosperity, which lasted several years and caused real estate in the city to go up to almost fabulous prices. The present year (1880), owing to the general revival of business throughout the country, with the projection or extension of several railroads in the vicinity, as well as the prospects of a bountiful harvest, promises to be very prosperous. In the earlier years of the settlement of the city there was a depression of business every winter. Merchandise was supplied almost entirely by ox-teams from the Missouri river, 1,000 miles east, which could travel only in the summer. Most of the staple goods thus brought were generally sold out by Christmas or soon after, so that the market was thenceforth bare of them until fresh supplies were obtained. A special business depression was occasioned by the advance of the United States troops into the

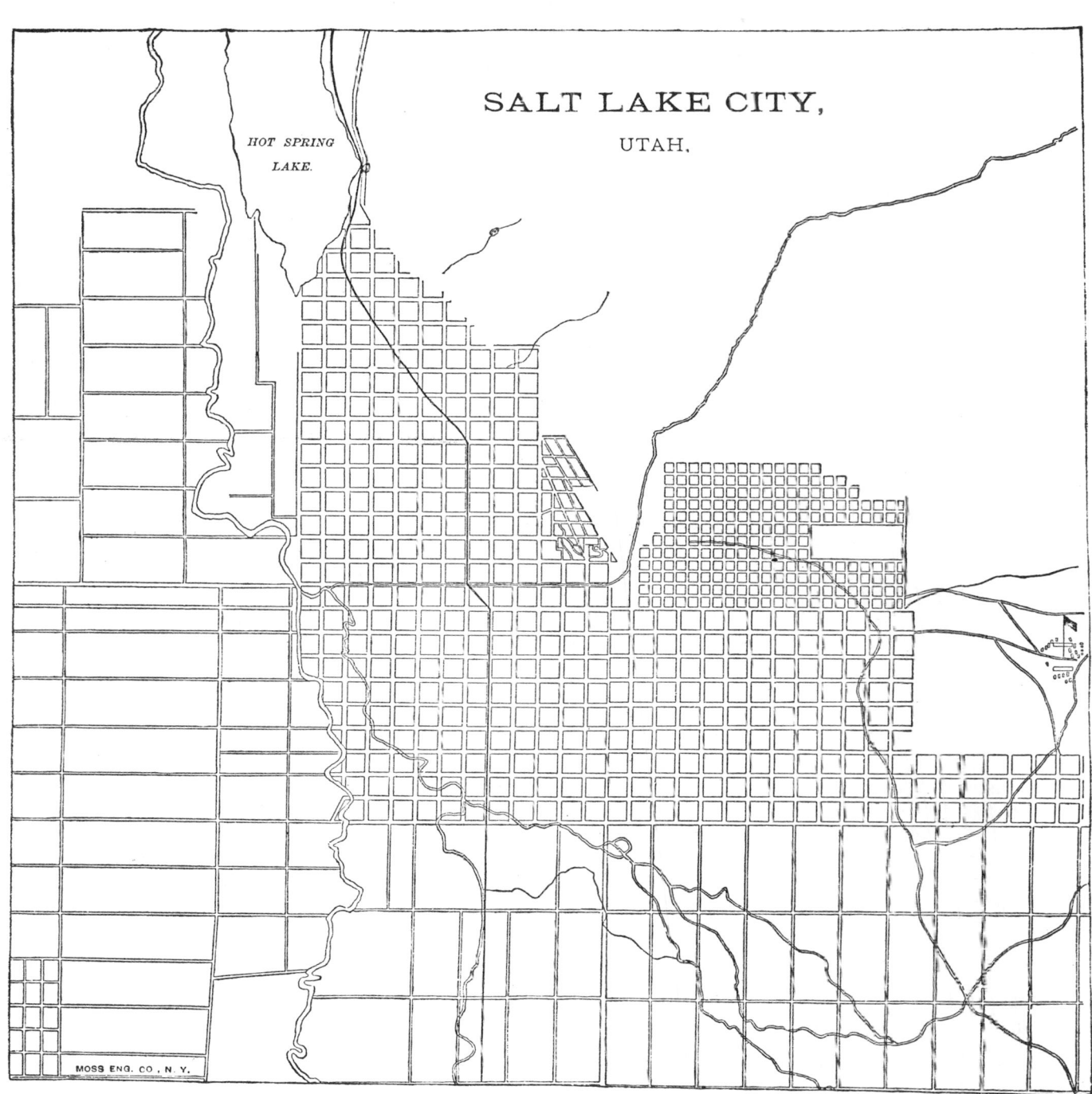

SALT LAKE CITY,

UTAH.

HOT SPRING LAKE.

MOSS ENG. CO., N. Y.

territory in 1857-'58, nearly all the people in the city and vicinity migrating to the south. The year 1869 was not a very prosperous year, and the city suffered also in common with the rest of the country during the financial depression in 1873-'79.

The city suffered more or less from floods in 1850, 1853, and 1862, from prolonged periods of droughts in 1848, 1855, and 1879, and from destructive insects in 1848, 1854, 1855, 1867, 1868, 1870, and 1873. Nearly every year since the settlement of the city the population has been increased by Mormon immigrants from the various states of the Union, as well as from Europe, and even Australia, in numbers varying from 1,000 to 6,000 per annum. These immigrants always come to the city first. Since the completion of the Central and Union Pacific railroads the influx of persons other than Mormons—men connected with mining, etc.—has been considerable. "As the religious sentiment of the Mormon people favors marriage and large families, the increase of population resultant therefrom has been proportionately large."

SALT LAKE CITY IN 1880.

The following statistical accounts, collected by the Census Office, indicate the present condition of Salt Lake City:

LOCATION.

Salt Lake City lies in latitude 40° 46' north, and longitude 111° 54' west from Greenwich, 11 miles from Salt lake, at the base of Wahsatch mountains, and occupies a most important position, not only in the territory but in the whole Rocky Mountain region. It has an altitude of 4,350 feet above the level of the sea, and the variation of the magnetic needle at the base meridian, as determined in 1878 by the United States Coast and Geodetic Survey, is 16° 32' east. The city is not on navigable water. Salt lake, or, as it used to be called, "Great Salt lake", the southern end of which is a few miles to the west of the city, is the principal body of water in the great Fremont basin, and one of the most remarkable lakes on the globe. It is 70 miles long by 45 miles wide, and the surface is 4,250 feet above mean sea-level. It has a mean depth of 12 feet, with a maximum depth of 60 feet. The specific gravity of the water is 1.17, or almost exactly that of the Dead sea; but unlike that sea it abounds in animal life. It is navigated by a line of steamers from Corinne on the north shore, to Black rock on the south shore.

RAILROAD COMMUNICATIONS.

The following railroad lines radiate from the city:

The Utah Central railroad, to Ogden, Utah, connecting there with the Central Pacific to San Francisco, the Union Pacific to Omaha, and the Utah Northern to Dillon, Idaho.

The Utah Western railway, to terminus, distant 37 miles.

The Utah Southern, to Frisco, Utah.

TRIBUTARY COUNTRY.

The country in the immediate vicinity of the city is agricultural, the settlements being small and rather scattered. Salt Lake City is the center of supply not only for this region but for the mining camps in western Utah as well as in Idaho.

TOPOGRAPHY.

The city is built somewhat in the shape of an irregular and broad-faced L, the angle, an obtuse one, being formed by a short western spur from the Wahsatch range, the city hugging the southwest corner of the spur. Indeed, of late years the houses have crept up the foot of the spur on to the *bench*, as it is called. The present corporate limits are a little over 9 miles from east to west, and about 6 miles from north to south. This includes the Fort Douglas military reservation, 2 miles square, directly east of the city. The city is divided into 5 municipal wards, and subdivided into 21 ecclesiastical, or bishop's, wards. Localities are better known by the ecclesiastical than by the municipal title. The interior ecclesiastical wards consist uniformly of squares of 9 blocks each. The exterior ecclesiastical wards are of irregular size, owing to the growth of the city, but are generally larger, some much larger, than the interior wards. The soil is alluvial. In the higher portions of the city it is of a light-brown color, interspersed with gravel and sand, with an occasional admixture of clay. In places there are streaks of a coarser gravel, and sometimes hard pan is found. In the lower parts of the city the soil is a black loam of great fertility, decidedly impregnated with salt and alkali, and in dry places is sometimes covered with efflorescent incrustations. In the western portion the subsoil is a drab-colored clay, from which a good class of *adobe* (sun-dried brick) is made. Most of the soil requires irrigation for profitable cultivation. The city is watered chiefly by a stream, known as City creek, that comes down through a cañon in the mountains, directly into the city, on the north side, and from there is dispersed in numerous divisions and subdivisions over a good portion of the corporate limits. Several small streams also flow from the Wahsatch range, and their waters are used for irrigation, the surplus finally passing into the Jordan river. The country within a radius of 5 miles is open. The warm springs, having a temperature of about 100° Fahrenheit, are at the foot of the spur on the northern border of the city. The water is therapeutic and is used for bathing purposes. About 1½ mile to the northwest are the hot springs, temperature 128° Fahrenheit, the water from which forms what is called Hot Spring lake, a shallow lake covering about 2 square miles, and extending from the base of the mountains nearly to the Jordan river.

CLIMATE.

Highest recorded summer temperature, 95°; lowest recorded winter temperature, —8°; mean annual temperature, 51.86°. The climate of Utah is naturally very dry. It is claimed, however, that the rainfall has greatly increased since the first settlement of the country.

STREETS.

But very little information was furnished on this subject. The streets are 137 feet wide, and the custom of tree-planting is quite general, rendering the city a conspicuous contrast with the surrounding country. The central portions of the city are supplied with water from City creek, through 10 miles of pipes, by gravity, the water being used for domestic purposes, fire, street-sprinkling, and, to a certain extent, for motive power. The central portions of the city are also lighted by gas, there being 6 miles of pipes laid in the streets. Several electric lamps, on the Brush system, are used in East Temple street, and also in some of the stores.

PUBLIC BUILDINGS.

No information on this subject was furnished.

PUBLIC PARKS AND PLEASURE-GROUNDS.

Salt Lake City has no large parks. There are four public squares, of 10 acres each, in different parts of the city that are intended for pleasure-grounds. Three of these were reserved for this purpose when the city was laid out, and one has since been purchased at a cost of $5,000. These squares have only been partially improved, the total cost of improvements, such as fencing, planting trees, etc., having been $10,000.

PLACES OF AMUSEMENT.

There is one theater in the city, but no information concerning it or other places of amusement was furnished.

DRAINAGE.

In reply to the schedule asking for information on this subject Mr. Caine says:

Salt Lake City has no sewers, nor has it yet adopted any plans looking to the early construction of sewers. It has depended entirely upon surface drainage, which has been greatly facilitated by the irrigation water-channels that run through all the streets of the city, being located at the outer edge of the sidewalks, as gutters are placed in the streets of other cities, and at the intersection of streets are carried across in covered culverts. All the surface water is conducted to these channels, and the flow of irrigating water through them usually keeps them clean and free from the accumulations of filth. Where this is insufficient to keep the channels open they are cleaned out by the property-owners, which cleaning is enforced by municipal authority. The waste water from these channels runs south and west, emptying into the Jordan river, which runs past the city on the west. This system, which heretofore has answered the purpose of drainage, and does yet where the city is thinly inhabited, is becoming quite inadequate to the wants of the business center, which is being rapidly built up in solid blocks, and the time is not far distant when some more perfect system of drainage will have to be adopted.

CEMETERIES.

There are 4 cemeteries within the corporate limits of Salt Lake City:
City Cemetery, area 100 acres.
Holy Cross Cemetery, area 1.5 acre
Hebrew Cemetery, 1.8 acre.
These are all situated together, between Birch, Willow, Mountain, and Wall streets.
Mount Olivet Cemetery, area 20 acres, on the Fort Douglas military reservation.
There are 2 small private burial grounds, one belonging to the family of Brigham Young, area 100 square rods, and the other to the family of Heber C. Kimball, area 25 square rods, in which burials are no longer made; they are both situated near the center of the city, not far from Temple block.
The total number of interments in the several cemeteries, so far as past records show, is: City cemetery from September 27, 1848, 9,423; Hebrew cemetery from October 31, 1867, 49; Holy Cross cemetery since March 25, 1873, 127; Mount Olivet cemetery from April 4, 1877, 184; Brigham Young's, 63, and Heber C. Kimball's, 51; making a total of 9,897. A full record of the person deceased is required to be furnished to the city sexton (who is *ex officio*

registrar of deaths) before interment. No limit of time is established between the time of death and of burial, the proper officer regulating this according to circumstances. Graves less than 4 feet 6 inches in length are required to be 4 feet 6 inches deep, and all graves over 4 feet 6 inches in length are required to be 6 feet deep.

The City cemetery is owned by the corporation of Salt Lake City. Lots one rod square are sold for $12 each, the corporation giving purchasers a warrantee title running to them, their heirs and assigns forever. Owing to the absence of water, no landscape-gardening has been attempted, owners improving their lots to a limited extent. Since 1860 there has been expended on improvements in this cemetery $12,623 63, and the revenue during the same period was $8,777 81. Mount Olivet cemetery was established by virtue of an act of Congress approved May 16, 1874, and is controlled by regulations published by the Secretary of War. Lots 18 feet square are sold at prices ranging from $10 to $50. The improvements mainly consist in fencing and the laying out and grading of roads. So far the total cost of improvements has been $4,035 91 and the revenue $3,902 40. The Hebrew cemetery belongs to the Hebrew Congregation B'nai Israel of Salt Lake City. Each head of a family belonging to the congregation is entitled to a lot 25½ by 31 feet. In former years the expenses were borne by voluntary contributions; but at the present time each lot is assessed $3 per annum. The total expenses so far have been $2,500. In the Holy Cross cemetery graves are furnished free of charge to persons dying in the faith of the Roman Catholic church. The annual interments in all the cemeteries during the past eleven years were as follows: 1870, 281; 1871, 368; 1872, 406; 1873, 431; 1874, 437; 1875, 391; 1876, 386; 1877, 392 (a); 1878, 497; 1879, 514; 1880, 204.

MARKETS.

There are no public or corporation markets in the city, except an open market for the sale of wood, coal, hay, and similar articles that are sold in bulk from wagons. All meats, poultry, fish, vegetables, fruits, etc., are sold at private stores or stands, while during the summer some fresh vegetables and fruits are peddled through the streets from country wagons. A few years ago an effort was made to establish public markets in different parts of the city, and to compel all retail dealers in meats, etc., to do their business therein; but the plan met with so much opposition that it was abandoned and the market buildings and grounds were sold.

SANITARY AUTHORITY.

There is no board of health in Salt Lake City. An ordinance provides that the city council shall appoint one or more quarantine physicians, who, associated with the mayor, shall form a board of quarantine. This board takes cognizance only of diseases of a contagious nature occurring within the city and in a district 12 miles around the corporate limits. The board can take all measures necessary to prevent epidemics on the introduction of disease. The city ordinances define nuisances and prohibit the same, but nothing is said as to who has the matter in charge. In case of small-pox, the board of quarantine can isolate patients by sending them to the pest-house, which is situated on a plateau southeast of the city. Vaccination is not compulsory, nor is it done at the public expense. Diseases and births are not recorded, but the city sexton keeps a record of all deaths and publishes a monthly mortuary report. Mr. Caine adds the following to the above information:

The city for its population probably covers a larger area of ground than any other in the Union. Outside of the business center the houses are detached. The streets are mostly 137 feet wide, and the sanitary regulations of compactly built cities have not, to the present time, been found necessary here.

MUNICIPAL CLEANSING.

Street-cleaning.—The streets are cleaned at the expense of the city, with its regular force and wholly by hand. The work is done under the direction of the street supervisor, according to the necessities of the case. The cost is included in the general street work, no separate account of the cleaning being kept. The sweepings are deposited in low places in grades of streets or on vacant lands outside the city. "The system is defective, and as the city becomes more densely populated a more effective one must be adopted."

Removal of garbage and ashes.—These are generally removed by the city with its own force. While awaiting removal the garbage is kept in boxes or barrels until called for by the city carts. Ashes and garbage are allowed to be kept in the same vessels. The garbage is deposited on vacant ground outside the city, while the ashes are disposed of in the same manner as the street-sweepings. The cost of the service is included in the regular street work. No injurious effects are reported from the manner of keeping, handling, or disposing of the garbage. "The system is defective, but answers the immediate wants of a new and sparsely inhabited city. The work is pretty thoroughly executed."

Dead animals.—The carcasses of all animals dying within the city limits are removed, under direction of the city marshal, and buried outside the corporate limits. No account is kept of the cost of the service or of the number of dead animals removed annually.

Liquid household wastes; human excreta.—There being no public sewers in the city, the liquid household wastes are either run into cesspools or thrown out on the surface of the ground, a small amount only reaching the street gutters. The cesspools are porous, are not provided with overflows, in some cases receive the wastes from water-closets, and are not governed by any regulations as to their cleansing. The number of water-closets and their proportion to privy-vaults was not stated. There are no regulations as to the construction or cleaning out of privy-vaults. The night-soil is either buried in the ground, used as manure, or hauled outside the city. "The water in many of the wells in that portion of the city built on lower ground than that where the bulk of the cesspools exist has been rendered unfit for use, and it is asserted that zymotic diseases have been engendered from using water from infected wells." The public water-supply comes from the mountains around the city, and is in no danger from contamination.

Manufacturing wastes.—There are no regulations governing this matter. There are only a few manufacturing establishments, and they are located on the outskirts of the city, where the solid wastes can be buried in the ground and the liquid carried off by the stream emptying into the Jordan river.

POLICE.

No information was furnished on this subject.

CITY GOVERNMENT. (a)

The municipal government of Salt Lake City is vested in the city council, composed of the mayor, 5 aldermen (1 from each of the 5 municipal wards) and 9 councilors, all qualified electors, and all elected biennially, by the qualified voters, on the second Monday in February in the even years. At the same election 1 marshal, 1 treasurer, 1 recorder, and 1 assessor and collector are elected. All the above officers hold office for two years, or until their successors are elected and qualified. The mayor and aldermen are conservators of the peace and justices of the peace in the city, having jurisdiction in municipal and territorial cases, civil and criminal. The city council has power to appoint other city officers, and remove them by a two-thirds vote at discretion; to remove elective city officials by a two-thirds vote for cause, after opportunity for hearing, and to fill vacancies; to prescribe the duties and powers of officers if not designated by law, or beyond those so designated, arrange their fees and determine their compensation; to purchase or dispose of property in behalf of the city, and control its finances; to control public grounds, streets, sidewalks, and bridges; to declare, define, and abate nuisances; to direct the location of buildings where dangerous, unhealthful, or unpleasant business is carried on; to license, tax, and regulate various pursuits, and restrain, punish, prohibit, or suppress same; to borrow money, generally to an amount the interest on which shall not exceed one-fourth of the taxes assessed the year previous; to levy and collect taxes not exceeding 5 mills on the dollar for contingent expenses, 5 mills for street improvements and repairs, and 1¼ mill for water control; to levy and collect poll- and ditch-taxes; to establish and regulate police; to provide for the election of trustees and appoint a board of school inspectors; to provide for public schools or other institutions of learning; to provide a school fund by direct tax or otherwise; to build and control hospitals, infirmaries, and medical colleges; to build a house of correction; to control the location of railroad tracks and depots, and the use of locomotive engines in the city; to control the location of gas-works, canals, telegraph poles, etc.; to levy special taxes for street and sidewalk improvements, making and repairing sewers and drains, and lighting streets in districts benefited thereby; to make regulations for the peace, convenience, cleanliness, and good order of the city, the protection of property therein, and the health, safety, and happiness of the inhabitants; to appoint quarantine physicians; to regulate street shade trees, fences, public pounds, pumps, wells, cisterns, hydrants, etc.; to provide for taking census of the inhabitants; to regulate the registration of births and deaths and the burying of the dead; to take care of, provide for, and educate destitute and neglected children; to appoint watchmen and policemen, also inspectors of various kinds, weighers, gaugers, and sealers of weights and measures, and prescribe their duties; to regulate the measuring of wood and the weighing of coal; to distribute and control the water flowing into the city; to supply the inhabitants with water, and for that purpose to construct and maintain the necessary canals, flumes, dams, reservoirs, and other water-works, and levy and collect special taxes in districts benefited by the water-works; to procure and control fire-engines, etc., and engine-houses for the same; to organize fire, hose, and ladder companies; to prevent and extinguish fires, define fire districts, and prevent the erection of wooden buildings therein; and must publish quarterly statements of receipts and disbursements of revenue.

The recorder keeps the records, papers, and seal of the city; keeps a list of licenses issued; records the proceedings of the council and all ordinances and resolutions passed by it; keeps a plat of surveys by the city; and administers oaths, and receives and approves official bonds.

The treasurer receives and disburses the funds of the city, and is the custodian of all property of the city not otherwise provided for, and reports yearly to the council.

The marshal, by himself or deputy, has charge of the city hall; attends the meetings of the council; acts as doorkeeper and sergeant-at-arms; preserves the peace and good order of the city and of public meetings; brings

---

a Salt Lake City being practically a Mormon city, and the headquarters of that sect, the following, as reported by Mr. Caine, is given entire.

disorderly persons to trial; serves processes; executes the orders and judgments of the mayor or council; visits and inspects slaughter-houses and examines the record books; and is the principal ministerial officer, with power to appoint deputies.

The assessor and collector assesses the taxable property in the city; collects the taxes; sells property of delinquents; may appoint deputies; and reports annually.

The following officials are appointed by the council: 1 auditor of public accounts, 1 supervisor of streets, 1 captain of police (the mayor appoints and controls the police force), 1 water-master, 1 sexton, 1 inspector of buildings, 1 sealer of weights and measures, 1 inspector of liquors, 1 inspector of provisions, 1 stock inspector, 1 jailor, 1 market-master, 1 surveyor, 1 attorney, and 1 chief engineer of the fire department. The duties of these officials are indicated by the titles, and are about the same as those performed by the same officers in other cities. The water-master is the only one peculiar to Salt Lake City; he regulates and distributes the water flowing into the city, and adjudicates difficulties in the distribution of the supply in the several wards; he reports quarterly to the council, and has several assistants.

MANUFACTURES.

The following is a summary of the statistics of the manufactures of Salt Lake City for 1880, being taken from tables prepared for the Tenth Census by A. A. Leonard, special agent :

Mechanical and manufacturing industries.	No. of establishments.	Capital.	AVERAGE NUMBER OF HANDS EMPLOYED.			Total amount paid in wages during the year.	Value of materials.	Value of products.
			Males above 16 years.	Females above 15 years.	Children and youths.			
All industries	166	$360,415	696	114	118	$125,537	$812,736	$1,610,133
Awnings and tents	3	900	6	4		3,437	7,000	13,800
Blacksmithing	12	7,200	22			12,971	7,904	35,164
Boots and shoes, including custom work and repairing	19	74,885	124	29	36	60,484	107,380	206,601
Bread and other bakery products	9	23,200	17	6	4	11,912	63,120	96,672
Brick and tile	6	53,325	28		26	7,967	5,111	24,612
Carpentering	4	10,650	14			8,910	14,300	29,800
Carriages and wagons	5	11,400	25		1	14,989	13,515	36,600
Confectionery	3	7,000	3	1		1,475	16,860	26,180
Dentistry, mechanical	6	8,100	4	2		2,250	2,850	18,950
Flouring- and grist-mill products	4	52,000	10			4,650	107,830	125,875
Foundery and machine-shop products	7	87,000	64	9	2	42,171	44,510	117,770
Furniture	4	25,350	22	4	4	13,250	18,325	49,387
Jewelry	3	2,690	7			6,783	9,150	19,362
Lime	3	36,000	16		2	7,180	3,040	16,770
Liquors, malt	3	100,500	32		1	16,125	60,125	108,020
Marble and stone work	3	4,400	5			3,868	3,300	9,400
Masonry, brick and stone	3	120	2			250	200	1,535
Painting and paperhanging	3	5,500	17		5	11,600	5,600	24,740
Photographing	5	6,600	8	4	2	5,633	3,170	16,300
Printing and publishing	6	154,660	114	11	17	91,861	64,054	202,625
Saddlery and harness	11	23,300	30		4	14,230	42,195	66,067
Tinware, copperware, and sheet-iron ware	3	32,000	24		5	21,200	47,400	85,070
All other industries (a)	41	128,725	102	44	9	62,350	155,707	278,833

a Embracing baking and yeast powders; baskets, rattan and willow ware; bluing; bookbinding and blank-book making; brass castings; clothing, men's; cordage and twine; iron railings, wrought; kaolin and ground earths; lasts; leather, curried; leather, dressed skins; leather, tanned; lock- and gun-smithing; mattresses and spring beds; mineral and soda waters; plumbing and gasfitting; sash, doors, and blinds; saws; soap and candles; stencils and brands; stone- and earthen-ware; tobacco, cigars and cigarettes; trunks and valises; upholstering; watch and clock repairing; wood, turned and carved; wooden ware; and woolen goods.

From the foregoing table it appears that the average capital of all establishments is $5,183 22; that the average wages of all hands employed is $458 55 per annum; and that the average outlay in wages, in materials, and in interest (at 6 per cent.) on capital employed is $7,770 46.

TABULATED INDEX

OF

CITIES AND SUBJECTS.

TABULATED INDEX OF CITIES AND SUBJECTS.

	City.	State.	Cemeteries.	Climate.	Commerce and navigation.	Distance chart.	Drainage.	Financial condition.	Fire department.	Garbage.	Gas.	History.	Infectious diseases.	Inspection.	Interments.	Location.
			Page.	Page.	Page.	Page.	Page.	Page.	Page.	Page.	Page.	Page.	Page.	Page.	Page.	Page.
1	Akron	Ohio	338	337		335	338	335			337	335, 336				336
2	Alexandria	Va	58			55	58	55			58	55–57	59			57
3	Atchison	Kans	754	753		751	754	751	756		754	751, 752	755			752, 753
4	Atlanta	Ga	160	159		157	160	157			160	157–159	161			159
5	Augusta	Ga	165, 166	165		163	165	163			165	163, 164	166			164
6	Aurora	Ill	479	478		477	479	477	480		478	477, 478	479			478
7	Austin	Tex	306	305		301	308	301		308		301–304	308	308	308	304
8	Baltimore	Md	19, 20	16	24	3	19	3	23, 24	21	17	3–15			20	15
9	Bay City	Mich				595		595				595	596			
10	Belleville	Ill	483	482		481	483	481			482	481, 482				482
11	Beloit	Wis	643	642		641	643	641			643	641				642
12	Bloomington	Ill	487	486		485	487	485			487	485, 486				486
13	Burlington	Iowa	709	708		707	709	707	711		709	707	710		710	708
14	Canton	Ohio				340		340				340				
15	Cedar Rapids	Iowa	713	713		712	713	712			713					712
16	Charleston	S. C.	100, 101	99	103, 104	95	100	95	103	102	99	95–98	102			98
17	Chattanooga	Tenn	138	136		135	137	135	139		137	135, 136	138			136
18	Chicago	Ill	506	494	510	489	498, 499	489	509		496	489–492	507		506	492
19	Chillicothe	Ohio	342			341	342	341			342	341				342
20	Cincinnati	Ohio	368–370	360, 361		344	364, 365	344	373		362	344–358	371, 372			358
21	Cleveland	Ohio	383, 384	380	387	377	382, 383	377	386		381	377, 378	384, 385		384	379
22	Columbia	S. C.	108	107		105	107	105		108	107	105, 106	108			106
23	Columbus	Ohio				390	392	390	393		391	390, 391				391
24	Council Bluffs	Iowa	717	716		715	717	715			717	715				716
25	Covington	Ky	114	113		111	114	111			113	111, 112	115			112
26	Dallas	Tex	313	312		311	313	311			313	311, 312	314			312
27	Davenport	Iowa	722	721		719	722	719			721	719, 720	722			720
28	Dayton	Ohio	399	398		394	399	394	401		398	394–397	400			397
29	Denver	Colo	770, 771	770		769		769			770		771			769, 770
30	Des Moines	Iowa	727, 728	726		725	727	725	729		727	725, 726				726
31	Detroit	Mich	610, 611	605	615	598	609, 610	598	614		608	598–603				604
32	Dubuque	Iowa		731		730		730			732	730				731
33	East Saginaw	Mich	621	619		617	620, 621	617	622		620	617, 618	622			618
34	Eau Claire	Wis				614		644				644				
35	Evansville	Ind	441	440		437	441	437			440	437–439	442			439
36	Fond du Lac	Wis	648	647		645	648	645	649		647	645, 646				646
37	Fort Wayne	Ind	446	445		444	446	444			446	444, 445	447	446	447	445
38	Galesburg	Ill	516	515		514	516	514			516	514, 515	517			515
39	Galveston	Tex	319	318	321	315	319	315	321		319	315–318	320			318
40	Georgetown	D. C.				53						53, 54				
41	Grand Rapids	Mich	625	625		623	625	623			625	623, 624	626			624
42	Hamilton	Ohio				403		403				403				
43	Hannibal	Mo	551	550		549	551	549			551	549, 550	552			550
44	Houston	Tex	325	325		323	325	323		326	325	323, 324	326		326	324
45	Indianapolis	Ind	452, 453	451		449	452	449	454		451	449, 450	453			450

TABULATED INDEX OF CITIES AND SUBJECTS.

Manufactures.	Markets.	Monuments.	Municipal cleansing.	Parks.	Penal reformatory, charitable, and healing institutions.	Places of amusement.	Police.	Population by decades, and by present division.	Public buildings.	Railroads.	Sanitary authority.	Schools and libraries (public).	Streets.	Topography.	Tributary country.	Water-courses, harbors, etc.	Water-works.	
Page.	Page.	Page.	Page.	Page.	Page.	Page.	Page.	Page.	Page.	Page.	Page.	Page.	Page.	Page.	Page.	Page.	Page.	
	338		338	337		337	339	335	337	336	338		337	337	336		337	1
	58		59	58		58	59	55	58	57	58		58	58	57		58	2
	754		755	754		754	755	751	754	753	754, 755	756	753, 754	753	753		754	3
162	161		161	160		160	162	157	160	159	161		159, 160	159	159		160	4
167, 168	166		166, 167	165		165	167	163	165	164	166		165	165	164		165	5
	479		479, 480	478		478	480	477	478	478	479		478	478	478		478	6
306, 307			308, 309	305	309	305	309	301	305	304	307		305	304, 305	304			7
24–26	20	18	21, 22	18, 19		19	23	3	17, 18	15, 16	20, 21		16, 17		16		17	8
597			596					595			596							9
	483		483, 484	482		483	484	481	482	482	483		482		482		482	10
	643		643	643		643		641	643	642	643		642	642	642		642	11
	487		488	487		487	488	485	487	486	487, 488	488	486, 487	483	486		487	12
	709		710, 711	709		709	711	707	709	708	709, 710		708	708	708		708, 709	13
								340										14
	714		714	713		713	714	712	713	712, 713	714		713	713	713		713	15
104	101		102, 103	100		100	103	95	100	98	101, 102	103	99	99	95	98	99	16
	138		139	137		137	139	135	137	136	138		137	136	136		137	17
511–513	506		507, 508	496–498		498	508, 509	489	496	492, 493	506	509, 510	494, 495	493	493		495, 496	18
	342		343	342		342	343	341	342	342	343		342				342	19
374–376	370, 371		372	362, 363		363, 364	372, 373	344	362	358, 359	371		361	359, 360	359		362	20
387–389	384		385	381, 382		382	385, 386	377	381	379	384	386, 387	380, 381	380	379, 380		381	21
	108		108	107		107	108	105	107	106, 107	108		107	107	107		107	22
393			392	391		392	392	390	391	391	392		391				391	23
	717		717, 718	717		717	718	715	717	716	717		716	716	716		716	24
116	114		115	113		113	115	111	113	112	114, 115		113	112, 113	112		113	25
	313		314	313		313	314	311	313	312	313		312	312	312		312, 313	26
723, 724	722		723	721		721	723	719	721	720	722		721	720, 721	720		721	27
402	399		400, 401	399		399	401	394	398	397, 398	399, 400	401	398	398	398		398	28
772			771	770		770		769	770	770	771		770				770	29
729	728		728	727		727	728, 729	725	727	726	728		726, 727	726	726		727	30
615, 616	611, 612		613	608, 609		609	614	598	608	604	612, 613	614	605, 606	604, 605	604		607	31
				732		732		730	732	731	731		731, 732	731	731		732	32
732, 733	621		622	620		620	622	617	620	618	621		619	619	619		619, 620	33
								644										34
443	447		442	440		441	442, 443	437	440	439, 440	441, 442		440	440	440		440	35
	648		648, 649	647		648	649	645	647	646	648	649	647	646, 647	646		647	36
446	446		447	446		446	447	444	446	445	446		445	445	445		445, 446	37
	516		517	516		516	518	514	516	515	517		515	515	515		515	38
322	319, 320		320, 321	319		319	321	315	319	318	320		318	318	318		319	39
								53										40
627	625		626, 627	625		625		623	625	624	626		625	624	624		625	41
								403										42
	551		552	551		551	553	549	551	550	551, 552		550	550	550		551	43
	325		326	325		325		323	325	324	325, 326		325	325	324		325	44
455, 456			453, 454	452		452	454	449	452	450	453	454	451	451	451		451	45

O

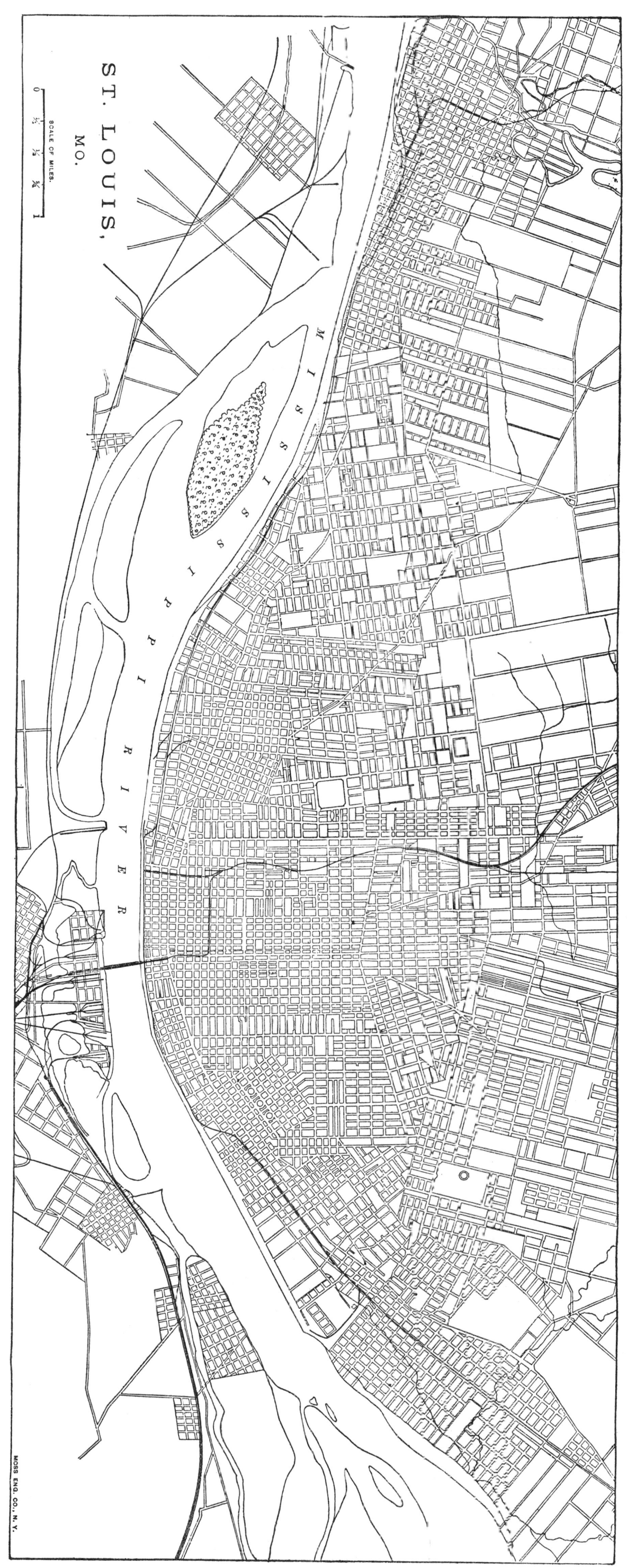

ST. LOUIS,
MO.

SCALE OF MILES.

MOSS ENG. CO., N. Y.